Baseball America
2018 ALMANAC

BASEBALL AMERICA INC. · DURHAM, N.C.

Baseball America

ESTABLISHED 1981
P.O. BOX 12877, DURHAM, NC 27709 • PHONE (919) 682-9635
EDITOR AND PUBLISHER B.J. Schecter
EXECUTIVE EDITORS J.J. Cooper, Matt Eddy
DIRECTOR OF BUSINESS DEVELOPMENT Ben Leigh

EDITORIAL
ASSOCIATE EDITORS Kegan Lowe @KeganLowe
Josh Norris @jnorris427
SENIOR WRITER Ben Badler @benbadler
NATIONAL WRITERS Teddy Cahill @tedcahill
Carlos Collazo @CarlosACollazo
Kyle Glaser @KyleAGlaser
Michael Lananna @mlananna
SPECIAL CONTRIBUTOR Tim Newcomb

PRODUCTION
DESIGN & PRODUCTION DIRECTOR Sara Hiatt McDaniel
MULTIMEDIA MANAGER Linwood Webb
DESIGN ASSISTANT James Alworth

ADVERTISING
ADVERTISING DIRECTOR George Shelton
DIGITAL SALES MANAGER Larry Sarzyniak

BUSINESS
DIRECTOR OF OPERATIONS Hailey Carpenter
TECHNOLOGY MANAGER Brent Lewis
CUSTOMER SERVICE Jonathan Smith

STATISTICAL SERVICE
MAJOR LEAGUE BASEBALL ADVANCED MEDIA

Alliance
BASEBALL

BASEBALL AMERICA ENTERPRISES
CHAIRMAN & CEO Gary Green
PRESIDENT Larry Botel
GENERAL COUNSEL Matthew Pace
DIRECTOR OF MARKETING Amy Heart
INVESTOR RELATIONS Michele Balfour
DIRECTOR OF OPERATIONS Joan Disalvo
PARTNERS Jon Ashley
Stephen Alepa
Martie Cordaro
Brian Rothschild
Andrew Fox
Maurice Haroche
Dan Waldman
Sonny Kalsi
Glenn Isaacson
Robert Hernreich
Craig Amazeen
Peter Ruprecht
Beryl Snyder
Tom Steiglehner

3STEP
MANAGING PARTNER David Geaslen
CHIEF CONTENT OFFICER Jonathan Segal
CHIEF FINANCIAL OFFICER Sue Murphy
DIRECTOR OF DIGITAL CONTENT Tom Johnson
DIRECTOR OF OPERATIONS, DATABASE/VIDEO Brendan Nolan

BASEBALL AMERICA (ISSN 0745-5372/USPS 591-210) is published bi-weekly with a double issue in August and December, 24 issues per year, by Baseball America Enterprises, LLC, 4319 South Alston Ave, Suite 103, Durham, NC 27713. Subscription rate is $92.95 for one year; Canada $118.95 (U.S. funds); all other foreign $144.95 per year (U.S. funds). Periodicals postage paid at Durham, NC, & additional mailing offices. Occasionally our subscriber list is made available to reputable firms offering goods and services we believe would be of interest to our readers. If you prefer to be excluded, please send your current address label and a note requesting to be excluded from these promotions to Baseball America Enterprises, LLC, 4319 South Alston Ave, Suite 103, Durham, NC 27713, Attn Privacy Coordinator.

EDITOR'S NOTE: Major league statistics are based on final, unofficial 2017 averages.

» The organization statistics, which begin on page 44, include all players who participated in at least one game during the 2017 season.

» Pitchers' batting statistics are not included, nor are the pitching statistics of field players who pitched in less than two games.

» For players who played with more than one team in the same league, the player's cumulative statistics appear on the line immediately after the player's statistics with each team.

» Innings pitched have been rounded off to the nearest full inning.

Baseball America
2018 ALMANAC

Editors
Kegan Lowe and J.J. Cooper

Assistant Editors
Ben Badler, Teddy Cahill, Carlos Collazo
Matt Eddy, Michael Lananna,
John Manuel, Josh Norris

Database and Application Development
Brent Lewis

Contributing Writers
John Perrotto, Tom Haudricourt

Photo Editor
Brendan Nolan

Design & Production
James Alworth, Sara Hiatt McDaniel, Linwood Webb

Programming & Technical Development
Brent Lewis

Cover Photo
Jose Altuve of the Houston Astros hits a three-run home run against the Los Angeles Dodgers in game five of the 2017 World Series in Houston, Texas. Photo by Christian Petersen/Getty Images.

For additional copies, visit our Website at BaseballAmerica.com or call 1-800-845-2726 to order.

US $23.95-$26.95, plus shipping and handling per order. Expedited shipping available.

Distributed by Simon & Schuster.
ISBN-13: 978-1-932391-75-6

Statistics provided by Major League Baseball Advanced Media and Compiled by Baseball America.

TABLE OF CONTENTS

Cody Bellinger

JAMIE SQUIRE/GETTY IMAGES

MAJOR LEAGUES 6

ORGANIZATION STATISTICS 44

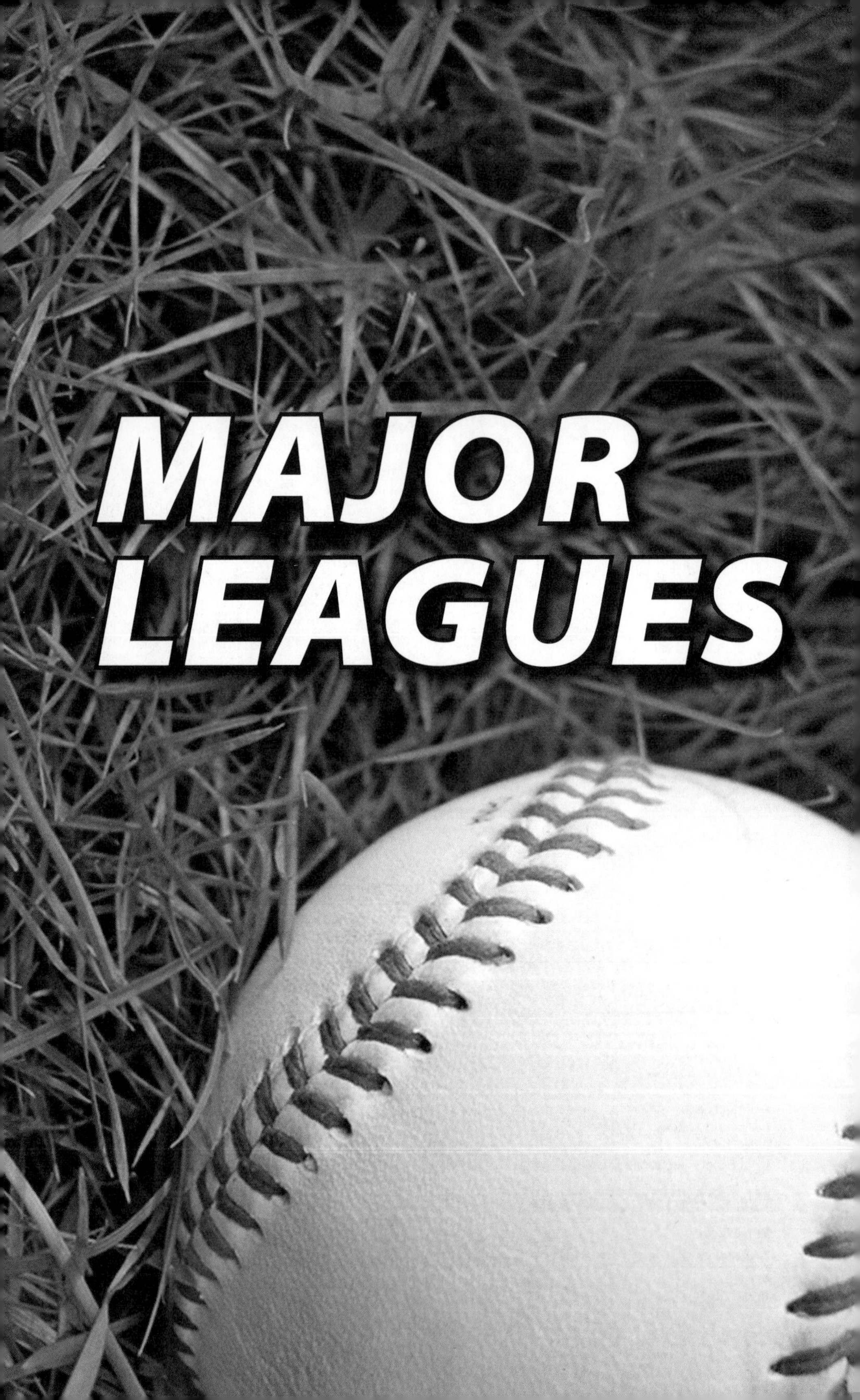
MAJOR LEAGUES

Remarkable Rookies Pace A Power Binge

BY JOHN PERROTTO

Aaron Judge was unsure of his season-opening destination with less than a week remaining in spring training.

The rookie was in competition with Aaron Hicks for the Yankees' starting right fielder's job. Judge got the nod and rewrote history.

Judge hit an American League-leading 52 home runs, breaking the major league rookie record of 49 set by the Athletics' Mark McGwire in 1987. Judge also won the All-Star Home Run Derby at Marlins Park in Miami and was one of several rookie sluggers who put themselves in the record book.

Dodgers first baseman Cody Bellinger's 39 home runs broke the National League rookie record of 38 set by the Braves' Wally Berger in 1930 and matched by Hall of Famer Frank Robinson with the 1956 Reds. Bellinger set the record despite not being called up from Triple-A Oklahoma City until April 25 when veteran first baseman Adrian Gonzalez went on the disabled list with a back injury.

Phillies first baseman Rhys Hoskins became the fastest player since at least 1913 to reach 11 home runs. He did so in his 18th game on Aug. 27 against the Cubs, 17 days after being called up from Triple-A Lehigh Valley. Hoskins also hit his first 11 homers in 17 fewer at-bats than anyone in history.

Pirates first baseman Josh Bell's 26 homers were the most by an NL switch-hitting rookie.

However, none of the rookies stood out like Judge, who broke McGwire's mark on Sept. 25 when he connected off another rookie, the Royals' Jakob Junis, at Yankee Stadium.

Judge also set the Yankees' rookie home run record on July 7 when he took Brewers rookie reliever Josh Hader deep. That mark had stood for 71 years since Hall of Famer Joe DiMaggio hit 29 homers in 1936.

A supplemental first-round draft pick of the Yankees in 2013 from Fresno State, Judge struggled in his first taste of the major leagues in 2016 when he batted .179 with four home runs while striking out 42 times in 84 at-bats. In 2017, however, Judge led the AL with 128 runs scored and 127 walks, despite a majors-worst 208 strikeouts in 542 at-bats.

JIM MCISAAC/GETTY IMAGES

Yankees outfielder Aaron Judge hit a MLB-rookie record 52 home runs.

The genial Judge seemingly won as many admirers for his disposition as his power feats.

"He's handled it with grace and humility, and he's never lost who he is and his ability to change someone's day," Yankees manager Joe Girardi after Judge hit his 50th homer. "He's a natural-born leader for me. It's almost like he's a big brother. He watches out over everyone. He waits for the players to come off the field. You got the whole package."

In most seasons, Bellinger would have been the game's best rookie.

The Dodgers' fourth-round draft pick in 2013 from Hamilton High School in Chandler, Ariz. became the fastest player in history to have four multi-homer games when he went deep twice June 13 against the Indians. Bob Horner did it in 63 games for the 1978 Braves. Bellinger also became the fastest player to 21 career homers when he connected on June 19 against the Mets' Zack Wheeler in his 51st game, beating the old mark by Berger in 1930.

Bellinger broke the NL rookie record on Sept. 22, taking the Giants' Jeff Samardzjia deep at

Dodger Stadium. What the made the homer extra special was that it broke a 1-1 tie in the seventh inning as the Dodgers claimed a 4-2 victory that clinched their fifth consecutive NL West title.

"The feeling running the base paths was awesome," Bellinger said during the postgame celebration. "This is so awesome. You see it on TV, and it looks fun. To actually be part of it, it's even better. I'm glad to be part of it."

With two home runs April 16 against the Blue Jays, Orioles left fielder Trey Mancini tied the major league record with seven home runs in his first 12 games. That matched Dino Restelli with the 1949 Pirates and Trevor Story with the 2016 Rockies. Mancini began his career by homering three times in five games at the end of the 2016 season.

Three Athletics rookies—right fielder Matt Olson, center fielder Jaycob Brugman and second baseman Franklin Barreto—became the first trio of teammates to hit their first career home runs in the same game, connecting June 24 off the White Sox's James Shields at Guaranteed Rate Field in Chicago.

Power Surge

Overall, the rookies played their part in a record-setting 6,105 home runs being hit in the major leagues in 2017. That easily surpassed the old mark in 5,963, set in 2000 at the height of the Steroids Era and four years before Major League Baseball instituted testing for performance-enhancing drugs.

The record was broken on Sept. 19 when Royals left fielder Alex Gordon homered off Blue Jays reliever Ryan Tepera.

There were many theories for why home runs were up. The most consistent was that hitters were intentionally trying to hit fly balls—focusing on the launch angle, as it is called in sabermetric terms—as a way to counteract the extreme infield shifts many teams had started to employ in recent seasons.

"My biggest take on it is that players are trying to hit more home runs," Giants manager Bruce Bochy said. "Their philosophy overall, a lot of these position players, is to get the ball in the air and also pull the ball and get the ball in the air and hit it as far as you can. So, you're increasing the launch angle, whatever you want to call this, stay away from the ground balls. And, so, they're sacrificing a little bit more contact to do a little bit more damage."

Marlins right fielder Giancarlo Stanton's 59 homers led the major leagues and were the most in a season since Barry Bonds connected 73 times for the Giants in 2001, a year in which Sammy Sosa went deep 64 times for the Cubs. Stanton also easily surpassed the Marlins' season-single record of 42 set by Gary Sheffield in 1996.

A total of 117 players hit at least 20 home runs, up from 111 in 2016, and 41 players hit at least 30 home runs, up from 38 the previous season.

Strikeouts increased in lockstep with home runs. The MLB record for whiffs was set for a 10th straight season with 40,104—an increase from 38,982 in 2016.

Angels DH Albert Pujols reached the biggest individual home run milestone of 2017, hitting the 600th home run of his career on June 3 with a fourth-inning grand slam off the Twins' Ervin Santana at Angel Stadium in Anaheim. Pujols became the ninth player to reach that milestone and first to join the club with a grand slam.

Pujols had gone homerless in three games since reaching No. 599. Prior to his at-bat against Santana, he checked his phone in the dugout and saw a text from his wife, Deidre, urging him to relax.

"I'm glad I listen to her once in a while," Pujols said. "At a moment like this, I always start putting pressure on myself. Usually she'll give me some encouragement. It was just a perfect time to check my phone, and I'm glad I did."

Pujols hit one of the seven grand slams that day, which set a major league record. Also connecting with the bases loaded were Cubs left fielder Kyle Schwarber, Brewers third baseman Travis Shaw, Dodgers center fielder Chris Taylor, Braves first baseman Matt Adams, Rockies first baseman Ian Desmond and Mariners catcher Mike Zunino.

Reds second baseman Scooter Gennett and Diamondbacks right fielder J.D. Martinez became the 17th and 18th players in major league history to hit four home runs in a game. Gennett performed the feat on June 6 against the Cardinals and Martinez matched the major league record on Sept. 4 versus the Dodgers.

Gennett, a Cincinnati native, hit a grand slam in the third inning, a two-run homer in the fourth, a solo shot in the sixth and another two-run homer in the eighth at Great American Ball Park. He became the first player in major league history with five hits, four homers and 10 RBIs in a game.

Prior to his eruption in Cincinnati, Gennett had just 38 career home runs over five seasons, 502 games and 1,637 at-bats.

"It's surreal, man. It really is," Gennett said. "I'm truly blessed. I'm from here, born here. Watching all those great Reds players of the past play when I was little. And to do something that's never been done is hard to put words on it."

Marlins outfielder Giancarlo Stanton led all of baseball with 59 home runs, which was the most anyone in baseball has hit since Barry Bonds hit 73 in 2001.

Martinez sandwiched a pair of two-run homers in the fourth and ninth innings around a pair of solo shots in the seventh and eighth in the game at Dodger Stadium. He became the first player since 1900 to hit home runs in the seventh, eighth and ninth innings of a game.

"We were part of history," Diamondbacks manager Torey Lovullo said. "You can't believe it after it keeps happening — second, third and finally the fourth time. It was amazing."

It marked just the second season in major league history with multiple four-home run games. In 2002, Shawn Green did it for the Dodgers and Mike Cameron for the White Sox.

First baseman Ryan Zimmerman set the Expos/Nationals franchise record for home runs with his 235th on July 17 against the Reds. The mark had previously been held by Vladimir Guerrero.

Blue Jays left fielder Steve Pearce tied the major league record for most walk-off grand slams in a season when he hit two. Both came in the span of three days—July 27 against the Athletics and July 30 against the Angels. Cy Williams accomplished the feat with the 1926 Phillies and Jim Presley did the same with the 1986 Mariners.

Astros center fielder George Springer set a major league record against the Mariners on April 11 when he hit his fourth leadoff homer in the first nine games of the season. Springer's teammate, Marwin Gonzalez became the first player in major league history to hit a home run in four consecutive games while playing four different positions. Gonzalez completed the feat from April 30-May 3 while manning third base, left field, first base and right field, respectively.

Even pitchers got into the home run act, as Giants lefthander Madison Bumgarner became the first pitcher to hit two home runs on Opening Day April 2 against the Diamondbacks.

The Twins became the first team to hit home runs in each of the first seven innings of a game in a 16-0 rout against the Padres on Sept. 12. Catcher Jason Castro connected twice while second baseman Brian Dozier, first baseman Kennys Vargas, shortstop Jorge Polanco, third baseman Eduardo Escobar and right fielder Eddie Rosario also went deep.

Milestones and More

Rangers third baseman Adrian Beltre became the 31st member of the 3,000-hit club on July 30 when he doubled in the fourth inning off Orioles

CONTINUED ON PAGE 11

PLAYER OF THE YEAR

Altuve Stands Above The Rest

BY JOHN MANUEL

Like a lot of good scouts, Al Pedrique remembers the sound off the bat. A hard sound. The sound of a hitter. It was the sound of the ball off Jose Altuve's bat, a sound that Altuve couldn't wait for Pedrique, then helping run the Astros' international program as a special assistant to general manager Ed Wade, to hear.

"I was supposed to be in Venezuela, but I got stuck in the Dominican (Republic) for an extra night when my flight got canceled," remembered Pedrique, who just wrapped the season managing Triple-A Scranton/Wilkes-Barre in the Yankees organization.

"Our scouts in Venezuela had about 25 or 30 guys ready for a tryout camp, and they had to send them home because I couldn't be there. Altuve told the scouts that he wanted to make sure he would get invited again. He wanted me to see him play. But our scouts told him to come back the next day. I got in early, around 7 or 8 o'clock, and he was there and ready to go."

At this February 2007 workout, Altuve, who was 16 years old going on 17, ran the 60-yard dash, turning in plus times. Pedrique remembers saying, "For a small guy, he can fly."

He recalls Altuve's defense was behind his bat, which was somewhat mitigated by that good sound in batting practice. He showed quick hands, surprising pop and the ability to drive the ball to right-center field. Pedrique asked the scouts in the area to arrange a scrimmage to make sure he could see Altuve face live pitching, and by the end of the week he saw the diminutive Venezuelan in a game.

PREVIOUS POY WINNERS

2007: Alex Rodriguez, ss, Yankees
2008: C.C. Sabathia, lhp, Indians/Brewers
2009: Joe Mauer, c, Twins
2010: Roy Halladay, rhp, Phillies
2011: Matt Kemp, of, Dodgers
2012: Mike Trout, Angels
2013: Mike Trout, Angels
2014: Clayton Kershaw, Angels
2015: Bryce Harper, Nationals
2016: Mike Trout, Angels
Full list: BaseballAmerica.com/awards

BILLIE WEISS/GETTY IMAGES

Astros second baseman Jose Altuve won his third batting title in 2017

"He had confidence," Pedrique remembers. "At the time, we thought he was a hot dog, but the more you watch him, that's just his personality. He has a lot of confidence. That's what got my attention—the confidence, his quick hands and how he swung the bat. I told the coaches at the workout, 'Keep this kid, he can swing it.'"

The Astros kept after it and signed Altuve in March 2007. Ten years later, the 27-year-old has just completed his fourth straight season with 200 or more hits, leading the American League each year. He won his third batting title, posting a career-best slash line of .346/.410/.547 and tied his career high with 24 home runs while stealing 32 bases—his sixth straight season with 30 or more thefts.

He's the confident 5-foot-6, 165-pound second baseman, in many ways the same traits Pedrique saw back in 2007. And now, after helping lead the Astros to a 101-win regular season and the organization's first World Series title, Altuve is Baseball America's 2017 Major League Player of the Year.

CONTINUED FROM PAGE 9

lefthander Wade Miley. Beltre also became the first player from the Dominican Republic to reach 3,000 hits.

After Beltre pulled into second base, his three children ran onto the field toward him at Globe Life Park in Arlington. They continued running to the wall in right-center field to help unveil a logo commemorating the occasion before returning to second base to hug their father.

"What happened today after the hit, it was the best moment in my life," Beltre said. "When I saw that, I felt like I was in the cloud, because I really saw the joy in their faces. It was a nice moment to enjoy with them, my family, my wife."

It was a year of milestones for Beltre, as the 38-year-old also hit his 450th home run on June 27 off Indians closer Cody Allen, then smacked his 600th double off Red Sox lefty David Price on July 4 before recoding his 5,000th total base on July 7 with a home run off Angels righthander Ricky Nolasco.

Tigers first baseman Miguel Cabrera also hit the 450th home run of his career in 2017, when he took Indians righthander Corey Kluber deep on May 2.

Meanwhile, Yankees DH Matt Holliday, Mets infielder Jose Reyes, Tigers DH Victor Martinez, Braves right fielder Nick Markakis, Dodgers first baseman Adrian Gonzalez and Angels second baseman Brandon Phillips all notched their 2,000th hits.

Reyes also stole the 500th base of his career while Mariners second baseman Robinson Cano hit his 500th double and Dodgers second baseman Chase Utley and Indians DH Edwin Encarnacion each reached 1,000 RBIs.

Marlins righthander Edinson Vólquez threw the season's only no-hitter, facing the minimum and needing just 98 pitches to beat the Diamondbacks 3-0 on June 3. He struck out 10, walked two and threw 65 strikes while tossing the sixth no-no in franchise history.

Three pitches into the game, Volquez felt a sharp pain in his right ankle after a collision at first base with Diamondbacks center fielder Rey Fuentes. Volquez received a mound visit from one of the Marlins' athletic trainers but stayed in the game. He briefly thought about asking manager Don Mattingly to remove him following the fifth inning, but ultimately decided to keep pitching.

"When I passed the seventh, I said, 'I'm going to go for it,'" Volquez said. "And I got it."

Vólquez dedicated the game to former Marlins pitcher José Fernández, who died on Sept. 25, 2016 in a boating accident, and Yordano Ventura, who died on Jan. 22, 2017 in a car crash. Volquez and Ventura were teammates as members of the Royals in 2015 and 2016.

Cubs lefthander Jon Lester reached two significant milestones over the course of the season. He recorded his 150th career win on June 13 against the Mets and then notched his 2,000th career strikeout on Aug. 1 by fanning Diamondbacks infielder Jack Reinheimer.

Also reaching 2,000 career strikeouts in 2017 were Dodgers lefty Clayton Kershaw, Nationals righthander Max Scherzer and White Sox righty James Shields.

CONTINUED ON PAGE 13

AMERICAN LEAGUE STANDINGS

EAST	W	L	PCT	GB	Manager	General Manager	Attendance	Average	Last Penn.
Boston Red Sox	93	69	.574	—	John Farrell	Dave Dombrowski	2,917,678	36,021	2013
* New York Yankees	91	71	.562	2	Joe Girardi	Brian Cashman	3,146,966	39,835	2009
Tampa Bay Rays	80	82	.494	13	Kevin Cash	Matthew Silverman	1,253,619	15,670	2008
Toronto Blue Jays	76	86	.469	17	John Gibbons	Ross Atkins	3,203,886	39,554	1993
Baltimore Orioles	75	87	.463	18	Buck Showalter	Dan Duquette	2,028,424	25,042	1983
CENTRAL	**W**	**L**	**PCT**	**GB**	**Manager**	**General Manager**	**Attendance**	**Average**	**Last Penn.**
Cleveland Indians	102	60	.630	—	Terry Francona	Mike Chernoff	2,048,138	25,286	2016
* Minnesota Twins	85	77	.525	17	Paul Molitor	Derek Falvey	2,051,279	25,641	1991
Kansas City Royals	80	82	.494	22	Ned Yost	Dayton Moore	2,220,370	27,412	2015
Chicago White Sox	67	95	.414	35	Rick Renteria	Rick Hahn	1,629,470	20,626	2005
Detroit Tigers	64	98	.395	38	Brad Ausmus	Al Avila	2,321,599	28,662	2012
WEST	**W**	**L**	**PCT**	**GB**	**Manager**	**General Manager**	**Attendance**	**Average**	**Last Penn.**
Houston Astros	101	61	.623	—	A.J. Hinch	Jeff Luhnow	2,403,671	29,675	2017
Los Angeles Angels	80	82	.494	21	Mike Scioscia	Billy Eppler	3,019,583	37,279	2002
Seattle Mariners	78	84	.481	23	Scott Servais	Jerry Dipoto	2,135,445	26,364	None
Texas Rangers	78	84	.481	23	Jeff Bannister	Jon Daniels	2,507,760	30,960	2011
Oakland Athletics	75	87	.463	26	Bob Melvin	David Forst	1,475,721	18,447	1990

Wild Card Game: Yankees defeated Twins. **Division Series:** Yankees defeated Indians 3-2 and Astros defeated Red Sox 3-1 in best-of-five series. **Championship Series:** Astros defeated Yankees 4-3 in a best-of-seven series.

ROOKIE OF THE YEAR

Judge Rules Over All Rookies

BY KYLE GLASER

Before Aaron Judge became the toast of New York, before his home runs became the nightly subjects of oohs and ahhs and Statcast GIFs, he had to come to a humbling realization. His swing needed to change.

"The biggest thing, the way I can explain it, was controlling my back hip," Judge said in May. "I watched the great hitters. They're into their back hip, and that's where the swing starts. They're in their legs. They're in that hip. For me it allows me to stay in and through the zone longer. I don't come around the zone."

The results of his change were evident. For all of his chiseled 6-foot-7, 282-pound physique and 80-grade raw power, Judge never hit more than 20 home runs or slugged above .490 in any minor league season. But as a rookie with the Yankees in 2017, Judge hit 52 home runs with a .627 slugging percentage.

"He's always been powerful, but I think he's learning to use his body more efficiently," said Yankees first baseman Greg Bird. "And then you're seeing him reap the rewards more than ever."

Judge, 25, reaped rewards and records indeed. His 52 home runs set a new rookie record, breaking Mark McGwire's mark of 49 in 1987. He walked 127 times to shatter the modern rookie record of 107 set by Ted Williams in 1939.

Judge hit .284/.422/.627 to finish second in the American League in on-base percentage, slugging percentage and RBIs (114). He was first in runs in scored (128), home runs and walks. His 95.6 mph average exit velocity was highest in the majors and the longest home run of the season (495 feet), as measured by Statcast, also belonged to Judge.

In one year, Judge accumulated the most career wins above replacement of any Yankees first-rounder since Ian Kennedy (2006).

The 2013 first-round pick from Fresno State made the all-star team, won the Home Run Derby with a jaw-dropping performance and, most importantly, carried the Yankees to their highest win total since 2012 and a berth in the ALCS against the Houston Astros.

Aaron Judge's 2017 season came after he tweaked his swing during the offseason.

For all that, Judge is the 2017 Baseball America Rookie of the Year.

And with the improvements Judge made to turn his raw power into game power, there figures to be a whole lot more to come for the Baby Bomber.

"Of course, his power has always been there. He's the biggest, strongest guy in baseball," outfielder Brett Gardner said. "I think that everybody knows what he's capable of doing and how far he is capable of hitting a baseball. It's just all about becoming a better hitter."

PREVIOUS ROY WINNERS

2007: Ryan Braun, 3b, Brewers
2008: Geovany Soto, c, Cubs
2009: Andrew McCutchen, of, Pirates
2010: Jason Heyward, of, Braves
2011: Jeremy Hellickson, rhp, Rays
2012: Mike Trout, of, Angels
2013: Jose Fernandez, rhp, Marlins
2014: Jose Abreu, 1b, White Sox
2015: Kris Bryant, 3b, Cubs
2016: Corey Seager, ss, Dodgers
Full list: BaseballAmerica.com/awards

CONTINUED FROM PAGE 11

The Orioles' Zach Britton set the AL record for most consecutive saves when he closed out his 55th game in a row on July 23 against the Astros. The streak got to 60 before the Athletics tagged the lefthander with a blown save on Aug. 13.

Also in the closers' market, the Dodgers' Kenley Jansen and Yankees' Aroldis Chapman both notched their 200th career saves in 2017.

The Cubs' Joe Maddon became the 63rd manager in major league history to reach 1,000 wins on May 15 when his team defeated the Reds.

Marlins outfielder Ichiro Suzuki became the all-time leader for hits for a player born outside of the United States on July 6 when he hit a single off the Cardinals' Michael Wacha. The single, which was the Japan native's 3,054th career hit, broke the previous record held by Hall of Famer Rod Carew.

Then, on June 25, the 43-year-old Suzuki hit leadoff and played center field against the Cubs, becoming the oldest player to start a game in center field since 1900.

Indians second baseman Jose Ramirez tied a major league record held by 12 others when he had five extra-base hits—three doubles and two home runs—on Sept. 3 against the Tigers.

Red Sox right fielder Mookie Betts tied the major league single-game record for RBIs by a leadoff hitter with eight on July 2 against the Blue Jays. Augie Bergamo set the mark with the 1945 Cardinals and it was later tied by the Indians' Bill Glynn in 1954, the Tigers' Jim Northrup in 1973 and the Rockies' Ronnie Belliard in 2003.

Nationals third baseman Anthony Rendon went 6-for-6 with three home runs, a three-run double, five runs scored and 10 RBIs on April 30 in a 23-5 victory over the Mets. He became the second player in major league history to collect six hits, three home runs and 10 RBIs in a game, joining Walker Cooper, who did it for the 1949 Reds.

Rendon also became the 13th player with at least 10 RBIs in a game, as well as the fourth player since 1900 to go 6-for-6 and have at least three home runs in a game, joining Ty Cobb (1925 Tigers), Edgardo Alfonzo (1999 Mets) and Shawn Green (2002 Dodgers). Green hit four homers.

The Tigers' Andrew Romine became the fifth player in major league history to play nine positions in a game, doing so on Sept. 30 against the Twins. The highlight was striking out the only batter he faced, third baseman Miguel Sano, to end the eighth inning and preserve a one-run lead in a game the Tigers won 3-2.

Leaders In The Clubhouse

Despite standing just 5-foot-6, Astros second baseman Jose Altuve had another big season in 2017, helping Houston win the American League pennant and, eventually, the first World Series in franchise history.

Altuve hit .346 to win his second straight American League batting title and third in four years. He also topped the AL in hits for a fourth consecutive season with 204.

"A little more special," Altuve said of his 2017 campaign just after the regular season ended. "This is the first time I won a batting title and the team is going to the playoffs."

Charlie Blackmon continued the Rockies' dominance of the National League batting crown. The center fielder hit .331 to become the second

NATIONAL LEAGUE STANDINGS

EAST	W	L	PCT	GB	Manager	General Manager	Attendance	Average	Last Penn.
Washington Nationals	97	65	.599	—	Dusty Baker	Mike Rizzo	2,524,980	31,173	Never
Miami Marlins	77	85	.475	20	Don Mattingly	Michael Hill	1,651,997	20,395	2003
Atlanta Braves	72	90	.444	25	Brian Snitker	John Coppolella	2,505,252	30,929	1999
New York Mets	70	92	.432	27	Terry Collins	Sandy Alderson	2,460,622	30,758	2015
Philadelphia Phillies	66	96	.407	31	Pete Mackanin	Matt Klentak	1,905,354	24,118	2009
CENTRAL	**W**	**L**	**PCT**	**GB**	**Manager**	**General Manager**	**Attendance**	**Average**	**Last Penn.**
Chicago Cubs	92	70	.640	—	Joe Maddon	Jed Hoyer	3,199,562	39,501	2016
Milwaukee Brewers	86	76	.531	6	Craig Counsell	David Stearns	2,558,722	31,589	1982 (AL)
St. Louis Cardinals	83	79	.484	9	Mike Matheny	Mike Girsch	3,447,937	42,567	2013
Pittsburgh Pirates	75	87	.451	17	Clint Hurdle	Neal Huntington	1,919,447	23,697	1979
Cincinnati Reds	68	94	.420	24	Bryan Price	Dick Williams	1,836,917	22,678	1990
WEST	**W**	**L**	**PCT**	**GB**	**Manager**	**General Manager**	**Attendance**	**Average**	**Last Penn.**
Los Angeles Dodgers	104	58	.562	—	Dave Roberts	Farhan Zaidi	3,765,856	46,492	2017
*Arizona Diamondbacks	93	69	.537	11	Torey Lovullo	Mike Hazen	2,134,375	26,350	2001
*Colorado Rockies	87	75	.463	17	Bud Black	Jeff Bridich	2,953,650	36,465	2007
San Diego Padres	71	91	.426	33	Andy Green	A.J. Preller	2,138,491	26,401	1998
San Francisco Giants	64	98	.420	40	Bruce Bochy	Bobby Evans	3,303,652	40,786	2014

Wild Card Game: Diamondbacks defeated Rockies. **Division Series:** Dodgers defeated Diamondbacks 3-0 and Cubs defeated Nationals 3-2 in best-of-five series. **Championship Series:** Dodgers defeated Cubs 4-1 in a best-of-seven series.

straight Colorado player to finish atop the league and the 10th in 20 years. Blackmon also led the major leagues with 213 hits and 137 runs scored.

Blackmon, helped by the thin air of Coors Field, joined a list of Rockies' batting champions over the past two decades that included Larry Walker (1998, 1999, 2001), Todd Helton (2000), Matt Holliday (2007), Carlos Gonzalez (2010), Michael Cuddyer (2013), Justin Morneau (2014) and D.J. LeMahieu (2016).

There were no 20-game winners for just the fourth time in a non-shortened season—the others were 1871, 2006 and 2009—as Dodgers lefthander Clayton Kershaw, Royals lefty Jason Vargas and Indians righthanders Carlos Carrasco and Corey Kluber tied for the major league lead with 18 victories.

In an era when managers were calling on their relievers earlier in games and more frequently, the record for fewest complete games was set for a third straight season. Pitchers went the distance just 59 times, down from 83 in 2016 and 104 in 2015.

There were also just 27 individual shutouts. That was the fewest since there were only 25 in 1878, back when there were only six major league teams.

"I think it's reflective of how bullpens are being used and how good the bullpens are," Padres lefthander Clayton Richard said. "They're so specialized and the numbers are so detailed that managers are able to match up earlier in the game."

Red Sox lefthander Chris Sale topped the majors with 308 strikeouts, the first pitcher to reach that mark since Randy Johnson and Curt Schilling both did so for the 2002 Diamondbacks. Nationals righthander Max Scherzer led the NL for a second straight season with 268 strikeouts.

Sale tied a major league record by striking out 10 or more batters in eight consecutive starts from April 10-May 19. He also became the fastest pitcher in major league history to reach 1,500 strikeouts, doing so in 1,290 innings when he fanned Blue Jays center fielder Kevin Pillar on Aug. 29. The old mark was 1,303 innings by Kerry Wood.

The Diamondbacks set a major league record as their pitching staff had nine consecutive games of 10-or-more strikeouts from April 24-May 3. A total of 14 pitches combined for 113 Ks in four games against the Padres, three against the Rockies and two more against the Nationals.

The Yankees and Cubs set the major league record for most strikeouts in a game with 48 on May 7 in an 18-inning affair. The previous mark had stood since 1971 when the Angels and Athletics combined for 43 whiffs in a 20-inning game.

G FIUME/GETTY IMAGES

Chris Sale was the first pitcher to reach 300 strikeouts in a season since 2002.

The Dodgers and Brewers set the NL record for most strikeouts in a game with 42 on June 2 in a game that lasted 12 innings. The Brewers tied the major league record with 26. They also had 26 strikeouts in a 2004 game against the Angels, tying the record the Angels established in the aforementioned 1971 game against the Athletics.

One-run strategies continued to decline as the 30 teams combined for 925 sacrifice bunts. That was the fewest since 1900 when eight major league teams combined for 806.

Furthermore, Royals second baseman Whit Merrifield's 34 stolen bases were the fewest to lead the AL since Hall of Famer Luis Aparicio had 31 for the 1961 White Sox. Marlins second baseman Dee Gordon paced the NL and the majors with 60 stolen bases.

The average runs per team per game rose from 4.48 to 4.65 in 2017, the highest mark since 2008.

Stanton led the major leagues with 132 RBIs, and Mariners DH Nelson Cruz was first in the American League with 119.

Kluber led the major leagues in ERA at 2.25, while Kershaw's ERA (2.31) was lowest in the NL for the fifth time in his career and first since 2014.

The Rays' Alex Colome led the major leagues with 47 saves, while the Rockies' Greg Holland and the Dodgers' Kenley Jansen shared the NL lead with 41. Those were the fewest saves for an NL leader since 1999.

Padres righty Luis Perdomo became the first

ALL-ROOKIE TEAM 2017

Pos	PLAYER, TEAM	AGE	AB	AVG	OBP	SLG	2B	HR	RBI	SB	RUNDOWN
C	Manny Pina, Brewers	30	417	.271	.327	.415	27	11	55	2	A defensive stalwart who also delivered at the plate
1B	Cody Bellinger, Dodgers	22	480	.267	.352	.581	26	39	97	10	NL rookie record for HRs, superb athlete at first base
2B	Ian Happ, Cubs	23	364	.253	.328	.514	17	24	68	8	Switch-hitting slugger, can play all over the field defensively
3B	Matt Chapman, Athletics	24	290	.234	.313	.472	23	14	40	0	Elite defense and big power, 39 extra-base hits in 86 games
SS	Paul DeJong, Cardinals	24	417	.285	.325	.532	26	25	65	1	Led team in HRs, .857 OPS third best among MLB shortstops
CF	Manuel Margot, Padres	23	487	.263	.313	.409	18	13	39	17	Sixth-best defensive WAR among MLB outfielders
OF	Aaron Judge, Yankees	25	542	.284	.422	.627	24	52	114	9	Led AL in HRs, walks (127), runs (128) and strikeouts (208)
OF	A. Benintendi, Red Sox	23	573	.271	.352	.424	26	20	90	20	First 20-20 rookie since 2012, 2nd in AL with 11 OF assists
DH	Rhys Hoskins, Phillies	24	170	.259	.396	.618	7	18	48	2	Fastest to hit 10 HRs in MLB history (17 games)

Pos	PITCHER, TEAM	AGE	W	L	SV	ERA	IP	SO	BB	RUNDOWN
SP	Luis Castillo, Reds	24	3	7	0	3.12	89	98	32	Led all rookie starters with 3.12 ERA, fastball sits 96-100
SP	Kyle Freeland, Rockies	24	11	11	0	4.10	156	107	63	Top five among rookies in wins, ERA and innings pitched
SP	German Marquez, Rockies	22	11	7	0	4.39	162	147	49	Led rookie starters with 147 strikeouts, tied for first in wins
SP	J. Montgomery, Yankees	24	9	7	0	3.88	155	144	51	2-0, 2.49 ERA in final five starts, helped Yankees to playoffs
SP	Trevor Williams, Pirates	25	7	9	0	4.07	150	117	52	Started in the bullpen, even better as durable rotation piece
RP	Josh Hader, Brewers	23	2	3	0	2.08	48	68	22	Limited opponents to a .154 average with a 0.99 WHIP

pitcher to hit four triples in a season since Hall of Famer Robin Roberts did so for the 1955 Phillies.

Winning Ways

No team had a run in 2017 quite like the Indians, who set the American League record for longest winning streak by running off 22 in a row from Aug. 24-Sept. 14.

The Indians broke the old mark of 20 by the 2002 Athletics—the team immortalized in the book and film version of "Moneyball"—on Sept. 13 with a 5-3 victory over the Tigers at Progressive Field in Cleveland. The Indians became just the second team in 101 years to have a streak that long, joining the 1935 Cubs.

The Indians, though, fell short of the major league record of 26 held by the 1916 Giants when they lost 4-3 to the visiting Royals on Sept. 15. However, the Indians did become the first team in major league history to have winning streaks of 14 or more games in consecutive seasons.

Not only was the streak historic but the Indians played at a historic pace throughout much of it. With their 11-0 blanking of the Tigers on Sept. 11, the Indians became the first team to have a +100 or better run differential in a 19-game span since the 1939 Yankees. The Indians were also the first team to allow 32 runs or fewer in a 19-game span since the 1916 Giants.

A day after their streak ended, the Indians clinched their second consecutive AL Central title. They finished with the best record in the American League at 102-60 and wound up 17 games ahead of the second-place Twins (85-77).

The Red Sox won their second straight AL East championship, finishing 93-69 and edging the rival Yankees (91-71) by two games.

The Astros (101-61) handily won the AL West by 21 games over the Angels (80-82) for their first division title since 2001 when they were still in the National League and captured the West Division.

The Yankees and Twins won the wild cards. The Twins reached the postseason a year after their 59-103 record was the worst in the major leagues. They became the first team in major league history to lose at least 100 games in one season and then make the playoffs the very next season.

The Dodgers had the best record in the major leagues at 104-58 and won their fifth straight NL West title. Though the Diamondbacks (93-69) and Rockies (87-75) finished 11 and 17 games behind the Dodgers, they won the NL's two wild cards.

The Nationals (97-65) won their second straight NL East title and the Cubs (92-70) made it back-to-back NL Central crowns. The Nationals won by a 20-game margin over the Marlins (77-85) while the Cubs wound up six games ahead of the Brewers (86-76).

It marked the first time since 2003 that there were three teams with at least 100 wins in the same regular season.

Jeter Takes Over The Marlins

Derek Jeter often said late in his legendary career with the Yankees that he would eventually like to run his own franchise.

The former Yankees shortstop received that chance on Oct. 3, the day after the regular season ended, when he was part of a group led by venture capitalist Bruce Sherman that bought the Marlins from Jeffrey Loria for $1.2 billion.

While Jeter's stake was just 4 percent, Sherman put him in charge of the Marlins with the title of chief executive officer. Jeter said he planned to focus more on big-picture ideas while retaining president of baseball operations Michael Hill to oversee day-to-day matters.

The Marlins had their eighth straight losing

season in 2017, the longest in the major leagues.

"I'm not coming in here thinking I know everything about team ownership. I do not," Jeter said. "One thing I'm good at is knowing what I do not know. I surround myself with people who are much smarter than I am.

"We have some wonderful people who are working in this organization now. We are going to add some quality people as well to help us turn this organization around."

Though Jeter lives in Tampa, he said he spends plenty of time in Miami.

"The vast majority of my time will be working for the Marlins," Jeter said. "You have to be present. You have to be involved."

Jeter also had his No. 2 retired by the Yankees on May 14. It was the 21st career number retired by the organization, including the last single-digit one.

Jeter made his debut with the Yankees in 1995 and spent 20 seasons with the franchise, including the last 12 years as team captain. Jeter won five World Series titles with the Yankees, had a lifetime batting average of .310 and his 3,485 hits are the most in franchise history.

"I want to thank my family for their love, support, honesty and more importantly their presence at everything I did both on and off the field," Jeter said during a three-minute speech that ended a 40-minute ceremony prior to the second game of a day-night doubleheader against the Astros. "And the fans—wow—I want to thank you guys for pushing me, for challenging me, making me accountable, more importantly for embracing me since day one."

Five other players also their numbers retired in 2017: Frank Robinson (No. 20, Indians), David Ortiz (No. 34, Red Sox), Mark Buehrle (No. 56, White Sox), Edgar Martinez (No. 11, Mariners) and Ivan Rodriguez (No. 7, Rangers).

Five More In The Hall Of Fame

The Hall of Fame class for 2017 included five men as Jeff Bagwell, Tim Raines and Ivan Rodriguez were immortalized in Cooperstown along with former commissioner Bud Selig and longtime front office executive John Schuerholz.

Bagwell spent his entire 15-year career as a first baseman with the Astros, one of the franchise's famed "Killer B's" along with fellow Hall of Famer Craig Biggio and Lance Berkman. Bagwell ended his career with 449 home runs and from 1996-2001 had at least 30 home runs, 100 runs scored and 100 RBIs each season. Bagwell was only the sixth player in major league history to reach those marks in at least six straight seasons.

"It's always emotional when you see the fans cheering for you, and my whole family in front of me," Bagwell said. "I'm an emotional person. It's a dream just to be part of this beautiful group. Now I have that plaque forever. It's unbelievable."

Raines, a switch-hitting outfielder, batted .294 and had a .385 on-base percentage in his 23-year career, finishing with 2,605 hits, 1,571 runs and 808 stolen bases. His stolen base total is the fifth-highest in major league history and included 70 or more steals in each season from 1981-86, a streak that stands alone in baseball history. And his 84.7 percent success rate tops the list among players with at least 400 steal attempts.

Raines began his career with the Expos from 1979-90. He also played for the White Sox, Yankees, Athletics, Orioles and Marlins in a career that spanned 23 seasons and ended in 2002.

Raines fought cocaine problems early in his career and said there was "no telling where I'd be," without former Expos teammate and Hall of Famer Andre Dawson.

"Thank you so much for making me the player I became," Raines said.

Rodriguez holds major league records for games caught (2,427) and putouts by a catcher (12,376). He hit 311 homers and batted .296 in his career. He's also only the second catcher elected on the first ballot, following in the footsteps of his childhood idol and former Reds star Johnny Bench.

A winner of 13 Gold Gloves in his 21-year career, Rodriguez spent his first 12 seasons with the Rangers from 1991-2002 before stops with the Tigers, Yankees, Astros and Nationals.

"This is such an incredible honor for me," Rodriguez said. "A little kid from Puerto Rico with a big dream. Never let them take your dream away from you."

Induction day was a special 83rd birthday for Selig, who served as commissioner for 22 years. During his time, he was instrumental in the approval of interleague play, the expansion of the postseason, splitting each league into three divisions with wild cards, instituting video review and revenue-sharing in an era that saw the construction of 20 new ballparks.

His tenure also included the Steroids Era and the cancellation of the 1994 World Series amid a players' strike.

Schuerholz was a general manager for 26 years with the Royals (1981-90) then the Braves (1990-2007). His teams won 16 division titles, six pennants and two World Series, one in each league, which was a first for a general manager.

Bagwell, in his seventh year on the ballot, received 86.2 percent of 442 votes from the

Baseball Writers Association of America, up from the 71.6 percent he received in 2016. Raines, in his 10th and final year on the ballot, received 86 percent of the votes, up from the 69.8 percent he received in 2016. Rodriguez received 76 percent of the vote in his first year on the ballot.

There were also a couple of Hall of Fame near-misses in 2017, as second-year candidate Trevor Hoffman just missed the 75-percent threshold for election by receiving 74.0 percent of the vote and Vladimir Guerrero had 71.1 percent of the vote.

Cain And Others Call It Quits

Matt Cain, dogged by injuries in recent season, decided to retire at the end of the season and he went out in the style.

The Giants righthander pitched five scoreless innings against the Padres on Oct. 1, the penultimate day of the season. Although the Giants wound up losing the game, Cain received a long ovation from the crowd at AT&T Park in San Francisco the day before his 33rd birthday.

"It was definitely an emotional roller-coaster as you walk out onto the field and take the bullpen mound," Cain said. "The first couple of innings were all adrenaline, the last three were just on the guys and the fans, the fans just willing me along."

Cain finished the season with a 3-11, 5.43 record in 27 games. He spent his entire 13-year career with the Giants and was 104-118, 3.68. Cain starred on World Series-winning teams in 2010 and 2012, threw a perfect game in 2012 and was a three-time All-Star before being beset by injured over his final five seasons.

Reds righthander Bronson Arroyo also retired following an injury-plagued season that saw him compile a 3-6, 7.35 record in 14 starts after missing the previous two seasons because of elbow and shoulder injuries. Arroyo pitched in the majors for 16 seasons, compiling a 148-137, 4.28 record.

Padres righthander Jered Weaver retired midway through his 12th season after going 0-5 with a 7.44 ERA in nine starts. Weaver spent his first 11 years with the Angels and concluded his career with a 150-98 record and 3.63 ERA. He was selected to three straight All-Star Games from 2010-12.

Another veteran righty, Jeremy Guthrie, also retired. He lost his lone start for the Nationals in 2017 and had a 91-109, 4.42 record in 13 seasons. Meanwhile, Joe Nathan was unable to crack the Nationals' Opening Day roster and the six-time all-star closer retired with 377 saves in a 16-year career.

Also announced their retirements were Brennan Boesch, Jed Bradley, Cory Luebke, Jeff Francoeur, Nolan Reimold, Joe Beimel, Paul Janish, Will Venable and Ryan Vogelsong.

AMERICAN LEAGUE BEST TOOLS

A Baseball America survey of American League managers, conducted at midseason 2017, ranked players with the best tools.

BEST HITTER
1. Mike Trout, Angels
2. Jose Altuve, Astros
3. Miguel Cabrera, Tigers

BEST POWER
1. Aaron Judge, Yankees
2. Joey Gallo, Rangers
3. Miguel Sano, Twins

BEST BUNTER
1. Jarrod Dyson, Mariners
2. Elvis Andrus, Rangers
3. Delino DeShields Jr., Rangers

BEST STRIKE-ZONE JUDGMENT
1. Joe Mauer, Twins
2. Miguel Cabrera, Tigers
3. Mookie Betts, Red Sox

BEST HIT-AND-RUN ARTIST
1. Jose Altuve, Astros
2. Elvis Andrus, Rangers
3. Xander Bogaerts, Red Sox

BEST BASERUNNER
1. Mookie Betts, Red Sox
2. Jarrod Dyson, Mariners
3. Mike Trout, Angels

FASTEST BASERUNNER
1. Byron Buxton, Twins
2. Jarrod Dyson, Mariners
3. Delino DeShields Jr., Rangers

MOST EXCITING PLAYER
1. Mike Trout, Angels
2. Aaron Judge, Yankees
3. Mookie Betts, Red Sox

BEST PITCHER
1. Chris Sale, White Sox
2. Corey Kluber, Indians
3. Dallas Keuchel, Astros

BEST FASTBALL
1. Aroldis Chapman, Yankees
2. Chris Sale, Red Sox
3. Craig Kimbrel, Red Sox

BEST CURVEBALL
1. Lance McCullers Jr., Astros
2. Dellin Betances, Yankees
3. Craig Kimbrel, Red Sox

BEST SLIDER
1. Chris Sale, Red Sox
2. Chris Archer, Rays
3. Corey Kluber, Indians

BEST CHANGEUP
1. Marco Estrada, Blue Jays
2. Dallas Keuchel, Astros
3. Chris Sale, Red Sox

BEST CONTROL
1. Josh Tomlin, Indians
2. Chris Sale, Red Sox
3. Dallas Keuchel, Astros

BEST PICKOFF MOVE
1. Alex Cobb, Rays
2. Wade Miley, Orioles
3. James Shields, White Sox

BEST RELIEVER
1. Craig Kimbrel, Red Sox
2. Andrew Miller, Indians
3. Dellin Betances, Yankees

BEST DEFENSIVE CATCHER
1. Salvador Perez, Royals
2. Martin Maldonado, Angels
3. Christian Vasquez, Red Sox

BEST DEFENSIVE 1B
1. Eric Hosmer, Royals
2. Mitch Moreland, Rangers
3. Logan Morrison, Rays

BEST DEFENSIVE 2B
1. Ian Kinsler, Tigers
2. Jose Altuve, Astros
3. Dustin Pedroia, Red Sox

BEST DEFENSIVE 3B
1. Manny Machado, Orioles
2. Adrian Beltre, Rangers
3. Evan Longoria, Rays

BEST DEFENSIVE SS
1. Andrelton Simmons, Angels
2. Francisco Lindor, Indians
3. Didi Gregorius, Yankees

BEST INFIELD ARM
1. Manny Machado, Orioles
2. Andrelton Simmons, Angels
3. Miguel Sano, Twins

BEST DEFENSIVE OF
1. Kevin Kiermaier, Rays
2. Jackie Bradley, Red Sox
3. Byron Buxton, Twins

BEST OUTFIELD ARM
1. Aaron Hicks, Yankees
2. Kevin Kiermaier, Rays
3. Alex Gordon, Royals

BEST MANAGER
1. Terry Francona, Indians
2. Joe Girardi, Yankees
3. Kevin Cash, Rays

Going Global

A record 29.8 percent of major league players

CONTINUED ON PAGE 19

ORGANIZATION OF THE YEAR

Dodgers Build Team To Last

BY KYLE GLASER

The Dodgers had won back-to-back National League West titles when they blew up their management structure after the 2014 season. Andrew Friedman and Farhan Zaidi were hired that fall and entered into a winning organization as the Dodgers' president of baseball operations and general manager, respectively.

A winning organization wasn't enough for a team with the highest payroll in baseball For Friedman, Zaidi, vice president of baseball operations Josh Byrnes and everyone else brought in, the charge was to make the Dodgers a championship organization.

After three years of tinkering and adjusting, they did just that.

The Dodgers won 104 games in 2017, their most victories since relocating from Brooklyn to Los Angeles. They cruised through the National League playoffs with an 8-1 record and made it to the World Series for the first time in 29 years, ultimately falling to the Astros in seven games.

It was a championship-worthy year made possible through shrewd drafts, astute trades, savvy free-agent signings and successful player development going back across two regimes. For that, the Dodgers are the 2017 Baseball America Organization of the Year.

The previous regime under general manager Ned Colletti and scouting director Logan White set the table. The drafting of Clayton Kershaw, Corey Seager, Cody Bellinger and Joc Pederson happened under them. So did the free agent signing of Justin Turner and international signings of Kenley Jansen, Yasiel Puig and Hyun Jin-Ryu.

PREVIOUS WINNERS

2007: Colorado Rockies
2008: Tampa Bay Rays
2009: Philadelphia Phillies
2010: San Francisco Giants
2011: St. Louis Cardinals
2012: Cincinnati Reds
2013: St. Louis Cardinals
2014: Kansas City Royals
2015: Pittsburgh Pirates
2016: Chicago Cubs
Full list: BaseballAmerica.com/awards

CHRISTIAN PETERSEN/GETTY IMAGES

Farhan Zaidi and the Dodgers front office made a number of astute trades.

But ineffective bullpens, trades for expensive and underperforming veterans and shorthanded starting rotations prevented the club from taking the next step and seriously contending for a World Series, which led to a change in leadership.

With many key cornerstones already in place, Friedman, Zaidi and Co. filled in the gaps with an array of successful moves.

They acquired Kike Hernandez and Austin Barnes in their first major trade just two months into the job. They traded for Alex Wood and signed Kenta Maeda within a year of taking over, elongating the rotation considerably. They took a weak spot, catcher, and make it a strength by acquiring Yasmani Grandal and unloading Matt Kemp's albatross contract while they were at it. A year later they acquired Rich Hill and Chris Taylor in lopsided trades. And at the 2017 trade deadline, knowing they were close, they brought in Yu Darvish, Tony Cingrani and Tony Watson. In all, 16 of the 25 players on the Dodgers' World Series roster were brought in under the Friedman-Zaidi management team.

What was once a winning organization became a championship-caliber one.

CONTINUED FROM PAGE 17

at the start of the season were born outside the 50 states, topping the previous high of 29.2 percent in 2005.

The Dominican Republic led with 93 players, followed by Venezuela (77) and Cuba (23), according to Major League Baseball. Venezuela topped its previous high of 66 in 2012 and Cuba matched its most, set in 2016.

Puerto Rico was fourth at 16, followed by Mexico (nine), Japan (eight), Canada (six), South Korea, Curacao and Nicaragua (four each), Panama (three), and Australia, Brazil and Colombia (two apiece). Aruba, Germany, Netherlands, Taiwan and the U.S. Virgin Islands had one each player representative in the majors in 2017.

The 19 nations and territories are records, topping 18 in 1998 and 2016.

On April 26, Pirates infielder Gift Ngoepe became the first African to reach the major leagues, singling in his first plate appearance in a 6-5 victory over the Cubs.

Ngoepe was recalled from Triple-A Indianapolis and entered the game in fourth inning as part of a double switch and finished 1-for-2 with a walk. The 27-year-old South African, who signed with the Pirates in 2008 as an amateur free agent, led off the fourth with a hit off Jon Lester.

"To accomplish this not only for me but for my country and my continent is something so special," Ngoepe said. "There are 1.62 billion people on our continent. To be the first person out of 1.62 billion to do this is amazing."

Ngoepe played in 28 games with the Pirates, hitting .222, before being optioned back to Indianapolis.

Rule Changes

In March, Major League Baseball and the Major League Baseball Players Association agreed to seven rule changes, most of which were designed to cut the average time of game and improve pace of play:

■ A no-pitch intentional walk, allowing the defensive team's manager to signal a decision to home plate without pitches being thrown. Following the signal, the umpire immediately awards first base to the batter.

■ A 30-second limit for a manager to decide whether to challenge a play and invoke video replay review. When a manager has exhausted his challenges for the game, umpiring crew chiefs may now invoke replay review for non-home run calls beginning in the eighth inning instead of the seventh inning.

■ A conditional two-minute guideline for replay officials to render a decision on review, allowing various exceptions.

■ A prohibition of the use of any markers on the field that could create a reference system for

CONTINUED ON PAGE 21

NATIONAL LEAGUE BEST TOOLS

A Baseball America survey of National League managers, conducted at midseason 2017, ranked players with the best tools.

BEST HITTER
1. Joey Votto, Reds
2. Paul Goldschmidt, D-backs
3. Daniel Murphy, Nationals

BEST POWER
1. Giancarlo Stanton, Marlins
2. Bryce Harper, Nationals
3. Cody Bellinger, Dodgers

BEST BUNTER
1. Dee Gordon, Marlins
2. Ender Inciarte, Braves
3. Cesar Hernandez, Phillies

BEST STRIKE-ZONE JUDGMENT
1. Joey Votto, Reds
2. Paul Goldschmidt, D-backs
3. Buster Posey, Giants

BEST HIT-AND-RUN ARTIST
1. Martin Prado, Marlins
2. D.J. LeMahieu, Rockies
3. Daniel Murphy, Nationals

BEST BASERUNNER
1. Billy Hamilton, Reds
2. Trea Turner, Nationals
3. Paul Goldschmidt, D-backs

FASTEST BASERUNNER
1. Billy Hamilton, Reds
2. Trea Turner, Nationals
3. Dee Gordon, Marlins

MOST EXCITING PLAYER
1. Bryce Harper, Nationals
2. Nolan Arenado, Rockies
3. Kris Bryant, Cubs

BEST PITCHER
1. Clayton Kershaw, Dodgers
2. Max Scherzer, Nationals
3. Zack Greinke, D-backs

BEST FASTBALL
1. Carlos Martinez, Cardinals
2. Noah Syndergaard, Mets
3. Max Scherzer, Nationals

BEST CURVEBALL
1. Clayton Kershaw, Dodgers
2. Stephen Strasburg, Nationals
3. Gio Gonzalez, Nationals

BEST SLIDER
1. Max Scherzer, Nationals
2. Clayton Kershaw, Dodgers
3. Noah Syndergaard, Mets

BEST CHANGEUP
1. Zack Greinke, Diamondbacks
2. Max Scherzer, Nationals
3. Kyle Hendricks, Cubs

BEST CONTROL
1. Clayton Kershaw, Dodgers
2. Zack Greinke, Diamondbacks
3. Kenley Jansen, Dodgers

BEST PICKOFF MOVE
1. Julio Teheran, Braves
2. Johnny Cueto, Giants
3. Clayton Richard, Padres

BEST RELIEVER
1. Kenley Jansen, Dodgers
2. Greg Holland, Rockies
3. Wade Davis, Cubs

BEST DEFENSIVE CATCHER
1. Buster Posey, Giants
2. Yadier Molina, Cardinals
3. Yasmani Grandal, Dodgers

BEST DEFENSIVE 1B
1. Paul Goldschmidt, D-backs
2. Anthony Rizzo, Cubs
3. Brandon Belt, Giants

BEST DEFENSIVE 2B
1. D.J. LeMahieu, Rockies
2. Cesar Hernandez, Phillies
3. Javier Baez, Cubs

BEST DEFENSIVE 3B
1. Nolan Arenado, Rockies
2. Anthony Rendon, Nationals
3. Justin Turner, Dodgers

BEST DEFENSIVE SS
1. Brandon Crawford, Giants
2. Nick Ahmed, D-backs
3. Addison Russell, Cubs

BEST INFIELD ARM
1. Nolan Arenado, Rockies
2. Brandon Crawford, Giants
3. Orlando Arcia, Brewers

BEST DEFENSIVE OF
1. Ender Inciarte, Braves
2. Jason Heyward, Cubs
3. Billy Hamilton, Reds

BEST OUTFIELD ARM
1. Yoenis Cespedes, Mets
2. Hunter Renfroe, Padres
3. Yasiel Puig, Dodgers

BEST MANAGER
1. Dave Roberts, Dodgers
2. Joe Maddon, Cubs
3. Craig Counsell, Brewers

MAJOR LEAGUE ALL-STARS

SELECTED BY BASEBALL AMERICA

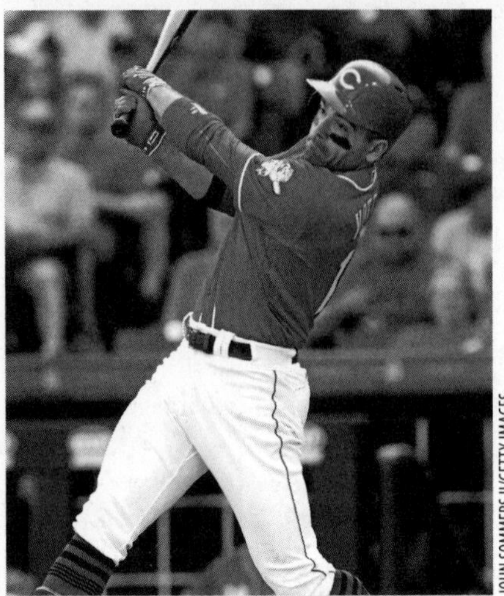

JOHN SOMMERS II/GETTY IMAGES

Joey Votto posted an MLB-best .454 on-base percentage in 2017.

MADDIE MEYER/GETTY IMAGES

Craig Kimbrel struck out 126 batters in only 69 innings.

FIRST TEAM

Pos	Player, Team	AVG	OBP	SLG	AB	R	H	2B	3B	HR	RBI	BB	SO	SB	CS
C	Buster Posey, Giants	.320	.400	462	494	62	158	34	0	12	67	61	66	6	1
1B	Joey Votto, Reds	.320	.454	.578	559	106	179	34	1	36	100	134	83	5	1
2B	Jose Altuve, Astros	.346	.410	.547	590	112	204	39	4	24	81	61	84	32	6
3B	Nolan Arenando, Rockies	.309	.373	.586	606	100	187	43	7	37	130	62	106	3	2
SS	Francisco Lindor, Indians	.273	.337	.505	651	99	178	44	4	33	89	60	93	15	3
CF	Mike Trout, Angels	.306	.442	.629	402	92	123	25	3	33	72	94	90	22	4
OF	Aaron Judge, Yankees	.284	.422	.627	542	128	154	24	3	52	114	127	208	9	4
OF	Giancarlo Stanton, Marlins	.281	.376	.631	597	122	168	32	0	59	132	85	163	2	2
DH	Jose Ramirez, Indians	.318	.374	.583	585	107	186	56	6	29	83	52	69	17	5

Pos	Player, Team	W	L	ERA	G	GS	SV	IP	H	R	ER	HR	BB	SO	WHIP
SP	Clayton Kershaw, Dodgers	18	4	2.31	27	27	0	175	136	49	45	23	30	202	0.95
SP	Corey Kluber, Indians	18	4	2.25	29	29	0	204	141	56	51	21	36	265	0.87
SP	Chris Sale, Red Sox	17	8	2.90	32	32	0	214	165	73	69	24	43	308	0.97
SP	Max Scherzer, Nationals	16	6	2.51	31	31	0	201	126	62	56	22	55	268	0.90
RP	Kenley Jansen, Dodgers	5	0	1.32	65	0	41	68	44	11	10	5	7	109	0.75
RP	Craig Kimbrel, Red Sox	5	0	1.43	67	0	35	69	33	11	11	6	14	126	0.68

SECOND TEAM

Pos	Player, Team	AVG	OBP	SLG	AB	R	H	2B	3B	HR	RBI	BB	SO	SB	CS
C	Gary Sanchez, Yankees	.278	.345	.531	471	79	131	20	0	33	90	40	120	2	1
1B	Paul Goldschmidt, Diamondbacks	.297	.404	.563	558	117	166	34	3	36	120	94	147	18	5
2B	Daniel Murphy, Nationals	.322	.384	.543	534	94	172	43	3	23	93	52	77	2	0
3B	Anthony Rendon, Nationals	.301	.403	.533	508	81	153	41	1	25	100	84	82	7	2
SS	Corey Seager, Dodgers	.295	.375	.479	539	85	159	33	0	22	77	67	131	4	2
CF	Charlie Blackmon, Rockies	.331	.399	.601	644	137	213	35	14	37	104	65	135	14	10
OF	J.D. Martinez, Tigers/Diamondbacks	.303	.376	.690	432	85	131	26	3	45	104	53	128	4	0
OF	Tommy Pham, Cardinals	.306	.411	.520	444	95	136	22	2	23	73	71	117	25	7
DH	Kris Bryant, Cubs	.295	.409	.537	549	111	162	38	4	29	73	95	128	7	5

Pos	Player, Team	W	L	ERA	G	GS	SV	IP	H	R	ER	HR	BB	SO	WHIP
SP	Stephen Strasburg, Nationals	15	4	2.52	28	28	0	175	131	55	49	13	47	204	1.02
SP	Justin Verlander, Tigers/Astros	15	8	3.36	33	33	0	206	170	80	77	27	72	219	1.18
SP	Luis Severino, Yankees	14	6	2.98	31	31	0	193	150	73	64	21	51	230	1.04
SP	Robbie Ray, Diamondbacks	15	5	2.89	28	28	0	162	116	57	52	23	71	218	1.15
SP	Gio Gonzalez, Nationals	15	9	2.96	32	32	0	201	158	69	66	21	79	188	1.18
RP	Corey Knebel, Brewers	1	4	1.78	48	0	39	76	48	15	15	6	40	126	1.16

EXECUTIVE OF THE YEAR

Brian Cashman

The temptation in New York is always to find the quick fix. The Yankees are not a team that embarks on long rebuilds. But as the team's veteran core aged, Brian Cashman and the front office didn't try to paper over the growing faults by trading away prospects. The result was four consecutive seasons where the Yankees failed to win 90 games. New York still managed to post a winning record in all four of those seasons, but that slight dip allowed the team to reload with the best young core the team has had in years. Homegrown stars Gary Sanchez, Aaron Judge and Luis Severino led New York to 91 wins in 2017 and a spot in the American League Championship Series. With one of the deepest farm systems in the game, the Yankees look poised to be a playoff contender for years to come.

PREVIOUS WINNERS

2007: Jack Zduriencik, Brewers
2008: Theo Epstein, Red Sox
2009: Dan O'Dowd, Rockies
2010: Jon Daniels, Rangers
2011: Doug Melvin, Brewers
2012: Billy Beane, Athletics
2013: Dan Duquette, Orioles
2014: Dan Duquette, Orioles
2015: Sandy Alderson, Mets
2016: Chris Antonetti, Indians
Full list: BaseballAmerica.com/awards

MANAGER OF THE YEAR

A.J. Hinch

A wide range of experiences prepared A.J. Hinch for this moment. After seven seasons playing in the majors, four years as a farm director with the Diamondbacks, three years as a pro scouting director with the Padres, and two years as a manager with the D'backs, Hinch saw the game through just about every lens. He took everything he learned with him to Houstion, and pressed all the right buttons to guide the Astros to their first World Series championship. "The goal was always to have a full understanding of how the organization operates, Hinch said. "I think more than anything I have an appreciation of what it takes to get here. To be able to tie it all together at this level and have appreciation for the people that helped us get here...it's part of my story, my journey."

PREVIOUS WINNERS

2007: Terry Francona, Red Sox
2008: Ron Gardenhire, Twins
2009: Mike Scioscia, Angels
2010: Bobby Cox, Braves
2011: Joe Maddon, Rays
2012: Buck Showalter, Orioles
2013: Clint Hurdle, Pirates
2014: Buck Showalter, Orioles
2015: Joe Maddon, Cubs
2016: Terry Francona, Indians
Full list: BaseballAmerica.com/awards

CONTINUED FROM PAGE 19

fielders.

■ An addition to Rule 5.07 formalizing an umpire interpretation by stipulating that a pitcher may not take a second step toward home plate with either foot or otherwise reset his pivot foot in his delivery of the pitch. If there is at least one runner on base, then such an action is called a balk under Rule 6.02(a). If the bases are unoccupied, it is considered an illegal pitch under Rule 6.02(b).

■ An amendment to Rule 5.03 that requires base coaches to position themselves behind the line of the coach's box closest to home plate and the front line that runs parallel to the foul line prior to each pitch. Once a ball is put in play, a base coach is allowed to leave the box to signal a player so long as the coach does not interfere with the play.

Despite the rule changes, the average time of a nine-inning game rose 4½ minutes this season to a record three hours, five minutes, 11 seconds. The average had dropped to 2:56 in 2015.

The 2017 season also marked the first year of the 10-day disabled list and use of the shortest DL increased by 21 percent from 2016.

There were 626 uses of the 10-day DL, up from 512 placements on the 15-day DL the previous season. Some clubs used the 10-day DL to add players around the time of the four-day All-Star break by disabling starting pitchers after their outings.

"I think the concept of a 10-day DL was a good one," Manfred said. "It gave clubs additional flexibility to deal with injuries. Unfortunately, and we saw some of this right around the All-Star break, any new rule, our guys figure out a way to manage to it."

A Brave New Stadium

The Braves moved from downtown Atlanta to the city's suburbs for the 2017 season and beyond, opening SunTrust Park on April 14 with a 5-2 victory over the Padres before a sellout crowd of 41,149 in the Cobb County city of Cumberland.

Braves center fielder Ender Inciarte hit the facility's first home run, a two-run, sixth-inning shot down the right-field line against Padres right-hander Craig Stammen. He also recorded the first out, had the first hit and scored the first run.

"It was a special night for me and for a lot of people," Inciarte said. "We were really pumped in the dugout. If the fans give us that every day, we'll do a lot of good things in this ballpark."

The Braves wound up a 37-44 home record on their way to a 72-90 season. The season attendance was 2,505,252, the franchise's highest total since their last playoff season in 2013 when they won the National League East.

Among those on hand for opening night were former President Jimmy Carter and Commissioner Rob Manfred, Hall of Fame pitchers Tom Glavine, Greg Maddux and John Smoltz as well as Braves legends Chipper Jones and Dale Murphy.

Two other Braves' legends and Hall of Famers formed a battery for the ceremonial first pitch with one-time home run king Hank Aaron pitching to Bobby Cox.

"Sometimes you take for granted what this organization has," Braves first baseman Freddie Freeman said. "To see everybody come back, you just kind of step back and realize what kind of organization you are a part of."

The first season in at SunTrust Park ended on a sour note, though, as general manager John Coppolella was forced to resign after an investigation by Major League Baseball revealed serious rules violations in the international player market.

Manager Madness

Each of the 30 managers made it through the entire season but there was plenty of turnover once it ended.

The Tigers announced in the next-to-last week of the season that Brad Ausmus' contract would not be renewed for 2018. With two days remaining in the season, the Phillies decided to shift Pete Mackanin to a front-office advisory role. The Mets' Terry Collins announced he was retiring the morning of his team's regular-season finale.

ELSA/GETTY IMAGES

Joe Girardi's 10 years with the Yankees ended after an ALCS loss.

Collins stepped away just two years after leading the Mets to a berth in the World Series. He compiled a 551-583 record in seven seasons and Mets finished 70-92 in an injury-plagued 2017.

The Tigers were 314-332 under Ausmus, including a major league-worst 64-98 in 2017. The Phillies finished the 2017 season with a 66-96 record and went 174-238 in Mackanin's three years on the job.

Three managers were fired after their teams lost in the postseason: The Red Sox's John Farrell, the Nationals' Dusty Baker and the Yankees' Joe Girardi.

The Red Sox fell in an American League Division Series for the second straight year, falling in four games to the eventual World Series champion Astros. In five seasons at the helm, Farrell had a 432-378 record and guided the Red Sox to a World Series title in his first year on the job in 2013.

The Nationals lost in five games to the Cubs in an National League Division Series, failing once again to win a postseason series since the franchise relocated to Washington from Montreal in 2005. Baker led the Nationals to NL East titles in each of his two seasons while compiling a 192-132 record.

CONTINUED ON PAGE 24

Cano Powers AL To 2-1 Win

BY J.J. COOPER

MIAMI

It no longer counted, per se, but the 2017 All-Star Game proved that home-field advantage wasn't needed to provide drama

The game, played in Miami, was the first midsummer classic to be played since Major League Baseball removed home-field advantage as an all-star incentive.

But the lack of any postseason stakes didn't seem to matter in a well-played game that saw wave after wave of power pitchers overmatch the game's best hitters for nine innings.

Carlos Martinez struck out four of the seven batters he faced to post the most dominant line, but there were few pitchers who didn't have their way.

The American League finally broke the scoreless tie when Jonathan Schoop doubled off Alex Wood in the fifth and Miguel Sano followed with an RBI single.

The National League tied the game back up an inning later when Yadier Molina homered off of Ervin Santana.

The game remained deadlocked 1-1 until extra innings.

Robinson Cano led off the 10th inning with a home run to right field off of Wade Davis.

Reliever Andrew Miller ensured that the one-run lead stood up as he danced around a Joey Votto walk by striking out Cody Bellinger to end the game.

Cano was named the game's MVP thanks to his home run. A pair of third basemen, Jose Ramirez and Nolan Arenado, and first baseman Yonder Alonso were the only batters to have two hits.

The game's signature moment may have occurred in the sixth inning. Coming to the plate, Mariners outfielder Nelson Cruz whipped out his phone and handed it to Molina, who took a photo of Cruz with home-plate umpire Joe West. Cruz then put the phone back in his back pocket and stepped into the batter's box.

The American League win evened the all-time series. The all-star slate is now 43-43-2 all-time.

ALL-STAR GAME

MIKE EHRMANN/GETTY IMAGES

Robinson Cano's extra-inning home run proved the difference for the AL.

2017 ALL-STAR GAME

JULY 11, 2017
AMERICAN LEAGUE 2, NATIONAL LEAGUE 1

American	AB	R	H	RBI	National	AB	R	H	RBI
Altuve, 2B	2	0	0	0	Blackmon, CF	3	0	0	0
Schoop, J, 2B	1	1	1	0	Inciarte, CF	2	0	0	0
Cano, PH-2B	2	1	1	1	Stanton, DH	3	0	0	0
Ramirez, Js, 3B	2	0	2	0	Votto, PH-DH	1	0	0	0
Sano, 3B	1	0	1	1	Harper, RF	1	0	1	0
Moustakas, 3B	2	0	0	0	Bellinger, RF	3	0	0	0
Judge, RF	3	0	0	0	Posey, C	1	0	0	0
Upton, J, RF	2	0	1	0	Molina, C	1	1	1	1
Springer, LF	3	0	0	0	Murphy, 2B	2	0	1	0
Brantley, LF	2	0	1	0	Harrison, 2B	2	0	0	0
Correa, SS	2	0	0	0	Arenado, 3B	2	0	2	0
Lindor, SS	2	0	0	0	Turner, 3B	2	0	0	0
Smoak, 1B	1	0	1	0	Lamb, J, 1B	1	0	0	0
Alonso, 1B	2	0	2	0	Zimmerman, 1B	2	0	0	0
Dickerson, C, DH	2	0	0	0	Goldschmidt, 1B	2	0	0	0
Cruz, PH-DH	2	0	0	0	Ozuna, LF	2	0	0	0
Perez, S, C	2	0	0	0	Conforto, LF	2	0	1	0
Sanchez, G, C	2	0	0	0	Cozart, SS	2	0	1	0
Betts, CF	2	0	0	0	Seager, C, SS	2	0	0	0
Garcia, A, CF	2	0	0	0					
Totals	**39**	**2**	**10**	**2**	**Totals**	**34**	**1**	**7**	**1**

2B: Schoop, J, (1, Wood, A). **HR:** Cano (1, 10th inning off Davis, W, 0 on, 0 out); Molina (1, 6th inning off Santana, 0 on, 1 out). **RBI:** Sano (1); Cano (1); Molina (1). **TB:** Schoop, J 2; Ramirez, Js 2; Cano 4; Smoak; Brantley; Upton, J; Alonso 2; Sano; Molina 4; Cozart; Harper; Murphy; Arenado 2; Conforto.

American	IP	H	R	SO	National	IP	H	R	SO
Sale	2.0	3	0	2	Scherzer	1.0	1	0	2
Betances	1.0	1	0	2	Neshek	1.0	1	0	0
Vargas, J	1.0	1	0	0	Martinez, C	2.0	1	0	4
Kintzler	1.0	0	0	0	Wood, A	1.0	2	1	0
Santana, E	1.0	1	1	1	Greinke	1.0	1	0	1
Osuna	1.0	1	0	0	Hand	1.0	0	0	1
Devenski	1.0	0	0	1	Holland, G	1.0	1	0	2
Kimbrel (W)	1.0	0	0	2	Jansen	1.0	1	0	3
Miller (S, 1)	1.0	0	0	1	Davis, W (L)	1.0	2	1	1

CONTINUED FROM PAGE 22

Girardi's 10-year stint with the Yankees ended with a seven-game loss to the Astros in the American League Championship Series. He had a 910-710 record and guided the Yankees to a World Series title in 2009.

Little League Goes Big

The inaugural Little League Classic was held on Aug. 20 when the Pirates played the Cardinals in Williamsport, Pa., which coincided with the Little League World Series in the same city.

Pirates rookie first baseman Josh Bell homered and drove in four runs to lead the Pirates to a 6-3 victory at renovated Bowman Field, a 91-year-old minor league ballpark located five miles from where the LLWS is held in Lamade Stadium. There was no public sale of tickets and only participants in the LLWS and Little League players from the nearby area attended as 2,596 crowded into the 2,366-seat venue.

After the final out of the first major league game in Williamsport, the Pirates shook hands on the field as usual following a victory. Then, in a nod to Little League, both teams lined up at home plate and shook hands with each other, throwing in some hugs and high-fives to finish off a day that began with players from both side attending LLWS games and participating in clinics.

"It was refreshing every once in a while to be able to look in the stands and see the kids watching the game," Pirates manager Clint Hurdle said. "It was one of the highlights of my career."

The event proved to be so popular that MLB plans to make it an annual event. The Mets and Phillies will face each other 2018.

"I think there's a relationship here with Little League that is really important to growing the game," Commissioner Rob Manfred said.

ALEX TRAUTWIG/GETTY IMAGES

The Little League Classic proved a hit for Matt Carpenter and everyone involved.

The Little League Classic turned out not to be the only unique game on the schedule as hurricanes forced the Astros, Rays and Marlins to move home games.

As a consequence of Hurricane Harvey damaging the Houston area, the three-game Lone Star Series between the Rangers and Astros from Aug. 29-31 was moved from Minute Maid Park to Tropicana Field in St. Petersburg, Fla.

The Rays' three-game series with the Yankees from Sept. 11-13 was moved from Tropicana Field to the Mets' Citi Field in New York because of Hurricane Irma's impending landfall on the Tampa Bay area.

Irma's damage to South Florida forced the Marlins' three-game set with the Brewers from Sept. 15-17 to move from Marlins Park in Miami and the Brewers' Miller Park in Milwaukee.

Prior to 2017, major league games had been relocated because of weather.

The Astros were involved as well in 2008, when two scheduled home games against the Cubs were moved to Miller Park because of Hurricane Ike. Three games between the Angels and Indians were played at Miller Park instead of Cleveland in 2007 because of snow. Two games between the Expos and Marlins were moved from Miami to what was then known as U.S. Cellular Field in Chicago in 2004 due to Hurricane Ivan.

ACTIVE LEADERS

Career leaders among players who played in a game in 2017. Batters require 3,000 plate appearances and pitchers 1,000 innings to qualify for percentage titles.

BATTERS			PITCHERS		
AVG	Miguel Cabrera	.317	ERA	Clayton Kershaw	2.36
OBP	Joey Votto	.428	SO/9	Chris Sale	10.55
SLG	Mike Trout	.566	BB/9	J. Zimmermann	1.93
OPS	Mike Trout	.976	HR/9	Clayton Kershaw	0.60
R	Albert Pujols	1,723	W	Bartolo Colon	240
H	Ichiro Suzuki	3,080	L	Bartolo Colon	176
2B	Albert Pujols	619	SV	F. Rodriguez	437
3B	Jose Reyes	128	IP	CC Sabathia	3,317
HR	Albert Pujols	614	SO	CC Sabathia	2,846
RBI	Albert Pujols	1,918	BB	CC Sabathia	1,009
BB	Albert Pujols	1,251	AVG	Clayton Kershaw	.206
SO	Ryan Howard	1,843	G	F. Rodriguez	948
XBH	Albert Pujols	1,249	GS	Bartolo Colon	528
SB	Jose Reyes	512	HR	Bartolo Colon	407

MAJOR LEAGUE DEBUTS

ARIZONA DIAMONDBACKS

Ildemaro Vargas	June 29
Anthony Banda	July 22
Jack Reinheimer	Aug. 1
Jimmie Sherfy	Aug. 20

ATLANTA BRAVES

Johan Camargo	April 11
Sean Newcomb	June 10
Ozzie Albies	Aug. 1
Lucas Sims	Aug. 1
Max Fried	Aug. 8
A.J. Minter	Aug. 23
David Freitas	Aug. 30
Luiz Gohara	Sept. 6

BALTIMORE ORIOLES

Stefan Crichton	April 16
Jimmy Yacabonis	June 11
David Washington	June 14
Anthony Santander	Aug. 18
Chance Sisco	Sept. 2
Richard Rodriguez	Sept. 2
Austin Hays	Sept. 7
Tanner Scott	Sept. 20

BOSTON RED SOX

Justin Haley	April 5
Ben Taylor	April 7
Hector Velazquez	May 18
Sam Travis	May 24
Austin Maddox	June 17
Tzu-Wei Lin	June 24
Kyle Martin	July 20
Rafael Devers	July 25

CHICAGO CUBS

Ian Happ	May 13
Mark Zagunis	June 22
Victor Caratini	June 28
Luke Farrell	July 1
Dillon Maples	Sept. 3
Taylor Davis	Sept. 8
Jen-Ho Tseng	Sept. 14

CHICAGO WHITE SOX

Jacob May	April 4
Dylan Covey	April 14
Willy Garcia	April 14
Adam Engel	May 27
Brad Goldberg	June 3
Aaron Bummer	July 27
Nicky Delmonico	August 1
Jace Fry	Sept. 5

CINCINNATI REDS

Barrett Astin	April 3
Rookie Davis	April 6
Stuart Turner	April 6
Amir Garrett	April 7
Jesse Winker	April 14
Sal Romano	April 16
Phillip Ervin	April 22
Ariel Hernandez	April 24
Luis Castillo	June 23
Kevin Shackelford	June 29
Jackson Stephens	July 1
Alejandro Chacin	Aug. 23
Tyler Mahle	Aug. 27
Chad Wallach	Aug. 27
Zach Vincej	Sept. 1
Deck McGuire	Sept. 12
Keury Mella	Sept. 20

CLEVELAND INDIANS

Yandy Diaz	April 3
Bradley Zimmer	May 16
Greg Allen	Sept. 1
Francisco Mejia	Sept. 1

COLORADO ROCKIES

Antonio Senzatela	April 6
Kyle Freeland	April 7
Shane Carle	April 14
Mike Tauchman	June 27
Ryan McMahon	Aug. 12

DETROIT TIGERS

Joe Jimenez	April 13
Chad Bell	May 10
Zac Reininger	Aug. 27
Jairo Labourt	Sept. 1
Myles Jaye	Sept. 2
Artie Lewicki	Sept. 4
Victor Alcantara	Sept. 5

HOUSTON ASTROS

Mike Hauschild	April 8
Reymin Guduan	May 31
Francis Martes	June 9
Derek Fisher	June 14
J.D. Davis	Aug. 5

KANSAS CITY ROYALS

Jakob Junis	April 12
Jorge Bonifacio	April 21
Sam Gaviglio	May 11
Eric Skoglund	May 30
Ramon Torres	June 7
Glenn Sparkman	June 30
Cam Gallagher	Aug. 6
Andres Machado	Sept. 2

LOS ANGELES ANGELS

Keynan Middleton	May 5
Nolan Fontana	May 22
Eduardo Paredes	June 23
Troy Scribner	July 29

LOS ANGELES DODGERS

Cody Bellinger	April 25
Jordan Jankowski	May 24
Edward Paredes	July 24
Kyle Farmer	July 30
Alex Verdugo	Sept. 1
Fabio Castillo	Sept. 2
O'Koyea Dickson	Sept. 2
Walker Buehler	Sept. 7
Tim Locastro	Sept. 29

MIAMI MARLINS

J.T. Riddle	April 11
Jarlin Garcia	April 14
Drew Steckenrider	May 24
Chris O'Grady	July 8
Brian Anderson	Sept. 1
Dillon Peters	Sept. 1

MILWAUKEE BREWERS

Brett Phillips	June 5
Josh Hader	June 10
Lewis Brinson	June 11
Tyler Webb	June 24
Brandon Woodruff	Aug. 4
Taylor Williams	Sept. 6
Aaron Wilkerson	Sept. 15

MINNESOTA TWINS

Randy Rosario	June 2
Nik Turley	June 11
Alan Busenitz	June 17
Trevor Hildenberger	June 23
Felix Jorge	July 1
Zack Granite	July 8
Dietrich Enns	Aug. 10
Aaron Slegers	Aug. 17
Mitch Garver	Aug. 19
John Curtiss	Aug. 25
Niko Goodrum	Sept. 2
Gabriel Moya	Sept. 12

NEW YORK METS

Paul Sewald	April 8
Tyler Pill	May 27
Chasen Bradford	June 25
Chris Flexen	July 27
Amed Rosario	Aug. 1
Dominic Smith	Aug. 11
Kevin McGowan	Aug. 22
Travis Taijeron	Aug. 26
Jamie Callahan	Sept. 2
Jacob Rhame	Sept. 2
Phillip Evans	Sept. 8
Tomas Nido	Sept. 13

NEW YORK YANKEES

Kyle Higashioka	April 10
Jordan Montgomery	April 12
Giovanny Gallegos	May 12
Domingo German	June 11
Ronald Herrera	June 14
Tyler Wade	June 27
Miguel Andujar	June 28
Clint Frazier	July 1
Garrett Cooper	July 14
Caleb Smith	July 17

OAKLAND ATHLETICS

Boog Powell	April 29
Bobby Wahl	May 3
Jaycob Brugman	June 9
Daniel Gossett	June 14
Matt Chapman	June 15
Michael Brady	June 20
Franklin Barreto	June 24
Dustin Fowler	June 29
Paul Blackburn	July 1
Sam Moll	Sept. 1

PHILADELPHIA PHILLIES

Brock Stassi	April 3
Andrew Knapp	April 6
Mark Leiter	April 28
Nick Pivetta	April 30
Ricardo Pinto	May 31
Ben Lively	June 3
Cameron Perkins	June 20
Hoby Milner	June 24
Nick Williams	June 30
Jesen Therrien	July 29
Drew Anderson	Aug. 1
Rhys Hoskins	Aug. 10
Yacksel Rios	Aug. 22
J.P. Crawford	Sept. 5
Victor Arano	Sept. 12

PITTSBURGH PIRATES

Jose Osuna	April 18
Dovydas Neverauskas	April 24
Gift Ngoepe	April 26
Danny Ortiz	April 29
John Bormann	April 30
Christopher Bostick	May 8
Edgar Santana	June 10
Jordan Luplow	July 28
Angel Sanchez	Aug. 24

SAN DIEGO PADRES

Allen Cordoba	April 3
Miguel Diaz	April 3
Luis Torrens	April 3
Dinelson Lamet	May 25
Franchy Cordero	May 27
Phil Maton	June 11
Jose Ruiz	July 24
Kyle Lloyd	July 25
Kyle McGrath	July 30
Christian Villanueva	Sept. 18

SAN FRANCISCO GIANTS

Christian Arroyo	April 24
Pierce Johnson	May 19
Austin Slater	June 2
Kyle Crick	June 22
Ryder Jones	June 24
Jae-Gyun Hwang	June 28
Dan Slania	June 30
Miguel Gomez	July 7
Roberto Gomez	Sept. 5
Reyes Moronta	Sept. 5

SEATTLE MARINERS

Chase De Jong	April 5
Casey Lawrence	April 8
Emilio Pagan	May 3
Seth Frankoff	June 9
Andrew Moore	June 22
Max Povse	June 22
Thyago Vieira	Aug. 14
Mike Marjama	Sept. 3
Jacob Hannemann	Sept. 9

ST. LOUIS CARDINALS

Magneuris Sierra	May 7
John Brebbia	May 28
Paul DeJong	May 28
Luke Voit	June 25
Alex Mejia	June 29
Harrison Bader	July 25
Josh Lucas	Aug. 19
Ryan Sherriff	Aug. 25
Jack Flaherty	Sept. 1
Sandy Alcantara	Sept. 3
Breyvic Valera	Sept. 5

TAMPA BAY RAYS

Austin Pruitt	April 2
Daniel Robertson	April 4
Chih-Wei Hu	April 24
Jose Alvarado	May 3
Ryne Stanek	May 14
Hunter Wood	May 30
Jake Faria	June 7
Adam Kolarek	June 29
Andrew Kittredge	July 18
Cesar Puello	Aug. 9

TEXAS RANGERS

Drew Robinson	April 5
Austin Bibens-Dirkx	May 17
Paolo Espino	May 19
Tyler Smith	June 2
Ricardo Rodriguez	Aug. 14
Nick Gardewine	Aug. 22
A.J. Jimenez	Sept. 6
Willie Calhoun	Sept. 12

TORONTO BLUE JAYS

Dwight Smith Jr.	May 18
Anthony Alford	May 19
Ian Parmley	June 23
Chris Smith	June 27
Taylor Cole	Aug. 9
Chris Rowley	Aug. 12
Tim Mayza	Aug. 15
Carlos Ramirez	Sept. 1
Richard Urena	Sept. 1
Luis Santos	Sept. 2

WASHINGTON NATIONALS

Rafael Bautista	April 30
Adrian Sanchez	June 30
Austin Adams	July 15
Andrew Stevenson	July 23
Erick Fedde	July 30
Raudy Read	Sept. 3
Victor Robles	Sept. 7

AMERICAN LEAGUE 2017 STATISTICS

CLUB BATTING

	AVG	G	AB	R	H	2B	3B	HR	RBI	BB	SO	SB	OBP	SLG
Houston	.282	162	5611	896	1581	346	20	238	854	509	1087	98	.346	.478
Cleveland	.263	162	5511	818	1449	333	29	212	780	604	1153	88	.339	.449
New York	.262	162	5594	858	1463	266	23	241	821	616	1386	90	.339	.447
Baltimore	.260	162	5650	743	1469	269	12	232	713	392	1412	32	.312	.435
Minnesota	.260	162	5557	815	1444	286	31	206	781	593	1342	95	.334	.434
Kansas City	.259	162	5536	702	1436	260	24	193	660	390	1166	91	.311	.420
Seattle	.259	162	5551	750	1436	281	17	200	714	487	1267	89	.325	.424
Detroit	.258	162	5556	735	1435	289	35	187	699	503	1313	65	.324	.424
Boston	.258	162	5669	785	1461	302	19	168	735	571	1224	106	.329	.407
Chicago	.256	162	5513	706	1412	256	37	186	670	401	1397	71	.314	.417
Oakland	.246	162	5464	739	1344	305	15	234	708	565	1491	57	.319	.436
Tampa Bay	.245	162	5478	694	1340	226	32	228	671	545	1538	88	.317	.422
Texas	.244	162	5430	799	1326	255	21	237	756	544	1493	113	.320	.430
Los Angeles	.243	162	5415	710	1314	251	14	186	678	523	1198	136	.315	.397
Toronto	.240	162	5499	693	1320	269	5	222	661	542	1327	53	.312	.412

CLUB PITCHING

	ERA	G	CG	SHO	SV	IP	H	R	ER	HR	BB	SO	AVG
Cleveland	3.30	162	7	3	37	1441	1267	564	529	163	406	1614	.236
Boston	3.70	162	5	1	39	1482	1384	668	610	195	465	1580	.245
New York	3.72	162	2	1	36	1449	1248	660	599	192	504	1560	.228
Tampa Bay	3.97	162	0	0	53	1445	1324	704	638	193	503	1352	.242
Houston	4.12	162	1	0	45	1446	1314	700	662	192	522	1593	.240
Los Angeles	4.20	162	1	1	43	1441	1373	709	672	224	470	1312	.252
Toronto	4.42	162	2	0	45	1465	1460	784	720	203	549	1372	.258
Seattle	4.46	162	1	0	39	1440	1399	772	713	237	490	1244	.254
Minnesota	4.59	162	6	3	42	1436	1487	788	732	224	483	1166	.266
Kansas City	4.61	162	1	1	39	1438	1480	791	737	196	519	1216	.265
Oakland	4.67	162	1	1	35	1431	1444	826	743	210	502	1202	.261
Texas	4.66	162	2	1	29	1434	1443	816	742	214	559	1107	.261
Chicago	4.78	162	0	0	25	1422	1384	820	755	242	632	1193	.254
Baltimore	4.97	162	1	1	35	1441	1505	841	795	242	579	1233	.269
Detroit	5.36	162	2	1	32	1420	1587	894	846	218	538	1202	.282

CLUB FIELDING

	PCT	PO	A	E	DP
Baltimore	.984	5305	1637	111	491
Boston	.983	5471	1418	122	359
Chicago	.980	5334	1581	138	428
Cleveland	.987	5151	1479	86	460
Detroit	.985	5381	1408	101	406
Houston	.984	5160	1551	108	416
Kansas City	.987	5396	1549	93	398
Los Angeles	.987	5397	1490	92	365
Minnesota	.987	5462	1499	95	399
New York	.984	5266	1489	110	277
Oakland	.980	5321	1619	142	439
Seattle	.983	5431	1456	122	416
Tampa Bay	.983	5364	1458	116	358
Texas	.982	5305	1651	129	482
Toronto	.985	5333	1598	105	404

INDIVIDUAL BATTING LEADERS

	AVG	G	AB	R	H	2B	3B	HR	RBI	BB	SO	SB
Altuve, Jose, Houston	.346	153	590	112	204	39	4	24	81	58	84	32
Garcia, Avisail, Chicago	.330	136	518	75	171	27	5	18	80	33	111	5
Hosmer, Eric, Kansas City	.318	162	603	98	192	31	1	25	94	66	104	6
Ramirez, Jose, Cleveland	.318	152	585	107	186	56	6	29	83	52	69	17
Reddick, Josh, Houston	.315	134	477	77	150	34	4	13	82	43	72	7
Trout, Mike, Los Angeles	.306	114	402	92	123	25	3	33	72	94	90	22
Mauer, Joe, Minnesota	.305	141	525	69	160	36	1	7	71	66	83	2
Abreu, Jose, Chicago	.304	156	621	95	189	43	6	33	102	35	119	3
Gonzalez, Marwin, Houston	.303	134	455	67	138	34	0	23	90	49	99	8
Cain, Lorenzo, Kansas City	.300	155	584	86	175	27	5	15	49	54	100	26

INDIVIDUAL PITCHING LEADERS

	W	L	ERA	G	GS	CG	SV	IP	H	R	ER	BB	SO
Kluber, Corey, Cleveland	18	4	2.25	29	29	5	0	204	141	56	51	36	265
Sale, Chris, Boston	17	8	2.90	32	32	1	0	214	165	73	69	43	308
Severino, Luis, New York	14	6	2.98	31	31	0	0	193	150	73	64	51	230
Stroman, Marcus, Toronto	13	9	3.09	33	33	2	0	201	201	82	69	62	164
Santana, Ervin, Minnesota	16	8	3.28	33	33	5	0	211	177	85	77	61	167
Carrasco, Carlos, Cleveland	18	6	3.29	32	32	1	0	200	173	73	73	46	226
Pomeranz, Drew, Boston	17	6	3.32	32	32	0	0	173	166	69	64	69	174
Verlander, Justin, Detroit/Houston	15	8	3.36	33	33	0	0	206	170	80	77	72	219
Cashner, Andrew, Texas	11	11	3.40	28	28	0	0	167	156	75	63	64	86
Gray, Sonny, Oakland/New York	10	12	3.55	27	27	1	0	162	139	79	64	57	153

AWARD WINNERS

Selected by Baseball Writers Association of America

MOST VALUABLE PLAYER

Player	1st	2nd	3rd	Total
Jose Altuve, Astros	27	3		405
Aaron Judge, Yankees	2	27	1	279
Jose Ramirez, Indians	1		22	237
Mike Trout, Angels			6	197
Francisco Lindor, Indians				143
Mookie Betts, Red Sox				110
Corey Kluber, Indians			1	101
Andrelton Simmons, Angels				60
Chris Sale, Red Sox				56
Nelson Cruz, Mariners				44
Brian Dozier, Twins				25
Jonathan Schoop, Orioles				19
George Springer, Astros				17
Jose Abreu, White Sox				16
Eric Hosmer, Royals				16
Justin Upton, Tigers/Angels				12
Carlos Correa, Astros				9
Byron Buxton, Twins				7
Marwin Gonzalez, Astros				6
Edwin Encarnacion, Indians				4
DiDi Gregorius, Yankees				4
Khris Davis, Athletics				1
Josh Donaldson, Blue Jays				1
Gary Sanchez, Yankees				1

CY YOUNG AWARD

Player	1st	2nd	3rd	Total
Corey Kluber, Indians	28	2		204
Chris Sale, Red Sox	2	28		126
Luis Severino, Yankees			20	73
Carlos Carrasco, Indians			1	43
Justin Verlander, Tigers/Astros			3	32
Craig Kimbrel, Red Sox			6	27
Ervin Santana, Twins				3
Marcus Stroman, Blue Jays				2

ROOKIE OF THE YEAR

Player	1st	2nd	3rd	Total
Aaron Judge, Yankees	30			150
Andrew Benintendi, Red Sox		23	6	75
Trey Mancini, Orioles		5	16	31
Matt Olson, Athletics		1	2	5
Yuli Gurriel, Astros			5	5
Jordan Montgomery, Yankees		1	1	4

MANAGER OF THE YEAR

Player	1st	2nd	3rd	Total
Paul Molitor, Twins	18	6	4	112
Terry Francona, Indians	11	9	8	90
A.J. Hinch, Astros	1	13	12	56
Joe Girardi, Yankees		2	6	12

GOLD GLOVE WINNERS

Selected by AL Managers

P—Marcus Stroman, Blue Jays. **C**—Martin Maldonado, Angels. **1B**—Eric Hosmer, Royals. **2B**—Brian Dozier, Twins. **3B**—Evan Longoria, Rays. **SS**—Andrelton Simmons, Angels. **LF**—Alex Gordon, Royals. **CF**—Bryon Buxton, Twins. **RF**—Mookie Betts, Red Sox.

AMERICAN LEAGUE

DEPARTMENT LEADERS

BATTING

GAMES
Alcides Escobar, Kansas City 162
Rougned Odor, Texas 162
Eric Hosmer, Kansas City 162
Jonathan Schoop, Baltimore 160
Francisco Lindor, Cleveland 159

AT-BATS
Francisco Lindor, Cleveland 651
Elvis Andrus, Texas 643
Manny Machado, Baltimore 630
Mookie Betts, Boston 628
Jonathan Schoop, Baltimore 622

PLATE APPERANCES
Francisco Lindor, Cleveland 723
Mookie Betts, Boston 712
Brian Dozier, Minnesota 705
Manny Machado, Baltimore 690
Elvis Andrus, Texas 689

RUNS
Aaron Judge, New York 128
Jose Altuve, Houston 112
George Springer, Houston 112
Jose Ramirez, Cleveland 107
Brian Dozier, Minnesota 106

HITS
Jose Altuve, Houston 204
Eric Hosmer, Kansas City 192
Elvis Andrus, Texas 191
Jose Abreu, Chicago 189
Jose Ramirez, Cleveland 186

TOTAL BASES
Jose Abreu, Chicago 343
Jose Ramirez, Cleveland 341
Aaron Judge, New York 340
Francisco Lindor, Cleveland 329
Jose Altuve, Houston 323

DOUBLES
Jose Ramirez, Cleveland 56
Jed Lowrie, Oakland 49
Mookie Betts, Boston 46
Justin Upton, Detroit, Los Angeles 44
Elvis Andrus, Texas 44
Francisco Lindor, Cleveland 44

TRIPLES
Nicholas Castellanos, Detroit 10
Yolmer Sanchez, Chicago 8
Xander Bogaerts, Boston 6
Bryon Buxton, Minnesota 6
Mikie Mahtook, Detroit 6
Jose Abreu, Chicago 6
Whit Merrifield, Kansas City 6
Jose Ramirez, Cleveland 6

EXTRA-BASE HITS
Jose Ramirez, Cleveland 91
Jose Abreu, Chicago 82
Francisco Lindor, Cleveland 81
Justin Upton, Detroit/Los Angeles 79
Aaron Judge, New York 79

HOME RUNS
Aaron Judge, New York 52
Khris Davis, Oakland 43
Joey Gallo, Texas 41
Nelson Cruz, Seattle 39
Justin Smoak, Toronto 38
Mike Moustakas, Kansas City 38

Jose Abreu

Edwin Encarnacion, Cleveland 38
Logan Morrison, Tampa 38

RUNS BATTED IN
Nelson Cruz, Seattle 119
Aaron Judge, New York 114
Khris Davis, Oakland 110
Justin Upton, Detroit, Los Angeles 109
Edwin Encarnacion, Cleveland 107

SACRIFICES
Delino DeShields, Texas 13
Martin Maldonado, Los Angeles 8
Adam Engel, Chicago 8
Yolmer Sanchez, Chicago 7
Jorge Polanco, Minnesota 7
Alcides Escobar, Kansas City 7

SACRIFICE FLIES
Josh Reddick, Houston 12
Evan Longoria, Tampa 12
Manny Machado, Baltimore 9
Eddie Rosario, Minnesota 8
Andrelton Simmons, Los Angeles 8
Andrew Benintendi, Boston 8
Danny Valencia, Seattle 8

HIT BY PITCHES
Carlos Gomez, Texas 19
Martin Maldonado, Los Angeles 18
Jose Abreu, Chicago 15
Todd Frazier, Chicago, New York 14
Alex Gordon, Kansas City 14

WALKS
Aaron Judge, New York 127
Edwin Encarnacion, Cleveland 104
Mike Trout, Los Angeles 94
Carlos Santana, Cleveland 88
Steven Souza Jr., Tampa 84
Jose Bautista, Toronto 84

STOLEN BASES
Whit Merrifield, Kansas City 34
Cameron Maybin, Los Angeles, Houston 33
Jose Altuve, Houston 32
Delino DeShields, Texas 29
Rajai Davis, Oakland, Boston 29
Byron Buxton, Minnesota 29

STOLEN BASE PERCENTAGE
Byron Buxton, Minnesota .967
Bradley Zimmer, Cleveland .947
Xander Bogaerts, Boston .938
Tim Anderson, Chicago .938
Lorenzo Cain, Kansas City .929

STRIKEOUTS
Aaron Judge, New York 208
Joey Gallo, Texas 196
Khris Davis, Oakland 195
Chris Davis, Baltimore 195
Justin Upton, Los Angeles 180

TOUGHEST TO STRIKE OUT
(At-bats per strikeout)
Andrelton Simmons, Los Angeles 8.79
Yuli Gurriel, Houston 8.53
Jose Ramirez, Cleveland 8.48
Melky Cabrera, Chicago, Kansas City 8.38
Mookie Betts, Boston 7.95

GROUNDED INTO DOUBLE PLAYS
Albert Pujols, Los Angeles 26
Salvador Perez, Kansas City 23
Kendrys Morales, Toronto 22
Jose Abreu, Chicago 21
Lorenzo Cain, Kansas City 20
Jonathan Schoop, Baltimore 20
Andrelton Simmons, Los Angeles 20
Eric Hosmer, Kansas City 20
Khris Davis, Oakland 20

MULTI-HIT GAMES
Jose Altuve, Houston 59
Jose Abreu, Chicago 58
Elvis Andrus, Texas 54
Eric Hosmer, Kansas City 53
Jonathan Schoop, Baltimore 53

ON-BASE PERCENTAGE
Mike Trout, Los Angeles .442
Aaron Judge, New York .422
Jose Altuve, Houston .410
Eric Hosmer, Kansas City .385
Joe Mauer, Minnesota .384

ON-BASE PLUS SLUGGING
Mike Trout, Los Angeles 1.071
Aaron Judge, New York 1.049
Jose Altuve, Houston .957
Jose Ramirez, Cleveland .957
Nelson Cruz, Seattle .924

PITCHING

WINS
Jason Vargas, Kansas City 18
Carlos Carrasco, Cleveland 18
Corey Kluber, Cleveland 18
Chris Sale, Boston 17
Drew Pomeranz, Boston 17
Trevor Bauer, Cleveland 17

LOSSES
Rick Porcello, Boston 17
Ricky Nolasco, Los Angeles 15
Jason Hammel, Kansas City 13
Martin Perez, Texas 12

Corey Kluber

JONATHAN DANIEL/GETTY IMAGES; STEPHEN BRASHEAR/GETTY IMAGES

AMERICAN LEAGUE DEPARTMENT LEADERS

Alex Colome

Sonny Gray, Oakland, New York 12
Chris Archer, Tampa 12
Michael Fulmer, Detroit 12
Tanaka, Masahiro, New York 12
Gausman, Kevin, Baltimore 12

GAMES
Peter Moylan, Kansas City 79
Bryan Shaw, Cleveland 79
Dan Jennings, Tampa Bay 77
Ryan Tepera, Toronto 73
Daniel Coulombe, Oakland 72

GAMES STARTED
Chris Archer, Tampa 34
Kevin Gausman, Baltimore 34
Ricky Nolasco, Los Angeles 33
Rick Porcello, Boston 33
Marcus Stroman, Toronto 33
Justin Verlander, Detroit, Houston 33
Ervin Santana, Minnesota 33
Marco Estrada, Toronto 33

GAMES FINISHED
Roberto Osuna, Toronto 58
Ken Giles, Houston 55
Cody Allen, Cleveland 55
Alex Colome, Tampa 53
Edwin Diaz, Seattle 52

COMPLETE GAMES
Corey Kluber, Cleveland 5
Ervin Santana, Minnesota 5
Marcus Stroman, Toronto 2
Rick Porcello, Boston 2
18 players 1

SHUTOUTS
Corey Kluber, Cleveland 3
Ervin Santana, Minnesota 3
8 players 1

SAVES
Alex Colome, Tampa 47
Roberto Osuna, Toronto 39
Craig Kimbrel, Boston 35
Ken Giles, Houston 34
Edwin Diaz, Seattle 34

INNINGS PITCHED
Chris Sale, Boston 214
Ervin Santana, Minnesota 211
Justin Verlander, Detroit, Houston 206
Corey Kluber, Cleveland 204
Rick Porcello, Boston 203

HITS ALLOWED
Rick Porcello, Boston 236
Martin Perez, Texas 221
Jason Hammel, Kansas City 209
Kevin Gausman, Baltimore 208
Ricky Nolasco, Los Angeles 205

RUNS ALLOWED
Rick Porcello, Boston 125
Jordan Zimmermann, Detroit 111
Jason Hammel, Kansas City 109
Ubaldo Jimenez, Baltimore 109
Martin Perez, Texas 108

HOME RUNS ALLOWED
Rick Porcello, Boston 38
Ariel Miranda, Seattle 37
Masahiro Tanaka, New York 35
Ricky Nolasco, Los Angeles 35
Ian Kennedy, Kansas City 34

WALKS ALLOWED
Wade Miley, Baltimore 93
Derek Holland, Chicago 75
Justin Verlander, Detroit, Houston 72
Kevin Gausman, Baltimore 71
Marco Estrada, Toronto 71

LOWEST WALKS PER NINE INNINGS
Corey Kluber, Cleveland 1.59
Chris Sale, Boston 1.81
Masahiro Tanaka, New York 2.07
Carlos Carrasco, Cleveland 2.07
Rick Porcello, Boston 2.12

HIT BATTERS
Mike Fiers, Houston 13
Charlie Morton, Houston 13
Jose Berrios, Minnesota 13
Lance McCullers Jr., Houston 11
Dellin Betances, New York 11
Cole Hamels, Texas 11

STRIKEOUTS
Chris Sale, Boston 308
Corey Kluber, Cleveland 265
Chris Archer, Tampa 249
Luis Severino, New York 230
Carlos Carrasco, Cleveland 226

STRIKEOUTS PER NINE INNINGS
Chris Sale, Boston 12.93
Corey Kluber, Cleveland 11.71
Chris Archer, Tampa 11.15
Luis Severino, New York 10.71
Carlos Carrasco, Cleveland 10.17

STRIKEOUT PER NINE INNINGS
(Relievers)
Craig Kimbrel, Boston 16.44
Chad Green, New York 13.44
David Robertson, Chicago 12.91
Cody Allen, Cleveland 12.30
Edwin Diaz, Seattle 12.14

DOUBLE PLAYS
Marcus Stroman, Toronto 34
Martin Perez, Texas 32
Kyle Gibson, Minnesota 26
Drew Pomeranz, Boston 23
Andrew Cashner, Texas 23
Dallas Keuchel, Houston 23

PICKOFFS
Alex Cobb, Tampa 5
Cole Hamels, Texas 4
Derek Holland, Chicago 4
Sean Manaea, Oakland 4
Wade Miley, Baltimore 4
Jason Vargas, Kansas City 4

WILD PITCHES
Chris Archer, Tampa 15
James Paxton, Seattle 15
Ervin Santana, Minnesota 12
Sonny Gray, Oakland, New York 11
Mike Fiers, Houston 11
Chris Tillman, Baltimore 11

WALKS PLUS HITS PER INNING
Corey Kluber, Cleveland 0.87
Chris Sale, Boston 0.97
Luis Severino, New York 1.04
Carlos Carrasco, Cleveland 1.10
Ervin Santana, Minnesota 1.13

OPPONENT AVERAGE
Corey Kluber, Cleveland .193
Chris Sale, Boston .208
Luis Severino, New York .208
Justin Verlander, Detroit, Houston .221
Ervin Santana, Minnesota .225

WORST ERA
Jason Hammel, Kansas City 5.29
Marco Estrada, Toronto 4.98
Ricky Nolasco, Los Angeles 4.92
Martin Perez, Texas 4.82
Masahiro Tanaka, New York 4.74

FIELDING

PITCHER

PCT	6 players	1.000
DP	Marcus Stroman, Toronto	6
E	Dallas Keuchel, Houston	5
A	Marcus Stroman, Toronto	37
PO	Kyle Gibson, Minnesota	19
	Ervin Santana, Minnesota	19

CATCHER

PCT	Martin Maldonado, Los Angeles	.998
E	Gary Sanchez, New York	13
PO	Martin Maldonado, Los Angeles	1046
CS	Martin Maldonado, Los Angeles	29
PB	Gary Sanchez, New York	16
A	Martin Maldonado, Los Angeles	65
DP	Welington Castillo, Baltimore	9

FIRST BASE

PCT	Miguel Cabrera, Detroit	.999
PO	Justin Smoak, Toronto	1244
A	Carlos Santana, Cleveland	95
DP	Jose Abreu, Chicago	130
E	Danny Valencia, Seattle	11

SECOND BASE

PCT	Brian Dozier, Minnesota	.993
PO	Jonathan Schoop, Baltimore	329
A	Jonathan Schoop, Baltimore	446
DP	Jonathan Schoop, Baltimore	132
E	Rougned Odor, Texas	19

THIRD BASE

PCT	Alex Bregman, Houston	.970
PO	Kyle Seager, Seattle	130
A	Kyle Seager, Seattle	310
DP	Kyle Seager, Seattle	46
E	Nick Castellanos, Detroit	18

SHORTSTOP

PCT	Jose Iglesias, Detroit	.987
PO	Elvis Andrus, Texas	245
A	Elvis Andrus, Texas	493
DP	Francisco Lindor, Cleveland	111
E	Tim Anderson, Chicago	28

OUTFIELD

PCT	Brett Gardner, New York	1.000
PO	Lorenzo Cain, Kansas City	430
A	Avisail Garcia, Chicago	13
DP	Jarrod Dyson, Seattle	6
E	Avisail Garcia, Chicago	9

MITCHELL LAYTON/GETTY IMAGES

NATIONAL LEAGUE 2017 STATISTICS

CLUB BATTING

	AVG	G	AB	R	H	2B	3B	HR	RBI	BB	SO	SB	OBP	SLG
Colorado	.273	162	5534	824	1510	293	38	192	793	519	1408	59	.338	.444
Miami	.267	162	5602	778	1497	271	31	194	743	486	1282	91	.331	.431
Washington	.266	162	5553	819	1477	311	31	215	796	542	1327	108	.332	.449
Atlanta	.263	162	5584	732	1467	289	26	165	706	474	1184	77	.326	.412
St. Louis	.256	162	5470	761	1402	284	28	196	728	593	1348	81	.334	.426
Chicago	.255	162	5496	822	1402	274	29	223	785	622	1401	62	.338	.437
Arizona	.254	162	5525	812	1405	314	39	220	776	578	1456	103	.329	.445
Cincinnati	.254	162	5484	753	1390	249	38	219	715	565	1329	120	.329	.433
New York	.250	162	5510	735	1379	286	28	224	713	529	1291	58	.320	.434
Philadelphia	.250	162	5535	690	1382	287	36	174	654	494	1417	59	.315	.409
Milwaukee	.249	162	5467	732	1363	267	22	224	695	547	1571	128	.322	.429
Los Angeles	.249	162	5408	770	1347	312	20	221	730	649	1380	77	.335	.437
San Francisco	.249	162	5551	639	1382	290	28	128	612	467	1204	76	.309	.381
Pittsburgh	.244	162	5458	668	1331	249	36	151	635	519	1213	67	.318	.386
San Diego	.234	162	5356	604	1251	227	31	189	576	460	1499	89	.299	.393

CLUB PITCHING

	ERA	G	CG	SHO	SV	IP	H	R	ER	HR	BB	SO	AVG
Los Angeles	3.38	162	2	0	51	1445	1226	580	543	184	442	1549	.228
Arizona	3.66	162	2	1	43	1441	1309	659	586	171	516	1482	.241
Washington	3.88	162	3	1	46	1447	1300	672	623	189	495	1457	.239
Chicago	3.95	162	2	1	38	1447	1294	695	636	194	554	1439	.238
Milwaukee	4.00	162	1	0	54	1446	1381	697	642	185	553	1346	.252
St. Louis	4.01	162	3	3	43	1450	1393	705	646	183	493	1351	.253
Pittsburgh	4.22	162	2	1	36	1441	1464	731	676	182	511	1262	.264
San Francisco	4.50	162	3	2	32	1452	1515	776	726	182	496	1234	.268
Colorado	4.51	162	1	1	47	1438	1453	757	721	190	532	1270	.264
Philadelphia	4.55	162	1	0	33	1441	1471	782	729	221	527	1309	.265
San Diego	4.67	162	2	1	45	1431	1417	816	742	226	554	1325	.259
Atlanta	4.72	162	0	0	36	1441	1463	821	756	192	584	1258	.263
Miami	4.82	162	1	1	34	1443	1450	822	772	193	627	1202	.263
New York	5.01	162	2	0	34	1435	1538	863	799	220	593	1374	.273
Cincinnati	5.17	162	2	1	33	1430	1442	869	821	248	631	1300	.263

CLUB FIELDING

	PCT	PO	A	E	DP
Miami	.988	5402	1575	83	415
Philadelphia	.987	5325	1527	91	403
Colorado	.987	5200	1748	93	466
Cincinnati	.986	5252	1663	100	361
San Francisco	.986	5401	1542	101	358
Washington	.985	5306	1465	100	377
Los Angeles	.985	5204	1386	98	355
Chicago	.985	5234	1680	106	382

	PCT	PO	A	E	DP
St. Louis	.985	5294	1617	107	467
Atlanta	.985	5358	1597	108	381
New York	.984	5318	1482	110	351
Pittsburgh	.984	5255	1695	113	439
Arizona	.982	5194	1624	124	394
San Diego	.981	5227	1654	136	491
Milwaukee	.981	5189	1653	136	445

INDIVIDUAL BATTING LEADERS

	AVG	G	AB	R	H	2B	3B	HR	RBI	BB	SO	SB
Blackmon, Charlie, Colorado	.331	159	644	137	213	35	14	37	104	65	135	14
Murphy, Daniel, Washington	.322	144	534	94	172	43	3	23	93	52	77	2
Turner, Justin, Los Angeles	.322	130	457	72	147	32	0	21	71	59	56	7
Votto, Joey, Cincinnati	.320	162	559	106	179	34	1	36	100	134	83	5
Posey, Buster, San Francisco	.320	140	494	62	158	34	0	12	67	61	66	6
Ozuna, Marcell, Miami	.312	159	613	93	191	30	2	37	124	64	144	1
LeMahieu, DJ, Colorado	.310	155	609	95	189	28	4	8	64	59	90	6
Arenado, Nolan, Colorado	.309	159	606	100	187	43	7	37	130	62	106	3
Gordon, Dee, Miami	.308	158	653	114	201	20	9	2	33	25	93	60
Freeman, Freddie, Atlanta	.307	117	440	84	135	35	2	28	71	65	95	8

INDIVIDUAL PITCHING LEADERS

	W	L	ERA	G	GS	CG	SV	IP	H	R	ER	BB	SO
Kershaw, Clayton, Los Angeles	18	4	2.31	27	27	1	0	175	136	49	45	30	202
Scherzer, Max, Washington	16	6	2.51	31	31	2	0	201	126	62	56	55	268
Strasburg, Stephen, Washington	15	4	2.51	28	28	1	0	175	131	55	49	47	204
Ray, Robbie, Arizona	15	5	2.89	28	28	1	0	162	116	57	52	71	218
Gonzalez, Gio, Washington	15	9	2.96	32	32	0	0	201	158	69	66	79	188
Greinke, Zack, Arizona	17	7	3.20	32	32	1	0	202	172	80	72	45	215
Lynn, Lance, St. Louis	11	8	3.43	33	33	0	0	186	151	80	71	78	153
Nelson, Jimmy, Milwaukee	12	6	3.49	29	29	1	0	175	171	75	68	48	199
Arrieta, Jake, Chicago	14	10	3.53	30	30	0	0	168	150	82	66	55	163
deGrom, Jacob, New York	15	10	3.53	31	31	1	0	201	180	87	79	59	239

AWARD WINNERS

Selected by Baseball Writers Association of America

MOST VALUABLE PLAYER

Player	1st	2nd	3rd	Total
Giancarlo Stanton, Marlins	10	10	5	302
Joey Votto, Reds	10	9	4	300
Paul Goldschmidt, D-backs	4	5	4	239
Nolan Arenado, Rockies	2	3	8	229
Charlie Blackmon, Rockies	3	3	7	205
Anthony Rendon, Nationals			1	141
Kris Bryant, Cubs	1		1	132
Justin Turner, Dodgers				43
Cody Bellinger, Dodgers				38
Max Scherzer, Nationals				34
Tommy Pham, Cardinals				24
Bryce Harper, Nationals				21
Anthony Rizzo, Cubs				17
J.D. Martinez, Diamondbacks				11
Kenley Jansen, Dodgers				8
Marcell Ozuna, Marlins				8
Clayton Kershaw, Dodgers				6
Corey Seager, Dodgers				6
Daniel Murphy, Nationals				3
Archie Bradley, Diamondbacks				1
Zack Greinke, Diamondbacks				1
Ryan Zimmerman, Nationals				1

CY YOUNG AWARD

Player	1st	2nd	3rd	Total
Max Scherzer, Nationals	27	3		201
Clayton Kershaw, Dodgers	3	25	1	126
Stephen Strasburg, Nationals		1	23	81
Zack Greinke, Diamondbacks		1	3	52
Kenley Jansen, Dodgers			2	22
Gio Gonzalez, Nationals			1	18
Robbie Ray, Diamondbacks				6
Jacob deGrom, Mets				2
Jimmy Nelson, Brewers				1
Alex Wood, Dodgers				1

ROOKIE OF THE YEAR

Player	1st	2nd	3rd	Total
Cody Bellinger, Dodgers	30			150
Paul DeJong, Cardinals		15	11	56
Josh Bell, Pirates		10	2	32
Rhys Hoskins, Phillies		1	9	12
German Marquez, Rockies		2	4	10
Manuel Margot, Padres		1	2	5
Kyle Freeland, Rockies		1		3
Luis Castillo, Reds			1	1
Ian Happ, Cubs			1	1

MANAGER OF THE YEAR

Player	1st	2nd	3rd	Total
Torey Lovullo, Diamondbacks	18	5	6	111
Dave Roberts, Dodgers	5	8	6	55
Bud Black, Rockies	3	6	10	43
Craig Counsell, Brewers	3	4	6	33
Dusty Baker, Nationals	1	6	2	25
Joe Maddon, Cubs		1		3

GOLD GLOVE WINNERS

Selected by NL Managers

P—Zack Greinke, Diamondbacks. **C**—Tucker Barnhart, Reds. **1B**—Paul Goldschmidt, Diamondbacks. **2B**—D.J. LeMahieu, Rockies. **3B**—Nolan Arenado, Rockies. **SS**—Brandon Crawford, Giants. **LF**—Marcell Ozuna, Marlins. **CF**—Ender Inciarte, Braves. **RF**—Jason Heyward, Cubs.

NATIONAL LEAGUE DEPARTMENT LEADERS

BATTING

GAMES

Joey Votto, Cincinnati	162
Freddy Galvis, Philadelphia	162
Nick Markakis, Atlanta	160
Marcell Ozuna, Miami	159
Charlie Blackmon, Colorado	159
Josh Bell, Pittsburgh	159
Giancarlo Stanton, Miami	159
Nolan Arenado, Colorado	159

AT-BATS

Ender Inciarte, Atlanta	662
Dee Gordon, Miami	653
Charlie Blackmon, Colorado	644
Marcell Ozuna, Miami	613
D.J. LeMahieu, Colorado	609

PLATE APPERANCES

Charlie Blackmon, Colorado	725
Ender Inciarte, Atlanta	718
Joey Votto, Cincinnati	707
Christian Yelich, Miami	695
Dee Gordon, Miami	695

RUNS

Charlie Blackmon, Colorado	137
Giancarlo Stanton, Miami	123
Paul Goldschmidt, Arizona	117
Dee Gordon, Miami	114
Kris Bryant, Chicago	111

HITS

Charlie Blackmon, Colorado	213
Ender Inciarte, Atlanta	201
Dee Gordon, Miami	201
Marcell Ozuna, Miami	191
D.J. LeMahieu, Colorado	189

TOTAL BASES

Charlie Blackmon, Colorado	387
Giancarlo Stanton, Miami	377
Nolan Arenado, Colorado	355
Marcell Ozuna, Miami	336
Joey Votto, Cincinnati	323

DOUBLES

Daniel Murphy, Washington	43
Nolan Arenado, Colorado	43
Odubel Herrera, Philadelphia	42
Anthony Rendon, Washington	41
Nick Markakis, Atlanta	39

TRIPLES

Charlie Blackmon, Colorado	14
Billy Hamilton, Cincinnati	11
Dee Gordon, Miami	9
Dexter Fowler, St. Louis	9
Zack Cozart, Cincinnati	7
Manuel Margot, San Diego	7
Jose Reyes, New York	7
Nolan Arenado, Colorado	7

EXTRA-BASE HITS

Giancarlo Stanton, Miami	91
Nolan Arenado, Colorado	87
Charlie Blackmon, Colorado	86
Paul Goldschmidt, Arizona	73
Joey Votto, Cincinnati	71
Kris Bryant, Chicago	71
Adam Duvall, Cincinnati	71

HOME RUNS

Giancarlo Stanton, Miami	59
Cody Bellinger, Los Angeles	39
Marcell Ozuna, Miami	37
Charlie Blackmon, Colorado	37
Nolan Arenado, Colorado	37

RUNS BATTED IN

Giancarlo Stanton, Miami	132
Nolan Arenado, Colorado	130
Marcell Ozuna, Miami	124
Paul Goldschmidt, Arizona	120
Anthony Rizzo, Chicago	109

SACRIFICES

Zach Davies, Milwaukee	14
Julio Teheran, Atlanta	12
Gerrit Cole, Pittsburgh	12
Ivan Nova, Pittsburgh	9
Zack Godley, Arizona	9

SACRIFICE FLIES

Adam Duvall, Cincinnati	11
Gerrado Parra, Colorado	9
Yadier Molina, St. Louis	9
Brandon Crawford, S.F.	9
Joe Panik, San Francisco	8

Dee Gordon

Charlie Blackmon

HIT BY PITCH

Anthony Rizzo, Chicago	24
Josh Harrison, Pittsburgh	23
Tyler Flowers, Atlanta	20
Justin Turner, Los Angeles	19
Derek Dietrich, Miami	18

WALKS

Joey Votto, Cincinnati	134
Matt Carpenter, St. Louis	109
Kris Bryant, Chicago	95
Paul Goldschmidt, Arizona	94
Anthony Rizzo, Chicago	91

STOLEN BASES

Dee Gordon, Miami	60
Billy Hamilton, Cincinnati	59
Trea Turner, Washington	46
Tommy Pham, St. Louis	25
Jose Reyes, New York	24

STOLEN BASE PERCENTAGE

Gregor Blanco, Arizona	.938
Christian Yelich, Miami	.889
Trea Turner, Washington	.852
Sterling Marte, Pittsburgh	.840
Billy Hamilton, Cincinnati	.819

STRIKEOUTS

Trevor Story, Colorado	191
Wil Myers, San Diego	180
D. Santana, Milwaukee	178
Mark Reynolds, Colorado	175
Keon Broxton, Milwaukee	175

TOUGHEST TO STRIKE OUT

(At-bats per strikeout)

Joe Panik, San Francisco	9.5
Justin Turner, Los Angeles	8.2
Brandon Phillips, Atlanta	8.2
Yangervis Solarte, San Diego	7.6
Buster Posey, San Francisco	7.5

GROUNDED INTO DOUBLE PLAYS

Matt Kemp, Atlanta	25
D.J. LeMahieu, Colorado	24
Tommy Joseph, Philadelphia	21
Anthony Rizzo, Chicago	21
Yasiel Puig, Los Angeles	21
Nolan Arenado, Colorado	21
Maikel Franco, Philadelphia	21

MULTI-HIT GAMES

Charlie Blackmon, Colorado	68
Marcell Ozuna, Miami	60
Dee Gordon, Miami	59
Ender Inciarte, Atlanta	57
Nolan Arenado, Colorado	52
D.J. LeMahieu, Colorado	52

ON-BASE PERCENTAGE

Joey Votto, Cincinnati	.454
Justin Turner, Los Angeles	.415
Tommy Pham, St. Louis	.411
Kris Bryant, Chicago	.409
Paul Goldschmidt, Arizona	.404

ON-BASE PLUS SLUGGING

Joey Votto, Cincinnati	1.032
Giancarlo Stanton, Miami	1.007
Charlie Blackmon, Colorado	1.000
Freedie Freeman, Atlanta	.989
Paul Goldschmidt, Arizona	.966

PITCHING

WINS

Clayton Kershaw, Los Angeles	18
Zack Greinke, Arizona	17
Zach Davies, Milwaukee	17
Max Scherzer, Washington	16
Alex Wood, Los Angeles	16

LOSSES

Clayton Richard, San Diego	15
Tyler Chatwood, Colorado	15
Matt Moore, San Francisco	15
Jeff Samardzija, San Francisco	15
Ivan Nova, Pittsburgh	14

GAMES

Juan Nicasio, Pittsburgh, Philadelphia, St. Louis	76
Corey Knebel, Milwaukee	76
Matt Bowman, St. Louis	75

DUSTIN BRADFORD/GETTY IMAGES; ROB FOLDY/MIAMI MARLINS VIA GETTY IMAGES

NATIONAL LEAGUE DEPARTMENT LEADERS

Max Scherzer

Jerry Blevins, New York	75
Hector Neris, Philadelphia	74

GAMES STARTED

Gerrit Cole, Pittsburgh	33
Dan Straily, Miami	33
Lance Lynn, St. Louis	33
Zach Davies, Milwaukee	33
9 players	32

GAMES FINISHED

Greg Holland, Colorado	58
Raisel Iglesias, Cincinnati	57
Kenley Jansen, Los Angeles	57
Hector Neris, Philadelphia	56
Wade Davis, Chicago	56

COMPLETE GAMES

Max Scherzer, Washington	2
Clayton Richard, San Diego	2
Ivan Nova, Pittsburgh	2
Carlos Martinez, St. Louis	2
19 players	1

SHUTOUTS

Carlos Martinez, St. Louis	2
11 players	1

SAVES

Greg Holland, Colorado	41
Kenley Jansen, Los Angeles	41
Fernando Rodney, Arizona	39
Corey Knebel, Milwaukee	39
Wade Davis, Chicago	32

INNINGS PITCHED

Jeff Samardzija, San Francisco	208
Carlos Martinez, St. Louis	205
Gerrit Cole, Pittsburgh	203
Zack Greinke, Arizona	202
Jacob deGrom, New York	201

HITS ALLOWED

Clayton Richard, San Diego	240
Patrick Corbin, Arizona	208
Jeff Samardzija, San Francisco	204
Zach Davies, Milwaukee	204
Ivan Nova, Pittsburgh	203

RUNS ALLOWED

Matt Moore, San Francisco	116
Clayton Richard, San Diego	114
Jeff Samardzija, San Francisco	107
Tanner Roark, Washington	105
Julio Teheran, Atlanta	103

HOME RUNS ALLOWED

John Lackey, Chicago	36
Gerrit Cole, Pittsburgh	31
Julio Teheran, Atlanta	31
Dan Straily, Miami	31
Jeff Samardzija, San Francisco	30

WALKS ALLOWED

Gio Gonzalez, Washington	79
Lance Lynn, St. Louis	78
Tyler Chatwood, Colorado	77
Jhoulys Chacin, San Diego	72
Chad Kuhl, Pittsburgh	72
Julio Teheran, Atlanta	72

FEWEST WALKS PER NINE INNINGS

Jeff Samardzija, San Francisco	1.39
Clayton Kershaw, Los Angeles	1.54
Ivan Nova, Pittsburgh	1.73
Zack Greinke, Arizona	2.00
Ty Blach, San Francisco	2.36

HIT BATTERS

Jose Urena, Miami	14
Jhoulys Chacin, San Diego	14
John Lackey, Chicago	12
Max Scherzer, Washington	11
5 players	10

STRIKEOUTS

Max Scherzer, Washington	268
Jacob deGrom, New York	239
Robbie Ray, Arizona	218
Carlos Martinez, St. Louis	217
Zack Greinke, Arizona	215

STRIKEOUTS PER NINE INNINGS

Robbie Ray, Arizona	12.11
Max Scherzer, Washington	12.02
Jacob DeGrom, New York	10.68
Stephen Strasburg, Washington	10.47
Clayton Kershaw, Los Angeles	10.39

STRIKEOUTS PER NINE INNINGS (RELIEVERS)

Corey Knebel, Milwaukee	14.92
Kenley Jansen, Los Angeles	14.36
Carl Edwards Jr., Chicago	12.75
Brad Hand, San Diego	11.80
Raisel Iglesias, Cincinnati	10.90

DOUBLE PLAYS

Clayton Richard, San Diego	32
Luis Perdomo, San Diego	32
Tyler Chatwood, Colorado	23
Ivan Nova, Pittsburgh	23
Zack Godley, Arizona	22
Zach Davies, Milwaukee	22
Ty Blach, San Francisco	22

PICKOFFS

Kyle Hendricks, Chicago	7
Clayton Richard, San Diego	6
R.A. Dickey, Atlanta	4
Rich Hill, Los Angeles	4
Julio Teheran, Atlanta	4

WILD PITCHES

Jake Arrieta, Chicago	14
R.A. Dickey, Atlanta	13
Zack Godley, Arizona	13
Michael Lorenzen, Cincinnati	12
Zack Greinke, Arizona	12
Tyler Chatwood, Colorado	12

WALKS PLUS HITS PER INNING

Max Scherzer, Washington	0.90
Clayton Kershaw, Los Angeles	0.95
Stephen Strasburg, Washington	1.02
Zack Greinke, Arizona	1.07
Jeff Samardzija, San Francisco	1.14

OPPONENT AVERAGE

Max Scherzer, Washington	.178
Robbie Ray, Arizona	.199
Stephen Strasburg, Washington	.204
Clayton Kershaw, Los Angeles	.212
Gio Gonzalez, Washington	.216

WORST ERA

Matt Moore, San Francisco	5.52
Clayton Richard, San Diego	4.79
Ty Blach, an Francisco	4.78
Luis Perdomo, San Diego	4.67
Tanner Roark, Washington	4.67

FIELDING

PITCHER

PCT	9 players	1.000
DP	Julio Teheran	6
E	4 players	4
A	R.A. Dickey	44
PO	John Lackey	27

CATCHER

PCT	Tucker Barnhart, Cincinnati	.999
E	Wilson Contreras, Chicago	13
PO	Yasmani Grandal, Los Angeles	1089
CS	Tucker Barnhart, Cincinnati	32
PB	Yasmani Grandal, Los Angeles	16
A	Tucker Barnhart	89
DP	Yadier Molina, St. Louis	13

FIRST BASE

PCT	Anthony Rizzo, Chicago	.998
PO	Wil Myers, San Diego	1295
A	Joey Votto, Cincinnati	165
DP	Wil Myers, San Diego	147
E	Ryan Zimmerman, Washington	12

SECOND BASE

PCT	D.J. LeMahieu, Colorado	.989
PO	Dee Gordon, Miami	266
A	D.J. LeMahieu, Colorado	470
DP	D.J. LeMahieu, Colorado	106
E	Jonathan Villar, Milwaukee	15

THIRD BASE

PCT	Anthony Rendon, Washington	.979
	Nolan Arenado, Colorado	.979
PO	Nolan Arenado, Colorado	103
	Maikel Franco, Philadelphia	103
	Eugenio Suarez, Cincinnati	103
A	Nolan Arenado, Colorado	311
DP	Nolan Arenado, Colorado	103
E	Kris Bryant, Chicago	18

SHORTSTOP

PCT	Freddy Galvis, Philadelphia	.989
PO	Orlando Arcia, Milwaukee	253
A	Orlando Arcia, Milwaukee	415
DP	Orlando Arcia, Milwaukee	103
E	Orlando Arica, Milwaukee	20
	Dansby Swanson, Atlanta	20

OUTFIELD

PCT	Jon Jay, Chicago	1.000
PO	Ender Inciartem Atlanta	410
A	Adam Duvall, Cincinnati	15
DP	Jason Heyward, Chicago	15
E	Hunter Renfroe, San Diego	9

WIN MCNAMEE/GETTY IMAGES

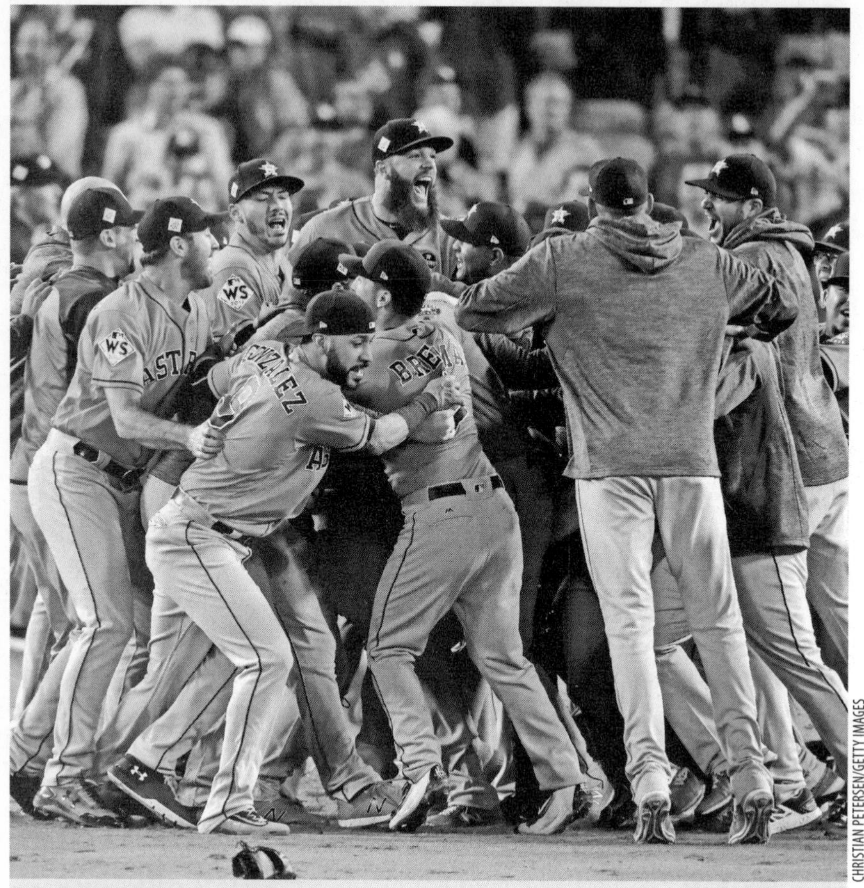
CHRISTIAN PETERSEN/GETTY IMAGES

Led by Jose Altuve and World Series MVP George Springer, the Astros won the World Series for the first time in franchise history.

Resilient Astros Prevail In A Classic World Series

BY JOHN PERROTTO

The Astros lost 106 games in 2011 then followed that with 107 losses in 2012 and a 111-loss season in 2013.

However, there were no more Lastros jokes in 2017.

The Astros won the first World Series title in franchise history, which dates back to 1962 when they entered the National League as expansion franchise known as the Colt .45s, by beating the Dodgers in seven games.

Behind a huge performance from center fielder George Springer and playing for a city that had been devastated by Hurricane Harvey in late August, the Astros rose to the top of the baseball in their second World Series appearance. In 2005, while still in the NL, the Astros were swept by the White Sox in four games.

The Astros made a thrilling series anticlimactic by scoring five runs in the first two innings of

Game 7 off Yu Darvish on their way to a 5-1 victory at Dodger Stadium. However, that did not dull the enthusiasm of Astros fans who packed Minute Maid Park in Houston to watch the television broadcast on the video board.

The Astros' players, who wore 'H Strong' patches on their jerseys in honor of the "Houston Strong" mantra the city adopted during the recovery. The players had the fans on their minds during their raucous postgame celebration.

"I always believed that we could make it," second baseman Jose Altuve said. "We did this for them."

"We're coming home a champion, Houston," Springer said after accepting the Willie Mays World Series MVP.

Astros star shortstop Carlos Correa made sure the night would be doubly memorable. Following a TV interview, he dropped to one knee asked his girlfriend, Daniella Rodriguez, to marry him. The former Miss Texas said yes.

It was only fitting that the Altuve made the play on the final out of the series, throwing Corey Seager out on a ground ball. Altuve was one of four players remaining from the 2013 team, which had switched to the American League from the National League prior to the the season, along with lefthander Dallas Keuchel, righthander Brad Peacock and utility player Marwin Gonzalez.

"I think it was the happiest moment of my life in baseball," Altuve said of the last out.

Meanwhile, there was disappointment on the other side. The Dodgers led the major leagues with 104 victories in the regular season with a $240 million payroll but came up short in their first World Series appearance since 1988.

"Obviously, this one hurts," manager Dave Roberts said. "And like I told the guys, when you put everything, every ounce of your being into something and you come up short, it hurts. And it's supposed to hurt."

Springer Rolls

It wasn't hard to pick a World Series MVP after George Springer came up big game after game after game.

The center fielder and leadoff hitter became just the third player to hit five home runs in one World Series, joining Reggie Jackson (1977 for the Yankees) and Chase Utley (2009 for the Phillies).

"The wildness of this series, the wackiness of this series, the emotional ups and downs, being able to play in this is something that I will never, ever forget, even if this is the only time I will ever get here," he told reporters afterward.

Springer homered in all of the final four games

EZRA SHAW/GETTY IMAGES

George Springer's five home runs tied the record for most in a World Series.

in the series. For the series overall, Springer hit .379/.471/.1.000 with a World Series-record eight extra-base hits. He was also the first player to hit home runs in four consecutive World Series games.

Springer's last home run was a two-run shot off Yu Darvish in Game Seven that chased the Dodgers righthander out of the game in the second inning.

"I just remember swinging and hearing the sound of the bat, and I knew it was a good sound," Springer told the Associated Press. "Then I saw the flight of the ball. And I got to first base and I rounded third, and got home and that's a crazy feeling. It's a very surreal feeling because this is Game Seveb. This is what you dream of as a kid. And for that to happen is indescribable."

If Springer was the star, Darvish, acquired in a deadline deal trade from the Rangers, had a Series to forget. He went 0-2, 21.60 in the World Series, lasting just 3.1 innings over two starts while allowing nine hits and nine runs, eight of which were earned. Darvish didn't strike out any of the 22 batters he faced in the World Series.

Springer struck out in four plate appearances in

a Game 1 loss to ace lefthander Clayton Kershaw. However, he bounced back to hit a tiebreaking two-run home run in the 11th inning of a Game Two win at Dodger Stadium as he went 11-for-25 over the final six games.

The 101-win Astros and Dodgers combined for a World Series-record 25 home runs while being the first 100-win teams to meet in the World Series since the Orioles defeated the Reds in 1970.

Paths To The Pennant

The Astros advanced to the World Series by going the distance in the American League Championship Series before beating the Yankees in seven games. The Dodgers dispatched the defending World Series champion Cubs in five games in the National League Championship Series.

The home team won all seven games in the ALCS, with the Astros capturing Games One and Two in Houston before the Yankees won the middle three games of the series at Yankee Stadium. Houston then rallied to win the final two games, including a 4-0 victory in Game Seven as Charlie Morton and Lance McCullers Jr. combined on a three-hit shutout while Jose Altuve and Evan Gattis homered.

Righthander Justin Verlander, acquired on Aug. 31 from the Tigers in a trade that was consumated just seconds before the deadline, was named ALCS MVP. The longtime Tigers star quickly took to his new team and a return to the postseason. He beat the Yankees in both starts, pitching a complete-game five-hitter with 13 strikeouts in Game Two then striking out eight during a seven-inning start in Game Six.

The ALCS had many thrilling moments, but Game Two was the most memorable. Carlos Correa homered off of Luis Severino to give Houston a 1-0 lead in the fourth. Todd Frazier quickly tied it back up by driving in Aaron Hicks in the top of the fifth.

The game remained tied 1-1 until the bottom of the ninth as a series of Yankees relievers matched Verlander's dominance.

In the ninth, Jose Altuve singled off of Aroldis Chapman and then scored from first on Correa's double, giving the Astros a thrilling 2-1 win.

The Yankees came up short in their bid to a win a record forty-first pennant, primarily because they struggled offensively at Minute Maid Park. In the four games in Houston, New York managed just three runs.

The series loss cost manager Joe Girardi his job as he was fired following 10 years in charge.

The Dodgers advanced to the World Series for the first time since 1988, ending the Cubs' hope of repeating as world champions with an 11-1 rout in Game Five at Wrigley Field in Chicago that included a three-home run, seven-RBI performance from utility man Enrique Hernandez.

Hernandez became the fourth player with a three-homer game in an LCS, joining Bob Robertson (Pirates, 1971 NLCS), George Brett (Royals, 1978 ALCS) and Adam Kennedy (Angels, 2002 ALCS). Hernandez's seven RBIs tied a postseason record shared by four other players, who all did it in a Division Series, most recently Troy O'Leary for the Red Sox in 1999 against the

AMERICAN LEAGUE CHAMPIONS, 1995-2017

American League postseason results in Wild Card Era, 1995-present, where (*) denotes wild card playoff entrant.

YEAR	CHAMPIONSHIP SERIES	ALCS MVP	DIVISION SERIES	DIVISION SERIES
2017	Houston 4, New York 3	Justin Verlander, RHP, Houston	New York* 3, Cleveland 2	Houston 3, Boston 1
2016	Cleveland 4, Toronto 1	Andrew Miller, LHP, Cleveland	Toronto* 3, Texas 0	Cleveland 3, Boston 0
2015	Kansas City 4, Toronto 2	Alcides Escobar, SS, Kansas City	Kansas City 3, Houston* 2	Baltimore 3, Texas 2
2014	Kansas City 4, Baltimore 0	Lorenzo Cain, OF, Kansas City	Kansas City 3, Los Angeles 0	Baltimore 3, Detroit 0
2013	Boston 4, Detroit 2	Koji Uehara, RHP, Boston	Boston 3, Tampa Bay* 1	Detroit, 3, Oakland 2
2012	Detroit 4, New York 0	Delmon Young, OF, Detroit	New York 3, Baltimore* 2	Detroit 3, Oakland 2
2011	Texas 4, Detroit 2	Nelson Cruz, OF, Texas	Detroit 3, New York 2	Texas 3, Tampa Bay* 1
2010	Texas 4, New York 2	Josh Hamilton, OF, Texas	Texas 3, Tampa Bay 2	New York* 3, Minnesota 0
2009	New York 4, Los Angeles 2	C.C. Sabathia, LHP, New York	New York 3, Minnesota 0	Los Angeles 3, Boston* 0
2008	Tampa Bay 4, Boston 3	Matt Garza, RHP, Tampa Bay	Boston* 3, Los Angeles 1	Tampa Bay 3, Chicago 1
2007	Boston 4, Cleveland 3	Josh Beckett, RHP, Boston	Boston 3, Los Angeles 0	Cleveland 3, New York* 1
2006	Detroit 4, Oakland 0	Placido Polanco, 2B, Detroit	Detroit* 3, New York 1	Oakland 3, Minnesota 0
2005	Chicago 4, Los Angeles 1	Paul Konerko, 1B, Chicago	Chicago 3, Boston* 0	Los Angeles 3, New York 2
2004	Boston 4, New York 3	David Ortiz, DH, Boston	Boston* 3, Anaheim 0	New York 3, Minnesota 1
2003	New York 4, Boston 3	Mariano Rivera, RHP, New York	New York 3, Minnesota 1	Boston* 3, Oakland 2
2002	Anaheim 4, Minnesota 1	Adam Kennedy, 2B, Anaheim	Anaheim* 3, New York 1	Minnesota 3, Oakland 2
2001	New York 4, Seattle 1	Andy Pettitte, LHP, New York	Seattle 3, Cleveland 2	New York 3, Oakland* 2
2000	New York 4, Seattle 2	David Justice, OF, New York	New York 3, Oakland 2	Seattle* 3, Chicago 0
1999	New York 4, Boston 1	Orlando Hernandez, RHP, New York	Boston* 3, Cleveland 2	New York 3, Texas 0
1998	New York 4, Cleveland 2	David Wells, LHP, New York	Cleveland 3, Boston* 1	New York 3, Texas 0
1997	Cleveland 4, Baltimore 2	Marquis Grissom, OF, Cleveland	Cleveland 3, New York* 2	Baltimore 3, Seattle 1
1996	New York 4, Baltimore 1	Bernie Williams, OF, New York	Baltimore* 3, Cleveland 1	New York 3, Texas 1
1995	Cleveland 4, Seattle 2	Orel Hershiser, RHP, Cleveland	Cleveland 3, Boston 0	Seattle 3, New York* 2

Indians in an ALDS.

It was a stunning display for Hernandez, who had just 28 career regular-season homers over four seasons and 967 plate appearances.

Third baseman Justin Turner and utility player Chris Taylor were named co-MVPs of the NLCS. Turner hit .333 with two home runs—including a walk-off shot in Game Two at Dodger Stadium—and seven RBIs while Taylor—who was acquired from the Mariners in a trade that cost the Dodgers only righthander Zach Lee— batted .316 with two homers.

Meanwhile, the Cubs batted just .156 and scored just eight runs, all coming on home runs.

In the Division Series round, the Astros defeat the Red Sox in four games and the Yankees rallied from a 2-0 deficit to defeat the Indians in five games in the AL while the Dodgers swept the Diamondbacks in three games and the Cubs outlasted the Nationals in five games in the NL.

Verlander won twice for the Astros against the Red Sox, including getting the decision in the decisive Game Four while making the first relief appearance of his career following 424 starts. The Yankees began their comeback from a 2-0 series deficit against the Indians with a pair of victories at Yankee Stadium before beating the Indians 5-2 in Game Five at Progressive Field in Cleveland behind a pair of Didi Gregorius home runs.

Cody Bellinger, who set the NL rookie record with 39 regular-season homers, helped the Dodgers finish off a sweep of the Diamondbacks by homering in a 3-1 victory in Game 3 at Chase Field in Arizona. The Cubs notched a wacky 9-8 victory over the Nationals in Game Five at Nationals Park in Washington with shortstop Addison Russell driving in the go-ahead runs with a two-run double in the fifth inning.

The Yankees beat the visiting Twins 7-3 in the AL wild card game, storming back from a 3-0 deficit in the top of the first inning as Gregorius hit a tying three-run home run in the bottom of the inning and rookie right fielder Aaron Judge later added a two-run shot. For the Twins, simply making the postseason was a very impressive feat—they went 59-103 in 2016 to post the worst record in the major leagues.

In the NL wild card game, the Diamondbacks outlasted the visiting Rockies 11-8. The Diamondbacks hit four triples, including one by relief pitcher Archie Bradley that drove in two runs, after he had gone 6-for-61 (.098) with no extra-base hits in his three-year career.

In the end, the Astros prevailed as they became the first team to win a pair of Game Sevens in the same postseason since the 1985 Royals. The patience shown by owner Jim Crane and general manager Jeff Luhnow paid off in the team's first title. Their willingness to stick with their plan, knowing it would mean years of 100-plus loss seasons while drawing the ire of fans and media alike, paid off in the best way possible.

"It's a crazy journey, man," Altuve said. "I was the only one in 2011, '12 and '13, those 100 losses, three years in a row. It's not easy. But I believed in the process. I believed in what Jeff Luhnow and Jim Crane used to (say) to me: 'Hey, we're going to be good. We're going to be good.'"

NATIONAL LEAGUE CHAMPIONS, 1995-2017

National League postseason results in Wild Card Era, 1995-present, where (*) denotes wild card playoff entrant.

YEAR	CHAMPIONSHIP SERIES	NLCS MVP	DIVISION SERIES	DIVISION SERIES
2017	Los Angeles 4, Chicago 1	Justin Turner, 3B/Chris Taylor, CF, L.A.	Los Angeles 3, Arizona* 0	Chicago 3, Washington 2
2016	Chicago 4, Los Angeles 2	Javier Baez, 2B/Jon Lester, LHP, Chicago	Chicago 3, San Francisco* 1	Los Angeles 3, Washington 2
2015	New York 4, Chicago 0	Daniel Murphy, 2B, New York	New York 3, Los Angeles 2	Chicago* 3, St. Louis 1
2014	San Francisco 4, St. Louis 1	Madison Bumgarner, LHP, San Francisco	San Francisco 3, Washington 1	St. Louis 3, Los Angeles 1
2013	St. Louis 4, Los Angeles 2	Michael Wacha, RHP, St. Louis	St. Louis 3, Pittsburgh* 2	Los Angeles 3, Atlanta 1
2012	San Francisco 4, St. Louis 3	Marco Scutaro, 2B, San Francisco	St. Louis* 3, Washington 2	San Francisco 3, Cincinnati 2
2011	St. Louis 4, Milwaukee 2	David Freese, 3B, St. Louis	St. Louis* 3, Philadelphia 2	Milwaukee 3, Arizona 2
2010	San Francisco 4, Philadelphia 2	Cody Ross, OF, San Francisco	Philadelphia 3, Cincinnati 0	San Francisco 3, Atlanta* 1
2009	Philadelphia 4, Los Angeles 1	Ryan Howard, 1B, Philadelphia	Los Angeles 3, St. Louis 0	Philadelphia 3, Colorado* 1
2008	Philadelphia 4, Los Angeles 1	Cole Hamels, LHP, Philadelphia	Los Angeles 3, Chicago 0	Philadelphia 3, Milwaukee* 1
2007	Colorado 4, Arizona 0	Matt Holliday, OF, Colorado	Arizona 3, Chicago 0	Colorado* 3, Philadelphia 0
2006	St. Louis 4, New York 3	Jeff Suppan, RHP, St. Louis	New York 3, Los Angeles* 0	St. Louis 3, San Diego 1
2005	Houston 4, St. Louis 2	Roy Oswalt, RHP, Houston	St. Louis 3, San Diego 0	Houston* 3, Atlanta 1
2004	St. Louis 4, Houston 3	Albert Pujols, 1B, St. Louis	St. Louis 3, Los Angeles 1	Houston* 3, Atlanta 2
2003	Florida 4, Chicago 3	Ivan Rodriguez, C, Florida	Florida* 3, San Francisco 1	Chicago 3, Atlanta 2
2002	San Francisco 4, St. Louis 1	Benito Santiago, C, San Francisco	San Francisco* 3, Atlanta 2	St. Louis 3, Arizona 0
2001	Arizona 4, Atlanta 1	Craig Counsell, SS, Arizona	Atlanta 3, Houston 0	Arizona 3, St. Louis* 2
2000	New York 4, St. Louis 1	Mike Hampton, LHP, New York	St. Louis 3, Atlanta 0	New York* 3, San Francisco 1
1999	Atlanta 4, New York 2	Eddie Perez, C, Atlanta	Atlanta 3, Houston 1	New York* 3, Arizona 1
1998	San Diego 4, Atlanta 2	Sterling Hitchcock, LHP, San Diego	Atlanta 3, Chicago* 0	San Diego 3, Houston 1
1997	Florida 4, Atlanta 2	Livan Hernandez, RHP, Florida	Florida* 3, San Francisco 0	Atlanta 3, Houston 0
1996	Atlanta 4, St. Louis 3	Javy Lopez, C, Atlanta	St. Louis 3, San Diego 0	Atlanta 3, Los Angeles* 0
1995	Atlanta 4, Cincinnati 0	Mike Devereaux, OF, Atlanta	Atlanta 3, Colorado* 1	Cincinnati 3, Los Angeles 0

THE WORLD SERIES YEAR-BY-YEAR

Year	Winner	Loser	Result
1903	Boston (AL)	Pittsburgh (NL)	5-3
1904	NO SERIES		
1905	New York (NL)	Philadelphia (AL)	4-1
1906	Chicago (AL)	Chicago (NL)	4-2
1907	Chicago (NL)	Detroit (AL)	4-0
1908	Chicago (NL)	Detroit (AL)	4-1
1909	Pittsburgh (NL)	Detroit (AL)	4-3
1910	Philadelphia (AL)	Chicago (NL)	4-1
1911	Philadelphia (AL)	New York (NL)	4-2
1912	Boston (AL)	New York (NL)	4-3-1
1913	Philadelphia (AL)	New York (NL)	4-1
1914	Boston (NL)	Philadelphia (AL)	4-0
1915	Boston (AL)	Philadelphia (NL)	4-1
1916	Boston (AL)	Brooklyn (NL)	4-1
1917	Chicago (AL)	New York (NL)	4-2
1918	Boston (AL)	Chicago (NL)	4-2
1919	Cincinnati (NL)	Chicago (AL)	5-3
1920	Cleveland (AL)	Brooklyn (NL)	5-2
1921	New York (NL)	New York (AL)	5-3
1922	New York (NL)	New York (AL)	4-0
1923	New York (AL)	New York (NL)	4-2
1924	Washington (AL)	New York (NL)	4-3
1925	Pittsburgh (NL)	Washington (AL)	4-3
1926	St. Louis (NL)	New York (AL)	4-3
1927	New York (AL)	Pittsburgh (NL)	4-0
1928	New York (AL)	St. Louis (NL)	4-0
1929	Philadelphia (AL)	Chicago (NL)	4-1
1930	Philadelphia (AL)	St. Louis (NL)	4-2
1931	St. Louis (NL)	Philadelphia (AL)	4-3
1932	New York (AL)	Chicago (NL)	4-0
1933	New York (NL)	Washington (AL)	4-1
1934	St. Louis (NL)	Detroit (AL)	4-3
1935	Detroit (AL)	Chicago (NL)	4-2
1936	New York (AL)	New York (NL)	4-2
1937	New York (AL)	New York (NL)	4-1
1938	New York (AL)	Chicago (NL)	4-0
1939	New York (AL)	Cincinnati (NL)	4-0
1940	Cincinnati (NL)	Detroit (AL)	4-3
1941	New York (AL)	Brooklyn (NL)	4-1
1942	St. Louis (NL)	New York (AL)	4-1
1943	New York (AL)	St. Louis (NL)	4-1
1944	St. Louis (NL)	St. Louis (AL)	4-2
1945	Detroit (AL)	Chicago (NL)	4-3
1946	St. Louis (NL)	Boston (AL)	4-3
1947	New York (AL)	Brooklyn (NL)	4-3
1948	Cleveland (AL)	Boston (NL)	4-2
1949	New York (AL)	Brooklyn (NL)	4-1
1950	New York (AL)	Philadelphia (NL)	4-0
1951	New York (AL)	New York (NL)	4-2
1952	New York (AL)	Brooklyn (NL)	4-3
1953	New York (AL)	Brooklyn (NL)	4-2
1954	New York (NL)	Cleveland (AL)	4-0
1955	Brooklyn (NL)	New York (AL)	4-3
1956	New York (AL)	Brooklyn (NL)	4-3
1957	Milwaukee (NL)	New York (AL)	4-3
1958	New York (AL)	Milwaukee (NL)	4-3
1959	Los Angeles (NL)	Chicago (AL)	4-2
1960	Pittsburgh (NL)	New York (AL)	4-3
1961	New York (AL)	Cincinnati (NL)	4-1
1962	New York (AL)	San Francisco (NL)	4-3
1963	Los Angeles (NL)	New York (AL)	4-0
1964	St. Louis (NL)	New York (AL)	4-3
1965	Los Angeles (NL)	Minnesota (AL)	4-3
1966	Baltimore (AL)	Los Angeles (NL)	4-0
1967	St. Louis (NL)	Boston (AL)	4-3
1968	Detroit (AL)	St. Louis (NL)	4-3
1969	New York (NL)	Baltimore (AL)	4-1
1970	Baltimore (AL)	Cincinnati (NL)	4-1
1971	Pittsburgh (NL)	Baltimore (AL)	4-3
1972	Oakland (AL)	Cincinnati (NL)	4-3
1973	Oakland (AL)	New York (NL)	4-3
1974	Oakland (AL)	Los Angeles (NL)	4-1
1975	Cincinnati (NL)	Boston (AL)	4-3
1976	Cincinnati (NL)	New York (AL)	4-0

ROB TRINGALI/MLB PHOTOS VIA GETTY IMAGES

Justin Verlander proved a vital acquisition.

Year	Winner	Loser	Result
1977	New York (AL)	Los Angeles (NL)	4-2
1978	New York (AL)	Los Angeles (NL)	4-2
1979	Pittsburgh (NL)	Baltimore (AL)	4-3
1980	Philadelphia (NL)	Kansas City (AL)	4-2
1981	Los Angeles (NL)	New York (AL)	4-2
1982	St. Louis (NL)	Milwaukee (AL)	4-3
1983	Baltimore (AL)	Philadelphia (NL)	4-1
1984	Detroit (AL)	San Diego (NL)	4-1
1985	Kansas City (AL)	St. Louis (NL)	4-3
1986	New York (NL)	Boston (AL)	4-3
1987	Minnesota (AL)	St. Louis (NL)	4-3
1988	Los Angeles (NL)	Oakland (AL)	4-1
1989	Oakland (AL)	San Francisco (NL)	4-0
1990	Cincinnati (NL)	Oakland (AL)	4-0
1991	Minnesota (AL)	Atlanta (NL)	4-3
1992	Toronto (AL)	Atlanta (NL)	4-2
1993	Toronto (AL)	Philadelphia (NL)	4-2
1994	NO SERIES		
1995	Atlanta (NL)	Cleveland (AL)	4-2
1996	New York (AL)	Atlanta (NL)	4-2
1997	Florida (NL)	Cleveland (AL)	4-3
1998	New York (AL)	San Diego (NL)	4-0
1999	New York (AL)	Atlanta (NL)	4-0
2000	New York (AL)	New York (NL)	4-1
2001	Arizona (NL)	New York (AL)	4-3
2002	Anaheim (AL)	San Francisco (NL)	4-3
2003	Florida (NL)	New York (AL)	4-2
2004	Boston (AL)	St. Louis (NL)	4-0
2005	Chicago (AL)	Houston (NL)	4-0
2006	St. Louis (NL)	Detroit (AL)	4-1
2007	Boston (AL)	Colorado (NL)	4-0
2008	Philadelphia (NL)	Tampa Bay (AL)	4-1
2009	New York (AL)	Philadelphia (NL)	4-2
2010	San Francisco (NL)	Texas (AL)	4-1
2011	St. Louis (NL)	Texas (AL)	4-3
2012	San Francisco (NL)	Detroit (AL)	4-0
2013	Boston (AL)	St. Louis (NL)	4-2
2014	San Francisco (NL)	Kansas City (AL)	4-3
2015	Kansas City (AL)	New York (NL)	4-1
2016	Chicago (NL)	Cleveland (AL)	4-3
2017	Houston (AL)	Los Angeles (NL)	4-3

WORLD SERIES BOX SCORES

GAME ONE *October 24, 2017*

LOS ANGELES DODGERS 3, HOUSTON ASTROS 1

HOUSTON	AB	R	H	RBI	BB	SO	LOB	AVG
Springer, CF	4	0	0	0	0	4	1	.000
Bregman, 3B	4	1	1	1	0	0	0	.250
Altuve, 2B	4	0	1	0	0	1	0	.250
Correa, SS	3	0	0	0	0	1	1	.000
Gurriel, 1B	3	0	0	0	0	2	1	.000
McCann, B, C	3	0	0	0	0	0	1	.000
Gonzalez, M, LF	3	0	0	0	0	1	0	.000
Reddick, RF	3	0	1	0	0	1	0	.333
Keuchel, P	2	0	0	0	0	2	1	.000
Peacock, P	0	0	0	0	0	0	0	.000
a-Beltran, PH	1	0	0	0	0	0	0	.000
Devenski, P	0	0	0	0	0	0	0	.000
TOTALS	**30**	**1**	**3**	**1**	**0**	**12**	**5**	

a-Grounded out for Peacock in the 8th. **HR:** Bregman (1, 4th inning off Kershaw, 0 on, 0 out). **TB:** Reddick; Bregman 4; Altuve. **RBI:** Bregman (1). **Team LOB:** 2.

LOS ANGELES	AB	R	H	RBI	BB	SO	LOB	AVG
Taylor, C, CF	3	2	1	1	1	0	1	.333
Turner, 3B	4	1	1	2	0	2	0	.250
Bellinger, 1B	3	0	0	0	0	1	0	.000
Puig, RF	3	0	0	0	0	0	0	.000
Hernandez, LF	3	0	1	0	0	1	0	.333
Seager, C, SS	3	0	2	0	0	0	1	.667
Forsythe, 2B	2	0	0	0	1	0	1	.000
Barnes, A, C	3	0	1	0	0	0	2	.333
Kershaw, P	1	0	0	0	0	0	0	.000
Morrow, P	0	0	0	0	0	0	0	.000
a-Culberson, PH	1	0	0	0	0	1	0	.000
Jansen, P	0	0	0	0	0	0	0	.000
TOTALS	**26**	**3**	**6**	**3**	**2**	**5**	**5**	

a-Struck out for Morrow in the 8th. **HR:** Taylor, C (1, 1st inning off Keuchel, 0 on, 0 out); Turner (1, 6th inning off Keuchel, 1 on, 2 out). **TB:** Hernandez; Taylor, C 4; Turner 4; Barnes, A; Seager, C 2. **RBI:** Taylor, C (1); Turner 2 (2). **Team LOB:** 2.

HOUSTON	IP	H	R	ER	BB	SO	HR	ERA
Keuchel (L, 0-1)	6.2	6	3	3	1	3	2	4.05
Peacock	0.1	0	0	0	1	0	0	0.00
Devenski	1.0	0	0	0	0	2	0	0.00
LOS ANGELES	**IP**	**H**	**R**	**ER**	**BB**	**SO**	**HR**	**ERA**
Kershaw (W, 1-0)	7.0	3	1	1	0	11	1	1.29
Morrow (H, 1)	1.0	0	0	0	0	0	0	0.00
Jansen (S, 1)	1.0	0	0	0	0	1	0	0.00

	1	2	3	4	5	6	7	8	9	R	H	E
HOUSTON	0	0	0	1	0	0	0	0	0	1	3	0
LA DODGERS	1	0	0	0	0	2	0	0	X	3	6	0

GAME TWO *October 25, 2017*

HOUSTON ASTROS 7, LOS ANGELES DODGERS 6

HOUSTON	AB	R	H	RBI	BB	SO	LOB	AVG
Springer, CF-RF	5	1	3	2	1	0	1	.333
Bregman, 3B	6	1	2	1	0	0	2	.300
Altuve, 2B	6	1	1	1	0	2	4	.200
Correa, SS	6	1	3	2	0	1	3	.333
Gurriel, 1B	4	0	1	0	1	0	2	.143
McCann, B, C	5	0	0	0	0	2	4	.000
Gonzalez, M, LF	3	1	1	1	2	2	1	.167
Reddick, RF	4	1	1	0	1	0	3	.286
Devenski, P	0	0	0	0	0	0	0	.000
Verlander, P	1	0	0	0	0	1	2	.000
a-Gattis, PH	1	0	1	0	0	0	0	1.000
Harris, P	0	0	0	0	0	0	0	.000
Musgrove, P	0	0	0	0	0	0	0	.000
b-Beltran, PH	1	0	0	0	0	0	0	.000
Giles, P	0	0	0	0	0	0	0	.000
Maybin, CF	1	1	1	0	0	0	0	1.000
TOTALS	**43**	**7**	**14**	**7**	**5**	**8**	**22**	

a-Singled for Verlander in the 7th. **b-**Flied out for Musgrove in the 9th. **2B:** Bregman (1, Morrow); Springer (1, Jansen); Gurriel (1, Fields, J). **HR:** Gonzalez, M (1, 9th inning off Jansen, 0 on, 0 out); Altuve (1, 10th inning off Fields, J, 0 on, 0 out); Correa (1, 10th inning off Fields, J, 0 on, 0 out); Springer (1, 11th inning off McCarthy, 1 on, 0 out). **TB:** Gonzalez, M 4; Maybin; Springer 7; Reddick; Gurriel 2; Gattis; Bregman 3; Correa 6; Altuve 4. **RBI:** Bregman (2); Correa 2 (2); Gonzalez, M (1); Altuve (1); Springer 2 (2). **Team LOB:** 9. **SB:** Maybin (1, 2nd base off McCarthy/Grandal). **E:** Bregman (1, throw).

LOS ANGELES	AB	R	H	RBI	BB	SO	LOB	AVG
Taylor, C, CF	3	1	0	0	2	1	1	.167
McCarthy, P	0	0	0	0	0	0	0	.000
Seager, C, SS	5	1	1	2	0	2	1	.375
Turner, 3B	5	0	0	0	0	0	1	.111
Bellinger, 1B	4	0	0	0	0	2	0	.000
Cingrani, P	0	0	0	0	0	0	0	.000
Culberson, LF	1	1	1	1	0	0	0	.500
Puig, RF	5	1	1	1	0	1	1	.125
Pederson, LF	3	1	1	1	0	2	1	.333
Jansen, P	0	0	0	0	0	0	0	.000
Fields, J, P	0	0	0	0	0	0	0	.000
Grandal, C	1	0	0	0	0	1	0	.000
Barnes, A, C-2B	4	0	0	0	0	2	1	.143
Utley, 2B	3	0	0	0	0	0	0	.000
Forsythe, 2B-1B	0	1	0	0	1	0	0	.000
Hill, R, P	1	0	0	0	0	0	0	.000
Maeda, P	0	0	0	0	0	0	0	.000
Watson, P	0	0	0	0	0	0	0	.000
a-Ethier, PH	1	0	0	0	0	0	0	.000
Stripling, P	0	0	0	0	0	0	0	.000
Morrow, P	0	0	0	0	0	0	0	.000
Hernandez, LF-CF	2	0	1	1	0	0	0	.400
TOTALS	**38**	**6**	**5**	**6**	**3**	**11**	**6**	

a-Flied out for Watson in the 6th. **HR:** Pederson (1, 5th inning off Verlander, 0 on, 2 out); Seager, C (1, 6th inning off Verlander, 1 on, 2 out); Puig (1, 10th inning off Giles, 0 on, 0 out); Culberson (1, 11th inning off Devenski, 0 on, 2 out). **TB:** Puig 4; Pederson 4; Hernandez; Culberson 4; Seager, C 4. **RBI:** Pederson (1); Seager, C 2 (2); Puig (1); Hernandez (1); Culberson (1). **Team LOB:** 2. **PB:** Barnes, A (1).

HOUSTON	IP	H	R	ER	BB	SO	HR	ERA
Verlander	6.0	2	3	3	2	5	2	4.50
Harris	1.0	0	0	0	0	2	0	0.00
Musgrove	1.0	0	0	0	0	0	0	0.00
Giles	1.2	2	2	2	1	3	1	10.80
Devenski (W, 1-0)	1.1	1	1	1	0	1	1	3.86
LOS ANGELES	**IP**	**H**	**R**	**ER**	**BB**	**SO**	**HR**	**ERA**
Hill, R	4.0	3	1	1	3	7	0	2.25
Maeda	1.1	1	0	0	0	0	0	0.00
Watson	0.2	0	0	0	0	0	0	0.00
Stripling	0.0	0	0	0	1	0	0	-
Morrow (H, 2)	1.0	2	1	1	0	0	0	4.50
Jansen (BS, 1)	2.0	3	1	1	0	1	1	3.00
Fields, J	0.0	3	2	2	0	0	2	-.--
Cingrani	1.0	0	0	0	1	0	0	0.00
McCarthy (L, 0-1)	1.0	2	2	2	0	0	1	18.00

Stripling pitched to 1 batter in the 7th.

				4	5	6	7	8	9	10	11	R	H	E
HOUSTON	0	0	1	0	0	0	0	1	1	2	2	7	14	1
LA DODGERS	0	0	0	0	1	2	0	0	0	2	1	6	5	0

GAME THREE *October 27, 2017*

HOUSTON ASTROS 5, LOS ANGELES DODGERS 3

LOS ANGELES	AB	R	H	RBI	BB	SO	LOB	AVG
Taylor, C, CF	3	0	0	0	1	0	2	.111
Seager, C, SS	3	1	0	0	1	1	2	.273
Turner, 3B	4	1	1	0	0	0	1	.154
Bellinger, 1B	4	0	0	0	0	4	2	.000
Puig, RF	4	0	1	1	0	1	1	.167
Forsythe, 2B	2	0	1	0	0	0	0	.250
a-Utley, PH-2B	2	0	0	0	0	0	0	.000
Barnes, A, C	2	0	0	0	0	0	1	.111
b-Grandal, PH-C	2	0	0	0	0	0	0	.000

Pederson, DH	2	1	1	0	1	1	0	.400
Hernandez, LF	1	0	0	0	1	0	1	.333
c-Ethier, PH-LF	0	0	0	0	1	0	0	.000
TOTALS	**29**	**3**	**4**	**1**	**5**	**7**	**10**	

a-Popped out for Forsythe in the 6th. **b**-Flied out for Barnes, A in the 7th. **c**-Walked for Hernandez in the 7th. **2B:** Pederson (1, McCullers Jr.); Turner (1, McCullers Jr.). **TB:** Puig; Turner 2; Pederson 2; Forsythe. **RBI:** Puig (2). **Team LOB:** 4. **SB:** Forsythe (1, 2nd base off McCullers Jr./McCann, B). **E:** Watson (1, throw); Turner (1, throw).

HOUSTON	AB	R	H	RBI	BB	SO	LOB	AVG
Springer, CF	5	0	1	0	0	1	6	.286
Bregman, 3B	3	0	0	1	1	1	2	.231
Altuve, 2B	5	0	1	0	0	2	4	.200
Correa, SS	5	0	1	0	0	1	5	.286
Gurriel, 1B	5	1	2	1	0	0	1	.250
Reddick, RF	4	2	2	0	0	0	1	.364
Gattis, DH	1	1	1	0	3	0	0	1.000
Gonzalez, M, LF	4	1	1	1	0	1	4	.200
McCann, B, C	4	0	3	1	0	0	0	.250
TOTALS	**36**	**5**	**12**	**4**	**4**	**6**	**23**	

2B: Springer (2, Darvish); Reddick (1, Darvish); Altuve (1, Darvish); Gurriel (2, Morrow). **HR:** Gurriel (1, 2nd inning off Darvish, 0 on, 0 out). **TB:** Springer 2; Reddick 3; Gurriel 6; Gonzalez, M; Gattis; Altuve 2; Correa; McCann, B 3. **RBI:** Gurriel (1); Gonzalez, M (2); McCann, B (1); Bregman (3). **Team LOB:** 12.

LOS ANGELES	IP	H	R	ER	BB	SO	HR	ERA
Darvish (L, 0-1)	1.2	6	4	4	1	0	1	21.60
Maeda	2.2	1	0	0	1	2	0	0.00
Watson	1.0	2	1	0	0	1	0	0.00
Morrow	0.2	1	0	0	1	2	0	3.38
Cingrani	0.2	1	0	0	1	0	0	0.00
Stripling	1.1	1	0	0	0	1	0	0.00
HOUSTON	**IP**	**H**	**R**	**ER**	**BB**	**SO**	**HR**	**ERA**
McCullers Jr. (W, 1-0)	5.1	4	3	3	4	3	0	5.06
Peacock (S, 1)	3.2	0	0	0	1	4	0	0.00

Morrow pitched to 1 batter in the 7th.

	1	2	3	4	5	6	7	8	9	R	H	E
LA DODGERS	**0**	**0**	**1**	**0**	**0**	**2**	**0**	**0**	**0**	**3**	**4**	**2**
HOUSTON	**0**	**4**	**0**	**0**	**1**	**0**	**0**	**0**	**X**	**5**	**12**	**0**

GAME FOUR *October 28, 2017*

LOS ANGELES DODGERS 6, HOUSTON ASTROS 2

LOS ANGELES	AB	R	H	RBI	BB	SO	LOB	AVG
Taylor, C, CF	4	0	1	0	0	1	2	.154
Seager, C, SS	4	1	1	0	0	1	3	.267
Turner, 3B	3	0	0	0	1	1	1	.125
1-Culberson, PR-2B	0	1	0	0	0	0	0	.500
Bellinger, 1B	4	2	2	1	0	1	0	.133
Puig, RF	4	0	0	0	0	1	3	.125
Forsythe, 2B-3B	3	1	1	1	1	1	0	.286
Barnes, A, C	2	0	0	1	0	0	1	.091
Pederson, DH	4	1	1	3	0	2	1	.333
Hernandez, LF	4	0	1	0	0	1	0	.300
TOTALS	**32**	**6**	**7**	**6**	**2**	**9**	**11**	

1-Ran for Turner in the 9th. **2B:** Bellinger 2 (2, Morton, Giles). **HR:** Pederson (2, 9th inning off Musgrove, 2 on, 2 out). **TB:** Hernandez; Taylor, C; Pederson 4; Forsythe; Seager, C; Bellinger 4. **RBI:** Forsythe (1); Bellinger (1); Barnes, A (1); Pederson 3 (4). **Team LOB:** 3. CS: Taylor, C (1, 2nd base by Morton/McCann, B). **DP:** (Turner-Forsythe-Bellinger).

HOUSTON	AB	R	H	RBI	BB	SO	LOB	AVG
Springer, CF	4	1	1	1	0	1	1	.278
Bregman, 3B	4	1	1	1	0	0	0	.235
Altuve, 2B	4	0	0	0	0	0	0	.158
Correa, SS	2	0	0	0	1	0	0	.250
Gurriel, 1B	3	0	0	0	0	1	1	.200
Reddick, RF	3	0	0	0	0	0	0	.286
Gattis, DH	3	0	0	0	0	0	0	.400
Gonzalez, M, LF	2	0	0	0	1	0	0	.167
McCann, B, C	3	0	0	0	0	2	1	.200
TOTALS	**28**	**2**	**2**	**2**	**2**	**4**	**3**	

HR: Springer (2, 6th inning off Wood, A, 2 out); Bregman (2, 9th inning off Jansen, 0 on, 2 out). **TB:** Springer 4; Bregman 4. **RBI:** Springer (3); Bregman (4). **2-out RBI:** Springer; Bregman. **Team LOB:** 1.

LOS ANGELES	IP	H	R	ER	BB	SO	HR	ERA
Wood, A	5.2	1	1	1	2	3	1	1.59
Morrow	1.1	0	0	0	0	0	0	2.25
Watson (W, 1-0)	1.0	0	0	0	0	0	0	0.00
Jansen	1.0	1	1	1	0	1	1	4.50
HOUSTON	**IP**	**H**	**R**	**ER**	**BB**	**SO**	**HR**	**ERA**
Morton	6.1	3	1	1	0	7	0	1.42
Harris (BS, 1)	0.2	1	0	0	0	0	0	0.00
Devenski	1.0	0	0	0	0	1	0	2.70
Giles (L, 0-1)	0.0	2	3	3	1	0	0	27.00
Musgrove	1.0	1	2	2	1	1	1	9.00

Giles pitched to 3 batters in the 9th.

	1	2	3	4	5	6	7	8	9	R	H	E
LA DODGERS	**0**	**0**	**0**	**0**	**0**	**0**	**1**	**0**	**5**	**6**	**7**	**0**
HOUSTON	**0**	**0**	**0**	**0**	**0**	**1**	**0**	**0**	**1**	**2**	**2**	**0**

GAME FIVE *October 29, 2017*

HOUSTON ASTROS 13, LOS ANGELES DODGERS 12

LOS ANGELES	AB	R	H	RBI	BB	SO	LOB	AVG
Taylor, C, CF-2B	5	1	2	1	0	1	3	.222
Seager, C, SS	5	1	1	1	1	2	3	.250
Turner, DH	4	2	1	0	2	0	2	.150
Hernandez, LF-2B	3	2	0	0	1	1	3	.231
b-Ethier, PH-LF	2	0	1	0	0	0	2	.333
Bellinger, 1B	5	2	2	4	1	2	4	.200
Forsythe, 3B	6	1	2	2	0	2	3	.308
Puig, RF	5	1	1	2	0	2	3	.143
Barnes, A, C	5	1	2	1	0	2	0	.188
Culberson, 2B	2	0	1	0	0	0	0	.500
a-Pederson, PH-LF-CF	2	1	1	0	1	0	1	.364
TOTALS	**44**	**12**	**14**	**11**	**6**	**12**	**24**	

a-Walked for Culberson in the 6th. **b**-Batted for Hernandez in the 8th. **2B:** Forsythe (1, Keuchel); Turner (2, Peacock); Pederson (2, Peacock); Seager, C (1, Harris); Barnes, A (1, Devenski). 3B: Bellinger (1, Peacock). **HR:** Bellinger (1, 5th inning off McHugh, 2 on, 1 out); Puig (2, 9th inning off Devenski, 1 on, 1 out). **TB:** Puig 4; Turner 2; Pederson 2; Bellinger 7; Culberson; Taylor, C 2; Ethier; Forsythe 3; Barnes, A 3; Seager, C 2. **RBI:** Forsythe 2 (3); Barnes, A (2); Bellinger 4 (5); Seager, C (3); Puig 2 (4); Taylor, C (2). **Team LOB:** 9. CS: Forsythe (1, 2nd base by Keuchel/McCann, B). **E:** Forsythe (1, throw).

HOUSTON	AB	R	H	RBI	BB	SO	LOB	AVG
Springer, CF-RF	3	3	2	1	3	0	0	.333
Bregman, 3B	5	2	2	1	1	0	2	.273
Altuve, 2B	5	3	3	4	0	1	0	.250
Correa, SS	5	2	3	3	0	0	0	.333
Gurriel, 1B	5	1	2	3	0	1	1	.250
1-Maybin, PR-CF	0	0	0	0	0	0	0	1.000
Reddick, RF-LF	5	0	0	0	0	2	1	.211
Gattis, DH	4	0	1	0	1	0	0	.333
Gonzalez, M, LF-1B	5	0	0	0	0	1	2	.118
McCann, B, C	4	1	1	1	0	1	1	.211
2-Fisher, PR	0	1	0	0	0	0	0	.000
TOTALS	**41**	**13**	**14**	**13**	**5**	**6**	**7**	

1-Ran for Gurriel in the 9th. **2**-Ran for McCann, B in the 10th. **2B:** Correa (1, Kershaw); Altuve (2, Morrow); Gurriel (3, Jansen). **HR:** Gurriel (2, 4th inning off Kershaw, 2 on, 1 out); Altuve (2, 5th inning off Maeda, 2 on, 2 out); Springer (3, 7th inning off Morrow, 0 out); Correa (2, 7th inning off Morrow, 1 on, 0 out); McCann, B (1, 8th inning off Cingrani, 0 on, 1 out). **TB:** Springer 5; Gurriel 6; Gattis; Bregman 2; Correa 7; Altuve 7; McCann, B 4. **RBI:** Correa 3 (5); Gurriel 3 (4); Altuve 4 (5); Springer (4); McCann, B (2); Bregman (5). **Team LOB:** 5. E: Gurriel (1, throw).

LOS ANGELES	IP	H	R	ER	BB	SO	HR	ERA
Kershaw	4.2	4	6	6	3	2	1	5.40
Maeda	0.2	2	1	1	1	1	1	1.93
Watson	0.2	0	0	0	0	0	0	0.00
Morrow (BS, 1)	0.0	4	4	4	0	0	2	11.25
Cingrani	1.1	1	1	1	0	2	1	3.00

	IP	H	R	ER	BB	SO	HR	ERA
Stripling	0.2	1	0	0	0	0	0	0.00
Jansen (L, 0-1)	1.2	2	1	1	1	1	0	4.76
HOUSTON	**IP**	**H**	**R**	**ER**	**BB**	**SO**	**HR**	**ERA**
Keuchel	3.2	5	4	3	2	4	0	5.23
Gregerson	0.1	0	0	0	0	1	0	0.00
McHugh	2.0	1	3	3	3	4	1	13.50
Peacock	1.1	3	2	2	0	2	0	3.38
Harris (H, 1)	0.1	1	0	0	0	0	0	0.00
Devenski (BS, 1)	1.1	3	3	3	1	1	1	7.71
Musgrove (W, 1-0)	1.0	1	0	0	0	0	0	6.00

Morrow pitched to 4 batters in the 7th.

	1	2	3	4	5	6	7	8	9	10	R	H	E
LA DODGERS	3	0	0	1	3	0	1	1	3	0	12	14	1
HOUSTON	0	0	0	4	3	0	4	1	0	1	13	14	1

Two out when winning run scored.

GAME SIX *October 31, 2017*

LOS ANGELES DODGERS 3, HOUSTON ASTROS 1

HOUSTON	AB	R	H	RBI	BB	SO	LOB	AVG
Springer, CF	3	1	2	1	1	1	0	.375
Bregman, 3B	4	0	1	0	0	0	5	.269
Altuve, 2B	4	0	0	0	0	1	3	.214
Correa, SS	4	0	0	0	0	1	1	.280
Gurriel, 1B	4	0	1	0	0	0	0	.250
McCann, B, C	3	0	1	0	0	1	0	.227
Gonzalez, M, LF	4	0	1	0	0	0	2	.143
Reddick, RF	3	0	0	0	1	2	2	.182
Verlander, P	2	0	0	0	0	2	2	.000
a-Gattis, PH	1	0	0	0	0	0	1	.300
1-Fisher, PR	0	0	0	0	0	0	0	.000
Musgrove, P	0	0	0	0	0	0	0	.000
Gregerson, P	0	0	0	0	0	0	0	.000
Liriano, P	0	0	0	0	0	0	0	.000
b-Beltran, PH	1	0	0	0	0	1	0	.000
TOTALS	**33**	**1**	**6**	**1**	**2**	**9**	**16**	

a-Batted for Verlander in the 7th. **b**-Struck out for Liriano in the 9th. **1**-Ran for Gattis in the 7th. **2B:** Gonzalez, M (1, Hill, R). **HR:** Springer (4, 3rd inning off Hill, R, 0 on, 2 out). **TB:** Gonzalez, M 2; Springer 5; Gurriel; Bregman; McCann, B. **RBI:** Springer (5). **Team LOB:** 8.

LOS ANGELES	AB	R	H	RBI	BB	SO	LOB	AVG
Taylor, C, CF	4	0	1	1	0	1	1	.227
Seager, C, SS	3	0	0	1	0	2	1	.217
Turner, 3B	3	0	0	0	1	1	1	.130
Bellinger, 1B	4	0	0	0	0	4	3	.167
Puig, RF	3	0	1	0	0	0	0	.167
Pederson, LF	3	1	1	1	0	1	1	.357
Forsythe, 2B	2	0	0	0	0	1	1	.267
Watson, P	0	0	0	0	0	0	0	.000
Maeda, P	0	0	0	0	0	0	0	.000
a-Ethier, PH	1	0	0	0	0	0	0	.250
Jansen, P	0	0	0	0	0	0	0	.000
Barnes, A, C	3	1	1	0	0	1	0	.211
Hill, R, P	1	0	0	0	0	1	0	.000
Morrow, P	0	0	0	0	0	0	0	.000
Utley, 2B	0	1	0	0	0	0	0	.000
Culberson, 2B	1	0	1	0	0	0	0	.600
TOTALS	**28**	**3**	**5**	**3**	**1**	**12**	**8**	

a-Batted for Maeda in the 7th. **2B:** Taylor, C (1, Verlander). **HR:** Pederson (3, 7th inning off Musgrove, 0 on, 1 out). **TB:** Puig; Pederson 4; Culberson; Taylor, C 2; Barnes, A. **RBI:** Taylor, C (3); Seager, C (4); Pederson (5). **Team LOB:** 4.

HOUSTON	IP	H	R	ER	BB	SO	HR	ERA
Verlander (L, 0-1)	6.0	3	2	2	0	9	0	3.75
Musgrove	1.0	1	1	1	0	1	1	6.75
Gregerson	0.2	1	0	0	1	1	0	0.00
Liriano	0.1	0	0	0	0	1	0	0.00
LOS ANGELES	**IP**	**H**	**R**	**ER**	**BB**	**SO**	**HR**	**ERA**
Hill, R	4.2	4	1	1	1	5	1	2.08
Morrow	1.0	1	0	0	0	1	0	9.00
Watson (W, 2-0)	0.1	0	0	0	1	0	0	0.00
Maeda (H, 1)	1.0	1	0	0	0	0	0	1.59
Jansen (S, 2)	2.0	0	0	0	0	3	0	3.52

Watson pitched to 1 batter in the 7th.

	1	2	3	4	5	6	7	8	9	R	H	E
HOUSTON	0	0	1	0	0	0	0	0	0	1	6	0
LA DODGERS	0	0	0	0	0	2	1	0	X	3	5	0

GAME SEVEN *November 1, 2017*

HOUSTON ASTROS 5, LOS ANGELES DODGERS 1

HOUSTON	AB	R	H	RBI	BB	SO	LOB	AVG
Springer, CF-RF	5	2	2	2	0	1	0	.379
Bregman, 3B	4	1	0	0	0	3	0	.233
Altuve, 2B	3	0	0	1	1	0	0	.194
Correa, SS	4	0	1	0	0	0	1	.276
Gurriel, 1B	4	0	0	0	0	1	1	.214
McCann, B, C	3	1	0	0	1	2	1	.200
Gonzalez, M, LF	3	1	2	0	1	0	0	.208
Reddick, RF	2	0	0	0	0	0	3	.167
a-Gattis, PH	0	0	0	0	1	0	0	.300
Morton, P	1	0	0	0	0	1	0	.000
McCullers Jr., P	1	0	0	1	0	0	1	.000
Peacock, P	1	0	0	0	0	0	1	.000
Liriano, P	0	0	0	0	0	0	0	.000
Devenski, P	0	0	0	0	0	0	0	.000
b-Maybin, PH-CF	2	0	0	0	0	1	3	.333
TOTALS	**33**	**5**	**5**	**4**	**4**	**9**	**11**	

a-Batted for Reddick in the 6th. **b**-Popped out for Devenski in the 6th. **2B:** Springer (3, Darvish); Gonzalez, M (2, Darvish). **HR:** Springer (5, 2nd inning off Darvish, 1 on, 2 out). **TB:** Gonzalez, M 3; Springer 6; Correa. **RBI:** Altuve (6); McCullers Jr. (1); Springer 2 (7). **Team LOB:** 5. **SB:** Bregman (1, 3rd base off Darvish/Barnes, A); Altuve (1, 2nd base off Jansen/Barnes, A).

LOS ANGELES	AB	R	H	RBI	BB	SO	LOB	AVG
Taylor, C, CF	5	0	1	0	0	1	4	.222
Seager, C, SS	4	0	1	0	1	1	3	.222
Turner, 3B	2	0	1	0	0	0	0	.160
Bellinger, 1B	4	0	0	0	0	3	6	.143
Puig, RF	3	0	0	0	0	0	4	.148
Pederson, LF	4	1	1	0	0	2	5	.333
Forsythe, 2B	3	0	1	0	1	0	0	.278
Barnes, A, C	4	0	0	0	0	0	3	.174
Darvish, P	0	0	0	0	0	0	0	.000
Morrow, P	0	0	0	0	0	0	0	.000
a-Hernandez, PH	0	0	0	0	0	0	0	.231
Kershaw, P	1	0	0	0	0	1	0	.000
b-Ethier, PH	1	0	1	1	0	0	0	.400
Jansen, P	0	0	0	0	0	0	0	.000
Wood, A, P	0	0	0	0	0	0	0	.000
c-Utley, PH	1	0	0	0	0	1	0	.000
TOTALS	**32**	**1**	**6**	**1**	**2**	**9**	**25**	

a-Hit by pitch for Morrow in the 2nd. **b**-Batted for Kershaw in the 6th. **c**-Struck out for Wood, A in the 9th. **2B:** Taylor, C (2, McCullers Jr.). **TB:** Turner; Pederson; Taylor, C 2; Ethier; Forsythe; Seager, C. **RBI:** Ethier (1). **Team LOB:** 10. E: Bellinger (1, throw).

HOUSTON	IP	H	R	ER	BB	SO	HR	ERA
McCullers Jr.	2.1	3	0	0	0	3	0	3.52
Peacock	2.0	1	0	0	1	2	0	2.45
Liriano	0.1	0	0	0	0	0	0	0.00
Devenski	0.1	0	0	0	0	0	0	7.20
Morton (W, 1-0)	4.0	2	1	1	1	4	0	1.74
LOS ANGELES	**IP**	**H**	**R**	**ER**	**BB**	**SO**	**HR**	**ERA**
Darvish (L, 0-2)	1.2	3	5	4	1	0	1	21.60
Morrow	0.1	0	0	0	0	1	0	8.44
Kershaw	4.0	2	0	0	2	4	0	4.02
Jansen	1.0	0	0	0	1	1	0	3.12
Wood, A	2.0	0	0	0	0	3	0	1.17

	1	2	3	4	5	6	7	8	9	R	H	E
HOUSTON	2	3	0	0	0	0	0	0	0	5	5	0
LA DODGERS	0	0	0	0	0	1	0	0	0	1	6	1

AMERICAN LEAGUE WILD CARD GAME

NEW YORK YANKEES 8, MINNESOTA TWINS 4

MINNESOTA	AB	R	H	RBI	BB	SO	LOB	AVG
Dozier, B, 2B	4	1	2	1	1	2	0	.500
Mauer, 1B	5	0	1	0	0	0	3	.200
Polanco, J, SS	4	2	1	0	1	2	1	.250
Rosario, E, LF-CF	3	1	1	2	1	1	0	.333
Escobar, E, 3B	4	0	2	0	0	0	2	.500
Kepler, RF	3	0	1	0	1	0	1	.333
Buxton, CF	2	0	0	1	0	1	4	.000
Granite, CF	2	0	1	0	0	0	0	.500
Gimenez, C	0	0	0	0	0	0	0	.000
Castro, J, C	3	0	0	0	0	3	5	.000
a-Adrianza, PH-LF	1	0	0	0	0	1	0	.000
Grossman, DH	4	0	0	0	0	3	1	.000
TOTALS	**35**	**4**	**9**	**4**	**4**	**13**	**17**	

a-Struck out for Castro, J in the 8th. **2B:** Kepler (1, Severino, L). **HR:** Dozier, B (1, 1st inning off Severino, L, 0 out); Rosario, E (1, 1st inning off Severino, L, 1 on, 1 out). **TB:** Escobar, E 2; Polanco, J; Granite; Kepler 2; Dozier, B 5; Mauer; Rosario, E 4. **RBI:** Dozier, B (1); Rosario, E 2 (2); Buxton (1). **Team LOB:** 8. SB: Buxton (1). **E:** Rosario, E (1, throw).

NEW YORK	AB	R	H	RBI	BB	SO	LOB	AVG
Gardner, LF	4	3	2	1	1	0	0	.500
Judge, RF	4	3	2	2	1	0	0	.500
Sanchez, G, C	4	1	2	0	0	0	2	.500
Gregorius, SS	3	1	1	3	1	1	1	.333
Castro, S, 2B	4	0	0	0	0	1	4	.000
Bird, 1B	3	0	1	1	1	2	3	.333
Hicks, CF	3	0	1	1	1	0	1	.333
Ellsbury, DH	4	0	0	0	0	0	5	.000
Frazier, T, 3B	4	0	0	0	0	1	0	.000
TOTALS BATTING	**33**	**8**	**9**	**8**	**5**	**5**	**16**	

2B: Sanchez, G (1, Berrios). **HR:** Gregorius (1, 1st inning off Santana, E, 2 on, 1 out); Gardner (1, 2nd inning off Santana, E, 0 on, 2 out); Judge (1, 4th inning off Berrios, 1 on, 1 out). **TB:** Judge 5; Hicks; Gardner 5; Gregorius 4; Sanchez, G 3; Bird. **RBI:** Gregorius 3 (3); Gardner (1); Bird (1); Judge 2 (2); Hicks (1). **Team LOB:** 6.

MINNESOTA	IP	H	R	ER	BB	SO	HR	ERA
Santana, E	2.0	3	4	4	2	0	2	18.00
Berrios (L, 0-1)	3.0	5	3	3	0	4	1	9.00
Hildenberger	1.1	1	1	1	2	0	0	6.75
Rogers	0.1	0	0	0	0	1	0	0.00
Busenitz	0.1	0	0	0	1	0	0	0.00
Belisle	1.0	0	0	0	0	0	0	0.00

NY YANKEES	IP	H	R	ER	BB	SO	HR	ERA
Severino, L	0.1	4	3	3	1	0	2	81.00
Green, C	2.0	1	1	1	2	4	0	4.50
Robertson (BS, 1)(W, 1-0)	3.1	3	0	0	1	5	0	0.00
Kahnle (H, 1)	2.1	0	0	0	0	1	0	0.00
Chapman	1.0	1	0	0	0	3	0	0.00

AMERICAN LEAGUE DIVISION SERIES

CLEVELAND INDIANS VS. NEW YORK YANKEES

NEW YORK	AVG	G	AB	R	H	2B	3B	HR	RBI	BB	SO	SB
Greg Bird, 1B	.222	5	18	3	4	0	0	2	3	3	7	0
Starlin Castro, 2B	.273	5	22	3	6	2	0	0	1	1	5	0
Jacoby Ellsbury, DH	.000	3	4	0	0	0	0	0	0	2	2	0
Todd Frazier, 3B	.235	5	17	3	4	1	0	0	1	2	5	0
Brett Gardner, LF	.286	5	21	2	6	1	0	0	2	1	3	1
Didi Gregorius, SS	.235	5	17	3	4	0	0	2	3	6	3	0
Chase Headley, DH	.000	5	12	0	0	0	0	0	0	1	6	0
Aaron Hicks, CF	.316	5	19	3	6	1	0	1	4	1	6	0
Aaron Judge, RF	.050	5	20	1	1	1	0	0	2	4	16	0
Gary Sanchez, C	.174	5	23	3	4	0	0	2	3	0	10	0
Ronald Torreyes, 3B	.000	1	1	0	0	0	0	0	0	0	1	0
Totals	**.201**	**5**	**174**	**21**	**35**	**6**	**0**	**7**	**19**	**21**	**64**	**1**

NEW YORK	W	L	ERA	G	GS	SV	IP	H	R	ER	BB	SO
Dellin Betances	0	1	3.00	3	0	0	3.0	1	1	1	3	5
Aroldis Chapman	0	0	0.00	3	0	2	5.2	4	0	0	2	10
Jaime Garcia	0	0	0.00	1	0	0	2.2	0	0	0	2	3
Sonny Gray	0	1	8.10	1	1	0	3.1	3	3	3	4	2
Chad Green	0	0	81.00	1	0	0	0.1	2	3	3	0	0
Tommy Kahnle	0	0	0.00	2	0	1	2.2	0	0	0	0	5
David Robertson	1	0	1.93	3	0	0	4.2	1	1	1	2	5
CC Sabathia	0	0	3.72	2	2	0	9.2	8	6	4	3	14
Luis Severino	1	0	3.86	1	1	0	7.0	4	3	3	1	9
Masahiro Tanaka	1	0	0.00	1	1	0	7.0	3	0	0	1	7
Adam Warren	0	0	9.00	1	0	0	1.0	2	1	1	0	1
Totals	**3**	**2**	**3.06**	**5**	**5**	**3**	**47.0**	**28**	**18**	**16**	**18**	**61**

CLEVELAND	AVG	G	AB	R	H	2B	3B	HR	RBI	BB	SO	SB
Michael Brantley, DH	.091	3	11	0	1	0	0	0	0	1	4	0
Jay Bruce, RF	.278	5	18	5	5	1	0	2	4	2	8	0
Lonnie Chisenhall, LF	.000	4	5	1	0	0	0	0	0	0	4	0
Edwin Encarnacion, DH	.000	3	7	1	0	0	0	0	0	1	3	0
Yan Gomes, C	.333	3	6	1	2	1	0	0	1	2	2	0
Erik Gonzalez, 3B	.000	2	2	0	0	0	0	0	0	0	0	0
Austin Jackson, LF	.214	5	14	3	3	0	0	0	0	1	6	1
Jason Kipnis, CF	.182	5	22	0	4	0	1	0	1	0	8	0
Francisco Lindor, SS	.111	5	18	2	2	0	0	1	4	4	6	0
Roberto Perez, C	.300	4	10	1	3	0	0	1	2	2	3	0
Jose Ramirez, 2B	.100	5	20	2	2	0	0	0	0	2	7	0
Carlos Santana, 1B	.211	5	19	2	4	0	0	1	4	3	4	0
Giovanny Urshela, 3B	.167	5	12	0	2	0	0	0	1	0	6	0
Totals	**.171**	**5**	**164**	**18**	**28**	**2**	**1**	**5**	**17**	**18**	**61**	**1**

CLEVELAND	W	L	ERA	G	GS	SV	IP	H	R	ER	BB	SO
Cody Allen	0	0	1.69	4	0	1	5.1	5	2	1	3	8
Trevor Bauer	1	1	0.00	2	2	0	8.1	6	4	0	3	11
Carlos Carrasco	0	0	0.00	1	1	0	5.2	3	0	0	3	7
Mike Clevinger	0	0	13.50	2	0	0	1.1	2	3	2	4	3
Corey Kluber	0	1	12.79	2	2	0	6.1	10	9	9	3	10
Andrew Miller	0	1	1.80	4	0	0	5.0	4	1	1	2	8
Tyler Olson	0	0	0.00	3	0	0	2.0	1	0	0	0	2
Danny Salazar	0	0	0.00	1	0	0	1.2	0	1	0	2	3
Bryan Shaw	0	0	1.50	3	0	0	6.0	4	1	1	0	5
Joe Smith	0	0	0.00	4	0	0	2.1	0	0	0	1	3
Josh Tomlin	1	0	0.00	2	0	0	3.0	0	0	0	0	4
Totals	**2**	**3**	**2.68**	**5**	**5**	**1**	**47.0**	**35**	**21**	**14**	**21**	**64**

SCORE BY INNINGS

New York 347 031 102 000 0—21
Cleveland 220 444 010 000 1—18

HOUSTON ASTROS VS. BOSTON RED SOX

BOSTON	AVG	G	AB	R	H	2B	3B	HR	RBI	BB	SO	SB
Andrew Benintendi, LF	.250	4	16	2	4	0	0	1	2	1	3	0
Mookie Betts, RF	.313	4	16	2	5	2	0	0	0	1	4	1
Xander Bogaerts, SS	.059	4	17	2	1	0	0	1	1	1	4	0
Jackie Bradley Jr., CF	.200	4	15	1	3	0	0	1	5	0	6	0
Rafael Devers, 3B	.364	4	11	3	4	0	0	2	5	2	4	0
Sandy Leon, C	.500	2	8	0	4	0	0	0	2	0	2	0
Deven Marrero, 3B	.000	1	2	0	0	0	0	0	0	0	2	0
Mitch Moreland, 1B	.385	4	13	4	5	2	0	0	0	2	2	0
Eduardo Nunez, DH	.000	1	1	0	0	0	0	0	0	0	0	0
Dustin Pedroia, 2B	.125	4	16	0	2	0	0	0	0	2	2	0
Hanley Ramirez, DH	.571	4	14	2	8	2	0	0	3	1	2	0
Christian Vazquez, C	.333	2	6	1	2	0	0	0	0	2	2	0
Chris Young, DH	.500	1	2	1	1	1	0	0	0	0	0	1
Totals	**.285**	**4**	**137**	**18**	**39**	**7**	**0**	**5**	**18**	**12**	**33**	**2**

BOSTON	W	L	ERA	G	GS	SV	IP	H	R	ER	BB	SO
Doug Fister	0	0	20.25	1	1	0	1.1	4	3	3	1	1
Joe Kelly	1	0	0.00	2	0	0	2.2	4	0	0	0	1
Craig Kimbrel	0	0	4.50	2	0	0	2.0	4	1	1	1	2
Austin Maddox	0	0	4.50	2	0	0	2.0	3	1	1	2	2
Drew Pomeranz	0	1	18.00	1	1	0	2.0	5	4	4	1	1
Rick Porcello	0	0	4.50	2	1	0	4.0	5	2	2	3	4
David Price	0	0	0.00	2	0	0	6.2	5	0	0	2	6
Addison Reed	0	0	7.71	3	0	0	2.1	3	2	2	1	0
Eduardo Rodriguez	0	0	—	1	0	0	0.0	1	2	2	0	0

	W	L	ERA	G	GS	SV	IP	H	R	ER	BB	SO
Chris Sale	0	2	8.38	2	1	0	9.2	13	9	9	1	12
Carson Smith	0	0	0.00	2	0	0	1.1	2	0	0	2	1
Totals	**1**	**3**	**6.35**	**4**	**4**	**0**	**34.0**	**49**	**24**	**24**	**14**	**30**

HOUSTON	AVG	G	AB	R	H	2B	3B	HR	RBI	BB	SO	SB
Jose Altuve, 2B	.533	4	15	5	8	0	0	3	4	4	2	0
Carlos Beltran, DH	.400	3	5	0	2	1	0	0	1	1	1	0
Alex Bregman, 3B	.222	4	18	3	4	1	0	2	2	0	3	0
Carlos Correa, SS	.235	4	17	3	4	1	0	2	6	2	4	0
Derek Fisher, DH	—	2	0	0	0	0	0	0	0	0	0	0
Evan Gattis, DH	.400	3	10	2	4	2	0	0	1	2	3	0
Marwin Gonzalez, LF	.200	4	15	2	3	1	0	0	2	0	6	0
Yuli Gurriel, 1B	.529	4	17	1	9	1	1	0	0	1	1	0
Cameron Maybin, CF	.000	2	1	1	0	0	0	0	0	0	0	0
Brian McCann, C	.125	4	16	0	2	0	0	0	2	0	4	0
Josh Reddick, RF	.375	4	16	3	6	0	0	0	2	2	2	0
George Springer, CF	.412	4	17	4	7	2	0	1	2	2	4	0
Totals	**.333**	**4**	**147**	**24**	**49**	**9**	**1**	**8**	**22**	**14**	**30**	**0**

HOUSTON	W	L	ERA	G	GS	SV	IP	H	R	ER	BB	SO
Chris Devenski	0	0	11.57	3	0	0	2.1	4	3	3	0	3
Ken Giles	0	0	6.00	2	0	1	3.0	3	2	2	0	2
Luke Gregerson	0	0	0.00	2	0	0	2.0	1	0	0	0	3
Will Harris	0	0	0.00	1	0	0	0.2	2	0	0	0	0
Dallas Keuchel	1	0	1.59	1	1	0	5.2	3	1	1	3	7
Francisco Liriano	0	1	13.50	2	0	0	0.2	2	1	1	0	0
Lance McCullers Jr.	0	0	6.00	1	0	0	3.0	3	2	2	2	4
Charlie Morton	0	0	4.15	1	1	0	4.1	7	2	2	2	6
Joe Musgrove	0	0	4.50	2	0	0	2.0	1	1	1	0	1
Brad Peacock	0	0	10.13	1	1	0	2.2	6	3	3	1	4
Justin Verlander	2	0	3.12	2	1	0	8.2	7	3	3	4	3
Totals	**3**	**1**	**4.63**	**4**	**4**	**1**	**35.0**	**39**	**18**	**18**	**12**	**33**

SCORE BY INNINGS

Boston	**133 120 602—18**
Houston	**812 216 121—24**

AMERICAN LEAGUE CHAMPIONSHIP SERIES

HOUSTON ASTROS VS. NEW YORK YANKEES

NEW YORK	AVG	G	AB	R	H	2B	3B	HR	RBI	BB	SO	SB
Greg Bird, 1B	.250	7	20	2	5	2	0	1	2	8	8	0
Starlin Castro, 2B	.208	7	24	2	5	1	0	0	0	1	8	0
Jacoby Ellsbury, PH	.000	2	1	1	0	0	0	0	0	0	1	0
Todd Frazier, 3B	.182	7	22	3	4	1	0	1	4	2	4	0
Brett Gardner, LF	.148	7	27	2	4	1	0	0	1	1	9	0
Didi Gregorius, SS	.250	7	28	2	7	1	1	0	1	0	8	0
Chase Headley, DH	.389	6	18	2	7	1	0	0	1	0	4	0
Aaron Hicks, CF	.083	7	24	2	2	1	0	0	0	2	8	0
Matt Holliday, DH	.000	1	3	0	0	0	0	0	0	0	0	0
Aaron Judge, RF	.250	7	24	5	6	2	0	3	7	4	11	0
Austin Romine, C	.000	2	2	0	0	0	0	0	0	0	0	0
Gary Sanchez, C	.192	7	26	1	5	1	0	1	5	1	9	0
Totals	**.205**	**7**	**219**	**22**	**45**	**11**	**1**	**6**	**21**	**19**	**70**	**0**

NEW YORK	W	L	ERA	G	GS	SV	IP	H	R	ER	BB	SO
Dellin Betances	0	0	9.00	2	0	0	1.0	1	1	1	2	1
Aroldis Chapman	0	1	6.75	2	0	1	1.1	2	1	1	0	3
Sonny Gray	0	0	1.80	1	1	0	5.0	1	2	1	2	4
Chad Green	1	0	0.00	3	0	0	6.1	3	1	0	1	7
Tommy Kahnle	0	0	4.26	4	0	0	6.1	6	3	3	2	4
David Robertson	0	0	9.00	4	0	0	5.0	7	5	5	1	6
CC Sabathia	1	1	0.96	2	2	0	9.1	8	1	1	7	5
Luis Severino	0	1	4.15	2	2	0	8.2	5	4	4	6	3
Masahiro Tanaka	1	1	1.38	2	2	0	13.0	7	2	2	2	11
Adam Warren	0	0	0.00	2	0	0	3.1	0	0	0	1	1
Totals	**3**	**4**	**2.73**	**7**	**7**	**1**	**59.1**	**40**	**20**	**18**	**24**	**45**

HOUSTON	AVG	G	AB	R	H	2B	3B	HR	RBI	BB	SO	SB
Jose Altuve, 2B	.320	7	25	5	8	0	0	2	4	4	5	1
Carlos Beltran, DH	.083	4	12	0	1	1	0	0	0	0	4	0
Alex Bregman, 3B	.167	7	24	2	4	1	0	0	3	3	3	0
Carlos Correa, SS	.333	7	27	4	9	3	0	1	3	1	5	0
Victor Robles, LF	—	1	0	0	0	0	0	0	0	1	0	0
Evan Gattis, DH	.100	4	10	2	1	0	0	1	2	2	2	0
Marwin Gonzalez, LF	.136	7	22	2	3	1	0	0	0	2	4	0
Yuli Gurriel, 1B	.250	7	24	2	6	3	0	0	4	2	4	0
Cameron Maybin, LF	.333	1	3	0	1	0	0	0	0	1	0	0
Brian McCann, C	.188	6	16	1	3	2	0	0	3	3	5	0
Josh Reddick, RF	.040	7	25	1	1	0	0	0	0	1	6	0
George Springer, CF	.115	7	26	1	3	0	0	0	0	4	7	0
Totals	**.187**	**7**	**214**	**20**	**40**	**11**	**0**	**4**	**19**	**24**	**45**	**1**

HOUSTON	W	L	ERA	G	GS	SV	IP	H	R	ER	BB	SO
Chris Devenski	0	0	13.50	2	0	0	0.2	1	1	1	2	0
Ken Giles	0	1	9.00	3	0	1	3.0	5	3	3	3	5
Luke Gregerson	0	0	0.00	1	0	0	0.2	0	0	0	1	0
Will Harris	0	0	6.75	2	0	0	1.1	2	1	1	1	1
Dallas Keuchel	1	1	3.09	2	2	0	11.2	11	4	4	2	18
Francisco Liriano	0	0	0.00	1	0	0	1.0	0	0	0	1	1
Lance McCullers Jr.	0	0	0.90	2	1	1	10.0	3	1	1	3	9
Collin McHugh	0	0	0.00	1	0	0	4.0	0	0	0	1	3
Charlie Morton	1	1	7.27	2	2	0	8.2	8	7	7	3	8
Joe Musgrove	0	0	27.00	1	0	0	0.2	2	2	2	0	0
Brad Peacock	0	0	7.71	2	0	0	2.1	3	2	2	0	4
Justin Verlander	2	0	0.56	2	2	0	16.0	10	1	1	2	21
Totals	**4**	**3**	**3.30**	**7**	**7**	**2**	**60.0**	**45**	**22**	**22**	**19**	**70**

SCORE BY INNINGS

New York	**041 530 351—22**
Houston	**000 463 142—20**

NATIONAL LEAGUE WILD CARD GAME

ARIZONA DIAMONDBACKS 11, COLORADO ROCKIES 8

COLORADO	AB	R	H	RBI	BB	SO	LOB	AVG
Blackmon, CF	4	0	0	1	0	1	4	.000
LeMahieu, 2B	5	0	0	0	0	2	3	.000
Gonzalez, C, RF	5	0	2	1	0	1	0	.400
Arenado, 3B	5	2	1	1	0	1	2	.200
Story, SS	4	2	2	1	0	0	0	.500
Parra, LF	4	1	2	1	0	0	0	.500
Reynolds, Ma, 1B	3	0	0	1	0	0	2	.000
Neshek, P	0	0	0	0	0	0	0	.000
McGee, P	0	0	0	0	0	0	0	.000
c-Valaika, PH	1	0	1	0	0	0	0	1.000
Estevez, P	0	0	0	0	0	0	0	.000
Holland, G, P	0	0	0	0	0	0	0	.000
Lucroy, C	3	2	2	1	1	0	1	.667
Gray, J, P	0	0	0	0	0	0	0	.000
Oberg, P	0	0	0	0	0	0	0	.000
a-Tapia, R, PH	1	0	1	0	0	0	0	1.000
Anderson, T, P	0	0	0	0	0	0	0	.000
b-Amarista, PH	1	0	1	1	0	0	0	1.000
Rusin, P	0	0	0	0	0	0	0	.000
Desmond, 1B	2	1	1	0	0	1	1	.500
TOTALS	**38**	**8**	**13**	**8**	**1**	**6**	**13**	

a-Singled for Oberg in the 3rd. **b-**Batted for Anderson, T in the 4th. **c-**Doubled for McGee in the 8th. **2B:** Lucroy 2 (2, Greinke, Ray); Valaika (1, Bradley, A). **HR:** Arenado (1, 8th inning off Bradley, A, 0 on, 1 out); Story (1, 8th inning off Bradley, A, 0 on, 1 out). **TB:** Arenado 4; Parra 2; Lucroy 4; Amarista; Tapia, R; Desmond; Story 5; Valaika 2; Gonzalez, C 2. RBI: Parra (1); Reynolds, Ma (1); Lucroy (1); Amarista (1); Blackmon (1); Arenado (1); Story (1); Gonzalez, C (1). **Team LOB:** 5.

ARIZONA	AB	R	H	RBI	BB	SO	LOB	AVG
Peralta, D, LF	5	2	3	0	0	0	1	.600
Marte, K, SS	5	1	3	1	0	2	1	.600
Goldschmidt, 1B	5	1	2	3	0	1	3	.400
Martinez, J, RF	4	1	0	0	1	2	3	.000
Lamb, J, 3B	5	3	4	0	0	0	2	.800
Pollock, CF	5	1	2	2	0	1	2	.400
Descalso, 2B	3	2	1	2	2	2	2	.333
Mathis, C	4	0	1	1	1	2	4	.250
Greinke, P	2	0	0	0	0	0	0	.000
Chafin, P	0	0	0	0	0	0	0	.000
Ray, P	1	0	0	0	0	1	1	.000
De La Rosa, J, P	0	0	0	0	0	0	0	.000
Bradley, A, P	1	0	1	2	0	0	0	1.000
a-Drury, PH	1	0	0	0	0	0	2	.000
Rodney, P	0	0	0	0	0	0	0	.000
TOTALS	**41**	**11**	**17**	**11**	**4**	**11**	**21**	

a-Grounded into a forceout for Bradley, A in the 8th. **2B:** Pollock (1, Gray, J). **3B:** Marte, K 2 (2, Gray, J, Rusin); Bradley, A (1, Neshek); Pollock (1, Holland, G). **HR:** Goldschmidt (1, 1st inning off Gray, J, 2 on, 0 out); Descalso (1, 3rd inning off Anderson, T, 1 on, 1 out). **TB:** Pollock 5; Lamb, J 4; Goldschmidt 5; Mathis; Descalso 4; Bradley, A 3; Peralta, D 3; Marte, K 7. **RBI:** Goldschmidt 3 (3); Marte, K (1); Descalso 2 (2); Bradley, A 2 (2); Pollock 2 (2); Mathis (1). **Team LOB:** 10.

COLORADO	IP	H	R	ER	BB	SO	HR	ERA
Gray, J (L, 0-1)	1.1	7	4	4	0	2	1	27.00
Oberg	0.2	0	0	0	0	2	0	0.00
Anderson, T	1.0	2	2	2	0	1	1	18.00
Rusin	2.1	2	0	0	2	3	0	0.00
Neshek	1.1	2	2	2	1	2	0	13.50
McGee	0.1	0	0	0	0	0	0	0.00
Estevez	0.1	1	1	1	0	1	0	27.00
Holland, G	0.2	3	2	2	1	0	0	27.00

ARIZONA	IP	H	R	ER	BB	SO	HR	ERA
Greinke	3.2	6	4	4	1	1	0	9.82
Chafin (W, 1-0)	0.1	0	0	0	0	0	0	0.00
Ray (H, 1)	2.1	2	1	1	0	3	0	3.86
De La Rosa, J (H, 1)	0.1	0	0	0	0	0	0	0.00
Bradley, A (H, 1)	1.1	3	2	2	0	0	2	13.50
Rodney	1.0	2	1	1	0	2	0	9.00

NATIONAL LEAGUE DIVISION SERIES

LOS ANGELES DODGERS VS. ARIZONA DIAMONDBACKS

ARIZONA	AVG	G	AB	R	H	2B	3B	HR	RBI	BB	SO	SB
Gregor Blanco, PH	.000	3	3	0	0	0	0	0	0	0	2	0
Daniel Descalso, 2B	.333	3	6	1	2	1	0	1	1	2	2	0
Brandon Drury, 2B	.200	2	5	1	1	0	0	1	3	0	2	0
Zack Godley, P	.000	1	2	0	0	0	0	0	0	0	1	0
Paul Goldschmidt, 1B	.091	3	11	1	1	0	0	1	2	1	3	0
Zack Greinke, P	.000	1	1	0	0	0	0	0	0	0	0	0
Chris Iannetta, C	.000	2	5	0	0	0	0	0	0	0	3	0
Jake Lamb, 3B	.250	3	8	1	2	0	0	0	0	0	2	0
Ketel Marte, SS	.333	3	12	3	4	0	0	1	1	0	3	0
J.D. Martinez, RF	.364	3	11	1	4	0	0	1	1	0	4	0
Jeff Mathis, C	.200	2	5	1	1	0	0	1	1	0	1	0
David Peralta, LF	.077	3	13	0	1	0	0	0	0	1	1	0
A.J. Pollock, CF	.111	3	9	2	1	0	0	1	1	2	3	0
Robbie Ray, P	.000	1	1	0	0	0	0	0	0	0	1	0
Adam Rosales, 3B	.000	1	2	0	0	0	0	0	0	1	0	0
Christian Walker, PH	1.000	2	1	0	1	0	0	0	0	0	0	0
Totals	**.189**	**3**	**95**	**11**	**18**	**1**	**0**	**7**	**10**	**7**	**28**	**0**

ARIZONA	W	L	ERA	G	GS	SV	IP	H	R	ER	BB	SO
Archie Bradley	0	0	0.00	2	0	0	4.2	3	1	0	3	5
Andrew Chafin	0	0	27.00	2	0	0	0.1	2	1	1	0	0
Jorge De La Rosa	0	0	0.00	2	0	0	2.0	4	0	0	0	2
Zack Godley	0	0	3.60	1	0	0	5.0	4	3	2	2	5
Zack Greinke	0	1	5.40	1	1	0	5.0	4	3	3	5	4
David Hernandez	0	0	0.00	2	0	0	1.2	1	0	0	0	1
Robbie Ray	0	1	8.31	1	1	0	4.1	4	4	4	4	6
Jimmie Sherfy	0	0	36.00	2	0	0	1.0	5	4	4	0	1
Taijuan Walker	0	1	36.00	1	1	0	1.0	4	4	4	2	3
Totals	**0**	**3**	**6.48**	**3**	**3**	**0**	**25.0**	**31**	**20**	**18**	**16**	**27**

LOS ANGELES	AVG	G	AB	R	H	2B	3B	HR	RBI	BB	SO	SB
Austin Barnes, C	.500	3	8	4	4	1	0	1	3	1	2	1
Cody Bellinger, 1B	.214	3	14	3	3	0	0	1	2	1	6	0
Yu Darvish, P	.000	1	2	0	0	0	0	0	0	0	1	0
Andre Ethier, LF	—	1	0	0	0	0	0	0	0	1	0	0
Kyle Farmer, PH	.000	1	1	0	0	0	0	0	0	0	1	0
Logan Forsythe, 2B	.444	3	9	4	4	0	0	0	1	1	0	1
Yasmani Grandal, C	.000	1	4	0	0	0	0	0	0	0	2	0
Curtis Granderson, LF	.125	3	8	1	1	0	0	0	0	0	4	0
Enrique Hernandez, LF	.333	3	3	1	1	1	0	0	0	1	0	0
Rich Hill, P	.000	1	1	0	0	0	0	0	0	0	1	0
Kenley Jansen, P	.000	3	1	0	0	0	0	0	0	0	1	0
Clayton Kershaw, P	.500	1	2	0	1	0	0	0	0	0	1	0
Kenta Maeda, P	.000	2	1	0	0	0	0	0	0	0	0	0
Yasiel Puig, RF	.455	3	11	0	5	1	1	0	4	2	1	0
Corey Seager, SS	.273	3	11	3	3	0	1	0	2	4	3	1
Chris Taylor, CF	.231	3	13	3	3	1	0	0	1	2	3	0
Justin Turner, 3B	.462	3	13	1	6	0	0	1	5	1	1	1
Chase Utley, 2B	.000	2	2	0	0	0	0	0	0	2	0	0
Totals	**.298**	**3**	**104**	**20**	**31**	**4**	**2**	**3**	**18**	**16**	**27**	**4**

LOS ANGELES	W	L	ERA	G	GS	SV	IP	H	R	ER	BB	SO
Tony Cingrani	0	0	0.00	2	0	0	1.0	0	0	0	0	0
Yu Darvish	1	0	1.80	1	1	0	5.0	2	1	1	0	7
Josh Fields	0	0	0.00	1	0	0	0.1	1	0	0	0	1
Rich Hill	0	0	4.50	1	1	0	4.0	3	2	2	3	4
Kenley Jansen	0	0	0.00	3	0	2	3.2	2	1	0	1	4
Clayton Kershaw	1	0	5.68	1	1	0	6.1	5	4	4	3	7
Kenta Maeda	1	0	0.00	2	0	0	2.0	0	0	0	0	4
Brandon Morrow	0	0	2.45	3	0	0	3.2	2	1	1	0	1
Tony Watson	0	0	18.00	2	0	0	1.0	3	2	2	0	0
Totals	**3**	**0**	**3.33**	**3**	**3**	**2**	**27.0**	**18**	**11**	**10**	**7**	**28**

SCORE BY INNINGS

Arizona	**201 011 501—11**
Los Angeles	**510 551 120—20**

WASHINGTON NATIONALS VS. CHICAGO CUBS

CHICAGO	AVG	G	AB	R	H	2B	3B	HR	RBI	BB	SO	SB
Albert Almora Jr., CF	.333	4	6	0	2	0	0	0	1	1	0	0
Jake Arrieta, P	.000	1	1	0	0	0	0	0	0	0	1	0
Javier Baez, 2B	.000	5	14	1	0	0	0	0	0	1	5	1
Kris Bryant, 3B	.200	5	20	3	4	2	0	0	2	1	10	0
Willson Contreras, C	.214	5	14	3	3	0	0	1	1	6	3	0
Ian Happ, LF	.000	2	3	0	0	0	0	0	0	1	2	0
Kyle Hendricks, P	.000	2	3	0	0	0	0	0	0	0	2	0
Jason Heyward, RF	.167	5	12	1	2	0	0	0	0	2	3	0
Jon Jay, CF	.273	5	11	2	3	2	0	0	1	0	2	0
Tommy La Stella, PH	—	2	0	0	0	0	0	0	0	1	0	0
Jon Lester, P	.000	2	2	0	0	0	0	0	0	0	1	0
Leonys Martin, CF	.000	3	2	1	0	0	0	0	0	0	1	0
Jose Quintana, P	.000	2	2	0	0	0	0	0	0	0	2	0
Anthony Rizzo, 1B	.200	5	20	1	4	1	0	1	6	1	6	0
Addison Russell, SS	.222	5	18	1	4	2	0	0	4	2	8	1
Kyle Schwarber, LF	.200	3	5	1	1	0	0	0	0	1	3	0
Ben Zobrist, LF	.235	5	17	3	4	2	0	0	0	1	3	0
Totals	**.180**	**5**	**150**	**17**	**27**	**9**	**0**	**2**	**15**	**18**	**52**	**2**

CHICAGO	W	L	ERA	G	GS	SV	IP	H	R	ER	BB	SO
Jake Arrieta	0	1	0.00	1	1	0	4.0	2	1	0	5	4
Wade Davis	0	0	4.15	4	0	3	4.1	4	2	2	3	5
Brian Duensing	1	0	0.00	2	0	0	1.1	0	0	0	1	1
Carl Edwards Jr.	1	1	23.14	5	0	0	2.1	2	6	6	4	4
Kyle Hendricks	1	0	3.27	2	2	0	11.0	11	4	4	4	13
Jon Lester	0	0	1.86	2	1	0	9.2	3	2	2	3	5
Mike Montgomery	0	0	27.00	2	0	0	1.0	4	3	3	2	1
Jose Quintana	0	0	0.00	2	1	0	6.1	3	1	0	2	7
Pedro Strop	0	0	2.70	3	0	0	3.1	1	1	1	1	1
Justin Wilson	0	0	0.00	1	0	0	0.2	0	0	0	0	0
Totals	**3**	**2**	**3.68**	**5**	**5**	**3**	**44.0**	**30**	**20**	**18**	**25**	**41**

WASHINGTON	AVG	G	AB	R	H	2B	3B	HR	RBI	BB	SO	SB
Wilmer Difo, PH	.000	1	1	0	0	0	0	0	0	0	0	0
Gio Gonzalez, P	.000	2	2	0	0	0	0	0	0	0	1	0
Bryce Harper, RF	.211	5	19	2	4	1	0	1	3	3	6	1
Howie Kendrick, LF	.000	3	2	0	0	0	0	0	0	1	1	0
Adam Lind, PH	.667	3	3	0	2	0	0	0	0	0	0	0
Jose Lobaton, C	.500	1	2	0	1	0	0	0	0	0	0	0
Daniel Murphy, 2B	.211	5	19	5	4	1	0	1	2	3	6	0
Anthony Rendon, 3B	.176	5	17	4	3	1	0	1	1	5	1	0
Victor Robles, LF	.000	2	1	1	0	0	0	0	0	0	1	0
Max Scherzer, P	.000	2	3	0	0	0	0	0	0	0	2	0
Stephen Strasburg, P	.000	2	4	0	0	0	0	0	0	0	0	0
Michael A. Taylor, CF	.333	5	15	3	5	0	0	2	8	3	4	0
Trea Turner, SS	.143	5	21	1	3	1	0	0	0	2	7	1
Jayson Werth, LF	.167	5	18	1	3	1	0	0	0	4	4	0
Matt Wieters, C	.143	5	14	2	2	0	0	0	0	2	4	0
Ryan Zimmerman, 1B	.150	5	20	1	3	1	0	1	4	2	4	1
Totals	**.186**	**5**	**161**	**20**	**30**	**6**	**0**	**6**	**18**	**25**	**41**	**3**

WASHINGTON	W	L	ERA	G	GS	SV	IP	H	R	ER	BB	SO
Matt Albers	0	0	0.00	2	0	0	2.1	1	0	0	1	0
Sean Doolittle	0	0	0.00	3	0	1	3.0	1	0	0	0	4
Gio Gonzalez	0	0	6.75	2	2	0	8.0	6	6	6	6	11
Brandon Kintzler	0	1	5.40	3	0	0	3.1	1	2	2	2	2
Ryan Madson	0	0	2.25	4	0	0	4.0	3	1	1	2	4
Oliver Perez	1	0	0.00	2	0	0	1.0	1	0	0	0	0
Max Scherzer	0	1	3.68	2	1	0	7.1	4	5	3	4	8
Sammy Solis	0	0	9.00	3	0	0	1.0	4	1	1	0	1
Stephen Strasburg	1	1	0.00	2	2	0	14.0	6	2	0	3	22
Totals	**2**	**3**	**2.66**	**5**	**5**	**1**	**44.0**	**27**	**17**	**13**	**18**	**52**

SCORE BY INNINGS

Chicago	**112 243 220—17**
Washington	**141 003 1(10)0—20**

NATIONAL LEAGUE CHAMPIONSHIP SERIES

LOS ANGELES DODGERS VS. CHICAGO CUBS

CHICAGO	AVG	G	AB	R	H	2B	3B	HR	RBI	BB	SO	SB
Albert Almora Jr., CF	.188	5	16	1	3	1	0	1	2	0	3	0
Jake Arrieta, P	.500	1	2	0	1	0	0	0	0	0	1	0
Alex Avila, C	1.000	1	1	0	1	0	0	0	0	0	0	0
Javier Baez, 2B	.167	5	12	2	2	0	0	2	2	1	6	1
Kris Bryant, 3B	.200	5	20	1	4	0	0	1	1	0	4	0
Willson Contreras, C	.222	5	18	2	4	0	0	1	1	0	8	0
Wade Davis, P	.000	1	1	0	0	0	0	0	0	0	1	0
Ian Happ, 2B	.250	3	4	0	1	0	0	0	0	0	3	0
Kyle Hendricks, P	.000	1	2	0	0	0	0	0	0	0	2	0
Jason Heyward, RF	.000	3	5	0	0	0	0	0	0	1	0	0
Jon Jay, LF	.083	4	12	0	1	0	0	0	0	0	4	0
Tommy La Stella, PH	.000	2	2	0	0	0	0	0	0	0	1	0
Jon Lester, P	.500	1	2	0	1	0	0	0	0	0	1	0
Leonys Martin, CF	.000	2	1	0	0	0	0	0	0	0	0	0
Jose Quintana, P	.500	2	2	0	1	0	0	0	0	0	1	0
Anthony Rizzo, 1B	.059	5	17	0	1	0	0	0	0	1	8	0
Addison Russell, SS	.125	5	16	1	2	0	0	1	1	0	5	0
Kyle Schwarber, LF	.167	4	12	1	2	0	0	1	1	2	2	0
Ben Zobrist, RF	.000	4	9	0	0	0	0	0	0	0	3	0
Totals	**.156**	**5**	**154**	**8**	**24**	**1**	**0**	**7**	**8**	**5**	**53**	**1**

CHICAGO	W	L	ERA	G	GS	SV	IP	H	R	ER	BB	SO
Jake Arrieta	1	0	1.35	1	1	0	6.2	3	1	1	5	9
Wade Davis	0	0	4.50	1	0	1	2.0	1	1	1	3	3
Brian Duensing	0	1	2.25	3	0	0	4.0	1	1	1	3	3
Carl Edwards Jr.	0	0	0.00	2	0	0	2.1	0	0	0	2	4
Kyle Hendricks	0	1	5.40	1	1	0	5.0	6	4	3	1	5
John Lackey	0	0	9.82	3	0	0	3.2	5	4	4	2	3
Jon Lester	0	0	1.93	1	1	0	4.2	3	1	1	5	2
Mike Montgomery	0	0	13.50	3	0	0	3.1	10	6	5	2	3
Jose Quintana	0	1	10.29	2	2	0	7.0	8	8	8	3	5
Hector Rondon	0	1	6.00	3	0	0	3.0	5	2	2	0	4
Pedro Strop	0	0	0.00	2	0	0	2.0	0	0	0	2	0
Totals	**1**	**4**	**5.36**	**5**	**5**	**1**	**43.2**	**42**	**28**	**26**	**28**	**41**

LOS ANGELES	AVG	G	AB	R	H	2B	3B	HR	RBI	BB	SO	SB
Austin Barnes, C	.133	5	15	2	2	0	0	0	0	3	3	0
Cody Bellinger, 1B	.318	5	22	3	7	2	0	1	2	1	6	1
Charlie Culberson, SS	.455	5	11	2	5	2	1	0	1	0	2	0
Yu Darvish, P	.000	1	2	0	0	0	0	0	1	1	1	0
Andre Ethier, LF	.250	2	8	1	2	0	0	1	1	0	3	0
Kyle Farmer, PH	.000	4	3	0	0	0	0	0	1	0	1	0
Logan Forsythe, 2B	.200	4	10	2	2	1	0	0	2	4	3	0
Yasmani Grandal, C	.000	1	1	0	0	0	0	0	0	3	0	0
Curtis Granderson, CF	.000	3	7	0	0	0	0	0	0	0	4	0
Enrique Hernandez, LF	.444	4	9	3	4	0	0	3	7	2	1	0
Rich Hill, P	.000	1	1	0	0	0	0	0	0	0	1	0
Clayton Kershaw, P	.000	2	4	0	0	0	0	0	0	0	1	0
Brandon Morrow, P	.000	4	1	0	0	0	0	0	0	0	0	0
Joc Pederson, LF	.200	5	5	1	1	1	0	0	0	0	2	0
Yasiel Puig, RF	.389	5	18	6	7	1	0	1	2	4	2	0
Chris Taylor, CF	.316	5	19	5	6	1	1	2	3	5	2	0
Justin Turner, 3B	.333	5	18	3	6	0	0	2	7	5	4	0
Chase Utley, 2B	.000	3	7	0	0	0	0	0	0	0	4	0
Alex Wood, P	.000	1	2	0	0	0	0	0	0	0	1	0
Totals	**.258**	**5**	**163**	**28**	**42**	**8**	**2**	**10**	**27**	**28**	**41**	**1**

LOS ANGELES	W	L	ERA	G	GS	SV	IP	H	R	ER	BB	SO
Tony Cingrani	0	0	0.00	2	0	0	1.0	1	0	0	0	1
Yu Darvish	1	0	1.42	1	1	0	6.1	6	1	1	1	7
Josh Fields	0	0	0.00	2	0	0	0.2	0	0	0	0	0
Rich Hill	0	0	1.80	1	1	0	5.0	3	1	1	1	8
Kenley Jansen	1	0	0.00	4	0	1	4.1	0	0	0	0	8
Clayton Kershaw	1	0	2.45	2	2	0	11.0	7	3	3	2	9
Kenta Maeda	1	0	0.00	3	0	0	3.0	0	0	0	0	3
Brandon Morrow	0	0	0.00	4	0	0	4.2	1	0	0	1	7
Ross Stripling	0	0	0.00	2	0	0	1.0	2	0	0	0	1
Tony Watson	0	0	0.00	4	0	0	2.1	0	0	0	0	2
Alex Wood	0	1	5.79	1	1	0	4.2	4	3	3	0	7
Totals	**4**	**1**	**1.64**	**5**	**5**	**1**	**44.0**	**24**	**8**	**8**	**5**	**53**

SCORE BY INNINGS

Chicago	**120 320 000—8**
Los Angeles	**127 242 235—28**

ORGANIZATION STATISTICS

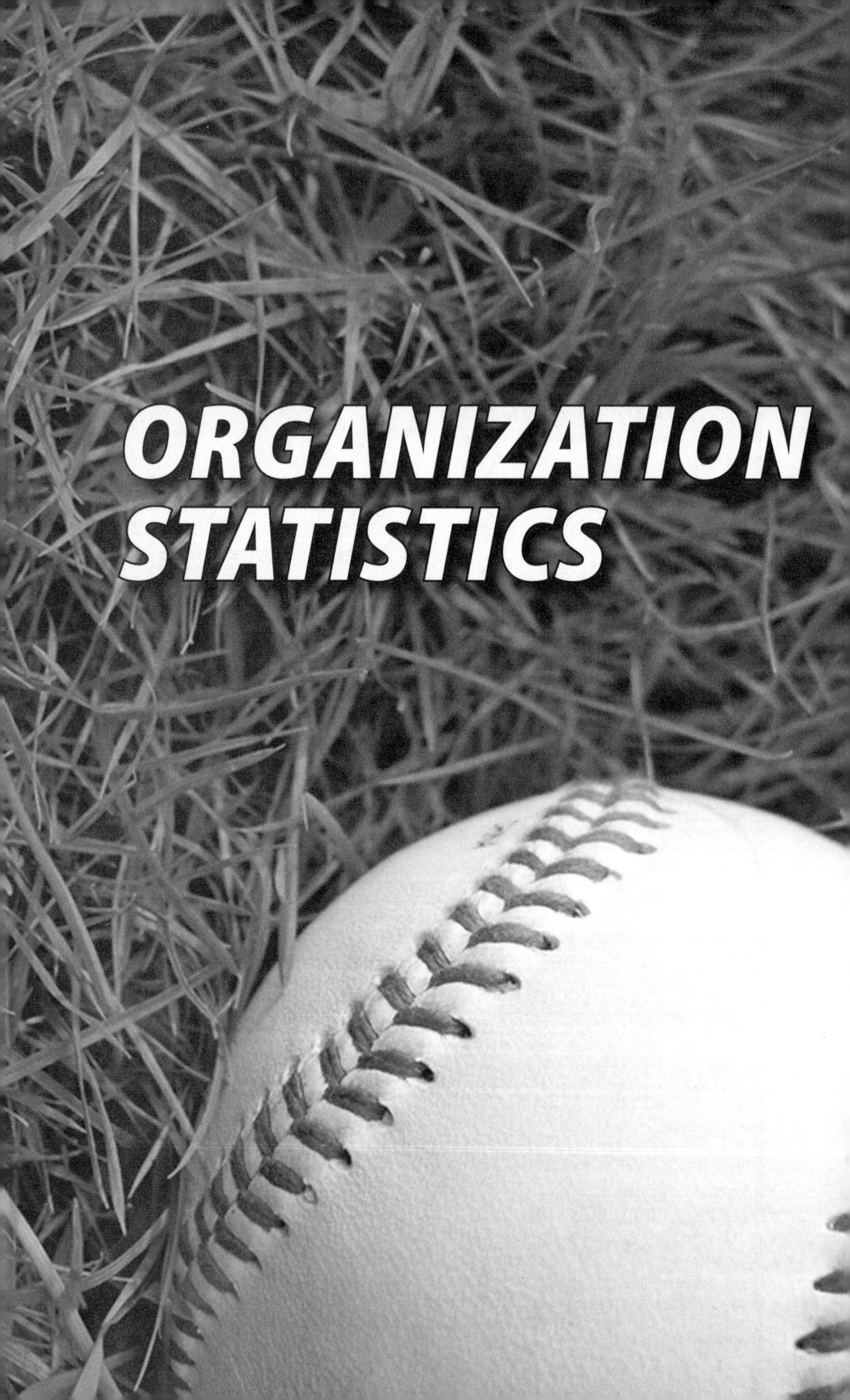

Arizona Diamondbacks

SEASON IN A SENTENCE: Mike Hazen's first year as GM proved to be a resounding success, as the D-backs outperformed all preseason expectations, with a 93-69 record, and reached the playoffs for the first time since 2011 with first-year manager Torey Lovullo.

HIGH POINT: Arizona's 11-8 wild-card game victory vs. the Rockies was certainly the most exciting moment of the year. The Diamondbacks got timely performances from several of their biggest contributors during the season: Paul Goldschmidt gave the Diamondbacks a 3-0 lead with a home run in the first inning, but the team also got a solid relief effort from Robbie Ray, a miraculous triple from righthander Archie Bradley and another triple from outfielder A.J. Pollock that sealed the victory.

LOW POINT: Getting swept by the Dodgers in three games during the National League Division Series certainly qualifies, and while making the playoffs is still a success, it certainly hurts to be forced out by a division rival that has over $148 million more than Arizona in Opening Day payroll and the same team that effectively won the NL West in mid-July.

NOTABLE ROOKIES: Lefthander Anthony Banda made his big league debut, but went just 1-3, 7.32 as a starter in four games before pitching out of the major league bullpen successfully in four appearances at the end of the season. While he threw just six innings out of the pen, he posted a 1.50 ERA and struck out six batters compared to just two walks.

KEY TRANSACTIONS: The J.D. Martinez trade worked out almost as well as the infamous Shelby Miller trade turned out poorly two years ago. The 29-year-old outfielder was the best available bat on the market and hit .302/.366/.741 in 62 games down the stretch for Arizona. The Tigers acquired Dawel Lugo, Sergio Alcantara and Jose King in the trade.

DOWN ON THE FARM: Reno had the third-best record in the Pacific Coast League, and won the Northern Division with an 80-62 record and the most runs scored per game (6.04) of any team in the league. Top performers include righthander Jon Duplantier (12-3, 1.39), who had a top-three ERA in both the Midwest and California Leagues and outfielder Marcus Wilson, who hit .295/.383/.446 in the Midwest League with added strength that has translated to more pop at the plate.

OPENING DAY PAYROLL: $93,257,600 (26th)

PLAYERS OF THE YEAR

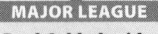

MAJOR LEAGUE

Paul Goldschmidt, 1B

.297/.404/.563
36 HR, 120 RBI
34 2B, 18 SB

MINOR LEAGUE

Jon Duplantier, RHP

(Low Class A/
High Class A)
12-3, 1.38

ORGANIZATION LEADERS

BATTING — ***Minimum 250 AB**

MAJORS

*	AVG	Paul Goldschmidt	.297
*	OPS	Paul Goldschmidt	.966
	HR	Paul Goldschmidt	36
	RBI	Paul Goldschmidt	120

MINORS

*	AVG	Ketel Marte, Reno	.338
*	OBP	Oswaldo Arcia, AZL D-backs, Reno	.404
*	SLG	Oswaldo Arcia, AZL D-backs, Reno	.623
*	OPS	Oswaldo Arcia, AZL D-backs, Reno	1.028
	R	Christian Walker, Reno	104
	H	Christian Walker, Reno	159
	TB	Christian Walker, Reno	307
	2B	Marty Herum, Visalia, Jackson	37
	3B	Kristopher Negron, Reno	11
	HR	Christian Walker, Reno	32
	RBI	Christian Walker, Reno	114
	BB	Evan Marzilli, Jackson, Reno	69
	SO	Grant Heyman, Visalia	161
	SB	Matt McPherson, Visalia	31

PITCHING — **#Minimum 75 IP**

MAJORS

	W	Zack Greinke	17
#	ERA	Robbie Ray	2.89
	SO	Robbie Ray	218
	SV	Fernando Rodney	39

MINORS

	W	Taylor Clarke, Jackson, Reno	12
	W	Jon Duplantier, Kane County, Visalia	12
	L	Bo Takahashi, Kane County, Visalia	12
#	ERA	Jon Duplantier, Kane County, Visalia	1.39
	G	Erik Davis, Reno	53
	G	Jared Miller, Jackson, Reno	53
	GS	Taylor Clarke, Jackson, Reno	27
	SV	Jimmie Sherfy, Reno	20
	IP	Frank Duncan, Reno, Jackson	152
	BB	Jose Almonte, Visalia	66
	SO	Ryan Atkinson, Visalia, Kane County, Jackson	167
#	AVG	Jon Duplantier, Kane County, Visalia	.192

2017 PERFORMANCE

General Manager: Mike Hazen. **Farm Director:** Mike Bell. **Scouting Director:** Deric Ladnier.

Class	Team	League	W	L	PCT	Finish	Manager
Majors	Arizona Diamondbacks	National	93	69	.574	3rd (15)	Torey Lovullo
Triple-A	Reno Aces	Pacific Coast	80	62	.563	3rd (16)	Jerry Narron
Double-A	Jackson Generals	Southern	71	69	.507	5th (10)	J.R. House
High-A	Visalia Rawhide	California	69	71	.493	5th (8)	Shelley Duncan
Low-A	Kane County Cougars	Midwest	72	65	.526	t-5th (16)	Butch Hobson
Short Season	Hillsboro Hops	Northwest	41	35	.539	2nd (8)	Shawn Roof
Rookie	Missoula Osprey	Pioneer	38	38	.5	t-3rd (8)	Mike Benjamin
Rookie	AZL D-backs	Arizona	24	32	.429	13th (15)	Javier Colina
Overall 2017 Minor League Record			395	372	.515	8th (30)	

ORGANIZATION STATISTICS

ARIZONA DIAMONDBACKS

NATIONAL LEAGUE

Batting	B-T	HT	WT	DOB	AVG	vLH	vRH	G	AB	R	H	2B	3B	HR	RBI	BB	HBP	SH	SF	SO	SB	CS	SLG	OBP
Ahmed, Nick	R-R	6-2	195	3-15-90	.252	.396	.193	53	167	24	42	8	1	6	21	10	1	0	0	39	3	4	.419	.298
Blanco, Gregor	L-L	5-11	175	12-24-83	.246	.217	.256	90	224	43	55	10	3	3	13	31	0	1	0	59	15	1	.357	.337
Descalso, Daniel	L-R	5-10	190	10-19-86	.233	.169	.251	130	344	47	80	16	5	10	51	48	4	0	2	89	4	0	.395	.332
Drury, Brandon	R-R	6-2	210	8-21-92	.267	.271	.266	135	445	41	119	37	2	13	63	28	5	0	2	103	1	1	.447	.317
Fuentes, Rey	L-L	6-0	160	2-12-91	.235	.191	.244	64	136	19	32	1	2	3	9	8	0	1	0	35	4	1	.338	.278
Goldschmidt, Paul	R-R	6-3	225	9-10-87	.298	.311	.293	155	558	117	166	34	3	36	120	94	8	0	4	147	18	5	.563	.404
Hazelbaker, Jeremy	L-R	6-3	190	8-14-87	.346	.364	.342	41	52	10	18	2	2	2	10	9	0	0	0	20	1	0	.577	.443
Herrmann, Chris	L-R	6-0	200	11-24-87	.181	.156	.188	106	226	35	41	7	0	10	27	29	0	0	1	67	5	0	.345	.273
Iannetta, Chris	R-R	6-0	230	4-8-83	.254	.300	.234	89	272	38	69	19	0	17	43	37	6	0	1	87	0	0	.511	.354
Lamb, Jake	L-R	6-3	215	10-9-90	.248	.144	.282	149	536	89	133	30	4	30	105	87	7	0	5	152	6	4	.487	.358
Marte, Ketel	B-R	6-1	165	10-12-93	.260	.242	.268	73	223	30	58	11	2	5	18	29	1	0	2	37	3	1	.395	.345
Martinez, J.D.	R-R	6-3	220	8-21-87	.302	.309	.299	62	232	47	70	13	1	29	65	24	0	0	1	74	2	0	.741	.366
Mathis, Jeff	R-R	6-0	205	3-31-83	.215	.213	.216	60	186	13	40	10	2	2	11	14	2	1	0	61	1	0	.323	.277
Murphy, John Ryan	R-R	5-11	205	5-13-91	.143	—	.143	5	7	0	1	1	0	0	1	0	0	0	0	1	0	0	.286	.143
Negron, Kristopher	R-R	6-0	190	2-1-86	.160	.083	.231	14	25	3	4	1	0	0	1	4	1	1	0	7	0	0	.200	.300
Owings, Chris	R-R	5-10	185	8-12-91	.268	.253	.273	97	362	41	97	25	1	12	51	17	1	2	4	87	12	2	.442	.300
Peralta, David	L-L	6-1	210	8-14-87	.293	.269	.302	140	525	82	154	31	3	14	57	43	6	0	3	94	8	4	.444	.352
Pollock, A.J.	R-R	6-1	195	12-5-87	.266	.277	.261	112	425	73	113	33	6	14	49	35	6	0	0	71	20	6	.471	.331
Reinheimer, Jack	R-R	6-1	185	7-19-92	.000	.000	.000	2	5	0	0	0	0	0	0	0	0	0	0	3	0	0	.000	.000
Rosales, Adam	R-R	6-2	200	5-20-83	.202	.200	.207	34	84	10	17	5	0	3	9	1	2	1	1	34	0	1	.369	.227
Tomas, Yasmany	R-R	6-2	250	11-14-90	.241	.185	.268	47	166	19	40	11	1	8	32	13	0	0	1	50	0	0	.464	.294
Vargas, Ildemaro	B-R	6-0	170	7-16-91	.308	.500	.222	12	13	4	4	1	0	0	4	0	0	0	0	3	0	0	.385	.308
Walker, Christian	R-R	6-0	220	3-28-91	.250	.333	.000	11	12	2	3	1	0	2	2	1	2	0	0	5	0	0	.833	.400

Pitching	B-T	HT	WT	DOB	W	L	ERA	G	GS	CG	SV	IP	H	R	ER	HR	BB	SO	AVG	vLH	vRH	K/9	BB/9
Banda, Anthony	L-L	6-2	190	8-10-93	2	3	5.96	8	4	0	0	26	26	17	17	1	10	25	.255	.158	.313	8.77	3.51
Barrett, Jake	R-R	6-2	240	7-22-91	1	1	5.00	28	0	0	0	27	27	18	15	7	15	26	.260	.238	.274	8.67	5.00
Bracho, Silvino	R-R	5-10	190	7-17-92	0	0	5.66	21	0	0	0	21	18	14	13	5	7	25	.225	.258	.204	10.89	3.05
Bradley, Archie	R-R	6-4	225	8-10-92	3	3	1.73	63	0	0	1	73	55	14	14	4	21	79	.207	.223	.193	9.74	2.59
Chafin, Andrew	R-L	6-2	225	6-17-90	1	0	3.51	71	0	0	0	51	48	21	20	5	21	61	.246	.222	.263	10.69	3.68
Corbin, Patrick	L-L	6-3	210	7-19-89	14	13	4.03	33	32	0	0	190	208	97	85	26	61	178	.276	.220	.292	8.45	2.89
De La Rosa, Jorge	L-L	6-1	215	4-5-81	3	1	4.21	65	0	0	0	51	46	24	24	7	21	45	.240	.194	.267	7.89	3.68
De La Rosa, Rubby	R-R	6-0	210	3-4-89	0	1	4.70	9	0	0	0	8	7	4	4	2	4	12	.233	.286	.217	14.09	4.70
Delgado, Randall	R-R	6-4	220	2-9-90	1	2	3.59	26	5	0	1	63	60	31	25	6	14	60	.251	.221	.274	8.62	2.01
Godley, Zack	R-R	6-3	240	4-21-90	8	9	3.37	26	25	0	0	155	124	61	58	15	53	165	.221	.219	.223	9.58	3.08
Greinke, Zack	R-R	6-2	200	10-21-83	17	7	3.20	32	32	1	0	202	172	80	72	25	45	215	.230	.242	.217	9.56	2.00
Hernandez, David	R-R	6-3	245	5-13-85	2	1	4.82	26	0	0	1	19	19	10	10	4	1	15	.268	.250	.279	7.23	0.48
Hoover, J.J.	R-R	6-3	240	8-13-87	3	1	3.92	52	0	0	0	41	47	20	18	7	26	54	.277	.279	.275	11.76	5.66
Koch, Matt	L-R	6-3	215	11-2-90	0	0	—	1	0	0	0	0	2	3	3	0	1	0	1.000	1.000	1.000	—	—
McFarland, T.J.	L-L	6-3	220	6-8-89	4	5	5.33	43	1	0	0	54	65	42	32	4	17	29	.300	.222	.338	4.83	2.83
Miller, Shelby	R-R	6-3	225	10-10-90	2	2	4.09	4	4	0	0	22	20	10	10	1	12	20	.230	.280	.162	8.18	4.91
Ray, Robbie	L-L	6-2	195	10-1-91	15	5	2.89	28	28	1	0	162	116	57	52	23	71	218	.199	.216	.195	12.11	3.94
Rodney, Fernando	R-R	5-11	230	3-18-77	5	4	4.23	61	0	0	39	55	40	29	26	3	26	65	.200	.233	.165	10.57	4.23
Sherfy, Jimmie	R-R	6-0	175	12-27-91	2	0	0.00	11	0	0	1	11	5	0	0	0	2	9	.143	.091	.167	7.59	1.69
Shipley, Braden	R-R	6-1	190	2-22-92	0	1	5.76	10	3	0	0	25	31	18	16	5	15	18	.301	.250	.353	6.48	5.40
Walker, Taijuan	R-R	6-4	235	8-13-92	9	9	3.49	28	28	0	0	157	148	76	61	17	61	146	.247	.230	.262	8.35	3.49
Wilhelmsen, Tom	R-R	6-6	220	12-16-83	1	1	4.44	27	0	0	0	26	25	13	13	4	12	17	.253	.242	.258	5.81	4.10

Fielding

Catcher	PCT	G	PO	A	E	DP	PB
Herrmann	.997	45	320	23	1	1	3
Iannetta	.991	78	617	36	6	1	5
Mathis	.994	58	489	44	3	6	4
Murphy	1.000	5	19	1	0	0	0

First Base	PCT	G	PO	A	E	DP
Descalso	1.000	19	84	6	0	6
Goldschmidt	.997	151	1254	103	4	116
Herrmann	.938	5	14	1	1	1
Negron	1.000	2	7	1	0	1
Rosales	1.000	6	17	2	0	3

	PCT	G	PO	A	E	DP
Walker	.917	1	11	0	1	2

Second Base	PCT	G	PO	A	E	DP
Descalso	.963	45	75	109	7	36
Drury	.977	114	154	276	10	61
Negron	.000	1	0	0	0	0
Owings	.986	22	26	42	1	8
Rosales	1.000	3	4	3	0	3
Vargas	1.000	3	1	3	0	2

Third Base	PCT	G	PO	A	E	DP
Descalso	.882	15	4	11	2	1
Drury	.800	1	1	3	1	0
Iannetta	.000	1	0	0	0	0
Lamb	.959	144	84	241	14	20
Marte	1.000	3	1	0	0	0
Rosales	.958	11	7	16	1	2
Vargas	.500	2	0	1	1	0

Shortstop	PCT	G	PO	A	E	DP
Ahmed	.974	48	44	140	5	29
Descalso	.000	1	0	0	0	0
Marte	.963	64	68	166	9	43
Negron	.944	5	3	14	1	5
Owings	.943	54	43	140	11	18
Reinheimer	1.000	1	0	2	0	1
Rosales	.972	10	10	25	1	6

Outfield	PCT	G	PO	A	E	DP
Blanco	.970	72	97	0	3	0
Descalso	.926	36	25	0	2	0
Fuentes	.969	53	62	1	2	0
Hazelbaker	1.000	24	17	1	0	1
Herrmann	1.000	24	27	1	0	0
Martinez	.980	60	99	1	2	0
Negron	1.000	5	3	0	0	0
Owings	.953	26	38	3	2	0
Peralta	.984	126	246	7	4	1
Pollock	.995	109	213	6	1	2
Tomas	1.000	42	44	0	0	0

RENO ACES — TRIPLE-A

PACIFIC COAST LEAGUE

Batting	B-T	HT	WT	DOB	AVG	vLH	vRH	G	AB	R	H	2B	3B	HR	RBI	BB	HBP	SH	SF	SO	SB	CS	SLG	OBP
Ahmed, Nick	R-R	6-2	195	3-15-90	.143	.000	.167	2	7	1	1	0	0	1	3	0	1	0	0	1	0	0	.571	.250
Arcia, Oswaldo	L-R	6-0	225	5-9-91	.326	.351	.318	93	341	79	111	25	5	24	87	45	8	0	6	86	0	0	.639	.410
Astudillo, Willians	R-R	5-9	225	10-14-91	.342	.238	.364	36	120	22	41	14	0	4	22	4	2	1	1	5	0	1	.558	.370
Blanco, Gregor	L-L	5-11	175	12-24-83	.400	.000	.500	1	5	2	2	0	0	0	0	1	0	0	0	1	0	0	.400	.500
Bonifacio, Emilio	B-R	5-10	210	4-23-85	.400	.333	.444	4	15	5	6	1	0	0	2	2	0	0	0	1	4	1	.467	.471
Borenstein, Zach	L-R	6-0	225	7-23-90	.279	.243	.287	122	384	80	107	27	7	24	91	45	0	0	4	126	2	1	.573	.351
Brito, Socrates	L-L	6-2	205	9-6-92	.291	.277	.295	78	292	43	85	15	8	5	44	22	0	0	4	64	6	1	.449	.337
Conger, Hank	R-B	6-2	220	1-29-88	.239	.191	.254	58	180	20	43	8	1	6	40	21	1	0	4	45	0	0	.394	.316
Flores, Rudy	L-R	6-3	205	12-12-90	.231	.273	.222	48	121	12	28	7	0	4	21	11	0	0	2	43	0	0	.388	.291
Franco, Angel	B-R	5-10	155	5-23-90	.275	.357	.231	12	40	5	11	1	0	0	3	3	0	0	0	7	0	0	.300	.326
Freeman, Ronnie	R-R	6-1	190	1-8-91	.257	.140	.285	70	222	35	57	13	1	3	27	19	1	1	0	50	0	1	.365	.318
Frias, Vladimir	B-R	6-2	170	9-6-86	.444	—	.444	3	9	2	4	1	0	0	0	2	0	0	0	1	0	0	.556	.546
Fuentes, Rey	L-L	6-0	160	2-12-91	.343	.475	.304	45	175	30	60	11	3	0	14	12	2	0	3	30	13	1	.440	.385
Hazelbaker, Jeremy	L-R	6-3	190	8-14-87	.279	.222	.297	52	190	31	53	13	5	6	25	19	0	0	2	57	11	0	.495	.341
Ijames, Stewart	R-L	6-0	220	8-21-88	.286	.500	.200	5	7	1	2	1	0	0	2	0	0	0	1	2	0	0	.429	.250
Marte, Ketel	B-R	6-1	165	10-12-93	.338	.324	.342	70	311	62	105	23	7	6	41	25	2	0	0	34	7	2	.515	.391
Marzilli, Evan	L-L	6-0	185	3-13-91	.264	.381	.235	32	106	14	28	5	2	2	18	15	1	0	2	27	1	0	.406	.355
Medrano, Kevin	L-R	6-1	155	5-21-90	.329	.167	.359	20	76	13	25	5	3	0	11	6	1	1	0	7	0	1	.474	.386
Murphy, John Ryan	R-R	5-11	205	5-13-91	.284	.417	.255	19	67	5	19	0	0	2	7	7	0	1	0	7	0	0	.373	.351
Negron, Kristopher	R-R	6-0	190	2-1-86	.300	.235	.318	120	387	70	116	17	11	13	64	35	7	5	3	88	13	3	.501	.366
Perez, Michael	L-R	5-11	180	8-7-92	.444	.750	.200	3	9	2	4	1	1	1	6	1	0	0	0	0	0	0	1.111	.500
Pollock, A.J.	R-R	6-1	195	12-5-87	.278	.500	.250	7	18	6	5	2	0	2	2	4	0	0	0	2	0	0	.722	.409
Reinheimer, Jack	R-R	6-1	185	7-19-92	.278	.268	.281	129	482	87	134	19	2	4	56	47	2	0	6	86	12	8	.351	.341
Renda, Tony	R-R	5-8	179	1-24-91	.185	.200	.182	8	27	3	5	2	0	0	1	1	0	0	0	4	1	0	.259	.214
Rivero, Carlos	R-R	6-3	230	5-20-88	.296	.273	.303	59	206	27	61	12	1	8	38	20	0	0	7	39	0	1	.481	.348
Vargas, Ildemaro	B-R	6-0	170	7-16-91	.312	.309	.313	113	487	87	152	35	4	10	65	30	7	3	8	40	8	3	.462	.355
Walker, Christian	R-R	6-0	220	3-28-91	.309	.299	.312	133	514	104	159	34	9	32	114	61	6	0	10	104	5	2	.597	.382

Pitching	B-T	HT	WT	DOB	W	L	ERA	G	GS	CG	SV	IP	H	R	ER	HR	BB	SO	AVG	vLH	vRH	K/9	BB/9
Acevedo, Andury	R-R	6-4	235	8-23-90	0	1	45.00	2	0	0	0	1	4	5	5	1	1	2	.571	.500	.667	18.00	9.00
2-team total (8 Iowa)					2	1	6.92	10	0	0	0	13	18	10	10	1	6	9	.327	.500	.667	6.23	4.15
Badamo, Tyler	R-R	6-1	220	8-8-92	0	0	6.75	1	1	0	0	5	9	4	4	0	0	2	.360	.000	.500	3.38	0.00
Baker, Nick	R-R	6-1	190	8-2-92	0	1	12.15	2	1	0	0	7	15	10	9	1	5	5	.484	.500	.462	6.75	6.75
Banda, Anthony	L-L	6-2	190	8-10-93	8	7	5.39	22	22	0	0	122	125	76	73	15	51	116	.266	.265	.267	8.56	3.76
Barrett, Jake	R-R	6-2	240	7-22-91	2	0	4.91	20	0	0	3	22	18	12	12	2	11	19	.225	.139	.296	7.77	4.50
Benitez, Anfernee	R-L	6-1	180	7-24-95	0	0	8.10	1	0	0	0	3	5	3	3	1	4	2	.333	.250	.429	5.40	10.80
Bracho, Silvino	R-R	5-10	190	7-17-92	3	2	4.08	33	0	0	8	35	25	17	16	8	17	48	.197	.241	.159	12.23	4.33
Bradley, J.R.	R-R	6-3	185	6-9-92	0	0	0.00	1	0	0	0	2	1	0	0	0	3	4	.143	.000	.200	15.43	11.57
Buchanan, Jake	R-R	6-0	235	9-24-89	5	0	4.26	11	11	0	0	61	61	29	29	2	9	38	.254	.294	.221	5.58	1.32
2-team total (8 Iowa)					7	2	4.46	19	19	0	0	103	110	55	51	7	28	67	.270	.294	.221	5.85	2.45
Burgos, Enrique	R-R	6-4	250	11-23-90	1	1	6.23	11	0	0	1	13	15	9	9	2	11	13	.300	.304	.296	9.00	7.62
Carpenter, David	R-R	6-3	250	7-15-85	0	0	9.90	7	0	0	0	10	18	11	11	2	6	7	.409	.389	.423	6.30	5.40
Clarke, Taylor	R-R	6-4	200	5-13-93	3	2	4.81	6	6	0	0	34	29	18	18	8	13	31	.225	.169	.281	8.29	3.48
Coleman, Louis	R-R	6-4	205	4-4-86	2	1	2.30	25	0	0	0	27	16	8	7	2	16	33	.172	.212	.150	10.87	5.27
Davis, Erik	R-R	6-3	205	10-8-86	8	2	4.38	53	0	0	3	64	69	32	31	8	31	72	.277	.293	.266	10.18	4.38
De La Rosa, Rubby	R-R	6-0	210	3-4-89	1	2	3.10	19	0	0	0	20	17	8	7	3	9	28	.224	.290	.178	12.39	3.98
Duncan, Frank	R-R	6-4	215	1-30-92	8	8	6.94	22	21	0	0	119	173	100	92	19	39	77	.340	.360	.327	5.81	2.94
Fleck, Kaleb	R-R	6-2	215	1-24-89	2	2	5.30	44	0	0	1	54	62	40	32	7	23	55	.287	.237	.325	9.11	3.81
Gibson, Daniel	R-L	6-3	215	10-16-91	0	1	9.24	11	0	0	0	13	21	14	13	2	15	6	.404	.471	.371	4.26	10.66
Godley, Zack	R-R	6-3	240	4-21-90	2	1	2.57	5	3	0	0	28	14	11	8	0	17	29	.154	.172	.121	9.32	5.46
Grey, Connor	R-R	6-0	180	5-6-94	0	0	6.75	2	1	0	0	7	7	5	5	1	1	8	.269	.429	.211	10.80	1.35
Hall, Brooks	R-R	6-5	235	6-26-90	0	0	1.80	2	0	0	0	5	4	1	1	1	1	5	.222	.400	.154	9.00	1.80
Hoover, J.J.	R-R	6-3	240	8-13-87	0	0	0.87	9	0	0	0	10	6	1	1	1	7	12	.177	.267	.105	10.45	6.10
Jokisch, Eric	R-L	6-2	205	7-29-89	8	8	4.21	28	21	0	0	135	139	70	63	12	42	91	.267	.302	.250	6.08	2.81
Koch, Matt	L-R	6-3	215	11-2-90	2	2	8.40	10	10	0	0	45	68	42	42	11	15	25	.347	.378	.321	5.00	3.00
Krehbiel, Joey	R-R	6-2	185	12-20-92	0	0	0.00	2	0	0	1	2	1	0	0	0	0	2	.167	.500	.000	10.80	0.00
Laffey, Aaron	L-L	5-11	190	4-15-85	5	3	5.42	21	13	0	0	80	96	50	48	8	27	44	.301	.205	.338	4.97	3.05

Long, Keegan	R-R	6-2	190	8-27-93	0	0	13.50	1	0	0	0	1	2	1	1	1	1	0	.500	.000	.667	0.00	13.50
Matusz, Brian	L-L	6-5	190	2-11-87	0	1	6.11	11	0	0	0	18	26	12	12	3	5	13	.333	.342	.324	6.62	2.55
McFarland, T.J.	L-L	6-3	220	6-8-89	0	0	0.00	7	0	0	1	11	6	0	0	0	4	9	.171	.118	.222	7.36	3.27
Miller, Jared	L-L	6-7	240	8-21-93	3	3	1.72	22	0	0	1	31	16	8	6	2	10	43	.147	.214	.105	12.35	2.87
Muren, Drew	L-R	6-6	225	11-22-88	0	0	0.00	4	0	0	1	8	3	0	0	0	4	7	.115	.143	.105	8.22	4.70
2-team total (1 Sacramento)					1	0	0.00	5	0	0	1	9	3	0	0	0	5	7	.103	.143	.105	7.27	5.19
Nakaushiro, Yuhei	L-L	6-0	160	9-17-89	0	0	6.75	2	0	0	0	3	5	3	2	0	0	2	.385	.200	.500	6.75	0.00
Payamps, Joel	R-R	6-2	170	4-7-94	2	0	3.00	2	2	0	0	12	13	4	4	0	3	10	.283	.360	.191	7.50	2.25
Pineyro, Ivan	R-R	6-1	200	9-29-91	0	2	9.82	4	2	0	0	15	22	18	16	3	4	10	.339	.333	.341	6.14	2.45
Sampson, Keyvius	R-R	6-2	225	1-6-91	4	3	6.75	12	9	0	0	43	55	38	32	5	30	46	.309	.262	.351	9.70	6.33
2-team total (14 New Orleans)					5	5	5.92	26	15	0	0	79	84	59	52	9	60	84	.272	.262	.351	9.57	6.84
Sherfy, Jimmie	R-R	6-0	175	12-27-91	2	1	3.12	44	0	0	20	49	37	17	17	6	10	61	.211	.317	.125	11.20	1.84
Shipley, Braden	R-R	6-1	190	2-22-92	7	6	5.66	19	19	1	0	105	129	68	66	18	42	69	.304	.340	.272	5.91	3.60
Sides, Grant	R-R	6-4	215	6-22-89	0	1	22.50	2	0	0	0	2	6	6	5	0	2	1	.500	.375	.750	4.50	9.00
Stites, Matt	R-R	5-11	205	5-28-90	1	1	5.93	23	0	0	0	27	43	22	18	2	22	16	.361	.349	.368	5.27	7.24
Winston, Jake	R-R	6-3	194	9-13-93	0	0	3.00	3	0	0	1	6	4	3	2	0	2	2	.200	.000	.364	3.00	3.00

Fielding

Catcher	PCT	G	PO	A	E	DP	PB
Astudillo	.978	19	161	15	4	0	4
Conger	.987	44	294	14	4	1	2
Freeman	.996	65	429	23	2	2	3
Murphy	.989	19	170	8	2	3	4
Perez	.966	3	25	3	1	1	0

First Base	PCT	G	PO	A	E	DP
Flores	.992	16	120	8	1	16
Negron	1.000	1	5	1	0	1
Rivero	1.000	11	92	8	0	16
Walker	.992	119	1025	41	9	98

Second Base	PCT	G	PO	A	E	DP
Franco	1.000	2	2	3	0	1
Marte	1.000	4	4	16	0	3
Medrano	.985	15	34	32	1	7
Negron	1.000	9	13	22	0	11
Reinheimer	.953	23	39	62	5	6
Vargas	.989	93	186	279	5	78

Third Base	PCT	G	PO	A	E	DP
Astudillo	.978	14	11	34	1	2
Bonifacio	.889	3	3	5	1	1
Franco	.947	9	4	14	1	2
Medrano	.917	4	3	8	1	1
Negron	.973	30	20	52	2	4
Reinheimer	.910	34	22	49	7	2
Renda	.870	8	4	16	3	1
Rivero	.973	43	26	82	3	9
Vargas	.917	4	3	8	1	2
Walker	.895	9	6	11	2	2

Shortstop	PCT	G	PO	A	E	DP
Ahmed	1.000	2	2	3	0	0
Frias	1.000	3	4	7	0	2
Marte	.977	59	97	194	7	53
Negron	.969	9	8	23	1	5
Reinheimer	.969	63	92	189	9	50
Vargas	.971	8	14	19	1	2

Outfield	PCT	G	PO	A	E	DP
Arcia	.953	57	98	3	5	2
Blanco	1.000	1	1	0	0	0
Bonifacio	1.000	1	3	0	0	0
Borenstein	.974	104	144	8	4	1
Brito	.974	75	149	1	4	1
Flores	1.000	5	5	0	0	0
Fuentes	.988	43	82	2	1	1
Hazelbaker	.956	49	82	4	4	1
Ijames	1.000	2	1	0	0	0
Marte	1.000	5	15	1	0	0
Marzilli	.986	31	71	1	1	1
Negron	.986	63	134	7	2	2
Pollock	1.000	7	11	0	0	0
Reinheimer	1.000	4	3	0	0	0
Rivero	.000	1	0	0	0	0
Vargas	.833	8	5	0	1	0
Walker	1.000	5	4	0	0	0

JACKSON GENERALS

DOUBLE-A

SOUTHERN LEAGUE

Batting	B-T	HT	WT	DOB	AVG	vLH	vRH	G	AB	R	H	2B	3B	HR	RBI	BB	HBP	SH	SF	SO	SB	CS	SLG	OBP
Bonifacio, Emilio	B-R	5-10	210	4-23-85	.286	.286	.286	24	91	15	26	5	2	1	5	4	0	4	1	15	5	4	.418	.313
Cribbs, Galli	L-R	6-0	170	10-8-92	.171	.000	.214	29	88	11	15	2	1	0	7	10	1	1	2	38	2	0	.216	.257
Cron, Kevin	R-R	6-5	245	2-17-93	.284	.243	.295	138	515	76	146	35	0	25	91	56	8	0	9	134	1	0	.497	.357
Denker, Travis	R-R	5-9	205	8-5-85	.296	.269	.306	77	186	24	55	11	0	7	28	31	5	0	6	38	0	0	.468	.399
Dugan, Kelly	L-R	6-3	210	9-18-90	.256	.177	.275	105	313	40	80	20	2	13	48	30	10	0	3	81	4	1	.457	.337
Flores, Raymel	B-R	5-9	155	9-22-94	.267	.000	.286	6	15	4	4	0	0	0	1	4	1	0	0	5	1	1	.267	.450
Flores, Rudy	L-R	6-3	205	12-12-90	.298	.239	.312	63	235	35	70	20	1	8	38	12	3	0	2	64	2	0	.494	.337
Franco, Angel	B-R	5-10	155	5-23-90	.286	.167	.318	15	56	7	16	3	0	0	5	3	0	0	0	10	1	2	.339	.322
Frias, Vladimir	B-R	6-2	170	9-6-86	.223	.111	.259	32	112	12	25	3	0	0	6	7	1	0	1	16	4	2	.250	.273
Hernandez, Oscar	R-R	6-1	230	7-9-93	.197	.205	.196	67	233	23	46	11	0	8	21	17	2	2	1	58	0	0	.348	.257
Herum, Marty	R-R	6-3	214	12-16-91	.284	.233	.296	43	162	11	46	10	2	2	19	7	1	0	2	26	1	0	.407	.314
Ijames, Stewart	R-L	6-0	220	8-21-88	.220	.194	.229	52	141	22	31	7	1	6	20	19	1	0	2	51	2	1	.411	.313
Leyba, Domingo	B-R	5-11	160	9-11-95	.276	.429	.189	17	58	11	16	4	0	2	9	5	1	0	0	6	0	0	.448	.344
Lockhart, Daniel	L-R	5-11	175	11-4-92	.205	.182	.209	23	78	14	16	6	0	1	8	11	0	1	1	11	3	0	.321	.300
Lopez, B.J.	R-R	5-9	185	9-29-94	.286	.500	.200	3	7	1	2	0	0	0	0	0	0	0	0	1	1	0	.286	.286
Lugo, Dawel	R-R	6-0	190	12-31-94	.282	.257	.288	88	341	40	96	21	4	7	43	21	3	0	4	51	1	0	.428	.325
Marzilli, Evan	L-L	6-0	185	3-13-91	.253	.263	.250	95	296	54	75	10	5	5	17	54	2	1	2	70	15	7	.372	.370
Meadows, Chaz	R-R	5-7	150	2-17-93	—	—	—	1	0	0	0	0	0	0	0	0	0	0	0	0	0	0	—	—
Medrano, Kevin	L-R	6-1	155	5-21-90	.321	.309	.325	70	262	42	84	21	0	3	32	25	1	10	0	46	1	0	.435	.382
Perez, Michael	L-R	5-11	180	8-7-92	.279	.283	.277	80	262	29	73	23	0	5	39	35	2	1	2	61	0	2	.424	.365
Queliz, Jose	R-R	6-2	224	8-7-92	.211	.000	.235	10	19	5	4	1	0	1	3	7	1	0	0	6	0	0	.421	.444
Reyes, Victor	B-R	6-3	170	10-5-94	.292	.238	.307	126	479	59	140	29	5	4	51	27	3	4	3	80	18	9	.399	.332
Walsh, Colin	B-R	6-1	200	9-26-89	.273	.178	.294	68	242	49	66	17	0	11	31	65	0	0	4	70	5	2	.479	.421
Westbrook, Jamie	R-R	5-9	170	6-18-95	.265	.293	.258	104	377	38	100	19	3	8	55	16	8	0	5	43	2	2	.395	.305

Pitching	B-T	HT	WT	DOB	W	L	ERA	G	GS	CG	SV	IP	H	R	ER	HR	BB	SO	AVG	vLH	vRH	K/9	BB/9
Acevedo, Andury	R-R	6-4	235	8-23-90	1	0	4.32	9	0	0	1	8	7	4	4	0	6	7	.259	.400	.177	7.56	6.48
2-team total (12 Tennessee)					2	0	1.54	21	0	0	4	23	16	4	4	0	11	13	.211	.400	.176	5.01	4.24
Aker, Mitchell	R-R	6-2	185	6-22-94	0	1	6.75	2	0	0	0	1	2	1	1	0	3	0	.333	1.000	.200	0.00	20.25
Atkinson, Ryan	R-R	6-3	218	5-10-93	4	2	3.22	7	7	0	0	36	26	14	13	3	24	33	.210	.196	.219	8.17	5.94
Badamo, Tyler	R-R	6-1	220	8-8-92	0	0	7.50	1	1	0	0	6	10	5	5	1	0	10	.385	.167	.450	15.00	0.00
Bellow, Kirby	L-L	6-1	220	11-14-91	0	1	4.85	11	0	0	0	13	10	7	7	1	10	15	.208	.059	.290	10.38	6.92
Bradley, J.R.	R-R	6-3	185	6-9-92	1	1	3.94	14	1	0	1	16	14	8	7	2	8	19	.222	.217	.225	10.69	4.50

Carpenter, David	R-R	6-3	250	7-15-85	0	0	10.13	3	0	0	0	3	5	3	3	0	2	2	.385	.500	.286	6.75	6.75
Clarke, Taylor	R-R	6-4	200	5-13-93	9	7	2.91	21	21	0	0	111	94	41	36	7	39	107	.232	.267	.195	8.65	3.15
Diaz, Miller	R-R	6-1	230	6-22-92	1	1	3.72	28	0	0	2	39	36	21	16	2	21	38	.254	.265	.243	8.84	4.89
Duncan, Frank	R-R	6-4	215	1-30-92	1	2	3.90	5	5	0	0	32	25	17	14	1	9	19	.216	.216	.215	5.29	2.51
Gibson, Daniel	R-L	6-3	215	10-16-91	0	0	0.40	16	0	0	3	22	18	4	1	0	5	19	.220	.389	.172	7.66	2.01
Hall, Brooks	R-R	6-5	235	6-26-90	2	4	5.60	15	8	0	0	55	67	35	34	2	16	40	.309	.270	.336	6.59	2.63
Hathaway, Steve	L-L	6-1	185	9-13-90	0	0	27.00	1	0	0	0	0	1	1	1	0	2	1	.500	1.000	.000	27.00	54.00
Jeter, Bud	R-R	6-3	205	10-27-91	0	0	12.86	4	0	0	0	7	11	10	10	2	4	9	.355	.471	.214	11.57	5.14
Jokisch, Eric	R-L	6-2	205	7-29-89	0	0	1.50	1	1	0	0	6	6	1	1	1	0	6	.261	.200	.278	9.00	0.00
Keller, Brad	R-R	6-5	230	7-27-95	10	9	4.68	26	26	0	0	131	142	73	68	7	57	111	.279	.272	.285	7.65	3.93
Krehbiel, Joey	R-R	6-2	185	12-20-92	2	4	3.27	44	0	0	4	55	45	23	20	3	27	74	.224	.244	.210	12.11	4.42
Long, Keegan	R-R	6-2	190	8-27-93	0	0	3.00	2	0	0	0	3	3	1	1	0	0	3	.250	.250	.250	9.00	0.00
McCullough, Mason	R-R	6-4	245	1-7-93	3	0	2.25	24	0	0	0	24	12	6	6	0	20	31	.150	.172	.137	11.63	7.50
Miller, Jared	L-L	6-7	240	8-21-93	0	3	3.89	31	0	0	2	39	33	19	17	2	18	51	.222	.171	.241	11.67	4.12
Moya, Gabriel	L-L	6-0	175	1-9-95	4	1	0.82	34	0	0	17	44	22	5	4	1	12	68	.148	.200	.128	14.02	2.47
2-team total (13 Chattanooga)					6	1	0.77	47	0	0	24	58	30	6	5	2	15	87	.150	.200	.128	13.42	2.31
Muren, Drew	L-R	6-6	225	11-22-88	2	2	4.70	19	0	0	0	23	16	13	12	1	17	27	.191	.177	.200	10.57	6.65
Nakaushiro, Yuhei	L-L	6-0	160	9-17-89	1	2	2.35	48	0	0	4	65	49	21	17	2	27	63	.203	.133	.235	8.72	3.74
Payamps, Joel	R-R	6-2	170	4-7-94	6	6	4.78	17	17	1	0	92	104	56	49	13	21	56	.282	.292	.274	5.46	2.05
Pineyro, Ivan	R-R	6-1	200	9-29-91	8	1	3.39	19	11	0	0	72	77	33	27	6	12	65	.276	.318	.238	8.16	1.51
Sides, Grant	R-R	6-4	215	6-22-89	0	0	3.27	6	0	0	1	11	12	5	4	0	5	8	.293	.389	.217	6.55	4.09
Simms, Trevor	R-R	6-4	220	3-15-92	1	0	4.50	1	0	0	0	4	4	2	2	1	4	4	.250	.111	.429	9.00	9.00
Speier, Gabe	L-L	6-0	175	4-12-95	2	6	4.30	36	4	0	2	69	81	47	33	4	31	50	.303	.288	.309	6.52	4.04
Taylor, Josh	L-L	6-5	225	3-2-93	4	7	5.01	33	14	0	1	97	115	59	54	7	46	91	.303	.264	.316	8.44	4.27
Young, Alex	L-L	6-2	205	9-9-93	9	9	3.68	27	24	0	0	137	125	67	56	12	58	103	.245	.209	.254	6.77	3.81

Fielding

Catcher	PCT	G	PO	A	E	DP	PB
Hernandez	.986	65	502	52	8	2	23
Lopez	1.000	2	20	4	0	0	0
Perez	.983	73	534	62	10	1	5
Queliz	1.000	6	51	4	0	1	1

First Base	PCT	G	PO	A	E	DP
Cron	.990	126	965	69	10	94
Denker	1.000	11	70	6	0	9
Flores	1.000	8	53	5	0	9
Herum	1.000	1	2	0	0	0

Second Base	PCT	G	PO	A	E	DP
Bonifacio	.867	5	8	5	2	1
Denker	.982	15	24	30	1	8
Franco	1.000	8	15	21	0	5
Frias	1.000	14	26	44	0	16
Lockhart	.983	13	19	39	1	13
Meadows	1.000	1	1	0	0	0
Medrano	.990	28	34	63	1	7
Walsh	.955	27	30	54	4	9
Westbrook	.959	39	54	88	6	20

Third Base	PCT	G	PO	A	E	DP
Bonifacio	1.000	2	1	3	0	0
Cron	.750	1	1	2	1	1
Denker	.889	2	1	7	1	1
Franco	1.000	1	1	0	0	0
Frias	1.000	2	2	2	0	1
Herum	.959	42	22	72	4	7
Lugo	.955	77	49	144	9	9
Medrano	1.000	5	3	4	0	1
Walsh	.897	14	8	18	3	3

Shortstop	PCT	G	PO	A	E	DP
Cribbs	.966	29	51	64	4	23
Denker	.000	1	0	0	0	0
Flores	.952	6	9	11	1	3
Franco	1.000	6	8	14	0	4
Frias	.945	18	35	51	5	16
Leyba	1.000	14	15	21	0	5
Lockhart	1.000	2	1	3	0	0
Lugo	.955	10	22	20	2	4
Medrano	.973	38	54	92	4	15
Walsh	.947	24	30	60	5	10

Outfield	PCT	G	PO	A	E	DP
Bonifacio	.964	17	26	1	1	0
Dugan	.967	82	141	4	5	3
Flores	.977	29	41	2	1	0
Ijames	.957	37	65	1	3	0
Lockhart	1.000	9	17	1	0	0
Marzilli	.996	93	219	3	1	1
Reyes	.997	124	297	11	1	5
Walsh	1.000	3	7	0	0	0
Westbrook	.929	52	76	2	6	0

VISALIA RAWHIDE — *HIGH CLASS A*

CALIFORNIA LEAGUE

Batting	B-T	HT	WT	DOB	AVG	vLH	vRH	G	AB	R	H	2B	3B	HR	RBI	BB	HBP	SH	SF	SO	SB	CS	SLG	OBP
Alcantara, Sergio	B-R	5-9	168	7-10-96	.279	.329	.264	86	340	44	95	15	2	3	28	34	0	3	1	57	11	10	.362	.344
Baker, Tyler	L-R	5-9	179	3-8-93	.238	.229	.241	61	210	26	50	11	1	6	15	21	5	0	0	67	1	2	.386	.322
Blanco, Gregor	L-L	5-11	175	12-24-83	.389	.600	.308	5	18	3	7	1	0	0	3	2	0	0	0	5	4	0	.444	.450
Bray, Colin	B-L	6-3	197	6-18-93	.244	.000	.268	13	45	10	11	1	0	0	1	4	0	0	0	14	3	0	.267	.306
Byler, Austin	L-R	6-3	225	10-15-92	.242	.238	.244	121	450	64	109	31	6	9	66	42	6	1	4	138	8	4	.398	.313
Castillo, Henry	B-R	5-11	189	12-8-94	.227	.215	.231	107	397	31	90	23	1	6	48	24	1	0	5	130	2	3	.335	.269
Christy, Francis	L-R	6-2	220	9-1-95	.211	.074	.237	48	175	12	37	5	1	0	8	11	1	0	2	58	1	2	.251	.259
Cribbs, Galli	L-R	6-0	170	10-8-92	.205	.143	.224	81	239	29	49	11	5	0	12	26	3	2	0	88	8	4	.293	.291
DeLuzio, Ben	R-R	6-3	190	8-9-94	.350	.452	.293	30	117	20	41	4	1	0	8	5	2	0	1	21	12	1	.402	.384
Flores, Jorge	R-R	5-5	160	11-25-91	.216	.167	.236	30	102	12	22	2	1	4	12	9	0	1	1	14	2	1	.373	.277
Flores, Raymel	B-R	5-9	155	9-22-94	.000	—	.000	4	5	1	0	0	0	0	0	0	1	0	0	2	1	0	.000	.167
Herum, Marty	R-R	6-3	214	12-16-91	.311	.338	.304	87	331	38	103	27	3	5	49	18	7	0	4	53	3	3	.456	.356
Heyman, Grant	L-R	6-4	222	11-7-93	.239	.231	.240	112	436	52	104	24	3	18	70	16	11	0	1	161	2	2	.431	.282
Jones, Matt	R-R	6-0	195	4-14-92	.237	.260	.225	88	283	37	67	8	1	10	40	37	5	1	3	55	0	3	.378	.332
Karaviotis, Mark	R-R	6-1	185	10-12-95	.250	.321	.221	28	96	15	24	4	1	4	15	10	3	0	1	26	1	0	.438	.336
Lockhart, Daniel	L-R	5-11	175	11-4-92	.220	.254	.210	82	273	27	60	14	4	4	26	18	3	3	2	40	7	3	.344	.274
Lopez, B.J.	R-R	5-9	185	9-29-94	.071	.000	.077	4	14	0	1	0	0	0	0	0	0	0	0	4	0	0	.071	.071
McPhearson, Matt	L-L	5-8	175	4-18-95	.278	.219	.297	111	406	48	113	15	5	0	29	30	4	3	2	86	31	11	.340	.333
Morozowski, Jason	R-R	6-2	190	6-10-94	.252	.280	.242	113	421	60	106	25	3	7	56	45	2	0	6	110	7	4	.375	.323
Nehrir, Zach	R-R	6-2	205	1-28-93	.152	.222	.125	11	33	3	5	1	1	0	1	5	1	0	0	12	0	1	.242	.282
Ozuna, Fernery	R-R	5-8	170	11-9-95	.217	.183	.230	70	258	36	56	12	2	6	29	16	2	0	1	76	6	1	.349	.267
Queliz, Jose	R-R	6-2	224	8-7-92	.143	—	.143	2	7	0	1	0	0	0	0	0	0	0	0	1	0	0	.143	.143
Sopilka, David	R-R	6-0	170	8-30-93	.100	.000	.125	4	10	1	1	1	0	0	4	2	0	1	0	3	0	0	.200	.250
Spivey, Seth	L-R	5-11	180	7-6-92	.265	.167	.279	16	49	5	13	3	0	1	2	7	0	0	0	15	1	0	.388	.357

Pitching	B-T	HT	WT	DOB	W	L	ERA	G	GS	CG	SV	IP	H	R	ER	HR	BB	SO	AVG	vLH	vRH	K/9	BB/9
Aguilar, Miguel	L-L	5-11	180	9-26-91	0	0	1.19	13	0	0	0	23	16	3	3	1	10	28	.195	.214	.185	11.12	3.97
Almonte, Jose	R-R	6-2	185	9-8-95	11	8	3.55	27	27	0	0	139	129	62	55	10	66	162	.243	.261	.232	10.46	4.26
Atkinson, Ryan	R-R	6-3	218	5-10-93	3	3	3.33	9	9	0	0	49	40	23	18	5	18	66	.222	.181	.267	12.21	3.33
Badamo, Tyler	R-R	6-1	220	8-8-92	1	1	5.68	3	3	0	0	19	23	12	12	5	2	9	.303	.316	.290	4.26	0.95
Baker, Nick	R-R	6-1	190	8-2-92	1	3	5.12	36	5	0	0	65	86	40	37	9	14	39	.322	.319	.324	5.40	1.94
Barrett, Jake	R-R	6-2	240	7-22-91	0	0	2.45	4	0	0	0	4	4	4	1	0	1	7	.250	.333	.200	17.18	2.45
Bellow, Kirby	L-L	6-1	220	11-14-91	3	1	2.81	16	0	0	0	26	11	8	8	0	9	31	.129	.030	.192	10.87	3.16
Benitez, Anfernee	R-L	6-1	180	7-24-95	0	0	0.00	2	0	0	0	1	0	0	0	0	1	2	.000	.000	.000	13.50	6.75
Bradley, J.R.	R-R	6-3	185	6-9-92	1	2	4.66	15	0	0	0	19	25	12	10	3	4	22	.309	.282	.333	10.24	1.86
Burr, Ryan	R-R	6-4	225	5-28-94	1	0	0.72	17	0	0	1	25	13	2	2	0	6	29	.161	.147	.170	10.44	2.16
Clark, Cody	R-R	6-2	215	7-22-93	1	0	9.27	19	0	0	1	22	33	23	23	7	14	33	.337	.370	.308	13.30	5.64
De La Rosa, Rubby	R-R	6-0	210	3-4-89	0	0	0.00	3	0	0	0	3	1	0	0	0	0	2	.111	.000	.125	6.00	0.00
Donatella, Justin	R-R	6-6	236	9-16-94	6	9	3.51	20	20	0	0	105	98	50	41	12	34	87	.251	.275	.232	7.46	2.91
Duplantier, Jon	L-R	6-4	225	7-11-94	6	2	1.56	12	12	0	0	63	46	13	11	2	27	87	.204	.212	.198	12.36	3.84
Eveld, Tommy	R-R	6-5	195	12-30-93	0	5	5.73	19	0	0	2	22	22	15	14	1	11	26	.262	.205	.311	10.64	4.50
Gann, Cameron	R-R	6-0	203	10-8-92	4	1	4.26	35	0	0	1	44	38	22	21	4	23	54	.226	.211	.239	10.96	4.67
Grey, Connor	R-R	6-0	180	5-6-94	0	1	7.36	1	1	0	0	4	3	3	3	0	2	3	.231	.143	.333	7.36	4.91
Huang, Wei-Chieh	R-R	6-1	170	9-26-93	1	0	2.19	10	0	0	1	25	15	7	6	0	10	32	.167	.133	.200	11.68	3.65
Jeter, Bud	R-R	6-3	205	10-27-91	3	4	3.12	32	0	0	17	35	28	12	12	3	13	49	.226	.265	.200	12.72	3.38
Lewis, Sam	R-R	6-4	195	10-9-91	1	3	2.70	7	7	0	0	40	42	14	12	3	11	40	.271	.227	.303	9.00	2.48
Long, Keegan	R-R	6-2	190	8-27-93	2	1	3.69	42	1	0	0	63	71	38	26	5	22	54	.281	.355	.238	7.67	3.13
Lopez, Yoan	R-R	6-3	185	1-2-93	2	0	0.88	20	0	0	4	31	16	3	3	2	9	56	.152	.167	.140	16.43	2.64
Mason, Austin	R-R	6-2	200	12-10-93	1	1	3.40	37	0	0	0	50	42	22	19	3	17	52	.221	.226	.217	9.30	3.04
McCullough, Mason	R-R	6-4	245	1-7-93	2	0	2.12	26	0	0	4	34	19	8	8	2	17	60	.164	.146	.177	15.88	4.50
Payamps, Joel	R-R	6-2	170	4-7-94	3	1	3.69	8	8	0	0	46	41	21	19	2	13	30	.238	.200	.259	5.83	2.53
Pineyro, Ivan	R-R	6-1	200	9-29-91	0	2	5.63	3	3	0	0	16	19	10	10	2	6	22	.292	.267	.300	12.38	3.38
Poche, Colin	L-L	6-3	185	1-17-94	1	1	1.40	18	0	0	2	26	14	5	4	0	13	37	.163	.182	.151	12.97	4.56
Ray, Robbie	L-L	6-2	195	10-1-91	0	1	3.86	1	1	0	0	5	4	2	2	0	2	11	.211	.429	.083	21.21	3.86
Reed, Cody	R-L	6-3	245	6-7-96	5	6	3.91	17	17	0	0	90	94	51	39	14	30	90	.272	.273	.271	9.03	3.01
Simms, Trevor	R-R	6-4	220	3-15-92	3	3	6.75	11	6	0	0	36	47	27	27	2	14	32	.318	.371	.279	8.00	3.50
Takahashi, Bo	R-R	6-0	197	1-23-97	7	10	5.33	20	20	0	0	110	107	70	65	13	37	93	.255	.250	.259	7.63	3.04

Fielding

Catcher	PCT	G	PO	A	E	DP	PB
Baker	.996	47	440	42	2	3	4
Christy	.997	34	312	60	1	5	7
Jones	.993	54	482	59	4	3	10
Lopez	.976	4	36	5	1	0	1
Queliz	1.000	2	15	2	0	0	1
Sopilka	1.000	4	30	2	0	0	2

First Base	PCT	G	PO	A	E	DP
Byler	.988	109	836	65	11	72
Cribbs	.000	1	0	0	1	0
Herum	.986	26	202	17	3	13
Jones	1.000	4	18	1	0	2
Karaviotis	1.000	2	12	1	0	2
Spivey	1.000	1	1	1	0	1

Second Base	PCT	G	PO	A	E	DP
Castillo	.940	27	51	59	7	23
Cribbs	.944	5	3	14	1	1
Flores	1.000	1	1	1	0	0
Karaviotis	.800	2	7	1	2	0
Lockhart	.982	68	113	158	5	32
Ozuna	.948	28	51	59	6	14
Spivey	1.000	15	21	37	0	4

Third Base	PCT	G	PO	A	E	DP
Castillo	.923	71	42	102	12	12
Cribbs	.800	5	1	3	1	0
Flores	1.000	2	2	1	0	1
Herum	.930	50	20	87	8	4
Ozuna	.952	18	15	25	2	4

Shortstop	PCT	G	PO	A	E	DP
Alcantara	.961	85	130	219	14	36
Castillo	1.000	1	1	0	0	0
Cribbs	.968	22	34	56	3	15
Flores	.969	30	48	78	4	14
Flores	.500	3	0	3	3	0
Ozuna	1.000	4	6	14	0	1

Outfield	PCT	G	PO	A	E	DP
Blanco	1.000	4	2	0	0	0
Bray	1.000	9	14	1	0	1
Cribbs	.972	49	66	4	2	1
DeLuzio	.957	30	43	1	2	0
Heyman	1.000	89	135	4	0	1
Jones	.000	1	0	0	0	0
Karaviotis	.000	1	0	0	0	0
Lockhart	1.000	10	16	0	0	0
McPhearson	.976	106	204	1	5	0
Morozowski	.985	109	190	11	3	1
Nehrir	.957	11	22	0	1	0
Ozuna	.920	21	21	2	2	0
Spivey	.750	2	3	0	1	0

KANE COUNTY COUGARS — *LOW CLASS A*

MIDWEST LEAGUE

Batting	B-T	HT	WT	DOB	AVG	vLH	vRH	G	AB	R	H	2B	3B	HR	RBI	BB	HBP	SH	SF	SO	SB	CS	SLG	OBP
Baker, Tyler	L-R	5-9	179	3-8-93	.250	—	.250	2	4	0	1	0	0	0	0	0	0	0	0	2	0	0	.250	.250
Basabe, Luis Alejandro	B-R	5-10	160	8-26-96	.229	.278	.207	53	175	21	40	13	0	2	7	22	1	3	0	54	8	4	.337	.318
Chisholm, Jasrado	L-R	5-11	165	2-1-98	.248	.200	.262	29	109	14	27	5	2	1	12	10	3	2	1	39	3	0	.358	.325
Christy, Francis	L-R	6-2	220	9-1-95	.180	.080	.226	21	78	7	14	1	0	0	2	1	0	0	0	25	3	0	.192	.190
De La Garza, Paxton	R-R	6-0	200	12-17-93	.224	.219	.226	37	125	13	28	8	0	4	19	15	0	1	1	41	1	1	.384	.305
DeLuzio, Ben	R-R	6-3	190	8-9-94	.317	.316	.318	46	186	20	59	14	3	0	18	13	2	0	1	33	13	7	.425	.366
Endris, Billy	L-L	6-2	190	10-18-93	.187	.273	.172	22	75	7	14	1	0	0	10	5	0	1	1	20	1	3	.200	.235
Flores, Raymel	B-R	5-9	155	9-22-94	.206	.278	.164	32	97	12	20	5	1	0	9	5	2	3	0	26	4	2	.278	.260
Grier, Anfernee	R-R	6-1	180	10-13-95	.251	.248	.252	123	475	69	119	20	3	4	36	58	8	3	3	114	30	11	.331	.340
Hernandez, Ramon	R-R	6-4	195	3-2-96	.294	.276	.302	114	445	46	131	21	2	13	72	20	11	0	4	87	3	6	.438	.338
Herrera, Jose	B-R	5-10	185	2-24-97	.208	.299	.169	58	221	14	46	15	0	1	22	16	0	0	1	32	0	0	.290	.261
Jefferson, Manny	R-R	6-3	170	3-5-95	.221	.239	.215	121	420	41	93	20	3	2	40	35	9	0	7	105	7	2	.298	.291
Karaviotis, Mark	R-R	6-1	185	10-12-95	.307	.268	.317	57	202	35	62	13	1	2	21	21	11	0	2	54	1	0	.411	.398
Lopez, B.J.	R-R	5-9	185	9-29-94	.281	.269	.286	28	82	9	23	6	0	0	9	16	0	2	1	9	0	1	.354	.394
Morozowski, Jason	R-R	6-2	190	6-10-94	.286	.286	.286	11	49	3	14	0	0	0	3	2	2	0	0	8	1	0	.286	.340
Nehrir, Zach	R-R	6-2	205	1-28-93	.111	.091	.143	6	18	3	2	0	0	0	0	3	1	0	0	8	0	2	.111	.273
Olmeda, Alexis	R-R	6-0	225	4-5-94	.183	.167	.188	33	104	12	19	3	0	0	6	14	0	1	1	27	2	3	.212	.277
Owings, Connor	R-L	5-10	190	5-11-94	.207	.000	.250	7	29	4	6	0	0	1	4	2	1	0	0	10	0	0	.310	.281

Ozuna, Fernery	R-R	5-8	170	11-9-95	.267	.250	.271	30	90	13	24	4	1	2	16	8	2	3	1	32	3	3	.400	.337
Queliz, Jose	R-R	6-2	224	8-7-92	.353	1.000	.313	5	17	3	6	1	0	0	1	2	0	0	0	4	0	0	.412	.421
Ramos, Eudy	R-R	6-1	195	2-19-96	.219	.200	.228	30	119	8	26	2	0	1	11	4	1	0	1	25	0	2	.261	.248
Sanchez, Yan	R-R	6-2	170	8-31-96	.203	.175	.222	33	138	18	28	6	2	2	13	4	1	0	0	32	2	4	.319	.231
Silverio, Luis	R-R	6-3	180	6-27-95	.270	.265	.273	101	385	62	104	22	6	5	37	26	5	0	2	83	10	5	.397	.323
Smith, Kyle	R-R	6-4	220	10-14-93	.182	.226	.162	26	99	11	18	8	0	4	14	7	0	0	1	50	0	0	.384	.234
Smith, Stephen	R-R	6-1	220	11-3-94	.286	.235	.320	42	126	19	36	10	2	2	19	27	4	0	0	41	2	3	.444	.427
Sopilka, David	R-R	6-0	170	8-30-93	.278	.125	.400	5	18	1	5	1	0	0	1	0	0	0	0	3	0	0	.333	.278
Spivey, Seth	L-R	5-11	180	7-6-92	.115	.000	.143	7	26	2	3	3	0	0	5	3	1	0	0	4	0	0	.231	.233
Thompson, Cole	R-R	6-3	190	4-11-94	.177	.313	.114	14	51	4	9	3	0	1	6	2	0	0	1	17	0	1	.294	.204
Walton, Adam	R-R	6-1	190	9-22-93	.266	.409	.208	72	244	26	65	15	1	2	25	17	3	1	1	60	6	2	.361	.321
Wilson, Marcus	R-R	6-3	175	8-15-96	.295	.239	.313	103	383	56	113	21	5	9	54	55	2	1	4	90	15	7	.447	.383

Pitching	B-T	HT	WT	DOB	W	L	ERA	G	GS	CG	SV	IP	H	R	ER	HR	BB	SO	AVG	vLH	vRH	K/9	BB/9
Aker, Mitchell	R-R	6-2	185	6-22-94	0	2	12.00	4	2	0	0	9	19	17	12	1	8	2	.413	.409	.417	2.00	8.00
Atkinson, Ryan	R-R	6-3	218	5-10-93	2	5	3.34	10	10	0	0	57	40	22	21	4	18	68	.201	.151	.239	10.80	2.86
Badamo, Tyler	R-R	6-1	220	8-8-92	1	0	2.57	1	1	0	0	7	10	2	2	0	0	3	.345	.375	.308	3.86	0.00
Becker, Cal	R-R	6-1	195	6-9-93	1	1	6.62	13	0	0	1	18	21	13	13	2	11	13	.296	.400	.239	6.62	5.60
Benitez, Anfernee	R-L	6-1	180	7-24-95	0	1	2.03	11	0	0	1	13	10	3	3	0	9	11	.208	.143	.235	7.43	6.08
Burr, Ryan	R-R	6-4	225	5-28-94	1	2	2.81	22	0	0	4	32	29	10	10	3	15	46	.244	.277	.222	12.94	4.22
Bustamante, Carlos	R-R	6-0	190	9-25-94	1	1	0.55	6	1	0	1	16	9	1	1	0	2	16	.164	.063	.205	8.82	1.10
Clark, Cody	R-R	6-2	215	7-22-93	0	2	4.44	19	0	0	3	24	25	13	12	5	7	28	.272	.282	.264	10.36	2.59
Duplantier, Jon	L-R	6-4	225	7-11-94	6	1	1.24	13	12	0	0	73	45	13	10	4	15	78	.180	.192	.171	9.66	1.86
Eveld, Tommy	R-R	6-5	195	12-30-93	1	0	0.33	22	0	0	14	28	10	3	1	0	8	33	.111	.152	.088	10.73	2.60
Garcia, Junior	L-L	5-11	220	10-1-95	2	3	2.45	18	0	0	3	26	14	9	7	1	14	38	.157	.118	.182	13.32	4.91
Ginkel, Kevin	R-R	6-4	210	3-24-94	1	1	14.85	6	0	0	0	7	8	11	11	1	9	5	.308	.500	.188	6.75	12.15
Gonzalez, Erbert	R-R	5-10	170	10-21-95	1	0	3.72	9	0	0	1	10	9	4	4	0	6	10	.243	.182	.269	9.31	5.59
Grey, Connor	R-R	6-0	180	5-6-94	3	1	2.11	7	7	2	0	47	36	14	11	2	1	39	.216	.247	.189	7.47	0.19
Hoover, J.J.	R-R	6-3	240	8-13-87	0	1	9.00	1	0	0	0	1	2	1	1	0	0	2	.500	.500	.500	18.00	0.00
Huang, Wei-Chieh	R-R	6-1	170	9-26-93	1	1	1.58	20	0	0	0	40	25	8	7	2	10	47	.172	.120	.200	10.58	2.25
Lemieux, Mack	L-L	6-3	205	9-6-96	7	5	4.69	19	19	0	0	102	111	56	53	4	34	80	.278	.306	.266	7.08	3.01
Lewis, Sam	R-R	6-4	195	10-9-91	3	3	3.80	27	5	0	1	66	66	37	28	6	13	61	.250	.220	.268	8.28	1.76
Mark, Tyler	R-R	6-1	195	10-18-94	5	3	3.76	39	2	0	3	65	55	28	27	5	24	54	.226	.276	.188	7.52	3.34
Martinez, Jose	R-R	6-1	160	4-14-94	1	1	10.61	10	0	0	0	9	12	11	11	2	13	9	.308	.154	.385	8.68	12.54
Mason, Austin	R-R	6-2	200	12-10-93	2	2	4.42	13	0	0	0	18	16	11	9	1	6	16	.242	.300	.194	7.85	2.95
McWilliams, Sam	R-R	6-7	190	9-4-95	11	6	2.84	25	25	0	0	133	112	46	42	5	31	98	.231	.249	.217	6.63	2.10
Mejia, Jeferson	R-R	6-7	195	8-2-94	1	1	6.08	18	0	0	0	24	22	17	16	1	22	27	.247	.343	.185	10.27	8.37
Poche, Colin	L-L	6-3	185	1-17-94	2	0	1.09	13	0	0	1	25	16	3	3	0	6	44	.186	.214	.172	16.05	2.19
Reed, Cody	R-L	6-3	245	6-7-96	3	2	1.74	8	8	1	0	47	29	11	9	1	11	49	.174	.256	.148	9.45	2.12
Simms, Trevor	R-R	6-4	220	3-15-92	3	3	2.87	22	0	0	4	31	35	21	10	4	16	30	.273	.291	.260	8.62	4.60
Smith, Riley	R-R	6-1	195	1-15-95	3	1	3.07	14	8	0	0	59	63	21	20	1	13	49	.278	.298	.263	7.52	1.99
Takahashi, Bo	R-R	6-0	197	1-23-97	0	2	3.86	4	4	0	0	16	16	13	7	3	5	14	.239	.179	.282	7.71	2.76
Taylor, Curtis	R-R	6-6	215	7-25-95	3	4	3.32	13	13	0	0	62	55	28	23	4	23	68	.235	.223	.244	9.82	3.32
Vargas, Emilio	R-R	6-3	200	8-12-96	5	7	4.02	21	20	0	1	101	85	46	45	8	43	98	.232	.252	.217	8.76	3.84
Winston, Jake	R-R	6-3	194	9-13-93	1	2	4.27	36	0	0	4	46	45	25	22	1	24	38	.268	.295	.244	7.38	4.66

Fielding

Catcher	PCT	G	PO	A	E	DP	PB
Baker	1.000	2	6	0	0	0	0
Christy	.991	13	97	10	1	1	1
Herrera	.991	57	469	56	5	2	7
Lopez	.985	27	238	27	4	1	3
Olmeda	.972	19	155	21	5	0	2
Ozuna	1.000	1	1	0	0	0	0
Queliz	.977	5	37	5	1	0	1
Sopilka	1.000	4	29	6	0	0	0
Thompson	.993	14	130	13	1	0	1

First Base	PCT	G	PO	A	E	DP
De La Garza	.992	16	111	14	1	9
Hernandez	.987	21	142	13	2	8
Karaviotis	.988	51	386	14	5	38
Olmeda	.989	10	82	9	1	9
Ramos	1.000	16	138	10	0	16
Smith	.995	22	184	11	1	12
Spivey	1.000	5	23	3	0	3

Second Base	PCT	G	PO	A	E	DP
Basabe	.972	36	45	95	4	18
De La Garza	1.000	3	5	6	0	1
Jefferson	.972	59	97	145	7	28
Owings	1.000	2	3	8	0	1
Ozuna	1.000	10	22	27	0	8
Spivey	.000	1	0	0	0	0
Walton	.979	36	61	77	3	14

Third Base	PCT	G	PO	A	E	DP
Basabe	.667	3	0	4	2	0
De La Garza	.923	7	1	11	1	0
Flores	.000	1	0	0	0	0
Hernandez	.938	90	61	136	13	10
Ozuna	.850	8	9	8	3	2
Ramos	.931	10	12	15	2	0
Walton	.943	24	21	29	3	2

Shortstop	PCT	G	PO	A	E	DP
Chisholm	.940	29	59	83	9	18
Flores	.925	28	35	64	8	12
Jefferson	.959	50	84	101	8	24
Ozuna	1.000	6	16	19	0	3
Sanchez	.961	31	50	97	6	21

Outfield	PCT	G	PO	A	E	DP
De La Garza	1.000	2	2	0	0	0
DeLuzio	.989	46	85	8	1	0
Endris	.975	21	37	2	1	2
Flores	1.000	2	2	0	0	0
Grier	.978	113	216	5	5	2
Jefferson	.000	1	0	0	0	0
Morozowski	1.000	11	31	1	0	0
Nehrir	1.000	6	6	1	0	0
Owings	1.000	2	2	0	0	0
Ozuna	1.000	7	9	0	0	0
Sanchez	1.000	3	3	0	0	0
Silverio	.964	79	125	7	5	1
Smith	1.000	38	63	6	0	0
Wilson	.980	93	188	7	4	3

HILLSBORO HOPS — *SHORT SEASON*

NORTHWEST LEAGUE

Batting	B-T	HT	WT	DOB	AVG	vLH	vRH	G	AB	R	H	2B	3B	HR	RBI	BB	HBP	SH	SF	SO	SB	CS	SLG	OBP
Araiza, Bryan	L-R	6-2	190	4-27-96	.212	.203	.215	62	241	31	51	10	3	2	29	37	2	1	4	71	9	4	.303	.317
De La Garza, Paxton	R-R	6-0	200	12-17-93	.255	.333	.225	14	55	8	14	2	1	0	2	6	2	0	0	14	1	0	.327	.349
Dobson, Ryan	R-R	6-0	175	5-2-95	.191	.231	.172	26	84	17	16	4	0	0	6	12	2	2	1	29	2	3	.238	.303

Duzenack, Camden	R-R	5-9	170	3-8-95	.288	.288	.289	58	222	43	64	16	1	3	34	18	8	0	7	31	8	4	.410	.353
Ellis, Drew	R-R	6-3	210	12-1-95	.227	.244	.221	48	181	35	41	8	0	8	23	24	3	0	0	45	3	1	.403	.327
Endris, Billy	L-L	6-2	190	10-18-93	.206	.263	.185	23	73	14	15	3	1	2	10	6	2	0	1	28	4	0	.356	.281
Grotjohn, Ryan	L-R	6-2	175	4-25-95	.261	.293	.248	38	142	21	37	8	2	0	27	12	4	1	5	24	3	3	.345	.325
Holmes, Tramayne	R-R	6-0	165	7-10-96	.193	.161	.210	52	181	32	35	5	0	3	23	21	9	1	1	64	12	5	.271	.307
Lara, Luis	B-R	6-0	190	5-6-95	.247	.241	.250	24	89	9	22	3	0	2	11	16	0	0	2	17	1	0	.348	.355
Leyba, Domingo	B-R	5-11	160	9-11-95	.286	.000	.381	6	28	4	8	1	0	1	6	4	0	0	0	2	0	0	.429	.375
Lowery, Luke	R-R	6-2	230	12-8-93	.000	.000	.000	7	17	1	0	0	0	0	2	5	0	0	0	3	0	0	.000	.227
Owings, Connor	R-L	5-10	190	5-11-94	.200	.125	.219	25	80	9	16	2	0	0	7	13	1	0	1	25	1	2	.225	.316
Perez, Jorge	L-L	5-8	165	1-18-98	.194	.120	.221	26	93	7	18	4	0	0	11	2	0	2	0	21	6	1	.237	.211
Ramos, Eudy	R-R	6-1	195	2-19-96	.315	.429	.279	40	178	27	56	9	1	4	30	13	0	0	2	45	0	0	.444	.358
Sanchez, Yan	R-R	6-2	170	8-31-96	.281	.220	.306	40	171	28	48	10	6	3	26	13	2	0	2	50	5	2	.462	.335
Smith, Kyle	R-R	6-4	220	10-14-93	.180	.167	.185	11	39	10	7	3	0	2	7	6	5	0	0	18	0	1	.410	.360
Smith, Pavin	L-L	6-2	210	2-6-96	.318	.323	.316	51	195	34	62	15	2	0	27	27	0	0	0	24	2	1	.415	.401
Smith, Stephen	R-R	6-1	220	11-3-94	.222	.250	.214	16	54	9	12	1	0	0	1	13	1	0	0	18	2	0	.241	.382
Stupienski, Gavin	L-R	6-1	220	3-12-94	.250	—	.250	1	4	1	1	0	0	0	2	0	0	0	0	1	0	0	.250	.250
Susnara, Tim	L-R	6-1	185	4-17-96	.210	.188	.217	36	124	7	26	7	1	0	9	20	2	0	0	36	0	1	.282	.329
Swain, Dan	R-R	5-11	192	9-30-94	.198	.143	.234	31	106	12	21	8	0	1	15	7	3	0	0	34	3	2	.302	.267
Thompson, Cole	R-R	6-3	190	4-11-94	.282	.333	.273	11	39	5	11	3	0	0	4	6	0	0	1	12	0	1	.359	.370
Tufts, Ryan	R-R	6-2	205	7-27-94	.214	.143	.238	12	28	4	6	2	0	0	2	2	2	0	1	4	1	0	.286	.303
Varsho, Daulton	L-R	5-10	190	7-2-96	.311	.262	.333	50	193	36	60	16	3	7	39	17	1	0	1	30	7	2	.534	.368

Pitching	B-T	HT	WT	DOB	W	L	ERA	G	GS	CG	SV	IP	H	R	ER	HR	BB	SO	AVG	vLH	vRH	K/9	BB/9
Aker, Mitchell	R-R	6-2	185	6-22-94	1	5	7.86	8	7	0	0	34	43	38	30	8	9	25	.299	.355	.256	6.55	2.36
Badamo, Tyler	R-R	6-1	220	8-8-92	1	2	5.13	6	6	0	0	33	41	19	19	0	5	20	.318	.283	.342	5.40	1.35
Becker, Cal	R-R	6-1	195	6-9-93	0	2	2.84	13	0	0	0	19	12	6	6	1	8	25	.182	.308	.100	11.84	3.79
Benitez, Anfernee	R-L	6-1	180	7-24-95	0	1	4.50	10	0	0	0	10	15	5	5	0	3	13	.357	.154	.448	11.70	2.70
Brill, Matt	R-R	6-2	190	10-25-94	1	1	0.89	18	0	0	2	20	12	3	2	0	12	25	.164	.267	.093	11.07	5.31
Castillo, Luis	R-R	6-2	180	3-10-95	1	0	2.91	19	0	0	1	34	28	11	11	3	14	35	.221	.278	.178	9.26	3.71
Clark, Cody	R-R	6-2	215	7-22-93	1	0	0.00	2	0	0	0	4	1	0	0	0	2	9	.083	.000	.143	20.25	4.50
Duran, Jhoan	R-R	6-5	175	1-8-98	6	3	4.24	11	11	0	0	51	44	28	24	5	17	36	.228	.212	.236	6.35	3.00
Garcia, Junior	L-L	5-11	220	10-1-95	2	0	0.57	6	0	0	0	16	7	1	1	1	3	18	.132	.067	.158	10.34	1.72
Ginkel, Kevin	R-R	6-4	210	3-24-94	0	1	3.48	20	0	0	0	34	26	13	13	1	11	49	.213	.148	.265	13.10	2.94
Gonzalez, Erbert	R-R	5-10	170	10-21-95	3	1	2.01	19	0	0	7	22	12	6	5	1	11	27	.158	.167	.152	10.88	4.43
Grey, Connor	R-R	6-0	180	5-6-94	6	2	2.74	8	8	0	0	46	35	16	14	4	5	41	.207	.235	.188	8.02	0.98
Hernandez, Carlos	R-R	5-9	171	4-26-94	0	0	4.50	1	1	0	0	4	5	2	2	1	4	6	.313	.333	.286	13.50	9.00
Keele, Tyler	R-R	6-3	195	8-17-93	5	5	4.32	15	14	0	0	75	63	44	36	7	27	72	.229	.252	.215	8.64	3.24
Koch, Matt	L-R	6-3	215	11-2-90	1	0	4.91	2	2	0	0	11	13	7	6	2	1	9	.302	.353	.269	7.36	0.82
Madero, Luis	R-R	6-3	175	4-15-97	1	1	8.24	4	4	0	0	20	28	22	18	2	5	17	.337	.364	.320	7.78	2.29
Martinez, Jose	R-R	6-1	160	4-14-94	0	0	7.50	5	0	0	0	6	3	6	5	1	12	7	.150	.125	.167	10.50	18.00
McCanna, Kevin	L-R	6-1	185	2-1-94	5	1	0.27	6	0	0	0	33	12	2	1	0	10	43	.111	.117	.104	11.61	2.70
Mejia, Jeferson	R-R	6-7	195	8-2-94	0	0	5.06	3	0	0	0	5	5	3	3	1	3	8	.250	.333	.182	13.50	5.06
Peacock, Matt	R-R	6-1	180	2-27-94	0	2	2.45	22	0	0	1	29	24	8	8	2	8	23	.229	.229	.229	7.06	2.45
Pujols, Rafael	R-R	6-6	175	8-21-95	0	0	1.93	10	0	0	0	14	11	7	3	0	2	17	.204	.053	.286	10.93	1.29
Ramirez, Nestor	R-R	6-4	195	9-4-95	0	0	0.00	1	0	0	0	1	1	0	0	0	0	0	.333	1.000	.000	0.00	0.00
Romero, Pierce	R-R	6-3	200	5-12-94	0	0	4.00	8	0	0	0	9	9	5	4	0	11	8	.257	.100	.320	8.00	11.00
Santana, Yeison	R-R	6-0	160	10-25-96	0	0	12.79	2	0	0	0	6	11	10	9	0	2	8	.379	.429	.364	11.37	2.84
Shaffer, Brian	R-R	6-5	200	8-12-96	0	0	3.43	11	8	0	0	21	18	8	8	0	1	21	.228	.270	.191	9.00	0.43
Smith, Riley	R-R	6-1	195	1-15-95	4	3	3.06	8	8	0	0	47	42	20	16	3	7	35	.232	.269	.211	6.70	1.34
Torres, Juan	R-R	6-2	180	5-25-95	1	0	3.38	8	0	0	0	16	17	6	6	1	6	19	.283	.286	.281	10.69	3.38
Vail, Tyler	R-R	6-1	208	11-3-91	1	5	5.06	7	7	0	0	37	44	26	21	2	14	33	.299	.362	.244	7.96	3.38
Ward, Tucker	R-R	6-6	230	5-10-92	0	0	0.00	3	0	0	0	3	1	0	0	0	2	1	.125	.333	.000	3.00	6.00
Watson, Jordan	L-L	6-0	185	9-14-93	0	0	0.00	3	0	0	0	3	1	0	0	0	2	6	.100	.000	.125	18.00	6.00
Williams, Breckin	R-R	6-0	200	9-5-93	1	0	2.63	13	0	0	2	14	7	4	4	0	3	21	.146	.150	.143	13.83	1.98

Fielding

C: Lowery 3, Stupienski 1, Susnara 31, Thompson 6, Varsho 36. **1B:** De La Garza 3, Lara 13, Ramos 9, Smith 7, Smith 42, Tufts 3. **2B:** De La Garza 4, Dobson 9, Duzenack 10, Grotjohn 30, Lara 2, Owings 8, Sanchez 12, Tufts 4. **3B:** De La Garza 3, Ellis 40, Grotjohn 3, Lara 4, Ramos 23, Sanchez 1, Tufts 3. **SS:** Dobson 6, Duzenack 47, Grotjohn 3, Leyba 6, Sanchez 17. **OF:** Araiza 60, Dobson 9, Endris 22, Holmes 52, Lowery 2, Owings 11, Perez 26, Sanchez 10, Smith 15, Swain 29.

MISSOULA OSPREY — *ROOKIE*

PIONEER LEAGUE

Batting	B-T	HT	WT	DOB	AVG	vLH	vRH	G	AB	R	H	2B	3B	HR	RBI	BB	HBP	SH	SF	SO	SB	CS	SLG	OBP
Araujo, Juan	R-R	6-2	195	6-24-98	.232	.293	.219	62	233	38	54	12	2	11	32	24	5	0	1	68	1	2	.442	.316
Bracho, Didimo	R-R	5-11	170	9-2-96	.500	—	.500	1	4	0	2	0	0	0	0	0	0	0	0	1	0	0	.500	.500
Caballero, Jose	R-R	5-10	185	8-30-96	.319	.409	.301	36	135	20	43	8	3	2	15	8	6	0	2	27	4	0	.467	.378
Connelly, Terence	L-R	6-2	225	3-7-94	.357	.167	.380	19	56	11	20	7	1	1	13	8	0	0	1	10	0	0	.571	.431
De La Trinidad, Ernie	L-L	5-9	165	1-3-96	.297	.250	.306	50	192	39	57	10	8	5	25	21	7	1	1	36	4	4	.510	.385
Diaz, Eduardo	R-R	6-2	175	7-19-97	.312	.271	.322	57	247	58	77	18	5	7	44	11	7	2	1	47	11	2	.510	.357
Gorman, William	L-R	6-4	210	11-8-94	.308	.539	.262	26	78	20	24	4	3	3	11	8	2	0	0	22	5	0	.551	.386
Grotjohn, Ryan	L-R	6-2	175	4-25-95	.227	—	.227	6	22	6	5	3	0	0	4	1	0	0	0	2	0	0	.364	.261
Hernandez, Eddie	B-R	5-9	160	4-18-99	.200	.000	.222	2	10	2	2	0	0	1	4	0	0	0	0	2	0	0	.500	.200
Lara, Luis	B-R	6-0	190	5-6-95	.295	.200	.313	26	95	15	28	8	2	4	20	13	0	0	0	20	0	0	.547	.380
Leyton, Brandon	R-R	5-10	165	12-17-98	.280	.242	.288	52	193	29	54	10	4	4	23	7	5	0	1	26	4	2	.435	.320

Lynch, Keshawn	R-R	5-6	155	10-12-96	.301	.342	.290	50	203	33	61	9	2	3	31	27	1	1	2	54	6	5	.409	.382
Maciel, Gabriel	B-R	5-10	170	1-10-99	.323	.316	.324	52	217	40	70	14	1	3	25	24	1	1	2	34	9	8	.438	.389
Martinez, Francis	B-R	6-4	187	6-28-97	.271	.308	.262	56	207	33	56	12	1	6	28	20	3	0	1	67	0	0	.425	.342
Miroglio, Dominic	R-R	6-0	203	3-10-95	.317	.276	.327	37	142	18	45	13	0	1	16	14	2	1	1	8	0	0	.430	.384
Novas, Joel	R-R	6-1	185	12-31-94	.257	.276	.252	38	140	14	36	5	0	0	20	13	0	0	0	31	1	1	.293	.320
Perez, Jorge	L-L	5-8	165	1-18-98	.125	—	.125	2	8	1	1	0	0	0	0	1	0	0	0	1	0	0	.125	.222
Rose, Joey	R-R	6-1	205	1-20-98	.312	.306	.313	49	199	32	62	15	2	9	39	13	4	0	1	56	2	0	.543	.364
Smith, Kyle	R-R	6-4	220	10-14-93	.214	.000	.222	8	28	4	6	2	0	1	3	3	1	0	0	9	0	0	.393	.313
Stupienski, Gavin	L-R	6-1	220	3-12-94	.359	.333	.368	20	78	13	28	9	0	3	16	6	2	0	2	17	0	0	.590	.409
Tejeda, Luis	R-R	6-3	195	7-11-95	.000	—	.000	1	3	0	0	0	0	0	0	1	0	0	0	1	0	0	.000	.250
Yerzy, Andy	L-R	6-3	215	7-5-98	.298	.310	.295	54	225	36	67	12	0	13	45	24	0	0	0	45	0	0	.524	.366

Pitching	B-T	HT	WT	DOB	W	L	ERA	G	GS	CG	SV	IP	H	R	ER	HR	BB	SO	AVG	vLH	vRH	K/9	BB/9
Aker, Mitchell	R-R	6-2	185	6-22-94	0	0	9.00	1	0	0	0	2	3	2	2	1	0	3	.375	.400	.333	13.50	0.00
Almonte, Abraham	L-L	5-11	195	12-3-93	1	0	2.86	19	0	0	11	22	21	7	7	2	9	31	.247	.273	.238	12.68	3.68
Bain, Jeff	R-R	6-4	200	3-3-96	3	1	4.09	14	0	0	0	22	22	11	10	2	5	27	.259	.304	.242	11.05	2.05
Bartlett, Cole	R-R	6-2	189	12-22-94	1	0	2.53	21	0	0	4	32	26	9	9	4	4	30	.222	.206	.229	8.44	1.13
Bustamante, Carlos	R-R	6-0	190	9-25-94	0	0	0.00	10	0	0	3	12	7	1	0	0	4	13	.175	.167	.179	9.75	3.00
Cruz, Wilfry	R-R	6-2	160	10-22-97	0	0	4.50	2	0	0	1	4	2	2	2	0	2	4	.154	.000	.250	9.00	4.50
Defrank, Damian	R-R	6-3	200	2-1-95	0	1	9.49	7	0	0	0	12	24	18	13	3	7	10	.400	.444	.381	7.30	5.11
Durruthy, Williams	R-R	6-4	225	10-11-94	0	0	8.68	7	0	0	0	9	12	9	9	0	11	6	.343	.333	.350	5.79	10.61
Gonzalez, Gabe	R-R	6-4	210	8-16-96	0	0	9.56	12	0	0	0	16	23	17	17	2	12	10	.354	.370	.342	5.63	6.75
Herman, Omar	R-R	5-10	170	3-21-97	0	0	7.71	2	0	0	0	5	4	4	4	0	2	4	.235	.250	.222	7.71	3.86
Hernandez, Kenny	L-L	6-2	185	6-24-98	0	0	0.00	1	0	0	0	2	3	0	0	0	2	2	.375	.000	.429	9.00	9.00
Herrera, Jhoendri	R-R	5-9	170	6-6-94	2	0	2.89	8	0	0	0	9	8	4	3	0	5	7	.211	.200	.214	6.75	4.82
Johnson, James	R-R	6-2	205	6-22-93	3	2	8.79	15	6	0	0	43	59	47	42	6	21	25	.332	.362	.317	5.23	4.40
Kulina, Casey	R-L	5-9	175	4-17-93	2	0	2.83	13	0	0	0	29	24	13	9	6	6	34	.218	.250	.211	10.67	1.88
Lin, Kai-Wei	R-R	5-11	165	3-19-96	0	6	8.28	13	11	0	0	54	78	57	50	15	19	47	.329	.299	.347	7.79	3.15
Luciano, Elvis	R-R	6-2	184	2-15-00	0	0	0.00	1	0	0	0	2	0	0	0	0	0	2	.000	.000	.000	9.00	0.00
Madero, Luis	R-R	6-3	175	4-15-97	3	1	3.99	5	5	0	0	29	29	16	13	3	6	28	.261	.314	.237	8.59	1.84
Martinez, Edgar	R-R	6-0	175	11-2-97	3	3	4.76	8	7	0	0	40	48	23	21	9	8	27	.300	.250	.324	6.13	1.82
Muller, Brady	L-L	6-1	185	7-3-92	7	7	5.22	15	15	0	0	79	96	61	46	12	22	73	.295	.338	.282	8.28	2.50
Ovalles, Melvin	R-R	6-2	180	11-21-96	0	0	20.25	2	0	0	0	1	3	7	3	1	3	0	.333	.333	.333	0.00	20.25
Pimentel, Cesilio	L-L	6-2	185	1-5-93	2	2	5.00	5	5	0	0	27	35	24	15	3	6	19	.313	.231	.323	6.33	2.00
Pujols, Rafael	R-R	6-6	175	8-21-95	1	2	3.78	13	0	0	0	17	18	13	7	0	7	12	.281	.438	.229	6.48	3.78
Ramirez, Nestor	R-R	6-4	195	9-4-95	3	0	7.71	8	0	0	1	14	16	14	12	3	7	15	.276	.333	.235	9.64	4.50
Romero, Pierce	R-R	6-3	200	5-12-94	0	2	12.50	14	0	0	0	18	42	27	25	4	8	11	.452	.303	.533	5.50	4.00
Santana, Yeison	R-R	6-0	160	10-25-96	1	2	6.75	18	0	0	0	32	45	32	24	2	8	30	.317	.425	.275	8.44	2.25
Soriano, Franklyn	L-L	6-2	173	7-21-95	3	5	6.64	15	15	0	0	60	77	50	44	12	31	52	.320	.348	.313	7.84	4.68
Stapler, Cole	R-R	6-4	240	12-22-94	1	2	2.83	14	5	0	1	35	28	15	11	3	7	41	.211	.114	.258	10.54	1.80
Tunnell, West	L-R	6-1	195	11-20-93	0	0	9.00	1	0	0	0	1	1	1	1	0	1	1	.250	.333	.000	9.00	9.00
Vail, Tyler	R-R	6-1	208	11-3-91	2	2	6.75	7	7	0	0	35	45	31	26	8	13	33	.304	.292	.310	8.57	3.38

Fielding

C: Miroglio 34, Stupienski 4, Tejeda 1, Yerzy 37. **1B:** Connelly 12, Lara 8, Martinez 52, Smith 7. **2B:** Bracho 1, Caballero 28, Grotjohn 1, Leyton 3, Lynch 34, Novas 12. **3B:** Connelly 6, Hernandez 1, Lara 4, Novas 22, Rose 46. **SS:** Caballero 8, Grotjohn 5, Leyton 49, Lynch 14. **OF:** Araujo 58, De La Trinidad 44, Diaz 57, Gorman 21, Maciel 50, Perez 2.

AZL D-BACKS — *ROOKIE*

ARIZONA LEAGUE

Batting	B-T	HT	WT	DOB	AVG	vLH	vRH	G	AB	R	H	2B	3B	HR	RBI	BB	HBP	SH	SF	SO	SB	CS	SLG	OBP
Ahmed, Nick	R-R	6-2	195	3-15-90	.000	.000	.000	4	10	1	0	0	0	0	1	3	0	0	0	4	0	1	.000	.231
Almond, Zachery	R-R	6-3	210	4-12-96	.260	.000	.361	19	50	5	13	2	0	0	5	11	0	0	1	14	1	1	.300	.387
Arcia, Oswaldo	L-R	6-0	225	5-9-91	.167	.500	.100	3	12	2	2	0	0	0	0	1	0	0	0	3	0	0	.167	.231
Bracho, Didimo	R-R	5-11	170	9-2-96	.271	.258	.275	38	140	25	38	10	5	4	19	13	2	0	0	34	2	2	.500	.342
Bray, Colin	B-L	6-3	197	6-18-93	.556	.667	.500	2	9	5	5	0	2	0	1	1	0	0	0	1	1	0	1.000	.600
Christy, Francis	L-R	6-2	220	9-1-95	.333	—	.333	5	15	2	5	0	1	0	3	4	0	0	1	1	1	0	.467	.450
Cintron, Jancarlos	R-R	5-8	170	12-1-94	.260	.214	.276	46	169	23	44	8	5	1	22	8	4	1	2	16	3	3	.385	.306
Connelly, Terence	L-R	6-2	225	3-7-94	.333	.333	.333	5	15	2	5	0	0	0	3	4	0	0	0	5	0	0	.333	.474
Dobson, Ryan	R-R	6-0	175	5-2-95	.287	.360	.258	22	87	11	25	3	0	0	5	10	0	1	1	27	8	1	.322	.357
Dugan, Kelly	L-R	6-3	210	9-18-90	.333	1.000	.000	1	3	1	1	1	0	0	2	0	1	0	0	2	0	0	.667	.500
Flores, Raymel	B-R	5-9	155	9-22-94	.200	.000	.250	1	5	0	1	0	0	0	1	0	0	0	0	1	0	0	.200	.200
Fuentes, Rey	L-L	6-0	160	2-12-91	.600	—	.600	2	5	1	3	2	0	0	2	0	1	0	0	0	0	0	1.000	.667
Gorman, William	L-R	6-4	210	11-8-94	.250	1.000	.000	1	4	1	1	0	1	0	3	0	0	0	0	0	0	0	.750	.250
Hazelbaker, Jeremy	L-R	6-3	190	8-14-87	.333	1.000	.000	1	3	1	1	0	0	0	0	1	0	0	0	1	1	1	.333	.500
Hernandez, Eddie	B-R	5-9	160	4-18-99	.301	.263	.311	24	93	15	28	5	4	2	12	3	1	0	2	22	2	1	.505	.323
Herrera, Jose	B-R	5-10	185	2-24-97	.429	.625	.308	8	21	4	9	4	0	0	7	6	0	0	0	3	0	0	.619	.556
Higuera, Walter	R-R	6-3	159	5-18-96	.230	.348	.195	33	100	15	23	3	0	0	5	9	5	1	0	20	7	1	.260	.325
Kennedy, Buddy	R-R	6-1	190	10-5-98	.270	.143	.309	50	178	29	48	9	8	0	20	19	2	0	2	47	7	2	.410	.343
King, Jose	L-R	6-0	160	1-16-99	.261	.500	.156	13	46	7	12	0	2	0	9	3	2	0	0	20	2	2	.348	.333
Marriaga, Jesus	R-R	6-0	170	12-17-98	.205	.178	.214	51	185	28	38	7	5	0	15	20	5	1	1	78	11	5	.297	.299
Martinez, Renae	R-R	6-1	185	4-15-94	.313	.265	.330	37	134	20	42	4	1	5	30	13	3	0	1	22	1	4	.470	.384
McArdle, Jordan	L-R	6-0	175	5-2-98	.191	.192	.191	33	115	10	22	2	0	0	11	17	0	0	1	47	0	2	.209	.293
Meadows, Chaz	R-R	5-7	150	2-17-93	.121	.133	.118	22	66	5	8	1	0	0	5	5	2	0	0	36	1	2	.136	.206
Munoz, Jesus	L-L	6-2	160	12-19-98	.167	.000	.188	4	18	2	3	0	0	0	1	0	0	0	1	1	0	0	.167	.158

Batting	B-T	HT	WT	DOB	AVG	vLH	vRH	G	AB	R	H	2B	3B	HR	RBI	BB	HBP	SH	SF	SO	SB	CS	SLG	OBP
Olmeda, Alexis	R-R	6-0	225	4-5-94	.267	.500	.231	4	15	2	4	1	0	0	2	0	0	0	0	5	0	0	.333	.267
Perez, Jorge	L-L	5-8	165	1-18-98	.269	.200	.298	18	67	8	18	5	2	1	4	10	0	1	1	7	1	2	.448	.359
Romero, Gerardo	R-B	5-9	160	10-5-95	.192	.286	.158	11	26	1	5	0	0	0	1	3	0	0	0	6	2	0	.192	.276
Swain, Dan	R-R	5-11	192	9-30-94	.000	—	.000	2	2	0	0	0	0	0	0	0	1	1	0	1	0	0	.000	.333
Tejeda, Luis	R-R	6-3	195	7-11-95	.119	.000	.175	18	59	5	7	3	0	1	3	2	0	0	1	29	0	1	.220	.145
Tomas, Yasmany	R-R	6-2	250	11-14-90	.286	.500	.200	3	7	1	2	1	0	1	1	0	0	0	0	2	0	0	.857	.286
Tufts, Ryan	R-R	6-2	205	7-27-94	.242	.200	.250	10	33	4	8	0	0	0	2	5	1	0	0	9	1	1	.242	.359
Van Rycheghem, Luke	L-R	6-3	210	2-9-98	.162	.177	.157	38	142	13	23	7	1	2	12	10	1	0	0	49	0	0	.268	.222
Vargas, Ildemaro	B-R	6-0	170	7-16-91	.375	—	.375	2	8	2	3	0	0	0	0	0	0	0	0	0	1	0	.375	.375
Watson Jr., Kevin	L-R	6-1	190	5-25-99	.174	.333	.118	9	23	0	4	1	0	0	0	2	0	0	0	7	2	0	.217	.240
Westbrook, Jamie	R-R	5-9	170	6-18-95	.286	.333	.250	2	7	1	2	0	0	1	1	0	0	0	0	0	0	0	.714	.286

Pitching	B-T	HT	WT	DOB	W	L	ERA	G	GS	CG	SV	IP	H	R	ER	HR	BB	SO	AVG	vLH	vRH	K/9	BB/9
Arroyo, Mailon	B-R	6-0	200	1-2-98	0	2	6.75	8	0	0	2	12	15	13	9	1	5	10	.306	.316	.300	7.50	3.75
Autry, Trent	R-R	6-2	215	8-12-97	1	0	5.00	6	3	0	0	9	10	6	5	0	4	6	.278	.250	.300	6.00	4.00
Bartlett, Cole	R-R	6-2	189	12-22-94	0	0	0.00	1	0	0	0	1	0	0	0	0	0	1	.000	.000	.000	9.00	0.00
Bellow, Kirby	L-L	6-1	220	11-14-91	0	0	9.00	1	0	0	0	1	0	1	1	0	1	1	.000	.000	.000	9.00	9.00
Bustamante, Carlos	R-R	6-0	190	9-25-94	0	0	0.00	1	0	0	0	1	0	0	0	0	0	3	.000	.000	.000	27.00	0.00
Cruz, Wilfry	R-R	6-2	160	10-22-97	5	7	4.95	14	9	0	1	56	57	37	31	3	32	52	.263	.232	.282	8.31	5.11
De La Rosa, Rubby	R-R	6-0	210	3-4-89	0	0	0.00	1	1	0	0	1	0	0	0	0	0	3	.000	.000	.000	27.00	0.00
Defrank, Damian	R-R	6-3	200	2-1-95	0	0	0.00	4	0	0	0	6	6	0	0	0	2	1	.273	.500	.188	1.50	3.00
Duran, Jhoan	R-R	6-5	175	1-8-98	0	2	7.15	3	3	0	0	11	19	13	9	0	4	13	.352	.400	.324	10.32	3.18
Francis, Harrison	R-R	6-2	195	10-26-98	0	1	9.00	3	3	0	0	3	5	5	3	0	2	5	.333	.600	.200	15.00	6.00
Gonzalez, Gabe	R-R	6-4	210	8-16-96	0	0	2.77	5	0	0	1	13	14	8	4	1	4	9	.286	.267	.294	6.23	2.77
Herman, Omar	R-R	5-10	170	3-21-97	3	1	4.19	13	5	0	0	43	29	23	20	0	31	35	.191	.216	.178	7.33	6.49
Hernandez, Juan	R-R	6-2	175	8-10-99	3	2	4.25	7	4	1	0	30	28	14	14	4	1	32	.239	.200	.256	9.71	0.30
Hernandez, Kenny	L-L	6-2	185	6-24-98	2	4	4.03	13	5	0	0	58	63	38	26	4	16	59	.266	.316	.250	9.16	2.48
Hiciano, Argenis	R-R	6-3	160	10-19-96	0	1	16.20	7	0	0	0	5	7	11	9	1	10	3	.333	.375	.308	5.40	18.00
Hoover, J.J.	R-R	6-3	240	8-13-87	0	0	0.00	1	1	0	0	1	0	0	0	0	0	1	.000	.000	.000	9.00	0.00
Kulina, Casey	R-L	5-9	175	4-17-93	1	1	0.96	6	0	0	3	9	4	1	1	0	2	13	.143	.200	.111	12.54	1.93
Lopez, Jose	R-R	6-0	181	12-15-96	0	0	22.50	3	0	0	0	2	4	6	5	0	3	1	.444	.500	.333	4.50	13.50
Lopez, Yoan	R-R	6-3	185	1-2-93	0	0	0.00	1	0	0	1	1	0	0	0	0	1	3	.000	.000	.000	27.00	9.00
Luciano, Elvis	R-R	6-2	184	2-15-00	1	0	2.76	4	2	0	1	16	16	10	5	0	3	9	.242	.318	.205	4.96	1.65
Martinez, Edgar	R-R	6-0	175	11-2-97	0	2	3.33	8	3	0	2	27	34	17	10	2	6	13	.312	.235	.347	4.33	2.00
Martinez, Jose	R-R	6-1	160	4-14-94	0	1	18.00	4	0	0	0	4	2	11	8	0	9	7	.125	.000	.182	15.75	20.25
Olivero, Deyni	R-R	6-1	165	1-7-98	3	0	1.75	6	3	0	0	26	28	8	5	1	9	15	.292	.265	.307	5.26	3.16
Ovalles, Melvin	R-R	6-2	180	11-21-96	1	0	3.33	13	0	0	1	27	22	14	10	2	14	15	.229	.257	.213	5.00	4.67
Ozuna, Bryan	R-R	6-1	215	3-13-94	0	1	27.00	1	0	0	0	0	1	1	1	0	3	0	1.000	1.000	—	0.00	81.00
Polancic, Jake	R-R	6-3	205	6-8-98	2	5	7.38	13	5	0	0	46	62	44	38	4	24	54	.313	.325	.305	10.49	4.66
Polanco, Oliver	R-R	6-3	210	5-13-97	0	0	10.26	12	0	0	0	17	20	23	19	3	16	14	.294	.304	.289	7.56	8.64
Ramirez, Nestor	R-R	6-4	195	9-4-95	2	0	2.76	10	0	0	3	16	12	9	5	0	2	20	.194	.191	.195	11.02	1.10
Rodriguez, Wesley	R-R	5-10	210	12-4-96	0	0	1.50	2	2	0	0	6	5	1	1	1	2	9	.217	.222	.214	13.50	3.00
Shaffer, Brian	R-R	6-5	200	8-12-96	0	0	3.00	2	2	0	0	3	1	1	1	1	0	5	.091	.000	.111	15.00	0.00
Shipley, Braden	R-R	6-1	190	2-22-92	0	0	9.00	1	1	0	0	4	5	4	4	1	0	5	.294	.333	.273	11.25	0.00
Tabor, Matt	R-R	6-2	160	7-14-98	0	1	1.93	4	4	0	0	5	8	3	1	0	0	9	.348	.200	.462	17.36	0.00
Taylor, Josh	L-L	6-5	225	3-2-93	0	0	0.00	1	0	0	1	1	0	0	0	0	0	1	.000	—	.000	9.00	0.00
Torres, Juan	R-R	6-2	180	5-25-95	0	1	3.52	5	0	0	0	8	8	3	3	0	1	8	.258	.500	.174	9.39	1.17
Tunnell, West	L-R	6-1	195	11-20-93	0	0	7.56	6	0	0	0	8	13	9	7	1	4	11	.351	.467	.273	11.88	4.32
Ward, Tucker	R-R	6-6	230	5-10-92	0	0	0.00	1	0	0	0	1	0	0	0	0	0	1	.000	.000	.000	9.00	0.00
Watson, Jordan	L-L	6-0	185	9-14-93	0	0	7.71	3	0	0	0	2	4	3	2	0	0	6	.333	.500	.300	23.14	0.00
Williams, Breckin	R-R	6-0	200	9-5-93	0	0	0.00	2	0	0	0	2	0	0	0	0	1	3	.000	.000	.000	13.50	4.50

Fielding

C: Almond 17, Christy 2, Herrera 4, Martinez 20, McArdle 3, Olmeda 3, Tejeda 14. **1B:** Connelly 4, Hernandez 1, Martinez 4, McArdle 26, Tufts 4, Van Rycheghem 20. **2B:** Bracho 3, Cintron 27, Dobson 2, Flores 1, Hernandez 18, King 2, Meadows 1, Romero 7, Westbrook 2. **3B:** Bracho 7, Cintron 3, Connelly 1, Hernandez 4, Kennedy 41, Tufts 2. **SS:** Ahmed 3, Cintron 16, Dobson 12, Flores 1, Hernandez 1, King 11, Meadows 15, Vargas 2. **OF:** Arcia 2, Bracho 27, Dobson 8, Fuentes 2, Gorman 1, Higuera 33, Marriaga 51, Meadows 5, Munoz 4, Perez 18, Romero 1, Swain 1, Tomas 3, Van Rycheghem 18, Watson Jr. 7.

DSL D-BACKS — *ROOKIE*

DOMINICAN SUMMER LEAGUE

Batting	B-T	HT	WT	DOB	AVG	vLH	vRH	G	AB	R	H	2B	3B	HR	RBI	BB	HBP	SH	SF	SO	SB	CS	SLG	OBP
Acosta, Enyor	R-L	6-2	165	1-28-99	.153	.177	.148	33	98	11	15	2	0	0	6	5	3	0	1	31	3	2	.174	.215
Andueza, Axel	R-R	6-0	163	10-27-98	.265	.267	.265	39	132	20	35	1	1	0	7	12	2	1	0	19	2	2	.288	.336
Arocha, Jose	R-R	6-0	160	1-24-00	.211	.182	.215	32	90	18	19	3	0	0	6	11	7	0	2	20	2	1	.244	.336
Bello, Jorge	L-L	6-0	175	12-2-99	.228	.267	.217	39	127	12	29	6	1	0	5	11	1	0	1	38	2	2	.291	.293
Bueno, Jonathan	R-R	6-1	168	10-4-98	.265	.125	.308	10	34	5	9	2	0	0	2	2	1	0	0	7	0	1	.324	.324
Caraballo, Richard	R-R	6-1	175	4-16-00	.147	.192	.139	44	156	16	23	3	0	2	16	9	3	0	2	47	3	0	.205	.206
Collie, Dominique	L-L	6-0	160	10-29-99	.245	.259	.240	37	102	18	25	2	3	0	6	24	1	2	0	34	2	3	.324	.394
Cordero, Andres	L-R	6-0	165	5-18-00	.238	.180	.259	46	151	13	36	1	0	2	16	19	0	0	1	27	1	2	.285	.322
Cossio, Luis	L-R	6-1	185	12-12-96	.266	.231	.274	44	143	27	38	5	3	1	19	34	2	1	1	46	6	4	.364	.411
Curpa, Jose	R-R	5-9	160	3-9-00	259	.317	.255	61	212	37	55	12	2	0	18	29	12	1	2	41	13	9	.335	.377
Diaz, Dalgeli	L-L	6-3	190	2-3-00	.239	.264	.229	51	197	23	47	5	3	2	28	15	4	0	3	55	17	4	.325	.301
Federico, Randy	R-R	6-3	210	4-28-98	.179	.269	.163	51	173	20	31	7	0	1	23	16	4	0	6	44	5	2	.237	.256
Garcia, Andy	R-R	6-0	179	5-27-99	.173	.130	.192	25	75	10	13	0	0	1	5	11	2	0	0	20	3	0	.213	.296

Gil, Juan	B-R	5-10	155	12-31-99	.234	.194	.250	39	124	17	29	4	0	0	12	12	4	1	1	26	6	4	.266	.319
Gonzalez, Luis	R-L	6-1	166	12-27-98	.146	.095	.159	35	103	17	15	4	2	0	7	26	2	0	0	43	3	1	.223	.328
Hernandez, Alexander	R-R	5-11	150	6-20-99	.260	.239	.266	49	185	17	48	9	1	1	23	20	1	1	1	53	6	4	.335	.333
Hernandez, Eddie	B-R	5-9	160	4-18-99	.343	.324	.348	43	169	20	58	7	4	3	34	11	3	1	3	20	4	4	.485	.387
Herrera, Eduardo	B-R	5-9	155	1-5-00	.181	.059	.218	27	72	9	13	1	0	0	6	10	5	1	0	19	3	1	.194	.322
Jaime, Ismael	L-L	6-0	179	11-30-99	.276	.350	.259	56	214	38	59	7	2	2	20	19	3	0	3	41	7	8	.355	.339
Jimenez, Rafael	L-R	6-6	215	8-25-99	.188	.182	.191	56	207	17	39	8	0	3	20	20	3	0	0	72	0	0	.271	.270
Lanza, Douglas	R-R	6-1	180	3-14-98	.246	.211	.253	39	114	7	28	1	2	1	11	6	7	1	1	28	2	2	.316	.320
Leyton, Brandon	R-R	5-10	165	12-17-98	.259	.000	.304	7	27	4	7	2	0	0	1	3	1	0	0	1	1	0	.333	.355
Lopez, Miguel	R-R	6-1	206	8-2-98	.106	.167	.098	19	47	2	5	2	1	0	3	5	2	0	2	22	0	1	.192	.214
Martinez, Sandy	R-R	6-4	195	5-9-00	.204	.121	.228	41	147	9	30	4	2	0	16	5	4	1	2	33	0	2	.259	.247
Noriega, Kevin	R-R	6-2	175	10-14-99	.225	.227	.224	38	129	10	29	1	1	1	17	14	1	1	0	25	3	3	.271	.306
Perdomo, Geraldo	R-R	6-2	184	10-22-99	.238	.405	.203	63	214	42	51	3	2	1	11	60	3	0	1	37	16	8	.285	.410
Porteles, Richard	R-R	5-10	165	1-9-99	.234	.189	.245	57	192	29	45	4	2	1	12	9	6	5	2	17	11	4	.292	.287
Reyes, Jose	R-R	5-9	160	10-11-98	.246	.210	.259	58	224	33	55	8	6	1	31	20	1	0	1	31	14	3	.348	.309
Sanchez, David	R-R	6-1	175	1-6-99	.314	.433	.285	41	153	27	48	4	2	3	31	13	1	0	3	20	3	2	.425	.365
Santana, Yordeni	R-R	6-5	198	10-8-99	.153	.214	.141	27	85	7	13	0	0	0	5	5	4	0	0	32	3	1	.153	.234
Santilien, Osvaldo	R-R	6-3	195	6-23-99	.287	.241	.299	39	136	20	39	14	1	1	14	14	3	0	2	43	4	2	.427	.361
Selmo, Jean	R-R	6-2	190	4-25-00	.232	.195	.244	45	164	24	38	10	2	3	17	22	3	0	1	51	6	0	.372	.332
Valbuena, Luvin	R-R	5-9	165	5-7-99	.258	.083	.296	22	66	4	17	0	0	0	2	6	1	0	0	11	1	0	.258	.329
Yanqui, Yoel	L-L	6-1	210	4-26-96	.373	.303	.390	50	169	31	63	13	5	2	28	29	1	0	3	34	11	1	.544	.460

Pitching	B-T	HT	WT	DOB	W	L	ERA	G	GS	CG	SV	IP	H	R	ER	HR	BB	SO	AVG	vLH	vRH	K/9	BB/9
Acosta, Elian	L-L	6-1	160	1-15-00	0	1	13.09	6	0	0	0	11	16	16	16	0	5	13	.340	.500	.326	10.64	4.09
Armas, Sergio	L-L	6-3	210	12-16-98	0	0	1.35	7	0	0	0	7	5	2	1	0	6	4	.208	.333	.191	5.40	8.10
Arroyo, Mailon	B-R	6-0	200	1-2-98	3	3	2.49	16	0	0	9	22	14	7	6	0	9	31	.182	.240	.154	12.88	3.74
Beriguete, Francis	L-L	6-3	165	8-11-99	1	1	6.10	3	2	0	0	10	10	7	7	1	8	10	.263	.222	.276	8.71	6.97
Bravo, Argenis	L-L	5-10	160	1-7-00	0	0	5.87	6	0	0	0	8	10	6	5	0	7	12	.333	.250	.346	14.09	8.22
Cardenas, Antonio	R-R	6-2	165	12-24-99	1	3	4.29	14	8	0	2	57	61	38	27	2	18	63	.272	.296	.261	10.01	2.86
Ceballos, Jesus	R-R	5-11	162	1-9-97	1	2	3.68	13	5	0	1	44	44	24	18	2	12	38	.262	.250	.333	7.77	2.45
Contreras, Christian	L-L	6-3	195	11-17-98	0	0	6.35	12	0	0	0	17	12	14	12	0	28	18	.207	.167	.212	9.53	14.82
Cuevas, Felix	R-R	5-11	170	3-27-97	2	2	4.88	18	0	0	2	28	18	16	15	0	22	23	.188	.172	.194	7.48	7.16
Custodio, Raibel	R-R	6-3	185	9-8-99	4	3	2.11	14	9	0	0	55	49	20	13	0	19	37	.239	.317	.191	6.02	3.09
De Jesus, Henler	L-L	6-4	170	6-15-98	2	2	3.03	18	0	0	5	33	33	13	11	0	18	34	.268	.154	.282	9.37	4.96
De La Cruz, Daniel	R-R	6-2	185	4-29-98	2	7	5.26	14	9	0	1	51	53	43	30	3	21	37	.262	.227	.279	6.49	3.68
De La Cruz, Ezequiel	L-L	6-2	180	1-21-99	4	4	3.44	14	8	0	0	55	59	32	21	1	23	57	.271	.270	.271	9.33	3.76
De Leon, Yonal	R-R	6-2	186	8-6-97	1	2	4.50	15	0	0	1	26	25	16	13	1	14	17	.263	.359	.196	5.88	4.85
Done, Dawry	R-R	6-3	175	3-17-98	0	1	10.13	11	0	0	0	16	14	24	18	0	25	9	.259	.188	.290	5.06	14.06
Fuenmayor, Liu	L-L	5-11	170	2-2-99	5	2	2.52	15	1	0	2	39	24	15	11	3	29	37	.182	.192	.179	8.47	6.64
Gomez, Jose	R-R	6-3	175	9-23-96	2	7	3.93	14	14	0	0	69	77	40	30	3	29	49	.291	.276	.296	6.42	3.80
Herrera, Jhoendri	R-R	5-9	170	6-6-94	0	1	1.59	4	0	0	2	6	7	3	1	0	3	4	.292	.333	.267	6.35	4.76
Hilario, Ismael	R-R	6-4	175	9-21-98	0	0	—	2	0	0	0	0	1	8	8	0	7	0	1.000	—	1.000	—	—
Jaquez, Jhonatan	R-R	6-2	175	9-10-96	0	1	13.50	6	0	0	0	7	12	15	11	0	12	10	.343	.500	.238	12.27	14.73
Javier, Joshua	L-L	6-3	185	12-16-98	7	2	1.44	12	10	0	0	56	37	19	9	1	19	52	.188	.278	.207	8.31	3.04
Leal, Jhairon	L-L	6-2	175	8-21-98	2	2	3.14	15	0	0	3	29	27	17	10	0	18	23	.255	.136	.286	7.22	5.65
Luciano, Elvis	R-R	6-2	184	2-15-00	3	1	2.98	11	6	0	0	48	42	20	16	2	15	41	.236	.226	.240	7.63	2.79
Martinez, Jose	R-R	6-1	174	2-2-00	0	1	2.23	15	0	0	0	36	35	15	9	2	22	25	.256	.240	.264	6.19	5.45
Martinez, Victor	L-L	6-1	190	8-16-99	2	2	3.44	18	0	0	2	34	34	24	13	1	21	39	.252	.333	.246	10.32	5.56
Mieses, Junior	R-R	6-1	168	10-15-99	0	2	5.14	4	3	0	0	14	17	9	8	0	13	12	.327	.250	.316	7.71	8.36
Ogando, Gerald	R-R	6-2	180	7-28-00	0	3	7.16	6	0	0	0	16	18	15	13	1	7	15	.281	.440	.180	8.27	3.86
Olivero, Deyni	R-R	6-1	165	1-7-98	3	2	3.58	10	10	0	0	50	62	25	20	3	12	33	.313	.379	.280	5.90	2.15
Quezada, Edwin	R-R	6-5	205	11-22-96	1	4	1.74	15	3	0	0	41	30	14	8	1	17	46	.206	.233	.194	10.02	3.70
Ratia, Eduardo	L-L	6-2	185	5-6-00	1	2	7.24	10	6	0	0	27	24	26	22	0	25	21	.240	.214	.244	6.91	8.23
Rodriguez, Joseph	R-R	6-1	180	9-5-98	1	2	4.44	12	0	0	2	26	20	13	13	0	11	19	.206	.313	.154	6.49	3.76
Rosario, Oliver	L-L	6-0	140	6-15-99	1	1	3.04	14	7	0	0	47	22	22	16	0	40	53	.147	.208	.137	10.08	7.61
Sanchez, Geraldo	R-R	6-2	193	8-19-97	4	3	4.04	14	14	0	0	69	67	33	31	3	37	63	.257	.240	.267	8.22	4.83
Tineo, Marcos	R-R	6-0	165	3-14-97	3	2	3.92	13	13	0	0	60	59	33	26	2	19	61	.260	.274	.252	9.20	2.87
Valdez, Jhonny	R-R	6-3	187	8-10-98	2	2	2.22	17	0	0	4	28	32	14	7	1	8	19	.296	.225	.338	6.04	2.54
Zorrilla, Pedro	L-L	6-2	168	4-30-96	2	8	3.95	14	14	0	0	73	84	39	32	1	7	48	.295	.361	.285	5.92	0.86

Fielding

C: Andueza 25, Cordero 4, Herrera 14, Garcia 20, Lanza 31, Lopez 15, Martinez 37, Valbuena 20. **1B:** Andueza 14, Bueno 6, Cordero 37, Federico 24, Garcia 4, Gonzalez 1, Hernandez 1, Herrera 2, Jimenez 14,Lanza 7, Noriega 1, Yanqui 40. **2B:** Curpa 40, Gil 38, Hernandez 8, Hernandez 23, Leyton 6, Porteles 22, Reyes 10. **3B:** Bueno 1, Curpa 17, Federico 30, Gonzalez 32, Hernandez 16, Hernandez 12, Herrera 4, Porteles 34, Reyes 2, Curpa 4, Hernandez 25, Hernandez 8, Leyton 1, Perdomo 63, Porteles 1, Reyes 45, Acosta 26, Arocha 24, Bello 30, Caraballo 34, Collie 32, Cossio 21, Diaz 51, Jaime 55, Jimenez 30, Noriega 31, Sanchez 31, Santana 19, Santilien 26, Selmo 34, Yanqui 6.

Atlanta Braves

SEASON IN A SENTENCE: A new ballpark is nice and brings in fans, but it will be nicer and draw more fans once the Braves start winning again.

HIGH POINT: Atlanta christened its brand-new stadium with a four-game sweep of the Padres in front of large crowds and less traffic than expected. That sweep got the Braves to .500 at 6-6. That was the last day of the season when the Braves didn't have a losing record.

LOW POINT: Nothing on the field could compare to the turmoil of the beginning of the offseason when GM John Coppolella resigned amid an MLB investigation into potential rules violations. The investigation threw the organization into a chaotic limbo as it prepared for a very important offseason. The remaining front office tried to continue with business as usual, but it's hard to make significant decisions until a team knows who is going to be running it in the long-term.

NOTABLE ROOKIES: SS Dansby Swanson struggled for much of the first half of the season and eventually was demoted to Triple-A before reclaiming the shortstop job in August. 2B Ozzie Albies had no such adjustment issues, hitting .286/.354/.456 with six home runs and eight steals in 57 games. He showed speed, a little power and solid defense to step in and replace veteran Brandon Phillips. LHP Sean Newcomb showcased power stuff and control problems, but was as productive as any Braves' starting pitcher. INF Johan Camargo showed a solid bat (.299/.331/.452) while displaying the ability to handle second, third base and shortstop.

KEY TRANSACTIONS: The Braves brought in a number of veterans on short-term deals to serve as the bridges to the prospects. It didn't work out all that well as RHP Bartolo Colon (8.14 ERA) and RHP Jim Johnson (5.56 ERA, 9 blown saves) struggled. Veterans RHP Jaime Garcia and 2B Brandon Phillips brought back modest returns in midseason trades.

DOWN ON THE FARM: This is where hope resides for Braves fans. Even after graduating Swanson, Albies, Newcomb and Lucas Sims, the Braves have one of the best farm systems in baseball, led by Minor League Player of the Year Ronald Acuna. Acuna, 3B Austin Riley, RHP Mike Soroka, LHP Kolby Allard and LHP A.J. Minter could all figure into the Braves' big league plans in 2018.

OPENING DAY PAYROLL: $112,437,541 (19th)

PLAYERS OF THE YEAR

MAJOR LEAGUE

Freddie Freeman
1B

.307/.403/.586
28 HR, 71 RBI
.280 ISO, 84 R

MINOR LEAGUE

Ronald Acuna
OF

(High Class A/ Double-A/ Triple-A)
.325/.374/.522

ORGANIZATION LEADERS

BATTING			***Minimum 250 AB**
MAJORS			
*	AVG	Freddie Freeman	.307
*	OPS	Freddie Freeman	.989
	HR	Freddie Freeman	28
	RBI	Nick Markakis	76
MINORS			
*	AVG	Ronald Acuna, Florida, Mississippi, Gwinnett	.325
*	OBP	Brett Cumberland, Rome, Florida	.409
*	SLG	Ronald Acuna, Florida, Mississippi, Gwinnett	.522
*	OPS	Ronald Acuna, Florida, Mississippi, Gwinnett	.896
	R	Ronald Acuna, Florida, Mississippi, Gwinnett	88
	H	Ronald Acuna, Florida, Mississippi, Gwinnett	181
	TB	Ronald Acuna, Florida, Mississippi, Gwinnett	291
	2B	Ronald Acuna, Florida, Mississippi, Gwinnett	31
	3B	Cristian Pache, Rome	8
		Ozzie Albies, Gwinnett	8
	HR	Ronald Acuna, Florida, Mississippi, Gwinnett	21
		Carlos Franco, Mississippi, Gwinnett	21
	RBI	Ronald Acuna, Florida, Mississippi, Gwinnett	82
	BB	Braxton Davidson, Florida	66
	SO	Connor Lien, Mississippi	160
	SB	Ronald Acuna, Florida, Mississippi, Gwinnett	44

PITCHING			**#Minimum 75 IP**
MAJORS			
	W	Julio Teheran	11
#	ERA	R.A. Dickey	4.26
	SO	Julio Teheran	151
	SV	Jim Johnson	22
MINORS			
	W	Andrew Albers, Gwinnett	12
	L	Touki Toussaint, Florida, Mississippi	13
#	ERA	Bryse Wilson, Rome	2.50
	G	David Peterson, Gwinnett	50
	GS	Kolby Allard, Mississippi	27
		Jeremy Walker, Rome	27
		Tyler Pike, Florida, Mississippi	27
	SV	Brandon White, Rome, Florida	10
	IP	Mike Soroka, Mississippi	154
	BB	Tyler Pike, Florida, Mississippi	90
	SO	Touki Toussaint, Florida, Mississippi	167
#	AVG	Joey Wentz, Rome	.209

2017 PERFORMANCE

General Manager: John Coppolella. **Farm Director:** Dave Trembley. **Scouting Director:** Brian Bridges.

Class	Team	League	W	L	PCT	Finish	Manager
Majors	Atlanta Braves	National	72	90	.444	10th (15)	Brian Snitker
Triple-A	Gwinnett Braves	International	71	71	.5	t-6th (14)	Damon Berryhill
Double-A	Mississippi Braves	Southern	58	80	.42	9th (10)	Luis Salazar
High-A	Florida Fire Frogs	Florida State	48	81	.372	12th (12)	Paul Runge / Rocket Wheeler
Low-A	Rome Braves	South Atlantic	74	65	.532	5th (14)	Randy Ingle
Rookie	Danville Braves	Appalachian	36	32	.529	4th (10)	Nestor Perez
Rookie	GCL Braves	Gulf Coast	31	28	.525	8th (17)	Barrett Kleinknecht
Overall 2017 Minor League Record			318	357	.471	23rd (30)	

ORGANIZATION STATISTICS

ATLANTA BRAVES

NATIONAL LEAGUE

Batting	B-T	HT	WT	DOB	AVG	vLH	vRH	G	AB	R	H	2B	3B	HR	RBI	BB	HBP	SH	SF	SO	SB	CS	SLG	OBP
Adams, Lane	R-R	6-3	220	11-13-89	.275	.143	.321	85	109	19	30	4	1	5	20	10	1	1	1	37	10	0	.468	.339
Adams, Matt	L-R	6-3	260	8-31-88	.272	.190	.292	100	291	42	79	20	1	19	58	19	1	0	3	71	0	0	.543	.315
2-team total (31 St. Louis)					.274	.000	.311	131	339	46	93	22	1	20	65	23	1	0	4	88	0	0	.522	.319
Albies, Ozzie	B-R	5-9	160	1-7-97	.286	.327	.273	57	217	34	62	9	5	6	28	21	3	1	2	36	8	1	.456	.354
Bonifacio, Emilio	B-R	5-10	210	4-23-85	.132	.000	.167	38	38	2	5	1	1	0	3	1	0	4	1	9	0	0	.211	.150
Camargo, Johan	B-R	6-0	160	12-13-93	.299	.403	.254	82	241	30	72	21	2	4	27	12	0	2	1	51	0	0	.452	.331
d'Arnaud, Chase	R-R	6-2	205	1-21-87	.375	.500	.000	11	8	5	3	0	0	0	0	2	0	0	0	3	0	0	.375	.500
2-team total (22 San Diego)					.175	.000	.233	33	57	10	10	2	0	1	3	4	0	0	0	20	5	1	.263	.230
Flowers, Tyler	R-R	6-4	260	1-24-86	.281	.283	.280	99	317	41	89	16	0	12	49	31	20	0	2	82	0	1	.445	.378
Freeman, Freddie	L-R	6-5	220	9-12-89	.307	.278	.319	117	440	84	135	35	2	28	71	65	7	0	2	95	8	5	.586	.403
Freitas, David	R-R	6-3	225	3-18-89	.235	.000	.286	6	17	2	4	2	0	0	2	0	0	0	0	4	0	0	.353	.235
Garcia, Adonis	R-R	5-9	205	4-12-85	.237	.231	.238	52	173	19	41	4	0	5	19	7	2	0	1	23	4	0	.347	.273
Inciarte, Ender	L-L	5-11	190	10-29-90	.304	.291	.307	157	662	93	201	27	5	11	57	49	0	3	4	94	22	9	.409	.350
Johnson, Micah	L-R	6-0	210	12-18-90	.200	—	.200	18	10	2	2	0	0	0	0	0	0	1	0	4	1	0	.200	.200
Kemp, Matt	R-R	6-4	210	9-23-84	.276	.250	.284	115	438	47	121	23	1	19	64	27	0	0	1	99	0	2	.464	.318
Markakis, Nick	L-L	6-1	215	11-17-83	.275	.265	.278	160	593	76	163	39	1	8	76	68	6	0	3	110	0	2	.385	.354
Peterson, Jace	L-R	6-0	215	5-9-90	.215	.177	.219	89	186	15	40	9	2	2	17	27	1	1	0	48	3	0	.317	.318
Phillips, Brandon	R-R	6-0	211	6-28-81	.292	.303	.288	120	470	68	137	27	1	11	52	19	8	1	1	57	10	8	.423	.329
Recker, Anthony	R-R	6-2	240	8-29-83	.143	.000	.167	6	7	1	1	0	0	0	0	0	0	0	0	1	0	0	.143	.143
Rodriguez, Sean	R-R	6-0	200	4-26-85	.162	.294	.050	15	37	6	6	1	0	2	3	8	1	1	0	19	1	0	.351	.326
2-team total (39 Pittsburgh)					.167	.194	.153	54	132	18	22	2	0	5	8	16	4	1	0	57	1	0	.296	.276
Ruiz, Rio	L-R	6-1	230	5-22-94	.193	.417	.174	53	150	22	29	5	0	4	19	19	1	0	3	41	1	0	.307	.283
Sanchez, Tony	R-R	5-11	220	5-20-88	.000	—	.000	1	1	0	0	0	0	0	0	0	0	0	0	1	0	0	.000	.000
Santana, Danny	B-R	5-11	185	11-7-90	.203	.133	.221	69	143	16	29	9	2	3	22	7	1	1	0	33	6	0	.357	.245
Suzuki, Kurt	R-R	5-11	205	10-4-83	.283	.345	.266	81	276	38	78	13	0	19	50	17	13	1	2	39	0	0	.536	.351
Swanson, Dansby	R-R	6-1	190	2-11-94	.232	.263	.224	144	488	59	113	23	2	6	51	59	0	0	4	120	3	3	.324	.312

Pitching	B-T	HT	WT	DOB	W	L	ERA	G	GS	CG	SV	IP	H	R	ER	HR	BB	SO	AVG	vLH	vRH	K/9	BB/9
Blair, Aaron	R-R	6-4	250	5-26-92	0	1	15.00	1	1	0	0	3	5	5	5	1	5	3	.417	.571	.200	9.00	15.00
Brothers, Rex	L-L	6-0	210	12-18-87	4	3	7.23	27	0	0	0	24	23	19	19	3	12	33	.250	.216	.273	12.55	4.56
Collmenter, Josh	R-R	6-3	240	2-7-86	0	2	9.00	11	0	0	0	17	29	19	17	7	6	18	.372	.250	.440	9.53	3.18
Colon, Bartolo	R-R	5-11	285	5-24-73	2	8	8.14	13	13	0	0	63	92	66	57	11	20	42	.338	.311	.365	6.00	2.86
Dickey, R.A.	R-R	6-3	215	10-29-74	10	10	4.26	31	31	0	0	190	193	99	90	26	67	136	.266	.243	.285	6.44	3.17
Foltynewicz, Mike	R-R	6-4	220	10-7-91	10	13	4.79	29	28	0	0	154	169	86	82	20	59	143	.277	.309	.248	8.36	3.45
Freeman, Sam	R-L	5-11	180	6-24-87	2	0	2.55	58	0	0	0	60	48	19	17	3	27	59	.216	.190	.236	8.85	4.05
Fried, Max	L-L	6-4	200	1-18-94	1	1	3.81	9	4	0	0	26	30	15	11	3	12	22	.286	.258	.297	7.62	4.15
Garcia, Jaime	L-L	6-2	215	7-8-86	4	7	4.30	18	18	0	0	113	108	58	54	12	41	85	.252	.242	.255	6.77	3.27
Gohara, Luiz	L-L	6-3	210	7-31-96	1	3	4.91	5	5	0	0	29	32	17	16	2	8	31	.283	.105	.319	9.51	2.45
Hursh, Jason	R-R	6-3	200	10-2-91	1	0	5.06	9	0	0	0	11	13	6	6	1	4	7	.317	.222	.391	5.91	3.38
Jackson, Luke	R-R	6-2	210	8-24-91	2	0	4.62	43	0	0	0	51	55	26	26	4	19	33	.278	.217	.322	5.86	3.38
Johnson, Jim	R-R	6-6	250	6-27-83	6	3	5.56	61	0	0	22	57	59	39	35	8	25	61	.260	.278	.244	9.69	3.97
Krol, Ian	L-L	6-1	210	5-9-91	2	2	5.33	51	0	0	0	49	50	34	29	8	21	44	.266	.291	.248	8.08	3.86
Minter, A.J.	L-L	6-0	205	9-2-93	0	1	3.00	16	0	0	0	15	13	5	5	1	2	26	.224	.191	.243	15.60	1.20
Morris, Akeel	R-R	6-1	195	11-14-92	0	0	1.23	8	0	0	0	7	6	1	1	0	4	9	.214	.200	.231	11.05	4.91
Motte, Jason	R-R	6-0	205	6-22-82	1	0	3.54	46	0	0	0	41	28	16	16	6	20	27	.199	.188	.204	5.98	4.43
Newcomb, Sean	L-L	6-5	255	6-12-93	4	9	4.32	19	19	0	0	100	100	51	48	10	57	108	.260	.261	.259	9.72	5.13
O'Flaherty, Eric	L-L	6-2	210	2-5-85	0	0	7.85	22	0	0	0	18	20	16	16	4	9	15	.278	.189	.371	7.36	4.42
Ramirez, Jose	R-R	6-1	215	1-21-90	2	3	3.19	68	0	0	0	62	45	26	22	9	29	56	.204	.180	.220	8.13	4.21
Roe, Chaz	R-R	6-5	190	10-9-86	0	0	9.00	3	0	0	0	2	3	4	2	0	2	1	.300	.500	.167	4.50	9.00
Sims, Lucas	R-R	6-2	220	5-10-94	3	6	5.62	14	10	0	0	58	64	37	36	9	23	44	.288	.305	.276	6.87	3.59
Teheran, Julio	R-R	6-2	205	1-27-91	11	13	4.49	32	32	0	0	188	186	103	94	31	72	151	.257	.241	.276	7.22	3.44
Vizcaino, Arodys	R-R	6-0	230	11-13-90	5	3	2.83	62	0	0	14	57	42	19	18	7	21	64	.199	.217	.185	10.05	3.30
Winkler, Dan	R-R	6-3	205	2-2-90	1	1	2.51	16	0	0	0	14	7	4	4	1	6	18	.152	.053	.222	11.30	3.77
Wisler, Matt	R-R	6-3	205	9-12-92	0	1	8.35	20	1	0	0	32	43	31	30	5	13	22	.323	.355	.296	6.12	3.62

Fielding

Catcher	PCT	G	PO	A	E	DP	PB
Flowers	.993	85	643	46	5	4	9
Freitas	1.000	6	48	3	0	0	0
Recker	.923	4	12	0	1	0	1
Suzuki	.995	77	553	42	3	2	10

First Base	PCT	G	PO	A	E	DP
Adams	.990	59	488	29	5	42
Freeman	.996	105	829	56	4	72
Peterson	1.000	7	56	3	0	6
Ruiz	.917	2	11	0	1	4

Second Base	PCT	G	PO	A	E	DP
Albies	.987	57	92	140	3	34
Camargo	1.000	9	9	14	0	5
Peterson	.967	15	23	35	2	7
Phillips	.984	88	135	223	6	55
Rodriguez	1.000	4	2	4	0	1
Santana	1.000	7	5	5	0	2

Third Base	PCT	G	PO	A	E	DP
Camargo	.968	43	30	61	3	7
d'Arnaud	.000	1	0	0	0	0
Freeman	.971	16	13	21	1	1
Garcia	.946	39	21	66	5	6
Peterson	.941	15	5	11	1	0
Phillips	1.000	25	5	40	0	3
Rodriguez	.833	5	0	10	2	1
Ruiz	.972	41	28	77	3	8
Santana	1.000	4	1	2	0	0

Shortstop	PCT	G	PO	A	E	DP
Camargo	.988	26	16	64	1	10
Peterson	.929	4	4	9	1	0
Swanson	.965	142	195	357	20	83

Outfield	PCT	G	PO	A	E	DP
Adams	.961	41	48	1	2	0
Adams	.900	13	18	0	2	0
Bonifacio	1.000	10	11	0	0	0
Camargo	.000	1	0	0	0	0
d'Arnaud	1.000	4	3	0	0	0
Garcia	.000	1	0	0	0	0
Inciarte	.993	156	410	7	3	0
Johnson	1.000	3	2	0	0	0
Kemp	.993	103	148	3	1	2
Markakis	.997	156	286	6	1	1
Peterson	.977	27	43	0	1	0
Rodriguez	1.000	5	8	0	0	0
Santana	.983	38	57	2	1	0

GWINNETT BRAVES — *TRIPLE-A*

INTERNATIONAL LEAGUE

Batting	B-T	HT	WT	DOB	AVG	vLH	vRH	G	AB	R	H	2B	3B	HR	RBI	BB	HBP	SH	SF	SO	SB	CS	SLG	OBP
Acuna, Ronald	R-R	6-0	180	12-18-97	.344	.378	.335	54	221	38	76	14	2	9	33	17	2	1	2	48	11	6	.548	.393
Adams, Lane	R-R	6-3	220	11-13-89	.264	.265	.264	48	178	21	47	10	2	7	30	15	0	0	1	60	15	3	.461	.320
Albies, Ozzie	B-R	5-9	160	1-7-97	.285	.370	.257	97	411	67	117	21	8	9	41	28	2	3	4	90	21	2	.440	.330
Avery, Xavier	L-L	6-0	190	1-1-90	.259	.239	.265	121	371	65	96	21	5	14	52	59	2	1	3	159	21	7	.456	.361
Camargo, Johan	B-R	6-0	160	12-13-93	.295	.345	.280	33	129	17	38	9	1	4	20	8	2	1	2	22	1	0	.473	.340
Franco, Carlos	L-R	6-3	220	12-20-91	.232	.231	.232	93	311	33	72	11	0	10	39	34	2	0	0	97	1	0	.363	.311
Freeman, Freddie	L-R	6-5	220	9-12-89	.667	—	.667	2	3	1	2	0	0	0	0	2	0	0	0	1	0	0	.667	.800
Freitas, David	R-R	6-3	225	3-18-89	.263	.355	.230	72	236	28	62	13	0	3	21	25	4	0	4	35	0	0	.356	.338
Garcia, Adonis	R-R	5-9	205	4-12-85	.316	1.000	.278	6	19	1	6	3	0	0	4	0	1	0	1	2	1	0	.474	.333
Gaylor, Stephen	L-R	6-1	195	10-4-91	.250	.278	.227	14	40	5	10	2	0	0	1	4	0	0	0	7	2	0	.300	.318
Giardina, Sal	B-R	6-4	215	4-30-92	.455	—	.455	6	11	3	5	0	0	0	2	3	2	0	0	2	0	0	.455	.625
Howard, Ryan	L-L	6-4	250	11-19-79	.184	.000	.241	11	38	1	7	0	0	1	5	2	1	0	1	11	0	0	.263	.238
Johnson, Micah	L-R	6-0	210	12-18-90	.289	.324	.277	40	135	19	39	6	3	1	15	18	1	1	0	38	6	4	.400	.377
Kazmar, Sean	R-R	5-9	180	8-5-84	.284	.299	.278	99	363	41	103	15	0	11	45	12	3	1	3	40	5	1	.416	.310
Kemp, Matt	R-R	6-4	210	9-23-84	.333	—	.333	1	3	0	1	0	0	0	1	0	0	0	1	1	0	0	.333	.250
Kubitza, Kyle	L-R	6-3	210	7-15-90	.241	.226	.248	91	286	46	69	5	5	5	25	39	2	1	3	89	5	5	.346	.333
Lalli, Blake	L-R	6-1	210	5-12-83	.167	.333	.143	16	48	5	8	2	0	1	6	4	0	0	1	9	0	0	.271	.226
Landoni, Emerson	R-R	5-11	189	2-19-89	.189	.263	.147	15	53	5	10	0	0	0	6	4	0	0	1	9	0	0	.189	.241
Loney, James	L-L	6-3	235	5-7-84	.143	.333	.000	2	7	0	1	0	0	0	0	1	0	0	0	1	0	0	.143	.250
2-team total (16 Toledo)					.218	.000	.256	18	55	6	12	1	0	0	2	14	0	0	1	8	0	0	.236	.371
Odom, Joe	R-R	6-2	225	1-9-92	.000	.000	.000	3	7	0	0	0	0	0	0	3	0	0	0	1	0	0	.000	.300
Peterson, Dustin	R-R	6-2	210	9-10-94	.248	.301	.232	87	314	35	78	17	1	1	30	27	5	0	0	78	1	2	.319	.318
Peterson, Jace	L-R	6-0	215	5-9-90	.258	.250	.260	34	128	20	33	5	1	2	26	25	0	0	2	26	6	1	.359	.374
Recker, Anthony	R-R	6-2	240	8-29-83	.223	.136	.263	41	139	20	31	8	1	4	10	11	5	0	1	48	1	0	.381	.301
2-team total (19 Rochester)					.244	.188	.315	60	209	29	51	17	1	4	18	15	7	0	3	63	1	0	.392	.312
Rodriguez, Sean	R-R	6-0	200	4-26-85	.056	.000	.077	5	18	1	1	0	0	0	2	4	1	0	2	5	0	0	.056	.240
Rojas Jr., Mel	R-B	6-2	225	5-24-90	.259	.292	.250	54	212	27	55	13	0	6	31	18	2	0	4	50	2	2	.406	.318
Ruiz, Rio	L-R	6-1	230	5-22-94	.247	.202	.264	103	388	48	96	25	2	16	56	42	1	0	1	110	1	2	.446	.322
Santana, Danny	B-R	5-11	185	11-7-90	.500	.500	.500	5	18	4	9	1	0	0	4	1	0	0	0	3	2	0	.556	.526
Schlehuber, Braeden	R-R	6-2	210	1-7-88	.267	.600	.100	6	15	3	4	0	0	1	3	0	0	0	0	7	0	0	.467	.267
Scivicque, Kade	R-R	6-0	225	3-22-93	.272	.333	.246	24	81	12	22	2	0	2	11	8	1	0	0	18	0	0	.370	.344
Swanson, Dansby	R-R	6-1	190	2-11-94	.237	.200	.242	11	38	5	9	1	0	1	5	6	1	0	0	9	1	0	.342	.356
Tuiasosopo, Matt	R-R	6-2	235	5-10-86	.207	.274	.183	114	363	51	75	10	1	8	45	55	5	1	3	139	1	0	.306	.317
Valenzuela, Luis	L-R	5-10	179	8-25-93	.382	.250	.423	13	34	8	13	2	1	0	7	3	0	0	0	7	0	0	.500	.432
Walker, Adam Brett	R-R	6-5	225	10-18-91	.128	.333	.037	10	39	3	5	3	0	1	4	4	0	0	1	16	2	0	.282	.205
3-team total (25 Louisville, 18 Norfolk)					.152	.148	.050	53	198	17	30	9	1	5	22	11	2	0	2	76	3	0	.283	.202

Pitching	B-T	HT	WT	DOB	W	L	ERA	G	GS	CG	SV	IP	H	R	ER	HR	BB	SO	AVG	vLH	vRH	K/9	BB/9
Albers, Andrew	R-L	6-1	200	10-6-85	12	3	2.61	26	17	0	0	121	120	38	35	6	19	115	.261	.246	.268	8.58	1.42
Barreda, Manny	R-R	5-11	195	10-8-88	3	1	1.83	7	7	1	0	39	27	12	8	2	19	33	.185	.207	.148	7.55	4.35
Blair, Aaron	R-R	6-4	250	5-26-92	7	9	5.02	25	25	2	0	127	135	72	71	10	56	104	.270	.281	.256	7.35	3.96
Brothers, Rex	L-L	6-0	210	12-18-87	0	0	2.57	7	0	0	1	7	4	2	2	0	1	8	.167	.143	.200	10.29	1.29
Burgos, Enrique	R-R	6-4	250	11-23-90	0	1	5.24	24	0	0	2	22	13	13	13	1	15	26	.167	.143	.194	10.48	6.04
Cabrera, Mauricio	R-R	6-3	245	9-22-93	2	2	7.86	24	0	0	3	26	26	23	23	1	25	20	.260	.213	.302	6.84	8.54
Chapman, Kevin	L-L	6-3	230	2-19-88	0	0	7.71	9	0	0	0	12	14	10	10	1	3	10	.311	.286	.323	7.71	2.31
2-team total (9 Rochester)					0	1	6.65	18	0	0	0	23	27	19	17	1	8	24	.297	.320	.238	9.39	3.13
Collmenter, Josh	R-R	6-3	240	2-7-86	1	1	3.60	5	4	0	0	20	20	8	8	3	5	21	.256	.205	.308	9.45	2.25
Cruz, Rhiner	R-R	6-2	210	11-1-86	1	5	2.84	40	0	0	5	51	43	17	16	3	24	63	.224	.235	.215	11.19	4.26
De La Cruz, Joel	R-B	6-1	240	6-9-89	0	0	7.27	6	0	0	0	9	12	9	7	1	5	3	.308	.313	.304	3.12	5.19
Dirks, Caleb	R-R	6-3	220	6-9-93	2	2	4.02	27	0	0	2	40	35	22	18	6	13	45	.235	.241	.231	10.04	2.90
Franco, Enderson	R-R	6-2	180	12-29-92	0	0	1.00	2	2	0	0	9	6	1	1	0	3	11	.188	.000	.200	11.00	3.00

Freeman, Sam	R-L	5-11	180	6-24-87	3	1	0.87	9	0	0	1	10	5	2	1	1	6	8	.147	.071	.200	6.97	5.23
Fried, Max	L-L	6-4	200	1-18-94	0	0	0.00	2	2	0	0	6	1	0	0	0	2	6	.056	.000	.077	9.00	3.00
Gohara, Luiz	L-L	6-3	210	7-31-96	2	2	3.31	7	7	0	0	35	31	16	13	4	16	48	.230	.318	.187	12.23	4.08
Hernandez, David	R-R	6-3	245	5-13-85	1	0	1.13	7	0	0	4	8	4	2	1	0	2	9	.148	.100	.177	10.13	2.25
Hursh, Jason	R-R	6-3	200	10-2-91	3	4	5.50	28	0	0	0	38	53	26	23	3	12	41	.323	.369	.293	9.80	2.87
Jackson, Luke	R-R	6-2	210	8-24-91	0	3	6.29	9	4	0	1	24	26	17	17	2	16	23	.271	.191	.333	8.51	5.92
Krol, Ian	L-L	6-1	210	5-9-91	1	0	0.00	1	0	0	0	1	0	0	0	0	2	0	.000	—	.000	0.00	18.00
Matthews, Kevin	R-L	5-11	180	11-29-92	0	1	2.25	1	1	0	0	4	2	1	1	0	4	3	.167	.000	.500	6.75	9.00
Medlen, Kris	B-R	5-10	190	10-7-85	3	7	5.42	16	16	1	0	95	105	61	57	15	23	84	.279	.259	.304	7.99	2.19
Minter, A.J.	L-L	6-0	205	9-2-93	1	2	4.70	17	0	0	0	15	15	11	8	1	10	17	.259	.182	.306	9.98	5.87
Morris, Akeel	R-R	6-1	195	11-14-92	1	3	3.09	30	0	0	1	47	38	18	16	3	23	53	.212	.239	.187	10.22	4.44
Motte, Jason	R-R	6-0	205	6-22-82	1	0	1.23	7	0	0	2	7	5	1	1	0	1	7	.192	.273	.133	8.59	1.23
Newcomb, Sean	L-L	6-5	255	6-12-93	3	3	2.97	11	11	0	0	58	45	23	19	3	33	74	.212	.262	.191	11.55	5.15
O'Flaherty, Eric	L-L	6-2	210	2-5-85	0	0	13.50	2	0	0	0	1	4	2	2	0	1	0	.500	.500	.500	0.00	6.75
Parsons, Wes	R-R	6-5	204	9-6-92	0	0	8.64	4	1	0	0	8	18	9	8	0	6	10	.429	.571	.286	10.80	6.48
Peterson, David	R-R	6-5	205	1-4-90	2	4	4.12	50	1	0	7	68	75	39	31	4	15	53	.279	.277	.280	7.05	2.00
Pfeifer, Philip	L-L	6-0	200	7-15-92	0	2	3.60	11	1	0	1	15	10	6	6	0	9	9	.192	.217	.172	5.40	5.40
Phillips, Evan	R-R	6-2	215	9-11-94	2	3	4.75	25	1	0	2	30	30	17	16	1	23	29	.268	.220	.307	8.60	6.82
Reynolds, Danny	R-R	6-0	190	5-2-91	0	0	0.00	2	0	0	0	3	2	0	0	0	1	2	.182	.500	.111	6.00	3.00
Roe, Chaz	R-R	6-5	190	10-9-86	0	1	27.00	1	0	0	0	1	3	3	3	0	1	1	.600	1.000	.000	9.00	9.00
2-team total (17 Durham)					0	4	4.09	18	0	0	4	22	21	11	10	1	6	36	.241	.256	.179	14.73	2.45
Santiago, Andres	R-R	6-1	220	10-26-89	2	0	0.00	4	0	0	0	10	7	0	0	0	1	7	.194	.333	.125	6.30	0.90
Sims, Lucas	R-R	6-2	220	5-10-94	7	4	3.75	20	19	0	0	115	95	49	48	19	36	132	.224	.273	.176	10.30	2.81
Vizcaino, Arodys	R-R	6-0	230	11-13-90	0	0	0.00	1	1	0	0	1	0	0	0	0	0	1	.000	.000	.000	9.00	0.00
Weigel, Patrick	R-R	6-6	240	7-8-94	3	2	5.27	8	8	0	0	41	42	24	24	5	17	30	.269	.250	.280	6.59	3.73
Winkler, Dan	R-R	6-3	205	2-2-90	1	0	6.30	10	0	0	0	10	14	7	7	2	1	12	.333	.381	.286	10.80	0.90
Wisler, Matt	R-R	6-3	205	9-12-92	7	5	3.56	18	14	1	0	94	101	44	37	7	20	64	.275	.250	.301	6.15	1.92

Fielding

Catcher	PCT	G	PO	A	E	DP	PB
Freitas	.998	62	510	35	1	3	1
Giardina	1.000	5	39	3	0	0	0
Lalli	1.000	11	70	9	0	0	0
Odom	1.000	3	26	1	0	1	0
Recker	.994	37	290	24	2	1	3
Schlehuber	1.000	3	31	3	0	0	0
Scivicque	.982	24	205	10	4	1	3

First Base	PCT	G	PO	A	E	DP
Franco	.990	51	359	25	4	44
Freitas	1.000	2	2	0	0	0
Howard	1.000	1	7	0	0	0
Kazmar	1.000	5	34	4	0	3
Kubitza	.975	4	38	1	1	5
Lalli	1.000	6	27	3	0	1
Loney	1.000	1	10	0	0	1
Ruiz	1.000	5	27	3	0	1
Tuiasosopo	.988	77	516	45	7	42

Second Base	PCT	G	PO	A	E	DP
Albies	.972	82	131	216	10	42
Kazmar	1.000	9	9	24	0	3
Kubitza	.966	23	36	48	3	13
Landoni	.980	12	16	32	1	3
Peterson	.955	7	16	26	2	8
Rodriguez	1.000	3	4	8	0	1
Santana	1.000	2	1	8	0	1
Swanson	1.000	2	7	2	0	1
Valenzuela	.929	5	4	9	1	2

Third Base	PCT	G	PO	A	E	DP
Camargo	1.000	2	1	3	0	1
Franco	.905	25	3	35	4	4
Freeman	1.000	2	0	1	0	0
Garcia	.750	5	3	3	2	0
Kazmar	.950	10	3	16	1	2
Kubitza	.900	10	3	15	2	3
Peterson	.900	4	3	6	1	0
Rodriguez	1.000	1	0	2	0	0
Ruiz	.971	91	56	146	6	19

Shortstop	PCT	G	PO	A	E	DP
Albies	.983	14	26	31	1	6
Camargo	.964	31	47	61	4	12
Kazmar	.966	69	99	154	9	33
Landoni	1.000	1	0	3	0	0
Peterson	.933	14	18	24	3	4
Rodriguez	1.000	1	0	2	0	0
Swanson	1.000	9	20	23	0	11
Valenzuela	1.000	7	6	11	0	3

Outfield	PCT	G	PO	A	E	DP
Acuna	.990	53	92	5	1	1
Adams	.992	44	114	3	1	2
Avery	.970	101	227	1	7	0
Garcia	1.000	1	1	0	0	0
Gaylor	1.000	12	38	0	0	0
Johnson	.986	31	69	1	1	0
Kazmar	1.000	1	1	0	0	0
Kemp	1.000	1	1	0	0	0
Kubitza	.975	44	76	3	2	0
Peterson	.988	77	163	1	2	0
Peterson	1.000	8	22	1	0	0
Rojas Jr.	.959	49	91	3	4	1
Santana	1.000	3	6	0	0	0
Tuiasosopo	1.000	4	8	0	0	0
Walker	.917	7	11	0	1	0

MISSISSIPPI BRAVES — *DOUBLE-A*

SOUTHERN LEAGUE

Batting	B-T	HT	WT	DOB	AVG	vLH	vRH	G	AB	R	H	2B	3B	HR	RBI	BB	HBP	SH	SF	SO	SB	CS	SLG	OBP
Acuna, Ronald	R-R	6-0	180	12-18-97	.326	.275	.337	57	221	29	72	14	1	9	30	18	1	0	3	56	19	11	.520	.375
Araiza, Armando	R-R	5-11	205	6-19-93	.143	.000	.152	11	35	5	5	2	0	1	2	1	0	1	0	11	0	0	.286	.167
Curcio, Keith	L-R	5-10	185	12-28-92	.220	.288	.203	120	401	44	88	14	6	4	21	43	1	3	4	67	10	5	.314	.294
Daniel, Andrew	R-R	6-1	195	1-27-93	.095	.000	.125	10	21	1	2	0	0	0	0	2	0	0	0	8	0	0	.095	.174
2-team total (49 Mobile)					.211	.159	.248	59	190	17	40	10	2	2	16	23	2	1	1	50	8	5	.316	.301
Demeritte, Travis	R-R	6-0	180	9-30-94	.231	.247	.228	124	458	62	106	21	6	15	45	49	1	1	2	134	5	7	.402	.306
Franco, Carlos	L-R	6-3	220	12-20-91	.293	.154	.307	41	150	20	44	7	0	11	38	14	1	0	0	45	0	0	.560	.358
Gaylor, Stephen	L-R	6-1	195	10-4-91	.180	.125	.191	21	50	8	9	1	0	0	2	4	0	2	0	9	1	1	.200	.241
Giardina, Sal	B-R	6-4	215	4-30-92	.248	.333	.226	38	105	13	26	5	0	1	11	9	3	0	2	29	1	0	.324	.319
Harper, Reed	R-R	6-2	200	12-21-90	.121	.100	.125	24	58	2	7	1	0	0	2	6	1	2	2	21	0	1	.138	.209
Hyams, Levi	R-L	6-2	210	10-6-89	.189	.000	.205	32	90	4	17	1	0	0	6	4	2	0	1	22	0	0	.200	.237
Jackson, Alex	R-R	6-2	215	12-25-95	.255	.438	.223	30	110	12	28	4	0	5	20	10	0	0	0	32	0	0	.427	.317
James, Jared	L-R	6-1	185	2-22-94	.279	.250	.285	113	340	39	95	19	6	5	34	33	7	0	3	61	1	2	.415	.353
Joe, Connor	R-R	6-0	205	8-16-92	.135	.077	.154	20	52	2	7	1	0	0	4	6	1	1	1	18	0	1	.154	.233
Landoni, Emerson	R-R	5-11	189	2-19-89	.173	.091	.195	18	52	6	9	0	0	0	2	4	1	0	0	13	0	0	.173	.246
Lien, Connor	R-R	6-3	225	3-15-94	.187	.205	.182	119	374	41	70	19	2	10	34	24	9	3	1	160	17	4	.329	.253
Meneses, Joey	R-R	6-3	220	5-6-92	.292	.270	.297	108	360	44	105	13	0	9	45	38	1	1	1	81	0	0	.403	.360
Moore, Dylan	R-R	6-0	200	8-2-92	.207	.207	.207	122	421	49	87	15	0	7	42	45	7	5	4	96	10	8	.292	.291

ATLANTA BRAVES

Batting	B-T	HT	WT	DOB	AVG	vLH	vRH	G	AB	R	H	2B	3B	HR	RBI	BB	HBP	SH	SF	SO	SB	CS	SLG	OBP
Morales, Jonathan	R-R	5-11	180	1-29-95	.169	.077	.192	39	130	8	22	4	0	1	12	7	2	3	1	20	0	0	.223	.221
Neslony, Tyler	L-R	6-1	190	2-13-94	.194	.200	.193	43	144	12	28	4	0	1	14	18	2	1	2	27	0	1	.243	.289
Obregon, Omar	B-R	5-10	150	4-18-94	.320	.500	.286	8	25	3	8	2	0	0	0	3	0	0	0	8	0	0	.400	.393
Odom, Joe	R-R	6-2	225	1-9-92	.298	.353	.275	25	57	5	17	3	0	1	8	3	0	2	0	16	0	0	.404	.333
Riley, Austin	R-R	6-3	220	4-2-97	.315	.310	.315	48	178	28	56	9	1	8	27	20	3	0	2	50	2	0	.511	.389
Rodriguez, Sean	R-R	6-0	200	4-26-85	.083	.000	.125	3	12	1	1	1	0	0	0	1	0	0	0	6	0	0	.167	.154
Scivicque, Kade	R-R	6-0	225	3-22-93	.269	.289	.264	68	234	19	63	11	1	3	25	16	2	1	2	46	0	1	.363	.319
Valenzuela, Luis	L-R	5-10	179	8-25-93	.259	.333	.241	62	232	26	60	15	4	2	20	12	4	1	2	40	4	5	.384	.304
Walker, Adam Brett	R-R	6-5	225	10-18-91	.122	.167	.116	14	49	5	6	1	0	4	12	4	0	0	2	23	0	0	.388	.182

Pitching	B-T	HT	WT	DOB	W	L	ERA	G	GS	CG	SV	IP	H	R	ER	HR	BB	SO	AVG	vLH	vRH	K/9	BB/9
Allard, Kolby	L-L	6-1	190	8-13-97	8	11	3.18	27	27	2	0	150	146	62	53	11	45	129	.258	.292	.246	7.74	2.70
Biddle, Jesse	L-L	6-5	230	10-22-91	2	4	2.90	27	0	0	2	50	48	22	16	3	16	53	.254	.400	.194	9.60	2.90
Brothers, Rex	L-L	6-0	210	12-18-87	0	0	2.79	10	0	0	1	10	7	4	3	0	5	18	.194	.200	.192	16.76	4.66
Cabrera, Mauricio	R-R	6-3	245	9-22-93	1	0	5.27	14	0	0	0	14	8	11	8	0	18	15	.163	.211	.133	9.88	11.85
Clouse, Corbin	B-L	6-0	230	6-26-95	3	4	2.86	16	0	0	1	22	21	8	7	2	13	26	.256	.250	.258	10.64	5.32
Fried, Max	L-L	6-4	200	1-18-94	2	11	5.92	19	19	0	0	87	88	61	57	8	43	85	.268	.208	.285	8.83	4.47
Gohara, Luiz	L-L	6-3	210	7-31-96	2	1	2.60	12	11	0	0	52	42	17	15	2	18	60	.218	.277	.199	10.38	3.12
Graham, Josh	R-R	6-1	215	10-14-93	0	1	1.38	10	0	0	2	13	10	2	2	0	9	10	.213	.105	.286	6.92	6.23
Hursh, Jason	R-R	6-3	200	10-2-91	0	0	1.23	10	0	0	5	15	10	2	2	0	5	10	.208	.238	.185	6.14	3.07
Mader, Michael	L-L	6-2	205	2-18-94	5	5	4.18	35	1	0	4	65	57	34	30	5	41	57	.235	.206	.246	7.93	5.71
Medlen, Kris	B-R	5-10	190	10-7-85	1	0	1.74	2	2	1	0	10	10	4	2	0	3	8	.238	.250	.227	6.97	2.61
Minter, A.J.	L-L	6-0	205	9-2-93	0	0	0.00	3	0	0	0	3	1	0	0	0	2	3	.111	.333	.000	9.00	6.00
Morris, Akeel	R-R	6-1	195	11-14-92	0	0	0.00	6	0	0	4	8	2	0	0	0	2	9	.080	.100	.067	10.57	2.35
Parsons, Wes	R-R	6-5	204	9-6-92	3	3	2.71	26	10	0	3	103	83	36	31	5	33	98	.219	.252	.198	8.56	2.88
Pfeifer, Philip	L-L	6-0	200	7-15-92	1	3	3.45	30	0	0	3	44	37	18	17	2	33	68	.227	.196	.239	13.80	6.70
Phillips, Evan	R-R	6-2	215	9-11-94	1	1	8.14	15	0	0	1	21	22	19	19	5	11	24	.279	.250	.294	10.29	4.71
Pike, Tyler	L-L	6-0	180	1-26-94	0	9	4.58	15	15	1	0	75	62	45	38	3	63	86	.228	.185	.239	10.37	7.59
Reynolds, Danny	R-R	6-0	190	5-2-91	1	3	3.26	39	0	0	3	58	50	25	21	0	31	52	.239	.275	.221	8.07	4.81
Rincon, Junior	R-R	6-2	185	12-7-91	0	1	4.76	3	0	0	0	6	3	4	3	0	5	8	.150	.000	.200	12.71	7.94
Rogers, Joe	L-L	6-1	205	2-18-91	0	1	11.57	3	0	0	0	2	4	3	3	0	3	1	.400	.000	.500	3.86	11.57
Roney, Bradley	R-R	6-2	200	9-1-92	4	1	3.75	15	0	0	2	24	17	12	10	4	17	36	.205	.231	.182	13.50	6.38
Santiago, Andres	R-R	6-1	220	10-26-89	0	2	6.11	5	3	0	0	18	29	14	12	1	10	9	.372	.441	.318	4.58	5.09
Sobotka, Chad	R-R	6-7	225	7-10-93	3	1	5.52	18	0	0	0	31	29	19	19	1	19	23	.252	.200	.286	6.68	5.52
Soroka, Mike	R-R	6-5	225	8-4-97	11	8	2.75	26	26	0	0	154	133	58	47	10	34	125	.233	.264	.209	7.32	1.99
Toussaint, Touki	R-R	6-3	185	6-20-96	3	4	3.18	7	7	1	0	40	30	19	14	3	22	44	.207	.136	.256	9.98	4.99
Watts, Devan	R-R	6-0	205	4-21-95	0	2	2.25	20	0	0	1	32	27	12	8	1	13	31	.223	.186	.244	8.72	3.66
Webb, Jacob	R-R	6-1	200	8-15-93	3	1	2.63	16	0	0	0	24	17	8	7	1	14	26	.202	.121	.255	9.75	5.25
Weigel, Patrick	R-R	6-6	240	7-8-94	3	0	2.89	7	7	0	0	37	32	13	12	2	11	38	.234	.210	.253	9.16	2.65
Withrow, Matt	R-R	6-5	235	9-23-93	1	3	4.47	10	10	0	0	48	39	26	24	8	22	44	.220	.239	.209	8.19	4.10

Fielding

Catcher	PCT	G	PO	A	E	DP	PB
Araiza	1.000	10	80	9	0	1	0
Giardina	.980	20	129	19	3	0	1
Hyams	1.000	1	4	1	0	0	0
Jackson	.990	23	189	17	2	1	3
Morales	.995	20	164	19	1	1	2
Odom	1.000	7	39	7	0	1	1
Scivicque	.994	65	566	46	4	2	8

First Base	PCT	G	PO	A	E	DP
Franco	.992	15	112	11	1	6
Giardina	.989	15	87	2	1	11
Hyams	1.000	15	129	9	0	11
Joe	1.000	4	20	3	0	4
Meneses	.989	82	578	47	7	63
Morales	.986	18	136	9	2	18

Second Base	PCT	G	PO	A	E	DP
Daniel	.909	7	6	14	2	5
Demeritte	.964	77	156	196	13	51
Harper	.957	5	14	8	1	4
Hyams	1.000	11	9	33	0	7
Landoni	.977	11	18	24	1	5
Moore	1.000	2	3	0	0	0
Obregon	.952	6	7	13	1	6
Rodriguez	1.000	1	3	2	0	0
Valenzuela	.992	26	53	66	1	18

Third Base	PCT	G	PO	A	E	DP
Demeritte	.935	43	21	80	7	6
Franco	.977	17	13	30	1	4
Giardina	1.000	2	5	2	0	0
Harper	.857	4	1	5	1	3
Hyams	.000	1	0	0	0	0
Joe	.000	1	0	0	1	0
Landoni	1.000	1	0	1	0	0
Moore	.667	3	1	1	1	0
Riley	.898	47	38	77	13	9
Rodriguez	1.000	1	0	3	0	0
Valenzuela	.955	24	16	48	3	2

Shortstop	PCT	G	PO	A	E	DP
Harper	.891	14	16	25	5	4
Landoni	1.000	2	1	4	0	2
Moore	.974	118	189	306	13	78
Obregon	.500	2	0	1	1	0
Rodriguez	1.000	1	2	2	0	0
Valenzuela	.892	9	12	21	4	4

Outfield	PCT	G	PO	A	E	DP
Acuna	.981	56	102	1	2	0
Curcio	.990	113	185	8	2	1
Gaylor	1.000	15	21	1	0	1
James	.990	80	96	5	1	0
Joe	1.000	12	18	1	0	0
Lien	.996	117	267	8	1	1
Neslony	.987	42	73	1	1	1
Walker	1.000	12	21	0	0	0

FLORIDA FIRE FROGS — *HIGH CLASS A*

FLORIDA STATE LEAGUE

Batting	B-T	HT	WT	DOB	AVG	vLH	vRH	G	AB	R	H	2B	3B	HR	RBI	BB	HBP	SH	SF	SO	SB	CS	SLG	OBP
Acuna, Ronald	R-R	6-0	180	12-18-97	.287	.267	.290	28	115	21	33	3	5	3	19	8	1	1	1	40	14	3	.478	.336
Castro, Carlos	R-R	6-1	195	5-24-94	.283	.313	.272	96	361	41	102	18	1	10	58	8	6	0	4	92	3	6	.421	.306
Cumberland, Brett	B-R	5-11	205	6-25-95	.269	.216	.290	56	182	14	49	12	1	1	21	18	16	0	0	62	0	2	.363	.384
Daniel, Andrew	R-R	6-1	195	1-27-93	.139	.111	.148	11	36	3	5	1	0	1	3	4	1	0	0	11	0	1	.250	.244
Davidson, Braxton	L-L	6-2	230	6-18-96	.213	.210	.214	111	362	41	77	13	1	7	36	66	4	0	2	155	2	4	.312	.339
Didder, Ray-Patrick	R-R	6-0	170	10-1-94	.230	.243	.225	118	418	51	96	17	5	5	44	44	21	8	4	123	25	13	.330	.331
Ellison, Justin	L-L	6-2	175	2-6-95	.196	.120	.220	30	107	8	21	3	2	2	7	4	1	1	1	33	1	1	.318	.230
Franklin, Kevin	R-R	6-1	220	11-24-94	.161	.211	.135	16	56	4	9	2	0	0	1	3	0	0	1	14	0	0	.196	.200
2-team total (13 Daytona)					.156	.154	.148	29	96	6	15	3	0	0	1	5	0	0	1	21	0	0	.188	.196

Gaylor, Stephen	L-R	6-1	195	10-4-91	.270	.211	.296	19	63	16	17	3	2	0	3	5	2	2	1	14	4	1	.381	.338
Giardina, Sal	B-R	6-4	215	4-30-92	.250	.000	.300	8	24	2	6	1	0	0	2	0	2	0	0	4	0	0	.292	.308
Gonzalez, Matt	R-R	5-11	193	11-30-93	.236	.327	.190	43	144	15	34	8	0	1	13	9	0	6	0	38	1	3	.313	.281
Jackson, Alex	R-R	6-2	215	12-25-95	.272	.283	.269	66	257	44	70	17	0	14	45	13	11	0	1	74	0	1	.502	.333
Lago, Alay	R-R	6-0	200	7-21-91	.303	.320	.298	113	416	47	126	20	4	6	46	22	5	4	4	65	6	6	.414	.342
Martinez, Carlos	R-R	5-11	204	5-2-95	.333	1.000	.000	1	3	0	1	1	0	0	0	0	0	0	0	0	0	0	.667	.333
Morales, Jonathan	R-R	5-11	180	1-29-95	.253	.361	.228	53	194	25	49	4	0	2	17	12	1	2	0	32	1	1	.304	.300
Moss, J.B.	R-R	6-0	185	6-21-93	.133	.000	.182	12	30	0	4	0	0	0	0	0	0	0	0	8	0	0	.133	.133
Murphy, Tanner	R-R	6-1	215	2-27-95	.189	.148	.206	30	90	6	17	3	0	1	5	6	3	0	0	20	0	0	.256	.263
Neslony, Tyler	L-R	6-1	190	2-13-94	.309	.296	.312	60	217	31	67	17	0	4	21	22	2	0	0	43	0	4	.442	.378
Nevarez, Wigberto	R-R	6-3	230	7-17-91	.217	.200	.222	16	46	7	10	2	0	1	5	3	1	0	0	17	1	0	.326	.280
Obregon, Omar	B-R	5-10	150	4-18-94	.257	.214	.263	33	113	10	29	5	2	0	8	10	0	3	1	19	1	4	.336	.315
Riley, Austin	R-R	6-3	220	4-2-97	.252	.258	.250	81	306	43	77	10	1	12	47	23	5	0	5	74	0	2	.409	.310
Salazar, Alejandro	R-R	6-0	170	10-5-96	.247	.250	.246	108	385	30	95	16	2	1	29	9	1	8	1	75	5	6	.307	.265
Schwartz, Garrison	L-L	6-1	205	1-22-96	.111	.000	.125	3	9	1	1	0	0	0	0	1	0	0	0	5	1	0	.111	.200
Seymour, Anfernee	B-R	5-11	165	6-24-95	.280	.291	.276	82	307	45	86	13	4	1	18	28	3	6	5	89	17	17	.358	.341

Pitching	B-T	HT	WT	DOB	W	L	ERA	G	GS	CG	SV	IP	H	R	ER	HR	BB	SO	AVG	vLH	vRH	K/9	BB/9
Cabrera, Mauricio	R-R	6-3	245	9-22-93	0	0	0.00	2	0	0	0	3	1	0	0	0	2	3	.100	.250	.000	9.00	6.00
Caicedo, Oriel L	L-L	5-11	190	1-14-94	2	5	3.58	12	11	1	0	60	61	31	24	2	15	41	.256	.305	.231	6.12	2.24
Clouse, Corbin	B-L	6-0	230	6-26-95	2	0	2.31	25	0	0	2	35	31	13	9	0	21	46	.228	.282	.206	11.83	5.40
Franco, Enderson	R-R	6-2	180	12-29-92	6	6	4.13	19	19	0	0	107	107	53	49	9	38	87	.262	.290	.230	7.34	3.21
Gohara, Luiz	L-L	6-3	210	7-31-96	3	1	1.98	7	7	0	0	36	33	8	8	0	10	39	.243	.325	.208	9.66	2.48
Graham, Josh	R-R	6-1	215	10-14-93	3	3	4.69	31	0	0	1	48	41	27	25	0	18	56	.228	.222	.232	10.50	3.38
Harrington, Drew	R-L	6-2	225	3-30-95	4	8	4.50	15	14	0	0	70	84	44	35	1	22	55	.298	.280	.304	7.07	2.83
Hellinger, Jaret	R-L	6-4	170	11-18-96	0	0	0.00	1	0	0	0	2	1	0	0	0	0	0	.167	.500	.000	0.00	0.00
Johnson-Mullins, Chase	L-L	6-8	270	7-19-94	1	5	3.07	25	0	0	4	44	44	18	15	2	16	50	.251	.215	.273	10.23	3.27
Krol, Ian	L-L	6-1	210	5-9-91	0	0	0.00	1	0	0	0	2	1	0	0	0	0	1	.167	.000	.200	4.50	0.00
Lewis, Taylor	R-R	6-1	170	10-4-93	0	1	8.87	16	0	0	1	23	33	23	23	2	14	21	.351	.405	.308	8.10	5.40
Matthews, Kevin	R-L	5-11	180	11-29-92	0	1	9.28	5	1	0	0	11	11	17	11	1	13	11	.250	.158	.320	9.28	10.97
McCreery, Adam	L-L	6-8	195	12-31-92	1	1	2.64	18	0	0	5	31	21	11	9	1	23	43	.191	.182	.197	12.62	6.75
McLaughlin, Sean	L-R	5-11	195	5-16-94	4	4	3.97	35	0	0	3	66	66	30	29	2	22	58	.272	.265	.277	7.95	3.02
Medlen, Kris	B-R	5-10	190	10-7-85	1	1	3.97	2	2	0	0	11	10	5	5	1	4	6	.238	.211	.261	4.76	3.18
Minter, A.J.	L-L	6-0	205	9-2-93	0	0	1.80	5	0	0	0	5	3	1	1	1	0	9	.167	.143	.182	16.20	0.00
Navarro, Raymar	R-R	6-1	205	3-19-91	2	2	3.70	8	3	0	0	24	20	11	10	0	12	19	.222	.192	.256	7.03	4.44
Pike, Tyler	L-L	6-0	180	1-26-94	5	2	2.20	12	12	0	0	70	56	21	17	2	27	68	.223	.202	.234	8.78	3.49
Rincon, Junior	R-R	6-2	185	12-7-91	1	1	4.84	7	2	0	0	22	28	15	12	2	8	20	.292	.333	.238	8.06	3.22
Roe, Chaz	R-R	6-5	190	10-9-86	0	1	27.00	3	1	0	0	2	6	6	6	0	2	3	.500	.500	.500	13.50	9.00
Rogers, Joe	L-L	6-1	205	2-18-91	0	2	6.61	8	3	0	0	16	22	14	12	1	11	18	.324	.308	.333	9.92	6.06
Roney, Bradley	R-R	6-2	200	9-1-92	0	2	27.00	3	0	0	0	2	5	8	6	0	4	3	.417	.250	.500	13.50	18.00
Salazar, Carlos	R-R	6-0	200	11-23-94	0	0	4.15	4	0	0	0	4	4	5	2	0	7	5	.222	.143	.273	10.38	14.54
Sanchez, Ricardo	L-L	5-11	170	4-11-97	4	12	4.95	22	21	0	0	100	117	65	55	10	46	101	.288	.305	.281	9.09	4.14
Santiago, Andres	R-R	6-1	220	10-26-89	2	6	7.19	15	4	0	0	41	52	38	33	4	15	51	.302	.293	.307	11.10	3.27
Sobotka, Chad	R-R	6-7	225	7-10-93	1	4	6.75	16	0	0	2	27	32	21	20	3	13	29	.314	.417	.222	9.79	4.39
Toussaint, Touki	R-R	6-3	185	6-20-96	3	9	5.04	19	19	0	0	105	101	61	59	8	42	123	.245	.284	.206	10.51	3.59
Watts, Devan	R-R	6-0	205	4-21-95	1	0	2.03	19	0	0	4	27	22	6	6	1	7	34	.222	.214	.228	11.48	2.36
Webb, Jacob	R-R	6-1	200	8-15-93	2	1	1.74	22	0	0	2	41	29	9	8	1	22	48	.203	.222	.191	10.45	4.79
White, Brandon S.	R-R	6-2	215	12-21-94	0	1	4.32	11	0	0	0	17	15	10	8	2	7	14	.238	.323	.156	7.56	3.78
Winkler, Dan	R-R	6-3	205	2-2-90	0	0	0.00	3	0	0	0	3	0	0	0	0	2	2	.000	.000	.000	6.00	6.00
Withrow, Matt	R-R	6-5	235	9-23-93	0	1	3.08	6	4	0	0	26	21	9	9	1	9	21	.228	.262	.200	7.18	3.08
Wright, Kyle	R-R	6-4	200	10-2-95	0	1	3.18	6	6	0	0	11	8	4	4	0	4	10	.205	.375	.087	7.94	3.18

Fielding

Catcher	PCT	G	PO	A	E	DP	PB
Cumberland	.980	29	223	25	5	1	4
Jackson	.973	33	328	30	10	5	4
Martinez	1.000	1	4	0	0	0	0
Morales	.983	35	257	35	5	3	4
Murphy	.995	29	192	23	1	1	2
Nevarez	.982	11	54	2	1	1	5

First Base	PCT	G	PO	A	E	DP
Castro	.981	92	713	53	15	68
Franklin	1.000	3	17	0	0	1
Giardina	.900	3	16	2	2	1
Gonzalez	.941	5	29	3	2	1
Neslony	.959	26	196	13	9	18
Nevarez	1.000	6	39	1	0	5

Second Base	PCT	G	PO	A	E	DP
Didder	.980	9	22	26	1	4
Gonzalez	1.000	1	1	3	0	1
Lago	.972	105	157	255	12	61
Morales	1.000	1	2	2	0	0
Obregon	.986	15	25	44	1	14
Salazar	1.000	2	2	4	0	2

Third Base	PCT	G	PO	A	E	DP
Daniel	.810	10	9	8	4	0
Franklin	.840	12	5	16	4	1
Giardina	.900	4	3	6	1	0
Gonzalez	.833	2	0	5	1	0
Obregon	.889	4	3	5	1	2
Riley	.965	80	53	138	7	9
Salazar	.932	19	15	26	3	4

Shortstop	PCT	G	PO	A	E	DP
Didder	.983	29	43	72	2	12
Obregon	.954	15	21	41	3	8
Salazar	.962	87	121	237	14	60

Outfield	PCT	G	PO	A	E	DP
Acuna	.960	28	47	1	2	0
Davidson	.994	103	154	8	1	1
Didder	.961	79	133	13	6	4
Ellison	.971	22	33	1	1	0
Gaylor	1.000	18	44	1	0	0
Gonzalez	1.000	27	50	2	0	1
Moss	1.000	11	16	0	0	0
Neslony	.938	30	43	2	3	0
Schwartz	1.000	3	2	0	0	0
Seymour	.946	79	154	5	9	1

ROME BRAVES — *LOW CLASS A*

SOUTH ATLANTIC LEAGUE

Batting	B-T	HT	WT	DOB	AVG	vLH	vRH	G	AB	R	H	2B	3B	HR	RBI	BB	HBP	SH	SF	SO	SB	CS	SLG	OBP
Baez, Leudys	B-R	6-0	160	6-26-96	.268	.267	.269	31	123	12	33	4	5	2	16	6	0	0	0	35	1	3	.431	.302
Bush, Austin	L-R	6-6	220	12-22-95	.216	.095	.247	31	102	7	22	6	0	2	11	9	2	0	0	38	0	0	.333	.292

Concepcion, Anthony	R-R	6-1	200	3-23-95	.228	.250	.218	98	289	37	66	6	4	5	35	33	9	2	5	78	10	2	.329	.321
Crowley, Alan	R-R	6-2	210	3-4-96	.185	.125	.211	8	27	0	5	2	0	0	1	1	0	0	0	11	0	0	.259	.214
Cruz, Derian	B-R	6-1	180	10-3-98	.167	.179	.163	29	114	14	19	6	1	0	13	3	3	3	1	35	3	2	.237	.207
Cumberland, Brett	B-R	5-11	205	6-25-95	.263	.282	.257	55	175	34	46	15	1	10	48	31	25	0	5	61	1	0	.531	.432
Delgado, Riley	R-R	5-10	175	2-22-95	.143	.200	.111	4	14	3	2	1	0	0	5	1	0	0	1	2	0	0	.214	.188
Ellison, Justin	L-L	6-2	175	2-6-95	.254	.200	.271	45	169	27	43	9	4	5	21	12	0	1	1	52	6	4	.444	.302
Gonzalez, Matt	R-R	5-11	193	11-30-93	.300	.333	.286	16	70	10	21	0	1	0	7	6	0	0	0	15	2	0	.329	.355
Grullon, Yeudi	R-B	6-1	170	7-18-94	.175	.067	.214	22	57	8	10	0	1	0	5	5	0	2	1	11	0	2	.211	.238
Herbert, Lucas	R-R	6-0	200	11-28-96	.243	.226	.249	101	375	40	91	21	1	8	50	26	10	2	1	74	3	0	.368	.308
Hoekstra, Kurt	L-R	6-2	190	6-27-93	.255	.254	.256	114	415	48	106	18	7	3	35	34	2	1	2	96	11	4	.354	.314
Johnson, Micah	L-R	6-0	210	12-18-90	.286	—	.286	2	7	0	2	0	0	0	1	0	0	0	0	1	0	0	.286	.286
Josephina, Kevin	B-R	6-0	170	10-2-96	.247	.221	.257	118	429	42	106	13	6	1	34	22	2	6	6	92	21	11	.312	.283
Keller, Bradley	R-R	6-1	195	12-15-96	.163	.273	.121	25	80	8	13	7	0	2	6	5	3	1	1	37	1	0	.325	.236
Lugbauer, Drew	L-R	6-3	220	8-23-96	.277	.278	.277	31	119	13	33	11	1	3	19	8	3	0	0	38	0	0	.462	.339
Martinez, Carlos	R-R	5-11	204	5-2-95	.270	.184	.309	51	159	12	43	1	0	0	11	16	5	1	1	19	1	1	.277	.354
Mooney, Marcus	R-R	5-7	160	1-20-94	.238	.173	.261	111	416	53	99	13	1	0	32	21	25	7	5	54	10	6	.274	.311
Murphy, Tanner	R-R	6-1	215	2-27-95	.227	.300	.200	23	75	6	17	4	0	1	11	17	0	2	2	17	2	0	.320	.362
Osuna, Ramon	L-R	6-2	245	6-27-95	.164	.125	.170	20	67	6	11	3	0	0	5	5	0	0	0	35	0	0	.209	.222
Pache, Cristian	R-R	6-2	185	11-19-98	.281	.259	.289	119	469	60	132	13	8	0	42	39	0	4	2	104	32	14	.343	.335
Rodgers, Jordan	R-R	6-1	185	5-9-95	.257	.312	.237	63	230	21	59	17	1	2	27	11	6	1	1	49	3	4	.365	.307
Rodriguez, Sean	R-R	6-0	200	4-26-85	.000	.000	—	1	4	0	0	0	0	0	0	0	0	0	0	1	0	0	.000	.000
Seymour, Anfernee	B-R	5-11	165	6-24-95	.287	.217	.306	28	108	17	31	5	1	0	6	7	3	4	1	22	8	3	.352	.345
Ventura, Randy	B-R	5-9	165	7-11-97	.294	.245	.312	95	381	46	112	7	1	1	16	24	2	5	1	83	29	12	.326	.338
Wilson, Israel	L-R	6-3	185	3-6-98	.262	.324	.246	43	168	28	44	3	3	2	20	18	3	0	2	52	9	3	.351	.340
Yepez, Juan	R-R	6-1	200	2-19-98	.275	.300	.265	36	142	15	39	13	0	1	15	8	0	0	2	32	4	1	.387	.309

Pitching	B-T	HT	WT	DOB	W	L	ERA	G	GS	CG	SV	IP	H	R	ER	HR	BB	SO	AVG	vLH	vRH	K/9	BB/9
Anderson, Ian	R-R	6-3	170	5-2-98	4	5	3.14	20	20	0	0	83	69	30	29	0	43	101	.232	.215	.243	10.95	4.66
Borkovich, Walter	L-R	6-5	217	7-3-95	1	1	2.38	6	0	0	1	11	13	4	3	0	1	16	.277	.286	.269	12.71	0.79
Burrows, Thomas	L-L	6-1	205	9-14-94	3	5	2.16	38	0	0	3	67	48	20	16	1	25	92	.198	.165	.215	12.42	3.38
Caicedo, Oriel L	L-L	5-11	190	1-14-94	5	2	3.20	13	3	0	1	45	42	19	16	2	6	31	.246	.157	.283	6.20	1.20
Conyers, Troy	L-L	6-5	230	4-11-94	4	0	2.86	10	0	0	0	28	26	9	9	3	10	24	.250	.194	.274	7.62	3.18
Custred, Matt	R-R	6-6	240	9-8-93	1	3	1.16	24	0	0	2	39	19	8	5	1	15	48	.144	.200	.104	11.17	3.49
Davidson, Tucker	L-L	6-2	215	3-25-96	5	4	2.60	31	12	0	2	104	96	45	30	4	30	101	.248	.180	.282	8.77	2.60
Deal, Hayden	L-L	6-4	210	11-4-94	1	0	0.00	1	0	0	0	4	1	0	0	0	1	4	.077	.125	.000	9.00	2.25
Franco, Enderson	R-R	6-2	180	12-29-92	0	0	3.18	2	0	0	0	6	7	3	2	0	2	5	.318	.546	.091	7.94	3.18
Hellinger, Jaret	R-L	6-4	170	11-18-96	0	2	9.49	6	1	0	0	12	17	14	13	0	9	6	.354	.273	.378	4.38	6.57
Hughes, Landon	R-R	6-5	198	9-20-94	0	0	6.75	1	0	0	0	1	2	2	1	0	3	1	.400	.000	.667	6.75	20.25
Kennedy, Jon	L-L	6-5	215	9-20-95	5	2	2.87	39	1	0	5	78	79	28	25	4	6	65	.262	.263	.261	7.47	0.69
Lawlor, Ryan	R-L	6-1	185	1-8-94	3	1	4.37	11	10	0	0	47	49	24	23	0	16	61	.266	.250	.273	11.60	3.04
Lewis, Taylor	R-R	6-1	170	10-4-93	2	2	2.75	18	0	0	3	39	38	16	12	4	17	38	.244	.275	.218	8.69	3.89
Matos, Bladimir	R-R	6-0	190	1-20-94	3	3	3.90	38	0	0	1	60	54	33	26	5	32	68	.237	.156	.278	10.20	4.80
Matthews, Kevin	R-L	5-11	180	11-29-92	1	0	0.93	5	0	0	0	10	9	1	1	0	5	8	.265	.273	.261	7.45	4.66
McCreery, Adam	L-L	6-8	195	12-31-92	2	0	2.84	20	0	0	2	32	26	17	10	0	15	47	.219	.184	.235	13.36	4.26
Minter, A.J.	L-L	6-0	205	9-2-93	0	0	0.00	1	0	0	0	1	1	0	0	0	0	1	.333	.000	.500	9.00	0.00
Mora, Luis	R-R	6-4	160	6-17-95	1	0	3.86	2	0	0	0	5	6	3	2	0	2	0	.300	.300	.300	0.00	3.86
Motte, Jason	R-R	6-0	205	6-22-82	0	0	0.00	1	0	0	0	1	0	0	0	0	0	1	.000	.000	.000	9.00	0.00
Navarro, Raymar	R-R	6-1	205	3-19-91	0	0	4.35	6	0	0	0	10	12	5	5	2	3	12	.286	.273	.290	10.45	2.61
Rangel, Alan	R-R	6-2	170	8-21-97	2	6	4.71	15	13	0	0	71	82	38	37	5	14	48	.299	.273	.320	6.11	1.78
Rogers, Joe	L-L	6-1	205	2-18-91	2	0	5.17	9	0	0	1	16	18	10	9	2	9	22	.305	.188	.349	12.64	5.17
Santiago, Andres	R-R	6-1	220	10-26-89	0	0	0.00	2	0	0	0	6	4	2	0	0	1	5	.167	.200	.143	7.11	1.42
Schlosser, Ryan	R-R	6-4	190	1-31-96	1	7	6.84	14	0	0	0	26	39	22	20	4	8	13	.361	.372	.354	4.44	2.73
Walker, Jeremy	R-R	6-5	205	6-12-95	7	11	3.97	27	27	2	0	138	159	76	61	7	30	100	.288	.297	.282	6.51	1.95
Wentz, Joey	L-L	6-5	210	10-6-97	8	3	2.60	26	26	0	0	132	99	44	38	4	46	152	.209	.215	.207	10.39	3.14
White, Brandon S.	R-R	6-2	215	12-21-94	2	0	1.82	25	0	0	10	40	36	13	8	1	10	37	.247	.372	.194	8.39	2.27
Wilson, Bryse	R-R	6-1	225	12-20-97	10	7	2.50	26	26	1	0	137	105	45	38	8	37	139	.211	.214	.209	9.13	2.43
Winkler, Dan	R-R	6-3	205	2-2-90	0	0	9.00	1	0	0	0	1	2	1	1	0	1	0	.400	—	.400	0.00	9.00

Fielding

Catcher	PCT	G	PO	A	E	DP	PB
Crowley	.963	4	22	4	1	0	0
Cumberland	.995	21	188	25	1	1	2
Herbert	.987	74	589	95	9	8	7
Lugbauer	1.000	5	50	5	0	0	0
Martinez	.989	32	241	30	3	2	2
Murphy	1.000	13	105	21	0	1	2

First Base	PCT	G	PO	A	E	DP
Bush	.995	26	208	13	1	19
Concepcion	.982	41	303	20	6	25
Hoekstra	.996	52	454	17	2	44
Lugbauer	.989	19	181	3	2	17
Osuna	.981	14	98	6	2	12
Yepez	1.000	1	20	3	0	1

Second Base	PCT	G	PO	A	E	DP
Gonzalez	.000	1	0	0	0	0
Grullon	.889	3	2	6	1	1
Josephina	.953	109	180	269	22	77
Mooney	.971	11	16	17	1	6
Rodgers	.972	18	25	44	2	11
Rodriguez	1.000	1	1	3	0	1

Third Base	PCT	G	PO	A	E	DP
Gonzalez	1.000	3	1	5	0	1
Grullon	.857	9	3	15	3	0
Hoekstra	.908	60	41	117	16	17
Josephina	.000	1	0	0	0	0
Lugbauer	.889	5	1	7	1	0
Martinez	.000	1	0	0	0	0
Mooney	1.000	8	5	13	0	1
Rodgers	.955	32	15	48	3	5
Yepez	.890	34	17	48	8	6

Shortstop	PCT	G	PO	A	E	DP
Cruz	.869	26	34	72	16	19
Delgado	.957	4	11	11	1	6
Grullon	.900	7	8	19	3	6
Hoekstra	1.000	1	3	3	0	2
Josephina	.000	1	0	0	0	0
Mooney	.980	92	117	281	8	44
Rodgers	.969	16	14	49	2	11

Outfield	PCT	G	PO	A	E	DP
Baez	.944	20	33	1	2	0
Concepcion	.962	59	74	1	3	0
Ellison	.983	44	57	0	1	0
Gonzalez	1.000	9	21	0	0	0
Johnson	1.000	2	3	0	0	0
Keller	.970	24	32	0	1	0
Mooney	.000	1	0	0	0	0
Pache	.981	118	288	17	6	8
Seymour	1.000	26	32	2	0	0
Ventura	.965	91	158	6	6	2
Wilson	.965	41	77	5	3	1

DANVILLE BRAVES — ROOKIE

APPALACHIAN LEAGUE

Batting	B-T	HT	WT	DOB	AVG	vLH	vRH	G	AB	R	H	2B	3B	HR	RBI	BB	HBP	SH	SF	SO	SB	CS	SLG	OBP
Baez, Leudys	B-R	6-0	160	6-26-96	.340	.191	.384	25	94	14	32	7	2	4	18	11	1	0	0	21	1	2	.585	.415
Benson, Griffin	B-R	6-5	210	9-28-97	.234	.194	.245	45	137	18	32	4	0	1	15	17	2	0	1	40	1	0	.285	.325
Bush, Austin	L-R	6-6	220	12-22-95	.273	.167	.283	18	66	9	18	8	0	3	11	9	1	0	0	23	0	0	.530	.368
Commings, Sanders	R-R	6-1	195	3-8-90	.154	.500	.000	6	13	5	2	1	0	0	1	1	1	0	0	9	0	0	.231	.267
Contreras, William	R-R	6-0	180	12-24-97	.290	.290	.290	45	169	29	49	10	1	4	25	24	2	0	3	30	1	0	.432	.379
Crowley, Alan	R-R	6-2	210	3-4-96	.211	.250	.206	13	38	7	8	3	0	2	5	3	1	1	0	10	1	0	.447	.286
Cruz, Derian	B-R	6-1	180	10-3-98	.235	.244	.233	50	213	32	50	9	1	2	22	14	1	2	3	61	11	5	.315	.281
Delgado, Riley	R-R	5-10	175	2-22-95	.232	.000	.254	22	69	5	16	1	0	0	6	7	0	1	1	9	0	0	.246	.299
Encarnacion, Jean Carlos	R-R	6-3	195	1-17-98	.290	.231	.313	23	93	14	27	3	0	1	6	3	1	0	1	21	3	5	.355	.316
Fernandez, Jeremy	R-R	6-1	185	7-11-97	.174	.250	.147	13	46	5	8	1	0	0	1	4	0	0	0	10	1	0	.196	.240
Keller, Bradley	R-R	6-1	195	12-15-96	.307	.333	.300	33	124	24	38	14	2	6	22	10	1	0	1	38	2	1	.597	.360
Lugbauer, Drew	L-R	6-3	220	8-23-96	.243	.182	.259	29	103	23	25	4	0	10	27	19	1	0	0	30	0	0	.573	.366
Maitan, Kevin	B-R	6-2	190	2-12-00	.221	.214	.222	33	127	10	28	5	1	2	15	9	1	0	2	39	1	0	.323	.273
Mejia, Luis	B-R	5-10	160	3-8-97	.297	.278	.301	30	91	14	27	3	0	0	5	8	0	4	0	13	5	0	.330	.354
Michel, Raysheandall	R-R	5-11	170	9-26-97	.326	.276	.340	35	132	23	43	9	2	0	11	11	0	2	0	30	7	4	.424	.378
Owenby, Hagen	R-R	6-1	211	7-21-95	.237	.152	.264	39	139	11	33	5	1	3	22	11	5	0	3	32	0	1	.353	.310
Ramos, Jefrey	R-R	6-1	185	2-10-99	.278	.294	.273	20	72	7	20	6	0	1	8	3	1	0	2	15	0	0	.403	.308
Schwartz, Garrison	L-L	6-1	205	1-22-96	.281	.267	.284	31	96	24	27	9	0	5	15	19	1	2	2	24	1	2	.531	.398
Shumpert, Nicholas	R-R	5-11	180	11-11-96	.216	.281	.196	43	134	14	29	4	2	0	14	6	2	1	1	52	5	2	.276	.259
Smith, Justin	R-R	6-2	205	2-29-96	.250	.407	.200	33	112	9	28	5	0	3	11	11	1	0	1	47	5	2	.375	.320
Waters, Drew	B-R	6-2	183	12-30-98	.255	.258	.254	36	149	20	38	11	1	2	14	16	1	0	0	59	4	2	.383	.331
Wilson, Israel	L-R	6-3	185	3-6-98	.250	.222	.254	17	68	11	17	2	3	4	12	9	0	0	0	18	2	0	.544	.338

Pitching	B-T	HT	WT	DOB	W	L	ERA	G	GS	CG	SV	IP	H	R	ER	HR	BB	SO	AVG	vLH	vRH	K/9	BB/9
Belinda, Jacob	R-R	6-0	190	9-24-94	6	0	3.64	12	1	0	0	30	24	12	12	2	14	22	.224	.310	.192	6.67	4.25
Borkovich, Walter	L-R	6-5	217	7-3-95	2	1	3.00	8	0	0	2	12	12	6	4	2	1	13	.261	.250	.267	9.75	0.75
Curtis, John	L-L	6-2	180	10-15-95	0	1	2.13	15	0	0	1	25	18	7	6	1	9	27	.202	.100	.232	9.59	3.20
De La Cruz, Jasseel	R-R	6-1	175	6-26-97	0	2	5.32	7	6	0	0	24	25	20	14	1	11	19	.260	.177	.307	7.23	4.18
Dyals, Cutter	R-R	5-11	205	8-10-95	2	4	2.05	17	0	0	0	22	17	9	5	0	9	21	.202	.208	.200	8.59	3.68
Hellinger, Jaret	R-L	6-4	170	11-18-96	4	2	3.64	13	7	0	1	54	44	23	22	4	20	41	.223	.129	.241	6.79	3.31
Heredia, Jesus	R-R	6-2	175	1-21-95	1	3	5.91	15	0	0	1	21	26	20	14	2	15	26	.286	.286	.286	10.97	6.33
Hughes, Landon	R-R	6-5	198	9-20-94	1	1	1.69	15	0	0	5	21	16	4	4	0	5	27	.203	.367	.102	11.39	2.11
Hyssong, Taylor	L-L	6-4	190	1-4-94	1	1	2.77	15	0	0	1	26	21	14	8	0	11	23	.219	.280	.197	7.96	3.81
Javier, Odalvi	R-R	6-0	180	9-4-96	4	2	3.14	13	13	0	0	63	61	22	22	3	22	50	.253	.226	.273	7.14	3.14
Johnstone, Connor	R-R	6-1	175	10-4-94	1	1	5.40	3	3	0	0	10	10	6	6	2	1	12	.250	.313	.208	10.80	0.90
Mejia, Dilmer	L-L	5-11	160	7-9-97	4	3	3.91	13	9	0	1	51	46	31	22	1	10	52	.232	.278	.222	9.24	1.78
Muller, Kyle	R-L	6-6	225	10-7-97	1	1	4.15	11	11	0	0	48	43	24	22	5	18	49	.232	.184	.245	9.25	3.40
Navarro, Raymar	R-R	6-1	205	3-19-91	0	1	5.94	8	0	0	2	17	28	17	11	2	6	11	.364	.333	.377	5.94	3.24
Rice, Zach	L-L	6-2	205	10-15-95	0	1	2.97	16	0	0	0	30	27	15	10	1	12	38	.229	.125	.267	11.27	3.56
Rodriguez, Kelvin	L-L	6-5	195	12-31-93	4	1	2.28	19	0	0	1	28	28	11	7	1	12	30	.255	.250	.256	9.76	3.90
Schlosser, Ryan	R-R	6-4	190	1-31-96	1	1	3.12	6	0	0	1	9	7	3	3	0	1	7	.219	.200	.227	7.27	1.04
Simmons, Connor	L-L	6-2	160	11-7-95	1	0	2.95	13	0	0	1	18	14	7	6	0	6	18	.206	.286	.185	8.84	2.95
Suarez, Gilbert	R-R	6-2	215	6-19-97	0	0	12.60	6	0	0	0	10	23	21	14	4	6	9	.426	.409	.438	8.10	5.40
Weisenberg, Keith	R-R	6-5	195	12-6-95	3	2	3.24	15	0	0	1	25	22	12	9	0	9	20	.234	.243	.228	7.20	3.24
Ynoa, Huascar	R-R	6-3	175	5-28-98	0	3	5.26	7	7	0	0	26	24	17	15	1	15	27	.238	.242	.235	9.47	5.26
2-team total (6 Elizabethton)					0	4	5.26	13	13	0	0	51	52	33	30	2	29	50	.257	.378	.219	8.77	5.08
Zimmermann, Bruce	L-L	6-2	215	2-9-95	0	1	3.09	11	11	0	0	23	21	8	8	0	9	28	.244	.231	.247	10.80	3.47

Fielding

C: Contreras 35, Crowley 11, Lugbauer 11, Owenby 17., **1B:** Benson 45, Bush 17, Lugbauer 6, Owenby 5., **2B:** Cruz 29, Delgado 6, Fernandez 13, Mejia 2, Shumpert 20., **3B:** Encarnacion 23, Lugbauer 9, Mejia 24, Shumpert 14., **SS:** Cruz 18, Delgado 17, Maitan 30, Mejia 3, Shumpert 4., **OF:** Baez 18, Commings 4, Keller 25, Michel 33, Ramos 16, Schwartz 30, Smith 28, Waters 35, Wilson 17.

GCL BRAVES — ROOKIE

GULF COAST LEAGUE

Batting	B-T	HT	WT	DOB	AVG	vLH	vRH	G	AB	R	H	2B	3B	HR	RBI	BB	HBP	SH	SF	SO	SB	CS	SLG	OBP
Baerga, Carlos	L-L	5-10	190	9-2-95	.208	.130	.227	40	120	17	25	7	0	0	6	15	4	5	0	12	0	1	.267	.317
Bermudez, Jose	B-R	6-2	160	7-9-97	.247	.289	.229	39	150	17	37	5	1	1	15	14	3	2	0	41	7	4	.313	.323
Camargo, Johan	B-R	6-0	160	12-13-93	.500	—	.500	1	4	1	2	0	0	0	0	0	0	0	0	0	0	0	.500	.500
Encarnacion, Jean Carlos	R-R	6-3	195	1-17-98	.350	.333	.353	27	103	16	36	8	4	2	16	4	0	0	0	22	4	2	.563	.374
Fernandez, Jeremy	R-R	6-1	185	7-11-97	.305	.273	.317	24	82	16	25	4	0	3	16	0	4	0	2	11	3	1	.463	.330
Garcia, Adonis	R-R	5-9	205	4-12-85	.167	.000	.250	2	6	1	1	0	0	0	0	0	0	0	0	0	0	0	.167	.167
Groesbeck, Adam	R-R	5-10	175	4-7-95	.069	.000	.077	15	29	7	2	1	0	0	1	7	1	2	0	11	0	0	.103	.270
Gutierrez, Abrahan	R-R	6-2	214	10-31-99	.264	.194	.290	35	129	15	34	9	0	1	12	10	1	0	1	21	0	0	.357	.319
Johnson, Micah	L-R	6-0	210	12-18-90	.429	.667	.250	3	7	2	3	0	0	0	2	3	0	0	0	2	5	0	.429	.600
Lopez, Yoeli	R-R	5-10	167	7-31-97	.241	.259	.235	35	108	21	26	6	2	1	7	9	6	1	0	40	7	3	.361	.333

Batting	B-T	HT	WT	DOB	AVG	vLH	vRH	G	AB	R	H	2B	3B	HR	RBI	BB	HBP	SH	SF	SO	SB	CS	SLG	OBP
Maitan, Kevin	B-R	6-2	190	2-12-00	.314	.429	.286	9	35	5	11	3	0	0	3	2	0	0	0	10	1	0	.400	.351
Michel, Raysheandall	R-R	5-11	170	9-26-97	.227	.000	.263	5	22	3	5	1	0	0	2	2	0	0	0	3	2	0	.273	.292
Morhardt, Justin	B-R	6-3	200	3-3-94	.182	.200	.179	26	77	4	14	2	0	0	5	12	0	1	2	27	1	0	.208	.286
Ovando, Luis	R-R	6-1	160	10-29-98	.176	.250	.155	29	91	16	16	1	1	1	15	13	3	1	2	31	5	1	.242	.294
Ramos, Jefrey	R-R	6-1	185	2-10-99	.325	.250	.337	30	117	22	38	7	1	6	30	8	3	0	3	27	1	0	.556	.374
Rodriguez, Ricardo	R-R	5-10	175	12-20-97	.238	.182	.253	29	105	8	25	6	1	1	12	3	1	0	3	11	0	0	.343	.259
Rodriguez, Sean	R-R	6-0	200	4-26-85	.200	.000	.333	2	5	0	1	0	0	0	0	0	0	0	0	0	0	0	.200	.200
Severino, Yunior	B-R	6-1	180	10-3-99	.286	.234	.303	48	189	27	54	17	2	3	27	16	1	0	0	61	0	1	.444	.345
Soria, Zack	R-R	5-10	192	10-29-93	.256	.333	.222	29	78	7	20	7	0	0	11	12	5	1	0	14	0	0	.346	.390
Soto, Livan	R-R	6-0	160	6-22-00	.225	.250	.217	47	173	24	39	5	0	0	14	27	2	3	3	26	7	3	.254	.332
Valenzuela, Luis	L-R	5-10	179	8-25-93	.364	.000	.500	3	11	3	4	2	0	0	2	0	0	0	1	1	1	0	.546	.333
Vasquez, Braulio	B-R	6-0	170	4-13-99	.270	.273	.269	47	152	22	41	3	3	0	16	21	4	1	1	36	12	3	.329	.371
Vizcaino, Nicholas	R-R	6-1	200	3-19-97	.259	.162	.296	40	135	11	35	10	1	0	11	12	3	0	2	37	0	0	.348	.329
Waters, Drew	B-R	6-2	183	12-30-98	.347	.500	.317	14	49	13	17	3	1	2	10	7	2	0	0	11	2	1	.571	.448

Pitching	B-T	HT	WT	DOB	W	L	ERA	G	GS	CG	SV	IP	H	R	ER	HR	BB	SO	AVG	vLH	vRH	K/9	BB/9
Allison, Tanner	L-L	6-1	200	5-23-95	1	1	2.20	11	0	0	2	16	14	6	4	0	2	15	.226	.063	.283	8.27	1.10
Aquino, Alex	R-R	6-2	165	7-6-96	0	1	7.56	7	0	0	1	8	7	7	7	0	11	5	.241	.100	.316	5.40	11.88
Bacon, Troy	R-R	6-0	165	9-26-96	1	1	3.44	13	0	0	2	18	11	7	7	1	7	22	.164	.174	.159	10.80	3.44
Becherer, Zach	R-R	6-4	220	9-4-95	1	1	4.00	16	0	0	0	18	17	9	8	0	17	24	.246	.250	.245	12.00	8.50
Borkovich, Walter	L-R	6-5	217	7-3-95	0	0	0.00	2	0	0	0	4	4	0	0	0	1	1	.250	.667	.154	2.25	2.25
Collmenter, Josh	R-R	6-3	240	2-7-86	1	0	1.50	2	0	0	0	6	4	1	1	0	1	6	.182	.111	.231	9.00	1.50
Contreras, Juan	R-R	6-2	180	9-8-99	2	1	6.27	9	7	0	0	19	17	14	13	1	21	11	.250	.200	.271	5.30	10.13
Conyers, Troy	L-L	6-5	230	4-11-94	3	0	0.00	8	0	0	1	14	7	1	0	0	2	19	.149	.400	.081	12.21	1.29
De La Cruz, Jasseel	R-R	6-1	175	6-26-97	2	1	1.89	4	4	0	0	19	13	4	4	1	7	17	.188	.179	.195	8.05	3.32
Deal, Hayden	L-L	6-4	210	11-4-94	2	2	3.71	13	0	0	2	27	29	17	11	1	8	23	.271	.179	.304	7.76	2.70
Del Rosario, Yefri	R-R	6-2	180	9-23-99	1	1	3.90	11	6	0	0	32	37	20	14	1	10	29	.285	.349	.253	8.07	2.78
Hodgson, Alger	R-R	6-2	190	4-10-99	2	2	6.47	9	6	0	0	32	35	27	23	3	19	22	.271	.326	.244	6.19	5.34
Jerez, Miguel	L-L	5-11	180	10-13-97	2	0	1.38	15	1	0	1	39	25	7	6	2	10	35	.181	.156	.189	8.08	2.31
Julian, Deyvis	R-R	6-2	165	4-10-96	3	2	3.35	13	2	0	0	40	36	17	15	2	21	29	.234	.216	.243	6.47	4.69
Krol, Ian	L-L	6-1	210	5-9-91	0	0	0.00	2	0	0	0	2	1	0	0	0	0	4	.125	.000	.167	18.00	0.00
Lourie, Jackson	R-R	6-3	190	10-10-94	2	0	3.10	14	0	0	0	20	15	7	7	0	12	12	.214	.240	.200	5.31	5.31
Montilla, Jose	R-R	6-1	170	6-4-98	0	1	3.24	2	2	0	0	8	9	4	3	0	2	6	.290	.357	.235	6.48	2.16
Noguera, Gabriel	L-L	6-2	175	5-31-96	1	0	2.66	5	3	0	0	20	14	7	6	1	11	17	.192	.333	.164	7.52	4.87
Roe, Chaz	R-R	6-5	190	10-9-86	0	0	0.00	1	1	0	0	1	0	1	0	0	1	1	.000	.000	.000	9.00	9.00
Sanchez, Filyer	L-L	6-1	175	2-8-97	1	0	1.35	2	0	0	0	7	5	1	1	0	1	2	.208	.143	.235	2.70	1.35
Sepulveda, Jhoniel	R-R	6-2	175	5-15-97	2	3	2.84	11	0	0	1	19	20	14	6	2	8	16	.263	.300	.239	7.58	3.79
Suarez, Gilbert	R-R	6-2	215	6-19-97	1	2	1.96	11	0	0	0	23	16	10	5	0	5	16	.188	.226	.167	6.26	1.96
Tarnok, Freddy	R-R	6-3	185	11-24-98	0	3	2.57	8	8	0	0	14	11	6	4	0	3	10	.208	.125	.243	6.43	1.93
Taveras, Ramon	R-R	6-1	200	8-31-95	1	2	3.90	17	0	0	1	32	44	22	14	0	6	33	.319	.327	.315	9.19	1.67
Vega, Bredio	R-R	6-3	185	4-8-96	0	0	0.00	3	0	0	0	4	3	0	0	0	5	2	.231	.400	.125	4.91	12.27
Volquez, Albinson	R-R	6-3	185	8-16-97	2	1	2.19	12	9	0	1	37	30	9	9	2	11	25	.222	.186	.239	6.08	2.68
Withrow, Matt	R-R	6-5	235	9-23-93	0	0	0.00	2	1	0	0	5	1	0	0	0	0	5	.077	.000	.125	9.00	0.00
Wright, Kyle	R-R	6-4	200	10-2-95	0	0	1.59	3	3	0	0	6	3	1	1	0	2	8	.150	.000	.231	12.71	3.18
Zuniga, Guillermo	R-R	6-3	195	10-10-98	0	3	5.06	8	6	0	0	21	28	18	12	0	11	13	.333	.400	.296	5.48	4.64

Fielding

C: Gutierrez 28, Morhardt 7, Rodriguez 18, Soria 18. **1B:** Encarnacion 14, Morhardt 12, Vasquez 1, Vizcaino 38. **2B:** Fernandez 6, Ovando 17, Rodriguez 1, Severino 33, Soto 3, Valenzuela 2, Vasquez 1. **3B:** Camargo 1, Encarnacion 15, Garcia 1, Ovando 3, Vasquez 44. **SS:** Bermudez 1, Maitan 5, Ovando 9, Rodriguez 1, Soto 44, Valenzuela 1, Vasquez 1. **OF:** Baerga 40, Bermudez 38, Fernandez 15, Garcia 1, Groesbeck 14, Johnson 3, Lopez 35, Michel 5, Ovando 1, Ramos 29, Soto 1, Waters 11.

DSL BRAVES — ROOKIE

DOMINICAN SUMMER LEAGUE

Batting	B-T	HT	WT	DOB	AVG	vLH	vRH	G	AB	R	H	2B	3B	HR	RBI	BB	HBP	SH	SF	SO	SB	CS	SLG	OBP
Adrianza, Andres	R-R	6-0	190	2-6-99	.225	.174	.242	25	89	9	20	4	0	0	13	3	1	1	1	18	0	0	.270	.255
Blanco, Reilys	B-R	5-10	150	7-30-96	.217	.182	.230	53	166	21	36	6	1	0	22	28	5	1	3	18	10	1	.265	.342
Carrillo, Franger	R-R	6-1	185	11-7-98	.258	.333	.240	10	31	4	8	2	0	0	4	2	0	0	2	9	1	1	.323	.286
Centeno, Carlos	R-R	5-9	180	11-19-97	.152	.167	.148	12	33	1	5	1	0	0	2	1	1	2	0	10	0	0	.182	.200
Cerrato, Wiston	B-R	5-10	170	4-9-99	.186	.250	.167	33	86	6	16	4	0	0	6	12	2	0	1	24	5	1	.233	.297
De Hoyos, Victor	R-R	5-9	170	2-23-98	.273	.000	.333	4	11	2	3	0	0	0	0	1	0	0	0	2	0	0	.273	.333
Encarnacion, Kimberling	R-R	6-0	180	11-22-99	.188	.500	.167	11	32	1	6	1	0	0	3	3	0	0	0	5	0	0	.219	.257
Guitian, Enmanuel	R-R	5-11	165	9-14-98	.192	.103	.220	44	120	14	23	3	0	0	16	25	9	1	0	28	2	0	.217	.370
Isea, Emmanuel	R-R	6-1	180	12-2-98	.241	.231	.244	15	54	5	13	1	0	0	3	3	0	0	0	16	2	0	.259	.281
Jimenez, Eric	R-R	5-9	165	5-6-97	.247	.235	.250	33	85	16	21	3	0	0	8	17	3	0	0	22	7	3	.282	.391
Juan, Manuel	L-L	6-4	200	10-24-99	.150	.133	.154	27	80	5	12	1	0	0	7	6	0	0	1	24	1	0	.163	.207
Lara, Yandri	R-R	6-0	190	5-31-00	.050	.000	.061	12	40	4	2	0	0	0	1	3	1	0	0	23	0	0	.050	.136
Lopez, Yoeli	R-R	5-10	167	7-31-97	.222	.375	.189	12	45	11	10	2	0	0	5	6	3	0	0	17	4	0	.267	.352
Lora, Eudis	L-R	6-2	180	10-8-97	.196	.167	.203	67	230	28	45	7	2	1	22	33	1	1	1	66	6	2	.257	.298
Morales, Juan	R-R	6-2	165	11-17-98	.250	.000	.500	2	4	1	1	0	0	0	0	0	1	0	0	0	0	0	.250	.400
Negret, Juan Carlos	R-R	6-1	190	6-19-99	.264	.162	.292	50	174	31	46	14	1	2	10	27	16	0	0	47	23	9	.391	.410
Ordonez, Sergio	R-R	6-0	175	4-21-99	.200	.000	.233	20	35	4	7	0	0	0	4	4	3	1	0	9	0	0	.200	.333
Palma, Jose	L-L	6-0	170	6-9-99	.246	.000	.320	40	65	9	16	1	1	0	4	9	0	2	0	12	5	2	.292	.338
Pena, Yenci	R-R	6-2	175	7-13-00	.230	.256	.222	45	165	20	38	8	1	2	19	24	0	1	0	31	7	6	.327	.328
Quintero, Henry	R-R	6-1	193	5-23-94	.333	.125	.409	9	30	6	10	5	1	0	9	3	2	0	1	7	0	0	.567	.417

Reyes, Charles	R-R	6-1	165	9-9-99	.216	.286	.193	61	222	19	48	7	2	0	29	20	3	0	4	66	6	2	.266	.285
Reyes, Joel	R-R	6-0	200	10-3-99	.169	.143	.182	21	65	8	11	5	0	0	3	5	2	0	0	16	0	2	.246	.250
Rojas, Luidemid	B-R	5-11	170	5-4-99	.143	.500	.000	2	7	2	1	0	0	0	1	0	0	0	0	0	0	0	.143	.143
Salazar, Danyer	R-R	6-1	180	2-19-98	.143	.167	.133	10	21	2	3	1	0	0	2	2	1	0	0	6	0	0	.191	.250
Santana, Gerardo	R-R	6-2	200	9-12-99	.169	.250	.151	23	65	5	11	1	0	0	3	8	1	0	0	19	1	1	.185	.270
Severino, Yunior	B-R	6-1	180	10-3-99	.189	.222	.179	10	37	6	7	2	1	0	2	8	1	0	0	6	0	0	.297	.348
Sucre, Antonio	R-R	5-11	185	11-8-99	.237	.240	.237	57	198	28	47	7	0	4	24	20	10	0	3	58	4	4	.333	.333

Pitching	**B-T**	**HT**	**WT**	**DOB**	**W**	**L**	**ERA**	**G**	**GS**	**CG**	**SV**	**IP**	**H**	**R**	**ER**	**HR**	**BB**	**SO**	**AVG**	**vLH**	**vRH**	**K/9**	**BB/9**
Abreu, Erick	L-L	6-3	180	1-1-98	1	0	0.00	1	0	0	0	3	1	0	0	0	1	1	.100	.000	.111	3.00	3.00
Asencio, Eudi	R-R	6-3	170	2-28-99	0	0	3.10	10	4	0	0	20	13	9	7	1	13	17	.183	.207	.167	7.52	5.75
Caminero, Carlos	L-L	6-4	185	9-17-97	1	2	5.60	18	0	0	0	35	48	35	22	2	15	32	.320	.323	.319	8.15	3.82
Ciriaco, Javier	R-R	6-3	185	1-1-96	1	5	4.91	19	0	0	0	29	27	25	16	0	34	24	.239	.261	.224	7.36	10.43
Colon, Madinson	R-R	6-1	198	2-15-98	0	3	18.41	8	0	0	0	7	9	16	15	0	16	4	.300	.364	.263	4.91	19.64
Contreras, Juan	R-R	6-2	180	9-8-99	0	0	0.00	1	1	0	0	1	0	0	0	0	0	1	.000	.000	.000	9.00	0.00
De Jesus, Luis	R-R	5-11	170	10-8-98	2	5	4.64	14	11	0	0	43	48	38	22	0	25	31	.293	.303	.284	6.54	5.27
Del Rosario, Yefri	R-R	6-2	180	9-23-99	0	0	1.80	2	2	0	0	5	1	2	1	0	4	7	.067	.000	.100	12.60	7.20
Diaz, Jhonny	L-L	6-0	180	6-22-96	2	6	4.79	15	0	0	1	41	56	37	22	3	14	21	.331	.410	.308	4.57	3.05
Hernandez, Servando	R-R	6-3	210	11-25-96	0	2	3.54	12	10	0	0	41	36	18	16	0	13	31	.237	.250	.229	6.86	2.88
Hodgson, Alger	R-R	6-2	190	4-10-99	0	0	1.13	3	2	0	0	8	4	5	1	0	3	3	.143	.083	.188	3.38	3.38
Jerez, Miguel	L-L	5-11	180	10-13-97	0	1	1.00	4	0	0	0	9	6	2	1	0	1	10	.188	.000	.200	10.00	1.00
Jimenez, Edwin	L-L	6-1	170	7-22-00	0	3	10.13	9	2	0	0	13	17	18	15	1	14	8	.327	.455	.293	5.40	9.45
Julian, Deyvis	R-R	6-2	165	4-10-96	0	1	7.36	4	3	0	0	7	7	7	6	0	4	6	.250	.222	.263	7.36	4.91
Lopez, Carlos	R-R	6-4	175	3-20-98	0	3	2.81	13	3	0	0	26	29	22	8	0	12	15	.276	.238	.302	5.26	4.21
Montilla, Jose	R-R	6-1	170	6-4-98	0	4	3.07	14	10	0	0	44	44	19	15	2	11	20	.264	.343	.206	4.09	2.25
Noguera, Gabriel	L-L	6-2	175	5-31-96	1	2	0.87	9	6	0	0	31	19	8	3	1	14	31	.179	.059	.202	9.00	4.06
Nunez, Oscar	R-R	6-0	190	6-16-00	0	2	5.17	12	0	0	0	16	10	14	9	1	15	10	.182	.154	.207	5.74	8.62
Olague, Jose	R-R	6-0	207	12-13-98	0	0	0.00	3	1	0	0	7	6	1	0	0	0	8	.231	.313	.100	10.29	0.00
Pena, Miguel	L-R	6-1	190	11-26-98	2	1	3.96	15	0	0	1	25	27	19	11	0	7	13	.267	.316	.238	4.68	2.52
Polanco, Walner	R-R	6-7	200	12-24-96	2	3	3.63	22	0	0	1	35	17	16	14	0	27	36	.149	.180	.133	9.35	7.01
Rodriguez, Estarlin	R-R	6-0	180	10-24-99	1	1	1.86	10	5	0	0	19	15	6	4	0	4	17	.214	.219	.211	7.91	1.86
Rodriguez, Kelvin	L-L	6-5	195	12-31-93	0	0	5.79	3	0	0	0	5	7	5	3	1	1	1	.318	.000	.350	1.93	1.93
Sanchez, Filyer	L-L	6-1	175	2-8-97	1	3	2.97	15	2	0	1	33	35	19	11	0	12	26	.267	.273	.266	7.02	3.24
Santos, Lisandro	L-L	6-1	170	7-24-98	2	0	3.00	20	0	0	1	30	29	18	10	0	18	35	.240	.048	.280	10.50	5.40
Vasquez, Willians	R-R	6-1	200	5-7-97	2	5	6.86	15	6	0	0	42	49	36	32	1	20	19	.303	.300	.305	4.07	4.29
Volquez, Albinson	R-R	6-3	185	8-16-97	0	1	5.79	3	3	0	0	9	10	10	6	0	6	4	.270	.250	.280	3.86	5.79

Fielding

C: Centeno 12, Cerrato 31, De Hoyos 4, Encarnacion 10, Guitian 22, Ordonez 3, Palma 1. **1B:** Adrianza 24, Guitian 21, Juan 23, Ordonez 13, Salazar 1. **2B:** Blanco 1, Cerrato 1, Jimenez 1, Jimenez 31, Lora 31, Rojas 2, Severino 10. **3B:** Blanco 33, Cerrato 1, Guitian 2, Jimenez 1, Lara 12, Lora 24, Salazar 8. **SS:** Blanco 17, Lora 11, Morales 2, Pena 44, Rojas 1. **OF:** Blanco 3, Carrillo 10, Isea 12, Lopez 10, Negret 48, Palma 34, Quintero 5, Reyes 54, Reyes 17, Santana 19, Sucre 23.

Baltimore Orioles

SEASON IN A SENTENCE: Despite a down year by team star Manny Machado, the Orioles contended into September before suffering a late-season collapse, losing 19 of their last 23 games to earn a losing record and last-place finish for the first time since 2011.

HIGH POINT: Baltimore was chasing the Yankees for a wild-card spot Sept. 5 when the Yankees came to Oriole Park at Camden Yards and put up a six spot in the third inning. The Orioles rallied, however, first against CC Sabathia, and finished the comeback on Manny Machado's walk-off homer in the ninth off Dellin Betances for a 7-6 victory, leaving them one game back in the wild-card standings.

LOW POINT: Starting pitching sunk the Orioles more than anything in 2017, and a lack of depth meant lefty Wade Miley had to make 32 starts, even while leading the American League with 93 walks. He got one out Sept. 14 in a 13-5 loss at Yankee Stadium as the Orioles' fall fade continued. The club lost all five of his September starts and finished with a 4.97 overall team ERA, second-worst in the American League.

NOTABLE ROOKIES: Trey Mancini struggled defensively at times in left field, but he showed a level of offensive consistency that most rookies cannot, grinding through a full season to hit .293/.338/.488 with 27 home runs, 78 RBIs and an .826 OPS. Righthanders Miguel Castro and Gabriel Ynoa and lefty Donnie Hart all showed they can contribute to the pitching staff going forward.

KEY TRANSACTIONS: General manager Dan Duquette surprised the industry, as the Orioles were buyers rather than sellers at the trade deadline. They added middle infielder Tim Beckham from the Rays (for 2016 draftee Tobias Myers) and righthander Jeremy Hellickson from the Phillies. Beckham took over at shortstop and hit 10 homers in two streaky months; Hellickson was not the answer in the rotation, though, and posted a 6.97 ERA in 10 starts.

DOWN ON THE FARM: Outfielder Austin Hays finished tied for second in the minors with 32 homers and 12th with a .593 slugging percentage, finishing the year as the first member of the 2016 draft class to reach the major leagues. Double-A Bowie and high Class A Frederick made their league playoffs and had most of the Orioles' better prospects on hand.

OPENING DAY PAYROLL: $163,676,616 (10th)

PLAYERS OF THE YEAR

MAJOR LEAGUE

Jonathan Schoop
2B
.293/.338/.503
32 HR, 105 RBI
92 R, .211 ISO

MINOR LEAGUE

Austin Hays
OF
(High Class A/
Double-A)
.329/.365/.593

ORGANIZATION LEADERS

BATTING *Minimum 250 AB

MAJORS			
*	AVG	Trey Mancini	.306
*	OPS	Jonathan Schoop	.841
	HR	Manny Machado	33
	RBI	Jonathan Schoop	105
MINORS			
*	AVG	Austin Hays, Frederick, Bowie	.329
*	OBP	Jay Gonzalez, Bowie, Frederick	.380
*	SLG	Austin Hays, Frederick, Bowie	.593
*	OPS	Austin Hays, Frederick, Bowie	.958
	R	Ryan Mountcastle, Frederick, Bowie	81
		Austin Hays, Frederick, Bowie	81
	H	Austin Hays, Frederick, Bowie	172
	TB	Austin Hays, Frederick, Bowie	310
	2B	Ryan Mountcastle, Frederick, Bowie	48
	3B	Frank Crinella, Delmarva	7
	HR	Austin Hays, Frederick, Bowie	32
	RBI	Austin Hays, Frederick, Bowie	95
	BB	D.J. Stewart, Bowie	65
	SO	Jake Ring, Delmarva, Frederick	141
	SB	Jay Gonzalez, Bowie, Frederick	31

PITCHING #Minimum 75 IP

MAJORS			
	W	Dylan Bundy	13
#	ERA	Mychal Givens	2.75
	SO	Kevin Gausman	179
	SV	Brad Brach	18
MINORS			
	W	David Hess, Bowie	11
		Alex Wells, Delmarva	11
	L	Lucas Humpal, Delmarva	11
#	ERA	Alex Wells, Delmarva	2.38
	G	Jake Bray, Delmarva	18
	GS	David Hess, Bowie	26
		Matthias Dietz, Delmarva	26
		Ofelky Peralta, Frederick	26
	SV	Jake Bray, Delmarva	18
	IP	David Hess, Bowie	154
	BB	Ofelky Peralta, Frederick	86
	SO	John Means, Bowie	124
#	AVG	Alex Wells, Delmarva	.222

2017 PERFORMANCE

General Manager: Dan Duquette. **Farm Director:** Brian Graham. **Scouting Director:** Gary Rajsich.

Class	Team	League	W	L	PCT	Finish	Manager
Majors	Baltimore Orioles	American	75	87	.463	t-12th (15)	Buck Showalter
Triple-A	Norfolk Tides	International	66	76	.465	10th (14)	Ron Johnson
Double-A	Bowie Baysox	Eastern	72	68	.514	t-4th (12)	Gary Kendall
High-A	Frederick Keys	Carolina	68	71	.489	6th (10)	Keith Bodie
Low-A	Delmarva Shorebirds	South Atlantic	59	78	.431	13th (14)	Ryan Minor
Short Season	Aberdeen IronBirds	New York-Penn	41	34	.547	5th (14)	Kevin Bradshaw
Rookie	GCL Orioles	Gulf Coast	28	32	.467	t-12th (17)	Carlos Tosca
Overall 2017 Minor League Record			334	359	.482	22nd (30)	

ORGANIZATION STATISTICS

BALTIMORE ORIOLES

AMERICAN LEAGUE

Batting	B-T	HT	WT	DOB	AVG	vLH	vRH	G	AB	R	H	2B	3B	HR	RBI	BB	HBP	SH	SF	SO	SB	CS	SLG	OBP
Alvarez, Pedro	R-L	6-3	250	2-6-87	.313	.667	.276	14	32	4	10	1	0	1	4	2	0	0	0	10	0	0	.438	.353
Beckham, Tim	R-R	6-1	205	1-27-90	.306	.261	.318	50	216	36	66	13	2	10	26	12	2	0	0	57	1	1	.523	.348
2-team total (87 Tampa Bay)					.278	.261	.318	137	533	67	148	18	5	22	62	36	4	1	1	167	6	5	.454	.328
Castillo, Welington	R-R	5-10	220	4-24-87	.282	.344	.258	96	341	44	96	11	0	20	53	22	0	0	2	97	0	0	.490	.323
Davis, Chris	L-R	6-3	230	3-17-86	.215	.208	.218	128	456	65	98	15	1	26	61	61	3	0	4	195	1	1	.423	.309
Flaherty, Ryan	R-L	6-3	220	7-27-86	.211	.125	.233	23	38	5	8	1	0	0	4	4	1	0	0	10	0	0	.237	.302
Gentry, Craig	R-R	6-2	190	11-29-83	.257	.271	.238	77	101	17	26	5	1	2	11	11	1	3	1	24	5	4	.386	.333
Giavotella, Johnny	R-R	5-8	185	7-10-87	.100	.000	.333	7	10	0	1	0	0	0	0	0	0	0	0	4	1	0	.100	.100
Hardy, J.J.	R-R	6-1	200	8-19-82	.217	.195	.227	73	254	24	55	13	1	4	24	12	1	1	0	48	0	1	.323	.255
Hays, Austin	R-R	6-1	195	7-5-95	.217	.214	.217	20	60	4	13	3	0	1	8	2	0	0	1	16	0	0	.317	.238
Janish, Paul	R-R	6-2	200	10-12-82	.077	—	.077	14	26	0	2	0	0	0	3	1	0	1	0	6	0	0	.077	.111
Jones, Adam	R-R	6-2	215	8-1-85	.285	.260	.293	147	597	82	170	28	1	26	73	27	7	1	3	113	2	1	.466	.322
Joseph, Caleb	R-R	6-3	180	6-18-86	.256	.258	.255	89	254	31	65	14	1	8	28	10	1	1	0	72	0	0	.413	.287
Kim, Hyun Soo	R-L	6-2	210	1-12-88	.232	.125	.239	56	125	11	29	4	0	1	10	12	2	0	2	27	0	0	.288	.305
Machado, Manny	R-R	6-3	185	7-6-92	.259	.269	.255	156	630	81	163	33	1	33	95	50	1	0	9	115	9	4	.471	.310
Mancini, Trey	R-R	6-4	215	3-18-92	.293	.293	.293	147	543	65	159	26	4	24	78	33	6	0	4	139	1	0	.488	.338
Pena, Francisco	R-R	6-2	230	10-12-89	.500	.286	1.000	5	10	3	5	0	0	2	2	0	0	0	0	3	0	0	1.100	.500
Rickard, Joey	R-L	6-1	185	5-21-91	.241	.279	.209	111	261	29	63	15	0	4	19	9	4	2	1	63	8	1	.345	.276
Santander, Anthony	B-R	6-2	190	10-19-94	.267	.125	.318	13	30	1	8	3	0	0	2	0	0	0	1	8	0	0	.367	.258
Schoop, Jonathan	R-R	6-1	225	10-16-91	.293	.300	.290	160	622	92	182	35	0	32	105	35	11	0	7	142	1	0	.503	.338
Sisco, Chance	L-R	6-2	195	2-24-95	.333	.000	.462	10	18	3	6	2	0	2	4	3	1	0	0	7	0	0	.778	.455
Smith, Seth	L-L	6-3	210	9-30-82	.258	.250	.258	111	330	50	85	19	0	13	32	36	6	0	1	79	2	0	.433	.341
Tejada, Ruben	R-R	5-11	200	10-27-89	.230	.267	.217	41	113	17	26	6	0	0	5	8	2	1	0	15	0	0	.283	.293
Trumbo, Mark	R-R	6-4	225	1-16-86	.234	.272	.221	146	559	79	131	22	0	23	65	42	1	0	1	149	1	0	.397	.289
Washington, David	L-L	6-5	260	11-20-90	.000	—	.000	3	6	0	0	0	0	0	0	0	0	0	0	5	0	0	.000	.000

Pitching	B-T	HT	WT	DOB	W	L	ERA	G	GS	CG	SV	IP	H	R	ER	HR	BB	SO	AVG	vLH	vRH	K/9	BB/9
Aquino, Jayson	L-L	6-1	225	11-22-92	1	2	7.43	4	2	0	0	13	15	12	11	4	6	13	.268	.313	.250	8.78	4.05
Asher, Alec	R-R	6-4	230	10-4-91	2	5	5.25	24	6	0	0	60	61	36	35	10	23	47	.263	.220	.301	7.05	3.45
Bleier, Richard	L-L	6-3	215	4-16-87	2	1	1.99	57	0	0	0	63	62	23	14	6	13	26	.257	.235	.273	3.69	1.85
Brach, Brad	R-R	6-6	215	4-12-86	4	5	3.18	67	0	0	18	68	51	27	24	7	26	70	.208	.212	.205	9.26	3.44
Britton, Zach	L-L	6-3	195	12-22-87	2	1	2.89	38	0	0	15	37	39	12	12	1	18	29	.277	.250	.286	6.99	4.34
Bundy, Dylan	B-R	6-1	200	11-15-92	13	9	4.24	28	28	1	0	170	152	82	80	26	51	152	.240	.261	.222	8.06	2.71
Castro, Miguel	R-R	6-7	205	12-24-94	3	3	3.53	39	1	0	0	66	53	29	26	8	28	38	.224	.272	.193	5.16	3.80
Crichton, Stefan	R-R	6-3	200	2-29-92	0	0	8.03	8	0	0	0	12	26	11	11	2	4	8	.456	.455	.457	5.84	2.92
Drake, Oliver	R-R	6-4	215	1-13-87	0	0	8.10	3	0	0	0	3	6	3	3	0	3	3	.400	.125	.714	8.10	8.10
Gausman, Kevin	L-R	6-3	190	1-6-91	11	12	4.68	34	34	0	0	187	208	99	97	29	71	179	.283	.275	.288	8.63	3.42
Givens, Mychal	R-R	6-0	210	5-13-90	8	1	2.75	69	0	0	0	79	57	24	24	10	25	88	.200	.184	.209	10.07	2.86
Hart, Donnie	L-L	5-11	180	9-6-90	2	0	3.71	51	0	0	0	44	48	19	18	5	13	29	.279	.273	.284	5.98	2.68
Hellickson, Jeremy	R-R	6-1	190	4-8-87	2	6	6.97	10	10	0	0	52	49	43	40	13	17	31	.243	.243	.242	5.40	2.96
Jackson, Edwin	R-R	6-2	215	9-9-83	0	0	7.20	3	0	0	0	5	11	7	4	2	4	2	.458	.500	.429	3.60	7.20
Jimenez, Ubaldo	R-R	6-5	210	1-22-84	6	11	6.81	31	25	0	0	143	169	109	108	33	58	139	.291	.295	.288	8.77	3.66
Miley, Wade	L-L	6-0	220	11-13-86	8	15	5.61	32	32	0	0	157	179	104	98	25	93	142	.287	.230	.298	8.12	5.32
Nuno, Vidal	L-L	5-11	210	7-26-87	0	1	10.43	12	0	0	0	15	23	17	17	7	10	13	.343	.357	.333	7.98	6.14
O'Day, Darren	R-R	6-4	220	10-22-82	2	3	3.43	64	0	0	2	60	41	24	23	8	24	76	.193	.183	.200	11.34	3.58
Rodriguez, Richard	R-R	6-4	205	3-4-90	0	0	14.29	5	0	0	0	6	12	9	9	4	3	3	.444	.000	.600	4.76	4.76
Scott, Tanner	R-L	6-2	220	7-22-94	0	0	10.80	2	0	0	0	2	2	2	2	0	2	2	.286	.000	.400	10.80	10.80
Tillman, Chris	R-R	6-5	200	4-15-88	1	7	7.84	24	19	0	0	93	125	86	81	24	51	63	.324	.329	.320	6.10	4.94
Verrett, Logan	R-R	6-2	190	6-19-90	2	0	4.22	4	0	0	0	11	11	6	5	3	3	9	.275	.267	.280	7.59	2.53
Wilson, Tyler	R-R	6-2	185	9-25-89	2	2	7.04	9	1	0	0	15	22	14	12	3	4	9	.344	.250	.400	5.28	2.35
Wright, Mike	R-R	6-6	215	1-3-90	0	0	5.76	13	0	0	0	25	26	16	16	5	7	28	.265	.286	.254	10.08	2.52
Yacabonis, Jimmy	R-R	6-3	205	3-21-92	2	0	4.35	14	0	0	0	21	18	10	10	2	14	8	.247	.240	.250	3.48	6.10
Ynoa, Gabriel	R-R	6-2	205	5-26-93	2	3	4.15	9	4	0	0	35	39	17	16	5	8	26	.289	.313	.265	6.75	2.08

Fielding

Catcher	PCT	G	PO	A	E	DP	PB
Castillo	.994	88	647	42	4	9	5
Joseph	.995	79	569	27	3	0	2
Pena	.944	5	16	1	1	0	0
Sisco	1.000	10	37	1	0	0	1

First Base	PCT	G	PO	A	E	DP
Alvarez	1.000	2	11	1	0	2
Davis	.994	125	1015	80	7	122
Mancini	.990	45	285	16	3	33
Trumbo	.909	2	8	2	1	3

Second Base	PCT	G	PO	A	E	DP
Flaherty	1.000	12	6	12	0	2
Giavotella	1.000	5	2	3	0	0
Schoop	.981	159	329	446	15	132
Tejada	1.000	4	2	0	0	0

Third Base	PCT	G	PO	A	E	DP
Davis	.000	2	0	0	0	0
Flaherty	.667	5	1	1	1	0
Joseph	1.000	8	1	1	0	0
Machado	.967	156	114	297	14	37
Tejada	1.000	6	2	8	0	0
Trumbo	.000	2	0	0	0	0

Shortstop	PCT	G	PO	A	E	DP
Beckham	.961	49	73	148	9	33
Flaherty	1.000	5	7	5	0	0
Hardy	.983	71	86	200	5	48
Janish	.976	14	14	26	1	13
Schoop	1.000	5	1	14	0	3
Tejada	.983	36	37	77	2	18

Outfield	PCT	G	PO	A	E	DP
Flaherty	1.000	2	8	1	0	0
Gentry	.959	68	68	2	3	1
Hays	.903	20	28	0	3	0
Jones	.985	147	331	5	5	1
Kim	1.000	42	54	3	0	1
Mancini	.982	90	156	5	3	2
Rickard	.986	107	135	5	2	2
Santander	1.000	12	16	0	0	0
Smith	1.000	91	140	4	0	0
Trumbo	.980	31	46	3	1	0
Washington	.000	2	0	0	0	0

NORFOLK TIDES — *TRIPLE-A*

INTERNATIONAL LEAGUE

Batting	B-T	HT	WT	DOB	AVG	vLH	vRH	G	AB	R	H	2B	3B	HR	RBI	BB	HBP	SH	SF	SO	SB	CS	SLG	OBP
Alvarez, Pedro	R-L	6-3	250	2-6-87	.240	.226	.245	138	547	60	131	31	1	26	89	42	2	0	4	137	1	0	.442	.294
Andino, Robert	R-R	5-11	185	4-25-84	.234	.370	.192	49	192	25	45	7	1	6	23	13	0	0	1	52	1	0	.375	.282
Araiza, Armando	R-R	5-11	205	6-19-93	.353	.375	.333	5	17	1	6	2	0	0	2	1	0	0	0	6	0	0	.471	.389
Bourn, Michael	R-L	5-11	190	12-27-82	.220	.182	.233	11	41	8	9	0	2	0	0	10	0	0	0	8	3	0	.317	.373
Castellanos, Alex	R-R	6-0	200	8-4-86	.141	.147	.136	25	78	8	11	3	0	2	5	5	2	0	0	24	0	0	.256	.212
Choice, Michael	R-R	6-0	230	11-10-89	.039	.000	.050	10	26	1	1	1	0	0	2	5	1	0	0	9	1	0	.077	.219
Dickerson, Chris	L-L	6-4	230	4-10-82	.244	.237	.246	81	283	46	69	14	4	7	26	49	5	0	0	90	7	2	.396	.365
Dosch, Drew	L-R	6-2	200	6-24-92	.265	.219	.278	120	430	58	114	36	2	8	47	36	3	0	4	113	3	1	.414	.324
Fajardo, Daniel	R-R	6-1	170	11-19-94	.250	.000	.333	1	4	1	1	0	0	0	0	0	0	0	0	1	0	0	.250	.250
Gentry, Craig	R-R	6-2	190	11-29-83	.243	.214	.255	37	148	16	36	6	2	1	16	11	3	0	0	36	6	3	.331	.309
Giavotella, Johnny	R-R	5-8	185	7-10-87	.306	.342	.295	83	333	43	102	22	4	5	45	34	3	1	8	41	4	3	.441	.368
Hardy, J.J.	R-R	6-1	200	8-19-82	.227	.000	.294	9	22	6	5	1	0	1	3	9	0	0	0	7	0	0	.409	.452
Janish, Paul	R-R	6-2	200	10-12-82	.256	.283	.249	73	223	23	57	10	1	3	28	24	7	2	2	37	1	0	.350	.344
Johnson, Chris	R-R	6-3	225	10-1-84	.301	.333	.287	62	249	32	75	17	2	10	36	11	1	0	3	75	1	0	.506	.330
Montero, Jesus	R-R	6-3	235	11-28-89	.143	.105	.167	13	49	1	7	1	0	0	3	2	0	0	0	14	0	1	.163	.177
Nathans, Tucker	R-L	6-0	200	11-6-88	.000	—	.000	1	1	0	0	0	0	0	0	0	0	0	0	0	0	0	.000	.000
O'Brien, Chris	B-R	5-11	225	7-24-89	.200	.000	.250	3	5	0	1	1	0	0	0	2	0	0	0	2	0	0	.400	.429
Pena, Francisco	R-R	6-2	230	10-12-89	.278	.311	.255	51	180	15	50	13	0	6	18	8	0	0	0	31	1	0	.450	.309
Perez, Audry	R-R	5-10	220	12-23-88	.200	.286	.000	4	10	0	2	1	0	0	0	0	0	0	0	0	0	0	.300	.200
Rickard, Joey	R-L	6-1	185	5-21-91	.192	.143	.212	13	47	8	9	1	0	1	4	11	0	0	0	9	0	0	.277	.345
Sardinas, Luis	B-R	6-1	180	5-16-93	.319	.264	.341	83	310	34	99	10	3	5	30	12	2	6	1	39	6	4	.419	.348
Schafer, Logan	L-L	6-1	200	9-8-86	.247	.209	.260	113	364	40	90	14	6	3	33	35	2	14	4	64	5	3	.343	.314
Schoop, Sharlon	R-R	6-2	190	4-15-87	.193	.167	.212	26	88	11	17	6	0	5	6	5	2	0	0	19	0	0	.432	.253
Sisco, Chance	L-R	6-2	195	2-24-95	.267	.231	.276	97	344	47	92	23	0	7	47	32	8	0	4	99	2	2	.395	.340
Tejada, Ruben	R-R	5-11	200	10-27-89	.311	.308	.313	13	45	9	14	3	0	0	2	4	2	0	0	4	0	0	.378	.392
2-team total (37 Scranton/Wilkes-Barre)					.280	.308	.313	50	175	31	49	10	0	6	23	19	3	0	2	21	0	2	.440	.357
Urrutia, Henry	L-R	6-5	200	2-13-87	.175	.067	.208	20	63	5	11	2	0	1	4	6	0	0	1	21	0	0	.254	.243
Walker, Adam Brett	R-R	6-5	225	10-18-91	.090	.148	.050	18	67	3	6	2	0	1	3	0	0	0	0	26	0	0	.164	.090
3-team total (10 Gwinnett, 25 Louisville)					.152	.148	.050	53	198	17	30	9	1	5	22	11	2	0	2	76	3	0	.283	.202
Washington, David	L-L	6-5	260	11-20-90	.264	.217	.282	102	368	49	97	23	1	18	42	27	1	0	1	137	7	3	.478	.315
Yastrzemski, Mike	L-L	5-11	180	8-23-90	.240	.171	.264	81	271	41	65	15	3	9	41	31	3	0	2	74	2	1	.417	.323

Pitching	B-T	HT	WT	DOB	W	L	ERA	G	GS	CG	SV	IP	H	R	ER	HR	BB	SO	AVG	vLH	vRH	K/9	BB/9
Aquino, Jayson	L-L	6-1	225	11-22-92	3	10	4.24	21	21	0	0	115	125	63	54	11	41	89	.277	.297	.269	6.99	3.22
Asher, Alec	R-R	6-4	230	10-4-91	3	3	4.65	10	10	0	0	50	62	26	26	6	15	36	.301	.310	.289	6.44	2.68
Barker, Brandon	R-R	6-3	210	8-20-92	0	0	0.00	1	1	0	0	5	4	1	0	0	1	6	.211	.267	.000	10.80	1.80
Berry, Tim	L-L	6-3	180	3-18-91	0	0	1.80	3	0	0	0	5	2	1	1	0	4	6	.118	.000	.222	10.80	7.20
Bleier, Richard	L-L	6-3	215	4-16-87	0	0	0.61	8	0	0	1	15	9	3	1	0	0	15	.173	.111	.206	9.20	0.00
Bradley, Jed	L-L	6-3	225	6-12-90	1	0	0.00	1	0	0	0	2	2	0	0	0	1	1	.286	.500	.200	4.50	4.50
Bridwell, Parker	R-R	6-4	185	8-2-91	0	0	18.00	2	0	0	0	4	10	8	8	3	1	6	.476	.556	.417	13.50	2.25
Bundy, Bobby	R-R	6-2	215	1-13-90	0	0	0.00	1	0	0	0	2	1	0	0	0	2	1	.167	.250	.000	4.50	9.00
Crichton, Stefan	R-R	6-3	200	2-29-92	7	2	3.02	29	0	0	2	48	47	16	16	2	11	50	.247	.247	.248	9.44	2.08
Faulkner, Andrew	R-L	6-3	205	9-12-92	3	0	2.79	34	0	0	0	39	30	13	12	1	24	35	.216	.208	.224	8.15	5.59
Fry, Paul	L-L	6-0	190	7-26-92	3	2	4.66	25	3	0	0	46	47	29	24	6	26	53	.264	.265	.264	10.29	5.05
Hart, Donnie	L-L	5-11	180	9-6-90	1	0	2.35	13	0	0	0	15	17	4	4	1	2	20	.283	.300	.267	11.74	1.17
Jackson, Edwin	R-R	6-2	215	9-9-83	0	0	3.10	12	1	0	2	20	20	7	7	1	10	17	.278	.316	.264	7.52	4.43
2-team total (5 Syracuse)					2	0	1.77	17	5	0	2	41	29	8	8	1	20	39	.206	.316	.264	8.63	4.43
Johnson, Steve	R-R	6-1	220	8-31-87	1	2	5.30	19	5	0	0	37	40	22	22	4	14	39	.278	.307	.256	9.40	3.38
2-team total (5 Charlotte)					2	4	6.44	24	10	0	0	59	64	42	42	10	23	60	.282	.306	.256	9.20	3.53
Kipper, Jordan	R-R	6-4	185	10-6-92	3	5	5.07	12	11	1	0	60	89	40	34	4	18	26	.352	.320	.382	3.88	2.69
Lee, Chris	L-L	6-3	180	8-17-92	5	6	5.11	27	20	0	0	116	144	76	66	11	54	83	.302	.285	.309	6.42	4.18
Luetge, Lucas	L-L	6-4	205	3-24-87	1	0	4.50	4	0	0	0	4	3	2	2	1	3	3	.200	.143	.250	6.75	6.75
2-team total (20 Louisville)					2	2	4.55	24	0	0	0	32	37	19	16	5	12	33	.291	.143	.250	9.38	3.41

Magnifico, Damien	R-R	6-1	195	5-24-91	1	0	9.95	5	0	0	0	6	13	8	7	0	3	5	.433	.467	.400	7.11	4.26
Martis, Shairon	R-R	6-1	225	3-30-87	0	1	4.38	8	0	0	0	12	16	7	6	3	4	8	.314	.381	.267	5.84	2.92
McGough, Scott	R-R	5-11	190	10-31-89	2	1	3.86	13	0	0	0	23	28	14	10	2	13	25	.292	.282	.298	9.64	5.01
Nuno, Vidal	L-L	5-11	210	7-26-87	1	3	4.05	19	0	0	0	27	24	12	12	1	7	30	.233	.212	.243	10.13	2.36
Rodriguez, Richard	R-R	6-4	205	3-4-90	4	4	2.42	42	1	0	10	71	56	20	19	5	18	80	.216	.215	.217	10.19	2.29
Stewart, Zach	R-R	6-2	205	9-28-86	0	3	7.41	7	3	0	0	17	20	15	14	4	10	13	.294	.250	.344	6.88	5.29
Tillman, Chris	R-R	6-5	200	4-15-88	0	1	9.00	1	1	0	0	5	5	5	5	4	2	6	.263	.375	.182	10.80	3.60
Verrett, Logan	R-R	6-2	190	6-19-90	2	6	5.10	40	2	0	5	60	56	40	34	9	22	49	.242	.230	.252	7.35	3.30
Wheeler, Jason	L-L	6-6	255	10-27-90	1	2	3.07	13	6	0	1	41	37	15	14	5	11	33	.240	.242	.239	7.24	2.41
2-team total (8 Rochester)					5	3	3.81	21	13	0	1	85	84	40	36	10	21	70	.257	.242	.239	7.41	2.22
Wilson, Tyler	R-R	6-2	185	9-25-89	7	8	4.74	20	20	0	0	114	128	64	60	10	35	68	.283	.298	.270	5.37	2.76
Wotherspoon, Matt	R-R	6-2	215	10-6-91	3	1	2.20	17	0	0	0	29	21	7	7	3	15	34	.202	.302	.131	10.67	4.71
2-team total (6 Scranton/Wilkes-Barre)					4	1	2.21	23	1	0	1	41	31	10	10	3	18	46	.211	.302	.131	10.18	3.98
Wright, Mike	R-R	6-6	215	1-3-90	4	6	3.69	16	16	1	0	83	81	41	34	6	26	71	.251	.277	.226	7.70	2.82
Yacabonis, Jimmy	R-R	6-3	205	3-21-92	4	0	1.32	41	0	0	11	61	30	9	9	0	28	48	.144	.143	.145	7.04	4.11
Ynoa, Gabriel	R-R	6-2	205	5-26-93	6	9	5.25	21	21	0	0	106	129	69	62	8	24	72	.297	.287	.305	6.09	2.03

Fielding

Catcher	PCT	G	PO	A	E	DP	PB
Araiza	1.000	5	32	2	0	0	0
Fajardo	.923	1	11	1	1	1	0
O'Brien	1.000	2	9	1	0	0	0
Pena	.991	44	299	26	3	0	3
Perez	1.000	3	24	0	0	0	0
Sisco	.987	94	677	32	9	3	4

First Base	PCT	G	PO	A	E	DP
Alvarez	.991	52	392	38	4	43
Castellanos	1.000	2	18	0	0	4
Johnson	1.000	13	97	3	0	9
Montero	1.000	6	35	2	0	2
Pena	1.000	5	28	2	0	0
Washington	.988	71	543	38	7	56

Second Base	PCT	G	PO	A	E	DP
Andino	.958	30	49	89	6	19
Castellanos	1.000	1	1	2	0	1
Giavotella	.987	43	93	128	3	25
Johnson	.961	13	16	33	2	6
Sardinas	.965	46	80	115	7	33
Schoop	.967	12	22	37	2	6
Tejada	.750	3	2	1	1	1

Third Base	PCT	G	PO	A	E	DP
Andino	1.000	1	1	0	0	0
Castellanos	.929	11	4	22	2	5
Dosch	.916	104	69	181	23	15
Giavotella	1.000	4	4	7	0	0
Johnson	.882	18	14	31	6	2
Sardinas	.800	3	1	3	1	0
Schoop	1.000	5	4	12	0	0
Tejada	1.000	4	1	8	0	0

Shortstop	PCT	G	PO	A	E	DP
Andino	.967	15	17	41	2	6
Hardy	.966	8	10	18	1	4
Janish	.976	73	118	207	8	42
Sardinas	.963	36	46	85	5	15
Schoop	.929	9	20	32	4	9
Tejada	1.000	10	6	19	0	4

Outfield	PCT	G	PO	A	E	DP
Alvarez	.972	42	65	4	2	1
Bourn	1.000	11	20	0	0	0
Castellanos	.947	10	18	0	1	0
Choice	.933	10	14	0	1	0
Dickerson	.963	68	151	7	6	0
Gentry	.989	37	89	5	1	2
Giavotella	1.000	6	9	0	0	0
Johnson	.875	2	6	1	1	0
Nathans	.000	1	0	0	0	0
Rickard	1.000	13	28	0	0	0
Sardinas	1.000	1	1	0	0	0
Schafer	.978	111	254	11	6	1
Urrutia	1.000	13	21	2	0	0
Walker	.967	18	27	2	1	1
Washington	1.000	26	41	0	0	0
Yastrzemski	.994	73	159	6	1	1

BOWIE BAYSOX — *DOUBLE-A*

EASTERN LEAGUE

Batting	B-T	HT	WT	DOB	AVG	vLH	vRH	G	AB	R	H	2B	3B	HR	RBI	BB	HBP	SH	SF	SO	SB	CS	SLG	OBP
Araiza, Armando	R-R	5-11	205	6-19-93	.267	.000	.571	4	15	1	4	1	0	0	2	3	0	0	0	4	0	0	.333	.389
Billingsley, Cole	L-L	5-10	165	5-29-94	.500	1.000	.333	3	4	0	2	0	0	0	0	1	0	0	0	0	0	0	.500	.600
Castillo, Welington	R-R	5-10	220	4-24-87	.200	.500	.125	4	10	0	2	0	0	0	0	1	1	0	0	2	0	0	.200	.333
Coyle, Sean	R-R	5-8	175	1-17-92	.187	.238	.163	42	134	15	25	11	1	1	8	16	0	0	0	36	2	4	.306	.273
Davis, Glynn	R-R	6-3	170	12-7-91	.235	.184	.267	28	98	9	23	5	1	1	6	4	1	1	0	24	1	2	.337	.272
Dosch, Drew	L-R	6-2	200	6-24-92	.424	.667	.400	9	33	6	14	3	1	0	9	5	1	1	0	7	1	0	.576	.513
Flaherty, Ryan	R-L	6-3	220	7-27-86	.395	.375	.409	12	38	18	15	3	0	2	6	10	1	0	0	3	0	0	.632	.531
Gassaway, Randolph	R-R	6-4	210	5-23-95	.185	.200	.182	9	27	4	5	0	0	0	3	5	0	0	0	2	0	0	.185	.313
Gonzalez, Jay	L-L	5-9	170	12-11-91	.284	.281	.284	44	134	21	38	7	3	0	10	27	0	3	3	33	13	3	.381	.396
Hays, Austin	R-R	6-1	195	7-5-95	.330	.432	.289	64	261	39	86	17	2	16	54	13	4	2	3	45	1	1	.594	.367
Kemp, Jeff	R-R	6-0	190	3-23-90	.256	.231	.269	22	78	8	20	2	0	2	8	9	0	1	1	23	1	0	.359	.330
Marin, Adrian	R-R	6-0	180	3-8-94	.266	.316	.243	110	433	58	115	23	3	2	38	26	2	6	3	90	8	1	.346	.308
Mercedes, Yermin	R-R	5-11	175	2-14-93	.296	.333	.281	12	44	5	13	3	0	1	7	2	0	0	0	8	1	0	.432	.326
Mountcastle, Ryan	R-R	6-3	195	2-18-97	.222	.302	.180	39	153	18	34	13	0	3	15	3	1	0	2	35	0	0	.366	.239
Mullins, Cedric	B-L	5-8	175	10-1-94	.265	.208	.293	76	309	53	82	19	1	13	37	27	0	4	6	58	9	7	.460	.319
Nathans, Tucker	R-L	6-0	200	11-6-88	.284	.231	.307	24	88	11	25	3	0	3	10	2	1	0	0	25	1	0	.421	.308
O'Brien, Chris	B-R	5-11	225	7-24-89	.203	.333	.151	23	74	9	15	2	0	2	8	13	2	0	1	19	0	0	.311	.333
Perez, Audry	R-R	5-10	220	12-23-88	.301	.345	.282	50	193	22	58	17	0	2	22	9	1	0	1	30	0	0	.420	.333
Rodriguez, Aderlin	R-R	6-3	210	11-18-91	.279	.303	.268	125	484	61	135	25	1	22	76	43	5	0	4	102	0	0	.471	.341
Rosa, Garabez	R-R	6-2	166	10-12-89	.310	.340	.297	124	523	75	162	24	2	14	91	17	2	0	2	98	1	5	.444	.333
Salcedo, Erick	B-R	5-10	155	6-28-93	.260	.276	.253	121	408	46	106	16	1	5	47	35	3	10	4	50	2	5	.341	.320
Santander, Anthony	B-R	6-2	190	10-19-94	.380	.278	.438	15	50	13	19	5	0	5	14	7	1	0	1	9	0	0	.780	.458
Schoop, Sharlon	R-R	6-2	190	4-15-87	.348	.222	.429	8	23	4	8	0	1	0	4	3	0	0	0	3	0	0	.435	.423
Stewart, D.J.	L-R	6-0	230	11-30-93	.278	.291	.272	126	457	80	127	26	2	21	79	65	12	0	6	87	20	4	.481	.378
Walker, Adam Brett	R-R	6-5	225	10-18-91	.426	.522	.333	12	47	13	20	5	0	6	12	2	0	0	0	13	0	1	.915	.449
Wilkerson, Steve	B-R	6-1	195	1-11-92	.294	.288	.296	71	245	34	72	13	0	6	30	20	4	2	2	53	5	2	.420	.354
Wynns, Austin	R-R	6-2	205	12-10-90	.281	.271	.286	105	370	54	104	19	1	10	46	52	7	2	3	64	1	0	.419	.377
Yastrzemski, Mike	L-L	5-11	180	8-23-90	.386	.500	.362	20	83	20	32	6	1	6	19	9	0	0	2	17	1	1	.699	.436

Pitching	B-T	HT	WT	DOB	W	L	ERA	G	GS	CG	SV	IP	H	R	ER	HR	BB	SO	AVG	vLH	vRH	K/9	BB/9
Barker, Brandon	R-R	6-3	210	8-20-92	7	5	4.67	25	14	0	0	118	128	65	61	10	44	103	.280	.274	.285	7.88	3.37
Berry, Tim	L-L	6-3	180	3-18-91	4	1	3.45	33	0	0	4	44	44	18	17	1	36	52	.265	.226	.289	10.56	7.31

Bradley, Jed	L-L	6-3	225	6-12-90	0	2	11.70	7	0	0	0	10	16	13	13	3	5	8	.356	.389	.333	7.20	4.50
Britton, Zach	L-L	6-3	195	12-22-87	0	0	4.91	4	0	0	0	4	4	2	2	1	2	5	.267	.400	.200	12.27	4.91
Bundy, Bobby	R-R	6-2	215	1-13-90	1	1	8.18	9	0	0	0	11	20	10	10	0	4	11	.400	.409	.393	9.00	3.27
Castro, Miguel	R-R	6-7	205	12-24-94	3	0	4.44	6	0	0	0	24	23	13	12	1	6	11	.258	.171	.315	4.07	2.22
Cleavinger, Garrett	R-L	6-1	210	4-23-94	2	4	6.28	27	0	0	3	39	38	29	27	4	23	42	.245	.245	.245	9.78	5.35
2-team total (11 Reading)					2	5	6.00	38	0	0	4	54	57	42	36	5	32	59	.265	.245	.245	9.83	5.33
Fry, Paul	L-L	6-0	190	7-26-92	0	0	0.75	7	0	0	1	12	7	1	1	0	5	18	.171	.125	.235	13.50	3.75
Garcia, Jason	R-R	6-0	185	11-21-92	6	4	5.26	38	0	0	0	75	85	47	44	6	40	74	.283	.323	.253	8.84	4.78
Grimes, Matthew	R-R	6-5	185	9-4-91	4	8	5.40	17	15	0	0	85	100	55	51	17	32	53	.297	.273	.318	5.61	3.39
Hernandez, Jefri	R-R	6-2	210	4-27-91	1	3	3.47	30	0	0	2	49	56	21	19	10	17	37	.295	.301	.289	6.75	3.10
Hess, David	R-R	6-2	180	7-10-93	11	9	3.85	27	26	0	0	154	137	75	66	16	53	123	.235	.263	.206	7.17	3.09
Keller, Jon	R-R	6-5	210	8-8-92	0	1	22.50	5	0	0	0	4	8	10	10	1	11	2	.421	.636	.125	4.50	24.75
Kipper, Jordan	R-R	6-4	185	10-6-92	2	1	3.29	9	3	0	0	41	47	16	15	5	11	22	.299	.309	.292	4.83	2.41
Lazo, Raudel	L-L	5-9	180	4-12-89	0	1	4.35	8	0	0	0	10	9	5	5	2	3	9	.243	.188	.286	7.84	2.61
Liranzo, Jesus	R-R	6-2	175	3-7-95	3	4	4.85	31	12	0	2	65	54	36	35	12	43	75	.224	.242	.207	10.38	5.95
Long, Lucas	R-R	6-0	195	10-7-92	9	6	2.95	31	14	2	5	128	124	45	42	7	33	106	.256	.323	.194	7.43	2.31
McGough, Scott	R-R	5-11	190	10-31-89	1	3	1.95	27	0	0	13	32	34	14	7	2	8	36	.266	.333	.211	10.02	2.23
Means, John	L-L	6-3	230	4-24-93	9	9	4.11	26	24	0	0	142	158	77	65	16	36	124	.274	.244	.287	7.84	2.28
Meisinger, Ryan	R-R	6-4	235	5-4-94	4	3	3.00	41	0	0	6	63	55	24	21	2	21	67	.232	.271	.200	9.57	3.00
Ramirez, Yefry	R-R	6-2	215	11-28-93	5	0	3.66	6	6	1	0	32	27	13	13	6	11	26	.241	.290	.180	7.31	3.09
2-team total (18 Trenton)					15	3	3.47	24	24	3	0	124	105	51	48	15	49	117	.232	.290	.180	8.47	3.55
Scott, Tanner	R-L	6-2	220	7-22-94	0	2	2.22	24	24	0	0	69	45	17	17	2	46	87	.188	.171	.195	11.35	6.00
Tillman, Chris	R-R	6-5	200	4-15-88	0	1	5.68	2	2	0	0	6	7	4	4	2	1	6	.280	.353	.125	8.53	1.42

Fielding

Catcher	PCT	G	PO	A	E	DP	PB
Araiza	.969	4	29	2	1	0	0
Castillo	1.000	2	8	1	0	0	0
Mercedes	.974	6	32	6	1	1	1
O'Brien	.978	7	41	4	1	0	0
Perez	1.000	34	240	18	0	3	3
Wynns	.998	92	740	63	2	3	5

First Base	PCT	G	PO	A	E	DP
O'Brien	1.000	3	18	0	0	2
Rodriguez	.988	105	815	38	10	84
Rosa	.980	32	225	21	5	26
Schoop	1.000	1	5	0	0	0
Wilkerson	1.000	1	7	0	0	1

Second Base	PCT	G	PO	A	E	DP
Coyle	1.000	14	32	34	0	10
Flaherty	1.000	4	6	8	0	4
Kemp	1.000	3	1	8	0	2
Marin	.977	72	82	178	6	35
Rosa	1.000	2	2	7	0	2
Salcedo	.987	19	32	45	1	16
Schoop	1.000	4	5	7	0	1
Wilkerson	.976	28	55	67	3	11

Third Base	PCT	G	PO	A	E	DP
Coyle	.957	11	6	16	1	1
Dosch	.926	9	8	17	2	1
Flaherty	1.000	4	0	3	0	3
Kemp	.976	17	10	31	1	4
Marin	.500	1	1	2	3	0
Mountcastle	.937	37	35	54	6	7
Rosa	.983	27	13	46	1	7
Schoop	.750	3	2	1	1	0
Wilkerson	.949	37	32	61	5	1

Shortstop	PCT	G	PO	A	E	DP
Flaherty	.909	2	5	5	1	2
Marin	.966	37	51	90	5	24
Salcedo	.966	104	149	246	14	54

Outfield	PCT	G	PO	A	E	DP
Billingsley	1.000	1	6	0	0	0
Davis	.984	28	60	1	1	1
Flaherty	1.000	1	4	0	0	0
Gassaway	1.000	6	18	0	0	0
Gonzalez	.987	44	74	4	1	0
Hays	.969	60	120	4	4	0
Mullins	1.000	72	196	3	0	1
Nathans	.962	12	25	0	1	0
Rosa	.969	56	117	6	4	3
Santander	1.000	10	10	1	0	0
Stewart	.988	116	238	6	3	0
Walker	1.000	3	4	0	0	0
Wilkerson	1.000	3	4	1	0	0
Yastrzemski	.976	18	39	1	1	0

FREDERICK KEYS — *HIGH CLASS A*

CAROLINA LEAGUE

Batting	B-T	HT	WT	DOB	AVG	vLH	vRH	G	AB	R	H	2B	3B	HR	RBI	BB	HBP	SH	SF	SO	SB	CS	SLG	OBP
Andujar, Ricardo	L-R	6-0	160	8-6-92	.250	.308	.234	82	236	39	59	13	2	2	20	16	7	7	1	54	5	4	.348	.315
Araiza, Armando	R-R	5-11	205	6-19-93	.238	.354	.208	71	240	28	57	11	0	9	41	25	3	1	1	72	1	0	.396	.316
Becker, Branden	L-R	6-1	175	9-13-96	.167	.000	.250	2	6	0	1	0	0	0	0	0	0	0	0	2	0	0	.167	.167
Clare, Chris	R-R	6-2	175	11-24-94	.260	.259	.260	42	127	19	33	2	0	2	9	19	3	1	2	26	3	1	.323	.364
Copeland, Garrett	B-R	5-11	190	2-22-95	.000	—	.000	1	4	1	0	0	0	0	0	0	0	0	0	1	0	0	.000	.000
Davis, Chris	L-R	6-3	230	3-17-86	.250	.000	.333	1	4	1	1	1	0	0	0	1	0	0	0	2	0	0	.500	.400
Davis, Glynn	R-R	6-3	170	12-7-91	.265	.295	.254	64	230	31	61	16	2	3	31	16	0	3	6	55	8	3	.391	.306
Fajardo, Daniel	R-R	6-1	170	11-19-94	.154	.200	.125	4	13	0	2	0	0	0	0	0	0	0	0	4	0	0	.154	.154
Flaherty, Ryan	R-L	6-3	220	7-27-86	.154	.000	.222	4	13	2	2	0	0	0	0	5	1	0	0	3	0	0	.154	.421
Gassaway, Randolph	R-R	6-4	210	5-23-95	.265	.287	.256	114	431	48	114	19	1	5	58	23	3	0	5	82	3	3	.348	.303
Gonzalez, Jay	L-L	5-9	170	12-11-91	.265	.256	.268	51	185	28	49	9	2	0	11	30	0	3	0	51	18	6	.335	.367
Hart, Josh	L-L	6-1	180	10-2-94	.263	.240	.273	25	80	9	21	9	0	1	7	6	2	0	0	24	2	1	.413	.330
Hays, Austin	R-R	6-1	195	7-5-95	.328	.390	.303	64	262	42	86	15	3	16	41	12	4	0	2	40	4	6	.592	.364
Hoelscher, Shane	R-R	6-0	195	9-21-91	.248	.333	.216	87	314	39	78	15	0	6	39	27	2	1	3	66	2	3	.354	.309
Jones, Markel	B-R	5-10	175	8-8-94	.000	.000	.000	5	9	0	0	0	0	0	0	2	0	0	0	5	0	0	.000	.182
Laurino, Steve	R-L	6-3	215	1-5-93	.190	.207	.179	49	153	12	29	5	0	3	17	12	2	2	1	48	0	1	.281	.256
Levy, Stuart	R-R	6-2	185	8-21-92	.246	.344	.211	39	122	14	30	11	0	2	19	15	3	2	0	27	2	2	.385	.343
Mercedes, Yermin	R-R	5-11	175	2-14-93	.274	.263	.278	98	336	48	92	17	0	15	55	33	4	0	5	59	4	3	.458	.341
Mountcastle, Ryan	R-R	6-3	195	2-18-97	.314	.376	.287	88	360	63	113	35	1	15	47	14	3	0	2	61	8	2	.542	.343
Murphy, Alex	R-R	5-11	210	10-5-94	.239	.266	.226	90	306	41	73	21	0	11	38	36	7	0	0	85	2	1	.415	.332
Perez, Brallan	R-R	5-10	165	1-27-96	.368	.375	.366	19	57	13	21	2	1	1	4	7	2	1	0	2	1	1	.491	.455
2-team total (46 Down East)					.270	.375	.366	65	215	29	58	4	1	2	12	22	4	4	0	23	9	6	.326	.349
Reyes, Jomar	R-R	6-3	220	2-20-97	.302	.356	.285	50	182	28	55	10	1	4	21	8	1	1	1	31	1	0	.434	.333
Rifaela, Ademar	L-L	5-10	180	11-20-94	.284	.265	.292	126	450	73	128	23	1	24	78	41	12	2	3	124	7	5	.500	.358
Ring, Jake	L-L	5-11	175	8-11-94	.125	.000	.167	3	8	1	1	0	0	1	2	1	1	0	0	1	1	0	.500	.300
Santander, Anthony	B-R	6-2	190	10-19-94	.400	.500	.000	1	5	0	2	0	0	0	0	0	0	0	0	1	0	0	.400	.400

	B-T	HT	WT	DOB	AVG	vLH	vRH	G	AB	R	H	2B	3B	HR	RBI	BB	HBP	SH	SF	SO	SB	CS	SLG	OBP
Turbin, Drew	L-R	5-11	200	4-24-93	.190	.267	.160	80	216	24	41	5	1	4	18	21	9	3	0	59	1	0	.278	.289
Wilkerson, Steve	B-R	6-1	195	1-11-92	.323	.373	.298	41	155	29	50	10	0	2	15	19	3	3	0	40	2	3	.426	.407

Pitching	B-T	HT	WT	DOB	W	L	ERA	G	GS	CG	SV	IP	H	R	ER	HR	BB	SO	AVG	vLH	vRH	K/9	BB/9
Akin, Keegan	L-L	6-0	225	4-1-95	7	8	4.14	21	21	0	0	100	89	50	46	12	46	111	.240	.269	.230	9.99	4.14
Alcantara, Mario	R-R	6-2	225	12-27-92	0	1	6.23	13	0	0	0	17	14	13	12	4	12	25	.219	.226	.212	12.98	6.23
Alvarado, Cristian	R-R	6-3	175	9-20-94	7	9	5.00	26	25	3	0	140	162	85	78	16	22	109	.286	.294	.278	6.99	1.41
Britton, Zach	L-L	6-3	195	12-22-87	0	0	0.00	2	0	0	0	2	1	0	0	0	1	2	.143	.333	.000	9.00	4.50
Bundy, Bobby	R-R	6-2	215	1-13-90	1	0	6.00	1	0	0	0	3	3	2	2	1	0	2	.250	.250	.250	6.00	0.00
Burke, Mike	R-R	6-2	200	8-27-92	4	1	3.88	32	0	0	3	60	46	28	26	9	21	56	.212	.221	.205	8.35	3.13
Chleborad, Tanner	R-R	6-6	185	11-4-92	1	4	3.29	37	0	0	17	52	57	25	19	2	19	47	.288	.276	.295	8.13	3.29
Flaa, Jay	R-R	6-3	225	6-10-92	4	3	3.29	38	0	0	4	55	37	21	20	2	36	78	.197	.187	.204	12.84	5.93
Gonzalez, Brian	R-L	6-3	230	10-25-95	5	7	4.91	21	21	1	0	106	132	65	58	9	52	85	.306	.328	.296	7.19	4.40
Gonzalez, Luis	L-L	6-2	170	1-17-92	6	2	2.47	36	0	0	5	62	39	22	17	3	24	75	.173	.241	.130	10.89	3.48
Grimes, Matthew	R-R	6-5	185	9-4-91	1	2	3.66	5	5	0	0	20	18	8	8	4	3	23	.250	.214	.300	10.53	1.37
Hernandez, Jefri	R-R	6-2	210	4-27-91	3	0	0.48	8	0	0	3	19	15	2	1	0	5	15	.221	.211	.233	7.23	2.41
Horacek, Mitch	L-L	6-5	185	12-3-91	5	3	3.88	32	0	0	0	53	58	26	23	8	24	68	.270	.235	.299	11.48	4.05
Jimenez, Francisco	R-R	6-1	160	10-4-94	1	0	0.00	1	0	0	0	4	3	0	0	0	0	3	.231	.200	.250	7.36	0.00
Jones, Cory	R-R	6-5	225	9-20-91	1	0	3.00	2	0	0	0	6	4	2	2	0	2	4	.182	.154	.222	6.00	3.00
Katz, Alex	L-L	5-11	195	10-12-94	3	2	5.57	25	0	0	0	42	43	30	26	3	35	34	.267	.233	.287	7.29	7.50
Keller, Jon	R-R	6-5	210	8-8-92	0	1	7.04	9	0	0	1	15	22	16	12	0	9	9	.344	.333	.351	5.28	5.28
Love, Reid	R-L	5-11	195	5-15-92	6	4	3.71	24	16	0	0	107	120	53	44	8	24	81	.286	.246	.306	6.83	2.03
McGranahan, Zeke	R-R	6-4	215	1-3-91	3	0	3.08	17	0	0	1	26	20	13	9	0	21	26	.211	.182	.235	8.89	7.18
Peralta, Ofelky	R-R	6-5	195	4-20-97	2	10	5.42	26	26	0	0	105	109	71	63	8	86	95	.269	.277	.263	8.17	7.39
Romero, Franderlin	R-R	6-1	190	2-21-93	1	6	5.44	16	4	0	0	45	48	33	27	6	23	38	.274	.257	.287	7.66	4.63
Sedlock, Cody	R-R	6-3	190	6-19-95	4	5	5.90	20	20	0	0	90	119	66	59	11	36	69	.313	.287	.339	6.90	3.60
Tillman, Chris	R-R	6-5	200	4-15-88	0	1	7.20	1	1	0	0	5	8	6	4	1	1	2	.364	.313	.500	3.60	1.80
Triana, Karl	R-R	6-0	180	10-7-92	2	2	5.95	10	0	0	0	20	24	14	13	4	10	22	.293	.360	.263	10.07	4.58
Turnipseed, Christian	R-R	5-11	214	5-30-92	1	0	4.15	7	0	0	2	13	8	6	6	0	11	13	.191	.118	.240	9.00	7.62

Fielding

Catcher	PCT	G	PO	A	E	DP	PB
Araiza	.996	65	501	62	2	4	14
Fajardo	.975	4	31	8	1	2	1
Levy	.990	34	265	38	3	4	4
Mercedes	.983	35	254	32	5	2	5
Murphy	.958	4	22	1	1	0	1

First Base	PCT	G	PO	A	E	DP
Araiza	1.000	2	6	0	0	1
Davis	1.000	1	13	0	0	2
Flaherty	1.000	1	1	0	0	1
Hoelscher	.987	19	142	10	2	15
Laurino	.997	43	281	13	1	31
Mercedes	.991	14	98	13	1	8
Murphy	.988	63	456	25	6	38
Wilkerson	1.000	2	11	2	0	2

Second Base	PCT	G	PO	A	E	DP
Andujar	.968	39	62	88	5	18
Copeland	1.000	1	2	2	0	0
Flaherty	1.000	1	7	1	0	1
Perez	.928	16	32	45	6	10
Turbin	.967	69	104	159	9	38
Wilkerson	.972	26	42	63	3	15

Third Base	PCT	G	PO	A	E	DP
Andujar	.871	18	10	17	4	1
Becker	.000	1	0	0	0	0
Clare	1.000	1	0	1	0	0
Flaherty	1.000	1	0	3	0	0
Hoelscher	.928	65	44	110	12	13
Perez	.875	1	3	4	1	1
Reyes	.899	47	37	79	13	7
Wilkerson	.950	8	5	14	1	3

Shortstop	PCT	G	PO	A	E	DP
Andujar	.932	19	32	36	5	6
Becker	1.000	1	2	2	0	2
Clare	.951	39	62	75	7	22
Flaherty	1.000	1	0	1	0	0
Mountcastle	.954	82	117	151	13	37
Perez	1.000	1	2	2	0	1
Wilkerson	.000	1	0	0	1	0

Outfield	PCT	G	PO	A	E	DP
Andujar	1.000	7	6	0	0	0
Davis	.987	59	140	7	2	2
Gassaway	.957	105	171	8	8	2
Gonzalez	.979	45	87	6	2	2
Hart	1.000	25	53	1	0	0
Hays	.994	61	154	4	1	1
Jones	1.000	5	1	0	0	0
Mercedes	1.000	2	1	0	0	0
Rifaela	.985	110	193	3	3	0
Ring	1.000	3	5	0	0	0
Santander	.000	1	0	0	0	0
Wilkerson	1.000	7	3	2	0	1

DELMARVA SHOREBIRDS — LOW CLASS A

SOUTH ATLANTIC LEAGUE

Batting	B-T	HT	WT	DOB	AVG	vLH	vRH	G	AB	R	H	2B	3B	HR	RBI	BB	HBP	SH	SF	SO	SB	CS	SLG	OBP
Billingsley, Cole	L-L	5-10	165	5-29-94	.282	.310	.273	120	461	66	130	24	3	3	31	44	6	5	5	97	27	12	.367	.349
Carrillo, Jean	R-R	6-0	200	6-16-97	.667	.667	—	1	3	0	2	0	0	0	0	0	0	0	0	1	0	0	.667	.667
Clare, Chris	R-R	6-2	175	11-24-94	.242	.225	.249	82	302	38	73	13	2	2	38	40	12	0	1	62	2	1	.318	.352
Crinella, Frank	R-R	5-11	188	6-9-94	.210	.167	.231	85	291	33	61	7	7	1	24	16	5	0	1	82	5	5	.292	.262
Davis, Chris	L-R	6-3	230	3-17-86	.000	—	.000	1	4	0	0	0	0	0	0	0	0	0	0	1	0	0	.000	.000
Fajardo, Daniel	R-R	6-1	170	11-19-94	.240	.148	.266	67	242	23	58	14	0	1	24	6	0	1	0	41	1	1	.310	.258
Gonzalez, Alfredo	R-R	6-0	165	12-14-95	.000	—	.000	1	4	0	0	0	0	0	0	0	0	0	0	0	0	0	.000	.000
Grim, Gerrion	R-R	6-2	190	9-17-93	.223	.248	.212	97	368	40	82	12	1	17	60	18	4	0	2	102	2	1	.400	.265
Juvier, Alejandro	L-R	6-1	180	1-20-96	.241	.226	.246	111	394	45	95	15	1	4	34	24	5	2	3	114	6	0	.315	.291
Kirk, Tanner	R-R	5-11	183	8-14-93	.184	.114	.208	48	141	16	26	4	0	2	5	14	4	0	0	47	2	1	.255	.277
Levy, Stuart	R-R	6-2	185	8-21-92	.241	.360	.207	33	112	10	27	4	0	0	5	11	1	1	1	37	0	0	.277	.312
McClanahan, Jerry	R-R	6-1	200	6-11-92	.130	.154	.118	23	77	3	10	2	0	1	6	7	0	0	1	19	0	0	.195	.200
McKenna, Ryan	R-R	5-11	185	2-14-97	.256	.284	.246	126	468	62	120	33	2	7	42	43	11	5	3	128	20	2	.380	.331
Ortega, Irving	R-R	6-2	165	10-30-96	.167	.000	.209	17	54	5	9	1	0	0	0	4	0	0	0	22	0	0	.185	.224
Palmeiro, Preston	L-R	5-11	180	1-22-95	.253	.199	.273	127	491	55	124	27	3	13	77	43	6	1	3	133	1	2	.399	.319
Ramirez, Wagner	R-R	5-11	170	12-11-94	.000	—	.000	1	1	0	0	0	0	0	0	0	0	0	0	0	0	0	.000	.000
Ramos, Milton	R-R	5-11	193	10-26-95	.239	.238	.239	48	180	16	43	7	1	2	17	7	2	0	0	44	6	3	.322	.275
2-team total (57 Columbia)					.233	.238	.239	105	361	35	84	14	2	2	35	18	3	2	2	85	15	3	.299	.273
Rickard, Joey	R-L	6-1	185	5-21-91	.300	.375	.000	3	10	2	3	0	0	0	0	0	0	0	0	2	0	0	.300	.300
Ring, Jake	L-L	5-11	175	8-11-94	.272	.220	.290	118	464	69	126	36	4	14	65	37	4	4	4	140	17	6	.457	.328

Batting	B-T	HT	WT	DOB	AVG	vLH	vRH	G	AB	R	H	2B	3B	HR	RBI	BB	HBP	SH	SF	SO	SB	CS	SLG	OBP
Shaw, Chris	R-R	6-1	215	4-25-94	.189	.125	.207	30	111	10	21	6	1	2	14	4	4	0	2	37	0	0	.315	.240
Torres, Alexis	R-R	6-0	183	12-12-97	.167	.000	.188	6	18	4	3	1	1	0	3	3	0	0	0	5	0	0	.333	.286
Woody, Collin	R-R	6-1	210	8-5-94	.226	.232	.223	115	420	47	95	23	5	8	47	20	35	3	4	129	2	0	.362	.313

Pitching	B-T	HT	WT	DOB	W	L	ERA	G	GS	CG	SV	IP	H	R	ER	HR	BB	SO	AVG	vLH	vRH	K/9	BB/9
Bray, Jake	R-R	6-1	185	12-8-92	2	5	3.88	43	0	0	18	51	50	25	22	2	14	82	.258	.250	.264	14.47	2.47
Britton, Zach	L-L	6-3	195	12-22-87	0	0	0.00	2	1	0	0	2	1	0	0	0	1	2	.167	.250	.000	9.00	4.50
Dietz, Matthias	R-R	6-5	220	9-20-95	3	10	4.93	26	26	0	0	130	144	83	71	6	50	92	.282	.273	.293	6.39	3.47
Dube, Cody	R-R	6-1	198	10-21-94	2	2	3.44	25	2	0	0	65	59	30	25	6	19	52	.244	.250	.238	7.16	2.62
Erwin, Tyler	L-L	6-0	185	8-29-94	2	2	2.68	26	0	0	1	47	50	16	14	1	9	39	.276	.355	.235	7.47	1.72
Groves, Kory	R-R	6-1	200	9-2-92	3	5	2.58	33	0	0	1	59	58	20	17	5	14	41	.260	.262	.258	6.22	2.12
Harvey, Hunter	R-R	6-3	175	12-9-94	0	1	2.08	3	3	0	0	9	4	2	2	0	3	14	.133	.231	.059	14.54	3.12
Humpal, Lucas	R-R	6-3	180	9-5-93	7	11	4.14	26	25	0	0	150	153	76	69	10	35	105	.262	.250	.273	6.30	2.10
Jimenez, Francisco	R-R	6-1	160	10-4-94	7	2	3.13	28	2	0	0	78	68	36	27	10	28	63	.238	.210	.264	7.30	3.24
Jobst, Nick	R-R	6-2	260	4-20-94	0	0	27.00	2	0	0	0	1	6	5	4	1	1	4	.546	.400	.667	27.00	6.75
Klimek, Steven	L-R	6-3	205	4-4-94	7	3	2.67	37	0	0	6	71	60	28	21	3	12	71	.225	.241	.212	9.04	1.53
MacNabb, Max	L-L	6-1	205	8-28-92	0	1	4.85	3	3	0	0	13	16	9	7	1	2	4	.308	.118	.400	2.77	1.38
Matson, Zach	L-L	6-3	225	10-24-95	0	1	4.05	3	0	0	0	7	5	3	3	1	4	4	.208	.333	.167	5.40	5.40
McGranahan, Zeke	R-R	6-4	215	1-3-91	0	2	4.82	6	0	0	0	9	9	5	5	1	7	9	.265	.250	.286	8.68	6.75
Muckenhirn, Zach	L-L	6-1	185	2-27-95	4	9	5.09	22	21	0	0	115	156	80	65	12	34	89	.321	.316	.323	6.97	2.66
Myers, Aaron	R-R	6-3	225	9-2-93	0	0	2.57	9	0	0	0	14	14	4	4	2	3	11	.250	.207	.296	7.07	1.93
Peluffo, Jhon	R-R	6-3	140	6-16-97	6	5	3.50	23	14	0	0	93	89	48	36	8	24	74	.254	.242	.268	7.19	2.33
Seabrooke, Travis	R-L	6-6	205	9-16-95	3	9	5.01	26	15	0	0	101	104	68	56	5	54	73	.274	.241	.292	6.53	4.83
Teague, James	R-R	6-0	185	8-29-94	0	1	6.35	5	0	0	0	6	12	8	4	3	4	5	.444	.556	.389	7.94	6.35
Trowbridge, Matt	L-L	5-10	175	3-24-93	2	4	3.50	28	0	0	3	44	34	17	17	1	24	53	.217	.255	.196	10.92	4.95
Vespi, Nick	L-L	6-3	215	10-10-95	0	0	9.00	1	0	0	0	1	0	1	1	0	2	0	.000	.000	.000	0.00	18.00
Wells, Alex	L-L	6-1	190	2-27-97	11	5	2.38	25	25	0	0	140	118	49	37	16	10	113	.222	.237	.215	7.26	0.64

Fielding

Catcher	PCT	G	PO	A	E	DP	PB
Carrillo	1.000	1	8	0	0	0	0
Fajardo	.992	66	442	87	4	4	8
Gonzalez	1.000	1	9	1	0	0	0
Levy	.997	33	267	35	1	1	3
McClanahan	.988	22	152	17	2	2	5
Shaw	.982	15	97	11	2	0	2

First Base	PCT	G	PO	A	E	DP
Palmeiro	.992	123	1028	53	9	86
Woody	.972	15	137	4	4	11

Second Base	PCT	G	PO	A	E	DP
Clare	.964	11	22	31	2	8
Crinella	.958	23	38	54	4	15
Juvier	.978	75	153	203	8	43
Kirk	.973	31	48	97	4	7
Torres	.818	3	5	4	2	1

Third Base	PCT	G	PO	A	E	DP
Clare	.867	8	5	8	2	1
Crinella	.250	1	1	0	3	0
Juvier	.924	27	16	45	5	5
Kirk	.778	4	2	5	2	1
Woody	.944	100	82	186	16	17

Shortstop	PCT	G	PO	A	E	DP
Clare	.956	64	102	156	12	26
Juvier	.933	9	12	16	2	2
Ortega	.882	17	18	42	8	9
Ramos	.922	47	66	122	16	29
Torres	1.000	3	4	1	0	0

Outfield	PCT	G	PO	A	E	DP
Billingsley	.996	117	233	8	1	1
Crinella	1.000	6	5	1	0	0
Grim	.943	50	79	3	5	1
Kirk	1.000	6	15	1	0	1
McKenna	.977	124	285	7	7	1
Rickard	1.000	1	3	0	0	0
Ring	.992	116	232	9	2	4

ABERDEEN IRONBIRDS — *SHORT SEASON*

NEW YORK-PENN LEAGUE

Batting	B-T	HT	WT	DOB	AVG	vLH	vRH	G	AB	R	H	2B	3B	HR	RBI	BB	HBP	SH	SF	SO	SB	CS	SLG	OBP
Baez, Carlos	R-R	6-3	175	11-22-97	.400	.333	.500	2	5	1	2	0	0	0	1	1	0	0	0	2	0	0	.400	.500
Becker, Branden	L-R	6-1	175	9-13-96	.292	.000	.304	6	24	1	7	2	0	1	3	0	0	0	0	2	0	0	.500	.292
Breazeale, Ben	L-R	6-0	208	10-21-94	.318	.234	.345	57	195	29	62	14	0	5	32	37	2	0	2	56	3	0	.467	.428
Carrillo, Jean	R-R	6-0	200	6-16-97	.184	.289	.132	44	136	16	25	6	0	0	17	10	1	0	3	34	0	1	.228	.240
Copeland, Garrett	B-R	5-11	190	2-22-95	.274	.156	.304	50	157	26	43	11	2	0	16	23	4	0	3	56	4	2	.369	.374
Craport, Trevor	R-R	5-11	201	8-12-96	.302	.213	.333	52	179	31	54	15	3	3	30	21	6	0	3	36	4	1	.469	.388
Curran, Seamus	L-R	6-6	245	9-6-97	.240	.300	.225	13	50	8	12	1	1	3	10	3	0	0	0	20	0	0	.480	.283
Diaz, Carlos	L-R	6-1	240	12-16-96	.125	.000	.143	2	8	1	1	0	0	0	1	0	0	0	0	3	0	0	.125	.125
Ferguson, Jaylen	R-R	6-2	180	7-21-97	.233	.255	.226	53	193	12	45	6	0	0	14	8	1	2	1	59	5	3	.264	.266
Graham, Tristan	R-R	6-4	215	7-21-95	.193	.265	.173	44	161	13	31	5	1	1	14	4	1	0	1	62	2	0	.255	.216
Hart, Josh	L-L	6-1	180	10-2-94	.346	.375	.333	7	26	6	9	2	1	0	2	2	0	0	1	3	1	1	.500	.379
Jarrett, Zach	R-R	6-4	220	12-8-94	.201	.303	.170	45	139	21	28	6	0	2	7	9	1	0	2	59	1	3	.288	.252
Johnson, Chris	R-R	6-3	225	10-1-84	.182	.000	.191	7	22	2	4	0	0	1	1	5	0	0	0	9	0	0	.318	.333
Jones, Markel	B-R	5-10	175	8-8-94	.220	.286	.197	25	82	12	18	5	1	0	6	12	1	1	0	36	5	1	.305	.326
Lizarraga, Jose	R-R	5-10	170	8-27-97	.250	.000	.500	1	4	1	1	0	0	0	1	0	0	0	0	2	0	0	.250	.250
McCoy, Mason	R-R	6-0	175	3-31-95	.301	.388	.270	53	186	34	56	11	3	1	29	26	1	3	4	28	4	3	.409	.383
Moesquit, Kirvin	B-R	5-8	165	3-10-95	.276	.232	.292	61	210	48	58	10	0	1	17	26	4	3	4	48	29	10	.338	.361
Nichting, T.J.	B-R	5-11	188	1-13-95	.271	.239	.283	62	240	27	65	12	2	3	35	10	4	1	3	39	13	4	.375	.307
Ortega, Irving	R-R	6-2	165	10-30-96	.216	.286	.193	35	111	14	24	3	3	1	11	10	3	3	0	28	3	0	.324	.298
Paez, Jose	R-B	6-0	165	8-11-93	.133	—	.133	4	15	3	2	0	0	1	1	3	0	0	0	7	0	0	.333	.278
Ringhofer, Luke	L-R	6-1	210	2-19-96	.225	.200	.230	43	120	9	27	6	1	0	22	28	2	0	4	28	0	1	.292	.370
Ripken, Ryan	L-L	6-6	205	7-26-93	.287	.244	.301	51	188	14	54	8	0	3	24	9	1	0	0	54	2	2	.378	.323
Robertson, Will	R-R	6-2	190	3-2-95	.000	.000	.000	3	6	0	0	0	0	0	1	0	1	0	0	3	0	0	.000	.143
Soto, Ronald	R-R	6-4	220	10-5-94	.000	—	.000	1	3	0	0	0	0	0	0	1	0	0	0	3	0	0	.000	.250

Pitching	B-T	HT	WT	DOB	W	L	ERA	G	GS	CG	SV	IP	H	R	ER	HR	BB	SO	AVG	vLH	vRH	K/9	BB/9
Baumann, Michael	R-R	6-4	225	9-10-95	4	2	1.31	10	9	0	0	41	25	13	6	2	19	41	.168	.203	.133	8.93	4.14
Bishop, Cameron	L-L	6-4	215	2-14-96	1	1	0.78	8	8	0	0	35	20	7	3	1	16	38	.165	.044	.194	9.87	4.15

Bonilla, Brandon	R-L	6-3	200	10-21-93	0	1	1.93	13	1	0	0	19	8	5	4	1	15	33	.129	.211	.093	15.91	7.23
Britton, Zach	L-L	6-3	195	12-22-87	0	0	0.00	1	1	0	0	1	0	0	0	0	1	1	.000	—	.000	9.00	9.00
Bruner, Layne	L-L	6-3	175	9-24-94	0	0	18.00	2	0	0	0	2	4	4	4	2	0	3	.400	1.000	.333	13.50	0.00
Burke, Scott	R-R	6-3	200	6-2-94	3	1	1.35	14	5	0	0	40	22	7	6	0	6	43	.162	.123	.190	9.68	1.35
Echevarria, Juan	R-R	6-3	195	6-25-97	0	0	0.00	1	0	0	0	1	1	0	0	0	0	2	.250	—	.250	18.00	0.00
Fenter, Gray	R-R	6-0	200	1-25-96	0	0	16.20	1	0	0	0	2	3	3	3	1	0	1	.375	.333	.400	5.40	0.00
Garcia, Ruben	R-R	6-4	220	8-2-96	1	2	7.79	15	0	0	1	17	20	16	15	0	16	23	.278	.280	.277	11.94	8.31
Gruener, Nick	R-R	6-0	185	5-16-95	0	4	6.75	13	3	0	0	36	58	35	27	3	17	32	.365	.373	.360	8.00	4.25
Guance, Hector	R-R	6-6	200	7-12-95	1	2	6.60	5	2	0	0	15	11	13	11	0	11	9	.196	.208	.188	5.40	6.60
Hanifee, Brenan	R-R	6-5	180	5-29-98	7	3	2.75	12	12	0	0	69	65	24	21	2	12	44	.249	.262	.237	5.77	1.57
Harvey, Hunter	R-R	6-3	175	12-9-94	0	0	0.00	2	2	0	0	5	1	0	0	0	3	10	.063	.000	.100	18.00	5.40
Hayes, William Reed	R-R	6-3	185	3-17-95	2	2	5.89	17	0	0	7	18	21	12	12	2	2	13	.288	.333	.256	6.38	0.98
Jobst, Nick	R-R	6-2	260	4-20-94	2	2	2.08	18	0	0	0	17	10	6	4	0	9	18	.172	.250	.132	9.35	4.67
Johnson, Joe	R-R	6-3	175	5-24-94	2	0	3.21	15	0	0	0	14	9	5	5	0	6	19	.177	.200	.167	12.21	3.86
Keaton, Josh	R-R	6-1	200	10-20-93	1	2	4.00	9	0	0	0	18	21	14	8	0	7	21	.296	.286	.300	10.50	3.50
Keller, Jon	R-R	6-5	210	8-8-92	2	0	0.55	10	0	0	1	16	5	1	1	0	4	17	.096	.125	.071	9.37	2.20
Knutson, Max	L-L	6-2	205	4-1-95	1	0	2.91	18	0	0	1	22	16	7	7	1	8	23	.208	.214	.204	9.55	3.32
Lowther, Zac	L-L	6-2	235	4-30-96	2	2	1.66	12	11	0	0	54	35	11	10	1	11	75	.182	.234	.166	12.42	1.82
Matson, Zach	L-L	6-3	225	10-24-95	0	0	4.15	13	0	0	0	17	20	11	8	0	6	22	.282	.345	.238	11.42	3.12
Ming, Cameron	L-L	6-1	177	5-2-96	2	1	2.92	10	7	0	0	37	39	15	12	1	4	30	.267	.264	.269	7.30	0.97
Muckenhirn, Zach	L-L	6-1	185	2-27-95	1	1	5.59	5	0	0	0	10	8	7	6	1	2	14	.222	.091	.280	13.03	1.86
Murphy, Jimmy	R-R	5-11	195	10-14-94	2	3	2.40	11	2	0	1	30	25	11	8	1	9	21	.225	.237	.219	6.30	2.70
Myers, Tobias	R-R	6-0	193	8-5-98	2	2	3.94	7	7	1	0	30	28	20	13	0	6	35	.235	.182	.302	10.62	1.82
2-team total (5 Hudson Valley)					4	2	3.54	12	12	1	0	56	45	29	22	1	10	73	.211	.182	.302	11.73	1.61
Naughton, Timothy	R-R	6-3	195	11-14-95	0	0	0.00	1	0	0	0	1	0	0	0	0	1	0	.000	—	.000	0.00	13.50
Rios, Willie	B-L	5-11	190	2-6-96	0	0	3.52	5	0	0	0	8	5	5	3	1	9	9	.185	.091	.250	10.57	10.57
Romero, Victor	R-R	6-3	170	2-17-95	0	0	9.00	1	0	0	0	1	2	2	1	0	0	1	.333	.000	.400	9.00	0.00
Teague, James	R-R	6-0	185	8-29-94	1	0	1.02	16	0	0	8	18	4	3	2	1	10	29	.066	.080	.056	14.77	5.09
Vespi, Nick	L-L	6-3	215	10-10-95	4	3	4.31	13	5	0	3	48	37	24	23	5	15	69	.209	.170	.229	12.94	2.81

Fielding

C: Breazeale 26, Carrillo 42, Lizarraga 1, Ringhofer 13, Soto 1. **1B:** Craport 3, Curran 12, Diaz 1, Ringhofer 18, Ripken 46. **2B:** Becker 4, Copeland 12, Moesquit 58, Ortega 5. **3B:** Becker 4, Copeland 31, Craport 42, Johnson 5. **SS:** Baez 2, Copeland 1, Craport 1, McCoy 48, Ortega 26. **OF:** Ferguson 51, Graham 43, Hart 4, Jarrett 42, Jones 23, Nichting 61, Paez 4, Robertson 2.

GCL ORIOLES — *ROOKIE*

GULF COAST LEAGUE

Batting	B-T	HT	WT	DOB	AVG	vLH	vRH	G	AB	R	H	2B	3B	HR	RBI	BB	HBP	SH	SF	SO	SB	CS	SLG	OBP
Arredondo, Bryndan	R-R	5-10	190	11-8-94	.286	.200	.320	13	35	5	10	0	0	1	7	10	2	0	0	7	0	0	.371	.468
Baez, Carlos	R-R	6-3	175	11-22-97	.267	.268	.266	47	180	21	48	11	0	3	24	3	2	1	1	50	3	1	.378	.285
Brown, Jacob	R-R	5-9	190	2-16-99	.242	.327	.202	43	153	16	37	6	2	5	22	11	3	1	1	46	2	0	.405	.304
Coolbaugh, Tyler	B-R	6-2	190	10-29-93	.128	.000	.162	14	47	4	6	1	0	0	0	7	1	0	0	12	1	0	.149	.255
DiBenedetto, Nick	R-R	6-0	200	1-5-94	.182	.167	.192	19	44	7	8	1	0	1	5	8	3	0	0	11	0	0	.273	.346
Escarra, J.C.	L-R	6-3	205	4-24-95	.224	.170	.248	58	192	23	43	18	0	2	34	40	9	0	2	40	0	1	.349	.379
Estrada, Jaime	L-R	5-10	170	12-15-95	.240	.214	.250	23	50	11	12	0	0	1	3	14	1	0	0	11	1	0	.300	.415
Gonzalez, Alfredo	R-R	6-0	165	12-14-95	.162	.250	.120	24	74	9	12	3	0	1	4	4	0	1	0	7	0	0	.243	.205
Hall, Adam	R-R	6-0	170	5-22-99	.667	.667	.667	2	9	4	6	1	1	0	2	0	0	0	0	2	1	0	1.000	.667
Hart, Josh	L-L	6-1	180	10-2-94	.200	.111	.273	6	20	3	4	1	1	0	4	1	2	0	0	3	1	0	.350	.304
Hogan, Max	L-R	5-11	195	9-24-93	.310	.294	.316	40	129	32	40	11	5	2	28	32	3	0	2	17	2	1	.519	.452
Lizarraga, Jose	R-R	5-10	170	8-27-97	.276	.438	.233	25	76	15	21	7	1	2	13	6	3	0	0	12	0	0	.474	.353
Montanez, Jose	R-R	6-1	200	7-13-98	.288	.409	.235	27	73	8	21	5	0	0	4	8	1	0	1	12	1	2	.356	.361
Reyes, Jomar	R-R	6-3	220	2-20-97	.464	.333	.526	7	28	6	13	1	0	0	4	1	1	0	1	3	0	0	.500	.484
Robertson, Will	R-R	6-2	190	3-2-95	.303	.344	.287	53	211	32	64	19	0	2	40	11	4	1	4	26	7	1	.422	.344
Shaw, Chris	R-R	6-1	215	4-25-94	.063	.000	.111	5	16	0	1	0	0	0	0	2	0	0	0	7	0	0	.063	.167
Sparks, Lamar	R-R	6-2	170	9-26-98	.241	.347	.188	42	145	31	35	7	2	0	9	33	1	2	0	39	11	3	.317	.386
Tavarez, Davis	R-R	6-2	190	1-7-99	.143	.250	.118	7	21	1	3	0	0	0	1	2	0	0	0	8	0	0	.143	.217
Thorburn, Robbie	L-R	5-11	175	3-30-95	.188	.263	.174	38	117	16	22	2	1	0	5	14	1	1	0	28	8	2	.222	.280
Torres, Alexis	R-R	6-0	183	12-12-97	.237	.233	.239	28	97	17	23	6	3	0	10	16	0	0	1	26	0	0	.361	.342
Xu, Guiyuan	L-L	6-0	188	1-29-96	.180	.000	.206	15	39	4	7	1	1	0	7	4	1	0	1	14	3	0	.256	.267
Yahn, Willy	R-R	5-11	185	11-7-95	.278	.278	.277	56	209	18	58	12	0	0	33	12	12	0	1	16	9	4	.335	.350

Pitching	B-T	HT	WT	DOB	W	L	ERA	G	GS	CG	SV	IP	H	R	ER	HR	BB	SO	AVG	vLH	vRH	K/9	BB/9
Baca, Tucker	L-L	6-4	193	6-17-96	0	0	4.50	13	0	0	0	12	15	8	6	0	7	10	.300	.250	.316	7.50	5.25
Baker, Patrick	R-R	6-3	215	8-15-93	0	0	54.00	3	0	0	0	1	1	6	6	0	9	3	.250	.500	.000	27.00	81.00
Baumann, Michael	R-R	6-4	225	9-10-95	0	0	0.00	1	1	0	0	1	2	0	0	0	0	2	.400	.667	.000	18.00	0.00
Bishop, Cameron	L-L	6-4	215	2-14-96	0	0	0.00	1	1	0	0	3	1	0	0	0	0	1	.111	.333	.000	3.00	0.00
Bruner, Layne	L-L	6-3	175	9-24-94	1	1	9.82	4	0	0	0	7	9	9	8	1	3	5	.300	.167	.333	6.14	3.68
Crichton, Stefan	R-R	6-3	200	2-29-92	0	1	2.45	3	1	0	0	4	0	1	1	0	5	2	.000	.000	.000	4.91	12.27
Diaz, Jose	R-R	6-3	185	8-1-96	4	2	3.69	15	5	0	0	46	46	22	19	1	19	23	.275	.395	.176	4.47	3.69
Echevarria, Juan	R-R	6-3	195	6-25-97	2	1	8.10	15	0	0	0	23	26	23	21	1	12	16	.283	.250	.313	6.17	4.63
Fenter, Gray	R-R	6-0	200	1-25-96	0	1	3.45	11	11	0	0	29	17	13	11	0	10	33	.172	.160	.184	10.36	3.14
Guance, Hector	R-R	6-6	200	7-12-95	0	1	7.83	8	3	0	0	23	27	23	20	1	13	11	.294	.478	.109	4.30	5.09
Hall, DL	L-L	6-0	180	9-19-98	0	0	6.97	5	5	0	0	10	10	9	8	1	10	12	.263	.091	.333	10.45	8.71
Hammonds, Matthew	L-L	6-4	205	5-23-95	0	0	3.52	4	1	0	0	8	14	9	3	1	1	12	.359	.333	.364	14.09	1.17
Harvey, Hunter	R-R	6-3	175	12-9-94	0	0	0.00	3	3	0	0	5	6	0	0	0	0	6	.300	.364	.222	10.80	0.00

Pitching	B-T	HT	WT	DOB	W	L	ERA	G	GS	CG	SV	IP	H	R	ER	HR	BB	SO	AVG	vLH	vRH	K/9	BB/9
Jones, Cory	R-R	6-5	225	9-20-91	1	0	1.13	7	0	0	0	8	6	1	1	0	0	8	.214	.143	.286	9.00	0.00
Keaton, Josh	R-R	6-1	200	10-20-93	0	0	0.00	1	0	0	0	2	1	0	0	0	0	2	.167	.000	.250	9.00	0.00
Leoncio, Tomas	R-R	6-2	180	3-3-95	0	2	7.36	13	1	0	0	18	26	18	15	1	5	12	.317	.188	.400	5.89	2.45
Leyva, Lazaro	R-R	6-2	190	8-8-94	0	1	7.04	5	0	0	0	8	12	6	6	1	4	5	.364	.200	.393	5.87	4.70
MacNabb, Max	L-L	6-1	205	8-28-92	1	0	0.00	2	1	0	0	5	1	0	0	0	0	9	.059	.000	.071	16.20	0.00
Marrugo, Yeizer	R-R	6-0	170	10-1-94	1	0	4.82	6	0	0	1	9	7	6	5	2	2	11	.206	.154	.238	10.61	1.93
Ming, Cameron	L-L	6-1	177	5-2-96	0	1	4.50	1	1	0	0	2	3	1	1	0	0	3	.375	1.000	.000	13.50	0.00
Murphy, Jimmy	R-R	5-11	195	10-14-94	0	0	0.00	1	1	0	0	2	2	0	0	0	0	2	.286	.500	.200	9.00	0.00
Naughton, Timothy	R-R	6-3	195	11-14-95	0	2	3.71	17	0	0	7	17	16	13	7	1	11	21	.242	.296	.205	11.12	5.82
Perez, Luis	R-R	6-0	175	5-3-95	2	2	3.61	16	7	0	0	42	30	21	17	5	10	41	.204	.231	.183	8.72	2.13
Rios, Willie	B-L	5-11	190	2-6-96	1	4	2.87	8	7	0	0	31	31	15	10	2	15	28	.261	.167	.292	8.04	4.31
Rodriguez, Paco	L-L	6-3	220	4-16-91	1	2	7.50	9	0	0	0	12	17	12	10	2	6	10	.333	.250	.371	7.50	4.50
Rodriguez, Yelin	L-L	6-3	200	11-3-98	2	0	3.79	17	2	0	1	40	37	20	17	0	12	41	.245	.333	.208	9.15	2.68
Romero, Franderlin	R-R	6-1	190	2-21-93	1	1	3.09	7	0	0	2	12	8	6	4	2	2	14	.186	.111	.240	10.80	1.54
Romero, Victor	R-R	6-3	170	2-17-95	3	2	1.65	17	0	0	2	33	20	9	6	0	13	35	.179	.180	.177	9.64	3.58
Stauffer, Adam	R-R	6-7	240	1-13-99	2	0	21.60	5	0	0	0	3	11	8	8	0	4	4	.579	.800	.500	10.80	10.80
Turnipseed, Christian	R-R	5-11	214	5-30-92	0	0	18.00	2	0	0	0	1	0	2	2	0	4	0	.000	—	.000	0.00	36.00
Vichio, Nick	R-R	6-0	190	4-21-95	4	1	3.92	18	0	0	0	21	19	10	9	0	7	27	.244	.212	.267	11.76	3.05
Wernet, Gillian	R-R	6-3	210	10-1-98	0	1	6.75	13	0	0	0	21	29	16	16	2	7	16	.333	.293	.370	6.75	2.95
Wilson, Ryan	L-L	6-1	190	11-6-96	1	5	4.40	12	8	0	0	47	53	26	23	2	14	54	.291	.292	.291	10.34	2.68
Wright, Mike	R-R	6-6	215	1-3-90	1	1	8.31	3	1	0	0	4	8	4	4	0	0	7	.400	.444	.364	14.54	0.00

Fielding

C: Arredondo 9, Gonzalez 24, Lizarraga 23, Montanez 14, Shaw 3. **1B:** Arredondo 2, DiBenedetto 2, Escarra 58, Estrada 1, Montanez 1. **2B:** Coolbaugh 8, Estrada 11, Hogan 28, Torres 12, Yahn 6. **3B:** Baez 8, Coolbaugh 1, DiBenedetto 7, Hogan 4, Reyes 3, Torres 1, Yahn 42. **SS:** Baez 39, Coolbaugh 5, Hall 2, Torres 16, Yahn 1. **OF:** Brown 41, DiBenedetto 1, Hart 5, Hogan 9, Robertson 53, Sparks 41, Tavarez 7, Thorburn 34, Xu 3.

DSL ORIOLES — *ROOKIE*

DOMINICAN SUMMER LEAGUE

Batting	B-T	HT	WT	DOB	AVG	vLH	vRH	G	AB	R	H	2B	3B	HR	RBI	BB	HBP	SH	SF	SO	SB	CS	SLG	OBP
Ayala, Fernando	R-R	5-10	175	3-31-97	.128	.077	.150	29	86	14	11	1	0	0	9	9	3	0	1	11	6	2	.140	.232
Barcenas, Richard	R-R	6-1	165	10-22-97	.236	.191	.252	47	165	16	39	6	2	1	12	8	0	0	1	44	4	5	.315	.270
Bautista, Welbin	R-R	6-0	180	5-7-98	.154	.000	.182	9	26	4	4	0	0	0	0	4	0	0	0	10	0	0	.154	.267
Ciriaco, Bryan	R-R	6-1	185	3-29-97	.177	.200	.169	37	102	8	18	3	0	0	7	13	5	1	0	34	1	1	.206	.300
Estevez, Marcos	R-R	6-0	185	7-12-95	.227	.308	.204	45	119	21	27	5	0	3	14	33	9	1	0	39	7	0	.345	.429
Gonzalez, Frank	L-R	5-11	170	3-5-97	.219	.191	.226	35	105	11	23	4	0	1	9	17	1	0	1	30	5	2	.286	.331
Grasso, Victor	R-R	6-2	245	8-28-96	.146	.250	.121	31	82	7	12	3	0	3	13	10	9	0	2	29	2	0	.293	.301
Hernandez, Luis	B-R	6-2	175	5-13-98	.205	.000	.245	36	112	8	23	1	0	2	11	21	0	0	0	33	1	2	.268	.331
Jimenez, Hansel	L-L	5-11	170	7-10-96	.212	.270	.193	50	156	18	33	1	2	0	10	27	1	2	3	39	6	6	.244	.326
Joubas, Malek	R-R	6-0	175	7-23-96	.156	.182	.147	32	45	5	7	2	0	0	0	2	1	1	0	10	1	1	.200	.208
Lizarraga, Jose	R-R	5-10	170	8-27-97	.375	.333	.385	5	16	3	6	1	0	0	4	1	0	0	1	4	1	1	.438	.389
Mendez, Carlos	R-R	6-4	215	2-15-98	.213	.000	.250	15	47	4	10	2	0	0	4	5	3	0	0	16	0	0	.255	.327
Montes, Juan	B-R	6-2	185	5-15-95	.251	.205	.265	64	191	33	48	8	0	1	19	30	19	0	1	42	25	7	.309	.403
Morillo, Antony	L-R	6-1	190	10-9-97	.194	.222	.185	44	144	11	28	3	1	0	14	13	4	1	0	56	3	1	.229	.280
Olivares, Oscar	R-R	6-1	185	9-3-98	.264	.105	.297	32	110	17	29	11	0	3	20	14	1	0	0	27	2	0	.446	.352
Rivero, Leisxonyer	R-R	6-1	165	2-12-97	.175	.227	.161	38	103	9	18	5	0	0	13	10	1	1	2	30	1	5	.223	.250
Rojas, Edidson	L-R	6-3	185	5-14-99	.232	.195	.243	52	185	31	43	9	2	2	17	28	7	0	2	51	15	6	.335	.351
Sanchez, Jose	R-R	6-0	165	12-8-95	.169	.161	.172	43	130	16	22	5	1	1	12	16	2	2	2	48	4	0	.246	.267
Tavarez, Davis	R-R	6-2	190	1-7-99	.273	.385	.242	33	121	16	33	8	2	1	15	9	4	0	2	28	2	2	.397	.338
Tolentino, Frank	R-R	6-1	170	8-5-99	.235	.100	.281	33	119	19	28	5	1	0	10	23	0	0	2	44	7	3	.294	.354

Pitching	B-T	HT	WT	DOB	W	L	ERA	G	GS	CG	SV	IP	H	R	ER	HR	BB	SO	AVG	vLH	vRH	K/9	BB/9
Alcantara, Jose	R-R	6-1	190	11-29-92	2	2	3.16	14	0	0	2	26	32	14	9	1	5	24	.305	.286	.314	8.42	1.75
Alcantara, Nichel	R-R	6-2	185	5-8-96	2	2	1.78	10	8	0	0	35	35	20	7	1	8	26	.245	.227	.253	6.62	2.04
Angomas, Cesar	L-L	6-3	200	4-19-00	1	4	3.49	9	9	0	0	28	34	27	11	0	16	22	.279	.400	.262	6.99	5.08
Bautista, Felix	R-R	6-5	190	6-20-95	4	3	2.01	15	14	0	0	67	53	24	15	1	22	75	.210	.232	.196	10.07	2.96
Bonilla, Miguel Angel	R-R	6-3	185	9-29-94	0	0	0.00	1	0	0	0	1	1	0	0	0	1	1	.250	.500	.000	9.00	9.00
Constante, Marlon	R-R	5-11	180	7-5-96	4	3	1.44	19	0	0	5	31	24	11	5	0	6	25	.212	.184	.227	7.18	1.72
Cruz, Oscar	R-R	6-1	170	8-25-94	2	1	5.58	17	0	0	0	31	38	24	19	2	18	22	.304	.273	.321	6.46	5.28
Daza, Manuel	R-R	6-1	175	9-22-96	2	0	4.06	15	1	0	0	31	28	14	14	1	8	25	.239	.273	.219	7.26	2.32
Diaz, Frandy	L-L	5-10	155	3-25-95	2	2	2.81	16	4	0	1	42	49	23	13	0	12	42	.283	.179	.303	9.07	2.59
Dominguez, Manuel	R-R	6-5	230	1-17-94	4	0	2.97	19	0	0	0	39	34	21	13	0	21	29	.224	.250	.210	6.64	4.81
Gonzalez, Miguel	R-R	6-3	185	9-29-95	1	1	6.56	15	0	0	0	23	22	21	17	1	20	20	.250	.226	.263	7.71	7.71
Jador, Junior	R-R	6-1	175	4-25-96	1	0	2.55	15	2	0	1	25	14	9	7	0	19	26	.165	.077	.203	9.49	6.93
Mena, Francisco	R-R	6-4	195	11-4-93	2	1	1.45	19	0	0	4	31	25	8	5	0	6	35	.225	.250	.211	10.16	1.74
Polanco, Miguel	L-L	6-4	200	1-28-94	0	6	5.27	14	7	0	0	41	59	35	24	0	15	19	.339	.394	.326	4.17	3.29
Rodriguez, Leonardo	R-R	6-7	215	11-25-97	1	5	2.49	11	11	0	0	51	40	18	14	1	13	50	.219	.286	.183	8.88	2.31
Rojas, Edwin	R-R	6-6	200	9-26-95	3	6	3.48	13	13	0	0	62	66	33	24	1	24	23	.276	.266	.281	3.34	3.48
Vizcaino, Dember	R-R	6-4	205	5-12-95	0	1	5.06	17	0	0	2	27	32	21	15	1	8	23	.288	.308	.278	7.76	2.70

Fielding

C: Ayala 24, Bautista 9, Grasso 27, Lizarraga 5, Mendez 15. **1B:** Ciriaco 14, Gonzalez 7, Grasso 7, Montes 30, Morillo 28, Rivero 1. **2B:** Gonzalez 11, Hernandez 22, Rivero 16, Sanchez 26. **3B:** Ciriaco 19, Gonzalez 17, Olivares 32, Rivero 8, Sanchez 3. **SS:** Hernandez 1, Rivero 10, Rojas 48, Sanchez 14. **OF:** Ayala 1, Barcenas 44, Estevez 23, Jimenez 48, Joubas 1, Montes 41, Rivero 3, Tavarez 31, Tolentino 33.

Boston Red Sox

SEASON IN A SENTENCE: The Red Sox won the American League East with 93 wins for the second straight year, but the season ended in the same spot with an exit in the AL Division Series.

HIGH POINT: The Red Sox played their best baseball at the end of the year, going 35-20 from Aug. 1 until the end of the regular season. That strong finish helped them pull past the Yankees to win the division by two games.

LOW POINT: Boston avoided any prolonged slumps during the season—their longest losing streak during the year was just four games. After losing to the Brewers on May 10, however, the Red Sox dropped to 17-16, putting them five games back in the AL East behind the Yankees (21-10) and Orioles (22-11).

NOTABLE ROOKIES: Andrew Benintendi entered the year as the No. 1 prospect in baseball and made an immediate impact in Boston. He wasn't a star right away, but he batted .271/.352/.424 and played above-average defense in left field. With the Red Sox in desperate need of an upgrade at third base after the all-star break, they called up 20-year-old Rafael Devers, who smashed his way to a .284/.338/.482 line and looked like a franchise centerpiece who will hit in the middle of their lineup for several years.

KEY TRANSACTIONS: The big moves for the Red Sox came before the season started, with the Winter Meetings blockbuster that brought ace Chris Sale to town in exchange for a prospect package of second baseman Yoan Moncada, righthanders Michael Kopech and Victor Diaz and outfielder Luis Alexander Basabe. In season, the Red Sox sent righthanders Shaun Anderson and Gregory Santos to the Giants for Eduardo Nunez, who hit .321/.353/.539 in 38 games with the Red Sox before a September knee injury limited him down the stretch.

DOWN ON THE FARM: What has typically been one of the game's best farm systems is now in the bottom tier, a combination of graduations and a slew of trades since president Dave Dombrowski took charge in 2015. Losing five players and getting banned from international signings for one year as a penalty for what MLB determined was circumvention of the international bonus pools also hurt the farm system. Third baseman Michael Chavis was a bright spot in the minor leagues, batting .282/.347/.563 between high Class A Salem and Double-A Portland.

OPENING DAY PAYROLL: $199,805,178 (3rd)

PLAYERS OF THE YEAR

MAJOR LEAGUE

Chris Sale
LHP
17-8, 2.90
308 SO in 214.1 IP
1st in AL in SO, IP

MINOR LEAGUE

Michael Chavis
3B
(High Class A/
Double-A)
.282/.347/.563

ORGANIZATION LEADERS

BATTING — *Minimum 250 AB

MAJORS			
*	AVG	Dustin Pedroia	.293
*	OPS	Mookie Betts	.803
	HR	Mookie Betts	24
	RBI	Mookie Betts	102
MINORS			
*	AVG	Rusney Castillo, Pawtucket	.314
*	OBP	Josh Ockimey, Salem, Portland	.385
*	SLG	Jeremy Barfield, Portland, Pawtucket	.589
*	OPS	Jeremy Barfield, Portland, Pawtucket	.957
	R	Michael Chavis, Salem, Portland	89
	H	Danny Mars, Portland	145
	TB	Michael Chavis, Salem, Portland	265
	2B	Jose Sermo, Salem	35
		Roldani Baldwin, Greenville	35
		Michael Chavis, Salem, Portland	35
	3B	Tate Matheny, Salem	7
	HR	Bryce Brentz, Pawtucket	31
		Michael Chavis, Salem, Portland	31
	RBI	Michael Chavis, Salem, Portland	94
	BB	Josh Ockimey, Salem, Portland	83
	SO	Jose Sermo, Salem	145
	SB	Tyler Hill, Greenville	42

PITCHING — #Minimum 75 IP

MAJORS			
	W	Chris Sale	17
		Drew Pomeranz	17
#	ERA	Chris Sale	2.90
	SO	Chris Sale	308
	SV	Craig Kimbrel	35
MINORS			
	W	Dedgar Jimenez, Salem, Portland	15
	L	Trey Ball, Portland	12
#	ERA	Hildemaro Requena, Greenville	1.98
	G	Bobby Poyner, Salem, Portland	43
	GS	Matthew Kent, Salem	28
	SV	Stephen Nogosek, Greenville, Salem, St. Lucie	19
	IP	Matthew Kent, Salem	164
	BB	Henry Owens, Pawtucket, Portland	115
	SO	Mike Shawaryn, Greenville, Salem	169
#	AVG	Daniel Gonzalez, Greenville, Salem	.210

2017 PERFORMANCE

President, Baseball Ops: Dave Dombrowski. **Farm Director:** Ben Crockett. **Scouting Director:** Mike Rikard.

Class	Team	League	W	L	PCT	Finish	Manager
Majors	Boston Red Sox	American	93	69	.574	3rd (15)	John Farrell
Triple-A	Pawtucket Red Sox	International	67	75	.472	9th (14)	Kevin Boles
Double-A	Portland Sea Dogs	Eastern	65	74	.468	6th (12)	Carlos Febles
High-A	Salem Red Sox	Carolina	73	66	.525	4th (10)	Joe Oliver
Low-A	Greenville Drive	South Atlantic	79	60	.568	1st (14)	Darren Fenster
Short Season	Lowell Spinners	New York-Penn	33	42	.44	11th (14)	Iggy Suarez
Rookie	GCL Red Sox	Gulf Coast	27	31	.466	14th (17)	Tom Kotchman
Overall 2017 Minor League Record			344	348	.497	15th (30)	

ORGANIZATION STATISTICS

BOSTON RED SOX

AMERICAN LEAGUE

Batting	B-T	HT	WT	DOB	AVG	vLH	vRH	G	AB	R	H	2B	3B	HR	RBI	BB	HBP	SH	SF	SO	SB	CS	SLG	OBP
Benintendi, Andrew	L-L	5-10	170	7-6-94	.271	.232	.280	151	573	84	155	26	1	20	90	70	6	1	8	112	20	5	.424	.352
Betts, Mookie	R-R	5-9	180	10-7-92	.264	.307	.254	153	628	101	166	46	2	24	102	77	2	0	5	79	26	3	.459	.344
Bogaerts, Xander	R-R	6-1	210	10-1-92	.273	.294	.268	148	571	94	156	32	6	10	62	56	6	0	2	116	15	1	.403	.343
Bradley Jr., Jackie	L-R	5-10	200	4-19-90	.245	.276	.235	133	482	58	118	19	3	17	63	48	9	0	2	124	8	3	.403	.324
d'Arnaud, Chase	R-R	6-2	205	1-21-87	1.000	—	1.000	2	1	2	1	0	0	0	0	0	0	0	0	0	0	0	1.000	1.000
Davis, Rajai	R-R	5-10	195	10-19-80	.250	.154	.304	17	36	7	9	2	0	0	2	1	1	0	0	13	3	1	.306	.290
2-team total (100 Athletics)					.235	.154	.304	117	336	56	79	19	2	5	20	27	1	1	1	83	29	7	.348	.293
Devers, Rafael	L-R	6-0	195	10-24-96	.284	.400	.250	58	222	34	63	14	0	10	30	18	0	0	0	57	3	1	.482	.338
Hernandez, Marco	L-R	6-0	200	9-6-92	.276	.313	.262	21	58	7	16	3	0	0	2	1	1	0	0	15	0	1	.328	.300
Holt, Brock	L-R	5-10	180	6-11-88	.200	.280	.183	64	140	20	28	6	0	0	7	19	3	0	2	34	2	1	.243	.305
Leon, Sandy	B-R	5-10	225	3-13-89	.225	.247	.217	85	271	32	61	14	0	7	39	25	1	1	3	74	0	0	.354	.290
Lin, Tzu-Wei	L-R	5-9	155	2-15-94	.268	.333	.260	25	56	7	15	0	2	0	2	9	0	1	0	17	1	1	.339	.369
Marrero, Deven	R-R	6-1	195	8-25-90	.211	.291	.172	71	171	32	36	9	0	4	27	12	0	3	2	61	5	0	.333	.260
Moreland, Mitch	L-L	6-2	230	9-6-85	.246	.247	.246	149	508	73	125	34	0	22	79	57	6	0	5	120	0	1	.443	.326
Nunez, Eduardo	R-R	6-0	195	6-15-87	.321	.273	.339	38	165	23	53	12	0	8	27	6	2	0	0	25	6	2	.539	.353
Pedroia, Dustin	R-R	5-9	175	8-17-83	.293	.344	.284	105	406	46	119	19	0	7	62	49	2	2	4	48	4	3	.392	.369
Ramirez, Hanley	R-R	6-2	235	12-23-83	.242	.179	.259	133	496	58	120	24	0	23	62	51	6	0	0	116	1	3	.429	.320
Rutledge, Josh	R-R	6-1	190	4-21-89	.224	.222	.225	37	107	10	24	2	1	0	9	9	2	0	0	31	1	0	.262	.297
Sandoval, Pablo	B-R	5-11	255	8-11-86	.212	.150	.228	32	99	10	21	2	0	4	12	8	0	0	1	24	0	1	.354	.269
Selsky, Steve	R-R	6-0	213	7-20-89	.111	.143	.000	8	9	0	1	1	0	0	0	0	0	0	0	5	0	0	.222	.111
Swihart, Blake	B-R	6-1	200	4-3-92	.200	—	.200	6	5	1	1	0	0	0	0	2	0	0	0	3	0	0	.200	.429
Travis, Sam	R-R	6-0	205	8-27-93	.263	.381	.118	33	76	13	20	6	0	0	1	6	1	0	0	23	1	0	.342	.325
Vazquez, Christian	R-R	5-9	195	8-21-90	.290	.278	.293	99	324	43	94	18	2	5	32	17	3	0	1	64	7	2	.404	.330
Young, Chris	R-R	6-2	200	9-5-83	.235	.200	.259	90	243	30	57	12	2	7	25	30	2	0	1	55	3	2	.387	.323

Pitching	B-T	HT	WT	DOB	W	L	ERA	G	GS	CG	SV	IP	H	R	ER	HR	BB	SO	AVG	vLH	vRH	K/9	BB/9
Abad, Fernando	L-L	6-1	220	12-17-85	2	1	3.30	48	0	0	1	44	40	18	16	4	14	37	.242	.227	.253	7.63	2.89
Barnes, Matt	R-R	6-4	210	6-17-90	7	3	3.88	70	0	0	1	70	57	31	30	7	28	83	.224	.261	.204	10.72	3.62
Boyer, Blaine	R-R	6-3	225	7-11-81	1	1	4.35	32	0	0	0	41	50	20	20	3	14	33	.311	.367	.286	7.19	3.05
Elias, Roenis	L-L	6-1	205	8-1-88	0	0	0.00	1	0	0	0	0	0	0	0	0	1	1	.000	—	.000	27.00	27.00
Fister, Doug	R-L	6-8	210	2-4-84	5	9	4.88	18	15	1	0	90	87	55	49	9	38	83	.254	.300	.208	8.27	3.79
Hembree, Heath	R-R	6-4	210	1-13-89	2	3	3.63	62	0	0	0	62	72	29	25	10	18	70	.289	.313	.280	10.16	2.61
Johnson, Brian	L-L	6-4	235	12-7-90	2	0	4.33	5	5	1	0	27	32	13	13	5	8	21	.283	.154	.300	7.00	2.67
Kelly, Joe	R-R	6-1	190	6-9-88	4	1	2.79	54	0	0	0	58	42	19	18	3	27	52	.202	.222	.191	8.07	4.19
Kendrick, Kyle	R-R	6-3	220	8-26-84	0	2	12.96	2	2	0	0	8	18	12	12	1	3	3	.429	.539	.379	3.24	3.24
Kimbrel, Craig	R-R	6-0	210	5-28-88	5	0	1.43	67	0	0	35	69	33	11	11	6	14	126	.140	.178	.109	16.43	1.83
Maddox, Austin	R-R	6-2	220	5-13-91	0	0	0.52	13	0	0	0	17	13	1	1	1	2	14	.200	.280	.150	7.27	1.04
Martin, Kyle	R-R	6-7	230	1-18-91	0	0	3.86	2	0	0	0	2	2	1	1	1	2	1	.222	.000	.333	3.86	7.71
Pomeranz, Drew	R-L	6-6	240	11-22-88	17	6	3.32	32	32	0	0	174	166	69	64	19	69	174	.252	.293	.240	9.02	3.58
Porcello, Rick	R-R	6-5	205	12-27-88	11	17	4.65	33	33	2	0	203	236	125	105	38	48	181	.286	.286	.287	8.01	2.12
Price, David	L-L	6-5	215	8-26-85	6	3	3.38	16	11	0	0	75	65	30	28	8	24	76	.227	.206	.232	9.16	2.89
Ramirez, Noe	R-R	6-3	205	12-22-89	0	0	3.86	2	0	0	0	5	3	2	2	2	1	4	.177	.500	.133	7.71	1.93
2-team total (10 Los Angeles)					0	0	2.77	12	0	0	0	13	6	5	4	2	5	14	.136	.286	.050	9.69	3.46
Reed, Addison	R-L	6-4	230	12-27-88	1	1	3.33	29	0	0	0	27	16	10	10	5	9	28	.168	.175	.164	9.33	3.00
Rodriguez, Eduardo	L-L	6-2	220	4-7-93	6	7	4.19	25	24	0	0	137	126	66	64	19	50	150	.241	.284	.230	9.83	3.28
Ross Jr., Robbie	L-L	5-11	215	6-24-89	0	0	7.00	8	0	0	0	9	12	7	7	0	5	9	.324	.263	.389	9.00	5.00
Sale, Chris	L-L	6-6	180	3-30-89	17	8	2.90	32	32	1	0	214	165	73	69	24	43	308	.208	.203	.209	12.93	1.81
Scott, Robby	B-L	6-3	220	8-29-89	2	1	3.79	57	0	0	0	36	22	16	15	7	13	31	.179	.121	.246	7.82	3.28
Smith, Carson	R-R	6-6	215	10-19-89	0	0	1.35	8	0	0	1	7	7	1	1	0	2	7	.280	.167	.316	9.45	2.70
Taylor, Ben	R-R	6-3	225	11-12-92	0	1	5.19	14	0	0	1	17	20	10	10	3	9	18	.282	.240	.304	9.35	4.67
Velazquez, Hector	R-R	6-0	180	11-26-88	3	1	2.92	8	3	0	0	25	21	8	8	4	7	19	.236	.290	.207	6.93	2.55
Workman, Brandon	R-R	6-5	235	8-13-88	1	1	3.18	33	0	0	0	40	37	17	14	7	11	37	.252	.296	.226	8.39	2.50
Wright, Steven	R-R	6-2	215	8-30-84	1	3	8.25	5	5	0	0	24	40	24	22	9	5	13	.377	.342	.397	4.88	1.88

Fielding

Catcher	PCT	G	PO	A	E	DP	PB
Leon	.993	84	767	42	6	2	7
Swihart	1.000	4	16	1	0	0	1
Vazquez	.991	95	794	47	8	2	11

First Base	PCT	G	PO	A	E	DP
Holt	.900	2	9	0	1	0
Marrero	.000	1	0	0	0	0
Moreland	.995	138	938	67	5	95
Ramirez	1.000	18	119	6	0	12
Rutledge	1.000	5	11	0	0	1
Travis	.992	21	114	4	1	10

Second Base	PCT	G	PO	A	E	DP
d'Arnaud	1.000	1	1	1	0	1
Hernandez	1.000	6	5	12	0	0
Holt	.978	31	40	51	2	9
Lin	1.000	10	4	12	0	3
Marrero	1.000	11	17	17	0	7
Nunez	.979	26	39	54	2	15
Pedroia	.995	98	156	208	2	59
Rutledge	.978	16	17	28	1	5
Sandoval	.000	1	0	0	0	0

Third Base	PCT	G	PO	A	E	DP
Devers	.906	56	28	107	14	12
Hernandez	.800	9	4	16	5	1
Holt	.944	9	5	12	1	4
Lin	.917	9	1	10	1	2
Marrero	.971	53	26	75	3	10
Nunez	.952	4	5	15	1	1
Rutledge	.939	20	18	28	3	1
Sandoval	.914	29	10	43	5	2
Selsky	1.000	2	0	1	0	0
Vazquez	.000	2	0	0	0	0

Shortstop	PCT	G	PO	A	E	DP
Bogaerts	.969	146	199	336	17	75
Hernandez	.938	5	5	10	1	5
Lin	1.000	6	2	16	0	2
Marrero	1.000	6	4	9	0	2
Nunez	.923	5	5	7	1	0

Outfield	PCT	G	PO	A	E	DP
Benintendi	.982	149	257	11	5	1
Betts	.987	153	366	8	5	1
Bradley Jr.	.987	132	300	6	4	1
Davis	.947	14	18	0	1	0
Holt	1.000	11	16	2	0	0
Selsky	1.000	1	2	0	0	0
Young	1.000	46	65	1	0	1

PAWTUCKET RED SOX — TRIPLE-A

INTERNATIONAL LEAGUE

Batting	B-T	HT	WT	DOB	AVG	vLH	vRH	G	AB	R	H	2B	3B	HR	RBI	BB	HBP	SH	SF	SO	SB	CS	SLG	OBP
Barfield, Jeremy	R-L	6-5	245	7-12-88	.455	.000	.714	3	11	3	5	0	0	1	1	4	0	0	0	1	0	0	.727	.600
Bogusevic, Brian	L-L	6-3	215	2-18-84	.278	.306	.269	76	291	43	81	15	2	12	40	21	3	0	2	57	4	4	.467	.331
Bradley Jr., Jackie	L-R	5-10	200	4-19-90	.200	—	.200	2	5	1	1	0	0	1	1	2	0	0	0	2	0	0	.800	.429
Brentz, Bryce	R-R	6-0	210	12-30-88	.271	.279	.269	120	450	75	122	21	1	31	85	42	1	0	1	109	1	1	.529	.334
Butler, Dan	R-R	5-10	210	10-17-86	.259	.255	.260	73	232	26	60	15	0	4	34	27	2	1	4	48	0	0	.375	.336
Castillo, Rusney	R-R	5-9	195	7-9-87	.314	.395	.287	87	347	52	109	22	0	15	43	11	9	0	2	51	14	2	.507	.350
Court, Ryan	R-R	6-2	210	5-28-88	.263	.321	.241	106	388	49	102	21	3	10	44	46	5	1	2	125	5	2	.410	.347
Craig, Allen	R-R	6-2	215	7-18-84	.253	.268	.248	47	158	18	40	7	0	1	14	22	2	0	0	40	0	2	.317	.352
Devers, Rafael	L-R	6-0	195	10-24-96	.400	.250	.444	9	35	6	14	1	0	2	4	3	0	0	0	8	0	0	.600	.447
Dominguez, Matt	R-R	6-2	220	8-28-89	.264	.266	.264	116	424	47	112	20	0	16	67	19	2	0	6	68	3	2	.425	.295
Holt, Brock	L-R	5-10	180	6-11-88	.214	.207	.220	20	70	9	15	1	0	3	9	6	1	0	0	14	0	0	.357	.286
Lake, Junior	R-R	6-2	230	3-27-90	.246	.400	.216	19	61	6	15	2	1	0	1	4	0	0	0	19	2	0	.312	.292
Lin, Tzu-Wei	L-R	5-9	155	2-15-94	.227	.107	.257	35	141	12	32	5	1	2	9	11	0	2	0	28	2	4	.319	.283
Marrero, Deven	R-R	6-1	195	8-25-90	.240	.278	.231	50	183	17	44	13	0	3	14	6	1	2	2	52	1	4	.361	.266
Meneses, Heiker	R-R	5-9	200	7-1-91	.291	.386	.261	68	237	34	69	10	2	1	16	6	3	1	0	70	9	2	.363	.317
Miller, Mike	R-R	5-9	170	9-27-89	.261	.279	.255	85	280	37	73	11	1	3	28	30	7	6	3	52	4	5	.339	.344
Peralta, Jhonny	R-R	6-2	225	5-28-82	.200	.500	.147	10	40	4	8	1	0	2	5	0	0	0	1	11	0	0	.375	.195
Roberson, Tim	R-R	5-10	215	7-19-89	.217	.250	.204	19	69	3	15	3	0	0	6	2	0	0	0	20	0	0	.261	.239
Romanski, Jake	R-R	5-11	200	12-22-90	.286	.333	.273	15	56	5	16	1	0	0	3	1	0	0	0	4	0	0	.304	.298
Rosario, Jose	R-R	5-11	190	11-29-91	.333	.000	1.000	1	3	0	1	0	0	0	0	0	0	0	0	0	0	0	.333	.333
Rutledge, Josh	R-R	6-1	190	4-21-89	.120	.143	.111	9	25	2	3	1	0	1	1	4	0	0	0	10	0	0	.280	.241
Sandoval, Pablo	B-R	5-11	255	8-11-86	.221	.130	.259	20	77	7	17	3	0	1	4	4	0	0	0	16	0	0	.299	.259
Selsky, Steve	R-R	6-0	213	7-20-89	.216	.276	.195	79	297	30	64	10	0	11	39	18	5	0	2	97	1	1	.360	.270
Swihart, Blake	B-R	6-1	200	4-3-92	.190	.128	.210	53	195	22	37	6	1	4	23	13	2	1	1	54	1	0	.292	.246
Tavarez, Aneury	L-R	5-9	175	4-14-92	.244	.282	.229	33	135	11	33	3	3	4	13	7	2	1	0	29	2	1	.400	.292
Travis, Sam	R-R	6-0	205	8-27-93	.270	.270	.270	82	304	40	82	14	0	6	24	37	1	0	0	57	6	2	.375	.351
Witte, Jantzen	R-R	6-2	195	1-4-90	.242	.159	.274	80	244	31	59	10	1	3	24	35	2	2	0	52	3	2	.328	.342

Pitching	B-T	HT	WT	DOB	W	L	ERA	G	GS	CG	SV	IP	H	R	ER	HR	BB	SO	AVG	vLH	vRH	K/9	BB/9
Beeks, Jalen	L-L	5-11	195	7-10-93	6	7	3.86	17	17	0	0	96	86	45	41	10	33	97	.236	.298	.212	9.13	3.10
Boyer, Blaine	R-R	6-3	225	7-11-81	0	2	2.93	11	0	0	2	15	13	5	5	0	7	12	.241	.286	.192	7.04	4.11
Buttrey, Ty	L-R	6-6	230	3-31-93	1	1	7.64	10	0	0	0	18	21	16	15	2	10	18	.296	.282	.313	9.17	5.09
Callahan, Jamie	R-R	6-2	230	8-24-94	1	1	4.03	22	0	0	4	29	28	14	13	2	13	36	.250	.236	.263	11.17	4.03
Cordier, Erik	R-R	6-4	215	2-25-86	0	1	5.40	6	0	0	1	8	4	5	5	0	9	15	.138	.133	.143	16.20	9.72
Elias, Roenis	L-L	6-1	205	8-1-88	1	4	6.62	7	7	0	0	34	43	25	25	9	9	25	.305	.262	.323	6.62	2.38
Haley, Justin	R-R	6-5	230	6-16-91	1	2	2.66	7	7	1	0	44	35	13	13	7	7	35	.219	.227	.212	7.16	1.43
2-team total (5 Rochester)					2	2	2.93	12	11	1	0	61	52	21	20	10	10	46	.230	.227	.212	6.75	1.47
Haviland, Shawn	R-R	6-2	200	11-10-85	6	8	4.33	23	17	2	0	127	119	63	61	22	41	99	.247	.268	.225	7.03	2.91
Jerez, Williams	L-L	6-4	200	5-16-92	0	2	3.75	9	0	0	0	12	9	7	5	3	6	10	.209	.071	.276	7.50	4.50
Johnson, Brian	L-L	6-4	235	12-7-90	3	4	3.09	17	17	0	0	90	82	32	31	10	28	70	.241	.212	.258	6.97	2.79
Kelly, Joe	R-R	6-1	190	6-9-88	0	0	0.00	1	0	0	0	1	0	0	0	0	0	1	.000	.000	.000	9.00	0.00
Kendrick, Kyle	R-R	6-3	220	8-26-84	5	7	5.67	18	18	2	0	102	114	67	64	24	16	67	.282	.271	.298	5.93	1.42
Maddox, Austin	R-R	6-2	220	5-13-91	2	2	3.50	27	0	0	6	36	22	14	14	2	21	38	.176	.191	.161	9.50	5.25
Martin, Kyle	R-R	6-7	230	1-18-91	0	4	4.36	33	0	0	1	54	56	26	26	7	26	50	.271	.202	.340	8.39	4.36
Olmos, Edgar	L-L	6-4	220	4-12-90	9	3	2.68	29	6	0	4	87	67	31	26	6	33	77	.213	.236	.198	7.94	3.40
Owens, Henry	L-L	6-6	220	7-21-92	4	5	3.91	14	14	0	0	69	57	32	30	6	60	72	.224	.215	.228	9.39	7.83
Price, David	L-L	6-5	215	8-26-85	0	0	9.53	2	2	0	0	6	12	9	6	1	2	8	.400	.500	.364	12.71	3.18
Ramirez, Noe	R-R	6-3	205	12-22-89	3	3	3.51	33	0	0	5	49	40	19	19	7	16	57	.225	.235	.215	10.54	2.96
Rodriguez, Eduardo	L-L	6-2	220	4-7-93	0	1	4.35	2	2	0	0	10	10	5	5	0	5	12	.263	.375	.182	10.45	4.35
Ross Jr., Robbie	L-L	5-11	215	6-24-89	1	0	1.50	6	0	0	0	6	1	1	1	0	3	7	.059	.111	.000	10.50	4.50
Scott, Robby	B-L	6-3	220	8-29-89	0	0	0.00	7	0	0	0	7	3	0	0	0	5	5	.130	.083	.182	6.14	6.14

Pitching	B-T	HT	WT	DOB	W	L	ERA	G	GS	CG	SV	IP	H	R	ER	HR	BB	SO	AVG	vLH	vRH	K/9	BB/9
Shepherd, Chandler	R-R	6-3	185	8-25-92	1	5	4.07	34	1	0	2	60	59	31	27	5	18	68	.259	.263	.255	10.26	2.72
Smith, Carson	R-R	6-6	215	10-19-89	1	1	4.15	10	0	0	0	9	10	5	4	0	3	6	.313	.462	.211	6.23	3.12
Smith, Josh	L-L	6-3	200	10-11-89	0	0	0.00	2	0	0	1	5	1	0	0	0	3	3	.067	.167	.000	5.06	5.06
Taylor, Ben	R-R	6-3	225	11-12-92	0	0	2.70	12	0	0	2	13	7	4	4	2	5	12	.156	.125	.191	8.10	3.38
Velazquez, Hector	R-R	6-0	180	11-26-88	8	4	2.21	19	19	0	0	102	78	27	25	7	24	79	.213	.193	.231	6.97	2.12
Walden, Marcus	R-R	6-0	195	9-13-88	10	6	3.92	29	15	1	0	106	102	52	46	4	36	86	.256	.239	.276	7.32	3.07
Workman, Brandon	R-R	6-5	235	8-13-88	4	1	1.55	18	0	0	2	29	16	6	5	1	13	35	.162	.154	.170	10.86	4.03

Fielding

Catcher	PCT	G	PO	A	E	DP	PB
Butler	.993	72	526	44	4	9	4
Roberson	1.000	13	116	5	0	1	1
Romanski	.993	15	124	9	1	2	0
Swihart	.997	43	353	20	1	1	7

First Base	PCT	G	PO	A	E	DP
Court	1.000	15	109	6	0	10
Craig	1.000	14	91	10	0	9
Dominguez	.990	13	93	3	1	3
Selsky	.991	14	94	11	1	13
Swihart	.952	3	18	2	1	2
Travis	.996	58	472	27	2	43
Witte	.996	31	215	17	1	24

Second Base	PCT	G	PO	A	E	DP
Court	.972	11	13	22	1	3
Holt	1.000	1	1	0	0	0
Lin	1.000	3	4	7	0	2
Marrero	.963	7	7	19	1	4
Meneses	.995	47	70	119	1	30
Miller	.995	51	83	105	1	27
Rutledge	1.000	3	4	7	0	1
Witte	.972	29	42	62	3	14

Third Base	PCT	G	PO	A	E	DP
Court	1.000	3	4	3	0	0
Devers	.810	8	8	9	4	1
Dominguez	.980	91	58	142	4	15
Holt	.923	4	4	8	1	1
Lin	1.000	4	2	3	0	0
Marrero	1.000	3	1	8	0	1
Meneses	1.000	1	0	1	0	0
Peralta	.857	3	2	4	1	0
Rutledge	1.000	3	2	2	0	0
Sandoval	.903	15	11	17	3	1
Witte	.959	21	12	35	2	3

Shortstop	PCT	G	PO	A	E	DP
Court	.982	41	64	102	3	28
Holt	1.000	1	0	2	0	0
Lin	1.000	9	9	25	0	3
Marrero	.980	40	62	86	3	25
Meneses	1.000	19	23	50	0	9
Miller	.968	36	54	68	4	16
Rosario	.000	1	0	0	0	0

Outfield	PCT	G	PO	A	E	DP
Barfield	1.000	3	3	0	0	0
Bogusevic	1.000	76	166	3	0	3
Bradley Jr.	1.000	2	3	0	0	0
Brentz	.956	98	170	5	8	1
Castillo	.990	80	196	3	2	0
Court	1.000	38	62	3	0	1
Craig	1.000	5	8	0	0	0
Holt	1.000	7	13	1	0	0
Lake	1.000	18	33	1	0	0
Lin	.964	20	53	0	2	0
Meneses	.000	1	0	0	0	0
Selsky	.991	59	104	1	1	1
Tavarez	.982	33	54	0	1	0

PORTLAND SEA DOGS

DOUBLE-A

EASTERN LEAGUE

Batting	B-T	HT	WT	DOB	AVG	vLH	vRH	G	AB	R	H	2B	3B	HR	RBI	BB	HBP	SH	SF	SO	SB	CS	SLG	OBP
Barfield, Jeremy	R-L	6-5	245	7-12-88	.288	.310	.282	92	344	62	99	21	0	27	75	30	9	0	1	89	1	0	.584	.359
Bethea, Danny	R-R	6-1	210	1-31-90	.239	.286	.217	22	67	9	16	3	0	2	11	7	0	1	0	17	0	0	.373	.311
Chavis, Michael	R-R	5-10	210	8-11-95	.250	.156	.271	67	248	39	62	18	0	14	39	20	3	0	3	56	1	0	.492	.310
De La Guerra, Chad	L-R	5-11	190	11-24-92	.270	.290	.267	52	196	34	53	15	0	4	23	23	2	1	0	48	2	1	.408	.353
DePew, Jake	R-R	6-1	210	3-1-92	.218	.222	.216	32	101	11	22	0	0	2	11	8	2	1	0	20	1	0	.277	.288
Devers, Rafael	L-R	6-0	195	10-24-96	.300	.282	.306	77	287	48	86	19	3	18	56	31	1	0	1	55	0	3	.575	.369
Holt, Brock	L-R	5-10	180	6-11-88	.250	.000	.273	4	12	2	3	0	0	0	1	2	0	0	0	1	0	0	.250	.357
Lin, Tzu-Wei	L-R	5-9	155	2-15-94	.302	.314	.298	48	159	31	48	9	3	5	19	20	1	2	2	27	8	2	.491	.379
Longhi, Nick	R-L	6-2	205	8-16-95	.262	.265	.260	62	237	26	62	15	0	6	33	13	2	0	0	40	0	1	.401	.306
Lopez, Deiner	B-R	6-0	165	5-30-94	.247	.185	.266	73	231	38	57	5	1	3	17	16	1	5	2	66	5	0	.316	.296
Lovullo, Nick	R-R	6-0	175	12-1-93	.294	.333	.286	6	17	0	5	0	0	0	2	3	0	0	0	5	0	0	.294	.400
Mars, Danny	B-R	6-0	195	1-22-94	.304	.353	.288	119	477	62	145	21	4	6	47	33	3	2	2	95	12	10	.403	.352
Meneses, Heiker	R-R	5-9	200	7-1-91	.229	.150	.260	20	70	8	16	3	0	0	4	7	0	2	1	14	2	2	.271	.295
Meyers, Mike	R-R	6-1	190	12-28-93	.083	.143	.000	3	12	1	1	1	0	0	0	0	0	0	0	4	0	0	.167	.083
Monge, Joseph	R-R	6-1	190	5-18-95	.238	.228	.243	55	193	26	46	10	1	2	19	10	9	2	0	49	5	2	.332	.307
Ockimey, Josh	L-R	6-1	215	10-18-95	.272	.286	.268	31	103	12	28	7	0	3	11	17	0	0	1	33	0	0	.427	.372
Olt, Mike	R-R	6-2	210	8-27-88	.245	.333	.222	113	392	51	96	23	2	16	57	48	4	1	2	117	0	0	.436	.332
Procyshen, Jordan	L-R	5-10	185	3-11-93	.200	.180	.205	68	215	25	43	9	0	4	21	27	2	4	0	67	0	3	.298	.295
Romanski, Jake	R-R	5-11	200	12-22-90	.233	.192	.245	33	120	13	28	3	0	1	8	2	0	0	0	19	0	1	.283	.246
Rosario, Jose	R-R	5-11	190	11-29-91	.140	.063	.177	16	50	3	7	1	0	0	3	2	1	2	0	13	0	1	.160	.189
Rutledge, Josh	R-R	6-1	190	4-21-89	.000	.000	.000	1	3	0	0	0	0	0	0	1	0	0	0	1	0	0	.000	.250
Sturgeon, Cole	L-L	6-0	180	9-17-91	.264	.220	.275	118	406	43	107	21	4	6	52	39	2	6	7	86	11	4	.379	.326
Tavarez, Aneury	L-R	5-9	175	4-14-92	.377	.294	.409	18	61	13	23	3	0	1	6	12	0	1	1	6	6	3	.475	.473
Tobias, Josh	B-R	5-9	195	11-23-92	.268	.324	.253	92	332	32	89	19	0	3	34	19	9	3	4	72	4	3	.352	.321
Tovar, Carlos	R-R	5-11	170	8-20-95	.000	.000	.000	1	5	0	0	0	0	0	0	0	0	0	0	1	0	0	.000	.000
Urrutia, Henry	L-R	6-5	200	2-13-87	.284	.273	.287	63	211	30	60	13	0	3	29	23	2	0	0	49	4	2	.389	.360

Pitching	B-T	HT	WT	DOB	W	L	ERA	G	GS	CG	SV	IP	H	R	ER	HR	BB	SO	AVG	vLH	vRH	K/9	BB/9
Ball, Trey	L-L	6-6	185	6-27-94	7	12	5.27	25	24	2	0	125	161	93	73	17	57	103	.322	.273	.342	7.44	4.11
Barnes, Matt	R-R	6-4	210	6-17-90	0	0	0.00	1	1	0	0	1	1	0	0	0	1	1	.250	.000	.500	9.00	9.00
Beeks, Jalen	L-L	5-11	195	7-10-93	5	1	2.19	9	9	1	0	49	35	12	12	3	22	58	.199	.127	.231	10.58	4.01
Buttrey, Ty	L-R	6-6	230	3-31-93	1	4	3.72	30	0	0	4	46	39	22	19	1	23	56	.234	.338	.162	10.96	4.50
Callahan, Jamie	R-R	6-2	230	8-24-94	4	1	1.38	10	0	0	2	13	8	2	2	0	0	20	.170	.250	.111	13.85	0.00
Cosart, Jake	R-R	6-2	175	2-11-94	5	2	3.10	38	0	0	2	49	28	23	17	5	41	52	.163	.227	.123	9.49	7.48
Dahlstrand, Jacob	R-R	6-5	205	3-26-92	5	4	6.66	29	8	0	0	77	93	60	57	9	46	38	.308	.343	.279	4.44	5.38
Drehoff, Jake	L-L	6-4	195	6-5-92	1	2	9.53	11	3	0	0	28	43	33	30	5	11	28	.353	.275	.390	8.89	3.49
Elias, Roenis	L-L	6-1	205	8-1-88	0	1	3.38	1	1	0	0	3	2	1	1	1	1	1	.200	.250	.167	3.38	3.38
Grover, Taylor	R-R	6-3	195	4-22-91	3	5	5.16	29	7	0	0	75	77	47	43	11	33	82	.263	.294	.240	9.84	3.96
Jerez, Williams	L-L	6-4	200	5-16-92	2	0	3.16	29	0	0	4	51	50	21	18	3	17	47	.258	.206	.282	8.24	2.98
Jimenez, Dedgar	L-L	6-3	240	3-6-96	5	0	2.91	8	8	0	0	46	45	16	15	4	18	25	.253	.311	.233	4.86	3.50
Kelley, Trevor	R-R	6-2	210	10-20-93	1	1	3.62	16	0	0	0	27	28	12	11	1	7	17	.267	.290	.254	5.60	2.30

Lakins, Travis	R-R	6-1	180	6-29-94	0	4	6.23	8	8	0	0	30	34	25	21	2	21	19	.301	.324	.290	5.64	6.23
Maddox, Austin	R-R	6-2	220	5-13-91	0	1	1.35	10	0	0	2	13	9	2	2	0	5	8	.205	.136	.273	5.40	3.38
McAvoy, Kevin	R-R	6-4	210	7-21-93	6	9	4.28	22	21	0	0	118	117	65	56	8	46	97	.260	.245	.272	7.42	3.52
Owens, Henry	L-L	6-6	220	7-21-92	3	6	4.58	12	12	0	0	57	40	34	29	2	55	49	.205	.238	.196	7.74	8.68
Pimentel, Yankory	R-R	6-2	210	9-29-93	1	0	6.00	4	0	0	1	6	5	4	4	2	3	6	.208	.111	.267	9.00	4.50
Poyner, Bobby	L-L	6-0	205	12-1-92	0	1	0.94	27	0	0	9	38	19	7	4	2	11	52	.142	.237	.104	12.21	2.58
Rodriguez, Eduardo	L-L	6-2	220	4-7-93	0	1	15.00	1	1	0	0	3	9	6	5	1	0	3	.529	—	.529	9.00	0.00
Smith, Carson	R-R	6-6	215	10-19-89	0	1	54.00	1	1	0	0	0	0	2	2	0	3	0	—	—	—	0.00	81.00
Smith, Josh	L-L	6-3	200	10-11-89	5	1	3.26	33	0	0	1	66	61	27	24	5	34	75	.243	.165	.288	10.18	4.61
Stankiewicz, Teddy	R-R	6-4	215	11-25-93	5	6	5.03	25	23	1	0	140	169	83	78	13	36	107	.303	.299	.307	6.89	2.32
Villanueva, Elih	R-R	6-2	230	7-27-86	5	5	7.85	14	12	0	0	57	85	53	50	12	15	48	.337	.348	.329	7.53	2.35
Ysla, Luis	L-L	6-1	185	4-27-92	1	5	5.05	29	0	0	1	46	47	28	26	2	32	44	.266	.216	.286	8.55	6.22

Fielding

Catcher	PCT	G	PO	A	E	DP	PB
Bethea	.991	16	108	7	1	1	0
DePew	.996	30	228	27	1	3	6
Procyshen	.987	67	490	42	7	4	7
Romanski	.983	29	206	27	4	2	3

First Base	PCT	G	PO	A	E	DP
Longhi	.997	48	365	23	1	37
Ockimey	.971	24	186	16	6	24
Olt	.993	58	427	28	3	45
Urrutia	.970	16	127	3	4	9

Second Base	PCT	G	PO	A	E	DP
De La Guerra	1.000	7	12	21	0	7
Lin	.900	2	5	4	1	0
Lopez	.988	19	29	51	1	15
Lovullo	.957	5	12	10	1	5
Meneses	1.000	10	19	30	0	7
Rosario	.932	9	16	25	3	5
Tobias	.974	89	166	209	10	60

Third Base	PCT	G	PO	A	E	DP
Chavis	.948	43	30	79	6	13
Devers	.930	64	35	124	12	8
Holt	1.000	1	0	2	0	0
Lopez	1.000	3	3	7	0	0
Olt	.908	33	14	45	6	7
Rosario	1.000	2	0	2	0	1
Rutledge	1.000	1	1	1	0	0

Shortstop	PCT	G	PO	A	E	DP
Chavis	1.000	1	0	1	0	0
De La Guerra	.949	42	48	121	9	23
Holt	1.000	1	0	2	0	0
Lin	.975	37	56	102	4	22
Lopez	.955	48	71	121	9	22
Lovullo	1.000	2	4	4	0	0
Meneses	.980	10	24	25	1	9
Rosario	.833	1	2	3	1	2
Tovar	.909	1	4	6	1	3

Outfield	PCT	G	PO	A	E	DP
Barfield	.980	80	140	5	3	0
Lin	1.000	7	23	0	0	0
Longhi	.941	7	16	0	1	0
Lopez	1.000	3	6	1	0	0
Mars	.995	115	204	8	1	1
Meyers	1.000	2	4	0	0	0
Monge	.983	55	114	1	2	0
Rosario	1.000	3	2	0	0	0
Sturgeon	.985	111	196	4	3	0
Tavarez	1.000	15	17	2	0	0
Urrutia	1.000	30	46	3	0	1

SALEM RED SOX

HIGH CLASS A

CAROLINA LEAGUE

Batting	B-T	HT	WT	DOB	AVG	vLH	vRH	G	AB	R	H	2B	3B	HR	RBI	BB	HBP	SH	SF	SO	SB	CS	SLG	OBP
Acosta, Victor	R-R	5-11	160	6-2-96	.304	.423	.263	31	102	8	31	7	0	2	16	10	0	0	0	14	3	3	.431	.366
Betts, Jordan	R-R	6-3	220	10-6-91	.262	.256	.264	98	340	54	89	24	0	13	51	40	1	1	7	104	5	1	.447	.335
Chavis, Michael	R-R	5-10	210	8-11-95	.318	.338	.309	59	223	50	71	17	2	17	55	19	7	0	1	57	1	0	.641	.388
De La Guerra, Chad	L-R	5-11	190	11-24-92	.294	.324	.280	58	218	47	64	16	3	5	36	25	2	3	2	40	5	2	.463	.368
Gregor, Conrad	L-R	6-3	225	2-27-92	.302	.281	.311	30	106	13	32	8	0	4	19	21	1	0	0	20	4	1	.491	.422
Hudson, Bryan	L-R	6-1	185	2-10-95	.233	.254	.225	80	249	37	58	5	0	0	15	38	0	1	2	72	22	6	.253	.332
Kemp, Trenton	R-R	6-2	195	9-30-95	.316	.368	.291	33	117	22	37	10	3	2	15	11	0	0	2	34	4	1	.504	.369
Lopez, Deiner	B-R	6-0	165	5-30-94	.257	.185	.298	19	74	11	19	2	1	2	10	2	0	1	0	9	7	3	.392	.276
Lovullo, Nick	R-R	6-0	175	12-1-93	.234	.175	.253	74	231	26	54	7	3	1	19	24	2	4	1	39	4	3	.303	.310
Madera, Chris	R-R	5-10	190	8-23-92	.233	.250	.228	59	219	19	51	5	2	0	14	22	1	6	0	35	9	6	.274	.306
Matheny, Tate	R-R	6-0	185	2-9-94	.266	.325	.243	114	429	78	114	26	7	7	46	44	4	8	3	119	27	7	.408	.338
McLean, Matt	L-R	5-11	190	9-15-93	.333	.333	.333	3	6	1	2	2	0	0	0	1	1	0	0	2	0	0	.667	.500
Meyers, Mike	R-R	6-1	190	12-28-93	.255	.299	.232	86	314	37	80	13	2	2	29	17	3	4	0	99	8	4	.328	.299
Miller, Derek	R-R	6-2	180	7-18-92	.091	.091	.091	8	22	5	2	1	0	0	1	6	1	0	0	8	1	0	.136	.310
Nunez, Jhon	B-R	5-9	165	12-5-94	.286	.321	.270	55	182	23	52	9	1	3	32	9	4	4	3	34	4	5	.396	.328
Ockimey, Josh	L-R	6-1	215	10-18-95	.275	.259	.282	100	349	56	96	20	2	11	63	66	3	0	7	110	1	4	.438	.388
Pacchioli, Justin	R-R	6-2	190	9-28-92	.000	.000	.000	5	15	1	0	0	0	0	0	4	2	0	0	2	1	0	.000	.286
Rei, Austin	R-R	6-0	185	10-27-93	.223	.220	.224	95	319	41	71	30	0	3	38	39	13	0	2	96	3	5	.345	.330
Reveles, Steven	R-R	5-8	170	1-8-93	.188	.000	.250	5	16	4	3	1	0	0	0	2	0	1	0	5	1	0	.250	.278
Reynoso, Eddy	R-R	6-0	195	8-7-94	.200	—	.200	3	5	0	1	0	0	0	0	1	0	0	0	1	0	0	.200	.333
Rivera, Jeremy	B-R	5-9	150	1-30-95	.246	.260	.242	84	325	28	80	22	0	2	24	15	3	13	2	66	3	4	.332	.284
Sermo, Jose	B-R	6-1	190	3-22-91	.250	.312	.226	110	384	55	96	35	0	14	58	40	2	2	3	145	8	0	.451	.322
Spoon, Tyler	R-R	5-11	190	9-28-92	.201	.241	.191	41	144	12	29	5	1	2	17	15	1	1	1	33	2	0	.292	.280
Studdard, Granger	L-R	6-1	200	2-14-95	.222	.125	.250	10	36	2	8	0	0	0	3	2	3	0	0	9	0	0	.222	.317
Tobias, Josh	B-R	5-9	195	11-23-92	.345	.444	.275	21	87	16	30	7	0	2	11	8	2	0	0	16	4	2	.494	.412
Washington, Kyri	R-R	5-11	220	7-11-94	.250	.105	.317	18	60	5	15	3	0	1	8	4	1	1	0	24	1	1	.350	.308

Pitching	B-T	HT	WT	DOB	W	L	ERA	G	GS	CG	SV	IP	H	R	ER	HR	BB	SO	AVG	vLH	vRH	K/9	BB/9
Anderson, Shaun	R-R	6-4	225	10-29-94	3	3	3.99	11	11	0	0	59	53	30	26	6	18	48	.236	.202	.281	7.36	2.76
Bautista, Gerson	R-R	6-2	170	5-31-95	3	2	5.16	27	0	0	4	45	54	33	26	2	28	53	.292	.298	.287	10.52	5.56
Boyd, Logan	L-L	6-2	205	11-26-93	3	1	2.56	12	7	0	1	56	49	16	16	2	24	46	.237	.222	.243	7.35	3.83
Brakeman, Marc	L-R	6-2	185	6-15-94	0	3	5.95	21	0	0	1	39	40	32	26	5	22	46	.260	.244	.278	10.53	5.03
Cooney, Harrison	R-R	6-2	175	3-23-92	0	2	4.15	8	0	0	0	13	15	7	6	1	13	10	.313	.286	.333	6.92	9.00
Elias, Roenis	L-L	6-1	205	8-1-88	0	1	15.75	1	1	0	0	4	10	9	7	1	2	1	.435	.333	.450	2.25	4.50
Glorius, Austin	R-R	6-3	205	5-10-93	4	5	4.85	33	0	0	0	56	52	32	30	7	48	64	.250	.216	.275	10.35	7.76
Goetze, Pat	R-R	6-6	200	3-3-94	0	1	5.40	7	0	0	0	13	18	8	8	0	5	6	.321	.375	.281	4.05	3.38
Gonzalez, Daniel	R-R	6-5	180	2-9-96	5	0	1.31	6	6	0	0	34	24	5	5	1	6	31	.195	.203	.188	8.13	1.57
Gorst, Matthew	R-R	6-1	205	8-24-94	1	2	1.20	9	0	0	0	15	15	2	2	0	8	14	.259	.250	.265	8.40	4.80
Hart, Kyle	L-L	6-5	170	11-23-92	2	3	2.49	9	9	0	0	51	45	15	14	5	23	52	.241	.211	.254	9.24	4.09

Pitching	B-T	HT	WT	DOB	W	L	ERA	G	GS	CG	SV	IP	H	R	ER	HR	BB	SO	AVG	vLH	vRH	K/9	BB/9
Jimenez, Dedgar	L-L	6-3	240	3-6-96	10	3	3.07	18	17	1	0	100	97	41	34	2	23	93	.259	.229	.273	8.40	2.08
Kelley, Trevor	R-R	6-2	210	10-20-93	1	0	1.34	22	0	0	7	34	23	5	5	1	8	32	.198	.113	.270	8.55	2.14
Kent, Matthew	L-L	6-0	180	9-13-92	7	7	4.23	28	28	0	0	164	186	90	77	12	38	142	.282	.246	.298	7.79	2.09
Lakins, Travis	R-R	6-1	180	6-29-94	5	0	2.61	7	7	0	0	38	32	12	11	2	13	43	.225	.262	.198	10.18	3.08
Lau, Adam	R-R	6-2	210	7-5-94	4	7	2.98	37	0	0	7	63	56	23	21	4	31	68	.241	.275	.220	9.66	4.41
McGrath, Daniel	R-L	6-3	205	7-7-94	4	9	4.98	34	11	0	4	85	100	60	47	5	51	87	.295	.250	.318	9.21	5.40
Nogosek, Stephen	R-R	6-2	205	1-11-95	2	1	4.08	13	0	0	6	18	15	8	8	3	10	18	.242	.233	.250	9.17	5.09
O'Linger, Durin	L-R	5-10	185	10-10-93	0	1	9.31	2	2	0	0	10	16	11	10	2	3	5	.356	.421	.308	4.66	2.79
Osnowitz, Mitchell	R-R	6-5	245	7-2-91	0	0	7.33	13	0	0	0	23	28	23	19	2	19	25	.295	.319	.271	9.64	7.33
Pimentel, Yankory	R-R	6-2	210	9-29-93	2	1	1.54	11	0	0	0	23	24	8	4	1	7	21	.267	.294	.250	8.10	2.70
Poyner, Bobby	L-L	6-0	205	12-1-92	2	0	2.45	16	0	0	6	22	20	7	6	2	6	32	.233	.267	.214	13.09	2.45
Raudes, Roniel	R-R	6-1	160	1-16-98	4	7	4.50	23	23	0	0	116	134	66	58	14	44	95	.297	.233	.356	7.37	3.41
Shawaryn, Mike	R-R	6-2	200	9-17-94	5	5	3.76	16	16	0	0	81	71	38	34	10	35	91	.232	.237	.226	10.07	3.87
Weems, Jordan	L-R	6-3	175	11-7-92	6	2	4.93	19	1	0	1	42	38	28	23	5	22	36	.250	.269	.230	7.71	4.71

Fielding

Catcher	PCT	G	PO	A	E	DP	PB
Nunez	.983	49	357	36	7	5	7
Rei	.988	88	740	74	10	5	11
Spoon	1.000	8	55	5	0	0	1

First Base	PCT	G	PO	A	E	DP
Betts	.970	23	151	13	5	21
Gregor	.992	29	226	12	2	21
Ockimey	.984	91	642	54	11	65

Second Base	PCT	G	PO	A	E	DP
De La Guerra	.985	14	24	42	1	8
Lovullo	.983	67	127	165	5	44
Madera	.000	1	0	0	0	0
Reveles	1.000	4	6	6	0	2
Rivera	1.000	7	8	21	0	5
Sermo	.949	33	44	67	6	20
Tobias	.976	19	34	49	2	13

Third Base	PCT	G	PO	A	E	DP
Acosta	1.000	1	2	2	0	0
Betts	.947	72	42	118	9	13
Chavis	.853	27	17	47	11	7
Lopez	1.000	6	5	2	0	0
Reveles	1.000	1	2	0	0	0
Sermo	.875	34	23	54	11	7

Shortstop	PCT	G	PO	A	E	DP
De La Guerra	.937	43	55	108	11	33
Lopez	.956	13	18	25	2	4
Lovullo	.970	8	9	23	1	5
Rivera	.975	77	119	151	7	29

Outfield	PCT	G	PO	A	E	DP
Acosta	1.000	18	32	1	0	1
Hudson	.990	62	97	2	1	0
Kemp	.952	32	57	2	3	1
Lopez	.500	2	1	0	1	0
Madera	.993	57	129	10	1	2
Matheny	.978	114	293	13	7	4
McLean	.000	3	0	0	0	0
Meyers	.950	79	130	3	7	2
Miller	.875	6	6	1	1	0
Pacchioli	1.000	5	10	1	0	1
Spoon	.977	28	40	2	1	1
Studdard	.958	10	22	1	1	0
Washington	.962	16	25	0	1	0

GREENVILLE DRIVE

LOW CLASS A

SOUTH ATLANTIC LEAGUE

Batting	B-T	HT	WT	DOB	AVG	vLH	vRH	G	AB	R	H	2B	3B	HR	RBI	BB	HBP	SH	SF	SO	SB	CS	SLG	OBP
Aybar, Yoan	L-L	6-2	165	7-3-97	.160	.227	.141	30	100	12	16	2	1	0	4	6	0	3	1	38	2	0	.200	.206
Baldwin, Roldani	R-R	5-11	175	3-16-96	.275	.184	.303	95	368	45	101	35	1	14	66	19	2	1	4	73	1	0	.489	.310
Castellanos, Pedro	R-R	6-3	195	12-11-97	.333	—	.333	2	9	1	3	1	0	0	1	0	0	0	0	2	0	0	.444	.333
Cedrola, Lorenzo	R-R	5-11	170	1-12-98	.285	.347	.262	92	354	47	101	18	3	4	34	11	9	3	2	48	19	7	.387	.322
Chatham, C.J.	R-R	6-4	185	12-22-94	.333	—	.333	1	3	0	1	0	0	0	2	0	0	0	0	0	0	1	.333	.333
Dalbec, Bobby	R-R	6-4	225	6-29-95	.247	.239	.249	78	284	48	70	15	0	13	39	36	7	1	1	123	4	5	.437	.345
Downs, Jerry	L-L	6-2	215	12-22-93	.274	.179	.303	34	117	16	32	9	1	3	17	11	7	0	1	33	1	0	.444	.368
Espinal, Santiago	R-R	5-10	175	11-13-94	.281	.302	.273	123	492	64	138	18	4	4	46	39	3	5	5	67	20	6	.358	.334
Gunsolus, Mitchell	L-R	6-0	200	1-23-93	.205	.247	.191	112	346	40	71	20	1	2	26	69	9	2	5	141	9	1	.286	.347
Hill, Tyler	R-R	6-0	195	3-4-96	.272	.320	.254	119	459	65	125	19	4	9	57	37	13	2	2	74	42	8	.390	.343
Lovullo, Nick	R-R	6-0	175	12-1-93	.329	.316	.333	27	76	19	25	6	0	1	11	14	2	4	1	12	1	0	.447	.441
Lucena, Isaias	B-R	5-11	180	11-15-94	.251	.265	.246	53	187	14	47	7	0	5	21	16	0	2	1	53	3	2	.369	.309
Madera, Chris	R-R	5-10	190	8-23-92	.276	.305	.262	48	185	34	51	6	0	5	22	21	2	1	1	39	12	2	.389	.354
Netzer, Brett	L-R	6-0	195	6-4-96	.260	.318	.244	26	100	15	26	4	0	0	13	9	2	1	2	24	5	1	.300	.327
Reveles, Steven	R-R	5-8	170	1-8-93	.199	.237	.185	43	146	11	29	2	0	0	8	7	0	3	0	35	2	1	.212	.235
Reynoso, Eddy	R-R	6-0	195	8-7-94	.214	.333	.125	4	14	0	3	0	0	0	2	0	1	0	0	4	0	0	.214	.267
Rusconi, Jagger	B-R	5-11	165	7-18-96	.198	.186	.202	45	167	13	33	3	1	2	11	5	1	0	0	52	4	3	.264	.225
Sciortino, Nick	R-R	5-9	197	7-21-95	.152	.286	.053	11	33	2	5	1	0	1	6	4	0	0	0	12	0	0	.273	.243
Scott, Ryan	L-R	6-2	195	7-6-93	.242	.278	.229	115	417	56	101	20	4	14	79	38	16	0	6	120	11	3	.410	.325
Spoon, Tyler	R-R	5-11	190	9-28-92	.318	.300	.326	19	66	10	21	4	1	0	8	1	1	0	2	8	0	0	.409	.329
Studdard, Granger	L-R	6-1	200	2-14-95	.230	.083	.261	44	139	19	32	5	0	2	10	16	5	1	0	62	2	1	.309	.331
Tovar, Carlos	R-R	5-11	170	8-20-95	.215	.244	.204	79	279	30	60	10	4	2	12	14	3	5	0	69	3	11	.301	.260
Tubbs, Tucker	R-R	6-3	212	9-11-92	.233	.198	.249	106	369	40	86	26	1	6	38	40	6	0	2	93	6	4	.358	.317

Pitching	B-T	HT	WT	DOB	W	L	ERA	G	GS	CG	SV	IP	H	R	ER	HR	BB	SO	AVG	vLH	vRH	K/9	BB/9
Anderson, Shaun	R-R	6-4	225	10-29-94	3	0	2.56	7	7	0	0	39	30	12	11	2	11	37	.216	.221	.211	8.61	2.56
Boyd, Logan	L-L	6-2	205	11-26-93	8	4	4.02	15	15	0	0	81	71	40	36	9	26	67	.238	.250	.231	7.48	2.90
Cooney, Harrison	R-R	6-2	175	3-23-92	1	2	6.59	8	0	0	0	14	15	14	10	2	10	19	.250	.333	.167	12.51	6.59
De Jesus, Enmanuel	L-L	6-3	190	12-10-96	0	1	6.17	2	2	0	0	12	16	8	8	0	0	10	.348	.273	.371	7.71	0.00
Diaz, Jhonathan	L-L	6-0	170	9-13-96	6	6	4.57	18	18	0	0	89	101	57	45	4	28	80	.289	.303	.283	8.12	2.84
Drehoff, Jake	L-L	6-4	195	6-5-92	0	0	0.00	2	0	0	0	6	5	0	0	0	1	6	.217	.200	.231	9.00	1.50
Florentino, Juan	R-R	5-10	182	9-8-96	0	0	2.12	10	0	0	3	17	18	5	4	0	4	18	.273	.385	.200	9.53	2.12
Goetze, Pat	R-R	6-6	200	3-3-94	2	1	1.85	23	0	0	1	49	51	15	10	1	10	38	.266	.355	.207	7.03	1.85
Gonzalez, Daniel	R-R	6-5	180	2-9-96	7	3	3.39	23	6	1	1	82	65	33	31	8	24	82	.217	.210	.225	8.96	2.62
Gorst, Matthew	R-R	6-1	205	8-24-94	6	3	3.19	27	0	0	4	54	47	21	19	9	11	46	.235	.267	.211	7.71	1.84
Groome, Jay	L-L	6-6	220	8-23-98	3	7	6.70	11	11	0	0	44	44	34	33	6	25	58	.257	.184	.287	11.77	5.08
Hart, Kyle	L-L	6-5	170	11-23-92	4	2	1.90	13	10	0	0	66	50	15	14	0	17	57	.211	.214	.209	7.73	2.31
Hernandez, Darwinzon	L-L	6-2	185	12-17-96	4	5	4.01	23	23	0	0	103	85	57	46	8	49	116	.221	.134	.251	10.10	4.27
Martinez, Algenis	R-R	6-1	185	9-12-93	4	1	2.48	26	0	0	3	62	56	21	17	7	18	70	.240	.271	.209	10.22	2.63

Martinez, Joan	R-R	6-3	195	8-29-96	1	0	0.60	8	0	0	1	15	7	1	1	0	5	18	.137	.120	.154	10.80	3.00
Mata, Bryan	R-R	6-3	160	5-3-99	5	6	3.74	17	17	1	0	77	75	34	32	3	26	74	.259	.257	.260	8.65	3.04
Nail, Brendan	L-L	6-0	190	12-9-96	1	0	0.00	1	0	0	0	1	0	0	0	0	0	0	.000	—	.000	0.00	0.00
Nogosek, Stephen	R-R	6-2	205	1-11-95	2	3	2.55	23	0	0	13	35	24	10	10	4	11	45	.197	.273	.134	11.46	2.80
Oliver, Jared	R-R	6-1	185	2-1-93	0	0	5.89	9	0	0	0	18	11	12	12	1	16	23	.175	.214	.143	11.29	7.85
Requena, Hildemaro	R-R	6-2	170	7-20-97	11	3	1.98	32	8	0	3	95	72	24	21	2	31	84	.212	.186	.235	7.93	2.93
Sexton, Robby	L-L	6-0	225	4-29-94	4	6	3.86	27	12	0	1	107	103	50	46	7	31	102	.249	.221	.261	8.55	2.60
Shawaryn, Mike	R-R	6-2	200	9-17-94	3	2	3.88	10	10	0	0	53	44	25	23	5	13	78	.222	.232	.212	13.16	2.19
Smith, Dakota	R-R	5-10	195	10-25-92	0	1	6.41	12	0	0	1	20	22	14	14	1	12	22	.286	.316	.256	10.07	5.49
Smith, Hunter	R-R	6-3	195	3-18-94	3	3	3.45	36	0	0	8	73	70	32	28	8	18	68	.254	.262	.247	8.38	2.22
Weems, Jordan	L-R	6-3	175	11-7-92	0	0	0.93	4	0	0	0	10	6	1	1	0	3	10	.177	.177	.177	9.31	2.79
Young, Lukas	R-R	6-2	190	7-26-96	0	0	5.23	5	0	0	1	10	13	7	6	2	1	9	.317	.438	.240	7.84	0.87

Fielding

Catcher	PCT	G	PO	A	E	DP	PB
Baldwin	.993	88	781	103	6	9	18
Lucena	.992	46	346	48	3	1	6
Sciortino	1.000	8	80	6	0	0	2
Spoon	1.000	1	1	0	0	0	0

First Base	PCT	G	PO	A	E	DP
Castellanos	1.000	1	9	0	0	2
Downs	.992	15	110	8	1	7
Gunsolus	.993	37	284	18	2	13
Tubbs	.997	97	848	42	3	64

Second Base	PCT	G	PO	A	E	DP
Espinal	.981	13	19	34	1	
4 Lovullo	.977	24	38	48	2	7
Netzer	.958	22	36	55	4	12
Reveles	.947	28	41	66	6	6
Rusconi	.989	24	40	47	1	10
Tovar	.993	33	49	86	1	16

Third Base	PCT	G	PO	A	E	DP
Dalbec	.935	67	45	114	11	6
Gunsolus	.976	58	36	84	3	9
Reveles	.909	9	5	15	2	0
Tovar	.955	11	7	14	1	0

Shortstop	PCT	G	PO	A	E	DP
Chatham	1.000	1	3	1	0	0
Espinal	.965	104	122	324	16	52
Lovullo	1.000	2	1	3	0	1
Tovar	.932	37	49	89	10	11

Outfield	PCT	G	PO	A	E	DP
Aybar	1.000	29	63	2	0	2
Castellanos	1.000	1	1	0	0	0
Cedrola	.981	88	148	6	3	1
Gunsolus	1.000	13	10	3	0	0
Hill	.976	100	157	8	4	0
Madera	.990	46	99	3	1	0
Reveles	1.000	6	10	1	0	0
Rusconi	.913	15	20	1	2	0
Scott	.968	94	144	7	5	1
Spoon	.889	4	8	0	1	0
Studdard	.984	40	59	1	1	0

LOWELL SPINNERS — *SHORT SEASON*

NEW YORK-PENN LEAGUE

Batting	B-T	HT	WT	DOB	AVG	vLH	vRH	G	AB	R	H	2B	3B	HR	RBI	BB	HBP	SH	SF	SO	SB	CS	SLG	OBP
Acosta, Victor	R-R	5-11	160	6-2-96	.333	.200	.364	9	27	6	9	1	0	0	3	3	0	0	2	4	1	0	.370	.375
Aybar, Yoan	L-L	6-2	165	7-3-97	.267	.260	.270	50	187	25	50	7	5	2	28	6	3	3	3	67	5	2	.390	.297
Barriento, Juan	R-R	6-2	201	4-28-96	.236	.234	.236	57	212	29	50	6	1	3	15	16	5	0	0	58	1	2	.316	.305
Benge, Garrett	L-R	6-0	205	12-28-95	.230	.283	.214	52	191	21	44	9	2	0	21	25	4	0	1	51	0	2	.298	.330
Brannen, Cole	L-R	6-0	170	8-4-98	.111	.143	.000	3	9	0	1	0	1	0	1	4	0	0	0	4	1	1	.333	.385
Campana, Marino	R-R	6-4	180	11-28-97	.235	.233	.236	45	166	17	39	9	1	4	28	8	3	0	0	50	1	0	.374	.283
Diaz, Imeldo	R-R	6-0	175	11-2-97	.208	.250	.200	7	24	4	5	3	0	0	4	2	0	0	0	4	0	1	.333	.269
2-team total (7 State College					.235	.250	.200	14	51	6	12	3	0	0	9	4	0	0	0	7	0	2	.294	.291
Espinal, Stanley	R-R	6-2	190	11-15-96	.185	.400	.136	7	27	1	5	2	0	0	3	2	0	0	0	6	0	0	.259	.241
2-team total (5 State College)					.171	.400	.136	12	41	1	7	2	0	0	4	4	0	0	0	11	0	1	.220	.244
Hamilton, Nicholos	R-R	5-11	170	12-4-97	.185	.139	.198	47	162	18	30	5	2	2	12	16	6	5	1	62	8	4	.278	.281
Lameda, Raiwinson	L-R	5-11	175	10-7-95	.240	.229	.243	51	192	15	46	7	3	2	24	8	1	1	4	37	4	2	.339	.268
Lozada, Everlouis	B-R	5-7	150	11-14-98	.583	.556	.667	3	12	0	7	0	0	0	1	0	0	0	0	1	0	1	.583	.583
Madden, Charlie	R-R	6-3	205	9-1-95	.177	.083	.205	19	51	4	9	3	0	1	5	9	1	1	0	18	0	0	.294	.312
Martinez, Alexander	R-R	6-0	170	9-6-96	.192	.154	.213	26	73	8	14	5	1	0	4	11	3	0	1	21	2	1	.288	.318
McLean, Matt	L-R	5-11	190	9-15-93	.222	.250	.200	3	9	1	2	0	0	0	1	2	1	0	0	3	1	0	.222	.417
Miranda, Samuel	L-R	6-1	175	8-21-97	.200	.206	.198	38	125	10	25	4	1	0	7	8	2	2	1	36	0	0	.248	.257
Monge, Joseph	R-R	6-1	190	5-18-95	.318	.333	.316	6	22	3	7	0	1	1	2	4	1	0	0	7	1	1	.546	.444
Netzer, Brett	L-R	6-0	195	6-4-96	.317	.360	.298	22	82	11	26	6	0	0	14	9	0	1	2	20	0	3	.390	.376
Nishioka, Tanner	R-R	5-11	180	10-22-94	.268	.250	.273	22	71	6	19	2	1	0	4	5	5	0	1	20	6	0	.324	.354
Osinski, Michael	R-R	6-2	195	8-4-95	.261	.263	.261	41	153	19	40	8	1	2	14	12	2	0	2	43	3	0	.366	.320
Reveles, Steven	R-R	5-8	170	1-8-93	.148	.182	.140	20	54	3	8	1	0	0	4	5	0	2	0	16	0	1	.167	.220
Rios, Frankie	R-R	5-10	185	5-27-95	.245	.225	.252	44	151	26	37	2	1	1	14	21	4	0	2	32	6	3	.291	.348
Sciortino, Nick	R-R	5-9	197	7-21-95	.224	.200	.231	22	67	12	15	1	0	2	5	13	0	1	0	25	0	1	.328	.350
Sterry, Zach	L-R	5-11	226	6-4-94	.203	.143	.220	20	64	5	13	3	0	0	8	10	2	0	0	13	0	2	.250	.329
Suarez, Kervin	B-R	5-11	165	12-19-98	.250	.286	.000	3	8	1	2	0	0	0	0	2	0	0	0	2	0	0	.250	.400
Tavarez, Aneury	L-R	5-9	175	4-14-92	.179	.333	.160	7	28	2	5	1	1	0	3	2	1	0	0	6	1	0	.286	.258
Valentin, Yomar	B-R	5-8	145	12-26-97	.200	.273	.180	47	150	17	30	6	0	0	7	22	2	4	0	24	5	3	.240	.310
Wren, Jordan	L-L	6-1	195	9-23-93	.183	.182	.184	24	71	4	13	1	0	0	6	6	2	0	0	30	1	0	.197	.266

Pitching	B-T	HT	WT	DOB	W	L	ERA	G	GS	CG	SV	IP	H	R	ER	HR	BB	SO	AVG	vLH	vRH	K/9	BB/9
Ahearn, Taylor	R-R	6-1	190	11-25-94	0	1	5.03	8	0	0	1	20	23	12	11	3	1	10	.291	.206	.356	4.58	0.46
Cooney, Harrison	R-R	6-2	175	3-23-92	0	0	13.50	1	0	0	0	2	2	3	3	0	0	4	.222	—	.222	18.00	0.00
Crawford, Kutter	R-R	6-1	192	4-1-96	0	0	0.00	1	1	0	0	1	1	0	0	0	1	2	.250	.333	.000	18.00	9.00
De Jesus, Enmanuel	L-L	6-3	190	12-10-96	3	3	3.40	12	12	0	0	53	62	27	20	2	20	45	.290	.240	.317	7.64	3.40
Duron, Nick	R-R	6-4	190	1-30-96	3	5	3.35	13	12	0	0	54	43	21	20	3	16	36	.221	.206	.230	6.04	2.68
Elias, Roenis	L-L	6-1	205	8-1-88	0	0	0.00	1	1	0	0	2	0	0	0	0	0	2	.000	.000	.000	9.00	0.00
Fisher, Devon	R-R	6-0	215	5-1-96	4	1	4.86	17	0	0	0	33	25	23	18	1	19	35	.202	.233	.185	9.45	5.13
Florentino, Juan	R-R	5-10	182	9-8-96	1	2	0.96	12	0	0	5	19	14	5	2	1	2	25	.200	.258	.154	12.05	0.96
Gomez, Rio	L-L	6-0	190	10-20-94	0	1	9.00	3	0	0	0	5	8	6	5	0	3	6	.364	.000	.400	10.80	5.40
Groome, Jay	L-L	6-6	220	8-23-98	0	2	1.64	3	3	0	0	11	5	4	2	0	5	14	.132	.125	.133	11.45	4.09
Houck, Tanner	R-R	6-5	220	6-29-96	0	3	3.63	10	10	0	0	22	21	14	9	0	8	25	.239	.244	.234	10.07	3.22

Pitching	B-T	HT	WT	DOB	W	L	ERA	G	GS	CG	SV	IP	H	R	ER	HR	BB	SO	AVG	vLH	vRH	K/9	BB/9
Johnson, Brian	L-L	6-4	235	12-7-90	0	0	3.38	1	1	0	0	3	2	2	1	0	2	4	.200	.000	.222	13.50	6.75
Lantigua, Marcos	R-R	6-3	200	12-14-95	0	0	0.00	1	0	0	0	2	2	1	0	0	1	0	.286	.333	.250	0.00	4.50
LoBrutto, Dominic	L-L	6-1	185	5-31-96	1	1	3.28	15	0	0	5	25	20	10	9	2	18	30	.215	.333	.159	10.95	6.57
Lopez-Soto, Francisco	R-R	6-5	220	12-18-96	0	0	0.00	1	0	0	0	1	1	0	0	0	0	3	.250	1.000	.000	27.00	0.00
Martinez, Joan	R-R	6-3	195	8-29-96	0	2	1.56	11	0	0	1	17	12	5	3	0	4	13	.197	.182	.214	6.75	2.08
McAvoy, Kevin	R-R	6-4	210	7-21-93	0	0	0.00	1	1	0	0	5	1	0	0	0	2	4	.071	.167	.000	7.20	3.60
Nail, Brendan	L-L	6-0	190	12-9-96	1	0	0.00	2	0	0	0	4	4	0	0	0	1	5	.250	.286	.222	11.25	2.25
O'Linger, Durin	L-R	5-10	185	10-10-93	4	1	2.03	13	3	0	1	49	42	14	11	1	14	49	.231	.278	.200	9.06	2.59
Oduber, Ryan	L-L	5-11	140	8-16-97	2	2	5.40	16	0	0	1	32	42	22	19	2	12	27	.321	.286	.333	7.67	3.41
Oliver, Jared	R-R	6-1	185	2-1-93	0	0	2.12	9	0	0	0	17	8	5	4	2	8	27	.131	.097	.167	14.29	4.24
Osnowitz, Mitchell	R-R	6-5	245	7-2-91	0	1	3.31	14	0	0	0	33	28	12	12	3	23	38	.233	.227	.237	10.47	6.34
Padron, Angel	L-L	5-11	175	9-16-97	0	2	5.14	4	3	0	0	14	16	10	8	2	4	13	.276	.000	.314	8.36	2.57
Pantoja, Yorvin	L-L	5-11	175	9-22-97	0	7	5.46	15	15	0	0	58	60	42	35	6	33	40	.274	.188	.298	6.24	5.15
Perez, Juan	R-R	6-1	198	8-30-96	0	0	30.86	1	0	0	0	2	8	8	8	0	1	0	.571	.333	.636	0.00	3.86
Reyes, Denyi	R-R	6-4	209	11-2-96	9	0	1.45	15	0	0	0	62	52	13	10	3	7	53	.221	.239	.210	7.69	1.02
Smith, Dakota	R-R	5-10	195	10-25-92	4	4	3.74	14	6	0	0	65	70	34	27	0	16	49	.268	.268	.269	6.78	2.22
Taylor, Ben	R-R	6-3	225	11-12-92	0	0	0.00	2	0	0	0	2	1	0	0	0	1	1	.167	.000	.200	3.86	3.86
Thompson, Jake	R-R	6-1	200	9-22-94	0	3	3.18	7	7	0	0	11	10	7	4	0	6	11	.238	.158	.304	8.74	4.76
Young, Lukas	R-R	6-2	190	7-26-96	1	1	4.50	10	0	0	1	20	19	11	10	1	4	25	.244	.308	.212	11.25	1.80

Fielding

C: Madden 19, Miranda 37, Sciortino 22. **1B:** Barriento 5, Lameda 51, Miranda 1, Sterry 20. **2B:** Diaz 1, Netzer 19, Nishioka 16, Reveles 8, Rios 2, Suarez 3, Valentin 27. **3B:** Benge 45, Espinal 7, Lozada 3, Osinski 16, Reveles 4. **SS:** Diaz 6, Osinski 14, Rios 39, Valentin 19. **OF:** Acosta 8, Aybar 50, Barriento 46, Brannen 3, Campana 34, Hamilton 47, Lameda 1, Martinez 26, McLean 2, Monge 5, Reveles 7, Tavarez 4.

GCL RED SOX — *ROOKIE*

GULF COAST LEAGUE

Batting	B-T	HT	WT	DOB	AVG	vLH	vRH	G	AB	R	H	2B	3B	HR	RBI	BB	HBP	SH	SF	SO	SB	CS	SLG	OBP
Abreu, Juan Carlos	R-R	6-0	175	5-30-97	.240	.290	.210	33	100	15	24	3	4	0	11	19	3	2	2	38	5	2	.350	.371
Arnold, Jecorrah	R-R	6-2	190	1-6-99	.197	.115	.250	25	66	6	13	0	0	1	12	7	8	1	2	19	1	0	.242	.337
Berroa, Ramfis	R-R	6-2	190	11-2-95	.274	.222	.294	27	95	11	26	3	1	3	16	9	2	0	1	38	3	0	.421	.346
Brannen, Cole	L-R	6-0	170	8-4-98	.231	.316	.198	39	134	23	31	2	0	0	7	30	3	1	0	37	9	1	.246	.383
Campana, Marino	R-R	6-4	180	11-28-97	.250	.250	.250	9	36	3	9	2	0	0	4	4	1	0	1	6	0	0	.306	.333
Castellanos, Pedro	R-R	6-3	195	12-11-97	.339	.391	.312	52	186	27	63	14	1	2	30	10	7	0	5	15	0	0	.457	.385
Chatham, C.J.	R-R	6-4	185	12-22-94	.313	.000	.455	6	16	5	5	0	0	1	3	2	0	0	0	1	0	0	.500	.389
Colon, Andre	R-R	6-0	180	2-12-99	.263	.308	.247	34	99	14	26	4	0	0	10	14	14	0	1	22	1	2	.303	.422
Conde, Eduard	L-R	5-9	155	2-13-98	.207	.286	.182	10	29	4	6	2	0	0	4	2	0	1	0	5	0	0	.276	.258
Cubillan, Ricardo	B-R	6-0	155	2-1-98	.271	.324	.242	34	96	21	26	0	0	0	11	30	0	4	0	20	6	1	.271	.444
Dalbec, Bobby	R-R	6-4	225	6-29-95	.259	.200	.294	7	27	3	7	1	0	0	2	5	0	0	0	9	1	0	.296	.375
Dearden, Tyler	L-R	6-2	185	7-6-98	.257	.357	.233	28	74	9	19	5	0	2	15	14	5	1	0	28	1	1	.405	.409
Downs, Jerry	L-L	6-2	215	12-22-93	.188	.000	.261	11	32	7	6	3	0	0	3	3	6	0	2	8	0	0	.281	.349
Durden, David	R-R	6-2	200	12-26-98	.220	.100	.279	30	91	7	20	1	0	0	9	6	7	0	2	33	1	0	.231	.311
Esplin, Tyler	L-R	6-4	225	7-6-99	.271	.286	.263	22	85	16	23	4	0	2	11	7	2	0	0	26	1	0	.388	.340
Ganns, Trey	L-L	6-2	225	10-28-95	.242	.333	.191	13	33	3	8	1	0	0	3	4	1	0	0	12	2	1	.273	.342
Hanna, Beau	R-R	6-1	210	7-10-98	.000	.000	.000	3	7	0	0	0	0	0	0	0	0	0	0	4	0	0	.000	.000
Hardy, Chad	R-R	6-2	175	5-22-97	.000	.000	—	1	3	0	0	0	0	0	0	0	0	0	0	2	0	0	.000	.000
Hernandez, Juan	L-R	5-10	155	4-9-96	.167	.200	.143	13	24	5	4	1	0	0	1	2	0	1	0	6	0	0	.208	.231
LeGrant, Xavier	R-R	6-0	175	4-19-97	.115	.222	.059	11	26	2	3	1	0	0	0	3	1	0	0	10	0	0	.154	.233
Lozada, Everlouis	B-R	5-7	150	11-14-98	.315	.289	.325	44	159	26	50	9	2	0	20	18	1	0	2	27	6	4	.396	.383
Marrero, Alan	R-R	5-10	195	2-28-98	.200	.105	.232	24	75	12	15	3	0	2	8	6	4	0	0	28	0	0	.320	.294
Osinski, Michael	R-R	6-2	195	8-4-95	.222	.000	.333	3	9	1	2	0	0	0	0	1	2	0	0	2	1	0	.222	.417
Pulido, Carlos	B-R	5-10	170	2-7-98	.100	.000	.167	11	20	2	2	0	0	0	4	6	1	0	0	4	0	0	.100	.333
Reynoso, Eddy	R-R	6-0	195	8-7-94	.185	.375	.105	9	27	3	5	3	0	1	5	4	0	0	0	1	0	0	.407	.290
Rusconi, Jagger	B-R	5-11	165	7-18-96	.308	.286	.316	7	26	5	8	3	0	0	3	4	0	0	0	10	2	0	.423	.400
Schmidt, Alberto	R-R	5-9	180	5-29-97	.108	.167	.080	16	37	2	4	0	0	0	4	10	4	1	0	11	0	0	.108	.353
Sterry, Zach	L-R	5-11	226	6-4-94	.188	.333	.100	5	16	0	3	0	0	0	1	0	1	0	0	6	0	0	.188	.235
Suarez, Kervin	B-R	5-11	165	12-19-98	.274	.322	.252	47	190	33	52	9	1	2	13	17	1	1	1	47	11	1	.363	.335
Swihart, Blake	B-R	6-1	200	4-3-92	.167	.200	.160	9	30	6	5	2	0	0	2	8	0	0	0	8	2	0	.233	.342

Pitching	B-T	HT	WT	DOB	W	L	ERA	G	GS	CG	SV	IP	H	R	ER	HR	BB	SO	AVG	vLH	vRH	K/9	BB/9
Adames, Rayniel	L-L	6-6	175	9-7-97	0	0	3.91	9	8	0	0	25	22	17	11	0	17	20	.242	.185	.266	7.11	6.04
Ahearn, Taylor	R-R	6-1	190	11-25-94	2	0	2.30	6	1	0	0	16	11	4	4	1	2	16	.196	.167	.219	9.19	1.15
Batista, Edilson	L-L	6-3	210	7-7-97	2	4	6.37	11	11	0	0	41	59	41	29	1	21	20	.328	.356	.319	4.39	4.61
Bazardo, Eduard	R-R	6-0	155	9-1-95	2	4	3.08	13	2	0	2	38	31	17	13	0	16	43	.223	.293	.194	10.18	3.79
Behenna, Kory	L-L	6-2	185	8-2-96	0	2	7.64	14	0	0	1	18	22	19	15	0	14	14	.314	.278	.327	7.13	7.13
Carber, Andrew	R-R	6-9	232	7-16-95	0	0	22.50	4	1	0	0	2	0	6	5	0	6	1	.000	.000	.000	4.50	27.00
Garcia, Victor	R-R	6-4	204	6-15-97	1	1	4.98	13	0	0	0	22	27	14	12	0	12	24	.307	.313	.304	9.97	4.98
Gomez, Rio	L-L	6-0	190	10-20-94	2	1	1.98	13	1	0	2	27	27	11	6	0	7	25	.252	.258	.250	8.23	2.30
Gonzalez, Jose	R-R	6-0	175	7-27-98	1	2	3.48	8	2	0	1	21	24	8	8	1	3	17	.293	.276	.302	7.40	1.31
Haworth, Hunter	R-R	6-4	210	10-2-96	3	0	1.50	6	0	0	0	12	9	2	2	1	5	10	.209	.250	.185	7.50	3.75
Lantigua, Marcos	R-R	6-3	200	12-14-95	1	1	4.94	17	0	0	3	24	24	16	13	0	9	21	.273	.222	.308	7.99	3.42
Lopez-Soto, Francisco	R-R	6-5	220	12-18-96	3	1	2.49	14	0	0	0	22	12	7	6	2	22	25	.164	.259	.109	10.38	9.14
Mendoza, Ritzi	R-R	6-2	175	1-10-96	3	3	3.52	13	2	0	1	38	41	17	15	0	10	34	.279	.349	.226	7.98	2.35
Mosqueda, Oddanier	L-L	5-10	155	5-6-99	0	5	7.38	11	10	0	0	39	48	34	32	3	22	31	.310	.250	.325	7.15	5.08
Padron, Angel	L-L	5-11	175	9-16-97	3	2	3.21	10	6	0	1	42	40	16	15	1	12	48	.248	.200	.265	10.29	2.57

Pitching	B-T	HT	WT	DOB	W	L	ERA	G	GS	CG	SV	IP	H	R	ER	HR	BB	SO	AVG	vLH	vRH	K/9	BB/9
Perez, Juan	R-R	6-1	198	8-30-96	2	3	4.50	11	8	0	0	44	51	25	22	2	11	36	.298	.325	.277	7.36	2.25
Raiburn, Tanner	L-L	5-9	175	12-28-94	2	1	3.98	17	0	0	4	20	16	9	9	0	10	16	.219	.000	.276	7.08	4.43
Rodriguez, Alejandro	L-L	6-1	160	10-30-96	0	1	2.73	9	3	0	0	26	30	14	8	1	4	26	.289	.321	.276	8.89	1.37
Rodriguez, Fernando	R-R	6-3	235	6-18-84	0	0	3.00	2	2	0	0	3	3	1	1	0	0	2	.250	.333	.167	6.00	0.00
Schellenger, Zach	R-R	6-5	210	1-9-96	0	0	6.00	3	1	0	0	3	1	2	2	0	6	4	.100	.000	.200	12.00	18.00
Weems, Jordan	L-R	6-3	175	11-7-92	0	0	0.00	1	0	0	0	1	2	0	0	0	0	0	.500	—	.500	0.00	0.00

Fielding

C: Conde 9, Hanna 3, Marrero 23, Pulido 10, Reynoso 7, Schmidt 16, Swihart 2. **1B:** Castellanos 43, Cubillan 1, Downs 5, Ganns 8, Reynoso 2, Sterry 3, Swihart 4. **2B:** Arnold 1, Colon 3, Conde 1, Cubillan 3, LeGrant 8, Lozada 3, Rusconi 4, Suarez 40. **3B:** Arnold 9, Colon 1, Conde 1, Cubillan 6, Dalbec 4, Durden 1, Lozada 41, Osinski 2. **SS:** Arnold 8, Chatham 4, Colon 28, Cubillan 24. **OF:** Abreu 30, Berroa 25, Brannen 38, Campana 9, Castellanos 1, Dearden 24, Durden 29, Esplin 15, Hernandez 11, Suarez 6.

DSL RED SOX — ROOKIE

DOMINICAN SUMMER LEAGUE

Batting	B-T	HT	WT	DOB	AVG	vLH	vRH	G	AB	R	H	2B	3B	HR	RBI	BB	HBP	SH	SF	SO	SB	CS	SLG	OBP
Andrade, Fabian	L-L	5-11	162	4-1-99	.211	.250	.198	44	128	15	27	3	1	0	13	13	4	1	3	22	5	2	.250	.297
Baez, Lewis	L-R	5-9	170	11-7-96	.127	.111	.135	17	55	3	7	2	1	0	2	1	0	0	2	14	1	4	.200	.138
Chacon, Jesus	R-R	5-11	167	5-27-99	.173	.091	.208	31	75	9	13	3	0	0	9	6	1	1	1	21	1	1	.213	.241
Conde, Eduard	L-R	5-9	155	2-13-98	.241	.263	.233	23	79	16	19	6	1	2	14	5	3	1	1	16	2	0	.418	.307
Diaz, Jonathan	L-R	5-11	170	7-7-99	.270	.263	.273	19	63	8	17	4	0	2	10	6	0	0	0	13	1	2	.429	.333
Figueroa, Willis	B-R	5-10	165	12-31-94	.356	.343	.361	46	132	33	47	3	2	0	10	32	5	2	1	24	10	6	.409	.494
Gonzalez, Angel	R-R	6-2	180	11-10-98	.202	.182	.211	32	109	14	22	2	0	0	10	6	10	1	0	24	4	4	.220	.304
Hernandez, Luis	R-R	6-1	165	10-7-98	.188	.139	.204	49	144	26	27	3	1	0	15	23	9	11	0	43	3	3	.222	.335
Houellemont, Ivan	B-R	6-2	170	9-10-98	.288	.333	.271	56	170	28	49	6	1	1	29	15	13	1	3	39	5	4	.353	.383
Jimenez, Ivan	R-R	6-4	215	4-17-98	.220	.273	.205	22	50	6	11	1	0	0	4	7	1	1	0	16	0	0	.240	.328
Marin, Freiberg	B-R	5-11	170	9-5-97	.279	.221	.308	57	201	21	56	4	0	0	29	24	4	4	3	20	5	5	.299	.362
Martinez, Alexander	R-R	6-0	170	9-6-96	.331	.432	.293	39	136	15	45	8	1	0	22	14	6	1	4	20	13	4	.404	.406
Martinez, Marcos	L-R	5-11	165	1-28-98	.268	.216	.287	44	138	21	37	5	1	0	18	10	3	2	3	29	2	2	.319	.325
Mejias, Jose	R-R	6-1	160	3-13-99	.205	.233	.190	29	88	5	18	1	0	0	5	3	2	1	1	17	2	2	.216	.245
Petit, Keibert	R-R	6-1	175	8-3-98	.270	.286	.262	67	226	34	61	11	1	2	33	34	3	0	4	45	16	4	.354	.367
Pulgar, Ronaldo	R-R	5-10	158	1-2-97	.136	.182	.119	32	81	6	11	2	0	0	4	15	3	1	0	14	3	1	.161	.293
Rincones, Rafael	B-R	6-0	159	7-1-99	.258	.169	.301	58	198	38	51	13	3	1	19	32	5	0	1	51	8	3	.369	.373
2-team total (2 DSL Athletics)					.265	.169	.301	60	204	40	54	14	3	1	22	32	5	0	1	51	8	3	.378	.376
Torres, Luis	R-R	5-11	174	9-29-98	.342	.333	.344	18	38	5	13	3	1	0	6	6	0	0	0	6	4	2	.474	.432
Ugueto, Reinaldo	R-R	5-11	165	12-9-97	.222	.122	.270	48	149	32	33	5	1	0	17	13	24	4	0	26	8	7	.269	.376

Pitching	B-T	HT	WT	DOB	W	L	ERA	G	GS	CG	SV	IP	H	R	ER	HR	BB	SO	AVG	vLH	vRH	K/9	BB/9
Bazardo, Eduard	R-R	6-0	155	9-1-95	1	0	1.00	4	0	0	0	18	9	2	2	0	1	24	.145	.083	.184	12.00	0.50
Calvo, Gary	R-R	6-3	180	10-4-96	0	0	0.00	1	1	0	0	0	0	0	0	0	0	1	.000	.000	—	27.00	0.00
Colmenares, Luis	L-L	6-0	180	4-22-98	2	2	3.77	14	9	0	0	43	38	20	18	0	29	43	.248	.222	.252	9.00	6.07
Cortes, Carlos	R-R	6-1	165	7-26-96	2	1	5.35	17	0	0	1	34	35	23	20	1	27	30	.285	.277	.290	8.02	7.22
Figueroa, Junior	R-R	6-4	176	8-16-99	0	1	8.59	5	0	0	0	7	11	9	7	0	4	7	.379	.400	.368	8.59	4.91
Franco, Alberto	R-R	5-11	165	8-16-94	1	0	0.75	11	0	0	3	12	3	2	1	0	6	20	.081	.167	.040	15.00	4.50
Gomez, Rafael	R-R	5-11	167	4-17-98	2	3	2.43	14	10	0	0	59	59	21	16	3	8	54	.263	.241	.276	8.19	1.21
Gutierrez, Ronald	R-R	6-2	175	4-22-99	0	1	10.50	3	3	0	0	6	11	8	7	0	1	7	.393	.364	.412	10.50	1.50
Jimenez, Andres	R-R	6-1	170	10-23-98	5	1	2.25	9	5	0	0	32	19	8	8	2	4	28	.167	.200	.145	7.88	1.13
Lacrus, Shair	R-R	6-1	170	12-22-96	2	1	3.55	12	0	0	2	25	21	15	10	4	14	25	.233	.216	.245	8.88	4.97
Larez, Jose	R-R	6-4	195	1-12-97	1	2	7.11	7	0	0	0	6	8	6	5	0	10	7	.333	.429	.294	9.95	14.21
Martinez, Johan	R-R	6-2	180	4-7-99	0	0	13.50	6	0	0	0	6	11	10	9	0	8	5	.458	.571	.412	7.50	12.00
Medina, Roberto	R-R	6-3	160	1-13-95	0	0	0.00	1	0	0	0	0	0	0	0	0	0	0	.000	—	.000	0.00	0.00
Montero, Alexander	R-R	6-3	180	9-21-97	0	0	4.11	5	4	0	0	15	15	7	7	0	6	15	.263	.292	.242	8.80	3.52
Moreno, Rayniel	L-L	6-1	165	9-11-98	5	2	2.12	13	13	1	0	64	53	19	15	1	11	50	.231	.200	.239	7.07	1.55
Morillo, Juan	R-R	6-2	176	9-27-96	1	0	0.96	9	1	0	0	28	25	4	3	0	9	18	.260	.219	.281	5.79	2.89
Pena, Jeison	R-R	6-2	185	5-15-98	1	0	4.91	7	0	0	0	15	15	8	8	0	5	5	.273	.357	.244	3.07	3.07
Perez, Geraldo	R-R	6-3	190	5-13-96	4	3	1.55	16	0	0	0	29	22	10	5	0	18	35	.214	.171	.235	10.86	5.59
Pinales, Isaac	R-R	6-0	172	8-15-95	0	0	1.61	7	5	0	0	28	16	7	5	0	3	27	.168	.094	.206	8.68	0.96
Police, Antonio	R-R	6-2	180	2-12-98	2	0	3.00	11	0	0	1	15	13	11	5	0	19	21	.245	.250	.242	12.60	11.40
Ramirez, Manuel	R-R	5-11	155	2-15-99	3	2	3.18	15	3	0	1	40	43	20	14	1	17	27	.274	.345	.232	6.13	3.86
Rivero, Luis	R-R	6-3	195	1-23-98	10	1	1.06	17	0	0	5	34	17	4	4	0	9	34	.160	.172	.156	9.00	2.38
Rodriguez, Alejandro	L-L	6-1	160	10-30-96	3	1	1.07	7	6	0	0	34	20	5	4	2	8	31	.170	.214	.164	8.29	2.14
Sanchez, Kelvin	L-L	6-3	196	5-12-97	0	0	0.00	2	2	0	0	7	3	1	0	0	2	5	.130	.500	.095	6.43	2.57
Santana, Yasel	R-R	6-1	180	12-14-96	0	2	3.32	10	1	0	0	22	16	10	8	0	9	17	.216	.167	.240	7.06	3.74
Santos, Gregory	R-R	6-2	190	8-28-99	2	0	0.89	8	8	0	0	30	22	6	3	0	15	24	.206	.237	.188	7.12	4.45
2-team total (4 DSL Giants)					3	0	1.29	12	12	0	0	49	43	11	7	2	20	41	.234	.237	.188	7.53	3.67
Zacarias, Jose	R-R	5-11	160	1-9-97	0	1	5.23	6	0	0	1	10	12	8	6	1	4	6	.316	.167	.385	5.23	3.48

Fielding

C: Conde 23, Diaz 9, Jimenez 6, Martinez 42. **1B:** Andrade 23, Diaz 1, Jimenez 11, Mejias 12, Petit 34. **2B:** Chacon 11, Marin 47, Pulgar 14, Ugueto 9. **3B:** Chacon 14, Hernandez 46, Houellemont 8, Marin 9. **SS:** Chacon 1, Hernandez 1, Houellemont 44, Ugueto 30. **OF:** Andrade 17, Baez 16, Figueroa 34, Gonzalez 29, Martinez 33, Mejias 12, Petit 29, Rincones 54, Torres 14.

Chicago Cubs

SEASON IN A SENTENCE: The third year of the Cubs being good wasn't as satisfying. While the 2015 club set the table with 97 wins and the '16 team ended the game's longest World Series drought, the '17 Cubs won the National League Central and a Division Series but petered out in the NL Championship Series.

HIGH POINT: After entering the all-star break down in the standings by 5 1/2 games, the Cubs stormed into the second half, winning 10 out of 12 to overtake the Brewers for first place. But they didn't sew up the division until after a three-game sweep at the hands of the Brewers with a season-long, seven-game September winning streak.

LOW POINT: The Cubs may have been spent by a grueling Division Series with the Nationals, but the gap between Chicago and the Dodgers seemed vast in the NLCS. The Cubs hit seven homers in the five-game series loss—six solo and one two-run shot—to account for all of their runs. The team hit just .156 in the series loss.

NOTABLE ROOKIES: Albert Almora and Ian Happ combined for 120-plus starts in center field, and Happ hit 24 home runs to rank fourth on the team while playing outfield and second base. Almora shined defensively while hitting .298. However, no rookies on the mound lost their prospect eligibility other than righty Felix Pena, who was removed from the 40-man roster after the season.

KEY TRANSACTIONS: Wade Davis (acquired in a deal for Jorge Soler) thrived as closer and shut the door on the Nationals in the NLDS. Chicago continued emptying the farm system to trade for big league talent. Acquiring lefthander Jose Quintana, with three more years of club control, cost top prospect Eloy Jimenez and top pitching prospect Dylan Cease. A late July deal with Detroit, bringing catcher Alex Avila and lefthander Justin Wilson, cost prospects Jeimer Candelario and Isaac Paredes.

DOWN ON THE FARM: Befitting an organization that has traded or graduated so much talent at the upper levels, the Cubs had their greatest success at the lower levels of the farm system. The Cubs won the Rookie-level Arizona League championship while short-season Eugene lost in the short-season Northwest League finals. Righthander Dillon Maples, a 2011 draftee, finally got healthy and together in a relief role, striking out 100 in 63.1 innings to earn a September callup.

OPENING DAY PAYROLL: $172,846,918 (8th)

PLAYERS OF THE YEAR

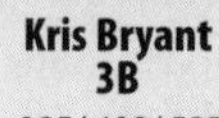

MAJOR LEAGUE

Kris Bryant
3B
.295/.409/.537
29 HR, .946 OPS
111 R, 95 BB

MINOR LEAGUE

Dillon Maples
RHP
(High Class A/
Double-A/Triple-A)
2.27 ERA in 63.1 IP

ORGANIZATION LEADERS

BATTING — *Minimum 250 AB

MAJORS

*	AVG	Albert Almora Jr.	.298
*	OPS	Kris Bryant	.946
	HR	Anthony Rizzo	32
	RBI	Anthony Rizzo	109

MINORS

*	AVG	Victor Caratini, Iowa	.342
*	OBP	Mark Zagunis, Iowa	.404
*	SLG	Victor Caratini, Iowa	.558
*	OPS	Victor Caratini, Iowa	.951
	R	Zack Short, South Bend, Myrtle Beach	84
	H	Vimael Machin, South Bend, Myrtle Beach	130
	TB	David Bote, Tennessee	206
	2B	Jacob Hannemann, Tennessee, Iowa	32
	3B	John Andreoli, Iowa	8
		D.J. Wilson, AZL Cubs, South Bend	8
	HR	Jason Vosler, Tennessee	21
	RBI	Jason Vosler, Tennessee	81
	BB	Zack Short, South Bend, Myrtle Beach	94
	SO	John Andreoli, Iowa	138
	SB	Jacob Hannemann, Tennessee, Iowa	29

PITCHING — #Minimum 75 IP

MAJORS

	W	Jake Arrieta	14
#	ERA	Kyle Hendricks	3.03
	SO	Jon Lester	180
	SV	Wade Davis	32

MINORS

	W	Manuel Rondon, South Bend	14
	L	Zach Hedges, Iowa, Tennessee	12
#	ERA	Daury Torrez, Tennessee	1.40
	G	Dillon Maples, Myrtle Beach, Tennessee, Iowa	52
	GS	Zach Hedges, Iowa, Tennessee	26
		Thomas Hatch, Myrtle Beach	26
		Manuel Rondon, South Bend	26
	SV	Wyatt Short, South Bend	16
	IP	Zach Hedges, Iowa, Tennessee	146
	BB	Manuel Rondon, South Bend	66
	SO	Thomas Hatch, Myrtle Beach	126
#	AVG	James Pugliese, Tennessee	.203

2017 PERFORMANCE

President, Baseball Ops: Theo Epstein. **Farm Director:** Jaron Madison. **Scouting Director:** Matt Dorey.

Class	Team	League	W	L	PCT	Finish	Manager
Majors	Chicago Cubs	National	92	70	.568	4th (15)	Joe Maddon
Triple-A	Iowa Cubs	Pacific Coast	67	72	.482	t-10th (16)	Marty Pevey
Double-A	Tennessee Smokies	Southern	68	70	.493	6th (10)	Mark Johnson
High-A	Myrtle Beach Pelicans	Carolina	73	67	.521	5th (10)	Buddy Bailey
Low-A	South Bend Cubs	Midwest	75	64	.54	3rd (16)	Jimmy Gonzalez
Short Season	Eugene Emeralds	Northwest	39	37	.513	t-4th (8)	Jesus Feliciano
Rookie	AZL Cubs	Arizona	25	31	.446	t-11th (15)	Carmelo Martinez
Overall 2017 Minor League Record			347	341	.504	t-11th (30)	

CHICAGO CUBS

ORGANIZATION STATISTICS

CHICAGO CUBS

NATIONAL LEAGUE

Batting	B-T	HT	WT	DOB	AVG	vLH	vRH	G	AB	R	H	2B	3B	HR	RBI	BB	HBP	SH	SF	SO	SB	CS	SLG	OBP
Almora Jr., Albert	R-R	6-2	190	4-16-94	.298	.342	.271	132	299	39	89	18	1	8	46	19	0	3	2	53	1	0	.445	.338
Avila, Alex	R-L	5-11	210	1-29-87	.239	.250	.236	35	92	11	22	2	1	3	17	19	0	1	0	40	0	0	.380	.369
Baez, Javier	R-R	6-0	190	12-1-92	.273	.315	.258	145	469	75	128	24	2	23	75	30	1	6	2	144	10	3	.480	.317
Bryant, Kris	R-R	6-5	230	1-4-92	.295	.298	.294	151	549	111	162	38	4	29	73	95	15	0	6	128	7	5	.537	.409
Candelario, Jeimer	B-R	6-1	210	11-24-93	.152	.286	.115	11	33	2	5	2	0	1	3	1	2	0	0	12	0	0	.303	.222
Caratini, Victor	B-R	6-1	215	8-17-93	.254	.500	.192	31	59	6	15	3	0	1	2	4	3	0	0	13	0	0	.356	.333
Contreras, Willson	R-R	6-1	210	5-13-92	.276	.279	.274	117	377	50	104	21	0	21	74	45	3	1	2	98	5	4	.499	.356
Davis, Taylor	R-R	5-10	200	11-28-89	.231	.000	.273	8	13	1	3	1	0	0	1	0	0	0	0	4	0	0	.308	.231
Freeman, Mike	L-R	6-0	190	8-4-87	.160	.000	.211	15	25	3	4	2	0	0	0	2	0	0	0	8	0	0	.240	.222
2-team total (4 Los Angeles)					.133	.000	.211	19	30	3	4	2	0	0	0	2	0	0	0	10	0	0	.200	.188
Happ, Ian	B-R	6-0	205	8-12-94	.253	.276	.243	115	364	62	92	17	3	24	68	39	4	2	4	129	8	4	.514	.329
Heyward, Jason	L-L	6-5	240	8-9-89	.259	.267	.256	126	432	59	112	15	4	11	59	41	3	2	2	67	4	4	.389	.326
Jay, Jon	L-L	5-11	195	3-15-85	.296	.318	.289	141	379	65	112	18	3	2	34	37	12	3	2	80	6	2	.375	.374
La Stella, Tommy	L-R	5-11	180	1-31-89	.288	.385	.277	73	125	18	36	8	0	5	22	20	2	0	2	18	0	0	.472	.389
Martin, Leonys	L-R	6-2	200	3-6-88	.154	.000	.182	15	13	2	2	1	0	0	1	3	0	0	0	4	1	0	.231	.313
Montero, Miguel	R-L	5-11	210	7-9-83	.286	.417	.267	44	98	12	28	3	0	4	8	11	2	0	1	24	1	0	.439	.366
Rivera, Rene	R-R	5-10	215	7-31-83	.341	.188	.429	20	44	8	15	5	0	2	12	5	0	1	0	16	0	0	.591	.408
2-team total (54 New York)					.252	.188	.429	74	218	23	55	9	0	10	35	14	3	1	1	70	0	1	.431	.305
Rizzo, Anthony	L-L	6-3	240	8-8-89	.273	.260	.277	157	572	99	156	32	3	32	109	91	24	0	4	90	10	4	.507	.392
Russell, Addison	R-R	6-0	200	1-23-94	.239	.264	.230	110	352	52	84	21	3	12	43	29	4	0	0	91	2	1	.418	.304
Schwarber, Kyle	L-R	6-0	235	3-5-93	.211	.171	.221	129	422	67	89	16	1	30	59	59	5	0	0	150	1	1	.467	.315
Szczur, Matt	R-R	6-0	200	7-20-89	.211	.222	.200	15	19	2	4	1	0	0	3	2	0	1	1	4	0	0	.263	.273
2-team total (104 San Diego)					.226	.222	.200	119	195	28	44	12	2	3	18	34	4	3	1	44	0	2	.354	.350
Zagunis, Mark	R-R	6-0	205	2-5-93	.000	.000	.000	7	14	0	0	0	0	0	1	4	0	0	0	6	2	0	.000	.222
Zobrist, Ben	B-R	6-3	210	5-26-81	.232	.179	.249	128	435	58	101	20	3	12	50	54	2	2	3	71	2	2	.375	.318

Pitching	B-T	HT	WT	DOB	W	L	ERA	G	GS	CG	SV	IP	H	R	ER	HR	BB	SO	AVG	vLH	vRH	K/9	BB/9
Anderson, Brett	L-L	6-3	230	2-1-88	2	2	8.18	6	6	0	0	22	34	22	20	2	12	16	.347	.500	.313	6.55	4.91
Arrieta, Jake	R-R	6-4	225	3-6-86	14	10	3.53	30	30	0	0	168	150	82	66	23	55	163	.236	.267	.209	8.71	2.94
Butler, Eddie	R-R	6-2	180	3-13-91	4	3	3.95	13	11	0	0	55	50	24	24	4	28	30	.244	.217	.262	4.94	4.61
Davis, Wade	R-R	6-5	225	9-7-85	4	2	2.30	59	0	0	32	59	39	16	15	6	28	79	.186	.156	.211	12.12	4.30
Duensing, Brian	L-L	6-0	200	2-22-83	1	1	2.74	68	0	0	0	62	58	19	19	6	18	61	.246	.258	.237	8.81	2.60
Edwards Jr., Carl	R-R	6-3	170	9-3-91	5	4	2.98	73	0	0	0	66	29	22	22	6	38	94	.134	.119	.148	12.75	5.16
Floro, Dylan	R-L	6-2	175	12-27-90	0	0	6.52	3	0	0	0	10	15	7	7	2	2	6	.357	.273	.387	5.59	1.86
Frankoff, Seth	R-R	6-5	210	8-27-88	0	1	9.00	1	0	0	0	2	4	2	2	1	0	2	.444	.667	.333	9.00	0.00
Grimm, Justin	R-R	6-3	210	8-16-88	1	2	5.53	50	0	0	1	55	47	34	34	12	27	59	.233	.238	.230	9.60	4.39
Hendricks, Kyle	R-R	6-3	190	12-7-89	7	5	3.03	24	24	0	0	140	126	49	47	17	40	123	.242	.241	.243	7.93	2.58
Johnson, Pierce	R-R	6-3	200	5-10-91	0	0	0.00	1	0	0	0	1	2	2	0	0	1	2	.333	.333	.333	18.00	9.00
Lackey, John	R-R	6-6	235	10-23-78	12	12	4.59	31	30	0	0	171	165	93	87	36	53	149	.252	.276	.230	7.86	2.79
Leathersich, Jack	R-L	6-0	205	7-14-90	0	0	27.00	1	0	0	0	1	1	2	2	0	4	1	.500	—	.500	13.50	54.00
2-team total (6 Pittsburgh)					0	0	3.60	7	0	0	0	5	4	2	2	0	6	7	.235	—	.500	12.60	10.80
Lester, Jon	L-L	6-4	240	1-7-84	13	8	4.33	32	32	1	0	181	179	101	87	26	60	180	.259	.205	.276	8.97	2.99
Maples, Dillon	R-R	6-2	225	5-9-92	0	0	10.13	6	0	0	0	5	6	6	6	0	6	11	.286	.250	.308	18.56	10.13
Montgomery, Mike	L-L	6-5	215	7-1-89	7	8	3.38	44	14	0	3	131	103	52	49	10	55	100	.219	.230	.215	6.89	3.79
Pena, Felix	R-R	6-2	185	2-25-90	1	0	5.24	25	0	0	0	34	35	21	20	8	18	37	.259	.226	.288	9.70	4.72
Quintana, Jose	R-L	6-1	220	1-24-89	7	3	3.74	14	14	1	0	84	72	37	35	9	21	98	.228	.170	.241	10.46	2.24
Rondon, Hector	R-R	6-3	230	2-26-88	4	1	4.24	61	0	0	0	57	50	30	27	10	20	69	.233	.230	.234	10.83	3.14
Rosscup, Zac	R-L	6-2	220	6-9-88	0	0	0.00	1	0	0	0	1	0	0	0	0	0	0	.000	.000	.000	0.00	0.00
2-team total (9 Colorado)					0	0	4.70	10	0	0	0	8	9	4	4	2	0	10	.290	.000	.000	11.74	0.00
Strop, Pedro	R-R	6-1	220	6-13-85	5	4	2.83	69	0	0	0	60	45	22	19	4	26	65	.206	.178	.227	9.70	3.88
Tseng, Jen-Ho	L-R	6-1	195	10-3-94	1	0	7.50	2	1	0	0	6	5	5	5	2	2	8	.227	.375	.143	12.00	3.00
Uehara, Koji	R-R	6-2	195	4-3-75	3	4	3.98	49	0	0	2	43	38	21	19	7	12	50	.232	.250	.217	10.47	2.51
Wilson, Justin	L-L	6-2	205	8-18-87	1	0	5.09	23	0	0	0	18	18	11	10	0	19	25	.254	.261	.250	12.74	9.68
Zastryzny, Rob	R-L	6-3	205	3-26-92	0	0	8.31	4	0	0	0	13	19	13	12	2	7	11	.352	.286	.362	7.62	4.85

Fielding

Catcher	PCT	G	PO	A	E	DP	PB
Avila	.991	28	210	15	2	2	4
Caratini	.977	12	76	10	2	1	0
Contreras	.985	108	782	86	13	7	7
Davis	1.000	1	6	0	0	0	0
Montero	.991	29	205	12	2	0	0
Rivera	1.000	19	127	6	0	0	2
Schwarber	1.000	4	9	0	0	0	0

First Base	PCT	G	PO	A	E	DP
Avila	1.000	3	8	1	0	1
Baez	1.000	4	1	0	0	1
Bryant	1.000	2	12	3	0	0
Candelario	1.000	1	6	1	0	1
Caratini	1.000	8	33	2	0	3
Contreras	1.000	5	17	3	0	4
Davis	1.000	2	9	0	0	0
La Stella	.000	1	0	0	0	0
Montero	1.000	1	2	0	0	0
Rizzo	.998	157	1222	150	3	112
Schwarber	.000	1	0	0	0	0
Zobrist	1.000	5	5	0	0	3

Second Base	PCT	G	PO	A	E	DP
Baez	.983	80	105	132	4	33
Freeman	1.000	3	1	0	0	0
Happ	.983	44	39	79	2	13
La Stella	.981	21	27	26	1	13
Rizzo	1.000	10	0	2	0	1
Zobrist	.988	81	99	147	3	35

Third Base	PCT	G	PO	A	E	DP
Baez	1.000	8	8	11	0	2
Bryant	.949	144	72	260	18	23
Candelario	.962	9	8	17	1	2
Contreras	1.000	1	0	1	0	0
Davis	1.000	2	0	2	0	0
Happ	1.000	4	3	5	0	2
La Stella	1.000	18	9	14	0	0
Rizzo	.000	1	0	0	0	0

Shortstop	PCT	G	PO	A	E	DP
Baez	.959	73	91	165	11	39
Freeman	.938	10	10	20	2	4
Russell	.969	101	113	258	12	49
Zobrist	1.000	5	2	2	0	1

Outfield	PCT	G	PO	A	E	DP
Almora Jr.	.994	105	161	4	1	0
Baez	.000	1	0	0	0	0
Bryant	1.000	9	18	0	0	0
Caratini	.000	1	0	0	0	0
Contreras	.750	6	3	0	1	0
Happ	.981	82	100	4	2	0
Heyward	.992	124	230	6	2	5
Jay	1.000	111	138	3	0	0
Martin	1.000	12	8	0	0	0
Rizzo	.000	1	0	0	0	0
Schwarber	.967	110	141	7	5	1
Szczur	1.000	7	6	0	0	0
Zagunis	1.000	4	5	0	0	0
Zobrist	1.000	61	82	0	0	0

IOWA CUBS — *TRIPLE-A*

PACIFIC COAST LEAGUE

Batting	B-T	HT	WT	DOB	AVG	vLH	vRH	G	AB	R	H	2B	3B	HR	RBI	BB	HBP	SH	SF	SO	SB	CS	SLG	OBP
Andreoli, John	R-R	6-1	210	6-9-90	.244	.315	.226	119	430	81	105	24	8	14	49	65	4	5	1	138	26	10	.435	.348
Brockmeyer, Cael	R-R	6-5	235	10-8-91	.444	.500	.429	2	9	3	4	2	0	1	2	0	0	1	1	1	0	0	1.000	.400
Bruno, Stephen	R-R	5-9	165	11-17-90	.265	.286	.258	96	219	28	58	10	0	9	37	7	11	2	4	43	7	0	.434	.315
Candelario, Jeimer	B-R	6-1	210	11-24-93	.266	.222	.278	81	286	39	76	27	3	12	52	41	2	0	1	72	0	0	.507	.361
Caratini, Victor	B-R	6-1	215	8-17-93	.343	.329	.347	83	292	50	100	27	3	10	61	27	1	0	6	48	1	0	.558	.393
Davis, Taylor	R-R	5-10	200	11-28-89	.297	.294	.298	102	357	41	106	27	1	6	62	37	1	3	8	45	0	3	.429	.357
Dominguez, Chris	R-R	6-4	235	11-22-86	.284	.318	.273	102	359	58	102	22	1	11	45	11	10	0	1	102	12	2	.443	.323
Freeman, Mike	L-R	6-0	190	8-4-87	.273	.250	.279	23	77	10	21	3	0	2	6	7	2	1	1	19	3	0	.390	.345
3-team total (41 Oklahoma City, 16 Tacoma)					.306	.250	.279	80	258	39	79	10	3	3	31	27	5	2	2	60	10	0	.403	.380
Glaesmann, Todd	R-R	6-4	225	10-24-90	.175	.200	.163	24	63	6	11	1	0	1	4	3	2	0	0	25	1	0	.238	.235
Hannemann, Jacob	L-L	6-1	200	4-29-91	.265	.250	.269	80	287	40	76	23	1	5	26	24	3	4	4	69	23	3	.404	.324
Happ, Ian	B-R	6-0	205	8-12-94	.298	.409	.268	26	104	21	31	6	0	9	25	11	0	0	1	27	2	1	.615	.362
La Stella, Tommy	L-R	5-11	180	1-31-89	.218	.191	.225	33	110	14	24	2	0	1	6	10	0	0	1	22	0	1	.264	.281
Martinez, Ozzie	R-R	5-10	200	5-7-88	.222	.233	.219	46	144	11	32	2	0	1	10	7	0	2	1	28	3	0	.257	.257
Rademacher, Bijan	L-L	6-0	200	6-15-91	.294	.290	.295	107	289	38	85	16	2	7	46	36	2	1	1	64	3	2	.436	.375
Russell, Addison	R-R	6-0	200	1-23-94	.333	—	.333	1	3	0	1	1	0	0	0	0	0	0	0	1	0	0	.667	.333
Schwarber, Kyle	L-R	6-0	235	3-5-93	.343	.353	.333	11	35	9	12	1	0	4	9	8	1	0	0	12	0	0	.714	.477
Solis, Ali	R-R	6-0	200	9-29-87	.253	.257	.252	58	158	18	40	13	0	3	19	8	2	0	0	48	1	0	.392	.298
Soto, Elliot	R-R	5-9	160	8-21-89	.238	.218	.243	81	244	28	58	15	2	2	29	26	1	7	5	49	5	2	.340	.308
Weeks, Jemile	B-R	5-9	170	1-26-87	.235	.246	.230	63	226	31	53	18	2	2	24	28	0	3	2	32	4	0	.358	.316
Young, Chesny	R-R	6-0	170	10-6-92	.257	.270	.253	120	425	56	109	20	0	1	33	33	4	6	7	70	7	6	.311	.311
Zagunis, Mark	R-R	6-0	205	2-5-93	.267	.319	.253	97	330	59	88	21	1	13	55	70	7	0	1	93	4	3	.455	.404

Pitching	B-T	HT	WT	DOB	W	L	ERA	G	GS	CG	SV	IP	H	R	ER	HR	BB	SO	AVG	vLH	vRH	K/9	BB/9
Acevedo, Andury	R-R	6-4	235	8-23-90	2	0	3.75	8	0	0	0	12	14	5	5	0	5	7	.292	.333	.267	5.25	3.75
2-team total (2 Reno)					2	1	6.92	10	0	0	0	13	18	10	10	1	6	9	.327	.500	.667	6.23	4.15
Berg, David	R-R	6-0	190	3-28-93	2	0	0.90	7	0	0	0	10	13	1	1	0	1	3	.325	.267	.360	2.70	0.90
Brooks, Aaron	R-R	6-4	225	4-27-90	8	9	6.20	24	24	0	0	138	181	102	95	27	28	105	.320	.342	.301	6.85	1.83
2-team total (2 Colorado Springs)					8	10	6.12	26	26	0	0	146	192	110	99	29	29	107	.321	.342	.301	6.61	1.79
Buchanan, Jake	R-R	6-0	235	9-24-89	2	2	4.75	8	8	0	0	42	49	26	22	5	19	29	.293	.269	.315	6.26	4.10
2-team total (11 Reno Aces)					7	2	4.46	19	19	0	0	103	110	55	51	7	28	67	.270	.294	.221	5.85	2.45
Butler, Eddie	R-R	6-2	180	3-13-91	2	0	2.17	8	8	0	0	46	49	12	11	1	12	30	.278	.281	.276	5.91	2.36
Carasiti, Matt	R-R	6-3	205	7-23-91	0	2	4.66	19	0	0	8	19	18	10	10	1	10	25	.254	.313	.205	11.64	4.66
2-team total (27 Albuquerque)					1	3	3.26	46	0	0	21	50	49	19	18	2	23	68	.259	.313	.205	12.32	4.17
Carroll, Scott	R-R	6-4	215	9-24-84	2	1	3.68	4	4	0	0	22	25	11	9	4	8	16	.291	.361	.240	6.55	3.27
Detwiler, Ross	L-R	6-3	210	3-6-86	0	1	9.00	5	0	0	0	9	14	9	9	3	7	10	.342	.231	.393	10.00	7.00
2-team total (14 Nashville)					0	2	7.43	19	0	0	1	23	29	19	19	4	15	22	.309	.231	.393	8.61	5.87
Duensing, Brian	L-L	6-0	200	2-22-83	0	0	0.00	2	0	0	0	3	1	0	0	0	0	5	.100	.000	.125	15.00	0.00
Floro, Dylan	R-L	6-2	175	12-27-90	3	2	3.88	25	2	0	1	49	54	28	21	9	8	26	.276	.241	.301	4.81	1.48
2-team total (8 Oklahoma City)					3	3	4.20	33	2	0	2	60	72	36	28	9	11	38	.294	.241	.301	5.70	1.65
Frankoff, Seth	R-R	6-5	210	8-27-88	2	8	4.40	24	21	0	0	117	102	61	57	18	47	119	.238	.215	.257	9.18	3.63
Garner, David	R-R	6-1	180	9-21-92	2	1	4.73	9	0	0	2	13	17	8	7	3	8	14	.315	.368	.286	9.45	5.40
Grimm, Justin	R-R	6-3	210	8-16-88	0	1	3.86	10	0	0	3	12	10	5	5	2	5	18	.227	.235	.222	13.89	3.86
Hancock, Justin	R-R	6-4	185	10-28-90	1	2	4.50	17	0	0	1	22	25	11	11	2	11	24	.278	.244	.306	9.82	4.50
Hedges, Zach	R-R	6-4	210	10-21-92	0	3	11.94	4	4	0	0	17	36	23	23	2	10	5	.419	.431	.400	2.60	5.19
Johnson, Pierce	R-R	6-3	200	5-10-91	3	2	4.31	43	1	0	9	54	52	26	26	3	27	74	.257	.203	.293	12.26	4.47
Kelly, Casey	R-R	6-3	215	10-4-89	5	2	4.65	12	11	1	1	60	72	33	31	9	23	43	.304	.316	.295	6.45	3.45

Pitching	B-T	HT	WT	DOB	W	L	ERA	G	GS	CG	SV	IP	H	R	ER	HR	BB	SO	AVG	vLH	vRH	K/9	BB/9
2-team total (7 Sacramento)					7	5	4.46	19	18	1	1	101	115	55	50	16	38	82	.290	.316	.295	7.31	3.39
Leathersich, Jack	R-L	6-0	205	7-14-90	2	4	2.84	41	0	0	1	44	25	19	14	3	28	72	.167	.224	.130	14.62	5.68
Maples, Dillon	R-R	6-2	225	5-9-92	1	2	1.96	17	0	0	4	18	12	7	4	1	11	28	.185	.167	.195	13.75	5.40
Markey, Brad	R-R	5-10	185	3-3-92	0	1	2.04	6	1	0	0	18	14	6	4	3	1	14	.212	.148	.256	7.13	0.51
Mejia, Miguel	R-R	6-2	210	1-19-88	2	0	6.55	14	0	0	0	22	25	17	16	4	11	11	.309	.333	.289	4.50	4.50
Mills, Alec	R-R	6-4	190	11-30-91	2	0	3.21	3	3	0	0	14	12	9	5	0	3	7	.231	.240	.222	4.50	1.93
Mullee, Conor	R-R	6-4	195	2-25-88	1	0	7.36	13	0	0	0	18	16	15	15	1	5	13	.232	.241	.225	6.38	2.45
Paniagua, Juan	R-R	6-1	200	4-4-90	0	3	5.65	11	4	0	0	29	38	19	18	2	18	20	.328	.296	.347	6.28	5.65
Parra, Manny	L-L	6-3	215	10-30-82	0	1	14.09	11	0	0	1	8	16	14	12	1	7	6	.410	.286	.480	7.04	8.22
Pena, Felix	R-R	6-2	185	2-25-90	2	1	5.54	24	0	0	6	39	42	24	24	6	14	46	.280	.258	.296	10.62	3.23
Perakslis, Stephen	R-R	6-1	185	1-15-91	0	1	3.43	8	3	0	0	21	19	8	8	1	10	23	.241	.290	.195	9.86	4.29
Perez, Williams	R-R	6-0	240	5-21-91	7	10	5.01	23	23	1	0	120	122	74	67	8	51	102	.268	.294	.249	7.63	3.81
Rodriguez, Fernando	R-R	6-3	235	6-18-84	1	0	3.09	9	0	0	1	12	9	5	4	2	1	13	.205	.263	.160	10.03	0.77
Rollins, David	L-L	6-1	210	12-21-89	3	4	5.79	32	2	0	2	42	39	30	27	7	24	39	.244	.276	.226	8.36	5.14
Rosario, Jose	R-R	6-1	170	8-29-90	0	0	18.00	6	0	0	0	4	7	8	8	3	7	1	.389	.286	.455	2.25	15.75
Rosscup, Zac	R-L	6-2	220	6-9-88	2	2	2.60	17	1	0	1	28	21	9	8	3	8	39	.208	.242	.191	12.69	2.60
2-team total (12 Albuquerque)					2	2	2.45	29	1	0	2	40	29	12	11	4	12	54	.197	.242	.191	12.05	2.68
Swarmer, Matt	R-R	6-5	175	9-25-93	1	0	0.00	1	1	0	0	7	5	0	0	0	1	8	.192	.167	.214	10.29	1.29
Thorpe, Tommy	L-L	6-0	185	9-20-92	0	0	0.00	1	0	0	0	2	1	0	0	0	0	1	.143	.000	.200	4.50	0.00
Tseng, Jen-Ho	L-R	6-1	195	10-3-94	6	1	1.80	9	9	0	0	55	48	15	11	5	14	39	.235	.231	.240	6.38	2.29
Williams, Ryan	R-R	6-4	220	11-1-91	1	3	11.85	6	2	0	0	14	28	18	18	3	4	12	.406	.567	.282	7.90	2.63
Zastryzny, Rob	R-L	6-3	205	3-26-92	2	3	5.94	14	7	0	1	47	50	32	31	7	14	40	.270	.222	.286	7.66	2.68

Fielding

Catcher	PCT	G	PO	A	E	DP	PB
Brockmeyer	1.000	2	22	2	0	0	0
Caratini	.990	50	344	39	4	7	5
Davis	.992	59	478	33	4	4	7
Solis	.992	31	231	19	2	1	1

First Base	PCT	G	PO	A	E	DP
Bruno	.000	1	0	0	0	0
Candelario	.990	16	94	4	1	13
Caratini	.992	30	227	18	2	23
Davis	1.000	26	227	16	0	13
Dominguez	.988	66	540	37	7	53
Solis	1.000	7	44	4	0	3
Young	1.000	12	72	5	0	9

Second Base	PCT	G	PO	A	E	DP
Bruno	.959	22	12	35	2	5
Freeman	1.000	5	9	12	0	4
Happ	.949	16	27	47	4	14
La Stella	.978	22	36	54	2	18
Martinez	1.000	5	6	11	0	4
Soto	1.000	4	8	9	0	2
Weeks	.975	40	57	102	4	25
Young	.979	52	78	106	4	19

Third Base	PCT	G	PO	A	E	DP
Bruno	.947	34	11	43	3	5
Candelario	.978	70	45	132	4	6
Caratini	.000	1	0	0	0	0
Davis	.000	2	0	0	0	0
Dominguez	.875	21	5	44	7	3
Freeman	1.000	7	3	7	0	1
La Stella	.769	4	4	6	3	1
Martinez	1.000	2	0	1	0	0
Weeks	.667	1	1	1	1	0
Young	.944	24	15	52	4	7

Shortstop	PCT	G	PO	A	E	DP
Bruno	1.000	3	0	1	0	0
Freeman	1.000	11	12	25	0	7
Martinez	.972	35	39	100	4	19
Russell	1.000	1	0	2	0	0
Soto	.965	76	109	222	12	50
Young	.981	30	31	70	2	15

Outfield	PCT	G	PO	A	E	DP
Andreoli	.983	115	221	5	4	2
Bruno	1.000	19	20	1	0	0
Carroll	.000	1	0	0	0	0
Dominguez	.889	12	8	0	1	0
Freeman	1.000	3	3	0	0	0
Glaesmann	.929	19	37	2	3	0
Hannemann	1.000	77	159	4	0	2
Happ	.967	13	28	1	1	0
Rademacher	.969	82	119	8	4	2
Schwarber	1.000	9	8	0	0	0
Weeks	1.000	10	10	1	0	0
Young	.950	17	19	0	1	0
Zagunis	.980	92	144	3	3	1

TENNESSEE SMOKIES — *DOUBLE-A*

SOUTHERN LEAGUE

Batting	B-T	HT	WT	DOB	AVG	vLH	vRH	G	AB	R	H	2B	3B	HR	RBI	BB	HBP	SH	SF	SO	SB	CS	SLG	OBP
Baez, Jeffrey	R-R	6-0	180	10-30-93	.217	.235	.209	81	276	38	60	14	1	10	27	26	3	2	2	59	7	5	.384	.290
Balaguert, Yasiel	R-R	6-2	215	1-9-93	.256	.306	.236	129	477	51	122	27	0	15	75	35	2	0	4	103	0	1	.407	.307
Bote, David	R-R	5-11	185	4-7-93	.272	.305	.260	127	470	65	128	30	3	14	59	49	12	0	4	101	5	2	.438	.353
Brockmeyer, Cael	R-R	6-5	235	10-8-91	.180	.210	.165	70	195	18	35	5	1	6	19	14	6	0	0	58	0	0	.308	.256
Burks, Charcer	R-R	6-0	170	3-9-95	.270	.250	.277	121	456	67	123	21	3	10	40	69	6	0	4	107	16	12	.395	.370
Caro, Roberto	B-R	6-0	185	9-25-93	.143	.182	.125	22	35	1	5	1	0	0	1	5	1	0	0	7	1	1	.171	.268
Castillo, Erick	R-R	5-11	178	2-25-93	.245	.200	.260	66	204	17	50	10	0	1	20	19	3	2	2	43	0	0	.309	.316
Cornelius, Kevin	R-R	6-1	180	8-28-92	.197	.171	.209	52	132	10	26	6	0	3	12	7	0	0	1	51	0	0	.311	.236
Ely, Andrew	L-R	5-11	180	1-23-93	.259	.205	.269	97	282	39	73	14	2	3	25	42	2	10	3	59	1	4	.355	.356
Hannemann, Jacob	L-L	6-1	200	4-29-91	.180	.133	.196	34	122	17	22	9	1	1	6	14	4	1	0	44	6	3	.295	.286
Martin, Trey	R-R	6-2	190	12-11-92	.265	.235	.276	84	317	29	84	17	2	5	35	12	6	1	1	89	6	6	.379	.304
Martinez, Ozzie	R-R	5-10	200	5-7-88	.292	.250	.306	15	48	5	14	4	0	1	2	3	0	0	0	2	0	0	.438	.333
Penalver, Carlos	R-R	6-0	170	5-17-94	.254	.295	.237	112	382	48	97	11	4	3	18	18	5	6	2	67	1	1	.327	.295
Rice, Ian	R-R	6-0	195	8-19-93	.230	.209	.237	119	331	40	76	11	1	17	52	60	3	0	0	90	0	1	.423	.353
Spingola, Daniel	L-L	6-1	180	5-5-93	.237	.211	.241	43	135	23	32	6	1	4	13	9	3	0	0	35	0	0	.385	.299
Vosler, Jason	L-R	6-1	190	9-6-93	.241	.265	.233	129	452	70	109	18	2	21	81	53	20	0	6	120	1	1	.429	.343
Zobrist, Ben	B-R	6-3	210	5-26-81	.500	.500	.500	2	6	2	3	0	0	0	0	2	0	0	0	0	0	0	.500	.625

Pitching	B-T	HT	WT	DOB	W	L	ERA	G	GS	CG	SV	IP	H	R	ER	HR	BB	SO	AVG	vLH	vRH	K/9	BB/9
Acevedo, Andury	R-R	6-4	235	8-23-90	1	0	0.00	12	0	0	3	15	9	0	0	0	5	6	.184	.158	.200	3.60	3.00
2-team total (9 Jackson)					2	0	1.54	21	0	0	4	23	16	4	4	0	11	13	.211	.400	.176	5.01	4.24
Alzolay, Adbert	R-R	6-0	179	3-1-95	0	3	3.03	7	7	0	0	33	27	12	11	0	12	30	.229	.263	.197	8.27	3.31
Anderson, Brett	L-L	6-3	230	2-1-88	2	2	4.61	6	5	0	0	27	34	17	14	2	9	15	.321	.310	.328	4.94	2.96
Araujo, Pedro	R-R	6-3	214	7-2-93	0	0	0.00	1	0	0	0	2	1	0	0	0	1	4	.125	.333	.000	18.00	4.50
Berg, David	R-R	6-0	190	3-28-93	1	1	5.11	11	0	0	0	12	17	8	7	2	3	7	.333	.308	.360	5.11	2.19
Bloomquist, Casey	R-R	6-3	190	1-25-94	1	0	3.75	2	2	0	0	12	16	5	5	1	2	6	.333	.350	.321	4.50	1.50

Pitching	B-T	HT	WT	DOB	W	L	ERA	G	GS	CG	SV	IP	H	R	ER	HR	BB	SO	AVG	vLH	vRH	K/9	BB/9
Brooks, Craig	R-R	5-10	180	9-23-92	0	1	4.46	33	0	0	7	40	30	22	20	1	29	58	.201	.203	.200	12.94	6.47
Clifton, Trevor	R-R	6-1	170	5-11-95	5	8	5.20	21	21	0	0	100	112	61	58	8	45	86	.286	.297	.276	7.71	4.04
Concepcion, Gerardo	L-L	6-2	200	2-29-92	1	0	5.87	7	0	0	0	8	9	5	5	2	5	5	.321	.250	.350	5.87	5.87
Corcino, Daniel	R-R	5-11	210	8-26-90	0	1	8.68	5	2	0	0	9	6	9	9	2	9	11	.177	.250	.111	10.61	8.68
Garner, David	R-R	6-1	180	9-21-92	2	2	2.61	26	0	0	1	31	23	10	9	3	17	37	.209	.286	.106	10.74	4.94
Hancock, Justin	R-R	6-4	185	10-28-90	1	2	4.41	16	0	0	3	16	19	12	8	0	8	16	.292	.325	.240	8.82	4.41
Hedges, Zach	R-R	6-4	210	10-21-92	9	9	3.49	22	22	2	0	129	143	61	50	11	30	71	.282	.294	.269	4.95	2.09
Hendricks, Kyle	R-R	6-3	190	12-7-89	0	0	1.08	2	2	0	0	8	2	1	1	0	1	5	.077	.059	.111	5.40	1.08
Maples, Dillon	R-R	6-2	225	5-9-92	1	1	3.29	14	0	0	6	14	11	5	5	0	11	28	.212	.226	.191	18.44	7.24
Markey, Brad	R-R	5-10	185	3-3-92	2	1	3.08	34	2	0	1	61	62	23	21	6	13	59	.261	.228	.297	8.66	1.91
McNeil, Ryan	R-R	6-3	210	2-1-94	1	3	5.79	28	0	0	3	28	29	23	18	3	20	32	.257	.254	.259	10.29	6.43
Medina, Jhondaniel	R-R	5-11	218	2-8-93	0	0	11.57	7	0	0	0	7	5	9	9	0	9	5	.192	.200	.182	6.43	11.57
2-team total (15 Mobile)					1	1	4.63	22	1	0	0	35	25	18	18	4	21	37	.197	.295	.123	9.51	5.40
Morrison, Preston	R-R	6-2	185	7-19-93	1	10	5.51	28	19	1	0	119	129	78	73	14	38	86	.278	.311	.242	6.49	2.87
Norwood, James	R-R	6-2	205	12-24-93	1	3	5.30	14	0	0	1	19	22	11	11	1	9	19	.301	.400	.211	9.16	4.34
Nunn, Chris	L-L	6-5	200	10-5-90	0	1	4.76	4	4	0	0	17	13	9	9	1	10	14	.206	.292	.154	7.41	5.29
Perakslis, Stephen	R-R	6-1	185	1-15-91	5	2	3.10	26	3	0	1	52	46	18	18	2	13	54	.235	.188	.284	9.29	2.24
Pugliese, James	R-R	6-3	220	8-12-92	7	2	1.84	40	7	0	1	78	56	17	16	5	33	48	.203	.200	.206	5.51	3.79
Rosario, Jose	R-R	6-1	170	8-29-90	0	1	2.00	6	0	0	0	9	6	2	2	0	4	7	.194	.177	.214	7.00	4.00
Stinnett, Jake	R-R	6-4	202	4-25-92	0	1	0.61	9	0	0	0	15	6	1	1	0	6	14	.130	.053	.185	8.59	3.68
Swarmer, Matt	R-R	6-5	175	9-25-93	0	2	13.00	2	2	0	0	9	19	16	13	2	4	8	.413	.344	.571	8.00	4.00
Thorpe, Tommy	L-L	6-0	185	9-20-92	1	0	0.00	4	0	0	0	7	2	0	0	0	1	4	.095	.000	.133	5.40	1.35
Torrez, Daury	R-R	6-3	170	6-11-93	6	4	1.40	43	1	0	1	77	58	17	12	6	13	56	.209	.233	.183	6.52	1.51
Tseng, Jen-Ho	L-R	6-1	195	10-3-94	7	3	2.99	15	15	0	0	90	79	38	30	7	24	83	.232	.212	.256	8.27	2.39
Underwood Jr., Duane	R-R	6-2	210	7-20-94	13	7	4.43	25	24	0	0	138	130	75	68	13	50	98	.250	.252	.247	6.39	3.26

Fielding

Catcher	PCT	G	PO	A	E	DP	PB
Brockmeyer	.995	32	197	16	1	3	1
Castillo	.994	64	447	54	3	3	6
Rice	.989	49	319	34	4	1	8

First Base	PCT	G	PO	A	E	DP
Balaguert	.993	94	751	56	6	75
Bote	1.000	4	28	2	0	2
Brockmeyer	.961	12	65	9	3	5
Cornelius	.981	27	193	13	4	17
Rice	.986	10	61	7	1	12

Second Base	PCT	G	PO	A	E	DP
Bote	.988	107	195	314	6	67
Ely	.992	29	38	84	1	22
Martinez	1.000	4	5	5	0	0
Penalver	1.000	1	2	3	0	0
Vosler	1.000	1	1	1	0	0
Zobrist	1.000	1	0	4	0	0

Third Base	PCT	G	PO	A	E	DP
Cornelius	.000	1	0	0	0	0
Ely	1.000	11	11	18	0	1
Martinez	1.000	3	0	3	0	0
Vosler	.973	127	72	185	7	20

Shortstop	PCT	G	PO	A	E	DP
Ely	.978	41	41	91	3	23
Martinez	.968	4	11	19	1	5
Penalver	.943	97	161	234	24	56

Outfield	PCT	G	PO	A	E	DP
Baez	.976	77	153	12	4	0
Balaguert	1.000	38	58	3	0	0
Bote	.964	12	25	2	1	0
Burks	.996	121	250	3	1	1
Caro	1.000	11	21	0	0	0
Ely	1.000	2	4	0	0	0
Hannemann	1.000	34	86	0	0	0
Martin	.991	83	207	3	2	0
Martinez	1.000	2	4	0	0	0
Penalver	.958	10	22	1	1	0
Spingola	.970	36	61	3	2	1
Zobrist	1.000	1	1	0	0	0

MYRTLE BEACH PELICANS — *HIGH CLASS A*

CAROLINA LEAGUE

Batting	B-T	HT	WT	DOB	AVG	vLH	vRH	G	AB	R	H	2B	3B	HR	RBI	BB	HBP	SH	SF	SO	SB	CS	SLG	OBP
Alamo, Tyler	R-R	6-4	200	5-2-95	.281	.294	.275	114	427	61	120	24	0	12	42	21	5	0	0	108	0	1	.422	.322
Caro, Roberto	B-R	6-0	185	9-25-93	.185	.156	.200	39	92	10	17	2	2	1	15	13	3	1	1	29	5	4	.283	.303
Flete, Bryant	L-R	5-10	146	1-31-93	.306	.254	.322	70	275	45	84	15	0	6	37	18	4	1	2	53	4	3	.426	.355
2-team total (45 Winston-Salem)					.276	.254	.322	115	442	63	122	25	2	7	49	32	5	1	3	81	5	5	.389	.330
Garcia, Robert	B-R	5-10	170	12-6-93	.248	.156	.275	108	339	42	84	6	3	2	31	26	5	4	4	100	16	12	.301	.308
Giambrone, Trent	R-R	5-8	175	12-20-93	.242	.219	.254	128	480	65	116	15	0	12	44	36	4	3	6	101	7	6	.348	.297
Higgins, P.J.	R-R	5-10	185	5-10-93	.237	.194	.255	98	342	32	81	9	0	4	23	43	5	10	5	47	3	1	.298	.327
Hodges, Jesse	R-R	6-1	212	3-29-94	.269	.264	.271	124	447	58	120	26	3	13	63	45	8	4	2	105	4	3	.427	.345
Jimenez, Eloy	R-R	6-4	205	11-27-96	.271	.264	.275	42	155	23	42	6	2	8	32	18	1	0	0	35	0	0	.490	.351
2-team total (29 Winston-Salem)					.302	.264	.275	71	265	43	80	17	3	16	58	30	1	0	0	56	0	2	.570	.375
Machin, Vimael	L-R	5-10	185	9-25-93	.274	.290	.269	45	157	19	43	6	0	1	15	16	0	0	0	31	0	2	.331	.341
Martinez, Eddy	R-R	6-1	195	1-18-95	.244	.226	.252	127	464	59	113	11	2	14	61	31	5	0	2	78	6	6	.366	.297
Monasterio, Andruw	R-R	6-0	175	5-30-97	.241	.148	.283	26	87	9	21	4	0	0	5	8	1	1	0	14	1	1	.287	.313
Myers, Connor	R-R	5-11	170	2-3-94	.188	.202	.179	95	298	29	56	13	2	0	24	16	3	12	3	97	7	3	.245	.234
Paula, Adonis	R-R	6-1	185	6-21-94	.272	.267	.276	51	147	12	40	4	0	2	18	16	3	1	1	52	1	1	.340	.353
Pearson, Tyler	R-R	6-0	185	4-15-92	.257	.364	.155	35	113	17	29	7	0	4	11	10	4	2	0	31	0	0	.425	.339
Rose, Matt	R-R	6-4	195	8-2-94	.228	.209	.235	65	233	30	53	15	1	14	38	15	3	1	2	63	0	0	.481	.281
2-team total (36 Winston-Salem)					.242	.209	.235	101	355	51	86	28	1	18	61	27	4	3	4	103	2	0	.479	.300
Sepulveda, Carlos	L-R	5-10	170	8-27-96	.196	.258	.173	28	112	13	22	2	0	0	7	11	1	0	1	19	0	1	.214	.272
Short, Zack	R-R	5-10	175	5-29-95	.263	.321	.230	65	232	34	61	11	3	6	21	40	2	0	3	50	3	5	.414	.372
Spingola, Daniel	L-L	6-1	180	5-5-93	.285	.305	.278	64	221	27	63	15	6	2	27	27	3	0	2	66	5	0	.434	.368

Pitching	B-T	HT	WT	DOB	W	L	ERA	G	GS	CG	SV	IP	H	R	ER	HR	BB	SO	AVG	vLH	vRH	K/9	BB/9
Alzolay, Adbert	R-R	6-0	179	3-1-95	7	1	2.98	15	15	1	0	82	65	29	27	8	22	78	.217	.180	.240	8.60	2.42
Araujo, Pedro	R-R	6-3	214	7-2-93	6	1	1.81	44	0	0	10	65	42	16	13	3	17	83	.177	.220	.151	11.55	2.37
Berg, David	R-R	6-0	190	3-28-93	1	3	6.28	22	0	0	1	39	36	33	27	3	14	34	.243	.362	.188	7.91	3.26
Bloomquist, Casey	R-R	6-3	190	1-25-94	4	5	6.14	27	9	1	2	73	99	53	50	9	15	56	.317	.274	.350	6.87	1.84
Brooks, Craig	R-R	5-10	180	9-23-92	1	0	0.44	12	0	0	3	20	9	1	1	1	6	30	.134	.129	.139	13.28	2.66

Pitching	B-T	HT	WT	DOB	W	L	ERA	G	GS	CG	SV	IP	H	R	ER	HR	BB	SO	AVG	vLH	vRH	K/9	BB/9
De La Cruz, Oscar	R-R	6-4	200	3-4-95	4	3	3.46	12	12	1	0	55	55	22	21	6	13	47	.263	.248	.283	7.74	2.14
Effross, Scott	R-R	6-1	195	12-28-93	5	2	3.40	42	2	0	9	79	80	35	30	1	26	74	.256	.279	.244	8.39	2.95
Hatch, Thomas	R-R	6-1	190	9-29-94	5	11	4.04	26	26	0	0	125	126	74	56	2	50	126	.264	.304	.234	9.10	3.61
Huberman, Marc	L-L	6-2	180	1-10-94	0	2	6.00	17	0	0	0	24	30	21	16	2	18	21	.303	.318	.299	7.88	6.75
Kellogg, Ryan	R-L	6-6	230	2-4-94	5	7	5.12	23	20	1	0	104	124	69	59	15	28	53	.300	.287	.304	4.60	2.43
Maples, Dillon	R-R	6-2	225	5-9-92	4	0	2.01	21	0	0	3	31	21	7	7	2	15	44	.188	.174	.197	12.64	4.31
Mekkes, Dakota	R-R	6-7	252	11-6-94	5	2	1.28	24	0	0	3	42	25	6	6	0	20	45	.171	.196	.160	9.57	4.25
Miller, Kyle	R-R	6-3	185	12-2-93	4	4	3.87	28	9	0	3	77	82	39	33	6	33	58	.272	.287	.264	6.81	3.87
Mills, Alec	R-R	6-4	190	11-30-91	0	1	3.00	2	2	0	0	9	8	3	3	0	1	7	.250	.100	.318	7.00	1.00
Minch, Jordan	L-L	6-3	180	7-16-93	1	3	6.38	29	0	0	1	37	33	27	26	6	25	29	.248	.279	.233	7.12	6.14
Norwood, James	R-R	6-2	205	12-24-93	3	0	2.31	27	0	0	6	39	32	11	10	1	16	41	.232	.256	.221	9.46	3.69
Null, Jeremy	R-R	6-7	200	9-27-93	0	1	11.74	3	0	0	0	8	12	10	10	4	2	8	.343	.214	.429	9.39	2.35
Robinson, Duncan	R-R	6-6	220	12-5-93	4	4	2.37	10	10	0	0	49	43	16	13	0	15	37	.242	.250	.237	6.75	2.74
Rucker, Michael	R-R	6-1	185	4-27-94	5	5	2.51	20	15	0	1	93	82	33	26	5	21	92	.235	.291	.211	8.87	2.03
Steele, Justin	L-L	6-2	195	7-11-95	6	7	2.92	20	20	0	0	99	100	42	32	6	36	82	.265	.229	.278	7.48	3.28
Stinnett, Jake	R-R	6-4	202	4-25-92	0	1	5.40	2	0	0	0	3	5	2	2	1	2	4	.385	.500	.200	10.80	5.40
Thorpe, Tommy	L-L	6-0	185	9-20-92	3	4	4.32	35	0	0	0	58	54	33	28	7	31	59	.246	.308	.219	9.10	4.78
Williamson, John	L-L	6-1	195	9-27-92	0	0	2.08	3	0	0	0	4	3	1	1	0	4	2	.200	.000	.333	4.15	8.31

Fielding

Catcher	PCT	G	PO	A	E	DP	PB
Alamo	.987	27	202	21	3	2	1
Higgins	.991	87	688	93	7	6	15
Pearson	.996	30	213	27	1	3	1

First Base	PCT	G	PO	A	E	DP
Alamo	.986	56	470	27	7	36
Machin	1.000	4	24	3	0	2
Paula	.984	26	175	11	3	16
Rose	.994	58	465	41	3	36

Second Base	PCT	G	PO	A	E	DP
Flete	.970	50	84	108	6	24
Giambrone	.973	55	63	118	5	25
Machin	.986	20	33	37	1	9
Monasterio	.957	4	7	15	1	2
Sepulveda	.986	18	23	47	1	14

Third Base	PCT	G	PO	A	E	DP
Giambrone	.944	5	5	12	1	0
Hodges	.934	118	82	200	20	15
Machin	.947	5	4	14	1	2
Paula	.872	13	9	25	5	0
Rose	1.000	2	2	1	0	0

Shortstop	PCT	G	PO	A	E	DP
Flete	.952	10	16	24	2	7
Giambrone	.925	51	63	123	15	18
Monasterio	.946	22	30	57	5	8
Short	.971	61	84	147	7	36

Outfield	PCT	G	PO	A	E	DP
Caro	.964	34	51	3	2	0
Garcia	.948	106	193	7	11	4
Giambrone	.938	13	28	2	2	1
Jimenez	.980	24	48	0	1	0
Martinez	.991	112	204	14	2	3
Myers	.987	94	207	14	3	4
Spingola	1.000	58	98	2	0	2

SOUTH BEND CUBS — *LOW CLASS A*

MIDWEST LEAGUE

Batting	B-T	HT	WT	DOB	AVG	vLH	vRH	G	AB	R	H	2B	3B	HR	RBI	BB	HBP	SH	SF	SO	SB	CS	SLG	OBP
Ademan, Aramis	L-R	5-11	160	9-13-98	.244	.160	.265	29	127	13	31	6	1	3	15	4	1	0	2	24	4	2	.378	.269
Ayala, Luis	L-R	6-0	176	12-21-95	.281	.264	.287	114	391	52	110	17	5	3	42	43	7	3	3	86	24	15	.373	.360
Caro, Roberto	B-R	6-0	185	9-25-93	.307	.387	.280	37	124	21	38	6	5	0	14	21	2	5	2	33	14	2	.436	.409
Cruz, Michael	L-R	5-11	210	1-13-96	.186	.000	.197	25	70	7	13	4	0	1	8	11	2	0	1	13	0	0	.286	.310
Cummins, Brandon	R-L	5-10	170	11-21-93	.195	.200	.194	25	82	18	16	2	0	1	6	10	0	5	1	32	7	1	.256	.280
Davis, Zach	B-R	5-11	175	6-29-94	.000	.000	.000	4	13	0	0	0	0	0	0	0	0	0	0	6	1	0	.000	.000
Galindo, Wladimir	R-R	6-3	210	11-6-96	.290	.241	.315	44	162	21	47	11	0	4	19	14	1	0	0	40	1	1	.432	.350
Heyward, Jason	L-L	6-5	240	8-9-89	.571	—	.571	3	7	2	4	0	0	0	2	1	0	0	0	0	0	0	.571	.625
Machin, Vimael	L-R	5-10	185	9-25-93	.320	.318	.320	72	272	46	87	17	1	10	57	24	0	6	3	33	4	2	.500	.371
Martarano, Joe	R-R	6-4	235	7-28-94	.208	.229	.197	32	106	9	22	4	1	1	9	6	2	1	0	35	0	0	.293	.263
Mineo, Alberto	L-R	5-10	170	7-23-94	.278	.351	.257	98	349	46	97	20	4	0	44	47	7	1	1	66	3	0	.358	.374
Mitchell, Kevonte	R-R	6-4	185	8-12-95	.245	.266	.237	115	408	54	100	19	5	11	59	38	6	3	4	108	21	6	.397	.316
Monasterio, Andruw	R-R	6-0	175	5-30-97	.281	.274	.284	58	231	42	65	13	2	1	23	22	4	2	2	38	7	4	.368	.351
Paredes, Isaac	R-R	5-11	175	2-18-99	.264	.298	.253	92	337	49	89	25	0	7	49	29	13	2	3	54	2	1	.401	.343
2-team total (32 West Michigan)					.252	.298	.253	124	452	65	114	28	0	11	70	42	18	2	3	67	2	1	.387	.338
Paula, Adonis	R-R	6-1	185	6-21-94	.174	.300	.139	12	46	3	8	3	0	0	4	0	0	0	1	14	0	0	.239	.170
Payne, Tyler	R-R	5-11	210	10-25-92	.245	.302	.215	53	184	21	45	7	0	6	32	18	1	1	2	39	0	0	.380	.312
Peguero, Yeiler	B-R	5-10	150	9-20-97	.233	.217	.241	107	377	54	88	21	5	2	40	46	2	9	3	75	9	9	.332	.318
Pereda, Jhonny	R-R	6-1	170	4-18-96	.249	.250	.249	92	317	33	79	13	0	0	29	37	4	1	0	60	2	3	.290	.335
Pieters, Chris	L-L	6-3	185	9-21-94	.254	.262	.252	86	307	51	78	14	7	4	31	35	6	1	2	73	13	9	.384	.340
Short, Zack	R-R	5-10	175	5-29-95	.237	.217	.244	66	236	50	56	17	3	7	26	54	7	2	1	54	15	5	.424	.393
Upshaw, Austin	L-R	6-0	175	7-28-96	.291	.378	.267	52	210	28	61	11	1	2	29	14	3	0	3	31	1	1	.381	.339
Wilson, D.J.	L-L	5-8	177	10-8-96	.229	.205	.239	88	310	56	71	16	8	9	45	33	3	2	0	89	15	7	.419	.309

Pitching	B-T	HT	WT	DOB	W	L	ERA	G	GS	CG	SV	IP	H	R	ER	HR	BB	SO	AVG	vLH	vRH	K/9	BB/9
Cease, Dylan	R-R	6-2	190	12-28-95	1	2	2.79	13	13	0	0	52	39	18	16	2	26	74	.214	.212	.217	12.89	4.53
Cheek, Jared	R-B	5-11	190	10-31-92	1	2	4.15	24	0	0	1	35	43	17	16	2	13	33	.305	.281	.325	8.57	3.38
Clark, Bailey	R-R	6-4	185	12-3-94	0	0	12.46	2	0	0	0	4	8	8	6	1	8	5	.471	.462	.500	10.38	16.62
Diaz, Elvis	R-R	6-3	185	2-6-93	2	0	8.64	6	0	0	0	8	13	8	8	1	3	9	.351	.353	.350	9.72	3.24
Gomez, Yapson	L-L	5-10	160	10-2-93	1	0	3.91	11	0	0	1	25	28	11	11	3	9	27	.286	.233	.309	9.59	3.20
Hockin, Chad	R-R	6-2	210	10-7-94	3	4	3.95	38	0	0	2	55	51	31	24	8	19	57	.238	.221	.252	9.38	3.13
Huberman, Marc	L-L	6-2	180	1-10-94	3	2	1.70	21	0	0	0	37	23	10	7	2	19	52	.183	.114	.209	12.65	4.62
Hudson, Bryan	L-L	6-8	220	5-8-97	9	3	3.91	24	24	0	0	124	128	65	54	10	52	81	.272	.338	.238	5.86	3.76
Knighton, Michael	R-R	6-2	190	4-30-94	2	2	5.66	14	0	0	0	21	30	18	13	5	7	16	.319	.340	.296	6.97	3.05
Malave, Mark	R-R	6-3	185	1-5-95	1	2	2.76	18	0	0	2	33	32	11	10	2	12	36	.256	.274	.238	9.92	3.31
Mekkes, Dakota	R-R	6-7	252	11-6-94	3	0	0.58	18	0	0	4	31	14	4	2	1	14	47	.133	.152	.119	13.65	4.06
Miller, Kyle	R-R	6-3	185	12-2-93	1	0	1.93	4	1	0	1	14	10	5	3	0	9	6	.204	.148	.273	3.86	5.79

Miller, Tyson	R-R	6-5	200	7-29-95	6	7	4.48	28	20	0	0	121	122	70	60	10	38	99	.259	.250	.266	7.38	2.83
Moreno, Erling	R-R	6-3	200	1-13-97	2	4	4.22	14	14	0	0	64	56	38	30	3	31	57	.248	.276	.218	8.02	4.36
Paulino, Jose	L-L	6-2	165	4-9-95	7	6	4.51	27	22	0	0	124	125	68	62	6	42	94	.265	.277	.260	6.84	3.06
Peyton, Tyler	R-R	6-3	200	3-31-94	3	3	3.19	18	4	0	1	68	68	28	24	6	25	42	.273	.258	.288	5.59	3.33
Robinson, Duncan	R-R	6-6	220	12-5-93	5	5	2.11	15	10	0	0	77	66	29	18	7	13	59	.232	.281	.195	6.93	1.53
Rodriguez, Manuel	R-R	5-11	205	8-6-96	0	0	5.40	4	0	0	2	7	8	5	4	2	5	5	.276	.250	.294	6.75	6.75
Romero, Jhon	R-R	5-10	195	1-17-95	0	1	0.35	13	0	0	3	26	7	2	1	0	5	34	.085	.118	.063	11.92	1.75
Rondon, Manuel	L-L	6-1	165	3-7-95	14	6	4.63	27	26	0	0	128	132	75	66	15	66	113	.273	.312	.255	7.92	4.63
Rucker, Michael	R-R	6-1	185	4-27-94	0	0	1.42	7	0	0	1	13	7	2	2	1	0	22	.156	.143	.161	15.63	0.00
Sands, Carson	L-L	6-3	205	3-28-95	0	3	24.16	3	3	0	0	6	12	17	17	1	14	5	.414	.375	.429	7.11	19.89
Short, Wyatt	L-L	5-8	180	10-14-94	4	3	3.19	40	0	0	16	62	64	25	22	2	20	62	.266	.290	.255	9.00	2.90
Silverio, Pedro	R-R	6-2	210	6-29-94	4	5	4.85	28	0	0	1	56	59	35	30	3	27	62	.271	.292	.256	10.02	4.37
Swarmer, Matt	R-R	6-5	175	9-25-93	3	3	5.33	14	2	0	2	49	54	31	29	6	9	52	.271	.340	.194	9.55	1.65

Fielding

Catcher	PCT	G	PO	A	E	DP	PB
Cruz	.947	9	64	7	4	2	0
Mineo	.992	54	408	71	4	3	7
Payne	.988	47	359	48	5	5	2
Pereda	.991	34	285	36	3	2	3

First Base	PCT	G	PO	A	E	DP
Galindo	.971	15	131	3	4	9
Machin	.976	19	147	18	4	18
Martarano	.962	12	95	6	4	14
Mineo	.990	26	194	10	2	19
Paula	.923	1	11	1	1	1
Pereda	.995	47	387	24	2	36
Pieters	.933	3	14	0	1	2
Upshaw	.996	25	229	19	1	20

Second Base	PCT	G	PO	A	E	DP
Machin	.975	7	15	24	1	9
Monasterio	.980	10	25	25	1	9
Paula	1.000	1	0	1	0	0
Peguero	.957	97	172	275	20	66
Short	1.000	12	17	33	0	9
Upshaw	.923	16	24	48	6	13

Third Base	PCT	G	PO	A	E	DP
Galindo	.880	25	14	52	9	4
Machin	.933	33	19	65	6	7
Martarano	.000	1	0	0	0	0
Monasterio	.930	38	23	83	8	10
Paredes	1.000	7	5	16	0	1
Paula	.833	7	4	11	3	1
Pereda	.800	2	1	3	1	1
Short	.906	23	21	37	6	6
Upshaw	.957	11	7	15	1	1

Shortstop	PCT	G	PO	A	E	DP
Ademan	.944	29	45	73	7	16
Machin	1.000	6	10	15	0	5
Monasterio	.962	12	22	28	2	11
Paredes	.977	70	98	195	7	46
Short	.911	26	43	69	11	12

Outfield	PCT	G	PO	A	E	DP
Ayala	.954	107	214	15	11	1
Caro	.980	35	48	1	1	0
Cummins	1.000	24	47	3	0	1
Davis	.900	4	8	1	1	1
Heyward	1.000	3	4	0	0	0
Machin	1.000	1	2	0	0	0
Martarano	1.000	8	12	1	0	0
Mitchell	.957	89	124	10	6	1
Pieters	.975	78	146	8	4	2
Wilson	.961	84	168	5	7	0

EUGENE EMERALDS — *SHORT SEASON*

NORTHWEST LEAGUE

Batting	B-T	HT	WT	DOB	AVG	vLH	vRH	G	AB	R	H	2B	3B	HR	RBI	BB	HBP	SH	SF	SO	SB	CS	SLG	OBP
Ademan, Aramis	L-R	5-11	160	9-13-98	.286	.267	.290	39	161	23	46	9	4	4	27	14	6	2	0	30	10	6	.466	.365
Amaya, Miguel	R-R	6-1	185	3-9-99	.228	.273	.217	58	228	21	52	14	1	3	26	11	2	0	3	49	1	0	.338	.266
Bethencourt, Jhonny	R-R	5-11	160	2-12-97	.272	.339	.247	63	228	44	62	12	6	1	21	31	1	0	3	50	17	6	.390	.357
Carrier, Chris	R-R	6-2	225	4-18-95	.208	.091	.238	17	53	5	11	2	0	1	4	4	5	1	0	31	3	0	.302	.323
Cruz, Michael	L-R	5-11	210	1-13-96	.282	.318	.275	35	124	20	35	9	1	8	28	14	6	0	1	18	0	0	.565	.379
Davis, Zach	B-R	5-11	175	6-29-94	.275	.348	.252	56	193	31	53	7	2	2	12	24	8	2	2	56	23	5	.363	.374
Filiere, Austin	R-R	6-1	190	9-1-95	.261	.262	.261	49	176	22	46	14	0	6	25	32	7	0	2	56	1	2	.443	.392
Filotei, Tolly	L-R	5-6	155	11-28-95	.193	.250	.171	15	57	6	11	1	0	0	2	0	2	0	0	19	5	1	.211	.220
Gonzalez, Jose	R-R	6-1	160	1-12-96	.203	.158	.214	54	192	17	39	8	5	0	17	13	1	2	1	51	5	3	.297	.256
Hughes, Brandon	B-L	6-2	215	12-1-95	.248	.296	.238	41	153	20	38	12	1	1	16	13	2	0	3	43	6	3	.360	.310
Kwon, Kwang-Min	L-L	6-2	210	12-12-97	.207	.177	.213	24	92	9	19	2	1	2	10	8	0	0	1	43	2	0	.315	.267
Martarano, Joe	R-R	6-4	235	7-28-94	.340	.250	.368	15	50	3	17	2	0	1	9	8	1	0	1	14	2	0	.440	.433
Myers, Connor	R-R	5-11	170	2-3-94	.238	.143	.286	6	21	4	5	1	0	0	1	3	1	0	0	5	4	0	.286	.360
Narea, Rafael	R-R	5-10	160	4-3-98	.237	.327	.204	57	207	27	49	7	0	0	11	26	2	6	0	42	6	11	.271	.328
Payne, Tyler	R-R	5-11	210	10-25-92	.243	.111	.286	10	37	6	9	3	0	1	5	6	0	0	1	9	0	0	.405	.341
Polanco, Gustavo	R-R	6-0	190	6-13-97	.281	.368	.256	64	260	26	73	12	3	2	32	10	4	0	2	76	2	1	.373	.315
Remillard, Will	R-R	6-1	195	9-18-92	.474	.333	.500	5	19	4	9	3	0	0	6	4	0	0	0	2	0	0	.632	.565
Romano, Ramsey	R-R	6-2	208	5-10-95	.161	.111	.182	19	62	7	10	0	0	0	6	5	1	0	1	14	1	0	.161	.232
Rondon, Edgar	R-L	5-7	170	1-14-95	.163	.200	.143	12	43	2	7	0	0	0	3	7	0	0	1	19	2	0	.163	.275
Singleton, Chris	R-R	6-0	175	7-5-96	.185	.200	.181	27	108	15	20	7	0	1	10	8	1	0	1	27	6	1	.278	.246
Young, Jared	L-R	6-2	185	7-9-95	.257	.177	.268	39	140	23	36	6	1	1	15	11	0	2	0	29	6	2	.336	.311

Pitching	B-T	HT	WT	DOB	W	L	ERA	G	GS	CG	SV	IP	H	R	ER	HR	BB	SO	AVG	vLH	vRH	K/9	BB/9
Abbott, Cory	R-R	6-2	210	9-20-95	0	0	3.86	5	5	0	0	14	14	8	6	1	3	18	.269	.238	.290	11.57	1.93
Albertos, Jose	R-R	6-1	185	11-7-98	2	1	2.86	8	8	0	0	35	24	16	11	0	14	42	.181	.259	.127	10.90	3.63
Aquino, Luis	R-R	6-1	170	6-30-93	2	4	1.99	22	0	0	8	32	23	8	7	0	17	49	.204	.308	.115	13.93	4.83
Assad, Javier	R-R	6-1	200	7-30-97	5	6	4.23	13	13	0	0	66	69	34	31	2	21	72	.275	.250	.296	9.82	2.86
Camargo, Jesus	R-R	5-11	170	11-23-95	3	1	2.39	14	8	0	0	60	40	21	16	0	22	73	.185	.214	.161	10.89	3.28
Cammack, Holden	R-R	6-0	195	6-14-93	0	0	6.75	6	0	0	0	5	8	7	4	0	8	5	.348	.125	.467	8.44	13.50
Clark, Bailey	R-R	6-4	185	12-3-94	2	4	3.83	11	11	0	0	45	45	32	19	1	28	44	.260	.277	.250	8.87	5.64
De Los Rios, Enrique	R-R	6-1	175	5-2-95	4	1	3.51	12	6	0	0	59	47	27	23	5	23	49	.223	.204	.237	7.47	3.51
Diaz, Andin	L-L	6-0	182	9-2-92	0	2	2.31	8	0	0	1	12	13	8	3	0	7	13	.260	.273	.256	10.03	5.40
Diaz, Elvis	R-R	6-3	185	2-6-93	3	0	1.72	16	0	0	0	31	24	8	6	0	8	32	.214	.214	.214	9.19	2.30
Garcia, Alonso	R-R	6-0	157	5-30-98	2	0	3.38	4	4	0	0	19	16	7	7	1	8	13	.225	.286	.167	6.27	3.86
Glowicki, Brian	R-R	5-11	190	10-19-94	1	3	4.57	18	0	0	3	22	25	14	11	1	8	26	.281	.342	.229	10.80	3.32
Gomez, Yapson	L-L	5-10	160	10-2-93	4	1	1.75	9	2	0	1	26	21	6	5	0	5	32	.219	.148	.246	11.22	1.75
Hecht, Ben	R-R	6-2	170	5-31-95	0	0	1.53	10	0	0	0	18	12	7	3	1	10	25	.182	.222	.154	12.74	5.09

Pitching	B-T	HT	WT	DOB	W	L	ERA	G	GS	CG	SV	IP	H	R	ER	HR	BB	SO	AVG	vLH	vRH	K/9	BB/9
Knighton, Michael	R-R	6-2	190	4-30-94	1	1	0.96	6	0	0	3	9	7	2	1	0	3	10	.212	.154	.250	9.64	2.89
Lacy, Rollie	R-R	6-4	195	7-17-95	0	2	5.59	3	1	0	1	10	11	6	6	0	2	10	.297	.385	.250	9.31	1.86
Lange, Alex	R-R	6-3	197	10-2-95	0	1	4.82	4	4	0	0	9	9	6	5	0	3	13	.243	.177	.300	12.54	2.89
Little, Brendon	L-L	6-1	195	8-11-96	0	2	9.37	6	6	0	0	16	21	18	17	2	9	12	.300	.200	.327	6.61	4.96
Malave, Mark	R-R	6-3	185	1-5-95	0	0	2.25	3	0	0	0	4	3	1	1	0	1	4	.200	.143	.250	9.00	2.25
Marte, Junior	R-R	6-0	170	6-6-95	0	2	3.60	7	0	0	0	10	8	10	4	2	5	6	.211	.188	.227	5.40	4.50
Rodriguez, Manuel	R-R	5-11	205	8-6-96	1	0	3.52	12	0	0	0	23	20	11	9	1	6	33	.222	.256	.196	12.91	2.35
Romero, Jhon	R-R	5-10	195	1-17-95	1	0	1.80	8	0	0	1	15	8	4	3	0	5	19	.151	.111	.171	11.40	3.00
Rondon, Andry	R-R	6-2	190	9-16-95	0	0	1.62	9	0	0	0	17	10	4	3	0	5	18	.170	.227	.135	9.72	2.70
Ryan, Casey	R-R	6-4	230	5-20-94	1	1	8.50	13	0	0	0	18	28	19	17	2	6	12	.342	.441	.271	6.00	3.00
Sands, Carson	L-L	6-3	205	3-28-95	1	0	13.50	1	0	0	0	2	2	3	3	1	2	1	.286	.000	.333	4.50	9.00
Steffens, Jake	R-R	6-4	215	6-24-94	1	1	1.54	16	0	0	2	23	15	4	4	0	7	22	.177	.290	.111	8.49	2.70
Swarmer, Matt	R-R	6-5	175	9-25-93	3	0	2.72	7	7	0	0	36	31	12	11	4	8	37	.230	.200	.250	9.17	1.98
Thomas, Ricky Tyler	R-L	6-1	175	12-22-95	1	0	2.33	11	0	0	0	19	15	5	5	1	13	24	.227	.211	.234	11.17	6.05
Thompson, Keegan	R-R	6-0	193	3-13-95	1	2	2.37	7	1	0	0	19	15	5	5	1	4	23	.214	.333	.088	10.89	1.89
Uelmen, Erich	R-R	6-3	185	5-19-96	0	2	2.04	7	0	0	0	18	18	11	4	2	9	23	.265	.348	.222	11.72	4.58

Fielding

C: Amaya 43, Cruz 18, Payne 7, Polanco 5, Remillard 4. **1B:** Amaya 8, Filiere 2, Martarano 4, Payne 2, Polanco 57, Remillard 1, Romano 6. **2B:** Bethencourt 29, Hughes 1, Narea 10, Rondon 8, Young 31. **3B:** Bethencourt 16, Filiere 36, Kwon 1, Narea 16, Romano 9. **SS:** Ademan 38, Bethencourt 7, Narea 30, Young 1. **OF:** Bethencourt 1, Carrier 17, Davis 54, Filotei 12, Gonzalez 52, Hughes 36, Kwon 22, Martarano 5, Myers 5, Narea 1, Rondon 1, Singleton 27.

AZL CUBS — ROOKIE

ARIZONA LEAGUE

Batting	B-T	HT	WT	DOB	AVG	vLH	vRH	G	AB	R	H	2B	3B	HR	RBI	BB	HBP	SH	SF	SO	SB	CS	SLG	OBP
Baez, Jeffrey	R-R	6-0	180	10-30-93	.214	.000	.231	5	14	2	3	1	0	0	3	2	0	0	2	3	2	1	.286	.278
Balego, Cam	R-R	5-11	205	6-12-95	.286	.379	.246	36	98	14	28	13	0	1	9	14	3	1	2	21	1	3	.449	.385
Carrier, Chris	R-R	6-2	225	4-18-95	.067	.000	.077	7	15	1	1	0	0	0	0	2	2	0	0	6	1	0	.067	.263
Cuevas, Yovanny	R-R	6-0	170	7-28-98	.235	.191	.250	33	81	13	19	6	1	0	8	9	1	0	2	15	4	0	.333	.312
Diaz, Carlos	R-R	5-11	175	3-10-95	.197	.353	.148	27	71	4	14	8	0	0	6	3	0	0	0	14	1	0	.310	.230
Filiere, Austin	R-R	6-1	190	9-1-95	.125	—	.125	2	8	0	1	0	0	0	1	0	0	0	0	4	0	0	.125	.125
Filotei, Tolly	L-R	5-6	155	11-28-95	.125	.000	.182	10	16	2	2	0	0	0	0	1	0	0	0	7	0	0	.125	.177
Gutierrez, Jose	B-R	5-11	185	11-9-98	.256	.235	.262	40	156	22	40	11	3	0	13	8	0	1	1	51	6	1	.365	.291
Hidalgo, Luis	R-R	6-1	190	2-23-96	.339	.364	.333	17	62	9	21	5	0	2	13	2	0	0	0	7	1	1	.516	.359
Kwon, Kwang-Min	L-L	6-2	210	12-12-97	.169	.278	.132	25	71	10	12	3	1	0	2	7	3	1	0	24	1	1	.239	.272
Mastrobuoni, Marcus	R-R	5-11	205	11-28-93	.308	.250	.327	41	133	25	41	13	0	6	22	19	0	0	2	18	1	1	.541	.390
Mejia, Fidel	B-R	5-11	160	8-30-98	.214	.188	.224	36	117	16	25	6	1	0	12	10	3	1	1	25	2	2	.282	.290
Mejia, Rafael	R-R	6-1	195	12-12-97	.209	.125	.242	25	86	7	18	3	1	4	8	4	1	0	0	20	2	1	.407	.253
Nunez, Richard	R-R	5-10	170	3-14-95	.121	.167	.111	17	33	5	4	0	0	0	3	5	1	1	0	14	0	0	.121	.256
Perlaza, Yonathan	B-R	5-10	195	11-10-98	.235	.310	.206	25	102	13	24	4	2	0	6	6	0	1	0	25	4	3	.314	.278
Remillard, Will	R-R	6-1	195	9-18-92	.167	.500	.000	3	6	0	1	1	0	0	0	1	1	0	0	1	0	0	.333	.375
Reyes, Ruben	L-L	5-11	170	10-1-95	.191	.000	.222	6	21	5	4	2	0	0	1	1	0	0	0	3	1	0	.286	.227
Romano, Ramsey	R-R	6-2	208	5-10-95	.359	.273	.393	11	39	2	14	2	0	0	5	0	0	0	2	4	0	2	.410	.342
Sepulveda, Carlos	L-R	5-10	170	8-27-96	.324	.167	.355	9	37	6	12	2	0	0	4	4	0	0	0	4	0	1	.378	.390
Sierra, Jonathan	L-L	6-3	190	10-17-98	.260	.222	.271	48	185	19	48	10	2	2	22	18	2	0	0	59	6	2	.368	.332
Singleton, Chris	R-R	6-0	175	7-5-96	.304	.214	.344	12	46	6	14	2	1	1	6	3	0	0	0	10	5	1	.457	.347
Upshaw, Austin	L-R	6-0	175	7-28-96	.313	—	.313	4	16	4	5	1	0	2	8	0	0	0	0	4	0	0	.750	.313
Vazquez, Luis	R-R	6-1	165	10-10-99	.185	.250	.165	29	103	7	19	4	0	0	9	6	0	2	0	23	4	1	.223	.229
Velazquez, Nelson	R-R	6-0	190	12-26-98	.236	.250	.233	32	110	26	26	5	2	8	17	15	1	0	0	39	5	2	.536	.333
Wilson, D.J.	L-L	5-8	177	10-8-96	.500	.500	.500	3	8	5	4	1	0	3	5	2	1	0	1	1	1	0	1.750	.583
Zamudio, Kevin	R-R	6-0	200	8-23-97	.110	.074	.121	34	118	7	13	3	0	1	7	13	0	0	0	52	0	0	.161	.199
Zinn, Delvin	R-R	5-10	170	5-29-97	.228	.250	.218	40	114	16	26	6	1	0	9	12	0	2	0	31	3	1	.298	.302

Pitching	B-T	HT	WT	DOB	W	L	ERA	G	GS	CG	SV	IP	H	R	ER	HR	BB	SO	AVG	vLH	vRH	K/9	BB/9
Albertos, Jose	R-R	6-1	185	11-7-98	0	0	4.32	2	2	0	0	8	6	4	4	0	3	6	.200	.000	.231	6.48	3.24
Barry, Sean	R-R	6-2	190	5-22-95	1	0	6.00	3	0	0	0	3	4	3	2	0	1	2	.308	.167	.429	6.00	3.00
Carrera, Faustino	L-L	5-10	165	3-9-99	2	4	3.88	10	9	0	0	51	48	26	22	2	9	30	.245	.265	.238	5.29	1.59
Carter, Jed	R-R	6-0	190	1-26-95	0	0	1.50	5	0	0	0	6	3	3	1	0	4	8	.143	.167	.133	12.00	6.00
Colorado, Alfredo	R-R	6-1	170	6-22-96	3	4	3.91	11	5	0	0	51	54	25	22	6	18	49	.274	.271	.277	8.70	3.20
Correa, Danis	R-R	5-11	155	8-26-99	0	1	2.16	2	0	0	0	8	9	5	2	0	3	6	.273	.333	.222	6.48	3.24
De La Cruz, Oscar	R-R	6-4	200	3-4-95	0	0	0.00	1	0	0	0	2	0	0	0	0	0	1	.000	.000	.000	4.50	0.00
Estrada, Jeremiah	B-R	6-1	185	11-1-98	0	0	1.42	4	0	0	0	6	5	1	1	0	6	6	.217	.400	.167	8.53	8.53
Ferrebus, Emilio	R-R	6-2	165	11-25-97	2	1	4.76	4	3	0	0	17	12	9	9	0	9	12	.207	.227	.194	6.35	4.76
Guerrero, Fauris	R-R	5-11	180	10-5-96	1	1	3.06	8	0	0	3	18	17	13	6	1	4	18	.239	.318	.204	9.17	2.04
Hecht, Ben	R-R	6-2	170	5-31-95	0	0	11.57	2	0	0	0	2	2	3	3	1	3	5	.222	.333	.000	19.29	11.57
King, Brendan	R-R	6-1	200	7-8-94	0	0	2.82	9	4	0	0	22	23	9	7	0	5	28	.253	.275	.235	11.28	2.01
Lacy, Rollie	R-R	6-4	195	7-17-95	1	1	0.92	8	0	0	1	20	13	7	2	1	2	17	.178	.200	.163	7.78	0.92
Leidenz, Jose	R-R	6-1	171	10-16-94	0	1	4.50	4	0	0	0	6	7	8	3	0	5	7	.269	.625	.111	10.50	7.50
Mac Donna, Jose	L-L	6-2	195	9-3-95	2	0	4.26	5	0	0	0	6	6	3	3	0	3	6	.240	.200	.250	8.53	4.26
Marquez, Brailyn	L-L	6-4	185	1-30-99	2	1	5.52	11	9	0	0	44	50	34	27	3	12	52	.275	.283	.271	10.64	2.45
Medina, Ivan	R-R	6-3	162	2-26-96	0	4	3.86	9	0	0	4	14	21	8	6	0	2	15	.375	.296	.448	9.64	1.29
Mills, Alec	R-R	6-4	190	11-30-91	0	0	0.00	2	2	0	0	5	2	0	0	0	1	6	.133	.000	.200	10.80	1.80
Mills, Alec	R-R	6-4	190	11-30-91	0	0	0.00	2	2	0	0	5	2	0	0	0	1	6	.133	.000	.200	10.80	1.80
Palma, Eugenio	L-L	5-11	170	11-26-96	5	1	2.40	16	0	0	1	41	31	14	11	1	6	44	.199	.125	.224	9.58	1.31
Passantino, Jeffrey	R-R	5-9	225	9-25-95	2	0	3.10	11	0	0	0	20	28	8	7	0	2	22	.333	.333	.333	9.74	0.89

Pitching	B-T	HT	WT	DOB	W	L	ERA	G	GS	CG	SV	IP	H	R	ER	HR	BB	SO	AVG	vLH	vRH	K/9	BB/9
Perez, Yunior	R-R	6-4	190	12-19-98	0	3	9.82	7	6	0	0	18	29	23	20	3	9	26	.341	.344	.340	12.76	4.42
Ramos, Eury	R-R	6-3	152	10-10-97	2	2	5.63	11	1	0	0	24	36	25	15	2	15	22	.346	.371	.333	8.25	5.63
Remy, Peyton	L-R	6-2	170	8-20-96	0	0	7.50	5	0	0	1	6	7	6	5	0	5	10	.292	.300	.286	15.00	7.50
Ridings, Stephen	R-R	6-8	220	8-19-95	0	2	4.09	12	8	0	0	22	17	11	10	1	20	26	.218	.161	.255	10.64	8.18
Romero, Jhon	R-R	5-10	195	1-17-95	0	0	0.00	1	0	0	0	1	0	0	0	0	1	0	.000	.000	.000	0.00	9.00
Rosario, Jose	R-R	6-1	170	8-29-90	1	1	6.23	4	0	0	0	4	4	3	3	2	3	7	.235	.500	.091	14.54	6.23
Sands, Carson	L-L	6-3	205	3-28-95	0	1	3.09	4	4	0	0	12	8	4	4	0	11	10	.195	.231	.179	7.71	8.49
Stinnett, Jake	R-R	6-4	202	4-25-92	0	0	0.00	3	0	0	0	5	4	0	0	0	0	9	.222	.400	.154	17.36	0.00
Stophel, Mitch	R-R	6-3	205	11-9-94	1	0	3.45	12	0	0	1	16	12	6	6	2	8	22	.214	.421	.108	12.64	4.60
Sweeney, Nathan	R-R	6-4	185	8-21-97	0	2	5.91	14	0	0	0	21	30	22	14	2	14	18	.319	.378	.265	7.59	5.91
Zastryzny, Rob	R-L	6-3	205	3-26-92	0	1	1.04	3	3	0	0	9	9	6	1	0	1	4	.243	.222	.250	4.15	1.04

Fielding

C: Diaz 11, Mastrobuoni 23, Nunez 12, Remillard 3, Zamudio 19. **1B:** Balego 2, Diaz 6, Hidalgo 17, Mastrobuoni 11, Mejia 18, Nunez 1, Romano 3, Zamudio 13. **2B:** Balego 7, Mejia 11, Perlaza 21, Sepulveda 8, Upshaw 2, Zinn 12. **3B:** Balego 24, Filiere 1, Mejia 25, Romano 7, Upshaw 1, Zinn 3. **SS:** Balego 3, Perlaza 3, Vazquez 29, Zinn 23. **OF:** Baez 5, Carrier 4, Cuevas 29, Filotei 6, Gutierrez 36, Kwon 17, Mejia 8, Reyes 6, Sierra 42, Singleton 10, Velazquez 25, Wilson 3.

DSL CUBS — *ROOKIE*

DOMINICAN SUMMER LEAGUE

Batting	B-T	HT	WT	DOB	AVG	vLH	vRH	G	AB	R	H	2B	3B	HR	RBI	BB	HBP	SH	SF	SO	SB	CS	SLG	OBP
Alfonzo, Carmelo	L-R	6-0	177	10-1-97	.166	.200	.155	55	169	22	28	3	1	1	8	22	4	3	1	57	10	4	.213	.276
Blanco, Santiago	B-R	5-11	165	10-14-99	.148	.044	.211	23	61	11	9	1	0	0	3	14	1	0	0	18	3	2	.164	.316
Brete, Jeinser	R-R	6-0	180	11-26-99	.209	.313	.169	41	115	13	24	3	0	0	12	12	6	0	0	29	2	3	.235	.316
Chacon, Miller	R-R	6-0	189	6-17-98	.221	.231	.216	50	163	13	36	9	1	1	17	10	5	0	0	36	6	3	.307	.287
Cruz, Rochest	L-R	5-11	150	6-24-99	.250	.125	.268	22	64	10	16	1	1	0	6	14	1	1	0	8	4	6	.297	.392
Diaz, Daniel	R-R	5-11	200	4-5-97	.270	.200	.275	43	74	17	20	3	1	2	12	11	5	0	0	20	1	1	.419	.400
Diaz, Luis	R-R	5-9	160	4-16-99	.273	.282	.271	64	238	43	65	10	6	8	34	34	5	1	1	50	25	12	.466	.374
Gaitan, Alonso	R-R	6-0	176	2-23-98	.280	.319	.262	38	150	30	42	8	2	0	14	10	2	1	2	21	14	2	.360	.329
Gonzalez, Erick	R-R	5-10	175	9-2-96	.178	.067	.198	48	101	11	18	4	1	0	15	10	2	0	0	22	1	3	.238	.266
Hidalgo, Luis	R-R	6-1	190	2-23-96	.353	.300	.363	54	190	34	67	17	0	5	44	16	8	0	3	21	7	5	.521	.419
Hinirio, Albert	B-R	6-2	170	5-15-98	.266	.154	.277	44	154	20	41	4	2	0	15	10	6	0	1	33	4	3	.318	.333
Huma, Josue	B-R	6-1	175	3-17-00	.238	.187	.260	64	248	41	59	4	7	1	24	29	1	0	2	28	20	5	.323	.318
Jules, Jose	R-R	6-2	170	10-13-97	.216	.318	.201	55	171	26	37	4	2	2	14	28	3	3	0	28	14	5	.298	.337
Kelli, Fernando	B-R	6-0	180	7-28-98	.320	.294	.324	67	244	61	78	11	5	3	39	37	20	1	8	53	58	15	.443	.437
Marchan, Ervis	L-L	5-11	175	8-16-99	.184	.286	.161	23	76	10	14	4	0	0	6	7	0	1	2	11	2	2	.237	.247
Matos, Fidel	R-R	6-0	200	2-6-95	.279	.143	.500	52	172	19	48	7	2	4	27	10	6	0	3	31	1	4	.413	.335
Morel, Christopher	R-R	6-0	140	6-24-99	.220	.237	.216	61	223	44	49	6	2	7	40	35	5	0	5	37	23	10	.359	.332
Nunez, Orian	R-R	5-10	160	9-3-98	.305	.242	.329	61	226	42	69	14	1	3	31	21	7	2	2	20	22	10	.416	.379
Otano, Ignacio	R-R	6-0	175	1-6-97	.216	.273	.218	30	88	15	19	4	0	1	9	10	1	1	1	13	10	2	.296	.300
Pacheco, Carlos	R-R	5-11	195	4-2-99	.232	.211	.237	67	224	45	52	10	3	9	40	46	4	1	5	70	10	7	.424	.366
Pedra, Henrry	R-R	5-11	175	4-26-94	.260	.250	.262	59	185	33	48	9	2	2	21	16	13	1	1	40	13	5	.362	.358
Pena, Raymond	R-R	5-10	160	4-7-97	.168	.250	.148	43	101	5	17	3	0	0	6	11	2	0	0	27	2	3	.198	.263
Perez, Henderson	R-R	5-11	160	6-10-99	.224	.182	.231	51	143	31	32	4	2	2	22	25	1	0	0	29	9	4	.322	.343
Perez, Herson	B-R	5-11	175	12-19-96	.290	.152	.319	61	190	36	55	5	1	0	16	23	2	2	1	27	16	10	.326	.370
Pina, Oswaldo	R-R	5-10	170	8-9-98	.200	.500	.000	3	5	0	1	0	0	0	0	0	0	0	0	0	1	0	.200	.200
Rijo, Tony	R-R	6-0	170	11-3-97	.059	.000	.083	6	17	4	1	0	0	0	4	8	0	0	1	4	5	1	.059	.346
Soto, Jonathan	L-R	5-9	143	7-9-98	.284	.284	.284	62	201	21	57	7	5	1	38	21	1	0	3	22	7	0	.383	.350
Tineo, Franklin	R-R	6-1	176	12-30-94	.295	.281	.302	62	193	36	57	21	0	5	29	39	7	1	2	42	11	8	.482	.427
Ubiera, Luis	R-R	6-2	170	9-17-96	.233	.225	.236	58	176	23	41	4	4	0	19	30	9	1	1	27	8	10	.301	.370
Verenzuela, Ricardo	L-R	6-0	170	1-14-00	.188	.119	.211	54	170	12	32	4	3	0	13	26	7	4	1	63	12	4	.247	.319

Pitching	B-T	HT	WT	DOB	W	L	ERA	G	GS	CG	SV	IP	H	R	ER	HR	BB	SO	AVG	vLH	vRH	K/9	BB/9
Aguiar, Maikel	R-R	6-0	185	11-20-96	3	2	4.55	8	8	0	0	32	33	17	16	0	21	39	.275	.321	.239	11.08	5.97
Arredondo, Keiber	R-R	6-0	178	10-9-97	3	4	5.48	12	12	1	0	48	48	35	29	6	24	41	.255	.333	.207	7.74	4.53
Beato, Anyel	R-R	6-3	175	3-3-96	0	3	5.65	8	0	0	0	14	18	13	9	3	5	10	.333	.412	.297	6.28	3.14
Bruzual, Jonathan	L-L	6-1	172	2-15-00	3	6	6.86	14	9	0	0	39	37	32	30	0	36	41	.253	.222	.258	9.38	8.24
Calderon, Fernando	R-R	6-0	170	10-22-96	4	1	1.80	20	0	0	4	40	26	15	8	0	10	45	.182	.208	.167	10.13	2.25
Carreno, Kleiber	R-R	6-2	165	10-11-98	1	2	8.83	13	0	0	1	17	17	23	17	1	26	25	.250	.238	.255	12.98	13.50
Correa, Danis	R-R	5-11	155	8-26-99	2	3	3.62	8	8	0	0	32	28	25	13	0	14	17	.224	.222	.225	4.73	3.90
Cruz, Yovanny	R-R	6-1	190	8-23-99	3	2	3.51	13	12	0	0	56	50	32	22	3	14	54	.234	.221	.242	8.63	2.24
De La Cruz, Yan	R-R	5-11	165	8-5-93	6	4	2.83	24	0	0	6	54	45	24	17	3	15	48	.227	.229	.227	8.00	2.50
Delgado, Wilfre	R-R	6-1	175	11-10-95	1	0	0.00	2	0	0	0	3	0	0	0	0	1	3	.000	.000	.000	9.00	3.00
Estevez, Miguel	R-R	6-3	160	10-31-93	3	1	3.10	14	0	0	2	29	22	14	10	1	17	22	.220	.200	.240	6.83	5.28
Feliz, Wander	R-R	6-2	185	9-7-97	3	1	5.73	16	0	0	0	33	26	25	21	0	23	33	.219	.294	.182	9.00	6.27
Fernandez, Riger	L-L	6-2	190	1-1-98	0	3	4.08	17	3	0	2	35	26	19	16	1	33	43	.206	.000	.159	10.95	8.41
Ferrebus, Emilio	R-R	6-2	165	11-25-97	5	3	1.54	12	12	0	0	64	52	18	11	1	19	58	.227	.316	.183	8.11	2.66
Garay, Francisco	R-R	6-2	170	3-19-98	0	0	0.00	1	0	0	0	1	0	0	0	0	1	1	.000	.000	.000	9.00	9.00
Garcia, Jean	R-R	6-5	220	12-7-96	1	0	3.63	10	0	0	4	17	18	13	7	0	11	13	.269	.250	.279	6.75	5.71
Gomez, Jose	R-R	6-2	165	3-15-97	2	0	4.45	16	0	0	0	28	27	19	14	0	23	16	.252	.259	.250	5.08	7.31
Gonzalez, Jose	R-R	6-2	173	12-5-97	1	2	5.77	16	4	0	0	44	48	32	28	3	17	29	.287	.316	.273	5.98	3.50
Gracia, Francisco	R-R	6-0	200	9-4-98	0	1	9.22	16	0	0	0	27	36	39	28	2	20	20	.303	.340	.275	6.59	6.59
Guerrero, Fauris	R-R	5-11	180	10-5-96	2	0	1.77	4	3	0	0	20	19	8	4	1	2	16	.244	.219	.261	7.08	0.89
Heredia, Ferrol	L-L	5-11	200	11-7-98	1	2	2.89	16	0	0	1	28	14	14	9	0	27	27	.152	.364	.124	8.68	8.68
Herrera, Elias	R-R	6-1	172	9-23-97	3	2	4.24	20	2	0	2	47	50	34	22	1	17	51	.269	.187	.324	9.84	3.28

Lopez, Ronaldo	R-R	6-1	160	5-22-98	0	0	2.03	9	0	0	1	13	12	7	3	1	6	6	.235	.294	.206	4.05	4.05
Marte, Junior	R-R	6-0	170	6-6-95	2	2	1.93	9	0	0	2	19	13	5	4	1	10	23	.206	.389	.133	11.09	4.82
Matos, Hector	R-R	6-0	175	9-25-98	2	0	1.48	7	4	0	0	24	14	6	4	0	4	19	.167	.156	.173	7.03	1.48
Medina, Ivan	R-R	6-3	162	2-26-96	3	0	2.05	12	0	0	3	31	20	8	7	1	8	32	.187	.179	.190	9.39	2.35
Molina, Bryan	R-R	6-1	187	3-21-95	2	1	5.28	18	0	0	1	29	23	25	17	3	24	26	.217	.108	.275	8.07	7.45
Novas, Edison	R-R	6-0	150	2-8-97	0	0	5.19	5	0	0	1	9	7	5	5	0	3	9	.226	.250	.211	9.35	3.12
Nunez, Eduarniel	R-R	6-2	174	6-7-99	1	1	3.31	5	5	0	0	16	14	9	6	1	7	14	.226	.278	.205	7.71	3.86
Paula, Carlos	R-R	6-0	195	1-29-00	0	4	3.20	12	11	0	0	45	40	25	16	4	24	24	.244	.239	.247	4.80	4.80
Ramos, Eury	R-R	6-3	152	10-10-97	0	0	2.25	2	2	0	0	8	2	2	2	1	4	7	.077	.200	.048	7.88	4.50
Rodriguez, Benjamin	R-R	6-1	165	7-27-99	0	2	7.11	8	3	0	0	13	15	11	10	0	18	7	.319	.294	.333	4.97	12.79
Rosario, Aneuris	R-R	6-0	165	3-4-95	1	0	0.00	7	0	0	0	13	5	0	0	0	1	18	.104	.118	.097	12.15	0.68
Silva, Luis	L-L	5-11	165	6-6-97	1	4	4.64	14	9	0	0	43	46	31	22	0	27	27	.284	.000	.233	5.70	5.70
Tejada, Jesus	R-R	6-1	168	10-24-96	5	7	2.64	14	14	1	0	75	61	28	22	1	18	59	.229	.277	.202	7.08	2.16
Tineo, Freddy	R-R	6-0	160	11-22-97	0	0	5.19	14	0	0	1	26	29	21	15	4	15	27	.287	.244	.317	9.35	5.19
Valdez, Sucre	R-R	6-2	180	9-1-93	0	1	7.59	7	0	0	2	11	14	10	9	0	2	13	.311	.467	.233	10.97	1.69
Vargas, Didier	R-L	6-0	175	3-13-99	4	2	0.99	14	14	0	0	64	44	19	7	1	23	55	.188	.137	.202	7.77	3.25
Vasquez, Edward	R-R	6-3	180	7-7-97	3	2	3.69	11	4	0	0	32	31	20	13	1	17	19	.254	.229	.270	5.40	4.83
Ventura, Omar	R-R	6-2	190	9-10-96	0	2	4.04	15	2	0	0	36	27	23	16	0	31	25	.213	.192	.225	6.31	7.82

Fielding

C: Chacon 21, Diaz 32, Gonzalez 44, Pena 38, Perez 42, Soto 37, Tineo 18. **1B:** Brete 5, Chacon 21, Diaz 9, Hidalgo 51, Marchan 9, Matos 2, Matos 12, Pedra 1, Pena 8, Soto 22, Tineo 29, Tineo 1. **2B:** Blanco 1, Brete 1, Cruz 15, Diaz 30, Huma 12, Matos 1, Nunez 34, Otano 8, Perez 26, Pedra 23, Pina 1, Tineo 3. **3B:** Brete 19, Diaz 19, Gonzalez 1, Huma 1, Matos 17, Morel 12, Nunez 6, Otano 18, Pedra 34, Perez 26, Pina 2, Ubiera 1. **SS:** Cruz 6, Diaz 17, Huma 49, Morel 49, Nunez 20, Otano 1, Pedra 1, Perez 1. OF: Alfonzo 54, Blanco 1, Gaitan 33, Hidalgo 2, Hinirio 24, Jules 50, Kelli 66, Marchan 12, Matos 2, Pacheco 64, Pedra 4, Pena 2, Rijo 6, Tineo 20, Ubiera 57, Verenzuela 50.

Chicago White Sox

SEASON IN A SENTENCE: What began in December at the Winter Meetings continued into the regular season, when the White Sox continued trading established veterans for high-end prospects with an eye toward the future.

HIGH POINT: The first wave of the White Sox's rebuild went as planned. Although neither was particularly dominant, righthander Lucas Giolito and second baseman Yoan Moncada each showed enough development in the major leagues to give the team and its fans realistic hope of playoff contention in the coming years.

LOW POINT: With a loss to the Indians on Sept. 29, the White Sox moved 35 games behind the Indians for first place in the division.

NOTABLE ROOKIES: After acquiring them in offseason deals for outfielder Adam Eaton and lefty Chris Sale, the White Sox summoned righties Giolito and Reynaldo Lopez and second baseman Moncada at various points during the season. Each was inconsistent but showed signs of promise at the same time. Moncada struggled with strikeouts, whiffing at a 32 percent clip in his short sample. Giolito found some semblance of the form he showed as a younger prospect and went 3-3, 2.38 but allowed eight home runs in 45.1 innings. Lopez, armed with dynamite pure stuff, struck out just 5.7 hitters per nine innings.

KEY TRANSACTIONS: The White Sox owned the month of July. They started with the Quintana deal, then followed it up by acquiring three prospects from the Yankees in exchange for third baseman Todd Frazier and righthanded relievers David Robertson and Tommy Kahnle. In return, Chicago got back outfielder Blake Rutherford, as well as outfielder Tito Polo, lefty Ian Clarkin and major league reliever Tyler Clippard. In addition, they won the bidding for Cuban wunderkind Luis Robert, who immediately jumped into the upper tier of their system.

DOWN ON THE FARM: With its three biggest prospects graduated, Jimenez easily moves into the top spot in the system. He crushed the ball after the trade, hitting .345/.410/.682 with eight home runs in 29 games before a promotion to Double-A. The White Sox also saw results from its three top arms—righthanders Michael Kopech, Alec Hansen and Dane Dunning. Kopech in particular was dazzling, working to a 9-8, 2.88 mark with 172 strikeouts, which tied him for fifth in the minors.

OPENING DAY PAYROLL: $99,096,770 (24th)

PLAYERS OF THE YEAR

MAJOR LEAGUE	MINOR LEAGUE
Jose Abreu	**Michael Kopech**
1B	**RHP**
.304/.354/.522	(Double-A/Triple-A)
Provided a spark on a	9-8, 3.38
decimated club	172 SO (5th, MiLB)

ORGANIZATION LEADERS

BATTING		*Minimum 250 AB
MAJORS		
* AVG	Avisail Garcia	.330
* OPS	Jose Abreu	.906
HR	Jose Abreu	33
RBI	Jose Abreu	102
MINORS		
* AVG	Craig Dedelow, Kannapolis, Great Falls	.306
* OBP	Cody Asche, Charlotte	.392
* SLG	Craig Dedelow, Kannapolis, Great Falls	.552
* OPS	Craig Dedelow, Kannapolis, Great Falls	.894
R	Joel Booker, Winston-Salem, Kannapolis	76
H	Mitch Roman, Kannapolis	131
TB	Seby Zavala, Kannapolis, Winston-Salem	193
	Jake Peter, Birmingham, Charlotte	192
2B	Jameson Fisher, Kannapolis, Winston-Salem	30
3B	Jameson Fisher, Kannapolis, Winston-Salem	6
HR	Seby Zavala, Kannapolis, Winston-Salem	21
RBI	Seby Zavala, Kannapolis, Winston-Salem	72
BB	Zack Collins, Winston-Salem, Birmingham	87
SO	Keon Barnum, Winston-Salem, Birmingham	151
SB	Jacob May, Charlotte	31

PITCHING		#Minimum 75 IP
MAJORS		
W	Miguel Gonzalez	7
	Derek Holland	7
# ERA	Miguel Gonzalez	4.31
SO	Jose Quintana	109
SV	David Robertson	13
MINORS		
W	Jimmy Lambert, Kannapolis, Winston-Salem	12
L	Spencer Adams, Birmingham	15
# ERA	Alec Hansen, Kannapolis, Winston-Salem, Birm.	2.80
G	Matt Purke, Charlotte	48
GS	Spencer Adams, Birmingham	26
	Alec Hansen, Kannapolis, Winston-Salem, Birm.	26
	Dane Dunning, Kannapolis, Winston-Salem	26
	Jimmy Lambert, Kannapolis, Winston-Salem	26
SV	Brandon Brennan, Birmingham, Charlotte	15
IP	Spencer Adams, Birmingham	153
BB	Carson Fulmer, Charlotte	65
	Michael Kopech, Birmingham, Charlotte	65
SO	Alec Hansen, Kannapolis, Winston-Salem, Birm.	191
# AVG	Michael Kopech, Birmingham, Charlotte	.193

2017 PERFORMANCE

General Manager: Rick Hahn. **Farm Director:** Chris Getz. **Scouting Director:** Nick Hostetler.

Class	Team	League	W	L	PCT	Finish	Manager
Majors	Chicago White Sox	American	67	95	.414	14th (15)	Rick Renteria
Triple-A	Charlotte Knights	International	61	81	.43	12th (14)	Mark Grudzielanek
Double-A	Birmingham Barons	Southern	53	85	.384	10th (10)	Julio Vinas
High-A	Winston-Salem Dash	Carolina	56	84	.400	10th (10)	Willie Harris
Low-A	Kannapolis Intimidators	South Atlantic	68	69	.496	8th (14)	Justin Jirschele
Rookie	Great Falls Voyagers	Pioneer	34	42	.447	6th (8)	Tim Esmay
Rookie	AZL White Sox	Arizona	30	26	.536	t-7th (15)	Ryan Newman
Overall 2017 Minor League Record			302	387	.438	30th (30)	

ORGANIZATION STATISTICS

CHICAGO WHITE SOX

AMERICAN LEAGUE

Batting	B-T	HT	WT	DOB	AVG	vLH	vRH	G	AB	R	H	2B	3B	HR	RBI	BB	HBP	SH	SF	SO	SB	CS	SLG	OBP
Abreu, Jose	R-R	6-3	255	1-29-87	.304	.356	.288	156	621	95	189	43	6	33	102	35	15	0	4	119	3	0	.552	.354
Anderson, Tim	R-R	6-1	185	6-23-93	.257	.321	.234	146	587	72	151	26	4	17	56	13	3	2	1	162	15	1	.402	.277
Asche, Cody	R-L	6-1	205	6-30-90	.105	.000	.115	19	57	5	6	1	0	1	4	3	2	0	0	21	0	0	.175	.177
Brantly, Rob	R-L	6-1	195	7-14-89	.290	.200	.308	13	31	4	9	1	0	2	5	3	2	0	0	14	0	0	.516	.389
Cabrera, Melky	L-B	5-10	210	8-11-84	.295	.296	.294	98	397	54	117	17	0	13	56	25	1	2	3	52	0	0	.436	.336
2-team total (58 Kansas City)					.286	.256	.272	156	620	78	177	30	2	17	85	36	2	2	6	74	1	2	.423	.324
Davidson, Matt	R-R	6-3	230	3-26-91	.220	.250	.209	118	414	43	91	16	1	26	68	19	5	0	5	165	0	1	.452	.260
Delmonico, Nicky	L-R	6-2	230	7-12-92	.262	.258	.264	43	141	25	37	4	0	9	23	23	2	0	0	31	2	0	.482	.374
Engel, Adam	R-R	6-2	210	12-9-91	.166	.217	.147	97	301	34	50	11	3	6	21	19	8	8	0	117	8	1	.282	.235
Frazier, Todd	R-R	6-3	220	2-12-86	.207	.203	.209	81	280	41	58	15	0	16	44	48	4	0	3	71	4	3	.432	.328
2-team total (66 New York)					.213	.203	.209	147	474	74	101	19	1	27	76	83	14	0	5	125	4	3	.428	.344
Garcia, Avisail	R-R	6-4	240	6-12-91	.330	.424	.298	136	518	75	171	27	5	18	80	33	9	0	1	111	5	3	.506	.380
Garcia, Leury	B-R	5-8	170	3-18-91	.270	.302	.257	87	300	41	81	15	2	9	33	13	8	3	2	69	8	5	.423	.316
Garcia, Willy	R-R	6-2	215	9-4-92	.238	.250	.232	44	105	15	25	5	3	2	12	11	0	1	2	31	0	0	.400	.305
Hanson, Alen	B-R	5-11	170	10-22-92	.231	.259	.226	69	160	28	37	9	1	4	10	10	1	1	3	43	9	2	.375	.276
Liriano, Rymer	R-R	6-0	230	6-20-91	.220	.167	.229	21	41	4	9	2	0	1	6	5	0	0	0	14	1	0	.342	.304
May, Jacob	B-R	5-10	180	1-23-92	.056	.100	.039	15	36	2	2	0	0	0	3	3	1	2	0	17	0	0	.056	.150
Moncada, Yoan	B-R	6-2	205	5-27-95	.231	.224	.235	54	199	31	46	8	2	8	22	29	3	0	0	74	3	2	.412	.338
Narvaez, Omar	L-R	5-11	215	2-10-92	.277	.233	.286	90	253	23	70	10	0	2	14	38	1	3	0	45	0	0	.340	.373
Saladino, Tyler	R-R	6-0	200	7-20-89	.178	.214	.160	79	253	23	45	9	2	0	10	23	3	2	0	67	5	4	.229	.255
Sanchez, Yolmer	B-R	5-11	185	6-29-92	.267	.248	.273	141	484	63	129	19	8	12	59	35	4	7	4	111	8	9	.413	.319
Smith, Kevan	R-R	6-4	230	6-28-88	.283	.243	.309	87	276	23	78	17	0	4	30	9	3	2	3	46	0	0	.388	.309
Soto, Geovany	R-R	6-1	225	1-20-83	.191	.308	.138	13	42	5	8	0	0	3	9	4	1	0	1	10	0	0	.405	.271

Pitching	B-T	HT	WT	DOB	W	L	ERA	G	GS	CG	SV	IP	H	R	ER	HR	BB	SO	AVG	vLH	vRH	K/9	BB/9
Alburquerque, Al	R-R	6-0	195	6-10-86	0	1	1.13	10	0	0	0	8	3	1	1	0	2	5	.111	.000	.158	5.63	2.25
2-team total (11 Kansas City)					0	2	2.50	21	0	0	0	18	10	5	5	0	8	14	.159	.154	.217	7.00	4.00
Beck, Chris	R-R	6-3	225	9-4-90	2	1	6.40	57	0	0	0	65	73	48	46	16	34	42	.290	.247	.315	5.85	4.73
Bummer, Aaron	L-L	6-3	200	9-21-93	1	3	4.50	30	0	0	0	22	13	11	11	4	15	17	.178	.171	.188	6.95	6.14
Clippard, Tyler	R-R	6-3	200	2-14-85	1	1	1.80	11	0	0	2	10	8	2	2	0	5	12	.211	.118	.286	10.80	4.50
3-team total (16 Houston, 40 New York)					2	8	4.77	67	0	0	5	60	47	33	32	10	31	72	.209	.269	.148	10.74	4.62
Covey, Dylan	R-R	6-2	195	8-14-91	0	7	7.71	18	12	0	0	70	83	60	60	20	34	41	.305	.275	.333	5.27	4.37
Danish, Tyler	R-R	6-0	200	9-12-94	1	0	0.00	1	1	0	0	5	3	0	0	0	6	6	.177	.167	.182	10.80	10.80
Farquhar, Danny	R-R	5-9	185	2-17-87	2	0	4.40	15	0	0	0	14	11	7	7	1	6	12	.208	.130	.267	7.53	3.77
2-team total (37 Tampa Bay)					4	2	4.20	52	0	0	0	49	39	23	23	3	28	45	.223	.207	.250	8.21	5.11
Fry, Jace	L-L	6-1	190	7-9-93	0	0	10.80	11	0	0	0	7	12	8	8	1	5	3	.387	.308	.444	4.05	6.75
Fulmer, Carson	R-R	6-0	195	12-13-93	3	1	3.86	7	5	0	0	23	16	10	10	4	13	19	.188	.163	.222	7.33	5.01
Giolito, Lucas	R-R	6-6	255	7-14-94	3	3	2.38	7	7	0	0	45	31	14	12	8	12	34	.190	.200	.181	6.75	2.38
Goldberg, Brad	R-R	6-4	220	2-21-90	0	0	8.25	11	0	0	0	12	14	11	11	2	14	3	.304	.222	.421	2.25	10.50
Gonzalez, Miguel	R-R	6-1	170	5-27-84	7	10	4.31	22	22	0	0	134	145	72	64	16	47	85	.273	.283	.263	5.72	3.16
2-team total (5 Texas)					8	13	4.62	27	27	0	0	156	167	88	80	22	55	100	.271	.314	.220	5.77	3.17
Holland, Derek	L-B	6-2	215	10-9-86	7	14	6.20	29	26	0	0	135	156	106	93	31	75	104	.290	.237	.305	6.93	5.00
Holmberg, David	L-R	6-3	245	7-19-91	2	4	4.68	37	7	0	0	58	63	37	30	12	34	33	.275	.286	.270	5.15	5.31
Infante, Gregory	R-R	6-2	215	7-10-87	2	1	3.13	52	0	0	0	55	45	20	19	4	20	49	.226	.231	.223	8.07	3.29
Jennings, Dan	L-L	6-3	210	4-17-87	3	1	3.45	48	0	0	0	44	35	20	17	6	19	38	.215	.169	.250	7.71	3.86
2-team total (29 Tampa Bay)					3	1	3.45	77	0	0	0	63	53	27	24	8	31	51	.228	.297	.212	7.32	4.45
Jones, Nate	R-R	6-5	220	1-28-86	1	0	2.31	11	0	0	0	12	9	3	3	1	6	15	.220	.174	.278	11.57	4.63
Kahnle, Tommy	R-R	6-1	235	8-7-89	1	3	2.50	37	0	0	0	36	28	12	10	3	7	60	.214	.289	.165	15.00	1.75
2-team total (32 New York)					2	4	2.59	69	0	0	0	63	53	20	18	4	17	96	.228	.288	.165	13.79	2.44
Lopez, Reynaldo	R-R	6-0	185	1-4-94	3	3	4.72	8	8	0	0	48	49	29	25	7	14	30	.258	.269	.247	5.66	2.64
Minaya, Juan	R-R	6-4	210	9-18-90	3	2	4.53	40	0	0	9	44	38	22	22	7	20	51	.239	.194	.268	10.51	4.12
Pelfrey, Mike	R-R	6-7	240	1-14-84	3	12	5.93	34	21	0	0	120	127	87	79	25	62	79	.270	.259	.279	5.93	4.65
Petricka, Jake	R-R	6-5	220	6-5-88	1	1	7.01	27	0	0	0	26	39	21	20	6	6	26	.342	.364	.329	9.12	2.10
Putnam, Zach	R-R	6-2	220	7-3-87	0	0	1.04	7	0	0	0	9	2	1	1	0	1	9	.074	.167	.000	9.35	1.04

Quintana, Jose	R-L	6-1	220	1-24-89	4	8	4.49	18	18	0	0	104	98	55	52	14	40	109	.246	.255	.243	9.40	3.45
Robertson, David	R-R	5-11	195	4-9-85	4	2	2.70	31	0	0	13	33	21	10	10	4	11	47	.177	.138	.213	12.69	2.97
2-team total (30 New York)					9	2	1.84	61	0	0	14	68	35	14	14	6	23	98	.148	.138	.213	12.91	3.03
Rodon, Carlos	L-L	6-3	235	12-10-92	2	5	4.15	12	12	0	0	69	64	35	32	12	31	76	.246	.286	.234	9.87	4.02
Shields, James	R-R	6-3	215	12-20-81	5	7	5.23	21	21	0	0	117	116	72	68	27	53	103	.253	.279	.228	7.92	4.08
Swarzak, Anthony	R-R	6-4	215	9-10-85	4	3	2.23	41	0	0	1	48	37	12	12	2	13	52	.216	.179	.235	9.68	2.42
Volstad, Chris	R-R	6-8	235	9-23-86	1	2	4.66	6	2	0	0	19	16	11	10	4	5	10	.232	.259	.214	4.66	2.33
Ynoa, Michael	R-R	6-7	210	9-24-91	1	0	5.90	22	0	0	0	29	28	22	19	4	22	23	.246	.255	.239	7.14	6.83

Fielding

Catcher	PCT	G	PO	A	E	DP	PB
Brantly	1.000	6	23	1	0	0	0
Narvaez	.989	83	513	36	6	2	6
Smith	.997	79	572	27	2	2	5
Soto	1.000	13	91	7	0	0	0

First Base	PCT	G	PO	A	E	DP
Abreu	.993	139	1135	78	8	130
Asche	1.000	2	19	0	0	1
Davidson	.974	19	140	7	4	11
Delmonico	1.000	4	29	1	0	4
Frazier	.900	4	8	1	1	1
Narvaez	.833	1	5	0	1	0
Saladino	1.000	3	3	1	0	0

Second Base	PCT	G	PO	A	E	DP
Garcia	1.000	3	2	6	0	0
Hanson	1.000	13	13	37	0	7
Moncada	.966	54	61	169	8	29
Saladino	.993	26	49	84	1	21
Sanchez	.981	78	132	184	6	53

Third Base	PCT	G	PO	A	E	DP
Asche	1.000	1	1	0	0	0
Davidson	.955	34	14	49	3	7
Frazier	.958	67	36	123	7	27
Hanson	1.000	1	0	2	0	0
Saladino	.958	22	18	51	3	7
Sanchez	.977	52	43	87	3	11

Shortstop	PCT	G	PO	A	E	DP
Anderson	.952	145	197	363	28	85
Garcia	.857	2	1	5	1	1
Saladino	1.000	13	19	32	0	7
Sanchez	1.000	4	6	10	0	3

Outfield	PCT	G	PO	A	E	DP
Asche	.000	1	0	0	0	0
Cabrera	.988	92	150	9	2	0
Delmonico	.985	27	66	1	1	0
Engel	.992	96	253	5	2	2
Garcia	.968	132	263	13	9	3
Garcia	.984	79	172	9	3	0
Garcia	.971	40	67	0	2	0
Hanson	.911	36	49	2	5	1
Liriano	1.000	19	24	1	0	0
May	1.000	15	24	0	0	0
Sanchez	1.000	1	1	0	0	0

CHARLOTTE KNIGHTS — *TRIPLE-A*

INTERNATIONAL LEAGUE

Batting	B-T	HT	WT	DOB	AVG	vLH	vRH	G	AB	R	H	2B	3B	HR	RBI	BB	HBP	SH	SF	SO	SB	CS	SLG	OBP
Alvarez, Eddy	B-R	5-9	180	1-30-90	.240	.200	.267	34	100	14	24	0	0	0	7	14	3	0	1	32	1	0	.240	.348
Asche, Cody	R-L	6-1	205	6-30-90	.292	.227	.311	87	291	42	85	15	1	14	57	49	2	0	5	75	4	1	.495	.392
Blair, Carson	R-R	6-2	210	10-18-89	.211	.277	.171	36	123	15	26	7	0	5	15	12	3	1	0	51	0	1	.390	.297
Bourgeois, Jason	R-R	5-9	195	1-4-82	.266	.234	.283	68	222	21	59	5	1	4	24	13	0	0	3	36	4	2	.351	.303
Brantly, Rob	R-L	6-1	195	7-14-89	.286	.368	.270	37	119	18	34	5	0	5	30	11	8	0	4	14	0	1	.454	.373
2-team total (46 Louisville)					.293	.132	.346	83	287	39	84	11	1	10	46	20	9	0	5	39	3	3	.443	.352
Bueno, Ronald	B-R	5-10	154	10-4-92	.222	.177	.243	58	162	20	36	8	2	6	24	17	1	2	0	40	0	4	.407	.300
Cabrera, Everth	R-B	5-10	190	11-17-86	.201	.244	.186	52	169	21	34	5	0	1	8	18	2	1	1	34	10	1	.249	.284
Davidson, Matt	R-R	6-3	230	3-26-91	.000	—	.000	1	3	0	0	0	0	0	0	0	0	0	0	3	0	0	.000	.000
Delmonico, Nicky	L-R	6-2	230	7-12-92	.262	.250	.267	99	378	55	99	18	3	12	45	46	4	0	1	73	4	2	.421	.347
Engel, Adam	R-R	6-2	210	12-9-91	.218	.188	.231	46	165	20	36	12	2	8	19	19	4	3	1	51	4	3	.461	.312
Garcia, Avisail	R-R	6-4	240	6-12-91	.000	.000	.000	1	4	0	0	0	0	0	0	0	0	0	0	2	0	0	.000	.000
Garcia, Leury	B-R	5-8	170	3-18-91	.000	—	.000	1	4	0	0	0	0	0	0	0	0	0	0	1	0	0	.000	.000
Garcia, Willy	R-R	6-2	215	9-4-92	.286	.406	.238	31	112	20	32	6	0	5	20	18	3	0	1	38	1	0	.473	.396
Gelalich, Jeff	L-R	6-0	210	3-16-91	.071	.000	.125	5	14	2	1	0	0	0	0	1	1	0	0	6	0	0	.071	.188
Gillaspie, Casey	B-L	6-4	240	1-25-93	.210	.108	.265	30	105	17	22	5	0	6	18	14	0	0	1	23	0	0	.429	.300
2-team total (95 Durham)					.223	.242	.219	125	458	62	102	20	2	15	62	50	1	0	6	100	1	1	.373	.297
Green, Grant	R-R	6-3	180	9-27-87	.211	.244	.184	28	90	9	19	7	0	1	10	10	0	0	1	19	0	1	.322	.287
2-team total (40 Syracuse)					.232	.242	.247	68	220	20	51	12	0	1	12	24	0	0	1	53	0	3	.300	.306
Hayes, Danny	L-R	6-4	230	9-21-90	.228	.189	.244	128	439	52	100	23	1	19	67	67	1	2	6	142	0	2	.415	.328
Ladendorf, Tyler	R-R	5-11	195	3-7-88	.250	.271	.239	60	200	24	50	14	0	2	21	18	4	0	0	40	4	1	.350	.324
Liriano, Rymer	R-R	6-0	230	6-20-91	.256	.300	.236	123	449	67	115	15	3	17	52	42	4	2	3	133	7	4	.417	.323
May, Jacob	B-R	5-10	180	1-23-92	.248	.188	.272	110	415	54	103	10	5	4	27	30	5	17	0	112	31	8	.325	.307
Moncada, Yoan	B-R	6-2	205	5-27-95	.282	.216	.308	80	309	57	87	9	3	12	36	49	0	0	3	102	17	8	.447	.377
O'Dowd, Chris	L-R	5-11	190	10-4-90	.143	—	.143	4	14	1	2	1	0	0	1	0	0	0	0	3	0	0	.214	.143
Pena, Roberto	R-R	6-0	225	6-8-92	.210	.262	.185	60	200	11	42	7	0	3	17	11	2	1	0	29	0	0	.290	.258
Peter, Jake	L-R	6-1	185	4-5-93	.292	.377	.239	45	178	28	52	7	2	9	28	15	1	0	0	44	2	2	.506	.351
Peterson, D.J.	R-R	6-1	210	12-31-91	.198	.258	.164	25	86	9	17	2	0	4	9	10	0	1	0	21	0	0	.361	.281
Raburn, Ryan	R-R	6-0	185	4-17-81	.277	.320	.259	27	83	11	23	2	1	3	13	20	1	0	1	29	1	0	.434	.419
2-team total (6 Syracuse)					.274	.125	.333	33	106	14	29	4	1	4	18	20	2	0	3	38	1	0	.443	.389
Saladino, Tyler	R-R	6-0	200	7-20-89	.350	.600	.267	6	20	3	7	1	0	1	4	3	0	0	0	7	0	0	.550	.435
Smith, Kevan	R-R	6-4	230	6-28-88	.377	.400	.364	14	53	10	20	6	0	0	15	6	1	0	2	9	0	0	.491	.436
Vinicio, Jose	B-R	5-11	150	7-10-93	.246	.273	.233	36	130	13	32	5	1	1	7	0	0	4	1	35	5	1	.323	.244

Pitching	B-T	HT	WT	DOB	W	L	ERA	G	GS	CG	SV	IP	H	R	ER	HR	BB	SO	AVG	vLH	vRH	K/9	BB/9
Alburquerque, Al	R-R	6-0	195	6-10-86	0	0	4.63	10	0	0	2	12	10	6	6	3	5	15	.233	.320	.111	11.57	3.86
Beatty, Max	R-R	6-2	225	3-27-91	1	0	8.10	2	0	0	0	3	5	3	3	0	4	2	.333	.375	.286	5.40	10.80
Beck, Chris	R-R	6-3	225	9-4-90	1	0	2.25	5	0	0	1	8	6	2	2	1	4	6	.207	.125	.238	6.75	4.50
Brennan, Brandon	R-R	6-4	220	7-26-91	0	0	3.06	14	0	0	6	18	16	6	6	0	9	16	.250	.167	.324	8.15	4.58
Bummer, Aaron	L-L	6-3	200	9-21-93	0	0	1.80	3	0	0	0	5	5	2	1	0	1	5	.263	.250	.273	9.00	1.80
Burdi, Zack	R-R	6-3	205	3-9-95	0	4	4.05	29	0	0	7	33	30	18	15	2	17	51	.231	.233	.229	13.77	4.59
Clark, Brian	R-L	6-3	225	4-27-93	6	1	4.01	36	0	0	2	49	59	26	22	4	13	44	.298	.287	.306	8.03	2.37

Covey, Dylan	R-R	6-2	195	8-14-91	0	0	3.00	2	0	0	0	6	5	2	2	1	1	3	.227	.333	.154	4.50	1.50
Danish, Tyler	R-R	6-0	200	9-12-94	4	14	5.47	26	25	1	0	138	175	107	84	18	47	71	.305	.292	.318	4.62	3.06
Dunning, Jake	R-R	6-4	190	8-12-88	2	0	10.43	8	0	0	0	15	25	18	17	2	8	12	.385	.375	.394	7.36	4.91
Farquhar, Danny	R-R	5-9	185	2-17-87	0	0	3.00	8	0	0	1	9	6	3	3	2	2	12	.188	.308	.105	12.00	2.00
2-team total (4 Durham)					0	1	4.26	12	0	0	1	13	8	6	6	2	5	16	.182	.286	.000	11.37	3.55
Fulmer, Carson	R-R	6-0	195	12-13-93	7	9	5.79	25	25	0	0	126	132	89	81	18	65	96	.268	.270	.266	6.86	4.64
Giolito, Lucas	R-R	6-6	255	7-14-94	6	10	4.48	24	24	2	0	129	122	66	64	17	59	134	.253	.274	.232	9.37	4.13
Goldberg, Brad	R-R	6-4	220	2-21-90	3	2	3.35	30	0	0	5	40	40	19	15	2	22	47	.263	.297	.231	10.49	4.91
Gonzalez, Miguel	R-R	6-1	170	5-27-84	0	0	5.79	1	1	0	0	5	7	3	3	0	0	1	.333	.286	.357	1.93	0.00
Hasler, Drew	R-R	6-6	245	8-14-93	0	0	0.00	2	0	0	0	6	4	1	0	0	1	1	.174	.154	.200	1.50	1.50
Holmberg, David	L-R	6-3	245	7-19-91	3	1	2.78	10	4	0	0	32	26	10	10	4	8	24	.222	.143	.267	6.68	2.23
Infante, Gregory	R-R	6-2	215	7-10-87	0	1	1.80	12	0	0	3	15	7	3	3	0	8	18	.143	.095	.179	10.80	4.80
Johnson, Steve	R-R	6-1	220	8-31-87	1	2	8.44	5	5	0	0	21	24	20	20	6	9	21	.289	.231	.387	8.86	3.80
2-team total (19 Norfolk)					2	4	6.44	24	10	0	0	59	64	42	42	10	23	60	.282	.306	.256	9.20	3.53
Kopech, Michael	R-R	6-3	205	4-30-96	1	1	3.00	3	3	0	0	15	15	5	5	0	5	17	.263	.229	.318	10.20	3.00
Lamb, Will	L-L	6-6	180	9-9-90	0	1	7.46	17	3	0	1	35	45	36	29	11	20	35	.302	.219	.365	9.00	5.14
Lopez, Reynaldo	R-R	6-0	185	1-4-94	6	7	3.79	22	22	0	0	121	101	56	51	16	49	131	.220	.235	.207	9.74	3.64
Lowe, Mark	R-L	6-3	210	6-7-83	0	0	8.38	8	0	0	0	10	12	9	9	3	3	6	.300	.438	.208	5.59	2.79
Luebke, Cory	L-R	6-4	210	3-4-85	0	0	3.60	2	1	0	0	5	6	3	2	1	0	5	.300	.111	.455	9.00	0.00
Machi, Jean	R-R	6-0	255	2-1-82	5	0	3.60	12	2	0	0	30	23	12	12	7	10	28	.215	.333	.107	8.40	3.00
Minaya, Juan	R-R	6-4	210	9-18-90	1	0	1.42	13	0	0	0	19	17	3	3	0	5	15	.236	.263	.206	7.11	2.37
Parnell, Bobby	R-R	6-3	205	9-8-84	3	3	11.48	12	0	0	1	13	25	17	17	1	5	12	.391	.393	.389	8.10	3.38
Pelfrey, Mike	R-R	6-7	240	1-14-84	0	2	7.50	2	2	0	0	6	10	5	5	2	3	4	.357	.500	.250	6.00	4.50
Petricka, Jake	R-R	6-5	220	6-5-88	0	0	2.57	5	0	0	0	7	6	2	2	0	2	4	.240	.091	.357	5.14	2.57
Purke, Matt	L-L	6-4	215	7-17-90	4	5	3.84	48	0	0	0	66	61	29	28	4	28	80	.251	.192	.292	10.96	3.84
Rodon, Carlos	L-L	6-3	235	12-10-92	0	3	9.22	3	3	0	0	14	17	15	14	0	7	11	.288	.286	.289	7.24	4.61
Shields, James	R-R	6-3	215	12-20-81	0	3	3.21	3	3	0	0	14	13	7	5	0	3	14	.250	.267	.227	9.00	1.93
Soto, Giovanni	L-L	6-2	210	5-18-91	0	0	5.33	16	0	0	0	25	24	15	15	4	11	32	.247	.282	.224	11.37	3.91
Turner, Colton	L-L	6-3	215	1-17-91	1	1	6.85	15	1	0	0	22	30	18	17	5	6	19	.309	.390	.250	7.66	2.42
Valerio, Kelvis	R-R	6-1	190	9-26-91	1	0	3.00	1	0	0	0	3	5	1	1	0	0	4	.385	.250	.600	12.00	0.00
Volstad, Chris	R-R	6-8	235	9-23-86	3	10	5.57	27	18	2	1	118	161	82	73	12	23	71	.332	.346	.319	5.42	1.75
Walsh, Connor	L-R	6-2	180	10-18-92	1	1	3.86	12	0	0	0	14	16	6	6	0	6	13	.308	.296	.320	8.36	3.86
Ynoa, Michael	R-R	6-7	210	9-24-91	1	0	5.40	8	0	0	1	8	7	5	5	2	6	10	.241	.222	.273	10.80	6.48

Fielding

Catcher	PCT	G	PO	A	E	DP	PB
Blair	.996	36	270	14	1	1	5
Brantly	.993	35	261	25	2	2	2
O'Dowd	1.000	4	26	0	0	0	0
Pena	.994	59	436	34	3	4	4
Smith	.992	13	116	6	1	1	2

First Base	PCT	G	PO	A	E	DP
Asche	.958	10	66	3	3	8
Delmonico	.958	3	23	0	1	1
Gillaspie	1.000	22	184	8	0	23
Green	1.000	1	11	0	0	0
Hayes	.993	105	880	60	7	95
Ladendorf	.962	6	25	0	1	2
Peterson	1.000	1	3	0	0	0

Second Base	PCT	G	PO	A	E	DP
Bueno	.960	8	7	17	1	1
Green	.000	1	0	0	0	0
Ladendorf	.967	7	12	17	1	4
Moncada	.969	80	123	226	11	58
Peter	.983	41	53	121	3	39
Saladino	.857	1	3	3	1	1
Vinicio	.970	7	13	19	1	6

Third Base	PCT	G	PO	A	E	DP
Asche	1.000	8	5	6	0	1
Bueno	.944	19	9	25	2	5
Cabrera	1.000	3	2	4	0	0
Delmonico	.902	73	40	116	17	14
Green	.949	15	12	25	2	4
Ladendorf	.806	13	6	19	6	4
Peterson	.977	22	14	29	1	2

Shortstop	PCT	G	PO	A	E	DP
Alvarez	.964	33	50	109	6	28
Bueno	.970	24	41	55	3	13
Cabrera	.944	48	58	126	11	28
Ladendorf	.955	16	22	42	3	10
Saladino	1.000	4	4	7	0	1
Vinicio	.900	24	32	58	10	18

Outfield	PCT	G	PO	A	E	DP
Asche	.986	39	68	0	1	0
Bourgeois	.989	56	83	4	1	0
Bueno	1.000	4	9	0	0	0
Delmonico	1.000	16	28	0	0	0
Engel	.982	46	107	1	2	1
Garcia	1.000	1	2	0	0	0
Garcia	1.000	1	3	0	0	0
Garcia	1.000	28	37	3	0	1
Gelalich	1.000	4	3	1	0	0
Green	.889	9	8	0	1	0
Ladendorf	1.000	7	13	0	0	0
Liriano	.974	104	178	10	5	2
May	.979	109	231	6	5	1
Peter	1.000	2	1	0	0	0
Raburn	.889	8	8	0	1	0
Vinicio	1.000	1	1	0	0	0

BIRMINGHAM BARONS — *DOUBLE-A*

SOUTHERN LEAGUE

Batting	B-T	HT	WT	DOB	AVG	vLH	vRH	G	AB	R	H	2B	3B	HR	RBI	BB	HBP	SH	SF	SO	SB	CS	SLG	OBP
Alvarez, Eddy	B-R	5-9	180	1-30-90	.234	.274	.223	92	329	45	77	16	2	4	32	55	4	6	4	73	7	5	.331	.347
Austin, Brett	B-R	6-1	210	11-24-92	.215	.273	.198	53	149	18	32	7	1	4	19	16	0	2	2	49	0	0	.356	.287
Barnum, Keon	L-L	6-5	225	1-16-93	.210	.164	.223	96	333	37	70	14	1	16	36	36	1	0	4	125	0	1	.402	.286
Basto, Nick	R-R	6-2	210	4-1-94	.247	.231	.252	129	477	38	118	25	1	14	51	44	3	3	4	133	0	1	.392	.313
Bueno, Ronald	B-R	5-10	154	10-4-92	.204	.200	.205	17	54	2	11	2	0	1	3	11	0	2	0	7	1	2	.296	.339
Collins, Zack	L-R	6-3	220	2-6-95	.235	.200	.241	12	34	7	8	2	0	2	5	11	0	0	0	11	0	0	.471	.422
Gelalich, Jeff	L-R	6-0	210	3-16-91	.293	.273	.297	28	75	9	22	2	0	1	8	7	2	2	0	19	4	1	.360	.369
Gonzalez, Alfredo	R-R	6-1	225	7-13-92	.208	.177	.218	71	216	22	45	6	1	4	24	29	2	1	1	41	4	4	.301	.307
Hawkins, Courtney	R-R	6-3	245	11-12-93	.190	.200	.186	80	295	33	56	8	1	10	27	21	4	0	2	105	0	0	.325	.252
Jimenez, Eloy	R-R	6-4	205	11-27-96	.353	.391	.333	18	68	11	24	5	0	3	7	5	0	0	0	16	1	1	.559	.397
Jones, Hunter	R-R	6-2	185	8-17-91	.222	.175	.238	121	410	36	91	22	5	7	44	36	12	4	2	86	11	3	.351	.302
Mendick, Danny	R-R	5-10	189	9-28-93	.197	.180	.204	41	147	14	29	5	0	3	21	17	0	1	0	27	1	2	.293	.281
Michalczewski, Trey	B-R	6-3	210	2-27-95	.234	.210	.243	106	368	40	86	14	2	9	38	39	5	3	4	125	8	1	.356	.313
Nash, Telvin	R-R	6-1	248	2-20-91	.177	—	.177	10	34	2	6	1	0	1	2	2	0	0	0	18	0	0	.294	.222

Batting	B-T	HT	WT	DOB	AVG	vLH	vRH	G	AB	R	H	2B	3B	HR	RBI	BB	HBP	SH	SF	SO	SB	CS	SLG	OBP
O'Dowd, Chris	L-R	5-11	190	10-4-90	.177	.167	.179	13	34	1	6	1	0	0	3	4	1	2	1	11	0	0	.206	.275
Peter, Jake	L-R	6-1	185	4-5-93	.270	.209	.281	75	285	35	77	12	1	4	21	26	5	4	2	80	9	4	.361	.340
Polo, Tito	R-R	5-10	195	8-23-94	.278	.360	.234	21	72	10	20	4	2	0	7	5	2	0	0	15	7	3	.389	.342
Robbins, Mason	L-L	6-0	200	2-1-93	.265	.227	.273	125	480	49	127	11	1	3	36	20	0	3	2	49	4	4	.310	.293
Rondon, Cleuluis	B-R	6-0	155	4-13-94	.205	.227	.192	38	122	6	25	4	0	0	8	7	0	4	1	28	0	3	.238	.246
2-team total (13 Jacksonville)					.204	.227	.192	51	162	9	33	7	0	0	9	8	0	6	2	43	1	3	.247	.238
Thomas, Toby	R-R	5-11	185	12-9-93	.216	.000	.262	20	51	4	11	6	0	1	5	3	0	2	0	11	0	0	.392	.259
Vinicio, Jose	B-R	5-11	150	7-10-93	.221	.382	.157	50	195	21	43	9	2	3	13	11	0	3	1	50	4	2	.333	.261

Pitching	B-T	HT	WT	DOB	W	L	ERA	G	GS	CG	SV	IP	H	R	ER	HR	BB	SO	AVG	vLH	vRH	K/9	BB/9
Adams, Spencer	R-R	6-3	171	4-13-96	7	15	4.42	26	26	2	0	153	171	80	75	19	40	113	.281	.320	.246	6.66	2.36
Banks, Tanner	L-L	6-1	195	10-24-91	3	8	6.18	12	11	0	0	55	76	45	38	8	16	41	.323	.267	.343	6.67	2.60
Brennan, Brandon	R-R	6-4	220	7-26-91	2	2	5.36	28	0	0	9	42	47	28	25	1	20	39	.283	.250	.309	8.36	4.29
Bummer, Aaron	L-L	6-3	200	9-21-93	1	3	3.00	17	1	0	3	33	29	11	11	2	16	34	.246	.182	.284	9.27	4.36
Chalas, Miguel	R-R	5-11	155	6-27-92	1	0	9.00	7	0	0	1	8	17	9	8	3	1	4	.415	.435	.389	4.50	1.13
Charleston, Jack	L-R	6-5	165	9-14-92	1	1	2.84	11	0	0	3	19	16	7	6	0	8	18	.239	.389	.184	8.53	3.79
Cooper, Matt	R-R	6-0	190	9-30-91	1	7	4.75	14	14	1	0	72	79	48	38	1	26	77	.276	.300	.256	9.63	3.25
Dunning, Jake	R-R	6-4	190	8-12-88	0	1	5.40	6	1	0	1	10	11	7	6	2	6	11	.282	.300	.263	9.90	5.40
Easterling, Brannon	R-R	6-4	240	8-1-90	1	1	3.86	10	4	0	0	30	40	14	13	2	10	12	.313	.404	.259	3.56	2.97
Fry, Jace	L-L	6-1	190	7-9-93	2	1	2.78	33	0	0	3	45	36	14	14	1	24	52	.217	.197	.229	10.32	4.76
Gonzalez, Miguel	R-R	6-1	170	5-27-84	0	0	10.38	1	1	0	0	4	7	5	5	0	0	5	.350	.556	.182	10.38	0.00
Guerrero, Jordan	L-L	6-3	195	5-31-94	7	12	4.18	25	25	2	0	146	150	71	68	8	43	136	.270	.248	.279	8.36	2.64
Hamilton, Ian	R-R	6-0	200	6-16-95	1	3	5.21	14	0	0	1	19	26	14	11	0	8	22	.317	.419	.255	10.42	3.79
Hansen, Alec	R-R	6-7	235	10-10-94	0	0	4.35	2	2	0	0	10	15	5	5	0	3	17	.333	.250	.351	14.81	2.61
Hasler, Drew	R-R	6-6	245	8-14-93	0	0	3.72	5	0	0	0	10	11	7	4	0	4	6	.282	.250	.304	5.59	3.72
Johansen, Jake	R-R	6-6	235	1-23-91	2	2	3.42	17	0	0	2	26	22	10	10	2	12	19	.234	.265	.217	6.49	4.10
Kopech, Michael	R-R	6-3	205	4-30-96	8	7	2.87	22	22	0	0	119	77	45	38	6	60	155	.184	.186	.182	11.69	4.53
Kubat, Kyle	L-L	6-1	195	12-4-92	2	0	1.35	7	1	0	2	20	10	5	3	2	2	17	.141	.091	.163	7.65	0.90
Lamb, Will	L-L	6-6	180	9-9-90	0	0	1.98	9	0	0	0	14	10	3	3	1	8	16	.213	.191	.231	10.54	5.27
Leyer, Robinson	R-R	6-2	175	3-13-93	2	4	3.55	38	0	0	4	58	49	29	23	2	33	62	.224	.307	.168	9.57	5.09
Lowry, Thaddius	R-R	6-4	215	10-4-94	3	4	6.26	28	9	0	1	82	100	64	57	11	32	61	.301	.292	.307	6.70	3.51
Muhammad, El'Hajj	R-R	6-2	219	7-7-91	0	0	8.44	7	0	0	2	11	19	13	10	1	6	5	.380	.391	.370	4.22	5.06
Seitzer, Cameron	L-R	6-5	220	1-11-90	0	0	0.00	1	0	0	0	1	1	0	0	0	0	1	.250	—	.250	9.00	0.00
Snodgress, Scott	L-L	6-6	235	9-20-89	0	2	4.86	23	4	0	1	37	35	22	20	2	25	46	.250	.160	.300	11.19	6.08
Stephens, Jordan	R-R	6-1	190	9-12-92	3	7	3.14	16	16	0	0	92	84	38	32	4	35	83	.249	.299	.202	8.15	3.44
Turner, Colton	L-L	6-3	215	1-17-91	4	2	2.45	20	1	0	1	33	27	10	9	1	10	37	.223	.286	.169	10.09	2.73
Walsh, Connor	L-R	6-2	180	10-18-92	2	2	3.19	27	0	0	3	42	24	18	15	1	27	50	.166	.186	.151	10.63	5.74

Fielding

Catcher	PCT	G	PO	A	E	DP	PB
Austin	.988	51	360	38	5	3	4
Collins	.963	11	74	3	3	0	0
Gonzalez	.993	71	604	62	5	4	12
O'Dowd	1.000	13	88	6	0	2	0

First Base	PCT	G	PO	A	E	DP
Austin	.000	1	0	0	0	0
Barnum	.983	69	552	33	10	51
Basto	.989	50	417	19	5	34
Nash	1.000	2	9	0	0	3
Seitzer	.994	19	137	16	1	13
Thomas	1.000	2	12	0	0	0

Second Base	PCT	G	PO	A	E	DP
Alvarez	.979	35	65	73	3	20
Bueno	1.000	3	3	9	0	2
Mendick	.935	7	24	19	3	7
Michalczewski	.950	5	7	12	1	3
Peter	.991	56	81	142	2	34
Thomas	1.000	5	10	10	0	1
Vinicio	.964	30	54	79	5	18

Third Base	PCT	G	PO	A	E	DP
Basto	.962	9	2	23	1	1
Bueno	1.000	14	14	26	0	5
Michalczewski	.944	96	62	141	12	15
Peter	1.000	8	2	21	0	3
Seitzer	.968	11	5	25	1	1
Thomas	1.000	1	0	2	0	0
Vinicio	1.000	1	0	1	0	0

Shortstop	PCT	G	PO	A	E	DP
Alvarez	.965	58	76	169	9	26
Mendick	.976	34	55	107	4	17
Rondon	.934	38	38	89	9	15
Vinicio	.967	12	22	36	2	8

Outfield	PCT	G	PO	A	E	DP
Basto	.958	34	44	2	2	0
Gelalich	.945	23	52	0	3	0
Hawkins	.926	61	84	4	7	0
Jimenez	1.000	15	24	1	0	1
Jones	.992	118	249	10	2	2
Peter	1.000	12	22	2	0	0
Polo	1.000	20	50	2	0	0
Robbins	.972	110	171	4	5	0
Seitzer	1.000	14	29	0	0	0
Thomas	1.000	11	12	1	0	0
Vinicio	.929	6	12	1	1	0

WINSTON-SALEM DASH — *HIGH CLASS A*

CAROLINA LEAGUE

Batting	B-T	HT	WT	DOB	AVG	vLH	vRH	G	AB	R	H	2B	3B	HR	RBI	BB	HBP	SH	SF	SO	SB	CS	SLG	OBP
Barnum, Keon	L-L	6-5	225	1-16-93	.262	.167	.286	19	61	7	16	1	0	2	9	13	0	0	1	26	0	0	.377	.387
Basabe, Luis Alexander	B-R	6-0	160	8-26-96	.221	.244	.210	107	375	52	83	12	5	5	36	49	6	4	1	104	17	6	.320	.320
Booker, Joel	R-R	6-1	190	11-1-93	.233	.250	.227	52	189	23	44	6	0	2	15	10	4	4	1	41	9	3	.296	.284
Bueno, Ronald	B-R	5-10	154	10-4-92	.303	.324	.292	28	99	11	30	6	2	1	11	11	1	1	1	17	1	2	.434	.375
Call, Alex	R-R	6-0	188	9-27-94	.244	.294	.208	10	41	2	10	3	1	0	5	3	1	0	0	11	2	1	.366	.311
Collins, Zack	L-R	6-3	220	2-6-95	.223	.167	.249	101	341	63	76	18	3	17	48	76	2	4	3	118	0	2	.443	.365
Conlan, Brady	R-R	6-1	207	8-21-93	.206	.219	.199	116	413	41	85	16	1	5	44	20	6	2	2	106	0	3	.286	.252
Cruz, Johan	R-R	6-2	188	10-8-95	.218	.182	.237	75	257	26	56	14	1	6	21	13	1	2	2	65	8	2	.350	.256
Dexter, Sam	R-R	5-11	185	3-7-94	.269	.273	.267	25	67	5	18	1	0	2	7	6	2	0	1	17	1	1	.373	.342
Dulin, Brandon	L-R	6-3	225	12-29-92	.173	.136	.180	43	139	18	24	6	2	6	13	18	4	1	0	48	0	1	.374	.286
Fincher, Jake	R-R	6-1	185	1-26-93	.215	.262	.190	44	121	15	26	8	0	2	9	6	2	2	0	29	3	5	.331	.264
Fisher, Jameson	L-R	6-2	200	12-18-93	.221	.221	.222	64	235	33	52	16	1	7	32	27	7	2	0	55	3	4	.387	.320
Flete, Bryant	L-R	5-10	146	1-31-93	.228	.212	.231	45	167	18	38	10	2	1	12	14	1	0	1	28	1	2	.329	.290
2-team total (70 Myrtle Beach)					.276	.254	.322	115	442	63	122	25	2	7	49	32	5	1	3	81	5	5	.389	.330

Forbes, Ti'Quan	R-R	6-3	180	8-26-96	.154	.167	.143	4	13	3	2	1	0	0	0	1	0	0	0	0	0	1	.231	.214
2-team total (51 Down East)					.222	.291	.200	55	198	23	44	7	0	3	11	14	1	1	1	54	2	5	.303	.276
Franco, J.J.	R-R	5-9	180	2-2-92	.233	.273	.211	12	30	1	7	3	0	0	2	7	0	0	0	9	1	1	.333	.378
Gelalich, Jeff	L-R	6-0	210	3-16-91	.111	.000	.182	10	36	2	4	0	0	0	2	4	0	0	0	17	0	0	.111	.200
Gonzalez, Daniel	R-R	6-1	190	12-6-95	.236	.273	.215	35	123	12	29	6	0	1	10	2	1	0	0	20	2	1	.309	.254
Hawkins, Courtney	R-R	6-3	245	11-12-93	.222	.000	.364	5	18	3	4	0	0	2	5	0	0	0	0	4	0	0	.556	.222
Jimenez, Eloy	R-R	6-4	205	11-27-96	.346	.462	.310	29	110	20	38	11	1	8	26	12	0	0	0	21	0	2	.682	.410
2-team total (42 Myrtle Beach)					.302	.264	.275	71	265	43	80	17	3	16	58	30	1	0	0	56	0	2	.570	.375
Lassiter, Landon	R-R	6-1	195	6-14-93	.262	.321	.216	39	130	17	34	11	1	2	19	10	4	2	2	37	3	0	.408	.329
Mendick, Danny	R-R	5-10	189	9-28-93	.289	.301	.283	84	263	45	76	18	4	7	30	31	6	2	3	40	11	4	.468	.373
Michalczewski, Trey	B-R	6-3	210	2-27-95	.294	.375	.269	19	68	12	20	4	1	4	12	6	0	0	2	19	1	0	.559	.342
Nash, Telvin	R-R	6-1	248	2-20-91	.214	.243	.200	32	112	16	24	8	0	5	13	19	3	0	1	44	0	0	.420	.341
Rose, Matt	R-R	6-4	195	8-2-94	.271	.355	.242	36	122	21	33	13	0	4	23	12	1	2	2	40	2	0	.475	.336
2-team total (65 Myrtle Beach)					.242	.209	.235	101	355	51	86	28	1	18	61	27	4	3	4	103	2	0	.479	.300
Schnurbusch, Aaron	L-L	6-5	235	1-21-94	.168	.218	.132	35	131	13	22	2	4	2	13	5	0	1	0	53	2	0	.290	.199
Silverio, Louis	R-R	6-3	215	12-15-93	.268	.298	.254	89	321	30	86	22	2	4	46	11	3	3	2	73	0	5	.386	.297
Sullivan, Tyler	L-L	5-9	180	11-21-92	.125	—	.125	2	8	1	1	0	0	0	2	0	0	0	0	1	1	0	.125	.125
Thomas, Toby	R-R	5-11	185	12-9-93	.261	.342	.209	68	211	28	55	18	2	0	19	25	0	4	3	47	5	1	.365	.335
Yrizarri, Yeyson	R-R	6-0	175	2-2-97	.295	.394	.253	31	112	12	33	1	0	1	11	2	0	2	1	21	1	4	.330	.304
2-team total (8 Down East)					.277	.167	.217	39	141	17	39	3	0	3	18	3	2	2	3	29	1	4	.362	.295
Zavala, Seby	R-R	5-11	205	8-28-93	.302	.424	.252	55	202	31	61	13	0	8	38	24	0	1	0	52	1	0	.485	.376

Pitching	**B-T**	**HT**	**WT**	**DOB**	**W**	**L**	**ERA**	**G**	**GS**	**CG**	**SV**	**IP**	**H**	**R**	**ER**	**HR**	**BB**	**SO**	**AVG**	**vLH**	**vRH**	**K/9**	**BB/9**
Banks, Tanner	L-L	6-1	195	10-24-91	7	3	3.05	14	14	1	0	86	75	32	29	2	21	72	.233	.243	.230	7.56	2.21
Beatty, Max	R-R	6-2	225	3-27-91	2	4	4.66	12	7	0	0	46	50	26	24	4	11	34	.272	.265	.277	6.60	2.14
Bummer, Aaron	L-L	6-3	200	9-21-93	0	2	4.91	8	0	0	2	11	10	6	6	2	3	15	.227	.267	.207	12.27	2.45
Burr, Ryan	R-R	6-4	225	5-28-94	0	0	0.00	6	0	0	1	8	5	1	0	0	5	13	.179	.182	.177	14.04	5.40
Charleston, Jack	L-R	6-5	165	9-14-92	2	1	2.18	23	0	0	9	33	23	11	8	1	15	18	.198	.191	.203	4.91	4.09
Clarkin, Ian	L-L	6-2	215	2-14-95	0	0	2.45	3	3	0	0	11	7	4	3	1	8	5	.194	.143	.207	4.09	6.55
Diaz, Victor	R-R	6-3	190	5-24-94	0	0	23.63	8	0	0	1	5	13	14	14	0	7	4	.464	.455	.471	6.75	11.81
Dunning, Dane	R-R	6-4	200	12-20-94	6	8	3.51	22	22	2	0	118	114	62	46	15	36	135	.250	.268	.237	10.30	2.75
Easterling, Brannon	R-R	6-4	240	8-1-90	6	5	4.61	18	18	0	0	96	105	51	49	11	33	79	.282	.296	.274	7.43	3.10
Elliott, Jake	R-R	6-7	230	3-22-95	0	0	18.00	1	0	0	0	1	2	2	2	0	1	0	.400	.000	.667	0.00	9.00
Flores, Bernardo	L-L	6-3	170	8-23-95	2	3	4.24	9	9	0	0	40	43	20	19	5	19	33	.267	.211	.285	7.36	4.24
Foster, Matt	R-R	6-0	195	1-27-95	0	2	0.68	10	0	0	1	13	8	3	1	0	3	14	.174	.167	.179	9.45	2.03
Hamilton, Ian	R-R	6-0	200	6-16-95	3	3	1.71	30	0	0	6	53	33	12	10	1	8	52	.179	.200	.167	8.89	1.37
Hansen, Alec	R-R	6-7	235	10-10-94	4	5	2.93	11	11	1	0	58	42	24	19	5	25	82	.203	.205	.202	12.65	3.86
Hasler, Drew	R-R	6-6	245	8-14-93	2	1	3.28	30	0	0	1	58	61	28	21	1	8	28	.271	.375	.204	4.37	1.25
Hobbs, Lane	R-R	6-5	235	5-22-95	1	0	9.00	1	0	0	0	1	1	1	1	0	1	1	.250	.500	.000	9.00	9.00
Johansen, Jake	R-R	6-6	235	1-23-91	1	1	6.30	7	0	0	0	10	13	8	7	1	3	10	.325	.444	.290	9.00	2.70
Kubat, Kyle	L-L	6-1	195	12-4-92	1	3	3.77	7	1	0	0	14	14	8	6	0	4	12	.259	.267	.256	7.53	2.51
Lambert, Jimmy	R-R	6-2	170	11-18-94	5	4	5.45	14	14	0	0	76	86	51	46	10	29	59	.290	.309	.272	6.99	3.43
Lechich, Louie	L-L	6-4	200	11-19-91	2	6	2.45	43	0	0	1	59	50	18	16	1	25	48	.238	.232	.241	7.36	3.84
Martinez, Luis	R-R	6-6	190	1-29-95	0	2	9.00	5	4	0	0	16	25	20	16	1	10	8	.362	.350	.367	4.50	5.63
McRee, Aron	R-R	6-0	180	10-29-93	1	6	5.00	10	9	0	0	45	45	30	25	4	17	36	.260	.265	.256	7.20	3.40
Morrison, Mike	R-R	6-2	195	9-22-93	2	3	5.03	19	0	0	2	34	36	21	19	2	18	33	.277	.259	.290	8.74	4.76
Peralta, Yelmison	R-R	6-2	210	3-3-95	0	2	4.97	19	0	0	0	29	17	20	16	2	25	25	.174	.194	.161	7.76	7.76
Puckett, A.J.	R-R	6-4	200	5-27-95	1	0	4.28	5	5	0	0	27	35	14	13	2	5	21	.327	.381	.292	6.91	1.65
2-team total (20 Wilmington)					10	7	3.98	25	25	0	0	136	142	67	60	9	51	119	.272	.276	.238	7.89	3.38
Riga, Ryan	R-L	6-0	190	10-22-92	1	4	5.17	29	1	0	3	38	44	24	22	2	14	38	.291	.260	.307	8.92	3.29
Rodon, Carlos	L-L	6-3	235	12-10-92	0	1	13.50	1	1	0	0	3	4	5	5	1	2	6	.286	.167	.375	16.20	5.40
Solorzano, Yosmer	R-R	6-2	181	2-11-97	0	1	3.86	1	1	0	0	5	4	2	2	1	4	2	.235	.143	.300	3.86	7.71
Thompson, Zach	R-R	6-7	230	10-23-93	2	7	5.50	33	14	0	0	93	102	74	57	8	50	73	.281	.278	.283	7.04	4.82
Valerio, Kelvis	R-R	6-1	190	9-26-91	4	5	5.12	21	6	0	0	63	61	43	36	7	22	41	.254	.278	.235	5.83	3.13
VanVossen, Mick	R-R	6-3	190	10-30-92	1	1	8.25	8	0	0	0	12	18	11	11	3	3	8	.340	.280	.393	6.00	2.25
Wheeler, Andre	L-L	6-1	170	9-27-91	0	1	6.91	19	0	0	0	29	40	23	22	4	15	25	.348	.372	.333	7.85	4.71

Fielding

Catcher	**PCT**	**G**	**PO**	**A**	**E**	**DP**	**PB**
Collins	.987	76	526	63	8	3	16
Gonzalez	.992	32	222	29	2	3	5
Zavala	.984	34	271	29	5	2	4

First Base	**PCT**	**G**	**PO**	**A**	**E**	**DP**
Barnum	.994	17	155	5	1	12
Conlan	1.000	20	147	9	0	11
Dulin	.990	35	277	14	3	26
Fisher	1.000	1	4	0	0	0
Nash	.992	26	240	11	2	16
Rose	1.000	17	138	10	0	19
Silverio	1.000	12	77	5	0	4
Thomas	.978	20	171	7	4	14

Second Base	**PCT**	**G**	**PO**	**A**	**E**	**DP**
Bueno	.977	10	18	24	1	4
Cruz	.958	7	11	12	1	3
Dexter	.875	5	3	11	2	2
Flete	.978	45	78	104	4	30
Franco	.973	9	14	22	1	8
Mendick	.991	45	81	133	2	23
Thomas	.925	30	45	54	8	18
Yrizarri	1.000	1	0	1	0	0

Third Base	**PCT**	**G**	**PO**	**A**	**E**	**DP**
Bueno	.952	9	3	17	1	1
Conlan	.928	83	48	172	17	12
Dexter	1.000	1	0	5	0	0
Mendick	.977	17	7	35	1	2
Michalczewski	.930	15	10	30	3	0
Rose	.969	15	10	21	1	2
Thomas	.786	5	4	7	3	0

Shortstop	**PCT**	**G**	**PO**	**A**	**E**	**DP**
Bueno	1.000	2	2	4	0	2
Cruz	.933	68	80	198	20	37
Dexter	.958	17	30	38	3	14
Forbes	1.000	4	6	11	0	1
Mendick	.967	25	23	65	3	10
Yrizarri	.981	30	34	70	2	15

Outfield	**PCT**	**G**	**PO**	**A**	**E**	**DP**
Basabe	.992	104	243	10	2	2
Booker	.965	49	107	4	4	1
Bueno	1.000	4	15	0	0	0
Call	.947	9	17	1	1	0
Fincher	1.000	35	44	2	0	0
Fisher	.971	63	101	1	3	0
Franco	1.000	1	2	0	0	0
Gelalich	1.000	9	15	1	0	0

Hawkins	1.000	3	5	0	0	0	Lassiter	1.000	31	57	1	0	0	Silverio	.942	60	77	4	5	1
Jimenez	.974	21	38	0	1	0	Schnurbusch	.984	34	59	3	1	1	Thomas	1.000	4	9	0	0	0

KANNAPOLIS INTIMIDATORS — *LOW CLASS A*

SOUTH ATLANTIC LEAGUE

Batting	B-T	HT	WT	DOB	AVG	vLH	vRH	G	AB	R	H	2B	3B	HR	RBI	BB	HBP	SH	SF	SO	SB	CS	SLG	OBP
Adolfo, Micker	R-R	6-3	200	9-11-96	.264	.244	.273	112	424	60	112	28	2	16	68	31	13	2	3	149	2	0	.453	.331
Booker, Joel	R-R	6-1	190	11-1-93	.301	.306	.299	71	286	53	86	11	2	3	29	17	10	6	2	66	14	5	.385	.359
Burger, Jake	R-R	6-2	210	4-10-96	.271	.292	.263	47	181	21	49	9	2	4	27	13	5	0	1	28	0	1	.409	.335
Cabrera, Everth	R-B	5-10	190	11-17-86	.100	.000	.111	3	10	1	1	0	0	0	0	1	0	0	0	3	0	0	.100	.182
Call, Alex	R-R	6-0	188	9-27-94	.248	.303	.232	38	145	24	36	9	1	3	22	16	3	3	1	33	2	2	.386	.333
Dedelow, Craig	L-R	6-4	195	11-15-94	.105	.500	.000	5	19	2	2	0	0	1	1	2	0	0	0	4	0	1	.263	.191
Dexter, Sam	R-R	5-11	185	3-7-94	.276	.385	.188	10	29	2	8	1	1	0	4	5	1	0	0	4	0	0	.379	.400
Dulin, Brandon	L-R	6-3	225	12-29-92	.245	.232	.251	71	257	39	63	8	0	12	42	25	8	5	0	64	0	1	.416	.331
Dutto, Max	L-R	6-0	205	11-2-93	.160	.083	.175	26	75	13	12	5	0	2	6	16	1	0	0	45	0	0	.307	.315
Fisher, Jameson	L-R	6-2	200	12-18-93	.269	.323	.248	60	223	35	60	14	5	3	36	31	5	2	4	59	2	2	.417	.365
Franco, J.J.	R-R	5-9	180	2-2-92	.306	.000	.393	12	36	2	11	1	0	0	6	5	0	1	0	6	0	1	.333	.390
2-team total (36 Columbia)					.283	.333	.255	48	173	19	49	7	0	0	16	28	0	3	0	33	3	2	.324	.383
Gonzalez, Daniel	R-R	6-1	190	12-6-95	.254	.286	.237	16	59	4	15	2	0	0	5	3	0	0	0	11	0	0	.288	.290
Gonzalez, Luis	L-L	6-1	185	9-10-95	.245	.254	.241	63	233	26	57	13	4	2	12	38	3	2	1	50	2	3	.361	.356
Hawkins, Courtney	R-R	6-3	245	11-12-93	.357	.231	.467	6	28	2	10	4	0	0	1	2	0	2	0	11	0	1	.500	.400
Massey, Grant	R-R	5-11	190	7-10-92	.246	.320	.212	98	330	34	81	16	2	0	36	12	5	6	4	71	5	4	.306	.279
Nolan, Nate	R-R	6-1	210	10-11-94	.053	.000	.087	14	38	2	2	0	0	0	1	8	0	0	0	22	0	0	.053	.217
Remillard, Zach	R-R	6-1	200	2-21-94	.246	.288	.228	133	484	54	119	27	2	7	50	19	7	13	6	124	4	3	.353	.281
Rodriguez, Antonio	R-R	6-4	230	5-7-95	.199	.146	.219	48	176	18	35	11	3	3	21	9	0	0	0	49	1	1	.347	.238
Rodriguez, Wilfredo	R-R	5-10	200	1-25-94	.200	.111	.273	6	20	1	4	1	0	0	3	3	0	0	1	3	0	0	.250	.292
Roman, Mitch	R-R	6-0	161	3-22-95	.254	.289	.241	132	516	53	131	14	2	3	45	31	7	9	1	120	8	5	.306	.305
Rutherford, Blake	L-R	6-3	195	5-2-97	.213	.364	.180	30	122	11	26	5	0	0	5	13	0	1	0	21	1	0	.254	.289
2-team total (71 Charleston)					.260	.364	.180	101	396	52	103	25	2	2	35	38	2	1	3	76	10	4	.349	.326
Schnurbusch, Aaron	L-L	6-5	235	1-21-94	.172	.159	.178	43	145	18	25	4	1	3	9	21	2	1	0	66	0	4	.276	.286
Schroeder, Casey	B-R	6-2	210	7-12-93	.202	.200	.202	42	134	17	27	7	3	4	14	11	4	2	0	47	0	0	.388	.282
Sheets, Gavin	L-L	6-4	230	4-23-96	.266	.238	.273	52	192	16	51	10	0	3	25	20	4	1	1	34	0	0	.365	.346
Skoug, Evan	L-R	5-11	200	10-21-95	.154	.000	.179	21	65	6	10	0	2	2	7	8	2	0	1	29	0	0	.308	.263
Sullivan, Tyler	L-L	5-9	180	11-21-92	.237	.149	.276	45	152	15	36	5	0	0	13	13	2	3	2	33	5	1	.270	.302
Zavala, Seby	R-R	5-11	205	8-28-93	.260	.196	.284	52	185	32	48	8	0	13	34	13	6	2	1	52	0	0	.514	.327

Pitching	B-T	HT	WT	DOB	W	L	ERA	G	GS	CG	SV	IP	H	R	ER	HR	BB	SO	AVG	vLH	vRH	K/9	BB/9
Boelter, Ryan	L-L	6-2	240	12-28-93	0	0	7.11	3	0	0	0	6	8	5	5	1	5	6	.320	.556	.188	8.53	7.11
Cease, Dylan	R-R	6-2	190	12-28-95	0	8	3.89	9	9	0	0	42	35	22	18	1	18	52	.229	.228	.230	11.23	3.89
Comito, Chris	R-R	6-6	240	6-25-96	0	0	5.71	4	4	0	0	17	28	17	11	1	5	6	.378	.393	.370	3.12	2.60
Davis, Andre	L-L	6-6	230	9-29-93	1	1	2.84	4	2	0	0	13	10	4	4	0	7	12	.217	.235	.207	8.53	4.97
2-team total (18 Lexington)					6	5	4.58	22	20	1	0	98	106	56	50	9	30	99	.273	.216	.302	9.06	2.75
Diaz, Victor	R-R	6-3	190	5-24-94	0	1	6.75	6	0	0	1	7	6	5	5	0	5	10	.240	.273	.214	13.50	6.75
Dopico, Danny	R-R	6-2	190	12-18-93	5	4	3.25	39	1	0	4	69	36	29	25	3	30	96	.148	.157	.141	12.46	3.89
Dunning, Dane	R-R	6-4	200	12-20-94	2	0	0.35	4	4	0	0	26	13	2	1	0	2	33	.143	.125	.157	11.42	0.69
Elliott, Jake	R-R	6-7	230	3-22-95	1	3	2.29	28	0	0	1	63	48	16	16	2	10	59	.215	.204	.223	8.43	1.43
Escorcia, Kevin	L-L	6-1	170	1-5-95	4	4	4.14	42	0	0	0	50	43	26	23	1	26	69	.236	.225	.245	12.42	4.68
Flores, Bernardo	L-L	6-3	170	8-23-95	8	4	3.00	14	14	0	0	78	73	29	26	5	13	70	.251	.227	.259	8.08	1.50
Foster, Matt	R-R	6-0	195	1-27-95	0	0	1.88	12	0	0	6	14	8	3	3	1	2	19	.163	.105	.200	11.93	1.26
Hansen, Alec	R-R	6-7	235	10-10-94	7	3	2.48	13	13	0	0	73	57	27	20	3	23	92	.207	.181	.228	11.39	2.85
Hickman, Blake	R-R	6-5	225	10-29-93	4	6	3.76	17	17	0	0	89	80	42	37	4	27	56	.245	.200	.280	5.68	2.74
Hobbs, Lane	R-R	6-5	235	5-22-95	4	1	4.52	37	4	0	1	76	85	39	38	5	16	61	.291	.360	.247	7.26	1.90
Johnson, Tyler	R-R	6-2	180	8-21-95	0	0	5.74	14	0	0	2	16	19	12	10	0	12	21	.302	.346	.270	12.06	6.89
Katz, Alex	L-L	5-11	195	10-12-94	0	1	4.40	10	0	0	0	14	15	10	7	1	8	17	.263	.267	.262	10.67	5.02
Kubat, Kyle	L-L	6-1	195	12-4-92	3	2	1.12	21	1	0	2	40	26	8	5	0	6	48	.177	.104	.212	10.71	1.34
Lambert, Jimmy	R-R	6-2	170	11-18-94	7	2	2.19	12	12	1	0	74	77	29	18	1	11	43	.274	.254	.289	5.23	1.34
Ledo, Luis	R-R	6-4	208	5-28-95	0	0	11.25	5	0	0	0	4	6	5	5	2	5	5	.316	.333	.300	11.25	11.25
Martinez, Luis	R-R	6-6	190	1-29-95	8	2	3.19	14	14	0	0	79	69	33	28	2	24	85	.232	.200	.261	9.68	2.73
McClure, Kade	R-R	6-7	230	2-12-96	0	0	0.00	5	0	0	1	6	2	0	0	0	1	8	.095	.250	.000	12.00	1.50
Morrison, Mike	R-R	6-2	195	9-22-93	1	0	0.53	23	0	0	10	34	9	2	2	1	6	42	.084	.132	.058	11.23	1.60
Olson, J.B.	R-R	6-2	195	2-12-95	1	1	3.20	13	0	0	1	20	19	8	7	2	4	18	.247	.148	.300	8.24	1.83
Peralta, Yelmison	R-R	6-2	210	3-3-95	3	4	5.06	13	12	0	0	53	47	33	30	3	30	41	.241	.260	.221	6.92	5.06
Solorzano, Yosmer	R-R	6-2	181	2-11-97	3	11	6.28	24	24	2	0	116	143	98	81	14	48	91	.305	.276	.325	7.06	3.72
Valerio, Kelvis	R-R	6-1	190	9-26-91	2	1	2.45	8	6	1	0	37	31	11	10	1	3	22	.230	.212	.246	5.40	0.74
VanVossen, Mick	R-R	6-3	190	10-30-92	1	1	1.52	17	0	0	1	24	18	5	4	1	5	30	.207	.237	.184	11.41	1.90
2-team total (12 Hagerstown)					4	1	2.72	29	0	0	1	50	40	18	15	3	17	58	.219	.182	.269	10.51	3.08
Wright, Ben	R-R	6-0	185	6-21-94	2	7	3.19	42	0	0	1	59	54	26	21	1	16	55	.242	.349	.179	8.34	2.43

Fielding

Catcher	PCT	G	PO	A	E	DP	PB
Gonzalez	.985	16	123	12	2	0	3
Nolan	.982	14	89	18	2	2	2
Rodriguez	.982	6	48	7	1	0	1
Schroeder	.989	40	342	11	4	2	5
Skoug	1.000	20	171	19	0	3	2
Zavala	.995	43	373	50	2	2	9

First Base	PCT	G	PO	A	E	DP
Dulin	.987	71	643	22	9	44
Massey	1.000	19	144	4	0	14
Schroeder	1.000	1	5	1	0	0
Sheets	.993	50	398	26	3	31

Second Base	PCT	G	PO	A	E	DP
Dexter	.941	7	15	17	2	5
Dutto	1.000	6	8	22	0	3
Franco	1.000	6	8	16	0	5
Massey	.981	11	20	31	1	5
Remillard	.994	38	64	109	1	21
Roman	.977	72	112	186	7	31

Third Base	PCT	G	PO	A	E	DP
Burger	.946	42	23	64	5	7
Massey	.750	6	1	5	2	1
Remillard	.943	90	71	178	15	10

Shortstop	PCT	G	PO	A	E	DP
Cabrera	1.000	2	4	4	0	0
Dexter	1.000	1	4	1	0	1
Dutto	.974	19	24	50	2	6
Massey	.956	63	81	177	12	28
Roman	.951	58	82	132	11	37

Outfield	PCT	G	PO	A	E	DP
Adolfo	.968	102	142	7	5	0
Booker	.971	69	161	4	5	1
Call	.955	33	62	2	3	0
Dedelow	1.000	4	9	0	0	0
Fisher	.989	52	86	4	1	1
Gonzalez	.953	50	102	0	5	0
Hawkins	1.000	2	3	0	0	0
Rodriguez	1.000	10	15	0	0	0
Roman	.857	4	5	1	1	0
Rutherford	1.000	23	41	2	0	0
Schnurbusch	.969	34	54	8	2	3
Sullivan	.958	30	43	3	2	0

GREAT FALLS VOYAGERS — *ROOKIE*

PIONEER LEAGUE

Batting	B-T	HT	WT	DOB	AVG	vLH	vRH	G	AB	R	H	2B	3B	HR	RBI	BB	HBP	SH	SF	SO	SB	CS	SLG	OBP
Blackman, Tate	R-R	6-0	195	9-7-94	.245	.188	.260	49	163	27	40	10	1	5	23	24	6	2	2	39	1	0	.411	.359
Brown, Nolan	L-L	5-11	175	1-13-94	.330	.318	.331	46	173	28	57	6	1	1	18	12	1	9	0	30	7	3	.393	.376
Cooper, Jacob	R-R	5-10	221	6-1-96	.291	.304	.288	30	103	11	30	4	2	3	13	7	5	2	0	36	2	0	.456	.365
Cronin, David	L-R	5-9	175	12-19-94	.303	.455	.282	26	89	25	27	2	0	0	11	5	2	2	0	7	5	1	.326	.354
Curbelo, Luis	R-R	6-3	185	11-10-97	.429	—	.429	3	14	4	6	1	0	1	2	1	2	0	0	4	0	0	.714	.529
Dedelow, Craig	L-R	6-4	195	11-15-94	.321	.341	.317	60	249	40	80	21	3	12	54	12	3	4	5	39	5	3	.574	.353
Dexter, Sam	R-R	5-11	185	3-7-94	.200	—	.200	1	5	1	1	0	0	0	1	0	0	0	0	1	0	0	.200	.200
Duarte, Mikey	R-R	5-11	195	4-8-94	.143	—	.143	2	7	1	1	0	0	0	1	1	0	0	0	1	0	0	.143	.250
Dutto, Max	L-R	6-0	205	11-2-93	.170	.129	.179	55	171	30	29	6	2	4	21	51	1	1	3	71	2	4	.298	.358
Frost, Tyler	L-R	5-10	183	11-21-95	.261	.357	.250	32	142	24	37	7	5	4	26	13	3	2	0	33	2	0	.465	.335
Gonzalez, Luis	L-L	6-1	185	9-10-95	.118	—	.118	4	17	3	2	1	0	0	3	4	0	1	0	3	0	0	.177	.286
Hadley, Tracy	R-R	6-1	190	6-29-95	.268	.136	.300	29	112	18	30	9	0	2	18	12	4	0	0	30	0	1	.402	.359
Mercedes, Felix	R-R	6-2	185	2-13-97	.268	.333	.263	13	41	9	11	3	0	1	6	7	5	0	0	12	0	0	.415	.434
Mota, Ricky	R-R	5-11	170	2-21-98	.273	.250	.276	8	33	3	9	0	0	0	2	1	0	0	0	11	1	0	.273	.294
Muno, JJ	L-R	5-11	190	12-21-93	.333	.667	.267	11	36	8	12	6	0	0	4	4	3	0	1	3	2	0	.500	.432
Nolan, Nate	R-R	6-1	210	10-11-94	.253	.185	.267	42	162	27	41	13	1	7	27	12	3	0	2	66	1	1	.475	.313
Nunez, Amado	R-R	6-2	178	10-10-97	.183	.143	.190	34	142	12	26	6	0	1	17	12	0	0	0	31	1	1	.247	.247
Otano, Hanleth	R-R	6-3	195	7-16-96	.200	.200	.200	12	45	2	9	2	0	1	8	1	2	1	1	13	1	1	.311	.245
Perez, Carlos	R-R	5-10	160	9-10-96	.263	.313	.255	28	114	9	30	3	1	0	8	5	0	2	2	8	0	0	.307	.289
Reyes, Franklin	R-R	6-4	205	9-11-98	.249	.242	.250	56	241	24	60	12	0	5	34	5	2	2	0	68	1	0	.361	.270
Taylor, Logan	R-R	5-9	175	6-21-94	.307	.345	.299	44	176	32	54	8	1	1	19	25	4	1	3	27	4	3	.381	.399
Villa, Anthony	R-R	6-3	220	3-29-94	.314	.394	.301	63	226	56	71	17	2	16	57	52	8	0	3	72	0	0	.620	.453
Yurchak, Justin	L-R	6-1	204	9-17-96	.345	.348	.345	60	223	46	77	13	1	8	27	43	0	1	2	33	1	0	.520	.448

Pitching	B-T	HT	WT	DOB	W	L	ERA	G	GS	CG	SV	IP	H	R	ER	HR	BB	SO	AVG	vLH	vRH	K/9	BB/9
Agar, Brandon	R-R	6-4	200	2-7-93	7	2	5.01	15	15	0	0	83	104	57	46	11	20	42	.313	.285	.330	4.57	2.18
Battenfield, Blake	R-R	6-3	220	8-22-94	1	4	4.88	21	0	0	0	31	35	19	17	2	8	40	.271	.378	.228	11.49	2.30
Boelter, Ryan	L-L	6-2	240	12-28-93	2	0	1.74	17	0	0	0	31	26	12	6	3	16	28	.232	.182	.244	8.13	4.65
Comito, Chris	R-R	6-6	240	6-25-96	3	7	5.09	15	15	0	0	76	100	59	43	4	24	41	.320	.296	.332	4.86	2.84
Erickson, Ryan	L-L	6-3	190	8-27-93	0	0	22.09	4	0	0	0	4	13	12	9	1	3	4	.520	.500	.526	9.82	7.36
Gallegos, Fernando	L-R	5-11	175	9-4-92	2	3	4.73	16	3	0	0	46	49	27	24	3	20	52	.277	.281	.275	10.25	3.94
Gerardo, Josue	R-R	6-3	180	3-27-93	1	2	9.40	21	0	0	0	30	45	39	31	3	31	39	.352	.326	.365	11.83	9.40
Henzman, Lincoln	R-R	6-2	205	7-4-95	0	3	4.00	10	7	0	0	27	27	13	12	0	9	16	.270	.194	.313	5.33	3.00
Johnson, Tyler	R-R	6-2	180	8-21-95	1	1	0.90	8	0	0	0	10	7	2	1	0	7	16	.194	.333	.095	14.40	6.30
Kincanon, Will	L-R	6-3	202	10-27-95	2	1	3.94	21	0	0	3	30	24	16	13	1	13	29	.220	.188	.234	8.80	3.94
Ledo, Luis	R-R	6-4	208	5-28-95	1	0	1.50	1	1	0	0	6	3	1	1	1	1	6	.150	.000	.177	9.00	1.50
McClure, Kade	R-R	6-7	230	2-12-96	1	0	2.25	4	0	0	0	4	1	1	1	1	2	8	.077	.000	.091	18.00	4.50
Mockbee, Joe	R-L	6-3	205	1-7-95	0	1	3.18	20	0	0	2	28	28	15	10	3	17	22	.250	.292	.239	6.99	5.40
Olson, J.B.	R-R	6-2	195	2-12-95	2	2	0.69	10	0	0	1	13	11	6	1	1	1	13	.216	.308	.184	9.00	0.69
Panayotovich, Adam	R-R	5-11	180	9-3-91	1	5	6.50	16	9	0	0	64	95	53	46	8	22	43	.347	.303	.371	6.08	3.11
Quijada, Jhoan	R-R	6-3	210	12-27-94	1	1	2.90	20	1	0	3	31	27	14	10	2	10	18	.229	.191	.250	5.23	2.90
Renzi, Sean	R-R	6-3	245	2-14-93	0	2	3.28	22	0	0	2	25	21	12	9	3	15	19	.233	.200	.250	6.93	5.47
Rigler, Parker	L-L	5-11	183	2-16-95	5	4	5.88	16	10	0	0	52	55	38	34	8	24	46	.282	.406	.258	7.96	4.15
Von Ruden, Kyle	R-R	6-0	195	5-21-94	4	4	4.27	15	15	0	0	86	95	57	41	8	17	63	.270	.310	.243	6.57	1.77

Fielding

C: Cooper 10, Nolan 40, Perez 27. **1B:** Reyes 40, Villa 21, Yurchak 19. **2B:** Blackman 45, Cronin 22, Dexter 1, Dutto 2, Hadley 6, Mota 1. **3B:** Blackman 1, Hadley 7, Mota 2, Nunez 33, Villa 24, Yurchak 12. **SS:** Blackman 1, Curbelo 3, Duarte 2, Dutto 53, Hadley 7, Mota 5, Muno 7, Nunez 1. **OF:** Brown 44, Cooper 19, Cronin 1, Dedelow 58, Frost 32, Gonzalez 4, Hadley 10, Mercedes 11, Muno 4, Otano 8, Taylor 44.

AZL WHITE SOX — *ROOKIE*

ARIZONA LEAGUE

Batting	B-T	HT	WT	DOB	AVG	vLH	vRH	G	AB	R	H	2B	3B	HR	RBI	BB	HBP	SH	SF	SO	SB	CS	SLG	OBP
Abbott, Sam	L-R	6-4	225	4-9-99	.226	.167	.238	31	102	14	23	5	0	0	7	17	2	1	1	38	0	0	.275	.344
Alfaro, Jhoandro	B-R	6-1	180	11-4-97	.220	.333	.192	29	91	14	20	2	1	0	8	12	2	2	0	25	0	0	.264	.324
Beltre, Ramon	R-R	5-11	160	10-18-96	.308	.368	.296	27	107	14	33	2	0	2	14	7	0	0	4	23	8	3	.383	.339
Burger, Jake	R-R	6-2	210	4-10-96	.154	.000	.200	4	13	4	2	1	0	1	2	1	3	0	0	2	0	0	.462	.353
Call, Alex	R-R	6-0	188	9-27-94	.059	.000	.068	13	51	8	3	1	0	0	6	7	1	0	2	5	1	0	.078	.180

Colina, Jose	B-R	6-0	180	3-26-98	.327	.250	.340	16	55	6	18	3	0	1	13	4	0	2	1	15	0	0	.436	.367
Coronado, Anthony	R-R	6-1	180	1-21-00	.308	.000	.333	4	13	1	4	1	0	0	0	1	0	0	0	5	0	0	.385	.357
Cronin, David	L-R	5-9	175	12-19-94	.243	.400	.219	13	37	3	9	1	1	0	7	10	0	2	0	7	2	0	.324	.404
Crutcher, Austin	R-R	6-2	205	4-17-93	.244	.286	.235	43	119	21	29	9	2	2	19	21	3	0	2	39	5	1	.403	.366
Destino, Alex	L-L	6-2	215	10-24-95	.290	.361	.272	49	183	28	53	13	2	3	23	38	0	2	2	40	1	2	.432	.408
Feliz, Maiker	R-R	6-0	195	8-17-97	.295	.467	.239	18	61	8	18	4	1	2	11	6	2	0	0	19	1	0	.492	.377
Garcia, Jose	R-R	6-0	210	7-25-95	.429	.000	.474	13	42	9	18	3	5	0	6	7	3	1	1	11	2	3	.738	.528
Garcia, Leury	B-R	5-8	170	3-18-91	.444	.333	.500	2	9	2	4	0	0	2	6	1	0	0	1	1	0	1	1.111	.455
Gelalich, Jeff	L-R	6-0	210	3-16-91	.400	.500	.389	5	20	4	8	0	1	0	2	1	2	0	0	5	2	0	.500	.478
Hickman, Michael	L-R	6-1	215	11-5-96	.270	.355	.253	49	189	33	51	7	4	2	21	26	2	2	1	54	3	1	.381	.362
Maloney, Alex	R-R	6-3	190	12-2-94	.254	.250	.254	23	71	14	18	1	0	0	4	15	0	0	0	11	1	2	.268	.384
McGinnis, Adam	R-R	5-11	225	10-4-94	.290	.462	.245	19	62	11	18	4	1	3	13	4	2	0	2	13	0	0	.532	.343
Montilla, Gerson	R-R	5-10	170	11-13-89	.000	—	.000	1	1	0	0	0	0	0	0	0	0	0	0	1	0	0	.000	.000
Mota, Ricky	R-R	5-11	170	2-21-98	.333	—	.333	2	3	0	1	0	0	0	1	0	0	0	0	0	0	0	.333	.333
Muno, JJ	L-R	5-11	190	12-21-93	.274	.400	.254	27	73	14	20	4	2	0	14	8	9	1	1	14	4	0	.384	.407
Nunez, Amado	R-R	6-2	178	10-10-97	.375	.000	.500	2	8	2	3	0	0	0	1	1	1	0	0	0	0	0	.375	.500
Rivera, Laz	R-R	6-1	185	9-20-94	.296	.378	.275	47	186	37	55	12	5	2	24	8	16	2	1	26	3	4	.446	.374
Rodriguez, Antonio	R-R	6-4	230	5-7-95	.300	.750	.231	8	30	6	9	1	1	0	5	4	0	0	1	5	0	1	.400	.371
Sheets, Gavin	L-L	6-4	230	4-23-96	.500	1.000	.400	4	12	3	6	2	0	1	3	3	1	1	0	0	0	0	.917	.625
Silverio, Louis	R-R	6-3	215	12-15-93	.318	.250	.357	5	22	5	7	1	0	1	7	1	1	0	0	4	1	0	.500	.375
Skoug, Evan	L-R	5-11	200	10-21-95	.529	.500	.533	4	17	6	9	1	1	1	3	3	0	0	0	7	0	0	.882	.600
Sosa, Lenyn	R-R	6-0	180	1-25-00	.270	.259	.273	42	159	19	43	4	2	2	23	14	1	4	2	24	3	4	.359	.330
Staudinger, Michael	L-L	6-3	193	9-5-94	.218	.182	.222	27	101	11	22	6	0	0	14	9	2	1	1	22	1	0	.277	.292
Taylor, Logan	R-R	5-9	175	6-21-94	.333	1.000	.263	5	21	7	7	1	1	1	2	5	0	1	0	2	1	0	.619	.462

Pitching	B-T	HT	WT	DOB	W	L	ERA	G	GS	CG	SV	IP	H	R	ER	HR	BB	SO	AVG	vLH	vRH	K/9	BB/9
Andrews, Ted	R-R	6-6	235	1-19-94	0	0	2.25	13	0	0	0	12	7	7	3	0	13	10	.180	.100	.207	7.50	9.75
Arias, Edinxon	R-R	6-2	155	12-5-97	1	4	7.82	10	9	0	0	38	47	37	33	5	30	21	.313	.353	.293	4.97	7.11
Arobio, Vince	R-R	6-0	185	3-31-95	2	3	4.03	15	0	0	3	29	21	13	13	3	5	27	.198	.207	.195	8.38	1.55
Benitez, Joseph	R-L	6-0	190	4-17-95	3	1	1.80	7	0	0	0	10	7	5	2	0	2	7	.194	.125	.214	6.30	1.80
Cashman, Pat	R-R	6-0	185	11-1-92	0	0	0.00	1	0	0	0	1	1	0	0	0	0	0	.333	.000	.500	0.00	0.00
Covey, Dylan	R-R	6-2	195	8-14-91	0	0	0.00	3	3	0	0	5	2	0	0	0	0	5	.133	.000	.182	9.00	0.00
De La Cruz, Leonardo	L-L	6-4	180	4-29-94	0	1	1.50	11	0	0	0	12	8	6	2	0	4	14	.205	.143	.219	10.50	3.00
Erickson, Ryan	L-L	6-3	190	8-27-93	0	0	7.31	12	0	0	2	16	29	15	13	1	6	16	.397	.536	.311	9.00	3.38
George, Kevin	L-L	5-10	180	4-11-95	3	4	2.05	15	0	0	1	22	19	9	5	1	6	26	.241	.278	.230	10.64	2.45
Henzman, Lincoln	R-R	6-2	205	7-4-95	0	0	0.00	1	0	0	0	1	0	0	0	0	0	1	.000	—	.000	9.00	0.00
Herron, Jr., Anthony	R-R	6-2	195	3-1-96	0	0	8.22	7	0	0	1	8	11	7	7	0	6	6	.333	.357	.316	7.04	7.04
Kiel, Hunter	R-R	6-3	229	7-18-96	0	0	8.18	12	0	0	0	11	11	11	10	1	18	16	.290	.546	.185	13.09	14.73
Ledo, Luis	R-R	6-4	208	5-28-95	1	0	5.79	4	0	0	0	5	5	3	3	0	3	6	.263	.143	.333	11.57	5.79
Lewis, Zach	R-R	6-3	205	5-24-95	6	1	2.72	12	8	1	0	53	46	18	16	2	13	45	.241	.143	.282	7.64	2.21
McClure, Kade	R-R	6-7	230	2-12-96	0	0	0.00	1	0	0	0	1	0	0	0	0	0	3	.000	—	.000	27.00	0.00
McCormick, Michael	L-R	6-3	190	12-8-93	2	3	2.68	16	5	0	0	44	36	16	13	2	13	41	.232	.240	.229	8.45	2.68
Minier, Greg	R-L	6-4	235	9-22-95	0	0	1.53	15	0	0	0	18	21	3	3	0	2	16	.304	.133	.352	8.15	1.02
Parke, John	L-L	6-4	205	1-3-95	3	2	2.77	14	10	0	0	68	65	27	21	2	9	46	.248	.186	.266	6.06	1.19
Percel, Eriberto	R-R	6-5	200	8-2-92	0	0	81.00	1	0	0	0	0	0	3	3	0	4	1	.000	—	.000	27.00	108.00
Riga, Ryan	R-L	6-0	190	10-22-92	4	0	0.00	9	0	0	1	12	6	0	0	0	4	13	.146	.111	.156	10.03	3.09
Sanchez, Andres	R-R	6-4	180	10-7-96	2	3	4.91	12	5	0	0	29	33	26	16	3	20	23	.277	.182	.314	7.06	6.14
Saucedo, Bryan	R-R	6-6	225	2-3-94	3	2	7.04	13	13	0	0	55	58	49	43	4	37	41	.266	.194	.295	6.71	6.05
Villarreal, Salvador	R-R	6-1	165	2-5-98	0	2	4.94	13	3	0	1	27	21	18	15	3	23	19	.212	.191	.218	6.26	7.57
Wheeler, Andre	L-L	6-1	170	9-27-91	0	0	3.38	8	0	0	0	8	9	3	3	1	0	11	.273	.222	.292	12.38	0.00

Fielding

C: Alfaro 28, Colina 15, Hickman 5, McGinnis 11, Skoug 2. **1B:** Abbott 16, Hickman 39, Sheets 3. **2B:** Beltre 8, Cronin 11, Maloney 2, Mota 1, Muno 4, Rivera 12, Sosa 20. **3B:** Beltre 19, Burger 3, Cronin 1, Feliz 10, Maloney 12, Mota 1, Muno 10, Nunez 1. **SS:** Rivera 34, Sosa 22. **OF:** Call 11, Coronado 4, Crutcher 41, Destino 45, Garcia 13, Garcia 2, Gelalich 5, Maloney 2, Muno 9, Rodriguez 7, Silverio 5, Staudinger 26, Taylor 5.

DSL WHITE SOX — *ROOKIE*

DOMINICAN SUMMER LEAGUE

Batting	B-T	HT	WT	DOB	AVG	vLH	vRH	G	AB	R	H	2B	3B	HR	RBI	BB	HBP	SH	SF	SO	SB	CS	SLG	OBP
Barreras, Robert	R-R	6-3	205	9-15-98	.200	.125	.222	13	35	5	7	1	0	0	4	6	0	0	0	11	0	0	.229	.317
Beltre, Ramon	R-R	5-11	160	10-18-96	.335	.367	.329	42	176	33	59	12	2	3	24	15	3	2	2	25	7	3	.477	.393
Betancourt, Jhoneiker	R-R	6-1	174	5-2-00	.268	.333	.255	18	56	7	15	3	0	0	7	2	3	0	0	13	2	0	.321	.328
Comas, Anderson	L-L	6-3	185	2-10-00	.291	.263	.300	63	237	29	69	5	2	0	17	8	1	0	1	45	1	1	.329	.316
Coronado, Anthony	R-R	6-1	180	1-21-00	.262	.186	.285	54	187	24	49	19	0	4	28	16	11	1	1	55	1	2	.428	.354
Felix, Enrique	R-R	6-3	188	1-7-99	.193	.200	.192	23	57	6	11	3	0	1	5	4	1	0	0	29	1	0	.298	.258
Garcia, Richard	R-R	6-1	185	9-20-98	.115	.083	.125	19	52	6	6	2	1	0	2	4	1	2	0	15	0	0	.192	.193
Gideon, Yolberth	R-R	5-11	155	2-6-96	.170	.364	.125	25	59	4	10	0	0	0	2	9	2	1	0	11	1	1	.170	.300
Guerrero, Josue	R-R	6-2	190	11-23-99	.222	.214	.224	55	207	33	46	13	2	3	25	16	5	1	3	54	5	0	.348	.290
Martinez, Omar	R-R	6-3	192	12-23-98	.140	.250	.122	31	57	13	8	0	0	0	2	5	2	0	0	24	3	1	.140	.234
Martinez, Ulises	R-R	6-1	190	3-2-99	.206	.214	.204	24	63	9	13	2	0	0	4	2	0	1	1	16	0	0	.238	.227
Mendoza, Harvin	L-L	6-2	185	2-18-99	.283	.262	.288	63	233	36	66	17	2	1	38	39	0	1	1	44	1	0	.386	.385
Mieses, Luis	L-L	6-3	180	5-31-00	.263	.244	.267	59	247	24	65	8	3	0	25	10	4	1	1	42	3	2	.320	.302
Nova, Brayant	B-R	6-1	170	8-25-98	.282	.150	.313	58	206	26	58	6	7	0	27	26	4	1	2	52	11	3	.379	.370
Robert, Luis	R-R	6-3	185	8-3-97	.310	.364	.301	28	84	17	26	8	1	3	14	22	8	0	0	23	12	3	.536	.491
Rosas, Jorgen	R-R	5-9	160	1-10-98	.229	.241	.226	45	153	24	35	11	2	1	15	13	3	2	2	42	1	0	.346	.298

Sanchez, Kleyder	R-R	5-10	170	12-13-99	.342	.417	.328	43	155	20	53	6	0	0	14	5	6	0	1	24	1	0	.381	.383
Vasquez, Santo	R-R	6-0	170	11-27-98	.249	.273	.243	56	181	40	45	7	3	5	28	24	4	1	2	52	12	5	.403	.346

Pitching	**B-T**	**HT**	**WT**	**DOB**	**W**	**L**	**ERA**	**G**	**GS**	**CG**	**SV**	**IP**	**H**	**R**	**ER**	**HR**	**BB**	**SO**	**AVG**	**vLH**	**vRH**	**K/9**	**BB/9**
Acosta, Hector	L-L	6-4	200	10-24-98	1	5	3.35	13	12	0	0	48	43	34	18	0	22	43	.232	.282	.219	8.01	4.10
Acosta, Nelson	R-R	6-3	195	8-22-97	1	3	9.10	19	1	0	0	30	30	32	30	3	30	26	.261	.304	.232	7.89	9.10
Batista, Cristopher	R-R	6-3	180	11-1-98	1	7	8.62	22	0	0	0	31	41	45	30	1	25	15	.325	.319	.329	4.31	7.18
Caraballo, Jendersson	R-R	6-3	190	10-27-99	2	2	2.11	14	14	0	0	64	52	26	15	1	29	38	.226	.225	.227	5.34	4.08
Caro, Fernando	R-R	6-3	192	2-25-97	1	1	5.61	20	0	0	1	34	32	25	21	2	27	26	.252	.222	.264	6.95	7.22
Coroba, Josbel	L-L	6-0	180	5-18-97	0	0	0.00	2	0	0	1	1	1	0	0	0	2	3	.250	.000	.500	27.00	18.00
Herrera, Antonio	R-R	6-4	195	9-26-94	3	1	3.11	26	0	0	2	38	39	22	13	1	24	23	.279	.275	.280	5.50	5.73
Herrera, Brayan	R-R	6-2	185	4-5-98	5	2	2.62	15	12	0	0	69	57	28	20	0	17	47	.221	.274	.190	6.16	2.23
Lara, Bryan	L-L	6-0	170	11-6-97	2	1	4.05	18	0	0	0	33	31	15	15	2	14	25	.248	.389	.224	6.75	3.78
Nin, Jose	R-R	6-2	170	6-20-95	6	3	2.68	28	0	0	12	40	37	15	12	0	9	28	.252	.333	.216	6.25	2.01
Perez, Erick	R-R	6-1	175	12-9-98	2	1	6.75	17	0	0	0	27	21	23	20	0	32	15	.214	.231	.203	5.06	10.80
Pineda, Ramon	R-R	6-3	200	2-3-98	4	3	3.76	14	14	0	0	67	64	29	28	3	18	46	.257	.277	.243	6.18	2.42
Ramos, Jordis	L-L	6-10	194	6-15-96	1	3	4.06	22	3	0	1	44	31	29	20	0	48	41	.203	.350	.181	8.32	9.74
Rodriguez, Ruddy	R-R	5-11	160	8-6-96	0	1	5.40	2	1	0	0	2	2	1	1	0	1	1	.286	.500	.200	5.40	5.40
Rosario, Yordi	R-R	6-2	185	1-30-99	4	2	2.26	14	14	0	0	72	56	23	18	0	26	64	.215	.185	.231	8.04	3.27
Silva, Yender	R-R	6-1	180	6-12-98	1	0	0.00	1	0	0	0	1	0	0	0	0	0	2	.000	—	.000	18.00	0.00
Yanes, Pablo	R-R	6-4	195	10-28-99	0	2	13.14	11	0	0	0	12	9	19	18	0	24	8	.225	.133	.280	5.84	17.51

Fielding

C: Betancourt 10, Garcia 16, Martinez 21, Sanchez 39. **1B:** Barreras 9, Martinez 9, Mendoza 60. **2B:** Beltre 2, Gideon 9, Nova 58, Rosas 10, Vasquez 3. **3B:** Beltre 19, Betancourt 5, Gideon 16, Martinez 1, Rosas 16, Vasquez 20. **SS:** Beltre 20, Gideon 1, Rosas 20, Vasquez 32. **OF:** Comas 50, Coronado 38, Felix 19, Guerrero 43, Martinez 18, Mieses 57, Robert 19.

Cincinnati Reds

SEASON IN A SENTENCE: Young pitchers can give hope for the future, but they can also make a manager feel very old, very quickly.

HIGH POINT: There weren't a lot of highlights in a third-consecutive fifth-place finish in the National League Central, but Reds fans did get to see history on June 6 when Scooter Gennett went 5-for-5 with a record-tying four home runs and an equally impressive 10 RBIs. Power was a key part of the Reds' offense all year—six different Reds hitters hit 24 or more home runs.

LOW POINT: The Reds came out of the all-star break with a thud, losing 14 of their first 16 games in the second half, turning what had been a rough first half into an even tougher second-half. Pitching was the problem, as the Reds allowed 6.8 runs per game during the losing stretch.

NOTABLE ROOKIES: Righthander Luis Castillo showed signs of being the Reds' ace of the future as he mixed a high-90s fastball, an excellent changeup and impressive feel to go 3-7, 3.12. Righthander Sal Romano went 5-8, 4.45 while spending half the season in the Reds' rotation. Righthander Robert Stephenson was 5-6, 4.68 as he mixed impressive stuff and imprecise command. Lefthander Amir Garrett had five quality starts in his first six MLB appearances. He had only one quality start in his next eight starts on his way to a 3-8, 7.39 rookie season.

KEY TRANSACTIONS: Castillo was acquired before the season in a pitcher-for-pitcher swap as Cincinnati sent Dan Straily to the Marlins. Straily was fine (10-9, 4.26) but Castillo outpitched him in 2017, is four years younger and is under club control for six more seasons. Gennett proved to be a very valuable waiver claim as he hit 27 home runs to earn the team's everyday second-base job.

DOWN ON THE FARM: While the big league team struggled, the minor league teams thrived. Third baseman Nick Senzel, the team's No. 1 pick in 2016, lived up to lofty expectations as he hit .321/.391/.514 between high Class A and Double-A. Righthander Tyler Mahle went 10-7, 2.06 and threw a perfect game. It was his second no-hitter in the past two seasons. Outfielder Jose Siri had a Midwest League record 39-game hitting streak. Siri's season was nearly as notable as he hit .293 with 24 home runs and 46 steals. Outfielder Taylor Trammell was just as effective for low Class A Dayton as he hit .281-13-77 with 41 stolen bases.

OPENING DAY PAYROLL: $112,437,541 (19th)

PLAYERS OF THE YEAR

MAJOR LEAGUE

Joey Votto
1B
.320/.454/.578
Led MLB with 134 BBs, .454 OBP

MINOR LEAGUE

Nick Senzel
3B
(High Class A/ Double-A)
.321/.391/.514

ORGANIZATION LEADERS

BATTING		*Minimum 250 AB
MAJORS		
* AVG	Joey Votto	.320
* OPS	Joey Votto	1.032
HR	Joey Votto	36
RBI	Joey Votto	100
MINORS		
* AVG	Jose Siri, Dayton	.321
* OBP	Jesse Winker, Louisville	.395
* SLG	Jose Siri, Dayton	.530
* OPS	Nick Senzel, Daytona, Pensacola	.905
R	Jose Siri, Dayton	92
H	Jose Siri, Dayton	146
	Nick Senzel, Daytona, Pensacola	146
TB	Jose Siri, Dayton	264
2B	Nick Senzel, Daytona, Pensacola	40
3B	Jose Siri, Dayton	11
HR	Jose Siri, Dayton	24
RBI	Gavin LaValley, Daytona, Pensacola	79
BB	Taylor Trammell, Dayton	71
SO	Aristides Aquino, Pensacola	145
SB	Jose Siri, Dayton	46

PITCHING		#Minimum 75 IP
MAJORS		
W	Michael Lorenzen	8
# ERA	Raisel Iglesias	2.49
SO	Tim Adleman	108
SV	Raisel Iglesias	28
MINORS		
W	Scott Moss, Dayton	13
L	Jonathan Crawford, Daytona	10
	Wendolyn Bautista, Dayton, Louisville	10
	Wennington Romero, Dayton	10
	Keury Mella, Pensacola	10
	Jackson Stephens, Louisville	10
# ERA	Tyler Mahle, Pensacola, Louisville	2.06
G	Tanner Rainey, Daytona, Pensacola	53
GS	Deck McGuire, Pensacola	27
SV	Jimmy Herget, Pensacola, Louisville	25
IP	Deck McGuire, Pensacola	168
BB	Jonathon Crawford, Daytona	79
SO	Deck McGuire, Pensacola	170
# AVG	Tyler Mahle, Louisville	.208

2017 PERFORMANCE

General Manager: Dick Williams. **Farm Director:** Jeff Graupe. **Scouting Director:** Chris Buckley.

Class	Team	League	W	L	PCT	Finish	Manager
Majors	Cincinnati Reds	National	68	94	.42	13th (15)	Bryan Price
Triple-A	Louisville Bats	International	56	86	.394	13th (14)	Delino DeShields
Double-A	Pensacola Blue Wahoos	Southern	74	66	.529	3rd (10)	Pat Kelly
High-A	Daytona Tortugas	Florida State	53	80	.398	11th (12)	Eli Marrero
Low-A	Dayton Dragons	Midwest	71	69	.507	7th (16)	Luis Bolivar
Rookie	Billings Mustangs	Pioneer	36	39	.48	5th (8)	Ray Martinez
Rookie	AZL Reds	Arizona	22	33	.4	14th (15)	Jose Nieves
Overall 2017 Minor League Record			312	373	.455	28th (30)	

ORGANIZATION STATISTICS

CINCINNATI REDS

NATIONAL LEAGUE

Batting	B-T	HT	WT	DOB	AVG	vLH	vRH	G	AB	R	H	2B	3B	HR	RBI	BB	HBP	SH	SF	SO	SB	CS	SLG	OBP
Alcantara, Arismendy	B-R	5-10	170	10-29-91	.171	.079	.224	70	105	13	18	3	1	1	7	2	0	1	0	38	2	0	.248	.187
Barnhart, Tucker	B-R	5-11	192	1-7-91	.270	.236	.279	121	370	26	100	24	2	7	44	42	3	5	3	68	4	0	.403	.347
Cozart, Zack	R-R	6-0	204	8-12-85	.297	.337	.285	122	438	80	130	24	7	24	63	62	3	0	4	78	3	0	.548	.385
Duvall, Adam	R-R	6-1	215	9-4-88	.249	.279	.239	157	587	78	146	37	3	31	99	39	10	0	11	170	5	3	.480	.301
Ervin, Phillip	R-R	5-10	207	7-15-92	.259	.412	.195	28	58	8	15	2	0	3	10	4	1	1	0	15	4	1	.448	.318
Gennett, Scooter	L-R	5-10	185	5-1-90	.295	.248	.310	141	461	80	136	22	3	27	97	30	4	0	2	114	3	2	.532	.342
Hamilton, Billy	B-R	6-0	160	9-9-90	.247	.219	.259	139	582	85	144	17	11	4	38	44	0	5	2	133	59	13	.335	.299
Kivlehan, Patrick	R-R	6-2	223	12-22-89	.208	.239	.187	115	178	23	37	5	1	9	26	22	3	0	1	61	1	2	.399	.304
Mesoraco, Devin	R-R	6-1	229	6-19-88	.213	.180	.231	56	141	17	30	5	1	6	14	18	5	0	1	38	1	0	.390	.321
Peraza, Jose	R-R	6-0	196	4-30-94	.259	.282	.250	143	487	50	126	9	4	5	37	20	7	3	1	70	23	8	.324	.297
Schebler, Scott	L-R	6-0	228	10-6-90	.233	.276	.215	141	473	63	110	25	2	30	67	39	14	0	5	125	5	3	.484	.307
Suarez, Eugenio	R-R	5-11	213	7-18-91	.260	.276	.256	156	534	87	139	25	2	26	82	84	9	0	5	147	4	5	.461	.367
Turner, Stuart	R-R	6-2	220	12-27-91	.134	.125	.140	37	82	4	11	3	0	2	7	5	0	1	1	22	0	0	.244	.182
Vincej, Zach	R-R	6-0	190	5-1-91	.111	.000	.143	9	9	2	1	0	0	0	0	1	2	0	0	5	0	0	.111	.333
Votto, Joey	L-R	6-2	220	9-10-83	.320	.292	.331	162	559	106	179	34	1	36	100	134	8	0	6	83	5	1	.578	.454
Wallach, Chad	R-R	6-3	230	11-4-91	.091	.000	.111	6	11	0	1	0	0	0	0	0	0	0	0	5	0	0	.091	.091
Winker, Jesse	L-L	6-3	215	8-17-93	.298	.120	.344	47	121	21	36	7	0	7	15	15	0	1	0	24	1	1	.529	.375

Pitching	B-T	HT	WT	DOB	W	L	ERA	G	GS	CG	SV	IP	H	R	ER	HR	BB	SO	AVG	vLH	vRH	K/9	BB/9
Adleman, Tim	R-R	6-5	225	11-13-87	5	11	5.52	30	20	0	0	122	124	79	75	29	51	108	.264	.269	.261	7.95	3.75
Arroyo, Bronson	R-R	6-4	190	2-24-77	3	6	7.35	14	14	0	0	71	94	59	58	23	19	45	.320	.297	.333	5.70	2.41
Astin, Barrett	R-R	6-1	225	10-22-91	0	0	6.75	6	0	0	0	8	9	6	6	2	7	2	.290	.286	.294	2.25	7.88
Bailey, Homer	R-R	6-4	223	5-3-86	6	9	6.43	18	18	0	0	91	112	67	65	11	42	67	.309	.277	.339	6.63	4.15
Bonilla, Lisalverto	R-R	6-0	225	6-18-90	1	3	8.10	10	4	1	0	37	42	33	33	8	22	28	.292	.349	.244	6.87	5.40
Brice, Austin	R-R	6-4	235	6-19-92	0	0	4.96	22	0	0	0	33	33	18	18	6	7	26	.264	.192	.308	7.16	1.93
Buchanan, Jake	R-R	6-0	235	9-24-89	0	0	8.16	5	0	0	0	14	24	13	13	1	7	4	.375	.400	.359	2.51	4.40
Castillo, Luis	R-R	6-2	190	12-12-92	3	7	3.12	15	15	0	0	89	64	32	31	11	32	98	.202	.185	.216	9.87	3.22
Chacin, Alejandro	R-R	6-0	204	6-24-93	0	0	10.50	6	0	0	0	6	11	7	7	2	4	6	.393	.462	.333	9.00	6.00
Cingrani, Tony	L-L	6-4	214	7-5-89	0	0	5.40	25	0	0	0	23	25	14	14	9	6	24	.272	.293	.255	9.26	2.31
2-team total (22 Los Angeles)					0	0	4.22	47	0	0	0	43	40	22	20	10	12	52	.247	.293	.255	10.97	2.53
Davis, Rookie	R-R	6-5	255	4-29-93	1	3	8.63	7	6	0	0	24	38	25	23	7	14	20	.365	.370	.362	7.50	5.25
Farrell, Luke	L-R	6-6	210	6-7-91	0	0	2.61	9	0	0	0	10	5	3	3	1	7	7	.139	.125	.150	6.10	6.10
Feldman, Scott	R-L	6-6	225	2-7-83	7	7	4.77	21	21	1	0	111	116	62	59	21	35	93	.274	.286	.262	7.52	2.83
Finnegan, Brandon	L-L	5-11	212	4-14-93	1	1	4.15	4	4	0	0	13	9	6	6	1	13	16	.196	.167	.200	11.08	9.00
Garrett, Amir	R-L	6-5	228	5-3-92	3	8	7.39	16	14	0	0	71	74	60	58	23	40	63	.269	.298	.262	8.02	5.09
Hernandez, Ariel	R-R	6-4	230	3-2-92	0	0	5.18	19	0	0	0	24	14	14	14	6	22	29	.165	.244	.091	10.73	8.14
Iglesias, Raisel	R-R	6-2	188	1-4-90	3	3	2.49	63	0	0	28	76	57	22	21	5	27	92	.207	.256	.163	10.89	3.20
Lorenzen, Michael	R-R	6-3	217	1-4-92	8	4	4.45	70	0	0	2	83	78	43	41	9	34	80	.244	.247	.242	8.67	3.69
Mahle, Tyler	R-R	6-3	210	9-29-94	1	2	2.70	4	4	0	0	20	19	6	6	0	11	14	.253	.286	.241	6.30	4.95
McGuire, Deck	R-R	6-6	220	6-23-89	1	1	2.63	6	2	0	0	14	10	6	4	1	2	11	.189	.185	.192	7.24	1.32
Mella, Keury	R-R	6-2	200	8-2-93	0	0	6.75	2	0	0	0	4	5	3	3	1	2	1	.294	.250	.333	2.25	4.50
Peralta, Wandy	L-L	6-0	220	7-27-91	3	4	3.76	69	0	0	0	65	53	28	27	8	24	57	.228	.214	.237	7.93	3.34
Reed, Cody	L-L	6-5	228	4-15-93	1	1	5.09	12	1	0	1	18	11	11	10	3	19	17	.183	.111	.214	8.66	9.68
Romano, Sal	L-R	6-5	270	10-12-93	5	8	4.45	16	16	0	0	87	91	49	43	9	37	73	.275	.274	.276	7.55	3.83
Shackelford, Kevin	R-R	6-5	210	4-7-89	0	0	4.70	26	0	0	0	31	30	16	16	6	13	38	.254	.275	.239	11.15	3.82
Stephens, Jackson	R-R	6-2	220	5-11-94	2	1	4.68	7	4	0	0	25	19	13	13	6	9	21	.209	.237	.189	7.56	3.24
Stephenson, Robert	R-R	6-2	200	2-24-93	5	6	4.68	25	11	0	1	85	81	52	44	12	53	86	.256	.250	.260	9.14	5.63
Storen, Drew	R-B	6-1	195	8-11-87	4	2	4.45	58	0	0	1	55	57	32	27	7	23	48	.271	.288	.262	7.90	3.79
Wojciechowski, Asher	R-R	6-4	235	12-21-88	4	3	6.50	25	8	0	0	62	71	48	45	14	19	64	.287	.317	.258	9.24	2.74
Wood, Blake	R-R	6-5	233	8-8-85	1	4	5.65	55	0	0	0	57	64	40	36	5	29	62	.284	.380	.218	9.73	4.55

Fielding

Catcher	PCT	G	PO	A	E	DP	PB
Barnhart	.999	110	863	89	1	9	4
Mesoraco	.993	40	260	22	2	6	4
Turner	.989	28	165	10	2	1	1
Wallach	.955	3	20	1	1	0	0

First Base	PCT	G	PO	A	E	DP
Duvall	1.000	3	9	0	0	0
Kivlehan	1.000	12	35	2	0	3
Votto	.997	162	1227	165	4	109
Wallach	.000	1	0	0	0	0

Second Base	PCT	G	PO	A	E	DP
Alcantara	.897	10	9	17	3	2
Gennett	.981	99	156	203	7	40
Peraza	.990	77	122	184	3	50
Vincej	1.000	1	1	1	0	0

Third Base	PCT	G	PO	A	E	DP
Alcantara	1.000	4	0	2	0	1
Gennett	.895	10	4	13	2	1
Kivlehan	1.000	7	5	15	0	0
Suarez	.976	153	103	267	9	30

Shortstop	PCT	G	PO	A	E	DP
Alcantara	1.000	6	2	9	0	1
Cozart	.975	112	146	288	11	65
Peraza	.972	55	47	125	5	19
Suarez	1.000	1	0	2	0	0
Vincej	1.000	3	2	4	0	0

Outfield	PCT	G	PO	A	E	DP
Alcantara	1.000	17	23	1	0	0
Duvall	.979	151	267	15	6	1
Ervin	.947	18	36	0	2	0
Gennett	1.000	15	24	0	0	0
Hamilton	.991	137	301	13	3	4
Kivlehan	.957	43	42	2	2	1
Peraza	1.000	2	3	0	0	0
Schebler	.979	133	225	7	5	2
Winker	.977	27	41	2	1	0

LOUISVILLE BATS — *TRIPLE-A*

INTERNATIONAL LEAGUE

Batting	B-T	HT	WT	DOB	AVG	vLH	vRH	G	AB	R	H	2B	3B	HR	RBI	BB	HBP	SH	SF	SO	SB	CS	SLG	OBP
Amaral, Beau	L-L	5-10	177	2-11-91	.220	.219	.221	53	168	24	37	7	1	0	12	18	2	1	1	40	3	1	.274	.302
Blandino, Alex	R-R	6-0	190	11-6-92	.270	.342	.252	63	196	29	53	14	1	6	20	32	7	1	1	37	1	3	.444	.390
Boulware, Garrett	R-R	6-2	200	9-9-92	.143	.000	.182	5	14	1	2	0	0	0	0	0	0	0	0	4	0	0	.143	.143
Brantly, Rob	R-L	6-1	195	7-14-89	.298	.132	.346	46	168	21	50	6	1	5	16	9	1	0	1	25	3	2	.435	.335
2-team total (37 Charlotte)					.293	.132	.346	83	287	39	84	11	1	10	46	20	9	0	5	39	3	3	.443	.352
Dixon, Brandon	R-R	6-2	215	1-29-92	.264	.327	.244	124	440	58	116	31	3	16	64	37	7	1	6	125	18	8	.457	.327
Duarte, Jose	R-R	6-2	222	4-23-93	.259	.500	.191	7	27	1	7	0	0	0	5	0	0	0	0	7	0	0	.259	.259
Elizalde, Sebastian	L-R	6-0	195	11-20-91	.277	.242	.288	134	506	39	140	15	6	8	60	35	7	6	5	70	4	2	.378	.329
Ervin, Phillip	R-R	5-10	207	7-15-92	.256	.214	.272	99	363	46	93	20	2	7	40	37	2	5	0	83	23	6	.380	.328
Goeddel, Tyler	R-R	6-4	180	10-20-92	.278	.314	.264	55	191	23	53	9	2	1	15	19	3	1	0	40	7	2	.361	.352
Herrera, Dilson	R-R	5-10	210	3-3-94	.264	.262	.264	68	239	31	63	9	1	7	42	15	3	4	3	61	2	4	.398	.312
Hunter, Cedric	L-L	5-11	200	3-10-88	.300	.429	.231	14	40	5	12	4	0	1	4	1	0	1	1	8	0	0	.475	.310
Iribarren, Hernan	L-R	6-1	202	6-29-84	.285	.206	.303	91	340	40	97	17	2	4	32	24	0	3	2	43	2	3	.382	.331
Jagielo, Eric	L-R	6-3	210	5-17-92	.161	.150	.163	42	118	8	19	4	0	0	6	15	5	1	0	30	0	1	.195	.283
Mejias-Brean, Seth	R-R	6-2	216	4-5-91	.262	.316	.238	16	61	6	16	1	0	0	1	3	2	0	0	9	0	1	.279	.318
Mesoraco, Devin	R-R	6-1	229	6-19-88	.143	—	.143	2	7	1	1	0	0	1	4	3	0	0	0	4	0	0	.571	.400
Nieto, Adrian	R-B	5-10	205	11-12-89	.204	.333	.185	27	93	7	19	3	0	0	6	5	1	1	1	17	0	1	.237	.250
O'Brien, Peter	R-R	6-4	235	7-15-90	.200	.000	.286	5	20	4	4	2	0	1	2	4	0	0	0	6	0	0	.450	.333
Ovalle, Gabriel	R-B	6-2	170	12-10-94	.000	.000	.000	5	12	0	0	0	0	0	1	0	0	0	1	0	0	0	.000	.000
Perez, Juan	L-R	5-11	185	11-1-91	.300	.348	.281	22	80	9	24	5	1	4	8	12	1	0	0	18	6	3	.538	.398
Renda, Tony	R-R	5-8	179	1-24-91	.260	.339	.221	51	181	16	47	7	1	1	19	12	1	1	3	18	2	3	.326	.305
Schebler, Scott	L-R	6-0	228	10-6-90	.333	.500	.200	3	9	1	3	1	0	0	1	2	0	0	0	1	0	0	.444	.455
Sweeney, Darnell	B-R	6-1	195	2-1-91	.281	.246	.290	81	324	48	91	18	3	7	29	35	3	0	1	76	11	13	.420	.355
Turner, Stuart	R-R	6-2	220	12-27-91	.237	.211	.250	15	59	2	14	0	0	0	3	3	2	0	0	14	0	1	.237	.297
Van Slyke, Scott	R-R	6-4	215	7-24-86	.146	.294	.065	15	48	5	7	3	0	1	3	7	1	0	1	12	2	0	.271	.263
Veras, Josciel	R-R	5-8	175	12-7-92	.000	.000	.000	1	2	0	0	0	0	0	0	1	0	0	0	1	0	0	.000	.333
Vincej, Zach	R-R	6-0	190	5-1-91	.270	.314	.257	110	378	36	102	21	4	3	38	28	4	8	2	49	4	3	.370	.325
Walker, Adam Brett	R-R	6-5	225	10-18-91	.207	.217	.203	25	92	11	19	4	1	3	15	7	2	0	1	34	1	0	.370	.275
3-team total (10 Gwinnett, 18 Norfolk)					.152	.148	.050	53	198	17	30	9	1	5	22	11	2	0	2	76	3	0	.283	.202
Wallach, Chad	R-R	6-3	230	11-4-91	.226	.225	.226	64	226	28	51	12	0	9	18	13	4	0	0	62	1	0	.398	.280
Walters, Zach	B-R	6-2	210	9-5-89	.174	.000	.222	11	46	3	8	3	0	0	2	1	1	0	0	14	0	0	.239	.208
Winker, Jesse	L-L	6-3	215	8-17-93	.314	.280	.326	85	299	33	94	22	0	2	41	38	5	0	5	46	2	4	.408	.395

Pitching	B-T	HT	WT	DOB	W	L	ERA	G	GS	CG	SV	IP	H	R	ER	HR	BB	SO	AVG	vLH	vRH	K/9	BB/9
Adleman, Tim	R-R	6-5	225	11-13-87	0	1	2.57	1	1	0	0	7	5	2	2	1	1	6	.185	.308	.071	7.71	1.29
Astin, Barrett	R-R	6-1	225	10-22-91	3	4	6.10	26	3	0	0	49	71	38	33	4	22	44	.341	.432	.291	8.14	4.07
Bailey, Homer	R-R	6-4	223	5-3-86	1	0	3.18	1	1	0	0	6	7	2	2	1	2	6	.304	.000	.333	9.53	3.18
Bautista, Wendolyn	R-R	6-0	185	3-27-93	0	2	14.90	4	3	0	0	10	25	18	16	2	3	5	.472	.480	.464	4.66	2.79
Bonilla, Lisalverto	R-R	6-0	225	6-18-90	3	4	3.59	18	8	0	2	63	61	31	25	6	23	59	.255	.281	.238	8.47	3.30
Brice, Austin	R-R	6-4	235	6-19-92	1	2	3.80	15	0	0	1	21	23	10	9	0	9	21	.281	.387	.216	8.86	3.80
Broussard, Geoff	R-R	6-0	185	9-21-90	0	0	4.91	4	0	0	0	7	7	4	4	1	1	9	.250	.300	.222	11.05	1.23
Buchanan, Jake	R-R	6-0	235	9-24-89	0	1	6.75	2	0	0	0	3	4	2	2	1	1	4	.333	.333	.333	13.50	3.38
Chacin, Alejandro	R-R	6-0	204	6-24-93	0	3	2.60	44	0	0	1	69	63	26	20	4	27	63	.243	.270	.226	8.18	3.50
Christiani, Nick	R-R	6-0	190	7-17-87	0	0	9.00	12	0	0	0	15	19	16	15	1	22	16	.317	.333	.310	9.60	13.20
Cingrani, Tony	L-L	6-4	214	7-5-89	0	0	0.00	2	0	0	0	2	0	0	0	0	2	1	.000	.000	.000	4.50	9.00
Coleman, Louis	R-R	6-4	205	4-4-86	2	1	2.21	25	0	0	2	37	28	10	9	1	16	44	.214	.186	.227	10.80	3.93
Davis, Rookie	R-R	6-5	255	4-29-93	4	4	4.77	11	11	1	0	60	68	34	32	10	13	54	.282	.306	.262	8.06	1.94
De Paula, Rafael	R-R	6-2	215	3-24-91	0	0	0.00	2	0	0	0	2	1	0	0	0	1	2	.200	1.000	.000	9.00	4.50
Farrell, Luke	L-R	6-6	210	6-7-91	1	2	9.82	4	3	0	0	15	14	16	16	2	11	18	.241	.286	.200	11.05	6.75
Finnegan, Brandon	L-L	5-11	212	4-14-93	0	0	7.20	1	1	0	0	5	4	4	4	2	2	5	.222	.400	.154	9.00	3.60
Garrett, Amir	R-L	6-5	228	5-3-92	2	4	5.72	14	14	1	0	68	79	50	43	7	24	61	.295	.328	.285	8.11	3.19
Guillon, Ismael	L-L	6-1	222	2-13-92	1	4	5.20	27	3	0	0	54	57	35	31	6	35	55	.274	.299	.262	9.22	5.87
Herget, Jimmy	R-R	6-3	170	9-9-93	3	1	3.06	28	0	0	9	32	30	11	11	4	9	28	.248	.304	.213	7.79	2.51
Hernandez, Ariel	R-R	6-4	230	3-2-92	1	2	5.29	15	0	0	0	17	14	10	10	1	19	19	.233	.292	.194	10.06	10.06
Luetge, Lucas	L-L	6-4	205	3-24-87	1	2	4.55	20	0	0	0	28	34	17	14	4	9	30	.304	.225	.347	9.76	2.93
2-team total (4 Norfolk)					2	2	4.55	24	0	0	0	32	37	19	16	5	12	33	.291	.143	.250	9.38	3.41
Mahle, Tyler	R-R	6-3	210	9-29-94	3	4	2.73	10	10	0	0	59	52	24	18	4	13	51	.233	.238	.229	7.74	1.97
Mazzaro, Vin	R-R	6-2	220	9-27-86	0	2	24.92	2	2	0	0	4	13	13	12	3	3	3	.500	.600	.438	6.23	6.23

McMyne, Kyle	R-R	5-11	212	10-18-89	4	1	6.75	41	1	0	1	63	76	54	47	6	40	42	.305	.354	.273	6.03	5.74
Mitchell, Evan	R-R	6-2	185	3-18-92	2	4	4.85	25	0	0	1	39	58	29	21	1	12	28	.347	.404	.318	6.46	2.77
Ogando, Nefi	R-R	6-0	230	6-3-89	0	0	4.15	4	0	0	0	4	4	2	2	0	1	4	.235	.600	.083	8.31	2.08
Reed, Cody	L-L	6-5	228	4-15-93	4	9	3.55	21	20	0	0	106	105	49	42	7	61	102	.261	.206	.278	8.63	5.16
Romano, Sal	L-R	6-5	270	10-12-93	1	4	3.47	10	10	1	0	49	49	26	19	1	17	32	.259	.242	.268	5.84	3.10
Ross, Austin	L-R	6-2	200	8-12-88	2	2	4.91	5	4	0	0	26	30	14	14	4	6	12	.286	.122	.391	4.21	2.10
Routt, Nick	L-L	6-4	215	8-28-90	2	5	7.57	21	3	0	0	36	54	34	30	5	15	23	.346	.246	.411	5.80	3.79
Shackelford, Kevin	R-R	6-5	210	4-7-89	3	1	1.53	35	0	0	12	47	33	11	8	2	18	61	.195	.188	.202	11.68	3.45
Stephens, Jackson	R-R	6-2	220	5-11-94	7	10	4.92	26	25	1	0	139	156	85	76	16	51	110	.281	.306	.262	7.12	3.30
Stephenson, Robert	R-R	6-2	200	2-24-93	1	2	3.79	8	7	0	0	40	27	17	17	8	13	45	.186	.222	.151	10.04	2.90
Tapia, Domingo	R-R	6-3	250	8-4-91	0	1	4.76	3	1	0	0	6	9	4	3	1	1	4	.360	.308	.417	6.35	1.59
Wojciechowski, Asher	R-R	6-4	235	12-21-88	2	0	2.05	8	5	0	0	31	24	8	7	2	8	35	.207	.220	.197	10.27	2.35
Wooten, Rob	R-R	6-1	200	7-21-85	1	3	6.94	6	6	0	0	23	34	18	18	6	5	26	.343	.438	.255	10.03	1.93

Fielding

Catcher	PCT	G	PO	A	E	DP	PB
Boulware	1.000	4	36	1	0	0	1
Brantly	.997	39	315	28	1	2	1
Duarte	.982	7	51	4	1	0	0
Mesoraco	1.000	2	17	1	0	0	0
Nieto	.984	27	177	12	3	2	5
Turner	1.000	11	85	6	0	0	0
Wallach	.994	57	452	37	3	4	5

First Base	PCT	G	PO	A	E	DP
Dixon	.985	17	124	4	2	21
Elizalde	.975	33	260	11	7	37
Iribarren	.996	28	207	21	1	25
Jagielo	.990	30	187	15	2	19
Mejias-Brean	1.000	11	80	6	0	5
O'Brien	1.000	2	11	0	0	2
Renda	.977	5	40	3	1	2
Van Slyke	.989	13	83	7	1	10
Wallach	1.000	8	48	2	0	5
Walters	.983	8	54	5	1	9

Second Base	PCT	G	PO	A	E	DP
Blandino	.991	29	49	65	1	15
Herrera	.973	55	115	139	7	48
Iribarren	.952	15	20	20	2	8
Ovalle	1.000	4	5	10	0	1
Perez	.963	6	12	14	1	4
Renda	.911	13	31	20	5	11
Sweeney	.969	30	48	78	4	15
Veras	1.000	1	3	1	0	1
Vincej	.920	3	10	13	2	4

Third Base	PCT	G	PO	A	E	DP
Blandino	.897	26	10	42	6	8
Dixon	.905	93	54	175	24	18
Herrera	1.000	3	0	3	0	0
Iribarren	.944	14	13	21	2	1
Jagielo	.000	1	0	0	0	0
Mejias-Brean	1.000	4	7	10	0	1
Renda	.861	14	8	23	5	5
Sweeney	.846	2	1	10	2	1

Shortstop	PCT	G	PO	A	E	DP
Blandino	.889	8	8	24	4	4
Iribarren	.930	11	16	24	3	6
Perez	.939	15	14	48	4	7
Sweeney	.926	8	8	17	2	3
Vincej	.984	106	139	298	7	72

Outfield	PCT	G	PO	A	E	DP
Amaral	1.000	49	102	1	0	1
Dixon	1.000	12	25	0	0	0
Elizalde	.978	91	171	3	4	0
Ervin	.977	96	201	9	5	1
Goeddel	1.000	52	104	4	0	0
Hunter	1.000	2	7	0	0	0
Iribarren	1.000	3	3	0	0	0
O'Brien	.000	1	0	0	0	0
Perez	1.000	1	2	0	0	0
Renda	1.000	6	8	0	0	0
Schebler	.800	2	4	0	1	0
Sweeney	.973	43	104	5	3	0
Walker	.923	21	36	0	3	0
Winker	.993	75	140	3	1	2

PENSACOLA BLUE WAHOOS — DOUBLE-A

SOUTHERN LEAGUE

Batting	B-T	HT	WT	DOB	AVG	vLH	vRH	G	AB	R	H	2B	3B	HR	RBI	BB	HBP	SH	SF	SO	SB	CS	SLG	OBP
Alcantara, Arismendy	B-R	5-10	170	10-29-91	.164	.182	.154	17	61	9	10	3	3	0	8	7	0	0	0	19	0	1	.312	.250
Aquino, Aristides	R-R	6-4	220	4-22-94	.216	.303	.185	131	459	54	99	20	6	17	56	39	4	0	2	145	9	3	.397	.282
Blandino, Alex	R-R	6-0	190	11-6-92	.259	.208	.278	62	197	31	51	22	0	6	31	32	5	1	1	49	3	4	.462	.375
Boulware, Garrett	R-R	6-2	200	9-9-92	.000	.000	.000	1	2	0	0	0	0	0	0	0	0	0	0	1	0	0	.000	.000
Chavez, Alberti	R-R	5-10	170	7-21-95	.141	.214	.120	33	64	3	9	2	0	0	5	7	0	0	0	26	0	1	.172	.225
Duarte, Jose	R-R	6-2	222	4-23-93	.200	.333	.000	3	5	0	1	0	0	0	0	0	0	0	0	3	0	0	.200	.200
Goeddel, Tyler	R-R	6-4	180	10-20-92	.243	.304	.222	62	214	30	52	15	1	5	21	33	9	0	0	44	9	3	.393	.367
Guerrero, Gabriel	R-R	6-3	215	12-11-93	.274	.292	.267	132	501	61	137	24	4	7	50	34	3	0	5	103	3	7	.379	.320
Gumbs, Angelo	R-R	6-0	175	10-13-92	.231	.298	.189	54	147	18	34	5	2	1	7	15	0	0	1	32	3	0	.313	.301
Hudson, Joe	R-R	6-1	205	5-21-91	.171	.150	.178	75	217	14	37	15	0	1	16	29	0	4	0	50	0	0	.254	.268
Jagielo, Eric	L-R	6-3	210	5-17-92	.230	.200	.236	61	191	19	44	8	0	5	19	30	5	1	1	53	0	0	.351	.348
Landry, Leon	R-L	5-11	185	9-20-89	.198	.333	.181	46	106	11	21	3	2	0	3	4	1	1	0	24	2	1	.264	.234
LaValley, Gavin	R-R	6-3	235	12-28-94	.251	.288	.239	67	247	24	62	16	0	3	34	19	2	0	4	67	0	0	.352	.305
Long, Shed	L-R	5-8	180	8-22-95	.227	.281	.211	42	141	13	32	6	2	3	14	19	0	0	0	31	3	1	.362	.319
Longhi, Nick	R-L	6-2	205	8-16-95	.316	—	.316	7	19	2	6	1	0	1	7	3	0	0	0	5	0	0	.526	.409
Medina, Reydel	L-L	6-0	220	2-14-93	.182	.250	.167	10	22	1	4	0	0	1	3	0	0	0	0	10	0	0	.318	.182
Mesoraco, Devin	R-R	6-1	229	6-19-88	.170	.000	.205	13	47	4	8	1	0	1	3	6	2	0	0	10	0	0	.255	.291
Nieto, Adrian	R-B	5-10	205	11-12-89	.250	.250	.250	41	124	11	31	4	2	3	15	9	1	0	0	39	0	0	.387	.306
O'Grady, Brian	L-R	6-2	215	5-17-92	.166	.243	.144	66	169	23	28	4	2	7	21	34	2	2	3	59	7	0	.337	.308
Reynoso, Jonathan	R-R	6-3	177	1-7-93	.282	.364	.245	27	71	13	20	3	0	2	8	6	1	0	1	15	6	2	.409	.342
Senzel, Nick	R-R	6-1	205	6-29-95	.340	.286	.353	57	209	40	71	14	1	10	34	26	0	0	0	43	5	4	.560	.413
Sparks, Taylor	R-R	6-4	200	4-3-93	.129	.100	.135	18	62	8	8	2	0	2	4	9	2	0	0	21	0	0	.258	.260
Trahan, Blake	R-R	5-9	180	9-5-93	.222	.191	.232	136	455	55	101	18	0	2	27	52	7	11	1	82	12	7	.275	.311
Tromp, Chadwick	R-R	5-9	180	3-21-95	.204	.167	.214	36	113	6	23	4	0	0	10	14	2	0	0	15	1	0	.239	.302
VanMeter, Josh	L-R	5-11	165	3-10-95	.255	.273	.249	132	475	45	121	29	1	5	54	53	1	1	7	100	15	3	.352	.327

Pitching	B-T	HT	WT	DOB	W	L	ERA	G	GS	CG	SV	IP	H	R	ER	HR	BB	SO	AVG	vLH	vRH	K/9	BB/9
Bailey, Homer	R-R	6-4	223	5-3-86	1	0	0.00	1	1	0	0	5	3	0	0	0	1	5	.200	.200	.200	9.00	1.80
Bernardino, Brennan	L-L	6-4	180	1-15-92	2	4	4.46	38	0	0	0	40	42	22	20	5	19	42	.275	.340	.245	9.37	4.24
Brice, Austin	R-R	6-4	235	6-19-92	1	0	0.00	3	0	0	0	3	1	0	0	0	1	3	.100	.000	.143	9.00	3.00
Broussard, Geoff	R-R	6-0	185	9-21-90	4	2	3.20	41	0	0	5	45	44	18	16	5	14	34	.257	.325	.202	6.80	2.80
Castillo, Luis	R-R	6-2	190	12-12-92	4	4	2.58	14	14	1	0	80	68	24	23	5	13	81	.233	.220	.240	9.07	1.46
Davis, Rookie	R-R	6-5	255	4-29-93	0	0	4.61	3	3	0	0	14	12	7	7	2	6	11	.231	.318	.167	7.24	3.95

Ehret, Jake	R-R	6-3	190	3-18-93	0	1	9.14	19	0	0	1	22	33	22	22	2	17	15	.359	.333	.377	6.23	7.06
Finnegan, Brandon	L-L	5-11	212	4-14-93	0	0	0.00	2	2	0	0	7	2	0	0	0	1	5	.087	.000	.105	6.43	1.29
Gonzalez, Carlos	R-R	6-1	213	6-12-90	2	5	4.04	26	0	0	5	36	31	17	16	3	16	26	.244	.208	.270	6.56	4.04
Guillon, Ismael	L-L	6-1	222	2-13-92	1	2	2.25	13	0	0	1	16	18	7	4	0	11	21	.269	.353	.240	11.81	6.19
Herget, Jimmy	R-R	6-3	170	9-9-93	1	3	2.73	24	0	0	16	30	22	9	9	1	12	44	.202	.147	.227	13.35	3.64
Hernandez, Ariel	R-R	6-4	230	3-2-92	2	0	2.18	24	0	0	1	33	18	8	8	0	20	39	.167	.200	.143	10.64	5.45
Lopez, Jose	R-R	6-1	185	9-1-93	7	2	2.43	17	15	1	0	96	64	30	26	9	35	95	.189	.210	.174	8.88	3.27
Mahle, Tyler	R-R	6-3	210	9-29-94	7	3	1.59	14	14	1	0	85	57	15	15	5	17	87	.190	.179	.196	9.21	1.80
McGuire, Deck	R-R	6-6	220	6-23-89	9	9	2.79	28	27	0	0	168	125	58	52	13	57	170	.208	.199	.215	9.11	3.05
McKirahan, Andrew	R-L	6-2	200	2-8-90	2	0	2.61	9	0	0	0	10	6	3	3	1	5	8	.171	.100	.200	6.97	4.35
Mella, Keury	R-R	6-2	200	8-2-93	4	10	4.30	27	26	1	1	134	135	73	64	14	43	109	.260	.256	.263	7.32	2.89
Ogando, Nefi	R-R	6-0	230	6-3-89	0	0	0.00	2	0	0	0	2	1	0	0	0	1	1	.143	.250	.000	4.50	4.50
Portuondo, Carlos	R-R	6-2	235	11-9-87	0	0	54.00	1	0	0	0	1	3	5	4	0	0	0	.600	1.000	.500	0.00	0.00
Powers, Alex	R-R	6-4	180	2-26-92	1	4	4.30	34	1	0	1	61	66	32	29	5	27	85	.277	.266	.285	12.61	4.01
Rainey, Tanner	R-R	6-2	235	12-25-92	1	1	1.59	14	0	0	4	17	8	4	3	2	11	27	.146	.191	.118	14.29	5.82
Reyes, Jesus	R-R	6-2	180	2-21-93	2	4	3.31	10	10	0	0	52	55	19	19	3	20	44	.282	.276	.286	7.66	3.48
Ross, Austin	L-R	6-2	200	8-12-88	9	0	1.87	18	18	0	0	101	86	23	21	3	31	68	.236	.212	.249	6.04	2.75
Stock, Robert	L-R	6-1	200	11-21-89	8	2	2.98	25	0	0	0	45	39	16	15	0	21	36	.247	.297	.213	7.15	4.17
Tapia, Domingo	R-R	6-3	250	8-4-91	4	6	4.03	35	9	0	1	83	93	37	37	8	25	81	.283	.303	.266	8.82	2.72
Weiss, Zack	R-R	6-3	210	6-16-92	2	4	2.89	24	0	0	9	28	22	15	9	2	11	37	.210	.244	.188	11.89	3.54

Fielding

Catcher	PCT	G	PO	A	E	DP	PB
Boulware	1.000	1	1	0	0	0	0
Duarte	1.000	2	6	1	0	0	0
Hudson	.997	73	557	51	2	7	7
Mesoraco	.991	11	99	9	1	2	4
Nieto	.987	39	279	22	4	4	3
Tromp	.996	28	235	9	1	1	2

First Base	PCT	G	PO	A	E	DP
Gumbs	.989	28	175	7	2	19
Jagielo	.994	42	302	17	2	25
LaValley	.996	57	462	32	2	50
Longhi	1.000	3	23	1	0	2
Medina	1.000	2	13	1	0	1
Nieto	.000	1	0	0	0	0
O'Grady	1.000	18	87	9	0	9
VanMeter	1.000	1	11	0	0	1

Second Base	PCT	G	PO	A	E	DP
Alcantara	1.000	12	21	27	0	6
Blandino	.994	39	77	89	1	24
Chavez	1.000	12	11	14	0	5
Gumbs	1.000	8	17	23	0	3
Long	.984	39	87	103	3	29
VanMeter	.953	41	57	84	7	24

Third Base	PCT	G	PO	A	E	DP
Alcantara	.900	3	0	9	1	0
Blandino	.977	18	17	25	1	4
Chavez	.778	5	3	4	2	1
Senzel	.971	56	38	94	4	11
Sparks	.979	18	5	41	1	3
VanMeter	.922	48	27	68	8	11

Shortstop	PCT	G	PO	A	E	DP
Alcantara	1.000	1	0	1	0	0
Blandino	.917	5	4	7	1	2
Chavez	1.000	4	4	8	0	2
Trahan	.982	135	154	345	9	73
VanMeter	1.000	2	3	2	0	1

Outfield	PCT	G	PO	A	E	DP
Aquino	.968	128	231	9	8	1
Chavez	1.000	3	4	0	0	0
Goeddel	1.000	60	105	1	0	0
Guerrero	.989	129	256	9	3	2
Gumbs	1.000	3	5	0	0	0
Landry	1.000	19	32	0	0	0
Longhi	1.000	3	6	0	0	0
Medina	1.000	4	6	0	0	0
O'Grady	.979	43	89	3	2	1
Reynoso	1.000	20	42	1	0	0
VanMeter	.951	33	37	2	2	0

DAYTONA TORTUGAS — HIGH CLASS A

FLORIDA STATE LEAGUE

Batting	B-T	HT	WT	DOB	AVG	vLH	vRH	G	AB	R	H	2B	3B	HR	RBI	BB	HBP	SH	SF	SO	SB	CS	SLG	OBP
Bell, Brantley	R-R	6-3	185	11-16-94	.223	.267	.207	62	215	13	48	6	0	1	21	9	9	2	6	51	14	2	.265	.276
Boulware, Garrett	R-R	6-2	200	9-9-92	.269	.277	.267	52	182	12	49	10	0	1	16	10	0	4	1	38	0	0	.341	.306
Butler, Blake	R-R	6-3	195	10-29-93	.212	.209	.214	94	306	38	65	7	1	4	22	22	6	3	1	92	6	4	.281	.278
Collymore, Malik	R-R	6-0	195	4-29-95	.375	.333	.381	7	24	4	9	1	0	1	5	2	0	0	0	6	1	0	.542	.423
Crook, Narciso	R-R	6-3	220	7-12-95	.213	.231	.206	36	136	8	29	6	1	4	17	10	2	0	1	41	3	2	.360	.275
Duarte, Jose	R-R	6-2	222	4-23-93	.083	.250	.000	3	12	1	1	0	0	0	1	0	0	0	0	5	0	0	.083	.083
Franklin, Kevin	R-R	6-1	220	11-24-94	.150	.154	.148	13	40	2	6	1	0	0	0	2	0	0	0	7	0	0	.175	.191
2-team total (16 Florida)					.156	.154	.148	29	96	6	15	3	0	0	1	5	0	0	1	21	0	0	.188	.196
Friedl, T.J.	L-L	5-10	170	8-14-95	.257	.211	.270	48	179	15	46	6	2	2	13	10	5	4	1	39	2	1	.346	.313
Gonzalez, Luis	R-R	6-0	175	7-28-94	.286	.325	.270	66	266	30	76	16	1	5	30	4	2	0	8	44	7	2	.410	.293
LaValley, Gavin	R-R	6-3	235	12-28-94	.288	.213	.314	61	236	38	68	14	0	15	45	15	3	0	5	49	0	0	.538	.332
Long, Shed	L-R	5-8	180	8-22-95	.312	.258	.330	62	247	37	77	16	1	13	36	27	2	0	3	63	6	3	.543	.380
Mardirosian, Shane	L-R	5-10	175	10-13-95	.292	.143	.338	26	89	15	26	5	0	2	8	13	0	1	3	22	1	2	.416	.371
McElroy, Satchel	R-R	5-10	170	8-13-96	.059	.000	.063	5	17	0	1	0	0	0	0	0	0	1	0	7	0	0	.059	.059
Medina, Reydel	L-L	6-0	220	2-14-93	.240	.242	.239	102	346	41	83	18	7	8	43	20	7	1	7	113	5	6	.402	.290
O'Grady, Brian	L-R	6-2	215	5-17-92	.245	.200	.273	16	53	4	13	2	1	1	6	7	0	1	0	13	1	1	.377	.333
Okey, Chris	R-R	5-11	195	12-29-94	.185	.240	.168	93	325	27	60	10	1	3	28	32	4	0	1	104	2	1	.249	.265
Ovalle, Gabriel	R-B	6-2	170	12-10-94	.152	.429	.077	11	33	5	5	0	0	0	2	5	1	0	1	13	0	0	.152	.275
Piatnik, Mitch	B-R	6-0	170	9-12-94	.176	.147	.186	85	262	26	46	9	3	2	12	13	3	8	0	120	11	5	.256	.223
Reynoso, Jonathan	R-R	6-3	177	1-7-93	.167	.182	.161	23	78	4	13	3	0	0	2	2	0	1	0	15	1	1	.205	.188
Rodriguez, Alfredo	R-R	6-0	190	6-17-94	.253	.202	.271	118	483	52	122	14	0	2	36	25	4	2	2	79	11	9	.294	.294
Senzel, Nick	R-R	6-1	205	6-29-95	.305	.230	.330	62	246	41	75	26	2	4	31	23	3	0	0	54	9	2	.476	.371
Sweet, Daniel	B-L	6-0	190	12-28-94	.270	.235	.281	96	348	48	94	9	2	2	29	42	15	4	1	84	22	9	.325	.372
Trees, Mitch	R-R	6-2	200	7-18-95	.250	.000	.286	2	8	0	2	0	0	0	0	0	0	0	0	3	0	0	.250	.250
Tromp, Chadwick	R-R	5-9	180	3-21-95	.311	.214	.341	33	119	11	37	9	0	1	24	8	1	1	3	23	0	0	.412	.351
Vasquez, James	L-L	6-0	220	11-8-92	.274	.292	.267	64	226	23	62	14	0	5	33	26	1	0	2	35	0	0	.403	.349
Veras, Josciel	R-R	5-8	175	12-7-92	.333	.400	.000	2	6	3	2	2	0	0	1	2	0	0	0	3	0	0	.667	.500

Pitching	B-T	HT	WT	DOB	W	L	ERA	G	GS	CG	SV	IP	H	R	ER	HR	BB	SO	AVG	vLH	vRH	K/9	BB/9
Armstrong, Mark	R-R	6-2	210	11-26-94	0	2	6.98	6	6	0	0	19	19	16	15	4	13	11	.271	.262	.286	5.12	6.05
Bautista, Wendolyn	R-R	6-0	185	3-27-93	2	8	4.49	19	19	0	0	108	114	58	54	7	33	68	.271	.282	.261	5.65	2.74
Bender, Joel	L-L	6-4	210	8-3-91	0	0	2.12	16	0	0	1	17	21	11	4	1	5	21	.280	.323	.250	11.12	2.65
Boyles, Ty	R-L	6-3	270	9-30-95	5	7	4.10	16	16	0	0	83	86	46	38	4	35	58	.261	.171	.287	6.26	3.78
Broussard, Geoff	R-R	6-0	185	9-21-90	0	0	0.00	4	0	0	3	6	5	0	0	0	2	7	.238	.000	.263	10.50	3.00
Crawford, Jonathon	R-R	6-2	205	11-1-91	0	10	5.65	22	22	1	0	88	93	70	55	11	79	44	.283	.323	.256	4.52	8.11
De Paula, Rafael	R-R	6-2	215	3-24-91	1	0	0.00	4	0	0	1	5	3	0	0	0	1	9	.188	.167	.200	17.36	1.93
Ehret, Jake	R-R	6-3	190	3-18-93	1	1	5.95	17	0	0	3	20	14	13	13	3	13	16	.200	.167	.225	7.32	5.95
Gutierrez, Vladimir	R-R	6-0	190	9-18-95	7	8	4.46	19	19	0	0	103	108	54	51	10	19	94	.267	.263	.270	8.21	1.66
Hendrix, Ryan	R-R	6-3	185	12-16-94	1	4	3.58	24	0	0	2	28	29	15	11	4	19	27	.266	.298	.242	8.78	6.18
Hunter, Brian	R-R	6-3	215	11-22-92	0	0	2.38	12	0	0	0	23	14	6	6	1	10	29	.175	.194	.159	11.51	3.97
Lopez, Jose	R-R	6-1	185	9-1-93	2	4	2.84	9	9	0	0	51	50	22	16	3	14	48	.262	.280	.255	8.53	2.49
Lugo, Sandy	R-R	6-0	170	3-26-94	4	6	5.32	42	0	0	0	64	51	43	38	5	40	82	.217	.256	.196	11.47	5.60
Martinez, Juan	L-L	6-2	175	7-15-92	3	3	4.08	40	2	1	0	82	84	39	37	4	26	61	.263	.250	.268	6.72	2.87
Ohanian, Sarkis	R-R	5-11	195	8-6-93	3	0	4.22	11	0	0	1	11	8	5	5	1	10	21	.205	.385	.115	17.72	8.44
Orewiler, Austin	R-R	6-2	220	5-18-93	5	4	3.58	41	0	0	0	78	71	41	31	7	32	71	.238	.290	.200	8.19	3.69
Ortiz, Braulio	R-R	6-7	253	12-20-91	0	0	0.00	4	0	0	0	4	2	0	0	0	8	3	.182	.000	.286	7.36	19.64
Paulson, Jake	R-R	6-7	210	2-17-92	4	4	4.13	40	3	0	0	89	99	49	41	4	17	87	.282	.321	.257	8.76	1.71
Quillen, Aaron	R-R	6-6	205	12-19-93	1	0	0.00	11	0	0	0	12	6	0	0	0	1	3	.154	.200	.125	2.19	0.73
Rainey, Tanner	R-R	6-2	235	12-25-92	2	2	3.80	39	0	0	9	45	21	19	19	4	22	77	.136	.208	.099	15.40	4.40
Reyes, Jesus	R-R	6-2	180	2-21-93	6	5	3.78	15	15	0	0	86	80	46	36	8	27	67	.250	.285	.219	7.04	2.84
Stock, Robert	L-R	6-1	200	11-21-89	1	3	2.52	16	0	0	2	25	18	7	7	1	8	25	.212	.304	.177	9.00	2.88
Strahan, Wyatt	R-R	6-3	220	4-18-93	2	6	3.84	14	14	0	0	73	71	36	31	4	14	56	.255	.277	.237	6.94	1.73
Varner, Seth	L-L	6-3	225	1-27-92	1	2	5.31	8	8	0	0	39	52	23	23	5	7	30	.329	.320	.333	6.92	1.62
Weiss, Zack	R-R	6-3	210	6-16-92	2	1	2.08	10	0	0	1	13	8	6	3	1	2	19	.178	.263	.115	13.15	1.38

Fielding

Catcher	PCT	G	PO	A	E	DP	PB
Boulware	.988	33	221	24	3	1	4
Butler	.000	1	0	0	0	0	0
Duarte	1.000	3	20	4	0	0	1
Okey	.987	82	627	83	9	4	5
Trees	1.000	2	17	4	0	0	2
Tromp	.986	15	120	16	2	1	1

First Base	PCT	G	PO	A	E	DP
Butler	1.000	18	106	9	0	9
Franklin	.966	7	49	8	2	5
LaValley	.991	61	561	21	5	58
Medina	1.000	9	39	1	0	2
Vasquez	.996	53	441	26	2	41

Second Base	PCT	G	PO	A	E	DP
Bell	.976	58	95	154	6	35
Butler	.913	8	16	26	4	8
Long	.970	62	108	183	9	47
Mardirosian	1.000	1	0	2	0	0
Ovalle	.917	6	6	16	2	1
Veras	1.000	1	2	8	0	1

Third Base	PCT	G	PO	A	E	DP
Butler	.966	18	12	45	2	6
Franklin	.000	1	0	0	0	0
Gonzalez	.927	54	41	98	11	11
LaValley	1.000	1	0	1	0	0
Ovalle	.917	4	3	8	1	2
Senzel	.947	60	47	132	10	16

Shortstop	PCT	G	PO	A	E	DP
Butler	.951	10	14	25	2	4
Gonzalez	.923	11	14	34	4	7
Ovalle	.000	1	0	0	0	0
Rodriguez	.967	115	143	325	16	66

Outfield	PCT	G	PO	A	E	DP
Bell	.000	1	0	0	0	0
Boulware	1.000	4	3	0	0	0
Butler	.983	35	57	1	1	1
Collymore	1.000	3	8	0	0	0
Crook	.986	36	66	5	1	2
Friedl	1.000	48	98	3	0	1
Mardirosian	.960	21	21	3	1	1
McElroy	1.000	5	11	0	0	0
Medina	.963	80	123	7	5	0
O'Grady	1.000	13	23	0	0	0
Okey	1.000	1	1	0	0	0
Piatnik	.985	82	187	7	3	0
Reynoso	.985	23	66	0	1	0
Sweet	.959	67	116	2	5	0
Vasquez	.000	1	0	0	0	0
Veras	1.000	1	1	0	0	0

DAYTON DRAGONS

LOW CLASS A

MIDWEST LEAGUE

Batting	B-T	HT	WT	DOB	AVG	vLH	vRH	G	AB	R	H	2B	3B	HR	RBI	BB	HBP	SH	SF	SO	SB	CS	SLG	OBP
Bell, Brantley	R-R	6-3	185	11-16-94	.240	.282	.222	63	229	25	55	13	1	2	32	21	3	0	3	72	15	5	.332	.309
Beltre, Michael	B-R	6-3	180	7-3-95	.238	.243	.237	117	407	51	97	14	6	3	36	49	2	7	0	89	9	9	.324	.323
Brown, Cassidy	R-R	6-3	215	7-21-94	.166	.191	.155	83	277	31	46	13	0	4	29	33	6	2	3	67	4	0	.256	.267
Collymore, Malik	R-R	6-0	195	4-29-95	.222	.188	.237	34	108	16	24	6	2	3	12	17	4	0	0	33	6	1	.398	.349
Franklin, Kevin	R-R	6-1	220	11-24-94	.205	.222	.192	14	44	3	9	1	0	1	5	2	1	0	0	9	0	0	.296	.255
Friedl, T.J.	L-L	5-10	170	8-14-95	.284	.238	.307	66	250	47	71	20	6	5	25	29	10	1	2	46	14	8	.472	.378
Gonzalez, Luis	R-R	6-0	175	7-28-94	.276	.244	.295	40	123	20	34	6	0	3	17	4	2	1	0	13	2	2	.398	.310
Lofstrom, Morgan	L-R	6-1	185	8-17-95	.300	.000	.375	3	10	1	3	0	0	0	0	1	0	0	0	2	0	0	.300	.364
Mardirosian, Shane	L-R	5-10	175	10-13-95	.188	.100	.215	27	85	8	16	3	1	1	10	7	3	0	0	27	3	1	.282	.274
Ovalle, Gabriel	R-B	6-2	170	12-10-94	.208	.083	.250	17	48	5	10	1	0	0	4	6	0	0	0	11	0	0	.229	.296
Piatnik, Mitch	B-R	6-0	170	9-12-94	.177	.182	.174	11	34	2	6	1	0	0	1	0	1	0	0	14	1	1	.206	.200
Rachal, Avain	R-R	6-0	195	2-11-94	.207	.182	.222	19	58	10	12	2	1	1	3	12	2	1	0	23	2	2	.328	.361
Rivero, Carlos	L-R	6-0	175	4-30-97	.180	.167	.183	38	122	15	22	6	0	0	6	16	0	6	1	49	3	0	.230	.273
Sansone, John	R-R	5-11	200	9-15-93	.216	.220	.214	107	375	54	81	22	1	13	59	48	14	1	7	128	3	1	.384	.322
Siri, Jose	R-R	6-2	175	7-22-95	.293	.305	.287	126	498	92	146	24	11	24	76	33	6	9	6	130	46	12	.530	.341
Sparks, Taylor	R-R	6-4	200	4-3-93	.226	.360	.192	33	124	16	28	5	1	7	22	12	5	0	0	47	0	0	.452	.319
Stephenson, Tyler	R-R	6-4	225	8-16-96	.278	.258	.288	80	295	39	82	22	0	6	50	44	4	0	5	58	2	1	.414	.374
Trammell, Taylor	L-L	6-2	195	9-13-97	.281	.264	.288	129	491	80	138	24	10	13	77	71	1	0	7	123	41	12	.450	.368
Trees, Mitch	R-R	6-2	200	7-18-95	.109	.000	.143	13	46	2	5	1	0	0	3	1	1	0	0	26	0	0	.130	.146
Vargas, Hector	R-R	6-2	170	1-27-95	.225	.217	.228	121	440	43	99	14	1	7	36	19	3	7	4	66	4	5	.309	.260
Vasquez, James	L-L	6-0	220	11-8-92	.236	.158	.247	46	161	21	38	10	0	5	26	15	3	0	3	23	0	1	.391	.308
Ventura, Randy	B-R	5-9	165	7-11-97	.276	.292	.272	26	105	22	29	8	1	1	10	11	0	1	1	20	9	2	.400	.342
Veras, Josciel	R-R	5-8	175	12-7-92	.250	.333	.200	2	8	0	2	0	0	0	0	0	0	0	0	1	0	0	.250	.250
White, Zeke	R-R	6-0	170	1-7-97	.000	.000	.000	1	5	0	0	0	0	0	0	0	0	0	0	0	0	0	.000	.000
Yari, Bruce	L-L	6-3	224	12-9-94	.252	.267	.246	88	329	46	83	17	0	13	54	41	1	0	3	98	2	0	.423	.334

Pitching	B-T	HT	WT	DOB	W	L	ERA	G	GS	CG	SV	IP	H	R	ER	HR	BB	SO	AVG	vLH	vRH	K/9	BB/9
Adams, Jesse	L-L	6-0	190	8-12-93	5	2	2.44	43	0	0	6	70	50	21	19	6	11	83	.201	.138	.239	10.67	1.41
Bailey, Homer	R-R	6-4	223	5-3-86	1	0	0.00	1	1	0	0	6	1	0	0	0	0	6	.053	.100	.000	9.00	0.00
Benenati, Lucas	R-R	6-2	215	5-27-93	1	1	6.75	19	0	0	0	29	35	23	22	6	6	27	.285	.286	.284	8.28	1.84
Blandino, Matt	R-R	6-1	180	7-30-95	4	4	5.48	14	12	0	0	66	88	47	40	5	8	40	.320	.366	.283	5.48	1.10
Boyles, Ty	R-L	6-3	270	9-30-95	5	2	3.99	10	10	1	0	56	59	26	25	6	10	40	.272	.205	.313	6.39	1.60
Cingrani, Tony	L-L	6-4	214	7-5-89	0	0	0.00	1	1	0	0	1	0	0	0	0	1	0	.000	.000	.000	0.00	9.00
Cox, Andy	R-L	6-2	185	10-23-93	3	1	1.64	22	0	0	3	22	18	4	4	0	11	33	.217	.231	.205	13.50	4.50
DeSclafani, Anthony	R-R	6-1	195	4-18-90	0	1	16.62	2	2	0	0	4	10	8	8	3	0	6	.435	.546	.333	12.46	0.00
Fossas, Aaron	R-R	6-2	200	9-2-92	4	1	2.43	44	0	0	6	67	61	20	18	1	16	49	.246	.265	.224	6.62	2.16
Hendrix, Ryan	R-R	6-3	185	12-16-94	4	1	2.36	23	0	0	6	34	19	11	9	2	10	61	.161	.132	.185	15.99	2.62
Hunter, Brian	R-R	6-3	215	11-22-92	0	0	3.00	5	0	0	4	6	5	3	2	0	1	8	.238	.167	.267	12.00	1.50
Jordan, Andrew	R-R	6-3	180	8-3-97	7	8	4.66	25	25	0	0	131	121	74	68	17	37	113	.245	.300	.195	7.74	2.54
Kuhnel, Joel	R-R	6-5	260	2-19-95	2	4	4.36	48	0	0	11	64	78	37	31	6	10	54	.296	.305	.288	7.59	1.41
Lugo, Sandy	R-R	6-0	170	3-26-94	0	1	1.59	2	0	0	0	6	4	2	1	1	2	6	.200	.273	.111	9.53	3.18
Machorro, Carlos	R-R	6-2	175	9-20-96	2	3	2.29	29	0	0	1	51	33	17	13	1	20	43	.177	.210	.140	7.59	3.53
Mena, Alfredo	R-R	6-3	205	12-6-93	0	0	6.52	7	0	0	0	10	14	8	7	0	7	13	.318	.333	.300	12.10	6.52
Moreta, Dauri	R-R	6-2	185	4-15-96	1	2	4.94	19	0	0	0	27	18	15	15	4	9	37	.186	.265	.104	12.18	2.96
Moss, Scott	L-L	6-5	215	10-6-94	13	6	3.45	26	26	0	0	136	114	62	52	11	48	156	.224	.217	.227	10.35	3.18
Nova, Moises	R-R	6-3	190	8-2-95	0	1	4.86	8	0	0	1	17	14	11	9	2	9	18	.219	.258	.182	9.72	4.86
Olson, Ryan	R-R	6-2	195	11-22-94	2	2	4.18	4	4	1	0	24	24	13	11	1	4	18	.270	.237	.333	6.85	1.52
Quillen, Aaron	R-R	6-6	205	12-19-93	0	0	11.25	1	0	0	0	4	8	5	5	1	2	1	.444	.000	.667	2.25	4.50
Riehl, Patrick	R-R	6-5	230	5-19-94	1	2	6.75	25	0	0	1	29	25	24	22	1	26	28	.232	.278	.185	8.59	7.98
Romero, Wennington	L-L	5-11	175	1-29-98	5	10	5.10	26	26	1	0	136	153	82	77	17	30	126	.284	.296	.278	8.34	1.99
Santillan, Tony	R-R	6-3	240	4-15-97	9	8	3.38	25	24	0	0	128	104	57	48	9	56	128	.222	.238	.203	9.00	3.94
Stallings, Jesse	R-R	6-2	198	10-27-94	1	4	4.57	45	0	0	1	63	70	37	32	5	21	39	.273	.283	.265	5.57	3.00
Webb, Alex	R-R	6-3	210	7-19-94	1	4	4.84	12	7	0	2	48	50	28	26	6	13	40	.262	.221	.302	7.45	2.42
Wotell, Max	R-L	6-3	190	9-13-96	0	1	8.10	2	2	0	0	7	10	6	6	2	5	7	.357	.500	.318	9.45	6.75

Fielding

Catcher	PCT	G	PO	A	E	DP	PB
Brown	.991	74	594	59	6	4	3
Lofstrom	1.000	3	15	1	0	0	0
Stephenson	.988	53	448	34	6	3	7
Trees	.985	13	110	20	2	3	4

First Base	PCT	G	PO	A	E	DP
Franklin	.974	5	33	4	1	2
Rachal	.984	17	119	8	2	16
Sansone	.976	6	40	1	1	1
Vasquez	.982	39	298	26	6	21
Yari	.993	77	555	38	4	34

Second Base	PCT	G	PO	A	E	DP
Bell	1.000	61	79	157	0	30
Collymore	.933	14	19	23	3	4
Gonzalez	.941	9	14	18	2	5
Mardirosian	.947	17	29	25	3	4
Ovalle	1.000	10	18	23	0	7
Sansone	.978	10	19	26	1	7
Vargas	.933	23	30	54	6	9

Third Base	PCT	G	PO	A	E	DP
Bell	.000	1	0	0	0	0
Franklin	.000	2	0	0	0	0
Gonzalez	1.000	10	5	13	0	1
Mardirosian	1.000	1	0	1	0	0
Ovalle	1.000	4	2	4	0	0
Sansone	.934	87	57	128	13	8
Sparks	.926	31	25	38	5	1
Vargas	.967	8	7	22	1	2
Veras	1.000	1	1	1	0	0

Shortstop	PCT	G	PO	A	E	DP
Gonzalez	.971	19	21	45	2	9
Ovalle	.833	2	3	2	1	1
Rivero	.963	38	44	86	5	11
Vargas	.939	87	126	181	20	41

Outfield	PCT	G	PO	A	E	DP
Beltre	.982	98	210	10	4	2
Collymore	.800	3	3	1	1	0
Franklin	1.000	2	2	0	0	0
Friedl	.974	55	110	1	3	0
Gonzalez	1.000	2	2	0	0	0
Mardirosian	1.000	1	1	0	0	0
Piatnik	1.000	10	18	0	0	0
Rachal	1.000	1	1	0	0	0
Sansone	.000	1	0	0	0	0
Siri	.973	112	310	10	9	2
Trammell	.988	118	239	3	3	2
Ventura	.931	24	53	1	4	0
White	1.000	1	7	0	0	0

BILLINGS MUSTANGS — *ROOKIE*

PIONEER LEAGUE

Batting	B-T	HT	WT	DOB	AVG	vLH	vRH	G	AB	R	H	2B	3B	HR	RBI	BB	HBP	SH	SF	SO	SB	CS	SLG	OBP
Azcona, Francis	B-R	5-10	155	11-20-95	.163	.000	.180	16	43	6	7	0	0	1	4	8	0	0	0	10	2	1	.233	.294
Clementina, Hendrik	R-R	6-0	165	6-17-97	.240	.310	.209	27	96	13	23	6	0	2	10	7	2	0	1	25	0	0	.365	.302
2-team total (24 Ogden)					.303	.310	.209	51	188	30	57	11	0	6	35	17	5	1	3	41	0	0	.457	.371
Cruz, Manny	R-R	5-11	170	8-21-95	.000	—	.000	1	2	0	0	0	0	0	0	1	1	0	0	0	0	0	.000	.500
Downs, Jeter	R-R	5-11	180	7-27-98	.267	.244	.275	50	172	31	46	3	3	6	29	27	4	1	5	32	8	5	.424	.370
Fairchild, Stuart	R-R	6-0	190	3-17-96	.304	.326	.298	56	204	36	62	5	4	3	23	19	11	0	0	35	12	4	.412	.393
Gordon, Miles	L-R	6-1	175	12-3-97	.319	.308	.321	61	232	40	74	15	5	8	37	27	1	1	2	55	7	3	.530	.389
Greene, Hunter	R-R	6-4	197	8-6-99	.233	.250	.227	7	30	1	7	2	1	0	3	0	0	0	0	8	0	0	.367	.233
Juaquin, Urwin	R-R	6-0	140	12-29-97	.205	.167	.212	17	39	5	8	0	0	0	2	4	0	0	1	12	0	1	.205	.273
Kolozsvary, Mark	R-R	5-8	180	9-4-95	.305	.286	.313	28	95	19	29	7	0	1	15	8	1	0	1	30	1	0	.411	.362
Ljatifi, Nadir	R-R	5-10	170	2-21-98	.246	.100	.306	28	69	9	17	3	1	2	12	7	1	0	2	18	1	0	.406	.317
Lofstrom, Morgan	L-R	6-1	185	8-17-95	.202	.125	.211	25	84	13	17	3	0	1	12	7	1	2	1	25	1	0	.274	.269
Lopez, Alejo	B-R	5-10	170	5-5-96	.300	.250	.313	67	220	49	66	10	6	4	33	30	6	6	7	28	11	4	.455	.388
Manzanero, Pabel	R-R	6-3	170	1-30-96	.242	.133	.290	30	99	13	24	6	0	3	16	3	2	0	0	22	0	0	.394	.279
Marshall, Montrell	R-R	6-5	215	4-2-96	.269	.235	.279	61	223	33	60	16	2	7	39	21	0	0	2	55	2	0	.453	.329
McElroy, Satchel	R-R	5-10	170	8-13-96	.237	.263	.231	29	97	23	23	1	2	2	5	9	3	2	0	14	6	2	.351	.321
Rivero, Carlos	L-R	6-0	175	4-30-97	.250	.462	.206	21	76	11	19	2	0	0	9	4	0	0	0	19	5	0	.276	.288
Salmon-Williams, J.D.	R-R	5-11	190	3-21-97	.225	.259	.211	35	98	19	22	2	0	4	11	8	2	0	0	19	4	0	.367	.296
Santana, Leandro	R-R	6-2	175	2-19-97	.281	.259	.287	67	246	38	69	6	2	11	43	22	3	0	0	70	1	1	.455	.347
Sugilio, Andy	B-R	6-2	170	10-26-96	.345	.347	.344	62	235	45	81	13	4	3	40	17	1	0	1	33	20	4	.472	.390
Trees, Mitch	R-R	6-2	200	7-18-95	.300	.500	.290	11	40	4	12	4	0	3	9	1	1	0	0	13	0	0	.625	.333
Turnbull, Jake	L-R	6-1	190	2-16-98	.200	.300	.189	36	100	8	20	2	1	2	13	6	0	0	0	41	1	0	.300	.245

Batting	B-T	HT	WT	DOB	AVG	vLH	vRH	G	AB	R	H	2B	3B	HR	RBI	BB	HBP	SH	SF	SO	SB	CS	SLG	OBP
Wallace, Raul	R-R	6-2	180	8-19-95	.286	.364	.250	11	35	8	10	4	0	1	5	2	2	0	0	10	2	0	.486	.359
White, Zeke	R-R	6-0	170	1-7-97	.206	.160	.221	41	102	17	21	3	2	2	11	14	1	1	1	39	8	2	.333	.305

Pitching	B-T	HT	WT	DOB	W	L	ERA	G	GS	CG	SV	IP	H	R	ER	HR	BB	SO	AVG	vLH	vRH	K/9	BB/9
Aguilar, Miguel	R-R	6-0	180	7-25-95	3	2	4.43	20	0	0	0	43	46	27	21	2	20	36	.271	.228	.292	7.59	4.22
Alecis, Luis	R-R	6-3	190	6-7-97	6	6	5.11	16	11	0	0	62	54	38	35	4	39	61	.241	.261	.228	8.90	5.69
Benenati, Lucas	R-R	6-2	215	5-27-93	1	0	2.25	6	0	0	0	8	7	3	2	0	5	10	.226	.250	.211	11.25	5.63
Bennett, Connor	R-R	5-9	190	4-10-97	0	1	3.20	22	0	0	0	39	27	15	14	4	23	62	.192	.214	.177	14.19	5.26
Blandino, Matt	R-R	6-1	180	7-30-95	3	0	3.27	4	4	0	0	22	24	9	8	2	2	14	.267	.270	.264	5.73	0.82
Buffett, Tyler	R-R	6-1	195	5-22-95	4	2	3.86	22	0	0	3	44	49	24	19	0	11	34	.285	.268	.293	6.90	2.23
Correll, Zac	R-R	6-6	230	1-28-96	3	0	4.34	9	0	0	0	19	18	12	9	0	10	19	.234	.276	.208	9.16	4.82
De Jesus, Jhon	R-R	6-4	180	1-9-97	2	4	5.79	15	15	0	0	61	62	42	39	7	30	58	.267	.278	.259	8.60	4.45
Escoboza, Edward	R-R	6-5	185	12-5-95	0	0	27.00	1	0	0	0	2	6	5	5	1	1	1	.546	1.000	.375	5.40	5.40
Ghyzel, John	R-R	6-5	200	5-18-96	0	0	9.26	8	0	0	0	12	16	17	12	1	6	11	.308	.318	.300	8.49	4.63
Heatherly, Jacob	L-L	6-2	208	5-20-98	0	1	12.00	3	3	0	0	9	17	12	12	0	4	5	.405	.500	.382	5.00	4.00
McKirahan, Andrew	R-L	6-2	200	2-8-90	0	0	6.75	4	0	0	0	5	9	4	4	2	2	10	.360	.200	.400	16.88	3.38
Mena, Alfredo	R-R	6-3	205	12-6-93	1	0	6.00	4	0	0	1	9	9	7	6	3	5	10	.250	.214	.273	10.00	5.00
Mondile, Tyler	L-R	6-1	190	11-4-97	4	4	4.35	15	12	0	0	68	82	40	33	4	23	48	.296	.337	.277	6.32	3.03
Moreta, Dauri	R-R	6-2	185	4-15-96	0	0	0.00	4	0	0	0	4	3	0	0	0	4	8	.200	.500	.091	18.00	9.00
Naughton, Packy	R-L	6-2	195	4-16-96	3	3	3.15	14	12	0	0	60	58	24	21	5	20	63	.256	.263	.253	9.45	3.00
Nova, Moises	R-R	6-3	190	8-2-95	1	1	3.13	12	1	0	1	32	22	12	11	0	12	36	.200	.242	.182	10.23	3.41
Nutof, Ryan	L-R	6-2	190	11-2-95	0	2	4.08	21	0	0	1	29	35	22	13	1	14	30	.294	.270	.305	9.42	4.40
Quillen, Aaron	R-R	6-6	205	12-19-93	1	0	8.74	5	2	0	0	11	21	13	11	1	3	6	.375	.364	.378	4.76	2.38
Reinoso, Gregory	L-L	6-1	170	11-17-95	1	0	9.95	10	0	0	0	13	18	15	14	2	11	10	.346	.286	.387	7.11	7.82
Ryan, Connor	R-R	6-1	180	11-20-94	0	4	4.71	18	0	0	8	21	19	11	11	0	8	23	.232	.280	.211	9.86	3.43
Santos, Yerry	R-R	6-4	180	11-30-94	0	1	11.00	10	0	0	0	9	8	11	11	2	19	11	.222	.182	.240	11.00	19.00
Sceroler, Mac	R-R	6-3	200	4-9-95	0	4	3.26	12	9	0	0	39	37	25	14	3	16	44	.240	.280	.221	10.24	3.72
Smith, Ricardo	R-R	6-2	175	2-16-96	0	0	4.50	1	1	0	0	4	4	2	2	0	3	4	.267	.000	.286	9.00	6.75
Thompson, Cory	R-R	5-11	180	9-23-94	3	1	3.62	21	0	0	1	32	29	13	13	3	18	32	.238	.239	.237	8.91	5.01
Wotell, Max	R-L	6-3	190	9-13-96	0	2	10.13	3	3	0	0	11	15	14	12	3	9	4	.349	.250	.359	3.38	7.59

Fielding

C: Clementina 16, Kolozsvary 24, Lofstrom 15, Manzanero 17, Trees 9. **1B:** Lofstrom 1, Manzanero 6, Marshall 60, Turnbull 19. **2B:** Azcona 11, Cruz 1, Juaquin 4, Ljatifi 18, Lopez 47, Rivero 5, Salmon-Williams 2, Santana 3. **3B:** Ljatifi 3, Lopez 17, Santana 60, Turnbull 2. **SS:** Azcona 3, Downs 50, Juaquin 13, Ljatifi 1, Lopez 2, Rivero 14. **OF:** Fairchild 51, Gordon 55, McElroy 28, Salmon-Williams 20, Sugilio 56, Wallace 10, White 33.

AZL REDS — *ROOKIE*

ARIZONA LEAGUE

Batting	B-T	HT	WT	DOB	AVG	vLH	vRH	G	AB	R	H	2B	3B	HR	RBI	BB	HBP	SH	SF	SO	SB	CS	SLG	OBP
Abreu, Hidekel	R-R	5-10	155	10-30-97	.500	—	.500	2	2	1	1	0	0	0	1	0	0	0	0	0	0	0	.500	.500
Bautista, Mariel	R-R	6-3	170	10-15-97	.320	.371	.304	36	147	29	47	9	1	0	20	5	3	1	1	24	16	1	.395	.353
Bellinger, Justin	L-L	6-6	230	8-18-95	.282	.417	.250	34	124	20	35	8	0	4	26	16	1	1	0	39	0	0	.444	.369
Case, Cash	L-R	6-1	190	5-12-99	.181	.200	.175	34	133	18	24	2	0	2	12	17	0	0	0	28	2	3	.241	.273
Conde, Mauro	R-R	6-0	20	6-1-97	.136	.286	.108	16	44	6	6	1	0	1	4	7	5	2	0	22	2	1	.227	.321
Hernandez, Miguel	R-R	6-0	170	4-13-99	.314	.320	.313	32	140	20	44	4	3	1	12	4	1	0	0	18	1	1	.407	.338
Juaquin, Urwin	R-R	6-0	140	12-29-97	.211	.211	.212	19	71	12	15	1	0	1	9	3	2	2	1	13	0	1	.268	.260
Juarez, Raul	R-R	6-1	165	5-21-98	.278	.300	.274	35	115	12	32	3	0	0	14	6	4	0	2	22	2	2	.304	.331
Liberatore, Ernesto	R-R	6-0	180	3-26-96	.238	.083	.275	21	63	9	15	2	0	1	5	9	1	0	0	16	0	0	.318	.343
Martinez, Juan	R-R	6-0	179	11-8-98	.220	.177	.234	40	141	25	31	10	1	0	19	13	9	0	1	43	2	1	.305	.323
Martinez, Valentin	R-R	6-0	175	9-21-96	.292	.389	.259	22	72	9	21	4	2	1	14	5	3	0	1	20	0	1	.444	.358
Munroe, Reshard	L-L	6-0	170	6-15-96	.290	.136	.324	36	124	31	36	5	1	3	15	22	1	1	0	28	6	3	.419	.401
Ozuna, Reniel	R-R	6-2	180	7-29-98	.288	.182	.329	35	118	14	34	7	3	0	14	11	1	0	1	30	8	2	.398	.351
Paulino, Alejandro	R-R	6-0	150	11-23-96	.256	.333	.233	24	78	16	20	8	1	0	8	6	0	0	0	16	2	2	.385	.310
Perez, Juan	L-R	5-11	185	11-1-91	.125	.000	.250	3	8	1	1	1	0	0	0	1	0	0	0	2	0	1	.250	.222
Reyes, Ermys	R-B	5-11	178	8-13-96	.308	1.000	.250	6	13	2	4	0	0	0	0	5	1	0	0	2	1	1	.308	.526
Reynoso, Jonathan	R-R	6-3	177	1-7-93	.393	.625	.300	7	28	6	11	1	0	1	1	4	0	0	0	3	5	3	.536	.469
Ruiz, Victor	R-R	6-1	190	10-20-99	.244	.100	.265	22	78	8	19	4	1	0	11	1	0	0	1	22	0	0	.321	.250
Scantlin, Nathaniel	L-R	6-1	180	2-17-99	.170	.000	.182	17	47	3	8	0	0	0	2	2	3	0	0	18	1	2	.170	.250
Sparks, Taylor	R-R	6-4	200	4-3-93	.250	.333	.235	6	20	2	5	2	0	1	3	3	1	0	0	5	0	0	.500	.375
Wallace, Raul	R-R	6-2	180	8-19-95	.281	.194	.309	33	128	13	36	7	6	0	16	4	1	0	3	44	9	0	.430	.302
Wiggins, Blake	R-R	6-1	195	3-1-96	.267	.091	.324	12	45	5	12	3	0	0	4	2	2	0	1	14	0	0	.333	.320
Willems, Jonathan	R-R	5-11	180	11-7-98	.234	.000	.259	23	64	7	15	3	0	0	4	2	3	0	0	19	7	2	.281	.290
Yon, Edwin	R-R	6-5	180	7-24-98	.165	.125	.174	24	85	6	14	2	2	0	13	8	1	0	2	44	0	0	.235	.240

Pitching	B-T	HT	WT	DOB	W	L	ERA	G	GS	CG	SV	IP	H	R	ER	HR	BB	SO	AVG	vLH	vRH	K/9	BB/9
Anesty, Isaac	L-L	6-2	190	6-6-97	0	2	7.13	18	0	0	0	18	19	20	14	1	14	14	.268	.389	.226	7.13	7.13
Astin, Barrett	R-R	6-1	225	10-22-91	0	0	0.00	3	2	0	0	4	2	0	0	0	0	4	.143	.125	.167	9.00	0.00
Bender, Joel	L-L	6-4	210	8-3-91	0	1	6.00	3	1	0	0	3	5	2	2	0	1	5	.357	.000	.417	15.00	3.00
Castillo, Jose	R-R	6-4	190	6-10-96	0	6	6.45	12	8	0	1	45	55	40	32	2	22	36	.302	.276	.321	7.25	4.43
Chacon, Adrian	R-R	6-0	205	3-8-95	1	2	6.46	13	1	0	0	15	20	16	11	0	9	20	.308	.333	.296	11.74	5.28
Correll, Zac	R-R	6-6	230	1-28-96	1	0	2.08	3	1	0	0	9	9	2	2	0	3	15	.265	.300	.250	15.58	3.12
Davis, Rookie	R-R	6-5	255	4-29-93	0	1	1.93	2	2	0	0	9	5	3	2	1	2	10	.161	.111	.182	9.64	1.93
DeLeon, Anderson	R-R	5-7	150	7-27-96	0	0	0.00	1	0	0	0	1	0	0	0	0	0	2	.000	.000	.000	18.00	0.00
DeSclafani, Anthony	R-R	6-1	195	4-18-90	0	0	7.71	1	1	0	0	2	3	3	2	0	1	3	.273	.000	.375	11.57	3.86
Diaz, Alexis	R-R	6-2	170	9-28-96	2	3	4.94	13	4	0	0	31	31	21	17	2	13	40	.248	.256	.244	11.61	3.77

Escoboza, Edward	R-R	6-5	185	12-5-95	2	0	4.33	14	1	0	1	44	40	22	21	4	9	59	.238	.179	.277	12.16	1.85
Ghyzel, John	R-R	6-5	200	5-18-96	1	0	1.74	9	0	0	3	10	7	4	2	0	3	15	.189	.231	.167	13.06	2.61
Harding, Junior	R-R	5-9	180	7-21-96	0	4	6.52	18	0	0	2	19	22	17	14	0	16	28	.297	.308	.292	13.03	7.45
Heatherly, Jacob	L-L	6-2	208	5-20-98	2	1	2.93	9	6	0	0	31	26	13	10	3	16	26	.224	.286	.205	7.63	4.70
Jones, Francis	R-R	6-4	200	12-6-96	3	1	6.48	16	0	0	0	33	42	30	24	2	19	33	.300	.271	.315	8.91	5.13
Karcher, Ricky	L-R	6-4	195	9-18-97	0	3	10.67	7	4	0	0	14	18	20	17	1	13	14	.295	.222	.353	8.79	8.16
Keller, Stephen	B-R	6-2	210	11-19-97	0	0	2.89	11	0	0	0	19	14	7	6	0	9	22	.212	.185	.231	10.61	4.34
McKirahan, Andrew	R-L	6-2	200	2-8-90	0	0	0.00	1	0	0	0	1	0	0	0	0	1	2	.000	.000	.000	18.00	9.00
Mitchell, Evan	R-R	6-2	185	3-18-92	0	0	1.59	5	1	0	0	6	5	2	1	0	2	3	.250	.333	.182	4.76	3.18
Ogando, Nefi	R-R	6-0	230	6-3-89	0	2	6.00	3	3	0	0	3	4	3	2	0	1	3	.286	.200	.333	9.00	3.00
Perez, Alexander	R-R	6-3	195	4-23-95	2	0	5.40	16	0	0	0	22	23	15	13	1	12	21	.274	.242	.294	8.72	4.98
Reinoso, Gregory	L-L	6-1	170	11-17-95	1	0	7.56	10	0	0	1	17	17	14	14	2	11	14	.270	.133	.313	7.56	5.94
Routt, Nick	L-L	6-4	215	8-28-90	0	0	7.36	3	2	0	0	4	4	3	3	0	0	4	.267	.250	.273	9.82	0.00
Santos, Yerry	R-R	6-4	180	11-30-94	0	1	18.00	6	0	0	0	4	7	9	8	0	7	7	.368	.444	.300	15.75	15.75
Shred, Darren	R-R	6-3	200	10-13-97	1	0	0.00	4	0	0	0	4	1	0	0	0	6	0	.083	.000	.111	0.00	14.73
Smith, Ricardo	R-R	6-2	175	2-16-96	4	4	3.33	13	6	0	0	54	63	34	20	2	17	61	.280	.247	.296	10.17	2.83
Solomon, Jared	R-R	6-2	180	6-10-97	2	2	4.26	11	6	0	0	38	39	21	18	2	16	43	.260	.277	.252	10.18	3.79
Varner, Seth	L-L	6-3	225	1-27-92	0	0	1.50	3	3	0	0	6	4	1	1	1	0	10	.174	.000	.200	15.00	0.00
Webb, Alex	R-R	6-3	210	7-19-94	0	0	3.52	3	3	0	0	8	7	6	3	1	2	9	.226	.429	.167	10.57	2.35

Fielding

C: Liberatore 18, Martinez 21, Ruiz 22. **1B:** Bellinger 15, Juarez 29, Liberatore 3, Paulino 1, Wiggins 11. **2B:** Abreu 1, Case 29, Juarez 1, Paulino 15, Reyes 5, Willems 9. **3B:** Juarez 5, Martinez 38, Paulino 3, Sparks 6, Willems 8. **SS:** Hernandez 32, Juaquin 19, Paulino 5, Perez 2, Willems 2. **OF:** Bautista 35, Conde 13, Munroe 32, Ozuna 33, Reynoso 4, Scantlin 14, Wallace 28, Yon 13.

DSL REDS — ROOKIE

DOMINICAN SUMMER LEAGUE

Batting	B-T	HT	WT	DOB	AVG	vLH	vRH	G	AB	R	H	2B	3B	HR	RBI	BB	HBP	SH	SF	SO	SB	CS	SLG	OBP
Abreu, Felix	R-R	6-1	180	12-26-97	.275	.200	.290	51	182	25	50	5	2	0	18	12	7	3	1	33	6	4	.324	.342
Aleixo, Axel	L-L	6-1	172	9-11-99	.233	.231	.234	56	193	28	45	4	3	3	19	34	2	0	4	27	8	4	.332	.348
Amador, Ranser	R-R	6-2	165	3-15-99	.210	.216	.208	55	167	18	35	5	1	1	11	16	2	2	1	48	8	2	.270	.285
Castro, Fidel	L-R	6-3	175	12-26-98	.216	.077	.333	48	139	16	30	8	1	1	22	17	2	0	1	43	3	2	.309	.308
Cuevas, Abel	R-R	6-0	180	9-13-96	.273	.229	.289	56	183	33	50	4	0	0	17	33	2	0	0	31	13	7	.295	.390
Diaz, Giovanni	R-R	6-1	150	5-5-99	.228	.192	.237	39	123	13	28	6	0	1	13	15	3	3	2	33	4	0	.301	.322
Finol, Claudio	R-R	5-11	150	4-13-00	.300	.298	.301	58	200	35	60	10	4	1	21	23	4	3	2	19	6	4	.405	.380
Gomez, Elvis	R-R	6-0	170	5-27-99	.238	.217	.244	35	101	12	24	3	0	0	5	8	4	0	0	11	1	1	.267	.319
Gonzalez, Victor	R-R	6-1	185	4-6-99	.200	.000	.250	9	20	3	4	1	0	0	2	5	1	0	0	1	1	0	.250	.385
Graterol, Jean	R-R	5-11	155	1-1-99	.287	.368	.275	45	136	18	39	8	3	2	27	10	2	0	3	39	6	2	.434	.338
Hernandez, Miguel	R-R	6-0	170	4-13-99	.285	.357	.268	37	151	31	43	10	2	1	18	11	2	1	2	24	9	3	.397	.337
Lantigua, Danny	B-R	6-1	165	3-7-99	.200	.200	.200	17	60	6	12	3	2	0	7	4	0	0	0	22	1	0	.317	.250
Lozano, Deybert	L-R	6-1	165	11-15-99	.217	.200	.257	36	120	17	26	4	0	0	3	13	2	2	0	23	5	6	.250	.304
Melo, Junior	R-R	6-2	175	5-10-97	.289	.269	.297	28	90	11	26	4	1	0	6	6	1	2	0	11	0	3	.356	.340
Nava, William	R-R	6-1	180	5-20-98	.164	.235	.143	33	73	9	12	0	1	0	5	1	0	2	1	16	3	1	.192	.173
Olivo, Cristian	L-L	6-2	170	9-30-98	.251	.136	.285	54	195	23	49	10	4	3	24	10	4	2	2	51	7	3	.390	.299
Ortiz, Leonardo	R-R	6-1	198	3-30-97	.296	.231	.314	57	176	21	52	14	1	2	23	16	8	2	1	23	1	0	.421	.378
Palacios, Aiverson	B-R	6-0	150	4-13-00	.148	.077	.171	43	108	8	16	3	1	0	8	12	1	2	2	59	2	5	.194	.236
Plaz, Peterson	L-L	5-10	155	3-6-99	.316	.227	.301	53	190	34	60	4	1	0	15	25	1	2	2	19	13	6	.347	.395
Reina, Carlos	B-R	6-0	175	12-11-98	.324	.286	.333	46	139	27	45	6	2	1	20	17	0	0	3	24	3	2	.417	.390
Remy, Danielito	R-R	6-1	170	5-5-98	.249	.250	.249	60	225	32	56	5	9	3	25	12	3	0	2	70	18	4	.391	.293
Reyes, Ermys	R-B	5-11	178	8-13-96	.178	.231	.149	29	73	14	13	1	1	0	6	9	3	2	1	24	4	2	.219	.291
Reyes, Reyny	R-R	6-2	185	3-20-99	.240	.103	.272	59	208	29	50	9	0	2	19	16	5	2	2	23	9	2	.313	.307
Rijo, Jeison	R-R	6-0	165	10-14-99	.310	.389	.297	42	129	17	40	14	0	2	20	12	5	1	0	25	2	1	.465	.390
Rivas, Moises	R-R	6-1	175	11-18-98	.133	.056	.150	36	98	10	13	2	2	2	11	9	1	1	0	49	7	0	.255	.213
Santana, Debby	R-R	6-2	185	8-24-00	.302	.297	.304	49	172	26	52	17	1	2	23	13	2	0	1	45	5	2	.448	.356
Sencion, Jorge	R-R	6-4	194	10-3-98	.178	.200	.174	37	118	10	21	6	0	2	13	4	5	0	0	55	2	1	.280	.236
Sequera, Jorge	R-R	6-0	175	3-20-99	.269	.444	.228	44	108	17	29	5	1	1	17	17	4	0	0	12	4	4	.361	.388
Silverio, Isaias	R-R	6-2	185	2-18-00	.262	.281	.220	59	202	39	53	18	1	5	40	25	9	0	2	52	4	1	.436	.366
Soto, Mario	B-R	5-10	162	2-12-98	.200	.243	.200	.344	38	107	15	26	4	2	1	11	8	0	2	4	25	54	.346	.286
Soto, Ronard	R-R	6-2	185	5-18-99	.212	.300	.191	46	156	22	33	7	0	3	27	11	11	0	0	57	2	2	.314	.309
Tello, Jose	R-R	6-0	170	5-21-98	.268	.289	.263	61	224	36	60	10	0	6	35	15	3	1	4	30	3	4	.393	.317

Pitching	B-T	HT	WT	DOB	W	L	ERA	G	GS	CG	SV	IP	H	R	ER	HR	BB	SO	AVG	vLH	vRH	K/9	BB/9
Abril, Juan Manuel	R-R	6-0	160	3-11-98	8	1	2.21	18	0	0	3	41	20	14	10	0	28	35	.152	.077	.183	7.75	6.20
Aranguren, Frainger	R-R	6-2	190	3-17-97	6	2	2.15	15	0	0	0	38	37	16	9	0	14	33	.250	.354	.200	7.88	3.35
Berroa, Samuel	R-R	6-7	200	10-12-98	0	2	9.49	16	2	0	1	30	32	34	32	1	35	12	.274	.289	.264	3.56	10.38
Cachutt, Manuel	R-R	6-0	185	6-7-97	4	1	2.00	14	8	0	1	54	37	19	12	1	15	49	.195	.123	.239	8.17	2.50
Carreno, Carlos	R-R	6-2	174	9-4-98	7	3	2.56	14	14	0	0	70	55	23	20	0	18	65	.218	.274	.199	8.32	2.30
Castillo, Jose	R-R	6-4	190	6-10-96	0	0	4.32	4	0	0	1	8	7	4	4	0	3	6	.241	.231	.250	6.48	3.24
Centeno, Jaccen	L-L	5-11	170	7-3-99	3	4	3.07	14	11	0	0	56	35	20	19	3	23	37	.183	.225	.172	5.98	3.72
Conoropo, Omar	B-L	5-10	165	5-27-98	2	5	3.38	13	13	1	0	64	78	34	24	5	14	56	.308	.366	.297	7.88	1.97
Cuevas, Andry	R-R	6-4	185	8-4-98	1	3	4.30	12	5	0	0	38	23	21	18	2	23	43	.173	.158	.184	10.27	5.50
Diaz, Yoel	R-R	6-1	190	1-9-99	2	1	5.90	14	0	0	3	29	25	22	19	3	19	24	.236	.750	.125	7.45	5.90
Escoboza, Edward	R-R	6-5	185	12-5-95	1	0	0.00	4	0	0	0	12	4	1	0	0	5	16	.108	.091	.115	12.34	3.86
German, Uarlim	R-R	6-5	215	8-2-96	2	3	3.38	19	0	0	3	37	22	17	14	1	24	29	.172	.167	.174	6.99	5.79
Hernandez, Raul	R-R	6-3	190	2-2-99	2	0	8.55	15	0	0	1	20	18	21	19	1	16	29	.234	.333	.180	13.05	7.20

Lantigua, Israel	R-R	6-3	190	2-9-99	0	0	6.62	12	0	0	0	18	14	15	13	3	19	13	.215	.188	.225	6.62	9.68
Mallen, Jorge	R-R	6-0	160	4-5-98	1	2	4.35	20	0	0	7	31	21	20	15	0	18	37	.194	.263	.157	10.74	5.23
Manuel, Maiker	R-R	6-2	175	7-29-98	3	3	5.63	15	8	0	0	46	49	32	29	3	25	37	.285	.259	.298	7.19	4.86
Mateo, Marvin	R-R	6-3	170	1-8-98	1	6	3.11	14	14	0	0	64	66	37	22	0	34	44	.267	.227	.293	6.22	4.81
Mendez, Dawrin	L-L	6-3	170	2-21-98	2	2	1.71	17	0	0	4	21	19	10	4	0	17	25	.235	.191	.250	10.71	7.29
Mojica, Ariel	R-R	6-2	185	9-20-98	4	5	4.54	20	0	0	2	38	40	22	19	2	11	35	.276	.246	.300	8.36	2.63
Mota, Reinardo	R-R	6-2	165	11-14-98	1	0	3.04	16	0	0	0	24	25	13	8	1	15	21	.284	.300	.276	7.99	5.70
Nino, Jeffry	R-R	6-4	170	9-26-96	1	4	5.26	15	3	0	3	39	43	33	23	2	22	27	.277	.268	.283	6.18	5.03
Noriega, Orlando	R-R	6-0	175	5-15-99	1	2	4.11	14	14	0	0	66	68	38	30	1	26	50	.273	.233	.290	6.85	3.56
Peguero, Francis	R-R	6-1	185	8-11-97	0	1	2.45	8	0	0	4	15	10	4	4	0	1	17	.189	.250	.162	10.43	0.61
Pichardo, Juan	R-R	6-5	170	4-25-97	5	3	4.26	16	1	0	1	38	38	25	18	1	24	20	.253	.293	.228	4.74	5.68
Salazar, Eduardo	R-R	6-2	165	5-5-98	4	4	2.70	12	12	0	0	60	54	22	18	1	10	47	.246	.212	.267	7.05	1.50
Santos, Carlos	R-R	6-1	180	7-12-98	0	0	5.25	16	0	0	1	24	16	17	14	0	29	23	.195	.000	.000	8.63	10.88
Severino, Moises	R-R	5-11	185	9-20-97	2	4	3.02	12	8	0	0	48	35	28	16	1	29	37	.202	.302	.146	6.99	5.48
Sparles, Luis	R-R	6-3	170	5-1-97	0	2	4.68	12	12	0	0	42	35	28	22	4	43	41	.229	.313	.169	8.72	9.14
Tavarez, Dannysmel	R-R	6-3	190	3-10-98	0	0	10.47	13	0	0	0	16	21	21	19	1	23	17	.304	.333	.292	9.37	12.67
Valenzuela, Jose	R-R	6-1	190	5-5-98	5	5	1.79	15	15	1	0	75	62	23	15	3	21	62	.221	.272	.192	7.41	2.51
Zorrilla, Jose	L-R	6-1	180	10-2-98	3	1	3.16	16	1	0	3	43	40	24	15	1	16	25	.252	.254	.250	5.27	3.38

Fielding

C: Gomez 34, Melo 10, Ortiz 21, Reina 39, Sequera 10, Tello 44. **1B:** Diaz 3, Finol 9, Gomez 1, Graterol 2, Melo 14, Ortiz 33, Reina 5, Rijo 12, Sencion 31, Sequera 34, Tello 16. **2B:** Amador 1, Diaz 2, Finol 12, Graterol 31, Palacios 21, Remy 40, Reyes 8, Reyes 19, Soto 24. **3B:** Amador 6, Diaz 11, Finol 29, Graterol 3, Reyes 22, Reyes 20, Rijo 21, Santana 31, Soto 36. **SS:** Amador 21, Diaz 23, Hernandez 36, Palacios 19, Remy 16, Reyes 18, Soto 1. OF: Abreu 40, Aleixo 56, Amador 25, Castro 39, Cuevas 52, Gonzalez 6, Lantigua 16, Lozano 36, Nava 33, Olivo 37, Plaz 51, Rivas 23, Sencion 1, Silverio 36.

Cleveland Indians

SEASON IN A SENTENCE: The Indians won 102 games in the regular season, the second most in franchise history, and set the AL record with a 22-game winning streak, but their season came to a disappointing end with a playoff loss to the Yankees in the AL Division Series.

HIGH POINT: The winning streak lasted from Aug. 24 to Sept. 15, eclipsing the 2002 Athletics' 20-game run for the longest in AL history. The final win of the streak came on a walk-off double from Jay Bruce.

LOW POINT: After taking a 2-0 lead on the Yankees in the ALDS, the Indians were unable to close out the series. They lost three straight games for the first time in more than two months to end their season.

NOTABLE ROOKIES: Outfielder Bradley Zimmer, the team's top prospect in 2016, debuted in mid-May and took over as the Indians' starting center fielder. He had some ups and downs at the plate before he broke his hand in September and had season-ending surgery. Third baseman Yandy Diaz made the team's Opening Day roster, but struggled to carve out a regular role in the Indians' crowded infield and was left off the playoff roster. Erik Gonzalez filled the role of utility man capably, appearing at four positions for the Tribe.

KEY TRANSACTIONS: In the offseason, the Indians signed free agent slugger Edwin Encarnacion to a three-year, $60 million contract, the largest free agent deal in club history. The team was not as active in the trade market as they were during 2016, but still swung two small but significant deals over the summer. At the trade deadline, they acquired righthander Joe Smith from the Blue Jays to shore up the bullpen. They traded for Jay Bruce about two weeks later, adding another power bat to their lineup. Encarnacion had the biggest impact of the newcomers, as he led the team in home runs (38), on-base percentage (.377) and RBIs (107).

DOWN ON THE FARM: Righthander Triston McKenzie went 12-6, 3.46 and ranked second among all minor leaguers with 186 strikeouts in 143 innings. He helped high Class A Lynchburg win a share the Carolina League title for the first time since 2012. While Diaz had an inconsistent season with Cleveland, he was outstanding for Triple-A Colubus and hit .350/.454/.460 to win the International League batting title.

OPENING DAY PAYROLL: $124,861,165 (17th)

PLAYERS OF THE YEAR

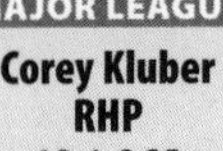

MAJOR LEAGUE

Corey Kluber
RHP
18-4, 2.25
265 SO in 203.2 IP
1st in MLB in W, ERA

RODGER WOOD

MINOR LEAGUE

Triston McKenzie
RHP
(High Class A)
12-6, 3.46
186 SO in 143 IP

ORGANIZATION LEADERS

BATTING — *Minimum 250 AB

MAJORS

*	AVG	Jose Ramirez	.318
*	OPS	Jose Ramirez	.957
	HR	Edwin Encarnacion	38
	RBI	Edwin Encarnacion	107

MINORS

*	AVG	Yandy Diaz, Columbus	.350
*	OBP	Yandy Diaz, Columbus	.454
*	SLG	Eric Haase, Akron, Columbus	.578
*	OPS	Eric Haase, Akron, Columbus	.930
	R	Conner Capel, Lake County	73
	H	Willi Castro, Lynchburg	136
	TB	Bobby Bradley, Akron	217
	2B	Ka'ai Tom, Lynchburg	31
	3B	Sam Haggerty, Lynchburg	13
	HR	Richie Shaffer, Columbus	30
	RBI	Richie Shaffer, Columbus	89
		Bobby Bradley, Akron	89
	BB	Mike Papi, Akron, Columbus	70
	SO	Richie Shaffer, Columbus	188
	SB	Sam Haggerty, Lynchburg	49

PITCHING — #Minimum 75 IP

MAJORS

	W	Corey Kluber	18
		Carlos Carrasco	18
#	ERA	Corey Kluber	2.25
	SO	Corey Kluber	265
	SV	Cody Allen	30

MINORS

	W	Aaron Civale, Lake County, Lynchburg	13
	L	Brady Aiken, Lake County	13
		Micah Miniard, Lake County	13
#	ERA	Ben Krauth, Lake County, Lynchburg	1.72
	G	Kyle Crockett, Columbus	51
	GS	Shane Bieber, Lake County, Lynchburg, Akron	28
	SV	Argenis Angulo, Lynchburg	15
	IP	Shane Bieber, Lake County, Lynchburg, Akron	173
	BB	Brady Aiken, Lake County	101
	SO	Triston McKenzie, Lynchburg	186
#	AVG	Ben Krauth, Lake County, Lynchburg	.192

2017 PERFORMANCE

President, Baseball Ops: Chris Antonetti. **Farm Director:** James Harris. **Scouting Director:** Brad Grant.

Class	Team	League	W	L	PCT	Finish	Manager
Majors	Cleveland Indians	American	102	60	.63	1st (15)	Terry Francona
Triple-A	Columbus Clippers	International	71	71	.500	t-6th (14)	Chris Tremie
Double-A	Akron RubberDucks	Eastern	69	71	.493	5th (12)	Mark Budzinski
High-A	Lynchburg Hillcats	Carolina	87	52	.626	1st (10)	Tony Mansolino
Low-A	Lake County Captains	Midwest	54	85	.388	16th (16)	Larry Day
Short Season	Mahoning Valley Scrappers	New York-Penn	44	29	.603	2nd (14)	Luke Carlin
Rookie	AZL Indians	Arizona	15	41	.268	15th (15)	Anthony Medrano
Overall 2017 Minor League Record			340	349	.493	18th (30)	

ORGANIZATION STATISTICS

CLEVELAND INDIANS

CLEVELAND INDIANS

AMERICAN LEAGUE

Batting	B-T	HT	WT	DOB	AVG	vLH	vRH	G	AB	R	H	2B	3B	HR	RBI	BB	HBP	SH	SF	SO	SB	CS	SLG	OBP
Allen, Greg	B-R	6-0	175	3-15-93	.229	.400	.160	25	35	7	8	1	0	1	6	2	1	0	1	8	1	0	.343	.282
Almonte, Abraham	B-R	5-9	210	6-27-89	.233	.200	.244	69	172	26	40	8	3	3	14	20	1	1	1	46	2	1	.366	.314
Brantley, Michael	L-L	6-2	200	5-15-87	.299	.288	.305	90	338	47	101	20	1	9	52	31	2	0	4	50	11	1	.444	.357
Bruce, Jay	L-L	6-3	225	4-3-87	.248	.193	.283	43	149	21	37	9	2	7	26	18	1	0	1	37	1	0	.477	.331
Chisenhall, Lonnie	L-R	6-2	190	10-4-88	.288	.340	.275	82	236	34	68	17	1	12	53	25	3	3	3	55	2	2	.521	.360
Diaz, Yandy	R-R	6-2	185	8-8-91	.263	.268	.260	49	156	25	41	8	1	0	13	21	1	0	1	35	2	0	.327	.352
Encarnacion, Edwin	R-R	6-1	230	1-7-83	.258	.249	.263	157	554	96	143	20	1	38	107	104	5	0	5	133	2	0	.504	.377
Gomes, Yan	R-R	6-2	215	7-19-87	.232	.245	.226	105	341	43	79	15	0	14	56	31	8	1	2	99	0	0	.399	.309
Gonzalez, Erik	R-R	6-3	195	8-31-91	.255	.222	.270	60	110	18	28	6	0	4	11	3	0	1	1	37	1	2	.418	.272
Guyer, Brandon	R-R	6-2	200	1-28-86	.236	.252	.204	70	165	23	39	7	1	2	20	15	8	2	2	43	2	0	.327	.326
Jackson, Austin	R-R	6-1	205	2-1-87	.318	.353	.291	85	280	46	89	19	3	7	35	33	1	0	4	64	3	1	.482	.387
Kipnis, Jason	L-R	5-11	195	4-3-87	.232	.207	.246	90	336	43	78	25	0	12	35	28	2	2	5	71	6	2	.414	.291
Lindor, Francisco	B-R	5-11	190	11-14-93	.273	.305	.257	159	651	99	178	44	4	33	89	60	4	5	3	93	15	3	.505	.337
Martinez, Michael	B-R	5-9	180	9-16-82	.364	.250	.429	14	11	1	4	1	0	0	0	2	0	1	0	5	0	1	.455	.462
2-team total (13 Tampa Bay)					.162	.250	.429	27	37	2	6	1	0	0	0	5	0	1	0	15	0	1	.189	.262
Mejia, Francisco	B-R	5-10	180	10-27-95	.154	.167	.143	11	13	1	2	0	0	0	1	1	0	0	0	3	0	0	.154	.214
Naquin, Tyler	L-R	6-2	195	4-24-91	.216	.250	.212	19	37	4	8	2	0	0	1	2	0	0	1	9	0	1	.270	.250
Perez, Roberto	R-R	5-11	220	12-23-88	.207	.229	.197	73	217	22	45	12	0	8	38	26	0	4	1	71	0	1	.373	.291
Ramirez, Jose	B-R	5-9	165	9-17-92	.318	.329	.312	152	585	107	186	56	6	29	83	52	3	0	5	69	17	5	.583	.374
Robertson, Daniel	R-R	5-8	205	9-30-85	.225	.286	.129	32	80	9	18	4	1	1	7	7	0	1	0	3	0	1	.338	.287
Santana, Carlos	R-B	5-11	210	4-8-86	.259	.255	.262	154	571	90	148	37	3	23	79	88	6	0	2	94	5	1	.455	.363
Urshela, Giovanny	R-R	6-0	215	10-11-91	.224	.228	.222	67	156	14	35	7	0	1	15	8	0	1	0	22	0	0	.289	.262
Zimmer, Bradley	L-R	6-5	220	11-27-92	.241	.243	.240	101	299	41	72	15	2	8	39	26	4	0	3	99	18	1	.385	.307

Pitching	B-T	HT	WT	DOB	W	L	ERA	G	GS	CG	SV	IP	H	R	ER	HR	BB	SO	AVG	vLH	vRH	K/9	BB/9
Allen, Cody	R-R	6-1	210	11-20-88	3	7	2.94	69	0	0	30	67	57	24	22	9	21	92	.221	.209	.230	12.30	2.81
Armstrong, Shawn	R-R	6-2	225	9-11-90	1	0	4.38	21	0	0	0	25	23	12	12	5	10	20	.237	.216	.250	7.30	3.65
Bauer, Trevor	R-R	6-1	190	1-17-91	17	9	4.19	32	31	0	0	176	181	84	82	25	60	196	.266	.276	.258	10.00	3.06
Breslow, Craig	L-L	6-0	190	8-8-80	0	0	4.15	7	0	0	0	4	3	2	2	0	2	5	.214	.286	.143	10.38	4.15
2-team total (30 Minnesota)					1	1	5.09	37	0	0	0	35	41	21	20	4	14	23	.297	.286	.143	5.86	3.57
Carrasco, Carlos	R-R	6-3	212	3-21-87	18	6	3.29	32	32	1	0	200	173	73	73	21	46	226	.235	.244	.228	10.17	2.07
Clevinger, Mike	R-R	6-4	210	12-21-90	12	6	3.11	27	21	0	0	122	92	46	42	13	60	137	.211	.257	.181	10.13	4.44
Crockett, Kyle	L-L	6-2	175	12-15-91	0	0	10.80	4	0	0	0	2	4	2	2	0	1	2	.444	.500	.333	10.80	5.40
Goody, Nick	R-R	5-11	195	7-6-91	1	2	2.80	56	0	0	0	55	39	20	17	7	20	72	.198	.188	.203	11.85	3.29
Kluber, Corey	R-R	6-4	215	4-10-86	18	4	2.25	29	29	5	0	204	141	56	51	21	36	265	.193	.200	.186	11.71	1.59
Logan, Boone	R-L	6-5	215	8-13-84	1	0	4.71	38	0	0	0	21	20	13	11	2	9	28	.250	.250	.250	12.00	3.86
McAllister, Zach	R-R	6-6	240	12-8-87	2	2	2.61	50	0	0	0	62	53	18	18	8	21	66	.235	.293	.189	9.58	3.05
Merritt, Ryan	L-L	6-0	180	2-21-92	2	0	1.74	5	4	0	0	21	26	6	4	0	4	7	.310	.455	.258	3.05	1.74
Miller, Andrew	L-L	6-7	205	5-21-85	4	3	1.44	57	0	0	2	63	31	11	10	3	21	95	.144	.164	.136	13.64	3.02
Olson, Tyler	R-L	6-3	195	10-2-89	1	0	0.00	30	0	0	1	20	13	0	0	0	6	18	.188	.162	.219	8.10	2.70
Otero, Dan	R-R	6-3	205	2-19-85	3	0	2.85	52	0	0	0	60	63	23	19	6	9	38	.273	.341	.231	5.70	1.35
Salazar, Danny	R-R	6-0	195	1-11-90	5	6	4.28	23	19	0	0	103	94	51	49	14	44	145	.242	.257	.230	12.67	3.84
Shaw, Bryan	R-B	6-1	220	11-8-87	4	6	3.52	79	0	0	3	77	71	36	30	5	22	73	.247	.234	.254	8.57	2.58
Smith, Joe	R-R	6-2	205	3-22-84	0	0	3.44	21	0	0	1	18	16	7	7	1	0	20	.229	.214	.232	9.82	0.00
2-team total (38 Toronto)					3	0	3.33	59	0	0	1	54	46	20	20	4	10	71	.229	.214	.232	11.83	1.67
Tomlin, Josh	R-R	6-1	190	10-19-84	10	9	4.98	26	26	1	0	141	166	80	78	23	14	109	.294	.307	.284	6.96	0.89

Fielding

Catcher	PCT	G	PO	A	E	DP	PB
Gomes	.991	103	938	60	9	5	4
Mejia	1.000	3	4	0	0	0	0
Perez	.997	71	664	33	2	6	5

First Base	PCT	G	PO	A	E	DP
Bruce	1.000	1	1	0	0	0
Chisenhall	1.000	7	14	1	0	4
Encarnacion	.994	23	152	10	1	16
Santana	.996	140	1055	95	5	129
Urshela	1.000	2	2	0	0	1

Second Base	PCT	G	PO	A	E	DP
Gonzalez	1.000	36	38	53	0	16
Kipnis	.975	75	107	171	7	41
Martinez	.917	3	3	8	1	1
Ramirez	.980	71	118	170	6	55
Urshela	.909	5	2	8	1	2

Third Base	PCT	G	PO	A	E	DP
Diaz	.972	40	19	50	2	8
Gonzalez	1.000	8	1	7	0	2
Martinez	1.000	6	0	1	0	0
Ramirez	.972	88	61	146	6	23
Urshela	.959	60	28	66	4	7

Shortstop	PCT	G	PO	A	E	DP
Gonzalez	.875	11	3	11	2	4
Lindor	.984	158	210	391	10	111
Martinez	1.000	1	0	1	0	0
Urshela	1.000	5	2	8	0	2

Outfield	PCT	G	PO	A	E	DP
Allen	1.000	25	26	0	0	0
Almonte	.986	58	70	2	1	0
Brantley	.993	87	135	8	1	1
Bruce	.967	41	56	2	2	0
Chisenhall	1.000	75	102	2	0	1
Diaz	.667	3	2	0	1	0
Gonzalez	1.000	1	1	0	0	0
Guyer	.974	65	73	2	2	1
Jackson	.985	81	124	4	2	1
Kipnis	1.000	11	14	0	0	0
Martinez	1.000	2	2	0	0	0
Naquin	1.000	17	15	0	0	0
Robertson	.972	27	32	3	1	1
Santana	1.000	7	9	1	0	1
Zimmer	1.000	97	168	8	0	1

COLUMBUS CLIPPERS — TRIPLE-A

INTERNATIONAL LEAGUE

Batting	B-T	HT	WT	DOB	AVG	vLH	vRH	G	AB	R	H	2B	3B	HR	RBI	BB	HBP	SH	SF	SO	SB	CS	SLG	OBP
Almonte, Abraham	B-R	5-9	210	6-27-89	.260	.185	.300	23	77	11	20	6	1	2	6	15	0	0	0	13	3	1	.442	.380
Chisenhall, Lonnie	L-R	6-2	190	10-4-88	.370	.364	.375	8	27	4	10	2	0	1	4	0	0	0	1	6	1	0	.556	.357
Colabello, Chris	R-R	6-4	210	10-24-83	.225	.179	.238	72	262	25	59	11	0	6	37	34	4	0	0	76	3	1	.336	.323
Diaz, Yandy	R-R	6-2	185	8-8-91	.350	.371	.341	85	309	56	108	17	1	5	33	60	1	2	2	56	1	2	.460	.454
Gonzalez, Erik	R-R	6-3	195	8-31-91	.256	.255	.257	40	160	21	41	4	3	6	13	7	0	2	1	53	5	1	.431	.286
Guyer, Brandon	R-R	6-2	200	1-28-86	.267	.333	.222	6	15	3	4	0	0	1	1	2	3	0	0	4	0	0	.467	.450
Haase, Eric	R-R	5-10	180	12-18-92	.333	—	.333	2	6	1	2	0	0	1	2	1	1	0	0	2	0	0	.833	.500
Hankins, Todd	R-R	5-9	180	11-18-90	.207	.250	.194	29	82	13	17	4	0	1	5	6	1	2	0	25	2	2	.293	.270
Jackson, Austin	R-R	6-1	205	2-1-87	.333	.250	.348	8	27	2	9	3	0	1	4	2	0	0	0	6	2	0	.556	.379
Kipnis, Jason	L-R	5-11	195	4-3-87	.182	.125	.214	6	22	1	4	2	1	0	2	1	0	0	0	4	0	0	.364	.217
Kratz, Erik	R-R	6-4	245	6-15-80	.270	.280	.266	86	282	38	76	16	1	13	37	32	8	1	1	64	5	1	.472	.359
Lough, David	L-L	5-10	175	1-20-86	.500	—	.500	4	12	1	6	1	0	0	0	0	0	0	0	0	0	1	.583	.500
2-team total (24 Toledo)					.225	—	.500	28	71	8	16	3	0	0	0	2	1	1	0	16	0	3	.268	.257
Lucas, Jeremy	R-R	6-1	205	1-10-91	.140	.167	.135	16	43	2	6	0	0	0	3	3	4	0	0	13	0	1	.140	.260
Marabell, Connor	L-R	6-1	195	3-28-94	.467	.286	.625	5	15	0	7	2	0	0	1	1	0	0	0	3	0	2	.600	.500
Martinez, Michael	B-R	5-9	180	9-16-82	.277	.233	.300	63	213	29	59	16	2	0	20	13	0	2	1	35	4	2	.371	.317
Medina, Jose	L-L	6-1	185	2-14-95	.000	.000	.000	1	3	0	0	0	0	0	0	0	0	0	0	3	0	0	.000	.000
Moore, Adam	R-R	6-3	220	5-8-84	.238	.206	.249	76	244	26	58	6	1	8	33	25	3	1	3	87	0	0	.369	.313
Naquin, Tyler	L-R	6-2	195	4-24-91	.298	.247	.323	80	295	42	88	14	4	10	51	30	0	1	4	71	5	2	.475	.359
Papi, Mike	L-R	6-3	215	9-19-92	.235	.382	.177	37	119	20	28	5	0	2	18	20	4	1	4	25	1	1	.328	.354
Robertson, Daniel	R-R	5-8	205	9-30-85	.321	.339	.313	57	209	29	67	8	0	1	16	21	0	1	0	35	12	6	.373	.383
Rodriguez, Nellie	R-R	6-2	225	6-12-94	.170	.167	.171	120	377	38	64	14	0	17	49	53	0	1	2	181	0	0	.342	.271
Rodriguez, Ronny	R-R	6-0	170	4-17-92	.291	.267	.299	117	447	60	130	18	2	17	64	23	1	7	5	92	15	5	.454	.324
Sever, Joe	R-R	6-0	205	8-12-90	.500	—	.500	2	2	2	1	0	0	0	0	0	1	0	0	1	0	0	.500	.667
Shaffer, Richie	R-R	6-3	230	3-15-91	.227	.191	.239	131	463	69	105	18	1	30	89	67	12	1	3	188	4	0	.464	.338
Smith, Jordan	L-R	6-4	235	7-5-90	.153	.114	.165	56	150	11	23	4	1	1	11	8	1	2	1	38	3	4	.213	.200
Stamets, Eric	R-R	6-0	190	9-25-91	.252	.241	.255	101	334	49	84	23	0	15	47	30	7	6	3	87	8	0	.455	.324
Urshela, Giovanny	R-R	6-0	215	10-11-91	.266	.222	.280	76	297	34	79	12	1	6	34	20	5	1	2	45	0	0	.374	.321
Wilson, Josh	R-R	6-0	175	3-26-81	.207	.114	.243	53	155	26	32	9	0	2	9	11	8	4	1	41	1	1	.303	.291
Zimmer, Bradley	L-R	6-5	220	11-27-92	.294	.323	.284	33	126	22	37	11	2	5	14	14	2	1	1	43	9	3	.532	.371

Pitching	B-T	HT	WT	DOB	W	L	ERA	G	GS	CG	SV	IP	H	R	ER	HR	BB	SO	AVG	vLH	vRH	K/9	BB/9
Armstrong, Shawn	R-R	6-2	225	9-11-90	1	1	3.07	28	0	0	10	29	27	10	10	3	11	36	.241	.296	.190	11.05	3.38
Aviles, Robbie	L-R	6-4	200	12-17-91	0	0	9.82	3	0	0	0	4	3	4	4	1	2	2	.214	.222	.200	4.91	4.91
Banwart, Travis	R-R	6-3	220	2-14-86	2	4	5.49	15	8	0	0	39	47	25	24	4	15	25	.298	.265	.333	5.72	3.43
Breslow, Craig	L-L	6-0	190	8-8-80	0	0	3.86	7	0	0	0	5	5	2	2	0	2	4	.278	.083	.667	7.71	3.86
2-team total (3 Rochester)					0	0	3.68	10	0	0	0	7	6	3	3	0	3	6	.222	.083	.667	7.36	3.68
Brown, D.J.	R-R	6-6	205	11-28-90	0	0	3.00	2	0	0	0	3	3	1	1	0	1	2	.250	.250	.250	6.00	3.00
Clevinger, Mike	R-R	6-4	210	12-21-90	3	2	2.65	7	7	0	0	34	28	10	10	3	14	38	.228	.250	.206	10.06	3.71
Colon, Joe	R-R	6-0	180	2-18-90	0	0	4.13	28	0	0	6	33	33	15	15	4	18	34	.260	.308	.227	9.37	4.96
Crockett, Kyle	L-L	6-2	175	12-15-91	5	5	3.38	51	0	0	4	48	42	23	18	2	11	49	.235	.176	.296	9.19	2.06
Frias, Carlos	R-R	6-4	195	11-13-89	1	1	8.05	30	1	0	0	38	46	34	34	8	22	21	.301	.413	.222	4.97	5.21
Garner, Perci	R-R	6-3	225	12-13-88	0	0	47.25	3	0	0	0	1	1	7	7	0	8	2	.200	.500	.000	13.50	54.00
Goody, Nick	R-R	5-11	195	7-6-91	1	0	0.00	3	0	0	0	4	2	0	0	0	1	10	.133	.286	.000	20.77	2.08
Grube, Jarrett	R-R	6-4	220	11-5-81	5	6	3.56	14	14	0	0	78	76	34	31	9	25	56	.255	.278	.234	6.43	2.87
2-team total (11 Buffalo)					7	9	4.63	25	25	0	0	134	139	77	69	19	46	103	.268	.278	.234	6.92	3.09
Head, Louis	R-R	6-1	180	4-23-90	3	2	3.23	50	0	0	7	61	50	22	22	2	28	65	.222	.224	.220	9.54	4.11
Hill, Cameron	R-R	6-1	185	5-24-94	0	0	0.00	2	0	0	0	2	2	0	0	0	1	0	.250	.333	.200	0.00	4.50
Holland, Neil	R-R	6-0	190	8-14-88	0	1	7.36	4	0	0	0	4	5	3	3	1	1	4	.333	.286	.375	9.82	2.45
Johnson, Jeff	R-R	6-0	185	2-9-90	2	1	3.27	50	0	0	3	55	44	22	20	3	37	65	.222	.205	.235	10.64	6.05
Martin, Josh	R-R	6-5	230	12-30-89	1	2	3.25	30	0	0	4	36	36	13	13	2	8	38	.257	.238	.273	9.50	2.00
Merritt, Ryan	L-L	6-0	180	2-21-92	10	5	3.03	19	18	1	0	116	116	40	39	19	25	85	.263	.264	.263	6.59	1.94
Merryweather, Julian	R-R	6-4	200	10-14-91	3	7	6.58	16	16	0	0	78	105	58	57	13	25	76	.327	.316	.340	8.77	2.88
Miller, Andrew	L-L	6-7	205	5-21-85	0	0	0.00	1	0	0	0	1	0	0	0	0	0	2	.000	—	.000	18.00	0.00
Moreno, Diego	R-R	6-1	180	7-21-87	1	0	0.73	9	0	0	0	12	8	1	1	1	2	10	.186	.158	.208	7.30	1.46
2-team total (11 Durham)					1	0	0.94	20	0	0	5	29	17	3	3	1	5	27	.170	.158	.208	8.48	1.57
Morimando, Shawn	L-L	6-0	200	11-20-92	10	9	4.41	26	26	4	0	159	177	91	78	22	57	128	.281	.318	.265	7.23	3.22
Narveson, Chris	L-L	6-3	205	12-20-81	6	7	3.41	20	17	0	0	103	98	45	39	11	44	62	.249	.193	.273	5.42	3.84
Olson, Tyler	R-L	6-3	195	10-2-89	2	0	3.21	34	0	0	2	42	28	16	15	7	12	54	.189	.127	.247	11.57	2.57
Pasquale, Nick	R-R	6-0	190	10-27-90	0	1	0.00	1	1	0	0	4	4	3	0	0	2	3	.308	.333	.250	7.36	4.91

Peoples, Michael	R-R	6-5	190	9-5-91	1	4	7.15	8	7	1	0	39	60	34	31	4	18	18	.364	.477	.241	4.15	4.15
Plutko, Adam	R-R	6-3	200	10-3-91	7	12	5.90	24	22	0	0	136	153	92	89	24	53	103	.295	.273	.320	6.83	3.52
Salazar, Danny	R-R	6-0	195	1-11-90	1	1	2.89	2	2	0	0	9	6	3	3	3	5	13	.188	.286	.111	12.54	4.82
Speer, David	L-L	6-1	185	8-14-92	1	0	0.00	4	1	0	0	6	6	0	0	0	4	2	.261	.222	.286	2.84	5.68
Sulser, Cole	R-R	6-0	190	3-12-90	2	0	2.63	35	0	0	2	48	47	15	14	3	26	59	.257	.222	.284	11.06	4.88
Tully, Tanner	L-L	6-0	200	11-30-94	1	0	3.86	1	1	0	0	7	8	3	3	0	1	3	.286	.200	.333	3.86	1.29
Whitehouse, Matt	L-L	6-1	175	4-13-91	1	0	12.00	2	1	0	0	6	9	9	8	0	4	3	.360	.500	.294	4.50	6.00

Fielding

Catcher	PCT	G	PO	A	E	DP	PB
Haase	1.000	2	14	1	0	0	0
Kratz	.997	78	558	37	2	9	3
Lucas	1.000	3	17	0	0	0	0
Moore	.996	68	518	34	2	4	5

First Base	PCT	G	PO	A	E	DP
Colabello	.995	28	196	13	1	23
Kratz	1.000	1	2	0	0	0
Medina	1.000	1	6	0	0	0
Rodriguez	.988	108	769	55	10	101
Rodriguez	1.000	3	9	1	0	3
Shaffer	1.000	26	102	5	0	10
Wilson	1.000	2	11	3	0	0

Second Base	PCT	G	PO	A	E	DP
Diaz	.000	1	0	0	0	0
Gonzalez	.979	9	23	24	1	9
Hankins	.974	16	30	45	2	14
Kipnis	1.000	6	10	11	0	2
Martinez	1.000	17	22	26	0	10
Robertson	1.000	2	1	0	0	0
Rodriguez	.993	62	121	173	2	47
Stamets	.966	10	12	16	1	2
Wilson	.960	46	75	95	7	28

Third Base	PCT	G	PO	A	E	DP
Diaz	.977	42	22	64	2	13
Gonzalez	1.000	3	1	6	0	0
Lucas	.000	1	0	0	0	0
Martinez	1.000	1	1	0	0	0
Rodriguez	.966	25	18	39	2	2
Sever	.000	1	0	0	0	0
Shaffer	.882	18	6	24	4	5
Urshela	.959	60	33	107	6	13
Wilson	1.000	4	2	1	0	0

Shortstop	PCT	G	PO	A	E	DP
Gonzalez	.978	26	36	54	2	17
Martinez	.978	12	16	29	1	11
Rodriguez	1.000	2	2	3	0	0
Stamets	.980	91	139	260	8	60
Urshela	1.000	16	16	37	0	6
Wilson	1.000	3	5	10	0	4

Outfield	PCT	G	PO	A	E	DP
Almonte	.917	14	22	0	2	0
Chisenhall	1.000	7	8	0	0	0
Colabello	1.000	22	28	0	0	0
Diaz	.966	30	54	3	2	0
Gonzalez	.800	4	4	0	1	0
Guyer	1.000	4	2	0	0	0
Hankins	1.000	16	26	0	0	0
Jackson	1.000	5	7	0	0	0
Lough	1.000	4	6	0	0	0
Marabell	.900	4	9	0	1	0
Martinez	.984	32	57	4	1	0
Naquin	1.000	69	162	5	0	2
Papi	1.000	36	65	3	0	1
Robertson	1.000	52	97	7	0	0
Rodriguez	1.000	24	41	6	0	3
Shaffer	.959	80	133	8	6	1
Smith	.989	50	88	2	1	0
Zimmer	1.000	33	88	2	0	1

AKRON RUBBERDUCKS — DOUBLE-A

EASTERN LEAGUE

Batting	B-T	HT	WT	DOB	AVG	vLH	vRH	G	AB	R	H	2B	3B	HR	RBI	BB	HBP	SH	SF	SO	SB	CS	SLG	OBP
Allen, Greg	B-R	6-0	175	3-15-93	.264	.356	.227	71	258	37	68	16	1	2	24	22	13	4	6	55	21	2	.357	.345
Bradley, Bobby	L-R	6-1	225	5-29-96	.251	.177	.276	131	467	66	117	25	3	23	89	55	4	1	5	122	3	3	.465	.332
Castillo, Ivan	B-R	5-9	173	5-30-95	.203	.063	.245	28	69	10	14	3	0	1	8	10	2	5	1	13	1	2	.290	.317
Chang, Yu-Cheng	R-R	6-1	175	8-18-95	.221	.198	.228	126	440	72	97	24	5	24	66	52	9	2	5	134	11	4	.461	.312
Chisenhall, Lonnie	L-R	6-2	190	10-4-88	.125	.125	.125	5	16	1	2	0	0	0	0	1	0	0	0	4	0	0	.125	.177
De La Cruz, Juan	B-R	6-1	195	8-5-93	.133	.250	.056	12	30	0	4	1	0	0	3	3	0	2	0	9	0	0	.167	.212
Haase, Eric	R-R	5-10	180	12-18-92	.258	.298	.245	95	333	59	86	17	5	26	59	44	3	0	1	116	4	2	.574	.349
Hankins, Todd	R-R	5-9	180	11-18-90	.228	.200	.235	73	232	28	53	7	1	2	19	21	0	4	3	70	15	5	.293	.289
Kipnis, Jason	L-R	5-11	195	4-3-87	.143	—	.143	5	14	1	2	0	0	1	1	0	1	0	0	6	0	0	.357	.200
Krieger, Tyler	B-R	6-2	170	1-16-94	.225	.208	.231	119	418	55	94	25	2	6	43	42	8	5	7	107	12	6	.337	.303
Laureano, Jonathan	R-R	6-1	200	12-21-95	.200	.000	.286	3	10	1	2	1	0	0	2	1	0	0	0	0	1	0	.300	.273
Marabell, Connor	L-R	6-1	195	3-28-94	.268	.222	.281	11	41	2	11	1	0	0	2	3	0	0	0	8	0	0	.293	.318
Mathias, Mark	R-R	6-0	200	8-2-94	.212	.167	.235	35	104	17	22	5	1	1	13	13	6	0	2	34	4	0	.308	.328
Medina, Yhoxian	R-R	5-10	165	5-11-90	.182	.222	.167	11	33	6	6	0	0	1	2	3	3	0	0	7	0	1	.273	.308
Mejia, Francisco	B-R	5-10	180	10-27-95	.297	.352	.277	92	347	52	103	21	2	14	52	24	5	1	6	53	7	2	.490	.346
Mendoza, Yonathan	B-R	5-11	167	2-10-94	.196	.091	.225	15	51	2	10	2	0	1	6	4	0	0	0	9	2	0	.294	.255
Murphy, Taylor	L-R	6-2	200	11-3-92	.203	.083	.224	25	79	13	16	1	0	3	13	13	4	0	0	29	3	1	.329	.344
Papi, Mike	L-R	6-3	215	9-19-92	.267	.304	.256	87	296	50	79	13	0	10	37	50	2	2	2	61	5	2	.412	.374
Paulino, Dorssys	R-R	6-0	175	11-21-94	.257	.233	.267	94	315	37	81	12	2	6	37	42	4	2	3	76	6	2	.365	.349
Rodriguez, Jorma	R-R	5-10	150	3-25-96	.238	.400	.188	7	21	2	5	0	0	0	0	0	0	1	0	6	0	0	.238	.238
Rodriguez, Luigi	L-R	5-11	160	11-13-92	.276	.220	.291	82	286	31	79	22	1	13	40	19	0	2	2	94	8	8	.497	.319
Salters, Daniel	L-R	6-3	210	2-5-93	.200	.000	.250	4	10	3	2	1	0	0	1	1	1	0	1	2	0	0	.300	.308
Sever, Joe	R-R	6-0	205	8-12-90	.282	.255	.290	118	440	46	124	21	2	7	54	32	4	0	5	82	5	2	.386	.333
Smith, Jordan	L-R	6-4	235	7-5-90	.268	.279	.263	41	157	23	42	6	0	2	13	19	1	1	1	37	5	5	.344	.348
Stamets, Eric	R-R	6-0	190	9-25-91	.325	.167	.353	14	40	7	13	3	1	1	5	8	0	1	1	13	2	0	.525	.429

Pitching	B-T	HT	WT	DOB	W	L	ERA	G	GS	CG	SV	IP	H	R	ER	HR	BB	SO	AVG	vLH	vRH	K/9	BB/9
Aviles, Robbie	L-R	6-4	200	12-17-91	7	4	3.12	38	0	0	3	58	51	22	20	3	13	35	.238	.217	.254	5.46	2.03
Baker, Dylan	R-R	6-2	205	4-6-92	0	1	2.84	13	0	0	0	13	15	4	4	1	1	10	.289	.240	.333	7.11	0.71
Baker, Dylan	R-R	6-2	205	4-6-92	0	1	2.84	13	0	0	0	13	15	4	4	1	1	10	.289	.240	.333	7.11	0.71
Banwart, Travis	R-R	6-3	220	2-14-86	1	1	5.73	3	2	0	0	11	17	7	7	1	2	8	.347	.471	.281	6.55	1.64
Bieber, Shane	R-R	6-3	195	5-31-95	2	1	2.32	9	9	0	0	54	56	15	14	2	5	49	.264	.273	.255	8.12	0.83
Brown, D.J.	R-R	6-6	205	11-28-90	1	7	4.72	29	5	0	1	74	76	45	39	9	20	63	.269	.321	.224	7.63	2.42
Brown, Mitch	R-R	6-1	195	4-13-94	1	2	6.33	33	0	0	4	48	41	36	34	3	39	40	.238	.238	.239	7.45	7.26
Chiang, Shao-Ching	R-R	6-0	175	11-10-93	1	2	6.61	6	6	0	0	33	43	24	24	4	11	20	.314	.363	.246	5.51	3.03
DeMasi, Dominic	R-R	6-3	190	5-18-93	1	0	1.80	1	1	0	0	5	2	1	1	0	1	6	.118	.167	.091	10.80	1.80
Esparza, Matt	R-R	6-2	195	8-22-94	5	5	4.94	17	17	0	0	95	90	55	52	16	36	72	.251	.246	.256	6.85	3.42
Garcia, Justin	R-R	6-1	180	9-16-92	1	0	0.00	1	0	0	0	3	1	0	0	0	1	2	.111	.000	.250	6.75	3.38
Garner, Perci	R-R	6-3	225	12-13-88	0	0	3.14	10	0	0	1	14	7	5	5	0	9	18	.146	.217	.080	11.30	5.65

Pitching	B-T	HT	WT	DOB	W	L	ERA	G	GS	CG	SV	IP	H	R	ER	HR	BB	SO	AVG	vLH	vRH	K/9	BB/9
Herrera, Alsis	L-L	5-11	180	5-25-92	0	0	9.00	1	0	0	0	2	8	2	2	0	0	4	.615	1.000	.583	18.00	0.00
Hill, Cameron	R-R	6-1	185	5-24-94	4	4	3.18	41	0	0	13	62	55	26	22	7	16	50	.235	.178	.271	7.22	2.31
Holland, Neil	R-R	6-0	190	8-14-88	3	1	4.85	26	0	0	5	30	34	19	16	4	3	21	.283	.353	.232	6.37	0.91
Kaminsky, Rob	R-L	5-11	190	9-2-94	0	1	9.00	1	1	0	0	5	6	5	5	0	2	1	.316	.167	.385	1.80	3.60
Kluber, Corey	R-R	6-4	215	4-10-86	1	0	0.00	1	1	0	0	5	1	0	0	0	0	1	.067	.000	.111	1.80	0.00
Lee, Jacob	R-R	6-1	190	10-25-89	1	1	9.18	14	0	0	0	17	25	17	17	2	11	10	.362	.433	.308	5.40	5.94
Linares, Leandro	R-R	6-3	205	1-27-94	2	2	3.78	23	0	0	3	33	39	19	14	2	21	37	.296	.273	.318	9.99	5.67
Lugo, Luis	L-L	6-5	200	3-5-94	8	7	4.35	26	25	1	0	134	140	74	65	19	55	93	.268	.265	.269	6.23	3.68
Merryweather, Julian	R-R	6-4	200	10-14-91	4	2	3.38	9	9	0	0	51	37	21	19	3	10	52	.196	.197	.195	9.24	1.78
Milbrath, Jordan	R-R	6-6	215	8-1-91	3	2	3.90	15	0	0	2	30	30	20	13	5	11	29	.259	.333	.194	8.70	3.30
Pannone, Thomas	L-L	6-0	195	4-28-94	6	1	2.62	14	14	1	0	82	67	27	24	5	21	81	.223	.193	.235	8.85	2.30
2-team total (6 New Hampshire)					7	3	2.92	20	20	1	0	117	98	43	38	14	29	110	.227	.193	.235	8.46	2.23
Pasquale, Nick	R-R	6-0	190	10-27-90	3	8	5.90	19	16	0	0	82	85	58	54	10	39	74	.267	.236	.292	8.09	4.26
Peoples, Michael	R-R	6-5	190	9-5-91	2	5	5.58	9	9	0	0	50	61	33	31	7	14	30	.298	.244	.336	5.40	2.52
Salazar, Danny	R-R	6-0	195	1-11-90	0	1	16.20	1	1	0	0	2	3	3	3	1	2	3	.375	.500	.250	16.20	10.80
Speer, David	L-L	6-1	185	8-14-92	2	3	5.60	38	2	0	5	53	69	38	33	2	18	47	.312	.302	.319	7.98	3.06
Sulser, Cole	R-R	6-0	190	3-12-90	1	1	2.93	10	0	0	1	15	12	7	5	2	4	11	.222	.250	.206	6.46	2.35
Tully, Tanner	L-L	6-0	200	11-30-94	1	1	4.32	3	3	0	0	17	25	12	8	2	5	4	.357	.278	.385	2.16	2.70
Whitehouse, Matt	L-L	6-1	175	4-13-91	8	8	4.47	28	19	1	1	111	118	69	55	15	27	87	.266	.223	.284	7.08	2.20

Fielding

Catcher	PCT	G	PO	A	E	DP	PB
De La Cruz	1.000	6	25	1	0	0	0
Haase	.987	60	410	52	6	4	4
Mejia	.991	72	471	86	5	4	7
Salters	1.000	4	24	2	0	0	1

First Base	PCT	G	PO	A	E	DP
Bradley	.993	125	1028	63	8	91
De La Cruz	1.000	2	3	0	0	0
Papi	1.000	1	6	0	0	0
Sever	.985	17	129	6	2	7

Second Base	PCT	G	PO	A	E	DP
Castillo	1.000	3	5	6	0	2
Hankins	.988	22	24	60	1	13
Kipnis	1.000	4	4	2	0	2
Krieger	.967	101	197	237	15	46
Mathias	.975	9	13	26	1	5
Medina	.857	2	0	6	1	0
Mendoza	1.000	4	5	14	0	2
Rodriguez	1.000	2	1	1	0	0

Third Base	PCT	G	PO	A	E	DP
Castillo	1.000	13	14	21	0	2
Hankins	1.000	8	2	10	0	0
Laureano	.833	3	1	4	1	1
Mathias	.932	22	15	40	4	2
Medina	.714	4	2	3	2	0
Mejia	1.000	1	1	0	0	0
Mendoza	1.000	7	2	16	0	2
Rodriguez	.889	4	9	7	2	1
Sever	.936	70	34	112	10	7
Stamets	.957	10	6	16	1	0

Shortstop	PCT	G	PO	A	E	DP
Castillo	1.000	9	5	21	0	6
Chang	.956	122	175	373	25	67
Mathias	.750	2	2	4	2	0
Mendoza	1.000	4	10	13	0	5
Rodriguez	1.000	1	3	1	0	1
Stamets	1.000	3	5	5	0	2

Outfield	PCT	G	PO	A	E	DP
Allen	.987	67	148	3	2	1
Chisenhall	1.000	3	3	0	0	0
Hankins	.986	37	71	1	1	1
Marabell	.955	11	20	1	1	0
Medina	1.000	4	7	2	0	0
Murphy	.979	24	47	0	1	0
Papi	.989	81	169	4	2	1
Paulino	.983	85	163	7	3	1
Rodriguez	.977	61	126	1	3	0
Sever	.962	16	23	2	1	0
Smith	1.000	41	101	2	0	0

LYNCHBURG HILLCATS — *HIGH CLASS A*

CAROLINA LEAGUE

Batting	B-T	HT	WT	DOB	AVG	vLH	vRH	G	AB	R	H	2B	3B	HR	RBI	BB	HBP	SH	SF	SO	SB	CS	SLG	OBP
Bautista, Claudio	R-R	5-11	170	11-29-93	.216	.150	.240	73	227	26	49	10	1	7	24	17	5	1	2	66	0	0	.361	.283
Brooks, Trenton	L-L	6-0	180	7-3-95	.000	.000	.000	3	7	0	0	0	0	0	0	0	0	0	0	1	0	0	.000	.000
Calica, Andrew	L-R	6-1	190	3-5-94	.274	.264	.278	103	376	64	103	22	3	6	40	43	15	4	4	84	14	9	.396	.368
Carter, Jodd	R-R	5-10	170	7-20-96	.239	.230	.244	115	385	51	92	17	4	11	46	47	4	5	2	125	9	5	.390	.327
Castillo, Ivan	B-R	5-9	173	5-30-95	.315	.222	.354	28	92	7	29	6	1	0	6	4	3	0	1	11	3	3	.402	.360
Castro, Willi	B-R	6-1	165	4-24-97	.290	.292	.289	123	469	69	136	24	3	11	58	28	7	2	4	90	19	9	.424	.337
Cervenka, Martin	R-R	6-1	175	8-3-92	.278	.272	.281	112	400	59	111	24	4	8	57	42	1	0	6	103	1	1	.418	.343
Collins, Gavin	R-R	5-11	205	7-17-95	.275	.389	.236	40	142	18	39	16	0	4	35	13	3	0	4	45	1	1	.472	.340
De La Cruz, Juan	B-R	6-1	195	8-5-93	.143	.000	.200	2	7	1	1	1	0	0	1	0	0	0	1	3	0	0	.286	.125
Haggerty, Sam	B-R	5-11	175	5-26-94	.253	.281	.240	112	427	72	108	27	13	3	32	67	2	3	2	103	49	13	.398	.355
Longo, Mitch	L-R	6-0	185	1-12-95	.563	.500	.571	5	16	8	9	2	0	0	3	4	0	0	0	2	2	0	.688	.650
Loopstok, Sicnarf	R-R	5-11	195	4-26-93	.249	.219	.266	119	421	67	105	28	4	17	65	52	13	2	6	132	11	8	.456	.346
Marabell, Connor	L-R	6-1	195	3-28-94	.238	.196	.255	97	362	43	86	15	1	6	45	31	1	2	3	57	8	5	.334	.297
Medina, Jose	L-L	6-1	185	2-14-95	.290	.273	.300	10	31	3	9	4	0	0	9	3	0	0	1	9	0	1	.419	.343
Mendoza, Yonathan	B-R	5-11	167	2-10-94	.307	.363	.277	72	257	35	79	6	2	2	30	30	1	2	0	31	5	2	.370	.382
Miller, Anthony	L-R	6-4	240	10-4-94	.242	.143	.276	61	194	17	47	15	0	3	28	18	1	0	1	83	0	0	.366	.308
Rodriguez, Jorma	R-R	5-10	150	3-25-96	.286	.000	.500	4	7	1	2	1	0	0	3	0	0	1	0	1	0	0	.429	.286
Salters, Daniel	L-R	6-3	210	2-5-93	.198	.188	.202	90	314	36	62	13	1	5	30	24	4	3	4	86	0	0	.293	.260
Sayles, Silento	R-R	5-9	185	8-28-95	—	—	—	2	0	0	0	0	0	0	0	2	0	0	0	0	0	0	—	1.000
Tom, Ka'ai	L-R	5-9	185	5-29-94	.254	.237	.262	126	457	68	116	31	7	10	65	59	4	2	7	100	23	6	.418	.340

Pitching	B-T	HT	WT	DOB	W	L	ERA	G	GS	CG	SV	IP	H	R	ER	HR	BB	SO	AVG	vLH	vRH	K/9	BB/9
Angulo, Argenis	R-R	6-3	220	2-26-94	5	2	2.29	41	0	0	15	55	31	15	14	1	27	68	.160	.257	.100	11.13	4.42
Bieber, Shane	R-R	6-3	195	5-31-95	6	1	3.10	14	14	0	0	90	95	35	31	5	4	82	.275	.275	.275	8.20	0.40
Brady, Sean	L-L	6-0	175	6-9-94	3	1	3.18	4	4	0	0	23	19	9	8	1	8	15	.221	.227	.219	5.96	3.18
Chiang, Shao-Ching	R-R	6-0	175	11-10-93	8	8	3.67	19	19	2	0	123	122	61	50	12	22	81	.261	.274	.249	5.94	1.61
Civale, Aaron	R-R	6-2	215	6-12-95	11	2	2.59	17	17	0	0	108	96	38	31	11	9	88	.238	.207	.260	7.36	0.75
DeMasi, Dominic	R-R	6-3	190	5-18-93	7	4	2.58	31	13	1	2	101	85	31	29	5	22	58	.230	.275	.203	5.17	1.96
Esparza, Matt	R-R	6-2	195	8-22-94	3	3	3.26	9	9	0	0	47	46	21	17	6	11	40	.251	.225	.282	7.66	2.11
Eubank, Luke	R-R	6-0	180	2-24-94	2	0	1.42	12	0	0	3	13	6	4	2	2	6	13	.128	.250	.065	9.24	4.26
Garcia, Justin	R-R	6-1	180	9-16-92	4	3	3.26	32	0	0	2	47	41	18	17	6	27	47	.234	.263	.211	9.00	5.17

Pitching	B-T	HT	WT	DOB	W	L	ERA	G	GS	CG	SV	IP	H	R	ER	HR	BB	SO	AVG	vLH	vRH	K/9	BB/9
Hartson, Brock	R-R	6-2	200	8-9-93	6	5	3.06	23	19	0	1	129	104	51	44	11	31	88	.220	.195	.233	6.12	2.16
Hendrix, Paul	R-R	6-2	190	11-18-91	0	2	7.48	20	0	0	0	28	32	24	23	3	17	27	.302	.275	.327	8.78	5.53
Herrera, Alsis	L-L	5-11	180	5-25-92	1	0	0.00	1	0	0	0	3	1	0	0	0	0	1	.083	.000	.125	2.70	0.00
Holland, Neil	R-R	6-0	190	8-14-88	0	0	2.08	4	0	0	1	4	5	2	1	0	1	4	.313	.286	.333	8.31	2.08
Krauth, Ben	L-L	6-0	180	3-10-94	1	0	1.59	10	1	0	4	17	8	3	3	1	9	20	.146	.130	.156	10.59	4.76
Linares, Leandro	R-R	6-3	205	1-27-94	2	1	0.78	19	0	0	5	23	19	6	2	2	11	20	.229	.226	.231	7.83	4.30
Lovegrove, Kieran	R-R	6-4	185	7-28-94	4	3	5.01	38	2	0	1	50	43	29	28	5	25	51	.231	.244	.222	9.12	4.47
Martinez, Henry	R-R	6-1	175	4-27-94	0	0	4.50	1	0	0	1	2	6	2	1	0	0	0	.546	.500	.571	0.00	0.00
McKenzie, Triston	R-R	6-5	165	8-2-97	12	6	3.46	25	25	0	0	143	105	62	55	14	45	186	.204	.239	.175	11.71	2.83
Milbrath, Jordan	R-R	6-6	215	8-1-91	2	1	2.03	15	0	0	2	27	18	10	6	0	14	34	.194	.178	.208	11.48	4.73
Pannone, Thomas	L-L	6-0	195	4-28-94	2	0	0.00	5	5	0	0	28	10	1	0	0	7	39	.111	.040	.139	12.69	2.28
Pasquale, Nick	R-R	6-0	190	10-27-90	3	0	5.19	8	3	0	0	17	16	10	10	0	13	21	.250	.194	.303	10.90	6.75
Robinson, Jared	R-R	6-0	190	11-20-94	3	4	3.86	35	4	0	3	61	60	29	26	4	26	39	.264	.237	.285	5.79	3.86
Strode, Billy	L-L	6-0	180	8-10-92	2	3	3.74	42	1	0	1	55	55	30	23	3	24	57	.258	.133	.339	9.27	3.90
Tully, Tanner	L-L	6-0	200	11-30-94	0	3	4.94	5	3	0	1	24	22	18	13	2	6	12	.250	.250	.250	4.56	2.28

Fielding

Catcher	PCT	G	PO	A	E	DP	PB
Cervenka	.994	56	431	47	3	3	2
Loopstok	.975	22	134	22	4	0	3
Salters	.991	64	505	57	5	6	15

First Base	PCT	G	PO	A	E	DP
Bautista	.947	3	15	3	1	3
De La Cruz	1.000	2	15	0	0	1
Loopstok	.985	59	434	32	7	40
Medina	.979	9	92	3	2	4
Mendoza	.993	14	127	7	1	7
Miller	.992	61	497	31	4	46

Second Base	PCT	G	PO	A	E	DP
Bautista	1.000	9	17	21	0	7
Castillo	.968	16	24	36	2	2
Haggerty	.980	96	179	212	8	53
Mendoza	.979	22	31	63	2	11
Rodriguez	1.000	2	5	6	0	3

Third Base	PCT	G	PO	A	E	DP
Bautista	.936	57	27	104	9	9
Castillo	1.000	5	3	8	0	0
Collins	.921	37	26	67	8	6
Loopstok	.971	13	11	23	1	4
Mendoza	.971	37	25	77	3	8

Shortstop	PCT	G	PO	A	E	DP
Castillo	.955	8	8	13	1	1
Castro	.953	122	166	340	25	69
Haggerty	.896	11	13	30	5	5

Outfield	PCT	G	PO	A	E	DP
Brooks	.750	3	3	0	1	0
Calica	.989	88	176	7	2	3
Carter	.996	109	228	9	1	2
Haggerty	1.000	3	4	0	0	0
Longo	1.000	3	4	0	0	0
Loopstok	.960	16	23	1	1	0
Marabell	.953	85	139	4	7	1
Tom	.991	116	225	6	2	1

LAKE COUNTY CAPTAINS — *LOW CLASS A*

MIDWEST LEAGUE

Batting	B-T	HT	WT	DOB	AVG	vLH	vRH	G	AB	R	H	2B	3B	HR	RBI	BB	HBP	SH	SF	SO	SB	CS	SLG	OBP
Bradley, Kevin	R-B	6-0	195	1-9-94	.237	.091	.296	13	38	2	9	2	0	0	4	5	0	0	2	17	0	2	.290	.311
Brooks, Trenton	L-L	6-0	180	7-3-95	.214	.281	.188	29	112	11	24	5	0	1	8	12	2	0	0	26	0	1	.286	.302
Capel, Conner	L-L	6-1	185	5-19-97	.246	.246	.246	119	439	73	108	22	7	22	61	43	4	2	4	108	15	10	.478	.316
Cerda, Erlin	R-R	5-9	170	5-5-94	.231	.250	.222	7	26	3	6	2	1	0	3	0	0	0	0	7	1	0	.385	.231
Chu, Li-Jen	R-R	5-11	200	3-13-94	.269	.302	.255	125	465	57	125	22	0	17	67	40	10	1	2	91	0	0	.426	.339
Collins, Gavin	R-R	5-11	205	7-17-95	.270	.267	.270	40	141	23	38	5	1	8	19	14	2	0	2	30	0	0	.489	.340
De La Cruz, Juan	B-R	6-1	195	8-5-93	.280	.500	.177	8	25	2	7	1	0	1	4	1	0	0	0	5	0	0	.440	.308
Eladio, Miguel	R-R	6-1	160	5-10-96	.242	.232	.247	95	355	39	86	11	4	7	28	11	3	1	1	103	2	2	.355	.270
Ice, Logan	B-R	5-10	195	5-27-95	.228	.194	.244	93	316	38	72	10	1	11	42	42	3	1	5	74	1	1	.370	.320
Isaacs, Todd	R-R	5-11	175	5-22-96	.224	.265	.208	82	295	30	66	14	2	9	33	12	3	1	2	103	18	3	.376	.260
Longo, Mitch	L-R	6-0	185	1-12-95	.361	.339	.372	55	202	37	73	18	2	4	25	23	4	0	3	35	18	1	.530	.431
Medina, Jose	L-L	6-1	185	2-14-95	.234	.333	.206	54	175	28	41	6	0	9	17	18	5	0	0	56	0	2	.423	.323
Mejia, Gabriel	B-R	5-11	160	7-30-95	.229	.250	.218	44	153	15	35	4	1	0	8	13	0	1	2	31	12	4	.268	.286
Pantoja, Alexis	L-R	5-11	150	1-18-96	.251	.261	.247	83	303	34	76	11	0	2	21	15	0	5	2	51	10	2	.307	.284
Perez, Elvis	B-R	6-0	165	1-10-96	.146	.071	.185	16	41	5	6	0	0	0	2	4	0	0	1	12	0	0	.146	.217
Rodriguez, Jorma	R-R	5-10	150	3-25-96	.201	.189	.205	88	294	39	59	14	2	3	16	23	4	4	2	78	8	8	.293	.266
Soto, Junior	R-R	6-3	175	1-21-97	.172	.191	.167	52	174	19	30	14	0	9	17	6	2	0	1	61	1	1	.408	.208
Tapia, Emmanuel	L-L	6-3	215	2-26-96	.213	.153	.240	124	461	53	98	20	0	29	71	35	4	0	5	180	1	0	.445	.271
Tinsley, Michael	L-R	6-0	195	5-10-95	.240	.257	.231	30	100	10	24	4	2	3	11	11	0	1	0	40	3	0	.410	.315
Vicente, Jose	R-R	5-11	175	11-13-95	.278	.214	.299	35	115	15	32	8	2	6	24	8	0	0	1	28	1	1	.539	.323
Wakamatsu, Luke	B-R	6-3	185	10-10-96	.239	.231	.243	100	377	49	90	17	3	12	53	32	4	1	5	100	8	5	.395	.301

Pitching	B-T	HT	WT	DOB	W	L	ERA	G	GS	CG	SV	IP	H	R	ER	HR	BB	SO	AVG	vLH	vRH	K/9	BB/9
Aiken, Brady	L-L	6-4	205	8-16-96	5	13	4.77	27	27	0	0	132	134	83	70	12	101	89	.277	.256	.289	6.07	6.89
Bieber, Shane	R-R	6-3	195	5-31-95	2	3	3.10	5	5	0	0	29	34	14	10	1	1	31	.291	.318	.259	9.62	0.31
Brady, Sean	L-L	6-0	175	6-9-94	1	0	1.00	4	4	0	0	18	12	2	2	0	1	13	.182	.294	.143	6.50	0.50
Civale, Aaron	R-R	6-2	215	6-12-95	2	4	4.58	10	10	0	0	57	64	34	29	2	5	53	.284	.295	.271	8.37	0.79
Colegate, Ryan	R-R	6-5	195	11-12-93	2	2	5.97	27	0	0	0	60	76	48	40	4	17	39	.305	.323	.286	5.82	2.54
Draper, Zack	L-L	6-3	200	10-18-94	0	0	5.40	1	0	0	0	2	4	1	1	0	0	3	.444	.000	.571	16.20	0.00
Eubank, Luke	R-R	6-0	180	2-24-94	0	0	0.00	3	0	0	0	4	2	0	0	0	2	3	.143	.000	.200	6.75	4.50
Garza, Justin	R-R	5-10	170	3-20-94	4	6	5.83	26	8	0	3	96	97	72	62	12	46	86	.265	.244	.283	8.09	4.33
Herrera, Alsis	L-L	5-11	180	5-25-92	6	2	3.69	28	0	0	0	61	57	30	25	3	28	46	.248	.193	.279	6.79	4.13
Hillman, Juan	L-L	6-2	185	5-15-97	7	10	6.08	26	26	0	0	138	158	102	93	22	48	101	.290	.305	.282	6.60	3.14
Jimenez, Domingo	R-R	6-3	175	8-29-93	0	0	8.18	9	0	0	0	11	16	10	10	1	8	4	.356	.300	.400	3.27	6.55
Jimenez, Luis	R-R	6-4	170	1-2-95	2	8	6.60	16	16	0	0	76	93	61	56	16	30	65	.294	.312	.277	7.66	3.54
Krauth, Ben	L-L	6-0	180	3-10-94	4	2	1.75	23	2	0	0	62	43	14	12	4	30	72	.205	.226	.191	10.51	4.38
Lee, Jacob	R-R	6-1	190	10-25-89	0	1	4.91	5	0	0	0	7	4	5	4	0	7	4	.160	.231	.083	4.91	8.59
Letkewicz, Michael	R-R	6-4	220	1-31-94	0	2	3.65	17	0	0	0	25	28	10	10	1	11	24	.275	.319	.236	8.76	4.01
Martinez, Henry	R-R	6-1	175	4-27-94	5	3	3.15	35	1	0	3	60	54	30	21	1	16	59	.238	.243	.234	8.85	2.40

Pitching	B-T	HT	WT	DOB	W	L	ERA	G	GS	CG	SV	IP	H	R	ER	HR	BB	SO	AVG	vLH	vRH	K/9	BB/9
Merritt, Ryan	L-L	6-0	180	2-21-92	1	0	2.57	1	1	0	0	7	7	2	2	0	1	4	.269	.250	.278	5.14	1.29
Mingo, Cameron	R-R	6-4	185	9-10-93	0	2	2.55	5	1	0	0	18	19	10	5	1	4	3	.260	.231	.294	1.53	2.04
Miniard, Micah	R-R	6-7	195	4-12-96	4	13	7.80	26	23	0	0	118	157	109	102	21	60	61	.320	.301	.340	4.67	4.59
Plesac, Zach	R-R	6-3	200	1-21-95	1	1	3.60	6	6	0	0	25	19	11	10	2	6	19	.211	.231	.196	6.84	2.16
Ryan, Ryder	R-R	6-2	205	5-11-95	3	4	4.79	33	0	0	6	41	44	28	22	4	17	49	.267	.230	.297	10.67	3.70
Siri, Dalbert	R-R	6-2	190	7-19-95	1	2	3.10	39	0	0	14	41	29	19	14	1	26	64	.192	.164	.218	14.16	5.75
Tully, Tanner	L-L	6-0	200	11-30-94	4	6	3.16	16	8	1	1	77	73	37	27	10	10	76	.243	.191	.272	8.88	1.17
Valladares, Randy	L-L	5-11	155	7-6-94	0	0	13.50	1	0	0	0	2	1	3	3	1	3	1	.143	.000	.333	4.50	13.50
Ventura, Cesar	R-R	6-0	195	3-14-95	0	1	4.89	16	1	0	0	39	49	23	21	5	20	32	.318	.357	.271	7.45	4.66

Fielding

Catcher	PCT	G	PO	A	E	DP	PB
Chu	.983	50	364	36	7	3	9
Collins	.982	7	49	7	1	0	3
De La Cruz	1.000	3	19	1	0	0	0
Ice	.990	81	555	60	6	3	5
Vicente	1.000	3	7	5	0	0	0

First Base	PCT	G	PO	A	E	DP
De La Cruz	.976	5	39	2	1	4
Medina	.965	12	78	4	3	4
Pantoja	1.000	2	8	0	0	1
Perez	1.000	1	1	0	0	0
Tapia	.982	100	860	50	17	91
Vicente	.982	27	202	12	4	23

Second Base	PCT	G	PO	A	E	DP
Bradley	.917	11	10	23	3	2
Cerda	.909	2	3	7	1	1
Eladio	.989	61	91	168	3	50
Mejia	.000	1	0	0	0	0
Pantoja	.978	45	83	137	5	28
Perez	1.000	5	8	13	0	4
Rodriguez	1.000	21	42	60	0	18

Third Base	PCT	G	PO	A	E	DP
Cerda	.909	5	5	5	1	0
Collins	.888	34	15	56	9	7
Eladio	.750	6	4	11	5	1
Pantoja	.982	25	17	39	1	4
Perez	.972	11	7	28	1	3
Rodriguez	.944	67	33	101	8	11

Shortstop	PCT	G	PO	A	E	DP
Eladio	.913	32	30	64	9	15
Pantoja	.950	11	17	21	2	6
Perez	1.000	1	1	3	0	2
Wakamatsu	.962	100	150	286	17	66

Outfield	PCT	G	PO	A	E	DP
Bradley	1.000	1	1	0	0	0
Brooks	.977	29	42	1	1	0
Capel	.987	111	213	11	3	1
Isaacs	.983	82	168	4	3	1
Longo	.981	48	98	3	2	0
Medina	.966	33	54	3	2	1
Mejia	.989	43	89	5	1	3
Pantoja	1.000	1	2	0	0	0
Soto	.978	52	127	6	3	2
Tinsley	.914	30	73	1	7	1

MAHONING VALLEY SCRAPPERS — *SHORT SEASON*

NEW YORK-PENN LEAGUE

Batting	B-T	HT	WT	DOB	AVG	vLH	vRH	G	AB	R	H	2B	3B	HR	RBI	BB	HBP	SH	SF	SO	SB	CS	SLG	OBP
Benson, Will	L-L	6-5	225	6-16-98	.238	.205	.247	56	202	29	48	8	5	10	36	31	3	0	0	80	7	1	.475	.348
Berardi, Jesse	L-R	5-10	185	1-13-96	.284	.378	.246	38	155	16	44	7	0	1	15	6	1	0	1	31	2	3	.348	.313
Cantu, Ulysses	R-R	5-11	220	5-1-98	.254	.262	.250	54	209	17	53	10	0	4	25	17	3	0	1	66	0	0	.359	.317
Clement, Ernie	R-R	6-0	170	3-22-96	.280	.275	.282	45	175	32	49	9	1	0	13	6	3	3	0	12	6	2	.343	.315
Friis, Tyler	B-R	5-9	180	2-12-96	.221	.143	.235	33	95	12	21	3	0	1	11	7	1	1	2	18	3	2	.284	.276
Gonzalez, Gian Paul	R-R	6-0	185	1-11-96	.125	.154	.114	32	96	6	12	1	0	0	7	9	3	0	1	29	0	0	.135	.220
Gonzalez, Oscar	R-R	6-2	180	1-10-98	.283	.310	.274	55	237	20	67	16	0	3	34	5	2	0	2	61	0	0	.388	.301
Jones, Nolan	L-R	6-4	185	5-7-98	.317	.214	.341	62	218	41	69	18	3	4	33	43	2	0	2	60	1	0	.482	.430
Laureano, Jonathan	R-R	6-1	200	12-21-95	.231	.273	.211	35	134	17	31	4	1	1	12	1	1	0	1	27	1	1	.299	.241
Lucas, Simeon	L-R	6-2	195	2-7-96	.262	.333	.246	43	164	16	43	7	0	3	25	7	4	0	1	55	0	0	.360	.307
Nelson, Hosea	L-L	6-0	210	11-22-96	.240	.250	.239	42	129	18	31	8	1	1	7	8	4	0	0	50	9	0	.341	.305
Perez, Elvis	B-R	6-0	165	1-10-96	.189	.167	.195	14	53	0	10	1	1	0	6	1	1	0	1	18	0	0	.245	.214
Persinger, Dillon	R-R	5-11	180	1-31-96	.208	.133	.228	22	72	9	15	4	0	2	4	9	4	2	1	22	1	1	.347	.326
Reeves, Mitch	R-R	6-2	210	11-18-94	.500	.500	.500	3	8	0	4	1	0	0	1	3	1	0	0	1	0	0	.625	.667
Rivera, Michael	R-R	5-10	200	12-12-95	.170	.300	.135	15	47	6	8	3	0	0	4	3	1	1	1	12	0	0	.234	.231
Rodriguez, Jason	R-R	5-11	180	1-11-95	.202	.167	.209	31	104	10	21	4	1	2	8	5	0	0	1	25	0	0	.317	.236
Sayles, Silento	R-R	5-9	185	8-28-95	.143	.091	.200	7	21	2	3	2	0	0	0	3	0	0	0	8	0	0	.238	.250
Scolamiero, Clark	L-L	6-0	175	1-24-96	.246	.160	.268	42	122	21	30	4	1	0	12	16	3	0	0	36	6	2	.295	.348
Taylor, Samad	R-R	5-10	160	7-11-98	.300	.243	.325	28	120	18	36	6	1	4	19	5	1	2	2	24	4	2	.467	.328
Wade, Austen	L-L	6-1	185	2-17-96	.256	.267	.252	36	137	21	35	5	2	1	10	14	0	0	1	30	3	2	.343	.322

Pitching	B-T	HT	WT	DOB	W	L	ERA	G	GS	CG	SV	IP	H	R	ER	HR	BB	SO	AVG	vLH	vRH	K/9	BB/9
Araujo, Luis	R-R	6-1	155	8-1-96	0	1	9.00	2	0	0	0	3	3	3	3	0	1	7	.273	.333	.250	21.00	3.00
Chen, Ping-Hsueh	R-R	6-2	195	7-8-94	1	0	4.66	23	0	0	2	29	30	20	15	2	19	26	.266	.275	.260	8.07	5.90
Draper, Zack	L-L	6-3	200	10-18-94	2	0	2.13	6	1	0	0	13	11	3	3	0	2	12	.225	.177	.250	8.53	1.42
Echols, Riley	R-R	6-4	205	4-12-95	1	1	3.86	23	0	0	2	33	33	18	14	0	12	23	.266	.310	.244	6.34	3.31
Hendrickson, Michael	R-L	6-3	205	9-13-95	1	0	6.23	4	0	0	0	4	4	3	3	1	3	9	.250	.167	.300	18.69	6.23
Hentges, Sam	L-L	6-6	245	7-18-96	0	1	2.04	5	5	0	0	18	5	7	4	1	12	23	.088	.000	.132	11.72	6.11
Hockin, Grant	R-R	6-4	200	3-5-96	2	4	4.36	8	8	0	0	33	40	22	16	2	8	18	.296	.245	.329	4.91	2.18
Jimenez, Domingo	R-R	6-3	175	8-29-93	0	0	5.65	10	0	0	1	14	11	11	9	1	12	16	.216	.211	.219	10.05	7.53
Karinchak, James	R-R	6-3	230	9-22-95	2	2	5.79	10	6	0	0	23	30	15	15	1	9	31	.319	.357	.289	11.96	3.47
Lopez, Francisco	R-R	5-11	170	2-13-94	0	0	9.00	2	0	0	0	2	1	2	2	0	3	4	.200	.500	.000	18.00	13.50
Manzanillo, Maiker	R-R	6-2	190	10-14-96	0	0	6.23	3	0	0	0	4	5	3	3	0	1	5	.313	.429	.222	10.38	2.08
McCarty, Kirk	L-L	5-10	185	10-12-95	2	2	1.85	13	6	0	0	34	27	12	7	3	10	33	.213	.143	.256	8.74	2.65
Mejia, Jean Carlos	R-R	6-4	205	8-26-96	1	0	0.00	11	0	0	3	23	6	0	0	0	5	31	.083	.100	.071	12.31	1.99
Mingo, Cameron	R-R	6-4	185	9-10-93	3	0	2.22	13	0	0	1	28	24	7	7	3	9	19	.242	.286	.219	6.04	2.86
Morgan, Elijah	R-R	5-10	190	5-13-96	3	2	1.03	13	5	0	0	35	24	9	4	0	9	58	.188	.143	.209	14.91	2.31
Nelson, Kyle	L-L	6-1	175	7-8-96	3	2	2.48	19	0	0	4	29	21	12	8	3	8	40	.193	.154	.214	12.41	2.48
Perez, Francisco	L-L	6-2	195	7-20-97	4	4	3.28	15	15	0	0	74	67	41	27	5	28	48	.238	.225	.244	5.84	3.41
Plesac, Zach	R-R	6-3	200	1-21-95	0	1	1.38	8	7	0	0	26	14	4	4	0	8	31	.161	.167	.157	10.73	2.77
Salazar, Danny	R-R	6-0	195	1-11-90	1	0	0.00	1	1	0	0	5	2	0	0	0	2	7	.125	.250	.000	12.60	3.60
Santos, Luis	R-R	6-4	180	9-18-94	0	0	9.00	2	0	0	0	2	3	2	2	1	1	3	.333	.333	.333	13.50	4.50

Pitching	B-T	HT	WT	DOB	W	L	ERA	G	GS	CG	SV	IP	H	R	ER	HR	BB	SO	AVG	vLH	vRH	K/9	BB/9
Tati, Felix	R-R	6-2	190	4-1-97	7	3	3.77	14	4	0	0	60	54	30	25	1	24	59	.241	.256	.231	8.90	3.62
Teaney, Jonathan	R-R	6-2	195	1-28-96	2	1	2.08	22	0	0	5	30	18	9	7	3	13	51	.171	.205	.152	15.13	3.86
Tomlin, Josh	R-R	6-1	190	10-19-84	0	0	2.45	1	1	0	0	4	8	5	1	1	0	4	.421	1.000	.353	9.82	0.00
Valladares, Randy	L-L	5-11	155	7-6-94	3	2	2.70	19	0	0	2	30	28	11	9	1	20	26	.252	.200	.282	7.80	6.00
Vasquez, Gregori	R-R	6-1	185	9-8-97	5	3	2.38	14	14	0	0	76	67	20	20	5	13	57	.238	.225	.248	6.78	1.55
Ventura, Cesar	R-R	6-0	195	3-14-95	1	0	1.10	8	0	0	3	16	10	2	2	0	8	22	.179	.059	.231	12.12	4.41

Fielding

C: Gonzalez 32, Lucas 4, Rivera 14, Rodriguez 31. **1B:** Cantu 53, Laureano 3, Lucas 16, Reeves 3. **2B:** Berardi 3, Clement 17, Friis 14, Laureano 1, Persinger 17, Taylor 21. **3B:** Friis 1, Jones 53, Laureano 20, Persinger 2. **SS:** Berardi 28, Clement 21, Friis 9, Perez 14, Taylor 1. **OF:** Benson 56, Gonzalez 54, Laureano 6, Nelson 33, Sayles 6, Scolamiero 36, Wade 32.

AZL INDIANS — *ROOKIE*

ARIZONA LEAGUE

Batting	B-T	HT	WT	DOB	AVG	vLH	vRH	G	AB	R	H	2B	3B	HR	RBI	BB	HBP	SH	SF	SO	SB	CS	SLG	OBP
Alfonseca, Pedro	R-R	6-0	178	9-4-97	.250	—	.250	2	8	2	2	0	1	0	0	0	0	0	0	3	1	0	.500	.250
Allen, Greg	B-R	6-0	175	3-15-93	.333	.333	.333	5	15	3	5	0	0	0	2	0	1	0	1	1	3	0	.333	.353
Cerda, Erlin	R-R	5-9	170	5-5-94	.267	.250	.273	5	15	2	4	2	0	0	1	1	1	0	0	4	1	0	.400	.353
Cooper, Michael	L-R	6-5	180	7-27-99	.219	.325	.186	45	169	19	37	9	4	3	27	17	2	0	2	33	1	0	.373	.295
Dominguez, Ronny	R-R	6-0	175	6-5-97	.215	.171	.228	43	149	22	32	5	3	3	12	12	0	0	0	52	4	2	.349	.273
Fermin, Jose	R-R	5-11	160	3-29-99	.229	.167	.246	45	166	24	38	11	1	1	14	5	7	2	2	19	5	2	.325	.278
Fernandez, Felix	R-R	6-0	185	12-9-96	.227	.333	.206	23	75	11	17	2	0	4	8	7	0	0	1	20	0	0	.413	.289
Freeman, Tyler	R-R	6-0	170	5-21-99	.297	.433	.255	36	128	19	38	9	0	2	14	7	7	1	1	12	5	1	.414	.364
Gantt, Tre	L-L	5-10	180	5-10-96	.197	.290	.163	37	117	15	23	2	3	2	15	19	3	0	1	46	2	2	.316	.321
Holmes, Quentin	R-R	6-3	175	7-7-99	.182	.143	.194	41	159	22	29	5	3	2	15	8	0	1	1	61	5	4	.289	.220
Jerez, Miguel	R-R	6-1	178	10-24-97	.218	.161	.241	30	110	11	24	8	0	1	12	8	1	0	0	37	1	0	.318	.277
Lopez Alvarez, Angel	R-R	5-10	194	3-14-97	.194	.167	.200	23	72	14	14	6	1	2	6	9	0	0	1	20	0	0	.389	.281
Mejia, Gabriel	B-R	5-11	160	7-30-95	.278	.250	.286	10	36	4	10	2	0	0	2	1	1	0	0	2	4	3	.333	.316
Murphy, Taylor	L-R	6-2	200	11-3-92	.304	.000	.368	7	23	3	7	0	1	0	3	2	1	0	0	4	0	0	.391	.385
Pujols, Henry	R-R	6-3	195	12-10-98	.239	.186	.256	52	180	35	43	13	0	8	29	11	8	0	1	77	0	1	.444	.310
Reeves, Mitch	R-R	6-2	210	11-18-94	.291	.243	.309	43	134	18	39	8	0	4	19	23	1	1	1	42	2	3	.440	.396
Rodriguez, Jhan	R-R	6-0	165	7-2-98	.121	.074	.141	28	91	5	11	0	0	0	5	2	1	0	2	44	1	1	.121	.146
Rodriguez, Johnathan	B-R	6-3	180	11-4-99	.250	.333	.227	31	96	13	24	4	2	0	11	21	0	1	1	23	0	1	.333	.381
Rolette, Joshua	L-R	5-11	195	5-21-96	.333	.000	.444	5	12	3	4	1	0	0	1	2	0	0	0	0	0	0	.417	.429
Santiago, Wilbis	L-R	6-0	180	1-20-96	.287	.308	.280	30	101	11	29	8	1	1	14	3	3	1	2	12	3	2	.416	.321
Tinsley, Michael	L-R	6-0	195	5-10-95	.283	.364	.257	15	46	10	13	1	2	2	10	11	0	0	0	12	1	0	.522	.421

Pitching	B-T	HT	WT	DOB	W	L	ERA	G	GS	CG	SV	IP	H	R	ER	HR	BB	SO	AVG	vLH	vRH	K/9	BB/9
Algarin, Erick	R-R	6-1	195	3-31-95	0	0	0.00	2	0	0	0	1	1	0	0	0	1	1	.250	—	.250	9.00	9.00
Araujo, Luis	R-R	6-1	155	8-1-96	0	4	8.54	16	0	0	0	26	39	29	25	1	14	29	.342	.311	.362	9.91	4.78
Arias, Skylar	L-L	6-3	190	6-30-97	0	0	1.23	5	0	0	0	7	2	2	1	1	4	14	.083	.000	.125	17.18	4.91
Baker, Dylan	R-R	6-2	205	4-6-92	1	0	2.25	4	2	0	0	4	5	2	1	0	0	6	.278	.000	.455	13.50	0.00
Baker, Dylan	R-R	6-2	205	4-6-92	1	0	2.25	4	2	0	0	4	5	2	1	0	0	6	.278	.000	.455	13.50	0.00
Brady, Sean	L-L	6-0	175	6-9-94	0	0	7.50	2	2	0	0	6	8	5	5	0	1	7	.320	.200	.350	10.50	1.50
Clemmer, Dakody	R-R	6-2	185	1-19-96	0	1	0.00	3	0	0	1	3	2	1	0	0	1	5	.182	.250	.143	15.00	3.00
Cooney, Tim	L-L	6-3	195	12-19-90	0	0	6.00	4	4	0	0	3	3	2	2	0	3	4	.250	.200	.286	12.00	9.00
DeJuneas, Tommy	R-R	6-1	175	10-24-95	0	3	2.42	17	0	0	0	26	27	16	7	2	15	34	.257	.293	.234	11.77	5.19
Draper, Zack	L-L	6-3	200	10-18-94	0	1	4.73	10	0	0	0	13	17	11	7	0	9	13	.340	.214	.389	8.78	6.08
Eubank, Luke	R-R	6-0	180	2-24-94	0	0	0.00	5	2	0	0	5	3	0	0	0	2	6	.158	.143	.167	10.13	3.38
Ferguson, Chandler	R-R	6-3	193	3-3-98	0	0	0.00	1	0	0	0	1	0	0	0	0	1	2	.000	.000	.000	18.00	9.00
Hendrickson, Michael	R-L	6-3	205	9-13-95	0	1	9.00	4	0	0	0	7	12	7	7	2	1	6	.375	.400	.364	7.71	1.29
Hentges, Sam	L-L	6-6	245	7-18-96	0	3	4.85	6	6	0	0	13	16	9	7	2	3	18	.296	.059	.405	12.46	2.08
Izaguirre, Alejandro	R-R	6-0	175	3-5-97	0	0	2.45	3	0	0	0	4	2	1	1	0	2	3	.182	.500	.111	7.36	4.91
Kery, Adoni	R-R	6-0	170	2-18-96	2	3	2.48	17	0	0	0	29	15	9	8	3	15	41	.155	.135	.167	12.72	4.66
Kime, Dace	R-R	6-4	200	3-6-92	0	0	13.50	3	0	0	0	2	4	3	3	0	2	1	.400	.500	.333	4.50	9.00
Lopez, Francisco	R-R	5-11	170	2-13-94	0	0	0.00	9	1	0	0	9	4	0	0	0	3	11	.138	.300	.053	11.42	3.12
Manzanillo, Maiker	R-R	6-2	190	10-14-96	1	1	2.45	13	1	0	1	37	26	14	10	2	5	37	.199	.239	.177	9.08	1.23
Marte, Randy	R-R	6-1	175	12-27-96	1	2	15.07	9	0	0	0	14	21	32	24	2	24	17	.323	.227	.372	10.67	15.07
Mejia, Jean Carlos	R-R	6-4	205	8-26-96	1	0	3.14	10	0	0	6	14	13	6	5	0	5	19	.228	.125	.268	11.93	3.14
Mendoza, Dante	R-R	6-5	186	12-16-98	0	0	6.00	3	2	0	0	3	5	6	2	0	2	2	.357	.250	.400	6.00	6.00
Mota, Juan	R-R	6-4	190	5-4-96	3	5	4.94	14	8	0	0	58	53	44	32	3	32	73	.235	.219	.242	11.26	4.94
Oviedo, Luis	R-R	6-4	170	5-15-99	4	2	7.14	14	7	0	0	52	62	49	41	2	22	70	.286	.274	.293	12.19	3.83
Polanco, Anderson	L-L	6-3	190	9-6-92	0	1	6.00	4	2	0	0	3	2	3	2	0	5	4	.182	.000	.222	12.00	15.00
Santos, Luis	R-R	6-4	180	9-18-94	0	0	9.00	5	0	0	0	6	11	8	6	1	5	7	.407	.539	.286	10.50	7.50
Scheftz, Jordan	R-R	6-3	190	8-31-95	1	2	6.33	19	0	0	0	27	30	20	19	0	15	31	.283	.263	.294	10.33	5.00
Thomas, Tahnaj	R-R	6-4	190	6-16-99	0	3	6.00	13	10	0	0	33	35	26	22	4	25	29	.282	.213	.325	7.91	6.82
Turner, Matt	L-L	6-4	180	8-4-99	1	2	6.75	10	3	0	2	24	36	23	18	1	8	22	.340	.375	.324	8.25	3.00
Valdez, Luis	R-R	6-3	170	10-14-96	0	7	7.24	13	6	0	0	51	63	50	41	2	36	35	.301	.265	.325	6.18	6.35
Wyatt, Jonas	R-R	6-1	185	9-16-97	0	0	27.00	2	0	0	0	1	1	3	3	0	2	2	.250	—	.250	18.00	18.00

Fielding

C: Fernandez 19, Jerez 20, Lopez Alvarez 22, Rolette 3. **1B:** Cooper 41, Reeves 11, Santiago 5. **2B:** Cerda 1, Fermin 18, Freeman 4, Rodriguez 27, Santiago 10. **3B:** Cerda 2, Pujols 46, Rodriguez 1, Santiago 13. **SS:** Fermin 27, Freeman 29, Santiago 1. **OF:** Alfonseca 2, Allen 3, Dominguez 32, Gantt 35, Holmes 37, Mejia 8, Murphy 4, Reeves 21, Rodriguez 29, Tinsley 10.

DSL INDIANS — ROOKIE

DOMINICAN SUMMER LEAGUE

Batting	B-T	HT	WT	DOB	AVG	vLH	vRH	G	AB	R	H	2B	3B	HR	RBI	BB	HBP	SH	SF	SO	SB	CS	SLG	OBP
Celesten, Nehemias	R-R	6-1	195	2-3-00	.241	.355	.215	49	166	22	40	10	1	3	19	29	4	0	1	47	0	1	.368	.365
Cespedes, Cristopher	R-R	6-3	200	5-18-98	.338	.308	.343	27	80	16	27	5	3	3	11	9	2	0	0	15	0	2	.588	.418
2-team total (25 Indians/Brewers)					.314	.308	.343	52	172	29	54	13	4	5	28	16	4	1	2	27	3	4	.523	.381
Contreras, Jeikol	L-R	6-0	175	4-14-00	.175	.097	.193	53	171	23	30	11	1	2	19	33	3	2	1	54	2	5	.287	.317
De Jesus, Christopher	R-R	5-11	170	9-24-96	.219	.250	.212	26	64	7	14	1	0	0	6	5	0	4	0	9	3	0	.234	.275
De Oleo, Henderson	R-R	6-4	210	2-11-98	.263	.207	.279	50	133	37	35	5	1	6	25	27	6	0	0	37	1	0	.451	.410
Diaz, Yainer	R-R	6-0	195	9-21-98	.294	.292	.295	42	153	12	45	8	1	1	21	3	4	0	2	18	0	1	.379	.321
Flores, Jothson	B-R	5-11	160	10-6-98	.143	.333	.125	14	35	4	5	0	1	0	2	3	2	0	0	6	1	1	.200	.250
Gonzalez, Marcos	R-R	5-11	165	10-12-99	.274	.235	.282	56	215	31	59	7	0	1	24	31	3	1	2	28	13	4	.321	.371
Jimenez, Pablo	R-R	6-2	175	2-6-99	.224	.191	.234	26	85	18	19	2	0	1	6	17	4	0	1	26	2	3	.282	.374
2-team total (25 Indians/Brewers)					.238	.190	.234	51	172	31	41	10	2	2	20	22	5	0	1	43	2	5	.355	.340
Lopez, Jonathan	B-R	6-2	175	8-13-99	.267	.244	.272	62	225	35	60	10	5	2	36	32	6	2	5	40	3	3	.382	.366
Maestre, Jesus	R-R	5-10	155	2-4-00	.059	.125	.039	12	34	4	2	2	0	0	1	6	2	0	0	6	0	1	.118	.238
2-team total (27 Indians/Brewers)					.110	.125	.038	39	109	14	12	2	0	0	4	18	5	0	0	25	6	2	.128	.265
Marmol, Roger	R-R	5-11	190	10-5-99	.243	.269	.237	40	140	14	34	7	1	2	17	12	3	0	1	37	0	1	.350	.314
Mateo, Franklin	R-R	6-2	180	5-24-98	.191	.182	.193	31	68	10	13	5	0	0	5	19	3	1	1	34	3	1	.265	.385
Montero, Jean	R-R	5-11	175	2-26-99	.272	.333	.260	54	147	43	40	9	2	3	13	29	7	1	0	39	14	6	.422	.415
Palacio, Gaspar	B-R	5-8	155	3-2-00	.169	.095	.194	23	83	9	14	3	1	1	6	11	1	0	0	29	2	3	.265	.274
2-team total (29 Indians/Brewers)					.173	.095	.194	52	168	21	29	7	3	1	12	22	2	1	1	51	7	8	.268	.275
Rodriguez, Henry	R-R	6-2	190	3-26-99	.067	.000	.083	6	15	2	1	0	0	0	0	4	1	0	0	8	1	0	.067	.300
Santiago, Wilbis	L-R	6-0	180	1-20-96	.333	.286	.343	11	42	8	14	3	2	0	5	0	2	0	1	5	1	0	.500	.356
Torres, Jhon	R-R	6-4	199	3-29-00	.255	.323	.242	54	184	25	47	7	3	5	35	28	7	0	7	41	4	4	.408	.363
Ventura, Carlos	L-R	6-0	180	2-22-98	.161	.167	.160	49	124	16	20	7	1	3	20	36	4	0	2	42	2	2	.307	.361

Pitching	B-T	HT	WT	DOB	W	L	ERA	G	GS	CG	SV	IP	H	R	ER	HR	BB	SO	AVG	vLH	vRH	K/9	BB/9
Cedeno, Orlando	R-R	6-2	195	9-16-97	0	0	9.28	6	0	0	0	11	11	13	11	0	12	6	.290	.250	.308	5.06	10.13
2-team total (13 Indians/Brewers)					0	0	9.09	19	0	0	1	35	44	43	35	1	35	17	.328	.250	.308	4.41	9.09
De La Cruz, Joel	R-R	6-2	190	11-9-96	4	0	2.76	17	0	0	3	29	26	11	9	1	6	18	.236	.229	.242	5.52	1.84
Feliz, Ignacio	R-R	6-1	180	10-23-99	2	4	4.39	13	13	0	0	55	47	36	27	4	41	42	.239	.275	.219	6.83	6.67
Figueroa, Hector	R-R	6-3	190	11-30-94	3	1	3.74	16	0	0	1	34	39	19	14	1	11	28	.296	.220	.330	7.49	2.94
Garcia, Henry	R-R	6-5	195	3-29-97	0	0	0.00	2	0	0	0	2	2	0	0	0	0	0	.286	.000	.333	0.00	0.00
2-team total (5 Indians/Brewers)					0	1	5.63	7	0	0	2	8	5	5	5	0	5	6	.200	.000	.333	6.75	5.63
Garcia, Luis C.	R-R	6-3	180	4-26-97	1	1	2.19	7	0	0	2	12	9	5	3	0	8	11	.205	.214	.200	8.03	5.84
2-team total (10 Indians/Brewers)					3	2	2.66	17	1	0	2	41	30	19	12	1	17	33	.195	.214	.200	7.30	3.76
Garcia, Luis D.	R-R	6-2	180	6-23-00	3	3	2.31	15	14	0	0	66	58	34	17	2	19	52	.236	.250	.227	7.06	2.58
Garcia, Mike	R-R	6-4	183	8-11-00	1	7	3.81	13	13	0	0	59	62	38	25	4	22	34	.274	.338	.242	5.19	3.36
Jimenez, Diarlin	R-R	6-5	180	3-18-00	4	6	4.98	14	10	0	0	65	79	52	36	2	20	47	.298	.273	.313	6.51	2.77
Meza, Wuilson	R-R	5-11	170	10-5-98	1	0	2.33	14	0	0	3	27	16	11	7	1	16	21	.178	.194	.167	7.00	5.33
Morillo, Sergio	R-R	6-3	190	9-13-99	0	3	5.79	6	1	0	0	9	10	9	6	1	8	7	.303	.231	.350	6.75	7.71
2-team total (1 Indians/Brewers)					0	4	12.10	7	2	0	0	10	14	16	13	1	10	7	.368	.231	.350	6.52	9.31
Oca, Jose	R-R	6-0	150	2-28-99	0	2	8.78	11	0	0	0	13	17	13	13	1	3	11	.315	.217	.387	7.43	2.03
Paredes, Juan	R-R	6-3	200	9-25-98	1	0	2.41	13	0	0	1	19	10	8	5	1	5	15	.154	.046	.209	7.23	2.41
Peguero, Luis	R-R	6-1	165	11-15-99	0	0	6.75	2	0	0	0	4	6	4	3	0	1	3	.333	.286	.364	6.75	2.25
Pereda, Leomar	R-R	6-1	160	9-27-97	1	2	4.00	12	0	0	0	18	16	12	8	0	13	15	.235	.280	.209	7.50	6.50
Perez, Eric	R-R	6-6	190	7-27-97	2	0	0.00	2	0	0	0	8	3	0	0	0	7	7	.111	.100	.118	7.88	7.88
2-team total (12 Indians/Brewers)					2	4	7.64	14	4	0	0	35	45	38	30	0	42	27	.315	.100	.118	6.88	10.70
Sanchez, Wilton	R-R	6-4	175	9-8-98	2	2	2.29	13	2	0	1	35	23	11	9	0	13	39	.186	.261	.141	9.93	3.31
Santana, Christophers	R-R	6-2	195	2-26-98	0	2	5.97	16	0	0	0	29	34	25	19	1	17	26	.309	.293	.319	8.16	5.34
Thomas, Luigence	R-R	6-3	160	10-12-94	3	2	4.81	16	0	0	1	24	25	20	13	0	15	30	.266	.258	.270	11.10	5.55
Thomas, Tahnaj	R-R	6-4	190	6-16-99	0	2	3.38	3	3	0	0	5	3	4	2	0	8	5	.167	.200	.154	8.44	13.50
Yannuzzi, Yeffersson	L-L	6-2	175	10-4-96	1	4	2.60	14	14	0	0	55	38	27	16	1	43	53	.202	.205	.201	8.62	6.99

Fielding

C: De Jesus 19, De Oleo 1, Diaz 31, Marmol 27. **1B:** Celesten 3, Cespedes 1, Contreras 2, De Jesus 5, De Oleo 47, Lopez 15, Santiago 5. **2B:** Contreras 19, Flores 12, Lopez 16, Maestre 7, Palacio 20, Santiago 4. **3B:** Celesten 33, Contreras 25, Flores 1, Lopez 18. **SS:** Gonzalez 55, Lopez 12, Maestre 3. **OF:** Cespedes 24, Jimenez 26, Mateo 29, Montero 53, Torres 48, Ventura 45.

DSL INDIANS/BREWERS — ROOKIE

DOMINICAN SUMMER LEAGUE

Batting	B-T	HT	WT	DOB	AVG	vLH	vRH	G	AB	R	H	2B	3B	HR	RBI	BB	HBP	SH	SF	SO	SB	CS	SLG	OBP
Cabrera, Julio	L-L	6-0	190	11-21-97	.217	.118	.238	32	97	11	21	2	3	2	16	9	2	0	1	22	3	0	.361	.294
Cespedes, Cristopher	R-R	6-3	200	5-18-98	.294	.217	.319	25	92	13	27	8	1	2	17	7	2	1	2	12	3	2	.467	.350
2-team total (27 Indians)					.314	.308	.343	52	172	29	54	13	4	5	28	16	4	1	2	27	3	4	.523	.381
De La Rosa, Luis	R-R	6-4	170	8-31-98	.146	.222	.138	30	89	9	13	4	0	2	7	11	2	0	1	23	0	0	.258	.252
Jimenez, Pablo	R-R	6-2	175	2-6-99	.253	.250	.253	25	87	13	22	8	2	1	14	5	1	0	0	17	0	2	.425	.301
2-team total (26 Indians)					.238	.190	.234	51	172	31	41	10	2	2	20	22	5	0	1	43	2	5	.355	.340
Kelkboom, M.	R-R	5-11	152	7-12-00	.207	.364	.191	34	121	8	25	6	2	0	13	12	1	2	1	29	2	8	.289	.282
Maestre, Jesus	R-R	5-10	155	2-4-00	.133	.308	.097	27	75	10	10	0	0	0	3	12	3	0	0	19	6	1	.133	.278
2-team total (12 Indians)					.110	.125	.038	39	109	14	12	2	0	0	4	18	5	0	0	25	6	2	.128	.265
Palacio, Gaspar	B-R	5-8	155	3-2-00	.177	.182	.176	29	85	12	15	4	2	0	6	11	1	1	1	22	5	5	.271	.276
2-team total (23 Indians)					.173	.095	.194	52	168	21	29	7	3	1	12	22	2	1	1	51	7	8	.268	.275

Perez, Derian	L-L	6-3	175	6-8-00	.224	.310	.205	56	156	21	35	5	2	1	12	27	9	2	1	35	9	14	.301	.368
Ramirez, Micael	R-R	5-11	170	6-8-99	.304	.450	.254	23	79	15	24	8	1	0	14	8	1	0	0	10	0	0	.430	.375

Pitching	**B-T**	**HT**	**WT**	**DOB**	**W**	**L**	**ERA**	**G**	**GS**	**CG**	**SV**	**IP**	**H**	**R**	**ER**	**HR**	**BB**	**SO**	**AVG**	**vLH**	**vRH**	**K/9**	**BB/9**
Cedeno, Orlando	R-R	6-2	195	9-16-97	0	0	9.00	13	0	0	1	24	33	30	24	1	23	11	.344	.306	.367	4.13	8.63
2-team total (6 Indians)					0	0	9.09	19	0	0	1	35	44	43	35	1	35	17	.328	.250	.308	4.41	9.09
Feliz, Daritzon	L-L	6-2	175	8-19-99	0	7	6.32	12	12	0	0	47	55	37	33	2	25	33	.307	.375	.293	6.32	4.79
Garcia, Henry	R-R	6-5	195	3-29-97	0	1	7.50	5	0	0	2	6	3	5	5	0	5	6	.167	.200	.154	9.00	7.50
2-team total (2 Indians)					0	1	5.63	7	0	0	2	8	5	5	5	0	5	6	.200	.000	.333	6.75	5.63
Garcia, Luis C.	R-R	6-3	180	4-26-97	2	1	2.86	10	1	0	0	28	21	14	9	1	9	22	.191	.135	.219	6.99	2.86
2-team total (7 Indians)					3	2	2.66	17	1	0	2	41	30	19	12	1	17	33	.195	.214	.200	7.30	3.76
Kery, Adoni	R-R	6-0	170	2-18-96	2	0	0.79	7	0	0	0	11	8	6	1	0	6	9	.186	.154	.200	7.15	4.76
Mejia, Wilmer	R-R	6-2	170	1-15-99	0	3	4.79	10	7	0	0	41	54	28	22	4	6	29	.320	.348	.300	6.31	1.31
Morillo, Sergio	R-R	6-3	190	9-13-99	0	1	189.00	1	1	0	0	0	4	7	7	0	2	0	.800	.750	1.000	0.00	54.00
2-team total (6 DSL Indians)					0	4	12.10	7	2	0	0	10	14	16	13	1	10	7	.368	.231	.350	6.52	9.31
Perez, Eric	R-R	6-6	190	7-27-97	0	4	9.88	12	4	0	0	27	42	38	30	0	35	20	.362	.357	.365	6.59	11.52
2-team total (2 Indians)					2	4	7.64	14	4	0	0	35	45	38	30	0	42	27	.315	.100	.118	6.88	10.70
Varela, Jahir	L-L	5-10	175	2-7-98	3	2	2.05	15	8	0	1	48	37	15	11	1	18	35	.218	.088	.250	6.52	3.35

Fielding

C: Ramirez 22. **1B:** Cabrera 1, Cespedes 13, De La Rosa 7, Jimenez 11. **2B:** Kelkboom 9, Maestre 18, Palacio 18. **3B:** Cabrera 1, Maestre 7, Palacio 8. **SS:** Kelkboom 23, Maestre 3, Palacio 1. **OF:** Cabrera 16, Cespedes 10, De La Rosa 12, Jimenez 15, Perez 50.

Colorado Rockies

SEASON IN A SENTENCE: Star turns by Nolan Arenado and Charlie Blackmon, plus a young, vastly improved and mostly homegrown rotation, pushed the Rockies to a fast start under new manager Bud Black and produced the club's fourth-ever playoff berth and first since 2009.

HIGH POINT: Colorado got off to a great start, then took it up a notch in June, winning 14 of its first 18 in the month to get to 21 games over .500 (47-26). The end of that hot streak included a four-game sweep of the Giants, bookended by walk-off wins, and a 4-3 win against the Diamondbacks that Arenado won with an eighth-inning, two-run triple off Zack Greinke.

LOW POINT: An eight-game June losing streak dropped the Rockies behind the streaking Diamondbacks in the wild-card chase, and a three-game sweep at Dodger Stadium ensured they'd never threaten the Dodgers for the National League West title. The sweep included a shutout loss and a 12-6 defeat in which the bullpen, an issue most of the second half of the season, gave up eight unanswered runs.

NOTABLE ROOKIES: Four rookie pitchers started a combined 93 games, with the Rockies going 53-40 in them. Three rookies—lefthander Kyle Freeland and righties German Marquez and Antonio Senzatela—won at least 10 games apiece. Freeland provided the highlight on July 9, taking a no-hitter into the ninth inning of a 10-0 win against the White Sox. Fellow rookie Jeff Hoffman got off to a fine start before foundering in the second half. Outfielder Raimel Tapia had his moments and could replace free agent Carlos Gonzalez, who had a poor season, in right field in 2018.

KEY TRANSACTIONS: While free-agent pickup Ian Desmond struggled with injuries and modest production, offseason pickup Mark Reynolds finished third on the club with 30 homers. The front office patched two holes with in-season veteran pickups at catcher, with Jonathan Lucroy, and in the bullpen, with 2017 all-star Pat Neshek.

DOWN ON THE FARM: Infielder Ryan McMahon (second) and shortstop Brendan Rodgers (sixth) both threatened for the minors' batting title. The Double-A Hartford affiliate, where both players spent time, opened its new Dunkin' Donuts Park finally, to much acclaim, while high Class A Lancaster had the best record in the California League.

OPENING DAY PAYROLL: $130,963,571 (16th)

PLAYERS OF THE YEAR

MAJOR LEAGUE

Charlie Blackmon
OF

.331/.399/.601
Led NL in hits (213), AVG (.331), runs (137)

MINOR LEAGUE

Brendan Rodgers
SS

(High Class A/ Double-A)
.336/.373/.567

ORGANIZATION LEADERS

BATTING		*Minimum 250 AB	
MAJORS			
*	AVG	Charlie Blackmon	.331
*	OPS	Charlie Blackmon	1.000
	HR	Nolan Arenado	37
		Charlie Blackmon	37
	RBI	Nolan Arenado	130
MINORS			
*	AVG	Raimel Tapia, Albuquerque	.369
*	OBP	Steven Linkous, Boise	.409
*	SLG	Ryan McMahon, Hartford, Albuquerque	.583
*	OPS	Ryan McMahon, Hartford, Albuquerque	.986
	R	Garrett Hampson, Lancaster	113
	H	Yonathan Daza, Lancaster	177
		Garrett Hampson, Lancaster	177
	TB	Ryan McMahon, Hartford, Albuquerque	274
	2B	Ryan McMahon, Hartford, Albuquerque	39
	3B	Garrett Hampson, Lancaster	12
		Noel Cuevas, Albuquerque	12
		Derrik Gibson, Albuquerque	12
	HR	Jordan Patterson, Albuquerque	26
	RBI	Jordan Patterson, Albuquerque	92
		Sam Hilliard, Lancaster	92
	BB	Brian Mundell, Lancaster, Hartford	60
	SO	Sam Hilliard, Lancaster	154
	SB	Wes Rogers, Lancaster	70

PITCHING		#Minimum 75 IP	
MAJORS			
	W	Kyle Freeland	11
		German Marquez	11
#	ERA	Chris Rusin	2.65
	SO	German Marquez	147
	SV	Greg Holland	41
MINORS			
	W	Jesus Tinoco, Lancaster	11
		Trey Killian, Lancaster	11
		Craig Schlitter, Lancaster, Hartford	11
	L	Ryan Castellani, Hartford	12
#	ERA	Alejandro Requena, Asheville, Lakewood	2.85
	G	Julian Fernandez, Asheville	51
	GS	Trey Killian, Lancaster	28
	SV	Shane Broyles, Hartford, Albuquerque	21
	IP	Ryan Castellani, Hartford	157.1
	BB	Riley Pint, Asheville	59
	SO	Ryan Carpenter, Albuquerque	161
#	AVG	Sam Howard, Hartford, Albuquerque	.236

2017 PERFORMANCE

General Manager: Jeff Bridich. **Farm Director:** Zach Wilson. **Scouting Director:** Bill Schmidt.

Class	Team	League	W	L	PCT	Finish	Manager
Majors	Colorado Rockies	National	87	75	.537	5th (15)	Bud Black
Triple-A	Albuquerque Isotopes	Pacific Coast	68	73	.482	t-10th (16)	Glenallen Hill
Double-A	Hartford Yard Goats	Eastern	62	77	.446	9th (12)	Jerry Weinstein
High-A	Lancaster JetHawks	California	79	61	.564	1st (8)	Fred Ocasio
Low-A	Asheville Tourists	South Atlantic	68	70	.493	t-9th (14)	Warren Schaeffer
Short Season	Boise Hawks	Northwest	37	39	.487	6th (8)	Scott Little
Rookie	Grand Junction Rockies	Pioneer	38	38	.500	t-3rd (8)	Frank Gonzales
Overall 2017 Minor League Record			352	358	.496	16th (30)	

ORGANIZATION STATISTICS

COLORADO ROCKIES

NATIONAL LEAGUE

Batting	B-T	HT	WT	DOB	AVG	vLH	vRH	G	AB	R	H	2B	3B	HR	RBI	BB	HBP	SH	SF	SO	SB	CS	SLG	OBP
Adames, Cristhian	B-R	6-0	185	7-26-91	.000	.000	.000	12	13	1	0	0	0	0	0	1	0	0	0	6	0	0	.000	.071
Amarista, Alexi	L-R	5-6	160	4-6-89	.238	.294	.232	96	168	22	40	10	0	3	19	7	0	1	0	38	1	0	.351	.269
Arenado, Nolan	R-R	6-2	205	4-16-91	.309	.420	.272	159	606	100	187	43	7	37	130	62	4	1	6	106	3	2	.586	.373
Blackmon, Charlie	L-L	6-3	210	7-1-86	.331	.333	.330	159	644	137	213	35	14	37	104	65	10	3	3	135	14	10	.601	.399
Cardullo, Stephen	R-R	6-0	215	8-31-87	.143	.191	.000	15	28	2	4	0	0	0	3	3	1	0	0	7	0	0	.143	.250
Desmond, Ian	R-R	6-3	215	9-20-85	.274	.250	.283	95	339	47	93	11	1	7	40	24	4	2	4	87	15	4	.375	.326
Garneau, Dustin	R-R	6-0	200	8-13-87	.206	.177	.235	22	68	5	14	7	0	1	6	4	1	1	0	24	0	0	.353	.260
Gonzalez, Carlos	L-L	6-1	220	10-17-85	.262	.206	.283	136	470	72	123	34	0	14	57	56	2	0	6	119	3	0	.423	.339
Hanigan, Ryan	R-R	6-0	225	8-16-80	.267	.467	.183	33	101	9	27	2	0	2	12	8	1	1	1	26	0	0	.347	.324
LeMahieu, DJ	R-R	6-4	215	7-13-88	.310	.362	.293	155	609	95	189	28	4	8	64	59	6	3	5	90	6	5	.409	.374
Lucroy, Jonathan	R-R	6-0	200	6-13-86	.310	.225	.343	46	142	18	44	6	3	2	13	27	4	0	2	19	0	0	.437	.429
McMahon, Ryan	L-R	6-2	185	12-14-94	.158	.000	.200	17	19	2	3	1	0	0	1	5	0	0	0	5	0	0	.211	.333
Murphy, Tom	R-R	6-1	220	4-3-91	.042	.059	.000	12	24	1	1	1	0	0	1	2	0	0	0	9	0	0	.083	.115
Parra, Gerardo	L-L	5-11	210	5-6-87	.309	.347	.296	115	392	56	121	24	1	10	71	20	4	0	9	67	2	5	.452	.341
Reynolds, Mark	R-R	6-2	220	8-3-83	.267	.231	.281	148	520	82	139	22	1	30	97	69	1	0	3	175	2	1	.487	.352
Story, Trevor	R-R	6-1	210	11-15-92	.239	.301	.216	145	503	68	120	32	3	24	82	49	2	0	1	191	7	2	.457	.308
Tapia, Raimel	L-L	6-2	160	2-4-94	.288	.227	.310	70	160	27	46	12	2	2	16	8	2	1	0	36	5	2	.425	.329
Tauchman, Mike	L-L	6-2	200	12-3-90	.222	.400	.182	31	27	2	6	0	1	0	2	5	0	0	0	10	1	2	.296	.344
Valaika, Pat	R-R	5-11	200	9-9-92	.258	.290	.236	110	182	28	47	11	0	13	40	7	0	5	1	53	0	0	.533	.284
Wolters, Tony	L-R	5-10	200	6-9-92	.240	.196	.253	83	229	30	55	8	1	0	16	33	2	2	0	55	0	1	.284	.341

Pitching	B-T	HT	WT	DOB	W	L	ERA	G	GS	CG	SV	IP	H	R	ER	HR	BB	SO	AVG	vLH	vRH	K/9	BB/9
Anderson, Tyler	L-L	6-4	210	12-30-89	6	6	4.81	17	15	0	0	86	88	48	46	16	26	81	.269	.221	.286	8.48	2.72
Bettis, Chad	R-R	6-1	200	4-26-89	2	4	5.05	9	9	0	0	46	52	27	26	8	11	30	.286	.256	.313	5.83	2.14
Carle, Shane	R-R	6-4	185	8-30-91	0	0	6.75	3	0	0	0	4	6	3	3	1	0	4	.316	.364	.250	9.00	0.00
Chatwood, Tyler	R-R	6-0	185	12-16-89	8	15	4.69	33	25	1	1	148	136	79	77	20	77	120	.251	.270	.230	7.31	4.69
Diaz, Jairo	R-R	6-0	200	5-27-91	0	0	9.00	4	0	0	0	5	12	6	5	0	5	2	.500	.500	.500	3.60	9.00
Dunn, Mike	L-L	6-0	215	5-23-85	5	1	4.47	68	0	0	0	50	43	25	25	8	28	57	.228	.244	.212	10.19	5.01
Estevez, Carlos	R-R	6-4	210	12-28-92	5	0	5.57	35	0	0	0	32	39	21	20	3	14	31	.293	.339	.260	8.63	3.90
Freeland, Kyle	L-L	6-3	170	5-14-93	11	11	4.10	33	28	0	0	156	169	78	71	17	63	107	.284	.283	.284	6.17	3.63
Gray, Jon	R-R	6-4	235	11-5-91	10	4	3.67	20	20	0	0	110	113	47	45	10	30	112	.266	.260	.274	9.14	2.45
Hoffman, Jeff	R-R	6-5	225	1-8-93	6	5	5.89	23	16	0	0	99	106	66	65	15	40	82	.273	.232	.314	7.43	3.62
Holland, Greg	R-R	5-10	205	11-20-85	3	6	3.61	61	0	0	41	57	40	24	23	7	26	70	.193	.157	.232	10.99	4.08
Lyles, Jordan	R-R	6-4	230	10-19-90	0	2	6.94	33	0	0	0	47	61	37	36	11	12	33	.316	.363	.283	6.36	2.31
2-team total (5 San Diego)					1	5	7.75	38	5	0	0	70	96	61	60	16	22	55	.325	.363	.283	7.11	2.84
Marquez, German	R-R	6-1	185	2-22-95	11	7	4.39	29	29	0	0	162	174	82	79	25	49	147	.274	.279	.270	8.17	2.72
McGee, Jake	L-L	6-3	230	8-6-86	0	2	3.61	62	0	0	3	57	47	23	23	4	16	58	.224	.260	.203	9.10	2.51
Neshek, Pat	R-B	6-3	220	9-4-80	2	1	2.45	28	0	0	0	22	20	8	6	1	1	24	.235	.303	.192	9.82	0.41
2-team total (43 Philadelphia)					5	3	1.59	71	0	0	1	62	48	13	11	3	6	69	.212	.303	.192	9.96	0.87
Oberg, Scott	R-R	6-2	205	3-13-90	0	1	4.94	66	0	0	0	58	70	35	32	4	24	55	.297	.294	.299	8.49	3.70
Ottavino, Adam	B-R	6-5	220	11-22-85	2	3	5.06	63	0	0	0	53	48	30	30	8	39	63	.244	.209	.262	10.63	6.58
Qualls, Chad	R-R	6-4	235	8-17-78	1	1	5.40	19	0	0	0	17	17	11	10	3	5	11	.258	.179	.316	5.94	2.70
Rosscup, Zac	R-L	6-2	220	6-9-88	0	0	5.14	9	0	0	0	7	9	4	4	2	0	10	.310	.000	.600	12.86	0.00
2-team total (1 Chicago Cubs)					0	0	4.70	10	0	0	0	8	9	4	4	2	0	10	.290	.000	.000	11.74	0.00
Rusin, Chris	L-L	6-2	195	10-22-86	5	1	2.65	60	0	0	2	85	75	31	25	9	19	71	.240	.268	.221	7.52	2.01
Senzatela, Antonio	R-R	6-1	180	1-21-95	10	5	4.68	36	20	0	0	135	128	72	70	18	47	102	.254	.240	.267	6.82	3.14

Fielding

Catcher	PCT	G	PO	A	E	DP	PB
Garneau	1.000	22	138	12	0	2	5
Hanigan	.996	30	239	14	1	1	2
Lucroy	.991	44	306	30	3	2	2
Murphy	1.000	8	46	4	0	1	2
Wolters	.997	77	528	43	2	5	7

First Base	PCT	G	PO	A	E	DP
Adames	1.000	1	2	0	0	0
Desmond	.995	27	200	5	1	12
McMahon	1.000	7	36	3	0	0
Parra	1.000	6	34	0	0	4
Reynolds	.995	138	1218	62	6	131
Valaika	1.000	5	10	2	0	4

Second Base	PCT	G	PO	A	E	DP
Adames	.000	1	0	0	0	0
Amarista	1.000	19	18	29	0	6
LeMahieu	.989	153	251	470	8	106

	PCT	G	PO	A	E	DP
McMahon	1.000	4	1	2	0	1
Valaika	.947	8	10	8	1	2
Wolters	1.000	4	2	5	0	1

Third Base	PCT	G	PO	A	E	DP
Amarista	.500	1	0	1	1	0
Arenado	.979	157	103	311	9	39
McMahon	1.000	3	0	1	0	0
Valaika	.962	19	10	15	1	3
Wolters	.000	1	0	0	0	0

Shortstop	PCT	G	PO	A	E	DP
Adames	1.000	1	1	1	0	0
Amarista	.902	18	7	30	4	6
Desmond	1.000	1	1	3	0	0
Story	.982	142	191	408	11	101
Valaika	.984	22	13	47	1	10

Outfield	PCT	G	PO	A	E	DP
Amarista	1.000	22	6	0	0	0
Blackmon	.988	158	339	4	4	3
Cardullo	1.000	8	13	0	0	0
Desmond	.973	67	106	2	3	0
Gonzalez	.986	125	201	3	3	1
Parra	.988	103	155	9	2	1
Reynolds	.000	1	0	0	0	0
Tapia	.952	46	60	0	3	0
Tauchman	.750	9	3	0	1	0
Valaika	1.000	5	4	0	0	0

ALBUQUERQUE ISOTOPES — TRIPLE-A

PACIFIC COAST LEAGUE

Batting	B-T	HT	WT	DOB	AVG	vLH	vRH	G	AB	R	H	2B	3B	HR	RBI	BB	HBP	SH	SF	SO	SB	CS	SLG	OBP
Adames, Cristhian	B-R	6-0	185	7-26-91	.263	.275	.261	89	323	47	85	19	6	11	52	29	0	2	8	68	3	4	.461	.317
Bemboom, Anthony	L-R	6-2	195	1-18-90	.278	.280	.278	45	133	20	37	8	2	4	20	24	1	1	1	30	0	0	.459	.390
Brown, Domonic	L-L	6-5	225	9-3-87	.304	.250	.312	48	158	23	48	10	2	3	21	8	0	0	5	23	0	2	.449	.328
Cardullo, Stephen	R-R	6-0	215	8-31-87	.308	.333	.304	8	26	6	8	3	0	0	5	4	1	0	0	4	1	1	.423	.419
Castro, Daniel	R-R	5-11	190	11-14-92	.306	.355	.297	115	395	43	121	25	1	3	45	24	1	5	5	43	1	3	.398	.344
Ciriaco, Juan	R-R	5-9	165	7-6-90	.278	.667	.200	12	18	0	5	0	0	0	0	0	0	1	0	4	2	1	.278	.278
Cuevas, Noel	R-R	6-2	210	10-2-91	.312	.424	.284	128	493	79	154	17	12	15	79	25	7	1	2	102	16	3	.487	.353
Dahl, David	L-R	6-2	195	4-1-94	.243	.286	.225	17	70	12	17	2	2	2	14	3	0	1	0	17	1	1	.414	.274
Denorfia, Chris	R-R	6-0	195	7-15-80	.275	.200	.293	20	51	7	14	0	2	0	2	9	0	1	0	13	4	0	.353	.383
Desmond, Ian	R-R	6-3	215	9-20-85	.333	.333	.333	3	9	1	3	1	0	1	1	1	0	0	0	1	0	0	.778	.400
Ferguson, Collin	L-L	6-2	215	2-9-93	.314	.200	.333	12	35	7	11	1	0	1	7	5	0	0	1	6	1	1	.429	.390
Garneau, Dustin	R-R	6-0	200	8-13-87	.281	.429	.252	36	128	24	36	9	2	10	26	13	1	0	2	22	0	1	.617	.347
Gibson, Derrik	R-R	6-1	195	12-5-89	.242	.306	.227	108	376	53	91	16	12	5	47	34	3	4	5	87	10	1	.388	.306
Hanigan, Ryan	R-R	6-0	225	8-16-80	.264	.250	.268	17	53	9	14	3	0	0	8	10	1	0	5	16	0	0	.321	.362
Herrera, Rosell	B-R	6-3	195	10-16-92	.278	.254	.284	103	320	59	89	20	4	3	27	35	2	4	2	69	20	6	.394	.351
Howard, Ryan	L-L	6-4	250	11-19-79	.192	.125	.222	16	52	5	10	4	0	3	8	0	0	0	2	17	0	0	.442	.185
McMahon, Ryan	L-R	6-2	185	12-14-94	.374	.304	.391	70	289	46	108	23	2	14	56	21	0	0	4	53	4	3	.613	.411
Murphy, Tom	R-R	6-1	220	4-3-91	.255	.400	.224	38	141	22	36	10	1	4	19	9	3	0	1	56	0	0	.426	.312
Parra, Gerardo	L-L	5-11	210	5-6-87	.200	.000	.222	3	10	0	2	0	0	0	0	1	0	0	0	3	0	0	.200	.273
Patterson, Jordan	L-L	6-4	215	2-12-92	.283	.287	.282	131	484	78	137	32	7	26	92	36	15	1	6	128	3	5	.539	.348
Perkins, Robbie	R-R	6-0	175	5-29-94	.200	.000	.500	2	5	0	1	0	0	0	0	0	0	0	0	1	0	0	.200	.200
Story, Trevor	R-R	6-1	210	11-15-92	.273	.400	.167	4	11	2	3	0	0	1	2	2	0	0	0	3	1	0	.546	.385
Tapia, Raimel	L-L	6-2	160	2-4-94	.369	.360	.371	58	263	45	97	20	8	2	30	13	0	0	1	42	12	2	.529	.397
Tauchman, Mike	L-L	6-2	200	12-3-90	.331	.370	.322	110	420	82	139	30	8	16	80	40	4	1	10	73	16	7	.555	.386
Thomas, Dillon	L-L	6-1	225	12-10-92	.000	.000	.000	3	2	0	0	0	0	0	1	0	0	0	1	0	0	0	.000	.000
Valaika, Pat	R-R	5-11	200	9-9-92	.267	.071	.355	11	45	6	12	2	1	1	11	4	0	1	0	11	0	0	.422	.327
Vazquez, Jan	B-R	5-10	165	4-29-91	.316	.167	.385	6	19	2	6	1	1	1	1	0	0	1	0	3	0	0	.632	.316
Wolters, Tony	L-R	5-10	200	6-9-92	.259	.333	.255	14	54	6	14	5	1	2	9	3	1	0	0	15	0	1	.500	.310
Ynoa, Rafael	B-R	6-0	190	8-7-87	.234	.270	.225	98	316	39	74	9	5	2	32	34	2	2	2	65	7	3	.313	.311

Pitching	B-T	HT	WT	DOB	W	L	ERA	G	GS	CG	SV	IP	H	R	ER	HR	BB	SO	AVG	vLH	vRH	K/9	BB/9
Almonte, Yency	B-R	6-3	205	6-4-94	3	1	4.89	8	7	0	0	35	41	20	19	7	21	22	.315	.345	.292	5.66	5.40
Anderson, Tyler	L-L	6-4	210	12-30-89	0	2	4.38	4	2	0	0	12	14	6	6	0	4	13	.304	.278	.321	9.49	2.92
Balog, Alex	R-R	6-5	210	7-16-92	0	0	5.40	1	0	0	0	2	2	1	1	0	1	1	.286	.250	.333	5.40	5.40
Bettis, Chad	R-R	6-1	200	4-26-89	0	3	4.82	4	4	0	0	19	22	13	10	2	6	11	.301	.297	.306	5.30	2.89
Broyles, Shane	R-R	6-1	180	8-19-91	0	0	0.00	1	0	0	0	1	0	0	0	0	0	0	.000	.000	—	0.00	0.00
Carasiti, Matt	R-R	6-3	205	7-23-91	1	1	2.37	27	0	0	13	30	31	9	8	1	13	43	.263	.240	.279	12.76	3.86
2-team total (19 Iowa)					1	3	3.26	46	0	0	21	50	49	19	18	2	23	68	.259	.313	.205	12.32	4.17
Carle, Shane	R-R	6-4	185	8-30-91	3	5	5.37	36	3	0	1	62	74	38	37	8	22	50	.300	.320	.286	7.26	3.19
Carpenter, Ryan	L-L	6-5	210	8-22-90	10	9	4.15	27	25	1	0	156	161	74	72	19	39	161	.269	.269	.269	9.29	2.25
Diaz, Jairo	R-R	6-0	200	5-27-91	0	1	5.00	20	0	0	3	18	16	10	10	1	7	17	.242	.212	.273	8.50	3.50
Enright, Barry	R-R	6-3	220	3-30-86	5	4	6.96	12	12	0	0	63	80	50	49	14	13	47	.305	.321	.295	6.68	1.85
Estevez, Carlos	R-R	6-4	210	12-28-92	1	4	1.34	33	0	0	4	34	23	6	5	2	10	34	.193	.235	.162	9.09	2.67
Farris, James	R-R	6-2	210	4-4-92	1	3	4.62	31	0	0	2	39	37	22	20	8	15	41	.243	.172	.296	9.46	3.46
Flemer, Matt	R-R	6-2	210	11-22-90	8	7	5.76	26	21	0	0	127	158	85	81	26	35	81	.311	.355	.278	5.76	2.49
Gonzalez, Nelson	R-R	6-1	170	2-15-90	0	1	4.18	16	0	0	0	32	26	16	15	4	18	24	.220	.220	.221	6.68	5.01
Gray, Jon	R-R	6-4	235	11-5-91	0	0	1.93	2	2	0	0	9	10	6	2	2	5	13	.270	.357	.217	12.54	4.82
Hoffman, Jeff	R-R	6-5	225	1-8-93	3	3	4.71	10	10	0	0	50	44	31	26	3	19	47	.233	.260	.202	8.52	3.44
House, Austin	R-R	6-4	200	1-24-91	8	2	1.85	49	0	0	3	68	56	16	14	2	23	53	.226	.170	.264	7.01	3.04
Howard, Sam	R-L	6-3	170	3-5-93	4	4	3.89	15	14	0	0	81	82	35	35	6	33	64	.264	.317	.238	7.11	3.67
Jemiola, Zach	L-R	6-3	200	4-6-94	5	5	6.83	16	15	0	0	82	104	65	62	13	38	40	.310	.306	.314	4.41	4.19
Jiminian, Johendi	R-R	6-3	170	10-14-92	1	2	5.04	18	1	0	0	30	28	19	17	3	22	17	.250	.298	.215	5.04	6.53
Lee, C.C.	R-R	5-11	190	10-21-86	2	2	5.54	27	0	0	0	37	37	23	23	4	16	53	.252	.225	.265	12.78	3.86
Marquez, German	R-R	6-1	185	2-22-95	0	0	2.70	3	2	0	0	10	8	3	3	2	0	18	.216	.250	.177	16.20	0.00
Moll, Sam	L-L	5-10	185	1-3-92	3	2	4.18	44	0	0	0	47	56	27	22	4	18	39	.292	.307	.285	7.42	3.42
2-team total (6 Nashville)					3	2	3.64	50	0	0	0	54	61	27	22	4	19	47	.280	.306	.285	7.79	3.15
Musgrave, Harrison	L-L	6-1	205	3-3-92	3	1	6.79	12	12	0	0	54	64	41	41	10	26	39	.301	.286	.306	6.46	4.31
Niebla, Luis	R-R	6-4	185	1-4-91	1	0	1.80	1	1	0	0	5	6	3	1	0	2	5	.300	.500	.278	9.00	3.60
Oberg, Scott	R-R	6-2	205	3-13-90	1	0	2.08	3	0	0	0	4	2	1	1	0	1	5	.143	.333	.000	10.38	2.08
Qualls, Chad	R-R	6-4	235	8-17-78	0	0	1.80	6	0	0	0	5	5	1	1	0	1	5	.278	.167	.333	9.00	1.80

Rosscup, Zac	R-L	6-2	220	6-9-88	0	0	2.13	12	0	0	1	13	8	3	3	1	4	15	.174	.313	.100	10.66	2.84
2-team total (17 Iowa)					2	2	2.45	29	1	0	2	40	29	12	11	4	12	54	.197	.242	.191	12.05	2.68
Rusin, Chris	L-L	6-2	195	10-22-86	1	0	0.00	1	0	0	0	3	2	0	0	0	0	3	.182	.000	.250	10.13	0.00
Senzatela, Antonio	R-R	6-1	180	1-21-95	0	0	2.70	1	1	0	0	3	4	1	1	0	1	2	.286	.333	.273	5.40	2.70
Vasto, Jerry	L-L	6-2	195	2-12-92	3	3	6.88	41	0	0	0	54	66	41	41	8	24	62	.301	.317	.293	10.40	4.02
Weber, Thad	R-R	6-2	205	9-28-84	1	7	7.85	16	9	0	0	55	92	51	48	14	11	39	.382	.358	.407	6.38	1.80

Fielding

Catcher	PCT	G	PO	A	E	DP	PB
Bemboom	.990	40	269	37	3	3	1
Garneau	.990	36	278	28	3	2	1
Hanigan	.986	16	126	12	2	1	0
Murphy	.986	34	252	24	4	3	1
Perkins	1.000	1	7	0	0	0	0
Vazquez	1.000	6	46	1	0	0	0
Wolters	.990	13	94	9	1	1	1

First Base	PCT	G	PO	A	E	DP
Cardullo	1.000	4	21	1	0	2
Desmond	1.000	2	14	0	0	0
Ferguson	.988	9	78	7	1	11
Howard	.986	10	70	2	1	5
McMahon	.993	36	269	18	2	26
Parra	1.000	1	9	1	0	0
Patterson	.988	84	688	52	9	64
Valaika	1.000	2	23	1	0	0

Second Base	PCT	G	PO	A	E	DP
Adames	.967	49	97	110	7	24
Castro	1.000	15	32	36	0	6
Ciriaco	.950	6	9	10	1	4
Gibson	.981	12	24	27	1	5
Herrera	.900	3	4	5	1	1
McMahon	.958	24	48	66	5	11
Ynoa	.995	43	89	113	1	32

Third Base	PCT	G	PO	A	E	DP
Adames	.952	33	26	54	4	4
Castro	.500	1	0	1	1	0
Gibson	.956	86	42	173	10	18
Herrera	.833	5	2	8	2	1
McMahon	.963	13	10	16	1	1
Ynoa	.875	7	2	5	1	1

Shortstop	PCT	G	PO	A	E	DP
Adames	1.000	7	12	17	0	1
Castro	.989	96	132	298	5	63
Desmond	1.000	1	1	3	0	0
Gibson	1.000	1	0	1	0	0
Story	.895	3	7	10	2	2
Valaika	1.000	9	10	25	0	3
Ynoa	.953	32	45	77	6	17

Outfield	PCT	G	PO	A	E	DP
Brown	1.000	26	45	3	0	0
Cardullo	1.000	4	2	1	0	0
Cuevas	.986	111	200	6	3	2
Dahl	1.000	15	25	0	0	0
Denorfia	.929	12	25	1	2	0
Desmond	1.000	1	1	0	0	0
Flemer	1.000	1	1	0	0	0
Herrera	.991	71	100	6	1	0
Parra	1.000	2	4	0	0	0
Patterson	.986	39	64	4	1	0
Tapia	.977	55	125	3	3	0
Tauchman	.988	102	241	7	3	1
Thomas	.000	1	0	0	0	0
Ynoa	1.000	6	9	0	0	0

COLORADO ROCKIES

HARTFORD YARD GOATS — *DOUBLE-A*

EASTERN LEAGUE

Batting	B-T	HT	WT	DOB	AVG	vLH	vRH	G	AB	R	H	2B	3B	HR	RBI	BB	HBP	SH	SF	SO	SB	CS	SLG	OBP
Cardullo, Stephen	R-R	6-0	215	8-31-87	.195	.205	.191	41	128	17	25	5	1	4	17	22	1	0	0	22	1	0	.344	.318
Carrizales, Omar	L-L	6-0	175	1-30-95	.248	.248	.248	120	432	47	107	20	5	5	41	48	5	4	3	96	12	12	.352	.328
Ciriaco, Juan	R-R	5-9	165	7-6-90	.196	.065	.262	33	92	5	18	2	0	2	9	3	0	3	1	15	3	2	.283	.219
Ferguson, Collin	L-L	6-2	215	2-9-93	.179	.250	.157	24	67	5	12	2	2	2	7	7	1	0	0	22	0	0	.358	.267
Fuentes, Josh	R-R	6-2	215	2-19-93	.307	.312	.305	122	414	48	127	28	7	15	72	24	6	4	2	92	8	5	.517	.352
Graeter, Ashley	R-R	6-1	190	10-3-89	.247	.258	.243	95	348	42	86	17	1	10	38	23	4	4	1	70	7	4	.388	.301
Jean, Luis	R-R	6-1	150	8-17-94	.213	.195	.221	61	136	13	29	3	1	0	11	6	1	2	1	20	6	3	.250	.250
McMahon, Ryan	L-R	6-2	185	12-14-94	.326	.159	.380	49	181	28	59	16	2	6	32	20	1	0	3	39	7	0	.536	.390
Metzler, Ryan	R-R	6-3	190	3-20-93	.250	.286	.233	17	44	6	11	1	0	0	6	3	0	0	1	15	1	2	.273	.292
Mundell, Brian	R-R	6-3	230	2-28-94	.302	.346	.282	52	172	30	52	12	0	3	19	25	3	0	3	26	1	1	.424	.394
Nunez, Dom	L-R	6-0	175	1-17-95	.202	.220	.195	95	297	37	60	10	1	11	28	53	8	3	3	83	7	1	.354	.335
Phillips, Anthony	R-R	5-9	160	4-11-90	.209	.204	.211	99	287	22	60	9	0	4	24	21	1	5	0	73	2	6	.282	.265
Prime, Correlle	R-R	6-5	222	2-18-94	.272	.297	.263	91	272	31	74	7	2	8	29	22	3	0	0	90	2	9	.401	.333
Rodgers, Brendan	R-R	6-0	180	8-9-96	.260	.286	.245	38	150	20	39	5	0	6	17	8	6	0	0	36	0	2	.413	.323
Soto, Elvin	R-B	5-10	210	2-12-92	.063	.000	.077	6	16	0	1	1	0	0	2	1	0	0	0	4	0	0	.125	.118
Thomas, Dillon	L-L	6-1	225	12-10-92	.229	.281	.213	83	271	33	62	14	1	6	37	23	6	0	2	101	9	5	.354	.301
Vazquez, Jan	B-R	5-10	165	4-29-91	.289	.357	.260	62	187	28	54	7	1	6	34	25	7	5	0	48	3	3	.433	.393
Weeks, Drew	R-R	6-2	200	6-9-93	.245	.303	.222	128	470	69	115	22	2	17	63	41	7	2	3	114	13	14	.409	.313
White, Max	L-L	6-2	175	10-10-93	.243	.234	.246	113	371	55	90	22	4	7	24	52	1	4	2	118	24	13	.380	.336

Pitching	B-T	HT	WT	DOB	W	L	ERA	G	GS	CG	SV	IP	H	R	ER	HR	BB	SO	AVG	vLH	vRH	K/9	BB/9
Additon, Nick	R-L	6-5	215	12-16-87	0	4	2.45	5	5	0	0	26	23	14	7	1	9	26	.242	.308	.232	9.12	3.16
Almonte, Yency	B-R	6-3	205	6-4-94	5	3	2.00	14	14	0	0	76	58	19	17	4	31	71	.213	.159	.259	8.37	3.66
Ascher, Steve	L-L	6-0	185	10-18-93	0	0	4.91	9	0	0	0	7	6	4	4	0	7	2	.240	.273	.214	2.45	8.59
Bettis, Chad	R-R	6-1	200	4-26-89	0	0	1.93	2	1	0	0	5	3	2	1	1	1	6	.167	.000	.250	11.57	1.93
Brazoban, Huascar	R-R	6-3	155	10-15-89	2	1	6.29	24	0	0	0	24	28	17	17	0	13	16	.286	.340	.235	5.92	4.81
Broyles, Shane	R-R	6-1	180	8-19-91	3	1	1.84	47	0	0	21	54	36	15	11	7	16	78	.186	.185	.186	13.08	2.68
Castellani, Ryan	R-R	6-4	220	4-1-96	9	12	4.81	27	27	1	0	157	163	94	84	16	47	132	.264	.287	.245	7.55	2.69
Farris, James	R-R	6-2	210	4-4-92	0	0	1.45	17	0	0	9	19	14	4	3	1	2	28	.203	.172	.225	13.50	0.96
French, Parker	L-R	6-2	225	3-19-93	8	11	6.37	24	24	1	0	129	154	108	91	22	52	69	.297	.305	.289	4.83	3.64
Frias, Edison	R-R	6-1	180	12-18-90	3	4	3.94	31	0	0	1	46	44	22	20	1	18	34	.243	.212	.271	6.70	3.55
Holman, David	R-R	6-6	220	5-31-90	1	1	6.14	16	0	0	0	22	26	15	15	4	12	20	.299	.308	.292	8.18	4.91
Howard, Sam	R-L	6-3	170	3-5-93	1	4	2.33	9	9	1	0	46	31	13	12	5	10	40	.185	.154	.194	7.77	1.94
Jiminian, Johendi	R-R	6-3	170	10-14-92	0	3	5.73	18	2	0	0	33	45	21	21	7	19	24	.319	.344	.299	6.55	5.18
Johnson, D.J.	L-R	6-4	235	8-30-89	1	1	2.80	43	0	0	4	64	53	24	20	4	24	51	.226	.235	.217	7.13	3.36
Lamb, Will	L-L	6-6	180	9-9-90	1	1	3.50	10	0	0	0	18	18	9	7	3	12	22	.269	.250	.279	11.00	6.00
Neiman, Troy	R-R	6-6	230	11-13-90	4	2	3.66	35	0	0	0	64	60	31	26	7	25	62	.247	.245	.248	8.72	3.52
Niebla, Luis	R-R	6-4	185	1-4-91	1	5	6.31	15	10	0	0	46	55	35	32	5	27	30	.309	.397	.240	5.91	5.32
Pierpont, Matt	R-R	6-2	215	1-25-91	8	1	2.02	28	0	0	2	62	38	14	14	5	13	55	.176	.181	.173	7.94	1.88
Ramirez, Luis	R-R	6-3	200	7-12-92	0	2	20.25	4	0	0	0	4	9	9	9	1	6	4	.474	.444	.500	9.00	13.50
Schlitter, Craig	R-R	6-0	195	5-16-92	1	3	10.64	9	8	0	0	35	56	44	41	7	19	37	.368	.375	.364	9.61	4.93

Wade, Konner	L-R	6-3	190	12-3-91	9	7	4.28	33	15	0	0	109	118	55	52	15	21	79	.278	.265	.288	6.50	1.73
Wright, Austin	L-L	6-4	235	9-26-89	0	0	5.40	7	0	0	0	7	6	5	4	1	7	5	.240	.400	.133	6.75	9.45
Wynkoop, Jack	L-L	6-5	200	11-2-93	5	11	4.44	24	24	2	0	150	170	80	74	17	22	80	.293	.279	.297	4.80	1.32

Fielding

Catcher	PCT	G	PO	A	E	DP	PB
Graeter	1.000	1	6	1	0	0	0
Nunez	.988	88	596	66	8	2	5
Soto	.977	5	39	4	1	1	0
Vazquez	.989	48	319	25	4	1	3

First Base	PCT	G	PO	A	E	DP
Cardullo	1.000	2	10	1	0	1
Ferguson	.966	15	132	10	5	9
Fuentes	1.000	3	9	0	0	1
Graeter	1.000	10	87	5	0	9
McMahon	.995	25	192	11	1	14
Mundell	.989	40	347	21	4	36
Prime	.990	57	458	24	5	46

Second Base	PCT	G	PO	A	E	DP
Ciriaco	.972	28	45	59	3	19
Graeter	.980	64	94	151	5	31
Jean	.959	20	39	32	3	9
McMahon	.963	15	30	49	3	10
Metzler	1.000	4	5	4	0	1
Phillips	1.000	33	56	68	0	22
Rodgers	.972	6	13	22	1	5

Third Base	PCT	G	PO	A	E	DP
Cardullo	.889	4	0	8	1	1
Ciriaco	.778	3	1	6	2	0
Fuentes	.965	113	77	252	12	28
Graeter	.900	11	0	9	1	0
Jean	.000	3	0	0	0	0
McMahon	1.000	13	9	24	0	1
Metzler	1.000	8	7	12	0	4

Shortstop	PCT	G	PO	A	E	DP
Ciriaco	.875	2	1	6	1	1
Jean	.903	31	33	51	9	7
Jimenez	.932	21	15	54	5	10
Metzler	1.000	7	8	17	0	7
Phillips	.980	69	84	162	5	29
Rodgers	.925	33	38	85	10	22

Outfield	PCT	G	PO	A	E	DP
Cardullo	1.000	31	47	3	0	0
Carrizales	.983	119	281	6	5	1
Ciriaco	1.000	1	2	0	0	0
Graeter	.000	3	0	0	0	0
Thomas	.965	73	128	8	5	1
Weeks	.958	124	194	11	9	1
White	.963	95	154	4	6	0

LANCASTER JETHAWKS — *HIGH CLASS A*

CALIFORNIA LEAGUE

Batting	B-T	HT	WT	DOB	AVG	vLH	vRH	G	AB	R	H	2B	3B	HR	RBI	BB	HBP	SH	SF	SO	SB	CS	SLG	OBP
Burcham, Scott	R-R	5-11	185	6-17-93	.251	.225	.262	70	235	33	59	14	0	3	26	14	4	9	3	48	9	5	.349	.301
Dahl, David	L-R	6-2	195	4-1-94	.429	—	.429	2	7	2	3	0	0	1	2	1	0	0	0	1	0	0	.857	.500
Daza, Yonathan	R-R	6-2	190	2-28-94	.341	.343	.340	125	519	93	177	34	11	3	87	30	5	5	10	88	31	8	.466	.376
Ferguson, Collin	L-L	6-2	215	2-9-93	.444	.308	.480	18	63	10	28	6	1	3	21	4	1	0	2	13	3	2	.714	.471
Hampson, Garrett	R-R	5-11	185	10-10-94	.327	.328	.326	127	533	113	174	24	12	8	70	56	2	4	8	77	51	14	.462	.387
Hilliard, Sam	L-L	6-5	225	2-21-94	.300	.284	.307	133	536	95	161	23	7	21	92	50	2	5	4	154	37	17	.487	.360
Jones, Mylz	R-R	6-1	185	4-13-94	.297	.308	.293	115	445	65	132	23	4	9	63	23	2	8	3	86	34	16	.427	.332
Marte, Hamlet	R-R	5-10	180	2-3-94	.309	.338	.297	64	243	48	75	20	2	9	43	21	0	0	1	63	2	0	.519	.362
Mundell, Brian	R-R	6-3	230	2-28-94	.299	.273	.306	67	264	44	79	16	1	12	59	35	0	0	2	44	0	1	.504	.379
Perkins, Robbie	R-R	6-0	175	5-29-94	.271	.368	.235	22	70	13	19	6	0	1	6	7	0	2	0	20	1	0	.400	.338
Rabago, Chris	R-R	5-11	185	4-22-93	.272	.224	.291	89	305	52	83	18	8	1	43	35	5	7	6	53	25	8	.393	.350
Ramos, Roberto	L-R	6-5	220	12-28-94	.297	.238	.318	122	478	72	142	29	1	13	68	41	1	0	4	124	3	2	.444	.351
Rodgers, Brendan	R-R	6-0	180	8-9-96	.387	.413	.381	51	222	44	86	21	3	12	47	6	4	0	4	35	2	1	.671	.407
Rogers, Wes	R-R	6-3	180	3-7-94	.319	.365	.304	123	461	94	147	37	7	9	82	45	3	4	8	85	70	12	.488	.377
Romero, Avery	R-R	5-11	195	5-11-93	.271	.308	.252	44	155	31	42	6	0	6	23	18	0	1	3	23	4	1	.426	.341
Soriano, Wilson	R-R	5-9	140	12-31-91	.281	.292	.278	76	263	34	74	14	3	1	37	11	1	8	2	32	30	7	.369	.311
Thomas, Dillon	L-L	6-1	225	12-10-92	.240	.000	.255	12	50	7	12	1	0	1	3	2	1	0	0	18	6	0	.320	.283
Wall, Forrest	L-R	6-0	176	11-20-95	.299	.294	.300	22	87	17	26	4	1	3	16	9	0	1	1	16	5	3	.471	.361

Pitching	B-T	HT	WT	DOB	W	L	ERA	G	GS	CG	SV	IP	H	R	ER	HR	BB	SO	AVG	vLH	vRH	K/9	BB/9
Brazoban, Huascar	R-R	6-3	155	10-15-89	0	0	4.91	13	0	0	5	15	11	8	8	1	9	16	.204	.185	.222	9.82	5.52
Cozart, Logan	R-R	6-2	215	1-27-93	4	3	4.48	44	0	0	1	60	76	33	30	5	23	61	.313	.283	.333	9.10	3.43
Culbreth, Ty	L-L	5-11	175	4-9-94	7	1	3.13	12	11	0	0	69	66	27	24	6	16	51	.259	.261	.258	6.65	2.09
Diaz, Jairo	R-R	6-0	200	5-27-91	0	0	9.00	2	0	0	0	2	3	2	2	1	0	3	.375	.000	.500	13.50	0.00
Drozd, Jonny	L-L	6-7	200	9-17-91	0	0	6.94	10	0	0	0	12	19	13	9	2	2	7	.365	.300	.406	5.40	1.54
Gold, Brandon	R-R	6-3	203	9-16-94	4	3	4.40	12	12	0	0	76	97	45	37	10	12	50	.307	.314	.302	5.95	1.43
Gray, Jon	R-R	6-4	235	11-5-91	0	0	0.00	1	1	0	0	4	4	0	0	0	1	5	.286	.286	.286	11.25	2.25
Griggs, Scott	R-R	6-4	215	5-13-91	0	3	12.60	10	0	0	3	10	9	15	14	0	15	11	.243	.200	.273	9.90	13.50
Guillen, Alexander	R-R	6-2	175	11-23-95	0	6	6.26	46	0	0	12	55	73	39	38	8	26	72	.317	.340	.298	11.85	4.28
Hammer, J.D.	R-R	6-3	215	7-12-94	0	1	5.25	12	0	0	6	12	10	7	7	0	9	18	.227	.105	.320	13.50	6.75
Holder, Heath	R-R	6-6	211	8-23-92	0	0	7.36	19	0	0	0	26	31	25	21	2	16	25	.295	.264	.327	8.77	5.61
Justo, Salvador	R-R	6-5	210	10-14-94	2	4	9.89	25	0	0	3	24	28	27	26	6	20	14	.292	.229	.354	5.32	7.61
Killian, Trey	R-R	6-3	190	3-24-94	11	9	6.34	28	28	0	0	153	191	116	108	27	46	130	.302	.323	.284	7.63	2.70
Lambert, Peter	R-R	6-2	185	4-18-97	9	8	4.17	26	26	0	0	142	147	75	66	18	30	131	.267	.246	.286	8.28	1.90
Magliaro, Marc	R-R	5-11	175	2-17-90	4	2	5.11	41	0	0	2	62	73	37	35	9	14	53	.294	.302	.288	7.74	2.04
Polanco, Carlos	R-R	6-2	175	2-18-94	5	5	6.24	37	5	0	0	66	60	52	46	9	54	56	.242	.244	.241	7.60	7.33
Quintin, Cristian	R-R	6-3	165	12-27-93	0	0	17.28	8	0	0	0	8	14	24	16	4	13	8	.350	.250	.450	8.64	14.04
Rodriguez, Helmis	L-L	5-11	155	6-10-94	4	2	4.21	24	5	0	1	58	54	31	27	7	27	36	.249	.265	.235	5.62	4.21
Schlitter, Craig	R-R	6-0	195	5-16-92	10	1	2.50	15	15	0	0	90	82	28	25	4	32	62	.244	.246	.242	6.20	3.20
Schreiber, Brad	R-R	6-3	225	2-13-91	2	1	5.06	11	0	0	0	16	12	10	9	3	5	19	.203	.250	.171	10.69	2.81
Schuh, Max	L-L	6-4	210	3-13-92	2	5	5.21	39	0	0	1	48	54	33	28	8	27	57	.276	.268	.281	10.61	5.03
Thoele, Sam	R-R	6-3	205	10-17-92	1	1	6.46	11	0	0	0	15	21	11	11	1	7	12	.328	.273	.387	7.04	4.11
Tinoco, Jesus	R-R	6-4	190	4-30-95	11	4	4.67	24	24	0	0	141	157	78	73	19	50	107	.285	.313	.260	6.85	3.20
Welmon, Colin	L-R	6-3	190	8-7-92	3	2	6.32	13	13	0	0	73	94	54	51	18	20	51	.309	.340	.280	6.32	2.48

Fielding

Catcher	PCT	G	PO	A	E	DP	PB
Marte	.979	43	296	35	7	3	9
Perkins	1.000	13	101	10	0	1	1
Rabago	.986	86	633	83	10	3	8

First Base	PCT	G	PO	A	E	DP
Ferguson	.971	7	67	1	2	4

Hilliard	1.000	5	35	3	0	3
Mundell	.980	52	412	37	9	36
Perkins	1.000	1	4	1	0	0
Ramos	.992	74	614	46	5	72
Soriano	.968	4	29	1	1	1

Second Base	PCT	G	PO	A	E	DP
Burcham	.975	24	56	60	3	20
Hampson	.988	71	125	204	4	41
Rodgers	1.000	4	7	11	0	2
Romero	.952	5	9	11	1	4
Soriano	.955	39	58	89	7	22
Wall	1.000	2	3	3	0	2

Third Base	PCT	G	PO	A	E	DP
Burcham	.912	16	12	19	3	1
Jones	.950	80	59	130	10	14
Romero	.943	34	17	65	5	8
Soriano	.932	14	12	29	3	3

Shortstop	PCT	G	PO	A	E	DP
Burcham	.991	31	36	75	1	18
Hampson	.984	56	80	163	4	34
Rodgers	.958	47	56	104	7	29
Soriano	.978	9	20	24	1	8

Outfield	PCT	G	PO	A	E	DP
Dahl	.000	1	0	0	0	0
Daza	.980	120	281	7	6	1
Hilliard	.992	119	242	13	2	2
Jones	1.000	35	68	5	0	0
Rogers	.960	115	230	7	10	0
Soriano	1.000	10	16	0	0	0
Thomas	.889	7	8	0	1	0
Wall	.939	19	44	2	3	0

ASHEVILLE TOURISTS — LOW CLASS A

SOUTH ATLANTIC LEAGUE

Batting	B-T	HT	WT	DOB	AVG	vLH	vRH	G	AB	R	H	2B	3B	HR	RBI	BB	HBP	SH	SF	SO	SB	CS	SLG	OBP
Abreu, Willie	L-L	6-4	225	3-21-95	.283	.285	.282	119	477	73	135	32	6	14	78	26	2	4	3	93	40	9	.463	.321
Anderson, Cole	R-R	5-11	190	2-7-97	.207	.188	.214	18	58	8	12	4	0	1	4	6	2	0	1	32	5	2	.328	.299
Bosiokovic, Jacob	R-R	6-5	240	12-21-93	.246	.255	.243	95	341	48	84	24	3	15	54	12	15	1	3	145	16	8	.466	.299
Castro, Luis	R-R	6-1	187	9-19-95	.244	.100	.290	12	41	3	10	6	0	0	9	0	2	0	0	5	2	1	.390	.279
Diaz, Joel	R-R	6-1	195	9-18-95	.257	.230	.268	72	257	31	66	21	0	0	34	21	1	3	2	45	4	1	.339	.313
Ferguson, Collin	L-L	6-2	215	2-9-93	.167	.000	.333	2	6	0	1	0	0	0	0	1	1	0	0	3	0	1	.167	.375
Fernandez, Vince	L-R	6-3	210	7-25-95	.269	.268	.270	100	375	57	101	23	1	16	59	44	5	2	2	122	12	8	.464	.352
George, Max	R-R	5-9	180	4-7-96	.252	.254	.252	117	416	65	105	27	3	13	47	46	14	13	3	82	30	10	.426	.345
Gomez, Jose	R-R	5-11	175	12-10-96	.324	.301	.332	81	318	54	103	20	2	4	33	18	8	6	1	57	18	11	.437	.374
Herrera, Carlos	L-R	6-0	145	9-23-96	.223	.215	.226	69	256	27	57	7	3	4	23	14	3	8	1	46	17	6	.320	.270
Johnson, Ben	R-R	6-0	185	5-4-94	.191	.182	.194	38	126	12	24	2	0	2	7	8	4	3	0	55	11	1	.254	.261
Melendez, Manuel	L-L	5-11	165	1-10-97	.266	.303	.250	115	488	78	130	21	4	11	59	10	8	7	2	84	32	11	.393	.291
Metzler, Ryan	R-R	6-3	190	3-20-93	.208	.211	.207	13	48	5	10	0	1	0	1	3	1	0	0	9	1	0	.250	.269
Nevin, Tyler	R-R	6-4	200	5-29-97	.305	.319	.299	76	298	45	91	18	3	7	47	27	4	0	6	56	10	5	.456	.364
Perkins, Robbie	R-R	6-0	175	5-29-94	.188	.238	.173	29	96	10	18	5	1	4	12	5	2	1	0	30	1	2	.385	.243
Rodriguez, Jose G.	L-R	5-10	160	2-23-96	.286	.250	.300	5	14	1	4	0	0	0	1	0	0	0	0	2	0	0	.286	.286
Serven, Brian	R-R	6-0	195	5-5-95	.280	.245	.296	49	168	22	47	14	1	1	19	20	6	3	2	29	3	4	.393	.372
Snyder, Taylor	R-R	6-2	165	9-28-94	.229	.242	.225	98	349	39	80	21	1	11	37	16	7	3	2	106	17	9	.390	.275
Toole, Eric	R-L	6-0	180	2-8-93	.224	.235	.220	19	58	6	13	4	0	1	6	5	1	4	0	15	1	2	.345	.297
Wear, Campbell	R-R	6-3	205	10-23-93	.111	.000	.200	6	18	2	2	0	0	0	0	3	0	0	0	7	1	0	.111	.238
Welker, Colton	R-R	6-2	195	10-9-97	.350	.369	.341	67	254	32	89	18	1	6	33	18	5	0	2	42	5	7	.500	.401
Wernes, Bobby	R-R	6-3	200	7-4-94	.290	.286	.292	66	252	42	73	25	0	5	34	30	6	3	2	43	3	2	.448	.376

Pitching	B-T	HT	WT	DOB	W	L	ERA	G	GS	CG	SV	IP	H	R	ER	HR	BB	SO	AVG	vLH	vRH	K/9	BB/9
Ascher, Steve	L-L	6-0	185	10-18-93	0	0	16.88	3	0	0	0	3	7	5	5	2	3	2	.467	.286	.625	6.75	10.13
Baker, Bryan	R-R	6-6	220	12-2-94	7	2	1.66	26	2	0	0	54	41	16	10	3	13	57	.208	.207	.210	9.44	2.15
Bunal, Mike	R-R	6-2	205	11-18-93	0	0	16.20	2	0	0	0	2	5	3	3	0	2	4	.556	.667	.500	21.60	10.80
Culbreth, Ty	L-L	5-11	175	4-9-94	2	2	3.05	19	6	0	0	59	54	27	20	3	8	50	.250	.283	.237	7.63	1.22
Dennis, Matt	R-R	6-1	210	1-3-95	8	6	3.35	41	9	1	0	97	86	42	36	4	18	85	.242	.255	.231	7.91	1.68
Eusebio, Breiling	L-L	6-1	175	10-21-96	3	3	4.46	8	8	0	0	40	44	22	20	3	16	31	.280	.167	.301	6.92	3.57
Fernandez, Julian	R-R	6-2	160	12-5-95	1	2	3.26	51	0	0	3	58	54	28	21	2	18	57	.241	.330	.169	8.84	2.79
Garcia, Rico	R-R	5-11	190	1-10-94	2	2	2.57	8	4	0	0	28	27	10	8	2	7	30	.246	.196	.296	9.64	2.25
Gesell, Jared	R-R	6-3	185	3-20-94	0	0	7.98	12	0	0	0	15	21	13	13	3	5	14	.328	.389	.250	8.59	3.07
Gold, Brandon	R-R	6-3	203	9-16-94	4	5	4.33	13	13	1	0	71	94	43	34	9	9	62	.318	.292	.342	7.90	1.15
Hammer, J.D.	R-R	6-3	215	7-12-94	4	1	1.20	24	0	0	7	30	17	4	4	0	5	47	.164	.078	.245	14.10	1.50
Holder, Heath	R-R	6-6	211	8-23-92	0	1	2.00	27	0	0	1	45	32	10	10	3	11	46	.207	.186	.224	9.20	2.20
Humphreys, Reid	R-R	6-1	205	11-21-94	1	3	2.56	43	0	0	13	46	32	14	13	3	6	47	.194	.176	.209	9.26	1.18
Julio, Erick	R-R	6-1	175	9-22-96	7	11	4.98	27	26	0	0	148	183	92	82	18	42	106	.311	.318	.305	6.43	2.55
Justo, Salvador	R-R	6-5	210	10-14-94	1	1	2.25	16	0	0	0	16	18	4	4	0	8	18	.305	.158	.375	10.13	4.50
Lawrence, Justin	R-R	6-3	220	11-25-94	0	2	1.65	16	0	0	6	16	10	4	3	1	4	20	.172	.208	.147	11.02	2.20
Longwith, Logan	R-R	6-3	170	3-30-94	2	0	0.98	4	1	0	0	18	22	10	2	1	4	13	.297	.308	.286	6.38	1.96
Luna, Ryan	R-R	5-11	190	9-21-93	0	0	13.50	9	0	0	0	9	20	14	14	2	3	8	.417	.636	.231	7.71	2.89
Moore, Austin	R-R	6-2	230	6-21-94	0	1	4.91	19	0	0	0	26	32	14	14	1	9	23	.314	.283	.339	8.06	3.16
Oakley, Kenny	R-R	6-3	195	8-30-93	5	3	3.86	45	1	0	1	68	72	35	29	4	17	76	.273	.209	.322	10.11	2.26
Pena, Juan	R-R	6-2	175	8-25-95	2	1	2.66	18	0	0	0	24	19	7	7	0	5	24	.221	.219	.222	9.13	1.90
Pint, Riley	R-R	6-4	195	11-6-97	2	11	5.42	22	22	0	0	93	96	67	56	3	59	79	.264	.294	.240	7.65	5.71
Requena, Alejandro	R-R	6-2	200	11-29-96	8	3	2.85	19	19	0	0	117	102	46	37	9	25	97	.239	.263	.223	7.46	1.92
2-team total (2 Lakewood BlueClaws)					9	4	2.74	21	21	0	0	128	109	49	39	9	25	104	.235	.263	.223	7.31	1.76
Santos, Antonio	R-R	6-3	180	10-6-96	9	10	5.39	27	27	1	0	147	200	101	88	17	26	106	.328	.259	.392	6.49	1.59

Fielding

Catcher	PCT	G	PO	A	E	DP	PB
Diaz	.992	57	418	49	4	0	7
Perkins	.976	27	223	25	6	2	5
Serven	.989	49	407	63	5	4	5
Wear	1.000	6	52	3	0	0	0

First Base	PCT	G	PO	A	E	DP
Bosiokovic	.977	40	328	18	8	27
Castro	.989	12	86	4	1	6
Diaz	.992	15	117	6	1	7
Ferguson	1.000	1	11	2	0	1
Nevin	.981	32	287	25	6	24
Perkins	1.000	1	3	2	0	1
Snyder	.978	22	202	22	5	22
Wernes	.976	19	159	6	4	17

Second Base	PCT	G	PO	A	E	DP
George	.981	86	169	240	8	48
Gomez	.965	12	16	39	2	4

	PCT	G	PO	A	E	DP
Herrera	.990	18	37	62	1	16
Metzler	1.000	4	5	14	0	3
Rodriguez	.880	5	13	9	3	2
Snyder	.976	9	18	22	1	5
Wernes	1.000	6	11	19	0	6

Third Base	PCT	G	PO	A	E	DP
George	.783	9	4	14	5	1
Gomez	1.000	10	5	21	0	0
Metzler	1.000	2	1	3	0	0
Nevin	.900	23	15	30	5	4
Snyder	.857	13	5	19	4	1
Welker	.938	52	30	61	6	5
Wernes	.950	34	33	63	5	5

Shortstop	PCT	G	PO	A	E	DP
George	1.000	2	4	5	0	2
Gomez	.954	49	70	156	11	43
Herrera	.944	38	53	117	10	22
Metzler	.935	7	9	20	2	4
Snyder	.959	44	68	117	8	22

Outfield	PCT	G	PO	A	E	DP
Abreu	.975	115	177	16	5	2
Anderson	.949	18	36	1	2	0
Bosiokovic	.962	42	72	3	3	1
Fernandez	.978	85	129	5	3	0
Johnson	1.000	38	70	3	0	1
Melendez	.966	107	240	12	9	0
Snyder	.000	2	0	0	0	0
Toole	1.000	17	31	1	0	0

BOISE HAWKS — *SHORT SEASON*

NORTHWEST LEAGUE

Batting	B-T	HT	WT	DOB	AVG	vLH	vRH	G	AB	R	H	2B	3B	HR	RBI	BB	HBP	SH	SF	SO	SB	CS	SLG	OBP
Anderson, Cole	R-R	5-11	190	2-7-97	.249	.260	.245	59	209	26	52	6	3	0	14	22	4	1	2	66	9	10	.306	.329
Bernard, Austin	B-R	5-10	195	3-14-96	.231	.231	.232	34	121	17	28	8	0	3	16	14	1	0	2	39	0	0	.372	.312
Boswell, Bret	L-R	6-1	180	10-4-94	.293	.275	.298	54	229	46	67	8	5	11	42	15	2	1	2	55	3	3	.515	.339
Bouchard, Sean	R-R	6-3	215	5-16-96	.290	.314	.279	39	155	31	45	11	0	6	27	25	1	1	1	41	6	2	.477	.390
Cardullo, Stephen	R-R	6-0	215	8-31-87	.242	.200	.261	8	33	8	8	2	0	1	5	5	0	0	0	5	0	1	.394	.342
Castro, Luis	R-R	6-1	187	9-19-95	.286	.407	.244	25	105	15	30	7	1	2	25	6	1	0	1	20	3	1	.429	.327
Correa, Christian	R-R	5-10	210	5-18-93	.083	.000	.143	4	12	0	1	0	0	0	1	1	0	0	0	1	0	0	.083	.154
Edgeworth, Danny	L-R	6-3	210	7-26-95	.303	.261	.314	61	234	32	71	14	0	3	47	21	6	0	9	56	6	1	.402	.363
Gonzalez, Hidekel	R-R	6-0	189	10-7-96	.272	.323	.253	28	114	19	31	6	1	4	17	1	2	0	0	37	1	1	.447	.291
Hale, Conner	R-R	6-1	190	10-10-92	.225	.444	.175	14	49	3	11	2	0	0	1	5	0	0	0	15	1	2	.265	.296
Hatch, LJ	R-R	5-11	175	5-18-94	.221	.350	.167	17	68	7	15	2	0	0	4	5	1	2	0	9	1	1	.250	.284
Haynie, Will	R-R	6-5	222	6-12-94	.172	.273	.149	16	58	5	10	2	1	1	5	1	0	0	0	33	0	0	.293	.186
Jipping, Daniel	R-R	6-2	232	4-10-96	.233	.289	.216	51	193	33	45	4	2	11	31	21	6	0	1	65	5	1	.446	.326
Linkous, Steven	L-R	6-0	171	9-28-94	.308	.409	.286	63	250	50	77	5	1	1	24	39	5	4	2	54	37	16	.348	.409
McCarty, Aubrey	B-B	6-3	205	1-24-95	.207	.278	.184	38	145	13	30	6	0	0	6	12	2	0	1	40	2	2	.248	.275
McLaughlin, Matt	R-R	6-1	185	2-2-96	.305	.244	.323	51	200	36	61	13	0	1	20	31	5	3	5	43	7	4	.385	.403
Metzler, Ryan	R-R	6-3	190	3-20-93	.286	.250	.299	33	119	19	34	4	1	3	15	12	0	1	1	29	5	3	.412	.349
Moss, J.B.	R-R	6-0	185	6-21-93	.255	.135	.289	46	165	26	42	10	1	7	30	14	2	1	1	50	5	2	.455	.319
Nevin, Tyler	R-R	6-4	200	5-29-97	.233	1.000	.207	6	30	4	7	3	0	1	5	0	0	0	0	9	0	1	.433	.233
Piron, Jonathan	R-L	6-0	195	11-14-94	.235	.500	.219	9	34	5	8	0	0	3	7	4	0	0	0	7	1	0	.500	.316
Rodriguez, Jose G.	L-R	5-10	160	2-23-96	.180	.000	.194	14	39	5	7	0	0	0	5	4	0	2	1	10	1	0	.180	.250
Romero, Avery	R-R	5-11	195	5-11-93	.136	.000	.167	6	22	3	3	1	0	1	4	2	0	0	1	1	1	0	.318	.200
Tidaback, Sam	R-R	6-0	210	10-6-93	.283	.286	.283	19	60	8	17	1	0	3	8	9	2	0	2	15	1	3	.450	.384
Wernes, Bobby	R-R	6-3	200	7-4-94	.385	.333	.400	4	13	2	5	1	0	1	1	1	0	0	0	1	0	0	.692	.429

Pitching	B-T	HT	WT	DOB	W	L	ERA	G	GS	CG	SV	IP	H	R	ER	HR	BB	SO	AVG	vLH	vRH	K/9	BB/9
Browning, Brian	L-L	6-3	200	4-28-95	1	2	6.89	11	0	0	0	16	24	13	12	0	5	12	.343	.333	.346	6.89	2.87
Bunal, Mike	R-R	6-2	205	11-18-93	1	3	2.65	25	0	0	7	37	25	16	11	2	12	41	.188	.218	.167	9.88	2.89
Byrd, Alec	L-L	6-3	175	3-31-95	4	1	3.00	14	4	0	0	36	33	16	12	1	19	33	.256	.212	.271	8.25	4.75
Calomeni, Justin	R-R	6-3	210	10-13-95	0	0	0.00	1	0	0	0	1	0	0	0	0	0	0	.000	.000	.000	0.00	0.00
Cedotal, Kyle	L-L	6-1	190	9-19-93	0	2	3.20	22	0	0	2	39	40	18	14	4	19	23	.265	.300	.252	5.26	4.35
Ceja, Moises	R-R	6-0	175	8-17-95	2	1	3.26	18	0	0	2	30	25	13	11	1	7	36	.221	.098	.292	10.68	2.08
Eusebio, Breiling	L-L	6-1	175	10-21-96	3	0	1.59	3	3	0	0	17	10	4	3	0	4	22	.175	.150	.189	11.65	2.12
Garcia, Rico	R-R	5-11	190	1-10-94	0	4	3.95	8	8	0	0	41	50	28	18	2	11	35	.305	.339	.286	7.68	2.41
Gesell, Jared	R-R	6-3	185	3-20-94	2	0	4.19	15	0	0	0	19	7	11	9	0	15	21	.108	.105	.109	9.78	6.98
Guzman, Luis	L-L	6-1	180	2-27-96	0	1	24.30	3	1	0	0	3	7	9	9	2	3	3	.438	.167	.600	8.10	8.10
Hanson, Tyler	R-R	6-2	220	7-29-94	0	0	4.50	10	0	0	0	20	28	13	10	2	3	12	.333	.350	.328	5.40	1.35
Harris, Nate	R-R	6-0	190	9-7-94	1	1	4.60	12	0	0	0	16	17	9	8	1	7	21	.279	.208	.324	12.06	4.02
Jemiola, Zach	L-R	6-3	200	4-6-94	1	0	3.97	3	3	0	0	11	13	5	5	0	5	8	.283	.177	.345	6.35	3.97
Justo, Salvador	R-R	6-5	210	10-14-94	2	0	1.08	5	0	0	0	8	6	3	1	0	3	7	.194	.000	.400	7.56	3.24
Kennedy, Nick	R-L	6-1	200	6-20-96	2	3	3.68	9	9	0	0	37	44	19	15	2	10	31	.306	.290	.310	7.61	2.45
Lepore, Jesse	R-R	6-4	210	6-15-96	2	0	6.75	17	0	0	0	25	23	19	19	3	12	22	.237	.207	.250	7.82	4.26
Luna, Ryan	R-R	5-11	190	9-21-93	4	4	4.41	13	10	0	0	69	82	46	34	4	18	50	.294	.348	.258	6.49	2.34
McMahan, Pearson	L-R	6-2	190	7-1-96	0	1	4.67	6	6	0	0	17	20	12	9	2	5	8	.294	.259	.317	4.15	2.60
Moore, Austin	R-R	6-2	230	6-21-94	0	0	5.06	5	0	0	0	11	12	9	6	2	3	10	.267	.083	.333	8.44	2.53
Olivares, Keinter	L-L	6-0	170	12-1-97	3	3	5.11	15	12	0	0	56	80	42	32	4	20	37	.328	.349	.320	5.91	3.20
Pena, Juan	R-R	6-2	175	8-25-95	1	1	2.61	9	0	0	2	10	7	3	3	0	1	13	.194	.231	.174	11.32	0.87
Quintin, Cristian	R-R	6-3	165	12-27-93	0	0	9.64	4	0	0	0	5	8	7	5	1	3	1	.348	.300	.385	1.93	5.79
Schilling, Garrett	R-R	6-2	185	10-25-95	0	3	5.54	10	10	0	0	39	55	30	24	3	9	23	.335	.293	.359	5.31	2.08
Thanopoulos, George	R-R	6-1	205	1-18-93	1	0	3.00	8	0	0	0	9	8	4	3	0	6	6	.235	.100	.292	6.00	6.00
Thoele, Sam	R-R	6-3	205	10-17-92	0	0	17.18	5	0	0	0	4	9	10	7	0	3	2	.450	.273	.667	4.91	7.36
Valek, John	L-L	6-0	175	1-31-94	3	6	5.84	16	10	0	0	62	83	45	40	3	21	32	.333	.307	.342	4.67	3.06
Westphal, Ethan	R-R	5-10	170	5-12-92	4	3	4.81	25	0	0	2	43	45	25	23	3	10	48	.268	.246	.280	10.05	2.09

Fielding

C: Bernard 30, Correa 4, Gonzalez 24, Haynie 3, Tidaback 18. **1B:** Bouchard 27, Cardullo 3, Castro 20, Edgeworth 2, Gonzalez 3, Hale 13, Metzler 6, Nevin 2, Wernes 1. **2B:** Boswell 53, Edgeworth 4, Hatch 4, Metzler 2, Rodriguez 13, Romero 2. **3B:** Bouchard 4, Edgeworth 50, Hatch 2, Metzler 11, Nevin 3, Romero 4, Wernes 3. **SS:** Hatch 11, McLaughlin 51, Metzler 14. **OF:** Anderson 57, Cardullo 4, Jipping 35, Linkous 61, McCarty 24, Moss 46, Piron 8.

GRAND JUNCTION ROCKIES — ROOKIE

PIONEER LEAGUE

Batting	B-T	HT	WT	DOB	AVG	vLH	vRH	G	AB	R	H	2B	3B	HR	RBI	BB	HBP	SH	SF	SO	SB	CS	SLG	OBP
Bartosic, Joey	R-R	6-0	190	7-29-94	.315	.389	.293	38	159	28	50	7	2	0	19	11	2	1	0	18	12	6	.384	.366
Bates, Tyler	R-R	5-8	165	6-1-94	.268	.263	.269	32	112	19	30	3	0	1	11	8	5	1	1	13	5	4	.321	.341
Bohling, Jeff	B-R	5-10	190	5-4-94	.273	.250	.276	9	33	4	9	1	0	1	2	2	0	0	0	10	1	3	.394	.314
Coronado, Nathaniel	R-R	6-3	205	6-5-92	.450	.500	.444	5	20	9	9	0	1	3	7	1	2	0	0	0	1	0	1.000	.522
Cunningham, Kyle	R-R	6-0	205	10-5-94	.250	.500	.231	8	28	6	7	2	0	0	5	3	1	0	0	6	0	0	.321	.344
Czinege, Todd	R-R	6-2	204	7-28-94	.304	.233	.324	52	191	36	58	13	1	10	31	20	2	0	1	50	2	1	.539	.374
Ebert, Jordan	R-R	6-1	180	7-7-93	.375	—	.375	2	8	1	3	0	0	0	1	0	1	1	0	2	0	2	.375	.444
Golden, Casey	R-R	6-2	185	9-1-94	.289	.275	.292	54	208	55	60	14	1	20	59	17	12	1	2	74	8	1	.654	.372
Gonzalez, Hidekel	R-R	6-0	189	10-7-96	.242	.250	.241	15	62	9	15	3	1	2	9	2	0	0	1	16	1	1	.419	.262
Gonzalez, Pedro	R-R	6-5	190	10-27-97	.321	.429	.302	45	187	28	60	16	6	3	28	18	3	0	1	53	11	6	.519	.388
Guevara, Javier	R-R	5-11	165	9-25-97	.268	.314	.258	47	198	23	53	8	3	0	14	8	1	0	1	47	2	1	.338	.298
Marcelino, Ramon	L-R	6-1	175	12-23-96	.318	.263	.328	61	242	45	77	13	6	19	55	9	5	1	1	62	1	4	.657	.354
McDowell, Kennard	R-R	6-3	195	9-15-93	.315	.500	.261	25	89	18	28	7	1	3	12	11	0	0	1	29	3	4	.517	.386
Mendoza, Shael	L-R	6-0	165	10-15-96	.364	.349	.367	55	231	54	84	13	4	5	35	20	1	4	3	38	25	9	.520	.412
Moberg, Jeff	R-R	5-9	170	7-18-94	.199	.207	.196	43	141	24	28	4	1	10	24	19	3	1	2	52	1	3	.454	.303
Motley, Nic	R-R	6-3	210	8-1-96	.198	.267	.176	36	121	23	24	7	2	5	14	23	1	0	0	51	0	1	.413	.331
Spanberger, Chad	L-R	6-3	235	11-1-95	.294	.160	.330	60	235	49	69	15	2	19	51	27	3	0	4	71	2	0	.617	.368
Stephens, Brett	L-R	6-0	190	3-18-95	.307	.273	.319	35	127	25	39	8	0	2	17	18	2	0	1	19	7	2	.417	.399
Trejo, Alan	R-R	6-2	185	5-30-96	.347	.303	.357	46	173	30	60	13	2	7	32	9	4	2	2	28	7	4	.567	.388
Vilade, Ryan	R-R	6-2	194	2-18-99	.308	.105	.347	33	117	23	36	3	2	5	21	27	1	0	1	31	5	5	.496	.438

Pitching	B-T	HT	WT	DOB	W	L	ERA	G	GS	CG	SV	IP	H	R	ER	HR	BB	SO	AVG	vLH	vRH	K/9	BB/9
Agis, Michael	R-R	5-11	190	9-6-94	1	2	3.55	19	0	0	0	25	28	17	10	4	4	29	.269	.242	.282	10.30	1.42
Amarista, Anderson	R-R	6-1	185	9-15-98	4	3	8.20	12	12	0	0	56	73	55	51	12	24	38	.316	.379	.272	6.11	3.86
Ascher, Steve	L-L	6-0	185	10-18-93	1	0	0.00	1	0	0	0	1	0	0	0	0	1	1	.000	.000	.000	9.00	9.00
Biechler, Reagan	L-L	6-1	195	11-9-94	0	1	6.30	6	0	0	0	10	9	9	7	5	2	10	.205	.167	.219	9.00	1.80
Doyle, Tommy	R-R	6-6	235	5-1-96	3	3	5.14	20	0	0	3	21	29	13	12	2	10	18	.319	.320	.318	7.71	4.29
Duarte, Aneudy	R-R	6-3	170	10-20-97	0	0	15.63	6	0	0	0	6	13	11	11	2	8	10	.394	.333	.417	14.21	11.37
Gaddis, Will	R-R	6-1	185	3-12-96	3	1	5.68	11	9	0	0	44	66	33	28	6	7	26	.353	.304	.374	5.28	1.42
Gilbreath, Lucas	L-L	6-1	185	3-5-96	2	3	4.60	12	10	0	0	43	39	24	22	3	27	32	.245	.258	.242	6.70	5.65
Hathcock, Colton	R-R	6-2	185	11-2-95	2	4	3.82	23	0	0	0	33	24	19	14	0	16	39	.195	.184	.203	10.64	4.36
Lambright, Brandon	L-R	6-3	205	8-26-94	1	2	8.86	17	0	0	0	21	25	22	21	3	21	21	.301	.333	.277	8.86	8.86
Longwith, Logan	R-R	6-3	170	3-30-94	2	3	6.56	10	10	0	0	47	64	40	34	12	11	28	.320	.333	.313	5.40	2.12
Lopez, Jan Carlos	R-R	6-2	187	4-24-96	0	0	8.67	20	0	0	1	27	43	31	26	6	16	23	.347	.302	.380	7.67	5.33
Martinez, Alexander	R-R	6-1	165	12-28-96	0	0	3.41	18	0	0	0	29	30	16	11	2	13	33	.263	.275	.257	10.24	4.03
Ocando, Jeffri	R-R	6-1	180	5-15-99	5	4	7.12	13	13	0	0	61	87	57	48	5	17	36	.332	.314	.344	5.34	2.52
Oviedo, Jorge	L-L	6-2	180	10-6-96	3	2	6.09	15	7	0	0	44	65	43	30	4	11	36	.340	.333	.343	7.31	2.23
Roberts, Hayden	R-R	6-0	187	8-22-95	3	0	4.93	21	0	0	0	35	46	23	19	1	13	45	.315	.283	.330	11.68	3.38
Smith, Shameko	R-R	6-1	190	6-4-97	0	0	6.00	9	0	0	1	12	17	11	8	1	2	7	.354	.438	.313	5.25	1.50
Valdespina, Justin	R-R	6-0	200	3-20-95	3	6	5.97	15	15	0	0	75	110	59	50	12	25	40	.351	.380	.338	4.78	2.99
Valdez, Jefry	R-R	6-1	165	8-20-95	2	3	4.20	27	0	0	10	30	27	18	14	4	8	48	.229	.273	.203	14.40	2.40
Watson, Derrik	R-R	6-2	175	8-21-94	1	1	8.15	14	0	0	0	18	20	19	16	0	9	14	.278	.286	.275	7.13	4.58
Williams, Hunter	L-L	6-1	220	2-7-96	2	0	2.33	20	0	0	0	27	27	7	7	0	11	30	.260	.118	.287	10.00	3.67
Zimmerman, Michael	L-L	6-3	185	8-13-96	0	0	3.86	1	0	0	0	2	3	1	1	0	0	3	.333	—	.333	11.57	0.00

Fielding

C: Cunningham 4, Gonzalez 6, Guevara 38, Motley 28. **1B:** Czinege 9, Gonzalez 7, Guevara 6, Spanberger 54. **2B:** Czinege 1, Mendoza 55, Moberg 15, Trejo 9. **3B:** Bohling 8, Coronado 2, Czinege 29, Moberg 23, Trejo 17. **SS:** Coronado 1, McDowell 25, Moberg 2, Trejo 21, Vilade 30. **OF:** Bartosic 36, Bates 32, Golden 44, Gonzalez 41, Marcelino 52, Stephens 29.

DSL ROCKIES — ROOKIE

DOMINICAN SUMMER LEAGUE

Batting	B-T	HT	WT	DOB	AVG	vLH	vRH	G	AB	R	H	2B	3B	HR	RBI	BB	HBP	SH	SF	SO	SB	CS	SLG	OBP
Alaniz, Bernnie	R-R	6-0	180	10-20-99	.239	.222	.241	45	134	17	32	5	1	1	17	16	11	3	1	35	1	5	.313	.364
Baptista, Jesus	L-R	6-0	160	1-12-99	.234	.286	.228	45	128	18	30	2	0	0	6	14	6	3	0	19	6	3	.250	.338
Blandin, Yeikel	L-R	6-0	160	1-9-00	.245	.269	.241	55	184	25	45	4	4	0	8	19	0	8	1	35	15	10	.310	.314
Cabrera, Walking	R-R	6-2	177	8-26-00	.235	.429	.194	23	81	7	19	4	1	0	9	6	1	0	0	18	4	3	.309	.296
Chal, Welington	L-R	6-1	170	11-18-97	.242	.600	.179	10	33	3	8	2	0	0	3	1	0	0	0	8	2	0	.303	.265
Diaz, Eddy	R-R	5-11	171	2-14-00	.311	.353	.304	36	132	22	41	7	4	0	10	19	2	1	1	21	30	6	.424	.403
Fana, Steven	R-R	6-1	180	6-23-99	.236	.304	.224	43	157	19	37	9	1	0	11	10	4	2	3	44	7	3	.306	.293
Garcia, Franklin	R-R	6-0	170	3-3-98	.259	.242	.261	63	232	29	60	11	2	0	24	9	8	5	1	37	6	5	.323	.308
Grullart, Jose	L-L	6-1	175	6-21-99	.151	.133	.155	27	86	11	13	5	0	1	7	5	3	2	1	30	1	1	.244	.221
Mezquita, Jonatan	R-R	6-0	180	1-11-99	.152	.400	.107	20	66	9	10	2	0	2	6	5	5	1	0	20	1	1	.273	.263
Montano, Daniel	L-R	6-1	170	3-31-99	.270	.276	.269	52	189	32	51	14	3	3	39	24	1	3	0	39	9	7	.423	.355
Navarro, Cristopher	R-R	6-0	152	6-14-99	.280	.250	.286	59	214	33	60	10	1	0	28	23	2	9	1	29	5	10	.336	.354
Ortiz, Francisco	R-R	6-0	160	9-15-99	.224	.179	.232	58	192	26	43	14	0	0	17	22	3	2	3	28	3	3	.297	.309
Pena, Yolki	L-L	6-2	165	3-30-00	.302	.207	.317	62	212	36	64	8	2	2	32	40	2	1	4	34	3	4	.387	.411
Quijada, Bryant	R-R	5-10	167	7-2-99	.322	.273	.333	21	59	11	19	7	0	0	12	14	2	1	3	19	0	1	.441	.449
Saldana, Enrique	R-R	5-11	155	6-26-99	.267	.381	.242	32	116	12	31	2	0	4	18	9	1	2	2	26	4	5	.388	.320
Santos, Adonis	R-R	6-1	165	9-11-99	.096	.286	.067	22	52	7	5	1	0	0	8	12	3	2	0	14	2	2	.115	.299

COLORADO ROCKIES

Pitching	B-T	HT	WT	DOB	W	L	ERA	G	GS	CG	SV	IP	H	R	ER	HR	BB	SO	AVG	vLH	vRH	K/9	BB/9
Alcantara, Jhosua	R-R	6-6	200	9-30-97	0	0	3.60	4	0	0	1	5	4	3	2	0	0	7	.211	.375	.091	12.60	0.00
Amarista, Anderson	R-R	6-1	185	9-15-98	1	1	5.28	3	3	0	0	15	19	10	9	0	5	14	.302	.091	.346	8.22	2.93
Bido, Anderson	R-R	6-3	184	5-7-99	2	1	2.85	10	10	0	0	41	41	22	13	2	9	39	.265	.146	.307	8.56	1.98
Blanco, Diego	R-R	6-2	165	9-14-99	2	2	4.13	18	1	0	0	28	28	15	13	2	5	32	.257	.294	.240	10.16	1.59
Cabrera, Wander	L-L	6-1	185	11-7-97	0	0	—	1	0	0	0	0	0	0	0	0	0	0	—	—	—	—	—
Castillo, Enrique	R-R	6-1	170	11-27-99	0	1	6.94	11	0	0	0	12	12	10	9	1	12	17	.273	.600	.177	13.11	9.26
Cespedes, Richard	R-R	6-0	185	8-29-97	0	1	1.59	3	0	0	0	6	4	1	1	0	0	6	.211	.222	.200	9.53	0.00
Duarte, Aneudy	R-R	6-3	170	10-20-97	1	0	0.79	21	0	0	10	23	13	3	2	0	6	29	.169	.261	.130	11.51	2.38
Encarnacion, Daniel	R-R	6-3	170	6-14-99	0	0	15.68	9	3	0	0	10	9	19	18	1	29	14	.250	.556	.148	12.19	25.26
Filpo, Eris	R-R	6-3	170	5-3-98	4	2	2.86	12	12	0	0	57	46	27	18	1	20	60	.220	.226	.218	9.53	3.18
Garcia, Alfredo	L-L	6-1	177	7-22-99	2	3	2.12	9	6	0	1	47	45	18	11	1	8	41	.256	.125	.285	7.91	1.54
Gonzalez, Carlos	R-R	6-2	180	12-11-98	4	5	3.12	18	2	0	0	58	63	27	20	3	7	44	.278	.300	.268	6.87	1.09
Guevara, Eliecer	R-R	6-2	191	4-5-99	3	2	3.67	8	4	0	0	27	28	17	11	1	11	27	.267	.281	.260	9.00	3.67
Martinez, Jaiver	R-R	6-1	175	9-16-98	3	2	3.44	26	0	0	5	34	27	15	13	0	17	29	.225	.314	.188	7.68	4.50
Mejia, Alejandro	L-L	6-1	168	7-2-98	4	0	1.42	13	8	0	0	44	36	12	7	1	20	36	.225	.333	.200	7.31	4.06
Mejia, Juan	R-R	6-1	181	7-4-00	3	1	2.84	16	1	0	0	32	24	19	10	3	11	27	.202	.294	.165	7.67	3.13
Moya, Ever	L-L	6-4	150	5-25-99	1	3	5.58	13	12	0	0	50	58	36	31	2	19	33	.292	.275	.296	5.94	3.42
Noguera, Luis	L-L	6-2	160	3-20-00	1	3	5.79	9	2	0	0	9	10	11	6	1	11	4	.278	.667	.242	3.86	10.61
Ocando, Jeffri	R-R	6-1	180	5-15-99	1	1	4.85	4	4	0	0	13	16	10	7	2	3	17	.291	.353	.263	11.77	2.08
Olivarez, Helcris	L-L	6-2	192	8-8-00	0	1	3.55	18	1	0	0	33	24	13	13	0	17	35	.200	.167	.206	9.55	4.64
Oviedo, Jorge	L-L	6-2	180	10-6-96	0	0	4.82	5	0	0	0	9	11	5	5	2	0	10	.297	.250	.303	9.64	0.00
Pilar, Anderson	R-R	6-2	175	3-2-98	1	3	3.24	26	0	0	4	25	29	12	9	0	8	15	.284	.235	.309	5.40	2.88
Rosa, Raymells	R-R	6-2	180	12-6-98	3	3	4.50	18	2	0	0	32	35	19	16	1	22	16	.282	.233	.309	4.50	6.19

Fielding

C: Alaniz 29, Garcia 12, Ortiz 29, Quijada 8. **1B:** Alaniz 15, Baptista 1, Garcia 20, Mezquita 4, Ortiz 27, Quijada 10, Santos 1. **2B:** Baptista 16, Diaz 13, Navarro 17, Saldana 12, Santos 17. **3B:** Baptista 21, Garcia 34, Mezquita 16, Saldana 4. **SS:** Diaz 23, Mezquita 1, Navarro 34, Saldana 18. **OF:** Blandin 48, Cabrera 20, Chal 4, Fana 25, Grullart 18, Montano 48, Pena 58.

Detroit Tigers

SEASON IN A SENTENCE: With an expensive veteran roster, the Tigers planned to go on one last October run led by 34-year-olds Miguel Cabrera and Justin Verlander, but Detroit faltered and entered sell mode in July, ultimately ending the season with 98 losses—and the No. 1 pick the 2018 draft.

HIGH POINT: The Tigers defeated the Rays 13-4 on June 16 to improve to 32-34 and move to within three games of first place in the American League Central. They then lost eight in a row.

LOW POINT: After selling veterans Alex Avila, J.D. Martinez, Justin Upton, Verlander and Justin Wilson in July, the Tigers limped to the finish line by going 17-41 (.293) and were outscored by 131 runs from Aug. 1 to the end. That performance helped cost manager Brad Ausmus his job.

NOTABLE ROOKIES: Many prospects debuted for the last-place Tigers, but no one made an impact even remotely close to 2016 AL Rookie of the Year Michael Fulmer. Third baseman Jeimer Candelario, an in-season trade pickup, hit .330 as a September callup while showing a disciplined hitting approach and gap power. John Hicks, a 2016 waiver claim, made starts at catcher and first base and provided roughly league-average production.

KEY TRANSACTIONS: Parting with franchise icon Verlander, whom Detroit drafted second overall in 2004, was a difficult but necessary move. He returned three prospects from the Astros—righthander Franklin Perez, outfielder Daz Cameron and catcher Jake Rogers—who could impact the future of the franchise. Low Class A shortstop Isaac Paredes, acquired from the Cubs for Avila and Wilson, also offers a high ceiling. The Tigers' other trades returned value, but not necessarily marquee names. At least the switch-hitting Candelario, righthander Grayson Long and third baseman Dawel Lugo are nearly big league ready. The Tigers will try to develop Lugo, who signed as a shortstop, at second base to better fit on the big league depth chart. Shortstop Jose King and righthander Elvin Rodriguez spent most of the summer in Rookie ball and are faraway wild cards.

DOWN ON THE FARM: Tigers affiliates finished with a middle-of-the-pack .502 winning percentage that ranked 13th in baseball. Low Class A West Michigan lost in the first round of the Midwest League playoffs and was Detroit's only postseason entrant.

OPENING DAY PAYROLL: $199,750,600 (4th)

PLAYERS OF THE YEAR

MAJOR LEAGUE

Michael Fulmer
RHP
10-12, 3.83
0.7 HR/9 led AL
First time all-star

MINOR LEAGUE

Christin Stewart
OF
(Double-A)
Led system with 28 HR, 86 RBIs

ORGANIZATION LEADERS

BATTING — *Minimum 250 AB

MAJORS			
*	AVG	Justin Upton	.279
*	OPS	Justin Upton	.904
	HR	Justin Upton	28
	RBI	Nichoas Castellanos	101
MINORS			
*	AVG	Mike Gerber, Lakeland, Erie, Toledo	.304
*	OBP	Jake Robson, West Michigan, Lakeland	.380
*	SLG	Christin Stewart, Erie	.501
*	OPS	Mike Gerber, Lakeland, Erie, Toledo	.869
	R	Danny Woodrow, West Michigan	73
	H	Blaise Salter, West Michigan, Lakeland	143
	TB	Christin Stewart, Erie	243
	2B	Blaise Salter, West Michigan, Lakeland	39
	3B	Cam Gibson, West Michigan, Lakeland	11
	HR	Christin Stewart, Erie	28
	RBI	Christin Stewart, Erie	86
	BB	Efren Navarro, Toledo	71
	SO	Zac Shepherd, Lakeland, West Michigan	171
	SB	Danny Woodrow, West Michigan	31

PITCHING — #Minimum 75 IP

MAJORS			
	W	Michael Fulmer	10
		Justin Verlander	10
#	ERA	Justin Verlander	3.82
	SO	Justin Verlander	176
	SV	Justin Wilson	13
MINORS			
	W	Artie Lewicki, Erie, Toledo	14
	L	Myles Jaye, Erie, Toledo	13
#	ERA	Austin Sodders, West Michigan, Lakeland	1.80
	G	Logan Kensing, Toledo	66
	GS	Anthony Vasquez, Erie, Toledo	27
		A.J. Ladwig, Lakeland, Erie, Toledo	27
	SV	Edward Mujica, Toledo	21
	IP	Anthony Vasquez, Erie, Toledo	165
	BB	Gregory Soto, West Mighigan, Lakeland	65
	SO	Matt Hall, Lakeland, Erie	149
#	AVG	Austin Sodders, West Michigan, Lakeland	.209

2017 PERFORMANCE

General Manager: Al Avila. **Farm Director:** Dave Owen. **Scouting Director:** Scott Pleis.

Class	Team	League	W	L	PCT	Finish	Manager
Majors	Detroit Tigers	American	64	98	.395	15th (15)	Brad Ausmus
Triple-A	Toledo Mud Hens	International	70	71	.496	8th (14)	Mike Rojas
Double-A	Erie SeaWolves	Eastern	65	75	.464	7th (12)	Lance Parrish
High-A	Lakeland Flying Tigers	Florida State	62	66	.484	9th (12)	Andrew Graham
Low-A	West Michigan Whitecaps	Midwest	91	45	.669	1st (16)	Mike Rabelo
Short Season	Connecticut Tigers	New York-Penn	37	35	.514	8th (14)	Gerald Laird
Rookie	GCL Tigers East	Gulf Coast	14	45	.237	17th (17)	Jesus Garces
Rookie	GCL Tigers West	Gulf Coast	29	28	.509	9th (17)	Rafael Gil
Overall 2017 Minor League Record			368	365	.502	13th (30))	

ORGANIZATION STATISTICS

DETROIT TIGERS

AMERICAN LEAGUE

Batting	B-T	HT	WT	DOB	AVG	vLH	vRH	G	AB	R	H	2B	3B	HR	RBI	BB	HBP	SH	SF	SO	SB	CS	SLG	OBP
Adduci, Jim	L-L	6-2	210	5-15-85	.241	.300	.233	29	83	14	20	6	2	1	10	10	0	0	0	27	1	1	.398	.323
Avila, Alex	R-L	5-11	210	1-29-87	.274	.177	.282	77	219	30	60	11	0	11	32	43	1	0	1	80	0	1	.475	.394
Cabrera, Miguel	R-R	6-4	240	4-18-83	.250	.326	.230	130	469	50	117	22	0	16	60	54	3	0	3	110	0	1	.399	.329
Candelario, Jeimer	B-R	6-1	210	11-24-93	.330	.375	.321	27	94	16	31	7	0	2	13	12	0	0	0	18	0	0	.468	.406
Castellanos, Nicholas	R-R	6-4	210	3-4-92	.272	.292	.266	157	614	73	167	36	10	26	101	41	5	0	5	142	4	5	.490	.320
Collins, Tyler	L-L	5-11	215	6-6-90	.193	.100	.200	49	150	18	29	4	1	5	14	18	0	0	1	55	0	4	.333	.278
den Dekker, Matt	L-L	6-2	210	8-10-87	.143	1.000	.000	4	7	1	1	0	0	0	0	1	0	0	0	4	0	0	.143	.250
Hicks, John	R-R	6-2	230	8-31-89	.266	.230	.286	60	173	25	46	12	0	6	22	13	3	0	1	51	2	1	.439	.326
Holaday, Bryan	R-R	6-0	205	11-19-87	.241	.200	.250	13	29	1	7	2	0	0	2	0	0	0	0	1	0	0	.310	.241
Iglesias, Jose	R-R	5-11	185	1-5-90	.255	.263	.253	130	463	56	118	33	1	6	54	21	1	3	1	65	7	4	.369	.288
Jones, JaCoby	R-R	6-2	205	5-10-92	.170	.158	.175	56	141	14	24	3	1	3	13	9	4	0	0	65	6	2	.270	.240
Kinsler, Ian	R-R	6-0	200	6-22-82	.236	.278	.225	139	551	90	130	25	3	22	52	55	7	0	0	86	14	5	.412	.313
Machado, Dixon	R-R	6-1	170	2-22-92	.259	.192	.286	73	166	17	43	5	1	1	11	10	1	2	2	32	1	0	.319	.302
Mahtook, Mikie	R-R	6-1	200	11-30-89	.276	.263	.283	109	348	50	96	15	6	12	38	23	6	0	2	79	6	0	.457	.330
Martinez, J.D.	R-R	6-3	220	8-21-87	.305	.474	.265	57	200	38	61	13	2	16	39	29	0	0	3	54	2	0	.630	.388
Martinez, Victor	B-R	6-2	210	12-23-78	.255	.255	.255	107	392	38	100	16	0	10	47	36	5	0	2	63	0	0	.372	.324
McCann, James	R-R	6-2	210	6-13-90	.253	.298	.234	106	352	39	89	14	2	13	49	26	9	1	3	89	1	0	.415	.318
Navarro, Efren	L-L	6-0	210	5-14-86	.230	.444	.192	23	61	9	14	1	1	2	2	8	0	0	0	21	0	1	.377	.319
Presley, Alex	L-L	5-10	195	7-25-85	.314	.267	.321	71	245	30	77	10	3	3	20	15	0	3	0	49	5	0	.416	.354
Romine, Andrew	B-R	6-1	200	12-24-85	.233	.262	.225	124	318	45	74	17	2	4	25	22	4	2	2	67	6	4	.337	.289
Upton, Justin	R-R	6-2	205	8-25-87	.279	.350	.258	125	459	81	128	37	0	28	94	57	3	0	1	147	10	5	.543	.362
2-team total (27 Los Angeles)					.273	.318	.224	152	557	100	152	44	0	35	109	74	3	0	1	180	14	5	.540	.361

Pitching	B-T	HT	WT	DOB	W	L	ERA	G	GS	CG	SV	IP	H	R	ER	HR	BB	SO	AVG	vLH	vRH	K/9	BB/9
Alcantara, Victor	R-R	6-2	190	4-3-93	0	0	8.59	6	0	0	0	7	12	7	7	1	4	5	.375	.444	.286	6.14	4.91
Bell, Chad	R-L	6-3	200	2-28-89	0	3	6.93	28	4	0	0	62	81	49	48	12	31	57	.313	.286	.324	8.23	4.48
Boyd, Matthew	L-L	6-3	215	2-2-91	6	11	5.27	26	25	1	0	135	157	84	79	18	53	110	.291	.282	.292	7.33	3.53
Cuevas, William	B-R	6-2	215	10-14-90	0	0	108.00	1	0	0	0	0	3	4	4	0	0	1	.750	1.000	.500	27.00	0.00
Farmer, Buck	L-R	6-4	225	2-20-91	5	5	6.75	11	11	0	0	48	55	38	36	9	20	49	.285	.291	.278	9.19	3.75
Ferrell, Jeff	R-R	6-4	205	11-23-90	0	0	6.75	11	0	0	0	9	17	7	7	2	5	6	.395	.267	.464	5.79	4.82
Fulmer, Michael	R-R	6-3	210	3-15-93	10	12	3.83	25	25	1	0	165	150	80	70	13	40	114	.243	.264	.225	6.23	2.19
Greene, Shane	R-R	6-4	210	11-17-88	4	3	2.66	71	0	0	9	68	50	21	20	6	34	73	.205	.235	.185	9.71	4.52
Hardy, Blaine	L-L	6-2	215	3-14-87	1	0	5.94	35	0	0	0	33	46	24	22	7	13	28	.331	.269	.368	7.56	3.51
Jaye, Myles	B-R	6-3	170	12-28-91	1	2	12.08	5	2	0	0	13	18	18	17	2	10	4	.321	.351	.263	2.84	7.11
Jimenez, Joe	R-R	6-3	220	1-17-95	0	2	12.32	24	0	0	0	19	31	28	26	4	9	17	.356	.206	.453	8.05	4.26
Labourt, Jairo	L-L	6-4	205	3-7-94	0	0	4.50	6	0	0	0	6	4	3	3	0	7	4	.200	.400	.133	6.00	10.50
Leon, Arcenio	R-R	6-3	222	9-22-86	0	0	12.15	6	0	0	0	7	7	9	9	0	6	2	.292	.286	.294	2.70	8.10
Lewicki, Artie	R-R	6-3	195	4-8-92	0	1	6.10	4	1	0	0	10	19	8	7	1	4	6	.396	.391	.400	5.23	3.48
Mujica, Edward	R-R	6-3	220	5-10-84	0	0	9.95	5	0	0	0	6	11	7	7	4	0	7	.393	.500	.350	9.95	0.00
Norris, Daniel	L-L	6-2	195	4-25-93	5	8	5.31	22	18	0	0	102	120	64	60	12	44	86	.295	.287	.297	7.61	3.90
Reininger, Zac	B-R	6-3	170	1-28-93	0	0	7.45	10	0	0	0	10	16	8	8	3	3	5	.372	.263	.458	4.66	2.79
Rodriguez, Francisco	R-R	6-0	195	1-7-82	2	5	7.82	28	0	0	7	25	31	23	22	9	11	23	.293	.340	.245	8.17	3.91
Rondon, Bruce	R-R	6-3	275	12-9-90	1	3	10.91	21	0	0	1	16	21	19	19	1	10	22	.328	.433	.235	12.64	5.74
Ryan, Kyle	L-L	6-5	215	9-25-91	0	0	7.94	8	0	0	0	6	9	5	5	0	7	1	.429	.444	.417	1.59	11.12
Sanchez, Anibal	R-R	6-0	205	2-27-84	3	7	6.41	28	17	0	0	105	139	81	75	26	29	104	.313	.284	.342	8.89	2.48
Saupold, Warwick	R-R	6-1	195	1-16-90	3	2	4.88	45	0	0	0	63	64	36	34	9	31	44	.267	.282	.258	6.32	4.45
Stumpf, Daniel	L-L	6-2	200	1-4-91	0	1	3.82	55	0	0	0	38	37	16	16	5	15	33	.266	.220	.300	7.88	3.58
VerHagen, Drew	R-R	6-6	230	10-22-90	0	3	5.77	24	2	0	0	34	42	22	22	10	9	25	.311	.317	.309	6.55	2.36
Verlander, Justin	R-R	6-5	225	2-20-83	10	8	3.82	28	28	0	0	172	153	76	73	23	67	176	.234	.220	.246	9.21	3.51
2-team total (5 Houston)					15	8	3.36	33	33	0	0	206	170	80	77	27	72	219	.221	.220	.246	9.57	3.15
Wilson, Alex	R-R	6-0	215	11-3-86	2	5	4.50	66	0	0	2	60	67	34	30	7	15	42	.279	.257	.298	6.30	2.25
Wilson, Justin	L-L	6-2	205	8-18-87	3	4	2.68	42	0	0	13	40	22	12	12	5	16	55	.157	.220	.131	12.27	3.57
Zimmermann, Jordan	R-R	6-2	225	5-23-86	8	13	6.08	29	29	0	0	160	204	111	108	29	44	103	.313	.322	.304	5.79	2.48

Fielding

Catcher	PCT	G	PO	A	E	DP	PB
Avila	.997	50	323	18	1	4	1
Hicks	.977	18	119	9	3	1	1
Holaday	1.000	11	44	1	0	0	1
McCann	.997	103	745	34	2	7	10
Romine	.000	1	0	0	0	0	1

First Base	PCT	G	PO	A	E	DP
Avila	1.000	16	71	2	0	10
Cabrera	.999	115	761	63	1	90
Hicks	.989	26	164	12	2	20
Navarro	1.000	20	114	8	0	12
Romine	1.000	22	56	4	0	3

Second Base	PCT	G	PO	A	E	DP
Holaday	.000	1	0	0	0	0
Kinsler	.983	135	263	327	10	95
Machado	.974	27	23	51	2	12
Romine	.988	27	29	50	1	11

Third Base	PCT	G	PO	A	E	DP
Candelario	.931	27	15	39	4	2
Castellanos	.939	129	77	202	18	21
Machado	1.000	5	5	6	0	1
Romine	.955	23	5	16	1	3

Shortstop	PCT	G	PO	A	E	DP
Iglesias	.987	130	199	332	7	83
Machado	.981	32	51	55	2	11
Romine	1.000	10	11	21	0	7

Outfield	PCT	G	PO	A	E	DP
Adduci	1.000	26	50	2	0	0
Castellanos	.963	21	26	0	1	0
Collins	.980	44	95	3	2	0
den Dekker	1.000	3	6	0	0	0
Jones	.992	51	132	0	1	0
Mahtook	.991	105	224	3	2	1
Martinez	.980	53	98	2	2	2
Presley	.991	65	107	1	1	0
Romine	.991	51	109	1	1	0
Upton	.976	124	273	7	7	0

TOLEDO MUD HENS — *TRIPLE-A*

INTERNATIONAL LEAGUE

Batting	B-T	HT	WT	DOB	AVG	vLH	vRH	G	AB	R	H	2B	3B	HR	RBI	BB	HBP	SH	SF	SO	SB	CS	SLG	OBP
Adduci, Jim	L-L	6-2	210	5-15-85	.288	.250	.306	55	215	32	62	13	1	4	27	20	0	0	4	59	10	3	.414	.343
Almanzar, Michael	R-R	6-3	190	12-2-90	.246	.333	.222	61	224	19	55	10	2	7	24	9	5	0	2	59	0	1	.402	.288
2-team total (44 Syracuse)					.254	.333	.222	105	366	31	93	17	2	9	43	16	5	0	3	92	0	1	.385	.292
Candelario, Jeimer	B-R	6-1	210	11-24-93	.265	.158	.313	29	121	13	32	9	1	3	19	5	1	0	1	32	1	0	.430	.297
Collins, Tyler	L-L	5-11	215	6-6-90	.289	.203	.316	74	260	29	75	14	2	9	46	29	2	0	5	72	11	2	.462	.358
den Dekker, Matt	L-L	6-2	210	8-10-87	.251	.180	.271	59	179	28	45	10	3	5	16	24	0	2	1	50	8	5	.425	.338
Diaz, Argenis	R-R	6-0	190	2-12-87	.244	.219	.253	69	234	21	57	9	0	2	16	21	2	3	1	50	1	2	.308	.310
Eaves, Kody	L-R	6-0	175	7-8-93	.259	.333	.250	8	27	3	7	1	1	0	1	2	0	0	0	6	0	0	.370	.310
Ficociello, Dominic	B-R	6-4	200	4-10-92	.235	.180	.263	35	115	12	27	6	0	2	12	11	1	1	0	32	2	1	.339	.307
Gerber, Mike	L-R	6-0	190	7-8-92	.412	1.000	.333	4	17	4	7	2	0	1	3	1	0	0	0	6	0	0	.706	.444
Gonzalez, Miguel	R-R	5-11	220	12-3-90	.192	.192	.192	24	73	2	14	1	0	0	2	3	0	0	1	18	1	0	.206	.221
Greiner, Grayson	R-R	6-6	220	10-11-92	.143	.400	.000	5	14	0	2	1	0	0	2	2	0	0	1	3	0	0	.214	.235
Hicks, John	R-R	6-2	230	8-31-89	.269	.377	.232	52	208	21	56	10	1	7	35	4	1	1	4	54	5	3	.428	.281
Holaday, Bryan	R-R	6-0	205	11-19-87	.269	.315	.250	93	309	31	83	20	0	12	50	22	6	5	5	54	0	3	.450	.325
Infante, Omar	R-R	5-11	195	12-26-81	.282	.390	.246	123	489	46	138	31	0	3	37	24	2	3	5	50	3	6	.364	.315
Jones, JaCoby	R-R	6-2	205	5-10-92	.245	.230	.250	90	351	57	86	19	2	9	44	33	3	5	1	104	12	4	.388	.314
Krizan, Jason	L-R	6-0	185	6-28-89	.264	.322	.246	107	371	41	98	22	4	4	37	40	0	1	2	53	4	5	.377	.334
Loney, James	L-L	6-3	235	5-7-84	.229	.000	.256	16	48	6	11	1	0	0	2	13	0	0	1	7	0	0	.250	.387
2-team total (2 Gwinnett)					.218	.000	.256	18	55	6	12	1	0	0	2	14	0	0	1	8	0	0	.236	.371
Lough, David	L-L	5-10	175	1-20-86	.170	.000	.222	24	59	7	10	2	0	0	0	2	1	1	0	16	0	2	.203	.210
2-team total (4 Columbus)					.225	—	.500	28	71	8	16	3	0	0	0	2	1	1	0	16	0	3	.268	.257
Martinez, J.D.	R-R	6-3	220	8-21-87	.067	.333	.000	4	15	1	1	0	0	1	2	2	0	0	1	6	0	0	.267	.167
McCann, James	R-R	6-2	210	6-13-90	.667	.333	1.000	2	6	1	4	0	0	0	3	1	0	0	0	1	0	0	.667	.714
McVaney, Jeff	R-R	6-2	210	1-16-90	.063	.125	.000	5	16	1	1	0	0	0	0	1	1	0	0	4	0	0	.063	.167
Moya, Steven	L-R	6-7	260	8-9-91	.166	.097	.183	46	151	12	25	2	2	7	15	11	0	0	0	61	3	0	.344	.222
Murton, Matt	R-R	6-1	220	10-3-81	.154	.167	.150	7	26	2	4	0	0	0	2	2	0	0	0	8	0	0	.154	.214
Navarro, Efren	L-L	6-0	210	5-14-86	.276	.217	.294	131	479	61	132	23	2	10	61	71	3	0	4	101	2	3	.395	.370
Perez, Juan	R-R	5-11	185	11-13-86	.204	.261	.176	39	137	11	28	5	2	1	17	10	1	1	3	35	10	1	.292	.258
Presley, Alex	L-L	5-10	195	7-25-85	.216	.172	.225	43	167	26	36	6	1	2	9	12	4	2	0	36	4	2	.299	.284
Rubio, Elvis	R-R	6-3	215	7-2-94	.000	—	.000	2	5	0	0	0	0	0	0	0	0	0	0	2	0	0	.000	.000
Ryan, Brendan	R-R	6-1	190	3-26-82	.236	.203	.246	112	356	46	84	20	0	4	28	45	2	3	2	74	5	7	.326	.324
Valdes, Luis	R-R	6-0	190	1-18-89	.241	.333	.217	9	29	5	7	1	0	0	4	1	0	0	0	5	0	0	.276	.267
Watkins, Logan	L-R	5-11	195	8-29-89	.257	.444	.192	13	35	3	9	0	0	0	1	2	0	0	0	8	1	0	.257	.297

Pitching	B-T	HT	WT	DOB	W	L	ERA	G	GS	CG	SV	IP	H	R	ER	HR	BB	SO	AVG	vLH	vRH	K/9	BB/9
Alaniz, Ruben	R-R	6-4	219	6-14-91	1	2	4.25	20	3	0	0	36	43	21	17	5	21	40	.301	.347	.277	10.00	5.25
Alcantara, Victor	R-R	6-2	190	4-3-93	0	1	4.05	9	1	0	0	20	22	13	9	0	12	16	.275	.257	.289	7.20	5.40
Bell, Chad	R-L	6-3	200	2-28-89	2	4	3.41	7	7	0	0	34	34	15	13	3	10	31	.264	.154	.291	8.13	2.62
Boyd, Matthew	L-L	6-3	215	2-2-91	3	3	2.82	8	8	1	0	51	35	16	16	7	13	53	.191	.063	.219	9.35	2.29
Crouse, Matt	L-L	6-4	190	7-1-90	1	3	6.40	6	6	0	0	32	38	23	23	3	12	22	.297	.333	.277	6.12	3.34
Cuevas, William	B-R	6-2	215	10-14-90	2	4	4.06	9	9	0	0	44	50	26	20	5	12	34	.273	.271	.276	6.90	2.44
Donatello, Sean	R-R	6-2	205	8-24-90	0	0	21.00	3	0	0	0	3	8	7	7	2	1	2	.444	.000	.500	6.00	3.00
Farmer, Buck	L-R	6-4	225	2-20-91	6	4	3.93	21	21	0	0	124	133	58	54	9	31	114	.275	.247	.302	8.30	2.26
Ferrell, Jeff	R-R	6-4	205	11-23-90	2	1	2.51	41	0	0	2	47	39	14	13	1	14	51	.223	.225	.221	9.84	2.70
Garcia, Bryan	R-R	6-1	203	4-19-95	1	0	4.05	14	0	0	0	13	10	6	6	1	8	12	.213	.083	.257	8.10	5.40
Hardy, Blaine	L-L	6-2	215	3-14-87	7	3	3.10	34	2	0	3	41	32	14	14	1	5	45	.221	.245	.207	9.96	1.11
Jaye, Myles	B-R	6-3	170	12-28-91	3	6	3.58	11	11	0	0	60	71	31	24	3	23	42	.298	.287	.306	6.27	3.43
Jimenez, Joe	R-R	6-3	220	1-17-95	1	1	1.44	26	0	0	4	25	19	4	4	1	12	36	.214	.160	.234	12.96	4.32
Kensing, Logan	R-R	6-1	190	7-3-82	3	3	2.54	66	0	0	0	74	71	23	21	3	25	57	.260	.268	.256	6.90	3.03
Labourt, Jairo	L-L	6-4	205	3-7-94	0	0	2.45	16	0	0	0	22	12	6	6	1	23	21	.158	.136	.167	8.59	9.41
Ladwig, A.J.	R-R	6-5	180	12-24-92	1	1	6.30	2	2	0	0	10	18	8	7	0	1	6	.391	.381	.400	5.40	0.90
Leon, Arcenio	R-R	6-3	222	9-22-86	1	2	5.24	26	0	0	10	22	15	14	13	2	13	21	.179	.220	.140	8.46	5.24
Lewicki, Artie	R-R	6-3	195	4-8-92	5	0	2.03	5	5	0	0	31	28	7	7	2	7	33	.248	.320	.191	9.58	2.03
Molleken, Dustin	R-L	6-4	230	8-21-84	2	1	2.76	13	1	0	0	16	15	7	5	1	10	21	.227	.233	.222	11.57	5.51
Mujica, Edward	R-R	6-3	220	5-10-84	1	1	2.57	56	0	0	21	56	51	17	16	4	9	46	.235	.250	.226	7.39	1.45

Pitching	B-T	HT	WT	DOB	W	L	ERA	G	GS	CG	SV	IP	H	R	ER	HR	BB	SO	AVG	vLH	vRH	K/9	BB/9
Nesbitt, Angel	R-R	6-1	240	12-4-90	1	1	6.48	7	0	0	0	8	7	6	6	3	6	8	.233	.091	.316	8.64	6.48
Norris, Daniel	L-L	6-2	195	4-25-93	0	4	12.21	6	6	0	0	14	22	20	19	3	16	18	.355	.364	.353	11.57	10.29
Reininger, Zac	B-R	6-3	170	1-28-93	1	0	1.59	9	0	0	1	11	7	2	2	0	4	5	.180	.231	.154	3.97	3.18
Rondon, Bruce	R-R	6-3	275	12-9-90	2	1	2.70	38	0	0	1	37	34	15	11	2	25	43	.241	.203	.273	10.55	6.14
Ryan, Kyle	L-L	6-5	215	9-25-91	3	1	4.96	48	0	0	0	45	55	26	25	5	27	39	.307	.300	.312	7.74	5.36
Sanchez, Anibal	R-R	6-0	205	2-27-84	0	2	4.60	4	4	0	0	16	17	9	8	3	5	20	.270	.324	.207	11.49	2.87
Saupold, Warwick	R-R	6-1	195	1-16-90	2	0	2.90	7	7	0	0	40	38	13	13	2	17	33	.255	.254	.256	7.36	3.79
Spomer, Kurt	B-R	6-2	215	7-10-89	0	0	2.25	2	0	0	0	4	3	1	1	0	0	2	.200	.000	.300	4.50	0.00
Stumpf, Daniel	L-L	6-2	200	1-4-91	1	2	3.38	24	0	0	0	21	19	8	8	3	5	26	.250	.200	.293	10.97	2.11
Turley, Josh	L-L	6-0	185	8-26-90	2	2	6.27	7	7	0	0	37	47	32	26	5	22	25	.305	.367	.290	6.03	5.30
Vasquez, Anthony	L-L	6-0	190	9-19-86	9	9	4.06	22	22	1	0	133	134	61	60	13	40	86	.262	.274	.258	5.82	2.71
VerHagen, Drew	R-R	6-6	230	10-22-90	7	7	4.90	19	19	0	0	97	108	59	53	7	43	69	.287	.320	.261	6.38	3.98
Voelker, Paul	R-R	5-10	185	8-19-92	0	0	3.00	2	0	0	0	3	5	1	1	0	1	4	.357	.250	.400	12.00	3.00
Zagurski, Mike	L-L	6-0	240	1-27-83	0	2	5.06	13	0	0	0	11	13	6	6	0	3	18	.310	.238	.381	15.19	2.53

Fielding

Catcher	PCT	G	PO	A	E	DP	PB
Gonzalez	.984	17	114	8	2	1	3
Greiner	1.000	4	19	0	0	0	2
Hicks	.993	37	287	17	2	1	2
Holaday	.986	90	701	56	11	11	7
McCann	1.000	2	12	1	0	0	0

First Base	PCT	G	PO	A	E	DP
Adduci	1.000	1	3	1	0	1
Ficociello	.988	17	150	8	2	15
Hicks	1.000	11	83	1	0	9
Krizan	1.000	4	20	2	0	2
Loney	.984	7	55	6	1	5
Navarro	.997	105	826	55	3	86

Second Base	PCT	G	PO	A	E	DP
Diaz	.981	15	21	30	1	8
Eaves	.900	2	2	7	1	1
Infante	.977	118	209	304	12	73
Krizan	.913	6	6	15	2	6
Perez	.958	5	10	13	1	1
Ryan	1.000	1	1	1	0	0
Valdes	.800	2	1	3	1	0

Third Base	PCT	G	PO	A	E	DP
Almanzar	.896	60	29	100	15	9
Candelario	.986	28	18	51	1	4
Diaz	.968	29	16	45	2	4
Eaves	1.000	6	3	8	0	0
Ficociello	.929	10	5	21	2	3
Holaday	1.000	3	1	1	0	0
Perez	.882	6	5	10	2	0
Watkins	.818	6	2	7	2	0

Shortstop	PCT	G	PO	A	E	DP
Almanzar	1.000	2	1	2	0	0
Diaz	.986	24	24	48	1	11
Infante	1.000	3	6	8	0	4
Ryan	.985	112	153	304	7	72
Valdes	1.000	7	10	12	0	6

Outfield	PCT	G	PO	A	E	DP
Adduci	.971	50	101	0	3	0
Collins	.979	68	139	1	3	1
den Dekker	.988	50	78	3	1	2
Gerber	1.000	4	9	0	0	0
Hicks	1.000	4	5	0	0	0
Jones	1.000	84	212	5	0	1
Krizan	.982	61	107	5	2	0
Lough	1.000	19	29	0	0	0
Martinez	.800	3	4	0	1	0
McVaney	.923	5	12	0	1	0
Moya	.971	21	33	0	1	0
Navarro	1.000	5	6	0	0	0
Perez	.980	25	48	1	1	0
Presley	.990	42	101	1	1	0
Rubio	1.000	2	3	0	0	0
Watkins	1.000	1	0	1	0	0

ERIE SEAWOLVES — *DOUBLE-A*

EASTERN LEAGUE

Batting	B-T	HT	WT	DOB	AVG	vLH	vRH	G	AB	R	H	2B	3B	HR	RBI	BB	HBP	SH	SF	SO	SB	CS	SLG	OBP
Allen, Will	R-R	6-3	220	3-25-92	.000	.000	.000	2	7	0	0	0	0	0	0	1	0	0	0	1	0	0	.000	.125
Castro, Harold	L-R	6-0	165	11-30-93	.290	.246	.306	106	414	51	120	16	4	1	30	18	6	6	5	53	20	9	.355	.325
Cox, Zack	L-R	5-11	225	5-9-89	.281	.247	.296	85	274	31	77	13	0	3	33	30	3	0	6	70	1	0	.361	.351
Diaz, Argenis	R-R	6-0	190	2-12-87	.083	.167	.000	4	12	1	1	0	0	1	1	1	0	0	0	2	0	0	.333	.154
Eaves, Kody	L-R	6-0	175	7-8-93	.272	.171	.302	88	305	48	83	18	2	13	41	31	2	0	0	74	7	3	.472	.343
Ficociello, Dominic	B-R	6-4	200	4-10-92	.306	.313	.303	90	330	53	101	21	2	7	39	42	0	1	5	87	10	2	.446	.379
Gerber, Mike	L-R	6-0	190	7-8-92	.291	.234	.313	92	350	62	102	22	2	13	45	39	2	0	3	85	10	6	.477	.363
Gonzalez, Miguel	R-R	5-11	220	12-3-90	.242	.194	.267	26	91	12	22	1	0	4	10	8	3	0	0	18	1	0	.385	.324
Greiner, Grayson	R-R	6-6	220	10-11-92	.241	.298	.218	98	328	34	79	20	1	14	42	38	3	0	2	72	0	0	.436	.324
Hinkle, Wade	L-L	6-0	230	9-5-89	.133	.000	.149	23	75	7	10	2	0	3	12	9	2	0	1	24	0	0	.280	.241
Kivett, Ross	R-R	6-1	195	10-19-91	.218	.323	.149	25	78	12	17	5	0	2	4	12	2	1	0	12	4	3	.359	.337
Krizan, Jason	L-R	6-0	185	6-28-89	.393	.467	.366	14	56	10	22	4	0	4	14	8	0	0	2	3	2	1	.679	.455
Lugo, Dawel	R-R	6-0	190	12-31-94	.269	.278	.265	43	175	18	47	6	1	6	22	12	0	0	1	21	2	1	.417	.314
Maddox, Will	L-R	5-10	180	6-11-92	.297	.188	.333	17	64	5	19	1	0	1	5	2	0	1	0	15	3	0	.359	.318
McVaney, Jeff	R-R	6-2	210	1-16-90	.234	.206	.241	42	171	19	40	8	2	3	19	16	7	0	0	34	3	3	.357	.325
Moya, Steven	L-R	6-7	260	8-9-91	.246	.203	.263	59	224	23	55	10	1	11	35	19	1	0	2	65	2	0	.446	.305
Nunez, Gustavo	B-R	5-11	189	2-8-88	.133	.000	.167	4	15	2	2	0	0	0	0	2	0	0	0	1	1	0	.133	.235
2-team total (78 Binghamton)					.263	.000	.167	82	259	26	68	11	2	1	24	16	0	2	3	40	9	5	.332	.302
Quintana, Gabriel	R-R	6-3	215	9-7-92	.265	.260	.267	118	434	61	115	30	3	22	73	20	4	1	7	124	1	0	.500	.299
Remes, Tim	R-R	6-0	205	6-17-92	.143	.136	.145	28	84	5	12	1	1	0	6	3	0	3	2	36	0	0	.179	.169
Simcox, A.J.	R-R	6-3	185	6-22-94	.250	.280	.237	125	436	55	109	22	5	8	36	27	1	6	4	72	12	5	.378	.293
Stewart, Christin	L-R	6-0	205	12-10-93	.256	.243	.261	136	485	67	124	29	3	28	86	56	6	0	8	138	3	0	.501	.335
Valdes, Luis	R-R	6-0	190	1-18-89	.200	.333	.000	6	20	2	4	1	0	0	0	1	0	1	0	8	0	0	.250	.238
Watkins, Logan	L-R	5-11	195	8-29-89	.240	.273	.227	72	238	36	57	6	2	2	20	34	7	4	2	44	4	6	.307	.349

Pitching	B-T	HT	WT	DOB	W	L	ERA	G	GS	CG	SV	IP	H	R	ER	HR	BB	SO	AVG	vLH	vRH	K/9	BB/9
Achter, A.J.	R-R	6-5	215	8-27-88	0	0	5.34	14	2	0	1	29	30	17	17	3	14	24	.266	.340	.212	7.53	4.40
Alaniz, Ruben	R-R	6-4	219	6-14-91	2	1	2.10	23	2	0	3	34	29	13	8	3	8	36	.221	.302	.182	9.44	2.10
Alcantara, Victor	R-R	6-2	190	4-3-93	1	2	3.46	30	2	0	1	55	46	26	21	1	34	57	.231	.265	.207	9.38	5.60
Alexander, Tyler	R-L	6-2	200	7-14-94	8	9	5.07	27	26	1	0	138	178	95	78	20	23	120	.309	.263	.324	7.81	1.50
Baez, Sandy	R-R	6-2	180	11-25-93	0	1	4.50	2	2	0	0	10	9	6	5	3	5	13	.237	.143	.353	11.70	4.50
Burrows, Beau	R-R	6-2	200	9-18-96	6	4	4.72	15	15	1	0	76	79	40	40	5	33	75	.269	.271	.267	8.84	3.89
Crouse, Matt	L-L	6-4	190	7-1-90	7	6	4.60	23	18	0	0	110	127	64	56	16	31	69	.286	.283	.287	5.66	2.54
Donatello, Sean	R-R	6-2	205	8-24-90	4	3	3.45	42	0	0	6	57	56	25	22	5	18	52	.263	.241	.278	8.16	2.83

Ecker, Mark	R-R	6-0	180	5-27-95	0	0	2.00	15	0	0	3	18	15	4	4	2	8	18	.242	.214	.265	9.00	4.00
Ferrell, Jeff	R-R	6-4	205	11-23-90	1	0	1.04	8	0	0	1	9	4	1	1	1	1	10	.133	.222	.095	10.38	1.04
Garcia, Bryan	R-R	6-1	203	4-19-95	1	1	0.96	17	0	0	8	19	7	2	2	1	8	24	.115	.077	.143	11.57	3.86
Garrido, Santiago	R-R	6-1	195	10-4-89	0	1	8.68	4	0	0	0	9	14	9	9	4	3	10	.350	.500	.286	9.64	2.89
Hall, Matt	L-L	6-0	200	7-23-93	1	0	3.09	6	6	0	0	35	30	16	12	2	21	39	.224	.192	.232	10.03	5.40
Jaye, Myles	B-R	6-3	170	12-28-91	1	7	4.29	14	14	1	0	71	77	41	34	8	23	73	.270	.311	.226	9.21	2.90
Joaquin, Waldis	R-R	6-3	230	12-25-86	2	4	6.06	12	1	0	0	16	23	12	11	3	6	14	.324	.333	.317	7.71	3.31
Labourt, Jairo	L-L	6-4	205	3-7-94	1	1	2.64	21	0	0	4	31	23	10	9	3	7	36	.215	.227	.206	10.57	2.05
Ladwig, A.J.	R-R	6-5	180	12-24-92	7	6	5.16	21	20	1	0	106	135	67	61	16	21	75	.308	.291	.328	6.35	1.78
Lewicki, Artie	R-R	6-3	195	4-8-92	9	4	3.76	20	20	0	0	110	107	53	46	5	24	90	.250	.215	.281	7.36	1.96
Long, Grayson	R-R	6-5	230	5-27-94	0	1	13.50	1	1	0	0	4	8	6	6	2	1	3	.444	.556	.333	6.75	2.25
Moreno, Gerson	R-R	6-0	175	9-10-95	0	3	6.43	20	0	0	0	28	23	20	20	4	17	36	.221	.293	.175	11.57	5.46
Navilhon, Joe	R-R	6-0	200	7-13-93	0	1	27.00	1	0	0	0	1	4	3	3	1	0	2	.571	.500	.667	18.00	0.00
Nesbitt, Angel	R-R	6-1	240	12-4-90	0	0	9.00	2	0	0	0	2	5	2	2	1	1	3	.455	.400	.500	13.50	4.50
Ravenelle, Adam	R-R	6-3	185	10-5-92	0	5	5.16	42	0	0	1	52	59	33	30	8	21	49	.291	.286	.295	8.43	3.61
Reininger, Zac	B-R	6-3	170	1-28-93	1	1	1.48	16	0	0	1	24	13	5	4	0	8	29	.167	.108	.220	10.73	2.96
Spomer, Kurt	B-R	6-2	215	7-10-89	6	4	4.50	40	0	0	2	46	42	26	23	1	23	33	.232	.327	.191	6.46	4.50
Thompson, Jeff	R-R	6-6	245	9-23-91	1	0	0.00	1	0	0	0	2	2	0	0	0	1	4	.250	.000	.500	18.00	4.50
Turley, Josh	L-L	6-0	185	8-26-90	0	2	5.56	5	2	0	0	11	12	8	7	1	10	8	.279	.182	.313	6.35	7.94
Turnbull, Spencer	R-R	6-3	215	9-18-92	0	3	6.20	4	4	0	0	20	22	16	14	1	8	22	.272	.191	.359	9.74	3.54
Vasquez, Anthony	L-L	6-0	190	9-19-86	3	1	2.84	5	5	0	0	32	34	12	10	3	5	18	.272	.306	.258	5.12	1.42
Voelker, Paul	R-R	5-10	185	8-19-92	1	2	2.17	28	0	0	7	29	23	7	7	3	7	30	.215	.289	.161	9.31	2.17
Zagurski, Mike	L-L	6-0	240	1-27-83	2	2	2.16	12	0	0	0	17	12	4	4	2	5	25	.203	.273	.162	13.50	2.70

Fielding

Catcher	PCT	G	PO	A	E	DP	PB
Allen	1.000	2	15	0	0	0	1
Gonzalez	1.000	24	192	14	0	1	3
Greiner	.992	93	703	60	6	4	6
Remes	.995	27	192	17	1	1	4

First Base	PCT	G	PO	A	E	DP
Ficociello	.992	61	486	22	4	41
Hinkle	.989	23	157	15	2	19
Krizan	1.000	1	8	1	0	1
Maddox	1.000	3	13	2	0	0
Quintana	.979	55	388	29	9	34
Watkins	.941	2	15	1	1	0

Second Base	PCT	G	PO	A	E	DP
Castro	.983	42	67	108	3	21
Cox	1.000	15	18	40	0	4
Diaz	1.000	2	4	1	0	0
Eaves	.985	33	54	77	2	19
Lugo	1.000	13	24	38	0	11
Maddox	.974	8	17	21	1	5
Nunez	.952	3	9	11	1	3
Simcox	.000	1	0	0	0	0
Watkins	.961	27	40	59	4	14

Third Base	PCT	G	PO	A	E	DP
Cox	.963	17	7	19	1	2
Diaz	.000	1	0	0	0	0
Eaves	.934	49	29	99	9	11
Ficociello	.957	9	7	15	1	2
Lugo	.930	29	13	40	4	4
Quintana	.918	24	22	34	5	1
Watkins	.923	15	5	19	2	0

Shortstop	PCT	G	PO	A	E	DP
Castro	.957	7	5	17	1	2
Diaz	.600	1	2	1	2	1
Lugo	1.000	2	5	1	0	0
Nunez	1.000	1	1	2	0	0
Simcox	.946	125	185	319	29	70
Valdes	1.000	4	4	11	0	2
Watkins	1.000	7	11	9	0	2

Outfield	PCT	G	PO	A	E	DP
Castro	.985	53	129	1	2	0
Ficociello	.967	13	26	3	1	1
Gerber	.995	87	214	1	1	0
Kivett	1.000	23	55	0	0	0
Krizan	1.000	9	18	1	0	0
McVaney	.962	38	72	4	3	0
Moya	.976	58	122	1	3	0
Remes	1.000	1	1	0	0	0
Stewart	.986	124	199	7	3	0
Watkins	1.000	18	26	1	0	0

LAKELAND FLYING TIGERS — *HIGH CLASS A*

FLORIDA STATE LEAGUE

Batting	B-T	HT	WT	DOB	AVG	vLH	vRH	G	AB	R	H	2B	3B	HR	RBI	BB	HBP	SH	SF	SO	SB	CS	SLG	OBP
Alcantara, Sergio	B-R	5-9	168	7-10-96	.230	.209	.241	35	126	18	29	4	1	0	7	14	0	3	0	23	4	3	.278	.307
Allen, Will	R-R	6-3	220	3-25-92	.245	.315	.216	86	310	33	76	16	2	9	40	24	6	0	5	81	0	0	.397	.307
Azocar, Jose	R-R	5-11	160	5-11-96	.220	.250	.209	119	431	38	95	10	6	3	37	14	2	5	4	122	12	6	.292	.246
Castro, Harold	L-R	6-0	165	11-30-93	.364	.286	.421	8	33	3	12	2	1	0	3	0	0	0	0	3	2	0	.485	.364
Cooper, Shane	R-R	5-11	185	12-19-94	.167	.143	.174	9	30	2	5	0	0	0	1	2	0	0	0	8	0	0	.167	.219
Escobar, Elys	R-R	6-0	190	9-21-96	.333	.000	.400	2	6	1	2	1	0	0	0	1	0	0	0	2	0	0	.500	.429
Frailey, Dustin	R-R	5-10	180	2-19-94	.348	.154	.429	27	89	14	31	2	0	1	8	16	4	2	0	20	3	2	.405	.468
Gerber, Mike	L-R	6-0	190	7-8-92	.444	.400	.500	5	18	3	8	2	1	0	2	2	0	0	0	7	0	0	.667	.500
Gibson, Cam	L-R	6-1	195	2-12-94	.240	.419	.191	44	146	21	35	10	4	3	13	22	1	3	2	46	7	2	.425	.339
Gonzalez, David	R-R	5-9	140	12-1-93	.159	.146	.164	49	157	13	25	3	1	0	7	12	2	3	3	18	6	4	.191	.224
Green, Austin	R-R	6-1	200	2-22-90	.231	.278	.206	14	52	2	12	0	1	1	7	3	0	1	0	9	1	0	.327	.273
Hill, Derek	R-R	6-2	195	12-30-95	.194	.000	.250	9	31	3	6	1	0	0	2	5	1	1	0	10	10	0	.226	.324
Hinkle, Wade	L-L	6-0	230	9-5-89	.241	.291	.225	68	237	28	57	14	0	3	28	45	5	0	1	68	1	1	.338	.372
Kivett, Ross	R-R	6-1	195	10-19-91	.270	.250	.276	41	159	19	43	8	0	2	9	14	2	3	1	32	13	1	.359	.335
Latimore, Quincy	R-R	5-11	175	2-3-89	.240	.270	.220	23	96	11	23	3	1	2	5	3	0	0	0	23	2	2	.354	.263
Ledezma, Junnell	R-R	5-9	165	11-9-95	.158	.313	.046	11	38	3	6	0	0	1	1	1	1	0	0	8	0	1	.237	.200
Lester, Josh	L-R	6-3	216	7-17-94	.265	.300	.250	44	166	17	44	12	1	4	24	10	0	1	3	41	2	1	.422	.302
Maddox, Will	L-R	5-10	180	6-11-92	.284	.230	.299	73	275	29	78	9	3	2	23	23	2	7	2	52	12	9	.360	.341
Martinez, J.D.	R-R	6-3	220	8-21-87	.375	—	.375	2	8	2	3	1	0	1	2	0	0	0	0	1	0	0	.875	.375
Pankake, Joey	R-R	6-2	185	11-23-92	.195	.216	.187	77	256	22	50	9	1	5	22	35	2	1	2	73	9	6	.297	.295
Pearce, Jordan	L-R	6-2	200	6-14-96	.000	.000	.000	2	8	0	0	0	0	0	0	0	0	0	0	3	0	0	.000	.000
Perez, Arvicent	R-R	5-10	180	1-14-94	.228	.234	.226	75	259	15	59	7	2	3	28	10	2	4	1	44	4	1	.305	.261
Policelli, Brady	R-R	5-11	195	6-24-95	.200	.333	.143	4	10	2	2	0	1	0	1	1	0	0	1	3	0	0	.400	.250
Remes, Tim	R-R	6-0	205	6-17-92	.188	.286	.111	6	16	2	3	1	0	0	1	4	0	1	0	9	0	0	.250	.350
Robson, Jake	L-R	5-10	175	11-20-94	.277	.193	.305	58	224	27	62	11	4	2	18	23	3	4	1	59	16	9	.388	.351
Rogers, Jake	R-R	6-1	190	4-18-95	.143	.333	.000	2	7	0	1	0	0	0	0	1	0	0	0	2	0	0	.143	.250
Rubio, Elvis	R-R	6-3	215	7-2-94	.250	.000	.261	6	24	2	6	1	0	2	4	1	0	0	0	8	0	0	.542	.280

Salas, Jose	R-R	6-0	160	4-17-97	.067	.333	.000	5	15	1	1	0	0	0	1	1	1	1	1	2	0	0	.067	.167
Salter, Blaise	R-R	6-5	245	6-25-93	.271	.298	.261	55	210	21	57	10	2	2	22	13	5	0	1	41	0	0	.367	.328
Sedio, Chad	L-R	6-3	205	3-30-94	.158	.000	.214	5	19	1	3	1	0	0	3	1	0	1	1	4	0	0	.211	.191
Serrano, Ariel	R-R	5-10	174	6-23-96	.156	.094	.190	27	90	2	14	2	1	1	7	7	0	1	1	18	1	0	.233	.214
Shepherd, Zac	R-R	6-3	185	9-14-95	.208	.245	.197	65	226	28	47	6	1	11	29	27	5	0	2	107	0	2	.389	.304
Valdes, Luis	R-R	6-0	190	1-18-89	.226	.250	.218	63	235	19	53	7	1	3	15	15	2	0	2	39	1	2	.302	.276
Valdez, Ignacio	R-R	6-3	195	7-16-95	.083	.125	.063	8	24	2	2	2	0	0	3	6	0	0	0	16	0	0	.167	.267
Verlander, Ben	R-R	6-4	200	1-31-92	.230	.175	.248	49	165	15	38	7	0	1	14	17	1	0	2	36	0	4	.291	.303
Warner, Cameron	R-R	6-2	188	3-4-94	.250	—	.250	1	4	0	1	0	0	0	0	0	0	0	0	0	0	0	.250	.250

Pitching	B-T	HT	WT	DOB	W	L	ERA	G	GS	CG	SV	IP	H	R	ER	HR	BB	SO	AVG	vLH	vRH	K/9	BB/9
Baez, Sandy	R-R	6-2	180	11-25-93	6	7	3.86	17	17	0	0	89	88	40	38	7	24	92	.257	.273	.242	9.34	2.44
Belisario, Johan	R-R	5-11	165	8-13-93	1	1	3.77	12	0	0	1	14	12	8	6	1	8	17	.211	.136	.257	10.67	5.02
Boardman, Toller	L-L	6-3	210	11-15-92	0	1	2.16	3	0	0	0	8	6	2	2	2	1	6	.207	.250	.191	6.48	1.08
Briceno, Endrys	R-R	6-5	175	2-7-92	1	4	3.59	27	6	0	1	58	65	28	23	3	25	36	.293	.298	.289	5.62	3.90
Burrows, Beau	R-R	6-2	200	9-18-96	4	3	1.23	11	11	0	0	59	45	9	8	3	11	62	.221	.258	.191	9.51	1.69
Dowdy, Kyle	R-R	6-1	195	2-3-93	8	12	3.83	25	22	0	0	134	142	68	57	8	28	121	.276	.265	.285	8.13	1.88
Ecker, Mark	R-R	6-0	180	5-27-95	2	4	3.50	36	0	0	7	44	37	17	17	3	17	63	.233	.344	.163	12.98	3.50
Foley, Jason	R-R	6-4	215	11-1-95	0	2	6.14	6	0	0	1	7	8	5	5	1	2	5	.267	.214	.313	6.14	2.45
Funkhouser, Kyle	R-R	6-2	220	3-16-94	1	1	1.72	5	5	1	0	31	23	6	6	1	6	34	.205	.143	.286	9.77	1.72
Garcia, Bryan	R-R	6-1	203	4-19-95	2	0	0.00	7	0	0	0	9	7	0	0	0	2	15	.233	.308	.177	15.58	2.08
Garrido, Santiago	R-R	6-1	195	10-4-89	1	0	4.02	9	0	0	1	16	10	7	7	2	4	16	.182	.222	.143	9.19	2.30
Gose, Anthony	L-L	6-1	190	8-10-90	0	2	7.59	11	0	0	0	11	7	9	9	0	6	14	.189	.125	.207	11.81	5.06
Hall, Matt	L-L	6-0	200	7-23-93	7	6	2.44	19	18	0	0	103	98	34	28	4	38	110	.250	.277	.241	9.58	3.31
Houston, Zac	R-R	6-5	250	11-30-94	0	1	0.77	8	0	0	4	12	3	1	1	0	8	20	.077	.000	.120	15.43	6.17
Jimenez, Eduardo	R-R	6-0	183	4-4-95	0	1	4.41	13	0	0	6	16	21	11	8	2	5	16	.323	.258	.382	8.82	2.76
Jimenez, Joe	R-R	6-3	220	1-17-95	0	0	0.00	1	1	0	0	1	1	0	0	0	0	1	.200	.000	.500	9.00	0.00
Joaquin, Waldis	R-R	6-3	230	12-25-86	0	1	6.00	3	0	0	0	3	5	2	2	0	1	1	.357	.429	.286	3.00	3.00
Labourt, Jairo	L-L	6-4	205	3-7-94	0	0	0.66	8	0	0	0	14	8	2	1	0	3	22	.167	.167	.167	14.49	1.98
Ladwig, A.J.	R-R	6-5	180	12-24-92	2	2	3.86	5	5	0	0	26	22	14	11	1	2	20	.225	.211	.233	7.01	0.70
Moreno, Gerson	R-R	6-0	175	9-10-95	1	0	2.01	21	0	0	8	22	19	6	5	1	8	30	.226	.238	.214	12.09	3.22
Navilhon, Joe	R-R	6-0	200	7-13-93	2	3	3.16	22	0	0	0	43	42	18	15	3	8	53	.261	.299	.234	11.18	1.69
Perez, Fernando	R-R	6-3	181	12-17-93	2	1	1.79	26	1	0	0	50	42	15	10	1	16	49	.222	.256	.194	8.76	2.86
Reininger, Zac	B-R	6-3	170	1-28-93	1	1	3.86	17	0	0	0	28	22	12	12	2	6	26	.218	.174	.255	8.36	1.93
Shull, Jake	R-R	5-10	190	4-26-94	0	0	3.60	6	0	0	0	10	12	5	4	1	2	4	.333	.368	.294	3.60	1.80
Smith, Blake	R-R	6-5	205	12-5-94	0	0	0.00	1	0	0	0	3	1	0	0	0	1	2	.100	.167	.000	6.00	3.00
Smith, Drew	R-R	6-2	190	9-24-93	1	0	0.77	7	0	0	0	12	4	2	1	0	4	12	.108	.105	.111	9.26	3.09
2-team total (20 Charlotte)					1	2	1.79	27	0	0	7	40	30	13	8	1	9	40	.206	.105	.111	8.93	2.01
Sodders, Austin	L-L	6-3	180	4-29-95	4	5	2.17	12	12	1	0	75	55	21	18	0	17	57	.203	.228	.193	6.87	2.05
Soto, Gregory	L-L	6-1	180	2-11-95	2	1	2.25	5	5	0	0	28	27	8	7	1	11	28	.267	.278	.262	9.00	3.54
Thompson, Jeff	R-R	6-6	245	9-23-91	5	2	3.59	29	0	0	0	53	47	25	21	4	23	56	.241	.205	.265	9.57	3.93
Turley, Josh	L-L	6-0	185	8-26-90	2	1	0.96	8	8	0	0	47	29	7	5	0	10	50	.180	.177	.182	9.64	1.93
Turnbull, Spencer	R-R	6-3	215	9-18-92	7	3	3.05	15	15	0	0	83	68	30	28	3	25	64	.230	.236	.225	6.97	2.72
Voelker, Paul	R-R	5-10	185	8-19-92	0	0	0.00	3	0	0	0	4	1	0	0	0	1	6	.083	.250	.000	13.50	2.25
Warner, Burris	R-R	6-0	190	10-15-94	0	0	4.50	1	0	0	0	2	3	1	1	0	1	1	.333	.400	.250	4.50	4.50
Watkins, Spenser	R-R	6-1	190	8-27-92	0	1	4.87	6	2	0	1	20	27	15	11	2	9	17	.314	.366	.267	7.52	3.98

Fielding

Catcher	PCT	G	PO	A	E	DP	PB
Allen	.996	29	259	14	1	5	7
Escobar	1.000	2	18	3	0	0	1
Green	.992	14	122	9	1	1	0
Perez	.988	74	639	80	9	8	13
Policelli	1.000	4	25	1	0	0	0
Remes	.984	6	53	10	1	0	0
Rogers	1.000	1	4	0	0	0	0

First Base	PCT	G	PO	A	E	DP
Allen	.994	21	165	12	1	16
Hinkle	1.000	48	405	31	0	32
Lester	1.000	6	41	4	0	3
Maddox	1.000	3	31	0	0	0
Pearce	1.000	1	7	0	0	2
Salter	.995	50	387	15	2	39

Second Base	PCT	G	PO	A	E	DP
Castro	1.000	6	14	16	0	3
Cooper	.933	7	7	21	2	0
Gonzalez	1.000	10	22	30	0	4
Ledezma	1.000	10	12	29	0	9
Maddox	.973	65	123	166	8	44
Pankake	.942	20	24	57	5	9
Salas	1.000	2	1	2	0	0
Sedio	.938	4	6	9	1	2
Valdes	.933	8	13	15	2	4

Third Base	PCT	G	PO	A	E	DP
Lester	.961	36	20	54	3	7
Pankake	.909	24	9	31	4	7
Pearce	1.000	1	1	2	0	0
Salas	1.000	4	1	4	0	0
Sedio	.500	1	0	1	1	0
Shepherd	.977	63	28	97	3	8
Valdes	1.000	1	1	2	0	1

Shortstop	PCT	G	PO	A	E	DP
Alcantara	.930	35	51	82	10	22
Castro	1.000	1	4	3	0	1
Cooper	1.000	2	3	4	0	0
Gonzalez	.964	38	54	105	6	23
Ledezma	1.000	1	3	3	0	2
Lester	1.000	1	2	3	0	0
Shepherd	.667	1	0	2	1	0
Valdes	.947	50	51	129	10	17

Outfield	PCT	G	PO	A	E	DP
Azocar	.977	119	242	9	6	0
Castro	.000	1	0	0	0	0
Frailey	1.000	27	41	2	0	0
Gerber	1.000	3	10	0	0	0
Gibson	.983	34	58	0	1	0
Gonzalez	.000	1	0	0	0	0
Hill	1.000	6	12	0	0	0
Kivett	.978	40	84	6	2	2
Latimore	.933	21	27	1	2	0
Martinez	1.000	1	3	0	0	0
Pankake	.900	16	18	0	2	0
Robson	1.000	49	126	3	0	2
Rubio	1.000	6	14	0	0	0
Serrano	.976	25	41	0	1	0
Valdez	1.000	3	5	0	0	0
Verlander	.955	43	60	4	3	0

WEST MICHIGAN WHITECAPS

LOW CLASS A

MIDWEST LEAGUE

Batting	B-T	HT	WT	DOB	AVG	vLH	vRH	G	AB	R	H	2B	3B	HR	RBI	BB	HBP	SH	SF	SO	SB	CS	SLG	OBP
Athmann, Austin	R-R	6-2	210	4-27-95	.268	.304	.251	90	343	44	92	16	0	3	35	18	1	2	2	69	1	0	.341	.305
Bauml, Cole	L-R	6-3	205	11-2-92	.268	.292	.259	125	488	61	131	25	3	1	55	46	4	1	3	98	13	6	.338	.335
Burch, Luke	L-L	6-2	185	4-18-94	.267	.500	.000	5	15	0	4	0	0	0	0	1	1	1	0	5	0	0	.267	.353
Burdeaux, Dylan	R-R	6-2	230	2-1-94	.260	.231	.270	43	150	23	39	10	1	2	22	15	1	0	1	33	2	1	.380	.329
Cameron, Daz	R-R	6-2	185	1-15-97	.250	.000	.333	3	8	1	2	0	0	0	1	3	0	0	0	4	0	1	.250	.455
2-team total (120 Quad Cities)					.271	.000	.333	123	454	80	123	29	8	14	74	48	12	1	7	112	32	13	.463	.351
Gibson, Cam	L-R	6-1	195	2-12-94	.274	.256	.283	65	263	49	72	10	7	10	34	25	2	7	6	45	12	4	.479	.335
Gonzalez, David	R-R	5-9	140	12-1-93	.259	.231	.268	21	54	13	14	0	1	0	7	8	0	2	2	5	0	0	.296	.344
Hill, Derek	R-R	6-2	195	12-30-95	.285	.297	.280	35	144	28	41	8	6	1	21	16	4	2	2	38	12	5	.444	.368
Lester, Josh	L-R	6-3	216	7-17-94	.276	.299	.266	66	265	30	73	17	1	9	42	12	3	0	5	46	1	1	.449	.309
Longley, Drew	R-R	6-3	215	10-5-88	.227	.255	.217	62	216	28	49	17	3	2	17	20	2	0	1	77	0	0	.361	.297
Machonis, Sam	L-B	6-1	195	6-16-94	.219	.158	.234	32	96	12	21	1	0	0	5	12	3	0	0	29	0	0	.229	.324
Paredes, Isaac	R-R	5-11	175	2-18-99	.217	.222	.215	32	115	16	25	3	0	4	21	13	5	0	0	13	0	0	.348	.323
2-team total (92 South Bend)					.252	.298	.253	124	452	65	114	28	0	11	70	42	18	2	3	67	2	1	.387	.338
Pereira, Anthony	R-R	6-0	170	11-28-96	.251	.209	.268	126	470	45	118	29	1	7	64	40	4	3	1	84	11	3	.362	.315
Pinero, Danny	R-R	6-5	210	5-2-94	.289	.341	.265	120	422	61	122	26	4	4	56	57	7	3	8	68	5	2	.398	.377
Quero, Jose	L-L	6-0	190	9-5-98	.118	.000	.191	9	34	2	4	0	0	0	0	1	0	0	0	11	0	0	.118	.143
Remes, Tim	R-R	6-0	205	6-17-92	.000	—	.000	2	5	0	0	0	0	0	0	1	0	0	0	4	0	0	.000	.167
Robson, Jake	L-R	5-10	175	11-20-94	.329	.295	.347	60	228	38	75	10	1	1	27	31	1	5	2	59	5	9	.395	.408
Rubio, Elvis	R-R	6-3	215	7-2-94	.096	.071	.105	15	52	3	5	0	0	0	4	6	5	0	2	16	1	0	.096	.246
Salter, Blaise	R-R	6-5	245	6-25-93	.330	.361	.315	66	261	39	86	29	0	6	53	17	6	0	5	47	2	0	.510	.377
Savage, Will	R-R	6-0	185	12-9-94	.215	.125	.255	25	79	9	17	3	1	0	5	9	0	1	1	20	4	2	.279	.292
Sedio, Chad	L-R	6-3	205	3-30-94	.268	.244	.278	80	272	41	73	16	3	11	41	21	10	1	3	52	1	1	.471	.340
Shepherd, Zac	R-R	6-3	185	9-14-95	.158	.162	.157	41	139	17	22	6	0	0	13	25	1	0	1	64	0	2	.201	.289
Warner, Cameron	R-R	6-2	188	3-4-94	.250	.273	.231	7	24	4	6	0	0	0	5	3	1	0	0	7	1	0	.250	.357
Woodrow, Danny	L-R	5-10	155	1-26-95	.271	.288	.263	116	469	73	127	17	4	0	47	51	2	13	6	93	31	11	.324	.341

Pitching	B-T	HT	WT	DOB	W	L	ERA	G	GS	CG	SV	IP	H	R	ER	HR	BB	SO	AVG	vLH	vRH	K/9	BB/9
Carlton, Drew	R-R	6-1	197	9-8-95	0	0	0.00	1	0	0	0	1	0	0	0	0	0	0	.000	.000	.000	0.00	0.00
Castro, Anthony	R-R	6-0	174	4-13-95	10	6	2.49	21	21	1	0	108	91	41	30	4	35	95	.226	.196	.264	7.89	2.91
de Blok, Tom	R-R	6-4	195	5-8-96	4	2	2.87	23	11	0	1	78	69	28	25	6	13	73	.232	.205	.261	8.39	1.49
Foley, Jason	R-R	6-4	215	11-1-95	3	1	1.55	18	0	0	5	29	20	7	5	0	5	36	.189	.163	.211	11.17	1.55
Funkhouser, Kyle	R-R	6-2	220	3-16-94	4	1	3.16	7	7	0	0	31	30	13	11	3	13	49	.254	.262	.245	14.07	3.73
Garcia, Bryan	R-R	6-1	203	4-19-95	1	2	3.14	14	0	0	9	14	12	6	5	0	4	27	.218	.130	.281	16.95	2.51
Gutierrez, Alfred	R-R	6-0	143	6-12-95	10	7	3.06	24	20	1	1	126	101	51	43	15	23	127	.213	.239	.181	9.05	1.64
Hill, Evan	L-L	6-5	210	8-18-93	2	0	3.58	16	0	0	1	28	22	12	11	1	15	36	.220	.263	.194	11.71	4.88
Houston, Zac	R-R	6-5	250	11-30-94	0	0	2.53	24	0	0	2	46	24	13	13	1	22	71	.148	.143	.152	13.79	4.27
Idrogo, Eudis	L-L	6-1	198	6-6-95	7	7	3.01	23	23	1	0	135	130	52	45	8	28	100	.255	.238	.262	6.68	1.87
Jimenez, Eduardo	R-R	6-0	183	4-4-95	1	1	1.05	21	0	0	6	34	21	6	4	0	10	44	.180	.184	.177	11.53	2.62
Manning, Matt	R-R	6-6	190	1-28-98	2	0	5.60	5	5	0	0	18	14	11	11	0	11	26	.209	.182	.235	13.25	5.60
Navilhon, Joe	R-R	6-0	200	7-13-93	2	2	2.70	11	0	0	1	23	15	8	7	0	5	28	.177	.237	.128	10.80	1.93
Perez, Fernando	R-R	6-3	181	12-17-93	0	1	2.84	5	0	0	0	13	11	5	4	1	3	14	.244	.263	.231	9.95	2.13
Pinto, Wladimir	R-R	5-11	170	2-12-98	0	0	0.00	1	0	0	0	0	1	0	0	0	0	0	.500	.000	1.000	0.00	0.00
Sanchez, Anibal	R-R	6-0	205	2-27-84	0	1	6.75	1	1	0	0	4	5	3	3	0	2	3	.333	.273	.500	6.75	4.50
Schmidt, Clate	R-R	6-1	190	12-10-93	1	0	6.55	9	0	0	0	22	28	19	16	2	5	13	.318	.357	.283	5.32	2.05
Schreiber, John	R-R	6-3	215	3-5-94	5	1	0.54	27	0	0	11	50	25	5	3	0	8	70	.147	.188	.111	12.52	1.43
Shull, Jake	R-R	5-10	190	4-26-94	2	1	4.68	21	0	0	1	33	38	17	17	5	10	25	.292	.333	.250	6.89	2.76
Sittinger, Brandyn	R-R	6-1	200	6-6-94	3	1	3.38	7	0	0	1	13	12	7	5	1	7	18	.226	.231	.222	12.15	4.73
Sodders, Austin	L-L	6-3	180	4-29-95	7	0	1.40	11	11	0	0	64	49	10	10	2	13	65	.217	.256	.196	9.09	1.82
Soto, Gregory	L-L	6-1	180	2-11-95	10	1	2.25	18	18	0	0	96	70	29	24	3	54	116	.204	.159	.220	10.88	5.06
St. John, Locke	L-L	6-3	180	1-31-93	1	5	2.94	27	1	0	2	64	54	23	21	6	17	74	.224	.130	.268	10.35	2.38
Szkutnik, Trent	R-L	6-0	195	8-21-93	6	2	2.72	34	2	0	4	89	78	29	27	6	18	74	.234	.239	.230	7.46	1.81
Warner, Burris	R-R	6-0	190	10-15-94	0	0	4.00	4	0	0	2	9	4	5	4	0	5	9	.133	.059	.231	9.00	5.00
Watkins, Spenser	R-R	6-1	190	8-27-92	9	3	3.22	16	16	0	0	89	89	38	32	8	32	66	.262	.253	.270	6.65	3.22

Fielding

Catcher	PCT	G	PO	A	E	DP	PB
Athmann	.988	77	698	67	9	5	17
Longley	.995	59	551	36	3	5	6
Remes	.941	2	15	1	1	1	0

First Base	PCT	G	PO	A	E	DP
Burdeaux	.990	36	288	14	3	28
Lester	1.000	6	43	4	0	5
Longley	1.000	3	20	3	0	1
Pinero	.975	15	108	9	3	10
Quero	1.000	9	67	4	0	6
Salter	.985	61	495	47	8	41
Sedio	.986	9	68	2	1	7

Second Base	PCT	G	PO	A	E	DP
Gonzalez	.984	19	29	33	1	8
Paredes	.933	3	7	7	1	2
Pereira	.962	61	87	164	10	34
Pinero	1.000	1	1	1	0	0
Savage	.948	23	40	51	5	12
Sedio	.950	30	40	94	7	17
Shepherd	.000	1	0	0	0	0
Warner	.931	6	10	17	2	2

Third Base	PCT	G	PO	A	E	DP
Lester	.952	56	34	84	6	10
Paredes	1.000	5	4	13	0	2
Pereira	.946	16	13	22	2	4
Pinero	.936	26	9	35	3	5
Sedio	1.000	3	4	5	0	1
Shepherd	.885	34	16	38	7	4

Shortstop	PCT	G	PO	A	E	DP
Paredes	.970	22	23	41	2	7
Pereira	.982	46	67	151	4	29
Pinero	.962	71	88	164	10	35

Outfield	PCT	G	PO	A	E	DP
Bauml	.981	91	154	2	3	1
Burch	1.000	5	10	0	0	0
Cameron	1.000	3	7	0	0	0
Gibson	.991	61	110	2	1	2
Hill	.966	23	55	1	2	0
Machonis	1.000	32	51	2	0	0

Pereira	1.000	1	1	0	0	0	Rubio	1.000	12	22	0	0	0	Sedio	1.000	22	39	1	0	1
Robson	.990	54	97	2	1	0	Savage	1.000	1	1	0	0	0	Woodrow	.984	108	232	7	4	1

CONNECTICUT TIGERS — *SHORT SEASON*

NEW YORK-PENN LEAGUE

Batting	B-T	HT	WT	DOB	AVG	vLH	vRH	G	AB	R	H	2B	3B	HR	RBI	BB	HBP	SH	SF	SO	SB	CS	SLG	OBP
Alcantara, Randel	L-R	6-1	220	5-13-97	.189	.107	.213	35	122	16	23	4	1	2	11	11	3	0	3	40	1	1	.287	.266
Bortles, Colby	R-R	6-5	225	5-28-95	.251	.395	.208	56	187	22	47	9	1	3	23	23	2	0	3	48	1	0	.358	.335
Burch, Luke	L-L	6-2	185	4-18-94	.261	.395	.219	42	157	20	41	2	1	0	11	16	1	3	2	31	8	1	.287	.330
Burdeaux, Dylan	R-R	6-2	230	2-1-94	.306	.250	.345	14	49	6	15	4	0	0	7	6	1	0	1	13	0	0	.388	.386
Coleman, Ro	B-R	5-5	150	11-22-94	.227	.227	.226	30	75	14	17	3	2	0	2	10	1	0	0	14	4	2	.320	.326
De La Cruz, Isrrael	R-R	6-0	150	6-15-97	.500	.667	.000	1	4	1	2	0	0	0	1	0	0	0	0	2	1	0	.500	.500
Escobar, Elys	R-R	6-0	190	9-21-96	.255	.200	.290	17	51	7	13	3	0	1	8	7	0	0	1	14	2	0	.373	.339
Garcia, Alexis	R-R	6-2	170	7-1-97	.231	.143	.333	3	13	0	3	0	0	0	3	0	0	0	0	3	0	0	.231	.231
Hoffman, Teddy	R-R	6-0	195	8-3-96	.156	.189	.141	37	122	18	19	2	0	3	10	16	2	0	0	52	5	0	.246	.264
Ledezma, Junnell	R-R	5-9	165	11-9-95	.303	.367	.250	20	66	7	20	3	0	0	4	9	1	0	1	21	2	1	.349	.390
Machonis, Sam	L-B	6-1	195	6-16-94	.667	1.000	.000	1	3	1	2	1	0	0	3	1	0	0	0	0	0	0	1.000	.750
Martinez, Hector	R-R	5-11	175	11-1-96	.221	.233	.217	50	181	21	40	8	0	1	20	9	1	1	2	56	3	1	.282	.259
Martinez, Julio	R-R	6-2	195	12-15-97	.125	.000	.200	2	8	0	1	0	0	0	0	0	0	0	0	7	0	0	.125	.125
McCain, Garrett	R-L	6-0	180	2-28-96	.259	.321	.236	53	193	26	50	6	1	3	22	20	4	0	1	41	5	2	.347	.339
Morgan, Joey	R-R	6-0	185	8-26-96	.250	.423	.198	34	112	14	28	5	0	1	10	9	5	0	2	25	0	0	.321	.328
Pearce, Jordan	L-R	6-2	200	6-14-96	.261	.343	.237	42	153	9	40	5	0	2	26	11	3	0	2	45	3	1	.333	.320
Peterson, Cole	L-R	5-11	160	8-2-95	.246	.229	.250	55	183	28	45	5	0	0	16	11	1	1	5	24	6	3	.273	.285
Rivera, Reynaldo	L-R	6-6	250	6-14-97	.187	.245	.165	52	182	16	34	9	1	2	26	18	2	0	5	55	3	1	.280	.261
Rosa, Dylan	R-R	6-2	200	6-27-96	.213	.292	.172	43	141	17	30	6	0	4	18	17	0	1	3	56	8	2	.340	.292
Savage, Will	R-R	6-0	185	12-9-94	.222	.227	.218	30	99	11	22	1	0	0	8	7	1	1	0	20	5	2	.232	.280
Serrano, Ariel	R-R	5-10	174	6-23-96	.222	.000	.400	3	9	2	2	0	1	0	2	2	1	0	0	1	0	0	.444	.417
Silverio, Gresuan	B-R	6-0	175	1-5-99	.000	—	.000	2	6	0	0	0	0	0	0	0	0	0	0	1	0	0	.000	.000
Sthormes, Andres	R-R	5-10	171	8-7-96	.254	.111	.306	19	67	9	17	1	3	1	7	0	0	0	0	15	0	2	.403	.254
Swilling, Hunter	R-R	5-11	190	12-26-94	.133	.133	.133	11	30	4	4	0	1	0	2	4	0	0	0	10	0	0	.200	.235
Tejeda, Bryan	R-R	6-0	190	1-17-96	.429	.000	.750	2	7	1	3	1	0	0	0	1	1	0	0	2	0	0	.571	.556
Valdez, Ignacio	R-R	6-3	195	7-16-95	.111	.143	.100	10	27	3	3	1	0	1	1	3	0	0	0	13	1	0	.259	.200
Warner, Cameron	R-R	6-2	188	3-4-94	.277	.063	.347	20	65	8	18	6	0	0	2	8	1	0	0	15	1	0	.369	.365

Pitching	B-T	HT	WT	DOB	W	L	ERA	G	GS	CG	SV	IP	H	R	ER	HR	BB	SO	AVG	vLH	vRH	K/9	BB/9
Aldridge, Dean	R-R	6-3	190	7-29-94	1	1	6.75	6	0	0	1	7	9	5	5	0	2	7	.333	.182	.438	9.45	2.70
Bass, Brad	R-R	6-6	250	2-15-96	1	2	3.00	7	6	0	0	21	23	11	7	0	6	18	.281	.257	.298	7.71	2.57
Carlton, Drew	R-R	6-1	197	9-8-95	1	0	1.29	13	0	0	10	14	8	2	2	1	2	20	.160	.143	.172	12.86	1.29
Castellanos, Ryan	R-R	6-3	215	4-15-94	5	5	4.12	14	14	0	0	74	86	44	34	6	17	28	.291	.346	.247	3.39	2.06
Castillo, Oswaldo	R-R	6-0	193	8-18-96	3	3	2.91	17	7	1	0	43	38	17	14	1	14	30	.239	.247	.233	6.23	2.91
de Blok, Tom	R-R	6-4	195	5-8-96	0	0	0.00	1	1	0	0	4	1	0	0	0	1	5	.083	.167	.000	12.27	2.45
Figueroa, Ken	R-R	6-0	190	5-30-96	2	2	3.52	7	6	0	0	31	38	18	12	1	11	18	.309	.240	.356	5.28	3.23
German, Francisco	R-R	6-2	160	12-26-96	0	2	20.25	4	0	0	0	5	15	15	12	0	8	8	.500	.471	.539	13.50	13.50
Gonzalez, Daniel	R-R	6-3	200	8-15-95	1	0	0.00	2	0	0	0	4	1	0	0	0	2	2	.091	.000	.143	4.50	4.50
Green, Max	L-L	6-1	175	5-28-96	1	2	2.81	21	0	0	1	26	28	14	8	1	11	28	.269	.318	.233	9.82	3.86
Hayes, John	R-R	6-6	225	1-7-93	1	0	4.43	17	0	0	0	22	32	12	11	1	11	18	.340	.386	.300	7.25	4.43
Lance, Carson	R-R	6-5	245	5-3-95	2	3	2.45	10	3	0	0	29	20	9	8	0	8	26	.191	.186	.194	7.98	2.45
Lescher, Billy	R-R	6-4	215	9-17-95	0	0	5.40	1	0	0	0	2	2	1	1	0	0	4	.286	.000	.333	21.60	0.00
Lopez, Jose	R-R	5-9	174	6-21-95	0	0	13.50	1	0	0	0	1	2	1	1	0	1	1	.667	1.000	.500	13.50	13.50
Manning, Matt	R-R	6-6	190	1-28-98	2	2	1.89	9	9	0	0	33	27	10	7	0	14	36	.223	.154	.275	9.72	3.78
Mateo, Jhonny	R-R	6-3	170	8-19-94	4	3	6.64	14	5	0	0	41	50	37	30	3	25	19	.301	.347	.266	4.20	5.53
Mueses, Victor	R-R	6-1	175	10-13-95	1	0	3.76	21	0	0	0	26	26	12	11	0	16	21	.260	.239	.278	7.18	5.47
Myers, Dane	R-R	6-2	205	3-8-96	1	2	2.33	13	12	0	0	46	31	14	12	2	10	29	.193	.186	.198	5.63	1.94
O'Connell, Colyn	R-R	6-5	215	7-19-93	1	3	3.82	20	0	0	0	31	30	14	13	0	16	38	.248	.289	.224	11.15	4.70
Pinto, Wladimir	R-R	5-11	170	2-12-98	1	0	0.00	8	0	0	4	10	2	0	0	0	0	18	.065	.111	.046	16.76	0.00
Schmidt, Clate	R-R	6-1	190	12-10-93	0	1	1.50	10	0	0	0	12	7	4	2	1	0	12	.156	.125	.172	9.00	0.00
Sittinger, Brandyn	R-R	6-1	200	6-6-94	1	0	1.06	11	0	0	2	17	13	2	2	0	6	21	.210	.259	.171	11.12	3.18
Stock, Dylan	R-R	6-4	195	7-21-96	0	0	0.00	1	0	0	0	1	0	0	0	0	1	0	.000	.000	.000	0.00	9.00
Vasquez, Jose	R-R	6-0	175	3-19-96	1	2	3.89	10	8	0	0	39	35	21	17	1	16	33	.230	.243	.220	7.55	3.66
Vest, Will	R-R	6-0	180	6-6-95	3	1	2.83	21	0	0	2	29	15	9	9	1	9	28	.156	.229	.115	8.79	2.83
Viloria, Felix	L-L	6-1	165	12-2-96	1	0	2.63	12	0	0	0	14	14	4	4	0	5	10	.259	.286	.242	6.59	3.29
Warner, Burris	R-R	6-0	190	10-15-94	3	1	4.15	14	1	0	0	26	27	14	12	0	8	27	.262	.163	.333	9.35	2.77

Fielding

C: Escobar 17, Morgan 34, Silverio 2, Sthormes 19, Tejeda 1. **1B:** Alcantara 24, Bortles 4, Burdeaux 9, Ledezma 2, Pearce 26, Rivera 12. **2B:** Garcia 1, Ledezma 7, Martinez 39, Savage 19, Warner 9. **3B:** Bortles 43, Garcia 1, Ledezma 1, Pearce 10, Savage 2, Swilling 11, Warner 12. **SS:** De La Cruz 1, Garcia 1, Ledezma 8, Peterson 54, Savage 9. **OF:** Burch 41, Coleman 22, Hoffman 30, Machonis 1, Martinez 2, McCain 52, Rivera 30, Rosa 34, Savage 1, Serrano 3, Valdez 8.

GCL TIGERS EAST — *ROOKIE*

GULF COAST LEAGUE

Batting	B-T	HT	WT	DOB	AVG	vLH	vRH	G	AB	R	H	2B	3B	HR	RBI	BB	HBP	SH	SF	SO	SB	CS	SLG	OBP
Arias, Franklin	R-R	6-0	165	1-9-97	.220	.100	.255	42	132	25	29	5	1	0	14	25	1	2	1	17	7	3	.273	.346
Bello, Moises	R-R	5-10	160	6-13-97	.279	.250	.286	39	129	19	36	3	1	1	13	9	1	3	0	9	7	4	.341	.331

Cortez, Johandry	R-R	5-10	170	5-24-98	.238	.158	.262	29	80	6	19	1	0	1	9	5	1	0	0	18	1	0	.288	.291
Escalona, Ildemaro	R-R	6-0	170	2-12-99	.248	.207	.258	47	149	8	37	4	2	0	12	8	1	0	1	29	2	3	.302	.289
Gonzalez, Cesar	R-R	6-2	175	5-31-95	.289	.455	.235	26	90	13	26	4	1	2	14	7	0	0	0	23	2	1	.422	.340
Gonzalez, Gerardo	R-R	5-9	170	12-21-98	.219	.250	.211	37	114	11	25	6	1	0	10	9	2	7	1	40	1	3	.290	.286
2-team total (2 Tigers West)					.240	.250	.211	39	121	12	29	6	1	0	12	9	2	7	2	41	1	3	.306	.299
Gonzalez, Jose	R-R	6-2	165	7-14-98	.171	.222	.154	11	35	9	6	1	0	0	1	3	3	1	0	8	2	0	.200	.293
Hurtado, Pedro	B-R	5-11	160	3-1-99	.188	.217	.178	32	96	7	18	2	2	1	9	9	1	3	0	22	0	1	.281	.264
Martinez, Julio	R-R	6-2	195	12-15-97	.260	.267	.258	49	158	19	41	9	2	3	15	11	4	1	1	39	3	0	.399	.322
Nunez, Moises	R-R	6-2	190	2-7-97	.186	.120	.205	37	113	12	21	4	0	0	8	15	5	1	2	27	3	0	.221	.304
Ramos, Melvin	B-R	5-11	155	12-26-98	.206	.214	.205	34	97	15	20	1	1	1	7	15	1	1	2	34	4	3	.268	.313
Santos, Allan	R-R	6-1	180	6-5-98	.172	.276	.141	40	128	10	22	9	1	1	12	16	1	1	3	40	2	1	.281	.264
Silverio, Gresuan	B-R	6-0	175	1-5-99	.331	.391	.319	42	136	10	45	8	1	2	29	22	1	0	2	23	1	1	.449	.422
Torres, Mike	R-R	5-10	140	2-10-98	.180	.177	.180	31	78	7	14	1	0	0	4	8	4	1	0	21	2	4	.192	.289
Vital, Santiago	R-R	6-2	145	1-15-99	.234	.216	.239	51	175	28	41	7	2	2	16	8	2	2	0	44	8	3	.331	.276
Ynirio, Jorge	R-R	5-11	170	10-19-97	.226	.130	.253	35	106	9	24	1	1	0	5	3	0	2	0	21	4	3	.255	.248

Pitching	B-T	HT	WT	DOB	W	L	ERA	G	GS	CG	SV	IP	H	R	ER	HR	BB	SO	AVG	vLH	vRH	K/9	BB/9
Baker, Jake	R-L	6-2	200	6-12-98	0	1	3.60	8	0	0	0	10	8	6	4	0	5	11	.222	.167	.233	9.90	4.50
Batista, Franchi	R-R	6-0	170	5-26-96	0	2	7.02	12	0	0	1	17	17	14	13	2	9	13	.262	.320	.225	7.02	4.86
De La Cruz, Sandel	R-R	6-2	185	8-6-96	0	6	4.89	10	10	0	0	46	47	32	25	2	22	41	.254	.310	.228	8.02	4.30
De La Rosa, Bairon	R-R	6-0	195	7-17-96	1	2	6.86	15	1	0	1	21	19	16	16	1	16	18	.247	.276	.229	7.71	6.86
De Pena, Enrique	R-R	6-2	175	2-19-96	0	3	6.98	11	1	0	0	19	29	17	15	2	8	9	.330	.412	.310	4.19	3.72
Escalona, Edgar	R-R	6-4	193	3-30-98	2	7	5.73	11	11	0	0	44	58	35	28	3	17	25	.319	.254	.357	5.11	3.48
Guante, Julio	R-R	6-3	180	5-29-97	0	5	7.04	14	1	0	0	31	44	37	24	1	12	16	.317	.289	.330	4.70	3.52
Guzman, Carlos	R-R	6-1	170	5-16-98	1	1	0.45	11	0	0	4	20	12	2	1	0	6	18	.179	.238	.152	8.10	2.70
2-team total (3 Tigers West)					1	1	0.70	14	0	0	4	26	16	4	2	0	6	25	.180	.238	.152	8.77	2.10
Lopez, Ronaldo	R-R	6-2	165	1-7-98	2	2	6.44	11	2	0	1	29	43	24	21	4	14	25	.339	.300	.364	7.67	4.30
Paulino, Miguel	R-R	6-1	185	8-21-98	1	1	7.25	11	0	0	0	22	15	19	18	1	32	24	.195	.111	.220	9.67	12.90
Rodriguez, Hector	R-R	6-4	210	12-4-96	0	0	6.20	14	0	0	0	20	15	15	14	3	24	11	.200	.214	.192	4.87	10.62
Rodriguez, Jesus	R-R	6-3	170	2-16-98	3	3	3.26	11	11	0	0	58	59	31	21	4	10	27	.257	.267	.252	4.19	1.55
Rodriguez, Perkyn	R-R	6-1	165	5-6-98	0	0	1.80	2	0	0	0	5	2	1	1	0	5	2	.143	.333	.000	3.60	9.00
Santana, Kilber	R-R	6-1	160	10-15-98	0	4	3.77	12	1	0	1	29	27	21	12	2	11	18	.237	.278	.218	5.65	3.45
Silva, Alfredo	L-L	6-3	180	7-27-98	0	5	4.71	11	11	0	0	50	66	31	26	3	16	30	.328	.425	.304	5.44	2.90
Terrero, Richard	L-L	6-6	220	9-9-97	1	1	3.55	9	9	0	0	33	33	14	13	2	21	35	.268	.296	.260	9.55	5.73
Tortosa, Cristhian	L-L	6-4	170	10-30-98	3	2	3.68	11	1	0	0	29	20	17	12	0	17	29	.198	.111	.217	8.90	5.22

Fielding

C: Hurtado 30, Nunez 14, Silverio 21. **1B:** Bello 4, Cortez 19, Hurtado 2, Nunez 22, Silverio 17, Ynirio 1. **2B:** Escalona 4, Gonzalez 18, Ramos 17, Torres 14, Ynirio 17. **3B:** Bello 26, Gonzalez 14, Ramos 1, Torres 17, Ynirio 10. **SS:** Bello 1, Escalona 43, Ramos 18, Ynirio 2. **OF:** Arias 42, Bello 10, Gonzalez 11, Martinez 49, Santos 30, Vital 49.

GCL TIGERS WEST — ROOKIE

GULF COAST LEAGUE

Batting	B-T	HT	WT	DOB	AVG	vLH	vRH	G	AB	R	H	2B	3B	HR	RBI	BB	HBP	SH	SF	SO	SB	CS	SLG	OBP
Alvarado, Darwin	L-R	6-1	170	11-10-98	.200	.185	.204	44	140	17	28	3	0	1	11	14	2	1	2	38	5	3	.243	.279
Aristigueta, Keyder	R-R	5-11	165	2-2-96	.266	.222	.276	47	154	20	41	6	0	1	17	18	7	0	2	36	8	1	.325	.365
Azuaje, Jheyser	R-R	5-9	165	2-12-97	.303	.273	.313	29	89	7	27	1	0	0	6	1	3	1	0	13	4	1	.315	.333
Bivens, Jake	L-R	6-1	185	5-25-95	.267	.000	.300	24	45	5	12	0	0	0	5	10	5	2	0	6	4	0	.267	.450
Bojarski, Ulrich	R-R	6-3	190	9-15-98	.225	.333	.195	38	111	14	25	7	1	1	13	7	5	0	1	35	1	0	.333	.298
Cooper, Shane	R-R	5-11	185	12-19-94	.255	.167	.268	21	47	10	12	3	0	1	5	6	0	0	1	7	3	0	.383	.333
De La Cruz, Isrrael	R-R	6-0	150	6-15-97	.297	.269	.304	46	128	23	38	5	2	0	8	8	1	1	1	33	16	10	.367	.341
Garcia, Alexis	R-R	6-2	170	7-1-97	.208	.333	.183	39	125	19	26	4	4	0	16	17	2	1	3	39	8	4	.304	.306
Gonzalez, Gerardo	R-R	5-9	170	12-21-98	.571	.500	.600	2	7	1	4	0	0	0	2	0	0	0	1	1	0	0	.571	.500
2-team total (37 Tigers East)					.240	.250	.211	39	121	12	29	6	1	0	12	9	2	7	2	41	1	3	.306	.299
Hill, Derek	R-R	6-2	195	12-30-95	.163	.250	.135	14	49	11	8	1	1	1	7	10	0	1	1	15	7	0	.286	.300
Karstetter, Ryan	R-R	6-4	200	1-30-97	.226	.300	.206	31	93	9	21	2	1	1	15	8	1	1	1	19	2	0	.301	.291
King, Jose	L-R	6-0	160	1-16-99	.321	.375	.307	28	112	18	36	3	1	0	6	6	0	0	0	29	8	9	.366	.356
McMillan, Sam	R-R	6-1	195	12-1-98	.288	.222	.301	37	111	24	32	5	1	3	25	19	12	0	1	17	1	1	.432	.441
Pearce, Jordan	L-R	6-2	200	6-14-96	.342	.600	.303	13	38	6	13	0	0	2	10	5	0	1	1	7	0	1	.500	.409
Quero, Jose	L-L	6-0	190	9-5-98	.256	.333	.238	40	156	25	40	6	0	6	26	13	2	0	2	32	0	1	.410	.318
Ramirez, Juan	L-L	5-9	160	4-9-99	.301	.360	.290	46	163	30	49	6	2	0	10	20	3	1	1	14	11	7	.362	.385
Rosa, Dylan	R-R	6-2	200	6-27-96	.000	—	.000	1	2	0	0	0	0	0	1	0	0	0	1	1	0	0	.000	.000
Salas, Jose	R-R	6-0	160	4-17-97	.272	.227	.284	34	103	15	28	3	0	1	5	8	4	0	0	16	4	2	.330	.348
Serrano, Ariel	R-R	5-10	174	6-23-96	.294	.400	.250	7	17	0	5	1	0	0	2	0	0	1	0	1	2	0	.353	.294
Tejeda, Bryan	R-R	6-0	190	1-17-96	.222	.143	.239	28	81	7	18	4	0	1	11	7	3	0	0	19	1	0	.309	.308
Torres, Bryan	R-R	6-2	180	11-20-97	.033	.000	.037	17	30	1	1	0	0	0	2	2	2	0	2	13	0	0	.033	.139
Valdez, Ignacio	R-R	6-3	195	7-16-95	.255	.111	.283	20	55	10	14	3	0	4	18	10	2	0	1	21	0	1	.527	.382
Warner, Cameron	R-R	6-2	188	3-4-94	.556	.500	.571	3	9	3	5	1	0	1	3	3	0	0	0	0	0	0	1.000	.667
Zeile, Shane	R-R	6-1	195	6-14-93	.306	.167	.333	9	36	5	11	2	0	0	6	3	0	0	0	8	2	0	.361	.359

Pitching	B-T	HT	WT	DOB	W	L	ERA	G	GS	CG	SV	IP	H	R	ER	HR	BB	SO	AVG	vLH	vRH	K/9	BB/9
Aldridge, Dean	R-R	6-3	190	7-29-94	0	0	3.52	7	0	0	0	8	5	4	3	0	6	9	.179	.000	.217	10.57	7.04
Arriera, Gio	R-R	6-2	220	6-7-98	0	2	4.61	11	11	0	0	27	30	18	14	3	14	28	.278	.333	.259	9.22	4.61
Belisario, Johan	R-R	5-11	165	8-13-93	1	0	5.40	5	0	0	1	8	8	5	5	0	1	8	.276	.214	.333	8.64	1.08
Carlton, Drew	R-R	6-1	197	9-8-95	0	0	0.90	6	0	0	2	10	10	2	1	0	1	9	.263	.273	.259	8.10	0.90
Crosby, Drew	R-L	6-0	196	11-16-95	0	0	4.00	16	0	0	0	27	34	17	12	0	12	29	.298	.385	.287	9.67	4.00

DETROIT TIGERS

Pitching	B-T	HT	WT	DOB	W	L	ERA	G	GS	CG	SV	IP	H	R	ER	HR	BB	SO	AVG	vLH	vRH	K/9	BB/9
Fernandez, Aaron	R-R	6-2	190	9-25-94	2	3	4.21	15	0	0	0	26	26	17	12	1	13	24	.263	.167	.284	8.42	4.56
Figueroa, Ken	R-R	6-0	190	5-30-96	1	1	1.88	6	5	0	0	29	23	12	6	0	8	21	.219	.209	.226	6.59	2.51
German, Francisco	R-R	6-2	160	12-26-96	1	2	2.49	12	0	0	1	22	21	8	6	0	13	24	.253	.333	.226	9.97	5.40
Gonzalez, Daniel	R-R	6-3	200	8-15-95	4	1	2.57	13	7	0	0	42	38	16	12	0	20	40	.241	.190	.270	8.57	4.29
Guzman, Carlos	R-R	6-1	170	5-16-98	0	0	1.59	3	0	0	0	6	4	2	1	0	0	7	.182	.143	.200	11.12	0.00
2-team total (11 Tigers East)					1	1	0.70	14	0	0	4	26	16	4	2	0	6	25	.180	.238	.152	8.77	2.10
Howe, Tyler	R-R	6-1	235	1-19-94	3	1	1.57	10	1	0	1	23	14	5	4	0	13	28	.192	.208	.184	10.96	5.09
Javier, Xavier	R-R	6-4	170	2-9-98	1	5	8.23	11	7	0	0	35	40	41	32	3	35	18	.292	.286	.295	4.63	9.00
Lescher, Billy	R-R	6-4	215	9-17-95	1	3	2.45	17	0	0	5	22	14	11	6	1	6	26	.173	.177	.172	10.64	2.45
Moreno, Dominic	R-R	5-11	197	3-12-93	0	0	0.00	1	0	0	0	0	0	0	0	0	1	1	.000	—	.000	27.00	27.00
Nesbitt, Angel	R-R	6-1	240	12-4-90	0	0	3.00	2	2	0	0	3	2	1	1	0	0	5	.200	.500	.125	15.00	0.00
Reuss, Grant	R-L	6-5	230	5-23-96	1	2	21.73	16	0	0	0	14	15	37	33	1	41	9	.289	.222	.302	5.93	27.00
Savarese, Mark	R-R	5-11	200	10-14-94	3	0	2.89	9	0	0	0	19	18	7	6	2	5	16	.254	.318	.225	7.71	2.41
Smith, Blake	R-R	6-5	205	12-5-94	2	2	2.18	10	1	0	1	21	15	11	5	0	7	15	.200	.105	.232	6.53	3.05
Stalsberg, Mitchell	L-L	6-0	215	1-13-96	0	2	3.94	9	8	0	0	30	24	14	13	2	11	34	.220	.191	.227	10.31	3.34
Stock, Dylan	R-R	6-4	195	7-21-96	2	2	1.35	17	0	0	4	27	13	6	4	1	7	34	.144	.179	.129	11.48	2.36
Thomas, Kyle	R-R	6-3	200	3-5-95	0	0	6.00	2	0	0	1	3	4	2	2	0	0	4	.308	.333	.300	12.00	0.00
Turnbull, Spencer	R-R	6-3	215	9-18-92	0	0	4.00	2	2	0	0	9	8	5	4	0	2	16	.242	.333	.233	16.00	2.00
Villarroel, Javier	R-R	6-1	180	10-31-97	3	2	3.69	10	10	0	0	46	50	29	19	0	14	30	.270	.200	.300	5.83	2.72
Viloria, Felix	L-L	6-1	165	12-2-96	2	0	5.87	8	0	0	1	15	17	10	10	1	2	12	.274	.125	.296	7.04	1.17
Weston, Drew	L-L	6-2	170	12-13-94	2	0	4.50	5	3	0	0	24	38	16	12	1	2	12	.349	.333	.351	4.50	0.75

Fielding

C: Azuaje 20, McMillan 27, Tejeda 15, Torres 9. **1B:** Aristigueta 19, Azuaje 5, Garcia 1, Pearce 9, Quero 25, Tejeda 10. **2B:** Aristigueta 14, Bivens 13, Cooper 5, De La Cruz 12, Garcia 20, Salas 9, Warner 3. **3B:** Aristigueta 7, Garcia 10, Gonzalez 2, Karstetter 30, Pearce 3, Salas 19. **SS:** Cooper 8, De La Cruz 16, Garcia 11, King 26, Salas 6. **OF:** Alvarado 43, Aristigueta 10, Bojarski 38, De La Cruz 10, Hill 7, Quero 17, Ramirez 45, Serrano 7, Valdez 20.

DSL TIGERS — ROOKIE

DOMINICAN SUMMER LEAGUE

Batting	B-T	HT	WT	DOB	AVG	vLH	vRH	G	AB	R	H	2B	3B	HR	RBI	BB	HBP	SH	SF	SO	SB	CS	SLG	OBP
Adames, Ernesto	L-L	6-1	180	12-29-99	.246	.429	.186	16	57	7	14	5	1	0	7	4	4	0	1	19	0	1	.368	.333
Alfonzo, Eliezer	B-R	5-10	155	9-23-99	.305	.357	.293	52	151	24	46	4	1	0	14	26	3	0	1	18	5	1	.344	.414
Batista, Enrique	R-R	5-9	170	2-10-00	.230	.286	.221	36	100	9	23	3	1	0	5	9	3	0	0	31	2	3	.280	.313
Chacon, Esney	R-R	6-1	160	3-17-00	.273	.375	.250	50	172	27	47	5	1	1	20	29	1	2	1	20	10	7	.331	.379
Figueroa, Gustavo	R-R	6-0	170	9-22-98	.264	.368	.239	55	197	24	52	5	2	0	26	11	3	2	0	18	1	5	.310	.313
Hernandez, Jhoan	R-R	6-0	145	4-21-99	.172	.217	.158	41	99	9	17	2	1	0	10	17	2	1	1	33	0	3	.212	.303
Laurencio, Luis	R-R	6-2	215	10-6-98	.249	.275	.241	64	225	18	56	11	1	4	37	22	3	0	3	72	2	4	.360	.320
Marte, Kendry	B-R	6-0	160	5-10-00	.140	.177	.132	36	93	12	13	1	0	0	9	11	2	2	1	31	4	4	.151	.243
Medrano, Carlos	L-R	5-11	170	11-11-99	.180	.250	.171	34	100	11	18	2	1	1	9	9	2	0	0	35	1	3	.250	.261
Mojica, Jimmy	R-R	6-0	175	5-4-00	.223	.170	.238	66	242	26	54	8	1	0	16	12	11	0	0	44	3	6	.265	.291
Moreno, Jhenrry	L-R	5-11	160	3-28-00	.233	.200	.241	30	73	14	17	4	1	1	4	19	4	0	1	24	7	3	.356	.412
Ortega, Marfrey	R-R	5-11	175	10-15-98	.246	.308	.228	41	118	13	29	5	4	2	19	25	6	0	0	29	6	5	.407	.403
Perez, Wenceel	B-R	5-11	170	10-30-99	.314	.182	.346	61	226	31	71	8	1	0	22	27	1	2	2	21	16	6	.358	.387
Perez, Yerjeni	R-R	6-1	165	2-6-00	.239	.250	.236	51	163	18	39	3	1	0	13	13	4	4	2	40	4	2	.270	.308
Sandoval, Jhon	R-R	6-2	172	11-14-99	.206	.240	.198	42	141	17	29	6	4	3	16	8	1	2	0	69	1	1	.369	.253
Veliz, Frank	R-R	5-11	160	9-10-99	.220	.214	.221	24	82	10	18	0	2	0	3	9	4	0	0	19	1	0	.268	.326

Pitching	B-T	HT	WT	DOB	W	L	ERA	G	GS	CG	SV	IP	H	R	ER	HR	BB	SO	AVG	vLH	vRH	K/9	BB/9
Appleton, Jose	R-R	6-3	170	7-2-97	0	1	12.27	4	4	0	0	4	4	5	5	1	3	4	.286	.750	.100	9.82	7.36
Burgos, Ronald	R-R	6-3	190	12-22-99	2	4	4.91	15	4	0	0	40	44	29	22	2	18	31	.279	.250	.294	6.92	4.02
Chavez, Alejandro	R-R	6-2	170	7-14-99	2	1	3.96	17	1	0	1	39	41	22	17	1	19	35	.275	.250	.286	8.15	4.42
Cortes, Maximo	R-R	6-1	170	11-18-99	2	1	4.84	19	0	0	3	22	28	14	12	1	9	19	.315	.103	.417	7.66	3.63
Dacosta, Francarlos	R-R	6-1	175	2-27-00	0	1	3.09	5	2	0	1	12	11	6	4	0	4	17	.229	.292	.167	13.11	3.09
De Jesus, Angel	R-R	6-4	185	2-13-97	4	4	2.20	14	8	1	0	61	44	19	15	2	18	45	.202	.171	.218	6.60	2.64
De Los Reyes, Raul	R-R	6-4	220	8-24-97	0	1	3.74	15	5	0	0	46	52	27	19	2	15	41	.281	.358	.221	8.08	2.96
Fajardo, Rodolfo	L-L	6-3	165	2-17-00	2	0	3.64	18	3	0	2	42	40	22	17	1	8	39	.247	.242	.248	8.36	1.71
Jimenez, Marco	R-R	6-0	165	12-6-99	1	2	8.64	3	0	0	0	8	7	8	8	0	4	9	.233	.267	.200	9.72	4.32
Montero, Keider	R-R	6-1	145	7-6-00	1	5	4.02	14	12	0	0	47	46	34	21	0	27	41	.251	.267	.244	7.85	5.17
Munoz, Dionis	R-R	5-11	155	6-5-97	4	2	3.38	19	0	0	2	24	25	15	9	2	11	22	.269	.357	.231	8.25	4.13
Ozuna, Angel	R-R	5-10	170	9-25-98	0	1	2.88	17	0	0	0	25	20	12	8	0	11	27	.217	.308	.182	9.72	3.96
Perez, Cleiverth	L-L	5-11	167	2-5-00	1	5	3.81	14	14	0	0	52	49	30	22	1	18	36	.250	.194	.263	6.23	3.12
Perez, Luis	L-L	6-1	165	10-10-99	1	1	4.66	6	0	0	0	10	9	5	5	0	6	7	.250	.400	.226	6.52	5.59
Salazar, Joseph	R-R	6-1	175	9-24-99	1	2	2.35	13	5	0	0	46	41	22	12	0	17	31	.232	.286	.207	6.07	3.33
Santana, Andy	R-R	6-3	190	10-27-99	1	6	5.23	14	10	0	0	41	52	31	24	2	22	38	.289	.241	.310	8.27	4.79
Silva, Ricardo	L-L	6-1	165	4-14-00	4	2	2.41	16	0	0	2	41	37	16	11	0	4	35	.227	.097	.258	7.68	0.88
Valderrey, Rafael	R-R	6-2	155	5-31-99	0	0	2.70	8	0	0	0	10	4	4	3	0	11	7	.118	.091	.130	6.30	9.90
Vazquez, Juan	L-L	6-2	165	7-2-99	0	5	5.40	15	2	0	1	30	38	26	18	0	12	29	.317	.320	.316	8.70	3.60

Fielding

C: Alfonzo 28, Figueroa 31, Medrano 20. **1B:** Adames 7, Alfonzo 18, Figueroa 10, Hernandez 2, Laurencio 37, Marte 1, Ortega 1. **2B:** Batista 26, Hernandez 15, Marte 12, Medrano 3, Perez 11, Veliz 16. **3B:** Alfonzo 3, Hernandez 18, Laurencio 1, Marte 16, Perez 39. **SS:** Batista 3, Hernandez 2, Perez 10, Perez 50, Veliz 9. **OF:** Adames 3, Chacon 49, Hernandez 5, Laurencio 4, Marte 4, Mojica 65, Moreno 27, Ortega 32, Sandoval 36.

Houston Astros

SEASON IN A SENTENCE: The pain had a payoff as the Astros' trip from laughingstocks to baseball power paid off in the team's first World Series title.

HIGH POINT: Houston won back-to-back Game Sevens thanks to heroic performances by Charlie Morton and Lance McCullers in Game Seven of the ALCS and Charlie Morton again in Game Seven of the World Series. George Springer won the World Series MVP award. He hit home runs in each of the final four World Series games.

LOW POINT: A 3-10 start to August kept Houston from finishing with the best record in the American League as the streaking Indians caught and passed them. In a dream season, that qualifies as a disappointing stretch.

NOTABLE ROOKIES: First baseman Yuli Gurriel hit .299/.322/.486 with 43 doubles and 18 home runs. Righthander Joe Musgrove struggled as a starter, but he became a useful member of the Astros' bullpen, going 3-0, 1.44 in 31.1 innings as a reliever. Righthander Francis Martes struggled as he bounced between the Astros' rotation and bullpen.

KEY TRANSACTIONS: The Astros had an astute offseason, as they added Brian McCann and Josh Reddick to bulk up the lineup. fter that, Houston didn't need to do much for quite a while. At the July 31 trade deadline, the Astros largely stood pat, as the only move they made was acquiring lefthander Francisco Liriano from the Blue Jays to bolster the bullpen. The team immediately went into a slump, and Houston responded by acquiring Tigers righthander Justin Verlander in the final seconds before the Aug. 31 waiver deadline in what proved to be one of the most significant trades of the year. The trade cost a trio of solid prospects in righthander Franklin Perez, catcher Jake Rogers and outfielder Daz Cameron, but Verlander made the trade pay off immediately. Verlander was 5-0, 1.06 in the regular season and went 4-1, 2.21 in the postseason during the team's run to the World Series.

DOWN ON THE FARM: Even with recent graduations and trades, the Astros' farm system remains deep. Righthander Forrest Whitley emerged as one of the best pitching prospects in the minors. Outfielder Kyle Tucker hit .274/.346/.528 with 25 home runs between high Class A and Double-A. Outfielder and first baseman Yordan Alvarez hit .304/.379/.481 in his stateside debut and earned a spot in the Futures Game.

OPENING DAY PAYROLL: $112,437,541 (19th)

PLAYERS OF THE YEAR

Jose Altuve
2B
.346/.410/.547
Won his third batting title in four years.

MINOR LEAGUE

Forrest Whitley
RHP
(Low Class A/High Class A/Double-A)
5-4, 2.83

ORGANIZATION LEADERS

BATTING — *Minimum 250 AB

MAJORS

*	AVG	Jose Altuve	.346
*	OPS	Jose Altuve	.957
	HR	George Springer	34
	RBI	Marwin Gonzalez	90

MINORS

*	AVG	Tony Kemp, Fresno	.329
*	OBP	Carmen Benedetti, Quad Cities, Buies Creek	.421
*	SLG	Derek Fisher, Fresno	.583
*	OPS	Derek Fisher, Fresno	.967
	R	Tony Kemp, Fresno	95
	H	Tony Kemp, Fresno	166
	TB	A.J. Reed, Fresno	250
	2B	Jason Martin, Buies Creek, Corpus Christi	35
	3B	Tony Kemp, Fresno	9
	HR	A.J. Reed, Fresno	34
	RBI	A.J. Reed, Fresno	104
	BB	Jon Singleton, Corpus Christi	107
	SO	A.J. Reed, Fresno	146
	SB	Myles Straw, Buies Creek, Corpus Christi	38

PITCHING — #Minimum 75 IP

MAJORS

	W	Dallas Keuchel	14
		Charlie Morton	14
#	ERA	Chris Decenski	2.68
	SO	Charlie Morton	163
	SV	Ken Giles	34

MINORS

	W	Carson LaRue, Quad Cities, Buies Creek	12
	L	David Martinez, Fresno	12
#	ERA	Rogelio Armenteros, Corpus Christi, Fresno	2.04
	G	Kevin Comer, Corpus Christi, Fresno	45
	GS	David Martinez, Fresno	23
	GS	Trent Thornton, Corpus Christi, Fresno	23
	SV	Nick Hernandez, Buies Creek, Corpus Christi	10
	SV	Jordan Jankowski, Fresno, Oklahoma City	10
	IP	David Martinez, Fresno	136
	BB	Hector Perez, Quad Cities, Buies Creek	78
	SO	Rogelio Armenteros, Corpus Christi, Fresno	146
#	AVG	Jorge Alcala, Quad Cities, Buies Creek	.188

2017 PERFORMANCE

General Manager: Jeff Luhnow. **Farm Director:** Pete Putila. **Scouting Director:** Mike Elias.

Class	Team	League	W	L	PCT	Finish	Manager
Majors	Houston Astros	American	101	61	.623	2nd (15)	A.J. Hinch
Triple-A	Fresno Grizzlies	Pacific Coast	77	65	.542	4th (16)	Tony DeFrancesco
Double-A	Corpus Christi Hooks	Texas	67	71	.486	t-4th (8)	Rodney Linares
High-A	Buies Creek Astros	Carolina	74	65	.532	2nd (10)	Omar Lopez
Low-A	Quad Cities River Bandits	Midwest	79	59	.572	2nd (16)	Russ Steinhorn
Short Season	Tri-City ValleyCats	New York-Penn	34	39	.466	10th (14)	Morgan Ensberg
Rookie	Greeneville Astros	Appalachian	33	34	.493	t-5th (10)	Danny Ortega
Rookie	GCL Astros	Gulf Coast	27	27	.5	10th (17)	Wladimir Sutil
Overall 2017 Minor League Record			391	360	0.521	7th (30)	

ORGANIZATION STATISTICS

HOUSTON ASTROS

AMERICAN LEAGUE

Batting	B-T	HT	WT	DOB	AVG	vLH	vRH	G	AB	R	H	2B	3B	HR	RBI	BB	HBP	SH	SF	SO	SB	CS	SLG	OBP
Altuve, Jose	R-R	5-6	165	5-6-90	.346	.353	.344	153	590	112	204	39	4	24	81	58	9	1	4	84	32	6	.548	.410
Aoki, Norichika	R-L	5-9	180	1-5-82	.272	.282	.270	70	202	28	55	12	1	2	19	15	2	1	4	29	5	2	.371	.323
2-team total (12 Toronto)					.274	.282	.270	82	234	32	64	13	1	5	27	16	2	1	5	34	5	2	.402	.319
Beltran, Carlos	R-B	6-1	215	4-24-77	.231	.185	.247	129	467	60	108	29	0	14	51	33	3	0	6	102	0	0	.383	.283
Bregman, Alex	R-R	6-0	180	3-30-94	.284	.331	.268	155	556	88	158	39	5	19	71	55	7	1	7	97	17	5	.475	.352
Centeno, Juan	L-R	5-9	195	11-16-89	.231	.333	.200	22	52	5	12	0	0	2	4	4	0	1	0	12	0	0	.346	.286
Correa, Carlos	R-R	6-4	215	9-22-94	.315	.391	.294	109	422	82	133	25	1	24	84	53	2	0	4	92	2	1	.550	.391
Davis, J.D.	R-R	6-3	225	4-27-93	.226	.217	.231	24	62	8	14	4	0	4	7	4	1	0	1	20	1	1	.484	.279
Fisher, Derek	L-R	6-3	205	8-21-93	.212	.241	.205	53	146	21	31	4	1	5	17	17	3	0	0	54	3	3	.356	.307
Gattis, Evan	R-R	6-4	270	8-18-86	.263	.241	.272	84	300	41	79	22	0	12	55	18	4	0	3	50	0	1	.457	.311
Gonzalez, Marwin	B-R	6-1	205	3-14-89	.303	.250	.322	134	455	67	138	34	0	23	90	49	6	3	2	99	8	3	.530	.377
Gurriel, Yuli	R-R	6-0	190	6-9-84	.299	.252	.317	139	529	69	158	43	1	18	75	22	7	0	6	62	3	2	.486	.332
Hernandez, Teoscar	R-R	6-2	180	10-15-92	—	—	—	1	0	0	0	0	0	0	0	0	0	0	0	0	0	0	—	—
2-team total (26 Toronto)					.261	—	—	27	88	16	23	6	0	8	20	6	0	0	1	36	0	1	.602	.305
Kemp, Tony	L-R	5-6	165	10-31-91	.216	.222	.214	17	37	6	8	1	0	0	4	1	1	0	0	5	1	0	.243	.256
Marisnick, Jake	R-R	6-4	220	3-30-91	.244	.266	.228	106	230	50	56	10	0	16	35	20	6	2	1	90	9	4	.496	.319
Maybin, Cameron	R-R	6-3	215	4-4-87	.186	.143	.200	21	59	6	11	1	1	4	13	3	0	1	0	16	4	3	.441	.226
2-team total (93 Los Angeles)					.228	.275	.218	114	395	63	90	20	2	10	35	51	2	1	1	94	33	8	.365	.319
McCann, Brian	L-R	6-3	225	2-20-84	.241	.227	.246	97	349	47	84	12	1	18	62	38	7	0	5	58	1	0	.436	.323
Moran, Colin	L-R	6-4	204	10-1-92	.364	.400	.333	7	11	3	4	0	1	1	3	1	0	0	0	1	0	0	.818	.417
Reddick, Josh	L-R	6-2	195	2-19-87	.315	.315	.314	134	477	77	150	34	4	13	82	43	0	1	12	72	7	3	.484	.363
Reed, A.J.	L-L	6-4	275	5-10-93	.000	.000	.000	2	6	0	0	0	0	0	0	0	0	0	0	1	0	0	.000	.000
Springer, George	R-R	6-3	215	9-19-89	.283	.301	.277	140	548	112	155	29	0	34	85	64	11	0	4	111	5	7	.522	.367
Stassi, Max	R-R	5-10	200	3-15-91	.167	.167	.167	14	24	5	4	1	0	2	4	6	0	0	1	4	0	0	.458	.323
White, Tyler	R-R	5-11	225	10-29-90	.279	.250	.283	22	61	7	17	6	0	3	10	4	1	0	1	16	0	1	.525	.328

Pitching	B-T	HT	WT	DOB	W	L	ERA	G	GS	CG	SV	IP	H	R	ER	HR	BB	SO	AVG	vLH	vRH	K/9	BB/9
Clippard, Tyler	R-R	6-3	200	2-14-85	0	2	6.43	16	0	0	2	14	11	10	10	3	7	18	.208	.269	.148	11.57	4.50
3-team total (11 Chicago, 40 New York)					2	8	4.77	67	0	0	5	60	47	33	32	10	31	72	.209	.269	.148	10.74	4.62
Devenski, Chris	R-R	6-3	210	11-13-90	8	5	2.68	62	0	0	4	81	50	26	24	11	26	100	.174	.111	.238	11.16	2.90
Diaz, Dayan	R-R	5-10	195	2-10-89	1	1	9.00	10	1	0	0	13	17	14	13	3	4	20	.315	.278	.333	13.85	2.77
Feliz, Michael	R-R	6-4	230	6-28-93	4	2	5.63	46	0	0	0	48	53	31	30	8	22	70	.276	.280	.274	13.13	4.13
Fiers, Mike	R-R	6-2	200	6-15-85	8	10	5.22	29	28	0	0	153	157	95	89	32	62	146	.266	.256	.275	8.57	3.64
Giles, Ken	R-R	6-2	205	9-20-90	1	3	2.30	63	0	0	34	63	44	16	16	4	21	83	.198	.196	.200	11.92	3.02
Gregerson, Luke	R-L	6-3	205	5-14-84	2	3	4.57	65	0	0	1	61	62	31	31	13	20	70	.257	.240	.269	10.33	2.95
Guduan, Reymin	L-L	6-4	205	3-16-92	0	0	7.88	22	0	0	0	16	24	14	14	1	12	16	.338	.270	.412	9.00	6.75
Gustave, Jandel	R-R	6-2	210	10-12-92	0	0	5.40	6	0	0	0	5	5	4	3	0	7	2	.278	.250	.300	3.60	12.60
Harris, Will	R-R	6-4	250	8-28-84	3	2	2.98	46	0	0	2	45	37	15	15	7	7	52	.218	.233	.206	10.32	1.39
Hoyt, James	R-R	6-6	230	9-30-86	1	0	4.38	43	0	0	0	49	51	24	24	7	14	66	.262	.284	.240	12.04	2.55
Jankowski, Jordan	R-R	6-1	225	5-17-89	1	0	12.46	3	0	0	0	4	7	6	6	3	2	5	.350	.385	.286	10.38	4.15
Keuchel, Dallas	L-L	6-3	205	1-1-88	14	5	2.90	23	23	1	0	146	116	50	47	15	47	125	.218	.146	.236	7.72	2.90
Liriano, Francisco	L-L	6-2	225	10-26-83	0	2	4.40	20	0	0	0	14	14	9	7	0	10	11	.269	.281	.250	6.91	6.28
2-team total (18 Toronto)					6	7	5.66	38	18	0	0	97	105	66	61	11	53	85	.279	.281	.250	7.89	4.92
Martes, Francis	R-R	6-1	225	11-24-95	5	2	5.80	32	4	0	0	54	51	40	35	7	31	69	.245	.253	.239	11.43	5.13
McCullers Jr., Lance	L-R	6-1	205	10-2-93	7	4	4.25	22	22	0	0	119	114	61	56	8	40	132	.250	.231	.264	10.01	3.03
McHugh, Collin	R-R	6-2	190	6-19-87	5	2	3.55	12	12	0	0	63	62	27	25	7	20	62	.253	.295	.218	8.81	2.84
Morton, Charlie	R-R	6-5	235	11-12-83	14	7	3.62	25	25	0	0	147	125	65	59	14	50	163	.228	.175	.273	10.00	3.07
Musgrove, Joe	R-R	6-5	265	12-4-92	7	8	4.77	38	15	0	2	109	117	59	58	18	28	98	.277	.268	.285	8.07	2.30
Paulino, David	R-R	6-7	215	2-6-94	2	0	6.52	6	6	0	0	29	36	21	21	8	7	34	.300	.317	.283	10.55	2.17
Peacock, Brad	R-R	6-1	210	2-2-88	13	2	3.00	34	21	0	0	132	100	46	44	10	57	161	.206	.249	.173	10.98	3.89
Sipp, Tony	L-L	6-0	190	7-12-83	0	1	5.79	46	0	0	0	37	36	25	24	8	16	39	.247	.247	.247	9.40	3.86
Tolliver, Ashur	L-L	6-0	170	1-24-88	0	0	3.60	3	0	0	0	5	4	2	2	0	4	5	.235	.125	.333	9.00	7.20
Verlander, Justin	R-R	6-5	225	2-20-83	5	0	1.06	5	5	0	0	34	17	4	4	4	5	43	.149	.225	.092	11.38	1.32
2-team total (28 Detroit)					15	8	3.36	33	33	0	0	206	170	80	77	27	72	219	.221	.220	.246	9.57	3.15

Fielding

Catcher	PCT	G	PO	A	E	DP	PB
Centeno	.988	22	151	8	2	1	6
Gattis	.982	49	473	14	9	2	4
McCann	.995	95	905	48	5	4	6
Stassi	.986	11	70	1	1	0	0

First Base	PCT	G	PO	A	E	DP
Davis	.000	2	0	0	0	0
Gattis	1.000	1	2	0	0	0
Gonzalez	.988	31	151	14	2	16
Gurriel	.993	131	991	90	8	116
Moran	.900	4	9	0	1	2
Reddick	1.000	1	2	0	0	0
Reed	1.000	1	3	1	0	0
Stassi	1.000	1	3	0	0	0
White	.974	19	110	4	3	11

Second Base	PCT	G	PO	A	E	DP
Altuve	.982	149	201	351	10	86
Bregman	1.000	4	0	5	0	2
Gonzalez	.986	22	24	45	1	17
Gurriel	1.000	1	1	2	0	1
White	1.000	4	1	2	0	0

Third Base	PCT	G	PO	A	E	DP
Bregman	.970	132	86	241	10	28
Davis	1.000	22	11	38	0	4
Gonzalez	.932	19	12	29	3	2
Gurriel	.941	7	6	10	1	1
Moran	.000	3	0	0	0	0

Shortstop	PCT	G	PO	A	E	DP
Bregman	.957	30	31	58	4	14
Correa	.978	108	127	282	9	62
Gonzalez	.984	38	39	88	2	23
Moran	1.000	1	0	2	0	0

Outfield	PCT	G	PO	A	E	DP
Aoki	1.000	67	77	6	0	1
Beltran	1.000	14	11	0	0	0
Fisher	.987	48	76	2	1	0
Gonzalez	1.000	48	48	2	0	0
Hernandez	1.000	1	1	0	0	0
Kemp	1.000	14	14	0	0	0
Marisnick	.985	102	131	3	2	0
Maybin	1.000	20	24	1	0	0
Reddick	.976	129	195	6	5	0
Springer	.996	131	243	5	1	2
White	1.000	2	2	0	0	0

FRESNO GRIZZLIES — *TRIPLE-A*

PACIFIC COAST LEAGUE

Batting	B-T	HT	WT	DOB	AVG	vLH	vRH	G	AB	R	H	2B	3B	HR	RBI	BB	HBP	SH	SF	SO	SB	CS	SLG	OBP
Aplin, Andrew	L-L	6-0	205	3-21-91	.250	.269	.241	30	84	14	21	3	1	1	13	16	2	1	2	21	1	1	.345	.375
2-team total (47 Tacoma)					.246	.269	.241	77	232	35	57	11	3	6	38	42	3	1	2	53	5	3	.397	.366
Brignac, Reid	L-R	6-3	210	1-16-86	.251	.198	.267	110	387	53	97	17	3	13	52	41	4	1	4	116	4	1	.411	.326
Centeno, Juan	L-R	5-9	195	11-16-89	.311	.404	.284	65	235	25	73	12	1	1	33	16	1	3	2	37	0	1	.383	.354
Correa, Carlos	R-R	6-4	215	9-22-94	.286	—	.286	4	14	1	4	0	0	0	4	1	0	0	1	4	0	0	.286	.313
Davis, J.D.	R-R	6-3	225	4-27-93	.295	.313	.289	16	61	10	18	5	0	5	18	9	0	0	3	18	0	0	.623	.370
De Goti, Alex	R-R	5-10	165	8-19-94	.182	.000	.200	5	11	0	2	1	0	0	0	1	0	0	0	6	0	0	.273	.250
de Oleo, Eduardo	R-R	5-10	180	1-25-93	.304	.250	.333	6	23	0	7	2	0	0	0	0	0	0	0	5	0	0	.391	.304
Ferguson, Drew	R-R	5-11	180	8-3-92	.223	.143	.244	29	103	11	23	7	0	1	9	12	0	0	0	21	3	1	.320	.304
Fisher, Derek	L-R	6-3	205	8-21-93	.318	.274	.332	84	343	63	109	26	1	21	66	35	3	1	2	74	16	10	.583	.384
Garcia, Alejandro	R-R	5-10	182	6-21-91	.269	.245	.279	50	160	27	43	11	0	1	19	5	5	3	0	16	4	3	.356	.312
Hernandez, Teoscar	R-R	6-2	180	10-15-92	.279	.163	.321	79	301	54	84	20	3	12	44	39	5	0	2	72	12	7	.485	.369
Johnson, Spencer	R-R	6-4	225	11-1-93	.125	.000	.167	4	8	0	1	0	0	0	0	1	0	0	0	4	0	0	.125	.222
Kemmer, Jon	L-L	6-2	230	11-17-90	.299	.287	.304	87	304	68	91	17	3	16	57	44	8	0	2	95	6	2	.533	.399
Kemp, Tony	L-R	5-6	165	10-31-91	.329	.397	.306	118	504	95	166	23	9	10	62	35	3	8	2	43	24	7	.470	.375
Mayfield, Jack	R-R	5-11	190	9-30-90	.273	.229	.293	42	154	28	42	12	0	6	23	10	1	0	0	30	3	0	.468	.321
Moran, Colin	L-R	6-4	204	10-1-92	.308	.287	.316	79	302	53	93	15	1	18	63	31	2	0	3	55	0	3	.543	.373
Noel, Rico	R-R	5-8	170	1-11-89	.250	.250	.250	18	68	11	17	4	1	0	2	2	2	1	0	15	2	2	.338	.292
Reed, A.J.	L-L	6-4	275	5-10-93	.261	.189	.287	127	476	89	124	24	0	34	104	72	3	0	5	146	0	0	.525	.358
Rojas, Josh	L-R	6-1	185	6-30-94	.333	.250	.375	4	12	2	4	0	0	0	0	4	0	0	0	3	0	0	.333	.500
Stassi, Max	R-R	5-10	200	3-15-91	.266	.338	.230	73	241	54	64	14	0	12	33	38	8	0	0	67	1	1	.473	.383
Stubbs, Garrett	L-R	5-10	175	5-26-93	.221	.385	.188	23	77	11	17	5	0	0	12	11	3	0	0	15	3	0	.286	.341
Tucker, Preston	L-L	6-0	215	7-6-90	.250	.274	.241	128	492	84	123	20	7	24	96	65	1	0	10	102	2	3	.465	.333
Walsh, Colin	B-R	6-1	200	9-26-89	.266	.235	.277	22	64	15	17	5	1	0	3	19	0	2	0	17	0	1	.375	.434
White, Tyler	R-R	5-11	225	10-29-90	.301	.302	.300	111	436	84	131	22	1	25	89	47	6	1	7	101	7	3	.528	.371
Woodward, Trent	B-R	6-2	215	2-4-92	.214	.333	.182	3	14	1	3	1	1	0	3	0	0	0	0	7	0	0	.429	.214

Pitching	B-T	HT	WT	DOB	W	L	ERA	G	GS	CG	SV	IP	H	R	ER	HR	BB	SO	AVG	vLH	vRH	K/9	BB/9
Armenteros, Rogelio	R-R	6-1	215	6-30-94	8	1	2.16	10	10	0	0	58	42	15	14	5	19	72	.203	.240	.171	11.11	2.93
Coleman, Casey	R-L	6-0	185	7-3-87	3	5	6.75	12	12	0	0	64	76	50	48	8	32	56	.297	.322	.275	7.88	4.50
Comer, Kevin	R-R	6-3	205	8-1-92	5	4	3.68	43	0	0	5	64	70	32	26	5	28	74	.278	.320	.250	10.46	3.96
Deetz, Dean	R-R	6-1	195	11-29-93	3	4	6.40	17	10	0	0	45	46	34	32	5	41	55	.267	.324	.231	11.00	8.20
Diaz, Dayan	R-R	5-10	195	2-10-89	4	3	4.13	35	0	0	2	48	47	22	22	3	18	52	.257	.317	.212	9.75	3.38
Diaz, Jumbo	R-R	6-4	315	2-27-84	1	0	2.92	12	0	0	3	12	11	4	4	1	5	11	.234	.053	.357	8.03	3.65
Dorris, Jacob	R-R	6-2	165	3-24-93	3	0	1.87	20	0	0	0	34	22	9	7	3	13	28	.185	.283	.106	7.49	3.48
Emanuel, Kent	L-L	6-3	225	6-4-92	1	2	7.71	9	8	0	1	42	71	39	36	7	20	28	.382	.375	.385	6.00	4.29
Frias, Edison	R-R	6-1	180	12-18-90	1	3	6.91	6	6	0	0	27	38	27	21	4	18	19	.328	.313	.338	6.26	5.93
Garza, Ralph	R-R	6-2	195	4-6-94	0	0	9.00	1	0	0	0	2	1	2	2	0	2	2	.143	.000	.167	9.00	9.00
Guduan, Reymin	L-L	6-4	205	3-16-92	5	7	5.87	39	0	0	1	46	61	33	30	4	14	47	.316	.301	.325	9.20	2.74
Harris, Will	R-R	6-4	250	8-28-84	0	0	18.00	1	0	0	0	1	2	2	2	0	1	1	.400	.333	.500	9.00	9.00
Hauschild, Mike	R-R	6-3	210	1-22-90	6	2	4.58	18	18	0	0	90	85	46	46	8	53	79	.252	.265	.242	7.87	5.28
Holmes, Brian	L-L	6-4	217	1-30-91	2	2	9.11	19	5	0	1	53	73	57	54	11	29	46	.319	.273	.337	7.76	4.89
Hoyt, James	R-R	6-6	230	9-30-86	2	0	1.93	13	0	0	4	14	10	3	3	1	6	18	.196	.150	.226	11.57	3.86
Jankowski, Jordan	R-R	6-1	225	5-17-89	2	3	5.13	37	0	0	10	40	39	24	23	4	23	53	.250	.344	.190	11.83	5.13
2-team total (4 Oklahoma City)					2	3	5.61	41	0	0	11	43	41	28	27	4	28	55	.246	.344	.189	11.42	5.82
Martes, Francis	R-R	6-1	225	11-24-95	0	2	5.29	8	8	0	0	32	40	24	19	5	28	38	.299	.355	.250	10.58	7.79
Martinez, David	R-R	6-2	220	8-4-87	7	12	4.69	25	23	0	0	136	143	77	71	19	47	101	.270	.309	.236	6.67	3.10
McCullers Jr., Lance	L-R	6-1	205	10-2-93	0	1	9.00	1	1	0	0	3	3	3	3	0	5	1	.300	.167	.500	3.00	15.00
McCurry, Brendan	R-R	5-10	170	1-7-92	4	2	4.43	35	0	0	6	45	51	29	22	6	12	52	.285	.247	.316	10.48	2.42
McHugh, Collin	R-R	6-2	190	6-19-87	0	0	27.00	1	1	0	0	1	3	3	3	0	1	1	.500	.750	.000	9.00	9.00
Mortensen, Jared	R-L	5-11	205	6-1-88	0	0	13.50	3	0	0	0	5	10	10	7	0	6	4	.417	.400	.429	7.71	11.57
Morton, Charlie	R-R	6-5	235	11-12-83	0	1	1.50	2	2	0	0	6	4	1	1	1	2	3	.200	.300	.100	4.50	3.00
Musgrove, Joe	R-R	6-5	265	12-4-92	1	0	0.00	1	1	0	0	7	1	0	0	0	2	7	.050	.000	.125	9.00	2.57

Pitching	B-T	HT	WT	DOB	W	L	ERA	G	GS	CG	SV	IP	H	R	ER	HR	BB	SO	AVG	vLH	vRH	K/9	BB/9
Paulino, David	R-R	6-7	215	2-6-94	0	1	4.50	3	3	0	0	14	11	8	7	3	9	13	.208	.269	.148	8.36	5.79
Perez, Tyson	R-R	6-3	215	12-27-89	3	0	5.48	31	0	0	3	44	57	28	27	6	11	27	.318	.243	.371	5.48	2.23
Rodgers, Brady	R-R	6-2	210	9-17-90	2	0	1.10	3	3	0	0	16	14	2	2	0	1	11	.241	.222	.250	6.06	0.55
Sipp, Tony	L-L	6-0	190	7-12-83	0	0	4.50	2	0	0	0	2	2	1	1	0	0	0	.222	.000	.500	0.00	0.00
Smith, Kyle	R-R	6-0	170	9-10-92	2	0	8.87	7	4	0	1	22	40	23	22	3	3	14	.404	.468	.346	5.64	1.21
Sneed, Cy	R-R	6-4	185	10-1-92	1	1	11.21	4	4	0	0	18	25	22	22	4	7	14	.329	.303	.349	7.13	3.57
Stutzman, Sean	L-L	5-9	175	7-8-93	0	0	3.12	4	0	0	0	9	10	3	3	0	5	3	.303	.250	.320	3.12	5.19
Thome, Andrew	R-R	6-3	215	1-13-93	0	0	7.50	8	0	0	0	12	17	11	10	0	7	7	.370	.435	.304	5.25	5.25
Thompson, Ryan	R-R	6-6	221	6-26-92	0	1	15.26	6	0	0	0	8	18	13	13	2	2	6	.462	.539	.423	7.04	2.35
Thornton, Trent	R-R	6-0	175	9-30-93	8	4	5.09	21	20	0	0	115	137	71	65	12	23	88	.295	.349	.240	6.89	1.80
Tolliver, Ashur	L-L	6-0	170	1-24-88	2	0	7.13	31	0	0	0	35	39	28	28	2	33	28	.289	.259	.312	7.13	8.41
West, Aaron	R-R	6-1	195	6-1-90	0	1	4.53	33	0	0	0	44	72	25	22	1	8	36	.377	.444	.327	7.42	1.65
Yuhl, Keegan	R-R	6-0	220	1-23-92	1	3	15.56	7	3	0	0	20	38	36	34	4	15	13	.409	.441	.390	5.95	6.86

Fielding

Catcher	PCT	G	PO	A	E	DP	PB
Centeno	.987	54	395	46	6	5	12
de Oleo	1.000	6	35	5	0	1	1
Stassi	.995	65	521	31	3	5	5
Stubbs	.989	19	176	8	2	0	2

First Base	PCT	G	PO	A	E	DP
Davis	1.000	4	23	1	0	3
Johnson	1.000	2	18	2	0	0
Moran	.983	15	113	6	2	12
Reed	.989	109	864	68	10	98
White	1.000	15	83	10	0	14

Second Base	PCT	G	PO	A	E	DP
Brignac	1.000	1	0	1	0	0
De Goti	1.000	2	2	2	0	0
Kemp	.977	97	189	238	10	74
Mayfield	.962	14	23	28	2	3
Rojas	1.000	4	7	12	0	4
Walsh	1.000	11	17	30	0	7
White	.968	21	29	62	3	16

Third Base	PCT	G	PO	A	E	DP
Centeno	1.000	1	0	1	0	0
Davis	.956	13	8	35	2	3
Mayfield	.951	17	8	31	2	4
Moran	.940	57	24	102	8	19
Walsh	1.000	4	5	11	0	3
White	.945	50	32	105	8	13
Woodward	.900	2	2	7	1	1

Shortstop	PCT	G	PO	A	E	DP
Brignac	.973	107	136	267	11	55
Correa	1.000	3	6	5	0	3
De Goti	1.000	2	3	3	0	1
Mayfield	.974	12	12	25	1	6
Moran	.000	1	0	0	0	0
Walsh	.929	4	3	10	1	2
White	.973	20	19	53	2	10

Outfield	PCT	G	PO	A	E	DP
Aplin	1.000	29	64	2	0	1
Ferguson	.982	29	52	3	1	0
Fisher	.994	74	177	2	1	0
Garcia	.980	49	94	3	2	0
Hernandez	.976	67	158	6	4	0
Kemmer	.975	66	113	4	3	0
Kemp	1.000	20	30	2	0	1
Moran	1.000	4	5	0	0	0
Noel	1.000	18	42	1	0	0
Tucker	.981	87	152	2	3	1
White	1.000	1	1	0	0	0

CORPUS CHRISTI HOOKS

DOUBLE-A

TEXAS LEAGUE

Batting	B-T	HT	WT	DOB	AVG	vLH	vRH	G	AB	R	H	2B	3B	HR	RBI	BB	HBP	SH	SF	SO	SB	CS	SLG	OBP
Bernal, Ihan	L-R	6-1	195	10-20-96	.000	.000	—	1	1	0	0	0	0	0	0	0	0	0	0	1	0	0	.000	.000
Birk, Ryne	L-R	5-10	185	11-11-94	.246	.316	.234	37	126	13	31	2	0	7	24	7	0	1	0	22	1	2	.429	.286
Boyd, Bobby	R-L	5-9	175	1-4-93	.186	.071	.208	26	86	8	16	3	1	2	7	7	1	2	1	24	3	0	.314	.253
Canelon, Carlos	B-R	5-11	170	12-14-94	.208	—	.208	8	24	4	5	0	0	1	1	3	0	0	0	8	0	0	.333	.296
Correa, Carlos	R-R	6-4	215	9-22-94	.300	.500	.250	2	10	2	3	1	0	0	1	0	0	0	0	1	0	0	.400	.300
Davis, J.D.	R-R	6-3	225	4-27-93	.279	.384	.245	87	351	49	98	18	0	21	60	31	3	0	3	90	5	2	.510	.340
De La Cruz, Bryan	R-R	6-2	175	12-16-96	.179	.286	.143	10	28	4	5	2	0	1	5	2	1	0	1	7	0	0	.357	.250
Ferguson, Drew	R-R	5-11	180	8-3-92	.292	.288	.293	84	312	55	91	18	0	8	32	45	5	1	0	77	15	5	.426	.390
Garcia, Alejandro	R-R	5-10	182	6-21-91	.203	.182	.208	42	163	13	33	7	2	3	16	4	5	2	0	29	2	4	.325	.244
Gattis, Evan	R-R	6-4	270	8-18-86	.000	—	.000	2	5	1	0	0	0	0	0	2	0	0	0	2	0	0	.000	.286
Hyde, Mott	R-R	5-10	190	3-10-92	.207	.200	.209	26	82	12	17	1	0	2	6	12	3	1	0	32	5	2	.293	.330
Johnson, Spencer	R-R	6-4	225	11-1-93	.158	.000	.214	5	19	1	3	0	0	0	1	0	0	0	0	8	0	0	.158	.158
Laureano, Ramon	R-R	5-11	185	7-15-94	.227	.295	.209	123	463	65	105	21	6	11	55	40	8	0	2	110	24	5	.369	.298
Marisnick, Jake	R-R	6-4	220	3-30-91	.429	.500	.333	2	7	2	3	1	0	1	2	0	0	0	0	2	0	0	1.000	.429
Martin, Jason	L-R	5-11	190	9-5-95	.273	.169	.302	79	300	38	82	24	3	11	37	19	1	0	0	82	7	6	.483	.319
Mayfield, Jack	R-R	5-11	190	9-30-90	.289	.355	.263	70	270	39	78	16	2	14	44	17	1	0	3	57	7	2	.519	.330
McCall!, Dexture	R-R	6-1	220	1-29-94	.242	.194	.261	37	128	17	31	3	1	6	13	6	0	0	0	39	0	0	.422	.276
Michelena, Arturo	R-R	5-11	165	10-15-94	.210	.121	.233	52	162	15	34	2	0	1	9	10	2	0	1	42	0	1	.241	.263
Muniz, Bryan	R-R	6-0	210	6-5-93	.203	.182	.208	32	118	11	24	5	0	1	6	4	1	0	0	30	0	0	.271	.236
Noel, Rico	R-R	5-8	170	1-11-89	.185	.000	.200	7	27	1	5	0	0	1	3	3	0	0	0	10	2	0	.296	.267
Nunez, Antonio	R-R	5-9	165	1-10-93	.223	.281	.206	114	363	34	81	7	2	2	25	45	5	4	2	100	8	6	.270	.316
Ritchie, Jamie	R-R	6-2	205	4-9-93	.256	.324	.228	76	242	27	62	8	1	3	20	45	5	0	1	44	3	0	.335	.382
Sanchez-Galan, Ozziel	R-R	5-11	160	10-30-97	—	—	—	1	0	1	0	0	0	0	0	0	0	0	0	0	0	0	—	—
Singleton, Jon	L-L	6-2	230	9-18-91	.205	.144	.224	117	385	55	79	20	0	18	62	107	2	0	6	132	3	0	.397	.376
Stassi, Max	R-R	5-10	200	3-15-91	.444	.750	.200	3	9	5	4	1	0	2	4	3	1	0	0	3	0	0	1.222	.615
Straw, Myles	R-R	5-10	180	10-17-94	.239	.125	.263	13	46	9	11	0	0	0	3	7	0	1	0	9	2	0	.239	.340
Stubbs, Garrett	L-R	5-10	175	5-26-93	.236	.167	.254	75	263	36	62	13	0	4	25	32	3	1	1	44	8	0	.331	.324
Trompiz, Kristian	R-R	6-1	184	12-2-95	.222	.375	.196	17	54	3	12	0	0	0	4	2	0	1	0	13	2	1	.222	.250
Tucker, Kyle	L-R	6-4	190	1-17-97	.265	.317	.251	72	287	39	76	21	1	16	47	22	5	0	3	64	8	4	.512	.325
Walsh, Colin	B-R	6-1	200	9-26-89	.146	.333	.114	12	41	5	6	2	0	1	4	10	1	0	0	14	0	0	.268	.327
Wolfe, Tyler	R-R	6-0	190	9-21-93	.152	.500	.103	12	33	5	5	1	0	2	6	1	1	0	0	12	0	0	.364	.200
Woodward, Trent	B-R	6-2	215	2-4-92	.259	.107	.296	44	143	17	37	6	0	4	20	21	3	1	0	41	0	0	.385	.365

Pitching	B-T	HT	WT	DOB	W	L	ERA	G	GS	CG	SV	IP	H	R	ER	HR	BB	SO	AVG	vLH	vRH	K/9	BB/9
Armenteros, Rogelio	R-R	6-1	215	6-30-94	2	3	1.93	14	10	0	1	65	49	15	14	3	19	74	.207	.160	.228	10.19	2.62
Bostick, Akeem	R-R	6-6	215	5-4-95	6	6	4.59	18	13	0	0	80	97	42	41	7	20	58	.299	.258	.324	6.50	2.24
Comer, Kevin	R-R	6-3	205	8-1-92	0	0	0.00	2	0	0	1	3	1	0	0	0	0	5	.100	.000	.167	15.00	0.00
Deemes, Ryan	R-R	6-2	205	6-11-93	0	0	7.71	1	0	0	0	2	3	2	2	1	0	3	.300	.667	.143	11.57	0.00

Deetz, Dean	R-R	6-1	195	11-29-93	4	2	1.82	8	6	0	0	40	27	8	8	3	9	42	.194	.167	.212	9.53	2.04
Dorris, Jacob	R-R	6-2	165	3-24-93	1	2	3.99	23	0	0	3	38	38	21	17	5	15	47	.259	.319	.230	11.03	3.52
Dykxhoorn, Brock	R-R	6-8	250	7-2-94	3	5	4.62	25	16	0	1	99	109	54	51	9	40	84	.279	.288	.274	7.61	3.62
Emanuel, Kent	L-L	6-3	225	6-4-92	5	5	4.60	16	11	0	0	74	95	42	38	7	17	63	.318	.321	.317	7.63	2.06
Feliz, Michael	R-R	6-4	230	6-28-93	0	0	0.00	1	0	0	0	1	0	0	0	0	1	1	.000	—	.000	9.00	9.00
Ferrell, Riley	R-R	6-2	200	10-18-93	2	2	3.81	36	0	0	4	52	51	24	22	2	14	55	.263	.273	.258	9.52	2.42
Freeman, Michael	L-R	6-8	235	10-7-91	2	0	3.15	14	0	0	1	20	21	9	7	1	16	14	.280	.333	.255	6.30	7.20
Garza, Ralph	R-R	6-2	195	4-6-94	1	1	4.97	15	0	0	0	25	23	14	14	4	18	23	.253	.290	.233	8.17	6.39
Harris, Will	R-R	6-4	250	8-28-84	0	0	0.00	1	0	0	0	1	0	0	0	0	0	1	.000	.000	.000	9.00	0.00
Hernandez, Nick	R-R	6-1	212	12-30-94	1	2	5.84	14	0	0	1	25	17	20	16	7	15	22	.187	.276	.145	8.03	5.47
Hill, Kevin	R-R	6-0	230	8-12-92	1	0	0.00	2	0	0	0	5	3	0	0	0	3	2	.158	.167	.154	3.38	5.06
Hiraldo, Carlos	L-L	5-10	175	7-15-96	0	0	3.68	3	0	0	0	7	10	3	3	1	5	5	.357	.250	.438	6.14	6.14
James, Josh	R-R	6-3	206	3-8-93	4	8	4.38	21	11	0	3	76	79	48	37	1	32	72	.263	.252	.270	8.53	3.79
Keuchel, Dallas	L-L	6-3	205	1-1-88	0	0	0.00	1	1	0	0	3	2	0	0	0	1	3	.182	.000	.200	9.00	3.00
McCullers Jr., Lance	L-R	6-1	205	10-2-93	1	0	3.60	1	1	0	0	5	5	2	2	0	1	2	.278	.000	.357	3.60	1.80
McHugh, Collin	R-R	6-2	190	6-19-87	0	0	3.60	4	4	0	0	15	18	10	6	1	4	11	.290	.357	.235	6.60	2.40
Minnis, Albert	L-R	6-0	190	11-5-91	0	0	0.00	3	0	0	0	3	2	1	0	0	0	1	.167	.000	.250	3.38	0.00
Morton, Charlie	R-R	6-5	235	11-12-83	0	0	0.00	1	1	0	0	4	1	2	0	0	2	5	.067	.000	.143	10.38	4.15
Perez, Cionel	L-L	5-11	170	4-21-96	0	0	5.54	4	3	0	0	13	15	8	8	1	5	10	.294	.167	.333	6.92	3.46
Perez, Franklin	R-R	6-3	197	12-6-97	2	1	3.09	7	6	0	1	32	33	13	11	2	11	25	.266	.240	.284	7.03	3.09
Peterson, Eric	R-R	6-4	195	3-8-93	1	2	12.15	8	0	0	0	13	29	19	18	3	4	9	.446	.444	.447	6.08	2.70
Quiala, Yoanys	R-R	6-3	235	1-15-94	4	4	2.86	12	7	0	0	50	65	26	16	3	11	33	.302	.341	.277	5.90	1.97
Ramirez, Yohan	R-R	6-4	190	5-6-95	0	0	1.93	1	1	0	0	5	3	1	1	1	1	8	.188	.143	.222	15.43	1.93
Sipp, Tony	L-L	6-0	190	7-12-83	0	0	0.00	1	1	0	0	1	0	0	0	0	1	2	.000	.000	.000	18.00	9.00
Smith, Kyle	R-R	6-0	170	9-10-92	2	1	2.33	12	8	0	2	54	44	19	14	1	15	46	.221	.237	.211	7.67	2.50
Sneed, Cy	R-R	6-4	185	10-1-92	9	5	5.01	22	14	0	1	97	117	61	54	12	33	81	.297	.337	.268	7.52	3.06
Stutzman, Sean	L-L	5-9	175	7-8-93	1	1	3.51	13	0	0	0	26	23	10	10	4	9	30	.237	.379	.177	10.52	3.16
Thome, Andrew	R-R	6-3	215	1-13-93	4	4	2.85	28	0	0	7	41	36	15	13	3	13	33	.232	.250	.222	7.24	2.85
Thompson, Ryan	R-R	6-6	221	6-26-92	2	3	2.59	31	0	0	6	59	59	24	17	3	11	55	.255	.319	.226	8.39	1.68
Thornton, Trent	R-R	6-0	175	9-30-93	1	2	6.06	4	3	0	0	16	25	14	11	2	0	13	.329	.313	.341	7.16	0.00
Valdez, Framber	L-L	5-11	170	11-19-93	5	5	5.88	12	9	0	0	49	60	33	32	4	23	53	.306	.299	.310	9.73	4.22
Walter, Andrew	R-R	6-4	200	10-18-90	1	0	6.28	9	0	0	1	14	23	12	10	1	2	14	.354	.419	.294	8.79	1.26
Whitley, Forrest	R-R	6-7	240	9-15-97	0	0	1.84	4	2	0	0	15	8	3	3	1	4	26	.157	.000	.235	15.95	2.45
Winkelman, Alex	L-L	6-2	180	2-8-94	2	7	4.04	18	10	0	0	71	85	54	32	6	29	64	.286	.267	.295	8.07	3.66

Fielding

Catcher	PCT	G	PO	A	E	DP	PB
Canelon	.986	8	67	4	1	1	1
Gattis	1.000	1	4	1	0	0	0
Ritchie	.981	57	449	28	9	3	3
Stassi	1.000	2	18	1	0	0	1
Stubbs	.995	64	512	45	3	6	1
Woodward	.988	11	67	13	1	2	2

First Base	PCT	G	PO	A	E	DP
Davis	1.000	3	12	2	0	0
Johnson	1.000	2	13	2	0	1
McCall	.993	33	263	13	2	34
Muniz	.990	23	182	10	2	28
Ritchie	1.000	3	28	0	0	1
Singleton	.987	77	600	63	9	70

Second Base	PCT	G	PO	A	E	DP
Birk	.957	33	37	73	5	16
Hyde	.984	15	32	31	1	11
Mayfield	.970	43	81	112	6	30
Michelena	.978	14	16	29	1	7
Muniz	.000	1	0	0	0	0
Nunez	.947	21	33	57	5	18
Walsh	.864	5	5	14	3	4
Wolfe	1.000	12	16	22	0	8
Woodward	1.000	3	1	5	0	0

Third Base	PCT	G	PO	A	E	DP
Birk	1.000	3	1	8	0	0
Davis	.937	73	50	143	13	21
Hyde	1.000	4	0	7	0	1
Mayfield	.867	6	3	10	2	1
Michelena	.945	34	19	50	4	10
Muniz	1.000	2	0	1	0	0
Sanchez-Galan	.000	1	0	0	0	0
Trompiz	1.000	2	0	1	0	1
Walsh	.941	5	5	11	1	1
Woodward	.944	18	13	21	2	4

Shortstop	PCT	G	PO	A	E	DP
Correa	.923	2	5	7	1	3
Hyde	.935	10	8	21	2	7
Mayfield	.961	20	22	51	3	9
Michelena	1.000	6	13	16	0	2
Nunez	.955	92	140	220	17	60
Trompiz	.914	15	18	46	6	10

Outfield	PCT	G	PO	A	E	DP
Boyd	.930	24	39	1	3	0
Davis	1.000	6	5	1	0	1
De La Cruz	.929	9	12	1	1	1
Ferguson	.994	79	151	4	1	1
Garcia	1.000	38	72	2	0	0
Johnson	1.000	3	9	0	0	0
Laureano	.984	123	233	16	4	6
Marisnick	.000	1	0	0	0	0
Martin	.989	57	86	1	1	0
Noel	1.000	7	13	0	0	0
Straw	1.000	13	26	1	0	0
Tucker	.993	65	130	4	1	1

BUIES CREEK ASTROS — HIGH CLASS A

CAROLINA LEAGUE

Batting	B-T	HT	WT	DOB	AVG	vLH	vRH	G	AB	R	H	2B	3B	HR	RBI	BB	HBP	SH	SF	SO	SB	CS	SLG	OBP
Alvarez, Yordan	L-L	6-5	225	6-27-97	.277	.364	.241	58	224	19	62	11	3	3	36	19	2	0	7	41	6	1	.393	.329
Ayarza, Rodrigo	B-R	5-8	145	2-20-95	.233	.257	.225	41	146	13	34	10	2	1	17	9	1	0	0	31	0	1	.349	.282
Benedetti, Carmen	L-L	6-2	215	10-29-94	.268	.286	.259	23	82	9	22	7	1	1	9	9	0	2	0	21	1	0	.415	.341
Birk, Ryne	L-R	5-10	185	11-11-94	.274	.202	.310	81	314	47	86	15	5	8	47	29	5	1	5	62	5	4	.430	.340
Cesar, Randy	R-R	6-1	180	1-11-95	.296	.385	.258	83	308	35	91	15	0	4	35	22	3	0	4	79	4	1	.383	.344
Correa, Christian	R-R	5-10	210	5-18-93	.208	.353	.129	16	48	4	10	5	0	1	4	4	2	0	0	9	0	0	.375	.296
Dawson, Ronnie	L-R	6-2	225	5-19-95	.327	.333	.324	13	52	7	17	3	1	0	5	4	0	0	1	9	1	3	.423	.368
De Goti, Alex	R-R	5-10	165	8-19-94	.227	.234	.224	70	238	29	54	13	0	5	24	28	4	1	1	65	3	2	.345	.317
de Oleo, Eduardo	R-R	5-10	180	1-25-93	.242	.200	.255	16	62	11	15	2	1	5	11	6	0	0	1	20	0	0	.548	.304
Duarte, Osvaldo	R-R	5-9	160	1-18-96	.190	.095	.215	28	100	7	19	3	2	0	8	7	1	0	0	38	3	4	.260	.250
Hermelyn, Anthony	R-R	6-1	210	11-18-93	.242	.225	.250	74	264	23	64	15	0	3	32	38	0	0	1	55	0	2	.333	.337
Johnson, Spencer	R-R	6-4	225	11-1-93	.198	.254	.171	55	192	25	38	6	4	6	18	22	2	0	1	70	1	2	.365	.286
Jones, Taylor	R-R	6-7	225	12-6-93	.225	.120	.262	55	191	17	43	5	1	2	17	28	1	0	3	51	0	0	.293	.323

Martin, Jason	L-R	5-11	190	9-5-95	.287	.302	.279	46	174	34	50	11	2	7	29	20	0	0	4	42	9	5	.494	.354
McCall, Dexture	R-R	6-1	220	1-29-94	.231	.183	.254	54	186	20	43	9	1	4	22	35	1	0	1	57	2	2	.355	.354
McCormick, Chas	R-L	6-0	190	4-19-95	.188	.333	.154	4	16	0	3	0	0	0	0	0	1	0	0	2	1	0	.188	.235
Michelena, Arturo	R-R	5-11	165	10-15-94	.230	.143	.282	32	113	13	26	5	1	0	10	10	1	1	0	28	1	1	.292	.298
Porter, Pat	L-L	6-0	215	6-10-93	.226	.246	.218	53	190	20	43	9	0	3	12	22	3	1	1	51	3	5	.321	.315
Rogers, Jake	R-R	6-1	190	4-18-95	.265	.286	.256	83	313	43	83	18	3	12	55	44	4	0	6	72	13	8	.457	.357
Sanchez-Galan, Ozziel	R-R	5-11	160	10-30-97	.333	—	.333	1	3	1	1	0	0	0	0	0	0	0	0	1	0	0	.333	.333
Sewald, Johnny	R-L	5-11	175	11-11-93	.208	.191	.216	21	72	11	15	6	0	1	5	3	1	2	0	27	3	2	.333	.250
Sierra, Anibal	R-R	6-1	190	2-15-94	.196	.180	.204	104	357	39	70	10	3	6	31	26	10	6	3	118	2	4	.291	.268
Straw, Myles	R-R	5-10	180	10-17-94	.295	.313	.286	114	437	81	129	17	7	1	41	87	2	4	3	70	36	9	.373	.412
Tucker, Kyle	L-R	6-4	190	1-17-97	.288	.319	.269	48	177	31	51	12	4	9	43	24	3	0	2	45	13	5	.554	.379
van der Meer, Stijn	R-L	6-3	170	5-1-93	.158	.250	.133	6	19	2	3	1	0	0	0	1	0	0	0	4	1	0	.211	.200
Vasquez, Randy	R-R	5-10	190	3-13-96	.231	.167	.286	4	13	1	3	0	0	0	0	1	0	1	0	3	0	0	.231	.286
Wolfe, Tyler	R-R	6-0	190	9-21-93	.250	.250	.250	3	12	4	3	0	0	0	0	1	0	0	0	1	0	0	.250	.308
Wrenn, Stephen	R-R	6-2	185	10-7-94	.242	.261	.234	83	306	36	74	7	4	4	25	32	3	8	4	66	10	5	.330	.316

Pitching	B-T	HT	WT	DOB	W	L	ERA	G	GS	CG	SV	IP	H	R	ER	HR	BB	SO	AVG	vLH	vRH	K/9	BB/9
Adcock, Brett	L-L	6-1	225	8-28-95	4	4	4.71	20	14	0	1	84	78	48	44	9	32	80	.245	.241	.245	8.57	3.43
Alcala, Jorge	R-R	6-3	180	7-28-95	5	6	3.45	16	14	1	0	78	55	33	30	7	33	60	.200	.144	.230	6.89	3.79
Blanco, Ronel	R-R	6-0	180	8-31-93	0	1	5.40	1	0	0	0	3	2	2	2	1	1	3	.182	.500	.000	8.10	2.70
Bostick, Akeem	R-R	6-6	215	5-4-95	2	1	1.86	4	3	0	0	19	10	4	4	0	6	16	.154	.125	.171	7.45	2.79
Bower, Matt	R-L	6-5	190	6-16-94	5	6	5.32	22	15	1	1	95	109	58	56	14	25	84	.288	.298	.284	7.99	2.38
Brey, Howie	L-L	5-11	195	5-22-94	1	2	6.26	15	0	0	1	23	25	22	16	5	11	25	.275	.333	.250	9.78	4.30
Carr, Devon	L-L	6-2	190	11-5-92	0	0	6.00	4	0	0	0	6	9	5	4	0	3	4	.360	.167	.539	6.00	4.50
Deemes, Ryan	R-R	6-2	205	6-11-93	2	0	5.40	6	0	0	2	10	14	6	6	1	3	14	.333	.316	.348	12.60	2.70
Ferrell, Justin	R-R	6-7	205	4-21-94	7	5	4.26	28	8	0	3	82	84	42	39	9	29	89	.259	.252	.264	9.73	3.17
Ferrell, Riley	R-R	6-2	200	10-18-93	0	0	0.00	2	0	0	2	2	0	0	0	0	0	5	.000	.000	.000	22.50	0.00
Garza, Ralph	R-R	6-2	195	4-6-94	2	2	3.44	20	0	0	3	37	36	15	14	2	16	43	.257	.294	.236	10.55	3.93
Harris, Will	R-R	6-4	250	8-28-84	0	0	0.00	1	1	0	0	1	0	0	0	0	0	2	.000	.000	.000	18.00	0.00
Hartman, Ryan	L-L	6-3	205	4-21-94	2	6	4.17	16	11	0	1	69	67	35	32	8	19	53	.254	.268	.250	6.91	2.48
Hernandez, Elieser	R-R	6-0	210	5-3-95	4	5	3.98	15	11	0	0	63	55	28	28	6	21	74	.235	.255	.219	10.52	2.98
Hernandez, Nick	R-R	6-1	212	12-30-94	0	1	1.59	24	0	0	9	34	18	6	6	1	11	48	.157	.156	.157	12.71	2.91
Hill, Kevin	R-R	6-0	230	8-12-92	1	0	1.05	10	0	0	2	34	21	8	4	0	8	36	.171	.152	.178	9.44	2.10
Javier, Cristian	R-R	6-1	170	3-26-97	1	0	0.00	2	0	0	0	6	2	0	0	0	3	9	.105	.143	.083	14.29	4.76
Kessay, Sebastian	L-L	6-2	215	6-19-93	6	3	3.58	26	0	0	3	50	43	24	20	2	23	55	.229	.218	.233	9.83	4.11
LaRue, Carson	R-R	6-1	175	3-6-96	0	3	5.12	4	3	0	0	19	30	11	11	2	2	10	.349	.250	.371	4.66	0.93
Perez, Cionel	L-L	5-11	170	4-21-96	2	1	2.84	5	4	0	0	25	27	10	8	1	5	18	.276	.177	.296	6.39	1.78
Perez, Franklin	R-R	6-3	197	12-6-97	4	2	2.98	12	10	1	2	54	38	20	18	4	16	53	.191	.191	.191	8.78	2.65
Perez, Hector	R-R	6-3	190	6-6-96	6	5	3.63	21	14	0	2	89	69	49	36	6	67	104	.218	.217	.219	10.48	6.75
Pinales, Erasmo	R-R	5-11	180	11-25-94	1	2	3.52	12	0	0	0	23	15	9	9	1	9	27	.181	.182	.180	10.57	3.52
Quiala, Yoanys	R-R	6-3	235	1-15-94	5	1	2.31	12	7	0	0	58	40	17	15	3	13	59	.191	.161	.211	9.10	2.01
Raftery, Devin	R-R	5-10	205	9-21-92	0	0	6.00	1	0	0	0	3	4	2	2	0	0	1	.333	—	.333	3.00	0.00
Ramirez, Yohan	R-R	6-4	190	5-6-95	0	0	1.80	2	0	0	1	5	5	1	1	0	1	4	.263	.000	.357	7.20	1.80
Saldana, Abdiel	R-R	5-11	195	3-13-96	2	1	5.52	4	3	0	0	15	13	9	9	1	7	13	.245	.200	.273	7.98	4.30
Sandoval, Patrick	L-L	6-3	190	10-18-96	0	1	10.13	1	0	0	0	3	4	3	3	0	1	2	.333	.000	.364	6.75	3.38
Sierra, Carlos	R-R	6-3	195	10-18-94	3	1	3.00	25	0	0	1	48	34	19	16	3	21	49	.192	.175	.200	9.19	3.94
Stutzman, Sean	L-L	5-9	175	7-8-93	2	1	1.10	16	0	0	3	33	16	7	4	2	9	39	.140	.129	.145	10.74	2.48
Thome, Andrew	R-R	6-3	215	1-13-93	0	1	5.68	4	0	0	1	6	8	6	4	1	2	6	.296	.400	.273	8.53	2.84
Valdez, Framber	L-L	5-11	170	11-19-93	2	3	2.79	13	9	0	1	61	41	24	19	3	29	73	.185	.169	.191	10.71	4.26
Valdez, Gabriel	R-R	6-2	185	10-25-95	0	0	3.86	2	1	0	0	7	8	3	3	0	0	6	.276	.231	.313	7.71	0.00
Walter, Andrew	R-R	6-4	200	10-18-90	0	0	3.18	4	0	0	1	6	6	3	2	1	3	3	.273	.273	.273	4.76	4.76
Whitley, Forrest	R-R	6-7	240	9-15-97	3	1	3.16	7	6	0	0	31	28	11	11	2	9	50	.237	.220	.247	14.36	2.59
Winkelman, Alex	L-L	6-2	180	2-8-94	2	0	1.39	8	5	0	0	32	22	7	5	0	6	46	.193	.160	.202	12.80	1.67

Fielding

Catcher	PCT	G	PO	A	E	DP	PB
Correa	1.000	15	145	17	0	0	1
de Oleo	.990	10	90	10	1	1	0
Hermelyn	1.000	51	431	35	0	2	3
Rogers	.994	63	586	58	4	8	5
Vasquez	1.000	1	8	1	0	1	0

First Base	PCT	G	PO	A	E	DP
Alvarez	1.000	15	111	6	0	8
Johnson	.995	27	205	10	1	17
Jones	.994	44	329	13	2	29
McCall	.991	41	323	14	3	21
Porter	1.000	12	93	5	0	5

Second Base	PCT	G	PO	A	E	DP
Ayarza	1.000	17	23	31	0	5
Birk	.974	72	106	152	7	37
De Goti	1.000	35	60	94	0	18
Duarte	.773	7	3	14	5	1
Michelena	1.000	3	3	10	0	1
Sanchez-Galan	1.000	1	1	1	0	0
van der Meer	1.000	1	1	0	0	0
Wolfe	1.000	3	3	4	0	1

Third Base	PCT	G	PO	A	E	DP
Ayarza	.667	2	1	1	1	0
Birk	1.000	4	1	8	0	0
Cesar	.933	81	57	124	13	13
De Goti	.938	10	8	22	2	1
Duarte	1.000	7	5	8	0	0
Michelena	.986	27	20	52	1	6
Sierra	.857	7	3	9	2	1
van der Meer	1.000	2	0	2	0	0

Shortstop	PCT	G	PO	A	E	DP
Ayarza	1.000	3	3	4	0	1
De Goti	.972	21	26	44	2	8
Duarte	.905	14	22	35	6	6
Michelena	1.000	2	2	4	0	0
Sierra	.931	97	93	205	22	35
van der Meer	.909	3	4	6	1	1

Outfield	PCT	G	PO	A	E	DP
Alvarez	1.000	28	39	5	0	1
Ayarza	.938	17	28	2	2	0
Benedetti	.974	21	32	6	1	1
Dawson	1.000	13	21	0	0	0
Johnson	1.000	21	27	0	0	0
Martin	.986	42	70	2	1	0
McCormick	1.000	4	10	0	0	0
Porter	.971	22	31	2	1	0
Sewald	1.000	18	30	1	0	0
Straw	.990	111	271	13	3	7
Tucker	.976	45	76	4	2	1
Wrenn	.995	82	199	7	1	1

QUAD CITIES RIVER BANDITS

LOW CLASS A

MIDWEST LEAGUE

Batting	B-T	HT	WT	DOB	AVG	vLH	vRH	G	AB	R	H	2B	3B	HR	RBI	BB	HBP	SH	SF	SO	SB	CS	SLG	OBP
Almonte, Marcos	R-R	5-10	163	3-28-96	.248	.323	.217	84	322	39	80	14	1	9	38	10	3	5	2	84	11	8	.382	.276
Alvarez, Yordan	L-L	6-5	225	6-27-97	.360	.350	.363	32	111	26	40	6	0	9	33	23	2	0	3	36	2	0	.658	.468
Arauz, Jonathan	B-R	6-0	150	8-3-98	.221	.154	.238	36	127	23	28	3	2	0	4	20	1	1	0	18	0	1	.276	.331
Ayarza, Rodrigo	B-R	5-8	145	2-20-95	.316	.265	.333	37	136	23	43	10	0	7	29	5	2	0	2	14	3	0	.544	.345
Benedetti, Carmen	L-L	6-2	215	10-29-94	.332	.381	.322	69	241	49	80	20	0	4	32	51	0	1	2	47	1	0	.465	.446
Bohanek, Cody	R-R	6-1	195	7-2-95	.278	.250	.286	10	36	5	10	1	0	0	1	2	1	0	0	14	0	1	.306	.333
Bracamonte, Gabriel	R-R	5-9	165	5-15-95	.177	.000	.188	12	34	2	6	1	0	0	2	0	0	0	1	10	0	0	.206	.171
Cameron, Daz	R-R	6-2	185	1-15-97	.271	.366	.240	120	446	79	121	29	8	14	73	45	12	1	7	108	32	12	.466	.349
2-team total (3 West Michigan)					.271	.000	.333	123	454	80	123	29	8	14	74	48	12	1	7	112	32	13	.463	.351
Cesar, Randy	R-R	6-1	180	1-11-95	.302	.267	.316	27	106	16	32	8	0	3	22	11	0	0	0	29	0	0	.462	.368
Dawson, Ronnie	L-R	6-2	225	5-19-95	.272	.192	.296	116	438	81	119	23	4	14	62	55	9	0	3	101	17	8	.438	.362
De Goti, Alex	R-R	5-10	165	8-19-94	.261	.303	.244	34	119	22	31	4	1	3	8	24	2	0	0	29	4	3	.387	.393
De La Cruz, Bryan	R-R	6-2	175	12-16-96	.270	.250	.276	10	37	6	10	2	0	0	2	3	0	0	0	7	1	1	.324	.325
Duarte, Osvaldo	R-R	5-9	160	1-18-96	.194	.139	.210	47	160	22	31	9	1	4	22	24	1	1	1	55	10	2	.338	.301
Franco, Wander	B-R	6-1	189	10-11-96	.230	.265	.220	64	226	25	52	9	1	6	30	18	0	0	2	66	1	1	.358	.285
Henderson, Raymond	R-R	5-9	188	12-27-95	.208	.255	.193	60	197	23	41	11	0	3	29	19	5	0	5	55	0	0	.310	.288
Johnson, Spencer	R-R	6-4	225	11-1-93	.253	.208	.275	20	75	16	19	5	2	3	16	7	0	0	1	23	0	1	.493	.313
Jones, Taylor	R-R	6-7	225	12-6-93	.218	.250	.209	50	174	23	38	8	0	5	28	17	6	1	4	50	0	0	.351	.304
Matijevic, J.J.	L-R	6-0	206	11-14-95	.125	.167	.083	6	24	2	3	0	0	1	4	1	1	0	0	9	0	1	.250	.192
McCormick, Chas	R-L	6-0	190	4-19-95	.262	.235	.273	39	122	21	32	6	1	2	18	11	0	1	2	16	1	3	.377	.319
Moran, Colin	L-R	6-4	204	10-1-92	.100	.000	.167	3	10	0	1	1	0	0	2	2	0	0	0	4	0	0	.200	.250
Payano, Luis	R-R	6-1	175	5-12-96	.253	.296	.232	24	83	10	21	6	0	2	12	7	2	0	0	18	1	1	.398	.326
Robinson, Chuckie	R-R	5-11	225	12-14-94	.274	.276	.274	108	430	69	118	32	2	15	77	31	5	0	1	98	7	1	.463	.330
Rogers, Jake	R-R	6-1	190	4-18-95	.255	.313	.229	27	102	17	26	7	1	6	15	9	4	0	1	28	1	0	.520	.336
Rojas, Josh	L-R	6-1	185	6-30-94	.256	.192	.280	52	195	33	50	5	5	10	40	15	2	0	7	43	0	0	.487	.306
Sieber, Troy	L-R	5-11	215	6-22-95	.290	.283	.292	55	190	34	55	11	0	7	33	37	1	0	2	47	0	1	.458	.404
Sierra, Anibal	R-R	6-1	190	2-15-94	.250	.600	.185	9	32	2	8	1	0	0	3	3	0	0	0	9	2	1	.281	.314
Toro-Hernandez, A.	B-R	6-1	190	12-20-96	.209	.205	.211	37	134	25	28	3	2	9	17	21	2	0	1	30	2	0	.463	.323
Trompiz, Kristian	R-R	6-1	184	12-2-95	.261	.275	.255	40	142	16	37	5	1	0	13	14	1	0	0	21	6	5	.310	.331
Wolfe, Tyler	R-R	6-0	190	9-21-93	.157	.000	.191	16	51	5	8	2	1	0	4	11	1	0	0	6	1	0	.235	.318
Wrenn, Stephen	R-R	6-2	185	10-7-94	.288	.182	.328	42	160	29	46	10	2	3	11	18	1	3	0	46	8	2	.431	.363

Pitching	B-T	HT	WT	DOB	W	L	ERA	G	GS	CG	SV	IP	H	R	ER	HR	BB	SO	AVG	vLH	vRH	K/9	BB/9
Adcock, Brett	L-L	6-1	225	8-28-95	1	0	1.14	5	4	0	0	24	15	4	3	0	7	37	.179	.143	.191	14.07	2.66
Alcala, Jorge	R-R	6-3	180	7-28-95	2	0	2.03	6	4	0	0	31	16	7	7	3	12	35	.155	.192	.118	10.16	3.48
Balaguer, Jesus	R-R	6-4	195	8-12-93	4	1	4.34	10	0	0	1	19	14	9	9	2	10	29	.212	.136	.250	13.98	4.82
Blanco, Ronel	R-R	6-0	180	8-31-93	6	4	3.30	22	11	0	0	85	80	44	31	6	46	76	.244	.261	.235	8.08	4.89
Britton, Tyler	R-R	6-0	195	3-6-94	0	0	6.75	1	1	0	0	4	7	4	3	1	1	2	.350	.800	.200	4.50	2.25
Carr, Devon	L-L	6-2	190	11-5-92	0	4	5.02	17	0	0	2	29	29	17	16	2	17	36	.259	.240	.264	11.30	5.34
Corniel, Robert	R-R	6-3	190	6-23-95	1	0	5.08	15	0	0	1	28	24	16	16	1	21	26	.226	.200	.239	8.26	6.67
Feliz, Michael	R-R	6-4	230	6-28-93	0	0	0.00	1	1	0	0	1	0	0	0	0	0	2	.000	.000	.000	18.00	0.00
Hartman, Ryan	L-L	6-3	205	4-21-94	3	1	2.72	9	5	0	1	40	32	12	12	4	14	37	.222	.143	.241	8.39	3.18
Hill, Kevin	R-R	6-0	230	8-12-92	2	1	3.60	14	0	0	3	25	19	10	10	0	10	30	.211	.286	.177	10.80	3.60
Hunt, Dustin	R-R	6-5	195	8-2-94	0	7	5.91	25	8	0	0	70	75	48	46	10	50	82	.276	.184	.328	10.54	6.43
Javier, Cristian	R-R	6-1	170	3-26-97	2	0	2.39	8	7	0	1	38	25	10	10	3	15	47	.188	.241	.152	11.23	3.58
Johnson, Reggie	R-R	6-4	205	10-28-93	0	0	10.00	5	0	0	0	9	12	10	10	2	6	3	.308	.400	.250	3.00	6.00
LaRue, Carson	R-R	6-1	175	3-6-96	12	4	2.86	20	16	0	1	101	76	37	32	7	28	95	.207	.244	.188	8.49	2.50
Montano, Salvador	L-L	6-3	150	7-14-94	8	4	2.89	36	0	0	5	53	35	21	17	2	41	68	.189	.146	.204	11.55	6.96
Paredes, Enoli	R-R	5-11	165	9-28-95	1	3	2.11	8	6	0	0	38	21	9	9	3	13	33	.163	.179	.151	7.75	3.05
Perez, Cionel	L-L	5-11	170	4-21-96	4	3	4.39	12	9	0	2	55	52	30	27	2	17	55	.254	.373	.214	8.95	2.77
Perez, Hector	R-R	6-3	190	6-6-96	1	1	2.50	4	3	0	0	18	9	5	5	2	11	24	.150	.158	.146	12.00	5.50
Pinales, Erasmo	R-R	5-11	180	11-25-94	3	1	3.32	21	0	0	6	38	28	16	14	2	17	36	.209	.222	.202	8.53	4.03
Ramirez, Yohan	R-R	6-4	190	5-6-95	4	5	5.07	17	10	0	1	66	59	40	37	4	44	53	.248	.274	.227	7.26	6.03
Rosado, Cesar	R-R	6-1	172	6-22-96	3	2	6.16	7	3	0	0	19	16	14	13	2	14	18	.235	.300	.184	8.53	6.63
Saldana, Abdiel	R-R	5-11	195	3-13-96	5	2	2.97	25	5	0	2	76	76	28	25	4	27	73	.261	.301	.242	8.68	3.21
Sanabria, Carlos	R-R	6-0	165	1-24-97	4	4	4.46	19	12	0	2	81	75	44	40	6	47	78	.246	.256	.239	8.70	5.24
Sandoval, Edgardo	R-R	6-0	170	7-9-96	2	1	3.71	6	1	0	0	17	13	8	7	3	4	16	.200	.083	.226	8.47	2.12
Sandoval, Patrick	L-L	6-3	190	10-18-96	2	2	3.83	9	7	0	1	40	38	25	17	1	16	48	.244	.273	.239	10.80	3.60
Scheetz, Kit	L-L	5-10	185	5-18-94	2	0	0.95	4	3	0	1	19	14	3	2	0	3	16	.203	.455	.155	7.58	1.42
Sierra, Carlos	R-R	6-3	195	10-18-94	0	1	1.93	4	0	0	1	9	5	2	2	1	3	11	.152	.091	.182	10.61	2.89
Thompson, Nathan	L-L	6-1	170	11-14-93	0	2	6.11	5	2	0	0	18	18	12	12	3	11	16	.273	.417	.241	8.15	5.60
Valdez, Gabriel	R-R	6-2	185	10-25-95	3	0	3.79	15	10	0	0	62	64	30	26	8	16	61	.270	.259	.276	8.90	2.34
Velazquez, Derick	R-R	6-4	200	11-28-93	1	2	3.38	5	0	0	1	8	9	4	3	0	2	3	.290	.400	.238	3.38	2.25
Whitley, Forrest	R-R	6-7	240	9-15-97	2	3	2.91	12	10	0	0	46	42	16	15	2	21	67	.247	.230	.260	13.01	4.08
Williams, Lucas	L-R	6-3	180	7-20-94	1	1	2.75	30	0	0	0	56	51	20	17	5	30	62	.238	.306	.204	10.02	4.85

Fielding

Catcher	PCT	G	PO	A	E	DP	PB
Bracamonte	1.000	12	90	5	0	0	2
Henderson	.977	23	162	10	4	1	2
Robinson	.996	80	709	82	3	9	13
Rogers	.996	21	201	28	1	2	3
Toro-Hernandez	.991	9	100	6	1	1	4

First Base	PCT	G	PO	A	E	DP
Alvarez	1.000	7	46	1	0	7
Franco	.988	14	77	4	1	8
Johnson	1.000	12	92	4	0	3

	PCT	G	PO	A	E	DP
Jones	.995	49	353	30	2	32
Robinson	.960	3	22	2	1	3
Sieber	.992	53	338	20	3	35
Trompiz	1.000	5	29	1	0	4

Second Base	PCT	G	PO	A	E	DP
Almonte	.940	36	60	66	8	21
Arauz	1.000	4	6	6	0	3
Ayarza	1.000	18	24	46	0	11
Bohanek	1.000	1	1	0	0	0
De Goti	1.000	13	25	27	0	3
Duarte	1.000	10	10	16	0	6
Henderson	.947	22	40	31	4	6
Rojas	.984	18	32	28	1	9
Toro-Hernandez	.667	1	1	1	1	1
Trompiz	1.000	11	25	19	0	9
Wolfe	.967	14	34	25	2	10

Third Base	PCT	G	PO	A	E	DP
Almonte	.750	4	4	5	3	0
Ayarza	.964	11	7	20	1	1
Cesar	.909	26	12	38	5	1
De Goti	1.000	2	3	4	0	0
Franco	.920	45	29	75	9	14
Henderson	.929	5	6	7	1	1
Moran	.875	2	1	6	1	0
Rojas	.964	30	32	48	3	7
Toro-Hernandez	.972	17	5	30	1	5

Shortstop	PCT	G	PO	A	E	DP
Almonte	.815	9	10	12	5	1
Arauz	.959	32	43	73	5	20
Ayarza	.952	5	5	15	1	0
Bohanek	.972	9	12	23	1	4
De Goti	.985	16	27	39	1	8
Duarte	.938	33	46	75	8	12
Rojas	.833	3	2	3	1	3
Sierra	.955	9	8	13	1	2
Trompiz	.947	24	34	38	4	5
Wolfe	1.000	2	2	7	0	0

Outfield	PCT	G	PO	A	E	DP
Almonte	.935	30	43	0	3	0
Alvarez	.947	13	17	1	1	0
Benedetti	.984	55	119	5	2	0
Cameron	.982	118	273	4	5	2
Dawson	.982	98	159	1	3	0
De La Cruz	1.000	10	22	1	0	1
Duarte	1.000	4	5	0	0	0
Henderson	.000	2	0	0	0	0
McCormick	1.000	39	72	1	0	0
Payano	.980	20	47	2	1	1
Rojas	1.000	1	2	2	0	1
Trompiz	1.000	1	2	0	0	0
Wrenn	1.000	37	78	1	0	0

TRI-CITY VALLEYCATS

SHORT SEASON

NEW YORK-PENN LEAGUE

Batting	B-T	HT	WT	DOB	AVG	vLH	vRH	G	AB	R	H	2B	3B	HR	RBI	BB	HBP	SH	SF	SO	SB	CS	SLG	OBP
Adams, Jake	R-R	6-2	250	12-23-95	.170	.180	.167	48	165	17	28	6	0	10	21	24	2	0	2	68	2	1	.388	.280
Arauz, Jonathan	B-R	6-0	150	8-3-98	.265	.308	.244	33	121	16	32	7	1	1	11	12	2	0	0	29	1	0	.364	.341
Bracamonte, Gabriel	R-R	5-9	165	5-15-95	.260	.357	.224	28	104	12	27	6	4	0	9	12	1	0	1	19	0	0	.394	.339
Canelon, Carlos	B-R	5-11	170	12-14-94	.140	.182	.128	16	50	3	7	0	0	0	3	7	0	0	1	17	1	0	.140	.241
Castro, Ruben	L-R	5-10	182	7-10-96	.500	.333	1.000	1	4	1	2	1	0	0	0	0	0	0	0	0	0	0	.750	.500
Davis, Kyle	R-R	6-0	195	12-30-95	.177	.194	.173	52	164	22	29	7	1	3	14	29	3	0	2	50	1	2	.287	.308
De La Cruz, Bryan	R-R	6-2	175	12-16-96	.250	.227	.259	40	156	16	39	6	2	1	14	9	1	0	3	23	4	1	.333	.290
Fernandez, Frankeny	R-R	6-1	170	12-7-96	.250	.500	.125	4	12	2	3	0	0	0	0	1	0	0	0	4	1	1	.250	.308
Heras, Bernardo	B-R	6-0	180	11-3-95	.100	.000	.143	3	10	0	1	0	0	0	0	0	0	0	0	4	0	0	.100	.100
Julks, Corey	R-R	6-1	185	2-27-96	.177	.222	.167	32	102	7	18	3	0	1	7	18	2	0	0	19	9	2	.235	.312
MacDonald, Connor	R-R	6-5	200	2-27-96	.182	.077	.203	24	77	8	14	4	0	3	11	6	1	0	1	35	0	0	.351	.247
Mathis, Patrick	L-L	6-1	190	3-23-96	.111	.000	.167	3	9	1	1	0	0	0	0	0	0	0	0	4	0	0	.111	.111
Matijevic, J.J.	L-R	6-0	206	11-14-95	.240	.220	.245	53	200	34	48	14	0	6	27	18	1	0	3	60	11	3	.400	.302
Mauricio, Joan	L-R	5-11	160	10-22-96	.000	.000	.000	2	3	0	0	0	0	0	0	1	1	0	0	0	2	1	.000	.400
Meyers, Jacob	R-L	6-0	200	6-18-96	.207	.114	.240	42	135	17	28	4	0	3	10	12	4	0	1	30	11	2	.304	.290
Papierski, Michael	B-R	6-4	225	2-26-96	.198	.310	.163	37	121	18	24	5	1	5	18	30	6	0	2	29	3	1	.380	.377
Payano, Luis	R-R	6-1	175	5-12-96	.246	.333	.231	20	61	11	15	5	1	3	6	2	1	0	0	14	0	3	.508	.281
Pineda, Andy	L-R	6-1	165	11-11-96	.222	.275	.203	51	158	20	35	2	7	1	16	8	0	5	0	37	19	1	.342	.259
Russell, Reid	R-R	6-3	223	8-22-95	.192	.300	.162	12	47	6	9	2	0	2	7	4	0	0	0	26	0	0	.362	.255
Sanchez, Vicente	L-R	5-11	170	10-4-96	.333	.500	.000	1	3	1	1	1	0	0	1	0	0	0	1	2	0	0	.667	.250
Shaver, Colton	R-R	6-1	210	9-18-95	.196	.083	.229	32	107	11	21	3	0	4	18	13	2	0	2	43	2	3	.336	.290
Sieber, Troy	L-R	5-11	215	6-22-95	.286	.667	.000	2	7	0	2	1	0	0	0	0	1	0	0	2	0	0	.429	.375
Sierra, Miguelangel	R-R	5-11	165	12-2-97	.178	.273	.149	57	185	15	33	8	1	4	13	17	4	0	2	62	6	1	.297	.260
Toro-Hernandez, Abraham	B-R	6-1	190	12-20-96	.293	.353	.281	32	106	21	31	8	0	6	16	19	3	0	0	21	1	3	.538	.414
Tovalin, Adrian	R-R	6-2	222	2-11-96	.197	.139	.219	36	132	19	26	5	1	5	23	12	2	0	2	50	0	1	.364	.270
Trompiz, Kristian	R-R	6-1	184	12-2-95	.338	.273	.349	25	77	11	26	6	0	0	5	10	0	0	0	16	14	2	.416	.414
Vasquez, Randy	R-R	5-10	190	3-13-96	.273	.000	.333	7	22	1	6	0	0	0	1	2	0	0	0	4	1	1	.273	.333

Pitching	B-T	HT	WT	DOB	W	L	ERA	G	GS	CG	SV	IP	H	R	ER	HR	BB	SO	AVG	vLH	vRH	K/9	BB/9
Almengo, Diogenes	R-R	6-2	190	6-2-95	1	4	4.96	18	0	0	1	33	26	23	18	2	24	27	.219	.200	.230	7.44	6.61
Balaguer, Jesus	R-R	6-4	195	8-12-93	1	1	1.23	5	0	0	2	7	3	1	1	0	3	10	.120	.188	.000	12.27	3.68
Bielak, Brandon	L-R	6-1	210	4-2-96	1	1	0.92	8	4	0	1	29	18	4	3	0	4	37	.171	.109	.220	11.35	1.23
Bleday, Adam	L-L	5-11	175	11-2-94	1	1	4.11	4	3	0	0	15	14	7	7	0	6	15	.250	.091	.353	8.80	3.52
Bukauskas, J.B.	R-R	6-0	196	10-11-96	0	0	4.50	2	2	0	0	6	4	3	3	0	4	6	.191	.100	.273	9.00	6.00
Castellanos, Humberto	R-R	5-11	170	4-3-98	1	0	0.00	3	0	0	0	4	4	0	0	0	0	2	.250	.200	.273	4.91	0.00
Castro, Ricardo	R-R	6-3	187	1-12-96	1	1	1.23	3	2	0	0	15	9	4	2	1	8	13	.196	.292	.091	7.98	4.91
Corniel, Robert	R-R	6-3	190	6-23-95	0	0	0.00	3	0	0	1	6	4	0	0	0	2	10	.182	.100	.250	14.21	2.84
Hardman, Ian	R-R	6-5	240	9-16-95	0	0	0.00	2	0	0	0	4	0	0	0	0	1	5	.000	.000	.000	10.38	2.08
Heredia, Angel	R-R	5-9	170	7-22-92	0	0	1.93	4	1	0	0	5	5	1	1	0	4	7	.263	.222	.300	13.50	7.71
Hiraldo, Carlos	L-L	5-10	175	7-15-96	1	6	6.79	15	10	0	0	50	68	45	38	3	23	57	.319	.333	.316	10.19	4.11
House, Alex	R-R	6-3	194	8-24-96	0	0	3.54	9	4	0	0	20	20	10	8	1	7	23	.250	.258	.245	10.18	3.10
Ivey, Tyler	R-R	6-4	195	5-12-96	0	3	5.94	11	7	0	0	36	41	26	24	2	12	41	.281	.298	.270	10.16	2.97
Javier, Cristian	R-R	6-1	170	3-26-97	0	0	2.70	4	2	0	0	17	11	7	5	0	9	24	.183	.243	.087	12.96	4.86
Johnson, Reggie	R-R	6-4	205	10-28-93	5	0	1.69	12	0	0	1	21	11	4	4	1	4	28	.151	.231	.106	11.81	1.69
Keuchel, Dallas	L-L	6-3	205	1-1-88	1	0	1.80	1	1	0	0	5	3	1	1	0	0	5	.167	.167	.167	9.00	0.00
Martin, Corbin	R-R	6-2	200	12-28-95	0	1	2.60	8	3	0	1	28	20	11	8	1	8	38	.202	.140	.250	12.36	2.60
Martin, Hunter	R-R	6-1	195	12-14-94	2	1	3.86	12	3	0	1	33	37	16	14	0	10	26	.285	.196	.351	7.16	2.76
McKee, Colin	R-R	6-3	225	6-21-94	2	4	3.51	17	0	0	4	41	19	20	16	2	33	53	.137	.100	.152	11.63	7.24
Mushinski, Parker	L-L	6-0	225	11-22-95	3	1	3.60	13	3	0	0	30	22	14	12	1	19	40	.212	.206	.214	12.00	5.70
Ramirez, Luis	L-L	5-10	160	11-27-95	1	3	2.91	16	0	0	4	22	16	7	7	0	13	18	.208	.259	.180	7.48	5.40
Robles, Juan	R-R	6-0	185	11-6-97	1	2	4.64	12	6	0	0	43	44	26	22	3	22	46	.267	.284	.253	9.70	4.64

Rodriguez, Leovanny	R-R	6-0	160	6-13-96	1	0	3.63	6	4	0	0	22	23	10	9	1	6	25	.264	.290	.245	10.07	2.42
Rosado, Cesar	R-R	6-1	172	6-22-96	1	0	0.00	2	2	0	0	10	2	0	0	0	1	13	.063	.167	.039	11.70	0.90
Ruppenthal, Matt	R-R	6-4	225	10-21-95	2	1	3.04	8	7	0	0	24	25	8	8	1	8	29	.281	.200	.364	11.03	3.04
Sandoval, Patrick	L-L	6-3	190	10-18-96	1	1	3.79	4	4	0	0	19	19	8	8	0	6	28	.257	.344	.191	13.26	2.84
Scheetz, Kit	L-L	5-10	185	5-18-94	0	3	2.91	6	4	0	2	22	21	8	7	0	6	24	.253	.208	.271	9.97	2.49
Smith, Ben	L-L	6-2	195	1-20-93	7	5	6.37	21	0	0	0	30	23	22	21	2	24	42	.213	.263	.186	12.74	7.28
Tejada, Felipe	R-R	6-1	190	2-27-98	0	0	0.00	1	0	0	0	1	1	0	0	0	2	2	.333	—	.333	27.00	27.00
Thompson, Nathan	L-L	6-1	170	11-14-93	0	0	1.41	10	1	0	1	32	24	5	5	1	21	43	.214	.262	.186	12.09	5.91

Fielding

C: Bracamonte 12, Canelon 16, Castro 1, Papierski 35, Toro-Hernandez 6, Vasquez 6. **1B:** Adams 42, De La Cruz 3, MacDonald 16, Matijevic 1, Shaver 17, Sieber 1. **2B:** Davis 51, Mauricio 1, Sierra 15, Trompiz 13. **3B:** Arauz 5, MacDonald 1, Mauricio 1, Shaver 2, Toro-Hernandez 25, Tovalin 35, Trompiz 8. **SS:** Arauz 28, Sierra 43, Trompiz 5. **OF:** De La Cruz 37, Fernandez 4, Julks 31, Mathis 3, Matijevic 44, Meyers 42, Payano 19, Pineda 49, Sanchez 1.
Greeneville Astros Rookie

HOUSTON ASTROS

GREENEVILLE ASTROS — ROOKIE

APPALACHIAN LEAGUE

Batting	B-T	HT	WT	DOB	AVG	vLH	vRH	G	AB	R	H	2B	3B	HR	RBI	BB	HBP	SH	SF	SO	SB	CS	SLG	OBP
Amador, Wilson	R-R	6-1	160	12-14-96	.270	.263	.272	52	174	26	47	8	2	1	20	8	2	1	1	43	20	6	.356	.308
Beltre, Reiny	R-R	6-0	180	7-16-96	.208	.292	.188	36	120	9	25	3	0	1	7	11	3	1	1	19	0	0	.258	.289
Benjamin, Jose	R-R	6-2	170	12-16-95	.230	.167	.244	29	100	13	23	2	2	0	10	3	1	2	2	15	1	0	.290	.255
Bohanek, Cody	R-R	6-1	195	7-2-95	.239	.111	.276	47	163	28	39	7	0	3	16	16	15	1	2	40	4	3	.337	.357
Campos, Oscar	R-R	5-10	170	12-8-96	.209	.154	.226	31	110	9	23	6	0	1	10	4	0	2	2	9	1	1	.291	.233
Castro, Ruben	L-R	5-10	182	7-10-96	.276	.133	.312	21	76	11	21	2	1	1	16	6	2	1	0	11	1	2	.368	.345
Celestino, Gilberto	R-L	6-0	170	2-13-99	.268	.231	.279	59	235	38	63	10	2	4	24	22	1	1	2	59	10	2	.379	.331
Fernandez, Frankeny	R-R	6-1	170	12-7-96	.240	.229	.244	46	154	25	37	7	0	1	21	21	2	0	1	34	4	4	.305	.337
Figueroa, Martin	R-B	5-11	200	12-14-95	.273	.563	.180	21	66	7	18	2	0	1	6	12	1	0	0	12	0	1	.349	.392
Garcia, Roman	R-R	6-1	210	11-22-95	.278	.313	.270	48	173	28	48	8	1	7	29	14	4	1	2	48	1	3	.457	.342
Machado, Carlos	R-R	6-2	170	6-5-98	.345	.400	.333	8	29	3	10	2	0	0	3	1	1	0	0	5	1	0	.414	.387
Mathis, Patrick	L-L	6-1	190	3-23-96	.238	.233	.240	46	164	25	39	7	0	3	19	18	3	0	2	53	2	2	.335	.321
Mauricio, Joan	L-R	5-11	160	10-22-96	.182	.040	.215	45	132	16	24	0	0	1	16	23	1	3	1	28	0	4	.205	.306
McCormick, Chas	R-L	6-0	190	4-19-95	.500	.200	.560	8	30	7	15	3	0	0	4	4	0	0	0	2	4	1	.600	.559
Mota, Vicente	R-R	6-3	195	6-8-94	.250	.333	.222	3	12	3	3	1	0	0	1	2	0	0	0	4	0	1	.333	.357
Pineda, Juan	R-R	5-10	145	1-31-98	.286	.167	.318	14	56	10	16	1	0	1	8	3	2	1	0	9	1	1	.357	.344
Russell, Reid	R-R	6-3	223	8-22-95	.137	.143	.135	18	51	4	7	2	0	0	4	8	4	0	0	23	0	0	.177	.302
Shaver, Colton	R-R	6-1	210	9-18-95	.250	.286	.238	17	56	16	14	1	0	6	15	12	3	0	1	20	0	0	.589	.403
Tovalin, Adrian	R-R	6-2	222	2-11-96	.262	.167	.283	18	65	11	17	1	0	4	11	8	0	0	0	15	0	0	.462	.343
Valdez, Enmanuel	L-R	5-9	171	12-28-98	.083	.000	.143	3	12	2	1	0	0	0	0	3	0	0	0	5	0	0	.083	.267
Westmoreland, Brody	R-R	6-3	185	8-22-95	.231	.245	.226	55	199	31	46	10	0	8	33	22	3	0	3	70	1	0	.402	.313

Pitching	B-T	HT	WT	DOB	W	L	ERA	G	GS	CG	SV	IP	H	R	ER	HR	BB	SO	AVG	vLH	vRH	K/9	BB/9
Abreu, Bryan	R-R	6-1	175	4-22-97	1	3	7.98	8	6	0	0	29	29	27	26	4	21	40	.259	.324	.227	12.27	6.44
Acosta, Yhoan	L-L	6-1	175	6-17-95	0	2	6.23	4	4	0	0	9	8	6	6	2	2	9	.235	.111	.280	9.35	2.08
Aquino, Dariel	R-R	6-1	190	1-30-96	2	1	4.63	15	0	0	0	23	18	13	12	1	17	29	.209	.242	.189	11.19	6.56
Arias, Johsson	R-R	6-1	178	4-3-94	1	3	7.98	8	0	0	0	15	21	14	13	0	8	20	.356	.444	.281	12.27	4.91
Balaguer, Jesus	R-R	6-4	195	8-12-93	0	0	0.00	3	0	0	1	7	3	0	0	0	2	14	.130	.200	.077	18.00	2.57
Bleday, Adam	L-L	5-11	175	11-2-94	1	1	3.03	9	2	0	1	30	27	12	10	1	10	35	.246	.231	.250	10.62	3.03
Bojorquez, Gerardo	R-R	6-3	195	10-23-97	3	3	4.92	13	7	0	0	53	55	35	29	7	21	42	.266	.250	.277	7.13	3.57
Caraballo, Jheyson	R-R	6-0	170	10-16-95	1	2	3.52	11	4	0	2	38	43	21	15	4	15	28	.277	.224	.318	6.57	3.52
Castellanos, Humberto	R-R	5-11	170	4-3-98	4	1	2.29	10	3	0	1	39	35	13	10	2	9	34	.233	.207	.250	7.78	2.06
Collado, Willy	R-R	6-2	165	3-30-98	2	1	6.94	16	0	0	2	23	28	18	18	0	10	30	.315	.237	.373	11.57	3.86
Corniel, Juan	R-R	6-2	175	1-2-96	1	1	3.00	6	0	0	1	9	9	3	3	0	3	6	.257	.235	.278	6.00	3.00
Donato, Chad	R-R	6-0	180	6-3-95	1	1	4.02	4	4	0	0	16	14	9	7	1	7	24	.222	.304	.175	13.79	4.02
Hardman, Ian	R-R	6-5	240	9-16-95	2	0	2.82	15	0	0	2	22	22	11	7	0	19	26	.256	.177	.308	10.48	7.66
Hardy, Tim	L-L	6-7	250	3-1-96	1	3	4.19	13	2	0	2	34	34	18	16	2	15	32	.262	.375	.225	8.39	3.93
Kerns, Austin	L-L	6-2	215	3-5-95	0	0	14.63	6	1	0	0	8	16	15	13	1	3	3	.390	.182	.467	3.38	3.38
Navas, Javier	L-L	5-11	165	2-3-98	0	0	3.00	1	0	0	0	3	2	2	1	1	1	2	.200	1.000	.111	6.00	3.00
Paulino, Hansel	R-R	6-2	170	1-3-96	4	3	3.48	13	10	0	0	54	53	27	21	5	15	54	.251	.309	.202	8.94	2.48
Pinto, Noel	L-L	6-2	220	12-26-95	0	1	5.00	7	3	0	0	9	9	6	5	0	6	11	.257	.091	.333	11.00	6.00
Robles, Juan	R-R	6-0	185	11-6-97	1	0	5.19	2	1	0	0	9	10	5	5	0	2	15	.286	.308	.273	15.58	2.08
Rodriguez, Leovanny	R-R	6-0	160	6-13-96	3	0	2.50	8	6	0	0	36	35	11	10	3	6	34	.252	.264	.239	8.50	1.50
Sepulveda, Maikel	L-L	6-1	165	12-31-96	0	2	6.23	4	2	0	0	13	17	10	9	1	7	11	.315	.417	.286	7.62	4.85
Solis, Jairo	R-R	6-2	160	12-22-99	1	1	1.93	4	2	0	0	14	12	4	3	0	6	17	.226	.400	.121	10.93	3.86
Tejada, Felipe	R-R	6-1	190	2-27-98	0	1	3.33	7	5	0	1	24	24	12	9	0	10	21	.245	.174	.308	7.77	3.70
Villegas, Francisco	L-L	6-2	175	8-31-97	2	1	2.66	9	3	0	0	24	21	13	7	3	8	22	.239	.120	.286	8.37	3.04
Watts, Cole	R-L	6-4	205	11-2-95	2	3	6.68	12	2	0	0	31	38	30	23	3	16	35	.299	.194	.341	10.16	4.65

Fielding

C: Campos 30, Castro 19, Figueroa 21. **1B:** Benjamin 14, Celestino 1, Garcia 35, Mota 2, Russell 7, Shaver 4, Tovalin 5, Westmoreland 2. **2B:** Beltre 27, Bohanek 16, Fernandez 6, Mauricio 17, Pineda 1, Valdez 3. **3B:** Beltre 8, Garcia 2, Mauricio 4, Tovalin 8, Westmoreland 47. **SS:** Bohanek 31, Mauricio 25, Pineda 13. **OF:** Amador 49, Benjamin 13, Celestino 53, Fernandez 36, Machado 7, Mathis 41, McCormick 8, Shaver 1.

GCL ASTROS

ROOKIE

GULF COAST LEAGUE

Batting	B-T	HT	WT	DOB	AVG	vLH	vRH	G	AB	R	H	2B	3B	HR	RBI	BB	HBP	SH	SF	SO	SB	CS	SLG	OBP
Angarita, Alfredo	B-R	5-10	155	11-16-96	.273	.333	.254	32	88	16	24	4	0	0	8	10	0	0	0	20	6	1	.318	.347
Benjamin, Jose	R-R	6-2	170	12-16-95	.377	.364	.383	19	69	17	26	3	5	3	17	3	3	0	2	13	5	1	.696	.416
Bernal, Ihan	L-R	6-1	195	10-20-96	.077	.143	.053	16	26	2	2	1	0	0	2	6	1	1	0	15	0	0	.115	.273
Carrillo, Jose	R-R	6-0	178	1-24-98	.133	.200	.100	8	15	0	2	0	0	0	1	1	0	0	0	2	0	0	.133	.188
Cortez, Cesar	R-R	6-0	165	4-1-99	.214	.214	.214	29	98	11	21	4	0	1	13	11	0	2	1	24	3	2	.286	.291
de Oleo, Eduardo	R-R	5-10	180	1-25-93	.143	.333	.000	4	14	1	2	0	0	1	3	0	0	0	0	4	0	0	.357	.143
Diaz, Carlos	L-L	6-2	175	7-15-99	.194	.059	.240	19	67	8	13	0	1	1	3	3	0	0	0	19	1	0	.269	.229
Franco, Wander	B-R	6-1	189	10-11-96	.326	.300	.333	12	46	9	15	5	0	3	11	6	0	0	1	12	1	0	.630	.396
Heras, Bernardo	B-R	6-0	180	11-3-95	.310	.417	.267	19	42	8	13	3	0	0	7	3	1	1	0	4	0	1	.381	.370
Machado, Carlos	R-R	6-2	170	6-5-98	.319	.286	.330	33	116	18	37	4	4	2	14	10	4	0	2	17	5	2	.474	.386
Marquez, Orlando	R-R	5-10	180	3-12-96	.268	.409	.204	28	71	7	19	5	0	1	8	6	3	0	1	10	0	0	.380	.346
Martinez, Hector	R-R	6-1	185	7-6-98	.269	.242	.277	43	134	21	36	5	0	2	16	21	7	0	1	47	3	1	.351	.393
Matute, Jonathan	R-R	6-0	170	4-28-97	.252	.207	.269	40	107	19	27	4	1	1	6	28	3	1	1	26	4	1	.336	.417
Muriel, Nestor	R-R	6-2	170	6-11-98	.143	.000	.200	2	7	0	1	0	0	0	0	1	1	0	0	5	0	0	.143	.333
Perry, Nathan	L-R	6-2	195	7-7-99	.229	.000	.262	27	70	4	16	3	0	2	11	10	1	0	2	14	0	0	.357	.325
Pineda, Juan	R-R	5-10	145	1-31-98	.261	.268	.258	36	134	12	35	8	3	2	20	3	4	0	3	19	2	1	.410	.292
Rafael, Ronny	R-R	6-2	185	10-14-97	.125	.188	.107	28	72	6	9	2	1	1	9	12	1	0	2	32	0	0	.222	.253
Rodriguez, Ramiro	L-L	5-10	145	2-2-98	.300	.333	.286	9	30	4	9	3	0	0	1	3	1	0	0	5	0	0	.400	.382
Sanchez, Vicente	L-R	5-11	170	10-4-96	.169	.158	.173	22	71	9	12	3	1	1	5	7	0	0	1	23	1	0	.282	.241
Sanchez-Galan, Ozziel	R-R	5-11	160	10-30-97	.275	.306	.260	35	109	18	30	9	1	1	10	14	4	1	0	27	2	2	.404	.378
Santana, Andres	R-R	6-1	180	11-5-98	.164	.118	.179	25	73	3	12	2	0	0	6	1	1	0	0	19	0	0	.192	.187
Slenker, Richard	R-R	5-11	200	12-22-94	.273	.400	.235	9	22	4	6	2	0	2	4	5	1	0	0	3	0	1	.636	.429
Tanielu, Nick	R-R	5-11	215	9-4-92	.400	—	.400	2	5	0	2	1	0	0	1	0	1	0	0	0	0	0	.600	.500
Tejeda, Angel	L-L	6-0	168	1-22-97	.200	.250	.186	17	55	10	11	1	1	0	4	4	1	0	1	14	1	1	.255	.262
Valdez, Enmanuel	L-R	5-9	171	12-28-98	.228	.146	.260	42	145	23	33	10	3	4	15	20	2	0	2	31	4	2	.421	.325
Woodward, Trent	B-R	6-2	215	2-4-92	.083	.000	.091	4	12	0	1	0	0	0	1	3	0	0	0	2	0	0	.083	.267

Pitching	B-T	HT	WT	DOB	W	L	ERA	G	GS	CG	SV	IP	H	R	ER	HR	BB	SO	AVG	vLH	vRH	K/9	BB/9
Arias, Johsson	R-R	6-1	178	4-3-94	0	1	7.36	5	0	0	0	11	17	10	9	1	5	9	.354	.375	.344	7.36	4.09
Bielak, Brandon	L-R	6-1	210	4-2-96	1	0	0.00	2	0	0	0	4	3	0	0	0	1	5	.188	.250	.167	10.38	2.08
Bukauskas, J.B.	R-R	6-0	196	10-11-96	0	0	0.00	1	1	0	0	4	3	0	0	0	1	3	.231	.000	.333	6.75	2.25
Caraballo, Jheyson	R-R	6-0	170	10-16-95	0	0	5.19	3	2	0	0	9	11	7	5	1	3	9	.290	.200	.348	9.35	3.12
Castellanos, Humberto	R-R	5-11	170	4-3-98	1	0	6.00	1	0	0	0	3	5	4	2	0	0	4	.455	1.000	.250	12.00	0.00
Corniel, Juan	R-R	6-2	175	1-2-96	2	0	3.00	5	1	0	0	15	10	5	5	2	7	20	.196	.182	.207	12.00	4.20
Donato, Chad	R-R	6-0	180	6-3-95	2	1	1.62	6	4	0	0	17	16	6	3	1	6	20	.250	.217	.268	10.80	3.24
Duncan, Tanner	R-R	6-2	205	8-12-94	1	2	2.17	11	6	0	1	37	26	12	9	1	8	31	.194	.177	.205	7.47	1.93
Feldmann, Brendan	R-R	6-4	205	4-7-94	2	1	0.54	12	0	0	2	17	10	3	1	0	1	21	.156	.150	.159	11.34	0.54
Garcia, Freylin	R-R	6-3	170	12-6-97	0	3	5.79	3	2	0	0	14	19	9	9	0	6	11	.322	.222	.366	7.07	3.86
Gonzalez, Diosward	R-R	6-0	180	7-7-95	2	2	2.61	7	1	0	0	21	12	8	6	0	17	25	.162	.000	.207	10.89	7.40
Guerrero, Fredis	R-R	6-3	175	2-16-96	1	0	1.80	3	3	0	0	15	16	5	3	0	4	13	.291	.294	.290	7.80	2.40
Heredia, Angel	R-R	5-9	170	7-22-92	0	0	0.00	3	1	0	0	3	2	0	0	0	1	3	.200	.250	.167	8.10	2.70
Hernandez, Elieser	R-R	6-0	210	5-3-95	1	0	1.80	3	2	0	0	10	6	2	2	0	1	14	.177	.250	.136	12.60	0.90
Ivey, Tyler	R-R	6-4	195	5-12-96	0	0	0.00	1	1	0	0	2	1	0	0	0	2	3	.167	.000	.333	13.50	9.00
Kerns, Austin	L-L	6-2	215	3-5-95	1	0	2.57	9	0	0	0	14	15	5	4	0	5	9	.289	.154	.333	5.79	3.21
Lopez, Juan Pablo	L-L	6-4	170	2-17-99	0	3	6.16	11	9	0	0	31	43	27	21	2	16	19	.316	.333	.313	5.58	4.70
Marrero, Ronaldo	R-R	6-0	160	2-7-96	0	0	6.43	4	1	0	0	7	11	7	5	1	5	6	.367	.385	.353	7.71	6.43
Martin, Corbin	R-R	6-2	200	12-28-95	0	0	0.00	2	1	0	0	5	0	0	0	0	1	5	.000	.000	.000	9.00	1.80
Martinez, Saul	R-R	6-2	185	6-21-95	1	1	3.72	12	0	0	1	19	18	9	8	1	7	13	.250	.238	.255	6.05	3.26
Merrill, Matthew	R-R	6-4	202	6-11-98	1	1	11.57	6	2	0	0	9	16	14	12	1	7	6	.381	.364	.387	5.79	6.75
Navas, Javier	L-L	5-11	165	2-3-98	1	3	4.20	11	4	0	0	30	30	22	14	2	24	24	.250	.194	.270	7.20	7.20
Nunez, Chauncey	R-R	5-10	185	12-10-98	0	1	8.49	11	0	0	0	12	17	15	11	2	11	10	.340	.286	.361	7.71	8.49
Pimentel, Carlos	R-R	6-3	225	4-11-94	1	2	4.66	14	0	0	3	19	18	12	10	2	6	21	.243	.200	.259	9.78	2.79
Raftery, Devin	R-R	5-10	205	9-21-92	2	0	1.15	10	0	0	2	16	8	6	2	0	6	21	.143	.158	.135	12.06	3.45
Ramirez, Luis	L-L	5-10	160	11-27-95	0	0	36.00	1	0	0	0	1	4	4	4	0	1	0	.571	.667	.500	0.00	9.00
Rodriguez, Nivaldo	R-R	6-1	170	4-16-97	1	2	3.48	9	3	0	0	31	32	15	12	1	11	34	.267	.161	.303	9.87	3.19
Scheetz, Kit	L-L	5-10	185	5-18-94	0	0	0.00	2	0	0	0	6	4	0	0	0	0	13	.191	.000	.211	18.47	0.00
Sepulveda, Maikel	L-L	6-1	165	12-31-96	4	3	2.34	9	4	0	1	35	30	15	9	2	12	21	.227	.205	.237	5.45	3.12
Serrano, Kyle	R-R	6-1	190	7-6-95	0	1	13.50	1	1	0	0	1	0	4	1	0	4	2	.000	.000	—	27.00	54.00
Solis, Jairo	R-R	6-2	160	12-22-99	1	0	3.00	5	4	0	0	21	19	13	7	1	7	24	.229	.300	.189	10.29	3.00
Solomon, Peter	R-R	6-4	201	8-16-96	0	0	0.00	1	1	0	0	1	0	0	0	0	0	0	.000	.000	.000	0.00	0.00
Villegas, Francisco	L-L	6-2	175	8-31-97	1	0	1.29	2	0	0	1	7	3	1	1	0	0	9	.125	.250	.100	11.57	0.00

Fielding

C: Bernal 14, Carrillo 7, de Oleo 2, Heras 19, Marquez 27, Matute 2, Perry 12, Woodward 2. **1B:** Benjamin 16, Bernal 3, Carrillo 1, Franco 1, Matute 19, Slenker 1, Tejeda 17. **2B:** Angarita 10, Matute 4, Pineda 4, Sanchez-Galan 5, Valdez 35. **3B:** Angarita 8, Franco 11, Matute 14, Pineda 2, Sanchez-Galan 13, Slenker 6, Valdez 5, Woodward 1. **SS:** Angarita 12, Pineda 29, Sanchez-Galan 17. **OF:** Benjamin 2, Cortez 27, Diaz 18, Machado 29, Martinez 35, Muriel 2, Rafael 21, Rodriguez 8, Sanchez 15, Santana 22.

DSL ASTROS — *ROOKIE*

DOMINICAN SUMMER LEAGUE

Batting	B-T	HT	WT	DOB	AVG	vLH	vRH	G	AB	R	H	2B	3B	HR	RBI	BB	HBP	SH	SF	SO	SB	CS	SLG	OBP
Abreu, Wilyer	L-L	6-0	180	6-24-99	.286	.355	.261	34	119	21	34	5	1	0	16	14	4	0	1	29	7	4	.345	.377
Alvarez, Jose	R-R	6-1	180	6-4-00	.204	.118	.215	51	152	27	31	2	0	0	11	25	2	3	0	34	4	6	.217	.324
Angarita, Alfredo	B-R	5-10	155	11-16-96	.200	.167	.211	9	25	7	5	2	1	0	4	8	0	0	0	6	3	1	.360	.394
Barajas, Luis	R-R	6-1	190	7-13-98	.211	.111	.220	43	109	13	23	7	0	0	13	20	1	0	1	19	1	0	.275	.336
Benavente, Brandon	B-R	5-10	200	9-3-97	.171	.071	.205	40	111	12	19	3	0	1	14	13	10	0	3	28	4	2	.225	.307
Caraballo, Samir	R-R	5-8	145	9-12-98	.194	.667	.139	41	134	22	26	0	1	0	5	16	5	2	2	22	6	5	.209	.299
Carrasco, Deury	L-R	5-9	165	9-20-99	.266	.292	.262	64	207	44	55	9	1	0	17	50	2	2	4	48	32	14	.319	.407
Carrillo, Jose	R-R	6-0	178	1-24-98	.250	.333	.232	44	152	21	38	7	0	0	21	13	5	0	2	16	2	2	.296	.326
Castillo, Gerry	R-R	5-10	170	10-3-97	.235	.208	.242	50	119	17	28	3	2	1	22	16	2	1	2	26	2	3	.319	.331
Castillo, Jeury	L-R	5-10	170	1-14-00	.136	.118	.139	51	132	15	18	4	3	1	18	22	2	2	4	44	9	2	.235	.263
Ceuta, Yorbin	B-R	6-0	165	1-14-00	.248	.296	.232	60	222	36	55	4	3	0	22	27	8	0	1	39	11	6	.293	.349
Chavez, Euclides	L-L	6-1	170	7-1-97	.210	.273	.198	48	143	19	30	5	1	0	23	17	0	0	4	43	3	3	.259	.287
Chirino, Freddy	R-R	5-10	180	12-15-99	.111	.071	.122	23	63	4	7	0	0	0	3	9	0	1	0	23	2	2	.111	.222
Coronel, Luis	B-R	5-11	150	7-11-97	.207	.219	.202	43	121	12	25	3	0	1	8	7	2	2	0	46	2	2	.256	.262
Cortez, Cesar	R-R	6-0	165	4-1-99	.227	.143	.243	12	44	11	10	0	1	1	7	8	0	1	2	9	3	0	.341	.333
Garcia, Michael	R-R	6-3	180	9-10-97	.250	.389	.222	50	108	18	27	8	1	0	10	29	9	0	1	34	6	2	.343	.442
Gonzalez, Leonardo	L-R	5-11	160	5-27-00	.226	.000	.241	59	177	24	40	4	0	0	19	31	5	1	1	53	11	8	.249	.355
Martinez, Hector	R-R	6-1	185	7-6-98	.100	.000	.120	9	30	4	3	2	0	0	3	6	1	0	0	13	1	0	.167	.270
Martis, Renaigel	L-L	6-2	170	11-26-97	.241	.269	.235	50	145	23	35	6	4	1	15	22	6	0	0	40	8	3	.359	.364
Matute, Jonathan	R-R	6-0	170	4-28-97	.083	.250	.000	3	12	0	1	0	0	0	0	1	0	0	0	6	0	0	.083	.154
Mendoza, Sean	B-R	5-8	150	6-2-00	.301	.200	.319	63	196	20	59	6	1	0	22	27	2	0	4	29	17	10	.342	.384
Moya, Kendy	B-R	5-10	150	12-14-98	.241	.254	.236	62	199	37	48	8	3	1	26	49	5	1	2	59	12	5	.327	.400
Nova, Freudis	R-R	6-1	180	1-12-00	.247	.182	.263	47	166	30	41	6	0	4	16	15	9	0	0	33	8	3	.355	.342
Perez, Kelvin	R-R	6-0	195	12-8-98	.216	.200	.218	40	102	12	22	3	0	0	13	6	3	0	0	16	0	1	.245	.279
Perfecto, Fildex	B-R	5-11	160	8-19-98	.214	.188	.218	40	126	14	27	4	2	0	12	11	4	2	1	29	7	6	.278	.296
Rafael, Ronny	R-R	6-2	185	10-14-97	.225	.250	.216	12	49	11	11	4	0	3	10	6	3	0	0	19	1	0	.490	.345
Ramirez, Yeuris	R-R	6-0	170	11-28-98	.219	.196	.228	57	178	31	39	10	1	3	29	35	18	0	1	54	4	5	.337	.397
Rodriguez, Anthony	R-R	6-2	195	7-23-96	.229	.174	.247	63	192	30	44	8	1	2	24	50	11	0	0	57	5	4	.313	.415
Rodriguez, Ramiro	L-L	5-10	145	2-2-98	.342	.455	.324	49	164	33	56	8	3	5	23	27	6	0	1	18	8	7	.518	.450
Rodriguez, Nerio	R-R	6-2	205	9-21-99	.203	.238	.189	44	153	27	31	10	0	4	23	24	1	0	5	55	1	0	.346	.306
Sanchez, Rhandall	R-R	6-1	170	11-29-98	.233	.283	.215	52	176	24	41	9	0	0	29	15	2	1	3	37	3	0	.284	.296
Sanchez-Galan, Ozziel	R-R	5-11	160	10-30-97	.208	.125	.250	7	24	5	5	0	2	0	1	2	0	0	0	8	0	0	.375	.269
Tejeda, Angel	L-L	6-0	168	1-22-97	.359	.269	.390	28	103	18	37	8	3	0	19	18	3	0	1	9	4	2	.495	.464
Urdaneta, Ronaldo	B-R	5-10	155	11-18-98	.312	.316	.310	57	199	42	62	6	4	3	27	35	3	2	1	44	27	8	.427	.420
Van Der Wijst, Marco	R-R	5-10	180	2-23-98	.273	.133	.298	35	99	11	27	6	0	2	14	23	1	0	1	20	2	3	.394	.411

Pitching	B-T	HT	WT	DOB	W	L	ERA	G	GS	CG	SV	IP	H	R	ER	HR	BB	SO	AVG	vLH	vRH	K/9	BB/9
Almonte, Gustavo	R-R	6-4	185	6-3-98	0	2	23.00	12	0	0	0	9	10	26	23	1	24	8	.294	.000	.455	8.00	24.00
Barcenas, Hecduar	R-R	6-3	185	7-21-98	2	1	11.68	9	0	0	0	12	14	16	16	1	15	16	.326	.167	.387	11.68	10.95
Bernaez, Jesus	R-R	6-0	170	5-6-97	2	6	4.70	12	6	0	0	38	33	28	20	1	32	37	.241	.294	.209	8.69	7.51
Betances, Jose	R-R	6-0	170	10-17-99	0	0	3.38	5	0	0	0	3	1	5	1	0	8	1	.125	.000	.143	3.38	27.00
Blanco, Alex	R-R	6-1	180	10-3-97	0	0	9.00	4	0	0	0	4	4	4	4	0	6	5	.235	.400	.250	11.25	13.50
Ceballos, Yeremi	L-L	6-2	165	12-21-98	1	0	6.43	3	1	0	0	7	6	6	5	0	8	8	.250	.000	.316	10.29	10.29
Chavez, Jervic	L-L	6-0	175	2-8-97	2	1	3.86	16	1	0	3	35	25	21	15	0	18	28	.198	.500	.318	7.20	4.63
De Paula, Luis	R-R	6-0	160	11-15-96	2	1	1.38	19	0	0	4	26	12	5	4	0	15	23	.148	.259	.093	7.96	5.19
Frontado, Yulian	R-R	6-2	175	12-29-97	1	3	4.00	14	1	0	1	27	23	14	12	0	15	8	.245	.267	.136	2.67	5.00
Garcia, Freylin	R-R	6-3	170	12-6-97	1	5	4.50	11	4	0	0	36	39	23	18	0	14	31	.281	.500	.000	7.75	3.50
Garcia, Luis	R-R	6-1	185	12-13-96	1	1	1.64	6	1	0	0	11	13	5	2	1	4	18	.310	.231	.345	14.73	3.27
Garcia, Ronny	R-R	6-3	170	12-2-99	0	3	9.27	20	0	0	1	22	24	27	23	0	20	23	.267	.258	.250	9.27	8.06
Gonzalez, Diosward	R-R	6-0	180	7-7-95	2	2	1.62	8	5	0	0	33	24	15	6	1	9	37	.189	.147	.204	9.99	2.43
Gonzalez, Flaer	R-R	5-10	160	9-27-96	3	1	2.81	9	3	0	0	26	20	8	8	0	14	19	.213	.200	.219	6.66	4.91
Guerrero, Fredis	R-R	6-3	175	2-16-96	3	1	2.23	10	5	0	2	40	31	11	10	1	8	36	.212	.143	.273	8.03	1.79
Hernandez, Jose Antonio	R-R	6-0	165	6-18-99	3	2	3.86	14	9	0	0	47	44	22	20	1	14	44	.249	.254	.246	8.49	2.70
Jaquez, Ernesto	R-R	6-2	190	6-11-99	0	1	1.35	5	2	0	0	13	10	7	2	1	8	16	.196	.091	.225	10.80	5.40
Javier, Christopher	R-R	6-4	170	7-16-98	2	1	2.31	15	0	0	5	23	9	8	6	0	23	17	.127	.053	.154	6.56	8.87
Lugo, Denilson	L-L	5-11	160	12-22-97	0	1	3.21	9	3	0	1	28	22	13	10	0	18	18	.214	.136	.235	5.79	5.79
Macuare, Angel	R-R	6-2	188	3-3-00	2	3	4.85	12	9	0	0	30	32	20	16	1	16	36	.271	.147	.321	10.92	4.85
Marrero, Ronaldo	R-R	6-0	160	2-7-96	2	0	1.47	4	3	0	0	18	10	5	3	1	3	13	.156	.053	.200	6.38	1.47
Matos, Angel	R-R	6-4	225	7-21-97	0	0	13.50	8	0	0	1	8	9	12	12	0	10	5	.265	.400	.208	5.63	11.25
Matos, Miguel	R-R	5-11	165	9-29-96	1	3	5.34	10	3	0	0	32	27	24	19	1	22	30	.227	.256	.213	8.44	6.19
Medina, Fredy	R-R	5-10	160	9-26-97	4	3	2.56	19	2	0	1	39	30	22	11	3	26	43	.214	.132	.245	10.01	6.05
Mejias, Christian	R-R	6-0	160	5-19-99	2	2	4.01	14	7	0	0	52	39	26	23	1	24	40	.219	.274	.190	6.97	4.18
Melendez, Cristofer	R-R	6-3	170	9-16-97	0	3	7.68	17	3	0	3	36	37	39	31	2	27	32	.259	.366	.216	7.93	6.69
Oberto, Wender	R-R	6-0	170	12-9-99	1	1	3.29	10	5	0	1	27	25	11	10	0	16	36	.234	.235	.233	11.85	5.27
Ochoa, Jonger	R-R	6-2	185	1-16-97	1	1	9.31	8	0	0	0	10	11	11	10	0	10	6	.314	.333	.304	5.59	9.31
Ortega, Angel	R-R	5-11	180	11-18-99	3	3	1.54	10	2	0	0	23	11	8	4	1	12	13	.145	.000	.167	5.01	4.63
Peralta, Kilvio	R-R	6-3	190	3-6-97	0	1	4.50	3	2	0	0	6	4	4	3	1	0	3	.167	.143	.177	4.50	0.00
Perdomo, Carlos	L-L	6-1	167	4-25-98	2	1	6.19	13	5	0	0	36	38	30	25	3	33	32	.277	.208	.292	7.93	8.17
Pujols, Antonio	L-L	6-3	195	1-27-98	4	2	1.65	14	6	0	0	55	35	13	10	2	16	49	.186	.225	.176	8.07	2.63
Quintero, Carlos	R-R	6-3	185	1-11-00	0	1	27.00	1	0	0	0	1	1	6	2	0	4	1	.250	.333	.000	13.50	54.00
Ramirez, Manny	R-R	5-11	170	11-21-99	2	1	3.44	8	1	0	0	18	14	9	7	0	12	18	.226	.300	.191	8.84	5.89

Reina, Fabricio	R-R	6-3	175	2-26-00	1	2	7.78	15	3	0	0	42	39	41	36	2	32	38	.257	.255	.278	8.21	6.91
Reyes, Jean	R-R	6-0	180	12-1-97	0	2	4.98	16	6	0	1	34	32	21	19	1	14	21	.254	.167	.298	5.50	3.67
Rivera, Jose Alberto	R-R	6-3	160	2-14-97	2	3	3.44	12	5	0	0	37	20	17	14	3	24	37	.158	.043	.225	9.08	5.89
Rodriguez, Elian	R-R	6-4	205	3-10-97	0	3	7.46	9	9	0	0	25	26	23	21	1	30	19	.313	.214	.364	6.75	10.66
Rodriguez, Nivaldo	R-R	6-1	170	4-16-97	3	0	0.35	6	4	0	1	26	17	4	1	0	6	29	.181	.177	.183	10.04	2.08
Santana, Mauricio	R-R	5-9	177	2-3-97	0	1	4.05	8	6	0	0	13	12	8	6	0	14	18	.235	.316	.188	12.15	9.45
Severino, Oscar	R-R	6-1	175	2-26-98	3	1	4.18	15	2	0	1	32	27	18	15	1	28	29	.227	.257	.214	8.07	7.79
Solano, Bryan	R-R	6-1	154	1-25-98	1	2	4.94	12	2	0	0	27	29	21	15	0	23	27	.274	.314	.254	8.89	7.57
Solis, Jairo	R-R	6-2	160	12-22-99	1	1	2.73	6	4	0	0	26	20	12	8	2	8	28	.220	.148	.250	9.57	2.73
Taveras, Diosmerky	R-R	6-3	180	9-23-99	0	0	2.35	5	0	0	1	8	7	4	2	0	6	5	.250	.125	.300	5.87	7.04
Ugarte, Renny	R-R	6-1	178	2-27-97	1	1	2.45	10	6	0	0	40	32	13	11	0	14	26	.218	.236	.207	5.80	3.12
Uribe, Asael	R-R	6-3	160	5-4-96	2	3	4.31	13	6	0	0	48	43	26	23	3	34	44	.242	.239	.236	8.25	6.38
Ventura, Nathanael	R-R	6-1	175	12-15-95	2	1	18.47	10	0	0	0	6	2	14	13	0	19	9	.105	.000	.125	12.79	27.00

Fielding

C: Alvarez 20, Barajas 13, Benavente 34, Carrillo 19, Castillo 33, Chirino 8, Perez 15, Rodriguez 19, Sanchez 16. **1B:** Alvarez 21, Barajas 12, Benavente 3, Carrillo 21, Garcia 27, Mendoza 1, Matute 1, Perez 7, Rodriguez 37, Sanchez 32, Tejeda 6. **2B:** Angarita 4, Caraballo 24, Carrasco 14, Castillo 3, Castillo 31, Ceuta 2, Matute 1, Mendoza 14, Moya 17, Ramirez 13, Sanchez-Galan 1, Urdaneta 19, Van Der Wijst 19. **3B:** Barajas 1, Caraballo 9, Carrasco 3, Carrillo 1, Castillo 17, Garcia 12, Matute 1, Mendoza 23, Moya 5, Nova 10, Ramirez 43, Rodriguez 21, Urdaneta 5, Van Der Wijst 8. **SS:** Caraballo 4, Carrasco 47, Carrillo 1, Castillo 1, Ceuta 56, Mendoza 8, Moya 3, Nova 21, Ramirez 1, Sanchez-Galan 4, Urdaneta 12. **OF:** Abreu 34, Alvarez 16, Angarita 5, Barajas 2, Caraballo 1, Carrasco 2, Castillo 1, Chavez 46, Chirino 2, Coronel 39, Cortez 12, Garcia 3, Gonzalez 57, Martinez 9, Martis 48, Mendoza 21, Moya 37, Perfecto 40, Rafael 11, Rodriguez 48, Tejeda 20, Urdaneta 23.

Kansas City Royals

SEASON IN A SENTENCE: Every good thing must come to an end.

HIGH POINT: A nine-game winning streak in a late July helped the Royals enter August only two games behind the Indians for the American League Central Division lead. After bringing in a number of reinforcements in trade, the hope was that the Royals were ready for one more postseason run led by impending free agents and past World Series heroes Mike Moustakas, Eric Hosmer and Lorenzo Cain.

LOW POINT: The Royals' pitching staff imploded in August, ending those playoff hopes. The nadir was a three-game sweep at the hands of the Indians that was punctuated by a 12-0 loss on Aug. 26, but the entire month was filled with blowouts. Royals opponents scored 10 runs or more on six different occasions.

NOTABLE ROOKIES: RHP Jakob Junis gave the Royals reliable innings as a back-of-the-rotation starter, going 9-3, 4.30. LHP Matt Strahm struggled in a relief role before heading to the disabled list with a patella tendon tear. He was eventually traded to the Padres in a midseason deal. RHP Scott Alexander went 5-4, 2.48 in a solid season as a middle reliever.

KEY TRANSACTIONS: Few of the free agent acquisitions or trades panned out for Kansas City in 2017. Free-agent outfielder Brandon Moss hit .207/.279/.428 while Jorge Soler, acquired by trading Wade Davis to Chicago, spent most of the year in Triple-A. The Royals tried to shore up a number of weaknesses through trades, but OF Melky Cabrera (.269/.303/.399), RHP Trevor Cahill (8.22 ERA), RHP Brandon Maurer (8.10) failed to provide the boost the club needed for a playoff push.

DOWN ON THE FARM: The Royals will head into 2018 looking to rebuild, but the minor league system is as thin as it has been in quite a while. SS Raul Mondesi, still only 21, did have a bounce-back season thanks to some time in Triple-A and he, Jorge Soler, Jorge Bonifacio and Whit Merrifield will have to help the team move forward in 2018 and beyond. Trades to bolster the World Series teams in 2014 and 2015 carried a long-term cost. But the team also has seen 2015 first-round pick Ashe Russell step away from the game while 2012 first-round pick Kyle Zimmer has continued to struggle to get onto the mound because of injuries.

OPENING DAY PAYROLL: $140,925,250 (15th)

PLAYERS OF THE YEAR

MAJOR LEAGUE

Eric Hosmer
1B

.318/.385/.498
25 HR, .882 OPS
4th Gold Glove

MINOR LEAGUE

Foster Griffin
LHP

(High Class A/ Double-A)
15-7, 3.35

ORGANIZATION LEADERS

BATTING — *Minimum 250 AB

MAJORS			
*	AVG	Eric Hosmer	.318
*	OPS	Eric Hosmer	.882
	HR	Mike Moustakas	38
	RBI	Eric Hosmer	94
MINORS			
*	AVG	Robby Rinn, Idaho Falls	.355
*	OBP	Robby Rinn, Idaho Falls	.429
*	SLG	Jorge Soler, Omaha	.564
*	OPS	Jorge Soler, Omaha	.952
	R	Amalani Fukofuka, Lexington, Idaho Falls	78
	H	Frank Schwindel, Northwest Arkansas, Omaha	174
	TB	Frank Schwindel, Northwest Arkansas, Omaha	286
	2B	Frank Schwindel, Northwest Arkansas, Omaha	43
	3B	Raul Mondesi, Omaha	8
		Nicky Lopez, Wilmington, Northwest Arkansas	8
		Wander Franco, Wilmington	8
	HR	Jorge Soler, Omaha	24
	RBI	Frank Schwindel, Northwest Arkansas, Omaha	97
	BB	Khalil Lee, Lexington	65
	SO	Khalil Lee, Lexington	171
	SB	Amalani Fukofuka, Lexington, Idaho Falls	33

PITCHING — #Minimum 75 IP

MAJORS			
	W	Jason Vargas	18
#	ERA	Mike Minor	2.55
	SO	Jason Hammel	145
	SV	Kelvin Herrera	26
MINORS			
	W	Foster Griffin, Wilmington, Northwest Arkansas	15
	L	Nolan Watson, AZL Royals, Burlington, Lexington	12
		Cristian Castillo, Wilmington	12
		Corey Ray, Northwest Arkansas	12
		Josh Staumont, Omaha, Northwest Arkansas	12
		Ofreidy Gomez, Lexington	12
#	ERA	Gerson Garabito, AZL Royals, Lexington	2.93
	G	Eric Stout, Omaha	45
	GS	Emilio Ogando, Wilmington, Omaha, NW Arkansas	29
		Corey Ray, Northwest Arkansas	29
	SV	Jake Newberry, Northwest Arkansas, Omaha	15
	IP	Emilio Ogando, Wilmington, Omaha, NW Arkansas	164
	BB	Josh Staumont, Omaha, Northwest Arkansas	97
	SO	Foster Griffin, Wilmington, Northwest Arkansas	141
#	AVG	Gerson Garabito, AZL Royals, Lexington	.196

KANSAS CITY ROYALS

2017 PERFORMANCE

General Manager: Dayton Moore. **Farm Director:** Ronnie Richardson. **Scouting Director:** Lonnie Goldberg.

Class	Team	League	W	L	PCT	Finish	Manager
Majors	Kansas City Royals	American	80	82	.494	t-6th (15)	Ned Yost
Triple-A	Omaha Storm Chasers	Pacific Coast	69	72	.489	t-8th (16)	Brian Poldberg
Double-A	Northwest Arkansas Naturals	Texas	67	73	.479	6th (8)	Vance Wilson
High-A	Wilmington Blue Rocks	Carolina	67	72	.482	7th (10)	Jamie Quirk
Low-A	Lexington Legends	South Atlantic	62	75	.453	12th (14)	Scott Thorman
Rookie	Burlington Royals	Appalachian	29	39	.426	9th (10)	Omar Ramirez
Rookie	Idaho Falls Chukars	Pioneer	33	43	.434	7th (8)	Justin Gemoll
Rookie	AZL Royals	Arizona	26	30	.464	t-9th (15)	Darryl Kennedy
Overall 2017 Minor League Record			353	404	.466	25th (30)	

ORGANIZATION STATISTICS

KANSAS CITY ROYALS

AMERICAN LEAGUE

Batting	B-T	HT	WT	DOB	AVG	vLH	vRH	G	AB	R	H	2B	3B	HR	RBI	BB	HBP	SH	SF	SO	SB	CS	SLG	OBP
Bonifacio, Jorge	R-R	6-1	195	6-4-93	.255	.246	.259	113	384	55	98	15	1	17	40	35	2	0	1	118	1	1	.432	.320
Burns, Billy	B-R	5-9	170	8-30-89	.167	.000	.250	7	6	1	1	0	0	0	0	0	0	0	0	1	0	1	.167	.167
Butera, Drew	R-R	6-1	200	8-9-83	.227	.208	.235	75	163	18	37	4	1	3	14	12	1	1	0	41	0	0	.319	.284
Cabrera, Melky	L-B	5-10	210	8-11-84	.269	.256	.272	58	223	24	60	13	2	4	29	11	1	0	3	22	1	2	.399	.303
2-team total (98 Chicago)					.286	.256	.272	156	620	78	177	30	2	17	85	36	2	2	6	74	1	2	.423	.324
Cain, Lorenzo	R-R	6-2	205	4-13-86	.300	.277	.306	155	584	86	175	27	5	15	49	54	5	0	2	100	26	2	.440	.363
Colon, Christian	R-R	5-10	185	5-14-89	.177	.143	.200	7	17	1	3	0	0	0	0	1	0	1	0	3	0	0	.177	.222
Cuthbert, Cheslor	R-R	6-1	190	11-16-92	.231	.216	.239	58	143	10	33	7	0	2	18	9	0	0	1	39	0	0	.322	.275
Escobar, Alcides	R-R	6-1	185	12-16-86	.250	.276	.243	162	599	71	150	36	5	6	54	15	4	7	4	102	4	7	.357	.272
Gallagher, Cam	R-R	6-3	230	12-6-92	.250	.500	.227	13	24	2	6	1	0	1	5	3	0	0	0	4	0	0	.417	.333
Gordon, Alex	L-R	6-1	220	2-10-84	.208	.202	.210	148	476	52	99	20	2	9	45	45	14	2	4	126	7	4	.315	.293
Gore, Terrance	R-R	5-7	165	6-8-91	.000	.000	.000	12	4	2	0	0	0	0	0	1	0	0	0	2	2	2	.000	.200
Hosmer, Eric	L-L	6-4	225	10-24-89	.318	.284	.335	162	603	98	192	31	1	25	94	66	0	0	2	104	6	1	.498	.385
Merrifield, Whit	R-R	6-0	195	1-24-89	.288	.273	.292	145	587	80	169	32	6	19	78	29	6	1	7	88	34	8	.460	.324
Mondesi, Raul	B-R	6-1	185	7-27-95	.170	.231	.150	25	53	4	9	1	0	1	3	3	0	4	0	22	5	2	.245	.214
Moss, Brandon	L-R	6-1	210	9-16-83	.207	.271	.192	118	362	41	75	14	0	22	50	37	0	0	2	128	2	0	.428	.279
Moustakas, Mike	R-L	6-0	215	9-11-88	.272	.270	.273	148	555	75	151	24	0	38	85	34	3	0	6	94	0	0	.521	.314
Orlando, Paulo	R-R	6-2	210	11-1-85	.198	.267	.183	39	86	9	17	3	0	2	6	1	2	0	0	20	1	1	.302	.225
Perez, Salvador	R-R	6-3	240	5-10-90	.268	.257	.272	129	471	57	126	24	1	27	80	17	5	0	5	95	1	0	.495	.297
Soler, Jorge	R-R	6-4	215	2-25-92	.144	.139	.148	35	97	7	14	5	0	2	6	12	1	0	0	36	0	0	.258	.246
Torres, Ramon	B-R	5-11	170	1-22-93	.243	.227	.250	33	74	9	18	3	0	0	4	4	1	0	0	12	1	0	.284	.291

Pitching	B-T	HT	WT	DOB	W	L	ERA	G	GS	CG	SV	IP	H	R	ER	HR	BB	SO	AVG	vLH	vRH	K/9	BB/9
Alburquerque, Al	R-R	6-0	195	6-10-86	0	1	3.60	11	0	0	0	10	7	4	4	0	6	9	.194	.154	.217	8.10	5.40
2-team total (10 Chicago)					0	2	2.50	21	0	0	0	18	10	5	5	0	8	14	.159	.154	.217	7.00	4.00
Alexander, Scott	L-L	6-2	190	7-10-89	5	4	2.48	58	0	0	4	69	62	23	19	3	28	59	.246	.250	.244	7.70	3.65
Almonte, Miguel	R-R	6-2	210	4-4-93	0	0	13.50	2	0	0	0	2	5	3	3	0	2	0	.556	.714	.000	0.00	9.00
Buchter, Ryan	L-L	6-4	258	2-13-87	1	0	2.67	29	0	0	0	27	16	10	8	3	8	18	.170	.179	.167	6.00	2.67
Cahill, Trevor	R-R	6-4	240	3-1-88	0	0	8.22	10	3	0	0	23	33	21	21	10	21	15	.344	.300	.375	5.87	8.22
Duffy, Danny	L-L	6-3	205	12-21-88	9	10	3.81	24	24	0	0	146	143	67	62	13	41	130	.257	.167	.278	8.00	2.52
Farrell, Luke	L-R	6-6	210	6-7-91	0	0	16.88	1	1	0	0	3	7	5	5	1	3	2	.467	.500	.429	6.75	10.13
Feliz, Neftali	R-R	6-3	235	5-2-88	1	0	4.74	20	0	0	0	19	17	11	10	1	8	16	.236	.290	.195	7.58	3.79
Flynn, Brian	L-L	6-7	250	4-19-90	0	0	3.86	1	0	0	0	2	3	1	1	0	0	0	.375	.400	.333	0.00	0.00
Garcia, Onelki	L-L	6-3	225	8-2-89	0	1	13.50	2	1	0	0	6	12	9	9	2	5	2	.444	.500	.435	3.00	7.50
Gaviglio, Sam	R-R	6-2	195	5-22-90	1	0	3.00	4	2	0	0	12	13	4	4	1	5	9	.271	.310	.211	6.75	3.75
2-team total (12 Seattle)					4	5	4.36	16	13	0	0	74	76	41	36	16	26	49	.271	.310	.211	5.93	3.15
Hammel, Jason	R-R	6-6	225	9-2-82	8	13	5.29	32	32	0	0	180	209	109	106	26	48	145	.284	.281	.287	7.24	2.40
Herrera, Kelvin	R-R	5-10	200	12-31-89	3	3	4.25	64	0	0	26	59	60	33	28	9	20	56	.255	.282	.229	8.49	3.03
Junis, Jakob	R-R	6-2	225	9-16-92	9	3	4.30	20	16	0	0	98	101	52	47	15	25	80	.264	.278	.250	7.32	2.29
Karns, Nate	R-R	6-3	225	11-25-87	2	2	4.17	9	8	0	0	45	41	21	21	9	13	51	.237	.250	.229	10.13	2.58
Kennedy, Ian	R-R	6-0	200	12-19-84	5	13	5.38	30	30	0	0	154	143	99	92	34	61	131	.246	.236	.254	7.66	3.56
Machado, Andres	R-R	6-0	175	4-22-93	0	0	22.09	2	0	0	0	4	10	9	9	2	3	1	.476	.333	.583	2.45	7.36
Maness, Seth	R-R	6-0	190	10-14-88	1	0	3.72	8	0	0	0	10	16	5	4	3	2	4	.381	.333	.417	3.72	1.86
Maurer, Brandon	R-R	6-5	230	7-3-90	2	2	8.10	26	0	0	2	20	34	18	18	4	11	21	.366	.350	.377	9.45	4.95
McCarthy, Kevin	R-R	6-3	200	2-22-92	1	0	3.20	33	0	0	0	45	50	23	16	4	13	27	.276	.314	.252	5.40	2.60
Minor, Mike	L-R	6-4	210	12-26-87	6	6	2.55	65	0	0	6	78	57	23	22	5	22	88	.204	.163	.223	10.20	2.55
Morin, Mike	R-R	6-4	220	5-3-91	0	0	7.94	6	0	0	0	6	8	5	5	0	3	6	.333	.500	.214	9.53	4.76
2-team total (10 Los Angeles)					0	0	7.20	16	0	0	0	20	29	16	16	3	5	16	.345	.407	.303	7.20	2.25
Moylan, Peter	R-R	6-2	225	12-2-78	0	0	3.49	79	0	0	0	59	40	26	23	4	25	46	.189	.316	.161	6.98	3.79
Skoglund, Eric	L-L	6-7	200	10-26-92	1	2	9.50	7	5	0	0	18	30	20	19	2	12	14	.375	.444	.366	7.00	6.00
Soria, Joakim	R-R	6-3	200	5-18-84	4	3	3.70	59	0	0	1	56	49	24	23	1	20	64	.233	.269	.205	10.29	3.21
Strahm, Matt	R-L	6-3	185	11-12-91	2	5	5.45	24	3	0	0	35	30	22	21	6	22	37	.236	.233	.237	9.61	5.71
Vargas, Jason	L-L	6-0	215	2-2-83	18	11	4.16	32	32	1	0	180	181	84	83	27	58	134	.264	.311	.253	6.71	2.91

Wood, Travis	R-L	5-11	175	2-6-87	1	3	6.91	28	3	0	0	42	56	33	32	4	20	29	.329	.250	.357	6.26	4.32
Young, Chris	R-R	6-10	255	5-25-79	0	0	7.50	14	2	0	0	30	47	27	25	7	14	22	.353	.383	.329	6.60	4.20

Fielding

Catcher	PCT	G	PO	A	E	DP	PB
Butera	.995	74	397	18	2	2	7
Gallagher	1.000	13	51	1	0	0	1
Perez	.994	115	784	46	5	3	3

First Base	PCT	G	PO	A	E	DP
Butera	1.000	4	13	1	0	1
Cuthbert	.952	6	19	1	1	2
Hosmer	.997	157	1235	75	4	124
Merrifield	1.000	1	3	0	0	0
Moss	1.000	14	62	2	0	9

Second Base	PCT	G	PO	A	E	DP
Colon	1.000	6	11	17	0	6
Cuthbert	1.000	3	4	1	0	1
Merrifield	.981	132	232	341	11	93
Mondesi	1.000	14	24	30	0	12
Torres	1.000	20	19	32	0	5

Third Base	PCT	G	PO	A	E	DP
Cuthbert	.945	44	21	65	5	6
Merrifield	1.000	1	0	1	0	0
Moustakas	.962	127	74	226	12	17
Torres	1.000	12	4	13	0	1

Shortstop	PCT	G	PO	A	E	DP
Escobar	.978	162	202	468	15	97
Mondesi	.941	9	7	9	1	1
Torres	1.000	3	1	6	0	1

Outfield	PCT	G	PO	A	E	DP
Bonifacio	.978	102	173	4	4	1
Burns	1.000	5	2	0	0	0
Cabrera	1.000	54	87	3	0	0
Cain	.984	151	430	6	7	3
Gordon	.993	147	276	8	2	0
Gore	1.000	2	2	0	0	0
Merrifield	.960	16	23	1	1	0
Moss	1.000	7	5	0	0	0
Orlando	1.000	38	49	1	0	0
Soler	1.000	22	36	1	0	0

OMAHA STORM CHASERS — *TRIPLE-A*

PACIFIC COAST LEAGUE

Batting	B-T	HT	WT	DOB	AVG	vLH	vRH	G	AB	R	H	2B	3B	HR	RBI	BB	HBP	SH	SF	SO	SB	CS	SLG	OBP
Anna, Dean	L-R	5-11	180	11-24-86	.285	.297	.283	112	386	53	110	14	3	5	33	43	5	5	0	51	6	4	.376	.364
Bonifacio, Jorge	R-R	6-1	195	6-4-93	.314	.400	.304	13	51	6	16	2	2	3	12	6	0	0	0	8	0	0	.608	.386
Burns, Billy	B-R	5-9	170	8-30-89	.285	.185	.308	99	354	50	101	7	4	0	22	44	4	9	2	60	24	11	.328	.369
Cecchini, Garin	L-R	6-3	220	4-20-91	.266	.279	.263	89	290	35	77	21	2	4	33	12	2	3	3	59	3	3	.393	.296
Cuthbert, Cheslor	R-R	6-1	190	11-16-92	.271	.250	.277	15	59	10	16	3	1	4	9	7	1	0	1	11	0	0	.559	.353
Diaz, Carlos	R-R	5-8	145	11-15-92	.286	1.000	.167	4	7	0	2	0	0	0	1	0	0	0	1	0	0	1	.286	.250
Dozier, Hunter	R-R	6-4	220	8-22-91	.226	.200	.230	24	84	11	19	6	1	4	12	9	2	0	1	37	1	1	.464	.313
Esposito, Nathan	R-R	5-11	180	6-25-93	.167	.000	.182	4	12	0	2	0	0	0	0	0	0	1	0	4	0	0	.167	.167
Gallagher, Cam	R-R	6-3	230	12-6-92	.292	.388	.270	73	260	26	76	13	0	5	37	18	0	2	2	33	0	1	.400	.336
Gore, Terrance	R-R	5-7	165	6-8-91	.247	.200	.260	65	166	29	41	3	3	1	10	16	3	5	2	38	13	3	.319	.321
Lopez, Jack	R-R	5-9	165	12-16-92	.145	.200	.128	18	62	2	9	2	0	0	1	4	0	1	0	18	1	1	.177	.197
McCray, Jonathan	B-R	5-10	180	1-8-95	.143	—	.143	2	7	0	1	0	0	0	0	0	0	0	0	1	0	0	.143	.143
Merrifield, Whit	R-R	6-0	195	1-24-89	.412	.300	.458	9	34	6	14	4	0	3	9	1	1	0	1	4	1	1	.794	.432
Mondesi, Raul	B-R	6-1	185	7-27-95	.305	.320	.301	85	321	52	98	20	8	13	52	18	2	10	6	86	21	3	.539	.340
Moon, Logan	R-R	6-2	195	2-15-92	.336	.450	.310	29	107	18	36	8	1	4	15	6	0	2	1	30	2	1	.542	.368
Morin, Parker	L-R	5-11	195	7-2-91	.167	.231	.153	23	72	4	12	3	0	1	10	1	1	0	1	15	0	0	.250	.187
O'Brien, Peter	R-R	6-4	235	7-15-90	.162	.118	.171	27	105	10	17	1	1	3	6	9	1	0	0	31	0	0	.276	.235
2-team total (13 Round Rock)					.170	.118	.170	40	153	16	26	2	1	5	13	15	1	0	1	50	0	0	.294	.247
O'Hearn, Ryan	L-L	6-3	200	7-26-93	.252	.275	.247	114	413	48	104	26	1	18	53	45	1	2	2	119	1	0	.450	.325
Orlando, Paulo	R-R	6-2	210	11-1-85	.293	.278	.296	30	116	14	34	10	0	2	19	9	3	0	1	26	2	2	.431	.357
Pena, Brayan	B-R	5-9	240	1-7-82	.274	.346	.255	38	124	8	34	3	0	0	15	6	1	1	2	7	1	0	.298	.308
Schwindel, Frank	R-R	6-1	205	6-29-92	.321	.292	.328	99	392	51	126	30	0	17	72	10	2	0	2	68	0	1	.528	.340
Soler, Jorge	R-R	6-4	215	2-25-92	.267	.426	.235	74	273	49	73	9	0	24	59	50	4	0	0	82	1	0	.564	.388
Sosa, Ruben	B-R	5-7	170	9-23-90	.222	.250	.211	43	153	20	34	8	1	2	13	16	0	3	2	32	11	2	.327	.292
Starling, Bubba	R-R	6-4	210	8-3-92	.248	.123	.286	80	278	35	69	14	1	7	21	19	3	3	0	65	5	4	.381	.303
Torres, Ramon	B-R	5-11	170	1-22-93	.292	.230	.308	75	295	43	86	10	1	6	41	15	1	3	3	32	17	4	.393	.325
Toups, Corey	R-R	5-10	170	2-12-93	.232	.191	.243	88	289	46	67	12	4	6	28	34	6	0	3	90	9	2	.363	.322
Villegas, Luis	R-R	5-10	170	12-2-92	.238	.167	.250	13	42	2	10	0	0	0	2	1	1	1	0	11	0	0	.238	.273
Walters, Zach	B-R	6-2	210	9-5-89	—	—	—	1	0	0	0	0	0	0	0	0	0	0	0	0	0	0	—	—

Pitching	B-T	HT	WT	DOB	W	L	ERA	G	GS	CG	SV	IP	H	R	ER	HR	BB	SO	AVG	vLH	vRH	K/9	BB/9
Alburquerque, Al	R-R	6-0	195	6-10-86	2	1	2.08	22	0	0	3	26	21	11	6	0	5	28	.212	.229	.203	9.69	1.73
Alexander, Scott	L-L	6-2	190	7-10-89	1	0	4.70	7	0	0	0	8	9	4	4	1	3	4	.290	.300	.286	4.70	3.52
Almonte, Miguel	R-R	6-2	210	4-4-93	0	1	1.50	9	3	0	0	18	20	3	3	1	7	17	.299	.333	.275	8.50	3.50
Binford, Christian	R-R	6-6	215	12-20-92	7	10	7.24	22	19	0	0	116	157	96	93	25	39	94	.323	.305	.335	7.31	3.03
Camp, Justin	R-R	5-11	230	5-17-93	0	0	67.50	1	0	0	0	1	3	5	5	0	4	1	.600	.500	.667	13.50	54.00
Caramo, Yender	R-R	6-0	175	8-25-91	3	7	5.04	25	12	0	2	84	107	54	47	12	12	32	.307	.326	.295	3.43	1.29
Culver, Malcom	R-R	6-1	205	2-9-90	1	2	4.10	32	0	0	9	37	40	17	17	1	19	34	.278	.404	.207	8.20	4.58
Duffy, Danny	L-L	6-3	205	12-21-88	0	1	3.68	2	2	0	0	7	6	3	3	1	1	8	.214	.000	.261	9.82	1.23
Dziedzic, Jonathan	R-L	6-1	190	2-4-91	3	3	4.73	9	9	0	0	46	45	24	24	8	15	38	.254	.298	.239	7.49	2.96
Edwards, Andrew	R-R	6-6	265	10-7-91	0	1	40.50	1	0	0	0	1	3	3	3	1	2	0	.750	.500	1.000	0.00	27.00
Farrell, Luke	L-R	6-6	210	6-7-91	7	4	4.07	17	16	0	0	97	89	48	44	13	33	94	.245	.231	.255	8.69	3.05
2-team total (1 Oklahoma City)					7	4	4.06	18	17	0	0	102	93	51	46	13	35	99	.244	.231	.255	8.74	3.09
Fernandez, Pedro	R-R	6-0	175	5-25-94	2	1	4.10	10	3	0	1	26	29	15	12	3	10	16	.287	.225	.328	5.47	3.42
Flynn, Brian	L-L	6-7	250	4-19-90	5	3	5.40	22	4	0	0	50	68	36	30	10	12	50	.316	.254	.340	9.00	2.16
Garcia, Onelki	L-L	6-3	225	8-2-89	7	3	5.04	20	10	0	0	75	84	51	42	6	32	63	.282	.235	.301	7.56	3.84
Hernandez, Arnaldo	R-R	6-0	175	2-9-96	1	0	1.74	2	2	0	0	10	9	2	2	0	4	6	.231	.200	.250	5.23	3.48
Junis, Jakob	R-R	6-2	225	9-16-92	3	5	2.92	12	12	0	0	71	61	24	23	6	15	86	.227	.283	.186	10.90	1.90
Kalish, Jake	B-L	6-2	210	7-9-91	1	0	2.35	3	3	0	0	15	18	4	4	1	5	16	.305	.200	.359	9.39	2.93
Lenik, Kevin	R-R	6-5	225	8-1-91	1	1	1.88	12	0	0	2	24	11	5	5	1	8	24	.134	.139	.130	9.00	3.00

Machado, Andres	R-R	6-0	175	4-22-93	2	2	3.63	7	7	0	0	35	30	17	14	6	17	38	.233	.262	.206	9.87	4.41
Maness, Seth	R-R	6-0	190	10-14-88	2	2	6.13	24	0	0	2	47	63	32	32	7	8	35	.326	.258	.362	6.70	1.53
McCarthy, Kevin	R-R	6-3	200	2-22-92	1	1	3.09	25	0	0	2	32	32	12	11	3	9	17	.274	.281	.267	4.78	2.53
Newberry, Jake	R-R	6-2	195	11-20-94	2	2	4.76	7	0	0	0	11	10	7	6	1	7	11	.213	.214	.212	8.74	5.56
Ogando, Emilio	L-L	6-2	180	8-13-93	0	0	1.80	1	1	0	0	5	4	1	1	0	3	2	.222	.667	.133	3.60	5.40
Parnell, Bobby	R-R	6-3	205	9-8-84	3	2	4.71	15	0	0	1	21	20	13	11	0	13	17	.244	.242	.245	7.29	5.57
Peterson, Mark	R-R	6-0	190	9-7-90	3	3	4.57	23	0	0	0	43	46	23	22	4	24	32	.282	.328	.253	6.65	4.98
Selman, Sam	R-L	6-3	190	11-14-90	0	1	2.22	18	0	0	3	28	13	9	7	1	19	38	.141	.241	.095	12.07	6.04
Skoglund, Eric	L-L	6-7	200	10-26-92	4	5	4.11	19	19	1	0	101	110	57	46	14	29	102	.274	.231	.289	9.12	2.59
Staumont, Josh	R-R	6-3	200	12-21-93	3	8	6.28	16	15	0	0	76	64	56	53	14	63	93	.227	.224	.229	11.01	7.46
Stout, Eric	L-L	6-3	185	3-27-93	5	2	2.99	45	1	0	5	69	58	26	23	4	29	56	.228	.193	.244	7.27	3.76
Strahm, Matt	R-L	6-3	185	11-12-91	0	0	0.00	4	0	0	0	5	2	0	0	0	0	7	.118	.000	.222	12.60	0.00
Vines, Jace	R-R	6-3	215	9-4-94	0	0	3.00	1	1	0	0	6	6	2	2	0	0	3	.250	.200	.286	4.50	0.00
Zimmer, Kyle	R-R	6-3	225	9-13-91	0	0	5.79	20	2	0	3	33	35	21	21	4	16	34	.271	.174	.325	9.37	4.41

Fielding

Catcher	PCT	G	PO	A	E	DP	PB
Esposito	.969	4	29	2	1	0	0
Gallagher	.990	71	582	33	6	3	3
Morin	1.000	23	143	16	0	1	0
Pena	.985	37	238	19	4	1	0
Villegas	1.000	13	114	5	0	0	1

First Base	PCT	G	PO	A	E	DP
Cecchini	1.000	5	21	0	0	1
Cuthbert	1.000	2	18	0	0	3
Dozier	1.000	4	31	3	0	3
O'Brien	.975	9	74	5	2	2
O'Hearn	.995	75	539	27	3	56
Schwindel	.995	54	380	24	2	36

Second Base	PCT	G	PO	A	E	DP
Anna	.984	64	92	154	4	39
Diaz	1.000	2	2	2	0	0
Merrifield	1.000	6	10	14	0	1
Mondesi	.961	10	18	31	2	8
Sosa	.957	14	18	27	2	5
Torres	.992	27	61	59	1	15
Toups	1.000	26	42	52	0	11

Third Base	PCT	G	PO	A	E	DP
Anna	.935	26	15	43	4	3
Cecchini	.945	76	52	102	9	9
Cuthbert	.950	10	3	16	1	2
Dozier	1.000	7	7	10	0	1
Merrifield	1.000	1	0	1	0	0
Sosa	.800	2	1	3	1	0
Torres	1.000	4	3	10	0	0
Toups	.909	28	17	43	6	4

Shortstop	PCT	G	PO	A	E	DP
Anna	.933	4	5	9	1	1
Diaz	1.000	1	2	3	0	0
Lopez	.944	18	28	39	4	7
Mondesi	.961	71	88	185	11	36
Torres	.953	47	59	105	8	25
Toups	.947	11	8	10	1	3

Outfield	PCT	G	PO	A	E	DP
Anna	.000	1	0	0	0	0
Bonifacio	1.000	12	20	1	0	1
Burns	.987	94	231	4	3	1
Dozier	1.000	10	22	0	0	0
Gore	.967	59	114	4	4	0
McCray	.750	2	3	0	1	0
Merrifield	1.000	2	2	0	0	0
Moon	1.000	29	64	2	0	1
O'Brien	1.000	10	27	1	0	0
O'Hearn	1.000	7	13	0	0	0
Orlando	.952	25	57	3	3	1
Soler	1.000	62	128	3	0	0
Sosa	1.000	24	47	0	0	0
Starling	.975	78	182	11	5	1
Toups	.930	28	40	0	3	0

NORTHWEST ARKANSAS NATURALS — DOUBLE-A

TEXAS LEAGUE

Batting	B-T	HT	WT	DOB	AVG	vLH	vRH	G	AB	R	H	2B	3B	HR	RBI	BB	HBP	SH	SF	SO	SB	CS	SLG	OBP
Arteaga, Humberto	R-R	6-1	160	1-23-94	.258	.282	.253	124	453	47	117	12	3	1	35	25	4	4	4	65	4	4	.305	.300
de San Miguel, Allan	R-R	5-9	205	2-1-88	.237	.185	.253	34	114	8	27	8	0	1	10	8	4	0	0	26	0	1	.333	.310
Dewees Jr., Donald	L-L	5-11	204	9-29-93	.272	.256	.275	126	464	67	126	24	6	9	52	46	5	4	5	81	20	8	.407	.340
Diaz, Carlos	R-R	5-8	145	11-15-92	.215	.211	.216	38	107	8	23	4	0	0	5	3	1	3	0	29	1	1	.252	.243
Dini, Nick	R-R	5-8	180	7-27-93	.310	.400	.287	64	216	22	67	9	0	2	25	17	9	1	2	26	8	2	.380	.381
Dozier, Hunter	R-R	6-4	220	8-22-91	.250	.000	.286	6	16	4	4	1	0	0	0	4	0	0	0	8	0	0	.313	.400
Duenez, Samir	L-R	6-1	195	6-11-96	.252	.189	.269	132	523	65	132	23	2	17	75	37	3	0	3	116	10	3	.402	.304
Escalera, Alfredo	R-R	6-1	186	2-17-95	.261	.290	.255	118	456	50	119	17	2	7	54	19	11	2	2	113	14	4	.353	.305
Evans, Zane	R-R	6-2	225	11-29-91	.205	.048	.238	33	122	11	25	1	0	4	15	2	0	0	0	31	2	0	.312	.218
Gore, Terrance	R-R	5-7	165	6-8-91	.254	.111	.280	19	59	9	15	1	0	0	1	2	0	1	0	13	8	0	.271	.279
Hernandez, Elier	R-R	6-3	197	11-21-94	.339	.000	.375	16	62	8	21	4	0	1	10	4	2	1	1	14	0	3	.452	.391
Jones, Cody	B-R	5-11	175	5-25-93	.235	.281	.214	41	102	11	24	2	0	1	11	14	1	0	1	24	8	1	.284	.331
Lopez, Jack	R-R	5-9	165	12-16-92	.281	.356	.266	95	363	42	102	12	2	5	29	20	8	7	0	86	19	7	.366	.333
Lopez, Nicky	L-R	5-11	175	3-13-95	.259	.246	.263	59	232	26	60	6	1	0	11	16	2	3	0	29	7	4	.293	.312
Miller, Anderson	L-L	6-3	208	5-6-94	.230	.269	.217	58	213	17	49	8	0	2	19	9	1	1	1	56	3	2	.296	.263
Moon, Logan	R-R	6-2	195	2-15-92	.241	.283	.230	78	266	29	64	14	1	4	24	17	0	0	1	85	4	1	.346	.285
Morin, Parker	L-R	5-11	195	7-2-91	.179	.100	.196	18	56	5	10	1	0	0	4	3	2	0	2	20	0	0	.196	.238
O'Hearn, Ryan	L-L	6-3	200	7-26-93	.258	.125	.300	19	66	7	17	1	1	4	11	10	0	0	0	20	0	0	.485	.355
Orlando, Paulo	R-R	6-2	210	11-1-85	.342	.500	.303	12	41	4	14	1	0	0	3	6	0	0	0	7	0	0	.366	.426
Ramos, Mauricio	R-R	6-1	185	2-2-92	.258	.172	.275	92	356	36	92	9	2	11	47	14	7	0	1	89	0	2	.388	.299
Sanchez, Jose	L-L	5-10	155	7-21-94	.138	.000	.154	11	29	2	4	1	0	0	1	2	0	1	0	5	0	0	.172	.194
Schwindel, Frank	R-R	6-1	205	6-29-92	.350	.412	.342	34	137	17	48	13	0	6	25	6	1	0	3	17	0	0	.577	.374
Sosa, Ruben	B-R	5-7	170	9-23-90	.261	.160	.289	35	115	21	30	5	4	2	15	13	1	3	0	30	6	1	.426	.341
Toups, Corey	R-R	5-10	170	2-12-93	.286	.462	.259	25	98	14	28	7	0	2	10	7	1	0	1	35	4	1	.418	.336
Villegas, Luis	R-R	5-10	170	12-2-92	.269	.000	.304	8	26	2	7	2	0	0	6	1	0	1	0	5	0	0	.346	.296
Walters, Zach	B-R	6-2	210	9-5-89	.211	.154	.234	24	90	12	19	3	0	1	8	5	0	0	1	21	1	0	.278	.250

Pitching	B-T	HT	WT	DOB	W	L	ERA	G	GS	CG	SV	IP	H	R	ER	HR	BB	SO	AVG	vLH	vRH	K/9	BB/9
Adam, Jason	R-R	6-4	225	8-4-91	0	0	7.11	5	0	0	0	6	3	5	5	0	4	11	.136	.143	.133	15.63	5.68
2-team total (1 San Antonio)					0	0	5.40	6	0	0	0	8	4	5	5	0	4	13	.138	.143	.133	14.04	4.32
Almonte, Miguel	R-R	6-2	210	4-4-93	1	0	1.86	7	6	0	0	29	22	7	6	2	6	35	.210	.195	.219	10.86	1.86
Beal, Evan	R-R	6-5	195	8-2-93	0	0	4.20	10	0	0	2	15	15	9	7	2	9	16	.238	.167	.255	9.60	5.40
Binford, Christian	R-R	6-6	215	12-20-92	1	0	1.99	5	5	0	0	32	29	7	7	3	7	23	.244	.256	.237	6.54	1.99
Edwards, Andrew	R-R	6-6	265	10-7-91	3	0	6.06	24	0	0	4	36	45	25	24	2	14	36	.310	.258	.349	9.08	3.53

Fernandez, Pedro	R-R	6-0	175	5-25-94	4	3	2.66	29	0	0	1	51	41	17	15	1	13	51	.216	.152	.250	9.06	2.31
Garcia, Onelki	L-L	6-3	225	8-2-89	0	0	2.61	2	2	0	0	10	11	3	3	2	1	6	.262	.263	.261	5.23	0.87
Goudeau, Ashton	R-R	6-6	205	7-23-92	3	7	5.37	21	7	0	1	57	78	39	34	7	17	43	.322	.304	.336	6.79	2.68
Griffin, Foster	R-L	6-3	200	7-27-95	11	5	3.61	18	18	0	0	105	108	46	42	11	34	81	.271	.206	.294	6.96	2.92
Hill, Tim	L-L	6-2	200	2-10-90	1	2	4.17	36	0	0	4	69	76	36	32	2	19	75	.279	.168	.339	9.78	2.48
Kalish, Jake	B-L	6-2	210	7-9-91	0	7	3.77	18	9	0	0	72	83	32	30	4	17	49	.293	.327	.272	6.15	2.13
Lovelady, Richard	L-L	6-0	175	7-7-95	3	2	2.16	21	0	0	3	33	28	12	8	1	13	36	.228	.162	.256	9.72	3.51
Lovvorn, Zach	R-R	6-0	185	5-26-94	4	9	4.83	31	18	0	0	117	142	72	63	8	34	93	.298	.279	.309	7.13	2.61
Machado, Andres	R-R	6-0	175	4-22-93	0	0	3.00	1	0	0	0	3	2	1	1	0	2	1	.182	.250	.143	3.00	6.00
Marte, Yunior	R-R	6-2	180	2-2-95	1	2	5.75	17	0	0	1	36	33	23	23	5	27	38	.246	.271	.227	9.50	6.75
Newberry, Jake	R-R	6-2	195	11-20-94	4	2	2.13	36	0	0	15	51	45	17	12	3	19	33	.237	.357	.167	5.86	3.38
Ogando, Emilio	L-L	6-2	180	8-13-93	10	10	3.45	23	23	0	0	133	130	62	51	15	36	83	.255	.239	.261	5.62	2.44
Peterson, Mark	R-R	6-0	190	9-7-90	0	1	1.42	5	0	0	2	6	3	1	1	1	0	5	.143	.000	.214	7.11	0.00
Ray, Corey	R-R	6-4	175	12-15-92	6	12	5.41	29	29	1	0	143	170	97	86	20	59	93	.298	.305	.292	5.85	3.71
Redman, Reid	R-R	6-0	180	11-22-88	2	1	5.55	16	0	0	1	24	24	15	15	7	2	29	.255	.235	.267	10.73	0.74
Rico, Luis	L-L	6-1	175	11-29-93	2	1	7.33	18	0	0	0	27	37	23	22	3	14	25	.327	.275	.356	8.33	4.67
Ruxer, Jared	R-R	6-3	200	7-29-92	0	0	16.50	3	1	0	0	6	9	11	11	4	7	1	.333	.400	.294	1.50	10.50
Selman, Sam	R-L	6-3	190	11-14-90	4	3	2.97	24	0	0	5	39	21	15	13	1	19	59	.156	.089	.189	13.50	4.35
Sheller, Walker	R-R	6-3	195	5-21-95	0	0	0.00	3	0	0	1	6	3	0	0	0	3	5	.136	.333	.000	7.50	4.50
Skoglund, Eric	L-L	6-7	200	10-26-92	0	0	2.70	1	1	0	0	3	5	1	1	0	3	1	.385	.000	.500	2.70	8.10
Sparkman, Glenn	B-R	6-2	210	5-11-92	0	0	2.61	3	2	0	0	10	11	3	3	0	5	5	.275	.333	.211	4.35	4.35
Staumont, Josh	R-R	6-3	200	12-21-93	3	4	4.44	10	10	0	0	49	42	25	24	2	34	45	.244	.282	.213	8.32	6.29
Tenuta, Matt	L-L	6-4	225	12-16-93	4	2	5.74	17	8	0	0	53	74	38	34	9	17	38	.338	.310	.348	6.41	2.87
Zimmer, Kyle	R-R	6-3	225	9-13-91	0	0	2.25	1	1	0	0	4	6	1	1	0	0	6	.375	.750	.250	13.50	0.00

Fielding

Catcher	PCT	G	PO	A	E	DP	PB
de San Miguel	.996	31	207	22	1	2	4
Dini	.987	58	408	44	6	6	5
Evans	.992	30	240	22	2	1	1
Morin	1.000	16	107	11	0	0	0
Villegas	1.000	8	51	4	0	0	0

First Base	PCT	G	PO	A	E	DP
de San Miguel	1.000	2	14	2	0	0
Duenez	.988	104	816	42	10	93
O'Hearn	.972	8	69	1	2	5
Ramos	.986	12	62	7	1	9
Schwindel	1.000	12	88	6	0	10
Walters	.941	5	32	0	2	2

Second Base	PCT	G	PO	A	E	DP
Arteaga	.946	19	31	39	4	15
Diaz	.959	17	36	34	3	15
Lopez	.991	44	94	115	2	38
Lopez	.992	25	45	75	1	24
Sosa	.956	22	40	46	4	12
Toups	.949	19	36	38	4	6

Third Base	PCT	G	PO	A	E	DP
Arteaga	.944	6	2	15	1	2
Diaz	.879	15	9	20	4	3
Dozier	.889	3	3	5	1	0
Lopez	.939	41	29	63	6	2
Ramos	.934	72	49	120	12	12
Toups	.500	1	0	1	1	0
Walters	.917	11	7	15	2	2

Shortstop	PCT	G	PO	A	E	DP
Arteaga	.961	96	134	265	16	69
Diaz	.667	2	0	2	1	0
Lopez	.979	12	16	31	1	9
Lopez	.992	33	43	87	1	20
Walters	1.000	1	2	1	0	0

Outfield	PCT	G	PO	A	E	DP
Dewees Jr.	.994	121	335	3	2	1
Dozier	1.000	1	5	0	0	0
Escalera	.985	103	191	8	3	0
Gore	1.000	17	33	3	0	1
Hernandez	.950	15	37	1	2	0
Jones	1.000	33	62	1	0	0
Miller	.978	52	127	6	3	2
Moon	.977	62	120	8	3	2
O'Hearn	.875	8	6	1	1	0
Orlando	1.000	7	13	0	0	0
Sanchez	1.000	10	13	0	0	0
Sosa	.941	8	15	1	1	0
Toups	1.000	6	11	0	0	0

WILMINGTON BLUE ROCKS

HIGH CLASS A

CAROLINA LEAGUE

Batting	B-T	HT	WT	DOB	AVG	vLH	vRH	G	AB	R	H	2B	3B	HR	RBI	BB	HBP	SH	SF	SO	SB	CS	SLG	OBP
Brontsema, John	R-R	6-2	187	12-13-94	.226	.286	.177	22	62	5	14	2	0	1	2	5	0	1	0	19	0	1	.307	.284
Burt, D.J.	R-R	5-9	160	10-13-95	.227	.217	.233	103	365	52	83	19	5	0	29	64	5	7	4	101	32	13	.307	.347
Collins, Roman	L-L	6-2	210	6-17-94	.227	.177	.251	131	480	48	109	24	5	8	53	44	2	0	4	117	4	2	.348	.293
DeVito, Chris	L-R	6-2	220	12-1-94	.240	.129	.304	103	387	38	93	21	2	10	53	23	3	0	1	91	0	0	.382	.287
Diaz, Carlos	R-R	5-8	145	11-15-92	.091	.000	.167	13	22	0	2	0	0	0	1	2	1	3	1	4	0	1	.091	.192
Downes, Brandon	R-R	6-3	195	9-29-92	.245	.333	.203	72	261	37	64	12	4	13	35	30	6	1	2	70	2	3	.471	.334
Dozier, Hunter	R-R	6-4	220	8-22-91	.364	1.000	.300	3	11	1	4	1	0	0	1	1	1	0	0	5	0	0	.455	.462
Esposito, Nathan	R-R	5-11	180	6-25-93	.225	.258	.200	68	227	14	51	7	1	0	16	8	6	2	0	38	0	0	.264	.270
Flores, Jecksson	R-R	5-11	145	10-28-93	.257	.259	.255	96	304	31	78	14	3	2	21	24	3	21	3	63	7	5	.342	.314
Frabasilio, Colton	R-R	6-2	205	4-18-93	.200	.170	.224	40	105	9	21	3	0	1	12	19	1	0	1	27	0	0	.257	.325
Franco, Wander	R-R	6-2	170	12-13-94	.279	.298	.268	129	481	52	134	19	8	4	46	25	5	2	3	92	5	3	.376	.319
Heath, Nick	L-L	6-1	187	11-27-93	.250	.243	.253	60	224	27	56	7	0	1	12	19	1	3	1	59	21	8	.295	.310
Hernandez, Elier	R-R	6-3	197	11-21-94	.307	.372	.272	30	124	15	38	7	3	4	27	4	2	0	1	35	1	0	.508	.336
Hutchins, Nick	R-R	6-1	200	11-17-95	.167	.000	.200	2	6	0	1	0	0	0	0	0	0	0	0	2	0	0	.167	.167
Jones, Cody	B-R	5-11	175	5-25-93	.236	.305	.194	52	157	26	37	4	2	3	10	22	3	3	2	34	7	2	.344	.337
Lopez, Nicky	L-R	5-11	175	3-13-95	.295	.291	.297	70	285	42	84	12	7	2	27	36	1	2	0	23	14	8	.407	.376
Maezes, Travis	R-L	6-0	195	12-10-93	.203	.136	.219	77	227	28	46	9	1	6	28	28	2	0	3	80	3	1	.330	.292
McCray, Jonathan	B-R	5-10	180	1-8-95	.186	.167	.197	35	102	10	19	6	0	2	8	7	1	0	2	23	0	0	.304	.241
Melo, Yeison	R-R	6-1	180	7-30-95	.081	.158	.000	12	37	2	3	2	0	0	0	2	0	0	0	9	0	0	.135	.128
Miller, Anderson	L-L	6-3	208	5-6-94	.290	.375	.243	70	269	37	78	11	4	7	37	36	2	0	0	60	15	2	.439	.378
Peterson, Kort	L-R	6-1	195	4-29-94	.333	.333	.333	11	39	7	13	3	2	1	1	2	0	0	0	8	0	0	.590	.366
Sanchez, Jose	L-L	5-10	155	7-21-94	.208	.000	.263	17	48	6	10	2	0	0	2	6	0	0	0	11	0	0	.250	.296
Stanley, Tanner	L-L	5-10	180	9-12-93	.143	.000	.171	19	49	1	7	2	0	1	3	5	0	0	0	11	0	0	.245	.222
Vallot, Chase	R-R	6-0	215	8-21-96	.231	.271	.211	89	281	34	65	22	0	12	37	64	6	0	4	127	0	0	.438	.380

Pitching	B-T	HT	WT	DOB	W	L	ERA	G	GS	CG	SV	IP	H	R	ER	HR	BB	SO	AVG	vLH	vRH	K/9	BB/9
Bender, Anthony	R-R	6-4	205	2-3-95	0	1	4.50	1	1	0	0	4	5	3	2	0	2	3	.333	.444	.167	6.75	4.50
Blewett, Scott	R-R	6-6	210	4-10-96	7	10	4.07	27	27	1	0	153	153	76	69	16	52	129	.262	.258	.265	7.60	3.07
Bodner, Jacob	R-R	5-10	185	1-31-93	5	1	3.29	29	1	0	3	55	47	25	20	2	20	70	.237	.250	.230	11.52	3.29
Camp, Justin	R-R	5-11	230	5-17-93	0	2	3.63	11	0	0	1	22	19	10	9	0	13	10	.244	.222	.250	4.03	5.24
Castillo, Cristian	L-L	6-0	190	9-25-94	7	12	4.13	26	26	0	0	142	155	79	65	11	48	105	.277	.239	.289	6.67	3.05
Cramer, Gabe	R-R	6-2	205	11-1-94	1	0	1.98	6	0	0	3	14	11	3	3	1	2	27	.216	.115	.320	17.78	1.32
Edwards, Andrew	R-R	6-6	265	10-7-91	1	0	1.59	3	0	0	0	6	5	1	1	0	3	9	.227	.111	.308	14.29	4.76
Gavin, Grant	R-R	6-2	185	7-10-95	2	0	1.93	17	0	0	3	33	26	7	7	1	11	34	.215	.234	.203	9.37	3.03
Griffin, Foster	R-L	6-3	200	7-27-95	4	2	2.86	10	10	0	0	57	43	19	18	2	20	60	.210	.246	.194	9.53	3.18
Hill, Tim	L-L	6-2	200	2-10-90	0	0	5.40	4	0	0	0	5	6	3	3	0	5	9	.286	.250	.308	16.20	9.00
Kalish, Jake	B-L	6-2	210	7-9-91	1	1	1.93	10	0	0	1	19	13	4	4	0	6	23	.191	.143	.225	11.09	2.89
Lovelady, Richard	L-L	6-0	175	7-7-95	1	0	1.08	21	0	0	7	33	18	5	4	0	4	41	.154	.205	.128	11.07	1.08
Machado, Andres	R-R	6-0	175	4-22-93	6	7	5.03	21	9	0	2	73	88	46	41	8	14	72	.292	.315	.272	8.84	1.72
Marte, Yunior	R-R	6-2	180	2-2-95	3	2	2.23	20	1	0	4	36	25	9	9	0	20	42	.203	.186	.219	10.40	4.95
Nesbit, Cody	R-R	6-3	175	3-5-96	0	0	12.00	2	0	0	0	3	4	4	4	0	1	2	.333	.500	.167	6.00	3.00
Ogando, Emilio	L-L	6-2	180	8-13-93	1	0	5.47	5	5	0	0	26	30	16	16	5	9	25	.291	.046	.358	8.54	3.08
Puckett, A.J.	R-R	6-4	200	5-27-95	9	7	3.90	20	20	0	0	108	107	53	47	7	46	98	.257	.276	.238	8.14	3.82
2-team total (5 Winston-Salem)					10	7	3.98	25	25	0	0	136	142	67	60	9	51	119	.272	.276	.238	7.89	3.38
Rico, Luis	L-L	6-1	175	11-29-93	0	2	4.11	16	0	0	2	31	28	16	14	2	14	34	.233	.308	.198	9.98	4.11
Rodgers, Colin	L-L	5-10	181	12-2-93	2	6	4.36	22	15	1	0	89	89	48	43	6	42	81	.267	.195	.291	8.22	4.26
Ruxer, Jared	R-R	6-3	200	7-29-92	5	7	3.45	24	17	0	0	110	113	54	42	11	29	84	.268	.263	.270	6.89	2.38
Sheller, Walker	R-R	6-3	195	5-21-95	4	1	4.02	18	0	0	0	31	30	16	14	2	14	34	.252	.143	.329	9.77	4.02
Tenuta, Matt	L-L	6-4	225	12-16-93	2	2	1.57	13	0	0	3	34	28	6	6	2	13	40	.224	.158	.253	10.49	3.41
Terrero, Franco	R-R	6-0	180	5-20-95	3	5	2.59	34	0	0	6	63	41	24	18	3	28	62	.193	.210	.183	8.90	4.02
Veras, Jose	R-R	6-1	170	7-15-94	0	1	1.80	7	0	0	0	15	12	3	3	0	3	13	.214	.177	.231	7.80	1.80
Vines, Jace	R-R	6-3	215	9-4-94	3	3	3.60	7	7	2	0	40	41	17	16	2	15	20	.277	.286	.271	4.50	3.38

Fielding

Catcher	PCT	G	PO	A	E	DP	PB
Esposito	.995	67	527	65	3	3	4
Frabasilio	.973	17	92	15	3	3	2
Hutchins	1.000	2	15	1	0	0	0
Vallot	.977	59	481	33	12	2	10

First Base	PCT	G	PO	A	E	DP
Collins	.980	24	189	11	4	15
DeVito	.993	92	706	41	5	68
Frabasilio	.974	10	69	6	2	5
Franco	1.000	3	12	0	0	2
Maezes	.984	17	117	6	2	10

Second Base	PCT	G	PO	A	E	DP
Brontsema	.940	17	38	40	5	10
Burt	.960	97	149	211	15	46
Diaz	.500	1	1	1	2	1
Flores	1.000	13	30	42	0	14
Maezes	.750	1	0	3	1	0
McCray	.951	14	24	34	3	11

Third Base	PCT	G	PO	A	E	DP
Brontsema	.000	1	0	0	0	0
Dozier	1.000	2	2	2	0	0
Flores	1.000	12	5	12	0	1
Franco	.938	116	56	214	18	13
Maezes	.914	21	5	27	3	1

Shortstop	PCT	G	PO	A	E	DP
Brontsema	.000	2	0	0	0	0
Diaz	.962	12	6	19	1	1
Flores	.963	70	96	189	11	39
Lopez	.973	66	89	166	7	41

Outfield	PCT	G	PO	A	E	DP
Collins	.978	98	169	5	4	0
Downes	.962	66	146	5	6	0
Dozier	1.000	1	4	0	0	0
Flores	1.000	4	8	0	0	0
Heath	.979	57	141	2	3	2
Hernandez	.952	28	59	1	3	0
Jones	1.000	50	97	3	0	0
McCray	1.000	7	16	1	0	1
Melo	1.000	8	18	0	0	0
Miller	.986	67	135	6	2	2
Peterson	1.000	11	13	0	0	0
Sanchez	.962	15	23	2	1	1
Stanley	1.000	16	24	0	0	0

LEXINGTON LEGENDS — *LOW CLASS A*

SOUTH ATLANTIC LEAGUE

Batting	B-T	HT	WT	DOB	AVG	vLH	vRH	G	AB	R	H	2B	3B	HR	RBI	BB	HBP	SH	SF	SO	SB	CS	SLG	OBP
Aracena, Ricky	B-R	5-8	160	10-2-97	.139	.135	.141	30	108	5	15	1	0	0	7	0	0	5	1	34	3	5	.148	.138
Bartlett, Max	R-R	5-11	165	1-14-95	.109	.333	.075	16	46	4	5	3	1	0	0	6	1	0	0	20	0	0	.217	.226
Brontsema, John	R-R	6-2	187	12-13-94	.323	.302	.331	52	161	31	52	12	1	4	21	17	10	0	2	41	6	2	.485	.416
Cancel, Gabriel	R-R	6-1	185	12-8-96	.277	.346	.251	103	401	70	111	30	2	14	49	23	6	1	2	99	9	8	.466	.324
Castellano, Angelo	R-R	6-0	170	1-13-95	.245	.277	.234	116	433	63	106	14	2	8	43	51	3	6	3	81	19	10	.342	.327
DeVito, Chris	L-R	6-2	220	12-1-94	.347	.324	.357	30	121	25	42	10	0	11	38	6	1	0	3	32	0	1	.703	.374
Dini, Nick	R-R	5-8	180	7-27-93	.283	.389	.214	24	92	19	26	10	0	2	11	5	1	0	1	8	2	0	.457	.323
Dudek, Joe	L-L	6-2	230	1-6-95	.204	.185	.209	77	265	38	54	16	0	9	39	36	0	0	3	93	0	0	.366	.296
Fukofuka, Amalani	R-R	6-1	180	9-25-95	.208	.189	.217	33	106	12	22	4	0	1	11	9	2	4	1	41	9	2	.274	.280
Gasparini, Marten	B-R	6-0	195	5-24-97	.227	.180	.244	122	406	48	92	19	3	9	50	27	1	12	4	121	18	11	.355	.274
Gigliotti, Michael	L-L	6-1	180	2-14-96	.302	.333	.297	22	86	14	26	5	1	1	8	8	3	2	1	20	7	5	.419	.378
Heath, Nick	L-L	6-1	187	11-27-93	.400	1.000	.250	2	5	1	2	0	0	0	1	0	0	0	0	1	1	0	.400	.400
Hutchins, Nick	R-R	6-1	200	11-17-95	.194	.250	.174	9	31	2	6	2	0	1	4	0	1	1	1	14	0	0	.355	.212
Lee, Khalil	L-L	5-10	170	6-26-98	.237	.199	.253	121	451	71	107	24	6	17	61	65	10	3	3	171	20	18	.430	.344
Martin, Rudy	L-L	5-7	150	1-31-96	.277	.250	.287	37	119	25	33	7	1	2	19	16	1	4	1	37	26	4	.403	.365
Melo, Yeison	R-R	6-1	180	7-30-95	.256	.286	.250	39	156	20	40	9	0	3	22	3	1	1	0	27	0	0	.372	.275
Olloque, Manny	R-R	6-2	165	5-11-96	.244	.233	.247	106	365	52	89	18	2	6	44	30	4	3	3	92	6	1	.353	.306
Peterson, Kort	L-R	6-1	195	4-29-94	.290	.283	.293	52	193	24	56	12	2	1	19	17	10	1	2	54	5	3	.389	.374
Rivera, Emmanuel	R-R	6-2	195	6-29-96	.310	.336	.301	122	464	60	144	27	5	12	72	31	10	0	3	87	8	10	.468	.364
Sanchez, Mark	L-R	5-10	197	8-17-94	.206	.273	.174	11	34	2	7	1	0	0	2	3	0	0	0	12	0	0	.235	.270
Villegas, Luis	R-R	5-10	170	12-2-92	.239	.200	.244	13	46	6	11	0	0	2	6	4	1	0	0	10	1	0	.370	.314
Viloria, Meibrys	L-R	5-11	175	2-15-97	.259	.233	.267	101	363	42	94	25	0	8	52	25	4	5	1	79	4	3	.394	.313
Vizcaino, Vance	L-R	6-3	215	8-1-94	.315	.185	.344	42	149	22	47	9	0	0	14	17	0	2	2	36	11	8	.376	.381

Pitching	B-T	HT	WT	DOB	W	L	ERA	G	GS	CG	SV	IP	H	R	ER	HR	BB	SO	AVG	vLH	vRH	K/9	BB/9
Bender, Anthony	R-R	6-4	205	2-3-95	5	5	3.93	23	8	0	4	73	69	35	32	9	20	74	.246	.272	.224	9.08	2.45
Bramblett, Geoffrey	R-R	6-2	200	4-26-95	3	1	6.57	8	2	0	0	25	30	18	18	4	14	20	.316	.407	.279	7.30	5.11
Camp, Justin	R-R	5-11	230	5-17-93	0	0	0.34	11	0	0	2	27	11	1	1	0	6	32	.124	.125	.123	10.80	2.03
Davila, Garrett	L-L	6-2	180	1-17-97	8	8	5.08	27	21	0	3	126	127	78	71	8	52	92	.265	.280	.258	6.59	3.72
Davis, Andre	L-L	6-6	230	9-29-93	5	4	4.83	18	18	1	0	86	96	52	46	9	23	87	.280	.216	.302	9.14	2.42
2-team total (4 Kannapolis)					6	5	4.58	22	20	1	0	98	106	56	50	9	30	99	.273	.216	.302	9.06	2.75
Eckert, Travis	R-R	6-2	190	12-28-93	6	9	5.65	28	19	1	0	124	142	82	78	7	46	85	.292	.271	.308	6.15	3.33
Fallwell, Tyler	R-R	6-5	210	11-8-95	0	0	12.51	9	0	0	0	14	23	19	19	3	6	12	.365	.357	.371	7.90	3.95
Garabito, Gerson	R-R	6-0	160	8-19-95	4	5	2.81	15	15	0	0	77	52	36	24	8	19	72	.191	.174	.203	8.42	2.22
Gavin, Grant	R-R	6-2	185	7-10-95	1	2	1.38	19	0	0	6	33	17	6	5	1	14	43	.152	.128	.164	11.85	3.86
Gomez, Ofreidy	R-R	6-3	190	7-6-95	7	12	5.18	28	22	0	1	137	162	92	79	12	46	108	.295	.302	.289	7.08	3.01
Hernandez, Arnaldo	R-R	6-0	175	2-9-96	2	1	3.63	15	5	1	1	57	63	29	23	9	8	58	.278	.253	.294	9.16	1.26
Lenik, Kevin	R-R	6-5	225	8-1-91	0	0	2.16	5	0	0	1	8	8	4	2	1	6	11	.267	.429	.125	11.88	6.48
McKay, David	R-R	6-3	205	3-31-95	0	0	13.03	6	0	0	0	10	19	14	14	4	5	11	.404	.409	.400	10.24	4.66
Nesbit, Cody	R-R	6-3	175	3-5-96	0	0	1.45	12	0	0	0	19	10	3	3	2	8	25	.167	.194	.138	12.05	3.86
Pinto, Julio	R-R	6-3	185	11-18-95	0	2	13.83	12	0	0	0	14	22	22	21	4	16	14	.349	.364	.342	9.22	10.54
Sheller, Walker	R-R	6-3	195	5-21-95	2	1	2.88	14	0	0	3	25	21	8	8	2	9	27	.233	.250	.224	9.72	3.24
Silva, Michael	R-R	6-1	190	11-22-94	1	0	1.98	8	0	0	0	14	8	3	3	0	8	9	.163	.095	.214	5.93	5.27
Snider, Collin	R-R	6-4	200	10-10-95	0	0	6.75	5	0	0	1	9	14	8	7	3	0	6	.333	.333	.333	5.79	0.00
Tatum, Vance	L-L	6-4	215	5-2-95	3	5	4.63	34	1	0	2	58	79	37	30	7	30	66	.321	.279	.341	10.18	4.63
Veras, Jose	R-R	6-1	170	7-15-94	2	1	4.53	26	0	0	4	56	65	31	28	5	11	54	.290	.247	.315	8.73	1.78
Vines, Jace	R-R	6-3	215	9-4-94	9	5	3.42	19	14	0	3	100	96	45	38	6	23	63	.255	.279	.239	5.67	2.07
Watson, Nolan	R-R	6-2	195	1-25-97	1	10	6.78	15	13	0	1	69	101	64	52	8	33	41	.345	.330	.354	5.35	4.30
Wynne, Matthew	R-R	6-4	235	7-5-93	3	4	5.40	28	0	0	2	47	59	33	28	5	13	26	.314	.305	.321	5.01	2.51
Zuber, Tyler	R-R	5-11	175	6-16-95	0	0	19.29	3	0	0	0	2	8	5	5	0	3	1	.571	.000	.800	3.86	11.57

Fielding

Catcher	PCT	G	PO	A	E	DP	PB
Dini	.989	21	148	29	2	1	2
Hutchins	.968	9	53	7	2	0	0
Sanchez	1.000	8	48	9	0	0	1
Villegas	.991	13	108	8	1	3	1
Viloria	.986	92	668	85	11	11	18

First Base	PCT	G	PO	A	E	DP
DeVito	.996	29	247	20	1	22
Dudek	.991	66	539	39	5	48
Olloque	.980	49	367	22	8	25

Second Base	PCT	G	PO	A	E	DP
Bartlett	.885	5	9	14	3	1
Brontsema	.939	30	46	78	8	23
Cancel	.959	94	154	246	17	53
Castellano	1.000	12	23	25	0	3
Olloque	1.000	3	2	3	0	1

Third Base	PCT	G	PO	A	E	DP
Bartlett	1.000	2	2	1	0	0
Brontsema	.882	5	6	9	2	0
Castellano	.941	8	3	13	1	1
Olloque	.892	16	12	21	4	2
Rivera	.925	114	70	190	21	13

Shortstop	PCT	G	PO	A	E	DP
Aracena	.922	30	36	71	9	15
Bartlett	.917	9	9	24	3	3
Brontsema	.897	6	11	15	3	5
Castellano	.972	96	131	247	11	53

Outfield	PCT	G	PO	A	E	DP
Fukofuka	1.000	33	63	3	0	0
Gasparini	.979	120	279	7	6	3
Gigliotti	1.000	18	50	1	0	0
Heath	1.000	2	4	0	0	0
Lee	.973	119	241	14	7	3
Martin	.951	37	71	6	4	0
Melo	.872	26	38	3	6	0
Peterson	.988	40	79	1	1	0
Vizcaino	1.000	32	50	2	0	0

BURLINGTON ROYALS — ROOKIE

APPALACHIAN LEAGUE

Batting	B-T	HT	WT	DOB	AVG	vLH	vRH	G	AB	R	H	2B	3B	HR	RBI	BB	HBP	SH	SF	SO	SB	CS	SLG	OBP
Arroyo, Michael	R-R	6-0	181	12-31-95	.000	.000	.000	7	22	0	0	0	0	0	0	1	0	0	0	12	0	0	.000	.044
Atencio, Jesus	R-R	5-10	165	8-22-96	.306	.343	.291	33	121	14	37	6	1	1	14	6	2	2	2	24	0	0	.397	.344
Bartlett, Max	R-R	5-11	165	1-14-95	.500	—	.500	2	2	1	1	0	0	0	0	3	0	0	0	0	0	1	.500	.800
Caraballo, Jose	R-R	6-1	180	1-7-97	.222	.200	.250	3	9	2	2	0	0	0	2	1	0	0	0	4	0	1	.222	.300
Carrasco, Dennicher	R-R	5-11	195	10-12-95	.288	.267	.298	61	236	34	68	14	3	10	41	12	2	0	5	38	1	0	.500	.322
Cash, Benji	L-L	6-5	227	1-19-95	.173	.211	.161	27	75	16	13	6	0	2	9	16	1	0	1	37	0	0	.333	.323
Dale, Ryan	R-R	6-3	180	3-16-96	.095	.097	.094	20	63	5	6	1	0	0	0	5	1	1	0	28	0	0	.111	.174
Gigliotti, Michael	L-L	6-1	180	2-14-96	.329	.333	.327	42	155	30	51	8	3	3	30	32	1	1	2	21	15	5	.477	.442
Gonzalez, Julio	L-R	5-10	185	6-14-95	.286	.154	.364	10	35	6	10	0	0	0	1	5	0	0	0	8	4	0	.286	.375
Guzman, Jeison	L-R	6-2	180	10-8-98	.207	.214	.204	54	193	21	40	4	2	0	15	21	2	9	4	45	3	3	.249	.286
Hutchins, Nick	R-R	6-1	200	11-17-95	.313	.300	.318	9	32	3	10	3	1	1	4	4	1	0	0	10	0	0	.563	.405
Jones, Cal	R-R	6-0	175	9-16-97	.224	.188	.237	59	241	33	54	12	3	6	31	12	4	2	0	77	8	2	.373	.272
Jones, Travis	R-R	6-4	210	9-29-95	.391	.250	.467	7	23	3	9	3	0	0	4	1	0	0	2	3	0	0	.522	.385
Marquez, Jose	B-R	6-0	175	10-7-97	.254	.233	.265	50	177	24	45	9	4	2	19	15	5	1	0	32	1	2	.384	.330
Matias, Seuly	R-R	6-3	200	9-4-98	.243	.229	.250	57	222	27	54	13	3	7	36	16	3	0	5	72	2	1	.423	.297
Nunez, Oliver	B-R	5-10	170	2-21-95	.321	.318	.323	59	221	44	71	10	3	2	20	22	3	2	1	36	19	4	.421	.389
Rivero, Sebastian	R-R	6-1	180	11-16-98	.265	.235	.275	48	189	18	50	8	1	4	28	6	1	0	2	30	0	0	.381	.288
Rohlman, Reed	L-L	6-1	190	1-5-95	.267	.258	.270	58	221	33	59	10	1	4	29	17	8	0	2	46	0	2	.376	.339
Sanchez, Jose	L-L	5-10	155	7-21-94	.364	.435	.326	19	66	13	24	1	0	0	5	8	0	0	2	17	2	1	.379	.421

Pitching	B-T	HT	WT	DOB	W	L	ERA	G	GS	CG	SV	IP	H	R	ER	HR	BB	SO	AVG	vLH	vRH	K/9	BB/9
Alcantara, Luis	R-R	6-0	150	11-1-97	0	4	3.98	16	0	0	3	32	34	23	14	3	9	34	.266	.321	.227	9.66	2.56
Austin, Michael	R-R	6-4	200	6-4-94	1	0	7.20	3	0	0	0	5	6	5	4	1	5	4	.286	.000	.400	7.20	9.00
Biasi, Sal	R-R	6-0	190	9-30-95	3	2	2.44	9	7	0	0	44	29	14	12	3	15	39	.186	.148	.211	7.92	3.05
Cloney, J.C.	L-L	6-1	226	8-3-94	3	1	3.77	12	7	0	0	43	44	19	18	4	3	35	.260	.294	.252	7.33	0.63
Fallwell, Tyler	R-R	6-5	210	11-8-95	1	0	2.45	4	0	0	0	11	12	6	3	0	4	17	.273	.000	.414	13.91	3.27
Familia, Felix	L-L	6-0	170	11-28-95	1	0	3.71	15	0	0	0	27	31	19	11	1	13	28	.279	.129	.338	9.45	4.39
Floyd, Jordan	L-L	6-3	240	2-23-95	2	3	2.20	14	0	0	1	29	35	10	7	1	9	18	.294	.364	.267	5.65	2.83

Pitching	B-T	HT	WT	DOB	W	L	ERA	G	GS	CG	SV	IP	H	R	ER	HR	BB	SO	AVG	vLH	vRH	K/9	BB/9
Garcia, Yerelmy	R-R	6-2	180	11-5-95	1	3	3.82	18	0	0	3	38	31	18	16	2	15	19	.230	.244	.223	4.54	3.58
Garmendia, Daniel	R-R	6-3	205	10-7-94	1	0	3.00	2	0	0	1	6	3	2	2	0	0	8	.158	.143	.167	12.00	0.00
Hernandez, Carlos	R-R	6-4	175	3-11-97	1	4	5.49	12	11	0	0	62	64	45	38	6	27	62	.266	.222	.296	8.95	3.90
Lenik, Kevin	R-R	6-5	225	8-1-91	0	0	0.00	2	0	0	1	5	3	0	0	0	0	4	.167	.000	.214	7.20	0.00
Maldonado, Ismael	R-R	6-4	170	9-28-95	0	3	10.13	4	4	0	0	16	21	21	18	4	16	13	.323	.346	.308	7.31	9.00
Markus, Joey	R-L	6-7	220	5-29-96	0	1	9.45	7	2	0	1	13	14	14	14	5	12	14	.269	.235	.286	9.45	8.10
Mayes, Connor	R-R	6-2	205	5-23-96	4	2	3.82	10	6	0	0	38	36	21	16	2	10	33	.242	.327	.192	7.88	2.39
Messier, Michael	R-L	6-6	205	5-12-95	1	6	5.92	13	5	0	1	49	59	34	32	7	20	48	.298	.359	.283	8.88	3.70
Ratliff, Tad	R-R	6-2	240	4-3-96	0	0	11.25	2	0	0	0	4	6	5	5	1	0	9	.333	.167	.417	20.25	0.00
Snider, Collin	R-R	6-4	200	10-10-95	3	0	1.85	12	0	0	1	24	26	15	5	1	6	16	.274	.333	.242	5.92	2.22
Sotillet, Andres	R-R	6-1	175	3-2-97	0	2	11.20	4	4	0	0	14	22	19	17	1	3	5	.367	.292	.417	3.29	1.98
Tillo, Daniel	L-L	6-5	215	6-13-96	3	2	3.48	7	7	0	0	31	35	14	12	1	6	25	.285	.318	.277	7.26	1.74
Watson, Nolan	R-R	6-2	195	1-25-97	0	1	7.36	3	3	0	0	11	15	9	9	0	3	10	.306	.267	.324	8.18	2.45
Webb, Nathan	R-R	6-2	215	8-20-97	3	5	5.28	12	12	1	0	58	61	42	34	5	22	44	.269	.344	.219	6.83	3.41
Zuber, Tyler	R-R	5-11	175	6-16-95	1	0	2.16	16	0	0	6	25	26	12	6	0	7	38	.265	.171	.318	13.68	2.52

Fielding

C: Arroyo 3, Atencio 19, Hutchins 5, Marquez 1, Rivero 41. **1B:** Carrasco 21, Cash 22, Dale 13, Jones 1, Rohlman 18. **2B:** Atencio 1, Gonzalez 4, Marquez 46, Nunez 17. **3B:** Carrasco 34, Dale 4, Gonzalez 3, Jones 2, Nunez 27. **SS:** Bartlett 1, Gonzalez 3, Guzman 51, Nunez 13. **OF:** Caraballo 3, Gigliotti 39, Jones 4, Jones 59, Matias 52, Nunez 1, Rohlman 30, Sanchez 19.

Idaho Falls Chukars Rookie

IDAHO FALLS CHUKARS — *ROOKIE*

PIONEER LEAGUE

Batting	B-T	HT	WT	DOB	AVG	vLH	vRH	G	AB	R	H	2B	3B	HR	RBI	BB	HBP	SH	SF	SO	SB	CS	SLG	OBP
Aracena, Ricky	B-R	5-8	160	10-2-97	.385	.167	.450	6	26	10	10	1	1	2	7	4	0	1	0	5	1	0	.731	.467
Collado, Offerman	L-R	5-10	140	6-10-96	.250	.185	.264	41	156	28	39	3	2	0	16	22	0	5	0	24	9	3	.295	.343
Fermin, Freddy	R-R	5-10	185	5-16-95	.282	.200	.305	47	163	30	46	5	2	1	39	31	4	0	3	21	0	2	.356	.403
Fukofuka, Amalani	R-R	6-1	180	9-25-95	.295	.315	.290	66	278	66	82	17	3	6	36	26	4	0	3	73	24	6	.442	.360
Gonzalez, Julio	L-R	5-10	185	6-14-95	.290	.240	.299	44	162	21	47	10	3	0	35	30	0	5	1	25	9	1	.389	.399
Gray, Logan	R-R	6-1	180	1-12-95	.253	.235	.258	43	154	28	39	8	2	6	26	16	2	1	1	71	1	1	.448	.330
Griffin, Dalton	L-L	6-3	200	9-2-97	.225	.143	.242	12	40	6	9	2	0	0	3	8	1	0	0	12	0	0	.275	.367
Hicklen, Brewer	R-R	6-2	208	2-9-96	.299	.250	.307	20	87	19	26	8	2	1	10	9	3	0	0	22	3	1	.471	.384
Hudgins, Chris	R-R	6-1	190	3-2-96	.305	.381	.286	29	105	21	32	11	1	3	23	10	3	1	2	30	0	0	.514	.375
Jones, Travis	R-R	6-4	210	9-29-95	.335	.290	.346	42	164	40	55	15	3	4	42	18	10	1	4	32	20	3	.537	.424
McCray, Jonathan	B-R	5-10	180	1-8-95	.323	.450	.288	22	93	19	30	4	4	4	14	5	0	0	1	17	1	3	.581	.354
Miller, Darrell	R-R	6-2	220	9-29-93	.376	.333	.385	48	186	45	70	18	0	5	43	25	6	0	3	25	0	0	.554	.459
Morales, Matt	B-R	5-11	170	11-26-96	.358	.407	.348	37	165	31	59	13	1	1	25	14	0	4	1	29	12	3	.467	.406
Rinn, Robby	L-L	6-1	205	10-17-92	.355	.295	.371	69	282	58	100	22	2	6	59	36	2	0	2	35	3	2	.511	.429
Straub, Tyler	R-R	6-4	205	7-8-93	.278	.296	.275	67	255	36	71	16	2	5	46	31	4	1	3	41	19	5	.416	.362
Vasquez, Cristhian	L-L	6-0	175	9-11-96	.260	.238	.265	60	231	42	60	7	5	1	24	20	7	1	2	40	11	5	.346	.335
Vizcaino, Vance	L-R	6-3	215	8-1-94	.287	.177	.314	22	87	17	25	5	2	2	16	7	1	0	1	20	10	3	.460	.344
Wakamatsu, Jake	R-L	6-0	180	5-18-92	.217	.238	.212	31	106	20	23	3	0	3	22	5	1	1	2	16	6	0	.330	.254

Pitching	B-T	HT	WT	DOB	W	L	ERA	G	GS	CG	SV	IP	H	R	ER	HR	BB	SO	AVG	vLH	vRH	K/9	BB/9
Acevedo, Randy	R-R	6-1	155	3-14-97	0	0	6.63	5	0	0	1	19	36	17	14	0	6	8	.414	.400	.418	3.79	2.84
Beckwith, Andrew	R-R	6-0	180	3-22-95	1	0	2.55	13	0	0	4	25	27	7	7	0	8	30	.281	.250	.297	10.95	2.92
Bramblett, Geoffrey	R-R	6-2	200	4-26-95	4	3	5.79	14	4	0	1	56	75	41	36	6	16	40	.333	.277	.356	6.43	2.57
Capps, Holden	R-L	6-2	180	3-24-95	1	3	5.49	9	9	0	0	41	52	33	25	2	15	34	.313	.259	.324	7.46	3.29
De Leon, Jose	R-R	5-11	175	4-19-95	1	0	9.35	5	0	0	0	9	12	12	9	0	8	7	.324	.417	.280	7.27	8.31
Drabble, Dillon	R-R	6-2	190	7-12-96	2	3	5.25	7	7	0	0	36	51	32	21	3	16	33	.327	.388	.299	8.25	4.00
Estevez, Emmanuel	R-R	6-3	210	8-22-96	0	0	2.70	2	0	0	0	3	3	1	1	0	2	1	.273	.000	.333	2.70	5.40
Garcia, Robert	R-L	6-4	225	6-14-96	1	5	10.65	11	10	0	0	49	75	65	58	9	25	40	.341	.389	.332	7.35	4.59
Gwinn, Jeremy	R-R	6-5	195	10-1-95	0	5	9.75	15	3	0	2	48	77	57	52	14	21	41	.365	.308	.384	7.69	3.94
Harris, Garrettson	R-R	6-3	220	3-21-94	2	0	8.13	17	0	0	2	31	39	29	28	3	20	35	.307	.423	.277	10.16	5.81
Hope, Carter	L-R	6-3	195	2-5-95	0	0	8.31	2	0	0	0	4	9	4	4	0	1	3	.429	.200	.500	6.23	2.08
Hrbek, Danny	L-R	5-11	195	12-27-94	0	1	8.41	12	0	0	0	20	28	21	19	4	17	28	.329	.250	.361	12.39	7.52
Lara, Janser	R-R	6-0	170	8-10-96	4	2	4.13	12	10	0	0	52	51	28	24	8	29	57	.253	.210	.271	9.80	4.99
Marte, Christopher	R-R	6-1	190	7-9-96	3	4	5.40	15	1	0	1	47	66	36	28	5	17	29	.332	.327	.333	5.59	3.28
McKay, David	R-R	6-3	205	3-31-95	6	5	6.49	14	14	0	0	79	104	62	57	13	18	68	.313	.318	.311	7.75	2.05
Mitchell, Josh	R-L	6-2	220	9-8-94	2	1	7.59	14	0	0	4	21	34	19	18	4	6	24	.354	.364	.351	10.13	2.53
Nesbit, Cody	R-R	6-3	175	3-5-96	2	0	4.66	3	0	0	0	10	10	6	5	0	4	8	.263	.273	.259	7.45	3.72
Olds, Damon	R-R	6-4	190	10-17-94	0	1	6.56	13	0	0	0	23	34	29	17	3	25	26	.324	.321	.325	10.03	9.64
Pinto, Julio	R-R	6-3	185	11-18-95	4	8	10.33	14	14	0	0	61	91	80	70	13	47	54	.338	.393	.314	7.97	6.93
Silva, Michael	R-R	6-1	190	11-22-94	0	0	3.44	9	0	0	1	18	27	16	7	0	9	15	.333	.440	.286	7.36	4.42
Sotillet, Andres	R-R	6-1	175	3-2-97	0	2	10.57	4	4	0	0	15	32	18	18	5	4	11	.427	.526	.393	6.46	2.35

Fielding

C: Fermin 36, Hudgins 27, Miller 15. **1B:** Griffin 1, Jones 2, Miller 2, Rinn 66, Straub 5. **2B:** Collado 22, Gonzalez 16, McCray 13, Morales 5, Wakamatsu 25. **3B:** Gonzalez 9, Gray 7, Jones 1, Straub 59, Wakamatsu 4. **SS:** Aracena 6, Collado 18, Gonzalez 20, Morales 32, Straub 3. **OF:** Fukofuka 64, Gray 24, Griffin 7, Hicklen 13, Jones 38, McCray 7, Vasquez 59, Vizcaino 21.

AZL ROYALS

ROOKIE

ARIZONA LEAGUE

Batting	B-T	HT	WT	DOB	AVG	vLH	vRH	G	AB	R	H	2B	3B	HR	RBI	BB	HBP	SH	SF	SO	SB	CS	SLG	OBP
Arroyo, Michael	R-R	6-0	181	12-31-95	.083	—	.083	4	12	0	1	0	0	0	2	0	0	0	0	6	0	0	.083	.083
Bartlett, Max	R-R	5-11	165	1-14-95	.278	.400	.231	6	18	5	5	1	0	1	3	5	0	0	0	2	0	2	.500	.435
Bradshaw, Montae	R-R	5-10	170	4-29-96	.241	.300	.224	28	87	13	21	3	1	0	11	8	2	6	3	17	0	0	.299	.310
Caraballo, Jose	R-R	6-1	180	1-7-97	.217	.290	.195	43	161	21	35	13	1	4	17	9	1	1	2	70	0	0	.385	.260
Cox, Brady	R-R	6-0	205	10-24-94	.146	.154	.143	23	55	14	8	0	1	1	4	10	6	0	0	16	1	0	.236	.338
Heath, Nick	L-L	6-1	187	11-27-93	.250	—	.250	4	16	3	4	1	0	0	3	3	0	0	0	2	3	0	.313	.368
Henry, Isaiah	R-R	6-3	185	3-22-99	.202	.177	.207	32	99	13	20	1	1	0	3	18	2	0	0	43	7	6	.232	.336
Hicklen, Brewer	R-R	6-2	208	2-9-96	.348	.533	.296	19	69	19	24	3	3	3	13	9	3	0	1	24	13	3	.609	.439
James, Tyler	R-R	5-10	162	9-14-96	.258	.313	.244	46	159	35	41	8	5	0	10	20	4	6	1	38	31	1	.371	.353
Jones, Travis	R-R	6-4	210	9-29-95	.485	.286	.539	9	33	10	16	1	1	0	6	4	4	0	0	2	4	2	.576	.585
Lopez, Raymond	B-R	6-1	155	12-4-98	.182	—	.182	3	11	1	2	1	1	0	2	1	0	0	0	6	0	0	.455	.250
Lovelady, Josh	R-R	5-11	214	9-20-93	.241	.308	.220	18	54	5	13	2	0	0	7	4	0	0	0	8	1	1	.278	.293
Martin, Andres	R-R	6-0	190	2-14-97	.274	.412	.232	21	73	7	20	0	1	0	6	8	0	1	0	17	2	4	.301	.346
Medina, Angel	R-R	6-1	180	11-2-98	.255	.206	.268	43	157	20	40	2	7	2	17	5	1	0	1	50	3	2	.395	.281
Melendez, MJ	L-R	6-1	185	11-29-98	.262	.171	.286	47	168	25	44	8	3	4	30	26	4	0	0	60	4	2	.417	.374
Morin, Parker	L-R	5-11	195	7-2-91	.280	.250	.286	7	25	3	7	2	1	1	6	1	0	0	0	2	0	0	.560	.308
Perez, Cristian	R-R	5-10	170	10-26-98	.270	.244	.277	48	196	28	53	15	0	1	23	16	2	2	3	31	6	6	.362	.327
Pratto, Nick	L-L	6-1	195	10-6-98	.248	.234	.252	52	198	25	49	15	3	4	34	24	3	0	5	58	10	4	.414	.330
Ramos, Mauricio	R-R	6-1	185	2-2-92	.429	.286	.571	4	14	3	6	1	0	0	3	1	1	0	0	1	0	0	.500	.500
Romero, Rafael	B-R	5-10	155	11-14-98	.200	.167	.205	16	50	8	10	2	0	0	9	5	1	1	2	15	0	0	.240	.276
Ruiz, Esteury	R-R	6-0	150	2-15-99	.419	.417	.419	21	86	22	36	10	6	3	23	4	0	0	1	20	9	0	.779	.440
2-team total (31 Padres)					.350	.417	.419	52	206	45	72	20	10	4	39	13	3	2	1	54	26	6	.602	.395
Smith, Isaiah	R-R	6-3	190	6-19-99	.148	.241	.123	37	135	17	20	5	1	2	14	7	3	1	1	39	4	0	.244	.206

Pitching	B-T	HT	WT	DOB	W	L	ERA	G	GS	CG	SV	IP	H	R	ER	HR	BB	SO	AVG	vLH	vRH	K/9	BB/9
Acevedo, Randy	R-R	6-1	155	3-14-97	4	3	3.13	8	2	1	0	37	36	19	13	2	13	22	.247	.273	.231	5.30	3.13
Austin, Michael	R-R	6-4	200	6-4-94	1	0	3.18	11	0	0	5	11	14	6	4	1	3	13	.311	.313	.310	10.32	2.38
Beckwith, Andrew	R-R	6-0	180	3-22-95	0	0	10.13	3	0	0	0	3	5	3	3	0	2	2	.385	.000	.417	6.75	6.75
Biasi, Sal	R-R	6-0	190	9-30-95	1	0	2.31	4	1	0	0	12	9	8	3	1	8	15	.205	.167	.231	11.57	6.17
Capps, Holden	R-L	6-2	180	3-24-95	0	1	3.00	4	2	0	0	12	12	6	4	0	4	11	.250	.167	.300	8.25	3.00
Caramo, Yender	R-R	6-0	175	8-25-91	0	0	0.00	1	1	0	0	1	0	0	0	0	0	1	.000	.000	.000	9.00	0.00
De Leon, Jose	R-R	5-11	175	4-19-95	3	1	7.16	9	0	0	0	16	20	14	13	0	11	12	.313	.231	.368	6.61	6.06
Drabble, Dillon	R-R	6-2	190	7-12-96	0	0	3.95	6	3	0	0	14	16	8	6	0	6	6	.302	.375	.270	3.95	3.95
Estevez, Emmanuel	R-R	6-3	210	8-22-96	0	2	3.38	10	0	0	0	21	16	8	8	3	13	20	.208	.103	.271	8.44	5.48
Ferguson, Andy	R-R	6-1	195	9-2-88	0	0	0.00	3	3	0	0	2	0	0	0	0	1	5	.000	.000	.000	19.29	3.86
Floyd, Jordan	L-L	6-3	240	2-23-95	0	0	0.00	2	0	0	2	3	1	0	0	0	2	5	.100	.000	.143	15.00	6.00
Garabito, Gerson	R-R	6-0	160	8-19-95	0	0	6.00	2	2	0	0	3	4	2	2	1	1	2	.333	.400	.286	6.00	3.00
Garcia, Robert	R-L	6-4	225	6-14-96	1	0	5.40	2	0	0	0	5	6	3	3	1	3	8	.286	.286	.286	14.40	5.40
Garmendia, Daniel	R-R	6-3	205	10-7-94	3	1	3.06	11	0	0	0	18	9	11	6	1	7	19	.145	.136	.150	9.68	3.57
Gonzalez, Kelvin	R-R	6-0	170	12-24-97	0	2	7.02	7	0	0	0	17	25	16	13	2	3	17	.333	.296	.354	9.18	1.62
Goudeau, Ashton	R-R	6-6	205	7-23-92	0	0	0.00	2	1	0	0	3	2	0	0	0	1	3	.200	.000	.250	9.00	3.00
Greenlees, Stephen	L-L	6-4	215	5-7-96	0	2	6.30	11	1	0	1	20	23	16	14	0	9	15	.281	.211	.302	6.75	4.05
Hope, Carter	L-R	6-3	195	2-5-95	1	0	3.75	7	0	0	0	12	15	6	5	1	0	8	.294	.150	.387	6.00	0.00
Hrbek, Danny	L-R	5-11	195	12-27-94	0	1	4.91	3	0	0	1	4	4	4	2	0	2	6	.250	.143	.333	14.73	4.91
Johnson, Bryar	R-R	6-3	200	8-17-99	1	3	6.35	12	2	0	0	23	29	26	16	1	11	20	.296	.344	.273	7.94	4.37
Klein, Jackson	R-R	6-2	185	7-13-94	0	1	9.00	9	0	0	0	14	15	14	14	2	13	8	.300	.310	.286	5.14	8.36
Magallanes, Kelvin	R-R	6-1	201	7-15-94	0	0	43.20	1	0	0	0	2	6	8	8	0	4	2	.600	1.000	.556	10.80	21.60
Maldonado, Ismael	R-R	6-4	170	9-28-95	1	2	5.95	9	3	0	0	39	44	31	26	6	20	36	.273	.289	.266	8.24	4.58
Markus, Joey	R-L	6-7	220	5-29-96	0	0	6.97	3	1	0	0	10	12	8	8	0	6	9	.286	.222	.303	7.84	5.23
Mayes, Connor	R-R	6-2	205	5-23-96	1	0	0.00	2	0	0	0	5	3	0	0	0	1	3	.188	.200	.182	5.06	1.69
Mitchell, Josh	R-L	6-2	220	9-8-94	1	0	9.58	4	2	0	0	10	17	12	11	1	0	11	.362	.316	.393	9.58	0.00
Neuweiler, Charlie	R-R	6-1	205	2-8-99	3	3	1.76	12	5	0	0	41	28	13	8	3	12	34	.192	.155	.216	7.46	2.63
Olds, Damon	R-R	6-4	190	10-17-94	0	0	0.00	2	0	0	0	2	0	0	0	0	1	3	.000	.000	.000	11.57	3.86
Schulewitz, Mitchell	R-R	5-10	165	12-24-94	0	1	2.40	11	0	0	1	15	13	4	4	0	2	15	.232	.250	.219	9.00	1.20
Sigman, Jackson	R-R	6-2	200	6-13-95	1	0	4.70	5	0	0	1	8	11	4	4	0	0	11	.324	.333	.316	12.91	0.00
Sotillet, Andres	R-R	6-1	175	3-2-97	3	0	2.28	5	4	0	0	28	27	7	7	1	6	26	.250	.319	.197	8.46	1.95
Steele, Evan	R-L	6-5	210	11-14-96	0	2	5.63	5	5	0	0	8	11	8	5	2	2	16	.306	.200	.346	18.00	2.25
Tejeda, Gustavo	R-R	6-0	185	8-2-95	0	0	1.50	5	0	0	0	6	3	1	1	0	3	10	.158	.000	.250	15.00	4.50
Tillo, Daniel	L-L	6-5	215	6-13-96	0	0	9.53	3	2	0	0	6	8	6	6	0	0	7	.333	.111	.467	11.12	0.00
Van Buren, Malcolm	R-R	6-4	185	7-5-98	0	3	7.12	12	11	0	0	30	36	31	24	3	19	25	.293	.364	.253	7.42	5.64
Watson, Nolan	R-R	6-2	195	1-25-97	0	1	25.07	4	2	0	0	5	15	13	13	0	4	2	.536	.500	.563	3.86	7.71
Willis, Marlin	L-L	6-4	190	6-5-98	1	1	3.80	8	3	0	0	21	22	12	9	0	5	13	.259	.250	.262	5.48	2.11

Fielding

C: Arroyo 3, Cox 14, Lovelady 12, Melendez 30, Morin 5. **1B:** Cox 6, Jones 1, Pratto 51. **2B:** Bartlett 1, Bradshaw 1, James 39, Romero 1, Ruiz 17. **3B:** Bartlett 2, Cox 1, Jones 4, Medina 42, Ramos 3, Romero 10. **SS:** Bartlett 3, Medina 1, Perez 48, Romero 6. **OF:** Bradshaw 27, Caraballo 43, Heath 3, Henry 28, James 4, Jones 7, Lopez 3, Martin 21, Smith 36.

DSL ROYALS

ROOKIE

DOMINICAN SUMMER LEAGUE

Batting	B-T	HT	WT	DOB	AVG	vLH	vRH	G	AB	R	H	2B	3B	HR	RBI	BB	HBP	SH	SF	SO	SB	CS	SLG	OBP
Aponte, Brayant	R-R	5-7	155	1-26-00	.184	.243	.164	50	147	10	27	3	0	0	9	9	7	6	1	24	8	5	.204	.262
Biegel, Daytan	R-R	6-0	175	2-4-00	.184	.200	.177	44	141	9	26	8	1	0	3	4	8	1	2	41	1	2	.255	.245
Familia, Felix	R-R	6-2	205	10-13-98	.207	.081	.250	44	145	13	30	9	0	0	18	11	4	0	4	45	2	0	.269	.274
Febres, Nicolas	R-R	5-11	178	10-11-98	.113	.000	.150	26	53	4	6	2	0	0	5	3	3	1	2	18	2	0	.151	.197
Garcia, Maikel	R-R	6-0	145	3-3-00	.223	.290	.202	48	157	14	35	1	1	0	7	12	0	3	1	13	9	3	.242	.277
Jaquez, Rubendy	B-R	5-11	174	2-13-99	.267	.254	.272	62	210	19	56	8	2	1	18	32	0	3	1	41	19	8	.338	.362
Mendez, Yenrrys	B-R	5-7	165	5-31-00	.077	.133	.060	30	65	8	5	0	0	0	5	9	3	2	0	15	1	1	.077	.221
Mondesi, Paul	R-R	6-0	215	7-7-98	.150	.278	.103	40	133	2	20	2	0	1	9	4	0	0	1	19	3	2	.188	.174
Nacero, Kember	R-R	5-11	155	3-5-00	.200	.167	.209	25	85	6	17	0	0	0	5	8	3	3	2	36	4	4	.200	.286
Pineda, Hector	R-R	5-10	160	8-22-98	.118	.059	.136	23	76	5	9	3	0	1	9	6	1	1	0	19	1	1	.197	.193
Reynoso, Reynin	L-L	5-11	160	11-25-99	.224	.195	.233	49	161	20	36	4	2	1	11	24	5	2	0	42	5	11	.292	.342
Rodriguez, Ismaldo	B-R	6-0	175	7-3-98	.223	.143	.252	58	184	22	41	8	0	5	22	23	15	1	0	66	17	6	.348	.356
Romero, Rafael	B-R	5-10	155	11-14-98	.203	.174	.214	28	79	7	16	2	0	0	1	8	3	0	0	14	2	1	.228	.300
Sanchez, Javier	R-R	5-11	160	10-27-99	.146	.167	.141	30	89	5	13	4	0	0	6	6	2	1	1	19	3	3	.191	.214
Soto, Edickson	R-R	5-11	165	2-28-00	.260	.342	.235	53	173	15	45	8	1	0	17	13	6	0	2	31	12	3	.318	.330
Vargas, Randor	L-L	5-10	160	12-9-99	.138	.063	.165	53	123	13	17	2	0	2	6	15	0	2	0	43	6	5	.203	.232
Vicente, Warling	R-R	5-10	165	6-8-99	.222	.226	.221	51	144	23	32	7	0	0	6	25	3	3	0	36	10	7	.271	.349

Pitching	B-T	HT	WT	DOB	W	L	ERA	G	GS	CG	SV	IP	H	R	ER	HR	BB	SO	AVG	vLH	vRH	K/9	BB/9
Abreu, Brian	R-R	6-2	194	6-3-99	0	1	6.26	13	0	0	0	27	26	19	19	0	20	16	.250	.171	.290	5.27	6.59
Alcantara, Adrian	R-R	6-1	178	8-29-99	3	2	2.38	13	0	0	3	34	24	12	9	1	14	33	.198	.170	.226	8.74	3.71
Auguste, Donato	R-R	6-2	201	1-19-98	0	2	3.20	13	1	0	0	25	18	13	9	0	15	19	.198	.231	.173	6.75	5.33
Cabrera, Rovaldis	L-L	5-10	176	11-22-99	1	1	2.21	9	8	0	0	37	38	13	9	1	4	26	.273	.370	.250	6.38	0.98
Capellan, Delvin	R-R	6-1	167	12-6-98	3	2	0.48	12	12	0	0	56	32	4	3	1	3	48	.164	.192	.148	7.71	0.48
Castillo, Adriam	R-R	6-0	190	11-19-98	4	1	2.22	13	6	0	1	45	24	12	11	0	13	37	.163	.177	.153	7.46	2.62
De Los Santos, Kelvin	R-R	6-4	215	2-13-98	1	1	5.40	9	0	0	0	12	15	7	7	0	7	5	.333	.300	.360	3.86	5.40
Fana, Jeisson	R-R	5-11	155	1-29-99	0	0	8.71	9	0	0	0	10	12	10	10	1	7	8	.293	.316	.273	6.97	6.10
Frias, Adan	L-L	5-9	163	5-18-99	0	5	4.26	14	14	0	0	51	47	35	24	2	17	52	.245	.238	.247	9.24	3.02
Gonzalez, Kelvin	R-R	6-0	170	12-24-97	4	1	0.36	9	0	0	2	25	20	6	1	0	8	16	.241	.222	.250	5.68	2.84
Jimenez, Wilmer	L-L	5-11	162	6-1-98	4	3	2.64	13	8	0	1	44	29	15	13	2	11	55	.188	.250	.179	11.17	2.23
Matos, Yonathan	R-R	6-3	194	7-6-98	0	3	7.76	14	0	0	0	29	30	28	25	2	26	21	.273	.326	.239	6.52	8.07
Medina, Victor	R-R	5-10	170	2-9-00	1	2	1.33	14	2	0	2	27	12	7	4	0	16	18	.129	.094	.148	6.00	5.33
Mendez, Leandro	R-R	5-11	181	4-21-00	3	4	2.16	15	2	0	3	33	23	11	8	1	15	23	.213	.225	.203	6.21	4.05
Morales, Austin	R-R	6-2	185	1-23-98	2	2	2.57	10	0	0	1	14	8	8	4	0	8	6	.170	.133	.188	3.86	5.14
Nunez, Braulio	L-L	6-1	178	12-21-99	0	2	6.08	9	1	0	0	13	15	11	9	0	9	8	.283	.091	.333	5.40	6.08
Pinales, Gerson	R-R	6-2	166	9-2-99	0	0	2.45	3	0	0	0	4	2	1	1	1	6	2	.200	.000	.400	4.91	14.73
Rodriguez, Diogenes	R-R	6-1	178	2-17-99	0	3	4.78	12	2	0	0	26	18	16	14	0	13	12	.198	.158	.226	4.10	4.44
Sanchez, Carlos	R-R	6-0	175	6-20-99	1	1	3.34	13	2	0	0	30	20	16	11	1	13	19	.192	.122	.238	5.76	3.94
Valdez, Albert	L-L	6-2	165	7-5-99	0	0	6.75	2	0	0	0	4	1	3	3	0	2	0	.083	.000	.091	0.00	4.50
Zerpa, Angel	L-L	6-0	175	9-27-99	3	4	1.84	14	12	0	0	64	47	15	13	0	11	39	.208	.128	.229	5.51	1.55

Fielding

C: Familia 32, Febres 11, Mondesi 39. **1B:** Febres 10, Jaquez 20, Pineda 6, Rodriguez 44. **2B:** Aponte 9, Garcia 11, Jaquez 41, Romero 3, Sanchez 12. **3B:** Aponte 40, Pineda 15, Romero 12, Sanchez 9. **SS:** Garcia 33, Nacero 25, Romero 14, Sanchez 8. **OF:** Biegel 26, Mendez 25, Reynoso 44, Rodriguez 19, Soto 32, Vargas 45, Vicente 48.

Los Angeles Angels

SEASON IN A SENTENCE: Mike Trout missed six weeks with a thumb injury and starters Garrett Richards, Tyler Skaggs, Andrew Heaney and Matt Shoemaker all spent at least half the season on the disabled list, as the Angels went 80-82 to post back-to-back losing seasons for the first time since 1993-94.

HIGH POINT: Trying to keep their slim playoff hopes alive, August trade acquisition Justin Upton homered twice off Rangers lefthander Cole Hamels to beat Texas 2-0 on Sept. 16 and put the Angels just one game back of the wild card. They would not get any closer however, going 4-10 after Upton's big-time performance.

LOW POINT: Trout was in the middle of his best season yet when he jammed his left thumb sliding into second base on May 28 at Miami. An MRI revealed a torn thumb ligament that required surgery. He ultimately missed 40 games.

NOTABLE ROOKIES: Righthander Parker Bridwell, acquired from the Orioles for cash in April, emerged as one of the top rookies of the season, going 10-3, 3.64 to help stabilize the Angels rotation after it was demolished by injuries. Righthander Alex Meyer posted a 3.74 ERA in 13 starts before he too was lost to injury, suffering a torn labrum that will keep him out all of 2018. Righthander Keynan Middleton showcased his 96-100 mph fastball and delivered a 3.86 ERA in 64 appearances out of the bullpen.

KEY TRANSACTIONS: The Angels continued to play for the present with two August waiver trade acquisitions in Upton and second baseman Brandon Phillips. The moves were necessitated by Cameron Maybin and Danny Espinosa, acquired in the offseason, failing to perform in left field and second base and getting shipped out before the year ended. Righthander David Hernandez performed well in relief before being traded to the Diamondbacks at the July 31 deadline.

DOWN OF THE FARM: A system largely bereft of talent finished with a .492 win percentage and saw only one team make the playoffs. There were positives on an individual level, as dymanic outfielder Jahmai Jones blossomed in Class A and 10th overall draft pick Jordon Adell dominated at the Rookie levels after signing. An intriguing crop of young, Latin American arms led by Jose Soriano and Wilkel Hernandez began to emerge as the Angels refocused on making international scouting a priority.

OPENING DAY PAYROLL: $160,375,333 (11th)

PLAYERS OF THE YEAR

MAJOR LEAGUE

Mike Trout
OF

.306/.442/.629
Led MLB in OPS
Career high BB%

BILL MITCHELL

MINOR LEAGUE

Jaime Barria
RHP

(High Class A/
Double-A/Triple-A)
7-9, 2.80, 1.07 WHIP

ORGANIZATION LEADERS

BATTING — *Minimum 250 AB

MAJORS			
*	AVG	Mike Trout	.306
*	OPS	Mike Trout	1.071
	HR	Mike Trout	33
	RBI	Albert Pujols	101
MINORS			
*	AVG	Carlos Perez, Salt Lake	.352
*	OBP	Carlos Perez, Salt Lake	.423
*	SLG	Jared Walsh, Mobile, Inland Empire	.506
*	OPS	Carlos Perez, Salt Lake	.925
	R	Jahmai Jones, Burlington, Inland Empire	86
	H	Brennon Lund, Burlington, Inland Empire, Mobile	151
	TB	Jahmai Jones, Burlington, Inland Empire	231
	2B	Jared Walsh, Mobile, Inland Empire	32
	3B	Troy Montgomery, Burlington, Inland Empire, Mobile	8
		Jo Adell, AZL Angels, Orem	8
	HR	Jeyson Sanchez, Burlington, Orem	15
	RBI	Rey Navarro, Salt Lake	82
	BB	Matt Thaiss, Inland Empire, Mobile	77
	SO	Jordan Zimmerman, Burlington, Inland Empire	120
	SB	Michael Hermosillo, Inland Empire, Mobile, Salt L.	35

PITCHING — #Minimum 75 IP

MAJORS			
	W	J.C. Ramirez	11
#	ERA	Yusmeiro Petit	2.76
	SO	J.C Ramirez	105
	SV	Bud Norris	19
MINORS			
	W	Troy Scribner, Salt Lake	11
	L	Luis Pena, Inland Empire, Mobile	13
#	ERA	Grayson Long, Inland Empire, Mobile, Erie	2.69
	G	Greg Mahle, Mobile, Salt Lake	50
	GS	Luis Pena, Inland Empire, Mobile	29
	SV	Samil De Los Santos, Burlington, Inland Empire	12
	IP	Luis Pena, Inland Empire, Mobile	151
	BB	Luis Pena, Inland Empire, Mobile	67
	SO	Luis Pena, Inland Empire, Mobile	167
#	AVG	Jaime Barria, Inland Empire, Mobile, Salt Lake	.227

2017 PERFORMANCE

General Manager: Billy Eppler. **Farm Director:** Mike Gallego. **Scouting Director:** Matt Swanson.

Class	Team	League	W	L	PCT	Finish	Manager
Majors	Los Angeles Angels	American	80	82	.494	t-6th (15)	Mike Scioscia
Triple-A	Salt Lake Bees	Pacific Coast	72	70	.507	7th (16)	Keith Johnson
Double-A	Mobile BayBears	Southern	64	75	.46	8th (10)	Sal Fasano
High-A	Inland Empire 66ers	California	65	75	.464	6th (8)	Chad Tracy
Low-A	Burlington Bees	Midwest	60	79	.432	14th (16)	Adam Melhuse
Rookie	Orem Owlz	Pioneer	49	26	.653	1st (8)	Tom Nieto
Rookie	AZL Angels	Arizona	30	26	.536	t-7th (15)	Dave Stapleton
Overall 2017 Minor League Record			340	351	.492	19th (30)	

ORGANIZATION STATISTICS

LOS ANGELES ANGELS

AMERICAN LEAGUE

Batting	B-T	HT	WT	DOB	AVG	vLH	vRH	G	AB	R	H	2B	3B	HR	RBI	BB	HBP	SH	SF	SO	SB	CS	SLG	OBP
Calhoun, Kole	L-L	5-10	205	10-14-87	.244	.223	.253	155	569	77	139	23	2	19	71	71	8	0	6	134	5	1	.392	.333
Cowart, Kaleb	B-R	6-3	225	6-2-92	.226	.167	.238	50	102	18	23	5	1	3	11	10	3	2	0	28	4	2	.382	.313
Cron, C.J.	R-R	6-4	235	1-5-90	.248	.233	.253	100	339	39	84	14	1	16	56	22	7	0	3	96	3	2	.437	.305
Escobar, Yunel	R-R	6-2	215	11-2-82	.274	.343	.246	89	350	43	96	20	1	7	31	29	2	0	0	51	1	4	.397	.333
Espinosa, Danny	R-B	6-0	205	4-25-87	.162	.163	.162	77	228	27	37	8	0	6	29	19	4	1	2	91	3	5	.276	.237
3-team total (8 Seattle, 8 Tampa Bay)					.173	.163	.162	93	266	30	46	10	0	6	31	21	5	1	2	109	4	5	.278	.245
Flores, Ramon	L-L	5-10	190	3-26-92	.125	.000	.143	3	8	0	1	0	0	0	1	0	0	0	1	1	0	0	.125	.111
Fontana, Nolan	L-R	5-11	195	6-6-91	.050	.000	.056	12	20	1	1	0	0	1	1	3	0	0	0	8	1	1	.200	.174
Franklin, Nick	B-R	6-1	190	3-2-91	.125	.000	.130	13	24	2	3	1	0	0	2	5	1	0	0	3	0	0	.167	.300
Graterol, Juan	R-R	6-1	205	2-14-89	.202	.148	.228	48	84	5	17	4	0	0	10	1	0	0	2	13	0	0	.250	.207
Maldonado, Martin	R-R	6-0	230	8-16-86	.221	.228	.219	138	429	43	95	19	1	14	38	15	18	8	1	119	0	2	.368	.277
Marte, Jefry	R-R	6-1	220	6-21-91	.173	.185	.161	45	127	10	22	5	0	4	14	13	4	0	1	34	1	0	.307	.269
Maybin, Cameron	R-R	6-3	215	4-4-87	.235	.275	.218	93	336	57	79	19	1	6	22	48	2	0	1	78	29	5	.351	.333
2-team total (21 Houston)					.228	.275	.218	114	395	63	90	20	2	10	35	51	2	1	1	94	33	8	.365	.319
Pennington, Cliff	R-B	5-11	195	6-15-84	.253	.246	.256	87	194	23	49	6	0	3	21	16	1	1	5	58	3	1	.330	.306
Perez, Carlos	R-R	6-0	210	10-27-90	.100	.000	.111	11	20	1	2	0	0	1	3	1	0	0	0	6	0	0	.250	.143
Phillips, Brandon	R-R	6-0	211	6-28-81	.255	.263	.253	24	102	13	26	7	0	2	8	2	0	1	0	16	1	0	.382	.269
Puello, Cesar	R-R	6-2	220	4-1-91	.250	.000	.333	1	4	0	1	0	0	0	1	0	0	0	0	1	2	0	.250	.250
2-team total (16 Tampa Bay)					.206	.000	.333	17	34	6	7	0	0	0	3	4	1	0	0	12	2	0	.206	.308
Pujols, Albert	R-R	6-3	240	1-16-80	.241	.230	.245	149	593	53	143	17	0	23	101	37	2	0	4	93	3	0	.386	.286
Revere, Ben	R-L	5-9	175	5-3-88	.275	.163	.298	109	291	37	80	13	2	1	20	15	0	0	2	25	21	6	.344	.308
Robinson, Shane	R-R	5-9	170	10-30-84	.194	.238	.100	20	31	7	6	0	0	0	1	3	0	0	1	5	2	0	.194	.257
Simmons, Andrelton	R-R	6-2	200	9-4-89	.278	.239	.291	158	589	77	164	38	2	14	69	47	3	0	8	67	19	6	.421	.331
Trout, Mike	R-R	6-2	235	8-7-91	.306	.281	.313	114	402	92	123	25	3	33	72	94	7	0	4	90	22	4	.629	.442
Upton, Justin	R-R	6-2	205	8-25-87	.245	.318	.224	27	98	19	24	7	0	7	15	17	0	0	0	33	4	0	.531	.357
2-team total (125 Detroit)					.273	.318	.224	152	557	100	152	44	0	35	109	74	3	0	1	180	14	5	.540	.361
Valbuena, Luis	L-R	5-10	215	11-30-85	.199	.105	.210	117	347	42	69	15	0	22	65	48	1	0	5	106	0	2	.432	.294
Young Jr., Eric	R-B	5-10	195	5-25-85	.264	.200	.293	47	110	24	29	5	0	4	16	5	7	3	0	31	12	3	.418	.336

Pitching	B-T	HT	WT	DOB	W	L	ERA	G	GS	CG	SV	IP	H	R	ER	HR	BB	SO	AVG	vLH	vRH	K/9	BB/9
Alvarez, Jose	L-L	5-11	190	5-6-89	0	3	3.88	64	0	0	1	49	50	23	21	7	12	45	.263	.245	.286	8.32	2.22
Bailey, Andrew	R-R	6-3	240	5-31-84	2	0	0.00	4	0	0	0	4	1	0	0	0	0	2	.077	.000	.125	4.50	0.00
Bedrosian, Cam	R-R	6-0	230	10-2-91	6	5	4.43	48	0	0	6	45	41	26	22	5	17	53	.240	.238	.242	10.68	3.43
Bridwell, Parker	R-R	6-4	185	8-2-91	10	3	3.64	21	20	0	0	121	115	52	49	19	30	73	.252	.252	.252	5.43	2.23
Chavez, Jesse	R-R	6-2	175	8-21-83	7	11	5.35	38	21	0	0	138	148	83	82	28	45	119	.276	.271	.280	7.76	2.93
Guerra, Deolis	R-R	6-5	245	4-17-89	2	2	4.68	19	0	0	0	25	20	13	13	4	12	22	.217	.234	.200	7.92	4.32
Gurka, Jason	L-L	6-0	170	1-10-88	0	0	0.00	3	0	0	0	1	2	0	0	0	1	0	.500	.667	.000	0.00	13.50
Heaney, Andrew	L-L	6-2	195	6-5-91	1	2	7.06	5	5	0	0	22	27	17	17	12	9	27	.300	.294	.301	11.22	3.74
Hernandez, David	R-R	6-3	245	5-13-85	1	0	2.23	38	0	0	1	36	29	10	9	0	8	37	.223	.175	.260	9.17	1.98
Magnifico, Damien	R-R	6-1	195	5-24-91	0	0	0.00	1	0	0	0	0	0	0	0	0	2	1	.000	.000	—	27.00	54.00
Meyer, Alex	R-R	6-9	225	1-3-90	4	5	3.74	13	13	0	0	67	48	30	28	6	42	75	.197	.228	.165	10.02	5.61
Middleton, Keynan	R-R	6-2	185	9-12-93	6	1	3.86	64	0	0	3	58	60	25	25	11	18	63	.266	.268	.264	9.72	2.78
Morin, Mike	R-R	6-4	220	5-3-91	0	0	6.91	10	0	0	0	14	21	11	11	3	2	10	.350	.407	.303	6.28	1.26
2-team total (6 Kansas City)					0	0	7.20	16	0	0	0	20	29	16	16	3	5	16	.345	.407	.303	7.20	2.25
Nolasco, Ricky	R-R	6-2	235	12-13-82	6	15	4.92	33	33	1	0	181	205	102	99	35	58	143	.286	.274	.298	7.11	2.88
Norris, Bud	R-R	6-0	215	3-2-85	2	6	4.21	60	3	0	19	62	56	29	29	8	27	74	.236	.188	.270	10.74	3.92
Paredes, Eduardo	R-R	6-1	170	3-6-95	0	1	4.43	18	0	0	1	22	21	11	11	2	6	17	.259	.226	.280	6.85	2.42
Parker, Blake	R-R	6-3	225	6-19-85	3	3	2.54	71	0	0	8	67	40	20	19	7	16	86	.172	.168	.177	11.50	2.14
Petit, Yusmeiro	R-R	6-1	255	11-22-84	5	2	2.76	60	1	0	4	91	69	32	28	9	18	101	.207	.237	.186	9.95	1.77
Pounders, Brooks	R-R	6-5	265	9-26-90	1	0	10.45	11	0	0	0	10	17	12	12	4	5	12	.362	.400	.333	10.45	4.35
Ramirez, JC	R-R	6-4	250	8-16-88	11	10	4.15	27	24	0	0	147	149	72	68	21	49	105	.267	.281	.254	6.41	2.99
Ramirez, Noe	R-R	6-3	205	12-22-89	0	0	2.16	10	0	0	0	8	3	3	2	0	4	10	.111	.286	.050	10.80	4.32
2-team total (2 Boston)					0	0	2.77	12	0	0	0	13	6	5	4	2	5	14	.136	.286	.050	9.69	3.46
Richards, Garrett	R-R	6-3	210	5-27-88	0	2	2.28	6	6	0	0	28	18	8	7	1	7	27	.180	.188	.173	8.78	2.28

Pitching	B-T	HT	WT	DOB	W	L	ERA	G	GS	CG	SV	IP	H	R	ER	HR	BB	SO	AVG	vLH	vRH	K/9	BB/9
Salas, Fernando	R-R	6-2	200	5-30-85	1	0	2.63	13	0	0	0	14	7	4	4	0	2	9	.167	.211	.130	5.93	1.32
Scribner, Troy	R-R	6-3	190	7-2-91	2	1	4.18	10	4	0	0	24	17	14	11	7	10	18	.195	.184	.204	6.85	3.80
Shoemaker, Matt	R-R	6-2	225	9-27-86	6	3	4.52	14	14	0	0	78	73	41	39	15	28	69	.251	.275	.229	8.00	3.24
Skaggs, Tyler	L-L	6-4	215	7-13-91	2	6	4.55	16	16	0	0	85	90	46	43	13	28	76	.274	.267	.276	8.05	2.96
Street, Huston	R-R	6-0	205	8-2-83	0	0	0.00	4	0	0	0	4	2	0	0	0	1	3	.143	.000	.222	6.75	2.25
Valdez, Jose	R-R	6-1	200	3-1-90	0	0	18.00	1	0	0	0	1	1	2	2	1	1	1	.250	.000	.500	9.00	9.00
Wood, Blake	R-R	6-5	233	8-8-85	2	0	4.76	17	0	0	0	17	20	9	9	3	4	22	.290	.258	.316	11.65	2.12
Wright, Daniel	R-R	6-2	205	4-3-91	0	1	4.58	5	2	0	0	20	21	12	10	1	8	11	.284	.278	.290	5.03	3.66
Yates, Kirby	L-R	5-10	210	3-25-87	0	0	18.00	1	0	0	0	1	2	2	2	2	0	1	.400	.333	.500	9.00	0.00

Fielding

Catcher	PCT	G	PO	A	E	DP	PB
Graterol	.996	47	233	22	1	1	0
Maldonado	.998	137	1046	65	2	2	8
Perez	.962	10	44	7	2	1	2

First Base	PCT	G	PO	A	E	DP
Cron	.995	98	745	61	4	63
Maldonado	.000	1	0	0	0	0
Marte	.989	28	172	12	2	21
Pujols	.932	6	38	3	3	6
Valbuena	1.000	48	316	24	0	33

Second Base	PCT	G	PO	A	E	DP
Cowart	.982	30	35	76	2	21
Espinosa	.993	71	114	162	2	37
Fontana	1.000	9	4	15	0	4
Franklin	1.000	8	15	25	0	6
Pennington	.977	47	41	86	3	23
Phillips	.988	24	28	54	1	11

Third Base	PCT	G	PO	A	E	DP
Cowart	1.000	24	3	9	0	1
Escobar	.938	87	54	126	12	12
Marte	1.000	10	3	16	0	1
Pennington	1.000	18	8	19	0	0
Valbuena	.947	59	33	92	7	8

Shortstop	PCT	G	PO	A	E	DP
Pennington	.966	18	7	21	1	5
Simmons	.980	158	235	436	14	99

Outfield	PCT	G	PO	A	E	DP
Calhoun	.988	154	312	10	4	1
Flores	1.000	3	6	0	0	0
Franklin	.000	3	0	0	0	0
Marte	1.000	3	3	0	0	0
Maybin	.986	89	208	5	3	0
Puello	1.000	1	4	0	0	0
Revere	.981	82	148	5	3	1
Robinson	1.000	17	28	0	0	0
Trout	.996	108	253	5	1	0
Upton	.979	27	45	2	1	0
Young Jr.	1.000	34	68	1	0	0

SALT LAKE BEES

TRIPLE-A

PACIFIC COAST LEAGUE

Batting	B-T	HT	WT	DOB	AVG	vLH	vRH	G	AB	R	H	2B	3B	HR	RBI	BB	HBP	SH	SF	SO	SB	CS	SLG	OBP
Ackley, Dustin	L-R	6-1	205	2-26-88	.261	.258	.262	116	441	66	115	27	3	6	59	54	2	2	6	71	3	2	.376	.340
Allday, Forrestt	L-L	5-11	190	4-24-91	.800	1.000	.750	1	5	2	4	1	0	0	1	0	0	0	0	0	0	0	1.000	.800
Arakawa, Tim	L-R	5-8	175	4-18-93	.333	—	.333	1	3	0	1	0	0	0	0	1	0	0	0	0	0	0	.333	.500
Arcia, Francisco	L-R	5-11	195	9-14-89	.192	.083	.225	15	52	4	10	1	0	0	1	3	2	0	0	10	1	0	.212	.263
Bourn, Michael	R-L	5-11	190	12-27-82	.260	.316	.247	23	96	15	25	2	1	2	9	8	0	2	0	16	4	5	.365	.317
Briceno, Jose	R-R	6-1	210	9-19-92	.200	—	.200	3	10	1	2	0	0	0	0	0	0	0	0	1	1	0	.200	.200
Cowart, Kaleb	B-R	6-3	225	6-2-92	.311	.352	.298	90	367	65	114	25	1	12	57	44	0	0	2	73	19	5	.482	.383
Cron, C.J.	R-R	6-4	235	1-5-90	.268	.333	.246	22	82	11	22	6	0	4	23	7	4	0	3	15	1	0	.488	.344
Fletcher, David	R-R	5-10	175	5-31-94	.254	.359	.229	47	205	27	52	6	1	2	17	6	3	3	0	25	8	1	.322	.285
Flores, Ramon	L-L	5-10	190	3-26-92	.312	.276	.324	115	413	65	129	21	5	10	71	68	2	6	4	70	12	2	.460	.409
Fontana, Nolan	L-R	5-11	195	6-6-91	.272	.230	.285	105	361	82	98	26	4	10	51	75	3	8	6	97	14	2	.449	.396
Franklin, Nick	B-R	6-1	190	3-2-91	.273	.000	.333	3	11	0	3	0	0	0	1	1	0	0	1	3	0	0	.273	.308
Hermosillo, Michael	R-R	5-11	190	1-17-95	.287	.348	.272	30	115	20	33	6	1	5	16	7	3	3	1	28	9	2	.487	.341
Houchins, Zach	R-R	6-2	210	9-16-92	.500	.000	.583	4	14	5	7	1	3	0	2	2	1	0	0	2	0	0	1.000	.588
Johnson, Sherman	L-R	5-10	190	7-15-90	.244	.197	.257	88	287	48	70	15	3	3	39	48	2	4	0	66	12	4	.348	.356
LaMarre, Ryan	L-R	6-1	210	11-21-88	.268	.214	.296	10	41	6	11	1	1	0	7	6	1	0	0	11	4	1	.342	.375
2-team total (41 Nashville)					.247	.214	.296	51	170	17	42	3	3	0	19	17	4	2	1	58	9	6	.300	.328
Marte, Jefry	R-R	6-1	220	6-21-91	.265	.276	.263	45	185	26	49	10	0	9	39	17	2	0	1	32	6	1	.465	.332
Maybin, Cameron	R-R	6-3	215	4-4-87	.286	—	.286	2	7	0	2	1	0	0	1	0	0	0	1	2	1	0	.429	.250
Navarro, Rey	B-R	5-10	185	12-22-89	.279	.324	.265	126	492	59	137	27	1	7	82	48	3	4	7	79	7	4	.380	.342
Perez, Carlos	R-R	6-0	210	10-27-90	.353	.360	.351	68	261	40	92	18	3	5	40	32	3	0	4	38	4	1	.502	.423
Puello, Cesar	R-R	6-2	220	4-1-91	.397	.324	.415	44	184	42	73	18	1	7	34	13	2	0	1	44	13	3	.620	.440
2-team total (43 Round Rock)					.327	.324	.415	87	346	66	113	26	2	13	61	25	5	0	3	82	18	4	.526	.377
Robinson, Shane	R-R	5-9	170	10-30-84	.319	.500	.275	86	348	64	111	21	5	2	47	28	3	1	5	37	15	1	.425	.370
Sanchez, Tony	R-R	5-11	220	5-20-88	.272	.255	.277	70	243	33	66	13	0	4	40	29	4	5	3	61	1	3	.375	.355
Way, Bo	L-L	6-0	180	11-17-91	.298	.214	.330	42	151	20	45	4	0	0	20	8	1	6	1	29	9	8	.325	.335
Williams, Matt	R-R	6-0	170	8-29-89	.268	.305	.255	63	224	30	60	10	2	6	33	21	1	5	1	28	9	8	.411	.332
Yacinich, Jake	L-R	6-2	195	3-2-93	.250	.333	.235	6	20	3	5	0	0	0	3	1	0	1	0	2	0	1	.250	.286
Young Jr., Eric	R-B	5-10	195	5-25-85	.305	.333	.297	83	341	67	104	15	5	8	52	33	6	4	1	56	20	7	.449	.375

Pitching	B-T	HT	WT	DOB	W	L	ERA	G	GS	CG	SV	IP	H	R	ER	HR	BB	SO	AVG	vLH	vRH	K/9	BB/9
Adams, Austin	R-R	5-11	200	8-19-86	0	1	4.15	5	0	0	1	4	5	2	2	0	6	4	.278	.250	.300	8.31	12.46
Alvarez, Jose	L-L	5-11	190	5-6-89	0	0	2.31	9	0	0	0	12	10	3	3	0	2	10	.227	.333	.154	7.71	1.54
Bailey, Andrew	R-R	6-3	240	5-31-84	0	2	8.10	7	0	0	0	7	9	9	6	3	1	4	.310	.500	.133	5.40	1.35
Banuelos, Manny	R-L	5-10	215	3-13-91	5	6	4.93	39	9	0	0	95	107	62	52	4	49	85	.282	.266	.291	8.05	4.64
Barria, Jaime	R-R	6-1	210	7-18-96	2	0	2.45	3	3	0	0	15	11	5	4	0	3	13	.208	.189	.250	7.98	1.84
Blackford, Alex	R-R	5-11	200	11-16-90	1	4	9.76	7	5	0	0	28	34	31	30	7	23	22	.312	.250	.368	7.16	7.48
Bridwell, Parker	R-R	6-4	185	8-2-91	2	3	4.28	6	5	0	0	27	26	16	13	2	8	24	.248	.289	.217	7.90	2.63
Campos, Vicente	R-R	6-3	230	7-27-92	0	2	8.27	6	5	0	0	16	23	16	15	2	12	9	.354	.281	.424	4.96	6.61
De Los Santos, Abel	R-R	6-2	195	11-21-92	0	0	0.00	1	0	0	0	1	0	0	0	0	0	1	.000	.000	.000	9.00	0.00
Diaz, Luis	R-R	6-4	209	4-9-92	4	11	5.44	24	18	0	0	94	110	69	57	13	41	87	.299	.302	.296	8.30	3.91
Dimock, Michael	R-R	6-2	195	10-26-89	0	0	4.91	2	0	0	0	4	5	2	2	0	2	2	.333	.333	.333	4.91	4.91
2-team total (6 El Paso)					0	1	10.97	8	0	0	0	11	21	13	13	2	5	9	.420	.333	.333	7.59	4.22
Ege, Cody	L-L	6-1	190	5-8-91	2	2	5.49	26	0	0	0	39	44	28	24	1	14	40	.293	.328	.272	9.15	3.20

Fister, Doug	R-L	6-8	210	2-4-84	1	0	4.02	3	3	0	0	16	16	7	7	0	5	10	.281	.286	.276	5.74	2.87
Gagnon, Drew	R-R	6-4	195	6-26-90	1	1	6.25	31	10	0	0	86	95	60	60	6	39	83	.284	.324	.253	8.65	4.07
Guerra, Deolis	R-R	6-5	245	4-17-89	4	1	1.98	31	0	0	2	41	26	9	9	3	8	41	.179	.191	.169	9.00	1.76
Gurka, Jason	L-L	6-0	170	1-10-88	3	1	2.12	30	0	0	1	34	29	11	8	1	11	36	.234	.125	.303	9.53	2.91
Heaney, Andrew	L-L	6-2	195	6-5-91	1	1	3.12	3	3	0	0	17	17	7	6	2	4	14	.266	.286	.260	7.27	2.08
Hofacket, Adam	R-R	6-1	195	2-18-94	0	2	6.75	11	0	0	0	15	20	11	11	2	2	9	.351	.348	.353	5.52	1.23
Isaac, Sean	R-R	6-4	225	12-17-92	0	0	1.69	3	0	0	0	5	4	1	1	1	5	5	.211	.250	.143	8.44	8.44
Kelly, Justin	L-L	6-1	175	4-22-93	0	0	11.25	2	0	0	0	4	7	5	5	1	1	4	.389	.400	.385	9.00	2.25
Klonowski, Alex	R-R	6-4	195	4-1-92	1	1	5.26	5	4	0	0	26	31	15	15	3	5	17	.301	.378	.241	5.96	1.75
Lamb, John	L-L	6-4	205	7-10-90	6	3	5.37	13	13	0	0	70	85	44	42	9	26	48	.307	.398	.265	6.14	3.33
Magnifico, Damien	R-R	6-1	195	5-24-91	4	2	6.82	31	0	0	4	34	42	28	26	2	24	34	.302	.339	.277	8.91	6.29
2-team total (2 Colorado Springs)					4	2	6.56	33	0	0	4	36	43	29	26	2	26	36	.297	.339	.277	9.08	6.56
Mahle, Greg	L-L	6-2	230	4-17-93	4	4	8.13	20	1	0	0	28	40	26	25	4	15	13	.354	.375	.343	4.23	4.88
Meyer, Alex	R-R	6-9	225	1-3-90	0	1	6.00	5	5	0	0	24	30	17	16	4	9	31	.306	.364	.259	11.63	3.38
Middleton, Keynan	R-R	6-2	185	9-12-93	0	0	2.84	10	0	0	2	13	11	5	4	0	4	8	.234	.200	.273	5.68	2.84
Miller, Justin	R-R	6-3	215	6-13-87	5	1	5.48	38	0	0	9	46	50	30	28	7	8	37	.273	.281	.266	7.24	1.57
Morales, Osmer	R-R	6-3	196	10-30-92	2	1	3.22	9	9	0	0	50	43	20	18	8	21	40	.231	.216	.245	7.15	3.75
Morin, Mike	R-R	6-4	220	5-3-91	0	1	3.20	22	1	0	1	39	34	14	14	5	7	25	.238	.258	.221	5.72	1.60
Nuss, Garrett	R-R	6-1	180	4-15-93	0	1	4.50	3	1	0	0	4	3	2	2	1	0	4	.200	.000	.300	9.00	0.00
Paredes, Eduardo	R-R	6-1	170	3-6-95	1	0	2.92	25	0	0	2	37	27	13	12	3	17	38	.203	.200	.206	9.24	4.14
Pinder, Branden	R-R	6-4	215	1-26-89	1	0	5.40	8	0	0	0	8	11	7	5	0	7	2	.324	.364	.250	2.16	7.56
Pounders, Brooks	R-R	6-5	265	9-26-90	2	2	2.63	38	2	0	6	51	42	18	15	6	15	49	.217	.264	.178	8.59	2.63
Ramirez, Noe	R-R	6-3	205	12-22-89	0	0	0.00	4	0	0	0	4	2	0	0	0	2	4	.133	.222	.000	8.31	4.15
Richards, Garrett	R-R	6-3	210	5-27-88	0	0	0.00	1	1	0	0	2	5	0	0	0	0	2	.556	.400	.750	9.00	0.00
Robichaux, Austin	R-R	6-6	175	11-23-92	1	0	3.29	3	3	0	0	14	12	7	5	0	9	8	.255	.238	.269	5.27	5.93
Salas, Fernando	R-R	6-2	200	5-30-85	0	0	0.00	3	0	0	0	3	1	0	0	0	2	5	.100	.000	.250	15.00	6.00
Scribner, Troy	R-R	6-3	190	7-2-91	11	4	4.35	20	19	0	0	103	100	52	50	13	38	103	.253	.253	.252	8.97	3.31
Skaggs, Tyler	L-L	6-4	215	7-13-91	0	1	8.10	3	3	0	0	10	14	10	9	0	6	7	.333	.500	.231	6.30	5.40
Smith, Nate	L-L	6-3	210	8-28-91	1	0	0.00	1	1	0	0	6	1	0	0	0	0	4	.056	.000	.071	6.35	0.00
Street, Huston	R-R	6-0	205	8-2-83	0	0	3.60	5	0	0	0	5	3	2	2	0	1	4	.177	.143	.200	7.20	1.80
Valdez, Jose	R-R	6-1	200	3-1-90	1	1	6.00	10	0	0	1	12	10	8	8	0	5	15	.222	.304	.136	11.25	3.75
2-team total (23 El Paso)					3	4	5.31	33	0	0	1	41	44	24	24	2	16	45	.270	.304	.136	9.96	3.54
Warmoth, Tyler	R-R	6-2	205	6-4-92	0	0	0.00	1	0	0	0	3	0	0	0	0	1	2	.000	.000	.000	6.75	3.38
Wright, Daniel	R-R	6-2	205	4-3-91	6	10	6.99	19	18	0	0	93	112	83	72	17	35	61	.296	.274	.312	5.92	3.40
Yates, Kirby	L-R	5-10	210	3-25-87	0	0	2.57	6	0	0	1	7	8	2	2	0	3	14	.276	.333	.261	18.00	3.86

Fielding

Catcher	PCT	G	PO	A	E	DP	PB
Arcia	1.000	15	109	8	0	0	2
Briceno	1.000	3	22	2	0	1	0
Perez	.983	58	428	40	8	6	5
Sanchez	.993	68	546	48	4	9	9

First Base	PCT	G	PO	A	E	DP
Ackley	.993	16	125	9	1	16
Cowart	.953	8	58	3	3	4
Cron	.982	19	151	13	3	14
Flores	.984	9	54	6	1	7
Houchins	1.000	1	9	0	0	0
Johnson	.995	52	382	31	2	34
Marte	.992	31	228	14	2	31
Sanchez	1.000	1	6	2	0	0
Williams	1.000	13	95	5	0	12

Second Base	PCT	G	PO	A	E	DP
Arakawa	1.000	1	2	3	0	0
Cowart	.979	35	50	89	3	25
Fletcher	.981	22	44	57	2	14
Fontana	1.000	37	66	92	0	27
Franklin	1.000	1	3	4	0	0
Johnson	1.000	6	16	17	0	9
Navarro	.989	43	65	110	2	17

Third Base	PCT	G	PO	A	E	DP
Cowart	.981	45	39	65	2	
Fontana	.976	29	14	66	2	10
Houchins	1.000	3	1	5	0	0
Johnson	.984	22	23	37	1	6
Marte	.818	11	6	12	4	3
Navarro	.963	37	30	47	3	3
Williams	1.000	2	1	1	0	0

Shortstop	PCT	G	PO	A	E	DP
Fletcher	.991	26	49	58	1	16
Fontana	.971	40	64	106	5	28
Franklin	1.000	2	2	3	0	0
Navarro	.958	37	52	107	7	35
Williams	.956	37	50	81	6	18
Yacinich	1.000	6	8	14	0	2

Outfield	PCT	G	PO	A	E	DP
Ackley	.929	7	13	0	1	0
Allday	1.000	1	1	0	0	0
Bourn	1.000	21	42	1	0	0
Flores	.971	101	193	6	6	2
Franklin	.000	1	0	0	0	0
Hermosillo	1.000	29	51	4	0	1
Johnson	.944	10	15	2	1	0
LaMarre	1.000	10	19	1	0	0
Maybin	1.000	2	4	1	0	0
Navarro	1.000	2	3	1	0	0
Puello	.981	43	101	4	2	0
Robinson	.985	81	194	8	3	1
Way	.981	41	98	6	2	2
Williams	.955	12	21	0	1	0
Young Jr.	.993	75	145	5	1	1

MOBILE BAYBEARS — *DOUBLE-A*

SOUTHERN LEAGUE

Batting	B-T	HT	WT	DOB	AVG	vLH	vRH	G	AB	R	H	2B	3B	HR	RBI	BB	HBP	SH	SF	SO	SB	CS	SLG	OBP
Adams, Caleb	R-R	5-10	185	1-26-93	.196	.211	.188	15	51	6	10	1	0	1	3	5	1	1	0	20	2	2	.275	.281
Allday, Forrestt	L-L	5-11	190	4-24-91	.290	.302	.284	91	297	35	86	9	0	1	32	53	7	3	4	43	11	9	.330	.404
Arakawa, Tim	L-R	5-8	175	4-18-93	.245	.270	.236	76	237	31	58	4	1	4	15	37	1	4	3	73	8	7	.321	.345
Arcia, Francisco	L-R	5-11	195	9-14-89	.238	.227	.241	28	80	15	19	3	0	0	3	9	5	1	0	17	1	2	.275	.351
Barash, Michael	R-R	6-1	200	10-12-94	.364	1.000	.300	3	11	1	4	0	0	0	2	2	0	0	0	2	1	0	.364	.462
Briceno, Jose	R-R	6-1	210	9-19-92	.194	.231	.181	92	351	34	68	12	2	9	41	23	0	2	2	73	7	2	.316	.242
Daniel, Andrew	R-R	6-1	195	1-27-93	.225	.159	.248	49	169	16	38	10	2	2	16	21	2	1	1	42	8	5	.343	.316
2-team total (10 Mississippi)					.211	.159	.248	59	190	17	40	10	2	2	16	23	2	1	1	50	8	5	.316	.301
Fletcher, David	R-R	5-10	175	5-31-94	.276	.213	.297	64	243	32	67	14	1	1	22	21	4	2	2	30	12	5	.354	.341
Gibbons, Zach	R-R	5-8	186	10-14-93	.236	.212	.243	79	301	31	71	18	0	3	31	25	1	1	2	47	6	2	.326	.295
Hermosillo, Michael	R-R	5-11	190	1-17-95	.248	.231	.255	77	278	40	69	13	2	4	26	40	12	5	5	73	21	9	.353	.361
Houchins, Zach	R-R	6-2	210	9-16-92	.251	.280	.240	125	474	46	119	28	4	14	77	37	2	1	4	82	7	8	.416	.306
Jenkins, Derek	R-R	5-8	155	2-11-94	.182	.000	.200	3	11	1	2	0	0	0	0	1	0	0	0	6	1	1	.182	.250

Johnson, Sherman	L-R	5-10	190	7-15-90	.296	.207	.329	32	108	14	32	6	0	2	18	15	2	1	0	22	2	1	.407	.392
Kerr, Stephen	R-R	5-10	165	12-22-94	.000	—	.000	1	2	0	0	0	0	0	0	1	0	0	0	1	0	0	.000	.333
Lund, Brennon	L-R	5-10	185	11-27-94	.287	.207	.312	29	122	17	35	3	0	1	6	3	2	0	2	33	1	2	.336	.310
McCann, Matt	R-R	5-9	170	1-12-95	.167	.500	.125	5	18	2	3	0	0	0	0	0	1	0	0	5	1	1	.167	.211
Montgomery, Troy	L-L	5-10	185	8-13-94	.235	.263	.225	20	68	15	16	2	0	0	3	10	2	2	0	12	4	0	.265	.350
Moyer, Hutton	B-R	6-1	185	4-30-93	.207	.250	.188	24	92	9	19	6	1	0	6	8	0	0	1	25	9	1	.294	.267
Rojas, Jose	L-R	6-0	200	2-24-93	.227	.132	.254	44	172	16	39	9	1	4	20	6	3	0	4	35	0	1	.361	.260
Rosa, Angel	R-R	6-2	185	9-19-92	.184	.111	.226	15	49	3	9	1	0	0	2	7	0	0	0	17	1	2	.204	.286
Sanger, Brendon	L-R	6-0	195	9-11-93	.182	.000	.286	3	11	0	2	2	0	0	2	2	0	0	0	5	0	0	.364	.308
Serena, Jordan	R-R	6-1	220	8-4-92	.333	.000	.429	3	9	2	3	2	0	1	1	1	0	0	0	3	0	0	.889	.400
Tejada, Luis	R-R	6-3	175	10-12-92	.199	.226	.186	48	171	16	34	3	1	3	15	14	1	1	0	38	2	3	.281	.263
Thaiss, Matt	L-R	6-0	195	5-6-95	.292	.326	.280	49	178	29	52	14	0	1	25	37	2	0	4	50	4	3	.388	.412
Triunfel, Alberto	R-R	5-11	160	2-1-94	.243	.207	.258	89	301	27	73	10	3	3	36	18	0	5	1	64	3	8	.326	.284
Walsh, Jared	L-L	6-1	210	7-30-93	.232	.222	.235	20	69	7	16	3	0	3	9	3	1	1	0	29	1	0	.406	.274
Ward, Taylor	R-R	6-1	200	12-14-93	.286	.222	.304	33	119	14	34	3	0	3	19	22	2	0	2	17	0	0	.387	.400
Wass, Wade	R-R	6-0	215	9-23-91	.257	.258	.256	59	191	36	49	8	1	11	24	23	10	1	1	69	9	4	.482	.364
Way, Bo	L-L	6-0	180	11-17-91	.221	.183	.235	67	213	25	47	6	3	1	20	20	4	7	3	35	12	6	.291	.296
Welz, Zach	R-R	6-1	190	5-7-92	.235	.205	.253	40	119	12	28	6	0	0	8	13	1	3	0	41	2	1	.286	.316

Pitching	B-T	HT	WT	DOB	W	L	ERA	G	GS	CG	SV	IP	H	R	ER	HR	BB	SO	AVG	vLH	vRH	K/9	BB/9
Anderson, Justin	L-R	6-3	220	9-28-92	3	2	5.06	42	0	0	1	59	56	35	33	7	29	36	.255	.216	.280	5.52	4.45
Barria, Jaime	R-R	6-1	210	7-18-96	1	6	3.21	12	12	1	0	62	62	27	22	8	15	47	.256	.240	.268	6.86	2.19
Blackford, Alex	R-R	5-11	200	11-16-90	1	3	4.58	8	8	0	0	39	34	22	20	3	12	31	.231	.246	.218	7.09	2.75
Bridwell, Parker	R-R	6-4	185	8-2-91	0	1	2.00	3	3	0	0	9	9	2	2	2	1	7	.257	.333	.177	7.00	1.00
Buckel, Cody	R-R	6-1	185	6-18-92	1	2	4.79	12	0	0	0	21	17	11	11	3	21	13	.236	.217	.269	5.66	9.15
Carpenter, Tyler	R-R	6-5	225	2-25-92	2	6	4.46	14	14	0	0	71	78	39	35	6	21	40	.282	.322	.250	5.09	2.67
Castillo, Jesus	R-R	6-2	165	8-27-95	0	2	3.04	5	5	0	0	24	27	14	8	2	6	22	.287	.292	.283	8.37	2.28
De Los Santos, Abel	R-R	6-2	195	11-21-92	4	2	2.95	25	0	0	4	37	29	13	12	3	13	41	.218	.175	.257	10.06	3.19
Diaz, Luis	R-R	6-4	209	4-9-92	2	0	0.00	3	3	0	0	17	8	1	0	0	6	21	.143	.194	.080	11.12	3.18
Dimock, Michael	R-R	6-2	195	10-26-89	1	3	3.12	22	0	0	4	26	21	10	9	2	9	29	.223	.167	.250	10.04	3.12
Fitzsimmons, Jon	R-R	6-2	205	11-29-91	1	1	2.25	11	0	0	0	16	13	4	4	0	6	14	.224	.179	.267	7.88	3.38
Grendell, Kevin	L-L	6-2	210	8-22-93	0	1	10.93	14	0	0	0	14	16	17	17	6	16	12	.291	.313	.282	7.71	10.29
Hernandez, Ivan	R-R	6-2	249	7-28-91	2	1	4.22	8	0	0	1	11	8	6	5	0	4	8	.205	.150	.263	6.75	3.38
Hofacket, Adam	R-R	6-1	195	2-18-94	1	2	2.79	26	0	0	6	39	38	13	12	3	8	37	.257	.283	.239	8.61	1.86
Jewell, Jake	R-R	6-3	200	5-16-93	7	8	4.84	24	23	1	0	125	136	73	67	14	41	81	.284	.306	.267	5.85	2.96
Karch, Eric	R-R	6-2	205	10-15-91	2	2	2.06	19	2	0	1	35	28	9	8	5	5	33	.222	.207	.235	8.49	1.29
Kelly, Justin	L-L	6-1	175	4-22-93	1	0	7.50	2	1	0	0	6	4	5	5	2	5	6	.191	.000	.286	9.00	7.50
Kipper, Jordan	R-R	6-4	185	10-6-92	2	1	1.74	5	5	0	0	31	21	8	6	2	8	18	.194	.275	.123	5.23	2.32
Klonowski, Alex	R-R	6-4	195	4-1-92	5	8	4.17	20	17	0	2	104	102	52	48	15	25	73	.255	.253	.257	6.34	2.17
Lillis-White, Conor	L-L	6-4	220	7-22-92	3	4	4.03	26	1	0	2	45	26	21	20	4	32	54	.167	.178	.162	10.88	6.45
Long, Grayson	R-R	6-5	230	5-27-94	8	6	2.52	23	23	0	0	122	100	38	34	7	38	111	.226	.229	.223	8.21	2.81
Magnifico, Damien	R-R	6-1	195	5-24-91	1	0	3.18	9	0	0	0	11	9	4	4	0	9	17	.209	.308	.167	13.50	7.15
Mahle, Greg	L-L	6-2	230	4-17-93	6	0	2.66	30	0	0	4	44	31	14	13	2	10	39	.203	.211	.198	7.98	2.05
Mathews, Simon	R-R	6-2	180	9-24-95	1	0	3.00	1	0	0	0	3	3	1	1	1	3	3	.250	.000	.333	9.00	9.00
Medina, Jhondaniel	R-R	5-11	218	2-8-93	1	1	2.89	15	1	0	0	28	20	9	9	4	12	32	.198	.296	.123	10.29	3.86
2-team total (7 Tennessee)					1	1	4.63	22	1	0	0	35	25	18	18	4	21	37	.197	.295	.123	9.51	5.40
Morales, Osmer	R-R	6-3	196	10-30-92	4	4	4.83	16	16	0	0	76	77	42	41	11	29	81	.268	.252	.283	9.55	3.42
Muck, Ronnie	R-R	6-0	195	8-23-91	0	2	4.60	11	0	0	1	16	13	8	8	2	9	10	.236	.222	.250	5.74	5.17
Nuss, Garrett	R-R	6-1	180	4-15-93	0	1	9.00	1	0	0	0	2	1	2	2	0	1	3	.143	.000	.200	13.50	4.50
Paredes, Eduardo	R-R	6-1	170	3-6-95	0	0	1.42	9	0	0	1	13	11	2	2	0	4	17	.225	.280	.167	12.08	2.84
Pena, Luis	R-R	5-11	190	8-24-95	1	3	3.15	4	4	0	0	20	16	9	7	3	9	19	.213	.333	.146	8.55	4.05
Peterson, Brandon	R-R	6-1	190	9-23-91	0	1	3.54	12	0	0	0	20	19	8	8	2	15	24	.241	.216	.262	10.62	6.64
Rhoades, Jeremy	R-R	6-4	225	2-12-93	1	0	6.08	20	0	0	0	27	29	20	18	4	14	23	.271	.386	.191	7.76	4.73
Warmoth, Tyler	R-R	6-2	205	6-4-92	1	2	3.44	33	1	0	1	50	46	22	19	6	18	49	.240	.224	.252	8.88	3.26
Zarubin, Jackson	R-R	6-2	190	1-8-93	1	0	0.00	1	0	0	0	3	1	0	0	0	2	2	.125	.000	.167	6.00	6.00

Fielding

Catcher	PCT	G	PO	A	E	DP	PB
Arcia	.993	21	129	9	1	1	3
Barash	1.000	2	15	0	0	0	0
Briceno	.982	77	556	82	12	8	9
Ward	.978	21	166	13	4	0	0
Wass	.994	21	163	13	1	0	3

First Base	PCT	G	PO	A	E	DP
Houchins	.993	36	260	20	2	26
Tejada	.992	44	356	28	3	31
Thaiss	.995	46	371	17	2	33
Walsh	.987	18	142	5	2	11

Second Base	PCT	G	PO	A	E	DP
Arakawa	.975	33	64	91	4	19
Daniel	.965	25	50	59	4	15
Fletcher	1.000	34	60	79	0	18
Johnson	1.000	16	29	34	0	8
Kerr	1.000	1	3	1	0	1
McCann	1.000	1	2	4	0	0
Moyer	.964	4	10	17	1	5
Rojas	.952	14	21	39	3	9
Rosa	.500	1	1	1	2	0
Triunfel	1.000	10	19	30	0	6

Third Base	PCT	G	PO	A	E	DP
Arakawa	.895	10	5	12	2	0
Daniel	.912	16	11	20	3	2
Houchins	.956	73	63	134	9	15
Rojas	.946	27	16	37	3	1
Rosa	1.000	9	5	9	0	1
Triunfel	1.000	10	5	13	0	2

Shortstop	PCT	G	PO	A	E	DP
Arakawa	.600	1	0	3	2	0
Fletcher	.990	28	35	68	1	12
Houchins	.962	6	7	18	1	2
Johnson	.985	13	18	49	1	8
McCann	.950	4	5	14	1	3
Moyer	.966	18	21	35	2	9
Rosa	.933	5	5	9	1	2
Triunfel	.966	68	106	178	10	43

Outfield	PCT	G	PO	A	E	DP
Adams	1.000	13	23	0	0	0
Allday	.982	81	155	7	3	1
Arakawa	.968	28	61	0	2	0
Briceno	.000	1	0	0	0	0
Gibbons	1.000	73	137	12	0	4
Hermosillo	.982	73	161	3	3	0
Jenkins	1.000	3	7	0	0	0
Lund	.981	26	50	1	1	0
Montgomery	1.000	18	49	0	0	0
Sanger	1.000	3	5	0	0	0

Serena	1.000	1	2	0	0	0	Walsh	.000	1	0	0	0	0	Welz	.970	40	92	6	3	1
Tejada	1.000	4	7	1	0	1	Wass	.833	3	4	1	1	0							
Triunfel	1.000	1	1	0	0	0	Way	.993	62	131	5	1	1							

INLAND EMPIRE 66ERS — *HIGH CLASS A*

CALIFORNIA LEAGUE

Batting	B-T	HT	WT	DOB	AVG	vLH	vRH	G	AB	R	H	2B	3B	HR	RBI	BB	HBP	SH	SF	SO	SB	CS	SLG	OBP
Anderson, Brad	R-R	6-4	210	1-10-94	.313	.000	.357	6	16	3	5	1	0	0	1	3	0	0	0	6	0	0	.375	.421
Barash, Michael	R-R	6-1	200	10-12-94	.237	.296	.220	84	321	43	76	19	0	10	42	43	1	1	1	76	0	0	.389	.328
Diaz, Brandon	R-R	5-11	175	4-14-95	.211	.238	.200	23	76	10	16	3	1	1	6	15	0	0	0	30	8	1	.316	.341
Escobar, Yunel	R-R	6-2	215	11-2-82	.250	.000	.400	3	8	0	2	0	0	0	1	0	0	0	0	3	0	0	.250	.250
Foster, Jared	R-R	6-1	200	11-2-92	.275	.267	.278	33	138	15	38	7	1	4	18	9	2	0	0	29	4	2	.428	.329
Gibbons, Zach	R-R	5-8	186	10-14-93	.339	.400	.326	27	115	20	39	6	3	1	10	12	0	0	1	15	5	0	.470	.398
Grieshaber, Keith	R-R	6-1	168	6-29-95	.295	.408	.246	45	163	20	48	10	1	2	27	13	5	1	2	25	13	3	.405	.361
Hermosillo, Michael	R-R	5-11	190	1-17-95	.321	.385	.300	13	53	5	17	6	0	0	2	9	2	0	0	15	5	2	.434	.438
Jenkins, Derek	R-R	5-8	155	2-11-94	.200	.150	.222	18	65	4	13	2	0	0	3	2	0	0	1	15	4	0	.231	.221
Jones, Jahmai	R-R	6-0	215	8-4-97	.302	.236	.333	41	172	32	52	11	3	5	17	13	5	1	0	43	9	6	.488	.368
Justus, Connor	R-R	6-0	190	11-2-94	.202	.194	.204	116	411	52	83	19	3	5	34	61	11	5	3	110	15	6	.299	.319
Kruger, Jack	R-R	6-1	185	10-26-94	.256	.297	.240	35	137	21	35	4	1	1	16	18	0	1	2	26	0	0	.321	.338
Leon, Julian	R-R	5-11	200	1-24-96	.196	.000	.237	14	46	6	9	1	0	1	3	6	0	0	1	18	0	0	.283	.283
Lund, Brennon	L-R	5-10	185	11-27-94	.321	.304	.327	46	196	26	63	11	0	3	23	16	5	0	1	41	5	4	.424	.385
McCann, Matt	R-R	5-9	170	1-12-95	.250	.333	.000	2	8	1	2	0	0	0	0	1	0	0	0	2	0	0	.250	.333
Montgomery, Troy	L-L	5-10	185	8-13-94	.282	.333	.267	65	262	41	74	10	7	6	31	26	1	6	1	58	9	5	.443	.348
Ramer, Cody	R-L	5-8	178	11-24-93	.231	.137	.257	72	238	32	55	11	3	1	21	37	1	2	1	72	7	1	.315	.336
Rojas, Jose	L-R	6-0	200	2-24-93	.319	.227	.343	79	317	44	101	20	5	7	50	17	2	1	2	64	4	8	.480	.355
Sandoval, Brandon	R-R	6-1	180	6-24-95	.385	.143	.474	7	26	5	10	0	0	1	7	2	0	0	0	4	0	1	.500	.429
Sanger, Brendon	L-R	6-0	195	9-11-93	.277	.308	.266	63	206	29	57	11	1	10	42	27	2	1	2	64	1	0	.485	.363
Sanjur, Mario	R-R	5-7	174	12-23-95	.000	—	.000	1	1	0	0	0	0	0	0	0	0	0	0	0	0	0	.000	.000
Serena, Jordan	R-R	6-1	220	8-4-92	.228	.327	.195	59	206	28	47	5	4	2	30	13	5	2	1	58	8	1	.320	.289
Survance Jr., Kyle	L-R	6-1	190	12-6-93	.207	.172	.216	76	305	39	63	16	4	4	37	20	3	1	2	107	17	2	.325	.261
Thaiss, Matt	L-R	6-0	195	5-6-95	.265	.246	.269	84	336	46	89	13	4	8	48	40	7	0	2	59	4	3	.399	.353
Trout, Mike	R-R	6-2	235	8-7-91	.222	.333	.167	4	9	5	2	1	1	0	0	4	1	0	0	2	0	0	.556	.500
Valbuena, Luis	L-R	5-10	215	11-30-85	.348	.250	.400	6	23	5	8	3	0	0	6	1	0	0	0	4	0	0	.478	.375
Walsh, Jared	L-L	6-1	210	7-30-93	.331	.300	.342	70	275	43	91	29	1	8	52	26	4	0	1	72	1	0	.531	.395
Ward, Taylor	R-R	6-1	200	12-14-93	.242	.149	.269	54	207	32	50	11	1	6	30	35	0	3	2	43	0	0	.391	.348
Yacinich, Jake	L-R	6-2	195	3-2-93	.264	.222	.276	92	326	43	86	10	6	5	31	21	5	5	2	90	13	5	.377	.316
Zimmerman, Jordan	R-R	6-1	195	11-21-94	.294	.308	.288	42	184	30	54	16	1	4	28	10	2	1	1	41	1	0	.457	.335

Pitching	B-T	HT	WT	DOB	W	L	ERA	G	GS	CG	SV	IP	H	R	ER	HR	BB	SO	AVG	vLH	vRH	K/9	BB/9
Alexander, Jason	R-R	6-3	200	3-1-93	0	0	6.75	2	0	0	0	5	8	7	4	0	1	2	.333	.333	.333	3.38	1.69
Anderson, Justin	L-R	6-3	220	9-28-92	0	0	5.06	4	0	0	1	5	4	4	3	0	2	6	.174	.333	.071	10.13	3.38
Barkell, Ty	R-R	6-3	225	3-12-93	0	1	0.00	3	0	0	0	6	3	1	0	0	3	6	.158	.000	.214	8.53	4.26
Barria, Jaime	R-R	6-1	210	7-18-96	4	3	2.48	11	11	0	0	65	48	20	18	6	13	57	.202	.244	.181	7.85	1.79
Bates, Nathan	R-R	6-8	205	3-1-94	0	5	6.53	33	0	0	7	51	65	38	37	5	22	58	.308	.299	.313	10.24	3.88
Bedrosian, Cam	R-R	6-0	230	10-2-91	0	0	7.36	4	1	0	0	4	5	3	3	1	0	7	.294	.286	.300	17.18	0.00
Belton, Greg	R-R	5-10	190	12-31-92	0	0	0.00	1	0	0	0	2	0	0	0	0	1	4	.000	.000	.000	18.00	4.50
Bertness, Nate	L-L	6-6	205	8-4-95	1	2	3.55	6	6	0	0	33	37	20	13	2	8	31	.280	.237	.298	8.45	2.18
Bethell, Max	L-L	6-3	225	5-8-94	0	0	8.25	6	0	0	0	12	19	13	11	1	7	9	.373	.421	.344	6.75	5.25
Campos, Vicente	R-R	6-3	230	7-27-92	0	1	16.20	1	1	0	0	2	3	3	3	2	3	3	.429	.333	.500	16.20	16.20
Castillo, Jesus	R-R	6-2	165	8-27-95	8	3	3.62	16	15	0	0	82	86	45	33	13	18	74	.270	.305	.246	8.12	1.98
Clark, Ryan	R-R	6-5	220	12-9-93	1	4	8.27	10	9	0	0	37	58	41	34	12	16	29	.356	.318	.381	7.05	3.89
De Los Santos, Samil	R-R	6-4	175	1-8-94	3	2	4.08	32	0	0	10	46	49	21	21	4	20	52	.272	.288	.262	10.10	3.88
Eregua, Greyfer	R-R	5-11	160	10-15-93	0	3	5.02	17	9	0	3	52	53	31	29	7	18	53	.265	.247	.277	9.17	3.12
Fitzsimmons, Jon	R-R	6-2	205	11-29-91	0	1	10.64	7	0	0	0	11	14	13	13	4	7	9	.304	.250	.333	7.36	5.73
Gatto, Joe	R-R	6-3	220	6-14-95	3	2	3.34	6	6	0	0	32	31	17	12	1	14	23	.258	.271	.250	6.40	3.90
Hofacket, Adam	R-R	6-1	195	2-18-94	2	0	2.20	10	0	0	0	16	12	5	4	1	3	16	.203	.222	.195	8.82	1.65
Holland, Sam	R-R	6-4	200	2-20-94	3	1	3.22	45	0	0	7	64	55	28	23	6	23	58	.228	.231	.227	8.11	3.22
Isaac, Sean	R-R	6-4	225	12-17-92	1	0	5.02	18	1	0	1	38	33	23	21	3	18	52	.234	.217	.242	12.42	4.30
Jewell, Jake	R-R	6-3	200	5-16-93	0	1	2.25	3	3	0	0	16	11	6	4	1	3	15	.183	.182	.184	8.44	1.69
Kaelin, Mike	R-R	5-9	185	3-30-94	1	1	4.76	20	0	0	2	34	36	19	18	3	15	36	.277	.346	.231	9.53	3.97
Karch, Eric	R-R	6-2	205	10-15-91	1	0	9.35	3	0	0	0	9	14	10	9	2	1	7	.368	.500	.333	7.27	1.04
Kelly, Justin	L-L	6-1	175	4-22-93	0	1	5.79	2	0	0	0	5	6	3	3	0	4	2	.353	.143	.500	3.86	7.71
Lavendier, Winston	L-L	6-2	225	8-7-92	4	2	6.16	39	0	0	0	57	63	39	39	7	29	60	.281	.240	.302	9.47	4.58
Lillis-White, Conor	L-L	6-4	220	7-22-92	2	0	3.63	13	0	0	0	22	16	9	9	3	5	27	.205	.050	.259	10.88	2.01
Long, Grayson	R-R	6-5	230	5-27-94	0	2	4.50	3	3	0	0	12	14	8	6	0	4	14	.286	.118	.375	10.50	3.00
Manoah, Erik	R-R	6-2	190	12-22-95	1	2	9.75	3	3	0	0	12	17	13	13	1	7	9	.347	.294	.375	6.75	5.25
Medina, Jhondaniel	R-R	5-11	218	2-8-93	0	0	8.00	7	0	0	0	9	16	8	8	3	3	15	.372	.286	.455	15.00	3.00
Norris, Bud	R-R	6-0	215	3-2-85	0	0	0.00	1	1	0	0	1	1	0	0	0	0	3	.250	.500	.000	27.00	0.00
Nuss, Garrett	R-R	6-1	180	4-15-93	5	2	5.36	28	0	0	1	49	71	44	29	6	18	49	.341	.343	.341	9.06	3.33
Pena, Luis	R-R	5-11	190	8-24-95	6	10	5.28	25	25	1	0	131	138	84	77	15	58	148	.267	.297	.248	10.14	3.97
Rhoades, Jeremy	R-R	6-4	225	2-12-93	3	3	7.31	19	0	0	5	32	39	26	26	4	6	35	.296	.326	.279	9.84	1.69
Robichaux, Austin	R-R	6-6	175	11-23-92	6	9	6.80	23	17	0	0	94	124	80	71	12	49	64	.326	.354	.308	6.13	4.69
Rodriguez, Jose	R-R	6-2	175	8-29-95	8	12	5.18	27	27	0	0	149	178	97	86	11	44	134	.295	.295	.296	8.08	2.65
Shoemaker, Matt	R-R	6-2	225	9-27-86	0	0	0.00	1	1	0	0	3	2	0	0	0	0	5	.200	.286	.000	15.00	0.00

Pitching	B-T	HT	WT	DOB	W	L	ERA	G	GS	CG	SV	IP	H	R	ER	HR	BB	SO	AVG	vLH	vRH	K/9	BB/9
Smith, Blake	R-R	6-5	240	8-12-92	0	0	2.66	12	0	0	0	20	14	6	6	2	11	18	.187	.152	.214	7.97	4.87
Street, Huston	R-R	6-0	205	8-2-83	0	1	81.00	1	1	0	0	0	2	3	3	0	2	0	.667	—	.667	0.00	54.00
Warmoth, Tyler	R-R	6-2	205	6-4-92	1	1	1.08	4	0	0	0	8	6	1	1	0	2	11	.207	.077	.313	11.88	2.16
Wesely, Jonah	L-L	6-1	215	12-8-94	1	0	4.05	12	0	0	0	20	27	9	9	1	5	28	.321	.212	.392	12.60	2.25

Fielding

Catcher	PCT	G	PO	A	E	DP	PB
Barash	.990	62	539	45	6	1	5
Kruger	.977	28	229	25	6	1	2
Leon	.986	9	66	5	1	1	3
Ward	.993	42	364	60	3	6	4

First Base	PCT	G	PO	A	E	DP
Anderson	1.000	3	14	0	0	3
Leon	1.000	2	17	1	0	0
Rojas	1.000	1	12	1	0	0
Serena	.979	6	43	3	1	1
Thaiss	.990	78	633	34	7	60
Valbuena	1.000	3	19	1	0	4
Walsh	.984	51	400	41	7	34

Second Base	PCT	G	PO	A	E	DP
Justus	1.000	2	1	7	0	0
McCann	1.000	1	0	1	0	0
Ramer	.974	68	118	144	7	39
Yacinich	.964	30	74	86	6	26
Zimmerman	.982	39	69	96	3	19

Third Base	PCT	G	PO	A	E	DP
Escobar	.750	3	2	1	1	0
Grieshaber	.889	29	24	56	10	5
McCann	1.000	1	1	0	0	0
Rojas	.960	73	46	146	8	18
Serena	.870	7	4	16	3	3
Valbuena	1.000	1	1	3	0	0
Yacinich	.938	29	20	56	5	5

Shortstop	PCT	G	PO	A	E	DP
Grieshaber	1.000	1	2	1	0	0
Justus	.954	113	145	268	20	59
Yacinich	.946	26	30	57	5	13

Outfield	PCT	G	PO	A	E	DP
Diaz	.979	23	45	1	1	0
Foster	.985	30	65	2	1	0
Gibbons	.983	23	57	2	1	1
Grieshaber	1.000	12	21	1	0	1
Hermosillo	.952	12	20	0	1	0
Jenkins	.971	18	34	0	1	1
Jones	.963	40	75	2	3	0
Lund	.968	45	85	5	3	2
Montgomery	.984	61	118	3	2	0
Sandoval	.867	7	13	0	2	0
Sanger	.957	56	87	3	4	0
Serena	.989	45	81	5	1	0
Survance Jr.	.988	40	79	1	1	0
Trout	1.000	2	4	0	0	0
Walsh	1.000	12	23	1	0	0

BURLINGTON BEES — *LOW CLASS A*

MIDWEST LEAGUE

Batting	B-T	HT	WT	DOB	AVG	vLH	vRH	G	AB	R	H	2B	3B	HR	RBI	BB	HBP	SH	SF	SO	SB	CS	SLG	OBP
Almao, Angel	R-R	5-10	145	11-5-94	.177	.167	.180	22	68	6	12	3	0	0	6	10	0	1	0	21	0	2	.221	.282
Baldoquin, Roberto	R-R	5-11	199	5-14-94	.253	.293	.241	52	178	19	45	8	1	4	12	12	2	4	0	42	6	4	.376	.307
Fecteau, Richard	L-R	5-10	190	3-17-94	.315	.296	.321	58	222	29	70	11	2	8	44	15	5	1	3	31	2	2	.491	.367
Grieshaber, Keith	R-R	6-1	168	6-29-95	.274	.276	.274	36	135	22	37	13	0	2	9	13	10	0	0	22	12	6	.415	.380
Gurwitz, Zane	R-R	5-8	185	12-1-94	.192	.167	.200	8	26	2	5	0	0	0	1	0	1	0	0	5	0	1	.192	.222
Jenkins, Derek	R-R	5-8	155	2-11-94	.288	.216	.306	52	184	15	53	3	1	0	11	17	3	4	0	43	13	4	.315	.358
Jones, Jahmai	R-R	6-0	215	8-4-97	.272	.333	.255	86	346	54	94	18	4	9	30	32	3	5	1	63	18	7	.425	.338
Kadkhodaian, Artemis	R-R	5-10	175	11-21-94	.228	.231	.227	44	158	17	36	5	0	3	14	14	5	0	2	37	8	1	.317	.307
Kerr, Stephen	R-R	5-10	165	12-22-94	.263	.389	.226	22	80	10	21	5	0	1	11	5	1	1	0	15	1	0	.363	.314
Kruger, Jack	R-R	6-1	185	10-26-94	.232	.231	.233	69	267	34	62	13	2	4	23	21	4	2	2	54	2	1	.341	.296
Leon, Julian	R-R	5-11	200	1-24-96	.304	.325	.298	44	161	21	49	14	0	5	23	17	5	0	1	41	0	0	.485	.386
Lund, Brennon	L-R	5-10	185	11-27-94	.306	.349	.292	46	173	25	53	7	4	2	18	24	3	1	0	26	14	3	.428	.400
McCann, Matt	R-R	5-9	170	1-12-95	.211	.500	.133	6	19	3	4	0	0	0	1	5	1	0	0	7	0	3	.211	.400
McDonnell, Sam	L-R	6-0	190	8-10-95	.247	.256	.244	104	369	41	91	13	5	6	42	44	3	0	3	84	8	4	.358	.329
Merrigan, Josh	R-L	6-2	172	9-15-93	.197	.167	.204	20	61	5	12	4	2	0	9	7	0	1	0	20	0	0	.328	.279
Montgomery, Troy	L-L	5-10	185	8-13-94	.256	.400	.212	15	43	6	11	1	1	2	4	12	0	1	0	4	2	1	.465	.418
Moreno, Juan	R-R	6-0	170	11-17-94	.164	.273	.133	93	299	27	49	8	0	1	21	21	2	7	4	65	5	5	.201	.221
Morgan, Brennan	R-R	6-4	230	4-13-94	.230	.238	.228	106	391	36	90	18	2	4	50	36	10	0	2	83	2	2	.317	.310
Navarro, Franklin	B-R	5-10	181	10-17-94	.257	.333	.236	22	70	9	18	5	0	0	9	6	0	1	0	15	0	0	.329	.316
Rivas, Leonardo	B-R	5-10	150	10-10-97	.267	.219	.293	26	90	24	24	5	0	0	7	20	3	2	1	22	8	1	.322	.412
Sanchez, Jeyson	R-R	5-10	174	7-4-94	.153	.139	.157	48	157	11	24	5	0	2	10	21	4	0	0	36	3	1	.223	.269
Sandoval, Brandon	R-R	6-1	180	6-24-95	.323	.286	.344	24	96	12	31	3	2	0	8	4	0	1	0	16	5	3	.396	.350
Sanjur, Mario	R-R	5-7	174	12-23-95	.149	.105	.164	22	74	3	11	2	0	0	7	5	1	0	0	18	0	0	.176	.213
Schuknecht, John	R-R	6-0	200	7-12-94	.171	.228	.154	96	346	40	59	12	1	10	37	32	9	0	2	119	3	3	.298	.257
Serena, Jordan	R-R	6-1	220	8-4-92	.091	.077	.097	13	44	2	4	1	0	1	5	1	2	0	0	15	0	1	.182	.149
Todd, Jonah	L-L	6-0	185	9-18-95	.257	.189	.287	44	175	20	45	7	0	0	17	17	2	4	0	40	0	4	.297	.330
Zimmerman, Jordan	R-R	6-1	195	11-21-94	.270	.325	.253	85	326	43	88	13	6	5	43	27	1	2	3	79	8	4	.393	.325

Pitching	B-T	HT	WT	DOB	W	L	ERA	G	GS	CG	SV	IP	H	R	ER	HR	BB	SO	AVG	vLH	vRH	K/9	BB/9
Almeida, Adrian	L-L	6-0	160	2-25-95	1	3	5.31	27	0	0	0	42	43	30	25	1	32	50	.265	.152	.310	10.63	6.80
Barkell, Ty	R-R	6-3	225	3-12-93	2	6	5.25	22	0	0	1	48	55	30	28	4	20	39	.299	.299	.299	7.31	3.75
Bates, Nathan	R-R	6-8	205	3-1-94	0	1	2.03	8	0	0	1	13	9	4	3	0	6	18	.188	.191	.185	12.15	4.05
Belton, Greg	R-R	5-10	190	12-31-92	1	2	4.55	17	0	0	3	30	33	15	15	3	7	43	.285	.235	.323	13.04	2.12
Bertness, Nate	L-L	6-6	205	8-4-95	5	9	5.15	21	19	0	0	94	108	68	54	10	39	84	.292	.236	.310	8.01	3.72
Bethell, Max	L-L	6-3	225	5-8-94	0	0	4.50	1	1	0	0	4	5	3	2	1	1	1	.294	.500	.231	2.25	2.25
Castillo, Jesus	R-R	6-2	165	8-27-95	1	1	2.37	4	4	0	0	19	13	5	5	1	2	22	.191	.222	.171	10.42	0.95
De Los Santos, Samil	R-R	6-4	175	1-8-94	0	0	0.00	8	0	0	2	14	5	0	0	0	3	18	.109	.105	.111	11.30	1.88
Eregua, Greyfer	R-R	5-11	160	10-15-93	0	0	3.00	3	0	0	0	9	8	3	3	1	0	9	.229	.222	.231	9.00	0.00
Gatto, Joe	R-R	6-3	220	6-14-95	5	7	3.46	21	21	0	0	96	90	42	37	2	45	78	.247	.265	.233	7.29	4.20
Glenn, Ronnie	L-L	6-3	230	7-15-93	2	2	5.09	26	1	0	1	58	57	38	33	6	25	44	.262	.275	.255	6.79	3.86
Halbohn, Kyle	R-R	6-8	230	1-19-93	1	1	5.83	20	0	0	1	29	31	19	19	0	15	36	.284	.275	.290	11.05	4.60
Herrin, Travis	R-R	6-2	220	4-29-95	2	4	3.61	10	6	0	2	42	41	18	17	6	11	51	.252	.235	.263	10.84	2.34
Isaac, Sean	R-R	6-4	225	12-17-92	0	0	0.81	11	0	0	3	22	14	4	2	0	9	33	.187	.233	.156	13.30	3.63
Kaelin, Mike	R-R	5-9	185	3-30-94	3	1	4.33	19	1	0	2	35	30	19	17	2	12	37	.234	.250	.224	9.42	3.06
Kelly, Justin	L-L	6-1	175	4-22-93	2	3	2.43	11	3	0	2	30	26	12	8	1	11	26	.230	.308	.207	7.89	3.34
Madero, Luis	R-R	6-3	175	4-15-97	1	2	7.76	6	6	0	0	27	42	24	23	3	9	18	.362	.380	.349	6.08	3.04

Manoah, Erik	R-R	6-2	190	12-22-95	5	8	3.81	23	20	0	0	104	88	53	44	8	56	84	.231	.232	.230	7.27	4.85
Pastrone, Sam	R-R	6-0	185	6-28-97	1	5	8.92	14	9	0	0	38	47	43	38	5	35	27	.313	.261	.358	6.34	8.22
Riley, Connor	R-R	6-0	185	5-7-95	0	2	6.11	9	1	0	0	18	24	15	12	0	6	23	.308	.292	.315	11.72	3.06
Rodriguez, Chris	R-R	6-2	185	7-20-98	1	2	5.84	6	6	0	0	25	32	17	16	1	7	24	.314	.372	.271	8.76	2.55
Rodriguez, Elvin	R-R	6-3	160	3-31-98	0	2	4.50	3	3	0	0	14	20	9	7	2	3	12	.345	.240	.424	7.71	1.93
Ryan, Zac	R-R	6-1	201	5-28-94	2	1	0.63	14	1	0	1	29	19	10	2	2	12	33	.181	.167	.188	10.36	3.77
Salazar, Carlos	R-R	6-0	200	11-23-94	2	0	3.34	20	0	0	1	32	23	13	12	2	24	48	.200	.225	.182	13.36	6.68
Smith, Blake	R-R	6-5	240	8-12-92	1	2	3.33	26	0	0	8	49	40	20	18	7	13	43	.221	.289	.163	7.95	2.40
Stevens, Tyler	R-R	6-0	215	4-4-96	0	1	2.40	7	0	0	0	15	8	4	4	1	1	18	.154	.095	.194	10.80	0.60
Suarez, Jose	L-L	5-10	170	1-3-98	5	1	3.62	12	12	0	0	55	49	25	22	7	18	71	.243	.270	.236	11.69	2.96
Vinson, Andrew	L-R	5-10	160	11-12-93	9	11	4.58	25	25	0	0	114	128	70	58	9	32	92	.284	.312	.261	7.26	2.53
Wesely, Jonah	L-L	6-1	215	12-8-94	1	1	4.32	23	0	0	2	42	32	21	20	0	24	49	.215	.118	.244	10.58	5.18
Zarubin, Jackson	R-R	6-2	190	1-8-93	6	1	2.07	32	0	0	2	61	63	22	14	2	16	54	.270	.315	.243	7.97	2.36

Fielding

Catcher	PCT	G	PO	A	E	DP	PB
Kruger	.990	63	535	80	6	3	5
Leon	.970	37	254	41	9	2	6
Navarro	1.000	22	191	14	0	2	2
Sanchez	1.000	2	15	2	0	0	0
Sanjur	.984	20	154	28	3	2	3

First Base	PCT	G	PO	A	E	DP
Fecteau	.991	14	109	5	1	7
Kerr	.981	6	51	2	1	6
Morgan	.985	96	752	49	12	91
Sanchez	.985	23	183	16	3	17

Second Base	PCT	G	PO	A	E	DP
Almao	.957	6	10	12	1	2
Baldoquin	1.000	5	10	6	0	1
Fecteau	1.000	2	4	4	0	0
Gurwitz	.962	6	11	14	1	1
Kadkhodaian	.957	26	56	56	5	14
Kerr	.964	5	11	16	1	8
McCann	1.000	1	4	2	0	2
Moreno	.946	15	33	37	4	13
Rivas	.947	4	10	8	1	4
Serena	1.000	2	4	5	0	0
Zimmerman	.974	69	119	175	8	52

Third Base	PCT	G	PO	A	E	DP
Almao	.879	11	10	19	4	2
Fecteau	.932	35	26	70	7	9
Grieshaber	.910	30	28	43	7	12
Kadkhodaian	1.000	1	1	0	0	0
Kerr	.824	10	4	10	3	1
McCann	1.000	3	0	6	0	0
Moreno	.928	25	19	45	5	7
Sanchez	.833	16	4	21	5	1
Serena	1.000	9	8	19	0	1

Shortstop	PCT	G	PO	A	E	DP
Almao	.952	3	11	9	1	5
Baldoquin	.957	45	57	141	9	25
Grieshaber	.893	6	12	13	3	6
Kadkhodaian	.956	11	26	17	2	6
Kerr	1.000	1	1	1	0	0
McCann	1.000	1	1	2	0	1
Moreno	.953	52	70	114	9	25
Rivas	.948	21	23	69	5	15

Outfield	PCT	G	PO	A	E	DP
Jenkins	.990	49	92	5	1	1
Jones	.982	81	160	6	3	1
Lund	.978	45	84	4	2	1
McDonnell	.966	78	135	7	5	1
Merrigan	.963	15	26	0	1	0
Montgomery	.960	15	24	0	1	0
Sandoval	1.000	21	42	3	0	2
Schuknecht	.979	78	128	10	3	3
Todd	.986	38	68	2	1	0

OREM OWLZ

ROOKIE

PIONEER LEAGUE

Batting	B-T	HT	WT	DOB	AVG	vLH	vRH	G	AB	R	H	2B	3B	HR	RBI	BB	HBP	SH	SF	SO	SB	CS	SLG	OBP
Adell, Jo	R-R	6-2	195	4-8-99	.377	.300	.400	18	85	25	32	5	2	1	9	4	1	0	0	17	3	2	.518	.411
Fecteau, Richard	L-R	5-10	190	3-17-94	.333	.250	.348	6	27	9	9	1	0	2	9	4	0	0	1	4	0	0	.593	.406
Garcia, Julio	B-R	6-0	175	7-31-97	.329	.333	.328	16	70	13	23	9	0	0	11	3	1	2	1	19	0	1	.457	.360
Griffin, Spencer	R-R	6-1	170	10-24-96	.206	.185	.213	26	102	17	21	5	2	1	6	8	3	1	1	37	3	1	.324	.281
Guzman, Manuel	B-R	5-9	160	2-10-95	.360	.310	.371	60	228	46	82	13	5	5	40	41	1	4	0	28	7	6	.526	.459
Hunter, Torii	R-R	6-2	180	6-7-95	.352	.500	.326	52	213	48	75	10	3	1	28	23	7	4	0	44	13	2	.441	.432
Kerr, Stephen	R-R	5-10	165	12-22-94	.229	.400	.184	14	48	9	11	3	0	1	6	10	0	0	0	13	0	2	.354	.362
MacKinnon, David	R-R	6-2	200	12-15-94	.398	.235	.427	33	113	29	45	7	2	2	27	25	6	0	4	11	1	0	.549	.514
Marsh, Brandon	L-R	6-4	210	12-18-97	.350	.324	.357	39	177	47	62	13	5	4	44	9	5	0	1	35	10	2	.548	.396
McCann, Matt	R-R	5-9	170	1-12-95	.261	.571	.204	41	134	26	35	5	0	1	13	26	4	1	3	26	5	1	.321	.389
Molina, Angel	R-R	6-0	175	8-20-97	.315	.227	.337	28	108	15	34	10	0	3	24	5	3	1	3	23	0	1	.491	.353
Navarro, Franklin	B-R	5-10	181	10-17-94	.314	.250	.323	11	35	7	11	2	0	0	6	7	0	0	1	9	0	0	.371	.419
Pina, Keinner	R-R	5-10	165	2-12-97	.292	.292	.292	48	185	34	54	7	0	0	33	23	8	0	3	19	1	0	.330	.388
Rivas, Leonardo	B-R	5-10	150	10-10-97	.299	.412	.283	35	137	37	41	6	4	2	29	39	4	1	2	22	11	0	.445	.462
Roper, Erven	L-R	6-0	205	2-28-95	.000	—	.000	2	5	0	0	0	0	0	0	0	0	0	0	5	0	0	.000	.000
Sanchez, Jeyson	R-R	5-10	174	7-4-94	.360	.476	.333	30	114	28	41	11	0	13	43	9	4	1	2	30	1	0	.798	.419
Sandoval, Brandon	R-R	6-1	180	6-24-95	.328	.316	.330	32	131	29	43	8	2	2	22	16	3	0	3	24	3	1	.466	.405
Santana, Yefry	R-R	6-1	170	11-8-95	.167	—	.167	5	18	2	3	0	0	1	2	1	0	0	0	8	1	0	.333	.211
Todd, Jonah	L-L	6-0	185	9-18-95	.306	.286	.308	25	98	25	30	6	3	0	22	25	0	0	2	12	1	0	.429	.440
Torres, Franklin	R-R	6-0	175	10-27-96	.292	.268	.296	66	271	47	79	20	1	5	47	21	1	2	5	34	4	0	.428	.339
Vega, Ryan	R-R	6-2	180	9-17-96	.313	.311	.314	64	268	55	84	12	3	5	58	37	6	0	6	52	6	5	.437	.401
Wenson, Harrison	R-R	6-3	235	4-21-95	.286	.261	.291	36	133	34	38	8	0	13	48	25	6	0	3	38	0	0	.639	.413
Williams, Cam	R-R	5-11	185	1-16-97	.292	.167	.333	8	24	10	7	1	0	1	5	6	1	0	1	9	1	1	.458	.438
Williams, Kevin	R-R	6-0	190	6-17-96	.322	.444	.300	15	59	15	19	3	0	4	8	5	1	1	0	16	1	0	.576	.385

Pitching	B-T	HT	WT	DOB	W	L	ERA	G	GS	CG	SV	IP	H	R	ER	HR	BB	SO	AVG	vLH	vRH	K/9	BB/9
Adams, Austin	R-R	5-11	200	8-19-86	0	0	0.00	1	0	0	0	1	1	0	0	0	0	0	.500	—	.500	0.00	0.00
Agosto, Edrick	R-R	6-4	245	11-28-96	0	1	6.00	14	10	0	0	48	60	37	32	7	31	38	.319	.278	.345	7.13	5.81
Alexander, Jason	R-R	6-3	200	3-1-93	1	0	1.02	6	0	0	1	18	10	2	2	0	1	16	.159	.200	.140	8.15	0.51
Beasley, Jeremy	R-R	6-3	215	11-20-95	2	1	3.12	13	0	0	1	26	21	12	9	3	12	31	.219	.367	.152	10.73	4.15
Bethell, Max	L-L	6-3	225	5-8-94	1	0	9.00	4	0	0	0	7	13	8	7	3	3	9	.382	.571	.333	11.57	3.86
Brady, Denny	R-R	6-1	200	1-18-97	1	1	4.43	13	0	0	0	20	23	14	10	2	4	24	.284	.207	.327	10.62	1.77
Carpenter, Tyler	R-R	6-5	225	2-25-92	1	1	3.21	4	4	0	0	14	11	5	5	3	1	11	.212	.136	.267	7.07	0.64
Duensing, Cole	L-R	6-4	175	6-16-98	3	5	10.74	9	9	0	0	33	42	39	39	9	17	22	.323	.273	.349	6.06	4.68
Gonzalez, Jorge	L-L	5-9	175	9-25-96	1	1	18.00	6	0	0	1	8	12	16	16	1	15	11	.333	.214	.409	12.38	16.88

Pitching	B-T	HT	WT	DOB	W	L	ERA	G	GS	CG	SV	IP	H	R	ER	HR	BB	SO	AVG	vLH	vRH	K/9	BB/9
Grendell, Kevin	L-L	6-2	210	8-22-93	0	0	5.63	8	1	0	0	8	4	5	5	1	13	13	.148	.091	.188	14.63	14.63
Hanewich, Brett	B-R	6-3	200	12-15-94	2	1	7.18	18	0	0	0	26	31	21	21	2	18	30	.290	.279	.297	10.25	6.15
Heredia, Andres	R-R	6-3	175	8-15-96	1	3	10.61	6	5	0	0	19	33	24	22	1	10	14	.393	.500	.339	6.75	4.82
Hernandez, Wilkel	R-R	6-3	160	4-13-99	1	0	3.00	1	0	0	0	3	2	1	1	0	2	2	.222	.200	.250	6.00	6.00
Kelly, Justin	L-L	6-1	175	4-22-93	3	0	1.86	8	2	0	0	19	14	5	4	0	8	19	.206	.333	.149	8.84	3.72
Lind, Luke	L-R	6-6	225	1-26-95	1	0	8.88	9	0	0	0	24	30	24	24	6	15	39	.297	.382	.254	14.42	5.55
Malmin, Jon	R-L	6-1	170	9-2-94	0	0	0.00	2	0	0	0	3	2	0	0	0	1	2	.222	.333	.167	6.75	3.38
Mathews, Simon	R-R	6-2	180	9-24-95	3	1	3.97	10	6	0	0	34	40	16	15	4	9	34	.290	.306	.281	9.00	2.38
Mattson, Isaac	R-R	6-3	205	7-14-95	1	0	1.35	17	0	0	6	27	16	4	4	4	10	40	.174	.160	.179	13.50	3.38
Mieses, Crusito	R-R	6-5	224	9-15-96	0	0	6.23	5	0	0	0	4	5	3	3	1	8	3	.294	.400	.250	6.23	16.62
Molina, Cristopher	R-R	6-3	170	6-10-97	1	3	11.12	8	5	0	0	28	43	41	35	10	20	40	.371	.500	.313	12.71	6.35
Morell, Johnny	R-R	6-2	200	10-30-97	1	0	5.40	2	1	0	0	7	8	5	4	1	4	1	.286	.333	.231	1.35	5.40
Perez, David	R-R	6-5	200	12-20-92	0	0	6.75	10	0	0	0	13	19	12	10	3	10	11	.339	.278	.368	7.43	6.75
Perez, Mayky	R-R	6-5	235	9-26-96	5	1	5.67	15	8	0	0	46	54	31	29	4	19	26	.302	.312	.294	5.09	3.72
Procopio, Daniel	R-R	6-0	190	9-18-95	2	2	2.49	16	0	0	3	22	14	7	6	1	14	32	.177	.250	.146	13.29	5.82
Riley, Connor	R-R	6-0	185	5-7-95	2	0	2.03	9	0	0	0	13	10	4	3	1	6	13	.196	.191	.200	8.78	4.05
Rodriguez, Chris	R-R	6-2	185	7-20-98	4	1	6.40	8	8	0	0	32	35	24	23	1	7	32	.271	.211	.319	8.91	1.95
Rodriguez, Elvin	R-R	6-3	160	3-31-98	5	1	2.50	11	11	0	0	54	45	18	15	5	11	49	.224	.254	.209	8.17	1.83
Rogalla, Keith	R-R	6-3	205	9-15-95	0	1	4.38	14	0	0	0	25	21	12	12	1	18	26	.228	.179	.250	9.49	6.57
Ryan, Zac	R-R	6-1	201	5-28-94	0	1	6.48	7	0	0	2	8	9	6	6	2	3	11	.273	.429	.158	11.88	3.24
Smith, Evan	L-R	6-5	190	8-17-95	1	0	9.78	12	0	0	0	19	26	21	21	4	9	20	.325	.364	.310	9.31	4.19
Soriano, Jose	R-R	6-3	168	10-20-98	0	0	2.70	1	1	0	0	3	4	1	1	0	4	2	.308	.200	.375	5.40	10.80
Stevens, Tyler	R-R	6-0	215	4-4-96	1	0	5.51	12	0	0	0	16	20	10	10	3	4	19	.299	.346	.268	10.47	2.20
Traver, Mitchell	R-R	6-7	255	5-3-94	0	1	7.20	4	4	0	0	15	22	13	12	2	5	14	.349	.389	.333	8.40	3.00
Ziemba, James	R-L	6-10	230	8-10-94	5	0	1.99	20	1	0	1	32	26	8	7	1	13	35	.224	.118	.268	9.95	3.69

Fielding

C: Navarro 9, Pina 43, Roper 1, Wenson 29. **1B:** Fecteau 1, MacKinnon 31, Molina 24, Navarro 1, Sanchez 12, Torres 12, Wenson 1. **2B:** Garcia 3, Guzman 23, Kerr 13, McCann 27, Rivas 8, Torres 9. **3B:** Fecteau 4, Garcia 1, Guzman 16, Kerr 2, Molina 3, Sanchez 12, Torres 46. **SS:** Garcia 13, Guzman 24, McCann 15, Rivas 28. **OF:** Griffin 23, Hunter 49, Marsh 37, Sandoval 27, Santana 5, Todd 21, Vega 50, Williams 7, Williams 12.

AZL ANGELS — *ROOKIE*

ARIZONA LEAGUE

Batting	B-T	HT	WT	DOB	AVG	vLH	vRH	G	AB	R	H	2B	3B	HR	RBI	BB	HBP	SH	SF	SO	SB	CS	SLG	OBP
Adell, Jo	R-R	6-2	195	4-8-99	.288	.381	.268	31	118	18	34	6	6	4	21	10	2	1	1	32	5	0	.542	.351
Arias, Kevin	R-R	5-7	160	2-18-99	.205	.200	.206	13	39	7	8	1	2	0	2	4	1	1	0	15	4	1	.333	.296
Barnes, Jimmy	R-R	6-4	190	6-16-97	.273	.259	.277	38	139	20	38	7	4	4	15	13	1	0	1	47	6	2	.468	.338
Blumenfeld, Dalton	R-R	6-3	210	11-14-96	.178	.148	.188	32	107	17	19	5	2	3	16	17	3	0	0	52	0	1	.346	.307
Del Valle, Francisco	L-L	6-1	187	8-18-98	.206	.139	.242	31	102	12	21	2	1	2	15	10	0	0	2	20	2	0	.304	.272
Fecteau, Richard	L-R	5-10	190	3-17-94	.286	.333	.250	4	14	0	4	0	0	0	0	2	1	0	0	6	0	0	.286	.412
Fitzsimons, Connor	R-R	5-10	190	8-29-94	.243	.227	.247	33	107	15	26	4	3	1	9	9	6	0	1	36	1	0	.365	.333
Foster, Jared	R-R	6-1	200	11-2-92	.111	.000	.125	3	9	2	1	0	0	0	2	1	0	0	1	1	1	0	.111	.182
Garcia, Julio	B-R	6-0	175	7-31-97	.283	.333	.267	47	159	31	45	10	4	1	23	21	0	2	4	34	3	2	.415	.359
Gibbons, Zach	R-R	5-8	186	10-14-93	.000	—	.000	1	1	0	0	0	0	0	0	0	0	0	0	0	0	0	.000	.000
Gurwitz, Zane	R-R	5-8	185	12-1-94	.386	.471	.366	23	88	15	34	7	2	2	17	7	3	0	0	11	7	2	.580	.449
Herazo, Manuel	B-R	5-10	175	3-17-95	.292	.250	.300	11	24	3	7	0	0	1	2	4	1	0	0	10	1	0	.417	.414
Kadkhodaian, Artemis	R-R	5-10	175	11-21-94	.222	.250	.214	5	18	4	4	2	1	0	4	1	0	1	0	5	1	0	.444	.263
Kerr, Stephen	R-R	5-10	165	12-22-94	.143	.250	.100	4	14	2	2	1	0	0	0	4	1	0	0	3	1	0	.214	.368
MacKinnon, David	R-R	6-2	200	12-15-94	.286	—	.286	2	7	0	2	0	0	0	0	0	0	0	0	2	0	0	.286	.286
Molina, Angel	R-R	6-0	175	8-20-97	.111	.143	.097	12	45	2	5	0	1	0	5	3	0	0	0	5	0	0	.156	.167
Morgan, Brennan	R-R	6-4	230	4-13-94	.120	.200	.100	9	25	2	3	2	0	0	0	3	0	0	0	8	1	0	.200	.214
Pearson, Jacob	L-R	6-1	185	6-1-98	.226	.177	.240	40	155	20	35	7	1	0	13	15	2	4	0	37	5	3	.284	.302
Pineda, Gleyvin	L-R	5-11	160	8-19-96	.316	.258	.333	40	133	20	42	7	1	0	14	18	0	2	0	29	4	3	.384	.397
Roper, Erven	L-R	6-0	205	2-28-95	.233	.077	.353	9	30	5	7	1	1	1	6	2	1	1	1	11	0	0	.433	.294
Rosario, Rayneldy	L-L	5-8	139	4-30-98	.203	.188	.208	25	64	7	13	0	0	0	5	3	0	1	0	12	3	3	.203	.239
Sala, Johan	R-R	6-1	175	12-17-97	.248	.324	.217	36	129	15	32	5	2	0	9	12	2	0	0	31	3	4	.318	.322
Sanger, Brendon	L-R	6-0	195	9-11-93	.148	.125	.158	7	27	3	4	1	0	1	2	2	0	0	0	10	0	0	.296	.207
Sanjur, Mario	R-R	5-7	174	12-23-95	.196	.231	.186	20	56	7	11	1	0	2	8	2	0	0	1	8	1	1	.321	.220
Scires, Caleb	L-L	6-0	195	9-1-98	.236	.000	.277	19	55	12	13	1	2	1	3	12	0	0	1	17	4	2	.382	.368
Wenson, Harrison	R-R	6-3	235	4-21-95	.200	.000	.333	2	5	1	1	0	0	0	1	1	1	0	1	0	0	0	.200	.375
Williams, Nonie	R-R	6-2	200	5-22-98	.220	.300	.195	43	168	22	37	3	2	1	15	14	2	0	1	53	11	3	.280	.287
Woods, Dylan	B-R	5-10	175	12-27-94	.257	.143	.286	11	35	4	9	3	0	0	4	4	1	0	0	12	1	1	.343	.350

Pitching	B-T	HT	WT	DOB	W	L	ERA	G	GS	CG	SV	IP	H	R	ER	HR	BB	SO	AVG	vLH	vRH	K/9	BB/9
Alexander, Jason	R-R	6-3	200	3-1-93	1	1	4.79	10	0	0	1	21	23	11	11	0	2	19	.277	.333	.240	8.27	0.87
Andress, Nick	R-R	6-1	180	1-23-94	2	1	6.17	14	0	0	0	23	24	19	16	1	15	25	.264	.414	.194	9.64	5.79
Aquino, Stiward	R-R	6-6	170	6-20-99	1	0	1.59	2	0	0	0	6	5	1	1	0	4	2	.250	.143	.308	3.18	6.35
Bailey, Andrew	R-R	6-3	240	5-31-84	0	0	0.00	1	1	0	0	1	0	0	0	0	0	1	.000	.000	.000	9.00	0.00
Beasley, Jeremy	R-R	6-3	215	11-20-95	1	0	3.18	4	0	0	0	6	3	2	2	0	0	6	.150	.182	.111	9.53	0.00
Campos, Vicente	R-R	6-3	230	7-27-92	0	0	5.40	4	3	0	0	5	6	4	3	0	2	7	.286	.333	.250	12.60	3.60
Clark, Ryan	R-R	6-5	220	12-9-93	1	1	4.38	4	1	0	0	12	15	7	6	0	4	11	.294	.267	.306	8.03	2.92
De La Cruz, Kida	R-R	6-5	240	8-10-94	2	2	4.64	18	0	0	2	21	16	14	11	1	14	30	.200	.211	.197	12.66	5.91
De Leon, Yoel	L-L	6-2	200	11-23-97	0	2	4.66	3	1	0	0	10	10	6	5	1	2	6	.256	.400	.235	5.59	1.86
De Los Santos, Abel	R-R	6-2	195	11-21-92	0	0	4.50	2	1	0	0	2	3	2	1	0	1	2	.333	.250	.400	9.00	4.50
Duensing, Cole	L-R	6-4	175	6-16-98	0	1	3.12	4	1	0	0	9	8	3	3	1	8	3	.242	.308	.200	3.12	8.31

Pitching	B-T	HT	WT	DOB	W	L	ERA	G	GS	CG	SV	IP	H	R	ER	HR	BB	SO	AVG	vLH	vRH	K/9	BB/9
Fuller, Sam	R-R	6-0	195	10-20-98	0	0	0.00	2	0	0	0	2	2	2	0	0	0	0	.250	.333	.200	0.00	0.00
Heaney, Andrew	L-L	6-2	195	6-5-91	0	1	1.74	3	3	0	0	10	11	3	2	0	1	15	.268	.182	.300	13.06	0.87
Hernandez, Ivan	R-R	6-2	249	7-28-91	0	0	0.00	2	1	0	0	2	2	0	0	0	0	1	.286	.333	.250	4.50	0.00
Hernandez, Wilkel	R-R	6-3	160	4-13-99	3	1	2.61	11	7	0	0	41	23	15	12	1	20	42	.161	.167	.158	9.15	4.35
Herrmann, Max	L-L	6-3	210	7-17-93	2	1	5.06	10	0	0	1	16	17	10	9	1	12	17	.283	.429	.239	9.56	6.75
Krzeminski, Austin	R-R	6-2	210	9-30-96	1	2	1.78	16	0	0	3	30	28	10	6	0	3	26	.250	.220	.268	7.71	0.89
Lind, Luke	L-R	6-6	225	1-26-95	0	2	1.98	9	0	0	1	14	11	4	3	1	0	23	.225	.250	.216	15.15	0.00
Malmin, Jon	R-L	6-1	170	9-2-94	4	1	3.24	16	0	0	1	25	19	16	9	1	14	26	.211	.133	.227	9.36	5.04
Mathews, Simon	R-R	6-2	180	9-24-95	3	0	0.64	6	0	0	0	14	7	2	1	0	3	18	.146	.167	.139	11.57	1.93
Mattson, Isaac	R-R	6-3	205	7-14-95	0	0	1.93	3	0	0	1	5	3	1	1	0	1	7	.177	.125	.222	13.50	1.93
Molina, Cristopher	R-R	6-3	170	6-10-97	0	1	11.42	4	3	0	0	9	7	11	11	1	6	10	.206	.111	.240	10.38	6.23
Morell, Johnny	R-R	6-2	200	10-30-97	1	0	1.95	10	5	0	0	28	17	8	6	1	15	24	.179	.242	.145	7.81	4.88
Natera, Jose	R-R	6-1	180	11-30-99	0	3	8.55	7	5	0	0	20	25	22	19	1	13	20	.305	.235	.354	9.00	5.85
Rivera, Jerryell	L-L	6-3	180	4-19-99	1	0	1.64	8	1	0	0	11	7	2	2	0	3	11	.175	.154	.185	9.00	2.45
Skaggs, Tyler	L-L	6-4	215	7-13-91	0	0	4.91	1	1	0	0	4	2	2	2	0	0	6	.154	.250	.111	14.73	0.00
Smith, Nate	L-L	6-3	210	8-28-91	0	0	0.00	3	3	0	0	9	3	0	0	0	2	10	.094	.154	.053	9.64	1.93
Soriano, Jose	R-R	6-3	168	10-20-98	2	2	2.94	12	10	0	0	49	43	23	16	2	14	37	.234	.230	.236	6.80	2.57
Suarez, Jose	L-L	5-10	170	1-3-98	1	0	1.93	3	3	0	0	14	10	3	3	1	4	19	.208	.071	.265	12.21	2.57
Swanda, John	R-R	6-2	185	3-18-99	1	2	9.31	7	1	0	0	10	13	10	10	1	6	6	.333	.308	.346	5.59	5.59
Tavarez, Jorge	R-R	5-10	150	8-4-95	1	0	1.99	19	0	0	3	23	23	9	5	1	6	35	.253	.229	.268	13.90	2.38
Tolleson, Sam	R-R	6-3	200	3-31-93	1	0	2.70	5	0	0	0	10	6	4	3	0	4	13	.167	.231	.130	11.70	3.60
Traver, Mitchell	R-R	6-7	255	5-3-94	1	1	9.00	4	0	0	0	7	10	7	7	1	3	4	.370	.429	.350	5.14	3.86
Walsh, Tyler	R-R	6-5	200	4-11-95	0	0	1.93	6	0	0	0	9	4	2	2	0	5	8	.138	.100	.158	7.71	4.82
Yan, Hector	L-L	5-11	180	4-26-99	0	1	4.96	10	5	0	1	16	10	10	9	0	11	21	.179	.182	.178	11.57	6.06

Fielding

C: Fitzsimons 26, Herazo 7, Roper 9, Sanjur 20, Wenson 2. **1B:** Blumenfeld 30, Fitzsimons 8, MacKinnon 2, Molina 8, Morgan 9, Walsh 1, Woods 3. **2B:** Arias 12, Gurwitz 18, Kerr 1, Pineda 28, Woods 1. **3B:** Fecteau 4, Garcia 39, Gurwitz 3, Molina 3, Pineda 8. **SS:** Arias 1, Garcia 9, Kadkhodaian 5, Kerr 3, Pineda 1, Williams 32, Woods 7. **OF:** Barnes 35, Del Valle 26, Foster 3, Gibbons 1, Herazo 1, Pearson 40, Rosario 21, Sala 35, Sanger 4, Scires 17.

DSL ANGELS — *ROOKIE*

DOMINICAN SUMMER LEAGUE

Batting	B-T	HT	WT	DOB	AVG	vLH	vRH	G	AB	R	H	2B	3B	HR	RBI	BB	HBP	SH	SF	SO	SB	CS	SLG	OBP
Arias, Kevin	R-R	5-7	160	2-18-99	.296	.000	.286	7	27	6	8	0	2	0	1	4	1	0	0	8	3	1	.444	.406
Bisay, Edwin	R-R	5-9	156	3-8-00	.168	.273	.161	33	95	15	16	3	0	0	5	18	6	0	0	42	3	1	.200	.336
Borges, Joel	R-R	6-0	196	7-13-98	.141	.067	.157	33	85	8	12	2	0	0	7	14	2	2	1	27	2	0	.165	.275
Carmona, Oliver	L-R	5-10	189	2-28-98	.281	.189	.302	68	231	29	65	9	3	3	31	43	4	3	7	39	14	9	.385	.393
Castillo, Oscateri	R-R	6-0	202	12-28-97	.255	.261	.254	50	157	23	40	6	2	2	21	23	4	1	2	45	14	7	.357	.360
De La Cruz, Julio	R-R	5-11	170	8-3-00	.249	.281	.235	57	181	31	45	7	7	2	28	34	4	1	1	61	11	8	.398	.377
De La Cruz, Miguel	B-R	5-11	170	12-4-97	.240	.279	.228	63	217	44	52	11	8	3	28	48	2	0	2	57	18	11	.406	.379
Diaz, Luis	L-R	5-11	186	1-13-00	.193	.250	.179	24	83	4	16	2	0	0	9	5	1	0	1	27	0	2	.217	.244
Gomez, Cristian	L-R	6-2	205	10-29-96	.249	.149	.276	70	261	31	65	13	2	4	35	19	9	0	1	48	12	6	.360	.321
Marcano, Marlon	R-R	5-10	180	9-14-99	.174	.133	.183	31	86	5	15	2	0	0	7	11	0	1	1	22	2	3	.198	.265
Mendoza, Willian	R-R	5-11	185	12-1-97	.206	.421	.159	37	107	10	22	2	0	1	11	8	2	1	1	25	2	5	.252	.271
Nunez, Jesus	R-R	5-11	150	12-25-99	.248	.231	.250	40	117	20	29	2	1	0	8	20	0	0	2	25	11	3	.282	.353
Oliva, Osvaldo	R-R	5-11	171	12-10-97	.259	.286	.245	58	205	30	53	6	1	0	13	15	2	2	1	35	13	3	.298	.314
Ozoria, Daniel	L-R	5-9	135	8-24-00	.247	.132	.266	60	219	31	54	6	3	0	22	23	6	2	2	42	21	10	.301	.332
Quezada, Jose	R-R	5-9	145	7-26-98	.267	.118	.304	22	86	13	23	2	2	0	7	10	1	0	1	22	10	4	.337	.347
Santana, Adderlin	B-R	5-8	154	5-31-00	.209	.000	.220	15	43	6	9	2	0	0	4	13	0	0	1	18	2	1	.256	.386

Pitching	B-T	HT	WT	DOB	W	L	ERA	G	GS	CG	SV	IP	H	R	ER	HR	BB	SO	AVG	vLH	vRH	K/9	BB/9
Agramonte, Galvi	R-R	5-11	184	5-19-98	2	2	5.14	12	0	0	1	21	25	17	12	2	12	17	.301	.300	.302	7.29	5.14
Antigua, Faustino	R-R	6-5	180	5-21-99	0	1	16.20	8	0	0	0	5	6	12	9	1	12	8	.300	.333	.286	14.40	21.60
Aquino, Stiward	R-R	6-6	170	6-20-99	0	2	4.56	7	4	0	0	24	25	14	12	1	9	29	.272	.355	.230	11.03	3.42
Arvelaez, Kiber	R-R	5-10	170	5-9-98	5	3	1.56	24	0	0	7	40	31	12	7	0	13	37	.221	.244	.212	8.26	2.90
Bonilla, Christopher	R-R	6-0	180	1-13-99	2	2	3.92	18	0	0	2	41	35	22	18	1	26	38	.240	.333	.206	8.27	5.66
De Leon, Yoel	L-L	6-2	200	11-23-97	2	1	2.58	12	11	0	0	45	35	15	13	1	17	50	.213	.111	.234	9.93	3.38
Espinal, Andersson	L-L	6-1	174	9-1-99	0	2	9.92	9	0	0	0	16	29	21	18	2	11	11	.392	.308	.410	6.06	6.06
Fortunato, Rafael	R-R	5-11	181	7-13-98	1	4	2.56	14	13	0	0	53	45	19	15	2	14	40	.233	.222	.237	6.84	2.39
Franco, Sadrac	R-R	6-0	155	6-4-00	1	3	3.45	7	1	0	0	16	15	8	6	0	3	14	.246	.125	.289	8.04	1.72
Guzman, Emilker	R-R	5-10	160	2-10-99	6	0	1.02	17	1	1	0	44	24	8	5	0	11	30	.162	.152	.167	6.14	2.25
Mendoza, Reyember	R-R	6-0	168	2-20-99	2	2	5.16	10	4	0	0	23	23	18	13	2	12	15	.281	.212	.327	5.96	4.76
Natera, Jose	R-R	6-1	180	11-30-99	2	0	2.57	7	4	0	0	28	24	12	8	0	4	33	.218	.162	.247	10.61	1.29
Nova, Luis	R-R	5-11	175	6-28-98	2	5	3.60	13	9	0	0	45	38	26	18	4	17	36	.230	.313	.197	7.20	3.40
Pena, Andres	R-R	6-1	160	10-22-99	4	1	3.20	18	3	0	0	39	33	16	14	1	15	29	.232	.147	.259	6.64	3.43
Pina, Robinson	R-R	6-4	180	11-26-98	1	2	3.68	15	11	0	0	51	35	26	21	0	24	47	.188	.259	.156	8.24	4.21
Pina, Shakiro	L-L	5-11	190	3-4-97	3	2	4.54	21	0	0	1	34	33	20	17	2	13	45	.260	.286	.253	12.03	3.48
Pineda, Roberto	R-R	6-3	190	6-2-96	2	0	2.57	8	0	0	0	14	18	9	4	0	4	12	.316	.333	.310	7.71	2.57
Santa Maria, Tulio	R-R	6-4	170	6-6-00	0	3	2.65	14	9	0	0	51	41	23	15	1	19	41	.230	.228	.231	7.24	3.35
Villar, Yogeiry	R-R	6-4	195	8-24-98	0	0	10.00	7	0	0	0	9	8	10	10	1	12	6	.250	.250	.250	6.00	12.00

Fielding

C: Bisay 19, Borges 15, Marcano 26, Mendoza 24. **1B:** Borges 17, Carmona 8, Mendoza 3, Nunez 1, Oliva 46. **2B:** Arias 3, Bisay 1, De La Cruz 39, Nunez 8, Oliva 4, Ozoria 7, Santana 9. **3B:** Arias 1, Carmona 59, De La Cruz 1, De La Cruz 6, Nunez 4, Ozoria 1. **SS:** Arias 3, De La Cruz 2, Nunez 19, Oliva 1, Ozoria 48, Quezada 2, Santana 1. **OF:** Castillo 41, De La Cruz 58, Diaz 16, Gomez 64, Mendoza 1, Nunez 2, Oliva 8, Ozoria 4, Quezada 20.

Los Angeles Dodgers

SEASON IN A SENTENCE: The Dodgers blitzed through a magical regular season in which they couldn't seem to lose, finishing with 104 wins and reaching with their first World Series in 29 years, where they fell to the Astros in seven games.

HIGH POINT: The entire summer was a dizzying array of dramatic walkoffs, dominant pitching performances and wild offensive outbursts. The peak was a 50-10 stretch that lasted nearly 12 weeks from June to August, and included winning streaks of nine, 10 and 11 games.

LOW POINT: The Dodgers came back against Justin Verlander in Game Six to force a Game Seven of the World Series, but with a championship on the line and the home crowd behind them, Yu Darvish got lit up for five runs in 1.2 innings and the offense went 1-for-13 with runners in scoring position. Overall, the Dodgers stranded 10 men on base as they meekly fell, 5-1.

NOTABLE ROOKIES: 1B Cody Bellinger assumed the cleanup spot in the Dodgers' order and set a National League rookie record with 39 home runs. OF Alex Verdugo and RHP Walker Buehler made their ML debuts in September and retain rookie eligibility for 2018. So do C Kyle Farmer, 2B Tim Locastro, OF O'Koyea Dickson and LHP Edward Paredes, all of whom made their big league debuts as well.

KEY TRANSACTIONS: The Dodgers signaled they were going for it when they made a blockbuster trade for Darvish minutes before the July 31 trade deadline, sending prospects Willie Calhoun, Brendon Davis and A.J. Alexy to the Rangers in return for the Japanese ace. Darvish pitched well for the Dodgers in the regular season and won his NLDS and NLCS starts before faltering with two poor outings in the World Series. The Dodgers also traded for lefties Tony Watson (Pirates) and Tony Cingrani (Reds) on July 31. Both became crucial bullpen pieces in their run to the World Series.

DOWN OF THE FARM: Buehler shot from high Class A all the way to the majors and established himself as one of the top pitching prospects in baseball. RHP Wilmer Font won Pacific Coast League Pitcher of the Year, 3B Matt Beatty was named MVP of the Double-A Texas League and OF D.J. Peters won California League MVP at high Class A Rancho Cucamonga. Overall Dodgers affiliates posted a .546 winning percentage, tied for third-best in the minors. Rookie-level Ogden was the only champion.

OPENING DAY PAYROLL: $242,065,828 (1st)

PLAYERS OF THE YEAR

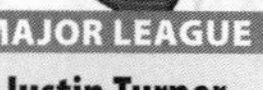

Justin Turner
3B
.322/.415/.530
32 2B, 21 HR, 71 RBI
59 BB, 56 SO

MINOR LEAGUE

Walker Buehler
RHP
(High Class A/
Double-A/Triple-A)
3.35 ERA, 12.7 SO/9

ORGANIZATION LEADERS

BATTING — *Minimum 250 AB

		MAJORS	
*	AVG	Justin Turner	.322
*	OPS	Justin Turner	.945
	HR	Cody Bellinger	39
	RBI	Cody Bellinger	97
		MINORS	
*	AVG	Romer Cuadrado, Ogden	.335
*	OBP	Max Muncy, Oklahoma City	.414
*	SLG	Willie Calhoun, Oklahoma City, Round Rock	.574
*	OPS	Romer Cuadrado, Ogden	.936
	R	Luke Raley, Rancho Cucamonga	102
	H	Edwin Rios, Tulsa, Oklahoma City	147
	TB	DJ Peters, Rancho Cucamonga	259
	2B	Edwin Rios, Tulsa, Oklahoma City	34
	3B	Luke Raley, Rancho Cucamonga	11
	HR	Ibandel Isabel, Rancho Cucamonga	28
	RBI	Edwin Rios, Tulsa, Oklahoma City	91
	BB	DJ Peters, Rancho Cucamonga	64
	SO	DJ Peters, Rancho Cucamonga	189
	SB	Tim Locastro, Tulsa, Oklahoma City	34

PITCHING — #Minimum 75 IP

		MAJORS	
	W	Clayton Kershaw	18
#	ERA	Clayton Kershaw	2.31
	SO	Clayton Kershaw	202
	SV	Kenley Jansen	41
		MINORS	
	W	Justin Masterson, Oklahoma City	11
	L	Leo Crawford, Great Lakes	10
#	ERA	Caleb Ferguson, Rancho Cucamonga	2.87
	G	Corey Copping, Tulsa	49
	GS	Scott Barlow, Oklahoma City, Tulsa	26
	SV	Corey Copping, Tulsa	18
	IP	Devin Smeltzer, Great Lakes, Rancho Cucamonga	142
	BB	Justin Masterson, Oklahoma City	66
	SO	Wilmer Font, Oklahoma City	178
#	AVG	Scott Barlow, Oklahoma City, Tulsa	.192

2017 PERFORMANCE

President, Baseball Ops: Andrew Friedman. **Farm Director:** Gabe Kapler. **Scouting Director:** Billy Gasparino.

Class	Team	League	W	L	PCT	Finish	Manager
Majors	Los Angeles Dodgers	National	104	58	.642	1st (15)	Dave Roberts
Triple-A	Oklahoma City Dodgers	Pacific Coast	72	69	.511	6th (16)	Bill Haselman
Double-A	Tulsa Drillers	Texas	77	63	.550	t-2nd (8)	R. Garko/S. Hennessey
High-A	Rancho Cucamonga Quakes	California	76	64	.543	2nd (8)	Drew Saylor
Low-A	Great Lakes Loons	Midwest	69	70	.496	t-8th (16)	Jeremy Rodriguez
Rookie	Ogden Raptors	Pioneer	47	29	.618	2nd (8)	Mark Kertenian
Rookie	AZL Dodgers	Arizona	37	19	.661	1st (15)	John Shoemaker
Overall 2017 Minor League Record			378	314	0.546	t-3rd (30)	

ORGANIZATION STATISTICS

LOS ANGELES DODGERS

NATIONAL LEAGUE

Batting	B-T	HT	WT	DOB	AVG	vLH	vRH	G	AB	R	H	2B	3B	HR	RBI	BB	HBP	SH	SF	SO	SB	CS	SLG	OBP
Barnes, Austin	R-R	5-10	190	12-28-89	.289	.257	.321	102	218	35	63	15	2	8	38	39	5	0	0	43	4	1	.486	.408
Bellinger, Cody	L-L	6-4	210	7-13-95	.267	.271	.265	132	480	87	128	26	4	39	97	64	1	0	3	146	10	3	.581	.352
Culberson, Charlie	R-R	6-0	200	4-10-89	.154	.143	.167	15	13	0	2	1	0	0	1	2	0	0	0	4	0	0	.231	.267
Dickson, O'Koyea	R-R	5-11	220	2-9-90	.143	.200	.000	7	7	0	1	0	0	0	0	2	0	0	0	2	0	0	.143	.333
Eibner, Brett	R-R	6-4	215	12-2-88	.182	.188	.177	17	33	3	6	0	0	2	6	2	1	0	0	17	0	0	.364	.250
Ethier, Andre	L-L	6-2	210	4-10-82	.235	.000	.258	22	34	3	8	1	0	2	3	4	0	0	0	10	0	0	.441	.316
Farmer, Kyle	R-R	6-0	214	8-17-90	.300	.250	.333	20	20	1	6	1	0	0	2	0	0	0	0	3	0	0	.350	.300
Forsythe, Logan	R-R	6-1	205	1-14-87	.224	.290	.190	119	361	56	81	19	0	6	36	69	4	0	5	109	3	2	.327	.351
Freeman, Mike	L-R	6-0	190	8-4-87	.000	.000	.000	4	5	0	0	0	0	0	0	0	0	0	0	2	0	0	.000	.000
2-team total (15 Chicago)					.133	.000	.211	19	30	3	4	2	0	0	0	2	0	0	0	10	0	0	.200	.188
Gonzalez, Adrian	L-L	6-2	215	5-8-82	.242	.192	.255	71	231	14	56	17	0	3	30	16	0	0	4	43	0	1	.355	.287
Grandal, Yasmani	B-R	6-1	235	11-8-88	.247	.233	.250	129	438	50	108	27	0	22	58	40	0	1	3	130	0	1	.459	.308
Granderson, Curtis	R-L	6-1	200	3-16-81	.161	.067	.175	36	112	16	18	2	0	7	12	18	2	0	0	33	2	0	.366	.288
2-team total (111 New York)					.212	.067	.175	147	449	74	95	24	3	26	64	71	4	0	3	123	6	2	.452	.323
Gutierrez, Franklin	R-R	6-2	200	2-21-83	.232	.195	.333	35	56	8	13	3	0	1	8	7	0	0	0	16	0	1	.339	.318
Hernandez, Enrique	R-R	5-11	200	8-24-91	.216	.270	.159	140	297	46	64	24	2	11	37	41	0	1	3	80	3	0	.421	.308
Locastro, Tim	R-R	6-1	200	7-14-92	.000	—	.000	3	1	0	0	0	0	0	0	0	0	0	0	0	1	0	.000	.000
Pederson, Joc	L-L	6-1	220	4-21-92	.213	.204	.214	102	273	44	58	20	0	11	35	39	10	0	1	68	4	3	.407	.331
Puig, Yasiel	R-R	6-2	240	12-7-90	.263	.183	.288	152	499	72	131	24	2	28	74	64	2	0	5	100	15	6	.487	.346
Seager, Corey	L-R	6-4	220	4-27-94	.295	.325	.281	145	539	85	159	33	0	22	77	67	4	0	3	131	4	2	.479	.375
Segedin, Rob	R-R	6-2	220	11-10-88	.200	.200	.200	13	20	3	4	2	0	0	1	0	0	0	0	7	0	0	.300	.200
Taylor, Chris	R-R	6-1	195	8-29-90	.288	.297	.285	140	514	85	148	34	5	21	72	50	3	0	1	142	17	4	.496	.354
Thompson, Trayce	R-R	6-3	217	3-15-91	.122	.080	.167	27	49	6	6	2	1	1	2	6	0	0	0	23	0	0	.265	.218
Toles, Andrew	L-R	5-9	192	5-24-92	.271	.400	.264	31	96	17	26	3	0	5	15	5	1	0	0	16	0	1	.458	.314
Turner, Justin	R-R	5-11	205	11-23-84	.322	.380	.295	130	457	72	147	32	0	21	71	59	19	1	7	56	7	1	.530	.415
Utley, Chase	R-L	6-1	195	12-17-78	.236	.167	.242	127	309	43	73	20	4	8	34	32	9	1	2	57	6	1	.405	.324
Van Slyke, Scott	R-R	6-4	215	7-24-86	.122	.138	.083	29	41	6	5	1	0	2	3	7	0	0	0	15	1	0	.293	.250
Verdugo, Alex	L-L	6-0	205	5-15-96	.174	.200	.167	15	23	1	4	0	0	1	1	2	0	0	0	4	0	1	.304	.240

Pitching	B-T	HT	WT	DOB	W	L	ERA	G	GS	CG	SV	IP	H	R	ER	HR	BB	SO	AVG	vLH	vRH	K/9	BB/9
Avilan, Luis	L-L	6-2	225	7-19-89	2	3	2.93	61	0	0	0	46	42	16	15	2	22	52	.246	.195	.292	10.17	4.30
Baez, Pedro	R-R	6-0	230	3-11-88	3	6	2.95	66	0	0	0	64	56	24	21	9	29	64	.225	.206	.238	9.00	4.08
Buehler, Walker	R-R	6-2	175	7-28-94	1	0	7.71	8	0	0	0	9	11	8	8	2	8	12	.306	.188	.400	11.57	7.71
Castillo, Fabio	R-R	6-1	235	2-19-89	0	0	13.50	2	0	0	0	1	3	2	2	0	1	2	.429	1.000	.333	13.50	6.75
Cingrani, Tony	L-L	6-4	214	7-5-89	0	0	2.79	22	0	0	0	19	15	8	6	1	6	28	.214	.188	.237	13.03	2.79
2-team total (25 Cincinnati)					0	0	4.22	47	0	0	0	43	40	22	20	10	12	52	.247	.293	.255	10.97	2.53
Darvish, Yu	R-R	6-5	220	8-16-86	4	3	3.44	9	9	0	0	50	44	20	19	7	13	61	.235	.293	.161	11.05	2.36
Dayton, Grant	L-L	6-2	215	11-25-87	1	1	4.94	29	0	0	0	24	19	13	13	5	12	20	.221	.171	.267	7.61	4.56
Fields, Josh	R-R	6-0	195	8-19-85	5	0	2.84	57	0	0	2	57	40	19	18	10	15	60	.194	.232	.169	9.47	2.37
Font, Wilmer	R-R	6-4	265	5-24-90	0	0	17.18	3	0	0	0	4	7	7	7	2	4	3	.389	.286	.455	7.36	9.82
Hatcher, Chris	R-R	6-1	200	1-12-85	0	1	4.66	26	0	0	0	37	37	20	19	7	12	43	.259	.224	.282	10.55	2.95
Hill, Rich	L-L	6-5	220	3-11-80	12	8	3.32	25	25	1	0	136	99	51	50	18	49	166	.203	.255	.190	11.01	3.25
Jansen, Kenley	B-R	6-5	275	9-30-87	5	0	1.32	65	0	0	41	68	44	11	10	5	7	109	.177	.236	.120	14.36	0.92
Kershaw, Clayton	L-L	6-4	228	3-19-88	18	4	2.31	27	27	1	0	175	136	49	45	23	30	202	.212	.248	.203	10.39	1.54
Liberatore, Adam	L-L	6-3	243	5-12-87	0	0	2.70	4	0	0	0	3	3	1	1	0	2	5	.231	.400	.125	13.50	5.40
Maeda, Kenta	R-R	6-1	175	4-11-88	13	6	4.22	29	25	0	1	134	121	68	63	22	34	140	.238	.263	.214	9.38	2.28
McCarthy, Brandon	R-R	6-7	235	7-7-83	6	4	3.98	19	16	0	0	93	89	43	41	5	27	72	.257	.254	.259	6.99	2.62
Morrow, Brandon	R-R	6-3	205	7-26-84	6	0	2.06	45	0	0	2	44	31	10	10	0	9	50	.194	.125	.231	10.31	1.85
Paredes, Edward	L-L	6-0	180	9-30-86	1	0	3.24	10	0	0	0	8	8	3	3	1	0	11	.258	.273	.222	11.88	0.00
Ravin, Josh	R-R	6-4	215	1-21-88	0	1	6.48	14	0	0	1	17	12	12	12	4	9	19	.197	.167	.216	10.26	4.86
Romo, Sergio	R-R	5-11	185	3-4-83	1	1	6.12	30	0	0	0	25	23	17	17	7	12	31	.240	.316	.221	11.16	4.32
Ryu, Hyun-Jin	R-L	6-3	250	3-25-87	5	9	3.77	25	24	0	1	127	128	58	53	22	45	116	.263	.326	.240	8.24	3.20
Stewart, Brock	L-R	6-3	210	10-3-91	0	0	3.41	17	4	0	1	34	28	18	13	4	19	29	.226	.236	.217	7.60	4.98

Name	B-T	HT	WT	DOB	W	L	ERA	G	GS	CG	SV	IP	H	R	ER	HR	BB	SO	AVG	vLH	vRH	K/9	BB/9
Stripling, Ross	R-R	6-3	210	11-23-89	3	5	3.75	49	2	0	2	74	69	31	31	10	19	74	.246	.198	.283	8.96	2.30
Urias, Julio	L-L	6-0	215	8-12-96	0	2	5.40	5	5	0	0	23	23	15	14	1	14	11	.271	.500	.200	4.24	5.40
Watson, Tony	L-L	6-4	220	5-30-85	2	1	2.70	24	0	0	0	20	15	6	6	2	6	18	.208	.212	.205	8.10	2.70
2-team total (47 Pittsburgh)					7	4	3.38	71	0	0	10	67	72	26	25	9	20	53	.278	.212	.205	7.16	2.70
Wood, Alex	R-L	6-4	215	1-12-91	16	3	2.72	27	25	0	0	152	123	50	46	15	38	151	.217	.229	.213	8.92	2.25

Fielding

Catcher	PCT	G	PO	A	E	DP	PB
Barnes	.994	55	497	16	3	4	3
Farmer	1.000	3	5	0	0	0	0
Grandal	.995	117	1089	54	6	4	16

First Base	PCT	G	PO	A	E	DP
Bellinger	.994	93	656	36	4	62
Farmer	1.000	1	10	1	0	1
Forsythe	1.000	1	7	1	0	0
Gonzalez	.996	60	414	31	2	41
Hernandez	1.000	3	16	0	0	1
Segedin	1.000	6	26	0	0	3
Utley	.989	17	83	4	1	7
Van Slyke	.971	9	29	5	1	7

Second Base	PCT	G	PO	A	E	DP
Barnes	.967	21	12	17	1	4
Culberson	1.000	2	2	3	0	0
Forsythe	.989	80	106	157	3	35
Hernandez	.941	9	7	9	1	2
Taylor	.944	22	33	52	5	16
Utley	.978	80	94	131	5	33

Third Base	PCT	G	PO	A	E	DP
Barnes	.000	1	0	0	0	0
Culberson	.000	1	0	0	0	0
Farmer	.000	4	0	0	0	0
Forsythe	.963	42	17	60	3	3
Freeman	.000	1	0	0	0	0
Hernandez	.955	14	6	15	1	1
Segedin	1.000	5	1	1	0	0
Taylor	.909	8	5	5	1	0
Turner	.969	121	69	184	8	16

Shortstop	PCT	G	PO	A	E	DP
Culberson	.957	11	6	16	1	5
Forsythe	1.000	2	0	1	0	0
Hernandez	.959	24	21	50	3	5
Seager	.979	138	185	324	11	77
Taylor	.941	14	11	37	3	8

Outfield	PCT	G	PO	A	E	DP
Bellinger	.986	46	69	2	1	0
Dickson	1.000	5	3	0	0	0
Eibner	1.000	11	11	0	0	0
Ethier	.875	8	7	0	1	0
Forsythe	1.000	3	1	0	0	0
Granderson	1.000	33	43	0	0	0
Gutierrez	1.000	17	13	0	0	0
Hernandez	.988	73	79	5	1	4
Locastro	1.000	2	1	0	0	0
Pederson	.993	96	135	1	1	0
Puig	.996	145	259	4	1	0
Segedin	.000	1	0	0	0	0
Taylor	.989	96	176	7	2	0
Thompson	.913	19	21	0	2	0
Toles	.977	28	42	0	1	0
Van Slyke	1.000	12	6	0	0	0
Verdugo	1.000	10	4	0	0	0

OKLAHOMA CITY DODGERS

TRIPLE-A

PACIFIC COAST LEAGUE

Batting	B-T	HT	WT	DOB	AVG	vLH	vRH	G	AB	R	H	2B	3B	HR	RBI	BB	HBP	SH	SF	SO	SB	CS	SLG	OBP
Ahmed, Michael	R-R	6-2	195	1-20-92	.194	.143	.208	11	31	2	6	0	0	0	1	8	0	1	0	7	0	0	.194	.359
Bellinger, Cody	L-L	6-4	210	7-13-95	.343	.222	.362	18	67	15	23	4	0	5	15	9	1	0	0	22	7	0	.627	.429
Calhoun, Willie	L-R	5-8	187	11-4-94	.298	.292	.299	99	373	64	111	24	5	23	67	36	1	0	4	49	3	2	.574	.358
2-team total (29 Round Rock)					.300	.292	.299	128	486	80	146	27	6	31	93	42	1	1	4	61	4	2	.572	.355
Culberson, Charlie	R-R	6-0	200	4-10-89	.250	.311	.228	108	384	37	96	13	4	4	32	26	1	2	1	68	7	3	.336	.299
Cunningham, Todd	B-R	6-0	205	3-20-89	.339	.357	.333	20	62	12	21	6	1	0	4	6	3	0	1	13	1	1	.468	.417
2-team total (76 Memphis)					.284	.357	.333	96	292	57	83	20	3	4	31	43	18	2	3	50	7	3	.414	.405
Dickson, O'Koyea	R-R	5-11	220	2-9-90	.246	.211	.257	116	403	70	99	22	1	24	76	44	7	0	4	97	4	1	.484	.328
Eibner, Brett	R-R	6-4	215	12-2-88	.231	.280	.217	37	117	18	27	4	1	4	14	9	1	0	1	34	0	1	.385	.289
Ethier, Andre	L-L	6-2	210	4-10-82	.286	.000	.667	2	7	0	2	1	0	0	0	1	0	0	0	1	0	0	.429	.375
Farmer, Kyle	R-R	6-0	214	8-17-90	.305	.322	.299	59	223	32	68	16	1	7	38	13	4	0	0	36	0	4	.480	.354
Fernandez, Jose Miguel	L-R	5-10	185	4-27-88	.300	—	.300	3	10	1	3	1	0	0	1	1	1	0	0	1	0	0	.400	.417
Freeman, Mike	L-R	6-0	190	8-4-87	.306	.370	.287	41	121	17	37	4	2	0	16	13	3	1	1	31	5	0	.372	.384
3-team total (23 Iowa, 16 Tacoma)					.306	.250	.279	80	258	39	79	10	3	3	31	27	5	2	2	60	10	0	.403	.380
Gonzalez, Adrian	L-L	6-2	215	5-8-82	.308	.333	.300	5	13	1	4	0	0	1	6	0	0	0	4	3	0	0	.539	.235
Holt, Tyler	R-R	5-10	200	3-10-89	.130	.000	.177	8	23	2	3	0	0	0	0	1	0	1	0	3	4	0	.130	.167
Landon, Logan	R-R	6-2	180	2-17-93	.200	1.000	.000	2	5	1	1	0	0	0	0	3	0	0	0	0	0	0	.200	.500
Locastro, Tim	R-R	6-1	200	7-14-92	.388	.462	.364	31	103	18	40	10	0	2	9	6	5	0	1	12	12	2	.544	.444
Maggi, Drew	R-R	6-0	192	5-16-89	.271	.273	.270	84	255	40	69	16	0	5	29	35	5	1	2	63	7	3	.392	.367
Mejia, Erick	B-R	5-11	155	11-9-94	—	—	—	1	0	0	0	0	0	0	0	0	0	0	0	0	0	0	—	—
Muncy, Max	L-R	6-0	210	8-25-90	.309	.258	.323	109	320	62	99	20	1	12	44	54	4	0	1	84	3	6	.491	.414
Murphy, Jack	B-R	6-4	235	4-6-88	.137	.103	.146	48	139	6	19	7	0	0	13	17	1	1	2	38	0	1	.187	.233
Pederson, Joc	L-L	6-1	220	4-21-92	.169	.286	.137	17	65	8	11	1	0	3	9	5	0	0	1	14	1	0	.323	.225
Ramos, Henry	B-R	6-2	220	4-15-92	.295	.174	.329	30	105	16	31	8	0	3	8	6	0	0	0	13	2	2	.457	.333
Rios, Edwin	L-R	6-3	220	4-21-94	.296	.167	.339	51	169	23	50	13	0	9	29	18	2	0	1	42	0	1	.533	.368
Scavuzzo, Jacob	R-R	6-4	185	1-15-94	.250	.000	.333	1	4	1	1	0	0	0	0	0	0	0	0	2	0	0	.250	.250
Segedin, Rob	R-R	6-2	220	11-10-88	.320	.231	.333	25	97	13	31	7	0	4	15	4	0	0	0	16	0	1	.516	.347
Sweeney, Darnell	B-R	6-1	195	2-1-91	.227	.200	.234	38	119	17	27	8	1	4	15	11	0	0	1	33	7	1	.412	.290
Taylor, Chris	R-R	6-1	195	8-29-90	.233	.429	.194	10	43	8	10	2	2	1	5	5	1	0	0	5	1	2	.442	.327
Thompson, Trayce	R-R	6-3	217	3-15-91	.212	.181	.223	95	339	44	72	12	6	9	33	26	1	1	2	93	3	5	.363	.269
Van Slyke, Scott	R-R	6-4	215	7-24-86	.242	.286	.226	55	182	30	44	12	0	5	20	19	6	0	1	54	1	1	.390	.332
Verdugo, Alex	L-L	6-0	205	5-15-96	.314	.277	.325	117	433	67	136	27	4	6	62	52	4	1	5	50	9	3	.437	.389
Whiting, Brant	L-R	5-9	190	2-6-92	.429	.000	.500	5	7	1	3	1	0	0	0	2	0	0	0	3	0	0	.571	.556
Wilson, Bobby	R-R	6-0	230	4-8-83	.243	.235	.245	75	243	34	59	12	0	11	45	25	3	1	3	55	0	0	.428	.318

Pitching	B-T	HT	WT	DOB	W	L	ERA	G	GS	CG	SV	IP	H	R	ER	HR	BB	SO	AVG	vLH	vRH	K/9	BB/9
Allie, Stetson	R-R	6-2	230	3-13-91	0	0	0.00	1	0	0	0	1	1	0	0	0	1	0	.333	.500	.000	0.00	9.00
Avilan, Luis	L-L	6-2	225	7-19-89	0	0	9.00	2	0	0	0	2	1	2	2	0	1	3	.143	.000	.167	13.50	4.50
Baez, Pedro	R-R	6-0	230	3-11-88	0	0	6.00	3	0	0	0	3	1	2	2	0	1	3	.100	.000	.167	9.00	3.00
Barlow, Scott	R-R	6-3	215	12-18-92	1	3	7.24	7	7	0	0	32	37	36	26	6	23	36	.276	.319	.253	10.02	6.40
Bleich, Jeremy	L-L	6-2	215	6-18-87	5	3	3.22	31	0	0	3	50	45	19	18	4	9	43	.238	.310	.206	7.69	1.61
Bray, Adam	R-R	6-3	210	4-14-93	0	0	0.00	1	0	0	1	3	1	0	0	0	0	2	.100	.000	.200	5.40	0.00
Broussard, Joe	R-R	6-1	220	1-28-91	4	1	3.57	44	0	0	3	58	57	23	23	7	20	67	.253	.220	.273	10.40	3.10

Buehler, Walker	R-R	6-2	175	7-28-94	1	1	4.63	12	3	0	1	23	19	12	12	1	11	34	.216	.227	.205	13.11	4.24
Castillo, Fabio	R-R	6-1	235	2-19-89	4	8	4.27	22	16	0	1	84	77	40	40	9	31	85	.245	.252	.241	9.07	3.31
Curry, Parker	R-R	6-0	185	11-21-93	0	0	9.00	1	0	0	0	2	3	2	2	0	2	3	.375	1.000	.286	13.50	9.00
Dayton, Grant	L-L	6-2	215	11-25-87	0	1	7.71	5	0	0	1	5	9	4	4	1	1	7	.391	.286	.438	13.50	1.93
Farrell, Luke	L-R	6-6	210	6-7-91	0	0	3.86	1	1	0	0	5	4	3	2	0	2	5	.211	.000	.235	9.64	3.86
2-team total (17 Omaha)					7	4	4.06	18	17	0	0	102	93	51	46	13	35	99	.244	.231	.255	8.74	3.09
Fields, Josh	R-R	6-0	195	8-19-85	0	0	0.00	3	0	0	0	3	1	0	0	0	0	3	.100	.333	.000	9.00	0.00
Floro, Dylan	R-L	6-2	175	12-27-90	0	1	5.56	8	0	0	1	11	18	8	7	0	3	12	.367	.348	.385	9.53	2.38
2-team total (25 Iowa)					3	3	4.20	33	2	0	2	60	72	36	28	9	11	38	.294	.241	.301	5.70	1.65
Font, Wilmer	R-R	6-4	265	5-24-90	10	8	3.42	25	25	0	0	134	114	52	51	11	35	178	.222	.221	.223	11.93	2.34
Gamboa, Eddie	R-R	6-1	215	12-21-84	3	1	5.40	6	6	0	0	32	36	21	19	7	13	19	.286	.271	.299	5.40	3.69
2-team total (14 Round Rock)					8	7	6.17	20	20	0	0	109	130	81	75	20	52	65	.300	.271	.299	5.35	4.28
Geltz, Steve	R-R	5-10	210	11-1-87	2	2	2.67	23	0	0	3	27	22	11	8	2	12	29	.218	.268	.183	9.67	4.00
Gunkel, Joe	R-R	6-5	225	12-30-91	0	0	4.00	3	1	0	1	9	12	5	4	1	0	6	.333	.286	.364	6.00	0.00
Hale, David	R-R	6-2	210	9-27-87	2	4	4.27	9	9	0	0	53	64	30	25	4	7	39	.302	.326	.283	6.66	1.20
Hatcher, Chris	R-R	6-1	200	1-12-85	0	0	0.00	3	0	0	0	4	2	0	0	0	1	6	.143	.286	.000	13.50	2.25
Heston, Chris	R-R	6-3	195	4-10-88	0	1	9.00	1	0	0	0	3	4	3	3	2	1	4	.308	.500	.273	12.00	3.00
2-team total (6 Tacoma)					2	2	3.89	7	6	1	0	35	30	15	15	4	12	32	.236	.500	.273	8.31	3.12
Hynes, Colt	L-L	5-11	200	6-28-85	0	0	5.68	3	0	0	0	6	13	5	4	1	2	1	.433	.444	.429	1.42	2.84
Jankowski, Jordan	R-R	6-1	225	5-17-89	0	0	12.00	4	0	0	1	3	2	4	4	0	5	2	.182	.500	.000	6.00	15.00
2-team total (37 Fresno)					2	3	5.61	41	0	0	11	43	41	28	27	4	28	55	.246	.344	.189	11.42	5.82
Jurrjens, Jair	R-R	6-1	200	1-29-86	4	3	4.64	11	10	0	0	54	63	30	28	6	18	44	.290	.351	.226	7.29	2.98
Kershaw, Clayton	L-L	6-4	228	3-19-88	0	1	1.80	1	1	0	0	5	2	1	1	1	0	8	.125	—	.125	14.40	0.00
Layne, Tommy	L-L	6-2	195	11-2-84	0	0	3.18	3	0	0	0	6	3	2	2	1	6	3	.158	.500	.067	4.76	9.53
Liberatore, Adam	L-L	6-3	243	5-12-87	0	1	2.31	10	0	0	0	12	9	3	3	0	1	10	.214	.167	.233	7.71	0.77
Marks, Justin	L-L	6-3	205	1-12-88	4	3	5.25	31	6	0	3	60	66	38	35	4	27	56	.277	.284	.275	8.40	4.05
Masterson, Justin	R-R	6-6	260	3-22-85	11	6	4.13	26	25	0	0	142	129	72	65	7	66	140	.244	.268	.225	8.89	4.19
Morrow, Brandon	R-R	6-3	205	7-26-84	0	5	7.20	20	0	0	6	20	25	18	16	5	5	22	.294	.200	.360	9.90	2.25
Oaks, Trevor	R-R	6-3	220	3-26-93	4	3	3.64	16	15	0	0	84	87	35	34	5	18	72	.277	.346	.225	7.71	1.93
Paredes, Edward	L-L	6-0	180	9-30-86	2	1	0.75	11	0	0	0	12	4	2	1	0	6	21	.100	.000	.154	15.75	4.50
Ravin, Josh	R-R	6-4	215	1-21-88	4	0	4.33	30	0	0	2	35	29	20	17	2	19	55	.220	.275	.185	14.01	4.84
Rhame, Jacob	R-R	6-1	215	3-16-93	0	2	4.31	41	0	0	2	48	52	24	23	6	10	55	.274	.243	.292	10.31	1.88
2-team total (4 Las Vegas)					0	3	4.00	45	0	0	2	54	54	25	24	6	10	66	.257	.243	.292	11.00	1.67
Schuster, Patrick	R-L	6-2	190	10-30-90	1	0	6.16	17	0	0	0	19	25	13	13	3	7	14	.325	.400	.289	6.63	3.32
2-team total (27 Nashville)					4	2	6.02	44	0	0	1	52	68	36	35	7	19	54	.313	.400	.288	9.29	3.27
Shibuya, Tim	R-R	6-1	190	9-14-89	0	1	43.88	1	1	0	0	3	14	13	13	2	0	4	.636	.800	.500	13.50	0.00
Sierra, Yaisel	R-R	6-1	170	6-5-91	0	1	4.22	13	0	0	0	21	22	10	10	2	15	20	.268	.323	.235	8.44	6.33
Somsen, Layne	R-R	6-0	190	6-5-89	2	0	2.35	20	0	0	0	31	26	14	8	3	13	32	.232	.163	.275	9.39	3.82
Stewart, Brock	L-R	6-3	210	10-3-91	0	1	3.12	5	5	0	0	17	19	6	6	2	3	25	.279	.269	.286	12.98	1.56
Stripling, Ross	R-R	6-3	210	11-23-89	1	1	0.00	3	0	0	0	3	3	1	0	0	1	4	.214	.200	.222	10.80	2.70
Urias, Julio	L-L	6-0	215	8-12-96	3	0	2.59	6	6	0	0	31	20	9	9	1	15	32	.185	.238	.172	9.19	4.31
Wheeler, Jason	L-L	6-6	255	10-27-90	0	1	10.38	3	1	0	0	9	16	11	10	1	2	3	.400	.385	.407	3.12	2.08
Younginer, Madison	R-R	6-4	205	11-3-90	4	5	4.76	40	3	0	8	62	69	34	33	8	26	70	.286	.317	.264	10.11	3.75

Fielding

Catcher	PCT	G	PO	A	E	DP	PB
Farmer	.996	32	239	17	1	1	4
Murphy	1.000	43	406	17	0	3	3
Whiting	1.000	2	13	1	0	0	0
Wilson	.999	72	628	44	1	6	4

First Base	PCT	G	PO	A	E	DP
Ahmed	1.000	2	13	0	0	1
Bellinger	1.000	16	101	10	0	10
Davis	1.000	20	121	9	0	12
Dickson	1.000	7	32	2	0	5
Eibner	1.000	5	31	1	0	5
Farmer	1.000	6	31	5	0	2
Freeman	1.000	1	2	0	0	1
Gonzalez	1.000	5	31	0	0	1
Muncy	.988	22	159	10	2	16
Murphy	1.000	1	3	0	0	1
Rios	.983	33	205	20	4	21
Segedin	1.000	8	59	5	0	2
Van Slyke	.991	38	305	19	3	25
Wilson	1.000	1	10	1	0	2

Second Base	PCT	G	PO	A	E	DP
Calhoun	.980	74	120	174	6	39
Cunningham	1.000	2	0	1	0	0
Farmer	1.000	5	3	6	0	2
Fernandez	.909	2	3	7	1	3
Freeman	1.000	4	5	4	0	2
Locastro	1.000	22	28	34	0	9
Maggi	.963	28	32	71	4	19
Muncy	1.000	9	18	16	0	2
Sweeney	.941	10	10	22	2	4
Taylor	1.000	2	1	0	0	0

Third Base	PCT	G	PO	A	E	DP
Ahmed	.947	10	6	12	1	1
Culberson	1.000	7	6	10	0	3
Farmer	.964	18	4	23	1	1
Freeman	.960	14	3	21	1	4
Maggi	.930	36	16	37	4	1
Mejia	.000	1	0	0	0	0
Muncy	.920	53	22	81	9	3
Rios	.688	9	4	7	5	1
Segedin	.926	9	10	15	2	1
Sweeney	.952	9	4	16	1	0
Taylor	1.000	1	1	1	0	0

Shortstop	PCT	G	PO	A	E	DP
Culberson	.980	97	137	261	8	58
Farmer	1.000	2	4	9	0	2
Freeman	.966	14	16	41	2	5
Maggi	.957	18	20	47	3	9
Sweeney	.932	10	18	23	3	8
Taylor	1.000	5	5	16	0	4

Outfield	PCT	G	PO	A	E	DP
Bellinger	1.000	3	5	0	0	0
Calhoun	1.000	12	10	0	0	0
Culberson	1.000	2	2	0	0	0
Cunningham	.971	17	33	1	1	0
Dickson	.985	82	125	7	2	1
Eibner	1.000	26	33	1	0	0
Ethier	1.000	2	4	0	0	0
Fernandez	1.000	1	1	0	0	0
Freeman	1.000	8	12	0	0	0
Holt	1.000	7	9	0	0	0
Landon	1.000	2	3	0	0	0
Locastro	1.000	9	10	0	0	0
Muncy	1.000	17	14	0	0	0
Pederson	1.000	14	21	2	0	1
Ramos	.983	25	54	4	1	0
Rios	1.000	9	19	0	0	0
Segedin	.778	4	6	1	2	0
Sweeney	1.000	9	14	0	0	0
Taylor	1.000	3	10	0	0	0
Thompson	.994	85	156	3	1	0
Van Slyke	1.000	8	11	0	0	0
Verdugo	1.000	111	198	9	0	1

TULSA DRILLERS

DOUBLE-A

TEXAS LEAGUE

LOS ANGELES DODGERS

Batting	B-T	HT	WT	DOB	AVG	vLH	vRH	G	AB	R	H	2B	3B	HR	RBI	BB	HBP	SH	SF	SO	SB	CS	SLG	OBP
Ahmed, Michael	R-R	6-2	195	1-20-92	.293	.294	.292	30	106	13	31	5	0	6	19	13	0	0	1	35	4	2	.509	.367
Beaty, Matt	L-R	6-0	210	4-28-93	.327	.250	.352	116	438	61	143	31	1	15	69	35	4	0	4	54	3	3	.505	.378
Diaz, Yusniel	R-R	6-1	195	10-7-96	.333	.345	.329	31	108	15	36	8	0	3	13	10	0	0	0	29	2	5	.491	.390
Ethier, Andre	L-L	6-2	210	4-10-82	.177	.000	.231	5	17	2	3	1	0	0	5	2	0	0	0	3	0	0	.235	.263
Farmer, Kyle	R-R	6-0	214	8-17-90	.339	.421	.324	33	124	21	42	7	0	3	18	16	0	0	1	13	1	0	.468	.411
Fernandez, Jose Miguel	L-R	5-10	185	4-27-88	.306	.267	.318	90	333	47	102	16	0	16	64	24	9	0	3	33	0	2	.499	.366
Gailen, Blake	L-L	5-9	180	3-27-85	.300	.452	.261	49	150	23	45	9	0	7	35	17	0	0	0	27	3	1	.500	.371
Garlick, Kyle	R-R	6-1	210	1-26-92	.239	.237	.239	74	268	45	64	9	0	17	42	30	4	0	3	78	1	0	.463	.321
Hoenecke, Paul	L-R	6-2	205	7-8-90	.220	.296	.206	48	173	13	38	11	0	7	16	7	2	0	2	44	1	0	.405	.255
Holt, Tyler	R-R	5-10	200	3-10-89	.171	.222	.156	12	41	4	7	0	0	0	0	6	0	0	0	14	2	1	.171	.277
Hope, Garrett	R-R	6-3	245	12-27-93	.000	.000	.000	2	8	0	0	0	0	0	0	0	0	0	0	1	0	0	.000	.000
Jackson, Drew	R-R	6-2	200	7-28-93	.234	.174	.250	29	111	22	26	5	1	1	10	11	8	0	0	28	7	2	.324	.346
Kennedy, Garrett	L-R	6-1	205	12-13-92	.195	.172	.202	37	123	12	24	5	1	4	16	14	1	1	2	29	0	0	.350	.279
Landon, Logan	R-R	6-2	180	2-17-93	.286	1.000	.211	6	21	3	6	0	0	1	1	0	0	0	0	2	1	0	.429	.286
Latimore, Quincy	R-R	5-11	175	2-3-89	.265	.200	.311	42	155	18	41	7	1	2	18	5	2	2	2	34	3	2	.361	.293
Locastro, Tim	R-R	6-1	200	7-14-92	.285	.350	.267	96	368	69	105	21	4	8	31	22	26	1	2	56	22	5	.429	.366
McKinstry, Zach	L-R	6-0	180	4-29-95	.256	.067	.375	15	39	5	10	1	1	0	2	6	0	0	0	8	0	0	.333	.356
Mejia, Erick	B-R	5-11	155	11-9-94	.289	.284	.291	102	356	61	103	17	3	7	30	37	2	5	3	78	25	4	.413	.357
Mieses, Johan	R-R	6-2	185	7-13-95	.160	.134	.167	90	294	34	47	7	0	16	36	27	7	0	1	116	0	0	.347	.246
Morales, Brayan	R-L	6-1	170	12-8-95	.177	.400	.083	11	17	1	3	0	1	0	0	1	0	1	0	5	0	1	.294	.222
Murphy, Jack	B-R	6-4	235	4-6-88	.167	.300	.071	9	24	0	4	0	0	0	0	3	0	0	0	6	0	0	.167	.259
O'Brien, Peter	R-R	6-4	235	7-15-90	.219	.264	.196	45	155	23	34	11	0	9	26	16	1	0	0	78	0	0	.465	.297
2-team total (3 Frisco)					.208	.264	.196	48	168	24	35	12	0	9	27	18	1	0	0	84	0	0	.441	.289
O'Connell, Sean	L-R	6-4	230	12-12-91	.261	.091	.417	11	23	3	6	0	0	1	2	2	0	0	0	7	0	0	.391	.320
Ortiz, Samuel	B-R	5-10	191	8-4-96	.200	.000	.333	3	10	0	2	0	0	0	1	0	0	0	0	3	0	0	.200	.200
Ramos, Henry	B-R	6-2	220	4-15-92	.416	.480	.391	25	89	18	37	4	1	5	17	10	0	0	2	15	1	0	.652	.465
Rios, Edwin	L-R	6-3	220	4-21-94	.317	.318	.317	77	306	47	97	21	0	15	62	17	5	0	4	69	1	1	.533	.358
Robinson, Errol	R-R	6-0	180	10-1-94	.273	.286	.269	57	227	35	62	8	2	2	14	29	1	0	1	50	11	3	.352	.357
Sawyer, Wynston	R-R	6-3	205	11-14-91	.277	.310	.268	54	184	16	51	14	1	4	17	13	3	0	1	42	1	2	.429	.333
Scavuzzo, Jacob	R-R	6-4	185	1-15-94	.237	.206	.246	72	274	32	65	12	0	16	52	13	3	0	4	81	3	1	.456	.276
Smith, Will	R-R	6-0	192	3-28-95	.000	—	.000	1	1	0	0	0	0	0	0	0	2	0	0	1	1	0	.000	.667
Tubbs, Darien	R-L	5-9	188	1-26-95	.290	.313	.273	12	38	7	11	3	0	0	5	4	1	2	0	6	4	1	.368	.372
Whiting, Brant	L-R	5-9	190	2-6-92	.364	.333	.375	4	11	3	4	1	0	0	0	1	1	0	0	4	0	0	.455	.462
Zarraga, Shawn	B-R	6-0	240	1-21-89	.278	.500	.214	6	18	4	5	3	0	1	3	2	0	0	0	2	0	0	.611	.350

Pitching	B-T	HT	WT	DOB	W	L	ERA	G	GS	CG	SV	IP	H	R	ER	HR	BB	SO	AVG	vLH	vRH	K/9	BB/9
Alvarez, Yadier	R-R	6-3	175	3-7-96	2	2	3.55	7	7	0	0	33	29	17	13	1	25	36	.234	.212	.250	9.82	6.82
Anderson, Isaac	R-R	6-2	185	9-4-93	0	8	8.74	12	11	0	0	45	64	46	44	8	19	32	.332	.385	.284	6.35	3.77
Barlow, Scott	R-R	6-3	215	12-18-92	6	3	2.10	19	19	0	0	107	60	33	25	9	37	124	.161	.203	.135	10.40	3.10
Bleich, Jeremy	L-L	6-2	215	6-18-87	0	1	6.17	7	0	0	0	12	17	8	8	0	5	9	.347	.389	.323	6.94	3.86
Broussard, Joe	R-R	6-1	220	1-28-91	1	0	0.00	4	0	0	2	5	0	0	0	0	0	6	.000	.000	.000	10.13	0.00
Buehler, Walker	R-R	6-2	175	7-28-94	2	2	3.49	11	11	0	0	49	40	19	19	5	15	64	.225	.241	.217	11.76	2.76
Cash, Ralston	R-R	6-3	215	8-20-91	3	2	5.28	31	0	0	1	44	51	30	26	4	17	61	.282	.266	.291	12.38	3.45
2-team total (5 Arkansas)					4	2	4.96	36	0	0	1	49	56	31	27	4	20	65	.281	.266	.291	11.94	3.67
Castillo, Fabio	R-R	6-1	235	2-19-89	0	1	1.29	3	0	0	0	7	10	1	1	0	3	3	.357	.143	.429	3.86	3.86
Copping, Corey	R-R	6-1	175	1-11-94	5	2	3.57	49	0	0	18	68	48	30	27	7	34	60	.200	.250	.169	7.94	4.50
Corcino, Daniel	R-R	5-11	210	8-26-90	0	0	2.70	4	0	0	1	7	8	3	2	1	0	7	.296	.364	.250	9.45	0.00
Cotton, Chris	L-R	5-10	166	11-21-90	0	1	11.57	3	0	0	0	2	5	5	3	1	3	0	.500	.500	.500	0.00	11.57
Curry, Parker	R-R	6-0	185	11-21-93	0	0	4.50	1	0	0	0	2	2	1	1	0	1	2	.333	1.000	.000	9.00	4.50
Gamboa, Eddie	R-R	6-1	215	12-21-84	2	1	2.14	4	3	0	0	21	14	5	5	1	9	17	.192	.220	.156	7.29	3.86
Hale, David	R-R	6-2	210	9-27-87	3	0	3.72	6	5	0	0	29	36	13	12	3	7	21	.303	.321	.288	6.52	2.17
Helsabeck, Wes	L-L	6-0	195	7-7-92	0	0	9.00	1	0	0	0	2	3	2	2	1	0	2	.333	.500	.286	9.00	0.00
Hynes, Colt	L-L	5-11	200	6-28-85	6	1	3.70	23	4	0	1	56	62	24	23	6	12	42	.277	.250	.292	6.75	1.93
Johnson, Michael	L-L	6-1	185	1-3-91	7	1	2.79	40	0	0	1	61	53	25	19	9	24	71	.222	.198	.235	10.42	3.52
Kowalczyk, Karch	R-R	6-1	215	3-31-91	5	7	3.18	44	0	0	0	62	63	24	22	5	23	46	.261	.296	.244	6.64	3.32
Moran, Brian	L-L	6-3	210	9-30-88	0	1	1.89	19	0	0	1	19	12	4	4	1	3	27	.182	.139	.233	12.79	1.42
Paredes, Edward	L-L	6-0	180	9-30-86	0	2	2.81	24	0	0	1	32	33	11	10	1	12	45	.273	.216	.314	12.66	3.38
Powell, Chris	R-R	6-2	170	9-21-92	0	0	1.50	3	0	0	0	6	4	2	1	0	3	6	.191	.200	.188	9.00	4.50
Rearick, Chris	L-L	6-3	200	12-5-87	0	1	6.94	5	5	0	0	23	32	22	18	4	10	19	.327	.300	.333	7.33	3.86
Santana, Dennis	R-R	6-2	160	4-12-96	3	1	5.51	7	7	0	0	33	32	23	20	2	23	37	.256	.298	.231	10.19	6.34
Sborz, Josh	R-R	6-3	225	12-17-93	8	8	3.86	24	24	0	0	117	106	60	50	8	56	81	.243	.249	.238	6.25	4.32
Shibuya, Tim	R-R	6-1	190	9-14-89	3	1	1.49	18	6	1	1	60	45	13	10	1	8	33	.203	.225	.186	4.92	1.19
Sierra, Yaisel	R-R	6-1	170	6-5-91	5	0	2.54	26	0	0	4	50	47	18	14	1	16	64	.244	.191	.272	11.60	2.90
Somsen, Layne	R-R	6-0	190	6-5-89	5	1	2.08	19	0	0	3	30	31	11	7	0	18	30	.256	.143	.317	8.90	5.34
Sopko, Andrew	R-R	6-2	205	8-7-94	5	7	4.13	23	23	0	0	105	104	53	48	11	45	74	.252	.274	.238	6.36	3.87
Spitzbarth, Shea	R-R	6-1	195	10-4-94	3	4	3.00	32	0	0	3	54	50	26	18	3	18	50	.239	.250	.233	8.33	3.00
Thurman, Andrew	R-R	6-3	225	12-10-91	1	1	4.32	5	0	0	0	8	7	5	4	0	7	5	.233	.235	.231	5.40	7.56
Urena, Miguel	R-R	6-8	210	2-27-95	0	0	9.00	1	0	0	0	2	4	2	2	0	0	1	.400	.600	.200	4.50	0.00
Vieitez, Ivan	R-L	6-2	170	5-8-93	1	3	4.97	11	8	0	0	38	44	24	21	2	19	21	.295	.306	.290	4.97	4.50
Wheeler, Jason	L-L	6-6	255	10-27-90	0	0	0.00	1	0	0	0	1	0	0	0	0	0	0	.000	.000	.000	0.00	0.00
White, Mitchell	R-R	6-4	207	12-28-94	1	1	2.57	7	7	0	0	28	17	8	8	2	13	31	.168	.146	.189	9.96	4.18
Ysla, Luis	L-L	6-1	185	4-27-92	0	0	6.17	7	0	0	0	12	13	8	8	1	7	8	.277	.267	.281	6.17	5.40

Fielding

Catcher	PCT	G	PO	A	E	DP	PB
Farmer	.988	19	146	15	2	2	2
Hoenecke	.996	29	214	27	1	1	10
Hope	.923	2	12	0	1	0	0
Kennedy	.994	36	312	24	2	1	5
Murphy	1.000	9	47	1	0	0	0
O'Connell	1.000	6	45	6	0	0	3
Sawyer	.993	37	280	20	2	2	6
Smith	1.000	1	7	0	0	0	0
Whiting	1.000	4	26	2	0	0	0
Zarraga	1.000	5	35	6	0	0	1

First Base	PCT	G	PO	A	E	DP
Ahmed	.966	3	27	1	1	2
Beaty	.991	55	404	40	4	39
Fernandez	.988	10	73	8	1	12
Garlick	1.000	3	5	0	0	2
Hoenecke	.975	13	103	12	3	12
O'Brien	.995	27	202	17	1	18
O'Connell	1.000	1	3	0	0	0
Rios	.991	28	210	17	2	13
Sawyer	.977	10	80	6	2	10

Second Base	PCT	G	PO	A	E	DP
Ahmed	1.000	5	7	18	0	4
Beaty	.000	1	0	0	0	0
Farmer	1.000	1	0	1	0	0
Fernandez	.970	57	92	135	7	34
Jackson	.978	23	31	59	2	4
Locastro	.988	24	41	44	1	9
McKinstry	1.000	5	8	11	0	5
Mejia	.955	22	46	61	5	13
Ortiz	1.000	3	2	7	0	2
Robinson	.980	11	22	26	1	8

Third Base	PCT	G	PO	A	E	DP
Ahmed	1.000	3	0	3	0	0
Beaty	.942	49	33	81	7	8
Farmer	.966	11	9	19	1	2
Fernandez	.875	4	3	4	1	2
Hoenecke	1.000	4	1	6	0	0
Jackson	1.000	2	2	1	0	0
McKinstry	.933	4	4	10	1	0
Mejia	.936	33	25	48	5	7
Rios	.859	38	22	63	14	5
Shibuya	.000	1	0	0	0	0

Shortstop	PCT	G	PO	A	E	DP
Ahmed	.977	18	33	51	2	14
Jackson	.933	4	3	11	1	1
Locastro	.900	31	49	59	12	15
McKinstry	.933	4	1	13	1	3
Mejia	.933	46	64	90	11	27
Robinson	.959	45	68	118	8	19

Outfield	PCT	G	PO	A	E	DP
Allie	.981	28	49	4	1	2
Beaty	1.000	5	10	0	0	0
Diaz	.918	30	43	2	4	0
Ethier	.857	5	6	0	1	0
Gailen	1.000	32	54	2	0	0
Garlick	1.000	63	108	5	0	1
Holt	.950	11	19	0	1	0
Landon	1.000	6	9	1	0	0
Latimore	1.000	35	56	2	0	0
Locastro	1.000	48	105	3	0	0
Mieses	.974	88	181	10	5	0
Morales	.909	8	10	0	1	0
O'Brien	1.000	6	9	0	0	0
Ramos	.927	23	37	1	3	0
Rios	1.000	2	2	0	0	0
Scavuzzo	.988	58	83	1	1	0
Tubbs	1.000	12	21	4	0	1

RANCHO CUCAMONGA QUAKES — *HIGH CLASS A*

CALIFORNIA LEAGUE

Batting	B-T	HT	WT	DOB	AVG	vLH	vRH	G	AB	R	H	2B	3B	HR	RBI	BB	HBP	SH	SF	SO	SB	CS	SLG	OBP
Brizuela, Jose	L-R	6-0	180	8-31-92	.353	.200	.370	16	51	9	18	4	0	0	4	6	1	0	1	14	0	1	.431	.424
Davis, Brendon	R-R	6-4	185	7-28-97	.200	.000	.207	8	30	2	6	3	0	1	8	3	0	0	0	13	0	0	.400	.273
Diaz, Yusniel	R-R	6-1	195	10-7-96	.278	.397	.250	83	331	42	92	15	3	8	39	35	1	1	6	73	7	9	.414	.343
Estevez, Omar	R-R	5-10	168	2-25-98	.256	.227	.264	120	457	56	117	24	3	4	47	33	4	3	4	97	2	2	.348	.309
Ethier, Andre	L-L	6-2	210	4-10-82	.250	.000	.400	3	8	0	2	0	0	0	1	1	0	0	0	4	0	0	.250	.333
Forsythe, Logan	R-R	6-1	205	1-14-87	.214	.000	.300	6	14	4	3	0	0	0	0	4	2	0	0	9	0	0	.214	.450
Gomez, Cristian	R-R	5-11	160	1-11-96	.444	1.000	.375	3	9	1	4	0	0	0	0	1	0	0	0	3	0	0	.444	.500
Gonzalez, Adrian	L-L	6-2	215	5-8-82	.208	.125	.250	6	24	4	5	2	0	0	2	3	0	0	0	2	0	0	.292	.296
Gutierrez, Franklin	R-R	6-2	200	2-21-83	.500	—	.500	2	6	2	3	0	0	1	3	1	0	0	0	0	0	0	1.000	.571
Hope, Garrett	R-R	6-3	245	12-27-93	.194	.167	.200	8	31	2	6	0	0	2	4	2	0	0	0	13	0	1	.387	.242
Isabel, Ibandel	R-R	6-4	225	6-20-95	.259	.291	.252	122	444	62	115	16	1	28	87	40	6	0	2	172	0	2	.489	.327
Jackson, Drew	R-R	6-2	200	7-28-93	.254	.275	.250	66	252	48	64	16	2	8	30	34	11	0	0	67	14	6	.429	.367
Kennedy, Garrett	L-R	6-1	205	12-13-92	.264	.286	.257	36	129	12	34	8	0	4	14	16	4	0	0	40	0	0	.419	.362
Landon, Logan	R-R	6-2	180	2-17-93	.276	.300	.271	20	58	13	16	4	0	3	7	8	0	1	0	11	5	0	.500	.364
Latimore, Quincy	R-R	5-11	175	2-3-89	.356	.267	.386	17	59	16	21	5	0	7	19	12	1	0	0	19	1	0	.797	.472
McKinstry, Zach	L-R	6-0	180	4-29-95	.226	.206	.231	82	319	39	72	13	0	3	28	29	5	1	1	87	5	2	.295	.299
Mejia, Erick	B-R	5-11	155	11-9-94	.230	.250	.227	24	87	14	20	4	1	1	11	8	0	1	1	19	3	0	.333	.292
Mieses, Johan	R-R	6-2	185	7-13-95	.353	.318	.362	28	116	25	41	17	0	8	27	10	2	0	1	38	0	0	.707	.411
Montgomery, Brandon	R-R	6-0	180	2-12-96	.252	.333	.228	98	326	30	82	13	3	2	45	14	3	1	8	61	5	3	.328	.282
Ortiz, Samuel	B-R	5-10	191	8-4-96	.238	.000	.250	5	21	1	5	1	0	0	4	1	0	0	0	9	1	1	.286	.273
Pederson, Joc	L-L	6-1	220	4-21-92	.143	.000	.250	3	7	0	1	0	0	0	0	3	0	0	0	3	0	0	.143	.400
Peters, DJ	R-R	6-6	225	12-12-95	.276	.252	.282	132	504	91	139	29	5	27	82	64	15	0	3	189	3	3	.514	.372
Raley, Luke	L-R	6-3	220	9-19-94	.295	.262	.306	123	478	102	141	21	11	14	62	43	19	0	1	124	9	1	.473	.375
Reks, Zach	L-R	6-2	190	11-12-93	.314	.160	.364	26	102	17	32	1	0	2	9	7	2	0	0	17	1	1	.382	.369
Roache, Victor	R-R	6-1	225	9-17-91	.192	.136	.204	35	125	18	24	8	1	6	17	10	1	0	0	59	0	1	.416	.257
Robinson, Errol	R-R	6-0	180	10-1-94	.286	.333	.261	16	70	13	20	4	3	2	8	5	1	0	0	17	5	1	.514	.342
Ruiz, Keibert	B-R	6-0	200	7-20-98	.315	.226	.339	38	149	24	47	7	1	6	27	7	1	0	3	23	0	0	.497	.344
Sandoval, Ariel	R-R	6-2	180	11-6-95	.214	.143	.229	61	192	27	41	7	0	8	22	17	1	0	0	75	4	3	.375	.281
Smith, Will	R-R	6-0	192	3-28-95	.232	.228	.233	72	250	38	58	15	3	11	43	37	13	1	4	71	6	2	.448	.355
Tubbs, Darien	R-L	5-9	188	1-26-95	.206	.200	.208	18	63	8	13	3	0	2	5	5	2	0	0	12	5	5	.349	.286
Turner, Justin	R-R	5-11	205	11-23-84	.333	—	.333	1	3	0	1	0	0	0	1	0	0	0	0	0	0	0	.333	.333
Walker, Jared	L-R	6-2	195	2-4-96	.224	.208	.233	20	67	6	15	4	0	1	5	10	0	0	0	35	1	0	.328	.325
Whiting, Brant	L-R	5-9	190	2-6-92	.286	.500	.235	12	42	6	12	2	0	1	6	4	4	0	0	13	0	0	.405	.400

Pitching	B-T	HT	WT	DOB	W	L	ERA	G	GS	CG	SV	IP	H	R	ER	HR	BB	SO	AVG	vLH	vRH	K/9	BB/9
Allie, Stetson	R-R	6-2	230	3-13-91	0	0	0.00	2	0	0	0	2	1	0	0	0	1	3	.143	.333	.000	13.50	4.50
Alvarez, Yadier	R-R	6-3	175	3-7-96	2	4	5.31	14	11	0	1	59	61	40	35	3	25	61	.263	.245	.277	9.25	3.79
Anderson, Isaac	R-R	6-2	185	9-4-93	0	1	10.13	5	1	0	0	11	16	13	12	0	4	9	.340	.316	.357	7.59	3.38
Boyle, Michael	R-L	6-3	200	4-12-94	5	6	4.75	19	7	0	0	53	56	33	28	4	17	37	.271	.250	.282	6.28	2.89
Bray, Adam	R-R	6-3	210	4-14-93	7	3	3.89	26	19	1	1	130	123	64	56	19	26	118	.247	.278	.222	8.19	1.80
Brown, Kevin	R-R	6-3	220	6-9-92	1	0	7.30	11	0	0	0	12	18	10	10	1	8	15	.353	.357	.348	10.95	5.84
Buehler, Walker	R-R	6-2	175	7-28-94	0	0	1.10	5	5	0	0	16	8	3	2	0	5	27	.143	.120	.161	14.88	2.76
Carter, James	R-R	6-3	185	3-10-94	0	0	5.40	1	0	0	0	2	1	1	1	1	3	2	.167	.500	.000	10.80	16.20

Corcino, Daniel	R-R	5-11	210	8-26-90	2	0	2.92	14	0	0	0	25	21	9	8	1	9	31	.219	.163	.264	11.31	3.28
Cotton, Chris	L-R	5-10	166	11-21-90	0	0	0.00	2	0	0	1	1	0	0	0	0	0	1	.000	.000	.000	6.75	0.00
Curry, Parker	R-R	6-0	185	11-21-93	2	8	4.31	27	3	0	3	48	54	25	23	4	16	62	.281	.229	.333	11.63	3.00
Dayton, Grant	L-L	6-2	215	11-25-87	0	0	0.00	2	1	0	0	2	0	0	0	0	0	4	.000	—	.000	18.00	0.00
Felix, Carlos	R-R	6-2	240	11-6-95	0	1	3.38	3	0	0	0	5	7	4	2	1	2	4	.304	.333	.286	6.75	3.38
Ferguson, Caleb	R-L	6-3	215	7-2-96	9	4	2.87	25	24	0	0	122	113	48	39	6	55	140	.246	.218	.261	10.30	4.05
Gonsolin, Tony	R-R	6-2	180	5-14-94	7	5	3.92	39	0	0	5	62	61	29	27	5	18	73	.254	.220	.279	10.60	2.61
Hartman, Zach	R-R	6-0	195	1-1-92	1	0	1.29	2	0	0	0	7	4	1	1	0	2	9	.167	.286	.118	11.57	2.57
Helsabeck, Wes	L-L	6-0	195	7-7-92	2	1	1.59	5	0	0	1	11	8	2	2	0	7	19	.195	.200	.192	15.09	5.56
Hermeling, Alex	R-R	6-5	230	3-22-93	5	0	3.08	38	0	0	1	61	53	22	21	5	20	55	.231	.242	.224	8.07	2.93
Hill, Rich	L-L	6-5	220	3-11-80	1	1	6.35	2	2	0	0	6	3	4	4	0	4	5	.167	.250	.143	7.94	6.35
Istler, Andrew	R-R	5-11	175	9-18-92	4	6	4.28	47	0	0	14	61	72	30	29	4	16	67	.303	.310	.297	9.89	2.36
Kazmir, Scott	L-L	6-0	195	1-24-84	1	0	4.50	4	3	0	0	12	12	6	6	2	6	6	.261	.364	.167	4.50	4.50
Kremer, Dean	R-R	6-3	180	1-7-96	1	4	5.18	33	6	0	3	80	86	55	46	6	34	96	.274	.247	.298	10.80	3.83
Liberatore, Adam	L-L	6-3	243	5-12-87	0	0	0.00	1	1	0	0	1	0	0	0	0	0	1	.000	.000	.000	9.00	0.00
Long, Nolan	R-R	6-10	255	1-19-94	2	0	2.00	13	0	0	1	18	13	5	4	0	8	19	.197	.125	.238	9.50	4.00
Maeda, Kenta	R-R	6-1	175	4-11-88	0	0	2.25	1	1	0	0	4	6	3	1	0	2	1	.316	.235	1.000	2.25	4.50
Mathewson, Chris	L-R	6-1	200	5-26-96	1	0	5.56	3	1	0	0	11	13	7	7	0	3	5	.296	.167	.344	3.97	2.38
May, Dustin	R-R	6-6	180	9-6-97	0	0	0.82	2	1	0	0	11	6	3	1	0	1	15	.150	.250	.107	12.27	0.82
McCarthy, Brandon	R-R	6-7	235	7-7-83	0	1	6.75	2	2	0	0	7	8	7	5	0	4	3	.308	.455	.200	4.05	5.40
Moseley, Ryan	R-R	6-3	190	10-6-94	0	1	3.26	10	3	0	1	30	25	12	11	0	17	20	.238	.260	.218	5.93	5.04
Osuna, Lenix	R-R	6-1	220	11-11-95	1	1	2.35	6	0	0	0	8	6	2	2	1	0	8	.214	.177	.273	9.39	0.00
Pittore, Gavin	R-R	6-3	230	9-18-93	0	0	1.80	4	0	0	0	5	2	1	1	0	2	5	.118	.250	.000	9.00	3.60
Powell, Chris	R-R	6-2	170	9-21-92	4	1	4.50	14	0	0	0	28	32	16	14	3	5	30	.281	.263	.298	9.64	1.61
Ravin, Josh	R-R	6-4	215	1-21-88	0	0	0.00	2	0	0	0	2	2	0	0	0	0	4	.286	.500	.000	18.00	0.00
Richman, Jason	L-L	6-4	210	10-15-93	2	2	2.66	14	0	0	0	24	17	7	7	2	7	19	.200	.111	.241	7.23	2.66
Romo, Sergio	R-R	5-11	185	3-4-83	0	0	3.00	2	2	0	0	3	3	1	1	0	0	2	.300	.200	.400	6.00	0.00
Santana, Dennis	R-R	6-2	160	4-12-96	5	6	3.57	17	14	0	0	86	87	44	34	5	22	92	.262	.279	.247	9.67	2.31
Schueller, Sven	R-R	6-3	205	1-17-96	1	0	5.25	12	0	0	0	24	17	14	14	4	16	21	.198	.310	.140	7.88	6.00
Sheffield, Jordan	R-R	5-10	190	6-1-95	0	2	8.00	5	4	0	0	18	23	17	16	2	15	18	.307	.368	.243	9.00	7.50
Smeltzer, Devin	R-L	6-3	195	9-7-95	5	4	4.40	16	15	0	0	90	107	56	44	10	18	102	.287	.259	.300	10.20	1.80
Spitzbarth, Shea	R-R	6-1	195	10-4-94	1	0	0.57	11	0	0	6	16	9	1	1	0	5	27	.164	.039	.276	15.51	2.87
Stewart, Brock	L-R	6-3	210	10-3-91	0	1	54.00	1	1	0	0	0	3	3	2	0	1	1	.600	.000	1.000	27.00	27.00
Thurman, Andrew	R-R	6-3	225	12-10-91	1	0	1.09	12	4	0	0	25	18	5	3	0	6	21	.200	.094	.259	7.66	2.19
Vieitez, Ivan	R-L	6-2	170	5-8-93	1	0	2.16	4	0	0	0	8	4	2	2	1	2	7	.138	.188	.077	7.56	2.16
White, Mitchell	R-R	6-4	207	12-28-94	2	1	3.72	9	9	0	0	39	26	23	16	0	16	49	.187	.239	.139	11.41	3.72

Fielding

Catcher	PCT	G	PO	A	E	DP	PB
Hope	1.000	5	46	1	0	0	2
Kennedy	.994	35	321	25	2	3	6
Ruiz	.992	37	329	38	3	1	5
Smith	.991	55	476	66	5	4	5
Whiting	.976	12	115	9	3	0	1

First Base	PCT	G	PO	A	E	DP
Brizuela	1.000	10	55	1	0	1
Gonzalez	1.000	4	29	4	0	3
Hope	1.000	2	18	1	0	0
Isabel	.981	113	816	49	17	72
Kennedy	.000	1	0	0	0	0
Raley	1.000	13	94	8	0	7
Walker	1.000	9	57	3	0	7

Second Base	PCT	G	PO	A	E	DP
Brizuela	.833	2	2	3	1	0
Davis	1.000	1	1	3	0	0
Estevez	.974	22	23	51	2	11
Forsythe	1.000	2	0	1	0	0
Gomez	1.000	3	5	3	0	1
Jackson	.964	25	50	58	4	10
McKinstry	.972	32	53	84	4	17
Mejia	.982	11	23	31	1	9
Montgomery	.966	32	46	69	4	15
Ortiz	1.000	2	5	5	0	0
Robinson	.942	11	18	31	3	8
Smith	.947	5	6	12	1	4

Third Base	PCT	G	PO	A	E	DP
Brizuela	.895	8	7	10	2	1
Davis	1.000	7	3	13	0	1
Forsythe	1.000	2	1	5	0	2
Jackson	.889	3	1	7	1	1
McKinstry	.900	44	32	76	12	7
Mejia	.917	7	4	7	1	0
Montgomery	.944	60	38	79	7	6
Ortiz	.500	1	2	1	3	0
Smith	.600	6	0	3	2	0
Turner	1.000	1	0	1	0	0
Walker	.880	12	9	13	3	1

Shortstop	PCT	G	PO	A	E	DP
Estevez	.962	98	123	236	14	40
Jackson	.909	29	40	70	11	11
McKinstry	.950	3	7	12	1	2
Mejia	.920	6	13	10	2	6
Ortiz	.833	2	3	2	1	0
Robinson	1.000	5	9	15	0	3

Outfield	PCT	G	PO	A	E	DP
Diaz	.945	71	152	4	9	2
Ethier	1.000	2	1	0	0	0
Gutierrez	1.000	2	3	0	0	0
Jackson	1.000	1	1	0	0	0
Landon	1.000	19	32	2	0	1
Latimore	.972	14	34	1	1	0
Mieses	.967	25	56	2	2	0
Montgomery	.917	3	11	0	1	0
Pederson	1.000	2	2	0	0	0
Peters	.976	114	231	11	6	5
Raley	.987	88	138	12	2	3
Reks	1.000	18	27	1	0	0
Roache	.978	23	38	6	1	1
Sandoval	.960	35	46	2	2	0
Tubbs	.933	17	26	2	2	1

GREAT LAKES LOONS — LOW CLASS A

MIDWEST LEAGUE

Batting	B-T	HT	WT	DOB	AVG	vLH	vRH	G	AB	R	H	2B	3B	HR	RBI	BB	HBP	SH	SF	SO	SB	CS	SLG	OBP
Adkison, Tyler	R-R	5-10	185	5-8-95	.208	.231	.200	15	48	8	10	6	0	0	7	11	0	0	3	21	3	0	.333	.339
Albert, Shakir	R-R	6-0	185	12-24-96	.231	.500	.182	4	13	2	3	2	0	0	2	2	0	0	0	5	2	0	.385	.333
Berman, Steve	R-R	6-2	225	11-28-94	.224	.184	.235	65	219	13	49	12	0	0	23	15	2	0	3	35	1	0	.279	.276
Carpenter, Brock	R-R	6-3	200	6-5-95	.261	1.000	.191	7	23	2	6	0	0	1	3	3	0	0	0	9	1	0	.391	.346
Cruz, Oneil	L-R	6-6	175	10-4-98	.240	.198	.259	89	342	51	82	9	1	8	36	28	0	0	5	110	8	7	.342	.293
Davis, Brendon	R-R	6-4	185	7-28-97	.245	.233	.250	86	310	39	76	19	3	8	35	47	8	0	2	107	3	7	.403	.357
Green, Gage	R-R	5-10	193	8-27-92	.213	.194	.224	28	94	12	20	8	0	0	14	6	3	0	4	18	0	0	.298	.271
Hansen, Mitchell	L-L	6-4	210	5-1-96	.198	.143	.218	74	263	32	52	9	3	5	25	32	2	0	2	75	11	3	.312	.288
Heredia, Starling	R-R	6-2	200	2-6-99	.212	.214	.211	26	99	14	21	6	1	1	8	10	1	0	0	38	5	1	.323	.291

Hope, Garrett	R-R	6-3	245	12-27-93	.250	.500	.000	1	4	0	1	1	0	0	1	0	0	0	0	0	0	0	.500	.250
Jenco, Saige	L-L	5-10	185	8-7-94	.242	.237	.244	90	293	53	71	16	6	4	28	47	4	1	1	75	12	8	.379	.354
Kendall, Jeren	L-R	6-0	190	2-4-96	.221	.171	.238	35	140	21	31	5	7	2	18	13	1	0	1	42	5	8	.400	.290
Lux, Gavin	L-R	6-2	190	11-23-97	.244	.165	.273	111	434	68	106	14	8	7	39	56	3	3	5	88	27	10	.362	.331
McKinstry, Zach	L-R	6-0	180	4-29-95	.308	.429	.289	17	52	10	16	7	0	1	3	17	0	0	0	10	2	1	.500	.478
Meza, Eric	L-L	6-1	245	3-5-98	.233	.259	.224	30	103	3	24	5	0	1	13	7	2	0	2	19	0	0	.311	.290
Montgomery, Brandon	R-R	6-0	180	2-12-96	.296	.500	.280	8	27	3	8	2	0	0	6	3	0	0	0	7	1	0	.370	.367
Morales, Brayan	R-L	6-1	170	12-8-95	.185	.154	.214	10	27	2	5	1	0	0	0	6	1	0	0	6	2	0	.222	.353
Paz, Luis	L-R	6-1	211	7-5-96	.196	.200	.194	39	143	16	28	4	1	3	17	10	0	0	0	41	0	1	.301	.248
Perez, Moises	R-R	6-0	160	7-18-97	.212	.300	.175	41	137	14	29	8	1	0	12	8	1	0	2	36	6	1	.285	.257
Pitre, Gersel	R-R	6-0	203	7-23-96	.247	.217	.258	27	85	12	21	5	0	0	5	7	0	1	0	20	0	1	.306	.304
Reks, Zach	L-R	6-2	190	11-12-93	.309	.125	.385	17	55	4	17	2	0	0	3	7	2	1	0	13	1	4	.346	.406
Rincon, Carlos	R-R	6-3	190	10-14-97	.198	.224	.189	87	334	41	66	13	1	18	48	32	2	0	2	143	6	1	.404	.270
Robinson, Errol	R-R	6-0	180	10-1-94	.247	.375	.189	22	77	13	19	5	1	3	13	6	0	0	3	21	6	1	.455	.291
Rodriguez, Ramon	R-R	5-11	185	10-30-98	.000	.000	.000	1	3	0	0	0	0	0	0	0	0	0	0	2	0	0	.000	.000
Ruiz, Keibert	B-R	6-0	200	7-20-98	.317	.246	.348	63	227	34	72	16	1	2	24	18	3	1	2	30	0	0	.423	.372
Santana, Cristian	R-R	6-2	175	2-24-97	.322	.465	.275	44	174	18	56	9	0	5	25	5	0	0	1	42	0	1	.460	.339
Thomas, Cody	L-R	6-4	211	10-8-94	.222	.225	.221	121	460	59	102	18	4	20	65	43	5	0	4	150	6	7	.409	.293
Tubbs, Darien	R-L	5-9	188	1-26-95	.137	.000	.167	16	51	6	7	1	0	0	5	7	0	0	2	12	2	1	.157	.233
Walker, Jared	L-R	6-2	195	2-4-96	.254	.310	.238	41	134	18	34	10	1	10	30	11	4	0	1	51	3	2	.567	.327
Wong, Connor	R-R	6-1	181	5-19-96	.278	.409	.240	27	97	19	27	6	0	5	18	7	2	0	1	26	1	1	.495	.336
Yarnall, Nick	L-L	6-0	200	10-17-94	.217	.240	.211	37	120	20	26	7	1	4	15	22	0	0	1	41	0	0	.392	.336

Pitching	B-T	HT	WT	DOB	W	L	ERA	G	GS	CG	SV	IP	H	R	ER	HR	BB	SO	AVG	vLH	vRH	K/9	BB/9
Abdullah, Imani	R-R	6-4	205	4-20-97	0	2	5.11	6	6	0	0	12	12	8	7	1	7	13	.250	.276	.211	9.49	5.11
Alexy, A.J.	R-R	6-4	195	4-21-98	2	6	3.67	19	19	0	0	74	46	32	30	3	37	86	.180	.184	.177	10.51	4.52
Carter, James	R-R	6-3	185	3-10-94	0	0	2.40	10	0	0	0	15	16	6	4	2	4	18	.276	.375	.154	10.80	2.40
Crawford, Leo	L-L	6-0	180	2-2-97	7	10	4.60	25	24	0	0	135	134	80	69	12	47	97	.255	.297	.237	6.47	3.13
Crouse, Logan	R-R	6-6	225	12-2-96	0	0	3.00	1	0	0	0	3	3	1	1	0	0	1	.250	.250	.250	3.00	0.00
Curry, Parker	R-R	6-0	185	11-21-93	1	1	1.88	5	1	0	1	14	8	5	3	2	3	17	.154	.208	.107	10.67	1.88
De Paula, Luis	L-L	6-1	170	4-23-92	0	2	24.75	3	0	0	0	4	9	11	11	1	4	5	.474	.167	.615	11.25	9.00
Duester, Patrick	R-R	6-6	225	12-24-93	2	0	4.71	15	0	0	1	21	19	11	11	3	7	20	.241	.270	.214	8.57	3.00
Felix, Carlos	R-R	6-2	240	11-6-95	1	1	3.86	3	2	0	0	14	19	9	6	1	3	14	.328	.333	.324	9.00	1.93
French, Austin	L-R	6-4	220	9-14-93	1	1	6.00	5	0	0	0	9	11	7	6	0	8	9	.297	.083	.400	9.00	8.00
German, Angel	R-R	6-4	185	5-25-96	1	0	1.91	21	0	0	7	33	22	9	7	0	14	37	.190	.128	.232	10.09	3.82
Gonsolin, Tony	R-R	6-2	180	5-14-94	0	1	3.38	3	0	0	1	8	8	3	3	2	0	12	.242	.278	.200	13.50	0.00
Grana, Kyle	R-R	6-4	245	4-26-91	0	0	3.86	2	0	0	0	2	1	1	1	0	1	2	.125	.000	.200	7.71	3.86
Harrison, Garrett	L-L	6-3	200	8-14-93	0	0	21.60	1	0	0	0	2	3	5	4	1	2	1	.375	.000	.429	5.40	10.80
Jagiello, Dan	R-R	6-3	180	5-23-95	2	0	4.26	12	0	0	3	19	13	9	9	1	9	21	.188	.071	.268	9.95	4.26
Jimenez, Melvin	B-R	6-0	170	7-23-99	2	1	2.57	9	4	0	1	28	19	8	8	1	12	36	.194	.208	.180	11.57	3.86
Kasowski, Marshall	L-R	6-3	215	3-10-95	1	1	6.00	5	3	0	0	6	10	6	4	1	9	6	.357	.385	.333	9.00	13.50
Long, Nolan	R-R	6-10	255	1-19-94	3	1	2.70	20	0	0	4	33	24	13	10	2	17	51	.191	.102	.269	13.77	4.59
Mathewson, Chris	L-R	6-1	200	5-26-96	5	4	3.11	21	12	2	0	101	95	44	35	7	37	102	.246	.279	.212	9.06	3.29
May, Dustin	R-R	6-6	180	9-6-97	9	6	3.88	23	23	0	0	123	121	60	53	8	26	113	.250	.272	.229	8.27	1.90
Montgomerie, Wills	R-R	6-3	205	6-2-95	0	0	4.91	3	0	0	0	4	5	3	2	0	3	3	.313	.429	.222	7.36	7.36
Moseley, Ryan	R-R	6-3	190	10-6-94	0	2	5.25	18	0	0	2	36	34	26	21	1	22	37	.248	.221	.275	9.25	5.50
Muhammad, Jeremiah	R-R	6-2	195	11-14-94	2	1	3.45	15	0	0	0	31	18	13	12	1	25	48	.168	.174	.164	13.79	7.18
Nealy, Colby	R-R	6-5	185	3-8-96	0	1	6.43	4	0	0	1	7	8	5	5	2	2	2	.286	.333	.200	2.57	2.57
Osuna, Lenix	R-R	6-1	220	11-11-95	0	1	9.00	5	1	0	0	11	14	13	11	0	6	10	.286	.333	.250	8.18	4.91
Ottesen, Riley	R-R	6-1	185	10-30-94	0	2	4.30	5	5	0	0	15	10	9	7	0	12	17	.192	.160	.222	10.43	7.36
Pittore, Gavin	R-R	6-3	230	9-18-93	0	0	2.45	2	0	0	0	4	4	1	1	0	1	3	.267	.333	.167	7.36	2.45
Ruibal, Evy	R-R	6-4	232	9-29-95	1	2	4.61	9	0	0	0	14	13	9	7	1	12	17	.250	.192	.308	11.20	7.90
Santarsiero, Vinny	R-R	6-7	185	12-10-93	3	1	3.33	24	0	0	0	51	51	24	19	3	20	26	.262	.244	.276	4.56	3.51
Santos, Jose	R-R	6-0	165	3-8-92	0	2	12.27	3	0	0	0	4	6	5	5	0	4	2	.375	.333	.429	4.91	9.82
Schueller, Sven	R-R	6-3	205	1-17-96	3	2	1.49	23	0	0	3	48	39	18	8	0	18	30	.219	.213	.226	5.59	3.35
Scrubb, Andre	R-R	6-4	265	1-13-95	6	2	1.74	31	1	0	2	52	33	14	10	2	33	55	.182	.135	.235	9.58	5.75
Sequera, Gregorio	R-R	6-1	165	12-9-97	0	0	6.75	5	0	0	0	8	10	10	6	0	9	6	.303	.273	.318	6.75	10.13
Sheffield, Jordan	R-R	5-10	190	6-1-95	3	7	4.03	20	20	0	0	89	86	50	40	9	42	91	.255	.285	.227	9.17	4.23
Smeltzer, Devin	R-L	6-3	195	9-7-95	2	3	3.78	10	10	0	0	52	40	23	22	6	12	57	.211	.188	.222	9.80	2.06
Soto, Willian	R-R	6-4	185	2-13-96	5	1	3.48	10	2	0	0	34	46	16	13	3	10	30	.329	.383	.288	8.02	2.67
Stolo, Christian	L-L	6-0	185	5-9-94	3	2	4.31	22	1	0	1	40	45	21	19	4	14	39	.296	.283	.304	8.85	3.18
Tavarez, Alfredo	R-R	6-5	190	11-27-97	0	2	5.40	5	5	0	0	20	18	13	12	2	13	19	.237	.281	.205	8.55	5.85
Urena, Miguel	R-R	6-8	210	2-27-95	3	0	2.14	16	0	0	4	34	26	11	8	2	14	24	.217	.250	.179	6.42	3.74
Uter, Kam	R-R	6-3	200	1-26-96	0	0	27.00	1	0	0	0	1	2	4	4	1	5	2	.333	.667	.000	13.50	33.75
Zabala, Aneurys	R-R	6-2	175	12-21-96	1	1	10.24	5	0	0	0	10	14	13	11	1	8	13	.333	.348	.316	12.10	7.45

Fielding

Catcher	PCT	G	PO	A	E	DP	PB
Berman	.993	62	526	55	4	3	4
Green	1.000	2	15	0	0	0	1
Hope	1.000	1	10	1	0	0	0
Rodriguez	1.000	1	10	0	0	0	0
Ruiz	.991	49	392	59	4	5	5
Wong	.981	27	238	20	5	2	4

First Base	PCT	G	PO	A	E	DP
Berman	1.000	2	3	0	0	0
Green	1.000	8	49	2	0	5
Hansen	1.000	2	10	4	0	0
Meza	.993	29	260	14	2	28
Paz	.989	34	269	8	3	23
Pitre	.985	7	62	3	1	6
Santana	.984	9	58	4	1	4
Walker	1.000	19	127	10	0	14
Yarnall	.990	37	291	17	3	32

Second Base	PCT	G	PO	A	E	DP
Davis	.975	24	41	76	3	19
Lux	.974	43	67	118	5	27
McKinstry	.966	12	31	25	2	6
Montgomery	1.000	7	14	21	0	5
Perez	.933	21	31	53	6	12
Pitre	.905	8	13	25	4	2

	PCT	G	PO	A	E	DP
Reks	.000	1	0	0	0	0
Robinson	.926	12	22	41	5	10
Santana	.889	2	2	6	1	1
Walker	1.000	13	29	24	0	7

Third Base	PCT	G	PO	A	E	DP
Berman	.000	1	0	0	0	0
Carpenter	.895	7	7	10	2	1
Cruz	.822	47	25	58	18	5
Davis	.875	27	18	38	8	1
McKinstry	1.000	5	2	9	0	0
Montgomery	.667	1	1	1	1	0
Perez	.882	9	11	19	4	2
Pitre	.769	7	4	6	3	3

	PCT	G	PO	A	E	DP
Robinson	1.000	1	0	1	0	0
Santana	.914	31	8	56	6	4
Walker	.882	8	8	7	2	2

Shortstop	PCT	G	PO	A	E	DP
Cruz	.919	30	32	70	9	15
Davis	.944	33	45	74	7	12
Lux	.933	65	87	178	19	37
Perez	.980	11	16	34	1	13
Robinson	.923	4	2	10	1	3

Outfield	PCT	G	PO	A	E	DP
Adkison	1.000	9	14	1	0	0
Albert	1.000	4	5	1	0	0
Green	1.000	17	26	3	0	1
Hansen	.969	59	93	2	3	0
Heredia	.967	19	28	1	1	0
Jenco	.994	79	156	4	1	1
Kendall	.974	29	71	5	2	1
Morales	1.000	9	15	1	0	1
Paz	.000	1	0	0	0	0
Pitre	1.000	4	5	0	0	0
Reks	1.000	12	24	2	0	0
Rincon	.948	65	107	2	6	1
Robinson	1.000	2	4	0	0	0
Thomas	.991	100	219	6	2	3
Tubbs	.964	15	25	2	1	0

OGDEN RAPTORS — ROOKIE

PIONEER LEAGUE

Batting	B-T	HT	WT	DOB	AVG	vLH	vRH	G	AB	R	H	2B	3B	HR	RBI	BB	HBP	SH	SF	SO	SB	CS	SLG	OBP
Adkison, Tyler	R-R	5-10	185	5-8-95	.343	.375	.337	30	102	25	35	11	1	1	20	19	3	0	4	23	1	4	.500	.445
Bannon, Rylan	R-R	5-10	180	4-22-96	.336	.333	.336	40	149	39	50	8	0	10	30	19	5	1	1	29	5	0	.591	.425
Brito, Ronny	R-R	6-0	165	3-22-99	.238	.200	.241	16	63	12	15	2	1	1	7	2	0	0	0	22	6	0	.349	.262
Carpenter, Brock	R-R	6-3	200	6-5-95	.214	.120	.238	39	126	13	27	2	1	4	20	20	1	0	1	39	5	2	.341	.324
Casey, Donovan	R-R	6-2	190	2-23-96	.396	.522	.371	33	139	37	55	5	2	7	23	9	3	0	0	18	5	2	.612	.444
Clementina, Hendrik	R-R	6-0	165	6-17-97	.370	.350	.375	24	92	17	34	5	0	4	25	10	3	1	2	16	0	0	.554	.439
2-team total (27 Billings)					.303	.310	.209	51	188	30	57	11	0	6	35	17	5	1	3	41	0	0	.457	.371
Cuadrado, Romer	R-R	6-4	185	9-12-97	.335	.293	.343	64	260	54	87	12	5	9	60	30	7	1	3	74	11	4	.523	.413
Gomez, Cristian	R-R	5-11	160	1-11-96	.235	.333	.214	4	17	5	4	3	0	1	1	1	0	0	0	6	0	0	.588	.278
Hansen, Mitchell	L-L	6-4	210	5-1-96	.329	.429	.311	34	140	27	46	11	4	7	33	16	0	0	2	29	4	3	.614	.392
Heady, Connor	R-R	5-11	158	7-3-94	.253	.154	.275	46	146	35	37	12	0	5	17	28	2	1	1	37	5	1	.438	.379
Heredia, Starling	R-R	6-2	200	2-6-99	.427	.154	.478	19	82	21	35	11	1	4	17	10	0	0	0	24	5	4	.732	.489
Hope, Garrett	R-R	6-3	245	12-27-93	.310	.250	.320	24	87	23	27	6	0	7	27	12	3	0	0	20	0	0	.621	.412
Jarrard, Jonah	R-R	6-0	215	6-26-94	.143	.333	.000	4	7	2	1	1	0	0	3	1	0	0	1	3	0	0	.286	.222
Kendall, Jeren	L-R	6-0	190	2-4-96	.455	1.000	.429	5	22	5	10	1	1	1	7	0	0	0	0	3	4	0	.727	.455
Lachance, Kevin	R-R	6-3	185	7-2-94	.258	.174	.273	50	155	27	40	6	1	0	17	30	4	0	2	31	10	6	.310	.387
Medina, Michael	R-R	6-4	210	8-24-96	.225	.294	.188	14	49	10	11	6	1	0	6	4	3	0	1	21	0	1	.388	.316
Meza, Eric	L-L	6-1	245	3-5-98	.172	.500	.148	8	29	5	5	1	0	1	1	2	0	0	0	6	0	0	.310	.226
Morales, Brayan	R-L	6-1	170	12-8-95	.297	.107	.342	41	145	35	43	8	0	0	12	18	2	3	2	29	29	7	.352	.377
Ortiz, Samuel	B-R	5-10	191	8-4-96	.236	.111	.261	18	55	10	13	1	0	2	12	10	0	0	3	18	1	0	.364	.338
Padilla, Daniel	R-R	6-2	175	2-16-97	.154	.000	.250	4	13	4	2	0	0	0	0	4	1	0	0	2	2	0	.154	.389
Paz, Luis	L-R	6-1	211	7-5-96	.319	.333	.316	60	238	48	76	17	1	18	63	25	2	0	3	67	1	2	.626	.384
Perez, Moises	R-R	6-0	160	7-18-97	.316	.290	.322	34	152	32	48	8	2	2	16	13	1	0	0	39	6	3	.434	.374
Peterson, Eric	R-R	5-11	190	9-22-93	.429	—	.429	9	28	7	12	3	1	0	8	4	2	0	0	8	0	0	.607	.529
Pitre, Gersel	R-R	6-0	203	7-23-96	.346	.400	.338	43	179	28	62	12	2	1	35	3	1	0	3	24	10	3	.453	.355
Reks, Zach	L-R	6-2	190	11-12-93	.400	—	.400	4	10	3	4	0	0	0	0	2	1	0	0	2	1	0	.400	.539
Rincon, Carlos	R-R	6-3	190	10-14-97	.275	.267	.278	14	51	8	14	4	0	3	13	1	0	0	0	16	0	0	.529	.289
Rodriguez, Ramon	R-R	5-11	185	10-30-98	.276	.333	.265	17	58	7	16	3	1	2	13	4	2	0	2	10	0	0	.466	.333
Santana, Cristian	R-R	6-2	175	2-24-97	.537	.667	.483	10	41	18	22	2	1	5	16	6	0	0	1	6	0	0	1.000	.583
Walker, Jared	L-R	6-2	195	2-4-96	.529	.750	.462	4	17	6	9	1	1	3	4	0	0	0	0	2	0	0	1.235	.529
Yarnall, Nick	L-L	6-0	200	10-17-94	.368	.280	.400	25	95	24	35	6	0	6	25	17	0	0	2	25	4	2	.621	.456

Pitching	B-T	HT	WT	DOB	W	L	ERA	G	GS	CG	SV	IP	H	R	ER	HR	BB	SO	AVG	vLH	vRH	K/9	BB/9
Carter, James	R-R	6-3	185	3-10-94	3	1	2.11	10	0	0	1	21	15	5	5	1	4	34	.185	.185	.185	14.34	1.69
Cespedes, Francis	L-L	6-4	185	9-28-94	4	0	11.79	21	0	0	0	24	28	34	31	0	36	31	.318	.286	.333	11.79	13.69
Cespedes, Yeison	R-R	6-1	178	3-5-98	0	0	9.00	1	0	0	0	2	2	2	2	1	1	1	.250	.333	.200	4.50	4.50
Costello, Conor	R-R	6-3	170	11-4-92	5	4	6.46	22	0	0	2	31	42	28	22	3	16	25	.321	.262	.348	7.34	4.70
Crouse, Logan	R-R	6-6	225	12-2-96	2	0	3.68	3	0	0	0	7	9	3	3	1	1	6	.310	.400	.263	7.36	1.23
Ditman, Matt	R-R	6-1	205	8-13-92	0	0	7.71	3	0	0	0	5	6	5	4	0	1	3	.353	.400	.333	5.79	1.93
Duester, Patrick	R-R	6-6	225	12-24-93	3	3	3.28	19	0	0	1	36	30	19	13	5	15	31	.227	.255	.210	7.82	3.79
Felix, Carlos	R-R	6-2	240	11-6-95	2	1	5.86	12	11	0	0	43	60	31	28	7	11	34	.330	.328	.331	7.12	2.30
French, Austin	L-R	6-4	220	9-14-93	2	0	7.71	3	0	0	0	5	8	4	4	1	7	6	.400	.200	.467	11.57	13.50
Hamilton, Austin	L-L	6-0	185	8-11-93	2	1	5.13	18	0	0	2	26	26	19	15	2	15	30	.250	.143	.290	10.25	5.13
Hartman, Zach	R-R	6-0	195	1-1-92	1	2	4.83	19	0	0	3	32	30	19	17	0	14	34	.242	.280	.216	9.66	3.98
Hemmerich, Devin	R-L	6-1	195	7-11-95	2	0	2.61	19	0	0	1	31	25	10	9	1	12	41	.221	.172	.238	11.90	3.48
Hoyt, Justin	L-L	6-0	210	4-30-95	1	0	4.03	19	0	0	2	29	26	19	13	1	11	39	.230	.216	.237	12.10	3.41
Jones, Matt	L-R	6-7	250	3-9-94	2	1	1.35	14	0	0	1	20	16	6	3	0	10	15	.213	.125	.255	6.75	4.50
Lewis, Justin	B-L	6-2	210	10-12-96	0	0	10.45	8	0	0	0	10	20	14	12	0	6	10	.417	.389	.433	8.71	5.23
Muhammad, Jeremiah	R-R	6-2	195	11-14-94	0	0	1.50	4	0	0	0	6	5	1	1	0	4	8	.227	.333	.154	12.00	6.00
Nealy, Colby	R-R	6-5	185	3-8-96	0	0	9.00	3	0	0	0	4	8	5	4	1	1	4	.400	.600	.333	9.00	2.25
Oaks, Trevor	R-R	6-3	220	3-26-93	0	0	7.94	2	2	0	0	6	12	6	5	1	1	6	.429	.500	.375	9.53	1.59
Pacheco, Jairo	L-L	6-0	165	7-6-96	1	0	4.63	7	1	0	0	12	21	12	6	0	6	12	.404	.529	.343	9.26	4.63
Paschke, Jeff	R-R	6-5	215	12-19-94	3	0	5.40	13	0	0	1	17	19	16	10	2	7	16	.288	.286	.290	8.64	3.78
Pena, Adalberto	R-R	6-2	173	3-11-95	0	3	5.63	14	13	0	0	48	55	32	30	2	27	47	.293	.365	.246	8.81	5.06
Ramirez, Osiris	R-R	6-3	185	9-14-95	2	4	6.65	15	15	0	0	47	57	43	35	3	37	44	.295	.307	.288	8.37	7.04
Santarsiero, Vinny	R-R	6-7	185	12-10-93	2	1	3.68	8	0	0	1	15	13	10	6	3	7	17	.232	.294	.205	10.43	4.30

Pitching	B-T	HT	WT	DOB	W	L	ERA	G	GS	CG	SV	IP	H	R	ER	HR	BB	SO	AVG	vLH	vRH	K/9	BB/9
Sequera, Gregorio	R-R	6-1	165	12-9-97	0	2	7.30	15	15	0	0	53	76	50	43	9	23	44	.342	.434	.295	7.47	3.91
Stolo, Christian	L-L	6-0	185	5-9-94	3	2	5.35	11	5	0	1	39	47	23	23	8	17	30	.309	.333	.298	6.98	3.96
Uceta, Edwin	R-R	6-0	155	1-9-98	2	3	6.59	14	14	0	0	56	63	45	41	8	14	62	.278	.314	.255	9.96	2.25
Urena, Miguel	R-R	6-8	210	2-27-95	3	0	2.96	19	0	0	6	27	25	12	9	1	14	30	.245	.310	.219	9.88	4.61
Uter, Kam	R-R	6-3	200	1-26-96	1	0	5.23	7	0	0	0	10	14	6	6	1	7	7	.326	.389	.280	6.10	6.10
Vargas, Jesus	R-R	6-2	175	8-18-98	1	0	6.75	1	0	0	0	4	7	3	3	0	0	3	.389	.625	.200	6.75	0.00
Washington, Mark	R-R	6-7	205	3-22-96	0	1	15.43	1	0	0	0	2	3	5	4	0	2	2	.273	.167	.400	7.71	7.71

Fielding

C: Clementina 23, Hope 20, Jarrard 4, Paz 9, Pitre 10, Rodriguez 17. **1B:** Carpenter 11, Casey 2, Hope 5, Meza 3, Paz 28, Pitre 9, Walker 2, Yarnall 20. **2B:** Brito 4, Carpenter 4, Heady 17, Lachance 34, Ortiz 7, Perez 3, Peterson 7, Pitre 8, Santana 3. **3B:** Bannon 34, Carpenter 23, Gomez 1, Heady 3, Ortiz 1, Paz 2, Perez 3, Peterson 2, Pitre 10, Santana 5, Walker 2. **SS:** Brito 8, Gomez 3, Heady 25, Lachance 6, Ortiz 10, Perez 28. **OF:** Adkison 20, Casey 27, Cuadrado 57, Hansen 29, Heredia 14, Kendall 4, Lachance 11, Medina 13, Morales 40, Padilla 4, Paz 11, Pitre 6, Reks 4, Rincon 3, Yarnall 1.

AZL DODGERS — *ROOKIE*

ARIZONA LEAGUE

Batting	B-T	HT	WT	DOB	AVG	vLH	vRH	G	AB	R	H	2B	3B	HR	RBI	BB	HBP	SH	SF	SO	SB	CS	SLG	OBP
Ahmed, Michael	R-R	6-2	195	1-20-92	.143	.333	.000	3	7	1	1	0	0	1	1	1	0	0	0	2	0	0	.571	.250
Albert, Shakir	R-R	6-0	185	12-24-96	.291	.250	.302	15	55	12	16	5	2	3	13	3	1	1	1	20	1	0	.618	.333
Amaya, Jacob	R-R	6-0	180	9-3-98	.254	.136	.281	34	118	17	30	4	1	2	14	19	2	0	1	25	4	2	.356	.364
Amon, Pascal	L-R	6-1	183	12-26-97	.230	.046	.275	41	113	19	26	8	1	2	15	11	1	1	0	38	2	3	.372	.304
Aponte, Kevin	R-R	6-2	175	10-26-97	.233	.313	.212	43	150	29	35	6	0	1	13	30	3	0	1	63	9	2	.293	.370
Arocho, Jeremy	B-R	5-10	165	10-6-98	.254	.300	.246	39	134	26	34	9	2	1	19	14	3	1	2	30	10	2	.373	.333
Arruebarrena, Erisbel	R-R	6-1	230	3-25-90	.519	.444	.556	8	27	8	14	2	2	2	10	2	0	0	0	6	0	0	.963	.552
Bellinger, Cody	L-L	6-4	210	7-13-95	.333	—	.333	1	3	1	1	0	0	1	4	0	0	0	1	1	0	0	1.333	.250
Brito, Ronny	R-R	6-0	165	3-22-99	.241	.154	.268	12	54	10	13	5	0	2	12	3	0	0	1	19	0	0	.444	.276
Camargo, Jair	R-R	5-10	150	7-1-99	.273	.214	.289	36	132	17	36	9	1	2	16	5	2	0	1	39	0	1	.402	.307
Casey, Donovan	R-R	6-2	190	2-23-96	.467	.750	.364	5	15	4	7	1	0	0	9	3	0	0	1	3	1	0	.533	.526
Chiu, Marcus	R-R	6-1	190	1-13-97	.297	.226	.316	45	148	30	44	15	0	3	22	11	11	0	2	40	5	0	.460	.384
Garlick, Kyle	R-R	6-1	210	1-26-92	.353	.500	.333	5	17	4	6	3	0	1	2	2	1	0	0	4	0	0	.706	.450
Grand Pre, Preston	R-R	6-4	175	7-15-95	.264	.333	.244	17	53	8	14	4	2	0	9	7	0	0	1	13	3	1	.415	.344
Heredia, Starling	R-R	6-2	200	2-6-99	.429	.714	.333	7	28	8	12	2	2	2	9	4	0	0	0	7	0	0	.857	.500
Jackson, Drew	R-R	6-2	200	7-28-93	.200	.000	.286	3	10	1	2	0	2	0	4	1	0	0	0	4	0	0	.600	.273
Jarrard, Jonah	R-R	6-0	215	6-26-94	.000	—	.000	4	7	0	0	0	0	0	0	2	1	0	0	1	0	1	.000	.300
Meza, Eric	L-L	6-1	245	3-5-98	.231	.130	.255	31	117	11	27	8	0	3	19	6	2	0	3	25	1	0	.376	.273
Ortiz, Samuel	B-R	5-10	191	8-4-96	.270	.091	.346	14	37	2	10	1	0	0	7	6	0	0	2	6	0	2	.297	.356
Osorio, Felix	R-R	6-4	195	11-13-96	.215	.194	.220	42	149	24	32	4	4	4	18	22	4	1	0	35	3	2	.376	.331
Padilla, Daniel	R-R	6-2	175	2-16-97	.214	.000	.231	5	14	3	3	0	1	0	2	2	0	0	0	4	0	0	.357	.313
Peterson, Eric	R-R	5-11	190	9-22-93	.239	.333	.194	21	46	11	11	1	1	0	8	10	1	1	1	8	4	1	.304	.379
Roberts, Jacob	R-R	6-0	200	2-2-96	.269	.000	.333	20	52	11	14	4	0	2	10	10	2	0	2	19	0	0	.462	.394
Rodriguez, Ramon	R-R	5-11	185	10-30-98	.383	.400	.378	14	47	10	18	5	0	0	11	6	0	0	1	5	0	0	.489	.444
Roller, Chris	R-R	6-0	190	10-8-96	.181	.185	.180	45	127	24	23	8	1	1	14	20	5	0	4	28	9	1	.284	.308
Rubi, Alvaro	R-R	6-2	185	2-16-97	.250	.478	.174	28	92	21	23	4	1	3	12	16	5	0	0	14	0	2	.413	.389
Sawyer, Wynston	R-R	6-3	205	11-14-91	.375	.333	.400	3	8	1	3	2	0	1	3	2	0	0	0	1	0	0	1.000	.500
Segedin, Rob	R-R	6-2	220	11-10-88	.333	.500	.000	2	3	1	1	0	0	0	1	1	0	0	0	0	0	0	.333	.500
Souffront, Jefrey	R-R	6-1	190	5-23-97	.299	.100	.340	39	117	23	35	5	2	5	24	19	2	0	0	25	2	1	.504	.406
Wong, Connor	R-R	6-1	181	5-19-96	.000	—	.000	1	1	0	0	0	0	0	0	0	0	0	0	1	0	0	.000	.000

Pitching	B-T	HT	WT	DOB	W	L	ERA	G	GS	CG	SV	IP	H	R	ER	HR	BB	SO	AVG	vLH	vRH	K/9	BB/9
Allie, Stetson	R-R	6-2	230	3-13-91	0	0	0.00	8	0	0	0	8	4	1	0	0	5	10	.143	.200	.111	11.25	5.63
Alvino, Jasiel	R-R	6-1	180	1-11-97	1	0	1.64	9	0	0	0	11	8	3	2	0	5	8	.200	.267	.160	6.55	4.09
Anderson, Isaac	R-R	6-2	185	9-4-93	0	0	6.00	1	1	0	0	3	4	3	2	0	0	4	.267	.000	.364	12.00	0.00
Castellanos, Saul	R-R	6-0	170	5-10-97	0	0	3.00	3	1	0	0	3	1	2	1	1	0	2	.091	.200	.000	6.00	0.00
Cespedes, Yeison	R-R	6-1	178	3-5-98	5	2	2.31	19	0	0	4	35	28	10	9	1	13	32	.207	.196	.214	8.23	3.34
Chacin, Jose	R-R	6-4	168	3-25-97	4	0	4.04	15	4	0	0	42	40	21	19	5	6	41	.248	.161	.303	8.72	1.28
Davis, Ike	L-L	6-4	220	3-22-87	0	0	0.00	6	1	0	0	6	3	0	0	0	4	6	.158	.000	.200	9.53	6.35
Dayton, Grant	L-L	6-2	215	11-25-87	0	0	0.00	1	1	0	0	1	0	0	0	0	1	2	.000	—	.000	18.00	9.00
Fernandez, Pablo	R-R	6-1	185	8-5-89	0	1	13.50	5	4	0	0	12	25	20	18	5	2	11	.397	.474	.364	8.25	1.50
Gamboa, Max	R-R	6-4	180	11-22-95	0	0	0.00	1	1	0	0	1	1	0	0	0	0	1	.250	.000	.333	9.00	0.00
Hatcher, Chris	R-R	6-1	200	1-12-85	0	0	4.50	2	2	0	0	2	2	1	1	0	0	3	.250	.000	.333	13.50	0.00
Inoa, Confesor	R-R	6-2	210	2-21-96	3	0	1.90	14	0	0	2	24	13	8	5	0	9	16	.161	.250	.123	6.08	3.42
Jagiello, Dan	R-R	6-3	180	5-23-95	0	1	2.84	4	0	0	0	6	2	2	2	0	2	10	.100	.000	.125	14.21	2.84
Jimenez, Melvin	B-R	6-0	170	7-23-99	1	0	1.64	5	0	0	0	11	3	2	2	1	4	18	.083	.143	.046	14.73	3.27
Kasowski, Marshall	L-R	6-3	215	3-10-95	0	0	0.00	4	0	0	0	5	1	0	0	0	3	9	.059	.000	.071	15.19	5.06
Lewis, Justin	B-L	6-2	210	10-12-96	1	0	3.48	6	0	0	2	10	8	5	4	0	1	16	.216	.000	.296	13.94	0.87
Liberatore, Adam	L-L	6-3	243	5-12-87	0	0	0.00	1	1	0	0	1	0	0	0	0	1	2	.000	.000	—	18.00	9.00
Malisheski, Kevin	R-R	6-3	200	9-7-97	2	1	3.82	10	4	0	0	38	39	21	16	2	10	25	.273	.245	.287	5.97	2.39
Marinan, James	R-R	6-5	220	10-10-98	2	0	1.59	9	6	0	0	17	14	5	3	0	14	14	.250	.429	.143	7.41	7.41
Mateo, Santos	R-R	6-3	185	2-22-97	1	1	11.20	14	0	0	0	14	15	23	17	2	22	14	.268	.211	.297	9.22	14.49
Montgomerie, Wills	R-R	6-3	205	6-2-95	0	0	0.00	3	0	0	0	3	0	0	0	0	0	6	.000	.000	.000	18.00	0.00
Nealy, Colby	R-R	6-5	185	3-8-96	2	1	0.47	13	0	0	2	19	9	2	1	0	4	18	.139	.182	.116	8.38	1.86
Nunez, Mateo	R-R	6-5	220	6-11-97	0	1	7.20	4	1	0	1	5	4	6	4	1	5	3	.200	.100	.300	5.40	9.00
Oaks, Trevor	R-R	6-3	220	3-26-93	0	0	0.00	1	1	0	0	2	0	0	0	0	0	3	.000	.000	.000	13.50	0.00
Osuna, Lenix	R-R	6-1	220	11-11-95	0	0	15.43	2	1	0	0	5	8	8	8	0	5	3	.421	.800	.286	5.79	9.64
Ottesen, Riley	R-R	6-1	185	10-30-94	0	1	2.25	8	6	0	0	16	9	4	4	2	2	16	.161	.125	.175	9.00	1.13

Pasen, Luis	R-R	6-0	175	1-14-95	0	0	2.42	16	0	0	4	22	15	7	6	2	10	34	.177	.211	.149	13.70	4.03
Pop, Zach	R-R	6-4	220	9-20-96	0	0	0.00	5	0	0	0	5	2	0	0	0	2	5	.125	.000	.222	9.00	3.60
Richert, Riley	R-R	6-3	200	1-28-97	0	0	3.38	2	0	0	0	3	0	1	1	0	1	2	.000	.000	.000	6.75	3.38
Ruibal, Evy	R-R	6-4	232	9-29-95	1	0	0.00	6	0	0	0	7	3	1	0	0	0	7	.125	.000	.188	9.45	0.00
Soto, Willian	R-R	6-4	185	2-13-96	0	1	6.14	5	3	0	0	7	11	5	5	1	4	8	.379	.500	.333	9.82	4.91
Tavarez, Alfredo	R-R	6-5	190	11-27-97	4	3	3.52	9	1	0	0	31	18	12	12	5	10	47	.170	.239	.117	13.79	2.93
Toribio, Joel	R-R	6-6	180	6-11-94	1	0	6.43	5	0	0	0	7	6	5	5	2	5	9	.240	.333	.154	11.57	6.43
Vargas, Jesus	R-R	6-2	175	8-18-98	4	3	3.38	14	11	0	0	59	51	30	22	6	9	49	.227	.189	.252	7.52	1.38
Washington, Mark	R-R	6-7	205	3-22-96	1	2	1.96	8	3	0	0	23	23	7	5	1	3	25	.256	.333	.222	9.78	1.17
White, Mitchell	R-R	6-4	207	12-28-94	0	0	0.00	3	3	0	0	7	2	1	0	0	2	8	.091	.111	.077	10.29	2.57
Witt, Nathan	R-R	6-4	210	4-19-96	1	0	1.80	5	0	0	0	5	5	1	1	0	1	3	.263	.000	.333	5.40	1.80
Zabala, Aneurys	R-R	6-2	175	12-21-96	3	1	6.00	10	0	0	0	15	19	14	10	1	10	12	.307	.333	.290	7.20	6.00

Fielding

C: Camargo 26, Roberts 16, Rodriguez 11, Rubi 8, Sawyer 3. **1B:** Amon 17, Meza 23, Ortiz 6, Peterson 6, Roberts 1, Rubi 14, Sawyer 1, Segedin 1, Souffront 6. **2B:** Ahmed 1, Amaya 7, Arocho 28, Brito 2, Chiu 19, Grand Pre 5, Jackson 1, Peterson 2, Souffront 3. **3B:** Amaya 1, Brito 1, Camargo 1, Chiu 21, Grand Pre 5, Ortiz 3, Peterson 3, Segedin 1, Souffront 31. **SS:** Ahmed 2, Amaya 25, Arocho 11, Arruebarrena 8, Brito 7, Chiu 1, Grand Pre 6, Jackson 1, Ortiz 4, Souffront 3. **OF:** Albert 15, Amon 24, Aponte 41, Casey 4, Garlick 3, Heredia 6, Ortiz 1, Osorio 39, Padilla 5, Peterson 7, Roller 43, Rubi 1.

DOMINICAN SUMMER LEAGUE

LEAGUE

Batting	B-T	HT	WT	DOB	AVG	vLH	vRH	G	AB	R	H	2B	3B	HR	RBI	BB	HBP	SH	SF	SO	SB	CS	SLG	OBP
Alcantara, Ismael	R-R	6-1	165	9-25-98	.267	.297	.261	64	221	38	59	6	6	1	26	31	7	1	2	55	18	8	.362	.372
Alvarez, Oscar	R-R	5-9	145	6-20-00	.156	.095	.186	19	64	5	10	2	0	0	5	4	1	0	1	12	1	0	.188	.214
Arias, Christopher	L-L	6-2	175	5-1-99	.164	.136	.171	39	110	21	18	2	2	2	8	23	5	0	1	38	3	2	.273	.331
Asencio, Luis	R-R	6-2	160	9-4-97	.111	.000	.141	34	81	10	9	0	1	0	6	6	1	0	1	25	4	0	.136	.180
Bastardo, Kiumel	R-R	6-0	180	1-12-00	.236	.095	.324	15	55	7	13	2	1	0	5	3	1	1	0	11	4	1	.309	.288
Bentura, Railison	R-R	5-10	155	1-16-00	.186	.185	.187	31	102	16	19	2	0	0	8	16	5	1	3	27	6	4	.206	.318
Betancourt, Kenneth	B-R	5-8	160	2-5-00	.255	.173	.282	65	208	28	53	9	3	1	23	26	1	5	2	27	19	6	.341	.338
Calderon, Jhoan	R-R	6-3	200	9-14-97	.234	.263	.224	32	77	14	18	7	0	2	12	9	3	1	0	40	6	2	.403	.337
Chalo, Wladimir	R-R	5-8	170	4-21-00	.243	.286	.236	33	103	13	25	2	0	0	8	7	1	1	0	21	0	0	.262	.297
Diaz, Luis Carlos	R-R	6-1	155	12-19-99	.172	.082	.201	64	198	32	34	7	1	0	31	44	11	0	7	36	7	8	.217	.342
Diaz, Luis Yanel	R-R	5-11	170	9-9-99	.236	.282	.225	60	212	29	50	12	5	2	29	15	5	0	1	64	7	5	.368	.300
Espinoza, Aldo	R-R	6-0	148	9-11-98	.373	.375	.371	16	51	6	19	2	2	0	7	5	2	0	0	7	3	0	.490	.448
Gonzalez, Bryan	R-R	5-9	180	12-6-99	.227	.154	.242	27	75	11	17	5	0	1	11	6	4	0	1	18	1	0	.333	.314
Hernandez, Marco	R-R	6-2	170	6-22-98	.279	.291	.275	63	208	35	58	12	1	2	19	26	13	1	2	22	4	10	.375	.390
Lao, Sauryn	R-R	6-2	182	8-14-99	.303	.286	.309	64	221	40	67	16	1	2	36	23	5	0	6	41	19	5	.412	.373
Lebron, Rolando	R-R	5-9	170	5-10-98	.343	.368	.339	50	143	34	49	8	2	3	24	15	8	1	0	33	12	6	.490	.434
Loaisiga, Mike	B-R	5-11	167	8-29-99	.196	.177	.200	38	112	14	22	1	3	0	15	18	2	0	0	21	2	1	.259	.318
Lozada, Jose	R-R	6-0	170	9-27-99	.187	.074	.225	43	107	19	20	5	0	0	8	18	9	2	0	23	4	3	.234	.351
Martinez, Hector	R-R	6-0	135	8-22-00	.171	.130	.180	40	140	17	24	7	3	0	18	15	7	0	1	23	1	3	.264	.282
Mateo, Edwin	L-L	5-9	160	11-18-98	.220	.167	.235	59	214	30	47	4	3	2	19	30	4	0	1	44	13	10	.294	.325
Mendoza, Cesar	R-R	5-11	175	2-28-97	.169	.118	.188	27	65	7	11	3	0	0	8	17	2	0	3	20	3	1	.215	.345
Perez, Jaime	R-R	6-1	178	4-5-00	.207	.364	.172	44	121	21	25	4	2	2	9	17	4	0	1	47	7	5	.322	.322
Pineda, Maikel	R-R	6-1	175	10-19-96	.236	.129	.256	60	199	23	47	12	2	1	33	25	3	2	3	34	4	5	.332	.326
Ramones, Gervin	R-R	6-2	180	5-15-99	.200	.125	.225	24	65	8	13	2	0	0	10	6	6	1	1	9	1	1	.231	.321
Rodriguez, Luis	B-R	6-0	150	3-2-99	.255	.167	.270	51	165	30	42	7	0	1	17	32	4	0	3	32	12	4	.315	.382
Romero, Mervin	B-R	5-11	138	8-7-99	.133	.143	.130	53	173	24	23	8	1	0	12	24	1	3	2	41	6	7	.191	.240
Sanchez, Frank	R-R	6-3	170	8-25-98	.256	.344	.234	49	160	23	41	10	2	2	17	15	2	0	3	36	8	8	.381	.322
Sarduy, Angel	L-L	5-10	160	11-5-96	.180	.214	.174	43	100	23	18	4	2	1	11	19	3	0	1	20	4	2	.290	.325
Suarez, Albert	L-R	5-11	150	11-30-99	.211	.083	.239	53	199	22	42	6	3	1	25	22	1	1	2	24	5	8	.286	.290
Valera, Leonel	R-R	6-1	165	7-9-99	.317	.367	.299	56	186	36	59	14	5	1	25	25	3	1	1	42	13	6	.462	.405
Vargas, Imanol	L-R	6-3	185	6-29-98	.211	.063	.255	25	71	15	15	5	0	2	11	16	2	0	0	25	2	3	.366	.371
Zabala, Juan	R-R	5-10	170	7-3-99	.242	.111	.269	51	161	31	39	7	2	0	11	36	7	0	0	21	6	4	.311	.402

Pitching	B-T	HT	WT	DOB	W	L	ERA	G	GS	CG	SV	IP	H	R	ER	HR	BB	SO	AVG	vLH	vRH	K/9	BB/9
Acosta, Aldry	R-R	6-4	200	9-7-99	3	1	1.26	14	14	0	0	57	37	10	8	0	10	48	.187	.261	.147	7.58	1.58
Alejo, Carlos	R-R	6-1	165	8-23-99	3	1	3.48	22	0	0	1	31	31	15	12	0	21	27	.265	.286	.253	7.84	6.10
Blanco, Leowis	R-R	5-11	190	3-20-95	1	2	5.03	16	0	0	2	20	22	14	11	1	17	15	.301	.222	.348	6.86	7.78
Cabrera, Luis	R-R	6-0	160	12-29-99	0	1	0.00	2	0	0	0	1	1	3	0	0	2	1	.200	.000	.333	9.00	18.00
Carrillo, Gerardo	R-R	6-0	154	9-13-98	5	2	2.79	14	10	0	0	48	44	18	15	1	14	32	.237	.319	.184	5.96	2.61
Castillo, Bryan	R-R	6-3	185	1-18-99	2	1	2.51	8	0	0	0	14	7	5	4	0	10	14	.143	.211	.100	8.79	6.28
Castro, Jeronimo	R-R	6-4	200	9-3-96	7	2	2.45	19	0	0	3	40	26	13	11	0	19	39	.191	.311	.132	8.70	4.24
Contreras, Nelfri	L-L	6-0	177	12-25-98	5	2	3.83	14	3	0	1	40	25	22	17	1	26	36	.184	.107	.204	8.10	5.85
Cuello, Edward	R-R	6-0	170	10-20-98	2	2	2.40	13	8	0	0	45	43	18	12	0	4	23	.250	.197	.283	4.60	0.80
De La Paz, Franklin	L-L	6-2	190	3-29-99	0	1	2.96	16	0	0	0	24	21	12	8	0	12	12	.253	.250	.254	4.44	4.44
De Paula, Reinaldo	R-R	5-11	17710-20-980		04.91		8	0	0	0	7	3	6	4	0	11	8	.130	.000	.000	9.82	13.50	
Gonzalez, Juan	R-R	6-0	165	6-24-00	3	2	2.49	14	4	0	1	43	32	19	12	2	12	30	.212	.226	.202	6.23	2.49
Hernandez, Antonio	L-L	5-8	187	9-27-99	4	2	2.40	12	9	1	0	49	41	13	13	1	6	33	.227	.159	.248	6.10	1.11
Hernandez, Jose	L-L	6-3	170	12-31-97	6	2	2.52	15	14	1	0	64	53	24	18	1	24	55	.226	.290	.213	7.69	3.36
Hernandez, Ricardo	R-R	6-1	205	2-4-98	6	1	2.13	19	2	0	2	38	27	10	9	0	7	30	.200	.000	.200	7.11	1.66
Inoa, Confesor	R-R	6-2	210	2-21-96	1	0	2.25	6	0	0	2	8	5	3	2	0	4	10	.179	.111	.250	11.25	4.50
Lantigua, Dawlyn	R-R	5-11	165	7-28-98	3	1	4.05	14	0	0	0	27	28	17	12	4	6	18	.286	.257	.302	6.08	2.03
Lara, Breidy	R-R	6-4	180	3-16-99	1	2	4.56	14	2	0	0	26	18	19	13	3	21	20	.194	.171	.207	7.01	7.36
Marcan, Enmanuel	R-R	6-1	185	12-4-98	4	1	4.96	13	5	0	0	33	39	20	18	1	12	20	.305	.298	.309	5.51	3.31

Martinez, Jose	R-R	6-0	175	4-23-99	2	3	2.56	13	11	0	0	53	54	18	15	1	8	30	.260	.237	.273	5.13	1.37
Mena, Johan	R-R	6-5	185	3-1-98	0	0	7.88	10	2	0	0	16	14	17	14	1	16	11	.246	.235	.250	6.19	9.00
Morillo, Juan	R-R	6-1	150	3-19-99	2	3	3.42	14	12	0	1	47	35	20	18	0	19	50	.201	.188	.209	9.51	3.61
Montilla, Carlos	R-R	5-11	165	7-24-99	3	2	3.94	14	6	0	1	48	47	27	21	7	12	44	.260	.233	.273	8.25	2.25
Navarro, Orlandy	R-R	6-2	175	6-3-99	3	0	0.87	13	11	0	0	52	43	10	5	0	15	51	.231	.290	.191	8.83	2.60
Nunez, Mateo	R-R	6-5	220	6-11-97	2	2	2.33	10	2	0	0	27	19	8	7	1	9	25	.198	.324	.129	8.33	3.00
Ortiz, Robinson	L-L	6-0	180	1-4-00	2	2	3.13	11	11	0	0	37	33	15	13	0	5	35	.229	.219	.232	8.44	1.21
Parra, Ronald	L-L	6-1	160	11-5-98	4	1	3.48	19	0	0	0	34	34	18	13	0	16	21	.270	.176	.287	5.61	4.28
Pasen, Luis	R-R	6-0	175	1-14-95	0	0	0.00	7	0	0	3	10	4	3	0	0	5	12	.121	.143	.105	10.45	4.35
Polanco, Oliver	R-R	6-2	180	3-3-96	1	0	2.84	12	0	0	1	19	14	11	6	1	13	12	.209	.304	.159	5.68	6.16
Puello, Yariel	R-R	6-4	200	8-29-97	0	1	3.18	2	0	0	0	6	8	2	2	0	3	5	.348	.400	.333	7.94	4.76
Rabsatt, Maykel	R-R	6-3	180	11-14-98	1	0	4.26	11	0	0	0	13	8	7	6	0	12	16	.186	.278	.120	11.37	8.53
Ramirez, Adolfo	R-R	6-0	165	6-1-99	2	1	0.79	17	4	0	6	34	23	6	3	0	8	33	.187	.188	.187	8.74	2.12
Rodulfo, Jose	R-R	6-0	165	8-20-00	3	2	3.21	14	13	0	0	56	50	27	20	2	15	42	.237	.275	.214	6.75	2.41
Romero, Jonny	R-R	6-2	170	3-5-99	1	0	0.79	9	0	0	1	11	9	5	1	0	8	5	.214	.429	.167	3.97	6.35
Serrano, Elio	R-R	5-11	160	8-2-98	3	4	2.67	23	0	0	7	30	26	10	9	0	8	37	.222	.279	.189	10.98	2.37
Tales, Raul	L-L	5-10	155	9-3-98	1	1	8.44	8	0	0	0	11	12	14	10	1	11	6	.279	.143	.306	5.06	9.28
Urbina, Andres	R-R	6-1	175	3-29-96	1	1	5.67	18	0	0	2	27	18	21	17	1	23	19	.186	.184	.192	6.33	7.67
Valdez, Joan	R-R	6-4	175	3-10-99	3	2	1.10	20	0	0	3	33	19	8	4	0	11	20	.192	.273	.152	5.51	3.03
Valenzuela, Ronald	R-R	6-0	190	3-8-97	1	1	1.80	16	0	0	2	20	21	8	4	0	15	18	.276	.200	.326	8.10	6.75

Fielding

C: Alvarez 10, Chalo 12, Gonzalez 20, Hernandez 26, Mendoza 21, Ramones 23, Zabala 47. **1B:** Alvarez 3, Asencio 10, Chalo 7, Gonzalez 1, Hernandez 26, Lao 37, Loaisiga 6, Mendoza 3, Pineda 51, Ramones 1, Sanchez 12, Sarduy 1. **2B:** Asencio 15, Bentura 13, Betancourt 12, Chalo 3, Espinoza 12, Loaisiga 15, Martinez 18, Pineda 7, Rodriguez 27, Romero 26, Suarez 7, Valera 1. **3B:** Asencio 4, Betancourt 37, Diaz 55, Lao 21, Loaisiga 16, Pineda 2, Rodriguez 5, Valera 15. **SS:** Betancourt 17, Diaz 2, Loaisiga 2, Martinez 12, Rodriguez 20, Romero 23, Suarez 37, Valera 36. OF: Alcantara 60, Arias 25, Asencio 5, Bastardo 13, Calderon 24, Chalo 1, Diaz 60, Lebron 48, Lozada 40, Mateo 56, Perez 39, Sanchez 33, Sarduy 30, Vargas 23.

Miami Marlins

SEASON IN A SENTENCE: Life without Jose Fernandez was a lot less fun for the Marlins, who contended for a National League wild card deep into August before fading in September in Jeffrey Loria's final season as owner. He did get to celebrate the All-Star Game at Marlins Park and a spectacular season by Giancarlo Stanton.

HIGH POINT: The Marlins went 17-12 in August to get into the playoff race, with Stanton carrying the team. He hit 18 homers that month—including a six-game streak with a home run—en route to 59 for the season, the most by any major leaguer since Barry Bonds' record-setting 73 in 2001. Stanton's final homer was his second-longest of the season at 473 feet.

LOW POINT: On Aug. 27, the Marlins were three games over .500. They lost 16 of their next 18 thereafter to fall out of the wild-card race, including a stretch with four walk-off losses in five games to the Braves (thrice) and Phillies, two of them in extra innings.

NOTABLE ROOKIES: Adeiny Hechavarria was injured and later traded, leaving playing time at shortstop that J.T. Riddle helped fill. He'd only played 15 games at Triple-A prior to his promotion. Lefthander Jarlin Garcia shifted into a relief specialist role and led the team with 68 appearances. Righty Drew Steckenrider struck out 14 batters per nine innings in 37 games, which could propel him into the closer role for 2018.

KEY TRANSACTIONS: The Marlins traded closer A.J. Ramos in late July to the Mets, which didn't preclude them from making a playoff run and adding prospect righthander Merandy Gonzalez. The biggest transaction was the sale of the team, for a reported $1.2 billion, in August to a group led by Derek Jeter and Bruce Sherman. Jeter will be running the front office and already had started making significant changes, letting go of assistant general manager Mike Berger and farm director Marc DelPiano, among others. More changes were expected throughout the offseason.

DOWN ON THE FARM: While Triple-A New Orleans struggled mightily (55-83), the rest of the system performed better than the 2016 season, though the Marlins still have a bottom-five farm system. The biggest news in the system was new nicknames for affiliates in New Orleans, now known as the Baby Cakes, and the Double-A Jacksonville Jumbo Shrimp. Jacksonville and low Class A Greensboro made their league playoffs.

OPENING DAY PAYROLL: $111,881,100 (20th)

PLAYERS OF THE YEAR

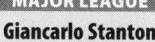

MAJOR LEAGUE

Giancarlo Stanton
OF

.281/.376/.631
59 HR, 132 RBIs
led NL in SLG (.631)

MINOR LEAGUE

Brian Anderson
3B

(Double-A/Triple-A)
.275/.361/.492
22 HR, 81 RBIs

ORGANIZATION LEADERS

BATTING			*Minimum 250 AB
MAJORS			
*	AVG	Marcell Ozuna	.312
*	OPS	Giancarlo Stanton	1.007
	HR	Giancarlo Stanton	59
	RBI	Giancarlo Stanton	132
MINORS			
*	AVG	James Nelson, Greensboro	.309
*	OBP	John Norwood, Jacksonville	.367
*	SLG	Brian Anderson, Jacksonville, New Orleans	.492
*	OPS	Brian Anderson, Jacksonville, New Orleans	.853
	R	Brian Anderson, Jacksonville, New Orleans	74
	H	John Norwood, Jacksonville	135
	TB	John Norwood, Jacksonville	217
	2B	Colby Lusignan, Greensboro, Jupiter	31
		James Nelson, Greensboro	31
	3B	Aaron Knapp, Greensboro	6
		Justin Twine, Greensboro, Jupiter	6
		Yefri Perez, Jacksonville	6
	HR	Brian Anderson, Jacksonville, New Orleans	22
	RBI	Brian Anderson, Jacksonville, New Orleans	81
	BB	Aaron Knapp, Greensboro	59
		John Norwood, Jacksonville	59
	SO	Colby Lusignan, Greensboro, Jupiter	165
	SB	Aaron Knapp, Greensboro	34

PITCHING			#Minimum 75 IP
MAJORS			
	W	Jose Urena	14
#	ERA	Jose Urena	3.82
	SO	Dan Straily	170
	SV	A.J. Ramos	20
MINORS			
	W	Matt Tomshaw, Jacksonville	13
	L	Trevor Richards, Jupiter, Jacksonville	11
		Scott Copeland, New Orleans	11
#	ERA	Michael Mertz, Greensboro	1.80
	G	Tyler Kinley, Jupiter, Jacksonville	50
	GS	Matt Tomshaw, Jacksonville	27
	SV	Tyler Kinley, Jupiter, Jacksonville	17
	IP	Matt Tomshaw, Jacksonville	163
	BB	Scott Copeland, New Orleans	53
	SO	Trevor Richards, Jupiter, Jacksonville	158
#	AVG	Michael Mertz, Greensboro	.184

2017 PERFORMANCE

President, Baseball Ops: Michael Hill. **Farm Director:** Marc DelPiano. **Scouting Director:** Stan Meek.

Class	Team	League	W	L	PCT	Finish	Manager
Majors	Miami Marlins	National	77	85	.475	8th (15)	Don Mattingly
Triple-A	New Orleans Baby Cakes	Pacific Coast	55	83	.399	15th (16)	Arnie Beyeler
Double-A	Jacksonville Jumbo Shrimp	Southern	69	71	.493	7th (10)	Randy Ready
High-A	Jupiter Hammerheads	Florida State	67	68	.496	7th (12)	Kevin Randel
Low-A	Greensboro Grasshoppers	South Atlantic	75	61	.551	2nd (14)	Todd Pratt
Short Season	Batavia Muckdogs	New York-Penn	30	45	.4	t-12th (14)	Mike Jacobs
Rookie	GCL Marlins	Gulf Coast	32	23	.582	5th (17)	John Pachot
Overall 2017 Minor League Record			328	351	.483	21st (30)	

MIAMI MARLINS

ORGANIZATION STATISTICS

MIAMI MARLINS

NATIONAL LEAGUE

Batting	B-T	HT	WT	DOB	AVG	vLH	vRH	G	AB	R	H	2B	3B	HR	RBI	BB	HBP	SH	SF	SO	SB	CS	SLG	OBP
Anderson, Brian	R-R	6-3	185	5-19-93	.262	.241	.273	25	84	11	22	7	1	0	8	10	0	0	1	28	0	0	.369	.337
Aviles, Mike	R-R	5-10	205	3-13-81	.233	.258	.218	37	86	5	20	2	0	1	8	6	2	3	0	15	0	0	.291	.298
Bour, Justin	L-R	6-3	265	5-28-88	.289	.253	.300	108	377	52	109	18	0	25	83	47	1	0	4	95	1	0	.536	.366
Colon, Christian	R-R	5-10	185	5-14-89	.152	.188	.118	17	33	3	5	1	0	0	0	4	0	1	0	7	0	0	.182	.243
Dietrich, Derek	L-R	6-0	205	7-18-89	.249	.307	.236	135	406	56	101	22	5	13	53	36	18	0	4	98	0	1	.424	.334
Ellis, A.J.	R-R	6-2	225	4-9-81	.210	.154	.231	51	143	17	30	5	0	6	14	12	6	2	0	29	0	0	.371	.298
Gordon, Dee	L-R	5-11	170	4-22-88	.308	.293	.314	158	653	114	201	20	9	2	33	25	10	2	4	93	60	16	.375	.341
Hechavarria, Adeiny	R-R	6-0	195	4-15-89	.277	.500	.226	20	65	8	18	2	1	1	6	1	0	1	0	9	0	0	.385	.288
Lombardozzi, Steve	R-B	6-0	195	9-20-88	.000	.000	.000	2	8	0	0	0	0	0	0	0	0	0	0	2	0	0	.000	.000
Moore, Tyler	R-R	6-2	220	1-30-87	.230	.192	.254	104	187	17	43	14	0	6	30	10	1	1	4	56	0	0	.401	.267
Ozuna, Marcell	R-R	6-1	225	11-12-90	.312	.305	.313	159	613	93	191	30	2	37	124	64	0	0	2	144	1	3	.548	.376
Prado, Martin	R-R	6-0	215	10-27-83	.250	.290	.239	37	140	13	35	9	0	2	12	6	0	0	1	22	0	0	.357	.279
Realmuto, J.T.	R-R	6-1	210	3-18-91	.278	.283	.277	141	532	68	148	31	5	17	65	36	8	0	3	106	8	2	.451	.332
Riddle, JT	L-R	6-1	180	10-12-91	.250	.262	.246	70	228	20	57	13	1	3	31	12	0	2	5	50	0	2	.355	.282
Rojas, Miguel	R-R	5-11	195	2-24-89	.290	.257	.303	90	272	37	79	16	2	1	26	27	4	1	2	32	2	1	.375	.361
Stanton, Giancarlo	R-R	6-6	245	11-8-89	.281	.323	.270	159	597	123	168	32	0	59	132	85	7	0	3	163	2	2	.632	.376
Suzuki, Ichiro	R-L	5-11	175	10-22-73	.255	.340	.228	136	196	19	50	6	0	3	20	17	1	1	0	35	1	1	.332	.318
Telis, Tomas	B-R	5-8	220	6-18-91	.240	.130	.272	48	104	13	25	5	3	0	9	3	3	0	1	10	0	0	.346	.279
Yelich, Christian	L-R	6-3	195	12-5-91	.282	.266	.288	156	602	100	170	36	2	18	81	80	6	0	6	137	16	2	.439	.369

Pitching	B-T	HT	WT	DOB	W	L	ERA	G	GS	CG	SV	IP	H	R	ER	HR	BB	SO	AVG	vLH	vRH	K/9	BB/9
Barraclough, Kyle	R-R	6-3	225	5-23-90	6	2	3.00	66	0	0	1	66	53	25	22	5	38	76	.222	.184	.263	10.36	5.18
Cervenka, Hunter	L-L	6-1	245	1-3-90	0	0	15.43	5	0	0	0	5	1	8	8	0	8	6	.083	.200	.000	11.57	15.43
Chen, Wei-Yin	R-L	6-0	200	7-21-85	2	1	3.82	9	5	0	0	33	25	14	14	3	9	25	.207	.212	.205	6.82	2.45
Conley, Adam	L-L	6-3	200	5-24-90	8	8	6.14	22	20	0	0	103	114	74	70	19	42	72	.283	.265	.289	6.31	3.68
Despaigne, Odrisamer	R-R	6-0	200	4-4-87	2	3	4.01	18	8	0	1	58	57	31	26	3	24	31	.256	.306	.196	4.78	3.70
Ellington, Brian	R-R	6-3	215	8-4-90	1	1	7.25	42	0	0	0	45	48	39	36	7	35	48	.270	.259	.280	9.67	7.05
Garcia, Jarlin	L-L	6-3	215	1-18-93	1	2	4.73	68	0	0	0	53	47	29	28	6	17	42	.235	.202	.267	7.09	2.87
Guerra, Javy	R-R	6-1	225	10-31-85	1	1	3.00	16	0	0	0	21	23	8	7	2	7	12	.288	.297	.279	5.14	3.00
Koehler, Tom	R-R	6-3	235	6-29-86	1	5	7.92	12	12	0	0	56	67	50	49	15	29	44	.302	.347	.266	7.11	4.69
Locke, Jeff	L-L	6-0	200	11-20-87	0	5	8.16	7	7	0	0	32	42	30	29	4	15	26	.311	.313	.311	7.31	4.22
McGowan, Dustin	R-R	6-3	235	3-24-82	8	2	4.75	63	0	0	0	78	77	42	41	13	27	64	.262	.281	.249	7.42	3.13
Nicolino, Justin	L-L	6-3	195	11-22-91	2	3	5.06	20	8	0	0	48	66	33	27	8	20	26	.324	.397	.295	4.88	3.75
O'Grady, Chris	R-L	6-4	225	4-17-90	2	1	4.36	13	6	0	0	33	33	16	16	4	18	30	.268	.167	.333	8.18	4.91
Peters, Dillon	L-L	5-9	195	8-31-92	1	2	5.17	6	6	0	0	31	32	18	18	3	19	27	.271	.423	.228	7.76	5.46
Phelps, David	R-R	6-2	200	10-9-86	2	4	3.45	44	0	0	0	47	42	20	18	5	21	51	.243	.258	.225	9.77	4.02
Ramos, AJ	R-R	5-10	200	9-20-86	2	4	3.63	40	0	0	20	40	30	17	16	4	22	47	.206	.173	.239	10.66	4.99
2-team total (21 New York)					2	4	3.99	61	0	0	27	59	49	27	26	7	34	72	.223	.238	.281	11.05	5.22
Steckenrider, Drew	R-R	6-5	215	1-10-91	1	1	2.34	37	0	0	1	35	30	13	9	4	18	54	.227	.260	.207	14.02	4.67
Straily, Dan	R-R	6-2	220	12-1-88	10	9	4.26	33	33	0	0	182	176	90	86	31	60	170	.256	.250	.263	8.42	2.97
Tazawa, Junichi	R-R	5-11	200	6-6-86	3	5	5.69	55	0	0	0	55	55	35	35	8	22	38	.261	.248	.274	6.18	3.58
Urena, Jose	R-R	6-2	200	9-12-91	14	7	3.82	34	28	0	0	170	152	77	72	26	64	113	.238	.241	.236	5.99	3.39
Volquez, Edinson	R-R	6-0	220	7-3-83	4	8	4.19	17	17	1	0	92	78	46	43	8	53	81	.236	.266	.203	7.90	5.17
Wittgren, Nick	R-R	6-2	210	5-29-91	3	1	4.68	38	0	0	0	42	46	22	22	5	13	43	.277	.353	.225	9.14	2.76
Worley, Vance	R-R	6-2	250	9-25-87	2	6	6.91	24	12	0	1	72	99	56	55	9	30	50	.339	.333	.345	6.28	3.77
Ziegler, Brad	R-R	6-4	220	10-10-79	1	4	4.79	53	0	0	10	47	57	29	25	1	16	26	.307	.259	.347	4.98	3.06

Fielding

Catcher	PCT	G	PO	A	E	DP	PB
Ellis	1.000	39	267	26	0	2	3
Realmuto	.994	126	929	87	6	11	9
Telis	.955	6	21	0	1	0	0

First Base	PCT	G	PO	A	E	DP
Aviles	1.000	2	2	0	0	0
Bour	.999	102	757	51	1	84
Dietrich	1.000	10	40	1	0	3
Moore	1.000	45	270	21	0	30
Realmuto	1.000	9	79	4	0	7
Rojas	1.000	2	4	0	0	1
Telis	.989	28	162	12	2	17

Second Base	PCT	G	PO	A	E	DP
Aviles	1.000	6	6	19	0	5
Colon	1.000	4	3	10	0	2

	PCT	G	PO	A	E	DP
Dietrich	1.000	10	13	21	0	5
Gordon	.982	153	266	390	12	96
Lombardozzi	1.000	2	6	4	0	1
Rojas	1.000	2	4	3	0	0

Third Base	PCT	G	PO	A	E	DP
Anderson	.944	25	20	31	3	2
Aviles	1.000	6	0	7	0	0
Colon	1.000	10	5	10	0	2
Dietrich	.957	103	55	144	9	19
Prado	.977	34	22	63	2	6
Rojas	1.000	15	2	9	0	0

Shortstop	PCT	G	PO	A	E	DP
Aviles	1.000	15	14	35	0	8
Gordon	1.000	3	1	7	0	1
Hechavarria	1.000	19	30	34	0	10
Riddle	.970	69	81	177	8	33
Rojas	.969	77	118	192	10	57

Outfield	PCT	G	PO	A	E	DP
Aviles	.000	1	0	0	0	0
Dietrich	1.000	5	3	0	0	0
Moore	1.000	13	3	0	0	0
Ozuna	.985	153	314	10	5	0
Stanton	.988	149	320	9	4	1
Suzuki	1.000	33	64	1	0	1
Yelich	.997	155	370	1	1	0

NEW ORLEANS BABY CAKES — *TRIPLE-A*

PACIFIC COAST LEAGUE

Batting	B-T	HT	WT	DOB	AVG	vLH	vRH	G	AB	R	H	2B	3B	HR	RBI	BB	HBP	SH	SF	SO	SB	CS	SLG	OBP
Anderson, Brian	R-R	6-3	185	5-19-93	.339	.474	.313	33	118	21	40	7	0	8	26	12	5	0	2	27	0	1	.602	.416
Arrojo, Junior	R-R	5-10	195	5-29-88	.250	.333	.167	3	12	1	3	1	0	0	2	1	0	1	0	2	0	0	.333	.308
Aviles, Mike	R-R	5-10	205	3-13-81	.292	.172	.315	55	178	22	52	8	2	1	24	10	1	3	4	24	1	2	.376	.326
Barnes, Brandon	R-R	6-2	210	5-15-86	.276	.325	.264	109	410	55	113	22	2	11	49	31	5	1	4	114	15	6	.420	.331
Cabrera, Ramon	B-R	5-8	195	11-5-89	.217	.189	.224	58	198	19	43	10	1	5	23	14	3	0	1	34	1	1	.354	.278
Colon, Christian	R-R	5-10	185	5-14-89	.302	.400	.277	49	149	17	45	8	0	1	13	16	3	8	1	26	6	3	.376	.379
den Dekker, Matt	L-L	6-2	210	8-10-87	.247	.200	.254	20	77	9	19	7	1	3	13	3	1	0	1	20	2	1	.481	.281
Elmore, Jake	R-R	5-10	180	6-15-87	.269	.333	.261	16	52	6	14	3	0	0	5	6	0	1	0	5	1	1	.327	.345
Galloway, Isaac	R-R	6-2	205	10-10-89	.280	.286	.279	26	75	12	21	0	0	7	16	7	1	0	0	21	5	0	.560	.349
Green, Grant	R-R	6-3	180	9-27-87	.304	.000	.326	14	46	4	14	1	0	0	8	3	0	0	1	9	1	1	.326	.340
Hinshaw, Chad	R-R	6-1	205	9-10-90	.229	.205	.234	81	258	32	59	15	1	4	24	26	4	4	0	75	6	3	.341	.309
Hood, Destin	R-R	6-2	205	4-3-90	.260	.136	.291	62	219	36	57	8	1	14	41	31	0	0	2	66	5	1	.498	.349
Jackson, Ryan	R-R	6-2	180	5-10-88	.262	.444	.212	14	42	4	11	0	0	0	4	8	0	0	0	9	0	0	.262	.380
2-team total (15 Tacoma)					.244	.100	.263	29	90	7	22	2	0	0	10	12	1	0	0	20	0	1	.267	.340
Juengel, Matt	R-R	6-2	185	1-13-90	.250	.257	.249	59	200	22	50	13	2	5	22	13	2	0	1	35	1	1	.410	.301
Kjerstad, Dexter	R-R	6-1	210	1-19-92	.000	.000	.000	3	6	0	0	0	0	0	0	0	0	0	0	2	0	0	.000	.000
Lombardozzi, Steve	R-B	6-0	195	9-20-88	.274	.213	.288	103	401	53	110	16	2	2	18	38	1	3	2	60	13	6	.339	.337
Mooney, Peter	L-R	5-6	155	8-19-90	.213	.200	.217	116	403	49	86	18	4	4	34	43	1	7	1	62	2	1	.308	.290
Moore, Tyler	R-R	6-2	220	1-30-87	.231	.500	.200	13	39	3	9	2	0	1	7	7	0	0	0	11	0	0	.359	.348
Nola, Austin	R-R	6-0	195	12-28-89	.202	.167	.208	29	89	7	18	4	0	1	6	10	1	4	1	16	0	0	.281	.287
Noonan, Nick	L-R	6-1	185	5-4-89	.156	.308	.125	23	77	13	12	2	0	1	8	8	1	1	1	24	2	0	.221	.241
2-team total (62 Colorado Springs)					.261	.308	.125	85	268	42	70	14	2	3	38	20	1	1	2	55	5	1	.362	.313
Parmelee, Chris	L-L	6-1	220	2-24-88	.273	.222	.292	13	33	5	9	3	0	1	4	13	0	0	1	7	0	0	.455	.468
2-team total (42 Nashville)					.213	.136	.211	55	169	26	36	9	0	6	18	29	0	0	2	53	0	1	.373	.325
Paulino, Carlos	R-R	6-0	175	9-24-89	.217	.375	.170	21	69	5	15	1	1	2	6	4	0	0	0	18	1	0	.348	.260
Perez, Eury	R-R	6-0	190	5-30-90	.375	.412	.368	27	104	15	39	9	1	0	12	5	2	3	1	17	9	3	.481	.411
Riddle, JT	L-R	6-1	180	10-12-91	.286	.111	.315	16	63	9	18	4	1	2	6	1	0	0	0	8	1	0	.476	.297
Serna, KC	R-R	6-0	185	10-15-89	.214	.167	.225	34	89	13	19	5	1	4	16	3	0	1	2	18	0	1	.427	.234
Sierra, Moises	R-R	6-1	220	9-24-88	.294	.284	.296	123	422	52	124	22	3	11	68	39	6	0	1	81	18	3	.438	.361
Telis, Tomas	B-R	5-8	220	6-18-91	.279	.271	.280	73	280	39	78	14	2	5	31	18	3	2	3	29	5	0	.396	.326
Towey, Cal	L-R	6-1	215	2-6-90	.237	.216	.243	76	236	29	56	14	2	4	24	42	7	0	1	73	2	1	.364	.367
Vidal, David	R-R	5-11	185	10-23-89	.200	.333	.164	24	85	9	17	1	0	2	11	6	1	0	0	19	0	0	.282	.261

Pitching	B-T	HT	WT	DOB	W	L	ERA	G	GS	CG	SV	IP	H	R	ER	HR	BB	SO	AVG	vLH	vRH	K/9	BB/9
Beckman, Ryan	R-R	6-4	185	1-2-90	0	0	20.25	3	0	0	0	3	5	7	6	1	3	3	.385	.500	.333	10.13	10.13
Bencomo, Omar	R-R	6-1	170	2-10-89	0	2	6.30	6	4	0	0	20	25	14	14	5	6	18	.325	.325	.324	8.10	2.70
Cervenka, Hunter	L-L	6-1	245	1-3-90	1	4	4.58	44	0	0	0	39	38	23	20	7	26	39	.257	.192	.292	8.92	5.95
Conley, Adam	L-L	6-3	200	5-24-90	3	3	5.49	12	12	0	0	62	69	41	38	7	25	41	.289	.279	.292	5.92	3.61
Copeland, Scott	R-R	6-3	220	12-15-87	9	11	4.97	26	26	0	0	138	158	78	76	20	53	118	.287	.292	.283	7.71	3.46
Cuevas, William	B-R	6-2	215	10-14-90	2	7	5.43	15	11	0	0	60	48	36	36	6	31	47	.224	.217	.231	7.09	4.68
Cunniff, Brandon	R-R	6-0	185	10-7-88	2	3	4.45	36	0	0	3	55	48	31	27	7	28	54	.242	.253	.235	8.89	4.61
Despaigne, Odrisamer	R-R	6-0	200	4-4-87	2	4	3.09	20	10	0	2	70	62	25	24	6	24	49	.243	.276	.212	6.30	3.09
Ellington, Brian	R-R	6-3	215	8-4-90	1	0	2.28	20	0	0	5	24	11	7	6	3	11	36	.136	.100	.157	13.69	4.18
Fife, Stephen	R-R	6-3	225	10-4-86	4	3	3.97	12	12	0	0	66	76	33	29	4	18	52	.293	.386	.221	7.13	2.47
Gonzalez, Severino	R-R	6-2	155	9-28-92	0	3	6.52	13	2	0	3	19	26	18	14	2	5	18	.313	.357	.291	8.38	2.33
Guerra, Javy	R-R	6-1	225	10-31-85	2	4	4.70	35	0	0	2	52	46	29	27	7	21	44	.242	.309	.193	7.66	3.66
Guerrero, Tayron	R-R	6-8	210	1-9-91	3	2	5.87	13	0	0	0	15	12	13	10	2	12	11	.207	.308	.125	6.46	7.04
Kickham, Mike	L-L	6-4	220	12-12-88	3	3	4.28	9	8	0	0	48	55	25	23	5	8	33	.291	.308	.282	6.14	1.49
Koehler, Tom	R-R	6-3	235	6-29-86	1	1	1.67	7	6	0	0	38	30	12	7	4	13	55	.213	.279	.151	13.14	3.11
Lazo, Raudel	L-L	5-9	180	4-12-89	0	2	4.35	8	0	0	0	10	13	5	5	2	2	8	.302	.667	.275	6.97	1.74
Lobstein, Kyle	L-L	6-3	220	8-12-89	0	2	2.21	27	0	0	1	37	31	13	9	3	18	24	.220	.192	.234	5.89	4.42
Marte, Kelvin	R-L	5-9	170	11-24-87	3	5	4.50	32	8	0	2	86	86	53	43	9	42	69	.268	.280	.262	7.22	4.40
Mortensen, Clayton	R-R	6-4	185	4-10-85	4	1	7.80	22	0	0	1	30	29	28	26	4	22	39	.246	.283	.222	11.70	6.60
Nappo, Greg	L-L	5-10	195	8-25-88	0	1	5.91	7	0	0	0	11	11	8	7	2	6	7	.250	.200	.265	5.91	5.06
Nicolino, Justin	L-L	6-3	195	11-22-91	5	5	3.19	14	14	0	0	79	75	34	28	10	24	51	.254	.275	.247	5.81	2.73
O'Grady, Chris	R-L	6-4	225	4-17-90	3	5	3.29	12	9	0	0	55	44	24	20	7	15	54	.219	.245	.210	8.89	2.47
Payano, Victor	L-L	6-5	185	10-17-92	4	3	3.42	28	2	0	0	53	37	21	20	5	32	59	.200	.188	.207	10.08	5.47
Sampson, Keyvius	R-R	6-2	225	1-6-91	1	2	4.95	14	6	0	0	36	29	21	20	4	30	38	.221	.215	.227	9.41	7.43
2-team total (12 Reno)					5	5	5.92	26	15	0	0	79	84	59	52	9	60	84	.272	.262	.351	9.57	6.84
Schlereth, Daniel	L-L	6-0	210	5-9-86	0	1	4.50	6	0	0	1	6	5	3	3	1	3	5	.238	.250	.231	7.50	4.50

Pitching	B-T	HT	WT	DOB	W	L	ERA	G	GS	CG	SV	IP	H	R	ER	HR	BB	SO	AVG	vLH	vRH	K/9	BB/9
Steckenrider, Drew	R-R	6-5	215	1-10-91	0	1	1.62	26	0	0	5	33	18	6	6	3	8	44	.155	.184	.134	11.88	2.16
Tazawa, Junichi	R-R	5-11	200	6-6-86	0	0	0.00	1	0	0	1	1	0	0	0	0	0	1	.000	.000	.000	9.00	0.00
Wittgren, Nick	R-R	6-2	210	5-29-91	0	0	0.00	5	0	0	0	5	3	0	0	0	0	6	.158	.143	.167	10.80	0.00
Worley, Vance	R-R	6-2	250	9-25-87	2	5	4.43	8	8	1	0	45	53	26	22	4	11	22	.305	.382	.245	4.43	2.22

Fielding

Catcher	PCT	G	PO	A	E	DP	PB
Cabrera	.992	47	364	16	3	1	3
Nola	.996	29	220	23	1	4	3
Paulino	.988	20	146	13	2	1	1
Telis	.995	45	344	24	2	2	1

First Base	PCT	G	PO	A	E	DP
Aviles	.962	9	48	2	2	5
Barnes	.962	16	112	15	5	9
den Dekker	1.000	2	14	2	0	3
Green	1.000	10	83	6	0	9
Juengel	1.000	21	169	19	0	16
Moore	.990	11	86	10	1	8
Parmelee	1.000	10	62	3	0	1
Telis	.992	15	119	4	1	12
Towey	.981	53	387	26	8	34

Second Base	PCT	G	PO	A	E	DP
Arrojo	.917	2	5	6	1	3
Aviles	.833	1	1	4	1	1
Colon	.974	16	32	43	2	9
Elmore	1.000	11	15	25	0	6
Jackson	1.000	5	9	11	0	4
Lombardozzi	.983	72	131	167	5	41
Mooney	.978	11	17	27	1	5
Noonan	1.000	5	5	8	0	2
Serna	.857	2	2	4	1	1
Vidal	.979	24	46	46	2	14

Third Base	PCT	G	PO	A	E	DP
Anderson	.939	30	22	55	5	4
Arrojo	.667	1	1	1	1	0
Aviles	.975	24	7	32	1	1
Colon	.973	17	18	18	1	2
Elmore	1.000	3	4	1	0	0
Green	1.000	2	1	2	0	0
Jackson	.909	4	1	9	1	0
Juengel	.927	20	15	36	4	3
Lombardozzi	.930	16	13	27	3	0
Mooney	.857	6	2	10	2	3
Noonan	.939	14	5	26	2	1
Serna	.958	15	6	17	1	1

Shortstop	PCT	G	PO	A	E	DP
Aviles	.938	5	7	8	1	2
Colon	1.000	7	5	8	0	1
Elmore	1.000	2	5	8	0	1
Green	1.000	1	2	4	0	1
Jackson	.933	5	4	10	1	2
Mooney	.970	96	118	272	12	49
Noonan	1.000	5	6	16	0	5
Riddle	.975	16	22	56	2	12
Serna	.971	7	9	25	1	5

Outfield	PCT	G	PO	A	E	DP
Aviles	1.000	9	12	0	0	0
Barnes	.990	89	201	4	2	2
den Dekker	.978	18	43	2	1	2
Elmore	1.000	1	1	1	0	0
Galloway	1.000	21	39	3	0	1
Hinshaw	.992	67	126	3	1	0
Hood	.978	55	86	4	2	0
Juengel	.952	13	18	2	1	0
Kjerstad	1.000	1	1	0	0	0
Lombardozzi	1.000	12	21	0	0	0
Parmelee	1.000	1	1	0	0	0
Perez	.967	25	53	5	2	1
Sierra	.985	103	194	6	3	1
Towey	1.000	18	26	2	0	1

JACKSONVILLE JUMBO SHRIMP — *DOUBLE-A*

SOUTHERN LEAGUE

Batting	B-T	HT	WT	DOB	AVG	vLH	vRH	G	AB	R	H	2B	3B	HR	RBI	BB	HBP	SH	SF	SO	SB	CS	SLG	OBP
Anderson, Brian	R-R	6-3	185	5-19-93	.251	.279	.244	87	311	53	78	14	3	14	55	36	9	0	5	71	1	1	.450	.341
Ard, Taylor	R-R	6-2	230	1-31-90	.215	.314	.184	124	368	36	79	21	0	12	49	31	10	0	4	115	3	1	.370	.291
Arrojo, Junior	R-R	5-10	195	5-29-88	.000	.000	.000	4	9	0	0	0	0	0	0	1	0	0	0	4	0	0	.000	.100
Barrett, Kyle	L-R	5-11	185	8-4-93	.230	.105	.252	48	126	15	29	5	1	0	6	9	1	4	1	33	2	1	.286	.285
Bour, Justin	L-R	6-3	265	5-28-88	.333	—	.333	3	9	1	3	0	0	1	1	0	0	0	0	1	0	0	.667	.333
Cordova, Rehiner	R-B	6-0	150	1-11-94	.133	.000	.143	10	15	1	2	0	0	0	0	3	0	0	0	3	0	0	.133	.278
Dean, Austin	R-R	6-1	190	10-14-93	.282	.304	.275	61	234	29	66	14	4	4	30	14	1	0	2	46	3	1	.427	.323
Diaz, Chris	R-R	5-10	190	11-9-90	.207	.171	.217	55	164	10	34	7	0	0	13	14	4	2	0	34	1	1	.250	.286
Galloway, Isaac	R-R	6-2	205	10-10-89	.405	.500	.389	10	42	4	17	5	0	0	3	6	1	0	0	8	5	2	.524	.490
Geiger, Dustin	R-R	6-2	180	12-2-91	.211	.192	.216	37	114	14	24	3	0	5	17	9	3	0	0	38	0	0	.368	.286
Glenn, Alex	L-L	5-11	180	6-11-91	.179	.200	.175	64	201	14	36	7	3	3	20	17	0	1	1	69	2	1	.289	.242
Hechavarria, Adeiny	R-R	6-0	195	4-15-89	.222	.333	.167	3	9	1	2	0	0	0	0	0	0	0	0	0	1	0	.222	.222
Hoo, Chris	R-R	5-9	190	2-19-92	.350	.429	.308	11	20	0	7	0	0	0	2	3	0	0	0	8	0	0	.350	.435
Lee, Braxton	L-R	5-10	185	8-23-93	.294	.289	.296	60	214	34	63	12	0	1	21	36	3	7	3	48	8	2	.365	.398
2-team total (67 Montgomery)					.309	.271	.339	127	476	81	147	21	3	3	37	65	5	11	4	104	20	13	.385	.395
Maron, Cam	L-R	6-1	195	1-20-91	.270	.278	.269	74	233	24	63	10	1	5	32	35	0	0	2	45	0	0	.386	.363
Nola, Austin	R-R	6-0	195	12-28-89	.250	.333	.234	54	168	21	42	7	0	2	25	25	2	1	1	26	3	2	.327	.352
Norwood, John	R-R	6-1	185	9-24-92	.285	.304	.281	135	473	68	135	17	4	19	62	59	4	0	3	134	4	4	.459	.367
Perez, Yefri	B-R	5-11	170	2-24-91	.169	.231	.148	76	248	31	42	6	6	0	15	37	1	7	0	57	10	4	.242	.280
Pineda, Jeremias	B-R	5-11	190	11-16-90	.229	.235	.228	65	170	20	39	5	5	0	9	19	1	1	0	56	9	2	.318	.311
Prado, Martin	R-R	6-0	215	10-27-83	.400	.500	.333	2	5	0	2	1	0	0	0	0	0	0	0	0	0	0	.600	.400
Rojas, Miguel	R-R	5-11	195	2-24-89	.143	—	.143	2	7	1	1	0	0	0	0	0	1	1	0	1	0	0	.143	.250
Rondon, Cleuluis	B-R	6-0	155	4-13-94	.200	.222	.194	13	40	3	8	3	0	0	1	1	0	2	1	15	1	0	.275	.214
2-team total (38 Birmingham)					.204	.227	.192	51	162	9	33	7	0	0	9	8	0	6	2	43	1	3	.247	.238
Serna, KC	R-R	6-0	185	10-15-89	.251	.346	.217	66	207	22	52	12	1	4	16	18	4	2	2	42	1	3	.377	.320
Towey, Cal	L-R	6-1	215	2-6-90	.177	.174	.179	26	79	9	14	5	0	1	11	13	2	0	1	37	0	0	.279	.305
Vidal, David	R-R	5-11	185	10-23-89	.285	.163	.318	107	376	53	107	26	1	10	41	45	4	5	2	70	1	0	.439	.365
Vigil, Rodrigo	R-R	6-0	165	1-3-93	.306	.300	.308	26	85	6	26	3	0	0	6	4	2	2	0	14	0	0	.341	.352
Yarbrough, Alex	B-R	6-0	200	8-3-91	.231	.161	.244	111	364	32	84	14	5	4	30	32	2	4	4	105	4	0	.330	.294

Pitching	B-T	HT	WT	DOB	W	L	ERA	G	GS	CG	SV	IP	H	R	ER	HR	BB	SO	AVG	vLH	vRH	K/9	BB/9
Adkins, Hunter	R-R	6-4	190	9-20-90	1	2	3.90	15	1	0	2	28	26	16	12	2	17	18	.252	.243	.258	5.86	5.53
2-team total (9 Montgomery)					2	3	4.03	24	6	0	2	58	58	30	26	5	28	37	.264	.310	.253	5.74	4.34
Alonzo, Eric	R-B	6-2	215	8-28-91	0	0	3.86	1	0	0	0	2	1	1	1	1	0	1	.125	.000	.167	3.86	0.00
Ballew, Travis	R-R	6-0	160	5-1-91	0	0	0.00	2	0	0	0	2	1	0	0	0	2	3	.143	.000	.250	13.50	9.00
Beckman, Ryan	R-R	6-4	185	1-2-90	3	0	6.62	15	0	0	3	18	24	13	13	1	15	14	.343	.462	.273	7.13	7.64
Beltre, Andy	R-R	6-4	195	7-6-93	4	0	3.44	28	0	0	0	34	32	16	13	2	15	45	.235	.189	.265	11.91	3.97
Bencomo, Omar	R-R	6-1	170	2-10-89	5	4	4.58	16	14	0	0	73	80	39	37	10	18	74	.278	.200	.330	9.17	2.23
Bremer, Tyler	R-R	6-2	210	12-7-89	0	2	9.00	6	0	0	0	5	6	5	5	0	7	7	.300	.222	.364	12.60	12.60
Buckelew, James	L-L	6-2	155	8-4-91	0	4	3.27	14	1	0	0	33	22	17	12	2	8	28	.183	.220	.165	7.64	2.18
De La Rosa, Esmerling	R-R	6-2	199	5-15-91	2	2	4.33	31	0	0	3	35	33	18	17	4	15	40	.252	.216	.275	10.19	3.82

Del Pozo, Miguel	L-L	6-1	180	10-14-92	1	0	2.25	5	0	0	0	4	3	1	1	0	5	3	.214	.400	.111	6.75	11.25
Garcia, Jarlin	L-L	6-3	215	1-18-93	0	0	0.00	3	0	0	0	4	3	0	0	0	3	2	.231	.667	.100	4.50	6.75
Gonzalez, Severino	R-R	6-2	155	9-28-92	5	5	4.28	31	5	0	3	61	59	32	29	9	12	38	.255	.286	.236	5.61	1.77
Guerrero, Tayron	R-R	6-8	210	1-9-91	0	1	3.38	17	0	0	0	16	14	7	6	3	14	22	.230	.177	.296	12.38	7.88
Gunkel, Joe	R-R	6-5	225	12-30-91	6	10	4.92	24	21	0	0	115	130	71	63	17	21	69	.288	.307	.274	5.38	1.64
Higgins, Tyler	R-R	6-3	215	4-22-91	3	3	3.43	34	1	0	0	60	62	26	23	7	17	47	.277	.258	.289	7.01	2.54
Kickham, Mike	L-L	6-4	220	12-12-88	5	7	3.33	18	17	2	0	97	88	36	36	9	16	86	.239	.304	.210	7.95	1.48
Kinley, Jeff	L-L	6-1	195	2-15-92	0	1	4.85	20	0	0	1	26	30	15	14	2	14	15	.291	.257	.309	5.19	4.85
Kinley, Tyler	R-R	6-4	205	1-31-91	1	2	5.19	27	0	0	8	26	29	19	15	2	16	34	.271	.325	.239	11.77	5.54
Lazo, Raudel	L-L	5-9	180	4-12-89	0	0	19.64	4	0	0	0	4	8	8	8	1	5	2	.444	.250	.500	4.91	12.27
Lobstein, Kyle	L-L	6-3	220	8-12-89	0	1	1.50	3	0	0	0	6	6	4	1	0	4	7	.261	.500	.211	10.50	6.00
Locke, Jeff	L-L	6-0	200	11-20-87	1	0	2.38	2	2	0	0	11	13	3	3	1	2	12	.296	.222	.314	9.53	1.59
Mazza, Chris	R-R	6-4	180	10-17-89	4	7	3.01	28	26	0	0	147	138	56	49	7	41	93	.251	.282	.226	5.71	2.52
Mortensen, Clayton	R-R	6-4	185	4-10-85	2	0	2.14	19	0	0	6	21	10	6	5	2	9	22	.143	.100	.175	9.43	3.86
Nappo, Greg	L-L	5-10	195	8-25-88	0	1	1.50	9	0	0	1	12	10	3	2	1	2	15	.217	.143	.231	11.25	1.50
Needy, James	R-R	6-6	230	3-30-91	0	1	4.50	2	2	0	0	10	10	5	5	1	3	10	.256	.154	.308	9.00	2.70
Payano, Victor	L-L	6-5	185	10-17-92	1	1	3.55	9	0	0	1	13	7	6	5	0	10	21	.156	.250	.121	14.92	7.11
Peters, Dillon	L-L	5-9	195	8-31-92	6	2	1.97	9	9	0	0	46	33	11	10	1	11	40	.200	.059	.237	7.88	2.17
Quijada, Jose	L-L	6-0	175	11-9-95	0	0	9.00	7	0	0	0	8	12	8	8	2	7	6	.333	.111	.407	6.75	7.88
Richards, Trevor	R-R	6-2	190	5-15-93	5	7	2.87	14	14	0	0	75	67	32	24	4	18	77	.231	.195	.258	9.20	2.15
Schlereth, Daniel	L-L	6-0	210	5-9-86	1	1	1.65	25	0	0	4	27	16	7	5	0	12	23	.172	.161	.177	7.57	3.95
Tazawa, Junichi	R-R	5-11	200	6-6-86	0	1	18.00	3	0	0	0	2	5	4	4	1	0	5	.455	.600	.333	22.50	0.00
Tomshaw, Matt	R-L	6-2	200	12-17-88	13	6	3.48	27	27	1	0	163	170	66	63	15	36	114	.268	.245	.275	6.29	1.99

Fielding

Catcher	PCT	G	PO	A	E	DP	PB
Hoo	1.000	6	30	5	0	0	0
Maron	.992	66	443	58	4	4	3
Nola	.994	46	306	41	2	2	10
Vigil	.990	26	180	18	2	3	1

First Base	PCT	G	PO	A	E	DP
Ard	.993	103	802	59	6	70
Bour	.962	3	25	0	1	1
Cordova	1.000	2	2	0	0	0
Geiger	.995	25	198	11	1	18
Nola	1.000	1	5	0	0	0
Rojas	1.000	1	8	2	0	1
Serna	1.000	1	1	1	0	0
Towey	1.000	9	74	7	0	6
Yarbrough	.987	9	68	6	1	5

Second Base	PCT	G	PO	A	E	DP
Arrojo	1.000	1	0	1	0	0
Cordova	.857	1	5	1	1	1
Perez	.977	15	13	29	1	2
Serna	.961	33	53	70	5	22
Vidal	.980	53	103	142	5	33
Yarbrough	.974	43	50	99	4	24

Third Base	PCT	G	PO	A	E	DP
Anderson	.961	82	54	168	9	20
Cordova	.800	3	2	2	1	0
Geiger	.000	1	0	0	0	0
Prado	1.000	2	0	2	0	0
Serna	.857	6	3	9	2	0
Towey	.000	1	0	0	0	0
Vidal	.971	51	41	95	4	7

Shortstop	PCT	G	PO	A	E	DP
Arrojo	1.000	1	2	1	0	0
Cordova	.923	3	4	8	1	1
Diaz	.964	55	65	122	7	26
Hechavarria	1.000	3	2	4	0	0
Perez	.920	6	10	13	2	4
Rojas	1.000	1	0	3	0	1
Rondon	.962	13	22	29	2	9
Serna	.937	23	23	51	5	8
Yarbrough	.927	45	36	91	10	15

Outfield	PCT	G	PO	A	E	DP
Ard	1.000	4	7	0	0	0
Barrett	1.000	28	56	0	0	0
Dean	1.000	55	86	3	0	1
Galloway	1.000	9	18	0	0	0
Glenn	.989	50	93	1	1	1
Lee	.987	58	147	9	2	3
Norwood	.975	124	225	10	6	3
Perez	.969	50	121	2	4	0
Pineda	.977	46	81	4	2	2
Towey	1.000	10	17	0	0	0

MIAMI MARLINS

JUPITER HAMMERHEADS — *HIGH CLASS A*

FLORIDA STATE LEAGUE

Batting	B-T	HT	WT	DOB	AVG	vLH	vRH	G	AB	R	H	2B	3B	HR	RBI	BB	HBP	SH	SF	SO	SB	CS	SLG	OBP
Arrojo, Junior	R-R	5-10	195	5-29-88	.244	.250	.241	24	82	9	20	5	0	0	7	16	7	2	0	22	4	3	.305	.410
Barrett, Kyle	L-R	5-11	185	8-4-93	.297	.244	.308	66	266	26	79	10	1	0	12	23	2	3	2	43	13	7	.342	.355
Bass, Corey	R-R	5-9	200	4-27-91	.188	.000	.214	6	16	1	3	1	0	0	1	4	0	1	0	8	0	0	.250	.350
Bird, Corey	L-L	6-1	185	8-11-95	.274	.297	.263	29	113	12	31	3	0	1	10	10	0	2	2	9	5	4	.327	.328
Bohn, Justin	R-R	6-0	180	11-2-92	.159	.133	.164	26	82	7	13	2	0	1	8	9	1	0	1	26	3	1	.220	.247
Bour, Justin	L-R	6-3	265	5-28-88	1.000	—	1.000	1	2	2	2	1	0	0	2	1	0	0	1	0	0	0	1.500	.750
Davis, Mason	B-R	5-9	175	1-11-93	.255	.292	.239	46	165	26	42	8	3	0	7	7	6	1	0	39	7	3	.339	.309
Dunand, Joe	R-R	6-2	205	9-20-95	.364	.250	.667	3	11	1	4	2	0	0	1	2	0	0	0	4	0	1	.546	.462
Galloway, Isaac	R-R	6-2	205	10-10-89	.333	.250	.400	2	9	1	3	0	0	0	0	0	0	0	0	1	1	0	.333	.333
Garrett, Stone	R-R	6-2	195	11-22-95	.212	.187	.218	94	373	37	79	24	1	4	29	21	2	2	1	126	8	1	.314	.257
Geiger, Dustin	R-R	6-2	180	12-2-91	.224	.327	.195	65	237	31	53	14	1	7	35	26	3	0	1	64	2	1	.380	.307
Gould, J.J.	R-R	6-0	195	8-22-93	.155	.290	.127	61	181	16	28	5	0	2	12	20	6	2	1	77	2	0	.216	.260
Haynal, Brad	R-R	6-3	215	8-21-91	.269	.200	.284	46	171	12	46	12	0	2	18	13	4	0	2	36	0	0	.374	.332
Hechavarria, Adeiny	R-R	6-0	195	4-15-89	.304	.143	.375	8	23	1	7	0	0	0	1	3	1	0	0	1	1	1	.304	.407
Ho, Shao-Pin	R-R	6-0	180	6-5-94	.667	—	.667	1	3	1	2	0	0	0	0	0	0	0	0	0	0	0	.667	.667
Hoo, Chris	R-R	5-9	190	2-19-92	.155	.086	.194	31	97	5	15	4	0	1	5	13	6	0	0	36	1	0	.227	.293
Juengel, Matt	R-R	6-2	185	1-13-90	.250	.000	.286	3	8	1	2	1	0	0	0	3	1	0	0	3	0	0	.375	.500
Kjerstad, Dexter	R-R	6-1	210	1-19-92	.213	.226	.209	60	230	22	49	7	0	4	20	17	3	1	1	64	0	4	.296	.275
Lombardozzi, Steve	R-B	6-0	195	9-20-88	.000	.000	.000	2	6	0	0	0	0	0	0	1	0	0	0	2	0	0	.000	.143
Lusignan, Colby	L-R	6-4	230	11-15-92	.285	.217	.327	46	179	20	51	12	0	6	25	17	2	0	3	48	2	1	.453	.348
Morales, Roy	R-R	6-2	195	6-25-95	.289	.357	.278	30	104	12	30	4	0	1	15	13	1	0	1	12	4	1	.356	.370
Pollman, Gunner	R-R	6-2	210	2-3-95	.184	.143	.198	32	109	8	20	5	0	1	10	8	3	2	1	49	0	0	.257	.256
Prado, Martin	R-R	6-0	215	10-27-83	.273	.400	.235	8	22	0	6	1	0	0	0	3	0	0	0	5	0	0	.318	.360
Reyes, Angel	R-R	6-0	175	5-6-95	.233	.258	.225	96	360	33	84	12	1	2	27	37	7	4	3	89	5	3	.289	.315
Rojas, Miguel	R-R	5-11	195	2-24-89	.308	.000	.348	8	26	3	8	2	0	0	2	3	1	0	0	1	0	1	.385	.400
Rondon, Cleuluis	B-R	6-0	155	4-13-94	.201	.111	.240	45	149	16	30	6	1	1	12	13	2	4	1	44	1	1	.275	.273

Schales, Brian	R-R	6-1	170	2-13-96	.251	.207	.266	111	367	41	92	13	3	6	42	39	7	0	6	95	0	4	.352	.329
Silviano, John	L-R	5-11	190	7-11-94	.245	.157	.277	103	384	48	94	17	5	13	55	37	1	0	2	127	4	0	.417	.311
Sullivan, Zach	R-R	6-3	180	11-26-95	.178	.173	.180	85	269	26	48	11	3	4	28	18	4	0	2	106	7	1	.286	.239
Twine, Justin	R-R	5-11	205	10-7-95	.242	.209	.260	32	120	14	29	6	1	1	4	3	3	0	0	30	4	1	.333	.278
Vazquez, Boo	L-R	6-4	220	4-4-93	.270	.220	.294	41	152	12	41	10	2	1	18	9	1	0	1	37	1	1	.382	.313
Vigil, Rodrigo	R-R	6-0	165	1-3-93	.244	.333	.216	39	135	15	33	6	0	0	9	6	3	2	0	15	2	1	.289	.292
Washington, Ty	R-R	5-9	174	9-1-93	.000	.000	.000	5	12	0	0	0	0	0	0	1	0	1	0	7	0	0	.000	.077
Wheat, Dalton	L-R	6-2	190	11-27-93	.205	.154	.226	13	44	5	9	1	1	0	4	2	0	1	0	10	2	2	.273	.239

Pitching	B-T	HT	WT	DOB	W	L	ERA	G	GS	CG	SV	IP	H	R	ER	HR	BB	SO	AVG	vLH	vRH	K/9	BB/9
Acosta, Horacio	R-R	5-11	195	10-24-90	0	0	7.71	2	0	0	0	2	6	3	2	0	1	1	.462	.500	.444	3.86	3.86
Alonzo, Eric	R-B	6-2	215	8-28-91	1	1	0.90	13	0	0	1	20	16	2	2	0	6	17	.219	.182	.235	7.65	2.70
Ballew, Travis	R-R	6-0	160	5-1-91	0	1	3.86	10	0	0	0	12	7	5	5	0	13	9	.189	.077	.250	6.94	10.03
Barraclough, Kyle	R-R	6-3	225	5-23-90	0	0	0.00	1	1	0	0	1	0	0	0	0	1	2	.000	.000	.000	18.00	9.00
Beal, Evan	R-R	6-5	195	8-2-93	1	2	1.50	5	0	0	0	6	6	8	1	0	6	5	.231	.455	.067	7.50	9.00
Beckman, Ryan	R-R	6-4	185	1-2-90	3	2	1.27	20	0	0	1	28	23	5	4	0	8	30	.217	.268	.185	9.53	2.54
Beltre, Andy	R-R	6-4	195	7-6-93	0	1	1.02	13	0	0	3	18	9	2	2	1	4	20	.148	.125	.156	10.19	2.04
Brigham, Jeff	R-R	6-0	200	2-16-92	4	2	2.90	11	11	0	0	59	49	23	19	2	20	53	.226	.261	.186	8.08	3.05
Buckelew, James	L-L	6-2	155	8-4-91	2	4	2.13	17	9	0	0	63	48	21	15	1	21	44	.212	.140	.232	6.25	2.98
Cavanerio, Jorgan	R-R	6-1	155	8-18-94	4	3	2.33	29	7	0	0	73	61	27	19	3	17	55	.229	.224	.233	6.75	2.09
Chen, Wei-Yin	R-L	6-0	200	7-21-85	0	0	0.00	2	1	0	0	4	4	0	0	0	1	2	.286	.250	.300	4.91	2.45
Cortright, Garrett	R-R	6-5	210	10-2-91	0	0	5.95	16	0	0	0	20	33	13	13	2	2	14	.384	.313	.426	6.41	0.92
Crescentini, Marcus	R-R	6-4	240	12-26-92	1	1	2.20	13	0	0	3	16	14	4	4	1	4	21	.219	.286	.186	11.57	2.20
De La Rosa, Esmerling	R-R	6-2	199	5-15-91	0	0	0.71	7	0	0	0	13	12	4	1	0	1	11	.240	.318	.179	7.82	0.71
Del Pozo, Miguel	L-L	6-1	180	10-14-92	2	0	0.54	12	0	0	0	17	12	3	1	0	5	17	.197	.250	.171	9.18	2.70
Despaigne, Odrisamer	R-R	6-0	200	4-4-87	0	0	0.00	1	1	0	0	4	0	0	0	0	1	7	.000	.000	.000	15.75	2.25
Farnworth, Steven	R-R	6-2	175	9-6-93	0	1	4.58	10	0	0	2	20	27	10	10	1	4	11	.333	.333	.333	5.03	1.83
Garcia, Javier	R-R	6-2	230	2-26-98	1	0	0.00	1	0	0	0	2	0	0	0	0	1	1	.000	.000	.000	5.40	5.40
Gonzalez, Felipe	R-R	6-1	200	8-15-91	9	8	4.15	34	11	0	5	89	96	46	41	10	31	92	.275	.285	.268	9.30	3.13
Gonzalez, Merandy	R-R	6-0	216	10-9-95	1	0	1.11	5	3	0	1	24	18	4	3	0	5	14	.212	.171	.240	5.18	1.85
2-team total (6 St. Lucie)					5	2	1.78	11	9	0	1	61	51	16	12	1	13	38	.225	.246	.222	5.64	1.93
Guerrero, Tayron	R-R	6-8	210	1-9-91	0	1	3.60	4	0	0	0	5	3	2	2	1	3	7	.177	.250	.154	12.60	5.40
Holmes, Ben	L-L	6-1	195	9-12-91	1	6	4.17	35	7	0	0	73	75	35	34	2	19	63	.266	.262	.267	7.73	2.33
Kinley, Jeff	L-L	6-1	195	2-15-92	2	0	1.30	21	0	0	6	28	21	6	4	1	7	28	.212	.310	.171	9.11	2.28
Kinley, Tyler	R-R	6-4	205	1-31-91	1	1	1.98	23	0	0	9	27	14	6	6	3	6	38	.151	.132	.164	12.51	1.98
Koehler, Tom	R-R	6-3	235	6-29-86	0	1	6.75	1	1	0	0	4	5	3	3	2	2	5	.278	.250	.333	11.25	4.50
Lakind, Jared	L-L	6-2	205	3-9-92	0	0	0.00	1	0	0	0	2	1	0	0	0	0	1	.200	—	.200	5.40	0.00
Locke, Jeff	L-L	6-0	200	11-20-87	0	0	1.00	2	2	0	0	9	7	1	1	1	0	10	.212	.429	.154	10.00	0.00
Lopez, Pablo	R-R	6-3	200	3-7-96	0	3	2.18	8	6	0	0	45	42	13	11	0	7	32	.252	.291	.210	6.35	1.39
Meyer, Ben	R-R	6-5	180	1-30-93	4	3	1.98	20	12	0	1	82	59	24	18	0	17	94	.201	.206	.197	10.32	1.87
Needy, James	R-R	6-6	230	3-30-91	3	2	1.73	7	7	0	0	36	23	8	7	0	12	33	.186	.255	.130	8.17	2.97
Neumann, Nick	R-R	6-3	205	4-26-91	2	0	6.98	13	0	0	0	19	25	18	15	2	10	6	.321	.303	.333	2.79	4.66
Newell, Ryan	R-R	6-2	215	6-18-91	2	0	1.42	5	0	0	0	13	5	2	2	0	2	15	.119	.125	.115	10.66	1.42
Nicolino, Justin	L-L	6-3	195	11-22-91	1	0	3.00	1	1	0	0	6	7	2	2	1	0	1	.304	.400	.278	1.50	0.00
Peters, Dillon	L-L	5-9	195	8-31-92	1	0	0.00	2	2	0	0	11	5	0	0	0	2	9	.139	.188	.100	7.59	1.69
Poteet, Cody	R-R	6-1	190	7-30-94	3	7	4.16	16	14	0	0	80	84	42	37	2	23	40	.282	.275	.287	4.50	2.59
Quijada, Jose	L-L	6-0	175	11-9-95	5	1	2.27	32	0	0	1	48	40	15	12	3	13	53	.225	.259	.210	10.01	2.45
Richards, Trevor	R-R	6-2	190	5-15-93	7	4	2.17	13	11	0	0	71	54	21	17	2	12	81	.204	.172	.228	10.32	1.53
Robinson, C.J.	R-R	6-0	215	5-11-93	0	1	1.69	3	0	0	0	5	7	2	1	0	6	4	.318	.375	.286	6.75	10.13
Schiraldi, Lukas	R-R	6-6	210	7-25-93	0	2	4.30	11	0	0	0	15	13	8	7	1	6	17	.245	.235	.250	10.43	3.68
Schlereth, Daniel	L-L	6-0	210	5-9-86	1	1	3.24	6	0	0	0	8	9	3	3	0	3	11	.300	.400	.280	11.88	3.24
Squier, Scott	R-L	6-5	185	9-17-92	5	9	3.82	28	26	1	0	132	143	65	56	15	26	102	.280	.252	.291	6.95	1.77
Tazawa, Junichi	R-R	5-11	200	6-6-86	0	0	0.00	1	1	0	0	2	1	0	0	0	0	2	.143	.250	.000	9.00	0.00
Ziegler, Brad	R-R	6-4	220	10-10-79	0	0	0.00	1	1	0	0	1	0	0	0	0	0	1	.000	—	.000	9.00	0.00

Fielding

Catcher	PCT	G	PO	A	E	DP	PB
Bass	.981	6	46	5	1	2	0
Hoo	.994	31	290	22	2	2	2
Morales	.992	30	238	20	2	2	3
Pollman	.996	32	231	35	1	2	5
Vigil	.990	39	269	30	3	2	3

First Base	PCT	G	PO	A	E	DP
Bohn	1.000	5	25	1	0	2
Bour	1.000	1	5	0	0	0
Geiger	.998	60	546	45	1	59
Haynal	1.000	24	208	15	0	22
Juengel	1.000	1	6	0	0	0
Lusignan	.978	45	415	22	10	38
Rojas	1.000	1	9	1	0	1
Silviano	1.000	3	25	1	0	0

Second Base	PCT	G	PO	A	E	DP
Arrojo	1.000	6	11	16	0	6
Bohn	1.000	6	9	21	0	5
Davis	.970	38	65	98	5	30
Lombardozzi	1.000	2	4	1	0	0
Reyes	.936	70	135	187	22	48
Rojas	1.000	3	10	8	0	4
Schales	1.000	1	2	0	0	1
Twine	.987	16	23	51	1	8
Washington	1.000	1	1	4	0	0

Third Base	PCT	G	PO	A	E	DP
Arrojo	.923	4	4	8	1	1
Bohn	.963	8	2	24	1	2
Davis	1.000	5	3	10	0	0
Lusignan	.000	1	0	0	0	0
Prado	1.000	8	3	13	0	1
Rojas	1.000	1	2	2	0	0
Schales	.947	110	50	217	15	20
Twine	.971	10	8	26	1	2
Washington	1.000	2	0	3	0	0

Shortstop	PCT	G	PO	A	E	DP
Arrojo	.889	12	9	39	6	10
Bohn	.968	9	8	22	1	5
Davis	1.000	1	0	1	0	0
Dunand	1.000	3	2	9	0	4
Gould	.933	61	65	145	15	23
Hechavarria	.944	8	10	24	2	4
Ho	1.000	1	1	5	0	2
Rojas	1.000	2	4	8	0	3
Rondon	.975	45	59	134	5	31
Twine	.938	5	5	10	1	2

Outfield	PCT	G	PO	A	E	DP
Barrett	.981	54	104	2	2	0
Bird	1.000	25	56	0	0	0
Galloway	1.000	2	5	0	0	0
Garrett	.980	82	140	10	3	2
Juengel	1.000	2	2	0	0	0
Kjerstad	.959	56	111	6	5	0

	PCT	G	PO	A	E	DP
Reyes	.875	9	7	0	1	0
Silviano	.978	57	83	4	2	3
Sullivan	.984	82	175	8	3	4
Vazquez	1.000	34	62	0	0	0
Wheat	1.000	12	15	3	0	0

GREENSBORO GRASSHOPPERS

LOW CLASS A

SOUTH ATLANTIC LEAGUE

Batting	B-T	HT	WT	DOB	AVG	vLH	vRH	G	AB	R	H	2B	3B	HR	RBI	BB	HBP	SH	SF	SO	SB	CS	SLG	OBP
Barnes, Jared	R-R	6-0	185	11-21-95	.235	.429	.100	6	17	3	4	0	0	0	0	3	1	0	0	5	0	0	.235	.381
Berry, Branden	R-R	6-4	225	5-19-93	.170	.208	.143	17	59	8	10	1	0	2	5	4	2	0	0	18	0	0	.288	.246
Bird, Corey	L-L	6-1	185	8-11-95	.294	.259	.309	81	279	41	82	13	5	1	30	28	3	17	4	59	23	9	.387	.360
Brown, Micah	R-R	6-2	200	5-9-96	.200	.267	.171	14	50	5	10	1	1	0	5	2	3	1	0	20	0	2	.260	.273
Cabrera, Rony	R-R	5-11	175	1-29-96	.215	.200	.220	50	172	9	37	9	1	2	15	6	0	1	2	56	1	1	.314	.239
Davis, Mason	B-R	5-9	175	1-11-93	.248	.172	.275	31	109	15	27	8	0	2	15	8	1	2	1	32	5	0	.376	.303
De La Rosa, Bryan	R-R	5-8	195	3-26-94	.179	.500	.125	9	28	5	5	1	0	1	2	5	0	0	0	11	1	0	.321	.303
Gutierrez, Eric	R-L	5-10	205	12-28-93	.259	.278	.249	90	325	48	84	14	0	7	49	34	10	1	6	53	5	1	.366	.341
Hill, Trenton	L-L	6-4	210	3-10-94	.254	.214	.259	33	122	13	31	3	0	2	17	15	1	0	2	44	0	0	.328	.336
Jones, Alex	R-R	6-2	215	2-16-93	.247	.154	.294	23	77	7	19	4	0	2	7	13	0	2	0	20	0	0	.377	.356
Knapp, Aaron	L-R	5-10	175	11-4-94	.218	.191	.227	119	427	59	93	9	6	5	36	59	6	10	7	142	34	14	.302	.317
Lara, Garvis	B-R	6-1	170	5-19-96	.233	.300	.200	20	60	9	14	3	0	2	5	6	0	1	0	19	8	1	.383	.303
Lusignan, Colby	L-R	6-4	230	11-15-92	.243	.169	.274	80	304	44	74	19	3	9	49	26	6	0	1	117	2	1	.415	.315
Mahan, Riley	L-R	6-3	185	12-31-95	.259	.167	.333	6	27	4	7	1	0	1	4	0	0	0	0	7	0	0	.407	.259
Millan, J.C.	R-R	6-0	185	1-18-96	.231	.227	.232	27	104	10	24	7	0	1	6	5	0	0	0	33	2	2	.327	.266
Miller, Brian	L-R	6-1	186	8-20-95	.322	.238	.353	57	233	42	75	17	1	1	28	23	1	0	1	35	21	6	.416	.384
Nelson, James	R-R	6-2	180	10-18-97	.309	.331	.300	102	395	41	122	31	3	7	59	26	5	0	6	106	6	2	.456	.354
Olis, Walker	R-R	6-2	190	5-4-94	.191	.192	.190	66	220	26	42	9	1	4	15	19	1	5	1	62	4	2	.296	.257
Pintor, Luis	R-R	5-9	170	6-6-95	.236	.225	.240	119	386	60	91	14	2	4	43	43	10	10	4	64	9	5	.314	.325
Pollman, Gunner	R-R	6-2	210	2-3-95	.229	.286	.191	11	35	4	8	2	0	1	5	1	0	0	1	13	0	0	.371	.243
Rindfleisch, Jarett	R-R	6-1	225	9-4-95	.243	.259	.237	89	288	39	70	13	1	6	45	32	23	7	5	83	2	1	.358	.359
Santos, Jhonny	R-R	6-0	160	10-2-96	.192	.071	.237	31	104	11	20	3	1	0	10	11	0	4	1	21	6	1	.240	.267
Twine, Justin	R-R	5-11	205	10-7-95	.186	.230	.167	66	248	29	46	6	5	3	31	18	5	1	4	76	3	2	.286	.251
Vazquez, Boo	L-R	6-4	220	4-4-93	.281	.293	.275	67	242	31	68	16	3	6	32	27	5	1	2	72	0	5	.446	.362
Wheat, Dalton	L-R	6-2	190	11-27-93	.242	.152	.275	36	124	21	30	6	1	1	16	11	5	2	0	27	3	0	.331	.329

Pitching	B-T	HT	WT	DOB	W	L	ERA	G	GS	CG	SV	IP	H	R	ER	HR	BB	SO	AVG	vLH	vRH	K/9	BB/9
Bautista, Nestor	L-L	6-3	200	5-13-92	1	2	1.62	14	0	0	3	17	15	7	3	0	2	20	.217	.154	.256	10.80	1.08
Beal, Evan	R-R	6-5	195	8-2-93	3	0	1.08	11	0	0	1	17	13	4	2	0	5	15	.217	.273	.184	8.10	2.70
Beggs, Dustin	R-R	6-3	180	6-14-93	10	6	3.86	26	26	1	0	149	150	71	64	23	31	107	.265	.243	.282	6.45	1.87
Brewster, LJ	R-R	6-2	205	5-2-94	4	7	4.59	20	9	0	1	65	60	35	33	6	25	34	.254	.243	.264	4.73	3.48
Bugg, Parker	R-R	6-6	210	10-26-94	2	3	5.04	18	0	0	1	30	37	21	17	3	9	35	.294	.263	.319	10.38	2.67
Clark, Ethan	R-R	6-5	235	10-26-94	3	2	2.05	11	11	0	0	53	41	14	12	4	26	57	.217	.241	.198	9.74	4.44
Cortright, Garrett	R-R	6-5	210	10-2-91	0	0	18.00	1	0	0	0	1	2	2	2	1	2	1	.400	.000	1.000	9.00	18.00
Crescentini, Marcus	R-R	6-4	240	12-26-92	2	0	1.03	26	0	0	0	35	16	5	4	1	12	47	.131	.151	.116	12.09	3.09
Del Pozo, Miguel	L-L	6-1	180	10-14-92	0	0	0.00	3	0	0	1	3	3	0	0	0	0	4	.231	.143	.333	12.00	0.00
Diaz, Carlos	L-L	6-3	190	2-3-92	0	0	0.00	3	0	0	0	4	2	0	0	0	3	6	.125	.000	.182	12.46	6.23
Duval, Max	R-R	6-5	235	4-15-91	4	0	2.09	6	6	2	0	39	28	9	9	3	5	38	.197	.196	.198	8.84	1.16
Garrett, Braxton	L-L	6-3	190	8-5-97	1	0	2.93	4	4	0	0	15	13	7	5	3	6	16	.220	.273	.208	9.39	3.52
Holloway, Jordan	R-R	6-4	190	6-13-96	1	2	5.22	11	11	0	0	50	41	31	29	10	22	50	.220	.200	.240	9.00	3.96
Hovis, Reilly	R-R	6-3	195	10-27-93	2	0	3.38	22	0	0	2	29	23	12	11	4	8	35	.205	.245	.175	10.74	2.45
Keller, Kyle	R-R	6-4	200	4-28-93	2	0	2.28	36	2	0	8	67	50	18	17	2	21	86	.208	.223	.197	11.55	2.82
King, Michael	R-R	6-3	204	5-25-95	11	9	3.14	26	25	2	0	149	141	55	52	14	21	106	.252	.266	.241	6.40	1.27
Lakind, Jared	L-L	6-2	205	3-9-92	1	1	4.24	14	0	0	0	17	22	8	8	1	4	11	.324	.321	.325	5.82	2.12
Lee, Dylan	L-L	6-4	210	8-1-94	4	10	4.85	19	19	0	0	98	104	56	53	13	23	73	.276	.283	.272	6.68	2.11
Lillie, Ryan	R-R	6-0	210	5-1-96	0	0	0.00	1	0	0	0	2	1	0	0	0	0	4	.143	.000	.200	18.00	0.00
MacEachern, Ryley	R-R	6-2	213	5-27-94	2	2	4.15	19	0	0	1	22	25	15	10	1	18	18	.275	.308	.250	7.48	7.48
Mahoney, Kolton	R-R	6-1	195	5-20-92	5	5	4.08	18	13	0	0	79	82	42	36	10	10	74	.266	.273	.261	8.39	1.13
2-team total (11 Charleston)					6	7	3.56	29	13	0	1	104	106	48	41	10	17	100	.263	.273	.261	8.68	1.48
Mateo, Alejandro	R-R	6-2	200	1-18-94	1	3	7.25	10	3	0	0	22	25	19	18	7	6	29	.281	.263	.294	11.69	2.42
Mertz, Michael	R-R	6-2	220	9-24-93	9	1	1.80	40	1	0	4	75	48	17	15	3	28	78	.184	.182	.185	9.36	3.36
Meyer, Ben	R-R	6-5	180	1-30-93	2	0	2.15	12	0	0	0	29	22	9	7	3	6	40	.218	.194	.231	12.27	1.84
Miller, Brandon	R-R	6-4	210	6-16-95	0	3	8.86	5	5	0	0	21	31	25	21	8	7	12	.326	.286	.359	5.06	2.95
Neubeck, Travis	L-R	6-2	180	3-13-95	0	1	12.86	3	0	0	0	7	15	11	10	1	3	9	.429	.546	.375	11.57	3.86
Neumann, Nick	R-R	6-3	205	4-26-91	0	1	3.24	4	1	0	0	8	10	5	3	1	1	4	.286	.500	.143	4.32	1.08
Peace, RJ	R-R	6-2	175	6-24-97	0	0	54.00	1	0	0	0	1	4	4	4	1	2	0	.800	1.000	.667	0.00	27.00
Perez, Sam	R-R	6-3	210	8-17-94	2	1	6.21	17	0	0	0	33	35	26	23	7	6	30	.267	.286	.253	8.10	1.62
Smith, Chad	R-R	6-4	200	6-8-95	3	2	2.93	34	0	0	7	46	42	20	15	3	14	52	.236	.222	.247	10.17	2.74

Fielding

Catcher	PCT	G	PO	A	E	DP	PB
Barnes	.979	6	44	3	1	0	1
De La Rosa	.989	9	80	9	1	0	7
Jones	.995	23	184	22	1	1	5
Pollman	1.000	11	58	8	0	1	3
Rindfleisch	.997	89	683	90	2	3	9

First Base	PCT	G	PO	A	E	DP
Berry	1.000	2	17	0	0	0
Cabrera	1.000	2	12	2	0	0
Gutierrez	.993	61	521	38	4	44
Hill	.992	14	116	4	1	6
Lusignan	.993	60	504	39	4	48

Second Base	PCT	G	PO	A	E	DP
Brown	1.000	1	2	1	0	1
Cabrera	.964	36	66	93	6	27
Davis	.975	18	31	48	2	7
Mahan	1.000	6	6	22	0	3
Millan	.944	16	21	30	3	3
Pintor	1.000	1	1	2	0	0
Twine	.981	58	93	161	5	38

Third Base	PCT	G	PO	A	E	DP
Berry	.923	9	6	6	1	0
Brown	.938	13	7	23	2	1
Cabrera	.875	11	3	18	3	1
Davis	1.000	5	2	10	0	1
Lusignan	.000	1	0	0	0	0
Millan	.870	9	5	15	3	3
Nelson	.910	80	51	141	19	5

Pintor	1.000	6	1	14	0	1
Twine	1.000	5	3	6	0	0

Shortstop	PCT	G	PO	A	E	DP
Cabrera	1.000	1	1	4	0	0
Davis	1.000	4	5	18	0	4
Lara	.924	20	28	57	7	11
Pintor	.967	112	190	307	17	68

Outfield	PCT	G	PO	A	E	DP
Bird	.994	79	149	7	1	2
Knapp	.985	112	195	6	3	2
Miller	.985	55	126	4	2	0
Olis	.989	57	87	1	1	0
Santos	.970	31	62	3	2	0
Vazquez	.988	50	85	0	1	0
Wheat	1.000	28	40	1	0	0

BATAVIA MUCKDOGS — *SHORT SEASON*

NEW YORK-PENN LEAGUE

Batting	B-T	HT	WT	DOB	AVG	vLH	vRH	G	AB	R	H	2B	3B	HR	RBI	BB	HBP	SH	SF	SO	SB	CS	SLG	OBP
Alonso, Lazaro	L-R	6-3	230	12-17-94	.255	.238	.262	58	204	25	52	13	0	2	30	37	0	0	2	56	0	0	.348	.366
Barnes, Jared	R-R	6-0	185	11-21-95	.321	.000	.409	8	28	5	9	5	0	2	6	2	0	0	0	4	0	0	.714	.367
Bennett, Terry	L-L	5-11	195	9-3-96	.268	.194	.299	36	123	13	33	3	1	1	20	15	1	0	0	40	3	4	.333	.353
Brooks, Mathew	L-R	6-0	185	3-21-96	.268	.250	.277	46	153	22	41	7	0	0	11	23	3	4	0	31	4	2	.314	.374
Brown, Micah	R-R	6-2	200	5-9-96	.271	.348	.234	20	70	12	19	5	0	1	8	10	3	0	1	16	3	2	.386	.381
Cabrera, Rony	R-R	5-11	175	1-29-96	.393	.556	.316	7	28	8	11	1	0	0	3	3	0	0	0	7	0	1	.429	.452
Castro, Samuel	B-R	5-10	160	10-16-97	.269	.283	.263	41	160	22	43	2	0	0	12	10	1	6	1	31	14	5	.281	.314
Cespedes, Ricardo	L-L	6-1	205	8-24-97	.190	.208	.182	19	79	4	15	2	0	0	4	1	0	1	0	21	0	1	.215	.200
2-team total (21 Brooklyn)					.208	.278	.210	40	159	7	33	2	0	1	16	5	0	3	0	37	1	2	.239	.232
Curtis, Tyler	R-R	6-3	220	2-14-94	.249	.211	.265	49	189	20	47	9	2	2	21	12	6	0	1	47	0	2	.349	.313
Daly, Zachary	L-L	6-3	175	12-13-93	.200	.143	.222	7	25	4	5	1	1	0	2	2	0	0	0	9	0	0	.320	.259
De La Rosa, Bryan	R-R	5-8	195	3-26-94	.200	.000	.250	3	10	2	2	1	0	0	2	2	1	0	0	5	0	0	.300	.385
Fisher, Ben	L-L	6-1	215	11-16-94	.191	.118	.217	33	126	10	24	2	0	1	8	13	0	0	0	28	0	0	.230	.266
Garzillo, Mike	R-R	5-11	185	2-11-94	.500	.000	.667	2	4	1	2	0	0	0	2	2	0	0	0	2	0	0	.500	.667
Gauntt, David	R-R	6-0	200	6-16-93	.121	.161	.096	29	83	10	10	2	0	0	5	24	2	1	0	49	1	0	.145	.330
Hernandez, Brayan	R-R	6-2	175	9-11-97	.271	.191	.316	15	59	9	16	2	3	0	3	2	1	1	1	14	0	0	.407	.302
Hernandez, Michael	R-R	5-10	195	5-24-95	.169	.136	.182	23	77	6	13	2	0	1	5	5	3	0	0	25	0	0	.234	.247
Ho, Shao-Pin	R-R	6-0	180	6-5-94	.184	.063	.273	11	38	2	7	1	0	0	2	3	0	0	1	6	0	1	.211	.238
Hollins, Bubba	R-R	6-1	200	12-6-95	.214	.200	.216	12	42	4	9	3	0	0	8	5	1	0	0	6	1	0	.286	.313
Jones, Alex	R-R	6-2	215	2-16-93	.211	.294	.175	15	57	5	12	3	0	0	6	7	0	0	0	10	1	0	.263	.297
Jones, Thomas	R-R	6-4	195	12-9-97	.181	.169	.186	68	238	31	43	10	4	2	21	34	14	3	3	94	7	6	.282	.315
Karas, Denis	R-R	5-11	180	11-27-95	.108	.083	.120	11	37	1	4	0	0	0	0	4	1	0	0	10	0	0	.108	.214
Millan, J.C.	R-R	6-0	185	1-18-96	.273	.125	.357	12	44	8	12	2	1	1	5	2	0	0	0	9	0	0	.432	.304
Reynolds, Sean	L-R	6-7	205	4-19-98	.176	.161	.186	20	74	11	13	3	1	4	10	4	0	0	0	41	2	0	.405	.218
Rivera, Marcos	R-R	6-1	160	5-13-97	.225	.233	.221	63	213	25	48	16	2	3	22	19	3	3	2	78	5	1	.362	.295
Santos, Jhonny	R-R	6-0	160	10-2-96	.276	.300	.265	30	123	18	34	11	0	1	10	6	1	2	1	21	8	0	.390	.313
Sims, Demetrius	R-R	6-2	200	7-14-95	.186	.217	.167	17	59	5	11	1	1	0	6	4	2	0	0	19	0	1	.237	.262
White, Harrison	L-R	5-11	175	11-18-94	.280	.097	.337	38	132	15	37	6	0	1	12	21	0	4	0	32	1	1	.349	.379

Pitching	B-T	HT	WT	DOB	W	L	ERA	G	GS	CG	SV	IP	H	R	ER	HR	BB	SO	AVG	vLH	vRH	K/9	BB/9
Acosta, Horacio	R-R	5-11	195	10-24-90	1	0	2.35	3	0	0	0	8	8	4	2	0	3	4	.286	.375	.250	4.70	3.52
Aiello, Vincenzo	R-R	6-3	220	8-6-94	1	1	2.33	13	0	0	4	19	15	7	5	2	6	31	.203	.156	.238	14.43	2.79
Alberius, Josh	R-R	5-11	170	11-19-94	1	1	10.03	8	0	0	0	12	23	15	13	3	6	8	.397	.440	.364	6.17	4.63
Bautista, Nestor	L-L	6-3	200	5-13-92	1	1	6.75	5	0	0	0	7	9	5	5	0	4	5	.333	.286	.350	6.75	5.40
Braley, Taylor	R-R	5-11	140	1-13-96	1	2	2.79	7	3	0	0	19	12	8	6	0	5	21	.164	.158	.171	9.78	2.33
Cabrera, Edward	R-R	6-4	175	4-13-98	1	3	5.30	13	6	0	0	36	42	27	21	1	8	32	.286	.265	.304	8.07	2.02
Cuello, Eliezer	R-R	6-2	195	11-18-96	0	1	27.00	2	0	0	0	1	4	8	3	2	1	0	.571	.667	.500	0.00	9.00
Frohwirth, Tyler	R-R	6-1	165	9-13-93	0	1	3.94	14	0	0	0	16	18	12	7	1	4	16	.269	.370	.200	9.00	2.25
2-team total (3 Williamsport)					0	2	3.44	17	0	0	0	18	20	13	7	1	4	18	.263	.500	.143	8.84	1.96
Garcia, Javier	R-R	6-2	230	2-26-98	0	0	9.00	2	0	0	0	3	5	3	3	0	2	4	.357	.500	.300	12.00	6.00
Guenther, Sean	L-L	5-11	194	12-29-95	1	4	3.83	9	9	0	0	40	43	18	17	3	4	33	.270	.290	.258	7.43	0.90
Guerrero, Alberto	R-R	6-3	192	12-13-97	0	0	7.88	6	1	0	0	8	10	7	7	1	5	10	.294	.231	.333	11.25	5.63
Gutierrez, Osman	R-R	6-4	220	12-15-94	1	1	3.18	3	3	0	0	17	15	6	6	3	3	18	.231	.286	.167	9.53	1.59
Hock, Colton	R-R	6-4	220	3-15-96	1	3	6.62	7	1	0	0	18	22	14	13	2	12	13	.324	.303	.343	6.62	6.11
Howe, Bryce	R-R	6-2	250	11-17-95	0	0	0.00	2	0	0	0	2	1	0	0	0	0	1	.143	.000	.333	4.50	0.00
Koplove, Kenny	R-R	6-2	170	8-2-93	3	2	4.15	16	0	0	1	17	16	12	8	0	12	23	.235	.214	.250	11.94	6.23
Lillie, Ryan	R-R	6-0	210	5-1-96	0	5	4.35	9	7	0	0	31	34	22	15	1	5	27	.264	.250	.274	7.84	1.45
Mateo, Alejandro	R-R	6-2	200	1-18-94	3	4	3.86	15	15	0	0	75	82	40	32	5	14	79	.275	.289	.262	9.52	1.69
McAree, Henry	R-R	6-1	205	8-31-93	0	0	0.00	2	0	0	0	4	2	0	0	0	1	7	.154	.000	.286	15.75	2.25
McKay, Ryan	R-R	6-4	195	9-20-96	1	1	4.50	17	0	0	1	30	31	22	15	2	11	18	.256	.288	.218	5.40	3.30
Neubeck, Travis	L-R	6-2	180	3-13-95	0	2	5.40	18	0	0	1	25	32	17	15	2	8	17	.308	.372	.262	6.12	2.88
Ovalle, Jeremy	R-R	6-3	185	1-17-97	1	0	4.44	16	0	0	0	24	28	14	12	2	12	27	.280	.250	.300	9.99	4.44
Peace, RJ	R-R	6-2	175	6-24-97	0	1	2.84	14	0	0	2	32	23	11	10	0	13	34	.207	.163	.242	9.66	3.69
Perez, Sam	R-R	6-3	210	8-17-94	4	2	2.21	14	14	0	0	77	69	20	19	3	13	53	.241	.228	.252	6.17	1.51
Puckett, Brady	R-R	6-8	220	7-31-95	0	0	4.50	1	0	0	0	2	2	1	1	1	0	3	.250	.000	.667	13.50	0.00
Reed, Remey	R-R	6-5	230	5-5-95	3	4	4.44	15	11	1	0	51	48	28	25	5	17	47	.246	.247	.245	8.35	3.02
Rodriguez, Manuel	L-L	6-2	160	12-23-96	1	2	9.00	9	3	0	0	17	23	19	17	2	8	18	.319	.323	.317	9.53	4.24
Sawczak, Shane	L-L	6-0	188	11-20-95	3	1	3.25	17	0	0	0	28	22	11	10	1	21	30	.225	.200	.235	9.76	6.83
Wells, Hunter	R-R	6-2	170	5-22-95	0	2	2.35	2	2	0	0	8	9	5	2	1	1	7	.273	.600	.130	8.22	1.17
Wheatley, Brent	R-R	6-4	210	8-31-93	2	1	4.44	16	0	0	5	24	19	14	12	1	15	25	.214	.162	.250	9.25	5.55

Fielding

C: Barnes 8, De La Rosa 3, Gauntt 29, Hernandez 22, Jones 14. **1B:** Alonso 22, Curtis 2, Fisher 31, Reynolds 20. **2B:** Brooks 1, Brown 4, Castro 40, Garzillo 2, Ho 8, Karas 7, Millan 4, Sims 12. **3B:** Brown 5, Cabrera 6, Curtis 46, Ho 2, Hollins 8, Karas 4, Millan 3, Rivera 1. **SS:** Brown 10, Ho 1, Millan 1, Rivera 60, Sims 5. **OF:** Bennett 14, Brooks 43, Cespedes 19, Daly 7, Hernandez 15, Jones 66, Santos 29, White 37.

GCL MARLINS — ROOKIE

GULF COAST LEAGUE

Batting	B-T	HT	WT	DOB	AVG	vLH	vRH	G	AB	R	H	2B	3B	HR	RBI	BB	HBP	SH	SF	SO	SB	CS	SLG	OBP
Arrojo, Junior	R-R	5-10	195	5-29-88	.400	1.000	.000	2	5	1	2	0	0	0	0	0	0	0	0	2	1	0	.400	.400
Baez, Igor	R-R	6-1	180	6-6-95	.000	—	.000	1	2	2	0	0	0	0	0	1	0	0	0	1	0	0	.000	.333
Baranek, Cameron	L-L	5-10	195	2-20-95	.234	.265	.221	29	111	14	26	6	2	1	22	9	3	0	1	30	6	3	.351	.307
Barnes, Jared	R-R	6-0	185	11-21-95	.333	.286	.348	10	30	7	10	3	1	1	4	4	0	1	0	7	0	1	.600	.412
Barzilli, Elliott	R-R	6-1	175	5-3-95	.254	.188	.277	19	63	8	16	4	1	2	8	4	0	0	0	7	1	0	.444	.299
Berry, Branden	R-R	6-4	225	5-19-93	.375	.000	.429	2	8	0	3	0	0	0	2	2	0	0	0	1	0	0	.375	.500
Cohen, Justin	R-R	6-0	190	9-26-96	.244	.240	.246	28	90	14	22	1	2	0	6	16	1	0	1	31	1	1	.300	.361
Dean, Austin	R-R	6-1	190	10-14-93	.412	.571	.300	4	17	3	7	2	0	1	7	0	0	0	0	2	0	0	.706	.412
Donadio, Michael	L-R	6-0	195	4-23-95	.278	.286	.276	31	97	17	27	6	1	1	13	16	5	0	0	23	2	1	.392	.407
Dunand, Joe	R-R	6-2	205	9-20-95	.375	.333	.385	5	16	4	6	3	0	1	3	3	1	0	1	4	0	0	.750	.476
Encarnacion, Yeral	R-R	6-4	219	10-22-97	.266	.189	.291	42	154	25	41	7	3	5	26	10	3	0	0	51	3	3	.448	.323
Fisher, Ben	L-L	6-1	215	11-16-94	.268	.444	.219	12	41	6	11	3	0	0	2	6	1	0	0	11	0	0	.342	.375
Galloway, Isaac	R-R	6-2	205	10-10-89	.333	.375	.320	11	33	5	11	1	0	3	10	3	1	0	1	7	3	0	.636	.395
Garcia, Pablo	B-R	5-10	170	9-26-96	.239	.091	.260	27	88	12	21	3	1	1	10	6	1	3	0	13	5	1	.330	.295
Guaimaro, Albert	R-R	6-0	180	1-17-99	.234	.273	.223	41	154	24	36	8	5	1	16	14	0	0	4	32	8	4	.370	.291
Hernandez, Brayan	R-R	6-2	175	9-11-97	.250	.000	.286	3	8	2	2	1	0	0	0	1	0	0	0	2	0	0	.375	.333
Hernandez, Michael	R-R	5-10	195	5-24-95	.323	.125	.391	10	31	10	10	0	1	3	9	4	2	0	1	11	0	0	.677	.421
Hill, Trenton	L-L	6-4	210	3-10-94	.400	.500	.368	7	25	4	10	3	1	0	8	7	0	0	1	6	0	0	.600	.515
Ho, Shao-Pin	R-R	6-0	180	6-5-94	.245	.231	.250	15	49	10	12	2	0	0	5	6	0	0	0	5	2	0	.286	.327
Karas, Denis	R-R	5-11	180	11-27-95	.171	.267	.141	38	129	20	22	5	0	2	15	14	4	0	1	42	3	0	.256	.270
Mercado, Jan	R-R	6-1	185	8-28-99	.079	.111	.050	11	38	1	3	0	0	0	2	4	0	0	0	15	0	1	.079	.167
Nunez, Gerardo	R-R	6-1	180	2-6-98	.287	.345	.271	37	136	19	39	5	1	0	14	9	3	0	1	32	16	3	.338	.342
Osborne, J.D.	R-R	6-1	215	7-13-95	.226	.188	.235	26	84	12	19	4	0	0	10	12	2	0	2	13	0	0	.274	.330
Reyna, Rosandel	B-R	5-10	165	6-5-97	.159	.167	.155	26	82	10	13	3	0	0	9	9	2	1	2	17	5	2	.195	.253
Reynolds, Sean	L-R	6-7	205	4-19-98	.214	.059	.290	31	103	19	22	5	1	1	14	14	0	0	2	44	1	1	.311	.303
Reynoso, Ronal	L-R	6-1	165	5-23-98	.161	.250	.122	32	118	12	19	2	2	0	8	9	0	4	1	40	3	1	.212	.219
Sims, Demetrius	R-R	6-2	200	7-14-95	.290	.438	.245	20	69	12	20	1	0	0	8	11	4	0	0	12	3	1	.304	.417

Pitching	B-T	HT	WT	DOB	W	L	ERA	G	GS	CG	SV	IP	H	R	ER	HR	BB	SO	AVG	vLH	vRH	K/9	BB/9
Aiello, Vincenzo	R-R	6-3	220	8-6-94	1	0	9.00	2	0	0	0	2	1	2	2	0	1	4	.143	.500	.000	18.00	4.50
Alberius, Josh	R-R	5-11	170	11-19-94	2	0	0.00	5	0	0	1	8	5	1	0	0	2	5	.172	.250	.143	5.63	2.25
Alcala, Elkin	R-R	5-11	175	8-2-97	2	0	2.03	5	0	0	0	13	11	3	3	0	3	5	.234	.231	.235	3.38	2.03
Anderson, Blake	R-R	6-3	180	1-5-96	0	1	5.59	9	0	0	0	10	9	6	6	2	7	12	.257	.200	.267	11.17	6.52
Barraclough, Kyle	R-R	6-3	225	5-23-90	0	0	0.00	1	0	0	0	1	1	0	0	0	0	1	.250	.500	.000	9.00	0.00
Bennett, Dakota	B-L	6-2	160	7-12-99	1	2	7.56	8	2	0	0	8	9	8	7	0	3	7	.257	.000	.300	7.56	3.24
Boone, Brandon	R-R	6-3	210	10-26-94	0	0	3.38	2	0	0	0	3	0	1	1	0	3	4	.000	.000	.000	13.50	10.13
Braley, Taylor	R-R	5-11	140	1-13-96	0	0	0.00	1	0	0	0	1	0	0	0	0	0	1	.000	.000	.000	9.00	0.00
Chen, Wei-Yin	R-L	6-0	200	7-21-85	0	0	0.00	1	1	0	0	1	2	0	0	0	0	1	.400	.000	.500	9.00	0.00
Craigie, Karl	L-L	6-1	215	1-22-95	3	0	4.86	12	0	0	0	17	21	10	9	1	6	17	.309	.278	.320	9.18	3.24
Cuello, Eliezer	R-R	6-2	195	11-18-96	0	1	5.40	2	1	0	0	5	4	5	3	0	4	1	.222	.400	.154	1.80	7.20
Cyphert, Dylan	L-L	6-0	186	9-10-96	1	1	4.50	11	0	0	0	16	13	11	8	0	13	5	.228	.313	.195	2.81	7.31
De Los Santos, Miguel	R-R	6-1	175	9-27-96	3	1	3.65	13	4	0	0	44	39	22	18	1	18	38	.224	.254	.209	7.71	3.65
Del Pozo, Miguel	L-L	6-1	180	10-14-92	0	0	0.00	2	2	0	0	2	3	0	0	0	0	3	.375	.000	.500	13.50	0.00
Diaz, Carlos	L-L	6-3	190	2-3-92	0	0	0.00	2	2	0	0	2	1	0	0	0	0	1	.143	.000	.250	4.50	0.00
Diaz, Obed	R-R	6-2	185	5-5-97	1	0	2.45	7	0	0	0	7	9	2	2	0	2	5	.321	.429	.286	6.14	2.45
Domnarski, Doug	L-L	5-11	190	7-8-94	0	0	1.59	14	0	0	2	17	14	6	3	0	11	12	.219	.214	.220	6.35	5.82
Estes, Evan	R-R	6-2	185	11-29-96	1	1	5.09	12	2	0	0	18	10	11	10	0	17	16	.167	.179	.156	8.15	8.66
Farjad, Kyle	L-L	5-11	205	11-2-96	1	0	5.11	10	0	0	0	12	15	7	7	1	8	10	.294	.364	.275	7.30	5.84
Frias, Julio	L-L	6-2	160	6-1-98	1	2	5.23	12	1	0	0	21	25	16	12	0	12	24	.298	.280	.305	10.45	5.23
Fritz, Gavin	R-R	6-2	195	2-26-96	1	2	5.00	12	0	0	0	18	14	10	10	2	7	11	.215	.238	.205	5.50	3.50
Garcia, Javier	R-R	6-2	230	2-26-98	3	1	4.30	13	0	0	3	23	24	15	11	1	8	25	.273	.368	.200	9.78	3.13
Givin, Matt	R-R	6-3	180	6-17-99	0	0	0.39	7	7	0	0	23	16	4	1	0	6	19	.198	.259	.167	7.33	2.31
Guenther, Sean	L-L	5-11	194	12-29-95	0	0	0.82	4	3	0	0	11	5	1	1	0	1	11	.125	.400	.086	9.00	0.82
Guerrero, Alberto	R-R	6-3	192	12-13-97	2	2	1.55	9	8	0	0	41	30	14	7	1	13	29	.196	.220	.181	6.42	2.88
Hock, Colton	R-R	6-4	220	3-15-96	0	1	7.00	4	1	0	0	9	8	7	7	1	0	10	.229	.182	.250	10.00	0.00
Howe, Bryce	R-R	6-2	250	11-17-95	1	3	1.53	14	0	0	4	18	15	8	3	0	11	12	.214	.316	.177	6.11	5.60
Johnson, Patrick	R-R	5-10	170	8-14-88	0	1	27.00	1	1	0	0	0	1	1	1	0	1	0	.500	.500	—	0.00	27.00
Kolek, Tyler	R-R	6-5	260	12-15-95	0	0	29.45	5	4	0	0	4	4	13	12	0	14	1	.286	.167	.375	2.45	34.36
Lara, Yeremin	R-R	6-1	160	11-6-98	0	0	12.27	2	0	0	0	4	5	5	5	0	4	1	.313	.000	.417	2.45	9.82
Lillie, Ryan	R-R	6-0	210	5-1-96	0	0	0.00	2	0	0	0	3	0	0	0	0	1	3	.000	.000	.000	10.13	3.38
MacEachern, Ryley	R-R	6-2	213	5-27-94	0	0	0.00	2	0	0	0	1	1	3	0	0	1	1	.200	.000	.250	6.75	6.75
Martinez, Edgar	R-R	6-1	170	7-13-97	0	0	10.03	7	0	0	0	12	18	14	13	1	7	7	.346	.391	.310	5.40	5.40
McAree, Henry	R-R	6-1	205	8-31-93	0	0	0.00	2	0	0	0	2	1	0	0	0	0	1	.143	.333	.000	4.50	0.00
Mercedes, Enmanuel	L-R	6-3	160	12-9-97	1	1	16.20	2	0	0	0	2	0	3	3	0	2	3	.000	.000	.000	16.20	10.80
Parsons, Montana	R-R	6-3	185	4-20-95	0	0	0.00	2	1	0	0	3	1	0	0	0	2	0	.100	.000	.111	0.00	6.00
Peters, Dillon	L-L	5-9	195	8-31-92	0	1	1.35	2	2	0	0	7	3	3	1	0	4	6	.130	.143	.125	8.10	5.40

Poteet, Cody	R-R	6-1	190	7-30-94	0	1	3.21	4	4	0	0	14	11	5	5	0	2	12	.200	.059	.263	7.71	1.29
Puckett, Brady	R-R	6-8	220	7-31-95	4	1	2.85	12	5	0	0	47	52	19	15	2	9	32	.281	.372	.254	6.08	1.71
Rodriguez, Manuel	L-L	6-2	160	12-23-96	3	0	2.61	7	3	0	0	21	25	7	6	0	3	15	.305	.177	.339	6.53	1.31
Silva, Geral	R-R	6-1	155	10-29-94	0	0	—	1	0	0	0	0	0	0	0	0	0	0	—	—	—	—	—
Ziegler, Brad	R-R	6-4	220	10-10-79	0	0	0.00	1	1	0	0	1	2	1	0	0	1	2	.333	.500	.250	18.00	9.00

Fielding

C: Baez 1, Barnes 3, Garcia 26, Hernandez 10, Mercado 11, Osborne 6. **1B:** Berry 1, Fisher 12, Hill 5, Osborne 14, Reynolds 23. **2B:** Ho 7, Karas 19, Nunez 27, Reynoso 3. **3B:** Barzilli 18, Berry 1, Ho 4, Karas 20, Nunez 10, Osborne 5. **SS:** Arrojo 2, Dunand 4, Ho 4, Reynoso 29, Sims 20. **OF:** Baranek 28, Cohen 17, Dean 3, Donadio 21, Encarnacion 31, Galloway 7, Guaimaro 41, Hernandez 2, Reyna 25.

DSL MARLINS — *ROOKIE*

DOMINICAN SUMMER LEAGUE

Batting	B-T	HT	WT	DOB	AVG	vLH	vRH	G	AB	R	H	2B	3B	HR	RBI	BB	HBP	SH	SF	SO	SB	CS	SLG	OBP
Alfonzo, Ezequiel	R-R	5-10	165	8-31-99	.256	.333	.230	28	82	15	21	0	0	0	6	10	3	3	1	10	3	2	.256	.354
Arcaya, Luis	R-R	6-1	170	2-26-99	.350	.333	.353	6	20	2	7	0	0	0	1	0	0	1	0	2	0	1	.350	.350
Caballero, Jorge	R-R	6-1	170	1-10-00	.268	.255	.273	61	198	40	53	10	1	2	32	27	12	3	4	33	10	3	.359	.382
Campos, Brhayan	R-R	6-1	185	9-17-98	.307	.529	.222	23	62	8	19	4	0	0	8	1	5	2	0	6	1	2	.371	.368
Espinal, Danyeli	L-L	6-2	190	11-11-98	.192	.333	.150	9	26	1	5	0	1	0	2	0	0	0	0	7	1	1	.269	.192
Espinal, Walner	R-R	6-0	170	12-21-99	.273	.173	.311	54	187	34	51	7	0	2	21	21	5	3	3	48	7	4	.342	.357
Garcia, Jhon	L-R	6-0	170	6-18-99	.117	.087	.127	35	94	13	11	2	0	0	6	18	0	3	2	33	0	2	.138	.254
Gilma, Joseph	B-R	5-9	145	3-18-99	.190	.333	.140	57	153	31	29	1	0	0	17	26	6	6	1	28	8	1	.196	.328
Heureaux, Danielsan	L-L	6-0	165	3-22-00	.187	.118	.207	30	75	12	14	0	1	0	7	11	2	1	0	16	1	3	.213	.307
Lebron, Omar	L-L	6-0	175	4-11-99	.249	.318	.225	67	241	60	60	7	4	3	34	46	10	2	0	40	29	11	.349	.391
Montero, Alvaro	L-R	5-11	155	6-27-00	.260	.300	.245	31	73	24	19	2	0	0	14	26	3	5	0	16	11	2	.288	.471
Paulino, Daniel	R-R	6-1	155	11-23-98	.319	.393	.294	64	226	39	72	8	6	0	37	34	7	1	2	43	16	9	.407	.420
Pena, Miguel	R-R	6-0	175	1-14-98	.293	.356	.273	56	188	27	55	4	0	0	36	13	4	1	2	20	2	7	.314	.348
Pineda, Bryan	R-R	6-3	165	2-28-00	.203	.111	.244	18	59	6	12	1	0	0	8	5	2	1	0	14	1	1	.220	.288
Prenza, Mario	R-R	6-0	160	2-3-99	.222	.200	.235	10	27	6	6	1	0	0	5	3	1	0	0	9	0	1	.259	.323
Rasquin, Wiklerman	L-L	5-9	145	12-5-98	.250	.318	.230	56	192	24	48	11	2	0	33	14	2	5	4	23	10	6	.328	.302
Rodriguez, Christopher	R-R	6-2	190	12-22-99	.278	.283	.276	51	162	19	45	9	0	2	26	30	6	2	2	36	1	0	.370	.405
Sosa, Maicol	R-R	6-2	185	2-9-99	.200	.385	.143	21	55	6	11	1	0	0	1	3	0	1	0	12	1	2	.218	.241
Urena, Juan	R-R	6-2	180	12-10-98	.215	.188	.230	34	93	17	20	5	1	0	16	16	5	3	0	33	3	0	.290	.360

Pitching	B-T	HT	WT	DOB	W	L	ERA	G	GS	CG	SV	IP	H	R	ER	HR	BB	SO	AVG	vLH	vRH	K/9	BB/9
Alcala, Elkin	R-R	5-11	175	8-2-97	7	0	0.75	13	0	0	2	24	10	5	2	1	4	16	.124	.111	.130	6.00	1.50
Baez, Gabriel	L-L	6-1	185	4-18-98	0	1	6.94	9	1	0	0	12	13	13	9	1	8	10	.277	.400	.243	7.71	6.17
Borges, Juan	R-R	6-2	160	1-6-98	2	1	1.44	14	5	0	0	44	33	10	7	0	17	45	.204	.283	.157	9.27	3.50
Brioso, Franklin	L-L	6-3	185	4-15-00	0	2	5.11	4	4	0	0	12	13	13	7	0	4	9	.265	.143	.286	6.57	2.92
Brito, Raul	R-R	6-1	180	5-23-97	6	2	4.02	18	0	0	1	31	37	18	14	0	16	28	.301	.327	.282	8.04	4.60
De Paula, Brayan	L-L	6-3	175	6-25-99	1	1	5.52	7	1	0	0	15	16	9	9	1	4	12	.286	.000	.356	7.36	2.45
Eysseric, Rafael	R-R	6-0	170	6-27-00	1	0	4.08	15	6	0	0	35	32	18	16	0	12	25	.252	.304	.222	6.37	3.06
Galindez, Geremy	R-R	6-1	170	4-29-98	0	0	5.63	2	2	0	0	8	12	5	5	1	1	5	.387	.455	.350	5.63	1.13
Lara, Yeremin	R-R	6-1	160	11-6-98	1	1	2.76	11	2	0	1	16	11	6	5	0	12	12	.200	.150	.229	6.61	6.61
Liriano, Edin	L-B	6-4	185	6-25-97	0	0	6.00	8	0	0	0	15	18	14	10	2	5	11	.295	.429	.278	6.60	3.00
Martinez, Edgar	R-R	6-1	170	7-13-97	1	1	4.15	8	0	0	0	9	16	8	4	0	3	8	.457	.500	.444	8.31	3.12
Martinez, Leudy	R-R	6-2	180	6-9-00	0	5	4.97	12	12	0	0	29	28	26	16	0	18	22	.252	.302	.221	6.83	5.59
Mercedes, Enmanuel	L-R	6-3	160	12-9-97	2	1	6.75	12	0	0	1	16	17	16	12	0	7	15	.274	.375	.211	8.44	3.94
Mora, Winston	R-R	6-1	180	10-17-96	0	2	3.00	15	1	0	0	30	19	14	10	0	11	20	.185	.135	.212	6.00	3.30
Palacios, Luis	L-L	6-2	160	7-1-00	4	0	2.70	15	4	0	0	47	38	21	14	1	15	43	.215	.207	.216	8.29	2.89
Quinonez, Yoilan	R-R	6-4	200	8-11-99	0	2	4.35	9	6	0	0	21	16	12	10	0	10	13	.208	.250	.184	5.66	4.35
Reyes, Juan	R-L	6-4	170	7-24-00	0	1	4.66	11	10	0	0	29	26	16	15	0	15	33	.230	.267	.225	10.24	4.66
Rodriguez, Eliezer	L-L	6-1	160	2-17-99	1	2	3.57	14	14	0	0	45	33	19	18	0	21	39	.212	.120	.229	7.74	4.17
Rosario, Jesus	R-R	6-1	180	10-25-99	1	2	8.62	9	0	0	0	16	22	23	15	0	12	13	.328	.348	.318	7.47	6.89
Sanchez, Jesus	R-R	5-11	150	4-8-99	3	2	4.76	12	1	0	1	23	22	15	12	0	17	14	.259	.321	.228	5.56	6.75
Suriel, Edison	L-L	5-10	160	10-24-98	4	1	1.59	17	0	0	1	40	21	12	7	0	14	56	.146	.200	.137	12.71	3.18
Valencio, Henry	R-R	6-1	170	5-11-99	1	1	7.20	5	0	0	0	5	6	6	4	0	3	3	.300	.167	.357	5.40	5.40
Vera, Anderson	R-R	6-3	185	10-14-97	1	0	3.41	18	0	0	5	32	33	19	12	0	12	27	.271	.318	.244	7.67	3.41
Villalobos, Jonaiker	L-L	6-0	160	7-11-99	4	1	1.13	15	0	0	2	40	26	10	5	1	12	24	.187	.273	.171	5.40	2.70

Fielding

C: Arcaya 6, Campos 19, Garcia 6, Pena 56. **1B:** Espinal 5, Garcia 21, Lebron 47, Rodriguez 2. **2B:** Alfonzo 5, Espinal 45, Garcia 1, Gilma 7, Montero 11, Urena 11. **3B:** Alfonzo 16, Espinal 7, Garcia 5, Rodriguez 40, Urena 8. **SS:** Alfonzo 1, Gilma 51, Montero 19, Urena 10. **OF:** Caballero 60, Heureaux 26, Lebron 10, Paulino 63, Pineda 16, Prenza 7, Rasquin 37, Sosa 15.

Milwaukee Brewers

SEASON IN A SENTENCE: Milwaukee was treated to games that mattered right down to the season's final weekend. The Brewers' 86 victories were the most for the franchise since the 2011 team that reached the National League Championship Series.

HIGH POINT: The Brewers peaked at 11 games over .500. One of those peaks came just after the all-star break when Travis Shaw hit an eighth-inning homer to beat the Phillies 3-2, pushing Milwaukee's lead over the Cubs to 5 1/2 games. Shaw went on to lead the team with 31 homers and 101 RBIs, while ace Jimmy Nelson struck out nine and closer Corey Knebel picked up one of his 39 saves.

LOW POINT: Milwaukee had two six-game losing skids, the worse one coming in early August, when the Cubs passed the Brewers to take over first place in the NL Central. The streak included (a) the game-deciding run scoring on a balk, (b) seven shutout innings against Milwaukee by 44-year-old Bartolo Colon and (c) a loss when 19-game winner Zach Davies started against Milwaukee rookie Dietrich Enns.

NOTABLE ROOKIES: Manny Pina, 30, solidified the catcher spot for much of the year until Stephen Vogt provided veteran reinforcement late. Pina made BA's All-Rookie team. Soft-tossing lefty Brent Suter provided 81 quality innings and 14 starts, while lefty Josh Hader was the biggest breakthrough among the club's top prospects. He shifted to a multi-inning bullpen role and averaged 12.8 strikeouts per nine innings over 35 outings, posting a 2.08 ERA.

KEY TRANSACTIONS: In the offseason, Milwaukee fleeced the Red Sox, acquiring Shaw, infielders Yeison Coca (in mid-June as the player to be named) and Mauricio Dubon and righthander Josh Pennington for reliever Tyler Thornburg, who wound up injured much of the season. In August, the Brewers bolstered their lineup by trading for second baseman Neil Walker, who posted a team-best .409 OBP for Milwaukee in its stretch run.

DOWN ON THE FARM: Triple-A Colorado Springs and high Class A Carolina were both loaded with key prospects, with the Sky Sox contributing several down the stretch to the big league club, such as outfielders Lewis Brinson and Brett Phillips and righthander Brandon Woodruff. Both teams, as well as Double-A Biloxi, finished with winning records.

OPENING DAY PAYROLL: $63,061,300 (30th)

PLAYERS OF THE YEAR

MAJOR LEAUGE	MINOR LEAGUE
Travis Shaw **3B**	**Corbin Burnes** **RHP**
.273/.349/.513	(High Class A/
31 HR, 101 RBI	Double-A)
10 SB, 0 CS	8-3, 1.67, 145.2 IP

ORGANIZATION LEADERS

BATTING — ***Minimum 250 AB**

MAJORS			
*	AVG	Manny Pina	.279
*	OPS	Eric Thames	.877
	HR	Eric Thames	31
		Travis Shaw	31
	RBI	Travis Shaw	101
MINORS			
*	AVG	Garrett Cooper, Colo. Springs, Scran./W-B, Trent.	.366
*	OBP	Garrett Cooper, Colo. Springs, Scran./W-B, Trent.	.428
*	SLG	Garrett Cooper, Colo. Springs, Scran./W-B, Trent.	.652
*	OPS	Garrett Cooper, Colo. Springs, Scran./W-B, Trent.	1.080
	R	Nate Orf, Colorado Springs	103
	H	Ivan De Jesus Jr., Colorado Springs	142
	TB	Jake Gatewood, Carolina, Biloxi	226
	2B	Jake Gatewood, Carolina, Biloxi	40
	3B	Nate Orf, Colorado Springs	11
	HR	Monte Harrison, Wisconsin, Carolina	21
	RBI	Lucas Erceg, Carolina, Colorado Springs	83
	BB	Trent Clark, Carolina	98
	SO	Jake Gatewood, Carolina, Biloxi	161
	SB	Johnny Davis, Biloxi	52

PITCHING — **#Minimum 75 IP**

MAJORS			
	W	Zach Davies	17
#	ERA	Corey Knebel	1.78
	SO	Jimmy Nelson	199
	SV	Corey Knebel	39
MINORS			
	W	Aaron Wilkerson, Biloxi	11
	L	Nattino Diplan, Wisconsin	10
#	ERA	Nick Ramirez, Biloxi, Colorado Springs	1.36
	G	Matt Ramsey, Colorado Springs, Biloxi	53
	GS	Corbin Burnes, Carolina, Biloxi	26
	SV	Nate Griep, Carolina	30
	IP	Corbin Burnes, Carolina, Biloxi	156
	BB	Marcos Diplan, Carolina	71
	SO	Freddy Peralta, Carolina, Biloxi	169
#	AVG	Freddy Peralta, Carolina, Biloxi	.178

MILWAUKEE BREWERS

2017 PERFORMANCE

General Manager: David Stearns. **Farm Director:** Tom Flanagan. **Scouting Director:** Tod Johnson.

Class	Team	League	W	L	PCT	Finish	Manager
Majors	Milwaukee Brewers	National	86	76	.531	6th (15)	Craig Counsell
Triple-A	Colorado Springs Sky Sox	Pacific Coast	80	57	.584	2nd (16)	Rick Sweet
Double-A	Biloxi Shuckers	Southern	71	66	.518	4th (10)	Mike Guerrero
High-A	Carolina Mudcats	Carolina	73	65	.529	3rd (10)	Joe Ayrault
Low-A	Wisconsin Timber Rattlers	Midwest	59	79	.428	15th (16)	Matt Erickson
Rookie	Helena Brewers	Pioneer	28	48	.368	8th (8)	Nestor Corredor
Rookie	AZL Brewers	Arizona	33	23	.589	3rd (15)	Rafael Neda
Overall 2017 Minor League Record			344	338	.504	t-11th (30)	

ORGANIZATION STATISTICS

MILWAUKEE BREWERS

NATIONAL LEAGUE

Batting	B-T	HT	WT	DOB	AVG	vLH	vRH	G	AB	R	H	2B	3B	HR	RBI	BB	HBP	SH	SF	SO	SB	CS	SLG	OBP
Aguilar, Jesus	R-R	6-3	250	6-30-90	.265	.301	.244	133	279	40	74	15	2	16	52	25	4	0	3	94	0	0	.505	.331
Arcia, Orlando	R-R	6-0	165	8-4-94	.277	.248	.285	153	506	56	140	17	2	15	53	36	1	2	3	100	14	7	.407	.324
Bandy, Jett	R-R	6-4	235	3-26-90	.207	.296	.190	60	169	14	35	6	0	6	18	15	4	0	0	51	1	0	.349	.287
Berry, Quintin	L-L	6-1	195	11-21-84	.000	.000	.000	7	3	0	0	0	0	0	0	0	0	0	0	2	2	1	.000	.000
Braun, Ryan	R-R	6-2	205	11-17-83	.268	.264	.270	104	380	58	102	28	2	17	52	38	3	0	4	76	12	4	.487	.337
Brinson, Lewis	R-R	6-3	195	5-8-94	.106	.200	.063	21	47	2	5	0	1	2	3	7	1	0	0	17	1	0	.277	.236
Broxton, Keon	R-R	6-3	195	5-7-90	.220	.226	.218	143	414	66	91	15	4	20	49	40	7	1	1	175	21	7	.420	.299
Franklin, Nick	B-R	6-1	190	3-2-91	.195	.000	.239	53	82	7	16	2	1	2	10	5	2	0	0	19	2	0	.317	.258
Nieuwenhuis, Kirk	R-L	6-3	225	8-7-87	.115	—	.115	16	26	3	3	1	0	1	1	4	1	0	0	15	0	0	.269	.258
Perez, Hernan	R-R	6-1	215	3-26-91	.259	.316	.239	136	432	47	112	19	3	14	51	20	0	2	4	79	13	4	.414	.290
Phillips, Brett	L-R	6-0	185	5-30-94	.276	.111	.295	37	87	9	24	3	0	4	12	9	1	1	0	34	5	0	.448	.351
Pina, Manny	R-R	6-0	215	6-5-87	.279	.287	.275	107	330	45	92	21	0	9	43	20	5	1	3	79	2	0	.424	.327
Rivera, Yadiel	R-R	6-3	185	5-2-92	.000	.000	—	1	2	0	0	0	0	0	0	0	0	0	0	1	0	0	.000	.000
Santana, Domingo	R-R	6-5	220	8-5-92	.278	.286	.276	151	525	88	146	29	0	30	85	73	6	0	3	178	15	4	.505	.371
Shaw, Travis	L-R	6-4	230	4-16-90	.273	.250	.281	144	538	84	147	34	1	31	101	60	4	1	3	138	10	0	.513	.349
Sogard, Eric	L-R	5-9	180	5-22-86	.273	.262	.275	94	249	37	68	15	1	3	18	45	4	1	0	37	3	3	.378	.393
Susac, Andrew	R-R	6-1	215	3-22-90	.083	—	.083	8	12	0	1	0	0	0	0	0	0	0	0	6	0	0	.083	.083
Thames, Eric	L-R	6-0	210	11-10-86	.247	.182	.265	138	469	83	116	26	4	31	63	75	7	0	0	163	4	2	.518	.359
Villar, Jonathan	B-R	6-1	215	5-2-91	.241	.214	.252	122	403	49	97	18	1	11	40	30	0	2	1	132	23	8	.372	.293
Vogt, Stephen	L-R	6-0	225	11-1-84	.254	.294	.248	45	122	13	31	7	0	8	20	5	0	1	1	25	0	0	.508	.281
Walker, Neil	R-B	6-3	210	9-10-85	.267	.231	.271	38	120	19	32	8	0	4	13	28	1	0	0	30	0	1	.433	.409
2-team total (73 New York)					.265	.211	.284	111	385	59	102	21	2	14	49	55	5	1	2	77	0	2	.439	.362

Pitching	B-T	HT	WT	DOB	W	L	ERA	G	GS	CG	SV	IP	H	R	ER	HR	BB	SO	AVG	vLH	vRH	K/9	BB/9
Anderson, Chase	R-R	6-1	200	11-30-87	12	4	2.74	25	25	0	0	141	113	47	43	14	41	133	.220	.212	.226	8.47	2.61
Barnes, Jacob	R-R	6-2	220	4-14-90	3	4	4.00	73	0	0	2	72	57	35	32	8	33	80	.215	.235	.199	10.00	4.13
Blazek, Michael	R-R	6-0	205	3-16-89	0	1	8.31	5	1	0	0	9	12	9	8	6	1	7	.343	.438	.263	7.27	1.04
Davies, Zach	R-R	6-0	155	2-7-93	17	9	3.90	33	33	0	0	191	204	90	83	20	55	124	.275	.265	.285	5.83	2.59
Drake, Oliver	R-R	6-4	215	1-13-87	3	5	4.44	61	0	0	1	53	57	28	26	6	22	59	.274	.257	.309	10.08	3.76
Espino, Paolo	R-R	5-10	215	1-10-87	0	0	6.11	6	2	0	0	18	17	13	12	5	8	13	.243	.273	.216	6.62	4.08
Feliz, Neftali	R-R	6-3	235	5-2-88	1	5	6.00	29	0	0	8	27	23	22	18	8	15	21	.232	.191	.263	7.00	5.00
Garza, Matt	R-R	6-4	220	11-26-83	6	9	4.94	24	22	0	0	115	121	72	63	17	45	79	.270	.270	.270	6.20	3.53
Goforth, David	R-R	5-10	205	10-11-88	0	0	0.00	1	0	0	0	1	0	0	0	0	1	0	.000	.000	.000	0.00	9.00
Guerra, Junior	R-R	6-0	205	1-16-85	1	4	5.12	21	14	0	0	70	61	44	40	18	43	67	.230	.235	.226	8.57	5.50
Hader, Josh	L-L	6-3	185	4-7-94	2	3	2.08	35	0	0	0	48	25	11	11	4	22	68	.156	.140	.165	12.84	4.15
Hughes, Jared	R-R	6-7	240	7-4-85	5	3	3.02	67	0	0	1	60	49	21	20	4	24	48	.231	.282	.206	7.24	3.62
Jeffress, Jeremy	R-R	6-0	205	9-21-87	4	0	3.65	22	1	0	0	25	24	10	10	2	15	22	.250	.226	.262	8.03	5.47
Jungmann, Taylor	R-R	6-6	210	12-18-89	0	0	13.50	1	0	0	0	1	2	1	1	0	1	1	.500	.000	.667	13.50	13.50
Knebel, Corey	R-R	6-4	220	11-26-91	1	4	1.78	76	0	0	39	76	48	15	15	6	40	126	.180	.156	.205	14.92	4.74
Lopez, Jorge	R-R	6-3	195	2-10-93	0	0	4.50	1	0	0	0	2	4	1	1	0	1	0	.444	.500	.400	0.00	4.50
Marinez, Jhan	R-R	6-1	200	8-12-88	0	2	5.40	15	0	0	0	17	23	12	10	2	11	14	.333	.375	.311	7.56	5.94
2-team total (24 Pittsburgh)					0	3	3.91	39	0	0	0	51	57	24	22	6	23	40	.289	.246	.284	7.11	4.09
Milone, Tommy	L-L	6-0	220	2-16-87	1	0	6.43	6	3	0	1	21	29	15	15	6	2	16	.319	.250	.343	6.86	0.86
2-team total (11 New York)					1	3	7.63	17	8	0	1	48	65	43	41	15	14	38	.317	.179	.360	7.08	2.61
Nelson, Jimmy	R-R	6-6	250	6-5-89	12	6	3.49	29	29	1	0	175	171	75	68	16	48	199	.257	.246	.267	10.21	2.46
Peralta, Wily	R-R	6-1	255	5-8-89	5	4	7.85	19	8	0	0	57	73	51	50	10	32	52	.315	.343	.290	8.16	5.02
Scahill, Rob	R-R	6-2	220	2-15-87	1	3	4.43	18	0	0	0	22	21	14	11	3	10	10	.256	.333	.186	4.03	4.03
Suter, Brent	L-L	6-5	195	8-29-89	3	2	3.42	22	14	0	0	82	83	33	31	8	22	64	.264	.192	.287	7.05	2.42
Swarzak, Anthony	R-R	6-4	215	9-10-85	2	1	2.48	29	0	0	1	29	21	9	8	4	9	39	.202	.225	.188	12.10	2.79
Torres, Carlos	R-R	6-1	180	10-22-82	4	4	4.21	67	0	0	1	73	78	37	34	10	33	56	.279	.261	.297	6.94	4.09
Wang, Wei-Chung	L-L	6-2	185	4-25-92	0	0	13.50	8	0	0	0	1	5	2	2	1	0	2	.556	.667	.333	13.50	0.00
Webb, Tyler	R-L	6-5	230	7-20-90	0	0	9.00	2	0	0	0	2	6	2	2	1	1	3	.500	.500	.500	13.50	4.50
Wilkerson, Aaron	R-R	6-3	190	5-24-89	1	0	3.48	3	2	0	0	10	6	4	4	1	1	7	.167	.091	.200	6.10	0.87
Williams, Taylor	B-R	5-11	195	7-21-91	0	0	1.93	5	0	0	0	5	4	1	1	0	2	4	.222	.300	.125	7.71	3.86
Woodruff, Brandon	L-R	6-4	215	2-10-93	2	3	4.81	8	8	0	0	43	43	23	23	5	14	32	.259	.345	.171	6.70	2.93

Fielding

Catcher	PCT	G	PO	A	E	DP	PB
Bandy	.995	50	362	26	2	3	5
Pina	.992	102	721	52	6	7	4
Susac	1.000	2	7	0	0	0	1
Vogt	.990	38	279	10	3	0	1

First Base	PCT	G	PO	A	E	DP
Aguilar	.988	77	455	44	6	65
Perez	1.000	2	1	1	0	0
Shaw	1.000	1	3	0	0	1
Thames	.993	108	805	71	6	79
Walker	.986	14	67	6	1	6

Second Base	PCT	G	PO	A	E	DP
Franklin	1.000	1	4	2	0	1
Perez	1.000	17	24	32	0	10
Sogard	.988	60	66	97	2	28
Villar	.963	98	155	237	15	56
Walker	.988	27	36	48	1	16

Third Base	PCT	G	PO	A	E	DP
Aguilar	.000	1	0	0	0	0
Perez	.938	31	13	48	4	6
Rivera	.000	1	0	0	0	0
Shaw	.975	143	90	255	9	32
Sogard	.857	7	2	4	1	0
Walker	1.000	2	2	3	0	0

Shortstop	PCT	G	PO	A	E	DP
Arcia	.971	152	253	415	20	103
Franklin	.000	1	0	0	0	0
Perez	.958	7	11	12	1	4
Sogard	1.000	26	29	54	0	9

Outfield	PCT	G	PO	A	E	DP
Berry	1.000	3	3	0	0	0
Braun	.987	95	146	7	2	0
Brinson	1.000	16	24	0	0	0
Broxton	.971	139	231	5	7	0
Franklin	.947	17	15	3	1	1
Nieuwenhuis	1.000	10	10	0	0	0
Perez	.975	88	113	5	3	0
Phillips	.983	30	53	4	1	1
Santana	.979	144	224	4	5	1
Sogard	1.000	1	1	0	0	0
Thames	.968	29	30	0	1	0
Villar	.750	6	2	1	1	0

COLORADO SPRINGS SKY SOX — TRIPLE-A

PACIFIC COAST LEAGUE

Batting	B-T	HT	WT	DOB	AVG	vLH	vRH	G	AB	R	H	2B	3B	HR	RBI	BB	HBP	SH	SF	SO	SB	CS	SLG	OBP
Bandy, Jett	R-R	6-4	235	3-26-90	.310	.267	.333	12	42	7	13	2	0	2	14	5	3	0	1	5	0	1	.500	.412
Berry, Quintin	L-L	6-1	195	11-21-84	.286	.222	.303	10	42	9	12	1	0	2	3	5	1	0	0	9	2	0	.452	.375
Bortnick, Tyler	R-R	5-11	185	7-3-87	.158	.000	.188	8	19	5	3	0	0	0	2	1	1	0	1	3	1	0	.158	.227
Brinson, Lewis	R-R	6-3	195	5-8-94	.331	.267	.353	76	299	66	99	22	4	13	48	32	5	0	4	62	11	5	.562	.400
Broxton, Keon	R-R	6-3	195	5-7-90	.385	—	.385	7	26	4	10	2	0	1	7	7	0	0	1	8	4	0	.577	.500
Colabello, Chris	R-R	6-4	210	10-24-83	.301	.364	.285	44	156	28	47	10	1	6	25	24	1	0	2	37	0	0	.494	.393
Cooper, Garrett	R-R	6-6	230	12-25-90	.366	.345	.371	75	279	64	102	29	0	17	82	33	2	0	6	48	0	0	.652	.428
Cordell, Ryan	R-R	6-4	195	3-31-92	.284	.282	.284	68	261	49	74	18	5	10	45	25	3	0	3	65	9	4	.506	.349
De Jesus Jr., Ivan	R-R	5-11	200	5-1-87	.345	.385	.332	112	412	67	142	30	4	7	65	33	12	6	3	75	3	2	.488	.407
Dubon, Mauricio	R-R	6-0	160	7-19-94	.272	.235	.283	58	224	40	61	15	0	6	33	14	2	3	1	34	7	6	.420	.320
Erceg, Lucas	L-R	6-3	200	5-1-95	.400	—	.400	3	10	2	4	2	0	0	2	1	0	0	0	1	0	0	.600	.455
Garcia, Rene	R-R	6-0	205	3-21-90	.347	.462	.316	34	121	13	42	6	0	3	28	4	0	1	1	11	0	0	.471	.365
Heineman, Tyler	B-R	5-11	205	6-19-91	.281	.321	.275	65	199	24	56	19	0	2	20	20	0	6	3	34	2	0	.407	.342
Nieuwenhuis, Kirk	R-L	6-3	225	8-7-87	.244	.256	.241	84	205	32	50	12	0	4	33	38	1	1	2	67	5	0	.361	.362
Noonan, Nick	L-R	6-1	185	5-4-89	.304	.237	.320	62	191	29	58	12	2	2	30	12	0	0	1	31	3	1	.419	.343
2-team total (23 New Orleans)					.261	.308	.125	85	268	42	70	14	2	3	38	20	1	1	2	55	5	1	.362	.313
Noriega, Gabriel	R-R	6-2	180	9-13-90	.247	.200	.259	35	73	9	18	2	0	0	6	4	0	1	0	21	0	0	.274	.286
Orf, Nate	R-R	5-9	180	2-1-90	.320	.344	.314	125	434	103	139	32	11	9	65	54	7	3	9	75	7	2	.507	.397
Phillips, Brett	L-R	6-0	185	5-30-94	.306	.340	.294	105	383	79	117	23	10	19	78	45	1	0	3	129	9	1	.567	.377
Rivera, Yadiel	R-R	6-3	185	5-2-92	.218	.145	.233	107	376	45	82	15	3	5	43	30	4	3	1	104	5	2	.314	.282
Sogard, Eric	L-R	5-9	180	5-22-86	.330	.333	.329	24	91	30	30	8	0	3	17	15	0	0	1	12	5	0	.517	.421
Susac, Andrew	R-R	6-1	215	3-22-90	.205	.250	.189	51	171	22	35	10	0	8	35	26	1	0	4	53	0	0	.404	.307
Vogt, Stephen	L-R	6-0	225	11-1-84	.250	—	.250	3	8	0	2	0	0	0	0	1	0	0	0	2	0	0	.250	.333
Weisenburger, Adam	R-R	5-10	185	12-13-88	.000	—	.000	2	2	1	0	0	0	0	0	2	0	0	0	2	0	0	.000	.500
Wren, Kyle	L-L	5-10	175	4-23-91	.286	.258	.292	128	476	80	136	20	10	5	62	54	5	5	0	77	26	5	.401	.365

Pitching	B-T	HT	WT	DOB	W	L	ERA	G	GS	CG	SV	IP	H	R	ER	HR	BB	SO	AVG	vLH	vRH	K/9	BB/9
Anderson, Chase	R-R	6-1	200	11-30-87	0	0	8.31	1	1	0	0	4	6	4	4	1	1	2	.353	.200	.417	4.15	2.08
Archer, Tristan	R-R	6-2	200	10-18-90	7	3	4.76	44	0	0	0	64	77	40	34	5	19	57	.290	.305	.281	7.97	2.66
Barbosa, Andrew	R-L	6-8	230	11-18-87	7	3	5.29	36	4	0	1	66	64	44	39	9	27	65	.256	.173	.296	8.82	3.66
Blazek, Michael	R-R	6-0	205	3-16-89	3	4	3.71	26	13	0	2	85	87	36	35	5	33	66	.269	.299	.247	6.99	3.49
Brooks, Aaron	R-R	6-4	225	4-27-90	0	1	4.70	2	2	0	0	8	11	8	4	2	1	2	.333	.412	.250	2.35	1.17
2-team total (24 Iowa)					8	10	6.12	26	26	0	0	146	192	110	99	29	29	107	.321	.342	.301	6.61	1.79
Burgos, Hiram	R-R	5-11	210	8-4-87	2	5	7.80	13	12	0	0	43	64	41	37	11	13	40	.350	.279	.412	8.44	2.74
Cravy, Tyler	R-R	6-2	220	7-13-89	6	5	6.24	42	0	0	3	53	61	38	37	9	24	38	.291	.324	.272	6.41	4.05
Derby, Bubba	L-R	5-11	185	2-24-94	5	0	3.55	12	12	0	0	63	59	27	25	7	17	49	.254	.299	.216	6.96	2.42
Dillard, Tim	R-R	6-4	220	7-19-83	3	2	5.17	34	2	0	1	63	68	41	36	3	27	49	.283	.289	.280	7.04	3.88
Espino, Paolo	R-R	5-10	215	1-10-87	4	2	4.52	16	14	0	0	76	86	40	38	12	14	73	.285	.217	.326	8.68	1.67
2-team total (1 Round Rock)					5	2	4.46	17	14	0	0	79	87	41	39	12	15	77	.280	.200	.000	8.81	1.72
Garza, Matt	R-R	6-4	220	11-26-83	0	0	1.80	1	1	0	0	5	2	1	1	1	2	4	.125	.250	.083	7.20	3.60
Goforth, David	R-R	5-10	205	10-11-88	3	4	3.98	48	0	0	5	54	57	25	24	7	26	38	.271	.243	.286	6.29	4.31
Gomez, Jeanmar	R-R	6-3	215	2-10-88	0	0	2.16	7	0	0	0	8	7	2	2	1	1	7	.250	.308	.200	7.56	1.08
2-team total (5 Tacoma)					1	0	1.93	12	0	0	1	14	10	3	3	2	3	11	.204	.182	.100	7.07	1.93
Guerra, Junior	R-R	6-0	205	1-16-85	2	2	2.10	6	6	0	0	30	27	8	7	0	12	20	.252	.200	.298	6.00	3.60
Hader, Josh	L-L	6-3	185	4-7-94	3	4	5.37	12	12	0	0	52	49	32	31	14	31	51	.253	.158	.276	8.83	5.37
Jungmann, Taylor	R-R	6-6	210	12-18-89	9	2	2.59	17	15	0	0	90	69	28	26	4	39	82	.216	.214	.217	8.17	3.89
Kohlscheen, Stephen	R-R	6-6	235	9-20-88	1	1	6.20	28	0	0	1	41	54	29	28	9	16	39	.320	.373	.284	8.63	3.54
Magnifico, Damien	R-R	6-1	195	5-24-91	0	0	0.00	2	0	0	0	1	1	1	0	0	2	2	.167	.500	.000	13.50	13.50
2-team total (31 Salt Lake)					4	2	6.56	33	0	0	4	36	43	29	26	2	26	36	.297	.339	.277	9.08	6.56
Oliver, Andy	L-L	6-3	215	12-3-87	0	0	7.59	16	1	0	0	21	31	20	18	6	15	20	.344	.400	.309	8.44	6.33
Peralta, Wily	R-R	6-1	255	5-8-89	1	0	3.38	13	0	0	1	16	13	12	6	0	10	10	.213	.292	.162	5.63	5.63
Ramirez, Nick	L-L	6-3	225	8-1-89	0	0	0.00	1	0	0	0	0	0	0	0	0	0	0	.000	—	.000	0.00	0.00
Ramsey, Matt	R-R	5-11	205	9-24-89	0	1	18.56	5	0	0	0	5	12	11	11	1	4	5	.462	.364	.533	8.44	6.75

Pitching	B-T	HT	WT	DOB	W	L	ERA	G	GS	CG	SV	IP	H	R	ER	HR	BB	SO	AVG	vLH	vRH	K/9	BB/9
Rodriguez, Wuilder	R-R	6-2	180	1-21-93	0	0	6.00	1	1	0	0	3	3	2	2	1	2	3	.250	.000	.300	9.00	6.00
Scahill, Rob	R-R	6-2	220	2-15-87	0	1	1.40	27	0	0	10	26	24	5	4	1	4	19	.247	.333	.203	6.66	1.40
Snow, Forrest	R-R	6-6	220	12-30-88	2	2	4.85	7	4	0	0	26	24	14	14	5	6	26	.247	.244	.250	9.00	2.08
Suter, Brent	L-L	6-5	195	8-29-89	3	1	4.42	10	8	0	0	37	42	18	18	5	8	38	.292	.462	.229	9.33	1.96
Ventura, Angel	R-R	6-2	185	4-7-93	6	4	4.06	14	13	1	0	78	72	37	35	6	25	52	.249	.244	.253	6.03	2.90
Wang, Wei-Chung	L-L	6-2	185	4-25-92	6	2	2.05	47	0	0	1	57	57	17	13	6	12	48	.257	.258	.256	7.58	1.89
Webb, Tyler	R-L	6-5	230	7-20-90	1	2	6.48	17	0	0	0	17	21	12	12	4	7	17	.318	.368	.298	9.18	3.78
Wilhelmsen, Tom	R-R	6-6	220	12-16-83	0	1	13.15	16	0	0	0	13	27	21	19	3	7	11	.436	.400	.469	7.62	4.85
Woodruff, Brandon	L-R	6-4	215	2-10-93	6	5	4.30	16	16	0	0	75	78	44	36	8	25	70	.266	.241	.282	8.36	2.99

Fielding

Catcher	PCT	G	PO	A	E	DP	PB
Bandy	1.000	9	52	5	0	0	0
Garcia	.978	30	206	20	5	5	3
Heineman	.998	52	406	42	1	5	2
Susac	.988	45	321	16	4	4	3
Vogt	1.000	2	7	1	0	0	0
Weisenburger	1.000	2	7	0	0	0	0

First Base	PCT	G	PO	A	E	DP
Colabello	.997	43	365	21	1	51
Cooper	.993	73	537	48	4	59
De Jesus Jr.	.989	23	159	13	2	15
Nieuwenhuis	1.000	7	46	1	0	4
Vogt	1.000	1	5	1	0	0

Second Base	PCT	G	PO	A	E	DP
Bortnick	1.000	3	9	9	0	3
De Jesus Jr.	.984	15	23	40	1	6
Dubon	.957	27	54	81	6	30
Noonan	.933	9	11	17	2	4
Noriega	1.000	2	4	4	0	1
Orf	.979	76	143	191	7	48
Rivera	.944	4	7	10	1	3
Sogard	.986	15	39	33	1	12

Third Base	PCT	G	PO	A	E	DP
Cordell	.895	12	5	12	2	1
De Jesus Jr.	.933	65	28	98	9	11
Erceg	.667	3	2	2	2	0
Noonan	.918	36	12	44	5	8
Noriega	.905	24	12	26	4	5
Orf	.970	16	11	21	1	0
Rivera	.909	7	2	8	1	0
Sogard	1.000	3	4	7	0	0

Shortstop	PCT	G	PO	A	E	DP
De Jesus Jr.	.929	8	11	15	2	4
Dubon	.963	30	47	82	5	22
Noonan	1.000	6	4	15	0	1
Noriega	1.000	5	1	7	0	2
Rivera	.976	96	122	277	10	58
Sogard	1.000	3	4	8	0	2

Outfield	PCT	G	PO	A	E	DP
Berry	1.000	9	31	0	0	0
Brinson	.960	73	165	5	7	2
Broxton	1.000	7	10	0	0	0
Colabello	1.000	2	1	0	0	0
Cordell	1.000	52	98	0	0	0
Nieuwenhuis	.980	43	47	1	1	0
Orf	1.000	31	50	9	0	3
Phillips	.967	102	197	10	7	1
Wren	.986	122	212	3	3	1

BILOXI SHUCKERS — *DOUBLE-A*

SOUTHERN LEAGUE

Batting	B-T	HT	WT	DOB	AVG	vLH	vRH	G	AB	R	H	2B	3B	HR	RBI	BB	HBP	SH	SF	SO	SB	CS	SLG	OBP
Allemand, Blake	B-R	5-10	175	7-1-92	.256	.250	.258	97	336	42	86	21	2	6	41	26	3	0	5	64	2	2	.384	.311
Betancourt, Javier	R-R	6-0	180	5-8-95	.243	.276	.231	107	338	40	82	18	3	6	22	21	0	1	1	50	3	2	.367	.286
Bortnick, Tyler	R-R	5-11	185	7-3-87	.133	.222	.000	5	15	0	2	0	0	0	0	1	1	0	0	5	0	0	.133	.235
Charles, Art	L-L	6-6	220	11-10-90	.176	.091	.186	43	108	8	19	6	0	2	17	11	0	1	2	42	0	0	.287	.248
Choice, Michael	R-R	6-0	230	11-10-89	.272	.300	.260	48	173	26	47	13	0	9	29	18	3	0	1	49	0	1	.503	.349
Coulter, Clint	R-R	6-3	225	7-30-93	.234	.200	.246	116	385	46	90	21	1	14	49	35	14	0	3	94	2	3	.403	.318
Davis, Johnny	B-R	5-10	180	4-26-90	.263	.248	.269	133	505	63	133	12	6	5	30	36	3	8	1	119	52	12	.341	.316
DeMuth, Dustin	L-R	6-3	200	7-30-91	.244	.239	.245	116	377	40	92	20	2	9	40	42	13	0	1	115	6	4	.379	.340
Dubon, Mauricio	R-R	6-0	160	7-19-94	.276	.282	.274	71	268	34	74	14	0	2	24	25	1	5	2	42	31	9	.351	.338
Garcia, Rene	R-R	6-0	205	3-21-90	.311	.350	.280	14	45	2	14	2	0	1	5	4	2	0	1	8	1	1	.422	.385
Gatewood, Jake	R-R	6-5	190	9-25-95	.239	.375	.211	23	92	9	22	4	2	4	9	8	0	0	0	29	3	0	.457	.300
Houle, Dustin	R-R	6-1	205	11-9-93	.225	.278	.208	46	142	11	32	9	0	1	18	17	1	2	1	34	0	1	.310	.311
Iskenderian, George	R-R	6-1	190	2-28-94	.086	.000	.111	14	35	1	3	0	0	0	1	2	1	0	0	16	0	0	.086	.158
Mejia, Natanael	R-R	6-0	175	7-10-92	.000	.000	—	1	1	0	0	0	0	0	0	0	0	0	0	1	0	0	.000	.000
Noriega, Gabriel	R-R	6-2	180	9-13-90	.234	.333	.194	47	137	11	32	5	0	2	15	2	0	0	1	27	0	0	.314	.243
Nottingham, Jacob	R-R	6-2	230	4-3-95	.209	.294	.170	101	325	37	68	21	2	9	48	37	20	1	2	87	7	3	.369	.326
Ortega, Angel	R-R	6-2	170	9-11-93	.248	.254	.246	129	471	48	117	15	1	9	50	23	3	5	1	88	14	9	.342	.287
Reed, Michael	R-R	6-0	215	11-18-92	.208	.290	.185	54	168	25	35	3	0	7	17	35	1	0	1	59	5	4	.351	.346
Rijo, Wendell	R-R	5-11	170	9-4-95	.185	.160	.196	41	81	16	15	3	0	0	5	7	3	0	0	22	2	1	.222	.275
Roache, Victor	R-R	6-1	225	9-17-91	.176	.294	.140	22	74	6	13	4	0	0	8	4	2	0	0	26	2	0	.230	.238
Stokes Jr., Troy	R-R	5-8	182	2-2-96	.252	.292	.243	35	135	19	34	9	0	6	18	16	1	0	1	34	9	3	.452	.333
Taylor, Tyrone	R-R	6-0	185	1-22-94	.247	.375	.197	25	85	15	21	6	1	1	6	8	1	0	1	18	2	1	.377	.316

Pitching	B-T	HT	WT	DOB	W	L	ERA	G	GS	CG	SV	IP	H	R	ER	HR	BB	SO	AVG	vLH	vRH	K/9	BB/9
Archer, Tristan	R-R	6-2	200	10-18-90	0	0	2.57	5	0	0	0	7	5	2	2	1	2	8	.192	.222	.177	10.29	2.57
Burgos, Hiram	R-R	5-11	210	8-4-87	2	0	2.29	5	3	0	0	20	13	6	5	0	7	24	.194	.158	.208	10.98	3.20
Burnes, Corbin	R-R	6-3	205	10-22-94	3	3	2.10	16	16	1	0	86	66	21	20	2	20	84	.212	.213	.211	8.82	2.10
Derby, Bubba	L-R	5-11	185	2-24-94	2	1	2.88	18	2	0	0	50	40	16	16	1	20	46	.224	.238	.212	8.28	3.60
Gainey, Preston	R-R	6-3	205	2-13-91	0	0	0.00	5	0	0	1	6	2	0	0	0	6	10	.111	.182	.000	14.21	8.53
Guerra, Junior	R-R	6-0	205	1-16-85	0	1	3.60	1	1	0	0	5	6	5	2	2	3	4	.333	.167	.417	7.20	5.40
Hissong, Travis	R-R	6-0	200	7-19-91	0	1	4.11	16	1	0	0	35	26	17	16	3	17	34	.217	.234	.206	8.74	4.37
Jungmann, Taylor	R-R	6-6	210	12-18-89	1	2	4.36	9	6	0	0	33	35	18	16	5	17	31	.280	.273	.286	8.45	4.64
Lopez, Jorge	R-R	6-3	195	2-10-93	8	8	4.25	39	13	1	7	104	92	53	49	7	38	105	.238	.255	.226	9.12	3.30
Ortiz, Luis	R-R	6-3	230	9-22-95	4	7	4.01	22	20	1	0	94	79	42	42	12	37	79	.227	.259	.206	7.54	3.53
Peralta, Freddy	R-R	5-11	175	6-4-96	2	5	2.26	13	11	0	1	64	38	18	16	2	31	91	.167	.140	.187	12.86	4.38
Perrin, Jon	R-R	6-5	220	5-23-93	5	3	2.91	23	12	0	1	105	103	42	34	9	21	91	.259	.272	.249	7.78	1.79
Ponce, Cody	R-R	6-6	265	4-25-94	2	1	1.53	3	3	0	0	18	10	4	3	0	5	9	.175	.100	.216	4.58	2.55
Ramirez, Nick	L-L	6-3	225	8-1-89	7	4	1.37	48	0	0	3	79	56	19	12	4	24	56	.199	.167	.215	6.38	2.73
Ramsey, Matt	R-R	5-11	205	9-24-89	3	3	3.65	48	0	0	27	44	42	21	18	4	18	58	.246	.320	.188	11.77	3.65
Rodriguez, Wuilder	R-R	6-2	180	1-21-93	0	0	12.91	3	0	0	0	8	17	11	11	1	4	7	.436	.563	.348	8.22	4.70
Salas, Javier	R-R	6-3	248	3-20-92	1	2	5.06	7	0	0	0	11	9	8	6	1	12	6	.237	.222	.250	5.06	10.13
Scott, Tayler	R-R	6-3	185	6-1-92	4	6	2.34	42	0	0	2	62	57	21	16	3	35	63	.245	.238	.250	9.19	5.11

Pitching	B-T	HT	WT	DOB	W	L	ERA	G	GS	CG	SV	IP	H	R	ER	HR	BB	SO	AVG	vLH	vRH	K/9	BB/9
Snow, Forrest	R-R	6-6	220	12-30-88	6	4	3.38	26	2	0	0	59	56	23	22	4	20	78	.248	.260	.238	11.97	3.07
Torres-Costa, Quintin	L-L	5-11	190	9-11-94	3	2	5.23	18	0	0	0	21	21	13	12	1	17	25	.273	.250	.286	10.89	7.40
Uhen, Josh	R-R	6-4	220	4-7-92	4	2	3.68	44	0	0	1	59	63	28	24	1	26	53	.275	.317	.253	8.13	3.99
Ventura, Angel	R-R	6-2	185	4-7-93	3	5	3.48	11	9	0	0	52	41	32	20	7	25	36	.215	.253	.190	6.27	4.35
Wilkerson, Aaron	R-R	6-3	190	5-24-89	11	4	3.16	24	24	2	0	142	117	54	50	12	36	143	.228	.236	.222	9.04	2.28
Williams, Taylor	B-R	5-11	195	7-21-91	0	2	3.09	22	14	0	0	47	42	22	16	2	21	57	.243	.317	.181	10.99	4.05

Fielding

Catcher	PCT	G	PO	A	E	DP	PB
Garcia	.981	12	99	6	2	1	1
Houle	.995	46	368	50	2	4	5
Nottingham	.989	83	692	84	9	6	9

First Base	PCT	G	PO	A	E	DP
Charles	.988	24	150	14	2	19
DeMuth	.991	107	797	56	8	67
Garcia	1.000	1	12	1	0	1
Noriega	.973	8	31	5	1	2
Nottingham	1.000	13	76	6	0	9
Ramirez	1.000	4	9	0	0	1
Rijo	1.000	2	11	0	0	1

Second Base	PCT	G	PO	A	E	DP
Allemand	.972	46	73	102	5	23
Betancourt	.959	62	87	125	9	38
Dubon	.989	20	35	51	1	11
Noriega	.000	1	0	0	0	0
Ortega	.923	5	8	16	2	5
Rijo	1.000	24	25	48	0	7

Third Base	PCT	G	PO	A	E	DP
Allemand	.875	10	11	10	3	3
Betancourt	.966	42	18	68	3	6
Bortnick	.667	2	0	2	1	0
Dubon	1.000	1	0	3	0	0
Gatewood	.925	21	15	34	4	4
Iskenderian	.750	12	4	5	3	0
Noriega	.922	19	13	34	4	6
Ortega	.977	45	30	56	2	6

Shortstop	PCT	G	PO	A	E	DP
Betancourt	.000	1	0	0	0	0
Dubon	.948	53	74	128	11	37
Noriega	1.000	13	3	31	0	4
Ortega	.952	81	103	172	14	34

Outfield	PCT	G	PO	A	E	DP
Allemand	1.000	20	24	3	0	2
Bortnick	1.000	3	2	1	0	0
Choice	1.000	40	60	2	0	1
Coulter	.961	107	163	10	7	2
Davis	.985	129	332	6	5	2
DeMuth	.000	2	0	0	0	0
Ortega	1.000	4	7	0	0	0
Reed	.979	54	93	2	2	1
Roache	1.000	17	33	2	0	0
Stokes Jr.	.985	34	66	1	1	0
Taylor	1.000	21	40	4	0	1

CAROLINA MUDCATS — *HIGH CLASS A*

CAROLINA LEAGUE

Batting	B-T	HT	WT	DOB	AVG	vLH	vRH	G	AB	R	H	2B	3B	HR	RBI	BB	HBP	SH	SF	SO	SB	CS	SLG	OBP
Aviles, Luis	R-R	6-1	170	3-16-95	.232	.217	.239	132	492	58	114	16	2	6	46	27	5	0	5	141	38	8	.309	.276
Belonis, Carlos	R-R	6-3	175	8-19-94	.273	.343	.234	33	99	15	27	2	0	0	8	8	1	2	1	29	4	1	.293	.330
Clark, Trent	L-L	6-0	205	11-1-96	.223	.180	.244	133	457	78	102	21	6	8	45	98	3	5	6	141	37	5	.348	.360
Cuas, Jose	R-R	6-3	195	6-28-94	.176	.175	.177	40	125	10	22	5	2	2	15	9	1	2	2	37	0	1	.296	.234
Diaz, Brandon	R-R	5-11	175	4-14-95	.185	.091	.250	8	27	2	5	1	0	1	4	0	0	1	0	13	0	0	.333	.185
Diaz, Isan	L-R	5-10	185	5-27-96	.222	.255	.201	110	383	59	85	20	0	13	54	62	5	0	5	121	9	3	.376	.334
Erceg, Lucas	L-R	6-3	200	5-1-95	.256	.253	.258	127	496	66	127	33	1	15	81	35	3	0	4	95	2	3	.417	.307
Gatewood, Jake	R-R	6-5	190	9-25-95	.269	.291	.257	111	420	66	113	36	1	11	53	43	4	0	3	132	7	5	.438	.340
Ghelfi, Mitch	B-R	5-11	185	9-24-92	.304	.368	.270	17	56	5	17	5	1	0	5	5	0	0	0	11	2	2	.429	.361
Harrison, Monte	R-R	6-3	220	8-10-95	.278	.320	.258	59	230	41	64	16	1	10	35	14	8	0	0	69	16	1	.487	.341
Hummel, Cooper	B-R	5-10	190	11-28-94	.244	.185	.266	59	197	26	48	11	2	4	25	38	2	0	2	42	2	2	.381	.368
McDowell, Max	R-R	6-0	208	1-12-94	.210	.171	.231	79	257	33	54	12	1	4	33	31	12	1	5	52	6	4	.311	.318
Meyer, Charlie	R-R	5-10	180	1-10-93	.250	.000	.400	3	8	1	2	1	0	0	0	1	1	0	0	5	0	0	.375	.400
Oquendo, Jonathan	B-R	6-3	170	3-21-96	.138	.111	.150	11	29	3	4	0	0	0	2	3	0	0	0	12	0	0	.138	.219
Ray, Corey	L-L	5-11	185	9-22-94	.238	.275	.220	112	449	56	107	29	4	7	48	48	1	2	3	156	24	10	.368	.311
Rijo, Wendell	R-R	5-11	170	9-4-95	.254	.273	.247	36	114	12	29	7	0	3	17	13	7	2	1	20	4	2	.395	.363
Stokes Jr., Troy	R-R	5-8	182	2-2-96	.250	.231	.261	100	364	60	91	19	5	14	56	47	7	4	4	77	21	9	.445	.344
Whalen, Caleb	R-R	6-2	195	10-19-92	.167	.083	.208	12	36	4	6	2	0	0	2	5	2	0	0	11	0	0	.222	.302
Wilson, Weston	R-R	6-3	195	9-11-94	.241	.203	.255	73	261	26	63	11	1	3	27	16	6	3	2	80	3	0	.326	.298

Pitching	B-T	HT	WT	DOB	W	L	ERA	G	GS	CG	SV	IP	H	R	ER	HR	BB	SO	AVG	vLH	vRH	K/9	BB/9
Barker, Luke	R-R	6-3	230	3-11-92	1	1	3.68	12	0	0	1	22	24	10	9	2	6	14	.276	.353	.257	5.73	2.45
Berberet, Parker	R-R	6-3	210	10-20-89	0	0	1.45	8	0	0	1	19	13	5	3	0	6	16	.191	.235	.177	7.71	2.89
Brown, Zack	R-R	6-1	180	12-15-94	3	0	2.16	4	4	0	0	25	24	6	6	1	2	23	.250	.267	.242	8.28	0.72
Burnes, Corbin	R-R	6-3	205	10-22-94	5	0	1.05	10	10	0	0	60	37	9	7	1	16	56	.181	.189	.175	8.40	2.40
Cross, Colton	R-R	6-1	200	3-24-93	0	2	15.68	8	0	0	0	10	18	20	18	1	11	9	.391	.353	.414	7.84	9.58
Diplan, Marcos	R-R	6-0	160	9-18-96	7	8	5.23	26	22	0	0	126	126	83	73	11	71	119	.266	.209	.294	8.52	5.08
Griep, Nate	R-R	6-2	190	10-11-93	3	1	2.37	45	0	0	30	49	31	14	13	3	24	41	.191	.109	.224	7.48	4.38
Grist, Scott	R-R	6-3	190	5-31-92	0	0	6.95	14	1	0	1	22	37	18	17	2	5	21	.378	.333	.394	8.59	2.05
Hanhold, Eric	R-R	6-5	220	11-1-93	8	3	3.94	30	3	0	2	64	71	33	28	3	21	60	.286	.325	.269	8.44	2.95
Harber, Conor	R-R	6-2	205	12-18-93	4	9	5.04	24	14	1	1	89	79	61	50	7	64	74	.240	.290	.216	7.46	6.45
Kuntz, Brad	L-L	6-0	180	5-14-92	3	4	3.30	36	1	0	0	60	55	28	22	6	18	58	.236	.273	.222	8.70	2.70
Lopez, Frank	L-L	6-1	175	2-18-94	3	3	5.85	12	5	0	0	40	49	30	26	4	21	30	.303	.308	.302	6.75	4.73
2-team total (6 Down East)					3	5	7.02	18	7	0	0	50	71	43	39	9	31	42	.335	.267	.514	7.56	5.58
Medeiros, Kodi	L-L	6-2	180	5-25-96	8	9	4.98	27	18	0	1	128	115	75	71	7	53	121	.241	.222	.245	8.49	3.72
Olczak, Jon	R-R	6-0	180	11-14-93	1	1	4.95	11	0	0	2	20	23	15	11	2	8	19	.295	.310	.286	8.55	3.60
Peralta, Freddy	R-R	5-11	175	6-4-96	1	3	3.04	12	8	0	0	56	39	30	19	6	31	78	.189	.108	.235	12.46	4.95
Ponce, Cody	R-R	6-6	265	4-25-94	8	8	3.38	22	22	1	0	120	130	64	45	14	25	94	.274	.284	.269	7.05	1.88
Rodriguez, Wuilder	R-R	6-2	180	1-21-93	0	1	1.63	27	1	0	2	61	36	11	11	1	23	65	.171	.226	.149	9.64	3.41
Supak, Trey	R-R	6-5	235	5-31-96	3	4	4.60	15	11	0	1	72	65	39	37	12	28	57	.241	.241	.241	7.09	3.48
Torres-Costa, Quintin	L-L	5-11	190	9-11-94	6	4	3.77	23	0	0	1	45	38	20	19	5	15	66	.228	.154	.261	13.10	2.98
Yamamoto, Jordan	R-R	6-0	185	5-11-96	9	4	2.51	22	18	2	1	111	91	36	31	8	30	113	.223	.225	.222	9.16	2.43

Fielding

Catcher	PCT	G	PO	A	E	DP	PB
Ghelfi	1.000	13	100	8	0	1	3
Hummel	.992	44	345	35	3	2	4
McDowell	.984	79	658	85	12	5	8
Meyer	1.000	3	21	1	0	0	0

First Base	PCT	G	PO	A	E	DP
Berberet	1.000	2	17	0	0	2
Cuas	.985	15	126	8	2	13
Gatewood	.977	80	568	37	14	70
Oquendo	1.000	1	2	0	0	0
Wilson	.997	42	339	19	1	39

Second Base	PCT	G	PO	A	E	DP
Aviles	.951	24	34	44	4	12
Cuas	.944	5	7	10	1	2
Diaz	.949	70	115	143	14	33
Oquendo	.958	10	9	14	1	4
Rijo	.986	29	65	74	2	30
Wilson	1.000	6	8	14	0	4

Third Base	PCT	G	PO	A	E	DP
Cuas	.974	13	7	31	1	6
Erceg	.937	97	58	179	16	18
Gatewood	1.000	14	7	26	0	1
Rijo	1.000	7	3	15	0	4
Wilson	.800	7	4	12	4	1

Shortstop	PCT	G	PO	A	E	DP
Aviles	.951	101	178	269	23	64
Cuas	1.000	6	7	21	0	3
Diaz	.932	32	37	59	7	18

Outfield	PCT	G	PO	A	E	DP
Belonis	.893	32	45	5	6	3
Clark	.968	117	201	14	7	5
Diaz	1.000	7	14	1	0	0
Harrison	.993	58	134	6	1	1
Ray	.989	103	264	10	3	2
Stokes Jr.	.981	84	150	3	3	0
Whalen	1.000	12	22	0	0	0
Wilson	1.000	4	4	1	0	0

WISCONSIN TIMBER RATTLERS — LOW CLASS A

MIDWEST LEAGUE

Batting	B-T	HT	WT	DOB	AVG	vLH	vRH	G	AB	R	H	2B	3B	HR	RBI	BB	HBP	SH	SF	SO	SB	CS	SLG	OBP
Aguilar, Ryan	L-L	6-2	168	9-11-94	.206	.310	.171	105	350	42	72	8	4	2	23	49	2	6	2	96	7	2	.269	.305
Bandy, Jett	R-R	6-4	235	3-26-90	.400	.333	.500	2	5	0	2	2	0	0	1	1	1	0	0	0	0	0	.800	.571
Belonis, Carlos	R-R	6-3	175	8-19-94	.211	.222	.203	26	95	10	20	2	1	0	4	8	2	1	0	37	4	2	.253	.286
Braun, Ryan	R-R	6-2	205	11-17-83	.250	.000	.286	3	8	2	2	0	0	1	2	2	0	0	1	1	0	0	.625	.364
Carroll, Dallas	R-R	6-0	205	5-18-94	.261	.242	.269	30	111	14	29	4	0	4	13	13	2	0	1	20	3	1	.405	.347
Clark, Zach	R-R	6-2	200	12-5-95	.176	.207	.161	27	91	10	16	4	1	3	10	12	1	1	3	43	4	2	.341	.271
Cuas, Jose	R-R	6-3	195	6-28-94	.195	.127	.227	54	174	23	34	8	4	3	13	21	7	1	0	54	5	3	.339	.307
Feliciano, Mario	R-R	6-1	195	11-20-98	.251	.230	.261	104	402	47	101	16	2	4	36	34	7	2	1	72	10	2	.331	.320
Ghelfi, Mitch	B-R	5-11	185	9-24-92	.211	.278	.180	17	57	4	12	4	0	0	7	3	3	0	2	12	0	0	.281	.277
Gideon, Ronnie	R-R	6-2	225	9-20-94	.228	.221	.231	113	390	42	89	28	1	14	55	39	4	0	5	133	6	4	.413	.301
Hairston, Devin	R-R	5-8	175	4-7-96	.210	.241	.192	44	157	13	33	3	0	2	12	16	1	1	2	46	5	5	.268	.284
Harrison, Monte	R-R	6-3	220	8-10-95	.265	.250	.272	63	223	32	59	12	1	11	32	29	5	2	2	70	11	3	.475	.359
Hiura, Keston	R-R	5-11	190	8-2-96	.333	.310	.349	27	105	14	35	11	2	0	15	7	1	0	2	24	2	0	.476	.374
Lara, Gilbert	R-R	6-4	198	10-30-97	.193	.152	.215	67	223	18	43	6	1	3	22	9	1	0	1	79	0	0	.269	.227
Morrison, Trever	L-R	6-0	175	4-21-95	.204	.234	.196	93	299	48	61	17	2	5	27	29	10	6	1	110	8	4	.324	.295
Murray, A.J.	R-R	6-2	215	4-4-93	.125	.200	.000	3	8	1	1	1	0	0	0	1	0	0	0	2	0	0	.250	.222
Neuhaus, Tucker	L-R	6-3	190	6-18-95	.245	.275	.233	87	323	45	79	26	1	13	47	20	6	1	5	99	4	5	.452	.297
Oquendo, Jonathan	B-R	6-3	170	3-21-96	.165	.207	.149	34	103	10	17	3	1	0	5	9	0	0	2	33	0	1	.214	.228
Orimoloye, Demi	R-R	6-4	225	1-6-97	.214	.252	.195	125	467	57	100	23	4	11	45	40	5	2	4	139	38	11	.351	.281
Rodriguez, Nathan	R-R	5-10	210	9-30-95	.221	.234	.216	51	163	13	36	6	0	1	15	16	0	1	2	37	7	3	.276	.287
Segovia, Joantgel	R-R	6-1	175	11-8-96	.220	.225	.218	111	413	33	91	11	0	1	34	22	2	5	2	67	11	2	.254	.262
Sogard, Eric	L-R	5-9	180	5-22-86	.000	.000	.000	2	5	1	0	0	0	0	0	2	0	0	0	1	0	0	.000	.286
Susac, Andrew	R-R	6-1	215	3-22-90	.429	.667	.250	2	7	2	3	0	0	1	2	1	0	0	0	0	0	0	.857	.500
Villar, Jonathan	B-R	6-1	215	5-2-91	.615	1.000	.583	4	13	2	8	1	1	0	6	1	0	0	1	3	0	1	.846	.600
Vogt, Stephen	L-R	6-0	225	11-1-84	.182	—	.182	3	11	1	2	2	0	0	1	0	0	0	0	1	0	0	.364	.182
Whalen, Caleb	R-R	6-2	195	10-19-92	.214	.282	.160	29	89	11	19	7	1	2	8	7	3	2	0	24	0	1	.382	.293
Wilson, Weston	R-R	6-3	195	9-11-94	.277	.268	.280	39	141	22	39	9	2	5	26	16	4	1	0	29	1	5	.475	.367
York, Trey	R-R	6-2	190	4-4-94	.200	.300	.150	11	30	4	6	2	0	0	2	6	0	0	0	9	0	0	.267	.333

Pitching	B-T	HT	WT	DOB	W	L	ERA	G	GS	CG	SV	IP	H	R	ER	HR	BB	SO	AVG	vLH	vRH	K/9	BB/9
Anderson, Chase	R-R	6-1	200	11-30-87	0	1	2.70	1	1	0	0	3	2	1	1	0	1	3	.182	.143	.250	8.10	2.70
Barker, Luke	R-R	6-3	230	3-11-92	1	4	2.84	22	0	0	5	32	30	12	10	2	8	34	.252	.282	.238	9.66	2.27
Benoit, Rodrigo	R-R	6-2	170	2-23-94	0	0	6.57	6	0	0	0	12	14	10	9	3	3	13	.275	.143	.324	9.49	2.19
Berberet, Parker	R-R	6-3	210	10-20-89	2	4	4.79	18	0	0	3	47	55	27	25	3	15	43	.306	.295	.311	8.23	2.87
Brown, Dalton	R-R	6-4	250	9-15-93	0	0	14.73	2	0	0	0	4	12	7	6	1	0	2	.571	.600	.563	4.91	0.00
Brown, Daniel	L-L	5-10	185	3-22-95	6	3	3.00	37	0	0	6	72	67	27	24	3	35	74	.257	.217	.275	9.25	4.38
Brown, Zack	R-R	6-1	180	12-15-94	4	5	3.39	18	13	0	0	85	78	33	32	7	34	84	.249	.229	.262	8.89	3.60
Burkhalter, David	R-R	6-3	190	7-25-95	0	4	6.75	10	5	0	1	32	45	28	24	6	7	18	.352	.333	.361	5.06	1.97
Cross, Colton	R-R	6-1	200	3-24-93	1	1	3.62	19	0	0	2	32	28	19	13	1	15	30	.230	.294	.205	8.35	4.18
Desguin, Jordan	R-R	6-1	195	10-30-93	5	5	5.13	30	10	0	0	88	101	54	50	17	23	69	.289	.269	.300	7.08	2.36
Diaz, Victor	R-R	6-1	170	10-6-93	2	6	5.81	21	17	0	0	79	99	56	51	12	31	55	.308	.320	.302	6.27	3.53
Diplan, Nattino	R-R	6-3	180	12-30-93	3	10	6.60	29	12	0	1	89	98	74	65	6	39	88	.278	.269	.283	8.93	3.96
Drossner, Jake	L-R	6-1	189	5-16-94	0	0	2.25	1	1	0	0	4	3	1	1	0	2	2	.231	.333	.200	4.50	4.50
Garza, Matt	R-R	6-4	220	11-26-83	0	1	6.35	1	1	0	0	6	9	5	4	1	2	8	.346	.167	.500	12.71	3.18
Herrera, Carlos	R-R	6-2	150	10-26-97	3	2	3.79	9	5	1	0	38	24	17	16	4	17	26	.181	.102	.226	6.16	4.03
Houser, Adrian	R-R	6-4	235	2-2-93	1	0	1.00	3	2	0	0	9	5	1	1	0	0	11	.156	.000	.217	11.00	0.00
Jankins, Thomas	R-R	6-3	200	7-2-95	9	8	3.62	27	24	0	0	142	141	66	57	14	32	121	.259	.291	.239	7.69	2.03
Kenilvort, Alec	R-R	6-6	230	1-7-93	2	0	7.27	11	0	0	1	17	24	18	14	1	6	26	.308	.250	.328	13.50	3.12
Myers, Aaron	R-R	6-3	225	9-2-93	2	0	4.37	17	0	0	3	35	37	19	17	4	17	37	.270	.213	.300	9.51	4.37
Owenby, Drake	L-L	6-2	205	1-7-94	0	1	3.35	11	6	0	0	38	27	15	14	5	10	48	.196	.250	.182	11.47	2.39
Pennington, Josh	R-R	6-0	175	7-6-95	1	3	2.97	9	9	0	0	30	24	13	10	4	8	29	.211	.184	.224	8.60	2.37
Roegner, Cameron	L-L	6-6	205	6-19-93	5	2	3.56	19	10	0	1	78	73	34	31	5	24	72	.254	.296	.240	8.27	2.76
Sanchez, Miguel	R-R	6-3	190	12-31-93	3	6	4.36	32	1	0	2	64	57	35	31	7	24	69	.236	.218	.245	9.70	3.38
Supak, Trey	R-R	6-5	235	5-31-96	2	2	1.76	8	7	0	0	41	21	9	8	1	10	53	.156	.245	.098	11.63	2.20
Suter, Brent	L-L	6-5	195	8-29-89	0	0	0.00	1	1	0	0	3	2	0	0	0	0	1	.182	.000	.200	3.00	0.00
Vernon, Andrew	R-R	6-4	232	1-17-94	0	4	5.90	22	0	0	1	29	34	20	19	3	17	30	.298	.262	.319	9.31	5.28
Webb, Braden	R-R	6-2	195	4-25-95	6	7	4.36	22	13	1	3	87	72	50	42	8	39	90	.222	.209	.232	9.35	4.05
Williams, Chase	R-R	6-6	210	11-23-92	1	0	1.35	5	0	0	1	7	7	1	1	0	3	5	.280	.286	.278	6.75	4.05

Fielding

Catcher	PCT	G	PO	A	E	DP	PB
Bandy	1.000	1	13	0	0	0	0
Feliciano	.988	78	667	58	9	4	10
Ghelfi	1.000	7	47	3	0	0	0
Murray	.957	3	20	2	1	1	1
Rodriguez	.995	51	366	51	2	2	4
Susac	1.000	2	17	0	0	0	0
Vogt	1.000	1	1	2	0	0	0

First Base	PCT	G	PO	A	E	DP
Aguilar	.997	38	303	19	1	31
Ghelfi	1.000	3	18	1	0	1
Gideon	.990	91	683	46	7	74
Oquendo	.000	1	0	0	0	0
Wilson	.987	10	73	4	1	4

Second Base	PCT	G	PO	A	E	DP
Hiura	1.000	3	1	0	0	0
Morrison	.943	42	54	78	8	16
Neuhaus	.959	68	122	159	12	45
Oquendo	.974	24	36	40	2	14
Sogard	1.000	2	3	6	0	0
Villar	.933	3	6	8	1	3
Wilson	1.000	1	0	4	0	2
York	1.000	6	16	13	0	8

Third Base	PCT	G	PO	A	E	DP
Carroll	.935	30	14	44	4	4
Cuas	.944	54	39	79	7	14
Lara	.936	17	16	28	3	1
Neuhaus	.955	7	8	13	1	1
Oquendo	.909	6	2	8	1	1
Wilson	.948	26	25	48	4	2

Shortstop	PCT	G	PO	A	E	DP
Hairston	.944	44	52	118	10	23
Lara	.928	50	48	132	14	26
Morrison	.964	46	60	127	7	27

Outfield	PCT	G	PO	A	E	DP
Aguilar	.981	69	151	3	3	0
Belonis	.966	24	56	1	2	0
Braun	1.000	2	1	0	0	0
Clark	1.000	27	80	2	0	1
Harrison	1.000	62	152	3	0	0
Morrison	1.000	1	1	0	0	
O Orimoloye	.967	110	195	10	7	0
Segovia	.971	99	161	7	5	2
Whalen	.958	27	44	2	2	1
Wilson	1.000	1	1	0	0	0

HELENA BREWERS — *ROOKIE*

PIONEER LEAGUE

Batting	B-T	HT	WT	DOB	AVG	vLH	vRH	G	AB	R	H	2B	3B	HR	RBI	BB	HBP	SH	SF	SO	SB	CS	SLG	OBP
Carroll, Dallas	R-R	6-0	205	5-18-94	.336	.261	.354	30	122	28	41	6	1	5	21	15	3	1	1	20	5	4	.525	.418
Clark, Zach	R-R	6-2	200	12-5-95	.263	.200	.272	30	118	24	31	4	2	4	16	18	2	2	0	38	6	4	.432	.370
Corey, Kenny	L-R	6-1	185	2-15-95	.286	.111	.325	23	98	10	28	6	0	0	7	5	0	0	0	27	1	2	.347	.320
Diaz, Brent	R-R	6-1	205	3-22-96	.267	.143	.290	12	45	5	12	3	0	0	3	4	2	0	0	13	0	1	.333	.353
Feliciano, Jay	R-R	6-2	215	9-28-95	.279	.300	.273	63	244	43	68	8	0	13	51	17	4	0	0	53	4	2	.471	.336
Garcia, Gabriel	R-R	6-3	185	12-16-97	.300	.326	.294	64	233	39	70	17	1	9	45	39	10	2	1	69	6	2	.498	.421
Gomez, Jose	R-R	5-3	184	11-17-93	.263	.237	.270	53	186	28	49	15	0	6	29	27	3	0	0	37	4	1	.441	.366
Guenette, Alexandre	R-R	5-10	200	6-12-95	.189	.143	.200	12	37	4	7	0	0	0	0	5	2	1	0	11	1	0	.189	.318
Harrison, KJ	R-R	6-0	208	8-11-96	.308	.302	.310	48	185	38	57	14	0	10	33	23	3	0	3	55	0	0	.546	.388
Henry, Payton	R-R	6-2	215	6-24-97	.242	.313	.229	55	207	38	50	17	1	7	33	30	3	0	1	69	1	0	.435	.344
Lara, Gilbert	R-R	6-4	198	10-30-97	.500	—	.500	1	4	0	2	0	0	0	1	0	0	0	0	1	0	0	.500	.500
Lutz, Tristen	R-R	6-3	210	8-22-98	.333	.267	.346	24	93	23	31	1	1	6	16	12	5	0	1	21	2	4	.559	.432
Mallen, Franly	R-R	6-1	160	5-27-97	.225	.242	.221	48	187	19	42	7	0	2	19	12	7	2	0	46	1	2	.294	.296
Martinez, Yerald	R-R	6-2	180	12-3-95	.213	.143	.225	26	94	11	20	3	0	5	19	11	0	0	0	43	1	2	.404	.295
McClanahan, Chad	L-R	6-5	200	12-22-97	.234	.263	.228	63	235	33	55	8	1	3	30	39	0	0	3	78	5	5	.315	.339
Mendez, Julio	R-R	5-10	140	10-24-96	.200	.000	.250	2	5	0	1	0	0	0	0	0	0	0	0	2	0	0	.200	.200
Meyer, Charlie	R-R	5-10	180	1-10-93	.167	.000	.200	6	6	2	1	0	0	0	0	2	2	0	0	3	0	0	.167	.500
Pierre, Nic	R-R	6-3	170	11-13-96	.287	.436	.247	52	185	20	53	6	1	2	16	11	3	2	1	34	0	2	.362	.335
Pinero, Antonio	B-R	6-1	155	3-15-99	.236	.341	.207	55	208	19	49	4	0	1	14	7	0	9	2	45	7	5	.269	.258
Roscetti, Nick	R-R	6-3	190	11-6-93	.264	.448	.228	45	174	30	46	9	3	1	17	7	0	2	2	33	5	1	.368	.290
Vasquez, Yoel	R-R	6-1	180	8-20-96	.200	—	.200	4	5	0	1	1	0	0	0	1	1	0	0	3	0	0	.400	.429

Pitching	B-T	HT	WT	DOB	W	L	ERA	G	GS	CG	SV	IP	H	R	ER	HR	BB	SO	AVG	vLH	vRH	K/9	BB/9
Bean, Parker	R-R	6-6	185	3-7-95	1	1	4.80	20	0	0	5	30	24	19	16	2	25	31	.218	.250	.197	9.30	7.50
Beckman, Cody	R-L	6-2	190	11-1-94	0	3	3.93	14	0	0	2	18	23	10	8	2	3	24	.299	.417	.245	11.78	1.47
Benoit, Rodrigo	R-R	6-2	170	2-23-94	1	4	6.31	11	1	0	0	26	38	20	18	1	3	28	.336	.350	.329	9.82	1.05
Bettinger, Alec	R-R	6-2	185	7-13-95	3	3	4.97	15	9	0	0	51	52	30	28	1	23	39	.274	.344	.238	6.93	4.09
Chirino, Harold	R-R	6-2	173	1-12-98	1	6	6.94	16	11	0	0	47	54	39	36	6	29	44	.283	.260	.297	8.49	5.59
Delgado, Roberto	R-R	6-5	240	7-27-96	1	2	7.27	14	0	0	0	26	36	27	21	5	10	16	.324	.381	.290	5.54	3.46
Diaz, Juan	R-R	6-0	185	9-24-92	2	2	4.76	11	0	0	0	17	21	12	9	0	10	16	.328	.208	.400	8.47	5.29
File, Dylan	R-R	6-1	180	6-4-96	1	2	4.02	12	7	0	0	47	51	32	21	7	13	37	.273	.250	.287	7.09	2.49
Friese, Gabe	L-R	6-3	180	5-5-95	3	1	3.82	7	6	0	0	33	39	15	14	4	3	26	.293	.283	.300	7.09	0.82
Hanes, Cameron	R-R	6-2	180	5-8-92	1	4	4.58	9	0	0	0	18	23	13	9	1	8	17	.311	.303	.317	8.66	4.08
Hardy, Matthew	L-R	6-0	160	7-15-95	1	0	7.53	15	0	0	1	29	37	27	24	5	6	27	.314	.390	.273	8.48	1.88
Hernandez, Nelson	R-R	6-2	170	3-13-97	5	4	5.22	14	12	0	0	60	81	36	35	9	15	38	.315	.350	.292	5.67	2.24
Herrera, Carlos	R-R	6-2	150	10-26-97	2	0	4.29	4	4	0	0	21	16	10	10	5	5	26	.219	.226	.214	11.14	2.14
Hitt, Robbie	R-R	6-2	185	6-21-96	0	0	4.88	13	0	0	0	24	30	17	13	2	10	24	.306	.333	.292	9.00	3.75
Lindell, Karsen	R-R	6-3	190	6-2-96	3	3	7.45	16	11	0	0	54	68	52	45	7	40	38	.313	.277	.336	6.29	6.63
Martin, Cody	R-R	6-2	165	3-27-96	1	1	11.16	16	0	0	1	25	42	37	31	4	18	19	.372	.362	.379	6.84	6.48
Ortiz, Braulio	R-R	6-7	253	12-20-91	0	2	13.97	9	0	0	0	10	7	15	15	2	13	10	.206	.000	.389	9.31	12.10
Petersen, Michael	R-R	6-7	195	5-16-94	1	3	6.41	15	9	0	0	46	51	36	33	5	31	48	.283	.354	.244	9.32	6.02
Presley, Brandon	R-L	6-7	205	11-21-96	0	1	3.43	11	0	0	1	21	17	11	8	2	16	23	.215	.100	.254	9.86	6.86
Rose, Jayson	R-R	6-0	180	2-20-96	1	4	5.97	10	6	0	2	32	34	25	21	9	9	37	.266	.290	.256	10.52	2.56
Texiera, Brandon	R-R	6-2	205	4-21-93	0	2	6.98	17	0	0	1	30	33	27	23	5	18	24	.297	.226	.325	7.28	5.46
Vernon, Andrew	R-R	6-4	232	1-17-94	0	0	0.00	4	0	0	1	8	4	0	0	0	3	12	.138	.214	.067	12.96	3.24

Fielding

C: Diaz 8, Guenette 10, Harrison 17, Henry 42, Meyer 4, Vasquez 1. **1B:** Carroll 2, Feliciano 4, Garcia 50, Guenette 1, Henry 1, McClanahan 20. **2B:** Carroll 2, Corey 13, Mallen 46, Mendez 1, Pinero 1, Roscetti 14. **3B:** Carroll 14, Corey 4, Garcia 13, McClanahan 42, Roscetti 9. **SS:** Corey 1, Lara 1, Pinero 54, Roscetti 23. **OF:** Clark 30, Corey 4, Feliciano 51, Garcia 2, Gomez 51, Lutz 22, Martinez 25, Pierre 50.

AZL BREWERS — ROOKIE

ARIZONA LEAGUE

Batting	B-T	HT	WT	DOB	AVG	vLH	vRH	G	AB	R	H	2B	3B	HR	RBI	BB	HBP	SH	SF	SO	SB	CS	SLG	OBP
Abreu, Pablo	R-R	6-0	170	10-19-99	.316	.333	.313	6	19	1	6	3	0	0	2	2	0	0	0	5	1	0	.474	.381
Beam, Kyle	R-R	6-1	220	2-4-95	.200	.000	.333	4	5	2	1	0	0	1	1	1	0	0	0	1	0	0	.800	.333
Carmona, Jean	B-R	6-1	183	10-31-99	.146	.154	.143	13	48	5	7	1	1	1	6	6	0	0	2	12	2	1	.271	.232
Castillo, Leugim	R-R	6-2	215	7-18-99	.178	.222	.167	12	45	4	8	0	1	0	2	2	0	0	0	19	1	1	.222	.213
Coca, Yeison	B-R	5-10	155	5-22-99	.238	.286	.225	34	126	14	30	3	0	0	15	8	0	0	1	36	6	2	.262	.282
Corey, Kenny	L-R	6-1	185	2-15-95	.371	.313	.383	29	97	31	36	13	2	0	11	19	5	0	0	22	5	2	.546	.496
Diaz, Brent	R-R	6-1	205	3-22-96	.368	.500	.333	18	57	15	21	6	1	0	9	9	3	0	0	11	4	0	.509	.478
Egnatuk, Nick	R-R	6-2	185	12-21-98	.224	.154	.244	33	116	17	26	5	0	0	9	20	5	0	0	33	0	4	.267	.362
Ghelfi, Mitch	B-R	5-11	185	9-24-92	.200	.500	.000	2	5	1	1	0	0	1	2	2	0	0	0	2	0	0	.800	.429
Guenette, Alexandre	R-R	5-10	200	6-12-95	.250	.000	.364	6	16	2	4	1	0	0	3	1	1	0	0	4	0	0	.313	.333
Henry, Robert	R-R	6-1	195	5-19-95	.261	.355	.234	43	142	32	37	4	3	1	17	33	7	2	1	30	17	5	.352	.421
Hiura, Keston	R-R	5-11	190	8-2-96	.436	.692	.367	15	62	18	27	3	5	4	18	6	3	0	1	13	0	2	.839	.500
Jarrard, Julian	R-R	6-1	210	8-8-92	.287	.242	.299	37	150	19	43	16	0	2	37	6	5	0	1	39	1	1	.433	.333
Lawrence, Tyler	R-R	5-9	200	11-6-94	.182	.188	.179	15	44	6	8	2	1	1	6	6	1	1	0	13	0	0	.341	.294
Lujano, Jesus	L-L	5-10	160	2-18-99	.255	.413	.212	50	216	50	55	6	3	1	21	20	1	1	0	38	29	5	.324	.321
Lutz, Tristen	R-R	6-3	210	8-22-98	.279	.278	.280	16	68	12	19	4	3	3	11	4	3	1	0	21	1	0	.559	.347
Martinez, Ernesto Wilson	L-L	6-6	225	6-20-99	.167	.300	.125	11	42	3	7	1	0	0	0	6	0	0	0	19	0	0	.191	.271
McInerney, Pat	R-R	6-5	245	9-14-94	.243	.233	.247	50	189	38	46	19	0	9	36	34	7	0	0	65	8	0	.487	.378
Mendez, Julio	R-R	5-10	140	10-24-96	.255	.219	.269	35	110	15	28	9	1	0	16	6	1	0	2	9	4	1	.355	.294
Mojica, Johan	R-R	6-1	220	8-16-95	.000	—	.000	3	4	1	0	0	0	0	0	0	1	0	0	1	0	0	.000	.200
Perez, Moises	R-R	6-1	190	8-17-98	.175	.214	.163	22	63	5	11	0	0	0	8	4	0	1	0	31	0	0	.175	.224
Rivera, Yadiel	R-R	6-3	185	5-2-92	.381	.600	.313	4	21	7	8	0	0	1	5	0	0	0	0	2	0	1	.524	.381
Rojas, Robie	R-R	5-7	185	12-3-94	.290	.238	.306	30	93	16	27	4	0	0	10	19	3	0	1	16	5	0	.333	.422
Taylor, Tyrone	R-R	6-0	185	1-22-94	.435	.400	.462	7	23	6	10	1	0	4	7	3	0	0	0	3	2	0	1.000	.500
Thomas, Francisco	B-R	6-2	195	8-27-98	.200	.214	.195	17	55	8	11	1	0	0	8	11	0	1	0	18	2	0	.218	.333
Ward, Je'Von	L-R	6-5	190	10-25-99	.276	.194	.310	32	123	15	34	6	0	0	15	9	0	0	0	39	2	7	.325	.326

Pitching	B-T	HT	WT	DOB	W	L	ERA	G	GS	CG	SV	IP	H	R	ER	HR	BB	SO	AVG	vLH	vRH	K/9	BB/9
Beckman, Cody	R-L	6-2	190	11-1-94	0	0	0.00	3	0	0	0	3	2	0	0	0	1	3	.200	.000	.250	9.00	3.00
Bickford, Phil	R-R	6-4	200	7-10-95	1	0	2.12	6	5	0	0	17	14	5	4	0	10	16	.215	.188	.225	8.47	5.29
Bullock, Justin	R-R	6-2	195	5-12-99	1	0	3.09	6	1	0	0	12	13	4	4	0	3	11	.289	.385	.250	8.49	2.31
De La Cruz, Joaquin	R-R	6-2	195	10-13-95	4	0	2.53	11	6	0	0	43	31	14	12	0	20	46	.201	.224	.188	9.70	4.22
Francis, Bowden	R-R	6-5	240	4-22-96	0	1	8.10	4	2	0	0	10	17	9	9	0	3	13	.362	.417	.343	11.70	2.70
Friese, Gabe	L-R	6-3	180	5-5-95	3	0	0.00	10	0	0	3	20	7	1	0	0	2	22	.108	.107	.108	9.74	0.89
Gomez, Jeanmar	R-R	6-3	215	2-10-88	0	0	0.00	1	1	0	0	1	1	0	0	0	0	2	.250	—	.250	18.00	0.00
Gonzalez, Michael	R-R	6-1	190	7-22-98	2	4	11.22	12	3	0	0	30	52	41	37	7	17	24	.382	.455	.333	7.28	5.16
Hanes, Cameron	R-R	6-2	180	5-8-92	1	0	1.69	5	0	0	1	5	5	2	1	0	1	5	.250	.250	.250	8.44	1.69
Hardy, Matthew	L-R	6-0	160	7-15-95	1	0	0.00	3	0	0	1	7	6	1	0	0	4	5	.222	.308	.143	6.43	5.14
Holifield, Landon	R-R	6-4	210	8-30-94	2	0	1.80	17	0	0	0	15	12	5	3	2	7	16	.218	.333	.147	9.60	4.20
Houser, Adrian	R-R	6-4	235	2-2-93	0	1	1.04	6	6	0	0	9	4	2	1	1	4	16	.129	.000	.182	16.62	4.15
Kenilvort, Alec	R-R	6-6	230	1-7-93	0	0	4.50	2	0	0	0	2	1	1	1	1	0	4	.143	.000	.200	18.00	0.00
Lazar, Max	R-R	6-3	165	6-3-99	0	2	5.93	7	1	0	0	14	16	11	9	2	1	14	.291	.231	.310	9.22	0.66
Lemons, Caden	R-R	6-6	175	12-2-98	0	1	6.75	3	3	0	0	3	2	2	2	1	0	1	.200	.250	.167	3.38	0.00
Morales, Karlos	L-L	6-3	170	8-10-99	1	0	8.38	5	1	0	0	10	13	10	9	1	4	9	.310	.200	.344	8.38	3.72
Murphy, Brendan	L-L	6-4	200	1-2-99	0	2	6.19	9	4	0	0	16	21	15	11	1	12	11	.318	.462	.283	6.19	6.75
Nunn, Branden	R-R	6-4	230	6-26-95	3	0	3.18	12	0	0	1	28	30	11	10	1	4	31	.268	.281	.263	9.85	1.27
Olczak, Jon	R-R	6-0	180	11-14-93	0	0	13.50	3	1	0	0	2	5	3	3	1	0	4	.455	.000	.556	18.00	0.00
Owenby, Drake	L-L	6-2	205	1-7-94	0	0	3.18	3	3	0	0	6	6	4	2	0	3	8	.250	.200	.286	12.71	4.76
Pennington, Josh	R-R	6-0	175	7-6-95	0	0	0.00	1	1	0	0	2	1	0	0	0	0	2	.167	.000	.500	9.00	0.00
Robinson, Cam	R-R	5-11	187	9-6-99	0	0	12.91	6	1	0	1	8	14	12	11	1	3	9	.389	.417	.375	10.57	3.52
Rock, Kody	R-R	6-4	220	5-17-94	2	0	3.66	12	0	0	4	20	26	12	8	0	3	17	.313	.348	.300	7.78	1.37
Rubick, Austin	R-R	6-3	210	8-11-97	2	2	6.14	14	5	0	1	37	48	29	25	2	25	29	.324	.339	.315	7.12	6.14
Salaman, Wilfred	L-L	5-11	210	10-5-97	3	3	5.23	14	5	0	0	52	65	36	30	3	21	35	.313	.316	.311	6.10	3.66
Serigstad, Scott	R-R	6-1	190	11-2-94	0	0	6.75	2	1	0	0	3	3	2	2	1	2	2	.273	.500	.143	6.75	6.75
Simmons, Kadon	R-R	6-1	195	4-21-95	1	2	5.64	16	0	0	5	22	24	15	14	2	12	26	.267	.333	.242	10.48	4.84
Smith, Jake	R-R	6-5	220	8-29-95	2	0	5.14	16	0	0	0	21	15	15	12	1	16	27	.192	.214	.180	11.57	6.86
Taugner, Christian	R-R	6-3	215	5-14-95	2	4	3.74	14	3	0	0	46	53	28	19	2	8	50	.278	.220	.298	9.85	1.58
Thorne, Tyler	R-R	6-4	205	11-8-94	2	0	4.18	13	0	0	1	28	32	16	13	1	6	26	.283	.306	.266	8.36	1.93
Williams, Chase	R-R	6-6	210	11-23-92	0	1	2.00	6	2	0	0	9	9	3	2	1	3	9	.250	.154	.304	9.00	3.00
Woodruff, Brandon	L-R	6-4	215	2-10-93	0	0	4.50	1	1	0	0	2	2	1	1	0	1	1	.250	.333	.200	4.50	4.50

Fielding

C: Beam 2, Diaz 14, Ghelfi 2, Guenette 6, Lawrence 11, Mojica 3, Perez 13, Rojas 24. **1B:** Beam 1, Martinez 10, McInerney 38, Perez 9. **2B:** Carmona 3, Coca 8, Corey 4, Jarrard 6, Mendez 23, Thomas 16. **3B:** Corey 1, Egnatuk 33, Jarrard 16, Mendez 10. **SS:** Carmona 10, Coca 26, Corey 11, Jarrard 9, Rivera 2, Thomas 2. **OF:** Abreu 6, Castillo 10, Corey 9, Henry 40, Lujano 50, Lutz 15, McInerney 6, Taylor 7, Ward 32.

DSL BREWERS — ROOKIE

DOMINICAN SUMMER LEAGUE

Batting	B-T	HT	WT	DOB	AVG	vLH	vRH	G	AB	R	H	2B	3B	HR	RBI	BB	HBP	SH	SF	SO	SB	CS	SLG	OBP
Abreu, Pablo	R-R	6-0	170	10-19-99	.256	.245	.260	59	203	29	52	10	2	2	23	23	6	0	3	52	7	6	.355	.345
Avalo, Luis	R-R	5-11	190	11-24-98	.268	.290	.262	51	153	14	41	9	0	3	18	3	6	1	1	17	1	0	.386	.307

Batting	B-T	HT	WT	DOB	AVG	vLH	vRH	G	AB	R	H	2B	3B	HR	RBI	BB	HBP	SH	SF	SO	SB	CS	SLG	OBP
Carmona, Jean	B-R	6-1	183	10-31-99	.302	.151	.377	47	159	37	48	9	7	0	18	22	8	0	3	39	8	7	.447	.406
Connell, Bryan	R-R	6-3	195	11-9-98	.177	.282	.144	56	164	9	29	12	0	1	16	19	6	0	2	69	1	2	.268	.283
Cruz, Jean	R-R	6-0	155	10-27-99	.160	.182	.154	50	150	8	24	7	0	0	8	17	5	1	2	51	4	4	.207	.264
Familia, Aaron	R-R	6-2	170	3-16-99	.289	.304	.284	59	187	32	54	14	1	5	38	35	11	0	4	70	3	2	.455	.422
Florentino, Francis	R-R	6-1	180	10-13-99	.251	.191	.270	52	179	22	45	8	2	0	13	11	5	1	1	29	14	3	.318	.311
Gonzalez, Elian	R-R	6-2	175	4-15-00	.000	—	.000	2	4	0	0	0	0	0	0	1	0	0	0	0	0	0	.000	.200
2-team total (28 Indians/Brewers)					.243	—	.000	30	74	8	18	1	1	1	5	6	0	1	0	22	2	4	.324	.300
Manon, Luis	B-R	5-11	160	1-5-99	.155	.186	.144	53	161	16	25	3	2	1	11	15	4	1	2	72	5	1	.217	.242
Maria, Victor	R-R	6-2	160	9-22-99	.191	.065	.239	62	225	19	43	9	0	2	19	16	8	0	0	57	6	3	.258	.269
Marte, Alejandro	R-R	6-2	180	5-23-00	.103	.167	.087	11	29	2	3	0	0	0	0	1	0	0	0	15	0	0	.103	.133
Martinez, Ernesto Wilson	L-L	6-6	225	6-20-99	.257	.235	.266	38	113	14	29	9	1	3	17	30	3	0	2	31	2	3	.434	.419
Melendez, Anderson	R-R	6-2	165	5-31-00	.232	.197	.244	66	246	25	57	11	1	1	11	8	4	3	1	47	7	2	.297	.266
Molina, Roberto	R-R	5-9	160	12-7-99	.186	.208	.180	39	113	14	21	4	0	0	3	14	1	0	0	26	2	0	.221	.281
Munoz, Joel	R-R	5-10	155	12-26-96	.178	.167	.185	16	45	3	8	1	0	0	3	6	0	0	0	10	0	0	.200	.275
Pacheco, Kelvin	R-R	5-11	180	11-23-97	.000	.000	.000	6	16	3	0	0	0	0	1	2	1	0	0	6	1	0	.000	.158
Valdez, Luis	R-R	6-3	195	9-12-99	.178	.091	.216	36	107	9	19	4	0	1	6	9	2	0	0	32	1	1	.243	.254

Pitching	B-T	HT	WT	DOB	W	L	ERA	G	GS	CG	SV	IP	H	R	ER	HR	BB	SO	AVG	vLH	vRH	K/9	BB/9
Adames, Freisis	R-R	6-3	175	11-18-96	5	6	3.13	14	13	1	0	75	63	37	26	1	21	80	.223	.279	.187	9.64	2.53
Batista, Nestor	R-R	6-5	200	4-13-97	1	1	5.63	9	0	0	0	16	18	10	10	0	9	13	.295	.400	.222	7.31	5.06
Berroa, Silvestre	L-L	6-0	175	5-13-97	3	1	1.50	11	0	0	1	24	11	6	4	0	6	15	.138	.143	.137	5.63	2.25
Brea, Jesus	R-R	6-3	194	12-25-95	2	4	2.43	24	0	0	10	41	34	19	11	3	15	36	.224	.214	.229	7.97	3.32
Brito, Oscar	R-R	6-5	195	12-25-95	0	1	6.00	16	0	0	0	27	31	22	18	3	17	13	.284	.171	.353	4.33	5.67
Colman, Jesus	R-R	6-1	175	3-11-98	0	0	5.06	4	0	0	0	5	5	3	3	0	3	3	.263	.200	.333	5.06	5.06
2-team total (7 Indians/Brewers)					0	1	3.93	11	0	0	1	18	16	13	8	0	13	10	.246	.200	.333	4.91	6.38
Dominguez, Johan	R-R	6-4	190	1-18-96	2	1	4.24	4	3	0	0	17	14	10	8	2	6	18	.212	.226	.200	9.53	3.18
Gonzalez, Davison	L-L	6-0	165	8-10-97	0	0	4.91	4	0	0	0	4	8	8	2	0	6	3	.381	.143	.500	7.36	14.73
Medina, Jeison	R-R	6-2	175	12-6-96	0	2	6.23	8	0	0	1	9	12	8	6	0	7	7	.324	.333	.318	7.27	7.27
Montas, Jenri	R-R	6-3	200	8-10-96	2	3	5.05	23	0	0	2	41	43	31	23	0	26	47	.267	.297	.247	10.32	5.71
Parra, Jose	R-R	6-3	180	3-18-97	1	5	2.60	14	6	0	0	62	54	32	18	1	21	53	.229	.219	.237	7.65	3.03
Paulino, Guillermo	R-R	6-4	180	3-30-97	1	0	7.36	13	0	0	0	15	11	13	12	0	18	10	.220	.250	.206	6.14	11.05
2-team total (1 Indians/Brewers)					1	0	8.10	14	0	0	0	17	13	16	15	0	22	11	.224	.250	.206	5.94	11.88
Perez, Wilber	R-R	6-2	170	11-3-97	0	0	3.45	9	0	0	0	16	18	7	6	1	9	16	.281	.259	.297	9.19	5.17
Pinto, Maiker	R-R	6-3	180	9-25-96	6	5	4.24	14	9	1	0	70	71	37	33	0	12	48	.254	.278	.240	6.17	1.54
Rodriguez, Jose A	R-R	6-1	190	12-27-95	0	0	5.79	9	0	0	0	9	6	9	6	0	12	7	.194	.111	.227	6.75	11.57
Romero, Jose	R-R	6-1	170	11-1-97	0	4	4.34	13	9	0	0	48	53	24	23	0	33	38	.291	.316	.274	7.17	6.23
Salaman, Wilfred	L-L	5-11	210	10-5-97	2	0	0.00	3	3	0	0	14	3	0	0	0	4	16	.071	.000	.107	10.29	2.57
Salaya, Brayan	R-R	6-1	178	2-13-00	2	6	4.60	13	13	0	0	47	44	25	24	1	36	23	.251	.212	.268	4.40	6.89
Vasquez, Victor	R-R	6-4	205	3-16-97	0	1	2.86	13	6	0	1	28	21	18	9	0	26	9	.210	.158	.242	2.86	8.26
Vassalotti, Michele	R-R	6-2	180	8-2-00	1	3	1.63	9	9	0	0	39	23	9	7	0	8	32	.178	.189	.171	7.45	1.86

Fielding

C: Avalo 38, Molina 35, Munoz 7. **1B:** Avalo 10, Familia 25, Maria 1, Martinez 32, Molina 2, Munoz 4, Pacheco 4. **2B:** Carmona 1, Cruz 3, Gonzalez 1, Manon 49, Maria 21. **3B:** Cruz 34, Familia 31, Maria 11. **SS:** Carmona 42, Manon 2, Maria 31. **OF:** Abreu 59, Connell 35, Florentino 50, Marte 7, Melendez 64, Valdez 20.

DSL INDIANS/BREWERS — ROOKIE

DOMINICAN SUMMER LEAGUE

Batting	B-T	HT	WT	DOB	AVG	vLH	vRH	G	AB	R	H	2B	3B	HR	RBI	BB	HBP	SH	SF	SO	SB	CS	SLG	OBP
Avila, Luis	R-R	5-11	150	3-5-99	.253	.171	.272	48	182	29	46	4	0	0	16	18	3	4	0	17	19	7	.275	.330
Brito, Rafael	R-R	6-2	180	10-25-98	.214	.233	.210	43	154	20	33	7	1	3	13	9	1	2	0	20	7	2	.331	.262
Castillo, Javier	R-R	5-11	160	4-4-98	.287	.250	.302	39	87	8	25	4	1	0	8	9	1	1	0	12	0	2	.356	.361
Dimas, Bryan	B-R	6-1	165	2-4-00	.151	.115	.157	56	166	25	25	3	5	1	10	32	3	2	1	92	17	8	.247	.297
Franco, Yorki	L-R	6-2	180	10-26-98	.274	.524	.228	40	135	8	37	10	2	0	18	8	0	1	1	18	0	5	.378	.313
Gonzalez, Elian	R-R	6-2	175	4-15-00	.257	.167	.276	28	70	8	18	1	1	1	5	5	0	1	0	22	2	4	.343	.307
2-team total (2 Brewers)					.243	—	.000	30	74	8	18	1	1	1	5	6	0	1	0	22	2	4	.324	.300
Pena, Jose	L-L	6-3	175	10-21-98	.264	.308	.259	40	125	17	33	6	1	0	12	12	4	0	2	37	2	4	.328	.343
Perez, Antonio	R-R	6-2	200	10-19-97	.162	.429	.134	30	74	8	12	3	0	2	6	7	2	0	1	34	0	0	.284	.250
Rosado, Ismael	R-R	5-11	185	12-14-96	.352	.500	.316	33	71	13	25	2	1	0	13	8	3	1	0	5	1	1	.409	.439
Sano, Edwin	B-R	5-9	160	12-12-98	.271	.364	.256	53	155	26	42	5	1	0	18	23	2	4	3	25	6	0	.316	.366
Torres, Bryan	L-R	5-11	165	7-2-97	.294	.353	.286	44	136	22	40	6	1	1	13	18	1	2	1	6	6	5	.375	.378

Pitching	B-T	HT	WT	DOB	W	L	ERA	G	GS	CG	SV	IP	H	R	ER	HR	BB	SO	AVG	vLH	vRH	K/9	BB/9
Acosta, Daniel	R-R	6-1	185	2-27-97	5	2	4.68	22	0	0	5	33	29	22	17	0	36	30	.246	.250	.243	8.27	9.92
Alberro, Jose	L-L	6-1	168	2-2-98	3	2	2.89	19	0	0	4	37	27	14	12	1	40	44	.213	.107	.242	10.61	9.64
Colman, Jesus	R-R	6-1	175	3-11-98	0	1	3.46	7	0	0	1	13	11	10	5	0	10	7	.239	.235	.241	4.85	6.92
2-team total (4 Brewers)					0	1	3.93	11	0	0	1	18	16	13	8	0	13	10	.246	.200	.333	4.91	6.38
Cordero, Luis	L-L	6-3	170	4-22-99	0	3	12.15	3	3	0	0	7	11	17	9	1	11	2	.344	.400	.333	2.70	14.85
De Jesus, Wilmy	R-R	6-0	170	2-26-00	1	5	5.61	19	5	0	0	51	69	49	32	1	23	31	.322	.318	.325	5.44	4.03
De La Cruz, Joaquin	R-R	6-2	195	10-13-95	1	1	2.50	4	4	0	0	18	12	6	5	0	7	17	.197	.182	.205	8.50	3.50
Gomez, Juan	L-R	6-3	185	5-1-97	1	4	5.85	16	10	0	0	52	64	40	34	5	24	38	.303	.203	.347	6.54	4.13
Mancebo, Jorge	R-R	6-2	195	4-25-95	0	1	5.40	3	0	0	0	2	1	1	1	0	7	0	.167	.000	.200	0.00	37.80
Medina, Henry	R-R	6-0	175	9-5-97	4	4	3.10	15	14	1	0	73	74	38	25	5	29	30	.266	.223	.288	3.72	3.59
Paulino, Guillermo	R-R	6-4	180	3-30-97	0	0	13.50	1	0	0	0	2	2	3	3	0	4	1	.250	.000	.500	4.50	18.00
2-team total (13 Brewers)					1	0	8.10	14	0	0	0	17	13	16	15	0	22	11	.224	.250	.206	5.94	11.88

Tamares, Jefry	R-R	6-2	190	7-31-97	1	0	5.54	16	0	0	0	26	25	18	16	0	18	15	.266	.185	.299	5.19	6.23
Velasquez, Ricardo	R-R	6-2	175	8-9-99	1	1	6.23	12	1	0	2	17	11	14	12	1	29	16	.204	.211	.200	8.31	15.06

Fielding

C: Rosado 23, Torres 38. **1B:** Brito 13, Castillo 24, Gonzalez 1, Perez 4, Rosado 6, Sano 6, Torres 2. **2B:** Avila 8, Castillo 12, Gonzalez 4, Sano 17, Torres 2. **3B:** Brito 30, Castillo 2, Gonzalez 7, Sano 29. **SS:** Avila 38, Gonzalez 13, Sano 1. **OF:** Castillo 1, Dimas 51, Franco 33, Pena 35, Perez 17, Torres 2.

Minnesota Twins

SEASON IN A SENTENCE: After losing 103 games in 2016, the Twins stormed back to relevance in the first year of the Derek Falvey/Thad Levine front office. With an offense full of emerging young players, Minnesota earn an American League wild card in its best season since 2010.

HIGH POINT: Byron Buxton's breakout coincided with the Twins' best month. He hit .324/.354/.619 with eight home runs and eight steals in August to help power Minnesota to a 20-10 month. (It also followed a players-only meeting in San Diego on Aug. 1.) Buxton capped an eight-game road trip with a three-homer effort at Toronto on Aug. 27 in a 7-2 victory as the Twins split the trip to maintain their hold on the wild-card spot.

LOW POINT: Minnesota wasn't at full strength for its wild-card matchup with the Yankees, with Miguel Sano out with a slow-healing shin injury. Homers by Brian Dozier and Eddie Rosario in the top of the first gave the Twins a 3-0 lead, but the Yankees stormed back with three in their half of the first off Ervin Santana and pounded their way to an 8-4 victory. It's the 13th straight playoff loss for the franchise since 2004, with 10 of those losses coming to the Yankees.

NOTABLE ROOKIES: Lefthander Adalberto Mejia made 21 starts for the club, finding success until a late fade. Two righthanders emerged as key relief options, with low-slot Trevor Hildenberger and hard-throwing Alan Busenitz earning high-leverage innings from manager Paul Molitor. Outfielder Zack Granite showed patience and a fourth-outfielder profile in 40 games.

KEY TRANSACTIONS: Catcher Jason Castro was the team's biggest free-agent signing. The Twins traded for lefthander Jaime Garcia in mid-July and he won his only start during an overall 2-8 stretch the club. He was traded away to the Yankees six days later, on July 30, and closer Brandon Kintzler was traded away to the Nationals a day later. The Twins rallied to make the playoffs nonetheless.

DOWN ON THE FARM: Every Twins affiliate had a winning record, and a 49-22 Dominican Summer League showing helped the organization edge the Yankees with a .592 winning percentage throughout the minors, best in baseball. Double-A Chattanooga won 91 games, tied for second-most in the minors, and was co-champion of the Southern League, while Elizabethton won the Rookie-level Appalachian League.

OPENING DAY PAYROLL: $108,077,500 (22nd)

PLAYERS OF THE YEAR

MAJOR LEAGUE

Brian Dozier
2B
.271/.359/.498
34 HR, 30 2B
First Gold Glove

MINOR LEAGUE

Mitch Garver
C
(Triple-A)
.291/.387/.541
17 HR, 29 2B

ORGANIZATION LEADERS

BATTING			***Minimum 250 AB**
MAJORS			
*	AVG	Joe Mauer	.305
*	OPS	Miguel Sano	.859
	HR	Brian Dozier	34
	RBI	Brian Dozier	93
MINORS			
*	AVG	Zack Granite, Fort Myers, Rochester	.340
*	OBP	Jonathan Rodriguez, Chattanooga, Rochester	.408
*	SLG	Mitch Garver, Rochester	.541
*	OPS	Mitch Garver, Rochester	.928
	R	Jonathan Rodriguez, Chattanooga, Rochester	89
	H	Matt Hague, Rochester	149
		Jermaine Palacios, Cedar Rapids, Fort Myers	149
	TB	Jonathan Rodriguez, Chattanooga, Rochester	234
	2B	Lewin Diaz, Cedar Rapids	33
	3B	Travis Blankenhorn, Cedar Rapids	11
	HR	Jonathan Rodriguez, Chattanooga, Rochester	22
	RBI	Jonathan Rodriguez, Chattanooga, Rochester	78
	BB	Jonathan Rodriguez, Chattanooga, Rochester	81
	SO	Jaylin Davis, Cedar Rapids, Fort Myers	147
	SB	Tanner English, Chattanooga, Fort Myers	35

PITCHING			**#Minimum 75 IP**
MAJORS			
	W	Ervin Santana	16
#	ERA	Ervin Santana	3.28
	SO	Ervin Santana	167
	SV	Brandon Kintzler	28
MINORS			
	W	Aaron Slegers, Rochester	15
	L	Lachlan Wells, GCL Twins, Fort Myers	10
#	ERA	Nik Turley, Chattanooga, Rochester	2.05
	G	Colton Davis, Cedar Rapids	44
		Nick Anderson, Fort Myers, Chattanooga	44
	GS	Felix Jorge, Chattanooga, Rochester	25
		Sean Poppen, Cedar Rapids, Fort Myers	25
	SV	John Curtiss, Chattanooga, Rochester	19
	IP	Felix Jorge, Chattanooga, Rochester	149
	BB	David Fischer, Fort Myers	55
		Eduardo Del Rosario, Cedar Rapids, Fort Myers	55
	SO	Nik Turley, Chattanooga, Rochester	124
#	AVG	Nik Turley, Chattanooga, Rochester	.198

2017 PERFORMANCE

Chief Baseball Officer: Derek Falvey. **Farm Director:** Brad Steil. **Scouting Director:** Sean Johnson.

Class	Team	League	W	L	PCT	Finish	Manager
Majors	Minnesota Twins	American	85	77	.525	5th (15)	Paul Molitor
Triple-A	Rochester Red Wings	International	80	62	.563	t-3rd (14)	Mike Quade
Double-A	Chattanooga Lookouts	Southern	91	49	.650	1st (10)	Jake Mauer
High-A	Fort Myers Miracle	Florida State	75	60	.556	2nd (12)	Doug Mientkiewicz
Low-A	Cedar Rapids Kernels	Midwest	75	65	.536	4th (16)	Tommy Watkins
Rookie	Elizabethton Twins	Appalachian	41	27	.603	3rd (10)	Ray Smith
Rookie	GCL Twins	Gulf Coast	35	23	.603	3rd (17)	Ramon Borrego
Overall 2017 Minor League Record			397	286	.581	2nd (30)	

ORGANIZATION STATISTICS

MINNESOTA TWINS

AMERICAN LEAGUE

Batting	B-T	HT	WT	DOB	AVG	vLH	vRH	G	AB	R	H	2B	3B	HR	RBI	BB	HBP	SH	SF	SO	SB	CS	SLG	OBP
Adrianza, Ehire	B-R	6-1	170	8-21-89	.265	.321	.236	70	162	30	43	9	2	2	24	16	1	1	6	25	8	1	.383	.324
Buxton, Byron	R-R	6-2	190	12-18-93	.253	.282	.242	140	462	69	117	14	6	16	51	38	4	5	2	150	29	1	.413	.314
Castro, Jason	L-R	6-3	215	6-18-87	.242	.263	.234	110	356	49	86	22	0	10	47	45	4	1	1	108	0	0	.388	.333
Dozier, Brian	R-R	5-11	200	5-15-87	.271	.331	.252	152	617	106	167	30	4	34	93	78	8	0	2	141	16	7	.498	.359
Escobar, Eduardo	B-R	5-10	185	1-5-89	.254	.255	.253	129	457	62	116	16	5	21	73	33	5	1	3	98	5	1	.449	.309
Garver, Mitch	R-R	6-1	220	1-15-91	.196	.238	.160	23	46	5	9	1	3	0	3	6	0	0	0	15	0	0	.348	.289
Gimenez, Chris	R-R	6-2	230	12-27-82	.220	.208	.229	74	186	28	41	9	0	7	16	33	4	2	0	60	1	0	.382	.350
Goodrum, Niko	B-R	6-3	198	2-28-92	.059	.000	.083	11	17	1	1	0	0	0	0	1	0	0	0	10	0	0	.059	.111
Granite, Zack	L-L	6-1	175	9-17-92	.237	.353	.211	40	93	14	22	2	0	1	13	12	0	1	1	9	2	2	.290	.321
Grossman, Robbie	B-L	6-0	215	9-16-89	.246	.238	.250	119	382	62	94	22	1	9	45	67	3	2	2	79	3	1	.380	.361
Kepler, Max	L-L	6-4	205	2-10-93	.243	.152	.272	147	511	67	124	32	2	19	69	47	6	1	3	114	6	1	.425	.312
Mauer, Joe	L-R	6-5	225	4-19-83	.305	.308	.304	141	525	69	160	36	1	7	71	66	3	0	3	83	2	1	.417	.384
Polanco, Jorge	B-R	5-11	200	7-5-93	.256	.249	.260	133	488	60	125	30	3	13	74	41	2	7	6	78	13	5	.410	.313
Rosario, Eddie	L-R	6-1	180	9-28-91	.290	.279	.295	151	542	79	157	33	2	27	78	35	0	4	8	106	9	8	.507	.328
Sano, Miguel	R-R	6-4	260	5-11-93	.264	.297	.254	114	424	75	112	15	2	28	77	54	4	0	1	173	0	0	.507	.352
Santana, Danny	B-R	5-11	185	11-7-90	.200	.000	.313	13	25	3	5	1	0	1	1	1	0	0	0	8	1	0	.360	.231
Vargas, Kennys	B-R	6-5	290	8-1-90	.253	.185	.278	78	241	33	61	13	0	11	41	20	2	0	1	77	0	0	.444	.314

Pitching	B-T	HT	WT	DOB	W	L	ERA	G	GS	CG	SV	IP	H	R	ER	HR	BB	SO	AVG	vLH	vRH	K/9	BB/9
Belisle, Matt	R-R	6-3	230	6-6-80	2	2	4.03	62	0	0	9	60	48	31	27	7	22	54	.218	.162	.247	8.06	3.28
Berrios, Jose	R-R	6-0	185	5-27-94	14	8	3.89	26	25	0	0	146	131	71	63	15	48	139	.239	.260	.222	8.59	2.97
Boshers, Buddy	L-L	6-3	205	5-9-88	1	0	4.89	38	0	0	0	35	37	20	19	7	10	28	.268	.224	.300	7.20	2.57
Breslow, Craig	L-L	6-0	190	8-8-80	1	1	5.23	30	0	0	0	31	38	19	18	4	12	18	.307	.200	.348	5.23	3.48
2-team total (7 Cleveland)					1	1	5.09	37	0	0	0	35	41	21	20	4	14	23	.297	.286	.143	5.86	3.57
Busenitz, Alan	R-R	6-1	180	8-22-90	1	1	1.99	28	0	0	0	32	22	9	7	4	9	23	.206	.225	.194	6.54	2.56
Colon, Bartolo	R-R	5-11	285	5-24-73	5	6	5.18	15	15	1	0	80	100	46	46	17	15	47	.302	.314	.291	5.29	1.69
Curtiss, John	R-R	6-4	200	4-5-93	0	0	8.31	9	0	0	0	9	9	8	8	2	2	10	.257	.294	.222	10.38	2.08
Duffey, Tyler	R-R	6-3	220	12-27-90	2	3	4.94	56	0	0	1	71	79	41	39	9	18	67	.275	.243	.294	8.49	2.28
Enns, Dietrich	L-L	6-1	210	5-16-91	0	0	6.75	2	1	0	0	4	7	4	3	2	1	2	.350	.500	.313	4.50	2.25
Garcia, Jaime	L-L	6-2	215	7-8-86	1	0	4.05	1	1	0	0	7	8	3	3	0	3	7	.308	.000	.348	9.45	4.05
2-team total (8 New York)					1	3	4.70	9	9	0	0	44	49	28	23	6	23	44	.283	.000	.348	9.00	4.70
Gee, Dillon	R-R	6-1	205	4-28-86	3	2	3.22	14	3	0	1	36	37	14	13	4	9	31	.268	.268	.268	7.68	2.23
2-team total (4 Texas)					3	2	3.47	18	4	0	1	49	54	24	19	8	15	41	.283	.385	.259	7.48	2.74
Gibson, Kyle	R-R	6-6	215	10-23-87	12	10	5.07	29	29	0	0	158	182	93	89	24	60	121	.292	.301	.282	6.89	3.42
Haley, Justin	R-R	6-5	230	6-16-91	0	0	6.00	10	0	0	1	18	22	12	12	3	6	14	.301	.360	.271	7.00	3.00
Heston, Chris	R-R	6-3	195	4-10-88	0	0	0.00	1	0	0	0	1	1	0	0	0	0	0	.250	—	.250	0.00	0.00
2-team total (2 Seattle)					0	1	16.50	3	1	0	0	6	15	12	11	3	5	3	.455	.385	.563	4.50	7.50
Hildenberger, Trevor	R-R	6-2	211	12-15-90	3	3	3.21	37	0	0	1	42	38	15	15	4	6	44	.241	.233	.245	9.43	1.29
Hughes, Phil	R-R	6-5	240	6-24-86	4	3	5.87	14	9	0	0	54	72	38	35	12	13	38	.316	.383	.269	6.37	2.18
Jorge, Felix	R-R	6-2	170	1-2-94	1	0	10.57	2	2	0	0	8	14	9	9	4	2	4	.412	.556	.360	4.70	2.35
Kintzler, Brandon	R-R	6-0	190	8-1-84	2	2	2.78	45	0	0	28	45	41	15	14	3	11	27	.246	.197	.286	5.36	2.18
Mejia, Adalberto	R-L	6-3	195	6-20-93	4	7	4.50	21	21	0	0	98	110	52	49	13	44	85	.281	.275	.283	7.81	4.04
Melville, Tim	R-R	6-4	225	10-9-89	0	1	13.50	1	1	0	0	3	4	5	5	1	3	4	.286	.143	.429	10.80	8.10
Moya, Gabriel	L-L	6-0	175	1-9-95	0	0	4.26	7	0	0	1	6	5	3	3	2	2	5	.208	.222	.200	7.11	2.84
Perkins, Glen	L-L	6-0	205	3-2-83	0	0	9.53	8	0	0	0	6	8	6	6	0	5	2	.320	.375	.294	3.18	7.94
Pressly, Ryan	R-R	6-3	210	12-15-88	2	3	4.70	57	0	0	0	61	52	34	32	10	19	61	.229	.281	.196	8.95	2.79
Rogers, Taylor	L-L	6-3	170	12-17-90	7	3	3.07	69	0	0	0	56	52	20	19	6	21	49	.246	.173	.287	7.92	3.40
Rosario, Randy	L-L	6-1	200	5-18-94	0	0	30.86	2	0	0	0	2	7	8	8	1	0	2	.500	.250	.600	7.71	0.00
Rucinski, Drew	R-R	6-2	190	12-30-88	0	0	10.38	2	0	0	0	4	10	5	5	2	2	5	.476	.500	.462	10.38	4.15
Santana, Ervin	R-R	6-2	175	12-12-82	16	8	3.28	33	33	5	0	211	177	85	77	31	61	167	.225	.215	.234	7.11	2.60
Santiago, Hector	L-R	6-0	215	12-16-87	4	8	5.63	15	14	0	0	70	70	44	44	15	31	51	.256	.478	.211	6.53	3.97
Slegers, Aaron	R-R	6-10	245	9-4-92	0	1	6.46	4	3	0	0	15	12	12	11	3	6	9	.211	.194	.231	5.28	3.52
Tepesch, Nick	R-R	6-4	240	10-12-88	0	1	5.40	1	1	0	0	2	5	7	1	1	2	2	.455	.500	.429	10.80	10.80
2-team total (3 Toronto)					1	2	5.17	4	4	0	0	16	22	15	9	6	9	9	.328	.281	.333	5.17	5.17

Tonkin, Michael	R-R	6-7	220	11-19-89	0	1	5.14	16	0	0	0	21	22	15	12	6	12	24	.265	.333	.226	10.29	5.14
Turley, Nik	L-L	6-4	195	9-11-89	0	2	11.21	10	3	0	0	18	30	22	22	5	8	13	.395	.385	.397	6.62	4.08
Wheeler, Jason	L-L	6-6	255	10-27-90	0	0	9.00	2	0	0	0	3	6	5	3	1	4	0	.429	.000	.462	0.00	12.00
Wilk, Adam	L-L	6-2	180	12-9-87	0	1	7.84	3	1	0	0	10	16	9	9	3	8	6	.356	.467	.300	5.23	6.97
Wimmers, Alex	R-L	6-2	215	11-1-88	0	0	4.91	6	0	0	0	7	8	4	4	2	8	7	.267	.308	.235	8.59	9.82

Fielding

Catcher	PCT	G	PO	A	E	DP	PB
Castro	.996	108	707	34	3	5	5
Escobar	.000	1	0	0	0	0	0
Garver	.983	13	54	3	1	0	1
Gimenez	.998	59	418	26	1	5	10

First Base	PCT	G	PO	A	E	DP
Adrianza	1.000	4	13	1	0	1
Garver	.952	3	18	2	1	2
Gimenez	1.000	7	18	1	0	1
Mauer	.998	125	947	63	2	90
Sano	.973	9	68	4	2	7
Vargas	.992	40	241	18	2	29

Second Base	PCT	G	PO	A	E	DP
Adrianza	.938	9	9	6	1	0
Dozier	.993	152	264	405	5	109
Escobar	1.000	9	10	20	0	5
Goodrum	1.000	8	4	3	0	1
Santana	.000	1	0	0	0	0

Third Base	PCT	G	PO	A	E	DP
Adrianza	1.000	9	4	21	0	1
Escobar	.963	79	31	127	6	15
Gimenez	1.000	1	0	1	0	0
Sano	.967	82	64	138	7	12
Santana	.000	1	0	0	0	0

Shortstop	PCT	G	PO	A	E	DP
Adrianza	.980	29	26	74	2	13
Escobar	1.000	16	14	31	0	12
Polanco	.964	130	154	335	18	70

Outfield	PCT	G	PO	A	E	DP
Adrianza	1.000	17	28	1	0	0
Buxton	.988	137	389	6	5	1
Escobar	.000	2	0	0	0	0
Garver	1.000	2	2	0	0	0
Gimenez	1.000	5	6	0	0	0
Goodrum	1.000	1	3	0	0	0
Granite	.986	32	71	1	1	0
Grossman	.955	53	83	1	4	0
Kepler	.993	143	290	7	2	3
Rosario	.985	150	265	5	4	1
Santana	.947	10	17	1	1	0

ROCHESTER RED WINGS — *TRIPLE-A*

INTERNATIONAL LEAGUE

Batting	B-T	HT	WT	DOB	AVG	vLH	vRH	G	AB	R	H	2B	3B	HR	RBI	BB	HBP	SH	SF	SO	SB	CS	SLG	OBP
Adrianza, Ehire	B-R	6-1	170	8-21-89	.216	.250	.200	10	37	1	8	0	0	0	3	6	0	1	0	11	0	1	.216	.326
Berry, Quintin	L-L	6-1	195	11-21-84	.194	.200	.194	14	36	5	7	1	1	0	0	4	0	0	0	11	1	2	.278	.275
Buxton, Byron	R-R	6-2	190	12-18-93	.417	.400	.500	3	12	3	5	0	0	2	3	1	0	0	0	3	0	0	.917	.462
Corcino, Edgar	B-R	6-1	210	6-7-92	.224	.167	.239	20	58	2	13	1	1	0	3	1	0	0	0	14	0	0	.276	.237
Field, Tommy	R-R	5-10	185	2-22-87	.231	.237	.230	115	402	50	93	29	0	6	32	30	8	4	3	89	4	0	.348	.296
Garver, Mitch	R-R	6-1	220	1-15-91	.291	.304	.286	88	320	56	93	29	0	17	45	50	1	0	1	85	2	0	.541	.387
Gonzalez, Bengie	B-R	5-11	160	1-16-90	.229	.098	.273	67	201	15	46	6	3	0	15	19	0	1	2	34	2	2	.289	.293
2-team total (31 Syracuse)					.237	.263	.254	98	291	24	69	9	3	0	20	28	0	1	2	44	2	2	.289	.302
Goodrum, Niko	B-R	6-3	198	2-28-92	.265	.333	.235	127	461	71	122	25	5	13	66	30	2	1	5	119	11	7	.425	.309
Granite, Zack	L-L	6-1	175	9-17-92	.338	.323	.346	71	284	46	96	16	4	5	29	24	1	4	0	34	15	6	.475	.392
Grossman, Robbie	B-L	6-0	215	9-16-89	.143	.500	.000	2	7	2	1	0	0	0	1	2	0	0	0	2	0	0	.143	.333
Hague, Matt	R-R	6-3	225	8-20-85	.297	.294	.298	136	502	64	149	30	0	10	65	61	6	0	10	75	8	2	.416	.373
Michael, Levi	R-R	5-10	180	2-9-91	.244	.294	.208	12	41	4	10	1	0	1	6	3	0	0	1	11	1	0	.342	.289
Murphy, John Ryan	R-R	5-11	205	5-13-91	.222	.260	.208	59	194	21	43	9	0	4	27	22	0	0	2	36	0	0	.330	.298
Palka, Daniel	L-L	6-2	220	10-28-91	.274	.343	.242	84	332	47	91	13	3	11	42	27	1	0	2	80	1	2	.431	.329
Park, ByungHo	R-R	6-1	220	7-10-86	.253	.242	.258	111	419	48	106	22	2	14	60	28	6	0	2	130	0	0	.415	.308
Paulino, Carlos	R-R	6-0	175	9-24-89	.063	.000	.333	5	16	2	1	0	0	0	0	1	0	2	0	8	0	0	.063	.118
Paulsen, Ben	R-L	6-4	210	10-27-87	.230	.053	.291	22	74	6	17	6	0	3	12	5	0	0	0	16	0	0	.432	.279
Recker, Anthony	R-R	6-2	240	8-29-83	.286	.188	.315	19	70	9	20	9	0	0	8	4	2	0	2	15	0	0	.414	.333
2-team total (41 Gwinnett)					.244	.188	.315	60	209	29	51	17	1	4	18	15	7	0	3	63	1	0	.392	.312
Reginatto, Leonardo	R-R	6-2	180	4-10-90	.303	.235	.332	86	277	28	84	15	0	3	38	30	1	3	4	52	0	4	.390	.369
Rodriguez, Jonathan	R-R	6-2	250	8-21-89	.167	.125	.200	5	18	2	3	0	0	1	2	1	1	0	0	5	0	0	.333	.250
Shuck, J.B.	L-L	5-11	195	6-18-87	.259	.234	.268	123	424	41	110	26	4	4	37	41	3	1	6	43	4	1	.368	.325
Strausborger, Ryan	R-R	6-0	185	3-4-88	.074	.000	.125	11	27	2	2	1	0	0	2	3	0	0	0	11	0	1	.111	.167
Vargas, Kennys	B-R	6-5	290	8-1-90	.253	.246	.256	51	178	26	45	8	1	9	28	31	0	0	2	53	0	0	.461	.360
Vielma, Engelb	B-R	5-11	155	6-22-94	.206	.192	.213	87	296	36	61	12	2	0	17	11	1	1	5	72	2	5	.260	.233
Walker, Ryan	L-R	6-1	157	3-26-92	.000	—	.000	2	3	0	0	0	0	0	0	0	0	0	0	0	0	0	.000	.000

Pitching	B-T	HT	WT	DOB	W	L	ERA	G	GS	CG	SV	IP	H	R	ER	HR	BB	SO	AVG	vLH	vRH	K/9	BB/9
Bard, Luke	R-R	6-3	202	11-13-90	0	0	3.46	8	0	0	0	13	13	5	5	1	4	21	.255	.533	.139	14.54	2.77
Baxendale, D.J.	R-R	6-2	190	12-8-90	1	3	2.98	29	4	0	1	54	54	24	18	2	15	40	.262	.189	.319	6.63	2.48
Berrios, Jose	R-R	6-0	185	5-27-94	3	0	1.13	6	6	0	0	40	24	8	5	2	8	39	.169	.159	.178	8.85	1.82
Boshers, Buddy	L-L	6-3	205	5-9-88	0	0	3.68	18	0	0	0	15	16	6	6	1	8	15	.281	.188	.400	9.20	4.91
Breslow, Craig	L-L	6-0	190	8-8-80	0	0	3.38	3	0	0	0	3	1	1	1	0	1	2	.111	.000	.143	6.75	3.38
2-team total (7 Columbus)					0	0	3.68	10	0	0	0	7	6	3	3	0	3	6	.222	.083	.667	7.36	3.68
Busenitz, Alan	R-R	6-1	180	8-22-90	3	0	1.78	24	0	0	2	35	19	7	7	0	10	39	.161	.233	.086	9.93	2.55
Chapman, Kevin	L-L	6-3	230	2-19-88	0	1	5.56	9	0	0	0	11	13	9	7	0	5	14	.283	.320	.238	11.12	3.97
2-team total (9 Gwinnett)					0	1	6.65	18	0	0	0	23	27	19	17	1	8	24	.297	.320	.238	9.39	3.13
Chargois, J.T.	B-R	6-3	200	12-3-90	0	0	0.00	2	0	0	1	3	1	0	0	0	1	2	.125	.167	.000	6.75	3.38
Colon, Bartolo	R-R	5-11	285	5-24-73	0	1	9.82	1	1	0	0	4	4	4	4	1	2	5	.267	.333	.167	12.27	4.91
Curtiss, John	R-R	6-4	200	4-5-93	0	0	1.85	18	0	0	6	24	11	5	5	0	10	33	.131	.098	.182	12.21	3.70
Eades, Ryan	R-R	6-2	200	12-15-91	2	0	1.13	2	1	0	0	8	6	1	1	0	2	9	.207	.200	.214	10.13	2.25
Enns, Dietrich	L-L	6-1	210	5-16-91	0	1	2.31	3	1	1	1	12	13	3	3	2	4	9	.289	.455	.235	6.94	3.09
2-team total (7 Scranton/Wilkes-Barre)					1	2	2.29	10	8	1	1	51	43	14	13	3	14	46	.226	.455	.235	8.12	2.47
Fernandez, Raul	R-R	6-2	180	6-22-90	0	0	3.72	7	0	0	0	10	11	4	4	2	1	6	.290	.400	.217	5.59	0.93
Gee, Dillon	R-R	6-1	205	4-28-86	3	1	2.00	5	5	0	0	27	24	6	6	1	3	20	.240	.250	.232	6.67	1.00
Gibson, Kyle	R-R	6-6	215	10-23-87	1	2	2.08	3	3	0	0	17	13	4	4	1	5	23	.206	.303	.100	11.94	2.60

Gonsalves, Stephen	L-L	6-5	213	7-8-94	1	2	5.56	5	4	0	0	23	27	14	14	4	8	22	.294	.188	.350	8.74	3.18
Haley, Justin	R-R	6-5	230	6-16-91	1	0	3.63	5	4	0	0	17	17	8	7	3	3	11	.258	.250	.269	5.71	1.56
2-team total (7 Pawtucket)					2	2	2.93	12	11	1	0	61	52	21	20	10	10	46	.230	.227	.212	6.75	1.47
Heston, Chris	R-R	6-3	195	4-10-88	0	3	10.00	8	6	0	0	27	56	32	30	8	15	12	.448	.436	.460	4.00	5.00
Hildenberger, Trevor	R-R	6-2	211	12-15-90	2	1	2.05	21	0	0	6	31	27	7	7	1	8	35	.235	.279	.208	10.27	2.35
Hughes, Phil	R-R	6-5	240	6-24-86	0	0	3.00	3	0	0	0	3	3	1	1	1	2	1	.250	.375	.000	3.00	6.00
Hurlbut, David	L-L	6-3	221	11-24-89	10	8	3.44	23	22	0	0	131	152	58	50	6	30	103	.292	.289	.294	7.09	2.07
Jorge, Felix	R-R	6-2	170	1-2-94	0	1	5.02	3	3	0	0	14	19	8	8	3	3	9	.339	.250	.429	5.65	1.88
Kohn, Michael	R-R	6-2	200	6-26-86	0	1	9.00	1	0	0	0	1	1	1	1	1	1	1	.333	.000	.500	9.00	9.00
Mejia, Adalberto	R-L	6-3	195	6-20-93	1	1	2.83	6	6	0	0	29	26	9	9	1	6	22	.241	.130	.271	6.91	1.88
Melotakis, Mason	R-L	6-2	220	6-28-91	2	0	4.07	21	0	0	1	24	22	11	11	1	12	23	.242	.238	.245	8.51	4.44
Melville, Tim	R-R	6-4	225	10-9-89	4	3	2.70	11	10	1	0	67	48	21	20	5	23	64	.199	.196	.202	8.64	3.11
Mickolio, Kam	R-R	6-9	255	5-10-84	0	1	4.00	7	0	0	1	9	4	4	4	1	4	3	.129	.133	.125	3.00	4.00
Pino, Yohan	R-R	6-2	190	12-26-83	0	5	4.89	10	5	1	0	35	39	19	19	7	7	25	.291	.271	.307	6.43	1.80
Pressly, Ryan	R-R	6-3	210	12-15-88	2	0	0.90	7	0	0	4	10	5	1	1	0	5	15	.152	.105	.214	13.50	4.50
Reed, Jake	R-R	6-2	190	9-29-92	1	0	2.05	22	0	0	5	31	24	7	7	1	11	25	.224	.186	.250	7.34	3.23
Rucinski, Drew	R-R	6-2	190	12-30-88	2	6	2.57	37	2	0	2	63	54	21	18	3	10	57	.231	.231	.231	8.14	1.43
Santiago, Hector	L-R	6-0	215	12-16-87	1	2	5.32	7	7	0	0	24	21	16	14	4	17	25	.233	.333	.203	9.51	6.46
Slegers, Aaron	R-R	6-10	245	9-4-92	15	4	3.40	24	24	1	0	148	154	59	56	11	29	119	.266	.290	.242	7.22	1.76
Stewart, Kohl	R-R	6-3	195	10-7-94	1	0	7.20	1	1	0	0	5	7	4	4	1	1	5	.333	.200	.455	9.00	1.80
Tepesch, Nick	R-R	6-4	240	10-12-88	1	3	5.59	6	5	0	0	29	36	24	18	6	9	27	.303	.288	.317	8.38	2.79
2-team total (4 Buffalo)					3	3	4.21	10	8	0	0	47	50	28	22	7	10	41	.270	.276	.162	7.85	1.91
Tonkin, Michael	R-R	6-7	220	11-19-89	4	2	1.73	31	0	0	5	42	31	8	8	1	13	61	.205	.242	.180	13.18	2.81
Tracy, Matt	L-L	6-3	215	11-26-88	2	2	7.64	4	3	0	0	18	25	15	15	4	8	15	.333	.417	.294	7.64	4.08
Turley, Nik	L-L	6-4	195	9-11-89	5	4	2.66	18	10	0	0	68	58	24	20	4	22	79	.236	.225	.240	10.51	2.93
Wheeler, Jason	L-L	6-6	255	10-27-90	4	1	4.50	8	7	0	0	44	47	25	22	5	10	37	.272	.280	.268	7.57	2.05
2-team total (13 Norfolk)					5	3	3.81	21	13	0	1	85	84	40	36	10	21	70	.257	.242	.239	7.41	2.22
Wilk, Adam	L-L	6-2	180	12-9-87	1	0	4.38	3	2	0	0	12	15	6	6	2	3	6	.300	.211	.355	4.38	2.19
Wimmers, Alex	R-L	6-2	215	11-1-88	7	3	3.23	34	0	0	7	47	33	17	17	5	11	48	.200	.197	.202	9.13	2.09

Fielding

Catcher	PCT	G	PO	A	E	DP	PB
Garver	.995	67	537	38	3	3	9
Murphy	.991	53	416	35	4	2	7
Paulino	.973	5	35	1	1	0	1
Recker	.994	19	161	8	1	2	0

First Base	PCT	G	PO	A	E	DP
Garver	.975	5	36	3	1	2
Goodrum	1.000	3	12	1	0	0
Hague	.995	47	346	18	2	25
Park	1.000	56	411	30	0	55
Paulsen	.974	8	71	4	2	8
Rodriguez	1.000	2	17	0	0	3
Vargas	1.000	29	208	6	0	13

Second Base	PCT	G	PO	A	E	DP
Adrianza	1.000	1	1	0	0	0
Field	.978	55	81	138	5	27
Gonzalez	.992	25	44	82	1	25
Goodrum	.957	37	64	70	6	21
Reginatto	.990	26	39	56	1	13
Vielma	.833	2	6	4	2	2
Walker	1.000	2	3	2	0	1

Third Base	PCT	G	PO	A	E	DP
Adrianza	.000	1	0	0	0	0
Field	.986	31	28	45	1	3
Gonzalez	1.000	7	2	8	0	0
Goodrum	1.000	20	10	25	0	1
Hague	.969	35	23	40	2	5
Reginatto	.954	59	33	91	6	6

Shortstop	PCT	G	PO	A	E	DP
Adrianza	1.000	2	3	8	0	1
Field	.982	15	20	36	1	9
Gonzalez	.986	33	48	93	2	16
Goodrum	.875	9	6	22	4	3
Reginatto	.923	2	3	9	1	3
Vielma	.981	84	134	231	7	58

Outfield	PCT	G	PO	A	E	DP
Adrianza	1.000	4	5	1	0	0
Berry	1.000	13	16	0	0	0
Buxton	1.000	3	11	0	0	0
Corcino	1.000	19	29	3	0	0
Field	1.000	9	10	2	0	0
Garver	1.000	14	24	0	0	0
Goodrum	.992	62	116	2	1	0
Granite	.995	70	180	5	1	0
Hague	.970	20	30	2	1	0
Michael	.958	12	23	0	1	0
Palka	.982	79	153	10	3	2
Park	1.000	2	2	0	0	0
Paulsen	1.000	13	17	0	0	0
Shuck	.986	119	208	11	3	0
Strausborger	1.000	11	14	1	0	0

CHATTANOOGA LOOKOUTS — DOUBLE-A

SOUTHERN LEAGUE

Batting	B-T	HT	WT	DOB	AVG	vLH	vRH	G	AB	R	H	2B	3B	HR	RBI	BB	HBP	SH	SF	SO	SB	CS	SLG	OBP
Corcino, Edgar	B-R	6-1	210	6-7-92	.302	.348	.284	102	401	54	121	19	1	6	50	38	2	1	5	66	4	3	.399	.361
English, Tanner	R-R	5-10	160	3-11-93	.129	.231	.102	24	62	11	8	2	1	0	3	8	1	2	1	26	6	1	.194	.236
Gamache, Dan	L-R	5-11	205	11-20-90	.206	.250	.196	54	199	16	41	10	2	0	29	23	0	1	2	46	0	0	.276	.286
Garcia, Kevin	B-R	5-9	190	9-17-92	.154	.000	.200	4	13	2	2	0	0	0	1	2	0	0	0	2	0	0	.154	.267
Gonzalez, Jose	R-R	6-1	215	6-23-87	.156	.067	.177	25	77	9	12	1	0	1	6	9	1	0	1	28	0	1	.208	.250
Gordon, Nick	L-R	6-0	160	10-24-95	.270	.174	.299	122	519	80	140	29	8	9	66	53	4	0	2	134	13	7	.409	.341
Harrison, Travis	R-R	6-1	215	10-17-92	.178	.127	.190	83	276	34	49	20	1	3	26	44	12	1	2	98	4	2	.290	.314
Michael, Levi	R-R	5-10	180	2-9-91	.264	.351	.235	88	295	45	78	14	1	6	43	33	12	1	0	85	7	4	.380	.362
Molina, Nelson	L-R	6-3	175	4-30-95	.273	.375	.000	3	11	0	3	0	0	0	0	1	0	0	0	2	0	0	.273	.333
Murphy, Max	R-R	5-11	195	11-17-92	.252	.321	.227	52	206	28	52	13	3	1	28	18	3	0	3	47	0	0	.359	.317
Navarreto, Brian	R-R	6-4	220	12-29-94	.206	.172	.219	29	102	11	21	2	0	2	10	9	2	2	1	18	0	0	.284	.281
Olson, Brian	R-R	6-0	171	1-21-93	.200	.250	.182	5	15	1	3	1	0	0	1	0	2	0	0	9	0	0	.267	.294
Paulino, Carlos	R-R	6-0	175	9-24-89	.350	.478	.298	26	80	11	28	5	0	0	11	12	2	1	2	12	0	0	.413	.438
Perez, Alex	L-R	5-10	180	10-24-92	.272	.177	.308	40	125	21	34	5	0	0	11	25	3	0	4	27	0	0	.312	.395
Rodriguez, Jonathan	R-R	6-2	250	8-21-89	.309	.253	.325	119	434	87	134	31	0	21	76	80	3	0	7	113	2	0	.525	.414
Rohlfing, Dan	R-R	6-0	205	2-12-89	.142	.184	.134	66	225	21	32	3	1	4	18	22	1	1	2	98	0	0	.218	.220
Strausborger, Ryan	R-R	6-0	185	3-4-88	.265	.370	.225	30	98	16	26	6	1	1	7	17	3	0	1	34	5	2	.378	.387
Vielma, Engelb	B-R	5-11	155	6-22-94	.286	.217	.302	34	119	7	34	5	0	0	18	14	2	3	3	13	1	3	.328	.362
Wade, LaMonte	L-L	6-1	189	1-1-94	.293	.313	.286	117	424	74	124	22	3	7	67	76	5	3	11	71	9	2	.408	.397
Walker, Ryan	L-R	6-1	157	3-26-92	.234	.161	.254	108	376	48	88	13	6	3	35	51	4	0	5	85	12	4	.325	.328

Batting	B-T	HT	WT	DOB	AVG	vLH	vRH	G	AB	R	H	2B	3B	HR	RBI	BB	HBP	SH	SF	SO	SB	CS	SLG	OBP
White, T.J.	R-R	5-10	200	1-24-92	.276	.245	.287	96	366	44	101	26	4	14	65	38	10	0	2	84	2	4	.484	.358
Wilkins, Andy	L-R	6-1	225	9-13-88	.254	.054	.292	61	232	39	59	15	0	12	44	37	2	0	3	70	2	0	.474	.358

Pitching	B-T	HT	WT	DOB	W	L	ERA	G	GS	CG	SV	IP	H	R	ER	HR	BB	SO	AVG	vLH	vRH	K/9	BB/9
Anderson, Nick	R-R	6-5	195	7-5-90	2	1	1.07	29	0	0	9	34	19	4	4	0	7	37	.165	.189	.145	9.89	1.87
Bard, Luke	R-R	6-3	202	11-13-90	4	3	2.58	33	0	0	5	52	50	16	15	4	20	78	.250	.262	.241	13.41	3.44
Baxendale, D.J.	R-R	6-2	190	12-8-90	0	0	1.27	6	3	0	0	21	20	4	3	0	4	17	.253	.256	.250	7.17	1.69
Burdi, Nick	R-R	6-5	220	1-19-93	2	0	0.53	14	0	0	1	17	9	1	1	1	4	20	.161	.120	.194	10.59	2.12
Clay, Sam	L-L	6-2	190	6-21-93	1	0	15.43	3	0	0	0	2	2	4	4	0	13	4	.250	.000	.286	15.43	50.14
Clemens, Paul	R-R	6-3	215	2-14-88	3	0	2.87	17	8	0	2	53	47	21	17	5	23	42	.240	.213	.259	7.09	3.88
Curtiss, John	R-R	6-4	200	4-5-93	2	0	0.72	21	0	0	13	25	12	3	2	0	12	35	.140	.135	.143	12.60	4.32
Eades, Ryan	R-R	6-2	200	12-15-91	4	3	3.63	28	8	0	0	79	59	33	32	3	31	58	.209	.207	.211	6.58	3.52
Fernandez, Raul	R-R	6-2	180	6-22-90	3	2	4.23	21	0	0	1	38	39	19	18	6	23	43	.273	.258	.286	10.10	5.40
Gonsalves, Stephen	L-L	6-5	213	7-8-94	8	3	2.68	15	15	0	0	87	67	28	26	7	23	96	.207	.241	.197	9.89	2.37
Jay, Tyler	L-L	6-1	185	4-19-94	0	0	4.50	2	0	0	0	2	1	1	1	1	3	2	.143	.000	.333	9.00	13.50
Jorge, Felix	R-R	6-2	170	1-2-94	10	3	3.54	22	22	0	0	135	142	57	53	11	37	99	.273	.281	.266	6.62	2.47
LeBlanc, Randy	R-R	6-4	185	3-7-92	5	4	3.99	19	11	0	0	79	89	38	35	1	24	49	.292	.285	.299	5.58	2.73
Littell, Zack	R-R	6-4	220	10-5-95	5	0	2.81	7	7	0	0	42	33	16	13	1	18	33	.223	.217	.228	7.13	3.89
McIver, Anthony	L-L	6-5	210	4-8-92	1	0	0.00	3	0	0	0	6	3	0	0	0	2	5	.136	.375	.000	7.50	3.00
Melotakis, Mason	R-L	6-2	220	6-28-91	3	1	2.42	21	0	0	5	26	15	9	7	2	9	31	.163	.161	.164	10.73	3.12
Moya, Gabriel	L-L	6-0	175	1-9-95	2	0	0.61	13	0	0	7	15	8	1	1	1	3	19	.157	.263	.094	11.66	1.84
2-team total (34 Jackson)					6	1	0.77	47	0	0	24	58	30	6	5	2	15	87	.150	.200	.128	13.42	2.31
Muren, Alex	R-R	6-3	200	11-6-91	2	0	3.00	8	0	0	0	15	16	5	5	2	4	13	.281	.158	.342	7.80	2.40
Perkins, Glen	L-L	6-0	205	3-2-83	0	1	6.75	3	0	0	0	3	1	2	2	0	3	3	.125	.000	.143	10.13	10.13
Pino, Yohan	R-R	6-2	190	12-26-83	1	1	2.57	3	1	0	0	7	5	2	2	1	0	8	.200	.200	.200	10.29	0.00
Reed, Jake	R-R	6-2	190	9-29-92	1	0	2.45	5	0	0	1	7	4	2	2	0	6	8	.154	.286	.000	9.82	7.36
Rodriguez, Dereck	R-R	6-1	180	6-5-92	5	4	3.94	15	13	0	0	75	74	36	33	9	27	62	.255	.283	.237	7.41	3.23
Romero, Fernando	R-R	6-0	215	12-24-94	11	9	3.53	24	23	1	0	125	124	59	49	4	45	120	.256	.276	.239	8.64	3.24
Rosario, Randy	L-L	6-1	200	5-18-94	1	0	4.08	32	0	0	1	57	57	29	26	4	23	45	.262	.170	.296	7.06	3.61
Stashak, Cody	R-R	6-2	169	6-4-94	0	0	0.00	3	0	0	0	6	4	0	0	0	0	10	.191	.273	.100	15.00	0.00
Steele, Keaton	R-R	6-3	225	10-30-91	0	0	1.29	4	0	0	1	7	7	3	1	0	2	3	.280	.000	.500	3.86	2.57
Stewart, Kohl	R-R	6-3	195	10-7-94	5	6	4.09	16	16	0	0	77	72	41	35	4	45	52	.253	.264	.244	6.08	5.26
Thorpe, Lewis	R-L	6-1	160	11-23-95	1	0	6.00	1	1	0	0	6	5	4	4	2	2	7	.217	.200	.222	10.50	3.00
Tracy, Matt	L-L	6-3	215	11-26-88	3	4	4.04	13	9	0	0	62	63	34	28	6	22	53	.269	.236	.279	7.65	3.18
Turley, Nik	L-L	6-4	195	9-11-89	0	1	0.37	5	3	1	0	24	6	1	1	0	7	45	.078	.067	.081	16.64	2.59
Van Steensel, Todd	R-R	6-1	215	1-14-91	5	3	1.38	36	0	0	0	59	42	9	9	0	25	59	.207	.198	.214	9.05	3.84

Fielding

Catcher	PCT	G	PO	A	E	DP	PB
Gonzalez	1.000	25	161	29	0	2	6
Navarreto	.988	29	224	22	3	0	1
Olson	1.000	4	36	1	0	0	0
Paulino	.992	25	209	27	2	0	2
Rohlfing	.993	63	529	45	4	3	9

First Base	PCT	G	PO	A	E	DP
Gamache	.991	13	105	4	1	3
Rodriguez	.991	94	748	50	7	76
Rohlfing	1.000	4	20	0	0	3
White	1.000	4	29	1	0	0
Wilkins	.996	29	255	12	1	23

Second Base	PCT	G	PO	A	E	DP
Gamache	1.000	1	1	3	0	0
Gordon	.949	14	22	34	3	10
Michael	1.000	14	13	32	0	3
Perez	.981	37	49	109	3	20
Vielma	.988	14	36	43	1	11
Walker	.984	62	99	142	4	41

Third Base	PCT	G	PO	A	E	DP
Gamache	.932	17	9	32	3	1
Molina	.700	3	2	5	3	0
Walker	.988	29	20	62	1	2
White	.959	93	75	156	10	15

Shortstop	PCT	G	PO	A	E	DP
Gordon	.957	104	160	268	19	66
Vielma	.949	19	30	45	4	9
Walker	.968	18	22	39	2	2

Outfield	PCT	G	PO	A	E	DP
Corcino	.994	93	154	7	1	1
English	1.000	22	44	2	0	0
Harrison	.978	57	87	2	2	1
LeBlanc	1.000	1	1	0	0	0
Michael	.988	69	160	3	2	0
Murphy	1.000	48	94	7	0	0
Strausborger	1.000	29	60	5	0	1
Wade	.996	105	223	8	1	1
Wilkins	1.000	3	8	0	0	0

FORT MYERS MIRACLE — HIGH CLASS A

FLORIDA STATE LEAGUE

Batting	B-T	HT	WT	DOB	AVG	vLH	vRH	G	AB	R	H	2B	3B	HR	RBI	BB	HBP	SH	SF	SO	SB	CS	SLG	OBP
Adrianza, Ehire	B-R	6-1	170	8-21-89	.400	.000	.429	3	15	5	6	2	0	0	1	0	0	0	0	0	1	0	.533	.400
Alvarez, Jhon	R-R	6-0	190	2-18-96	.000	.000	.000	1	3	0	0	0	0	0	0	0	0	0	0	0	0	0	.000	.000
Arraez, Luis	L-R	5-10	155	4-9-97	.385	.600	.250	3	13	1	5	0	1	0	1	0	0	0	0	0	0	0	.539	.385
Cronin, Joe	R-R	5-10	185	5-15-94	.333	—	.333	1	3	0	1	0	0	0	0	0	0	0	0	1	0	0	.333	.333
Davis, Jaylin	R-R	6-1	190	7-1-94	.237	.207	.248	59	215	26	51	8	2	3	25	12	4	0	2	70	1	1	.335	.288
English, Tanner	R-R	5-10	160	3-11-93	.215	.301	.187	92	298	49	64	16	4	8	42	42	10	4	2	113	29	4	.376	.330
Garcia, Kevin	B-R	5-9	190	9-17-92	.254	.255	.253	58	193	22	49	0	1	0	16	18	1	2	2	22	3	1	.264	.318
Granite, Zack	L-L	6-1	175	9-17-92	.368	.250	.400	5	19	2	7	1	1	0	1	2	0	0	0	2	3	0	.526	.429
Hazard, Justin	R-L	6-3	195	9-9-93	.125	—	.125	2	8	0	1	0	0	0	0	0	0	0	0	1	0	0	.125	.125
Hutcheon, Dane	L-R	5-9	177	7-14-94	.000	.000	.000	4	9	0	0	0	0	0	0	0	0	0	0	2	0	0	.000	.000
Kennedy, Shane	R-R	6-3	205	1-31-92	.209	.212	.208	42	139	22	29	5	2	2	14	20	3	0	1	60	10	4	.317	.319
Kihle, Daniel	L-R	6-0	190	10-1-93	.206	.188	.211	44	141	10	29	8	0	4	18	13	3	0	2	39	2	0	.348	.283
Kranson, Mitchell	L-R	5-9	210	1-11-94	.254	.207	.271	58	213	26	54	8	0	4	27	20	2	1	3	32	0	1	.347	.319
Lopez, Brandon	R-R	6-1	190	9-9-93	.263	.255	.265	59	213	29	56	9	1	0	26	30	7	3	4	56	0	1	.315	.366
Miller, Sean	R-R	5-11	175	10-10-94	.262	.202	.280	122	451	51	118	17	2	2	38	23	3	3	4	81	3	7	.322	.299
Molina, Nelson	L-R	6-3	175	4-30-95	.243	.218	.249	84	284	35	69	8	4	4	33	14	3	1	1	45	4	2	.342	.285
Montesino, Ariel	B-R	5-10	170	9-21-95	.400	.333	.500	2	5	0	2	0	0	0	1	1	0	0	0	1	0	0	.400	.500

Murphy, Max	R-R	5-11	195	11-17-92	.307	.308	.306	78	300	52	92	16	3	5	34	30	12	0	2	76	9	2	.430	.390
Navarreto, Brian	R-R	6-4	220	12-29-94	.210	.189	.217	65	219	20	46	11	0	2	18	11	3	2	2	45	1	1	.288	.255
Olson, Brian	R-R	6-0	171	1-21-93	.300	1.000	.125	3	10	1	3	0	0	0	0	0	0	0	0	3	0	0	.300	.300
Palacios, Jermaine	R-R	6-0	145	7-19-96	.269	.238	.280	62	245	30	66	8	4	2	28	10	3	2	3	53	11	7	.359	.303
Paul, Chris	R-R	6-2	200	10-12-92	.328	.429	.297	61	238	35	78	18	2	4	32	15	7	1	3	44	1	5	.471	.380
Perez, Alex	L-R	5-10	180	10-24-92	.253	.265	.248	56	202	26	51	7	1	0	15	26	2	0	0	49	1	3	.297	.344
Rooker, Brent	R-R	6-3	215	11-1-94	.280	.250	.291	40	143	23	40	6	0	11	35	16	3	0	0	47	0	0	.552	.364
Scoggins, Casey	L-L	5-10	185	3-14-94	.213	.222	.212	17	61	8	13	3	0	0	4	11	0	0	0	12	3	3	.262	.333
Strong, Bradley	R-L	5-8	175	7-1-92	.250	.308	.241	25	92	11	23	4	0	2	10	8	0	1	0	28	5	1	.359	.310
Valera, Rafael P	R-R	5-11	180	8-15-94	.212	.192	.216	42	137	18	29	3	4	1	11	14	4	2	2	38	1	2	.314	.299
Vavra, Trey	R-R	6-2	185	9-17-91	.132	.077	.150	32	106	11	14	2	0	1	8	12	7	0	1	31	0	0	.179	.262
Wiel, Zander	R-R	6-3	232	1-11-93	.250	.236	.254	128	452	59	113	30	6	13	67	62	6	0	6	104	8	2	.429	.344

Pitching	B-T	HT	WT	DOB	W	L	ERA	G	GS	CG	SV	IP	H	R	ER	HR	BB	SO	AVG	vLH	vRH	K/9	BB/9
Anderson, Brady	L-R	6-0	185	11-10-92	6	8	4.06	27	18	0	0	113	133	57	51	16	25	58	.294	.300	.287	4.62	1.99
Anderson, Chris	R-R	6-3	245	7-29-92	0	1	18.90	3	3	0	0	10	29	22	21	2	6	8	.527	.568	.444	7.20	5.40
Anderson, Nick	R-R	6-5	195	7-5-90	2	0	0.89	15	0	0	2	20	13	2	2	0	3	20	.186	.189	.182	8.85	1.33
Beeker, Clark	R-R	6-3	205	11-22-92	1	1	7.80	3	3	0	0	15	27	13	13	3	6	9	.391	.355	.421	5.40	3.60
Booser, Cam	L-L	6-3	225	5-4-92	0	0	3.38	3	0	0	0	3	0	1	1	0	7	0	.000	.000	.000	0.00	23.63
Clay, Sam	L-L	6-2	190	6-21-93	8	0	1.38	40	0	0	9	65	42	11	10	0	32	63	.190	.254	.162	8.72	4.43
Del Rosario, Eduardo	R-R	6-0	145	5-19-95	1	2	7.04	5	4	0	0	23	21	19	18	4	14	11	.247	.314	.200	4.30	5.48
Drozd, Jonny	L-L	6-7	200	9-17-91	1	0	2.83	18	0	0	3	29	32	14	9	0	8	19	.294	.281	.299	5.97	2.51
Fischer, David	R-R	6-5	175	4-10-90	4	8	4.29	22	15	0	0	80	64	40	38	6	55	67	.228	.194	.257	7.57	6.21
Hackimer, Tom	R-R	5-11	190	6-28-94	4	0	1.93	27	0	0	7	37	19	10	8	0	19	43	.148	.182	.123	10.37	4.58
Haley, Justin	R-R	6-5	230	6-16-91	0	0	0.00	1	1	0	0	2	1	0	0	0	1	2	.200	.333	.000	9.00	4.50
Jay, Tyler	L-L	6-1	185	4-19-94	3	0	1.50	3	0	0	0	6	4	1	1	0	0	10	.182	.000	.286	15.00	0.00
Kohn, Michael	R-R	6-2	200	6-26-86	1	0	0.00	7	0	0	1	7	5	0	0	0	2	10	.192	.182	.200	12.86	2.57
LeBlanc, Randy	R-R	6-4	185	3-7-92	2	2	2.82	8	8	0	0	45	49	14	14	0	11	32	.288	.319	.250	6.45	2.22
Marzi, Anthony	L-L	6-1	205	11-27-92	0	1	1.50	1	1	0	0	6	4	1	1	0	2	5	.182	.333	.125	7.50	3.00
McIver, Anthony	L-L	6-5	210	4-8-92	5	2	2.26	28	6	0	1	64	73	18	16	0	21	50	.285	.262	.292	7.07	2.97
Muren, Alex	R-R	6-3	200	11-6-91	2	2	2.25	25	0	0	4	36	34	10	9	1	10	37	.250	.290	.216	9.25	2.50
Perkins, Glen	L-L	6-0	205	3-2-83	0	0	10.13	3	1	0	0	3	4	3	3	1	1	4	.333	.000	.444	13.50	3.38
Poppen, Sean	R-R	6-4	195	3-15-94	3	2	3.63	11	11	0	0	52	57	23	21	0	8	41	.277	.315	.246	7.10	1.38
Ramirez, Williams	R-R	6-1	200	8-8-92	3	1	2.98	39	0	0	0	60	43	20	20	0	34	65	.211	.191	.226	9.70	5.07
Robinson, Alex	L-L	6-3	217	8-11-94	4	0	4.67	13	0	0	0	17	14	9	9	1	13	27	.233	.056	.310	14.02	6.75
Rodriguez, Dereck	R-R	6-1	180	6-5-92	5	2	2.51	11	11	1	0	68	59	22	19	7	11	59	.238	.236	.239	7.81	1.46
Rosario, Randy	L-L	6-1	200	5-18-94	0	0	0.00	2	0	0	0	4	2	0	0	0	0	3	.182	—	.182	7.36	0.00
Stashak, Cody	R-R	6-2	169	6-4-94	3	4	3.89	16	16	0	0	83	72	40	36	7	20	72	.236	.260	.220	7.78	2.16
Steele, Keaton	R-R	6-3	225	10-30-91	2	6	5.24	17	8	0	0	57	75	35	33	5	14	30	.323	.307	.336	4.76	2.22
Theofanopoulos, Michael	L-L	6-1	185	8-5-92	5	2	3.76	37	0	0	2	67	62	28	28	4	24	77	.245	.186	.282	10.34	3.22
Thorpe, Lewis	R-L	6-1	160	11-23-95	3	4	2.69	16	15	0	0	77	62	27	23	3	31	84	.226	.241	.218	9.82	3.62
Vasquez, Andrew	L-L	6-6	228	9-14-93	3	1	1.51	23	0	0	2	36	32	9	6	0	11	52	.241	.209	.256	13.12	2.78
Wells, Lachlan	L-L	6-1	185	2-27-97	4	10	3.98	16	14	1	0	81	76	42	36	11	19	68	.243	.236	.245	7.52	2.10

Fielding

Catcher	PCT	G	PO	A	E	DP	PB
Alvarez	1.000	1	8	0	0	0	0
Garcia	.995	49	374	35	2	4	6
Hazard	.938	2	13	2	1	0	0
Kranson	.988	22	149	18	2	0	3
Navarreto	.994	61	454	55	3	7	3
Olson	1.000	3	17	2	0	0	0
Valera	1.000	3	14	2	0	0	3

First Base	PCT	G	PO	A	E	DP
Kranson	1.000	12	98	3	0	14
Molina	.000	1	0	0	0	0
Navarreto	1.000	1	1	0	0	0
Paul	.991	14	103	9	1	9
Rooker	.988	11	74	5	1	3
Valera	1.000	1	11	1	0	1
Vavra	.988	20	152	15	2	16
Wiel	.985	80	656	48	11	64

Second Base	PCT	G	PO	A	E	DP
Adrianza	1.000	1	1	1	0	0
Arraez	1.000	3	5	9	0	1
Hutcheon	1.000	1	0	1	0	0
Lopez	.900	4	4	14	2	2
Miller	.987	54	92	136	3	27
Molina	.994	36	57	96	1	24
Montesino	1.000	1	3	1	0	2
Perez	.975	40	55	100	4	15
Valera	.929	4	5	8	1	2

Third Base	PCT	G	PO	A	E	DP
Adrianza	1.000	1	1	3	0	0
Kennedy	.875	5	7	7	2	0
Lopez	.986	55	38	102	2	13
Molina	.928	26	25	52	6	4
Paul	.871	33	21	33	8	2
Perez	.750	2	0	3	1	0
Valera	.939	17	8	23	2	5

Shortstop	PCT	G	PO	A	E	DP
Adrianza	1.000	1	2	5	0	1
Kennedy	.750	2	2	4	2	0
Miller	.973	68	86	169	7	38
Molina	.895	7	6	11	2	3
Palacios	.961	62	86	138	9	33

Outfield	PCT	G	PO	A	E	DP
Cronin	1.000	1	2	1	0	0
Davis	.990	58	91	10	1	3
English	.995	92	206	9	1	6
Granite	1.000	5	15	0	0	0
Hutcheon	1.000	2	2	0	0	0
Kennedy	.979	22	45	2	1	0
Kihle	.989	42	81	6	1	1
Miller	1.000	3	6	0	0	0
Molina	1.000	17	28	1	0	1
Montesino	1.000	1	4	0	0	0
Murphy	1.000	77	173	11	0	2
Paul	.889	6	8	0	1	0
Perez	.962	13	22	3	1	1
Rooker	1.000	16	18	0	0	0
Scoggins	.944	17	32	2	2	0
Strong	.969	19	30	1	1	0
Valera	.929	6	11	2	1	1
Wiel	.917	18	31	2	3	1

CEDAR RAPIDS KERNELS

LOW CLASS A

MIDWEST LEAGUE

Batting	B-T	HT	WT	DOB	AVG	vLH	vRH	G	AB	R	H	2B	3B	HR	RBI	BB	HBP	SH	SF	SO	SB	CS	SLG	OBP
Blankenhorn, Travis	L-R	6-2	208	8-3-96	.251	.228	.261	118	438	68	110	22	11	13	69	47	17	1	5	119	13	2	.441	.343
Cabbage, Trey	L-R	6-3	204	5-3-97	.224	.245	.213	47	161	12	36	7	1	2	13	15	0	0	2	57	0	2	.317	.287
Carrier, Shane	R-R	6-2	220	6-3-96	.239	.308	.215	55	201	16	48	12	0	7	23	7	3	0	0	55	0	1	.403	.275

Cavaness, Christian	L-L	6-2	190	3-16-94	.240	.246	.238	89	292	37	70	12	8	6	38	32	2	2	2	106	9	9	.397	.317
Cronin, Joe	R-R	5-10	185	5-15-94	.195	.213	.184	48	159	23	31	6	2	4	12	27	4	2	1	51	1	2	.333	.325
Davis, Jaylin	R-R	6-1	190	7-1-94	.267	.348	.236	66	251	36	67	13	3	12	41	16	3	0	2	77	9	2	.486	.316
Diaz, Lewin	L-L	6-3	180	11-19-96	.292	.268	.300	122	466	47	136	33	1	12	68	25	6	0	11	80	2	1	.444	.329
Gore, Jordan	B-R	6-0	165	8-3-94	.221	.120	.262	27	86	13	19	3	2	1	4	10	0	0	1	33	1	0	.337	.299
Hamilton, Caleb	R-R	6-0	185	2-5-95	.222	.269	.197	92	307	51	68	18	4	9	42	54	3	1	2	97	3	4	.394	.342
Jernigan, Andre	R-R	6-0	205	11-16-93	.157	.313	.086	16	51	7	8	3	0	1	5	4	0	1	1	23	0	0	.275	.214
Kennedy, Shane	R-R	6-3	205	1-31-92	.250	.154	.316	10	32	3	8	1	0	1	2	9	1	0	0	14	0	0	.375	.429
Kerrigan, Jimmy	R-R	6-1	215	3-16-94	.250	.356	.190	31	124	14	31	2	4	5	20	1	3	1	2	30	1	2	.452	.269
Kranson, Mitchell	L-R	5-9	210	1-11-94	.268	.239	.276	57	220	24	59	15	1	3	21	14	2	0	0	41	0	0	.386	.318
Lewis, Royce	R-R	6-2	188	6-5-99	.296	.323	.275	18	71	16	21	2	1	1	10	6	2	0	1	16	3	1	.394	.363
Lopez, Brandon	R-R	6-1	190	9-9-93	.276	.256	.281	53	185	22	51	4	2	0	13	11	2	1	1	32	1	0	.319	.322
Marrero, Lean	L-R	5-10	160	9-19-97	.200	.182	.207	11	40	1	8	1	1	0	2	3	0	0	0	7	1	1	.275	.256
Minier, Amaurys	R-B	6-2	190	1-30-96	.144	.129	.149	35	118	7	17	7	0	3	16	18	3	0	1	48	0	0	.280	.271
Montesino, Ariel	B-R	5-10	170	9-21-95	.185	.159	.196	45	151	14	28	7	2	0	5	16	0	3	3	40	3	3	.258	.259
Morrison, Hank	R-R	6-2	225	3-25-94	.217	.259	.198	53	184	21	40	6	1	4	10	10	8	0	1	41	2	0	.326	.286
Munoz, Gorge	R-R	6-1	180	6-21-96	.240	.360	.197	29	96	8	23	3	1	2	12	5	3	2	1	27	4	2	.354	.295
Palacios, Jermaine	R-R	6-0	145	7-19-96	.321	.304	.326	62	259	52	83	13	6	11	39	12	5	0	0	46	9	8	.544	.362
Rortvedt, Ben	L-R	5-10	190	9-25-97	.224	.312	.202	89	308	33	69	16	0	4	30	22	4	1	1	60	1	0	.315	.284
Whitefield, Aaron	R-R	6-4	200	9-2-96	.262	.227	.276	117	413	66	108	18	6	11	57	31	7	1	8	118	33	9	.414	.318

Pitching	B-T	HT	WT	DOB	W	L	ERA	G	GS	CG	SV	IP	H	R	ER	HR	BB	SO	AVG	vLH	vRH	K/9	BB/9
Anderson, Brady	L-R	6-0	185	11-10-92	0	1	1.42	2	0	0	1	6	4	1	1	0	1	4	.174	.200	.167	5.68	1.42
Barnes, Charlie	L-L	6-2	160	10-1-95	2	1	3.86	6	6	0	0	26	23	12	11	4	8	23	.230	.200	.238	8.06	2.81
Beardsley, Tyler	R-R	6-4	225	5-17-94	4	9	5.38	16	15	1	0	85	99	53	51	9	20	43	.292	.333	.268	4.54	2.11
Beeker, Clark	R-R	6-3	205	11-22-92	11	3	2.03	20	20	2	0	129	102	34	29	11	17	84	.217	.231	.208	5.88	1.19
Carlini, Domenick	L-L	6-2	175	11-19-93	4	8	5.18	17	16	0	0	83	96	56	48	12	29	66	.288	.346	.271	7.13	3.13
Cordy, Max	R-R	6-4	220	6-9-93	2	4	3.54	39	4	0	3	69	56	37	27	3	43	67	.225	.200	.238	8.78	5.64
Davis, Colton	R-R	6-1	190	1-5-94	6	3	3.43	44	1	0	3	63	51	25	24	4	26	60	.222	.152	.258	8.57	3.71
Del Rosario, Eduardo	R-R	6-0	145	5-19-95	7	6	4.11	23	18	0	1	105	92	49	48	8	41	94	.237	.248	.231	8.06	3.51
Dobnak, Randy	R-R	6-1	210	1-17-95	0	0	2.57	1	1	0	0	7	6	2	2	0	1	1	.240	.400	.200	1.29	1.29
Grogan, Quin	R-R	6-2	190	6-11-93	0	0	0.00	2	0	0	1	2	5	0	0	0	1	3	.417	.667	.333	11.57	3.86
Hackimer, Tom	R-R	5-11	190	6-28-94	3	1	1.50	16	0	0	6	24	11	5	4	0	3	28	.133	.188	.098	10.50	1.13
Jax, Griffin	R-R	6-2	195	11-22-94	2	1	2.39	4	4	0	0	26	19	7	7	1	7	13	.200	.163	.239	4.44	2.39
Lombana, Logan	R-R	6-3	225	7-17-94	1	2	2.60	36	0	0	0	66	57	21	19	4	17	55	.238	.286	.215	7.54	2.33
Lujan, Hector	R-R	6-3	230	8-23-94	3	1	1.33	42	0	0	17	54	41	15	8	3	8	54	.215	.216	.214	9.00	1.33
Marzi, Anthony	L-L	6-1	205	11-27-92	5	2	1.98	9	9	0	0	55	42	16	12	3	14	36	.211	.250	.201	5.93	2.30
Mason, Ryan	R-R	6-7	215	10-4-94	1	2	2.01	29	0	0	0	49	54	15	11	1	11	43	.280	.291	.275	7.84	2.01
McGuff, Patrick	L-R	6-2	200	3-30-94	3	2	2.49	27	1	0	1	51	39	16	14	2	19	53	.216	.143	.254	9.41	3.38
Poppen, Sean	R-R	6-4	195	3-15-94	6	2	2.90	14	14	0	0	87	76	40	28	5	17	81	.226	.235	.220	8.38	1.76
Robinson, Alex	L-L	6-3	217	8-11-94	2	5	2.84	28	0	0	2	38	29	12	12	2	15	51	.207	.091	.243	12.08	3.55
Sammons, Bryan	L-L	6-4	235	4-27-95	3	1	3.51	6	5	0	0	26	22	13	10	2	11	35	.222	.143	.235	12.27	3.86
Sanders, Evan	L-L	6-2	200	10-14-93	2	4	5.94	14	5	0	0	36	34	25	24	2	30	29	.260	.129	.300	7.18	7.43
Schick, Alex	R-R	6-7	210	12-1-94	1	1	6.10	2	2	0	0	10	14	7	7	1	2	10	.326	.400	.261	8.71	1.74
Tillery, Zack	R-R	6-3	210	1-12-93	0	0	6.43	6	0	0	0	7	5	5	5	0	14	8	.200	.222	.188	10.29	18.00
Vasquez, Andrew	L-L	6-6	228	9-14-93	1	0	1.61	14	0	0	0	22	15	4	4	0	10	33	.190	.182	.193	13.30	4.03
Watson, Tyler	R-L	6-5	200	5-22-97	1	3	4.28	5	5	0	0	27	28	15	13	4	8	18	.264	.227	.274	5.93	2.63
Wells, Tyler	R-R	6-8	265	8-26-94	5	3	3.11	14	14	0	0	75	63	28	26	6	22	92	.221	.228	.217	10.99	2.63

Fielding

Catcher	PCT	G	PO	A	E	DP	PB
Hamilton	.976	40	290	32	8	3	18
Kranson	1.000	17	127	13	0	4	3
Rortvedt	.992	86	650	84	6	5	15

First Base	PCT	G	PO	A	E	DP
Cabbage	1.000	3	19	1	0	5
Diaz	.987	110	940	59	13	78
Hamilton	1.000	12	82	8	0	9
Kranson	.982	8	52	3	1	5
Minier	.980	11	96	4	2	5

Second Base	PCT	G	PO	A	E	DP
Blankenhorn	.989	43	82	101	2	31
Cronin	.971	14	31	35	2	9
Gore	1.000	6	14	16	0	6
Hamilton	.875	4	6	8	2	3
Lopez	.990	47	93	108	2	29
Montesino	.990	21	45	54	1	8
Munoz	.938	7	15	15	2	3

Third Base	PCT	G	PO	A	E	DP
Blankenhorn	.916	55	44	87	12	8
Cabbage	.898	14	8	36	5	3
Cronin	.942	18	15	34	3	4
Gore	1.000	8	2	21	0	4
Hamilton	.919	22	15	53	6	4
Jernigan	.944	14	4	30	2	2
Kennedy	1.000	1	0	1	0	0
Kranson	.750	3	1	5	2	1
Lopez	.000	1	0	0	0	0
Montesino	.885	8	7	16	3	0

Shortstop	PCT	G	PO	A	E	DP
Cronin	.982	14	18	38	1	8
Gore	.955	13	13	50	3	12
Hamilton	1.000	2	2	2	0	0
Lewis	.963	17	22	55	3	9
Lopez	1.000	2	1	3	0	0
Montesino	.896	10	8	35	5	6
Munoz	.910	22	20	61	8	10
Palacios	.961	62	87	158	10	27

Outfield	PCT	G	PO	A	E	DP
Cabbage	1.000	22	37	2	0	1
Carrier	1.000	40	63	6	0	3
Cavaness	.986	84	132	4	2	0
Cronin	1.000	3	8	0	0	0
Davis	.983	60	110	9	2	3
Hamilton	.941	12	16	0	1	0
Kennedy	1.000	4	5	0	0	0
Kerrigan	1.000	31	77	1	0	0
Marrero	1.000	11	27	0	0	0
Montesino	1.000	5	11	1	0	0
Morrison	.975	46	75	2	2	1
Whitefield	.985	109	257	9	4	3

ELIZABETHTON TWINS — ROOKIE

APPALACHIAN LEAGUE

Batting	B-T	HT	WT	DOB	AVG	vLH	vRH	G	AB	R	H	2B	3B	HR	RBI	BB	HBP	SH	SF	SO	SB	CS	SLG	OBP
Albanese, Matt	R-R	6-2	200	7-26-95	.296	.308	.291	39	142	19	42	6	0	3	19	12	2	0	3	40	2	1	.401	.352
Baddoo, Akil	L-L	5-11	185	8-16-98	.357	.375	.351	33	126	39	45	15	2	3	19	27	3	0	1	19	5	4	.579	.478
Bechtold, Andrew	R-R	6-1	185	4-18-96	.299	.316	.293	43	144	33	43	10	1	2	19	27	1	0	3	40	0	0	.424	.406
Cabbage, Trey	L-R	6-3	204	5-3-97	.240	.250	.235	13	50	10	12	3	1	2	10	11	0	0	0	16	1	0	.460	.377
Carrier, Shane	R-R	6-2	220	6-3-96	.348	.324	.356	32	138	19	48	10	0	5	32	1	2	0	1	30	3	2	.529	.359
Contreras, Mark	L-R	6-0	185	1-24-95	.275	.262	.279	43	171	27	47	9	2	4	24	8	4	0	2	52	5	1	.421	.319
Cosgrove, Andrew	R-R	6-2	200	7-31-96	.221	.273	.200	21	77	9	17	2	0	1	8	6	5	0	0	20	0	0	.286	.318
Crites, Carson	R-R	6-0	195	1-18-95	.300	.282	.306	38	150	29	45	11	0	4	30	10	3	0	3	28	4	3	.453	.349
Dixon, T.J.	L-L	5-11	180	10-14-94	.259	.207	.274	40	135	25	35	3	2	1	19	20	1	1	1	28	4	6	.333	.357
Gore, Jordan	B-R	6-0	165	8-3-94	.389	.333	.400	18	72	14	28	5	0	1	16	6	1	1	0	21	1	0	.500	.443
Javier, Wander	R-R	6-1	165	12-29-98	.299	.277	.309	41	157	34	47	13	1	4	22	19	3	0	1	49	4	3	.471	.383
Jernigan, Andre	R-R	6-0	205	11-16-93	.000	.000	.000	4	10	0	0	0	0	0	1	3	0	0	0	4	0	0	.000	.231
Kendrick, Kolton	L-R	6-3	215	8-10-96	.231	.382	.169	35	117	24	27	6	0	4	18	22	0	0	3	45	0	0	.385	.345
Miranda, Jose	R-R	6-2	180	6-29-98	.283	.232	.299	54	223	43	63	8	2	11	43	16	5	0	3	24	2	3	.484	.340
Molina, Robert	B-R	5-11	175	9-16-96	.253	.150	.286	25	83	8	21	3	1	2	12	3	0	1	1	11	0	0	.386	.276
Montesino, Ariel	B-R	5-10	170	9-21-95	.257	.286	.244	35	113	21	29	5	1	3	19	16	0	0	2	18	2	2	.398	.344
Munoz, Gorge	R-R	6-1	180	6-21-96	.290	.333	.269	11	38	6	11	1	0	1	7	1	2	1	0	12	0	0	.395	.342
Robinson, J.J.	L-R	6-2	215	10-11-92	.264	.225	.278	40	148	22	39	3	1	9	36	12	6	0	3	44	1	0	.480	.337
Rooker, Brent	R-R	6-3	215	11-1-94	.282	.321	.263	22	85	19	24	5	0	7	17	11	1	0	2	21	2	2	.588	.364
Silva, Rainis	R-R	6-1	185	3-20-96	.356	.244	.433	30	101	16	36	4	1	1	7	17	1	2	2	8	1	0	.446	.446
Waltner, Colton	R-R	6-2	185	8-13-95	.234	.227	.238	19	64	15	15	5	0	1	9	16	1	0	0	12	2	1	.359	.395

Pitching	B-T	HT	WT	DOB	W	L	ERA	G	GS	CG	SV	IP	H	R	ER	HR	BB	SO	AVG	vLH	vRH	K/9	BB/9
Acosta, Melvi	R-R	6-1	188	6-2-95	5	3	6.22	11	9	0	1	51	62	43	35	4	20	33	.300	.241	.342	5.86	3.55
Barnes, Charlie	L-L	6-2	160	10-1-95	2	1	1.19	6	5	0	0	23	14	5	3	1	10	23	.165	.118	.177	9.13	3.97
Broussard, Christian	R-R	6-3	260	10-21-96	0	1	6.23	4	1	0	0	9	10	6	6	1	4	3	.323	.182	.400	3.12	4.15
Brown, Nick	R-R	6-1	190	11-20-94	3	1	3.93	11	7	0	1	50	49	25	22	8	15	54	.259	.312	.234	9.66	2.68
Clemensia, Taylor	L-L	6-1	185	2-20-97	1	0	0.00	2	0	0	0	5	0	0	0	0	2	3	.000	.000	.000	5.79	3.86
Colina, Edwar	R-R	5-11	182	5-3-97	3	5	3.34	12	11	0	0	59	48	26	22	6	29	56	.219	.281	.183	8.49	4.40
Dobnak, Randy	R-R	6-1	210	1-17-95	2	0	2.39	5	3	0	1	26	19	7	7	3	6	22	.198	.250	.154	7.52	2.05
Faucher, Calvin	R-R	6-0	170	9-22-95	3	0	1.23	5	0	0	1	7	4	1	1	1	3	13	.148	.250	.067	15.95	3.68
Finkel, Jared	R-R	6-3	205	4-27-96	2	1	2.18	17	0	0	3	33	33	13	8	0	7	29	.256	.231	.273	7.91	1.91
Gamez, Juan	R-R	5-11	220	3-7-94	1	1	6.33	15	0	0	2	27	25	20	19	1	16	21	.253	.294	.231	7.00	5.33
Gomez, Moises	R-R	6-1	192	2-8-97	4	1	4.99	12	6	0	0	49	49	34	27	6	25	51	.261	.250	.267	9.43	4.62
Graterol, Brusdar	R-R	6-1	180	8-26-98	2	1	3.92	5	5	0	0	21	16	9	9	1	9	24	.213	.138	.261	10.45	3.92
Jax, Griffin	R-R	6-2	195	11-22-94	0	1	3.86	1	1	0	0	5	6	5	2	1	0	7	.300	.500	.278	13.50	0.00
Lakso, Blair	R-R	6-2	225	8-23-94	1	4	7.09	16	0	0	1	33	32	27	26	4	24	32	.254	.167	.308	8.73	6.55
Martinez, Jose	R-R	6-2	175	10-29-96	5	1	3.34	17	0	0	0	32	32	13	12	2	7	27	.252	.325	.218	7.52	1.95
Moran, Jovani	L-L	6-1	167	4-24-97	3	1	0.36	11	0	0	0	25	12	2	1	1	6	45	.145	.158	.141	16.42	2.19
Ober, Bailey	R-R	6-8	215	7-12-95	2	2	3.21	6	4	0	0	28	24	10	10	2	3	35	.229	.286	.191	11.25	0.96
Ramirez, Rickey	R-R	6-0	170	10-20-96	0	0	5.52	15	0	0	2	29	26	21	18	2	13	21	.234	.220	.243	6.44	3.99
Sammons, Bryan	L-L	6-4	235	4-27-95	2	0	1.46	7	3	0	0	25	14	6	4	1	7	31	.161	.188	.155	11.31	2.55
Suniaga, Carlos	R-R	6-2	187	5-26-97	0	0	0.00	1	0	0	0	3	1	0	0	0	0	4	.083	.200	.000	10.80	0.00
Widell, Ryley	L-L	6-3	180	6-1-97	0	2	2.43	8	7	0	0	30	25	14	8	1	20	41	.229	.278	.220	12.44	6.07
Ynoa, Huascar	R-R	6-3	175	5-28-98	0	1	5.26	6	6	0	0	26	28	16	15	1	14	23	.277	.378	.219	8.06	4.91
2-team total (7 Danville)					0	4	5.26	13	13	0	0	51	52	33	30	2	29	50	.257	.378	.219	8.77	5.08

Fielding

C: Cosgrove 21, Molina 24, Silva 25, Waltner 2. **1B:** Kendrick 34, Robinson 37. **2B:** Crites 29, Miranda 37, Montesino 3. **3B:** Bechtold 39, Cabbage 4, Crites 1, Jernigan 3, Miranda 1, Montesino 20. **SS:** Gore 18, Javier 36, Montesino 4, Munoz 11. **OF:** Albanese 37, Baddoo 28, Cabbage 6, Carrier 29, Contreras 41, Dixon 38, Montesino 3, Rooker 17, Waltner 8.

GCL TWINS — ROOKIE

GULF COAST LEAGUE

Batting	B-T	HT	WT	DOB	AVG	vLH	vRH	G	AB	R	H	2B	3B	HR	RBI	BB	HBP	SH	SF	SO	SB	CS	SLG	OBP
Akins, Jared	L-R	6-3	195	12-12-96	.253	.206	.277	33	99	18	25	5	1	3	16	11	1	0	1	35	5	2	.414	.330
Alvarez, Jhon	R-R	6-0	190	2-18-96	.205	.167	.238	18	39	3	8	0	0	0	1	7	1	1	0	9	0	0	.205	.340
Arias, Jean Carlos	L-L	5-11	170	1-14-98	.298	.255	.316	48	168	30	50	7	4	5	32	14	2	1	0	42	10	3	.476	.359
Baddoo, Akil	L-L	5-11	185	8-16-98	.267	.269	.265	20	75	18	20	4	3	1	10	9	2	0	0	13	4	0	.440	.361
Burns, Colton	L-R	6-2	195	10-19-95	.282	.167	.333	27	78	14	22	5	0	1	7	16	3	1	0	23	8	3	.385	.423
Camacho, Kerby	B-R	5-10	175	11-24-97	.246	.267	.239	21	61	6	15	5	0	0	10	13	0	0	0	10	3	0	.328	.378
Cuesto, Darling	R-R	6-0	175	10-12-97	.136	.100	.167	7	22	1	3	1	0	0	2	3	0	0	0	6	0	1	.182	.240
De La Torre, Ricky	R-R	6-2	175	7-21-99	.268	.359	.220	42	153	25	41	3	1	3	12	16	1	0	0	39	5	6	.360	.341
Grzelakowski, Taylor	L-R	5-11	245	12-20-93	.222	.313	.150	12	36	3	8	2	0	1	7	3	0	1	1	7	1	0	.361	.275
Herrera, Edgar	L-L	6-0	170	4-19-97	.152	.273	.091	12	33	1	5	1	0	0	6	0	0	0	2	7	0	2	.182	.143
Hutcheon, Dane	L-R	5-9	177	7-14-94	.200	.133	.267	13	30	8	6	1	1	0	7	4	1	0	1	8	1	1	.300	.306
Kennedy, Shane	R-R	6-3	205	1-31-92	.214	.200	.222	5	14	3	3	1	2	0	3	5	0	0	1	3	1	0	.571	.400
Lewis, Royce	R-R	6-2	188	6-5-99	.271	.322	.230	36	133	38	36	6	2	3	17	19	7	0	0	17	15	2	.414	.390
Maldonado, Humberto	B-R	6-3	202	12-30-97	.233	.261	.220	26	73	7	17	6	1	1	10	7	1	0	0	32	0	2	.384	.309
Morel, Emmanuel	B-R	5-10	150	5-4-97	.260	.357	.214	38	131	29	34	10	0	0	7	15	4	1	0	37	12	4	.336	.353
Olson, Brian	R-R	6-0	171	1-21-93	.156	.200	.136	11	32	1	5	1	1	0	6	2	1	0	0	7	0	0	.250	.229

Batting	B-T	HT	WT	DOB	AVG	vLH	vRH	G	AB	R	H	2B	3B	HR	RBI	BB	HBP	SH	SF	SO	SB	CS	SLG	OBP
Palka, Daniel	L-L	6-2	220	10-28-91	.278	.400	.231	6	18	4	5	0	0	1	2	2	0	0	0	1	1	0	.444	.350
Paul, Chris	R-R	6-2	200	10-12-92	.167	.000	.286	3	12	2	2	1	0	0	0	1	0	0	0	2	0	1	.250	.231
Robles, Alex	R-R	6-0	200	7-7-95	.324	.382	.290	50	182	30	59	6	0	3	29	8	6	1	2	14	10	4	.407	.369
Rodriguez, Benjamin	R-R	6-6	235	11-9-94	.290	.431	.212	50	162	27	47	11	2	4	40	22	8	0	1	43	4	2	.457	.399
Salva, Kidany	B-R	5-11	185	8-24-98	.159	.077	.194	17	44	5	7	1	0	0	0	8	0	0	0	10	2	2	.182	.289
Tademo, Victor	R-R	6-1	170	7-9-99	.199	.260	.168	47	151	20	30	4	2	2	22	11	3	1	3	53	5	2	.291	.262
Tapia, Roni	R-R	6-3	175	4-3-97	.171	.063	.240	24	82	6	14	6	1	1	11	3	2	1	0	31	1	1	.305	.218

Pitching	B-T	HT	WT	DOB	W	L	ERA	G	GS	CG	SV	IP	H	R	ER	HR	BB	SO	AVG	vLH	vRH	K/9	BB/9
Balan, Petru	L-L	6-0	185	2-22-96	1	3	7.23	9	5	0	1	24	27	22	19	0	19	23	.290	.476	.236	8.75	7.23
Balan, Vadim	R-R	6-1	195	5-25-93	1	1	2.31	9	0	0	4	12	9	9	3	0	7	9	.205	.118	.259	6.94	5.40
Balazovic, Jordan	R-R	6-4	175	9-17-98	1	3	4.91	10	3	0	0	40	47	25	22	5	20	29	.298	.254	.326	6.47	4.46
Beardsley, Tyler	R-R	6-4	225	5-17-94	0	0	0.00	2	2	0	0	5	4	0	0	0	0	5	.222	.125	.300	9.00	0.00
Benninghoff, Tyler	R-R	6-4	180	9-17-97	0	1	9.00	4	4	0	0	4	3	4	4	1	4	6	.200	.250	.143	13.50	9.00
Bermudez, Jose	R-R	6-4	190	1-8-98	2	0	6.91	8	0	0	0	14	21	11	11	1	9	11	.356	.231	.391	6.91	5.65
Bizzle, Austin	R-R	6-1	205	3-16-95	1	0	1.86	7	2	0	0	10	5	2	2	0	3	8	.156	.000	.294	7.45	2.79
Centeno, Henry	R-R	6-2	200	8-24-94	0	1	2.89	5	3	0	0	9	6	3	3	0	4	8	.182	.158	.214	7.71	3.86
Clemensia, Taylor	L-L	6-1	185	2-20-97	1	3	4.50	9	4	0	0	20	16	16	10	2	25	22	.205	.217	.200	9.90	11.25
Cruz, Amilcar	R-R	6-2	190	3-28-96	1	1	4.76	12	0	0	1	28	29	16	15	1	23	28	.274	.258	.280	8.89	7.31
Enlow, Blayne	R-R	6-3	170	3-21-99	3	0	1.33	6	1	0	0	20	10	4	3	1	4	19	.141	.138	.143	8.41	1.77
Featherstone, Zach	L-L	6-2	215	12-18-95	0	2	2.93	12	0	0	2	15	14	9	5	0	7	11	.233	.235	.233	6.46	4.11
Garcia, Pedro	R-R	6-2	180	7-21-95	6	2	2.59	10	3	0	0	49	26	15	14	1	17	41	.152	.167	.144	7.58	3.14
Gerics, David	R-R	6-0	185	6-12-95	1	0	14.54	5	0	0	0	4	4	8	7	0	6	4	.235	.167	.273	8.31	12.46
Graterol, Brusdar	R-R	6-1	180	8-26-98	2	0	1.40	5	2	0	0	19	10	3	3	1	4	21	.152	.100	.194	9.78	1.86
Haley, Justin	R-R	6-5	230	6-16-91	0	0	0.00	1	1	0	0	1	1	0	0	0	0	1	.333	.000	.500	9.00	0.00
Heston, Chris	R-R	6-3	195	4-10-88	0	1	5.40	1	1	0	0	5	7	3	3	0	0	5	.318	.385	.222	9.00	0.00
Jay, Tyler	L-L	6-1	185	4-19-94	0	0	4.91	3	1	0	0	4	6	4	2	1	1	7	.353	.500	.308	17.18	2.45
Jones, Matt	R-L	6-2	150	10-16-98	2	1	3.94	11	2	0	2	32	29	17	14	0	19	19	.242	.148	.269	5.34	5.34
Jones, Zack	R-R	6-1	195	12-4-90	0	0	0.00	1	1	0	0	1	0	0	0	0	0	2	.000	.000	.000	18.00	0.00
Kohn, Michael	R-R	6-2	200	6-26-86	0	0	1.80	5	4	0	0	5	2	1	1	0	1	7	.125	.125	.125	12.60	1.80
Leach, Landon	R-R	6-4	220	7-12-99	2	0	3.38	5	2	0	0	13	11	9	5	0	6	10	.220	.227	.214	6.75	4.05
Marnon, Kevin	R-L	6-7	245	3-16-94	1	0	0.54	7	0	0	1	17	14	7	1	0	4	17	.219	.250	.208	9.18	2.16
Mojica, Juan	R-R	6-3	195	7-27-95	3	0	7.24	8	1	0	0	14	17	12	11	1	14	7	.315	.400	.282	4.61	9.22
Molina, Derek	L-R	6-3	195	7-27-97	1	0	1.08	10	2	0	4	17	12	2	2	0	3	21	.203	.125	.257	11.34	1.62
Perkins, Glen	L-L	6-0	205	3-2-83	0	0	0.00	2	2	0	0	2	1	0	0	0	1	3	.143	.500	.000	13.50	4.50
Rosenstein, Joe	R-R	6-7	220	3-21-96	1	1	9.00	6	0	0	1	9	10	10	9	0	13	4	.303	.308	.300	4.00	13.00
Schutte, Matz	R-R	6-3	185	10-4-97	0	0	9.00	6	0	0	2	11	7	13	11	2	12	7	.189	.125	.207	5.73	9.82
Stashak, Cody	R-R	6-2	169	6-4-94	1	0	3.18	3	0	0	0	6	5	2	2	0	0	8	.238	.250	.231	12.71	0.00
Suniaga, Carlos	R-R	6-2	187	5-26-97	4	0	1.69	11	6	0	1	48	36	11	9	2	12	38	.208	.203	.212	7.13	2.25
Tepesch, Nick	R-R	6-4	240	10-12-88	0	1	11.25	3	3	0	0	8	11	10	10	0	3	6	.324	.286	.350	6.75	3.38
Tracy, Matt	L-L	6-3	215	11-26-88	0	0	2.25	1	1	0	0	4	2	1	1	0	0	6	.143	.250	.100	13.50	0.00
Wells, Lachlan	L-L	6-1	185	2-27-97	0	0	2.25	1	1	0	0	4	2	1	1	0	0	6	.143	.500	.083	13.50	0.00
Wells, Tyler	R-R	6-8	265	8-26-94	0	2	2.63	4	1	0	0	14	10	7	4	0	5	16	.200	.235	.182	10.54	3.29

Fielding

C: Alvarez 17, Camacho 14, Cuesto 6, Grzelakowski 9, Olson 9, Rodriguez 5, Salva 9. **1B:** Camacho 3, Robles 13, Rodriguez 45, Tapia 1. **2B:** De La Torre 15, Hutcheon 5, Morel 34, Robles 2, Tademo 5. **3B:** De La Torre 3, Hutcheon 1, Paul 2, Robles 8, Tademo 38, Tapia 11. **SS:** De La Torre 22, Lewis 32, Tademo 5. **OF:** Akins 32, Arias 47, Baddoo 8, Burns 24, Herrera 10, Hutcheon 4, Kennedy 3, Maldonado 20, Palka 4, Robles 26, Salva 3, Tapia 8.

DSL TWINS — *ROOKIE*

DOMINICAN SUMMER LEAGUE

Batting	B-T	HT	WT	DOB	AVG	vLH	vRH	G	AB	R	H	2B	3B	HR	RBI	BB	HBP	SH	SF	SO	SB	CS	SLG	OBP
Calcano, Mariano	R-R	6-3	222	9-19-96	.239	.167	.266	33	109	19	26	7	0	2	17	14	5	0	2	39	3	3	.358	.346
Cuesto, Darling	R-R	6-0	175	10-12-97	.286	.333	.276	10	35	7	10	1	0	1	5	2	1	0	0	11	1	0	.400	.342
De La Cruz, Yeremi	R-R	5-11	185	7-15-97	.286	.429	.254	24	77	12	22	5	1	2	15	9	0	0	1	15	1	4	.455	.356
Encarnacion, Yeltsin	L-R	5-11	170	6-28-98	.318	.308	.320	47	151	29	48	9	8	2	21	22	1	3	0	20	6	5	.523	.408
Feliz, Jesus	R-R	6-0	180	6-7-00	.248	.229	.255	42	141	19	35	8	5	1	18	6	8	1	0	43	6	5	.397	.316
Henriquez, Zaino	R-R	6-0	180	6-7-98	.211	.273	.200	24	76	13	16	1	1	0	7	9	2	5	0	14	1	0	.250	.310
Heredia, Victor	R-R	6-2	230	6-1-00	.257	.300	.250	24	74	10	19	4	0	1	9	10	2	1	1	19	1	0	.351	.356
Marte, Agustin	B-R	6-0	180	12-9-98	.299	.487	.246	45	167	29	50	11	3	1	29	16	2	2	1	43	11	3	.419	.366
Martinez, Francisco	B-R	6-5	220	4-25-99	.255	.300	.238	39	145	25	37	8	0	3	17	13	1	0	0	56	2	2	.372	.321
Martinez, Juan	R-R	6-0	210	9-30-96	.273	.364	.245	44	139	23	38	10	2	0	24	17	4	0	3	30	1	1	.374	.362
Nunez, Alberoni	R-R	6-1	180	2-17-99	.352	.415	.331	48	165	35	58	9	7	3	38	20	3	0	5	35	11	8	.546	.420
Perez, Yeison	R-R	5-11	200	4-9-96	.224	.226	.224	35	107	15	24	2	1	2	18	9	4	0	1	9	2	0	.318	.306
Pimentel, Davinson	R-R	5-9	170	2-12-97	.242	.143	.269	9	33	6	8	3	0	1	5	5	2	0	0	6	1	0	.424	.375
Reyes, Felix	L-L	6-0	180	3-1-99	.250	.400	.207	36	112	19	28	7	3	1	13	13	5	1	1	47	5	3	.393	.351
Salazar, Cesar	L-L	6-1	185	3-4-00	.232	.368	.197	30	95	13	22	3	1	0	7	15	3	1	0	30	4	4	.284	.354
Santana, Ruben	B-R	5-9	160	11-30-97	.340	.324	.344	46	159	36	54	10	4	0	18	18	5	1	2	18	6	5	.453	.419
Urena, Estamy	R-R	6-0	175	5-27-99	.306	.271	.320	46	173	32	53	7	3	3	36	19	1	0	5	26	4	4	.434	.369
Valdez, Wander	R-R	6-2	200	11-22-99	.264	.244	.270	49	167	32	44	12	4	1	22	21	2	0	3	37	4	2	.401	.347
Vasquez, Samuel	L-L	5-10	155	1-15-97	.301	.212	.323	51	166	44	50	4	3	2	17	24	2	4	0	34	26	12	.398	.396

Pitching	B-T	HT	WT	DOB	W	L	ERA	G	GS	CG	SV	IP	H	R	ER	HR	BB	SO	AVG	vLH	vRH	K/9	BB/9
Bellorin, Luis	L-L	6-1	175	9-18-97	4	3	2.95	17	3	0	0	37	43	23	12	0	18	36	.295	.296	.294	8.84	4.42
Bermudez, Jose	R-R	6-4	190	1-8-98	0	1	4.32	6	0	0	1	8	7	6	4	0	2	9	.226	.375	.174	9.72	2.16

Berroa, Prelander	R-R	5-11	170	4-18-00	2	0	5.60	9	3	0	0	18	26	17	11	0	11	16	.361	.471	.327	8.15	5.60
Castro, Cristian	R-R	6-1	205	4-21-98	4	2	3.97	22	0	0	1	34	25	21	15	0	25	37	.214	.310	.182	9.79	6.62
Cruz, Steven	R-R	6-2	185	6-15-99	4	0	3.68	16	3	0	1	29	26	14	12	0	14	26	.241	.333	.214	7.98	4.30
De La Cruz, Luciano	L-L	5-11	165	2-4-99	0	1	4.40	11	0	0	2	14	15	9	7	0	5	11	.259	.154	.289	6.91	3.14
Garcia, Yeremi	R-R	6-2	185	11-16-99	3	2	5.13	18	0	0	2	26	24	26	15	1	19	14	.245	.308	.222	4.78	6.49
German, Osiris	R-R	6-1	170	11-2-98	1	2	3.13	15	3	0	0	32	22	14	11	0	11	30	.204	.177	.216	8.53	3.13
Gil, Luis	R-R	6-3	176	6-3-98	0	2	2.59	14	14	0	0	42	31	15	12	2	20	49	.205	.264	.174	10.58	4.32
Gutierrez, Robert	R-R	5-11	210	6-16-98	3	0	6.14	11	0	0	1	22	24	17	15	3	14	21	.270	.273	.269	8.59	5.73
Marin, Andriu	R-R	6-2	205	7-6-98	4	1	2.09	11	10	0	0	47	48	20	11	1	10	44	.270	.277	.267	8.37	1.90
Mojica, Juan	R-R	6-3	195	7-27-95	1	0	3.86	6	0	0	0	9	8	5	4	0	5	10	.222	.333	.185	9.64	4.82
Montero, Michael	R-R	6-3	190	1-6-00	4	1	2.78	13	13	1	0	58	44	21	18	3	12	64	.208	.174	.224	9.87	1.85
Navas, Junior	R-R	6-4	185	9-8-99	4	0	0.00	11	2	0	2	19	14	5	0	0	10	14	.206	.133	.226	6.75	4.82
Rivas, Elvis	R-R	6-0	200	2-16-96	2	1	6.39	15	0	0	2	25	26	24	18	0	23	31	.263	.172	.300	11.01	8.17
Sanchez, Fernando	R-R	5-9	155	2-20-00	2	4	7.55	21	1	0	2	39	56	38	33	2	18	21	.350	.333	.357	4.81	4.12
Soto, Fredderi	L-L	6-1	180	6-29-98	1	1	1.34	15	10	0	0	54	47	12	8	0	10	28	.234	.292	.226	4.70	1.68
Toledo, Jesus	L-L	5-11	180	8-25-99	4	1	2.38	14	9	0	0	45	40	14	12	1	17	30	.248	.196	.270	5.96	3.38
Torres, Frandy	R-R	5-10	160	8-4-95	6	0	0.72	23	0	0	10	38	25	9	3	0	13	34	.194	.143	.208	8.12	3.11

Fielding

C: Cuesto 5, De La Cruz 19, Heredia 16, Perez 30, Pimentel 9. **1B:** Calcano 22, Encarnacion 1, Henriquez 4, Martinez 21, Santana 22, Valdez 3. **2B:** Encarnacion 15, Feliz 8, Henriquez 13, Marte 10, Santana 10, Urena 21. **3B:** Encarnacion 18, Feliz 1, Marte 3, Santana 7, Urena 2, Valdez 43. **SS:** Encarnacion 3, Feliz 26, Marte 28, Santana 2, Urena 17. **OF:** Calcano 10, Martinez 22, Martinez 35, Nunez 46, Reyes 34, Salazar 30, Vasquez 48.

New York Mets

SEASON IN A SENTENCE: The Mets entered 2017 with high expectations, but, fueled by injuries to stars such as Yoenis Cespedes, Noah Syndergaard and Jeurys Familia, they dropped to seventh in the NL wild card race and entered sell mode in July on their way to 92 losses.

HIGH POINT: Third-year outfielder Michael Conforto hit .279/.384/.555 with 27 home runs and made his first all-star team. The breakout was bittersweet because he missed the final five weeks of the season after dislocating his shoulder while swinging the bat in an Aug. 24 game.

LOW POINT: With the exception of Jacob deGrom, the vaunted rotation that carried the Mets to the 2015 World Series failed to stay healthy. Matt Harvey, Steven Matz and Syndergaard combined for just 190 innings and a 5.88 ERA. Overall, the Mets recorded a 5.01 ERA and 85 ERA+ that both ranked third-worst in baseball.

NOTABLE ROOKIES: Shortstop Amed Rosario, who ranked as the system's No. 1 prospect coming into the year and No. 1 in the Triple-A Pacific Coast League at the end of it, made his big league debut on Aug. 1. The 21-year-old showed flashes of brilliance at bat, in the field and on the basepaths. Outfielder Brandon Nimmo fashioned a .379 on-base percentage in his first crack at extended play the majors. First baseman Dominic Smith produced nine home runs in 49 games but hit just .198. On the heels of a promising cup of coffee in 2016, righthander Robert Gsellman ran up a 5.19 ERA in 120 innings.

KEY TRANSACTIONS: The Mets traded pending free agents Jay Bruce, Lucas Duda, Curtis Granderson, Addison Reed and Neil Walker, targeting one specific demographic in return: young power relievers. Two of those relievers, Jamie Callahan and Jacob Rhame, made their big league debuts as September callups and averaged 95 mph. Meanwhile, Gerson Bautista hit 101 mph at high Class A and Drew Smith showed off a high-spin, swing-and-miss curveball at Double-A. Though they are farther from the majors, relievers Eric Hanhold, Steve Nogosek and Ryder Ryan all sit in the mid-90s with riding life on their fastballs.

DOWN ON THE FARM: Just three organizations had lower winning percentages by minor league affiliates than the Mets (.456). Only Double-A Binghamton qualified for the playoffs, led by starters Corey Oswalt—the Eastern League pitcher of the year—Marcos Molina and P.J. Conlon.

OPENING DAY PAYROLL: $155,187,460 (12th)

PLAYERS OF THE YEAR

MAJOR LEAGUE

Michael Conforto
OF
.279/.384/.555
27 HR, 145 OPS+
First all-star team

MINOR LEAGUE

Dominic Smith
1B
(Triple-A)
.330/.386/.519
16 HR, 76 RBIs

ORGANIZATION LEADERS

BATTING			*Minimum 250 AB
MAJORS			
*	AVG	Yoenis Cespedes	.292
*	OPS	Michael Conforto	.939
	HR	Jay Bruce	29
	RBI	Jay Bruce	75
MINORS			
*	AVG	Dominic Smith, Las Vegas	.330
*	OBP	Patrick Mazeika, St. Lucie, Binghamton	.389
*	SLG	Travis Taijeron, Las Vegas	.525
*	OPS	Travis Taijeron, Las Vegas	.907
	R	Dominic Smith, Las Vegas	77
		Jhoan Urena, St. Lucie, Las Vegas	77
	H	Dominic Smith, Las Vegas	151
	TB	Dominic Smith, Las Vegas	237
	2B	Dominic Smith, Las Vegas	34
		Jhoan Urena, St. Lucie, Las Vegas	34
	3B	Amed Rosario, Las Vegas	7
	HR	Travis Taijeron, Las Vegas	25
	RBI	Travis Taijeron, Las Vegas	78
	BB	Luis Guillorme, Binghamton	72
	SO	Travis Taijeron, Las Vegas	146
	SB	Champ Stuart, Binghamton	35

PITCHING			#Minimum 75 IP
MAJORS			
	W	Jacob deGrom	15
#	ERA	Jacob deGrom	3.53
	SO	Jacob deGrom	239
	SV	Addison Reed	19
MINORS			
	W	Corey Oswalt, Binghamton	12
		Merandy Gonzalez, Columbia, St. Lucie, Jupiter	12
		Andrew Church, Binghamton, St. Lucie	12
	L	Ricky Knapp, Las Vegas, Binghamton	13
		Nabil Crismatt, St. Lucie	13
		Wilfredo Boscan, Las Vegas	13
#	ERA	Merandy Gonzalez, Columbia, St. Lucie, Jupiter	1.78
	G	Ben Rowen, Las Vegas	54
	GS	Ricky Knapp, Las Vegas, Binghamton	29
	SV	Cory Burns, Las Vegas, Binghamton	19
	IP	Ricky Knapp, Las Vegas, Binghamton	172
	BB	Casey Delgado, Binghamton	55
	SO	Nabil Crismatt, St. Lucie	142
#	AVG	Jordan Humphreys, Columbia, St. Lucie	.197

2017 PERFORMANCE

General Manager: Sandy Alderson. **Farm Director:** Ian Levin. **Scouting Director:** Marc Tramuta.

Class	Team	League	W	L	PCT	Finish	Manager
Majors	New York Mets	National	70	92	.432	12th (15)	Terry Collins
Triple-A	Las Vegas 51s	Pacific Coast	56	86	.394	16th (16)	Pedro Lopez
Double-A	Binghamton Rumble Ponies	Eastern	85	54	.612	2nd (12)	Luis Rojas
High-A	St. Lucie Mets	Florida State	63	75	.457	10th (12)	Chad Kreuter
Low-A	Columbia Fireflies	South Atlantic	68	70	.493	t-9th (14)	Jose Leger
Short Season	Brooklyn Cyclones	New York-Penn	24	52	.316	14th (14)	Edgardo Alfonzo
Rookie	Kingsport Mets	Appalachian	29	37	.439	8th (10)	Luis Rivera
Rookie	GCL Mets	Gulf Coast	19	37	.339	16th (17)	Jose Carreno
Overall 2017 Minor League Record			344	411	.456	t-26th (30)	

ORGANIZATION STATISTICS

NEW YORK METS

NATIONAL LEAGUE

Batting	B-T	HT	WT	DOB	AVG	vLH	vRH	G	AB	R	H	2B	3B	HR	RBI	BB	HBP	SH	SF	SO	SB	CS	SLG	OBP
Aoki, Norichika	R-L	5-9	180	1-5-82	.284	.077	.315	27	102	16	29	7	1	0	8	13	1	0	0	10	5	0	.373	.371
Bruce, Jay	L-L	6-3	225	4-3-87	.256	.237	.264	103	406	61	104	20	0	29	75	39	1	0	2	102	0	1	.520	.321
Cabrera, Asdrubal	B-R	6-0	205	11-13-85	.280	.392	.240	135	479	66	134	32	0	14	59	50	5	1	5	83	3	2	.434	.351
Cecchini, Gavin	R-R	6-2	196	12-22-93	.208	.280	.173	32	77	4	16	2	0	1	7	4	1	0	0	19	0	1	.273	.256
Cespedes, Yoenis	R-R	5-10	220	10-18-85	.292	.256	.305	81	291	46	85	17	2	17	42	26	2	0	2	61	0	1	.540	.352
Conforto, Michael	L-R	6-1	215	3-1-93	.279	.212	.303	109	373	72	104	20	1	27	68	57	8	0	2	113	2	0	.555	.384
d'Arnaud, Travis	R-R	6-2	210	2-10-89	.244	.302	.225	112	348	39	85	19	1	16	57	23	2	0	3	59	0	0	.443	.293
Duda, Lucas	R-L	6-4	255	2-3-86	.246	.224	.253	75	252	30	62	21	0	17	37	37	2	0	0	73	0	0	.532	.347
Evans, Phillip	R-R	5-10	223	9-10-92	.303	.250	.320	19	33	4	10	2	0	0	1	4	1	0	0	8	0	0	.364	.395
Flores, Wilmer	R-R	6-3	205	8-6-91	.271	.291	.262	110	336	42	91	17	1	18	52	17	3	0	6	54	1	1	.488	.307
Granderson, Curtis	R-L	6-1	200	3-16-81	.229	.225	.230	111	337	58	77	22	3	19	52	53	2	0	3	90	4	2	.481	.334
2-team total (36 Los Angeles)					.212	.067	.175	147	449	74	95	24	3	26	64	71	4	0	3	123	6	2	.452	.323
Kelly, Ty	R-L	6-0	180	7-20-88	.000	—	.000	1	1	0	0	0	0	0	0	0	0	0	0	1	0	0	.000	.000
2-team total (69 Philadelphia)					.191	—	.000	70	89	11	17	7	0	2	14	8	1	4	3	25	0	0	.337	.257
Lagares, Juan	R-R	6-1	215	3-17-89	.250	.218	.264	94	252	37	63	16	2	3	15	14	3	2	1	56	7	3	.365	.296
Nido, Tomas	R-R	6-0	210	4-12-94	.300	.000	.333	5	10	0	3	1	0	0	3	0	0	0	0	2	0	0	.400	.300
Nimmo, Brandon	L-R	6-3	207	3-27-93	.260	.191	.282	69	177	26	46	11	1	5	21	33	2	1	2	60	2	0	.418	.379
Plawecki, Kevin	R-R	6-2	210	2-26-91	.260	.231	.270	37	100	11	26	5	0	3	13	14	3	0	1	17	1	0	.400	.364
Reyes, Jose	R-B	6-0	195	6-11-83	.246	.267	.239	145	501	75	123	25	7	15	58	50	2	5	3	79	24	6	.413	.315
Reynolds, Matt	R-R	6-1	198	12-3-90	.230	.233	.229	68	113	12	26	1	2	1	5	14	2	1	0	37	0	1	.301	.326
Rivera, Rene	R-R	5-10	215	7-31-83	.230	.250	.224	54	174	15	40	4	0	8	23	9	3	0	1	54	0	1	.391	.278
2-team total (20 Chicago)					.252	.188	.429	74	218	23	55	9	0	10	35	14	3	1	1	70	0	1	.431	.305
Rivera, T.J.	R-R	6-1	203	10-27-88	.290	.260	.299	73	214	27	62	13	1	5	27	9	5	1	2	32	1	0	.430	.330
Rosario, Amed	R-R	6-2	189	11-20-95	.249	.297	.234	46	165	16	41	4	4	4	10	3	2	0	0	49	7	3	.394	.271
Smith, Dominic	L-L	6-0	239	6-15-95	.198	.129	.213	49	167	17	33	6	0	9	26	14	1	0	1	49	0	0	.395	.262
Taijeron, Travis	R-R	6-2	224	1-20-89	.173	.182	.167	26	52	3	9	2	0	1	3	5	2	0	0	24	0	0	.269	.271
Walker, Neil	R-B	6-3	210	9-10-85	.264	.211	.284	73	265	40	70	13	2	10	36	27	4	1	2	47	0	1	.442	.339
2-team total (38 Milwaukee)					.265	.211	.284	111	385	59	102	21	2	14	49	55	5	1	2	77	0	2	.439	.362

Pitching	B-T	HT	WT	DOB	W	L	ERA	G	GS	CG	SV	IP	H	R	ER	HR	BB	SO	AVG	vLH	vRH	K/9	BB/9
Blevins, Jerry	L-L	6-6	190	9-6-83	6	0	2.94	75	0	0	1	49	43	16	16	4	24	69	.229	.197	.288	12.67	4.41
Bradford, Chasen	R-R	6-1	229	8-5-89	2	0	3.74	28	0	0	0	34	30	17	14	3	13	27	.233	.273	.191	7.22	3.48
Callahan, Jamie	R-R	6-2	230	8-24-94	0	0	4.05	9	0	0	0	7	7	4	3	0	1	5	.250	.143	.357	6.75	1.35
deGrom, Jacob	L-R	6-4	180	6-19-88	15	10	3.53	31	31	1	0	201	180	87	79	28	59	239	.238	.247	.229	10.68	2.64
Edgin, Josh	L-L	6-1	245	12-17-86	0	1	3.65	46	0	0	1	37	39	16	15	3	18	27	.273	.280	.265	6.57	4.38
Familia, Jeurys	R-R	6-3	240	10-10-89	2	2	4.38	26	0	0	6	25	21	14	12	1	15	25	.231	.282	.192	9.12	5.47
Flexen, Chris	R-R	6-3	250	7-1-94	3	6	7.88	14	9	0	0	48	62	44	42	11	35	36	.321	.286	.353	6.75	6.56
Gilmartin, Sean	L-L	6-2	206	5-8-90	0	0	13.50	2	0	0	0	3	8	5	5	2	1	4	.500	.400	.546	10.80	2.70
Goeddel, Erik	R-R	6-3	191	12-20-88	0	1	5.28	33	0	0	0	29	28	17	17	8	11	33	.257	.326	.212	10.24	3.41
Gsellman, Robert	R-R	6-4	205	7-18-93	8	7	5.19	25	22	1	0	120	138	85	69	17	42	82	.280	.276	.284	6.17	3.16
Harvey, Matt	R-R	6-4	215	3-27-89	5	7	6.70	19	18	0	0	93	110	70	69	21	47	67	.295	.331	.264	6.51	4.56
Lugo, Seth	R-R	6-4	225	11-17-89	7	5	4.71	19	18	0	0	101	114	57	53	13	25	85	.284	.293	.273	7.55	2.22
Matz, Steven	R-L	6-2	200	5-29-91	2	7	6.08	13	13	0	0	67	83	46	45	12	19	48	.305	.295	.308	6.48	2.57
McGowan, Kevin	R-R	6-5	233	10-18-91	0	0	5.19	8	0	0	0	9	8	5	5	2	6	8	.235	.222	.250	8.31	6.23
Milone, Tommy	L-L	6-0	220	2-16-87	0	3	8.56	11	5	0	0	27	36	28	26	9	12	22	.316	.179	.361	7.24	3.95
2-team total (6 Milwaukee)					1	3	7.63	17	8	0	1	48	65	43	41	15	14	38	.317	.179	.360	7.08	2.61
Montero, Rafael	R-R	6-0	185	10-17-90	5	11	5.52	34	18	0	0	119	141	75	73	12	67	114	.306	.300	.311	8.62	5.07
Pill, Tyler	L-R	6-1	199	5-29-90	0	3	5.32	7	3	0	0	22	22	16	13	3	10	16	.268	.303	.245	6.55	4.09
Ramirez, Neil	R-R	6-4	215	5-25-89	0	1	6.43	20	0	0	0	21	20	15	15	4	17	26	.247	.194	.289	11.14	7.29
2-team total (9 San Francisco)					0	1	7.18	29	0	0	0	31	35	30	25	6	21	44	.273	.194	.289	12.64	6.03
Ramos, AJ	R-R	5-10	200	9-20-86	0	0	4.74	21	0	0	7	19	19	10	10	3	12	25	.257	.238	.281	11.84	5.68
2-team total (40 Miami)					2	4	3.99	61	0	0	27	59	49	27	26	7	34	72	.223	.238	.281	11.05	5.22
Reed, Addison	R-L	6-4	230	12-27-88	1	2	2.57	48	0	0	19	49	49	14	14	6	6	48	.255	.263	.250	8.82	1.10

Rhame, Jacob	R-R	6-1	215	3-16-93	1	1	9.00	9	0	0	0	9	12	9	9	2	7	7	.333	.313	.350	7.00	7.00
Robles, Hansel	R-R	5-11	185	8-13-90	7	5	4.92	46	0	0	0	57	47	31	31	10	29	60	.226	.189	.246	9.53	4.61
Salas, Fernando	R-R	6-2	200	5-30-85	1	2	6.00	48	0	0	0	45	60	35	30	7	20	47	.321	.279	.341	9.40	4.00
Sewald, Paul	R-R	6-3	207	5-26-90	0	6	4.55	57	0	0	0	65	58	36	33	8	21	69	.237	.290	.204	9.51	2.89
Smoker, Josh	L-L	6-2	246	11-26-88	1	2	5.11	54	0	0	0	56	64	34	32	10	32	68	.282	.281	.283	10.86	5.11
Syndergaard, Noah	L-R	6-6	240	8-29-92	1	2	2.97	7	7	0	0	30	29	14	10	0	3	34	.246	.186	.305	10.09	0.89
Wheeler, Zack	L-R	6-4	195	5-30-90	3	7	5.21	17	17	0	0	86	97	53	50	15	40	81	.284	.275	.290	8.44	4.17
Wilk, Adam	L-L	6-2	180	12-9-87	0	1	12.27	1	1	0	0	4	8	6	5	3	1	2	.444	.286	.546	4.91	2.45

Fielding

Catcher	PCT	G	PO	A	E	DP	PB
d'Arnaud	.995	93	759	44	4	9	2
Nido	1.000	3	18	0	0	0	0
Plawecki	1.000	29	191	11	0	1	2
Rivera	.998	52	441	29	1	3	3

First Base	PCT	G	PO	A	E	DP
Bruce	.976	11	76	6	2	7
Duda	.996	69	528	36	2	43
Flores	1.000	29	158	6	0	16
Plawecki	1.000	2	15	1	0	0
Reynolds	1.000	3	6	0	0	0
Rivera	1.000	1	2	1	0	0
Rivera	.993	20	128	12	1	16
Smith	.994	46	327	26	2	32
Walker	1.000	3	10	0	0	1

Second Base	PCT	G	PO	A	E	DP
Cabrera	1.000	32	60	85	0	23
Cecchini	1.000	20	33	33	0	10
d'Arnaud	1.000	1	1	0	0	0
Evans	1.000	2	3	10	0	1
Flores	.976	12	19	22	1	6
Reyes	1.000	28	39	54	0	14
Reynolds	1.000	8	2	10	0	1
Rivera	1.000	12	18	18	0	2
Walker	.981	68	105	152	5	34

Third Base	PCT	G	PO	A	E	DP
Cabrera	.931	44	19	62	6	6
d'Arnaud	.000	1	0	0	0	0
Evans	1.000	6	5	5	0	0
Flores	.929	55	23	81	8	8
Reyes	.939	36	18	59	5	3
Reynolds	1.000	23	6	21	0	2
Rivera	.925	28	17	45	5	5
Walker	1.000	2	1	2	0	0

Shortstop	PCT	G	PO	A	E	DP
Cabrera	.940	45	49	124	11	31
Reyes	.988	80	75	182	3	34
Reynolds	.955	10	6	15	1	2
Rosario	.965	45	59	107	6	22

Outfield	PCT	G	PO	A	E	DP
Aoki	.979	27	47	0	1	0
Bruce	.990	92	195	3	2	0
Cespedes	.960	74	137	6	6	1
Conforto	.984	97	175	5	3	2
Granderson	.988	89	166	3	2	0
Lagares	.983	85	162	7	3	1
Nimmo	.991	50	108	2	1	0
Reyes	.000	2	0	0	0	0
Reynolds	1.000	8	8	0	0	0
Rivera	1.000	3	1	0	0	0
Taijeron	1.000	15	15	0	0	0

LAS VEGAS 51S — *TRIPLE-A*

PACIFIC COAST LEAGUE

Batting	B-T	HT	WT	DOB	AVG	vLH	vRH	G	AB	R	H	2B	3B	HR	RBI	BB	HBP	SH	SF	SO	SB	CS	SLG	OBP
Berrios, Arnaldo	B-R	5-9	154	1-15-96	.154	.250	.111	5	13	0	2	1	0	0	1	1	0	0	0	8	0	0	.231	.214
Boyd, Jayce	R-R	6-1	219	12-30-90	.297	.267	.304	92	246	39	73	18	1	11	46	26	4	0	2	47	3	0	.512	.371
Burdick, Dale	R-R	6-1	223	10-12-95	.182	.000	.222	5	11	1	2	2	0	0	0	2	0	0	0	4	0	0	.364	.308
Carrillo, Xorge	R-R	6-1	235	4-12-89	.270	.300	.262	70	252	24	68	12	0	9	44	17	2	0	1	62	0	0	.425	.320
Cecchini, Gavin	R-R	6-2	196	12-22-93	.267	.250	.271	110	453	68	121	27	3	6	39	40	2	2	0	61	5	4	.380	.329
Cruzado, Victor	B-R	6-0	199	6-30-92	.263	.216	.272	94	301	34	79	12	2	7	23	39	0	0	0	75	3	4	.385	.347
d'Arnaud, Travis	R-R	6-2	210	2-10-89	.231	.250	.222	4	13	1	3	2	0	0	1	0	0	0	0	2	0	0	.385	.231
Decker, Cody	R-R	5-11	218	1-17-87	.238	.269	.230	46	126	20	30	4	0	8	21	12	0	0	1	51	0	0	.460	.302
Evans, Phillip	R-R	5-10	223	9-10-92	.279	.237	.290	127	466	58	130	26	3	11	56	42	2	0	0	79	2	3	.419	.341
Flores, Wilmer	R-R	6-3	205	8-6-91	.500	—	.500	1	4	1	2	1	0	0	1	0	0	0	0	0	0	0	.750	.500
Glenn, Jeff	R-R	6-3	221	9-22-91	.234	.167	.257	18	47	5	11	2	0	1	6	6	0	0	0	16	0	0	.340	.321
Jennings, Desmond	R-R	6-2	210	10-30-86	.237	.268	.229	55	207	32	49	5	4	8	25	20	0	0	2	43	3	3	.416	.301
Mazzilli, L.J.	R-R	6-1	205	9-6-90	.217	.286	.188	16	46	5	10	3	0	1	4	7	0	1	0	13	2	0	.348	.321
McNeil, Jeff	L-R	6-0	195	4-8-92	.254	.391	.188	18	71	12	18	5	0	1	6	3	2	0	2	10	2	0	.366	.295
Mier, Jio	R-R	6-2	204	8-26-90	.224	.281	.206	47	134	12	30	7	0	2	14	6	2	0	2	29	0	0	.321	.264
Mora, John	L-L	5-11	195	5-31-93	.167	.333	.095	9	30	2	5	3	1	0	0	3	0	0	0	7	1	0	.333	.242
Nimmo, Brandon	L-R	6-3	207	3-27-93	.227	.222	.228	42	163	23	37	12	1	3	17	33	2	0	0	49	0	0	.368	.364
Plawecki, Kevin	R-R	6-2	210	2-26-91	.328	.280	.340	64	247	37	81	17	1	9	45	16	6	0	6	38	0	0	.514	.375
Reynolds, Matt	R-R	6-1	198	12-3-90	.320	.417	.310	33	128	27	41	9	0	4	14	16	0	0	0	30	2	2	.484	.396
Rivera, T.J.	R-R	6-1	203	10-27-88	.286	.500	.235	5	21	3	6	1	0	1	4	1	0	0	0	3	0	0	.476	.318
Rodriguez, Josh	R-R	6-0	192	12-18-84	.242	.237	.243	106	352	40	85	12	3	12	44	27	2	0	0	95	2	1	.395	.299
Rosario, Amed	R-R	6-2	189	11-20-95	.328	.357	.320	94	393	66	129	19	7	7	58	23	4	0	5	67	19	6	.466	.367
Smith, Dominic	L-L	6-0	239	6-15-95	.330	.247	.353	114	457	77	151	34	2	16	76	39	3	0	1	87	1	1	.519	.386
Snider, Travis	L-L	6-0	235	2-2-88	.308	.250	.342	17	65	9	20	2	1	1	8	7	0	0	0	15	0	1	.415	.375
2-team total (100 Round Rock)					.296	.250	.341	117	426	59	126	26	1	10	52	56	0	0	3	106	2	3	.432	.375
Taijeron, Travis	R-R	6-2	224	1-20-89	.272	.296	.267	125	448	75	122	32	3	25	78	70	12	0	3	146	2	1	.525	.383
Urena, Jhoan	B-R	6-1	220	9-1-94	.227	.154	.258	13	44	5	10	0	1	3	8	4	0	0	0	16	1	0	.477	.292
Walker, Neil	R-B	6-3	210	9-10-85	.263	.000	.294	5	19	4	5	1	0	0	1	1	0	0	0	1	0	0	.316	.300

Pitching	B-T	HT	WT	DOB	W	L	ERA	G	GS	CG	SV	IP	H	R	ER	HR	BB	SO	AVG	vLH	vRH	K/9	BB/9
Albaladejo, Jonathan	R-R	6-5	270	10-30-82	2	4	4.50	9	8	1	0	52	64	29	26	4	8	36	.305	.385	.226	6.23	1.38
Atkins, Mitch	R-R	6-4	225	10-1-85	4	8	5.65	14	14	0	0	78	90	53	49	13	27	57	.282	.257	.303	6.58	3.12
Baldonado, Alberto	L-L	6-4	247	2-1-93	0	4	6.65	39	0	0	2	43	47	33	32	9	23	39	.273	.215	.308	8.10	4.78
Beavan, Blake	R-R	6-7	255	1-17-89	0	2	7.45	4	3	0	0	19	32	17	16	1	11	13	.386	.400	.368	6.05	5.12
Boscan, Wilfredo	R-R	6-2	228	10-26-89	4	13	5.44	26	26	0	0	126	171	85	76	11	41	72	.335	.379	.300	5.16	2.94
Bradford, Chasen	R-R	6-1	229	8-5-89	1	1	4.04	33	0	0	11	36	47	20	16	3	7	28	.313	.353	.281	7.07	1.77
Burns, Cory	R-R	6-1	205	10-9-87	0	0	6.75	10	0	0	0	13	16	10	10	0	10	14	.291	.296	.286	9.45	6.75
Callahan, Jamie	R-R	6-2	230	8-24-94	1	1	1.80	9	0	0	1	10	12	5	2	2	4	10	.293	.348	.222	9.00	3.60
Edgin, Josh	L-L	6-1	245	12-17-86	0	1	2.70	3	0	0	0	3	2	1	1	0	3	2	.167	.143	.200	5.40	8.10
Gilmartin, Sean	L-L	6-2	206	5-8-90	2	2	7.05	8	8	0	0	37	52	30	29	6	14	31	.331	.209	.377	7.54	3.41
2-team total (8 Memphis)					2	3	6.70	16	9	0	1	50	67	38	37	8	16	39	.319	.209	.377	7.07	2.90

Goeddel, Erik	R-R	6-3	191	12-20-88	2	4	6.67	25	0	0	0	30	35	23	22	7	12	25	.297	.296	.297	7.58	3.64
Gorzelanny, Tom	R-L	6-3	218	7-12-82	0	0	0.00	4	0	0	0	3	1	0	0	0	2	5	.100	.000	.167	13.50	5.40
Gsellman, Robert	R-R	6-4	205	7-18-93	0	0	7.50	1	1	0	0	6	10	7	5	1	3	3	.385	.444	.353	4.50	4.50
Hand, Donovan	R-R	6-3	238	4-20-86	4	6	7.60	17	17	0	0	90	138	85	76	18	28	59	.356	.317	.398	5.90	2.80
Knapp, Ricky	R-R	6-0	217	5-20-92	6	13	5.97	25	25	0	0	145	184	104	96	16	35	75	.308	.347	.271	4.67	2.18
Mateo, Luis	R-R	6-3	205	3-22-90	1	0	5.85	18	4	0	0	32	39	21	21	5	12	29	.300	.282	.322	8.07	3.34
Matz, Steven	R-L	6-2	200	5-29-91	0	1	6.75	3	3	0	0	13	13	10	10	3	2	17	.255	.286	.243	11.48	1.35
McGowan, Kevin	R-R	6-5	233	10-18-91	6	5	4.15	47	1	0	4	65	63	35	30	8	25	57	.243	.231	.254	7.89	3.46
Montero, Rafael	R-R	6-0	185	10-17-90	0	2	2.48	5	5	0	0	29	18	9	8	3	12	37	.180	.239	.130	11.48	3.72
Peterson, Tim	R-R	6-1	215	2-22-91	0	0	16.88	2	0	0	0	3	5	5	5	1	2	2	.385	.375	.400	6.75	6.75
Pill, Tyler	L-R	6-1	199	5-29-90	4	3	3.47	13	13	0	0	80	83	38	31	8	22	50	.267	.289	.247	5.60	2.46
Regnault, Kyle	L-L	6-2	228	12-13-88	5	0	3.28	34	0	0	0	49	48	19	18	1	22	48	.247	.259	.239	8.76	4.01
Rhame, Jacob	R-R	6-1	215	3-16-93	0	1	1.50	4	0	0	0	6	2	1	1	0	0	11	.100	.083	.125	16.50	0.00
2-team total (41 Oklahoma City)					0	3	4.00	45	0	0	2	54	54	25	24	6	10	66	.257	.243	.292	11.00	1.67
Robles, Hansel	R-R	5-11	185	8-13-90	0	1	5.79	18	0	0	4	23	27	16	15	5	14	22	.287	.354	.217	8.49	5.40
Roseboom, David	L-L	6-3	215	5-17-92	0	2	8.31	18	0	0	0	17	21	19	16	2	10	12	.304	.241	.350	6.23	5.19
Rowen, Ben	R-R	6-4	203	11-15-88	3	3	4.41	54	0	0	0	63	80	35	31	6	13	52	.315	.309	.319	7.39	1.85
Secrest, Kelly	L-L	6-0	225	9-13-91	0	0	2.57	5	0	0	0	7	8	3	2	1	4	5	.276	.300	.263	6.43	5.14
Sewald, Paul	R-R	6-3	207	5-26-90	1	0	2.08	8	0	0	4	9	7	2	2	1	2	12	.206	.200	.208	12.46	2.08
Smoker, Josh	L-L	6-2	246	11-26-88	0	0	1.04	2	2	0	0	9	4	2	1	0	2	8	.138	.400	.083	8.31	2.08
Taylor, Logan	R-R	6-5	248	12-13-91	2	1	4.57	26	4	0	0	45	46	26	23	7	20	34	.269	.322	.210	6.75	3.97
Wagner, Neil	R-R	6-0	215	1-1-84	2	0	0.00	8	0	0	0	10	4	0	0	0	4	11	.114	.188	.053	9.58	3.48
Wheeler, Beck	R-R	6-3	213	12-13-88	4	5	8.18	41	2	0	0	58	80	61	53	12	35	51	.321	.355	.278	7.87	5.40
Wilk, Adam	L-L	6-2	180	12-9-87	2	3	5.91	6	6	0	0	32	40	22	21	5	5	29	.305	.368	.257	8.16	1.41

Fielding

Catcher	PCT	G	PO	A	E	DP	PB
Carrillo	.992	66	441	37	4	1	2
d'Arnaud	1.000	3	21	3	0	2	0
Glenn	.988	12	75	6	1	0	1
Plawecki	1.000	63	442	32	0	3	5

First Base	PCT	G	PO	A	E	DP
Decker	1.000	19	148	11	0	13
Mier	.857	1	5	1	1	1
Rivera	1.000	1	10	0	0	1
Rodriguez	.980	6	44	6	1	7
Smith	.992	107	917	94	8	93
Urena	.976	10	75	8	2	8

Second Base	PCT	G	PO	A	E	DP
Burdick	1.000	1	1	2	0	1
Cecchini	.977	80	135	204	8	47
Evans	.974	29	64	85	4	22
Mazzilli	1.000	4	10	18	0	6
McNeil	.970	17	20	45	2	11
Mier	.973	8	11	25	1	4
Reynolds	1.000	3	4	8	0	2
Rivera	1.000	1	1	2	0	0
Rodriguez	1.000	3	5	7	0	1
Walker	1.000	3	3	1	0	0

Third Base	PCT	G	PO	A	E	DP
Burdick	1.000	3	2	7	0	0
Carrillo	1.000	1	0	1	0	0
Evans	.926	66	56	119	14	15
Flores	1.000	1	0	4	0	0
Mazzilli	1.000	3	6	3	0	1
McNeil	1.000	1	2	1	0	0
Mier	.926	29	21	42	5	4
Reynolds	.818	7	8	10	4	0
Rivera	1.000	2	2	2	0	0
Rodriguez	.953	38	31	70	5	12
Rosario	.882	6	6	9	2	0
Urena	1.000	1	0	2	0	0
Walker	.667	1	1	1	1	0

Shortstop	PCT	G	PO	A	E	DP
Cecchini	.960	30	46	75	5	20
Evans	.927	18	31	45	6	11
Mier	1.000	2	1	5	0	1
Reynolds	.833	5	5	10	3	1
Rodriguez	1.000	1	1	2	0	0
Rosario	.953	88	90	251	17	49

Outfield	PCT	G	PO	A	E	DP
Berrios	.889	3	8	0	1	0
Boyd	1.000	38	66	0	0	0
Cruzado	.986	80	205	3	3	1
Decker	.923	7	12	0	1	0
Evans	1.000	17	24	1	0	0
Jennings	1.000	51	110	5	0	0
Mazzilli	1.000	8	11	1	0	0
Mora	1.000	9	15	0	0	0
Nimmo	.989	41	89	2	1	1
Reynolds	.976	22	38	2	1	0
Rivera	1.000	1	2	0	0	0
Rodriguez	.984	39	60	2	1	1
Snider	1.000	15	20	2	0	0
Taijeron	.984	119	237	6	4	2
Urena	1.000	1	1	0	0	0

BINGHAMTON RUMBLE PONIES — DOUBLE-A

EASTERN LEAGUE

Batting	B-T	HT	WT	DOB	AVG	vLH	vRH	G	AB	R	H	2B	3B	HR	RBI	BB	HBP	SH	SF	SO	SB	CS	SLG	OBP
Alonso, Peter	R-R	6-3	245	12-7-94	.311	.353	.286	11	45	7	14	4	1	2	5	2	0	0	0	7	0	0	.578	.340
Biondi, Patrick	L-R	5-8	171	1-9-91	.235	.180	.248	94	264	36	62	3	2	2	19	34	2	2	1	59	26	10	.284	.326
Burdick, Dale	R-R	6-1	223	10-12-95	.227	.250	.216	31	75	15	17	1	1	2	9	10	1	0	1	25	1	0	.347	.322
Cabrera, Asdrubal	B-R	6-0	205	11-13-85	.400	1.000	.250	2	5	0	2	0	0	0	0	0	0	0	0	0	0	0	.400	.400
Decker, Cody	R-R	5-11	218	1-17-87	.263	.290	.250	37	114	18	30	9	0	7	24	15	2	0	3	37	0	0	.526	.351
Guillorme, Luis	L-R	5-9	199	9-27-94	.283	.258	.291	128	481	70	136	20	0	1	43	72	1	2	2	55	4	3	.331	.376
Kaczmarski, Kevin	L-R	6-0	192	12-31-91	.274	.187	.301	128	452	66	124	18	5	5	52	61	10	4	4	84	15	8	.370	.370
Lagares, Juan	R-R	6-1	215	3-17-89	.241	.100	.316	8	29	3	7	0	0	0	0	0	0	0	0	6	0	0	.241	.241
Mazeika, Patrick	L-R	6-3	208	10-14-93	.333	.143	.429	6	21	3	7	5	0	0	5	2	0	0	0	6	0	0	.571	.391
Mazzilli, L.J.	R-R	6-1	205	9-6-90	.259	.308	.240	94	324	45	84	20	1	4	36	40	3	1	3	53	7	2	.364	.343
Mier, Jio	R-R	6-2	204	8-26-90	.240	.258	.233	32	104	9	25	9	0	2	19	6	1	0	2	29	2	2	.385	.283
Moore, Tyler	L-R	6-0	209	8-8-93	.188	.375	.161	29	64	6	12	3	0	0	7	9	0	0	2	20	0	1	.234	.280
Nido, Tomas	R-R	6-0	210	4-12-94	.232	.269	.216	102	367	41	85	19	1	8	60	30	1	0	6	63	0	0	.354	.287
Nunez, Gustavo	B-R	5-11	189	2-8-88	.271	.250	.277	78	244	24	66	11	2	1	24	14	0	2	3	39	8	5	.344	.307
2-team total (4 Erie)					.263	.000	.167	82	259	26	68	11	2	1	24	16	0	2	3	40	9	5	.332	.302
Oberste, Matt	R-R	6-2	240	8-9-91	.284	.285	.283	129	455	59	129	27	3	5	62	52	5	0	4	106	3	1	.389	.361
Plaia, Colton	R-R	6-2	219	9-25-90	.241	.357	.211	42	137	19	33	7	0	1	20	19	2	0	0	31	0	0	.314	.342
Rodriguez, J.C.	B-R	6-1	190	9-3-92	.286	.000	.400	3	7	2	2	0	0	0	0	1	0	0	0	1	0	0	.286	.375
Stuart, Champ	R-R	6-0	181	10-11-92	.222	.236	.215	101	320	43	71	16	2	5	34	38	4	7	3	122	35	6	.331	.310
Taylor, Kevin	L-R	6-0	197	7-13-91	.292	.252	.310	114	383	44	112	20	1	3	46	54	1	1	7	53	2	1	.373	.375
Thompson, David	R-R	6-0	210	8-28-93	.263	.310	.246	133	476	62	125	29	1	16	68	40	7	0	6	92	8	6	.429	.325

Pitching	B-T	HT	WT	DOB	W	L	ERA	G	GS	CG	SV	IP	H	R	ER	HR	BB	SO	AVG	vLH	vRH	K/9	BB/9
Baldonado, Alberto	L-L	6-4	247	2-1-93	0	0	0.00	11	0	0	6	17	8	0	0	0	5	25	.146	.100	.171	13.50	2.70
Bashlor, Tyler	R-R	6-0	197	4-16-93	1	0	0.00	12	0	0	3	15	7	0	0	0	4	23	.143	.182	.111	14.11	2.45
Beavan, Blake	R-R	6-7	255	1-17-89	1	1	3.72	3	3	0	0	19	18	8	8	2	4	14	.247	.216	.278	6.52	1.86
Burns, Cory	R-R	6-1	205	10-9-87	2	2	4.02	36	0	0	19	40	40	19	18	1	14	49	.267	.303	.238	10.93	3.12
Church, Andrew	R-R	6-2	205	10-7-94	0	1	19.29	1	1	0	0	5	10	10	10	2	6	3	.500	.571	.462	5.79	11.57
Conlon, P.J.	L-L	5-11	192	11-11-93	8	9	3.38	28	22	3	1	136	130	53	51	14	38	108	.253	.252	.254	7.15	2.51
Delgado, Casey	R-R	5-10	187	6-15-90	11	6	4.59	23	19	0	0	114	124	63	58	7	55	80	.283	.326	.241	6.33	4.35
Familia, Jeurys	R-R	6-3	240	10-10-89	0	0	0.00	1	0	0	0	1	0	0	0	0	0	1	.000	.000	.000	9.00	0.00
Flexen, Chris	R-R	6-3	250	7-1-94	6	1	1.66	7	7	2	0	49	28	10	9	4	7	50	.165	.161	.169	9.25	1.29
Griset, Ben	L-L	6-0	198	3-12-92	4	1	2.39	35	0	0	0	49	33	13	13	2	22	36	.193	.143	.228	6.61	4.04
Gsellman, Robert	R-R	6-4	205	7-18-93	1	0	2.92	4	4	0	0	12	15	7	4	0	5	9	.306	.308	.304	6.57	3.65
Hand, Donovan	R-R	6-3	238	4-20-86	3	2	3.08	8	8	1	0	50	40	19	17	3	12	33	.216	.163	.257	5.98	2.17
Harvey, Matt	R-R	6-4	215	3-27-89	0	0	5.87	2	2	0	0	8	9	7	5	1	2	5	.281	.467	.118	5.87	2.35
Jannis, Mickey	R-R	5-9	195	12-16-87	8	7	3.60	21	21	2	0	122	115	56	49	10	38	83	.252	.239	.266	6.11	2.80
Knapp, Ricky	R-R	6-0	217	5-20-92	1	0	2.00	4	4	1	0	27	25	6	6	1	3	22	.240	.149	.316	7.33	1.00
Lugo, Seth	R-R	6-4	225	11-17-89	1	1	2.77	2	2	1	0	13	14	4	4	1	2	15	.286	.346	.217	10.38	1.38
Mateo, Luis	R-R	6-3	205	3-22-90	1	0	4.50	18	0	0	0	22	20	14	11	3	14	23	.233	.314	.177	9.41	5.73
Milone, Tommy	L-L	6-0	220	2-16-87	1	0	4.95	4	4	0	0	20	26	11	11	8	2	11	.313	.229	.375	4.95	0.90
Molina, Marcos	R-R	6-3	206	3-8-95	3	7	3.92	13	12	2	0	78	77	37	34	5	21	63	.260	.239	.279	7.27	2.42
Oswalt, Corey	R-R	6-5	250	9-3-93	12	5	2.28	24	24	2	0	134	118	40	34	9	40	119	.236	.228	.246	7.97	2.68
Peterson, Tim	R-R	6-1	215	2-22-91	5	3	1.14	41	0	0	7	55	33	8	7	1	10	53	.176	.180	.172	8.62	1.63
Pill, Tyler	L-R	6-1	199	5-29-90	1	0	0.00	2	2	0	0	10	11	2	0	0	1	3	.282	.462	.192	2.61	0.87
Regnault, Kyle	L-L	6-2	228	12-13-88	2	0	1.17	11	0	0	1	15	8	2	2	0	6	18	.157	.235	.118	10.57	3.52
Reyes, Scarlyn	R-R	6-2	222	12-10-89	2	0	4.02	23	3	0	0	40	37	18	18	4	13	27	.243	.218	.258	6.02	2.90
Secrest, Kelly	L-L	6-0	225	9-13-91	1	1	4.03	25	1	0	0	38	45	17	17	3	18	46	.285	.254	.305	10.89	4.26
Smith, Drew	R-R	6-2	190	9-24-93	3	2	1.80	11	0	0	0	15	8	4	3	1	5	17	.151	.174	.133	10.20	3.00
Smoker, Josh	L-L	6-2	246	11-26-88	0	0	0.00	1	0	0	0	1	2	0	0	0	0	2	.400	.500	.333	18.00	0.00
Taylor, Corey	R-R	5-11	252	1-8-93	5	5	3.61	42	0	0	3	62	69	28	25	3	14	47	.290	.300	.283	6.79	2.02
Taylor, Logan	R-R	6-5	248	12-13-91	0	0	16.20	2	0	0	0	2	3	3	3	0	2	0	.429	.333	.500	0.00	10.80
Uceta, Adonis	R-R	6-1	228	5-10-94	2	0	4.50	4	0	0	1	6	6	3	3	1	1	5	.250	.222	.267	7.50	1.50

Fielding

Catcher	PCT	G	PO	A	E	DP	PB
Decker	1.000	1	7	1	0	0	0
Mazeika	1.000	2	13	2	0	0	0
Moore	1.000	12	77	8	0	0	1
Nido	.993	85	612	51	5	2	6
Plaia	.994	42	280	40	2	2	16

First Base	PCT	G	PO	A	E	DP
Alonso	.981	5	47	4	1	4
Burdick	1.000	2	6	0	0	0
Decker	.987	17	140	12	2	10
Moore	1.000	7	44	4	0	4
Oberste	.997	103	840	57	3	68
Taylor	1.000	11	73	5	0	6

Second Base	PCT	G	PO	A	E	DP
Burdick	.976	21	29	54	2	8
Guillorme	.983	72	110	184	5	33
Mazzilli	.978	44	74	151	5	23
Mier	.929	3	5	8	1	3
Nunez	1.000	7	10	20	0	4
Rodriguez	1.000	2	5	3	0	2

Third Base	PCT	G	PO	A	E	DP
Burdick	1.000	3	2	1	0	0
Guillorme	.000	3	0	0	0	0
Mier	1.000	5	2	6	0	1
Nunez	1.000	2	1	4	0	0
Thompson	.963	129	82	228	12	21

Shortstop	PCT	G	PO	A	E	DP
Cabrera	.833	2	3	2	1	0
Guillorme	.968	58	69	144	7	28
Mier	.964	22	30	51	3	14
Nunez	.970	64	69	155	7	22

Outfield	PCT	G	PO	A	E	DP
Biondi	.995	85	200	7	1	0
Kaczmarski	.981	124	207	3	4	0
Lagares	1.000	7	10	1	0	0
Mazzilli	1.000	47	87	8	0	1
Rodriguez	.000	1	0	0	0	0
Stuart	.995	93	188	10	1	0
Taylor	1.000	76	140	0	0	0

ST. LUCIE METS — *HIGH CLASS A*

FLORIDA STATE LEAGUE

Batting	B-T	HT	WT	DOB	AVG	vLH	vRH	G	AB	R	H	2B	3B	HR	RBI	BB	HBP	SH	SF	SO	SB	CS	SLG	OBP
Alonso, Peter	R-R	6-3	245	12-7-94	.286	.370	.250	82	308	45	88	23	0	16	58	25	12	0	1	64	3	4	.516	.361
Becerra, Wuilmer	R-R	6-3	243	10-1-94	.267	.271	.265	128	469	49	125	16	2	4	44	36	11	1	2	132	16	5	.335	.332
Berrios, Arnaldo	B-R	5-9	154	1-15-96	.167	.182	.164	22	66	9	11	3	0	1	5	5	1	0	0	23	2	0	.258	.236
Burdick, Dale	R-R	6-1	223	10-12-95	.214	.242	.204	42	131	18	28	5	1	5	13	14	3	0	0	45	1	2	.382	.304
Byrd, Leon	R-B	5-7	192	2-27-94	.118	.167	.107	10	34	4	4	1	0	0	3	4	0	1	0	4	0	1	.147	.211
Cabrera, Asdrubal	B-R	6-0	205	11-13-85	.375	—	.375	2	8	1	3	0	0	0	1	0	0	0	0	0	0	0	.375	.375
Cespedes, Yoenis	R-R	5-10	220	10-18-85	.000	—	.000	2	6	1	0	0	0	0	0	1	0	0	0	0	0	0	.000	.143
Conforto, Michael	L-R	6-1	215	3-1-93	.750	—	.750	1	4	1	3	1	0	0	1	1	0	0	0	1	0	0	1.000	.800
d'Arnaud, Travis	R-R	6-2	210	2-10-89	.250	.333	.200	2	8	0	2	0	0	0	0	0	0	0	0	1	0	0	.250	.250
Diehl, Jeff	R-R	6-5	235	9-30-93	.280	.320	.265	29	93	9	26	5	0	3	15	12	3	0	1	39	2	1	.430	.376
Dimino, Anthony	L-R	5-11	174	8-5-93	.318	.250	.331	54	189	22	60	6	1	0	14	22	3	2	1	28	9	4	.360	.395
Duda, Lucas	R-L	6-4	255	2-3-86	.250	.333	.231	5	16	5	4	0	0	2	3	3	0	0	0	6	0	0	.625	.368
Flores, Wilmer	R-R	6-3	205	8-6-91	.375	.500	.333	2	8	4	3	1	0	1	2	0	1	0	0	2	0	0	.875	.444
Garcia, Eudor	R-L	6-0	240	5-17-94	.357	.500	.333	5	14	3	5	1	0	0	3	1	0	0	0	3	0	2	.429	.400
Garcia, Jose	L-R	6-0	227	11-3-94	.272	.219	.293	40	114	8	31	3	0	1	10	10	5	0	2	42	0	0	.325	.351
Lagares, Juan	R-R	6-1	215	3-17-89	.364	—	.364	3	11	3	4	1	1	0	1	0	0	0	0	1	0	0	.636	.364
Mazeika, Patrick	L-R	6-3	208	10-14-93	.287	.319	.275	100	352	45	101	21	0	7	50	48	12	0	2	53	2	2	.406	.389
McNeil, Jeff	L-R	6-0	195	4-8-92	.324	.440	.288	30	105	13	34	7	0	3	15	7	4	0	0	19	2	2	.476	.388
Medina, Jose Miguel	R-R	6-3	180	10-21-96	.444	.000	.571	3	9	5	4	1	1	0	0	2	0	0	0	2	1	0	.778	.546
Mora, John	L-L	5-11	195	5-31-93	.265	.213	.285	124	502	60	133	22	5	3	43	40	6	4	4	100	19	15	.347	.324
Moscote, Victor	R-R	6-1	230	5-10-94	.111	.000	.125	2	9	0	1	1	0	0	2	0	0	0	0	3	0	0	.222	.111
Nimmo, Brandon	L-R	6-3	207	3-27-93	.222	.000	.333	5	18	4	4	2	0	1	4	5	0	0	0	4	0	0	.500	.391
Paez, Michael	R-R	5-7	175	12-8-94	.200	.203	.199	63	215	24	43	9	0	2	23	32	9	0	3	42	1	5	.270	.324

Rizzie, Dan	R-R	6-2	204	11-26-93	.153	.238	.105	20	59	2	9	1	0	0	1	9	1	0	1	13	0	0	.170	.271
Rodriguez, J.C.	B-R	6-1	190	9-3-92	.214	.216	.213	127	453	49	97	26	6	4	40	31	3	8	6	111	16	9	.325	.266
Sergakis, Nick	R-R	5-8	178	4-6-93	.252	.264	.246	65	206	33	52	17	1	6	27	30	10	4	2	58	12	3	.432	.371
Siena, Vinny	R-R	5-10	197	12-24-93	.157	.171	.152	47	147	15	23	8	1	1	16	16	1	1	2	58	0	2	.245	.241
Strom, Ian	R-L	6-1	209	12-12-94	.270	.300	.259	8	37	3	10	0	0	1	1	0	0	0	0	8	0	1	.351	.270
Tebow, Tim	L-L	6-3	250	8-14-87	.232	.239	.228	62	216	21	50	10	1	5	29	19	5	1	1	57	2	1	.357	.307
Urena, Jhoan	B-R	6-1	220	9-1-94	.282	.292	.277	122	458	72	129	34	2	11	62	60	1	0	3	114	17	3	.437	.364
Woodmansee, Colby	R-R	6-3	206	8-27-94	.213	.154	.235	14	47	6	10	3	0	1	2	4	0	0	0	13	0	0	.340	.275
Wright, David	R-R	6-0	205	12-20-82	.100	.000	.125	3	10	0	1	0	0	0	0	0	0	0	0	5	0	0	.100	.100
Zabala, Enmanuel	R-R	6-0	202	9-29-94	.209	.254	.189	67	206	16	43	6	0	0	17	14	5	2	2	55	6	7	.238	.273
Zanon, Jacob	R-R	6-0	180	6-25-95	.224	.333	.175	15	58	5	13	5	1	0	2	4	1	0	0	10	1	2	.345	.286

Pitching	B-T	HT	WT	DOB	W	L	ERA	G	GS	CG	SV	IP	H	R	ER	HR	BB	SO	AVG	vLH	vRH	K/9	BB/9
Atkins, Adam	R-R	6-3	221	9-8-93	0	0	7.71	5	0	0	0	7	14	6	6	1	3	8	.424	.583	.333	10.29	3.86
Bashlor, Tyler	R-R	6-0	197	4-16-93	2	2	4.89	34	0	0	10	35	33	21	19	1	21	61	.248	.302	.213	15.69	5.40
Bautista, Gerson	R-R	6-2	170	5-31-95	0	1	1.26	10	0	0	5	14	10	3	2	0	3	20	.204	.273	.148	12.56	1.88
Brantley, Justin	R-R	6-0	192	3-5-91	3	2	5.12	23	1	0	0	32	33	22	18	1	23	32	.256	.244	.261	9.09	6.54
Campos, Yeizo	R-R	5-9	172	4-29-96	1	1	5.06	3	3	0	0	16	17	9	9	1	3	8	.266	.348	.220	4.50	1.69
Campusano, Briam	R-R	6-2	174	3-26-96	0	0	2.00	2	1	0	0	9	5	2	2	0	4	6	.167	.120	.400	6.00	4.00
Canelon, Kevin	L-L	6-0	181	1-16-94	3	4	2.97	32	10	0	1	79	83	37	26	6	16	78	.279	.316	.260	8.92	1.83
Church, Andrew	R-R	6-2	205	10-7-94	12	8	4.62	25	25	1	0	152	183	85	78	13	25	95	.297	.305	.290	5.63	1.48
Crismatt, Nabil	R-R	6-1	222	12-25-94	6	13	3.95	26	25	1	0	146	161	82	64	17	36	142	.278	.323	.247	8.77	2.22
Dunn, Justin	R-R	6-2	195	9-22-95	5	6	5.00	20	16	0	0	95	101	66	53	5	48	75	.273	.345	.239	7.08	4.53
Familia, Jeurys	R-R	6-3	240	10-10-89	0	0	0.00	3	0	0	0	3	1	0	0	0	2	5	.111	.250	.000	15.00	6.00
Flexen, Chris	R-R	6-3	250	7-1-94	0	0	2.13	3	3	0	0	13	12	6	3	1	3	13	.245	.111	.323	9.24	2.13
Gibbons, Mike	R-R	6-4	218	4-24-93	0	3	8.62	3	3	0	0	16	26	15	15	0	5	12	.371	.425	.300	6.89	2.87
Gonzalez, Harol	R-R	5-11	178	3-2-95	0	1	3.18	3	3	0	0	11	10	7	4	2	3	9	.222	.261	.182	7.15	2.38
Gonzalez, Merandy	R-R	6-0	216	10-9-95	4	2	2.23	6	6	0	0	36	33	12	9	1	8	24	.232	.246	.222	5.94	1.98
2-team total (5 Jupiter)					5	2	1.78	11	9	0	1	61	51	16	12	1	13	38	.225	.246	.222	5.64	1.93
Gorzelanny, Tom	R-L	6-3	218	7-12-82	0	0	23.14	3	0	0	1	2	5	6	6	1	1	3	.417	.200	.571	11.57	3.86
Griffin, Cameron	R-R	6-0	212	6-25-91	0	3	5.94	12	0	0	0	17	20	12	11	3	11	16	.278	.355	.220	8.64	5.94
Gutierrez, Miguel	L-L	6-0	189	12-3-94	1	0	0.00	3	0	0	0	5	3	0	0	0	1	3	.167	.200	.154	5.06	1.69
Huertas, Joel	B-L	6-3	236	2-14-96	0	0	6.00	1	0	0	0	3	3	2	2	0	1	4	.300	.000	.375	12.00	3.00
Humphreys, Jordan	R-R	6-2	223	6-11-96	0	0	4.09	2	2	0	0	11	17	6	5	1	3	3	.340	.414	.238	2.45	2.45
Ingram, Chase	R-R	6-3	210	4-17-95	0	0	6.75	1	1	0	0	4	4	4	3	0	3	5	.267	.333	.222	11.25	6.75
Lugo, Seth	R-R	6-4	225	11-17-89	0	1	8.10	2	1	0	0	7	9	7	6	2	1	4	.310	.556	.200	5.40	1.35
Magliozzi, Johnny	R-R	5-8	205	7-21-91	5	1	3.19	44	0	0	6	68	61	25	24	3	14	61	.248	.233	.259	8.11	1.86
Matz, Steven	R-L	6-2	200	5-29-91	0	0	3.00	1	1	0	0	3	2	1	1	0	2	3	.182	.500	.111	9.00	6.00
McGeorge, Austin	R-R	6-2	215	11-27-94	2	2	1.89	25	0	0	2	38	24	12	8	1	13	50	.183	.208	.167	11.84	3.08
McIlraith, Thomas	R-R	6-3	214	2-17-94	1	1	6.75	4	4	0	0	12	17	9	9	1	3	7	.333	.375	.314	5.25	2.25
Missigman, Craig	R-R	6-2	195	8-5-93	3	3	5.13	34	1	0	0	53	64	32	30	8	21	62	.294	.235	.342	10.59	3.59
Molina, Marcos	R-R	6-3	206	3-8-95	2	3	1.26	5	5	0	0	29	17	6	4	1	5	23	.174	.171	.175	7.22	1.57
Nogosek, Stephen	R-R	6-2	205	1-11-95	1	1	5.06	9	0	0	0	16	16	9	9	0	8	15	.262	.222	.294	8.44	4.50
Olivo, Aneury	L-L	6-0	174	10-24-94	0	1	2.57	2	0	0	1	7	6	2	2	0	5	7	.250	.188	.375	9.00	6.43
Palsha, Alex	R-R	6-1	190	5-10-92	3	3	3.77	42	1	0	5	60	58	31	25	3	26	57	.243	.191	.284	8.60	3.92
Ramos, Darwin	R-R	6-2	192	11-23-95	0	0	6.23	5	0	0	0	9	9	9	6	2	5	11	.243	.154	.292	11.42	5.19
Reyes, Scarlyn	R-R	6-2	222	12-10-89	1	2	5.76	6	6	0	0	30	40	24	19	5	10	26	.313	.449	.153	7.89	3.03
Shaw, Joe	R-R	6-3	228	12-20-93	7	5	4.97	18	18	1	0	100	113	59	55	9	35	83	.291	.333	.261	7.49	3.16
Smoker, Josh	L-L	6-2	246	11-26-88	0	1	4.15	4	1	0	0	4	6	2	2	0	0	3	.316	.333	.300	6.23	0.00
Torres, Joshua	R-R	6-0	168	4-26-94	1	4	3.14	41	1	0	4	63	54	31	22	2	22	77	.226	.258	.204	11.00	3.14
Uceta, Adonis	R-R	6-1	228	5-10-94	0	0	0.84	8	0	0	2	11	5	1	1	1	3	15	.143	.191	.071	12.66	2.53

Fielding

Catcher	PCT	G	PO	A	E	DP	PB
d'Arnaud	1.000	2	19	0	0	0	0
Dimino	1.000	18	133	15	0	0	4
Garcia	.988	31	234	18	3	3	5
Mazeika	.993	76	600	66	5	5	4
Moscote	1.000	2	16	1	0	0	1
Rizzie	.975	19	138	18	4	2	7

First Base	PCT	G	PO	A	E	DP
Alonso	.972	78	537	77	18	49
Becerra	.987	9	72	5	1	5
Dimino	1.000	11	68	1	0	3
Duda	.952	3	18	2	1	2
Flores	1.000	1	6	0	0	0
Mazeika	1.000	12	97	4	0	9
McNeil	1.000	1	8	1	0	2
Urena	.995	25	174	17	1	13
Woodmansee	.974	4	35	2	1	1

Second Base	PCT	G	PO	A	E	DP
Burdick	.984	18	28	34	1	10
Byrd	1.000	2	4	5	0	1
Dimino	1.000	2	3	7	0	0
McNeil	.942	18	31	34	4	9
Paez	.980	52	72	124	4	27
Rodriguez	.964	9	9	18	1	4
Sergakis	.917	6	9	13	2	3
Siena	.968	41	75	105	6	18

Third Base	PCT	G	PO	A	E	DP
Burdick	.943	14	7	26	2	4
Byrd	.769	4	3	7	3	0
Dimino	1.000	1	0	2	0	0
Flores	1.000	1	1	0	0	0
Garcia	.500	2	1	1	2	0
McNeil	.833	4	2	8	2	0
Paez	1.000	3	4	6	0	0
Rodriguez	1.000	2	0	2	0	0
Sergakis	.976	21	9	31	1	3
Siena	.000	1	0	0	1	0
Urena	.908	89	55	162	22	14
Woodmansee	.941	7	2	14	1	2
Wright	.800	2	1	3	1	0

Shortstop	PCT	G	PO	A	E	DP
Burdick	1.000	11	9	17	0	3
Cabrera	1.000	1	2	1	0	0
Paez	.963	9	12	14	1	4
Rodriguez	.937	118	183	278	31	55
Woodmansee	.857	4	7	11	3	2

Outfield	PCT	G	PO	A	E	DP
Becerra	.971	83	131	2	4	0
Berrios	.978	20	43	2	1	0
Byrd	1.000	4	11	1	0	0
Cespedes	1.000	2	3	0	0	0
Conforto	.500	1	1	0	1	0
Diehl	.980	28	46	2	1	0
Dimino	1.000	5	9	0	0	0
Lagares	1.000	2	1	0	0	0
McNeil	1.000	3	8	0	0	0
Medina	1.000	3	4	1	0	0
Mora	.994	124	311	6	2	1
Nimmo	1.000	4	11	0	0	0
Sergakis	.947	25	32	4	2	0
Strom	.955	8	21	0	1	0

Tebow	.952	36	59	1	3	0
Urena	1.000	10	11	1	0	0
Zabala	.958	62	133	5	6	0
Zanon	.950	15	37	1	2	0

COLUMBIA FIREFLIES — *LOW CLASS A*

SOUTH ATLANTIC LEAGUE

Batting	B-T	HT	WT	DOB	AVG	vLH	vRH	G	AB	R	H	2B	3B	HR	RBI	BB	HBP	SH	SF	SO	SB	CS	SLG	OBP
Berrios, Arnaldo	B-R	5-9	154	1-15-96	.193	.127	.218	57	202	15	39	8	3	1	14	14	1	3	1	72	4	3	.277	.248
Brodey, Quinn	L-L	6-1	200	12-1-95	.229	.400	.160	9	35	4	8	1	1	1	7	4	0	0	1	14	0	0	.400	.300
Brosher, Brandon	R-R	6-2	237	2-17-95	.221	.226	.220	67	217	28	48	7	0	13	31	30	12	0	1	103	8	3	.433	.346
Carpio, Luis	R-R	5-11	190	7-11-97	.232	.286	.211	125	474	53	110	18	3	3	36	53	2	0	6	95	17	5	.302	.308
Cespedes, Ricardo	L-L	6-1	205	8-24-97	.417	.250	.500	5	12	1	5	1	0	0	3	0	0	0	0	3	0	0	.500	.417
Cone, Gene	L-L	6-0	173	9-21-94	.219	.126	.259	84	315	41	69	11	3	0	29	48	2	2	3	70	6	3	.273	.323
Dimino, Anthony	L-R	5-11	174	8-5-93	.700	1.000	.667	3	10	4	7	1	0	0	0	2	0	0	0	0	1	1	.800	.750
Franco, J.J.	R-R	5-9	180	2-2-92	.277	.333	.255	36	137	17	38	6	0	0	10	23	0	2	0	27	3	1	.321	.381
2-team total (12 Kannapolis)						.283	.333	.255	48	173	19	49	7	0	0	16	28	0	3	0	33	3	2	.324
.383																								
Gamache, Reed	R-R	6-0	195	1-3-94	.237	.213	.250	42	131	13	31	5	1	1	12	15	4	0	2	28	0	1	.313	.329
Gimenez, Andres	L-R	5-11	176	9-4-98	.265	.275	.261	92	347	50	92	9	4	4	31	28	16	6	2	61	14	8	.349	.346
Jabs, Jay	L-R	6-0	195	9-30-94	.206	.182	.214	90	320	38	66	18	3	7	35	31	1	1	0	100	4	0	.347	.278
Lindsay, Desmond	R-R	5-11	196	1-15-97	.220	.171	.243	65	214	40	47	10	1	8	30	33	2	0	2	77	4	2	.388	.327
Medina, Jose Miguel	R-R	6-3	180	10-21-96	.205	.191	.209	25	88	13	18	1	0	0	3	3	1	1	0	26	3	1	.216	.239
Paez, Michael	R-R	5-7	175	12-8-94	.290	.333	.270	64	224	32	65	21	2	8	43	27	7	0	5	56	8	5	.509	.376
Pascual, Oliver	B-R	5-9	178	11-16-96	.286	.400	.222	5	14	1	4	0	0	0	2	1	0	0	1	2	0	0	.286	.313
Ramos, Milton	R-R	5-11	193	10-26-95	.227	.260	.214	57	181	19	41	7	1	0	18	11	1	2	2	41	9	0	.276	.272
2-team total (48 Delmarva)					.233	.238	.239	105	361	35	84	14	2	2	35	18	3	2	2	85	15	3	.299	.273
Ramos, Natanael	R-R	5-11	216	6-19-93	.227	.214	.233	12	44	4	10	2	0	0	3	1	2	0	0	9	0	1	.273	.277
Rizzie, Dan	R-R	6-2	204	11-26-93	.261	.102	.319	52	184	8	48	8	0	0	15	15	0	3	0	38	0	0	.304	.317
Sanchez, Ali	R-R	6-1	196	1-20-97	.231	.300	.197	56	182	20	42	3	0	1	15	13	2	2	1	26	2	3	.264	.288
Siena, Vinny	R-R	5-10	197	12-24-93	.194	.143	.207	22	72	7	14	3	2	0	6	5	3	0	0	30	1	0	.292	.275
Strom, Ian	R-L	6-1	209	12-12-94	.294	.205	.327	41	143	23	42	7	4	3	17	11	7	0	1	29	11	1	.462	.370
Tebow, Tim	L-L	6-3	250	8-14-87	.220	.136	.252	64	214	29	47	14	1	3	23	24	5	0	1	69	0	1	.336	.312
Tiberi, Blake	L-R	6-0	205	2-16-95	.167	.400	.077	5	18	3	3	1	0	0	2	4	0	0	0	5	1	0	.222	.318
Winningham, Dash	L-L	6-1	225	10-11-95	.237	.263	.225	114	426	42	101	15	1	13	70	37	6	0	5	104	3	2	.369	.304
Woodmansee, Colby	R-R	6-3	206	8-27-94	.132	.143	.129	37	121	10	16	4	0	0	3	9	1	0	1	42	0	0	.165	.197
Zanon, Jacob	R-R	6-0	180	6-25-95	.246	.268	.239	50	179	26	44	8	2	1	16	24	2	0	2	43	28	3	.330	.338

Pitching	B-T	HT	WT	DOB	W	L	ERA	G	GS	CG	SV	IP	H	R	ER	HR	BB	SO	AVG	vLH	vRH	K/9	BB/9
Aldridge, Keaton	R-L	6-1	198	7-20-92	1	1	6.62	12	0	0	0	18	27	17	13	0	4	9	.351	.483	.271	4.58	2.04
Anderson, Martin	L-R	6-1	175	1-13-93	0	5	6.89	7	7	0	0	31	46	34	24	6	16	36	.338	.343	.337	10.34	4.60
Atkins, Adam	R-R	6-3	221	9-8-93	3	0	0.86	23	0	0	0	31	23	4	3	0	6	29	.209	.189	.219	8.33	1.72
Blackham, Matt	R-R	5-10	169	1-7-93	4	2	1.43	40	0	0	8	57	37	11	9	0	19	82	.185	.247	.139	13.02	3.02
Brantley, Justin	R-R	6-0	192	3-5-91	2	4	5.18	9	9	0	0	49	54	29	28	3	20	45	.286	.272	.299	8.32	3.70
Cornish, Gary	R-R	6-2	207	1-21-94	1	3	3.07	5	5	0	0	29	30	10	10	1	5	20	.273	.275	.271	6.14	1.53
Ford, Aaron	L-L	5-11	190	9-9-94	0	0	12.71	4	0	0	0	6	7	9	8	3	3	9	.269	.400	.188	14.29	4.76
Gonzalez, Harol	R-R	5-11	178	3-2-95	9	8	3.56	20	20	3	0	126	123	56	50	11	37	91	.257	.254	.260	6.48	2.64
Gonzalez, Merandy	R-R	6-0	216	10-9-95	8	1	1.55	11	11	0	0	70	50	16	12	3	13	65	.200	.198	.201	8.40	1.68
Griffin, Cameron	R-R	6-0	212	6-25-91	1	2	3.05	28	0	0	1	41	41	16	14	3	10	40	.252	.259	.248	8.71	2.18
Henry, Taylor	L-L	6-2	200	7-6-93	4	0	4.33	39	0	0	1	60	73	35	29	5	20	39	.290	.235	.316	5.82	2.98
Holderman, Colin	R-R	6-7	240	10-8-95	2	3	4.94	7	7	0	0	31	24	20	17	2	11	25	.209	.250	.183	7.26	3.19
Huertas, Joel	B-L	6-3	236	2-14-96	0	2	10.80	3	1	0	0	8	12	10	10	0	4	6	.353	.273	.391	6.48	4.32
Humphreys, Jordan	R-R	6-2	223	6-11-96	10	1	1.42	11	11	2	0	70	41	12	11	2	9	80	.168	.142	.197	10.33	1.16
Ingram, Chase	R-R	6-3	210	4-17-95	1	4	4.63	5	5	1	0	23	18	14	12	0	18	16	.209	.273	.170	6.17	6.94
Kuhns, Max	R-R	6-2	209	8-11-94	1	0	2.10	17	0	0	5	26	13	6	6	0	10	37	.149	.158	.143	12.97	3.51
Llanes, Gabriel	R-R	6-4	200	1-15-96	6	11	4.48	24	24	2	0	143	166	90	71	8	38	67	.294	.301	.289	4.23	2.40
McGeorge, Austin	R-R	6-2	215	11-27-94	0	0	1.42	6	0	0	0	13	9	4	2	0	4	16	.192	.059	.267	11.37	2.84
McIlraith, Thomas	R-R	6-3	214	2-17-94	2	1	2.22	4	4	0	0	24	19	7	6	0	8	15	.211	.245	.171	5.55	2.96
Medina, Jose Carlos	L-L	6-3	215	8-25-96	1	1	2.70	4	4	0	0	23	27	9	7	0	7	17	.294	.318	.286	6.56	2.70
Pobereyko, Matt	R-R	6-3	230	12-24-91	2	2	3.15	23	0	0	2	34	26	16	12	2	14	53	.205	.260	.169	13.89	3.67
Ramos, Darwin	R-R	6-2	192	11-23-95	2	3	4.81	12	5	0	0	39	47	24	21	2	19	27	.309	.356	.280	6.18	4.35
Ryan, Ryder	R-R	6-2	205	5-11-95	0	0	2.08	8	0	0	0	13	6	3	3	1	5	13	.133	.133	.133	9.00	3.46
Simon, Jake	L-L	6-2	189	1-21-97	2	2	4.70	4	2	0	0	15	14	9	8	1	7	12	.280	.227	.321	7.04	4.11
Szapucki, Thomas	R-L	6-2	181	6-12-96	1	2	2.79	6	6	0	0	29	24	10	9	0	10	27	.231	.226	.233	8.38	3.10
Taylor, Blake	L-L	6-2	230	8-17-95	1	9	4.94	18	17	0	0	86	83	64	47	6	49	72	.253	.241	.259	7.56	5.15
Uceta, Adonis	R-R	6-1	228	5-10-94	4	0	1.26	29	0	0	11	43	23	7	6	0	16	47	.158	.145	.167	9.84	3.35
Zanghi, Joseph	R-R	6-0	254	12-1-94	0	3	2.19	41	0	0	4	62	51	29	15	2	26	64	.220	.231	.211	9.34	3.79

Fielding

Catcher	PCT	G	PO	A	E	DP	PB
Brosher	.979	34	255	30	6	0	11
Dimino	1.000	1	14	2	0	0	1
Ramos	1.000	7	49	5	0	0	0
Rizzie	.991	46	295	42	3	1	8
Sanchez	.992	55	431	43	4	3	5

First Base	PCT	G	PO	A	E	DP
Brosher	.957	12	82	8	4	6
Dimino	1.000	1	8	1	0	0
Gamache	.974	21	147	5	4	5
Ramos	.875	2	5	2	1	1
Rizzie	1.000	2	9	0	0	1
Siena	.982	7	53	2	1	0
Winningham	.992	100	833	38	7	73

Second Base	PCT	G	PO	A	E	DP
Carpio	.970	97	174	249	13	46
Franco	.969	16	26	37	2	5
Gamache	1.000	1	1	1	0	1
Jabs	1.000	1	0	1	0	0

	PCT	G	PO	A	E	DP
Paez	.919	17	25	32	5	5
Pascual	1.000	1	1	1	0	1
Ramos	1.000	4	3	8	0	1
Siena	.932	8	13	28	3	8

Third Base	PCT	G	PO	A	E	DP
Brosher	1.000	1	2	0	0	0
Franco	.889	16	10	22	4	1
Gamache	.942	18	10	39	3	1
Jabs	.880	11	8	14	3	2
Paez	.980	20	17	32	1	3
Ramos	.915	41	27	59	8	3

	PCT	G	PO	A	E	DP
Siena	.867	6	5	8	2	0
Tiberi	.857	3	2	4	1	0
Woodmansee	.916	31	26	50	7	4

Shortstop	PCT	G	PO	A	E	DP
Carpio	.929	27	40	64	8	14
Gimenez	.971	89	147	257	12	49
Paez	.909	16	16	24	4	1
Pascual	.923	4	3	9	1	1
Ramos	1.000	8	6	14	0	2

Outfield	PCT	G	PO	A	E	DP
Berrios	.977	56	122	6	3	0
Brodey	1.000	9	24	0	0	0
Cespedes	1.000	5	6	0	0	0
Cone	1.000	77	139	6	0	0
Franco	1.000	1	1	0	0	0
Jabs	.959	61	114	4	5	0
Lindsay	.959	62	137	5	6	0
Medina	1.000	22	34	1	0	0
Ramos	.000	1	0	0	0	0
Strom	.949	38	91	3	5	0
Tebow	.879	44	50	1	7	0
Zanon	1.000	47	96	3	0	0

BROOKLYN CYCLONES

SHORT SEASON

NEW YORK-PENN LEAGUE

Batting	B-T	HT	WT	DOB	AVG	vLH	vRH	G	AB	R	H	2B	3B	HR	RBI	BB	HBP	SH	SF	SO	SB	CS	SLG	OBP
Aybar, Cecilio	R-R	5-11	172	11-23-93	.194	.136	.220	26	72	8	14	3	0	0	1	3	1	1	0	25	3	2	.236	.237
Brodey, Quinn	L-L	6-1	200	12-1-95	.257	.302	.242	54	210	20	54	9	2	2	30	14	1	0	3	49	10	3	.348	.303
Byrd, Leon	R-B	5-7	192	2-27-94	.234	.222	.238	38	137	14	32	6	0	0	9	21	4	1	1	34	5	4	.277	.350
Cespedes, Ricardo	L-L	6-1	205	8-24-97	.225	.278	.210	21	80	3	18	0	0	1	12	4	0	2	0	16	1	1	.263	.262
2-team total (19 Batavia)					.208	.278	.210	40	159	7	33	2	0	1	16	5	0	3	0	37	1	2	.239	.232
Correa, Franklin	R-R	5-8	195	1-1-96	.234	.182	.246	51	171	20	40	6	1	1	12	9	1	3	1	63	4	2	.298	.275
Fermin, Edgardo	R-R	6-0	171	5-28-98	.219	.333	.173	23	73	7	16	1	1	1	5	8	0	0	0	22	3	0	.301	.296
Gamache, Reed	R-R	6-0	195	1-3-94	.255	.194	.271	42	149	15	38	9	0	0	15	23	4	0	1	18	1	1	.315	.367
Granadillo, Guillermo	R-R	5-11	197	2-12-97	.236	.083	.279	19	55	6	13	1	0	0	2	5	0	1	0	12	5	2	.255	.300
Lagrange, Wagner	R-R	5-11	187	9-6-95	.308	.500	.241	13	39	4	12	1	2	0	4	5	0	0	1	8	1	1	.436	.378
Manea, Scott	R-R	5-11	216	12-21-95	.223	.148	.247	37	112	10	25	3	0	1	11	18	11	0	1	18	0	1	.277	.380
Maria, Jose	R-R	5-10	227	11-30-94	.221	.257	.209	39	145	11	32	7	0	5	13	4	2	0	0	36	0	1	.372	.252
Medina, Jose Miguel	R-R	6-3	180	10-21-96	.262	.325	.249	63	225	20	59	9	2	1	20	19	3	0	2	63	25	6	.333	.325
Rasquin, Walter	R-R	5-9	200	3-21-96	.300	.274	.309	63	243	41	73	21	1	1	19	13	4	1	4	40	32	8	.407	.341
Sanchez, Carlos	R-R	6-0	203	6-6-96	.175	.250	.156	37	137	4	24	4	2	0	7	12	0	0	0	40	0	0	.234	.242
Snypes, Dylan	L-R	6-2	180	5-1-96	.180	.222	.168	37	122	15	22	3	1	0	3	18	3	1	0	52	3	3	.221	.301
Stajduhar, Carl	R-R	6-1	215	4-29-96	.137	.191	.119	52	168	12	23	6	0	3	15	16	4	0	3	76	1	1	.226	.225
Strom, Ian	R-L	6-1	209	12-12-94	.095	.000	.100	8	21	3	2	0	0	0	3	6	3	0	1	5	2	1	.095	.355
Vasquez, Jeremy	L-L	6-1	205	7-17-96	.226	.143	.257	31	102	11	23	7	0	1	8	15	2	0	1	34	0	0	.324	.333
Winaker, Matt	L-L	6-1	195	11-29-95	.268	.417	.237	21	71	10	19	1	0	0	3	15	1	0	0	11	2	0	.282	.402
Wolf, Jeremy	R-L	6-1	213	11-2-93	.241	.133	.265	26	83	6	20	6	0	0	10	6	2	0	0	20	1	1	.313	.308
Zanon, Jacob	R-R	6-0	180	6-25-95	.250	—	.250	1	4	1	1	1	0	0	0	1	0	0	0	1	1	0	.500	.400

Pitching	B-T	HT	WT	DOB	W	L	ERA	G	GS	CG	SV	IP	H	R	ER	HR	BB	SO	AVG	vLH	vRH	K/9	BB/9
Aldridge, Keaton	R-L	6-1	198	7-20-92	1	0	5.63	9	0	0	2	8	10	5	5	0	6	6	.313	.357	.278	6.75	
6.75 Anderson, Martin	L-R	6-1	175	1-13-93	0	1	2.50	4	3	0	0	18	11	5	5	0	8	27	.172	.095	.209	13.50	4.00
Campos, Yeizo	R-R	5-9	172	4-29-96	0	0	4.91	1	0	0	0	4	6	2	2	1	0	6	.375	—	.375	14.73	0.00
Campusano, Briam	R-R	6-2	174	3-26-96	0	1	1.64	2	2	1	0	11	3	3	2	1	2	13	.083	.000	.130	10.64	1.64
Chadwick, Cannon	R-R	6-0	195	12-2-94	1	1	1.33	18	0	0	1	27	23	7	4	0	14	40	.232	.217	.245	13.33	4.67
Cobb, Trey	R-R	6-1	190	6-24-94	1	2	2.63	20	0	0	1	27	21	12	8	1	10	30	.212	.119	.281	9.88	3.29
De Los Santos, Luis	R-R	5-10	175	1-27-94	0	5	11.00	6	5	0	0	18	32	24	22	2	11	16	.372	.351	.388	8.00	5.50
Debora, Nicolas	R-R	6-4	189	12-6-93	1	4	2.33	14	7	0	1	54	58	24	14	5	15	56	.271	.309	.239	9.33	2.50
Dibrell, Tony	R-R	6-3	190	11-8-95	1	1	5.03	12	0	0	0	20	19	13	11	4	8	28	.253	.167	.333	12.81	3.66
Estevez, Gregorix	R-R	6-5	231	4-12-94	3	1	3.77	21	0	0	3	31	23	19	13	2	26	26	.202	.204	.200	7.55	7.55
Familia, Jeurys	R-R	6-3	240	10-10-89	0	0	0.00	2	0	0	0	2	1	0	0	0	0	1	.143	.000	.200	4.50	0.00
Geraldo, Jose	R-R	6-0	200	7-14-95	1	3	2.33	6	6	0	0	27	23	13	7	2	10	22	.232	.308	.183	7.33	3.33
Gibbons, Mike	R-R	6-4	218	4-24-93	0	2	7.59	3	3	0	0	11	14	9	9	0	6	12	.318	.308	.333	10.13	5.06
Harvey, Matt	R-R	6-4	215	3-27-89	0	0	2.25	2	2	0	0	4	2	1	1	0	1	3	.167	.333	.000	6.75	2.25
Holderman, Colin	R-R	6-7	240	10-8-95	0	0	7.20	2	2	0	0	5	5	5	4	1	4	5	.263	.375	.182	9.00	7.20
Horne, Kurtis	L-L	6-4	205	8-5-96	0	0	11.37	7	0	0	1	6	14	9	8	3	4	3	.438	.600	.364	4.26	5.68
Ingram, Chase	R-R	6-3	210	4-17-95	1	0	2.25	3	1	0	0	8	6	2	2	1	3	6	.214	.357	.071	6.75	3.38
Johnson, Trent	R-R	6-5	205	8-12-96	3	5	5.95	15	7	0	0	62	79	44	41	3	20	37	.306	.341	.271	5.37	2.90
Kines, Gunnar	L-L	6-3	210	7-25-93	2	2	3.00	7	3	0	0	33	28	11	11	4	5	32	.228	.231	.227	8.73	1.36
McAuliffe, Ryan	R-R	6-4	195	6-19-95	0	0	2.84	4	2	0	0	13	11	4	4	1	4	11	.239	.188	.267	7.82	2.84
McIlraith, Thomas	R-R	6-3	214	2-17-94	1	0	0.00	1	1	0	0	5	2	0	0	0	1	4	.111	—	.111	7.20	1.80
Medina, Jose Carlos	L-L	6-3	215	8-25-96	1	5	3.53	10	8	1	1	51	57	29	20	3	7	30	.274	.277	.273	5.29	1.24
Napolitano, Joe	R-R	6-2	217	2-10-92	1	3	6.17	16	0	0	0	23	24	23	16	3	14	21	.253	.282	.232	8.10	5.40
O'Neil, Conner	R-R	6-2	195	9-25-94	1	2	3.28	19	0	0	3	25	24	9	9	1	9	28	.273	.222	.308	10.22	3.28
Peterson, David	L-L	6-6	240	9-3-95	0	0	2.45	3	3	0	0	4	4	1	1	0	1	6	.267	.000	.308	14.73	2.45
Ramos, Darwin	R-R	6-2	192	11-23-95	2	3	3.86	8	6	0	0	33	29	19	14	0	16	37	.230	.310	.162	10.19	4.41
Renteria, Marcel	R-R	5-11	185	9-27-94	1	2	9.53	9	0	0	1	11	15	12	12	0	7	17	.300	.177	.364	13.50	5.56
Simon, Jake	L-L	6-2	189	1-21-97	1	4	6.53	14	9	0	0	40	53	33	29	2	27	27	.321	.344	.308	6.08	6.08
Syndergaard, Noah	L-R	6-6	240	8-29-92	0	1	13.50	1	1	0	0	2	3	3	3	0	2	2	.375	.667	.200	9.00	9.00
Torres, Placido	L-L	5-11	165	5-17-93	0	0	3.60	7	0	0	0	10	7	4	4	1	7	8	.219	.111	.261	7.20	6.30
Viall, Chris	R-R	6-9	253	9-28-95	0	3	3.42	9	5	0	0	26	17	12	10	2	14	31	.187	.212	.172	10.59	4.78
Villines, Stephen	R-R	6-2	175	7-15-95	1	1	1.89	11	0	0	1	19	13	5	4	1	1	30	.186	.077	.250	14.21	0.47

Fielding

C: Manea 32, Maria 14, Sanchez 31. **1B:** Gamache 10, Maria 16, Vasquez 30, Winaker 21, Wolf 1. **2B:** Byrd 9, Correa 14, Fermin 19, Gamache 10, Rasquin 28. **3B:** Correa 3, Gamache 22, Stajduhar 51. **SS:** Byrd 15, Correa 34, Fermin 4, Snypes 24. **OF:** Aybar 23, Brodey 53, Byrd 15, Cespedes 20, Granadillo 19, Lagrange 13, Medina 62, Strom 8, Wolf 22, Zanon 1.

KINGSPORT METS — *ROOKIE*

APPALACHIAN LEAGUE

Batting	B-T	HT	WT	DOB	AVG	vLH	vRH	G	AB	R	H	2B	3B	HR	RBI	BB	HBP	SH	SF	SO	SB	CS	SLG	OBP
Adon, Ranfy	R-R	6-3	177	8-2-97	.333	1.000	.200	1	6	3	2	0	1	0	3	0	0	0	0	2	2	0	.667	.333
De Aza, Yeffry	R-R	5-11	210	1-14-97	.217	.429	.180	17	46	6	10	2	0	0	0	8	1	1	0	16	2	0	.261	.346
Dirocie, Anthony	R-R	5-11	175	4-24-97	.245	.219	.254	61	237	31	58	19	3	11	48	14	0	0	0	93	3	2	.490	.287
Fermin, Edgardo	R-R	6-0	171	5-28-98	.352	.692	.276	17	71	19	25	7	0	0	10	9	0	0	0	14	1	2	.451	.425
Garay, Gavin	R-R	6-2	205	6-18-97	.246	.238	.250	36	130	22	32	5	0	3	13	10	2	0	1	47	1	0	.354	.308
Gladu, Raphael	L-R	6-2	195	6-23-95	.269	.216	.290	36	130	17	35	5	1	2	14	14	1	0	1	15	2	2	.369	.343
Hall, Kevin	R-R	6-2	210	11-13-93	.246	.357	.213	17	61	11	15	0	0	2	8	5	0	0	1	21	1	1	.344	.299
Hoy, Danny	R-R	5-10	191	7-1-93	.188	.143	.203	26	80	12	15	1	1	3	15	10	3	1	0	20	0	0	.338	.301
Jimenez, Grabiel	L-L	6-1	196	1-16-95	.205	.158	.214	34	122	17	25	8	0	0	10	11	1	0	1	27	1	1	.271	.274
Lagrange, Wagner	R-R	5-11	187	9-6-95	.335	.373	.321	45	185	27	62	10	1	4	40	15	0	0	3	18	2	2	.465	.379
Manzanarez, Angel	R-R	5-10	160	5-19-97	.234	.250	.229	51	192	29	45	3	2	1	13	20	1	3	2	25	0	2	.287	.307
Moreno, Hansel	B-R	6-4	180	11-3-96	.261	.167	.299	41	165	32	43	10	1	4	23	15	2	5	1	52	9	3	.406	.328
Moscote, Victor	R-R	6-1	230	5-10-94	.215	.278	.192	18	65	6	14	4	1	0	11	2	1	0	0	17	0	0	.308	.250
Pascual, Oliver	B-R	5-9	178	11-16-96	.296	.357	.267	12	44	7	13	2	0	0	3	4	0	1	0	11	0	0	.341	.354
Paulino, Dionis	L-L	6-1	223	6-20-94	.290	.250	.305	51	183	26	53	7	3	2	21	23	0	1	0	45	10	4	.393	.369
Terrazas, Rigoberto	B-R	6-1	185	4-11-96	.348	.381	.333	54	210	45	73	16	2	3	24	25	1	1	4	31	1	0	.486	.413
Uriarte, Juan	R-R	6-0	182	9-17-97	.305	.322	.298	52	200	36	61	13	1	5	36	15	8	0	3	31	0	0	.455	.372
Vasquez, Jeremy	L-L	6-1	205	7-17-96	.296	.219	.320	36	135	18	40	8	0	7	30	22	1	0	2	26	0	0	.511	.394
Vientos, Mark	R-R	6-4	185	12-11-99	.294	.250	.308	4	17	1	5	2	0	0	2	1	0	0	0	4	0	0	.412	.333

Pitching	B-T	HT	WT	DOB	W	L	ERA	G	GS	CG	SV	IP	H	R	ER	HR	BB	SO	AVG	vLH	vRH	K/9	BB/9
Bryant, Garrison	L-R	6-3	189	12-3-98	0	5	8.76	12	5	0	0	37	52	43	36	5	18	33	.331	.328	.333	8.03	4.38
Campusano, Briam	R-R	6-2	174	3-26-96	0	2	3.65	2	2	0	0	12	11	7	5	0	3	14	.234	.333	.188	10.22	2.19
Cavallaro, Joe	R-R	6-4	190	7-19-95	3	1	2.34	11	5	0	0	35	23	13	9	1	10	35	.183	.222	.153	9.09	2.60
Colon, Yeudy	R-R	6-1	230	6-9-95	0	2	3.90	17	0	0	2	28	26	18	12	2	23	29	.248	.156	.317	9.43	7.48
De Los Santos, Luis	R-R	5-10	175	1-27-94	0	0	4.50	3	1	0	0	6	4	3	3	0	4	9	.191	.300	.091	13.50	6.00
Ford, Aaron	L-L	5-11	190	9-9-94	1	2	1.17	10	0	0	2	15	8	4	2	0	4	24	.151	.250	.122	14.09	2.35
Geraldo, Jose	R-R	6-0	200	7-14-95	3	1	4.71	8	8	0	0	42	45	25	22	4	14	28	.268	.239	.289	6.00	3.00
German, Edwin	R-R	6-3	174	9-10-92	1	1	2.45	8	1	0	1	15	11	4	4	0	7	14	.212	.294	.171	8.59	4.30
Hernandez, Carlos	R-R	5-11	172	11-3-94	3	3	4.62	12	11	0	0	64	64	45	33	7	28	59	.259	.258	.260	8.25	3.92
James, Christian	R-R	6-3	210	5-24-98	2	3	4.18	11	11	0	0	52	54	29	24	3	16	58	.267	.273	.265	10.10	2.79
Lozer, Mac	R-R	6-1	200	7-18-95	2	1	4.30	16	0	0	3	23	29	13	11	2	9	20	.302	.270	.322	7.83	3.52
Mateo, Luis	R-R	6-6	178	4-7-93	0	0	13.50	1	0	0	0	2	3	3	3	2	1	2	.333	.400	.250	9.00	4.50
McAuliffe, Ryan	R-R	6-4	195	6-19-95	1	0	0.00	1	0	0	0	3	2	0	0	0	1	1	.200	.000	.250	3.00	3.00
Montijo, Marbin	R-R	6-3	181	7-4-96	3	2	5.46	17	0	0	0	28	26	17	17	1	19	37	.248	.257	.243	11.89	6.11
Olivo, Aneury	L-L	6-0	174	10-24-94	1	1	5.65	6	6	0	0	29	32	19	18	1	15	18	.283	.250	.294	5.65	4.71
Oxford, Billy	R-R	6-1	215	10-22-95	2	1	3.75	14	0	0	1	24	21	11	10	2	8	29	.244	.265	.231	10.88	3.00
Payne, Joshua	R-R	6-6	260	10-3-94	0	1	3.31	9	0	0	0	16	10	6	6	0	4	25	.170	.158	.175	13.78	2.20
Perez, Pedro	R-R	6-1	218	8-31-94	3	1	12.94	12	0	0	0	16	27	24	23	2	19	17	.380	.448	.333	9.56	10.69
Sanchez, Ronald	R-R	6-5	195	9-20-93	0	4	5.86	13	4	0	1	35	44	27	23	4	20	31	.295	.254	.326	7.90	5.09
Selmer, Ryan	R-R	6-8	220	5-20-94	0	1	2.14	14	0	0	2	21	21	8	5	1	11	8	.284	.375	.240	3.43	4.71
Villines, Stephen	R-R	6-2	175	7-15-95	2	1	1.08	8	0	0	0	8	10	1	1	0	0	11	.313	.286	.333	11.88	0.00
Zabaleta, Ezequiel	R-R	6-0	175	8-20-95	2	3	6.68	12	12	0	0	62	82	51	46	10	26	40	.320	.290	.342	5.81	3.77

Fielding

C: Hall 15, Moscote 10, Uriarte 44. **1B:** Garay 27, Moscote 3, Paulino 8, Terrazas 4, Vasquez 27. **2B:** Gladu 2, Hoy 14, Manzanarez 46, Pascual 7, Terrazas 1. **3B:** De Aza 9, Hoy 6, Moreno 4, Terrazas 50. **SS:** Fermin 15, Hoy 1, Manzanarez 7, Moreno 37, Pascual 5, Vientos 4. **OF:** Adon 1, Dirocie 61, Gladu 28, Jimenez 24, Lagrange 44, Paulino 43.

GCL METS — *ROOKIE*

GULF COAST LEAGUE

Batting	B-T	HT	WT	DOB	AVG	vLH	vRH	G	AB	R	H	2B	3B	HR	RBI	BB	HBP	SH	SF	SO	SB	CS	SLG	OBP
Adon, Ranfy	R-R	6-3	177	8-2-97	.280	.294	.273	11	50	9	14	4	2	0	1	4	0	0	0	16	1	0	.440	.333
Bautista, Kenneth	R-R	6-2	225	8-7-97	.264	.353	.232	43	129	18	34	13	1	3	20	22	3	0	0	43	1	1	.450	.383
Beracierta, Raul	R-R	6-0	211	5-24-99	.253	.227	.263	49	162	14	41	8	0	1	16	11	2	0	1	42	2	3	.321	.307
Cespedes, Ricardo	L-L	6-1	205	8-24-97	.200	.250	.182	4	15	0	3	0	0	0	0	0	0	0	0	3	0	0	.200	.200
Dimino, Anthony	L-R	5-11	174	8-5-93	.231	.400	.125	3	13	1	3	0	0	0	2	1	0	0	0	1	1	1	.231	.286
Espino, Sebastian	R-R	6-2	176	5-29-00	.177	.000	.214	4	17	1	3	2	1	0	2	1	0	0	0	6	0	0	.412	.222
Foley, Matthew	R-R	6-4	230	4-15-94	.290	.389	.255	23	69	11	20	7	0	1	7	6	0	0	0	20	0	0	.435	.347
Granadillo, Guillermo	R-R	5-11	197	2-12-97	.301	.333	.290	42	156	26	47	8	2	1	11	16	4	0	1	23	17	4	.397	.379
Guerrero, Gregory	R-R	6-0	186	1-20-99	.217	.220	.216	38	143	17	31	3	1	0	12	7	1	2	1	27	1	3	.252	.257
Hernandez, Kenny	L-R	6-0	194	8-13-98	.208	.188	.215	51	183	15	38	6	0	1	20	22	3	1	2	40	3	3	.257	.300
Kidwell, Robby	L-R	6-3	200	10-21-97	.172	.200	.163	21	64	3	11	1	0	0	4	5	0	0	0	22	0	0	.188	.232
Lebron, Luis	R-R	5-10	197	1-6-97	.226	.111	.286	17	53	8	12	2	0	0	3	3	0	2	1	10	0	2	.264	.263
Martinez, Domingo	R-R	5-10	214	4-2-95	.244	.368	.191	36	127	14	31	7	0	1	16	16	2	0	2	31	0	2	.323	.333
Montero, Luis	R-R	6-0	196	1-16-96	.233	.316	.205	46	150	12	35	6	4	0	15	15	2	0	0	22	2	1	.327	.311

Batting	B-T	HT	WT	DOB	AVG	vLH	vRH	G	AB	R	H	2B	3B	HR	RBI	BB	HBP	SH	SF	SO	SB	CS	SLG	OBP
Moreno, Hansel	B-R	6-4	180	11-3-96	.387	.273	.450	16	62	16	24	3	2	0	8	7	0	2	1	9	5	1	.500	.443
Peroza, Jose	R-R	6-1	214	6-15-00	.177	.200	.167	5	17	1	3	0	0	0	1	1	0	1	0	8	0	1	.177	.222
Ramos, Natanael	R-R	5-11	216	6-19-93	.091	.000	.111	3	11	0	1	0	0	0	0	0	0	0	0	2	0	0	.091	.091
Reyes, Wilmer	R-R	6-0	161	12-22-97	.333	.353	.324	13	54	7	18	5	0	0	7	6	0	1	1	8	7	2	.426	.393
Schneider, Jack	R-R	6-0	190	1-22-98	.000	.000	.000	3	3	1	0	0	0	0	0	0	1	0	0	0	0	0	.000	.250
Valdez, Edinson	R-R	6-2	212	1-22-99	.215	.182	.228	25	79	9	17	3	0	0	6	3	1	0	0	21	1	2	.253	.253
Ventura, Pedro	R-R	5-11	188	3-14-97	.194	.148	.212	30	93	9	18	3	0	2	5	10	2	3	0	22	1	0	.290	.286
Vientos, Mark	R-R	6-4	185	12-11-99	.259	.250	.262	47	174	22	45	12	0	4	24	14	2	0	3	42	0	2	.397	.316
Woodmansee, Colby	R-R	6-3	206	8-27-94	.091	.000	.111	3	11	1	1	0	0	0	1	1	0	0	1	3	0	0	.091	.154

Pitching	B-T	HT	WT	DOB	W	L	ERA	G	GS	CG	SV	IP	H	R	ER	HR	BB	SO	AVG	vLH	vRH	K/9	BB/9
Acosta, Daison	R-R	6-2	160	8-24-98	0	2	3.27	6	4	0	0	22	18	8	8	0	7	19	.237	.297	.180	7.77	2.86
Bard, Daniel	R-R	6-4	215	6-25-85	0	0	54.00	1	0	0	0	1	0	4	4	0	5	0	.000	.000	—	0.00	67.50
Campos, Yeizo	R-R	5-9	172	4-29-96	1	4	3.52	8	7	0	0	46	35	21	18	1	14	49	.213	.212	.214	9.59	2.74
Campusano, Briam	R-R	6-2	174	3-26-96	2	3	3.27	7	4	0	0	33	32	15	12	0	11	30	.244	.255	.238	8.18	3.00
Cleveland, Matt	R-R	6-3	187	3-18-98	1	0	2.55	7	4	0	0	25	13	8	7	0	12	17	.151	.182	.132	6.20	4.38
Felipe, Yom	L-L	5-10	180	9-18-96	0	0	10.80	4	0	0	0	2	1	2	2	0	7	2	.143	.000	.200	10.80	37.80
Flores, Yadiel	R-R	6-2	165	7-31-99	0	0	5.19	8	0	0	1	9	12	9	5	0	7	6	.324	.300	.353	6.23	7.27
German, Edwin	R-R	6-3	174	9-10-92	0	0	0.00	1	0	0	0	1	0	0	0	0	1	1	.000	—	.000	9.00	9.00
Gibbons, Mike	R-R	6-4	218	4-24-93	0	0	20.25	1	1	0	0	1	2	3	3	1	1	2	.333	.000	.400	13.50	6.75
Gorzelanny, Tom	R-L	6-3	218	7-12-82	0	0	0.00	2	2	0	0	2	2	0	0	0	0	1	.286	.000	.333	4.50	0.00
Gutierrez, Miguel	L-L	6-0	189	12-3-94	1	2	5.91	15	0	0	0	21	13	14	14	0	14	23	.186	.294	.151	9.70	5.91
Holderman, Colin	R-R	6-7	240	10-8-95	0	0	0.00	1	0	0	0	1	0	0	0	0	2	0	.000	—	.000	0.00	18.00
Hutchinson, Bryce	R-R	6-6	245	10-21-98	0	0	4.70	5	2	0	0	8	7	7	4	0	6	6	.219	.167	.250	7.04	7.04
Ingram, Chase	R-R	6-3	210	4-17-95	0	0	4.50	1	1	0	0	2	2	1	1	0	1	1	.286	.200	.500	4.50	4.50
Mateo, Luis	R-R	6-6	178	4-7-93	1	3	5.30	18	0	0	1	19	16	16	11	3	12	21	.232	.296	.191	10.13	5.79
McAuliffe, Ryan	R-R	6-4	195	6-19-95	0	1	7.45	6	1	0	0	10	11	11	8	1	5	9	.275	.278	.273	8.38	4.66
McCall, Liam	R-R	6-4	180	2-19-99	0	3	7.88	8	1	0	1	8	10	10	7	2	11	5	.303	.286	.316	5.63	12.38
Milone, Tommy	L-L	6-0	220	2-16-87	0	1	10.80	1	1	0	0	2	2	2	2	0	1	3	.286	—	.286	16.20	5.40
Moreno, Jose	R-R	6-4	165	7-31-96	2	3	3.12	10	5	0	1	40	31	18	14	1	25	36	.205	.164	.233	8.03	5.58
Nunez, Dedniel	R-R	5-11	210	6-5-96	1	3	5.24	10	8	0	0	45	51	32	26	3	16	46	.283	.377	.225	9.27	3.22
Nunez, Noah	R-R	6-4	210	12-28-98	1	2	7.15	8	0	0	0	11	15	11	9	3	2	5	.319	.235	.367	3.97	1.59
Olivo, Aneury	L-L	6-0	174	10-24-94	1	0	3.29	3	2	0	0	14	16	6	5	1	6	17	.320	.000	.390	11.20	3.95
Peden, Nate	R-R	6-4	170	10-16-98	1	1	6.35	8	1	0	0	11	19	9	8	2	5	9	.388	.429	.357	7.15	3.97
Rivera, Dariel	R-R	6-1	186	10-1-97	0	1	5.63	7	0	0	0	8	5	6	5	1	3	4	.167	.200	.150	4.50	3.38
Sierra, Jose	L-L	6-3	190	2-22-96	1	1	0.00	11	0	0	1	11	8	2	0	0	12	10	.211	.357	.125	7.94	9.53
Syndergaard, Noah	L-R	6-6	240	8-29-92	0	0	0.00	1	1	0	0	1	1	2	0	0	0	2	.167	.333	.000	18.00	0.00
Taylor, Jr., Ronnie	R-R	6-3	220	10-6-98	0	1	14.40	5	0	0	0	5	5	8	8	0	7	5	.278	.375	.200	9.00	12.60
Torres, Placido	L-L	5-11	165	5-17-93	0	0	0.00	2	0	0	0	1	2	1	0	0	1	1	.333	.000	.400	6.75	6.75
Vilera, Jaison	R-R	6-0	188	6-19-97	3	1	1.88	11	8	1	0	62	43	18	13	3	17	56	.195	.178	.206	8.09	2.45
Villanueva, Eric	R-R	6-0	179	3-19-98	0	3	5.63	18	1	0	0	16	19	13	10	0	24	8	.307	.423	.222	4.50	13.50
Walker, Joshua	L-L	6-6	225	12-1-94	2	1	9.42	14	0	0	2	14	21	18	15	1	6	13	.333	.438	.298	8.16	3.77
Wilson, Kyle	R-R	6-1	185	9-27-96	1	1	1.50	7	2	0	1	18	13	4	3	0	7	19	.197	.154	.225	9.50	3.50

Fielding

C: Dimino 2, Foley 10, Kidwell 20, Lebron 15, Martinez 15, Ramos 3. **1B:** Foley 6, Martinez 21, Montero 33. **2B:** Guerrero 20, Moreno 8, Reyes 12, Ventura 19. **3B:** Hernandez 29, Montero 4, Moreno 4, Peroza 3, Ventura 4, Vientos 14, Woodmansee 2. **SS:** Espino 4, Guerrero 16, Hernandez 17, Moreno 2, Reyes 1, Vientos 19. **OF:** Adon 11, Bautista 40, Beracierta 49, Cespedes 3, Granadillo 41, Montero 12, Reyes 2, Schneider 1, Valdez 23.

DSL METS — *ROOKIE*

DOMINICAN SUMMER LEAGUE

Batting	B-T	HT	WT	DOB	AVG	vLH	vRH	G	AB	R	H	2B	3B	HR	RBI	BB	HBP	SH	SF	SO	SB	CS	SLG	OBP
Araujo, Yordin	R-R	6-1	156	3-30-96	.215	.222	.214	45	135	26	29	9	2	2	15	21	6	4	1	43	6	6	.356	.344
Astudillo, Wilfred	B-R	5-11	209	3-14-00	.291	.189	.317	52	182	28	53	12	1	0	23	17	2	1	4	20	4	6	.368	.351
Bohorquez, Anderson	R-R	5-11	180	10-3-97	.272	.393	.253	61	206	40	56	8	3	1	22	16	8	1	4	23	14	5	.354	.342
De La Rosa, Juan	R-R	6-3	207	6-22-98	.250	.000	.273	8	24	4	6	0	1	1	6	2	0	0	0	3	2	1	.458	.308
Espino, Sebastian	R-R	6-2	176	5-29-00	.267	.273	.265	64	240	36	64	16	9	2	35	22	5	0	2	60	6	5	.433	.338
Espinoza, Gilberto	R-R	6-1	215	11-8-98	.212	.286	.198	42	137	14	29	4	1	3	22	7	5	1	4	43	4	2	.321	.268
Garcia, Tulio	R-L	6-2	206	7-3-98	.202	.353	.169	35	94	18	19	3	1	1	15	21	2	1	3	27	4	6	.287	.350
Gonzalez, Moises	R-R	5-11	163	6-10-00	.286	.389	.269	42	126	20	36	2	3	0	13	21	1	1	0	25	4	4	.349	.392
Lozano, David	R-R	5-11	177	5-11-98	.313	.182	.347	50	160	28	50	9	1	0	18	20	7	2	0	22	14	5	.381	.412
Marquez, Alexis	R-R	6-0	181	6-1-99	.219	.308	.200	27	73	10	16	3	1	0	6	11	0	1	0	8	3	1	.288	.321
Martinez, Jorge	R-R	5-10	192	7-23-96	.247	.244	.248	50	178	22	44	10	0	0	23	19	2	0	3	22	1	1	.303	.322
Medina, Alejandro	R-R	5-11	183	4-7-00	.263	.200	.279	25	76	11	20	2	0	0	7	10	4	1	0	27	0	0	.290	.378
Mena, Jose	R-R	6-0	208	12-22-96	.211	.294	.195	34	95	13	20	2	1	1	8	14	6	0	0	12	5	5	.284	.348
Newton, Shervyen	B-R	6-4	180	4-24-99	.311	.316	.310	66	241	51	75	11	9	1	31	50	4	5	3	57	10	4	.444	.433
Pena, Ezequiel	R-R	6-0	190	5-25-99	.104	.105	.104	36	96	8	10	5	0	0	8	6	9	2	1	47	4	1	.156	.223
Peroza, Jose	R-R	6-1	214	6-15-00	.301	.387	.286	57	213	29	64	21	1	2	28	17	0	0	2	55	7	3	.437	.349
Pujols, Cristopher	R-R	6-2	180	8-19-97	.349	.300	.359	16	63	9	22	5	1	0	13	5	0	0	2	8	5	2	.460	.386
Regnault, Andres	R-R	6-0	251	12-21-98	.270	.240	.278	36	115	13	31	4	0	3	13	12	4	1	0	28	3	2	.383	.359
Rene, Julio	R-R	6-2	182	11-6-97	.251	.286	.244	58	211	35	53	8	2	0	14	12	8	1	1	78	12	12	.308	.315
Reyes, Wilmer	R-R	6-0	161	12-22-97	.242	.214	.249	59	215	39	52	11	3	2	26	25	8	1	3	29	13	6	.349	.339
Rodriguez, Jeison	R-R	6-2	204	1-27-98	.195	.237	.186	58	210	29	41	13	1	6	37	35	3	0	3	65	2	6	.352	.315
Romero, Yoel	R-R	6-0	180	4-10-98	.364	.298	.380	67	239	47	87	10	4	2	35	31	4	3	4	32	17	7	.464	.439
Saez, Jhoander	B-R	6-0	165	3-24-98	.320	.242	.343	68	275	56	88	8	4	0	25	32	4	5	1	66	20	4	.378	.397

Sanchez, Eulises	R-R	6-1	172	3-7-97	.195	.194	.196	50	128	23	25	2	4	0	10	15	3	1	0	36	7	4	.273	.295
Santana, Luis	R-R	5-8	175	7-20-99	.325	.377	.310	65	237	47	77	12	8	3	52	34	11	3	2	22	16	4	.481	.430
Soto, Jean Carlos	L-L	6-0	165	4-3-00	.265	.233	.270	52	189	23	50	8	5	0	20	19	2	0	2	31	4	3	.360	.335
Torres, Kevin	R-R	6-0	169	5-4-99	.226	.381	.188	35	106	15	24	4	0	0	15	14	3	4	2	26	2	1	.264	.328
Valdez, Rafael	R-R	5-11	167	4-19-97	.246	.394	.214	59	183	17	45	9	1	1	23	10	0	5	4	25	7	6	.322	.279
Valdez, Wilmy	R-R	6-6	206	7-3-97	.186	.174	.189	38	129	19	24	4	2	1	14	11	0	0	0	38	3	4	.271	.250
Ventura, Pedro	R-R	5-11	188	3-14-97	.231	.200	.244	21	65	12	15	3	0	1	9	8	0	1	1	6	1	0	.323	.311

Pitching	**B-T**	**HT**	**WT**	**DOB**	**W**	**L**	**ERA**	**G**	**GS**	**CG**	**SV**	**IP**	**H**	**R**	**ER**	**HR**	**BB**	**SO**	**AVG**	**vLH**	**vRH**	**K/9**	**BB/9**
Advincola, Gregori	R-R	6-3	174	2-18-98	1	2	2.16	11	0	0	1	17	11	4	4	1	8	11	.216	.125	.233	5.94	4.32
Angela, Nelmerson Xavier	L-L	6-1	170	2-20-98	2	0	1.90	10	5	0	0	24	19	7	5	0	7	21	.218	.357	.192	7.99	2.66
Baez, Darling	R-R	6-1	198	6-26-97	0	0	3.60	12	0	0	1	15	17	6	6	1	3	12	.283	.053	.390	7.20	1.80
Butto, Jose	R-R	6-1	152	3-19-98	1	1	1.44	15	8	0	1	50	48	11	8	0	9	41	.258	.246	.264	7.38	1.62
Cespedes, Jorge	L-R	6-0	215	6-26-96	6	2	2.03	13	13	0	0	62	60	24	14	2	14	49	.256	.237	.263	7.11	2.03
Chalas, Angel	R-R	6-1	230	7-6-96	0	0	—	1	0	0	0	0	0	3	3	0	3	0	—	—	—	—	—
Correa, Marcos	R-R	6-3	195	1-31-00	2	1	4.32	15	2	0	2	33	42	19	16	0	16	35	.309	.273	.326	9.45	4.32
De Jesus, Jender	R-R	6-2	165	1-3-98	4	0	3.60	15	3	0	1	35	32	19	14	0	13	37	.242	.182	.273	9.51	3.34
Dominguez, Christofer	L-L	6-2	222	1-3-00	0	3	2.76	14	2	0	1	33	35	15	10	2	12	37	.276	.250	.283	10.19	3.31
Escalona, Jhonfran	R-R	5-10	159	4-8-99	1	1	3.86	15	0	0	3	21	20	9	9	2	3	17	.253	.217	.268	7.29	1.29
Escorcha, Jefferson	L-L	5-11	178	10-4-99	3	2	1.86	21	0	0	5	29	24	10	6	0	16	28	.233	.294	.221	8.69	4.97
Felipe, Yom	L-L	5-10	180	9-18-96	0	0	2.25	3	0	0	0	4	2	1	1	0	4	2	.200	.500	.125	4.50	9.00
German, Andres	R-R	6-1	150	5-16-97	2	2	4.01	13	6	0	1	43	45	20	19	3	15	23	.287	.324	.314	4.85	3.16
Guerrero, Jose	R-R	6-2	160	5-10-96	4	1	1.04	11	0	0	0	26	16	9	3	2	10	19	.178	.128	.216	6.58	3.46
Guzman, Daniel	L-L	6-1	194	2-16-98	5	2	2.61	21	0	0	6	31	26	13	9	0	7	26	.228	.227	.228	7.55	2.03
Guzman, Ramon	R-R	6-4	154	10-16-96	1	1	1.25	13	3	0	4	43	33	10	6	1	11	34	.209	.254	.182	7.06	2.28
Isturiz, Victor	R-R	6-2	208	3-8-97	1	2	5.67	15	5	0	0	27	29	18	17	0	13	23	.274	.206	.306	7.67	4.33
Jean, Ivan	L-L	6-1	211	9-14-93	7	3	2.14	13	11	0	0	59	33	20	14	0	34	60	.168	.170	.167	9.15	5.19
Jimenez, Jurgen	R-R	6-2	197	1-14-96	5	2	2.40	14	7	0	0	49	31	18	13	1	17	33	.180	.200	.174	6.10	3.14
Leon, Nelson	R-R	6-1	154	3-1-95	8	3	2.06	14	12	0	0	70	60	24	16	0	11	52	.234	.247	.228	6.69	1.41
Madera, Christopher	R-R	6-2	188	10-1-96	0	0	3.00	2	0	0	0	3	2	1	1	1	0	2	.182	.000	.286	6.00	0.00
Martinez, Juan	R-R	6-1	187	2-14-96	0	3	2.03	12	0	0	5	13	11	15	3	0	13	6	.234	.235	.233	4.05	8.78
Martinez, Michael	L-L	6-3	169	6-30-97	1	0	3.55	10	0	0	0	13	13	8	5	0	9	8	.302	.273	.313	5.68	6.39
Mata, Miguel	R-R	6-6	191	5-5-97	0	0	7.47	9	1	0	0	16	20	14	13	0	5	9	.308	.344	.273	5.17	2.87
Mena, Malky	R-R	6-0	164	10-3-96	3	3	2.13	13	10	0	1	55	45	15	13	0	7	50	.220	.224	.217	8.18	1.15
Moreno, Jose	R-R	6-4	165	7-31-96	1	1	2.49	5	5	0	0	22	17	6	6	0	9	26	.215	.267	.203	10.80	3.74
Nieves, Kerwin	L-L	6-2	179	10-22-95	0	0	—	1	0	0	0	0	0	1	1	0	2	0	—	—	—	—	—
Pena, Jasson	R-R	6-3	171	6-9-98	2	3	2.29	12	2	0	2	39	24	17	10	1	10	39	.174	.146	.189	8.92	2.29
Pena, Luis	L-L	6-0	178	2-8-97	0	0	4.82	7	0	0	0	9	7	5	5	0	10	6	.200	.273	.167	5.79	9.64
Pinedo, Miguel	R-R	6-2	190	4-17-98	3	0	0.47	15	0	0	6	19	9	2	1	0	10	19	.139	.095	.159	8.84	4.66
Ramirez, Miguel	R-R	6-1	140	3-10-97	6	2	1.76	14	14	0	0	67	57	18	13	1	3	53	.227	.211	.237	7.16	0.41
Rodriguez, Hector	L-L	6-2	166	12-27-97	3	0	1.86	13	0	0	4	39	21	12	8	0	21	55	.156	.095	.167	12.80	4.89
Rojas, Oscar	R-R	5-11	200	5-5-99	1	2	2.18	7	7	0	0	33	27	9	8	0	2	35	.223	.220	.225	9.55	0.55
Romero, Joel	R-R	6-1	195	2-13-97	5	3	2.70	15	0	0	0	27	21	11	8	1	10	14	.223	.189	.246	4.73	3.38
Sanchez, Boris	L-R	6-2	180	6-20-97	4	0	2.88	14	9	0	0	66	55	23	21	2	8	59	.231	.202	.247	8.09	1.10
Sosa, Felix	R-R	6-0	169	3-13-98	0	0	6.92	11	1	0	1	13	12	11	10	0	17	12	.245	.200	.300	8.31	11.77
Taveras, Willy	R-R	5-11	158	1-20-98	8	3	2.31	15	13	1	0	70	58	26	18	3	6	63	.229	.271	.213	8.10	0.77
Valencia, Williams	R-R	6-0	167	7-21-00	1	0	0.66	10	0	0	0	14	5	1	1	0	15	9	.116	.071	.138	5.93	9.88
Vasquez, Luis	R-R	6-3	197	8-25-97	3	0	3.00	14	3	0	2	45	37	19	15	0	23	28	.231	.236	.229	5.60	4.60

Fielding

C: Astudillo 47, Marquez 9, Martinez 18, Medina 3, Mena 22, Regnault 22, Torres 33. **1B:** Astudillo 5, Bohorquez 33, Espinoza 1, Lozano 27, Martinez 28, Marquez 18, Mena 13, Valdez 33. **2B:** Bohorquez 12, Lozano 11, Reyes 47, Romero 6, Santana 61, Valdez 18. **3B:** Garcia 1, Lozano 13, Newton 5, Peroza 44, Pujols 12, Reyes 3, Romero 37, Valdez 31, Ventura 11. **SS:** Espino 63, Espinoza 1, Newton 60, Pujols 3, Reyes 8, Romero 6, Saez 1, Santana 4, Valdez 1, Ventura 2. **OF:** Araujo 41, Bohorquez 16, De La Rosa 6, Espinoza 19, Garcia 28, Gonzalez 39, Pena 19, Rene 55, Reyes 1, Rodriguez 54, Romero 24, Saez 68, Sanchez 43, Soto 45, Valdez 1, Valdez 3.

New York Yankees

SEASON IN A SENTENCE: Thanks to breakout seasons from righthander Luis Severino and rookie outfielder Aaron Judge, the Yankees, expected to spend most of the year in rebuilding mode, made the playoffs and finished a win away from their first World Series appearance since 2009.

HIGH POINT: Thanks to a vintage performance from righty Masahiro Tanaka, the Yankees topped the Astros in Game Five of the ALCS and put themselves a win away from a date with the Dodgers in the World Series.

LOW POINT: On Aug. 12, 3.5 games back of the Red Sox in the AL East and with Severino starting, the Yankees lost the first of two straight games. Severino got bombarded in the first game, and closer Aroldis Chapman surrendered a tying home run to Boston rookie Rafael Devers the next night. The two-game skein put the Yankees 5.5 games back in the division, their lowest point all year.

NOTABLE ROOKIES: After striking out in 50 percent of his at-bats in 2016, Judge exploded for a league-best 52 home runs and put himself squarely in the conversation for both the rookie of the year and AL MVP. He also led the AL in runs (128) and walks (127) and led the majors in strikeouts (208). Beyond Judge, the Yankees also got solid work all season long from lefthander Jordan Montgomery, who won a rotation spot in spring training and went 9-7, 3.88 over 155.1 innings.

KEY TRANSACTIONS: The Yankees bolstered their roster for the stretch run with a trio of deals. First, they acquired third baseman Todd Frazier and righthanded relievers David Robertson and Tommy Kahnle for outfielders Blake Rutherford and Tito Polo, lefthander Ian Clarkin and major league reliever Tyler Clippard. They then added rotation help when they flipped a pair of injured prospects in righthander James Kaprielian and outfielder Dustin Fowler as well as shortstop prospect Jorge Mateo to the Athletics in exchange for righthander Sonny Gray. They also added lefthander Jaime Garcia from the Twins for righthanders Zack Littell and Dietrich Enns.

DOWN ON THE FARM: Shortstop Gleyber Torres, the Yankees' top prospect, looked near the major leagues before a collision at home plate required Tommy John surgery on his left elbow. Outfielder Estevan Florial, in his first full season, broke out. He showed a wealth of tools in going from low Class A Charleston all the way to a playoff cameo with Double-A Trenton.

OPENING DAY PAYROLL: $201,539,699 (2nd)

PLAYERS OF THE YEAR

MAJOR LEAGUE

Aaron Judge
OF

.284/.422/.627
Fifty-two home runs paced the AL

MINOR LEAGUE

Estevan Florial
of

(Low Class A/High Class A)
.298/.372/.479

ORGANIZATION LEADERS

BATTING		***Minimum 250 AB**
MAJORS		
* AVG	Starlin Castro	.300
* OPS	Aaron Judge	1.049
HR	Aaron Judge	52
RBI	Aaron Judge	114
MINORS		
* AVG	Miguel Andujar, Trenton, Scranton/Wilkes-Barre	.315
* OBP	Jeff Hendrix, Tampa, Trenton	.411
* SLG	Dustin Fowler, Scarnton/Wilkes-Barre	.542
* OPS	Ji-Man Choi, Scranton/Wilkes-Barre	.911
R	Mike Ford, Scranton/Wilkes-Barre, Trenton	80
	Isiah Gilliam, Charleston	80
H	Miguel Andujar, Trenton, Scranton/Wilkes-Barre	151
TB	Miguel Andujar, Trenton, Scranton/Wilkes-Barre	239
2B	Miguel Andujar, Trenton, Scranton/Wilkes-Barre	36
3B	Jorge Mateo, Tampa, Trenton, Midland	11
HR	Jake Cave, Trenton, Scranton/Wilkes-Barre	20
	Mike Ford, Scranton/Wilkes-Barre, Trenton	20
RBI	Mike Ford, Scranton/Wilkes-Barre, Trenton	86
BB	Mike Ford, Scranton/Wilkes-Barre, Trenton	94
SO	Estevan Florial, Charleston, Tampa	148
SB	Jorge Mateo, Tampa, Trenton, Midland	39

PITCHING		**#Minimum 75 IP**
MAJORS		
W	Luis Severino	14
	C.C. Sabathia	14
# ERA	Luis Severino	2.98
SO	Luis Severino	230
SV	Aroldis Chapman	22
MINORS		
W	Chance Adams, Trenton, Scranton/Wilkes-Barre	15
L	Nick Nelson, Charleston	12
# ERA	Zack Littell, Tampa, Trenton, Chattanooga	1.87
G	Cale Coshow, Trenton, Scranton/Wilkes-Barre	45
GS	Chance Adams, Trenton, Scranton/Wilkes-Barre	27
	Taylor Widener, Tampa	27
SV	Cale Coshow, Trenton, Scranton/Wilkes-Barre	15
IP	Chance Adams, Trenton, Scranton/Wilkes-Barre	150
BB	Jio Orozco, Charleston, Pulaski, Staten Island	65
SO	Brian Keller, Charleston, Tampa	157
# AVG	Jose Mesa, Tampa, Trenton	.166

2017 PERFORMANCE

General Manager: Brian Cashman. **Farm Director:** Gary Denbo. **Scouting Director:** Damon Oppenheimer.

Class	Team	League	W	L	PCT	Finish	Manager
Majors	New York Yankees	American	91	71	.562	4th (15)	Joe Girardi
Triple-A	Scranton/Wilkes-Barre RailRiders	International	86	55	.610	1st (14)	Al Pedrique
Double-A	Trenton Thunder	Eastern	92	48	.657	1st (12)	Bobby Mitchell
High-A	Tampa Yankees	Florida State	85	50	.630	1st (12)	Jay Bell
Low-A	Charleston RiverDogs	South Atlantic	76	63	.547	3rd (14)	Pat Osborn
Short Season	Staten Island Yankees	New York-Penn	46	29	.613	1st (14)	Julio Mosquera
Rookie	Pulaski Yankees	Appalachian	41	26	.612	2nd (10)	Luis Dorante
Rookie	GCL Yankees East	Gulf Coast	33	27	.550	6th (17)	Luis Sojo
Rookie	GCL Yankees West	Gulf Coast	32	27	.542	7th (17)	Marc Bombard
Overall 2017 Minor League Record			491	325	.602	1st (30)	

ORGANIZATION STATISTICS

NEW YORK YANKEES

AMERICAN LEAGUE

Batting	B-T	HT	WT	DOB	AVG	vLH	vRH	G	AB	R	H	2B	3B	HR	RBI	BB	HBP	SH	SF	SO	SB	CS	SLG	OBP
Andujar, Miguel	R-R	6-0	215	3-2-95	.571	.667	.500	5	7	0	4	2	0	0	4	1	0	0	0	0	1	0	.857	.625
Austin, Tyler	R-R	6-2	220	9-6-91	.225	.385	.148	20	40	4	9	2	0	2	8	4	0	0	2	17	0	0	.425	.283
Bird, Greg	L-R	6-4	220	11-9-92	.191	.286	.168	48	147	20	28	7	0	9	28	19	2	0	2	42	0	0	.422	.288
Carter, Chris	R-R	6-4	245	12-18-86	.201	.179	.211	62	184	20	37	5	1	8	26	20	2	0	2	76	0	0	.370	.284
Castro, Starlin	R-R	6-2	230	3-24-90	.300	.321	.294	112	443	66	133	18	1	16	63	23	4	0	3	93	2	0	.454	.338
Choi, Ji-Man	R-L	6-1	230	5-19-91	.267	.000	.308	6	15	2	4	1	0	2	5	2	0	0	1	5	0	0	.733	.333
Cooper, Garrett	R-R	6-6	230	12-25-90	.326	.368	.292	13	43	3	14	5	1	0	6	1	0	0	1	12	0	0	.488	.333
Ellsbury, Jacoby	L-L	6-1	195	9-11-83	.264	.240	.274	112	356	65	94	20	4	7	39	41	5	2	0	63	22	3	.402	.348
Fowler, Dustin	L-L	6-0	195	12-29-94	—	—	—	1	0	0	0	0	0	0	0	0	0	0	0	0	0	0	—	—
Frazier, Clint	R-R	6-1	190	9-6-94	.231	.257	.222	39	134	16	31	9	4	4	17	7	0	0	1	43	1	0	.448	.268
Frazier, Todd	R-R	6-3	220	2-12-86	.222	.213	.225	66	194	33	43	4	1	11	32	35	10	0	2	54	0	0	.423	.365
2-team total (81 Chicago)					.213	.203	.209	147	474	74	101	19	1	27	76	83	14	0	5	125	4	3	.428	.344
Gardner, Brett	L-L	5-11	195	8-24-83	.264	.210	.283	151	594	96	157	26	4	21	63	72	8	5	3	122	23	5	.428	.350
Gregorius, Didi	L-R	6-3	205	2-18-90	.287	.264	.295	136	534	73	153	27	0	25	87	25	3	0	7	70	3	1	.478	.318
Headley, Chase	B-R	6-2	215	5-9-84	.273	.260	.279	147	512	77	140	30	1	12	61	60	6	1	7	132	9	2	.406	.352
Hicks, Aaron	B-R	6-1	202	10-2-89	.266	.312	.240	88	301	54	80	18	0	15	52	51	3	1	5	67	10	5	.475	.372
Higashioka, Kyle	R-R	6-1	200	4-20-90	.000	.000	.000	9	18	2	0	0	0	0	0	2	0	0	0	6	0	0	.000	.100
Holliday, Matt	R-R	6-4	240	1-15-80	.231	.267	.220	105	373	50	86	18	0	19	64	46	3	0	5	114	1	0	.432	.316
Judge, Aaron	R-R	6-7	282	4-26-92	.284	.230	.298	155	542	128	154	24	3	52	114	127	5	0	4	208	9	4	.627	.422
Kozma, Pete	R-R	6-0	190	4-11-88	.111	.200	.000	11	9	2	1	0	0	0	0	1	0	0	0	2	0	0	.111	.200
2-team total (28 Texas)					.111	.188	.050	39	45	6	5	0	0	1	2	3	2	1	0	20	0	1	.178	.200
Kratz, Erik	R-R	6-4	245	6-15-80	1.000	1.000	1.000	4	2	0	2	1	0	0	2	0	0	0	0	0	0	0	1.500	1.000
Refsnyder, Rob	R-R	6-0	200	3-26-91	.135	.100	.148	20	37	3	5	1	1	0	0	3	0	0	0	8	2	0	.216	.200
2-team total (32 Toronto)					.171	.056	.273	52	88	8	15	2	1	0	0	8	1	0	0	17	4	1	.216	.247
Romine, Austin	R-R	6-1	220	11-22-88	.218	.143	.243	80	229	19	50	9	1	2	21	16	2	2	3	57	0	0	.293	.272
Sanchez, Gary	R-R	6-2	230	12-2-92	.278	.266	.282	122	471	79	131	20	0	33	90	40	10	0	4	120	2	1	.531	.345
Torreyes, Ronald	R-R	5-8	151	9-2-92	.292	.338	.278	108	315	35	92	15	1	3	36	11	1	5	4	43	2	0	.375	.314
Wade, Tyler	L-R	6-1	185	11-23-94	.155	.091	.170	30	58	7	9	4	0	0	2	5	0	0	0	19	1	1	.224	.222
Williams, Mason	L-R	6-1	185	8-21-91	.250	.200	.273	5	16	3	4	0	0	0	1	1	0	0	0	2	2	0	.250	.294

Pitching	B-T	HT	WT	DOB	W	L	ERA	G	GS	CG	SV	IP	H	R	ER	HR	BB	SO	AVG	vLH	vRH	K/9	BB/9
Betances, Dellin	R-R	6-8	265	3-23-88	3	6	2.87	66	0	0	10	60	29	20	19	3	44	100	.142	.122	.159	15.08	6.64
Cessa, Luis	R-R	6-0	205	4-25-92	0	3	4.75	10	5	0	0	36	36	21	19	7	17	30	.257	.172	.317	7.50	4.25
Chapman, Aroldis	L-L	6-4	212	2-28-88	4	3	3.22	52	0	0	22	50	37	20	18	3	20	69	.200	.175	.211	12.34	3.58
Clippard, Tyler	R-R	6-3	200	2-14-85	1	5	4.95	40	0	0	1	36	28	21	20	7	19	42	.209	.220	.202	10.40	4.71
3-team total (11 Chicago, 16 Houston)					2	8	4.77	67	0	0	5	60	47	33	32	10	31	72	.209	.269	.148	10.74	4.62
Gallegos, Giovanny	R-R	6-2	210	8-14-91	0	1	4.87	16	0	0	0	20	21	12	11	3	5	22	.263	.267	.260	9.74	2.21
Garcia, Jaime	L-L	6-2	215	7-8-86	0	3	4.82	8	8	0	0	37	41	25	20	6	20	37	.279	.297	.273	8.92	4.82
2-team total (1 Minnesota)					1	3	4.70	9	9	0	0	44	49	28	23	6	23	44	.283	.000	.348	9.00	4.70
German, Domingo	R-R	6-2	175	8-4-92	0	1	3.14	7	0	0	0	14	11	6	5	1	9	18	.216	.192	.240	11.30	5.65
Gray, Sonny	R-R	5-10	190	11-7-89	4	7	3.72	11	11	1	0	65	55	31	27	11	27	59	.222	.219	.224	8.13	3.72
2-team total (16 Oakland)					10	12	3.55	27	27	1	0	162	139	79	64	19	57	153	.226	.222	.236	8.48	3.16
Green, Chad	L-R	6-3	210	5-24-91	5	0	1.83	40	1	0	0	69	34	14	14	4	17	103	.147	.121	.162	13.43	2.22
Heller, Ben	R-R	6-3	205	8-5-91	1	0	0.82	9	0	0	0	11	5	1	1	0	6	9	.139	.263	.000	7.36	4.91
Herrera, Ronald	R-R	5-11	185	5-3-95	0	1	6.00	2	0	0	0	3	3	2	2	1	1	3	.250	.000	.429	9.00	3.00
Holder, Jonathan	R-R	6-2	235	6-9-93	1	1	3.89	37	0	0	0	39	45	17	17	5	8	40	.283	.361	.260	9.15	1.83
Kahnle, Tommy	R-R	6-1	235	8-7-89	1	1	2.70	32	0	0	0	27	25	8	8	1	10	36	.248	.350	.180	12.15	3.38
2-team total (37 Chicago)					2	4	2.59	69	0	0	0	63	53	20	18	4	17	96	.228	.288	.165	13.79	2.44
Layne, Tommy	L-L	6-2	195	11-2-84	0	0	7.62	19	0	0	0	13	16	12	11	1	8	9	.296	.304	.290	6.23	5.54
Mitchell, Bryan	L-R	6-3	210	4-19-91	1	1	5.79	20	1	0	1	33	42	24	21	2	13	17	.302	.273	.316	4.68	3.58
Montgomery, Jordan	L-L	6-6	225	12-27-92	9	7	3.88	29	29	0	0	155	140	72	67	21	51	144	.237	.195	.244	8.34	2.95
Pineda, Michael	R-R	6-7	260	1-18-89	8	4	4.39	17	17	0	0	96	103	55	47	20	21	92	.269	.253	.281	8.60	1.96

Pitching	B-T	HT	WT	DOB	W	L	ERA	G	GS	CG	SV	IP	H	R	ER	HR	BB	SO	AVG	vLH	vRH	K/9	BB/9
Robertson, David	R-R	5-11	195	4-9-85	5	0	1.03	30	0	0	1	35	14	4	4	2	12	51	.119	.143	.101	13.11	3.09
2-team total (31 Chicago)					9	2	1.84	61	0	0	14	68	35	14	14	6	23	98	.148	.138	.213	12.91	3.03
Sabathia, CC	L-L	6-6	300	7-21-80	14	5	3.69	27	27	0	0	149	139	64	61	21	50	120	.246	.253	.244	7.26	3.03
Severino, Luis	R-R	6-2	215	2-20-94	14	6	2.98	31	31	0	0	193	150	73	64	21	51	230	.208	.221	.198	10.71	2.37
Shreve, Chasen	L-L	6-4	195	7-12-90	4	1	3.77	44	0	0	0	45	35	20	19	8	25	58	.205	.164	.227	11.51	4.96
Smith, Caleb	R-L	6-2	205	7-28-91	0	1	7.71	9	2	0	0	19	21	16	16	4	10	18	.280	.360	.240	8.68	4.82
Tanaka, Masahiro	R-R	6-3	215	11-1-88	13	12	4.74	30	30	1	0	178	180	100	94	35	41	194	.257	.252	.261	9.79	2.07
Warren, Adam	R-R	6-1	224	8-25-87	3	2	2.35	46	0	0	1	57	35	19	15	4	15	54	.173	.208	.152	8.48	2.35
Webb, Tyler	R-L	6-5	230	7-20-90	0	0	4.50	7	0	0	0	6	3	3	3	1	4	5	.158	.143	.167	7.50	6.00

Fielding

Catcher	PCT	G	PO	A	E	DP	PB
Higashioka	1.000	8	55	2	0	0	1
Kratz	1.000	2	2	0	0	0	0
Romine	.998	67	524	43	1	1	4
Sanchez	.987	104	935	60	13	4	16

First Base	PCT	G	PO	A	E	DP
Austin	1.000	8	49	1	0	1
Bird	1.000	46	302	12	0	20
Carter	.990	56	391	22	4	31
Choi	.973	6	35	1	1	3
Cooper	1.000	13	101	5	0	8
Headley	.997	45	285	19	1	16
Holliday	.964	8	47	6	2	4
Mitchell	.500	1	1	0	1	0
Refsnyder	1.000	4	23	0	0	2
Romine	1.000	12	46	9	0	5
Sanchez	1.000	2	7	0	0	1

Second Base	PCT	G	PO	A	E	DP
Castro	.973	109	175	226	11	46
Headley	.000	1	0	0	0	0
Kozma	.000	1	0	0	0	0
Refsnyder	1.000	2	1	1	0	0
Torreyes	.990	54	90	105	2	19
Wade	.974	15	21	17	1	6

Third Base	PCT	G	PO	A	E	DP
Andujar	1.000	3	1	1	0	0
Frazier	.962	66	35	117	6	12
Headley	.947	86	56	175	13	17
Torreyes	.980	26	9	39	1	3

Shortstop	PCT	G	PO	A	E	DP
Gregorius	.982	135	144	360	9	47
Kozma	.923	9	4	8	1	4
Torreyes	.989	36	28	62	1	12
Wade	1.000	7	3	3	0	0

Outfield	PCT	G	PO	A	E	DP
Austin	1.000	7	2	0	0	0
Carter	.000	2	0	0	0	0
Ellsbury	.985	97	193	1	3	0
Fowler	.000	1	0	0	0	0
Frazier	.962	37	50	0	2	0
Gardner	1.000	138	241	12	0	2
Hicks	.987	84	152	3	2	1
Judge	.982	141	265	5	5	2
Refsnyder	.857	11	6	0	1	0
Torreyes	1.000	1	1	0	0	0
Wade	.600	7	3	0	2	0
Williams	1.000	5	7	0	0	0

SCRANTON/WILKES-BARRE RAILRIDERS — *TRIPLE-A*

INTERNATIONAL LEAGUE

Batting	B-T	HT	WT	DOB	AVG	vLH	vRH	G	AB	R	H	2B	3B	HR	RBI	BB	HBP	SH	SF	SO	SB	CS	SLG	OBP
Andujar, Miguel	R-R	6-0	215	3-2-95	.317	.379	.292	58	227	36	72	13	1	9	30	17	2	0	4	33	3	0	.502	.364
Austin, Tyler	R-R	6-2	220	9-6-91	.275	.378	.238	47	171	29	47	14	1	10	32	18	0	0	1	52	0	0	.544	.342
Avelino, Abiatal	R-R	5-11	205	2-14-95	.213	.177	.227	20	61	5	13	1	1	0	6	5	1	1	0	10	3	1	.262	.284
Bird, Greg	L-R	6-4	220	11-9-92	.298	.417	.257	15	47	12	14	4	0	3	7	11	0	0	1	9	0	0	.575	.424
Bolasky, Devyn	L-L	5-11	185	1-24-93	.200	.200	.200	4	15	1	3	0	0	1	2	0	0	0	0	2	0	0	.400	.200
Castillo, Wilkin	B-R	6-0	215	6-1-84	.192	.194	.191	45	146	12	28	4	0	2	10	8	1	1	1	22	1	1	.260	.237
Castro, Starlin	R-R	6-2	230	3-24-90	.333	.167	.389	6	24	4	8	0	0	1	2	1	0	0	0	4	0	0	.458	.360
Cave, Jake	L-L	6-0	200	12-4-92	.324	.188	.383	72	278	47	90	13	3	15	38	18	1	0	0	82	1	3	.554	.367
Choi, Ji-Man	R-L	6-1	230	5-19-91	.288	.279	.291	87	288	42	83	25	1	15	69	39	4	0	7	86	3	1	.538	.373
Cooper, Garrett	R-R	6-6	230	12-25-90	.000	.000	.000	2	7	0	0	0	0	0	0	0	0	0	0	1	0	0	.000	.000
Culver, Cito	R-R	6-0	205	8-26-92	.224	.247	.215	103	349	41	78	19	3	12	48	31	0	3	6	110	1	1	.398	.282
Diaz, Francisco	B-R	5-11	185	3-21-90	.231	.167	.286	4	13	0	3	2	0	0	4	1	0	1	0	3	0	0	.385	.286
Diaz, Jonathan	R-R	5-9	155	4-10-85	.243	.174	.275	28	74	8	18	2	0	2	5	14	3	1	2	14	1	1	.351	.376
2-team total (37 Buffalo)					.210	.258	.140	65	162	20	34	5	1	2	11	32	8	3	3	38	2	2	.290	.361
Ellsbury, Jacoby	L-L	6-1	195	9-11-83	.375	.333	.500	2	8	1	3	2	0	0	2	0	0	0	0	0	1	0	.625	.375
Fleming, Billy	R-R	6-1	210	9-20-92	.268	.200	.306	16	56	4	15	3	0	1	6	1	0	0	0	6	1	0	.375	.281
Ford, Mike	L-R	6-0	225	7-4-92	.266	.346	.235	25	94	19	25	5	0	7	21	18	1	0	2	16	0	0	.543	.383
Fowler, Dustin	L-L	6-0	195	12-29-94	.293	.286	.296	70	297	49	87	19	8	13	43	15	1	0	0	63	13	5	.542	.329
Frazier, Clint	R-R	6-1	190	9-6-94	.256	.286	.246	74	273	46	70	19	2	12	42	37	3	0	7	69	9	2	.473	.344
Hicks, Aaron	B-R	6-1	202	10-2-89	.375	.333	.429	5	16	4	6	2	1	0	1	2	0	0	0	2	1	0	.625	.444
Higashioka, Kyle	R-R	6-1	200	4-20-90	.264	.375	.216	14	53	5	14	4	0	2	11	4	0	0	0	7	0	0	.453	.316
Holliday, Matt	R-R	6-4	240	1-15-80	.278	.222	.333	5	18	5	5	0	0	0	1	3	0	0	0	2	0	0	.278	.381
McKinney, Billy	L-L	6-1	205	8-23-94	.306	.347	.285	55	209	32	64	13	3	10	35	9	2	1	3	49	0	0	.541	.336
Payton, Mark	L-L	5-8	190	12-7-91	.272	.157	.313	80	268	33	73	14	2	6	22	24	2	0	2	51	4	5	.407	.335
Refsnyder, Rob	R-R	6-0	200	3-26-91	.312	.350	.296	38	138	20	43	11	2	2	12	15	4	0	2	30	2	1	.464	.390
2-team total (4 Buffalo)					.320	.250	.500	42	150	23	48	12	2	2	14	18	4	0	2	32	2	1	.467	.402
Rodriguez, Eddy	R-R	6-0	220	12-1-85	.177	.192	.170	83	272	19	48	9	0	8	31	17	1	2	1	134	1	1	.298	.227
Sanchez, Gary	R-R	6-2	230	12-2-92	.385	.250	.444	3	13	3	5	2	0	1	3	0	0	0	0	3	0	0	.769	.385
Solano, Donovan	R-R	5-10	205	12-17-87	.282	.246	.297	99	373	44	105	29	0	4	48	24	4	1	3	60	1	0	.391	.329
Tejada, Ruben	R-R	5-11	200	10-27-89	.269	.344	.245	37	130	22	35	7	0	6	21	15	1	0	2	17	0	2	.462	.345
2-team total (13 Norfolk)					.280	.308	.313	50	175	31	49	10	0	6	23	19	3	0	2	21	0	2	.440	.357
Torres, Gleyber	R-R	6-1	175	12-13-96	.309	.211	.339	23	81	9	25	4	1	2	16	13	1	0	1	26	2	2	.457	.406
Wade, Tyler	L-R	6-1	185	11-23-94	.310	.301	.314	85	339	68	105	22	4	7	31	38	4	1	4	75	26	5	.460	.382
Williams, Mason	L-R	6-1	185	8-21-91	.263	.297	.249	106	399	44	105	10	3	2	30	28	1	3	6	66	19	5	.318	.309

Pitching	B-T	HT	WT	DOB	W	L	ERA	G	GS	CG	SV	IP	H	R	ER	HR	BB	SO	AVG	vLH	vRH	K/9	BB/9
Acevedo, Domingo	R-R	6-7	250	3-6-94	1	1	4.38	2	2	0	0	12	12	6	6	0	8	8	.255	.280	.227	5.84	5.84
Adams, Chance	R-R	6-1	210	8-10-94	11	5	2.89	21	21	0	0	115	81	39	37	9	43	103	.197	.198	.196	8.04	3.36
Barbato, Johnny	R-R	6-1	235	7-11-92	0	1	4.50	1	1	0	0	4	5	2	2	2	2	5	.357	.600	.222	11.25	4.50
2-team total (26 Indianapolis)					0	2	3.20	27	3	0	4	39	33	14	14	9	13	41	.226	.236	.195	9.38	2.97
Brewer, Colten	R-R	6-4	230	10-29-92	0	0	11.70	6	0	0	1	10	17	16	13	2	4	11	.347	.263	.400	9.90	3.60

Camarena, Daniel	L-L	6-0	210	11-9-92	4	2	3.28	7	7	0	0	36	30	14	13	3	11	30	.224	.182	.238	7.57	2.78
Cessa, Luis	R-R	6-0	205	4-25-92	4	6	3.45	14	13	0	0	78	75	37	30	7	26	67	.253	.225	.271	7.70	2.99
Cortes, Nestor	R-L	5-11	205	12-10-94	2	4	1.49	11	6	1	0	48	40	13	8	0	11	57	.219	.227	.213	10.61	2.05
Coshow, Cale	R-R	6-5	270	7-16-92	0	1	3.18	4	0	0	0	6	8	2	2	0	2	4	.348	.300	.385	6.35	3.18
Enns, Dietrich	L-L	6-1	210	5-16-91	1	1	2.29	7	7	0	0	39	30	11	10	1	10	37	.207	.157	.234	8.47	2.29
2-team total (3 Rochester)					1	2	2.29	10	8	1	1	51	43	14	13	3	14	46	.226	.455	.235	8.12	2.47
Feyereisen, J.P.	R-R	6-2	215	2-7-93	2	3	3.53	24	0	0	1	43	35	20	17	3	20	42	.224	.257	.198	8.72	4.15
Frieri, Ernesto	R-R	6-0	205	7-19-85	2	0	3.00	17	0	0	7	21	13	8	7	3	9	24	.173	.143	.192	10.29	3.86
Gallegos, Giovanny	R-R	6-2	210	8-14-91	4	2	2.08	28	0	0	5	43	28	12	10	4	11	69	.180	.162	.195	14.33	2.28
German, Domingo	R-R	6-2	175	8-4-92	7	2	2.83	14	13	0	0	76	59	26	24	5	22	81	.210	.226	.199	9.55	2.59
Gomez, Anyelo	R-R	6-1	185	3-1-93	0	0	0.00	1	0	0	0	2	0	0	0	0	0	2	.000	.000	.000	9.00	0.00
Graham, J.R.	R-R	5-11	195	1-14-90	0	1	6.64	18	0	0	1	20	32	19	15	3	11	23	.352	.333	.361	10.18	4.87
Green, Chad	L-R	6-3	210	5-24-91	2	1	4.73	5	5	0	0	27	32	15	14	1	11	33	.286	.255	.316	11.14	3.71
Gurka, Jason	L-L	6-0	170	1-10-88	0	0	5.40	13	0	0	0	17	25	14	10	4	2	20	.343	.303	.375	10.80	1.08
Heller, Ben	R-R	6-3	205	8-5-91	5	4	2.88	41	0	0	6	56	34	21	18	6	21	82	.172	.114	.210	13.10	3.36
Herrera, Ronald	R-R	5-11	185	5-3-95	0	0	4.35	2	2	0	0	10	6	7	5	2	3	6	.158	.158	.158	5.23	2.61
Holder, Jonathan	R-R	6-2	235	6-9-93	0	0	1.69	12	0	0	1	16	15	3	3	1	8	21	.250	.185	.303	11.81	4.50
Jones, Tyler	R-R	6-4	240	9-5-89	6	4	4.38	44	0	0	3	64	61	32	31	6	20	76	.250	.246	.254	10.74	2.83
Lail, Brady	R-R	6-2	205	8-9-93	6	5	5.17	26	22	0	2	132	139	80	76	19	42	94	.266	.289	.239	6.39	2.86
Layne, Tommy	L-L	6-2	195	11-2-84	0	0	2.70	6	0	0	1	7	4	2	2	1	2	4	.167	.167	.167	5.40	2.70
Mantiply, Joe	R-L	6-4	215	3-1-91	6	5	2.83	35	6	0	1	70	72	27	22	3	18	62	.264	.268	.261	7.97	2.31
Mitchell, Bryan	L-R	6-3	210	4-19-91	3	3	3.25	14	13	0	0	64	59	26	23	1	13	66	.243	.250	.235	9.33	1.84
Montgomery, Jordan	L-L	6-6	225	12-27-92	0	0	3.00	1	1	0	0	3	2	1	1	0	0	3	.200	.500	.125	9.00	0.00
Pena, Jose	R-R	6-0	190	3-22-91	0	1	9.95	3	1	0	0	6	8	7	7	2	5	6	.320	.353	.250	8.53	7.11
Rosa, Adonis	R-R	6-1	160	11-17-94	1	0	1.50	2	2	0	0	12	9	2	2	1	1	7	.205	.095	.304	5.25	0.75
Rumbelow, Nick	R-R	6-0	190	9-6-91	5	1	0.62	17	0	0	5	29	16	4	2	0	8	30	.158	.209	.121	9.31	2.48
Ruth, Eric	R-R	6-0	195	9-26-90	0	0	12.00	1	1	0	0	3	7	4	4	2	1	1	.500	.714	.286	3.00	3.00
Shreve, Chasen	L-L	6-4	195	7-12-90	1	0	1.59	9	0	0	1	11	7	2	2	0	3	19	.175	.211	.143	15.09	2.38
Smith, Caleb	R-L	6-2	205	7-28-91	9	1	2.39	18	17	1	0	98	75	34	26	7	28	97	.210	.210	.210	8.91	2.57
Webb, Tyler	R-L	6-5	230	7-20-90	3	1	3.24	21	0	0	1	33	33	12	12	3	3	47	.250	.200	.276	12.69	0.81
Wotherspoon, Matt	R-R	6-2	215	10-6-91	1	0	2.25	6	1	0	1	12	10	3	3	0	3	12	.233	.250	.211	9.00	2.25
2-team total (17 Norfolk)					4	1	2.21	23	1	0	1	41	31	10	10	3	18	46	.211	.302	.131	10.18	3.98

Fielding

Catcher	PCT	G	PO	A	E	DP	PB
Castillo	.998	44	391	23	1	1	7
Diaz	1.000	4	36	3	0	1	1
Higashioka	.971	14	129	5	4	0	2
Rodriguez	.992	83	655	67	6	1	3
Sanchez	1.000	2	13	2	0	0	0

First Base	PCT	G	PO	A	E	DP
Austin	.995	23	183	12	1	16
Bird	1.000	10	69	7	0	5
Castillo	1.000	1	8	1	0	3
Choi	.985	57	378	27	6	41
Cooper	1.000	2	16	2	0	0
Culver	.990	25	189	12	2	11
Fleming	1.000	2	9	0	0	1
Ford	.994	19	167	9	1	16
Refsnyder	1.000	9	72	1	0	4
Solano	1.000	1	6	0	0	0

Second Base	PCT	G	PO	A	E	DP
Avelino	1.000	3	3	5	0	2
Castro	.923	4	5	7	1	0
Culver	.926	12	10	15	2	2
Diaz	1.000	13	13	32	0	5
Fleming	.950	12	16	22	2	8
Refsnyder	.967	18	28	30	2	8
Solano	.975	59	76	154	6	39
Tejada	.952	8	18	22	2	6
Torres	.938	5	6	9	1	2
Wade	.986	13	27	42	1	12

Third Base	PCT	G	PO	A	E	DP
Andujar	.943	57	30	85	7	5
Avelino	1.000	6	5	8	0	1
Culver	.919	17	8	26	3	3
Fleming	1.000	1	2	1	0	0
Solano	.985	28	16	49	1	7
Tejada	.917	14	7	26	3	1
Torres	.917	9	4	18	2	4
Wade	.913	12	9	33	4	5

Shortstop	PCT	G	PO	A	E	DP
Avelino	.975	11	14	25	1	6
Culver	.956	46	55	119	8	24
Diaz	.981	15	22	29	1	5
Tejada	.949	12	14	23	2	6
Torres	.947	9	11	25	2	5
Wade	.953	54	75	126	10	20

Outfield	PCT	G	PO	A	E	DP
Austin	1.000	4	10	1	0	0
Bolasky	1.000	3	7	0	0	0
Cave	1.000	66	129	1	0	0
Culver	1.000	5	5	1	0	0
Ellsbury	1.000	1	1	0	0	0
Fowler	.970	65	130	1	4	0
Frazier	.965	67	107	4	4	2
Hicks	1.000	3	6	0	0	0
McKinney	.960	52	92	3	4	0
Payton	.968	51	89	3	3	0
Refsnyder	1.000	7	17	0	0	0
Wade	1.000	6	13	1	0	1
Williams	1.000	99	223	6	0	0

TRENTON THUNDER

DOUBLE-A

EASTERN LEAGUE

Batting	B-T	HT	WT	DOB	AVG	vLH	vRH	G	AB	R	H	2B	3B	HR	RBI	BB	HBP	SH	SF	SO	SB	CS	SLG	OBP
Andujar, Miguel	R-R	6-0	215	3-2-95	.312	.304	.315	67	253	30	79	23	1	7	52	12	2	0	5	38	2	3	.494	.342
Austin, Tyler	R-R	6-2	220	9-6-91	.429	.000	.462	5	14	5	6	1	2	0	1	2	1	0	0	2	0	0	.786	.529
Avelino, Abiatal	R-R	5-11	205	2-14-95	.270	.255	.274	69	230	35	62	12	4	3	28	14	2	1	2	33	4	0	.396	.315
Bichette, Dante	R-R	6-1	210	9-26-92	.262	.227	.275	72	244	27	64	8	1	4	33	35	0	0	2	49	0	1	.353	.352
Bolasky, Devyn	L-L	5-11	185	1-24-93	.217	.191	.221	43	143	18	31	6	3	0	17	11	1	3	1	31	1	0	.301	.276
Castillo, Wilkin	B-R	6-0	215	6-1-84	.209	.250	.205	14	43	6	9	4	0	1	3	3	0	1	0	2	0	0	.372	.261
Castro, Starlin	R-R	6-2	230	3-24-90	.286	.333	.250	2	7	0	2	1	0	0	0	0	0	0	0	2	0	0	.429	.286
Cave, Jake	L-L	6-0	200	12-4-92	.266	.286	.258	31	128	19	34	13	2	5	18	10	0	1	1	33	1	0	.516	.317
Conde, Vicente	R-R	6-0	195	10-13-93	.133	.167	.123	31	83	12	11	4	0	1	11	16	2	1	0	31	1	0	.217	.287
Cooper, Garrett	R-R	6-6	230	12-25-90	.400	.667	.286	6	20	5	8	1	0	1	2	3	0	0	0	6	0	0	.600	.478
Crawford, Rashad	L-R	6-3	225	10-15-93	.210	.180	.221	106	376	57	79	13	4	5	32	28	3	9	3	92	16	4	.306	.268
Diaz, Francisco	B-R	5-11	185	3-21-90	.228	.265	.211	46	158	17	36	5	0	0	14	10	1	2	1	24	0	0	.260	.277
Estrada, Thairo	R-R	5-10	185	2-22-96	.301	.252	.317	122	495	72	149	19	4	6	48	34	8	1	4	56	8	11	.392	.353
Fleming, Billy	R-R	6-1	210	9-20-92	.255	.261	.253	76	259	41	66	12	3	9	51	19	4	0	7	35	3	2	.429	.308

Ford, Mike	L-R	6-0	225	7-4-92	.272	.273	.271	101	335	61	91	19	1	13	65	76	4	0	2	56	1	0	.451	.410
Hendrix, Jeff	L-R	6-0	195	7-16-93	.333	.250	.364	32	120	12	40	3	1	0	3	13	5	1	1	25	5	1	.375	.417
Hicks, Aaron	B-R	6-1	202	10-2-89	.250	—	.250	2	8	3	2	1	0	1	2	1	0	0	0	1	0	0	.750	.333
Jackson, Jhalan	R-R	6-4	240	2-12-93	.302	.304	.302	29	86	11	26	5	1	3	12	14	3	0	0	27	1	2	.488	.418
Mateo, Jorge	R-R	6-0	190	6-23-95	.300	.333	.287	30	120	26	36	9	3	4	26	15	2	1	2	32	11	7	.525	.381
McBroom, Ryan	R-L	6-3	240	4-9-92	.257	.297	.243	38	140	11	36	5	0	4	16	13	2	0	1	35	1	1	.379	.327
2-team total (96 New Hampshire)					.247	.316	.222	134	486	56	120	24	0	16	70	43	14	0	5	112	1	3	.395	.323
McKinney, Billy	L-L	6-1	205	8-23-94	.250	.242	.253	69	232	34	58	16	4	6	29	30	5	2	7	45	2	1	.431	.339
Othman, Sharif	B-R	5-11	190	3-23-89	.275	.286	.273	15	51	4	14	2	0	2	5	1	0	0	0	12	0	0	.431	.289
Payton, Mark	L-L	5-8	190	12-7-91	.179	.177	.180	14	56	6	10	1	3	0	1	2	0	0	1	16	0	1	.304	.203
Polo, Tito	R-R	5-10	195	8-23-94	.382	.333	.400	14	55	14	21	4	1	1	17	6	2	1	0	8	7	1	.546	.460
Saez, Jorge	R-R	5-10	200	8-28-90	.249	.286	.237	67	201	32	50	8	0	9	34	33	1	0	5	63	1	0	.423	.350
Snyder, Matt	L-R	6-5	230	6-17-90	.167	.000	.182	3	12	0	2	0	0	0	1	0	0	0	0	3	0	0	.167	.167
Solak, Nick	R-R	5-11	175	1-11-95	.286	.424	.233	30	119	16	34	9	1	2	9	10	1	1	1	24	1	1	.429	.344
Torres, Gleyber	R-R	6-1	175	12-13-96	.273	.275	.272	32	121	22	33	10	1	5	18	17	1	0	0	21	5	4	.496	.367
Wilson, Wes	R-R	6-0	220	8-18-89	.050	.167	.000	6	20	0	1	0	0	0	0	0	0	0	0	8	0	0	.050	.050
Zehner, Zack	R-R	6-4	215	8-8-92	.260	.248	.264	128	431	63	112	23	4	11	68	64	1	3	2	125	8	3	.408	.355

Pitching	B-T	HT	WT	DOB	W	L	ERA	G	GS	CG	SV	IP	H	R	ER	HR	BB	SO	AVG	vLH	vRH	K/9	BB/9
Acevedo, Domingo	R-R	6-7	250	3-6-94	5	1	2.38	14	14	1	0	79	65	23	21	8	17	82	.223	.216	.229	9.30	1.93
Adams, Chance	R-R	6-1	210	8-10-94	4	0	1.03	6	6	0	0	35	23	6	4	2	15	32	.183	.204	.167	8.23	3.86
Brewer, Colten	R-R	6-4	230	10-29-92	3	1	1.31	29	0	0	11	41	37	10	6	0	11	43	.231	.239	.226	9.36	2.40
Camarena, Daniel	L-L	6-0	210	11-9-92	2	4	3.81	15	15	1	0	83	89	46	35	5	20	48	.276	.309	.266	5.23	2.18
Carroll, Cody	R-R	6-5	210	10-15-92	2	5	2.66	26	0	0	5	47	36	15	14	4	22	59	.212	.160	.253	11.22	4.18
Carter, Will	L-R	6-3	195	1-18-93	3	1	3.26	15	6	0	0	47	53	19	17	3	13	23	.285	.268	.298	4.40	2.49
Chapman, Aroldis	L-L	6-4	212	2-28-88	0	0	13.50	1	1	0	0	1	0	1	1	0	2	2	.000	.000	.000	27.00	27.00
Cortes, Nestor	R-L	5-11	205	12-10-94	5	0	2.60	18	7	0	0	52	35	15	15	3	20	45	.192	.224	.177	7.79	3.46
Coshow, Cale	R-R	6-5	270	7-16-92	2	5	3.81	41	0	0	15	54	63	30	23	4	22	72	.288	.247	.315	11.93	3.64
Espinal, Raynel	R-R	6-3	199	10-6-91	2	0	0.46	9	2	0	0	20	7	2	1	1	8	28	.105	.147	.061	12.81	3.66
Feyereisen, J.P.	R-R	6-2	215	2-7-93	0	0	2.70	13	0	0	3	20	14	6	6	2	8	18	.206	.257	.152	8.10	3.60
Frare, Caleb	L-L	6-1	220	7-8-93	2	2	4.28	24	0	0	0	34	19	16	16	2	34	42	.173	.188	.167	11.23	9.09
German, Domingo	R-R	6-2	175	8-4-92	1	4	3.00	6	6	1	0	33	32	13	11	4	10	38	.248	.300	.186	10.36	2.73
Gomez, Anyelo	R-R	6-1	185	3-1-93	3	1	1.72	17	1	0	0	37	26	10	7	1	11	43	.202	.203	.200	10.55	2.70
Graham, J.R.	R-R	5-11	195	1-14-90	0	0	0.00	5	0	0	1	9	4	0	0	0	1	9	.125	.077	.158	8.68	0.96
Haynes, Kyle	R-R	6-2	200	2-11-91	1	0	0.00	3	1	0	0	6	6	0	0	0	2	7	.261	.222	.286	11.12	3.18
Herrera, Ronald	R-R	5-11	185	5-3-95	8	0	1.13	9	9	0	0	56	34	10	7	2	12	42	.174	.181	.167	6.75	1.93
Hissong, Travis	R-R	6-0	200	7-19-91	1	1	5.28	11	0	0	1	15	20	10	9	2	12	21	.318	.458	.231	12.33	7.04
Koerner, Brody	R-R	6-2	220	10-17-93	6	3	4.08	12	12	0	0	71	84	32	32	7	20	45	.292	.299	.286	5.73	2.55
Lail, Brady	R-R	6-2	205	8-9-93	1	0	2.13	2	2	0	0	13	12	3	3	0	4	6	.267	.320	.200	4.26	2.84
Littell, Zack	R-R	6-4	220	10-5-95	5	0	2.05	7	7	0	0	44	37	14	10	3	8	52	.224	.233	.219	10.64	1.64
Marsh, Matt	R-R	6-3	210	7-10-91	2	2	3.68	10	0	0	0	15	14	9	6	0	9	16	.233	.167	.278	9.82	5.52
McNamara, Dillon	R-R	6-5	230	10-6-91	0	2	6.17	10	0	0	1	12	13	9	8	2	8	12	.271	.222	.333	9.26	6.17
2-team total (8 Richmond)					0	5	5.73	18	6	0	1	33	32	23	21	5	20	23	.250	.156	.343	6.27	5.45
Mesa, Jose	R-R	6-4	230	8-13-93	4	0	0.79	8	5	0	0	34	15	3	3	0	17	39	.132	.154	.102	10.22	4.46
Pena, Jose	R-R	6-0	190	3-22-91	0	0	1.50	2	0	0	0	6	2	1	1	1	0	6	.100	.000	.333	9.00	0.00
Pinder, Branden	R-R	6-4	215	1-26-89	1	0	0.00	3	0	0	1	4	3	0	0	0	4	3	.200	.000	.300	6.23	8.31
Ramirez, Yefry	R-R	6-2	215	11-28-93	10	3	3.41	18	18	2	0	92	78	38	35	9	38	91	.229	.247	.217	8.87	3.70
2-team total (6 Bowie)					15	3	3.47	24	24	3	0	124	105	51	48	15	49	117	.232	.290	.180	8.47	3.55
Reeves, James	R-L	6-3	195	6-7-93	2	0	0.00	6	0	0	2	10	7	0	0	0	2	10	.194	.222	.185	8.71	1.74
Rogers, Josh	L-L	6-3	210	7-10-94	4	2	4.62	7	7	0	0	39	35	20	20	5	8	29	.240	.243	.239	6.69	1.85
Rumbelow, Nick	R-R	6-0	190	9-6-91	0	0	2.38	8	0	0	1	11	5	3	3	0	3	15	.128	.000	.200	11.91	2.38
Rutckyj, Evan	L-R	6-5	225	1-31-92	0	0	13.50	1	0	0	0	1	2	1	1	0	0	1	.500	.500	.500	13.50	0.00
Ruth, Eric	R-R	6-0	195	9-26-90	0	2	8.44	4	0	0	0	5	5	5	5	1	4	10	.238	.333	.111	16.88	6.75
Schwaab, Andrew	R-R	6-1	210	2-8-93	2	0	2.57	13	0	0	2	21	21	6	6	0	8	21	.256	.294	.229	9.00	3.43
Sheffield, Justus	L-L	5-11	200	5-13-96	7	6	3.18	17	17	1	0	93	94	43	33	14	33	82	.258	.217	.276	7.91	3.18
Smith, Caleb	R-L	6-2	205	7-28-91	0	0	3.38	1	0	0	0	3	1	1	1	1	3	5	.143	.200	.000	16.88	10.13
Sosebee, David	R-R	6-1	200	8-25-93	0	0	6.35	3	0	0	1	6	12	4	4	1	2	7	.429	.444	.400	11.12	3.18
Tarpley, Stephen	R-L	6-1	220	2-17-93	1	0	3.48	4	0	0	0	10	10	4	4	0	2	6	.278	.182	.320	5.23	1.74
Tate, Dillon	R-R	6-2	195	5-1-94	1	2	3.24	4	4	1	0	25	23	9	9	3	9	17	.253	.241	.270	6.12	3.24
Wotherspoon, Matt	R-R	6-2	215	10-6-91	2	1	1.67	15	0	0	3	27	21	5	5	2	7	33	.214	.250	.185	11.00	2.33

Fielding

Catcher	PCT	G	PO	A	E	DP	PB
Castillo	1.000	14	96	6	0	0	0
Diaz	.991	46	420	26	4	3	3
Othman	.980	14	97	3	2	0	1
Saez	.998	66	488	52	1	5	3
Wilson	.982	6	54	1	1	0	0

First Base	PCT	G	PO	A	E	DP
Austin	1.000	2	10	1	0	0
Bichette	.984	23	167	16	3	22
Conde	1.000	5	21	6	0	1
Cooper	1.000	2	16	0	0	1
Fleming	1.000	26	185	16	0	12
Ford	.989	55	411	30	5	42
McBroom	.996	32	243	22	1	21
Saez	.923	1	12	0	1	0
Zehner	1.000	2	17	0	0	2

Second Base	PCT	G	PO	A	E	DP
Avelino	.957	39	69	109	8	25
Castro	1.000	2	7	6	0	4
Conde	.978	21	45	45	2	11
Estrada	1.000	23	41	50	0	10
Fleming	.983	17	22	35	1	8
Mateo	.929	6	11	15	2	5
Solak	.950	30	47	87	7	19
Torres	1.000	5	8	8	0	6

Third Base	PCT	G	PO	A	E	DP
Andujar	.917	58	37	73	10	7
Avelino	.920	9	3	20	2	1
Bichette	.918	39	22	68	8	7
Conde	1.000	5	3	3	0	0
Estrada	1.000	3	2	4	0	0
Fleming	.932	21	10	31	3	5
Ford	1.000	1	1	2	0	0
Torres	1.000	6	3	11	0	2

Shortstop	PCT	G	PO	A	E	DP
Avelino	.938	16	19	41	4	8
Conde	.000	1	0	0	0	0
Estrada	.952	90	106	234	17	59
Mateo	.962	17	25	51	3	6
Torres	1.000	19	30	49	0	8

Outfield	PCT	G	PO	A	E	DP
Austin	1.000	1	2	0	0	0
Bolasky	1.000	40	63	5	0	0
Cave	1.000	24	40	2	0	1
Crawford	.987	102	224	5	3	0
Hendrix	1.000	32	57	0	0	0
Jackson	.941	22	31	1	2	1
Mateo	1.000	7	16	0	0	0
McKinney	.981	65	153	5	3	2
Payton	.962	11	24	1	1	0
Polo	1.000	13	18	1	0	0
Zehner	.979	109	183	5	4	0

TAMPA YANKEES — *HIGH CLASS A*

FLORIDA STATE LEAGUE

Batting	B-T	HT	WT	DOB	AVG	vLH	vRH	G	AB	R	H	2B	3B	HR	RBI	BB	HBP	SH	SF	SO	SB	CS	SLG	OBP
Afenir, Austin	R-R	6-2	215	2-15-92	.143	.143	.143	12	35	2	5	0	0	0	0	2	1	0	0	11	0	0	.143	.211
Aguilar, Angel	R-R	6-0	170	6-13-95	.199	.205	.196	41	141	19	28	5	0	3	20	7	1	4	1	39	1	3	.298	.240
Alvarez, Mandy	R-R	6-1	205	7-14-94	.228	.308	.200	41	149	8	34	5	1	0	10	3	1	1	0	18	3	1	.275	.248
Amburgey, Trey	R-R	6-2	210	10-24-94	.236	.287	.218	121	461	63	109	19	3	14	57	33	8	0	4	115	13	3	.382	.296
Aune, Austin	R-L	6-2	190	9-6-93	.154	.105	.168	51	175	13	27	8	0	2	6	17	0	2	1	78	1	2	.234	.228
Avelino, Abiatal	R-R	5-11	205	2-14-95	.219	.200	.227	9	32	1	7	1	0	0	2	2	0	0	0	5	4	0	.250	.265
Barrios, Daniel	R-R	5-11	183	4-18-95	.200	.300	.133	13	50	4	10	0	0	0	2	4	0	0	0	10	0	0	.200	.259
Bird, Greg	L-R	6-4	220	11-9-92	.353	.000	.429	6	17	2	6	2	0	0	3	5	0	0	0	1	0	0	.471	.500
Bolasky, Devyn	L-L	5-11	185	1-24-93	.260	.167	.273	14	50	7	13	3	1	1	7	4	0	2	1	10	0	0	.420	.309
Conde, Vicente	R-R	6-0	195	10-13-93	.273	1.000	.200	3	11	2	3	1	0	1	2	1	0	0	0	7	0	1	.636	.333
Diaz, Cesar	B-R	5-10	165	4-12-93	.000	.000	.000	5	13	1	0	0	0	0	0	3	0	0	0	3	0	1	.000	.188
Diaz, Francisco	B-R	5-11	185	3-21-90	.364	.000	.421	6	22	2	8	2	0	1	7	2	1	0	0	1	1	0	.591	.440
Fleming, Billy	R-R	6-1	210	9-20-92	.217	.400	.167	7	23	1	5	2	0	0	4	1	0	0	0	3	0	0	.304	.250
Florial, Estevan	L-R	6-1	185	11-25-97	.303	.308	.302	19	76	13	23	2	2	2	14	9	0	0	2	24	6	1	.461	.368
Gittens, Chris	R-R	6-4	250	2-9-94	.266	.260	.268	73	248	35	66	12	0	13	43	37	5	0	0	79	1	1	.472	.372
Gregorius, Didi	L-R	6-3	205	2-18-90	.444	—	.444	5	18	2	8	1	0	1	2	1	0	0	0	1	1	0	.667	.474
Hendrix, Jeff	L-R	6-0	195	7-16-93	.271	.260	.276	67	236	28	64	7	1	2	12	47	8	2	1	65	13	7	.335	.408
Holder, Kyle	L-R	6-1	185	5-25-94	.271	.213	.289	104	406	41	110	16	2	4	44	26	2	6	2	62	4	3	.350	.317
Holliday, Matt	R-R	6-4	240	1-15-80	.240	.000	.273	7	25	1	6	1	0	0	5	3	1	0	1	5	0	0	.280	.333
Jackson, Jhalan	R-R	6-4	240	2-12-93	.226	.157	.250	65	199	19	45	9	0	8	33	23	2	1	3	65	2	2	.392	.308
Katoh, Gosuke	L-R	6-2	180	10-8-94	.293	.280	.298	84	300	44	88	20	3	6	43	40	1	3	2	72	11	7	.440	.376
Lynch, Tim	L-R	6-2	220	6-3-93	.310	.146	.367	57	213	28	66	15	1	13	40	17	3	0	1	42	0	3	.573	.368
Mateo, Jorge	R-R	6-0	190	6-23-95	.240	.282	.226	69	275	39	66	16	8	4	11	16	3	2	1	79	28	3	.400	.288
Othman, Sharif	B-R	5-11	190	3-23-89	.208	.271	.185	57	178	15	37	5	0	5	17	10	3	1	2	39	2	2	.320	.259
Palma, Alexander	R-R	6-0	201	10-18-95	.278	.180	.317	47	173	29	48	15	1	3	19	11	1	1	1	25	5	5	.428	.323
Park, Hoy Jun	L-R	6-1	175	4-7-96	.213	.333	.190	24	94	20	20	6	1	1	5	13	1	0	0	14	7	0	.330	.315
Polo, Tito	R-R	5-10	195	8-23-94	.289	.261	.301	60	235	42	68	10	6	4	20	16	5	2	1	62	20	6	.434	.346
Saez, Jorge	R-R	5-10	200	8-28-90	.222	—	.222	2	9	0	2	0	0	0	2	0	0	0	0	3	0	0	.222	.222
Sands, Donny	R-R	6-2	190	5-16-96	.307	.444	.283	17	62	9	19	5	0	2	10	5	0	0	1	10	1	1	.484	.353
Scott, Jordan	B-R	6-0	210	5-23-97	.250	.000	.333	1	4	0	1	1	0	0	0	0	0	0	0	2	0	0	.500	.250
Skinner, Keith	L-R	6-1	200	4-14-94	.139	.100	.154	9	36	1	5	1	0	0	1	2	0	0	0	8	0	0	.167	.184
Snyder, Matt	L-R	6-5	230	6-17-90	.239	.308	.224	22	71	6	17	6	0	3	11	5	2	0	0	22	0	0	.451	.308
Solak, Nick	R-R	5-11	175	1-11-95	.301	.326	.291	100	346	56	104	17	4	10	44	53	4	0	3	76	13	4	.460	.397
Surum, Ricky	R-R	5-10	170	12-7-94	.000	.000	.000	1	4	0	0	0	0	0	0	0	0	0	0	1	0	0	.000	.000
Wilson, Wes	R-R	6-0	220	8-18-89	.179	.133	.194	39	123	9	22	6	0	0	9	7	2	1	1	33	1	0	.228	.233

Pitching	B-T	HT	WT	DOB	W	L	ERA	G	GS	CG	SV	IP	H	R	ER	HR	BB	SO	AVG	vLH	vRH	K/9	BB/9
Abreu, Albert	R-R	6-2	175	9-26-95	1	3	4.19	9	9	0	0	34	33	17	16	2	15	31	.252	.254	.250	8.13	3.93
Acevedo, Domingo	R-R	6-7	250	3-6-94	0	4	4.57	7	7	0	0	41	49	29	21	5	9	52	.290	.316	.269	11.32	1.96
Brewer, Colten	R-R	6-4	230	10-29-92	0	0	0.00	6	0	0	2	9	3	0	0	0	1	15	.091	.000	.120	14.46	0.96
Carroll, Cody	R-R	6-5	210	10-15-92	1	0	2.25	13	0	0	2	20	10	7	5	1	8	30	.141	.160	.130	13.50	3.60
Clarkin, Ian	L-L	6-2	215	2-14-95	4	5	2.62	15	14	0	0	76	71	24	22	4	25	58	.254	.329	.226	6.90	2.97
Cortes, Nestor	R-L	5-11	205	12-10-94	0	0	2.08	1	0	0	0	4	6	1	1	1	1	3	.333	.000	.400	6.23	2.08
Espinal, Raynel	R-R	6-3	199	10-6-91	0	1	1.69	8	1	0	1	16	9	3	3	1	3	21	.173	.143	.194	11.81	1.69
Foley, Jordan	R-R	6-4	215	7-12-93	1	1	2.32	25	0	0	6	31	26	9	8	1	18	49	.220	.209	.227	14.23	5.23
Frare, Caleb	L-L	6-1	220	7-8-93	1	2	3.72	15	0	0	1	29	29	16	12	4	18	36	.282	.306	.269	11.17	5.59
Frawley, Matt	R-R	6-1	195	8-8-95	1	1	2.21	12	0	0	1	20	20	5	5	0	6	20	.256	.125	.348	8.85	2.66
Gomez, Anyelo	R-R	6-1	185	3-1-93	2	2	2.55	10	0	0	2	18	15	5	5	1	6	19	.221	.174	.244	9.68	3.06
Green, Chad	L-R	6-3	210	5-24-91	0	1	2.25	1	0	0	0	4	2	1	1	1	0	5	.154	.200	.125	11.25	0.00
Harris, Hobie	R-R	6-3	200	6-23-93	2	3	2.89	16	0	0	1	28	26	9	9	2	15	28	.239	.233	.242	9.00	4.82
Harvey, Joe	R-R	6-2	220	1-9-92	1	0	1.05	18	0	0	4	26	13	3	3	2	8	29	.148	.146	.149	10.17	2.81
Haynes, Kyle	R-R	6-2	200	2-11-91	0	0	0.00	1	1	0	0	4	1	0	0	0	1	3	.091	.000	.167	6.75	2.25
Hebert, Chaz	L-L	6-2	180	9-4-92	2	1	5.27	7	5	0	0	27	30	19	16	2	9	19	.283	.276	.286	6.26	2.96
Hissong, Travis	R-R	6-0	200	7-19-91	1	0	3.97	7	0	0	3	11	9	6	5	2	2	13	.205	.278	.154	10.32	1.59
Keller, Brian	R-R	6-3	170	6-21-94	5	3	2.90	10	10	2	0	62	59	21	20	2	11	67	.253	.272	.239	9.73	1.60
Koerner, Brody	R-R	6-2	220	10-17-93	4	1	2.45	6	6	1	0	37	32	12	10	2	9	26	.229	.233	.224	6.38	2.21
Lane, Trevor	L-L	5-11	185	4-26-94	2	2	3.15	13	0	0	1	20	21	11	7	1	2	20	.259	.233	.275	9.00	0.90
Littell, Zack	R-R	6-4	220	10-5-95	9	1	1.77	13	11	2	0	71	65	17	14	4	15	57	.251	.242	.259	7.19	1.89
Marsh, Matt	R-R	6-3	210	7-10-91	1	0	0.00	5	0	0	0	7	2	2	0	1	1	12	.083	.091	.077	15.43	1.29
Martin, Chad	R-R	6-4	215	1-2-94	1	0	0.00	2	0	0	1	3	1	0	0	0	2	0	.125	.000	.200	0.00	6.00
McNamara, Dillon	R-R	6-5	230	10-6-91	1	0	1.17	16	0	0	8	23	12	3	3	0	4	17	.154	.158	.150	6.65	1.57
Mendez, Bringnel	R-R	6-0	239	1-31-94	1	0	0.00	1	0	0	0	3	1	0	0	0	1	1	.100	.000	.167	3.00	3.00
Mesa, Jose	R-R	6-4	230	8-13-93	1	1	2.72	21	3	0	3	50	33	15	15	4	15	62	.188	.208	.172	11.23	2.72
Montgomery, Jordan	L-L	6-6	225	12-27-92	0	0	0.00	1	1	0	0	5	3	1	0	0	1	8	.177	.000	.231	14.40	1.80

Morris, Christian	R-R	6-4	195	1-23-94	0	0	0.00	1	0	0	0	4	3	0	0	0	0	2	.200	.143	.250	4.50	0.00
Palladino, David	R-R	6-8	235	3-15-93	1	0	0.00	2	0	0	0	4	2	0	0	0	1	5	.133	.000	.167	11.25	2.25
Pena, Jose	R-R	6-0	190	3-22-91	3	2	2.47	27	0	0	1	51	35	14	14	5	27	64	.191	.275	.140	11.29	4.76
Reeves, James	R-L	6-3	195	6-7-93	2	0	2.52	20	0	0	1	36	34	14	10	0	7	41	.246	.152	.294	10.35	1.77
Roeder, Josh	R-R	6-0	175	12-2-92	0	0	6.48	5	0	0	0	8	8	6	6	1	2	7	.258	.444	.182	7.56	2.16
Rogers, Josh	L-L	6-3	210	7-10-94	4	3	2.22	8	8	0	0	53	45	16	13	3	8	51	.231	.319	.203	8.72	1.37
Rosa, Adonis	R-R	6-1	160	11-17-94	3	0	4.32	3	3	0	0	17	15	8	8	1	4	16	.242	.267	.219	8.64	2.16
Schwaab, Andrew	R-R	6-1	210	2-8-93	4	2	3.93	26	0	0	5	37	36	16	16	1	12	32	.259	.304	.229	7.85	2.95
Sosebee, David	R-R	6-1	200	8-25-93	0	0	0.00	1	0	0	0	1	1	0	0	0	0	1	.250	.000	1.000	9.00	0.00
Swanson, Erik	R-R	6-3	220	9-4-93	7	3	3.95	20	20	0	0	100	115	46	44	10	14	84	.291	.310	.279	7.53	1.26
Tarpley, Stephen	R-L	6-1	220	2-17-93	6	0	0.00	14	0	0	0	31	8	0	0	0	16	36	.083	.083	.082	10.57	4.70
Tate, Dillon	R-R	6-2	195	5-1-94	6	0	2.62	9	9	0	0	58	48	19	17	4	15	46	.221	.213	.229	7.10	2.31
Widener, Taylor	L-R	6-0	195	10-24-94	7	8	3.39	27	27	0	0	119	87	53	45	5	50	129	.206	.218	.196	9.73	3.77

Fielding

Catcher	PCT	G	PO	A	E	DP	PB
Afenir	.989	12	79	7	1	0	1
Diaz	1.000	6	61	2	0	2	0
Othman	.988	57	474	41	6	4	3
Saez	1.000	2	33	2	0	0	1
Sands	.984	17	162	18	3	2	3
Skinner	1.000	9	79	10	0	2	0
Wilson	.979	38	285	36	7	0	2

First Base	PCT	G	PO	A	E	DP
Alvarez	.976	15	116	7	3	11
Bird	.968	4	28	2	1	3
Gittens	.987	57	424	35	6	24
Holliday	1.000	1	3	2	0	0
Katoh	.994	19	145	12	1	7
Lynch	1.000	40	327	35	0	30
Snyder	.987	9	76	1	1	6

Second Base	PCT	G	PO	A	E	DP
Avelino	1.000	2	4	3	0	0
Barrios	1.000	1	2	3	0	1
Conde	1.000	1	0	6	0	0
Fleming	1.000	3	5	3	0	1
Holder	.962	14	19	32	2	5
Katoh	1.000	14	26	37	0	8
Mateo	1.000	2	2	1	0	0
Park	.979	11	17	29	1	2
Solak	.974	92	144	230	10	42

Third Base	PCT	G	PO	A	E	DP
Aguilar	.931	27	22	32	4	1
Alvarez	.920	26	8	38	4	2
Avelino	.950	8	4	15	1	1
Barrios	.923	10	6	18	2	2
Conde	1.000	1	0	3	0	1
Fleming	1.000	4	1	6	0	0
Holder	.973	26	11	60	2	5
Katoh	.978	43	24	65	2	3

Shortstop	PCT	G	PO	A	E	DP
Aguilar	.968	13	23	38	2	11
Conde	1.000	1	2	3	0	1
Gregorius	.923	4	5	7	1	0
Holder	.964	64	77	137	8	25
Katoh	.957	7	10	12	1	0
Mateo	.947	42	60	100	9	19
Park	.976	13	19	22	1	5

Outfield	PCT	G	PO	A	E	DP
Amburgey	.989	106	165	7	2	1
Aune	.957	45	86	4	4	3
Bolasky	1.000	14	25	0	0	0
Diaz	1.000	5	8	0	0	0
Florial	1.000	18	47	0	0	0
Hendrix	1.000	61	121	0	0	0
Jackson	.988	45	78	4	1	2
Katoh	1.000	1	2	0	0	0
Mateo	.981	22	51	1	1	0
Palma	.988	44	74	5	1	0
Polo	.990	50	93	2	1	0
Scott	.000	1	0	0	0	0

CHARLESTON RIVERDOGS — LOW CLASS A

SOUTH ATLANTIC LEAGUE

Batting	B-T	HT	WT	DOB	AVG	vLH	vRH	G	AB	R	H	2B	3B	HR	RBI	BB	HBP	SH	SF	SO	SB	CS	SLG	OBP
Aguilar, Angel	R-R	6-0	170	6-13-95	.265	.270	.261	66	253	23	67	16	1	3	32	15	3	0	4	46	6	5	.372	.309
Alvarez, Mandy	R-R	6-1	205	7-14-94	.261	.318	.227	35	119	11	31	8	0	0	11	8	1	0	1	19	0	0	.328	.310
Blaser, Dalton	L-L	6-1	200	1-31-94	.277	.238	.288	31	101	16	28	9	0	3	9	10	2	0	0	19	0	0	.455	.354
Bolasky, Devyn	L-L	5-11	185	1-24-93	.444	.500	.400	3	9	0	4	0	0	0	0	1	0	0	0	2	1	1	.444	.500
Cabrera, Oswaldo	B-R	5-10	145	3-1-99	.242	.217	.252	89	318	37	77	11	0	4	37	26	1	4	4	46	6	0	.315	.298
Castillo, Diego	R-R	6-0	170	10-28-97	.264	.285	.254	118	463	66	122	15	3	1	42	31	1	13	2	51	9	5	.315	.310
Conde, Vicente	R-R	6-0	195	10-13-93	.130	.111	.137	22	69	6	9	4	0	1	3	11	0	1	0	23	0	0	.232	.250
Florial, Estevan	L-R	6-1	185	11-25-97	.297	.313	.287	91	344	64	102	21	5	11	43	41	2	0	2	124	17	7	.483	.373
Garcia, Dermis	R-R	6-3	200	1-7-98	.227	.191	.236	30	110	12	25	6	1	8	20	14	0	0	1	42	0	0	.518	.312
Gilliam, Isiah	B-R	6-3	220	7-23-96	.275	.317	.254	125	444	80	122	33	4	15	85	55	5	0	7	111	9	5	.469	.356
Hess, Chris	R-R	6-2	195	12-3-94	.140	.167	.121	19	57	8	8	2	2	0	5	3	2	0	0	19	0	0	.246	.210
Lidge, Ryan	B-R	6-2	216	10-27-94	.383	.583	.314	16	47	2	18	1	0	0	5	9	2	0	0	9	0	0	.404	.500
Molina, Leonardo	R-R	6-2	180	7-31-97	.186	.200	.179	23	86	5	16	3	1	0	7	2	0	0	1	23	2	2	.244	.202
Navas, Eduardo	B-R	5-10	180	4-5-96	.211	.204	.214	49	161	11	34	7	0	1	12	3	2	0	1	46	0	0	.273	.234
Olivares, Pablo	R-R	6-0	160	1-27-98	.160	.083	.179	36	119	10	19	3	0	1	6	9	3	1	2	40	4	1	.210	.233
Palma, Alexander	R-R	6-0	201	10-18-95	.296	.400	.235	7	27	6	8	2	0	1	4	1	0	0	0	7	0	0	.482	.321
Park, Hoy Jun	L-R	6-1	175	4-7-96	.262	.231	.277	86	324	53	85	6	5	6	34	39	9	1	0	63	18	7	.367	.358
Ruta, Ben	L-R	6-3	195	6-8-94	.273	.297	.259	53	172	24	47	3	1	0	13	13	0	1	1	24	11	5	.302	.323
Rutherford, Blake	L-R	6-3	195	5-2-97	.281	.265	.290	71	274	41	77	20	2	2	30	25	2	0	3	55	9	4	.391	.342
2-team total (30 Kannapolis)					.260	.364	.180	101	396	52	103	25	2	2	35	38	2	1	3	76	10	4	.349	.326
Sands, Donny	R-R	6-2	190	5-16-96	.269	.333	.237	76	286	31	77	17	0	2	45	21	3	1	3	53	0	5	.350	.323
Scott, Jordan	B-R	6-0	210	5-23-97	.000	.000	.000	2	7	0	0	0	0	0	0	1	1	0	0	5	0	0	.000	.222
Sensley, Steven	L-L	6-1	220	9-6-95	.259	.000	.296	21	81	10	21	5	0	4	22	5	1	0	0	20	0	0	.469	.310
Skinner, Keith	L-R	6-1	200	4-14-94	.250	.000	.500	1	4	1	1	0	0	0	2	0	0	0	0	0	0	0	.250	.250
Thompson-Williams, Dom	L-L	6-0	185	4-21-95	.188	.231	.179	23	80	6	15	2	0	0	6	9	0	1	0	15	2	2	.213	.270
Vidal, Carlos	L-L	5-11	160	11-29-95	.308	.246	.332	69	253	32	78	13	2	1	27	17	3	1	0	42	5	5	.387	.359
Wagner, Brandon	L-R	6-0	210	8-24-95	.277	.200	.307	110	372	55	103	20	1	7	51	57	7	0	3	116	1	0	.393	.380

Pitching	B-T	HT	WT	DOB	W	L	ERA	G	GS	CG	SV	IP	H	R	ER	HR	BB	SO	AVG	vLH	vRH	K/9	BB/9
Abreu, Albert	R-R	6-2	175	9-26-95	1	0	1.84	3	2	0	0	15	9	3	3	1	3	22	.180	.238	.138	13.50	1.84
Bristo, Braden	R-R	6-0	180	11-1-94	1	1	3.97	6	0	0	1	11	13	5	5	1	7	10	.302	.429	.241	7.94	5.56
Cedeno, Luis	R-R	5-11	154	7-14-94	6	0	1.00	15	0	0	0	18	12	3	2	1	2	14	.182	.238	.156	7.00	1.00
DeCarr, Austin	R-R	6-3	218	3-14-95	2	1	5.87	13	5	0	0	31	29	22	20	1	29	32	.238	.111	.338	9.39	8.51
Diehl, Phillip	L-L	6-2	180	7-16-94	9	3	3.16	28	5	0	2	85	76	31	30	4	26	101	.238	.207	.250	10.65	2.74

Espinal, Raynel	R-R	6-3	199	10-6-91	2	1	1.16	10	0	0	0	39	22	7	5	1	4	44	.161	.269	.094	10.24	0.93
Frawley, Matt	R-R	6-1	195	8-8-95	2	0	1.00	9	0	0	0	18	18	6	2	0	2	24	.247	.120	.313	12.00	1.00
2-team total (19 West Virginia)					5	1	1.40	28	0	0	3	51	39	13	8	1	6	56	.209	.222	.137	9.82	1.05
Garcia, Rony	R-R	6-3	200	12-19-97	2	3	2.24	11	11	0	0	64	52	22	16	3	15	45	.219	.220	.217	6.30	2.10
Gomez, Anyelo	R-R	6-1	185	3-1-93	0	0	1.93	10	0	0	7	14	10	3	3	0	4	23	.189	.087	.267	14.79	2.57
Green, Nick	R-R	6-1	165	3-25-95	8	9	4.49	26	26	1	0	126	131	74	63	7	39	112	.268	.201	.310	7.98	2.78
Harris, Hobie	R-R	6-3	200	6-23-93	1	0	2.36	18	0	0	1	27	19	8	7	0	8	37	.196	.125	.231	12.49	2.70
Hodson, Chase	R-R	6-1	205	7-10-92	0	0	0.00	5	0	0	1	7	5	1	0	0	3	9	.172	.091	.222	11.05	3.68
Keller, Brian	R-R	6-3	170	6-21-94	6	5	3.29	14	14	2	0	82	77	34	30	4	17	90	.248	.292	.211	9.88	1.87
Lane, Trevor	L-L	5-11	185	4-26-94	4	2	0.79	24	0	0	2	45	29	6	4	0	13	49	.184	.216	.168	9.73	2.58
Mahoney, Kolton	R-R	6-1	195	5-20-92	1	2	1.85	11	0	0	1	24	24	6	5	0	7	26	.253	.262	.245	9.62	2.59
2-team total (18 Greensboro)					6	7	3.56	29	13	0	1	104	106	48	41	10	17	100	.263	.273	.261	8.68	1.48
Morris, Christian	R-R	6-4	195	1-23-94	6	2	2.73	23	1	0	0	53	42	17	16	2	14	58	.212	.191	.223	9.91	2.39
Mundell, Garrett	R-R	6-6	245	2-16-93	1	4	2.64	35	0	0	11	48	34	16	14	2	12	70	.194	.152	.220	13.22	2.27
Nelson, Nick	R-R	6-1	195	12-5-95	3	12	4.56	22	22	0	0	101	103	54	51	5	50	110	.270	.287	.259	9.83	4.47
Orozco, Jio	R-R	6-1	210	8-15-97	3	5	4.95	12	12	0	0	56	61	37	31	3	34	48	.286	.389	.211	7.67	5.43
Perez, Freicer	R-R	6-8	190	3-14-96	10	3	2.84	24	24	0	0	124	96	53	39	5	45	117	.213	.220	.209	8.51	3.27
Rosa, Adonis	R-R	6-1	160	11-17-94	4	3	3.04	21	8	0	2	83	77	35	28	8	14	79	.245	.246	.245	8.57	1.52
Sosebee, David	R-R	6-1	200	8-25-93	2	3	2.20	35	0	0	13	65	50	16	16	0	15	76	.216	.239	.195	10.47	2.07
Trieglaff, Brian	R-R	6-1	190	6-13-94	0	1	2.08	5	0	0	0	9	10	4	2	0	2	8	.278	.267	.286	8.31	2.08
Vargas, Alexander	R-R	6-4	203	7-24-97	2	3	3.17	9	9	0	0	48	41	18	17	6	5	34	.229	.240	.217	6.33	0.93
Wivinis, Matthew	R-R	6-0	170	7-24-93	0	0	0.90	7	0	0	5	10	3	2	1	1	0	14	.091	.250	.040	12.60	0.00

Fielding

Catcher	PCT	G	PO	A	E	DP	PB
Lidge	.994	16	148	20	1	0	2
Navas	.990	49	349	57	4	2	6
Sands	.994	76	700	76	5	4	22
Skinner	1.000	1	7	2	0	0	0

First Base	PCT	G	PO	A	E	DP
Alvarez	1.000	9	74	9	0	1
Blaser	.988	10	79	3	1	10
Conde	.935	6	42	1	3	3
Garcia	1.000	5	43	2	0	3
Gilliam	.976	10	76	6	2	5
Wagner	.988	99	804	52	10	49

Second Base	PCT	G	PO	A	E	DP
Aguilar	1.000	14	27	36	0	7
Cabrera	.962	29	55	73	5	12
Castillo	.977	53	79	138	5	24
Conde	.875	4	6	8	2	2
Hess	.950	6	8	11	1	0
Park	.969	34	44	81	4	16

Third Base	PCT	G	PO	A	E	DP
Aguilar	.950	46	36	79	6	4
Alvarez	.906	22	15	43	6	2
Cabrera	.975	35	27	51	2	4
Castillo	.000	1	0	0	0	0
Conde	1.000	9	6	21	0	0
Garcia	.939	19	13	33	3	3
Hess	1.000	8	3	10	0	2

Shortstop	PCT	G	PO	A	E	DP
Cabrera	.946	24	30	57	5	13
Castillo	.938	65	85	158	16	21
Conde	1.000	1	0	3	0	0
Park	.925	49	68	117	15	19

Outfield	PCT	G	PO	A	E	DP
Blaser	1.000	17	27	1	0	0
Bolasky	1.000	3	4	0	0	0
Conde	.000	1	0	0	0	0
Florial	.976	83	157	6	4	2
Gilliam	.948	84	142	4	8	0
Molina	.875	20	26	2	4	0
Olivares	.970	35	63	2	2	1
Palma	1.000	5	8	2	0	0
Ruta	.985	36	62	2	1	0
Rutherford	.990	63	99	2	1	0
Sensley	.960	14	22	2	1	0
Thompson-Williams	.979	22	47	0	1	0
Vidal	.973	42	67	6	2	1

STATEN ISLAND YANKEES

SHORT SEASON

NEW YORK-PENN LEAGUE

Batting	B-T	HT	WT	DOB	AVG	vLH	vRH	G	AB	R	H	2B	3B	HR	RBI	BB	HBP	SH	SF	SO	SB	CS	SLG	OBP
Argomaniz, Manny	R-R	6-0	200	4-4-93	.257	.294	.241	38	113	15	29	8	0	1	12	14	4	0	1	28	2	2	.354	.356
Barrios, Daniel	R-R	5-11	183	4-18-95	.111	.000	.143	3	9	1	1	1	0	0	2	2	0	0	0	3	0	0	.222	.273
Blaser, Dalton	L-L	6-1	200	1-31-94	.225	.216	.230	36	111	14	25	4	1	1	10	11	2	0	1	17	2	3	.306	.304
Brown, Cody	L-R	5-11	190	4-1-94	.186	.107	.217	37	97	12	18	6	0	2	8	12	1	0	1	28	1	1	.309	.279
Cabrera, Oswaldo	B-R	5-10	145	3-1-99	.289	.333	.270	23	90	12	26	3	1	0	16	4	3	0	1	11	2	1	.344	.337
Coleman, Kendall	L-L	6-4	190	5-22-95	.212	.148	.238	63	208	20	44	12	1	3	25	22	4	1	4	65	2	7	.322	.294
Diaz, Andy	L-L	5-11	190	11-21-95	.195	.222	.186	24	77	10	15	7	0	2	7	4	0	2	0	28	4	0	.364	.235
Diaz, Cesar	B-R	5-10	165	4-12-93	.198	.333	.148	42	111	17	22	4	0	0	6	22	1	1	2	22	8	2	.234	.331
Diaz, Francisco	B-R	5-11	185	3-21-90	.833	.800	1.000	2	6	1	5	0	0	0	2	1	0	0	0	1	0	0	.833	.857
Garcia, Wilkerman	B-R	6-0	176	4-1-98	.222	.208	.228	67	257	27	57	10	3	1	20	12	1	4	3	72	8	9	.296	.256
Gomez, Nelson	R-R	6-1	220	10-8-97	.128	.069	.158	27	86	5	11	1	0	1	5	12	5	0	1	37	0	0	.174	.269
Hess, Chris	R-R	6-2	195	12-3-94	.154	.667	.000	4	13	2	2	1	1	0	0	3	0	0	0	2	0	0	.385	.313
Higashioka, Kyle	R-R	6-1	200	4-20-90	.438	.500	.417	5	16	7	7	2	0	4	8	2	0	0	0	5	0	0	1.313	.500
Krill, Ryan	L-R	6-4	205	3-17-93	.243	.237	.246	49	148	25	36	8	3	2	19	29	3	0	1	36	0	0	.378	.376
Lopez, Jason	R-R	5-9	172	3-16-98	.240	.225	.246	49	150	21	36	6	1	1	10	24	0	1	0	36	2	0	.313	.345
Mateo, Welfrin	R-R	5-10	170	9-8-95	.256	.214	.274	32	90	7	23	4	0	0	10	4	2	1	2	19	3	2	.300	.296
Molina, Leonardo	R-R	6-2	180	7-31-97	.238	.171	.273	28	101	10	24	5	1	0	8	9	0	0	1	29	5	1	.307	.297
Perez, Danienger	R-R	5-10	155	11-6-96	.211	.206	.214	28	90	10	19	2	0	1	9	2	2	2	1	35	1	0	.267	.242
Polonia, Jose	R-R	5-11	175	12-11-95	.258	.286	.250	29	89	2	23	0	0	0	5	11	0	0	1	20	1	3	.258	.337
Reyes, Brian	R-R	6-0	190	6-28-95	.161	.125	.174	11	31	3	5	0	0	0	1	0	0	0	0	8	0	0	.161	.161
Robinson, Timmy	R-R	6-1	225	6-17-94	.219	.220	.218	55	192	27	42	10	0	7	23	20	8	0	0	55	3	3	.380	.318
Skinner, Keith	L-R	6-1	200	4-14-94	.306	.238	.333	21	72	6	22	5	0	0	6	6	0	0	1	10	0	0	.375	.354
Thompson-Williams, D.	L-L	6-0	185	4-21-95	.277	.298	.266	41	141	17	39	7	0	3	22	18	2	1	0	30	7	6	.390	.367
Vidal, Carlos	L-L	5-11	160	11-29-95	.294	.200	.333	6	17	2	5	1	0	0	4	3	2	1	0	4	0	1	.353	.455

Pitching	B-T	HT	WT	DOB	W	L	ERA	G	GS	CG	SV	IP	H	R	ER	HR	BB	SO	AVG	vLH	vRH	K/9	BB/9
Alvarez, Daniel	R-R	6-3	228	6-28-96	3	4	4.16	13	12	0	0	71	64	39	33	6	19	73	.236	.196	.257	9.21	2.40
Bisacca, Alex	R-R	6-2	205	6-23-93	1	0	3.60	15	0	0	0	20	16	8	8	0	14	15	.225	.321	.163	6.75	6.30
Bristo, Braden	R-R	6-0	180	11-1-94	3	1	1.86	10	0	0	3	19	10	5	4	0	3	26	.152	.200	.122	12.10	1.40

Brito, Jhony	R-R	6-2	160	2-17-98	1	0	0.00	3	3	0	0	8	8	2	0	0	2	8	.258	.444	.000	9.39	2.35
Cedeno, Luis	R-R	5-11	154	7-14-94	0	0	0.00	2	0	0	1	3	1	0	0	0	0	5	.100	.333	.000	15.00	0.00
De Paula, Juan	R-R	6-3	165	9-22-97	5	5	2.90	12	11	0	0	62	42	28	20	0	25	53	.191	.200	.184	7.69	3.63
DeCarr, Austin	R-R	6-3	218	3-14-95	0	1	7.71	2	0	0	0	5	7	4	4	1	3	5	.368	.429	.333	9.64	5.79
Degano, Jeff	R-L	6-4	215	10-30-92	0	0	63.00	5	0	0	0	1	3	7	7	0	9	2	.600	—	.600	18.00	81.00
Finley, Drew	R-R	6-3	200	7-10-96	0	3	6.48	8	7	0	0	33	43	26	24	4	16	35	.305	.358	.257	9.45	4.32
Guzman, Jorge	R-R	6-2	182	1-28-96	5	3	2.30	13	13	1	0	67	51	21	17	4	18	88	.212	.236	.197	11.88	2.43
Hodson, Chase	R-R	6-1	205	7-10-92	1	1	1.53	12	0	0	0	18	13	3	3	0	2	28	.200	.156	.242	14.26	1.02
Jones, Will	R-R	6-1	190	3-15-93	3	2	1.55	16	0	0	0	29	27	9	5	0	6	17	.241	.233	.246	5.28	1.86
Kamplain, Justin	R-L	6-0	175	2-13-93	3	1	1.41	18	1	0	5	32	18	6	5	0	9	33	.162	.192	.153	9.28	2.53
Loaisiga, Jonathan	R-R	5-11	165	11-2-94	1	0	0.53	4	4	0	0	17	7	2	1	0	1	18	.121	.208	.059	9.53	0.53
Morris, Christian	R-R	6-4	195	1-23-94	0	0	0.00	4	1	0	0	8	4	1	0	0	2	3	.138	.231	.063	3.52	2.35
Orozco, Jio	R-R	6-1	210	8-15-97	3	1	2.04	8	8	0	0	35	29	12	8	2	21	37	.223	.170	.268	9.42	5.35
Ort, Kaleb	R-R	6-4	230	2-5-92	1	0	2.31	8	0	0	2	12	7	4	3	0	5	16	.171	.167	.172	12.34	3.86
Otto, Glenn	R-R	6-5	240	3-11-96	3	0	1.59	7	2	0	0	17	12	3	3	0	5	25	.194	.258	.129	13.24	2.65
Palladino, David	R-R	6-8	235	3-15-93	1	1	1.14	13	0	0	0	24	20	6	3	0	3	33	.217	.256	.189	12.55	1.14
Pinder, Branden	R-R	6-4	215	1-26-89	0	0	0.00	5	0	0	0	7	3	1	0	0	2	8	.125	.125	.125	9.82	2.45
Rivera, Eduardo	R-R	6-5	190	9-24-92	3	2	1.90	19	0	0	6	24	12	6	5	1	13	33	.150	.125	.167	12.55	4.94
Roeder, Josh	R-R	6-0	175	12-2-92	0	0	2.19	12	0	0	1	25	25	6	6	1	7	29	.250	.200	.283	10.58	2.55
Stephan, Trevor	R-R	6-4	210	11-25-95	1	1	1.39	10	9	0	0	32	20	7	5	0	6	43	.177	.196	.158	11.97	1.67
Trieglaff, Brian	R-R	6-1	190	6-13-94	2	1	2.04	13	0	0	6	18	14	5	4	1	1	16	.212	.333	.128	8.15	0.51
Vargas, Alexander	R-R	6-4	203	7-24-97	4	0	1.88	4	4	0	0	24	20	6	5	0	3	14	.235	.212	.250	5.25	1.13
Weissert, Greg	R-R	6-2	215	2-4-95	2	2	4.13	19	0	0	4	28	21	13	13	1	9	34	.204	.205	.203	10.80	2.86
Young, Paul	R-R	6-2	205	3-15-93	0	0	7.71	1	0	0	0	2	2	2	2	0	1	5	.222	.000	.400	19.29	3.86

Fielding

C: Argomaniz 16, Diaz 1, Higashioka 3, Lopez 43, Reyes 8, Skinner 13. **1B:** Argomaniz 7, Blaser 28, Gomez 1, Krill 36, Skinner 5. **2B:** Barrios 1, Brown 28, Cabrera 11, Garcia 1, Hess 4, Mateo 11, Perez 16, Polonia 12. **3B:** Argomaniz 8, Barrios 2, Cabrera 6, Gomez 25, Mateo 17, Perez 7, Polonia 17. **SS:** Cabrera 6, Garcia 65, Mateo 2, Perez 4, Polonia 3. **OF:** Blaser 1, Brown 7, Coleman 56, Diaz 23, Diaz 31, Molina 26, Robinson 47, Thompson-Williams 39, Vidal 3.

PULASKI YANKEES — *ROOKIE*

APPALACHIAN LEAGUE

Batting	B-T	HT	WT	DOB	AVG	vLH	vRH	G	AB	R	H	2B	3B	HR	RBI	BB	HBP	SH	SF	SO	SB	CS	SLG	OBP
Alexander, Evan	L-L	6-2	175	2-26-98	.234	.292	.208	25	77	12	18	4	1	1	11	10	2	1	0	23	4	1	.351	.337
Bastidas, Jesus	R-R	5-10	145	9-14-98	.196	.122	.224	40	148	22	29	4	0	0	14	9	5	2	0	27	4	2	.223	.265
Cabrera, Leobaldo	R-R	6-1	170	1-21-98	.221	.279	.193	40	131	25	29	4	0	1	9	17	3	2	1	31	6	1	.275	.322
Chaparro, Andres	R-R	6-1	200	5-4-99	.237	.173	.265	46	169	27	40	9	0	7	24	17	0	2	1	41	2	1	.414	.305
Corredera, Yeison	R-R	5-11	175	1-30-94	.180	.119	.213	39	117	14	21	3	1	1	11	11	1	0	1	28	4	1	.248	.254
Cuevas, Frederick	L-L	5-11	185	10-27-97	.312	.300	.316	43	154	24	48	11	1	3	17	14	1	5	0	34	6	6	.455	.373
Diaz, Andy	L-L	5-11	190	11-21-95	.167	.191	.156	21	66	10	11	1	0	2	10	8	1	0	1	30	2	1	.273	.263
Emery, Brayan	L-R	6-3	185	3-15-98	.200	.235	.180	26	95	8	19	6	1	2	14	9	4	0	1	36	1	0	.347	.294
Garcia, Dermis	R-R	6-3	200	1-7-98	.270	.306	.253	33	115	24	31	5	1	9	25	24	1	0	1	39	6	0	.565	.397
Higashioka, Kyle	R-R	6-1	200	4-20-90	.800	—	.800	2	5	3	4	1	0	3	4	1	0	0	1	0	0	0	2.800	.714
Lidge, Ryan	B-R	6-2	216	10-27-94	.150	.000	.167	7	20	3	3	0	0	0	2	6	0	0	0	7	0	0	.150	.346
Olivares, Pablo	R-R	6-0	160	1-27-98	.363	.310	.392	23	80	21	29	5	1	1	8	16	6	1	1	14	4	2	.488	.495
Perez, Danienger	R-R	5-10	155	11-6-96	.326	.438	.267	13	46	7	15	2	0	1	7	6	1	0	0	11	3	1	.435	.415
Rey, Victor	R-R	6-2	178	6-29-95	.280	.179	.323	27	93	13	26	5	0	1	10	11	0	0	0	26	0	0	.366	.356
Scott, Jordan	B-R	6-0	210	5-23-97	.250	.167	.300	5	16	1	4	1	0	0	2	0	1	0	0	9	0	0	.313	.294
Sensley, Steven	L-L	6-1	220	9-6-95	.316	.360	.301	27	98	23	31	8	0	9	23	12	2	0	0	27	2	1	.674	.402
Surum, Ricky	R-R	5-10	170	12-7-94	.219	.191	.233	20	64	9	14	3	0	1	9	4	2	1	1	13	2	0	.313	.282
Torrealba, Eduardo	R-R	5-8	140	3-26-99	.208	.196	.212	52	183	30	38	6	0	1	15	17	3	6	1	35	10	3	.257	.284
Torres, Saul	R-R	6-2	190	2-19-99	.174	.170	.176	46	178	16	31	6	0	6	23	10	3	0	0	69	0	1	.309	.230
Unda, Dario	L-L	5-11	168	5-24-96	.314	.421	.275	21	70	7	22	4	0	3	12	8	0	2	0	15	2	2	.500	.385
Vazquez, Charles	R-R	6-1	200	9-24-93	.130	.100	.154	10	23	1	3	0	0	0	2	2	0	0	0	16	0	0	.130	.200
Wagaman, Eric	R-R	6-4	210	8-14-97	.264	.254	.269	59	212	23	56	12	0	5	29	19	3	0	2	65	3	1	.392	.331

Pitching	B-T	HT	WT	DOB	W	L	ERA	G	GS	CG	SV	IP	H	R	ER	HR	BB	SO	AVG	vLH	vRH	K/9	BB/9
Blanton, Bryan	R-R	6-0	190	12-19-95	0	1	9.00	1	0	0	0	1	2	2	1	0	2	1	.500	.000	.667	9.00	18.00
Caceres, Wellington	R-R	5-11	185	1-29-96	2	2	6.25	9	5	0	1	32	40	24	22	5	12	30	.318	.321	.314	8.53	3.41
De la Rosa, Simon	R-R	6-3	185	5-11-93	0	0	5.00	8	0	0	0	9	5	5	5	2	4	14	.179	.273	.118	14.00	4.00
Duarte, Abel	R-R	6-1	190	5-20-94	6	1	1.53	11	0	0	0	29	20	5	5	1	7	31	.198	.268	.150	9.51	2.15
Espinal, Carlos	R-R	5-11	175	10-21-96	2	1	3.55	7	3	0	0	25	23	11	10	1	7	24	.245	.175	.296	8.53	2.49
Garcia, Deivi	R-R	5-10	163	5-19-99	2	1	4.50	6	5	0	0	28	23	14	14	3	13	43	.232	.293	.190	13.82	4.18
Garcia, Rony	R-R	6-3	200	12-19-97	0	0	3.97	2	2	0	0	11	11	7	5	1	2	11	.262	.333	.233	8.74	1.59
Hebert, Chaz	L-L	6-2	180	9-4-92	1	0	2.25	3	0	0	0	8	5	3	2	0	1	10	.161	.167	.158	11.25	1.13
Honahan, Tyler	R-L	6-2	175	1-5-94	1	0	7.27	7	0	0	1	9	12	7	7	1	4	11	.333	.429	.273	11.42	4.15
Jimenez, Juan	R-R	6-2	190	10-6-93	1	1	6.14	12	0	0	1	22	28	16	15	0	17	37	.308	.350	.275	15.14	6.95
Lehnen, Dalton	L-L	6-3	222	5-16-96	1	0	4.31	10	10	0	0	31	38	20	15	3	9	42	.297	.429	.271	12.06	2.59
Martin, Chad	R-R	6-4	215	1-2-94	2	2	1.54	12	0	0	0	23	14	7	4	0	11	21	.187	.219	.163	8.10	4.24
Martinez, Dallas	R-R	6-0	175	10-28-94	2	1	5.64	16	0	0	3	22	24	19	14	5	8	25	.261	.267	.255	10.07	3.22
Martinez, Nolan	R-R	6-2	165	6-30-98	0	0	0.00	1	1	0	0	4	2	0	0	0	0	2	.154	.000	.333	4.50	0.00
Medina, Luis	R-R	6-1	175	5-3-99	1	1	5.09	6	6	0	0	23	14	14	13	1	14	22	.171	.121	.204	8.61	5.48
Orozco, Jio	R-R	6-1	210	8-15-97	2	0	2.36	5	4	0	0	27	25	9	7	3	10	26	.263	.250	.275	8.78	3.38
Ort, Kaleb	R-R	6-4	230	2-5-92	2	0	0.63	12	0	0	8	14	5	1	1	0	4	23	.111	.217	.000	14.44	2.51
Pujols, Jose	R-R	6-6	183	11-19-92	1	2	6.30	14	0	0	0	20	19	21	14	3	21	25	.247	.200	.286	11.25	9.45

Ramos, Daniel	R-R	5-11	184	3-6-95	2	3	3.81	11	8	0	1	52	51	26	22	4	16	56	.260	.310	.220	9.69	2.77
Severino, Anderson	L-L	5-10	165	9-17-94	1	1	2.61	8	0	0	0	10	10	6	3	1	4	10	.238	.000	.303	8.71	3.48
Seyler, Mark	R-R	6-3	190	2-2-94	0	0	6.85	15	0	0	2	24	21	24	18	1	12	22	.231	.306	.182	8.37	4.56
Troya, Gilmael	R-R	6-0	196	4-4-97	4	2	4.22	12	11	0	0	53	41	31	25	8	23	54	.211	.220	.205	9.11	3.88
Vizcaino, Alexander	R-R	6-2	160	5-22-97	3	5	5.79	12	11	0	0	51	69	40	33	9	23	49	.321	.321	.321	8.59	4.03
Whitlock, Garrett	R-R	6-4	192	6-11-96	1	0	7.94	2	0	0	0	6	10	5	5	1	0	8	.400	.462	.333	12.71	0.00
Wivinis, Matthew	R-R	6-0	170	7-24-93	3	0	0.87	12	0	0	6	21	14	3	2	0	4	32	.189	.200	.184	13.94	1.74
Zurak, Kyle	R-R	6-1	192	11-28-94	1	2	3.10	7	1	0	1	20	17	8	7	2	8	25	.233	.158	.259	11.07	3.54

Fielding

C: Higashioka 2, Lidge 7, Rey 17, Torres 39, Vazquez 6. **1B:** Chaparro 11, Garcia 5, Rey 4, Vazquez 1, Wagaman 49. **2B:** Bastidas 7, Corredera 16, Perez 9, Surum 14, Torrealba 21. **3B:** Chaparro 22, Corredera 21, Garcia 21, Surum 5, Torrealba 1. **SS:** Bastidas 33, Perez 4, Torrealba 30. **OF:** Alexander 20, Cabrera 39, Cuevas 40, Diaz 18, Emery 25, Olivares 20, Scott 4, Sensley 21, Unda 17.

GCL Yankees East Rookie

GCL YANKEES EAST — ROOKIE

GULF COAST LEAGUE

Batting	B-T	HT	WT	DOB	AVG	vLH	vRH	G	AB	R	H	2B	3B	HR	RBI	BB	HBP	SH	SF	SO	SB	CS	SLG	OBP
Alvarez, Nelson	L-L	6-3	210	3-10-96	.181	.097	.204	48	144	12	26	2	1	0	9	31	4	0	1	37	5	1	.208	.339
Amundaray, Jonathan	R-R	6-2	215	5-11-98	.140	.154	.136	15	57	3	8	1	0	0	3	1	1	0	0	15	1	1	.158	.170
2-team total (20 Yankees West)					.193	.263	.237	35	114	11	22	3	0	1	11	5	1	0	0	26	1	3	.246	.233
Barrios, Daniel	R-R	5-11	183	4-18-95	.286	.250	.300	6	14	3	4	1	0	0	2	4	1	0	0	1	0	1	.357	.474
2-team total (13 Yankees West)					.244	.500	.207	19	45	9	11	1	0	1	3	12	2	2	0	9	0	2	.333	.424
Blanco, Lisandro	R-R	6-1	180	1-13-97	.202	.304	.174	33	109	10	22	4	1	2	8	9	3	0	1	38	2	0	.312	.279
Carrera, Jose	B-R	5-2	155	10-22-94	.276	.160	.306	41	123	20	34	6	1	1	19	20	5	1	1	15	11	3	.366	.396
Del Orbe, Malvin	R-R	5-10	197	3-2-97	.188	.222	.174	22	64	3	12	4	0	0	5	2	0	0	1	14	0	0	.250	.209
Devers, Jose	L-R	6-0	155	12-7-99	.246	.348	.226	42	138	17	34	7	2	1	9	18	8	2	3	21	15	3	.348	.359
Diaz, Pedro	R-R	6-2	202	11-6-97	.180	.000	.243	19	50	7	9	2	1	3	9	5	2	0	1	12	1	0	.440	.276
Gallardo, Carlos	R-R	5-10	160	1-26-97	.174	.286	.146	25	69	10	12	0	1	1	7	18	2	1	1	26	0	0	.246	.356
Graterol, Jesus	R-R	5-11	175	4-11-97	.150	.185	.140	38	113	9	17	3	1	0	6	7	1	3	0	29	6	2	.195	.207
Javier, Robert	R-R	5-8	173	2-1-99	.262	.296	.252	53	191	28	50	6	3	1	26	19	6	5	1	55	10	9	.340	.346
Jimenez, Brayan	R-R	6-0	140	5-31-99	.500	—	.500	2	4	1	2	0	0	0	1	0	0	0	0	0	0	0	.500	.500
2-team total (14 Yankees West)					.327	.167	.361	16	52	6	17	1	1	0	8	1	1	0	0	2	0	0	.385	.352
Mendez, Borinquen	B-R	5-11	165	2-1-98	.236	.267	.228	24	72	12	17	2	1	0	6	11	1	1	0	15	7	1	.292	.345
2-team total (19 Yankees West)					.212	.143	.176	43	113	22	24	3	1	1	9	17	1	1	1	25	13	1	.283	.318
Moreno, Raymundo	R-R	6-1	185	3-9-98	.248	.333	.227	49	161	16	40	12	0	1	15	18	6	0	1	31	3	4	.342	.344
Moronta, Jhon	R-R	6-4	215	5-17-99	.261	.302	.248	51	184	19	48	9	1	0	27	21	1	1	1	38	2	2	.321	.338
Pena, Ysaac	L-R	5-9	180	6-19-98	.235	.250	.231	5	17	2	4	1	0	0	0	2	0	0	0	4	0	1	.294	.316
Rosario, Hemmanuel	R-R	6-2	200	8-8-00	.111	.000	.136	14	27	3	3	1	0	0	1	9	3	1	0	15	1	1	.148	.385
Sensley, Steven	L-L	6-1	220	9-6-95	.333	.000	.400	2	6	4	2	2	0	0	1	3	0	0	0	2	0	0	.667	.556
Smith, Canaan	L-R	6-0	215	4-30-99	.289	.283	.291	57	187	29	54	10	0	5	28	46	2	0	2	44	5	3	.423	.430
Surum, Ricky	R-R	5-10	170	12-7-94	.259	.300	.237	21	58	9	15	0	0	0	6	5	6	1	2	13	3	2	.259	.366
Vazquez, Charles	R-R	6-1	200	9-24-93	.167	.000	.500	2	6	1	1	0	0	0	1	1	0	0	0	0	1	0	.167	.286

Pitching	B-T	HT	WT	DOB	W	L	ERA	G	GS	CG	SV	IP	H	R	ER	HR	BB	SO	AVG	vLH	vRH	K/9	BB/9
Abreu, Albert	R-R	6-2	175	9-26-95	0	0	2.08	2	2	0	0	4	3	3	1	0	0	8	.177	.000	.333	16.62	0.00
Baez, Yancarlos	B-R	6-2	165	9-21-95	0	2	3.51	8	5	0	0	26	24	14	10	1	7	16	.250	.265	.242	5.61	2.45
Bryson, Woody	R-L	6-3	201	2-19-93	1	0	0.00	6	0	0	0	8	2	0	0	0	4	10	.080	.000	.095	10.80	4.32
Contreras, Roansy	R-R	6-0	175	11-7-99	4	1	4.26	8	5	0	0	32	35	22	15	2	12	17	.276	.277	.275	4.83	3.41
Cortijo, Harold	R-R	6-2	180	4-27-98	1	0	4.98	10	0	0	1	22	19	13	12	2	7	25	.238	.100	.283	10.38	2.91
Diaz, Deivi	L-L	6-0	160	6-9-99	0	0	1.96	10	1	0	3	23	18	8	5	0	14	20	.207	.154	.216	7.83	5.48
Diaz, Wellington	R-R	6-4	190	4-25-97	2	5	3.43	10	8	0	0	45	51	23	17	1	8	29	.285	.275	.289	5.84	1.61
Enns, Dietrich	L-L	6-1	210	5-16-91	1	0	0.00	1	0	0	0	6	2	0	0	0	0	10	.095	—	.095	15.00	0.00
Hebert, Chaz	L-L	6-2	180	9-4-92	0	0	0.00	1	0	0	0	2	0	0	0	0	1	2	.000	.000	.000	9.00	4.50
2-team total (3 Yankees West)					0	0	4.32	4	2	0	0	8	3	4	4	2	4	12	.103	.000	.143	12.96	4.32
Hernandez, Tony	L-L	6-2	215	8-8-96	3	5	3.44	11	9	0	0	52	52	27	20	4	14	45	.251	.250	.251	7.74	2.41
Herrera, Ronald	R-R	5-11	185	5-3-95	0	1	4.00	3	3	0	0	9	13	4	4	0	0	9	.361	.417	.333	9.00	0.00
Higgins, Dalton	R-R	6-1	185	8-8-95	1	0	2.41	10	0	0	1	19	21	10	5	1	4	18	.284	.200	.315	8.68	1.93
Honahan, Tyler	R-L	6-2	175	1-5-94	0	1	5.68	5	0	0	0	6	5	4	4	0	4	8	.217	.667	.150	11.37	5.68
2-team total (3 Yankees West)					0	1	6.10	8	1	0	0	10	9	7	7	0	7	14	.225	.000	.333	12.19	6.10
Junk, Janson	R-R	6-1	177	1-15-96	1	0	0.84	8	0	0	0	11	14	5	1	0	4	7	.318	.286	.333	5.91	3.38
2-team total (3 Yankees West)					1	2	0.71	11	0	0	0	13	16	7	1	0	6	10	.302	.000	.286	7.11	4.26
Loaisiga, Jonathan	R-R	5-11	165	11-2-94	0	1	2.63	6	6	0	0	14	10	5	4	1	2	15	.196	.182	.200	9.88	1.32
2-team total (1 Yankees West)					0	1	2.30	7	7	0	0	16	10	5	4	1	2	15	.175	.000	.000	8.62	1.15
Marinaccio, Ron	R-R	6-2	205	7-1-95	3	0	2.30	13	0	0	5	16	12	4	4	0	6	15	.211	.467	.119	8.62	3.45
Martin, Chad	R-R	6-4	215	1-2-94	1	0	0.00	2	0	0	1	1	0	0	0	0	0	3	.000	—	.000	20.25	0.00
McGarity, Aaron	R-R	6-2	170	1-31-95	2	2	2.18	7	1	0	0	21	19	5	5	0	2	27	.244	.450	.172	11.76	0.87
Morales, Brett	R-R	6-1	200	1-10-95	0	0	0.00	2	2	0	0	7	3	0	0	0	0	9	.130	.333	.100	11.57	0.00
2-team total (2 Yankees West)					0	0	0.93	4	4	0	0	10	6	3	1	0	1	13	.171	.286	.200	12.10	0.93
Ojeda, Luis	R-R	5-11	180	1-10-97	1	5	7.01	10	6	0	0	35	40	29	27	7	11	25	.290	.353	.253	6.49	2.86
Otto, Glenn	R-R	6-5	240	3-11-96	0	0	0.00	1	1	0	0	2	1	0	0	0	0	3	.143	.250	.000	13.50	0.00
2-team total (1 Yankees West)					0	0	0.00	2	2	0	0	3	1	0	0	0	0	5	.100	.000	.000	15.00	0.00
Paredes, Edward	R-R	5-11	170	1-7-99	1	0	1.35	8	0	0	0	13	12	2	2	0	3	6	.245	.500	.162	4.05	2.03
Peguero, Elvis	R-R	6-5	208	3-20-97	1	1	3.00	3	3	0	0	12	6	4	4	0	5	5	.146	.200	.129	3.75	3.75
Pomeroy, Curtiss	R-R	6-1	200	5-5-93	0	0	0.00	2	0	0	0	3	1	2	0	0	2	3	.091	.000	.125	9.00	6.00

Pitching	B-T	HT	WT	DOB	W	L	ERA	G	GS	CG	SV	IP	H	R	ER	HR	BB	SO	AVG	vLH	vRH	K/9	BB/9
Reynoso, Anderson	R-R	6-2	180	11-25-97	0	0	0.00	2	0	0	0	2	0	0	0	0	0	1	.000	.000	.000	4.50	0.00
2-team total (7 Yankees West)					1	1	4.42	9	2	0	0	18	19	12	9	1	6	16	.260	.474	.208	7.85	2.95
Rijo, Luis	R-R	5-11	165	9-6-98	4	3	3.50	11	7	1	0	54	51	23	21	2	9	55	.253	.215	.270	9.17	1.50
Rodriguez, Carlos	R-R	5-10	155	12-13-98	0	0	0.00	1	0	0	0	2	3	0	0	0	1	2	.333	.333	.333	9.00	4.50
Semple, Shawn	R-R	6-1	195	10-9-95	4	0	1.00	13	0	0	2	18	16	3	2	0	1	22	.239	.167	.265	11.00	0.50
Severino, Anderson	L-L	5-10	165	9-17-94	2	0	0.77	6	0	0	0	12	8	1	1	0	8	14	.200	.250	.194	10.80	6.17
Soto, Wandy	R-R	6-0	187	1-27-96	0	0	7.36	9	0	0	0	11	10	9	9	1	15	12	.256	.417	.185	9.82	12.27
Stephan, Trevor	R-R	6-4	210	11-25-95	0	0	0.00	1	1	0	0	2	0	0	0	0	0	1	.000	.000	.000	4.50	0.00
Zurak, Kyle	R-R	6-1	192	11-28-94	0	0	0.00	1	0	0	0	1	0	0	0	0	0	1	.000	.000	.000	9.00	0.00
2-team total (3 Yankees West)					0	0	0.00	4	0	0	1	6	4	2	0	0	1	8	.167	.000	.267	12.00	1.50

Fielding

C: Del Orbe 8, Diaz 16, Gallardo 25, Moreno 1, Pena 4, Rosario 14, Vazquez 1. **1B:** Alvarez 48, Blanco 6, Del Orbe 6, Vazquez 1. **2B:** Carrera 15, Graterol 26, Jimenez 2, Mendez 16, Surum 4. **3B:** Barrios 6, Blanco 24, Carrera 23, Graterol 10, Surum 1. **SS:** Carrera 2, Devers 39, Mendez 8, Surum 14. **OF:** Amundaray 10, Blanco 1, Carrera 1, Javier 51, Moreno 39, Moronta 34, Sensley 2, Smith 47.

GCL YANKEES WEST — ROOKIE

GULF COAST LEAGUE

Batting	B-T	HT	WT	DOB	AVG	vLH	vRH	G	AB	R	H	2B	3B	HR	RBI	BB	HBP	SH	SF	SO	SB	CS	SLG	OBP
Alexander, Evan	L-L	6-2	175	2-26-98	.264	.100	.313	25	87	15	23	4	1	3	10	12	1	0	1	25	5	2	.437	.356
Amundaray, Jonathan	R-R	6-2	215	5-11-98	.246	.263	.237	20	57	8	14	2	0	1	8	4	0	0	0	11	0	2	.333	.295
2-team total (15 Yankees East)					.193	.263	.237	35	114	11	22	3	0	1	11	5	1	0	0	26	1	3	.246	.233
Arias, Antonio	R-R	6-2	180	6-12-98	.000	.000	.000	1	2	0	0	0	0	0	0	1	0	0	0	0	0	0	.000	.333
Barrios, Daniel	R-R	5-11	183	4-18-95	.226	.500	.207	13	31	6	7	0	0	1	1	8	1	2	0	8	0	1	.323	.400
2-team total (6 Yankees East)					.244	.500	.207	19	45	9	11	1	0	1	3	12	2	2	0	9	0	2	.333	.424
Campero, Gustavo	B-R	5-6	182	9-20-97	.292	.185	.333	30	96	20	28	7	3	3	16	26	1	0	1	21	11	0	.521	.444
De La Cruz, Samuel	R-R	5-11	180	10-18-97	.275	.667	.243	17	40	3	11	3	0	0	3	8	0	0	0	12	0	0	.350	.396
De Leon, Juan	R-R	6-2	185	9-13-97	.229	.209	.237	47	157	21	36	4	0	3	20	19	13	0	1	59	3	4	.312	.358
Flames, Miguel	R-R	6-2	210	9-14-97	.247	.225	.255	53	190	25	47	9	2	2	25	19	4	0	5	40	0	3	.347	.321
Garabito, Griffin	R-R	5-11	180	8-2-97	.253	.259	.250	52	190	26	48	11	1	5	32	10	3	0	1	44	2	0	.400	.299
Hess, Chris	R-R	6-2	195	12-3-94	.245	.412	.156	16	49	6	12	3	1	0	8	7	1	1	1	9	0	1	.347	.345
Jimenez, Brayan	R-R	6-0	140	5-31-99	.313	.167	.361	14	48	5	15	1	1	0	7	1	1	0	0	2	0	0	.375	.340
2-team total (2 Yankees East)					.327	.167	.361	16	52	6	17	1	1	0	8	1	1	0	0	2	0	0	.385	.352
Luaces, Edel	R-R	6-5	205	5-14-94	.182	.333	.125	4	11	1	2	1	0	0	1	1	0	0	0	7	1	0	.273	.250
Martinez, Luis	R-R	5-11	170	11-24-98	.192	.258	.162	30	99	12	19	4	1	3	8	10	1	0	0	38	3	2	.343	.273
Mendez, Borinquen	B-R	5-11	165	2-1-98	.171	.143	.177	19	41	10	7	1	0	1	3	6	0	0	1	10	6	0	.268	.271
2-team total (24 Yankees East)					.212	.143	.176	43	113	22	24	3	1	1	9	17	1	1	1	25	13	1	.283	.318
Metzgar, David	R-R	5-8	170	12-10-94	.278	.360	.207	20	54	9	15	2	1	0	8	3	0	0	0	5	2	1	.352	.316
Narvaez, Carlos	R-R	6-0	190	11-26-98	.255	.250	.256	32	106	13	27	1	0	1	11	15	2	0	1	22	0	0	.293	.355
Peraza, Oswald	R-R	6-0	176	6-15-00	.266	.192	.292	48	184	34	49	10	1	0	24	16	12	1	0	36	12	2	.332	.363
Polonia, Jose	R-R	5-11	175	12-11-95	.048	.000	.067	7	21	0	1	0	0	0	1	1	0	0	0	3	0	0	.048	.091
Robertson, Terrance	L-L	6-0	175	11-18-96	.264	.317	.243	42	144	25	38	11	1	0	16	24	4	1	1	43	10	4	.354	.382
Scott, Jordan	B-R	6-0	210	5-23-97	.260	.385	.218	32	104	25	27	2	2	7	19	24	0	0	0	26	7	0	.519	.398
Tatis, Carlos	R-R	6-5	211	12-19-96	.250	.348	.215	24	88	8	22	3	0	2	13	5	2	0	3	15	1	0	.352	.296
Unda, Dario	L-L	5-11	168	5-24-96	.231	.375	.205	16	52	7	12	4	1	2	13	3	0	0	0	12	1	0	.462	.273
Vergel, David	R-R	6-0	165	1-13-97	.150	.313	.042	21	40	10	6	1	0	0	3	9	2	0	1	12	0	0	.175	.327

Pitching	B-T	HT	WT	DOB	W	L	ERA	G	GS	CG	SV	IP	H	R	ER	HR	BB	SO	AVG	vLH	vRH	K/9	BB/9
Barrios, Pedro	R-R	6-1	199	3-27-99	4	2	4.23	10	8	0	0	45	49	26	21	2	8	26	.278	.258	.290	5.24	1.61
Blanton, Bryan	R-R	6-0	190	12-19-95	1	1	0.56	16	0	0	5	16	8	2	1	0	0	19	.143	.105	.162	10.69	0.00
Burgos, Havid	L-L	6-0	186	8-6-94	1	0	1.83	16	0	0	0	20	25	8	4	1	7	25	.294	.286	.297	11.44	3.20
Calderon, Daniel	L-L	6-1	170	10-13-97	2	1	5.79	8	3	0	0	19	14	15	12	1	13	18	.203	.500	.175	8.68	6.27
Correa, Nelvin	R-R	6-1	170	1-25-97	5	1	2.14	10	3	0	0	42	41	17	10	2	10	32	.253	.220	.268	6.86	2.14
Espinola, Pedro	R-R	6-4	207	2-1-96	1	5	4.03	10	7	0	0	38	27	22	17	1	25	37	.197	.275	.151	8.76	5.92
Garcia, Deivi	R-R	5-10	163	5-19-99	3	0	3.24	4	2	0	0	17	9	6	6	3	4	24	.155	.067	.186	12.96	2.16
Garcia, Jairo	R-R	5-11	182	1-25-95	1	2	8.02	15	0	0	0	21	28	19	19	5	17	13	.311	.387	.271	5.48	7.17
Gardner, Austin	R-R	6-2	215	12-2-94	1	1	2.35	16	0	0	0	23	19	6	6	2	4	22	.229	.136	.262	8.61	1.57
Gomez, Yoendrys	R-R	6-3	175	10-15-99	0	0	12.00	1	1	0	0	3	5	4	4	0	6	1	.417	.000	.556	3.00	18.00
Hebert, Chaz	L-L	6-2	180	9-4-92	0	0	5.68	3	2	0	0	6	3	4	4	2	3	10	.130	.000	.143	14.21	4.26
2-team total (1 Yankees East)					0	0	4.32	4	2	0	0	8	3	4	4	2	4	12	.103	.000	.143	12.96	4.32
Honahan, Tyler	R-L	6-2	175	1-5-94	0	0	6.75	3	1	0	0	4	4	3	3	0	3	6	.235	.000	.333	13.50	6.75
2-team total (5 Yankees East)					0	1	6.10	8	1	0	0	10	9	7	7	0	7	14	.225	.000	.333	12.19	6.10
Junk, Janson	R-R	6-1	177	1-15-96	0	2	0.00	3	0	0	0	2	2	2	0	0	2	3	.222	.000	.286	13.50	9.00
2-team total (8 Yankees East)					1	2	0.71	11	0	0	0	13	16	7	1	0	6	10	.302	.000	.286	7.11	4.26
Lehnen, Dalton	L-L	6-3	222	5-16-96	1	0	0.00	1	0	0	0	2	2	0	0	0	0	1	.250	.000	.333	4.50	0.00
Loaisiga, Jonathan	R-R	5-11	165	11-2-94	0	0	0.00	1	1	0	0	2	0	0	0	0	0	0	.000	.000	.000	0.00	0.00
2-team total (6 Yankees East)					0	1	2.30	7	7	0	0	16	10	5	4	1	2	15	.175	.000	.000	8.62	1.15
Luna, Anyelo	R-R	6-3	184	12-16-97	0	0	3.38	1	0	0	0	5	4	2	2	0	1	2	.211	.167	.231	3.38	1.69
Martinez, Nolan	R-R	6-2	165	6-30-98	0	0	0.93	5	4	0	0	10	6	1	1	0	3	12	.171	.083	.217	11.17	2.79
Mauricio, Alex	R-R	6-0	180	9-24-96	2	1	3.24	9	0	0	0	17	19	7	6	1	4	17	.279	.400	.229	9.18	2.16
Mejias, Alex	R-R	5-11	185	11-26-96	0	2	4.50	15	0	0	3	20	20	15	10	0	8	18	.263	.300	.250	8.10	3.60
Mendez, Bringnel	R-R	6-0	239	1-31-94	2	0	0.66	14	0	0	1	27	20	5	2	0	9	23	.217	.227	.214	7.57	2.96
Montas, Kenlly	R-R	6-0	187	5-31-96	0	1	5.82	4	3	0	0	17	21	13	11	4	6	19	.304	.429	.273	10.06	3.18
Morales, Brett	R-R	6-1	200	1-10-95	0	0	3.38	2	2	0	0	3	3	3	1	0	1	4	.250	.286	.200	13.50	3.38
2-team total (2 Yankees East)					0	0	0.93	4	4	0	0	10	6	3	1	0	1	13	.171	.286	.200	12.10	0.93

Munoz, Jhonatan	R-R	5-10	200	8-10-99	3	3	5.40	11	8	0	0	43	52	28	26	5	16	46	.297	.255	.313	9.55	3.32
Otto, Glenn	R-R	6-5	240	3-11-96	0	0	0.00	1	1	0	0	1	0	0	0	0	0	2	.000	.000	.000	18.00	0.00
2-team total (1 Yankees East)					0	0	0.00	2	2	0	0	3	1	0	0	0	0	5	.100	.000	.000	15.00	0.00
Reynoso, Anderson	R-R	6-2	180	11-25-97	1	1	4.96	7	2	0	0	16	19	12	9	1	6	15	.284	.474	.208	8.27	3.31
2-team total (2 Yankees East)					1	1	4.42	9	2	0	0	18	19	12	9	1	6	16	.260	.474	.208	7.85	2.95
Roeder, Josh	R-R	6-0	175	12-2-92	0	0	0.00	2	0	0	2	2	2	0	0	0	0	2	.222	.000	.400	7.71	0.00
Sauer, Matt	R-R	6-4	195	1-21-99	0	2	5.40	6	6	0	0	12	13	9	7	0	8	12	.271	.200	.303	9.26	6.17
Sheffield, Justus	L-L	5-11	200	5-13-96	0	1	1.93	2	2	0	0	5	4	1	1	0	1	6	.235	.250	.231	11.57	1.93
Vargas, Daris	R-R	6-3	195	8-12-92	1	1	3.57	13	0	0	2	23	22	14	9	1	6	18	.256	.214	.276	7.15	2.38
Whitlock, Garrett	R-R	6-4	192	6-11-96	0	0	1.04	3	3	0	0	9	4	2	1	0	0	14	.138	.375	.048	14.54	0.00
Whitmer, Chad	R-R	6-3	190	5-11-95	3	0	3.79	14	0	0	1	19	24	11	8	2	2	22	.312	.250	.333	10.42	0.95
Zurak, Kyle	R-R	6-1	192	11-28-94	0	0	0.00	3	0	0	1	5	4	2	0	0	1	7	.191	.000	.267	12.60	1.80
2-team total (1 Yankees East)					0	0	0.00	4	0	0	1	6	4	2	0	0	1	8	.167	.000	.267	12.00	1.50

Fielding

C: Campero 18, De La Cruz 5, Narvaez 27, Vergel 16. **1B:** De La Cruz 6, Flames 43, Tatis 14, Vergel 5. **2B:** Barrios 1, Garabito 24, Hess 6, Jimenez 7, Mendez 1, Mendez 14, Metzgar 15. **3B:** Barrios 7, Flames 11, Garabito 30, Hess 9, Jimenez 5, Polonia 7. **SS:** Barrios 6, Jimenez 3, Mendez 4, Metzgar 3, Peraza 47. **OF:** Alexander 22, Amundaray 19, Arias 1, De Leon 38, Luaces 4, Martinez 29, Robertson 39, Scott 27, Unda 12.

DSL YANKEES — ROOKIE

DOMINICAN SUMMER LEAGUE

Batting	B-T	HT	WT	DOB	AVG	vLH	vRH	G	AB	R	H	2B	3B	HR	RBI	BB	HBP	SH	SF	SO	SB	CS	SLG	OBP
Alvarez, Asdrubal	R-R	6-0	160	10-10-99	.212	.200	.216	41	132	14	28	6	1	0	14	16	2	0	4	32	10	3	.273	.299
Andrade, Christian	L-R	6-0	215	4-14-99	.242	.175	.264	47	165	19	40	9	4	2	24	22	2	0	1	55	2	1	.382	.337
Arias, Antonio	R-R	6-2	180	6-12-98	.376	.500	.349	40	157	36	59	6	3	4	26	22	3	1	1	23	9	2	.529	.459
Campero, Gustavo	B-R	5-6	182	9-20-97	.375	.333	.385	6	16	5	6	1	2	0	4	1	2	0	1	2	2	1	.688	.450
Capellan, Jonathan	R-R	5-10	165	3-26-99	.171	.214	.162	29	82	8	14	2	0	0	1	7	2	3	1	41	3	1	.195	.250
Del Orbe, Malvin	R-R	5-10	197	3-2-97	.231	.000	.333	4	13	1	3	0	0	0	2	0	0	0	0	2	0	0	.231	.231
Devers, Jose	L-R	6-0	155	12-7-99	.239	.000	.297	11	46	4	11	2	1	0	7	0	1	0	0	16	1	0	.326	.255
Duran, Ezequiel	R-R	5-11	185	5-22-99	.393	.357	.404	15	61	12	24	5	4	3	11	3	0	0	1	15	4	1	.754	.415
Espinosa, Roberto	R-R	5-10	170	12-28-98	.220	.273	.200	29	82	8	18	3	1	1	13	4	3	0	4	16	1	1	.317	.269
Garabito, Griffin	R-R	5-11	180	8-2-97	.364	.500	.333	9	33	9	12	0	2	1	7	2	0	0	0	4	0	0	.576	.400
Hernandez, Victor	L-R	5-11	165	1-31-99	.158	.083	.178	17	57	5	9	2	2	0	4	6	1	1	0	18	4	1	.263	.250
Javier, Robert	R-R	5-8	173	2-1-99	.265	.167	.279	11	49	5	13	1	0	0	2	0	1	0	0	11	1	1	.286	.280
Lopez, Jason	R-R	5-9	172	3-16-98	.100	—	.100	6	20	3	2	1	0	0	2	4	1	0	0	4	0	1	.150	.280
Mendez, Borinquen	B-R	5-11	165	2-1-98	.385	.500	.364	3	13	2	5	0	1	0	4	0	0	0	0	3	1	0	.539	.385
Mendez, Erick	R-R	6-0	185	4-7-96	.071	.000	.083	5	14	0	1	0	0	0	0	1	0	0	0	9	1	1	.071	.133
Mora, Gabriel	R-R	5-11	155	6-1-00	.181	.250	.164	28	83	7	15	3	1	0	9	10	2	1	0	13	0	0	.241	.284
Moronta, Jhon	R-R	6-4	215	5-17-99	.278	.400	.258	10	36	6	10	3	0	1	7	2	0	0	0	5	0	0	.444	.316
Mota, Sandy	R-R	6-0	170	9-25-96	.257	.276	.250	29	113	20	29	12	0	3	9	2	0	0	0	32	8	1	.443	.270
Paulino, Starlin	R-R	6-1	170	2-24-00	.281	.279	.282	50	185	33	52	8	3	1	30	19	3	0	2	33	9	3	.373	.354
Pena, Enrique	R-R	5-10	170	2-23-99	.107	.200	.083	27	75	12	8	2	1	0	4	13	2	0	1	33	1	1	.160	.253
Peraza, Oswald	R-R	6-0	176	6-15-00	.361	.167	.400	10	36	10	13	3	2	0	10	7	1	0	1	2	1	0	.556	.467
Polonia, Jose	R-R	5-11	175	12-11-95	.182	—	.182	3	11	2	2	0	0	0	0	0	1	0	0	1	0	0	.182	.250
Pujols, Alfred	R-R	6-2	10	11-5-98	.077	.000	.100	4	13	0	1	0	0	0	0	1	1	0	0	7	0	0	.077	.200
Rodriguez, Meure	B-R	6-2	200	5-20-99	.171	.091	.204	27	76	9	13	2	0	0	4	17	0	0	0	17	4	1	.197	.323
Santana, Alexander	R-R	6-0	175	7-7-00	.274	.250	.281	57	215	36	59	16	3	5	28	21	9	0	1	70	4	4	.447	.362
Santos, Luis	R-R	5-8	160	1-4-00	.216	.174	.227	30	111	16	24	6	2	0	7	9	5	0	1	17	9	6	.306	.302
Severino, Jesus	R-R	6-0	186	6-7-00	.140	.172	.131	45	136	29	19	4	0	2	10	29	13	0	0	55	15	3	.213	.343
Tatis, Carlos	R-R	6-5	211	12-19-96	.310	.294	.315	42	158	31	49	8	1	7	33	20	4	0	5	34	5	3	.506	.390
Torres, Miguel	R-R	6-0	170	3-3-00	.138	.000	.167	27	80	4	11	1	1	0	5	6	2	0	0	13	0	1	.175	.216
Villa, Jose	R-R	6-1	170	11-16-98	.311	.357	.300	19	74	11	23	1	1	2	13	10	2	0	0	15	5	3	.432	.407

Pitching	B-T	HT	WT	DOB	W	L	ERA	G	GS	CG	SV	IP	H	R	ER	HR	BB	SO	AVG	vLH	vRH	K/9	BB/9
Abreu, Joensy	R-R	6-1	190	12-29-97	0	1	7.29	10	3	0	0	21	30	25	17	0	12	8	.341	.536	.250	3.43	5.14
Arguello, Marcos	L-L	6-2	180	11-10-97	0	1	5.06	5	0	0	0	11	10	10	6	2	5	9	.238	.143	.257	7.59	4.22
Barrios, Pedro	R-R	6-1	199	3-27-99	0	1	5.91	3	2	0	0	11	14	12	7	1	5	10	.311	.267	.333	8.44	4.22
Barrios, Wilser	R-R	6-2	160	3-21-98	0	0	0.00	2	0	0	0	3	5	2	0	0	1	2	.357	.286	.429	6.75	3.38
Calderon, Daniel	L-L	6-1	170	10-13-97	0	0	0.00	1	0	0	0	2	1	0	0	0	1	2	.200	.500	.000	9.00	4.50
Carderon, Juan	R-R	6-0	172	8-1-98	3	2	4.13	13	2	0	0	33	24	23	15	1	14	40	.195	.263	.165	11.02	3.86
Contreras, Roansy	R-R	6-0	175	11-7-99	0	3	3.68	6	6	0	0	22	25	15	9	2	5	17	.278	.375	.257	6.95	2.05
Cordero, Diego	R-R	6-0	160	10-21-99	1	4	4.58	10	3	0	0	37	33	27	19	5	14	37	.232	.250	.226	8.92	3.38
Correa, Nelvin	R-R	6-1	170	1-25-97	1	0	3.65	3	1	0	0	12	15	6	5	0	1	12	.300	.333	.281	8.76	0.73
Diaz, Deivi	L-L	6-0	160	6-9-99	0	0	4.50	1	1	0	0	4	3	2	2	0	3	4	.200	.000	.231	9.00	6.75
Espana, Carfred	R-R	6-0	155	1-3-00	0	1	10.80	7	0	0	0	12	19	16	14	1	12	15	.346	.267	.375	11.57	9.26
Espinola, Pedro	R-R	6-4	207	2-1-96	1	0	0.00	4	2	0	1	16	9	0	0	0	1	18	.164	.167	.161	10.34	0.57
Estevez, Abel	R-R	6-1	170	1-17-00	0	1	6.46	7	0	0	0	15	17	20	11	1	7	8	.262	.333	.227	4.70	4.11
Garcia, Deivi	R-R	5-10	163	5-19-99	1	1	1.17	3	3	0	0	15	10	3	2	1	2	18	.196	.177	.206	10.57	1.17
Garcia, Rodrigo	R-R	6-2	192	3-13-99	2	2	2.25	14	0	0	3	20	19	6	5	2	3	17	.247	.286	.225	7.65	1.35
Gomez, Yoendrys	R-R	6-3	175	10-15-99	0	3	4.78	10	8	0	0	32	36	22	17	2	12	32	.288	.321	.278	9.00	3.38
Gonzalez, Gabriel	R-R	5-10	174	10-13-98	0	0	18.00	8	0	0	1	7	9	15	14	2	9	10	.310	.462	.188	12.86	11.57
Hernandez, Albert	L-L	6-1	150	12-1-99	0	0	15.75	4	0	0	0	4	4	7	7	1	6	2	.308	.000	.333	4.50	13.50
Herrera, Argelis	L-L	6-5	165	10-17-98	0	2	20.25	6	0	0	0	7	11	18	15	0	11	6	.367	.600	.320	8.10	14.85
Luna, Anyelo	R-R	6-3	184	12-16-97	3	1	2.74	14	10	0	1	62	52	22	19	3	14	53	.223	.192	.239	7.65	2.02
Manzano, Daison	R-R	6-0	180	7-6-98	0	1	4.91	7	3	0	0	22	17	13	12	0	15	16	.227	.200	.236	6.55	6.14

Marten, Daniel	R-R	6-0	179	5-7-97	3	4	4.18	16	0	0	3	24	28	15	11	3	8	27	.292	.310	.284	10.27	3.04
Medina, Luis	R-R	6-1	175	5-3-99	1	1	5.74	4	3	0	0	16	17	15	10	0	10	17	.270	.182	.317	9.77	5.74
Mejias, Alex	R-R	5-11	185	11-26-96	2	1	3.68	4	0	0	0	7	8	5	3	1	2	6	.286	.250	.313	7.36	2.45
Montas, Kenlly	R-R	6-0	187	5-31-96	1	1	3.47	5	3	0	0	23	26	14	9	2	3	22	.268	.294	.254	8.49	1.16
Munoz, Jhonatan	R-R	5-10	200	8-10-99	2	0	2.89	2	1	0	0	9	6	3	3	0	2	12	.182	.143	.192	11.57	1.93
Ojeda, Luis	R-R	5-11	180	1-10-97	1	0	0.64	3	3	0	0	14	15	2	1	1	1	13	.273	.294	.263	8.36	0.64
Padilla, Isaac	R-R	6-4	277	6-14-96	4	4	4.55	10	1	0	0	30	28	21	15	1	12	30	.252	.306	.227	9.10	3.64
Paredes, Edward	R-R	5-11	170	1-7-99	0	1	0.00	4	0	0	2	5	5	1	0	0	1	4	.278	.143	.364	7.20	1.80
Peguero, Elvis	R-R	6-5	208	3-20-97	0	3	8.76	7	3	0	0	25	35	27	24	1	10	16	.337	.333	.338	5.84	3.65
Peguero, Jose	R-R	6-2	180	8-8-98	0	1	7.16	10	0	0	0	16	24	21	13	3	8	15	.308	.191	.351	8.27	4.41
Reynoso, Anderson	R-R	6-2	180	11-25-97	1	0	0.00	2	1	0	0	5	3	1	0	0	0	6	.167	.000	.300	10.80	0.00
Rodriguez, Carlos	R-R	5-10	155	12-13-98	2	2	3.00	13	12	0	1	63	60	25	21	1	9	37	.253	.238	.261	5.29	1.29
Severino, Anderson	L-L	5-10	165	9-17-94	0	0	0.00	1	0	0	0	1	0	0	0	0	0	0	.000	—	.000	0.00	0.00
Soto, Wandy	R-R	6-0	187	1-27-96	0	0	9.82	3	0	0	0	4	4	4	4	0	3	3	.286	.400	.222	7.36	7.36

Fielding

C: Campero 3, Del Orbe 1, Espinosa 9, Lopez 5, Mora 19, Rodriguez 24, Torres 27. **1B:** Del Orbe 2, Espinosa 15, Mora 5, Mota 9, Rodriguez 2, Tatis 40. **2B:** Alvarez 27, Devers 3, Duran 9, Garabito 1, Mendez 3, Mota 11, Pena 14, Peraza 2, Santos 2. **3B:** Alvarez 5, Garabito 8, Mota 3, Paulino 21, Pena 12, Polonia 3, Pujols 4, Villa 17. **SS:** Alvarez 7, Devers 7, Duran 4, Paulino 25, Peraza 7, Santos 23. **OF:** Andrade 38, Arias 32, Capellan 24, Hernandez 12, Javier 9, Mendez 4, Moronta 8, Mota 2, Santana 47, Severino 42, Tatis 1.

Oakland Athletics

SEASON IN A SENTENCE: The Athletics finished last in the AL West for the third straight season, but showed some reason for optimism in the second half as rookies such as Matt Olson and Matt Chapman shined and plans for a long-awaited new stadium were unveiled.

HIGH POINT: Olson homered in five straight games (a franchise rookie record) in September. In the final game of the streak, he wasted no time and homered in his first plate appearance, with Chapman following two batters later with his own homer. The A's went on to beat the Tigers, 9-8, thanks to a comeback capped by Jed Lowrie's eighth-inning grand slam.

LOW POINT: The A's were swept at home at the start of July by the Braves. In the final game of the three-game series, former A's catcher Kurt Suzuki homered twice for the Braves, who won, 4-3, in 12 innings.

NOTABLE ROOKIES: Olson fully embraced the Year of the Homer, as he hit 24 in 59 games. In addition to his five-game homer streak, he became the first rookie ever to hit 15 homers in 21 games and added 23 homers in the minor leagues. Olson is a part of a group of exciting infielders breaking in together, as Chapman, Franklin Barreto and Chad Pinder. Chapman and Pinder also showed off their power, hitting 14 and 15 home runs in 84 and 87 games, respectively. Righthanders Jharel Cotton and Daniel Gossett both took over spots in the rotation, starting a combined 42 games.

KEY TRANSACTIONS: As the A's again fell out of contention, Billy Beane and David Forst were active on the trade market. Their biggest deals of the summer were to send relievers Sean Doolittle and Ryan Madson to the Nationals and Sonny Gray to the Yankees. Oakland received three minor leaguers in both trades, bolstering its farm system.

DOWN ON THE FARM: Barreto, Chapman and Olson showed off their power at Triple-A Nashville, as all three hit at least 15 home runs. Renato Nunez outdid them all, however, with 32 home runs to rank second in the circuit. Lefthander A.J. Puk, the sixth overall pick in 2016, had an outstanding first full professional season and struck out 184 batters in 125 innings. Puk was a part of a solid group of prospects that reached Double-A Midland in time to help the RockHounds win their fourth straight Texas League championship.

OPENING DAY PAYROLL: $81,738,333 (27th)

PLAYERS OF THE YEAR

MAJOR LEAGUE

Khris Davis
OF

.247/.336/.528
43 HR second in AL
130 OPS+

MINOR LEAGUE

A.J. Puk
LHP

(High Class A/
Double-A)
6-10, 4.03, 184 SO

ORGANIZATION LEADERS

BATTING		*Minimum 250 AB
MAJORS		
* AVG	Jed Lowrie	.277
* OPS	Yonder Alonso	.896
HR	Khris Davis	43
RBI	Khris Davis	110
MINORS		
* AVG	B.J. Boyd, Midland	.323
* OBP	Jermaine Curtis, Nashville, Midland	.412
* SLG	Matt Olson, Nashville	.568
* OPS	Matt Olson, Nashville	.935
R	B.J. Boyd, Midland	82
H	B.J. Boyd, Midland	172
TB	Seth Brown, Stockton	262
2B	Eli White, Stockton	32
3B	Trace Loehr, Beloit	8
	Joey Wendle, Nashville	8
HR	Renato Nunez, Nashville	32
RBI	Viosergy Rosa, Midland	110
BB	Tyler Ramirez, Stockton, Midland	73
SO	JaVon Shelby, Beloit	164
SB	Mike Martin, Vermont, Beloit	27

PITCHING		#Minimum 75 IP
MAJORS		
W	Sean Manaea	12
# ERA	Sonny Gray	3.43
SO	Sean Manaea	140
SV	Santiago Casilla	16
MINORS		
W	Heath Fillmyer, Midland	11
	Grant Holmes, Midland	11
L	Grant Holmes, Midland	12
	Evan Manarino, Midland, Stockton	12
# ERA	Zack Erwin, Beloit	2.08
G	Lou Trivino, Midland, Nashville	48
GS	Heath Fillmyer, Midland	29
SV	Nolan Blackwood, Stockton	19
IP	Heath Fillmyer, Midland	150
BB	Grant Holmes, Midland	61
SO	A.J. Puk, Stockton, Midland	184
# AVG	Brandon Bailey, Beloit, Stockton	.206

2017 PERFORMANCE

Executive VP, Baseball Ops: Billy Beane. **Farm Director:** Keith Lieppman. **Scouting Director:** Eric Kubota.

Class	Team	League	W	L	PCT	Finish	Manager
Majors	Oakland Athletics	American	75	87	0.463	t-12th (15)	Bob Melvin
Triple-A	Nashville Sounds	Pacific Coast	68	71	0.489	t-8th (16)	Ryan Christenson
Double-A	Midland RockHounds	Texas	67	71	0.486	t-4th (8)	Fran Riordan
High-A	Stockton Ports	California	71	69	0.507	4th (8)	Rick Magnante
Low-A	Beloit Snappers	Midwest	65	73	0.471	11th (16)	Scott Steinmann
Short Season	Vermont Lake Monsters	New York-Penn	42	33	0.56	4th (14)	Aaron Nieckula
Rookie	AZL Athletics	Arizona	26	30	0.464	t-9th (15)	Webster Garrison
Overall 2017 Minor League Record			339	347	0.494	17th (30)	

ORGANIZATION STATISTICS

OAKLAND ATHLETICS

AMERICAN LEAGUE

Batting	B-T	HT	WT	DOB	AVG	vLH	vRH	G	AB	R	H	2B	3B	HR	RBI	BB	HBP	SH	SF	SO	SB	CS	SLG	OBP
Alonso, Yonder	R-L	6-1	230	4-8-87	.267	.188	.286	100	319	52	85	17	0	22	49	50	2	0	0	88	1	0	.527	.369
2-team total (42 Seattle)					.266	.188	.286	142	451	72	120	22	0	28	67	68	2	0	0	118	2	0	.501	.365
Barreto, Franklin	R-R	5-10	190	2-27-96	.197	.091	.245	25	71	10	14	1	2	2	6	5	0	0	0	33	2	0	.352	.250
Brugman, Jaycob	L-L	6-0	195	1-18-92	.266	.167	.280	48	143	12	38	2	0	3	12	18	0	0	1	38	1	2	.343	.346
Canha, Mark	R-R	6-2	210	2-15-89	.208	.203	.212	57	173	16	36	13	1	5	14	7	6	0	1	56	2	0	.382	.262
Chapman, Matt	R-R	6-0	210	4-28-93	.235	.244	.231	84	290	39	68	23	2	14	40	32	2	0	2	92	0	3	.472	.313
Davis, Khris	R-R	5-10	195	12-21-87	.247	.213	.257	153	566	91	140	28	1	43	110	73	6	0	7	195	4	0	.528	.336
Davis, Rajai	R-R	5-10	195	10-19-80	.233	.255	.222	100	300	49	70	17	2	5	18	26	0	1	1	70	26	6	.353	.294
2-team total (17 Boston)					.235	.154	.304	117	336	56	79	19	2	5	20	27	1	1	1	83	29	7	.348	.293
Decker, Jaff	L-L	5-9	190	2-23-90	.200	.375	.167	17	50	4	10	1	1	0	1	8	1	3	0	17	1	1	.260	.322
Garneau, Dustin	R-R	6-0	200	8-13-87	.159	.269	.000	19	44	5	7	1	0	1	3	8	0	0	0	12	0	0	.250	.289
Healy, Ryon	R-R	6-5	225	1-10-92	.271	.314	.257	149	576	66	156	29	0	25	78	23	4	0	2	142	0	1	.451	.303
Joyce, Matt	L-R	6-2	205	8-3-84	.243	.186	.253	141	469	78	114	33	0	25	68	66	2	0	7	113	4	1	.473	.335
LaMarre, Ryan	L-R	6-1	210	11-21-88	.000	.000	.000	3	7	0	0	0	0	0	0	1	0	0	0	3	0	0	.000	.125
Lavarnway, Ryan	R-R	6-4	240	8-7-87	.273	.222	.500	6	11	0	3	1	0	0	2	1	1	0	0	3	0	0	.364	.385
Lowrie, Jed	B-R	6-0	180	4-17-84	.277	.258	.283	153	567	86	157	49	3	14	69	73	2	0	3	100	0	1	.448	.360
Maxwell, Bruce	L-R	6-1	250	12-20-90	.237	.188	.246	76	219	21	52	12	0	3	22	31	0	1	2	63	0	0	.333	.329
Nunez, Renato	R-R	6-1	220	4-4-94	.200	.182	.250	8	15	1	3	0	0	1	3	1	0	0	0	8	0	0	.400	.250
Olson, Matt	L-R	6-5	230	3-29-94	.259	.196	.280	59	189	33	49	2	0	24	45	22	5	0	0	60	0	0	.651	.352
Phegley, Josh	R-R	5-10	230	2-12-88	.201	.215	.191	57	149	14	30	11	0	3	10	9	2	0	1	26	0	1	.336	.255
Pinder, Chad	R-R	6-2	195	3-29-92	.238	.247	.234	87	282	36	67	15	1	15	42	18	5	0	3	92	2	1	.457	.292
Plouffe, Trevor	R-R	6-2	215	6-15-86	.214	.294	.183	58	182	22	39	5	0	7	14	16	0	0	1	58	1	1	.357	.276
2-team total (42 Tampa Bay)					.198	.294	.183	100	283	31	56	7	0	9	19	28	1	0	1	88	1	2	.318	.272
Powell, Boog	L-L	5-10	185	1-14-93	.321	.167	.333	29	81	18	26	5	0	3	10	9	0	0	2	21	0	1	.494	.380
2-team total (23 Seattle)					.282	.167	.333	52	117	24	33	5	0	3	12	15	0	1	2	30	0	1	.402	.358
Rosales, Adam	R-R	6-2	200	5-20-83	.234	.276	.218	71	205	15	48	11	0	4	27	10	2	3	3	66	1	1	.346	.273
Semien, Marcus	R-R	6-0	195	9-17-90	.249	.225	.258	85	342	53	85	19	1	10	40	38	2	1	3	85	12	1	.398	.325
Smolinski, Jake	R-R	5-11	205	2-9-89	.259	.455	.125	16	27	1	7	1	0	0	0	1	1	0	0	6	0	0	.296	.310
Vogt, Stephen	L-R	6-0	225	11-1-84	.217	.077	.229	54	157	12	34	8	1	4	20	16	0	0	1	31	0	1	.357	.287
Wendle, Joey	L-R	6-1	190	4-26-90	.308	—	.308	8	13	3	4	1	0	1	5	1	0	0	0	3	0	0	.615	.357

Pitching	B-T	HT	WT	DOB	W	L	ERA	G	GS	CG	SV	IP	H	R	ER	HR	BB	SO	AVG	vLH	vRH	K/9	BB/9
Alcantara, Raul	R-R	6-4	220	12-4-92	1	2	7.13	8	4	0	0	24	22	21	19	5	12	12	.239	.238	.240	4.50	4.50
Axford, John	R-R	6-5	220	4-1-83	0	1	6.43	22	0	0	0	21	27	16	15	3	17	21	.310	.400	.250	9.00	7.29
Blackburn, Paul	R-R	6-1	195	12-4-93	3	1	3.22	10	10	0	0	59	58	22	21	5	16	22	.262	.226	.294	3.38	2.45
Brady, Michael	R-R	6-0	195	3-21-87	0	0	5.68	16	0	0	0	32	33	22	20	7	6	24	.271	.216	.294	6.82	1.71
Casilla, Santiago	R-R	6-0	210	7-25-80	4	5	4.27	63	0	0	16	59	58	29	28	8	22	57	.259	.256	.261	8.69	3.36
Castro, Simon	R-R	6-5	230	4-9-88	1	3	4.38	26	0	0	0	37	32	20	18	7	14	35	.235	.180	.280	8.51	3.41
Cotton, Jharel	R-R	5-11	195	1-19-92	9	10	5.58	24	24	0	0	129	133	91	80	28	53	105	.267	.257	.275	7.33	3.70
Coulombe, Daniel	L-L	5-10	190	10-26-89	2	2	3.48	72	0	0	0	52	46	22	20	4	22	39	.240	.214	.270	6.79	3.83
Doolittle, Sean	L-L	6-2	210	9-26-86	1	0	3.38	23	0	0	3	21	12	8	8	3	2	31	.158	.000	.226	13.08	0.84
Dull, Ryan	R-R	5-9	175	10-2-89	2	2	5.14	49	0	0	0	42	37	30	24	7	16	45	.236	.300	.206	9.64	3.43
Gossett, Daniel	R-R	6-2	185	11-13-92	4	11	6.11	18	18	0	0	91	116	67	62	21	31	72	.306	.319	.296	7.09	3.05
Graveman, Kendall	R-R	6-2	200	12-21-90	6	4	4.19	19	19	0	0	105	114	50	49	12	32	70	.280	.238	.315	5.98	2.73
Gray, Sonny	R-R	5-10	190	11-7-89	6	5	3.43	16	16	0	0	97	84	48	37	8	30	94	.229	.222	.236	8.72	2.78
2-team total (11 New York)					10	12	3.55	27	27	1	0	162	139	79	64	19	57	153	.226	.222	.236	8.48	3.16
Hahn, Jesse	R-R	6-4	215	7-30-89	3	6	5.30	14	13	0	0	70	78	46	41	4	27	55	.283	.289	.277	7.11	3.49
Hatcher, Chris	R-R	6-1	200	1-12-85	1	1	3.52	23	0	0	1	23	21	9	9	3	9	20	.236	.194	.259	7.83	3.52
Hendriks, Liam	R-R	6-0	200	2-10-89	4	2	4.22	70	0	0	1	64	57	34	30	7	23	78	.229	.206	.243	10.97	3.23
Madson, Ryan	L-R	6-6	225	8-28-80	2	4	2.06	40	0	0	1	39	25	9	9	2	6	39	.188	.204	.177	8.92	1.37
Manaea, Sean	R-L	6-5	245	2-1-92	12	10	4.37	29	29	0	0	159	167	88	77	18	55	140	.268	.227	.279	7.94	3.12
Mengden, Daniel	R-R	6-2	190	2-19-93	3	2	3.14	7	7	1	0	43	36	16	15	6	9	29	.229	.268	.187	6.07	1.88
Moll, Sam	L-L	5-10	185	1-3-92	0	0	10.80	11	0	0	0	7	13	8	8	2	3	7	.406	.375	.500	9.45	4.05
Montas, Frankie	R-R	6-2	255	3-21-93	1	1	7.03	23	0	0	0	32	39	25	25	10	20	36	.302	.364	.257	10.13	5.63
Neal, Zach	R-R	6-3	220	11-9-88	0	0	7.98	6	0	0	0	15	19	13	13	5	1	10	.302	.258	.344	6.14	0.61

Pitching	B-T	HT	WT	DOB	W	L	ERA	G	GS	CG	SV	IP	H	R	ER	HR	BB	SO	AVG	vLH	vRH	K/9	BB/9
Smith, Chris	R-R	6-0	190	4-9-81	0	4	6.79	14	9	0	0	56	60	45	42	16	22	31	.268	.269	.267	5.01	3.56
Smith, Josh	R-R	6-2	220	8-7-87	2	1	4.89	26	0	0	0	35	35	20	19	3	15	25	.259	.281	.244	6.43	3.86
Treinen, Blake	R-R	6-5	225	6-30-88	3	4	2.13	35	0	0	13	38	32	11	9	3	12	42	.225	.271	.181	9.95	2.84
Triggs, Andrew	R-R	6-4	220	3-16-89	5	6	4.27	12	12	0	0	65	68	42	31	9	19	50	.266	.215	.302	6.89	2.62
Valdez, Cesar	R-R	6-2	200	3-17-85	0	0	9.64	4	1	0	0	9	14	10	10	4	4	5	.350	.412	.304	4.82	3.86
2-team total (7 Toronto Blue Jays)					1	1	7.63	11	4	0	0	31	41	29	26	7	11	21	.320	.412	.304	6.16	3.23
Wahl, Bobby	R-R	6-2	210	3-21-92	0	0	4.70	7	0	0	0	8	8	4	4	0	4	8	.258	.333	.211	9.39	4.70

Fielding

Catcher	PCT	G	PO	A	E	DP	PB
Garneau	.990	18	98	6	1	0	3
Lavarnway	.970	5	31	1	1	0	0
Maxwell	1.000	74	454	31	0	8	3
Phegley	.984	56	356	25	6	2	8
Vogt	.980	43	279	8	6	1	2

First Base	PCT	G	PO	A	E	DP
Alonso	.992	96	728	52	6	77
Canha	1.000	3	6	2	0	0
Healy	.993	39	269	27	2	24
Olson	.995	43	352	29	2	41

Second Base	PCT	G	PO	A	E	DP
Barreto	.971	10	12	21	1	2
Lowrie	.991	136	199	344	5	98
Pinder	.983	16	25	34	1	7
Rosales	.963	8	12	14	1	5
Wendle	1.000	5	6	7	0	3

Third Base	PCT	G	PO	A	E	DP
Chapman	.955	84	72	203	13	34
Healy	.857	34	9	57	11	2
Lowrie	1.000	1	0	1	0	0
Nunez	1.000	1	0	1	0	0
Plouffe	.954	52	33	91	6	9
Rosales	1.000	4	2	2	0	0

Shortstop	PCT	G	PO	A	E	DP
Barreto	.942	11	16	33	3	10
Pinder	.952	22	29	51	4	9
Rosales	.965	55	70	148	8	36
Semien	.976	85	125	241	9	45

Outfield	PCT	G	PO	A	E	DP
Brugman	.977	43	85	1	2	1
Canha	.953	53	101	1	5	0
Davis	.995	116	212	2	1	1
Davis	.988	98	160	5	2	2
Decker	.946	15	33	2	2	1
Joyce	.973	133	249	5	7	2
LaMarre	1.000	3	3	0	0	0
Nunez	1.000	3	1	0	0	0
Olson	1.000	12	21	3	0	1
Pinder	.987	41	77	1	1	0
Powell	.985	28	62	2	1	0
Rosales	.000	1	0	0	0	0
Smolinski	1.000	11	22	0	0	0
Vogt	1.000	1	2	0	0	0

NASHVILLE SOUNDS — *TRIPLE-A*

PACIFIC COAST LEAGUE

Batting	B-T	HT	WT	DOB	AVG	vLH	vRH	G	AB	R	H	2B	3B	HR	RBI	BB	HBP	SH	SF	SO	SB	CS	SLG	OBP
Barreto, Franklin	R-R	5-10	190	2-27-96	.290	.259	.297	111	469	63	136	19	7	15	54	27	9	3	2	141	15	8	.456	.339
Brugman, Jaycob	L-L	6-0	195	1-18-92	.275	.273	.275	38	153	17	42	5	1	1	9	19	0	0	0	28	3	1	.340	.355
Canha, Mark	R-R	6-2	210	2-15-89	.283	.213	.298	75	272	52	77	25	3	12	50	34	7	1	3	62	4	0	.529	.373
Carter, Chris	R-R	6-4	245	12-18-86	.252	.261	.250	36	131	21	33	5	1	9	22	19	3	0	1	49	0	0	.512	.357
Chapman, Matt	R-R	6-0	210	4-28-93	.257	.320	.247	49	175	30	45	6	2	16	30	25	1	0	3	63	5	4	.589	.348
Curtis, Jermaine	R-R	5-11	190	7-10-87	.254	.188	.275	22	67	3	17	2	0	0	4	9	2	1	0	15	0	0	.284	.359
Decker, Jaff	L-L	5-9	190	2-23-90	.274	.266	.275	93	351	41	96	13	1	6	36	38	1	3	5	93	15	5	.368	.342
LaMarre, Ryan	L-R	6-1	210	11-21-88	.240	.182	.252	41	129	11	31	2	2	0	12	11	3	2	1	47	5	5	.287	.313
2-team total (10 Salt Lake)					.247	.214	.296	51	170	17	42	3	3	0	19	17	4	2	1	58	9	6	.300	.328
Lambo, Andrew	L-L	6-3	220	8-11-88	.133	.100	.143	12	45	3	6	2	0	0	0	1	0	1	0	17	0	0	.178	.152
Lavarnway, Ryan	R-R	6-4	240	8-7-87	.239	.214	.245	82	264	33	63	9	0	6	26	31	5	1	3	65	0	2	.341	.327
Maxwell, Bruce	L-R	6-1	250	12-20-90	.286	.200	.322	25	84	11	24	9	0	2	14	8	0	0	1	14	0	0	.464	.344
McBride, Matt	R-R	6-2	215	5-23-85	.231	.255	.225	79	251	30	58	19	1	10	49	21	6	1	6	47	1	1	.434	.299
Mercedes, Melvin	B-R	5-8	170	1-13-92	.238	.143	.266	62	181	30	43	5	2	0	14	29	5	3	2	36	5	2	.287	.355
Munoz, Yairo	R-R	6-1	165	1-23-95	.289	.213	.306	65	256	30	74	9	1	7	42	11	1	0	4	46	10	4	.414	.316
Nunez, Renato	R-R	6-1	220	4-4-94	.250	.283	.242	126	473	74	118	27	2	32	78	47	5	0	8	141	2	1	.518	.319
Olson, Matt	L-R	6-5	230	3-29-94	.272	.194	.293	79	294	56	80	16	1	23	60	45	1	0	3	83	3	0	.568	.367
Parmelee, Chris	L-L	6-1	220	2-24-88	.199	.136	.211	42	136	21	27	6	0	5	14	16	0	0	1	46	0	1	.353	.281
2-team total (13 New Orleans)					.213	.136	.211	55	169	26	36	9	0	6	18	29	0	0	2	53	0	1	.373	.325
Phegley, Josh	R-R	5-10	230	2-12-88	.310	.333	.304	8	29	2	9	2	0	1	4	2	2	0	1	5	0	0	.483	.382
Pinder, Chad	R-R	6-2	195	3-29-92	.266	.250	.267	17	64	3	17	2	1	1	2	6	1	0	0	23	2	1	.375	.338
Powell, Boog	L-L	5-10	185	1-14-93	.250	.000	.286	3	16	1	4	1	0	0	0	1	0	0	0	5	0	0	.313	.294
2-team total (58 Tacoma)					.333	.000	.286	61	222	47	74	10	2	6	33	29	1	1	3	32	11	5	.478	.408
Semien, Marcus	R-R	6-0	195	9-17-90	.286	.000	.333	3	14	4	4	0	0	1	3	1	0	0	0	1	0	0	.500	.333
Smolinski, Jake	R-R	5-11	205	2-9-89	.129	.286	.083	6	31	4	4	1	0	0	1	0	1	0	0	8	0	0	.161	.156
Taylor, Beau	L-R	6-0	205	2-13-90	.289	.120	.325	41	142	26	41	6	0	3	17	20	0	0	1	32	0	1	.394	.374
Wendle, Joey	L-R	6-1	190	4-26-90	.285	.280	.286	118	478	67	136	29	8	8	54	19	12	0	1	82	13	4	.429	.328
Wilson, Kenny	R-R	6-0	205	1-30-90	.237	.194	.253	71	232	22	55	6	2	1	18	15	7	0	2	67	12	7	.293	.301

Pitching	B-T	HT	WT	DOB	W	L	ERA	G	GS	CG	SV	IP	H	R	ER	HR	BB	SO	AVG	vLH	vRH	K/9	BB/9
Alcantara, Raul	R-R	6-4	220	12-4-92	1	2	2.67	18	3	0	4	34	36	10	10	0	7	22	.273	.292	.254	5.88	1.87
Axford, John	R-R	6-5	220	4-1-83	0	0	0.00	3	0	0	0	3	2	0	0	0	0	4	.182	.200	.000	10.80	0.00
Bassitt, Chris	R-R	6-5	220	2-22-89	4	2	6.21	17	2	0	0	38	41	26	26	3	16	31	.283	.286	.281	7.41	3.82
Bawcom, Logan	R-R	6-2	220	11-2-88	1	2	5.19	11	0	0	0	17	18	10	10	1	6	9	.273	.259	.282	4.67	3.12
2-team total (36 El Paso)					2	5	3.31	47	0	0	2	71	66	33	26	5	31	63	.248	.259	.282	8.02	3.95
Blackburn, Paul	R-R	6-1	195	12-4-93	5	6	3.05	15	14	0	0	80	69	34	27	6	26	56	.231	.247	.216	6.33	2.94
Bracewell, Ben	R-R	6-0	195	9-19-90	5	2	4.60	13	12	0	0	63	69	38	32	3	23	44	.279	.240	.305	6.32	3.30
Brady, Michael	R-R	6-0	195	3-21-87	3	1	3.21	17	8	0	0	53	45	22	19	5	6	51	.222	.224	.220	8.61	1.01
Castro, Simon	R-R	6-5	230	4-9-88	3	5	3.32	33	0	0	4	38	24	21	14	3	21	63	.177	.190	.167	14.92	4.97
Cotton, Jharel	R-R	5-11	195	1-19-92	3	0	2.95	4	3	0	0	21	15	8	7	3	4	28	.195	.194	.195	11.81	1.69
Detwiler, Ross	L-R	6-3	210	3-6-86	0	1	6.43	14	0	0	1	14	15	10	10	1	8	12	.283	.207	.375	7.71	5.14
2-team total (5 Iowa)					0	2	7.43	19	0	0	1	23	29	19	19	4	15	22	.309	.231	.393	8.61	5.87
Doolittle, Sean	L-L	6-2	210	9-26-86	0	0	0.00	1	0	0	0	1	0	0	0	0	0	2	.000	.000	.000	18.00	0.00
Doubront, Felix	L-L	6-2	240	10-23-87	2	3	3.86	29	2	0	1	42	40	26	18	5	19	50	.244	.259	.236	10.71	4.07
Dull, Ryan	R-R	5-9	175	10-2-89	0	0	0.00	2	0	0	0	3	1	0	0	0	1	2	.111	.000	.125	6.75	3.38
Finnegan, Kyle	R-R	6-2	170	9-4-91	1	1	4.94	17	0	0	3	24	25	18	13	4	17	21	.275	.257	.286	7.99	6.46

Pitching	B-T	HT	WT	DOB	W	L	ERA	G	GS	CG	SV	IP	H	R	ER	HR	BB	SO	AVG	vLH	vRH	K/9	BB/9
Gossett, Daniel	R-R	6-2	185	11-13-92	4	4	3.66	14	14	0	0	76	70	35	31	6	24	71	.239	.250	.230	8.37	2.83
Graveman, Kendall	R-R	6-2	200	12-21-90	0	1	7.20	3	3	0	0	10	18	12	8	1	4	7	.383	.423	.333	6.30	3.60
Gray, Sonny	R-R	5-10	190	11-7-89	1	0	0.00	1	1	0	0	6	2	0	0	0	0	7	.095	.250	.000	10.50	0.00
Hahn, Jesse	R-R	6-4	215	7-30-89	2	0	4.32	6	5	0	0	25	28	14	12	1	14	18	.289	.250	.321	6.48	5.04
Healy, Tucker	L-R	6-1	210	6-15-90	1	2	4.64	35	0	0	1	43	46	23	22	3	22	34	.279	.339	.240	7.17	4.64
Hurlbutt, Dustin	R-R	6-1	195	11-5-92	0	1	15.00	1	1	0	0	3	7	5	5	1	2	2	.467	1.000	.333	6.00	6.00
Jensen, Chris	R-R	6-4	200	9-30-90	5	1	5.95	30	7	0	1	85	102	59	56	8	29	56	.294	.241	.327	5.95	3.08
Kurcz, Aaron	R-R	6-0	175	8-8-90	3	3	7.24	22	0	0	0	27	35	22	22	4	9	28	.313	.388	.254	9.22	2.96
Manaea, Sean	R-L	6-5	245	2-1-92	0	0	2.25	1	1	0	0	4	4	2	1	0	1	5	.250	.286	.222	11.25	2.25
Mengden, Daniel	R-R	6-2	190	2-19-93	2	4	4.17	9	9	0	0	41	40	20	19	5	18	40	.255	.200	.305	8.78	3.95
Moll, Sam	L-L	5-10	185	1-3-92	0	0	0.00	6	0	0	0	7	5	0	0	0	1	8	.192	.200	.191	10.29	1.29
2-team total (44 Albuquerque)					3	2	3.64	50	0	0	0	54	61	27	22	4	19	47	.280	.306	.285	7.79	3.15
Montas, Frankie	R-R	6-2	255	3-21-93	0	2	5.22	9	8	0	0	29	25	17	17	4	7	37	.223	.250	.188	11.35	2.15
Neal, Zach	R-R	6-3	220	11-9-88	4	8	4.82	21	16	0	0	99	115	54	53	9	10	43	.297	.296	.298	3.91	0.91
Sanchez, Jake	R-R	6-1	205	8-19-89	1	2	1.47	14	0	0	3	18	15	5	3	0	4	19	.227	.333	.167	9.33	1.96
Sawyer, Dalton	L-L	6-5	210	11-22-93	0	1	11.42	2	2	0	0	9	12	11	11	3	6	2	.343	.250	.355	2.08	6.23
Schuster, Patrick	R-L	6-2	190	10-30-90	3	2	5.94	27	0	0	1	33	43	23	22	4	12	40	.307	.255	.333	10.80	3.24
2-team total (17 Oklahoma City)					4	2	6.02	44	0	0	1	52	68	36	35	7	19	54	.313	.400	.288	9.29	3.27
Seddon, Joel	R-R	6-1	165	7-13-92	0	0	2.25	1	1	0	0	4	5	1	1	0	3	5	.333	.000	.500	11.25	6.75
Smith, Chris	R-R	6-0	190	4-9-81	4	3	3.16	15	12	0	0	74	76	27	26	5	20	64	.265	.245	.284	7.78	2.43
Smith, Josh	R-R	6-2	220	8-7-87	4	1	3.70	19	2	0	1	41	33	17	17	4	11	44	.220	.222	.219	9.58	2.40
Sturdevant, Tyler	R-R	6-0	185	12-20-85	1	2	4.39	18	0	0	0	27	35	21	13	1	13	13	.310	.346	.276	4.39	4.39
Trivino, Lou	R-R	6-5	225	10-1-91	1	2	3.60	25	0	0	4	35	33	15	14	0	11	31	.244	.321	.190	7.97	2.83
Valdez, Cesar	R-R	6-2	200	3-17-85	1	0	2.70	2	2	0	0	10	8	3	3	1	0	12	.211	.059	.333	10.80	0.00
Wahl, Bobby	R-R	6-2	210	3-21-92	1	1	4.15	11	0	0	3	13	13	8	6	3	5	22	.245	.286	.219	15.23	3.46
Walter, Corey	R-R	6-3	215	8-11-92	2	6	5.20	21	11	2	1	73	97	45	42	4	23	46	.321	.371	.287	5.70	2.85

Fielding

Catcher	PCT	G	PO	A	E	DP	PB
Lavarnway	.987	61	446	18	6	4	7
Maxwell	1.000	19	140	12	0	1	1
McBride	.985	27	183	12	3	1	2
Phegley	1.000	6	37	3	0	0	1
Taylor	.996	37	261	19	1	3	4

First Base	PCT	G	PO	A	E	DP
Carter	.986	24	211	7	3	23
Curtis	.987	9	67	7	1	6
Lavarnway	1.000	1	1	0	0	0
McBride	1.000	23	175	8	0	16
Nunez	.960	5	23	1	1	3
Olson	.997	73	610	35	2	63
Parmelee	1.000	11	88	4	0	6

Second Base	PCT	G	PO	A	E	DP
Barreto	.969	25	36	59	3	8
Mercedes	1.000	27	56	68	0	17
Nunez	.923	2	4	8	1	3
Pinder	1.000	8	10	18	0	1
Wendle	.973	82	165	229	11	60

Third Base	PCT	G	PO	A	E	DP
Chapman	.956	49	44	108	7	15
Curtis	.941	10	7	9	1	1
Mercedes	1.000	2	2	4	0	0
Munoz	.940	15	15	32	3	3
Nunez	.916	44	15	72	8	4
Olson	1.000	1	0	4	0	1
Wendle	.978	24	21	67	2	8

Shortstop	PCT	G	PO	A	E	DP
Barreto	.950	83	117	223	18	49
Mercedes	.968	23	38	54	3	11
Munoz	.946	24	40	83	7	18
Pinder	.875	4	7	7	2	0
Semien	.800	2	2	6	2	2
Wendle	.864	5	3	16	3	1

Outfield	PCT	G	PO	A	E	DP
Brugman	1.000	36	65	0	0	0
Canha	.993	71	134	4	1	0
Decker	.994	86	161	7	1	4
LaMarre	.990	39	98	4	1	0
Lambo	.952	11	20	0	1	0
McBride	.941	21	31	1	2	0
Mercedes	1.000	5	9	0	0	0
Munoz	1.000	27	56	3	0	0
Nunez	.984	48	61	2	1	1
Parmelee	.926	17	24	1	2	0
Pinder	.800	4	4	0	1	0
Powell	1.000	3	7	0	0	0
Wilson	.986	69	140	6	2	2

MIDLAND ROCKHOUNDS — *DOUBLE-A*

TEXAS LEAGUE

Batting	B-T	HT	WT	DOB	AVG	vLH	vRH	G	AB	R	H	2B	3B	HR	RBI	BB	HBP	SH	SF	SO	SB	CS	SLG	OBP
Bennie, Joe	R-R	6-0	200	5-7-91	.238	.200	.243	22	80	7	19	4	1	1	3	12	0	0	0	25	0	2	.350	.337
Boyd, B.J.	L-R	5-11	230	7-16-93	.323	.298	.329	130	533	82	172	29	6	5	56	34	5	1	5	74	16	5	.428	.366
Cogswell, Branden	L-R	6-1	180	1-12-93	.225	.100	.246	24	71	6	16	2	0	0	3	7	0	1	0	15	1	1	.254	.295
Curtis, Jermaine	R-R	5-11	190	7-10-87	.310	.346	.297	56	203	28	63	14	1	1	28	37	7	0	3	42	2	1	.404	.428
Marincov, Tyler	R-R	6-2	205	10-20-91	.266	.294	.257	79	286	42	76	20	2	9	54	30	5	0	6	95	5	4	.444	.339
Martin, Richie	R-R	5-11	190	12-22-94	.224	.192	.231	86	286	43	64	11	3	3	27	24	11	1	3	57	12	3	.315	.306
Mateo, Jorge	R-R	6-0	190	6-23-95	.292	.457	.235	30	137	25	40	5	7	4	20	9	0	0	1	33	13	3	.518	.333
Mercedes, Melvin	B-R	5-8	170	1-13-92	.300	.200	.333	5	20	5	6	1	0	0	2	3	0	0	0	0	0	0	.350	.391
Munoz, Yairo	R-R	6-1	165	1-23-95	.316	.367	.298	47	190	35	60	17	3	6	26	10	1	1	3	35	12	1	.532	.348
Murphy, Sean	R-R	6-3	215	10-10-94	.209	.205	.211	53	191	25	40	7	0	4	22	21	1	2	2	34	0	0	.309	.288
Neuse, Sheldon	R-R	6-0	195	12-10-94	.373	.308	.389	18	67	9	25	4	0	0	6	6	1	0	1	21	0	0	.433	.427
Paz, Andy	R-R	6-0	170	1-5-93	.251	.118	.283	53	179	14	45	4	0	0	19	14	0	2	2	37	3	0	.274	.303
Raga, Argenis	R-R	6-1	176	7-22-94	.200	.313	.177	28	95	11	19	5	0	2	13	8	0	0	2	25	0	0	.316	.257
Ramirez, Tyler	L-L	5-9	185	2-21-95	.308	.279	.315	58	208	29	64	11	1	4	24	28	4	0	3	53	3	3	.428	.395
Rodriguez, J.C.	R-R	5-10	170	1-12-96	.235	.500	.200	8	17	1	4	1	1	0	2	0	0	0	0	6	0	0	.412	.235
Rosa, Viosergy	L-L	6-3	185	6-16-90	.255	.328	.232	135	517	62	132	28	1	18	110	56	2	0	10	137	0	1	.418	.325
Schrock, Max	L-R	5-8	180	10-12-94	.321	.302	.327	106	417	55	134	19	1	7	46	34	5	0	1	42	4	2	.422	.379
Sportman, J.P.	R-R	5-9	190	1-26-92	.275	.276	.275	130	513	71	141	27	5	12	74	36	5	1	3	113	14	8	.417	.327
Tarsovich, Jordan	R-R	5-10	180	6-20-91	.241	.250	.238	104	341	56	82	15	3	3	30	48	3	3	4	79	13	5	.328	.336
Taylor, Beau	L-R	6-0	205	2-13-90	.309	.273	.326	21	68	10	21	4	1	2	7	9	0	0	1	17	0	0	.485	.385
Vertigan, Brett	L-L	5-9	175	8-21-90	.285	.225	.300	67	249	39	71	18	2	1	21	35	2	4	1	59	7	2	.386	.376
Wilson, Kenny	R-R	6-0	205	1-30-90	.250	.227	.262	19	64	13	16	1	1	2	8	10	2	0	0	14	3	2	.391	.368

Pitching	B-T	HT	WT	DOB	W	L	ERA	G	GS	CG	SV	IP	H	R	ER	HR	BB	SO	AVG	vLH	vRH	K/9	BB/9
Bracewell, Ben	R-R	6-0	195	9-19-90	2	1	6.30	15	8	0	0	50	61	35	35	5	22	29	.311	.356	.292	5.22	3.96

Pitching	B-T	HT	WT	DOB	W	L	ERA	G	GS	CG	SV	IP	H	R	ER	HR	BB	SO	AVG	vLH	vRH	K/9	BB/9
Bragg, Sam	R-R	6-2	190	3-23-93	4	1	3.03	45	0	0	6	68	69	25	23	4	16	56	.264	.259	.267	7.38	2.11
Fillmyer, Heath	R-R	6-1	180	5-16-94	11	5	3.49	29	29	0	0	150	158	66	58	19	51	115	.272	.279	.269	6.92	3.07
Finnegan, Kyle	R-R	6-2	170	9-4-91	1	3	3.19	29	0	0	9	37	36	13	13	4	8	36	.254	.281	.235	8.84	1.96
Friedrichs, Kyle	R-R	6-1	195	1-22-92	1	4	6.00	18	3	0	1	51	58	38	34	7	17	36	.280	.143	.350	6.35	3.00
Graves, Brett	R-R	6-1	170	1-30-93	1	1	5.97	7	6	0	0	32	48	22	21	1	10	28	.353	.313	.365	7.96	2.84
Holmes, Grant	L-R	6-1	215	3-22-96	11	12	4.49	29	24	0	0	148	149	82	74	15	61	150	.262	.189	.309	9.10	3.70
Hurlbutt, Dustin	R-R	6-1	195	11-5-92	3	2	3.55	9	8	0	0	46	33	19	18	5	25	32	.195	.185	.202	6.31	4.93
Kurcz, Aaron	R-R	6-0	175	8-8-90	2	1	3.09	17	0	0	0	23	18	8	8	2	8	11	.220	.206	.229	4.24	3.09
Manarino, Evan	L-L	6-1	195	12-28-92	1	4	8.10	5	5	0	0	27	45	25	24	4	6	12	.388	.360	.396	4.05	2.03
Mann, Brandon	L-L	6-2	200	5-16-84	3	8	4.40	46	2	0	2	76	66	46	37	6	36	81	.231	.177	.258	9.63	4.28
Meisner, Casey	R-R	6-7	190	5-22-95	4	4	4.12	12	12	0	0	59	55	27	27	4	27	37	.249	.274	.237	5.64	4.12
Naile, James	R-R	6-4	185	2-8-93	2	3	3.21	14	10	0	0	62	55	30	22	5	17	42	.239	.284	.218	6.13	2.48
Navas, Carlos	R-R	6-1	170	8-13-92	3	4	3.25	33	2	0	4	53	49	23	19	4	15	48	.246	.281	.230	8.20	2.56
Puk, A.J.	L-L	6-7	220	4-25-95	2	5	4.36	13	13	0	0	64	64	34	31	2	25	86	.256	.226	.266	12.09	3.52
Sanchez, Jake	R-R	6-1	205	8-19-89	0	0	1.13	9	0	0	3	8	4	1	1	0	2	14	.148	.125	.158	15.75	2.25
Seddon, Joel	R-R	6-1	165	7-13-92	3	4	5.00	33	6	0	2	94	107	56	52	8	31	70	.294	.349	.265	6.73	2.98
Stull, Cody	L-L	6-2	160	3-23-92	2	2	5.27	26	1	0	0	43	52	28	25	4	24	26	.301	.294	.303	5.48	5.06
Sturdevant, Tyler	R-R	6-0	185	12-20-85	2	4	3.74	25	0	0	4	34	32	18	14	5	7	31	.246	.143	.309	8.29	1.87
Trivino, Lou	R-R	6-5	225	10-1-91	7	1	2.43	23	0	0	1	33	31	9	9	0	10	34	.246	.263	.239	9.18	2.70
Twomey, Kyle	L-L	6-3	165	12-29-93	0	1	31.50	1	0	0	0	2	6	7	7	1	2	1	.600	1.000	.500	4.50	9.00
Walter, Corey	R-R	6-3	215	8-11-92	2	1	2.44	10	9	0	0	44	45	16	12	0	12	30	.265	.250	.275	6.09	2.44
Zambrano, Jesus	R-R	5-11	170	8-23-96	0	0	22.50	1	0	0	0	2	5	5	5	2	1	3	.455	.500	.444	13.50	4.50

Fielding

Catcher	PCT	G	PO	A	E	DP	PB
Murphy	.995	51	412	30	2	3	2
Paz	.997	47	315	37	1	5	3
Raga	.990	25	185	15	2	4	7
Taylor	1.000	18	116	11	0	3	2

First Base	PCT	G	PO	A	E	DP
Bennie	1.000	5	39	6	0	5
Curtis	1.000	7	55	6	0	10
Neuse	1.000	1	2	1	0	0
Rosa	.992	125	1076	71	9	130
Tarsovich	.000	1	0	0	0	0
Vertigan	1.000	1	9	1	0	1

Second Base	PCT	G	PO	A	E	DP
Cogswell	1.000	8	9	12	0	2
Mercedes	1.000	1	2	1	0	1
Munoz	1.000	2	2	7	0	1
Rodriguez	1.000	2	0	4	0	0
Schrock	.986	101	173	257	6	83
Sportman	.972	21	37	67	3	20
Tarsovich	.971	7	12	21	1	6

Third Base	PCT	G	PO	A	E	DP
Cogswell	.889	13	7	17	3	2
Curtis	1.000	8	2	18	0	2
Mercedes	.600	2	0	3	2	0
Munoz	.889	21	9	39	6	2
Neuse	.979	18	12	35	1	4
Raga	.600	2	0	3	2	0
Rodriguez	.778	4	2	5	2	0
Tarsovich	.932	81	55	165	16	13

Shortstop	PCT	G	PO	A	E	DP
Cogswell	1.000	2	0	4	0	0
Martin	.981	86	133	228	7	74
Mateo	.952	30	43	95	7	23
Mercedes	1.000	1	2	3	0	1
Munoz	.960	22	34	61	4	17
Rodriguez	.800	2	0	4	1	1

Outfield	PCT	G	PO	A	E	DP
Boyd	.988	109	238	5	3	2
Marincov	.974	58	110	4	3	2
Munoz	.000	1	0	0	0	0
Raga	.000	1	0	0	0	0
Ramirez	1.000	58	106	3	0	0
Sportman	.985	104	189	5	3	0
Tarsovich	.931	13	26	1	2	0
Vertigan	1.000	58	101	5	0	1
Wilson	.971	18	32	1	1	1

STOCKTON PORTS — *HIGH CLASS A*

CALIFORNIA LEAGUE

Batting	B-T	HT	WT	DOB	AVG	vLH	vRH	G	AB	R	H	2B	3B	HR	RBI	BB	HBP	SH	SF	SO	SB	CS	SLG	OBP
Akau, Iolana	R-R	5-11	180	8-31-95	.236	.100	.267	16	55	6	13	2	0	0	4	3	2	0	0	17	1	1	.273	.300
Barrera, Luis	L-L	6-0	180	11-15-95	.228	.087	.264	35	114	15	26	2	0	4	16	8	0	1	1	25	3	1	.351	.276
Bolt, Skye	B-R	6-3	190	1-15-94	.243	.244	.243	114	432	76	105	24	7	15	66	53	3	4	4	134	9	8	.435	.327
Brown, Seth	L-L	6-3	220	7-13-92	.270	.258	.273	135	518	80	140	18	7	30	109	56	1	0	4	146	7	7	.506	.340
Chapman, Matt	R-R	6-0	210	4-28-93	.000	.000	.000	2	7	0	0	0	0	0	0	1	0	0	0	3	0	0	.000	.125
Chavez, Santiago	R-R	5-11	175	8-5-95	.192	.303	.164	52	167	12	32	10	0	2	11	10	1	1	1	58	2	1	.287	.240
Cogswell, Branden	L-R	6-1	180	1-12-93	.282	.231	.296	71	255	32	72	15	1	0	23	34	1	2	1	48	4	2	.349	.368
Diaz, Edwin	R-R	6-2	195	8-25-95	.089	.000	.114	13	45	2	4	0	1	0	3	4	0	1	1	15	0	0	.133	.160
Gilbert, Trent	R-L	6-1	175	3-17-93	.278	.400	.260	31	115	16	32	7	1	3	13	3	2	1	0	32	1	0	.435	.308
Harris, James	R-R	6-1	180	8-7-93	.244	.227	.250	21	82	11	20	5	0	1	9	7	0	0	0	20	2	1	.342	.303
Iriart, Chris	R-R	6-2	230	10-7-94	.203	.160	.217	58	202	20	41	7	0	10	29	15	4	0	1	89	0	0	.386	.270
Martin, Richie	R-R	5-11	190	12-22-94	.266	.250	.273	23	94	16	25	2	3	1	6	8	1	0	0	21	1	1	.383	.330
Mondou, Nate	L-R	5-10	205	3-24-95	.278	.244	.286	59	223	38	62	8	4	2	27	28	3	0	3	57	8	5	.377	.362
Murphy, Sean	R-R	6-3	215	10-10-94	.297	.333	.285	45	165	22	49	11	0	9	26	11	1	0	1	33	0	0	.527	.343
Neuse, Sheldon	R-R	6-0	195	12-10-94	.386	.444	.369	22	83	21	32	3	0	7	22	9	2	0	0	25	2	0	.675	.457
Pimentel, Sandber	L-L	6-3	220	9-12-94	.279	.211	.300	70	244	40	68	8	0	14	42	36	1	0	0	78	0	0	.484	.374
Raga, Argenis	R-R	6-1	176	7-22-94	.259	.194	.275	47	162	24	42	11	0	6	20	13	0	0	1	40	0	0	.438	.313
Ramirez, Tyler	L-L	5-9	185	2-21-95	.301	.309	.299	76	279	51	84	12	2	7	39	45	2	0	2	80	5	2	.434	.399
Semien, Marcus	R-R	6-0	195	9-17-90	.353	.250	.444	5	17	2	6	3	0	1	5	0	0	0	3	2	0	0	.706	.300
Siddall, Brett	L-L	6-1	210	10-3-94	.300	.227	.318	117	440	78	132	23	0	21	68	33	14	0	3	104	3	1	.496	.365
Smolinski, Jake	R-R	5-11	205	2-9-89	.250	.000	.353	7	24	5	6	1	0	1	10	5	1	0	2	4	0	1	.417	.375
Vidales, Josh	B-R	5-8	164	8-6-93	.206	.208	.205	62	243	20	50	7	0	1	20	23	0	3	2	59	3	6	.247	.272
White, Eli	R-R	6-2	175	6-26-94	.270	.247	.276	115	448	71	121	32	6	4	36	41	9	2	2	121	12	5	.395	.342
White, Mikey	R-R	6-1	200	9-3-93	.261	.237	.268	115	440	59	115	27	4	17	73	40	6	1	1	121	4	0	.457	.331

Pitching	B-T	HT	WT	DOB	W	L	ERA	G	GS	CG	SV	IP	H	R	ER	HR	BB	SO	AVG	vLH	vRH	K/9	BB/9
Bailey, Brandon	R-R	5-10	175	10-19-94	2	1	4.24	9	6	0	1	34	28	16	16	4	10	47	.217	.148	.279	12.44	2.65
Bassitt, Chris	R-R	6-5	220	2-22-89	0	1	2.77	7	7	0	0	13	9	4	4	0	4	14	.192	.273	.120	9.69	2.77
Biegalski, Boomer	R-R	6-2	165	7-13-94	3	2	5.12	19	7	0	2	51	52	30	29	12	18	64	.265	.221	.294	11.29	3.18

Blackwood, Nolan	R-R	6-5	185	3-16-95	1	5	3.00	44	0	0	19	57	42	25	19	2	18	48	.205	.253	.167	7.58	2.84
Butler, Brendan	L-R	6-3	217	5-2-93	4	5	6.21	14	7	0	0	58	72	49	40	5	30	51	.308	.328	.280	7.91	4.66
Cochran-Gill, Trey	R-R	5-10	190	12-10-92	0	0	16.20	1	0	0	0	2	4	3	3	0	1	1	.444	.333	.667	5.40	5.40
Doolittle, Sean	L-L	6-2	210	9-26-86	0	0	0.00	2	0	0	0	2	0	0	0	0	0	3	.000	.000	.000	13.50	0.00
Duno, Angel	R-R	6-0	180	1-10-94	8	9	5.40	29	22	0	0	140	187	96	84	25	26	126	.317	.349	.289	8.10	1.67
Friedrichs, Kyle	R-R	6-1	195	1-22-92	2	2	2.98	16	4	0	1	54	44	22	18	7	12	42	.218	.245	.194	6.96	1.99
Gilbert, Will	L-L	5-11	170	2-9-94	1	1	6.86	9	0	0	0	20	23	16	15	2	9	14	.303	.214	.354	6.41	4.12
Gorman, John	R-R	6-1	230	2-19-92	0	0	6.00	4	0	0	0	6	7	4	4	1	2	4	.318	.286	.333	6.00	3.00
Graves, Brett	R-R	6-1	170	1-30-93	0	0	2.55	7	4	0	0	25	18	9	7	3	3	29	.196	.188	.200	10.58	1.09
Gray, Sonny	R-R	5-10	190	11-7-89	1	0	0.00	1	1	0	0	5	1	0	0	0	0	6	.063	.250	.000	10.80	0.00
Hahn, Jesse	R-R	6-4	215	7-30-89	0	0	3.38	1	1	0	0	5	4	2	2	1	1	4	.211	.000	.267	6.75	1.69
Hurlbutt, Dustin	R-R	6-1	195	11-5-92	2	2	3.23	15	8	0	0	70	52	25	25	7	16	74	.199	.227	.183	9.56	2.07
Jefferies, Daulton	R-L	6-0	180	8-2-95	0	0	2.57	2	1	0	0	7	7	6	2	0	1	6	.241	.375	.191	7.71	1.29
Jensen, Chris	R-R	6-4	200	9-30-90	0	0	1.69	2	0	0	1	5	1	1	1	1	0	6	.056	.000	.125	10.13	0.00
Lyons, Jared	L-L	6-0	190	5-18-93	2	3	4.63	33	0	0	1	47	51	35	24	4	22	47	.280	.266	.288	9.06	4.24
Manarino, Evan	L-L	6-1	195	12-28-92	7	8	4.89	25	13	0	0	103	129	62	56	13	11	93	.301	.267	.317	8.13	0.96
Marsonek, Brandon	L-L	6-1	190	6-12-94	0	1	2.82	11	0	0	1	22	13	9	7	2	15	17	.159	.095	.180	6.85	6.04
Meisner, Casey	R-R	6-7	190	5-22-95	6	5	3.98	16	12	0	0	75	73	36	33	9	20	80	.254	.232	.273	9.64	2.41
Naile, James	R-R	6-4	185	2-8-93	0	0	5.14	2	2	0	0	7	9	5	4	0	1	4	.290	.375	.200	5.14	1.29
Navas, Carlos	R-R	6-1	170	8-13-92	3	0	0.50	12	0	0	2	18	6	2	1	1	4	28	.100	.083	.111	14.00	2.00
Puk, A.J.	L-L	6-7	220	4-25-95	4	5	3.69	14	11	0	0	61	44	28	25	1	23	98	.196	.230	.183	14.46	3.39
Romero, Miguel	R-R	6-2	180	4-23-94	3	1	6.87	8	1	0	0	18	22	16	14	4	9	25	.301	.344	.268	12.27	4.42
Ruiz, Armando	R-R	5-9	185	7-19-93	3	1	4.87	27	0	0	2	44	40	24	24	5	19	46	.235	.260	.215	9.34	3.86
Ruiz, Norge	R-R	6-0	185	3-15-94	3	1	5.71	8	8	0	0	35	47	26	22	4	12	24	.326	.367	.277	6.23	3.12
Sawyer, Dalton	L-L	6-5	210	11-22-93	5	5	3.68	13	11	0	0	66	67	29	27	12	20	74	.253	.105	.312	10.09	2.73
Sergey, Matt	R-R	6-4	180	7-29-89	1	0	3.48	8	0	0	0	10	7	6	4	1	4	11	.189	.250	.143	9.58	3.48
Shore, Logan	R-R	6-2	215	12-28-94	2	5	4.09	17	14	0	1	73	81	38	33	5	16	74	.277	.237	.303	9.17	1.98
Stull, Cody	L-L	6-2	160	3-23-92	1	0	2.76	10	0	0	2	16	14	6	5	1	4	14	.230	.263	.214	7.71	2.20
Tomasovich, Andrew	L-L	6-4	215	9-24-93	3	3	4.72	29	0	0	0	34	33	21	18	3	18	42	.254	.289	.235	11.01	4.72
Wagman, Joey	L-R	6-0	185	7-25-91	4	2	4.86	37	0	0	1	54	56	33	29	5	31	48	.269	.289	.252	8.05	5.20
Wahl, Bobby	R-R	6-2	210	3-21-92	0	0	0.00	2	0	0	0	2	0	0	0	0	3	6	.000	.000	.000	27.00	13.50

Fielding

Catcher	PCT	G	PO	A	E	DP	PB
Akau	.980	16	139	9	3	0	8
Chavez	.983	50	420	41	8	4	8
Murphy	.992	40	369	25	3	3	7
Raga	.994	45	334	27	2	1	8

First Base	PCT	G	PO	A	E	DP
Brown	.987	23	141	15	2	12
Cogswell	1.000	2	2	1	0	0
Iriart	.998	57	438	19	1	26
Pimentel	.985	59	420	50	7	35
White	.985	9	58	7	1	6

Second Base	PCT	G	PO	A	E	DP
Cogswell	.994	46	72	101	1	13
Diaz	.944	4	5	12	1	3
Mondou	.988	55	95	150	3	34
Vidales	.981	35	64	88	3	14
White	1.000	1	2	1	0	1

Third Base	PCT	G	PO	A	E	DP
Chapman	1.000	1	1	2	0	0
Cogswell	.930	13	9	31	3	5
Diaz	.905	7	7	12	2	3
Gilbert	1.000	18	8	13	0	0
Neuse	1.000	10	7	13	0	0
Vidales	.946	17	15	20	2	0
White	.901	75	33	122	17	3

Shortstop	PCT	G	PO	A	E	DP
Diaz	1.000	2	6	4	0	1
Martin	.956	14	29	36	3	4
Neuse	.902	8	15	22	4	3
Semien	.917	3	5	6	1	3
Vidales	1.000	1	0	3	0	0
White	.929	92	129	200	25	33
White	.962	22	21	55	3	12

Outfield	PCT	G	PO	A	E	DP
Barrera	.938	33	56	4	4	0
Bolt	.981	111	254	8	5	3
Brown	.975	114	219	13	6	2
Harris	.968	18	28	2	1	0
Ramirez	1.000	70	116	1	0	1
Siddall	.957	72	108	2	5	1
Vidales	1.000	4	6	0	0	0
White	1.000	9	11	0	0	0

BELOIT SNAPPERS

LOW CLASS A

MIDWEST LEAGUE

Batting	B-T	HT	WT	DOB	AVG	vLH	vRH	G	AB	R	H	2B	3B	HR	RBI	BB	HBP	SH	SF	SO	SB	CS	SLG	OBP
Barrera, Luis	L-L	6-0	180	11-15-95	.277	.275	.278	73	278	41	77	13	7	3	22	16	3	1	3	61	13	7	.407	.320
Diaz, Edwin	R-R	6-2	195	8-25-95	.255	.349	.230	89	302	49	77	12	3	10	45	43	2	2	2	91	0	0	.414	.350
Goldstein, Jason	R-R	5-11	195	3-9-94	.203	.175	.212	72	241	23	49	9	0	3	21	21	4	1	3	42	0	0	.278	.275
Gruber, Cole	L-L	6-0	190	3-31-94	.182	.000	.200	18	55	7	10	3	0	0	2	9	1	1	0	22	2	0	.236	.308
Loehr, Trace	L-R	5-10	175	5-23-95	.267	.211	.281	94	363	47	97	10	8	3	36	19	0	7	2	63	10	6	.364	.302
Lopez, Jesus	R-R	5-11	170	10-5-96	.280	.195	.319	38	132	15	37	6	1	2	13	8	1	2	1	19	4	1	.386	.324
Marinez, Eric	B-R	6-1	160	9-12-95	.278	.200	.303	114	410	40	114	18	3	3	30	39	1	4	2	86	6	2	.359	.341
Martin, Mike	R-R	6-0	175	9-29-92	.300	.309	.297	73	263	46	79	16	1	1	27	22	5	3	3	41	24	4	.380	.362
Mercedes, Miguel	R-R	6-4	255	9-12-95	.230	.167	.249	119	452	46	104	26	0	16	59	31	6	0	4	126	0	2	.394	.286
Mondou, Nate	L-R	5-10	205	3-24-95	.296	.304	.294	66	247	31	73	16	3	0	32	31	2	2	6	43	8	3	.385	.371
Nowlin, Kyle	R-R	6-0	240	3-4-94	.248	.281	.239	123	416	52	103	28	0	11	66	69	3	0	2	133	2	2	.394	.357
Persico, Luke	R-R	6-3	180	10-4-95	.260	.225	.270	117	446	61	116	25	4	5	64	46	2	1	7	80	7	4	.368	.327
Rodriguez, J.C.	R-R	5-10	170	1-12-96	.244	.309	.217	62	193	22	47	13	0	4	21	28	4	2	2	33	0	1	.373	.348
Shelby, JaVon	R-R	6-1	190	5-6-95	.198	.155	.210	114	374	40	74	14	0	8	39	41	4	1	2	164	7	8	.300	.283
Theroux, Collin	R-R	6-2	220	3-10-94	.147	.154	.144	84	273	34	40	11	0	13	30	38	0	0	0	143	1	0	.330	.251
Vidales, Josh	B-R	5-8	164	8-6-93	.256	.250	.259	45	160	26	41	4	2	2	17	21	1	2	0	21	3	4	.344	.346

Pitching	B-T	HT	WT	DOB	W	L	ERA	G	GS	CG	SV	IP	H	R	ER	HR	BB	SO	AVG	vLH	vRH	K/9	BB/9
Alejo, Yordys	R-R	6-2	186	11-13-93	4	3	4.56	32	0	0	4	49	60	29	25	6	19	40	.305	.293	.312	7.30	3.47
Altamirano, Xavier	R-R	6-3	195	7-20-94	8	6	3.59	31	14	0	2	118	106	53	47	8	31	95	.245	.223	.258	7.27	2.37
Bailey, Brandon	R-R	5-10	175	10-19-94	1	1	2.68	15	11	0	0	57	40	17	17	4	21	73	.199	.150	.231	11.53	3.32
Biegalski, Boomer	R-R	6-2	165	7-13-94	0	0	3.38	2	2	0	0	8	7	4	3	1	2	6	.241	.182	.278	6.75	2.25

Pitching	B-T	HT	WT	DOB	W	L	ERA	G	GS	CG	SV	IP	H	R	ER	HR	BB	SO	AVG	vLH	vRH	K/9	BB/9
Bowers, Heath	R-R	6-4	190	7-25-93	5	0	2.22	32	0	0	4	81	66	26	20	1	42	53	.228	.229	.227	5.89	4.67
Butler, Brendan	L-R	6-3	217	5-2-93	2	3	2.32	12	9	0	0	54	42	22	14	1	13	64	.208	.222	.194	10.60	2.15
Camacho, Joseph	R-R	5-9	175	6-23-94	3	3	2.75	18	1	0	1	39	38	15	12	1	8	34	.248	.170	.298	7.78	1.83
Chalmers, Dakota	R-R	6-3	175	10-8-96	2	2	4.34	10	5	0	0	29	15	14	14	1	29	47	.155	.135	.167	14.59	9.00
Damron, Ty	L-L	6-2	200	7-28-94	5	5	4.53	18	5	0	2	46	58	27	23	1	22	47	.314	.292	.321	9.26	4.34
Erwin, Zack	L-L	6-5	195	1-24-94	6	4	2.08	19	19	0	0	95	74	30	22	4	29	91	.213	.192	.219	8.59	2.74
Gilbert, Will	L-L	5-11	170	2-9-94	2	0	1.04	6	0	0	0	9	7	2	1	0	1	6	.233	.333	.208	6.23	1.04
Gorman, John	R-R	6-1	230	2-19-92	1	0	0.93	13	0	0	2	19	8	2	2	1	1	24	.121	.167	.095	11.17	0.47
Highberger, Nick	R-R	5-10	190	11-4-93	1	1	6.60	10	0	0	1	15	21	16	11	2	4	10	.318	.407	.256	6.00	2.40
Hurtado, Jhenderson	L-L	6-1	180	3-28-96	0	1	6.75	1	0	0	0	3	4	2	2	0	2	2	.333	.000	.444	6.75	6.75
Jordan, Mitchell	R-R	6-2	205	4-10-95	2	10	5.78	25	7	0	1	76	97	52	49	12	31	66	.317	.361	.289	7.78	3.66
Martinez, Seth	R-R	6-2	200	8-29-94	5	10	3.49	20	10	0	1	95	90	46	37	9	19	73	.248	.294	.218	6.89	1.79
Mendoza, Abdiel	R-R	5-10	135	9-19-98	0	0	15.43	1	1	0	0	2	3	4	4	1	3	2	.333	.250	.400	7.71	11.57
Milburn, Matt	R-R	6-3	210	7-29-93	7	11	4.34	28	22	0	0	141	153	73	68	7	32	136	.281	.306	.263	8.68	2.04
Murray, Michael	R-R	6-3	215	9-26-93	0	1	2.54	8	4	0	0	28	30	15	8	3	8	27	.263	.291	.237	8.58	2.54
Romero, Miguel	R-R	6-2	180	4-23-94	0	0	2.25	3	3	0	0	8	6	2	2	0	2	7	.200	.231	.177	7.88	2.25
Sawyer, Dalton	L-L	6-5	210	11-22-93	4	3	2.25	12	8	1	1	56	34	15	14	3	21	64	.178	.067	.199	10.29	3.38
Sheehan, Sam	R-R	6-2	195	8-8-93	3	2	2.21	29	0	0	6	41	26	14	10	3	27	54	.181	.196	.172	11.95	5.98
Tomasovich, Andrew	L-L	6-4	215	9-24-93	1	0	0.00	6	0	0	0	9	4	0	0	0	0	13	.125	.125	.125	13.00	0.00
Twomey, Kyle	L-L	6-3	165	12-29-93	2	4	4.12	15	14	0	0	68	81	40	31	5	20	60	.292	.397	.258	7.98	2.66
Zambrano, Jesus	R-R	5-11	170	8-23-96	1	2	6.06	27	3	0	4	65	68	46	44	5	29	58	.271	.190	.325	7.99	3.99

Fielding

Catcher	PCT	G	PO	A	E	DP	PB
Goldstein	.995	65	522	38	3	2	5
Theroux	.988	76	645	75	9	12	6

First Base	PCT	G	PO	A	E	DP
Mercedes	.979	84	658	43	15	71
Nowlin	.985	42	312	15	5	27
Persico	.993	23	131	5	1	12

Second Base	PCT	G	PO	A	E	DP
Loehr	.985	27	56	78	2	22
Lopez	.972	25	42	64	3	14
Mondou	.965	58	104	141	9	38
Rodriguez	.939	10	13	18	2	5
Vidales	.989	23	34	52	1	7

Third Base	PCT	G	PO	A	E	DP
Diaz	1.000	29	22	58	0	6
Loehr	.942	53	42	105	9	17
Lopez	.885	8	6	17	3	0
Marinez	.946	36	26	62	5	9
Mondou	.900	4	3	6	1	1
Rodriguez	.893	12	10	15	3	0
Vidales	.600	2	1	2	2	0

Shortstop	PCT	G	PO	A	E	DP
Diaz	.945	56	71	154	13	34
Loehr	.906	6	9	20	3	4
Lopez	1.000	2	4	7	0	2
Marinez	.927	76	111	181	23	42

Outfield	PCT	G	PO	A	E	DP
Barrera	.985	70	127	6	2	0
Gruber	.842	17	13	3	3	1
Martin	1.000	70	128	6	0	2
Nowlin	.000	1	0	0	0	0
Persico	.967	102	186	16	7	1
Rodriguez	.970	40	59	5	2	0
Shelby	.968	113	235	10	8	2
Vidales	1.000	19	35	7	0	2

VERMONT LAKE MONSTERS

SHORT SEASON

NEW YORK-PENN LEAGUE

Batting	B-T	HT	WT	DOB	AVG	vLH	vRH	G	AB	R	H	2B	3B	HR	RBI	BB	HBP	SH	SF	SO	SB	CS	SLG	OBP
Akau, Iolana	R-R	5-11	180	8-31-95	.173	.250	.145	32	104	8	18	3	0	0	7	4	3	3	0	35	0	0	.202	.225
Arruda, Aaron	R-R	6-3	215	6-21-95	.191	.200	.188	45	157	17	30	8	0	4	15	11	2	1	1	66	0	1	.319	.252
Bennie, Robert	R-R	6-1	205	1-20-94	.000	.000	.000	4	17	2	0	0	0	0	0	0	0	0	0	7	0	0	.000	.000
Churlin, Anthony	R-R	6-1	190	5-27-97	.265	.316	.250	49	166	26	44	11	3	3	19	11	3	2	1	53	3	0	.422	.320
Costa, Jarrett	R-R	5-11	225	4-23-93	.180	.345	.131	42	128	12	23	4	1	2	12	19	1	0	2	35	0	0	.273	.287
Deichmann, Greg	L-R	6-2	190	5-31-95	.274	.270	.276	46	164	31	45	10	4	8	30	28	2	0	1	40	4	1	.531	.385
Devencenzi, Jordan	R-R	5-11	190	6-26-93	.277	.289	.272	50	170	20	47	5	0	1	16	20	5	1	1	16	2	0	.324	.367
Farrar, Logan	L-R	5-10	180	4-16-95	.313	.293	.319	47	179	27	56	13	0	3	26	14	7	1	1	33	5	0	.436	.383
Godard, Javier	R-R	6-0	170	12-13-95	.187	.267	.165	40	139	15	26	3	1	0	15	18	1	3	1	29	1	1	.223	.283
Gonzalez, Roger	R-B	5-9	190	11-2-93	.182	.200	.179	10	33	4	6	0	1	1	3	7	0	0	0	6	0	0	.333	.325
Gridley, Ryan	R-R	5-8	180	5-4-95	.262	.320	.244	56	210	25	55	12	0	1	24	28	4	3	2	33	6	2	.333	.357
Hargrove, Hunter	R-R	6-0	215	9-9-94	.237	.211	.246	20	76	4	18	3	0	1	7	3	0	0	0	15	0	0	.316	.266
Lage, Jesus	R-R	6-1	155	12-1-97	.233	.150	.261	47	159	18	37	8	3	1	16	5	3	3	1	52	2	3	.340	.268
Lopez, Jesus	R-R	5-11	170	10-5-96	.227	.385	.161	12	44	4	10	2	0	1	9	3	0	0	0	10	2	0	.341	.277
Martin, Mike	R-R	6-0	175	9-29-92	.238	.167	.267	5	21	4	5	0	1	0	3	1	0	0	0	4	3	0	.333	.273
McCray, Jeramiah	R-R	5-10	160	3-3-98	.174	.308	.121	17	46	4	8	0	0	0	1	0	1	0	1	10	1	3	.174	.188
McDonald, Mickey	B-R	6-4	180	6-2-95	.130	.167	.111	16	54	4	7	1	0	0	6	4	0	0	0	20	2	0	.148	.190
Meggs, Jack	L-L	6-1	175	4-18-95	.290	.177	.327	20	69	9	20	2	0	3	11	9	1	0	2	14	2	1	.449	.370
Merrell, Kevin	L-R	6-1	180	12-14-95	.320	.323	.319	31	125	27	40	5	1	2	9	9	1	2	3	22	10	3	.424	.362
Quintin, Christopher	R-R	6-0	135	6-7-99	.000	.000	.000	2	5	1	0	0	0	0	0	2	0	0	0	1	0	0	.000	.286
Squier, Payton	L-R	6-0	185	10-29-95	.262	.300	.255	33	122	10	32	4	1	0	20	4	0	4	3	22	0	1	.312	.279
Terrell, James	R-R	6-0	165	1-10-97	.221	.172	.238	40	113	9	25	2	1	2	12	4	1	3	1	32	2	1	.310	.252
Toffey, Will	L-R	6-2	205	12-31-94	.263	.352	.232	57	209	38	55	11	2	1	22	38	2	1	3	45	2	2	.349	.377

Pitching	B-T	HT	WT	DOB	W	L	ERA	G	GS	CG	SV	IP	H	R	ER	HR	BB	SO	AVG	vLH	vRH	K/9	BB/9
Andueza, Ivan	L-L	5-11	180	2-7-95	6	3	2.75	14	7	2	0	72	59	31	22	3	22	50	.228	.268	.213	6.25	2.75
Berube, Marc	L-R	6-2	180	2-12-93	2	2	3.92	14	1	0	1	21	24	12	9	3	9	18	.282	.306	.265	7.84	3.92
Blanco, Argenis	R-R	6-1	165	5-23-96	5	7	5.30	14	11	0	0	70	79	46	41	10	25	48	.283	.331	.248	6.20	3.23
Charles, Wandisson	R-R	6-6	220	9-7-96	2	0	3.43	15	0	0	5	21	15	10	8	1	18	29	.203	.294	.125	12.43	7.71
Conley, Bryce	R-R	6-3	200	8-22-94	0	3	6.12	15	4	0	0	25	21	18	17	2	23	28	.239	.290	.200	10.08	8.28
Danielak, Michael	R-R	6-4	215	3-16-94	3	0	1.20	17	0	0	4	30	23	4	4	2	9	35	.205	.191	.214	10.50	2.70
Donica, Heath	R-R	6-2	200	5-20-94	0	0	0.00	3	0	0	1	7	5	0	0	0	0	4	.217	.111	.286	5.40	0.00
Dunshee, Parker	R-R	6-1	205	2-12-95	1	0	0.00	12	9	0	0	38	15	0	0	0	8	45	.119	.083	.152	10.57	1.88

Gorman, John	R-R	6-1	230	2-19-92	0	0	1.80	2	0	0	0	5	3	1	1	0	0	8	.167	.200	.154	14.40	0.00
Howard, Brian	R-R	6-9	185	4-25-95	2	1	1.15	11	6	0	1	31	22	5	4	0	1	29	.200	.213	.191	8.33	0.29
Hurtado, Jhenderson	L-L	6-1	180	3-28-96	1	0	3.77	5	1	0	0	14	11	6	6	1	4	15	.212	.263	.182	9.42	2.51
Jones, Malik	R-R	6-1	185	3-14-96	1	2	3.29	11	1	0	0	14	10	6	5	0	11	15	.189	.100	.242	9.88	7.24
Kelliher, Branden	R-R	5-11	175	12-11-95	2	2	2.81	17	0	0	3	32	26	12	10	1	20	27	.226	.208	.239	7.59	5.63
Luzardo, Jesus	L-L	6-1	205	9-30-97	1	0	2.00	5	5	0	0	18	12	5	4	1	4	20	.188	.250	.167	10.00	2.00
Marks, Wyatt	R-R	6-3	205	6-28-95	3	0	2.68	11	5	0	0	37	29	14	11	7	12	49	.209	.193	.220	11.92	2.92
Martinez, Seth	R-R	6-2	200	8-29-94	0	1	1.80	1	1	0	0	5	7	1	1	0	0	3	.318	.600	.235	5.40	0.00
Mejia, Jeferson	R-R	6-7	195	8-2-94	1	1	1.54	9	0	0	1	12	4	2	2	0	11	13	.100	.111	.091	10.03	8.49
Mendoza, Abdiel	R-R	5-10	135	9-19-98	2	3	3.82	7	6	0	0	31	26	14	13	1	8	17	.234	.241	.228	4.99	2.35
Mora, Jose	R-R	6-3	185	10-1-97	0	1	17.36	3	0	0	1	5	11	9	9	1	1	8	.478	.556	.429	15.43	1.93
Morban, Richard	R-R	6-2	162	12-24-97	1	0	5.40	3	1	0	0	10	11	6	6	3	3	6	.282	.316	.250	5.40	2.70
Poche', Jared	R-L	6-1	215	11-21-94	0	0	0.00	1	1	0	0	2	3	0	0	0	0	2	.333	.250	.400	9.00	0.00
Reagan, Josh	B-L	6-1	185	10-2-94	1	1	2.21	12	0	0	1	20	15	5	5	1	2	21	.203	.222	.196	9.30	0.89
Ruiz, Jean	R-R	6-1	165	9-6-96	1	0	1.38	15	8	0	0	52	35	11	8	1	9	42	.187	.195	.182	7.22	1.55
Salow, Logan	L-L	6-1	185	9-27-94	2	3	1.61	15	0	0	1	22	14	7	4	0	14	28	.177	.174	.179	11.28	5.64
Sanchez, Carlos	R-R	5-11	150	12-26-97	1	0	18.00	2	0	0	0	4	8	8	8	3	2	1	.400	.429	.385	2.25	4.50
Tovar, Oscar	R-R	6-1	160	3-19-98	3	2	3.46	15	8	0	2	65	58	29	25	4	26	45	.242	.248	.237	6.23	3.60

Fielding

C: Akau 31, Costa 23, Devencenzi 22, Gonzalez 7. **1B:** Arruda 42, Costa 18, Devencenzi 3, Hargrove 18. **2B:** Godard 18, Gridley 33, Lage 17, Lopez 9, Quintin 1. **3B:** Costa 1, Godard 21, Lage 3, Toffey 53. **SS:** Gridley 22, Lage 25, Merrell 28, Quintin 1. **OF:** Bennie 4, Churlin 39, Deichmann 35, Farrar 40, Godard 2, Martin 4, McCray 14, McDonald 15, Meggs 16, Squier 32, Terrell 32.

AZL ATHLETICS — *ROOKIE*

ARIZONA LEAGUE

Batting	B-T	HT	WT	DOB	AVG	vLH	vRH	G	AB	R	H	2B	3B	HR	RBI	BB	HBP	SH	SF	SO	SB	CS	SLG	OBP
Allen, Nick	R-R	5-9	155	10-8-98	.254	.325	.225	35	138	26	35	3	2	1	14	13	1	2	0	28	7	3	.326	.322
Armenteros, Lazaro	R-R	6-0	182	5-22-99	.289	.314	.276	41	156	24	45	9	4	4	22	16	7	0	2	48	10	1	.474	.376
Beck, Austin	R-R	6-1	200	11-21-98	.211	.262	.191	41	152	23	32	7	4	2	28	17	2	0	3	51	7	1	.349	.293
Brito, Marcos	B-R	6-0	160	3-6-00	.234	.261	.224	44	171	30	40	4	2	1	17	21	1	0	1	42	4	1	.298	.320
Diaz, Jordan	R-R	5-10	175	8-13-00	.185	.400	.136	8	27	2	5	0	0	0	2	0	0	0	1	4	1	0	.185	.179
Farrar, Logan	L-R	5-10	180	4-16-95	.486	.333	.539	9	35	10	17	6	1	1	6	5	1	0	0	5	0	0	.800	.561
Goldby, Cooper	R-R	5-9	185	1-18-95	.189	.200	.184	22	53	8	10	1	0	0	3	10	4	1	0	24	0	0	.208	.358
Hargrove, Hunter	R-R	6-0	215	9-9-94	.299	.353	.280	17	67	6	20	8	0	0	13	4	2	0	0	11	1	0	.418	.356
Iriart, Chris	R-R	6-2	230	10-7-94	.212	.000	.259	10	33	9	7	2	0	0	2	8	2	0	1	14	0	0	.273	.386
Jones, Justin	L-R	5-11	190	3-7-94	.216	.235	.211	25	74	10	16	2	0	3	11	9	1	0	2	18	1	0	.365	.302
Lumley, Jake	L-R	6-1	178	2-13-95	.333	.395	.309	35	135	20	45	7	4	0	25	12	0	0	0	22	3	2	.444	.388
McCray, Jeramiah	R-R	5-10	160	3-3-98	.156	.167	.152	17	64	5	10	1	1	0	4	8	1	0	0	13	5	2	.203	.260
McDonald, Mickey	B-R	6-4	180	6-2-95	.278	.333	.259	20	72	18	20	0	2	2	9	6	0	0	1	9	7	2	.417	.329
Medina, Alonzo	R-R	6-2	190	2-2-99	.197	.115	.218	36	127	7	25	7	1	2	8	19	0	0	2	48	0	0	.315	.297
Monserratt, Jesus	R-R	6-0	180	1-3-97	.000	.000	.000	6	11	0	0	0	0	0	0	1	0	1	0	1	0	0	.000	.083
Pantoja, Enrry	R-R	6-0	199	9-27-96	.244	.167	.273	29	90	8	22	2	1	0	10	13	3	1	1	18	6	1	.289	.355
Quintin, Christopher	R-R	6-0	135	6-7-99	.000	.000	.000	4	10	1	0	0	0	0	1	1	0	0	0	2	0	0	.000	.091
Rodriguez, Jhonny	L-L	6-3	170	7-20-96	.194	.100	.231	21	72	8	14	1	3	2	9	14	1	0	1	28	0	0	.375	.330
Sanchez, Santis	R-R	6-1	199	8-21-98	.253	.348	.224	30	99	10	25	6	0	0	10	8	0	0	1	31	0	1	.313	.306
Spitz, Adrian	R-R	5-11	185	10-21-93	.160	.167	.154	19	25	5	4	3	0	0	5	4	0	0	0	9	0	1	.280	.276
Spitznagel, Ben	L-R	5-11	170	8-30-94	.337	.261	.362	29	92	27	31	7	2	0	6	18	3	2	0	13	6	1	.457	.460
Vargas, Yerdel	R-R	6-0	170	2-17-00	.208	.186	.218	39	144	13	30	6	4	0	13	6	4	1	2	36	3	4	.306	.256
Weber, Skyler	L-R	5-10	176	6-6-95	.186	.100	.212	13	43	10	8	4	1	0	3	2	1	0	1	12	1	0	.326	.234

Pitching	B-T	HT	WT	DOB	W	L	ERA	G	GS	CG	SV	IP	H	R	ER	HR	BB	SO	AVG	vLH	vRH	K/9	BB/9
Alcantara, Raul	R-R	6-4	220	12-4-92	0	0	0.00	4	2	0	0	5	2	0	0	0	1	7	.118	.000	.167	11.81	1.69
Berrios, Osvaldo	R-R	6-2	200	11-29-99	2	3	8.00	13	7	0	0	27	39	27	24	2	8	25	.342	.302	.366	8.33	2.67
Damron, Ty	L-L	6-2	200	7-28-94	0	2	9.00	3	0	0	0	4	9	4	4	0	1	6	.409	.375	.429	13.50	2.25
Danielak, Michael	R-R	6-4	215	3-16-94	0	0	13.50	1	1	0	0	1	4	3	1	0	0	1	.571	.333	.750	13.50	0.00
Donica, Heath	R-R	6-2	200	5-20-94	2	1	5.79	13	1	0	0	23	26	17	15	1	5	35	.263	.147	.323	13.50	1.93
Duchene, Kevin	L-L	6-2	220	12-10-93	0	1	5.40	2	2	0	0	5	2	3	3	0	5	4	.125	.000	.182	7.20	9.00
Dull, Ryan	R-R	5-9	175	10-2-89	0	0	0.00	1	1	0	0	1	0	0	0	0	0	1	.000	—	.000	9.00	0.00
Dunshee, Parker	R-R	6-1	205	2-12-95	0	0	13.50	1	0	0	0	2	5	3	3	1	0	3	.455	.400	.500	13.50	0.00
Evans, Caleb	R-R	6-8	220	3-4-95	0	1	2.61	13	0	0	2	21	18	6	6	1	9	25	.243	.240	.245	10.89	3.92
Falk, Josh	R-R	6-2	217	5-19-95	0	3	6.91	9	4	0	0	14	18	13	11	1	5	10	.316	.235	.350	6.28	3.14
Hurtado, Jhenderson	L-L	6-1	180	3-28-96	3	0	2.35	10	1	0	1	31	28	12	8	0	13	29	.237	.143	.277	8.51	3.82
Jones, Malik	R-R	6-1	185	3-14-96	0	0	3.60	2	0	0	0	5	2	2	2	0	0	4	.125	.000	.154	7.20	0.00
Kelly, Rafael	R-R	6-3	190	6-9-97	1	2	2.38	6	2	0	0	23	20	9	6	1	2	23	.238	.265	.220	9.13	0.79
Kelly, Zack	R-R	6-3	205	3-3-95	1	0	3.77	13	0	0	1	29	28	16	12	1	6	23	.252	.316	.219	7.22	1.88
Kohler, Chris	L-L	6-3	210	5-4-95	4	3	4.01	14	10	0	0	43	44	27	19	4	12	24	.260	.294	.252	5.06	2.53
Krall, Pat	L-L	6-6	220	8-27-94	3	5	3.18	16	0	0	1	28	34	16	10	0	3	23	.293	.290	.294	7.31	0.95
Lee, Slater	R-R	6-0	220	3-5-95	2	0	3.86	17	0	0	4	21	21	14	9	0	6	21	.244	.258	.236	9.00	2.57
Luzardo, Jesus	L-L	6-1	205	9-30-97	0	1	1.54	4	3	0	0	12	9	2	2	0	1	13	.205	.182	.212	10.03	0.77
Marks, Wyatt	R-R	6-3	205	6-28-95	0	0	0.00	2	2	0	0	5	3	0	0	0	2	7	.177	1.000	.067	12.60	3.60
Marsonek, Brandon	L-L	6-1	190	6-12-94	0	0	0.93	7	0	0	0	10	7	3	1	0	4	18	.189	.000	.259	16.76	3.72
Martinez, Jorge	L-L	5-11	170	1-5-96	1	1	3.18	15	0	0	2	23	16	12	8	0	8	25	.203	.292	.164	9.93	3.18
Mengden, Daniel	R-R	6-2	190	2-19-93	0	0	0.00	2	2	0	0	5	1	0	0	0	3	9	.063	.000	.083	16.20	5.40
Mora, Jose	R-R	6-3	185	10-1-97	2	1	5.70	13	5	0	0	36	29	24	23	0	24	45	.212	.231	.200	11.15	5.94

Morban, Richard	R-R	6-2	162	12-24-97	2	0	3.96	12	6	0	0	36	35	20	16	3	14	43	.254	.342	.217	10.65	3.47
Naile, James	R-R	6-4	185	2-8-93	0	0	1.80	2	2	0	0	5	4	1	1	1	0	11	.211	.125	.273	19.80	0.00
Puckett, Cody	R-L	6-1	210	3-29-95	0	1	3.05	15	0	0	1	21	17	14	7	0	13	29	.221	.217	.222	12.63	5.66
Reagan, Josh	B-L	6-1	185	10-2-94	1	1	8.10	2	0	0	0	3	3	3	3	0	2	5	.250	.000	.273	13.50	5.40
Reuss, Adam	R-R	6-4	185	3-14-95	1	1	6.52	14	1	0	1	19	20	15	14	0	16	25	.267	.276	.261	11.64	7.45
Romero, Miguel	R-R	6-2	180	4-23-94	0	0	4.50	1	0	0	0	2	3	1	1	0	0	3	.333	.333	.333	13.50	0.00
Ruiz, Norge	R-R	6-0	185	3-15-94	0	1	11.25	1	1	0	0	4	5	5	5	0	2	4	.278	.200	.308	9.00	4.50
Salow, Logan	L-L	6-1	185	9-27-94	0	0	0.00	1	0	0	1	2	1	0	0	0	1	1	.200	.000	.250	5.40	5.40
Sanchez, Carlos	R-R	5-11	150	12-26-97	0	0	3.38	1	0	0	0	3	3	1	1	1	0	0	.300	1.000	.222	0.00	0.00
Shore, Logan	R-R	6-2	215	12-28-94	0	0	0.00	3	3	0	0	8	2	0	0	0	0	13	.077	.143	.053	14.63	0.00
Withers, Brandon	R-R	6-1	205	7-4-94	1	2	3.60	9	0	0	0	15	10	6	6	0	8	10	.204	.238	.179	6.00	4.80

Fielding

C: Goldby 22, Jones 1, Monserratt 5, Sanchez 27, Weber 13. **1B:** Hargrove 16, Iriart 9, Jones 3, Lumley 2, Medina 29, Monserratt 1. **2B:** Brito 34, Jones 6, Quintin 1, Vargas 15. **3B:** Brito 4, Diaz 8, Jones 8, Lumley 29, Quintin 1, Vargas 9. **SS:** Allen 33, Brito 5, Lumley 3, Quintin 1, Vargas 17. **OF:** Armenteros 30, Beck 33, Farrar 5, McCray 17, McDonald 18, Medina 4, Pantoja 27, Rodriguez 9, Spitz 13, Spitznagel 27.

DSL ATHLETICS — ROOKIE

DOMINICAN SUMMER LEAGUE

Batting	B-T	HT	WT	DOB	AVG	vLH	vRH	G	AB	R	H	2B	3B	HR	RBI	BB	HBP	SH	SF	SO	SB	CS	SLG	OBP
Agelvis, Javier	R-R	6-1	170	8-18-97	.154	.222	.118	15	26	7	4	0	0	0	4	10	2	2	0	2	7	2	.154	.421
Almanzar, Luis	B-R	6-1	170	5-11-99	.256	.304	.236	47	156	23	40	6	2	0	14	14	4	1	1	25	5	6	.321	.331
Alvarez, Wilson	R-R	5-10	150	5-19-98	.304	.303	.305	43	115	16	35	2	0	0	8	11	5	6	0	18	8	8	.322	.389
Arias, Jhoan	R-R	5-11	150	9-7-98	.182	.000	.267	11	22	0	4	0	0	0	3	2	0	0	0	5	1	0	.182	.250
Armenteros, Lazaro	R-R	6-0	182	5-22-99	.167	.000	.200	6	18	6	3	0	0	0	1	3	4	0	1	9	2	2	.167	.385
Bell, George	R-R	6-2	170	1-3-00	.140	.154	.135	39	100	11	14	1	0	0	4	11	3	0	2	31	6	1	.150	.241
Brito, Marcos	B-R	6-0	160	3-6-00	.178	.000	.235	14	45	3	8	1	0	0	8	13	0	0	4	8	5	0	.200	.339
Diaz, Cesar	R-R	6-0	170	1-8-97	.213	.222	.208	30	75	15	16	1	0	2	4	9	3	1	1	29	8	2	.307	.318
Diaz, Jordan	R-R	5-10	175	8-13-00	.256	.359	.214	42	137	14	35	7	0	0	18	6	3	0	3	22	2	0	.307	.295
Gonzalez, Yhoelnys	R-R	6-0	170	10-30-96	.279	.327	.262	65	190	38	53	8	1	0	19	31	5	4	3	40	26	7	.332	.389
Gordon, Jorge	R-R	5-10	175	10-28-97	.250	.294	.233	41	120	8	30	2	0	0	15	8	1	1	1	17	5	2	.267	.300
Hiciano, Carlos	R-R	6-2	175	10-29-96	.163	.147	.168	46	129	18	21	3	1	0	7	11	2	0	1	34	6	6	.202	.238
Monserratt, Jesus	R-R	6-0	180	1-3-97	.125	.250	.063	8	24	2	3	2	0	0	2	5	2	0	0	4	1	0	.208	.323
Mordock, Erick	R-R	5-11	165	9-9-97	.108	.143	.097	45	93	13	10	4	0	0	7	9	5	6	0	13	1	1	.151	.224
Pantoja, Enrry	R-R	6-0	199	9-27-96	.256	.333	.233	12	39	8	10	1	1	0	7	2	4	0	1	10	2	2	.333	.348
Paula, Jose	R-R	6-1	185	4-18-99	.224	.273	.204	32	76	8	17	2	0	0	1	17	1	0	0	28	5	3	.250	.372
Quintin, Christopher	R-R	6-0	135	6-7-99	.190	.211	.183	28	79	11	15	3	1	0	5	11	2	2	0	18	4	3	.253	.304
Richards, Kevin	R-R	6-2	160	1-8-00	.248	.179	.274	35	101	16	25	0	4	0	10	11	2	1	2	29	10	5	.327	.328
Rigby, Gean	R-R	6-0	180	1-7-97	.268	.298	.253	50	142	15	38	4	1	1	14	19	3	1	1	25	4	7	.331	.364
Rincones, Rafael	B-R	6-0	159	7-1-99	.500	—	.500	2	6	2	3	1	0	0	3	0	0	0	0	0	0	0	.667	.500
2-team total (58 Red Sox)					.265	.169	.301	60	204	40	54	14	3	1	22	32	5	0	1	51	8	3	.378	.376
Rivas, Jose	R-R	5-11	190	8-5-98	.248	.233	.254	36	101	12	25	3	1	0	9	12	4	0	0	10	2	2	.297	.350
Serrano, Iraj	L-L	5-11	165	2-19-99	.329	.250	.359	47	146	24	48	5	2	0	17	27	5	4	2	22	10	3	.390	.444
Urena, Rafioby	L-L	6-4	210	9-22-98	.244	.235	.247	62	197	12	48	8	0	2	35	20	2	0	1	46	0	2	.315	.318
Vargas, Yerdel	R-R	6-0	170	2-17-00	.173	.154	.180	13	52	6	9	0	0	0	6	0	2	1	1	15	1	0	.173	.200

Pitching	B-T	HT	WT	DOB	W	L	ERA	G	GS	CG	SV	IP	H	R	ER	HR	BB	SO	AVG	vLH	vRH	K/9	BB/9
Alvarez, Miguel	L-L	6-5	192	6-13-96	1	0	4.00	7	4	0	0	18	21	11	8	1	9	15	.284	.214	.300	7.50	4.50
Aquino, Ismael	R-R	6-2	170	9-2-98	2	1	3.13	13	10	0	0	46	33	21	16	0	35	44	.200	.188	.208	8.61	6.85
Aquino, Ruber	R-R	6-2	185	12-29-96	1	2	1.69	21	0	0	9	27	19	11	5	0	5	32	.204	.035	.281	10.80	1.69
Arias, Tomy	R-R	6-2	185	3-4-97	0	0	1.74	5	0	0	0	10	7	2	2	0	4	9	.194	.286	.136	7.84	3.48
Benjamin-Garnett, Mario	R-R	6-4	190	11-22-99	1	3	4.71	13	1	0	1	21	20	13	11	0	17	25	.263	.250	.273	10.71	7.29
Calderon, Alexander	L-L	6-3	170	2-23-96	6	1	1.35	14	9	0	0	60	40	16	9	0	20	56	.191	.111	.207	8.40	3.00
Cruz, Andy	R-R	6-4	200	9-16-96	1	1	2.79	14	0	0	0	19	16	9	6	1	15	22	.246	.435	.143	10.24	6.98
De La Cruz, Frederick	R-R	6-3	170	9-13-96	1	6	8.35	7	5	0	0	18	25	24	17	0	12	12	.313	.343	.289	5.89	5.89
Hernandez, Marcelo	R-R	6-1	160	1-23-99	2	2	1.62	18	1	0	3	33	27	9	6	1	8	19	.223	.116	.282	5.13	2.16
Herrera, Dennis	L-L	6-0	165	9-28-98	3	3	2.21	14	10	0	0	53	46	21	13	0	20	50	.240	.133	.259	8.49	3.40
Infante, Angello	R-R	6-1	180	4-16-99	3	1	1.06	14	9	1	0	68	59	11	8	0	5	54	.240	.237	.242	7.18	0.67
Kelly, Rafael	R-R	6-3	190	6-9-97	4	1	2.53	10	6	0	0	43	28	16	12	1	10	47	.184	.186	.183	9.91	2.11
Manzanillo, Manuel	R-R	5-10	170	3-21-98	3	3	4.72	14	8	1	0	48	42	29	25	1	27	41	.240	.188	.270	7.74	5.10
Martinez, Jorge	L-L	5-11	170	1-5-96	1	1	1.08	5	0	0	2	8	1	3	1	0	6	11	.039	.000	.046	11.88	6.48
Montilla, David	L-L	6-0	170	5-29-98	2	0	2.01	15	0	0	0	22	13	5	5	0	10	18	.173	.167	.175	7.25	4.03
Ramirez, Eliel	R-R	6-0	165	9-27-97	3	1	2.11	13	0	0	0	21	16	9	5	1	6	9	.208	.192	.216	3.80	2.53
Rodriguez, Santiago	R-R	6-3	190	3-9-97	0	1	0.00	4	0	0	1	2	1	1	0	0	5	0	.125	.000	.167	0.00	22.50
Romero, Miguel	R-R	6-2	180	4-23-94	0	0	0.00	2	1	0	0	3	0	0	0	0	0	7	.000	.000	.000	21.00	0.00
Ruiz, Norge	R-R	6-0	185	3-15-94	2	0	0.47	4	4	0	0	19	9	1	1	0	1	14	.141	.177	.128	6.63	0.47
Sanchez, Carlos	R-R	5-11	150	12-26-97	1	0	0.73	13	0	0	4	25	15	4	2	0	7	20	.167	.238	.104	7.30	2.55
Sanchez, Livan	L-L	7-0	265	10-21-97	1	1	3.09	7	4	0	0	23	20	11	8	0	9	15	.220	.091	.238	5.79	3.47
Sullivan, Enmanuel	R-R	6-3	195	6-24-96	2	3	3.44	15	0	0	0	18	14	11	7	1	17	23	.215	.333	.159	11.29	8.35

Fielding

C: Diaz 18, Diaz 1, Gordon 40, Monserratt 4, Rivas 27. **1B:** Agelvis 1, Arias 1, Gonzalez 1, Gordon 1, Hiciano 10, Mordock 1, Rigby 13, Rivas 1, Serrano 37, Urena 19. **2B:** Agelvis 2, Almanzar 4, Alvarez 34, Arias 6, Brito 6, Hiciano 17, Quintin 9, Vargas 6. **3B:** Agelvis 9, Almanzar 10, Arias 1, Bell 11, Diaz 1, Diaz 40, Hiciano 14. **SS:** Agelvis 1, Almanzar 32, Alvarez 7, Brito 7, Hiciano 6, Pantoja 1, Quintin 20, Vargas 7. **OF:** Armenteros 6, Bell 18, Gonzalez 64, Hiciano 1, Mordock 37, Pantoja 11, Paula 30, Richards 33, Rigby 37, Rincones 1, Serrano 8, Vargas 1.

Philadelphia Phillies

SEASON IN A SENTENCE: The Phillies logged their fifth consecutive losing year and had the third-worst record in baseball, but rookie callups in season provided signs of hope for the future.

HIGH POINT: Once the calendar flipped to September, the Phillies went 16-13 the rest of the season. While that finish cost them an opportunity to pick No. 1 overall in the draft, the Phillies were getting contributions from first baseman/outfielder Rhys Hoskins, outfielder Nick Williams and infielder J.P. Crawford, three players who will play key roles in the organization's rebuilding efforts.

LOW POINT: The Phillies played a lot of bad baseball, especially in the first half. It got especially ugly in May, when the team went just 6-22 for the month, and it didn't get much better the next month either when they went 9-18.

NOTABLE ROOKIES: The 2017 season was less about the major league team's record and more about the development of the team's young talent to build on for the future. After a disappointing 2016 season in Triple-A, Williams made his major league debut on June 30 and hit .288/.338/.473. Hoskins became one of the biggest stories in baseball once he arrived in August, smashing 18 home runs in just 50 games. Crawford and catcher Jorge Alfaro also contributed as September callups and retained their rookie eligibility.

KEY TRANSACTIONS: On July 26, the Phillies traded reliever Pat Neshek to the Rockies in exchange for middle infielder Jose Gomez and righthanders J.D. Hammer and Alejandro Requena. Three days later, they dumped Jeremy Hellickson on the Orioles and got back outfielder Hyun-Soo Kim and lefthander Garrett Cleavinger.

DOWN ON THE FARM: The Phillies continued to boast one of the deepest farm systems, with a good balance of prospects at the upper and lower levels. After a slow start, Crawford tore up the Triple-A International League in the second half. His double play partner, second baseman Scott Kingery, looks poised to contribute in Philadelphia in 2018. Righthander Sixto Sanchez is one of the game's best pitching prospects, earning No. 1 prospect honors in the low Class A South Atlantic League and reaching high Class A Clearwater as a 19-year-old. Righthander Adonis Medina and lefthander Jojo Romero also took big leaps forward on the mound, although center fielder Mickey Moniak, the No. 1 overall pick in the 2016 draft, fell flat with a disappointing first full season.

OPENING DAY PAYROLL: $111,378,000 (21st)

PLAYERS OF THE YEAR

MAJOR LEAGUE

Aaron Nola
RHP

12-11, 3.54
184 SO in 168 IP
119 ERA+

MINOR LEAGUE

Rhys Hoskins
1B

(Triple-A)
.284/.385/.581
.966 OPS (5th in AAA)

ORGANIZATION LEADERS

BATTING — *Minimum 250 AB

MAJORS

*	AVG	Cesar Hernandez	.294
*	OPS	Aaron Altherr	.856
	HR	Maikel Franco	24
	RBI	Maikel Franco	76

MINORS

*	AVG	Damek Tomscha, Clearwater, GCL, Reading	.307
*	OBP	Damek Tomscha, Clearwater, GCL, Reading	.386
*	SLG	Rhys Hoskins, Lehigh Valley	.581
*	OPS	Rhys Hoskins, Lehigh Valley	.966
	R	Scott Kingery, Reading, Lehigh Valley	103
	H	Scott Kingery, Reading, Lehigh Valley	165
	TB	Scott Kingery, Reading, Lehigh Valley	288
	2B	Andrew Pullin, Reading, Lehigh Valley	43
	3B	Scott Kingery, Reading, Lehigh Valley	8
	HR	Darick Hall, Lakewood, Clearwater	29
	HR	Rhys Hoskins, Lehigh Valley	29
	RBI	Darick Hall, Lakewood, Clearwater	101
	BB	J.P. Crawford, Lehigh Valley	79
	SO	Dylan Cozens, Lehigh Valley	194
	SB	Zachary Coppola, Clearwater, Reading	39

PITCHING — #Minimum 75 IP

MAJORS

	W	Aaron Nola	12
#	ERA	Aaron Nola	3.54
	SO	Aaron Nola	184
	SV	Hector Neris	26

MINORS

	W	Tom Eshelman, Reading, Lehigh Valley	13
	L	Jake Thompson, Lehigh Valley	14
#	ERA	Harold Arauz, Lakewood, Reading, Clearwater	1.97
	G	Pedro Beato, Clearwater, Lehigh Valley	54
	GS	Tyler Viza, Reading	26
	SV	Pedro Beato, Clearwater, Lehigh Valley	33
	IP	Jose Taveras, Clearwater, Reading, Lehigh Valley	154
	BB	Alberto Tirado, Reading, GCL Phillies, Clearwater	60
	SO	Jose Taveras, Clearwater, Reading, Lehigh Valley	140
#	AVG	Harold Arauz, Lakewood, Reading, Clearwater	.196

2017 PERFORMANCE

General Manager: Matt Klentak. **Farm Director:** Joe Jordan. **Scouting Director:** Johnny Almaraz.

Class	Team	League	W	L	PCT	Finish	Manager
Majors	Philadelphia Phillies	National	66	96	.407	14th (15)	Pete Mackanin
Triple-A	Lehigh Valley IronPigs	International	80	62	.563	t-3rd (14)	Dusty Wathan
Double-A	Reading Fightin Phils	Eastern	72	68	.514	t-4th (12)	Greg Legg
High-A	Clearwater Threshers	Florida State	67	71	.486	8th (12)	Shawn Williams
Low-A	Lakewood BlueClaws	South Atlantic	73	66	.525	6th (14)	Marty Malloy
Short Season	Williamsport Crosscutters	New York-Penn	37	37	.500	9th (14)	Pat Borders
Rookie	GCL Phillies	Gulf Coast	36	22	.621	1st (17)	Roly de Armas
Overall 2017 Minor League Record			365	326	.528	6th (30)	

ORGANIZATION STATISTICS

PHILADELPHIA PHILLIES

NATIONAL LEAGUE

Batting	B-T	HT	WT	DOB	AVG	vLH	vRH	G	AB	R	H	2B	3B	HR	RBI	BB	HBP	SH	SF	SO	SB	CS	SLG	OBP
Alfaro, Jorge	R-R	6-2	225	6-11-93	.318	.200	.375	29	107	12	34	6	0	5	14	3	4	0	0	33	0	0	.514	.360
Altherr, Aaron	R-R	6-5	215	1-14-91	.272	.239	.285	107	372	58	101	24	5	19	65	32	7	0	1	104	5	4	.516	.340
Blanco, Andres	R-B	5-10	195	4-11-84	.192	.195	.191	80	130	10	25	4	0	3	13	12	0	0	2	34	1	0	.292	.257
Crawford, J.P.	L-R	6-2	180	1-11-95	.214	.087	.277	23	70	8	15	4	1	0	6	16	0	0	1	22	1	0	.300	.356
Florimon, Pedro	B-R	6-2	185	12-10-86	.348	.455	.314	15	46	6	16	4	1	0	6	3	0	0	0	16	0	0	.478	.388
Franco, Maikel	R-R	6-1	215	8-26-92	.230	.210	.237	154	575	66	132	29	1	24	76	41	2	0	5	95	0	0	.409	.281
Galvis, Freddy	B-R	5-10	185	11-14-89	.255	.255	.255	162	608	71	155	29	6	12	61	45	4	2	4	111	14	5	.382	.309
Hernandez, Cesar	B-R	5-10	160	5-23-90	.294	.281	.299	128	511	85	150	26	6	9	34	61	4	0	1	104	15	5	.421	.373
Herrera, Odubel	L-R	5-11	205	12-29-91	.281	.288	.279	138	526	67	148	42	3	14	56	31	4	0	2	126	8	5	.453	.325
Hoskins, Rhys	R-R	6-4	225	3-17-93	.259	.171	.287	50	170	37	44	7	0	18	48	37	3	0	2	46	2	0	.618	.396
Joseph, Tommy	R-R	6-1	255	7-16-91	.240	.211	.251	142	495	51	119	27	1	22	69	33	2	0	3	129	1	0	.432	.289
Kelly, Ty	R-L	6-0	180	7-20-88	.193	.179	.200	69	88	11	17	7	0	2	14	8	1	4	3	24	0	0	.341	.260
2-team total (1 New York)					.191	—	.000	70	89	11	17	7	0	2	14	8	1	4	3	25	0	0	.337	.257
Kendrick, Howie	R-R	5-11	220	7-12-83	.340	.342	.340	39	141	16	48	8	1	2	16	11	3	0	1	30	8	3	.454	.397
2-team total (52 Washington)					.315	.308	.286	91	305	40	96	16	3	9	41	22	5	0	2	68	12	5	.475	.368
Kim, Hyun Soo	R-L	6-2	210	1-12-88	.230	.143	.238	40	87	9	20	4	1	0	4	10	0	0	0	19	0	0	.299	.309
Knapp, Andrew	B-R	6-1	195	11-9-91	.257	.216	.269	56	171	26	44	8	1	3	13	31	0	0	2	56	1	0	.368	.368
Nava, Daniel	L-B	5-11	200	2-22-83	.301	.188	.341	80	183	21	55	8	1	4	21	26	3	0	2	38	1	0	.421	.393
Perkins, Cameron	R-R	6-5	195	9-27-90	.182	.238	.130	42	88	9	16	5	0	1	8	5	2	0	2	23	0	0	.273	.237
Rupp, Cameron	R-R	6-2	260	9-28-88	.217	.267	.195	88	295	35	64	17	0	14	34	34	1	0	1	114	1	0	.417	.299
Saunders, Michael	R-L	6-4	225	11-19-86	.205	.193	.210	61	200	25	41	9	2	6	20	13	1	0	0	51	0	1	.360	.257
Stassi, Brock	L-L	6-2	190	8-7-89	.167	.071	.188	51	78	6	13	2	1	2	7	12	0	0	0	22	0	0	.295	.278
Williams, Nick	L-L	6-3	195	9-8-93	.288	.274	.293	83	313	45	90	14	4	12	55	20	6	0	4	97	1	2	.473	.338

Pitching	B-T	HT	WT	DOB	W	L	ERA	G	GS	CG	SV	IP	H	R	ER	HR	BB	SO	AVG	vLH	vRH	K/9	BB/9
Alvarez, Henderson	R-R	6-0	205	4-18-90	0	1	4.30	3	3	0	0	15	14	7	7	2	11	6	.250	.207	.296	3.68	6.75
Anderson, Drew	R-R	6-3	185	3-22-94	0	0	23.14	2	0	0	0	2	6	7	6	0	1	2	.500	.714	.200	7.71	3.86
Arano, Victor	R-R	6-2	200	2-7-95	1	0	1.69	10	0	0	0	11	6	2	2	0	4	13	.158	.222	.138	10.97	3.38
Beato, Pedro	R-R	6-6	230	10-27-86	0	0	0.00	1	0	0	0	1	0	0	0	0	0	1	.000	.000	.000	13.50	0.00
Benoit, Joaquin	R-R	6-4	250	7-26-77	1	4	4.07	44	0	0	2	42	32	19	19	5	16	43	.207	.214	.197	9.21	3.43
2-team total (8 Pittsburgh)					1	6	4.65	52	0	0	2	50	43	28	26	7	22	46	.228	.375	.278	8.23	3.93
Buchholz, Clay	R-L	6-3	190	8-14-84	0	1	12.27	2	2	0	0	7	16	10	10	1	3	5	.457	.500	.400	6.14	3.68
Curtis, Zac	L-L	5-9	190	7-4-92	0	0	2.45	3	0	0	0	4	3	1	1	0	2	4	.250	.000	.375	9.82	4.91
Eflin, Zach	R-R	6-6	215	4-8-94	1	5	6.16	11	11	0	0	64	79	45	44	16	12	35	.309	.306	.312	4.90	1.68
Eickhoff, Jerad	R-R	6-4	245	7-2-90	4	8	4.71	24	24	0	0	128	142	74	67	16	53	118	.281	.314	.243	8.30	3.73
Fien, Casey	R-R	6-2	210	10-21-83	0	1	10.50	4	0	0	0	6	14	7	7	2	2	4	.467	.444	.476	6.00	3.00
Garcia, Luis	R-R	6-3	230	1-30-87	2	5	2.65	66	0	0	2	71	61	22	21	3	26	60	.229	.280	.184	7.57	3.28
Gomez, Jeanmar	R-R	6-3	215	2-10-88	3	2	7.25	18	0	0	2	22	31	19	18	7	7	21	.348	.404	.286	8.46	2.82
Hellickson, Jeremy	R-R	6-1	190	4-8-87	6	5	4.73	20	20	0	0	112	111	62	59	22	30	65	.261	.254	.266	5.21	2.40
Leiter, Mark	R-R	6-0	195	3-13-91	3	6	4.96	27	11	0	0	91	90	59	50	18	31	84	.254	.258	.251	8.34	3.08
Lively, Ben	R-R	6-4	190	3-5-92	4	7	4.26	15	15	1	0	89	90	45	42	13	24	52	.269	.286	.252	5.28	2.44
Milner, Hoby	L-L	6-2	165	1-13-91	0	0	2.01	37	0	0	0	31	30	7	7	2	16	22	.259	.159	.377	6.32	4.60
Morgan, Adam	L-L	6-1	200	2-27-90	3	3	4.12	37	0	0	0	55	51	25	25	10	18	63	.242	.193	.276	10.37	2.96
Neris, Hector	R-R	6-2	215	6-14-89	4	5	3.01	74	0	0	26	75	68	26	25	9	26	86	.239	.270	.204	10.37	3.13
Neshek, Pat	R-B	6-3	220	9-4-80	3	2	1.12	43	0	0	1	40	28	5	5	2	5	45	.199	.185	.207	10.04	1.12
2-team total (28 Colorado)					5	3	1.59	71	0	0	1	62	48	13	11	3	6	69	.212	.303	.192	9.96	0.87
Nicasio, Juan	R-R	6-4	252	8-31-86	1	0	0.00	2	0	0	0	1	0	0	0	0	0	1	.000	.000	.000	6.75	0.00
3-team total (65 Pittsburgh, 9 St. Louis)					5	5	2.61	76	0	0	6	72	58	22	21	5	20	72	.217	.202	.238	8.96	2.49
Nola, Aaron	R-R	6-2	195	6-4-93	12	11	3.54	27	27	0	0	168	154	67	66	18	49	184	.241	.255	.228	9.86	2.63
Pinto, Ricardo	R-R	6-0	165	1-20-94	1	2	7.89	25	0	0	0	30	39	28	26	7	17	25	.317	.339	.299	7.58	5.16
Pivetta, Nick	R-R	6-5	220	2-14-93	8	10	6.02	26	26	0	0	133	144	91	89	25	57	140	.281	.253	.308	9.47	3.86
Ramos, Edubray	R-R	6-0	160	12-19-92	2	7	4.21	59	0	0	0	58	57	29	27	4	28	75	.253	.299	.219	11.71	4.37
Rios, Yacksel	R-R	6-3	185	6-27-93	1	0	4.41	13	0	0	0	16	15	8	8	4	9	17	.238	.258	.219	9.37	4.96
Rodriguez, Joely	L-L	6-1	200	11-14-91	1	2	6.33	26	0	0	0	27	37	26	19	4	15	18	.325	.352	.300	6.00	5.00

Pitching	B-T	HT	WT	DOB	W	L	ERA	G	GS	CG	SV	IP	H	R	ER	HR	BB	SO	AVG	vLH	vRH	K/9	BB/9
Siegrist, Kevin	L-L	6-5	230	7-20-89	0	0	3.60	7	0	0	0	5	4	2	2	1	2	7	.211	.300	.111	12.60	3.60
2-team total (39 St. Louis)					1	1	4.81	46	0	0	1	39	39	21	21	5	22	43	.264	.240	.291	9.84	5.03
Therrien, Jesen	R-R	6-2	200	3-18-93	0	0	8.35	15	0	0	0	18	24	17	17	5	7	10	.308	.378	.244	4.91	3.44
Thompson, Jake	R-R	6-4	225	1-31-94	3	2	3.88	11	8	0	0	46	50	27	20	9	22	35	.276	.219	.308	6.80	4.27
Velasquez, Vince	R-R	6-3	205	6-7-92	2	7	5.13	15	15	0	0	72	74	44	41	15	34	68	.270	.287	.255	8.50	4.25

Fielding

Catcher	PCT	G	PO	A	E	DP	PB
Alfaro	.991	28	220	12	2	3	3
Knapp	.991	53	408	22	4	4	3
Rupp	.989	88	688	50	8	4	11

First Base	PCT	G	PO	A	E	DP
Alfaro	1.000	2	8	2	0	1
Blanco	1.000	11	17	2	0	3
Franco	1.000	2	14	1	0	2
Hoskins	.985	27	185	18	3	17
Joseph	.992	130	948	58	8	99
Kendrick	1.000	1	2	0	0	0
Knapp	.000	1	0	0	0	0
Nava	1.000	4	13	1	0	0
Perkins	.000	1	0	0	0	0
Stassi	1.000	21	109	10	0	8

Second Base	PCT	G	PO	A	E	DP
Blanco	.957	15	12	32	2	3
Crawford	1.000	4	4	9	0	1
Florimon	1.000	1	2	3	0	0
Hernandez	.981	127	224	337	11	79
Kelly	1.000	14	15	23	0	5
Kendrick	.960	10	17	31	2	8

Third Base	PCT	G	PO	A	E	DP
Blanco	1.000	16	4	11	0	0
Crawford	1.000	13	14	29	0	6
Florimon	.000	1	0	0	0	0
Franco	.955	144	103	215	15	23
Kelly	1.000	4	1	1	0	0

Shortstop	PCT	G	PO	A	E	DP
Blanco	1.000	4	5	1	0	1
Crawford	1.000	6	8	20	0	5
Florimon	1.000	2	1	5	0	0
Galvis	.989	155	226	404	7	94
Hernandez	1.000	1	0	2	0	0

Outfield	PCT	G	PO	A	E	DP
Altherr	.986	106	211	7	3	4
Florimon	1.000	11	18	1	0	0
Galvis	1.000	2	5	0	0	0
Herrera	.994	133	323	6	2	3
Hoskins	.979	30	44	2	1	0
Kelly	1.000	11	5	1	0	1
Kendrick	.977	24	43	0	1	0
Kim	1.000	23	35	2	0	2
Nava	.988	49	79	3	1	1
Perkins	1.000	28	37	0	0	0
Saunders	.990	52	91	4	1	0
Stassi	1.000	3	1	0	0	0
Williams	1.000	80	110	4	0	1

LEHIGH VALLEY IRONPIGS

TRIPLE-A

INTERNATIONAL LEAGUE

Batting	B-T	HT	WT	DOB	AVG	vLH	vRH	G	AB	R	H	2B	3B	HR	RBI	BB	HBP	SH	SF	SO	SB	CS	SLG	OBP
Aguila, Osmel	R-R	6-0	185	7-18-89	.233	.364	.188	16	43	4	10	1	0	0	0	4	0	0	0	10	0	0	.256	.298
Alfaro, Jorge	R-R	6-2	225	6-11-93	.241	.279	.223	84	324	34	78	13	2	7	43	16	8	0	2	113	1	1	.358	.291
Cozens, Dylan	L-L	6-6	235	5-31-94	.210	.194	.217	135	476	68	100	12	3	27	75	58	5	0	3	194	8	3	.418	.301
Crawford, J.P.	L-R	6-2	180	1-11-95	.243	.234	.246	127	474	75	115	20	6	15	63	79	1	1	1	97	5	4	.405	.351
Featherston, Taylor	R-R	6-1	185	10-8-89	.270	.261	.275	46	137	22	37	8	0	3	20	21	2	0	2	34	6	0	.394	.370
2-team total (31 Durham)					.237	.200	.200	77	257	34	61	13	0	7	35	28	3	0	3	92	8	0	.370	.316
Flores, Jorge	R-R	5-5	160	11-25-91	.260	.546	.180	23	50	7	13	2	0	0	6	3	1	0	2	15	0	0	.300	.304
Florimon, Pedro	B-R	6-2	185	12-10-86	.265	.317	.246	90	310	32	82	13	1	10	33	34	6	1	2	94	4	3	.410	.347
Gomez, Hector	R-R	6-2	195	3-5-88	.236	.200	.248	74	212	26	50	15	2	7	27	7	1	0	3	44	0	1	.425	.260
Herrera, Odubel	L-R	5-11	205	12-29-91	.250	—	.250	1	4	1	1	0	0	0	0	0	0	0	0	0	0	0	.250	.250
Hoskins, Rhys	R-R	6-4	225	3-17-93	.284	.273	.289	115	401	78	114	24	4	29	91	64	5	0	5	75	4	2	.581	.385
Kelly, Ty	R-L	6-0	180	7-20-88	.286	.200	.333	4	14	4	4	1	0	1	3	3	0	0	0	0	0	0	.571	.412
2-team total (2 Buffalo)					.273	.000	.400	6	22	4	6	2	0	1	4	3	1	0	0	2	0	0	.500	.385
Kendrick, Howie	R-R	5-11	220	7-12-83	.167	.000	.200	4	12	3	2	1	0	0	0	1	2	0	0	5	0	0	.250	.333
Kingery, Scott	R-R	5-10	180	4-29-94	.294	.269	.301	63	265	41	78	11	3	8	21	13	5	1	2	58	10	2	.449	.337
Marrero, Christian	L-L	6-1	185	7-30-86	.182	.000	.250	4	11	2	2	0	0	0	3	3	0	0	0	3	0	0	.182	.357
Martinez, Harold	R-R	6-3	210	5-3-90	.138	.333	.087	12	29	4	4	0	1	0	0	0	1	0	0	13	0	0	.207	.167
Moore, Logan	L-R	6-3	220	8-22-90	.233	.133	.261	64	210	26	49	7	1	6	31	25	0	1	4	72	0	1	.362	.310
Mora, Angelo	B-R	5-11	150	2-25-93	.280	.227	.295	27	100	12	28	5	0	0	8	2	0	1	1	19	1	0	.330	.291
Nava, Daniel	L-B	5-11	200	2-22-83	1.000	1.000	—	1	2	1	2	1	0	0	1	1	0	0	0	0	0	0	1.500	1.000
Perkins, Cameron	R-R	6-5	195	9-27-90	.288	.304	.281	76	257	37	74	18	1	7	27	30	6	1	1	47	3	2	.448	.374
Pullin, Andrew	L-R	6-0	190	9-25-93	.231	.196	.241	67	238	22	55	21	2	6	23	13	3	0	0	50	3	1	.412	.280
Quinn, Roman	B-R	5-10	170	5-14-93	.274	.268	.277	45	175	24	48	8	3	2	13	18	1	2	1	49	10	4	.389	.344
Rickles, Nick	R-R	6-3	220	2-2-90	.250	.182	.294	9	28	2	7	1	0	0	5	2	0	0	0	9	0	0	.286	.300
Rodriguez, Herlis	L-L	6-0	170	6-10-94	.216	.265	.202	48	148	16	32	6	0	3	8	5	4	2	1	36	3	2	.318	.260
Stassi, Brock	L-L	6-2	190	8-7-89	.249	.163	.277	50	173	18	43	4	0	4	22	18	2	0	3	42	0	0	.341	.321
Tocci, Carlos	R-R	6-2	160	8-23-95	.189	.250	.171	17	53	2	10	0	0	1	4	1	0	0	0	11	0	0	.245	.204
Tromp, Jiandido	R-R	5-11	175	9-27-93	.222	.400	.000	3	9	0	2	1	0	0	2	1	0	0	0	2	0	0	.333	.300
Valentin, Jesmuel	B-R	5-9	180	5-12-94	.229	.310	.167	29	96	9	22	3	0	1	7	6	1	1	0	16	0	0	.292	.282
Williams, Matt	R-R	6-0	170	8-29-89	.120	.235	.061	19	50	2	6	3	0	0	0	3	1	0	0	10	1	0	.180	.185
Williams, Nick	L-L	6-3	195	9-8-93	.280	.250	.292	78	282	43	79	16	2	15	44	16	5	1	2	90	5	4	.511	.328

Pitching	B-T	HT	WT	DOB	W	L	ERA	G	GS	CG	SV	IP	H	R	ER	HR	BB	SO	AVG	vLH	vRH	K/9	BB/9
Alvarez, Henderson	R-R	6-0	205	4-18-90	2	0	2.84	3	3	0	0	19	19	7	6	1	6	8	.268	.250	.277	3.79	2.84
Anderson, Drew	R-R	6-3	185	3-22-94	0	0	1.35	1	1	0	0	7	5	2	1	1	2	7	.208	.333	.133	9.45	2.70
Appel, Mark	R-R	6-5	220	7-15-91	5	4	5.27	17	17	0	0	82	91	51	48	9	53	60	.284	.326	.253	6.59	5.82
Beato, Pedro	R-R	6-6	230	10-27-86	1	3	2.75	52	0	0	33	56	41	17	17	4	20	42	.202	.222	.186	6.79	3.23
Bergjans, Tommy	R-R	6-1	190	12-1-92	0	1	7.20	1	1	0	0	5	3	4	4	1	3	3	.167	.333	.133	5.40	5.40
DeNato, Joey	L-L	5-10	175	3-17-92	1	1	5.50	11	3	0	0	18	18	13	11	3	10	9	.261	.267	.256	4.50	5.00
Eflin, Zach	R-R	6-6	215	4-8-94	1	4	4.57	8	7	0	0	43	48	22	22	3	15	38	.289	.375	.209	7.89	3.12
Eshelman, Tom	R-R	6-3	210	6-20-94	10	3	2.23	18	18	3	0	121	101	36	30	8	13	80	.227	.236	.218	5.95	0.97
Fien, Casey	R-R	6-2	210	10-21-83	0	1	5.06	14	0	0	0	16	15	9	9	3	3	13	.254	.250	.258	7.31	1.69
Garcia, Luis	R-R	6-3	230	1-30-87	0	0	5.79	4	1	0	1	5	5	3	3	0	5	7	.263	.250	.273	13.50	9.64
Leibrandt, Brandon	L-L	6-4	190	12-13-92	5	3	3.94	12	12	0	0	64	59	29	28	8	24	53	.244	.299	.223	7.45	3.38
Leiter, Mark	R-R	6-0	195	3-13-91	2	1	4.20	7	5	0	0	30	27	15	14	5	6	38	.233	.293	.172	11.40	1.80

Lively, Ben	R-R	6-4	190	3-5-92	7	5	3.15	16	16	1	0	97	91	39	34	3	22	82	.243	.327	.174	7.61	2.04
Mariot, Michael	R-R	6-0	190	10-20-88	7	2	4.42	45	0	0	2	57	56	32	28	5	21	63	.257	.241	.267	9.95	3.32
Milner, Hoby	L-L	6-2	165	1-13-91	1	2	2.60	22	0	0	0	28	24	8	8	1	4	27	.235	.200	.263	8.78	1.30
Morgan, Adam	L-L	6-1	200	2-27-90	0	1	4.67	12	0	0	0	17	19	9	9	1	5	14	.288	.231	.325	7.27	2.60
Murray, Colton	R-R	6-0	195	4-22-90	2	2	5.53	33	0	0	0	41	49	27	25	6	15	45	.301	.294	.305	9.96	3.32
Nola, Aaron	R-R	6-2	195	6-4-93	1	0	0.87	2	2	0	0	10	6	1	1	0	1	10	.167	.211	.118	8.71	0.87
Perez, Wander	L-L	6-3	160	1-5-85	0	0	5.63	6	0	0	0	8	10	8	5	1	7	5	.294	.364	.261	5.63	7.88
Peterson, Mark	R-R	6-0	190	9-7-90	0	0	8.00	5	0	0	0	9	18	9	8	1	5	5	.450	.412	.478	5.00	5.00
Pinto, Ricardo	R-R	6-0	165	1-20-94	5	3	3.86	19	8	0	1	61	61	35	26	4	18	46	.263	.274	.256	6.82	2.67
Pivetta, Nick	R-R	6-5	220	2-14-93	5	0	1.41	5	5	1	0	32	25	6	5	1	2	37	.208	.304	.186	10.41	0.56
Ramos, Cesar	L-L	6-2	200	6-22-84	5	4	4.00	40	11	0	1	92	91	51	41	10	31	74	.259	.272	.252	7.21	3.02
Ramos, Edubray	R-R	6-0	160	12-19-92	2	0	1.54	10	0	0	1	12	7	3	2	0	4	10	.171	.217	.111	7.71	3.09
Richy, John	R-R	6-4	215	7-28-92	0	0	4.76	2	1	0	0	6	9	3	3	0	1	1	.360	.273	.429	1.59	1.59
Rios, Yacksel	R-R	6-3	185	6-27-93	0	1	1.96	13	1	0	1	18	10	4	4	3	4	17	.159	.100	.212	8.35	1.96
Rivero, Alexis	R-R	6-0	180	10-18-94	1	1	7.00	8	0	0	0	9	14	7	7	2	4	6	.350	.278	.409	6.00	4.00
Taveras, Jose	L-R	6-4	210	11-6-93	3	1	1.32	7	7	0	0	41	26	7	6	5	15	37	.176	.127	.221	8.12	3.29
Therrien, Jesen	R-R	6-2	200	3-18-93	0	0	1.57	18	0	0	2	29	25	7	5	2	6	26	.227	.240	.217	8.16	1.88
Thompson, Jake	R-R	6-4	225	1-31-94	5	14	5.25	22	22	0	0	118	136	83	69	12	47	90	.293	.265	.318	6.85	3.57
Velasquez, Vince	R-R	6-3	205	6-7-92	0	0	4.50	1	1	0	0	2	1	1	1	0	1	0	.200	.000	.333	0.00	4.50
Venditte, Pat	L-B	6-1	185	6-30-85	9	5	3.36	52	0	0	2	70	54	28	26	7	36	69	.217	.218	.216	8.91	4.65

Fielding

Catcher	PCT	G	PO	A	E	DP	PB
Alfaro	.997	77	590	42	2	2	9
Moore	.991	58	395	32	4	4	5
Rickles	1.000	9	53	2	0	0	2

First Base	PCT	G	PO	A	E	DP
Featherston	.000	2	0	0	0	0
Hoskins	.991	105	801	48	8	76
Marrero	1.000	1	8	1	0	0
Martinez	1.000	2	18	0	0	1
Moore	1.000	1	1	0	0	0
Perkins	1.000	4	31	2	0	2
Stassi	1.000	32	232	16	0	20

Second Base	PCT	G	PO	A	E	DP
Crawford	1.000	5	6	8	0	3
Featherston	1.000	6	13	7	0	3
Flores	.985	16	23	43	1	6
Florimon	.993	33	63	74	1	19
Kelly	1.000	1	1	1	0	0
Kingery	.988	54	111	138	3	32
Mora	.972	8	9	26	1	5
Valentin	.969	26	42	53	3	14

Third Base	PCT	G	PO	A	E	DP
Crawford	1.000	6	6	12	0	1
Featherston	.962	33	19	57	3	3
Florimon	.966	25	15	41	2	5
Gomez	.937	57	30	88	8	8
Kelly	1.000	3	1	6	0	1
Kendrick	.667	2	2	0	1	0
Kingery	1.000	4	1	9	0	0
Martinez	.900	5	1	8	1	1
Mora	.963	12	7	19	1	2
Williams	.875	7	7	7	2	2

Shortstop	PCT	G	PO	A	E	DP
Crawford	.960	113	124	279	17	60
Flores	.667	1	1	1	1	1
Florimon	.980	15	12	38	1	5
Kingery	1.000	2	2	8	0	1
Mora	.941	7	13	19	2	5
Valentin	.857	2	1	5	1	0
Williams	1.000	3	6	6	0	2

Outfield	PCT	G	PO	A	E	DP
Aguila	.955	12	20	1	1	1
Cozens	.984	109	239	9	4	2
Featherston	.882	7	14	1	2	0
Florimon	.960	14	23	1	1	0
Herrera	1.000	1	3	0	0	0
Hoskins	1.000	3	9	0	0	0
Kendrick	1.000	2	5	0	0	0
Marrero	1.000	1	2	0	0	0
Nava	.000	1	0	0	0	0
Perkins	.970	61	125	3	4	0
Pullin	.979	45	92	0	2	0
Quinn	.962	44	100	2	4	1
Rodriguez	.985	45	126	4	2	1
Stassi	1.000	12	22	1	0	0
Tocci	1.000	15	31	2	0	1
Tromp	1.000	3	6	0	0	0
Williams	1.000	7	6	0	0	0
Williams	.980	64	141	5	3	0

READING FIGHTIN PHILS

DOUBLE-A

EASTERN LEAGUE

Batting	B-T	HT	WT	DOB	AVG	vLH	vRH	G	AB	R	H	2B	3B	HR	RBI	BB	HBP	SH	SF	SO	SB	CS	SLG	OBP
Aguila, Osmel	R-R	6-0	185	7-18-89	.244	.255	.229	25	82	10	20	5	1	3	13	11	1	0	3	15	0	0	.439	.330
Antequera, Jose	R-R	5-10	160	8-1-95	.250	—	.250	2	4	1	1	0	0	0	0	0	0	1	0	0	0	0	.250	.250
Bossart, Austin	R-R	6-2	210	7-4-93	.250	.000	1.000	1	4	0	1	0	0	0	0	0	0	0	0	1	0	0	.250	.250
Campbell, Derek	R-R	6-0	175	6-28-91	.162	.188	.143	13	37	3	6	1	0	1	2	0	1	0	0	10	0	0	.270	.184
Canelo, Malquin	R-R	5-10	156	9-5-94	.226	.273	.203	112	389	50	88	22	2	6	34	42	1	1	3	113	12	5	.339	.301
Coppola, Zachary	L-R	5-10	160	5-9-94	.252	.267	.247	85	325	46	82	9	1	0	24	38	1	5	3	61	29	9	.286	.330
Fisher, Joel	R-R	6-3	235	1-8-93	.154	.231	.077	9	26	3	4	0	0	1	2	5	0	0	0	11	0	0	.269	.290
Flores, Jorge	R-R	5-5	160	11-25-91	.231	.250	.214	9	26	1	6	2	0	0	4	1	0	1	2	7	0	0	.308	.241
Green, Zach	R-R	6-3	210	3-7-94	.222	.313	.172	15	45	3	10	2	0	1	5	3	2	0	1	20	0	0	.333	.294
Grullon, Deivi	R-R	6-1	180	2-17-96	.229	.375	.194	23	83	10	19	3	0	4	13	5	0	0	1	19	0	0	.410	.270
Herrera, Odubel	L-R	5-11	205	12-29-91	1.000	—	1.000	1	2	2	2	0	0	1	2	1	0	0	0	0	0	0	2.500	1.000
Kendrick, Howie	R-R	5-11	220	7-12-83	.250	.333	.000	1	4	2	1	0	0	1	1	0	0	0	0	0	0	0	1.000	.250
Kingery, Scott	R-R	5-10	180	4-29-94	.313	.324	.305	69	278	62	87	18	5	18	44	28	4	3	4	51	19	3	.608	.379
Marrero, Christian	L-L	6-1	185	7-30-86	.400	.200	.480	10	35	5	14	2	0	2	7	4	0	0	0	5	0	0	.629	.462
Martin, Kyle	L-L	6-2	240	11-13-92	.193	.163	.208	123	436	60	84	15	1	22	68	50	10	1	4	134	2	1	.383	.288
Martinez, Harold	R-R	6-3	210	5-3-90	.232	.290	.197	38	99	17	23	6	0	1	6	10	1	0	0	20	0	0	.323	.309
Mora, Angelo	B-R	5-11	150	2-25-93	.295	.320	.284	80	298	42	88	19	3	9	47	24	0	0	0	60	4	2	.470	.348
Nava, Daniel	L-B	5-11	200	2-22-83	.250	.250	—	1	4	1	1	0	0	0	0	0	0	0	0	0	0	0	.250	.250
Numata, Chace	B-R	6-0	175	8-14-92	.249	.240	.254	84	305	32	76	17	1	4	28	30	2	0	3	37	0	1	.351	.318
Pullin, Andrew	L-R	6-0	190	9-25-93	.308	.295	.317	67	266	40	82	22	1	14	46	22	5	0	3	43	2	0	.556	.368
Rickles, Nick	R-R	6-3	220	2-2-90	.274	.194	.322	26	95	9	26	8	0	4	12	5	0	0	2	9	1	0	.484	.304
2-team total (2 Harrisburg)					.260	.000	.000	28	100	9	26	8	0	4	12	5	0	0	2	11	1	0	.460	.290
Rodriguez, Herlis	L-L	6-0	170	6-10-94	.280	.400	.250	9	25	2	7	2	0	1	3	0	0	0	0	8	0	0	.480	.280
Sandberg, Cord	L-L	6-3	215	1-2-95	.263	.167	.293	33	99	11	26	6	0	4	11	3	0	1	1	30	1	0	.444	.282
Stankiewicz, Drew	L-R	5-9	160	6-18-93	.302	.324	.296	53	149	19	45	6	1	4	16	21	1	1	0	29	1	1	.436	.392

Batting	B-T	HT	WT	DOB	AVG	vLH	vRH	G	AB	R	H	2B	3B	HR	RBI	BB	HBP	SH	SF	SO	SB	CS	SLG	OBP
Stassi, Brock	L-L	6-2	190	8-7-89	.333	.250	.500	2	6	1	2	0	0	0	1	1	0	0	0	0	0	0	.333	.429
Tocci, Carlos	R-R	6-2	160	8-23-95	.307	.308	.307	113	430	59	132	19	7	2	48	29	10	2	3	66	4	5	.398	.362
Tomscha, Damek	R-R	6-2	200	8-27-91	.315	.356	.298	48	159	22	50	5	0	4	17	11	4	1	0	18	1	0	.421	.374
Tromp, Jiandido	R-R	5-11	175	9-27-93	.285	.354	.248	122	456	64	130	31	3	18	62	28	3	1	3	112	10	7	.485	.329
Walding, Mitch	L-R	6-3	190	9-10-92	.237	.229	.240	99	351	52	83	15	4	25	62	44	4	0	2	127	1	1	.516	.327

Pitching	B-T	HT	WT	DOB	W	L	ERA	G	GS	CG	SV	IP	H	R	ER	HR	BB	SO	AVG	vLH	vRH	K/9	BB/9
Anderson, Drew	R-R	6-3	185	3-22-94	9	4	3.59	21	21	0	0	108	81	49	43	13	40	86	.207	.209	.205	7.19	3.34
Arano, Victor	R-R	6-2	200	2-7-95	1	2	4.19	32	0	0	9	39	39	20	18	7	11	38	.264	.284	.247	8.84	2.56
Arauz, Harold	R-R	6-2	185	5-29-95	0	0	0.00	1	0	0	0	2	3	0	0	0	2	3	.300	.000	.500	11.57	7.71
Bergjans, Tommy	R-R	6-1	190	12-1-92	1	6	6.57	12	11	0	0	51	64	41	37	13	14	40	.314	.275	.353	7.11	2.49
Casimiro, Ranfi	R-R	6-8	200	7-16-92	1	5	3.57	20	4	0	1	45	43	22	18	5	12	31	.252	.206	.278	6.15	2.38
Cleavinger, Garrett	R-L	6-1	210	4-23-94	0	1	5.28	11	0	0	1	15	19	13	9	1	9	17	.317	.273	.342	9.98	5.28
2-team total (27 Bowie)					2	5	6.00	38	0	0	4	54	57	42	36	5	32	59	.265	.245	.245	9.83	5.33
Davis, Austin	L-L	6-4	245	2-3-93	4	2	2.87	32	0	0	1	47	45	17	15	3	20	46	.257	.241	.265	8.81	3.83
DeNato, Joey	L-L	5-10	175	3-17-92	5	1	1.09	22	0	0	0	33	27	4	4	0	22	24	.233	.154	.273	6.55	6.00
Eickhoff, Jerad	R-R	6-4	245	7-2-90	0	1	1.80	1	1	0	0	5	2	1	1	1	1	5	.118	.000	.182	9.00	1.80
Eshelman, Tom	R-R	6-3	210	6-20-94	3	0	3.10	5	5	0	0	29	27	11	10	6	5	22	.257	.229	.281	6.83	1.55
Garcia, Elniery	L-L	6-0	155	12-24-94	2	1	1.75	5	5	0	0	26	17	8	5	0	17	10	.193	.261	.169	3.51	5.96
Hockenberry, Matt	R-R	6-3	220	8-30-91	0	0	30.38	4	0	0	0	3	7	9	9	0	5	3	.539	.333	.714	10.13	16.88
Hollands, Mario	L-L	6-5	230	8-26-88	1	0	4.15	10	0	0	1	13	15	9	6	1	12	9	.289	.278	.294	6.23	8.31
Irvin, Cole	L-L	6-4	180	1-31-94	5	3	4.06	13	13	0	0	84	72	41	38	12	24	66	.228	.148	.255	7.04	2.56
Kilome, Franklyn	R-R	6-6	175	6-25-95	1	3	3.64	5	5	0	0	30	25	15	12	2	15	20	.238	.327	.161	6.07	4.55
Leibrandt, Brandon	L-L	6-4	190	12-13-92	6	2	3.34	13	13	0	0	73	77	29	27	4	23	52	.284	.241	.296	6.44	2.85
Murray, Colton	R-R	6-0	195	4-22-90	0	0	1.46	8	0	0	3	12	9	2	2	0	1	18	.209	.200	.214	13.14	0.73
Nunez, Miguel	R-R	6-6	215	10-27-92	1	4	3.57	24	2	0	3	35	31	14	14	4	20	25	.244	.237	.250	6.37	5.09
Richy, John	R-R	6-4	215	7-28-92	1	3	7.16	10	6	0	0	33	51	28	26	3	10	22	.362	.352	.371	6.06	2.76
Rios, Yacksel	R-R	6-3	185	6-27-93	1	2	1.89	24	0	0	2	38	22	12	8	2	10	47	.168	.232	.120	11.13	2.37
Rivero, Alexis	R-R	6-0	180	10-18-94	4	3	4.08	35	1	0	2	57	55	29	26	7	23	46	.257	.276	.244	7.22	3.61
Sanchez, Mario	R-R	6-1	166	10-31-94	4	2	2.88	19	7	0	0	56	52	20	18	7	13	32	.251	.264	.237	5.11	2.08
Singer, Jeff	L-L	6-0	200	9-13-93	0	2	5.54	12	0	0	2	13	11	9	8	1	9	12	.220	.143	.250	8.31	6.23
Taveras, Jose	L-R	6-4	210	11-6-93	0	1	3.97	2	2	0	0	11	10	5	5	2	1	11	.233	.250	.211	8.74	0.79
Therrien, Jesen	R-R	6-2	200	3-18-93	2	1	1.26	21	0	0	7	29	14	5	4	1	3	39	.149	.140	.157	12.24	0.94
Tirado, Alberto	R-R	6-0	180	12-10-94	0	0	6.75	10	0	0	0	12	13	9	9	0	19	8	.283	.333	.250	6.00	14.25
Velasquez, Vince	R-R	6-3	205	6-7-92	0	0	6.00	1	1	0	0	3	3	3	2	1	1	4	.250	.000	.273	12.00	3.00
Viza, Tyler	R-R	6-3	170	10-21-94	10	10	5.22	26	26	1	0	140	152	90	81	20	48	100	.277	.294	.265	6.44	3.09
Waguespack, Jacob	R-R	6-6	225	11-5-93	3	2	3.65	7	6	0	0	37	37	17	15	2	16	35	.262	.239	.286	8.51	3.89
Watson, Shane	R-R	6-4	200	8-13-93	4	5	4.10	33	11	0	1	83	97	42	38	12	40	45	.299	.322	.279	4.86	4.32
Windle, Tom	L-L	6-4	215	3-10-92	3	2	4.24	36	0	0	2	51	37	26	24	4	21	44	.200	.183	.211	7.76	3.71

Fielding

Catcher	PCT	G	PO	A	E	DP	PB
Bossart	1.000	1	5	2	0	0	1
Fisher	.984	9	56	4	1	1	2
Grullon	.977	23	150	19	4	1	1
Numata	.988	83	603	71	8	5	11
Rickles	.988	24	142	16	2	2	1

First Base	PCT	G	PO	A	E	DP
Green	1.000	6	53	3	0	7
Marrero	1.000	1	5	0	0	1
Martin	.993	116	965	73	7	102
Martinez	.972	15	92	13	3	12
Stassi	1.000	1	7	1	0	1
Tomscha	.983	8	54	4	1	5

Second Base	PCT	G	PO	A	E	DP
Antequera	1.000	2	0	4	0	0
Campbell	.950	8	16	22	2	6
Kingery	.989	59	104	170	3	43
Mora	.963	39	90	90	7	21
Stankiewicz	.972	38	77	97	5	25

Third Base	PCT	G	PO	A	E	DP
Campbell	1.000	2	1	2	0	0
Green	1.000	1	1	2	0	0
Martinez	.952	8	4	16	1	1
Mora	.943	12	9	24	2	3
Stankiewicz	1.000	4	0	4	0	1
Tomscha	.942	24	12	53	4	4
Walding	.943	96	59	188	15	26

Shortstop	PCT	G	PO	A	E	DP
Canelo	.955	112	184	304	23	60
Flores	1.000	8	12	18	0	9
Mora	.976	18	32	49	2	13
Stankiewicz	.842	3	7	9	3	4

Outfield	PCT	G	PO	A	E	DP
Aguila	.923	8	11	1	1	0
Brown	.967	24	53	5	2	1
Campbell	1.000	3	3	0	0	0
Coppola	.990	83	185	9	2	2
Herrera	.667	1	2	0	1	0
Kendrick	.000	1	0	0	0	0
Marrero	1.000	6	6	0	0	0
Mora	1.000	4	4	0	0	0
Pullin	.988	50	78	2	1	1
Rodriguez	1.000	6	8	0	0	0
Sandberg	.931	26	26	1	2	1
Tocci	.992	108	246	6	2	1
Tomscha	1.000	13	19	0	0	0
Tromp	1.000	106	190	4	0	1

CLEARWATER THRESHERS — *HIGH CLASS A*

FLORIDA STATE LEAGUE

Batting	B-T	HT	WT	DOB	AVG	vLH	vRH	G	AB	R	H	2B	3B	HR	RBI	BB	HBP	SH	SF	SO	SB	CS	SLG	OBP
Antequera, Jose	R-R	5-10	160	8-1-95	.171	.182	.167	29	88	6	15	2	1	0	2	6	0	1	0	17	3	0	.216	.223
Bossart, Austin	R-R	6-2	210	7-4-93	.244	.264	.236	54	180	14	44	10	0	2	18	8	3	2	2	42	2	0	.333	.285
Cabral, Edgar	R-R	5-11	210	9-12-95	.310	.385	.276	24	84	16	26	5	0	2	12	9	1	0	1	23	0	0	.441	.379
Campbell, Derek	R-R	6-0	175	6-28-91	.263	.100	.321	30	114	14	30	6	0	2	9	9	2	0	0	27	0	2	.368	.328
Coppola, Zachary	L-R	5-10	160	5-9-94	.350	.225	.392	45	160	23	56	5	1	1	12	17	1	4	1	26	10	6	.413	.413
Cumana, Grenny	R-R	5-5	145	11-10-95	.243	.310	.217	88	301	28	73	9	0	2	22	12	5	8	1	41	16	10	.292	.282
Duran, Carlos	R-R	6-2	170	11-22-94	.181	.194	.176	40	127	11	23	4	0	2	9	12	1	0	0	32	7	2	.260	.257
Encarnacion, Luis	R-R	6-2	185	8-9-97	.385	1.000	.333	4	13	1	5	1	0	0	2	1	0	1	0	5	0	0	.462	.429
Garcia, Wilson	B-R	5-11	160	1-11-94	.275	.265	.278	121	477	39	131	28	2	13	60	14	3	0	3	53	0	0	.424	.298
Gomez, Jose	R-R	5-11	175	12-10-96	.250	.273	.243	22	92	8	23	2	0	0	3	4	1	1	0	19	0	1	.272	.289
Green, Zach	R-R	6-3	210	3-7-94	.221	.241	.216	38	140	13	31	7	1	5	15	7	4	0	1	51	0	0	.393	.276

Grullon, Deivi	R-R	6-1	180	2-17-96	.255	.270	.250	71	271	31	69	14	0	8	24	12	1	0	2	61	0	1	.395	.287
Guzman, Jonathan	R-R	6-0	156	8-17-99	.000	.000	.000	1	3	0	0	0	0	0	0	0	0	0	0	3	0	0	.000	.000
Hall, Darick	L-R	6-4	236	7-25-95	.231	.143	.263	7	26	4	6	2	0	2	5	0	0	0	0	7	0	0	.539	.231
Hernandez, Cesar	B-R	5-10	160	5-23-90	.143	.000	.250	4	7	2	1	0	0	0	1	9	1	0	0	2	0	0	.143	.647
Hernandez, Jan	R-R	6-1	195	1-3-95	.212	.309	.179	90	316	42	67	10	3	16	35	26	7	2	0	114	5	3	.415	.287
Laird, Mark	L-L	6-2	180	3-29-93	.286	.250	.297	105	406	56	116	16	5	2	27	29	3	6	0	65	11	3	.365	.338
Marrero, Emmanuel	B-R	5-11	169	5-16-93	.252	.215	.265	109	365	39	92	16	4	5	32	26	5	7	1	83	11	4	.359	.310
Muzziotti, Simon	L-L	6-1	175	12-27-98	.286	.000	.333	2	7	2	2	0	0	0	0	0	0	0	0	2	1	0	.286	.286
Pujols, Jose	R-R	6-3	175	9-29-95	.194	.172	.202	90	325	24	63	10	1	8	29	23	1	0	3	150	2	2	.305	.247
Randolph, Cornelius	L-R	5-11	205	6-2-97	.250	.230	.258	122	440	47	110	18	5	13	55	55	6	4	5	125	7	3	.402	.338
Rodriguez, Herlis	L-L	6-0	170	6-10-94	.272	.208	.294	52	184	20	50	8	2	7	23	22	3	5	0	39	7	3	.451	.359
Sandberg, Cord	L-L	6-3	215	1-2-95	.277	.091	.315	18	65	7	18	7	0	2	6	6	1	1	0	16	0	0	.477	.347
Stankiewicz, Drew	L-R	5-9	160	6-18-93	.263	.191	.285	54	179	19	47	9	1	5	19	20	2	2	2	42	2	1	.408	.340
Tomscha, Damek	R-R	6-2	200	8-27-91	.304	.359	.284	57	201	28	61	10	0	7	33	27	4	1	0	38	2	1	.458	.397

Pitching	B-T	HT	WT	DOB	W	L	ERA	G	GS	CG	SV	IP	H	R	ER	HR	BB	SO	AVG	vLH	vRH	K/9	BB/9
Arauz, Harold	R-R	6-2	185	5-29-95	4	4	2.03	20	6	1	0	71	49	19	16	6	11	74	.191	.185	.195	9.38	1.39
Beato, Pedro	R-R	6-6	230	10-27-86	0	1	18.00	2	0	0	0	2	6	5	4	0	1	2	.500	.800	.286	9.00	4.50
Bettencourt, Trevor	R-R	6-0	195	7-21-94	2	0	1.57	16	0	0	2	23	13	4	4	2	4	22	.157	.147	.163	8.61	1.57
Brown, Aaron	L-L	6-2	220	6-20-92	0	1	5.27	10	0	0	0	14	17	12	8	1	11	14	.309	.267	.325	9.22	7.24
Casimiro, Ranfi	R-R	6-8	200	7-16-92	2	2	3.16	17	0	0	1	37	27	17	13	4	10	33	.202	.225	.188	8.03	2.43
Davis, Austin	L-L	6-4	245	2-3-93	2	0	2.01	10	0	0	1	22	19	5	5	1	3	29	.226	.286	.206	11.69	1.21
Dominguez, Seranthony	R-R	6-1	185	11-25-94	4	4	3.61	15	13	0	0	62	51	28	25	6	30	75	.230	.312	.186	10.83	4.33
Eflin, Zach	R-R	6-6	215	4-8-94	1	0	0.00	1	1	0	0	5	1	0	0	0	0	6	.059	.000	.125	10.80	0.00
Fien, Casey	R-R	6-2	210	10-21-83	0	0	0.00	2	0	0	0	2	1	0	0	0	1	1	.167	.000	.250	4.50	4.50
Frohwirth, Tyler	R-R	6-1	165	9-13-93	0	0	0.00	1	0	0	0	1	1	0	0	0	0	1	.333	1.000	.000	9.00	0.00
Garcia, Edgar	R-R	6-1	180	10-4-96	3	4	4.47	27	15	0	0	89	95	53	44	10	31	89	.271	.310	.240	9.03	3.15
Gilbert, Tyler	L-L	6-3	190	12-22-93	1	6	2.95	35	1	0	3	61	64	22	20	5	15	52	.271	.263	.275	7.67	2.21
Hammer, J.D.	R-R	6-3	215	7-12-94	2	0	0.57	12	0	0	0	16	8	1	1	0	2	20	.154	.217	.103	11.49	1.15
Hibbs, Will	R-R	6-7	245	10-27-93	0	0	7.88	5	0	0	0	8	11	7	7	2	7	7	.333	.385	.300	7.88	7.88
Hockenberry, Matt	R-R	6-3	220	8-30-91	2	0	4.60	21	0	0	0	31	34	17	16	5	9	27	.274	.314	.247	7.76	2.59
Irvin, Cole	L-L	6-4	180	1-31-94	4	6	2.55	12	11	0	0	67	68	26	19	2	14	52	.265	.268	.263	6.99	1.88
Kilome, Franklyn	R-R	6-6	175	6-25-95	6	4	2.59	19	19	0	0	97	96	33	28	5	37	83	.265	.272	.259	7.67	3.42
Leftwich, Luke	L-R	6-3	205	6-9-94	1	6	2.70	42	0	0	8	80	69	30	24	2	21	98	.232	.183	.264	11.03	2.36
McGarry, Seth	R-R	6-0	180	1-5-94	0	4	5.14	13	0	0	5	14	14	9	8	1	6	17	.255	.231	.276	10.93	3.86
2-team total (31 Bradenton)					1	4	2.32	44	0	0	19	54	34	15	14	2	20	55	.177	.197	.099	9.11	3.31
Mills, McKenzie	L-L	6-4	205	11-19-95	0	1	4.60	3	3	0	0	16	21	8	8	1	0	16	.323	.280	.350	9.19	0.00
Quinn, Blake	R-R	6-4	222	4-29-94	4	2	4.38	30	7	0	0	74	75	41	36	9	43	71	.272	.221	.298	8.64	5.23
Romero, JoJo	L-L	6-0	190	9-9-96	5	2	2.24	10	10	0	0	52	43	17	13	2	15	49	.223	.215	.227	8.43	2.58
Sanchez, Sixto	R-R	6-0	185	7-29-98	0	4	4.55	5	5	1	0	28	27	16	14	1	9	20	.252	.273	.231	6.51	2.93
Singer, Jeff	L-L	6-0	200	9-13-93	5	2	2.34	37	0	0	19	50	30	13	13	4	28	66	.171	.188	.165	11.88	5.04
Suarez, Ranger	L-L	6-1	180	8-26-95	2	4	3.82	8	8	0	0	38	43	18	16	1	11	38	.293	.386	.252	9.08	2.63
Taveras, Jose	L-R	6-4	210	11-6-93	6	4	2.38	16	16	1	0	102	86	28	27	13	23	92	.228	.204	.248	8.12	2.03
Tirado, Alberto	R-R	6-0	180	12-10-94	5	4	3.69	15	12	0	0	63	59	33	26	8	38	58	.250	.273	.237	8.24	5.40
Velasquez, Vince	R-R	6-3	205	6-7-92	0	1	1.80	1	1	0	0	5	2	1	1	1	1	5	.125	.100	.167	9.00	1.80
Waguespack, Jacob	R-R	6-6	225	11-5-93	6	5	3.29	24	10	0	1	68	63	29	25	3	24	73	.245	.274	.228	9.61	3.16

Fielding

Catcher	PCT	G	PO	A	E	DP	PB
Bossart	.988	50	442	54	6	2	6
Cabral	.979	21	164	20	4	2	0
Garcia	1.000	1	6	1	0	0	0
Grullon	.987	69	550	75	8	4	9

First Base	PCT	G	PO	A	E	DP
Garcia	.996	87	694	45	3	63
Green	.990	13	92	7	1	7
Hall	1.000	3	27	0	0	2
Rodriguez	.976	6	37	3	1	2
Sandberg	1.000	1	1	0	0	0
Tomscha	1.000	34	254	14	0	19

Second Base	PCT	G	PO	A	E	DP
Antequera	1.000	16	25	39	0	7
Campbell	1.000	7	11	16	0	3
Cumana	.961	68	116	155	11	43
Hernandez	1.000	4	7	11	0	4
Marrero	.905	6	7	12	2	1
Stankiewicz	.977	43	58	114	4	19

Third Base	PCT	G	PO	A	E	DP
Antequera	.667	2	1	1	1	0
Bossart	1.000	1	1	0	0	0
Campbell	.935	19	3	26	2	1
Green	.964	24	8	46	2	2
Hernandez	.835	46	21	65	17	3
Marrero	.905	16	6	13	2	0
Stankiewicz	.875	10	4	10	2	3
Tomscha	.865	24	11	34	7	3

Shortstop	PCT	G	PO	A	E	DP
Antequera	.936	11	13	31	3	8
Cumana	.974	20	22	54	2	11
Gomez	.968	22	32	59	3	9
Guzman	1.000	1	2	2	0	1
Marrero	.964	87	119	234	13	47

Outfield	PCT	G	PO	A	E	DP
Campbell	1.000	4	7	0	0	0
Coppola	.991	42	100	5	1	2
Duran	.989	39	83	5	1	1
Hernandez	1.000	23	29	5	0	0
Laird	1.000	98	223	3	0	1
Muzziotti	1.000	2	6	1	0	1
Pujols	.984	64	117	4	2	0
Randolph	.988	108	154	5	2	1
Rodriguez	.983	26	56	3	1	1
Sandberg	1.000	13	27	0	0	0

LAKEWOOD BLUECLAWS — *LOW CLASS A*

SOUTH ATLANTIC LEAGUE

Batting	B-T	HT	WT	DOB	AVG	vLH	vRH	G	AB	R	H	2B	3B	HR	RBI	BB	HBP	SH	SF	SO	SB	CS	SLG	OBP
Alastre, Jesus	R-R	6-1	155	11-25-96	.307	.242	.327	43	137	20	42	9	1	1	16	5	4	2	0	31	4	2	.409	.349
Antequera, Jose	R-R	5-10	160	8-1-95	.194	.219	.180	33	93	7	18	2	0	0	14	5	4	6	1	19	0	0	.215	.262
Barbier, Brett	R-R	5-11	190	12-6-93	.229	.231	.227	49	175	23	40	9	0	4	21	17	11	1	2	57	1	0	.349	.332
Brito, Daniel	L-R	6-1	155	1-23-98	.239	.262	.232	112	447	54	107	15	1	6	32	33	5	4	2	95	12	9	.318	.298
Cabral, Edgar	R-R	5-11	210	9-12-95	.243	.170	.267	67	235	19	57	12	1	2	14	23	3	0	2	39	0	0	.328	.316

Batting	B-T	HT	WT	DOB	AVG	vLH	vRH	G	AB	R	H	2B	3B	HR	RBI	BB	HBP	SH	SF	SO	SB	CS	SLG	OBP
Duran, Carlos	R-R	6-2	170	11-22-94	.230	.224	.233	57	196	23	45	9	4	1	17	16	1	7	0	47	4	7	.332	.291
Fitch, Colby	L-R	5-11	205	7-27-95	.217	.200	.222	22	69	12	15	2	0	2	5	16	2	0	0	17	0	0	.333	.379
Gamboa, Arquimedes	B-R	6-0	175	9-23-97	.261	.227	.274	79	307	44	80	12	3	6	29	33	0	5	5	52	8	0	.378	.328
Garcia, Enmanuel	R-R	6-0	180	7-23-94	.271	.381	.211	17	59	9	16	4	1	2	6	2	3	0	0	20	1	2	.475	.328
Hall, Darick	L-R	6-4	236	7-25-95	.272	.265	.275	114	426	64	116	28	1	27	96	29	17	0	5	110	0	0	.533	.340
Haseley, Adam	L-L	6-1	195	4-12-96	.258	.231	.264	18	66	15	17	3	1	1	6	6	0	1	1	13	0	1	.379	.315
Lartigue, Henri	B-R	6-0	205	2-24-95	.248	.163	.277	94	339	38	84	23	4	8	44	20	2	2	2	87	2	1	.410	.292
Listi, Austin	R-R	6-0	218	11-5-93	.242	.357	.207	31	120	16	29	7	2	4	11	4	2	1	1	30	0	0	.433	.276
Luis, Juan	L-R	6-4	175	3-23-96	.151	.105	.177	16	53	5	8	0	0	3	5	1	0	0	0	14	3	1	.321	.167
Martinelli, David	L-R	6-2	209	12-30-94	.205	.197	.208	98	302	32	62	15	2	6	26	21	1	1	2	92	4	1	.328	.258
Moniak, Mickey	L-R	6-2	185	5-13-98	.236	.180	.255	123	466	53	110	22	6	5	44	28	6	2	7	109	11	7	.341	.284
Rivas, Raul	B-R	5-10	160	10-27-96	.282	.321	.266	70	262	32	74	6	1	0	25	14	3	8	4	54	10	5	.313	.322
Rivero, Gregori	B-R	5-11	195	5-27-96	.266	.348	.244	30	109	7	29	8	1	1	12	3	2	0	1	20	0	0	.385	.296
Sandberg, Cord	L-L	6-3	215	1-2-95	.268	.213	.292	54	198	19	53	15	2	3	25	11	3	1	4	57	3	1	.409	.310
Williams, Luke	R-R	6-1	180	8-9-96	.216	.242	.206	115	402	41	87	16	0	1	27	28	2	7	3	83	29	2	.264	.269
Wojciechowski, Alex	R-R	6-5	230	3-17-94	.203	.269	.163	18	69	5	14	3	0	0	5	2	1	0	0	17	0	0	.246	.236
Zardon, Danny	R-R	6-0	200	9-30-94	.196	.222	.184	18	56	5	11	2	1	1	4	7	0	1	0	15	0	0	.321	.286

Pitching	B-T	HT	WT	DOB	W	L	ERA	G	GS	CG	SV	IP	H	R	ER	HR	BB	SO	AVG	vLH	vRH	K/9	BB/9
Arauz, Harold	R-R	6-2	185	5-29-95	1	2	1.99	8	0	0	0	23	16	5	5	0	3	16	.200	.200	.200	6.35	1.19
Armas, Gustavo	R-R	6-1	195	1-15-96	1	1	6.00	10	4	0	0	30	35	22	20	5	6	26	.294	.377	.207	7.80	1.80
Bettencourt, Trevor	R-R	6-0	195	7-21-94	3	2	3.28	25	0	0	8	36	32	14	13	1	5	55	.239	.250	.232	13.88	1.26
Brown, Casey	R-L	6-1	190	4-27-93	2	2	2.95	22	0	0	0	43	41	21	14	2	11	25	.247	.224	.263	5.27	2.32
Cabrera, Ismael	R-R	6-1	185	6-19-94	8	5	3.63	33	0	0	2	57	50	25	23	6	19	57	.242	.231	.250	9.00	3.00
Carrasco, Luis	R-R	6-3	170	9-11-94	1	3	4.43	4	4	0	0	20	21	11	10	2	10	11	.280	.278	.282	4.87	4.43
Falter, Bailey	R-L	6-4	175	4-24-97	8	7	2.99	21	21	0	0	114	117	41	38	7	23	105	.270	.331	.231	8.27	1.81
Fanti, Nick	L-L	6-2	185	12-30-96	9	2	2.54	21	21	1	0	120	87	37	34	5	28	121	.200	.211	.193	9.05	2.09
Hallead, Tyler	R-R	6-5	190	5-17-95	1	1	5.05	27	0	0	1	41	32	24	23	3	22	49	.216	.258	.183	10.76	4.83
Hennigan, Jonathan	L-L	6-4	185	8-27-94	1	3	5.84	30	0	0	3	49	47	35	32	3	27	67	.245	.293	.209	12.22	4.93
Hibbs, Will	R-R	6-7	245	10-27-93	6	4	1.77	40	0	0	20	61	29	12	12	2	17	73	.137	.154	.124	10.77	2.51
Kelzer, Jake	R-R	6-8	230	6-30-93	1	1	3.74	14	0	0	0	22	19	9	9	2	6	19	.235	.243	.227	7.89	2.49
Koplove, Kenny	R-R	6-2	170	8-2-93	0	0	27.00	2	0	0	0	3	5	10	10	0	8	3	.357	.500	.333	8.10	21.60
Llovera, Mauricio	R-R	5-11	200	4-17-96	2	4	3.35	30	10	0	0	86	81	43	32	2	33	94	.250	.276	.226	9.84	3.45
Medina, Adonis	R-R	6-1	185	12-18-96	4	9	3.01	22	22	0	0	120	103	47	40	7	39	133	.227	.258	.200	10.00	2.93
Morris, Zach	L-L	6-5	245	3-6-93	2	2	6.23	12	0	0	1	17	23	16	12	4	15	14	.311	.381	.283	7.27	7.79
Paulino, Felix	R-R	6-1	170	3-24-95	5	9	4.53	28	15	0	0	97	100	52	49	5	29	87	.269	.285	.255	8.04	2.68
Requena, Alejandro	R-R	6-2	200	11-29-96	1	1	1.64	2	2	0	0	11	7	3	2	0	0	7	.189	.118	.250	5.73	0.00
2-team total (19 Asheville)					9	4	2.74	21	21	0	0	128	109	49	39	9	25	104	.235	.263	.223	7.31	1.76
Romero, JoJo	L-L	6-0	190	9-9-96	5	1	2.11	13	13	1	0	77	61	25	18	2	21	79	.223	.161	.254	9.27	2.47
Russ, Addison	R-R	6-1	190	10-29-94	1	2	3.49	15	0	0	1	28	26	17	11	2	8	36	.241	.260	.224	11.44	2.54
Sanchez, Sixto	R-R	6-0	185	7-29-98	5	3	2.41	13	13	1	0	67	46	19	18	1	9	64	.191	.193	.189	8.55	1.20
Suarez, Ranger	L-L	6-1	180	8-26-95	6	2	1.59	14	14	1	0	85	52	17	15	4	24	90	.177	.080	.218	9.53	2.54

Fielding

Catcher	PCT	G	PO	A	E	DP	PB
Barbier	1.000	1	12	0	0	0	0
Cabral	.989	66	584	58	7	3	2
Fitch	1.000	19	178	15	0	0	4
Lartigue	.994	36	321	22	2	0	12
Rivero	.980	19	141	8	3	0	4

First Base	PCT	G	PO	A	E	DP
Barbier	1.000	29	246	18	0	14
Hall	.988	71	548	52	7	48
Lartigue	1.000	3	23	0	0	1
Listi	1.000	12	80	8	0	2
Rivero	1.000	7	49	6	0	2
Wojciechowski	.976	13	114	8	3	6
Zardon	.980	6	46	2	1	1

Second Base	PCT	G	PO	A	E	DP
Antequera	1.000	1	3	4	0	1
Brito	.977	107	176	253	10	43
Rivas	.967	26	33	56	3	10
Zardon	.958	7	12	11	1	4

Third Base	PCT	G	PO	A	E	DP
Antequera	1.000	2	0	2	0	0
Rivas	.952	17	12	28	2	5
Williams	.948	115	76	216	16	7
Zardon	.895	6	6	11	2	1

Shortstop	PCT	G	PO	A	E	DP
Antequera	.973	30	33	74	3	10
Brito	.917	6	10	12	2	3
Gamboa	.953	79	105	182	14	33
Rivas	.928	26	31	72	8	10

Outfield	PCT	G	PO	A	E	DP
Alastre	.970	42	60	4	2	1
Duran	.951	56	94	3	5	0
Garcia	1.000	17	27	1	0	0
Haseley	1.000	16	37	1	0	1
Listi	1.000	20	34	1	0	0
Luis	.971	16	31	2	1	0
Martinelli	.993	90	136	5	1	1
Moniak	.986	115	212	7	3	2
Sandberg	.988	49	73	6	1	0
Wojciechowski	1.000	4	3	0	0	0

WILLIAMSPORT CROSSCUTTERS — *SHORT SEASON*

NEW YORK-PENN LEAGUE

Batting	B-T	HT	WT	DOB	AVG	vLH	vRH	G	AB	R	H	2B	3B	HR	RBI	BB	HBP	SH	SF	SO	SB	CS	SLG	OBP
Alastre, Jesus	R-R	6-1	155	11-25-96	.263	.333	.200	7	19	2	5	0	0	0	1	2	1	0	0	2	1	2	.263	.364
Azuaje, Jesus	R-R	5-9	165	8-11-97	.141	.174	.127	24	78	5	11	0	0	0	3	2	1	2	1	14	3	0	.141	.171
Duran, Rodolfo	R-R	5-9	170	2-19-98	.252	.276	.238	48	159	14	40	9	3	0	6	8	3	0	1	36	0	1	.346	.298
Encarnacion, Luis	R-R	6-2	185	8-9-97	.161	.160	.162	21	62	5	10	1	0	2	5	7	1	1	0	24	0	0	.274	.257
Fitch, Colby	L-R	5-11	205	7-27-95	.350	.300	.367	12	40	8	14	2	0	2	7	3	4	0	1	6	1	0	.550	.438
Gurrola, Yahir	R-R	6-0	190	3-19-96	.237	.154	.268	25	97	6	23	7	0	1	12	1	1	0	1	24	3	1	.340	.250
Guzman, Jonathan	R-R	6-0	156	8-17-99	.263	.250	.267	6	19	2	5	0	0	1	2	4	0	0	0	3	0	1	.421	.391
Haseley, Adam	L-L	6-1	195	4-12-96	.270	.343	.245	37	137	18	37	9	0	2	18	14	4	1	2	28	5	3	.380	.350
Henriquez, Jesus	B-R	6-0	168	4-7-98	.250	—	.250	1	4	1	1	1	0	0	2	0	0	0	0	1	0	0	.500	.250
Listi, Austin	R-R	6-0	218	11-5-93	.293	.375	.255	22	75	14	22	5	0	3	17	8	2	0	1	16	3	0	.480	.372
Lovett, James	R-R	6-3	200	5-27-94	.000	—	.000	1	2	0	0	0	0	0	0	0	0	0	0	2	0	0	.000	.000

Luis, Juan	L-R	6-4	175	3-23-96	.129	.000	.160	12	31	3	4	1	0	0	4	3	1	0	0	8	1	0	.161	.229
Martinez, Nerluis	L-R	6-2	175	4-10-96	.155	.111	.163	17	58	3	9	2	1	0	1	2	0	0	0	11	0	1	.224	.183
Maton, Nick	L-R	6-2	165	2-18-97	.252	.158	.288	58	210	34	53	9	1	2	13	30	3	0	3	47	10	5	.333	.350
Matos, Malvin	R-R	6-3	170	8-19-96	.254	.315	.228	57	177	20	45	15	1	3	19	20	6	0	2	39	4	3	.401	.346
Mims, Brian	R-R	5-11	185	3-14-96	.190	.167	.200	34	121	9	23	5	2	0	6	4	5	0	1	42	1	0	.265	.244
Ortiz, Jhailyn	R-R	6-3	215	11-18-98	.302	.396	.261	47	159	27	48	15	1	8	30	18	9	0	1	47	5	1	.560	.401
Pickett, Greg	L-R	6-4	215	10-30-96	.272	.309	.259	62	221	23	60	11	0	6	25	25	0	0	2	70	1	0	.403	.343
Rivas, Raul	B-R	5-10	160	10-27-96	.196	.267	.171	13	56	4	11	3	0	0	4	3	2	1	0	8	2	2	.250	.262
Rivero, Gregori	B-R	5-11	195	5-27-96	.286	.333	.280	8	28	2	8	4	0	1	6	0	0	0	1	1	0	0	.536	.276
Scheiner, Jake	R-R	6-1	200	8-13-95	.250	.200	.271	61	236	32	59	14	2	4	19	16	7	0	0	54	5	7	.377	.317
Stephen, Josh	L-L	6-0	185	9-22-97	.247	.192	.260	64	239	23	59	12	5	2	28	12	0	1	1	50	4	3	.364	.282
Stobbe, Cole	R-R	6-1	200	8-30-97	.203	.315	.161	55	197	28	40	8	1	8	22	17	4	0	0	67	2	3	.376	.280

Pitching	**B-T**	**HT**	**WT**	**DOB**	**W**	**L**	**ERA**	**G**	**GS**	**CG**	**SV**	**IP**	**H**	**R**	**ER**	**HR**	**BB**	**SO**	**AVG**	**vLH**	**vRH**	**K/9**	**BB/9**
Alcantara, Randy	R-R	5-11	150	11-9-96	2	1	2.23	19	0	0	5	44	34	14	11	1	14	40	.207	.200	.213	8.12	2.84
Armas, Gustavo	R-R	6-1	195	1-15-96	0	3	4.09	5	3	0	1	22	22	13	10	2	4	22	.253	.209	.296	9.00	1.64
Brogdon, Connor	R-R	6-6	185	1-29-95	3	1	2.34	16	0	0	3	35	22	10	9	2	18	45	.177	.174	.180	11.68	4.67
Brown, Andrew	R-R	6-1	180	10-24-97	4	4	3.11	13	10	0	0	64	56	26	22	4	19	47	.236	.274	.206	6.64	2.69
Carrasco, Luis	R-R	6-3	170	9-11-94	2	0	2.61	6	6	0	0	31	23	13	9	1	14	20	.198	.275	.139	5.81	4.06
Dohy, Kyle	L-L	6-2	180	9-17-96	2	1	3.60	13	0	0	0	20	12	8	8	0	20	22	.182	.207	.162	9.90	9.00
Frohwirth, Tyler	R-R	6-1	165	9-13-93	0	1	0.00	3	0	0	0	2	2	1	0	0	0	2	.222	.500	.143	7.71	0.00
2-team total (14 Batavia)					0	2	3.44	17	0	0	0	18	20	13	7	1	4	18	.263	.500	.143	8.84	1.96
Garcia, Julian	L-R	6-3	185	5-13-95	4	5	3.90	13	13	0	0	60	47	28	26	3	29	82	.217	.258	.188	12.30	4.35
Howard, Spencer	R-R	6-3	205	7-28-96	1	1	4.45	9	9	0	0	28	22	15	14	0	18	40	.214	.211	.217	12.71	5.72
Jones, Damon	L-L	6-5	225	9-30-94	2	3	4.85	13	0	0	3	26	23	14	14	0	20	38	.240	.263	.224	13.15	6.92
Kelzer, Jake	R-R	6-8	230	6-30-93	0	0	6.43	4	0	0	0	7	7	6	5	1	5	5	.292	.364	.231	6.43	6.43
Melendez, Orestes	L-L	5-11	180	6-8-95	0	2	6.29	14	0	0	1	24	26	18	17	0	15	30	.271	.237	.293	11.10	5.55
Miller, Justin	R-R	6-4	183	5-17-98	0	0	9.00	1	0	0	0	2	2	2	2	0	1	0	.286	.000	.400	0.00	4.50
Nunez, Jhon	L-L	6-0	155	11-27-97	1	2	4.76	16	0	0	0	23	26	17	12	0	12	20	.296	.177	.370	7.94	4.76
Parkinson, David	R-L	6-2	210	12-14-95	1	3	2.48	11	3	0	0	33	30	12	9	2	9	42	.242	.327	.181	11.57	2.48
Ramirez, Luis	R-R	5-11	175	9-14-97	1	3	2.27	23	0	0	11	32	26	10	8	2	16	23	.226	.211	.241	6.54	4.55
Rosso, Ramon	R-R	6-4	215	6-9-96	1	0	3.00	4	4	0	0	18	13	6	6	0	9	23	.206	.226	.188	11.50	4.50
Russ, Addison	R-R	6-1	190	10-29-94	0	0	8.10	2	0	0	0	3	5	3	3	0	1	4	.333	.600	.200	10.80	2.70
Seabold, Connor	R-R	6-3	190	1-24-96	2	0	0.90	5	0	0	0	10	5	1	1	0	2	13	.143	.118	.167	11.70	1.80
Stewart, Will	L-L	6-2	175	7-14-97	4	2	4.18	13	13	0	0	60	64	37	28	3	25	58	.267	.258	.272	8.65	3.73
Warren, Zach	L-L	6-5	200	6-9-96	0	3	3.00	16	0	0	0	33	29	14	11	0	15	40	.236	.149	.290	10.91	4.09
Young, Kyle	L-L	6-10	205	12-2-97	7	2	2.77	13	13	0	0	65	58	22	20	1	15	72	.237	.231	.240	9.97	2.08

Fielding

C: Duran 47, Fitch 8, Lovett 1, Martinez 15, Rivero 7. **1B:** Encarnacion 3, Listi 15, Martinez 3, Mims 14, Pickett 43. **2B:** Azuaje 16, Henriquez 1, Mims 19, Rivas 9, Scheiner 31. **3B:** Scheiner 24, Stobbe 51. **SS:** Azuaje 8, Guzman 6, Maton 57, Rivas 4. **OF:** Alastre 5, Gurrola 23, Haseley 31, Listi 4, Luis 8, Matos 55, Mims 3, Ortiz 42, Stephen 59.

GCL PHILLIES — *ROOKIE*

GULF COAST LEAGUE

Batting	**B-T**	**HT**	**WT**	**DOB**	**AVG**	**vLH**	**vRH**	**G**	**AB**	**R**	**H**	**2B**	**3B**	**HR**	**RBI**	**BB**	**HBP**	**SH**	**SF**	**SO**	**SB**	**CS**	**SLG**	**OBP**
Azuaje, Jesus	R-R	5-9	165	8-11-97	.000	.000	.000	3	6	1	0	0	0	0	0	1	0	0	0	1	0	0	.000	.143
Bocio, Keudy	R-R	5-10	161	11-15-98	.278	.316	.271	39	115	22	32	8	0	0	18	18	2	0	4	21	7	1	.348	.374
Buhner, Gunnar	R-R	6-2	200	5-11-95	.122	.375	.073	24	49	6	6	2	0	0	3	5	2	0	0	15	2	0	.163	.232
Campbell, Derek	R-R	6-0	175	6-28-91	.600	—	.600	1	5	1	3	1	0	0	2	1	0	0	0	0	0	0	.800	.667
Eldridge, Caleb	L-L	6-3	235	7-3-95	.222	.000	.250	4	9	0	2	2	0	0	0	1	0	0	0	3	0	0	.444	.300
Gomez, Jose	R-R	5-11	175	12-10-96	.500	.500	.500	2	6	1	3	0	0	0	1	0	0	0	0	0	0	0	.500	.500
Gonzalez, Brayan	R-R	5-11	172	1-14-00	.269	.227	.277	38	134	23	36	10	0	2	24	12	2	1	3	33	6	0	.388	.331
Green, Zach	R-R	6-3	210	3-7-94	.308	.250	.333	4	13	6	4	1	0	3	6	3	0	0	1	4	0	0	1.077	.412
Gurrola, Yahir	R-R	6-0	190	3-19-96	.333	.375	.326	35	105	25	35	6	0	0	18	14	6	0	1	18	12	5	.391	.437
Guthrie, Dalton	R-R	5-11	160	12-23-95	.182	.400	.118	9	22	5	4	1	0	1	3	5	0	1	0	1	1	1	.364	.333
Guzman, Jonathan	R-R	6-0	156	8-17-99	.248	.179	.264	38	153	17	38	4	2	1	13	11	0	1	0	24	5	1	.320	.299
Haseley, Adam	L-L	6-1	195	4-12-96	.583	.000	.778	3	12	3	7	1	1	0	4	2	0	0	0	3	1	1	.833	.643
Henriquez, Jesus	B-R	6-0	168	4-7-98	.258	.261	.258	28	89	10	23	2	0	0	9	7	1	1	3	12	1	0	.281	.310
Holmes, Jake	R-R	6-3	185	7-2-98	.252	.278	.247	32	107	19	27	5	0	2	14	11	2	1	1	17	5	1	.355	.331
Marchan, Rafael	R-R	5-9	170	2-25-99	.238	.222	.242	30	84	10	20	5	0	0	10	4	3	0	2	8	1	0	.298	.290
Markham, Kevin	L-R	6-0	195	4-14-94	.250	.208	.259	41	140	32	35	8	2	1	17	22	5	0	1	9	7	2	.357	.369
Martinez, Nerluis	L-R	6-2	175	4-10-96	.143	.000	.154	7	14	1	2	0	0	0	1	1	0	0	0	1	0	0	.143	.200
Mayer, Danny	R-R	6-5	245	6-25-95	.255	.235	.258	31	106	15	27	9	0	2	18	12	2	0	0	33	1	0	.396	.342
Moore, Kipp	R-R	6-1	215	2-27-96	.250	.200	.261	32	56	13	14	3	1	0	7	3	5	0	0	16	0	0	.339	.344
Muzziotti, Simon	L-L	6-1	175	12-27-98	.269	.167	.291	33	134	20	36	4	6	0	14	7	0	0	0	8	8	3	.388	.305
Nieporte, Quincy	R-R	6-1	225	7-29-94	.299	.273	.306	41	154	19	46	13	1	5	35	12	3	0	3	17	0	0	.494	.355
Pelletier, Ben	R-R	6-2	190	8-22-98	.333	.212	.362	46	171	21	57	13	1	3	26	8	0	0	1	30	1	0	.474	.361
Rodriguez, Edwin	L-L	6-1	170	6-8-97	.211	.167	.217	33	95	15	20	5	0	3	20	5	2	0	3	12	0	0	.358	.257
Rodriguez, Lenin	R-R	5-9	165	3-26-98	.262	.188	.289	32	61	11	16	2	0	1	7	14	1	0	0	6	1	1	.344	.408
Stewart, D.J.	R-R	6-2	205	2-2-99	.195	.000	.242	16	41	4	8	1	0	1	5	4	0	0	0	12	1	0	.293	.267
Tomscha, Damek	R-R	6-2	200	8-27-91	.286	.500	.250	4	14	3	4	1	0	0	2	0	2	0	0	1	0	0	.357	.375
Walding, Mitch	L-R	6-3	190	9-10-92	.500	.000	.667	2	8	3	4	2	1	0	1	0	0	0	0	2	0	0	1.000	.500
Zoellner, Jack	L-R	6-2	205	10-29-94	.258	.250	.259	11	31	4	8	1	0	0	1	3	0	0	0	6	0	1	.290	.324

Pitching	B-T	HT	WT	DOB	W	L	ERA	G	GS	CG	SV	IP	H	R	ER	HR	BB	SO	AVG	vLH	vRH	K/9	BB/9
Appel, Mark	R-R	6-5	220	7-15-91	0	0	0.00	2	0	0	0	2	1	0	0	0	1	0	.143	1.000	.000	0.00	4.50
Brown, Aaron	L-L	6-2	220	6-20-92	0	0	3.38	4	0	0	0	5	2	3	2	0	8	6	.118	.000	.133	10.13	13.50
Brown, Ben	R-R	6-6	210	9-9-99	0	0	2.57	10	0	0	0	14	14	4	4	0	6	10	.269	.286	.263	6.43	3.86
Carvajal, Rafael	R-R	6-0	170	11-13-96	2	2	2.55	14	0	0	1	25	26	10	7	0	4	19	.255	.273	.246	6.93	1.46
Cummings, Bailey	R-R	6-3	200	12-20-97	0	0	10.13	3	0	0	0	3	3	3	3	0	5	3	.273	.333	.200	10.13	16.88
De Los Santos, Jesus	R-R	6-2	165	12-23-95	0	0	3.60	3	0	0	0	5	6	2	2	0	1	3	.300	.400	.267	5.40	1.80
Dominguez, Seranthony	R-R	6-1	185	11-25-94	0	0	5.06	2	2	0	0	5	5	3	3	0	4	7	.250	.333	.235	11.81	6.75
Eflin, Zach	R-R	6-6	215	4-8-94	0	0	1.29	2	2	0	0	7	5	1	1	0	0	6	.200	.100	.267	7.71	0.00
Garcia, Elniery	L-L	6-0	155	12-24-94	0	0	0.00	2	2	0	0	5	3	1	0	0	2	3	.167	.000	.200	5.40	3.60
Hernandez, Jakob	L-L	6-4	260	5-19-96	1	0	1.64	9	0	0	1	11	9	3	2	0	0	15	.237	.375	.200	12.27	0.00
Jimenez, Jose	L-L	5-11	175	9-25-97	2	2	5.59	10	6	0	0	39	44	28	24	3	18	24	.293	.257	.304	5.59	4.19
Kuznetsov, Anton	R-L	6-1	185	5-26-98	2	1	0.36	15	1	0	5	25	16	2	1	0	4	24	.184	.083	.200	8.53	1.42
Lindow, Ethan	R-L	6-3	180	10-15-98	2	2	4.55	8	8	0	0	28	26	15	14	2	12	34	.241	.250	.239	11.06	3.90
Marcelino, Oscar	R-R	6-3	166	6-8-97	4	2	2.25	17	0	0	2	28	14	7	7	2	15	22	.154	.296	.094	7.07	4.82
Martinez, Denny	B-L	6-0	157	11-1-96	3	2	2.49	15	0	0	0	22	15	9	6	2	9	21	.192	.278	.167	8.72	3.74
Martinez, Robinson	R-R	6-0	190	3-20-98	2	1	3.52	13	0	0	0	23	22	10	9	1	12	13	.250	.440	.175	5.09	4.70
Mezquita, Jhordany	L-L	6-1	185	1-30-98	3	0	0.72	9	9	0	0	38	20	6	3	0	12	35	.160	.222	.155	8.36	2.87
Miller, Justin	R-R	6-4	183	5-17-98	1	2	5.21	13	0	0	0	19	23	11	11	1	16	13	.307	.421	.268	6.16	7.58
Morales, Francisco	R-R	6-4	185	10-27-99	3	2	3.05	10	9	0	0	41	34	18	14	1	20	44	.225	.255	.210	9.58	4.35
Nunez, Miguel	R-R	6-6	215	10-27-92	0	0	0.00	1	0	0	0	1	1	0	0	0	0	0	.250	1.000	.000	0.00	0.00
Rosario, Sandro	R-R	6-3	185	1-23-96	1	4	4.22	11	7	0	0	49	66	29	23	3	19	37	.330	.333	.329	6.80	3.49
Rosso, Ramon	R-R	6-4	215	6-9-96	0	0	1.00	2	1	0	0	9	6	1	1	0	3	13	.188	.071	.278	13.00	3.00
Santa Cruz, Sati	R-R	6-3	230	9-3-96	1	1	5.63	8	0	0	0	8	6	5	5	1	10	11	.214	.429	.143	12.38	11.25
Silva, Manuel	L-L	6-2	145	12-18-98	6	0	2.60	9	9	0	0	45	42	17	13	2	14	30	.261	.235	.268	6.00	2.80
Sobil, Victor	R-R	6-2	215	7-17-96	3	1	3.09	10	2	0	1	32	27	17	11	0	18	34	.221	.273	.210	9.56	5.06
Tirado, Alberto	R-R	6-0	180	12-10-94	0	0	0.00	2	0	0	0	2	1	0	0	0	3	1	.200	—	.200	4.50	13.50

Fielding

C: Marchan 29, Martinez 7, Moore 32, Rodriguez 29. **1B:** Eldridge 3, Green 2, Henriquez 1, Nieporte 29, Rodriguez 29, Tomscha 1. **2B:** Bocio 1, Buhner 10, Gonzalez 38, Henriquez 13. **3B:** Bocio 21, Buhner 8, Green 2, Henriquez 13, Stewart 11, Tomscha 3, Walding 2, Zoellner 9. **SS:** Azuaje 3, Buhner 2, Gomez 2, Guthrie 8, Guzman 35, Holmes 18. **OF:** Bocio 14, Campbell 1, Gurrola 30, Haseley 2, Markham 40, Mayer 25, Muzziotti 27, Pelletier 44, Rodriguez 3.

DSL PHILLIES — *ROOKIE*

DOMINICAN SUMMER LEAGUE

Batting	B-T	HT	WT	DOB	AVG	vLH	vRH	G	AB	R	H	2B	3B	HR	RBI	BB	HBP	SH	SF	SO	SB	CS	SLG	OBP
Alfonso, Victor	B-R	5-11	140	8-27-99	.204	.097	.236	53	137	20	28	6	2	0	10	13	3	2	0	28	2	1	.277	.288
Aparicio, Juan	R-R	5-11	175	5-26-00	.228	.235	.239	45	136	4	31	4	1	1	19	13	2	0	3	19	1	1	.294	.299
Barreto, Freddy	R-R	6-0	155	9-27-99	.222	.360	.169	37	90	8	20	1	0	0	8	8	0	0	1	29	0	0	.233	.283
De La Rosa, Maximo	R-R	6-2	205	9-15-99	.237	.229	.240	45	139	15	33	13	0	1	13	9	0	0	3	30	3	4	.353	.278
Feliz, Alexito	R-R	5-11	160	8-6-96	.296	.292	.297	69	247	33	73	10	3	4	35	14	2	2	4	29	20	10	.409	.333
Francisco, Julio	L-L	6-1	140	3-19-98	.318	.318	.318	68	242	51	77	10	10	0	20	28	5	6	1	22	22	7	.442	.399
Garcia, Wilbert	R-R	5-11	179	1-20-00	.208	.154	.229	41	96	21	20	4	3	2	5	10	7	1	0	30	10	5	.375	.327
Gonzalez, Pedro	R-R	5-11	176	11-23-98	.154	.091	.167	20	65	5	10	3	0	1	6	2	1	1	0	20	0	2	.246	.191
Gonzalez, Ronaldo	R-R	5-11	178	10-14-98	.177	.182	.177	31	62	7	11	1	0	1	2	2	7	0	0	28	2	2	.242	.282
Gutierrez, Dixon	B-R	5-11	165	6-30-98	.230	.250	.225	44	135	15	31	0	1	0	16	17	3	0	1	19	9	4	.244	.327
Herrera, Juan	R-R	6-3	165	12-14-99	.206	.333	.167	40	102	9	21	2	1	1	9	2	3	1	1	37	2	0	.275	.241
Hernandez, Jevi	R-R	6-0	140	3-2-99	.232	.296	.216	61	211	21	49	16	3	1	31	10	3	1	1	32	11	6	.351	.276
Made, Edgar	B-R	5-10	145	12-15-99	.242	.238	.243	53	178	29	43	9	5	1	20	25	4	5	1	35	14	7	.365	.346
Matos, Luis	B-R	6-0	175	12-17-99	.230	.265	.221	60	174	28	40	5	1	0	9	23	2	2	0	48	15	8	.270	.327
Medina, Leandro	L-R	6-0	150	7-8-99	.153	.125	.163	51	124	11	19	3	0	0	6	9	2	4	3	29	2	4	.177	.217
Mendez, Juan	L-R	5-10	165	2-27-99	.379	.444	.356	39	140	19	53	4	7	3	26	8	1	0	2	19	3	3	.571	.411
Mora, Raymond	R-R	6-0	155	7-29-00	.242	.333	.208	67	211	27	51	4	1	0	20	20	4	5	4	52	5	5	.270	.314
Mujica, Luiggi	B-R	5-10	155	11-25-99	.161	.235	.150	42	124	14	20	3	0	0	8	14	2	2	1	39	9	3	.186	.255
Oropeza, Carlos	R-R	6-0	170	12-22-98	.271	.259	.306	64	218	20	59	12	2	1	30	20	6	0	8	25	7	1	.358	.337
Rivera, Jose	R-R	5-10	165	5-26-99	.284	.083	.346	36	102	19	29	3	1	0	10	21	7	1	2	22	6	4	.333	.432
Rojas, Luis	R-R	5-9	150	4-19-00	.261	.280	.255	56	207	27	54	7	3	0	27	13	1	1	5	29	14	4	.324	.301
Rondon, Enny	R-R	6-0	170	7-31-98	.222	.300	.210	51	144	18	32	10	1	1	15	16	9	1	0	33	4	1	.326	.337
Serra, Frailin	R-R	6-1	170	12-29-97	.264	.150	.308	27	72	11	19	2	0	0	6	5	1	1	1	6	5	5	.292	.317
Smith, Juan Carlos	R-R	6-1	188	8-22-97	.262	.300	.255	18	65	7	17	3	1	0	3	3	0	1	0	18	6	2	.339	.294
Tabares, Yorbys	R-R	6-0	165	1-24-97	.500	—	.500	2	4	2	2	0	0	0	1	0	0	0	0	1	0	0	.500	.500
Torrealba, Ronald	R-R	6-1	154	1-27-99	.212	.200	.214	34	85	4	18	1	0	0	8	9	5	3	2	17	2	2	.224	.317
Torres, Nicolas	R-R	5-10	155	9-23-99	.333	.333	.333	69	240	40	80	13	4	0	28	11	9	8	1	31	11	7	.421	.383
Tortolero, Jose	R-R	5-11	154	12-31-99	.206	.161	.224	67	218	28	45	10	3	1	20	21	5	2	1	40	12	7	.294	.290
Trejo, Yerwin	R-R	6-0	170	1-3-97	.272	.279	.270	59	191	29	52	6	3	1	20	27	7	2	1	28	21	4	.351	.381
Valerio, Christian	R-R	6-1	155	2-27-00	.248	.378	.211	58	206	28	51	10	2	0	18	26	5	4	1	39	14	6	.316	.345
Vasquez, Rusbel	B-R	5-11	165	11-14-98	.174	.192	.167	31	86	7	15	2	0	0	7	10	0	1	0	24	4	1	.198	.260

Pitching	B-T	HT	WT	DOB	W	L	ERA	G	GS	CG	SV	IP	H	R	ER	HR	BB	SO	AVG	vLH	vRH	K/9	BB/9
Alcala, Bryan	R-R	6-5	215	8-14-97	6	2	2.15	14	13	0	0	67	56	20	16	1	19	53	.231	.179	.265	7.12	2.55
Aponte, Leonel	R-R	6-4	144	7-2-99	7	1	0.77	15	13	1	1	81	55	10	7	1	9	69	.194	.107	.188	7.64	1.00
Aponte, Ruben	R-R	6-0	180	5-18-97	1	1	2.25	11	2	0	0	20	22	10	5	0	16	22	.279	.375	.236	9.90	7.20
Aris, Abdallah	R-L	5-11	155	10-8-96	3	3	2.45	23	1	0	8	37	32	14	10	2	14	51	.229	.154	.246	12.52	3.44
Avendano, Eudiver	R-R	6-3	200	2-1-99	2	4	4.36	18	0	0	0	43	36	23	21	2	24	46	.224	.226	.222	9.55	4.98
Benitez, Alfredo	L-L	5-10	165	8-13-96	2	2	2.82	16	0	0	2	22	15	10	7	0	8	33	.183	.214	.177	13.30	3.22

Blanco, Jeison	R-R	6-1	180	1-3-98	0	0	9.00	1	0	0	0	2	2	2	2	0	2	1	.286	.500	.200	4.50	9.00
Canizales, Antonio	R-R	6-1	160	1-24-98	3	5	2.89	14	13	1	0	65	53	29	21	1	21	48	.220	.233	.214	6.61	2.89
Conopoima, Jose	R-R	6-0	157	3-1-00	1	1	2.04	14	5	0	1	35	26	13	8	0	13	24	.206	.143	.231	6.11	3.31
Coveri, Ludovico	R-R	6-2	195	3-6-97	6	4	1.51	24	2	0	5	54	45	20	9	1	10	37	.230	.119	.277	6.20	1.68
De La Cruz, Jonas	R-R	6-3	175	1-1-98	5	6	3.71	15	14	0	0	63	60	31	26	4	33	60	.260	.264	.257	8.57	4.71
Francisco, Carlos	R-R	6-2	179	3-28-98	1	5	2.70	12	11	0	0	50	46	27	15	0	20	41	.247	.257	.241	7.38	3.60
Heredia, Erick	R-R	6-4	175	3-17-97	0	6	3.67	13	12	0	0	49	54	36	20	0	26	39	.274	.255	.282	7.16	4.78
Herrera, Alexis	R-R	6-3	180	5-6-99	0	0	18.00	6	0	0	2	5	6	10	10	0	8	4	.300	.200	.333	7.20	14.40
Liendo, Wilberson	R-R	6-3	160	9-13-99	2	2	3.55	19	3	0	0	38	33	23	15	0	24	43	.244	.389	.205	10.18	5.68
Made, Alejandro	R-R	6-4	190	12-29-97	0	2	12.00	6	0	0	0	6	8	11	8	0	9	3	.320	.200	.350	4.50	13.50
Mendoza, Roimy	L-L	6-3	170	12-18-96	5	1	5.59	19	0	0	1	37	41	25	23	0	23	31	.285	.222	.299	7.54	5.59
Nolasco, Moises	R-R	6-4	170	2-2-97	2	2	2.45	23	0	0	4	44	33	17	12	2	23	35	.208	.275	.176	7.16	4.70
Nunez, Anderson	R-R	5-10	180	5-24-94	0	0	0.00	1	0	0	1	1	0	1	0	0	0	0	.000	—	.000	0.00	0.00
Pacheco, Luis	R-R	6-2	185	4-22-99	0	0	2.57	2	2	0	0	7	3	2	2	0	1	7	.125	.000	.188	9.00	1.29
Parra, Anderson	L-L	6-2	185	4-17-99	4	2	5.36	15	5	0	0	42	50	28	25	0	23	28	.305	.303	.305	6.00	4.93
Perez, Jose	R-R	6-3	170	8-16-98	0	0	4.24	14	1	0	3	23	16	11	11	1	17	19	.195	.118	.250	7.33	6.56
Prada, Santy	R-L	6-2	187	8-12-99	3	2	4.50	14	0	0	0	24	19	17	12	0	17	20	.214	.207	.217	7.50	6.38
Rivas, Aldemar	R-R	6-1	170	1-21-99	2	0	2.59	12	2	0	0	31	18	13	9	0	14	35	.164	.188	.154	10.05	4.02
Romero, Jorbin	R-R	6-2	175	6-7-99	0	1	20.61	12	1	0	0	13	12	30	29	2	27	11	.240	.177	.273	7.82	19.18
Rosario, Dalvin	R-R	6-1	167	6-15-00	0	1	—	2	0	0	0	0	3	10	10	0	6	0	1.000	1.000	1.000	—	—
Rosso, Ramon	R-R	6-4	215	6-9-96	6	1	0.74	9	9	0	0	49	33	8	4	0	13	69	.190	.162	.210	12.76	2.40
Salazar, Carlos	R-R	6-1	155	11-19-96	4	1	1.57	19	0	0	6	46	35	11	8	0	12	40	.205	.220	.196	7.83	2.35
Sanchez, Yeison	R-R	6-0	170	11-13-97	2	1	9.45	12	0	0	2	20	32	23	21	1	8	24	.348	.450	.269	10.80	3.60
Santos, Juan	R-R	6-3	173	8-30-96	2	4	4.43	14	14	0	0	61	65	43	30	2	26	44	.273	.290	.265	6.49	3.84
Santos, Victor	R-R	6-1	191	7-12-00	4	2	2.57	12	9	0	0	49	52	16	14	1	5	38	.268	.273	.266	6.98	0.92
Soto, Ramiro	R-R	6-1	180	7-30-99	1	0	4.97	10	2	0	0	29	31	19	16	4	13	30	.277	.275	.278	9.31	4.03
Suarez, Luis	L-L	6-1	155	11-1-99	0	0	8.10	10	0	0	0	13	20	13	12	1	10	8	.328	.273	.340	5.40	6.75
Tejada, Junior	L-L	6-1	170	5-23-97	1	2	3.51	8	4	0	0	26	33	17	10	0	4	15	.308	.222	.338	5.26	1.40
Valdez, Jean Carlos	R-R	6-2	185	8-30-97	1	1	3.16	11	4	0	0	31	34	16	11	1	12	31	.272	.290	.264	8.90	3.45
Yanez, Gabriel	L-L	6-3	168	7-22-99	0	0	0.00	3	0	0	0	4	2	0	0	0	0	1	.154	.333	.000	2.25	0.00

Fielding

C: Aparicio 25, Barreto 32, Feliz 3, Gonzalez 32, Mendez 20, Oropeza 43, Torrealba 16. **1B:** Alfonso 10, Aparicio 6, De La Rosa 29, Feliz 54, Herrera 7, Matos 1, Medina 1, Mendez 1, Oropeza 17, Rondon 33, Serra 2, Torrealba 15. **2B:** Alfonso 15, Made 21, Medina 5, Mujica 36, Rivera 13, Rojas 2, Rondon 1, Serra 3, Torres 58, Tortolero 6. **Valerio 5. 3B:** Alfonso 19, Feliz 1, Herrera 33, Made 7, Medina 38, Mora 1. **Rojas 52, Rondon 7, Serra 8. SS:** Alfonso 9, Made 21, Medina 4, Rojas 3, Serra 4, Torres 6, Tortolero 62, Valerio 46. **OF:** De La Rosa 14, Feliz 27, Francisco 66, Garcia 34, Gutierrez 40, Hernandez 59, Matos 57, Mora 63, Rondon 7, Salazar 1, Serra 3, Smith 15, Tabares 1, Torres 1, Trejo 56, Vasquez 26.

Pittsburgh Pirates

SEASON IN A SENTENCE: Not much went right for the Pirates in 2017 as the team finished fourth in the NL Central with a 75-87 record—its worst mark since 2011—and one of the worst offenses in the league with just 668 runs scored (28th) and a .704 on-base plus slugging (28th).

HIGH POINT: Andrew McCutchen didn't return to his perennial top-five MVP candidate form of 2012-2015, but he did bounce back from an abysmal 2016 season with a 3.7 WAR campaign. The highest point, though, might be closer Felipe Rivero who was one of the best relievers in baseball. Rivero posted a 1.67 ERA in 75.1 innings and was a large part of Pittsburgh's respectable bullpen (3.84 team ERA for relievers).

LOW POINT: Take your pick: center fielder Starling Marte was suspended for performance enhancing drugs (Nandrolone) and lost 80 games during what should be the prime of his career; infielder Jung Ho Kang didn't play in a single game after a third drunken-driving arrest in South Korea; top prospects Ausin Meadows and Tyler Glasnow had an injury-riddled season and a disappointing major league stint, respectively.

NOTABLE ROOKIES: First baseman Josh Bell had a solid first full season at the plate, with a .255/.334/.466 triple slash and 26 home runs, giving the Pirates some much-needed power production to go along with McCutchen (28). The aforementioned Glasnow was hit hard (2-7, 7.69 ERA) but righthander Trevor Williams was solid with a 4.07 ERA over 150.1 IP and was better during the final three months where he posted a 3.49 ERA.

KEY TRANSACTIONS: Gerrit Cole and McCutchen were both involved in trade rumors during the year, but Neal Huntington didn't pull off any deals of that caliber, with both stars staying put. However, the Pirates did get a pair of low-level, lottery ticket-type prospects in shortstop Oneil Cruz and righthander Angel German after trading reliever Tony Watson to the Dodgers.

DOWN ON THE FARM: Each of the Pirates full -season minor league affiliates experienced winning seasons, with Triple-A Indianapolis posting the best record of the bunch (79-63) and winning the West Division of the International League. Lefthander Steven Brault won the IL Pitcher of the Year award after going 10-5, 1.94, while outfielder Jordan Luplow hit .325/.401/.513. Righthander Mitch Keller posted a 3.03 ERA across three leagues and finished the year in Double-A.

OPENING DAY PAYROLL: $100,575,946 (23rd)

PLAYERS OF THE YEAR

MAJOR LEAGUE

Andrew McCutchen
OF

.279/.363/.486
28 HR, 88 RBI
30 2B, 11 SB

MINOR LEAGUE

Steven Brault
LHP

(Triple-A)
10-5, 1.94
109 SO in 120.1 IP

ORGANIZATION LEADERS

BATTING *Minimum 250 AB

MAJORS

*	AVG	Andrew McCutchen	.279
*	OPS	Andrew McCutchen	.849
	HR	Andrew McCutchen	28
	RBI	Josh Bell	90

MINORS

*	AVG	Jordan George, Bradenton, Altoona	.302
*	OBP	Jordan George, Bradenton, Altoona	.386
*	SLG	Jordan Luplow, Altoona, Indianapolis	.527
*	OPS	Jordan Luplow, Altoona, Indianapolis	.907
	R	Christopher Bostick, Indianapolis	75
	H	Edwin Espinal, Altoona, Indianapolis	146
	TB	Edwin Espinal, Altoona, Indianapolis	222
	2B	Christopher Bostick, Indianapolis	33
	3B	Cole Tucker, Bradenton, Altoona	11
	HR	Jordan Luplow, Altoona, Indianapolis	23
	RBI	Edwin Espinal, Altoona, Indianapolis	86
	BB	Will Craig, Bradenton	62
	SO	Casey Hughston, Bradenton, Altoona	150
	SB	Cole Tucker, Bradenton, Altoona	47

PITCHING #Minimum 75 IP

MAJORS

	W	Gerrit Cole	12
#	ERA	Felipe Rivero	1.67
	SO	Gerrit Cole	196
	SV	Felipe Rivero	21

MINORS

	W	Clay Holmes, Indianapolis	10
		Alex McRae, Altoona	10
		Nick Kingham, Bradenton, Indianapolis	10
		Luis Escobar, West Virginia	10
		Tanner Anderson, Altoona	10
		Steven Brault, Indianapolis	10
	L	Cam Vieaux, West Virginia, Bradenton	10
#	ERA	Tyler Glasnow, Indianapolis	1.93
	G	Tate Scioneaux, Altoona	47
	GS	Drew Hutchinson, Indianapolis	26
	SV	Montana DuRapau, Altoona, Indianapolis	15
	IP	Drew Hutchinson, Indianapolis	159
	BB	Luis Escobar, West Virginia	60
	SO	Luis Escobar, West Virginia	168
#	AVG	Tyler Glasnow, Indianapolis	.176

2017 PERFORMANCE

General Manager: Neal Huntington. **Farm Director:** Larry Broadway. **Scouting Director:** Joe Delli Carri.

Class	Team	League	W	L	PCT	Finish	Manager
Majors	Pittsburgh Pirates	National	75	87	.463	9th (15)	Clint Hurdle
Triple-A	Indianapolis Indians	International	79	63	.556	5th (14)	Andy Barkett
Double-A	Altoona Curve	Eastern	74	66	.529	3rd (12)	Michael Ryan
High-A	Bradenton Marauders	Florida State	70	62	.530	4th (12)	Gerardo Alvarez
Low-A	West Virginia Power	South Atlantic	69	67	.507	7th (14)	Wyatt Toregas
Short Season	West Virginia Black Bears	New York-Penn	40	35	.533	t-6th (14)	Brian Esposito
Rookie	Bristol Pirates	Appalachian	17	49	.258	10th (10)	Miguel Perez
Rookie	GCL Pirates	Gulf Coast	26	34	.433	15th (17)	Bob Herold / Dave Turgeon
Overall 2017 Minor League Record			375	376	.499	14th (30)	

ORGANIZATION STATISTICS

PITTSBURGH PIRATES

NATIONAL LEAGUE

Batting	B-T	HT	WT	DOB	AVG	vLH	vRH	G	AB	R	H	2B	3B	HR	RBI	BB	HBP	SH	SF	SO	SB	CS	SLG	OBP
Bell, Josh	B-R	6-2	230	8-14-92	.255	.242	.259	159	549	75	140	26	6	26	90	66	1	0	4	117	2	4	.466	.334
Bormann, John	R-R	6-0	205	4-4-93	.000	.000	—	1	1	0	0	0	0	0	0	0	0	0	0	1	0	0	.000	.000
Bostick, Christopher	R-R	5-10	190	3-24-93	.296	.250	.316	20	27	6	8	2	0	0	1	4	1	0	0	9	0	1	.370	.406
Cervelli, Francisco	R-R	6-1	210	3-6-86	.249	.237	.252	81	265	31	66	13	2	5	31	32	6	0	1	65	0	2	.370	.342
Diaz, Elias	R-R	6-1	215	11-17-90	.223	.261	.211	64	188	18	42	14	0	1	19	11	0	0	1	38	1	0	.314	.265
Frazier, Adam	L-R	5-9	185	12-14-91	.276	.304	.271	121	406	55	112	20	6	6	53	36	8	1	3	57	9	5	.399	.344
Freese, David	R-R	6-2	220	4-28-83	.263	.308	.248	130	426	44	112	16	0	10	52	58	15	0	4	116	0	1	.371	.368
Gosselin, Phil	R-R	6-1	200	10-3-88	.150	.125	.167	28	40	3	6	1	0	0	2	2	0	0	0	9	0	1	.175	.191
Hanson, Alen	B-R	5-11	170	10-22-92	.193	.286	.180	37	57	8	11	0	2	0	1	2	0	0	0	9	2	1	.263	.220
Harrison, Josh	R-R	5-8	180	7-8-87	.272	.286	.267	128	486	66	132	26	2	16	47	28	23	2	3	90	12	4	.432	.339
Jaso, John	R-L	6-2	202	9-19-83	.211	.200	.212	126	256	28	54	19	0	10	35	40	5	0	1	66	1	1	.402	.328
Luplow, Jordan	R-R	6-1	195	9-26-93	.205	.154	.231	27	78	6	16	3	1	3	11	6	2	0	1	22	0	1	.385	.276
Marte, Starling	R-R	6-1	190	10-9-88	.275	.162	.311	77	309	48	85	7	2	7	31	20	8	0	2	63	21	4	.379	.333
McCutchen, Andrew	R-R	5-10	195	10-10-86	.279	.336	.263	156	570	94	159	30	2	28	88	73	4	0	3	116	11	5	.486	.363
Mercer, Jordy	R-R	6-3	210	8-27-86	.255	.248	.257	145	502	52	128	24	5	14	58	51	3	0	2	88	0	4	.406	.326
Moroff, Max	B-R	5-10	185	5-13-93	.200	.219	.193	56	120	19	24	4	1	3	21	16	2	1	1	43	0	1	.325	.302
Ngoepe, Gift	R-R	5-8	200	1-18-90	.222	.091	.256	28	54	10	12	2	1	0	6	8	0	1	0	26	0	0	.296	.323
Ortiz, Danny	L-L	5-11	190	1-5-90	.083	1.000	.000	9	12	1	1	0	0	0	0	1	0	0	0	1	0	0	.083	.154
Osuna, Jose	R-R	6-3	240	12-12-92	.233	.253	.216	104	215	31	50	13	4	7	30	9	2	0	1	40	0	0	.428	.269
Polanco, Gregory	L-L	6-5	235	9-14-91	.251	.231	.257	108	379	39	95	20	0	11	35	27	3	0	1	60	8	1	.391	.305
Rodriguez, Sean	R-R	6-0	200	4-26-85	.168	.194	.153	39	95	12	16	1	0	3	5	8	3	0	0	38	0	0	.274	.255
2-team total (15 Atlanta)					.167	.194	.153	54	132	18	22	2	0	5	8	16	4	1	0	57	1	0	.296	.276
Stallings, Jacob	R-R	6-5	220	12-22-89	.357	.400	.333	5	14	3	5	2	0	0	3	2	0	0	0	2	0	0	.500	.438
Stewart, Chris	R-R	6-4	200	2-19-82	.183	.094	.212	51	131	8	24	1	2	0	4	9	1	3	0	22	0	0	.221	.241

Pitching	B-T	HT	WT	DOB	W	L	ERA	G	GS	CG	SV	IP	H	R	ER	HR	BB	SO	AVG	vLH	vRH	K/9	BB/9
Barbato, Johnny	R-R	6-1	235	7-11-92	0	1	4.08	24	0	0	0	29	25	13	13	4	18	23	.227	.321	.130	7.22	5.65
Bastardo, Antonio	L-L	5-11	202	9-21-85	0	1	15.00	9	0	0	0	9	16	15	15	5	9	8	.372	.333	.387	8.00	9.00
Benoit, Joaquin	R-R	6-4	250	7-26-77	0	2	7.56	8	0	0	0	8	11	9	7	2	6	3	.324	.375	.278	3.24	6.48
2-team total (44 Philadelphia)					1	6	4.65	52	0	0	2	50	43	28	26	7	22	46	.228	.375	.278	8.23	3.93
Brault, Steven	L-L	6-0	200	4-29-92	1	0	4.67	11	4	0	1	35	41	21	18	3	14	23	.287	.235	.303	5.97	3.63
Cole, Gerrit	R-R	6-4	225	9-8-90	12	12	4.26	33	33	0	0	203	199	98	96	31	55	196	.254	.268	.241	8.69	2.44
Glasnow, Tyler	L-R	6-8	220	8-23-93	2	7	7.69	15	13	0	0	62	81	61	53	13	44	56	.319	.323	.315	8.13	6.39
Hudson, Daniel	R-R	6-3	225	3-9-87	2	7	4.38	71	0	0	0	62	57	34	30	7	33	66	.248	.255	.242	9.63	4.82
Kontos, George	R-R	6-3	215	6-12-85	1	1	1.84	15	0	0	1	15	9	3	3	1	3	15	.177	.158	.188	9.20	1.84
2-team total (50 San Francisco)					1	6	3.39	65	0	0	1	66	61	27	25	9	20	70	.242	.158	.188	9.50	2.71
Kuhl, Chad	R-R	6-3	216	9-10-92	8	11	4.35	31	31	0	0	157	159	81	76	17	72	142	.269	.285	.253	8.12	4.12
Leathersich, Jack	R-L	6-0	205	7-14-90	0	0	0.00	6	0	0	0	4	3	0	0	0	2	6	.200	.000	.333	12.46	4.15
2-team total (1 Chicago)					0	0	3.60	7	0	0	0	5	4	2	2	0	6	7	.235	—	.500	12.60	10.80
LeBlanc, Wade	L-L	6-3	205	8-7-84	5	2	4.50	50	0	0	1	68	64	35	34	10	17	54	.243	.296	.217	7.15	2.25
Lindblom, Josh	R-R	6-4	240	6-15-87	0	0	7.84	4	0	0	0	10	18	9	9	0	3	10	.375	.364	.385	8.71	2.61
Marinez, Jhan	R-R	6-1	200	8-12-88	0	1	3.18	24	0	0	0	34	34	12	12	4	12	26	.266	.246	.284	6.88	3.18
2-team total (15 Milwaukee)					0	3	3.91	39	0	0	0	51	57	24	22	6	23	40	.289	.246	.284	7.11	4.09
Neverauskas, Dovydas	R-R	6-3	215	1-14-93	1	1	3.91	24	0	0	0	25	24	11	11	4	8	17	.253	.262	.245	6.04	2.84
Nicasio, Juan	R-R	6-4	252	8-31-86	2	5	2.85	65	0	0	2	60	49	20	19	4	18	60	.222	.202	.238	9.00	2.70
3-team total (2 Philadelphia, 9 St. Louis)					5	5	2.61	76	0	0	6	72	58	22	21	5	20	72	.217	.202	.238	8.96	2.49
Nova, Ivan	R-R	6-5	245	1-12-87	11	14	4.14	31	31	2	0	187	203	96	86	29	36	131	.277	.309	.249	6.30	1.73
Rivero, Felipe	L-L	6-2	210	7-5-91	5	3	1.67	73	0	0	21	75	47	19	14	4	20	88	.171	.082	.211	10.51	2.39
Runzler, Dan	L-L	6-4	210	3-30-85	0	0	4.50	8	0	0	0	4	7	4	2	2	2	4	.389	.333	.444	9.00	4.50
Sanchez, Angel	R-R	6-1	190	11-28-89	1	0	8.76	8	0	0	0	12	16	12	12	5	1	10	.308	.375	.250	7.30	0.73
Santana, Edgar	R-R	6-2	180	10-16-91	0	0	3.50	19	0	0	0	18	16	8	7	2	12	20	.239	.357	.154	10.00	6.00
Schugel, A.J.	R-R	6-0	200	6-27-89	4	0	1.97	32	0	0	0	32	31	8	7	3	14	27	.258	.250	.263	7.59	3.94
Taillon, Jameson	R-R	6-5	225	11-18-91	8	7	4.44	25	25	0	0	134	152	69	66	11	46	125	.290	.313	.270	8.42	3.10

Pitching	B-T	HT	WT	DOB	W	L	ERA	G	GS	CG	SV	IP	H	R	ER	HR	BB	SO	AVG	vLH	vRH	K/9	BB/9
Watson, Tony	L-L	6-4	220	5-30-85	5	3	3.66	47	0	0	10	47	57	20	19	7	14	35	.305	.308	.303	6.75	2.70
2-team total (24 Los Angeles)					7	4	3.38	71	0	0	10	67	72	26	25	9	20	53	.278	.212	.205	7.16	2.70
Williams, Trevor	R-R	6-3	230	4-25-92	7	9	4.07	31	25	0	0	150	145	73	68	14	52	117	.255	.286	.225	7.00	3.11

Fielding

Catcher	PCT	G	PO	A	E	DP	PB
Cervelli	.991	78	500	47	5	6	7
Diaz	.990	55	356	37	4	4	3
Stallings	.964	5	26	1	1	0	1
Stewart	.985	48	379	26	6	1	4

First Base	PCT	G	PO	A	E	DP
Bell	.992	147	1139	86	10	116
Freese	1.000	3	13	1	0	3
Gosselin	1.000	1	3	0	0	0
Jaso	1.000	29	110	3	0	11
Osuna	.992	23	116	4	1	12
Rodriguez	1.000	2	2	0	0	0

Second Base	PCT	G	PO	A	E	DP
Bostick	1.000	3	8	7	0	0
Frazier	.951	42	69	85	8	21
Gosselin	.939	11	17	14	2	5
Hanson	.980	15	20	30	1	7
Harrison	.981	83	147	212	7	52
Moroff	1.000	28	34	45	0	16
Ngoepe	1.000	20	27	37	0	9
Rodriguez	.935	8	7	22	2	6

Third Base	PCT	G	PO	A	E	DP
Frazier	1.000	1	0	4	0	0
Freese	.960	116	66	222	12	29
Gosselin	1.000	1	0	1	0	0
Hanson	.000	1	0	0	0	0
Harrison	.966	49	39	75	4	12
Moroff	1.000	6	2	8	0	3
Ngoepe	1.000	3	0	1	0	0
Rodriguez	1.000	9	5	21	0	0

Shortstop	PCT	G	PO	A	E	DP
Frazier	.800	1	2	2	1	0
Hanson	1.000	2	3	2	0	2
Mercer	.982	144	176	359	10	88
Moroff	1.000	16	13	42	0	4
Ngoepe	1.000	6	6	6	0	1
Rodriguez	.917	6	8	14	2	3

Outfield	PCT	G	PO	A	E	DP
Bostick	1.000	3	4	0	0	0
Frazier	.992	67	114	3	1	0
Hanson	.000	2	0	0	0	0
Harrison	1.000	9	13	0	0	0
Jaso	.977	61	83	1	2	0
Luplow	.976	23	40	1	1	0
Marte	.994	76	157	8	1	0
McCutchen	.987	152	290	9	4	2
Ortiz	.833	9	5	0	1	0
Osuna	.963	36	48	4	2	0
Polanco	.988	96	163	6	2	3
Rodriguez	1.000	14	16	1	0	0

INDIANAPOLIS INDIANS — *TRIPLE-A*

INTERNATIONAL LEAGUE

Batting	B-T	HT	WT	DOB	AVG	vLH	vRH	G	AB	R	H	2B	3B	HR	RBI	BB	HBP	SH	SF	SO	SB	CS	SLG	OBP
Barnes, Barrett	R-R	5-11	209	7-29-91	.247	.243	.250	31	93	13	23	8	0	1	10	10	7	2	2	34	1	0	.366	.357
Bormann, John	R-R	6-0	205	4-4-93	.500	—	.500	2	4	1	2	0	0	0	0	0	0	0	0	0	0	0	.500	.500
Bostick, Christopher	R-R	5-10	190	3-24-93	.294	.275	.303	126	486	75	143	33	3	7	57	45	8	7	3	97	8	9	.418	.362
Diaz, Elias	R-R	6-1	215	11-17-90	.266	.276	.263	57	218	19	58	10	0	2	27	9	1	1	0	36	3	0	.339	.298
Espinal, Edwin	R-R	6-2	250	1-27-94	.323	.405	.290	35	130	12	42	6	0	0	14	4	0	0	1	22	1	0	.369	.341
Feliz, Anderson	B-R	6-0	175	5-11-92	.209	.180	.233	44	134	13	28	7	0	3	22	9	0	1	1	41	3	1	.328	.257
Frazier, Adam	L-R	5-9	185	12-14-91	.400	.000	.500	3	10	2	4	1	0	0	1	3	0	0	0	1	1	0	.500	.539
Gosselin, Phil	R-R	6-1	200	10-3-88	.266	.385	.222	63	241	27	64	10	2	1	26	14	0	1	2	46	3	2	.336	.304
Luplow, Jordan	R-R	6-1	195	9-26-93	.325	.361	.315	44	160	29	52	7	1	7	19	16	5	0	1	36	4	1	.513	.401
Maffei, Justin	R-R	5-11	173	8-27-91	.333	.333	.333	12	30	5	10	1	0	0	3	5	1	1	0	8	1	1	.367	.444
Marte, Starling	R-R	6-1	190	10-9-88	.333	.385	.304	9	36	4	12	1	0	1	3	2	2	0	0	8	3	0	.444	.400
Meadows, Austin	L-L	6-3	200	5-3-95	.250	.239	.257	72	284	48	71	19	0	4	36	24	2	0	2	50	11	3	.359	.311
Morales, Tomas	R-R	6-0	190	7-30-91	.182	.333	.125	3	11	1	2	1	0	0	1	0	0	0	0	3	0	0	.273	.182
Moroff, Max	B-R	5-10	185	5-13-93	.254	.233	.264	51	185	31	47	10	0	13	37	41	1	0	1	59	5	2	.519	.390
Newman, Kevin	R-R	6-1	180	8-4-93	.283	.306	.274	40	166	23	47	11	2	0	11	7	1	3	1	22	7	1	.374	.314
Ngoepe, Gift	R-R	5-8	200	1-18-90	.220	.242	.208	77	264	33	58	15	5	6	27	28	3	1	3	91	2	4	.383	.299
Ortiz, Danny	L-L	5-11	190	1-5-90	.270	.216	.288	110	411	47	111	30	1	15	63	19	3	2	6	80	5	2	.457	.303
Osuna, Jose	R-R	6-3	240	12-12-92	.250	.100	.308	10	36	6	9	5	0	0	1	5	0	0	0	9	1	1	.389	.342
Perez, Eury	R-R	6-0	190	5-30-90	.336	.390	.312	50	134	26	45	6	2	1	12	12	3	5	1	23	22	5	.433	.400
Rogers, Jason	R-R	6-1	260	3-13-88	.289	.240	.309	69	253	35	73	9	1	9	34	27	2	0	0	44	3	2	.439	.362
Stallings, Jacob	R-R	6-5	220	12-22-89	.301	.317	.292	62	216	35	65	16	0	4	38	17	4	3	3	30	1	2	.431	.358
Terdoslavich, Joey	B-R	6-2	200	9-9-88	.278	.306	.264	105	346	42	96	22	0	7	47	42	3	1	5	59	3	2	.402	.356
Weiss, Erich	L-R	6-2	200	9-11-91	.274	.198	.299	104	332	50	91	23	4	6	43	38	4	0	3	67	6	2	.422	.353
Williams, Jackson	R-R	5-11	200	5-14-86	.192	.091	.220	30	104	7	20	2	0	1	3	8	1	1	0	26	0	0	.240	.257
Wood, Eric	R-R	6-2	195	11-22-92	.238	.244	.235	120	416	58	99	25	5	16	61	45	3	1	8	125	7	1	.438	.311

Pitching	B-T	HT	WT	DOB	W	L	ERA	G	GS	CG	SV	IP	H	R	ER	HR	BB	SO	AVG	vLH	vRH	K/9	BB/9
Barbato, Johnny	R-R	6-1	235	7-11-92	0	1	3.06	26	2	0	4	35	28	12	12	7	11	36	.212	.236	.195	9.17	2.80
2-team total (1 Scranton/Wilkes-Barre)					0	2	3.20	27	3	0	4	39	33	14	14	9	13	41	.226	.236	.195	9.38	2.97
Bastardo, Antonio	L-L	5-11	202	9-21-85	2	0	3.18	12	1	0	0	11	11	5	4	2	8	9	.244	.105	.346	7.15	6.35
Brault, Steven	L-L	6-0	200	4-29-92	10	5	1.94	21	20	0	0	120	85	26	26	5	44	109	.199	.155	.217	8.15	3.29
Cumpton, Brandon	R-R	6-2	215	11-16-88	1	1	4.05	5	0	0	0	7	5	3	3	1	3	6	.217	.167	.235	8.10	4.05
Dickson, Cody	L-L	6-3	180	4-27-92	4	3	4.73	24	6	0	0	40	42	22	21	2	28	34	.276	.255	.287	7.65	6.30
DuRapau, Montana	R-R	5-11	175	3-27-92	1	0	3.24	15	0	0	1	17	7	6	6	2	6	23	.125	.261	.030	12.42	3.24
Eppler, Tyler	R-R	6-6	220	1-5-93	8	9	4.89	27	21	1	0	136	159	83	74	23	33	96	.292	.341	.259	6.34	2.18
Glasnow, Tyler	L-R	6-8	220	8-23-93	9	2	1.93	15	15	0	0	93	57	21	20	6	32	140	.176	.182	.170	13.50	3.09
Holmes, Clay	R-R	6-5	230	3-27-93	10	5	3.36	25	24	0	0	113	96	45	42	4	59	99	.238	.223	.251	7.91	4.71
Hutchison, Drew	R-L	6-3	205	8-22-90	9	9	3.56	28	26	1	0	159	149	69	63	14	57	124	.248	.249	.246	7.00	3.22
Kingham, Nick	R-R	6-5	225	11-8-91	9	6	4.13	20	19	1	0	113	119	59	52	8	29	93	.271	.267	.273	7.39	2.30
Light, Pat	R-R	6-5	220	3-29-91	3	0	3.76	22	0	0	4	26	23	12	11	1	15	20	.242	.177	.279	6.84	5.13
Lindblom, Josh	R-R	6-4	240	6-15-87	0	2	4.06	17	4	0	0	38	37	17	17	5	8	33	.257	.242	.268	7.88	1.91
McKinney, Brett	R-R	6-2	225	11-19-90	3	1	3.47	40	1	0	1	62	58	30	24	7	26	56	.245	.235	.252	8.09	3.75
Neverauskas, Dovydas	R-R	6-3	215	1-14-93	1	2	2.86	40	0	0	13	50	47	20	16	1	21	46	.253	.237	.264	8.23	3.75
Runzler, Dan	L-L	6-4	210	3-30-85	1	4	3.05	40	0	0	7	41	43	15	14	3	22	36	.276	.215	.319	7.84	4.79
Sadler, Casey	R-R	6-4	225	7-13-90	1	1	6.38	10	1	0	0	18	28	16	13	0	7	12	.364	.308	.421	5.89	3.44
Sanchez, Angel	R-R	6-1	190	11-28-89	3	5	3.74	39	0	0	1	55	51	23	23	4	15	65	.242	.226	.252	10.57	2.44
Santana, Edgar	R-R	6-2	180	10-16-91	1	3	2.79	44	0	0	8	58	62	19	18	4	12	54	.281	.298	.268	8.38	1.86

Pitching	B-T	HT	WT	DOB	W	L	ERA	G	GS	CG	SV	IP	H	R	ER	HR	BB	SO	AVG	vLH	vRH	K/9	BB/9
Schugel, A.J.	R-R	6-0	200	6-27-89	3	1	4.17	26	0	0	0	37	37	18	17	4	13	36	.268	.258	.276	8.84	3.19
Taillon, Jameson	R-R	6-5	225	11-18-91	0	1	4.09	2	2	0	0	11	12	6	5	0	2	15	.261	.136	.375	12.27	1.64

Fielding

Catcher	PCT	G	PO	A	E	DP	PB
Bormann	.800	1	3	1	1	0	0
Diaz	.998	50	409	43	1	6	2
Morales	1.000	3	20	4	0	0	0
Stallings	.996	60	480	35	2	0	1
Williams	.989	29	251	15	3	1	2

First Base	PCT	G	PO	A	E	DP
Espinal	1.000	27	208	18	0	22
Feliz	.000	1	0	0	0	0
Osuna	.981	6	50	1	1	6
Rogers	.994	37	308	18	2	34
Stallings	1.000	1	7	0	0	2
Terdoslavich	.986	49	375	34	6	34
Weiss	1.000	10	56	5	0	4
Wood	.995	26	171	14	1	18

Second Base	PCT	G	PO	A	E	DP
Bostick	.967	33	55	63	4	17
Feliz	.949	6	18	19	2	7
Frazier	1.000	1	4	1	0	0
Gosselin	1.000	26	37	67	0	14
Moroff	.990	18	45	59	1	15
Ngoepe	.986	14	30	43	1	11
Weiss	.983	55	85	149	4	34

Third Base	PCT	G	PO	A	E	DP
Bostick	1.000	6	3	7	0	1
Gosselin	.980	21	14	35	1	4
Moroff	.727	3	1	7	3	0
Ngoepe	.979	21	13	33	1	2
Weiss	.970	30	16	48	2	4
Wood	.930	73	39	120	12	10

Shortstop	PCT	G	PO	A	E	DP
Feliz	.959	19	19	51	3	9
Gosselin	.966	19	20	37	2	9
Moroff	.930	29	39	81	9	13
Newman	.988	38	54	106	2	27
Ngoepe	.983	42	56	118	3	30

Outfield	PCT	G	PO	A	E	DP
Barnes	.982	27	52	2	1	0
Bostick	.987	83	146	1	2	0
Feliz	.955	12	20	1	1	1
Frazier	1.000	2	2	0	0	0
Luplow	.957	40	64	3	3	1
Maffei	1.000	11	16	0	0	0
Marte	1.000	7	10	1	0	0
Meadows	1.000	70	118	3	0	0
Ortiz	.991	109	208	5	2	0
Osuna	1.000	3	9	0	0	0
Perez	1.000	44	64	2	0	0
Terdoslavich	.938	27	42	3	3	1
Wood	.941	19	28	4	2	0

ALTOONA CURVE — *DOUBLE-A*

EASTERN LEAGUE

Batting	B-T	HT	WT	DOB	AVG	vLH	vRH	G	AB	R	H	2B	3B	HR	RBI	BB	HBP	SH	SF	SO	SB	CS	SLG	OBP
Chavez, Zane	R-L	5-10	200	12-30-86	.111	.188	.085	19	63	5	7	1	0	0	5	5	0	0	2	9	0	0	.127	.171
Diaz, Chris	R-R	5-10	190	11-9-90	.375	.444	.333	10	24	6	9	1	2	0	3	6	0	1	0	6	1	0	.583	.500
Escobar, Elvis	L-L	5-8	169	9-6-94	.277	.299	.271	116	383	42	106	12	5	3	32	25	0	2	3	69	5	7	.358	.319
Espinal, Edwin	R-R	6-2	250	1-27-94	.283	.290	.281	95	367	41	104	25	0	15	72	18	6	0	6	48	0	1	.474	.322
Feliz, Anderson	B-R	6-0	175	5-11-92	.246	.300	.224	48	175	23	43	9	3	2	21	26	0	3	0	46	9	4	.366	.343
George, Jordan	B-R	6-2	200	7-16-92	.302	.320	.296	30	106	14	32	9	0	1	18	8	2	0	3	12	1	0	.415	.353
Hill, Logan	R-R	6-3	230	5-26-93	.279	.231	.302	22	79	12	22	5	0	2	9	14	1	0	2	21	0	0	.418	.385
Hughston, Casey	L-R	6-2	200	6-9-94	.200	.000	.250	2	5	0	1	0	1	0	2	0	0	0	0	3	0	0	.600	.200
Jhang, Jin-De	L-R	5-11	220	5-17-93	.231	.205	.236	72	273	29	63	9	2	3	25	17	2	3	1	24	1	0	.311	.280
Joe, Connor	R-R	6-0	205	8-16-92	.240	.273	.227	74	242	29	58	11	4	5	30	34	3	1	2	40	2	4	.380	.338
Kramer, Kevin	L-R	6-1	190	10-3-93	.297	.273	.306	53	202	31	60	17	3	6	27	17	12	0	3	50	7	2	.500	.380
Luplow, Jordan	R-R	6-1	195	9-26-93	.287	.338	.269	73	254	45	73	15	0	16	37	29	4	0	1	45	1	3	.535	.368
Maffei, Justin	R-R	5-11	173	8-27-91	.258	.206	.291	32	89	15	23	3	0	0	4	16	5	0	0	16	4	1	.292	.400
Mathisen, Wyatt	R-R	6-0	227	12-30-93	.272	.276	.270	114	375	43	102	16	2	5	31	44	7	1	3	75	3	2	.365	.357
Morales, Tomas	R-R	6-0	190	7-30-91	.188	.182	.192	36	117	7	22	6	0	2	14	6	0	3	0	24	2	0	.291	.228
Newman, Kevin	R-R	6-1	180	8-4-93	.260	.255	.261	82	343	42	89	18	2	4	30	22	4	3	2	40	4	2	.359	.310
Ratledge, Logan	R-R	5-11	190	7-20-92	.108	.000	.148	15	37	2	4	1	0	0	0	3	0	0	0	10	0	0	.135	.175
Reyes, Pablo	R-R	5-10	150	9-5-93	.274	.248	.287	115	420	62	115	21	3	10	50	51	4	5	3	70	21	14	.410	.356
Schwind, Jonathan	R-R	6-0	185	5-30-90	.353	.571	.200	12	17	4	6	2	0	2	5	1	0	1	0	4	1	0	.824	.389
Simpson, Chase	R-B	6-1	210	2-17-92	.176	.118	.185	43	125	13	22	5	1	4	13	9	1	1	0	42	1	2	.328	.237
Suchy, Michael	R-R	6-3	228	4-15-93	.200	.127	.225	78	250	31	50	8	1	4	17	21	5	2	2	95	2	2	.288	.273
Suiter, Jerrick	R-R	6-4	230	3-4-93	.285	.260	.296	100	347	47	99	20	3	10	58	47	2	1	2	83	7	2	.447	.372
Tolman, Mitchell	L-R	5-11	195	6-8-94	.222	.000	.250	3	9	1	2	1	0	1	5	0	0	1	1	2	0	0	.667	.200
Tucker, Cole	B-R	6-3	185	7-3-96	.258	.341	.228	42	167	25	43	4	5	2	18	21	3	2	1	31	11	3	.377	.349
Williams, Jackson	R-R	5-11	200	5-14-86	.212	.154	.237	25	85	9	18	1	0	1	7	9	2	0	1	18	0	0	.259	.299

Pitching	B-T	HT	WT	DOB	W	L	ERA	G	GS	CG	SV	IP	H	R	ER	HR	BB	SO	AVG	vLH	vRH	K/9	BB/9
Agrazal, Dario	R-R	6-3	216	12-28-94	0	1	4.50	1	1	0	0	4	3	2	2	0	2	2	.231	.286	.167	4.50	4.50
Anderson, Tanner	R-R	6-2	195	5-27-93	10	8	3.38	30	19	0	0	133	134	54	50	6	33	97	.263	.311	.218	6.55	2.23
Borden, Buddy	R-R	6-3	210	4-29-92	5	1	2.37	23	0	0	1	38	25	13	10	1	25	36	.187	.152	.236	8.53	5.92
Brentz, Jake	L-L	6-2	195	9-14-94	0	1	5.79	14	0	0	0	14	7	9	9	3	15	16	.146	.091	.162	10.29	9.64
Brubaker, J.T.	R-R	6-4	175	11-17-93	7	6	4.44	26	24	0	0	130	150	73	64	9	45	109	.291	.285	.296	7.57	3.12
Coley, Austin	R-R	6-2	203	7-14-92	6	4	3.01	29	23	0	0	144	144	49	48	10	31	114	.261	.245	.276	7.14	1.94
Cumpton, Brandon	R-R	6-2	215	11-16-88	3	3	4.50	13	0	0	1	20	24	12	10	2	9	18	.289	.229	.333	8.10	4.05
Dickson, Cody	L-L	6-3	180	4-27-92	2	4	5.85	12	6	0	0	32	39	22	21	8	20	31	.298	.189	.340	8.63	5.57
DuRapau, Montana	R-R	5-11	175	3-27-92	2	2	1.49	27	0	0	14	36	28	7	6	0	14	39	.209	.181	.242	9.66	3.47
Garcia, Yeudy	R-R	6-2	203	10-6-92	4	7	5.25	29	11	0	5	72	76	48	42	8	46	67	.273	.321	.227	8.38	5.75
Hellweg, Johnny	R-R	6-7	235	10-29-88	0	1	4.50	4	0	0	0	6	5	3	3	2	1	6	.238	.333	.167	9.00	1.50
Heredia, Luis	R-R	6-5	251	8-10-94	3	3	3.10	36	0	0	2	52	41	18	18	3	31	43	.211	.263	.158	7.39	5.33
Keller, Mitch	R-R	6-3	195	4-4-96	2	2	3.12	6	6	0	0	35	25	14	12	2	11	45	.197	.191	.203	11.68	2.86
Keselica, Sean	L-L	6-2	210	6-14-93	4	2	3.54	42	3	0	3	74	67	34	29	2	39	72	.245	.174	.282	8.80	4.76
Kuchno, John	R-R	6-5	210	5-21-91	0	1	8.38	6	0	0	1	10	18	10	9	0	3	9	.400	.520	.250	8.38	2.79
Lakind, Jared	L-L	6-2	205	3-9-92	1	1	6.81	22	0	0	2	36	49	29	27	3	17	38	.322	.368	.295	9.59	4.29
McRae, Alex	R-R	6-3	185	4-6-93	10	5	3.61	27	25	1	0	150	170	71	60	9	36	89	.291	.317	.261	5.35	2.16
Rosario, Miguel	R-R	6-0	185	1-30-93	3	1	1.80	27	0	0	3	45	36	12	9	1	35	43	.221	.268	.185	8.60	7.00
Sadler, Casey	R-R	6-4	225	7-13-90	2	3	3.91	10	6	1	0	48	49	21	21	5	3	40	.259	.235	.279	7.45	0.56
Scioneaux, Tate	R-R	6-1	200	12-14-92	6	5	2.39	47	0	0	14	83	67	27	22	4	15	67	.219	.227	.211	7.27	1.63
Taillon, Jameson	R-R	6-5	225	11-18-91	0	0	0.00	1	1	0	0	3	1	0	0	0	1	6	.100	.167	.000	18.00	3.00

	B-T	HT	WT	DOB	W	L	ERA	G	GS	CG	SV	IP	H	R	ER	HR	BB	SO	AVG	vLH	vRH	K/9	BB/9
Waddell, Brandon	L-L	6-3	180	6-3-94	3	3	3.55	15	15	0	0	66	60	28	26	3	27	56	.240	.243	.239	7.64	3.68
Zamora, Daniel	L-L	6-3	190	4-15-93	0	0	0.00	2	0	0	0	3	2	0	0	0	2	2	.200	.000	.400	6.00	6.00

Fielding

Catcher	PCT	G	PO	A	E	DP	PB
Chavez	.970	18	114	15	4	0	3
Jhang	.993	65	490	66	4	11	6
Morales	.974	34	249	17	7	1	1
Williams	.990	25	169	20	2	1	1

First Base	PCT	G	PO	A	E	DP
Espinal	1.000	81	698	67	0	70
George	.979	10	83	12	2	7
Joe	.995	24	189	24	1	17
Simpson	1.000	7	51	3	0	5
Suiter	.996	24	213	15	1	17

Second Base	PCT	G	PO	A	E	DP
Diaz	1.000	6	7	19	0	6
Feliz	.978	10	14	31	1	4
Kramer	.972	48	69	140	6	31
Mathisen	1.000	1	0	3	0	0
Ratledge	.943	7	13	20	2	7
Reyes	.992	71	137	219	3	42
Tolman	1.000	3	7	9	0	2

Third Base	PCT	G	PO	A	E	DP
Espinal	.750	2	0	3	1	0
Feliz	.927	16	10	28	3	2
Joe	1.000	1	1	0	0	0
Luplow	.000	1	0	0	0	0
Mathisen	.939	108	62	184	16	18
Simpson	1.000	21	14	35	0	3

Shortstop	PCT	G	PO	A	E	DP
Diaz	1.000	3	3	6	0	2
Newman	.980	81	127	222	7	49
Reyes	.972	15	32	37	2	9
Tucker	.952	42	54	126	9	28

Outfield	PCT	G	PO	A	E	DP
Escobar	.982	108	216	3	4	1
Feliz	1.000	21	34	3	0	1
George	1.000	5	6	0	0	0
Hill	.967	20	29	0	1	0
Hughston	1.000	2	2	0	0	0
Joe	.985	33	64	2	1	0
Luplow	1.000	65	120	6	0	1
Maffei	.980	28	48	1	1	1
Ratledge	1.000	5	11	0	0	0
Reyes	.987	31	75	2	1	0
Schwind	1.000	3	2	0	0	0
Suchy	.984	70	119	5	2	1
Suiter	.957	51	85	3	4	1

BRADENTON MARAUDERS — HIGH CLASS A

FLORIDA STATE LEAGUE

Batting	B-T	HT	WT	DOB	AVG	vLH	vRH	G	AB	R	H	2B	3B	HR	RBI	BB	HBP	SH	SF	SO	SB	CS	SLG	OBP
Alemais, Stephen	R-R	6-0	190	4-12-95	.317	.259	.338	30	101	10	32	6	0	1	20	14	0	5	2	14	5	2	.406	.393
Arribas, Daniel	R-R	6-0	212	9-30-92	.168	.269	.136	33	107	14	18	3	1	0	8	19	2	2	1	33	5	2	.215	.302
Bastardo, Alexis	R-R	5-11	190	2-26-94	.180	.111	.200	13	39	3	7	1	0	0	0	3	1	0	0	11	2	0	.205	.256
Bormann, John	R-R	6-0	205	4-4-93	.183	.321	.141	39	120	11	22	6	0	0	10	15	2	3	2	26	0	3	.233	.281
Craig, Will	R-R	6-3	212	11-16-94	.271	.349	.241	123	458	59	124	26	1	6	61	62	16	0	6	106	1	3	.371	.373
George, Jordan	B-R	6-2	200	7-16-92	.302	.186	.348	69	248	41	75	15	2	9	43	40	2	4	3	45	1	1	.488	.399
Hayes, Ke'Bryan	R-R	6-1	210	1-28-97	.278	.236	.292	108	421	66	117	16	7	2	43	41	4	12	4	76	27	5	.363	.345
Hill, Logan	R-R	6-3	230	5-26-93	.266	.269	.265	71	267	44	71	14	2	16	52	31	5	0	2	73	3	3	.513	.351
Hughston, Casey	L-R	6-2	200	6-9-94	.248	.219	.258	114	400	52	99	16	9	8	41	29	2	9	3	147	15	8	.393	.300
Kelley, Christian	R-R	5-11	185	9-23-93	.243	.275	.233	92	325	27	79	11	0	2	39	39	9	8	1	80	1	6	.295	.340
Krause, Kevin	R-R	6-2	200	11-23-92	.276	.329	.254	86	283	36	78	18	2	10	43	40	3	4	1	47	7	4	.459	.370
Marte, Starling	R-R	6-1	190	10-9-88	.200	.000	.250	3	10	2	2	0	0	0	0	0	0	0	0	2	1	0	.200	.200
Moore, Ty	L-R	6-0	190	7-26-93	.290	.340	.270	52	190	20	55	10	0	5	26	17	4	6	2	26	6	3	.421	.357
Munoz, Carlos	L-L	5-11	225	6-29-94	.154	.048	.226	15	52	4	8	2	0	0	2	7	1	0	1	6	0	0	.192	.262
Ratledge, Logan	R-R	5-11	190	7-20-92	.257	.218	.277	62	226	30	58	14	1	3	19	14	4	6	2	40	11	2	.367	.309
Reyes, Alfredo	R-R	6-2	160	10-4-93	.232	.242	.228	109	362	43	84	13	5	2	23	19	1	10	0	106	24	8	.312	.272
Suiter, Jerrick	R-R	6-4	230	3-4-93	.237	.429	.194	10	38	4	9	2	0	0	4	5	1	0	0	9	1	0	.290	.341
Tam Sing, Trace	R-R	6-0	175	12-7-91	.191	.167	.200	7	21	2	4	1	0	1	3	2	0	0	0	7	0	1	.381	.261
Tolman, Mitchell	L-R	5-11	195	6-8-94	.268	.308	.252	115	415	66	111	19	3	9	62	58	7	10	4	85	14	5	.393	.364
Tucker, Cole	B-R	6-3	185	7-3-96	.285	.257	.295	68	277	46	79	15	6	4	32	34	1	3	1	70	36	12	.426	.364

Pitching	B-T	HT	WT	DOB	W	L	ERA	G	GS	CG	SV	IP	H	R	ER	HR	BB	SO	AVG	vLH	vRH	K/9	BB/9
Agrazal, Dario	R-R	6-3	216	12-28-94	5	3	2.91	14	13	0	0	80	73	34	26	4	10	63	.243	.266	.222	7.06	1.12
Amedee, Jess	R-R	6-2	205	9-5-93	5	5	2.80	35	0	0	0	55	41	18	17	3	32	61	.207	.223	.192	10.04	5.27
Brentz, Jake	L-L	6-2	195	9-14-94	1	2	3.81	19	0	0	2	26	23	13	11	0	9	33	.230	.259	.219	11.42	3.12
Cumpton, Brandon	R-R	6-2	215	11-16-88	1	0	2.53	6	0	0	0	11	12	3	3	0	5	9	.308	.300	.316	7.59	4.22
Eusebio, Julio	R-R	6-1	202	6-2-92	0	0	0.00	1	0	0	0	1	0	0	0	0	0	1	.000	.000	.000	9.00	0.00
Hartlieb, Geoff	R-R	6-6	210	12-9-93	1	4	3.48	19	0	0	3	31	29	15	12	3	9	36	.250	.278	.226	10.45	2.61
Hearn, Taylor	L-L	6-5	210	8-30-94	4	6	4.12	18	17	0	0	87	65	41	40	8	37	106	.207	.221	.203	10.92	3.81
Helton, Bret	R-R	6-3	215	7-25-93	8	3	3.25	30	14	0	0	116	110	43	42	7	37	89	.255	.307	.217	6.89	2.86
Hinsz, Gage	R-R	6-4	210	4-20-96	5	5	5.61	20	19	0	0	95	112	60	59	9	31	52	.296	.335	.264	4.94	2.95
Jess, Jordan	L-L	6-3	240	1-29-93	0	0	9.24	8	0	0	0	13	18	13	13	1	5	7	.340	.353	.333	4.97	3.55
Keller, Mitch	R-R	6-3	195	4-4-96	6	3	3.14	15	15	0	0	77	57	29	27	5	20	64	.207	.236	.184	7.45	2.33
Kemp, Shane	R-R	6-3	180	7-12-94	0	0	0.00	1	0	0	0	1	0	0	0	0	1	1	.000	.000	.000	9.00	9.00
Kingham, Nick	R-R	6-5	225	11-8-91	1	0	0.00	1	1	0	0	5	1	0	0	0	0	0	.063	.167	.000	0.00	0.00
Marvel, James	R-R	6-4	210	9-17-93	1	0	1.50	4	4	0	0	24	19	7	4	0	5	16	.216	.216	.216	6.00	1.88
McGarry, Seth	R-R	6-0	180	1-5-94	1	0	1.34	31	0	0	14	40	20	6	6	1	14	38	.146	.197	.099	8.48	3.12
2-team total (13 Clearwater)					1	4	2.32	44	0	0	19	54	34	15	14	2	20	55	.177	.197	.099	9.11	3.31
Montero, Yunior	R-R	6-4	175	2-9-93	6	4	5.13	33	0	0	0	54	46	35	31	6	38	69	.229	.275	.191	11.43	6.29
Rosario, Miguel	R-R	6-0	185	1-30-93	0	1	4.85	9	0	0	0	13	10	7	7	2	11	12	.222	.381	.083	8.31	7.62
Sadler, Casey	R-R	6-4	225	7-13-90	2	0	0.75	6	0	0	0	12	5	1	1	0	2	14	.119	.200	.074	10.50	1.50
Sendelbach, Logan	R-R	6-3	185	5-5-94	5	6	3.58	31	11	0	2	88	90	39	35	9	24	62	.274	.290	.261	6.34	2.45
Street, Sam	R-R	6-3	215	3-18-92	4	2	2.74	31	1	0	2	69	67	26	21	3	14	51	.255	.271	.241	6.65	1.83
Vasquez, Pedro	R-R	6-4	190	9-23-95	9	7	3.73	26	24	0	0	138	135	57	57	13	30	107	.254	.276	.234	7.00	1.96
Vieaux, Cam	L-L	6-4	200	12-5-93	3	7	4.69	13	13	0	0	79	89	44	41	8	23	48	.286	.256	.298	5.49	2.63
Zamora, Daniel	L-L	6-3	190	4-15-93	2	4	1.86	37	0	0	9	53	48	17	11	2	17	61	.237	.250	.230	10.29	2.87

Fielding

Catcher	PCT	G	PO	A	E	DP	PB
Bormann	1.000	34	236	32	0	2	1
Kelley	.991	89	653	97	7	5	9
Krause	.965	12	74	9	3	1	3

First Base	PCT	G	PO	A	E	DP
Arribas	1.000	9	101	6	0	6

	PCT	G	PO	A	E	DP
Bormann	1.000	1	8	0	0	0
Craig	.993	93	855	78	7	75
George	1.000	18	168	4	0	15
Munoz	.979	10	83	10	2	6
Reyes	1.000	1	2	0	0	0
Suiter	1.000	1	12	0	0	1

Second Base	PCT	G	PO	A	E	DP
Ratledge	.971	12	32	34	2	8
Reyes	.990	21	40	60	1	12
Tolman	.978	102	172	323	11	59

Third Base	PCT	G	PO	A	E	DP
Arribas	1.000	1	0	2	0	0
George	1.000	1	1	2	0	0
Hayes	.974	108	54	245	8	25
Reyes	1.000	12	8	17	0	2
Tam Sing	1.000	2	0	5	0	1
Tolman	.929	9	5	21	2	0

Shortstop	PCT	G	PO	A	E	DP
Alemais	.964	29	34	72	4	13
Reyes	.961	40	48	100	6	25
Tucker	.975	66	92	182	7	33

Outfield	PCT	G	PO	A	E	DP
Arribas	1.000	16	25	0	0	0
Bastardo	.955	10	18	3	1	0
Bormann	1.000	2	1	0	0	0
George	1.000	2	6	0	0	0
Hill	.988	64	83	1	1	0
Hughston	.985	112	256	5	4	1
Krause	.980	64	96	2	2	1
Marte	1.000	3	4	0	0	0
Moore	.986	41	67	2	1	0
Ratledge	1.000	49	100	4	0	3
Reyes	.987	36	70	7	1	0
Suiter	1.000	7	11	0	0	0
Tam Sing	1.000	1	2	0	0	0

WEST VIRGINIA POWER

LOW CLASS A

SOUTH ATLANTIC LEAGUE

Batting	B-T	HT	WT	DOB	AVG	vLH	vRH	G	AB	R	H	2B	3B	HR	RBI	BB	HBP	SH	SF	SO	SB	CS	SLG	OBP
Alemais, Stephen	R-R	6-0	190	4-12-95	.223	.182	.239	29	121	14	27	6	2	3	12	5	2	3	0	32	5	3	.380	.266
Arbet, Trae	R-R	6-0	185	7-1-94	.232	.258	.222	88	323	44	75	17	4	9	50	13	12	0	1	93	3	3	.393	.287
Bastardo, Alexis	R-R	5-11	190	2-26-94	.253	.260	.250	49	166	16	42	6	1	3	19	9	2	5	1	34	11	2	.355	.298
Baur, Albert	L-R	6-4	215	3-22-92	.299	.295	.300	106	392	56	117	31	0	8	65	41	4	0	5	84	0	0	.439	.367
Brown, Garrett	L-R	6-0	185	3-3-93	.275	.309	.261	58	193	27	53	5	2	1	20	9	2	8	0	38	15	4	.337	.314
Cruz, Oneil	L-R	6-6	175	10-4-98	.218	.182	.227	16	55	9	12	2	1	2	8	8	0	0	0	22	0	0	.400	.318
Eagan, Clark	L-R	6-1	195	3-13-95	.262	.271	.258	119	436	62	114	21	5	8	59	28	10	2	6	58	5	8	.388	.317
Fernandez, Victor	R-R	5-11	175	10-17-94	.228	.211	.238	52	158	22	36	4	4	1	10	10	3	6	1	35	8	3	.323	.285
Gibbs, Brent	R-R	6-1	215	9-27-94	.229	.326	.188	40	144	15	33	7	0	3	11	6	5	0	1	49	0	0	.340	.282
Gonzalez, Yoel	R-R	6-1	180	8-1-96	.248	.367	.200	30	105	13	26	6	0	5	19	4	1	2	0	30	0	0	.448	.282
Harvey, Chris	R-R	6-5	220	3-10-93	.208	.188	.216	15	53	4	11	3	1	0	5	4	1	0	0	25	0	0	.302	.276
Hernandez, Raul	R-R	6-0	182	12-20-95	.188	.000	.250	5	16	0	3	0	0	0	1	1	0	1	0	3	0	0	.188	.235
King, Nick	R-R	6-0	190	11-12-93	.167	.111	.182	13	42	1	7	2	0	0	3	2	2	2	0	14	0	0	.214	.239
Mahala, Kevin	R-R	6-3	180	7-19-94	.230	.267	.216	98	317	37	73	11	1	4	27	35	4	3	4	94	3	2	.309	.311
Moore, Ty	L-R	6-0	190	7-26-93	.266	.157	.298	61	229	27	61	15	0	2	32	26	5	3	3	48	4	2	.358	.350
Munoz, Carlos	L-L	5-11	225	6-29-94	.275	.326	.257	100	349	46	96	23	1	5	49	54	11	5	3	41	0	2	.390	.386
Nagle, Ryan	L-R	6-1	200	8-7-94	.272	.167	.295	51	169	23	46	7	0	3	17	10	1	1	1	34	0	0	.367	.315
Owen, Hunter	R-R	6-0	195	9-22-93	.292	.319	.279	83	291	49	85	21	4	11	45	24	24	0	4	68	3	2	.505	.388
Pabst, Arden	R-R	6-1	202	3-14-95	.242	.212	.255	67	231	24	56	12	0	4	24	18	2	4	3	50	0	1	.346	.299
Ratledge, Logan	R-R	5-11	190	7-20-92	.234	.217	.238	28	107	19	25	5	0	3	12	15	1	0	2	19	4	4	.365	.328
Rosario, Henrry	L-L	5-9	180	4-5-93	.268	.250	.273	12	41	4	11	1	0	2	7	1	0	1	0	10	1	0	.439	.286
Santos, Sandy	R-R	6-3	185	4-20-94	.181	.182	.181	40	116	16	21	4	0	4	10	17	3	4	0	55	7	4	.319	.302
Valerio, Adrian	R-R	5-11	150	3-13-97	.273	.240	.288	81	326	55	89	18	2	11	34	11	4	7	4	63	8	7	.442	.301
Walker, Andrew	R-R	6-1	169	2-13-94	.274	.250	.281	26	84	9	23	1	0	0	7	8	1	0	0	25	2	1	.286	.344

Pitching	B-T	HT	WT	DOB	W	L	ERA	G	GS	CG	SV	IP	H	R	ER	HR	BB	SO	AVG	vLH	vRH	K/9	BB/9
Agustin, Ronny	L-L	6-2	185	9-18-94	3	0	3.06	20	0	0	1	35	21	15	12	1	17	52	.174	.122	.200	13.25	4.33
Anderson, Matt	R-R	6-2	200	7-29-94	8	5	3.10	25	11	0	1	81	58	34	28	7	35	90	.198	.254	.156	9.96	3.87
Cederlind, Blake	R-R	6-3	190	1-14-96	2	3	7.76	25	7	0	0	58	67	54	50	9	34	55	.289	.312	.268	8.53	5.28
Eckelman, Matt	R-R	6-4	240	10-6-93	5	6	4.63	37	3	0	1	72	72	40	37	7	26	63	.260	.236	.279	7.88	3.25
Escobar, Luis	R-R	6-1	155	5-30-96	10	7	3.83	26	25	1	0	132	97	60	56	9	60	168	.200	.217	.184	11.48	4.10
Eusebio, Julio	R-R	6-1	202	6-2-92	1	1	1.00	19	0	0	6	27	16	7	3	0	13	34	.167	.135	.186	11.33	4.33
Frawley, Matt	R-R	6-1	195	8-8-95	3	1	1.62	19	0	0	3	33	21	7	6	1	4	32	.184	.222	.137	8.64	1.08
2-team total (9 Charleston)					5	1	1.40	28	0	0	3	51	39	13	8	1	6	56	.209	.222	.137	9.82	1.05
Garcia, Hector	L-L	6-0	170	10-4-95	1	0	1.93	5	0	0	0	9	9	3	2	0	1	11	.257	.333	.241	10.61	0.96
German, Angel	R-R	6-4	185	5-25-96	0	0	1.80	9	0	0	1	10	9	2	2	0	8	9	.237	.191	.294	8.10	7.20
Hartlieb, Geoff	R-R	6-6	210	12-9-93	1	2	0.83	20	0	0	6	33	22	7	3	1	6	26	.191	.267	.109	7.16	1.65
Jess, Jordan	L-L	6-3	240	1-29-93	0	4	2.92	30	0	0	2	49	45	23	16	4	11	59	.242	.200	.265	10.76	2.01
Kemp, Shane	R-R	6-3	180	7-12-94	0	0	6.75	2	0	0	0	5	5	5	4	1	3	4	.294	.375	.222	6.75	5.06
Marvel, James	R-R	6-4	210	9-17-93	6	8	3.99	20	20	0	0	95	92	52	42	10	29	75	.254	.258	.251	7.13	2.76
Mazzoccoli, Pasquale	B-R	6-5	200	3-28-92	3	1	1.75	14	0	0	1	26	12	6	5	1	7	22	.143	.122	.163	7.71	2.45
Meyer, Stephan	R-R	6-4	190	5-11-94	3	1	2.84	6	6	1	0	38	31	14	12	2	16	26	.231	.268	.191	6.16	3.79
Nunez, Oddy	L-L	6-8	230	12-20-96	5	8	3.71	25	24	0	0	114	102	55	47	9	32	94	.239	.160	.272	7.42	2.53
Potter, Andrew	R-R	6-0	210	2-9-94	1	1	5.87	6	0	0	0	8	5	7	5	1	7	5	.179	.100	.222	5.87	8.22
Prohoroff, Dylan	R-R	6-3	215	11-29-94	2	2	4.76	40	0	0	4	59	57	35	31	5	25	65	.257	.226	.283	9.97	3.84
Vera, Eduardo	R-R	6-2	185	7-3-94	8	7	3.33	27	19	3	3	132	133	54	49	13	14	109	.258	.287	.233	7.41	0.95
Vieaux, Cam	L-L	6-4	200	12-5-93	2	3	2.73	11	11	0	0	63	61	20	19	1	13	33	.272	.300	.257	4.74	1.87
Wallace, Mike	R-R	6-5	180	5-21-94	5	6	3.47	26	10	1	1	99	89	46	38	9	27	77	.241	.246	.237	7.02	2.46

Fielding

Catcher	PCT	G	PO	A	E	DP	PB
Gibbs	.992	31	223	36	2	2	4
Gonzalez	.974	30	233	25	7	1	5
Harvey	.992	14	107	14	1	1	4
Hernandez	1.000	5	24	3	0	0	1
Pabst	.989	60	470	73	6	3	4

First Base	PCT	G	PO	A	E	DP
Baur	.994	92	748	67	5	62
Mahala	1.000	4	25	1	0	6
Munoz	.998	41	382	27	1	23

Second Base	PCT	G	PO	A	E	DP
Alemais	1.000	1	4	4	0	0
Arbet	.970	61	86	171	8	36
King	1.000	2	2	5	0	1
Mahala	.975	63	92	141	6	24
Ratledge	1.000	4	5	9	0	1
Valerio	1.000	2	3	6	0	0
Walker	.976	11	17	24	1	1

PITTSBURGH PIRATES

Third Base	PCT	G	PO	A	E	DP
Arbet	.922	24	11	36	4	0
Cruz	.840	15	8	34	8	1
King	1.000	3	3	5	0	0
Mahala	.909	7	2	8	1	1
Owen	.931	82	65	151	16	13
Ratledge	.667	2	1	1	1	1
Walker	.941	10	7	9	1	2

Shortstop	PCT	G	PO	A	E	DP
Alemais	.952	26	40	60	5	16
Cruz	.000	1	0	0	0	0
King	.952	8	7	13	1	3
Mahala	.938	18	14	46	4	9
Ratledge	1.000	4	3	6	0	1
Valerio	.957	79	87	201	13	40
Walker	.833	5	9	11	4	2

Outfield	PCT	G	PO	A	E	DP
Bastardo	.978	43	85	4	2	1
Brown	.969	57	126	1	4	0
Eagan	.991	117	206	8	2	3
Fernandez	.976	49	81	2	2	0
Moore	.981	61	100	4	2	1
Nagle	1.000	46	78	3	0	0
Owen	1.000	1	1	0	0	0
Ratledge	.941	10	16	0	1	0
Santos	.978	38	87	3	2	2

WEST VIRGINIA BLACK BEARS — SHORT SEASON

NEW YORK-PENN LEAGUE

Batting	B-T	HT	WT	DOB	AVG	vLH	vRH	G	AB	R	H	2B	3B	HR	RBI	BB	HBP	SH	SF	SO	SB	CS	SLG	OBP
Barraza, Jose	L-R	6-1	220	7-28-94	.221	.267	.198	38	136	21	30	11	1	2	23	24	2	0	0	48	3	0	.360	.346
Brown, Garrett	L-R	6-0	185	3-3-93	.273	.333	.250	5	11	2	3	0	0	0	2	2	1	0	0	2	2	2	.273	.429
Busby, Dylan	R-R	6-3	190	11-28-95	.188	.204	.180	41	160	20	30	8	0	1	14	11	6	2	0	48	7	4	.256	.266
De La Cruz, Julio	R-R	6-1	190	10-5-95	.200	.167	.222	34	120	9	24	4	1	2	13	11	0	0	1	43	0	2	.300	.265
De La Cruz, Michael	L-L	6-1	165	7-10-96	.200	.211	.196	17	65	6	13	1	0	0	6	6	0	2	0	20	1	3	.215	.268
Delay, Jason	R-R	5-11	185	3-7-95	.063	.000	.100	5	16	3	1	1	0	0	0	0	1	0	0	2	0	0	.125	.118
Diorio, Matt	L-R	6-1	195	7-24-95	.143	.167	.125	4	14	3	2	0	1	0	3	1	1	0	0	3	0	0	.286	.250
Fuentes, Huascar	R-R	6-2	195	6-2-92	.143	.200	.111	6	14	3	2	0	0	0	1	1	2	1	1	2	0	0	.143	.278
Glendinning, Robbie	R-R	6-2	196	10-6-95	.198	.235	.177	29	96	10	19	3	0	0	6	17	4	2	0	41	2	3	.229	.342
Gonzalez, Yoel	R-R	6-1	180	8-1-96	.333	.333	.333	11	39	4	13	4	1	0	8	0	0	2	1	11	0	1	.487	.325
Gray, Tristan	L-R	6-3	185	3-22-96	.269	.274	.267	53	208	28	56	12	6	7	37	19	1	3	3	32	5	7	.486	.329
Hernandez, Raul	R-R	6-0	182	12-20-95	.259	.250	.263	18	58	5	15	2	1	0	3	2	2	0	2	11	1	1	.328	.297
Joe, Connor	R-R	6-0	205	8-16-92	.250	—	.250	3	12	2	3	1	0	0	0	1	0	0	0	4	0	0	.333	.308
King, Nick	R-R	6-0	190	11-12-93	.200	.111	.250	7	25	1	5	0	1	0	3	3	0	0	0	5	0	1	.280	.286
Kramer, Kevin	L-R	6-1	190	10-3-93	.231	.333	.143	3	13	1	3	0	0	0	2	0	1	0	0	2	1	0	.231	.286
Madris, Bligh	L-R	6-2	200	2-28-96	.270	.271	.269	56	226	36	61	13	4	5	31	22	4	3	1	43	2	5	.429	.344
Meadows, Austin	L-L	6-3	200	5-3-95	.238	.333	.167	5	21	2	5	1	0	0	3	3	0	0	0	3	0	0	.286	.333
Nagle, Ryan	L-R	6-1	200	8-7-94	.231	.000	.333	4	13	2	3	1	0	0	1	2	0	0	1	0	0	0	.308	.313
Ngoepe, Gift	R-R	5-8	200	1-18-90	.286	.667	.000	2	7	2	2	0	0	1	1	0	1	0	0	2	0	0	.714	.375
Oliva, Jared	R-R	6-3	187	11-27-95	.266	.297	.253	56	222	30	59	10	7	0	17	17	4	9	2	57	15	4	.374	.327
Owen, Hunter	R-R	6-0	195	9-22-93	.083	.000	.111	3	12	1	1	0	0	1	1	2	0	0	0	6	0	0	.333	.214
Pope, Brett	L-R	6-0	180	5-28-96	.205	.333	.168	39	122	13	25	4	0	0	10	16	0	5	1	21	8	4	.238	.295
Santos, Sandy	R-R	6-3	185	4-20-94	.231	.185	.258	43	147	20	34	6	4	3	19	10	1	1	2	42	3	2	.388	.281
Schwind, Jonathan	R-R	6-0	185	5-30-90	.571	.500	.600	3	7	2	4	2	0	0	0	1	0	0	0	0	0	0	.857	.625
Sharpe, Chris	R-R	6-1	195	6-6-96	.234	.290	.217	39	158	19	37	8	1	3	15	19	4	3	1	49	6	6	.354	.330
Siri, Raul	R-R	5-9	175	10-21-94	.241	.295	.216	55	195	30	47	8	1	3	19	28	3	7	0	50	15	13	.339	.345
Stafford, Deon	R-R	6-0	202	3-17-96	.280	.298	.272	45	182	22	51	11	1	4	28	15	1	1	4	53	3	1	.418	.332
Suchy, Michael	R-R	6-3	228	4-15-93	.200	.500	.000	2	5	0	1	0	0	0	0	3	0	0	0	3	0	1	.200	.500
Tancas, Lucas	R-R	6-2	220	11-12-93	.276	.269	.280	51	199	24	55	9	1	4	19	8	7	2	0	38	3	5	.392	.327
Walker, Andrew	R-R	6-1	169	2-13-94	.171	.273	.133	13	41	3	7	1	0	0	4	7	1	2	0	9	3	1	.195	.306

Pitching	B-T	HT	WT	DOB	W	L	ERA	G	GS	CG	SV	IP	H	R	ER	HR	BB	SO	AVG	vLH	vRH	K/9	BB/9
Bingel, Brandon	R-R	5-10	185	2-2-95	0	2	4.88	17	0	0	0	24	24	14	13	3	7	15	.261	.289	.234	5.63	2.63
Cesar, Joel	R-R	5-11	191	1-26-96	1	1	3.67	22	0	0	7	27	16	12	11	2	18	27	.165	.209	.130	9.00	6.00
Cubilete, Sergio	R-R	6-4	185	3-19-95	3	7	5.12	15	14	0	0	63	74	43	36	1	24	45	.293	.293	.292	6.39	3.41
Economos, Nicholas	R-R	6-6	215	6-27-95	2	2	5.61	19	0	0	0	34	32	23	21	4	14	38	.241	.283	.218	10.16	3.74
Eusebio, Julio	R-R	6-1	202	6-2-92	0	0	0.00	3	0	0	2	4	2	0	0	0	2	5	.154	.333	.000	11.25	4.50
Fernandez, Yoandy	R-R	6-1	190	3-29-88	5	0	2.95	18	0	0	2	37	37	14	12	2	9	53	.262	.302	.231	13.01	2.21
Garcia, Hector	L-L	6-0	170	10-4-95	0	1	6.75	11	0	0	1	12	20	11	9	0	5	6	.357	.379	.333	4.50	3.75
Hightower, Scooter	R-R	6-6	215	10-15-93	4	1	1.94	16	15	0	0	88	77	30	19	3	9	80	.230	.262	.199	8.18	0.92
Keller, Mitch	R-R	6-3	195	4-4-96	0	0	0.00	2	2	0	0	4	2	0	0	0	1	7	.143	.167	.125	15.75	2.25
Kemp, Shane	R-R	6-3	180	7-12-94	3	2	3.68	14	0	0	0	22	26	9	9	1	4	22	.292	.214	.362	9.00	1.64
Mazzoccoli, Pasquale	B-R	6-5	200	3-28-92	0	0	0.00	5	0	0	0	9	2	0	0	0	1	13	.067	.111	.000	13.00	1.00
McDonald, Chris	R-R	6-6	220	10-7-94	0	0	0.00	1	0	0	0	1	2	0	0	0	0	0	.500	.667	.000	0.00	0.00
Meyer, Stephan	R-R	6-4	190	5-11-94	1	1	3.72	8	7	0	0	39	42	19	16	4	9	33	.276	.263	.292	7.68	2.09
Oller, Adam	R-R	6-4	225	10-17-94	5	3	1.59	17	2	0	1	45	30	10	8	1	9	50	.188	.177	.198	9.93	1.79
Piechota, Evan	R-R	6-1	225	10-19-93	0	0	0.00	1	0	0	0	1	2	0	0	0	0	0	.400	.500	.333	0.00	0.00
Potter, Andrew	R-R	6-0	210	2-9-94	0	0	3.00	2	0	0	0	3	2	1	1	0	1	5	.182	.000	.333	15.00	3.00
Quinones, Hector	R-R	6-3	227	6-7-94	0	1	4.86	8	0	0	0	17	20	9	9	1	6	12	.299	.281	.314	6.48	3.24
Schlabach, Ike	R-L	6-5	185	12-27-96	6	4	2.83	14	14	1	0	70	53	24	22	5	22	49	.205	.220	.199	6.30	2.83
Seelinger, Matt	R-R	6-0	205	4-19-95	0	1	1.80	20	0	0	4	30	17	7	6	1	9	37	.168	.205	.140	11.10	2.70
Sulser, Beau	R-R	6-2	195	5-5-94	2	4	5.31	18	6	0	1	41	54	26	24	4	7	33	.309	.279	.333	7.30	1.55
Waddell, Brandon	L-L	6-3	180	6-3-94	1	0	1.00	2	2	0	0	9	5	1	1	1	3	11	.167	.200	.150	11.00	3.00
Wallace, Gavin	R-R	6-5	210	11-14-95	3	2	2.65	15	13	0	0	68	60	26	20	0	5	41	.229	.242	.217	5.43	0.66
Weiman, Blake	R-L	6-4	208	11-5-95	4	3	3.78	21	0	0	1	33	36	15	14	2	4	35	.273	.225	.301	9.45	1.08

Fielding

C: Barraza 4, Delay 5, Gonzalez 11, Hernandez 18, Stafford 39. **1B:** Barraza 28, De La Cruz 10, De La Cruz 1, Fuentes 5, Joe 1, Tancas 32. **2B:** Gray 26, King 1, Kramer 2, Pope 7, Siri 40, Walker 1. **3B:** Busby 37, De La Cruz 21, Glendinning 7, King 3, Owen 2, Siri 5, Walker 1. **SS:** Glendinning 15, Gray 18, King 2, Ngoepe 2, Pope 28, Walker 11. **OF:** Brown 5, De La Cruz 16, Diorio 2, Joe 2, Madris 46, Meadows 5, Nagle 2, Oliva 53, Santos 43, Schwind 3, Sharpe 38, Suchy 2, Tancas 15.

BRISTOL PIRATES — ROOKIE

APPALACHIAN LEAGUE

Batting	B-T	HT	WT	DOB	AVG	vLH	vRH	G	AB	R	H	2B	3B	HR	RBI	BB	HBP	SH	SF	SO	SB	CS	SLG	OBP
Bengtson, Ben	R-R	6-0	205	7-28-95	.257	.250	.260	40	140	22	36	5	1	4	19	20	8	0	0	49	2	2	.393	.381
Benitez, Luis	R-R	5-10	165	8-12-93	.224	.091	.277	30	116	14	26	4	1	0	10	2	3	0	0	28	14	6	.276	.256
Brands, Paul	R-R	6-1	185	5-13-97	.220	.182	.235	32	118	18	26	7	1	3	15	16	0	0	1	49	1	0	.373	.311
Contreras, Yondry	R-R	5-11	180	9-11-97	.229	.250	.221	48	188	27	43	7	1	2	16	18	3	7	1	81	5	1	.309	.305
De Jesus, Johan	B-R	6-0	165	8-1-96	.214	.341	.171	47	173	18	37	9	4	2	26	20	0	0	2	55	3	3	.347	.292
Delay, Jason	R-R	5-11	185	3-7-95	.252	.308	.235	29	107	13	27	5	0	1	12	13	8	0	0	13	0	0	.327	.375
Diorio, Matt	L-R	6-1	195	7-24-95	.265	.069	.318	41	136	23	36	12	0	3	22	26	3	0	1	31	3	2	.419	.392
Fuentes, Huascar	R-R	6-2	195	6-2-92	.256	.171	.284	36	137	20	35	13	0	0	16	7	6	0	1	31	1	2	.350	.318
Granberry, Mikell	R-R	6-1	190	8-19-95	.250	—	.250	1	4	1	1	1	0	0	1	0	0	0	0	2	0	0	.500	.250
Hernandez, Raul	R-R	6-0	182	12-20-95	.192	.333	.174	6	26	3	5	1	1	0	6	0	0	0	1	4	0	0	.308	.185
Herrera, Jhoan	L-R	6-1	185	6-14-95	.353	.000	.546	4	17	2	6	2	0	1	3	3	0	0	0	5	0	1	.647	.450
Jimenez, Melvin	B-R	5-10	170	9-9-95	.280	.143	.320	43	157	21	44	2	1	0	20	24	0	1	3	15	6	2	.306	.370
Jorge, Nelson	R-R	5-11	175	12-14-95	.250	.179	.281	30	92	12	23	6	1	2	12	13	5	0	0	33	4	4	.402	.373
Lantigua, Edison	L-L	6-0	175	1-9-97	.307	.262	.321	48	176	28	54	14	2	4	18	30	1	0	0	62	8	2	.477	.411
Ngoepe, Victor	R-R	5-8	150	2-9-98	.000	—	.000	1	3	1	0	0	0	0	0	1	0	0	0	2	0	0	.000	.250
Perez, Luis	L-R	5-10	170	1-18-94	.216	.177	.222	38	116	12	25	5	1	0	12	20	4	2	3	25	7	5	.276	.343
Peurifoy, Ryan	R-R	6-2	206	3-26-95	.305	.344	.293	36	131	16	40	10	0	2	23	9	2	2	2	31	3	0	.428	.354
Rosario, Henrry	L-L	5-9	180	4-5-93	.327	.231	.357	33	110	21	36	7	2	5	22	13	2	1	2	27	5	2	.564	.402
Valaika, Nick	R-R	5-11	185	12-7-95	.151	.146	.153	34	126	9	19	3	0	1	11	10	0	1	2	42	1	2	.198	.210
Vinicio, Felix	L-L	5-10	175	10-28-94	.429	.500	.400	2	7	0	3	2	0	0	0	2	0	0	0	3	0	1	.714	.556
Watson, Kyle	R-R	6-3	195	1-14-96	.224	.207	.229	40	134	22	30	7	1	1	14	21	3	1	2	56	5	2	.313	.338

Pitching	B-T	HT	WT	DOB	W	L	ERA	G	GS	CG	SV	IP	H	R	ER	HR	BB	SO	AVG	vLH	vRH	K/9	BB/9
Delgado, Jose	R-R	6-3	195	12-19-94	0	0	0.00	1	0	0	0	1	0	2	0	0	2	1	.000	.000	.000	9.00	18.00
Fischer, Drew	R-R	6-3	205	6-3-96	3	1	5.00	17	0	0	1	27	28	19	15	3	20	31	.267	.310	.238	10.33	6.67
Hernandez, Dany	R-R	6-5	215	6-9-91	0	2	14.85	6	0	0	0	7	13	15	11	0	4	5	.406	.417	.400	6.75	5.40
Hernandez, Miguel	R-R	6-5	175	11-3-95	1	4	10.13	20	0	0	1	24	32	34	27	5	19	17	.323	.395	.279	6.38	7.13
Kranick, Max	R-R	6-3	175	7-21-97	1	0	2.31	2	2	0	0	12	10	4	3	1	2	9	.233	.200	.242	6.94	1.54
MacGregor, Travis	R-R	6-3	180	10-15-97	1	4	7.84	12	12	0	0	41	61	41	36	3	20	32	.339	.392	.297	6.97	4.35
Manasa, Alex	L-R	6-4	195	1-6-98	2	1	3.76	17	1	0	1	38	46	21	16	6	7	35	.295	.309	.287	8.22	1.64
McDonald, Chris	R-R	6-6	220	10-7-94	0	2	3.79	16	0	0	0	38	42	24	16	0	20	30	.286	.278	.290	7.11	4.74
Muhl, Eddie	R-R	6-4	224	6-20-95	0	2	2.13	18	0	0	1	25	29	13	6	2	6	12	.279	.400	.203	4.26	2.13
Ogle, Braeden	L-L	6-2	170	7-30-97	2	3	3.14	10	10	0	0	43	40	17	15	1	16	35	.242	.250	.241	7.33	3.35
Pichardo, Adonis	R-R	6-3	195	4-9-96	1	2	9.58	7	0	0	0	10	13	15	11	2	7	8	.296	.286	.300	6.97	6.10
Piechota, Evan	R-R	6-1	225	10-19-93	1	2	2.95	16	7	0	1	58	58	22	19	5	6	51	.260	.217	.286	7.91	
0.93 Quinones, Hector	R-R	6-3	227	6-7-94	0	1	7.11	3	0	0	0	6	6	5	5	2	0	5	.261	.182	.333	7.11	0.00
Reed, Will	R-R	6-2	190	11-3-95	0	0	9.00	1	0	0	0	2	4	2	2	0	1	1	.500	1.000	.429	4.50	4.50
Robles, Domingo	L-L	6-2	170	4-29-98	4	8	4.83	14	14	0	0	69	75	49	37	5	16	51	.265	.229	.277	6.65	2.09
Romano, Argenis	R-R	6-1	190	6-16-95	1	6	5.90	19	0	0	0	40	50	33	26	5	6	36	.298	.379	.245	8.17	1.36
Sepulveda, Eumir	R-R	6-2	170	2-14-96	0	0	0.00	2	0	0	0	3	3	5	0	0	1	2	.231	.000	.300	6.75	3.38
Sousa, Brian	R-R	6-3	180	8-7-97	0	0	37.80	2	0	0	0	2	8	8	7	0	2	1	.571	.600	.556	5.40	10.80
Stratton, Hunter	R-R	6-4	225	11-17-96	0	2	4.81	12	11	0	0	43	36	26	23	3	32	38	.228	.241	.220	7.95	6.70
Taylor, Jacob	R-R	6-3	205	7-5-95	0	6	8.35	12	9	0	0	37	50	38	34	5	22	25	.329	.404	.284	6.14	5.40
Valdes, Ryan	R-R	5-11	185	8-22-93	0	2	5.19	10	0	0	0	17	14	12	10	5	12	22	.219	.200	.231	11.42	6.23
Ward, Mason	L-L	6-4	170	7-5-95	0	1	3.80	17	0	0	1	24	21	12	10	1	7	25	.236	.207	.250	9.51	2.66

Fielding

C: Brands 32, Delay 28, Granberry 1, Hernandez 6. **1B:** De Jesus 29, Fuentes 20, Herrera 4, Perez 2, Watson 14. **2B:** Jimenez 26, Jorge 10, Perez 6, Valaika 27. **3B:** Bengtson 36, De Jesus 16, Jimenez 8, Jorge 5, Perez 4. **SS:** Jimenez 11, Ngoepe 1, Perez 25, Valaika 6, Watson 25. **OF:** Benitez 26, Contreras 48, Diorio 24, Jorge 5, Lantigua 38, Peurifoy 36, Rosario 25, Vinicio 1.

GCL PIRATES — ROOKIE

GULF COAST LEAGUE

Batting	B-T	HT	WT	DOB	AVG	vLH	vRH	G	AB	R	H	2B	3B	HR	RBI	BB	HBP	SH	SF	SO	SB	CS	SLG	OBP
Alemais, Stephen	R-R	6-0	190	4-12-95	.259	.500	.240	8	27	6	7	3	0	0	2	4	0	0	0	5	0	0	.370	.355
Barnes, Barrett	R-R	5-11	209	7-29-91	.154	.000	.333	4	13	1	2	0	0	0	0	1	0	0	0	2	0	0	.154	.214
Bejerano, Manny	R-R	6-3	185	5-14-97	.188	.267	.171	29	85	10	16	1	0	2	5	9	3	0	0	24	0	0	.271	.289
Brito, Gabriel	R-R	5-9	170	11-3-97	.259	.207	.277	35	112	13	29	6	2	0	16	9	4	0	2	28	0	1	.348	.331
Castro, Rodolfo	B-R	6-0	170	5-21-99	.277	.366	.252	53	188	27	52	12	4	6	32	16	4	2	1	47	4	3	.479	.345
Granberry, Mikell	R-R	6-1	190	8-19-95	.209	.241	.200	40	129	13	27	8	5	0	16	17	3	1	3	31	2	2	.349	.309
Hernandez, Raul	R-R	6-0	182	12-20-95	.000	—	.000	1	2	0	0	0	0	0	0	0	0	0	0	1	0	0	.000	.000
King, Nick	R-R	6-0	190	11-12-93	.193	.174	.206	20	57	9	11	2	0	0	3	11	2	2	1	12	5	0	.228	.338
Kramer, Kevin	L-R	6-1	190	10-3-93	.000	—	.000	1	2	0	0	0	0	0	1	0	0	0	1	1	0	0	.000	.000
Martin, Mason	L-R	6-0	201	6-2-99	.307	.344	.295	39	127	37	39	8	0	11	22	32	4	2	1	41	2	2	.630	.457
Meadows, Austin	L-L	6-3	200	5-3-95	.539	1.000	.455	4	13	3	7	2	1	1	7	1	0	0	0	2	0	0	1.077	.571
Medrano, Jesse	R-R	5-11	200	3-27-95	.259	.316	.231	20	58	8	15	2	2	0	8	5	0	5	1	10	0	0	.362	.313
Mepris, Francisco	B-R	5-11	165	10-10-97	.212	.278	.194	28	85	7	18	3	1	1	7	8	0	2	0	18	5	1	.306	.280
Mitchell, Calvin	L-L	6-0	190	3-8-99	.245	.242	.246	43	159	17	39	11	0	2	20	24	2	0	0	35	2	3	.352	.351
Ngoepe, Victor	R-R	5-8	150	2-9-98	.235	.244	.232	51	179	22	42	4	1	1	16	16	3	3	2	52	5	2	.285	.305
Owen, Hunter	R-R	6-0	195	9-22-93	.300	.200	.400	3	10	4	3	2	0	1	3	1	0	0	0	0	0	0	.800	.364
Perez, Cristopher	R-R	6-1	170	8-7-97	.250	.259	.248	43	140	9	35	5	0	0	10	6	4	2	0	25	1	2	.286	.300

PITTSBURGH PIRATES

Batting	B-T	HT	WT	DOB	AVG	vLH	vRH	G	AB	R	H	2B	3B	HR	RBI	BB	HBP	SH	SF	SO	SB	CS	SLG	OBP
Portorreal, Jeremias	L-L	6-3	195	8-7-97	.263	.217	.278	52	190	23	50	6	5	5	31	21	2	0	0	59	0	3	.426	.343
Sanchez, Lolo	R-R	6-0	150	4-23-99	.284	.309	.275	51	204	42	58	11	2	4	20	21	4	3	2	19	14	7	.417	.359
Uselton, Conner	R-R	6-3	185	5-20-98	.429	—	.429	2	7	0	3	1	0	0	1	0	0	0	0	1	0	0	.571	.429
Vinicio, Felix	L-L	5-10	175	10-28-94	.195	.143	.212	32	113	5	22	5	2	0	10	6	1	1	4	15	1	2	.274	.234
Vizcaino, Eddy	L-L	5-11	165	7-19-96	.233	.182	.245	22	60	4	14	2	1	0	3	10	0	0	0	7	5	2	.300	.343

Pitching	B-T	HT	WT	DOB	W	L	ERA	G	GS	CG	SV	IP	H	R	ER	HR	BB	SO	AVG	vLH	vRH	K/9	BB/9
Baz, Shane	R-R	6-3	190	6-17-99	0	3	3.80	10	10	0	0	24	26	12	10	2	14	19	.289	.344	.259	7.23	5.32
Bolton, Cody	R-R	6-3	185	6-19-98	0	2	3.16	9	9	0	0	26	23	11	9	1	8	22	.240	.333	.183	7.71	2.81
Delgado, Jose	R-R	6-3	195	12-19-94	1	1	12.91	16	0	0	0	15	19	23	22	2	22	14	.322	.400	.296	8.22	12.91
Deyzel, Vince	R-R	6-2	180	2-9-98	1	0	5.46	16	0	0	3	28	22	17	17	1	16	13	.218	.200	.224	4.18	5.14
Garcia, Hector	L-L	6-0	170	10-4-95	0	0	0.00	3	0	0	0	4	0	0	0	0	0	4	.000	.000	.000	9.00	0.00
Garcia, Yeudy	R-R	6-2	203	10-6-92	1	0	0.00	2	0	0	0	3	1	1	0	0	2	4	.100	.000	.143	12.00	6.00
Hearn, Taylor	L-L	6-5	210	8-30-94	0	0	0.00	1	1	0	0	2	0	0	0	0	0	3	.000	—	.000	13.50	0.00
Hernandez, Dany	R-R	6-5	215	6-9-91	1	0	0.00	2	0	0	0	3	1	0	0	0	0	3	.091	.000	.125	8.10	0.00
Jennings, Steven	R-R	6-2	175	11-13-98	0	2	4.10	10	10	0	0	26	31	18	12	2	10	13	.282	.257	.293	4.44	3.42
Kranick, Max	R-R	6-3	175	7-21-97	0	0	0.00	3	3	0	0	13	12	6	0	0	4	9	.255	.375	.194	6.39	2.84
Lee, David	R-R	6-4	195	9-13-95	0	1	5.82	12	0	0	2	17	22	13	11	0	5	15	.306	.238	.333	7.94	2.65
Lopez, Junior	R-R	6-2	165	6-27-91	0	0	19.29	3	0	0	1	2	5	6	5	0	1	4	.385	.333	.400	15.43	3.86
Manzanillo, Yeudry	R-R	6-3	175	12-7-98	3	4	4.11	12	7	0	0	46	59	25	21	3	15	29	.311	.347	.298	5.67	2.93
Pichardo, Adonis	R-R	6-3	195	4-9-96	0	1	4.24	9	0	0	1	23	27	17	11	1	8	9	.300	.300	.300	3.47	3.09
Pina, Leandro	R-R	6-3	174	9-23-98	1	2	4.50	7	5	0	0	28	36	17	14	2	5	23	.305	.371	.277	7.39	1.61
Quinones, Hector	R-R	6-3	227	6-7-94	0	3	3.65	4	1	0	0	12	11	6	5	1	0	2	.239	.308	.212	1.46	0.00
Reyes, Samuel	R-R	5-11	180	3-13-96	1	1	2.65	16	0	0	3	34	30	16	10	2	4	24	.229	.256	.216	6.35	1.06
Santana, Roger	L-L	6-1	168	9-26-97	2	4	4.83	12	9	0	0	41	49	29	22	3	16	31	.293	.185	.314	6.80	3.51
Scotti, Claudio	R-R	6-4	210	7-8-98	1	1	2.70	8	0	0	0	13	12	7	4	1	10	5	.231	.091	.268	3.38	6.75
Sepulveda, Eumir	R-R	6-2	170	2-14-96	1	2	5.33	17	0	0	3	25	20	17	15	3	9	19	.220	.161	.250	6.75	3.20
Shields, Austin	L-R	6-5	220	11-23-97	4	1	4.43	12	4	0	0	41	23	23	20	1	33	22	.163	.125	.174	4.87	7.30
Sousa, Brian	R-R	6-3	180	8-7-97	5	0	3.66	13	0	0	0	39	37	22	16	0	27	26	.250	.242	.252	5.95	6.18
Stoffel, Jason	R-R	6-1	230	9-15-88	0	1	16.88	4	0	0	0	3	3	5	5	0	3	4	.250	.000	.429	13.50	10.13
Valdes, Ryan	R-R	5-11	185	8-22-93	1	0	0.00	5	0	0	1	7	4	0	0	0	2	11	.154	.000	.211	13.50	2.45
Vasquez, Angel	R-R	6-0	185	4-13-94	2	4	9.40	15	1	0	2	30	50	37	31	4	10	22	.376	.353	.384	6.67	3.03
Waddell, Brandon	L-L	6-3	180	6-3-94	1	0	0.00	1	0	0	0	3	1	0	0	0	0	4	.100	.000	.125	12.00	0.00
Webb, Jacob	R-R	6-4	200	6-5-99	0	1	6.43	5	0	0	0	7	8	6	5	1	4	2	.267	.000	.381	2.57	5.14

Fielding

C: Bejerano 25, Brito 31, Granberry 9, Hernandez 1. **1B:** Bejerano 2, Granberry 26, King 1, Martin 26, Perez 10, Sepulveda 1. **2B:** Castro 15, King 8, Kramer 1, Medrano 1, Mepris 12, Ngoepe 15, Perez 16. **3B:** Castro 17, Granberry 3, King 11, Medrano 12, Mepris 15, Owen 3, Perez 11. **SS:** Alemais 8, Castro 19, Medrano 2, Mepris 1, Ngoepe 35. **OF:** Barnes 3, King 3, Martin 13, Meadows 4, Medrano 5, Mitchell 40, Perez 1, Portorreal 41, Sanchez 49, Uselton 1, Vinicio 11, Vizcaino 22.

DSL PIRATES — *ROOKIE*

DOMINICAN SUMMER LEAGUE

Batting	B-T	HT	WT	DOB	AVG	vLH	vRH	G	AB	R	H	2B	3B	HR	RBI	BB	HBP	SH	SF	SO	SB	CS	SLG	OBP
Acuna, Francisco	R-R	5-7	150	1-12-00	.201	.310	.181	58	189	40	38	5	3	2	22	53	5	7	2	41	19	3	.291	.386
Alcime, Larry	R-R	6-2	207	10-15-98	.179	.259	.159	39	140	15	25	4	1	0	15	11	2	2	2	44	1	3	.221	.245
Apostel, Sherten	R-R	6-4	213	3-11-99	.258	.138	.278	61	198	43	51	12	4	9	48	56	2	1	2	49	4	5	.495	.423
Babilonia, Yair	R-R	6-2	215	8-25-97	.259	.250	.261	23	58	8	15	2	0	0	7	5	4	1	0	16	0	0	.293	.358
Calderon, Williams	B-R	6-0	182	12-22-97	.258	.227	.265	44	120	16	31	7	5	0	27	21	4	1	2	32	7	7	.400	.381
Castillo, Pedro	L-L	6-2	170	4-23-00	.205	.250	.198	37	122	13	25	4	1	0	15	17	2	3	2	22	1	1	.254	.308
Eusebio, Jean	L-R	6-1	170	8-22-00	.191	.194	.191	50	178	26	34	7	2	0	10	35	2	2	0	42	13	2	.253	.330
Garcia, Carlos	L-L	5-10	180	4-7-99	.208	.214	.207	38	101	19	21	3	2	3	15	22	5	1	1	28	6	6	.366	.372
Gonzalez, Ruben	R-R	5-8	191	9-13-97	.207	.053	.239	41	111	12	23	4	0	0	15	9	3	1	0	33	1	0	.243	.285
Inoa, Samuel	R-R	5-10	211	10-6-98	.316	.450	.289	34	117	28	37	10	2	2	18	21	7	0	5	21	1	3	.487	.433
Lantigua, John	L-R	6-1	170	8-26-97	.214	.091	.233	28	84	18	18	0	0	0	7	14	2	3	2	12	7	4	.214	.333
Mercedes, Matthew	R-R	6-1	195	8-26-98	.237	.148	.264	39	118	12	28	7	0	0	11	10	5	1	0	18	0	3	.297	.323
Paulino, Ronaldo	R-R	6-4	223	9-30-98	.222	.136	.233	56	185	30	41	12	0	3	24	26	4	1	4	80	2	3	.335	.324
Rodriguez, Rayvi	L-L	5-11	142	4-16-98	.154	.267	.127	39	78	22	12	0	2	0	6	12	5	0	0	17	7	1	.205	.305
Rosario, Ivan	R-R	6-2	155	11-9-98	.113	.000	.133	26	53	8	6	0	0	0	4	12	0	0	0	16	2	2	.113	.277
Simmons, Kyle	R-R	5-11	181	12-12-96	.207	.222	.204	53	164	32	34	4	0	0	18	42	14	1	3	49	12	9	.232	.404
Soto, Emison	R-L	5-7	167	4-1-96	.268	.200	.282	54	142	29	38	6	1	1	22	36	10	2	4	13	14	11	.345	.438

Pitching	B-T	HT	WT	DOB	W	L	ERA	G	GS	CG	SV	IP	H	R	ER	HR	BB	SO	AVG	vLH	vRH	K/9	BB/9
Arrieta, Luis	R-R	6-2	180	6-21-99	2	1	2.56	14	4	0	0	53	38	21	15	1	17	35	.202	.254	.176	5.98	2.91
Bido, Osvaldo	R-R	6-3	175	10-18-95	1	8	5.33	15	13	0	0	51	53	37	30	1	36	41	.270	.191	.313	7.28	6.39
Contreras, Wilmer	R-R	6-4	213	2-5-98	6	1	3.18	20	0	0	3	34	22	16	12	0	14	23	.193	.209	.183	6.09	3.71
De La Cruz, Saul	R-R	6-4	174	10-26-97	1	0	3.50	16	1	0	0	36	29	26	14	1	22	35	.209	.286	.157	8.75	5.50
De Los Santos, Yerry	R-R	6-2	160	12-12-97	1	0	1.04	5	0	0	0	9	7	3	1	0	3	4	.226	.231	.222	4.15	3.12
Del Orbe, Francis	R-R	6-4	173	10-9-98	3	2	2.43	19	0	0	3	30	30	19	8	2	12	33	.242	.205	.259	10.01	3.64
Diaz, Luis	L-L	6-2	190	6-25-97	0	0	38.57	4	0	0	0	2	6	10	10	0	8	2	.462	1.000	.417	7.71	30.86
Florez, Santiago	R-R	6-5	222	5-9-00	2	5	4.56	14	14	0	0	53	43	38	27	2	38	30	.222	.206	.231	5.06	6.41
Garcia, Oliver	R-R	6-3	213	1-8-98	2	2	2.15	11	11	0	0	54	44	17	13	0	16	46	.225	.189	.246	7.62	2.65
Gonzalez, Julio	R-R	6-2	215	5-10-95	2	0	1.86	14	0	0	1	19	15	8	4	0	4	18	.203	.200	.204	8.38	1.86
Jimenez, Randy	L-L	6-2	200	6-21-98	2	2	8.59	16	0	0	1	22	20	23	21	1	24	27	.247	.143	.283	11.05	9.82
Machado, Kleiner	R-R	5-10	169	3-8-99	2	2	3.12	20	0	0	3	35	31	25	12	3	16	27	.231	.271	.209	7.01	4.15

Marcano, Jose	L-L	6-2	193	3-10-99	2	2	3.69	14	11	0	0	63	58	31	26	3	16	48	.239	.283	.226	6.82	2.27
Martinez, Angel	L-L	6-3	198	11-14-96	0	0	0.00	4	0	0	0	4	0	1	0	0	2	3	.000	.000	.000	7.36	4.91
Reyes, Samuel	R-R	5-11	180	3-13-96	2	1	4.66	5	0	0	1	10	13	6	5	0	1	10	.382	.467	.316	9.31	0.93
Rosario, Julio	R-R	6-2	194	6-5-99	1	2	9.25	15	2	0	0	24	27	29	25	2	26	16	.276	.231	.305	5.92	9.62
Santana, Pablo	R-R	6-1	186	2-28-99	5	2	3.60	15	1	0	1	40	30	20	16	2	16	32	.201	.103	.264	7.20	3.60
Toribio, Noe	R-R	6-2	194	8-25-99	2	2	4.13	13	13	1	0	57	63	39	26	7	26	49	.273	.306	.248	7.78	4.13
Vasquez, Angel	R-R	6-0	185	4-13-94	0	2	5.14	5	0	0	1	7	10	8	4	0	4	8	.345	.222	.400	10.29	5.14

Fielding

C: Babilonia 19, Gonzalez 1, Gonzalez 38, Inoa 26. **1B:** Calderon 10, Mercedes 27, Paulino 47, Soto 1. **2B:** Calderon 16, Mercedes 1, Rosario 19, Simmons 45. **3B:** Apostel 59, Calderon 6, Paulino 6, Simmons 2. **SS:** Acuna 56, Calderon 10, Rosario 3, Simmons 6. **OF:** Alcime 32, Calderon 1, Castillo 34, Eusebio 48, Garcia 33, Garcia 1, Lantigua 20, Rodriguez 27, Soto 38.

St. Louis Cardinals

SEASON IN A SENTENCE: A 33-40 start sunk the Cardinals early as injuries and poor veteran performances racked the team, and a late surge wasn't enough to prevent them from missing the postseason for the second straight year.

HIGH POINT: With their season heading toward disaster, the Cardinals won 10 of 12 from Aug. 31 through Sept. 12, vaulting into second place in the NL Central and into the thick of the playoff race.

LOW POINT: Just two games back of a wild-card spot on the morning of Sept. 23, the Cardinals dropped three straight and six of their next seven. The ultimate indignity was they were officially eliminated by the rival Cubs, dropping a 2-1, 11-inning decision at home.

NOTABLE ROOKIES: Paul DeJong made his debut May 28, seized the starting shortstop job and ultimately led the team with 24 home runs. First baseman Jose Martinez, 28, emerged as the Cardinals' most reliable bench player with a .309/.379/.518 slash line and 14 home runs. Righthander Luke Weaver ensconced himself in the rotation moving forward by going 7-2, 3.88 after his July callup. Rightander John Brebbia did the same in the bullpen after posting a 2.44 ERA in 50 appearances. Outfielders Harrison Bader and Magneuris Sierra and righthanders Jack Flaherty and Sandy Alcantara were top prospects who all made their MLB debuts during the year.

KEY TRANSACTIONS: In an effort to shore up center field for the long-term, the Cardinals signed Dexter Fowler to a five-year, $82.5 million deal before the season. Fowler was limited to 118 games by injury but still posted an .851 OPS. The Matt Adams era came to an end when they Cardinals sent him to the Braves for minor league infielder Juan Yepez in May, and the Cardinals swung a pair of notable trades with the Mariners during the summer. They first acquired slugging outfield prospect Tyler O'Neill in exchange for lefthander Marco Gonzales in July, and cleared some payroll by sending out struggling righthander Mike Leake for minor league shortstop Rayder Ascanio in an August waiver trade.

DOWN OF THE FARM: Triple-A Memphis won 91 games and the Pacific Coast League title with contributions from Weaver, Flaherty, Bader and others who later made their MLB debuts. High Class A Palm Beach shared the Florida State League title after the league championship series was washed out by Hurricane Irma.

OPENING DAY PAYROLL: $151,680,000 (14th)

PLAYERS OF THE YEAR

MAJOR LEAGUE

Tommy Pham
OF

.306/.411/.520
23 HR, 25 SB
3rd in NL in OBP

MINOR LEAGUE

Jack Flaherty
RHP

(Double-A/Triple-A)
14-4, 2.18
1.04 WHIP, 8.8 SO/9

ORGANIZATION LEADERS

BATTING			***Minimum 250 AB**
MAJORS			
*	AVG	Jose Martinez	.309
*	OPS	Tommy Pham	.931
	HR	Paul DeJong	25
	RBI	Yadier Molina	82
MINORS			
*	AVG	Luke Voit, Memphis	.327
*	OBP	Luke Voit, Memphis	.407
*	SLG	Luke Voit, Memphis	.565
*	OPS	Luke Voit, Memphis	.972
	R	Oscar Mercado, Springfield	76
	H	Oscar Mercado, Springfield	137
	TB	Patrick Wisdom, Memphis	231
	2B	Jose Adolis Garcia, Springfield, Memphis	34
	3B	Darren Seferina, Palm Beach, Springfield	10
	HR	Patrick Wisdom, Memphis	31
	RBI	Patrick Wisdom, Memphis	89
	BB	Nick Martini, Springfield, Memphis	66
	SO	Patrick Wisdom, Memphis	149
	SB	Oscar Mercado, Springfield	38

PITCHING			**#Minimum 75 IP**
MAJORS			
	W	Carlos Martinez	12
		Michael Wacha	12
		Adam Wainwright	12
#	ERA	Lance Lynn	3.43
	SO	Carlos Martinez	217
	SV	Seung Hwan Oh	20
MINORS			
	W	Matt Pearce, Springfield, Memphis	14
		Jack Flaherty, Springfield, Memphis	14
	L	Chris Ellis, Memphis, Springfield	12
#	ERA	Jack Flaherty, Springfield, Memphis	2.18
	G	Landon Beck, Palm Beach, Springfield	50
	GS	Matt Pearce, Springfield, Memphis	27
	SV	Josh Lucas, Memphis	17
	IP	Matt Pearce, Springfield, Memphis	164
	BB	Sandy Alcantara, Springfield	54
	SO	Jack Flaherty, Springfield, Memphis	147
#	AVG	Ryan Helsley, Palm Beach, Springfield, Memphis	.215

2017 PERFORMANCE

General Manager: John Mozeliak. **Farm Director:** Gary LaRocque. **Scouting Director:** Randy Flores.

Class	Team	League	W	L	PCT	Finish	Manager
Majors	St. Louis Cardinals	National	83	79	.512	7th (15)	Mike Matheny
Triple-A	Memphis Redbirds	Pacific Coast	91	50	.645	1st (16)	Stubby Clapp
Double-A	Springfield Cardinals	Texas	77	63	.550	t-2nd (8)	Johnny Rodriguez
High-A	Palm Beach Cardinals	Florida State	74	60	.552	3rd (12)	Dann Bilardello
Low-A	Peoria Chiefs	Midwest	69	70	.496	t-8th (16)	Chris Swauger
Short Season	State College Spikes	New York-Penn	40	35	.533	t-6th (14)	Joe Kruzel
Rookie	Johnson City Cardinals	Appalachian	33	34	.493	t-5th (10)	Roberto Espinoza
Rookie	GCL Cardinals	Gulf Coast	26	29	.473	11th (17)	S. Turco/E. Almonte
Overall 2017 Minor League Record			410	341	.546	t-3rd (30)	

ORGANIZATION STATISTICS

ST. LOUIS CARDINALS

NATIONAL LEAGUE

Batting	B-T	HT	WT	DOB	AVG	vLH	vRH	G	AB	R	H	2B	3B	HR	RBI	BB	HBP	SH	SF	SO	SB	CS	SLG	OBP
Adams, Matt	L-R	6-3	260	8-31-88	.292	.000	.311	31	48	4	14	2	0	1	7	4	0	0	1	17	0	0	.396	.340
2-team total (100 Atlanta)					.274	.000	.311	131	339	46	93	22	1	20	65	23	1	0	4	88	0	0	.522	.319
Bader, Harrison	R-R	6-0	195	6-3-94	.235	.400	.185	32	85	10	20	3	0	3	10	5	1	0	1	24	2	1	.377	.283
Carpenter, Matt	L-R	6-3	205	11-26-85	.241	.202	.253	145	497	91	120	31	2	23	69	109	9	2	5	125	2	1	.451	.384
DeJong, Paul	R-R	6-1	195	8-2-93	.285	.288	.285	108	417	55	119	26	1	25	65	21	4	0	1	124	1	0	.532	.325
Diaz, Aledmys	R-R	6-1	195	8-1-90	.259	.236	.264	79	286	31	74	17	0	7	20	13	0	1	1	42	4	1	.392	.290
Fowler, Dexter	B-R	6-5	195	3-22-86	.264	.252	.268	118	420	68	111	22	9	18	64	63	4	0	4	101	7	3	.488	.363
Fryer, Eric	R-R	6-2	215	8-26-85	.155	.000	.180	34	71	7	11	3	0	0	3	11	1	0	0	18	0	0	.197	.277
Garcia, Greg	L-R	6-0	190	8-8-89	.253	.086	.282	133	241	27	61	9	2	2	20	37	6	5	1	64	2	1	.332	.365
Grichuk, Randal	R-R	6-1	205	8-13-91	.238	.204	.248	122	412	53	98	25	3	22	59	26	2	0	2	133	6	1	.473	.285
Gyorko, Jedd	R-R	5-10	215	9-23-88	.272	.327	.255	125	426	52	116	21	2	20	67	47	1	0	7	105	6	2	.472	.341
Huffman, Chad	R-R	6-1	215	4-29-85	.286	.333	.250	12	14	3	4	0	1	0	0	1	0	0	0	6	0	0	.429	.333
Kelly, Carson	R-R	6-2	220	7-14-94	.174	.100	.186	34	69	5	12	3	0	0	6	5	1	0	0	11	0	0	.217	.240
Martinez, Jose	R-R	6-6	215	7-25-88	.309	.407	.282	106	272	47	84	13	1	14	46	32	0	1	2	60	4	0	.518	.379
Mejia, Alex	R-R	6-1	200	1-18-91	.109	.200	.065	29	46	6	5	0	0	1	3	2	0	1	0	13	0	0	.174	.146
Molina, Yadier	R-R	5-11	205	7-13-82	.274	.266	.276	136	501	60	137	27	1	18	82	28	4	1	9	74	9	4	.439	.312
Peralta, Jhonny	R-R	6-2	225	5-28-82	.204	.125	.267	21	54	3	11	0	0	0	0	4	0	0	0	13	0	0	.204	.259
Pham, Tommy	R-R	6-1	210	3-8-88	.306	.292	.310	128	444	95	136	22	2	23	73	71	10	2	3	117	25	7	.520	.411
Piscotty, Stephen	R-R	6-3	210	1-14-91	.235	.234	.235	107	341	40	80	16	1	9	39	52	5	0	3	87	3	6	.367	.342
Rosario, Alberto	R-R	5-10	190	1-10-87	.000	—	.000	3	3	0	0	0	0	0	0	0	0	0	0	1	0	0	.000	.000
Sierra, Magneuris	L-L	5-11	160	4-7-96	.317	.462	.277	22	60	10	19	0	0	0	5	4	0	0	0	14	2	2	.317	.359
Valera, Breyvic	B-R	5-11	160	1-8-92	.100	.000	.111	5	10	0	1	0	0	0	0	1	0	0	0	0	0	0	.100	.182
Voit, Luke	R-R	6-3	225	2-13-91	.246	.258	.241	62	114	18	28	9	0	4	18	7	3	0	0	31	0	0	.430	.307
Wong, Kolten	L-R	5-9	185	10-10-90	.285	.274	.288	108	354	55	101	27	3	4	42	41	12	1	3	60	8	2	.412	.376

Pitching	B-T	HT	WT	DOB	W	L	ERA	G	GS	CG	SV	IP	H	R	ER	HR	BB	SO	AVG	vLH	vRH	K/9	BB/9
Alcantara, Sandy	R-R	6-4	170	9-7-95	0	0	4.32	8	0	0	0	8	9	6	4	2	6	10	.273	.333	.200	10.80	6.48
Bowman, Matt	R-R	6-0	175	5-31-91	3	6	3.99	75	0	0	2	59	52	29	26	4	18	46	.239	.242	.236	7.06	2.76
Brebbia, John	L-R	6-1	185	5-30-90	0	0	2.44	50	0	0	0	52	37	15	14	8	11	51	.193	.208	.183	8.88	1.92
Broxton, Jonathan	R-R	6-4	285	6-16-84	0	1	6.89	20	0	0	0	16	23	12	12	2	11	16	.371	.524	.293	9.19	6.32
Cecil, Brett	R-L	6-3	235	7-2-86	2	4	3.88	73	0	0	1	67	67	31	29	7	16	66	.262	.343	.208	8.82	2.14
Duke, Zach	L-L	6-2	210	4-19-83	1	1	3.93	27	0	0	0	18	13	8	8	3	6	12	.197	.231	.148	5.89	2.95
Flaherty, Jack	R-R	6-4	205	10-15-95	0	2	6.33	6	5	0	0	21	23	15	15	4	10	20	.284	.342	.225	8.44	4.22
Gant, John	R-R	6-3	200	8-6-92	0	1	4.67	7	2	0	0	17	17	9	9	4	10	11	.266	.259	.270	5.71	5.19
Gonzales, Marco	L-L	6-1	195	2-16-92	0	0	13.50	1	1	0	0	3	6	5	5	3	0	2	.375	.500	.357	5.40	0.00
Leake, Mike	R-R	5-10	170	11-12-87	7	12	4.21	26	26	0	0	154	169	83	72	19	35	103	.282	.297	.267	6.02	2.05
Lucas, Josh	R-R	6-6	185	11-5-90	0	0	3.68	5	0	0	0	7	7	3	3	2	4	7	.259	.333	.222	8.59	4.91
Lynn, Lance	R-R	6-5	280	5-12-87	11	8	3.43	33	33	0	0	186	151	80	71	27	78	153	.223	.245	.203	7.39	3.77
Lyons, Tyler	L-L	6-4	210	2-21-88	4	1	2.83	50	0	0	3	54	39	17	17	3	20	68	.206	.178	.224	11.33	3.33
Martinez, Carlos	R-R	6-0	190	9-21-91	12	11	3.64	32	32	2	0	205	179	93	83	27	71	217	.232	.262	.204	9.53	3.12
Mayers, Mike	R-R	6-3	200	12-6-91	0	0	11.57	3	0	0	0	5	8	8	6	2	4	3	.421	.500	.333	5.79	7.71
Nicasio, Juan	R-R	6-4	252	8-31-86	2	0	1.64	9	0	0	4	11	9	2	2	1	2	11	.214	.250	.182	9.00	1.64
3-team total (2 Philadelphia, 65 Pittsburgh)					5	5	2.61	76	0	0	6	72	58	22	21	5	20	72	.217	.202	.238	8.96	2.49
Oh, Seung Hwan	R-R	5-10	205	7-15-82	1	6	4.10	62	0	0	20	59	68	31	27	10	15	54	.285	.333	.250	8.19	2.28
Rosenthal, Trevor	R-R	6-2	230	5-29-90	3	4	3.40	50	0	0	11	48	37	20	18	3	20	76	.210	.225	.195	14.35	3.78
Sherriff, Ryan	L-L	6-1	185	5-25-90	2	1	3.14	13	0	0	0	14	13	5	5	2	4	15	.236	.080	.367	9.42	2.51
Siegrist, Kevin	L-L	6-5	230	7-20-89	1	1	4.98	39	0	0	1	34	35	19	19	4	20	36	.271	.240	.291	9.44	5.24
2-team total (7 Philadelphia)					1	1	4.81	46	0	0	1	39	39	21	21	5	22	43	.264	.240	.291	9.84	5.03
Socolovich, Miguel	R-R	6-1	205	7-24-86	0	1	8.68	15	0	0	1	19	27	20	18	4	4	14	.338	.406	.292	6.75	1.93
Tuivailala, Sam	R-R	6-3	225	10-19-92	3	3	2.55	37	0	0	0	42	35	12	12	4	11	34	.223	.222	.223	7.23	2.34
Wacha, Michael	R-R	6-6	215	7-1-91	12	9	4.13	30	30	1	0	166	170	82	76	17	55	158	.267	.252	.280	8.58	2.99
Wainwright, Adam	R-R	6-7	235	8-30-81	12	5	5.11	24	23	0	0	123	140	73	70	14	45	96	.286	.289	.282	7.01	3.28
Weaver, Luke	R-R	6-2	170	8-21-93	7	2	3.88	13	10	0	0	60	59	27	26	7	17	72	.254	.210	.288	10.74	2.54

Fielding

Catcher	PCT	G	PO	A	E	DP	PB
Fryer	1.000	26	141	5	0	1	1
Kelly	.994	31	150	8	1	0	0
Molina	.994	133	1082	55	7	13	6

First Base	PCT	G	PO	A	E	DP
Adams	1.000	3	11	3	0	1
Carpenter	.993	120	895	74	7	103
Gyorko	.975	10	33	6	1	2
Martinez	.992	33	232	16	2	28
Mejia	1.000	1	1	0	0	0
Molina	1.000	1	4	0	0	0
Voit	1.000	31	154	15	0	15

Second Base	PCT	G	PO	A	E	DP
Carpenter	.922	13	15	32	4	9
DeJong	.965	20	30	53	3	15
Diaz	1.000	1	2	2	0	1
Garcia	.978	34	60	73	3	20
Gyorko	1.000	5	5	15	0	3
Mejia	1.000	7	2	8	0	2
Valera	1.000	3	2	3	0	1
Wong	.979	106	191	276	10	78

Third Base	PCT	G	PO	A	E	DP
Carpenter	.939	16	5	26	2	5
Diaz	1.000	4	2	3	0	1
Garcia	.971	41	14	52	2	3
Gyorko	.967	109	53	212	9	27
Mejia	.950	13	4	15	1	4
Peralta	.941	15	11	21	2	1

Shortstop	PCT	G	PO	A	E	DP
DeJong	.975	86	111	233	9	56
Diaz	.974	68	81	147	6	41
Garcia	.968	12	9	21	1	7
Mejia	1.000	7	6	12	0	6

Outfield	PCT	G	PO	A	E	DP
Adams	1.000	6	7	0	0	0
Bader	.962	27	49	1	2	0
Diaz	1.000	3	2	0	0	0
Fowler	.996	109	222	5	1	1
Grichuk	.985	107	193	4	3	1
Gyorko	1.000	1	2	0	0	0
Huffman	1.000	1	2	0	0	0
Martinez	.982	40	54	0	1	0
Pham	.996	119	220	8	1	1
Piscotty	.988	99	162	5	2	0
Sierra	.909	17	30	0	3	0

MEMPHIS REDBIRDS — *TRIPLE-A*

PACIFIC COAST LEAGUE

Batting	B-T	HT	WT	DOB	AVG	vLH	vRH	G	AB	R	H	2B	3B	HR	RBI	BB	HBP	SH	SF	SO	SB	CS	SLG	OBP
Bader, Harrison	R-R	6-0	195	6-3-94	.283	.389	.255	123	431	74	122	18	1	20	55	34	10	1	3	118	15	9	.469	.347
Caldwell, Bruce	L-R	5-11	175	11-27-91	.194	.167	.200	13	31	4	6	1	0	0	3	2	0	2	1	14	0	0	.226	.235
Cunningham, Todd	B-R	6-0	205	3-20-89	.270	.273	.269	76	230	45	62	14	2	4	27	37	15	2	2	37	6	2	.400	.401
2-team total (20 Oklahoma City)					.284	.357	.333	96	292	57	83	20	3	4	31	43	18	2	3	50	7	3	.414	.405
DeJong, Paul	R-R	6-1	195	8-2-93	.299	.222	.319	48	177	27	53	9	0	13	34	9	2	1	1	46	0	2	.571	.339
Diaz, Aledmys	R-R	6-1	195	8-1-90	.253	.206	.265	46	170	19	43	9	1	4	26	10	4	0	3	30	3	3	.388	.305
Garcia, Anthony	R-R	6-0	180	1-4-92	.180	.286	.156	14	39	1	7	1	0	1	3	3	1	0	0	6	1	1	.282	.256
Garcia, Jose Adolis	R-R	6-1	180	3-2-93	.302	.378	.273	40	136	21	41	11	2	3	10	7	2	1	1	31	3	1	.478	.343
Grichuk, Randal	R-R	6-1	205	8-13-91	.270	.500	.204	14	63	11	17	3	0	6	9	3	1	0	0	20	0	0	.603	.313
Huffman, Chad	R-R	6-1	215	4-29-85	.247	.290	.235	59	174	27	43	13	1	6	25	32	8	0	1	39	1	0	.437	.386
Jenner, Jesse	R-R	6-0	205	7-18-93	.667	—	.667	1	3	2	2	1	0	0	0	1	0	0	0	0	0	0	1.000	.750
Kelly, Carson	R-R	6-2	220	7-14-94	.283	.293	.280	68	244	37	69	13	0	10	41	33	3	0	0	40	0	2	.459	.375
Lino, Gabriel	R-R	6-3	200	5-17-93	.236	.467	.175	22	72	4	17	5	0	1	8	9	0	0	1	21	0	0	.347	.317
Martinez, Jeremy	R-R	5-11	195	12-29-94	.333	—	.333	1	3	4	1	0	0	0	0	2	0	0	0	0	0	0	.333	.600
Martini, Nick	L-L	5-11	205	6-27-90	.303	.358	.290	98	360	60	109	20	5	6	55	55	4	0	7	77	5	1	.436	.394
Mejia, Alex	R-R	6-1	200	1-18-91	.335	.283	.353	55	206	25	69	15	0	4	33	14	2	1	1	30	1	1	.466	.381
O'Neill, Tyler	R-R	5-11	210	6-22-95	.253	.133	.285	37	146	23	37	5	1	12	39	10	2	0	3	43	5	0	.548	.304
2-team total (93 Tacoma)					.247	.302	.224	130	495	77	122	26	3	31	95	54	3	0	5	151	14	2	.499	.321
Peralta, Jhonny	R-R	6-2	225	5-28-82	.364	—	.364	3	11	2	4	1	0	0	2	1	0	0	0	1	0	0	.455	.417
Pham, Tommy	R-R	6-1	210	3-8-88	.283	.200	.299	25	92	17	26	8	0	4	19	13	0	1	0	21	6	3	.500	.371
Piscotty, Stephen	R-R	6-3	210	1-14-91	.313	.333	.308	8	32	7	10	3	0	4	7	6	0	0	0	7	0	0	.781	.421
Ravelo, Rangel	R-R	6-1	225	4-24-92	.314	.250	.336	89	306	49	96	25	1	8	41	31	5	0	3	56	1	2	.480	.383
Rosario, Alberto	R-R	5-10	190	1-10-87	.247	.195	.262	50	190	20	47	6	0	0	23	11	1	1	1	31	3	0	.279	.291
Schafer, Jordan	L-L	6-1	205	9-4-86	.450	.000	.529	6	20	4	9	2	0	0	5	1	0	0	0	2	1	0	.550	.476
Tovar, Wilfredo	R-R	5-10	180	8-11-91	.253	.290	.240	111	360	44	91	19	0	6	31	27	1	2	1	64	19	7	.356	.306
Valera, Breyvic	B-R	5-11	160	1-8-92	.314	.241	.331	117	424	68	133	22	6	8	41	38	1	3	4	34	11	11	.451	.368
Voit, Luke	R-R	6-3	225	2-13-91	.327	.305	.333	74	269	35	88	23	1	13	50	29	8	0	1	53	1	1	.565	.407
Wisdom, Patrick	R-R	6-2	220	8-27-91	.243	.248	.242	127	456	68	111	25	1	31	89	38	8	0	4	149	2	2	.507	.310

Pitching	B-T	HT	WT	DOB	W	L	ERA	G	GS	CG	SV	IP	H	R	ER	HR	BB	SO	AVG	vLH	vRH	K/9	BB/9
Bray, Tyler	R-R	6-5	200	10-3-91	1	0	11.12	3	0	0	0	6	12	8	7	0	1	6	.429	.455	.412	9.53	1.59
Brebbia, John	L-R	6-1	185	5-30-90	1	1	1.69	15	1	0	3	27	16	5	5	2	5	29	.172	.146	.200	9.79	1.69
Duke, Zach	L-L	6-2	210	4-19-83	0	0	0.00	6	0	0	0	6	2	0	0	0	1	6	.100	.000	.250	9.00	1.50
Echemendia, Pedro	R-R	6-2	185	6-14-91	1	0	0.00	1	0	0	0	3	2	0	0	0	2	0	.200	.143	.333	0.00	6.00
Ellis, Chris	L-R	6-5	205	9-22-92	2	3	7.88	11	5	0	0	32	42	31	28	7	15	31	.321	.356	.292	8.72	4.22
Flaherty, Jack	R-R	6-4	205	10-15-95	7	2	2.74	15	15	0	0	85	73	26	26	10	24	85	.233	.215	.249	8.96	2.53
Gallen, Zac	R-R	6-2	191	8-3-95	1	1	3.48	4	4	0	0	21	18	9	8	2	6	23	.237	.345	.170	10.02	2.61
Gant, John	R-R	6-3	200	8-6-92	6	5	3.83	18	18	0	0	103	109	47	44	10	25	99	.272	.288	.257	8.62	2.18
Gilmartin, Sean	L-L	6-2	206	5-8-90	0	1	5.68	8	1	0	1	13	15	8	8	2	2	8	.283	.318	.258	5.68	1.42
2-team total (8 Las Vegas)					2	3	6.70	16	9	0	1	50	67	38	37	8	16	39	.319	.209	.377	7.07	2.90
Gonzales, Marco	L-L	6-1	195	2-16-92	6	4	2.90	11	11	0	0	68	54	25	22	6	17	57	.220	.159	.240	7.51	2.24
2-team total (2 Tacoma)					8	4	3.14	13	13	0	0	80	62	33	28	6	22	66	.215	.100	.219	7.39	2.46
Harris, Mitch	R-R	6-4	240	11-7-85	0	0	9.00	2	0	0	0	2	3	2	2	0	0	0	.375	.333	.400	0.00	0.00
Helsley, Ryan	R-R	6-1	195	7-18-94	0	0	3.60	1	1	0	0	5	7	2	2	0	3	5	.350	.333	.375	9.00	5.40
Herget, Kevin	L-R	5-10	185	4-3-91	4	2	4.62	22	9	0	0	62	68	35	32	7	21	60	.280	.212	.339	8.66	3.03
Heyer, Kurt	R-L	6-2	185	1-23-91	0	0	16.20	1	0	0	0	2	3	3	3	0	4	2	.429	.250	.667	10.80	21.60
Hudson, Dakota	R-R	6-5	215	9-15-94	1	1	4.42	7	7	0	0	39	36	20	19	2	15	19	.252	.306	.197	4.42	3.49
Lee, Thomas	R-R	6-1	190	10-20-89	0	1	54.00	1	0	0	0	1	5	4	4	1	1	0	.714	.750	.667	0.00	13.50
Lucas, Josh	R-R	6-6	185	11-5-90	8	1	3.15	47	0	0	17	60	58	23	21	3	12	68	.251	.281	.230	10.20	1.80
Lyons, Tyler	L-L	6-4	210	2-21-88	0	0	2.55	4	4	0	0	18	17	5	5	2	3	17	.250	.214	.259	8.66	1.53
Mayers, Mike	R-R	6-3	200	12-6-91	5	6	3.28	31	15	0	0	110	117	44	40	12	32	97	.270	.267	.272	7.96	2.63
Montgomery, Mark	R-R	6-0	200	8-30-90	5	1	2.43	46	0	0	5	67	46	19	18	4	15	73	.193	.281	.134	9.86	2.03

Morales, Andrew	R-R	6-0	185	1-16-93	0	0	5.40	4	0	0	0	3	6	2	2	1	1	2	.429	.500	.375	5.40	2.70
Nielsen, Trey	R-R	6-1	190	9-1-91	1	0	1.65	18	0	0	0	33	30	7	6	1	8	19	.254	.255	.254	5.23	2.20
Pearce, Matt	R-R	6-3	205	2-24-94	5	3	6.00	10	10	0	0	54	72	38	36	7	10	33	.327	.298	.353	5.50	1.67
Phillips, Zach	L-L	6-1	200	9-21-86	1	4	5.04	19	0	0	0	30	38	22	17	1	14	31	.304	.389	.270	9.20	4.15
Poncedeleon, Daniel	R-R	6-4	185	1-16-92	2	0	2.17	6	6	0	0	29	20	7	7	2	13	25	.196	.232	.152	7.76	4.03
Reyes, Arturo	R-R	5-11	185	4-6-92	5	5	4.41	22	6	1	1	63	63	34	31	5	17	41	.259	.279	.242	5.83	2.42
Sherriff, Ryan	L-L	6-1	185	5-25-90	5	1	3.19	48	0	0	6	54	40	22	19	2	13	47	.207	.198	.215	7.88	2.18
Socolovich, Miguel	R-R	6-1	205	7-24-86	2	1	4.15	30	1	0	1	39	35	19	18	4	9	29	.248	.241	.253	6.69	2.08
Tuivailala, Sam	R-R	6-3	225	10-19-92	1	0	1.27	18	0	0	6	21	13	3	3	2	3	21	.176	.120	.204	8.86	1.27
Weaver, Luke	R-R	6-2	170	8-21-93	10	2	2.55	15	15	0	0	78	63	24	22	3	19	76	.222	.206	.234	8.81	2.20
Wick, Rowan	L-R	6-3	220	11-9-92	2	1	5.40	14	0	0	1	17	16	11	10	2	7	17	.242	.214	.263	9.18	3.78
Zeid, Josh	R-R	6-4	220	3-24-87	9	4	5.19	33	12	0	0	102	117	61	59	18	48	95	.288	.285	.291	8.36	4.22

Fielding

Catcher	PCT	G	PO	A	E	DP	PB
Jenner	1.000	1	11	0	0	0	0
Kelly	.993	68	559	34	4	5	2
Lino	.982	22	146	14	3	2	1
Martinez	1.000	1	2	0	0	0	0
Rosario	.989	50	437	21	5	2	6

First Base	PCT	G	PO	A	E	DP
Huffman	1.000	18	102	18	0	9
Martini	1.000	8	78	3	0	14
Mejia	1.000	1	8	1	0	0
Ravelo	.995	52	376	26	2	45
Voit	.991	62	485	42	5	34
Wisdom	1.000	8	65	5	0	12

Second Base	PCT	G	PO	A	E	DP
Caldwell	1.000	6	9	12	0	4
Cunningham	1.000	4	3	7	0	1
DeJong	.958	5	10	13	1	1
Diaz	.968	6	9	21	1	7
Mejia	1.000	25	38	77	0	20
Tovar	1.000	26	40	61	0	19
Valera	.985	78	133	188	5	42

Third Base	PCT	G	PO	A	E	DP
Caldwell	1.000	5	0	3	0	0
DeJong	.833	3	2	3	1	0
Diaz	1.000	9	4	17	0	1
Mejia	.955	7	5	16	1	1
Peralta	1.000	2	0	4	0	0
Tovar	.895	9	6	11	2	3
Valera	1.000	1	1	1	0	0
Wisdom	.944	113	73	181	15	26

Shortstop	PCT	G	PO	A	E	DP
Caldwell	.000	1	0	0	0	0
DeJong	.956	39	44	85	6	8
Diaz	.973	28	39	68	3	17
Mejia	1.000	16	20	51	0	9
Peralta	1.000	1	1	6	0	2
Tovar	.963	67	91	167	10	35

Outfield	PCT	G	PO	A	E	DP
Bader	.990	117	301	7	3	3
Cunningham	1.000	59	102	6	0	1
Garcia	1.000	11	16	0	0	0
Garcia	1.000	34	70	5	0	0
Grichuk	1.000	10	17	3	0	0
Huffman	1.000	27	35	0	0	0
Martini	.993	80	147	4	1	0
O'Neill	.968	34	56	4	2	0
Pham	.959	25	45	2	2	0
Piscotty	1.000	6	12	0	0	0
Ravelo	.929	15	25	1	2	0
Schafer	1.000	4	11	1	0	1
Valera	1.000	26	43	5	0	1

SPRINGFIELD CARDINALS — *DOUBLE-A*

TEXAS LEAGUE

Batting	B-T	HT	WT	DOB	AVG	vLH	vRH	G	AB	R	H	2B	3B	HR	RBI	BB	HBP	SH	SF	SO	SB	CS	SLG	OBP
Alvarez, Eliezer	L-R	5-11	165	10-15-94	.247	.211	.257	54	186	29	46	11	1	4	26	16	5	0	2	56	8	3	.382	.321
Arozarena, Randy	R-R	5-11	170	2-28-95	.252	.228	.264	51	163	34	41	10	1	3	9	27	3	1	1	34	8	3	.380	.366
Caldwell, Bruce	L-R	5-11	175	11-27-91	.247	.221	.255	92	308	47	76	12	1	14	54	52	6	0	1	105	2	1	.429	.365
Cruz, Luis	R-R	6-2	225	5-26-93	.250	.167	.267	9	36	4	9	2	0	0	3	1	1	0	0	10	0	0	.306	.290
Diekroeger, Danny	R-L	6-2	205	5-25-92	.231	.333	.209	22	52	3	12	2	1	0	4	4	0	1	0	11	0	2	.308	.286
Drake, Blake	R-R	6-1	175	7-11-93	.220	.000	.290	12	41	4	9	1	0	2	4	5	0	1	0	7	1	1	.390	.304
Edman, Tommy	B-R	5-10	180	5-9-95	.247	.279	.232	63	219	20	54	12	2	2	26	16	1	1	2	34	5	2	.347	.298
Garcia, Anthony	R-R	6-0	180	1-4-92	.294	.372	.265	101	347	57	102	18	2	15	69	40	5	1	5	72	8	2	.487	.370
Garcia, Jose Adolis	R-R	6-1	180	3-2-93	.285	.276	.288	84	309	43	88	23	0	12	55	26	2	0	5	77	12	8	.476	.339
Grayson, Casey	L-L	6-1	215	8-24-91	.246	.260	.241	61	195	20	48	6	0	3	12	25	0	0	0	63	0	0	.323	.332
Grichuk, Randal	R-R	6-1	205	8-13-91	.250	.333	.000	1	4	1	1	0	0	1	3	0	0	0	0	2	0	0	1.000	.250
Jenner, Jesse	R-R	6-0	205	7-18-93	.254	.367	.216	36	118	14	30	4	0	4	18	8	0	1	1	27	0	0	.390	.299
Knizner, Andrew	R-R	6-1	200	2-3-95	.324	.409	.297	51	182	27	59	13	0	4	22	14	2	0	4	27	0	1	.462	.371
Lino, Gabriel	R-R	6-3	200	5-17-93	.267	.292	.259	58	191	21	51	15	1	4	28	17	6	0	4	59	0	0	.419	.339
Martinez, Jeremy	R-R	5-11	195	12-29-94	.000	—	.000	1	2	0	0	0	0	0	0	1	0	0	0	0	0	0	.000	.333
Martini, Nick	L-L	5-11	205	6-27-90	.263	.294	.256	23	99	13	26	5	0	2	15	11	0	0	0	16	1	0	.374	.336
Mejia, Alex	R-R	6-1	200	1-18-91	.251	.291	.238	63	227	24	57	17	0	3	24	16	3	2	3	36	1	1	.366	.305
Mercado, Oscar	R-R	6-2	175	12-16-94	.287	.226	.309	120	477	76	137	20	4	13	46	32	9	1	4	112	38	19	.428	.341
Nogowski, John	R-L	6-2	210	1-5-93	.295	.364	.270	59	207	32	61	12	0	2	21	27	2	0	2	25	2	0	.382	.378
O'Keefe, Brian	R-R	6-0	210	7-15-93	.400	—	.400	1	5	1	2	1	0	0	1	0	0	0	0	2	0	0	.600	.400
Pina, Leobaldo	R-R	6-2	160	6-29-94	.167	.250	.125	4	12	1	2	0	0	0	0	0	0	0	0	3	0	0	.167	.167
Piscotty, Stephen	R-R	6-3	210	1-14-91	.143	.500	.000	3	7	0	1	0	0	0	1	1	0	0	0	1	0	0	.143	.250
Seferina, Darren	L-R	5-9	175	1-24-94	.278	.263	.282	48	173	31	48	6	1	5	16	21	1	1	1	42	10	3	.410	.357
Sierra, Magneuris	L-L	5-11	160	4-7-96	.269	.318	.251	81	327	32	88	18	3	1	35	20	2	2	2	59	17	5	.352	.313
Sosa, Edmundo	R-R	5-11	170	3-6-96	.000	—	.000	1	4	0	0	0	0	0	0	1	0	0	0	0	0	0	.000	.200
Spitz, Thomas	R-R	6-1	180	4-16-92	.167	.000	.231	11	18	1	3	1	0	0	1	0	0	0	0	8	1	0	.222	.167
Thon, Dickie Joe	R-R	6-2	190	11-16-91	.237	.310	.213	52	169	14	40	8	2	4	15	11	0	3	1	56	1	0	.379	.282
Turgeon, Casey	R-R	5-10	160	9-28-92	.225	.357	.197	30	80	15	18	4	1	1	5	16	1	1	0	19	3	0	.338	.361
Wilson, Jacob	R-R	5-11	205	7-29-90	.248	.318	.224	129	432	63	107	20	1	17	66	50	12	1	8	97	2	3	.417	.337
Wong, Kolten	L-R	5-9	185	10-10-90	.400	.250	.455	4	15	3	6	2	0	1	4	2	0	0	0	1	0	0	.733	.471
Young, Andy	R-R	6-0	195	5-10-94	.667	1.000	.500	2	3	2	2	0	0	0	1	1	1	0	0	1	0	0	.667	.800

Pitching	B-T	HT	WT	DOB	W	L	ERA	G	GS	CG	SV	IP	H	R	ER	HR	BB	SO	AVG	vLH	vRH	K/9	BB/9
Alcantara, Sandy	R-R	6-4	170	9-7-95	7	5	4.31	25	22	0	0	125	125	64	60	13	54	106	.262	.249	.272	7.61	3.88
Baker, Corey	R-R	6-1	170	11-23-89	2	1	2.48	25	0	0	6	40	40	12	11	2	11	32	.272	.333	.233	7.20	2.48
Bard, Daniel	R-R	6-4	215	6-25-85	0	1	10.38	10	0	0	0	9	6	10	10	0	19	7	.222	.143	.250	7.27	19.73
Beck, Landon	R-R	6-3	215	12-9-92	1	4	3.76	37	0	0	6	41	41	24	17	3	17	44	.252	.290	.228	9.74	3.76
Bowen, Brady	R-L	6-1	160	7-24-92	0	0	0.00	1	0	0	0	2	0	0	0	0	0	2	.000	.000	.000	7.71	0.00

Bray, Tyler	R-R	6-5	200	10-3-91	8	0	2.91	37	0	0	2	53	49	21	17	2	29	46	.248	.342	.189	7.86	4.96
Carter, Eric	R-R	5-11	202	7-7-92	0	0	0.00	3	0	0	0	2	1	0	0	0	2	1	.125	.000	.167	3.86	7.71
Echemendia, Pedro	R-R	6-2	185	6-14-91	2	4	4.25	38	3	0	5	72	81	40	34	9	16	41	.295	.339	.258	5.13	2.00
Ellis, Chris	L-R	6-5	205	9-22-92	5	9	4.45	19	17	0	0	99	98	51	49	7	32	95	.256	.262	.251	8.64	2.91
Evans, Jacob	L-L	6-2	215	11-27-93	1	3	2.55	14	0	0	0	18	20	11	5	2	8	21	.274	.294	.256	10.70	4.08
Flaherty, Jack	R-R	6-4	205	10-15-95	7	2	1.42	10	10	0	0	63	47	10	10	2	11	62	.205	.220	.196	8.81	1.56
Gallen, Zac	R-R	6-2	191	8-3-95	4	5	3.79	13	13	0	0	71	76	33	30	8	19	42	.270	.317	.224	5.30	2.40
Gomber, Austin	L-L	6-5	235	11-23-93	10	7	3.34	26	26	0	0	143	116	64	53	17	51	140	.219	.248	.208	8.81	3.21
Hawkins, Chandler	L-L	6-1	170	2-28-93	0	1	3.92	16	0	0	0	21	16	12	9	4	13	13	.211	.258	.178	5.66	5.66
Helsley, Ryan	R-R	6-1	195	7-18-94	3	1	2.67	6	6	0	0	34	25	12	10	4	15	41	.200	.179	.217	10.96	4.01
Herget, Kevin	L-R	5-10	185	4-3-91	1	2	1.86	13	0	0	5	19	17	4	4	1	3	21	.258	.238	.267	9.78	1.40
Hudson, Dakota	R-R	6-5	215	9-15-94	9	4	2.53	18	18	1	0	114	111	38	32	5	34	77	.255	.284	.227	6.08	2.68
Jones, Connor	R-R	6-3	200	10-10-94	1	0	2.70	1	1	0	0	7	6	2	2	1	3	2	.261	.286	.250	2.70	4.05
Littrell, Corey	L-L	6-3	185	3-21-92	1	2	4.15	28	0	0	0	35	28	18	16	2	20	26	.219	.156	.281	6.75	5.19
Lyons, Tyler	L-L	6-4	210	2-21-88	1	0	3.60	1	1	0	0	5	3	2	2	1	0	3	.167	.000	.214	5.40	0.00
Martinez, Dailyn	R-R	6-2	170	4-19-93	0	1	5.93	7	1	0	0	14	23	9	9	1	6	3	.404	.375	.424	1.98	3.95
McKinney, Ian	L-L	5-11	185	11-18-94	1	0	5.16	14	2	0	0	23	28	13	13	3	11	10	.311	.351	.283	3.97	4.37
McKnight, Blake	R-R	6-1	185	2-13-91	1	5	6.92	24	1	0	2	39	52	37	30	5	19	22	.323	.375	.289	5.08	4.38
Morales, Andrew	R-R	6-0	185	1-16-93	2	1	3.13	19	0	0	2	23	24	8	8	1	11	28	.270	.158	.353	10.96	4.30
Nielsen, Trey	R-R	6-1	190	9-1-91	1	0	7.02	10	2	0	1	17	21	14	13	6	5	13	.300	.294	.306	7.02	2.70
Pearce, Matt	R-R	6-3	205	2-24-94	9	5	3.11	17	17	2	0	110	99	39	38	10	20	66	.239	.224	.249	5.40	1.64
Reed, Jimmy	L-L	5-11	185	12-18-90	0	0	8.10	3	0	0	0	7	7	7	6	1	3	4	.269	.333	.235	5.40	4.05
Siegrist, Kevin	L-L	6-5	230	7-20-89	0	0	9.00	2	0	0	0	2	4	2	2	0	1	2	.400	.500	.333	9.00	4.50
Vance, Ross	L-L	6-0	180	12-7-91	0	0	0.00	2	0	0	0	2	2	0	0	0	1	0	.286	.333	.250	0.00	4.50
Wick, Rowan	L-R	6-3	220	11-9-92	0	0	2.08	16	0	0	5	22	16	5	5	1	11	17	.208	.294	.140	7.06	4.57

Fielding

Catcher	PCT	G	PO	A	E	DP	PB
Cruz	.984	9	59	4	1	1	4
Jenner	.982	33	205	11	4	2	2
Knizner	.993	49	383	24	3	2	1
Lino	.997	49	329	43	1	0	3
Martinez	.889	1	8	0	1	0	0
O'Keefe	1.000	1	12	0	0	0	0

First Base	PCT	G	PO	A	E	DP
Caldwell	.964	4	24	3	1	4
Diekroeger	1.000	6	43	4	0	6
Grayson	.996	59	443	40	2	53
Lino	1.000	3	3	0	0	2
Nogowski	.996	57	479	49	2	52
Wilson	.994	21	158	18	1	18

Second Base	PCT	G	PO	A	E	DP
Alvarez	.933	45	70	96	12	24
Caldwell	.993	31	56	89	1	32
Seferina	.993	28	49	84	1	15
Thon	.964	33	37	71	4	21
Turgeon	.962	7	16	9	1	3
Wilson	1.000	3	3	5	0	2
Wong	1.000	4	3	4	0	0

Third Base	PCT	G	PO	A	E	DP
Caldwell	.910	33	25	46	7	5
Diekroeger	.833	5	3	2	1	0
Pina	1.000	2	0	2	0	1
Seferina	.868	14	10	23	5	2
Thon	.667	1	1	1	1	1
Turgeon	1.000	10	5	8	0	1
Wilson	.967	89	67	167	8	20
Young	1.000	1	0	4	0	0

Shortstop	PCT	G	PO	A	E	DP
Edman	.982	61	105	167	5	43
Mejia	.968	62	101	174	9	52
Pina	.750	1	1	2	1	0
Seferina	.857	3	5	7	2	2
Sosa	1.000	1	8	3	0	3
Wilson	.984	17	27	34	1	6

Outfield	PCT	G	PO	A	E	DP
Arozarena	1.000	47	84	2	0	0
Drake	.900	10	16	2	2	1
Garcia	.980	65	97	2	2	0
Garcia	.971	80	155	12	5	2
Grichuk	1.000	1	3	0	0	0
Martini	1.000	19	43	2	0	0
Mercado	.978	115	263	1	6	0
Piscotty	1.000	2	3	0	0	0
Sierra	.982	78	161	6	3	3
Spitz	1.000	6	6	0	0	0
Thon	1.000	4	5	0	0	0
Turgeon	1.000	10	19	1	0	0
Wilson	.500	2	1	0	1	0

PALM BEACH CARDINALS — HIGH CLASS A

FLORIDA STATE LEAGUE

Batting	B-T	HT	WT	DOB	AVG	vLH	vRH	G	AB	R	H	2B	3B	HR	RBI	BB	HBP	SH	SF	SO	SB	CS	SLG	OBP
Arozarena, Randy	R-R	5-11	170	2-28-95	.276	.345	.242	70	265	38	73	22	3	8	40	13	12	1	4	53	10	4	.472	.333
Ascanio, Rayder	B-R	5-11	155	3-17-96	.091	.000	.100	3	11	2	1	0	0	0	1	2	0	0	0	4	0	0	.091	.231
Bautista, Ricardo	L-R	6-0	185	12-27-95	.111	.500	.000	3	9	1	1	0	1	0	4	1	0	0	1	4	0	0	.333	.182
Billings, Shane	R-L	5-11	190	12-14-94	.281	.391	.232	59	224	22	63	11	1	0	12	11	1	1	1	38	3	2	.339	.317
Chinea, Chris	R-R	5-11	220	5-3-94	.260	.248	.265	123	466	48	121	24	0	6	48	34	5	3	3	93	0	1	.350	.315
Diekroeger, Danny	R-L	6-2	205	5-25-92	.248	.255	.245	55	198	19	49	9	2	2	21	12	1	3	5	40	1	0	.343	.287
Drake, Blake	R-R	6-1	175	7-11-93	.245	.247	.244	82	314	32	77	15	2	7	27	21	4	7	1	70	6	3	.373	.300
Dykstra, Luke	R-R	6-1	195	11-7-95	.250	.229	.260	81	268	29	67	9	0	2	27	14	8	2	2	32	4	3	.306	.305
Edman, Tommy	B-R	5-10	180	5-9-95	.257	.321	.214	18	70	7	18	2	1	1	11	7	2	2	1	18	0	1	.357	.338
Godoy, Jose	L-R	5-11	180	10-13-94	.265	.200	.276	69	238	21	63	14	0	4	41	16	3	6	2	36	1	2	.374	.317
Grayson, Casey	L-L	6-1	215	8-24-91	.250	.450	.194	25	92	13	23	1	1	1	13	15	2	1	0	21	2	0	.315	.367
Grichuk, Randal	R-R	6-1	205	8-13-91	.333	.500	.000	1	3	1	1	0	1	0	1	1	0	0	0	1	0	0	1.000	.500
Herrera, Juan	R-R	5-11	165	6-28-93	.143	.111	.167	7	21	5	3	0	0	0	0	1	0	1	0	2	0	0	.143	.182
Hudzina, Danny	R-R	5-11	185	2-27-94	.000	.000	.000	4	3	2	0	0	0	0	0	2	0	0	0	2	0	0	.000	.400
Jackson, Vince	L-L	6-4	190	2-4-94	.200	.111	.214	19	65	7	13	2	0	0	5	6	0	0	0	18	1	1	.231	.268
Martinez, Jeremy	R-R	5-11	195	12-29-94	.189	.180	.195	60	201	16	38	3	0	0	15	21	3	3	2	26	1	0	.204	.273
Martinez, Jose	R-R	6-6	215	7-25-88	.333	.200	.429	3	12	4	4	2	0	1	4	2	0	0	0	1	1	0	.750	.429
Martinez, Jose	B-R	5-10	150	8-15-96	.223	.173	.244	48	175	25	39	8	0	2	17	18	0	1	3	35	3	2	.303	.291
O'Keefe, Brian	R-R	6-0	210	7-15-93	.250	.333	.222	3	12	0	3	1	0	0	1	0	0	0	0	3	0	0	.333	.250
Peralta, Jhonny	R-R	6-2	225	5-28-82	.250	.667	.000	3	8	0	2	0	0	0	0	0	0	0	0	4	0	0	.250	.250
Pina, Leobaldo	R-R	6-2	160	6-29-94	.265	.264	.265	99	359	39	95	18	1	5	37	17	1	9	2	76	6	1	.362	.298
Rodriguez, Julio	R-R	6-0	197	6-11-97	.000	.000	.000	1	3	0	0	0	0	0	0	0	0	0	0	0	0	0	.000	.000
Seferina, Darren	L-R	5-9	175	1-24-94	.278	.116	.333	70	270	36	75	11	9	2	29	33	0	1	0	61	9	4	.407	.356
Sierra, Magneuris	L-L	5-11	160	4-7-96	.272	.208	.298	20	81	16	22	3	4	0	9	7	1	0	0	15	3	5	.407	.337

Sosa, Edmundo	R-R	5-11	170	3-6-96	.285	.278	.288	51	193	25	55	10	1	0	14	12	1	4	1	34	3	0	.347	.329
Spitz, Thomas	R-R	6-1	180	4-16-92	.253	.215	.269	101	360	57	91	16	2	5	27	46	3	2	3	88	11	4	.350	.340
Thomas, Lane	R-R	6-1	210	8-23-95	.257	.273	.250	9	35	5	9	0	1	0	3	3	0	0	1	10	2	2	.314	.308
2-team total (73 Dunedin)					.252	.273	.250	82	309	39	78	12	7	4	41	30	2	1	5	94	10	9	.375	.318
Turgeon, Casey	R-R	5-10	160	9-28-92	.220	.239	.211	60	209	20	46	3	0	5	21	31	4	1	2	44	2	0	.306	.329
Wilson, Austin	R-R	6-4	250	2-7-92	.168	.161	.171	37	119	8	20	0	0	0	11	8	2	0	0	39	0	1	.168	.233
Young, Andy	R-R	6-0	195	5-10-94	.265	.246	.273	57	196	24	52	9	0	5	20	10	10	1	4	49	3	0	.388	.327

Pitching	B-T	HT	WT	DOB	W	L	ERA	G	GS	CG	SV	IP	H	R	ER	HR	BB	SO	AVG	vLH	vRH	K/9	BB/9
Arias, Estarlin	R-R	6-1	175	5-22-94	1	1	2.48	28	0	0	6	33	33	11	9	1	9	41	.260	.372	.202	11.30	2.48
Beck, Landon	R-R	6-3	215	12-9-92	0	1	3.77	13	0	0	7	14	15	7	6	2	5	13	.289	.286	.290	8.16	3.14
Bowen, Brady	R-L	6-1	160	7-24-92	1	1	2.51	20	0	0	1	32	29	11	9	0	13	28	.259	.310	.229	7.79	3.62
Bray, Tyler	R-R	6-5	200	10-3-91	1	0	3.18	4	0	0	1	6	5	2	2	0	0	10	.238	.273	.200	15.88	0.00
Carter, Eric	R-R	5-11	202	7-7-92	1	0	0.77	9	0	0	4	12	9	1	1	1	4	16	.209	.188	.222	12.34	3.09
Ciavarella, Anthony	L-L	6-0	180	8-13-93	0	0	21.60	2	0	0	0	2	5	4	4	1	4	0	.556	.500	.571	0.00	21.60
De La Cruz, Steven	R-R	6-1	185	4-26-93	1	0	13.50	6	0	0	0	9	10	13	13	1	10	5	.278	.417	.208	5.19	10.38
Duke, Zach	L-L	6-2	210	4-19-83	0	0	0.00	1	0	0	0	1	1	0	0	0	0	1	.250	1.000	.000	9.00	0.00
Evans, Jacob	L-L	6-2	215	11-27-93	3	3	1.88	16	0	0	3	24	11	6	5	0	6	27	.141	.107	.160	10.13	2.25
Fernandez, Junior	R-R	6-1	180	3-2-97	5	3	3.69	16	16	1	0	90	82	41	37	5	39	58	.249	.299	.209	5.78	3.89
Gallen, Zac	R-R	6-2	191	8-3-95	5	2	1.62	9	9	1	0	56	44	14	10	1	10	56	.215	.175	.232	9.05	1.62
Gonzales, Marco	L-L	6-1	195	2-16-92	0	0	1.50	1	1	0	0	6	2	1	1	1	0	7	.100	.000	.125	10.50	0.00
Gonzalez, Derian	R-R	6-3	190	1-31-95	4	7	4.33	18	15	1	0	79	78	40	38	5	30	72	.259	.317	.221	8.20	3.42
Guillory, Evan	R-R	6-3	210	1-6-96	0	1	5.14	1	1	0	0	7	7	4	4	0	2	7	.280	.000	.350	9.00	2.57
Hamann, Kevin	R-R	6-4	180	11-24-93	1	0	0.00	1	0	0	0	2	3	0	0	0	0	2	.375	1.000	.167	9.00	0.00
Hawkins, Chandler	L-L	6-1	170	2-28-93	3	1	1.93	9	0	0	0	14	15	3	3	0	4	13	.289	.231	.346	8.36	2.57
Helsley, Ryan	R-R	6-1	195	7-18-94	8	2	2.69	17	16	1	0	94	72	30	28	3	30	91	.213	.235	.197	8.74	2.88
Hicks, Jordan	R-R	6-2	185	9-6-96	0	1	1.00	8	5	0	1	27	21	3	3	0	6	32	.214	.280	.146	10.67	2.00
Jones, Connor	R-R	6-3	200	10-10-94	8	5	3.97	24	21	0	1	113	120	60	50	3	49	76	.275	.282	.268	6.04	3.89
Leitao, Brennan	R-R	6-1	205	6-21-93	3	2	2.85	25	1	0	1	41	48	15	13	5	9	29	.296	.263	.314	6.37	1.98
Martinez, Dailyn	R-R	6-2	170	4-19-93	3	1	2.93	29	0	0	4	46	39	18	15	0	17	34	.238	.245	.235	6.65	3.33
McKinney, Ian	L-L	5-11	185	11-18-94	3	3	2.02	26	1	0	4	49	35	12	11	1	24	48	.205	.210	.202	8.82	4.41
Mendoza, Hector	R-R	6-2	176	3-5-94	0	6	5.54	19	0	0	0	26	29	18	16	2	11	27	.279	.296	.267	9.35	3.81
Morales, Andrew	R-R	6-0	185	1-16-93	0	0	3.52	6	0	0	0	8	7	5	3	0	2	6	.219	.364	.143	7.04	2.35
Nicacio, Winston	R-R	6-2	180	12-29-96	0	1	4.50	2	0	0	0	6	4	3	3	0	4	6	.182	.200	.177	9.00	6.00
O'Reilly, Mike	R-R	5-11	180	9-3-94	3	1	3.29	9	9	0	0	55	65	23	20	9	9	43	.300	.287	.309	7.08	1.48
Perez, Juan	R-R	6-2	195	7-22-95	1	0	3.58	20	0	0	1	28	26	11	11	1	16	18	.250	.296	.217	5.86	5.20
Reyes, Arturo	R-R	5-11	185	4-6-92	1	0	0.00	1	0	0	0	2	0	0	0	0	1	1	.000	.000	.000	4.50	4.50
Santos, Ramon	R-R	6-2	160	9-20-94	5	3	2.81	27	6	0	3	64	66	28	20	3	19	44	.281	.275	.285	6.19	2.67
Sexton, Austin	R-R	6-2	185	7-17-94	0	0	1.50	2	0	0	0	6	3	1	1	0	2	2	.143	.182	.100	3.00	3.00
Shew, Anthony	R-R	6-2	191	11-3-93	0	0	15.00	1	0	0	0	3	6	5	5	0	1	4	.400	.286	.500	12.00	3.00
Siegrist, Kevin	L-L	6-5	230	7-20-89	0	1	3.00	3	3	0	0	3	3	1	1	0	2	3	.250	.400	.143	9.00	6.00
Tewes, Sam	R-R	6-5	200	2-6-95	3	2	3.09	10	6	0	1	44	52	23	15	3	6	34	.296	.258	.318	7.01	1.24
Vance, Ross	L-L	6-0	180	12-7-91	2	6	5.31	38	3	0	1	59	76	41	35	1	27	64	.309	.226	.360	9.71	4.10
Warner, Austin	L-L	5-11	185	6-27-94	1	0	0.00	1	0	0	0	3	2	0	0	0	1	3	.200	.000	.250	9.00	3.00
Whitley, Kodi	R-R	6-4	220	2-21-95	0	0	0.00	1	0	0	0	3	1	0	0	0	1	3	.100	.000	.111	9.00	3.00
Woodford, Jake	R-R	6-4	210	10-28-96	7	6	3.10	23	21	0	0	119	128	57	41	7	39	72	.280	.283	.278	5.45	2.95

Fielding

Catcher	PCT	G	PO	A	E	DP	PB
Chinea	1.000	14	89	6	0	1	1
Godoy	.995	67	495	63	3	4	7
Martinez	.995	56	375	45	2	8	6
O'Keefe	1.000	2	13	2	0	0	0
Rodriguez	1.000	1	12	0	0	0	0

First Base	PCT	G	PO	A	E	DP
Chinea	.994	96	853	44	5	88
Diekroeger	.993	14	129	14	1	11
Grayson	.988	16	140	19	2	18
Martinez	.917	1	11	0	1	1
Pina	.989	13	79	14	1	14
Turgeon	.000	1	0	0	0	0

Second Base	PCT	G	PO	A	E	DP
Dykstra	.973	65	112	171	8	37
Edman	1.000	3	8	9	0	1
Herrera	1.000	1	0	3	0	1
Martinez	.929	2	3	10	1	4
Pina	1.000	1	2	2	0	1
Seferina	.966	30	44	96	5	27
Sosa	.968	7	11	19	1	7
Turgeon	1.000	2	2	1	0	0
Young	.971	30	51	85	4	24

Third Base	PCT	G	PO	A	E	DP
Diekroeger	.934	20	16	41	4	2
Hudzina	1.000	3	0	1	0	0
Peralta	1.000	2	1	4	0	0
Pina	.966	80	42	130	6	12
Seferina	.978	21	11	34	1	6
Sosa	1.000	1	0	3	0	1
Turgeon	.913	15	13	29	4	6
Young	1.000	8	4	7	0	0

Shortstop	PCT	G	PO	A	E	DP
Ascanio	1.000	2	2	6	0	1
Edman	.909	15	18	42	6	10
Herrera	.966	6	7	21	1	6
Martinez	.967	47	52	155	7	42
Pina	.818	11	7	20	6	1
Seferina	.944	3	11	6	1	3
Sosa	.938	41	44	121	11	28
Young	1.000	13	20	35	0	6

Outfield	PCT	G	PO	A	E	DP
Arozarena	.980	69	144	5	3	0
Bautista	1.000	3	2	1	0	0
Billings	.966	56	109	6	4	1
Diekroeger	1.000	5	3	0	0	0
Drake	.990	79	186	13	2	2
Jackson	.964	19	24	3	1	0
Martinez	1.000	2	2	0	0	0
Sierra	.977	19	38	4	1	1
Spitz	.981	99	195	13	4	4
Thomas	1.000	7	14	1	0	0
Turgeon	1.000	37	64	2	0	0
Wilson	.977	17	41	2	1	0

PEORIA CHIEFS — *LOW CLASS A*

MIDWEST LEAGUE

Batting	B-T	HT	WT	DOB	AVG	vLH	vRH	G	AB	R	H	2B	3B	HR	RBI	BB	HBP	SH	SF	SO	SB	CS	SLG	OBP
Aikin, Craig	L-L	5-10	175	8-19-93	.077	.000	.100	4	13	0	1	0	0	0	0	0	0	1	0	5	0	0	.077	.077
Billings, Shane	R-L	5-11	190	12-14-94	.310	.360	.288	46	168	26	52	3	3	1	11	7	1	3	1	27	14	5	.381	.339
Carlson, Dylan	B-L	6-3	195	10-23-98	.240	.225	.246	115	383	63	92	18	1	7	42	52	9	4	3	116	6	6	.347	.342

Davis, J.R.	R-R	5-10	190	8-10-94	.245	.326	.214	87	343	28	84	18	2	4	32	10	2	0	3	58	8	2	.344	.268
Davis, Matt	R-R	5-10	175	12-8-94	.192	.188	.193	25	73	8	14	3	0	2	7	10	2	0	0	28	2	0	.315	.306
Denton, Bryce	R-R	6-0	190	8-1-97	.157	.143	.161	19	70	2	11	4	0	1	4	4	0	0	1	18	2	1	.257	.200
Edman, Tommy	B-R	5-10	180	5-9-95	.284	.314	.275	38	155	24	44	8	5	2	18	15	1	1	2	19	8	2	.439	.347
Fennell, Mick	L-R	5-10	190	4-30-94	.254	.303	.243	46	173	14	44	4	0	1	25	13	1	1	1	29	5	4	.295	.309
Fiedler, Matt	R-R	5-10	195	3-22-95	.257	.273	.250	49	175	21	45	7	2	2	13	19	3	0	2	42	4	4	.354	.337
Hudzina, Danny	R-R	5-11	185	2-27-94	.252	.279	.243	74	270	28	68	12	0	8	32	22	1	1	1	53	1	1	.385	.310
Jackson, Vince	L-L	6-4	190	2-4-94	.266	.230	.277	72	256	33	68	16	3	8	32	28	1	0	4	71	0	2	.445	.336
Knizner, Andrew	R-R	6-1	200	2-3-95	.279	.306	.273	44	179	18	50	10	1	8	29	9	3	0	0	22	1	1	.480	.325
Martinez, Jose	B-R	5-10	150	8-15-96	.239	.235	.241	42	142	12	34	5	0	0	9	11	0	1	2	27	1	3	.275	.290
McCarvel, Ryan	R-R	6-2	180	12-23-94	.230	.161	.256	94	343	50	79	21	3	16	53	41	2	0	4	113	1	4	.449	.313
Mendoza, Evan	R-R	6-2	200	6-28-96	.270	.227	.289	18	74	9	20	6	1	1	8	2	0	0	1	15	2	0	.419	.286
O'Keefe, Brian	R-R	6-0	210	7-15-93	.260	.259	.260	97	373	43	97	20	0	15	46	34	1	0	3	89	7	3	.434	.321
Ortega, Dennis	R-R	6-2	180	6-11-97	.389	.250	.429	6	18	5	7	1	0	0	0	5	1	0	0	7	0	0	.444	.542
Piscotty, Stephen	R-R	6-3	210	1-14-91	.200	.333	.111	4	15	0	3	2	0	0	3	0	0	0	0	3	1	0	.333	.200
Plummer, Nick	L-L	5-10	200	7-31-96	.198	.200	.197	92	278	36	55	11	1	4	17	53	14	0	1	109	8	9	.288	.353
Robertson, Kramer	R-R	5-10	166	9-20-94	.270	.259	.274	54	215	34	58	12	0	3	13	21	6	0	0	36	10	4	.367	.351
Trosclair, Stefan	R-R	6-2	195	7-23-94	.272	.330	.251	111	404	61	110	18	6	15	59	56	13	2	6	111	14	4	.458	.374
Wong, Kolten	L-R	5-9	185	10-10-90	.143	.000	.167	3	7	2	1	0	0	1	1	1	1	0	0	1	1	0	.571	.333
Yepez, Juan	R-R	6-1	200	2-19-98	.260	.281	.252	80	304	33	79	16	1	7	47	19	3	0	2	72	6	1	.388	.308
Young, Andy	R-R	6-0	195	5-10-94	.284	.280	.286	58	211	31	60	11	4	12	38	22	10	1	0	54	5	2	.545	.379

Pitching	B-T	HT	WT	DOB	W	L	ERA	G	GS	CG	SV	IP	H	R	ER	HR	BB	SO	AVG	vLH	vRH	K/9	BB/9
Almonte, Max	R-R	6-1	205	3-4-92	2	4	3.40	32	0	0	2	45	39	18	17	3	19	44	.231	.196	.246	8.80	3.80
Arias, Estarlin	R-R	6-1	175	5-22-94	1	1	1.42	10	0	0	1	13	5	2	2	1	5	12	.122	.154	.107	8.53	3.55
Bowen, Brady	R-L	6-1	160	7-24-92	0	2	3.26	24	0	0	4	30	25	11	11	2	4	31	.221	.211	.227	9.20	1.19
Carter, Eric	R-R	5-11	202	7-7-92	3	1	2.51	33	0	0	9	43	33	14	12	4	17	50	.212	.194	.223	10.47	3.56
Dobzanski, Bryan	R-R	6-4	220	8-31-95	2	5	3.70	31	12	0	0	90	96	50	37	6	34	69	.278	.246	.297	6.90	3.40
Farinaro, Steven	R-R	6-0	170	8-18-95	1	4	7.71	8	8	0	0	42	58	39	36	9	12	23	.330	.330	.329	4.93	2.57
Hicks, Jordan	R-R	6-2	185	9-6-96	8	2	3.35	14	14	0	0	78	75	36	29	3	39	63	.260	.264	.258	7.27	4.50
Kilichowski, John	L-L	6-5	217	5-17-94	0	6	7.06	11	10	1	0	43	60	36	34	8	30	41	.335	.227	.370	8.52	6.23
Kruczynski, Evan	L-L	6-5	215	3-31-95	4	3	3.41	14	13	0	0	69	70	27	26	7	15	55	.264	.257	.267	7.21	1.97
Lyons, Tyler	L-L	6-4	210	2-21-88	0	1	6.75	1	1	0	0	3	4	2	2	0	0	1	.364	.333	.400	3.38	0.00
Martinez, Dailyn	R-R	6-2	170	4-19-93	1	0	8.10	3	0	0	0	7	11	6	6	1	1	6	.393	.800	.304	8.10	1.35
Medina, Yeison	R-R	6-2	210	10-2-92	5	0	2.03	32	0	0	11	44	37	11	10	1	21	74	.227	.259	.210	15.02	4.26
O'Reilly, Mike	R-R	5-11	180	9-3-94	9	2	1.75	15	12	2	0	88	49	17	17	10	11	89	.160	.146	.167	9.14	1.13
Oxnevad, Ian	R-L	6-4	205	10-3-96	3	10	4.09	24	23	1	0	132	134	72	60	17	34	84	.265	.203	.286	5.73	2.32
Parra, Frederis	R-R	6-3	162	10-22-94	5	6	3.74	25	10	1	0	89	108	42	37	8	24	49	.306	.327	.290	4.96	2.43
Perez, Dewin	L-L	6-0	175	9-29-94	3	6	3.89	31	0	0	2	44	36	21	19	1	28	42	.229	.265	.213	8.59	5.73
Perez, Juan	R-R	6-2	195	7-22-95	2	2	2.51	5	5	0	0	29	18	11	8	2	7	16	.173	.143	.184	5.02	2.20
Santos, Ramon	R-R	6-2	160	9-20-94	2	1	3.54	11	0	0	0	20	20	8	8	2	7	15	.267	.250	.277	6.64	3.10
Sexton, Austin	R-R	6-2	185	7-17-94	4	2	2.49	23	5	0	1	47	45	19	13	2	12	51	.256	.193	.286	9.77	2.30
Shew, Anthony	R-R	6-2	191	11-3-93	5	0	2.95	10	9	0	0	58	49	21	19	6	11	58	.225	.267	.197	9.00	1.71
Siomkin, Keaton	R-R	5-11	205	6-17-92	0	0	4.00	7	0	0	0	9	8	4	4	0	6	11	.235	.200	.250	11.00	6.00
Tewes, Sam	R-R	6-5	200	2-6-95	1	0	3.86	1	1	0	0	7	6	3	3	2	0	4	.222	.200	.227	5.14	0.00
Thomson, Colton	L-L	6-0	190	7-22-92	1	1	4.15	12	0	0	1	17	15	8	8	2	7	26	.231	.167	.255	13.50	3.63
Tilley, Leland	R-R	6-3	215	1-9-92	0	0	0.47	13	0	0	1	19	7	2	1	1	4	19	.108	.083	.122	8.84	1.86
Tomchick, Greg	R-R	6-4	200	12-30-92	0	0	9.75	8	0	0	0	12	17	13	13	3	10	6	.333	.200	.419	4.50	7.50
Trayner, Spencer	R-R	6-0	160	12-22-94	0	1	5.56	9	0	0	0	11	17	7	7	1	4	12	.347	.385	.304	9.53	3.18
Warner, Austin	L-L	5-11	185	6-27-94	2	4	3.00	9	9	0	0	48	43	21	16	4	14	51	.236	.200	.248	9.56	2.63
Williams, Ronnie	R-R	6-0	170	1-6-96	4	6	6.94	36	7	0	1	83	91	65	64	12	46	95	.288	.328	.264	10.30	4.99

Fielding

Catcher	PCT	G	PO	A	E	DP	PB
Knizner	1.000	26	207	17	0	1	2
McCarvel	.991	38	293	26	3	2	5
O'Keefe	.992	71	564	51	5	3	6
Ortega	1.000	6	62	5	0	0	0

First Base	PCT	G	PO	A	E	DP
Hudzina	1.000	1	7	0	0	1
Knizner	1.000	3	27	2	0	4
McCarvel	.996	29	213	14	1	24
Trosclair	.991	79	596	58	6	61
Yepez	.992	30	238	11	2	22

Second Base	PCT	G	PO	A	E	DP
Davis	.971	72	133	173	9	43
Hudzina	.964	8	14	13	1	7
Martinez	1.000	4	6	9	0	3
Trosclair	.953	27	45	56	5	18
Wong	1.000	3	2	5	0	1
Young	1.000	28	49	65	0	20

Third Base	PCT	G	PO	A	E	DP
Davis	1.000	6	5	7	0	2
Hudzina	.928	64	57	124	14	8
Martinez	.870	6	6	14	3	3
Mendoza	.900	13	9	27	4	6
Yepez	.887	37	16	70	11	8
Young	1.000	15	9	28	0	3

Shortstop	PCT	G	PO	A	E	DP
Edman	.968	38	54	95	5	28
Hudzina	1.000	2	4	3	0	0
Martinez	.980	32	44	104	3	22
Mendoza	.750	1	0	3	1	0
Robertson	.947	54	92	139	13	23
Young	.966	14	19	37	2	5

Outfield	PCT	G	PO	A	E	DP
Aikin	1.000	4	7	1	0	0
Billings	1.000	45	101	3	0	0
Carlson	.983	114	223	14	4	2
Davis	1.000	5	12	1	0	1
Davis	.969	17	29	2	1	0
Denton	.969	19	29	2	1	0
Fennell	.978	46	87	4	2	0
Fiedler	1.000	37	71	5	0	0
Jackson	.970	50	92	4	3	0
McCarvel	.900	4	9	0	1	0
Piscotty	.917	4	11	0	1	0
Plummer	.977	83	165	2	4	0
Young	1.000	1	1	0	0	0

STATE COLLEGE SPIKES

SHORT SEASON

NEW YORK-PENN LEAGUE

Batting	B-T	HT	WT	DOB	AVG	vLH	vRH	G	AB	R	H	2B	3B	HR	RBI	BB	HBP	SH	SF	SO	SB	CS	SLG	OBP
Bautista, Ricardo	L-R	6-0	185	12-27-95	.199	.146	.220	49	166	17	33	7	1	4	20	20	0	0	0	58	0	2	.325	.285
Benson, Brandon	R-R	6-1	195	6-13-94	.256	.333	.220	51	180	29	46	9	1	4	30	18	1	0	3	35	1	0	.383	.322
Crowe, J.D.	L-R	6-0	210	8-17-92	.273	.269	.274	33	110	16	30	6	1	0	12	11	0	3	0	13	1	1	.346	.339
Davis, Matt	R-R	5-10	175	12-8-94	.248	.250	.247	41	121	13	30	7	0	1	9	6	4	0	0	30	0	2	.331	.305
Denton, Bryce	R-R	6-0	190	8-1-97	.268	.268	.268	56	213	27	57	6	3	2	21	17	2	2	2	56	2	2	.352	.325
Diaz, Imeldo	R-R	6-0	175	11-2-97	.259	.250	.267	7	27	2	7	0	0	0	5	2	0	0	0	3	0	1	.259	.310
2-team total (7 Lowell)					.235	.250	.200	14	51	6	12	3	0	0	9	4	0	0	0	7	0	2	.294	.291
Espinal, Stanley	R-R	6-2	190	11-15-96	.143	.400	.000	5	14	0	2	0	0	0	1	2	0	0	0	5	0	1	.143	.250
2-team total (7 Lowell)					.171	.400	.136	12	41	1	7	2	0	0	4	4	0	0	0	11	0	1	.220	.244
Fennell, Mick	L-R	5-10	190	4-30-94	.250	.333	.200	8	32	2	8	3	0	0	6	4	2	1	0	7	1	0	.344	.368
Fiedler, Matt	R-R	5-10	195	3-22-95	.333	.000	.500	1	3	0	1	0	0	0	0	1	0	0	0	0	0	0	.333	.500
Figuera, Edwin	R-R	5-10	160	9-2-97	.284	.339	.256	56	194	36	55	11	1	1	19	6	8	1	1	27	12	2	.366	.330
Garcia, Erik	R-R	5-11	215	3-23-93	.214	.000	.300	4	14	4	3	1	0	0	3	1	0	0	0	4	0	0	.286	.267
Gomez, Joe	B-R	6-0	190	12-3-94	.125	.143	.100	10	24	3	3	1	0	0	3	0	3	1	0	5	0	0	.167	.222
Gonzalez, Yariel	B-R	6-1	190	6-1-94	.305	.288	.314	56	213	27	65	12	0	2	42	18	2	0	5	33	2	2	.390	.357
Hudzina, Danny	R-R	5-11	185	2-27-94	.500	.000	1.000	1	2	0	1	0	0	0	0	1	1	0	0	0	0	0	.500	.750
Hurst, Scott	L-R	5-10	175	3-25-96	.282	.273	.286	55	213	36	60	11	6	3	21	22	3	2	2	58	6	4	.432	.354
Kirtley, Zach	R-R	6-1	190	10-1-96	.223	.221	.225	51	188	28	42	11	0	2	20	30	4	0	1	40	0	0	.314	.341
Lancaster, Tyler	L-R	6-4	195	8-1-94	.255	.296	.239	29	94	12	24	5	0	2	17	14	2	0	1	17	0	0	.372	.360
Lopes, Caleb	R-R	5-8	195	7-21-95	.264	.382	.211	34	110	18	29	5	0	0	8	18	4	1	2	10	3	1	.309	.381
Lopez, Irving	L-R	5-10	170	6-30-95	.250	.500	.000	1	4	0	1	1	0	0	1	1	0	0	0	1	1	0	.500	.400
Lopez, Joshua	R-R	5-10	188	3-4-96	.285	.218	.313	52	186	21	53	11	0	5	27	15	4	1	2	44	0	0	.425	.348
Martin, Danny	R-R	5-11	180	8-5-94	.150	.000	.250	5	20	3	3	1	0	0	3	2	0	0	0	4	0	0	.200	.227
Mendoza, Evan	R-R	6-2	200	6-28-96	.370	.302	.395	41	162	34	60	14	3	3	28	16	2	1	1	33	1	2	.549	.431
Myers, Wood	L-R	5-10	180	10-11-94	.225	.182	.243	39	147	13	33	5	2	1	14	4	1	1	1	21	4	2	.306	.248
Newman, Hunter	R-R	6-2	210	12-20-93	.250	.000	.300	3	12	2	3	1	0	0	1	0	0	0	0	2	0	0	.333	.250
Ortega, Dennis	R-R	6-2	180	6-11-97	.213	.270	.189	39	127	12	27	5	0	0	11	12	1	2	1	23	0	0	.252	.284
Wilson, Alexis	R-R	5-10	168	8-13-96	.000	.000	.000	1	3	1	0	0	0	0	0	1	0	0	0	2	0	0	.000	.250

Pitching	B-T	HT	WT	DOB	W	L	ERA	G	GS	CG	SV	IP	H	R	ER	HR	BB	SO	AVG	vLH	vRH	K/9	BB/9
Balestrieri, Paul	R-R	6-0	210	9-4-94	3	4	6.49	14	12	0	0	53	68	46	38	1	28	40	.313	.284	.336	6.84	4.78
Calvano, Robert	R-R	6-2	225	2-27-93	0	0	6.75	4	0	0	0	5	8	4	4	0	4	3	.348	.400	.308	5.06	6.75
Castano, Daniel	L-L	6-4	230	9-17-94	9	3	2.57	14	14	1	0	91	87	33	26	3	13	81	.251	.307	.228	8.01	1.29
Ciavarella, Anthony	L-L	6-0	180	8-13-93	0	1	8.44	6	1	0	0	11	17	10	10	1	11	13	.378	.333	.400	10.97	9.28
Cruz, Jesus	R-R	6-1	225	4-15-95	1	0	1.93	5	0	0	1	5	4	1	1	0	0	8	.235	.143	.300	15.43	0.00
Fagalde, Alex	R-R	6-3	225	4-29-94	1	2	2.61	8	0	0	0	10	15	6	3	1	4	12	.326	.235	.379	10.45	3.48
Farinaro, Steven	R-R	6-0	170	8-18-95	2	1	4.93	18	1	0	0	38	38	26	21	3	25	25	.257	.322	.214	5.87	5.87
Gonzalez, Noel	R-R	5-11	190	2-27-94	0	0	2.79	21	0	0	3	29	29	10	9	1	14	32	.264	.283	.250	9.93	4.34
Gordon, Robbie	R-R	6-2	205	6-8-93	1	6	2.86	20	0	0	2	35	26	15	11	2	15	47	.205	.204	.205	12.20	3.89
Latcham, Will	R-R	6-2	200	1-26-96	3	1	2.05	18	0	0	4	31	26	11	7	3	11	41	.232	.192	.262	12.03	3.23
MaVorhis, Levi	R-R	6-2	215	7-31-94	1	1	2.06	17	3	0	2	44	36	11	10	4	11	39	.222	.224	.221	8.04	2.27
Mulford, Jonathon	R-R	6-2	210	8-16-94	2	5	3.95	15	15	0	0	73	87	40	32	4	45	61	.306	.305	.307	7.52	5.55
Oviedo, Johan	R-R	6-6	210	3-2-98	2	2	4.56	8	8	0	0	47	53	30	24	3	18	39	.285	.352	.221	7.42	3.42
Shew, Anthony	R-R	6-2	191	11-3-93	2	2	3.38	4	4	0	0	24	20	9	9	1	2	27	.227	.171	.277	10.13	0.75
Siomkin, Keaton	R-R	5-11	205	6-17-92	0	0	0.00	2	0	0	0	3	2	0	0	0	0	3	.167	.125	.250	8.10	0.00
Summerville, Andrew	L-L	6-3	195	9-4-95	4	1	1.64	13	10	0	1	60	44	13	11	4	26	52	.206	.172	.220	7.76	3.88
Tewes, Sam	R-R	6-5	200	2-6-95	3	3	3.83	7	7	0	0	42	51	25	18	3	9	31	.300	.304	.297	6.59	1.91
Thomson, Colton	L-L	6-0	190	7-22-92	0	0	2.45	8	0	0	0	11	12	5	3	0	3	20	.267	.188	.310	16.36	2.45
Tilley, Leland	R-R	6-3	215	1-9-92	1	0	0.66	9	0	0	0	14	8	5	1	0	5	14	.174	.308	.121	9.22	3.29
Trayner, Spencer	R-R	6-0	160	12-22-94	5	1	2.52	17	0	0	5	25	23	9	7	2	14	25	.253	.349	.167	9.00	5.04
Zgardowski, Jason	R-R	6-5	190	9-27-93	0	2	4.61	11	0	0	2	14	15	8	7	1	2	11	.273	.300	.240	7.24	1.32

Fielding

C: Garcia 1, Gomez 9, Lancaster 4, Lopez 34, Ortega 36, Wilson 1. **1B:** Davis 17, Gonzalez 32, Kirtley 3, Lancaster 24, Newman 3. **2B:** Davis 1, Figuera 3, Gonzalez 2, Kirtley 45, Lopes 20, Lopez 1, Martin 3, Myers 4. **3B:** Davis 7, Espinal 2, Figuera 12, Gonzalez 18, Hudzina 1, Mendoza 38. **SS:** Diaz 7, Figuera 40, Lopes 9, Myers 29. **OF:** Bautista 38, Benson 50, Crowe 23, Davis 7, Denton 54, Fennell 8, Hurst 53.

JOHNSON CITY CARDINALS

ROOKIE

APPALACHIAN LEAGUE

Batting	B-T	HT	WT	DOB	AVG	vLH	vRH	G	AB	R	H	2B	3B	HR	RBI	BB	HBP	SH	SF	SO	SB	CS	SLG	OBP
Balbuena, Starlin	R-R	6-2	175	3-4-98	.145	.231	.122	20	62	7	9	5	0	0	2	1	1	1	1	21	1	0	.226	.169
Bandes, Luis	R-R	6-1	200	5-15-96	.301	.359	.280	50	196	24	59	13	0	10	49	8	1	0	3	33	2	0	.520	.327
Diaz, Imeldo	R-R	6-0	175	11-2-97	.296	.390	.243	33	115	20	34	4	0	5	13	11	4	0	0	21	2	0	.461	.377
Espinal, Stanley	R-R	6-2	190	11-15-96	.203	.211	.200	22	69	7	14	5	1	2	8	7	2	0	0	13	0	0	.391	.295
Knight, Cameron	R-R	6-0	205	11-15-94	.184	.400	.107	13	38	4	7	1	0	1	3	5	2	0	0	13	0	0	.290	.311
Lopez, Irving	L-R	5-10	170	6-30-95	.287	.209	.311	50	178	37	51	7	2	5	27	19	9	3	3	25	5	3	.433	.378
Murders, J.D.	L-R	6-2	180	10-6-97	.195	.233	.184	38	128	17	25	1	1	0	8	10	1	1	2	33	2	0	.219	.255
Myers, Wood	L-R	5-10	180	10-11-94	.410	.385	.417	19	61	11	25	4	0	0	3	7	1	0	0	9	1	0	.475	.478
Perez, Delvin	R-R	6-3	175	11-24-98	.184	.143	.188	23	76	7	14	1	1	0	4	12	2	0	0	14	3	4	.224	.311
Pinder, Chase	R-R	6-1	190	3-16-96	.320	.417	.281	50	169	35	54	9	1	3	21	31	7	1	1	39	5	3	.438	.442
Rivera, Jonathan	R-R	6-1	185	4-27-97	.162	.171	.156	31	99	11	16	7	0	1	9	4	0	0	2	24	0	0	.263	.191

Robbins, Walker	L-L	6-3	215	11-18-97	.174	.071	.202	40	132	14	23	9	0	2	11	14	0	0	3	48	1	0	.288	.248
Rodriguez, Carlos	R-R	6-2	215	1-6-97	.200	.189	.205	36	125	15	25	3	0	3	11	14	6	0	0	57	2	0	.296	.310
Rodriguez, Julio	R-R	6-0	197	6-11-97	.280	.256	.288	47	182	28	51	14	1	5	36	17	1	0	1	31	0	0	.451	.343
Talavera, Carlos	B-R	6-1	175	9-20-96	.212	.133	.230	54	156	30	33	1	1	2	10	26	1	5	1	48	5	6	.269	.326
Whalen, Brady	B-R	6-4	180	1-15-98	.221	.089	.262	53	190	36	42	12	2	7	34	34	4	0	2	37	2	2	.416	.348
Wilson, Alexis	R-R	5-10	168	8-13-96	.255	.348	.228	30	102	7	26	7	1	2	17	15	1	0	2	16	0	0	.402	.350
Ynfante, Wadye	R-R	6-0	160	8-15-97	.299	.360	.274	43	167	27	50	11	0	7	23	17	3	0	0	51	11	3	.491	.374

Pitching	B-T	HT	WT	DOB	W	L	ERA	G	GS	CG	SV	IP	H	R	ER	HR	BB	SO	AVG	vLH	vRH	K/9	BB/9
Alvarez, Juan	R-R	6-4	180	12-28-96	2	2	5.63	16	0	0	0	24	22	21	15	2	22	12	.242	.265	.228	4.50	8.25
Blanco, Fabian	L-L	6-0	165	12-22-97	0	2	2.91	20	0	0	5	34	38	18	11	3	12	42	.277	.206	.301	11.12	3.18
Calvano, Robert	R-R	6-2	225	2-27-93	0	3	5.23	6	0	0	0	10	14	7	6	0	6	14	.342	.250	.379	12.19	5.23
Casadilla, Franyel	R-R	6-3	175	4-5-97	1	6	8.57	13	10	0	0	48	74	47	46	10	20	37	.352	.305	.383	6.89	3.72
Changarotty, Will	R-R	6-0	165	10-19-95	3	2	3.40	18	1	0	0	40	50	20	15	4	10	41	.307	.400	.259	9.30	2.27
Dahlberg, Jake	L-L	6-0	205	12-1-93	2	0	4.96	19	0	0	0	33	34	21	18	4	10	32	.256	.300	.243	8.82	2.76
Gonzalez, Junior	R-R	6-3	175	11-7-96	0	0	5.40	1	1	0	0	5	4	3	3	2	4	4	.222	.300	.125	7.20	7.20
Guillory, Evan	R-R	6-3	210	1-6-96	2	1	2.80	16	6	0	0	45	41	16	14	2	7	35	.241	.265	.226	7.00	1.40
Oviedo, Johan	R-R	6-6	210	3-2-98	2	1	4.88	6	6	0	0	28	22	17	15	0	18	31	.220	.290	.177	10.08	5.86
Patterson, Jacob	R-L	6-2	200	10-30-95	1	3	1.93	23	0	0	9	23	15	8	5	1	7	33	.185	.200	.179	12.73	2.70
Perez, Enrique	L-L	6-2	180	8-10-97	0	0	9.00	1	0	0	0	2	1	2	2	0	2	1	.200	.500	.000	4.50	9.00
Prendergast, Zach	R-R	6-2	175	5-6-95	3	0	2.20	6	6	0	0	33	26	10	8	1	6	44	.217	.205	.224	12.12	1.65
Ramirez, Edwar	R-R	6-3	190	3-15-98	3	7	7.39	13	11	0	0	56	83	54	46	10	27	43	.350	.351	.350	6.91	4.34
Rondon, Angel	R-R	6-2	185	12-1-97	0	0	6.75	1	1	0	0	4	6	3	3	2	3	5	.353	.300	.429	11.25	6.75
Rowland, Champ	R-R	5-11	185	2-28-92	0	0	3.38	2	0	0	0	3	3	1	1	0	1	5	.273	.000	.375	16.88	3.38
Salazar, Paul	B-R	6-2	195	5-23-97	0	0	10.80	15	0	0	0	15	14	25	18	2	30	9	.259	.280	.241	5.40	18.00
Schlesener, Jacob	L-L	6-3	175	10-8-96	2	3	4.33	12	11	0	0	44	31	28	21	2	38	61	.200	.147	.215	12.57	7.83
Seeburger, Brett	L-L	6-2	205	1-19-95	1	0	2.33	12	2	0	2	27	26	7	7	0	3	28	.260	.310	.239	9.33	1.00
Seijas, Alvaro	R-R	5-8	175	10-10-98	4	3	4.97	12	12	0	0	63	79	42	35	2	20	63	.306	.306	.306	8.95	2.84
St. Clair, Thomas	R-R	6-1	186	5-16-94	2	1	3.22	20	0	0	4	22	11	11	8	1	15	32	.143	.188	.111	12.90	6.04
Walsh, Jake	R-R	6-1	192	7-20-95	5	0	0.95	16	0	0	0	28	12	8	3	1	10	39	.126	.270	.035	12.39	3.18

Fielding

C: Knight 10, Rodriguez 36, Wilson 25. **1B:** Bandes 34, Rodriguez 29, Rodriguez 7. **2B:** Balbuena 1, Lopez 34, Murders 33, Myers 4. **3B:** Balbuena 9, Espinal 9, Lopez 3, Whalen 50. **SS:** Balbuena 7, Diaz 29, Lopez 9, Myers 7, Perez 22. **OF:** Bandes 1, Espinal 1, Pinder 48, Rivera 25, Robbins 38, Rodriguez 8, Talavera 48, Ynfante 42.

GCL CARDINALS — ROOKIE

GULF COAST LEAGUE

Batting	B-T	HT	WT	DOB	AVG	vLH	vRH	G	AB	R	H	2B	3B	HR	RBI	BB	HBP	SH	SF	SO	SB	CS	SLG	OBP
Alvarez, Eliezer	L-R	5-11	165	10-15-94	.250	.250	.250	7	24	4	6	2	0	1	2	2	0	0	1	3	1	0	.458	.296
Brdar, Michael	R-R	6-1	175	4-7-94	.235	.281	.208	31	85	9	20	4	0	0	10	10	2	1	0	12	1	2	.282	.330
Brodbeck, Andrew	R-L	5-10	185	1-22-93	.333	.250	.400	7	18	2	6	1	1	0	2	3	1	0	1	3	2	1	.500	.435
Bryant, Taylor	R-R	6-1	180	12-16-94	.324	.354	.307	43	136	22	44	11	1	1	21	27	1	0	1	27	2	0	.441	.436
Castillo, Moises	R-R	6-1	170	7-14-99	.248	.323	.218	37	109	19	27	6	1	1	11	10	4	2	0	27	2	0	.349	.333
Cedeno, Leandro	R-R	6-2	195	8-22-98	.351	.357	.348	9	37	8	13	4	0	4	12	1	0	0	1	7	0	0	.784	.359
Coman, Robbie	R-R	6-1	220	10-20-93	.353	.278	.394	18	51	8	18	6	0	1	9	2	1	0	1	5	0	0	.529	.382
Flores, Luis	B-R	6-0	190	10-22-96	.192	.175	.203	34	99	16	19	3	2	1	9	9	2	1	2	19	4	2	.293	.268
Fuller, Terry	L-R	6-4	210	12-5-98	.161	.185	.154	37	118	13	19	3	1	3	11	12	1	0	1	49	3	0	.280	.242
Gomez, Dariel	L-R	6-4	190	7-15-96	.240	.241	.240	35	104	16	25	4	0	2	12	17	3	0	2	30	0	0	.337	.357
Gomez, Joe	B-R	6-0	190	12-3-94	.167	.500	.000	2	6	2	1	0	0	0	0	1	0	0	0	1	0	0	.167	.286
Grayson, Casey	L-L	6-1	215	8-24-91	.412	.400	.417	6	17	8	7	4	1	0	9	6	0	0	0	3	0	0	.765	.565
Jackson, Zach	L-R	6-3	215	5-24-98	.098	.077	.107	14	41	2	4	0	0	0	5	10	0	0	1	20	0	0	.098	.269
Knight, Cameron	R-R	6-0	205	11-15-94	.191	.111	.212	15	42	3	8	2	0	0	2	7	1	0	0	16	0	0	.238	.320
Luna, Andres	R-R	5-10	175	7-17-97	.288	.364	.271	18	59	7	17	2	1	1	6	6	1	0	0	13	3	0	.407	.364
Machado, Jonathan	L-L	5-9	155	1-21-99	.323	.424	.286	35	124	27	40	8	0	2	20	8	5	0	2	13	8	2	.436	.381
Montero, Elehuris	R-R	6-3	195	8-17-98	.278	.259	.287	52	173	30	48	16	1	5	36	22	7	0	6	33	0	2	.468	.370
Perez, Delvin	R-R	6-3	175	11-24-98	.238	.625	.147	11	42	7	10	1	2	0	5	5	1	0	2	10	2	1	.357	.320
Rosendo, Sanel	R-R	6-2	205	5-7-97	.202	.242	.183	37	104	19	21	4	0	4	16	20	1	0	1	34	1	3	.356	.333
Sanchez, Brian	R-R	6-2	180	4-18-96	.200	.152	.224	33	100	10	20	4	2	1	11	10	1	0	1	30	0	0	.310	.277
Schafer, Jordan	L-L	6-1	205	9-4-86	.250	.400	.200	7	20	8	5	2	1	0	2	6	0	0	0	5	1	1	.450	.423
Sosa, Edmundo	R-R	5-11	170	3-6-96	.364	.333	.368	6	22	7	8	1	0	1	2	1	0	0	0	2	0	0	.546	.391
Soto, Carlos	L-R	6-2	220	4-27-99	.239	.220	.250	35	113	11	27	2	0	0	12	11	1	0	0	20	0	0	.257	.312
Williams, Donivan	R-R	6-0	190	7-25-99	.204	.160	.219	33	98	17	20	1	2	1	16	11	3	0	3	25	2	3	.286	.296
Zavala, Stephen	R-R	5-8	175	5-2-93	.667	—	.667	1	3	1	2	0	0	0	2	0	0	0	0	0	0	0	.667	.667

Pitching	B-T	HT	WT	DOB	W	L	ERA	G	GS	CG	SV	IP	H	R	ER	HR	BB	SO	AVG	vLH	vRH	K/9	BB/9
Alvarez, Juan	R-R	6-4	180	12-28-96	0	0	0.00	2	0	0	0	2	1	0	0	0	0	1	.167	.200	.000	4.50	0.00
Cruz, Jesus	R-R	6-1	225	4-15-95	0	0	5.40	1	0	0	0	2	4	1	1	0	0	3	.500	.800	.000	16.20	0.00
Dayton, Patrick	L-L	6-0	170	7-20-95	2	2	3.86	15	0	0	2	16	23	17	7	0	9	19	.319	.346	.304	10.47	4.96
De Jesus, Noel	R-R	6-3	181	1-8-97	2	1	2.94	10	5	0	0	34	35	13	11	1	9	20	.263	.209	.289	5.35	2.41
Diaz, Oneiver	R-R	6-2	160	8-28-96	0	2	14.73	3	1	0	0	7	13	13	12	1	2	4	.382	.417	.364	4.91	2.45
Duke, Zach	L-L	6-2	210	4-19-83	0	0	0.00	2	2	0	0	2	1	0	0	0	0	3	.143	.250	.000	13.50	0.00
Fagalde, Alex	R-R	6-3	225	4-29-94	2	1	2.25	6	1	0	0	12	12	3	3	1	0	14	.255	.267	.250	10.50	0.00
Gentner, Gabriel	R-R	6-1	235	9-6-95	2	2	2.04	15	0	0	0	18	23	7	4	1	3	19	.311	.458	.240	9.68	1.53
Gilmartin, Sean	L-L	6-2	206	5-8-90	0	0	4.76	5	5	0	0	6	3	3	3	0	0	7	.150	.143	.154	11.12	0.00

Pitching	B-T	HT	WT	DOB	W	L	ERA	G	GS	CG	SV	IP	H	R	ER	HR	BB	SO	AVG	vLH	vRH	K/9	BB/9
Gonzalez, Derian	R-R	6-3	190	1-31-95	0	0	3.00	2	2	0	0	3	5	2	1	0	0	6	.385	.667	.300	18.00	0.00
Gonzalez, Junior	R-R	6-3	175	11-7-96	2	2	4.70	12	8	0	0	59	75	41	31	3	19	29	.307	.267	.331	4.40	2.88
Hamann, Kevin	R-R	6-4	180	11-24-93	1	1	3.26	14	2	0	2	19	19	10	7	1	2	15	.253	.217	.269	6.98	0.93
Hunt, Chris	R-R	6-3	210	1-15-95	2	2	4.09	13	0	0	0	22	27	11	10	2	3	17	.294	.152	.373	6.95	1.23
Malcom, Cory	R-R	6-0	190	1-31-95	0	0	3.18	12	0	0	2	11	13	4	4	0	2	14	.296	.250	.321	11.12	1.59
Nicacio, Winston	R-R	6-2	180	12-29-96	4	3	2.61	11	8	0	0	52	57	24	15	4	16	39	.285	.227	.320	6.79	2.79
Perez, Enrique	L-L	6-2	180	8-10-97	1	2	8.14	18	1	0	0	24	24	24	22	0	27	31	.250	.177	.290	11.47	9.99
Pirela, Brian	R-R	6-2	221	1-19-98	3	4	4.50	11	8	0	0	54	60	33	27	8	23	37	.290	.339	.269	6.17	3.83
Reyes, Arturo	R-R	5-11	185	4-6-92	0	1	2.25	4	1	0	0	4	3	1	1	0	0	4	.200	.250	.143	9.00	0.00
Rivera, Wilberto	R-R	6-3	207	4-26-99	0	0	5.79	9	0	0	0	9	12	9	6	0	6	8	.308	.278	.333	7.71	5.79
Rondon, Angel	R-R	6-2	185	12-1-97	3	3	2.64	11	8	0	0	48	46	20	14	2	17	41	.254	.276	.238	7.74	3.21
Saylor, C.J.	R-R	5-11	195	10-14-93	1	2	7.30	10	0	0	2	12	16	14	10	1	5	14	.314	.214	.351	10.22	3.65
Voyles, Jim	R-R	6-7	205	3-20-95	0	1	8.18	8	1	0	1	11	13	10	10	1	2	7	.283	.313	.267	5.73	1.64
Warner, Austin	L-L	5-11	185	6-27-94	1	0	0.77	3	2	0	0	12	9	2	1	0	0	19	.209	.222	.206	14.66	0.00
Whitley, Kodi	R-R	6-4	220	2-21-95	0	0	1.84	12	0	0	2	15	15	4	3	0	3	19	.283	.278	.286	11.66	1.84
Wick, Rowan	L-R	6-3	220	11-9-92	0	0	0.00	4	0	0	0	4	0	0	0	0	1	8	.000	.000	.000	18.00	2.25

Fielding

C: Brdar 1, Coman 5, Gomez 2, Jackson 11, Knight 15, Soto 28, Zavala 1. **1B:** Bryant 9, Cedeno 8, Coman 4, Gomez 30, Grayson 4, Soto 4. **2B:** Alvarez 7, Brdar 21, Brodbeck 3, Castillo 20, Flores 11, Sosa 1, Williams 2. **3B:** Bryant 7, Flores 2, Montero 41, Williams 8. **SS:** Brdar 1, Brodbeck 4, Bryant 22, Castillo 17, Flores 4, Perez 9, Sosa 3. **OF:** Brdar 4, Flores 18, Fuller 35, Gomez 5, Luna 13, Machado 34, Rosendo 32, Sanchez 28, Schafer 4, Williams 14.

DSL CARDINALS — *ROOKIE*

DOMINICAN SUMMER LEAGUE

Batting	B-T	HT	WT	DOB	AVG	vLH	vRH	G	AB	R	H	2B	3B	HR	RBI	BB	HBP	SH	SF	SO	SB	CS	SLG	OBP
De Jesus, Freddy	R-R	6-1	200	10-15-99	.277	.242	.281	52	184	24	51	7	0	7	27	22	6	0	3	62	0	1	.429	.367
Del Rio, Diomedes	R-R	5-10	160	9-15-97	.250	.177	.263	41	112	20	28	3	3	0	13	13	4	5	2	24	6	3	.330	.344
Garcia, Joyser	R-R	5-10	165	10-14-99	.253	.250	.254	25	79	10	20	3	0	0	9	4	1	0	0	17	0	1	.291	.298
Garcia, Victor	R-R	6-3	235	9-16-99	.250	.167	.270	28	92	11	23	5	0	1	15	8	5	0	1	16	0	0	.337	.340
Gomez, Pablo	R-R	5-11	170	9-4-99	.300	.216	.322	50	190	29	57	8	1	1	16	10	1	3	1	27	8	4	.368	.337
Hernandez, Francisco	R-R	5-11	190	10-8-99	.200	.177	.206	27	90	14	18	1	0	3	10	3	4	0	2	26	1	3	.311	.253
Herrera, Ivan	R-R	6-0	180	6-1-00	.335	.371	.316	49	170	21	57	15	0	1	27	18	10	1	2	36	2	2	.441	.425
Jimenez, William	R-R	5-10	171	1-23-96	.308	.306	.319	45	156	24	48	11	4	1	25	22	4	1	2	36	8	6	.449	.402
Longa, Cristhian	R-R	5-11	180	4-28-00	.284	.273	.287	34	109	20	31	7	1	1	14	12	3	3	0	16	0	0	.395	.371
Montano, Luis	L-R	6-2	170	4-10-00	.208	.192	.214	54	159	23	33	8	3	3	16	22	1	1	0	54	1	3	.352	.308
Ozuna, Raffy	R-R	6-3	196	9-6-98	.253	.308	.239	58	198	38	50	13	4	4	28	46	2	1	0	86	1	2	.419	.398
Pena, Erik	B-R	5-8	140	1-6-00	.213	.177	.215	44	127	16	27	5	0	0	12	16	4	0	2	30	2	4	.252	.315
Rosario, Yowelfy	R-R	6-3	165	6-9-00	.216	.200	.220	35	111	14	24	3	1	0	15	9	0	4	1	31	2	0	.261	.273
Samuel, Alexander	R-R	6-3	190	3-24-00	.192	.227	.188	36	125	21	24	4	1	1	14	11	4	0	2	37	0	0	.264	.275
Soler, Carlos	L-R	6-2	163	10-29-99	.238	.222	.247	54	202	33	48	7	8	1	23	23	7	1	3	51	7	9	.366	.332
Soto, Franklin	R-R	5-11	168	9-23-99	.280	.342	.266	55	211	31	59	13	1	1	19	17	3	3	4	42	8	2	.365	.336

Pitching	B-T	HT	WT	DOB	W	L	ERA	G	GS	CG	SV	IP	H	R	ER	HR	BB	SO	AVG	vLH	vRH	K/9	BB/9
Avelino, Rodard	R-R	6-1	170	6-3-99	1	1	10.47	14	0	0	1	16	22	21	19	1	18	15	.314	.333	.300	8.27	9.92
Benitez, Allinson	R-R	6-4	200	11-4-99	0	3	8.44	9	6	0	0	21	23	20	20	0	17	32	.277	.182	.340	13.50	7.17
Cordero, Diego	L-L	6-2	171	9-8-97	4	4	3.09	13	11	0	0	67	70	31	23	1	13	49	.270	.255	.275	6.58	1.75
Cruz, Jesus	R-R	6-1	225	4-15-95	3	0	0.71	9	0	0	2	13	5	3	1	0	4	19	.119	.000	.143	13.50	2.84
Diaz, Oneiver	R-R	6-2	160	8-28-96	1	2	4.84	13	1	0	2	22	25	16	12	1	10	9	.278	.267	.283	3.63	4.03
Garcia, Roy	R-R	6-0	190	8-28-00	2	4	7.44	20	0	0	0	33	38	31	27	0	22	28	.299	.326	.286	7.71	6.06
Geronimo, Jose	R-R	6-3	239	10-26-97	1	2	6.05	16	0	0	0	19	18	14	13	0	17	18	.254	.250	.255	8.38	7.91
Madera, Wilman	R-R	6-2	200	3-10-99	0	0	7.77	16	0	0	1	24	42	22	21	1	6	17	.400	.297	.456	6.29	2.22
Mendoza, Hector	R-R	6-2	176	3-5-94	0	0	2.57	3	0	0	0	7	2	3	2	0	5	10	.091	.000	.154	12.86	6.43
Moreno, Jose	R-R	6-1	170	8-20-00	1	3	3.18	12	11	0	0	51	47	20	18	2	14	32	.244	.241	.244	5.65	2.47
Pereira, Wilfredo	R-R	5-11	197	4-26-99	1	7	3.16	12	10	0	0	51	51	21	18	1	20	38	.268	.240	.279	6.66	3.51
Pirela, Brian	R-R	6-2	221	1-19-98	1	0	2.08	3	2	0	0	13	10	4	3	0	5	13	.213	.167	.229	9.00	3.46
Prada, Nelson	L-L	6-2	170	5-6-00	0	0	4.11	12	0	0	1	15	15	10	7	0	10	12	.254	.333	.227	7.04	5.87
Rondon, Angel	R-R	6-2	185	12-1-97	0	1	4.76	2	2	0	0	6	4	3	3	0	3	6	.211	.286	.167	9.53	4.76
Solano, Enmanuel	R-R	6-1	160	9-23-98	4	2	3.28	12	9	0	0	49	39	29	18	0	11	36	.214	.157	.237	6.57	2.01
Soriano, Larimel	R-R	5-11	160	1-28-00	1	0	4.66	8	0	0	1	10	13	7	5	1	5	7	.333	.300	.345	6.52	4.66
Soto, Hector	R-R	6-1	175	3-2-99	3	2	3.30	15	2	0	0	30	27	13	11	0	7	27	.241	.233	.244	8.10	2.10
Taveras, Leonardo	R-R	6-5	190	9-7-98	1	0	10.13	14	0	0	0	19	25	25	21	2	20	14	.329	.276	.362	6.75	9.64
Trompiz, Anthony	R-R	6-3	214	11-20-97	2	3	4.38	19	0	0	0	25	32	22	12	2	13	16	.320	.391	.299	5.84	4.74
Ventura, Francis	R-R	6-2	195	7-22-99	2	2	3.74	12	12	0	0	53	58	30	22	0	19	35	.274	.304	.256	5.94	3.23
Zamora, Dionis	R-R	6-2	193	8-2-96	2	4	2.56	21	4	0	6	39	34	15	11	1	20	42	.241	.306	.219	9.78	4.66
Zapata, Cristoffer	L-L	6-1	150	10-30-98	0	0	7.62	14	0	0	0	13	17	12	11	0	23	10	.309	.273	.318	6.92	15.92

Fielding

C: Garcia 25, Herrera 49, Longa 6. **1B:** De Jesus 46, Longa 28, Montano 1. **2B:** Gomez 23, Pena 27, Soto 24. **3B:** Gomez 21, Hernandez 26, Longa 1, Rosario 25. **SS:** Gomez 4, Ozuna 46, Rosario 1, Soto 24. **OF:** Del Rio 37, Garcia 13, Jimenez 41, Montano 52, Pena 2, Samuel 31, Soler 54.

San Diego Padres

SEASON IN A SENTENCE: A squad of rookies, including three Rule 5 draft picks, and inexpensive veterans surpassed expectations by not finishing with the worst record in baseball, winning 71 games in the organization's first full season completely dedicated to a rebuild.

HIGH POINT: Hunter Renfroe set a new Padres rookie record for home runs in a season when he hit his 25th longball of the year off Dodgers LHP Alex Wood on Sept. 26. Renfroe, who finished with 26 homers, broke a 48-year-old franchise record held by Nate Colbert.

LOW POINT: An undermanned pitching staff suffered its worst indignity on Sept. 12 in Minnesota. The Twins hit seven home runs, one in each of the first seven innings, to bash to the Padres 16-0. Four days later, the Padres lost 16-0 again—this time to the Rockies.

NOTABLE ROOKIES: Outfielder Manuel Margot opened as the Padres center fielder and held the job throughout the year, showing excellent defense, great speed and unexpected power. Righthander Dinelson Lamet became the rotation's most electric starter after his May callup and struck out 139 batters in 114.1 innings. Carlos Asuaje hit .270 and was the starting second baseman by the end of the year. Lefhander Jose Torres and righthander Phil Maton developed into bullpen mainstays. The three Rule 5 picks—shortstop/outfielder Allen Cordoba, catcher Luis Torrens and righthander Miguel Diaz—contributed little but remained on the roster throughout the year.

KEY TRANSACTIONS: The Padres' strip-mining of any veteran talent continued when they traded pitchers Trevor Cahill, Ryan Buchter and Brandon Maurer to the Royals for lefty Travis Wood and prospects Matt Strahm and Esteury Ruiz in July. Veteran righthander Jered Weaver retired after going 0-5, 7.44 in nine starts and being placed on the disabled list.

DOWN OF THE FARM: Triple-A El Paso reached the Pacific Coast League championship series for the second straight year, led by outfielder Franchy Cordero. Double-A San Antonio reached the Texas League semifinals behind a strong prospect group including infielders Fernando Tatis Jr., Luis Urias and lefthander Joey Lucchesi. Low Class A Fort Wayne reached the Midwest League championship series behind the strong pitching of righthanders Michel Baez and Reggie Lawson. Overall the system posted a .505 win percentage.

OPENING DAY PAYROLL: $71,624,200 (28th)

PLAYERS OF THE YEAR

MAJOR LEAGUE

Wil Myers
1B

.243/.328/.464
30 HR, 74 RBI
29 2B, 20 SB

MINOR LEAGUE

Fernando Tatis, Jr.
SS

(Low Class
A/ Double-A)
.278/.379/.498

ORGANIZATION LEADERS

BATTING — ***Minimum 250 AB**

MAJORS			
*	AVG	Jose Pirela	.288
*	OPS	Jose Pirela	.837
	HR	Wil Myers	30
	RBI	Wil Myers	74
MINORS			
*	AVG	Nick Buss, El Paso	..348
*	OBP	Luis Urias, San Antonio	.398
*	SLG	Franchy Cordero, El Paso	.603
*	OPS	Franchy Cordero, El Paso	.972
	R	Fernando Tatis Jr., Fort Wayne, San Antonio	84
		Michael Gettys, Lake Elsinore	84
	H	Fernando Tatis Jr., Fort Wayne, San Antonio	135
	TB	Fernando Tatis Jr., Fort Wayne, San Antonio	242
	2B	Austin Allen, Lake Elsinore	31
		Rafael Ortega, El Paso	31
	3B	Franchy Cordero, El Paso	18
	HR	Franmil Reyes, San Antonio	25
	RBI	Franmil Reyes, San Antonio	102
	BB	Fernando Tatis Jr., Fort Wayne, San Antonio	77
	SO	Michael Gettys, Lake Elsinore	191
	SB	Eguy Rosario, Fort Wayne, AZL Padres 2	33

PITCHING — **#Minimum 75 IP**

MAJORS			
	W	Jhoulys Chacin	13
#	ERA	Brad Hand	2.16
	SO	Jhoulys Chacin	153
	SV	Brad Hand	21
MINORS			
	W	Brett Kennedy, San Antonio	13
	L	Cal Quantrill, Lake Elsinore, San Antonio	10
#	ERA	T.J. Weir, Lake Elsinore, San Antonio	2.09
	G	Jason Jester, El Paso	53
	GS	Kyle Lloyd, San Antonio, El Paso	27
	SV	Trey Wingenter, San Antonio	20
	IP	Enyel De Los Santos, San Antonio	150
	BB	Michael Kelly, San Antonio, El Paso	56
	SO	Pedro Avila, Lake Elsinore, Fort Wayne	170
#	AVG	Joey Lucchesi, Lake Elsinore, San Antonio	.200

2017 PERFORMANCE

General Manager: A.J. Preller. **Farm Director:** Sam Geaney. **Scouting Director:** Mark Conner.

Class	Team	League	W	L	PCT	Finish	Manager
Majors	San Diego Padres	National	71	91	.438	11th (15)	Andy Green
Triple-A	El Paso Chihuahuas	Pacific Coast	73	69	.514	5th (16)	Rod Barajas
Double-A	San Antonio Missions	Texas	78	62	.557	1st (8)	Phillip Wellman
High-A	Lake Elsinore Storm	California	64	76	.457	7th (8)	Edwin Rodriguez
Low-A	Fort Wayne TinCaps	Midwest	68	72	.486	10th (16)	Anthony Contreras
Short Season	Tri-City Dust Devils	Northwest	40	36	.526	3rd (8)	Ben Fritz
Rookie	AZL Padres	Arizona	25	31	.446	t-11th (15)	Shaun Cole
Rookie	AZL Padres 2	Arizona	30	25	.545	t-5th (15)	Michael Collins
Overall 2017 Minor League Record			378	371	.505	t-9th (30)	

ORGANIZATION STATISTICS

SAN DIEGO PADRES

NATIONAL LEAGUE

Batting	B-T	HT	WT	DOB	AVG	vLH	vRH	G	AB	R	H	2B	3B	HR	RBI	BB	HBP	SH	SF	SO	SB	CS	SLG	OBP
Asuaje, Carlos	L-R	5-9	158	11-2-91	.270	.230	.283	89	307	28	83	14	1	4	21	28	2	5	1	76	0	1	.362	.334
Aybar, Erick	R-B	5-10	195	1-14-84	.234	.244	.231	108	333	37	78	15	1	7	22	28	4	3	2	57	11	4	.348	.300
Blash, Jabari	R-R	6-5	235	7-4-89	.213	.290	.158	61	164	24	35	6	0	5	16	28	2	0	1	66	1	2	.342	.333
Coleman, Dusty	R-R	6-2	205	4-20-87	.227	.077	.264	27	66	6	15	3	0	4	9	2	2	0	1	33	1	0	.455	.268
Cordero, Franchy	L-R	6-3	175	9-2-94	.228	.188	.237	30	92	15	21	3	3	3	9	6	0	1	0	44	1	1	.424	.276
Cordoba, Allen	R-R	6-1	175	12-6-95	.208	.095	.238	100	202	17	42	2	2	4	15	18	4	0	3	54	2	2	.297	.282
d'Arnaud, Chase	R-R	6-2	205	1-21-87	.143	.000	.233	22	49	5	7	2	0	1	3	2	0	0	0	17	5	1	.245	.177
2-team total (11 Atlanta)					.175	.000	.233	33	57	10	10	2	0	1	3	4	0	0	0	20	5	1	.263	.230
Gale, Rocky	R-R	6-1	185	2-22-88	.100	.500	.000	3	10	1	1	0	0	1	2	0	0	0	0	2	0	0	.400	.100
Hedges, Austin	R-R	6-1	206	8-18-92	.215	.214	.215	120	387	36	83	17	0	18	55	23	3	1	3	122	4	1	.398	.262
Jankowski, Travis	L-R	6-2	185	6-15-91	.187	.125	.203	27	75	10	14	2	0	0	1	9	1	2	0	28	4	0	.213	.282
Margot, Manuel	R-R	5-11	180	9-28-94	.263	.285	.256	126	487	53	128	18	7	13	39	35	2	1	4	106	17	7	.409	.313
Myers, Wil	R-R	6-3	205	12-10-90	.243	.235	.246	155	567	80	138	29	3	30	74	70	5	0	7	180	20	6	.464	.328
Pirela, Jose	R-R	6-0	220	11-21-89	.289	.305	.283	83	312	43	90	25	4	10	40	27	2	1	2	71	4	3	.490	.347
Renfroe, Hunter	R-R	6-1	220	1-28-92	.232	.316	.202	122	445	51	103	25	1	26	58	27	6	0	1	140	3	0	.467	.284
Sanchez, Hector	B-R	6-0	235	11-17-89	.219	.212	.221	75	137	14	30	4	0	8	25	5	0	0	1	41	0	0	.423	.245
Sardinas, Luis	B-R	6-1	180	5-16-93	.163	.238	.107	29	49	3	8	0	0	0	1	4	0	0	0	11	1	0	.163	.226
Schimpf, Ryan	L-R	5-9	180	4-11-88	.158	.163	.156	53	165	24	26	2	0	14	25	27	3	0	2	70	0	0	.424	.284
Solarte, Yangervis	B-R	5-11	205	7-7-87	.255	.211	.272	128	466	49	119	21	0	18	64	37	5	0	4	61	3	0	.416	.315
Spangenberg, Cory	L-R	6-0	195	3-16-91	.264	.197	.289	129	444	57	117	18	2	13	46	34	5	2	1	128	11	3	.401	.322
Szczur, Matt	R-R	6-0	200	7-20-89	.227	.196	.240	104	176	26	40	11	2	3	15	32	4	2	0	40	0	2	.364	.359
2-team total (15 Chicago)					.226	.222	.200	119	195	28	44	12	2	3	18	34	4	3	1	44	0	2	.354	.350
Torrens, Luis	R-R	6-0	175	5-2-96	.163	.216	.140	56	123	7	20	3	1	0	7	12	1	3	0	30	0	0	.203	.243
Villanueva, Christian	R-R	5-11	210	6-19-91	.344	.385	.316	12	32	5	11	1	0	4	7	0	0	0	0	10	0	0	.750	.344

Pitching	B-T	HT	WT	DOB	W	L	ERA	G	GS	CG	SV	IP	H	R	ER	HR	BB	SO	AVG	vLH	vRH	K/9	BB/9
Baumann, Buddy	L-L	5-11	198	12-9-87	2	1	2.55	23	0	0	0	18	11	5	5	4	7	21	.177	.148	.200	10.70	3.57
Bethancourt, Christian	R-R	6-2	213	9-2-91	0	0	14.73	4	0	0	0	4	6	9	6	1	8	2	.353	.375	.333	4.91	19.64
Buchter, Ryan	L-L	6-4	258	2-13-87	3	3	3.05	42	0	0	1	38	28	15	13	7	18	47	.199	.175	.214	11.03	4.23
Cahill, Trevor	R-R	6-4	240	3-1-88	4	3	3.69	11	11	0	0	61	58	29	25	6	24	72	.247	.219	.269	10.62	3.54
Capps, Carter	R-R	6-5	230	8-7-90	0	0	6.57	11	0	0	0	12	12	9	9	2	2	7	.261	.350	.192	5.11	1.46
Chacin, Jhoulys	R-R	6-3	215	1-7-88	13	10	3.89	32	32	0	0	180	157	82	78	19	72	153	.235	.256	.217	7.64	3.59
Cosart, Jarred	R-R	6-3	206	5-25-90	0	2	4.88	7	6	0	0	24	26	15	13	0	19	15	.283	.378	.218	5.63	7.13
Diaz, Miguel	R-R	6-1	175	11-28-94	1	1	7.34	31	3	0	0	42	44	35	34	11	25	33	.275	.338	.228	7.13	5.40
Esch, Jake	R-R	6-3	205	3-27-90	0	0	—	1	0	0	0	0	0	0	0	0	2	0	—	—	—	—	—
Hand, Brad	L-L	6-3	228	3-20-90	3	4	2.16	72	0	0	21	79	54	20	19	9	20	104	.192	.150	.208	11.80	2.27
Lamet, Dinelson	R-R	6-4	187	7-18-92	7	8	4.57	21	21	0	0	114	88	63	58	18	54	139	.210	.263	.155	10.94	4.25
Lee, Zach	R-R	6-4	227	9-13-91	1	0	5.63	3	1	0	0	8	8	5	5	1	8	6	.250	.286	.222	6.75	9.00
Lloyd, Kyle	R-R	6-4	220	10-16-90	0	0	9.00	1	1	0	0	4	6	4	4	1	2	2	.333	.300	.375	4.50	4.50
Lyles, Jordan	R-R	6-4	230	10-19-90	1	3	9.39	5	5	0	0	23	35	24	24	5	10	22	.343	.357	.326	8.61	3.91
2-team total (33 Colorado)					1	5	7.75	38	5	0	0	70	96	61	60	16	22	55	.325	.363	.283	7.11	2.84
Maton, Phil	R-R	6-3	220	3-25-93	3	2	4.19	46	0	0	1	43	41	23	20	10	14	46	.249	.300	.211	9.63	2.93
Maurer, Brandon	R-R	6-5	230	7-3-90	1	4	5.72	42	0	0	20	39	39	25	25	4	8	38	.257	.224	.282	8.69	1.83
Mazzoni, Cory	R-R	6-1	210	10-19-89	0	0	13.50	6	0	0	0	8	17	16	12	5	4	4	.415	.360	.500	4.50	4.50
McGrath, Kyle	L-L	6-2	185	7-31-92	0	0	2.84	17	0	0	0	19	14	6	6	2	6	16	.209	.167	.233	7.58	2.84
Melville, Tim	R-R	6-4	225	10-9-89	0	0	7.71	2	0	0	0	2	3	3	2	0	3	3	.333	.200	.500	11.57	11.57
Overton, Dillon	L-L	6-2	175	8-17-91	0	1	7.71	1	1	0	0	5	9	4	4	2	2	3	.429	.500	.385	5.79	3.86
Perdomo, Luis	R-R	6-2	185	5-9-93	8	11	4.67	29	29	0	0	164	182	97	85	17	65	118	.285	.305	.267	6.49	3.57
Quackenbush, Kevin	R-R	6-4	235	11-28-88	0	2	7.86	20	0	0	0	26	32	23	23	5	16	23	.299	.239	.344	7.86	5.47
Richard, Clayton	L-L	6-5	240	9-12-83	8	15	4.79	32	32	2	0	197	240	114	105	24	59	151	.308	.286	.315	6.89	2.69
Ruiz, Jose	R-R	6-1	190	10-21-94	0	0	0.00	1	0	0	0	1	0	0	0	0	1	1	.000	.000	.000	9.00	9.00
Stammen, Craig	R-R	6-4	230	3-9-84	2	3	3.14	60	0	0	0	80	68	29	28	12	28	74	.229	.264	.202	8.29	3.14
Torres, Jose	L-L	6-2	175	9-24-93	7	4	4.21	62	0	0	1	68	63	34	32	13	16	63	.244	.258	.236	8.30	2.11

Pitching	B-T	HT	WT	DOB	W	L	ERA	G	GS	CG	SV	IP	H	R	ER	HR	BB	SO	AVG	vLH	vRH	K/9	BB/9
Valdez, Jose	R-R	6-1	200	3-1-90	0	0	7.94	13	0	0	0	17	20	16	15	7	4	16	.294	.172	.385	8.47	2.12
Weaver, Jered	R-R	6-7	210	10-4-82	0	5	7.44	9	9	0	0	42	51	41	35	16	12	23	.295	.281	.308	4.89	2.55
Wood, Travis	R-L	5-11	175	2-6-87	3	4	6.71	11	11	0	0	52	62	44	39	15	25	36	.295	.333	.287	6.19	4.30
Yates, Kirby	L-R	5-10	210	3-25-87	4	5	3.72	61	0	0	1	56	42	26	23	10	19	87	.206	.235	.185	14.07	3.07

Fielding

Catcher	PCT	G	PO	A	E	DP	PB
Gale	.947	3	18	0	1	0	0
Hedges	.990	115	921	56	10	9	3
Sanchez	.987	25	144	4	2	3	2
Torrens	.993	51	260	15	2	1	3

First Base	PCT	G	PO	A	E	DP
Asuaje	.000	1	0	0	0	0
d'Arnaud	.000	1	0	0	0	0
Myers	.994	154	1295	72	8	147
Pirela	.967	5	29	0	1	6
Sanchez	.958	6	21	2	1	2
Solarte	1.000	8	47	2	0	8

Second Base	PCT	G	PO	A	E	DP
Asuaje	.992	84	143	218	3	68
Bethancourt	.000	1	0	0	0	0
Cordoba	.000	1	0	0	0	0
d'Arnaud	.889	3	2	6	1	2
Myers	.000	1	0	0	0	0
Pirela	1.000	7	2	9	0	1
Sardinas	1.000	7	7	6	0	1
Solarte	.989	79	93	187	3	53
Spangenberg	1.000	7	12	13	0	3

Third Base	PCT	G	PO	A	E	DP
Cordoba	.500	3	0	1	1	0
d'Arnaud	1.000	2	1	3	0	1
Pirela	1.000	1	0	2	0	0
Sardinas	1.000	4	1	6	0	0
Schimpf	.950	50	21	113	7	8
Solarte	.947	22	16	38	3	5
Spangenberg	.944	96	47	173	13	20
Villanueva	1.000	9	4	11	0	2

Shortstop	PCT	G	PO	A	E	DP
Aybar	.977	99	117	273	9	63
Coleman	.960	27	28	67	4	16
Cordoba	.941	28	26	38	4	13
d'Arnaud	.943	10	17	16	2	6
Sardinas	.920	5	8	15	2	5
Solarte	.956	28	32	55	4	18

Outfield	PCT	G	PO	A	E	DP
Blash	.941	49	75	5	5	1
Cordero	.957	26	43	2	2	1
Cordoba	1.000	49	49	1	0	0
d'Arnaud	1.000	1	1	0	0	0
Jankowski	1.000	24	40	0	0	0
Margot	.989	123	273	6	3	0
Pirela	.977	71	120	5	3	2
Renfroe	.959	120	204	9	9	1
Spangenberg	1.000	32	32	1	0	1
Szczur	.990	74	98	2	1	1

EL PASO CHIHUAHUAS — *TRIPLE-A*

PACIFIC COAST LEAGUE

Batting	B-T	HT	WT	DOB	AVG	vLH	vRH	G	AB	R	H	2B	3B	HR	RBI	BB	HBP	SH	SF	SO	SB	CS	SLG	OBP
Asuaje, Carlos	L-R	5-9	158	11-2-91	.250	.240	.253	62	228	44	57	9	5	3	35	40	4	3	2	33	1	1	.373	.369
Blash, Jabari	R-R	6-5	235	7-4-89	.285	.273	.289	72	235	53	67	16	1	20	62	48	7	0	1	88	3	2	.617	.419
Buss, Nick	L-R	6-2	190	12-15-86	.348	.341	.351	114	353	53	123	19	8	11	55	27	4	0	6	54	9	2	.541	.395
Coleman, Dusty	R-R	6-2	205	4-20-87	.208	.203	.210	94	327	43	68	17	6	15	48	32	2	1	8	125	11	3	.434	.276
Cordero, Franchy	L-R	6-3	175	9-2-94	.326	.227	.358	93	390	68	127	21	18	17	64	23	4	2	0	118	15	4	.603	.369
Cowgill, Collin	L-R	5-9	190	5-22-86	.235	.180	.253	58	200	34	47	8	1	7	24	17	1	1	1	59	4	3	.390	.297
Cruz, Tony	R-R	5-11	215	8-18-86	.280	.381	.246	51	168	25	47	9	0	7	27	12	4	0	1	43	0	0	.458	.341
d'Arnaud, Chase	R-R	6-2	205	1-21-87	.297	.180	.344	45	172	39	51	8	1	4	19	17	2	1	2	33	12	1	.424	.363
Gale, Rocky	R-R	6-1	185	2-22-88	.278	.253	.286	103	342	43	95	20	2	2	37	24	4	2	5	55	0	0	.366	.328
Goris, Diego	R-R	5-10	200	11-8-90	.285	.279	.287	125	439	59	125	23	1	11	56	28	0	0	3	92	5	2	.417	.326
Jankowski, Travis	L-R	6-2	185	6-15-91	.266	.316	.248	35	139	20	37	5	1	0	11	18	0	0	0	28	8	1	.317	.350
Margot, Manuel	R-R	5-11	180	9-28-94	.150	.143	.154	5	20	1	3	0	1	0	4	3	0	0	0	4	2	0	.250	.261
Ortega, Rafael	L-R	5-11	160	5-15-91	.317	.327	.314	121	419	69	133	31	7	6	53	46	1	2	4	49	26	7	.468	.383
Pirela, Jose	R-R	6-0	220	11-21-89	.332	.359	.324	48	181	37	60	10	3	13	42	15	2	2	1	26	8	3	.635	.387
Renfroe, Hunter	R-R	6-1	220	1-28-92	.509	.813	.385	14	55	18	28	7	1	4	18	6	0	0	0	7	1	0	.891	.557
Romak, Jamie	R-R	6-2	220	9-30-85	.347	.316	.355	25	95	24	33	8	1	11	25	6	1	0	0	25	2	1	.800	.392
Rondon, Jose	R-R	6-1	195	3-3-94	.282	.345	.250	22	85	9	24	8	0	1	14	6	0	0	0	16	1	0	.412	.330
Sanchez, Hector	B-R	6-0	235	11-17-89	.269	.000	.304	7	26	2	7	2	0	2	6	2	0	0	0	8	0	0	.577	.321
Schimpf, Ryan	L-R	5-9	180	4-11-88	.203	.194	.206	69	242	44	49	7	1	19	44	36	3	0	2	105	0	0	.475	.311
Schulz, Nick	R-R	6-3	210	5-3-91	.182	.160	.191	29	88	13	16	2	1	4	8	8	1	0	1	20	1	0	.364	.255
Solarte, Yangervis	B-R	5-11	205	7-7-87	.286	—	.286	2	7	1	2	0	0	0	2	1	0	0	0	2	0	0	.286	.375
Spangenberg, Cory	L-R	6-0	195	3-16-91	.349	.412	.327	17	66	8	23	3	1	1	7	4	2	0	0	8	3	2	.470	.403
Stevens, River	L-R	6-0	185	1-10-92	.417	.600	.286	5	12	3	5	1	0	0	2	1	1	0	0	2	0	0	.500	.500
Van Gansen, Peter	L-R	5-9	175	3-4-94	.274	.381	.220	21	62	12	17	4	0	0	9	7	0	0	1	17	1	0	.339	.343
Villanueva, Christian	R-R	5-11	210	6-19-91	.297	.276	.303	109	398	69	118	28	2	20	86	43	6	1	6	83	4	2	.528	.369

Pitching	B-T	HT	WT	DOB	W	L	ERA	G	GS	CG	SV	IP	H	R	ER	HR	BB	SO	AVG	vLH	vRH	K/9	BB/9
Baumann, Buddy	L-L	5-11	198	12-9-87	0	0	1.59	3	0	0	1	6	4	1	1	1	1	7	.191	.333	.083	11.12	1.59
Bawcom, Logan	R-R	6-2	220	11-2-88	1	3	2.70	36	0	0	2	53	48	23	16	4	25	54	.240	.255	.226	9.11	4.22
2-team total (11 Nashville)					2	5	3.31	47	0	0	2	71	66	33	26	5	31	63	.248	.259	.282	8.02	3.95
Bethancourt, Christian	R-R	6-2	213	9-2-91	3	2	8.21	34	1	0	0	42	50	40	38	8	33	23	.296	.279	.313	4.97	7.13
Cahill, Trevor	R-R	6-4	240	3-1-88	0	1	6.00	1	1	0	0	3	4	2	2	1	1	4	.333	.286	.400	12.00	3.00
Capps, Carter	R-R	6-5	230	8-7-90	1	1	2.81	24	0	0	2	26	18	15	8	1	9	28	.188	.196	.178	9.82	3.16
Cimber, Adam	R-R	6-4	180	8-15-90	4	1	2.92	37	2	0	4	65	51	21	21	10	8	52	.216	.205	.228	7.24	1.11
Cosart, Jarred	R-R	6-3	206	5-25-90	1	0	0.00	1	0	0	0	4	2	0	0	0	1	4	.143	.000	.200	9.00	2.25
De Paula, Rafael	R-R	6-2	215	3-24-91	2	1	5.40	14	0	0	0	22	25	16	13	4	11	20	.301	.302	.300	8.31	4.57
Dimock, Michael	R-R	6-2	195	10-26-89	0	1	14.14	6	0	0	0	7	16	11	11	2	3	7	.457	.588	.333	9.00	3.86
2-team total (2 Salt Lake)					0	1	10.97	8	0	0	0	11	21	13	13	2	5	9	.420	.333	.333	7.59	4.22
Esch, Jake	R-R	6-3	205	3-27-90	0	1	7.71	1	1	0	0	5	7	4	4	1	0	3	.368	.400	.333	5.79	0.00
Fisher, Carlos	R-R	6-4	220	2-22-83	0	3	8.41	18	0	0	0	20	25	19	19	2	12	20	.305	.342	.268	8.85	5.31
Frank, Trevor	R-R	6-0	195	6-23-91	0	1	11.57	2	0	0	0	2	5	3	3	0	1	2	.417	.500	.400	7.71	3.86
Friedrich, Christian	L-R	6-4	222	7-8-87	0	1	18.00	1	1	0	0	3	6	6	6	2	2	4	.400	.833	.111	12.00	6.00
Hessler, Keith	L-L	6-4	244	3-15-89	2	2	4.57	41	0	0	1	45	52	25	23	7	23	36	.292	.333	.266	7.15	4.57
Huffman, Chris	R-R	6-1	205	11-25-92	3	1	3.31	7	7	0	0	33	35	12	12	6	9	27	.273	.315	.218	7.44	2.48
Jenkins, Tyrell	R-R	6-4	180	7-20-92	4	8	7.76	17	16	0	0	82	111	75	71	16	52	56	.337	.338	.337	6.12	5.68
Jester, Jason	R-R	5-11	205	5-4-91	4	2	5.91	53	0	0	3	67	79	45	44	9	27	41	.296	.317	.278	5.51	3.63

Pitching	B-T	HT	WT	DOB	W	L	ERA	G	GS	CG	SV	IP	H	R	ER	HR	BB	SO	AVG	vLH	vRH	K/9	BB/9
Kelly, Michael	R-R	6-4	185	9-6-92	3	2	6.64	13	7	0	0	42	47	33	31	6	26	37	.285	.314	.263	7.93	5.57
Lamet, Dinelson	R-R	6-4	187	7-18-92	3	2	3.23	8	8	0	0	39	32	17	14	2	20	50	.222	.258	.195	11.54	4.62
Lee, Zach	R-R	6-4	227	9-13-91	2	5	7.12	16	14	0	0	67	89	55	53	11	34	43	.320	.390	.242	5.78	4.57
Lloyd, Kyle	R-R	6-4	220	10-16-90	1	4	7.02	12	12	1	0	58	79	49	45	8	27	56	.335	.331	.339	8.74	4.21
Lockett, Walker	R-R	6-5	225	5-3-94	5	2	4.39	10	10	0	0	55	67	37	27	9	13	33	.289	.266	.309	5.37	2.11
Lyles, Jordan	R-R	6-4	230	10-19-90	1	1	4.50	5	5	0	0	20	20	11	10	1	8	20	.260	.200	.324	9.00	3.60
Magill, Matt	R-R	6-3	210	11-10-89	6	5	3.95	19	17	0	0	96	105	47	42	13	41	73	.285	.292	.279	6.87	3.86
Maton, Phil	R-R	6-3	220	3-25-93	1	1	2.84	23	0	0	13	25	22	10	8	1	8	31	.234	.250	.220	11.01	2.84
Mazzoni, Cory	R-R	6-1	210	10-19-89	1	0	0.89	14	0	0	1	20	18	2	2	0	3	31	.231	.250	.217	13.72	1.33
McGrath, Kyle	L-L	6-2	185	7-31-92	0	0	1.50	5	0	0	0	6	3	1	1	1	0	5	.143	.154	.125	7.50	0.00
Melville, Tim	R-R	6-4	225	10-9-89	1	0	4.66	2	2	0	0	10	7	8	5	0	10	8	.194	.118	.263	7.45	9.31
Nina, Aroni	R-R	6-4	180	4-9-90	0	0	9.00	1	0	0	0	1	2	1	1	0	0	1	.400	.250	1.000	9.00	0.00
Overton, Dillon	L-L	6-2	175	8-17-91	6	4	5.63	12	12	0	0	64	77	41	40	12	17	30	.294	.359	.273	4.22	2.39
2-team total (7 Tacoma)					7	6	6.73	19	18	0	0	91	111	69	68	21	29	52	.296	.359	.273	5.14	2.87
Quackenbush, Kevin	R-R	6-4	235	11-28-88	4	1	3.90	22	0	0	4	28	28	15	12	4	9	24	.277	.327	.225	7.81	2.93
Rienzo, Andre	R-R	6-2	195	7-5-88	3	0	2.83	21	5	0	0	41	37	18	13	3	27	39	.243	.239	.247	8.49	5.88
Rodriguez, Bryan	R-R	6-5	180	7-6-91	8	8	4.90	26	20	1	0	127	157	76	69	9	37	63	.308	.345	.270	4.48	2.63
Smith, Jake	R-R	6-4	190	6-2-90	0	0	0.00	2	0	0	0	4	2	0	0	0	4	4	.167	.000	.286	9.82	9.82
Valdez, Jose	R-R	6-1	200	3-1-90	2	3	5.02	23	0	0	0	29	34	16	16	2	11	30	.288	.237	.339	9.42	3.45
2-team total (10 Salt Lake)					3	4	5.31	33	0	0	1	41	44	24	24	2	16	45	.270	.304	.136	9.96	3.54
Vargas, Cesar	R-R	6-2	220	12-30-91	1	0	15.09	10	0	0	0	11	18	20	19	1	13	12	.375	.370	.381	9.53	10.32
Weaver, Jered	R-R	6-7	210	10-4-82	0	1	9.00	1	1	0	0	3	5	3	3	0	1	0	.357	.400	.250	0.00	3.00
Wieck, Brad	L-L	6-9	255	10-14-91	0	0	10.29	9	0	0	0	7	11	9	8	1	10	8	.344	.455	.286	10.29	12.86
Yardley, Eric	R-R	6-0	165	8-18-90	0	1	2.00	5	0	0	0	9	7	2	2	2	1	8	.226	.286	.177	8.00	1.00

Fielding

Catcher	PCT	G	PO	A	E	DP	PB
Cruz	.979	46	302	28	7	5	4
Gale	.995	99	687	64	4	2	9
Sanchez	1.000	4	17	1	0	1	0

First Base	PCT	G	PO	A	E	DP
Buss	1.000	15	97	11	0	6
Cruz	1.000	1	14	0	0	0
d'Arnaud	.990	16	95	6	1	11
Goris	1.000	37	270	33	0	32
Pirela	.969	26	196	20	7	18
Romak	.988	18	158	10	2	21
Sanchez	1.000	1	8	1	0	0
Villanueva	.987	43	352	24	5	42

Second Base	PCT	G	PO	A	E	DP
Asuaje	.989	59	92	166	3	40
Coleman	1.000	10	16	34	0	4
d'Arnaud	.953	19	39	43	4	7
Goris	.977	28	46	79	3	17
Pirela	.857	4	2	10	2	1
Rondon	1.000	3	9	9	0	3
Schimpf	.925	12	14	23	3	8
Solarte	1.000	1	2	5	0	2
Stevens	.909	2	2	8	1	1
Van Gansen	.968	16	28	32	2	7

Third Base	PCT	G	PO	A	E	DP
Coleman	1.000	1	0	2	0	0
d'Arnaud	1.000	2	2	0	0	1
Goris	.936	20	15	29	3	1
Romak	1.000	3	0	3	0	0
Schimpf	.973	50	19	90	3	11
Spangenberg	.939	17	13	33	3	4
Stevens	.667	1	2	2	2	1
Villanueva	.984	59	36	84	2	6

Shortstop	PCT	G	PO	A	E	DP
Coleman	.964	78	128	222	13	58
d'Arnaud	.912	9	10	21	3	2
Goris	.958	38	64	94	7	27
Rondon	.970	18	20	45	2	11
Solarte	1.000	1	1	1	0	0
Van Gansen	.960	4	6	18	1	2

Outfield	PCT	G	PO	A	E	DP
Blash	.984	59	119	6	2	2
Buss	.993	59	131	5	1	1
Coleman	1.000	5	7	0	0	0
Cordero	.986	89	202	3	3	0
Cowgill	1.000	49	106	1	0	2
d'Arnaud	1.000	2	1	0	0	0
Jankowski	.983	29	58	0	1	0
Margot	.923	4	12	0	1	0
Ortega	.990	101	194	10	2	2
Pirela	1.000	12	23	0	0	0
Renfroe	.929	12	24	2	2	0
Schulz	1.000	24	29	1	0	0

SAN ANTONIO MISSIONS — *DOUBLE-A*

TEXAS LEAGUE

Batting	B-T	HT	WT	DOB	AVG	vLH	vRH	G	AB	R	H	2B	3B	HR	RBI	BB	HBP	SH	SF	SO	SB	CS	SLG	OBP
Blanco, Felipe	R-R	6-1	175	12-9-93	.158	.000	.200	5	19	4	3	0	0	1	1	2	0	0	0	2	0	0	.316	.238
Bousfield, Auston	R-R	5-11	185	7-5-93	.229	.271	.216	93	297	35	68	11	1	4	30	30	5	2	3	52	15	6	.313	.308
France, Ty	R-R	6-0	205	7-13-94	.276	.259	.281	97	363	42	100	20	1	5	39	22	15	0	2	68	1	0	.377	.341
Guerra, Javier	L-R	5-11	155	9-25-95	.212	.152	.232	39	132	18	28	6	0	3	15	8	1	4	0	46	0	3	.326	.262
Kennedy, A.J.	R-R	6-0	190	1-23-94	.069	.154	.040	27	101	4	7	1	0	2	8	5	3	1	1	36	1	0	.139	.136
Martinez, Alberth	R-R	6-1	170	1-23-91	.241	.281	.227	113	395	45	95	24	2	10	45	25	7	1	2	82	6	2	.387	.296
McGee, Stephen	R-R	6-3	215	2-7-91	.252	.218	.263	78	230	34	58	15	0	7	31	48	3	0	1	68	0	0	.409	.387
Naylor, Josh	L-L	6-0	225	6-22-97	.250	.216	.261	42	156	18	39	9	0	2	19	16	1	0	2	36	2	1	.346	.320
Perez, Fernando	L-R	6-0	210	9-13-93	.212	.133	.234	63	212	20	45	8	1	3	18	16	4	0	1	64	0	2	.302	.279
Perio, Noah	L-R	6-0	170	11-14-91	.281	.283	.281	112	430	53	121	15	4	4	36	30	2	2	2	60	7	5	.363	.330
Reyes, Franmil	R-R	6-5	240	7-7-95	.258	.147	.292	135	507	79	131	27	1	25	102	48	3	0	8	134	4	4	.464	.322
Rivas, Webster	R-R	6-2	218	8-8-90	.287	.267	.293	39	136	21	39	9	1	1	23	12	0	0	1	35	0	0	.390	.342
Rondon, Jose	R-R	6-1	195	3-3-94	.293	.321	.284	51	215	30	63	12	3	4	28	16	1	1	1	43	2	1	.433	.343
Schulz, Nick	R-R	6-3	210	5-3-91	.251	.290	.240	88	311	36	78	17	1	14	41	44	6	0	2	96	7	4	.447	.353
Stevens, River	L-R	6-0	185	1-10-92	.215	.139	.239	43	149	16	32	7	1	0	9	12	1	4	1	29	0	2	.275	.276
Tatis Jr., Fernando	R-R	6-3	185	1-2-99	.255	.267	.250	14	55	6	14	1	0	1	6	2	0	0	0	17	3	0	.327	.281
Torres, Nick	R-R	6-1	220	6-30-93	.277	.333	.258	119	437	59	121	16	1	11	61	24	4	0	2	108	3	5	.394	.319
Urias, Luis	R-R	5-9	160	6-3-97	.296	.313	.292	118	442	77	131	20	4	3	38	68	8	6	2	65	7	5	.380	.398
Van Gansen, Peter	L-R	5-9	175	3-4-94	.121	.143	.115	10	33	0	4	0	0	0	0	3	0	0	0	8	1	1	.121	.194

Pitching	B-T	HT	WT	DOB	W	L	ERA	G	GS	CG	SV	IP	H	R	ER	HR	BB	SO	AVG	vLH	vRH	K/9	BB/9
Adam, Jason	R-R	6-4	225	8-4-91	0	0	0.00	1	0	0	0	2	1	0	0	0	0	2	.143	.000	.250	9.00	0.00
2-team total (5 Northwest Arkansas)					0	0	5.40	6	0	0	0	8	4	5	5	0	4	13	.138	.143	.133	14.04	4.32
Baumann, Buddy	L-L	5-11	198	12-9-87	0	0	5.40	4	0	0	0	3	4	2	2	0	2	3	.286	.400	.222	8.10	5.40
Brasoban, Yimmi	R-R	6-1	185	6-22-94	0	1	4.71	22	0	0	1	29	34	16	15	4	20	20	.293	.250	.333	6.28	6.28

Castillo, Jose	L-L	6-4	200	1-10-96	1	0	2.89	8	0	0	0	9	8	3	3	1	4	10	.235	.313	.167	9.64	3.86
Cimber, Adam	R-R	6-4	180	8-15-90	1	1	2.81	12	0	0	1	16	12	5	5	1	2	13	.203	.238	.184	7.31	1.13
De Horta, Adrian	R-R	6-3	185	3-13-95	1	0	2.25	1	0	0	0	4	2	1	1	1	2	6	.143	.167	.125	13.50	4.50
De Los Santos, Enyel	R-R	6-3	170	12-25-95	10	6	3.78	26	24	0	0	150	131	69	63	12	48	138	.237	.239	.236	8.28	2.88
De Paula, Rafael	R-R	6-2	215	3-24-91	2	1	2.05	15	0	0	0	26	17	9	6	2	7	27	.185	.209	.163	9.23	2.39
Dorminy, Thomas	L-L	6-0	190	6-1-92	0	0	0.00	2	0	0	0	4	3	0	0	0	2	6	.214	.000	.429	14.73	4.91
Enright, Barry	R-R	6-3	220	3-30-86	0	0	2.92	2	2	0	0	12	13	5	4	1	2	9	.260	.222	.281	6.57	1.46
Esch, Jake	R-R	6-3	205	3-27-90	0	3	2.86	6	4	1	0	35	37	17	11	2	16	19	.278	.250	.301	4.93	4.15
Friedrich, Christian	L-R	6-4	222	7-8-87	0	0	6.48	3	3	0	0	8	11	6	6	0	5	6	.306	.167	.375	6.48	5.40
Hancock, Justin	R-R	6-4	185	10-28-90	0	2	6.23	10	0	0	0	13	17	13	9	0	7	11	.327	.438	.278	7.62	4.85
Huffman, Chris	R-R	6-1	205	11-25-92	4	4	3.13	11	11	0	0	69	72	26	24	6	15	59	.268	.278	.261	7.70	1.96
Keel, Jerry	L-L	6-6	240	9-26-93	1	2	1.02	3	2	0	0	18	14	3	2	0	5	14	.222	.143	.245	7.13	2.55
Kelly, Michael	R-R	6-4	185	9-6-92	7	2	2.98	15	15	0	0	85	68	31	28	6	30	91	.222	.265	.195	9.67	3.19
Kennedy, Brett	R-R	6-0	200	8-4-94	13	7	3.70	26	26	0	0	141	133	62	58	16	38	134	.248	.281	.226	8.55	2.43
Lauer, Eric	R-L	6-3	205	6-3-95	4	3	3.93	10	9	0	0	55	52	25	24	6	17	48	.251	.222	.261	7.85	2.78
Lloyd, Kyle	R-R	6-4	220	10-16-90	7	5	3.71	15	15	1	0	90	78	40	37	2	24	89	.229	.250	.214	8.93	2.41
Lucchesi, Joey	L-L	6-5	204	6-6-93	5	3	1.79	10	9	0	1	60	46	17	12	3	14	53	.208	.129	.239	7.91	2.09
McGrath, Kyle	L-L	6-2	185	7-31-92	1	1	2.66	20	0	0	0	24	16	10	7	2	4	27	.182	.172	.186	10.27	1.52
Nading, Charles	R-R	6-5	225	7-9-87	0	2	4.50	21	0	0	5	22	28	15	11	1	14	23	.304	.405	.236	9.41	5.73
Nina, Aroni	R-R	6-4	180	4-9-90	2	2	3.30	23	0	0	2	30	30	13	11	1	10	22	.263	.130	.353	6.60	3.00
Nix, Jacob	R-R	6-4	220	1-9-96	1	2	5.53	6	6	0	0	28	32	21	17	0	9	22	.281	.263	.298	7.16	2.93
Quantrill, Cal	L-R	6-2	165	2-10-95	1	5	4.04	8	8	0	0	42	52	24	19	5	16	34	.296	.217	.336	7.23	3.40
Rodriguez, Bryan	R-R	6-5	180	7-6-91	0	0	3.18	2	2	0	0	11	10	4	4	0	2	5	.233	.177	.269	3.97	1.59
Smith, Jake	R-R	6-4	190	6-2-90	0	1	2.70	4	0	0	0	3	1	1	1	0	3	2	.091	.000	.143	5.40	8.10
Torres, Wilmer	R-R	6-3	190	5-31-96	1	0	0.00	1	0	0	0	2	2	0	0	0	0	3	.286	.000	.400	13.50	0.00
Vargas, Cesar	R-R	6-2	220	12-30-91	3	3	3.61	33	2	0	0	57	49	24	23	2	25	66	.229	.242	.220	10.36	3.92
Weir, T.J.	R-R	6-0	205	9-15-91	5	2	2.17	36	2	0	0	58	48	18	14	4	15	57	.219	.258	.192	8.84	2.33
Wieck, Brad	L-L	6-9	255	10-14-91	2	1	2.64	31	0	0	7	31	21	12	9	1	13	51	.191	.222	.169	14.97	3.82
Wingenter, Trey	R-R	6-7	200	4-15-94	2	1	2.45	49	0	0	20	48	33	16	13	6	19	64	.193	.192	.194	12.08	3.59
Yardley, Eric	R-R	6-0	165	8-18-90	3	1	2.05	44	0	0	6	61	52	18	14	2	12	52	.227	.267	.203	7.63	1.76

Fielding

Catcher	PCT	G	PO	A	E	DP	PB
Kennedy	.978	27	240	31	6	1	6
McGee	.990	75	651	36	7	1	12
Rivas	.991	38	291	29	3	3	3

First Base	PCT	G	PO	A	E	DP
France	.970	7	63	1	2	4
Naylor	.982	40	315	20	6	32
Perez	.996	54	444	29	2	34
Perio	.996	31	237	21	1	18
Torres	.992	12	113	5	1	10

Second Base	PCT	G	PO	A	E	DP
Blanco	1.000	2	3	6	0	2
Guerra	1.000	2	5	4	0	1
Perio	.990	66	112	177	3	31
Rondon	.977	11	16	26	1	3
Stevens	.957	4	16	6	1	2
Tatis Jr.	1.000	1	3	0	0	0
Torres	.000	1	0	0	0	0
Urias	.978	55	85	133	5	27
Van Gansen	1.000	2	2	5	0	0

Third Base	PCT	G	PO	A	E	DP
Blanco	.500	1	0	1	1	0
France	.952	85	55	125	9	14
Guerra	.875	4	5	9	2	1
Perio	1.000	6	1	3	0	1
Rondon	1.000	8	3	11	0	1
Stevens	.925	37	31	55	7	3
Tatis Jr.	.000	3	0	0	0	0
Van Gansen	1.000	1	0	2	0	0

Shortstop	PCT	G	PO	A	E	DP
Blanco	1.000	1	0	1	0	0
Guerra	.938	31	51	85	9	17
Rondon	.966	32	40	101	5	17
Stevens	1.000	1	3	4	0	2
Tatis Jr.	.861	9	9	22	5	5
Torres	.000	1	0	0	0	0
Urias	.946	60	83	162	14	25
Van Gansen	1.000	7	12	25	0	5

Outfield	PCT	G	PO	A	E	DP
Bousfield	.990	90	194	8	2	0
Martinez	.983	94	167	3	3	0
McGee	.000	1	0	0	0	0
Reyes	.978	89	169	5	4	2
Schulz	1.000	81	154	5	0	1
Torres	.968	75	116	5	4	1

LAKE ELSINORE STORM — *HIGH CLASS A*

CALIFORNIA LEAGUE

Batting	B-T	HT	WT	DOB	AVG	vLH	vRH	G	AB	R	H	2B	3B	HR	RBI	BB	HBP	SH	SF	SO	SB	CS	SLG	OBP
Allen, Austin	L-R	6-4	225	1-16-94	.283	.219	.300	121	463	71	131	31	1	22	81	44	7	0	2	109	0	1	.497	.353
Baker, Chris	R-R	6-1	180	11-29-94	.210	.203	.212	101	376	36	79	16	3	6	37	27	5	3	3	112	5	2	.317	.270
Belen, Carlos	R-R	6-1	213	2-28-96	.238	.299	.219	89	319	40	76	23	2	11	46	28	5	0	2	121	1	1	.426	.308
Bousfield, Auston	R-R	5-11	185	7-5-93	.256	.125	.286	11	43	8	11	4	0	2	3	7	1	0	0	9	0	2	.488	.373
Boykin, Rod	R-R	6-1	175	4-17-95	.314	.271	.331	43	172	30	54	9	5	6	20	16	1	0	0	62	7	1	.529	.376
Burgos, Aldemar	R-R	6-0	165	1-23-97	.000	.000	.000	2	7	1	0	0	0	0	0	0	0	0	0	5	0	0	.000	.000
De La Cruz, Wilfri	R-R	5-11	180	12-29-93	.227	.367	.164	28	97	11	22	5	0	2	11	1	1	0	0	30	0	0	.340	.242
Del Castillo, Miguel	R-R	5-10	170	10-14-91	.245	.125	.267	15	53	5	13	3	0	1	5	7	0	0	0	15	0	0	.359	.333
Easley, Nate	R-R	5-10	170	1-11-96	.059	.143	.000	4	17	1	1	0	0	0	1	0	0	0	0	2	0	0	.059	.059
Flores, Yuniet	L-L	5-10	175	3-15-86	.247	.053	.300	24	89	8	22	5	0	0	6	10	0	1	0	16	2	2	.303	.323
France, Ty	R-R	6-0	205	7-13-94	.288	.294	.287	30	111	10	32	4	2	0	19	7	12	0	1	16	1	0	.360	.389
Gettys, Michael	R-R	6-1	203	10-22-95	.254	.318	.239	116	457	84	116	22	4	17	51	46	6	2	2	191	22	8	.431	.329
Giron, Ruddy	R-R	5-11	175	1-4-97	.233	.151	.255	117	450	50	105	26	2	7	36	33	3	1	1	119	13	2	.347	.290
Guerra, Javier	L-R	5-11	155	9-25-95	.226	.221	.228	89	349	38	79	18	5	6	38	19	1	2	2	113	2	1	.358	.267
Kohlwey, Taylor	L-L	6-3	200	7-20-94	.244	.232	.248	92	303	40	74	15	5	1	25	27	5	6	3	81	2	2	.337	.314
Lambert, Greg	R-R	6-0	190	9-27-95	.167	.500	.000	3	6	0	1	0	0	0	0	1	0	0	0	1	0	1	.167	.286
Magee, Josh	R-R	5-10	185	2-13-97	.000	—	.000	1	3	0	0	0	0	0	0	0	0	0	0	2	0	0	.000	.000
Moreno, Edwin	L-L	6-1	190	10-27-93	.267	.250	.271	100	405	59	108	20	10	11	52	18	7	1	0	135	4	2	.447	.309
Naylor, Josh	L-L	6-0	225	6-22-97	.297	.232	.313	72	283	41	84	16	2	8	45	27	2	0	1	48	7	1	.452	.361
Overstreet, Kyle	R-R	5-11	205	9-4-93	.321	.333	.318	53	190	25	61	13	0	4	29	20	1	0	4	31	1	0	.453	.381
Perez, Fernando	L-R	6-0	210	9-13-93	.281	.263	.286	47	185	29	52	8	2	10	33	10	0	0	2	37	0	0	.508	.315

Selesky, Tyler	L-R	6-0	192	10-6-93	.209	.174	.222	28	86	8	18	5	0	0	7	9	1	0	1	24	0	0	.267	.289
Stevens, River	L-R	6-0	185	1-10-92	.287	.182	.319	23	94	13	27	3	1	1	9	9	0	0	0	11	2	1	.372	.350
Van Gansen, Peter	L-R	5-9	175	3-4-94	.242	.381	.200	51	182	17	44	9	2	1	25	15	0	0	2	28	1	0	.330	.297
White, Boomer	R-R	5-10	195	7-28-93	.219	.000	.280	10	32	5	7	1	1	0	5	3	1	0	1	10	1	0	.313	.297

Pitching	B-T	HT	WT	DOB	W	L	ERA	G	GS	CG	SV	IP	H	R	ER	HR	BB	SO	AVG	vLH	vRH	K/9	BB/9
Allen, Logan	R-L	6-3	200	5-23-97	2	5	3.97	11	10	0	0	57	60	29	25	2	18	57	.272	.338	.234	9.05	2.86
Avila, Pedro	R-R	5-11	170	1-14-97	1	4	4.98	10	9	0	0	43	50	31	24	2	18	53	.284	.367	.217	11.01	3.74
Barnette, Tyler	R-R	6-3	190	5-28-92	0	1	6.08	9	0	0	0	13	21	9	9	0	8	9	.382	.440	.333	6.08	5.40
Bednar, David	L-R	6-1	205	10-10-94	0	3	3.58	21	0	0	2	28	27	12	11	1	9	31	.257	.372	.177	10.08	2.93
Blueberg, Colby	R-R	6-0	195	5-11-93	7	2	2.85	45	0	0	10	60	50	21	19	3	25	74	.224	.233	.218	11.10	3.75
Boushley, Caleb	R-R	6-3	180	10-1-93	0	0	4.15	1	0	0	0	4	6	2	2	0	1	3	.316	.333	.308	6.23	2.08
Cahill, Trevor	R-R	6-4	240	3-1-88	0	1	6.75	1	1	0	0	3	3	4	2	0	1	3	.231	.250	.200	10.13	3.38
Capps, Carter	R-R	6-5	230	8-7-90	0	0	0.00	2	1	0	0	2	0	0	0	0	2	2	.000	.000	.000	9.00	9.00
Castillo, Jose	L-L	6-4	200	1-10-96	3	2	2.87	39	0	0	1	47	38	19	15	0	22	49	.220	.197	.235	9.38	4.21
Cosart, Jarred	R-R	6-3	206	5-25-90	1	0	4.50	1	0	0	0	2	3	1	1	0	2	1	.375	.500	.333	4.50	9.00
Cosme, Jean	R-R	6-2	155	5-24-96	0	3	7.43	6	6	0	0	23	35	19	19	1	12	17	.357	.297	.393	6.65	4.70
Cunningham, Alex	R-R	6-0	195	6-21-94	0	0	18.00	1	1	0	0	2	7	4	4	0	1	4	.583	.667	.333	18.00	4.50
De Horta, Adrian	R-R	6-3	185	3-13-95	3	1	4.89	8	7	0	0	35	35	26	19	4	11	42	.248	.154	.303	10.80	2.83
Diaz, Miguel	R-R	6-1	175	11-28-94	0	0	3.68	2	2	0	0	7	8	3	3	0	3	5	.296	.250	.333	6.14	3.68
Dorminy, Thomas	L-L	6-0	190	6-1-92	2	3	4.13	29	4	0	0	61	76	35	28	3	20	58	.309	.266	.336	8.56	2.95
Esch, Jake	R-R	6-3	205	3-27-90	1	4	5.74	7	7	1	0	42	56	32	27	5	8	31	.320	.341	.298	6.59	1.70
Frank, Trevor	R-R	6-0	195	6-23-91	4	4	4.23	43	0	0	7	55	55	27	26	7	9	66	.254	.270	.239	10.73	1.46
Friedrich, Christian	L-R	6-4	222	7-8-87	0	0	3.52	2	2	0	0	8	5	3	3	1	2	7	.192	.111	.235	8.22	2.35
Galindo, Jose	R-R	6-4	225	5-16-95	0	0	0.00	1	0	0	0	1	0	0	0	0	0	2	.000	.000	.000	18.00	0.00
Headean, Will	R-L	6-4	230	10-11-93	0	1	3.38	2	1	0	0	3	3	1	1	0	1	3	.273	.400	.167	10.13	3.38
Huffman, Chris	R-R	6-1	205	11-25-92	1	3	3.16	8	6	1	0	43	45	22	15	3	6	30	.266	.225	.324	6.33	1.27
Keel, Jerry	L-L	6-6	240	9-26-93	3	4	4.48	12	9	1	1	60	59	32	30	4	13	60	.261	.198	.304	8.95	1.94
Kulman, Spencer	R-R	6-1	195	3-29-95	0	0	0.00	2	0	0	0	2	2	0	0	0	1	2	.250	.000	.400	9.00	4.50
Lauer, Eric	R-L	6-3	205	6-3-95	2	5	2.79	12	12	0	0	68	65	25	21	4	19	84	.250	.247	.251	11.17	2.53
Lemond, Zech	R-R	6-1	170	10-9-92	2	3	4.39	44	0	0	1	66	79	40	32	5	17	68	.295	.325	.273	9.32	2.33
Lucchesi, Joey	L-L	6-5	204	6-6-93	6	4	2.52	14	14	0	0	79	56	26	22	9	19	95	.194	.179	.201	10.87	2.17
Megill, Trevor	L-R	6-8	235	12-5-93	1	0	13.50	2	0	0	0	3	5	4	4	0	2	3	.385	.600	.250	10.13	6.75
Nix, Jacob	R-R	6-4	220	1-9-96	4	3	4.32	11	10	1	0	67	78	40	32	5	10	51	.297	.264	.319	6.89	1.35
Quantrill, Cal	L-R	6-2	165	2-10-95	6	5	3.67	14	14	0	0	74	78	35	30	5	24	76	.273	.270	.275	9.29	2.93
Ramirez, Emmanuel	R-R	6-2	190	7-15-94	2	2	3.82	6	6	0	0	33	34	15	14	2	12	37	.274	.245	.296	10.09	3.27
Reyes, Gerardo	R-R	5-11	160	5-13-93	3	3	2.63	47	0	0	5	62	54	22	18	3	31	65	.240	.292	.206	9.49	4.52
Ruiz, Jose	R-R	6-1	190	10-21-94	1	2	5.98	44	0	0	2	50	57	34	33	7	25	45	.291	.273	.303	8.15	4.53
Scholtens, Jesse	R-R	6-4	230	4-6-94	6	7	3.98	19	18	1	0	111	124	52	49	10	24	86	.283	.308	.263	6.99	1.95
Smith, Jake	R-R	6-4	190	6-2-90	1	0	2.89	9	0	0	0	9	8	5	3	1	4	13	.211	.231	.200	12.54	3.86
Torres, Wilmer	R-R	6-3	190	5-31-96	1	0	0.00	1	0	0	0	1	0	0	0	0	0	1	.000	.000	.000	9.00	0.00
Weir, T.J.	R-R	6-0	205	9-15-91	1	0	1.86	10	0	0	0	19	14	6	4	0	5	22	.200	.214	.191	10.24	2.33

Fielding

Catcher	PCT	G	PO	A	E	DP	PB
Allen	.989	85	732	65	9	5	6
De La Cruz	.982	17	149	19	3	1	2
Del Castillo	.994	15	144	13	1	0	4
Overstreet	.991	27	207	14	2	1	5
Stevens	1.000	1	1	0	0	0	0

First Base	PCT	G	PO	A	E	DP
Allen	1.000	1	7	0	0	0
Belen	1.000	31	236	17	0	20
De La Cruz	1.000	3	10	0	0	0
France	.991	13	98	8	1	7
Naylor	.983	42	327	20	6	37
Overstreet	.990	11	92	5	1	11
Perez	.989	41	325	21	4	34
Selesky	1.000	1	7	0	0	0
Stevens	1.000	1	1	0	0	0
Van Gansen	1.000	1	9	1	0	1

Second Base	PCT	G	PO	A	E	DP
Baker	.981	88	134	232	7	55
Giron	.919	8	13	21	3	4
Overstreet	1.000	1	3	1	0	1
Perez	1.000	1	1	1	0	0
Selesky	.000	1	0	0	1	0
Stevens	.963	7	12	14	1	2
Van Gansen	.981	31	29	75	2	9
White	1.000	9	10	34	0	9

Third Base	PCT	G	PO	A	E	DP
Baker	.000	1	0	0	0	0
Belen	.929	48	39	79	9	8
France	1.000	4	3	7	0	1
Giron	.905	73	45	107	16	10
Overstreet	.938	5	5	10	1	1
Stevens	1.000	3	1	2	0	1
Van Gansen	.923	12	10	14	2	2
White	.750	1	2	1	1	0

Shortstop	PCT	G	PO	A	E	DP
Baker	.980	13	16	33	1	6
Giron	.956	35	46	83	6	17
Guerra	.968	89	144	246	13	60
Stevens	.000	1	0	0	0	0
Van Gansen	1.000	5	5	10	0	4

Outfield	PCT	G	PO	A	E	DP
Baker	1.000	1	1	1	0	0
Bousfield	1.000	11	26	1	0	0
Boykin	.981	43	99	2	2	0
Burgos	1.000	2	1	0	0	0
De La Cruz	.000	1	0	0	1	0
Easley	1.000	4	7	0	0	0
Flores	.975	22	36	3	1	0
France	1.000	1	1	0	0	0
Garcia	1.000	9	25	1	0	0
Gettys	.968	115	261	9	9	0
Giron	.000	1	0	0	0	0
Kohlwey	.976	89	157	8	4	1
Lambert	.750	3	3	0	1	0
Magee	1.000	1	3	0	0	0
Moreno	.929	88	131	12	11	2
Selesky	.944	25	33	1	2	0
Stevens	1.000	11	14	2	0	0
Van Gansen	.800	2	4	0	1	0

FORT WAYNE TINCAPS — *LOW CLASS A*

MIDWEST LEAGUE

Batting	B-T	HT	WT	DOB	AVG	vLH	vRH	G	AB	R	H	2B	3B	HR	RBI	BB	HBP	SH	SF	SO	SB	CS	SLG	OBP
Anguizola, Luis	R-R	5-11	210	2-27-94	.500	—	.500	1	2	1	1	0	0	0	0	0	0	0	0	1	0	0	.500	.500
Arias, Gabriel	R-R	6-1	185	2-27-00	.242	.111	.264	16	62	8	15	1	0	0	4	2	0	0	0	16	1	0	.258	.266
Benson, Tyler	L-R	5-11	180	6-17-96	.172	.250	.160	13	29	2	5	2	0	0	4	5	0	0	0	6	0	2	.241	.294
Boykin, Rod	R-R	6-1	175	4-17-95	.249	.286	.235	69	205	31	51	10	3	6	20	23	2	4	1	77	7	4	.415	.329

Easley, Nate	R-R	5-10	170	1-11-96	.261	.238	.268	77	257	39	67	14	4	4	25	41	2	4	0	64	14	4	.393	.367
Greene Jr., Marcus	R-R	5-11	195	8-19-94	.270	.307	.250	84	285	48	77	21	0	11	45	40	5	0	3	59	3	2	.460	.366
Ilarraza, Reinaldo	B-R	5-10	150	1-12-99	.229	.234	.227	126	480	58	110	17	2	4	45	40	6	1	3	149	26	7	.298	.295
Kennedy, A.J.	R-R	6-0	190	1-23-94	.138	.108	.149	42	138	11	19	4	0	2	11	5	4	1	1	52	1	0	.210	.189
Ona, Jorge	R-R	6-0	220	12-31-96	.277	.278	.277	107	415	54	115	18	1	11	64	40	8	0	2	115	8	2	.405	.351
Overstreet, Kyle	R-R	5-11	205	9-4-93	.327	.429	.313	17	55	10	18	6	0	2	6	11	1	0	0	8	0	1	.546	.448
Potts, Hudson	R-R	6-3	205	10-28-98	.253	.237	.259	125	491	67	124	23	4	20	69	23	6	0	2	140	0	1	.438	.293
Reed, Buddy	B-R	6-4	210	4-27-95	.234	.245	.229	88	316	48	74	17	8	6	35	23	3	1	3	97	12	8	.396	.290
Rivas, Webster	R-R	6-2	218	8-8-90	.232	.000	.296	23	69	3	16	3	0	1	7	9	0	0	0	13	0	0	.319	.321
Rosario, Eguy	R-R	5-9	150	8-25-99	.206	.204	.206	50	180	15	37	9	2	0	13	20	3	1	0	51	17	5	.278	.296
Seagle, Chandler	R-R	6-0	190	5-23-96	.148	.167	.143	10	27	1	4	1	0	0	4	0	0	0	1	12	0	0	.185	.143
Selesky, Tyler	L-R	6-0	192	10-6-93	.164	.150	.170	25	73	10	12	3	0	1	5	13	1	0	2	25	0	0	.247	.292
Suwinski, Jack	L-L	6-2	200	7-29-98	.227	.200	.237	125	462	64	105	21	4	9	41	55	9	2	4	139	6	5	.349	.319
Tatis Jr., Fernando	R-R	6-3	185	1-2-99	.281	.279	.282	117	431	78	121	26	7	21	69	75	6	0	6	124	29	15	.520	.390
Young, G.K.	L-R	6-1	225	10-27-94	.241	.192	.256	91	324	34	78	13	3	11	47	29	1	0	1	104	1	0	.401	.304
Zunica, Brad	L-R	6-6	254	10-21-95	.250	.300	.230	84	276	44	69	16	0	18	51	43	7	0	4	102	1	1	.504	.361

Pitching	B-T	HT	WT	DOB	W	L	ERA	G	GS	CG	SV	IP	H	R	ER	HR	BB	SO	AVG	vLH	vRH	K/9	BB/9
Allen, Logan	R-L	6-3	200	5-23-97	5	4	2.11	13	13	0	0	68	49	16	16	1	26	85	.201	.205	.199	11.20	3.42
Avila, Pedro	R-R	5-11	170	1-14-97	7	1	3.05	14	14	0	0	86	74	31	29	3	15	117	.231	.270	.193	12.29	1.58
Bachar, Lake	R-R	6-3	210	6-3-95	4	1	4.06	7	6	0	0	38	33	21	17	6	6	28	.239	.194	.282	6.69	1.43
Baez, Michel	R-R	6-8	220	1-21-96	6	2	2.45	10	10	0	0	59	41	16	16	8	8	82	.192	.182	.202	12.58	1.23
Bednar, David	L-R	6-1	205	10-10-94	1	1	1.87	24	0	0	9	34	18	7	7	1	11	50	.154	.172	.136	13.37	2.94
Bolanos, Ronald	R-R	6-2	195	8-23-96	5	2	4.41	16	11	1	0	69	65	38	34	3	34	51	.253	.269	.239	6.62	4.41
De Horta, Adrian	R-R	6-3	185	3-13-95	1	0	4.15	5	5	0	0	26	23	12	12	3	14	21	.237	.308	.156	7.27	4.85
Distasio, Louis	R-R	6-4	195	2-5-94	1	0	7.56	4	0	0	0	8	17	7	7	2	0	10	.415	.526	.318	10.80	0.00
Erb, Dalton	R-R	6-8	250	5-13-94	0	0	2.25	2	0	0	0	4	3	1	1	0	1	2	.231	.500	.000	4.50	2.25
Galindo, Jose	R-R	6-4	225	5-16-95	1	1	3.32	14	0	0	1	22	18	12	8	1	14	25	.217	.194	.234	10.38	5.82
Guerrero, Jordan	R-R	6-5	260	8-1-96	0	1	2.77	11	0	0	0	13	11	5	4	0	10	18	.239	.200	.269	12.46	6.92
Headean, Will	R-L	6-4	230	10-11-93	1	5	4.41	30	7	0	0	86	98	49	42	6	29	88	.289	.250	.315	9.25	3.05
Hernandez, Osvaldo	L-L	6-0	175	5-15-98	1	2	5.27	3	2	0	0	14	13	9	8	1	4	16	.250	.238	.258	10.54	2.63
Keel, Jerry	L-L	6-6	240	9-26-93	3	2	2.96	8	8	0	0	49	39	19	16	4	14	50	.219	.123	.274	9.25	2.59
Lawson, Reggie	R-R	6-4	205	8-2-97	4	6	5.30	17	17	0	0	73	65	44	43	8	35	89	.236	.221	.248	10.97	4.32
Lopez, Diomar	R-R	6-0	165	12-15-96	2	2	4.46	25	0	0	2	42	41	23	21	2	13	44	.250	.247	.253	9.35	2.76
McDade, Jim	L-R	6-5	190	12-1-92	3	4	3.95	17	7	0	2	68	73	39	30	8	4	61	.266	.261	.270	8.03	0.53
Miller, Evan	R-R	6-2	185	5-23-95	1	1	6.48	12	0	0	0	25	31	21	18	0	11	18	.301	.225	.349	6.48	3.96
Monroe, Nick	R-R	6-4	235	3-6-94	1	1	8.41	17	0	0	0	35	40	33	33	6	13	26	.290	.329	.242	6.62	3.31
Morejon, Adrian	L-L	6-0	165	2-27-99	1	2	4.23	6	6	0	0	28	28	14	13	2	13	23	.264	.192	.322	7.48	4.23
Munoz, Andres	R-R	6-2	165	1-16-99	0	0	3.86	3	0	0	0	2	2	1	1	0	2	3	.222	.200	.250	11.57	7.71
Ramirez, Emmanuel	R-R	6-2	190	7-15-94	0	2	3.63	7	0	0	1	17	21	12	7	4	8	24	.300	.333	.250	12.46	4.15
Rodriguez, Hansel	R-R	6-2	170	2-27-97	7	9	3.80	35	10	0	10	90	76	44	38	6	31	103	.224	.247	.203	10.30	3.10
Rogers, Blake	R-R	6-2	200	2-23-94	2	4	5.91	24	0	0	0	35	44	30	23	3	13	29	.293	.317	.278	7.46	3.34
Scholtens, Jesse	R-R	6-4	230	4-6-94	1	2	2.45	6	6	0	0	37	29	11	10	2	9	37	.223	.250	.200	9.08	2.21
Sheckler, Ben	L-L	6-8	240	5-12-95	2	3	5.63	13	0	0	1	24	31	19	15	1	11	34	.295	.261	.322	12.75	4.13
Smith, Austin	R-R	6-4	220	7-9-96	2	3	6.64	11	8	0	0	39	36	31	29	1	28	33	.242	.230	.253	7.55	6.41
Stillman, Will	R-R	6-4	175	11-2-93	1	2	8.27	5	3	0	0	16	19	15	15	4	9	20	.292	.350	.200	11.02	4.96
Thompson, Mason	R-R	6-7	186	2-20-98	2	4	4.67	7	7	0	0	27	23	17	14	2	12	28	.237	.279	.204	9.33	4.00
Torres, Wilmer	R-R	6-3	190	5-31-96	3	2	3.71	18	0	0	2	27	22	13	11	2	14	21	.218	.208	.226	7.09	4.73
Valdez, Dauris	R-R	6-8	221	10-22-95	0	1	2.38	7	0	0	0	11	7	3	3	0	7	14	.171	.250	.095	11.12	5.56
Zimmerman, Mark	L-R	6-0	195	3-29-94	0	2	4.89	24	0	0	1	42	45	30	23	2	22	52	.274	.265	.281	11.06	4.68

Fielding

Catcher	PCT	G	PO	A	E	DP	PB
Anguizola	1.000	1	1	3	0	0	0
Greene Jr.	.993	62	532	65	4	6	8
Kennedy	.987	42	401	46	6	2	1
Overstreet	1.000	8	71	15	0	0	2
Rivas	.985	22	167	31	3	2	3
Seagle	.978	10	81	10	2	0	1
Young	1.000	1	6	0	0	0	0

First Base	PCT	G	PO	A	E	DP
Overstreet	1.000	7	37	5	0	3
Selesky	1.000	1	4	0	0	0
Young	.982	68	488	44	10	21
Zunica	.984	72	525	25	9	38

Second Base	PCT	G	PO	A	E	DP
Easley	.952	23	24	55	4	2
Ilarraza	.952	94	147	212	18	34
Overstreet	1.000	2	1	3	0	1
Rosario	.941	22	27	53	5	6

Third Base	PCT	G	PO	A	E	DP
Arias	1.000	2	1	1	0	0
Ilarraza	1.000	3	1	6	0	1
Overstreet	1.000	1	0	2	0	0
Potts	.962	116	69	156	9	8
Rivas	.000	1	0	0	0	0
Rosario	.976	18	10	30	1	1
Selesky	1.000	1	0	1	0	0
Young	1.000	2	0	2	0	0

Shortstop	PCT	G	PO	A	E	DP
Arias	.981	14	24	28	1	7
Easley	.000	1	0	0	0	0
Ilarraza	.935	17	16	42	4	2
Potts	1.000	2	0	6	0	1
Tatis Jr.	.942	109	163	243	25	42

Outfield	PCT	G	PO	A	E	DP
Benson	1.000	5	8	0	0	0
Boykin	.985	65	129	5	2	2
Easley	.966	44	80	5	3	0
Garcia	1.000	12	20	4	0	0
Ona	.992	78	114	4	1	0
Reed	.990	85	198	4	2	0
Selesky	1.000	16	18	0	0	0
Suwinski	.972	123	236	6	7	0

TRI-CITY DUST DEVILS — *SHORT SEASON*

NORTHWEST LEAGUE

Batting	B-T	HT	WT	DOB	AVG	vLH	vRH	G	AB	R	H	2B	3B	HR	RBI	BB	HBP	SH	SF	SO	SB	CS	SLG	OBP
Almanzar, Luis	R-R	6-0	180	11-1-99	.230	.281	.216	67	261	36	60	10	1	2	21	25	1	0	1	85	10	5	.299	.299
Anguizola, Luis	R-R	5-11	210	2-27-94	.250	.308	.227	27	92	10	23	4	1	1	13	15	0	0	0	27	0	0	.348	.355
Aragon, Bryant	L-R	6-2	160	4-10-98	.213	.182	.219	43	150	12	32	7	1	1	10	12	0	0	2	41	0	0	.293	.268

Asuncion, Luis	R-R	6-4	205	2-27-97	.267	.346	.245	66	255	36	68	14	3	4	29	17	3	0	1	66	6	1	.392	.319
Batten, Matthew	R-R	5-11	175	6-22-95	.206	.600	.083	20	63	8	13	2	0	0	6	12	1	0	1	17	4	1	.238	.338
Bean, Steve	R-L	6-2	205	9-15-93	.308	.000	.400	3	13	3	4	0	0	0	3	1	0	0	0	1	0	0	.308	.357
Benson, Tyler	L-R	5-11	180	6-17-96	.304	.231	.321	21	69	8	21	4	0	0	10	13	2	0	1	21	9	1	.362	.424
Blanco, Felipe	R-R	6-1	175	12-9-93	.159	.188	.143	22	44	4	7	0	0	1	5	5	1	0	1	16	3	3	.227	.255
Burgos, Aldemar	R-R	6-0	165	1-23-97	.239	.156	.273	47	155	22	37	7	0	3	14	8	3	8	0	37	3	2	.342	.289
Carter, Tre	L-R	6-2	181	3-22-97	.230	.268	.220	68	261	25	60	6	11	3	32	27	1	1	1	95	16	2	.372	.303
De La Cruz, Wilfri	R-R	5-11	180	12-29-93	.182	.000	.222	3	11	0	2	1	0	0	0	1	0	0	0	4	0	0	.273	.250
Lambert, Greg	R-R	6-0	190	9-27-95	.375	.250	.500	4	8	1	3	0	0	0	1	0	0	0	1	4	0	0	.375	.333
Lezama, Jose	B-R	5-10	195	2-19-98	.278	.500	.250	6	18	1	5	0	0	0	4	2	0	0	0	6	0	0	.278	.350
Lopez, Justin	B-R	6-2	170	5-9-00	.246	.307	.228	66	281	25	69	16	0	2	22	17	2	1	2	80	1	2	.324	.291
Magdaleno, Westhers	R-R	6-1	190	10-30-96	.220	.364	.180	16	50	8	11	3	0	0	2	8	0	0	0	18	0	0	.280	.328
Magee, Josh	R-R	5-10	185	2-13-97	.218	.077	.246	29	78	10	17	4	1	0	9	22	2	1	1	29	7	4	.295	.398
Mattison, Chris	R-R	6-4	215	4-16-94	.225	.143	.259	34	120	17	27	10	2	4	19	7	3	0	0	60	0	1	.442	.285
Melean, Kelvin	R-R	6-0	165	9-5-98	.229	.167	.243	59	231	26	53	5	1	0	17	26	3	1	4	47	3	4	.260	.311
Pennell, Tucker	R-R	6-2	200	4-7-94	.600	.500	.625	3	10	3	6	2	0	0	4	4	1	0	0	3	2	0	.800	.733
Podorsky, Robbie	R-R	5-7	170	1-27-95	.302	.361	.283	37	149	22	45	6	2	1	13	11	7	1	1	12	16	5	.389	.375
Seagle, Chandler	R-R	6-0	190	5-23-96	.229	.333	.200	24	83	7	19	4	0	1	8	6	4	1	0	21	1	1	.313	.312
Washington, Jalen	R-R	5-11	190	2-28-95	.182	.188	.180	42	148	15	27	10	3	0	8	13	4	0	1	38	4	1	.291	.265
White, Boomer	R-R	5-10	195	7-28-93	.320	.250	.333	7	25	11	8	2	0	0	5	8	0	0	0	3	1	0	.400	.485

Pitching	**B-T**	**HT**	**WT**	**DOB**	**W**	**L**	**ERA**	**G**	**GS**	**CG**	**SV**	**IP**	**H**	**R**	**ER**	**HR**	**BB**	**SO**	**AVG**	**vLH**	**vRH**	**K/9**	**BB/9**
Ashbeck, Elliot	L-R	6-3	215	11-16-93	0	0	1.69	7	0	0	1	11	7	2	2	1	0	13	.180	.222	.143	10.97	0.00
Clase, Emmanuel	R-R	6-2	150	3-18-98	0	1	13.50	1	0	0	0	3	9	5	5	1	0	4	.474	.500	.462	10.80	0.00
Cosgrove, Thomas	L-L	6-2	190	6-14-96	1	4	3.48	11	6	0	0	41	40	22	16	0	16	36	.248	.231	.254	7.84	3.48
Cunningham, Alex	R-R	6-0	195	6-21-94	0	1	5.79	4	0	0	0	5	3	3	3	1	3	4	.177	.111	.250	7.71	5.79
Erb, Dalton	R-R	6-8	250	5-13-94	0	2	2.59	16	0	0	0	31	29	15	9	2	15	37	.250	.227	.264	10.63	4.31
Ford, Chasen	R-R	6-3	200	7-18-95	0	2	6.63	14	0	0	0	19	21	16	14	1	10	16	.276	.360	.235	7.58	4.74
Galindo, Jose	R-R	6-4	225	5-16-95	1	0	0.00	11	0	0	1	15	5	0	0	0	6	29	.100	.200	.057	17.02	3.52
Guerrero, Jordan	R-R	6-5	260	8-1-96	1	1	1.69	13	0	0	0	21	13	5	4	0	7	34	.173	.143	.192	14.34	2.95
Henry, Henry	R-R	6-4	178	12-17-98	2	5	3.48	12	11	0	0	52	52	24	20	0	14	43	.260	.261	.259	7.49	2.44
Hernandez, Osvaldo	L-L	6-0	175	5-15-98	2	3	5.33	8	8	0	0	27	37	20	16	0	8	31	.319	.316	.320	10.33	2.67
Leasher, Aaron	L-L	6-3	190	4-28-96	0	1	2.08	4	4	0	0	13	5	5	3	0	8	10	.119	.267	.037	6.92	5.54
Lopez, Diomar	R-R	6-0	165	12-15-96	0	0	0.00	1	0	0	0	2	0	0	0	0	0	3	.000	.000	.000	13.50	0.00
Margevicius, Nick	L-L	6-5	220	6-18-96	3	0	1.24	6	6	0	0	29	20	5	4	1	4	32	.189	.233	.171	9.93	1.24
McDade, Jim	L-R	6-5	190	12-1-92	1	0	0.00	2	2	0	0	14	10	4	0	1	0	14	.200	.316	.129	9.22	0.00
Megill, Trevor	L-R	6-8	235	12-5-93	3	0	0.98	16	0	0	2	18	10	2	2	0	2	35	.149	.167	.135	17.18	0.98
Miller, Evan	R-R	6-2	185	5-23-95	2	3	1.33	12	0	0	1	20	17	6	3	1	3	18	.239	.296	.205	7.97	1.33
Morejon, Adrian	L-L	6-0	165	2-27-99	2	2	3.57	7	7	0	0	35	37	14	14	2	3	35	.266	.167	.281	8.92	0.76
Munoz, Andres	R-R	6-2	165	1-16-99	3	0	3.80	21	0	0	1	24	15	13	10	2	16	35	.177	.188	.170	13.31	6.08
Radke, Travis	L-L	6-4	200	3-6-93	0	0	1.80	14	1	0	1	20	12	5	4	2	1	27	.179	.111	.204	12.15	0.45
Ramirez, Emmanuel	R-R	6-2	190	7-15-94	2	1	2.48	8	8	0	0	54	42	17	15	1	10	53	.214	.261	.176	8.78	1.66
Rogers, Blake	R-R	6-2	200	2-23-94	2	0	3.00	9	0	0	0	15	9	5	5	0	4	15	.177	.217	.143	9.00	2.40
Schlichtholz, Fred	R-L	6-3	215	9-18-95	4	2	0.81	16	0	0	2	22	16	6	2	0	9	23	.200	.191	.203	9.27	3.63
Sheckler, Ben	L-L	6-8	240	5-12-95	3	3	2.60	13	12	0	0	73	70	32	21	2	19	60	.248	.203	.262	7.43	2.35
Smith, Austin	R-R	6-4	220	7-9-96	1	0	5.14	19	0	0	2	21	20	14	12	2	11	24	.260	.138	.333	10.29	4.71
Stillman, Will	R-R	6-4	175	11-2-93	2	4	5.85	8	8	0	0	32	38	22	21	4	10	43	.286	.315	.266	11.97	2.78
Torres, Elias	R-R	6-1	176	2-22-92	3	0	5.14	18	0	0	0	21	24	16	12	1	10	35	.273	.167	.370	15.00	4.29
Torres, Wilmer	R-R	6-3	190	5-31-96	0	0	2.45	4	0	0	0	4	4	2	1	0	4	1	.286	.222	.400	2.45	9.82
Valdez, Dauris	R-R	6-8	221	10-22-95	1	1	4.30	10	3	0	0	23	20	12	11	3	5	31	.233	.276	.211	12.13	1.96
Zimmerman, Mark	L-R	6-0	195	3-29-94	1	0	0.69	11	0	0	1	13	4	1	1	0	3	23	.098	.067	.115	15.92	2.08

Fielding

C: Anguizola 1, Bean 2, De La Cruz 3, Lezama 6, Pennell 2, Seagle 24, Washington 40. **1B:** Anguizola 11, Aragon 42, Blanco 5, Mattison 25. **2B:** Almanzar 1, Batten 15, Blanco 7, Lopez 37, Magdaleno 1, Melean 18. **3B:** Almanzar 31, Batten 2, Blanco 4, Magdaleno 12, Melean 26, White 3. **SS:** Almanzar 32, Lopez 30, Melean 16. **OF:** Asuncion 52, Benson 12, Burgos 46, Carter 64, Lambert 3, Magee 22, Podorsky 34.

AZL PADRES — *ROOKIE*

ARIZONA LEAGUE

Batting	**B-T**	**HT**	**WT**	**DOB**	**AVG**	**vLH**	**vRH**	**G**	**AB**	**R**	**H**	**2B**	**3B**	**HR**	**RBI**	**BB**	**HBP**	**SH**	**SF**	**SO**	**SB**	**CS**	**SLG**	**OBP**
Aybar, Erick	R-B	5-10	195	1-14-84	.200	—	.200	2	5	0	1	1	0	0	1	2	0	0	0	0	0	0	.400	.429
Barley, Jordy	R-R	6-0	175	12-3-99	.242	.302	.223	49	182	34	44	11	6	4	28	11	2	0	0	65	7	2	.434	.292
Batten, Matthew	R-R	5-11	175	6-22-95	.263	.304	.250	29	99	22	26	6	2	1	14	11	0	0	0	22	1	0	.394	.336
Benson, Tyler	L-R	5-11	180	6-17-96	.177	.000	.333	5	17	1	3	0	0	0	1	3	0	0	0	7	0	1	.177	.300
Bono, Christoph	L-R	6-1	190	10-6-92	.189	.286	.151	22	74	5	14	5	0	0	4	5	1	4	0	22	1	3	.257	.250
Campusano, Luis	R-R	6-0	195	9-29-98	.278	.059	.329	24	90	3	25	4	0	1	13	6	1	0	1	14	0	1	.356	.327
2-team total (13 Padres 2)					.269	.059	.329	37	134	8	36	4	0	4	25	15	1	0	1	25	0	2	.388	.344
Cantu, Michael	R-R	6-3	225	8-28-95	.333	.333	.333	3	6	1	2	1	0	0	3	2	0	0	0	1	1	0	.500	.500
Cowgill, Collin	L-R	5-9	190	5-22-86	.250	.000	.273	4	12	1	3	1	0	0	3	1	0	0	0	2	0	0	.333	.308
2-team total (1 Padres 2)					.333	.000	.273	5	15	2	5	3	0	0	5	1	0	0	1	3	0	0	.533	.353
Fernandez, Juan	R-R	5-11	180	3-7-99	.250	.400	.211	8	24	5	6	1	0	1	3	0	1	0	0	0	0	0	.417	.280
2-team total (27 Padres 2)					.295	.400	.211	35	112	23	33	9	2	3	18	9	4	0	0	14	3	1	.491	.368
Gowdy, Denzell	R-R	5-11	185	11-30-96	.217	.250	.203	35	92	14	20	3	1	2	7	21	1	0	1	37	6	1	.337	.365
Hedges, Austin	R-R	6-1	206	8-18-92	.000	—	.000	1	3	0	0	0	0	0	0	0	0	0	0	2	0	0	.000	.000
Homza, Jonny	R-R	6-0	185	6-13-99	.228	.340	.190	52	184	28	42	13	0	0	20	16	5	1	2	54	0	4	.299	.304

Hunt, Blake	R-R	6-3	185	11-10-98	.214	.111	.263	8	28	7	6	2	0	1	4	3	1	0	0	13	0	0	.393	.313
2-team total (22 Padres 2)					.241	.111	.263	30	116	21	28	9	2	2	19	8	5	0	1	42	1	0	.405	.315
Jankowski, Travis	L-R	6-2	185	6-15-91	.286	.000	.333	2	7	3	2	1	0	0	0	2	1	0	0	1	1	0	.429	.500
2-team total (3 Padres 2)					.278	.000	.333	5	18	5	5	2	0	0	2	2	2	0	0	5	1	1	.389	.409
Lambert, Greg	R-R	6-0	190	9-27-95	.253	.250	.253	27	95	16	24	5	1	0	10	5	1	0	0	22	2	0	.326	.297
Lezama, Jose	B-R	5-10	195	2-19-98	.313	.267	.333	25	48	9	15	1	1	0	5	17	0	2	1	10	0	1	.375	.485
Olmo, Dayon	B-R	5-11	165	11-15-96	.276	.344	.255	44	134	21	37	6	3	2	26	8	2	0	2	39	6	2	.410	.322
Perez, Blinger	R-R	6-0	170	8-21-98	.250	.250	.250	4	16	3	4	0	0	0	1	1	0	0	0	7	0	0	.250	.294
Pineda, Jason	R-R	6-2	202	11-22-99	.223	.316	.181	38	121	13	27	7	0	2	16	14	1	0	2	45	2	1	.331	.304
Roman, Luis	L-R	6-0	215	12-19-94	.333	.000	.500	2	3	0	1	0	0	0	0	0	0	0	0	2	0	0	.333	.333
2-team total (31 Padres 2)					.190	.000	.500	33	100	15	19	4	0	1	10	11	1	0	3	28	1	0	.260	.270
Rondon, Jose	R-R	6-1	195	3-3-94	.250	.333	.222	3	12	1	3	0	0	1	4	1	0	0	1	2	0	0	.500	.286
2-team total (2 AZL Padres 2)					.353	.333	.222	5	17	5	6	0	0	2	7	4	0	0	1	3	1	0	.706	.455
Rosario, Jeisson	L-L	6-1	175	10-22-99	.300	.362	.279	52	187	31	56	10	0	1	24	33	1	1	2	36	8	6	.369	.404
Ruiz, Agustin	L-R	6-2	175	9-23-99	.208	.154	.225	18	53	10	11	2	1	0	3	7	1	0	1	22	1	1	.283	.307
Ruiz, Esteury	R-R	6-0	150	2-15-99	.300	.320	.295	31	120	23	36	10	4	1	16	9	3	2	0	34	17	6	.475	.364
2-team total (21 Royals)					.350	.417	.419	52	206	45	72	20	10	4	39	13	3	2	1	54	26	6	.602	.395
Rutherford, Cole	R-R	6-4	250	12-7-93	.128	.385	.029	22	47	3	6	0	0	0	1	4	0	0	0	16	0	0	.128	.196
Santos, Angel	L-R	6-4	170	1-13-96	.310	.313	.310	35	87	23	27	2	2	6	16	15	0	0	1	31	9	1	.586	.408
Williams, Jaquez	L-R	6-3	215	11-16-97	.203	.194	.205	43	143	21	29	7	0	6	24	25	4	0	1	52	1	0	.378	.335

Pitching	**B-T**	**HT**	**WT**	**DOB**	**W**	**L**	**ERA**	**G**	**GS**	**CG**	**SV**	**IP**	**H**	**R**	**ER**	**HR**	**BB**	**SO**	**AVG**	**vLH**	**vRH**	**K/9**	**BB/9**
Acevedo, Angel	R-R	6-1	180	9-19-98	0	2	9.98	14	3	0	0	31	55	43	34	4	13	25	.379	.400	.365	7.34	3.82
Adam, Jason	R-R	6-4	225	8-4-91	0	0	5.79	5	0	0	0	5	5	3	3	0	0	8	.250	.143	.308	15.43	0.00
2-team total (2 Padres 2)					1	0	4.05	7	0	0	0	7	6	3	3	0	2	12	.222	.143	.308	16.20	2.70
Anderson, Korey	R-R	6-2	205	9-11-94	0	1	5.82	12	0	0	1	17	16	12	11	1	6	19	.232	.174	.261	10.06	3.18
Ashbeck, Elliot	L-R	6-3	215	11-16-93	1	1	0.00	4	0	0	0	5	2	3	0	0	2	7	.111	.333	.067	13.50	3.86
2-team total (2 Padres 2)					1	1	0.00	6	0	0	0	8	4	3	0	0	2	11	.138	.333	.067	12.91	2.35
Bachar, Lake	R-R	6-3	210	6-3-95	1	0	1.00	5	0	0	0	9	5	1	1	1	6	15	.156	.182	.143	15.00	6.00
2-team total (1 AZL Padres 2)					1	0	1.38	6	1	0	0	13	7	2	2	1	8	19	.156	.182	.143	13.15	5.54
Baez, Michel	R-R	6-8	220	1-21-96	1	0	3.60	1	1	0	0	5	2	2	2	1	2	7	.133	.000	.182	12.60	3.60
Baumann, Buddy	L-L	5-11	198	12-9-87	0	1	27.00	1	1	0	0	0	1	3	1	0	2	0	.500	—	.500	0.00	54.00
2-team total (3 Padres 2)					0	1	2.25	4	2	0	0	4	3	3	1	0	2	4	.200	—	.500	9.00	4.50
Boushley, Caleb	R-R	6-3	180	10-1-93	2	2	6.03	10	9	0	0	37	42	28	25	2	13	34	.284	.386	.240	8.20	3.13
Cabrera, Jose	L-L	6-0	170	9-26-98	1	0	6.83	16	0	0	0	28	32	23	21	1	25	25	.294	.346	.277	8.13	8.13
Cosgrove, Thomas	L-L	6-2	190	6-14-96	0	0	0.00	2	0	0	1	3	2	0	0	0	0	5	.167	.000	.182	13.50	0.00
Cunningham, Alex	R-R	6-0	195	6-21-94	0	0	0.00	3	0	0	1	4	2	0	0	0	1	8	.143	.167	.125	16.62	2.08
Dallas, Dan	L-L	6-2	180	12-24-97	0	2	9.00	4	4	0	0	10	12	10	10	2	6	16	.308	.154	.385	14.40	5.40
De Paula, Rafael	R-R	6-2	215	3-24-91	0	0	0.00	1	0	0	1	1	0	0	0	0	0	3	.000	.000	.000	27.00	0.00
Diaz, Miguel	R-R	6-1	175	11-28-94	1	0	0.00	1	0	0	0	2	0	0	0	0	1	2	.000	.000	.000	9.00	4.50
Erb, Dalton	R-R	6-8	250	5-13-94	1	0	0.00	1	0	0	0	2	2	0	0	0	0	2	.250	—	.250	9.00	0.00
Gore, MacKenzie	L-L	6-3	180	2-24-99	0	1	1.27	7	7	0	0	21	14	5	3	0	7	34	.184	.100	.214	14.34	2.95
Guzman, Jonathan	R-R	5-10	180	2-8-95	1	2	5.90	20	0	0	2	29	31	24	19	2	22	33	.272	.238	.292	10.24	6.83
Hernandez, Osvaldo	L-L	6-0	175	5-15-98	0	1	6.00	1	1	0	0	6	4	4	4	2	2	11	.182	.000	.200	16.50	3.00
2-team total (1 Padres 2)					0	1	3.97	2	2	0	0	11	8	5	5	2	2	20	.195	.000	.200	15.88	1.59
Keating, Sam	R-R	6-3	190	8-31-98	0	3	6.87	7	7	0	0	18	32	21	14	0	5	16	.377	.353	.392	7.85	2.45
Kulman, Spencer	R-R	6-1	195	3-29-95	1	0	1.21	13	0	0	4	22	13	5	3	0	10	22	.161	.231	.127	8.87	4.03
Lopez, Diomar	R-R	6-0	165	12-15-96	0	0	1.50	4	0	0	1	6	2	3	1	0	1	5	.105	.000	.143	7.50	1.50
2-team total (2 Padres 2)					1	0	2.70	6	0	0	1	10	7	5	3	0	2	8	.200	.000	.143	7.20	1.80
Lorenzini, Braxton	R-R	6-4	172	4-5-95	1	0	7.71	5	0	0	0	5	3	6	4	0	10	6	.177	.143	.200	11.57	19.29
Margevicius, Nick	L-L	6-5	220	6-18-96	1	1	1.42	5	4	0	1	19	19	7	3	0	4	30	.250	.263	.246	14.21	1.89
Martinez, Adrian	R-R	6-2	195	12-10-96	2	3	4.50	13	4	0	1	30	31	17	15	3	9	37	.256	.302	.221	11.10	2.70
Mazzoni, Cory	R-R	6-1	210	10-19-89	1	0	0.00	7	0	0	0	8	7	0	0	0	0	15	.233	.500	.136	16.88	0.00
2-team total (2 Padres 2)					1	0	0.00	9	0	0	0	10	7	0	0	0	0	17	.189	.500	.136	15.30	0.00
Megill, Trevor	L-R	6-8	235	12-5-93	1	0	2.84	3	0	0	0	6	4	2	2	0	3	6	.174	.125	.200	8.53	4.26
Miliano, Michell	R-R	6-3	185	12-22-99	1	3	6.60	7	5	0	0	15	17	16	11	1	8	18	.270	.313	.255	10.80	4.80
Newman, Chandler	R-R	6-2	175	2-5-97	1	0	13.50	9	0	0	0	7	10	10	10	0	17	5	.370	.444	.333	6.75	22.95
Patino, Luis	R-R	6-0	150	10-26-99	2	1	2.48	9	8	0	0	40	32	14	11	2	16	43	.213	.250	.192	9.68	3.60
Rivera, Carlos	R-R	6-3	190	6-8-95	1	1	7.50	16	0	0	0	24	27	21	20	1	14	21	.287	.367	.250	7.88	5.25
Rogers, Blake	R-R	6-2	200	2-23-94	0	1	0.00	2	0	0	0	2	2	1	0	0	2	2	.286	.250	.333	9.00	9.00
Sexton, Danny	R-L	6-0	195	6-30-95	1	3	6.75	13	2	0	0	31	36	31	23	2	11	35	.279	.316	.264	10.27	3.23
Solano, Eduardo	L-L	6-3	203	5-22-97	1	1	2.30	11	0	0	0	16	13	5	4	0	14	16	.224	.250	.214	9.19	8.04
2-team total (8 Padres 2)					3	2	5.27	19	0	0	0	27	27	19	16	1	28	25	.260	.250	.214	8.23	9.22
Taccolini, Dominic	R-R	6-0	230	9-28-94	0	1	12.71	5	0	0	0	6	7	10	8	1	5	9	.269	.429	.083	14.29	7.94
Vela, Noel	L-L	6-1	165	12-1-98	2	0	3.46	7	0	0	0	13	6	7	5	1	15	18	.133	.400	.057	12.46	10.38

Fielding

C: Campusano 17, Cantu 2, Fernandez 8, Hedges 1, Homza 19, Hunt 3, Lezama 24. **1B:** Perez 2, Pineda 15, Rutherford 20, Williams 32. **2B:** Batten 18, Benson 1, Gowdy 12, Homza 2, Ruiz 28. **3B:** Batten 1, Gowdy 21, Homza 24, Pineda 19, Roman 2. **SS:** Aybar 2, Barley 43, Batten 11, Homza 4, Rondon 2. **OF:** Benson 3, Bono 22, Cowgill 3, Jankowski 1, Lambert 25, Olmo 43, Rosario 51, Ruiz 10, Santos 28.

AZL PADRES 2

ROOKIE

ARIZONA LEAGUE

Batting	B-T	HT	WT	DOB	AVG	vLH	vRH	G	AB	R	H	2B	3B	HR	RBI	BB	HBP	SH	SF	SO	SB	CS	SLG	OBP
Alarcon, Kelvin	L-R	6-1	155	3-6-99	.202	.310	.167	35	119	21	24	2	0	1	17	23	3	0	1	28	0	1	.244	.343
Arias, Gabriel	R-R	6-1	185	2-27-00	.275	.302	.264	37	153	18	42	6	3	0	13	10	3	1	1	51	4	6	.353	.329
Basabe, Olivier	R-R	5-11	190	7-15-97	.272	.303	.264	42	162	31	44	14	1	1	24	14	6	1	2	24	3	2	.389	.348
Campusano, Luis	R-R	6-0	195	9-29-98	.250	.250	.250	13	44	5	11	0	0	3	12	9	0	0	0	11	0	1	.455	.377
2-team total (24 Padres)					.269	.059	.329	37	134	8	36	4	0	4	25	15	1	0	1	25	0	2	.388	.344
Castro, Luis	L-L	5-11	155	6-15-98	.168	.280	.132	36	101	13	17	1	0	0	12	23	0	0	2	47	1	1	.178	.318
Cowgill, Collin	L-R	5-9	190	5-22-86	.667	—	.667	1	3	1	2	2	0	0	2	0	0	0	1	1	0	0	1.333	.500
2-team total (4 Padres)					.333	.000	.273	5	15	2	5	3	0	0	5	1	0	0	1	3	0	0	.533	.353
Feight, Nick	R-R	5-11	200	11-4-95	.247	.189	.266	40	150	30	37	12	1	2	19	18	4	0	1	33	1	0	.380	.341
Fernandez, Juan	R-R	5-11	180	3-7-99	.307	.421	.275	27	88	18	27	8	2	2	15	9	3	0	0	14	3	1	.511	.390
2-team total (8 Padres)					.295	.400	.211	35	112	23	33	9	2	3	18	9	4	0	0	14	3	1	.491	.368
House, Mason	B-L	6-3	190	9-10-98	.293	.318	.283	39	164	28	48	6	8	2	33	13	3	0	1	68	3	0	.463	.354
Hunt, Blake	R-R	6-3	185	11-10-98	.250	.333	.224	22	88	14	22	7	2	1	15	5	4	0	1	29	1	0	.409	.316
2-team total (8 Padres)					.241	.111	.263	30	116	21	28	9	2	2	19	8	5	0	1	42	1	0	.405	.315
Jankowski, Travis	L-R	6-2	185	6-15-91	.273	.333	.250	3	11	2	3	1	0	0	2	0	1	0	0	4	0	1	.364	.333
2-team total (2 Padres)					.278	.000	.333	5	18	5	5	2	0	0	2	2	2	0	0	5	1	1	.389	.409
Jarmon, Hunter	R-R	6-0	195	3-2-95	.247	.231	.250	23	77	13	19	2	1	0	9	12	0	0	0	24	2	0	.299	.348
Ornelas, Tirso	L-R	6-4	180	3-11-00	.276	.250	.285	53	196	46	54	11	3	3	26	40	1	0	1	61	0	0	.408	.399
Paulsen, Justin	L-R	6-1	220	1-3-95	.291	.364	.270	44	148	27	43	10	1	2	25	27	4	0	2	38	1	0	.412	.409
Podorsky, Robbie	R-R	5-7	170	1-27-95	.400	.500	.355	11	45	13	18	3	2	0	8	5	1	0	0	3	3	1	.556	.471
Roman, Luis	L-R	6-0	215	12-19-94	.186	.067	.239	31	97	15	18	4	0	1	10	11	1	0	3	26	1	0	.258	.268
2-team total (2 Padres)					.190	.000	.500	33	100	15	19	4	0	1	10	11	1	0	3	28	1	0	.260	.270
Rondon, Jose	R-R	6-1	195	3-3-94	.600	.000	.750	2	5	4	3	0	0	1	3	3	0	0	0	1	1	0	1.200	.750
2-team total (3 Padres)					.353	.333	.222	5	17	5	6	0	0	2	7	4	0	0	1	3	1	0	.706	.455
Rosario, Eguy	R-R	5-9	150	8-25-99	.282	.254	.293	50	206	36	58	12	7	1	33	24	3	0	1	43	16	7	.422	.363
Villalobos, Janigson	R-R	5-9	195	5-10-97	.275	.261	.281	27	80	12	22	7	1	0	18	14	0	0	4	23	1	0	.388	.367

Pitching	B-T	HT	WT	DOB	W	L	ERA	G	GS	CG	SV	IP	H	R	ER	HR	BB	SO	AVG	vLH	vRH	K/9	BB/9
Adam, Jason	R-R	6-4	225	8-4-91	1	0	0.00	2	0	0	0	2	1	0	0	0	2	4	.143	.500	.000	18.00	9.00
2-team total (5 Padres)					1	0	4.05	7	0	0	0	7	6	3	3	0	2	12	.222	.143	.308	16.20	2.70
Ashbeck, Elliot	L-R	6-3	215	11-16-93	0	0	0.00	2	0	0	0	3	2	0	0	0	0	4	.182	.250	.143	12.00	0.00
2-team total (4 Padres)					1	1	0.00	6	0	0	0	8	4	3	0	0	2	11	.138	.333	.067	12.91	2.35
Bachar, Lake	R-R	6-3	210	6-3-95	0	0	2.25	1	1	0	0	4	2	1	1	0	2	4	.154	.000	.182	9.00	4.50
2-team total (5 Padres)					1	0	1.38	6	1	0	0	13	7	2	2	1	8	19	.156	.182	.143	13.15	5.54
Baumann, Buddy	L-L	5-11	198	12-9-87	0	0	0.00	3	1	0	0	4	2	0	0	0	0	4	.154	.000	.200	9.82	0.00
2-team total (1 Padres)					0	1	2.25	4	2	0	0	4	3	3	1	0	2	4	.200	—	.500	9.00	4.50
Bellinger, Cole	R-R	6-1	175	10-12-99	0	0	0.68	9	0	0	0	13	8	2	1	1	5	15	.174	.050	.269	10.13	3.38
Bencomo, Edwuin	R-R	6-2	165	4-14-99	0	1	3.18	18	0	0	7	17	14	11	6	1	6	23	.222	.316	.182	12.18	3.18
Cantillo, Joey	L-L	6-4	225	12-18-99	1	0	4.50	7	0	0	0	8	5	4	4	0	6	14	.179	.182	.177	15.75	6.75
Clase, Emmanuel	R-R	6-2	150	3-18-98	2	4	5.30	9	6	0	0	36	40	29	21	4	22	42	.276	.262	.282	10.60	5.55
Colletti, Tom	R-R	6-3	220	6-22-95	2	1	4.26	13	0	0	0	19	26	11	9	1	7	30	.321	.368	.307	14.21	3.32
Cordero, Starlin	R-R	6-7	220	7-21-98	1	0	4.97	12	0	0	1	13	10	9	7	0	15	14	.196	.200	.192	9.95	10.66
Esch, Jake	R-R	6-3	205	3-27-90	0	1	4.50	1	1	0	0	4	5	2	2	0	1	7	.278	.750	.143	15.75	2.25
Fernandez, Omar	L-L	5-11	160	4-20-99	3	2	7.75	10	10	0	0	41	55	41	35	5	22	31	.329	.310	.339	6.86	4.87
Garcia, Alan	L-L	6-0	220	1-31-97	1	0	12.79	8	0	0	0	6	11	10	9	0	5	5	.367	.125	.455	7.11	7.11
Guzman, Manny	R-R	6-4	180	11-1-99	1	2	6.57	9	8	0	0	37	50	32	27	2	15	36	.323	.349	.304	8.76	3.65
Henry, Henry	R-R	6-4	178	12-17-98	1	0	1.50	1	1	0	0	6	4	1	1	1	0	6	.182	.200	.177	9.00	0.00
Hernandez, Osvaldo	L-L	6-0	175	5-15-98	0	0	1.69	1	1	0	0	5	4	1	1	0	0	9	.211	.333	.000	15.19	0.00
2-team total (1 Padres)					0	1	3.97	2	2	0	0	11	8	5	5	2	2	20	.195	.000	.200	15.88	1.59
Kuzia, Nick	R-R	6-4	190	2-7-96	3	1	4.35	16	0	0	3	21	24	17	10	2	12	24	.293	.393	.241	10.45	5.23
Leasher, Aaron	L-L	6-3	190	4-28-96	1	2	5.56	7	7	0	0	23	31	20	14	1	11	23	.333	.379	.313	9.13	4.37
Lebron, Jaimito	R-R	6-2	175	10-20-96	1	2	9.72	16	1	0	0	25	43	37	27	0	13	26	.381	.297	.421	9.36	4.68
Lockett, Walker	R-R	6-5	225	5-3-94	0	1	5.40	4	4	0	0	10	11	8	6	1	4	12	.262	.500	.167	10.80	3.60
Lopez, Diomar	R-R	6-0	165	12-15-96	1	0	4.50	2	0	0	0	4	5	2	2	0	1	3	.313	.167	.400	6.75	2.25
2-team total (4 Padres)					1	0	2.70	6	0	0	1	10	7	5	3	0	2	8	.200	.000	.143	7.20	1.80
Machuca, Cristian	L-L	6-1	165	4-24-97	0	0	0.00	7	0	0	0	10	4	0	0	0	5	7	.118	.100	.125	6.30	4.50
Magill, Matt	R-R	6-3	210	11-10-89	0	0	0.00	1	1	0	0	2	1	0	0	0	1	5	.143	.000	.250	22.50	4.50
Mazzoni, Cory	R-R	6-1	210	10-19-89	0	0	0.00	2	0	0	0	2	0	0	0	0	0	2	.000	.000	.000	9.00	0.00
2-team total (7 Padres)					1	0	0.00	9	0	0	0	10	7	0	0	0	0	17	.189	.500	.136	15.30	0.00
Miller, Vijay	L-R	6-3	190	11-8-97	1	0	3.75	15	0	0	0	24	19	11	10	3	10	30	.216	.185	.230	11.25	3.75
Ochoa, Duilio	R-R	6-0	180	8-2-98	3	0	5.00	10	5	0	0	36	44	28	20	5	15	29	.301	.400	.250	7.25	3.75
Perez, Ramon	L-L	6-1	190	7-2-99	2	2	2.66	12	9	0	0	51	37	21	15	0	33	48	.208	.211	.207	8.53	5.86
Polanco, Anderson	L-L	6-3	175	2-5-98	2	3	5.54	16	0	0	0	26	29	20	16	0	13	21	.276	.143	.343	7.27	4.50
Smith, Jake	R-R	6-4	190	6-2-90	0	0	4.35	10	0	0	0	10	7	5	5	2	3	14	.184	.444	.103	12.19	2.61
Smith, Jeremy	R-R	6-1	195	12-23-93	1	1	2.89	12	0	0	1	19	12	8	6	0	8	26	.185	.182	.186	12.54	3.86
Solano, Eduardo	L-L	6-3	203	5-22-97	2	1	9.26	8	0	0	0	12	14	14	12	1	14	9	.304	.273	.314	6.94	10.80
2-team total (11 Padres)					3	2	5.27	19	0	0	0	27	27	19	16	1	28	25	.260	.250	.214	8.23	9.22
Wieck, Brad	L-L	6-9	255	10-14-91	0	0	0.00	1	0	0	0	1	0	0	0	0	0	2	.000	—	.000	18.00	0.00

Fielding

C: Campusano 10, Fernandez 26, Roman 1, Villalobos 27. **1B:** Feight 18, Paulsen 38, Roman 3. **2B:** Alarcon 22, Basabe 12, Rosario 27. **3B:** Alarcon 6, Arias 2, Basabe 1, Roman 27, Rondon 1, Rosario 26. **SS:** Alarcon 9, Arias 33, Basabe 19, Rondon 1. **OF:** Basabe 12, Castro 36, Cowgill 1, Feight 6, House

38, Jankowski 3, Jarmon 18, Ornelas 51, Podorsky 11, Roman 1.

DSL PADRES — ROOKIE

DOMINICAN SUMMER LEAGUE

Batting	B-T	HT	WT	DOB	AVG	vLH	vRH	G	AB	R	H	2B	3B	HR	RBI	BB	HBP	SH	SF	SO	SB	CS	SLG	OBP
Antunez, Adrian	R-R	6-3	195	1-17-99	.182	.235	.173	37	121	15	22	6	1	1	11	11	4	0	2	51	5	2	.273	.268
Araujo, Ydie	R-R	6-3	210	4-28-98	.138	.111	.145	31	87	10	12	2	0	2	8	11	2	0	1	27	0	2	.230	.248
Batista, Carlos	L-L	6-2	177	10-30-99	.194	.111	.202	37	93	15	18	4	1	1	8	21	6	0	0	39	0	0	.290	.375
Burgos, Edward	L-L	6-2	175	8-24-96	.174	.250	.158	16	46	3	8	0	0	0	3	5	0	0	1	16	0	0	.174	.250
Francisco, Yordi	L-R	6-1	175	3-14-97	.275	.293	.272	65	247	29	68	12	3	3	31	14	9	0	1	49	6	1	.385	.336
Garcia, Jaffe	R-R	6-1	175	3-13-96	.186	.345	.140	50	129	22	24	5	2	1	25	43	2	1	0	42	1	1	.279	.397
Guzman, Luis	R-R	6-2	175	6-20-98	.236	.333	.219	63	225	34	53	6	1	4	28	32	6	0	0	30	0	3	.324	.346
Luis, Carlos	L-R	6-2	160	9-4-99	.286	.000	.320	7	28	5	8	3	0	1	3	2	0	0	0	4	0	0	.500	.333
Marcano, Tucupita	L-R	6-0	165	9-16-99	.206	.286	.190	49	170	17	35	4	2	0	15	34	1	1	3	15	10	3	.253	.337
Molina, Miguel	R-R	6-1	195	1-6-97	.255	.444	.236	35	98	10	25	3	1	2	17	11	0	1	1	22	2	1	.367	.327
Perez, Blinger	R-R	6-0	170	8-21-98	.270	.208	.281	48	163	21	44	12	0	2	24	23	3	0	1	28	0	2	.380	.368
Quintero, Alison	R-R	5-11	175	4-24-00	.174	.500	.159	15	46	5	8	2	1	0	4	6	1	0	1	15	0	0	.261	.278
Sabala, Elvis	R-R	6-1	178	9-26-97	.204	.233	.199	64	201	30	41	6	1	2	14	46	3	0	2	57	5	1	.274	.357
Torres, Bryan	R-R	5-9	165	12-11-99	.228	.270	.220	68	246	42	56	10	1	1	26	41	3	4	8	31	2	5	.289	.336
Tovar, Danny	L-L	5-11	180	11-2-98	.266	.167	.284	51	158	20	42	6	2	2	18	29	1	3	0	41	5	1	.367	.383
Vasquez, Juan	R-R	5-11	180	9-7-99	.133	.167	.125	12	30	1	4	1	0	0	1	1	0	0	0	7	0	0	.167	.161
Vizcarra, Gilberto	R-R	5-10	180	3-1-99	.225	.412	.185	53	191	26	43	10	1	2	28	17	11	0	2	29	0	0	.319	.321

Pitching	B-T	HT	WT	DOB	W	L	ERA	G	GS	CG	SV	IP	H	R	ER	HR	BB	SO	AVG	vLH	vRH	K/9	BB/9
Bencomo, Edwuin	R-R	6-2	165	4-14-99	0	2	5.00	6	0	0	1	9	9	11	5	0	5	7	.237	.100	.389	7.00	5.00
Bracamonte, Daniel	L-L	6-1	170	1-12-99	0	4	7.59	10	0	0	0	11	10	10	9	0	13	9	.250	.375	.219	7.59	10.97
Carrasco, Martin	R-R	6-0	165	11-22-99	1	4	2.64	13	13	0	0	61	53	24	18	1	7	31	.228	.217	.235	4.55	1.03
De La Cruz, Daniel	R-R	6-6	208	2-1-98	1	2	6.14	15	3	0	0	22	25	24	15	3	21	15	.272	.313	.250	6.14	8.59
Eusebio, Luis	R-R	6-0	180	3-15-96	1	6	3.77	14	14	0	0	57	50	39	24	2	31	37	.235	.292	.210	5.81	4.87
Garcia, Jeferson	R-R	6-0	165	2-4-00	0	0	0.00	1	0	0	0	1	1	0	0	0	0	0	.333	1.000	.000	0.00	0.00
Garcia, Jose	L-L	5-11	169	2-19-98	0	0	2.40	11	0	0	0	15	13	5	4	1	4	11	.228	.077	.273	6.60	2.40
Gonzalez, Cesar	R-R	6-1	160	2-24-99	1	0	5.75	13	0	0	0	20	23	14	13	1	9	14	.277	.212	.320	6.20	3.98
Guerra, Jorge	L-L	5-10	157	7-13-99	1	2	5.55	19	0	0	0	24	26	16	15	2	12	19	.283	.350	.264	7.03	4.44
Lezama, Aaron	L-L	6-5	180	4-22-97	4	1	3.13	14	0	0	0	23	22	10	8	1	14	20	.256	.118	.290	7.83	5.48
Lugo, Moises	R-R	6-1	185	1-20-99	2	2	1.97	13	13	0	0	64	50	20	14	1	17	54	.217	.239	.204	7.59	2.39
Medina, Diego	L-L	6-1	170	6-9-99	0	2	5.56	17	0	0	0	23	33	21	14	3	8	18	.340	.261	.365	7.15	3.18
Morales, Gabriel	L-L	6-3	175	4-14-99	1	6	3.40	14	10	0	0	48	40	23	18	4	23	31	.226	.250	.224	5.85	4.34
Nin, Luis	R-R	6-2	185	11-30-96	1	1	5.00	15	0	0	3	18	14	13	10	0	9	18	.209	.333	.163	9.00	4.50
Ochoa, Duilio	R-R	6-0	180	8-2-98	1	0	3.00	6	0	0	1	12	9	4	4	0	8	11	.220	.368	.091	8.25	6.00
Patino, Luis	R-R	6-0	150	10-26-99	2	1	1.69	4	4	0	0	16	11	5	3	0	2	15	.193	.320	.094	8.44	1.13
Pena, Ramon	R-R	6-4	190	8-24-97	0	3	6.21	12	5	0	2	29	27	25	20	2	21	19	.252	.308	.221	5.90	6.52
Perez, Enzo	R-R	5-11	180	6-7-00	2	1	7.12	18	0	0	0	30	40	29	24	2	17	22	.320	.359	.302	6.53	5.04
Polanco, Anderson	L-L	6-3	175	2-5-98	1	0	0.00	4	0	0	0	10	4	1	0	0	1	10	.118	.000	.138	8.71	0.87
Powell, Evan	R-R	6-9	246	11-18-96	0	1	8.53	7	0	0	0	6	5	8	6	0	9	1	.227	.200	.235	1.42	12.79
Roman, Miguel	R-R	6-1	170	2-23-97	3	1	1.98	21	0	0	1	27	26	9	6	0	15	17	.280	.250	.298	5.60	4.94
Rosario, Brayan	L-L	6-3	175	8-3-98	0	1	16.50	10	0	0	0	6	7	14	11	0	14	4	.292	.250	.313	6.00	21.00
Santana, Adonis	R-R	6-1	160	9-10-98	0	1	12.06	14	0	0	0	16	22	22	21	0	13	9	.339	.450	.289	5.17	7.47
Suarez, Luis	R-R	6-2	205	6-21-99	0	2	7.11	7	0	0	0	6	5	8	5	0	5	4	.200	.400	.067	5.68	7.11
Valenzuela, Carlos	L-L	5-9	155	6-2-00	2	4	3.86	9	9	0	0	44	45	24	19	2	6	30	.263	.231	.273	6.09	1.22

Fielding

C: Molina 16, Perez 5, Quintero 11, Vasquez 9, Vizcarra 42. **1B:** Araujo 15, Garcia 1, Guzman 1, Molina 7, Perez 29, Sabala 30. **2B:** Guzman 24, Marcano 41, Molina 2, Perez 1, Sabala 4, Torres 8. **3B:** Araujo 5, Guzman 34, Luis 5, Perez 5, Sabala 33. **SS:** Guzman 12, Marcano 3, Torres 60. **OF:** Antunez 33, Batista 28, Burgos 14, Francisco 58, Garcia 47, Molina 1, Perez 1, Tovar 48.

San Francisco Giants

SEASON IN A SENTENCE: It's a fairly easy argument to say the Giants were the most disappointing team of the 2017 season. San Francisco began the year with real postseason expectations and finished with just 64 wins—the worst full-season win total for the Giants since 1985.

HIGH POINT: Buster Posey. On a team with exceedingly few bright spots, the best catcher in baseball continued to be Posey, who hit .320/.400/.462 and has now hit over .300 in five of his seven full major league seasons. His 2017 campaign actually raised his career batting average from .307 to .308.

LOW POINT: The entire season could be the right answer here. It probably is. But let's go with the final game of the season, a 5-4 win over the Padres on Oct. 1. A win would normally be a good thing, but in this instance the Giants were just one loss away from the first pick of the 2018 MLB Draft. However, Pablo Sandoval's ninth-inning walk-off home run gave the Giants the same record as the Tigers, and with the draft tie-breaker going back to the 2016 season, the Giants were stuck with the second pick.

NOTABLE ROOKIES: Outfielder Austin Slater performed well in the Pacific Coast League before getting called up the the majors on June 2, where he hit .290/.343/.430 and played mostly left field before a groin injury a month later sidelined him during August. Lefthander Ty Blach started 24 games, but postd just a 4.78 ERA. Righthander Reyes Moronta spent most os his year in the minors but had a great major league debut in San Francisco's bullpen (6.2 innings, 2.12 ERA).

KEY TRANSACTIONS: The biggest trade the Giants made was likely a deal that sent third baseman Eduardo Nunez to the Red Sox in exchange for righthanders Shaun Anderson and Gregory Santos. Anderson was a reliever in college but has transitioned well to a starting role in the minors, while Santos has an exciting arm but is years away.

DOWN ON THE FARM: Giants fans couldn't look to the minor league system for a taste of winning baseball either, as all four of San Francisco's full season affiliates finished with losing records. Top prospect Chris Shaw could soon help improve a woeful Giants outfield after hitting .292/.346/.525 between Double-A and Triple-A with 24 home runs and improved bat control. Top pitching prospect, RHP Tyler Beede, experienced the PCL as well, but did so with a 6-7 record and 4.79 ERA.

OPENING DAY PAYROLL: $172,354,611 (7th)

PLAYERS OF THE YEAR

MAJOR LEAGUE

Buster Posey
C

.320/.400/.462
12 HR, 67 RBI
38% CS rate

MINOR LEAGUE

Chris Shaw
OF

(Double-A/Triple-A)
.292/.346/.525
24 HR, 35 2B

ORGANIZATION LEADERS

BATTING — *Minimum 250 AB

MAJORS			
*	AVG	Buster Posey	.320
*	OPS	Buster Posey	.861
	HR	Brandon Belt	18
	RBI	Brandon Crawford	77
MINORS			
*	AVG	Bryan Reynolds, San Jose	.312
*	OBP	Tim Federowicz, Sacramento	.366
*	SLG	Chris Shaw, Richmond, Sacramento	.525
*	OPS	Chris Shaw, Richmond, Sacramento	.871
	R	Bryan Reynolds, San Jose	72
	H	Ryan Howard, San Jose	161
	TB	Chris Shaw, Richmond, Sacramento	246
	2B	Jonah Arenado, San Jose	36
	3B	Bryan Reynolds, San Jose	9
	HR	Chris Shaw, Richmond, Sacramento	24
	RBI	Chris Shaw, Richmond, Sacramento	79
	BB	Slade Heathcott, Richmond, Sacramento	48
	SO	Dillon Dobson, San Jose	146
	SB	Cristian Paulino, Augusta, San Jose	34

PITCHING — #Minimum 75 IP

MAJORS			
	W	Jeff Samardzija	9
#	ERA	Brandon Crawford	3.32
	SO	Jeff Samardzija	205
	SV	Sam Dyson	14
MINORS			
	W	Andrew Suarez, Richmond, Sacramento	10
	L	Mark Reyes, San Jose, Sacramento	13
#	ERA	Garrett Williams, Augusta, San Jose	2.32
	G	Dylan Rheault, San Jose	55
		Tyler Rogers, Sacramento	55
	GS	Matt Gage, Richmond, Sacramento	25
		Dan Slania, Sacramento, Richmond	25
	SV	Dylan Rheault, San Jose	21
	IP	Andrew Suarez, Richmond, Sacramento	156
	BB	Mark Reyes, San Jose, Sacramento	79
	SO	Andrew Suarez, Richmond, Sacramento	135
#	AVG	Dusten Knight, San Jose, Sacramento	.207

2017 PERFORMANCE

Executive VP, Baseball Ops: Brian Sabean. **Farm Director:** Shane Turner. **Scouting Director:** John Barr.

Class	Team	League	W	L	PCT	Finish	Manager
Majors	San Francisco Giants	National	64	98	.395	15th (15)	Bruce Bochy
Triple-A	Sacramento River Cats	Pacific Coast	64	77	.454	14th (16)	Dave Brundage
Double-A	Richmond Flying Squirrels	Eastern	63	77	.450	8th (12)	Kyle Haines
High-A	San Jose Giants	California	62	78	.443	8th (8)	Nestor Rojas
Low-A	Augusta GreenJackets	South Atlantic	55	80	.407	14th (14)	Carlos Valderrama
Short Season	Salem-Keizer Volcanoes	Northwest	29	47	.382	8th (8)	Jolbert Cabrera
Rookie	AZL Giants	Arizona	34	22	.607	2nd (15)	Henry Cotto / Hector Borg
Overall 2017 Minor League Record			307	381	.446	29th (30)	

ORGANIZATION STATISTICS

SAN FRANCISCO GIANTS

NATIONAL LEAGUE

Batting	B-T	HT	WT	DOB	AVG	vLH	vRH	G	AB	R	H	2B	3B	HR	RBI	BB	HBP	SH	SF	SO	SB	CS	SLG	OBP
Arroyo, Christian	R-R	6-1	180	5-30-95	.192	.235	.162	34	125	9	24	5	0	3	14	8	1	0	1	32	1	2	.304	.244
Belt, Brandon	L-L	6-5	220	4-20-88	.241	.223	.250	104	382	63	92	27	3	18	51	66	2	0	1	104	3	2	.469	.355
Calixte, Orlando	R-R	5-11	180	2-3-92	.143	.154	.139	29	49	5	7	1	0	0	6	3	0	1	2	16	1	0	.163	.185
Crawford, Brandon	L-R	6-2	215	1-21-87	.253	.239	.258	144	518	58	131	34	1	14	77	42	1	0	9	113	3	5	.404	.305
Federowicz, Tim	R-R	5-10	215	8-5-87	.231	.111	.500	13	13	3	3	0	0	2	3	1	0	0	0	4	0	0	.692	.286
Gillaspie, Conor	R-L	6-1	195	7-18-87	.163	.182	.159	44	80	8	13	4	0	2	8	5	1	0	1	10	0	0	.288	.218
Gomez, Miguel	B-R	5-10	185	12-17-92	.242	.200	.278	22	33	3	8	2	0	0	2	0	0	0	1	6	0	0	.303	.235
Hernandez, Gorkys	R-R	6-1	190	9-7-87	.255	.237	.269	128	310	40	79	20	1	0	22	31	3	2	2	73	12	4	.326	.327
Hill, Aaron	R-R	5-11	200	3-21-82	.132	.154	.119	34	68	7	9	2	1	1	7	11	0	0	1	13	0	0	.235	.250
Hundley, Nick	R-R	6-1	205	9-8-83	.244	.305	.214	101	287	27	70	23	0	9	35	12	0	2	2	81	0	0	.418	.272
Hwang, Jae-Gyun	R-R	6-0	215	7-28-87	.154	.250	.094	18	52	2	8	1	0	1	5	5	0	0	0	15	0	0	.231	.228
Jones, Ryder	L-R	6-3	215	6-7-94	.173	.161	.177	53	150	12	26	5	2	2	5	10	4	0	0	52	1	0	.273	.244
Marrero, Chris	R-R	6-3	229	7-2-88	.132	.167	.100	15	38	2	5	0	0	1	5	2	0	0	1	9	0	0	.211	.171
Moncrief, Carlos	R-L	6-0	220	11-3-88	.211	.000	.229	28	38	4	8	1	0	0	5	3	0	0	2	15	0	0	.237	.256
Morse, Michael	R-R	6-5	245	3-22-82	.194	.182	.200	24	36	1	7	1	0	1	3	3	0	0	1	14	0	0	.306	.250
Nunez, Eduardo	R-R	6-0	195	6-15-87	.308	.299	.312	76	302	37	93	21	0	4	31	12	1	1	2	29	18	5	.417	.334
Panik, Joe	L-R	6-1	190	10-30-90	.288	.290	.287	138	511	60	147	28	5	10	53	46	5	3	8	54	4	1	.421	.347
Parker, Jarrett	L-L	6-4	210	1-1-89	.247	.250	.246	51	166	14	41	12	2	4	23	10	1	0	0	54	2	1	.416	.294
Pence, Hunter	R-R	6-4	220	4-13-83	.260	.286	.249	134	493	55	128	13	5	13	67	40	2	0	4	102	2	3	.385	.315
Posey, Buster	R-R	6-1	215	3-27-87	.320	.360	.304	140	494	62	158	34	0	12	67	61	8	0	5	66	6	1	.462	.400
Ruggiano, Justin	R-R	6-1	210	4-12-82	.217	.238	.205	19	60	2	13	1	0	2	4	1	1	0	1	17	1	1	.333	.238
Sandoval, Pablo	B-R	5-11	255	8-11-86	.225	.150	.250	47	160	17	36	9	0	5	20	8	1	0	2	29	0	0	.375	.263
Slater, Austin	R-R	6-2	215	12-13-92	.282	.333	.259	34	117	15	33	3	1	3	16	8	2	0	0	29	0	0	.402	.339
Span, Denard	L-L	6-0	210	2-27-84	.272	.226	.284	129	497	73	135	31	5	12	43	40	3	1	1	69	12	7	.427	.329
Stubbs, Drew	R-R	6-4	205	10-4-84	.091	.091	.091	10	22	0	2	0	0	0	0	2	0	0	0	9	0	0	.091	.167
Tomlinson, Kelby	R-R	6-3	180	6-16-90	.258	.270	.250	104	194	32	50	4	2	1	11	23	0	2	3	46	9	1	.314	.332
Williamson, Mac	R-R	6-4	240	7-15-90	.235	.353	.196	28	68	8	16	2	0	3	6	5	0	0	0	25	1	1	.397	.288

Pitching	B-T	HT	WT	DOB	W	L	ERA	G	GS	CG	SV	IP	H	R	ER	HR	BB	SO	AVG	vLH	vRH	K/9	BB/9
Blach, Ty	R-L	6-2	200	10-20-90	8	12	4.78	34	24	1	0	164	179	91	87	17	43	73	.283	.250	.295	4.01	2.36
Bumgarner, Madison	R-L	6-5	250	8-1-89	4	9	3.32	17	17	1	0	111	101	41	41	17	20	101	.238	.206	.245	8.19	1.62
Cain, Matt	R-R	6-3	230	10-1-84	3	11	5.43	27	23	0	0	124	157	85	75	18	49	75	.310	.312	.308	5.43	3.55
Crick, Kyle	L-R	6-4	220	11-30-92	0	0	3.06	30	0	0	0	32	22	13	11	2	17	28	.191	.220	.169	7.79	4.73
Cueto, Johnny	R-R	5-11	220	2-15-86	8	8	4.52	25	25	0	0	147	160	77	74	22	53	136	.277	.286	.268	8.31	3.24
Dyson, Sam	R-R	6-1	205	5-7-88	3	4	4.03	38	0	0	14	38	36	18	17	2	18	27	.245	.169	.305	6.39	4.26
Gearrin, Cory	R-R	6-3	200	4-14-86	4	3	1.99	68	0	0	0	68	50	16	15	4	35	64	.208	.205	.210	8.47	4.63
Gomez, Roberto	B-R	6-5	180	8-3-89	0	0	8.44	4	0	0	0	5	9	5	5	0	1	6	.360	.300	.400	10.13	1.69
Kontos, George	R-R	6-3	215	6-12-85	0	5	3.83	50	0	0	0	52	52	24	22	8	17	55	.259	.275	.250	9.58	2.96
2-team total (15 Pittsburgh)					1	6	3.39	65	0	0	1	66	61	27	25	9	20	70	.242	.158	.188	9.50	2.71
Law, Derek	R-R	6-2	210	9-14-90	4	1	5.06	41	0	0	4	37	45	21	21	5	14	35	.304	.323	.291	8.44	3.38
Melancon, Mark	R-R	6-2	210	3-28-85	1	2	4.50	32	0	0	11	30	37	16	15	3	6	29	.301	.246	.362	8.70	1.80
Moore, Matt	L-L	6-3	210	6-18-89	6	15	5.52	32	31	0	0	174	200	116	107	27	67	148	.283	.363	.258	7.64	3.46
Moronta, Reyes	R-R	6-0	175	1-6-93	0	0	2.70	7	0	0	0	7	6	2	2	1	3	11	.231	.143	.263	14.85	4.05
Morris, Bryan	R-L	6-3	220	3-28-87	2	0	6.43	20	0	0	0	21	24	16	15	1	11	15	.304	.433	.225	6.43	4.71
Okert, Steven	L-L	6-3	210	7-9-91	1	1	5.67	44	0	0	0	27	24	18	17	3	11	22	.242	.263	.214	7.33	3.67
Osich, Josh	L-L	6-2	230	9-3-88	3	2	6.23	54	0	0	0	43	48	32	30	7	27	43	.279	.247	.303	8.93	5.61
Ramirez, Neil	R-R	6-4	215	5-25-89	0	0	8.71	9	0	0	0	10	15	15	10	2	4	18	.319	.250	.355	15.68	3.48
2-team total (20 New York)					0	1	7.18	29	0	0	0	31	35	30	25	6	21	44	.273	.194	.289	12.64	6.03
Samardzija, Jeff	R-R	6-5	225	1-23-85	9	15	4.42	32	32	1	0	208	204	107	102	30	32	205	.255	.252	.258	8.88	1.39
Slania, Dan	R-R	6-5	275	5-24-92	0	0	0.00	1	0	0	0	1	0	0	0	0	0	0	.000	.000	—	0.00	0.00
Stratton, Chris	R-R	6-3	190	8-22-90	4	4	3.68	13	10	0	1	59	59	25	24	5	28	51	.266	.295	.239	7.82	4.30
Strickland, Hunter	R-R	6-4	220	9-24-88	4	3	2.64	68	0	0	1	61	59	20	18	4	29	58	.253	.333	.203	8.51	4.26
Suarez, Albert	R-R	6-3	235	10-8-89	0	3	5.12	18	0	0	1	32	28	18	18	4	11	34	.230	.255	.211	9.66	3.13

Fielding

Catcher	PCT	G	PO	A	E	DP	PB
Federowicz	1.000	6	17	2	0	0	0
Hundley	.987	82	510	30	7	3	5
Posey	.995	99	724	52	4	2	1

First Base	PCT	G	PO	A	E	DP
Belt	.998	98	771	64	2	74
Federowicz	.000	1	0	0	0	0
Gillaspie	1.000	4	7	1	0	0
Hwang	.947	3	17	1	1	3
Jones	.987	30	207	15	3	14
Morse	1.000	10	38	2	0	2
Posey	.992	38	223	25	2	19
Sandoval	1.000	9	55	1	0	8

Second Base	PCT	G	PO	A	E	DP
Arroyo	1.000	2	4	7	0	2
Gomez	1.000	6	7	7	0	1
Hill	1.000	7	5	16	0	4
Panik	.985	137	249	332	9	86
Tomlinson	.958	20	30	39	3	9

Third Base	PCT	G	PO	A	E	DP
Arroyo	.966	22	14	43	2	5
Calixte	1.000	5	1	1	0	0
Gillaspie	1.000	20	11	20	0	3
Hill	.875	7	3	11	2	0
Hwang	1.000	15	11	22	0	1
Jones	.969	18	5	26	1	2
Nunez	.934	49	23	91	8	8
Sandoval	.961	38	23	50	3	4
Slater	1.000	1	0	1	0	0
Tomlinson	.972	24	6	29	1	2

Shortstop	PCT	G	PO	A	E	DP
Arroyo	.969	10	12	19	1	3
Calixte	1.000	4	5	2	0	0
Crawford	.982	138	221	374	11	85
Nunez	.969	11	11	20	1	1
Tomlinson	.958	11	5	18	1	4

Outfield	PCT	G	PO	A	E	DP
Belt	.909	15	20	0	2	0
Calixte	.882	11	15	0	2	0
Hernandez	.989	113	184	4	2	0
Hill	1.000	6	3	0	0	0
Jones	.000	1	0	0	0	0
Marrero	1.000	12	14	0	0	0
Moncrief	1.000	10	11	1	0	0
Morse	1.000	1	1	0	0	0
Nunez	1.000	20	40	1	0	0
Parker	.976	47	76	4	2	1
Pence	.996	125	256	5	1	0
Ruggiano	1.000	17	27	1	0	0
Slater	.984	33	60	2	1	0
Span	.993	123	276	1	2	0
Stubbs	1.000	10	15	0	0	0
Tomlinson	1.000	9	11	0	0	0
Williamson	.949	21	36	1	2	0

SACRAMENTO RIVER CATS — *TRIPLE-A*

PACIFIC COAST LEAGUE

Batting	B-T	HT	WT	DOB	AVG	vLH	vRH	G	AB	R	H	2B	3B	HR	RBI	BB	HBP	SH	SF	SO	SB	CS	SLG	OBP
Arnold, Jeff	R-R	6-2	205	1-13-88	.177	.100	.208	9	34	3	6	1	0	1	2	2	0	0	0	15	0	0	.294	.222
Arroyo, Christian	R-R	6-1	180	5-30-95	.396	.417	.392	25	91	18	36	7	0	4	16	6	5	0	0	12	2	0	.604	.461
Bennett, T.J.	L-R	6-3	215	7-22-92	.286	.000	.308	6	14	1	4	0	0	1	2	4	0	1	0	4	0	0	.500	.444
Bernard, Wynton	R-R	6-2	195	9-24-90	.254	.327	.225	82	193	28	49	8	2	2	14	12	2	3	1	41	13	1	.347	.303
Blanks, Kyle	R-R	6-6	265	9-11-86	.232	.364	.211	35	82	11	19	4	0	3	12	7	3	0	0	28	0	0	.390	.315
Brown, Trevor	R-R	6-2	195	11-15-91	.163	.158	.165	58	196	11	32	4	0	1	9	9	2	5	0	43	2	0	.199	.208
Brown, Tyler	R-R	6-1	180	1-18-95	.000	—	.000	1	1	0	0	0	0	0	0	0	0	0	0	0	0	0	.000	.000
Calixte, Orlando	R-R	5-11	180	2-3-92	.243	.200	.257	97	378	48	92	15	5	14	43	21	0	2	0	84	19	4	.421	.283
Castillo, Ali	R-R	5-10	165	6-19-89	.254	.316	.235	70	244	23	62	10	3	1	18	10	1	2	2	23	4	2	.332	.284
Ciriaco, Juan	R-R	6-0	160	8-15-83	.277	.269	.279	75	235	28	65	13	2	4	30	16	0	2	2	46	7	0	.400	.320
Duggar, Steven	L-R	6-2	195	11-4-93	.261	.462	.182	13	46	7	12	1	0	2	6	8	0	0	0	12	3	2	.413	.370
Federowicz, Tim	R-R	5-10	215	8-5-87	.300	.359	.283	77	283	34	85	19	0	9	43	30	0	0	1	65	3	0	.463	.366
Gillaspie, Conor	R-L	6-1	195	7-18-87	.311	.333	.307	29	90	13	28	7	0	0	4	3	0	0	0	8	3	2	.389	.333
Heathcott, Slade	L-L	6-1	205	9-28-90	.290	.375	.264	26	69	8	20	2	1	2	8	11	2	2	0	22	3	1	.435	.402
Hill, Aaron	R-R	5-11	200	3-21-82	.235	.000	.250	5	17	5	4	0	1	1	3	2	2	0	0	7	0	0	.529	.381
Hwang, Jae-Gyun	R-R	6-0	215	7-28-87	.285	.354	.264	98	351	44	100	21	4	10	55	27	1	0	7	83	7	1	.453	.332
Jones, Ryder	L-R	6-3	215	6-7-94	.312	.294	.315	64	237	44	74	19	2	13	44	29	5	0	2	53	7	0	.574	.396
Lollis, Ryan	L-L	6-1	190	12-16-86	.292	.256	.303	56	185	16	54	14	0	1	22	11	1	1	2	19	1	0	.384	.332
Marrero, Chris	R-R	6-3	229	7-2-88	.207	.091	.234	17	58	7	12	4	0	2	11	6	2	0	1	12	0	0	.379	.299
Moncrief, Carlos	R-L	6-0	220	11-3-88	.287	.421	.270	71	171	17	49	17	0	2	18	17	0	1	1	45	4	2	.421	.349
Morse, Michael	R-R	6-5	245	3-22-82	.273	—	.273	3	11	1	3	1	0	0	2	1	0	0	0	3	0	0	.364	.333
Panik, Joe	L-R	6-1	190	10-30-90	.000	.000	—	1	2	0	0	0	0	0	0	0	0	0	0	1	0	0	.000	.000
Parker, Jarrett	L-L	6-4	210	1-1-89	.232	.136	.256	30	112	22	26	5	0	3	8	21	0	0	0	31	1	1	.357	.353
Polonius, John	R-R	6-1	160	1-13-91	.400	—	.400	3	5	2	2	0	1	0	1	0	0	1	0	0	0	0	.800	.400
Querecuto, Juniel	B-R	5-9	155	9-19-92	.232	.171	.254	94	293	26	68	11	0	2	27	26	3	3	3	63	6	2	.290	.299
Ruggiano, Justin	R-R	6-1	210	4-12-82	.280	.351	.258	45	157	23	44	13	0	6	21	9	2	0	1	33	1	2	.478	.325
Sandoval, Pablo	B-R	5-11	255	8-11-86	.207	.143	.227	9	29	4	6	1	0	1	3	5	1	0	2	3	0	0	.345	.324
Shaw, Chris	L-R	6-4	235	10-20-93	.289	.284	.290	88	336	42	97	25	1	18	50	20	1	0	3	106	0	0	.530	.328
Slater, Austin	R-R	6-2	215	12-13-92	.321	.361	.311	50	184	28	59	12	0	5	27	15	3	2	2	39	4	3	.467	.378
Stubbs, Drew	R-R	6-4	205	10-4-84	.256	.200	.265	10	39	6	10	1	0	2	7	6	0	0	1	16	1	0	.436	.348
2-team total (75 Round Rock)					.292	.200	.265	85	312	52	91	17	2	9	42	52	3	0	1	104	10	6	.446	.397
Tomlinson, Kelby	R-R	6-3	180	6-16-90	.296	.375	.274	26	108	17	32	6	0	0	8	13	1	0	0	12	9	2	.352	.377
Upton Jr., Melvin	R-R	6-3	185	8-21-84	.244	.375	.216	12	45	4	11	1	0	1	4	4	0	0	0	14	0	0	.333	.306
Williamson, Mac	R-R	6-4	240	7-15-90	.244	.274	.234	94	352	54	86	21	0	14	50	25	4	0	1	100	4	1	.423	.301
Winn, Matt	R-R	6-1	210	8-5-92	.333	—	.333	6	18	4	6	3	0	1	5	1	0	0	1	7	0	0	.667	.350
Zambrano, Eliezer	B-R	5-11	195	9-16-86	.417	.500	.375	4	12	2	5	0	0	0	1	2	0	0	0	2	0	0	.417	.500

Pitching	B-T	HT	WT	DOB	W	L	ERA	G	GS	CG	SV	IP	H	R	ER	HR	BB	SO	AVG	vLH	vRH	K/9	BB/9
Balester, Collin	R-R	6-4	190	6-6-86	1	0	5.79	14	0	0	0	23	31	15	15	2	7	25	.316	.222	.396	9.64	2.70
Beede, Tyler	R-R	6-3	210	5-23-93	6	7	4.79	19	19	0	0	109	121	68	58	14	39	83	.282	.288	.275	6.85	3.22
Blackburn, Clayton	L-R	6-3	230	1-6-93	0	0	15.00	1	1	0	0	3	6	5	5	1	1	1	.400	.375	.429	3.00	3.00
2-team total (19 Round Rock)					6	2	4.97	20	19	0	0	96	105	54	53	5	26	79	.280	.375	.429	7.41	2.44
Bumgarner, Madison	R-L	6-5	250	8-1-89	0	0	9.82	1	1	0	0	4	7	4	4	0	1	1	.438	.500	.333	2.45	2.45
Crick, Kyle	L-R	6-4	220	11-30-92	1	2	2.76	24	0	0	6	29	24	9	9	1	13	39	.220	.157	.276	11.97	3.99
Cueto, Johnny	R-R	5-11	220	2-15-86	0	0	0.00	1	1	0	0	3	3	0	0	0	0	1	.250	.222	.333	3.00	0.00
Flores, Jose	R-R	6-3	250	6-4-89	2	4	4.04	12	12	0	0	65	64	31	29	4	24	65	.260	.295	.231	9.05	3.34
Gage, Matt	R-L	6-4	240	2-11-93	2	7	5.75	13	12	0	0	67	99	49	43	3	20	40	.350	.299	.372	5.35	2.67
Gomez, Roberto	B-R	6-5	180	8-3-89	3	9	4.07	38	13	0	0	97	100	52	44	8	38	89	.265	.293	.237	8.23	3.51
Gregorio, Joan	R-R	6-7	180	1-12-92	4	4	3.04	13	13	0	0	74	63	33	25	9	35	61	.235	.314	.184	7.42	4.26

Johnson, Chase	R-R	6-3	190	1-9-92	0	2	4.35	6	0	0	0	10	11	5	5	2	0	9	.268	.400	.063	7.84	0.00
Kelly, Casey	R-R	6-3	215	10-4-89	2	3	4.17	7	7	0	0	41	43	22	19	7	15	39	.270	.297	.247	8.56	3.29
2-team total (12 Iowa)					7	5	4.46	19	18	1	1	101	115	55	50	16	38	82	.290	.316	.295	7.31	3.39
Knight, Dusten	R-R	6-0	200	9-2-90	3	2	3.43	31	3	0	0	60	51	28	23	6	31	59	.230	.213	.246	8.80	4.62
LaMarche, Will	R-R	6-3	220	8-7-91	0	0	67.50	1	0	0	0	1	5	5	5	1	1	0	.714	.667	.750	0.00	13.50
Law, Derek	R-R	6-2	210	9-14-90	1	1	2.48	25	0	0	10	33	32	9	9	1	12	26	.262	.246	.277	7.16	3.31
Melancon, Mark	R-R	6-2	210	3-28-85	0	0	0.00	1	1	0	0	1	0	0	0	0	1	0	.000	—	.000	0.00	9.00
Moronta, Reyes	R-R	6-0	175	1-6-93	3	0	2.12	13	0	0	0	17	13	4	4	1	8	17	.210	.185	.229	9.00	4.24
Morris, Bryan	R-L	6-3	220	3-28-87	0	0	0.00	3	0	0	0	3	2	0	0	0	1	2	.182	.000	.250	6.00	3.00
Muren, Drew	L-R	6-6	225	11-22-88	1	0	0.00	1	0	0	0	1	0	0	0	0	1	0	.000	.000	.000	0.00	9.00
2-team total (4 Reno)					1	0	0.00	5	0	0	1	9	3	0	0	0	5	7	.103	.143	.105	7.27	5.19
Okert, Steven	L-L	6-3	210	7-9-91	3	0	3.20	24	0	0	6	25	15	10	9	4	8	21	.179	.143	.196	7.46	2.84
Osich, Josh	L-L	6-2	230	9-3-88	1	1	7.71	9	0	0	2	9	12	11	8	0	3	8	.308	.333	.296	7.71	2.89
Owen, David	L-R	6-0	210	10-21-93	0	0	0.00	1	0	0	0	1	1	0	0	0	0	3	.200	.000	.333	20.25	0.00
Reyes, Mark	R-L	6-1	225	10-8-92	0	0	3.00	1	0	0	0	3	3	1	1	0	2	2	.231	.000	.333	6.00	6.00
Reynolds, Matt	L-L	6-5	240	10-2-84	2	1	3.86	29	0	0	0	30	28	15	13	3	6	27	.239	.214	.262	8.01	1.78
Rogers, Tyler	R-R	6-5	187	12-17-90	4	4	2.37	55	0	0	10	76	65	26	20	2	28	43	.236	.223	.245	5.09	3.32
Romero, Ricky	R-L	6-1	210	11-6-84	0	2	6.75	4	4	0	0	15	16	12	11	1	16	13	.286	.300	.278	7.98	9.82
Roth, Michael	L-L	6-1	210	2-15-90	4	4	4.68	15	11	0	1	67	89	44	35	6	18	42	.317	.312	.319	5.61	2.41
Sitton, Kraig	L-L	6-5	190	7-13-88	6	4	3.74	47	2	0	0	65	70	29	27	5	16	46	.279	.351	.234	6.37	2.22
Slania, Dan	R-R	6-5	275	5-24-92	0	8	7.82	12	12	0	0	61	78	54	53	14	31	57	.325	.331	.317	8.41	4.57
Slatton, Heath	L-R	6-3	210	9-17-93	0	0	12.60	4	0	0	0	5	8	8	7	1	6	3	.348	.444	.286	5.40	10.80
Snelten, D.J.	L-L	6-7	245	5-29-92	4	0	2.42	36	0	0	0	52	38	20	14	4	18	43	.197	.152	.221	7.44	3.12
Stratton, Chris	R-R	6-3	190	8-22-90	4	5	5.11	15	15	0	0	79	94	49	45	10	22	71	.290	.274	.305	8.05	2.50
Suarez, Albert	R-R	6-3	235	10-8-89	0	0	0.00	1	1	0	0	3	3	0	0	0	0	5	.250	.250	.250	15.00	0.00
Suarez, Andrew	L-L	6-2	205	9-11-92	6	6	3.55	15	13	0	0	89	94	39	35	7	27	80	.270	.355	.223	8.12	2.74
Webb, Ryan	R-R	6-6	245	2-5-86	1	0	3.98	17	0	0	2	20	22	12	9	3	12	13	.275	.349	.189	5.75	5.31

Fielding

Catcher	PCT	G	PO	A	E	DP	PB
Arnold	.984	9	56	7	1	0	0
Brown	.996	54	409	42	2	3	4
Federowicz	.991	73	518	49	5	7	6
Winn	1.000	6	40	4	0	0	0
Zambrano	1.000	4	19	1	0	0	0

First Base	PCT	G	PO	A	E	DP
Blanks	1.000	18	110	10	0	12
Ciriaco	.990	11	94	8	1	15
Federowicz	.933	2	13	1	1	1
Gillaspie	.993	18	125	8	1	13
Hwang	.982	34	252	18	5	39
Jones	.992	15	120	3	1	16
Lollis	.998	49	390	22	1	32
Marrero	.991	13	102	6	1	10
Morse	1.000	1	9	0	0	1

Second Base	PCT	G	PO	A	E	DP
Arroyo	1.000	5	9	8	0	3
Bennett	.882	5	8	7	2	1
Brown	1.000	3	5	5	0	3
Calixte	1.000	12	25	26	0	9
Castillo	.979	56	106	170	6	50
Ciriaco	.975	38	55	100	4	28
Hill	1.000	2	5	5	0	2
Panik	1.000	1	0	2	0	0
Querecuto	.976	25	37	44	2	10
Tomlinson	.981	17	37	64	2	14

Third Base	PCT	G	PO	A	E	DP
Arroyo	.909	4	3	7	1	1
Bennett	.000	1	0	0	0	0
Calixte	.981	20	18	34	1	4
Castillo	1.000	9	6	15	0	2
Ciriaco	.897	20	11	24	4	2
Gillaspie	1.000	7	2	11	0	0
Hill	1.000	1	2	4	0	1
Hwang	.938	58	34	103	9	20
Jones	.939	34	18	59	5	10
Sandoval	1.000	7	3	15	0	2

Shortstop	PCT	G	PO	A	E	DP
Arroyo	.963	16	29	50	3	12
Calixte	.957	55	94	129	10	28
Castillo	.944	9	10	24	2	4
Jones	.000	1	0	0	0	0
Polonius	1.000	3	2	5	0	1
Querecuto	.972	65	97	184	8	50
Tomlinson	1.000	5	7	10	0	0

Outfield	PCT	G	PO	A	E	DP
Bernard	.982	57	108	3	2	0
Calixte	1.000	15	20	0	0	0
Duggar	1.000	12	39	0	0	0
Heathcott	1.000	22	40	2	0	1
Hill	1.000	1	2	0	0	0
Hwang	1.000	2	6	0	0	0
Jones	.972	22	34	1	1	0
Lollis	1.000	1	4	0	0	0
Marrero	1.000	1	1	1	0	0
Moncrief	.929	45	60	5	5	0
Morse	1.000	2	1	0	0	0
Parker	.980	26	48	0	1	0
Ruggiano	1.000	36	72	2	0	0
Shaw	.980	76	97	1	2	0
Slater	.966	47	83	2	3	2
Stubbs	.967	9	26	3	1	0
Tomlinson	1.000	5	14	0	0	0
Upton Jr.	1.000	10	20	0	0	0
Williamson	.947	79	121	5	7	1

RICHMOND FLYING SQUIRRELS — DOUBLE-A

EASTERN LEAGUE

Batting	B-T	HT	WT	DOB	AVG	vLH	vRH	G	AB	R	H	2B	3B	HR	RBI	BB	HBP	SH	SF	SO	SB	CS	SLG	OBP
Arnold, Jeff	R-R	6-2	205	1-13-88	.184	.196	.180	61	185	19	34	10	1	6	22	29	3	1	3	70	0	1	.346	.300
Bednar, Brandon	R-R	6-4	195	3-21-92	.280	.227	.296	117	411	54	115	24	1	1	34	26	4	3	4	63	2	2	.350	.326
Bennett, T.J.	L-R	6-3	215	7-22-92	.242	.158	.277	24	66	11	16	6	1	1	4	6	1	0	0	12	0	0	.409	.315
Carbonell, Daniel	R-R	6-3	200	3-29-91	.242	.204	.257	55	190	21	46	11	1	4	22	11	2	1	2	39	5	2	.374	.288
Castillo, Ali	R-R	5-10	165	6-19-89	.297	.191	.325	34	101	1	30	3	0	0	7	6	1	0	2	9	1	2	.327	.336
Cole, Hunter	R-R	6-1	190	10-3-92	.249	.299	.234	83	281	29	70	20	5	7	34	31	2	0	5	64	2	1	.431	.323
Crawford, Brandon	L-R	6-2	215	1-21-87	.500	1.000	.429	2	8	1	4	1	0	0	0	0	0	0	0	0	0	0	.625	.500
Davis, Dylan	R-R	6-0	205	7-20-93	.217	.256	.205	99	327	32	71	17	0	10	38	26	3	1	1	92	0	0	.361	.280
Garcia, Aramis	R-R	6-2	220	1-12-93	.282	.333	.263	22	78	11	22	12	0	0	8	9	1	0	1	21	0	0	.436	.360
Garcia, Carlos	B-R	5-10	172	3-18-92	.242	.229	.247	47	132	15	32	4	1	2	12	3	2	0	2	20	6	3	.333	.266
Gindl, Caleb	L-L	5-7	210	8-31-88	.284	.222	.313	44	169	27	48	4	7	8	25	14	0	0	2	35	0	1	.533	.335
Gomez, Miguel	B-R	5-10	185	12-17-92	.305	.333	.298	78	308	43	94	19	2	8	38	12	0	1	1	36	0	0	.458	.330
Heathcott, Slade	L-L	6-1	205	9-28-90	.262	.198	.284	93	347	52	91	20	2	12	33	37	4	5	1	88	8	6	.435	.339
Hinojosa, C.J	R-R	5-10	175	7-15-94	.265	.313	.249	99	373	47	99	16	0	4	35	31	2	6	5	42	5	4	.341	.321
Hobson, K.C.	L-L	6-2	230	8-22-90	.246	.283	.233	56	203	26	50	5	1	11	35	17	1	0	2	55	1	0	.443	.305
Horan, Tyler	R-L	6-2	230	12-2-90	.218	.231	.215	33	78	6	17	3	1	1	9	7	0	0	1	22	0	2	.321	.279
Lollis, Ryan	L-L	6-1	190	12-16-86	.230	.214	.234	57	165	9	38	4	0	0	13	10	1	0	1	25	1	1	.255	.277

Moreno, Rando	B-R	5-11	165	6-6-92	.200	.244	.186	68	185	13	37	5	0	0	16	12	0	1	1	25	3	3	.227	.248
Nunez, Eduardo	R-R	6-0	195	6-15-87	.333	1.000	.000	1	3	1	1	1	0	0	0	0	0	0	0	1	0	0	.667	.333
Sands, Jerry	R-R	6-4	225	9-28-87	.298	.471	.244	64	215	30	64	17	4	5	28	38	0	0	1	44	3	1	.484	.402
Schroder, Myles	B-R	5-11	180	8-1-87	.259	.258	.260	89	332	47	86	22	4	7	30	36	12	5	0	76	4	1	.413	.353
Shaw, Chris	L-R	6-4	235	10-20-93	.301	.263	.307	37	133	16	40	10	0	6	29	18	2	0	1	26	0	0	.511	.390
Sonabend, Adam	R-R	6-0	200	5-12-92	.231	.167	.286	4	13	1	3	1	0	0	2	1	0	1	0	2	0	0	.308	.286
Winn, Matt	R-R	6-1	210	8-5-92	.125	.000	.139	12	40	3	5	0	0	0	0	7	0	0	0	17	0	0	.125	.255
Zambrano, Eliezer	B-R	5-11	195	9-16-86	.200	.115	.225	35	115	4	23	2	1	0	4	3	0	0	0	19	0	1	.235	.220

Pitching	B-T	HT	WT	DOB	W	L	ERA	G	GS	CG	SV	IP	H	R	ER	HR	BB	SO	AVG	vLH	vRH	K/9	BB/9
Alvarado, Carlos	R-R	6-4	175	10-22-89	1	4	3.22	43	0	0	2	59	50	21	21	6	28	70	.235	.279	.193	10.74	4.30
Balester, Collin	R-R	6-4	190	6-6-86	1	4	2.75	12	1	0	1	20	15	7	6	1	3	21	.211	.148	.250	9.61	1.37
Black, Vic	R-R	6-4	210	5-23-88	1	1	5.28	19	0	0	0	29	27	20	17	2	28	16	.246	.217	.280	4.97	8.69
Cabrera, Yordy	R-R	6-1	205	9-3-90	0	1	7.04	11	0	0	0	15	25	15	12	3	10	11	.368	.379	.359	6.46	5.87
Coonrod, Sam	R-R	6-2	225	9-22-92	4	11	4.69	24	18	0	0	104	96	62	54	7	42	94	.249	.242	.258	8.16	3.65
Cyr, Tyler	R-R	6-3	200	5-5-93	5	2	2.19	47	0	0	18	49	50	20	12	3	20	57	.260	.179	.340	10.40	3.65
Flores, Jose	R-R	6-3	250	6-4-89	3	1	2.09	19	7	0	0	47	33	12	11	0	15	45	.194	.194	.194	8.56	2.85
Gage, Matt	R-L	6-4	240	2-11-93	4	4	2.88	13	13	1	0	78	77	25	25	5	20	55	.261	.274	.257	6.35	2.31
Hall, Cody	R-R	6-4	235	1-6-88	4	2	2.79	25	0	0	1	29	23	10	9	3	12	40	.215	.185	.262	12.41	3.72
Halstead, Ryan	L-R	6-5	220	5-13-92	2	0	4.56	26	0	0	0	24	28	13	12	3	7	21	.295	.321	.262	7.99	2.66
Herb, Tyler	R-R	6-2	175	4-28-92	2	3	2.76	10	10	1	0	65	61	27	20	5	18	48	.246	.227	.267	6.61	2.48
Johnson, Jordan	R-R	6-3	200	9-15-93	4	6	4.48	21	15	0	0	92	89	51	46	12	37	65	.259	.273	.244	6.34	3.61
Johnson, Stephen	R-R	6-5	230	2-21-91	0	1	9.82	6	0	0	0	4	3	5	4	2	3	4	.200	.143	.250	9.82	7.36
Jones, Christian	L-L	6-3	210	1-27-91	0	3	5.33	20	0	0	1	25	34	16	15	2	12	24	.330	.326	.333	8.53	4.26
Lujan, Matt	L-L	6-1	210	8-23-88	4	5	4.99	15	11	0	0	70	88	39	39	8	18	55	.307	.159	.348	7.04	2.30
Martin, Jarret	L-L	6-3	230	8-14-89	4	2	2.04	37	1	0	1	40	22	9	9	0	30	40	.167	.158	.173	9.08	6.81
Martinez, Rodolfo	R-R	6-2	180	4-4-94	0	0	5.63	8	0	0	0	8	12	7	5	0	5	5	.364	.412	.313	5.63	5.63
McNamara, Dillon	R-R	6-5	230	10-6-91	0	3	5.48	8	6	0	0	21	19	14	13	3	12	11	.238	.156	.343	4.64	5.06
2-team total (10 Trenton)					0	5	5.73	18	6	0	1	33	32	23	21	5	20	23	.250	.156	.343	6.27	5.45
Moronta, Reyes	R-R	6-0	175	1-6-93	0	1	4.00	19	0	0	5	18	15	9	8	1	12	26	.217	.212	.222	13.00	6.00
Pino, Luis	R-R	6-0	175	11-4-94	0	0	11.66	9	0	0	0	15	26	19	19	0	8	10	.394	.346	.425	6.14	4.91
Reed, Nate	L-L	6-3	180	12-1-87	3	2	6.40	11	8	0	0	52	62	39	37	6	26	44	.300	.358	.271	7.62	4.50
Rosin, Seth	R-R	6-6	265	11-2-88	2	1	4.67	22	1	0	0	27	31	14	14	6	7	26	.304	.309	.298	8.67	2.33
Slania, Dan	R-R	6-5	275	5-24-92	5	3	3.59	13	13	1	0	80	81	35	32	5	28	55	.266	.254	.284	6.16	3.14
Snelten, D.J.	L-L	6-7	245	5-29-92	4	1	1.66	15	0	0	0	22	19	6	4	0	5	28	.226	.172	.255	11.63	2.08
Suarez, Andrew	L-L	6-2	205	9-11-92	4	4	2.96	11	11	0	0	67	72	30	22	3	15	55	.276	.266	.280	7.39	2.01
Taylor, Cory	R-R	6-2	255	12-14-93	4	11	4.30	25	24	2	0	128	125	66	61	9	58	100	.258	.249	.267	7.05	4.09
Young, Pat	R-R	6-7	240	3-24-92	0	1	8.59	5	1	0	0	7	11	7	7	0	9	4	.344	.389	.286	4.91	11.05

Fielding

Catcher	PCT	G	PO	A	E	DP	PB
Arnold	.996	59	428	62	2	4	5
Garcia	.982	20	150	16	3	3	1
Schroder	.989	13	75	11	1	0	3
Sonabend	1.000	4	28	5	0	0	0
Winn	.977	12	125	5	3	0	1
Zambrano	.992	34	224	12	2	5	4

First Base	PCT	G	PO	A	E	DP
Bednar	.992	30	223	13	2	24
Garcia	1.000	2	5	0	0	0
Hobson	.995	39	356	24	2	31
Lollis	1.000	21	139	9	0	9
Sands	.994	35	337	15	2	27
Schroder	1.000	1	9	1	0	0
Shaw	.993	18	130	9	1	16

Second Base	PCT	G	PO	A	E	DP
Bednar	.984	16	29	34	1	6
Garcia	.981	14	16	36	1	10
Gomez	.962	72	110	191	12	43
Hinojosa	.972	15	29	41	2	12
Moreno	1.000	1	0	2	0	0
Schroder	.985	27	34	96	2	16

Third Base	PCT	G	PO	A	E	DP
Bednar	.956	62	32	98	6	10
Bennett	.898	22	13	31	5	4
Castillo	.931	22	17	37	4	4
Davis	.636	2	5	2	4	0
Hinojosa	.975	21	12	27	1	2
Moreno	1.000	3	2	2	0	0
Nunez	1.000	1	0	1	0	0
Sands	1.000	1	0	3	0	0
Schroder	.944	23	20	48	4	4

Shortstop	PCT	G	PO	A	E	DP
Bednar	.958	8	10	13	1	7
Castillo	.960	8	10	14	1	3
Crawford	1.000	2	1	3	0	1
Garcia	.857	4	7	11	3	3
Hinojosa	.977	69	85	172	6	38
Moreno	.967	58	77	127	7	31
Schroder	1.000	9	7	35	0	4

Outfield	PCT	G	PO	A	E	DP
Carbonell	.960	45	91	6	4	2
Castillo	1.000	2	2	1	0	1
Cole	.986	77	133	8	2	4
Davis	.991	67	103	2	1	0
Garcia	1.000	18	24	0	0	0
Gindl	.989	41	91	3	1	1
Heathcott	.981	88	196	7	4	1
Hobson	1.000	8	15	2	0	0
Horan	1.000	19	36	3	0	0
Lollis	.981	24	49	2	1	1
Sands	1.000	9	15	1	0	0
Schroder	1.000	16	27	2	0	0
Shaw	1.000	18	26	0	0	0

SAN JOSE GIANTS — *HIGH CLASS A*

CALIFORNIA LEAGUE

Batting	B-T	HT	WT	DOB	AVG	vLH	vRH	G	AB	R	H	2B	3B	HR	RBI	BB	HBP	SH	SF	SO	SB	CS	SLG	OBP
Amion, Junior	R-R	5-10	190	2-24-93	.200	.000	.286	4	10	0	2	1	0	0	0	0	0	0	0	2	0	0	.300	.200
Arenado, Jonah	R-R	6-4	230	2-3-95	.268	.221	.283	129	488	67	131	36	4	13	73	26	4	0	4	104	1	1	.439	.308
Bennett, T.J.	L-R	6-3	215	7-22-92	.195	.444	.167	29	87	5	17	3	1	1	5	8	1	0	1	31	2	4	.287	.268
Bernal, Michael	R-R	5-11	210	9-6-92	.250	.200	.257	11	40	9	10	1	0	0	5	5	0	0	0	10	0	0	.275	.333
Bono, Christoph	L-R	6-1	190	10-6-92	.125	.167	.100	4	16	0	2	0	0	0	3	0	0	0	0	9	0	0	.125	.125
Brusa, Gio	B-R	6-3	235	7-26-93	.237	.291	.224	113	426	58	101	28	2	17	55	33	4	0	4	124	1	2	.432	.296
Carbonell, Daniel	R-R	6-3	200	3-29-91	.304	.250	.317	39	148	22	45	13	1	4	25	5	3	0	1	31	3	2	.487	.338
Castillo, Ali	R-R	5-10	165	6-19-89	.154	.250	.111	3	13	0	2	1	0	0	1	0	0	0	0	4	0	0	.231	.154
Dobson, Dillon	L-R	6-2	220	8-21-93	.234	.213	.238	110	428	56	100	21	3	15	68	35	4	0	5	146	3	1	.402	.295
Duggar, Steven	L-R	6-2	195	11-4-93	.270	.303	.256	29	115	22	31	11	0	4	20	17	0	0	1	42	7	0	.470	.361
Fargas, Johneshwy	R-R	6-1	180	12-15-94	.194	.353	.163	31	103	15	20	4	2	2	11	3	1	0	1	24	5	1	.330	.222

Garcia, Aramis	R-R	6-2	220	1-12-93	.272	.261	.275	81	324	43	88	20	1	17	65	15	6	0	2	73	0	0	.497	.314
Gillaspie, Conor	R-L	6-1	195	7-18-87	.286	.222	.400	5	14	1	4	1	0	0	1	1	0	0	0	3	0	0	.357	.333
Hill, Aaron	R-R	5-11	200	3-21-82	.250	.000	.286	3	8	4	2	2	0	0	0	3	1	0	0	5	0	0	.500	.500
Howard, Ryan	R-R	6-2	195	7-25-94	.306	.292	.310	127	526	59	161	21	0	9	50	23	8	3	5	81	7	2	.397	.342
Jebavy, Ronnie	R-R	6-2	205	5-17-94	.251	.205	.268	77	307	35	77	14	4	4	20	12	6	0	2	96	15	0	.362	.291
Miller, Jalen	R-R	5-11	190	12-19-96	.227	.274	.214	117	431	61	98	25	4	6	44	31	3	2	2	100	6	4	.346	.283
Morse, Michael	R-R	6-5	245	3-22-82	.222	.000	.250	3	9	2	2	0	0	0	1	1	0	0	0	2	0	0	.222	.300
Nunez, Eduardo	R-R	6-0	195	6-15-87	.200	—	.200	2	5	1	1	0	0	0	0	1	0	0	0	2	0	0	.200	.333
Panik, Joe	L-R	6-1	190	10-30-90	.000	—	.000	1	3	0	0	0	0	0	0	1	0	0	0	1	0	0	.000	.250
Pare, Matt	L-R	6-0	205	11-17-90	.191	.200	.189	15	42	3	8	2	0	1	3	7	4	1	1	12	1	0	.310	.352
Paulino, Cristian	R-R	5-10	190	9-4-91	.340	.471	.267	11	47	8	16	2	0	1	3	1	1	1	0	11	4	2	.447	.367
Pence, Hunter	R-R	6-4	220	4-13-83	.300	—	.300	3	10	3	3	0	0	0	0	2	0	0	0	2	0	0	.300	.417
Polonius, John	R-R	6-1	160	1-13-91	.265	.333	.247	36	102	16	27	5	0	2	10	7	3	1	1	22	2	3	.373	.327
Quinn, Heath	R-R	6-2	190	6-7-95	.228	.190	.238	75	272	24	62	9	0	10	29	20	4	0	1	86	0	0	.371	.290
Reynolds, Bryan	B-R	6-3	205	1-27-95	.312	.365	.295	121	491	72	153	26	9	10	63	37	6	1	5	106	5	3	.462	.364
Riley, John	R-R	6-0	210	2-14-94	.000	.000	.000	1	4	0	0	0	0	0	0	0	0	0	0	4	0	0	.000	.000
Sabanosh, Connor	R-R	6-0	200	8-6-93	.200	.143	.226	15	45	2	9	0	0	0	1	1	0	1	0	13	0	0	.200	.217
Sandoval, Pablo	B-R	5-11	255	8-11-86	.222	.333	.167	3	9	0	2	0	0	0	1	2	0	0	0	0	0	0	.222	.364
Span, Denard	L-L	6-0	210	2-27-84	.333	.000	.500	2	6	0	2	0	0	0	0	1	0	0	0	0	0	0	.333	.429
Vizcaino, Jose Jr.	R-R	6-2	220	4-5-94	.214	.125	.232	29	98	12	21	3	0	2	12	11	1	1	0	30	1	0	.306	.300
Williamson, Mac	R-R	6-4	240	7-15-90	.167	.000	.200	2	6	1	1	0	0	0	0	1	0	0	0	3	0	0	.167	.286
Winn, Matt	R-R	6-1	210	8-5-92	.215	.172	.230	71	251	32	54	17	1	6	23	25	2	0	3	96	0	0	.363	.288

Pitching	B-T	HT	WT	DOB	W	L	ERA	G	GS	CG	SV	IP	H	R	ER	HR	BB	SO	AVG	vLH	vRH	K/9	BB/9
Anderson, Shaun	R-R	6-4	225	10-29-94	3	3	3.51	6	5	0	0	26	19	13	10	1	4	22	.198	.267	.167	7.71	1.40
Bumgarner, Madison	R-L	6-5	250	8-1-89	0	1	8.10	2	2	0	0	10	11	10	9	4	2	13	.268	.143	.294	11.70	1.80
Cabrera, Yordy	R-R	6-1	205	9-3-90	0	1	4.25	14	0	0	0	30	39	15	14	1	16	23	.331	.314	.343	6.98	4.85
Cederoth, Michael	R-R	6-6	195	11-25-92	0	0	3.20	16	0	0	0	25	18	13	9	4	15	33	.200	.217	.182	11.72	5.33
Connolly, Mike	R-R	6-1	205	10-31-91	4	8	4.85	18	15	0	0	95	117	55	51	12	21	60	.312	.321	.306	5.70	2.00
Cueto, Johnny	R-R	5-11	220	2-15-86	0	1	6.75	2	2	0	0	7	11	8	5	1	1	8	.367	.353	.385	10.80	1.35
Diaz, Carlos	L-L	6-2	225	11-18-93	2	2	2.47	34	0	0	1	58	45	18	16	2	23	67	.214	.202	.222	10.34	3.55
Halstead, Ryan	L-R	6-5	220	5-13-92	0	0	1.11	22	0	0	8	24	24	5	3	0	2	27	.247	.308	.207	9.99	0.74
Kaden, Connor	R-R	6-4	215	10-27-92	4	0	4.34	21	0	0	0	37	35	19	18	3	31	24	.245	.308	.192	5.79	7.47
Knight, Dusten	R-R	6-0	200	9-2-90	2	0	1.10	8	0	0	1	16	6	2	2	0	1	24	.111	.129	.087	13.22	0.55
Krook, Matt	L-L	6-4	225	10-21-94	4	9	5.12	25	17	0	0	91	75	67	52	4	66	105	.217	.185	.231	10.35	6.50
LaMarche, Will	R-R	6-3	220	8-7-91	4	2	3.46	30	0	0	2	42	38	18	16	1	8	49	.241	.193	.267	10.58	1.73
Martinez, Rodolfo	R-R	6-2	180	4-4-94	2	0	4.05	10	0	0	0	13	14	6	6	2	1	12	.269	.231	.308	8.10	0.68
Mazza, Domenic	R-L	6-1	195	7-29-94	0	2	7.71	2	2	0	0	12	18	12	10	1	3	4	.360	.385	.351	3.09	2.31
McCasland, Jake	R-R	6-2	225	9-13-91	5	11	4.78	20	20	0	0	102	125	71	54	9	30	95	.299	.310	.288	8.41	2.66
Melancon, Mark	R-R	6-2	210	3-28-85	0	0	13.50	3	3	0	0	3	6	4	4	1	0	4	.462	.500	.429	13.50	0.00
Menez, Conner	L-L	6-3	195	5-29-95	7	7	4.41	23	22	0	0	114	127	64	56	5	50	99	.282	.243	.299	7.79	3.94
Morris, Bryan	R-L	6-3	220	3-28-87	1	0	0.00	2	0	0	0	3	0	0	0	0	1	1	.000	.000	.000	3.38	3.38
Muren, Drew	L-R	6-6	225	11-22-88	0	0	2.70	4	0	0	0	7	6	3	2	0	3	11	.231	.167	.286	14.85	4.05
Owen, David	L-R	6-0	210	10-21-93	3	1	5.76	27	0	0	0	66	86	45	42	4	19	50	.315	.363	.281	6.85	2.60
Reyes, Mark	R-L	6-1	225	10-8-92	4	13	6.08	25	21	0	0	111	128	82	75	9	77	60	.299	.301	.298	4.86	6.24
Rheault, Dylan	R-R	6-9	245	3-21-92	2	1	2.70	55	0	0	21	60	51	23	18	4	22	46	.229	.230	.228	6.90	3.30
Simpson, Caleb	R-R	6-3	230	9-15-91	1	5	4.68	44	0	0	0	60	43	34	31	8	39	80	.199	.265	.144	12.07	5.88
Slatton, Heath	L-R	6-3	210	9-17-93	3	3	7.93	22	6	0	1	48	63	45	42	8	26	54	.325	.286	.359	10.20	4.91
Smith, Caleb	R-L	6-2	210	10-4-92	0	1	7.27	7	0	0	0	9	10	7	7	0	14	6	.294	.500	.208	6.23	14.54
Solter, Matt	R-R	6-3	220	6-4-93	5	2	4.08	14	7	0	0	57	57	29	26	5	18	46	.262	.188	.325	7.22	2.83
Suarez, Albert	R-R	6-3	235	10-8-89	0	0	3.00	2	2	0	0	6	4	2	2	0	1	3	.191	.167	.200	4.50	1.50
Watson, Grant	L-L	6-0	185	7-2-93	4	3	3.96	14	11	0	0	75	83	37	33	8	29	69	.283	.244	.310	8.28	3.48
Williams, Garrett	L-L	6-1	205	9-15-94	2	2	2.45	6	5	0	0	33	28	11	9	3	10	38	.221	.229	.215	10.36	2.73

Fielding

Catcher	PCT	G	PO	A	E	DP	PB
Garcia	.989	50	388	44	5	5	8
Pare	.972	8	66	4	2	1	1
Riley	1.000	1	11	1	0	0	0
Sabanosh	1.000	14	95	11	0	0	3
Winn	.989	70	554	62	7	4	22

First Base	PCT	G	PO	A	E	DP
Arenado	.989	30	243	16	3	29
Dobson	.986	77	672	48	10	59
Garcia	1.000	17	136	10	0	17
Vizcaino	1.000	20	159	9	0	19

Second Base	PCT	G	PO	A	E	DP
Bennett	.936	8	17	27	3	5
Bernal	1.000	5	5	10	0	2
Castillo	1.000	3	4	8	0	4
Dobson	.952	30	59	101	8	27
Miller	.963	83	140	198	13	42
Panik	1.000	1	1	4	0	0
Paulino	.929	3	4	9	1	2
Polonius	.963	14	19	33	2	6

Third Base	PCT	G	PO	A	E	DP
Arenado	.922	97	61	198	22	16
Bennett	1.000	7	7	7	0	3
Bernal	.833	3	1	4	1	1
Gillaspie	.833	3	2	3	1	0
Howard	.879	23	14	37	7	4
Nunez	1.000	1	0	1	0	0
Paulino	1.000	2	1	6	0	1
Polonius	.963	13	6	20	1	2
Sandoval	1.000	1	0	2	0	0

Shortstop	PCT	G	PO	A	E	DP
Bennett	.900	2	2	7	1	1
Bernal	1.000	4	4	13	0	2
Howard	.969	102	147	261	13	63
Miller	.936	28	47	70	8	22
Polonius	.975	8	17	22	1	4

Outfield	PCT	G	PO	A	E	DP
Amion	1.000	1	2	0	0	0
Bennett	1.000	8	9	0	0	0
Bono	1.000	3	4	0	0	0
Brusa	.960	74	119	2	5	0
Carbonell	.945	33	48	4	3	1
Duggar	.944	23	33	1	2	0
Fargas	.987	30	71	5	1	1
Jebavy	1.000	76	185	4	0	3
Morse	1.000	2	2	0	0	0
Paulino	.875	5	7	0	1	0
Pence	1.000	3	1	0	0	0
Quinn	.966	60	82	3	3	0
Reynolds	.982	109	207	10	4	2
Span	1.000	2	3	0	0	0
Williamson	.000	1	0	0	0	0

AUGUSTA GREENJACKETS

LOW CLASS A

SOUTH ATLANTIC LEAGUE

Batting	B-T	HT	WT	DOB	AVG	vLH	vRH	G	AB	R	H	2B	3B	HR	RBI	BB	HBP	SH	SF	SO	SB	CS	SLG	OBP
Albertson, Will	R-R	5-11	190	6-26-94	.206	.258	.190	42	131	12	27	2	0	1	12	15	8	0	0	29	0	0	.244	.325
Angomas, Jean	L-R	6-0	170	6-5-95	.292	.278	.295	70	264	31	77	8	3	1	22	19	1	3	3	27	10	9	.356	.338
Beltre, Kelvin	R-R	5-11	170	9-25-96	.253	.287	.243	118	423	65	107	24	2	6	37	47	2	2	3	96	15	6	.362	.328
Bernal, Michael	R-R	5-11	210	9-6-92	.267	.388	.233	69	225	22	60	13	2	2	28	19	10	2	1	61	1	2	.369	.349
Bono, Christoph	L-R	6-1	190	10-6-92	.100	.250	.063	5	20	3	2	2	0	0	0	2	1	0	0	8	1	0	.200	.217
Bowers, Zack	R-R	6-2	215	10-14-93	.082	.000	.085	16	49	2	4	0	0	0	0	2	2	1	0	28	0	0	.082	.151
Brown, Tyler	R-R	6-1	180	1-18-95	.208	.083	.250	16	48	8	10	4	0	0	0	6	2	0	0	12	3	1	.292	.321
De La Rosa, Frandy	B-R	6-1	180	1-24-96	.231	.273	.219	56	199	21	46	9	2	5	19	15	1	1	3	66	2	4	.372	.284
Dunston Jr., Shawon	L-R	6-2	195	2-5-93	.241	.258	.237	50	170	17	41	5	2	2	13	14	1	7	1	30	13	5	.329	.301
Ewing, Skyler	R-R	6-1	225	8-22-92	.246	.193	.258	88	297	48	73	21	1	13	47	36	18	0	3	73	1	1	.455	.359
Fabian, Sandro	R-R	6-1	180	3-6-98	.277	.351	.259	122	480	51	133	30	0	11	61	10	5	4	4	88	5	4	.408	.297
Fargas, Johneshwy	R-R	6-1	180	12-15-94	.205	.333	.186	37	117	14	24	6	1	1	10	6	7	1	0	24	10	7	.299	.285
Fulmer, Ashford	R-R	6-1	175	6-29-93	.236	.227	.238	70	250	30	59	14	2	1	22	28	6	2	1	54	13	3	.320	.326
Garcia, Carlos	B-R	5-10	172	3-18-92	.221	.217	.222	33	122	15	27	5	0	4	8	17	3	4	0	24	7	3	.361	.331
Geraldo, Manuel	B-R	6-1	170	9-23-96	.165	.273	.140	30	115	13	19	2	1	3	10	3	2	0	0	34	5	0	.278	.200
Heyward, Jacob	R-R	6-3	210	8-1-95	.223	.230	.221	107	359	40	80	16	0	10	45	42	8	2	1	110	5	7	.351	.317
Kirby, Ryan	L-R	6-2	180	1-25-95	.220	.400	.194	23	82	8	18	5	2	1	8	9	1	0	1	34	0	0	.366	.301
Marks, Anthony	L-L	5-8	175	4-15-94	.182	.083	.200	20	77	8	14	3	0	0	9	8	0	1	1	15	5	2	.221	.256
Paulino, Cristian	R-R	5-10	190	9-4-91	.271	.348	.251	62	229	31	62	9	1	4	19	23	2	4	0	49	30	7	.371	.343
Rivera, Kevin	B-R	5-11	170	6-12-96	.214	.200	.217	24	84	8	18	3	1	1	5	5	0	0	0	17	2	1	.310	.258
Sonabend, Adam	R-R	6-0	200	5-12-92	.211	.286	.189	31	95	5	20	5	0	0	9	9	4	3	3	36	0	0	.263	.297
Van Horn, Brandon	R-R	6-2	175	12-18-93	.262	.271	.260	81	282	28	74	11	0	3	27	15	1	3	4	68	11	7	.333	.298
Vizcaino, Jose Jr.	R-R	6-2	220	4-5-94	.262	.177	.286	84	309	34	81	17	2	3	34	18	5	1	5	87	10	3	.359	.309

Pitching	B-T	HT	WT	DOB	W	L	ERA	G	GS	CG	SV	IP	H	R	ER	HR	BB	SO	AVG	vLH	vRH	K/9	BB/9
Adon, Melvin	R-R	6-3	195	6-9-94	3	11	4.35	23	19	0	0	99	110	65	48	5	35	89	.277	.299	.253	8.06	3.17
Avila-Leeper, Cameron	L-L	5-11	150	2-21-96	1	2	14.85	7	1	0	0	13	26	24	22	2	10	8	.406	.450	.386	5.40	6.75
Baragar, Caleb	R-L	6-3	210	4-9-94	5	7	4.63	22	22	0	0	115	127	75	59	8	35	81	.286	.333	.263	6.36	2.75
Bostic, Alex	L-L	6-3	195	11-14-94	0	1	7.71	6	0	0	0	9	9	10	8	0	13	10	.243	.200	.294	9.64	12.54
Brody, Greg	R-R	6-2	185	10-22-91	0	1	5.40	11	0	0	0	13	14	10	8	0	2	13	.246	.200	.281	8.78	1.35
Burke, Jeff	R-R	6-5	210	6-7-93	1	1	4.56	36	0	0	1	51	61	32	26	3	20	31	.298	.356	.252	5.44	3.51
Cabrera, Sandro	L-L	6-2	175	6-22-95	1	2	4.14	42	1	0	0	67	68	42	31	4	36	72	.258	.232	.276	9.62	4.81
Cabrera, Yordy	R-R	6-1	205	9-3-90	2	3	3.44	8	6	0	0	34	28	17	13	1	14	24	.228	.268	.194	6.35	3.71
Kaden, Connor	R-R	6-4	215	10-27-92	3	0	0.43	6	2	0	1	21	12	1	1	0	3	21	.164	.147	.180	9.00	1.29
Mazza, Domenic	R-L	6-1	195	7-29-94	7	9	3.01	19	19	3	0	120	109	47	40	4	20	97	.244	.258	.238	7.30	1.50
Medina, Hengerber	R-R	5-11	160	10-12-94	0	1	6.14	3	0	0	0	7	11	5	5	2	1	4	.379	.333	.429	4.91	1.23
Morel, Jose	R-R	6-2	190	9-6-93	3	2	4.11	39	2	0	0	70	72	38	32	4	21	47	.262	.314	.221	6.04	2.70
Myers, D.J.	L-R	6-5	255	12-24-94	3	8	4.37	22	12	0	0	78	100	51	38	4	22	66	.316	.338	.296	7.58	2.53
Pope, Matt	R-R	6-6	225	7-5-94	1	1	6.75	7	0	0	0	8	8	6	6	1	12	3	.296	.625	.158	3.38	13.50
Riggs, Nolan	R-R	6-8	235	5-22-93	3	6	2.13	44	0	0	3	68	55	23	16	0	15	69	.219	.183	.245	9.18	2.00
Ruotolo, Patrick	R-R	5-10	218	1-15-95	4	2	1.68	44	0	0	17	48	28	10	9	3	12	69	.167	.211	.130	12.85	2.23
Santos, Wilson	R-R	6-2	200	10-20-91	0	2	6.20	15	0	0	1	20	21	16	14	2	9	11	.263	.294	.239	4.87	3.98
Smith, Caleb	R-L	6-2	210	10-4-92	1	2	5.14	24	0	0	0	35	30	22	20	3	27	27	.238	.225	.247	6.94	6.94
Solter, Matt	R-R	6-3	220	6-4-93	2	1	3.98	7	5	0	0	32	30	16	14	2	18	35	.248	.367	.167	9.95	5.12
Vizcaino, Raffi	R-R	6-1	195	12-2-95	5	7	4.98	16	12	0	0	78	75	48	43	4	28	74	.259	.246	.268	8.58	3.24
Williams, Garrett	L-L	6-1	205	9-15-94	4	3	2.25	12	11	0	0	64	59	22	16	0	25	58	.234	.192	.251	8.16	3.52
Woods, Stephen	R-R	6-2	200	6-10-95	6	7	2.95	23	23	0	0	110	93	46	36	3	64	113	.226	.211	.244	9.25	5.24
Yanez, Cesar	R-R	6-5	175	9-30-94	0	1	9.00	9	0	0	0	11	7	12	11	1	19	7	.194	.385	.087	5.73	15.55

Fielding

Catcher	PCT	G	PO	A	E	DP	PB
Albertson	.984	42	289	24	5	3	14
Bowers	1.000	15	126	8	0	0	2
Ewing	.972	53	371	51	12	5	14
Fargas	.000	1	0	0	0	0	0
Sonabend	.992	30	227	21	2	2	4

First Base	PCT	G	PO	A	E	DP
Bowers	.000	1	0	0	0	0
De La Rosa	.986	33	259	18	4	16
Ewing	.972	24	193	13	6	16
Geraldo	1.000	3	18	2	0	3
Kirby	.979	17	128	9	3	16
Rivera	.929	1	12	1	1	0
Vizcaino	.977	60	469	31	12	38

Second Base	PCT	G	PO	A	E	DP
Angomas	1.000	6	9	5	0	0
Beltre	.963	114	199	289	19	56
Bernal	.957	10	12	33	2	5
Brown	1.000	5	8	9	0	3
De La Rosa	1.000	1	1	3	0	1
Rivera	.826	4	7	12	4	0

Third Base	PCT	G	PO	A	E	DP
Angomas	.667	3	1	3	2	1
Bernal	.882	45	14	61	10	4
Brown	.778	3	4	3	2	1
De La Rosa	.929	9	3	10	1	0
Geraldo	.886	21	6	33	5	0
Paulino	.943	46	43	72	7	3
Rivera	.889	12	5	19	3	2

Shortstop	PCT	G	PO	A	E	DP
Bernal	.967	16	23	35	2	5
Brown	1.000	4	6	10	0	2
Garcia	.971	33	55	78	4	22
Geraldo	.700	4	1	6	3	0
Van Horn	.967	81	137	214	12	47

Outfield	PCT	G	PO	A	E	DP
Angomas	.990	51	103	0	1	0
Bono	1.000	5	7	0	0	0
Dunston Jr.	.980	26	49	0	1	0
Fabian	.958	113	258	15	12	4
Fargas	.963	31	73	5	3	1
Fulmer	.978	64	121	11	3	1
Heyward	.955	90	163	6	8	2
Kirby	.667	2	2	0	1	0
Marks	1.000	18	33	1	0	0
Paulino	.975	17	39	0	1	0

SALEM-KEIZER VOLCANOES — SHORT SEASON

NORTHWEST LEAGUE

Batting	B-T	HT	WT	DOB	AVG	vLH	vRH	G	AB	R	H	2B	3B	HR	RBI	BB	HBP	SH	SF	SO	SB	CS	SLG	OBP
Amion, Junior	R-R	5-10	190	2-24-93	.326	.240	.359	25	89	11	29	4	0	1	13	2	0	0	1	11	5	6	.405	.337
Baldwin, Logan	L-L	6-0	170	4-9-96	.342	.469	.316	50	184	38	63	11	2	3	25	13	5	2	3	42	17	10	.473	.395
Bono, Christoph	L-R	6-1	190	10-6-92	.136	.000	.143	9	22	1	3	0	0	0	0	2	1	1	0	10	3	2	.136	.240
Brown, Tyler	R-R	6-1	180	1-18-95	.200	.200	.200	5	10	1	2	1	1	0	4	1	0	0	1	2	1	0	.500	.250
Burks, Christopher	L-R	5-10	180	6-24-94	.077	.000	.091	10	13	3	1	1	0	0	0	1	0	1	0	4	2	0	.154	.143
Cabrera, Gustavo	R-R	6-2	190	1-23-96	.294	.389	.242	16	51	4	15	2	1	3	10	3	1	0	0	13	1	2	.549	.346
Calabrese, Rob	R-R	6-1	205	10-3-95	.277	.292	.271	32	94	19	26	5	1	1	7	12	3	0	2	31	1	0	.383	.369
Combs, Dalton	L-L	6-3	200	10-29-94	.208	.200	.209	23	48	6	10	2	0	1	11	6	1	0	0	10	1	1	.313	.309
Corbett, Chris	R-R	6-1	195	7-7-94	.150	.000	.182	16	40	2	6	0	0	0	1	4	0	1	1	7	0	0	.150	.222
De La Rosa, Frandy	B-R	6-1	180	1-24-96	.150	.333	.071	8	20	1	3	0	0	0	1	1	0	0	0	7	0	0	.150	.191
Edie, Mikey	R-R	5-11	175	7-3-97	.174	.400	.111	13	23	4	4	1	0	0	0	1	0	0	0	7	2	0	.217	.208
Garcia, Orlando	R-R	6-2	190	12-31-95	.268	.417	.234	54	190	33	51	10	0	6	33	26	6	3	5	46	1	4	.416	.366
Geraldo, Manuel	B-R	6-1	170	9-23-96	.301	.321	.296	73	276	38	83	8	1	3	40	12	5	3	3	77	23	12	.370	.338
Johnson, Bryce	B-R	6-2	180	10-27-95	.329	.289	.339	57	222	41	73	5	2	0	16	17	10	0	1	52	25	10	.369	.400
Kirby, Ryan	L-R	6-2	180	1-25-95	.279	.344	.261	75	276	51	77	16	0	8	65	35	5	0	8	58	10	5	.424	.361
Manwaring, Dylan	R-R	6-3	210	9-27-94	.207	.250	.194	30	92	12	19	6	0	0	4	10	3	2	1	36	2	3	.272	.302
Matheny, Shane	L-R	6-1	205	6-5-96	.284	.353	.271	34	102	13	29	5	0	0	12	15	1	0	0	20	4	2	.333	.381
Medrano, Robinson	R-R	6-3	180	4-20-96	.286	.467	.185	27	84	16	24	6	1	2	10	5	0	0	0	29	1	3	.452	.326
Melendez, Rene	R-R	6-1	190	1-20-95	.071	.000	.100	6	14	0	1	0	0	0	1	1	0	0	0	7	0	1	.071	.133
Murray, Byron	R-R	5-10	195	7-26-95	.205	.143	.219	12	39	4	8	2	0	1	4	5	0	0	0	13	1	1	.333	.296
Parra, Jeffry	R-R	6-0	195	1-24-98	.173	.000	.205	17	52	3	9	2	1	0	4	4	0	3	0	9	1	1	.250	.232
Ramirez, A.J.	R-R	6-0	190	4-4-93	.100	.200	.067	9	20	2	2	0	0	1	3	2	1	0	1	7	1	0	.250	.208
Riley, John	R-R	6-0	210	2-14-94	.286	.556	.083	8	21	1	6	1	0	0	3	5	0	0	0	9	2	0	.333	.423
Rivera, Kevin	B-R	5-11	170	6-12-96	.272	.258	.276	41	136	18	37	6	4	1	18	13	0	1	2	30	2	4	.397	.331
Rodriguez, Juan	R-R	6-0	175	8-29-94	.239	.300	.218	33	117	10	28	1	1	1	15	6	1	1	1	35	5	1	.291	.280
Sexton, Michael	R-L	6-1	200	1-4-95	.218	.174	.227	38	133	12	29	5	0	1	17	13	0	1	2	40	1	3	.278	.284
Ziegler, Malique	R-R	6-2	170	9-8-96	.240	.246	.239	64	254	46	61	9	5	5	24	28	7	4	3	66	26	9	.374	.329

Pitching	B-T	HT	WT	DOB	W	L	ERA	G	GS	CG	SV	IP	H	R	ER	HR	BB	SO	AVG	vLH	vRH	K/9	BB/9
Bahr, Jason	R-R	6-5	190	2-15-95	3	2	3.55	13	7	0	0	33	31	16	13	0	11	36	.248	.200	.286	9.82	3.00
Benitez, Julio	R-R	6-3	185	11-1-94	1	7	4.30	14	14	1	0	69	85	44	33	4	12	35	.301	.339	.278	4.57	1.57
Black, Vic	R-R	6-4	210	5-23-88	0	0	5.14	6	0	0	1	7	6	4	4	0	7	11	.222	.091	.313	14.14	9.00
Bostic, Alex	L-L	6-3	195	11-14-94	0	2	8.79	13	5	0	0	29	29	29	28	4	22	22	.284	.273	.288	6.91	6.91
Cave, Garrett	R-R	6-4	200	7-18-96	1	1	5.85	14	0	0	3	20	19	13	13	0	12	29	.260	.321	.222	13.05	5.40
De La Rosa, Alejandro	R-R	6-0	165	2-14-95	3	3	4.01	16	8	0	0	49	53	25	22	4	24	57	.275	.227	.299	10.40	4.38
Deeg, Nick	L-L	6-5	225	6-26-95	1	1	4.22	10	0	0	1	21	25	13	10	1	11	21	.301	.286	.304	8.86	4.64
Diaz, Alvaro	R-R	6-3	190	6-13-93	0	0	6.75	2	0	0	0	3	2	3	2	0	5	1	.200	.000	.286	3.38	16.88
Duprey, Sidney	L-L	6-3	230	11-15-96	0	1	12.15	2	2	0	0	7	10	10	9	0	5	1	.345	.143	.409	1.35	6.75
Harasta, Logan	R-R	6-7	235	8-29-96	0	1	18.00	1	0	0	0	1	2	2	2	1	0	2	.400	.500	.333	18.00	0.00
Jacknewitz, Greg	L-L	6-3	210	6-26-95	0	2	7.47	4	4	0	0	16	23	16	13	2	4	10	.329	.526	.255	5.74	2.30
Kaden, Connor	R-R	6-4	215	10-27-92	1	1	3.60	3	0	0	0	5	5	2	2	0	0	6	.250	.333	.182	10.80	0.00
Lannoo, Peter	R-R	6-6	220	11-13-94	1	3	4.28	14	5	0	1	40	46	26	19	7	12	26	.281	.323	.253	5.85	2.70
Lujan, Matt	L-L	6-1	210	8-23-88	0	1	3.38	2	2	0	0	8	8	3	3	1	2	6	.258	.167	.280	6.75	2.25
Marte, Jose	R-R	6-3	180	6-14-96	2	5	5.33	14	14	0	0	54	61	42	32	2	34	42	.281	.258	.297	7.00	5.67
Medina, Hengerber	R-R	5-11	160	10-12-94	1	1	7.15	4	0	0	0	11	15	11	9	2	8	13	.333	.333	.333	10.32	6.35
Melo, Kendry	R-R	6-3	210	1-7-94	1	0	0.00	5	0	0	1	9	4	0	0	0	2	13	.138	.231	.063	13.50	2.08
Phillips, Aaron	R-R	6-5	215	10-11-96	3	0	4.45	14	0	0	1	28	20	15	14	2	13	36	.191	.167	.206	11.44	4.13
Pino, Luis	R-R	6-0	175	11-4-94	1	2	4.13	21	2	0	0	48	41	25	22	3	22	37	.230	.262	.212	6.94	4.13
Pope, Matt	R-R	6-6	225	7-5-94	0	0	10.80	4	0	0	0	8	17	10	10	1	5	9	.436	.250	.519	9.72	5.40
Rohloff, Andy	R-R	6-2	180	7-16-96	0	2	12.96	7	0	0	1	8	14	14	12	1	6	11	.368	.400	.333	11.88	6.48
Russell, John	R-R	6-3	170	10-17-95	1	2	1.99	16	0	0	4	23	13	7	5	1	7	37	.165	.103	.200	14.69	2.78
Schimpf, Tyler	R-R	6-4	210	8-7-95	0	2	4.50	15	0	0	0	24	29	21	12	3	12	25	.293	.310	.281	9.38	4.50
Slatton, Heath	L-R	6-3	210	9-17-93	2	1	7.04	3	0	0	0	8	8	6	6	2	3	9	.267	.375	.227	10.57	3.52
Timmins, John	R-R	6-6	215	1-20-94	1	4	7.02	22	1	0	0	33	54	32	26	5	16	24	.372	.373	.372	6.48	4.32
Webb, Logan	R-R	6-2	195	11-18-96	2	0	2.89	15	0	0	0	28	26	10	9	1	7	31	.241	.359	.174	9.96	2.25
Woods, Stetson	R-R	6-8	200	1-15-95	3	2	3.36	14	12	0	0	64	59	29	24	4	21	48	.246	.226	.259	6.72	2.94
Yan, Weilly	R-R	6-0	175	1-30-96	1	0	0.00	2	0	0	0	3	1	0	0	0	2	4	.091	.000	.167	10.80	5.40
Yanez, Cesar	R-R	6-5	175	9-30-94	0	1	8.50	10	0	0	1	18	20	17	17	1	26	20	.286	.300	.275	10.00	13.00

Fielding

C: Calabrese 30, Corbett 16, Manwaring 19, Melendez 6, Parra 17, Riley 3. **1B:** De La Rosa 1, Kirby 70, Medrano 6, Ramirez 1, Riley 3, Sexton 2. **2B:** Amion 7, Brown 1, Garcia 43, Ramirez 2, Rivera 27. **3B:** Amion 11, Brown 1, De La Rosa 1, Matheny 33, Murray 10, Ramirez 6, Rivera 9, Sexton 15. **SS:** Brown 3, De La Rosa 1, Garcia 4, Geraldo 70, Rivera 2. **OF:** Amion 6, Baldwin 48, Bono 5, Burks 7, Cabrera 7, Combs 15, Edie 11, Johnson 55, Medrano 6, Riley 1, Rodriguez 32, Ziegler 63.

AZL GIANTS — ROOKIE

ARIZONA LEAGUE

Batting	B-T	HT	WT	DOB	AVG	vLH	vRH	G	AB	R	H	2B	3B	HR	RBI	BB	HBP	SH	SF	SO	SB	CS	SLG	OBP
Almanzar, Angeddy	R-R	6-2	180	6-30-98	.197	.308	.172	24	71	9	14	2	0	2	6	9	4	0	0	26	1	1	.310	.321
Angulo, Andres	R-R	5-10	181	9-5-97	.232	.222	.237	17	56	9	13	3	1	1	8	2	0	3	1	12	1	0	.375	.254
Antunez, Robert	R-R	5-10	160	3-22-96	.278	.571	.207	13	36	6	10	1	1	1	3	5	1	2	0	10	2	1	.444	.381

Bond, Aaron	L-R	6-5	195	2-16-97	.306	.115	.347	41	147	26	45	8	3	8	31	14	1	0	1	50	5	3	.565	.368
Brickhouse, Cody	R-R	6-3	210	12-23-96	.000	—	.000	1	1	0	0	0	0	0	0	0	0	0	0	0	0	0	.000	.000
Brown, Tyler	R-R	6-1	180	1-18-95	.268	.125	.303	15	41	8	11	2	0	0	6	8	2	0	0	14	2	0	.317	.412
Burks, Christopher	L-R	5-10	180	6-24-94	.000	.000	.000	3	6	0	0	0	0	0	0	2	0	0	0	1	1	0	.000	.250
Corbett, Chris	R-R	6-1	195	7-7-94	.333	.500	.308	5	15	2	5	2	0	0	2	1	0	0	0	2	1	0	.467	.375
Coronado, Mecky	R-R	6-0	180	12-13-96	.133	.200	.100	6	15	2	2	1	0	0	1	2	1	0	0	9	0	0	.200	.278
Duggar, Steven	L-R	6-2	195	11-4-93	.000	—	.000	2	3	0	0	0	0	0	0	2	0	0	0	0	0	0	.000	.400
Edie, Mikey	R-R	5-11	175	7-3-97	.394	.667	.367	26	66	16	26	2	1	0	6	3	3	3	0	12	10	3	.455	.444
Edwards, Woody	R-R	5-10	155	4-2-95	.000	.000	.000	2	4	0	0	0	0	0	0	0	0	0	0	0	0	0	.000	.000
Garcia, Orlando	R-R	6-2	190	12-31-95	.000	—	.000	1	2	0	0	0	0	0	0	0	0	0	0	1	0	0	.000	.000
Genoves, Ricardo	R-R	6-2	190	5-14-99	.252	.095	.281	39	135	20	34	6	1	2	19	12	3	0	0	28	0	1	.356	.327
Giarratano, Nico	B-R	5-11	172	12-15-94	.253	.308	.242	35	79	16	20	5	1	0	10	9	7	3	1	13	8	1	.342	.375
Gonzalez, Jacob	R-R	6-3	190	6-26-98	.339	.300	.348	46	168	23	57	15	1	1	21	16	8	0	2	23	0	1	.458	.418
Hill, Nick	R-R	6-4	190	8-2-94	.217	.211	.220	27	69	17	15	3	3	0	9	11	6	1	0	22	9	1	.348	.372
Javier, Nathanael	R-R	6-3	185	10-10-95	.290	.207	.308	42	162	20	47	14	2	1	17	1	1	1	0	23	2	1	.420	.299
Lacen, Luis	R-R	6-3	195	10-13-96	.000	—	.000	1	2	0	0	0	0	0	0	1	0	0	0	1	0	0	.000	.333
Layer, Jose	R-R	6-0	160	5-28-97	.375	.429	.364	15	40	6	15	4	0	0	7	7	0	2	0	5	2	2	.475	.468
Marks, Anthony	L-L	5-8	175	4-15-94	.000	.000	—	2	1	0	0	0	0	0	0	0	0	0	0	0	0	0	.000	.000
McPherson, Kyle	R-R	5-11	180	2-9-96	.236	.500	.192	29	55	9	13	3	2	0	7	3	1	2	1	10	2	0	.364	.283
Medina, Francisco	R-R	6-1	165	3-20-98	.206	.160	.221	40	102	13	21	3	1	1	7	9	0	2	0	37	1	2	.284	.270
Mendoza, Beicker	R-R	6-2	185	2-14-98	.236	.546	.180	23	72	8	17	7	1	1	10	2	1	0	0	25	0	1	.403	.267
Munguia, Ismael	L-L	5-10	158	10-19-98	.331	.258	.351	42	142	31	47	7	4	1	19	17	0	3	2	18	8	4	.458	.398
Parra, Jeffry	R-R	6-0	195	1-24-98	.219	.600	.148	12	32	3	7	1	0	0	2	4	0	0	0	8	0	0	.250	.306
Ramos, Heliot	R-R	6-2	185	9-7-99	.348	.214	.382	35	138	33	48	11	6	6	27	10	3	0	0	48	10	2	.645	.404
Rincones, Diego	R-R	6-0	175	6-14-99	.308	.206	.336	47	159	19	49	8	1	3	34	14	4	0	3	20	0	1	.428	.372
Rivero, Jose	L-R	5-11	158	4-30-98	.284	.211	.309	24	74	18	21	2	0	0	5	8	0	0	1	14	1	2	.311	.349
Santiago, Hector	R-R	6-3	185	11-18-97	.000	.000	.000	14	13	0	0	0	0	0	0	0	0	0	0	7	0	0	.000	.000
Tona, Jesus	R-R	5-10	170	3-30-96	.273	—	.273	5	11	0	3	0	0	0	0	0	0	0	0	3	0	0	.273	.273

Pitching	B-T	HT	WT	DOB	W	L	ERA	G	GS	CG	SV	IP	H	R	ER	HR	BB	SO	AVG	vLH	vRH	K/9	BB/9
Bartlett, Keenan	R-R	6-1	170	9-27-95	4	0	1.53	15	0	0	1	29	19	5	5	1	12	34	.185	.256	.141	10.43	3.68
Bazar, Reagan	R-R	6-7	250	6-27-95	3	1	4.43	13	1	0	0	22	23	12	11	2	17	17	.258	.189	.308	6.85	6.85
Black, Ray	R-R	6-5	225	6-26-90	0	0	3.86	3	0	0	0	2	2	1	1	0	3	7	.222	.400	.000	27.00	11.57
Bolivar, Deiyerbert	L-L	5-11	155	4-3-96	0	2	4.82	10	7	0	0	28	33	17	15	0	14	25	.295	.258	.309	8.04	4.50
Bumgarner, Madison	R-L	6-5	250	8-1-89	0	0	0.00	1	1	0	0	3	0	0	0	0	1	2	.000	.000	.000	6.00	3.00
Corry, Seth	L-L	6-2	195	11-3-98	0	2	5.55	13	10	0	0	24	14	18	15	1	22	21	.163	.208	.145	7.77	8.14
Diaz, Alvaro	R-R	6-3	190	6-13-93	1	0	2.08	4	0	0	0	9	7	3	2	0	3	6	.241	.167	.294	6.23	3.12
Doval, Camilo	R-R	6-2	185	7-4-97	1	2	3.90	17	0	0	1	32	23	16	14	0	13	51	.197	.200	.194	14.20	3.62
Duprey, Sidney	L-L	6-3	230	11-15-96	4	4	5.17	14	4	0	0	47	61	32	27	4	16	35	.311	.352	.296	6.70	3.06
Falwell, Chris	L-L	6-7	210	4-14-95	0	0	18.00	1	0	0	0	1	3	2	2	0	1	0	.600	1.000	.333	0.00	9.00
Figueroa, Miguel	R-R	6-2	165	8-9-97	0	1	5.24	13	11	0	0	45	58	44	26	1	13	38	.297	.392	.240	7.66	2.62
Gavin, John	R-L	6-6	230	10-10-95	2	1	0.00	12	0	0	1	16	8	2	0	0	7	22	.151	.158	.147	12.38	3.94
Greenwalt, Jake	R-R	6-1	175	4-30-98	2	6	6.98	13	11	0	0	49	70	39	38	10	9	41	.332	.289	.359	7.53	1.65
Jacknewitz, Greg	L-L	6-3	210	6-26-95	0	0	6.08	7	1	0	0	13	15	9	9	2	4	9	.300	.429	.250	6.08	2.70
Johnson, Stephen	R-R	6-5	230	2-21-91	0	0	0.00	1	0	0	0	1	1	1	0	0	0	0	.250	.000	.500	0.00	0.00
Lujan, Matt	L-L	6-1	210	8-23-88	0	0	7.71	2	2	0	0	5	7	5	4	0	2	5	.333	.143	.429	9.64	3.86
Marciano, Joey	L-L	6-5	250	1-11-95	4	1	1.57	15	3	0	0	29	22	10	5	1	12	26	.212	.241	.200	8.16	3.77
Marshall, Mac	R-L	6-0	181	1-27-96	0	0	0.00	2	0	0	0	2	0	0	0	0	3	1	.000	.000	.000	5.40	16.20
Marte, Jose	R-R	6-3	180	6-14-96	0	0	0.00	1	0	0	0	1	0	0	0	0	0	2	.000	.000	.000	18.00	0.00
Martinez, Rodolfo	R-R	6-2	180	4-4-94	0	0	0.00	2	0	0	0	2	2	0	0	0	0	2	.250	.000	.333	9.00	0.00
Medina, Hengerber	R-R	5-11	160	10-12-94	0	0	0.00	2	0	0	0	2	0	0	0	0	1	3	.000	.000	.000	13.50	4.50
Moronta, Reyes	R-R	6-0	175	1-6-93	0	0	0.00	2	0	0	0	2	0	0	0	0	0	4	.000	.000	.000	18.00	0.00
Parra, Olbis	R-R	6-2	180	10-1-94	1	0	3.93	20	0	0	7	18	21	9	8	2	4	22	.276	.267	.283	10.80	1.96
Rohloff, Andy	R-R	6-2	180	7-16-96	1	0	1.50	5	0	0	0	6	5	3	1	0	1	10	.217	.250	.211	15.00	1.50
Rubio, Frank	R-R	6-0	190	4-23-95	1	0	3.45	12	0	0	0	16	17	7	6	1	1	14	.262	.154	.333	8.04	0.57
Russell, John	R-R	6-3	170	10-17-95	0	0	0.00	1	0	0	0	2	1	0	0	0	2	1	.200	.000	.333	4.50	9.00
Suarez, Albert	R-R	6-3	235	10-8-89	0	1	9.64	3	3	0	0	5	5	6	5	2	2	3	.250	.000	.385	5.79	3.86
Van Gurp, Franklin	R-R	6-1	210	10-26-95	5	1	0.92	17	0	0	2	29	17	8	3	1	7	41	.165	.200	.143	12.58	2.15
Yan, Weilly	R-R	6-0	175	1-30-96	3	0	3.21	12	2	0	1	34	29	17	12	2	21	43	.234	.213	.247	11.50	5.61
Yanez, Cesar	R-R	6-5	175	9-30-94	0	0	0.00	1	0	0	0	1	0	0	0	0	0	0	.000	—	.000	0.00	0.00
Young, Pat	R-R	6-7	240	3-24-92	1	0	2.25	8	0	0	0	8	6	6	2	0	4	10	.194	.222	.182	11.25	4.50

Fielding

C: Angulo 17, Brickhouse 1, Corbett 5, Genoves 27, Parra 12, Tona 3. **1B:** Almanzar 20, Coronado 1, Javier 26, Mendoza 17. **2B:** Antunez 13, Brown 9, Giarratano 14, McPherson 25, Rivero 12, Santiago 3. **3B:** Brown 3, Gonzalez 39, Javier 12, Medina 12, Santiago 2. **SS:** Brown 6, Garcia 1, Giarratano 24, Medina 31, Rivero 13, Santiago 3. **OF:** Bond 34, Burks 2, Duggar 2, Edie 16, Edwards 1, Hill 18, Layer 12, Marks 1, Munguia 36, Ramos 29, Rincones 34.

DSL GIANTS — *ROOKIE*

DOMINICAN SUMMER LEAGUE

Batting	B-T	HT	WT	DOB	AVG	vLH	vRH	G	AB	R	H	2B	3B	HR	RBI	BB	HBP	SH	SF	SO	SB	CS	SLG	OBP
Alcantara, Ismael	L-R	6-3	190	4-15-00	.333	—	.333	3	6	1	2	0	0	0	2	1	0	0	0	2	0	0	.333	.429
Alvarado, Luis	R-R	5-11	175	11-23-99	.219	.250	.213	26	73	7	16	2	1	0	6	3	5	3	1	6	0	2	.274	.293
Batista, Robinson	B-R	5-11	167	10-11-98	.370	.286	.385	18	46	15	17	2	1	1	4	5	0	5	0	4	9	4	.522	.431
Cairo, Victor	R-R	6-0	180	9-10-97	.225	.300	.205	33	49	7	11	1	0	0	4	9	6	1	1	9	0	0	.245	.400
Canario, Alexander	R-R	6-1	165	5-7-00	.294	.298	.292	66	235	42	69	17	4	5	45	33	5	0	1	40	18	10	.464	.391

Caraballo, Andrew	R-R	6-0	175	4-29-00	.204	.031	.257	48	137	18	28	7	0	0	18	33	1	2	2	30	4	5	.256	.358
De Leon, Wascar	B-R	5-11	180	1-8-98	.275	.226	.288	53	142	22	39	8	2	1	19	24	2	4	2	31	3	8	.380	.382
Doria, Martin	R-R	5-10	155	4-20-99	.271	.286	.268	42	85	17	23	1	0	0	9	14	2	1	2	10	7	6	.282	.379
Gutierrez, Nishell	B-R	5-10	165	5-4-99	.208	.238	.200	39	106	12	22	2	2	0	9	19	2	1	0	17	4	1	.264	.339
Gutierrez, Raiber	R-R	5-10	165	12-10-99	.275	.265	.278	56	149	38	41	3	1	0	13	24	12	6	0	21	18	8	.309	.416
Jorge, Samuel	R-R	6-2	190	9-9-99	.232	.370	.200	44	142	13	33	4	2	2	14	13	5	0	1	35	3	4	.331	.317
Labour, Franklin	R-R	6-1	190	5-11-98	.317	.311	:319	55	186	35	59	10	4	5	35	26	6	0	3	30	13	8	.495	.412
Medina, Omar	B-R	5-11	170	12-20-99	.214	.293	.190	55	178	30	38	2	0	0	25	22	6	1	0	22	10	5	.225	.320
Mejias, Keyberth	R-R	6-0	170	9-24-99	.190	.250	.167	31	58	4	11	2	1	0	0	6	1	2	0	12	1	2	.259	.277
Patino, Jose	B-R	6-0	160	12-11-97	.234	.281	.224	61	175	29	41	5	0	0	16	16	7	4	1	20	16	5	.263	.322
Pichardo, Luigi	R-R	5-10	185	9-4-99	.259	.500	.205	16	54	5	14	1	0	0	7	2	0	0	3	9	2	0	.278	.271
Santos, Ghordy	B-R	6-1	177	9-2-99	.218	.179	.227	52	156	24	34	9	3	1	20	38	1	4	1	40	15	9	.333	.372
Sivira, Anyesber	R-R	5-9	155	1-9-00	.222	.229	.219	64	194	43	43	6	1	0	20	23	15	1	2	17	20	11	.263	.346
Watts, Enoc	B-R	6-0	160	12-2-99	.134	.071	.151	28	67	6	9	3	1	0	4	4	2	0	0	12	2	1	.209	.206

Pitching	B-T	HT	WT	DOB	W	L	ERA	G	GS	CG	SV	IP	H	R	ER	HR	BB	SO	AVG	vLH	vRH	K/9	BB/9
Acosta, Aneudy	R-R	5-11	180	4-7-96	3	2	4.12	13	13	0	0	55	48	34	25	2	20	53	.231	.280	.203	8.73	3.29
Adames, Abel	R-R	6-5	190	12-8-95	4	0	1.67	26	0	0	3	38	24	12	7	0	26	33	.181	.250	.136	7.88	6.21
De Pena, Brayan	L-L	6-4	240	11-19-97	0	0	9.00	5	0	0	0	5	5	7	5	1	4	5	.238	.000	.250	9.00	7.20
Fermin, Janly	R-R	6-2	195	7-7-97	0	1	9.00	13	0	0	1	16	16	18	16	1	17	12	.271	.286	.267	6.75	9.56
Gonzalez, Marco	L-L	6-1	180	12-8-97	4	5	1.83	13	13	0	0	69	48	25	14	2	21	74	.192	.203	.188	9.65	2.74
Gudino, Norwith	R-R	6-2	200	11-22-95	6	1	1.82	13	13	0	0	74	62	18	15	1	10	83	.221	.207	.229	10.05	1.21
Labrador, Jorge	R-R	6-1	180	3-9-99	4	5	3.15	26	0	0	0	40	38	25	14	2	14	23	.245	.283	.229	5.18	3.15
Lopez, Lylon	R-R	6-1	190	3-1-97	0	0	2.45	14	1	0	0	18	13	11	5	0	11	20	.203	.143	.233	9.82	5.40
Maita, Jose	L-L	5-11	180	12-23-97	1	2	3.90	25	0	0	1	28	29	17	12	1	12	24	.259	.111	.329	7.81	3.90
Moreno, Luis	R-R	6-2	174	8-3-98	4	1	3.23	13	13	0	0	64	61	31	23	4	19	38	.245	.217	.259	5.34	2.67
Moronta, Yovanny	R-R	6-1	175	5-22-96	0	0	15.43	7	0	0	0	2	6	4	4	0	13	1	.500	.600	.429	3.86	50.14
Pena, Francis	R-R	6-3	175	6-2-97	2	3	3.22	13	13	0	0	59	67	32	21	0	18	60	.283	.238	.306	9.20	2.76
Pinto, Oliver	R-R	6-0	175	9-4-96	4	0	3.30	21	0	0	1	30	23	13	11	2	14	37	.213	.185	.222	11.10	4.20
Quiroz, Orleny	L-L	6-3	180	7-21-93	3	2	2.25	30	0	0	13	36	34	16	9	1	12	52	.250	.242	.252	13.00	3.00
Santos, Gregory	R-R	6-2	190	8-28-99	1	0	1.93	4	4	0	0	19	21	5	4	2	5	17	.273	.300	.263	8.20	2.41
2-team total (8 Red Sox)					3	0	1.29	12	12	0	0	49	43	11	7	2	20	41	.234	.237	.188	7.53	3.67
Severino, Jerson	R-R	6-3	191	7-30-98	4	4	4.78	21	1	0	1	32	35	24	17	0	24	27	.278	.265	.283	7.59	6.75
Suarez, Willian	R-R	6-3	175	3-21-98	0	0	13.50	4	0	0	0	2	7	5	3	0	1	4	.539	.600	.500	18.00	4.50
Veras, Yoel	R-R	6-0	175	10-2-96	1	0	1.50	10	0	0	0	12	7	4	2	0	5	10	.171	.300	.129	7.50	3.75
Yan, Jose	R-R	6-0	170	12-12-97	0	4	3.05	20	0	0	5	21	19	10	7	0	16	17	.250	.286	.236	7.40	6.97

Fielding

C: Alvarado 18, Cairo 32, Gutierrez 24, Mejias 29. **1B:** Alcantara 2, Alvarado 3, Gutierrez 11, Jorge 1, Labour 12, Medina 53. **2B:** Batista 5, Caraballo 17, De Leon 17, Doria 25, Santos 1, Sivira 22, Watts 3. **3B:** Caraballo 16, Doria 14, Gutierrez 1, Jorge 35, Santos 5, Sivira 12, Watts 7. **SS:** Caraballo 13, Santos 38, Sivira 14, Watts 19. **OF:** Alcantara 1, Cairo 1, Canario 53, De Leon 9, Doria 1, Gutierrez 55, Labour 40, Patino 60, Pichardo 15, Sivira 11.

Seattle Mariners

SEASON IN A SENTENCE: A year after winning 86 games and challenging for an American League wild card, the Mariners executed more than a dozen trades to try to push the Robinson Cano-Nelson Cruz-Felix Hernandez edition of the club into October—but the plan didn't work.

HIGH POINT: The Mariners defeated the Yankees 6-3 on Aug. 25 to move to 66-63 and to within half a game of the Twins for the second AL wild card. General manager Jerry Dipoto traded for righthander Mike Leake five days later.

LOW POINT: Even after adding starter Leake and first baseman Yonder Alonso in August, the Mariners faltered badly in September by going 12-16 and losing a season-high six games in a row from Sept. 15-21. Seattle finished 78-84 and seven games out of a wild card.

NOTABLE ROOKIES: Left fielder Ben Gamel and right fielder Mitch Haniger, a pair of offseason trade pickups by Dipoto, played well in regular roles. Haniger hit .282/.352/.491 with 16 home runs in between stints on the disabled list. He ranked among the most productive rookie hitters in baseball not named Aaron Judge or Cody Bellinger. Gamel spent most of the season batting first or second in the order and produced a .275/.322/.413 batting line with 11 home runs. Righthander Andrew Moore went 1-5, 5.34 in 11 games (nine starts) and didn't miss many bats with 4.7 strikeouts per nine innings.

KEY TRANSACTIONS: After a hectic offseason of trade activity, Dipoto kept dealing all season. The Mariners sent four lower-level players to the Marlins for righthander David Phelps on July 18, but Phelps made just 10 appearances before he came down with a season-ending elbow injury. A few days later, Dipoto traded preseason No. 2 prospect Tyler O'Neill, a power-hitting Triple-A outfielder, to the Cardinals for lefthander Marco Gonzales in an attempt to repair a patchwork rotation that lost Hernandez, Hisashi Iwakuma and Drew Smyly to the disabled list. Seattle added righthander Erasmo Ramirez on July 28 for the same reason.

DOWN ON THE FARM: A year after ranking second among all organizations in minor league winning percentage (.581), the Mariners slipped to 20th with a .487 mark. High Class A Modesto, however, claimed the California League title by sweeping Lancaster. Righthander Nick Neidert claimed the Cal League's pitcher of the year award.

OPENING DAY PAYROLL: $154,268,842 (13th)

PLAYERS OF THE YEAR

MAJOR LEAGUE

Nelson Cruz
OF
.288/.375/.549
39 HR, 146 OPS+
119 RBIs led AL

MINOR LEAGUE

Nick Neidert
RHP
(High Class A/ Double-A)
11-6, 3.45

ORGANIZATION LEADERS

BATTING		*Minimum 250 AB	
MAJORS			
*	AVG	Jean Segura	.300
*	OPS	Nelson Cruz	.924
	HR	Nelson Cruz	39
	RBI	Nelson Cruz	119
MINORS			
*	AVG	Eric Filia, Modesto	.326
*	OBP	Eric Filia, Modesto	.407
*	SLG	Leonys Martin, Tacoma	.492
*	OPS	Daniel Vogelbach, Tacoma	.844
	R	Braden Bishop, Modesto, Arkansas	89
	H	Eric Fillia, Modesto	160
	TB	Eric Fillia, Modesto	213
	2B	Joey Curletta, Modesto	37
	3B	Luis Liberato, Clinton, Modesto	14
	HR	Tyler O'Neill, Tacoma, Memphis	19
	RBI	Daniel Vogelbach, Tacoma	83
	BB	Daniel Vogelbach, Tacoma	76
	SO	Gareth Morgan, Clinton	185
	SB	Ian Miller, Arkansas, Tacoma	43

PITCHING		#Minimum 75 IP	
MAJORS			
	W	James Paxton	12
#	ERA	James Paxton	2.98
	SO	James Paxton	156
	SV	Edwin Diaz	34
MINORS			
	W	Reggie McClain, Modesto	12
	L	Danny Garcia, Clinton	13
#	ERA	Robert Dugger, Clinton, Modesto	2.75
	G	Dean Kiekhefer, Tacoma	49
	GS	Reggie McClain, Modesto	27
	SV	Zac Curtis, Arkansas	13
	IP	Lindsey Caughel, Arkansas	158
	BB	Nick Wells, Clinton	43
	SO	Reggie McClain, Modesto	127
#	AVG	Andrew Moore, Arkansas, Tacoma	.231

2017 PERFORMANCE

General Manager: Jerry Dipoto. **Farm Director:** Andy McKay. **Scouting Director:** Scott Hunter.

Class	Team	League	W	L	PCT	Finish	Manager
Majors	Seattle Mariners	American	78	84	.481	t-9th (15)	Scott Servais
Triple-A	Tacoma Rainiers	Pacific Coast	66	76	.465	13th (16)	Pat Listach
Double-A	Arkansas Travelers	Texas	65	75	.464	7th (8)	Daren Brown
High-A	Modesto Nuts	California	74	66	.529	3rd (8)	Mitch Canham
Low-A	Clinton LumberKings	Midwest	64	73	.467	12th (16)	P. Shine / D. Macias / T. Arnerich
Short Season	Everett AquaSox	Northwest	36	40	.474	7th (8)	Jose Moreno
Rookie	AZL Mariners	Arizona	31	24	.564	4th (15)	Zac Livingston
Overall 2017 Minor League Record			336	354	.487	20th (30)	

ORGANIZATION STATISTICS

SEATTLE MARINERS

AMERICAN LEAGUE

Batting	B-T	HT	WT	DOB	AVG	vLH	vRH	G	AB	R	H	2B	3B	HR	RBI	BB	HBP	SH	SF	SO	SB	CS	SLG	OBP
Alonso, Yonder	R-L	6-1	230	4-8-87	.265	.125	.274	42	132	20	35	5	0	6	18	18	0	0	0	30	1	0	.439	.353
2-team total (100 Oakland)					.266	.188	.286	142	451	72	120	22	0	28	67	68	2	0	0	118	2	0	.501	.365
Beckham, Gordon	R-R	6-0	190	9-16-86	.177	—	.177	11	17	2	3	0	0	0	0	1	0	0	0	2	1	0	.177	.222
Cano, Robinson	L-R	6-0	210	10-22-82	.280	.208	.312	150	592	79	166	33	0	23	97	49	4	0	3	85	1	0	.453	.338
Cruz, Nelson	R-R	6-2	230	7-1-80	.288	.229	.306	155	556	91	160	28	0	39	119	70	12	0	7	140	1	1	.549	.375
Dyson, Jarrod	R-L	5-10	165	8-15-84	.251	.146	.272	111	346	56	87	13	3	5	30	28	10	4	2	55	28	7	.350	.324
Espinosa, Danny	R-B	6-0	205	4-25-87	.188	.200	.182	8	16	2	3	2	0	0	2	1	0	0	0	7	1	0	.313	.235
3-team total (77 Los Angeles, 8 Tampa Bay)					.173	.163	.162	93	266	30	46	10	0	6	31	21	5	1	2	109	4	5	.278	.245
Freeman, Mike	L-R	6-0	190	8-4-87	.067	.000	.069	16	30	3	2	0	0	1	1	4	0	0	0	9	0	0	.167	.177
Gamel, Ben	L-L	5-11	185	5-17-92	.275	.275	.275	134	509	68	140	27	5	11	59	36	1	1	3	122	4	1	.413	.322
Gosewisch, Tuffy	R-R	5-11	200	8-17-83	.071	.077	.067	11	28	1	2	0	0	0	0	1	0	2	0	14	0	0	.071	.103
Haniger, Mitch	R-R	6-2	215	12-23-90	.282	.250	.292	96	369	58	104	25	2	16	47	31	9	1	0	93	5	4	.491	.352
Hannemann, Jacob	L-L	6-1	200	4-29-91	.150	.000	.167	11	20	3	3	0	0	1	1	0	0	0	0	4	0	1	.300	.150
Heredia, Guillermo	R-L	5-10	180	1-31-91	.249	.310	.218	123	386	43	96	16	0	6	24	27	11	1	1	64	1	5	.337	.315
Marjama, Mike	R-R	6-2	205	7-20-89	.333	1.000	.250	5	9	1	3	1	0	1	1	0	0	0	0	1	0	0	.778	.333
Martin, Leonys	L-R	6-2	200	3-6-88	.174	.263	.156	34	115	12	20	2	1	3	8	5	2	0	0	29	6	4	.287	.221
Motter, Taylor	R-R	6-1	195	9-18-89	.198	.153	.215	92	258	29	51	12	0	7	26	21	0	0	1	62	12	1	.326	.257
Powell, Boog	L-L	5-10	185	1-14-93	.194	.333	.182	23	36	6	7	0	0	0	2	6	0	1	0	9	0	0	.194	.310
2-team total (29 Oakland)					.282	.167	.333	52	117	24	33	5	0	3	12	15	0	1	2	30	0	1	.402	.358
Ruiz, Carlos	R-R	5-10	215	1-22-79	.216	.172	.229	53	125	14	27	8	0	3	11	14	4	1	1	38	1	0	.352	.313
Seager, Kyle	L-R	6-0	210	11-3-87	.249	.249	.249	154	578	72	144	33	1	27	88	58	8	0	6	110	2	1	.450	.323
Segura, Jean	R-R	5-10	205	3-17-90	.300	.317	.294	125	524	80	157	30	2	11	45	34	6	0	1	83	22	8	.428	.349
Smith, Tyler	R-R	6-0	195	7-1-91	.188	.286	.111	10	16	2	3	1	0	0	1	1	1	0	1	8	0	0	.250	.263
Valencia, Danny	R-R	6-2	210	9-19-84	.256	.264	.252	130	450	54	115	19	3	15	66	40	2	0	8	122	2	2	.411	.314
Vogelbach, Daniel	L-R	6-0	250	12-17-92	.214	.250	.208	16	28	0	6	1	0	0	2	3	0	0	0	9	0	0	.250	.290
Zunino, Mike	R-R	6-2	220	3-25-91	.251	.253	.250	124	387	52	97	25	0	25	64	39	8	0	1	160	1	0	.509	.331

Pitching	B-T	HT	WT	DOB	W	L	ERA	G	GS	CG	SV	IP	H	R	ER	HR	BB	SO	AVG	vLH	vRH	K/9	BB/9
Albers, Andrew	R-L	6-1	200	10-6-85	5	1	3.51	9	6	0	1	41	43	22	16	6	10	37	.262	.316	.246	8.12	2.20
Altavilla, Dan	R-R	5-11	200	9-8-92	1	1	4.24	41	0	0	0	47	43	27	22	9	20	52	.242	.265	.227	10.03	3.86
Bergman, Christian	R-R	6-1	195	5-4-88	4	5	5.00	13	8	0	0	54	61	31	30	12	15	33	.295	.290	.298	5.50	2.50
Cishek, Steve	R-R	6-6	215	6-18-86	1	1	3.15	23	0	0	1	20	13	7	7	3	7	15	.183	.150	.196	6.75	3.15
2-team total (26 Tampa Bay)					3	2	2.01	49	0	0	1	45	26	10	10	3	14	41	.167	.150	.196	8.26	2.82
Cloyd, Tyler	R-R	6-3	210	5-16-87	1	0	0.00	1	0	0	0	1	2	0	0	0	0	1	.500	.000	1.000	9.00	0.00
Curtis, Zac	L-L	5-9	190	7-4-92	0	0	0.00	3	0	0	0	5	3	3	0	1	1	2	.167	.000	.214	3.86	1.93
De Jong, Chase	L-R	6-4	205	12-29-93	0	3	6.35	7	4	0	0	28	31	20	20	5	13	13	.282	.309	.255	4.13	4.13
Diaz, Edwin	R-R	6-3	165	3-22-94	4	6	3.27	66	0	0	34	66	44	28	24	10	32	89	.183	.185	.183	12.14	4.36
Fien, Casey	R-R	6-2	210	10-21-83	0	0	15.00	6	0	0	0	6	9	10	10	3	4	6	.360	.500	.294	9.00	6.00
Gallardo, Yovani	R-R	6-2	205	2-27-86	5	10	5.72	28	22	0	1	131	138	84	83	24	60	94	.271	.257	.285	6.47	4.13
Garton, Ryan	R-R	5-10	190	12-5-89	0	0	1.54	13	0	0	0	12	5	2	2	1	1	7	.125	.273	.069	5.40	0.77
2-team total (7 Tampa Bay)					0	1	4.91	20	0	0	0	22	18	12	12	4	6	16	.220	.273	.069	6.55	2.45
Gaviglio, Sam	R-R	6-2	195	5-22-90	3	5	4.62	12	11	0	0	62	63	37	32	15	21	40	.270	.243	.292	5.78	3.03
2-team total (4 Kansas City)					4	5	4.36	16	13	0	0	74	76	41	36	16	26	49	.271	.310	.211	5.93	3.15
Gonzales, Marco	L-L	6-1	195	2-16-92	1	1	5.40	10	7	0	0	37	53	22	22	5	11	30	.340	.317	.348	7.36	2.70
Hernandez, Felix	R-R	6-3	225	4-8-86	6	5	4.36	16	16	0	0	87	86	46	42	17	26	78	.258	.306	.222	8.10	2.70
Heston, Chris	R-R	6-3	195	4-10-88	0	1	19.80	2	1	0	0	5	14	12	11	3	5	3	.483	.385	.563	5.40	9.00
2-team total (1 Minnesota)					0	1	16.50	3	1	0	0	6	15	12	11	3	5	3	.455	.385	.563	4.50	7.50
Iwakuma, Hisashi	R-R	6-3	210	4-12-81	0	2	4.35	6	6	0	0	31	27	16	15	7	12	16	.237	.340	.156	4.65	3.48
Lawrence, Casey	R-R	6-2	170	10-28-87	2	0	5.57	23	0	0	0	42	56	27	26	9	14	45	.318	.378	.275	9.64	3.00
2-team total (4 Toronto)					2	3	6.34	27	2	0	0	55	77	41	39	11	25	52	.328	.378	.275	8.46	4.07
Leake, Mike	R-R	5-10	170	11-12-87	3	1	2.53	5	5	0	0	32	32	10	9	1	2	27	.258	.246	.270	7.59	0.56
Machi, Jean	R-R	6-0	255	2-1-82	1	0	1.17	5	0	0	0	8	7	2	1	1	4	4	.269	.300	.250	4.70	4.70
Marshall, Evan	R-R	6-2	225	4-18-90	0	0	9.39	6	0	0	0	8	12	8	8	1	5	4	.364	.467	.278	4.70	5.87
Martin, Cody	R-R	6-3	230	9-4-89	0	0	13.50	1	0	0	0	2	5	4	3	0	2	0	.455	.400	.500	0.00	9.00

Miranda, Ariel	L-L	6-2	190	1-10-89	8	7	5.12	31	29	1	0	160	140	93	91	37	63	137	.233	.241	.231	7.71	3.54
Moore, Andrew	R-R	6-0	185	6-2-94	1	5	5.34	11	9	0	0	59	60	36	35	14	8	31	.261	.265	.258	4.73	1.22
Overton, Dillon	L-L	6-2	175	8-17-91	0	0	6.38	9	1	0	0	18	21	15	13	4	2	8	.280	.200	.300	3.93	0.98
Pagan, Emilio	L-R	6-3	210	5-7-91	2	3	3.22	34	0	0	0	50	39	20	18	7	8	56	.212	.258	.189	10.01	1.43
Paxton, James	L-L	6-4	235	11-6-88	12	5	2.98	24	24	0	0	136	113	47	45	9	37	156	.223	.198	.229	10.32	2.45
Pazos, James	R-L	6-2	235	5-5-91	4	5	3.86	59	0	0	0	54	51	30	23	7	24	65	.248	.218	.266	10.90	4.02
Phelps, David	R-R	6-2	200	10-9-86	2	1	3.12	10	0	0	0	9	9	3	3	0	5	11	.265	.400	.158	11.42	5.19
Povse, Max	R-R	6-8	185	8-23-93	0	0	7.36	3	0	0	0	4	9	5	3	1	1	2	.450	.400	.500	4.91	2.45
Ramirez, Erasmo	R-R	5-10	215	5-2-90	1	3	3.92	11	11	0	0	62	57	31	27	12	15	54	.243	.278	.217	7.84	2.18
2-team total (26 Tampa Bay)					5	6	4.39	37	19	0	1	131	123	70	64	22	31	109	.248	.278	.217	7.47	2.12
Rzepczynski, Marc	L-L	6-2	220	8-29-85	2	2	4.02	64	0	0	1	31	29	16	14	2	20	25	.252	.253	.250	7.18	5.74
Scribner, Evan	R-R	6-3	190	7-19-85	0	2	11.05	8	0	0	0	7	13	9	9	3	0	6	.394	.385	.400	7.36	0.00
Simmons, Shae	R-R	5-11	190	9-3-90	0	2	7.04	9	0	0	0	8	4	6	6	1	4	8	.167	.000	.267	9.39	4.70
Vieira, Thyago	R-R	6-2	210	7-1-93	0	0	0.00	1	0	0	0	1	0	0	0	0	0	1	.000	.000	.000	9.00	0.00
Vincent, Nick	R-R	6-0	185	7-12-86	3	3	3.20	69	0	0	0	65	62	23	23	3	13	50	.257	.281	.243	6.96	1.81
Weber, Ryan	R-R	6-1	180	8-12-90	0	0	2.45	1	1	0	0	4	3	1	1	0	0	0	.214	.125	.333	0.00	0.00
Whalen, Rob	R-R	6-2	220	1-31-94	0	1	6.14	2	1	0	0	7	7	5	5	1	2	2	.259	.308	.214	2.45	2.45
Zych, Tony	R-R	6-3	190	8-7-90	6	3	2.66	45	0	0	1	41	30	12	12	2	21	35	.208	.239	.194	7.75	4.65

Fielding

Catcher	PCT	G	PO	A	E	DP	PB
Gosewisch	1.000	10	75	1	0	1	0
Marjama	1.000	5	21	1	0	0	0
Ruiz	.997	47	282	19	1	2	5
Zunino	.993	120	894	56	7	5	10

First Base	PCT	G	PO	A	E	DP
Alonso	.984	39	236	11	4	19
Espinosa	.889	2	8	0	1	1
Freeman	1.000	3	18	4	0	4
Gamel	1.000	1	1	0	0	0
Gosewisch	.000	1	0	0	0	0
Motter	.986	15	69	1	1	9
Ruiz	.000	1	0	0	0	0
Valencia	.989	118	897	64	11	98
Vogelbach	.973	7	31	5	1	2

Second Base	PCT	G	PO	A	E	DP
Beckham	1.000	5	5	5	0	4
Cano	.983	150	254	339	10	97
Espinosa	1.000	1	1	5	0	1
Freeman	.857	3	3	3	1	2
Motter	.979	18	19	27	1	4
Smith	1.000	3	2	2	0	0

Third Base	PCT	G	PO	A	E	DP
Beckham	1.000	1	2	3	0	1
Espinosa	1.000	3	3	4	0	0
Freeman	1.000	2	1	3	0	0
Motter	1.000	6	2	4	0	1
Seager	.969	154	130	310	14	46
Valencia	1.000	1	1	2	0	1

Shortstop	PCT	G	PO	A	E	DP
Beckham	1.000	4	2	3	0	0
Espinosa	.800	2	0	4	1	0
Motter	.983	39	42	76	2	18
Segura	.962	124	136	298	17	61
Smith	1.000	6	5	17	0	4

Outfield	PCT	G	PO	A	E	DP
Cruz	1.000	5	7	0	0	0
Dyson	.988	108	236	11	3	6
Gamel	.980	131	238	7	5	3
Haniger	.969	96	213	6	7	1
Hannemann	.941	9	16	0	1	0
Heredia	.993	117	270	6	2	1
Martin	.987	30	75	1	1	1
Motter	1.000	19	27	2	0	0
Powell	1.000	8	14	0	0	0
Valencia	1.000	10	14	1	0	0

TACOMA RAINIERS

TRIPLE-A

PACIFIC COAST LEAGUE

Batting	B-T	HT	WT	DOB	AVG	vLH	vRH	G	AB	R	H	2B	3B	HR	RBI	BB	HBP	SH	SF	SO	SB	CS	SLG	OBP
Aplin, Andrew	L-L	6-0	205	3-21-91	.243	.130	.264	47	148	21	36	8	2	5	25	26	1	0	0	32	4	2	.426	.360
2-team total (30 Fresno)					.246	.269	.241	77	232	35	57	11	3	6	38	42	3	1	2	53	5	3	.397	.366
Ascanio, Rayder	B-R	5-11	155	3-17-96	.000	.000	.000	3	9	0	0	0	0	0	0	0	0	0	0	1	0	0	.000	.000
Baron, Steven	R-R	6-0	205	12-7-90	.256	.205	.275	54	164	16	42	6	0	2	17	20	1	1	1	42	0	0	.329	.339
Beckham, Gordon	R-R	6-0	190	9-16-86	.262	.200	.281	83	328	37	86	16	0	9	45	20	5	0	2	58	3	2	.393	.313
Capriata, Alexander	R-R	5-11	190	8-3-92	.286	.000	.333	4	7	0	2	0	0	0	0	1	0	0	0	1	1	0	.286	.375
Freeman, Mike	L-R	6-0	190	8-4-87	.350	.353	.349	16	60	12	21	3	1	1	9	7	0	0	0	10	2	0	.483	.418
3-team total (23 Iowa, 41 Oklahoma City)					.306	.250	.279	80	258	39	79	10	3	3	31	27	5	2	2	60	10	0	.403	.380
Gamel, Ben	L-L	5-11	185	5-17-92	.300	.400	.280	19	60	6	18	1	1	1	8	12	2	0	1	11	1	1	.400	.427
Gosewisch, Tuffy	R-R	5-11	200	8-17-83	.229	.328	.202	85	279	27	64	22	0	4	33	29	7	2	4	68	1	0	.351	.314
Grebeck, Austin	R-R	5-8	155	8-8-94	.200	.000	.214	4	15	2	3	0	0	1	1	0	0	0	0	4	0	1	.400	.200
Haniger, Mitch	R-R	6-2	215	12-23-90	.256	.357	.200	11	39	6	10	2	0	3	6	7	1	0	1	5	0	0	.539	.375
Helder, Eugene	R-R	5-11	165	2-26-96	.167	1.000	.118	5	18	2	3	0	1	0	1	0	0	0	0	2	0	0	.278	.167
Hernandez, Brayan	R-R	6-2	175	9-11-97	.400	.667	.000	3	5	0	2	0	0	0	0	0	0	1	0	0	1	0	.400	.400
Jackson, Ryan	R-R	6-2	180	5-10-88	.229	.100	.263	15	48	3	11	2	0	0	6	4	1	0	0	11	0	1	.271	.302
2-team total (14 New Orleans)					.244	.100	.263	29	90	7	22	2	0	0	10	12	1	0	0	20	0	1	.267	.340
Marjama, Mike	R-R	6-2	205	7-20-89	.167	.000	.210	21	78	5	13	3	1	3	12	7	1	0	0	15	0	0	.346	.244
Martin, Leonys	L-R	6-2	200	3-6-88	.306	.320	.300	88	360	63	110	24	5	11	39	21	3	0	3	89	25	6	.492	.346
Mejias-Brean, Seth	R-R	6-2	216	4-5-91	.271	.250	.278	19	70	15	19	6	1	1	7	7	0	0	0	13	1	0	.429	.338
Miller, Ian	L-R	6-0	175	2-21-92	.268	.406	.235	41	168	22	45	4	2	0	6	5	2	2	0	33	13	1	.316	.297
Motter, Taylor	R-R	6-1	195	9-18-89	.350	.444	.329	25	100	24	35	6	1	7	18	14	1	0	2	12	6	3	.640	.427
Muno, Danny	B-R	6-1	195	2-9-89	.273	.200	.290	90	293	47	80	20	1	8	33	53	2	0	1	91	12	8	.430	.387
O'Malley, Shawn	B-R	5-11	175	12-28-87	.205	.105	.237	20	78	8	16	3	0	1	5	4	1	0	1	17	0	1	.282	.250
O'Neill, Tyler	R-R	5-11	210	6-22-95	.244	.302	.224	93	349	54	85	21	2	19	56	44	1	0	2	108	9	2	.479	.328
2-team total (37 Memphis)					.247	.302	.224	130	495	77	122	26	3	31	95	54	3	0	5	151	14	2	.499	.321
Peterson, D.J.	R-R	6-1	210	12-31-91	.264	.276	.261	103	382	47	101	17	2	12	54	32	3	0	4	75	6	2	.414	.323
Pizzano, Dario	L-R	5-11	200	4-25-91	.229	.250	.224	44	140	16	32	8	1	5	16	11	3	0	1	19	1	0	.407	.297
Powell, Boog	L-L	5-10	185	1-14-93	.340	.267	.360	58	206	46	70	9	2	6	33	28	1	1	3	27	11	5	.490	.416
2-team total (3 Nashville)					.333	.000	.286	61	222	47	74	10	2	6	33	29	1	1	3	32	11	5	.478	.408
Ramsey, James	R-L	6-0	200	12-19-89	—	—	—	1	0	0	0	0	0	0	0	0	0	0	0	0	0	0	—	—
Rosa, Joseph	B-R	5-10	165	3-6-97	.071	.000	.111	4	14	0	1	1	0	0	0	0	0	0	0	0	0	0	.143	.071
Santa, Kevin	L-R	5-11	175	3-9-95	.286	.000	.333	2	7	1	2	1	0	0	0	1	0	0	0	2	0	0	.429	.375

Scott, Ryan	R-R	6-1	180	2-7-95	.125	—	.125	4	8	0	1	0	0	0	0	1	0	0	0	3	0	0	.125	.222
Segura, Jean	R-R	5-10	205	3-17-90	.125	.000	.167	2	8	2	1	0	0	0	0	0	0	0	0	2	0	0	.125	.125
Shank, Zach	R-R	6-1	180	1-6-91	.215	.233	.209	115	368	41	79	18	5	2	43	33	4	6	7	94	14	2	.307	.282
Smith, Tyler	R-R	6-0	195	7-1-91	.239	.207	.251	84	285	34	68	13	0	6	28	37	3	3	2	65	4	5	.347	.330
2-team total (13 Round Rock)					.231	.207	.251	97	333	39	77	15	0	6	29	40	5	3	2	76	4	6	.330	.321
Taylor, Logan	R-R	6-1	200	9-22-93	.182	.000	.222	3	11	1	2	0	0	1	3	0	0	0	0	2	0	1	.455	.182
Vogelbach, Daniel	L-R	6-0	250	12-17-92	.290	.234	.310	125	459	65	133	25	0	17	83	76	1	0	5	98	3	1	.455	.388
Waldrop, Kyle	L-L	6-2	215	11-26-91	.220	.000	.273	13	41	5	9	2	0	0	6	7	0	0	1	10	0	0	.268	.327
Wawoe, Gianfranco	R-R	5-11	170	7-25-94	.000	—	.000	2	6	0	0	0	0	0	0	0	0	0	0	1	0	0	.000	.000
Wong, Joey	L-R	5-10	185	4-12-88	.222	.000	.229	12	36	4	8	1	0	1	5	6	0	0	0	6	0	0	.333	.333
Zunino, Mike	R-R	6-2	220	3-25-91	.293	.000	.364	12	41	7	12	2	0	5	11	4	0	0	0	5	0	0	.707	.356

Pitching	**B-T**	**HT**	**WT**	**DOB**	**W**	**L**	**ERA**	**G**	**GS**	**CG**	**SV**	**IP**	**H**	**R**	**ER**	**HR**	**BB**	**SO**	**AVG**	**vLH**	**vRH**	**K/9**	**BB/9**
Altavilla, Dan	R-R	5-11	200	9-8-92	2	0	1.54	20	0	0	6	23	17	4	4	1	15	36	.205	.250	.177	13.89	5.79
Aro, Jonathan	R-R	6-0	235	10-10-90	6	1	3.16	25	1	0	0	43	31	16	15	5	11	48	.204	.160	.247	10.13	2.32
Ash, Brett	R-R	6-2	195	5-27-91	1	0	9.82	1	0	0	0	4	6	4	4	1	0	4	.353	.375	.333	9.82	0.00
Bannister, Nathan	R-R	6-3	224	12-17-93	1	0	4.37	4	3	0	0	23	23	11	11	5	5	18	.258	.340	.154	7.15	1.99
Bergman, Christian	R-R	6-1	195	5-4-88	9	4	5.34	16	16	1	0	86	102	53	51	7	18	63	.288	.291	.286	6.59	1.88
Castellanos, Chris	L-L	5-10	185	5-8-95	0	2	12.46	2	1	0	0	4	8	6	6	1	1	3	.381	.200	.438	6.23	2.08
Cishek, Steve	R-R	6-6	215	6-18-86	1	0	0.00	3	1	0	0	3	2	0	0	0	3	3	.222	.000	1.000	10.13	10.13
Cloyd, Tyler	R-R	6-3	210	5-16-87	1	1	5.67	19	14	0	1	60	64	41	38	8	17	48	.263	.267	.259	7.16	2.54
De Jong, Chase	L-R	6-4	205	12-29-93	3	6	6.00	15	15	0	0	84	99	61	56	18	27	61	.291	.295	.287	6.54	2.89
Delaplane, Sam	R-R	5-11	175	3-27-95	0	0	4.50	1	0	0	0	2	3	1	1	0	1	3	.333	.000	.500	13.50	4.50
Evans, Bryan	R-R	6-2	200	2-25-87	0	0	1.80	1	1	0	0	5	5	1	1	0	1	8	.263	.182	.375	14.40	1.80
Fien, Casey	R-R	6-2	210	10-21-83	0	1	3.38	5	0	0	1	5	7	2	2	0	0	3	.280	.375	.235	5.06	0.00
Frieri, Ernesto	R-R	6-0	205	7-19-85	1	2	5.25	7	0	0	0	12	9	7	7	1	9	18	.209	.136	.286	13.50	6.75
2-team total (7 Round Rock)					1	3	3.93	14	0	0	0	18	14	8	8	1	12	28	.215	.136	.286	13.75	5.89
Fry, Paul	L-L	6-0	190	7-26-92	0	1	18.00	1	0	0	0	2	6	4	4	0	1	1	.500	.000	.546	4.50	4.50
Garton, Ryan	R-R	5-10	190	12-5-89	0	2	6.00	7	0	0	0	12	11	11	8	0	8	15	.234	.167	.304	11.25	6.00
Gaviglio, Sam	R-R	6-2	195	5-22-90	3	6	3.88	13	13	1	0	72	72	35	31	5	12	57	.259	.212	.294	7.13	1.50
Gomez, Jeanmar	R-R	6-3	215	2-10-88	1	0	1.59	5	0	0	1	6	3	1	1	1	2	4	.143	.182	.100	6.35	3.18
2-team total (7 Colorado Springs)					1	0	1.93	12	0	0	1	14	10	3	3	2	3	11	.204	.182	.100	7.07	1.93
Gonzales, Marco	L-L	6-1	195	2-16-92	2	0	4.50	2	2	0	0	12	8	8	6	0	5	9	.191	.100	.219	6.75	3.75
2-team total (11 Memphis)						8	43.14		13	13	0	0	80	62	33	28	6	22	66	.215	.100	.219	7.39
2.46																							
Hagadone, Nick	L-L	6-5	230	1-1-86	3	3	3.51	28	0	0	0	33	26	13	13	3	13	35	.213	.315	.132	9.45	3.51
Harper, Ryne	R-R	6-3	215	3-27-89	3	2	3.88	37	0	0	3	46	42	21	20	5	21	45	.243	.197	.275	8.74	4.08
Hernandez, Felix	R-R	6-3	225	4-8-86	2	0	4.15	3	3	0	0	13	9	6	6	1	3	16	.192	.238	.154	11.08	2.08
Heston, Chris	R-R	6-3	195	4-10-88	2	1	3.41	6	6	1	0	32	26	12	12	2	11	28	.228	.324	.182	7.96	3.13
2-team total (1 Oklahoma City)					2	2	3.89	7	6	1	0	35	30	15	15	4	12	32	.236	.500	.273	8.31	3.12
Hunter, Kyle	L-L	6-2	210	6-18-89	3	0	3.05	8	2	0	0	21	23	8	7	1	4	14	.288	.188	.354	6.10	1.74
Hutchison, Austin	R-R	6-1	205	4-9-95	0	1	10.80	1	0	0	0	2	3	2	2	1	1	1	.375	.500	.250	5.40	5.40
Iwakuma, Hisashi	R-R	6-3	210	4-12-81	0	1	18.00	1	1	0	0	2	4	4	4	1	2	3	.400	.500	.250	13.50	9.00
Kelly, Ryan	R-R	6-2	180	10-30-87	1	1	5.74	15	0	0	0	16	14	10	10	1	3	19	.226	.290	.161	10.91	1.72
Kerski, Kody	R-R	5-10	185	4-18-92	0	0	0.00	1	0	0	0	0	0	0	0	0	0	0	.000	—	.000	0.00	0.00
Kiekhefer, Dean	L-L	6-0	175	6-7-89	3	3	4.47	49	0	0	3	44	53	27	22	3	19	42	.290	.227	.384	8.53	3.86
Kuzminsky, Scott	R-R	6-2	195	11-1-91	0	0	3.38	2	0	0	0	3	4	2	1	0	1	2	.364	.286	.500	6.75	3.38
Lawrence, Casey	R-R	6-2	170	10-28-87	2	4	4.08	11	7	1	0	57	50	26	26	7	10	41	.236	.248	.224	6.44	1.57
Light, Pat	R-R	6-5	220	3-29-91	1	2	5.34	20	0	0	0	29	28	17	17	2	19	14	.255	.276	.231	4.40	5.97
Lowe, Mark	R-L	6-3	210	6-7-83	3	4	6.23	32	0	0	1	39	49	31	27	6	20	37	.303	.274	.320	8.54	4.62
Machi, Jean	R-R	6-0	255	2-1-82	2	4	3.44	29	3	0	10	37	39	15	14	2	8	29	.281	.250	.307	7.12	1.96
Marshall, Evan	R-R	6-2	225	4-18-90	1	0	4.15	13	1	0	1	22	28	12	10	4	7	26	.311	.303	.316	10.80	2.91
Martin, Cody	R-R	6-3	230	9-4-89	0	2	4.13	20	7	0	1	57	59	27	26	7	14	67	.269	.235	.308	10.64	2.22
Moore, Andrew	R-R	6-0	185	6-2-94	3	4	3.48	15	14	0	0	75	68	30	29	9	13	66	.236	.245	.227	7.92	1.56
Overton, Dillon	L-L	6-2	175	8-17-91	1	2	9.33	7	6	0	0	27	34	28	28	9	12	22	.301	.302	.300	7.33	4.00
2-team total (12 El Paso)					7	6	6.73	19	18	0	0	91	111	69	68	21	29	52	.296	.359	.273	5.14	2.87
Paez, Paul	L-L	5-7	210	4-29-92	0	1	1.29	3	1	0	0	7	2	2	1	0	1	4	.091	.000	.125	5.14	1.29
Pagan, Emilio	L-R	6-3	210	5-7-91	2	1	2.56	23	0	0	5	32	19	9	9	0	8	36	.171	.195	.157	10.23	2.27
Pineda, Rafael	L-R	6-6	210	2-3-91	0	1	67.50	1	1	0	0	1	5	5	5	1	1	1	.833	.667	1.000	13.50	13.50
Povse, Max	R-R	6-8	185	8-23-93	1	4	7.39	13	5	0	0	32	41	28	26	3	12	29	.315	.379	.250	8.24	3.41
Ratliff, Lane	L-L	6-3	185	3-22-95	0	0	9.00	2	0	0	0	3	3	3	3	1	3	2	.250	.000	.600	6.00	9.00
Ridings, Steven	R-R	6-4	210	2-28-94	0	0	13.50	1	0	0	0	2	5	3	3	0	0	1	.556	.250	.800	4.50	0.00
Rivera, Michael	R-R	6-3	220	6-19-97	0	0	36.00	1	0	0	0	1	5	4	4	0	0	0	.625	.000	.833	0.00	0.00
Scribner, Evan	R-R	6-3	190	7-19-85	0	0	0.00	3	0	0	0	3	0	0	0	0	0	3	.000	.000	.000	9.00	0.00
Simmons, Shae	R-R	5-11	190	9-3-90	0	0	3.68	9	0	0	0	7	5	4	3	1	6	6	.192	.133	.273	7.36	7.36
Unsworth, Dylan	R-R	6-1	175	9-23-92	0	1	3.12	2	2	0	0	9	10	3	3	0	2	4	.323	.429	.292	4.15	2.08
Vieira, Thyago	R-R	6-2	210	7-1-93	0	1	4.58	12	0	0	2	18	18	9	9	1	7	11	.261	.375	.162	5.60	3.57
Weber, Ryan	R-R	6-1	180	8-12-90	2	0	0.85	6	5	0	0	32	20	3	3	1	4	19	.180	.098	.229	5.40	1.14
Whalen, Rob	R-R	6-2	220	1-31-94	0	7	6.58	10	10	1	0	53	61	44	39	9	20	43	.285	.278	.293	7.26	3.38
Zych, Tony	R-R	6-3	190	8-7-90	0	0	20.25	2	1	0	0	1	5	3	3	1	0	3	.556	—	.556	20.25	0.00

Fielding

Catcher	**PCT**	**G**	**PO**	**A**	**E**	**DP**	**PB**
Baron	.995	51	359	21	2	2	4
Capriata	1.000	3	11	3	0	0	0
Gosewisch	.993	73	555	37	4	4	2
Marjama	.969	14	120	4	4	1	2
Scott	1.000	3	10	1	0	0	0
Zunino	1.000	7	43	6	0	0	0

First Base	PCT	G	PO	A	E	DP
Gosewisch	1.000	4	12	2	0	2
Marjama	1.000	1	7	0	0	0
Motter	1.000	2	18	1	0	2
O'Malley	1.000	1	6	0	0	0
Peterson	.995	51	415	17	2	33
Pizzano	1.000	1	8	1	0	0
Shank	1.000	3	27	3	0	4
Vogelbach	.986	81	576	45	9	42
Waldrop	1.000	1	7	2	0	0
Wong	1.000	1	6	0	0	1

Second Base	PCT	G	PO	A	E	DP
Beckham	.974	63	104	155	7	32
Freeman	1.000	9	14	21	0	5
Motter	1.000	1	1	1	0	0
Muno	.945	17	18	34	3	7
O'Malley	.978	7	18	26	1	2
Rosa	1.000	4	8	13	0	6
Shank	1.000	34	50	84	0	11
Smith	1.000	4	4	8	0	1
Wawoe	1.000	2	2	8	0	1
Wong	.969	6	9	22	1	5

Third Base	PCT	G	PO	A	E	DP
Beckham	.938	7	3	12	1	0
Freeman	.950	6	3	16	1	2
Mejias-Brean	.964	19	11	43	2	5
Motter	.857	2	1	5	1	0
Muno	.936	50	38	79	8	11
O'Malley	1.000	2	1	0	0	0
Peterson	.938	43	33	57	6	5
Shank	.914	12	9	23	3	2
Smith	1.000	1	1	1	0	0
Taylor	1.000	3	2	2	0	1

Shortstop	PCT	G	PO	A	E	DP
Ascanio	.889	3	2	6	1	0
Beckham	1.000	3	2	7	0	0
Helder	.950	5	4	15	1	3
Jackson	.853	15	10	19	5	3
Motter	.974	19	24	52	2	10
O'Malley	1.000	8	11	15	0	2
Santa	1.000	2	1	5	0	1
Segura	.000	2	0	0	0	0
Shank	.889	4	6	10	2	1
Smith	.974	79	84	215	8	35
Wong	1.000	5	5	7	0	0

Outfield	PCT	G	PO	A	E	DP
Aplin	.979	44	89	4	2	1
Gamel	1.000	19	26	0	0	0
Gosewisch	1.000	1	1	0	0	0
Grebeck	1.000	4	5	1	0	0
Haniger	.909	6	9	1	1	1
Hernandez	.750	3	3	0	1	0
Kiekhefer	.000	2	0	0	0	0
Martin	.979	82	219	9	5	1
Miller	1.000	41	104	2	0	1
Motter	1.000	1	2	0	0	0
Muno	1.000	16	24	2	0	1
O'Malley	.000	1	0	0	0	0
O'Neill	.980	82	148	1	3	0
Peterson	1.000	1	1	0	0	0
Pizzano	.893	18	25	0	3	0
Powell	.975	57	113	2	3	0
Ramsey	.000	1	0	0	0	0
Shank	.977	62	121	5	3	3
Waldrop	.905	12	19	0	2	0

SEATTLE MARINERS

ARKANSAS TRAVELERS

DOUBLE-A

TEXAS LEAGUE

Batting	B-T	HT	WT	DOB	AVG	vLH	vRH	G	AB	R	H	2B	3B	HR	RBI	BB	HBP	SH	SF	SO	SB	CS	SLG	OBP
Argo, Willie	R-R	6-1	220	10-15-89	.179	.267	.154	19	67	8	12	6	0	2	7	4	0	0	0	28	0	0	.358	.225
Baron, Steven	R-R	6-0	205	12-7-90	.196	.133	.222	16	51	2	10	1	0	1	5	4	2	0	0	12	0	0	.275	.281
Baum, Jay	R-R	6-0	190	10-25-92	.192	.191	.193	27	104	10	20	4	0	1	8	4	1	0	0	28	3	0	.260	.229
Bishop, Braden	R-R	6-1	190	8-22-93	.336	.375	.327	31	125	18	42	9	1	1	11	15	3	1	1	15	6	1	.448	.417
Casteel, Ryan	R-R	5-11	205	6-6-91	.273	.260	.277	100	389	47	106	25	0	12	61	31	0	0	4	84	1	0	.429	.323
De La Cruz, Keury	L-L	5-11	170	11-28-91	.238	.273	.225	32	122	10	29	3	1	0	11	5	0	0	0	24	5	1	.279	.268
Hebert, Brock	R-R	5-10	180	5-11-91	.171	.200	.160	22	70	6	12	1	0	2	6	4	3	1	0	20	1	1	.271	.247
Kobernus, Jeff	R-R	6-2	190	6-30-88	.222	.317	.181	44	135	11	30	4	0	0	11	9	2	3	1	30	9	3	.252	.279
Law, Adam	R-R	6-0	195	2-5-90	.222	.316	.182	17	63	4	14	3	0	0	3	1	0	1	0	22	0	2	.270	.234
Littlewood, Marcus	B-R	6-3	195	3-18-92	.242	.353	.207	73	281	30	68	11	0	9	35	14	0	1	4	67	1	0	.377	.274
Mack, Chantz	L-L	5-10	205	5-4-91	.184	.100	.209	29	87	10	16	3	0	1	8	21	0	0	0	22	0	0	.253	.343
Mariscal, Chris	R-R	5-10	170	4-26-93	.245	.316	.222	40	155	15	38	3	2	1	14	14	2	0	0	30	0	1	.310	.316
Marlette, Tyler	R-R	5-11	195	1-23-93	.245	.272	.236	97	368	47	90	22	2	11	65	31	4	0	2	89	0	1	.405	.309
Mejias-Brean, Seth	R-R	6-2	216	4-5-91	.268	.306	.256	74	291	31	78	8	2	3	42	22	6	0	4	71	4	1	.340	.328
Miller, Ian	L-R	6-0	175	2-21-92	.326	.337	.322	83	344	63	112	18	3	4	29	28	6	2	4	69	30	4	.430	.382
O'Malley, Shawn	B-R	5-11	175	12-28-87	.250	.273	.235	8	28	5	7	1	0	1	3	8	0	0	0	7	0	0	.393	.417
Petty, Kyle	R-R	6-5	215	3-1-91	.252	.194	.282	34	107	8	27	5	0	0	14	13	3	0	3	37	2	0	.299	.341
Pizzano, Dario	L-R	5-11	200	4-25-91	.294	.306	.290	72	272	40	80	12	1	8	41	28	8	0	2	27	2	1	.434	.374
Rosa, Joseph	B-R	5-10	165	3-6-97	.286	—	.286	2	7	0	2	0	0	0	0	1	0	0	0	2	0	0	.286	.375
Scott, Ryan	R-R	6-1	180	2-7-95	.400	—	.400	1	5	1	2	0	0	0	1	0	0	0	0	2	0	0	.400	.400
Seager, Justin	R-R	6-1	215	5-15-92	.214	.091	.258	14	42	3	9	3	0	1	3	3	0	0	0	17	0	0	.357	.267
Segura, Jean	R-R	5-10	205	3-17-90	.091	.000	.100	3	11	1	1	0	0	0	0	1	0	0	0	0	0	0	.091	.167
Taylor, Chuck	B-L	5-9	190	9-21-93	.274	.286	.270	122	471	74	129	25	3	9	58	66	6	0	2	90	10	2	.397	.369
Waldrop, Kyle	L-L	6-2	215	11-26-91	.303	.253	.319	109	412	61	125	28	0	10	68	37	8	0	6	86	4	3	.444	.367
Ward, Nelson	L-R	5-11	175	8-6-92	.265	.203	.285	82	264	32	70	12	1	1	22	26	4	2	1	74	8	3	.330	.339
Wawoe, Gianfranco	R-R	5-11	170	7-25-94	.241	.273	.234	14	58	8	14	5	0	0	7	2	0	0	1	8	2	0	.328	.262
Wong, Joey	L-R	5-10	185	4-12-88	.241	.182	.261	118	390	62	94	10	1	2	29	66	8	6	3	79	0	1	.287	.360

Pitching	B-T	HT	WT	DOB	W	L	ERA	G	GS	CG	SV	IP	H	R	ER	HR	BB	SO	AVG	vLH	vRH	K/9	BB/9
Ash, Brett	R-R	6-2	195	5-27-91	5	10	7.48	20	14	0	0	77	114	65	64	12	28	42	.348	.348	.347	4.91	3.27
Boches, Scott	R-R	6-5	205	10-17-94	1	0	9.00	5	0	0	0	10	16	10	10	1	8	2	.400	.364	.444	1.80	7.20
Cash, Ralston	R-R	6-3	215	8-20-91	1	0	1.93	5	0	0	0	5	5	1	1	0	3	4	.278	.300	.250	7.71	5.79
2-team total (31 Tulsa)					4	2	4.96	36	0	0	1	49	56	31	27	4	20	65	.281	.266	.291	11.94	3.67
Caughel, Lindsey	R-R	6-3	205	8-13-90	10	10	3.71	27	26	2	0	158	148	66	65	18	38	116	.248	.264	.237	6.62	2.17
Cishek, Steve	R-R	6-6	215	6-18-86	0	0	5.40	4	1	0	0	3	4	2	2	0	1	4	.286	.167	.375	10.80	2.70
Curtis, Zac	L-L	5-9	190	7-4-92	1	2	3.51	41	0	0	13	51	43	21	20	3	19	60	.226	.242	.219	10.52	3.33
De Jong, Chase	L-R	6-4	205	12-29-93	1	3	5.97	5	5	0	0	29	32	20	19	3	10	18	.288	.313	.279	5.65	3.14
DeFratus, Justin	B-R	6-4	225	10-21-87	5	7	4.85	17	16	0	0	98	118	61	53	15	14	53	.294	.298	.292	4.85	1.28
Evans, Bryan	R-R	6-2	200	2-25-87	4	2	3.47	6	6	0	0	36	39	15	14	5	6	39	.273	.343	.211	9.66	1.49
Gerber, David	R-R	6-1	200	9-24-94	0	0	0.00	1	0	0	0	1	0	0	0	0	0	0	.000	—	.000	0.00	0.00
Gillies, Darin	R-R	6-4	220	11-6-92	3	3	3.32	39	0	0	3	60	52	23	22	4	25	47	.231	.191	.255	7.09	3.77
Harper, Ryne	R-R	6-3	215	3-27-89	1	0	0.00	4	0	0	0	7	2	0	0	0	0	10	.083	.077	.091	12.27	0.00
Herb, Tyler	R-R	6-2	175	4-28-92	6	4	3.31	16	16	0	0	98	97	40	36	5	30	88	.264	.289	.249	8.08	2.76
Horstman, Ryan	L-L	6-1	185	7-20-92	2	0	5.71	13	0	0	0	17	15	11	11	2	12	23	.246	.286	.225	11.94	6.23
Hunter, Kyle	L-L	6-2	210	6-18-89	1	0	4.73	23	3	0	0	51	66	28	27	8	14	40	.307	.352	.285	7.01	2.45
Hutchison, Austin	R-R	6-1	205	4-9-95	0	0	1.69	3	0	0	0	11	9	3	2	0	5	9	.225	.177	.261	7.59	4.22

Pitching	B-T	HT	WT	DOB	W	L	ERA	G	GS	CG	SV	IP	H	R	ER	HR	BB	SO	AVG	vLH	vRH	K/9	BB/9
Kelly, Ryan	R-R	6-2	180	10-30-87	1	0	0.00	14	0	0	6	15	5	0	0	0	4	13	.102	.188	.061	7.98	2.45
Knigge, Tyler	L-R	6-4	215	10-27-88	1	1	5.68	17	0	0	0	19	23	13	12	1	12	23	.303	.222	.347	10.89	5.68
Kober, Collin	R-R	6-1	185	9-8-94	0	0	6.23	4	0	0	0	4	5	3	3	1	3	3	.313	.286	.333	6.23	6.23
Kubitza, Austin	R-R	6-5	225	11-16-91	0	0	9.42	10	1	0	0	14	18	16	15	0	13	7	.305	.440	.206	4.40	8.16
Marshall, Evan	R-R	6-2	225	4-18-90	0	0	13.50	3	0	0	0	3	7	4	4	0	1	1	.500	.429	.571	3.38	3.38
Misiewicz, Anthony	R-L	6-1	190	11-1-94	3	3	4.35	7	7	0	0	41	40	20	20	4	11	32	.270	.256	.275	6.97	2.40
Moore, Andrew	R-R	6-0	185	6-2-94	1	2	2.08	6	5	0	0	35	28	8	8	4	9	33	.219	.244	.205	8.57	2.34
Neidert, Nick	R-R	6-1	180	11-20-96	1	3	6.56	6	6	0	0	23	33	21	17	4	5	13	.324	.229	.407	5.01	1.93
Paez, Paul	L-L	5-7	210	4-29-92	0	0	4.70	5	1	0	0	8	6	4	4	2	4	7	.214	.375	.150	8.22	4.70
Paxton, James	L-L	6-4	235	11-6-88	0	0	4.50	1	1	0	0	4	5	2	2	1	0	5	.313	.000	.385	11.25	0.00
Perry, Blake	R-R	6-5	190	2-3-92	1	4	5.66	40	0	0	3	62	66	43	39	5	33	67	.268	.330	.234	9.73	4.79
Povse, Max	R-R	6-8	185	8-23-93	3	2	3.46	9	8	0	0	39	34	17	15	1	14	32	.235	.333	.186	7.38	3.23
Ridings, Steven	R-R	6-4	210	2-28-94	0	1	10.80	1	0	0	0	3	4	4	4	0	3	4	.308	.333	.300	10.80	8.10
Simmons, Shae	R-R	5-11	190	9-3-90	0	0	10.13	3	0	0	0	3	6	3	3	0	1	4	.462	.667	.400	13.50	3.38
Tago, Peter	R-R	6-3	215	7-5-92	0	3	2.54	28	0	0	4	39	23	13	11	1	24	48	.167	.136	.181	11.08	5.54
Tolliver, Ashur	L-L	6-0	170	1-24-88	1	0	3.38	5	0	0	0	8	7	3	3	0	2	7	.241	.200	.286	7.88	2.25
Unsworth, Dylan	R-R	6-1	175	9-23-92	9	8	3.31	20	20	1	0	120	112	49	44	9	20	86	.240	.216	.254	6.47	1.50
Vieira, Thyago	R-R	6-2	210	7-1-93	2	3	3.72	29	0	0	2	36	30	18	15	1	15	35	.224	.262	.207	8.67	3.72
West, Aaron	R-R	6-1	195	6-1-90	1	4	2.59	9	4	0	0	24	30	10	7	1	5	13	.316	.357	.283	4.81	1.85

Fielding

Catcher	PCT	G	PO	A	E	DP	PB
Baron	1.000	10	62	10	0	2	0
Littlewood	.997	47	350	33	1	3	1
Marlette	.995	83	553	55	3	3	6
Scott	1.000	1	7	0	0	0	0

First Base	PCT	G	PO	A	E	DP
Casteel	.991	91	731	38	7	68
Mejias-Brean	1.000	4	30	1	0	1
Petty	1.000	20	160	4	0	16
Seager	1.000	4	21	2	0	5
Waldrop	1.000	23	175	14	0	21

Second Base	PCT	G	PO	A	E	DP
Baum	1.000	2	5	6	0	1
Hebert	1.000	16	31	34	0	9
Kobernus	.969	37	62	92	5	23
Law	1.000	8	18	21	0	7
Mariscal	1.000	11	17	25	0	5
O'Malley	1.000	4	10	14	0	2
Rosa	.923	2	3	9	1	3
Ward	.972	52	89	122	6	32
Wawoe	.957	14	34	33	3	11
Wong	1.000	2	5	5	0	1

Third Base	PCT	G	PO	A	E	DP
Baum	.929	25	26	39	5	3
Hebert	.909	5	3	7	1	1
Law	1.000	6	3	6	0	1
Mariscal	1.000	5	5	6	0	0
Mejias-Brean	.991	69	79	131	2	14
Seager	.571	3	1	3	3	1
Ward	.939	30	19	58	5	11

Shortstop	PCT	G	PO	A	E	DP
Kobernus	1.000	3	3	3	0	0
Law	.857	2	3	3	1	1
Mariscal	.984	17	24	38	1	6
O'Malley	.750	1	2	1	1	0
Segura	1.000	2	0	5	0	0
Wong	.980	117	157	343	10	69

Outfield	PCT	G	PO	A	E	DP
Argo	1.000	19	54	1	0	0
Bishop	.990	31	95	3	1	1
De La Cruz	1.000	28	40	1	0	0
Kobernus	1.000	2	2	0	0	0
Law	1.000	2	5	0	0	0
Littlewood	1.000	2	4	0	0	0
Mack	.953	21	40	1	2	1
Mariscal	1.000	6	10	0	0	0
Miller	.981	80	200	3	4	1
Pizzano	.986	40	70	0	1	0
Taylor	.986	109	204	3	3	1
Waldrop	1.000	85	175	9	0	2

MODESTO NUTS

HIGH CLASS A

CALIFORNIA LEAGUE

Batting	B-T	HT	WT	DOB	AVG	vLH	vRH	G	AB	R	H	2B	3B	HR	RBI	BB	HBP	SH	SF	SO	SB	CS	SLG	OBP
Argo, Willie	R-R	6-1	220	10-15-89	.234	.226	.237	54	201	25	47	14	1	6	30	22	4	0	5	60	13	3	.403	.315
Ascanio, Rayder	B-R	5-11	155	3-17-96	.223	.242	.216	66	233	25	52	16	1	4	24	26	2	5	2	40	3	4	.352	.304
Baum, Jay	R-R	6-0	190	10-25-92	.257	.333	.231	9	35	3	9	2	2	1	8	2	0	0	0	8	1	1	.514	.297
Bishop, Braden	R-R	6-1	190	8-22-93	.296	.276	.302	88	355	71	105	25	3	2	32	45	7	4	1	65	16	4	.400	.385
Cowan, Jordan	L-R	6-0	160	4-13-95	.271	.274	.270	121	468	67	127	20	2	2	39	50	4	8	3	88	18	5	.336	.345
Curletta, Joey	R-R	6-4	245	3-8-94	.256	.261	.254	121	454	72	116	37	1	15	68	62	3	0	9	136	13	1	.441	.343
DeCarlo, Joe	R-R	5-10	210	9-13-93	.240	.273	.228	96	325	45	78	14	2	13	46	42	12	0	2	99	1	2	.415	.347
Eusebio, Ricky	R-R	5-11	195	11-25-93	.215	.130	.235	32	121	22	26	11	1	4	9	9	2	0	0	34	0	1	.422	.280
Filia, Eric	L-R	6-0	189	7-6-92	.326	.307	.332	128	491	63	160	28	5	5	59	65	6	0	5	45	9	6	.434	.407
Grebeck, Austin	R-R	5-8	155	8-8-94	.128	.167	.111	16	39	7	5	1	0	0	1	10	0	0	1	17	4	1	.154	.300
Lewis, Kyle	R-R	6-4	210	7-13-95	.255	.277	.245	38	149	20	38	4	0	6	24	15	1	0	2	38	2	1	.403	.323
Liberato, Luis	L-L	6-1	175	12-18-95	.257	.152	.293	68	257	41	66	11	5	8	28	21	1	3	1	80	7	4	.432	.314
Mariscal, Chris	R-R	5-10	170	4-26-93	.305	.305	.305	85	325	52	99	13	6	7	49	44	6	2	5	75	6	5	.446	.392
Nieto, Arturo	R-R	6-2	195	12-9-92	.237	.213	.244	78	266	35	63	12	1	5	27	25	4	0	2	73	1	1	.346	.310
Rizzo, Joe	L-R	5-9	194	3-31-98	.200	.200	.200	5	20	1	4	0	1	0	1	1	0	0	0	8	0	0	.300	.238
Santa, Kevin	L-R	5-11	175	3-9-95	.244	.222	.250	15	45	5	11	0	0	1	5	4	1	0	0	4	1	3	.311	.320
Scott, Ryan	R-R	6-1	180	2-7-95	.100	.071	.115	14	40	3	4	1	0	0	2	3	0	0	0	15	1	0	.125	.163
Taylor, Logan	R-R	6-1	200	9-22-93	.241	.210	.251	82	316	37	76	26	3	8	59	24	9	1	8	107	4	4	.418	.305
Torres, Daniel	R-R	6-0	175	5-29-92	.181	.182	.180	25	83	9	15	1	0	0	8	7	2	1	1	21	0	1	.193	.258
Walton, Donnie	L-R	5-10	184	5-25-94	.269	.167	.302	67	242	37	65	16	1	2	24	27	3	0	0	49	6	6	.368	.349
Wawoe, Gianfranco	R-R	5-11	170	7-25-94	.270	.269	.271	97	374	36	101	17	6	2	62	23	4	6	4	59	15	8	.364	.316

Pitching	B-T	HT	WT	DOB	W	L	ERA	G	GS	CG	SV	IP	H	R	ER	HR	BB	SO	AVG	vLH	vRH	K/9	BB/9
Anderson, Jack	R-R	6-3	210	1-10-94	0	3	4.43	16	0	0	1	20	22	10	10	0	9	21	.279	.389	.186	9.30	3.98
Bannister, Nathan	R-R	6-3	224	12-17-93	8	7	4.33	23	23	0	0	121	130	60	58	17	16	99	.271	.248	.291	7.38	1.19
Bonnell, Bryan	L-R	6-5	210	9-28-93	3	2	3.64	32	2	0	3	59	62	31	24	6	17	51	.268	.301	.242	7.74	2.58
Dugger, Robert	R-R	6-2	180	7-3-95	2	5	3.94	9	9	0	0	46	49	25	20	4	16	47	.272	.319	.221	9.26	3.15
Festa, Matthew	R-R	6-2	195	3-11-93	4	2	3.23	42	1	0	6	70	61	30	25	7	19	99	.229	.215	.241	12.79	2.45
Gorgas, Marvin	R-R	5-9	185	1-19-96	4	2	3.21	23	0	0	4	42	36	23	15	4	26	55	.221	.244	.198	11.79	5.57
Hammond, Ted	R-R	6-2	195	12-17-93	0	0	4.50	1	0	0	0	2	1	1	1	0	2	1	.167	.000	.333	4.50	9.00
Herrmann, Spencer	L-L	6-4	235	8-6-93	4	6	3.53	36	13	0	2	105	103	41	41	10	29	103	.260	.226	.278	8.86	2.49

Pitching	B-T	HT	WT	DOB	W	L	ERA	G	GS	CG	SV	IP	H	R	ER	HR	BB	SO	AVG	vLH	vRH	K/9	BB/9
Hutchison, Austin	R-R	6-1	205	4-9-95	0	0	0.00	1	0	0	0	3	3	1	0	0	2	2	.231	.333	.200	5.40	5.40
Iwakuma, Hisashi	R-R	6-3	210	4-12-81	0	0	0.00	1	1	0	0	4	1	0	0	0	0	4	.077	.200	.000	9.00	0.00
Jackson, Tyler	R-R	6-6	210	10-22-93	2	2	3.60	9	9	0	0	45	46	22	18	1	9	36	.261	.225	.299	7.20	1.80
Kerski, Kody	R-R	5-10	185	4-18-92	1	2	10.45	7	0	0	1	10	16	13	12	1	2	13	.340	.308	.381	11.32	1.74
Knigge, Tyler	L-R	6-4	215	10-27-88	0	0	4.50	3	0	0	0	4	4	2	2	0	2	4	.267	.200	.300	9.00	4.50
Lopez, Pablo	R-R	6-3	200	3-7-96	5	8	5.04	19	18	0	0	100	113	63	56	6	13	89	.279	.294	.262	8.01	1.17
McClain, Reggie	R-R	6-2	180	11-16-92	12	9	4.75	27	27	1	0	153	164	85	81	15	35	127	.276	.262	.291	7.45	2.05
Misiewicz, Anthony	R-L	6-1	190	11-1-94	5	2	4.96	16	16	0	0	78	82	47	43	6	27	85	.265	.323	.227	9.81	3.12
Neidert, Nick	R-R	6-1	180	11-20-96	10	3	2.76	19	19	0	0	104	95	33	32	7	17	109	.244	.217	.274	9.40	1.47
Paez, Paul	L-L	5-7	210	4-29-92	0	0	0.00	1	0	0	0	2	0	0	0	0	0	1	.000	.000	.000	5.40	0.00
Pierce, Rohn	R-R	6-3	210	1-21-93	0	0	5.19	4	0	0	0	9	12	5	5	0	6	9	.364	.450	.231	9.35	6.23
Pistorese, Joe	L-L	6-2	175	10-15-92	0	2	3.89	28	1	0	0	42	36	21	18	2	19	49	.226	.267	.202	10.58	4.10
Ridings, Steven	R-R	6-4	210	2-28-94	0	0	9.00	1	0	0	0	2	1	2	2	0	2	3	.143	.000	.250	13.50	9.00
Rivera, Michael	R-R	6-3	220	6-19-97	0	0	7.20	2	0	0	0	5	6	5	4	0	2	3	.333	.250	.400	5.40	3.60
Santiago, Jose	R-R	6-1	190	3-1-94	0	1	18.00	1	0	0	0	2	3	4	4	1	2	1	.333	.500	.286	4.50	9.00
Schiraldi, Lukas	R-R	6-6	210	7-25-93	2	1	4.58	28	0	0	3	37	29	21	19	1	27	63	.213	.209	.217	15.19	6.51
Strain, Joey	R-R	6-1	200	1-17-94	3	3	5.96	37	1	0	0	74	104	51	49	5	10	51	.340	.311	.373	6.20	1.22
Walker, Matt	R-R	6-6	201	9-28-94	4	5	4.19	42	0	0	6	58	59	31	27	6	28	69	.260	.267	.254	10.71	4.34
Warren, Art	R-R	6-3	230	3-23-93	3	1	3.06	43	0	0	8	65	58	25	22	5	25	67	.247	.252	.242	9.32	3.48

Fielding

Catcher	PCT	G	PO	A	E	DP	PB
DeCarlo	.993	49	360	47	3	1	18
Nieto	.987	71	633	65	9	1	8
Scott	1.000	4	46	2	0	1	0
Torres	.995	22	177	22	1	1	0

First Base	PCT	G	PO	A	E	DP
Curletta	.995	104	883	56	5	66
DeCarlo	1.000	18	106	9	0	8
Filia	1.000	12	89	1	0	9
Scott	.986	8	62	6	1	9
Torres	1.000	3	28	2	0	2
Walton	.000	1	0	0	0	0

Second Base	PCT	G	PO	A	E	DP
Baum	.889	2	5	3	1	1
Cowan	1.000	33	55	87	0	19
Mariscal	.972	51	69	142	6	19
Santa	1.000	5	9	11	0	3
Walton	.986	16	19	52	1	10
Wawoe	.969	34	51	75	4	14

Third Base	PCT	G	PO	A	E	DP
Baum	.889	4	2	6	1	0
Cowan	.963	59	48	109	6	11
DeCarlo	.900	4	3	6	1	0
Mariscal	.952	8	11	9	1	1
Rizzo	1.000	4	2	6	0	1
Santa	1.000	5	2	9	0	0
Taylor	.935	42	34	67	7	4
Wawoe	.884	15	15	23	5	2

Shortstop	PCT	G	PO	A	E	DP
Ascanio	.971	65	84	183	8	36
Cowan	.982	14	21	33	1	7
Mariscal	.955	14	13	29	2	7
Santa	.833	2	3	2	1	1
Walton	.955	47	57	136	9	23

Outfield	PCT	G	PO	A	E	DP
Argo	.972	50	104	1	3	0
Baum	1.000	1	2	0	0	0
Bishop	.990	84	190	8	2	2
Curletta	.920	16	23	0	2	0
Eusebio	1.000	32	55	4	0	2
Filia	.984	107	183	4	3	1
Grebeck	.947	15	35	1	2	0
Lewis	.960	13	23	1	1	1
Liberato	.987	65	148	6	2	1
Taylor	.968	35	58	2	2	0
Wawoe	.913	13	21	0	2	0

SEATTLE MARINERS

CLINTON LUMBERKINGS — *LOW CLASS A*

MIDWEST LEAGUE

Batting	B-T	HT	WT	DOB	AVG	vLH	vRH	G	AB	R	H	2B	3B	HR	RBI	BB	HBP	SH	SF	SO	SB	CS	SLG	OBP
Ascanio, Rayder	B-R	5-11	155	3-17-96	.220	.243	.212	42	150	23	33	9	0	5	20	17	0	4	2	44	9	4	.380	.296
Boyd, Louis	R-R	5-11	169	5-4-94	.261	.267	.259	19	69	7	18	2	0	0	2	3	0	0	0	16	5	1	.290	.292
Brigman, Bryson	R-R	5-11	180	6-19-95	.235	.238	.235	120	463	55	109	14	4	2	36	44	5	2	4	74	16	8	.296	.306
Brito, Kristian	R-R	6-5	240	12-20-94	.200	.239	.181	41	140	16	28	5	1	4	15	12	0	0	0	52	0	0	.336	.263
Cooke, Billy	R-R	5-10	175	9-26-95	.156	.211	.131	42	122	13	19	1	0	2	9	18	2	0	1	45	6	5	.213	.273
Hale, Conner	R-R	6-1	190	10-10-92	.213	.111	.237	13	47	6	10	3	1	1	4	4	0	0	0	11	0	0	.383	.275
Jimenez, Anthony	R-R	5-11	165	10-21-95	.298	.328	.287	64	228	43	68	17	2	7	33	19	5	2	2	73	24	10	.483	.362
Liberato, Luis	L-L	6-1	175	12-18-95	.230	.065	.283	57	191	34	44	5	9	6	22	23	0	6	3	51	5	4	.445	.309
Morales, Jhombeyker	R-R	6-0	170	7-17-94	.245	.254	.243	77	273	28	67	20	0	1	31	19	4	3	4	72	7	6	.330	.300
Morgan, Gareth	R-R	6-4	220	4-12-96	.230	.178	.244	118	405	55	93	21	3	17	61	53	2	0	2	185	14	5	.422	.320
Ojeda, Dimas	L-L	6-1	195	9-19-95	.248	.145	.272	106	363	26	90	17	1	4	35	18	1	2	2	80	2	2	.333	.284
Quevedo, Yojhan	R-R	6-1	215	11-6-93	.273	.282	.270	101	396	36	108	24	1	7	46	12	5	0	4	51	5	1	.391	.300
Rengifo, Luis	B-R	5-10	165	2-26-97	.250	.290	.236	102	400	65	100	24	4	11	44	33	8	6	3	80	29	14	.413	.318
2-team total (23 Bowling Green)					.250	.290	.235	125	496	79	124	27	5	12	52	41	8	6	3	97	34	17	.397	.316
Rizzo, Joe	L-R	5-9	194	3-31-98	.254	.297	.238	110	410	47	104	17	0	7	50	63	3	0	4	113	3	1	.346	.354
Rosa, Joseph	B-R	5-10	165	3-6-97	.214	.000	.231	4	14	3	3	0	0	0	0	4	0	0	0	1	3	1	.214	.389
Scott, Ryan	R-R	6-1	180	2-7-95	.194	.286	.167	19	62	9	12	5	0	0	7	6	1	1	0	11	1	1	.274	.275
Slater, Johnny	L-L	6-1	190	8-9-95	.215	.231	.210	52	177	17	38	6	3	2	9	18	2	3	1	54	5	4	.316	.293
Thurman, Nick	L-R	6-2	210	9-9-93	.236	.230	.237	91	310	35	73	11	1	5	27	27	4	1	0	98	4	0	.326	.305
Zammarelli III, Nick	L-R	6-1	195	7-30-94	.282	.270	.286	109	401	48	113	26	3	6	44	36	6	0	3	111	6	4	.407	.348

Pitching	B-T	HT	WT	DOB	W	L	ERA	G	GS	CG	SV	IP	H	R	ER	HR	BB	SO	AVG	vLH	vRH	K/9	BB/9
Anderson, Jack	R-R	6-3	210	1-10-94	3	2	1.75	27	0	0	3	51	42	18	10	0	13	54	.221	.265	.197	9.47	2.28
Clancy, Matt	B-L	5-11	180	4-1-94	1	0	9.26	8	0	0	0	12	18	12	12	0	5	16	.367	.333	.378	12.34	3.86
Dominguez, Ronald	R-R	6-2	180	1-13-94	0	6	3.72	18	3	0	2	56	52	35	23	3	12	44	.242	.247	.239	7.11	1.94
Dugger, Robert	R-R	6-2	180	7-3-95	4	1	2.00	22	9	1	2	72	55	19	16	4	16	69	.206	.167	.226	8.63	2.00
Elledge, Seth	R-R	6-3	230	5-20-96	3	0	3.00	15	0	0	5	21	14	8	7	1	6	35	.182	.167	.192	15.00	2.57
Garcia, Danny	L-L	6-1	195	2-21-94	7	13	5.74	28	25	0	0	132	168	99	84	11	39	108	.307	.259	.324	7.38	2.67
Gorgas, Marvin	R-R	5-9	185	1-19-96	1	1	0.93	12	0	0	3	19	13	2	2	1	9	23	.188	.107	.244	10.71	4.19
Inman, Ryne	R-R	6-5	215	5-13-96	2	4	6.28	9	8	0	0	39	42	28	27	3	26	35	.296	.289	.299	8.15	6.05
Kerski, Kody	R-R	5-10	185	4-18-92	0	0	0.00	2	0	0	0	2	1	0	0	0	0	3	.125	.250	.000	13.50	0.00
Koval, Michael	R-R	6-1	180	4-20-95	4	6	2.84	40	0	0	3	73	68	25	23	3	21	65	.247	.302	.213	8.01	2.59

Pitching	B-T	HT	WT	DOB	W	L	ERA	G	GS	CG	SV	IP	H	R	ER	HR	BB	SO	AVG	vLH	vRH	K/9	BB/9
Medina, Jeffeson	R-R	6-2	184	5-31-94	7	0	1.94	35	0	0	3	70	47	21	15	2	31	58	.191	.126	.226	7.49	4.00
Miller, Brandon	R-R	6-4	210	6-16-95	9	4	3.65	18	18	0	0	101	96	46	41	11	23	94	.254	.245	.260	8.38	2.05
Mills, Wyatt	R-R	6-3	175	1-25-95	0	1	1.35	11	0	0	4	13	5	2	2	0	6	18	.111	.133	.100	12.15	4.05
Moyers, Steven	R-L	6-0	190	9-23-93	2	3	4.06	25	2	0	1	58	61	26	26	6	13	38	.274	.267	.276	5.93	2.03
Newsome, Ljay	R-R	5-11	210	11-8-96	8	9	4.10	25	25	0	0	130	131	68	59	14	16	111	.259	.323	.212	7.70	1.11
Ratliff, Lane	L-L	6-3	185	3-22-95	2	2	4.45	10	5	0	0	28	35	18	14	4	14	21	.304	.194	.354	6.67	4.45
Ridings, Steven	R-R	6-4	210	2-28-94	2	3	3.55	9	9	0	0	46	43	20	18	2	19	38	.243	.258	.235	7.49	3.74
Rivera, Michael	R-R	6-3	220	6-19-97	1	0	10.13	2	0	0	0	3	4	3	3	1	2	3	.364	.000	.571	10.13	6.75
Roman, Fabian	R-R	6-0	200	11-22-91	0	0	9.35	8	0	0	0	9	15	11	9	1	7	11	.395	.563	.273	11.42	7.27
Sears, JP	R-L	5-11	180	2-19-96	0	1	0.00	10	0	0	3	17	7	2	0	0	9	29	.127	.133	.125	15.35	4.76
Viehoff, Tim	L-L	6-4	200	12-17-93	1	6	4.40	30	8	0	0	88	89	49	43	8	36	79	.262	.311	.244	8.08	3.68
Watson, Tyler	L-L	5-11	175	6-9-93	1	0	3.70	14	0	0	0	24	26	13	10	1	10	29	.277	.286	.274	10.73	3.70
Wells, Nick	L-L	6-5	185	2-21-96	6	10	6.15	25	25	0	0	123	154	90	84	17	43	95	.312	.316	.311	6.95	3.15
Wilcox, Kyle	R-R	6-3	195	6-14-94	0	1	3.78	21	0	0	3	33	26	16	14	4	21	52	.210	.209	.210	14.04	5.67

Fielding

Catcher	PCT	G	PO	A	E	DP	PB
Quevedo	.981	77	615	54	13	7	10
Scott	.990	13	95	8	1	0	2
Thurman	.989	55	422	43	5	4	16

First Base	PCT	G	PO	A	E	DP
Brito	.992	27	243	9	2	19
Hale	1.000	5	38	1	0	2
Morales	1.000	5	23	0	0	1
Quevedo	1.000	18	151	8	0	10
Scott	1.000	5	44	1	0	6
Thurman	.921	6	55	3	5	6
Zammarelli III	.992	76	589	20	5	49

Second Base	PCT	G	PO	A	E	DP
Boyd	.960	7	13	11	1	3
Brigman	.994	80	128	199	2	50
Morales	.984	27	55	66	2	21
Rengifo	.964	25	34	73	4	13
Rosa	.818	3	5	4	2	0

Third Base	PCT	G	PO	A	E	DP
Boyd	.900	2	1	8	1	1
Hale	1.000	1	2	0	0	0
Morales	.917	18	10	34	4	1
Rengifo	.961	21	18	31	2	6
Rizzo	.917	97	58	185	22	19
Zammarelli III	.833	4	3	2	1	0

Shortstop	PCT	G	PO	A	E	DP
Ascanio	.943	40	53	112	10	21
Boyd	.981	10	16	37	1	6
Brigman	.986	35	43	96	2	12
Morales	.927	23	26	50	6	11
Rengifo	.912	31	50	74	12	20

Outfield	PCT	G	PO	A	E	DP
Cooke	1.000	42	88	5	0	3
Jimenez	.976	59	116	6	3	1
Liberato	.987	55	143	8	2	0
Morales	1.000	3	7	0	0	0
Morgan	.983	113	223	11	4	5
Ojeda	.977	73	118	8	3	1
Rengifo	.972	23	34	1	1	0
Slater	1.000	50	90	3	0	0
Zammarelli III	.941	10	15	1	1	1

EVERETT AQUASOX — *SHORT SEASON*

NORTHWEST LEAGUE

Batting	B-T	HT	WT	DOB	AVG	vLH	vRH	G	AB	R	H	2B	3B	HR	RBI	BB	HBP	SH	SF	SO	SB	CS	SLG	OBP
Adams, Johnny	R-R	6-0	200	9-2-94	.316	.300	.320	52	209	39	66	12	0	5	37	17	5	0	4	44	4	3	.445	.375
Andrade, Greifer	R-R	6-0	170	1-27-97	.295	.262	.303	55	207	28	61	11	0	5	35	5	0	2	5	57	0	0	.420	.304
Banuelos, David	R-R	6-0	205	10-1-96	.236	.286	.226	36	127	24	30	8	0	4	26	16	2	1	0	40	1	1	.394	.331
Boyd, Louis	R-R	5-11	169	5-4-94	.250	.000	.333	6	20	2	5	1	0	0	5	3	2	0	1	3	0	0	.300	.385
Camacho, Juan	R-R	6-3	215	4-19-96	.236	.293	.220	47	182	25	43	12	0	5	19	4	2	1	0	46	1	1	.385	.261
Cooke, Billy	R-R	5-10	175	9-26-95	.167	1.000	.000	3	12	1	2	0	0	0	1	1	1	1	0	3	0	0	.167	.286
Dixon, Troy	L-R	6-2	205	4-26-95	.196	.188	.198	28	97	15	19	2	0	2	6	9	1	1	0	28	0	0	.278	.271
Grebeck, Austin	R-R	5-8	155	8-8-94	.227	.300	.210	55	154	30	35	5	3	2	22	31	2	3	1	47	7	3	.338	.362
Gregorio, Osmy	R-R	6-2	175	5-27-98	.222	.250	.214	5	18	1	4	0	0	0	3	2	0	0	0	10	1	0	.222	.300
Helder, Eugene	R-R	5-11	165	2-26-96	.304	.302	.305	70	286	44	87	14	5	2	43	19	2	2	5	44	7	3	.409	.346
Hernandez, Brayan	R-R	6-2	175	9-11-97	.252	.333	.232	28	103	9	26	2	4	2	15	7	1	1	0	26	4	1	.408	.306
Lantigua, Jonas	R-L	6-5	205	12-15-94	.231	.429	.188	12	39	3	9	5	0	0	3	2	0	0	0	11	0	0	.359	.268
Montilla, Geoandry	R-R	6-0	165	5-14-96	.250	.000	.286	2	8	0	2	1	0	0	0	0	0	0	0	3	0	0	.375	.250
Pazos, Manny	R-R	5-11	190	1-23-95	.122	.000	.172	13	41	3	5	2	1	0	4	4	0	0	1	15	0	1	.220	.196
Pena, Onil	R-R	6-0	180	11-6-96	.270	.340	.250	71	241	42	65	13	2	10	31	33	5	0	0	78	5	0	.465	.369
Rivera, Jansiel	L-L	6-1	205	8-28-98	.192	.174	.200	25	73	6	14	5	2	2	9	5	0	0	0	32	0	0	.397	.244
Rosa, Joseph	B-R	5-10	165	3-6-97	.296	.229	.313	44	179	32	53	16	4	6	28	22	1	0	1	46	4	5	.531	.374
Rosario, Ronald	L-L	6-2	165	2-8-97	.294	.207	.320	40	126	22	37	6	2	6	17	11	1	0	0	40	1	0	.516	.355
Slater, Johnny	L-L	6-1	190	8-9-95	.357	—	.357	3	14	5	5	0	0	3	5	1	0	0	0	6	1	0	1.000	.400
Stroosma, Aaron	R-R	6-2	205	5-16-94	.213	.200	.217	30	75	11	16	2	1	1	9	11	1	0	0	26	2	0	.307	.322
Torres, Chris	B-R	5-11	170	2-6-98	.238	.296	.222	48	193	44	46	8	6	6	22	25	0	1	1	64	13	3	.435	.324
Venturino, Joe	R-R	6-0	185	7-18-94	.212	.280	.190	57	208	28	44	8	1	1	24	8	5	2	1	31	3	2	.274	.257
White, Evan	R-L	6-3	205	4-26-96	.277	.417	.229	14	47	6	13	1	1	3	12	6	0	0	2	6	1	1	.532	.346

Pitching	B-T	HT	WT	DOB	W	L	ERA	G	GS	CG	SV	IP	H	R	ER	HR	BB	SO	AVG	vLH	vRH	K/9	BB/9
Bell, Randy	R-R	5-10	190	2-11-95	0	2	4.94	13	13	0	0	31	41	22	17	1	5	29	.308	.318	.300	8.42	1.45
Boches, Scott	R-R	6-5	205	10-17-94	0	0	3.00	1	0	0	0	3	2	1	1	1	3	0	.182	.143	.250	0.00	9.00
Bonilla, Feliberto	R-R	6-2	165	4-21-98	0	0	4.15	2	0	0	0	4	1	2	2	0	4	1	.077	.000	.100	2.08	8.31
Castellanos, Chris	L-L	5-10	185	5-8-95	2	0	3.09	5	0	0	0	12	9	4	4	1	4	15	.214	.200	.219	11.57	3.09
Chandler, Clay	R-R	6-3	180	4-27-94	0	1	3.38	3	2	0	0	13	10	5	5	0	5	12	.222	.154	.250	8.10	3.38
Clancy, Matt	B-L	5-11	180	4-1-94	0	1	2.76	22	0	0	7	33	28	16	10	2	13	49	.215	.244	.202	13.50	3.58
Cloyd, Tyler	R-R	6-3	210	5-16-87	0	0	0.00	1	1	0	0	1	1	0	0	0	0	0	.250	.000	.333	0.00	0.00
Covelle, Paul	R-R	6-0	205	9-12-93	0	0	3.57	14	0	0	2	23	17	13	9	4	6	18	.195	.086	.269	7.15	2.38
De la Cruz, Adonis	R-R	6-2	170	12-20-94	2	2	3.28	18	0	0	0	36	38	21	13	3	17	32	.273	.294	.261	8.07	4.29
Elledge, Seth	R-R	6-3	230	5-20-96	0	0	4.50	4	0	0	0	4	2	2	2	0	2	7	.154	.000	.333	15.75	4.50
Ellingson, David	R-R	6-2	200	1-23-95	2	3	5.23	16	0	0	3	21	26	16	12	1	6	21	.296	.344	.268	9.15	2.61
Gerber, David	R-R	6-1	200	9-24-94	0	0	3.38	5	0	0	3	5	5	2	2	1	1	8	.238	.333	.167	13.50	1.69
Hammond, Ted	R-R	6-2	195	12-17-93	1	2	4.45	20	0	0	1	30	43	25	15	1	8	18	.323	.354	.306	5.34	2.37

Pitching	B-T	HT	WT	DOB	W	L	ERA	G	GS	CG	SV	IP	H	R	ER	HR	BB	SO	AVG	vLH	vRH	K/9	BB/9
Hernandez, Anjul	R-R	6-2	192	1-2-96	2	2	6.28	8	6	0	0	29	36	21	20	4	17	34	.305	.315	.297	10.67	5.34
Hernandez, Carlos	R-R	6-3	195	2-8-96	0	0	2.08	2	0	0	0	4	3	1	1	0	1	3	.188	.167	.200	6.23	2.08
Hesslink, David	L-R	6-2	190	4-12-95	0	2	5.60	15	0	0	0	27	38	30	17	6	14	22	.314	.432	.262	7.24	4.61
Inman, Ryne	R-R	6-5	215	5-13-96	2	4	4.79	7	6	0	0	36	33	21	19	5	10	37	.241	.222	.257	9.34	2.52
Jaskie, Oliver	L-L	6-3	210	11-17-95	0	1	6.82	13	10	0	0	30	43	27	23	5	13	33	.333	.429	.307	9.79	3.86
Kuzminsky, Scott	R-R	6-2	195	11-1-91	1	0	1.08	7	0	0	3	8	7	1	1	0	1	10	.219	.267	.177	10.80	1.08
McAfee, Brian	R-R	6-3	210	9-30-92	0	1	4.18	6	6	0	0	24	36	15	11	1	4	14	.350	.439	.290	5.32	1.52
Mills, Wyatt	R-R	6-3	175	1-25-95	0	1	2.57	7	0	0	2	7	3	2	2	0	3	11	.120	.182	.071	14.14	3.86
Mobley, Cody	R-R	6-3	190	9-23-96	1	1	12.46	2	1	0	0	4	5	6	6	0	2	3	.294	.143	.400	6.23	4.15
Ratliff, Lane	L-L	6-3	185	3-22-95	1	0	6.00	2	1	0	0	9	12	6	6	0	5	10	.316	.556	.241	10.00	5.00
Ridings, Steven	R-R	6-4	210	2-28-94	1	2	3.25	6	2	0	0	28	26	11	10	3	13	28	.250	.349	.180	9.11	4.23
Rivera, Michael	R-R	6-3	220	6-19-97	2	2	3.38	11	0	0	0	21	19	9	8	1	9	21	.244	.200	.271	8.86	3.80
Roman, Fabian	R-R	6-0	200	11-22-91	1	1	9.88	11	0	0	0	14	23	17	15	1	7	14	.383	.346	.412	9.22	4.61
Santiago, Jose	R-R	6-1	190	3-1-94	3	6	5.82	15	8	0	0	65	66	51	42	6	36	50	.263	.340	.214	6.92	4.98
Sears, JP	R-L	5-11	180	2-19-96	1	1	1.69	7	0	0	0	11	6	4	2	0	3	22	.154	.333	.100	18.56	2.53
Suarez, Michael	L-L	6-2	180	3-21-95	7	2	4.87	13	5	0	0	57	68	33	31	4	19	57	.301	.283	.307	8.95	2.98
Torres, Andres	R-R	6-3	185	10-31-95	7	2	3.65	15	15	0	0	74	82	36	30	6	22	64	.278	.370	.198	7.78	2.68
Watson, Tyler	L-L	5-11	175	6-9-93	0	1	6.00	6	0	0	0	12	17	12	8	0	4	21	.321	.333	.314	15.75	3.00

Fielding

C: Banuelos 27, Camacho 35, Dixon 15, Montilla 2. **1B:** Camacho 2, Helder 5, Lantigua 9, Pena 61, White 8. **2B:** Adams 10, Boyd 3, Helder 7, Pazos 5, Rosa 33, Venturino 22. **3B:** Adams 25, Helder 49, Pazos 6, Torres 1, Venturino 4. **SS:** Adams 20, Boyd 4, Gregorio 5, Helder 1, Rosa 9, Torres 44. **OF:** Andrade 50, Banuelos 1, Cooke 3, Dixon 1, Grebeck 53, Helder 12, Hernandez 26, Pazos 4, Rivera 24, Rosario 39, Slater 3, Stroosma 14, Venturino 28.

AZL MARINERS — *ROOKIE*

ARIZONA LEAGUE

Batting	B-T	HT	WT	DOB	AVG	vLH	vRH	G	AB	R	H	2B	3B	HR	RBI	BB	HBP	SH	SF	SO	SB	CS	SLG	OBP
Aplin, Andrew	L-L	6-0	205	3-21-91	.333	—	.333	2	3	2	1	0	0	0	0	1	0	0	0	0	0	0	.333	.500
Boyd, Louis	R-R	5-11	169	5-4-94	.321	.385	.286	28	109	20	35	14	1	0	25	9	1	0	0	19	4	2	.468	.378
Contreras, Danny	L-L	6-3	195	5-21-98	.056	.200	.000	6	18	0	1	0	0	0	0	1	0	0	0	9	0	0	.056	.105
Costello, Ryan	L-R	6-2	200	6-13-96	.331	.297	.343	44	142	31	47	13	3	8	38	26	1	0	3	38	3	1	.634	.430
Eldridge, Caleb	L-L	6-3	235	7-3-95	.298	.300	.297	38	131	19	39	8	2	4	21	12	1	0	1	50	1	0	.481	.359
Garcia, Ryan	L-L	6-2	205	7-8-95	.228	.182	.242	51	197	27	45	14	3	5	44	19	4	0	4	50	3	4	.406	.304
Gregorio, Osmy	R-R	6-2	175	5-27-98	.220	.302	.196	50	191	28	42	7	3	2	23	17	2	6	3	70	14	1	.319	.286
Hoover, Connor	L-R	5-10	185	7-18-96	.267	.262	.270	49	131	40	35	6	3	2	19	43	11	0	0	46	16	4	.405	.481
Jimenez, Anthony	R-R	5-11	165	10-21-95	.333	.500	.286	4	9	1	3	1	1	0	1	0	0	0	0	2	0	0	.667	.333
Larsen, Jack	L-L	6-1	195	1-13-95	.312	.364	.299	34	109	28	34	4	6	3	23	33	0	0	0	33	5	4	.541	.472
Lewis, Kyle	R-R	6-4	210	7-13-95	.263	.333	.217	11	38	9	10	2	1	1	7	4	2	0	2	14	1	0	.447	.348
Lovett, James	R-R	6-3	200	5-27-94	.186	.111	.206	17	43	5	8	3	0	0	4	6	2	0	0	14	1	0	.256	.314
Montilla, Geoandry	R-R	6-0	165	5-14-96	.218	.281	.198	37	133	23	29	10	2	3	15	18	3	1	1	49	4	2	.391	.323
Moses, DeAires	L-L	5-9	170	11-30-95	.283	.302	.276	48	159	36	45	3	5	0	15	15	2	2	0	49	24	6	.365	.352
Mota, Ismerling	R-R	6-1	185	9-2-97	.228	.214	.232	39	127	13	29	4	1	1	12	11	3	0	2	19	0	0	.299	.301
O'Malley, Shawn	B-R	5-11	175	12-28-87	.385	.333	.400	5	13	6	5	0	1	1	2	4	1	0	0	2	1	0	.769	.556
Pazos, Manny	R-R	5-11	190	1-23-95	.256	.412	.213	31	78	12	20	5	2	0	11	16	1	2	2	23	0	1	.372	.381
Rivera, Jansiel	L-L	6-1	205	8-28-98	.172	.167	.177	12	29	3	5	1	0	0	4	8	0	0	0	11	0	0	.207	.351
Rosario, Ronald	L-L	6-2	165	2-8-97	.232	.077	.279	13	56	5	13	6	0	1	8	2	0	0	0	19	0	1	.393	.259
Sandoval, Jose	R-R	6-2	195	10-23-96	.204	.226	.194	38	103	17	21	1	1	2	11	11	4	3	1	35	4	0	.291	.303
Santa, Kevin	L-R	5-11	175	3-9-95	.394	.083	.463	19	66	20	26	2	1	2	12	10	3	1	2	9	8	2	.546	.482
Taylor, Logan	R-R	6-1	200	9-22-93	.286	1.000	.167	3	7	1	2	0	0	0	0	2	0	0	0	1	0	0	.286	.444
Torres, Chris	B-R	5-11	170	2-6-98	.222	.286	.000	4	9	1	2	0	2	0	1	3	0	0	0	5	1	0	.667	.417
Valle, Sebastian	R-R	6-1	215	7-24-90	.000	—	.000	1	1	0	0	0	0	0	0	0	0	0	0	0	0	0	.000	.000
Walton, Donnie	L-R	5-10	184	5-25-94	.313	.667	.231	5	16	2	5	0	0	2	5	1	0	0	0	0	2	0	.688	.353

Pitching	B-T	HT	WT	DOB	W	L	ERA	G	GS	CG	SV	IP	H	R	ER	HR	BB	SO	AVG	vLH	vRH	K/9	BB/9
Benitez, Jorge	L-L	6-2	155	6-1-99	1	0	7.82	13	10	0	0	25	28	25	22	1	20	24	.280	.250	.290	8.53	7.11
Boches, Scott	R-R	6-5	205	10-17-94	0	0	3.55	5	0	0	0	13	11	7	5	0	5	13	.229	.182	.269	9.24	3.55
Bonilla, Feliberto	R-R	6-2	165	4-21-98	1	3	9.40	9	4	0	0	30	48	38	31	4	23	15	.356	.340	.364	4.55	6.98
Capen, George	R-R	6-3	185	12-23-94	0	1	9.82	6	0	0	0	7	16	8	8	0	3	9	.432	.500	.400	11.05	3.68
Carlson, Sam	R-R	6-4	195	12-3-98	0	0	3.00	2	2	0	0	3	4	1	1	0	0	3	.364	.000	.444	9.00	0.00
Castellanos, Chris	L-L	5-10	185	5-8-95	0	1	2.53	10	0	0	0	21	21	9	6	1	1	37	.241	.286	.227	15.61	0.42
Chandler, Clay	R-R	6-3	180	4-27-94	0	2	3.86	11	6	0	0	35	35	18	15	5	7	39	.257	.211	.276	10.03	1.80
Delaplane, Sam	R-R	5-11	175	3-27-95	2	1	2.90	14	0	0	0	31	27	14	10	2	8	47	.223	.196	.240	13.65	2.32
Fairchild, Michael	R-R	6-2	220	9-20-94	2	0	3.00	8	1	0	0	24	22	11	8	0	8	11	.256	.267	.250	4.13	3.00
Fortunato, Ivan	R-R	6-1	170	12-1-98	1	0	5.40	4	3	0	0	5	4	3	3	1	2	7	.222	.143	.273	12.60	3.60
Franks, AJ	R-R	6-2	170	6-25-95	2	0	0.71	7	0	0	1	13	9	3	1	0	1	11	.196	.333	.107	7.82	0.71
Gerber, David	R-R	6-1	200	9-24-94	1	1	1.50	3	0	0	1	6	3	3	1	0	1	8	.150	.000	.200	12.00	1.50
Hernandez, Anjul	R-R	6-2	192	1-2-96	3	2	3.34	7	4	0	0	30	29	18	11	3	12	32	.250	.318	.208	9.71	3.64
Horstman, Ryan	L-L	6-1	185	7-20-92	0	0	0.00	1	1	0	0	1	1	0	0	0	0	1	.250	.000	.333	9.00	0.00
Hutchison, Austin	R-R	6-1	205	4-9-95	2	1	2.08	9	2	0	0	22	20	6	5	2	4	24	.260	.148	.320	9.97	1.66
Jackson, Tyler	R-R	6-6	210	10-22-93	0	0	1.35	4	0	0	0	7	3	1	1	1	0	10	.125	.000	.177	13.50	0.00
Kerr, Raymond	L-L	6-2	185	9-10-94	0	0	0.00	1	0	0	0	1	0	0	0	0	0	2	.000	.000	.000	18.00	0.00
Kober, Collin	R-R	6-1	185	9-8-94	3	3	3.06	13	0	0	3	18	12	7	6	1	5	21	.197	.280	.139	10.70	2.55
Marshall, Evan	R-R	6-2	225	4-18-90	0	0	0.00	1	1	0	0	1	0	0	0	0	0	0	.000	.000	.000	0.00	0.00
Martinez, Edwin	R-R	6-6	240	7-31-95	2	0	4.43	5	1	0	0	20	20	10	10	3	13	13	.256	.294	.227	5.75	5.75
McCaughan, Darren	R-R	6-1	195	3-18-96	0	1	3.75	9	0	0	2	12	9	5	5	0	3	18	.205	.083	.250	13.50	2.25

Pitching	B-T	HT	WT	DOB	W	L	ERA	G	GS	CG	SV	IP	H	R	ER	HR	BB	SO	AVG	vLH	vRH	K/9	BB/9
Mobley, Cody	R-R	6-3	190	9-23-96	2	1	5.79	7	3	0	0	28	34	24	18	3	16	18	.306	.429	.265	5.79	5.14
Munoz, Luis	R-R	6-1	220	11-4-96	0	0	3.86	2	2	0	0	2	3	1	1	0	0	2	.333	.333	.333	7.71	0.00
Paez, Paul	L-L	5-7	210	4-29-92	0	0	0.00	2	1	0	0	3	2	0	0	0	0	2	.200	.333	.143	6.75	0.00
Perez, Ulises	R-R	6-3	160	7-14-97	0	1	18.00	2	2	0	0	2	5	4	4	0	1	2	.455	.000	.833	9.00	4.50
Pistorese, Joe	L-L	6-2	175	10-15-92	0	0	0.00	2	0	0	0	3	2	0	0	0	1	4	.222	.000	.250	13.50	3.38
Razo, Orlando	L-L	5-11	185	2-7-95	1	2	8.56	14	1	0	1	27	41	29	26	0	14	26	.357	.409	.344	8.56	4.61
Rivera, Michael	R-R	6-3	220	6-19-97	1	0	0.00	2	0	0	0	3	2	0	0	0	0	3	.182	.143	.250	9.00	0.00
Roberts, Max	L-L	6-6	190	7-23-97	1	1	5.18	10	7	0	0	24	32	17	14	2	9	18	.314	.333	.306	6.66	3.33
Romero, Tommy	L-R	6-2	225	7-8-97	5	1	2.08	13	2	0	0	43	27	12	10	0	15	51	.188	.115	.228	10.59	3.12
Scribner, Evan	R-R	6-3	190	7-19-85	0	0	0.00	1	1	0	0	1	1	0	0	0	0	0	.250	.000	.333	0.00	0.00
Simmons, Shae	R-R	5-11	190	9-3-90	0	0	0.00	1	1	0	0	1	1	0	0	0	0	2	.333	.500	.000	18.00	0.00
Suarez, Michael	L-L	6-2	180	3-21-95	0	0	1.42	2	0	0	1	6	4	2	1	0	4	8	.167	.200	.158	11.37	5.68
Surrey, Elliot	L-L	6-0	190	2-22-94	0	0	0.00	1	1	0	0	1	0	0	0	0	1	0	.000	—	.000	0.00	9.00
Viydo, Mitch	R-R	6-4	210	6-12-93	1	1	4.50	6	0	0	0	8	6	6	4	0	8	5	.231	.091	.333	5.63	9.00
Wade, Jamal	R-R	6-0	205	2-8-96	0	1	1.83	13	0	0	2	20	11	4	4	0	7	27	.159	.217	.130	12.36	3.20

Fielding

C: Lovett 9, Montilla 28, Mota 21, Pazos 8, Valle 1. **1B:** Contreras 6, Costello 5, Eldridge 32, Garcia 19. **2B:** Boyd 7, Gregorio 5, Hoover 38, O'Malley 2, Pazos 7, Santa 5, Walton 3. **3B:** Boyd 15, Costello 34, Gregorio 13, Hoover 1, Taylor 1. **SS:** Boyd 6, Gregorio 34, Hoover 9, Santa 12, Torres 3. **OF:** Aplin 1, Boyd 1, Garcia 31, Jimenez 1, Larsen 32, Lewis 8, Moses 45, Pazos 9, Rivera 12, Rosario 13, Sandoval 35.

DSL MARINERS — ROOKIE

DOMINICAN SUMMER LEAGUE

Batting	B-T	HT	WT	DOB	AVG	vLH	vRH	G	AB	R	H	2B	3B	HR	RBI	BB	HBP	SH	SF	SO	SB	CS	SLG	OBP
Batista, Freuddy	R-R	6-0	182	12-12-99	.268	.160	.299	34	112	11	30	5	2	1	8	14	3	0	0	30	1	1	.375	.364
Branche, Steve	R-R	6-1	165	9-1-97	.167	.177	.165	35	102	13	17	7	0	0	5	7	2	1	1	36	2	1	.235	.232
Campos, Alexander	R-R	6-0	178	2-20-00	.290	.227	.307	59	207	37	60	10	0	2	26	41	3	2	1	39	7	10	.367	.413
Cano, Jose	R-R	5-11	190	12-18-96	.000	—	.000	2	3	0	0	0	0	0	0	0	0	0	0	1	0	0	.000	.000
Contreras, Danny	L-L	6-3	195	5-21-98	.182	.231	.167	19	55	9	10	2	0	1	9	17	0	0	0	8	1	0	.273	.375
Garcia, Jepherson	R-R	6-2	185	4-19-99	.211	.205	.213	50	166	21	35	4	0	3	18	15	6	0	0	58	1	3	.289	.300
Izturis Jr., Cesar	B-R	5-11	145	11-11-99	.269	.212	.290	63	249	34	67	7	1	0	21	19	5	5	2	42	7	2	.305	.331
Joseph, Luis	B-R	5-9	160	9-20-96	.243	.377	.189	55	185	23	45	4	0	0	18	9	1	0	0	28	5	3	.265	.282
Munoz, Oberto	R-R	6-0	170	2-18-97	.200	.205	.198	43	130	20	26	5	1	0	17	27	4	0	0	35	2	0	.254	.354
Ochoa, Sebastian	R-R	6-1	180	5-8-98	.298	.377	.270	65	235	34	70	10	1	1	25	21	8	4	0	39	5	3	.362	.375
Perez, Miguel	R-R	6-2	170	8-21-00	.149	.250	.129	27	74	8	11	3	1	0	5	15	1	1	1	29	2	1	.216	.297
Perez, Nolan	B-R	6-1	190	5-9-99	.277	.255	.283	57	206	27	57	11	1	4	40	21	5	2	3	33	2	1	.398	.353
Perez, Robert	R-R	6-1	170	6-26-00	.217	.250	.206	66	249	27	54	14	0	4	35	19	5	0	4	68	6	2	.321	.282
Santos, Daniel	R-R	6-2	175	1-25-99	.207	.241	.198	44	140	18	29	8	1	1	14	16	11	1	3	31	2	2	.300	.329
Veloz, Luis	R-R	6-4	180	12-15-99	.180	.244	.162	60	189	21	34	1	0	0	11	21	1	3	0	43	1	4	.185	.265

Pitching	B-T	HT	WT	DOB	W	L	ERA	G	GS	CG	SV	IP	H	R	ER	HR	BB	SO	AVG	vLH	vRH	K/9	BB/9
Alcantara, Luis	R-R	6-0	180	9-30-99	1	0	9.35	7	0	0	0	9	10	9	9	2	4	3	.294	.333	.280	3.12	4.15
Arias, Dayeison	R-R	6-1	160	1-7-97	2	3	3.41	25	0	0	8	29	22	13	11	1	9	36	.222	.229	.219	11.17	2.79
Bonilla, Feliberto	R-R	6-2	165	4-21-98	0	1	1.64	3	2	0	0	11	10	3	2	0	3	5	.263	.273	.259	4.09	2.45
Canela, Jose	R-R	6-0	167	12-10-95	0	1	6.58	24	0	0	0	40	46	33	29	6	13	24	.288	.286	.288	5.45	2.95
Cruz, Aronny	L-L	6-2	175	7-23-95	2	5	4.05	22	0	0	2	33	41	23	15	3	9	29	.304	.393	.280	7.83	2.43
Cuenca, Saul	R-R	6-5	195	3-22-98	2	1	1.63	15	0	0	2	28	16	7	5	1	15	21	.170	.129	.191	6.83	4.88
Escobar, Melquiades	R-R	6-1	175	1-31-00	0	1	4.66	6	0	0	0	10	8	6	5	2	3	10	.229	.250	.217	9.31	2.79
Espinal, Erik	R-R	5-9	155	11-14-96	5	2	1.40	20	5	0	2	58	44	12	9	1	6	51	.207	.162	.230	7.91	0.93
Espino, Elias	R-R	6-2	195	4-19-97	4	2	1.90	11	10	0	0	47	37	15	10	0	13	38	.208	.175	.223	7.23	2.47
Guzman, Carlos	R-L	6-1	170	1-28-97	1	0	4.63	23	0	0	0	23	19	14	12	1	13	27	.221	.125	.243	10.41	5.01
Marte, Cristhopher	R-R	6-2	170	4-2-99	2	6	3.64	14	14	0	0	59	56	29	24	0	25	36	.250	.197	.275	5.46	3.79
Martinez, Edwin	R-R	6-6	240	7-31-95	3	2	3.73	16	6	0	0	51	53	28	21	2	19	31	.282	.294	.275	5.51	3.38
Mercedes, Juan	R-R	6-2	190	4-3-00	1	2	2.43	10	2	0	0	30	26	10	8	0	4	20	.243	.280	.232	6.07	1.21
Nunez, Kelvin	R-R	6-1	170	12-10-99	1	4	3.54	15	13	0	0	56	51	25	22	1	20	40	.234	.192	.255	6.43	3.21
Ozoria, Jesus	R-R	6-2	195	6-1-98	0	2	6.75	6	5	0	0	16	19	13	12	0	7	14	.284	.148	.375	7.88	3.94
Pedrol, Christian	R-R	5-11	190	6-15-00	1	1	2.25	4	0	0	0	8	3	2	2	0	0	10	.111	.111	.111	11.25	0.00
Perez, Daury	R-R	6-4	170	11-3-98	0	0	13.50	7	0	0	0	7	9	10	10	0	14	4	.321	.357	.286	5.40	18.90
Then, Juan	R-R	6-1	155	2-7-00	2	2	2.64	13	13	0	0	61	50	23	18	3	15	56	.220	.228	.216	8.22	2.20
Trinidad, Edinson	R-R	6-2	186	5-12-95	3	4	3.90	25	0	0	0	30	28	26	13	1	9	24	.237	.302	.200	7.20	2.70

Fielding

C: Batista 28, Munoz 10, Santos 39. **1B:** Branche 15, Cano 1, Contreras 18, Garcia 17, Munoz 25. **2B:** Branche 9, Campos 3, Izturis Jr. 41, Joseph 20. **3B:** Branche 9, Campos 5, Izturis Jr. 1, Joseph 10, Perez 53. **SS:** Campos 48, Izturis Jr. 21, Perez 4. **OF:** Garcia 10, Joseph 18, Ochoa 61, Perez 58, Perez 23, Veloz 57.

Tampa Bay Rays

SEASON IN A SENTENCE: The Rays won 80 games for the second time in three seasons thanks to a team-record 228 home runs. Nevertheless, they faded from contention in the second half and wound up with their fourth consecutive losing season.

HIGH POINT: The Rays weren't streaky; they never won more than four games in a row. They won six of seven bookending the all-star break to get to a season-best seven games over .500 on July 18, including winning four of their first five on a West Coast road trip. Closer Alex Colome, who led the majors with 47 saves, locked up three of the victories, all of the one-run variety. Adeiny Hechavarria, a July trade pickup, and Shane Peterson had ninth-inning, RBI singles in Oakland in the last win of the streak, a 4-3 victory.

LOW POINT: The fading Rays were essentially finished off by the Red Sox in a 13-6 loss in Tampa, as Boston scored three in the ninth to tie the game (aided by a Danny Espinosa error). Boston scored seven in the 15th to finish it off.

NOTABLE ROOKIES: Righthander Jake Faria became the latest Rays prospect to break through into the rotation, and was the team's best starter before an abdominal strain slowed him in the second half. Infielder Daniel Robertson made the Opening Day roster as a utility player, then got regular playing time at second base before injuries disrupted his season.

KEY TRANSACTIONS: When it was contending in the first half, Tampa's new-look front office, featuring president Matt Silverman, GM Erik Neander and senior vice president Chaim Bloom, decided to go for it. The Rays traded prospects to acquire big leaguers, picking up Lucas Duda from the Mets to be a DH (he hit .175 with 13 homers), and acquired Hechavarria from the Marlins to shore up shortstop. Hechavarria's acquisition helped prompt the Rays to trade 2008 No. 1 pick Tim Beckham to the Orioles for 2016 draftee Tobias Myers.

DOWN ON THE FARM: Triple-A Durham won the International League and Triple-A National Championship behind a prospect-laden team led by righthander Brent Honeywell, shortstop Willy Adames and first baseman Jake Bauers. First-round pick Brendan McKay helped lead short-season Hudson Valley to the New York-Penn League championship, while Double-A Montgomery and low Class A Bowling Green made their playoffs.

OPENING DAY PAYROLL: $69,962,532 (29th)

PLAYERS OF THE YEAR

MAJOR LEAGUE

Chris Archer
RHP
10-12, 4.07
Led AL with 34 starts
11.1 SO/9, 3.40 WHIP

MINOR LEAGUE

Brent Honeywell
RHP
(Triple-A)
13-9, 3.82
172 SO, 136 IP

ORGANIZATION LEADERS

BATTING — *Minimum 250 AB

MAJORS			
*	AVG	Corey Dickerson	.282
*	OPS	Logan Morrison	.868
	HR	Logan Morrison	38
	RBI	Evan Longoria	86
MINORS			
*	AVG	Michael Brosseau, Bowling Green, Charlotte	.321
*	OBP	Joe McCarthy, Montgomery	.409
*	SLG	Shane Peterson, Durham	.504
*	OPS	Brandon Lowe, Charlotte, Montgomery	.867
	R	Jesus Sanchez, Bowling Green	81
	H	Jesus Sanchez, Bowling Green	145
	TB	Jesus Sanchez, Bowling Green	227
	2B	Brandon Lowe, Charlotte, Montgomery	39
	3B	Joe McCarthy, Montgomery	8
	HR	Jesus Sanchez, Bowling Green	15
	RBI	Jesus Sanchez, Bowling Green	82
	BB	Joe McCarthy, Montgomery	90
	SO	Josh Lowe, Bowling Green	144
	SB	Cade Gotta, Durham, Montgomery	40

PITCHING — #Minimum 75 IP

MAJORS			
	W	Alex Cobb	12
#	ERA	Jake Faria	3.43
	SO	Chris Archer	249
	SV	Alex Colome	47
MINORS			
	W	Jose Mujica, Charlotte, Montgomery	14
	L	Eduar Lopez, Charlotte	9
	L	Brent Honeywell, Montgomery, Durham	9
	L	Genesis Cabrera, Charlotte, Montgomery	9
	L	Adrian Navas, Bowling Green	9
#	ERA	Travis Ott, Bowling Green, Charlotte	2.06
	G	Kyle Bird, Durham, Montgomery	54
	GS	Jose Mujica, Charlotte, Montgomery	27
	SV	Diego Castillo, Montgomery, Durham	15
	IP	Yonny Chirinos, Montgomery, Durham	168
	BB	Yoel Espinal, Durham, Montgomery, Charlotte	55
	SO	Brent Honeywell, Montgomery, Durham	172
#	AVG	Travis Ott, Bowling Green, Charlotte	.191

2017 PERFORMANCE

President, Baseball Ops: Matt Silverman. **Farm Director:** Mitch Lukevics. **Scouting Director:** Rob Metzler.

Class	Team	League	W	L	PCT	Finish	Manager
Majors	Tampa Bay Rays	American	80	82	.494	t-6th (15)	Kevin Cash
Triple-A	Durham Bulls	International	86	56	.606	2nd (14)	Jared Sandberg
Double-A	Montgomery Biscuits	Southern	76	64	.543	2nd (10)	Brady Williams
High-A	Charlotte Stone Crabs	Florida State	69	66	.511	6th (12)	Michael Johns
Low-A	Bowling Green Hot Rods	Midwest	72	65	.526	t-5th (16)	Reinaldo Ruiz
Short Season	Hudson Valley Renegades	New York-Penn	44	32	.579	3rd (14)	Craig Albernaz
Rookie	Princeton Rays	Appalachian	31	36	.463	7th (10)	Danny Sheaffer
Rookie	GCL Rays	Gulf Coast	28	32	.467	t-12th (17)	Jim Morrison
Overall 2017 Minor League Record			406	351	.536	5th (30)	

ORGANIZATION STATISTICS

TAMPA BAY RAYS

AMERICAN LEAGUE

Batting	B-T	HT	WT	DOB	AVG	vLH	vRH	G	AB	R	H	2B	3B	HR	RBI	BB	HBP	SH	SF	SO	SB	CS	SLG	OBP
Beckham, Tim	R-R	6-1	205	1-27-90	.259	.256	.260	87	317	31	82	5	3	12	36	24	2	1	1	110	5	4	.407	.314
2-team total (50 Baltimore)					.278	.261	.318	137	533	67	148	18	5	22	62	36	4	1	1	167	6	5	.454	.328
Bourjos, Peter	R-R	6-1	175	3-31-87	.223	.260	.179	100	188	27	42	9	3	5	15	12	1	1	1	53	5	4	.383	.272
Casali, Curt	R-R	6-3	235	11-9-88	.333	.500	.200	9	9	2	3	0	0	1	3	3	0	0	1	3	0	0	.667	.462
Dickerson, Corey	L-R	6-1	200	5-22-89	.282	.308	.273	150	588	84	166	33	4	27	62	35	3	0	2	152	4	3	.490	.325
Duda, Lucas	R-L	6-4	255	2-3-86	.175	.140	.188	52	171	20	30	7	0	13	27	23	4	0	2	62	0	0	.444	.285
Espinosa, Danny	R-B	6-0	205	4-25-87	.273	.231	.333	8	22	1	6	0	0	0	0	1	1	0	0	11	0	0	.273	.333
3-team total (77 Los Angeles, 8 Seattle)					.173	.163	.162	93	266	30	46	10	0	6	31	21	5	1	2	109	4	5	.278	.245
Featherston, Taylor	R-R	6-1	185	10-8-89	.180	.143	.200	17	39	6	7	1	0	2	6	5	1	0	2	15	1	0	.359	.277
Hechavarria, Adeiny	R-R	6-0	195	4-15-89	.257	.214	.272	77	265	29	68	12	4	7	24	12	1	1	2	58	4	1	.411	.289
Kiermaier, Kevin	L-R	6-1	215	4-22-90	.276	.255	.289	98	380	56	105	15	3	15	39	31	5	4	1	99	16	7	.450	.338
Longoria, Evan	R-R	6-2	210	10-7-85	.261	.217	.277	156	613	71	160	36	2	20	86	46	6	0	12	109	6	1	.424	.313
Martinez, Michael	B-R	5-9	180	9-16-82	.077	.000	.091	13	26	1	2	0	0	0	0	3	0	0	0	10	0	0	.077	.172
2-team total (14 Cleveland)					.162	.250	.429	27	37	2	6	1	0	0	0	5	0	1	0	15	0	1	.189	.262
Miller, Brad	L-R	6-2	215	10-18-89	.201	.220	.195	110	338	43	68	13	3	9	40	63	2	0	4	110	5	3	.337	.327
Morrison, Logan	L-L	6-3	245	8-25-87	.246	.233	.251	149	512	75	126	22	1	38	85	81	5	0	3	149	2	0	.516	.353
Norris, Derek	R-R	6-0	235	2-14-89	.201	.191	.204	53	179	21	36	5	0	9	24	12	3	0	4	48	1	0	.380	.258
Peterson, Shane	L-L	6-0	225	2-11-88	.253	.167	.260	30	79	9	20	5	0	2	11	5	2	0	1	21	2	0	.392	.310
Plouffe, Trevor	R-R	6-2	215	6-15-86	.168	.222	.106	42	101	9	17	2	0	2	5	12	1	0	0	30	0	1	.248	.263
2-team total (58 Oakland)					.198	.294	.183	100	283	31	56	7	0	9	19	28	1	0	1	88	1	2	.318	.272
Puello, Cesar	R-R	6-2	220	4-1-91	.200	.158	.273	16	30	6	6	0	0	0	2	4	1	0	0	11	0	0	.200	.314
2-team total (1 Los Angeles)					.206	.000	.333	17	34	6	7	0	0	0	3	4	1	0	0	12	2	0	.206	.308
Ramos, Wilson	R-R	6-1	260	8-10-87	.260	.310	.240	64	208	19	54	6	0	11	35	10	0	0	3	36	0	0	.447	.290
Rasmus, Colby	L-L	6-2	195	8-11-86	.281	.182	.291	37	121	17	34	7	1	9	23	7	0	0	1	45	1	0	.579	.318
Robertson, Daniel	R-R	5-11	200	3-22-94	.206	.185	.216	75	218	22	45	7	2	5	19	29	4	1	2	73	1	1	.326	.308
Smith, Mallex	L-R	5-10	180	5-6-93	.270	.268	.270	81	256	33	69	8	4	2	12	23	0	2	1	62	16	5	.356	.329
Souza Jr., Steven	R-R	6-4	225	4-24-89	.239	.262	.230	148	523	78	125	21	2	30	78	84	7	2	1	179	16	4	.459	.351
Sucre, Jesus	R-R	6-0	200	4-30-88	.256	.231	.263	62	176	20	45	6	0	7	29	7	3	2	4	35	2	0	.409	.290
Weeks Jr., Rickie	R-R	6-0	210	9-13-82	.217	.177	.261	37	97	13	21	6	0	2	8	12	3	0	0	49	1	0	.340	.321

Pitching	B-T	HT	WT	DOB	W	L	ERA	G	GS	CG	SV	IP	H	R	ER	HR	BB	SO	AVG	vLH	vRH	K/9	BB/9
Alvarado, Jose	L-L	6-2	245	5-21-95	0	3	3.64	35	0	0	0	30	24	12	12	1	9	29	.216	.298	.156	8.80	2.73
Andriese, Matt	R-R	6-2	225	8-28-89	5	5	4.50	18	17	0	1	86	90	48	43	16	28	76	.264	.216	.301	7.95	2.93
Archer, Chris	R-R	6-2	195	9-26-88	10	12	4.07	34	34	0	0	201	193	101	91	27	60	249	.246	.263	.232	11.15	2.69
Boxberger, Brad	R-R	6-2	205	5-27-88	4	4	3.38	30	0	0	0	29	23	11	11	4	11	40	.215	.214	.216	12.27	3.38
Cedeno, Xavier	L-L	5-11	210	8-26-86	1	1	12.00	9	0	0	0	3	7	5	4	3	4	0	.438	.444	.429	0.00	12.00
Cishek, Steve	R-R	6-6	215	6-18-86	2	1	1.09	26	0	0	0	25	13	3	3	0	7	26	.153	.250	.105	9.49	2.55
2-team total (23 Seattle)					3	2	2.01	49	0	0	1	45	26	10	10	3	14	41	.167	.150	.196	8.26	2.82
Cobb, Alex	R-R	6-3	205	10-7-87	12	10	3.66	29	29	0	0	179	175	78	73	22	44	128	.254	.225	.274	6.42	2.21
Colome, Alex	R-R	6-1	220	12-31-88	2	3	3.24	65	0	0	47	67	57	27	24	4	23	58	.232	.227	.236	7.83	3.11
De Leon, Jose	R-R	6-1	220	8-7-92	1	0	10.13	1	0	0	0	3	4	3	3	1	3	2	.333	.500	.167	6.75	10.13
Diaz, Jumbo	R-R	6-4	315	2-27-84	1	4	5.70	31	0	0	0	30	32	20	19	4	15	28	.271	.300	.256	8.40	4.50
Faria, Jake	R-R	6-4	235	7-30-93	5	4	3.43	16	14	0	0	87	71	35	33	11	31	84	.225	.174	.248	8.72	3.22
Farquhar, Danny	R-R	5-9	185	2-17-87	2	2	4.11	37	0	0	0	35	28	16	16	2	22	33	.230	.207	.250	8.49	5.66
2-team total (15 Chicago)					4	2	4.20	52	0	0	0	49	39	23	23	3	28	45	.223	.207	.250	8.21	5.11
Garton, Ryan	R-R	5-10	190	12-5-89	0	1	8.71	7	0	0	0	10	13	10	10	3	5	9	.310	.263	.348	7.84	4.35
2-team total (13 Seattle)					0	1	4.91	20	0	0	0	22	18	12	12	4	6	16	.220	.273	.069	6.55	2.45
Hu, Chih-Wei	R-R	6-0	220	11-4-93	1	1	2.70	6	0	0	0	10	5	4	3	2	4	9	.143	.143	.143	8.10	3.60
Hunter, Tommy	R-R	6-3	250	7-3-86	3	5	2.61	61	0	0	1	59	43	18	17	6	14	64	.202	.171	.224	9.82	2.15
Jennings, Dan	L-L	6-3	210	4-17-87	0	0	3.44	29	0	0	0	18	18	7	7	2	12	13	.257	.297	.212	6.38	5.89
2-team total (48 Chicago)					3	1	3.45	77	0	0	0	63	53	27	24	8	31	51	.228	.297	.212	7.32	4.45
Kittredge, Andrew	R-R	6-1	200	3-17-90	0	1	1.76	15	0	0	0	15	13	4	3	2	6	14	.220	.200	.231	8.22	3.52
Kolarek, Adam	L-L	6-3	205	1-14-89	1	0	6.48	12	0	0	0	8	9	6	6	2	4	4	.290	.364	.250	4.32	4.32

Name	B-T	HT	WT	DOB	W	L	ERA	G	GS	CG	SV	IP	H	R	ER	HR	BB	SO	AVG	vLH	vRH	K/9	BB/9
Marks, Justin	L-L	6-3	205	1-12-88	0	0	6.75	1	0	0	0	1	2	1	1	1	1	1	.333	—	.333	6.75	6.75
Moreno, Diego	R-R	6-1	180	7-21-87	0	1	4.76	5	0	0	0	6	6	4	3	1	2	6	.261	.200	.308	9.53	3.18
Odorizzi, Jake	R-R	6-2	190	3-27-90	10	8	4.14	28	28	0	0	143	117	80	66	30	61	127	.220	.210	.228	7.97	3.83
Pruitt, Austin	R-R	5-10	180	8-31-89	7	5	5.31	30	8	0	1	83	103	55	49	11	22	66	.300	.250	.340	7.16	2.39
Ramirez, Erasmo	R-R	5-10	215	5-2-90	4	3	4.80	26	8	0	1	69	66	39	37	10	16	55	.252	.263	.245	7.14	2.08
2-team total (11 Seattle)					5	6	4.39	37	19	0	1	131	123	70	64	22	31	109	.248	.278	.217	7.47	2.12
Roe, Chaz	R-R	6-5	190	10-9-86	0	0	1.04	9	0	0	0	9	4	1	1	1	3	12	.143	.100	.167	12.46	3.12
Romo, Sergio	R-R	5-11	185	3-4-83	2	0	1.47	25	0	0	0	31	19	6	5	2	7	28	.178	.194	.169	8.22	2.05
Snell, Blake	L-L	6-4	200	12-4-92	5	7	4.04	24	24	0	0	129	113	65	58	15	59	119	.234	.182	.243	8.28	4.11
Stanek, Ryne	R-R	6-4	215	7-26-91	0	0	5.85	21	0	0	0	20	26	13	13	6	12	29	.317	.278	.348	13.05	5.40
Whitley, Chase	R-R	6-4	220	6-14-89	2	1	4.08	41	0	0	2	57	48	29	26	4	16	43	.222	.227	.219	6.75	2.51
Wood, Hunter	R-R	6-1	165	8-12-93	0	0	0.00	1	0	0	0	0	0	0	0	0	0	0	.000	.000	—	0.00	0.00

Fielding

Catcher	PCT	G	PO	A	E	DP	PB
Casali	1.000	8	42	5	0	0	0
Norris	.986	53	414	19	6	2	6
Ramos	.992	62	469	38	4	1	5
Sucre	1.000	61	435	21	0	3	4

First Base	PCT	G	PO	A	E	DP
Duda	.989	24	165	10	2	9
Featherston	1.000	2	3	1	0	0
Morrison	.993	126	1015	59	8	91
Plouffe	.987	11	70	8	1	11
Weeks Jr.	1.000	12	70	4	0	8

Second Base	PCT	G	PO	A	E	DP
Beckham	.968	17	28	32	2	11
Espinosa	.895	6	9	8	2	1
Featherston	.943	11	10	23	2	3
Martinez	.969	8	13	18	1	5
Miller	.969	98	133	213	11	58
Plouffe	1.000	3	0	2	0	0
Robertson	.993	41	47	86	1	20

Third Base	PCT	G	PO	A	E	DP
Beckham	1.000	1	1	0	0	0
Espinosa	.000	1	0	0	0	0
Featherston	1.000	2	0	1	0	0
Longoria	.968	142	96	267	12	33
Martinez	1.000	3	0	2	0	0
Plouffe	.929	12	15	11	2	1
Robertson	.971	17	10	24	1	6

Shortstop	PCT	G	PO	A	E	DP
Beckham	.963	70	67	169	9	33
Espinosa	1.000	2	0	2	0	0
Featherston	1.000	3	1	1	0	0
Hechavarria	.987	77	89	205	4	36
Robertson	.961	24	26	48	3	6

Outfield	PCT	G	PO	A	E	DP
Bourjos	1.000	86	119	3	0	
O Dickerson	.995	93	182	4	1	2
Kiermaier	.976	97	242	5	6	1
Martinez	1.000	1	1	0	0	0
Peterson	1.000	20	37	1	0	0
Puello	1.000	9	10	1	0	0
Rasmus	1.000	30	54	4	0	1
Robertson	.000	1	0	0	0	0
Smith	.980	78	142	2	3	2
Souza Jr.	.976	139	242	5	6	1

DURHAM BULLS — *TRIPLE-A*

INTERNATIONAL LEAGUE

Batting	B-T	HT	WT	DOB	AVG	vLH	vRH	G	AB	R	H	2B	3B	HR	RBI	BB	HBP	SH	SF	SO	SB	CS	SLG	OBP
Adames, Willy	R-R	6-0	200	9-2-95	.277	.319	.260	130	506	74	140	30	5	10	62	65	3	1	3	132	11	5	.415	.361
Bauers, Jake	L-L	6-1	195	10-6-95	.263	.279	.257	132	486	79	128	31	1	13	63	78	5	1	5	112	20	3	.412	.368
Brett, Ryan	R-R	5-9	180	10-9-91	.250	.200	.280	12	40	2	10	5	0	0	3	0	0	0	0	7	1	0	.375	.250
Casali, Curt	R-R	6-3	235	11-9-88	.263	.235	.274	85	300	36	79	10	0	5	48	37	4	1	1	65	0	0	.347	.351
Featherston, Taylor	R-R	6-1	185	10-8-89	.200	.200	.200	31	120	12	24	5	0	4	15	7	1	0	1	58	2	0	.342	.248
2-team total (46 Lehigh Valley)					.237	.200	.200	77	257	34	61	13	0	7	35	28	3	0	3	92	8	0	.370	.316
Field, Johnny	R-R	5-10	180	2-20-92	.261	.290	.248	111	445	62	116	35	1	12	57	26	3	2	4	98	12	7	.425	.303
Gillaspie, Casey	B-L	6-4	240	1-25-93	.227	.242	.219	95	353	45	80	15	2	9	44	36	1	0	5	77	1	1	.357	.296
2-team total (30 Charlotte)					.223	.242	.219	125	458	62	102	20	2	15	62	50	1	0	6	100	1	1	.373	.297
Goetzman, Granden	R-R	6-4	200	11-14-92	.314	.368	.294	17	70	10	22	3	1	1	13	3	0	0	0	17	5	1	.429	.343
Gotta, Cade	R-R	6-4	205	8-1-91	.267	.292	.258	27	90	14	24	6	1	0	5	2	1	0	1	17	9	3	.356	.287
Hager, Jake	R-R	6-1	170	3-4-93	.229	.267	.218	73	271	29	62	9	3	4	26	13	5	0	2	43	3	4	.328	.275
Kay, Grant	R-R	6-0	185	5-29-93	.357	1.000	.250	5	14	3	5	1	0	0	0	2	0	0	0	4	0	0	.429	.438
Leonard, Patrick	R-R	6-4	225	10-20-92	.268	.224	.285	131	503	69	135	32	1	12	70	40	6	0	4	131	15	2	.408	.327
Marjama, Mike	R-R	6-2	205	7-20-89	.274	.240	.287	72	263	32	72	16	1	9	51	21	7	0	1	53	3	3	.445	.343
McKenry, Michael	R-R	5-10	205	3-4-85	.209	.230	.201	73	225	28	47	14	0	4	25	42	3	0	2	73	0	1	.324	.338
Miller, Brad	L-R	6-2	215	10-18-89	.429	1.000	.333	2	7	1	3	0	0	1	1	1	0	0	0	2	0	0	.857	.500
O'Conner, Justin	R-R	6-0	190	3-31-92	.194	.118	.220	20	67	3	13	4	0	1	3	1	2	0	1	21	0	0	.299	.225
Peterson, Shane	L-L	6-0	225	2-11-88	.286	.247	.302	76	280	39	80	19	3	12	40	11	2	2	4	63	10	0	.504	.313
Plouffe, Trevor	R-R	6-2	215	6-15-86	.227	.125	.286	7	22	4	5	1	0	0	1	5	0	0	1	5	0	0	.273	.357
Ramos, Wilson	R-R	6-1	260	8-10-87	.250	.154	.333	8	28	4	7	2	0	2	5	2	0	0	0	1	0	0	.536	.300
Robertson, Daniel	R-R	5-11	200	3-22-94	.372	.231	.433	11	43	7	16	2	0	1	1	3	1	0	0	7	0	1	.488	.426
Smith, Mallex	L-R	5-10	180	5-6-93	.263	.241	.273	45	186	26	49	7	4	3	10	17	0	2	0	45	21	8	.393	.325
Sole, Alec	R-L	6-2	200	6-1-93	.183	.129	.225	22	71	5	13	1	0	0	1	4	1	0	0	28	1	1	.197	.237
Varona, Dayron	R-R	5-11	185	2-24-88	.268	.273	.267	19	71	11	19	3	3	2	9	5	1	0	0	19	3	1	.479	.325
Weeks Jr., Rickie	R-R	6-0	210	9-13-82	.167	.000	.222	4	12	4	2	0	0	1	2	3	0	0	0	5	0	0	.417	.333
Wong, Kean	L-R	5-11	190	4-17-95	.265	.293	.255	105	377	44	100	21	0	5	44	34	2	2	2	78	14	9	.361	.328

Pitching	B-T	HT	WT	DOB	W	L	ERA	G	GS	CG	SV	IP	H	R	ER	HR	BB	SO	AVG	vLH	vRH	K/9	BB/9
Adkins, Hunter	R-R	6-4	190	9-20-90	0	1	9.00	2	2	0	0	9	9	9	9	4	6	5	.257	.136	.462	5.00	6.00
Alvarado, Jose	L-L	6-2	245	5-21-95	0	2	3.93	16	0	0	1	18	11	8	8	1	13	26	.162	.138	.180	12.76	6.38
Ames, Jeff	R-R	6-4	220	1-31-91	1	1	3.98	46	2	0	2	63	54	29	28	6	35	78	.229	.238	.218	11.08	4.97
Andriese, Matt	R-R	6-2	225	8-28-89	0	0	2.08	1	1	0	0	4	5	1	1	0	0	6	.294	.364	.167	12.46	0.00
Bird, Kyle	L-L	6-2	175	4-12-93	0	0	0.00	1	0	0	0	3	1	3	0	1	1	2	.083	.125	.000	5.40	2.70
Boxberger, Brad	R-R	6-2	205	5-27-88	0	0	2.45	4	0	0	0	4	2	1	1	0	5	7	.154	.200	.125	17.18	12.27
Broadway, Mike	R-R	6-5	215	3-30-87	1	1	0.60	6	4	0	0	15	5	1	1	1	2	18	.100	.037	.174	10.80	1.20
2-team total (13 Syracuse)					1	2	5.85	19	4	0	0	32	31	22	21	5	11	37	.242	.387	.298	10.30	3.06
Castillo, Diego	R-R	6-3	240	1-18-94	3	2	3.38	30	1	0	7	43	38	18	16	2	13	58	.235	.238	.231	12.23	2.74
Chirinos, Yonny	R-R	6-2	170	12-26-93	12	5	2.74	23	22	1	0	141	116	50	43	10	22	120	.227	.244	.209	7.66	1.40
De Leon, Jose	R-R	6-1	220	8-7-92	0	2	6.75	3	3	0	0	12	14	9	9	1	6	14	.292	.417	.167	10.50	4.50

Espinal, Yoel	R-R	6-2	200	11-7-92	2	1	5.96	12	2	0	0	23	16	16	15	2	23	28	.203	.220	.184	11.12	9.13
Faria, Jake	R-R	6-4	235	7-30-93	6	1	3.07	11	11	0	0	59	44	23	20	7	22	84	.204	.182	.232	12.89	3.38
Farquhar, Danny	R-R	5-9	185	2-17-87	0	1	7.36	4	0	0	0	4	2	3	3	0	3	4	.167	.286	.000	9.82	7.36
2-team total (8 Charlotte)					0	1	4.26	12	0	0	1	13	8	6	6	2	5	16	.182	.286	.000	11.37	3.55
Fierro, Edwin	R-R	6-1	200	8-30-93	0	0	11.81	3	0	0	0	5	11	7	7	1	2	4	.458	.462	.455	6.75	3.38
Franco, Mike	R-R	5-11	200	11-30-91	0	0	0.00	1	1	0	0	4	1	0	0	0	6	4	.071	.000	.100	8.31	12.46
Garton, Ryan	R-R	5-10	190	12-5-89	2	0	1.64	24	1	0	4	33	18	6	6	2	16	46	.162	.172	.151	12.55	4.36
Guerrieri, Taylor	R-R	6-2	210	12-1-92	1	0	2.89	2	2	0	0	9	7	3	3	0	2	12	.200	.174	.250	11.57	1.93
Honeywell, Brent	R-R	6-2	180	3-31-95	12	8	3.64	24	24	0	0	124	130	55	50	11	31	152	.268	.257	.280	11.06	2.26
Hu, Chih-Wei	R-R	6-0	220	11-4-93	4	1	3.06	31	4	0	2	62	59	28	21	9	12	57	.251	.289	.211	8.32	1.75
Kittredge, Andrew	R-R	6-1	200	3-17-90	6	1	1.45	41	2	0	2	68	49	14	11	2	16	78	.200	.206	.193	10.27	2.11
Kolarek, Adam	L-L	6-3	205	1-14-89	3	4	1.65	41	0	0	2	44	37	9	8	0	16	46	.226	.225	.226	9.48	3.30
Lawson, Brandon	R-R	6-3	205	12-13-94	0	0	0.00	1	0	0	0	2	0	0	0	0	1	3	.000	.000	.000	13.50	4.50
Marks, Justin	L-L	6-3	205	1-12-88	4	1	4.60	9	1	0	0	16	10	8	8	1	9	15	.182	.160	.200	8.62	5.17
Moreno, Diego	R-R	6-1	180	7-21-87	0	0	1.10	11	0	0	5	16	9	2	2	0	3	17	.158	.182	.125	9.37	1.65
2-team total (9 Columbus)					1	0	0.94	20	0	0	5	29	17	3	3	1	5	27	.170	.158	.208	8.48	1.57
Pike, Chris	R-R	6-1	180	10-11-92	0	0	4.91	1	0	0	1	4	4	2	2	1	2	2	.286	.167	.375	4.91	4.91
Pruitt, Austin	R-R	5-10	180	8-31-89	0	1	2.55	9	4	0	1	25	17	9	7	2	2	33	.189	.222	.139	12.04	0.73
Roe, Chaz	R-R	6-5	190	10-9-86	0	3	3.00	17	0	0	4	21	18	8	7	1	5	35	.220	.256	.180	15.00	2.14
2-team total (1 Gwinnett)					0	4	4.09	18	0	0	4	22	21	11	10	1	6	36	.241	.256	.179	14.73	2.45
Roth, Michael	L-L	6-1	210	2-15-90	2	4	5.08	10	9	0	0	44	50	28	25	11	11	37	.276	.271	.279	7.51	2.23
Schultz, Jaime	R-R	5-10	200	6-20-91	1	0	3.86	13	0	0	0	12	10	5	5	1	4	21	.222	.280	.150	16.20	3.09
Smith, Burch	R-R	6-4	215	4-12-90	2	1	1.65	3	3	0	0	16	9	3	3	2	4	19	.161	.167	.154	10.47	2.20
Smith, Drew	R-R	6-2	190	9-24-93	0	0	0.00	1	0	0	0	1	1	0	0	0	0	0	.333	.500	.000	0.00	0.00
Snell, Blake	L-L	6-4	200	12-4-92	5	0	2.66	7	7	0	0	44	43	13	13	5	15	61	.254	.184	.283	12.48	3.07
Stanek, Ryne	R-R	6-4	215	7-26-91	3	0	1.21	37	0	0	8	45	26	6	6	0	16	60	.167	.221	.100	12.09	3.22
Venters, Jonny	L-L	6-3	200	3-20-85	0	0	0.00	1	0	0	0	1	1	0	0	0	1	2	.250	.000	1.000	18.00	9.00
Wagner, Neil	R-R	6-0	215	1-1-84	0	1	3.07	32	1	0	3	44	37	17	15	3	14	41	.224	.279	.174	8.39	2.86
Whitley, Chase	R-R	6-4	220	6-14-89	0	3	13.00	5	2	0	0	9	13	13	13	6	4	8	.351	.348	.357	8.00	4.00
Winkler, Kyle	R-R	5-11	195	6-18-90	0	2	7.20	8	1	0	0	10	13	8	8	3	7	10	.342	.438	.273	9.00	6.30
Wood, Hunter	R-R	6-1	165	8-12-93	3	1	4.39	19	6	0	0	53	54	28	26	8	20	47	.258	.268	.247	7.93	3.38
Yarbrough, Ryan	R-L	6-5	205	12-31-91	13	6	3.43	26	26	0	0	157	144	65	60	20	39	159	.243	.217	.256	9.10	2.23

Fielding

Catcher	PCT	G	PO	A	E	DP	PB
Casali	.996	53	518	30	2	6	2
Marjama	.985	48	472	41	8	4	0
McKenry	.986	24	200	8	3	0	1
O'Conner	.994	17	164	13	1	1	4
Ramos	1.000	6	48	2	0	0	1

First Base	PCT	G	PO	A	E	DP
Bauers	.984	52	391	30	7	37
Gillaspie	.997	86	715	29	2	65
Leonard	1.000	5	48	0	0	5
Plouffe	1.000	1	6	0	0	2
Weeks Jr.	1.000	2	4	2	0	0

Second Base	PCT	G	PO	A	E	DP
Adames	.979	11	18	29	1	3
Brett	1.000	6	7	16	0	3
Featherston	1.000	4	6	8	0	5
Hager	.993	31	55	94	1	17
McKenry	1.000	1	0	1	0	0
Miller	1.000	1	3	2	0	1
Robertson	1.000	2	1	12	0	1
Wong	.975	90	111	243	9	58

Third Base	PCT	G	PO	A	E	DP
Featherston	.941	7	3	13	1	0
Hager	.939	22	7	24	2	5
Kay	1.000	3	0	3	0	0
Leonard	.962	84	53	124	7	16
McKenry	.000	1	0	0	0	0
Plouffe	.500	2	0	1	1	0
Robertson	.889	3	3	5	1	0
Sole	1.000	14	8	18	0	1
Wong	.913	10	6	15	2	2

Shortstop	PCT	G	PO	A	E	DP
Adames	.949	117	141	307	24	74
Featherston	1.000	3	2	7	0	1
Hager	.946	15	13	40	3	6
Leonard	1.000	1	0	1	0	0
Robertson	1.000	4	7	13	0	4
Sole	.955	5	9	12	1	1

Outfield	PCT	G	PO	A	E	DP
Bauers	.970	74	127	4	4	0
Brett	1.000	6	17	0	0	0
Featherston	.962	15	24	1	1	0
Field	.991	110	227	4	2	2
Goetzman	.935	17	28	1	2	0
Gotta	1.000	26	45	2	0	1
Kay	1.000	2	1	0	0	0
Leonard	.969	39	59	3	2	1
McKenry	1.000	25	15	1	0	0
Peterson	.990	69	96	8	1	1
Smith	1.000	44	81	4	0	3
Varona	.848	17	26	2	5	0

MONTGOMERY BISCUITS — *DOUBLE-A*

SOUTHERN LEAGUE

Batting	B-T	HT	WT	DOB	AVG	vLH	vRH	G	AB	R	H	2B	3B	HR	RBI	BB	HBP	SH	SF	SO	SB	CS	SLG	OBP
Ciuffo, Nick	L-R	6-1	205	3-7-95	.245	.200	.261	102	371	42	91	29	1	7	42	42	0	0	4	95	2	0	.385	.319
Cronenworth, Jake	L-R	6-1	185	1-21-94	.285	.258	.291	38	158	15	45	6	0	1	20	19	1	0	1	19	1	1	.342	.363
Goetzman, Granden	R-R	6-4	200	11-14-92	.225	.167	.239	24	89	13	20	4	3	3	15	6	0	0	0	22	6	1	.438	.274
Gotta, Cade	R-R	6-4	205	8-1-91	.282	.310	.272	94	341	47	96	17	2	5	47	46	0	0	3	65	31	10	.387	.364
James, Mac	R-R	6-1	195	6-2-93	.240	.225	.246	48	154	14	37	5	0	1	12	13	1	2	2	30	0	3	.292	.300
Kay, Grant	R-R	6-0	185	5-29-93	.261	.261	.262	110	417	62	109	36	5	7	54	44	6	0	5	88	14	4	.422	.337
Kelly, Dalton	L-L	6-3	180	8-4-94	.302	.250	.314	53	192	34	58	18	1	7	35	30	6	2	1	58	6	1	.516	.411
Lee, Braxton	L-R	5-10	185	8-23-93	.321	.271	.339	67	262	47	84	9	3	2	16	29	2	4	1	56	12	11	.401	.391
2-team total (60 Jacksonville)					.309	.271	.339	127	476	81	147	21	3	3	37	65	5	11	4	104	20	13	.385	.395
Lowe, Brandon	L-R	6-0	185	7-6-94	.253	.333	.230	24	95	8	24	5	1	2	12	2	1	1	2	26	1	1	.390	.270
Lukes, Nathan	L-R	5-11	185	7-12-94	.270	.239	.277	98	359	46	97	15	5	3	35	32	3	4	6	71	6	8	.365	.330
McCarthy, Joe	L-L	6-3	225	2-23-94	.284	.255	.292	127	454	76	129	31	8	7	56	90	7	0	2	94	20	5	.434	.409
O'Conner, Justin	R-R	6-0	190	3-31-92	.236	.236	.235	65	242	27	57	15	1	7	41	20	6	1	5	72	3	0	.393	.304
Rasmus, Colby	L-L	6-2	195	8-11-86	.100	.000	.154	6	20	3	2	1	0	1	2	2	0	0	1	7	0	0	.300	.174
Russell, Michael	R-R	6-2	200	1-30-93	.246	.287	.233	106	386	56	95	24	3	6	43	28	7	1	9	85	20	6	.371	.302
Sole, Alec	R-L	6-2	200	6-1-93	.194	.000	.265	22	67	5	13	1	0	0	8	5	1	1	1	25	0	0	.209	.257
Sullivan, Brett	L-R	6-1	195	2-22-94	.272	.313	.263	24	92	12	25	5	0	0	7	3	1	0	0	11	4	0	.326	.302

TAMPA BAY RAYS

Batting	B-T	HT	WT	DOB	AVG	vLH	vRH	G	AB	R	H	2B	3B	HR	RBI	BB	HBP	SH	SF	SO	SB	CS	SLG	OBP
Unroe, Riley	B-R	5-10	180	8-3-95	.225	.242	.219	75	245	33	55	10	3	2	30	41	2	7	3	69	6	5	.314	.337
Velazquez, Andrew	B-R	5-10	160	7-14-94	.235	.205	.245	108	374	49	88	17	4	9	37	30	3	6	0	112	18	9	.374	.297
Williams, Justin	L-R	6-2	215	8-20-95	.301	.297	.302	96	366	53	110	21	3	14	72	37	2	0	4	69	6	2	.489	.364
Wong, Kean	L-R	5-11	190	4-17-95	.222	.167	.242	12	45	5	10	1	0	0	4	3	0	1	0	9	3	0	.244	.271

Pitching	B-T	HT	WT	DOB	W	L	ERA	G	GS	CG	SV	IP	H	R	ER	HR	BB	SO	AVG	vLH	vRH	K/9	BB/9
Adkins, Hunter	R-R	6-4	190	9-20-90	1	1	4.15	9	5	0	0	30	32	14	14	3	11	19	.274	.310	.253	5.64	3.26
2-team total (15 Jacksonville)					2	3	4.03	24	6	0	2	58	58	30	26	5	28	37	.264	.310	.253	5.74	4.34
Alvarado, Jose	L-L	6-2	245	5-21-95	2	1	2.38	9	0	0	0	11	4	3	3	1	5	14	.111	.125	.107	11.12	3.97
Askew, Ryan	R-R	6-6	245	12-7-94	0	1	9.00	1	0	0	0	2	5	2	2	0	1	2	.500	.333	.750	9.00	4.50
Baez, Fernando	R-R	6-1	190	2-1-92	1	4	4.42	22	4	0	0	37	27	22	18	5	38	48	.208	.214	.203	11.78	9.33
Bird, Kyle	L-L	6-2	175	4-12-93	4	2	3.03	53	0	0	0	71	64	31	24	2	29	68	.247	.206	.276	8.58	3.66
Brashears, Tyler	L-R	6-1	165	2-24-94	2	2	5.84	11	6	0	0	37	40	27	24	6	24	24	.290	.329	.250	5.84	5.84
Broadway, Mike	R-R	6-5	215	3-30-87	0	1	4.50	17	0	0	1	18	12	10	9	2	12	10	.188	.150	.205	5.00	6.00
Cabrera, Genesis	L-L	6-1	170	10-10-96	5	4	3.62	12	12	0	0	65	75	32	26	6	27	51	.292	.288	.293	7.10	3.76
Castillo, Diego	R-R	6-3	240	1-18-94	1	3	1.86	21	0	0	8	29	20	8	6	1	7	32	.189	.208	.170	9.93	2.17
Chirinos, Yonny	R-R	6-2	170	12-26-93	1	0	2.63	4	4	0	0	27	22	9	8	5	4	21	.225	.239	.212	6.91	1.32
Darnell, Logan	L-L	6-2	220	2-2-89	5	3	3.98	12	12	0	0	75	94	41	33	11	16	54	.306	.303	.307	6.51	1.93
Espinal, Yoel	R-R	6-2	200	11-7-92	1	3	9.00	15	2	0	1	21	16	23	21	2	23	26	.216	.040	.306	11.14	9.86
Fierro, Edwin	R-R	6-1	200	8-30-93	6	4	3.11	30	9	0	1	84	81	35	29	4	21	63	.262	.311	.224	6.75	2.25
Franco, Mike	R-R	5-11	200	11-30-91	5	2	3.15	26	13	0	0	86	66	31	30	8	43	76	.215	.200	.228	7.98	4.52
Gibaut, Ian	R-R	6-3	250	11-19-93	6	1	2.22	43	0	0	10	53	33	21	13	6	26	63	.174	.161	.185	10.77	4.44
Harris, Greg	R-R	6-2	170	8-17-94	3	8	4.90	29	16	0	0	97	93	57	53	15	42	93	.252	.233	.269	8.60	3.88
Harrison, Jordan	R-L	6-1	180	4-9-91	3	3	3.28	53	0	0	2	58	43	22	21	2	43	49	.213	.193	.228	7.65	6.71
Honeywell, Brent	R-R	6-2	180	3-31-95	1	1	2.08	2	2	0	0	13	4	3	3	1	4	20	.100	.000	.174	13.85	2.77
Misiewicz, Anthony	R-L	6-1	190	11-1-94	3	1	3.49	5	5	1	0	28	26	12	11	3	5	24	.239	.211	.254	7.62	1.59
Moss, Benton	R-R	6-2	193	2-21-93	4	5	3.58	13	12	0	0	70	72	37	28	10	18	56	.260	.277	.243	7.17	2.30
Mujica, Jose	R-R	6-2	235	6-29-96	13	8	3.03	25	25	0	0	154	128	56	52	18	44	86	.225	.229	.220	5.02	2.57
Schreiber, Brad	R-R	6-3	225	2-13-91	2	0	6.31	31	1	0	0	41	46	30	29	2	25	38	.282	.313	.260	8.27	5.44
Smith, Drew	R-R	6-2	190	9-24-93	0	0	0.00	3	0	0	0	4	1	0	0	0	0	0	.091	.000	.111	0.00	0.00
Venters, Jonny	L-L	6-3	200	3-20-85	0	0	4.70	8	0	0	0	8	5	4	4	0	4	10	.192	.111	.235	11.74	4.70
Winkler, Kyle	R-R	5-11	195	6-18-90	3	2	3.12	41	0	0	14	43	38	17	15	2	22	42	.238	.295	.202	8.72	4.57
Wood, Hunter	R-R	6-1	165	8-12-93	4	4	4.76	12	12	0	0	70	68	38	37	7	24	68	.259	.274	.242	8.74	3.09

Fielding

Catcher	PCT	G	PO	A	E	DP	PB
Ciuffo	.990	70	521	52	6	2	13
James	.952	14	74	6	4	1	1
O'Conner	.983	45	369	28	7	0	12
Sullivan	.990	14	91	12	1	1	1

First Base	PCT	G	PO	A	E	DP
James	.986	10	71	2	1	11
Kay	.988	18	155	12	2	20
Kelly	.995	49	404	22	2	43
McCarthy	.994	61	439	23	3	40
Russell	1.000	8	64	4	0	6

Second Base	PCT	G	PO	A	E	DP
Kay	.979	10	14	33	1	5
Lowe	.962	24	40	61	4	17
Russell	1.000	22	30	48	0	13
Sole	.972	8	12	23	1	5
Unroe	.974	70	105	200	8	49
Velazquez	1.000	6	16	16	0	6
Wong	1.000	2	8	5	0	1

Third Base	PCT	G	PO	A	E	DP
James	1.000	1	0	1	0	0
Kay	.927	71	52	112	13	15
Russell	.922	51	39	80	10	13
Sole	1.000	9	4	14	0	3
Unroe	1.000	4	5	5	0	0
Velazquez	1.000	2	1	0	0	1
Wong	1.000	8	4	11	0	3

Shortstop	PCT	G	PO	A	E	DP
Cronenworth	.966	35	49	91	5	24
Russell	.927	21	36	53	7	8
Sole	.917	3	3	8	1	0
Velazquez	.964	82	113	210	12	47

Outfield	PCT	G	PO	A	E	DP
Goetzman	1.000	23	36	0	0	0
Gotta	.981	82	203	9	4	4
James	1.000	1	3	0	0	0
Kay	.900	4	9	0	1	0
Lee	.989	67	174	9	2	0
Lukes	.990	92	188	13	2	2
McCarthy	.992	62	122	3	1	0
Rasmus	1.000	4	4	0	0	0
Russell	1.000	2	1	0	0	0
Velazquez	1.000	16	36	2	0	0
Williams	.971	86	158	9	5	0

CHARLOTTE STONE CRABS — *HIGH CLASS A*

FLORIDA STATE LEAGUE

Batting	B-T	HT	WT	DOB	AVG	vLH	vRH	G	AB	R	H	2B	3B	HR	RBI	BB	HBP	SH	SF	SO	SB	CS	SLG	OBP
Boldt, Ryan	L-R	6-2	210	11-22-94	.296	.374	.268	120	440	60	130	22	6	5	62	39	7	2	6	89	23	6	.407	.358
Bourjos, Peter	R-R	6-1	175	3-31-87	.083	.000	.091	3	12	1	1	0	0	1	1	0	0	0	0	2	0	0	.333	.083
Brett, Ryan	R-R	5-9	180	10-9-91	.324	.231	.381	8	34	8	11	3	0	2	2	3	0	0	0	9	3	0	.588	.378
Brosseau, Michael	R-R	5-10	210	3-15-94	.333	.385	.302	19	69	13	23	3	0	1	10	5	6	0	0	15	4	3	.420	.425
Cronenworth, Jake	L-R	6-1	185	1-21-94	.268	.202	.293	87	328	58	88	16	5	2	29	47	3	1	1	69	12	5	.366	.364
Duffy, Matt	R-R	6-2	170	1-15-91	.250	.333	.200	3	8	0	2	0	0	0	0	0	0	0	0	1	0	0	.250	.250
Eureste, Matt	R-L	6-1	175	7-29-93	.100	.000	.200	3	10	1	1	0	0	0	1	0	0	0	0	4	1	0	.100	.100
Fox, Lucius	B-R	6-1	175	7-2-97	.235	.281	.217	30	115	19	27	3	0	1	12	12	3	0	1	33	3	3	.287	.321
Fraley, Jake	L-L	6-0	195	5-25-95	.170	.192	.162	26	94	6	16	3	1	1	12	7	2	0	2	24	1	3	.255	.238
Goetzman, Granden	R-R	6-4	200	11-14-92	.250	.000	.273	3	12	1	3	1	0	0	2	0	0	0	0	2	0	0	.333	.250
Haley, Jim	R-R	6-1	195	2-23-95	.224	.255	.205	42	125	8	28	4	0	0	16	7	1	1	1	31	9	1	.256	.269
Heim, Jonah	B-R	6-4	225	6-27-95	.218	.357	.171	16	55	3	12	3	0	0	8	3	1	0	2	17	1	0	.273	.262
Kelly, Dalton	L-L	6-3	180	8-4-94	.305	.346	.294	69	236	39	72	17	1	2	32	29	5	4	2	55	5	8	.411	.390
Kiermaier, Kevin	L-R	6-1	215	4-22-90	.125	.000	.188	7	24	2	3	1	1	0	1	2	0	0	0	7	0	1	.250	.192
Lowe, Brandon	L-R	6-0	185	7-6-94	.311	.293	.318	90	315	62	98	34	3	9	46	47	3	0	2	65	6	3	.524	.403
Lowe, Nathaniel	L-R	6-4	235	7-7-95	.249	.109	.299	52	173	21	43	10	1	2	24	28	1	0	1	53	1	1	.353	.355
Lukes, Nathan	L-R	5-11	185	7-12-94	.400	.200	.467	6	20	3	8	1	0	0	3	2	0	0	0	4	1	2	.450	.455
Maris, Peter	L-R	5-10	175	9-16-93	.290	.304	.286	104	359	52	104	13	3	6	33	39	1	10	2	42	13	5	.393	.359
Miller, Brad	L-R	6-2	215	10-18-89	.273	.250	.286	4	11	1	3	3	0	0	0	2	0	0	0	2	0	0	.546	.385

Milone, Thomas	L-L	5-11	190	1-26-95	.242	.283	.231	68	215	25	52	14	1	1	17	21	1	1	2	45	2	5	.330	.310
Moreno, Angel	R-R	6-2	200	7-31-96	.229	.250	.219	71	240	22	55	10	2	0	16	19	2	2	1	44	5	5	.288	.290
Olmedo-Barrera, David	L-R	6-1	195	6-22-94	.248	.273	.238	119	440	46	109	17	4	5	46	26	4	1	5	90	19	16	.339	.293
Padlo, Kevin	R-R	6-2	205	7-15-96	.223	.241	.216	64	220	28	49	13	3	6	34	35	0	0	4	60	4	5	.391	.324
Parrett, David	R-R	6-0	200	1-17-94	.333	1.000	.000	2	6	2	2	0	0	1	1	0	0	0	0	2	0	0	.833	.333
Ramos, Wilson	R-R	6-1	260	8-10-87	.143	.000	.200	5	14	0	2	1	0	0	0	1	0	0	0	3	0	0	.214	.200
Rapacz, Josh	R-R	6-1	205	7-10-90	.167	.143	.174	13	30	0	5	0	0	0	5	2	1	1	0	10	0	0	.167	.242
Rasmus, Colby	L-L	6-2	195	8-11-86	.000	—	.000	1	3	0	0	0	0	0	1	0	0	0	0	0	0	0	.000	.000
Robertson, Daniel	R-R	5-11	200	3-22-94	.556	1.000	.500	4	9	3	5	1	0	1	3	1	1	0	0	1	0	0	1.000	.636
Rodriguez, David	R-R	6-1	215	2-25-96	.201	.230	.190	91	303	23	61	12	1	0	24	22	8	1	4	73	1	3	.248	.270
Sanchez, Manny	R-R	6-2	225	10-6-95	.177	.174	.178	19	68	4	12	1	0	0	4	0	0	0	1	18	1	0	.191	.174
Smith, Mallex	L-R	5-10	180	5-6-93	.286	.333	.250	2	7	1	2	0	1	0	0	0	0	0	0	0	0	1	.571	.286
Sole, Alec	R-L	6-2	200	6-1-93	.182	.200	.175	18	55	8	10	1	1	1	4	6	2	1	0	13	5	2	.291	.286
Sullivan, Brett	L-R	6-1	195	2-22-94	.301	.276	.308	83	326	44	98	19	5	8	67	14	2	0	3	29	14	4	.463	.330
Unroe, Riley	B-R	5-10	180	8-3-95	.141	.227	.102	20	71	8	10	3	1	1	2	7	1	2	0	25	3	0	.254	.228

Pitching	B-T	HT	WT	DOB	W	L	ERA	G	GS	CG	SV	IP	H	R	ER	HR	BB	SO	AVG	vLH	vRH	K/9	BB/9
Adkins, Hunter	R-R	6-4	190	9-20-90	0	0	5.06	2	0	0	0	5	8	3	3	0	1	2	.381	.400	.375	3.38	1.69
Andriese, Matt	R-R	6-2	225	8-28-89	0	0	6.00	2	2	0	0	3	5	2	2	1	1	2	.357	.500	.250	6.00	3.00
Baez, Fernando	R-R	6-1	190	2-1-92	2	2	2.35	10	0	0	0	15	11	5	4	1	9	27	.193	.211	.184	15.85	5.28
Bivens, Blake	R-R	6-2	205	8-11-95	2	3	3.78	10	10	0	0	52	58	28	22	4	17	46	.283	.247	.305	7.91	2.92
Bonnell, Bryan	L-R	6-5	210	9-28-93	0	2	4.09	9	0	0	4	11	11	5	5	2	1	10	.275	.177	.348	8.18	0.82
Boxberger, Brad	R-R	6-2	205	5-27-88	0	1	11.25	4	4	0	0	4	6	5	5	1	2	6	.353	.286	.400	13.50	4.50
Brashears, Tyler	L-R	6-1	165	2-24-94	3	4	7.33	16	7	1	0	47	58	39	38	4	22	37	.304	.333	.285	7.14	4.24
Burke, Brock	L-L	6-4	200	8-4-96	5	6	4.64	13	13	0	0	66	75	43	34	6	16	49	.291	.211	.313	6.68	2.18
Cabrera, Genesis	L-L	6-1	170	10-10-96	4	5	2.84	13	12	0	0	70	45	25	22	3	25	60	.185	.149	.194	7.75	3.23
De Leon, Jose	R-R	6-1	220	8-7-92	1	0	1.88	4	3	0	0	14	11	3	3	0	9	18	.216	.280	.154	11.30	5.65
Diaz, Jumbo	R-R	6-4	315	2-27-84	0	0	0.00	1	1	0	0	1	1	0	0	0	0	0	.333	.333	—	0.00	0.00
Espinal, Yoel	R-R	6-2	200	11-7-92	0	0	0.00	4	0	0	0	6	1	0	0	0	4	7	.059	.000	.077	10.50	6.00
Gibaut, Ian	R-R	6-3	250	11-19-93	1	0	2.16	5	0	0	2	8	5	2	2	0	1	14	.172	.125	.191	15.12	1.08
Hawkins, Taylor	R-R	6-0	205	9-17-93	1	4	6.85	18	2	0	2	43	49	36	33	3	37	21	.287	.267	.297	4.36	7.68
Hunter, Tommy	R-R	6-3	250	7-3-86	0	0	18.00	1	1	0	0	1	3	2	2	0	0	3	.429	.333	.500	27.00	0.00
Jones, Spencer	R-R	6-5	205	9-22-94	2	1	1.71	18	0	0	1	32	19	6	6	0	8	30	.173	.128	.206	8.53	2.27
Karalus, Reece	R-R	6-3	245	6-14-94	4	1	4.18	23	0	0	3	47	49	23	22	5	16	37	.266	.333	.223	7.04	3.04
Lawson, Brandon	R-R	6-3	205	12-13-94	5	5	4.41	35	8	0	4	86	85	45	42	5	20	52	.262	.257	.265	5.46	2.10
Lopez, Eduar	R-R	6-0	180	2-21-95	9	9	3.63	27	21	0	0	144	152	67	58	11	40	82	.275	.243	.300	5.14	2.51
Maisto, Greg	L-L	6-1	180	11-17-94	2	1	4.70	12	0	0	0	15	9	8	8	0	14	8	.173	.118	.200	4.70	8.22
Moats, Dalton	L-L	6-3	195	5-24-95	6	1	2.21	25	0	0	11	41	25	10	10	2	10	26	.185	.122	.213	5.75	2.21
Moreno, Diego	R-R	6-1	180	7-21-87	0	0	0.00	1	1	0	0	1	1	0	0	0	0	2	.250	.000	.500	18.00	0.00
Moss, Benton	R-R	6-2	193	2-21-93	1	1	0.82	2	2	0	0	11	8	4	1	1	1	10	.182	.191	.174	8.18	0.82
Mozingo, Zack	L-R	6-1	215	4-26-94	0	0	0.00	1	0	0	0	3	0	0	0	0	0	1	.000	.000	.000	3.38	0.00
Mujica, Jose	R-R	6-2	235	6-29-96	1	0	3.18	2	2	0	0	11	11	4	4	1	1	4	.250	.211	.280	3.18	0.79
Munoz, Jairo	R-R	6-5	175	8-12-91	0	1	15.00	5	0	0	0	6	9	10	10	1	5	8	.333	.250	.368	12.00	7.50
Odorizzi, Jake	R-R	6-2	190	3-27-90	0	1	6.00	1	1	0	0	3	3	2	2	0	0	6	.250	.286	.200	18.00	0.00
Ott, Travis	L-L	6-4	175	6-29-95	6	1	2.04	20	14	0	2	79	50	21	18	5	35	94	.177	.154	.189	10.66	3.97
Ramirez, Roel	R-R	6-1	210	5-26-95	2	3	5.52	26	6	0	0	59	69	38	36	7	22	53	.299	.283	.309	8.13	3.38
Rodriguez, Noel	R-R	6-3	190	6-17-94	0	1	3.00	14	0	0	0	18	20	8	6	0	6	17	.274	.227	.294	8.50	3.00
Santos, Michael	R-R	6-4	205	5-29-95	4	2	4.03	22	4	0	1	67	84	35	30	2	13	42	.309	.288	.323	5.64	1.75
Schultz, Jaime	R-R	5-10	200	6-20-91	0	1	6.23	3	0	0	1	4	4	3	3	1	2	7	.250	.250	.250	14.54	4.15
Serrapica, Joe	L-R	6-1	215	5-25-94	1	0	7.36	16	0	0	0	22	27	20	18	3	12	20	.297	.303	.293	8.18	4.91
Smith, Burch	R-R	6-4	215	4-12-90	3	1	2.43	9	8	0	0	37	26	12	10	1	20	33	.200	.238	.164	8.03	4.86
Smith, Drew	R-R	6-2	190	9-24-93	0	2	2.20	20	0	0	7	29	26	11	7	1	5	28	.239	.195	.265	8.79	1.57
2-team total (7 Lakeland)					1	2	1.79	27	0	0	7	40	30	13	8	1	9	40	.206	.105	.111	8.93	2.01
Tapia, Alexis	R-R	6-2	240	8-10-95	0	0	1.35	2	2	0	0	7	3	1	1	1	3	9	.130	.100	.154	12.15	4.05
Velasquez, Michael	L-L	6-1	215	2-28-93	4	7	4.58	23	11	0	1	88	110	56	45	10	26	53	.304	.310	.301	5.40	2.65
Venters, Jonny	L-L	6-3	200	3-20-85	0	0	1.80	10	0	0	0	10	5	2	2	0	5	11	.156	.375	.083	9.90	4.50
Vogel, Matt	R-R	6-0	185	7-27-95	0	0	9.00	2	0	0	0	4	1	4	4	0	7	6	.083	.000	.143	13.50	15.75

Fielding

Catcher	PCT	G	PO	A	E	DP	PB
Heim	.984	15	109	16	2	1	1
Parrett	1.000	1	3	0	0	0	0
Ramos	1.000	3	14	3	0	0	1
Rapacz	.875	4	7	0	1	0	0
Rodriguez	.996	68	449	57	2	4	19
Sullivan	.992	51	347	43	3	5	12

First Base	PCT	G	PO	A	E	DP
Brosseau	1.000	3	18	4	0	3
Haley	1.000	1	11	0	0	0
Kelly	.991	65	536	35	5	53
Lowe	.998	51	454	22	1	43
Maris	.990	14	94	7	1	8
Olmedo-Barrera	.919	3	32	2	3	3

Second Base	PCT	G	PO	A	E	DP
Brett	.950	5	6	13	1	1
Brosseau	1.000	2	6	6	0	0
Haley	.821	6	7	16	5	5
Lowe	.958	75	131	189	14	50
Maris	.946	28	57	65	7	20
Miller	1.000	3	6	5	0	1
Robertson	.000	1	0	0	0	0
Sole	1.000	1	2	4	0	2
Unroe	.967	20	34	53	3	9

Third Base	PCT	G	PO	A	E	DP
Brosseau	1.000	7	3	14	0	0
Cronenworth	1.000	3	1	2	0	0
Eureste	.875	3	1	6	1	1
Haley	.934	33	20	37	4	4
Lowe	1.000	2	1	2	0	0
Maris	.898	31	12	41	6	4
Padlo	.921	60	45	107	13	12
Robertson	1.000	1	1	1	0	0
Sole	.938	6	6	9	1	1

Shortstop	PCT	G	PO	A	E	DP
Cronenworth	.963	79	119	219	13	54
Duffy	1.000	3	3	2	0	0
Fox	.962	29	39	89	5	13
Maris	.976	21	28	53	2	12
Robertson	1.000	1	0	1	0	0
Sole	.980	10	19	29	1	8

Outfield	PCT	G	PO	A	E	DP
Boldt	.991	108	215	11	2	1

Bourjos	1.000	2	4	0	0	0
Brett	1.000	2	4	0	0	0
Fraley	.950	26	57	0	3	0
Goetzman	1.000	3	4	0	0	0
Kiermaier	1.000	3	3	0	0	0
Lukes	1.000	5	5	0	0	0
Maris	1.000	5	4	0	0	0
Milone	1.000	66	169	3	0	1
Moreno	.993	69	147	5	1	3
Olmedo-Barrera	.990	111	187	3	2	0
Rasmus	1.000	1	1	0	0	0
Sanchez	.977	17	41	1	1	0
Smith	1.000	2	4	0	0	0

BOWLING GREEN HOT RODS

LOW CLASS A

MIDWEST LEAGUE

Batting	B-T	HT	WT	DOB	AVG	vLH	vRH	G	AB	R	H	2B	3B	HR	RBI	BB	HBP	SH	SF	SO	SB	CS	SLG	OBP
Brosseau, Michael	R-R	5-10	210	3-15-94	.318	.360	.297	80	302	50	96	21	2	6	32	26	12	3	1	48	5	7	.460	.393
Cabrera, Eleardo	L-R	5-11	195	11-8-95	.247	.284	.234	80	279	28	69	11	5	1	24	21	14	5	3	81	4	7	.333	.328
De La Calle, Daniel	R-R	6-3	220	9-18-92	.239	.200	.255	20	67	9	16	5	0	1	13	3	1	0	2	21	0	0	.358	.274
Fox, Lucius	B-R	6-1	175	7-2-97	.278	.209	.308	77	302	45	84	13	3	2	27	33	7	2	1	80	27	10	.361	.362
Gustave, Emilio	R-R	6-2	200	1-26-95	.238	.184	.269	31	105	13	25	3	0	5	19	8	1	1	1	32	5	3	.410	.296
Haley, Jim	R-R	6-1	195	2-23-95	.320	.351	.302	27	100	9	32	6	0	1	14	4	2	0	3	17	2	0	.410	.349
Heim, Jonah	B-R	6-4	225	6-27-95	.268	.298	.254	77	291	45	78	17	1	9	53	27	0	0	3	57	0	1	.426	.327
Lowe, Josh	L-R	6-4	205	2-2-98	.268	.229	.285	118	456	60	122	26	2	8	55	42	0	4	5	144	22	8	.386	.326
Lowe, Nathaniel	L-R	6-4	235	7-7-95	.293	.183	.342	63	229	34	67	13	0	5	35	36	1	0	3	53	0	1	.415	.387
Mastrobuoni, Miles	L-R	5-11	175	10-31-95	.264	.253	.268	104	379	61	100	17	3	3	39	51	0	3	6	66	18	7	.348	.346
Melley, Bobby	L-R	6-3	230	4-10-94	.252	.172	.269	47	159	22	40	6	0	3	23	22	2	0	3	33	0	0	.346	.344
Pinto, Rene	R-R	5-11	195	11-2-96	.283	.375	.249	70	269	30	76	16	2	2	36	17	3	0	4	41	1	0	.379	.328
Rengifo, Luis	B-R	5-10	165	2-26-97	.250	.200	.268	23	96	14	24	3	1	1	8	8	0	0	0	17	5	3	.333	.308
2-team total (102 Clinton)					.250	.290	.235	125	496	79	124	27	5	12	52	41	8	6	3	97	34	17	.397	.316
Roach, Joey	L-R	6-0	205	8-27-93	.111	.143	.091	5	18	1	2	1	0	0	0	0	0	0	0	1	0	0	.167	.111
Rondon, Adrian	R-R	6-1	190	7-7-98	.221	.262	.201	107	394	53	87	12	2	9	48	33	5	1	5	129	4	2	.330	.286
Sanchez, Jesus	L-R	6-3	210	10-7-97	.305	.287	.313	117	475	81	145	29	4	15	82	32	1	0	4	91	7	2	.478	.348
Tenerowicz, Robbie	R-R	6-1	185	1-6-95	.295	.317	.284	94	349	43	103	25	3	11	37	32	8	0	1	67	4	3	.479	.367
Whitley, Garrett	R-R	6-1	195	3-13-97	.249	.271	.239	104	358	65	89	18	4	13	61	57	7	3	1	122	21	4	.430	.362

Pitching	B-T	HT	WT	DOB	W	L	ERA	G	GS	CG	SV	IP	H	R	ER	HR	BB	SO	AVG	vLH	vRH	K/9	BB/9
Bayer, Peter	R-R	6-4	195	3-6-94	2	3	4.84	25	4	0	1	67	57	37	36	5	48	95	.229	.177	.272	12.76	6.45
Burke, Brock	L-L	6-4	200	8-4-96	6	0	1.10	10	10	0	0	57	37	9	7	0	20	59	.181	.094	.221	9.26	3.14
Busfield, J.D.	R-R	6-7	235	5-5-95	5	8	3.38	22	19	1	0	109	111	54	41	12	20	76	.268	.300	.242	6.26	1.65
Clark, Ethan	R-R	6-5	235	10-26-94	3	2	3.11	12	9	0	0	55	37	22	19	2	18	50	.196	.150	.247	8.18	2.95
Clayton, Porter	L-L	6-4	215	5-22-93	1	1	6.23	8	0	0	1	17	24	13	12	0	7	8	.343	.400	.320	4.15	3.63
Jones, Spencer	R-R	6-5	205	9-22-94	0	3	2.72	18	0	0	4	36	38	14	11	0	13	44	.260	.254	.265	10.90	3.22
Long, Sam	L-L	6-1	185	7-8-95	0	0	1.08	6	0	0	0	8	7	2	1	0	10	7	.212	.071	.316	7.56	10.80
Maisto, Greg	L-L	6-1	180	11-17-94	1	0	5.64	15	2	0	2	30	36	22	19	4	14	22	.293	.192	.355	6.53	4.15
McAfee, Brian	R-R	6-3	210	9-30-92	0	3	2.79	11	0	0	1	19	20	7	6	1	8	11	.267	.324	.220	5.12	3.72
McKinley, Jayson	R-R	6-4	210	1-18-94	4	1	4.38	18	0	0	1	39	36	20	19	3	16	39	.243	.197	.276	9.00	3.69
Mendez, Deivy	R-R	6-2	190	10-27-95	2	5	5.53	34	0	0	2	55	48	36	34	6	44	84	.232	.212	.250	13.66	7.16
Moats, Dalton	L-L	6-3	195	5-24-95	0	0	1.21	12	0	0	2	22	14	3	3	1	2	27	.169	.242	.120	10.88	0.81
Moran, Spencer	R-R	6-6	200	4-2-96	1	2	3.70	21	7	0	1	58	62	28	24	2	31	43	.273	.290	.258	6.63	4.78
Navas, Adrian	R-R	6-2	200	4-13-96	12	9	4.73	24	22	0	0	126	117	70	66	18	46	123	.248	.189	.300	8.81	3.29
Ortiz, Willy	R-R	6-1	180	7-20-95	8	3	3.06	16	16	0	0	85	78	32	29	4	35	63	.246	.242	.250	6.64	3.69
Ott, Travis	L-L	6-4	175	6-29-95	4	2	2.09	7	7	0	0	39	30	12	9	1	17	38	.219	.245	.205	8.84	3.96
Pike, Chris	R-R	6-1	180	10-11-92	4	5	5.17	13	13	0	0	71	76	47	41	10	30	43	.285	.266	.305	5.43	3.79
Ramirez, Roel	R-R	6-1	210	5-26-95	1	0	3.00	2	0	0	1	6	5	2	2	1	3	7	.227	.556	.000	10.50	4.50
Ramos, Reimin	R-R	6-1	190	4-27-96	4	2	2.61	28	0	0	6	59	43	19	17	3	25	49	.210	.204	.214	7.52	3.84
Romero, Orlando	R-R	6-0	211	9-26-96	1	4	4.14	24	0	0	7	41	35	24	19	3	24	48	.224	.243	.209	10.45	5.23
Rosenberg, Kenny	L-L	6-1	195	7-9-95	7	7	4.28	24	20	0	1	114	118	62	54	15	40	133	.270	.347	.230	10.53	3.17
Serrapica, Joe	L-R	6-1	215	5-25-94	2	1	2.61	15	0	0	4	21	18	7	6	5	7	21	.240	.258	.227	9.15	3.05
Torres, Elias	R-R	6-1	176	2-22-92	1	2	6.06	11	0	0	1	16	13	11	11	0	10	20	.213	.200	.222	11.02	5.51
Yepez, Angel	R-R	6-1	225	4-27-95	2	1	1.72	5	5	0	0	16	15	4	3	1	2	12	.263	.217	.294	6.89	1.15
York, Mikey	R-R	6-2	190	2-24-96	1	1	1.06	3	3	0	0	17	7	2	2	1	3	16	.127	.200	.067	8.47	1.59

Fielding

Catcher	PCT	G	PO	A	E	DP	PB
De La Calle	.958	19	143	18	7	3	4
Heim	.988	61	506	61	7	5	6
Pinto	.986	54	449	57	7	3	9
Roach	1.000	5	30	2	0	1	0

First Base	PCT	G	PO	A	E	DP
Brosseau	1.000	13	94	7	0	7
Haley	.967	5	27	2	1	1
Lowe	.997	49	338	21	1	30
Melley	.997	40	306	19	1	30
Tenerowicz	.988	33	246	11	3	21

Second Base	PCT	G	PO	A	E	DP
Brosseau	.985	30	52	80	2	22
Haley	1.000	9	9	28	0	3
Mastrobuoni	.992	63	101	134	2	33
Tenerowicz	.953	36	66	96	8	18

Third Base	PCT	G	PO	A	E	DP
Brosseau	.963	31	21	57	3	11
Haley	.912	12	12	19	3	5
Mastrobuoni	1.000	1	0	2	0	0
Rondon	.919	90	47	124	15	11
Tenerowicz	1.000	4	3	5	0	1

Shortstop	PCT	G	PO	A	E	DP
Brosseau	1.000	4	8	8	0	2
Fox	.953	71	112	153	13	30
Haley	1.000	1	1	4	0	1
Mastrobuoni	.964	40	64	95	6	20
Rengifo	.974	23	25	49	2	12

Outfield	PCT	G	PO	A	E	DP
Cabrera	.982	77	151	12	3	4
Gustave	.968	29	59	2	2	0
Haley	1.000	1	1	0	0	0
Lowe	.982	112	269	7	5	0
Sanchez	.981	98	191	11	4	2
Tenerowicz	.000	1	0	0	1	0
Whitley	.985	95	186	9	3	1

HUDSON VALLEY RENEGADES — SHORT SEASON

NEW YORK-PENN LEAGUE

Batting	B-T	HT	WT	DOB	AVG	vLH	vRH	G	AB	R	H	2B	3B	HR	RBI	BB	HBP	SH	SF	SO	SB	CS	SLG	OBP
Benard, Isaac	L-R	5-10	225	1-2-96	.243	.143	.254	46	152	15	37	6	3	0	11	22	1	1	1	48	1	1	.322	.341
Bridgman, Justin	R-R	5-11	175	6-20-95	.286	.250	.308	6	21	2	6	0	0	0	0	1	0	0	0	5	1	0	.286	.318
Brujan, Vidal	B-R	5-9	155	2-9-98	.285	.279	.286	67	260	51	74	15	5	3	20	34	5	3	0	36	16	8	.415	.378
Chester, Carl	R-R	6-0	200	12-12-95	.293	.263	.303	39	147	26	43	7	2	0	17	12	3	0	1	31	8	2	.367	.356
Dacey, Matt	R-L	6-2	205	3-31-94	.255	.250	.256	13	47	6	12	2	2	1	10	5	2	0	0	12	0	0	.447	.352
Eureste, Matt	R-L	6-1	175	7-29-93	.163	.261	.144	46	141	17	23	6	1	1	9	11	8	2	0	46	3	3	.241	.263
Gustave, Emilio	R-R	6-2	200	1-26-95	.252	.320	.233	29	115	17	29	2	0	3	16	10	4	0	1	34	4	3	.348	.331
Law, Zacrey	R-R	6-0	190	7-8-96	.241	.175	.263	60	232	20	56	12	0	3	27	12	10	0	3	38	3	3	.332	.304
Lorenzo, Rafelin	R-R	6-2	218	1-15-97	.250	.233	.255	51	200	30	50	14	1	3	25	9	3	0	1	43	0	1	.375	.291
McKay, Brendan	L-L	6-2	212	12-18-95	.232	.107	.268	36	125	16	29	4	1	4	22	21	2	0	1	33	2	0	.376	.349
Melley, Bobby	L-R	6-3	230	4-10-94	.160	.125	.177	6	25	3	4	0	0	0	1	3	0	0	0	8	0	0	.160	.250
Perez, Angel	R-R	6-2	200	1-10-95	.291	.310	.284	59	220	31	64	6	3	3	19	12	2	0	2	51	3	3	.386	.331
Pujols, Bill	R-R	5-11	160	7-19-94	.214	.147	.231	51	168	21	36	5	1	1	13	14	1	1	0	52	0	0	.274	.279
Ramirez, Jean	R-R	6-0	210	4-27-93	.133	.154	.123	28	83	10	11	2	0	2	6	12	3	0	0	28	0	0	.229	.265
Rojas, Oscar	R-R	5-11	165	7-5-96	.259	.208	.275	61	224	24	58	8	3	2	28	13	3	0	5	46	7	6	.348	.302
Tansel, Deion	R-R	5-8	155	6-4-94	.278	.327	.259	53	191	23	53	11	2	3	33	11	7	0	2	21	7	2	.403	.337
Walls, Taylor	B-R	5-10	180	7-10-96	.213	.241	.207	46	164	22	35	9	0	1	21	29	1	0	3	53	5	4	.287	.330

Pitching	B-T	HT	WT	DOB	W	L	ERA	G	GS	CG	SV	IP	H	R	ER	HR	BB	SO	AVG	vLH	vRH	K/9	BB/9
Disla, Jose	R-R	6-2	165	3-11-96	0	1	5.17	10	0	0	1	16	16	9	9	2	7	7	.262	.172	.344	4.02	4.02
Franklin, Austin	R-R	6-3	215	10-2-97	4	2	2.21	13	13	0	0	69	51	21	17	4	31	71	.207	.228	.189	9.22	4.02
Fulenchek, Garrett	R-R	6-4	205	6-7-96	3	1	5.55	18	0	0	2	24	25	17	15	1	21	29	.272	.355	.230	10.73	7.77
Gist, Andrew	R-L	5-10	192	3-28-95	3	1	2.81	16	1	0	0	32	36	15	10	3	15	29	.293	.268	.305	8.16	4.22
Letkeman, Reign	R-L	6-3	180	5-12-95	1	0	5.79	2	0	0	0	5	2	3	3	0	5	3	.167	.000	.222	5.79	9.64
Linares, Resly	L-L	6-2	170	12-11-97	3	3	2.35	13	12	0	0	61	36	20	16	2	23	60	.171	.133	.181	8.80	3.38
Long, Sam	L-L	6-1	185	7-8-95	1	0	2.70	14	0	0	1	23	20	9	7	0	8	22	.241	.250	.235	8.49	3.09
Lopez, Hector	R-R	6-4	190	6-10-95	2	6	4.38	15	6	0	1	39	33	24	19	0	24	32	.232	.274	.188	7.38	5.54
Maisto, Greg	L-L	6-1	180	11-17-94	1	0	0.00	2	0	0	0	3	1	0	0	0	0	3	.100	.000	.143	9.00	0.00
Mozingo, Zack	L-R	6-1	215	4-26-94	1	2	1.59	16	0	0	10	23	18	12	4	0	6	31	.212	.308	.130	12.31	2.38
Myers, Tobias	R-R	6-0	193	8-5-98	2	0	3.08	5	5	0	0	26	17	9	9	1	4	38	.181	.226	.159	12.99	1.37
2-team total (7 Aberdeen)					4	2	3.54	12	12	1	0	56	45	29	22	1	10	73	.211	.182	.302	11.73	1.61
Padilla, Nicholas	R-R	6-2	220	12-24-96	3	2	2.38	11	7	0	0	34	34	14	9	0	10	29	.262	.224	.292	7.68	2.65
Pelaez, Ivan	L-L	5-11	155	2-1-94	0	0	0.00	4	0	0	0	9	5	0	0	0	2	10	.167	.000	.185	10.00	2.00
Pflughaupt, Blake	L-L	6-0	210	9-4-96	1	0	5.12	12	0	0	1	19	27	15	11	1	6	19	.325	.464	.255	8.84	2.79
Rosillo, Eduard	R-R	6-4	210	12-22-93	2	3	10.17	18	0	0	0	26	28	32	29	1	19	29	.272	.250	.288	10.17	6.66
Salinas, Jhonleider	R-R	6-7	215	9-25-95	3	1	3.49	13	9	0	0	57	47	24	22	3	29	63	.226	.255	.202	10.01	4.61
Schryver, Hunter	L-L	6-1	198	4-3-95	4	0	3.12	20	0	0	6	35	35	13	12	2	5	38	.252	.205	.270	9.87	1.30
Strotman, Drew	R-R	6-3	195	9-3-96	2	3	1.78	11	7	0	0	51	29	13	10	0	9	42	.168	.183	.157	7.46	1.60
Thompson, Dylan	L-R	6-2	180	9-16-96	0	0	3.18	2	0	0	0	6	6	2	2	0	2	3	.273	.357	.125	4.76	3.18
Valverde, Alex	R-R	6-2	185	9-26-96	2	1	1.93	3	2	0	0	14	11	4	3	0	7	13	.229	.313	.188	8.36	4.50
Vogel, Matt	R-R	6-0	185	7-27-95	1	5	5.06	18	0	0	1	32	26	22	18	0	20	41	.217	.365	.103	11.53	5.63
York, Mikey	R-R	6-2	190	2-24-96	4	1	0.82	8	8	0	0	44	28	5	4	2	8	37	.180	.139	.221	7.57	1.64

Fielding

C: Law 50, Lorenzo 14, Ramirez 13. **1B:** Bridgman 3, Dacey 10, Eureste 31, McKay 21, Melley 6, Ramirez 8. **2B:** Bridgman 2, Brujan 65, Pujols 7, Tansel 4. **3B:** Bridgman 1, Dacey 3, Eureste 15, Pujols 38, Tansel 21. **SS:** Pujols 6, Tansel 28, Walls 42. **OF:** Benard 46, Chester 39, Gustave 29, Perez 58, Rojas 59.

PRINCETON RAYS — ROOKIE

APPALACHIAN LEAGUE

Batting	B-T	HT	WT	DOB	AVG	vLH	vRH	G	AB	R	H	2B	3B	HR	RBI	BB	HBP	SH	SF	SO	SB	CS	SLG	OBP
Aranda, Jonathan	L-R	5-10	173	5-23-98	.000	—	.000	1	4	0	0	0	0	0	0	0	0	0	0	3	0	0	.000	.000
Bridgman, Justin	R-R	5-11	175	6-20-95	.301	.298	.302	42	163	21	49	5	0	1	18	11	3	1	1	17	11	2	.350	.354
Brown, Bryce	R-R	6-1	185	7-23-96	.239	.229	.246	51	184	21	44	3	1	0	21	17	10	2	2	53	14	5	.266	.333
Chester, Carl	R-R	6-0	200	12-12-95	.345	.273	.372	29	119	36	41	6	4	0	12	20	5	0	1	12	8	4	.462	.455
Davis, Devin	R-R	6-3	215	2-14-97	.294	.333	.271	54	218	34	64	20	1	10	47	27	2	0	3	48	2	1	.532	.372
Gomez, Moises	R-R	5-11	200	8-27-98	.275	.308	.260	53	211	37	58	11	0	5	28	13	4	0	1	52	10	1	.398	.328
Hair, Trey	L-R	5-10	185	4-21-95	.286	.222	.312	58	217	42	62	18	3	10	49	29	8	0	1	48	5	1	.535	.388
Hernandez, Ronaldo	R-R	6-1	185	11-11-97	.332	.346	.324	54	223	42	74	22	1	5	40	16	4	0	3	39	2	2	.507	.382
King, Billy	L-L	6-3	200	4-30-95	.186	.231	.178	24	86	8	16	3	1	0	5	13	0	1	0	20	0	0	.244	.293
Miller, Andrew	L-R	6-1	200	3-19-97	.169	.182	.165	36	136	19	23	8	1	2	14	12	5	1	0	60	1	1	.287	.261
Roach, Joey	L-R	6-0	205	8-27-93	.305	.357	.294	21	82	13	25	5	0	1	11	10	1	1	1	11	0	1	.402	.383
Rutherford, Zach	R-R	6-2	180	3-13-96	.266	.293	.250	52	218	44	58	16	1	7	35	20	3	3	4	40	4	0	.445	.331
Santana, Yerson	R-R	6-3	195	12-2-96	.000	—	.000	1	4	0	0	0	0	0	0	0	0	0	0	2	0	0	.000	.000
Santiago, Kevin	B-R	6-0	170	9-28-97	.208	.097	.257	30	101	13	21	5	1	2	15	10	4	0	1	47	6	0	.337	.302
Seibert, Mac	R-R	6-0	195	11-17-93	.214	.000	.250	15	42	6	9	1	0	0	2	1	0	0	0	16	1	0	.238	.233
Smith, Michael	L-L	5-11	165	5-30-97	.268	.214	.296	31	123	20	33	2	1	0	10	14	4	0	0	24	6	2	.301	.362
Tonton, Jose	R-R	6-1	205	4-4-96	.193	.103	.241	26	83	14	16	2	3	3	12	5	1	0	1	33	1	1	.398	.244
Whalen, Seaver	R-R	6-2	185	2-5-95	.248	.263	.241	37	121	19	30	7	0	2	10	7	13	1	1	17	3	1	.355	.352

Pitching	B-T	HT	WT	DOB	W	L	ERA	G	GS	CG	SV	IP	H	R	ER	HR	BB	SO	AVG	vLH	vRH	K/9	BB/9
Anderson, Garrett	R-R	6-2	195	3-9-95	0	1	3.55	19	0	0	4	33	35	19	13	3	8	25	.269	.333	.228	6.82	2.18

Arias, Juan Carlos	R-R	6-3	228	9-16-95	1	1	8.10	10	0	0	0	17	17	16	15	0	15	18	.279	.381	.225	9.72	8.10
Askew, Ryan	R-R	6-6	245	12-7-94	3	2	3.18	17	0	0	1	40	39	19	14	0	5	20	.255	.250	.258	4.54	1.13
Day, Tyler	R-R	6-1	185	1-22-94	4	2	2.38	15	0	0	1	34	26	9	9	4	12	25	.220	.200	.233	6.62	3.18
Disla, Jose	R-R	6-2	165	3-11-96	1	0	7.36	6	0	0	0	11	15	9	9	3	7	6	.349	.313	.370	4.91	5.73
Fleming, Josh	R-L	6-2	190	5-18-96	1	2	5.40	12	9	0	0	35	42	23	21	5	7	26	.300	.308	.298	6.69	1.80
Goodbrand, Kyle	R-R	6-2	198	4-22-95	7	1	3.04	11	0	0	1	27	18	9	9	4	6	36	.192	.182	.197	12.15	2.03
Lebron, Thomas	R-R	6-2	160	8-8-95	0	0	13.50	4	0	0	0	9	19	14	14	5	6	8	.404	.375	.435	7.71	5.79
McGee, Easton	R-R	6-6	205	12-26-97	1	3	4.30	11	11	0	0	52	70	27	25	6	7	29	.329	.337	.323	4.99	1.20
Moncada, Luis	L-L	6-1	150	2-28-98	4	2	5.59	13	6	0	0	39	46	27	24	6	18	28	.297	.321	.291	6.52	4.19
Montero, Reynier	R-R	6-2	165	10-29-96	0	1	4.82	5	0	0	1	9	9	7	5	1	10	5	.257	.111	.308	4.82	9.64
O'Brien, Riley	R-R	6-4	170	2-6-95	1	0	2.20	11	10	0	0	41	28	10	10	1	17	40	.211	.216	.207	8.78	3.73
Ortiz, Jesus	R-R	6-2	185	8-4-97	0	1	9.95	4	0	0	0	6	7	9	7	1	6	6	.250	.200	.278	8.53	8.53
Peguero, Joel	R-R	5-11	160	5-5-97	3	5	8.12	13	10	0	0	44	67	43	40	5	11	31	.347	.320	.364	6.29	2.23
Rosa, Jeffrey	R-R	6-3	189	6-5-95	0	0	10.13	13	0	0	0	21	27	26	24	2	24	22	.307	.269	.323	9.28	10.13
Sanchez, Cristopher	L-L	6-5	165	12-12-96	1	6	10.01	13	7	0	0	39	61	48	43	8	16	30	.353	.349	.354	6.98	3.72
Sanders, Phoenix	R-R	5-10	184	6-5-95	2	3	4.42	14	5	0	0	39	42	24	19	7	10	40	.282	.250	.306	9.31	2.33
Thompson, Dylan	L-R	6-2	180	9-16-96	2	2	5.57	11	6	0	0	32	36	22	20	4	20	24	.281	.171	.333	6.68	5.57
Trageton, Zack	R-R	6-1	225	9-2-98	0	4	8.77	11	3	0	0	26	40	29	25	3	12	28	.370	.286	.424	9.82	4.21
Zombro, Tyler	R-R	6-1	190	9-2-94	0	0	3.86	13	0	0	1	26	24	11	11	2	8	23	.245	.355	.194	8.06	2.81

Fielding

C: Hernandez 43, Miller 12, Roach 10, Seibert 7. **1B:** Davis 45, King 21, Seibert 1. **2B:** Aranda 1, Bridgman 11, Hair 51, Santiago 4. **3B:** Bridgman 16, Santiago 18, Whalen 35. **SS:** Bridgman 9, Rutherford 50, Santiago 9. **OF:** Brown 49, Chester 28, Gomez 53, Miller 19, Santana 1, Smith 31, Tonton 24.

GCL RAYS — *ROOKIE*

GULF COAST LEAGUE

Batting	B-T	HT	WT	DOB	AVG	vLH	vRH	G	AB	R	H	2B	3B	HR	RBI	BB	HBP	SH	SF	SO	SB	CS	SLG	OBP
Alvarez, Alexander	R-R	5-11	200	9-14-96	.180	.235	.152	18	50	9	9	4	0	1	9	7	1	0	1	10	2	2	.320	.288
Alvarez, Roberto	R-R	5-11	151	7-28-99	.221	.241	.207	39	136	15	30	5	1	0	13	7	4	2	1	22	2	0	.272	.277
Aranda, Jonathan	L-R	5-10	173	5-23-98	.293	.298	.291	49	174	24	51	9	1	0	15	14	3	0	2	28	14	4	.356	.352
Betts, Chris	L-R	6-2	215	3-10-97	.429	.500	.333	3	7	1	3	2	0	0	1	1	0	0	0	1	1	0	.714	.500
Byrd, Vincent	L-R	6-7	240	10-8-97	.257	.216	.276	34	113	10	29	7	0	1	19	14	2	0	4	52	2	0	.345	.338
Diaz, Pedro	R-R	6-3	210	1-9-99	.177	.250	.137	48	158	18	28	5	0	5	14	7	10	1	0	50	8	4	.304	.257
Fraley, Jake	L-L	6-0	195	5-25-95	.467	.400	.500	4	15	6	7	3	0	1	2	2	0	0	0	3	3	1	.867	.529
Goetzman, Granden	R-R	6-4	200	11-14-92	.233	.182	.263	10	30	3	7	2	0	0	6	7	1	0	1	6	3	0	.300	.385
Leon, Luis	B-R	6-0	175	9-10-98	.205	.215	.200	49	185	24	38	8	2	1	14	12	0	3	0	28	7	1	.287	.254
Muffley, Jordyn	R-R	6-1	195	4-14-97	.150	.177	.130	14	40	6	6	2	0	0	2	3	5	1	0	5	2	1	.200	.292
Ostberg, Erik	L-R	5-10	225	10-12-95	.188	.240	.167	28	85	12	16	3	0	0	4	15	3	1	2	30	1	0	.224	.324
Padlo, Kevin	R-R	6-2	205	7-15-96	.118	.000	.133	5	17	3	2	0	1	0	1	3	1	0	0	1	1	0	.235	.286
Parrett, David	R-R	6-0	200	1-17-94	.000	.000	.000	1	2	1	0	0	0	0	0	1	0	0	0	1	0	0	.000	.333
Pedroza, Cristhian	R-R	5-10	173	2-14-99	.203	.200	.203	26	79	11	16	4	0	0	10	11	2	0	0	19	5	1	.253	.315
Pena, Tony	R-R	5-11	180	9-24-97	.138	.111	.155	33	94	5	13	3	0	0	6	11	2	1	0	39	2	3	.170	.243
Pinto, Rene	R-R	5-11	195	11-2-96	.429	.571	.286	4	14	4	6	1	0	1	3	3	0	0	0	1	0	0	.714	.529
Polanco, Sabriel	R-R	5-11	180	4-4-95	.244	.290	.216	22	82	7	20	2	3	0	9	2	1	0	0	8	3	3	.342	.271
Santana, Yerson	R-R	6-3	195	12-2-96	.237	.382	.159	33	97	11	23	5	1	1	11	13	4	1	2	48	5	3	.340	.345
Smith, Michael	L-L	5-11	165	5-30-97	.381	.273	.500	6	21	5	8	2	1	0	5	3	1	0	0	3	0	1	.571	.480
Smoot, Allen	L-R	6-2	200	4-6-94	.223	.300	.181	36	112	11	25	2	3	0	7	9	4	0	1	24	1	3	.295	.302
Stone, Jake	L-R	6-0	200	1-31-95	.301	.409	.255	45	146	24	44	11	2	2	14	19	3	0	2	34	10	3	.445	.388
Vargas, Carlos	R-R	6-3	170	3-18-99	.245	.156	.290	54	188	21	46	13	0	5	27	19	5	0	0	37	2	2	.394	.330

Pitching	B-T	HT	WT	DOB	W	L	ERA	G	GS	CG	SV	IP	H	R	ER	HR	BB	SO	AVG	vLH	vRH	K/9	BB/9
Arias, Juan Carlos	R-R	6-3	228	9-16-95	1	0	0.00	2	0	0	0	3	4	0	0	0	2	3	.364	.500	.333	9.00	6.00
Bastardo, Armando	R-R	6-0	175	7-11-94	0	0	0.00	2	1	0	0	3	1	0	0	0	1	0	.091	.000	.143	0.00	3.00
Bivens, Blake	R-R	6-2	205	8-11-95	0	0	1.29	2	2	0	0	7	5	2	1	0	0	7	.200	.308	.083	9.00	0.00
Campbell, Paul	L-R	6-0	190	7-26-95	1	0	2.29	9	1	0	1	20	16	6	5	1	6	19	.222	.152	.282	8.69	2.75
Carden, Chris	R-R	6-4	225	8-5-94	1	1	3.86	15	0	0	4	21	18	12	9	0	12	15	.234	.229	.238	6.43	5.14
Charpie, Trevor	R-R	6-1	195	12-30-93	5	1	1.67	14	0	0	1	27	17	8	5	0	6	27	.179	.237	.140	9.00	2.00
De Leon, Jose	R-R	6-1	220	8-7-92	1	0	0.75	3	2	0	0	12	4	1	1	1	1	12	.103	.091	.118	9.00	0.75
Espinal, Yoel	R-R	6-2	200	11-7-92	1	0	0.00	7	1	0	1	11	6	1	0	0	5	14	.154	.222	.095	11.45	4.09
Felipe, Angel	R-R	6-5	190	8-30-97	0	2	14.25	10	0	0	1	12	19	19	19	1	18	14	.359	.400	.304	10.50	13.50
Garcia, Wilson	R-R	6-3	205	10-14-96	4	4	3.78	11	10	0	0	48	53	24	20	3	15	27	.283	.278	.289	5.10	2.83
Goodbrand, Kyle	R-R	6-2	198	4-22-95	0	0	0.00	1	0	0	0	1	0	0	0	0	1	1	.000	.000	.000	9.00	9.00
Hernandez, Ronal	R-R	6-1	175	7-8-94	0	2	5.06	13	0	0	2	27	16	17	15	3	19	19	.170	.209	.137	6.41	6.41
Kirsch, Chris	L-L	6-2	185	11-15-91	0	0	0.00	1	1	0	0	2	1	0	0	0	0	2	.143	.500	.000	9.00	0.00
Lara, Miguel	R-R	5-11	165	7-17-97	2	3	2.59	11	8	0	1	42	25	21	12	3	21	42	.168	.203	.129	9.07	4.54
Lebron, Thomas	R-R	6-2	160	8-8-95	0	0	27.00	1	0	0	0	1	2	2	2	0	1	0	.667	1.000	.000	0.00	13.50
Linares, Wanderson	R-R	6-1	160	9-28-96	2	2	2.70	11	9	0	1	43	32	15	13	1	21	40	.207	.211	.202	8.31	4.36
Marsden, Justin	R-R	6-4	175	1-27-97	0	1	3.68	3	1	0	0	7	7	3	3	0	4	1	.250	.300	.222	1.23	4.91
Mercado, Michael	R-R	6-4	160	4-15-99	0	0	1.69	8	8	0	0	21	21	4	4	1	4	14	.256	.225	.286	5.91	1.69
Montero, Reynier	R-R	6-2	165	10-29-96	1	1	5.27	7	0	0	0	14	12	8	8	2	9	11	.222	.207	.240	7.24	5.93
Mozingo, Zack	L-R	6-1	215	4-26-94	0	0	0.00	2	0	0	0	2	0	0	0	0	1	1	.000	.000	.000	3.86	3.86
Mujica, Arturo	L-L	6-3	181	6-4-96	1	5	2.59	12	3	0	0	31	25	12	9	1	12	31	.216	.214	.216	8.90	3.45
Ortiz, Jesus	R-R	6-2	185	8-4-97	0	1	3.15	8	1	0	0	20	16	8	7	1	5	11	.225	.130	.271	4.95	2.25
Pelaez, Ivan	L-L	5-11	155	2-1-94	3	0	1.80	11	1	0	2	30	26	7	6	0	7	23	.232	.233	.232	6.90	2.10
Pflughaupt, Blake	L-L	6-0	210	9-4-96	0	2	3.86	2	0	0	0	5	4	2	2	0	1	4	.222	.000	.308	7.71	1.93

Rodriguez, Angel	R-R	6-5	229	1-28-98	5	2	4.38	12	1	0	0	39	31	21	19	6	17	35	.212	.183	.233	8.08	3.92
Rosa, Jeffrey	R-R	6-3	189	6-5-95	0	0	5.40	2	1	0	0	5	6	5	3	0	3	7	.286	.375	.231	12.60	5.40
Sanchez, Francisco	L-L	6-1	180	4-24-98	0	3	15.75	6	2	0	0	12	23	21	21	0	11	8	.426	.364	.442	6.00	8.25
Schultz, Jaime	R-R	5-10	200	6-20-91	0	0	0.00	3	1	0	0	4	3	1	0	0	0	4	.200	.143	.250	9.82	0.00
Smith, Burch	R-R	6-4	215	4-12-90	0	1	6.00	1	1	0	0	3	4	2	2	0	0	4	.364	.500	.200	12.00	0.00
Valverde, Alex	R-R	6-2	185	9-26-96	0	1	3.18	4	3	0	0	11	8	5	4	1	2	11	.182	.174	.191	8.74	1.59
Venters, Jonny	L-L	6-3	200	3-20-85	0	0	0.00	5	2	0	0	5	4	0	0	0	1	6	.211	.000	.267	10.80	1.80
Yepez, Angel	R-R	6-1	225	4-27-95	0	0	2.57	2	0	0	0	7	10	3	2	0	0	8	.313	.364	.286	10.29	0.00
Zombro, Tyler	R-R	6-1	190	9-2-94	0	0	0.00	1	0	0	0	1	1	0	0	0	0	1	.250	.500	.000	6.75	0.00

Fielding

C: Alvarez 15, Alvarez 27, Betts 2, Muffley 10, Ostberg 6, Pinto 3. **1B:** Byrd 31, Ostberg 8, Smoot 23. **2B:** Aranda 49, Pedroza 11. **3B:** Leon 9, Padlo 5, Pedroza 14, Smoot 11, Vargas 23. **SS:** Leon 36, Vargas 25. **OF:** Diaz 47, Fraley 3, Goetzman 6, Pena 32, Polanco 22, Santana 30, Smith 6, Stone 44.

DSL RAYS — *ROOKIE*

DOMINICAN SUMMER LEAGUE

Batting	B-T	HT	WT	DOB	AVG	vLH	vRH	G	AB	R	H	2B	3B	HR	RBI	BB	HBP	SH	SF	SO	SB	CS	SLG	OBP
Arcendo, Luis	L-R	6-1	160	11-1-99	.267	.205	.281	59	206	36	55	3	6	1	22	30	4	8	2	39	16	5	.354	.368
Arias, Amador	R-R	5-11	143	8-25-00	.127	.137	.121	48	142	11	18	3	0	0	14	10	4	1	4	42	7	3	.148	.200
Arias, Luis	R-R	6-1	165	10-7-98	.193	.250	.170	53	166	12	32	4	0	0	11	13	2	1	1	70	4	4	.217	.258
Arrendoll, Johampher	L-R	6-2	165	10-15-98	.206	.226	.202	56	165	27	34	8	3	1	19	29	6	5	1	44	2	7	.309	.343
Balbuena, Alfredo	R-R	5-9	178	11-25-98	.237	.371	.172	59	190	18	45	6	4	2	16	24	3	2	0	38	13	5	.342	.332
Bolivar, Roimer	R-R	6-0	175	12-10-99	.184	.230	.161	57	179	18	33	3	1	1	15	21	5	2	1	56	11	8	.229	.286
Brito, Raider	R-R	6-1	164	5-17-99	.225	.235	.220	67	249	21	56	12	1	3	24	14	3	0	1	46	19	4	.317	.273
Chevez, Freddvil	R-R	6-4	200	3-13-00	.221	.122	.244	61	217	27	48	11	1	3	32	25	5	0	3	51	3	1	.323	.312
Del Palacio, Jose	L-R	6-0	185	10-14-98	.188	.139	.216	52	176	18	33	6	1	2	20	15	5	1	2	60	3	1	.267	.268
Garcia, Juan	R-R	6-0	191	1-6-99	.129	.222	.091	9	31	2	4	1	0	0	3	2	0	1	1	4	1	3	.161	.177
Infante, Diego	R-R	6-2	178	10-22-99	.255	.276	.250	43	161	25	41	10	2	0	15	14	0	1	0	33	10	1	.342	.314
Lopez, Angel	R-R	5-11	160	11-14-99	.224	.114	.250	55	183	33	41	6	2	2	18	31	6	1	2	48	5	2	.312	.351
Lopez, Johan	R-R	5-10	167	7-28-00	.219	.265	.196	59	201	24	44	9	1	1	13	17	7	2	0	41	11	6	.289	.302
Martinez, Yunior	B-R	6-1	166	12-24-98	.265	.296	.252	50	189	25	50	1	2	1	5	10	3	2	0	52	35	13	.307	.312
Meza, Julio	R-R	6-0	165	5-4-99	.216	.389	.184	37	116	16	25	8	1	0	8	12	6	3	1	15	1	2	.302	.319
Nelo, Angel	R-R	5-7	164	3-29-00	.235	.171	.263	46	136	11	32	2	0	0	8	11	2	2	0	18	3	1	.250	.302
Pedroza, Cristhian	R-R	5-10	173	2-14-99	.271	.083	.319	16	59	15	16	2	1	1	14	12	2	0	2	8	7	0	.390	.400
Pereira, Jose	R-R	5-11	153	3-3-99	.235	.263	.221	59	179	20	42	2	1	0	14	16	0	6	0	34	10	4	.257	.297
Perez, Luis	R-R	6-0	241	6-16-97	.178	.136	.203	39	118	8	21	5	0	0	7	12	4	1	1	28	4	2	.220	.274
Ramirez, Abiezel	B-R	5-11	160	1-26-00	.217	.211	.219	54	198	25	43	6	4	1	14	27	1	0	0	55	8	7	.303	.314
Sanchez, Aldenis	R-R	6-1	165	9-26-98	.333	.370	.327	50	189	33	63	8	0	1	21	14	3	1	2	33	23	7	.392	.385
Santos, Bryan	L-L	6-0	165	5-4-99	.213	.196	.221	59	183	13	39	13	1	0	15	29	4	3	5	52	1	7	.295	.326
Tejeda, Gioser	R-R	5-11	204	9-23-97	.233	.053	.274	33	103	15	24	8	0	0	15	18	2	0	3	16	1	3	.311	.349
Torrealba, Jose	R-R	6-2	171	10-15-97	.285	.368	.266	58	207	23	59	8	5	0	26	26	7	0	2	49	19	7	.372	.380
Valera, Robert	R-R	6-0	165	9-6-98	.225	.219	.227	51	182	30	41	6	1	0	16	16	6	1	1	20	4	6	.269	.307
Vargas, Jhosner	B-R	5-11	158	1-24-99	.260	.286	.256	27	104	13	27	4	2	0	14	8	0	1	1	24	4	3	.337	.310
Verbel, Dewins	B-R	5-11	160	12-24-99	.152	.160	.150	48	138	13	21	2	0	0	10	28	4	2	2	39	6	2	.167	.308
Villasmil, Fermin	R-R	6-0	165	2-4-00	.273	—	.273	4	11	0	3	0	0	0	1	1	0	0	0	3	0	1	.273	.333

Pitching	B-T	HT	WT	DOB	W	L	ERA	G	GS	CG	SV	IP	H	R	ER	HR	BB	SO	AVG	vLH	vRH	K/9	BB/9
Alejandro, Jose	R-R	6-3	190	6-20-95	1	2	1.59	17	0	0	5	28	11	8	5	0	18	33	.115	.108	.119	10.48	5.72
Alfonzo, Emilio	R-R	6-6	170	8-2-00	5	0	1.71	15	1	0	0	32	10	8	6	0	24	24	.102	.000	.000	6.82	6.82
Arauz, Jaime	R-R	6-0	160	1-31-99	0	0	27.00	1	0	0	0	0	1	1	1	0	3	0	1.000	—	1.000	0.00	81.00
Barrios, Yariel	R-R	6-2	155	4-23-00	0	0	9.00	2	0	0	0	2	1	2	2	0	3	0	.143	.000	.200	0.00	13.50
Casilla, Marquito	R-R	6-2	180	11-12-99	0	1	12.15	12	0	0	0	13	12	22	18	0	24	12	.250	.263	.241	8.10	16.20
Cedeno, Jhoanbert	R-R	6-6	170	2-12-98	3	5	3.26	18	0	0	5	30	30	13	11	1	13	30	.263	.282	.253	8.90	3.86
Cespedes, Ender	R-R	5-11	206	5-30-96	2	4	6.98	17	0	0	2	30	31	31	23	2	21	31	.267	.286	.333	9.40	6.37
Cordero, Dauris	R-R	6-3	186	7-18-99	2	0	5.06	9	2	0	0	16	19	9	9	0	8	9	.307	.217	.359	5.06	4.50
Cuevas, Johan	R-R	6-2	180	5-8-00	1	0	1.86	6	0	0	0	10	5	3	2	0	2	5	.152	.143	.158	4.66	1.86
Dacosta, Franklin	L-L	5-11	162	2-27-00	0	2	4.13	14	3	0	0	33	27	18	15	0	14	27	.223	.238	.220	7.44	3.86
Duran, Luis	R-R	6-1	160	3-4-00	3	2	5.14	17	0	0	0	28	39	19	16	2	11	17	.342	.390	.315	5.46	3.54
Fernandez, Christian	R-R	6-2	170	8-11-99	0	5	3.41	14	14	0	0	61	45	33	23	2	24	52	.216	.133	.263	7.71	3.56
Galan, Jeremy	R-R	6-2	190	10-30-98	3	1	2.17	13	1	0	0	29	22	11	7	2	9	27	.212	.125	.266	8.38	2.79
Garcia, Wilson	R-R	6-3	205	10-14-96	3	0	0.86	5	4	0	0	21	8	4	2	2	2	23	.116	.120	.114	9.86	0.86
Gomez, Carlos	R-R	6-0	170	9-30-99	0	2	5.08	13	0	0	0	28	25	19	16	0	17	13	.253	.263	.246	4.13	5.40
Gonzalez, Edisson	R-R	5-10	160	10-2-99	2	1	2.23	14	7	0	0	44	21	13	11	6	13	60	.138	.106	.152	12.18	2.64
Gonzalez, Ender	R-R	6-2	175	2-26-97	5	3	3.09	18	1	0	3	32	27	15	11	2	14	27	.235	.302	.194	7.59	3.94
Gonzalez, Luis	R-R	6-2	190	4-27-96	1	3	6.53	12	0	0	1	21	24	22	15	0	13	20	.282	.324	.244	8.71	5.66
Herrera, Bryan	R-R	6-2	175	4-22-98	1	3	2.70	13	13	0	0	57	35	19	17	0	36	34	.184	.143	.205	5.40	5.72
Linares, Wanderson	R-R	6-1	160	9-28-96	1	0	1.06	4	4	0	0	17	14	6	2	1	4	15	.212	.250	.200	7.94	2.12
Lopez, Dauris	R-R	6-3	185	10-20-98	2	4	6.53	14	9	0	0	41	32	38	30	4	46	32	.213	.278	.177	6.97	10.02
Lopez, Edward	R-R	6-1	165	1-28-99	0	1	7.98	10	0	0	0	15	15	16	13	1	22	14	.259	.400	.184	8.59	13.50
Lopez, Janick	R-R	6-3	187	4-24-99	4	1	7.71	15	0	0	0	23	25	23	20	3	24	16	.287	.161	.357	6.17	9.26
Lopez, Jose	L-L	6-1	200	2-15-99	2	5	3.08	15	4	0	0	38	21	19	13	1	28	38	.162	.097	.182	9.00	6.63
Lugo, Enyerbeth	R-R	6-3	159	1-4-98	0	0	3.52	19	0	0	6	31	23	17	12	1	20	27	.213	.216	.211	7.92	5.87
Melo, Fernando	L-L	6-6	200	12-31-99	0	1	35.10	5	0	0	0	3	11	17	13	0	7	2	.524	1.000	.412	5.40	18.90
Medina, Luis	R-R	6-2	175	6-18-95	1	2	2.86	16	0	0	1	28	18	15	9	0	19	23	.186	.222	.164	7.31	6.04
Peguero, Matthew	R-R	6-2	200	1-12-00	1	4	3.86	14	6	0	0	35	25	17	15	1	21	25	.203	.293	.178	6.43	5.40

Perez, Eduardo	L-L	6-1	165	9-27-97	0	1	9.00	13	0	0	2	16	15	17	16	1	19	13	.263	.357	.233	7.31	10.69
Prensa, Rafael	R-R	6-4	190	2-15-98	2	6	3.93	14	14	0	0	55	57	29	24	0	19	38	.262	.327	.202	6.22	3.11
Ramirez, Angel	R-R	6-2	180	12-25-96	0	2	4.50	7	6	0	0	24	22	15	12	0	13	24	.234	.205	.255	9.00	4.88
Ramirez, Wikelman	R-R	6-0	183	8-9-00	1	1	1.02	13	9	0	1	35	25	6	4	0	9	29	.200	.150	.224	7.39	2.29
Roca, Jose	R-R	6-0	195	8-27-96	3	0	3.12	14	8	0	2	49	34	20	17	1	30	32	.209	.254	.180	5.88	5.51
Rodriguez, Aldor	R-R	6-1	182	7-4-97	3	6	3.41	14	13	0	0	61	54	29	23	0	24	46	.233	.265	.215	6.82	3.56
Sabino, Stanly	L-L	6-0	150	9-26-97	1	3	2.14	13	12	0	0	55	29	16	13	3	30	57	.154	1.000	.125	9.38	4.94
Sanchez, Leonardo	R-R	6-3	187	12-16-98	0	2	6.04	14	0	0	0	22	24	16	15	0	15	13	.282	.424	.192	5.24	6.04
Sanchez, Rodolfo	R-R	5-10	165	1-12-00	5	1	3.73	17	1	0	4	31	26	16	13	3	15	33	.230	.308	.189	9.48	4.31
Santana, Daniel	R-R	6-2	193	4-16-98	0	0	7.58	13	0	0	0	19	25	16	16	1	11	12	.333	.361	.308	5.68	5.21
Santos, Fraylin	R-R	6-3	195	10-3-98	2	3	1.94	14	10	0	0	51	40	13	11	0	14	32	.222	.277	.191	5.65	2.47
Trinidad, Luis	R-R	6-0	165	5-16-98	1	0	3.00	11	0	0	1	15	10	10	5	0	17	16	.200	.105	.258	9.60	10.20
Ventura, Heriberto	R-R	6-0	160	8-10-98	2	1	3.00	10	0	0	0	18	16	7	6	1	18	6	.246	.409	.163	3.00	9.00

Fielding

C: Meza 33, Nelo 45, Perez 27, Tejeda 25, Valera 15, Villasmil 3. **1B:** Chevez 52, Del Palacio 36, Nelo 1, Pedroza 1, Pereira 1, Perez 12, Santos 24, Tejeda 1, Valera 17, Vargas 1. **2B:** Arias 11, Arias 13, Arcendo 5, Balbuena 40, Garcia 2, Lopez 33, Pedroza 2, Pereira 8, Ramirez 11, Vargas 6, Verbel 16. **3B:** Arias 15, Arias 21, Arcendo 7, Balbuena 18, Lopez 18, Pedroza 6, Pereira 19, Valera 1, Vargas 18, Verbel 26. **SS:** Arcendo 36, Arias 16, Arias 13, Garcia 3, Lopez 42, Pereira 2, Ramirez 34. **OF:** Arrendoll 56, Bolivar 57, Brito 62, Del Palacio 8, Infante 43, Martinez 46, Meza 1, Pedroza 5, Pereira 31, Sanchez 45, Santos 17, Torrealba 56, Valera 11.

Texas Rangers

SEASON IN A SENTENCE: After winning 95 games and topping the American League West in 2016, the Rangers sputtered in 2017, dropping below .500 for just the third time in the last 10 years as several key players regressed.

HIGH POINT: Beginning on May 9, the Rangers won 10 straight games. After a May 21 victory, the Rangers were 24-21, an impressive turnaround after a sluggish start had them at 13-20 to begin the year.

LOW POINT: Righthander Yu Darvish took the mound against the Marlins on July 26 in his last start with the Rangers, but left after allowing 10 runs in 3.2 innings. The Marlins continued with the slaughter, beating the Rangers 22-10. On a broader level, several players either didn't break out or simply went backward. Nomar Mazara's offensive performance was below league-average, Rougned Odor cratered and veterans Jonathan Lucroy and Mike Napoli were holes in the Rangers' lineup.

NOTABLE ROOKIES: The Rangers didn't get much value from their rookies in 2017, in part because some of the players who could have contributed were dealt away in previous years, such as Nick Williams who helped get Cole Hamels from the Phillies. Righthanded reliever Jose LeClerc flashed great stuff to strike out 60 batters in 45.2 innings, but also showed an inability to control where it's going, as he also walked 40.

KEY TRANSACTIONS: At the trade deadline, the Rangers sent Darvish to the Dodgers. They got back second baseman/outfielder Willie Calhoun—a lefthanded hitter with a promising combination of power and bat control—as well as righthander A.J. Alexy and shortstop Brendon Davis from the Dodgers' low Class A club. The Rangers also sent Lucroy to the Rockies in exchange for Pedro Gonzalez, a 6-foot-6 outfielder who had been playing in the Rookie-level Pioneer League.

DOWN ON THE FARM: Not much went right for the Rangers in the minor leagues either. First baseman Ronald Guzman should be ready to make his major league debut in 2018 after hitting .298/.372/.434 in Triple-A Round Rock. The most exciting player in the system, center fielder Leody Taveras, played in low Class A Hickory at 18 and held his own as one of the youngest players in the South Atlantic League. Adding Calhoun helped, but the system remains thin on players who project as everyday regulars in the future.

OPENING DAY PAYROLL: $175,909,063 (6th)

PLAYERS OF THE YEAR

MAJOR LEAGUE
Elvis Andrus
SS
.297/.337/.471
20 HR, 25 SB here
.808 OPS (career best)

MINOR LEAGUE
Yohander Mendez
LHP
(Double-A)
7-8, 3.79 ERA
1.14 WHIP (8th in AA)

ORGANIZATION LEADERS

BATTING		*Minimum 250 AB
MAJORS		
* AVG	Adrian Beltre	.312
* OPS	Adrian Beltre	.915
HR	Joey Gallo	41
RBI	Nomar Mazara	101
MINORS		
* AVG	Carlos Garay, Hickory, Down East	.336
* OBP	Drew Stubbs, Sacramento, Round Rock	.404
* SLG	Will Middlebrooks, Round Rock	.529
* OPS	Drew Robinson, Round Rock	.863
R	Scott Heineman, Frisco	82
H	Isiah Kiner-Falefa, Frisco	148
TB	Ronald Guzman, Round Rock	204
2B	Isiah Kiner-Falefa, Frisco	31
3B	Anderson Tejeda, Hickory	9
HR	Will Middlebrooks, Round Rock	23
RBI	Yanio Perez, Hickory, Down East	66
BB	Eric Aguilera, Frisco	53
SO	LeDarious Clark, Down East	143
SB	Michael O'Neill, Down East, Frisco	28

PITCHING		#Minimum 75 IP
MAJORS		
W	Martin Perez	13
# ERA	Alex Claudio	2.50
SO	Yu Darvish	148
SV	Alex Claudio	11
MINORS		
W	Wes Benjamin, Down East	10
L	Collin Wiles, Frisco	12
# ERA	Kyle Cody, Hickory, Down East	2.64
G	Adam Lowen, Frisco, Round Rock	50
GS	Ariel Jurado, Frisco	27
SV	Ricardo Rodriguez, Down East, Frisco	17
IP	Ariel Jurado, Frisco	157
BB	Pedro Payano, Down East, Frisco	64
SO	Jeffrey Springs, Down East	146
# AVG	Kaleb Fontenot, Hickory	.214

2017 PERFORMANCE

General Manager: Jon Daniels. **Farm Director:** Jayce Tingler. **Scouting Director:** Kip Fagg.

Class	Team	League	W	L	PCT	Finish	Manager
Majors	Texas Rangers	American	78	84	.481	t-9th (15)	Jeff Banister
Triple-A	Round Rock Express	Pacific Coast	66	72	.478	12th (16)	Jason Wood
Double-A	Frisco RoughRiders	Texas	60	80	.429	8th (8)	Joe Mikulik
High-A	Down East Wood Ducks	Carolina	62	77	.446	9th (10)	Howard Johnson
Low-A	Hickory Crawdads	South Atlantic	64	76	.457	11th (14)	Spike Owen
Short Season	Spokane Indians	Northwest	39	37	.513	t-4th (8)	Matt Hagen
Rookie	AZL Rangers	Arizona	30	25	.545	t-5th (15)	Matt Siegel
Overall 2017 Minor League Record			321	367	.467	24th (30)	

ORGANIZATION STATISTICS

TEXAS RANGERS

AMERICAN LEAGUE

Batting	B-T	HT	WT	DOB	AVG	vLH	vRH	G	AB	R	H	2B	3B	HR	RBI	BB	HBP	SH	SF	SO	SB	CS	SLG	OBP
Andrus, Elvis	R-R	6-0	200	8-26-88	.297	.294	.298	158	643	100	191	44	4	20	88	38	3	1	4	101	25	10	.471	.337
Beltre, Adrian	R-R	5-11	220	4-7-79	.312	.388	.293	94	340	47	106	22	1	17	71	39	4	0	6	52	1	0	.532	.383
Calhoun, Willie	L-R	5-8	187	11-4-94	.265	.273	.261	13	34	3	9	0	0	1	4	2	1	0	0	7	0	0	.353	.324
Chirinos, Robinson	R-R	6-1	210	6-5-84	.255	.366	.214	88	263	46	67	13	1	17	38	34	10	1	1	79	1	0	.506	.360
Choo, Shin-Soo	L-L	5-11	210	7-13-82	.261	.287	.254	149	544	96	142	20	1	22	78	77	7	3	5	134	12	3	.423	.357
DeShields, Delino	R-R	5-9	200	8-16-92	.269	.250	.277	120	376	75	101	15	2	6	22	44	3	13	4	109	29	8	.367	.347
Gallo, Joey	L-R	6-5	235	11-19-93	.209	.226	.204	145	449	85	94	18	3	41	80	75	8	0	0	196	7	2	.537	.333
Gomez, Carlos	R-R	6-3	220	12-4-85	.255	.227	.264	105	368	51	94	23	1	17	51	31	19	3	5	127	13	5	.462	.340
Gosselin, Phil	R-R	6-1	200	10-3-88	.125	.000	.167	12	8	0	1	1	0	0	0	0	0	0	0	3	0	0	.250	.125
Hoying, Jared	L-R	6-3	205	5-18-89	.222	.308	.203	36	72	13	16	3	0	1	7	4	0	0	1	23	3	0	.306	.260
Jimenez, A.J.	R-R	6-0	195	5-1-90	.083	.000	.200	7	12	0	1	0	0	0	0	0	0	1	0	7	0	0	.083	.083
Kozma, Pete	R-R	6-0	190	4-11-88	.111	.188	.050	28	36	4	4	0	0	1	2	2	2	1	0	18	0	1	.194	.200
2-team total (11 New York)					.111	.188	.050	39	45	6	5	0	0	1	2	3	2	1	0	20	0	1	.178	.200
Lucroy, Jonathan	R-R	6-0	200	6-13-86	.242	.254	.238	77	281	27	68	15	0	4	27	19	4	0	2	32	1	0	.338	.297
Mazara, Nomar	L-L	6-4	215	4-26-95	.253	.228	.260	148	554	64	140	30	2	20	101	55	4	0	3	127	2	2	.422	.323
Middlebrooks, Will	R-R	6-3	220	9-9-88	.211	.417	.115	22	38	5	8	2	2	0	3	1	0	0	0	14	0	0	.368	.231
Napoli, Mike	R-R	6-1	225	10-31-81	.193	.196	.192	124	425	60	82	11	1	29	66	49	7	0	3	163	1	2	.428	.285
Nicholas, Brett	L-R	6-2	220	7-18-88	.238	.091	.269	21	63	7	15	4	0	2	11	2	0	0	0	13	0	0	.397	.262
Odor, Rougned	L-R	5-11	195	2-3-94	.204	.145	.225	162	607	79	124	21	3	30	75	32	8	0	4	162	15	6	.397	.252
Profar, Jurickson	B-R	6-0	190	2-20-93	.172	.200	.170	22	58	8	10	2	0	0	5	9	1	2	0	14	1	1	.207	.294
Robinson, Drew	L-R	6-1	200	4-20-92	.224	.333	.202	48	107	11	24	5	0	6	13	14	0	0	0	42	0	2	.439	.314
Rua, Ryan	R-R	6-2	205	3-11-90	.217	.262	.177	63	129	17	28	6	0	3	12	14	0	1	0	52	2	2	.333	.294

Pitching	B-T	HT	WT	DOB	W	L	ERA	G	GS	CG	SV	IP	H	R	ER	HR	BB	SO	AVG	vLH	vRH	K/9	BB/9
Alvarez, Dario	L-L	6-1	170	1-17-89	2	0	2.76	20	0	0	0	16	19	8	5	1	14	17	.292	.250	.324	9.37	7.71
Barnette, Tony	R-R	6-1	190	11-9-83	2	1	5.49	50	0	0	2	57	64	36	35	7	22	57	.288	.319	.273	8.95	3.45
Bass, Anthony	R-R	6-2	200	11-1-87	0	0	14.29	2	0	0	0	6	14	9	9	1	0	1	.467	.471	.462	1.59	0.00
Bibens-Dirkx, Austin	R-R	6-1	210	4-29-85	5	2	4.67	24	6	0	0	69	74	36	36	14	20	38	.270	.252	.284	4.93	2.60
Bush, Matt	R-R	5-9	180	2-8-86	3	4	3.78	57	0	0	10	52	57	30	22	7	19	58	.264	.284	.250	9.97	3.27
Cashner, Andrew	R-R	6-6	235	9-11-86	11	11	3.40	28	28	0	0	167	156	75	63	15	64	86	.250	.243	.256	4.64	3.46
Claiborne, Preston	R-R	6-2	225	1-21-88	0	0	13.50	1	0	0	0	2	5	3	3	0	0	2	.500	.500	.500	9.00	0.00
Claudio, Alex	L-L	6-3	180	1-31-92	4	2	2.50	70	1	0	11	83	71	26	23	5	15	56	.235	.147	.275	6.10	1.63
Darvish, Yu	R-R	6-5	220	8-16-86	6	9	4.01	22	22	0	0	137	115	63	61	20	45	148	.226	.249	.204	9.72	2.96
Diekman, Jake	L-L	6-4	200	1-21-87	0	0	2.53	11	0	0	1	11	4	3	3	1	10	13	.121	.154	.100	10.97	8.44
Dyson, Sam	R-R	6-1	205	5-7-88	1	6	10.80	17	0	0	0	17	31	23	20	6	12	7	.392	.517	.320	3.78	6.48
Espino, Paolo	R-R	5-10	215	1-10-87	0	0	5.68	6	0	0	0	6	6	4	4	2	2	7	.240	.333	.211	9.95	2.84
Frieri, Ernesto	R-R	6-0	205	7-19-85	0	1	5.14	6	0	0	0	7	6	4	4	0	6	5	.250	.364	.154	6.43	7.71
Gardewine, Nick	R-R	6-1	179	8-15-93	0	0	5.63	12	0	0	0	8	10	8	5	1	7	3	.303	.417	.238	3.38	7.88
Gee, Dillon	R-R	6-1	205	4-28-86	0	0	4.15	4	1	0	0	13	17	10	6	4	6	10	.321	.385	.259	6.92	4.15
2-team total (14 Minnesota)					3	2	3.47	18	4	0	1	49	54	24	19	8	15	41	.283	.385	.259	7.48	2.74
Gonzalez, Miguel	R-R	6-1	170	5-27-84	1	3	6.45	5	5	0	0	22	22	16	16	6	8	15	.259	.314	.220	6.04	3.22
2-team total (22 Chicago)					8	13	4.62	27	27	0	0	156	167	88	80	22	55	100	.271	.314	.220	5.77	3.17
Griffin, A.J.	R-R	6-5	230	1-28-88	6	6	5.94	18	15	1	0	77	76	52	51	20	28	61	.253	.242	.261	7.10	3.26
Grilli, Jason	R-R	6-5	235	11-11-76	0	1	5.59	20	0	0	0	19	22	13	12	3	9	25	.279	.269	.283	11.64	4.19
2-team total (26 Toronto Blue Jays)					2	5	6.30	46	0	0	1	40	46	30	28	12	18	48	.279	.269	.283	10.80	4.05
Hamels, Cole	L-L	6-4	205	12-27-83	11	6	4.20	24	24	1	0	148	125	74	69	18	53	105	.228	.161	.247	6.39	3.22
Hauschild, Mike	R-R	6-3	210	1-22-90	0	0	11.25	4	0	0	0	8	14	10	10	5	2	7	.389	.375	.393	7.88	2.25
Jeffress, Jeremy	R-R	6-0	205	9-21-87	1	2	5.31	39	0	0	0	41	49	25	24	8	19	29	.304	.310	.303	6.42	4.20
Kela, Keone	R-R	6-1	215	4-16-93	4	1	2.79	39	0	0	2	39	18	12	12	4	17	51	.135	.170	.113	11.87	3.96
Leclerc, Jose	R-R	6-0	190	12-19-93	2	3	3.94	47	0	0	2	46	23	21	20	4	40	60	.147	.203	.108	11.82	7.88
Marinez, Jhan	R-R	6-1	200	8-12-88	0	0	2.35	4	0	0	0	8	7	2	2	0	3	5	.250	.250	.250	5.87	3.52
Martinez, Nick	L-R	6-1	200	8-5-90	3	8	5.66	23	18	0	0	111	124	74	70	26	28	67	.279	.284	.275	5.42	2.26
Mendez, Yohander	L-L	6-5	200	1-17-95	0	1	5.11	7	0	0	0	12	13	9	7	3	3	7	.271	.188	.313	5.11	2.19
Perez, Martin	L-L	6-0	200	4-4-91	13	12	4.82	32	32	0	0	185	221	108	99	23	63	115	.301	.264	.310	5.59	3.06

Pitching	B-T	HT	WT	DOB	W	L	ERA	G	GS	CG	SV	IP	H	R	ER	HR	BB	SO	AVG	vLH	vRH	K/9	BB/9
Rodriguez, Ricardo	R-R	6-2	220	8-31-92	0	1	6.23	16	0	0	1	13	17	9	9	3	4	11	.315	.188	.368	7.62	2.77
Ross, Tyson	R-R	6-6	245	4-22-87	3	3	7.71	12	10	0	0	49	53	46	42	7	37	36	.275	.237	.313	6.61	6.80
Scheppers, Tanner	R-R	6-4	200	1-17-87	0	1	6.75	5	0	0	0	4	5	3	3	0	3	5	.294	.375	.222	11.25	6.75

Fielding

Catcher	PCT	G	PO	A	E	DP	PB
Chirinos	.990	85	559	24	6	2	4
Jimenez	1.000	5	16	1	0	0	0
Lucroy	.998	66	452	33	1	3	4
Nicholas	1.000	19	106	7	0	2	0

First Base	PCT	G	PO	A	E	DP
Gallo	.996	59	458	17	2	48
Kozma	.889	4	8	0	1	1
Lucroy	1.000	1	4	0	0	1
Middlebrooks	1.000	1	7	0	0	2
Napoli	.991	95	748	44	7	92
Profar	1.000	2	1	0	0	0
Rua	.994	23	153	13	1	18

Second Base	PCT	G	PO	A	E	DP
Gosselin	1.000	5	0	1	0	0
Kozma	1.000	4	6	8	0	4
Odor	.975	158	321	429	19	129
Profar	1.000	1	1	3	0	1
Robinson	1.000	7	9	17	0	3

Third Base	PCT	G	PO	A	E	DP
Beltre	.974	65	50	135	5	13
Gallo	.930	72	47	126	13	18
Gosselin	.000	2	0	0	0	0
Kozma	.947	14	6	12	1	1
Middlebrooks	.944	19	9	25	2	2
Profar	1.000	3	0	6	0	0
Robinson	.947	20	13	23	2	3

Shortstop	PCT	G	PO	A	E	DP
Andrus	.977	157	245	493	17	107
Gosselin	1.000	3	0	4	0	0
Kozma	1.000	5	1	5	0	2
Profar	1.000	4	3	14	0	3
Robinson	1.000	6	3	2	0	0

Outfield	PCT	G	PO	A	E	DP
Calhoun	.923	11	11	1	1	0
Choo	.975	77	151	7	4	0
DeShields	.991	106	208	9	2	3
Gallo	.973	18	34	2	1	1
Gomez	.983	102	229	5	4	1
Hoying	.979	36	46	0	1	0
Mazara	.976	131	232	8	6	0
Profar	1.000	12	20	1	0	1
Robinson	.931	20	26	1	2	0
Rua	1.000	38	45	1	0	0

ROUND ROCK EXPRESS — TRIPLE-A

PACIFIC COAST LEAGUE

Batting	B-T	HT	WT	DOB	AVG	vLH	vRH	G	AB	R	H	2B	3B	HR	RBI	BB	HBP	SH	SF	SO	SB	CS	SLG	OBP
Alberto, Hanser	R-R	5-11	215	10-17-92	.444	.250	.600	2	9	2	4	0	0	1	2	0	0	0	0	1	0	0	.778	.444
Beck, Preston	L-R	6-2	190	10-26-90	.245	.208	.256	66	229	30	56	10	2	1	29	26	2	0	4	45	2	2	.319	.322
Bernier, Doug	R-R	6-1	185	6-24-80	.247	.410	.212	61	223	24	55	7	0	3	17	18	4	7	2	53	0	1	.318	.312
Calhoun, Willie	L-R	5-8	187	11-4-94	.310	.233	.337	29	113	16	35	3	1	8	26	6	0	1	0	12	1	0	.566	.345
2-team total (99 Oklahoma City)					.300	.292	.299	128	486	80	146	27	6	31	93	42	1	1	4	61	4	2	.572	.355
Cantwell, Patrick	R-R	6-2	210	4-10-90	.133	.167	.125	7	30	1	4	0	0	0	1	0	2	0	0	11	1	0	.133	.188
Cardona, Jose	R-R	6-1	175	3-16-94	.177	.250	.154	4	17	4	3	0	0	0	0	2	0	0	0	3	2	0	.177	.263
Castillo, Elio	R-R	6-1	160	3-1-94	.118	.000	.133	5	17	1	2	0	0	0	0	1	0	0	0	5	0	0	.118	.167
Gomez, Carlos	R-R	6-3	220	12-4-85	.250	.500	.167	2	8	0	2	0	0	0	1	1	0	0	0	3	0	0	.250	.333
Gosselin, Phil	R-R	6-1	200	10-3-88	.219	.250	.214	10	32	3	7	1	0	0	3	2	0	0	0	9	0	0	.250	.265
Guzman, Ronald	L-L	6-5	205	10-20-94	.298	.259	.315	125	470	78	140	22	3	12	62	47	9	0	1	85	4	1	.434	.372
Hayes, Brett	R-R	6-1	210	2-13-84	.211	.302	.181	66	213	20	45	10	0	4	21	17	2	0	2	67	0	0	.315	.274
Hoying, Jared	L-R	6-3	205	5-18-89	.262	.211	.279	95	366	55	96	24	2	10	44	31	2	0	0	80	16	6	.421	.323
Jimenez, A.J.	R-R	6-0	195	5-1-90	.245	.415	.200	51	196	18	48	9	0	7	16	7	2	0	2	45	1	0	.398	.275
Kozma, Pete	R-R	6-0	190	4-11-88	.300	.100	.367	11	40	8	12	4	0	0	2	2	0	0	0	8	1	0	.400	.333
Lipka, Matt	R-R	6-1	190	4-15-92	.250	.333	.000	1	4	0	1	0	0	0	1	0	0	0	0	1	0	0	.250	.250
Marte, Luis	R-R	6-1	188	12-15-93	.257	.191	.275	52	191	12	49	7	2	1	17	1	1	0	0	33	6	0	.330	.264
Martinson, Jason	R-R	6-1	210	10-15-88	.208	.235	.197	50	183	28	38	7	0	7	27	18	2	1	0	76	0	3	.361	.286
Matta, Shaq	B-R	5-8	175	4-9-94	.000	—	.000	1	1	0	0	0	0	0	0	0	0	0	0	0	0	0	.000	.000
Mendez, Luis	B-R	5-10	188	1-1-93	.000	—	.000	1	4	0	0	0	0	0	0	0	0	0	0	0	0	0	.000	.000
Middlebrooks, Will	R-R	6-3	220	9-9-88	.258	.303	.244	78	306	51	79	14	0	23	64	31	2	0	3	88	0	1	.529	.328
Nicholas, Brett	L-R	6-2	220	7-18-88	.311	.310	.312	69	273	35	85	18	2	7	38	13	5	1	1	59	2	1	.469	.353
O'Brien, Peter	R-R	6-4	235	7-15-90	.188	.158	.207	13	48	6	9	1	0	2	7	6	0	0	1	19	0	0	.333	.273
2-team total (27 Omaha)					.170	.118	.170	40	153	16	26	2	1	5	13	15	1	0	1	50	0	0	.294	.247
Perez, Brallan	R-R	5-10	165	1-27-96	.000	.000	.000	2	5	0	0	0	0	0	0	0	0	0	0	0	0	0	.000	.000
Profar, Jurickson	B-R	6-0	190	2-20-93	.288	.386	.251	87	327	50	94	25	0	7	45	43	8	4	1	33	5	0	.428	.383
Puello, Cesar	R-R	6-2	220	4-1-91	.247	.316	.226	43	162	24	40	8	1	6	27	12	3	0	2	38	5	1	.420	.307
2-team total (44 Salt Lake)					.327	.324	.415	87	346	66	113	26	2	13	61	25	5	0	3	82	18	4	.526	.377
Robinson, Drew	L-R	6-1	200	4-20-92	.268	.171	.303	66	265	48	71	19	4	11	40	42	1	0	1	74	7	4	.494	.369
Rua, Ryan	R-R	6-2	205	3-11-90	.266	.271	.264	46	177	27	47	7	2	8	28	10	1	0	0	55	3	0	.463	.309
Smith, Tyler	R-R	6-0	195	7-1-91	.188	.231	.171	13	48	5	9	2	0	0	1	3	2	0	0	11	0	1	.229	.264
2-team total (84 Tacoma)					.231	.207	.251	97	333	39	77	15	0	6	29	40	5	3	2	76	4	6	.330	.321
Snider, Travis	L-L	6-0	235	2-2-88	.294	.245	.311	100	361	50	106	24	0	9	44	49	0	0	3	91	2	2	.435	.375
2-team total (17 Las Vegas 51s)					.296	.250	.341	117	426	59	126	26	1	10	52	56	0	0	3	106	2	3	.432	.375
Stubbs, Drew	R-R	6-4	205	10-4-84	.297	.250	.315	75	273	46	81	16	2	7	35	46	3	0	0	88	9	6	.447	.404
2-team total (10 Sacramento)					.292	.200	.265	85	312	52	91	17	2	9	42	52	3	0	1	104	10	6	.446	.397
Torres, Kevin	L-R	6-3	195	2-24-90	.300	.000	.353	6	20	3	6	1	0	1	1	2	0	0	0	6	0	0	.500	.364
Wilson, Josh	R-R	6-0	175	3-26-81	.329	.177	.375	22	73	11	24	4	0	4	16	4	2	1	2	15	0	1	.548	.370

Pitching	B-T	HT	WT	DOB	W	L	ERA	G	GS	CG	SV	IP	H	R	ER	HR	BB	SO	AVG	vLH	vRH	K/9	BB/9
Alvarez, Dario	L-L	6-1	170	1-17-89	2	0	2.33	18	1	0	0	27	24	7	7	3	10	36	.240	.182	.269	12.00	3.33
Alvarez, R.J.	R-R	6-2	225	6-8-91	1	2	4.43	45	0	0	7	45	37	24	22	2	30	57	.220	.212	.226	11.49	6.04
Barnette, Tony	R-R	6-1	190	11-9-83	0	0	0.00	2	0	0	0	3	0	0	0	0	1	3	.000	.000	.000	9.00	3.00
Bass, Anthony	R-R	6-2	200	11-1-87	3	4	4.18	18	12	0	0	75	79	43	35	7	28	87	.271	.276	.266	10.39	3.35
Bibens-Dirkx, Austin	R-R	6-1	210	4-29-85	0	2	3.04	6	3	0	0	24	22	9	8	3	7	20	.247	.205	.280	7.61	2.66
Blackburn, Clayton	L-R	6-3	230	1-6-93	6	2	4.65	19	18	0	0	93	99	49	48	4	25	78	.275	.259	.286	7.55	2.42
2-team total (1 Sacramento)					6	2	4.97	20	19	0	0	96	105	54	53	5	26	79	.280	.375	.429	7.41	2.44
Chapman, Jaye	R-R	6-0	195	5-22-87	2	2	6.89	27	0	0	0	31	37	24	24	5	20	22	.289	.220	.322	6.32	5.74
Claiborne, Preston	R-R	6-2	225	1-21-88	3	1	1.89	38	0	0	16	38	37	9	8	2	15	42	.259	.250	.266	9.95	3.55

Cook, Clayton	R-R	6-3	215	7-23-90	0	0	36.00	1	0	0	0	1	5	4	4	2	0	1	.625	.800	.333	9.00	0.00
Diekman, Jake	L-L	6-4	200	1-21-87	0	0	0.00	1	0	0	0	1	0	0	0	0	0	2	.000	.000	.000	13.50	0.00
Dragmire, Brady	R-R	6-1	185	2-5-93	0	4	5.70	20	1	0	0	36	43	28	23	6	15	18	.301	.246	.342	4.46	3.72
Dykstra, James	R-R	6-4	195	11-22-90	2	9	7.33	21	13	0	0	74	116	63	60	5	29	51	.361	.374	.352	6.23	3.54
Dyson, Sam	R-R	6-1	205	5-7-88	0	0	4.50	2	0	0	0	2	2	1	1	0	1	2	.250	.400	.000	9.00	4.50
Espino, Paolo	R-R	5-10	215	1-10-87	1	0	3.00	1	0	0	0	3	1	1	1	0	1	4	.111	.200	.000	12.00	3.00
2-team total (16 Colorado Springs Sky Sox)					5	2	4.46	17	14	0	0	79	87	41	39	12	15	77	.280	.200	.000	8.81	1.72
Frieri, Ernesto	R-R	6-0	205	7-19-85	0	1	1.42	7	0	0	0	6	5	1	1	0	3	10	.227	.308	.111	14.21	4.26
2-team total (7 Tacoma)					1	3	3.93	14	0	0	0	18	14	8	8	1	12	28	.215	.136	.286	13.75	5.89
Gamboa, Eddie	R-R	6-1	215	12-21-84	5	6	6.49	14	14	0	0	78	94	60	56	13	39	46	.305	.298	.311	5.33	4.52
2-team total (6 Oklahoma City)					8	7	6.17	20	20	0	0	109	130	81	75	20	52	65	.300	.271	.299	5.35	4.28
Gee, Dillon	R-R	6-1	205	4-28-86	3	4	3.88	9	9	0	0	51	53	25	22	5	13	43	.261	.253	.267	7.59	2.29
Griffin, A.J.	R-R	6-5	230	1-28-88	0	1	10.80	3	3	0	0	7	13	8	8	4	3	9	.394	.364	.409	12.15	4.05
Kela, Keone	R-R	6-1	215	4-16-93	0	0	2.25	4	0	0	1	4	5	1	1	0	1	8	.294	.286	.300	18.00	2.25
Ledbetter, David	L-R	5-11	190	2-13-92	3	4	4.31	13	13	0	0	71	66	34	34	13	36	46	.254	.320	.196	5.83	4.56
Loewen, Adam	L-L	6-6	245	4-9-84	6	0	4.02	32	0	0	0	31	24	17	14	4	29	42	.207	.219	.202	12.06	8.33
Lopez, Frank	L-L	6-1	175	2-18-94	0	0	0.00	4	0	0	0	9	7	3	0	0	3	7	.206	.111	.240	7.27	3.12
Martinez, Nick	L-R	6-1	200	8-5-90	4	0	2.15	7	6	1	0	38	27	9	9	3	7	23	.194	.177	.208	5.50	1.67
Palmquist, Cody	R-R	6-5	190	4-8-94	0	0	0.00	2	0	0	0	5	3	0	0	0	0	3	.177	.250	.111	5.40	0.00
Reyes, Jimmy	L-L	5-10	200	3-7-89	4	5	4.11	36	5	1	0	66	69	33	30	10	21	43	.279	.306	.269	5.89	2.88
Rodriguez, Joely	L-L	6-1	200	11-14-91	2	0	6.33	22	0	0	0	27	31	20	19	6	18	21	.293	.313	.284	7.00	6.00
Ross, Tyson	R-R	6-6	245	4-22-87	2	1	7.71	4	4	0	0	19	23	16	16	3	11	11	.324	.375	.282	5.30	5.30
Sampson, Adrian	R-R	6-2	210	10-7-91	1	0	0.90	2	2	0	0	10	10	1	1	0	1	7	.263	.316	.211	6.30	0.90
Scheppers, Tanner	R-R	6-4	200	1-17-87	1	3	4.84	31	1	0	3	48	56	28	26	9	14	39	.281	.281	.282	7.26	2.61
Scott, Tayler	R-R	6-3	185	6-1-92	0	1	7.62	12	0	0	1	13	17	12	11	3	5	13	.298	.348	.265	9.00	3.46
Slack, Ryne	L-L	6-2	239	7-22-92	1	0	10.38	5	0	0	0	9	15	10	10	2	9	13	.366	.500	.310	13.50	9.35
Torres, Christian	L-L	6-0	160	9-7-93	1	1	4.76	5	1	0	0	6	7	4	3	2	3	6	.304	.182	.417	9.53	4.76
Valdespina, Jose	R-R	6-6	220	3-22-92	1	1	16.50	5	0	0	0	6	16	11	11	2	4	5	.485	.600	.389	7.50	6.00
Wagner, Tyler	R-R	6-3	205	1-24-91	3	11	6.25	29	21	0	3	125	149	92	87	20	56	88	.302	.304	.300	6.32	4.02
Webster, Allen	R-R	6-2	190	2-10-90	4	4	6.79	12	11	0	0	58	77	44	44	14	20	44	.329	.360	.306	6.79	3.09
Wolff, Sam	R-R	6-1	204	4-14-91	2	2	2.38	24	0	0	0	23	17	9	6	2	9	32	.205	.276	.167	12.71	3.57
Wright, Wesley	L-R	5-10	185	1-28-85	3	1	4.88	30	0	0	0	31	36	17	17	2	16	22	.290	.184	.337	6.32	4.60

Fielding

Catcher	PCT	G	PO	A	E	DP	PB
Cantwell	1.000	3	33	6	0	2	0
Hayes	.998	51	381	28	1	6	2
Jimenez	.997	38	281	30	1	2	4
Nicholas	.994	44	302	19	2	6	2
Torres	1.000	6	35	4	0	0	0

First Base	PCT	G	PO	A	E	DP
Beck	.958	3	21	2	1	0
Guzman	.993	118	922	71	7	118
Hayes	1.000	6	51	2	0	7
Middlebrooks	1.000	2	13	0	0	2
Nicholas	1.000	8	48	7	0	2
O'Brien	1.000	1	1	0	0	0
Profar	1.000	1	12	1	0	0
Rua	1.000	1	6	1	0	1

Second Base	PCT	G	PO	A	E	DP
Alberto	1.000	1	5	4	0	2
Bernier	.985	29	63	71	2	28
Calhoun	1.000	3	8	6	0	0
Castillo	.950	4	7	12	1	3
Gosselin	1.000	6	7	13	0	3
Kozma	1.000	1	1	5	0	1
Marte	.955	15	30	33	3	9
Martinson	.978	19	35	54	2	13
Middlebrooks	1.000	1	1	2	0	0
Perez	1.000	2	2	5	0	0
Profar	1.000	3	4	4	0	2
Robinson	.978	39	84	96	4	28
Rua	1.000	3	0	6	0	1
Smith	1.000	6	11	16	0	4
Wilson	.980	12	17	33	1	10

Third Base	PCT	G	PO	A	E	DP
Bernier	1.000	1	0	2	0	0
Gosselin	1.000	5	2	3	0	0
Hayes	1.000	4	3	8	0	0
Kozma	1.000	4	2	5	0	0
Marte	.976	30	21	60	2	9
Martinson	.980	16	17	32	1	6
Mendez	1.000	1	0	2	0	0
Middlebrooks	.964	54	38	96	5	7
Nicholas	1.000	3	1	7	0	1
O'Brien	.000	1	0	0	0	0
Robinson	.865	13	8	24	5	4
Smith	.846	6	5	6	2	0
Wilson	.909	6	3	7	1	1

Shortstop	PCT	G	PO	A	E	DP
Alberto	1.000	1	0	2	0	0
Bernier	.979	30	58	83	3	21
Kozma	1.000	5	5	15	0	5
Marte	1.000	6	8	11	0	3
Martinson	.946	15	23	47	4	13
Profar	.968	78	131	201	11	54
Robinson	.000	1	0	0	1	0
Smith	1.000	1	2	1	0	1
Wilson	.938	4	6	9	1	2

Outfield	PCT	G	PO	A	E	DP
Beck	.987	49	74	2	1	0
Calhoun	1.000	24	42	3	0	1
Cantwell	1.000	4	9	1	0	0
Cardona	1.000	4	16	0	0	0
Castillo	.000	1	0	0	0	0
Hoying	.990	84	193	0	2	0
Kozma	1.000	2	2	0	0	0
Lipka	1.000	1	2	0	0	0
Marte	.000	1	0	0	0	0
Matta	.000	1	0	0	0	0
Middlebrooks	1.000	1	2	0	0	0
O'Brien	1.000	8	14	2	0	0
Paul	1.000	1	1	0	0	0
Profar	.000	1	0	0	0	0
Puello	.967	41	81	7	3	2
Robinson	1.000	17	36	1	0	0
Rua	.981	29	50	2	1	0
Snider	.993	83	143	4	1	2
Stubbs	.993	70	135	2	1	0

FRISCO ROUGHRIDERS — *DOUBLE-A*

TEXAS LEAGUE

Batting	B-T	HT	WT	DOB	AVG	vLH	vRH	G	AB	R	H	2B	3B	HR	RBI	BB	HBP	SH	SF	SO	SB	CS	SLG	OBP
Aguilera, Eric	L-L	6-2	218	7-3-90	.222	.195	.229	111	387	52	86	18	0	15	51	53	5	0	3	120	1	2	.385	.321
Alberto, Hanser	R-R	5-11	215	10-17-92	.273	.000	.300	3	11	2	3	1	0	0	0	1	0	0	0	2	0	0	.364	.333
Bolinger, Royce	R-R	6-2	200	8-12-90	.234	.225	.237	91	325	38	76	18	1	9	38	15	7	0	2	102	0	0	.379	.281
Cardona, Jose	R-R	6-1	175	3-16-94	.277	.277	.278	109	429	46	119	19	3	7	47	22	5	3	6	48	14	10	.385	.316
De Leon, Michael	B-R	6-1	160	1-14-97	.223	.247	.217	112	394	29	88	16	1	2	35	18	1	2	3	48	3	2	.284	.257
Gomez, Carlos	R-R	6-3	220	12-4-85	.167	—	.167	2	6	1	1	0	0	1	2	0	1	0	0	0	0	0	.667	.286
Heineman, Scott	R-R	6-1	215	12-4-92	.284	.279	.286	117	468	82	133	26	7	9	44	50	9	0	2	121	12	9	.427	.363
Hernandez, Yonny	B-R	5-9	140	5-4-98	.000	—	.000	3	3	0	0	0	0	0	0	0	0	0	0	1	0	0	.000	.000
Ibanez, Andy	R-R	5-10	170	4-3-93	.265	.278	.261	82	310	33	82	14	2	8	29	25	3	4	3	48	6	1	.400	.323

Kiner-Falefa, Isiah	R-R	5-10	176	3-23-95	.289	.262	.295	129	513	58	148	31	3	5	48	41	10	1	4	72	17	6	.390	.350
Lipka, Matt	R-R	6-1	190	4-15-92	.160	.130	.169	33	94	16	15	4	1	0	6	3	4	0	1	32	5	1	.223	.216
Marte, Luis	R-R	6-1	188	12-15-93	.231	.244	.227	47	169	19	39	7	1	6	25	5	0	1	3	23	3	3	.391	.249
Mendez, Luis	B-R	5-10	188	1-1-93	.100	.000	.125	8	20	2	2	1	0	0	3	9	0	0	0	7	2	0	.150	.379
Napoli, Mike	R-R	6-1	225	10-31-81	.000	—	.000	1	4	0	0	0	0	0	0	0	0	0	0	2	0	0	.000	.000
O'Brien, Peter	R-R	6-4	235	7-15-90	.077	.000	.143	3	13	1	1	1	0	0	1	2	0	0	0	6	0	0	.154	.200
2-team total (45 Tulsa)					.208	.264	.196	48	168	24	35	12	0	9	27	18	1	0	0	84	0	0	.441	.289
O'Neill, Michael	R-R	6-1	195	6-12-92	.262	.200	.282	74	271	31	71	9	4	8	22	26	9	1	1	82	12	3	.413	.345
Profar, Juremi	R-R	6-1	185	1-30-96	.263	.198	.285	109	415	38	109	13	2	10	40	19	1	0	0	58	1	2	.376	.297
Tendler, Luke	L-R	5-11	190	8-25-91	.245	.272	.239	113	420	51	103	24	2	13	49	41	2	0	1	104	1	2	.405	.315
Torres, Kevin	L-R	6-3	195	2-24-90	.133	.200	.125	16	45	1	6	0	0	0	3	1	0	0	1	10	0	0	.133	.149
Trevino, Jose	R-R	5-11	211	11-28-92	.241	.270	.233	105	402	39	97	12	0	7	42	19	0	1	1	44	1	2	.323	.275
Vettleson, Drew	R-L	6-1	185	7-19-91	.190	.200	.188	26	100	6	19	3	0	3	9	3	1	2	0	36	5	1	.310	.221

Pitching	B-T	HT	WT	DOB	W	L	ERA	G	GS	CG	SV	IP	H	R	ER	HR	BB	SO	AVG	vLH	vRH	K/9	BB/9
Chapman, Jaye	R-R	6-0	195	5-22-87	1	0	6.23	3	0	0	0	4	5	3	3	0	0	4	.294	.000	.417	8.31	0.00
Cook, Clayton	R-R	6-3	215	7-23-90	2	2	6.37	27	0	0	1	30	35	24	21	4	20	31	.289	.262	.304	9.40	6.07
Davis, Tyler	R-R	5-10	185	1-5-93	4	2	2.32	12	12	1	0	81	61	22	21	8	9	46	.213	.183	.227	5.09	1.00
Diekman, Jake	L-L	6-4	200	1-21-87	1	0	1.80	5	1	0	0	5	3	1	1	0	0	6	.177	.333	.143	10.80	0.00
Dykstra, James	R-R	6-4	195	11-22-90	0	1	1.46	8	2	0	2	25	16	5	4	1	4	19	.188	.172	.196	6.93	1.46
Feigl, Brady	R-L	6-4	195	12-27-90	1	1	5.45	27	0	0	0	35	46	23	21	3	10	37	.301	.255	.327	9.61	2.60
Filomeno, Joe	R-L	5-11	235	12-31-92	0	3	8.10	29	0	0	0	37	50	39	33	8	22	35	.319	.380	.290	8.59	5.40
Gardewine, Nick	R-R	6-1	179	8-15-93	1	2	2.21	33	0	0	6	37	35	10	9	2	12	53	.252	.264	.244	13.01	2.95
Garrett, Reed	R-R	6-2	210	1-2-93	2	5	4.98	44	4	0	10	69	69	41	38	10	31	70	.265	.280	.258	9.17	4.06
Griffin, A.J.	R-R	6-5	230	1-28-88	0	0	0.00	1	1	0	0	5	4	0	0	0	2	5	.211	.222	.200	9.00	3.60
Hamels, Cole	L-L	6-4	205	12-27-83	1	0	1.04	2	2	0	0	9	3	1	1	1	2	8	.107	.250	.050	8.31	2.08
Jurado, Ariel	R-R	6-1	180	1-30-96	9	11	4.59	27	27	0	0	157	188	93	80	16	37	95	.302	.342	.278	5.45	2.12
Leclerc, Jose	R-R	6-0	190	12-19-93	0	0	0.00	2	0	0	0	2	1	0	0	0	0	3	.143	.250	.000	13.50	0.00
Ledbetter, David	L-R	5-11	190	2-13-92	1	4	5.72	16	4	0	1	39	41	30	25	4	18	39	.265	.231	.282	8.92	4.12
Loewen, Adam	L-L	6-6	245	4-9-84	0	1	3.48	18	0	0	1	21	19	8	8	0	12	25	.247	.136	.291	10.89	5.23
McCain, Shane	L-L	6-1	210	8-4-91	2	2	5.51	36	0	0	1	51	62	32	31	10	8	38	.304	.288	.315	6.75	1.42
Mendez, Yohander	L-L	6-5	200	1-17-95	7	8	3.79	24	24	1	0	138	114	60	58	23	43	124	.229	.229	.228	8.11	2.81
Palmquist, Cody	R-R	6-5	190	4-8-94	1	1	4.50	32	2	0	1	48	41	24	24	8	13	34	.228	.254	.214	6.38	2.44
Payano, Pedro	R-R	6-2	170	9-27-94	4	5	3.63	17	16	0	0	84	76	37	34	4	42	77	.247	.222	.264	8.22	4.48
Pena, Richelson	R-R	6-1	170	9-29-93	2	3	3.24	5	5	0	0	33	34	14	12	3	6	23	.262	.250	.271	6.21	1.62
Rodriguez, Ricardo	R-R	6-2	220	8-31-92	2	0	1.20	12	0	0	5	15	9	2	2	1	1	17	.177	.200	.161	10.20	0.60
Ross, Tyson	R-R	6-6	245	4-22-87	1	1	2.31	2	2	0	0	12	11	5	3	0	4	10	.256	.421	.125	7.71	3.09
Sadzeck, Connor	R-R	6-7	240	10-1-91	4	8	6.25	38	13	0	0	94	104	67	65	13	39	111	.283	.273	.288	10.67	3.75
Slack, Ryne	L-L	6-2	239	7-22-92	2	2	2.52	27	0	0	3	36	30	13	10	2	17	30	.224	.149	.264	7.57	4.29
Valdespina, Jose	R-R	6-6	220	3-22-92	0	1	4.50	3	0	0	0	4	3	2	2	0	0	3	.200	.000	.250	6.75	0.00
Wiles, Collin	R-R	6-4	222	5-30-94	9	12	4.86	28	25	1	0	150	177	92	81	22	28	107	.294	.296	.292	6.42	1.68
Wolff, Sam	R-R	6-1	204	4-14-91	2	3	3.54	16	0	0	3	20	20	9	8	3	10	27	.244	.348	.203	11.95	4.43

Fielding

Catcher	PCT	G	PO	A	E	DP	PB
Kiner-Falefa	.985	33	250	21	4	1	4
Torres	.990	16	91	7	1	0	0
Trevino	.996	99	762	64	3	4	3

First Base	PCT	G	PO	A	E	DP
Aguilera	.991	92	782	32	7	93
Bolinger	.988	39	317	16	4	32
Profar	.982	14	105	7	2	15

Second Base	PCT	G	PO	A	E	DP
Alberto	1.000	1	3	3	0	2
De Leon	1.000	5	9	17	0	5
Hernandez	.000	1	0	0	0	0
Ibanez	.985	70	132	201	5	52
Kiner-Falefa	.983	37	64	111	3	36
Lipka	1.000	9	19	25	0	9
Marte	.957	6	10	12	1	4
Mendez	1.000	5	6	15	0	2
Profar	.976	9	16	24	1	4

Third Base	PCT	G	PO	A	E	DP
De Leon	1.000	1	1	3	0	0
Ibanez	.846	4	5	6	2	0
Kiner-Falefa	.948	50	33	112	8	12
Lipka	.000	1	0	0	0	0
Marte	.969	17	10	21	1	1
Mendez	1.000	3	0	6	0	2
Profar	.950	72	53	139	10	17

Shortstop	PCT	G	PO	A	E	DP
Alberto	.800	2	2	2	1	0
De Leon	.961	105	167	329	20	82
Kiner-Falefa	.925	10	11	26	3	4
Marte	.971	25	35	67	3	20

Outfield	PCT	G	PO	A	E	DP
Bolinger	.980	47	93	6	2	1
Cardona	.993	105	266	9	2	1
Gomez	1.000	2	4	1	0	0
Heineman	.990	113	194	5	2	0
Kiner-Falefa	.667	1	2	0	1	0
Lipka	1.000	17	27	2	0	0
O'Brien	1.000	1	1	1	0	0
O'Neill	1.000	70	119	3	0	0
Tendler	.935	59	84	3	6	0
Vettleson	.941	13	13	3	1	0

DOWN EAST WOOD DUCKS — *HIGH CLASS A*

CAROLINA LEAGUE

Batting	B-T	HT	WT	DOB	AVG	vLH	vRH	G	AB	R	H	2B	3B	HR	RBI	BB	HBP	SH	SF	SO	SB	CS	SLG	OBP
Altmann, Josh	R-R	6-3	190	7-6-94	.244	.219	.257	118	397	51	97	22	1	10	38	42	8	3	0	88	14	5	.380	.329
Arroyo, Carlos	R-L	5-11	150	6-28-93	.173	.259	.143	29	104	8	18	1	0	0	6	1	1	1	0	23	0	3	.183	.189
Castillo, Elio	R-R	6-1	160	3-1-94	.118	.125	.111	6	17	1	2	0	0	0	1	0	0	1	0	5	0	0	.118	.118
Clark, LeDarious	R-R	5-10	185	12-27-93	.228	.189	.245	119	404	55	92	24	3	13	48	52	3	3	2	143	20	8	.399	.319
De La Rosa, Frandy	B-R	6-1	180	1-24-96	.107	.083	.125	8	28	3	3	2	0	0	0	5	0	0	0	13	0	0	.179	.242
Forbes, Ti'Quan	R-R	6-3	180	8-26-96	.227	.291	.200	51	185	20	42	6	0	3	11	13	1	1	1	54	2	4	.308	.280
2-team total (4 Winston-Salem)					.222	.291	.200	55	198	23	44	7	0	3	11	14	1	1	1	54	2	5	.303	.276
Garay, Carlos	R-R	6-0	210	10-5-94	.321	.371	.302	69	262	22	84	9	0	1	21	12	6	1	1	30	2	1	.366	.363
La O, Luis	R-R	6-0	178	12-9-91	.292	.255	.311	124	476	57	139	23	2	8	53	21	12	4	3	50	11	10	.399	.336
Lara, Arturo	R-R	5-10	185	2-22-91	.192	.282	.142	69	219	10	42	8	1	2	22	9	1	5	3	46	1	1	.265	.224

Lipka, Matt	R-R	6-1	190	4-15-92	.265	.323	.239	83	325	45	86	16	4	9	43	28	7	6	4	68	20	5	.422	.332
Matta, Shaq	B-R	5-8	175	4-9-94	.333	1.000	.200	2	6	0	2	0	0	0	0	1	0	0	0	2	0	0	.333	.429
Mendez, Luis	B-R	5-10	188	1-1-93	.212	.214	.211	9	33	4	7	2	1	1	4	1	1	0	1	12	1	1	.424	.250
Moorman, Chuck	R-R	5-11	200	1-9-94	.253	.241	.259	98	340	34	86	20	0	5	40	23	3	3	3	72	0	1	.356	.304
Morgan, Josh	R-R	5-11	185	11-16-95	.270	.250	.277	106	408	56	110	21	3	6	45	26	5	2	4	54	3	0	.380	.318
O'Neill, Michael	R-R	6-1	195	6-12-92	.273	.367	.233	45	165	21	45	12	2	7	19	9	3	0	1	42	16	2	.497	.320
Perez, Brallan	R-R	5-10	165	1-27-96	.234	.283	.214	46	158	16	37	2	0	1	8	15	2	3	0	21	8	5	.266	.309
2-team total (19 Frederick)					.270	.375	.366	65	215	29	58	4	1	2	12	22	4	4	0	23	9	6	.326	.349
Perez, Yanio	R-R	6-2	205	8-10-95	.253	.272	.245	74	281	31	71	14	2	5	36	20	6	0	5	66	3	1	.370	.311
Pinto, Eduard	L-L	5-11	150	10-23-94	.311	.347	.297	46	177	30	55	10	1	4	18	10	3	1	0	21	7	3	.446	.358
Rollin, Franklin	R-R	5-11	165	8-26-95	.139	.333	.074	9	36	4	5	2	0	0	1	3	0	0	0	7	1	0	.194	.205
Sanchez, Tyler	R-R	6-2	190	5-30-93	.187	.138	.217	23	75	5	14	3	0	2	11	10	4	1	0	18	0	0	.307	.315
Scott, Preston	R-R	6-2	210	11-15-93	.256	.234	.267	73	238	32	61	14	2	5	24	23	10	3	1	54	5	3	.395	.346
Silva, Luis	R-R	5-11	170	6-30-95	.000	.000	.000	7	18	0	0	0	0	0	0	0	0	0	0	1	0	1	.000	.000
Van Hoosier, Evan	R-R	5-11	185	12-24-93	.230	.143	.253	29	100	14	23	3	1	2	13	8	4	0	0	23	5	0	.340	.313
Yrizarri, Yeyson	R-R	6-0	175	2-2-97	.207	.167	.217	8	29	5	6	2	0	2	7	1	2	0	2	8	0	0	.483	.265
2-team total (31 Winston-Salem)					.277	.167	.217	39	141	17	39	3	0	3	18	3	2	2	3	29	1	4	.362	.295

Pitching	B-T	HT	WT	DOB	W	L	ERA	G	GS	CG	SV	IP	H	R	ER	HR	BB	SO	AVG	vLH	vRH	K/9	BB/9
Bass, Blake	R-R	6-7	250	6-3-93	1	1	4.91	6	0	0	1	11	15	10	6	1	4	5	.326	.360	.286	4.09	3.27
Benjamin, Wes	R-L	6-1	180	7-26-93	10	7	3.94	22	22	0	0	119	133	53	52	8	34	101	.287	.293	.284	7.66	2.58
Beras, Jairo	R-R	6-6	195	12-25-94	0	0	0.00	1	0	0	0	1	0	0	0	0	0	0	.000	.000	.000	0.00	0.00
Bruce, Steven	R-R	6-0	190	3-7-92	3	4	5.00	15	7	0	0	54	55	32	30	4	10	44	.263	.228	.285	7.33	1.67
Choplick, Adam	L-L	6-9	250	11-18-92	4	3	2.93	42	0	0	9	55	34	22	18	2	32	76	.174	.191	.165	12.36	5.20
Cody, Kyle	R-R	6-7	245	8-9-94	3	0	2.05	5	5	0	0	31	25	7	7	0	10	35	.225	.356	.136	10.27	2.93
Davis, Tyler	R-R	5-10	185	1-5-93	0	2	8.00	13	4	0	0	36	48	33	32	6	10	22	.324	.303	.342	5.50	2.50
Fairbanks, Peter	R-R	6-6	215	12-16-93	2	1	5.79	9	1	0	0	19	22	14	12	1	13	10	.301	.357	.267	4.82	6.27
Feigl, Brady	R-L	6-4	195	12-27-90	3	0	1.48	14	0	0	0	24	26	4	4	2	6	22	.289	.324	.268	8.14	2.22
Ferguson, Tyler	R-R	6-4	225	10-5-93	2	6	7.76	24	0	0	0	31	34	32	27	9	20	31	.266	.256	.270	8.90	5.74
Hernandez, Jonathan	R-R	6-2	175	7-6-96	3	6	3.44	14	13	0	0	65	66	32	25	2	31	64	.271	.260	.278	8.82	4.27
Juan, Johan	R-R	6-1	180	4-14-94	0	1	6.52	5	0	0	0	10	12	7	7	2	2	4	.293	.308	.286	3.72	1.86
Lopez, Frank	L-L	6-1	175	2-18-94	0	2	11.70	6	2	0	0	10	22	13	13	5	10	12	.440	.267	.514	10.80	9.00
2-team total (12 Carolina)					3	5	7.02	18	7	0	0	50	71	43	39	9	31	42	.335	.267	.514	7.56	5.58
Lopez, Omarlin	R-R	6-3	175	10-8-93	0	1	6.43	13	0	0	0	21	29	16	15	2	14	20	.326	.394	.286	8.57	6.00
Martin, Brett	L-L	6-4	190	4-28-95	4	8	4.70	16	16	0	0	84	94	52	44	7	35	90	.287	.290	.285	9.60	3.74
Martinez, Emerson	R-R	6-0	190	1-11-95	3	10	4.19	20	19	0	0	116	124	59	54	9	27	93	.270	.279	.262	7.22	2.09
Palumbo, Joe	L-L	6-1	168	10-26-94	1	0	0.66	3	3	0	0	14	4	3	1	0	4	22	.087	.111	.081	14.49	2.63
Payano, Pedro	R-R	6-2	170	9-27-94	2	3	4.26	9	9	0	0	51	36	25	24	5	22	41	.199	.196	.203	7.28	3.91
Pena, Richelson	R-R	6-1	170	9-29-93	8	4	2.92	20	17	1	1	102	82	36	33	15	23	87	.219	.204	.229	7.70	2.04
Pettibone, Austin	R-R	6-3	180	9-10-92	0	1	9.82	3	0	0	0	4	5	4	4	0	2	4	.313	.429	.222	9.82	4.91
Richman, Jason	L-L	6-4	210	10-15-93	1	0	4.44	15	0	0	0	26	32	14	13	1	9	25	.299	.385	.250	8.54	3.08
Rodriguez, Ricardo	R-R	6-2	220	8-31-92	3	1	1.41	23	0	0	12	32	15	5	5	0	9	44	.136	.143	.132	12.38	2.53
Sampson, Adrian	R-R	6-2	210	10-7-91	0	1	5.19	2	2	0	0	9	13	7	5	1	1	7	.325	.231	.370	7.27	1.04
Shortslef, Jacob	R-R	6-5	235	12-29-94	0	5	4.88	28	2	0	1	59	63	35	32	8	20	73	.273	.304	.252	11.14	3.05
Springs, Jeffrey	L-L	6-3	180	9-20-92	2	8	3.69	31	17	0	2	112	104	48	46	13	37	146	.245	.308	.224	11.70	2.96
Valdespina, Jose	R-R	6-6	220	3-22-92	0	0	3.22	15	0	0	1	22	22	9	8	1	5	17	.259	.290	.241	6.85	2.01
Vasquez, Kelvin	R-R	6-4	195	4-6-93	2	1	6.35	20	0	0	1	28	23	24	20	3	28	27	.226	.278	.197	8.58	8.89
Williams, Scott	R-R	6-2	200	11-17-93	3	0	0.64	30	0	0	7	42	20	5	3	1	12	38	.140	.167	.124	8.14	2.57
Wiper, Cole	R-R	6-4	185	6-3-92	0	0	1.80	3	0	0	0	5	6	2	1	1	1	6	.300	.143	.385	10.80	1.80
Zawadzki, Grant	R-R	5-10	200	4-27-92	1	0	2.10	14	0	0	0	26	18	6	6	1	9	25	.198	.184	.208	8.77	3.16

Fielding

Catcher	PCT	G	PO	A	E	DP	PB
Garay	.991	25	211	20	2	3	2
Matta	1.000	2	13	2	0	0	0
Moorman	.991	63	532	33	5	3	5
Morgan	.985	36	305	24	5	1	5
Sanchez	1.000	13	118	4	0	0	3
Silva	1.000	1	5	1	0	0	0

First Base	PCT	G	PO	A	E	DP
Altmann	.994	41	301	9	2	30
Arroyo	.974	5	36	1	1	5
De La Rosa	1.000	7	54	7	0	4
Forbes	1.000	8	58	3	0	7
Garay	.996	34	243	19	1	16
Mendez	1.000	1	10	1	0	1
Moorman	.986	19	133	9	2	14
Perez	.995	22	181	6	1	13
Sanchez	1.000	5	38	2	0	4
Scott	1.000	3	29	1	0	1
Van Hoosier	1.000	1	5	0	0	1

Second Base	PCT	G	PO	A	E	DP
Altmann	1.000	1	2	3	0	1
Castillo	.944	5	7	10	1	2
La O	.982	64	111	155	5	34
Lara	.962	15	20	31	2	6
Mendez	1.000	5	10	19	0	5
Perez	.983	32	50	69	2	17
Silva	1.000	1	3	3	0	1
Van Hoosier	.934	14	20	37	4	5
Yrizarri	.938	4	5	10	1	2

Third Base	PCT	G	PO	A	E	DP
Altmann	.901	39	31	78	12	9
Arroyo	.917	4	3	8	1	0
Castillo	.000	1	0	0	0	0
Forbes	.964	27	18	63	3	6
La O	.905	41	21	55	8	5
Mendez	1.000	1	0	1	0	0
Morgan	.833	2	0	5	1	0
Perez	.800	2	2	2	1	0
Perez	.917	23	13	42	5	2
Silva	.800	2	2	2	1	0

Shortstop	PCT	G	PO	A	E	DP
Forbes	.927	17	19	32	4	6
Lara	.963	53	75	134	8	33
Morgan	.951	62	79	156	12	28
Perez	.958	7	4	19	1	2
Yrizarri	.923	4	6	6	1	0

Outfield	PCT	G	PO	A	E	DP
Altmann	.987	37	72	2	1	0
Arroyo	.967	13	26	3	1	2
Beras	.972	26	31	4	1	0
Clark	.972	112	241	5	7	0
Lipka	.995	81	206	7	1	2
Mendez	1.000	2	3	0	0	0
O'Neill	1.000	41	77	3	0	0
Perez	1.000	2	3	0	0	0
Perez	1.000	25	51	2	0	1
Pinto	.971	41	61	5	2	0
Rollin	1.000	9	17	2	0	0
Scott	1.000	42	76	3	0	1

HICKORY CRAWDADS — LOW CLASS A

SOUTH ATLANTIC LEAGUE

Batting	B-T	HT	WT	DOB	AVG	vLH	vRH	G	AB	R	H	2B	3B	HR	RBI	BB	HBP	SH	SF	SO	SB	CS	SLG	OBP
Almonte, Jose	R-R	6-3	205	9-9-96	.185	.188	.184	66	227	24	42	4	2	6	19	13	7	0	0	66	1	1	.300	.251
Aparicio, Miguel	L-L	6-0	165	3-17-99	.177	.136	.191	25	85	6	15	2	2	0	9	7	2	0	0	18	1	2	.247	.255
Bolin, Travis	R-R	5-11	208	10-18-94	.171	.077	.214	10	41	2	7	3	0	0	4	2	0	0	0	15	0	0	.244	.209
Castillo, Elio	R-R	6-1	160	3-1-94	.205	.167	.238	13	39	3	8	0	0	0	6	2	0	0	0	9	0	0	.205	.244
Cordero, Andretty	R-R	6-1	170	5-3-97	.281	.333	.266	44	178	23	50	8	1	4	25	9	1	0	0	38	2	1	.405	.319
Davis, Brendon	R-R	6-4	185	7-28-97	.182	.235	.167	25	77	8	14	1	0	2	6	12	1	0	0	28	0	0	.273	.300
Dorow, Ryan	R-R	6-0	195	8-21-95	.333	—	.333	1	3	0	1	1	0	0	0	0	0	0	0	2	0	0	.667	.333
Forbes, Ti'Quan	R-R	6-3	180	8-26-96	.242	.202	.257	80	302	36	73	10	2	8	34	12	6	0	0	76	3	0	.368	.284
Garay, Carlos	R-R	6-0	210	10-5-94	.362	.290	.386	41	152	18	55	10	0	1	25	4	2	0	2	15	0	0	.447	.381
Gardner, Tanner	L-R	6-0	210	9-28-95	.217	.200	.220	44	143	17	31	10	1	1	13	16	2	0	0	38	1	0	.322	.304
Jenkins, Eric	L-R	6-1	170	1-30-97	.207	.130	.224	73	256	35	53	10	4	1	16	19	1	1	1	82	10	0	.289	.264
Kowalczyk, Alex	R-R	6-3	205	10-17-93	.305	.314	.302	90	334	51	102	21	0	9	56	24	15	0	3	83	2	1	.449	.375
Leblanc, Charles	R-R	6-3	195	6-3-96	.262	.170	.291	54	195	27	51	7	0	4	19	19	1	0	2	33	3	0	.359	.327
Matta, Shaq	B-R	5-8	175	4-9-94	.250	.000	.286	3	8	0	2	0	0	0	2	0	0	0	0	3	0	0	.250	.250
Perez, Brallan	R-R	5-10	165	1-27-96	.359	.378	.342	21	78	12	28	1	0	2	10	7	0	1	1	11	0	1	.449	.407
Perez, Yanio	R-R	6-2	205	8-10-95	.322	.364	.304	49	180	27	58	9	1	9	30	18	4	0	2	34	3	0	.533	.392
Pozo, Yohel	R-R	6-0	175	6-14-97	.338	.371	.327	39	142	19	48	8	2	2	15	7	1	0	0	8	0	0	.465	.373
Prescott, Blaine	R-R	5-10	175	7-28-95	.235	.274	.222	95	370	44	87	13	2	9	29	22	8	1	4	85	8	5	.354	.290
Quiroz, Isaias	R-R	5-10	195	10-22-96	.086	.083	.087	11	35	1	3	1	1	0	6	4	2	0	1	19	0	0	.171	.214
Rollin, Franklin	R-R	5-11	165	8-26-95	.235	.270	.219	92	315	42	74	12	5	5	35	9	6	1	2	67	16	9	.352	.268
Scott, Preston	R-R	6-2	210	11-15-93	.254	.235	.260	20	67	10	17	6	1	3	7	9	3	0	1	22	4	0	.508	.363
Taveras, Leody	B-R	6-1	170	9-8-98	.249	.250	.249	134	522	73	130	20	7	8	50	47	2	3	3	92	20	6	.360	.312
Tejeda, Anderson	L-R	5-11	185	5-1-98	.247	.140	.279	115	401	68	99	24	9	8	53	36	2	3	4	132	10	7	.412	.309
Valencia, Ricardo	R-R	6-0	185	1-13-93	.259	.270	.255	71	255	33	66	15	0	5	37	21	3	1	6	78	0	0	.377	.316
Yrizarri, Yeyson	R-R	6-0	175	2-2-97	.264	.281	.257	74	269	22	71	17	1	5	30	5	5	1	3	49	5	4	.390	.287

Pitching	B-T	HT	WT	DOB	W	L	ERA	G	GS	CG	SV	IP	H	R	ER	HR	BB	SO	AVG	vLH	vRH	K/9	BB/9
Alexy, A.J.	R-R	6-4	195	4-21-98	1	1	3.05	5	5	0	0	21	13	7	7	3	15	27	.178	.103	.227	11.76	6.53
Anderson, Reid	R-R	6-3	185	8-22-95	1	11	5.30	28	13	0	0	88	96	60	52	8	32	65	.272	.289	.256	6.62	3.26
Arredondo, Edgar	R-R	6-3	190	5-16-97	6	6	3.86	22	21	0	0	110	118	58	47	8	21	105	.272	.293	.256	8.62	1.72
Ball, Matt	R-R	6-5	200	1-23-95	0	1	5.67	11	5	0	3	33	39	26	21	4	10	38	.283	.328	.239	10.26	2.70
Beltre, Dario	R-R	6-3	170	11-19-92	1	0	2.60	11	0	0	0	17	14	7	5	0	6	19	.209	.188	.229	9.87	3.12
Beras, Jairo	R-R	6-6	195	12-25-94	0	1	5.40	13	0	0	0	13	11	8	8	2	9	14	.220	.118	.273	9.45	6.08
Cody, Kyle	R-R	6-7	245	8-9-94	6	6	2.83	18	18	0	0	95	77	44	30	4	33	101	.218	.229	.207	9.53	3.12
Davis, Tyler	R-R	5-10	185	1-5-93	0	0	4.66	4	1	0	0	10	8	5	5	1	7	6	.242	.111	.292	5.59	6.52
Dignacco, Nick	L-L	6-3	185	4-1-92	2	0	5.74	11	0	0	2	16	18	12	10	1	10	15	.281	.258	.303	8.62	5.74
Evans, Demarcus	R-R	6-4	240	10-22-96	2	5	4.85	12	6	0	0	30	22	18	16	1	25	46	.198	.234	.172	13.96	7.58
Ferguson, Tyler	R-R	6-4	225	10-5-93	0	0	4.41	12	0	0	1	16	14	8	8	0	6	26	.230	.276	.188	14.33	3.31
Fontenot, Kaleb	R-R	6-1	180	6-23-93	5	4	3.06	41	0	0	6	85	66	34	29	10	25	96	.214	.239	.199	10.13	2.64
Hernandez, Jonathan	R-R	6-2	175	7-6-96	2	5	4.86	9	9	0	0	46	55	32	25	5	13	46	.306	.321	.294	8.94	2.53
Kuzia, Joseph	R-R	6-5	190	10-3-93	1	1	12.79	4	0	0	0	6	9	10	9	1	2	7	.360	.286	.389	9.95	2.84
Lanphere, Luke	R-R	6-2	175	9-30-95	3	0	8.10	9	0	0	0	23	35	22	21	3	13	21	.343	.405	.308	8.10	5.01
Lemoine, Jacob	R-R	6-5	220	11-28-93	3	4	2.96	39	0	0	4	70	65	31	23	2	33	59	.246	.268	.234	7.59	4.24
Lopez, Ismel	R-R	6-1	190	8-24-94	0	0	5.51	7	0	0	0	16	20	10	10	1	8	16	.318	.267	.364	8.82	4.41
Martinez, Emerson	R-R	6-0	190	1-11-95	2	1	1.69	3	3	0	0	16	15	6	3	2	4	12	.250	.258	.241	6.75	2.25
Matuella, Michael	R-R	6-6	220	6-3-94	4	6	4.20	21	20	0	0	75	88	42	35	6	23	60	.297	.299	.296	7.20	2.76
Mendez, Sal	R-L	6-4	180	2-25-95	6	6	4.71	25	9	0	0	94	114	61	49	8	28	71	.298	.316	.288	6.82	2.69
Pelham, C.D.	L-L	6-6	235	2-21-95	4	2	3.18	37	0	0	13	62	47	28	22	6	26	75	.204	.188	.213	10.83	3.75
Phillips, Tyler	R-R	6-5	200	10-27-97	1	2	6.39	7	4	0	0	25	28	21	18	2	9	15	.280	.340	.213	5.33	3.20
Rodriguez, Argenis	R-R	6-3	190	3-7-96	0	3	13.80	5	4	0	0	15	30	24	23	4	6	10	.429	.441	.417	6.00	3.60
Sanburn, Parker	R-R	6-1	195	11-12-94	0	1	1.69	3	0	0	0	5	5	1	1	1	2	6	.238	.167	.267	10.13	3.38
Sanmartin, Reiver	L-L	6-2	160	4-15-96	4	1	2.62	7	6	0	0	34	36	11	10	1	6	28	.263	.256	.265	7.34	1.57
Smoral, Matthew	L-L	6-8	220	3-18-94	0	1	6.43	12	0	0	0	14	9	12	10	0	21	25	.180	.238	.138	16.07	13.50
Torres, Christian	L-L	6-0	160	9-7-93	4	2	2.50	31	2	0	5	79	62	25	22	1	18	72	.213	.151	.249	8.17	2.04
Weickel, Walker	R-R	6-6	195	11-14-93	5	4	3.01	15	14	0	0	75	60	28	25	7	15	62	.221	.196	.238	7.47	1.81
Zawadzki, Grant	R-R	5-10	200	4-27-92	0	1	7.71	7	0	0	0	9	15	11	8	2	8	7	.357	.389	.333	6.75	7.71

Fielding

Catcher	PCT	G	PO	A	E	DP	PB
Kowalczyk	.969	31	256	21	9	2	5
Matta	.917	2	11	0	1	1	0
Pozo	.989	34	251	29	3	1	2
Quiroz	1.000	11	96	7	0	1	6
Valencia	.990	65	506	62	6	4	7

First Base	PCT	G	PO	A	E	DP
Castillo	.983	8	55	3	1	9
Cordero	.983	43	388	19	7	33
Forbes	1.000	13	95	10	0	10
Garay	.994	23	144	17	1	12
Gardner	1.000	7	64	1	0	5
Perez	.983	29	219	14	4	17
Pozo	1.000	1	5	1	0	0
Scott	.965	18	154	11	6	13

Second Base	PCT	G	PO	A	E	DP
Davis	.927	11	8	30	3	6
Dorow	1.000	1	2	4	0	0
Gardner	1.000	1	1	0	0	0
Leblanc	1.000	1	2	0	0	0
Perez	.941	11	19	29	3	8
Prescott	.976	56	102	137	6	32
Rollin	1.000	1	2	0	0	0
Tejeda	.957	30	50	83	6	14
Yrizarri	.976	31	48	74	3	16

Third Base	PCT	G	PO	A	E	DP
Castillo	.909	5	4	6	1	0
Cordero	1.000	1	1	1	0	0
Davis	1.000	4	2	4	0	2
Forbes	.931	63	47	115	12	10
Leblanc	.922	51	33	109	12	8
Perez	1.000	1	0	1	0	0
Perez	.875	4	2	5	1	0
Prescott	.839	13	9	17	5	2

Shortstop	PCT	G	PO	A	E	DP
Davis	.918	9	13	32	4	6
Perez	.906	6	9	20	3	4
Tejeda	.932	82	112	217	24	40
Yrizarri	.972	43	64	107	5	21

Outfield	PCT	G	PO	A	E	DP
Almonte	1.000	65	110	8	0	2
Aparicio	1.000	24	38	2	0	0
Bolin	1.000	5	6	1	0	1
Gardner	1.000	31	44	4	0	0
Jenkins	.964	72	129	3	5	1
Kowalczyk	1.000	8	6	0	0	0
Perez	.958	15	22	1	1	0
Prescott	.952	15	20	0	1	0
Rollin	.977	70	123	6	3	2
Taveras	.989	128	273	9	3	3

SPOKANE INDIANS — *SHORT SEASON*

NORTHWEST LEAGUE

Batting	B-T	HT	WT	DOB	AVG	vLH	vRH	G	AB	R	H	2B	3B	HR	RBI	BB	HBP	SH	SF	SO	SB	CS	SLG	OBP
Aparicio, Miguel	L-L	6-0	165	3-17-99	.293	.276	.298	70	294	47	86	12	3	4	33	16	2	5	0	39	2	8	.395	.333
Cordero, Andretty	R-R	6-1	170	5-3-97	.277	.276	.278	31	119	16	33	9	0	8	24	6	3	0	0	25	0	2	.555	.328
Enright, Kole	B-R	6-1	175	1-21-98	.233	.276	.218	67	232	29	54	8	2	3	20	24	4	3	1	55	4	2	.323	.314
Gonzalez, Pedro	R-R	6-5	190	10-27-97	.000	.000	.000	6	17	2	0	0	0	0	0	2	0	0	0	8	0	0	.000	.105
Hernandez, Yonny	B-R	5-9	140	5-4-98	.250	.364	.222	18	56	13	14	2	0	1	9	12	1	2	1	12	4	3	.339	.386
Inoa, Cristian	R-R	5-10	165	7-4-99	.213	.320	.178	60	207	21	44	10	1	4	31	13	3	2	5	48	2	1	.329	.263
Kaye, Nick	L-L	6-2	180	10-18-96	.129	.222	.115	34	70	8	9	2	0	0	5	12	3	0	1	33	1	0	.157	.279
Leblanc, Charles	R-R	6-3	195	6-3-96	.191	.217	.175	17	63	8	12	4	0	0	2	6	1	0	0	12	2	2	.254	.271
McReynolds, Jonah	R-R	5-11	165	12-16-95	.132	.077	.146	38	68	10	9	0	2	0	4	1	3	0	0	24	0	2	.191	.181
Middleton, Clayton	R-R	6-0	205	10-8-93	.263	.316	.253	39	118	15	31	4	1	4	17	11	1	0	3	34	0	1	.415	.323
Novoa, Melvin	R-R	5-11	200	6-17-96	.282	.233	.295	38	135	14	38	11	1	4	15	7	5	1	1	24	1	1	.467	.338
O'Banion, Austin	R-R	6-3	215	7-12-95	.250	.349	.221	54	188	23	47	17	1	5	24	13	14	0	4	73	0	4	.431	.338
Pozo, Yohel	R-R	6-0	175	6-14-97	.288	.353	.262	15	59	11	17	7	0	2	10	1	0	0	1	3	0	0	.509	.295
Quiroz, Isaias	R-R	5-10	195	10-22-96	.171	.100	.194	19	41	7	7	3	0	0	2	10	1	0	0	11	0	1	.244	.346
Ratliff, Tyler	R-R	6-2	210	11-2-95	.264	.333	.243	49	197	27	52	13	0	6	25	17	3	0	1	44	2	1	.421	.330
Rollin, Franklin	R-R	5-11	165	8-26-95	.000	—	.000	1	3	0	0	0	0	0	0	0	0	0	0	2	0	0	.000	.000
Seise, Chris	R-R	6-2	175	1-6-99	.222	.138	.257	24	99	10	22	3	1	0	9	4	0	0	1	30	1	1	.273	.250
Smith, Chad	L-L	6-2	200	9-30-97	.277	.314	.264	39	141	24	39	15	0	3	13	16	1	0	0	50	11	3	.447	.354
Taylor, Kobie	R-R	6-1	175	8-13-98	.214	.308	.182	34	103	13	22	4	4	2	7	3	3	0	0	40	1	0	.388	.257
Terry, Curtis	R-R	6-2	255	10-6-96	.258	.368	.221	61	229	26	59	12	0	12	30	7	8	0	0	60	3	0	.467	.303
Whatley, Matt	R-R	5-10	200	1-7-96	.289	.382	.261	39	149	23	43	6	0	6	25	16	4	0	1	28	3	4	.450	.371

Pitching	B-T	HT	WT	DOB	W	L	ERA	G	GS	CG	SV	IP	H	R	ER	HR	BB	SO	AVG	vLH	vRH	K/9	BB/9
Advocate, Josh	R-R	6-1	195	1-18-94	1	2	3.50	15	0	0	4	18	21	7	7	2	3	15	.292	.240	.319	7.50	1.50
Barlow, Joe	R-R	6-3	195	9-28-95	6	1	2.00	16	0	0	0	45	28	13	10	0	28	64	.177	.162	.189	12.80	5.60
Beltre, Dario	R-R	6-3	170	11-19-92	0	2	3.09	7	0	0	0	12	11	4	4	1	3	13	.244	.350	.160	10.03	2.31
Bremer, Noah	R-R	6-5	200	5-13-96	1	0	1.35	11	0	0	0	20	10	4	3	1	4	30	.152	.148	.154	13.50	1.80
Bruce, Steven	R-R	6-0	190	3-7-92	0	1	1.69	4	0	0	0	5	3	2	1	0	3	6	.158	.200	.143	10.13	5.06
Bueno, Hever	R-R	6-2	179	11-23-94	0	0	5.57	6	6	0	0	21	20	16	13	1	16	26	.244	.238	.250	11.14	6.86
Carvajal, Ronny	R-R	6-3	180	10-9-95	0	0	7.53	10	0	0	2	14	19	16	12	0	5	8	.312	.345	.281	5.02	3.14
Eubanks, Alex	R-R	6-2	180	9-13-95	3	0	1.17	10	0	0	3	15	7	2	2	0	2	23	.143	.067	.177	13.50	1.17
Evans, Demarcus	R-R	6-4	240	10-22-96	0	2	2.59	5	5	0	0	24	15	10	7	0	9	25	.171	.161	.175	9.25	3.33
Jacobsen, Lucas	L-L	6-5	190	7-1-95	3	0	1.64	10	0	0	1	11	5	2	2	0	6	18	.143	.222	.115	14.73	4.91
Juan, Johan	R-R	6-1	180	4-14-94	0	0	4.70	3	0	0	0	8	11	6	4	1	4	8	.324	.267	.368	9.39	4.70
Kuzia, Joseph	R-R	6-5	190	10-3-93	1	1	2.59	16	0	0	5	31	28	16	9	2	3	45	.222	.217	.225	12.93	0.86
Lopez, Ismel	R-R	6-1	190	8-24-94	2	2	4.76	14	0	0	1	28	30	18	15	1	19	38	.270	.239	.292	12.07	6.04
Lopez, Luis	R-R	6-4	185	7-25-96	1	4	7.41	13	4	0	1	34	49	30	28	3	15	25	.345	.404	.311	6.62	3.97
Phillips, Tyler	R-R	6-5	200	10-27-97	4	2	3.45	13	13	0	0	73	78	33	28	6	11	78	.265	.219	.301	9.62	1.36
Ragans, Cole	L-L	6-4	190	12-12-97	3	2	3.61	13	13	0	0	57	50	27	23	5	35	87	.234	.326	.211	13.66	5.49
Rodriguez, Argenis	R-R	6-3	190	3-7-96	0	0	6.15	12	0	0	1	26	24	19	18	2	15	36	.240	.267	.218	12.30	5.13
Rogers, Jacob	R-L	6-4	220	8-23-89	0	0	10.00	6	0	0	0	9	11	11	10	4	5	15	.282	.444	.233	15.00	5.00
Sanburn, Parker	R-R	6-1	195	11-12-94	0	1	2.70	6	0	0	0	10	5	3	3	0	10	10	.152	.143	.158	9.00	9.00
Sanmartin, Reiver	L-L	6-2	160	4-15-96	3	1	2.27	7	5	0	0	32	38	12	8	2	3	28	.282	.258	.289	7.96	0.85
Speas, Alex	R-R	6-4	180	3-4-98	1	6	6.15	16	7	0	1	34	29	31	23	5	25	45	.223	.143	.272	12.03	6.68
Thompson, Tyree	R-R	6-4	165	6-12-97	5	1	3.15	13	13	0	0	69	63	25	24	7	22	44	.245	.301	.208	5.77	2.88
Tiedemann, Tai	R-R	6-6	195	5-31-96	4	4	3.83	13	10	0	0	52	58	31	22	2	26	43	.286	.256	.308	7.49	4.53
Vivas, Samir	R-R	5-11	170	2-1-95	0	2	4.26	11	0	0	2	13	14	8	6	1	5	19	.259	.207	.320	13.50	3.55
Wiper, Cole	R-R	6-4	185	6-3-92	0	1	3.60	4	0	0	1	5	5	3	2	0	2	5	.263	.000	.417	9.00	3.60
Wynn, Sterling	L-B	6-2	175	11-23-93	0	1	8.22	7	0	0	0	8	8	8	7	1	8	6	.258	.500	.143	7.04	9.39
Zawadzki, Grant	R-R	5-10	200	4-27-92	1	1	9.00	2	0	0	0	3	4	3	3	1	2	1	.286	.667	.182	3.00	6.00

Fielding

C: Middleton 17, Novoa 17, Pozo 8, Quiroz 16, Whatley 25. **1B:** Cordero 13, Middleton 11, Ratliff 4, Terry 54. **2B:** Enright 44, Hernandez 12, Inoa 19, Leblanc 3, McReynolds 1. **3B:** Cordero 14, Enright 25, Hernandez 1, Leblanc 10, McReynolds 1, Ratliff 28. **SS:** Hernandez 6, Inoa 40, Leblanc 4, McReynolds 8, Seise 23. **OF:** Aparicio 69, Kaye 29, McReynolds 18, O'Banion 47, Quiroz 1, Ratliff 16, Rollin 1, Smith 37, Taylor 31.

AZL RANGERS — *ROOKIE*

ARIZONA LEAGUE

Batting	B-T	HT	WT	DOB	AVG	vLH	vRH	G	AB	R	H	2B	3B	HR	RBI	BB	HBP	SH	SF	SO	SB	CS	SLG	OBP
Almonte, Juan	R-R	6-0	168	4-13-97	.040	.000	.056	11	25	2	1	0	0	0	1	0	1	1	0	2	1	0	.040	.077
Bernier, Doug	R-R	6-1	185	6-24-80	.400	—	.400	2	5	3	2	1	0	0	0	3	0	0	0	0	0	0	.600	.625
Day, Darius	L-L	5-11	175	8-25-94	.333	.000	.389	10	21	6	7	3	0	0	5	13	0	0	0	9	1	0	.476	.588
Diaz, Willy	R-R	6-3	200	4-19-94	.040	.000	.056	9	25	3	1	0	0	0	3	6	0	0	0	14	1	0	.040	.226
Dorow, Ryan	R-R	6-0	195	8-21-95	.296	.419	.255	40	125	17	37	7	2	0	17	15	3	2	1	27	7	2	.384	.382

Batting	B-T	HT	WT	DOB	AVG	vLH	vRH	G	AB	R	H	2B	3B	HR	RBI	BB	HBP	SH	SF	SO	SB	CS	SLG	OBP
Hernandez, Yonny	B-R	5-9	140	5-4-98	.231	.320	.207	32	117	25	27	7	0	0	12	24	3	0	2	11	13	2	.291	.370
Huff, Sam	R-R	6-4	215	1-14-98	.249	.138	.295	49	197	34	49	9	2	9	31	24	1	0	3	66	3	2	.452	.329
Jacobs, Justin	L-R	6-1	195	10-25-95	.326	.213	.366	48	181	37	59	9	2	2	27	33	4	0	1	37	8	5	.431	.438
Joseph, Starling	R-R	6-3	180	8-1-98	.256	.321	.220	21	78	13	20	2	3	3	14	4	1	0	0	28	2	2	.474	.301
Lohr, Stephen	R-R	6-0	208	3-2-95	.257	.333	.225	36	113	11	29	7	0	3	10	19	2	1	0	38	0	1	.398	.373
Mack, Marcus	L-L	6-2	185	8-1-98	.207	.133	.231	41	121	21	25	4	7	1	19	20	1	2	1	53	11	2	.380	.322
McKisic, Myles	R-R	6-2	185	11-3-97	.194	.083	.218	25	67	10	13	3	0	0	3	6	1	0	0	33	2	2	.239	.270
Mendoza, Kevin	B-R	5-10	155	8-16-95	.295	.150	.366	18	61	8	18	1	2	0	7	5	2	0	0	11	2	1	.377	.368
Ratliff, Tyler	R-R	6-2	210	11-2-95	.500	.556	.480	8	34	13	17	4	0	0	9	3	0	0	0	5	0	0	.618	.541
Reed, Tyreque	R-R	6-2	260	6-6-97	.350	.171	.424	35	120	35	42	13	2	5	29	22	2	0	1	26	3	1	.617	.455
Ricumstrict, Obie	R-R	6-2	175	7-20-98	.225	.158	.250	39	138	17	31	6	0	0	18	15	3	0	2	44	9	1	.268	.310
Seise, Chris	R-R	6-2	175	1-6-99	.336	.342	.333	27	116	23	39	5	3	3	27	9	3	0	1	30	5	0	.509	.395
Taylor, Kobie	R-R	6-1	175	8-13-98	.225	.429	.182	13	40	7	9	2	0	0	4	2	0	0	0	15	2	2	.275	.262
Thompson, Bubba	R-R	6-2	180	6-9-98	.257	.346	.230	30	113	23	29	7	2	3	12	6	4	0	0	28	5	5	.434	.317
Ventura, Francisco	R-R	5-9	175	11-19-98	.300	.241	.317	34	130	13	39	5	0	0	23	12	0	0	0	32	0	0	.339	.359
Ventura, Juan	R-R	6-0	165	6-15-98	.200	.000	.268	16	55	8	11	3	0	1	6	3	1	0	0	16	0	1	.309	.254
Whatley, Matt	R-R	5-10	200	1-7-96	.353	.667	.286	5	17	5	6	0	1	0	3	2	0	0	0	3	0	1	.471	.421

Pitching	B-T	HT	WT	DOB	W	L	ERA	G	GS	CG	SV	IP	H	R	ER	HR	BB	SO	AVG	vLH	vRH	K/9	BB/9
Advocate, Josh	R-R	6-1	195	1-18-94	0	1	4.15	3	0	0	0	4	4	2	2	0	1	2	.250	.000	.444	4.15	2.08
Bass, Anthony	R-R	6-2	200	11-1-87	0	1	4.00	3	2	0	0	9	11	5	4	1	2	9	.306	.263	.353	9.00	2.00
Bice, Dylan	L-R	6-4	220	8-17-97	1	2	4.58	10	6	0	0	39	31	22	20	2	21	40	.217	.225	.213	9.15	4.81
Bremer, Noah	R-R	6-5	200	5-13-96	0	0	40.50	1	0	0	0	1	3	3	3	0	1	1	.600	1.000	.333	13.50	13.50
Bueno, Hever	R-R	6-2	179	11-23-94	2	1	3.94	5	2	0	0	16	16	14	7	0	10	18	.250	.286	.233	10.13	5.63
Casanova, Jean	R-R	6-3	155	3-4-97	5	2	2.70	11	5	0	0	37	34	17	11	0	18	47	.241	.283	.221	11.54	4.42
Chapman, Jaye	R-R	6-0	195	5-22-87	0	0	0.00	1	1	0	0	1	0	0	0	0	1	2	.000	—	.000	18.00	9.00
Crouse, Hans	L-R	6-4	180	9-15-98	0	0	0.45	10	6	0	0	20	7	2	1	1	7	30	.109	.130	.098	13.50	3.15
Cruz, Israel	R-R	6-1	170	6-1-97	3	2	5.91	12	3	0	0	32	36	24	21	1	16	42	.288	.321	.261	11.81	4.50
Dease, Ryan	R-R	6-3	175	4-15-99	3	1	2.05	11	4	0	0	22	18	5	5	2	2	19	.228	.194	.250	7.77	0.82
Eubanks, Alex	R-R	6-2	180	9-13-95	0	0	0.00	1	0	0	0	1	1	0	0	0	0	2	.250	.500	.000	18.00	0.00
Evans, Demarcus	R-R	6-4	240	10-22-96	0	1	11.12	3	3	0	0	6	6	7	7	0	6	10	.273	.250	.286	15.88	9.53
Griffin, A.J.	R-R	6-5	230	1-28-88	0	0	0.00	1	1	0	0	3	0	0	0	0	0	2	.000	.000	.000	6.00	0.00
Heffel, Derek	R-R	6-6	225	4-13-96	2	3	2.84	11	6	0	1	44	40	16	14	1	14	50	.242	.208	.269	10.15	2.84
Iseneker, Marc	R-R	6-2	200	8-24-95	0	0	7.00	7	0	0	0	9	12	7	7	1	3	4	.324	.333	.318	4.00	3.00
Jacobsen, Lucas	L-L	6-5	190	7-1-95	0	0	10.80	3	0	0	0	3	5	5	4	1	1	7	.333	.000	.417	18.90	2.70
Jarneski, Joseph	R-R	6-0	170	10-28-99	0	0	9.00	8	0	0	0	6	10	6	6	0	7	7	.370	.500	.294	10.50	10.50
Jones, James	L-L	6-4	200	9-24-88	0	0	5.40	4	1	0	0	3	3	4	2	0	4	3	.273	.000	.333	8.10	10.80
Keith, Kyle	L-R	6-0	180	11-20-94	1	0	8.74	11	0	0	0	11	16	14	11	1	11	13	.333	.294	.355	10.32	8.74
LaFromboise, Bobby	L-L	6-4	225	6-25-86	0	0	0.00	2	2	0	0	3	1	0	0	0	2	4	.100	.250	.000	12.00	6.00
Latz, Jake	R-L	6-2	185	4-8-96	0	1	6.75	2	0	0	0	3	3	2	2	0	2	5	.273	.000	.500	16.88	6.75
Leal, Werner	R-R	6-1	160	7-8-95	2	3	5.01	12	6	0	0	41	46	27	23	1	13	43	.274	.241	.291	9.36	2.83
Martinez, Greidy	R-R	6-0	155	4-2-94	2	1	1.59	13	0	0	4	17	18	7	3	0	4	23	.265	.355	.189	12.18	2.12
Mendoza, Kenny	R-L	6-4	215	3-12-98	1	0	2.57	2	1	0	0	7	5	4	2	0	6	5	.208	.250	.200	6.43	7.71
Moore, Xavier	R-R	6-2	175	1-7-99	0	0	3.60	12	0	0	2	15	15	8	6	0	8	17	.250	.125	.296	10.20	4.80
Morris, Chris	R-R	6-2	180	1-11-96	2	1	5.49	11	0	0	0	20	20	12	12	1	14	20	.286	.172	.366	9.15	6.41
Nordlin, Seth	R-R	6-4	205	9-4-97	3	0	2.49	12	0	0	0	22	12	6	6	0	5	34	.164	.222	.130	14.12	2.08
Paul, Xavier	L-R	6-0	205	2-25-85	0	0	0.00	7	0	0	0	9	4	0	0	0	3	6	.154	.222	.118	6.23	3.12
Pena, Domingo	R-R	6-2	171	4-7-98	0	2	5.06	6	2	0	0	16	15	11	9	4	6	20	.242	.269	.222	11.25	3.38
Robertson, Wes	R-R	6-2	190	3-11-96	0	0	4.50	9	0	0	0	8	10	4	4	0	7	9	.303	.154	.400	10.13	7.88
Sampson, Adrian	R-R	6-2	210	10-7-91	1	1	4.26	4	4	0	0	13	11	7	6	0	1	7	.239	.385	.182	4.97	0.71
Snyder, Nick	R-R	6-4	190	10-10-95	0	0	1.29	5	0	0	0	7	6	2	1	0	0	6	.214	.400	.174	7.71	0.00
Urena, Joel	L-L	6-5	235	8-17-99	1	1	1.53	12	0	0	1	18	14	5	3	0	8	14	.222	.118	.261	7.13	4.08
Valdespina, Jose	R-R	6-6	220	3-22-92	0	0	4.50	2	0	0	0	2	3	1	1	0	1	2	.333	.500	.000	9.00	4.50
Vanasco, Ricky	R-R	6-3	180	10-13-98	0	1	0.00	10	0	0	0	9	8	2	0	0	5	16	.229	.273	.208	16.00	5.00
Vivas, Samir	R-R	5-11	170	2-1-95	1	0	0.00	2	0	0	0	5	3	0	0	0	1	8	.177	.200	.167	15.43	1.93
Wiper, Cole	R-R	6-4	185	6-3-92	0	0	0.00	3	0	0	0	4	1	0	0	0	1	5	.091	.167	.000	11.25	2.25

Fielding

C: Huff 30, Mendoza 3, Ventura 1, Ventura 19, Whatley 3. **1B:** Diaz 3, Jacobs 2, Lohr 29, Mendoza 4, Reed 28. **2B:** Almonte 1, Bernier 2, Dorow 26, Hernandez 13, Jacobs 7, McKisic 10, Ventura 1. **3B:** Almonte 2, Diaz 4, Dorow 4, Hernandez 2, Jacobs 12, Lohr 1, Mendoza 3, Ratliff 4, Ricumstrict 16, Ventura 13. **SS:** Almonte 3, Hernandez 18, McKisic 1, Ricumstrict 12, Seise 24, Ventura 2. **OF:** Almonte 3, Day 9, Dorow 11, Jacobs 30, Joseph 21, Mack 39, McKisic 12, Mendoza 1, Ratliff 3, Reed 9, Ricumstrict 12, Taylor 11, Thompson 27.

DSL RANGERS — *ROOKIE*

DOMINICAN SUMMER LEAGUE

Batting	B-T	HT	WT	DOB	AVG	vLH	vRH	G	AB	R	H	2B	3B	HR	RBI	BB	HBP	SH	SF	SO	SB	CS	SLG	OBP
Almonte, Juan	R-R	6-0	168	4-13-97	.324	.316	.325	44	176	45	57	9	3	1	32	10	5	2	4	10	11	6	.426	.369
Alonzo, Yimmelvyn	R-R	6-1	185	3-10-97	.204	.286	.195	54	142	25	29	6	5	4	17	40	3	1	0	49	6	3	.401	.389
Aponte, Angel	R-R	6-0	170	2-3-00	.261	.289	.250	60	184	36	48	11	3	3	24	22	8	0	1	41	14	3	.402	.363
Arias, Diosbel	R-R	6-2	190	7-21-96	.419	.500	.391	8	31	4	13	4	0	0	8	1	0	0	0	6	0	0	.548	.438
Barrios, Ciro	R-R	6-0	178	9-27-96	.320	.250	.333	16	25	4	8	2	0	0	4	4	1	0	0	10	1	0	.400	.433
Bidau, Juan	R-R	5-9	155	12-29-99	.238	.280	.224	39	101	18	24	4	2	1	11	14	1	2	0	18	6	2	.347	.336
Cabrera, Wanderley	R-R	5-10	180	2-27-95	.216	.333	.200	26	51	3	11	4	1	0	7	3	0	2	1	9	1	0	.333	.255
Cardozo, Jose	R-R	6-2	180	9-8-99	.154	.200	.125	19	39	3	6	0	0	0	1	3	1	1	0	11	0	1	.154	.233
Caygua, Yeyker	R-R	5-10	155	5-3-99	.103	.200	.083	14	29	1	3	0	0	0	0	2	0	0	0	6	3	1	.103	.161

Chirinos, Michael	B-R	5-10	155	10-11-99	.211	.182	.222	51	152	25	32	4	3	1	25	21	0	5	2	16	9	3	.296	.303
Damian, Rayner	B-R	6-0	155	4-29-97	.296	.000	.325	21	44	13	13	1	2	0	5	9	2	0	1	12	3	1	.409	.429
Drullard, Danny	L-L	6-1	175	5-8-00	.278	.160	.330	47	162	35	45	6	4	8	34	25	0	0	4	32	6	1	.512	.367
Favela, Samuel	R-R	5-11	160	5-15-98	.086	.000	.097	24	35	4	3	0	0	0	3	3	2	1	1	9	0	1	.086	.195
Garcia, David	B-R	5-11	160	2-6-00	.215	.143	.246	58	186	27	40	7	1	1	26	25	6	1	4	49	1	0	.280	.321
Guanipa, Osman	R-R	5-10	155	3-17-99	.095	.000	.105	12	21	3	2	0	0	0	1	2	1	0	0	12	0	0	.095	.208
Guardo, Jose	R-R	6-0	180	2-6-99	.261	.083	.324	14	46	6	12	2	0	1	3	6	3	0	1	14	2	1	.370	.375
Gutierrez, Beder	R-R	6-0	180	1-13-97	.290	.385	.281	47	152	32	44	10	1	5	33	27	4	3	3	31	9	3	.467	.403
Gutierrez, Jember	R-R	5-11	160	9-8-99	.276	.308	.264	59	181	26	50	9	2	0	24	37	2	2	3	27	6	5	.348	.399
Guzman, Yaniery	B-R	5-11	185	5-30-98	.285	.279	.287	49	158	21	45	6	3	4	21	22	2	0	1	26	0	2	.437	.377
Leon, Isaias	R-R	6-2	182	8-23-99	.180	.105	.208	47	139	25	25	5	0	1	13	11	11	1	3	54	5	4	.237	.287
Leon, Sergio	R-R	6-1	170	9-25-99	.115	.200	.095	11	26	1	3	0	0	0	0	1	0	0	0	10	0	0	.115	.148
Linares, Angel	R-R	5-11	175	1-21-98	.276	.333	.261	16	29	6	8	1	0	0	4	7	1	0	1	6	1	1	.310	.421
Liriano, Welin	R-R	6-2	160	10-18-98	.228	.227	.228	49	158	33	36	7	3	4	24	31	2	1	5	52	1	7	.386	.352
Martinez, Stanley	R-R	6-0	176	1-5-97	.287	.400	.273	59	192	35	55	11	2	6	37	26	9	1	5	32	5	1	.458	.388
Mejia, Leuri	B-R	6-0	150	8-30-00	.174	.203	.161	63	196	50	34	11	9	2	24	51	7	1	3	81	15	3	.352	.358
Mendoza, Edilberto	L-R	6-0	180	7-2-99	.207	.214	.206	32	87	17	18	2	0	1	7	22	3	0	2	21	0	0	.264	.377
Morales, Maxwell	R-R	6-0	190	9-28-97	.246	.400	.229	56	199	37	49	8	0	11	36	23	4	0	3	65	4	2	.452	.332
Odor, Rougned	R-R	5-8	140	10-17-97	.232	.154	.240	47	138	23	32	5	0	0	16	25	4	2	3	35	7	6	.268	.359
Ogando, Pedro	L-R	6-0	175	6-10-94	.255	.348	.237	43	141	32	36	2	4	0	11	18	3	2	2	18	16	2	.326	.348
Pena, Andrison	L-R	6-0	165	10-27-96	.344	.143	.362	48	163	29	56	17	3	4	37	31	1	0	2	18	4	3	.558	.447
Pernalete, Adrian	B-R	6-0	165	9-14-98	.171	.083	.207	19	41	6	7	3	0	0	3	3	0	0	0	8	2	0	.244	.227
Perozo, Rehybell	B-R	6-3	180	11-6-99	.210	.233	.202	55	167	16	35	3	1	1	19	25	1	0	3	49	2	2	.258	.311
Pineda, Edgar	R-R	5-11	140	2-12-98	.152	.071	.162	40	125	19	19	2	0	1	9	19	5	2	3	33	3	3	.192	.283
Quiceno, Daniel	L-R	6-1	165	2-8-00	.300	.333	.286	3	10	1	3	0	0	0	0	1	0	0	0	3	1	0	.300	.364
Rivera, Eudys	R-R	6-1	152	6-3-97	.262	.286	.260	48	141	25	37	3	3	0	11	17	4	2	1	23	11	3	.326	.356
Rodriguez, Josue	R-R	5-10	160	12-27-99	.091	.000	.100	8	11	1	1	0	0	0	1	1	2	0	0	5	0	0	.091	.286
Valdez, Fernando	B-R	6-0	175	11-14-98	.200	.333	.181	58	190	30	38	7	3	6	28	21	6	0	3	60	2	1	.363	.296
Velasquez, Emir	B-R	5-8	160	3-10-00	.247	.329	.209	65	223	38	55	8	3	1	29	42	3	3	2	27	17	10	.323	.370
Villa, Ramon Ulises	L-R	5-9	170	12-2-95	.241	.235	.234	32	79	17	19	2	1	0	10	25	1	0	2	23	2	0	.291	.421
Zacarias, Oswaldo	R-R	5-11	165	1-20-99	.312	.320	.309	25	93	12	29	3	1	0	10	3	1	0	1	8	5	2	.366	.337

Pitching	B-T	HT	WT	DOB	W	L	ERA	G	GS	CG	SV	IP	H	R	ER	HR	BB	SO	AVG	vLH	vRH	K/9	BB/9
Beard, Aneudis	R-R	6-1	185	1-30-98	3	5	3.40	15	7	0	1	48	50	27	18	3	18	34	.287	.280	.290	6.42	3.40
Betances, Emmanuel	R-R	6-5	189	2-5-96	2	2	4.83	18	0	0	3	32	40	22	17	1	13	18	.305	.231	.337	5.12	3.69
Buitimea, Martin	R-R	6-1	155	4-14-98	2	1	3.18	16	1	0	4	40	40	18	14	2	13	33	.260	.243	.265	7.49	2.95
Castillo, Juan	R-R	6-3	166	9-18-95	5	1	1.65	11	11	1	0	60	42	12	11	1	19	35	.202	.171	.220	5.25	2.85
Civil, Henrry	R-R	6-5	194	12-14-94	0	0	0.00	3	0	0	0	5	3	0	0	0	2	3	.177	.000	.231	5.40	3.60
Cruz, Edwin	L-L	6-4	195	7-26-94	1	2	4.73	10	7	0	1	32	35	19	17	1	15	28	.280	.333	.263	7.79	4.18
Cruz, Juan	R-R	6-6	215	12-5-97	4	1	2.25	16	0	0	3	32	27	12	8	1	10	28	.225	.205	.237	7.88	2.81
Encarnacion, Ediberto	R-R	5-11	170	2-9-94	1	0	3.94	15	0	0	2	30	25	17	13	0	15	25	.229	.282	.200	7.58	4.55
Encarnacion, Yohan	R-R	6-3	180	1-19-96	2	2	5.27	15	0	0	2	27	23	21	16	1	13	24	.230	.200	.250	7.90	4.28
Escalona, Maikol	L-L	5-10	170	10-19-98	3	1	2.70	18	0	0	6	43	38	15	13	1	26	33	.248	.211	.254	6.85	5.40
Fernandez, Jeuyson	R-R	6-2	185	6-9-98	0	3	5.25	6	0	0	0	12	16	13	7	1	6	17	.340	.294	.367	12.75	4.50
Hernandez, Alexander	L-L	6-1	170	3-20-98	2	1	8.44	6	3	0	0	16	21	16	15	3	8	10	.323	.000	.462	5.63	4.50
Inojosa, Rosmer	R-R	6-3	165	8-10-99	4	3	3.75	16	10	0	1	60	65	29	25	3	9	45	.275	.271	.278	6.75	1.35
Jasco, Yeison	R-R	6-0	160	8-5-96	1	0	3.86	9	0	0	2	19	22	13	8	1	7	7	.286	.250	.317	3.38	3.38
Lacle, Wily	R-R	6-2	175	5-30-96	1	3	6.00	15	0	0	0	24	23	22	16	0	25	17	.258	.216	.289	6.38	9.38
Linarez, Jesus	R-R	6-4	216	1-10-97	5	1	2.93	12	12	0	0	61	64	22	20	1	14	66	.272	.255	.286	9.68	2.05
Lopez, Abrahan	R-R	5-10	160	9-27-99	3	1	2.22	15	0	0	6	28	23	9	7	2	9	16	.237	.250	.228	5.08	2.86
Mavo, Daniel	L-L	5-10	170	7-20-95	2	2	2.30	15	0	0	3	27	25	17	7	0	18	21	.248	.333	.229	6.91	5.93
Medrano, Miguel	R-R	6-0	165	1-4-98	5	1	2.59	12	10	0	0	59	53	18	17	2	7	61	.243	.174	.275	9.31	1.07
Mejia, Juan	L-L	5-11	160	1-9-99	6	2	2.42	12	12	0	0	67	58	22	18	2	12	48	.234	.233	.234	6.45	1.61
Naveda, Carlos	R-R	6-2	190	7-5-99	5	1	2.43	14	12	0	1	56	44	15	15	3	19	66	.218	.188	.233	10.67	3.07
Nunez, Jeifry	R-R	5-11	160	4-1-98	3	1	5.28	9	3	0	0	31	34	19	18	3	8	30	.288	.368	.250	8.80	2.35
Ontiveros, Felipe	R-R	6-2	185	9-2-93	1	0	2.77	8	0	0	0	13	6	7	4	1	11	10	.154	.313	.044	6.92	7.62
Pacheco, Sergio	R-R	6-1	170	8-17-99	3	1	2.86	14	7	1	0	57	65	24	18	1	8	33	.293	.254	.311	5.24	1.27
Pena, Domingo	R-R	6-2	171	4-7-98	1	0	0.00	4	3	0	0	14	7	1	0	0	2	16	.149	.000	.259	10.29	1.29
Rodriguez, Eury	R-R	6-1	195	9-17-97	1	2	4.29	11	0	0	0	21	17	11	10	2	15	15	.221	.179	.245	6.43	6.43
Rodriguez, Yerry	R-R	6-2	180	10-15-97	1	0	0.00	2	1	0	0	6	6	0	0	0	1	3	.286	.500	.235	4.50	1.50
Rosario, Luis	R-R	5-11	165	2-8-97	2	3	1.69	10	9	0	0	48	34	23	9	1	3	43	.182	.242	.152	8.06	0.56
Rovain, Hector	R-R	6-1	165	5-5-98	1	1	15.00	11	0	0	0	9	16	16	15	0	12	5	.421	.462	.400	5.00	12.00
Santiago, Manuel	L-L	6-0	175	10-15-99	4	4	3.65	13	11	0	0	62	62	31	25	4	6	47	.263	.234	.270	6.86	0.88
Suarez, Sergio	L-L	6-0	160	5-24-95	3	2	3.11	17	0	0	0	38	47	22	13	0	17	26	.313	.346	.307	6.21	4.06
Torres, Darel	R-R	5-11	160	1-5-99	3	2	1.99	14	5	0	4	50	44	12	11	2	5	36	.238	.224	.246	6.52	0.91
Urriola, Elvis	L-L	5-11	180	9-9-97	6	0	1.96	11	11	1	0	55	36	20	12	2	20	41	.180	.146	.189	6.71	3.27
Volquez, Rafael	R-R	6-5	200	4-25-95	2	4	4.09	9	6	0	0	33	35	22	15	2	9	26	.271	.346	.216	7.09	2.45

Fielding

C: Cabrera 8, Favela 19, Garcia 41, Guardo 8, Leon 6, Mendoza 30, Morales 33, Pernalete 17, Rodriguez 2, Zacarias 9. **1B:** Alonzo 1, Barrios 2, Bidau 1, Cabrera 7, Chirinos 16, Guanipa 5, Gutierrez 12, Guzman 33, Leon 1, Liriano 2, Martinez 46, Morales 8, Pena 17, Perozo 4, Pineda 1, Valdez 1, Villa 5, Zacarias 8. **2B:** Almonte 1, Arias 1, Barrios 14, Bidau 20, Caygua 7, Chirinos 11, Guanipa 1, Gutierrez 5, Liriano 2, Odor 35, Pena 11, Pineda 11, Valdez 25, Velasquez 36, Villa 5. **3B:** Almonte 4, Bidau 2, Caygua 2, Chirinos 9, Guanipa 4, Gutierrez 17, Liriano 37, Martinez 8, Pena 6, Perozo 39, Velasquez 3, Villa 3. **SS:** Almonte 37, Arias 8, Bidau 10, Caygua 4, Chirinos 12, Guanipa 2, Gutierrez 18, Liriano 4, Perozo 11, Pineda 24, Velasquez 23, Villa 1. **OF:** Alonzo 51, Aponte 58, Cardozo 18, Damian 18, Drullard 37, Gutierrez 43, Leon 41, Linares 12, Martinez 1, Mejia 61, Ogando 40, Pena 1, Perozo 1, Quiceno 3, Rivera 39, Valdez 27, Villa 16, Zacarias 4.

Toronto Blue Jays

SEASON IN A SENTENCE: Injuries to key performers, offseason departures and the decline of aging stars helped end Toronto's postseason streak at two years.

HIGH POINT: The Blue Jays got as close to contending as they would get in late May and early June; a 7-5 win against the Yankees improved them to 26-27 and included a pair of homers by Josh Donaldson and one of Justin Smoak's team-high team-high 38 homers.

LOW POINT: The Jays got off to a miserable start, losing 17 of their first 23. But if there were any thoughts of the Jays' being a contender, they were answered around the all-star break. They lost two of three to the Astros just before the break, including 12-2 and 19-1 drubbings, then lost seven of 10 coming out of the break, capped by a three-game sweep in Cleveland to old friend Edwin Encarnacion and the Indians.

NOTABLE ROOKIES: Righthander Danny Barnes was the club's most prominent rookie, logging 66 relief innings. His 60 appearances ranked second among American League rookies. Righty Chris Rowley became the first big leaguer out of West Point since the 1920s when he made six appearances, including three starts for Toronto.

KEY TRANSACTIONS: In the offseason, Toronto acted quickly, signing DH Kendrys Morales to replace Encarnacion. Morales had his moments, with 38 home runs while hitting just .250/.308/.445. In July, Toronto sold, shedding Francisco Liriano's contract to Houston in a deal that brought back toolsy outfielder Teoscar Hernandez, among others. Hernandez hit eight homers in 26 games in September. Toronto also traded righty Joe Smith to Cleveland and acquired struggling starter Tom Koehler from the Marlins in August.

DOWN ON THE FARM: Big league progeny and teammates Bo Bichette, a second-round pick in 2016, and Vladimir Guerrero Jr. combined to take the minor leagues by storm at two stops, playing together on the left side of the infield. They started together in low Class A Lansing and finished with high Class A Dunedin, neither known as a hitter's paradise. Bichette hit .362/.423/.565 overall to lead the minors in batting, while Guerrero led in on-base percentage during a .323/.425/.485 season. Meanwhile, short-season Vancouver was the lone Jays affiliate to win a championship, winning its fourth Northwest League crown since 2011.

OPENING DAY PAYROLL: $177,795,368 (5th)

PLAYERS OF THE YEAR

MAJOR LEAGUE

Marcus Stroman
RHP
13-9, 3.09
164 SO, 201 IP
First Gold Glove

MINOR LEAGUE

Bo Bichette
SS
(Low Class A/
High Class A)
.362/.423/.565

ORGANIZATION LEADERS

BATTING			*Minimum 250 AB
MAJORS			
*	AVG	Ezequiel Carrera	.282
*	OPS	Josh Donaldson	1.143
	HR	Justin Smoak	38
	RBI	Justin Smoak	90
MINORS			
*	AVG	Bo Bichette, Lansing, Dunedin	.362
*	OBP	Vladimir Guerrero Jr., Lansing, Dunedin	.425
*	SLG	Bo Bichette, Lansing, Dunedin	.565
*	OPS	Bo Bichette, Lansing, Dunedin	.988
	R	Edward Olivares, Lansing, Dunedin	93
	H	Bo Bichette, Lansing, Dunedin	162
	TB	Bo Bichette, Lansing, Dunedin	253
	2B	Bo Bichette, Lansing, Dunedin	41
	3B	Edward Olivares, Lansing, Dunedin	10
	HR	Connor Panas, Dunedin	18
	RBI	Vladimir Guerrero Jr., Lansing, Dunedin	76
	BB	Vladimir Guerrero Jr., Lansing, Dunedin	76
	SO	J.B. Woodman, Lansing	157
	SB	Roemon Fields, New Hampshire, Buffalo	50

PITCHING			#Minimum 75 IP
MAJORS			
	W	Marcus Stroman	13
#	ERA	Marcus Stroman	3.09
	SO	Marco Estrada	176
	SV	Roberto Osuna	39
MINORS			
	W	Sean Reid-Foley, New Hampshire	10
	L	Luis Santos, New Hampshire, Buffalo	13
#	ERA	Chris Rowley, New Hampshire, Buffalo	2.24
	G	Andrew Case, Dunedin, Buffalo, New Hampshire	50
	GS	Sean Reid-Foley, New Hampshire	27
	SV	Jackson McClelland, Lansing, Dunedin	15
	IP	Conor Fisk, Dunedin	152
	BB	Conner Greene, New Hampshire	83
	SO	Ryan Borucki, Dunedin, New Hampshire, Buffalo	157
#	AVG	Chris Rowley, New Hampshire, Buffalo	.218

2017 PERFORMANCE

General Manager: Ross Atkins. **Farm Director:** Gil Kim. **Scouting Director:** Steve Sanders.

Class	Team	League	W	L	PCT	Finish	Manager
Majors	Toronto Blue Jays	American	76	86	.469	11th (15)	John Gibbons
Triple-A	Buffalo Bisons	International	65	76	.461	11th (14)	Bob Meacham
Double-A	New Hampshire Fisher Cats	Eastern	59	80	.424	11th (12)	Gary Allenson
High-A	Dunedin Blue Jays	Florida State	72	66	.522	5th (12)	John Schneider
Low-A	Lansing Lugnuts	Midwest	63	73	.463	13th (16)	Cesar Martin
Short Season	Vancouver Canadians	Northwest	43	33	.566	1st (8)	Rich Miller
Rookie	Bluefield Blue Jays	Appalachian	46	22	.676	1st (10)	Dennis Holmberg
Rookie	GCL Blue Jays	Gulf Coast	35	25	.583	4th (17)	Luis Hurtado
Overall 2017 Minor League Record			383	375	.505	t-9th (30)	

ORGANIZATION STATISTICS

TORONTO BLUE JAYS

AMERICAN LEAGUE

Batting	B-T	HT	WT	DOB	AVG	vLH	vRH	G	AB	R	H	2B	3B	HR	RBI	BB	HBP	SH	SF	SO	SB	CS	SLG	OBP
Alford, Anthony	R-R	6-1	215	7-20-94	.125	.000	.250	4	8	0	1	1	0	0	0	0	0	0	0	3	0	0	.250	.125
Aoki, Norichika	R-L	5-9	180	1-5-82	.281	.000	.310	12	32	4	9	1	0	3	8	1	0	0	1	5	0	0	.594	.294
2-team total (70 Houston)					.274	.282	.270	82	234	32	64	13	1	5	27	16	2	1	5	34	5	2	.402	.319
Barney, Darwin	R-R	5-10	180	11-8-85	.232	.244	.225	129	336	34	78	14	0	6	25	18	2	5	1	64	7	2	.327	.275
Bautista, Jose	R-R	6-0	205	10-19-80	.203	.201	.203	157	587	92	119	27	0	23	65	84	8	0	7	170	6	3	.366	.308
Carrera, Ezequiel	L-L	5-11	185	6-11-87	.282	.086	.310	131	287	38	81	10	1	8	20	30	3	5	0	75	10	1	.408	.356
Ceciliani, Darrell	L-L	6-1	220	6-22-90	.400	—	.400	3	5	2	2	1	0	1	3	0	0	0	0	0	0	0	1.200	.400
Coghlan, Chris	R-L	6-0	195	6-18-85	.200	.000	.211	36	75	7	15	2	0	1	5	9	2	1	1	22	0	0	.267	.299
Donaldson, Josh	R-R	6-1	210	12-8-85	.270	.271	.270	113	415	65	112	21	0	33	78	76	3	0	2	111	2	2	.559	.385
Goins, Ryan	L-R	5-10	180	2-13-88	.237	.246	.235	143	418	37	99	21	1	9	62	31	0	5	5	96	3	2	.357	.286
Hernandez, Teoscar	R-R	6-2	180	10-15-92	.261	.192	.290	26	88	16	23	6	0	8	20	6	0	0	1	36	0	1	.602	.305
2-team total (1 Houston)					.261	—	—	27	88	16	23	6	0	8	20	6	0	0	1	36	0	1	.602	.305
Lopez, Raffy	L-R	5-9	200	10-2-87	.222	.091	.256	24	54	9	12	1	0	4	12	7	0	0	1	21	0	0	.463	.307
Maile, Luke	R-R	6-3	225	2-6-91	.146	.195	.124	46	130	10	19	5	0	2	7	3	2	0	1	35	1	0	.231	.177
Martin, Russell	R-R	5-10	205	2-15-83	.222	.154	.240	91	307	49	68	12	0	13	35	50	7	1	0	83	1	2	.388	.343
Montero, Miguel	R-L	5-11	210	7-9-83	.138	.067	.153	32	87	12	12	3	0	2	8	12	1	0	1	23	0	0	.241	.248
Morales, Kendrys	B-R	6-1	225	6-20-83	.250	.362	.216	150	557	67	139	25	0	28	85	43	5	0	3	132	0	0	.445	.308
Ohlman, Mike	R-R	6-5	240	12-14-90	.231	.000	.333	7	13	1	3	0	0	0	1	0	0	0	0	3	0	0	.231	.231
Parmley, Ian	L-L	5-11	175	12-19-89	.000	—	.000	3	3	0	0	0	0	0	0	0	0	1	0	1	0	0	.000	.000
Pearce, Steve	R-R	5-11	200	4-13-83	.252	.207	.270	92	313	38	79	17	1	13	37	27	5	0	3	68	0	0	.438	.319
Pillar, Kevin	R-R	6-0	205	1-4-89	.256	.336	.230	154	587	72	150	37	1	16	42	33	6	3	3	95	15	6	.404	.301
Refsnyder, Rob	R-R	6-0	200	3-26-91	.196	.056	.273	32	51	5	10	1	0	0	0	5	1	0	0	9	2	1	.216	.281
2-team total (20 New York)					.171	.056	.273	52	88	8	15	2	1	0	0	8	1	0	0	17	4	1	.216	.247
Saltalamacchia, Jarrod	R-B	6-4	235	5-2-85	.040	.000	.067	10	25	1	1	0	0	0	0	1	0	0	0	16	0	0	.040	.077
Saunders, Michael	R-L	6-4	225	11-19-86	.167	—	.167	12	18	1	3	0	0	0	1	2	0	0	0	4	0	0	.167	.250
Smith Jr., Dwight	L-R	5-11	195	10-26-92	.370	.250	.421	12	27	2	10	2	0	0	1	1	1	0	0	10	1	0	.444	.414
Smoak, Justin	B-L	6-4	220	12-5-86	.270	.331	.252	158	560	85	151	29	1	38	90	73	2	0	2	128	0	1	.529	.355
Travis, Devon	R-R	5-9	190	2-21-91	.260	.323	.247	50	185	22	48	18	0	5	24	7	2	1	2	38	4	2	.438	.291
Tulowitzki, Troy	R-R	6-3	205	10-10-84	.249	.169	.278	66	241	16	60	10	0	7	26	17	1	0	1	40	0	1	.378	.300
Urena, Richard	B-R	6-0	185	2-26-96	.206	.250	.192	21	68	6	14	4	0	1	4	6	0	1	0	28	1	0	.309	.270

Pitching	B-T	HT	WT	DOB	W	L	ERA	G	GS	CG	SV	IP	H	R	ER	HR	BB	SO	AVG	vLH	vRH	K/9	BB/9
Anderson, Brett	L-L	6-3	230	2-1-88	2	2	5.13	7	7	0	0	33	39	19	19	3	9	22	.302	.381	.287	5.94	2.43
Barnes, Danny	L-R	6-1	195	10-21-89	3	6	3.55	60	0	0	0	66	48	26	26	11	24	62	.200	.172	.218	8.45	3.27
Beliveau, Jeff	L-L	6-1	190	1-17-87	1	1	7.47	19	0	0	0	16	17	14	13	4	6	17	.283	.269	.294	9.77	3.45
Biagini, Joe	R-R	6-5	240	5-29-90	3	13	5.34	44	18	0	1	120	125	78	71	15	42	97	.265	.279	.256	7.30	3.16
Bolsinger, Mike	R-R	6-1	215	1-29-88	0	3	6.31	11	5	0	0	41	48	32	29	9	27	39	.298	.167	.405	8.49	5.88
Campos, Leonel	R-R	6-2	215	7-17-87	0	0	2.63	13	0	0	0	14	11	6	4	2	8	15	.216	.208	.222	9.88	5.27
Cole, Taylor	R-R	6-1	200	8-20-89	0	0	36.00	1	0	0	0	1	6	4	4	0	1	1	.750	.667	.800	9.00	9.00
Dermody, Matt	R-L	6-5	190	7-4-90	2	0	4.43	23	0	0	0	22	23	13	11	6	5	15	.264	.195	.326	6.04	2.01
Estrada, Marco	R-R	6-0	180	7-5-83	10	9	4.98	33	33	0	0	186	186	104	103	31	71	176	.256	.217	.289	8.52	3.44
Grilli, Jason	R-R	6-5	235	11-11-76	2	4	6.97	26	0	0	1	21	24	17	16	9	9	23	.279	.250	.293	10.02	3.92
2-team total (20 Texas)					2	5	6.30	46	0	0	1	40	46	30	28	12	18	48	.279	.269	.283	10.80	4.05
Happ, J.A.	L-L	6-5	205	10-19-82	10	11	3.53	25	25	0	0	145	145	64	57	18	46	142	.252	.198	.265	8.79	2.85
Harrell, Lucas	R-B	6-2	205	6-3-85	0	0	7.11	4	0	0	0	6	10	5	5	1	4	6	.345	.167	.391	8.53	5.68
House, TJ	L-R	6-1	205	9-29-89	0	0	4.50	2	0	0	0	2	3	1	1	0	1	1	.333	.250	.400	4.50	4.50
Howell, J.P.	L-L	6-0	180	4-25-83	1	1	7.36	16	0	0	0	11	13	9	9	2	7	6	.289	.273	.304	4.91	5.73
Koehler, Tom	R-R	6-3	235	6-29-86	0	2	2.65	15	1	0	0	17	16	5	5	1	6	18	.242	.044	.349	9.53	3.18
Latos, Mat	R-R	6-6	245	12-9-87	0	1	6.60	3	3	0	0	15	19	11	11	5	8	10	.312	.350	.293	6.00	4.80
Lawrence, Casey	R-R	6-2	170	10-28-87	0	3	8.78	4	2	0	0	13	21	14	13	2	11	7	.356	.435	.306	4.73	7.43
2-team total (23 Seattle)					2	3	6.34	27	2	0	0	55	77	41	39	11	25	52	.328	.378	.275	8.46	4.07
Leone, Dominic	R-R	5-11	210	10-26-91	3	0	2.56	65	0	0	1	70	51	22	20	6	23	81	.202	.183	.211	10.36	2.94
Liriano, Francisco	L-L	6-2	225	10-26-83	6	5	5.88	18	18	0	0	83	91	57	54	11	43	74	.280	.230	.292	8.06	4.68

2-team total (20 Houston)					6	7	5.66	38	18	0	0	97	105	66	61	11	53	85	.279	.281	.250	7.89	4.92
Loup, Aaron	L-L	5-11	210	12-19-87	2	3	3.75	70	0	0	0	58	59	27	24	4	29	64	.262	.280	.250	9.99	4.53
Mayza, Tim	L-L	6-3	220	1-15-92	1	0	6.88	19	0	0	0	17	24	15	13	3	4	27	.320	.206	.415	14.29	2.12
Osuna, Roberto	R-R	6-2	215	2-7-95	3	4	3.38	66	0	0	39	64	46	26	24	3	9	83	.197	.204	.191	11.67	1.27
Ramirez, Carlos	R-R	6-5	205	4-24-91	0	0	2.70	12	0	0	0	17	6	5	5	3	3	14	.111	.235	.054	7.56	1.62
Rowley, Chris	R-R	6-2	195	8-14-90	1	2	6.75	6	3	0	0	19	24	14	14	4	10	11	.304	.250	.359	5.30	4.82
Sanchez, Aaron	R-R	6-4	215	7-1-92	1	3	4.25	8	8	0	0	36	42	24	17	6	20	24	.288	.211	.337	6.00	5.00
Santos, Luis	R-R	6-0	185	2-11-91	0	1	2.70	10	0	0	1	17	15	5	5	4	4	16	.234	.207	.257	8.64	2.16
Smith, Chris	R-R	6-2	205	8-19-88	0	0	5.40	4	0	0	0	5	7	3	3	1	1	1	.318	.286	.333	1.80	1.80
Smith, Joe	R-R	6-2	205	3-22-84	3	0	3.28	38	0	0	0	36	30	13	13	3	10	51	.229	.255	.211	12.87	2.52
2-team total (21 Cleveland)					3	0	3.33	59	0	0	1	54	46	20	20	4	10	71	.229	.214	.232	11.83	1.67
Sparkman, Glenn	B-R	6-2	210	5-11-92	0	0	63.00	2	0	0	0	1	9	7	7	0	1	1	.818	.667	.875	9.00	9.00
Stroman, Marcus	R-R	5-8	180	5-1-91	13	9	3.09	33	33	2	0	201	201	82	69	21	62	164	.264	.251	.275	7.34	2.78
Tepera, Ryan	R-R	6-2	195	11-3-87	7	1	3.59	73	0	0	2	78	57	35	31	7	31	81	.205	.194	.211	9.39	3.59
Tepesch, Nick	R-R	6-4	240	10-12-88	1	1	5.14	3	3	0	0	14	17	8	8	5	7	7	.304	.281	.333	4.50	4.50
2-team total (1 Minnesota)					1	2	5.17	4	4	0	0	16	22	15	9	6	9	9	.328	.281	.333	5.17	5.17
Valdez, Cesar	R-R	6-2	200	3-17-85	1	1	6.75	7	3	0	0	21	27	19	16	3	7	16	.307	.250	.354	6.75	2.95
2-team total (4 Oakland)					1	1	7.63	11	4	0	0	31	41	29	26	7	11	21	.320	.412	.304	6.16	3.23

Fielding

Catcher	PCT	G	PO	A	E	DP	PB
Lopez	.979	24	138	5	3	1	0
Maile	.989	46	343	15	4	0	4
Martin	.996	83	646	41	3	3	3
Montero	.981	27	192	12	4	3	1
Ohlman	.939	6	29	2	2	0	0
Saltalamacchia	1.000	7	52	0	0	0	0

First Base	PCT	G	PO	A	E	DP
Bautista	1.000	1	2	0	0	0
Morales	.991	12	104	3	1	6
Pearce	1.000	10	60	2	0	4
Refsnyder	.000	2	0	0	0	0
Smoak	.998	151	1244	66	2	127

Second Base	PCT	G	PO	A	E	DP
Barney	.992	73	87	166	2	40
Coghlan	1.000	3	2	10	0	1
Goins	.984	56	70	111	3	23
Refsnyder	.957	18	25	42	3	8
Travis	.981	50	93	117	4	34
Urena	1.000	1	3	4	0	1

Third Base	PCT	G	PO	A	E	DP
Barney	.957	44	14	74	4	8
Bautista	1.000	8	4	10	0	2
Coghlan	.875	18	6	22	4	3
Donaldson	.949	105	64	195	14	13
Goins	1.000	8	0	4	0	1
Lopez	.000	1	0	0	0	0
Martin	1.000	10	5	16	0	1

Shortstop	PCT	G	PO	A	E	DP
Barney	.926	10	12	13	2	4
Donaldson	1.000	4	4	2	0	0
Goins	.988	87	104	212	4	49
Tulowitzki	.970	64	68	188	8	41
Urena	.974	20	34	42	2	12

Outfield	PCT	G	PO	A	E	DP
Alford	1.000	4	4	0	0	0
Aoki	1.000	10	9	1	0	0
Barney	1.000	4	1	0	0	0
Bautista	.983	143	274	10	5	2
Carrera	.973	121	140	5	4	0
Ceciliani	1.000	2	2	0	0	0
Coghlan	1.000	8	7	0	0	0
Hernandez	.975	25	38	1	1	0
Parmley	1.000	2	3	0	0	0
Pearce	.985	85	132	2	2	0
Pillar	.997	153	316	8	1	0
Refsnyder	1.000	3	3	0	0	0
Saunders	1.000	6	6	1	0	1
Smith Jr.	1.000	10	3	0	0	0

BUFFALO BISONS — *TRIPLE-A*

INTERNATIONAL LEAGUE

Batting	B-T	HT	WT	DOB	AVG	vLH	vRH	G	AB	R	H	2B	3B	HR	RBI	BB	HBP	SH	SF	SO	SB	CS	SLG	OBP
Alford, Anthony	R-R	6-1	215	7-20-94	.333	—	.333	3	12	1	4	1	0	0	0	1	0	0	0	2	0	0	.417	.385
Barreto, Deiferson	R-R	5-10	165	5-19-95	.000	—	.000	1	2	0	0	0	0	0	0	0	0	0	0	0	0	0	.000	.000
Berti, Jon	R-R	5-10	195	1-22-90	.205	.217	.200	62	215	26	44	8	4	3	20	20	0	1	1	53	23	4	.321	.271
Carrera, Ezequiel	L-L	5-11	185	6-11-87	.500	.500	—	1	2	0	1	0	0	0	1	2	0	0	0	0	1	0	.500	.750
Ceciliani, Darrell	L-L	6-1	220	6-22-90	.156	.191	.143	22	77	5	12	1	0	0	3	3	1	0	0	21	1	0	.169	.198
Coghlan, Chris	R-L	6-0	195	6-18-85	.217	.333	.091	7	23	2	5	2	0	0	4	5	0	0	0	3	0	2	.304	.357
Diaz, Jonathan	R-R	5-9	155	4-10-85	.182	.258	.140	37	88	12	16	3	1	0	6	18	5	2	1	24	1	1	.239	.348
2-team total (28 Scranton/Wilkes-Barre)					.210	.258	.140	65	162	20	34	5	1	2	11	32	8	3	3	38	2	2	.290	.361
Elmore, Jake	R-R	5-10	180	6-15-87	.231	.225	.233	94	308	23	71	6	2	1	36	38	5	2	4	54	11	7	.273	.321
Fields, Roemon	L-L	5-11	180	11-28-90	.291	.213	.320	103	347	49	101	11	5	0	29	32	3	5	1	65	43	14	.352	.355
Graterol, Juan	R-R	6-1	205	2-14-89	.429	.667	.364	4	14	2	6	0	0	0	0	0	0	0	0	1	0	0	.429	.429
Guillotte, Andrew	R-R	5-8	170	3-30-93	.304	.455	.167	8	23	6	7	2	1	0	0	4	0	0	0	9	0	1	.478	.407
Hernandez, Teoscar	R-R	6-2	180	10-15-92	.222	.357	.169	26	99	14	22	6	2	6	22	8	2	0	0	30	4	1	.505	.294
Jacob, David	L-L	6-4	225	6-19-95	.000	.000	.000	1	4	0	0	0	0	0	0	0	0	0	0	2	0	0	.000	.000
Jansen, Danny	R-R	6-2	225	4-15-95	.328	.333	.327	21	67	8	22	4	1	3	10	11	0	0	0	7	0	0	.552	.423
Kelly, Ty	R-L	6-0	180	7-20-88	.250	.000	.400	2	8	0	2	1	0	0	1	0	1	0	0	2	0	0	.375	.333
2-team total (4 Lehigh Valley)					.273	.000	.400	6	22	4	6	2	0	1	4	3	1	0	0	2	0	0	.500	.385
Leblebijian, Jason	R-R	6-2	205	5-13-91	.258	.283	.248	120	427	56	110	22	4	11	60	35	8	0	3	124	3	2	.405	.324
Lopes, Christian	R-R	6-0	185	10-1-92	.261	.364	.218	92	333	48	87	25	2	6	40	43	4	0	4	52	18	4	.402	.349
Lopez, Raffy	L-R	5-9	200	10-2-87	.293	.244	.306	59	198	31	58	13	1	12	34	21	3	0	1	46	0	0	.551	.368
Maile, Luke	R-R	6-3	225	2-6-91	.167	.294	.108	16	54	5	9	0	0	0	1	4	0	0	0	12	0	0	.167	.224
Monsalve, Alex	R-R	6-2	225	4-22-92	.250	.235	.256	19	56	5	14	3	0	1	7	3	0	0	1	10	0	0	.357	.283
Montero, Miguel	R-L	5-11	210	7-9-83	.000	—	.000	1	3	0	0	0	0	0	0	0	0	0	0	1	0	0	.000	.000
Ohlman, Mike	R-R	6-5	240	12-14-90	.216	.255	.194	90	282	35	61	16	0	12	38	48	2	0	0	115	4	0	.401	.334
Opitz, Shane	L-R	6-1	180	1-10-92	.252	.205	.261	84	246	19	62	15	1	1	20	18	3	3	4	37	6	4	.333	.306
Parmley, Ian	L-L	5-11	175	12-19-89	.260	.321	.242	79	246	35	64	12	0	1	22	15	2	3	2	59	11	2	.321	.306
Pearce, Steve	R-R	5-11	200	4-13-83	.286	—	.286	2	7	2	2	0	0	0	1	0	1	0	0	2	0	0	.286	.375
Petit, Gregorio	R-R	5-10	200	12-10-84	.253	.217	.270	73	281	26	71	19	1	4	30	10	0	2	4	48	2	1	.370	.275
Pompey, Dalton	B-R	6-2	195	12-11-92	.118	.125	.111	5	17	0	2	1	0	0	1	0	0	0	0	5	0	0	.177	.118
Refsnyder, Rob	R-R	6-0	200	3-26-91	.417	.250	.500	4	12	3	5	1	0	0	2	3	0	0	0	2	0	0	.500	.533
2-team total (38 Scranton/Wilkes-Barre)					.320	.250	.500	42	150	23	48	12	2	2	14	18	4	0	2	32	2	1	.467	.402
Saltalamacchia, Jarrod	R-B	6-4	235	5-2-85	.162	.125	.183	33	111	8	18	6	0	1	5	17	0	0	1	51	0	0	.243	.271

Batting	B-T	HT	WT	DOB	AVG	vLH	vRH	G	AB	R	H	2B	3B	HR	RBI	BB	HBP	SH	SF	SO	SB	CS	SLG	OBP
Saunders, Michael	R-L	6-4	225	11-19-86	.274	.256	.282	35	146	22	40	11	1	2	12	9	1	0	0	30	1	0	.404	.321
Smith Jr., Dwight	L-R	5-11	195	10-26-92	.273	.321	.255	108	395	56	108	21	1	8	46	47	2	1	4	71	8	8	.392	.350
Tellez, Rowdy	L-L	6-4	220	3-16-95	.223	.148	.251	122	445	45	99	29	1	6	56	47	2	0	7	94	6	1	.333	.295

Pitching	B-T	HT	WT	DOB	W	L	ERA	G	GS	CG	SV	IP	H	R	ER	HR	BB	SO	AVG	vLH	vRH	K/9	BB/9
Anderson, Brett	L-L	6-3	230	2-1-88	1	1	0.93	2	2	0	0	10	4	1	1	0	2	3	.121	.000	.182	2.79	1.86
Barnes, Danny	L-R	6-1	195	10-21-89	0	1	3.00	4	0	0	2	6	6	2	2	0	0	8	.250	.231	.273	12.00	0.00
Beliveau, Jeff	L-L	6-1	190	1-17-87	4	1	3.04	29	1	0	2	50	34	18	17	5	26	60	.193	.174	.206	10.73	4.65
Biagini, Joe	R-R	6-5	240	5-29-90	1	1	3.12	4	4	0	0	17	13	6	6	2	6	14	.210	.143	.244	7.27	3.12
Bolsinger, Mike	R-R	6-1	215	1-29-88	4	2	1.70	16	5	0	1	48	42	9	9	2	8	42	.246	.317	.180	7.93	1.51
Borucki, Ryan	L-L	6-4	175	3-31-94	0	0	0.00	1	1	0	0	6	6	0	0	0	1	6	.273	.250	.278	9.00	1.50
Browning, Wil	R-R	6-3	190	9-8-88	4	3	6.55	39	0	0	1	58	71	44	42	5	36	57	.300	.287	.309	8.90	5.62
Campos, Leonel	R-R	6-2	215	7-17-87	3	0	1.65	26	0	0	9	33	20	6	6	2	14	39	.171	.148	.191	10.74	3.86
Carkuff, Jared	R-R	6-3	180	8-25-93	1	0	0.00	1	0	0	0	3	1	0	0	0	1	1	.091	.000	.111	2.70	2.70
Case, Andrew	R-R	6-2	230	1-6-93	0	0	5.87	4	0	0	0	8	7	5	5	2	3	3	.241	.091	.333	3.52	3.52
Cole, Taylor	R-R	6-1	200	8-20-89	0	0	0.00	4	0	0	0	6	0	0	0	0	1	7	.000	.000	.000	11.12	1.59
Dermody, Matt	R-L	6-5	190	7-4-90	5	1	3.56	33	1	0	1	43	48	21	17	6	11	39	.278	.234	.303	8.16	2.30
Girodo, Chad	L-L	6-1	190	2-6-91	2	4	3.02	30	1	0	4	48	55	19	16	3	17	35	.288	.224	.330	6.61	3.21
Glaude, Griffin	R-R	5-9	175	4-6-92	0	1	0.00	2	0	0	0	2	2	1	0	0	1	0	.250	.500	.167	0.00	5.40
Grube, Jarrett	R-R	6-4	220	11-5-81	2	3	6.14	11	11	0	0	56	63	43	38	10	21	47	.286	.285	.289	7.60	3.40
2-team total (14 Columbus)					7	9	4.63	25	25	0	0	134	139	77	69	19	46	103	.268	.278	.234	6.92	3.09
Harrell, Lucas	R-B	6-2	205	6-3-85	0	1	2.08	7	6	0	0	30	27	7	7	1	13	24	.233	.207	.259	7.12	3.86
House, TJ	L-R	6-1	205	9-29-89	9	11	4.32	24	24	1	0	133	149	73	64	11	63	108	.283	.264	.291	7.29	4.25
Howell, J.P.	L-L	6-0	180	4-25-83	0	1	6.43	8	0	0	0	7	9	6	5	1	3	6	.310	.091	.444	7.71	3.86
Latos, Mat	R-R	6-6	245	12-9-87	1	1	3.81	6	5	0	0	26	27	13	11	3	13	24	.276	.177	.383	8.31	4.50
Lawrence, Casey	R-R	6-2	170	10-28-87	1	0	0.90	3	3	0	0	10	9	2	1	1	1	7	.231	.261	.188	6.30	0.90
Leone, Dominic	R-R	5-11	210	10-26-91	0	0	4.50	4	0	0	0	4	4	2	2	0	1	4	.267	.400	.000	9.00	2.25
Liriano, Francisco	L-L	6-2	225	10-26-83	0	0	4.15	1	1	0	0	4	3	3	2	0	2	7	.188	.000	.300	14.54	4.15
Mayza, Tim	L-L	6-3	220	1-15-92	1	1	0.93	11	0	0	0	19	16	2	2	0	7	16	.216	.150	.241	7.45	3.26
Oberholtzer, Brett	L-L	6-1	225	7-1-89	4	8	4.12	24	24	1	0	131	157	66	60	7	44	81	.299	.287	.304	5.56	3.02
Ramirez, Carlos	R-R	6-5	205	4-24-91	1	0	0.00	7	0	0	0	14	6	0	0	0	3	16	.128	.118	.133	10.29	1.93
Rowley, Chris	R-R	6-2	195	8-14-90	3	5	2.66	12	8	0	0	64	60	21	19	2	17	46	.247	.240	.252	6.44	2.38
Sanchez, Aaron	R-R	6-4	215	7-1-92	0	1	8.31	1	1	0	0	4	5	4	4	0	3	4	.333	.333	.333	8.31	6.23
Santos, Luis	R-R	6-0	185	2-11-91	3	12	4.07	24	21	0	0	108	91	52	49	13	44	98	.227	.203	.250	8.14	3.66
Shafer, Justin	R-R	6-2	195	9-18-92	0	0	2.25	2	0	0	0	4	3	1	1	0	1	4	.200	.143	.250	9.00	2.25
Smith, Chris	R-R	6-2	205	8-19-88	2	3	4.46	29	0	0	9	34	36	17	17	6	6	24	.273	.310	.243	6.29	1.57
Smith, Joe	R-R	6-2	205	3-22-84	0	0	3.86	3	0	0	0	2	3	1	1	0	0	3	.333	.000	.429	11.57	0.00
Smith, Murphy	R-R	6-3	210	8-25-87	4	5	3.50	37	8	0	3	82	80	38	32	9	18	53	.252	.200	.289	5.79	1.97
Sparkman, Glenn	B-R	6-2	210	5-11-92	1	2	2.25	4	1	0	1	8	7	3	2	1	1	3	.250	.353	.091	3.38	1.13
Stilson, John	R-R	6-3	205	7-28-90	2	4	3.14	34	0	0	2	49	41	20	17	6	20	46	.224	.250	.206	8.51	3.70
Tepesch, Nick	R-R	6-4	240	10-12-88	2	0	2.00	4	3	0	0	18	14	4	4	1	1	14	.212	.276	.162	7.00	0.50
2-team total (6 Rochester)					3	3	4.21	10	8	0	0	47	50	28	22	7	10	41	.270	.276	.162	7.85	1.91
Valdez, Cesar	R-R	6-2	200	3-17-85	3	3	3.23	11	10	1	0	61	56	25	22	3	12	44	.242	.293	.185	6.46	1.76

Fielding

Catcher	PCT	G	PO	A	E	DP	PB
Graterol	1.000	3	25	0	0	0	
O Jansen	1.000	21	140	6	0	3	1
Lopez	.997	49	338	24	1	3	4
Maile	1.000	13	104	5	0	2	0
Monsalve	1.000	14	87	5	0	1	2
Montero	1.000	1	6	0	0	0	0
Ohlman	.997	47	297	19	1	0	7
Saltalamacchia	.950	3	19	0	1	0	0

First Base	PCT	G	PO	A	E	DP
Leblebijian	.988	11	74	10	1	6
Monsalve	.800	1	4	0	1	0
Ohlman	.985	8	60	6	1	4
Opitz	1.000	11	79	5	0	8
Tellez	.989	115	888	67	11	95

Second Base	PCT	G	PO	A	E	DP
Barreto	1.000	1	4	0	0	1
Berti	.970	47	77	153	7	32
Coghlan	1.000	2	2	7	0	1
Diaz	.980	8	22	27	1	6
Elmore	.978	16	23	22	1	5
Leblebijian	.975	31	46	72	3	14
Lopes	.968	30	42	79	4	14
Opitz	1.000	6	5	14	0	4
Petit	.938	4	7	8	1	0
Refsnyder	1.000	3	6	5	0	3

Third Base	PCT	G	PO	A	E	DP
Coghlan	1.000	2	2	2	0	0
Elmore	.907	13	15	24	4	1
Guillotte	1.000	1	0	1	0	0
Leblebijian	.976	66	42	119	4	11
Lopes	.973	51	34	73	3	6
Lopez	1.000	1	1	1	0	1
Opitz	.944	7	1	16	1	4
Petit	1.000	3	3	3	0	0

Shortstop	PCT	G	PO	A	E	DP
Berti	1.000	1	1	1	0	0
Diaz	.975	27	45	74	3	12
Elmore	1.000	3	4	4	0	2
Leblebijian	.938	4	8	7	1	1
Opitz	.948	49	69	96	9	26
Petit	.969	64	105	181	9	41

Outfield	PCT	G	PO	A	E	DP
Alford	1.000	3	8	1	0	0
Berti	.950	13	18	1	1	0
Ceciliani	1.000	19	36	1	0	0
Coghlan	.900	4	9	0	1	0
Elmore	1.000	55	93	5	0	0
Fields	.978	101	259	4	6	2
Guillotte	1.000	7	8	0	0	0
Hernandez	.986	23	64	4	1	1
Kelly	1.000	2	3	0	0	0
Leblebijian	1.000	2	3	0	0	0
Lopes	1.000	1	2	0	0	0
Ohlman	.000	1	0	0	0	0
Opitz	1.000	9	9	0	0	0
Parmley	.963	74	151	7	6	1
Pearce	1.000	2	5	0	0	0
Pompey	1.000	4	7	0	0	0
Saunders	.952	20	40	0	2	0
Smith Jr.	.977	99	163	5	4	1

NEW HAMPSHIRE FISHER CATS — *DOUBLE-A*

EASTERN LEAGUE

Batting	B-T	HT	WT	DOB	AVG	vLH	vRH	G	AB	R	H	2B	3B	HR	RBI	BB	HBP	SH	SF	SO	SB	CS	SLG	OBP
Alford, Anthony	R-R	6-1	215	7-20-94	.310	.281	.320	68	245	41	76	14	0	5	24	35	6	1	2	45	18	3	.429	.406
Cantwell, Patrick	R-R	6-2	210	4-10-90	.250	—	.250	2	4	0	1	1	0	0	2	0	0	0	0	1	0	0	.500	.250
Cardenas, J.C.	B-R	6-0	185	6-27-94	.200	.273	.158	9	30	3	6	0	0	0	1	2	0	1	0	10	1	1	.200	.250

Davis, J.D.	R-R	5-8	190	5-12-92	.249	.276	.239	128	446	75	111	20	4	10	45	69	13	11	6	110	20	14	.379	.361
De La Cruz, Michael	B-R	5-10	190	5-15-93	.500	.000	.579	7	22	5	11	3	0	1	2	4	0	0	0	3	0	0	.773	.577
Dean, Matt	R-R	6-3	220	12-22-92	.196	.216	.183	33	97	8	19	3	0	4	14	12	0	1	1	39	0	0	.351	.282
Diaz, Jonathan	R-R	5-9	155	4-10-85	.273	.250	.286	5	11	3	3	0	0	1	1	7	0	0	0	3	0	0	.546	.556
Fields, Roemon	L-L	5-11	180	11-28-90	.237	.444	.200	16	59	7	14	2	1	0	5	3	0	0	0	9	7	0	.305	.274
Guerrero, Emilio	R-R	6-4	189	8-21-92	.263	.247	.269	74	266	31	70	14	2	4	28	18	1	0	1	57	2	1	.376	.311
Guillotte, Andrew	R-R	5-8	170	3-30-93	.244	.262	.237	64	213	28	52	4	1	3	10	20	3	2	1	43	8	7	.315	.317
Gurriel, Lourdes	R-R	6-2	185	10-19-93	.241	.218	.252	46	170	20	41	10	0	4	28	10	2	0	3	30	2	0	.371	.287
Heidt, Gunnar	R-R	6-0	200	9-12-92	.229	.300	.202	126	432	62	99	20	1	13	48	45	2	3	3	138	10	5	.370	.303
Hissey, Ryan	L-R	6-0	190	4-8-94	.100	.500	.000	3	10	0	1	0	0	0	2	0	0	0	0	1	0	0	.100	.100
Jansen, Danny	R-R	6-2	225	4-15-95	.291	.395	.257	52	179	23	52	15	1	2	20	22	5	1	3	19	1	0	.419	.378
Lopes, Tim	R-R	5-11	180	6-24-94	.271	.237	.284	128	469	49	127	27	4	7	50	49	2	0	6	86	19	9	.390	.338
Lopez, Raffy	L-R	5-9	200	10-2-87	.262	.125	.294	14	42	7	11	1	1	4	11	8	0	0	0	15	0	0	.619	.380
Loveless, Derrick	L-R	6-1	200	3-7-93	.253	.300	.240	69	190	35	48	9	1	1	23	38	2	2	2	55	2	5	.326	.379
McBroom, Ryan	R-L	6-3	240	4-9-92	.243	.316	.222	96	346	45	84	19	0	12	54	30	12	0	4	77	0	2	.402	.321
2-team total (38 Trenton)					.247	.316	.222	134	486	56	120	24	0	16	70	43	14	0	5	112	1	3	.395	.323
McGuire, Reese	L-R	5-11	215	3-2-95	.278	.256	.290	34	115	19	32	5	1	6	20	16	1	2	2	19	2	1	.496	.366
Monsalve, Alex	R-R	6-2	225	4-22-92	.284	.269	.291	24	81	9	23	3	0	0	5	1	2	0	0	7	0	0	.321	.310
Pearce, Steve	R-R	5-11	200	4-13-83	.000	.000	.000	4	15	0	0	0	0	0	0	1	0	0	0	3	0	0	.000	.063
Ramirez, Harold	R-R	5-10	220	9-6-94	.266	.240	.276	121	444	46	118	19	2	6	53	32	6	2	5	65	5	3	.358	.320
Reeves, Mike	R-L	6-2	195	9-16-90	.286	.111	.417	7	21	1	6	2	0	0	2	2	1	1	0	5	0	0	.381	.375
Sotillo, Andres	R-R	5-11	180	12-28-93	.200	.250	.167	3	10	1	2	1	0	1	2	1	0	0	0	5	0	0	.600	.273
Thomas, Jake	L-R	5-10	190	7-21-93	.182	.000	.188	14	33	2	6	2	0	0	2	9	0	0	0	8	0	0	.242	.357
Urena, Richard	B-R	6-0	185	2-26-96	.247	.248	.247	129	510	44	126	36	3	5	60	30	1	3	7	100	0	1	.359	.287

Pitching	B-T	HT	WT	DOB	W	L	ERA	G	GS	CG	SV	IP	H	R	ER	HR	BB	SO	AVG	vLH	vRH	K/9	BB/9
Borucki, Ryan	L-L	6-4	175	3-31-94	2	3	1.94	7	7	0	0	46	31	11	10	2	8	42	.187	.125	.202	8.16	1.55
Case, Andrew	R-R	6-2	230	1-6-93	4	0	1.58	32	0	0	8	40	31	7	7	1	10	23	.210	.200	.217	5.18	2.25
Dawson, Shane	R-L	6-1	200	9-9-93	4	9	6.16	27	18	1	0	111	145	82	76	20	48	62	.317	.286	.330	5.03	3.89
DeGraaf, Josh	R-R	6-4	195	1-28-93	0	0	3.45	9	1	0	0	16	15	6	6	1	10	11	.263	.320	.219	6.32	5.74
Fernandez, Jose	L-L	6-3	170	2-13-93	1	2	5.44	41	0	0	4	46	52	30	28	4	26	48	.278	.293	.268	9.32	5.05
Glaude, Griffin	R-R	5-9	175	4-6-92	0	1	3.86	2	0	0	0	2	2	1	1	0	2	3	.250	.250	.250	11.57	7.71
Gonzalez, Alonzo	L-L	6-5	212	1-15-92	1	4	7.49	25	0	0	0	34	40	33	28	5	23	25	.290	.255	.308	6.68	6.15
Greene, Conner	R-R	6-3	185	4-4-95	5	10	5.29	26	25	0	0	133	141	86	78	7	83	92	.275	.290	.260	6.24	5.63
Harris, Jon	R-R	6-4	175	10-16-93	7	11	5.41	26	26	0	0	143	169	97	86	20	47	113	.292	.253	.333	7.11	2.96
Herdenez, Yonardo	R-R	6-1	170	9-20-95	0	0	2.25	2	0	0	0	4	4	1	1	0	1	1	.286	.333	.273	2.25	2.25
Isaacs, Dusty	R-R	6-1	190	8-7-91	4	3	3.79	41	0	0	4	62	47	26	26	7	28	76	.214	.238	.193	11.09	4.09
Mayza, Tim	L-L	6-3	220	1-15-92	1	1	4.59	29	0	0	4	33	32	18	17	5	15	42	.252	.288	.221	11.34	4.05
McFarland, Blake	R-R	6-5	230	2-28-88	0	0	1.42	5	0	0	0	6	4	1	1	0	2	7	.174	.250	.133	9.95	2.84
Pannone, Thomas	L-L	6-0	195	4-28-94	1	2	3.63	6	6	0	0	35	31	16	14	9	8	29	.237	.250	.232	7.53	2.08
2-team total (14 Akron)					7	3	2.92	20	20	1	0	117	98	43	38	14	29	110	.227	.193	.235	8.46	2.23
Ramirez, Carlos	R-R	6-5	205	4-24-91	2	0	0.00	18	0	0	3	24	10	2	0	0	7	29	.124	.211	.047	11.03	2.66
Reid-Foley, Sean	R-R	6-3	220	8-30-95	10	11	5.09	27	27	0	0	133	145	82	75	22	53	122	.278	.270	.286	8.28	3.60
Rios, Francisco	R-R	6-1	180	5-6-95	3	9	4.29	23	17	0	0	86	90	57	41	10	39	63	.270	.284	.257	6.59	4.08
Robson, Tom	R-R	6-4	210	6-27-93	0	0	2.45	2	0	0	0	4	2	1	1	1	1	1	.154	.250	.111	2.45	2.45
Rowley, Chris	R-R	6-2	195	8-14-90	3	2	1.73	17	5	0	1	52	33	10	10	4	9	49	.179	.128	.233	8.48	1.56
Santos, Luis	R-R	6-0	185	2-11-91	0	1	5.68	4	0	0	0	6	6	4	4	1	3	4	.240	.273	.214	5.68	4.26
Shafer, Justin	R-R	6-2	195	9-18-92	5	2	3.41	37	0	0	1	58	45	23	22	6	26	48	.214	.286	.173	7.45	4.03
Smith, Murphy	R-R	6-3	210	8-25-87	0	0	8.10	2	0	0	0	3	4	3	3	0	1	3	.286	.143	.429	8.10	2.70
Sparkman, Glenn	B-R	6-2	210	5-11-92	1	1	3.12	2	2	0	0	9	6	3	3	2	3	6	.194	.188	.200	6.23	3.12
Stilson, John	R-R	6-3	205	7-28-90	0	1	3.60	4	0	0	0	5	4	2	2	0	2	5	.235	.333	.125	9.00	3.60
Straka, John	L-R	6-2	215	1-19-90	1	2	8.18	3	2	1	0	11	20	10	10	1	3	9	.408	.318	.482	7.36	2.45
Villegas, Kender	R-R	6-2	170	6-8-93	2	4	4.73	20	3	0	1	40	41	23	21	3	24	26	.265	.258	.270	5.85	5.40
Young, Danny	L-L	6-3	200	5-27-94	2	1	3.86	21	0	0	0	33	30	15	14	2	14	23	.236	.151	.297	6.34	3.86

Fielding

Catcher	PCT	G	PO	A	E	DP	PB
Cantwell	1.000	2	3	1	0	0	0
De La Cruz	1.000	7	51	2	0	0	1
Hissey	.955	3	18	3	1	0	0
Jansen	.994	52	329	25	2	1	2
Lopez	.989	13	86	6	1	0	1
McGuire	1.000	34	230	33	0	3	3
Monsalve	.979	23	170	17	4	1	5
Reeves	.981	7	50	2	1	1	0
Sotillo	1.000	3	14	2	0	0	2

First Base	PCT	G	PO	A	E	DP
Dean	1.000	22	196	12	0	17
Guerrero	.977	36	280	17	7	32
Heidt	1.000	7	49	10	0	3
McBroom	.997	76	623	43	2	51

Second Base	PCT	G	PO	A	E	DP
Cardenas	.978	8	18	26	1	9
Diaz	1.000	2	3	7	0	0
Guillotte	1.000	13	18	34	0	7
Gurriel	.951	22	35	62	5	7
Heidt	.967	27	41	77	4	15
Lopes	.976	58	82	159	6	30
Urena	.984	11	24	36	1	9

Third Base	PCT	G	PO	A	E	DP
Dean	.667	3	1	1	1	0
Guerrero	.911	21	13	38	5	4
Guillotte	.750	3	0	3	1	0
Heidt	.905	63	47	115	17	11
Lopes	.905	52	24	90	12	8

Shortstop	PCT	G	PO	A	E	DP
Cardenas	.833	1	2	3	1	1
Diaz	1.000	2	2	4	0	1
Guillotte	1.000	2	5	4	0	2
Gurriel	.971	17	24	43	2	15
Lopes	.714	2	2	3	2	1
Urena	.960	115	154	276	18	57

Outfield	PCT	G	PO	A	E	DP
Alford	.949	59	145	5	8	2
Davis	.994	125	305	5	2	0
Fields	.971	14	31	2	1	1
Guerrero	1.000	3	1	0	0	0
Guillotte	.989	47	90	4	1	2
Heidt	.917	7	11	0	1	0
Loveless	.991	60	102	4	1	1
Pearce	1.000	2	1	0	0	0
Ramirez	.989	98	168	4	2	2
Thomas	1.000	9	10	0	0	0

DUNEDIN BLUE JAYS

HIGH CLASS A

FLORIDA STATE LEAGUE

Batting	B-T	HT	WT	DOB	AVG	vLH	vRH	G	AB	R	H	2B	3B	HR	RBI	BB	HBP	SH	SF	SO	SB	CS	SLG	OBP
Abbadessa, Dominic	R-R	5-10	185	12-8-97	.000	.000	.000	1	4	0	0	0	0	0	0	0	0	0	0	3	0	0	.000	.000
Alford, Anthony	R-R	6-1	215	7-20-94	.143	.000	.177	6	21	1	3	0	0	0	2	0	1	0	0	8	1	0	.143	.182
Almonte, Josh	R-R	6-3	210	1-28-94	.221	.298	.187	49	154	14	34	3	2	1	15	10	1	1	1	45	5	1	.286	.271
Barreto, Deiferson	R-R	5-10	165	5-19-95	.211	.238	.194	18	57	3	12	1	0	0	2	0	1	0	0	6	0	0	.228	.224
Berti, Jon	R-R	5-10	195	1-22-90	.182	.000	.250	3	11	2	2	0	0	0	0	1	0	0	0	4	1	0	.182	.250
Bichette, Bo	R-R	6-0	200	3-5-98	.323	.278	.346	40	164	28	53	9	1	4	23	14	2	0	2	26	10	4	.463	.379
Biggio, Cavan	L-R	6-1	203	4-11-95	.233	.250	.227	127	463	75	108	17	5	11	60	74	6	6	7	140	11	7	.363	.342
Cardenas, J.C.	B-R	6-0	185	6-27-94	.206	.125	.238	71	228	21	47	6	2	1	23	17	1	4	2	77	1	0	.263	.262
Ceciliani, Darrell	L-L	6-1	220	6-22-90	.389	.600	.308	6	18	3	7	1	0	0	0	1	1	0	0	6	0	0	.444	.450
Coghlan, Chris	R-L	6-0	195	6-18-85	.500	1.000	.455	4	12	2	6	3	0	0	2	1	0	0	0	0	0	0	.750	.539
Davis, D.J.	L-R	6-1	180	7-25-94	.258	.244	.262	112	349	57	90	9	4	2	33	35	4	6	2	92	32	11	.324	.331
De La Cruz, Michael	B-R	5-10	190	5-15-93	.246	.211	.261	58	199	27	49	11	0	2	30	19	0	1	3	47	2	2	.332	.308
Dean, Matt	R-R	6-3	220	12-22-92	.247	.133	.297	40	146	15	36	6	1	2	20	16	2	0	2	51	2	0	.343	.325
Donaldson, Josh	R-R	6-1	210	12-8-85	.400	.667	.000	2	5	0	2	0	0	0	1	1	1	0	0	2	0	0	.400	.571
Guerrero Jr., Vladimir	R-R	6-1	200	3-16-99	.333	.469	.277	48	168	31	56	7	1	6	31	36	2	0	3	28	2	2	.494	.450
Guillotte, Andrew	R-R	5-8	170	3-30-93	.293	.271	.304	39	150	34	44	10	0	2	14	15	3	0	3	25	14	3	.400	.363
Gurriel, Lourdes	R-R	6-2	185	10-19-93	.197	.191	.200	18	66	6	13	1	0	1	8	2	0	0	1	13	1	0	.258	.217
Hissey, Ryan	L-R	6-0	190	4-8-94	.171	.000	.194	14	41	5	7	2	0	0	5	7	0	0	1	16	1	0	.220	.286
Jansen, Danny	R-R	6-2	225	4-15-95	.369	.316	.393	31	122	19	45	6	0	5	18	8	4	1	1	14	0	0	.541	.422
Jones, Bradley	R-R	6-1	180	6-12-95	.156	.182	.151	17	64	4	10	1	0	1	5	4	0	0	0	30	0	0	.219	.206
Kelly, Juan	B-R	5-10	218	7-16-94	.272	.209	.298	130	481	68	131	29	4	10	68	51	4	1	8	111	1	3	.412	.342
Knight, Nash	B-R	6-0	195	9-20-92	.227	.182	.273	6	22	0	5	2	0	0	2	2	0	0	0	6	0	0	.318	.292
Lopes, Christian	R-R	6-0	185	10-1-92	.500	.429	.667	2	10	5	5	1	0	0	1	1	0	0	0	2	1	0	.600	.546
Loveless, Derrick	L-R	6-1	200	3-7-93	.293	.179	.362	20	75	14	22	10	0	0	10	14	1	0	0	18	3	0	.427	.411
Maile, Luke	R-R	6-3	225	2-6-91	.177	.200	.167	5	17	1	3	0	0	0	2	0	0	0	0	1	0	0	.177	.177
McGuire, Reese	L-R	5-11	215	3-2-95	.250	.250	.250	3	12	1	3	1	0	0	1	1	0	0	0	2	0	0	.333	.308
Navarro, Jesus	R-R	5-11	160	1-13-98	.000	—	.000	1	1	0	0	0	0	0	0	0	0	0	0	0	0	0	.000	.000
Olivares, Edward	R-R	6-2	186	3-6-96	.221	.250	.212	19	68	11	15	1	1	0	7	8	1	0	0	17	2	2	.265	.312
Panas, Connor	L-R	6-0	218	2-11-93	.276	.224	.295	114	402	64	111	20	3	18	55	41	15	0	1	99	4	0	.475	.364
Pentecost, Max	R-R	6-2	191	3-10-93	.276	.322	.256	71	286	34	79	14	2	9	54	23	2	1	2	62	0	1	.434	.332
Petit, Gregorio	R-R	5-10	200	12-10-84	.455	.667	.375	3	11	1	5	1	0	0	0	1	0	0	0	2	0	0	.546	.500
Pinto, Eduard	L-L	5-11	150	10-23-94	.149	.167	.143	15	47	4	7	1	0	0	5	2	2	2	2	7	1	1	.170	.208
Pompey, Dalton	B-R	6-2	195	12-11-92	.259	.500	.217	8	27	5	7	1	1	0	5	5	0	0	0	3	1	0	.370	.375
Reeves, Mike	R-L	6-2	195	9-16-90	.169	.167	.170	27	83	9	14	2	0	2	6	15	1	0	1	21	1	0	.265	.300
Silva, Luis	R-R	5-11	170	6-30-95	.100	—	.100	3	10	1	1	0	0	0	0	0	2	0	0	1	0	1	.100	.250
Smith, Ridge	R-R	5-10	190	4-26-95	.000	.000	.000	2	4	0	0	0	0	0	0	0	0	0	0	1	0	0	.000	.000
Sotillo, Andres	R-R	5-11	180	12-28-93	.250	.500	.192	13	32	6	8	1	0	0	6	4	3	0	1	6	0	1	.281	.375
Spiwak, Owen	L-R	6-2	185	5-23-95	—	—	—	1	0	0	0	0	0	0	0	0	0	0	0	0	0	0	—	—
Thomas, Jake	L-R	5-10	190	7-21-93	.255	.286	.240	34	110	18	28	5	0	1	12	21	0	1	0	35	1	2	.327	.374
Thomas, Lane	R-R	6-1	210	8-23-95	.252	.262	.249	73	274	34	69	12	6	4	38	27	2	1	4	84	8	7	.383	.319
2-team total (9 Palm Beach)					.252	.273	.250	82	309	39	78	12	7	4	41	30	2	1	5	94	10	9	.375	.318
Tulowitzki, Troy	R-R	6-3	205	10-10-84	.286	.429	.143	5	14	2	4	0	0	1	3	3	0	0	0	3	0	0	.500	.412
Vicuna, Kevin	R-R	6-0	140	1-14-98	.202	.185	.211	26	84	10	17	1	1	0	4	3	3	2	0	19	0	0	.238	.256
Wise, Carl	R-R	6-1	215	5-25-94	.172	.211	.162	24	87	7	15	3	0	0	8	3	0	0	1	27	0	0	.207	.198

Pitching	B-T	HT	WT	DOB	W	L	ERA	G	GS	CG	SV	IP	H	R	ER	HR	BB	SO	AVG	vLH	vRH	K/9	BB/9
Borucki, Ryan	L-L	6-4	175	3-31-94	6	5	3.58	19	18	0	0	98	95	49	39	5	27	109	.255	.214	.271	10.01	2.48
Campos, Leonel	R-R	6-2	215	7-17-87	0	1	9.00	1	1	0	0	1	1	1	1	1	0	2	.250	.500	.000	18.00	0.00
Cardona, Adonys	R-R	6-2	200	1-16-94	5	7	7.26	43	0	0	0	48	66	47	39	1	40	46	.339	.407	.290	8.57	7.45
Carkuff, Jared	R-R	6-3	180	8-25-93	1	2	5.14	10	0	0	1	21	24	12	12	3	6	15	.296	.351	.250	6.43	2.57
Case, Andrew	R-R	6-2	230	1-6-93	3	1	4.42	14	0	0	4	18	18	9	9	3	3	17	.273	.273	.273	8.35	1.47
Cole, Taylor	R-R	6-1	200	8-20-89	0	0	0.00	2	1	0	0	3	4	0	0	0	0	3	.308	.500	.222	9.00	0.00
Cook, Ryan	R-R	6-1	210	5-4-93	5	1	2.31	30	1	0	0	51	34	14	13	6	25	43	.189	.179	.195	7.64	4.44
DeGraaf, Josh	R-R	6-4	195	1-28-93	7	4	3.32	26	15	0	0	89	84	37	33	8	19	75	.252	.248	.254	7.56	1.91
Diaz, Denis	R-R	6-1	180	11-20-94	0	0	0.00	1	1	0	0	4	1	0	0	0	5	3	.083	—	.083	6.75	11.25
Eller, Connor	R-R	6-2	195	1-23-94	1	1	5.12	12	0	0	0	19	19	13	11	2	18	9	.264	.250	.271	4.19	8.38
Encina, Geno	R-L	6-4	220	7-7-94	0	0	11.25	2	0	0	0	4	9	5	5	2	0	2	.474	.600	.333	4.50	0.00
Eveld, Bobby	L-R	6-5	200	12-4-91	0	0	0.00	1	0	0	0	1	0	0	0	0	0	2	.000	.000	.000	18.00	0.00
Fisk, Conor	R-R	6-2	210	4-4-92	8	11	3.84	28	22	2	1	152	153	81	65	19	33	112	.258	.284	.239	6.62	1.95
Girodo, Chad	L-L	6-1	190	2-6-91	0	0	0.00	1	0	0	0	1	0	0	0	0	1	0	.000	.000	.000	0.00	9.00
Gonzalez, Alonzo	L-L	6-5	212	1-15-92	2	1	3.28	15	0	0	0	25	22	13	9	2	9	16	.237	.107	.292	5.84	3.28
Happ, J.A.	L-L	6-5	205	10-19-82	0	0	9.00	1	1	0	0	3	7	3	3	0	0	3	.438	.800	.273	9.00	0.00
Harrell, Lucas	R-B	6-2	205	6-3-85	0	0	2.84	2	2	0	0	6	6	2	2	0	2	5	.261	.143	.313	7.11	2.84
Hartman, Nick	R-R	6-2	180	10-24-94	1	0	0.00	4	0	0	1	7	0	0	0	0	1	5	.000	.000	.000	6.14	1.23
Howell, J.P.	L-L	6-0	180	4-25-83	0	0	0.00	2	2	0	0	2	1	0	0	0	0	5	.111	.250	.000	22.50	0.00
Jackson, Zach	R-R	6-4	215	12-25-94	1	2	2.03	27	0	0	4	31	19	7	7	0	18	43	.171	.170	.172	12.48	5.23
Lietz, Dan	L-L	6-2	200	6-1-94	1	2	6.75	16	0	0	1	20	23	15	15	0	19	9	.291	.345	.260	4.05	8.55
Manzueta, Danilo	R-R	6-3	188	1-18-97	0	0	0.00	1	0	0	0	1	0	0	0	0	0	1	.000	.000	.000	13.50	0.00
McClelland, Jackson	R-R	6-5	220	7-19-94	2	2	1.07	29	0	0	7	34	27	8	4	0	8	25	.218	.231	.208	6.68	2.14
Murphy, Patrick	R-R	6-4	220	6-10-95	0	1	7.00	2	2	0	0	9	14	7	7	0	3	5	.368	.353	.381	5.00	3.00
Nova, Jose	L-L	6-1	170	4-6-95	0	0	0.00	1	0	0	0	2	2	0	0	0	0	2	.250	—	.250	9.00	0.00

Ouellette, William	R-R	6-1	195	6-30-93	1	0	1.42	3	0	0	0	6	3	1	1	0	3	4	.136	.154	.111	5.68	4.26
Perdomo, Angel	L-L	6-6	200	5-7-94	5	6	3.70	16	16	0	0	75	74	38	31	7	43	65	.257	.233	.267	7.77	5.14
Robson, Tom	R-R	6-4	210	6-27-93	1	3	3.12	27	0	0	1	35	29	18	12	1	11	30	.216	.225	.212	7.79	2.86
Romano, Jordan	R-R	6-4	200	4-21-93	7	5	3.39	28	26	0	0	138	141	65	52	2	54	138	.263	.352	.192	9.00	3.52
Sanchez, Aaron	R-R	6-4	215	7-1-92	0	0	7.36	1	1	0	0	4	6	3	3	0	2	3	.400	.167	.556	7.36	4.91
Saucedo, Tayler	L-L	6-5	185	6-18-93	2	1	4.47	16	10	0	0	56	61	29	28	0	29	48	.274	.250	.284	7.67	4.63
Shafer, Justin	R-R	6-2	195	9-18-92	0	0	0.00	5	0	0	0	9	7	0	0	0	2	13	.226	.333	.182	12.54	1.93
Smith, Chris	R-R	6-2	205	8-19-88	0	0	0.00	1	1	0	0	1	0	0	0	0	0	2	.000	.000	.000	18.00	0.00
Snead, Kirby	L-L	6-0	200	10-7-94	3	1	1.36	26	0	0	8	33	27	7	5	0	12	26	.235	.214	.247	7.09	3.27
Sparkman, Glenn	B-R	6-2	210	5-11-92	0	1	0.00	1	1	0	0	3	3	3	0	0	1	3	.200	.000	.273	8.10	2.70
Straka, John	L-R	6-2	215	1-19-90	3	1	3.41	5	5	0	0	29	33	13	11	1	6	15	.282	.269	.300	4.66	1.86
Villegas, Kender	R-R	6-2	170	6-8-93	2	1	3.20	14	1	0	3	20	14	7	7	2	12	19	.197	.296	.136	8.69	5.49
Walby, Philip	L-R	6-2	190	7-24-92	0	2	5.76	34	0	0	0	50	55	36	32	4	24	38	.281	.300	.267	6.84	4.32
Wandling, Jon	R-R	6-3	205	5-28-92	0	0	13.50	2	0	0	0	3	3	4	4	1	2	1	.300	.400	.200	3.38	6.75
Young, Danny	L-L	6-3	200	5-27-94	2	0	2.08	26	0	0	4	30	22	7	7	1	9	27	.200	.194	.203	8.01	2.67
Zeuch, T.J.	R-R	6-7	225	8-1-95	3	4	3.38	12	11	0	0	59	63	35	22	3	17	46	.266	.270	.262	7.06	2.61

Fielding

Catcher	PCT	G	PO	A	E	DP	PB
De La Cruz	.994	48	308	26	2	4	7
Hissey	.976	12	77	4	2	0	1
Jansen	.992	25	220	19	2	3	1
Kelly	1.000	3	16	6	0	0	1
Maile	.958	4	20	3	1	0	0
McGuire	1.000	3	23	2	0	0	0
Pentecost	1.000	19	138	18	0	3	3
Reeves	.984	23	166	16	3	0	2
Smith	1.000	2	7	2	0	0	0
Sotillo	.986	13	63	8	1	0	3
Spiwak	.000	1	0	0	0	0	0

First Base	PCT	G	PO	A	E	DP
Dean	1.000	12	94	6	0	11
Hissey	1.000	2	20	1	0	4
Jones	1.000	5	28	3	0	4
Kelly	.978	85	680	44	16	56
Knight	1.000	2	14	0	0	1
Panas	.984	13	116	9	2	16
Pentecost	.991	22	206	8	2	17

Second Base	PCT	G	PO	A	E	DP
Barreto	1.000	4	4	8	0	3
Berti	1.000	1	1	4	0	0
Biggio	.976	116	205	330	13	76
Cardenas	.976	12	13	27	1	1
Coghlan	1.000	2	0	1	0	0
Guillotte	1.000	4	10	9	0	3
Gurriel	1.000	1	1	2	0	0
Jones	.917	2	5	6	1	2
Lopes	1.000	1	1	2	0	0

Third Base	PCT	G	PO	A	E	DP
Barreto	.941	6	3	13	1	4
Berti	1.000	1	1	2	0	0
Biggio	.750	6	2	7	3	0
Cardenas	1.000	2	1	2	0	0
Dean	.885	28	16	38	7	1
Donaldson	.909	2	3	7	1	1
Guerrero Jr.	.936	41	29	74	7	7
Jones	.900	7	3	15	2	1
Kelly	.893	29	11	39	6	6
Knight	.857	4	2	4	1	1
Petit	1.000	1	1	3	0	1
Reeves	1.000	2	2	1	0	1
Silva	.909	3	2	8	1	1
Wise	.922	14	9	38	4	3

Shortstop	PCT	G	PO	A	E	DP
Barreto	.941	8	12	20	2	7
Bichette	.937	35	58	91	10	19
Cardenas	.943	53	76	140	13	24
Guillotte	.947	10	11	25	2	9
Gurriel	.837	11	18	23	8	5
Petit	1.000	1	0	3	0	0
Tulowitzki	.944	4	7	10	1	4
Vicuna	.888	26	38	65	13	13

Outfield	PCT	G	PO	A	E	DP
Alford	1.000	3	4	0	0	0
Almonte	.968	47	88	4	3	2
Biggio	1.000	2	6	0	0	0
Ceciliani	.889	3	8	0	1	0
Coghlan	1.000	1	2	0	0	0
Davis	.969	104	186	4	6	0
Guillotte	.972	24	58	11	2	2
Kelly	1.000	4	9	1	0	1
Loveless	.905	19	19	0	2	0
Olivares	.950	17	37	1	2	0
Panas	.977	89	159	10	4	1
Pinto	.958	13	21	2	1	1
Pompey	1.000	5	9	2	0	0
Thomas	.980	29	48	2	1	0
Thomas	.983	71	160	11	3	3

LANSING LUGNUTS

LOW CLASS A

MIDWEST LEAGUE

Batting	B-T	HT	WT	DOB	AVG	vLH	vRH	G	AB	R	H	2B	3B	HR	RBI	BB	HBP	SH	SF	SO	SB	CS	SLG	OBP
Bichette, Bo	R-R	6-0	200	3-5-98	.384	.414	.368	70	284	60	109	32	3	10	51	28	5	0	0	55	12	3	.623	.448
De La Cruz, Michael	B-R	5-10	190	5-15-93	.200	.217	.182	13	45	4	9	2	0	0	5	5	1	0	1	7	1	0	.244	.289
De Los Santos, Luis	R-R	6-1	160	6-9-98	.143	.000	.158	6	21	1	3	0	0	0	1	0	0	2	1	6	0	0	.143	.136
Gudino, Yeltsin	R-R	6-0	150	1-17-97	.259	.288	.246	115	413	44	107	14	2	2	42	35	11	2	4	63	2	3	.317	.331
Guerrero Jr., Vladimir	R-R	6-1	200	3-16-99	.316	.333	.306	71	269	53	85	21	1	7	45	40	5	0	4	34	6	2	.480	.409
Hernandez, Javier	R-R	6-1	180	7-21-96	.224	.370	.187	35	134	12	30	5	0	2	10	8	1	0	0	39	0	0	.306	.273
Hissey, Ryan	L-R	6-0	190	4-8-94	.254	.227	.270	33	118	19	30	4	1	2	23	10	2	0	4	21	1	1	.356	.313
Jacob, David	L-L	6-4	225	6-19-95	.288	.286	.289	18	73	9	21	2	0	3	14	6	2	0	0	19	0	0	.438	.358
Jones, Bradley	R-R	6-1	180	6-12-95	.326	.364	.305	49	184	33	60	10	3	9	39	21	1	0	2	47	3	2	.560	.394
Knight, Nash	B-R	6-0	195	9-20-92	.261	.244	.268	87	318	37	83	17	2	3	54	51	3	2	2	64	4	0	.355	.366
Morgan, Matt	R-R	6-1	190	1-27-96	.250	—	.250	1	4	0	1	0	0	0	0	0	0	0	0	3	0	0	.250	.250
Nay, Mitch	R-R	6-3	200	9-20-93	.222	.300	.192	61	252	26	56	9	2	10	40	15	2	0	6	57	0	0	.393	.266
Olivares, Edward	R-R	6-2	186	3-6-96	.277	.253	.289	101	426	82	118	26	9	17	65	22	13	0	3	82	18	7	.500	.330
Orozco, Rodrigo	B-R	5-11	155	4-2-95	.282	.313	.270	70	284	42	80	19	2	1	29	39	1	3	3	52	8	4	.373	.367
Palacios, Joshua	L-R	6-1	193	7-30-95	.280	.252	.297	91	368	65	103	18	3	2	39	42	6	0	3	78	12	6	.361	.360
Romanin, Mattingly	R-R	5-10	185	2-27-93	.204	.222	.200	31	108	9	22	10	0	0	10	8	1	3	2	29	0	1	.296	.261
Silva, Luis	R-R	5-11	170	6-30-95	.196	.086	.233	38	138	14	27	6	0	0	8	7	1	1	0	25	0	0	.239	.240
Sinay, Nick	R-R	5-10	175	11-4-93	.215	.197	.223	79	219	44	47	4	1	1	16	32	38	4	0	58	23	10	.256	.405
Smith, Ridge	R-R	5-10	190	4-26-95	.247	.184	.274	51	166	22	41	15	1	2	26	23	2	0	5	38	2	0	.386	.337
Sotillo, Andres	R-R	5-11	180	12-28-93	.261	.286	.250	22	69	5	18	2	0	0	5	10	3	1	0	21	0	1	.290	.378
Thomas, Jake	L-R	5-10	190	7-21-93	.275	.220	.304	37	120	15	33	6	2	0	16	40	2	0	2	33	9	3	.358	.457
Vicuna, Kevin	R-R	6-0	140	1-14-98	.340	.308	.351	12	50	6	17	1	1	0	4	2	2	0	0	13	3	2	.400	.389
Williams, Christian	L-R	6-3	210	9-14-94	.263	.306	.239	66	240	39	63	14	1	3	35	26	4	0	2	78	1	0	.367	.342
Woodman, J.B.	L-R	6-2	195	12-13-94	.240	.232	.244	96	362	44	87	19	5	7	45	40	5	2	5	157	8	4	.379	.320

Pitching	B-T	HT	WT	DOB	W	L	ERA	G	GS	CG	SV	IP	H	R	ER	HR	BB	SO	AVG	vLH	vRH	K/9	BB/9
Burgos, Miguel	L-L	5-9	155	6-16-95	0	0	1.93	4	0	0	0	5	3	1	1	0	5	6	.214	.143	.286	11.57	9.64
Carkuff, Jared	R-R	6-3	180	8-25-93	1	2	3.79	21	0	0	7	36	32	18	15	1	8	32	.232	.219	.246	8.07	2.02
Cuevas, Adams	R-R	6-0	192	2-2-96	0	0	4.50	1	0	0	0	2	2	1	1	0	1	0	.333	.400	.000	0.00	4.50
Deramo, Andrew	R-R	6-6	210	5-26-95	0	3	6.24	28	0	0	0	49	68	37	34	3	29	43	.329	.368	.287	7.90	5.33
Diaz, Denis	R-R	6-1	180	11-20-94	0	5	7.84	26	11	0	0	70	79	68	61	8	56	59	.292	.311	.272	7.59	7.20
Diaz, Yennsy	R-R	6-1	160	11-15-96	5	2	4.79	16	16	0	0	77	71	41	41	10	41	82	.249	.270	.216	9.58	4.79
Ellenbest, Mike	R-R	6-4	220	8-20-94	8	8	6.53	27	25	0	0	123	157	91	89	17	56	93	.322	.321	.323	6.82	4.11
Eller, Connor	R-R	6-2	195	1-23-94	1	4	4.17	21	0	0	2	37	37	24	17	3	19	25	.257	.179	.325	6.14	4.66
Encina, Geno	R-L	6-4	220	7-7-94	4	2	4.26	29	2	0	2	76	85	48	36	16	29	55	.286	.287	.286	6.51	3.43
Eveld, Bobby	L-R	6-5	200	12-4-91	0	0	1.80	2	0	0	0	5	3	2	1	0	2	3	.200	.333	.000	5.40	3.60
Fishman, Jake	L-L	6-3	195	2-8-95	0	1	4.05	4	0	0	0	7	6	3	3	2	0	15	.222	.308	.143	20.25	0.00
Glaude, Griffin	R-R	5-9	175	4-6-92	4	3	5.48	24	0	0	1	48	47	29	29	9	19	47	.257	.264	.250	8.87	3.59
Gutierrez, Osman	R-R	6-4	220	12-15-94	4	11	7.85	18	18	0	0	78	89	72	68	9	52	71	.288	.347	.218	8.19	6.00
Gutierrez, Osman	R-R	6-4	220	12-15-94	4	11	7.85	18	18	0	0	78	89	72	68	9	52	71	.288	.347	.218	8.19	6.00
Hall, Chris	R-R	6-2	212	1-27-94	1	2	8.74	6	0	0	0	11	20	12	11	3	7	9	.400	.346	.458	7.15	5.56
Hartman, Nick	R-R	6-2	180	10-24-94	2	2	3.29	32	0	0	2	38	40	21	14	2	15	37	.267	.295	.236	8.69	3.52
Herdenez, Yonardo	R-R	6-1	170	9-20-95	0	1	4.13	9	1	0	0	24	21	11	11	2	10	17	.233	.286	.171	6.38	3.75
Higuera, Juliandry	L-L	6-1	180	9-6-94	4	0	4.74	18	2	0	0	44	46	26	23	3	15	51	.271	.236	.296	10.51	3.09
Jackson, Zach	R-R	6-4	215	12-25-94	1	0	3.15	15	0	0	1	20	13	7	7	2	8	25	.181	.128	.242	11.25	3.60
Lietz, Dan	L-L	6-2	200	6-1-94	2	1	2.50	22	0	0	1	40	31	14	11	2	21	29	.220	.125	.282	6.58	4.76
Maese, Justin	R-R	6-3	190	10-24-96	5	3	4.84	12	12	3	0	71	78	46	38	3	26	60	.279	.260	.299	7.64	3.31
Manzueta, Danilo	R-R	6-3	188	1-18-97	0	0	16.20	1	0	0	0	2	5	3	3	0	0	2	.500	.400	.600	10.80	0.00
McClelland, Jackson	R-R	6-5	220	7-19-94	1	2	1.80	16	0	0	8	20	13	8	4	0	10	17	.194	.250	.154	7.65	4.50
Murphy, Patrick	R-R	6-4	220	6-10-95	4	3	2.94	15	15	0	0	89	87	38	29	5	33	57	.263	.247	.285	5.79	3.35
Ramirez, Gaudy	R-R	6-2	175	9-11-97	0	1	9.00	1	0	0	0	1	2	1	1	0	1	0	.667	1.000	.500	0.00	9.00
Ravel, Andy	R-R	6-2	165	10-12-94	6	9	7.56	25	22	0	0	114	159	104	96	16	38	75	.340	.361	.319	5.90	2.99
Rodriguez, Dalton	R-R	6-1	180	8-20-96	1	1	8.04	3	3	0	0	16	20	15	14	1	6	10	.313	.300	.324	5.74	3.45
Saucedo, Tayler	L-L	6-5	185	6-18-93	3	2	4.50	17	3	0	1	40	44	25	20	4	16	37	.272	.308	.247	8.33	3.60
Snead, Kirby	L-L	6-0	200	10-7-94	4	1	2.42	16	0	0	0	22	15	6	6	0	13	30	.197	.105	.290	12.09	5.24
Walby, Philip	L-R	6-2	190	7-24-92	2	0	4.66	7	0	0	0	10	7	5	5	2	5	9	.189	.227	.133	8.38	4.66
Weatherly, Kyle	R-R	6-4	200	10-3-94	0	4	6.75	6	6	0	0	23	30	18	17	4	13	11	.319	.390	.264	4.37	5.16

Fielding

Catcher	PCT	G	PO	A	E	DP	PB
De La Cruz	1.000	13	84	14	0	0	2
Hernandez	.980	34	271	23	6	3	1
Hissey	.988	29	218	20	3	1	0
Knight	1.000	1	2	0	0	0	0
Morgan	1.000	1	11	2	0	0	0
Silva	1.000	1	6	2	0	0	0
Smith	.975	46	296	56	9	5	3
Sotillo	.993	20	125	15	1	3	1

First Base	PCT	G	PO	A	E	DP
Hissey	1.000	1	1	0	0	0
Jacob	1.000	14	92	6	0	14
Jones	1.000	8	64	3	0	7
Knight	.988	43	325	15	4	24
Nay	.978	18	166	15	4	19
Williams	.988	57	457	30	6	50
Woodman	1.000	1	1	0	0	0

Second Base	PCT	G	PO	A	E	DP
Bichette	.971	14	15	52	2	7
Gudino	.984	51	112	140	4	38
Jones	.958	20	40	75	5	19
Knight	.954	14	23	39	3	5
Romanin	.941	22	32	48	5	13
Silva	.984	16	24	36	1	5
Vicuna	1.000	1	2	2	0	1

Third Base	PCT	G	PO	A	E	DP
Guerrero Jr.	.941	61	40	87	8	14
Jones	.906	13	10	19	3	3
Knight	.976	17	21	20	1	1
Nay	.984	28	19	42	1	4
Romanin	.810	6	7	10	4	1
Silva	.897	14	7	19	3	0
Williams	.000	1	0	0	0	0

Shortstop	PCT	G	PO	A	E	DP
Bichette	.949	51	68	138	11	32
De Los Santos	1.000	6	11	16	0	6
Gudino	.964	66	105	212	12	42
Silva	1.000	5	9	14	0	2
Vicuna	.952	10	21	19	2	4

Outfield	PCT	G	PO	A	E	DP
Olivares	.967	88	192	14	7	5
Orozco	1.000	61	121	6	0	3
Palacios	.955	87	187	4	9	2
Romanin	1.000	1	2	0	0	0
Sinay	1.000	61	129	3	0	0
Thomas	1.000	25	47	2	0	0
Woodman	.972	87	166	7	5	1

VANCOUVER CANADIANS

SHORT SEASON

NORTHWEST LEAGUE

Batting	B-T	HT	WT	DOB	AVG	vLH	vRH	G	AB	R	H	2B	3B	HR	RBI	BB	HBP	SH	SF	SO	SB	CS	SLG	OBP
Adams, Riley	R-R	6-4	225	6-26-96	.305	.271	.316	52	203	26	62	16	1	3	35	18	5	0	1	50	1	1	.438	.374
Barreto, Deiferson	R-R	5-10	165	5-19-95	.249	.189	.265	48	173	18	43	6	2	0	14	6	2	4	1	21	3	4	.306	.280
Clemens, Kacy	L-R	6-2	200	7-27-94	.274	.265	.276	62	230	32	63	14	3	4	45	38	1	0	0	52	4	0	.413	.379
Hernandez, Javier	R-R	6-1	180	7-21-96	.316	.400	.286	5	19	3	6	1	2	0	6	1	0	0	0	5	0	0	.579	.350
Jacob, David	L-L	6-4	225	6-19-95	.267	.400	.250	23	90	11	24	3	0	4	22	7	1	0	1	22	0	0	.433	.323
Jones, Lance	R-R	5-11	175	11-10-92	.423	.667	.294	8	26	6	11	2	0	0	5	2	1	1	1	5	1	0	.500	.467
Large, Cullen	B-R	6-0	175	1-22-96	.246	.182	.260	34	126	16	31	8	1	0	7	18	4	2	1	28	3	0	.325	.356
Lizardo, Bryan	B-R	6-0	205	7-26-97	.212	.180	.220	54	203	17	43	6	2	1	16	17	1	1	0	65	2	1	.276	.276
Lundquist, Brock	L-R	5-11	190	1-23-96	.251	.314	.237	51	183	28	46	13	2	2	19	26	7	0	1	39	6	4	.377	.364
Morgan, Matt	R-R	6-1	190	1-27-96	.141	.095	.155	29	92	13	13	3	1	2	8	12	2	0	0	42	1	0	.261	.255
O'Brien, Cam	B-R	6-0	215	8-9-92	.216	.182	.231	11	37	3	8	1	0	0	0	1	2	0	0	12	0	0	.243	.275
Obeso, Norberto	L-R	6-0	175	7-9-95	.252	.200	.263	62	210	24	53	8	1	2	23	34	3	3	0	38	3	2	.329	.364
Polizzi, Brandon	R-R	5-10	170	3-16-96	.198	.265	.169	38	111	15	22	4	1	1	12	10	1	1	0	33	6	0	.279	.271
Pruitt, Reggie	R-R	6-0	169	5-7-97	.229	.246	.225	72	279	49	64	9	2	2	13	23	4	4	0	80	28	8	.298	.297
Rodriguez, Francisco	R-R	6-1	220	9-22-94	.000	.000	.000	3	6	0	0	0	0	0	0	1	0	0	0	2	0	0	.000	.143
Rodriguez, Yorman	R-R	5-10	160	7-23-97	.191	.000	.222	5	21	1	4	1	0	0	0	1	0	0	0	2	0	1	.238	.227
Romanin, Mattingly	R-R	5-10	185	2-27-93	.200	.214	.196	26	70	11	14	3	0	0	7	13	7	0	0	24	2	1	.243	.378
Severino, Jesus	R-R	6-1	175	6-11-97	.000	.000	.000	2	6	0	0	0	0	0	0	1	0	0	0	2	0	0	.000	.143

Spiwak, Owen	L-R	6-2	185	5-23-95	.211	.154	.220	28	95	9	20	5	0	1	11	13	1	1	0	39	2	1	.295	.312
Taylor, Samad	R-R	5-10	160	7-11-98	.294	.278	.300	19	68	7	20	3	0	2	8	5	1	2	2	18	2	2	.427	.342
Vicuna, Kevin	R-R	6-0	140	1-14-98	.280	.241	.288	46	189	34	53	3	1	0	17	11	5	2	2	36	14	7	.307	.333
Warmoth, Logan	R-R	6-0	190	9-6-95	.306	.257	.320	39	160	18	49	11	2	1	20	7	6	0	1	33	5	2	.419	.356
Young, Chavez	B-R	6-2	180	8-8-97	.308	.667	.200	5	13	3	4	1	1	0	5	0	2	0	0	5	0	0	.539	.400

Pitching	B-T	HT	WT	DOB	W	L	ERA	G	GS	CG	SV	IP	H	R	ER	HR	BB	SO	AVG	vLH	vRH	K/9	BB/9
Aleton, Wilfri	L-L	6-3	165	11-18-95	3	6	5.07	13	6	0	0	55	69	34	31	2	18	41	.314	.275	.322	6.71	2.95
Alicea, Angel	R-R	6-1	200	8-29-94	0	0	4.50	2	0	0	0	4	6	2	2	0	1	1	.353	.429	.300	2.25	2.25
Bergen, Travis	L-L	6-1	205	10-8-93	1	0	2.89	3	1	0	0	9	8	3	3	0	5	14	.222	.167	.233	13.50	4.82
Bouchey, Brayden	R-R	6-6	212	9-20-95	1	1	4.20	24	0	0	0	30	20	14	14	4	12	36	.194	.216	.182	10.80	3.60
Burgos, Miguel	L-L	5-9	155	6-16-95	3	0	4.68	14	0	0	0	25	28	17	13	3	13	17	.298	.304	.296	6.12	4.68
Carkuff, Jared	R-R	6-3	180	8-25-93	0	0	0.00	2	0	0	0	3	2	0	0	0	0	3	.200	.000	.333	9.00	0.00
DiBenedetto, Joe	L-L	5-9	180	5-25-95	0	1	5.68	4	0	0	0	6	6	4	4	0	6	4	.273	.000	.353	5.68	8.53
Dillon, Justin	R-R	6-3	225	9-5-93	2	1	1.96	13	5	0	0	23	17	7	5	0	4	28	.207	.231	.196	10.96	1.57
Espada, Jose	R-R	6-0	170	2-22-97	1	3	5.14	13	10	0	0	49	46	31	28	5	15	51	.249	.324	.205	9.37	2.76
Eveld, Bobby	L-R	6-5	200	12-4-91	2	0	11.17	16	0	0	0	19	35	24	24	5	7	13	.398	.421	.380	6.05	3.26
Fishman, Jake	L-L	6-3	195	2-8-95	1	0	1.17	14	0	0	1	23	20	4	3	1	4	23	.235	.174	.258	9.00	1.57
Hall, Chris	R-R	6-2	212	1-27-94	1	0	1.49	20	0	0	1	36	26	10	6	2	11	42	.200	.222	.184	10.40	2.72
Herdenez, Yonardo	R-R	6-1	170	9-20-95	0	0	2.08	6	0	0	0	13	9	5	3	1	5	8	.192	.179	.211	5.54	3.46
Higuera, Juliandry	L-L	6-1	180	9-6-94	1	0	0.00	2	0	0	0	4	3	0	0	0	1	9	.200	.200	.200	18.69	2.08
Huffman, Grayson	L-L	6-2	195	5-6-95	2	2	3.93	22	0	0	1	34	29	21	15	2	19	27	.234	.214	.240	7.08	4.98
Jimenez, Dany	R-R	6-3	190	12-23-93	2	3	5.30	6	3	0	0	19	13	15	11	3	4	23	.183	.120	.217	11.09	1.93
Laws, Colton	R-R	6-7	215	11-20-95	0	0	2.25	3	3	0	0	4	4	2	1	0	0	4	.250	.300	.167	9.00	0.00
Logue, Zach	L-L	6-0	165	4-23-96	3	1	1.75	9	4	0	0	26	19	6	5	0	6	28	.209	.105	.236	9.82	2.10
Nunez, Juan	R-R	6-2	185	1-23-96	2	8	5.05	14	12	0	0	62	57	45	35	4	30	53	.240	.253	.230	7.65	4.33
Ouellette, William	R-R	6-1	195	6-30-93	3	0	3.00	24	0	0	13	30	23	10	10	3	7	35	.204	.220	.194	10.50	2.10
Pascual, Orlando	R-R	6-3	210	11-7-95	2	0	2.18	24	0	0	6	33	25	8	8	3	10	45	.210	.116	.263	12.27	2.73
Pearson, Nate	R-R	6-6	245	8-20-96	0	0	0.95	7	7	0	0	19	6	2	2	0	5	24	.097	.150	.071	11.37	2.37
Reyes, Marcus	L-L	5-11	180	3-10-95	0	0	1.80	3	0	0	0	5	7	1	1	0	1	2	.333	.250	.353	3.60	1.80
Rodning, Brody	R-L	6-1	185	1-14-96	4	1	4.64	10	4	0	0	33	37	23	17	2	18	30	.280	.233	.294	8.18	4.91
Rodriguez, Dalton	R-R	6-1	180	8-20-96	5	4	4.15	11	9	0	0	56	56	30	26	4	17	37	.249	.229	.264	5.91	2.72
Sellers, Donnie	R-R	6-1	190	7-26-95	3	1	3.90	12	7	0	0	30	34	14	13	0	13	26	.291	.255	.323	7.80	3.90
Shannon, Matt	R-R	6-3	220	5-31-95	0	0	0.00	3	1	0	0	4	1	0	0	0	0	4	.077	.000	.125	9.00	0.00
Weatherly, Kyle	R-R	6-4	200	10-3-94	1	1	2.05	4	4	0	0	22	17	10	5	3	7	18	.205	.125	.237	7.36	2.86

Fielding

C: Adams 34, Hernandez 4, Morgan 25, O'Brien 2, Rodriguez 2, Spiwak 14. **1B:** Clemens 53, Jacob 9, Lizardo 10, O'Brien 2, Rodriguez 2, Rodriguez 3, Romanin 1. **2B:** Barreto 13, Large 28, Romanin 7, Taylor 19, Vicuna 13. **3B:** Barreto 24, Lizardo 44, Romanin 12, Severino 1. **SS:** Barreto 10, Vicuna 34, Warmoth 35. **OF:** Barreto 2, Jacob 4, Jones 8, Large 1, Lundquist 49, Obeso 61, Polizzi 36, Pruitt 72, Romanin 5, Young 4.

BLUEFIELD BLUE JAYS — *ROOKIE*

APPALACHIAN LEAGUE

Batting	B-T	HT	WT	DOB	AVG	vLH	vRH	G	AB	R	H	2B	3B	HR	RBI	BB	HBP	SH	SF	SO	SB	CS	SLG	OBP
Contreras, Mc Gregory	R-R	6-1	170	8-30-98	.279	.293	.275	51	190	36	53	8	2	5	33	12	4	1	0	55	4	3	.421	.335
Fuentes, Antony	R-R	5-11	160	9-26-95	.284	.327	.262	45	155	30	44	8	2	4	26	10	6	1	2	34	4	2	.439	.347
Gold, Ryan	L-R	5-9	188	10-10-97	.302	.300	.303	39	139	24	42	11	1	4	34	15	3	0	0	33	1	2	.482	.382
Grudzielanek, Brandon	R-R	6-0	205	5-26-95	.295	.303	.292	38	146	26	43	5	2	2	27	11	0	2	2	26	3	3	.397	.340
Guzman, Sterling	R-R	5-11	175	2-2-98	.304	.100	.361	15	46	8	14	2	0	1	8	10	0	2	0	13	2	0	.413	.429
Johnson, Reilly	R-R	5-9	170	9-26-96	.232	.286	.204	25	82	9	19	2	1	0	10	12	1	1	1	16	2	0	.281	.333
Kirwer, Tanner	R-R	6-0	160	3-15-96	.224	.080	.283	25	85	14	19	4	1	1	10	5	8	4	1	27	3	0	.329	.323
Navarro, Jesus	R-R	5-11	160	1-13-98	.204	.085	.248	52	172	22	35	1	1	0	17	15	0	10	0	30	0	2	.221	.267
Noda, Ryan	L-L	6-3	217	3-30-96	.365	.310	.378	66	214	62	78	18	3	7	39	59	3	0	0	60	7	4	.575	.507
Polizzi, Brandon	R-R	5-10	170	3-16-96	.357	.500	.333	7	28	8	10	4	1	0	2	1	3	0	0	7	1	0	.571	.438
Rodriguez, Francisco	R-R	6-1	220	9-22-94	.183	.250	.157	25	71	5	13	3	0	0	3	8	3	0	0	33	0	0	.225	.293
Rodriguez, Freddy	L-R	6-1	180	11-15-96	.308	.286	.312	28	91	17	28	2	2	3	16	12	0	1	0	21	0	0	.473	.388
Rodriguez, Yorman	R-R	5-10	160	7-23-97	.346	.404	.328	57	240	36	83	11	0	3	36	7	6	0	4	25	2	4	.429	.374
Severino, Jesus	R-R	6-1	175	6-11-97	.228	.212	.233	43	136	17	31	8	0	2	21	13	2	4	1	29	1	1	.331	.303
Smith, Kevin	R-R	6-1	188	7-4-96	.271	.217	.287	61	262	43	71	25	1	8	43	16	1	1	3	70	9	0	.466	.312
Taylor, Samad	R-R	5-10	160	7-11-98	.250	.250	.250	5	16	1	4	0	0	0	3	3	0	0	1	6	1	0	.250	.350
Young, Chavez	B-R	6-2	180	8-8-97	.282	.340	.266	62	252	52	71	14	7	4	25	13	8	4	4	58	4	5	.441	.332

Pitching	B-T	HT	WT	DOB	W	L	ERA	G	GS	CG	SV	IP	H	R	ER	HR	BB	SO	AVG	vLH	vRH	K/9	BB/9
Barrett, Jordan	L-L	6-3	215	6-24-95	3	2	2.80	11	5	0	1	35	24	19	11	2	13	46	.183	.107	.204	11.72	3.31
Burgos, Miguel	L-L	5-9	155	6-16-95	0	0	0.00	3	0	0	0	3	2	0	0	0	1	5	.182	.333	.125	15.00	3.00
Castillo, Maximo	R-R	6-1	200	5-4-99	6	0	3.80	10	10	0	0	47	54	23	20	4	7	52	.284	.258	.309	9.89	1.33
Cheshire, Jonathan	L-R	6-1	185	11-15-94	0	0	1.80	3	0	0	0	5	1	1	1	1	0	6	.063	.125	.000	10.80	0.00
DiBenedetto, Joe	L-L	5-9	180	5-25-95	3	1	4.24	16	0	0	1	23	25	17	11	5	9	18	.269	.107	.339	6.94	3.47
Espinal, Joel	R-R	6-2	185	8-15-96	1	4	5.51	12	5	0	1	47	53	37	29	4	14	37	.294	.257	.318	7.04	2.66
Galindo, Alvaro	R-R	6-2	170	2-25-98	4	4	4.94	12	8	0	0	47	54	34	26	4	21	29	.286	.317	.264	5.51	3.99
Herdenez, Yonardo	R-R	6-1	170	9-20-95	0	0	7.71	4	0	0	1	7	12	6	6	1	0	6	.375	.500	.300	7.71	0.00
Jose, Kelyn	L-L	6-4	195	5-19-95	2	0	3.12	19	0	0	0	26	15	9	9	1	25	36	.165	.273	.130	12.46	8.65
Larkins, Turner	R-R	6-3	200	11-6-95	3	1	2.04	10	6	0	0	35	33	8	8	0	11	30	.252	.222	.273	7.64	2.80
Law, Connor	R-R	6-4	195	4-27-94	1	0	0.00	3	0	0	0	5	3	0	0	0	1	7	.177	.167	.182	12.60	1.80
Laws, Colton	R-R	6-7	215	11-20-95	1	0	0.82	6	3	0	0	11	9	1	1	0	1	11	.237	.167	.300	9.00	0.82

Logue, Zach	L-L	6-0	165	4-23-96	1	0	0.00	3	2	0	0	5	2	0	0	0	0	5	.125	.000	.167	9.00	0.00
McKown, Mitch	R-R	6-4	195	5-21-96	3	1	3.55	16	0	0	0	25	18	12	10	0	15	24	.198	.212	.190	8.53	5.33
Nova, Jose	L-L	6-1	170	4-6-95	2	2	9.97	16	0	0	0	22	31	26	24	1	8	16	.320	.231	.352	6.65	3.32
Olander, Tyler	L-L	6-9	280	7-9-92	2	0	8.14	16	0	0	0	21	31	23	19	2	12	17	.341	.400	.324	7.29	5.14
Pondler, Randy	L-L	6-2	160	11-8-96	4	1	2.51	12	11	0	0	57	46	20	16	4	11	42	.220	.333	.194	6.59	1.73
Reyes, Marcus	L-L	5-11	180	3-10-95	2	0	1.77	13	0	0	3	20	19	8	4	2	2	25	.238	.222	.245	11.07	0.89
Silva, Elio	L-L	5-11	160	8-21-95	4	2	3.77	11	7	0	0	45	53	22	19	3	5	41	.283	.297	.280	8.14	0.99
Spraker, Graham	R-R	6-3	200	3-19-95	1	1	1.62	19	0	0	7	33	20	8	6	0	6	39	.168	.271	.099	10.53	1.62
Tice, Ty	L-R	5-9	170	7-4-96	1	1	1.05	23	0	0	12	26	18	7	3	2	11	35	.190	.171	.204	12.27	3.86
Winckowski, Josh	R-R	6-3	185	6-28-98	2	2	5.33	12	11	0	0	54	61	41	32	8	24	45	.282	.287	.279	7.50	4.00

Fielding

C: Gold 25, Johnson 18, Rodriguez 27. **1B:** Noda 49, Rodriguez 19, Rodriguez 5. **2B:** Grudzielanek 11, Guzman 10, Navarro 44, Taylor 5. **3B:** Grudzielanek 24, Guzman 6, Johnson 1, Severino 40. **SS:** Navarro 9, Severino 2, Smith 58. **OF:** Contreras 51, Fuentes 41, Kirwer 25, Noda 12, Polizzi 6, Rodriguez 25, Young 58.

GCL BLUE JAYS — *ROOKIE*

GULF COAST LEAGUE

Batting	B-T	HT	WT	DOB	AVG	vLH	vRH	G	AB	R	H	2B	3B	HR	RBI	BB	HBP	SH	SF	SO	SB	CS	SLG	OBP
Abbadessa, Dominic	R-R	5-10	185	12-8-97	.340	.333	.342	39	147	30	50	4	3	0	10	7	9	0	1	14	11	6	.408	.402
Daniels, D.J.	R-R	6-3	205	12-17-97	.157	.094	.176	44	140	14	22	5	0	1	6	8	9	0	0	57	1	2	.214	.248
Danner, Hagen	R-R	6-2	185	9-30-98	.160	.138	.167	34	125	10	20	5	0	2	20	5	3	1	2	36	3	1	.248	.207
De Los Santos, Luis	R-R	6-1	160	6-9-98	.288	.227	.307	49	184	26	53	11	3	1	28	6	6	1	3	42	7	0	.397	.327
Grudzielanek, Brandon	R-R	6-0	205	5-26-95	.667	—	.667	1	3	1	2	0	0	0	0	0	0	0	0	1	0	0	.667	.667
Guerra, Andres	R-R	5-11	175	6-3-97	.114	.091	.121	14	44	5	5	3	0	0	2	5	0	1	0	13	0	0	.182	.204
Guerrero, Emilio	R-R	6-4	189	8-21-92	.429	.200	.556	4	14	2	6	2	0	0	3	1	0	0	0	3	0	0	.571	.467
Hissey, Ryan	L-R	6-0	190	4-8-94	.500	1.000	.400	2	6	1	3	0	0	1	1	0	0	0	0	2	1	0	1.000	.500
Jacob, David	L-L	6-4	225	6-19-95	1.000	—	1.000	1	1	1	1	0	0	1	2	0	0	0	0	0	0	0	4.000	1.000
Kelly, Yhordegny	R-R	6-3	205	3-5-97	.239	.125	.271	35	109	11	26	7	1	1	14	18	2	0	0	44	1	0	.349	.357
Kirk, Alejandro	R-R	5-9	220	11-6-98	.000	—	.000	1	2	0	0	0	0	0	0	0	1	0	0	0	0	0	.000	.333
Lopes, Christian	R-R	6-0	185	10-1-92	.333	1.000	.200	2	6	3	2	0	1	1	5	2	0	0	0	1	0	0	1.167	.500
Lopez, Otto	R-R	5-10	160	10-1-98	.275	.186	.304	51	178	30	49	6	3	1	15	19	5	1	0	23	7	3	.360	.361
McDonald, Evan	R-R	6-1	185	6-30-94	.125	.000	.143	6	16	1	2	0	0	0	1	4	0	1	0	7	3	0	.125	.300
McGuire, Reese	L-R	5-11	215	3-2-95	.409	.667	.368	8	22	4	9	2	0	0	7	3	0	0	1	1	0	1	.500	.462
Molina, Jonelvy	R-R	6-0	180	3-18-97	.240	.095	.296	23	75	8	18	4	0	2	9	4	0	1	0	11	0	0	.373	.279
Morris, Patrick	L-L	6-1	195	11-30-98	.259	.125	.316	18	54	3	14	3	0	0	4	6	0	0	1	15	0	0	.315	.328
Neal, DJ	R-R	6-3	201	1-11-97	.297	.436	.250	42	155	23	46	7	2	3	20	8	3	0	1	26	8	2	.426	.341
Negron, Ricky	R-R	6-2	205	5-19-95	.039	.000	.048	8	26	2	1	0	0	0	0	2	0	0	0	12	0	0	.039	.107
Ovando, Aldo	R-R	6-5	195	4-6-97	.181	.065	.207	46	166	18	30	2	3	1	18	10	4	0	2	59	1	0	.247	.242
Pentecost, Max	R-R	6-2	191	3-10-93	.000	—	.000	1	2	0	0	0	0	0	0	0	0	0	0	0	0	0	.000	.000
Reyes, Joseph	L-R	6-3	195	1-24-98	.241	.171	.260	48	158	16	38	5	2	0	20	23	1	0	5	55	2	0	.298	.332
Schneider, Davis	R-R	5-10	190	1-26-99	.238	.180	.256	50	168	30	40	12	1	4	23	36	2	0	4	36	3	1	.393	.371
Theran, Jose	R-R	5-10	155	6-2-98	.270	.171	.297	46	163	18	44	10	1	0	15	18	2	2	2	35	3	0	.344	.346
Warmoth, Logan	R-R	6-0	190	9-6-95	.273	.250	.278	6	22	3	6	0	0	1	3	1	0	0	0	2	1	0	.409	.304

Pitching	B-T	HT	WT	DOB	W	L	ERA	G	GS	CG	SV	IP	H	R	ER	HR	BB	SO	AVG	vLH	vRH	K/9	BB/9
Alicea, Angel	R-R	6-1	200	8-29-94	1	1	9.82	3	1	0	0	4	3	4	4	0	1	9	.214	.143	.286	22.09	2.45
Bergen, Travis	L-L	6-1	205	10-8-93	0	1	3.00	6	6	0	0	9	7	4	3	2	3	8	.212	.125	.240	8.00	3.00
Buffo, Maverik	R-R	6-2	200	9-15-95	5	1	0.53	11	6	1	0	34	28	6	2	0	2	36	.222	.211	.227	9.53	0.53
Castaneda, Felipe	R-R	6-1	194	1-4-00	2	4	4.08	9	6	0	0	35	43	20	16	1	19	31	.295	.281	.303	7.90	4.84
Cheshire, Jonathan	L-R	6-1	185	11-15-94	2	0	1.40	13	0	0	6	19	9	4	3	1	1	25	.136	.167	.119	11.64	0.47
Cole, Taylor	R-R	6-1	200	8-20-89	0	0	0.00	3	3	0	0	4	2	0	0	0	1	6	.133	.167	.111	13.50	2.25
Concepcion, Jol	R-R	6-5	195	9-17-98	2	2	3.78	9	7	0	0	33	24	17	14	2	28	29	.195	.139	.218	7.83	7.56
Cuevas, Adams	R-R	6-0	192	2-2-96	3	2	2.08	16	0	0	3	26	19	9	6	0	9	23	.211	.200	.217	7.96	3.12
De Los Santos, Alvery	R-R	6-4	180	7-18-99	2	1	6.53	6	4	0	0	21	28	16	15	5	4	15	.318	.375	.286	6.53	1.74
Estevez, Mike	R-L	6-0	170	9-27-92	0	0	13.50	2	0	0	0	1	3	2	2	1	1	1	.429	.000	.600	6.75	6.75
Eveld, Bobby	L-R	6-5	200	12-4-91	0	1	2.25	3	0	0	0	4	4	1	1	0	3	4	.267	.400	.200	9.00	6.75
Fishman, Jake	L-L	6-3	195	2-8-95	0	0	0.00	1	1	0	0	1	1	0	0	0	0	1	.250	.000	.500	9.00	0.00
Galva, Claudio	L-L	6-2	169	10-9-96	3	1	3.08	9	2	0	0	38	40	16	13	1	3	23	.272	.367	.248	5.45	0.71
Gunter, Matthew	L-L	6-1	190	2-7-95	1	0	0.94	10	4	0	0	38	27	6	4	0	4	36	.197	.261	.184	8.45	0.94
Hernandez, Roither	R-R	6-4	185	3-5-98	1	0	0.79	3	3	0	0	11	9	1	1	0	2	9	.214	.294	.160	7.15	1.59
Hinojosa, Yunior	R-R	6-2	190	12-21-99	0	1	1.93	3	0	0	0	5	3	2	1	0	2	2	.200	.667	.083	3.86	3.86
Jimenez, Dany	R-R	6-3	190	12-23-93	0	0	9.00	1	0	0	0	1	1	2	1	0	0	1	.200	.000	.250	9.00	0.00
Jimenez, Emerson	B-R	6-1	160	12-16-94	1	0	0.00	9	0	0	0	15	6	0	0	0	5	23	.125	.071	.147	13.80	3.00
Law, Connor	R-R	6-4	195	4-27-94	2	1	1.54	14	0	0	2	23	19	6	4	1	5	15	.218	.276	.190	5.79	1.93
Maese, Justin	R-R	6-3	190	10-24-96	0	0	5.00	3	3	0	0	9	13	6	5	1	1	9	.333	.467	.250	9.00	1.00
Manzueta, Danilo	R-R	6-3	188	1-18-97	1	1	2.55	14	0	0	0	18	20	12	5	1	7	13	.286	.304	.277	6.62	3.57
Medrano, Elieser	R-R	6-2	180	8-17-98	3	0	3.52	6	2	0	0	23	18	11	9	0	16	26	.222	.154	.255	10.17	6.26
Meza, Juan	R-R	6-2	172	2-4-98	0	0	2.33	16	0	0	0	19	19	6	5	0	6	14	.253	.290	.227	6.52	2.79
Monsion, Rafael	L-L	6-3	185	8-16-99	0	0	4.50	3	0	0	1	4	2	2	2	0	3	1	.143	.333	.091	2.25	6.75
Murphy, Patrick	R-R	6-4	220	6-10-95	1	0	0.00	3	2	0	0	9	7	0	0	0	1	15	.212	.300	.174	15.00	1.00
Nunez, Anderson	R-R	6-1	190	12-23-97	1	2	4.03	14	2	0	0	29	30	16	13	0	16	17	.286	.273	.292	5.28	4.97
Pearson, Nate	R-R	6-6	245	8-20-96	0	0	0.00	1	1	0	0	1	1	0	0	0	0	2	.250	.000	.500	18.00	0.00
Price, Brennan	R-R	6-9	265	7-15-95	0	0	10.80	3	0	0	0	3	4	4	4	1	3	3	.308	.167	.429	8.10	8.10
Ramirez, Gaudy	R-R	6-2	175	9-11-97	1	0	1.21	12	0	0	1	22	11	6	3	0	7	27	.145	.174	.132	10.88	2.82

Reyes, Emmanuel	L-L	6-0	185	12-14-97	1	0	5.48	14	0	0	0	21	26	15	13	2	13	12	.292	.200	.304	5.06	5.48
Reyes, Marcus	L-L	5-11	180	3-10-95	0	0	0.00	1	0	0	0	2	1	0	0	0	0	4	.143	—	.143	18.00	0.00
Rodning, Brody	R-L	6-1	185	1-14-96	0	0	9.00	1	1	0	0	1	0	2	1	0	2	1	.000	.000	.000	9.00	18.00
Watts, Justin	R-R	6-3	215	9-8-93	2	4	3.62	17	3	0	2	32	30	20	13	1	8	34	.246	.220	.259	9.46	2.23
Zeuch, T.J.	R-R	6-7	225	8-1-95	0	2	5.14	3	3	0	0	7	9	6	4	1	2	5	.321	.333	.313	6.43	2.57

Fielding

C: Danner 30, Guerra 13, Hissey 1, McGuire 4, Molina 19, Pentecost 1. **1B:** Kelly 19, Morris 18, Reyes 30, Schneider 1. **2B:** Lopez 19, McDonald 1, Theran 42. **3B:** De Los Santos 1, Guerrero 3, Lopes 1, Lopez 10, Negron 5, Reyes 2, Schneider 43. **SS:** De Los Santos 46, Grudzielanek 1, Lopez 6, McDonald 5, Theran 3, Warmoth 5. **OF:** Abbadessa 34, Daniels 42, Lopez 15, Neal 37, Ovando 43, Reyes 14.

DSL BLUE JAYS — *ROOKIE*

DOMINICAN SUMMER LEAGUE

Batting	B-T	HT	WT	DOB	AVG	vLH	vRH	G	AB	R	H	2B	3B	HR	RBI	BB	HBP	SH	SF	SO	SB	CS	SLG	OBP
Berroa, Steward	B-R	5-10	178	6-5-99	.261	.316	.247	54	188	37	49	3	7	1	22	25	3	2	3	49	20	12	.367	.352
Briceno, Jose	R-R	6-2	185	10-14-97	.203	.280	.183	38	118	16	24	2	1	0	7	12	9	0	0	32	8	5	.237	.324
Cardona, Hugo	R-R	5-11	145	9-5-99	.249	.282	.240	57	193	38	48	5	1	0	13	24	4	1	1	51	15	6	.285	.342
Estevez, Yeison	R-R	6-0	180	4-29-96	.212	.143	.234	44	146	20	31	4	3	0	17	14	1	1	2	28	2	4	.281	.282
Figuereo, Victor	R-B	6-1	180	5-24-97	.215	.421	.181	41	135	15	29	8	2	2	21	14	0	0	2	48	2	4	.348	.285
Guerrero, Hector	L-R	6-0	155	9-11-97	.286	.200	.308	57	196	37	56	2	0	1	16	32	0	3	0	19	9	4	.311	.386
Lantigua, Rafael	R-R	5-8	153	4-28-98	.284	.250	.290	59	218	36	62	8	6	0	23	33	2	0	3	32	11	12	.376	.379
Martinez, Andres	R-R	6-1	165	9-15-97	.285	.256	.292	58	200	28	57	7	0	0	27	36	3	0	2	33	4	8	.320	.398
Mauricio, Kenny	L-R	5-9	150	3-16-00	.206	.143	.221	45	141	12	29	10	0	0	10	21	1	0	1	34	4	4	.277	.311
Moreno, Gabriel	R-R	5-11	160	2-14-00	.248	.161	.277	32	125	9	31	4	1	0	17	6	0	0	4	5	5	4	.296	.274
Perez, Yhon	R-R	5-9	150	5-5-00	.249	.313	.236	55	193	32	48	8	4	0	24	25	2	1	4	21	8	4	.332	.335
Saavedra, William	R-R	6-1	190	2-12-98	.149	.154	.148	29	94	5	14	6	0	0	8	11	2	0	1	16	0	3	.213	.250
Valdez, Warnel	L-L	5-10	150	3-16-99	.224	.216	.226	46	170	18	38	7	0	1	17	7	0	0	2	40	4	3	.282	.251
Ventura, Leonicio	R-R	5-10	170	4-7-97	.290	.250	.299	33	93	14	27	6	3	0	15	12	1	1	2	14	8	5	.419	.370

Pitching	B-T	HT	WT	DOB	W	L	ERA	G	GS	CG	SV	IP	H	R	ER	HR	BB	SO	AVG	vLH	vRH	K/9	BB/9
Alvarez, Luis	R-R	6-0	170	2-8-00	2	1	4.97	12	3	0	0	29	35	16	16	0	9	20	.297	.308	.291	6.21	2.79
Caballero, Elixon	R-R	5-9	160	7-9-00	0	0	0.84	17	4	0	7	32	23	8	3	0	13	36	.187	.256	.155	10.13	3.66
Concepcion, Jol	R-R	6-5	195	9-17-98	1	0	1.06	4	4	0	0	17	8	2	2	0	3	17	.140	.136	.143	9.00	1.59
Contreras, Jeison	L-R	6-4	185	1-7-00	3	0	5.54	9	0	0	0	13	14	9	8	0	7	6	.269	.313	.250	4.15	4.85
De La Cruz, Moises	R-R	6-1	175	7-23-99	0	0	5.79	4	0	0	0	5	2	3	3	0	3	2	.143	.200	.111	3.86	5.79
Diaz, Juan	L-L	6-0	175	6-19-98	3	1	1.67	16	5	0	1	38	23	7	7	1	17	38	.177	.133	.183	9.08	4.06
Hinojosa, Yunior	R-R	6-2	190	12-21-99	3	3	3.38	20	0	0	11	24	25	19	9	1	5	16	.266	.222	.284	6.00	1.88
Jimenez, Geremy	R-R	6-2	185	9-9-99	1	1	9.35	16	0	0	0	17	19	21	18	0	21	6	.284	.143	.348	3.12	10.90
Jimenez, Juan	R-R	6-2	180	8-12-97	0	0	5.40	14	0	0	0	17	16	17	10	1	16	9	.246	.250	.244	4.86	8.64
Magdaniel, Ronald	R-R	6-1	170	11-15-96	2	3	3.19	13	6	0	1	37	39	15	13	2	8	31	.273	.241	.294	7.61	1.96
Martir, Yohandy	R-R	6-4	200	10-27-99	1	2	3.66	11	1	0	0	20	17	11	8	2	5	20	.233	.100	.283	9.15	2.29
Medina, Nicolas	L-L	5-10	160	1-15-00	3	3	6.00	20	0	0	2	24	25	18	16	1	9	26	.269	.211	.284	9.75	3.38
Mejia, Brayan	R-R	6-2	165	6-1-00	1	1	3.57	16	0	0	1	23	13	10	9	1	17	10	.176	.115	.208	3.97	6.75
Mendoza, Luis	R-R	6-3	175	10-4-95	4	0	1.66	17	0	0	3	22	19	4	4	0	12	15	.253	.259	.250	6.23	4.98
Molina, Adolfo	R-R	6-4	200	4-26-98	3	3	3.42	18	0	0	1	26	28	17	10	1	13	17	.277	.355	.243	5.81	4.44
Molina, Alexander	R-R	6-1	155	2-17-00	1	0	3.70	15	0	0	0	24	20	12	10	0	13	15	.220	.303	.172	5.55	4.81
Monsion, Rafael	L-L	6-3	185	8-16-99	1	2	2.30	13	10	0	0	43	37	13	11	1	16	34	.234	.167	.246	7.12	3.35
Paulino, Naswell	L-L	5-11	160	4-17-00	4	2	2.26	13	13	0	0	56	43	16	14	2	18	52	.210	.227	.205	8.41	2.91
Pena, Luis	R-R	6-4	246	3-31-98	1	0	5.79	3	0	0	0	5	5	3	3	0	0	7	.250	.200	.267	13.50	0.00
Perez, Nathanael	R-R	6-1	160	6-5-98	7	1	1.42	13	13	0	0	57	47	11	9	1	7	55	.218	.286	.180	8.68	1.11
Ramirez, Gaudy	R-R	6-2	175	9-11-97	0	0	2.84	3	0	0	0	6	2	2	2	0	7	9	.095	.111	.083	12.79	9.95
Victorino, Jhon	R-R	6-3	200	10-1-98	2	0	1.93	15	0	0	0	23	13	5	5	1	12	10	.167	.333	.105	3.86	4.63
Vizcaino, Emanuel	R-R	6-5	180	8-24-99	1	3	2.06	14	11	0	0	48	44	19	11	0	18	38	.243	.304	.205	7.13	3.38

Fielding

C: Moreno 24, Saavedra 23, Ventura 28. **1B:** Estevez 33, Figuereo 28, Guerrero 7, Saavedra 3. **2B:** Lantigua 33, Mauricio 23, Perez 18. **3B:** Estevez 8, Guerrero 50, Lantigua 4, Mauricio 10. **SS:** Cardona 56, Estevez 1, Lantigua 13. **OF:** Berroa 52, Briceno 35, Figuereo 8, Martinez 52, Perez 29, Valdez 38.

Washington Nationals

SEASON IN A SENTENCE: The Nationals once again won the National League East, with a 97-65 record—just one win shy of tying the franchise-best mark of 98-64 set in 2012. However, after losing to the Cubs, 3-2, in the NLDS the team is still searching for its first postseason series victory.

HIGH POINT: Homegrown ace and draft icon Stephen Strasburg finally seemed to put everything together over a full season, going 15-4, 2.52 with the fourth-best ERA in baseball among starters. To top it off, Strasburg struck out 12 batters over seven innings in a must-win game four vs. the Cubs—perhaps the most important start of his career. Despite reaching the playoffs, the team fired manager Dusty Baker after the season and hire Dave Martinez in his place.

LOW POINT: One game after Strasburg's game four performance, the Nationals dropped a wild, 9-8 Game Five to the defending champion Cubs, which included Jose Lobaton getting picked off at first after an instant replay review. Over the last six years the Nationals have averaged a 92.5-69.5 record but have no playoff success to show for it.

NOTABLE ROOKIES: Wilmer Difo entered the season with 46 major league games under his belt, finally exceeding his rookie status in 2017 after parts of two seasons with the Nationals in 2015 and 2016. He primarily played the middle infield, but got time at every position aside from first base and catcher, hitting .286/.331/.401 as a starter. Righthander A.J. Cole started eight games for the Nationals and posted a 3.81 ERA.

KEY TRANSACTIONS: Hoping to improve a bullpen that was ranked last in the majors in ERA in mid-July, Washington traded for Athletics relievers Sean Doolittle and Ryan Madson. Doolittle posted a 2.40 ERA while serving as the team's closer and Madson posted a 1.37 mark while striking out 12.81 batters per nine innings as the setup man. The Athletics acquired Blake Treinen, Sheldon Neuse and Jesus Luzardo in the trade.

DOWN ON THE FARM: Top prospect Victor Robles cruised through the Carolina and Eastern Leagues—ranking as the No. 2 overall prospect in both—before earning his big league debut on September 7 and making the team's postseason roster a few weeks later. Catchers Raudy Read and Taylor Gushue showed some pop on the farm with the former hitting 17 homers in the Eastern League and the latter hitting 18 in the Carolina League—tied for second most in the league.

OPENING DAY PAYROLL: $167,846,918 (9th)

PLAYERS OF THE YEAR

MAJOR LEAGUE

Max Scherzer
RHP
16-6, 2.51
268 SO in 200.2 IP
Led NL SO, WHIP

MITCHELL LAYTON/GETTY IMAGES

MINOR LEAGUE

Victor Robles
OF
(High Class A/
Double-A)
.300/.382/.493

ORGANIZATION LEADERS

BATTING — *Minimum 250 AB

MAJORS

*	AVG	Daniel Murphy	.322
*	OPS	Bryce Harper	1.008
	HR	Ryan Zimmerman	36
	RBI	Ryan Zimmerman	108

MINORS

*	AVG	Neftali Soto, Harrisburg, Syracuse	.311
*	OBP	Victor Robles, Potomac, Harrisburg	.382
*	SLG	Neftali Soto, Harrisburg, Syracuse	.528
*	OPS	Neftali Soto, Harrisburg, Syracuse	.892
	R	Blake Perkins, Hagerstown	105
	H	Neftali Soto, Harrisburg, Syracuse	160
	TB	Neftali Soto, Harrisburg, Syracuse	272
	2B	Victor Robles, Potomac, Harrisburg	37
	3B	Victor Robles, Potomac, Harrisburg	8
	HR	Neftali Soto, Harrisburg, Syracuse	24
	RBI	Neftali Soto, Harrisburg, Syrcause	82
	BB	Blake Perkins, Hagerstown	72
	SO	Drew Ward, Harrisburg	131
	SB	Blake Perkins, Hagerstown	31

PITCHING — #Minimum 75 IP

MAJORS

	W	Max Scherzer	16
#	ERA	Max Scherzer	2.51
	SO	Max Scherzer	268
	SV	Sean Doolittle	21

MINORS

	W	McKenzie Mills, Hagerstown, Potomac	12
	L	Luis Reyes, Potomac	13
	L	Greg Ross, Syracuse, Harrisburg	13
#	ERA	Hayden Howard, Hagerstown	2.95
	G	Wander Suero, Harrisburg, Syraucse	54
	GS	John Simms, Harrisburg, Syracuse	27
	SV	Wander Suero, Harrisburg, Syracuse	20
	IP	Jaron Long, Harrisburg, Syracuse	164
	BB	Joan Baez, GCL Nationals, Potomac	71
	SO	Luis Reyes, Potomac	133
#	AVG	McKenzie Mills, Hagerstown, Potomac	.204

2017 PERFORMANCE

General Manager: Mike Rizzo. **Farm Director:** Doug Harris. **Scouting Director:** Kris Kline.

Class	Team	League	W	L	PCT	Finish	Manager
Majors	Washington Nationals	National	97	65	.599	2nd (15)	Dusty Baker
Triple-A	Syracuse Chiefs	International	54	87	.383	14th (14)	Billy Gardner
Double-A	Harrisburg Senators	Eastern	60	80	.429	10th (12)	Matthew LeCroy
High-A	Potomac Nationals	Carolina	63	77	.450	8th (10)	Tripp Keister
Low-A	Hagerstown Suns	South Atlantic	73	63	.537	4th (14)	Patrick Anderson
Short Season	Auburn Doubledays	New York-Penn	30	45	.400	t-12th (14)	Jerad Head
Rookie	GCL Nationals	Gulf Coast	34	22	.607	2nd (17)	Josh Johnson
Overall 2017 Minor League Record			314	374	.456	t-26th (30)	

WASHINGTON NATIONALS

ORGANIZATION STATISTICS

WASHINGTON NATIONALS

NATIONAL LEAGUE

Batting	B-T	HT	WT	DOB	AVG	vLH	vRH	G	AB	R	H	2B	3B	HR	RBI	BB	HBP	SH	SF	SO	SB	CS	SLG	OBP
Bautista, Rafael	R-R	6-2	165	3-8-93	.160	.250	.118	17	25	2	4	0	0	0	0	2	0	0	0	5	0	0	.160	.222
De Aza, Alejandro	L-L	6-0	195	4-11-84	.194	.154	.204	28	62	8	12	2	3	0	9	3	0	3	2	16	1	0	.323	.224
Difo, Wilmer	B-R	5-11	200	4-2-92	.271	.310	.258	124	332	47	90	10	4	5	21	24	1	5	3	74	10	1	.371	.319
Drew, Stephen	R-L	6-0	200	3-16-83	.253	.400	.244	46	95	9	24	7	0	1	17	8	0	0	3	21	0	0	.358	.302
Eaton, Adam	L-L	5-8	185	12-6-88	.297	.182	.313	23	91	24	27	7	1	2	13	14	1	0	1	18	3	1	.462	.393
Goodwin, Brian	L-R	6-0	205	11-2-90	.251	.341	.232	74	251	41	63	21	1	13	30	23	1	0	3	69	6	0	.498	.313
Green, Grant	R-R	6-3	180	9-27-87	.000	—	.000	2	3	0	0	0	0	0	0	0	0	0	0	2	0	0	.000	.000
Harper, Bryce	L-R	6-3	215	10-16-92	.319	.311	.322	111	420	95	134	27	1	29	87	68	1	0	3	99	4	2	.595	.413
Heisey, Chris	R-R	6-1	220	12-14-84	.162	.238	.132	38	74	8	12	3	1	1	5	5	0	0	0	22	0	0	.270	.215
Kendrick, Howie	R-R	5-11	220	7-12-83	.293	.308	.286	52	164	24	48	8	2	7	25	11	2	0	1	38	4	2	.494	.343
2-team total (39 Philadelphia)					.315	.308	.286	91	305	40	96	16	3	9	41	22	5	0	2	68	12	5	.475	.368
Lind, Adam	L-L	6-2	195	7-17-83	.303	.310	.303	116	267	39	81	14	0	14	59	28	0	0	6	47	1	0	.513	.362
Lobaton, Jose	R-B	6-1	205	10-21-84	.170	.184	.165	51	141	11	24	3	0	4	11	14	1	1	1	35	0	0	.277	.248
Murphy, Daniel	L-R	6-1	220	4-1-85	.322	.291	.332	144	534	94	172	43	3	23	93	52	4	0	3	77	2	0	.543	.385
Raburn, Ryan	R-R	6-0	185	4-17-81	.262	.185	.316	25	65	7	17	1	2	2	6	4	0	0	0	25	0	1	.431	.304
Read, Raudy	R-R	6-0	170	10-29-93	.273	.667	.125	8	11	1	3	0	0	0	0	0	0	0	0	3	0	0	.273	.273
Rendon, Anthony	R-R	6-1	210	6-6-90	.301	.337	.292	147	508	81	153	41	1	25	100	84	7	0	6	82	7	2	.534	.403
Robles, Victor	R-R	6-0	185	5-19-97	.250	.000	.273	13	24	2	6	1	2	0	4	0	2	1	0	6	0	1	.458	.308
Sanchez, Adrian	R-R	6-0	160	8-16-90	.268	.294	.259	34	71	6	19	7	0	0	11	1	1	2	0	25	0	2	.366	.288
Severino, Pedro	R-R	6-0	215	7-20-93	.172	.286	.136	17	29	0	5	1	0	0	3	2	0	0	0	10	0	0	.207	.226
Stevenson, Andrew	L-L	6-0	185	6-1-94	.158	.000	.205	37	57	5	9	2	0	0	1	7	0	2	0	20	1	0	.193	.250
Taylor, Michael A.	R-R	6-3	210	3-26-91	.271	.308	.260	118	399	55	108	23	3	19	53	29	1	1	2	137	17	7	.486	.320
Turner, Trea	R-R	6-1	185	6-30-93	.284	.245	.296	98	412	75	117	24	6	11	45	30	4	0	1	80	46	8	.452	.338
Werth, Jayson	R-R	6-5	235	5-20-79	.226	.239	.223	70	252	35	57	10	1	10	29	35	1	0	1	69	4	3	.393	.322
Wieters, Matt	B-R	6-5	230	5-21-86	.225	.244	.221	123	422	43	95	20	0	10	52	38	1	0	4	94	1	0	.344	.288
Zimmerman, Ryan	R-R	6-3	225	9-28-84	.303	.331	.295	144	524	90	159	33	0	36	108	44	3	0	5	126	1	0	.573	.358

Pitching	B-T	HT	WT	DOB	W	L	ERA	G	GS	CG	SV	IP	H	R	ER	HR	BB	SO	AVG	vLH	vRH	K/9	BB/9
Adams, Austin	R-R	6-2	225	5-5-91	0	0	3.60	6	0	0	0	5	4	4	2	0	8	10	.211	.222	.200	18.00	14.40
Albers, Matt	R-L	6-1	225	1-20-83	7	2	1.62	63	0	0	2	61	35	12	11	6	17	63	.166	.171	.163	9.30	2.51
Blanton, Joe	R-R	6-3	225	12-11-80	2	4	5.68	51	0	0	0	44	53	29	28	10	13	39	.296	.323	.281	7.92	2.64
Cole, A.J.	R-R	6-5	215	1-5-92	3	5	3.81	11	8	0	0	52	51	23	22	8	27	44	.262	.320	.196	7.62	4.67
Doolittle, Sean	L-L	6-2	210	9-26-86	1	0	2.40	30	0	0	21	30	22	10	8	2	8	31	.204	.333	.178	9.30	2.40
Fedde, Erick	R-R	6-4	180	2-25-93	0	1	9.39	3	3	0	0	15	25	16	16	5	8	15	.385	.297	.500	8.80	4.70
Glover, Koda	R-R	6-5	225	4-13-93	0	1	5.12	23	0	0	8	19	20	11	11	1	4	17	.267	.265	.268	7.91	1.86
Gonzalez, Gio	R-L	6-0	205	9-19-85	15	9	2.96	32	32	0	0	201	158	69	66	21	79	188	.216	.183	.226	8.42	3.54
Gott, Trevor	R-R	6-0	185	8-26-92	1	0	30.00	4	0	0	0	3	11	10	10	1	3	3	.550	.600	.500	9.00	9.00
Grace, Matt	L-L	6-4	215	12-14-88	1	0	4.32	40	1	0	2	50	50	25	24	3	18	31	.266	.235	.290	5.58	3.24
Guthrie, Jeremy	R-R	6-1	205	4-8-79	0	1	135.00	1	1	0	0	1	6	10	10	0	4	0	1.000	1.000	1.000	0.00	54.00
Jackson, Edwin	R-R	6-2	215	9-9-83	5	6	5.07	13	13	0	0	71	75	46	40	18	25	58	.269	.257	.280	7.35	3.17
Kelley, Shawn	R-R	6-2	230	4-26-84	3	2	7.27	33	0	0	4	26	29	21	21	12	11	25	.266	.196	.318	8.65	3.81
Kintzler, Brandon	R-R	6-0	190	8-1-84	2	1	3.46	27	0	0	1	26	25	10	10	2	5	12	.253	.192	.319	4.15	1.73
Madson, Ryan	L-R	6-6	225	8-28-80	3	0	1.37	20	0	0	1	20	13	3	3	0	3	28	.186	.205	.154	12.81	1.37
Perez, Oliver	L-L	6-3	225	8-15-81	0	0	4.64	50	0	0	1	33	32	17	17	4	12	39	.254	.227	.283	10.64	3.27
Roark, Tanner	R-R	6-2	235	10-5-86	13	11	4.67	32	30	0	0	181	178	105	94	23	64	166	.254	.284	.224	8.24	3.18
Romero, Enny	R-L	6-3	215	1-24-91	2	4	3.56	53	0	0	2	56	55	26	22	7	23	65	.254	.295	.230	10.51	3.72
Ross, Joe	R-R	6-4	225	5-21-93	5	3	5.01	13	13	0	0	74	88	44	41	16	20	68	.297	.310	.284	8.31	2.44
Scherzer, Max	R-R	6-3	210	7-27-84	16	6	2.51	31	31	2	0	201	126	62	56	22	55	268	.178	.215	.137	12.02	2.47
Solis, Sammy	R-L	6-5	250	8-10-88	1	0	5.88	30	0	0	1	26	22	17	17	4	13	28	.222	.227	.218	9.69	4.50
Strasburg, Stephen	R-R	6-4	235	7-20-88	15	4	2.52	28	28	1	0	175	131	55	49	13	47	204	.204	.193	.215	10.47	2.41
Treinen, Blake	R-R	6-5	225	6-30-88	0	2	5.73	37	0	0	3	38	48	24	24	3	13	32	.320	.339	.308	7.65	3.11
Turner, Jacob	R-R	6-5	215	5-21-91	2	3	5.08	18	2	0	0	39	43	23	22	8	15	23	.281	.219	.326	5.31	3.46

Fielding

Catcher	PCT	G	PO	A	E	DP	PB
Lobaton	.985	50	386	20	6	5	3
Read	1.000	3	12	1	0	0	1
Severino	.986	10	65	4	1	1	1
Wieters	.993	118	1023	43	8	5	5

First Base	PCT	G	PO	A	E	DP
Kendrick	1.000	3	9	0	0	1
Lind	.980	39	226	23	5	25
Zimmerman	.989	143	1005	49	12	100

Second Base	PCT	G	PO	A	E	DP
Difo	.983	25	22	35	1	6
Drew	1.000	2	3	7	0	1
Green	1.000	2	1	2	0	1
Kendrick	1.000	5	10	7	0	2
Murphy	.984	139	218	353	9	86
Sanchez	1.000	10	13	14	0	1

Third Base	PCT	G	PO	A	E	DP
Difo	1.000	6	0	8	0	2
Drew	1.000	11	7	7	0	1
Rendon	.979	145	83	244	7	28
Sanchez	1.000	7	1	13	0	3

Shortstop	PCT	G	PO	A	E	DP
Difo	.976	57	76	165	6	24
Drew	.973	13	11	25	1	2
Sanchez	.966	8	10	18	1	4
Turner	.979	95	134	234	8	57

Outfield	PCT	G	PO	A	E	DP
Bautista	1.000	13	11	0	0	0
De Aza	.935	23	27	2	2	1
Difo	1.000	6	10	0	0	0
Eaton	1.000	23	50	2	0	0
Goodwin	.984	69	118	5	2	2
Harper	.989	110	173	8	2	2
Heisey	1.000	24	33	1	0	0
Kendrick	1.000	39	57	0	0	0
Lind	1.000	25	45	1	0	0
Raburn	1.000	22	15	2	0	0
Robles	1.000	10	14	1	0	1
Stevenson	1.000	28	38	0	0	0
Taylor	.985	113	259	8	4	1
Werth	.967	67	116	1	4	0

SYRACUSE CHIEFS — *TRIPLE-A*

INTERNATIONAL LEAGUE

Batting	B-T	HT	WT	DOB	AVG	vLH	vRH	G	AB	R	H	2B	3B	HR	RBI	BB	HBP	SH	SF	SO	SB	CS	SLG	OBP
Almanzar, Michael	R-R	6-3	190	12-2-90	.268	.255	.274	44	142	12	38	7	0	2	19	7	0	0	1	33	0	0	.359	.300
2-team total (61 Toledo)					.254	.333	.222	105	366	31	93	17	2	9	43	16	5	0	3	92	0	1	.385	.292
Bautista, Rafael	R-R	6-2	165	3-8-93	.250	.220	.259	43	176	23	44	9	1	0	11	9	1	2	0	26	7	4	.313	.290
Burriss, Emmanuel	B-R	6-0	190	1-17-85	.253	.292	.235	42	146	16	37	3	0	0	18	5	1	1	0	11	3	2	.274	.283
Butler, Joey	R-R	6-2	220	3-12-86	.215	.192	.226	28	79	8	17	3	0	2	8	11	0	0	0	21	0	0	.329	.311
Collier, Zach	L-L	6-2	200	9-8-90	.259	.278	.250	31	108	23	28	6	0	5	12	13	0	0	0	27	4	2	.454	.339
De Aza, Alejandro	L-L	6-0	195	4-11-84	.280	.312	.264	56	186	30	52	11	0	4	19	25	1	0	0	30	2	0	.403	.368
Difo, Wilmer	B-R	5-11	200	4-2-92	.175	.143	.192	10	40	5	7	2	0	0	1	5	0	0	0	6	0	0	.225	.267
Falu, Irving	B-R	5-9	185	6-6-83	.280	.266	.286	119	382	41	107	19	1	9	44	32	0	4	3	43	6	4	.406	.333
Gonzalez, Bengie	B-R	5-11	160	1-16-90	.256	.263	.254	31	90	9	23	3	0	0	5	9	0	0	0	10	0	0	.289	.323
2-team total (67 Rochester)					.237	.263	.254	98	291	24	69	9	3	0	20	28	0	1	2	44	2	2	.289	.302
Goodwin, Brian	L-R	6-0	205	11-2-90	.256	.120	.308	25	90	9	23	4	0	2	11	10	0	2	1	29	2	1	.367	.327
Green, Grant	R-R	6-3	180	9-27-87	.246	.242	.247	40	130	11	32	5	0	0	2	14	0	0	0	34	0	2	.285	.319
2-team total (28 Charlotte)					.232	.242	.247	68	220	20	51	12	0	1	12	24	0	0	1	53	0	3	.300	.306
Heisey, Chris	R-R	6-1	220	12-14-84	.294	.000	.357	5	17	4	5	2	0	1	3	0	0	0	0	6	0	0	.588	.294
Huffman, Chad	R-R	6-1	215	4-29-85	.203	.130	.235	28	74	6	15	5	0	1	5	7	3	1	1	20	0	0	.311	.294
Jackson, Ryan	R-R	6-2	180	5-10-88	.125	.500	.071	5	16	0	2	0	0	0	0	3	0	0	0	3	0	0	.125	.263
Joseph, Corban	L-R	6-0	185	10-28-88	.232	.105	.258	34	108	8	25	7	0	0	13	8	0	0	1	15	1	1	.296	.282
Kieboom, Spencer	R-R	6-0	210	3-16-91	.275	.379	.252	47	160	17	44	9	0	3	19	15	0	0	1	30	0	0	.388	.335
Lisson, Mario	R-R	6-2	220	5-31-84	.000	.000	—	1	1	0	0	0	0	0	0	1	0	0	0	0	0	0	.000	.500
Perez, Stephen	B-R	5-11	185	12-16-90	.167	.222	.148	14	36	1	6	2	0	0	3	4	0	0	1	9	0	1	.222	.244
Raburn, Ryan	R-R	6-0	185	4-17-81	.261	.125	.333	6	23	3	6	2	0	1	5	0	1	0	2	9	0	0	.478	.269
2-team total (27 Charlotte)					.274	.125	.333	33	106	14	29	4	1	4	18	20	2	0	3	38	1	0	.443	.389
Ramsey, Caleb	R-L	6-2	215	10-7-88	.246	.238	.249	78	232	21	57	11	0	1	16	24	1	0	2	51	0	1	.306	.317
Robinson, Clint	L-L	6-5	240	2-16-85	.242	.260	.234	132	443	49	107	25	1	18	74	45	4	0	3	121	0	0	.424	.315
Sanchez, Adrian	R-R	6-0	160	8-16-90	.244	.208	.260	72	258	37	63	15	1	4	18	19	1	2	3	47	4	1	.357	.295
Severino, Pedro	R-R	6-0	215	7-20-93	.242	.175	.266	59	211	17	51	4	0	5	29	15	0	0	1	43	1	1	.332	.291
Skole, Matt	L-R	6-4	220	7-30-89	.222	.200	.231	64	212	38	47	16	0	11	29	26	0	0	3	61	0	0	.453	.303
Snyder, Brandon	R-R	6-2	225	11-23-86	.263	.240	.273	121	418	72	110	24	1	23	77	52	11	0	5	127	4	4	.490	.356
Solano, Jhonatan	R-R	5-9	205	8-12-85	.241	.255	.234	42	145	11	35	6	1	2	19	6	4	0	2	14	0	0	.338	.287
Soto, Neftali	R-R	6-1	210	2-28-89	.293	.293	.293	68	263	43	77	15	1	14	38	18	3	0	2	50	0	0	.517	.343
Stevenson, Andrew	L-L	6-0	185	6-1-94	.252	.220	.266	79	309	38	78	7	4	2	26	19	1	2	0	72	10	1	.320	.298
Turner, Trea	R-R	6-1	185	6-30-93	.000	—	.000	3	9	0	0	0	0	0	0	1	0	0	0	4	0	0	.000	.100
Werth, Jayson	R-R	6-5	235	5-20-79	.286	—	.286	3	7	1	2	0	0	0	0	2	1	0	0	2	0	0	.286	.500

Pitching	B-T	HT	WT	DOB	W	L	ERA	G	GS	CG	SV	IP	H	R	ER	HR	BB	SO	AVG	vLH	vRH	K/9	BB/9
Adams, Austin	R-R	6-2	225	5-5-91	6	2	2.14	44	0	0	5	59	44	22	14	2	37	91	.199	.239	.171	13.88	5.64
Antolin, Dustin	R-R	6-2	230	8-9-89	2	4	6.30	24	4	0	0	50	60	36	35	3	32	43	.313	.320	.305	7.74	5.76
Arias, Gabriel	R-R	6-2	185	12-6-89	0	0	3.38	2	1	0	0	5	6	2	2	1	0	2	.273	.417	.100	3.38	0.00
Broadway, Mike	R-R	6-5	215	3-30-87	0	1	10.38	13	0	0	0	17	26	21	20	4	9	19	.333	.387	.298	9.87	4.67
2-team total (6 Durham)					1	2	5.85	19	4	0	0	32	31	22	21	5	11	37	.242	.387	.298	10.30	3.06
Cole, A.J.	R-R	6-5	215	1-5-92	4	5	5.88	18	18	0	0	93	127	65	61	7	36	79	.330	.371	.295	7.62	3.47
Cotts, Neal	L-L	6-2	200	3-25-80	1	3	3.94	52	0	0	2	48	37	22	21	4	17	57	.215	.197	.229	10.69	3.19
Fedde, Erick	R-R	6-4	180	2-25-93	1	2	4.76	12	6	0	0	34	37	18	18	3	5	25	.276	.315	.250	6.62	1.32
Gott, Trevor	R-R	6-0	185	8-26-92	2	0	3.86	30	0	0	4	37	39	19	16	2	13	35	.264	.215	.301	8.44	3.13
Grace, Matt	L-L	6-4	215	12-14-88	1	3	3.66	13	1	0	0	20	21	9	8	2	8	21	.269	.259	.275	9.61	3.66
Hill, Taylor	R-R	6-3	230	3-12-89	3	5	7.25	9	9	0	0	50	70	41	40	12	10	24	.337	.347	.327	4.35	1.81
Jackson, Edwin	R-R	6-2	215	9-9-83	2	0	0.44	5	4	0	0	20	9	1	1	0	10	22	.130	.114	.147	9.74	4.43
2-team total (12 Norfolk)					2	0	1.77	17	5	0	2	41	29	8	8	1	20	39	.206	.316	.264	8.63	4.43
Jepsen, Kevin	R-R	6-3	235	7-26-84	0	1	5.32	19	0	0	1	24	22	17	14	5	10	29	.237	.270	.214	11.03	3.80
Kelley, Shawn	R-R	6-2	230	4-26-84	1	1	8.10	8	2	0	0	7	8	6	6	3	2	9	.286	.417	.188	12.15	2.70
Long, Jaron	R-R	6-0	190	8-28-91	4	6	4.43	14	13	0	0	85	90	44	42	13	16	63	.274	.328	.241	6.64	1.69
Martin, Rafael	R-R	6-3	225	5-16-84	4	2	4.60	52	0	0	2	63	63	32	32	6	17	62	.260	.309	.230	8.90	2.44
McGowin, Kyle	R-R	6-3	195	11-27-91	1	6	6.31	9	9	1	0	46	51	34	32	3	20	27	.288	.279	.296	5.32	3.94

	B-T	HT	WT	DOB	W	L	ERA	G	GS	CG	SV	IP	H	R	ER	HR	BB	SO	AVG	vLH	vRH	K/9	BB/9
Nathan, Joe	R-R	6-4	230	11-22-74	0	2	6.19	17	0	0	4	16	19	13	11	3	8	15	.292	.270	.321	8.44	4.50
O'Sullivan, Sean	R-R	6-1	245	9-1-87	1	2	5.80	10	8	0	0	36	43	24	23	6	19	23	.295	.226	.333	5.80	4.79
Ramirez, Neil	R-R	6-4	215	5-25-89	2	1	6.14	14	0	0	1	15	23	10	10	3	8	20	.354	.379	.333	12.27	4.91
Rogers, Esmil	R-R	6-3	200	8-14-85	3	2	3.18	7	7	0	0	40	42	16	14	3	6	41	.268	.243	.287	9.30	1.36
Romero, Enny	R-L	6-3	215	1-24-91	0	1	4.26	7	0	0	0	6	6	5	3	0	1	8	.222	.167	.267	11.37	1.42
Ross, Greg	R-R	6-3	205	9-6-89	3	9	6.40	16	13	0	0	77	91	58	55	12	33	36	.299	.280	.317	4.19	3.84
Ross, Joe	R-R	6-4	225	5-21-93	2	2	4.88	5	5	0	0	28	33	16	15	3	8	22	.297	.267	.318	7.16	2.60
Satterwhite, Cody	R-R	6-4	235	1-27-87	1	3	4.35	24	2	0	0	50	55	25	24	6	18	43	.278	.277	.278	7.79	3.26
Self, Derek	R-R	6-3	205	1-14-90	1	0	2.70	1	0	0	0	3	3	1	1	0	2	1	.250	.143	.400	2.70	5.40
Simms, John	R-R	6-3	205	1-17-92	2	4	5.40	8	8	1	0	45	54	27	27	7	16	35	.298	.342	.265	7.00	3.20
Solis, Sammy	R-L	6-5	250	8-10-88	1	3	6.39	13	1	0	0	13	13	9	9	5	6	8	.271	.333	.233	5.68	4.26
Suero, Wander	R-R	6-3	195	9-15-91	3	1	1.70	36	0	0	10	42	33	10	8	1	14	42	.212	.154	.253	8.93	2.98
Turner, Jacob	R-R	6-5	215	5-21-91	2	6	5.21	14	14	0	0	66	72	38	38	5	33	53	.285	.318	.252	7.26	4.52
Valdez, Phillips	R-R	6-2	160	11-16-91	0	3	6.75	10	3	0	0	24	30	18	18	1	5	19	.306	.429	.214	7.13	1.88
Voth, Austin	R-R	6-2	215	6-26-92	1	7	6.38	13	13	1	0	66	85	50	47	12	34	42	.310	.333	.291	5.70	4.61

Fielding

Catcher	PCT	G	PO	A	E	DP	PB
Kieboom	1.000	45	351	20	0	2	4
Severino	.993	58	404	37	3	5	8
Solano	.997	40	266	20	1	2	1

First Base	PCT	G	PO	A	E	DP
Butler	.000	1	0	0	0	0
Green	1.000	1	1	0	0	0
Robinson	.998	54	406	29	1	48
Skole	.992	36	246	18	2	30
Snyder	.993	22	138	11	1	12
Soto	.989	38	333	20	4	29

Second Base	PCT	G	PO	A	E	DP
Burriss	.983	17	22	35	1	6
Falu	.993	67	106	169	2	45
Green	.969	8	12	19	1	7
Joseph	.989	21	35	59	1	13
Perez	1.000	9	8	23	0	4
Sanchez	1.000	11	21	30	0	5
Snyder	.985	19	23	43	1	9

Third Base	PCT	G	PO	A	E	DP
Almanzar	.962	41	28	73	4	9
Falu	1.000	19	7	44	0	1
Green	.935	30	13	45	4	7
Jackson	1.000	1	0	1	0	0
Lisson	1.000	1	0	5	0	1
Sanchez	.889	13	5	19	3	2
Skole	.962	26	16	34	2	1
Snyder	.957	20	16	28	2	5
Soto	.833	6	3	2	1	0

Shortstop	PCT	G	PO	A	E	DP
Burriss	.949	23	35	76	6	19
Difo	.952	9	15	25	2	5
Falu	1.000	30	37	65	0	17
Gonzalez	.981	27	41	65	2	14
Green	1.000	2	3	2	0	1
Jackson	1.000	4	2	7	0	0
Perez	1.000	2	3	8	0	1
Sanchez	.954	52	71	135	10	33
Turner	1.000	3	4	6	0	2

Outfield	PCT	G	PO	A	E	DP
Bautista	.961	43	98	1	4	0
Butler	1.000	19	22	0	0	0
Collier	1.000	30	48	2	0	1
De Aza	.990	54	95	5	1	0
Difo	.000	2	0	0	0	0
Falu	1.000	1	3	0	0	0
Gonzalez	1.000	3	5	0	0	0
Goodwin	.982	25	54	2	1	0
Heisey	1.000	5	10	0	0	0
Huffman	1.000	21	35	1	0	0
Perez	1.000	2	3	0	0	0
Raburn	.875	4	7	0	1	0
Ramsey	.966	74	111	2	4	0
Snyder	.989	52	88	3	1	0
Soto	.980	29	47	1	1	0
Stevenson	.990	79	196	2	2	0
Werth	.667	3	2	0	1	0

HARRISBURG SENATORS — *DOUBLE-A*

EASTERN LEAGUE

Batting	B-T	HT	WT	DOB	AVG	vLH	vRH	G	AB	R	H	2B	3B	HR	RBI	BB	HBP	SH	SF	SO	SB	CS	SLG	OBP
Abreu, Osvaldo	R-R	6-0	170	6-13-94	.246	.262	.240	125	431	40	106	16	4	5	42	27	7	7	3	107	1	6	.336	.299
Ballou, Isaac	R-L	6-2	205	3-17-90	.194	.286	.157	49	124	13	24	4	2	2	7	15	1	1	1	44	2	0	.307	.284
Collier, Zach	L-L	6-2	200	9-8-90	.278	.200	.306	30	97	16	27	8	1	2	8	8	1	0	0	32	1	0	.443	.340
Gamache, Dan	L-R	5-11	205	11-20-90	.296	.283	.300	50	186	24	55	12	1	5	27	17	1	0	0	46	0	0	.452	.358
Gushue, Taylor	B-R	6-1	215	12-19-93	.083	1.000	.000	4	12	0	1	0	0	0	0	1	0	0	0	1	0	0	.083	.154
Heisey, Chris	R-R	6-1	220	12-14-84	.000	—	.000	2	4	0	0	0	0	0	0	0	1	0	0	2	0	0	.000	.200
Hernandez, Yadiel	L-R	5-9	185	10-9-87	.292	.336	.276	120	397	57	116	21	1	12	59	56	1	3	3	66	5	2	.441	.379
Joseph, Corban	L-R	6-0	185	10-28-88	.299	.194	.321	55	201	28	60	10	0	7	27	19	1	2	3	23	0	4	.453	.357
Keller, Alec	L-R	6-2	200	5-13-92	.264	.173	.296	77	288	41	76	13	2	3	18	18	4	1	0	60	6	1	.354	.316
Kieboom, Spencer	R-R	6-0	210	3-16-91	.183	.238	.154	19	60	6	11	5	0	2	6	10	0	0	0	13	0	0	.367	.300
Lisson, Mario	R-R	6-2	220	5-31-84	.192	.267	.137	65	203	23	39	11	0	7	28	24	0	0	1	50	3	0	.350	.276
Lowery, Jake	L-R	6-0	200	7-21-90	.214	.167	.237	19	56	6	12	4	0	0	5	10	0	0	0	16	0	0	.286	.333
Marmolejos, Jose	L-L	6-1	185	1-2-93	.288	.303	.281	107	400	68	115	18	4	14	66	44	5	0	5	79	0	2	.458	.361
Norfork, Khayyan	R-R	5-10	190	1-19-89	.268	.284	.257	95	280	38	75	11	0	3	22	27	6	3	1	64	2	1	.339	.344
Perez, Stephen	B-R	5-11	185	12-16-90	.213	.190	.221	82	230	30	49	6	1	4	20	30	5	8	1	69	9	2	.300	.316
Read, Raudy	R-R	6-0	170	10-29-93	.265	.280	.260	108	411	44	109	25	1	17	61	27	2	0	2	79	2	0	.455	.312
Rickles, Nick	R-R	6-3	220	2-2-90	.000	.000	.000	2	5	0	0	0	0	0	0	0	0	0	0	2	0	0	.000	.000
2-team total (26 Reading)					.260	.000	.000	28	100	9	26	8	0	4	12	5	0	0	2	11	1	0	.460	.290
Robles, Victor	R-R	6-0	185	5-19-97	.324	.200	.358	37	139	24	45	12	1	3	14	12	4	3	0	22	11	3	.489	.394
Sanchez, Adrian	R-R	6-0	160	8-16-90	.250	.333	.231	5	16	4	4	0	0	1	3	1	0	0	0	3	0	0	.438	.294
Sandford, Darian	R-B	5-9	170	4-28-87	.226	.235	.221	50	146	20	33	2	0	0	5	19	1	3	0	37	21	7	.240	.319
Soto, Neftali	R-R	6-1	210	2-28-89	.329	.319	.333	67	252	33	83	19	2	10	44	25	0	0	3	53	0	0	.540	.386
Stevenson, Andrew	L-L	6-0	185	6-1-94	.350	.348	.351	20	80	14	28	5	1	0	12	11	0	0	0	19	1	3	.438	.429
Taylor, Michael A.	R-R	6-3	210	3-26-91	.154	.333	.130	6	26	3	4	2	0	1	4	2	0	0	0	8	3	0	.346	.214
Ward, Drew	L-R	6-3	215	11-25-94	.235	.192	.253	121	413	47	97	20	0	10	53	55	4	0	8	131	0	0	.356	.325

Pitching	B-T	HT	WT	DOB	W	L	ERA	G	GS	CG	SV	IP	H	R	ER	HR	BB	SO	AVG	vLH	vRH	K/9	BB/9
Bacus, Dakota	R-R	6-2	200	4-2-91	1	2	2.41	11	0	0	2	19	18	5	5	2	4	17	.247	.323	.191	8.20	1.93
Blackmar, Mark	R-R	6-3	215	4-28-92	3	3	6.89	8	6	0	0	31	42	24	24	4	11	14	.331	.370	.309	4.02	3.16
Blanton, Joe	R-R	6-3	225	12-11-80	0	0	0.00	1	1	0	0	1	0	0	0	0	0	2	.000	.000	.000	18.00	0.00
Brinley, Ryan	L-R	6-1	200	4-9-93	4	4	4.60	37	0	0	7	45	48	26	23	2	13	40	.265	.279	.253	8.00	2.60
Collins, Tim	L-L	5-7	170	8-21-89	1	1	14.54	10	0	0	0	9	12	14	14	2	10	8	.333	.273	.360	8.31	10.38
Cordero, Jimmy	R-R	6-3	215	10-19-91	2	6	6.84	41	0	0	0	51	52	47	39	7	38	40	.264	.234	.291	7.01	6.66

Crownover, Matthew	R-L	5-11	205	3-5-93	1	7	4.50	17	14	0	1	84	90	43	42	11	34	45	.280	.353	.254	4.82	3.64
Dragmire, Brady	R-R	6-1	185	2-5-93	5	1	3.13	18	5	0	2	46	53	21	16	2	21	21	.298	.323	.271	4.11	4.11
Eitel, Derek	R-R	6-4	200	11-21-87	3	2	3.63	12	7	1	0	45	36	19	18	3	28	41	.221	.275	.153	8.26	5.64
Estevez, Wirkin	R-R	6-1	170	3-15-92	4	1	3.63	11	11	0	0	62	65	30	25	3	27	36	.286	.301	.274	5.23	3.92
Fedde, Erick	R-R	6-4	180	2-25-93	3	3	3.04	17	7	0	0	56	45	21	19	4	18	54	.215	.181	.250	8.63	2.88
Glover, Koda	R-R	6-5	225	4-13-93	0	0	0.00	1	0	0	0	1	1	0	0	0	0	1	.250	.333	.000	9.00	0.00
Hill, Taylor	R-R	6-3	230	3-12-89	4	6	5.28	18	17	1	0	104	120	72	61	16	27	49	.293	.306	.281	4.24	2.34
Johansen, Jake	R-R	6-6	235	1-23-91	0	0	6.17	10	0	0	0	12	11	8	8	1	8	13	.250	.143	.348	10.03	6.17
Lara, Braulio	R-L	6-1	180	12-20-88	3	2	4.08	34	0	0	1	40	45	24	18	6	32	47	.287	.298	.280	10.66	7.26
Long, Jaron	R-R	6-0	190	8-28-91	5	6	2.73	13	13	1	0	79	78	28	24	8	15	51	.259	.232	.282	5.81	1.71
McGowin, Kyle	R-R	6-3	195	11-27-91	1	5	6.54	8	8	0	0	43	58	35	31	12	16	39	.317	.287	.354	8.23	3.38
Orlan, R.C.	R-L	6-0	185	9-28-90	1	3	5.09	25	0	0	0	23	26	14	13	5	10	24	.277	.195	.340	9.39	3.91
Robinson, Andrew	R-R	6-1	185	2-13-88	1	2	3.69	38	0	0	13	39	29	19	16	5	13	47	.197	.213	.181	10.85	3.00
Rodriguez, Francisco	R-R	6-0	195	1-7-82	0	0	3.00	3	0	0	0	3	2	2	1	0	1	2	.182	.200	.167	6.00	3.00
Ross, Greg	R-R	6-3	205	9-6-89	5	4	5.97	10	10	1	0	57	71	41	38	8	17	39	.311	.355	.271	6.12	2.67
Schepel, Kyle	L-R	6-1	230	8-7-90	0	0	7.62	10	0	0	0	13	16	11	11	2	10	11	.291	.333	.240	7.62	6.92
Self, Derek	R-R	6-3	205	1-14-90	4	3	3.86	36	2	0	1	58	58	27	25	7	18	36	.262	.247	.273	5.55	2.78
Simms, John	R-R	6-3	205	1-17-92	5	6	3.54	19	19	0	0	112	96	46	44	9	28	87	.235	.219	.248	6.99	2.25
Suero, Wander	R-R	6-3	195	9-15-91	0	1	1.96	18	0	0	10	23	18	8	5	2	5	23	.205	.184	.220	9.00	1.96
Valdez, Phillips	R-R	6-2	160	11-16-91	0	2	2.72	25	0	0	1	43	37	14	13	1	13	34	.233	.268	.205	7.12	2.72
Voth, Austin	R-R	6-2	215	6-26-92	3	4	5.13	10	10	0	0	54	63	34	31	8	13	44	.288	.347	.240	7.29	2.15
Williams, Austen	R-R	6-3	220	12-19-92	1	6	6.85	10	10	0	0	46	67	38	35	6	11	34	.340	.378	.313	6.65	2.15

Fielding

Catcher	PCT	G	PO	A	E	DP	PB
Gushue	.960	3	19	5	1	0	0
Kieboom	1.000	19	130	11	0	2	0
Lowery	1.000	18	114	11	0	2	2
Read	.986	104	634	77	10	5	14

First Base	PCT	G	PO	A	E	DP
Gamache	.990	40	365	32	4	41
Joseph	1.000	1	10	2	0	4
Lisson	1.000	19	155	13	0	16
Marmolejos	.985	37	300	24	5	27
Soto	.997	42	322	32	1	35
Ward	1.000	3	22	0	0	1

Second Base	PCT	G	PO	A	E	DP
Gamache	1.000	1	1	1	0	0
Joseph	.985	38	84	109	3	30
Lisson	.938	5	7	8	1	2
Norfork	.978	53	72	153	5	40
Perez	.976	39	67	95	4	25
Sanchez	.944	5	6	11	1	1
Soto	.952	10	18	22	2	2

Third Base	PCT	G	PO	A	E	DP
Gamache	1.000	3	2	6	0	0
Lisson	.895	12	7	27	4	7
Norfork	1.000	7	3	12	0	0
Perez	1.000	6	5	16	0	2
Soto	.000	1	0	0	0	0
Ward	.952	114	76	202	14	17

Shortstop	PCT	G	PO	A	E	DP
Abreu	.946	123	187	320	29	81
Norfork	1.000	1	2	3	0	0
Perez	.951	20	27	50	4	12

Outfield	PCT	G	PO	A	E	DP
Ballou	1.000	32	54	1	0	0
Collier	1.000	25	65	1	0	0
Heisey	1.000	1	1	0	0	0
Hernandez	.980	112	192	8	4	2
Joseph	1.000	1	3	0	0	0
Keller	.994	73	164	5	1	2
Lisson	1.000	8	11	0	0	0
Marmolejos	.990	52	94	4	1	1
Norfork	.977	25	39	3	1	0
Perez	1.000	11	15	2	0	0
Robles	.969	35	92	3	3	2
Sandford	.990	40	98	1	1	0
Soto	1.000	1	1	0	0	0
Stevenson	1.000	19	33	0	0	0
Taylor	1.000	5	15	1	0	0

POTOMAC NATIONALS — *HIGH CLASS A*

CAROLINA LEAGUE

Batting	B-T	HT	WT	DOB	AVG	vLH	vRH	G	AB	R	H	2B	3B	HR	RBI	BB	HBP	SH	SF	SO	SB	CS	SLG	OBP
Agustin, Telmito	L-L	5-10	160	10-9-96	.206	.310	.164	33	102	12	21	4	0	1	14	6	1	5	0	27	3	2	.275	.257
Beckwith, Tyler	R-R	6-2	195	7-18-94	.207	.250	.191	10	29	4	6	0	1	1	3	2	0	0	1	11	0	0	.379	.250
Carey, Dale	R-R	6-3	185	11-14-91	.229	.261	.205	67	205	25	47	10	2	3	21	40	1	2	1	60	1	2	.342	.356
Davidson, Austin	L-R	6-0	180	1-3-93	.272	.260	.276	102	379	48	103	22	4	7	53	45	5	0	3	80	9	4	.406	.354
Gamache, Dan	L-R	5-11	205	11-20-90	.444	.500	.389	9	36	5	16	1	0	2	5	3	0	0	0	5	0	0	.639	.487
Gushue, Taylor	B-R	6-1	215	12-19-93	.242	.205	.255	91	323	38	78	9	0	18	67	41	4	0	8	88	0	0	.437	.327
Gutierrez, Kelvin	R-R	6-3	185	8-28-94	.288	.262	.299	58	222	34	64	10	6	2	16	19	2	0	2	59	3	0	.414	.347
Johnson, Daniel	L-L	5-10	185	7-11-95	.294	.250	.314	42	170	22	50	13	0	5	20	13	1	0	1	30	10	2	.459	.346
Lora, Edwin	R-R	6-1	150	9-14-95	.230	.161	.264	111	353	49	81	18	2	3	27	33	7	13	2	100	12	5	.317	.306
Lowery, Jake	L-R	6-0	200	7-21-90	.153	.222	.094	19	59	7	9	1	1	2	11	8	0	0	2	31	0	0	.305	.246
Masters, David	R-R	6-1	185	4-23-93	.241	.262	.229	89	295	40	71	14	1	8	41	36	3	1	3	62	0	1	.376	.326
Mejia, Bryan	B-R	6-1	170	3-2-94	.234	.233	.234	115	385	38	90	16	1	5	40	19	1	9	3	104	7	10	.320	.270
Noll, Jake	R-R	6-2	195	3-8-94	.190	.222	.175	17	58	5	11	2	1	1	7	5	0	1	1	12	0	1	.310	.250
Page, Matthew	L-L	6-3	210	10-22-91	.221	.289	.195	52	163	18	36	10	0	2	10	21	0	1	0	51	2	1	.319	.310
Reetz, Jakson	R-R	6-1	195	1-3-96	.236	.194	.259	26	89	8	21	6	0	2	11	9	3	1	0	32	2	1	.371	.327
Reistetter, Matt	L-R	5-10	180	5-5-92	.200	.000	.333	9	25	3	5	0	1	0	1	2	0	1	0	8	0	0	.280	.259
Robles, Victor	R-R	6-0	185	5-19-97	.289	.356	.259	77	291	49	84	25	7	7	33	25	17	4	1	62	16	7	.495	.377
Sagdal, Ian	L-R	6-3	190	1-6-93	.258	.266	.254	123	473	51	122	29	4	10	69	33	3	1	6	116	7	1	.400	.307
Sundberg, Jack	L-R	5-11	195	7-21-93	.277	.272	.280	110	393	56	109	14	1	1	28	52	2	11	4	110	24	8	.326	.361
Taylor, Michael A.	R-R	6-3	210	3-26-91	.158	.000	.231	6	19	2	3	0	0	0	0	2	0	0	0	7	1	0	.158	.238
Turner, Trea	R-R	6-1	185	6-30-93	.167	.000	.182	4	12	1	2	1	0	0	1	0	0	0	1	3	0	1	.250	.154
Werth, Jayson	R-R	6-5	235	5-20-79	.167	—	.167	3	6	0	1	1	0	0	0	2	0	0	0	2	0	0	.333	.375
Wiseman, Rhett	L-R	6-0	200	6-22-94	.229	.238	.226	123	432	55	99	21	5	13	55	34	1	1	6	97	2	4	.391	.283

Pitching	B-T	HT	WT	DOB	W	L	ERA	G	GS	CG	SV	IP	H	R	ER	HR	BB	SO	AVG	vLH	vRH	K/9	BB/9
Bacus, Dakota	R-R	6-2	200	4-2-91	1	0	1.27	12	0	0	3	21	21	6	3	1	3	16	.259	.276	.250	6.75	1.27
Baez, Joan	R-R	6-3	190	12-26-94	4	8	3.87	17	17	1	0	79	64	45	34	3	66	65	.229	.260	.203	7.41	7.52
Borne, Grant	L-L	6-5	205	4-6-94	4	4	2.50	14	10	0	2	72	60	23	20	2	19	60	.222	.143	.246	7.50	2.38
Collins, Tim	L-L	5-7	170	8-21-89	0	0	0.00	2	0	0	0	2	0	0	0	0	2	2	.000	—	.000	9.00	9.00
Crownover, Matthew	R-L	5-11	205	3-5-93	3	1	1.94	10	6	0	0	46	38	10	10	2	11	42	.224	.263	.204	8.16	2.14

Estevez, Wirkin	R-R	6-1	170	3-15-92	4	3	3.88	11	11	1	0	65	67	30	28	7	20	42	.270	.248	.289	5.82	2.77
Fuentes, Steven	R-R	6-2	175	5-4-97	0	1	7.71	2	1	0	0	2	2	2	2	0	4	0	.250	1.000	.143	0.00	15.43
Guilbeau, Taylor	L-L	6-4	180	5-12-93	4	5	5.89	23	15	0	0	99	128	72	65	9	24	78	.317	.250	.341	7.07	2.17
Held, Sam	R-R	6-5	190	8-24-94	0	2	3.72	5	0	0	0	10	7	4	4	0	8	7	.219	.313	.125	6.52	7.45
Mayberry, Whit	R-R	6-1	200	5-29-90	0	1	4.09	6	0	0	0	11	15	5	5	0	3	8	.333	.407	.222	6.55	2.45
McGowin, Kyle	R-R	6-3	195	11-27-91	1	1	1.80	2	2	0	0	10	10	2	2	1	4	9	.263	.267	.261	8.10	3.60
Mendez, Gilberto	R-R	6-0	165	11-17-92	3	4	4.47	35	0	0	11	52	43	26	26	9	12	42	.223	.259	.196	7.22	2.06
Mills, Jordan	L-L	6-5	215	5-11-92	2	2	4.20	18	1	0	2	30	30	14	14	1	7	26	.270	.391	.239	7.80	2.10
Orlan, R.C.	R-L	6-0	185	9-28-90	2	1	3.21	19	0	0	5	28	20	11	10	4	6	29	.196	.154	.222	9.32	1.93
Pantoja, Jorge	R-R	6-5	215	3-26-94	1	3	2.06	28	0	0	1	48	51	17	11	2	10	34	.267	.333	.230	6.38	1.88
Pena, Ronald	R-R	6-4	195	9-19-91	2	3	5.70	31	0	0	1	47	56	32	30	3	21	45	.292	.353	.258	8.56	3.99
Peterson, Tommy	R-R	6-1	205	10-11-93	0	0	2.81	12	0	0	1	16	6	5	5	0	8	14	.113	.000	.162	7.88	4.50
Reyes, Luis	R-R	6-2	175	9-26-94	8	13	4.33	26	26	0	0	143	149	77	69	19	56	133	.268	.277	.262	8.35	3.52
Rivera, Mariano	R-R	5-11	155	10-4-93	1	2	4.00	31	0	0	1	54	52	26	24	3	16	38	.254	.237	.264	6.33	2.67
Rodriguez, Francisco	R-R	6-0	195	1-7-82	0	0	0.00	1	0	0	0	1	1	3	0	0	2	0	.250	—	.250	0.00	18.00
Rodriguez, Jefry	R-R	6-5	185	7-26-93	4	3	3.32	12	10	0	0	57	44	25	21	2	19	51	.220	.175	.250	8.05	3.00
Sanburn, Nolan	R-R	6-1	205	7-21-91	4	3	4.87	17	8	0	1	65	69	38	35	8	27	56	.276	.247	.293	7.79	3.76
Schepel, Kyle	L-R	6-1	230	8-7-90	2	4	2.57	24	0	0	2	42	28	15	12	1	14	54	.188	.217	.169	11.57	3.00
Sharp, Sterling	R-R	6-4	170	5-30-95	2	2	4.78	6	5	0	0	32	39	19	17	4	13	26	.307	.360	.273	7.31	3.66
Silvestre, Hector	L-L	6-3	180	12-14-92	8	5	4.24	18	18	0	0	93	104	49	44	12	29	74	.276	.253	.284	7.14	2.80
Skulina, Tyler	R-R	6-5	230	9-18-91	1	1	5.60	10	0	0	0	18	18	11	11	1	16	19	.265	.231	.286	9.68	8.15
Strasburg, Stephen	R-R	6-4	235	7-20-88	0	0	1.80	1	1	0	0	5	3	1	1	0	1	5	.167	.375	.000	9.00	1.80
Williams, Austen	R-R	6-3	220	12-19-92	2	5	4.17	9	9	0	0	45	54	22	21	2	11	42	.286	.241	.321	8.34	2.18

Fielding

Catcher	PCT	G	PO	A	E	DP	PB
Gushue	.991	88	628	67	6	5	11
Lowery	.986	19	125	21	2	1	1
Reetz	.986	26	180	37	3	1	3
Reistetter	1.000	9	57	11	0	2	0

First Base	PCT	G	PO	A	E	DP
Beckwith	.911	5	39	2	4	2
Davidson	1.000	3	28	1	0	4
Masters	.986	10	66	5	1	7
Page	.978	21	163	16	4	13
Sagdal	.996	105	837	52	4	71

Second Base	PCT	G	PO	A	E	DP
Beckwith	.941	5	7	9	1	3
Davidson	.945	48	98	110	12	26
Gamache	1.000	1	2	4	0	0
Masters	.889	2	3	5	1	1
Mejia	.973	71	129	190	9	49
Noll	.985	16	29	37	1	8

Third Base	PCT	G	PO	A	E	DP
Davidson	.875	3	2	5	1	0
Gamache	.941	7	6	10	1	1
Gutierrez	.971	57	50	115	5	9
Masters	.969	39	43	81	4	10
Mejia	.895	27	27	58	10	7
Sagdal	.926	13	6	19	2	0

Shortstop	PCT	G	PO	A	E	DP
Lora	.938	102	113	218	22	41
Masters	.975	36	55	102	4	22
Mejia	.875	7	5	16	3	3
Turner	1.000	3	1	7	0	1

Outfield	PCT	G	PO	A	E	DP
Agustin	.962	31	50	1	2	1
Carey	.991	64	104	3	1	0
Johnson	1.000	37	80	3	0	2
Mejia	.000	1	0	0	0	0
Page	1.000	8	9	1	0	0
Robles	.995	77	209	12	1	4
Sundberg	.988	91	155	9	2	2
Taylor	.714	3	5	0	2	0
Werth	1.000	3	4	0	0	0
Wiseman	.991	116	214	14	2	3

HAGERSTOWN SUNS

LOW CLASS A

SOUTH ATLANTIC LEAGUE

Batting	B-T	HT	WT	DOB	AVG	vLH	vRH	G	AB	R	H	2B	3B	HR	RBI	BB	HBP	SH	SF	SO	SB	CS	SLG	OBP
Agustin, Telmito	L-L	5-10	160	10-9-96	.277	.310	.269	80	296	45	82	18	4	9	37	13	1	3	2	74	9	4	.456	.308
Banks, Nick	L-L	6-1	215	11-18-94	.252	.344	.216	122	440	52	111	24	4	7	58	31	3	5	4	90	14	7	.373	.303
Barrera, Tres	R-R	6-0	215	9-15-94	.279	.464	.221	67	237	28	66	18	1	8	27	23	6	0	2	58	1	0	.464	.355
Beckwith, Tyler	R-R	6-2	195	7-18-94	.218	.143	.254	30	87	16	19	1	1	2	5	19	0	0	0	34	3	0	.322	.359
Boggetto, Branden	R-R	6-0	190	11-10-93	.231	.000	.273	15	52	0	12	2	0	0	4	2	2	0	2	11	0	0	.269	.276
Corredor, Aldrem	L-L	6-0	202	10-27-95	.261	.207	.279	120	449	53	117	30	4	5	55	47	4	4	2	109	4	1	.379	.335
Franco, Anderson	R-R	6-3	190	8-15-97	.201	.232	.190	120	408	57	82	23	2	11	63	41	1	0	6	100	3	1	.348	.272
Johnson, Daniel	L-L	5-10	185	7-11-95	.300	.264	.314	88	327	61	98	16	4	17	52	22	11	1	3	70	12	9	.529	.361
Kieboom, Carter	R-R	6-2	190	9-3-97	.296	.321	.285	48	179	36	53	12	0	8	26	28	3	0	0	40	2	2	.497	.400
La Bruna, Angelo	R-R	5-10	175	4-15-92	.218	.246	.209	77	248	25	54	10	2	0	18	14	0	7	3	54	2	2	.274	.257
Neuse, Sheldon	R-R	6-0	195	12-10-94	.291	.317	.281	77	292	40	85	19	3	9	51	25	2	0	2	66	12	5	.469	.349
Noll, Jake	R-R	6-2	195	3-8-94	.270	.298	.258	108	400	51	108	19	2	16	67	20	8	2	8	64	12	4	.448	.312
Ortiz, Oliver	L-L	6-0	170	5-6-96	.199	.167	.205	41	136	14	27	6	1	3	14	10	2	3	0	41	1	2	.324	.264
Panaccione, Paul	R-R	5-10	190	12-6-93	.202	.250	.185	33	89	12	18	6	0	2	13	12	2	2	1	26	1	2	.337	.308
Perkins, Blake	B-R	6-1	165	9-10-96	.255	.277	.246	129	482	105	123	27	4	8	48	72	5	7	6	118	31	8	.378	.354
Reetz, Jakson	R-R	6-1	195	1-3-96	.238	.410	.157	37	122	16	29	7	0	2	11	15	5	1	0	41	1	2	.344	.345
Reistetter, Matt	L-R	5-10	180	5-5-92	.143	.000	.152	11	35	4	5	1	0	2	5	3	1	0	0	7	1	0	.343	.231
Ruiz, Adderling	R-R	6-1	175	5-3-91	.275	.125	.313	13	40	8	11	3	0	0	7	6	0	0	1	19	0	1	.350	.362
Soto, Juan	L-L	6-1	185	10-25-98	.361	.444	.322	23	86	15	31	5	0	3	14	10	0	0	0	8	1	2	.523	.427
Tillero, Jorge	R-R	5-11	160	12-21-93	.421	.313	.500	10	38	5	16	6	0	0	7	1	0	0	0	6	0	0	.579	.436

Pitching	B-T	HT	WT	DOB	W	L	ERA	G	GS	CG	SV	IP	H	R	ER	HR	BB	SO	AVG	vLH	vRH	K/9	BB/9
Acevedo, Carlos	R-R	6-3	200	9-27-94	0	0	2.08	2	2	0	0	9	5	2	2	0	1	8	.161	.182	.150	8.31	1.04
Barnett, Jake	L-L	6-2	190	7-30-94	1	1	3.86	9	0	0	0	16	18	9	7	0	3	14	.273	.276	.270	7.71	1.65
Bogucki, A.J.	R-R	6-3	187	5-2-95	4	2	3.56	20	5	0	1	56	55	25	22	3	17	50	.267	.194	.340	8.08	2.75
Bourque, James	R-R	6-4	190	7-9-93	5	7	5.07	23	20	0	0	114	123	76	64	8	35	90	.273	.283	.261	7.13	2.77
Braymer, Ben	L-L	6-2	215	4-28-94	3	2	5.26	7	7	0	0	38	46	25	22	3	8	37	.295	.327	.277	8.84	1.91
Davis, Weston	R-R	6-3	185	7-6-96	4	5	5.88	9	9	1	0	41	47	27	27	7	15	23	.294	.325	.263	5.01	3.27
DeRosier, Matthew	R-R	6-2	200	7-13-94	3	4	3.60	12	8	0	0	55	52	25	22	4	13	52	.245	.217	.283	8.51	2.13
Fuentes, Steven	R-R	6-2	175	5-4-97	4	3	4.41	25	1	0	2	63	80	33	31	9	13	53	.308	.317	.300	7.53	1.85
Held, Sam	R-R	6-5	190	8-24-94	2	4	5.29	22	0	0	3	32	44	24	19	2	9	26	.319	.393	.260	7.24	2.51

Player	B-T	HT	WT	DOB	W	L	ERA	G	GS	CG	SV	IP	H	R	ER	HR	BB	SO	AVG	vLH	vRH	K/9	BB/9
Hill, Brigham	R-R	6-0	185	7-8-95	0	1	6.07	6	6	0	0	30	41	22	20	4	5	30	.318	.313	.323	9.10	1.52
Howard, Hayden	R-L	6-5	193	3-26-94	4	2	2.95	31	2	0	5	76	77	38	25	6	23	74	.253	.182	.294	8.72	2.71
Howell, Jacob	R-R	6-3	180	8-9-95	0	1	9.72	5	0	0	0	8	12	9	9	1	7	9	.333	.286	.364	9.72	7.56
Klobosits, Gabe	L-R	6-7	270	5-16-95	0	0	1.80	3	0	0	1	5	1	1	1	0	1	11	.063	.143	.000	19.80	1.80
Mills, Jordan	L-L	6-5	215	5-11-92	4	3	3.03	20	0	0	4	30	26	11	10	0	8	26	.236	.262	.221	7.89	2.43
Mills, McKenzie	L-L	6-4	205	11-19-95	12	2	3.01	18	18	0	0	105	77	36	35	12	22	118	.204	.256	.181	10.15	1.89
Morse, Phil	R-R	6-2	195	5-23-94	0	4	6.53	19	0	0	5	21	30	15	15	1	7	31	.341	.325	.354	13.50	3.05
Pantoja, Jorge	R-R	6-5	215	3-26-94	1	0	0.93	5	0	0	1	10	8	1	1	0	2	6	.235	.583	.046	5.59	1.86
Pena, Carlos	R-R	6-6	240	4-3-94	6	6	5.00	23	18	1	0	99	96	63	55	9	41	79	.252	.293	.221	7.18	3.73
Peterson, Tommy	R-R	6-1	205	10-11-93	0	1	2.42	16	0	0	9	22	20	9	6	2	5	25	.238	.171	.286	10.07	2.01
Ramirez, Yonathan	L-L	5-11	165	4-13-97	1	2	5.29	14	6	0	0	48	55	30	28	6	20	23	.302	.307	.300	4.34	3.78
Ramos, David	R-R	6-0	175	9-13-91	1	0	10.57	6	0	0	0	8	14	9	9	3	3	11	.400	.294	.500	12.91	3.52
Rodriguez, Francisco	R-R	6-0	195	1-7-82	0	0	0.00	1	1	0	0	1	1	0	0	0	0	0	.333	.500	.000	0.00	0.00
Sharp, Sterling	R-R	6-4	170	5-30-95	4	9	3.69	18	17	1	0	93	100	46	38	8	14	69	.271	.272	.270	6.70	1.36
Simonds, Kyle	R-R	6-4	205	5-17-93	5	0	5.46	30	0	0	1	61	80	43	37	13	9	57	.300	.345	.264	8.41	1.33
Troop, Alex	L-L	6-5	210	7-19-96	0	0	1.80	2	0	0	0	5	2	1	1	1	0	4	.125	.111	.143	7.20	0.00
VanVossen, Mick	R-R	6-3	190	10-30-92	3	0	3.81	12	0	0	0	26	22	13	11	2	12	28	.229	.182	.269	9.69	4.15
2-team total (17 Kannapolis Intimidators)					4	1	2.72	29	0	0	1	50	40	18	15	3	17	58	.219	.182	.269	10.51	3.08
Watson, Tyler	R-L	6-5	200	5-22-97	6	4	4.35	18	17	0	0	93	92	50	45	7	24	98	.258	.291	.240	9.48	2.32

Fielding

Catcher	PCT	G	PO	A	E	DP	PB
Barrera	.995	67	539	43	3	1	3
Reetz	.997	37	269	36	1	0	11
Reistetter	.986	11	56	13	1	2	2
Ruiz	1.000	13	93	15	0	1	3
Tillero	.987	10	68	8	1	0	0

First Base	PCT	G	PO	A	E	DP
Beckwith	.900	2	9	0	1	1
Corredor	.993	107	829	45	6	74
Franco	.985	29	246	13	4	13

Second Base	PCT	G	PO	A	E	DP
Beckwith	1.000	8	17	18	0	7
Boggetto	.965	14	25	30	2	7
La Bruna	.990	26	48	53	1	10
Noll	.978	88	134	227	8	48
Panaccione	1.000	5	4	8	0	4

Third Base	PCT	G	PO	A	E	DP
Beckwith	.838	13	10	21	6	0
Franco	.886	72	47	108	20	11
La Bruna	.955	10	6	15	1	2
Neuse	.972	33	28	77	3	10
Panaccione	.929	12	7	19	2	0

Shortstop	PCT	G	PO	A	E	DP
Beckwith	.800	2	0	4	1	0
Kieboom	.961	45	55	119	7	19
La Bruna	.993	36	53	88	1	22
Neuse	.965	43	66	98	6	26
Panaccione	.909	14	16	34	5	2

Outfield	PCT	G	PO	A	E	DP
Agustin	.951	62	114	3	6	0
Banks	.994	92	167	5	1	0
Corredor	1.000	1	3	0	0	0
Johnson	.972	77	136	5	4	1
Ortiz	.983	33	55	3	1	1
Perkins	.975	128	304	9	8	6
Soto	.944	21	34	0	2	0

AUBURN DOUBLEDAYS

SHORT SEASON

NEW YORK-PENN LEAGUE

Batting	B-T	HT	WT	DOB	AVG	vLH	vRH	G	AB	R	H	2B	3B	HR	RBI	BB	HBP	SH	SF	SO	SB	CS	SLG	OBP
Baez, Jeyner	R-R	6-1	175	7-25-95	.250	.077	.317	39	140	12	35	12	0	1	19	4	0	1	0	30	4	0	.357	.271
Boggetto, Branden	R-R	6-0	190	11-10-93	.313	.333	.306	41	166	26	52	9	0	2	24	12	2	3	2	33	2	2	.404	.363
Choruby, Nick	L-R	6-0	190	11-8-94	.226	.163	.256	39	133	21	30	5	2	0	4	23	3	2	1	32	10	3	.293	.350
Collier, Zach	L-L	6-2	200	9-8-90	.421	.556	.300	7	19	8	8	1	2	1	4	4	2	0	0	3	1	0	.842	.560
Encarnacion, Randy	R-R	6-3	180	7-31-94	.233	.059	.286	20	73	7	17	2	0	1	11	10	1	0	1	17	3	1	.301	.329
Esthay, Kameron	L-L	6-0	215	12-5-94	.273	.263	.276	52	209	25	57	12	1	5	30	14	1	0	1	60	4	2	.412	.320
Guibor, Austin	L-R	5-9	185	4-29-95	.263	.161	.313	26	95	10	25	3	2	0	12	14	1	0	1	27	1	3	.337	.360
Kieboom, Carter	R-R	6-2	190	9-3-97	.250	.333	.227	7	28	4	7	1	0	1	4	1	0	0	0	2	1	0	.393	.276
Martinez, Andres	R-R	6-1	170	7-7-95	.241	.191	.262	45	145	22	35	4	1	1	18	24	2	1	2	41	2	1	.303	.353
Meregildo, Omar	R-R	6-1	185	8-18-97	.214	.268	.195	55	210	26	45	7	1	8	18	12	3	1	0	70	0	1	.371	.267
Merrill, Ryan	R-L	5-11	185	8-22-94	.118	.231	.048	10	34	1	4	0	0	0	3	1	1	0	0	7	0	1	.118	.167
Mota, Israel	R-R	6-2	165	1-3-96	.182	.000	.200	5	11	3	2	0	0	1	2	1	0	0	0	5	0	0	.455	.250
Ortiz, Oliver	L-L	6-0	170	5-6-96	.286	.208	.309	25	105	11	30	7	0	4	17	8	3	1	1	29	0	0	.467	.350
Panaccione, Paul	R-R	5-10	190	12-6-93	.267	.111	.316	18	75	11	20	5	1	3	9	5	0	0	1	16	0	0	.480	.309
Pascal, Juan	R-R	6-1	175	11-6-97	.164	.278	.108	17	55	4	9	2	0	0	5	2	1	1	0	19	3	0	.200	.207
Perdomo, Luis	L-L	5-11	170	5-21-97	.091	.000	.125	4	11	0	1	0	0	0	0	0	0	0	0	1	0	0	.091	.091
Perkins, Nic	R-R	6-4	215	2-19-96	.205	.194	.209	32	117	10	24	6	0	0	9	4	1	0	0	25	0	0	.256	.238
Peroni, Anthony	R-R	5-11	175	12-12-96	.500	—	.500	2	2	0	1	0	0	0	0	0	0	0	0	0	0	0	.500	.500
Pryor, Jonathan	L-L	6-1	190	4-28-94	.259	.273	.252	41	147	14	38	4	1	2	18	13	6	0	4	35	6	1	.340	.335
Ramirez, Joshual	R-R	6-2	185	5-20-96	.244	.239	.246	45	164	19	40	3	2	1	13	5	2	0	2	29	3	2	.305	.272
Scudder, Jake	L-R	6-0	210	3-23-95	.239	.288	.219	52	205	18	49	12	0	1	25	14	2	0	1	36	0	1	.312	.293
Severino, Pedro	R-R	6-0	215	7-20-93	.364	.500	.286	4	11	4	4	0	1	0	0	0	1	0	0	1	0	0	.546	.417
Shepard, Chance	R-R	6-1	210	11-8-94	.249	.317	.229	54	181	31	45	15	1	7	17	34	2	0	1	64	5	2	.459	.372
Simonetti, Conner	L-L	6-1	205	2-10-95	.160	.200	.150	6	25	4	4	0	0	1	5	3	0	0	0	13	1	1	.280	.250
Skole, Matt	L-R	6-4	220	7-30-89	.192	.222	.177	9	26	5	5	2	0	1	2	3	0	0	0	8	0	0	.385	.276
Upshaw, Armond	B-L	6-0	190	6-20-96	.180	.132	.197	60	195	26	35	6	1	1	10	41	9	6	0	62	11	5	.236	.347
Vilorio, Luis	R-R	6-1	180	8-28-93	.296	.429	.250	9	27	3	8	1	0	0	1	1	0	0	0	11	1	0	.333	.321

Pitching	B-T	HT	WT	DOB	W	L	ERA	G	GS	CG	SV	IP	H	R	ER	HR	BB	SO	AVG	vLH	vRH	K/9	BB/9
Alastre, Tomas	R-R	6-4	170	6-11-98	0	1	5.63	2	2	0	0	8	11	6	5	0	6	6	.367	.467	.267	6.75	6.75
Baltrip, Joseph	R-R	6-1	220	2-15-95	0	1	7.50	4	0	0	0	6	7	7	5	2	6	6	.292	.250	.333	9.00	9.00
Barnett, Jake	L-L	6-2	190	7-30-94	3	2	1.50	10	0	0	2	18	16	3	3	0	1	13	.250	.214	.260	6.50	0.50
Brasher, Jared	R-R	6-1	200	1-3-95	1	2	4.50	17	0	0	2	26	21	17	13	3	18	28	.221	.342	.140	9.69	6.23
Braymer, Ben	L-L	6-2	215	4-28-94	2	0	2.28	6	6	0	0	28	24	10	7	1	13	39	.226	.290	.200	12.69	4.23
Butler, Daniel	R-R	6-6	215	4-13-95	0	0	1.69	3	0	0	0	5	9	3	1	0	0	5	.360	.429	.333	8.44	0.00
Chu, Gilberto	L-L	5-11	160	11-19-97	2	1	3.86	7	0	0	0	19	18	10	8	1	6	12	.243	.350	.204	5.79	2.89

Cousins, Jake	R-R	6-4	185	7-14-94	2	2	2.43	15	0	0	2	30	27	12	8	0	7	23	.239	.304	.194	6.98	2.12
Crowe, Wil	R-R	6-2	240	9-9-94	0	0	2.61	7	7	0	0	21	18	6	6	3	3	15	.234	.188	.267	6.53	1.31
Davis, Weston	R-R	6-3	185	7-6-96	0	0	0.00	2	2	0	0	9	5	0	0	0	0	8	.156	.059	.267	8.00	0.00
DeRosier, Matthew	R-R	6-2	200	7-13-94	1	1	2.45	6	6	0	0	33	29	13	9	0	4	28	.225	.260	.203	7.64	1.09
Engelbrekt, Max	L-L	6-3	197	9-30-93	2	1	4.06	15	0	0	0	31	35	20	14	1	7	21	.280	.244	.298	6.10	2.03
Eusebio, Diomedes	R-R	6-0	185	9-8-92	0	1	10.80	4	0	0	0	5	9	6	6	0	4	1	.429	.300	.546	1.80	7.20
German, Jhonatan	R-R	6-4	215	1-24-95	0	1	6.75	2	2	0	0	9	7	7	7	0	8	5	.212	.200	.217	4.82	7.71
Guillen, Angel	R-R	6-2	150	1-24-97	0	3	4.30	5	2	0	0	15	17	16	7	5	2	14	.279	.136	.359	8.59	1.23
Hill, Brigham	R-R	6-0	185	7-8-95	0	1	2.63	4	3	0	0	14	12	7	4	0	3	9	.214	.200	.222	5.93	1.98
Johnson, Jared	R-L	6-4	185	9-1-95	1	2	5.23	11	1	0	1	21	26	12	12	1	13	15	.317	.313	.320	6.53	5.66
Johnston, Kyle	R-R	6-0	190	7-17-96	0	2	3.43	14	7	0	0	45	41	21	17	2	23	32	.241	.250	.235	6.45	4.63
Klobosits, Gabe	L-R	6-7	270	5-16-95	0	0	1.66	15	0	0	5	22	19	4	4	0	6	18	.244	.214	.260	7.48	2.49
McKinney, Jeremy	R-R	6-0	190	12-8-94	1	2	6.39	15	0	0	2	25	34	21	18	5	12	29	.318	.381	.277	10.30	4.26
O'Sullivan, Sean	R-R	6-1	245	9-1-87	0	0	0.00	1	1	0	0	2	2	0	0	0	0	1	.250	.333	.200	4.50	0.00
Pena, Malvin	R-R	6-2	180	6-24-97	0	0	3.86	2	0	0	1	7	10	3	3	0	4	5	.357	.167	.500	6.43	5.14
Ramirez, Yonathan	L-L	5-11	165	4-13-97	4	3	3.86	10	7	0	0	47	52	27	20	5	10	30	.277	.277	.276	5.79	1.93
Raquet, Nick	R-L	6-0	215	12-12-95	3	2	2.45	11	11	0	0	51	56	19	14	2	7	22	.283	.265	.289	3.86	1.23
Reid, Jonny	L-L	5-10	165	6-28-95	0	0	9.00	5	0	0	0	7	14	11	7	1	2	8	.378	.417	.360	10.29	2.57
Rishwain, Michael	R-R	6-3	220	6-27-94	1	4	5.11	16	0	0	0	37	46	26	21	4	10	25	.295	.310	.286	6.08	2.43
Romero, Seth	L-L	6-3	240	4-19-96	0	1	5.40	6	6	0	0	20	19	12	12	0	6	32	.244	.364	.196	14.40	2.70
Smith, David	R-R	6-4	210	10-20-94	3	4	6.69	15	0	0	0	36	52	30	27	3	7	28	.327	.302	.344	6.94	1.73
Taveras, Felix	R-R	6-2	155	7-11-95	0	0	6.00	1	0	0	0	3	2	2	2	0	3	5	.200	.000	.333	15.00	9.00
Tetreault, Jackson	R-R	6-5	170	6-3-96	2	2	2.58	11	6	0	0	38	32	15	11	1	16	36	.216	.229	.205	8.45	3.76
Troop, Alex	L-L	6-5	210	7-19-96	2	4	3.13	10	3	0	0	32	30	12	11	3	9	23	.246	.207	.258	6.54	2.56
Turnbull, Kylin	L-R	6-5	205	9-12-89	0	0	0.00	2	2	0	0	5	2	0	0	0	4	4	.133	.200	.100	7.71	7.71
Voth, Austin	R-R	6-2	215	6-26-92	0	1	13.50	1	1	0	0	2	4	3	3	0	1	2	.400	.286	.667	9.00	4.50

Fielding

C: Baez 39, Perkins 31, Peroni 2, Severino 4, Vilorio 9. **1B:** Encarnacion 3, Esthay 1, Martinez 2, Ramirez 4, Scudder 36, Shepard 30, Simonetti 5, Skole 4. **2B:** Boggetto 30, Martinez 25, Meregildo 7, Merrill 2, Ramirez 16. **3B:** Boggetto 3, Martinez 6, Meregildo 48, Panaccione 1, Ramirez 14, Scudder 8, Skole 4. **SS:** Boggetto 10, Kieboom 6, Martinez 12, Merrill 7, Panaccione 17, Pascal 17, Ramirez 10. **OF:** Choruby 39, Collier 6, Encarnacion 14, Esthay 40, Guibor 22, Mota 4, Ortiz 16, Perdomo 4, Pryor 34, Shepard 1, Upshaw 58.

GCL NATIONALS — *ROOKIE*

GULF COAST LEAGUE

Batting	B-T	HT	WT	DOB	AVG	vLH	vRH	G	AB	R	H	2B	3B	HR	RBI	BB	HBP	SH	SF	SO	SB	CS	SLG	OBP
Antuna, Yasel	B-R	6-0	170	10-26-99	.301	.143	.341	48	173	25	52	8	3	1	17	23	1	0	2	29	5	5	.399	.382
Bautista, Rafael	R-R	6-2	165	3-8-93	.296	.222	.314	13	44	7	13	2	1	0	3	5	3	0	0	5	2	1	.386	.404
Blash, Jamori	R-R	6-4	225	11-9-95	.253	.278	.247	28	95	18	24	3	1	1	8	11	2	0	1	26	2	3	.337	.339
Cabello, Jose	R-R	5-11	185	12-12-96	.245	.222	.250	20	49	8	12	1	1	1	10	15	1	0	0	12	1	0	.367	.431
Carrillo, Adalberto	R-R	5-11	185	6-1-95	.091	.000	.095	11	22	0	2	0	0	0	0	3	1	0	0	9	0	0	.091	.231
Caulfield, Phil	L-R	5-8	170	12-30-94	.250	.400	.217	18	56	6	14	1	0	0	6	7	1	0	1	12	2	0	.268	.339
Connell, Justin	R-R	6-1	185	3-11-99	.323	.444	.295	30	96	17	31	4	0	0	7	14	1	0	2	10	5	2	.365	.407
Cramer, Jackson	B-R	6-4	230	12-7-94	.235	.136	.258	34	115	20	27	6	0	2	8	18	2	0	0	38	1	0	.339	.348
Dunlap, Alex	R-R	6-2	195	10-6-94	.239	.143	.263	24	71	10	17	1	0	3	12	8	6	0	1	12	0	1	.380	.361
Evangelista, Juan	R-R	5-11	165	5-28-98	.240	.211	.247	33	104	20	25	6	0	3	12	8	3	0	2	18	0	1	.385	.308
Falcon, Santo	R-R	6-0	190	3-28-97	.253	.333	.230	29	79	9	20	7	0	0	11	4	4	2	1	19	0	2	.342	.318
Garcia, Luis	L-R	6-0	190	5-16-00	.302	.184	.329	49	199	25	60	8	3	1	22	9	0	2	1	32	11	2	.387	.330
Guibor, Austin	L-R	5-9	185	4-29-95	.238	.500	.211	7	21	7	5	0	2	0	1	4	0	0	0	3	0	1	.429	.360
Gutierrez, Kelvin	R-R	6-3	185	8-28-94	.212	.400	.179	10	33	6	7	3	1	0	1	4	0	0	0	7	2	0	.364	.297
Kieboom, Carter	R-R	6-2	190	9-3-97	.417	.000	.455	6	12	1	5	3	0	0	5	3	1	0	0	0	0	0	.667	.563
Mendez, Ricardo	L-L	6-0	155	1-24-00	.252	.192	.264	44	151	20	38	6	2	1	19	13	2	4	0	43	7	3	.338	.319
Pascal, Juan	R-R	6-1	175	11-6-97	.196	.105	.219	30	92	9	18	4	0	0	10	7	1	3	2	17	3	0	.239	.255
Perdomo, Luis	L-L	5-11	170	5-21-97	.167	—	.167	2	6	0	1	0	0	0	0	1	0	0	0	1	0	0	.167	.286
Pineda, Israel	R-R	5-11	190	4-3-00	.288	.625	.235	17	59	10	17	5	2	0	12	4	0	0	2	13	0	0	.441	.323
Sanchez, Jose	R-R	5-11	155	7-12-00	.209	.182	.216	48	158	22	33	3	0	1	20	14	2	3	1	26	0	2	.247	.280
Senior, Eric	R-R	6-2	170	9-29-97	.267	—	.267	6	15	3	4	0	0	1	2	2	1	0	1	4	1	0	.467	.368
Silva, Alian	R-R	5-8	174	5-29-94	.200	.500	.091	4	15	1	3	1	0	0	0	0	1	0	0	5	0	0	.267	.250
Soto, Juan	L-L	6-1	185	10-25-98	.320	.250	.333	9	25	3	8	1	1	0	4	2	0	0	0	1	0	0	.440	.370
Ventura, Edwin	R-R	6-1	180	8-27-97	.193	.167	.200	35	109	9	21	3	0	0	7	3	1	2	0	18	2	0	.220	.221

Pitching	B-T	HT	WT	DOB	W	L	ERA	G	GS	CG	SV	IP	H	R	ER	HR	BB	SO	AVG	vLH	vRH	K/9	BB/9
Acevedo, Carlos	R-R	6-3	200	9-27-94	0	0	1.13	3	3	0	0	8	4	1	1	0	0	7	.143	.250	.100	7.88	0.00
Adler, Sean	L-L	6-2	220	3-18-94	3	0	3.31	10	0	0	0	16	17	10	6	0	5	17	.250	.333	.226	9.37	2.76
Alastre, Tomas	R-R	6-4	170	6-11-98	3	1	2.55	9	6	0	0	42	29	15	12	3	14	43	.192	.143	.216	9.14	2.98
Baez, Joan	R-R	6-3	190	12-26-94	2	0	1.47	4	3	0	0	18	9	4	3	0	5	23	.150	.167	.146	11.29	2.45
Brasher, Jared	R-R	6-1	200	1-3-95	0	0	0.00	1	0	0	1	1	0	0	0	0	1	0	.000	—	.000	0.00	9.00
Butler, Daniel	R-R	6-6	215	4-13-95	1	1	2.70	6	0	0	1	10	6	3	3	1	1	6	.177	.000	.273	5.40	0.90
Chu, Gilberto	L-L	5-11	160	11-19-97	1	1	2.84	9	0	0	0	19	19	7	6	1	5	24	.241	.000	.322	11.37	2.37
Collins, Tim	L-L	5-7	170	8-21-89	0	1	1.35	6	2	0	0	7	5	3	1	0	2	13	.217	.167	.235	17.55	2.70
Cousins, Jake	R-R	6-4	185	7-14-94	0	0	3.00	3	0	0	0	3	3	2	1	0	3	4	.231	.143	.333	12.00	9.00
Crowe, Wil	R-R	6-2	240	9-9-94	0	0	4.91	2	2	0	0	4	3	2	2	0	1	2	.250	.167	.333	4.91	2.45
Davis, Weston	R-R	6-3	185	7-6-96	0	0	6.75	1	1	0	0	4	4	4	3	0	2	4	.250	.333	.231	9.00	4.50
De Los Santos, Jose	R-R	6-3	190	1-14-97	3	1	5.75	15	0	0	1	20	23	17	13	2	11	15	.281	.273	.286	6.64	4.87
Engelbrekt, Max	L-L	6-3	197	9-30-93	0	0	0.00	1	0	0	0	1	0	0	0	0	0	2	.000	.000	.000	18.00	0.00

Galindez, Nelson	L-L	6-3	220	7-26-98	2	2	3.79	12	7	0	0	38	25	20	16	1	27	27	.188	.222	.179	6.39	6.39
German, Jhonatan	R-R	6-4	215	1-24-95	1	4	3.27	8	8	0	0	33	22	18	12	1	17	27	.179	.150	.193	7.36	4.64
Guillen, Angel	R-R	6-2	150	1-24-97	2	1	3.42	11	1	0	1	24	23	9	9	1	5	19	.264	.250	.271	7.23	1.90
Infante, Darly	L-L	6-2	165	10-20-96	0	2	4.43	13	0	0	0	22	17	17	11	1	14	26	.205	.167	.215	10.48	5.64
Jimenez, Jose	L-L	6-1	190	12-7-96	3	0	1.35	15	0	0	2	27	25	9	4	1	5	11	.248	.281	.232	3.71	1.69
Johnson, Jared	R-L	6-4	185	9-1-95	1	1	0.64	7	2	0	1	14	8	1	1	0	3	14	.167	.000	.235	9.00	1.93
Johnston, Kyle	R-R	6-0	190	7-17-96	0	0	0.00	1	0	0	0	2	0	0	0	0	2	1	.000	.000	.000	4.50	9.00
Klobosits, Gabe	L-R	6-7	270	5-16-95	1	0	0.00	2	0	0	0	4	3	1	0	0	1	5	.214	.333	.182	11.25	2.25
Lee, Andrew	L-R	6-5	225	12-2-93	0	0	0.00	1	1	0	0	2	0	0	0	0	1	1	.000	.000	.000	5.40	5.40
Lee, Nick	L-L	5-11	205	1-13-91	0	0	0.00	3	1	0	0	3	4	0	0	0	0	1	.500	—	.500	3.38	0.00
Luzardo, Jesus	L-L	6-1	205	9-30-97	1	0	1.32	3	3	0	0	14	14	2	2	1	0	15	.259	.133	.308	9.88	0.00
Martin, J.D.	R-R	6-4	220	1-2-83	1	0	4.50	1	0	0	0	2	2	1	1	0	1	1	.286	.250	.333	4.50	4.50
McKinney, Jeremy	R-R	6-0	190	12-8-94	0	0	0.00	2	0	0	1	3	2	0	0	0	0	4	.182	.167	.200	12.00	0.00
Morales, Jose	R-R	6-3	180	2-12-95	0	1	0.75	5	1	0	0	12	5	3	1	0	3	13	.125	.095	.158	9.75	2.25
Peguero, Jairon	L-L	6-0	177	6-14-97	1	1	5.56	5	0	0	0	11	13	8	7	1	4	9	.283	.111	.324	7.15	3.18
Pena, Malvin	R-R	6-2	180	6-24-97	1	3	5.44	10	7	0	0	41	45	29	25	7	18	39	.274	.265	.278	8.49	3.92
Ramirez, Nector	R-R	6-0	170	9-4-96	3	1	5.23	14	0	0	1	21	28	18	12	3	4	12	.301	.333	.290	5.23	1.74
Raquet, Nick	R-L	6-0	215	12-12-95	0	0	0.00	1	1	0	0	2	2	0	0	0	0	2	.250	.000	.333	9.00	0.00
Romero, Seth	L-L	6-3	240	4-19-96	0	0	0.00	1	1	0	0	2	0	0	0	0	2	3	.000	.000	.000	13.50	9.00
Smith, David	R-R	6-4	210	10-20-94	1	0	0.00	1	0	0	0	1	1	0	0	0	0	0	.250	.500	.000	0.00	0.00
Stoeckinger, Jackson	L-L	6-3	210	2-13-96	2	0	4.73	8	5	0	0	27	28	14	14	1	7	31	.269	.222	.286	10.46	2.36
Tetreault, Jackson	R-R	6-5	170	6-3-96	0	0	4.50	1	0	0	0	2	1	1	1	1	1	2	.143	.000	.167	9.00	4.50
Troop, Alex	L-L	6-5	210	7-19-96	0	0	0.00	1	1	0	0	2	0	0	0	0	0	2	.000	.000	.000	9.00	0.00
Zwetsch, Connor	R-R	6-5	230	5-6-95	1	1	0.79	10	0	0	3	11	9	2	1	0	0	6	.209	.385	.133	4.76	0.00

Fielding

C: Cabello 20, Carrillo 7, Dunlap 23, Pineda 16. **1B:** Blash 26, Cramer 32. **2B:** Caulfield 18, Garcia 25, Pascal 3, Sanchez 14, Silva 1. **3B:** Antuna 15, Cramer 2, Gutierrez 8, Pascal 21, Sanchez 15. **SS:** Antuna 21, Garcia 17, Kieboom 5, Pascal 2, Sanchez 18. **OF:** Bautista 10, Connell 25, Evangelista 28, Falcon 27, Guibor 6, Mendez 43, Perdomo 1, Senior 6, Silva 3, Soto 9, Ventura 30.

DSL NATIONALS

ROOKIE

DOMINICAN SUMMER LEAGUE

Batting	B-T	HT	WT	DOB	AVG	vLH	vRH	G	AB	R	H	2B	3B	HR	RBI	BB	HBP	SH	SF	SO	SB	CS	SLG	OBP
Alvarado, Elvis	R-R	6-4	183	2-23-99	.139	.167	.131	45	158	19	22	6	1	2	9	10	2	2	1	70	0	1	.228	.199
Aquino, Luis	R-R	6-1	157	4-28-99	.270	.242	.276	52	178	32	48	4	5	1	24	15	3	3	4	52	19	11	.365	.330
Bencosme, Bryan	R-R	6-1	196	12-18-97	.259	.283	.253	61	224	27	58	13	3	3	29	24	2	3	2	53	4	3	.384	.333
Diaz, Geraldi	L-R	6-0	196	7-8-00	.229	.290	.212	51	175	20	40	12	1	1	18	25	4	0	2	30	0	0	.326	.335
Escobar, David	L-L	6-0	184	7-3-99	.204	.217	.201	49	162	18	33	7	1	1	17	16	9	2	2	18	3	3	.278	.307
Liriano, Adrian	R-R	5-11	157	1-4-00	.237	.231	.239	39	114	23	27	8	1	0	12	15	7	1	1	33	2	2	.325	.358
Mesa, Brailin	R-R	6-3	185	11-2-97	.125	.000	.143	13	40	4	5	2	0	0	1	4	3	0	0	14	0	1	.175	.255
Morales, Jesus	R-R	5-10	173	12-22-97	.290	.296	.288	52	183	28	53	7	3	0	23	17	7	0	2	37	4	3	.361	.368
Pena, Landerson	R-R	6-1	194	10-14-97	.261	.324	.244	51	157	32	41	3	4	2	15	12	6	4	0	39	13	10	.369	.337
Perez, Wilmer	R-R	5-10	186	4-16-98	.313	.275	.321	61	224	34	70	17	4	3	34	20	7	0	3	38	5	3	.464	.382
Porte, Cesar	R-R	6-0	180	10-31-98	.219	.226	.217	46	160	14	35	5	2	2	19	13	3	1	2	38	3	3	.313	.287
Sanfler, Caldioli	L-R	6-2	185	12-7-97	.237	.217	.242	61	224	41	53	8	4	1	26	37	4	1	5	54	19	6	.321	.348
Santana, Luis	R-R	6-1	160	6-3-99	.232	.238	.231	39	125	15	29	5	0	0	7	8	3	0	2	24	0	0	.272	.290
Sosa, Ronaldy	L-R	6-0	184	11-2-98	.262	.297	.254	58	206	23	54	10	1	0	21	19	5	1	2	31	2	2	.320	.336

Pitching	B-T	HT	WT	DOB	W	L	ERA	G	GS	CG	SV	IP	H	R	ER	HR	BB	SO	AVG	vLH	vRH	K/9	BB/9
Adon, Joan	R-R	6-2	185	8-12-98	2	1	3.54	13	0	0	1	28	24	13	11	1	9	31	.240	.333	.194	9.96	2.89
Amoroso, Thony	R-R	6-0	154	8-2-98	1	1	3.86	15	0	0	1	19	22	15	8	1	14	14	.293	.539	.242	6.75	6.75
Constanzo, Francisco	R-R	6-1	180	10-4-96	1	3	4.71	17	0	0	6	21	16	14	11	0	20	25	.232	.320	.182	10.71	8.57
Cuello, Carlos	R-R	6-5	190	2-26-99	0	3	5.68	13	0	0	1	19	21	14	12	1	13	5	.296	.316	.289	2.37	6.16
De La Cruz, Gerald	L-L	6-3	180	8-19-96	1	3	7.71	14	0	0	0	19	25	24	16	0	19	18	.305	.375	.297	8.68	9.16
Duran, Warner	R-R	5-11	165	3-25-98	0	1	7.20	2	0	0	0	5	5	4	4	0	1	6	.278	.167	.333	10.80	1.80
Gomez, Niomar	R-R	6-3	173	9-9-98	1	3	4.07	12	12	0	0	55	49	29	25	2	21	53	.241	.349	.190	8.62	3.42
Gomez, Rafael	R-R	6-0	178	6-15-98	6	3	4.09	11	11	0	0	55	56	31	25	1	14	47	.265	.161	.309	7.69	2.29
Gonzalez, Pedro	R-R	6-2	183	7-16-00	1	3	5.30	12	12	0	0	53	65	35	31	2	21	44	.300	.292	.303	7.52	3.59
Hernandez, Alfonso	L-L	5-11	162	8-3-99	1	1	2.10	12	12	0	0	56	43	17	13	0	22	61	.216	.156	.234	9.86	3.56
Martinez, Adrian	R-R	6-0	192	8-2-98	1	1	3.71	6	1	0	0	17	12	10	7	0	7	12	.200	.333	.156	6.35	3.71
Melendez, Rafael	R-R	6-4	196	12-13-97	0	1	8.44	10	0	0	0	11	8	12	10	0	14	7	.216	.182	.231	5.91	11.81
Michel, Edwin	L-L	6-2	168	4-22-99	1	0	6.65	15	0	0	1	23	32	20	17	0	11	15	.327	.211	.354	5.87	4.30
Peguero, Jairon	L-L	6-0	177	6-14-97	1	1	1.84	9	9	0	0	44	40	11	9	1	9	37	.238	.035	.281	7.57	1.84
Pena, Eric	R-R	6-0	155	6-29-99	3	2	3.55	16	0	0	2	33	30	20	13	1	17	22	.252	.211	.272	6.00	4.64
Perez, Fray	R-R	5-11	170	8-22-96	1	6	4.75	15	0	0	1	30	37	18	16	2	7	31	.306	.233	.346	9.20	2.08
Ramirez, Hector	R-R	6-4	206	2-25-98	1	1	7.64	12	0	0	1	18	20	18	15	0	15	15	.318	.333	.308	7.64	7.64
Romero, Carlos	R-R	6-6	179	7-15-99	4	0	5.12	14	2	0	2	32	29	24	18	0	16	23	.238	.258	.231	6.54	4.55
Segura, Fausto	R-R	6-3	191	10-24-96	1	3	2.96	8	3	0	0	24	16	13	8	0	16	19	.191	.208	.183	7.03	5.92
Severino, Wilson	R-R	6-4	188	6-7-98	1	0	2.41	13	0	0	0	19	17	6	5	0	13	7	.233	.292	.204	3.38	6.27
Vallejo, Alejandro	R-R	6-3	184	11-4-98	0	6	8.90	11	9	0	0	31	32	42	31	1	29	40	.254	.211	.273	11.49	8.33

Fielding

C: Diaz 41, Perez 20, Santana 13. **1B:** Mesa 1, Perez 14, Santana 15, Sosa 46. **2B:** Aquino 13, Liriano 19, Morales 35, Porte 3, Sosa 8. **3B:** Bencosme 53, Morales 12, Porte 9. **SS:** Aquino 14, Bencosme 6, Liriano 22, Morales 2, Porte 33. **OF:** Alvarado 42, Aquino 23, Escobar 45, Mesa 4, Pena 46, Sanfler 59, Sosa 2.

MINOR
LEAGUES

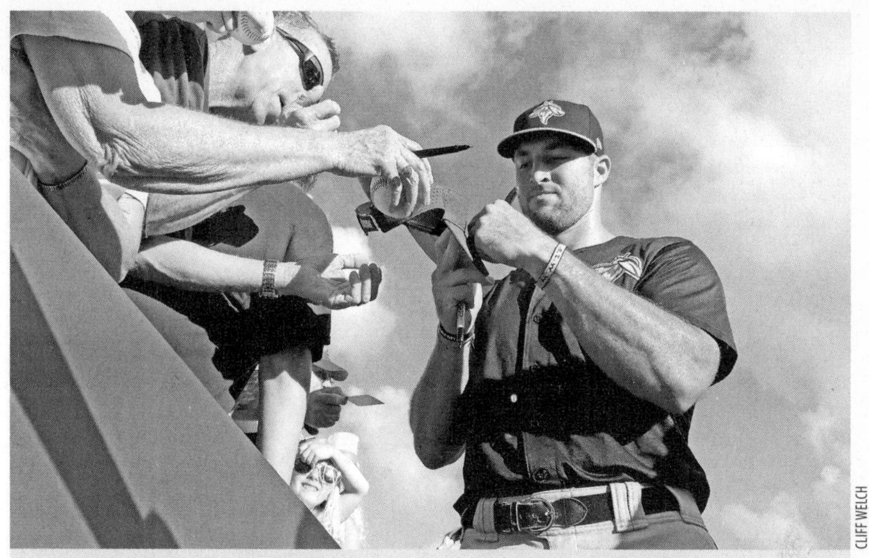
CLIFF WELCH

Tim Tebow was a fan favorite and proved to be the best draw in the minors.

MINOR LEAGUES

Tebow Takes Over the Minor Leagues

BY JOSH NORRIS

Unquestionably, the year in the minor leagues was about one man: Tim Tebow. Sure, the Carolina League gained two contracted California League franchises, the Hartford Yard Goats opened their brand-new ballpark after a year-long boondoggle, re-branding continued to go through the roof and a hurricane derailed the playoffs in several leagues, but the year belonged to Tebow.

The 30-year-old former NFL quarterback stole the show night in and night out from the moment he was assigned to low Class A Columbia until his last game of the season. Just as they did in the Arizona Fall League a few months earlier, fans lined up early, stayed late and packed normally barren parks to get a chance to see arguably the greatest attraction in the history of the minor leagues.

The St. Lucie Mets, for whom Tebow played in the second half of the season, saw a 37.1 percent increase from their 2016 attendance (96,556) to their 2017 figure (132,359). Columbia, in its second year of existence after moving from Savannah, Ga., got a 20.6 percent boost with the help of Tebow, jumping from 261,134 fans in 2016 to 315,034 fans in 2017.

Opponents of Tebow's teams, too, were big winners when Columbia or St. Lucie were in town. Low Class A Hagerstown, for instance, drew 22,078 fans over a four-game set with Tebow and Columbia. That series alone helped lift the Suns out of last place in attendance in the SAL for the first time since 2010. Moreover, the total attendance for that series accounted for most of the league's 0.9 percent increase overall from 2016.

"It was packed outside our office in the overflow of our parking lot," Hagerstown manager Patrick Anderson said. "It was lines everywhere. They were there early for BP for as much (of Tebow) as they could see. It was crazy."

The fans didn't stop pouring through the gates when Tebow got promoted to the Florida State League, either. Four teams—Charlotte, Fort Myers, Florida and Tampa—set season-high attendance marks when Tebow was in town. The FSL as a whole saw a 9.8 percent increase in attendance from the year prior, a figure which can almost solely be attributed to Tebow's half-season presence.

There were plenty of reasons fans turned out for Tebow. Some were autograph hounds who rushed through the stadium gates the minute they opened in the hopes of getting the man of the moment's signature on anything from baseballs to footballs to jerseys to magazine covers. If it was signable, they wanted it signed.

Others were hardcore fans of Tebow's alma mater, the Florida Gators, and were happy to simply watch the hero again.

Still others, such as Bobby VanSweden, were parents who saw Tebow as a strong role model for their children and wanted to take them out to a game to see him in person.

"He's a great role model for young people, for young ballplayers," VanSweden said. "My son's a ballplayer. We're big Florida fans. Carson's dream is to play for coach (Kevin) O'Sullivan at Florida. So we wanted to come out and support Tim, but also see the Tampa Yankees play as well.

"He was a phenomenal player. He's the kind of guy who puts his mind to something and he does it. Just like right now. It's kind of the same as (Michael) Jordan. He's just trying to live out a dream like Jordan did. They were both baseball players but they chose a different sport as profession to begin with, and when they retired they tried to live out a dream."

All of that extra attendance was quantifiable at the cash register as well. Minor league executives estimate that each fan, through the cost of tickets, concessions and merchandise, is worth $22 to a team. When he was promoted from low Class A to high Class A on June 26, BA's estimates calculated that he was worth roughly $1.6 million extra for that two-plus months alone.

On the field, Tebow didn't exactly tear the cover off the ball, but he did perform better than expected. He hit .226/.309/.347 between Columbia and St. Lucie, with eight home runs and 52 RBIs. That's better than NBA Hall of Famer Michael Jordan did in his one-year stint in the minor leagues in 1994, when he hit .202/.289/.266 with three home runs and 51 RBIs with Double-A Birmingham. Jordan's manager that year, by the way? None other than current Indians skipper Terry Francona.

The most notable on-field performance of Tebow's first season as a minor leaguer, however, came on his first day. Facing Augusta righthander Domenic Mazza (who threw a nine-inning perfect game later in the season), Tebow connected on an opposite-field home run.

"All of my sports experiences helped me for moments like that," Tebow told ESPN after the Fireflies' 14-7 victory over the GreenJackets that evening. "Playing in The Swamp or Death Valley or in Mile High Stadium in the playoffs, they all helped.

WHAT'S IN A NAME?

Five minor league teams changed their names and branding heading into the 2017 season

TRIPLE-A

TEAM (LEAGUE)	NEW NAME	OLD NAME
New Orleans (PCL)	Baby Cakes	Zephyrs

DOUBLE-A

TEAM (LEAGUE)	NEW NAME	OLD NAME
Binghamton (EL)	Rumble Ponies	Mets
Jacksonville (SL)	Jumbo Shrimp	Suns

HIGH CLASS A

TEAM (LEAGUE)	NEW NAME	OLD NAME
Brevard County (FSL)*	Fire Frogs	Manatees
Down East (CL)*	Wood Ducks	Mavericks

** These teams' new names came as the product of a move to a new city. Down East moved from Adelanto, Calif., to Kinston, N.C. and Brevard County moved to Kissimmee, Fla.*

"So much about sports is handling moments and handling pressure."

This was just season one of Tebow's career, and he returned to football broadcasting after the year, but he made clear during press conferences in various stops toward season's end that he fully intends to be back in 2018 to keep working toward his goal of bucking the odds and making the major leagues.

If he does return for a second go-round, fans and minor league executives alike will be very happy to welcome him back.

Contraction Action

After years of rumors and legal battles, the inevitable finally happened in 2017 when Minor League Baseball announced it was contracting two California League franchises and moving them to the Carolina League.

The two franchises—Bakersfield (Mariners) and High Desert (Rangers) had been the subject of much scrutiny over the past few years. High Desert in particular had been the subject of a legal battle in which the city of Adelanto, Calif., had claimed the team's rent of just $1 per year amounted to a gift of public funds and tried to evict the team from Stater Bros. Stadium before the 2016 season.

Instead, the Astros purchased Bakersfield, the Rangers purchased High Desert and both moved their teams to North Carolina. The Rangers' club became the Down East Wood Ducks and moved into Grainger Stadium in Kinston, N.C., the former home of the Kinston Indians.

Bakersfield's route was a little trickier. They picked up and left without a stadium to call home. Scheduled to move into a new stadium in Fayetteville, N.C. (on which ground was broken in August), in 2019, the team needed a landing spot for 2017 and 2018.

After surveying the state, the Astros settled on Jim Perry Stadium at Campbell University.

"The Astros are excited to be affiliated with the city of Fayetteville. It's a city with rich history, friendly people and a background in baseball," Astros president Reid Ryan said at a press confernce announcing the deal with Campbell for 2017 and 2018. "This agreement will be part of a dynamic revitalization of downtown Fayetteville, which will bring great crowds and a major league environment for our players to develop. Player development is a huge part of the Astros' success and Fayetteville will be a home for the club's top prospects."

Named for the Campbell alumnus who won the 1970 AL Cy Young award, Perry Stadium represented nearly the starkest contrast possible when compared with where the team will play beginning in 2019.

While their final home will seat nearly 4,800 people and cost $33 million to build, Perry Stadium seats just 630 fans when filled to capacity. Concessions at the new stadium are sure to fit the off-the-wall standards of the modern minor leagues. At Perry Stadium, where the team plays as the Buies Creek Astros, only the basics are offered. That means peanuts, Cracker Jack, hot dogs, hamburgers, candy and soft drinks. Most notably, because Campbell is a dry campus, no beer is sold at the stadium.

In exchange for use of its field for two seasons (with an option for a third if construction should hit a snag), the Astros paid to install a turf field at Perry Stadium. All money collected at games goes to Campbell.

The California and Carolina Leagues also saw another split for the 2017 season. For the first time since 1995, the leagues played separate all-star games instead of the traditional interleague affair that rotated between sites in each league.

"It's a matter of travel, and logistics got a bit much," California League president Charlie Blaney said in June 2016, when the split was announced. "It was time to make a break and go our separate ways."

Blaney also cited the desire for fans in each league to see prospects from their own league rather than players who play in cities thousands of miles away on the opposite coast, even though the interleague format gave fans in 2014 the chance to see a Corey Seager and Carlos Correa—two future rookies of the year and the starting shortstops in the 2017 World Series—on the same field in Wilmington, Del.

The first all-star games in the return to the single-league format were played at the homes of the Inland Empire 66ers and the Salem Red Sox, respectively.

The Carolina League game provided one of the summer's indelible moments, when Myrtle Beach outfielder Eloy Jimenez hit a ball in the home run derby that—in a scene straight out of "The Natural"—shattered one of the bulbs of the light tower in deep left field.

ORGANIZATION STANDINGS

Cumulative domestic farm club records for major league organizations, with winning percentages going back five years. Most organizations have six affiliates.

	2017						
	W	L	PCT	2016	2015	2014	2013
1. Yankees	491	325	.602	.595	.542	.435	.468
2. Twins	397	286	.581	.581	.435	.475	.497
3. Dodgers	378	314	.546	.527	.529	.458	.486
4. Cardinals	410	341	.546	.520	.512	.545	.494
5. Rays	406	351	.536	.529	.502	.505	.524
6. Phillies	365	326	.528	.595	.542	.435	.468
7. Astros	391	360	.521	.513	.565	.519	.570
8. D-backs	395	372	.515	.507	.509	.561	.510
9. Blue Jays	383	375	.505	.507	.485	.495	.493
10. Padres	378	371	.505	.463	.476	.472	.496
11. Brewers	344	338	.504	.443	.439	.508	.449
12. Cubs	347	341	.504	.539	.540	.522	.504
13. Tigers	368	365	.502	.474	.472	.516	.484
14. Pirates	375	376	.499	.490	.547	.450	.515
15. Red Sox	344	348	.497	.526	.469	.529	.504
16. Rockies	352	358	.496	.477	.466	.466	.482
17. Athletics	339	347	.494	.488	.483	.513	.497
18. Indians	340	349	.493	.550	.509	.495	.529
19. Angels	340	351	.492	.451	.459	.486	.501
20. Mariners	336	354	.487	.581	.435	.475	.497
21. Marlins	328	351	.483	.454	.427	.498	.497
22. Orioles	334	359	.482	.455	.524	.465	.481
23. Braves	318	357	.471	.468	.489	.493	.485
24. Rangers	321	367	.467	.491	.518	.546	.528
25. Royals	353	404	.466	.452	.497	.450	.463
26. Nationals	314	374	.456	.508	.469	.514	.550
27. Mets	344	411	.456	.480	.532	.568	.546
28. Reds	312	373	.456	.502	.512	.489	.426
29. Giants	307	381	.446	.483	.504	.509	.564
30. White Sox	302	387	.438	.427	.504	.456	.488

POSTSEASON RESULTS

LEAGUE	CHAMPION	RUNNER-UP
International	Durham	Scranton/W-B
Pacific Coast	Memphis	El Paso
Eastern	Altoona	Trenton
Southern	Pensacola/Chattanooga	N/A
Texas	Midland	Tulsa
California	Modesto	Lancaster
Carolina	Down East/Lynchburg	N/A
Florida State	Dunedin/Palm Beach	N/A
Midwest	Quad Cities	Fort Wayne
South Atlantic	Greenville	Kannapolis
New York-Penn	Hudson Valley	Vermont
Northwest	Vancouver	Eugene
Appalachian	Elizabethton	Pulaski
Pioneer	Ogden	Great Falls
Arizona	Cubs	Giants
Gulf Coast	Yankees	Nationals

Re-Brands Aplenty

Were it not for Tebow's appearance, the story of the minor league season would undoubtedly have belonged to the continuing trend of branding and re-branding, both for single games and for the long-term.

Five teams changed their names for the 2017 season. After moving from the California League, the High Desert Mavericks became the Down East Wood Ducks. After their move to Kissimmee, Fla., the former Brevard County Manatees became the Florida Fire Frogs. The latter change is particularly notable because it represented the only team in the Atlanta chain to have a nickname other than "Braves." They'll have company in 2018, when Gwinnett changes its name to one of six choices—the Buttons, the Gobblers, the Big Mouths, the Hush Puppies, the Lamb Chops or the Sweet Teas.

The Binghamton Mets became the Rumble Ponies, the New Orleans Zephyrs became the Baby Cakes and the Jacksonville Suns became the Jumbo Shrimp.

As an odd aside, the Gobblers, a finalist for the Gwinnett franchise's new name, was also in the running to be Binghamton's new name.

As is always the case when a minor league team changes its name, each team was met with plenty of online scorn. Fans on social media scorched them all, but the merchandise still moved off the shelves at a rapid pace.

Jacksonville owner Ken Babby—who also owns Double-A Akron and oversaw its name change from Aeros to RubberDucks in 2014—saw similarities between the two processes.

"The rebranding process in Akron was different—every community is different. You would never come into Jacksonville and try to operate it like we do in Akron, but there are some core principles in terms of listening to what our fans want and presenting it every night in an experience that is fun for families and affordable with something for everyone," Babby said. "In both communities we've put in picnic areas like our tiki terrace (in Jacksonville) and built great fan experiences with exceptional food yet found ways to keep the costs very affordable. There are similar elements that you'd find if you walked into both ballparks, but really each community is different and we recognized the uniqueness of both markets."

After the name change in Akron, attendance at Canal Park went up 18.7 percent the next season. Similarly, the Jumbo Shrimp's attendance was up 23.2 percent from 2016 (from 264,401 fans in 2016 to 325,743 fans in 2017).

Binghamton saw a 10.1 percent increase after its name change, and the Baby Cakes got 3.1 percent more fans. All three teams that changed names without moving to a different stadium saw their attendance jump.

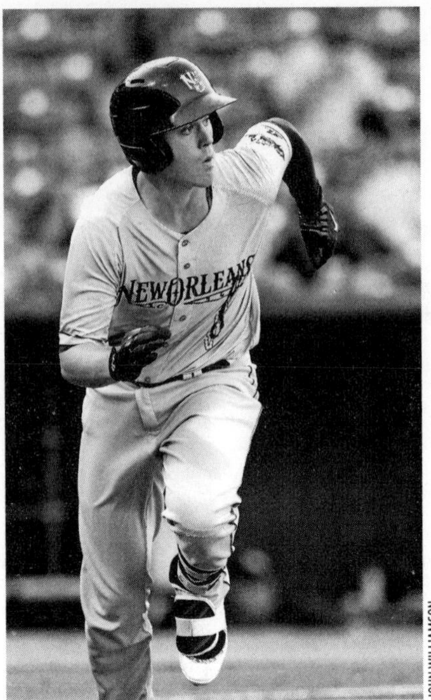

JOHN WILLIAMSON

The New Orleans Baby Cakes saw attendance spike after a rebranding effort.

Besides the full rebrands, there were scores of one-night name changes in the minor leagues this year, too. The Fresno Grizzlies kept their highly successful Tacos alter-ego rolling, and plenty of other teams followed suit with food themed one-offs. The Lakewood BlueClaws became the Pork Rolls. The Sacramento River Cats became the Tomatoes. The Reading Fightin' Phils became the Whoopie Pies. The Aberdeen IronBirds became the Stone Crabs. The Staten Island Yankees (who almost had a name change of their own for 2017) became the Cannolis. And that's just the beginning.

According to records provided by Minor League Baseball, there were 478 specialty jerseys approved for the 2017 season across its 160 clubs. That works out to an average of nearly three per team, and doesn't count each team's traditional uniforms.

So while it might lead to negative comments online, name changes do tend to pay off where they matter most—at the cash register.

CONTINUED ON PAGE 358

'Advanced' Acuna Breaks Out

BY KYLE GLASER

PLAYER OF THE YEAR

It took Damon Berryhill just two at-bats to realize Ronald Acuna was special.

It was July 13. Berryhill, the manager of the Braves' Triple-A Gwinnett affiliate, had just received the touted Acuna after his promotion from Double-A Mississippi. Berryhill placed Acuna in Gwinnett's leadoff spot immediately, eager to see how the precocious Venezuelan would fare.

"His first game, we're facing Charlotte and he swung at (consecutive) sliders to strike out his first at-bat," Berryhill said. "He was probably excited; it was the one time I did see him chase out of the zone. But his next at-bat, he walked up and first slider (in the zone) he saw, he hit it over the right-field wall for a home run. Right then, I knew, this is what they've been telling me."

Ronald Acuna

Acuna delivered a minor league season for the record books in 2017. At the tender age of 19, he shot from high Class A to Double-A to Triple-A, and managed to perform better at every level. Overall he hit .325 with 21 home runs, 82 RBIs and 44 stolen bases. He did it all while showcasing top-flight speed, strong defense in center field and a big arm.

For a historic season not even he saw coming, Acuna is Baseball America's 2017 Minor League Player of the Year.

"Before the season started my goal this year was 45 stolen bases and 15 home runs, but I got 20 home runs already, so that was cool," Acuna said through a translator. "I didn't expect it to be in Triple-A. When I got called up from high A to Double-A I wasn't surprised because they told me it was going to be one month in high A. When I got called up from Double-A to Triple-A, that was a surprise. I did not expect that at all."

The Braves front office didn't either.

Acuna was limited to just 40 games last season at low Class A Rome because of a broken thumb, and his numbers at high Class A Florida to start this season—.287 with an .814 OPS—were solid but not jaw-dropping.

But Braves player development personnel saw something beyond the stat line, something they felt would allow Acuna to do the improbable and actually perform better as the competition level improved.

"It was the approach," Braves assistant farm director Jonathan Schuerholz said. "You see him laying off breaking balls out of the zone, he's swinging at fastballs, he's hitting balls hard when he is getting pitches to hit. He's playing plus defense. He's doing everything we look at that aren't necessarily stat-driven markers . . . His approach was such, it was an advanced approach for that level."

Advanced for the level is a common theme with Acuna, who became a force in the minors and made the Braves front office dig into their past to learn how to handle best.

"Talking internally about how we were going to handle this season, it took us back to the days of Andruw Jones," Schuerholz said. "I'm not trying to make a comparison there at all, because I don't think it's fair to do that. But in terms of a very talented player and how he progresses through, we went back to (former scouting director) Paul Snyder and the days when they were bringing Andruw through and the common thread was, 'When he shows you he's ready at a level, move him up. Don't let him just sit at a level and get bored, because he's one of those special players who will rise to the challenge and will shine at every level if you let him.' And as you can tell, he did that."

PREVIOUS 10 WINNERS

2006: Alex Gordon, 3b, Wichita (Royals)
2007: Jay Bruce, of, Sarasota/Chattanooga/Louisville (Reds)
2008: Matt Wieters, c, Frederick/Bowie (Orioles)
2009: Jason Heyward, Myrtle Beach/Mississippi (Braves)
2010: Jeremy Hellickson, Montgomery/Durham (Rays)
2011: Mike Trout, Arkansas (Angels)
2012: Wil Myers, Northwest Arkansas/Omaha (Royals)
2013: Byron Buxton, Cedar Rapids/Fort Myers (Twins)
2014: Kris Bryant, Iowa (Cubs)
2015: Blake Snell, Charlotte/Montgomery/Durham (Rays)
2016: Yoan Moncada, Salem/Portland (Red Sox)

Full list: BaseballAmerica.com/awards

Keur Takes His Magic To The FSL

For three consecutive seasons, Ryan Keur was the best the Appalachian League had to offer. He won the league's executive of the year award in each of his three seasons as the general manager of the Burlington Royals. The industry took notice.

Keur jumped from the Appy League to the Florida State League in 2017 when he joined the Daytona Tortugas as the team's president. He took over a team that ranked third in the FSL in attendance and helped boost in to second place, behind only the Clearwater Threshers, who have led the league in attendance every year since 2011.

In Keur's first year, the Tortugas added more than 24,000 more fans to their season total. Even more impressively, the team added all those extra fans without the benefit of an appearance from St. Lucie and Tim Tebow, which was shown all year to draw fans in droves.

Keur helped spearhead two of the best promotions in the minor leagues: Bob Ross bobblehead night, which included a painting lesson like the late artist would have given on television. The other big hit involved a tribute to the late NBA analyst Craig Sager, a resident of the Daytona area, and included spectacularly colorful jerseys and an appearance from NBA all-star Vince Carter.

EXECUTIVE OF THE YEAR

PREVIOUS WINNERS

2006: Alan Ledford, Sacramento River Cats (Pacific Coast)
2007: Mike Moore, Minor League Baseball
2008: Naomi Silver, Rochester Red Wings (International)
2009: Ken Young, Norfolk Tides (International)
2010: Monty Hoppel, Midland Rockhounds (Texas)
2011: Todd Parnell, Richmond Flying Squirrels (Eastern)
2012: Bob Richmond, Northwest League
2013: Martie Cordaro, Omaha Storm Chasers (Pacific)
2014: Sam Bernabe, Iowa Cubs (Pacific Coast)
2015: Dave Oster, Lake Elsinore (California)
2016: Tom Kayser, President of the Texas League

Full list: BaseballAmerica.com/awards

CONTINUED FROM PAGE 356

Hurricane Scuttles Playoffs

This year has produced some particularly disastrous weather that has affected nearly every part of the country. Minor League Baseball wasn't immune to its effects.

When Hurricane Irma made landfall in the southeastern part of the country, the playoffs were just getting started, but the minds of the players, coaches and fans were understandably elsewhere, so the impacted leagues took action.

The Florida State League made the first move by cancelling its championship series altogether. That meant that the winners of each division series would be awarded shares of the title.

"I'm just really afraid of what's happening here," Florida State League president Ken Carson said. "I didn't meet any resistance at all, so that was a good thing."

The move left Dunedin (which topped Tampa) and Palm Beach (which beat Fort Myers) with the first shared FSL championship since 2004, when a hurricane also interfered.

Similar action was taken in the Southern League, where Pensacola and Chattanooga split the title because of their division series victories.

Southern League president Lori Webb also adjusted the Southern Division Series logistics because of damage Irma did to Florida's west coast.

Although Pensacola swept Jacksonville in three games at Blue Wahoos Stadium, there were no plans to head back to Jacksonville if the series had required decisive fourth and fifth games. Instead, the series would have been moved to Biloxi's MGM Stadium.

The Carolina League took similar action as well when it shortened its Division Series and awarded Down East and Lynchburg shares of its championship because Irma had begun moving up the coast toward CL territory.

"This was not an easy decision," CL president John Hopkins said at the time. "While much remains uncertain with this storm, it seems clear that there will be major damage wherever it goes, as there already has been in some Caribbean nations. Our immediate area remains at risk, too.

"Our game has a number of people who call Florida and the Caribbean home. With the prospect of potentially devastating impact, it just felt right to call it a season after this weekend's first round."

It was the first co-championship in the CL since 1999.

Memphis Flips For Clapp

Unless he's a Hall of Fame player, the announcement of a minor league managerial assignment barely gets noticed.

But Stubby Clapp's ties to Memphis were anything but normal. Clapp's return to Memphis was a perfect match of team and manager, as fans were thrilled to see a fan favorite return.

The Ontario native first played in Memphis in 1999. He spent much of the next four years playing for the Redbirds and becoming the most recognizable player on the team, thanks to his hard-nosed approach and the Ozzie Smith-style backflips he'd do before the game.

Clapp was such a part of Memphis lore that the team retired his No. 10 when he hung up his cleats. The team has also released multiple Stubby Clapp bobbleheads.

After his retirement, Clapp became a manager and coach in the Astros organization before becoming a hitting coach in the Blue Jays' organization. But this year, he and the Cardinals reunited in a move that worked out wonderfully for both sides.

MANAGER OF THE YEAR

PREVIOUS 10 WINNERS

2006: Todd Claus, Portland (Red Sox)
2007: Matt Wallbeck, Erie (Tigers)
2008: Rocket Wheeler, Myrtle Beach (Braves)
2009: Charlie Montoyo, Durham (Rays)
2010: Mike Sarbaugh, Columbus (Indians)
2011: Ryne Sandberg, Lehigh Valley (Phillies)
2012: Dave Miley, Scranton/Wilkes-Barre (Yankees)
2013: Gary DiSarcina, Pawtucket (Red Sox)
2014: Mark Johnson, Kane County (Cubs)
2015: Tony DeFrancesco, Fresno (Astros)
2016: Dave Wallace, Akron (Indians)

Full list: BaseballAmerica.com/awards

Under Clapp, Memphis won a club-record 91 games, finishing 91-50 to win the Southern Division by 22 games. Memphis then knocked off Colorado Springs and El Paso to win the Redbirds' third-ever Pacific Coast League title.

Memphis then fell in the Triple-A championship game to Durham.

Fanti Among Year's Best

There were some pretty amazing feats on the field this year, too. Chief among them was Nick Fanti throwing 17.1 innings of no-hit ball across two starts with low Class A Lakewood.

The lefthander came one out short of a solo no-hitter on May 6 against Columbia. He threw 113 pitches before being removed for closer Trevor Bettencourt, who put the finishing touches on Lakewood's fifth franchise no-hitter.

Fanti got another chance to finish the job on July 17 against Charleston, and this time he was up to the task. He struck out 12 RiverDogs during a matinee and allowed just a walk all afternoon.

Like any no-hitter, however, when Fanti got the last out—a flyball to center fielder Mickey Moniak—there was an overwhelming sense of relief.

"I'm really excited about it," he said, "and it was nice to finally finish one."

Not to be outdone the GCL Nationals threw no-hitters in both ends of their doubleheader against the GCL Marlins on July 17. Four pitchers combined for the back-to-back no-nos.

A year after Indians prospect Francisco Mejia put together a 50-game hitting streak, another prospect with an Ohio-based parent club went on a tear.

Dayton outfielder Jose Siri hit in 39 straight games, a run that ended on Aug. 4 with a bit of controversy attached. Great Lakes reliever Ryan Moseley threw behind Siri in his final at-bat en route to a streak-ending walk.

Short-season Eugene and Boise gave fans a little more than they bargained for on July 4 when the teams combined for a 20-inning game that lasted more than six hours. Even though the holiday had passed, the Emeralds still shot off fireworks afterward.

Elsewhere in the Northwest League, the Salem-Keizer Volcanoes became the first team to delay a game because of a total solar eclipse. In a promotion a year in the making, the team opened its gates at 5 a.m., hosted breakfast for its fans, and then started their game at 9:30 a.m. with the plan of delaying the action as soon as eclipse reached totality over their park.

A host of teams across the country held similar events in conjunction with the eclipse as well, including in Columbia, Charleston and Nashville.

With plenty of action and oddities both on the field and off, 2017 made itself one to remember in the minor leagues.

CLASSIFICATION ALL-STARS

TRIPLE-A

Pos	Player	Age	AVG	OBP	SLG	G	AB	H	2B	3B	HR	BB	SO	SB
C	Mitch Garver, Rochester (Twins)	26	.291	.387	.541	88	320	93	29	0	17	50	85	2
1B	Rhys Hoskins, Lehigh Valley (Phillies)	24	.284	.385	.581	115	401	114	24	4	29	64	75	4
2B	Yoan Moncada, Charlotte (White Sox)	22	.282	.377	.447	80	309	87	9	3	12	49	102	17
3B	Ryan McMahon, Albuquerque (Rockies)	22	.374	.411	.612	70	289	108	23	2	14	21	53	4
SS	Amed Rosario, Las Vegas (Mets)	21	.328	.367	.466	94	393	129	19	7	7	23	67	19
OF	Lewis Brinson, Colo. Springs (Brewers)	23	.331	.400	.562	76	299	99	22	4	13	32	62	11
OF	Franchy Cordero, El Paso (Padres)	22	.326	.369	.603	93	390	127	21	18	17	23	118	15
OF	Derek Fisher, Fresno (Astros)	23	.318	.384	.583	84	343	109	26	1	21	35	74	16
DH	Willie Calhoun, Round Rock (Rangers)	22	.300	.355	.572	128	486	146	27	6	31	42	61	4

Pos	Pitcher	Age	W	L	ERA	G	GS	SV	IP	HR	BB	SO	AVG	SO/9
SP	Chance Adams, Scranton/W-B (Yankees)	22	11	5	2.89	21	21	0	115	9	43	103	.197	8.0
SP	Steven Brault, Indianapolis (Pirates)	25	10	5	1.94	21	20	0	120	5	44	109	.199	8.2
SP	Yonny Chirinos, Durham (Rays)	23	12	5	2.74	23	22	0	141	10	22	120	.227	7.7
SP	Tom Eshelman, Lehigh Valley (Phillies)	23	10	3	2.23	18	18	0	121	8	13	80	.227	6.0
SP	Wilmer Font, Oklahoma City (Dodgers)	27	10	8	3.42	25	25	0	134	11	35	178	.222	11.9
RP	Jimmie Sherfy, Reno (D-backs)	25	2	1	3.12	44	0	20	49	6	10	61	.211	11.2

DOUBLE-A

Pos	Player	Age	AVG	OBP	SLG	G	AB	H	2B	3B	HR	BB	SO	SB
C	Francisco Mejia, Akron (Indians)	21	.297	.346	.490	92	347	103	21	2	14	24	53	7
1B	Kevin Cron, Jackson (D-backs)	24	.283	.357	.497	138	515	146	35	0	25	56	134	1
2B	Scott Kingery, Reading (Phillies)	23	.313	.379	.608	69	278	87	18	5	18	28	51	19
3B	Rafael Devers, Portland (Red Sox)	20	.300	.369	.575	77	287	86	19	3	18	31	55	0
SS	Jorge Mateo, Midland (Athletics)	22	.296	.357	.521	60	257	76	14	10	8	24	65	24
OF	Austin Hays, Bowie (Orioles)	21	.330	.367	.594	64	261	86	17	2	16	13	45	1
OF	D.J. Stewart, Bowie (Orioles)	23	.278	.378	.481	126	457	127	26	2	21	65	87	20
OF	Justin Williams, Montgomery (Rays)	21	.301	.364	.489	96	366	110	21	3	14	37	69	6
DH	Edwin Rios, Tulsa (Dodgers)	23	.317	.358	.533	77	306	97	21	0	15	17	69	1

Pos	Pitcher	Age	W	L	ERA	G	GS	SV	IP	HR	BB	SO	AVG	SO/9
SP	Corbin Burnes, Biloxi (Brewers)	22	3	3	2.10	16	16	0	86	2	20	84	.212	8.8
SP	Michael Kopech, Birmingham (White Sox)	21	8	7	2.87	22	22	0	119	6	60	155	.184	11.7
SP	Tyler Mahle, Pensacola (Reds)	22	7	3	1.59	14	14	0	85	5	17	87	.190	9.2
SP	Corey Oswalt, Binghamton (Mets)	23	12	5	2.28	24	24	0	134	9	40	119	.236	8.0
SP	Mike Soroka, Mississippi (Braves)	19	11	8	2.75	26	26	0	154	10	34	125	.233	7.3
RP	Gabriel Moya, Chattanooga (Twins)	22	6	1	0.77	47	0	24	58	2	15	87	.150	13.4

HIGH CLASS A

Pos	Player	Age	AVG	OBP	SLG	G	AB	H	2B	3B	HR	BB	SO	SB
C	Alex Jackson, Florida (Braves)	21	.272	.333	.502	66	257	70	17	0	14	13	74	0
1B	Pete Alonso, St. Lucie (Mets)	22	.286	.361	.516	82	308	88	23	0	16	25	64	3
2B	Brandon Lowe, Charlotte (Rays)	22	.311	.403	.524	90	315	98	34	3	9	47	65	6
3B	Michael Chavis, Salem (Red Sox)	21	.318	.388	.641	59	223	71	17	2	17	19	57	1
SS	Brendan Rodgers, Lancaster (Rockies)	20	.387	.407	.671	51	222	86	21	3	12	6	35	2
OF	Eloy Jimenez, Winston-Salem (White Sox)	20	.302	.375	.570	71	265	80	17	3	16	30	56	0
OF	D.J. Peters, Rancho Cucamonga (Dodgers)	21	.276	.372	.514	132	504	139	29	5	27	64	189	3
OF	Victor Robles, Potomac (Nationals)	20	.289	.377	.495	77	291	84	25	7	7	25	62	16
DH	Ryan Mountcastle, Frederick (Orioles)	20	.314	.343	.542	88	360	113	35	1	15	14	61	8

Pos	Pitcher	Age	W	L	ERA	G	GS	SV	IP	HR	BB	SO	AVG	SO/9
SP	Jose Almonte, Visalia (D-backs)	21	11	8	3.55	27	27	0	139	10	66	162	.243	10.5
SP	Caleb Ferguson, Rancho Cucamonga (Dodgers)	20	9	4	2.87	25	24	0	122	6	55	140	.246	10.3
SP	Matt Hall, Lakeland (Tigers)	23	7	6	2.44	19	18	0	103	4	38	110	.250	9.6
SP	Triston McKenzie, Lynchburg (Indians)	19	12	6	3.46	25	25	0	143	14	45	186	.203	11.7
SP	Nick Neidert, Modesto (Mariners)	20	10	3	2.76	19	19	0	104	7	17	109	.244	9.4
RP	Nate Griep, Carolina (Brewers)	23	3	1	2.37	45	0	30	49	3	24	41	.191	7.5

CLASSIFICATION ALL-STARS

LOW CLASS A

Pos	Player	Age	AVG	OBP	SLG	G	AB	H	2B	3B	HR	BB	SO	SB
C	Keibert Ruiz, Great Lakes (Dodgers)	18	.317	.372	.423	63	227	72	16	1	2	18	30	0
1B	Darick Hall, Lakewood (Phillies)	21	.272	.340	.533	114	426	116	28	1	27	29	110	0
2B	Bo Bichette, Lansing (Blue Jays)	19	.384	.448	.623	70	284	109	32	3	10	28	55	12
3B	Vladimir Guerrero Jr., Lansing (Blue Jays)	18	.316	.409	.480	71	269	85	21	1	7	40	34	6
SS	Fernando Tatis Jr., Fort Wayne (Padres)	18	.281	.390	.520	117	431	121	26	7	21	75	124	29
OF	Estevan Florial, Charleston (Yankees)	19	.297	.373	.483	91	344	102	21	5	11	41	124	17
OF	Jose Siri, Dayton (Reds)	21	.293	.341	.530	126	498	146	24	11	24	33	130	46
OF	Taylor Trammell, Dayton (Reds)	19	.281	.368	.450	129	491	138	24	10	13	71	123	41
DH	Jesus Sanchez, Bowling Green (Rays)	19	.305	.348	.478	117	475	145	29	4	15	32	91	7

Pos	Pitcher	Age	W	L	ERA	G	GS	SV	IP	HR	BB	SO	AVG	SO/9
SP	Luis Escobar, West Virginia (Pirates)	21	10	7	3.83	26	25	0	132	9	60	168	.200	11.5
SP	Nick Fanti, Lakewood (Phillies)	20	9	2	2.54	21	21	0	120	5	28	121	.200	9.1
SP	Alex Wells, Delmarva (Orioles)	20	11	5	2.38	25	25	0	140	16	10	113	.222	7.3
SP	Joey Wentz, Rome (Braves)	19	8	3	2.60	26	26	0	132	4	46	152	.209	10.4
SP	Bryse Wilson, Rome (Braves)	19	10	7	2.50	26	26	0	137	8	37	139	.211	9.1
RP	Tommy Eveld, Kane County (D-backs)	23	1	0	0.33	22	0	14	28	0	8	33	.111	10.7

SHORT-SEASON

Pos	Player	Age	AVG	OBP	SLG	G	AB	H	2B	3B	HR	BB	SO	SB
C	Daulton Varsho, Hillsboro (D-backs)	20	.311	.368	.534	50	193	60	16	3	7	17	30	7
1B	Pavin Smith, Hillsboro (D-backs)	21	.318	.401	.415	51	195	62	15	2	0	27	24	2
2B	Joseph Rosa, Everett (Mariners)	20	.296	.374	.531	44	179	53	16	4	6	22	46	4
3B	Evan Mendoza, State College (Cardinals)	21	.370	.431	.549	41	162	60	14	3	3	16	33	1
SS	Nolan Jones, Mahoning Valley (Indians)	19	.313	.429	.477	61	214	67	17	3	4	43	59	1
OF	Greg Deichmann, Vermont (Athletics)	22	.283	.392	.547	44	159	45	10	4	8	27	37	4
OF	Scott Hurst, State College (Cardinals)	21	.294	.368	.451	53	204	60	11	6	3	22	51	6
OF	Jhailyn Ortiz, Williamsport (Phillies)	18	.302	.401	.560	47	159	48	15	1	8	18	47	5
DH	Ben Breazeale, Aberdeen (Orioles)	22	.323	.433	.474	56	192	62	14	0	5	37	56	3

Pos	Pitcher	Age	W	L	ERA	G	GS	SV	IP	HR	BB	SO	AVG	SO/9
SP	Parker Dunshee, Vermont (Athletics)	22	1	0	0.00	12	9	0	38	0	8	45	.119	10.6
SP	Austin Franklin, Hudson Valley (Rays)	19	4	2	2.21	13	13	0	69	4	31	71	.207	9.2
SP	Jorge Guzman, Staten Island (Yankees)	21	5	3	2.30	13	13	0	67	4	18	88	.212	11.9
SP	Zac Lowther, Aberdeen (Orioles)	21	2	2	1.79	11	11	0	50	1	10	66	.194	11.8
SP	Cole Ragans, Spokane (Rangers)	19	3	2	3.61	13	13	0	57	5	35	87	.234	13.7
RP	Denyi Reyes, Lowell (Red Sox)	20	9	0	1.45	15	0	0	62	3	7	53	.221	7.7

ROOKIE

Pos	Player	Age	AVG	OBP	SLG	G	AB	H	2B	3B	HR	BB	SO	SB
C	Ronaldo Hernandez, Princeton (Rays)	19	.332	.382	.507	54	223	74	22	1	5	16	39	2
1B	Ryan Noda, Bluefield (Blue Jays)	21	.364	.507	.575	66	214	78	18	3	7	59	60	7
2B	Esteury Ruiz, AZL Padres	18	.350	.395	.602	52	206	72	20	10	4	13	54	26
3B	Rylan Bannon, Ogden (Dodgers)	21	.333	.422	.598	36	132	44	5	0	10	16	25	4
SS	Royce Lewis, GCL Twins	18	.271	.390	.414	36	133	36	6	2	3	19	17	15
OF	Akil Baddoo, Elizabethton (Twins)	18	.323	.436	.527	53	201	65	19	5	4	36	32	9
OF	Michael Gigliotti, Burlington (Royals)	21	.329	.442	.477	42	155	51	8	3	3	32	21	15
OF	Heliot Ramos, AZL Giants	17	.348	.404	.645	35	138	48	11	6	6	10	48	10
DH	Mason Martin, GCL Pirates	18	.307	.457	.630	39	127	39	8	0	11	32	41	2

Pos	Pitcher	Age	W	L	ERA	G	GS	SV	IP	HR	BB	SO	AVG	SO/9
SP	Sal Biasi, Burlington (Royals)	21	4	2	2.41	13	8	0	56	4	23	54	.186	8.7
SP	Maverik Buffo, GCL Blue Jays	21	5	1	0.53	11	6	0	34	0	2	36	.222	9.5
SP	Hans Crouse, AZL Rangers	18	0	0	0.45	10	6	0	20	1	7	30	.109	13.5
SP	MacKenzie Gore, AZL Padres	18	0	1	1.27	7	7	0	21	0	7	34	.184	14.3
SP	Jhordany Mezquita, GCL Phillies	19	3	0	0.72	9	9	0	38	0	12	35	.160	8.4
RP	Jovani Moran, Elizabethton (Twins)	20	3	1	0.36	11	0	0	25	1	6	45	.145	16.4

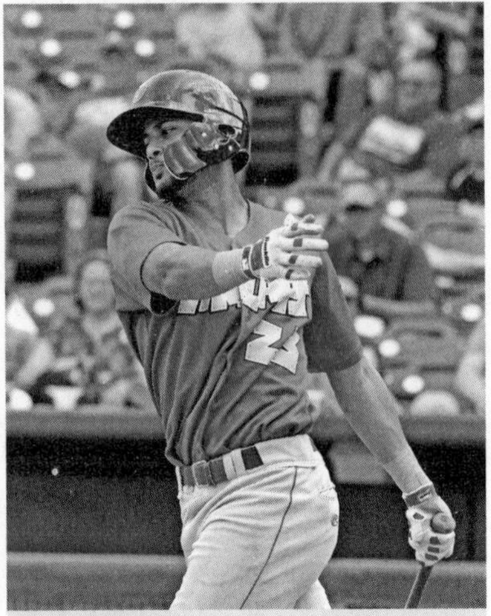

Padres shortstop Fernando Tatis Jr., hit 22 home runs as an 18-year-old.

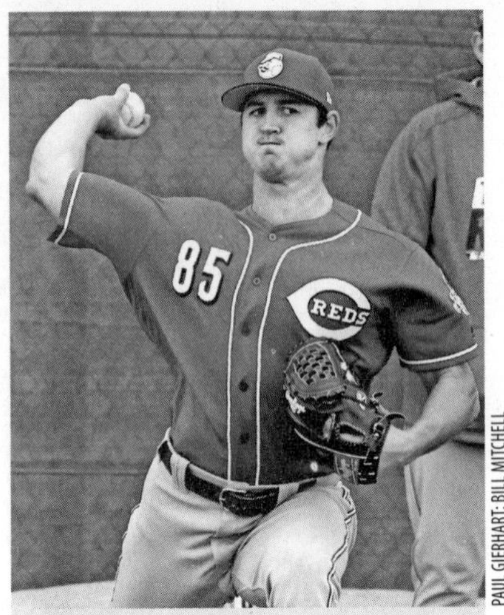

Reds righthander Tyler Mahle held hitters to a .208 average in 2017.

PAUL GIERHART; BILL MITCHELL

FIRST TEAM

Pos	Player, Organization (Highest Level)	Age	AVG	OBP	SLG	AB	R	H	HR	RBI	BB	SO
C	Danny Jansen, Blue Jays (AAA)	22	.323	.400	.484	368	50	119	10	48	41	40
1B	Rhys Hoskins, Phillies (AAA)	24	.284	.385	.581	401	78	114	29	91	64	75
2B	Bo Bichette, Blue Jays (HiA)	19	.362	.423	.565	448	88	162	14	74	42	81
3B	Nick Senzel, Reds (AA)	22	.321	.391	.514	455	81	146	14	65	49	97
SS	Fernando Tatis Jr., Padres (AA)	18	.278	.379	.498	486	84	135	22	75	77	141
OF	Ronald Acuna, Braves (AAA)	19	.325	.374	.522	557	88	181	21	82	43	144
OF	Austin Hays, Orioles (AA)	22	.329	.365	.593	523	81	172	32	95	25	85
OF	Eloy Jimenez, White Sox (AA)	20	.312	.379	.568	333	54	104	19	65	35	72
DH	Vladimir Guerrero Jr., Blue Jays (HiA)	18	.323	.425	.485	437	84	141	13	76	76	62

Pos	Pitcher, Organization (Highest Level)	Age	W	L	ERA	G	GS	IP	H	BB	SO	AVG
SP	Jon Duplantier, Diamondbacks (HiA)	23	12	3	1.39	25	24	136	91	42	165	.192
SP	Corbin Burnes, Brewers (AA)	22	8	3	1.67	26	26	146	103	36	140	.200
SP	Jack Flaherty, Cardinals (AAA)	21	14	4	2.18	25	25	149	120	35	147	.221
SP	Chance Adams, Yankees (AAA)	23	15	5	2.45	27	27	150	104	58	135	.193
SP	Tyler Mahle, Reds (AAA)	22	10	7	2.06	24	24	144	109	30	138	.208
RP	Gabriel Moya, Twins (AA)	22	6	1	0.77	47	0	58	30	15	87	.150

SECOND TEAM

Pos	Player (High Level)	Age	AVG	OBP	SLG	AB	R	H	HR	RBI	BB	SO
C	Francisco Mejia, Indians (AA)	21	.297	.346	.490	347	52	103	14	52	24	53
1B	Ryan McMahon, Rockies (AAA)	22	.355	.403	.583	470	74	167	20	88	41	92
2B	Scott Kingery, Phillies (AAA)	23	.304	.359	.530	543	103	165	26	65	41	109
3B	Rafael Devers, Red Sox (AAA)	20	.311	.377	.578	322	54	100	20	60	34	63
SS	Amed Rosario, Mets (AAA)	21	.328	.367	.466	393	66	129	7	58	23	67
OF	Derek Fisher, Astros (AAA)	24	.318	.384	.583	343	63	109	21	66	35	74
OF	Estevan Florial, Yankees (HiA)	19	.298	.372	.479	420	77	125	13	57	50	148
OF	Victor Robles, Nationals (AA)	20	.300	.382	.493	430	73	129	10	47	37	84
DH	Willie Calhoun, Rangers (AAA)	22	.300	.355	.572	486	80	146	31	93	42	61

Pos	Pitcher (Highest Level)	Age	W	L	ERA	G	GS	IP	H	BB	SO	AVG
SP	Michael Kopech, White Sox (AAA)	21	9	8	2.88	25	25	134	92	65	172	.193
SP	Alec Hansen, White Sox (AA)	22	11	8	2.80	26	26	141	114	51	191	.216
SP	Merandy Gonzalez, Marlins (HiA)	21	13	3	1.66	22	20	130	101	26	103	.212
SP	Zack Littell, Twins (AA)	21	19	1	2.12	27	25	157	135	41	142	.236
SP	Joey Lucchesi, Padres (AA)	24	11	7	2.20	24	23	139	102	33	148	.200
RP	Jimmy Herget, Reds (AAA)	23	4	4	2.90	52	0	62	52	21	72	.226

Midland Goes Four-For-Four

TEAM OF THE YEAR

When the Midland RockHounds arrived to begin the 2017 season, there was a message on the clubhouse whiteboard reminding them of their responsibility.

Midland's 2014, 2015 and 2016 teams had all won Texas League titles. No one wanted to be the team that broke the streak.

"There was some pride in wanting to defend the title and win four in a row. We did have eight or nine players who had some hand in last year's championship," Midland manager Fran Riordan said. "Winning three in a row is pretty special, but to have a chance to compete for a fourth, guys weren't shy about bringing it up."

BILL MITCHELL
A.J. Puk

In each of the past three seasons, Midland had clearly been one of the top teams in the league. The 2017 champs survived every test by the narrowest of margins.

Midland lost six consecutive games in the final 10 days of the season, washing away any margin of error it had in its battle with Corpus Christi for the South Division's wild card spot. But the RockHounds then won three of their last four regular season games. That was just enough to get them into a tie with the Hooks at 67-71. Midland's 17-13 record against Corpus Christi was the tiebreaker that earned them a playoff spot.

In the playoffs, Midland fell behind San Antonio 2-1 in the best-of-5 semifinal series, but rallied to win back-to-back elimination games to advance to the finals. In the finals, Tulsa jumped out to a 2-0 lead in the best-of-5 series, but Midland rallied once again, winning back-to-back-to-back elimination games to win its fourth straight Texas League title.

In the deciding Game 5, Visosergy Rosa drove in Jorge Mateo with an RBI single in the first and five Midland pitchers combined for a shutout as Midland held on for a 1-0 win.

Midland faced seven must-win games in the final two weeks of its 2017 season. It won them all.

"I think reslience is the first thing that comes to mind," Riordan said. "It was just an example of guys playing their best baseball when they needed it the most. From the last day of the regular season to the last game, we had six elimination games. Each time there was a positive response."

The RockHounds streak was probably in most jeopardy in Game Three of the championship series. Tulsa sent rehabbing big leaguer Brandon McCarthy to the mound. McCarthy was effective, but Heath Fillmyer and the Midland bullpen combined for a shutout in a 2-0 win.

"That gave us a lot of cofidence becaue we beat a quality big leaguer," Riordan said.

The fourth straight title is the longest streak in the Texas League in nearly a century (Fort Worth won six straight from 1920-25). It's the longest streak in pro baseball in nearly 20 years (Harrisburg won four straight Eastern League titles from 1996-1999).

More than 40 Midland players played on two of the championship teams. Ryan Doolittle, Kyle Finnegan, Chris Jensen and Jake Sanchez played on three different title teams and catcher Beau Taylor earned four rings.

Midland's streak stretches far enough that now Cubs' shortstop Addison Russell played for the first of the four championship teams in the year he was traded to the Cubs.

A.J. Puk, Jorge Mateo and Max Schrock were among the notable prospects who played for Midland during the 2017 season.

PREVIOUS 10 WINNERS

2006: Tucson/Pacific Coast (Diamondbacks)
2007: San Antonio/Texas (Padres)
2008: Frisco/Texas (Rangers)
2009: Akron/Eastern (Indians)
2010: Northwest Arkansas/Texas (Royals)
2011: Mobile BayBears/Southern (Diamondbacks)
2012: Springfield Cardinals/Texas (Cardinals)
2013: Daytona Cubs/Florida State (Cubs)
2014: Portland Sea Dogs/Eastern League (Red Sox)
2015: Biloxi Shuckers/Southern League (Brewers)
2016: Rome Braves/South Atlantic League (Braves)

Full list: BaseballAmerica.com/awards

ALL-STAR FUTURES GAME

BY J.J. COOPER

MIAMI

Every Futures Game leaves a memory.

It can be a young Angels outfielder introducing himself to the world a couple of years before everyone else caught up on the greatness of Mike Trout.

It can be Carlos Correa showing off his all-around game, or Giancarlo Stanton giving a sneak peek at his power.

Last year Yoan Moncada and Eloy Jimenez burst onto the national scene with standout performances, helping the World top the U.S. for the first time in seven years.

This year, the U.S. got its revenge, as a well-rounded lineup pounded hit after hit in the early innings, then hung on for a 7-6 win.

But this game didn't have one or two players who took the game and made it theirs. Rays righthander and U.S. starting pitcher Brent Honeywell came the closest. He was named the game's MVP after striking out four in two scoreless innings of work.

When it comes to memories, a game with no one clear star reminded us more than anything that baseball is in very good hands when it comes to young talent.

Honeywell showed his five pitches in two electric innings; White Sox righthander Michael Kopech blew hitters away with a lively, easy 100-plus mph fastball; Braves center fielder Ronald Acuna got to display his plus arm.

And Blue Jays third baseman Vladimir Guerrero Jr., the youngest player in the game, looked very much at ease, finishing as one of just three players to get two hits. Guerrero turned around 99 mph from Orioles lefthander Tanner Scott and made it look easy.

The crisply played game was not lacking for standout efforts. They were just spread around the park.

Marlins third baseman Brian Anderson had two hits; So did Mets catcher Tomas Nido; Tigers righthander Beau Burrows struck out two of the three batters he faced in a perfect inning.

In many ways, this Futures Game was a perfect representation of where the game is in 2017. Almost every pitcher threw really hard. On Sunday, a pitcher throwing 95 mph was routine. There were 19 fastballs thrown at 100 mph or harder and 39 pitches of 99 and up. There were just nine fastballs all game clocked at less than 93 mph.

"I don't think I saw a pitch under 93, fastball-wise" Rockies infielder Ryan McMahon said.

FUTURES GAME BOX SCORE

U.S. 7, WORLD 6
JULY 9 IN MIAMI

World	AB	R	H	RBI	U.S.	AB	R	H	RBI
Moncada, 2B	2	0	0	0	Gordon, SS	3	1	1	0
Dubon, 2B	3	1	1	0	a-Bichette, PH-SS	2	0	0	0
Verdugo, LF	2	0	0	0	Brinson, CF-LF	4	1	1	1
Robles, LF-CF	1	0	0	1	Fisher, LF	2	1	1	2
Rosario, SS	2	0	0	0	Ray, LF-CF	2	0	0	0
Fox, SS	2	0	0	1	Hoskins, 1B	2	0	1	0
Devers, 3B	4	0	1	0	McMahon, 1B	1	0	0	0
Acuna, CF-LF	4	0	0	0	Senzel, 3B	4	1	1	1
Jimenez, RF	2	0	0	0	Tucker, RF	3	0	1	1
Florial, RF	1	1	0	0	Reynolds, RF	0	0	0	0
Guerrero, DH-3B	4	2	2	0	Anderson, DH-3B	4	1	2	0
Naylor, 1B	2	0	1	1	Sisco, C	3	1	1	1
Alvarez, 1B	1	1	1	1	Collins, C	1	0	0	0
Mejia, F, C	2	1	1	0	Rodgers, 2B	1	1	1	1
Nido, C	2	0	2	2	Kingery, 2B	1	0	0	0
Totals	**34**	**6**	**9**	**6**	**Totals**	**33**	**7**	**10**	**7**

a-Flied out for Gordon in the 5th.

WORLD	**000**	**012**	**102**	**6**	**9**	**1**
UNITED STATES	**121**	**300**	**000**	**7**	**10**	**1**

World: 2B: Dubon (1, Flaherty). **RBI:** Naylor (1); Robles (1); Fox (1); Nido 2 (2); Alvarez (1). **Team RISP:** 4-for-8. **Team LOB:** 4. **E:** Moncada (1, throw).

U.S.: 2B: Anderson (1, Quantrill); Tucker (1, Soroka); Brinson (1, Acevedo); Fisher (1, Acevedo). **3B:** Sisco (1, Quantrill). **RBI:** Senzel (1); Sisco (1); Rodgers (1); Tucker (1); Brinson (1); Fisher 2 (2). **Team RISP:** 5-for-15. **Team LOB:** 9. **SB:** Brinson (1, 2nd base off Quantrill/Mejia, F); Fisher (1, 3rd base off Acevedo/Mejia, F). **Outfield assists:** Tucker (Naylor at 2nd base).

World	IP	H	R	ER	BB	SO	U.S.	IP	H	R	ER	BB	SO
Alvarez, Y (L)	1	2	1	1	1	1	Honey. (W)	2	1	0	0	0	4
Quantrill	1	2	2	2	1	0	Kopech	1	0	0	0	0	1
Soroka	1	1	1	0	0	1	Burrows	1	0	0	0	0	2
Acevedo	1	4	3	3	0	1	Scott	1	2	1	1	0	2
Escobar	1	0	0	0	1	0	Flaherty	1	2	2	2	0	1
Barria	1	0	0	0	1	2	Griffin	0.2	0	0	0	0	1
Vieira	0.2	1	0	0	1	1	Duplant.	0.1	2	1	1	1	0
Labourt	0.1	0	0	0	0	1	Herget	1	0	0	0	0	0
Guerrero	0.2	0	0	0	0	0	McKenzie	0.1	0	0	0	0	0
Hernandez	0.1	0	0	0	0	0	Puk	0.2	2	2	1	1	0
Totals	8	10	7	6	5	7	Totals	9	9	6	5	2	11

Game Scores: Alvarez, Y 38; Honeywell 54.

WP: Honeywell; Scott.

HBP: Hoskins (by Soroka).

Pitches-strikes: Alvarez, Y: 23-12; Quantrill 19-12; Soroka 13-9; Acevedo 22-18; Escobar 16-7; Barria 19-9; Vieira 16-8; Labourt 6-4; Guerrero 6-4; Hernandez 2-1; Honeywell 34-23; Kopech 9-8; Burrows 15-9; Scott 21-12; Flaherty 17-14; Griffin 10-5; Duplantier 9-4; Herget 12-9; McKenzie 2-1; Puk 17-10.

Inherited runners-scored: Labourt 2-0.

Weather: 75 degrees, roof closed. **Wind:** 0 mph, None.
First pitch: 4:09 p.m.

T: 2:59

MINOR LEAGUE ALL-STAR GAMES

TRIPLE-A: Athletics prospect Renato Nunez, who finished in a three-way tie for second in the minor leagues in home runs in 2017, hit a three-run home run that helped lift the Pacific Coast League past the International League, 6-4, in the annual interleague game, held this year at Cheney Stadium in Tacoma, Wash.

Richie Shaffer (Indians) homered for the IL in the loss, and Colin Moran (Astros) added a shot of his own for the PCL. Madison Younginer (Dodgers) got the win in relief of starter Wilmer Font. In an oddity, Font, who led MiLB in strikeouts, did not whiff a hitter in the game.

EASTERN LEAGUE: The game went the standard nine innings, but the Eastern Division only needed its seven-run sixth inning to score a 7-1 win over the Western Division.

Ryan McBroom (Blue Jays) got the scoring started with an RBI single, and Zack Zehner (Yankees) added a two-run knock a batter later. Danny Mars (Red Sox) followed with another RBI single, and Gunnar Heidt (Blue Jays) drove home two more with a double. Carlos Tocci capped the scoring with an RBI single.

SOUTHERN LEAGUE: A torrential rain in Pensacola, Fla., kept this game from being played.

TEXAS LEAGUE: The South topped the North in this game, held at Frisco's Dr. Pepper Ballpark, courtesy of a seven-run fourth inning en route to a 10-3 win.

Max Schrock (Athletics), J.D. Davis (Astros), Drew Ferguson (Astros) and J.P. Sportman (Athletics) each notched two hits in the win. Ariel Jurado (Rangers) earned the victory with a scoreless fourth inning before his team's offensive outburst.

Chuck Taylor (Angels) and Edwin Rios (Dodgers) each added home runs in the loss.

FLORIDA STATE LEAGUE: After a rainstorm cut short the pregame home run derby, Gavin LaValley (Reds) hit a pair of two-run longballs for the North in its 5-2 win over the South at Lakeland's newly renovated Joker Marchant Stadium.

LaValley's teammate Shed Long had two hits and scored twice in the win. Starter Jose Taveras, who pitched a scoreless first inning, was awarded the win.

CAROLINA: In its first season as its own all-star game after separating from the California League, the North team scored a 2-0 victory over its rivals from the South. All the offense in the game came early, on a two-run single from Michael Chavis (Red Sox) in the first inning off of starter Adbert Alzolay (Cubs).

STEPHEN GREEN PHOTOGRAPHY

Adbert Azolay

CALIFORNIA: Mariners prospect Braden Bishop stole the show in the North's 5-3 win over the South. Bishop went 4-for-4 with three runs and two stolen bases in the win, and finished a home run short of the cycle. His effort buoyed a pitching staff led by Bo Takahashi (Diamondbacks), who struck out three in two scoreless innings and earned the win in relief.

MIDWEST LEAGUE: At a rain-soaked Dow Diamond, the West got past the East by a 5-2 score. Monte Harrison (Brewers) was the game's biggest star, swatting two home runs and driving in three in the win. Brendon Davis (Dodgers) went deep for the East in the loss. Jordan Hicks (Cardinals) struck out the only two hitters he faced, and Braden Webb (Brewers) finished earned the win.

SOUTH ATLANTIC LEAGUE: A late rainstorm forced this game, held at Columbia's Spirit Communications Park, to end in a 3-3 tie. First baseman Aldrem Corredor (Nationals) drove in two runs for the North and hometown favorite Dash Winningham (Mets) did the same for the South.

NORTHWEST/PIONEER: The Northwest League exploded for five runs in the fifth inning, giving it the margin of victory for a 5-4 win over the Pioneer League. The tying and go-ahead runs were scored on bases-loaded walks to Daulton Varsho (Diamondbacks) and Steven Linkous (Rockies).

NEW YORK-PENN: The South Division scored a 5-2 win over the North with a three-run ninth inning. The go-ahead runs were plated on a two-run single from Joshua Lopez (Cardinals).

*Full-season teams only

2017 OVERALL MINOR LEAGUE DEPARTMENT LEADERS

TEAM

WINS

Trenton (Eastern)	92
Memphis (Pacific Coast)	91
Chattanooga (Southern)	91
West Michigan (Midwest)	91
Lynchburg (Carolina)	87

LONGEST WINNING STREAK

Lehigh Valley (International)	12
Fresno (Pacific Coast)	12
Trenton (Eastern)	12
Memphis (Pacific Coast)	11
Tampa (Florida State)	11
Rome (South Atlantic)	11

LOSSES

Syracuse (International)	87
Las Vegas (Pacific Coast)	86
Louisville (International)	86
Lake County (Midwest)	85
Birmingham (Southern)	85

LONGEST LOSING STREAK*

Wisconsin (Midwest)	12
Delmarva (South Atlantic)	12
Charlotte (Florida State)	11
Buffalo (International)	10
Corpus Christi (Texas)	10
Daytona (Florida State)	10
Bowling Green (Midwest)	10
Great Lakes (Midwest)	10

BATTING AVERAGE*

Lancaster (California)	.308
Colorado Springs (Pacific Coast)	.291
Salt Lake (Pacific Coast)	.290
Reno (Pacific Coast)	.290
Albuquerque (Pacific Coast)	.287

RUNS

Lancaster (California)	867
Reno (Pacific Coast)	858
Fresno (Pacific Coast)	853
Colorado Springs (Pacific Coast)	818
El Paso (Pacific Coast)	804

HOME RUNS

Fresno (Pacific Coast)	200
El Paso (Pacific Coast)	179
Tulsa (Texas)	168
Memphis (Pacific Coast)	164
Rancho Cucamonga (California)	160

STOLEN BASES

Lancaster (California)	313
Asheville (South Atlantic)	229
Cubs1 (Dominican Summer)	180
Carolina (Carolina)	175
Salt Lake (Pacific Coast)	173

EARNED RUN AVERAGE*

West Michigan (Midwest)	2.78
Tampa (Florida State)	2.83
Jupiter (Florida State)	2.84
Trenton (Eastern)	2.86
Lakeland (Florida State)	2.95

STRIKEOUTS

Durahm (International)	1421
Visalia (California)	1346
Rancho Cucamonga (California)	1314
Fort Wayne (Midwest)	1307
Oklahoma City (Pacific Coast)	1277

INDIVIDUAL BATTING

BATTING AVERAGE

Bichette, Bo (Lansing, Dunedin)	.384
Diaz, Yandy (Columbus)	.350
Buss, Nick (El Paso)	.348
De Jesus Jr., Ivan (Colorado Springs)	.345
Daza, Yonathan (Lancaster)	.341

RUNS

Hampson, Garrett (Lancaster)	113
Perkins, Blake (Hagerstown)	105
Walker, Christian (Reno)	104
Kingery, Scott (Reading, Lehigh Valley)	103
Orf, Nate (Colorado Springs)	103

HITS

Acuna, Ronald (Florida, Mississippi, Gwinnett)	181
Daza, Yonathan (Lancaster)	177
Hampson, Garrett (Lancaster)	174
Schwindel, Frank (NW Arkansas, Omaha)	174
Hays, Austin (Frederick, Bowie)	172
Boyd, B.J. (Midland)	172

TOP HITTING STREAKS

Siri, Jose (Dayton)	39
Jones, Jahmai (Inland Empire)	25
Kemp, Tony (Fresno)	24
Nelson, James (Greensboro)	24
Kingery, Scott (Lehigh Valley)	23
Ferguson, Drew (Corpus Christi)	23
Rojas, Jose (Inland Empire)	23
Rodgers, Brendan (Lancaster)	23
Gatewood, Jake (Carolina)	23

MOST HITS (ONE GAME)

Cowart, Kaleb (Salt Lake)	6
Daza, Yonathan (Lancaster)	6
Podorsky, Robbie (AZL Padres, Tri-City)	6
Tovar, Danny (DSL Padres)	6
Zimmerman, Jordan (Burlington, Inland Empire)	6

TOTAL BASES

Hays, Austin (Frederick, Bowie)	310
Walker, Christian (Reno)	307
Acuna, Ronald (Florida, Mississippi, Gwinnett)	291
Kingery, Scott (Reading, Lehigh Valley)	288
Schwindel, Frank (NW Arkansas, Omaha)	286

EXTRA-BASE HITS

Walker, Christian (Reno)	75
Hays, Austin (Frederick, Bowie)	69
Chavis, Michael (Salem, Portland)	68
Mountcastle, Ryan (Frederick, Bowie)	67
Schwindel, Frank (NW Arkansas, Omaha)	66
Pullin, Andrew (Reading, Lehigh Valley)	66

DOUBLES

Mountcastle, Ryan (Frederick, Bowie)	48
Pullin, Andrew (Reading, Lehigh Valley)	43
Schwindel, Frank (NW Arkansas, Omaha)	43
Bichette, Bo (Lansing, Dunedin)	41
Senzel, Nick (Daytona, Pensacola)	40
Gatewood, Jake (Carolina, Biloxi)	40

TRIPLES

Mateo, Jorge (Tampa, Trenton, Midland)	18
Cordero, Franchy (El Paso)	18
Liberato, Luis (Clinton, Modesto)	14
Haggerty, Sam (Lynchburg)	13
Hampson, Garrett (Lancaster)	12
Gibson, Derrik (Albuquerque)	12
Cuevas, Noel (Albuquerque)	12

HOME RUNS

Reed, A.J. (Fresno)	34
Walker, Christian (Reno)	32
Nunez, Renato (Nashville)	32
Hays, Austin (Frederick, Bowie)	32
Chavis, Michael (Salem, Portland)	31
Brentz, Bryce (Pawtucket)	31
O'Neill, Tyler (Tacoma, Memphis)	31
Wisdom, Patrick (Memphis)	31
Calhoun, Willie (Okla. City, Round Rock)	31

RUNS BATTED IN

Walker, Christian (Reno)	114
Rosa, Viosergy (Midland)	110
Brown, Seth (Stockton)	109
Reed, A.J. (Fresno)	104
Reyes, Franmil (San Antonio)	102

MOST RBIS (ONE GAME)

Feliciano, Jay (Helena)	9
Rodriguez, Aderlin (Bowie)	9
Rosa, Viosergy (Midland)	8
Calhoun, Willie (Okla. City, Round Rock)	8
Latimore, Quincy (Rancho Cucamonga)	8
Isabel, Ibandel (Rancho Cucamonga)	8
Castro, Carlos (Florida)	8

WALKS

Singleton, Jon (Corpus Christi)	107
Clark, Trent (Carolina)	98
Ford, Mike (Scranton/Wilkes-Barre, Trenton)	94
Straw, Myles (Buies Creek, Corpus Christi)	94
Short, Zack (Sound Bend, Myrtle Beach)	94
Walsh, Colin (Jackson, Corpus Christi, Fresno)	)94

INTENTIONAL WALKS

Ockimey, Josh (Salem, Portland)	10
Rios, Edwin (Tulsa, Oklahoma City)	8
Sermo, Jose (Salem)	8
Singleton, Jon (Corpus Christi)	7
Lee, Braxton (Montgomery, Jacksonville)	)6
Loopstok, Sicnarf (Lynchburg)	6
Jimenez, Eloy (Myrtle Beach, Winston-Salem, Birmingham)	6

STRIKEOUTS

Cozens, Dylan (Lehigh Valley)	194
Gettys, Michael (Lake Elsinore)	191
Peters, DJ (Rancho Cucamonga)	189
Shaffer, Richie (Columbus)	188
Morgan, Gareth (Clinton)	185

STOLEN BASES

Rogers, Wes (Lancaster)	70
Kelli, Fernando (DSL Cubs1)	58
Davis, Johnny (Biloxi)	52
Mateo, Jorge (Tampa, Trenton, Midland)	52
Hampson, Garrett (Lancaster)	51

CAUGHT STEALING

Seymour, Anfernee (Rome, Florida)	20
Acuna, Ronald (Florida, Mississippi, Gwinnett)	20
Mercado, Oscar (Springfield)	19
Robson, Jake (West Michigan, Lakeland)	18
Lee, Khalil (Lexington)	18

ON-BASE PERCENTAGE*

Guerrero Jr., Vladimir (Lansing, Dunedin)	.425
Bichette, Bo (Lansing, Dunedin)	.423
Benedetti, Carmen (Quad Cities, Buies Creek)	.421
Walsh, Colin (Jackson, Corpus Christi, Fresno)	.413
Hendrix, Jeff (Tampa, Trenton)	.411

SLUGGING PERCENTAGE*

Arcia, Oswaldo (Reno)	.639
Cordero, Franchy (El Paso)	.603
Walker, Christian (Reno)	.597
Hays, Austin (Frederick, Bowie)	.593
Barfield, Jeremy (Portland, Pawtucket)	.589

ON-BASE PLUS SLUGGING (OPS)*

Arcia, Oswaldo (Reno)	1.049
Bichette, Bo (Lansing, Dunedin)	.988
McMahon, Ryan (Hartford, Albuquerque)	.986
Walker, Christian (Reno)	.980
Cordero, Franchy (El Paso)	.972

HIT BY PITCH

Cumberland, Brett (Rome, Florida)	41
Sinay, Nick (Lansing)	38
Woody, Collin (Delmarva)	35
Locastro, Tim (Tulsa, Oklahoma City)	31
France, Ty (Lake Elsinore, San Antonio)	27

SACRIFICE BUNTS

Flores, Jecksson (Wilmington)	21
Bird, Corey (Greensboro, Jupiter)	19
May, Jacob (Charlotte)	17
Schafer, Logan (Norfolk)	14
George, Max (Asheville)	13
Castillo, Diego (Charleston)	13
Woodrow, Danny (West Michigan)	13
Rivera, Jeremy (Salem)	13
Lora, Edwin (Potomac)	13
Way, Bo (Salt Lake, Mobile)	13
Remillard, Zach (Kannapolis)	13

SACRIFICE FLIES

Wade, LaMonte (Chattanooga)	11
Diaz, Lewin (Cedar Rapids)	11
Alvarez, Yordan (Quad Cities, Buies Creek)	10
Walker, Christian (Reno)	10
Hague, Matt (Rochester)	10
Rosa, Viosergy (Midland)	10
Tauchman, Mike (Albuquerque)	10
McKinney, Billy (Trenton, Scranton/Wilkes-Barre)	10
Tucker, Preston (Fresno)	10
Daza, Yonathan (Lancaster)	10

GROUNDED INTO DOUBLE PLAY

Soto, Neftali (Harrisburg, Syracuse)	30
Nido, Tomas (Binghamton)	27
Herum, Marty (Visalia, Jackson)	23
Cuevas, Noel (Albuquerque)	22
Bauml, Cole (West Michigan)	21
Goris, Diego (El Paso)	21
Sportman, J.P. (Midland)	21
Roman, Mitch (Kannapolis)	21

BATTING AVERAGE

** By Position*

CATCHERS

Jansen, Danny (Buffalo, Dunedin, New Hampshire)	.323
Ruiz, Keibert (Great Lakes, Rancho Cucamonga)	.317
Knizner, Andrew (Springfield, Peoria)	.302
Davis, Taylor (Iowa)	.297
Mejia, Francisco (Akron)	.297

FIRST BASEMEN

Smith, Dominic (Las Vegas)	.330
Schwindel, Frank (Northwest Arkansas, Omaha)	.329
Beaty, Matt (Tulsa)	.327
Walsh, Jared (Inland Empire, Mobile)	.311
Soto, Neftali (Harrisburg, Syracuse)	.311

SECOND BASEMEN

Kemp, Tony (Fresno)	.329
Hampson, Garrett (Lancaster)	.327
Medrano, Kevin (Jackson, Reno)	.323
Schrock, Max (Midland)	.321
Orf, Nate (Colorado Springs)	.320

THIRD BASEMEN

De Jesus Jr., Ivan (Colorado Springs)	.345
Guerrero Jr., Vladimir (Dunedin, Lansing)	.323
Neuse, Sheldon (Hagerstown, Midland, Stockton)	.321
Senzel, Nick (Daytona, Pensacola)	.321
Andujar, Miguel (Scranton/Wilkes-Barre, Trenton)	.315

SHORTSTOPS

Bichette, Bo (Dunedin, Lansing)	.362
Rodgers, Brendan (Lancaster, Hartford)	.336
Rosario, Amed (Las Vegas)	.328
Mountcastle, Ryan (Frederick, Bowie)	.314
Wade, Tyler (Scranton/Wilkes-Barre)	.310

OUTFIELDERS

Buss, Nick (El Paso)	.348
Daza, Yonathan (Lancaster)	.341
Tauchman, Mike (Albuquerque)	.331
Filia, Eric (Modesto)	.326
Cordero, Franchy (El Paso)	.326

DESIGNATED HITTERS

Cervenka, Martin (Lynchburg)	.278
Mercedes, Yermin (Frederick, Bowie)	.274
Chu, Li-Jen (Lake County)	.269
Krizan, Jason (Toledo, Erie)	.264
Ackley, Dustin (Salt Lake)	.261

INDIVIDUAL PITCHING

EARNED RUN AVERAGE*

Duplantier, Jon (Kane County, Visalia)	1.39
Gonzalez, Merandy (Columbia, St. Lucie, Jupiter)	1.66
Burnes, Corbin (Carolina, Biloxi)	1.67
Sodders, Austin (West Michigan, Lakeland)	1.81
Brault, Steven (Indianapolis)	1.94

WORST ERA*

Miniard, Micah (Lake County)	7.80
Ravel, Andy (Lansing)	7.56
Ellenbest, Mike (Lansing)	6.53
French, Parker (Hartford)	6.37
Killian, Trey (Lancaster)	6.34

WINS

Littell, Zack (Tampa, Trenton, Chattanooga)	19
Griffin, Foster (Wilmington, Northwest Arkansas)	15
Jimenez, Dedgar (Salem, Portland)	15
Slegers, Aaron (Rochester)	15
Ramirez, Yefry (Trenton, Bowie)	15
Adams, Chance (Trenton, Scranton/Wilkes-Barre)	15

LOSSES

Adams, Spencer (Birmingham)	15
Thompson, Jake (Lehigh Valley)	14
Danish, Tyler (Charlotte)	14
Santos, Luis (New Hampshire, Buffalo)	13
Boscan, Wilfredo (Las Vegas)	13
Crismatt, Nabil (St. Lucie)	13
Miniard, Micah (Lake County)	13
Garcia, Danny (Clinton)	13
Jaye, Myles (Erie, Toledo)	13
Ross, Greg (Syracuse, Harrisburg)	13
Reyes, Mark (San Jose, Sacramento)	13
Pena, Luis (Inland Empire, Mobile)	13
Reyes, Luis (Potomac)	13
Aiken, Brady (Lake County)	13
Toussaint, Touki (Florida, Mississippi)	13
Knapp, Ricky (Las Vegas, Binghamton)	13

GAMES

Kensing, Logan (Toledo)	66
Mujica, Edward (Toledo)	56
Rogers, Tyler (Sacramento)	55
Rheault, Dylan (San Jose)	55
Scott, Tayler (Biloxi, Round Rock)	54
Beato, Pedro (Clearwater, Lehigh Valley)	54
Rowen, Ben (Las Vegas)	54
Suero, Wander (Harrisburg, Syracuse)	54
Bird, Kyle (Durham, Montgomery)	54

GAMES STARTED

Ogando, Emilio (Wilmington, Omaha, NW Arkansas)	29
Fillmyer, Heath (Midland)	29
Ray, Corey (Northwest Arkansas)	29
Pena, Luis (Inland Empire, Mobile)	29
Knapp, Ricky (Las Vegas, Binghamton)	29

COMPLETE GAMES

Morimando, Shawn (Columbus)	4
Keller, Brian (Charleston, Tampa)	4
Vera, Eduardo (West Virginia)	3
Ramirez, Yefry (Trenton, Bowie)	3
Conlon, P.J. (Binghamton)	3
Eshelman, Tom (Reading, Lehigh Valley)	3
Mazza, Domenic (Augusta, San Jose)	3
Alvarado, Cristian (Frederick)	3
Maese, Justin (GCL Blue Jays, Lansing)	3
Gonzalez, Harol (Columbia, St. Lucie)	3

SHUTOUTS

Morimando, Shawn (Columbus)	3
Conlon, P.J. (Binghamton)	3
O'Reilly, Mike (Peoria, Palm Beach)	2
Wilkerson, Aaron (Biloxi)	2
Dunning, Dane (Kannapolis, Winston-Salem)	2
Mazza, Domenic (Augusta, San Jose)	2
Beeker, Clark (Cedar Rapids, Fort Myers)	2
Giolito, Lucas (Charlotte)	2

GAMES FINISHED

Beato, Pedro (Clearwater, Lehigh Valley)	48
Rheault, Dylan (San Jose)	45
Herget, Jimmy (Pensacola, Louisville)	45
Suero, Wander (Harrisburg, Syracuse)	45
Ramsey, Matt (Colorado Springs, Biloxi)	43
Ruotolo, Patrick (Augusta)	43
Griep, Nate (Carolina)	43

HOLDS

Kiekhefer, Dean (Tacoma)	16
McCullough, Mason (Visalia, Jackson)	16
Purke, Matt (Charlotte)	14
Snelten, D.J. (Richmond, Sacramento)	14
Coleman, Louis (Louisville, Reno)	14

SAVES

Beato, Pedro (Clearwater, Lehigh Valley)	33
Griep, Nate (Carolina)	30
Ramsey, Matt (Colorado Springs, Biloxi)	27
Herget, Jimmy (Pensacola, Louisville)	25
Moya, Gabriel (Jackson, Chattanooga)	24

INNINGS PITCHED

Bieber, Shane (Lake County, Lynchburg, Akron)	173
Knapp, Ricky (Las Vegas, Binghamton)	172
Chirinos, Yonny (Montgomery, Durham)	168
McGuire, Deck (Pensacola)	168
Mujica, Jose (Charlotte, Montgomery)	166

WALKS

Pearce, Matt (Springfield, Memphis)	164
Owens, Henry (Pawtucket, Portland)	115
Aiken, Brady (Lake County)	101
Staumont, Josh (Omaha, Northwest Arkansas)	97
Pike, Tyler (Florida, Mississippi)	90

STRIKEOUTS

Hansen, Alec (Kannapolis, W-S, Birmingham)	191
McKenzie, Triston (Lynchburg)	186
Puk, A.J. (Stockton, Midland)	184
Font, Wilmer (Oklahoma City)	178
Honeywell, Brent (Montgomery, Durham)	172
Kopech, Michael (Birmingham, Charlotte)	172

HITS ALLOWED

Knapp, Ricky (Las Vegas, Binghamton)	209
Santos, Antonio (Asheville)	200
Duncan, Frank(Reno, Jackson)	198
Church, Andrew (Binghamton, St. Lucie)	193
Brooks, Aaron (Iowa, Colorado Springs)	192

HOME RUNS ALLOWED

Brooks, Aaron (Iowa, Colorado Springs)	29
Binford, Christian (Northwest Arkansas, Omaha)	28
Hill, Taylor (Syracuse, Harrisburg)	28
Killian, Trey (Lancaster)	27
Flemer, Matt (Albuquerque)	26

STRIKEOUTS PER NINE INNINGS (STARTERS)*

Puk, A.J. (Stockton, Midland)	13.25
Peralta, Freddy (Carolina, Biloxi)	12.68
Hansen, Alec (Kannapolis, W-S, Birmingham)	12.16
Font, Wilmer (Oklahoma City)	11.93
Avila, Pedro (Lake Elsinore, Fort Wayne)	11.86

STRIKEOUT PER NINE INNINGS (RELIEVERS)*

Rainey, Tanner (Daytona, Penacola)	15.10
Maples, Dillon (Myrtle Beach, Tennessee, Iowa)	14.21
McCullough, Mason (Visalia, Jackson)	14.12
Houston, Zac (West Michigan, Lakeland)	14.12
Whitley, Forrest (Quad Cities, Buies Creek, C. Christi)	13.94

BATTING AVERAGE AGAINST (STARTERS)*

Peralta, Freddy (Carolina, Biloxi)	.178
Ott, Travis (Bowling Green, Charlotte)	.191
Duplantier, Jon (Kane County, Visalia)	.192
Barlow, Scott (Oklahoma City, Tulsa)	.192
Kopech, Michael (Birmingham, Charlotte)	.193
Adams, Chance (Trenton, Scranton/Wilkes-Barre)	.193

BATTING AVERAGE AGAINST (RELIEVERS)*

Houston, Zac (West Michigan, Lakeland)	.134
Rainey, Tanner (Daytona, Penacola)	.139
Hackimer, Tom (Cedar Rapids, Fort Myers)	.142
Yacabonis, Jimmy (Norfolk)	.144
Dopico, Danny (Kannapolis)	.148
Espinal, Raynel (Charleston, Tampa, Trenton)	.148

MOST STRIKEOUTS (ONE GAME)

Avila, Pedro (Fort Wayne)	17
Font, Wilmer (Oklahoma City)	15
Hansen, Alec (Kannapolis)	15
Turley, Nik (Rochester)	15
Herget, Kevin (Memphis)	15

WILD PITCHES

Pint, Riley (Asheville)	26
Escobar, Luis (West Virginia)	25
Green, Nick (Charleston)	23
Ramos, Jordis (DSL White Sox	23
Santana, Adonis (DSL Padres)	21
Krook, Matt (San Jose)	21
Santos, Carlos (DSL Reds, DSL Rojos)	21
Robichaux, Austin (Salt Lake, Inland Empire)	21

BALKS

Manoah, Erik (Burlington, Inland Empire)	9
Orozco, Jio (Charleston, Pulaski, Staten Island)	8
Sanchez, Ricardo (Florida)	7
Bolanos, Ronald (Fort Wayne)	5
Santos, Antonio (Asheville)	5
Natera, Jose (DSL Angels, AZL Angels)	5
Paulino, Jose (South Bend)	5
Crawford, Leo (Great Lakes)	5
Mateo, Alejandro (Greensboro, Batavia)	5
Speas, Alex (Spokane)	5
Torres, Andres (Everett	5
Gallen, Zac (Palm Beach, Springfield, Memphis)	5
Del Rosario, Yefri (DSL Braves, GCL Braves)	5
Garner, David (Tennessee, Iowa)	5
Morales, Francisco (GCL Phillies)	5

HIT BATTERS

Payano, Pedro (Down East, Frisco)	25
Masterson, Justin (Oklahoma City)	23
Medeiros, Kodi (Carolina)	20
Davila, Garrett (Lexington)	18
Almonte, Jose (Visalia)	17
Owens, Henry (Pawtucket, Portland)	17

GROUND BALL DOUBLE PLAYS

Reyes, Jesus (Daytona, Penacola)	26
Herb, Tyler (Arkansas, Richmond)	24
Aiken, Brady (Lake County)	24
Civale, Aaron (Lake County, Lynchburg)	23
Gage, Matt (Richmond, Sacramento)	22
Lopez, Eduar (Charlotte)	22
Hudson, Dakota (Springfield, Memphis)	22
Kipper, Jordan (Mobile, Norfolk, Bowie)	22

INDIVIDUAL FIELDING

ERRORS

Cruz, Derian (Danville, Rome)	36
Cruz, Oneil (Great Lakes, West Virginia)	35
Rodriguez, J.C. (Binghamton, St. Lucie)	32
Barley, Jordy (AZL Padres)	30
Tejeda, Anderson (Hickory)	30
Tatis Jr., Fernando (San Antonio, Fort Wayne)	30

INTERNATIONAL LEAGUE TRIPLE-A

BY CARLOS CALLOZO

A horde of talented prospects called the International League home during the 2017 season, headlined by Minor League Player of the Year Ronald Acuna, the top-ranked player to start the season, Yoan Moncada, and league MVP and Rookie of the Year Rhys Hoskins.

From a team perspective, Scranton/Wilkes-Barre once again had the best record in the league, following up a 91-52 championship season with an 86-55 record in 2017, barely edging out Durham (86-56). Scraton/Wilkes-Barre placed four players on the IL top 20 prospects list—RHP Chance Adams, 3B Miguel Andujar, OF Clint Frazier and OF Dustin Fowler—while president and general manager Josh Olerud was named the league's executive of the year.

Despite their regular season success, the Bulls managed to top the RailRiders in the Governor's Cup, winning the series 3-1. Durham went on to win the Triple-A National League Championship Game with a 5-3 victory over Memphis, keeping the biggest trophy in the minors with an IL team for the second straight year.

The Bulls finished the season among the top three teams in the league in runs per game (4.53) and ERA (3.37) thanks in part to full-season contributions from Rays top prospects, righthander Brent Honeywell and shortstop Will Adames, who were the fourth and fifth ranked prospects in the league respectively.

Honeywell went 12-8, 3.64 while three of Durham's pitchers (including Honeywell) finished in the top five in wins for the IL. Lefthander Ryan Yarbrough went 13-6, 3.43 while righthander Yonny Chirinos went 12-5, 2.74. That doesn't even include Durham's top starter by ERA, lefthander Blake Snell, who posted a 2.66 IL ERA in seven starters before being promoted to the majors where he started 24 more games and posted a 4.04 ERA.

But the most impressive callup from the IL was Hoskins, who finished second in the league with 29 home runs—behind Pawtucket outfielder Bryce Bentz (31)—and led the league with 91 RBI before going on to hit an unprecedented 18 home runs in his first 50 games with the Phillies.

Indianapolis lefty Steven Brault was named the IL pitcher of the year after going 10-5 with a 1.94 ERA for an Indianapolis team that won the West Division with a 79-63 record.

A year after finishing second in the IL in average, Columbus third baseman Yandy Diaz took the batting title home with a .350/.454/.460 line. Buffalo outfielder Roemon Fields paced the league with 43 stolen bases.

TOP 20 PROSPECTS

1. Ronald Acuna, OF, Gwinnett (Braves)
2. Yoan Moncada, 2B, Charlotte (White Sox)
3. Rhys Hoskins, 1B/OF, Lehigh Valley (Phillies)
4. Brent Honeywell, RHP, Durham (Rays)
5. Willy Adames, SS, Durham (Rays)
6. Ozzie Albies, 2B/SS, Gwinnett (Braves)
7. Bradley Zimmer, OF, Columbus (Indians)
8. Scott Kingery, 2B, Lehigh Valley (Phillies)
9. Chance Adams, RHP, Scranton/Wilkes-Barre (Yankees)
10. J.P. Crawford, SS, Lehigh Valley (Phillies)
11. Sean Newcomb, LHP, Gwinnett (Braves)
12. Tyler Glasnow, RHP, Indianapolis (Pirates)
13. Lucas Giolito, RHP, Charlotte (White Sox)
14. Jacob Faria, RHP, Durham (Rays)
15. Miguel Andujar, 3B, Scranton/Wilkes-Barre (Yankees)
16. Clint Frazier, OF, Scranton/Wilkes-Barre (Yankees)
17. Dustin Fowler, OF, Scranton/Wilkes-Barre (Yankees)
18. Lucas Sims, RHP, Gwinnett (Braves)
19. Jake Bauers, OF/1B, Durham (Rays)
20. Chance Sisco, C, Norfolk (Orioles)

OVERALL STANDINGS

North Division	W	L	PCT	GB	Manager(s)	Attendance	Average	Last Pennant
Scranton/W-B RailRiders (Yankees)	86	55	.610	—	Al Pedrique	439,412	6,462	2016
Lehigh Valley IronPigs (Phillies)	80	62	.563	6½	Dusty Wathan	555,146	8,541	1995
Rochester Red Wings (Twins)	80	62	.563	6½	Mike Quade	445,581	6,553	1997
Pawtucket Red Sox (Red Sox)	67	75	.472	19½	Kevin Boles	409,960	6,406	2014
Buffalo Bisons (Blue Jays)	65	76	.461	21	Bob Meacham	526,574	8,101	2004
Syracuse Chiefs (Nationals)	54	87	.383	32	Billy Gardner	292,054	4,636	1976
South Division								
Durham Bulls (Rays)	86	56	.606	—	Jared Sandberg	547,841	7,716	2017
Gwinnett Braves (Braves)	71	71	.500	15	Damon Berryhill	210,075	3,135	2007
Norfolk Tides (Orioles)	66	76	.465	20	Ron Johnson	359,263	5,443	1999
Charlotte Knights (White Sox)	61	81	.430	25	Mark Grudzielanek	628,526	9,109	1985
West Division								
Indianapolis Indians (Pirates)	79	63	.556	—	Andy Barkett	641,141	9,159	2000
Columbus Clippers (Indians)	71	71	.500	8	Chris Tremie	616,059	9,060	2015
Toledo Mud Hens (Tigers)	70	71	.496	8½	Mike Rojas	533,014	7,614	2006
Louisville Bats (Reds)	56	86	.394	23	Delino DeShields	467,024	6,868	2001

Semifinals: Durham defeated Indianapolis 3-1 and Scranton/W-B defeated Lehigh Valley 3-1 in best-of-five series. **Finals:** Durham defeated Scranton/W-B 3-1 in a best-of-five series.

INTERNATIONAL LEAGUE STATISTICS

CLUB BATTING

	AVG	G	AB	R	H	2B	3B	HR	RBI	BB	SO	SB	OBP	SLG
Scranton/W-B	.272	141	4737	664	1290	272	36	153	629	426	1104	93	.334	.442
Indianapolis	.268	142	4794	647	1283	279	27	104	607	441	1065	101	.334	.402
Rochester	.262	142	4689	587	1226	259	26	103	541	435	1009	51	.326	.394
Louisville	.259	142	4831	541	1253	238	30	87	510	419	995	92	.325	.375
Pawtucket	.258	142	4758	590	1229	216	16	137	552	381	1094	58	.318	.397
Durham	.258	142	4850	643	1251	272	26	111	599	458	1161	131	.326	.393
Gwinnett	.257	142	4717	634	1211	219	33	117	581	483	1258	106	.329	.392
Columbus	.256	142	4773	635	1224	226	21	151	603	499	1297	84	.333	.408
Norfolk	.254	142	4805	591	1222	265	32	125	555	425	1175	51	.319	.401
Toledo	.253	141	4736	541	1196	238	24	93	515	423	1066	83	.316	.372
Syracuse	.251	141	4578	555	1151	222	11	110	527	407	977	44	.315	.377
Charlotte	.250	142	4637	614	1157	195	25	142	574	513	1204	95	.329	.394
Lehigh Valley	.249	142	4658	624	1158	217	31	152	585	449	1242	64	.321	.406
Buffalo	.247	141	4548	544	1123	239	28	78	507	462	1032	143	.320	.363

CLUB PITCHING

	ERA	G	CG	SHO	SV	IP	H	R	ER	HR	BB	SO	AVG
Scranton/W-B	3.33	141	2	1	37	1226	1079	521	454	101	382	1249	.233
Durham	3.37	142	1	1	42	1271	1099	524	476	126	417	1421	.231
Rochester	3.39	142	4	1	42	1228	1174	507	462	102	350	1128	.252
Indianapolis	3.48	142	3	0	39	1245	1163	529	482	103	453	1142	.249
Buffalo	3.58	141	3	0	35	1209	1177	535	481	102	421	993	.255
Lehigh Valley	3.72	142	5	2	44	1224	1167	578	506	111	410	1022	.251
Pawtucket	3.84	142	6	3	30	1229	1109	562	524	140	454	1101	.241
Toledo	3.89	141	2	1	42	1248	1263	595	540	101	478	1101	.263
Gwinnett	4.02	142	5	2	32	1231	1187	606	550	105	470	1184	.252
Norfolk	4.14	142	2	0	32	1241	1297	639	571	111	450	1028	.268
Columbus	4.33	142	6	3	38	1248	1289	644	600	152	486	1074	.268
Louisville	4.56	142	4	2	29	1256	1357	731	636	124	521	1129	.276
Charlotte	4.79	142	5	2	31	1216	1298	730	647	148	475	1090	.273
Syracuse	5.03	141	3	0	29	1187	1315	709	664	137	454	1017	.281

CLUB FIELDING

	PCT	PO	A	E	DP
Buffalo	.980	4506	1324	118	328
Charlotte	.976	4428	1387	141	393
Columbus	.985	4641	1373	94	420
Durham	.981	4558	1333	116	340
Gwinnett	.980	4614	1226	121	288
Indianapolis	.982	4515	1446	108	349
Lehigh Valley	.980	4636	1309	124	308

	PCT	PO	A	E	DP
Louisville	.975	4675	1377	153	398
Norfolk	.976	4627	1426	149	335
Pawtucket	.987	4552	1202	78	320
Rochester	.986	4522	1300	82	316
Scranton/W-B	.980	4506	1243	116	287
Syracuse	.983	4386	1342	98	347
Toledo	.982	4632	1320	109	356

INDIVIDUAL BATTING

Batter, Club	AVG	G	AB	R	H	2B	3B	HR	RBI	BB	SO	SB
Diaz, Yandy, Columbus	.350	85	309	56	108	17	1	5	33	60	56	1
Wade, Tyler, Scranton/W-B	.310	85	339	68	105	22	4	7	31	38	75	26
Hague, Matt, Rochester	.297	136	502	64	149	30	0	10	65	61	75	8
Bostick, Christopher, Indianapolis	.294	126	486	75	143	33	3	7	57	45	97	8
Fields, Roemon, Buffalo	.291	103	347	49	101	11	5	0	29	32	65	43
Rodriguez, Ronny, Columbus	.291	117	447	60	130	18	2	17	64	23	92	15
Albies, Ozzie, Gwinnett	.285	97	411	67	117	21	8	9	41	28	90	21
Hoskins, Rhys, Lehigh Valley	.284	115	401	78	114	24	4	29	91	64	75	4
Infante, Omar, Toledo	.282	123	489	46	138	31	0	3	37	24	50	3
Solano, Donovan, Scranton/W-B	.282	99	373	44	105	29	0	4	48	24	60	1

INDIVIDUAL PITCHING

Pitcher, Club	W	L	ERA	G	GS	CG	SV	IP	H	R	ER	BB	SO
Brault, Steven, Indianapolis	10	5	1.94	21	20	0	0	120	85	26	26	44	109
Eshelman, Tom, Lehigh Valley	10	3	2.23	18	18	3	0	121	101	36	30	13	80
Albers, Andrew, Gwinnett	12	3	2.61	26	17	0	0	121	120	38	35	19	115
Chirinos, Yonny, Durham	12	5	2.74	23	22	1	0	141	116	50	43	22	120
Adams, Chance, Scranton/W-B	11	5	2.89	21	21	0	0	115	81	39	37	43	103
Merritt, Ryan, Columbus	10	5	3.03	19	18	1	0	116	116	40	39	25	85
Slegers, Aaron, Rochester	15	4	3.40	24	24	1	0	148	154	59	56	29	119
Yarbrough, Ryan, Durham	13	6	3.43	26	26	0	0	157	144	65	60	39	159
Hurlbut, David, Rochester	10	8	3.44	23	22	0	0	131	152	58	50	30	103
Hutchison, Drew, Indianapolis	9	9	3.56	28	26	1	0	159	149	69	63	57	124

ALL-STAR TEAM

C: Mitch Garver, Rochester. **1B:** Rhys Hoskins, Lehigh Valley. **2B:** Ozzie Albies, Gwinnett. **3B:** Yandy Diaz, Columbus. **SS:** Tyler Wade, Scranton/W-B. **OF:** Bryce Brentz, Pawtucket; Rusney Castillo, Pawtucket; Zach Granite, Rochester. **DH:** Pedro Alvarez, Norfolk. **UT:** Ronny Rodriguez, Columbus.
SP: Steven Brault, Indianapolis. **RP:** Pedro Beato, Lehigh Valley.

Most Valuable Player: Rhys Hoskins, Lehigh Valley
Most Valuable Pitcher: Steven Brault, Indianapolis
Rookie of the Year: Rhys Hoskins, Lehigh Valley
Manager of the Year: Al Pedrique, Scranton/Wilkes-Barre

DEPARTMENT LEADERS

BATTING

OBP	Diaz, Yandy, Columbus	.454
SLG	Hoskins, Rhys, Lehigh Valley	.581
OPS	Hoskins, Rhys, Lehigh Valley	.966
R	Bauers, Jake, Durham	79
H	Hague, Matt, Rochester	149
TB	Alvarez, Pedro, Norfolk	242
XBH	Alvarez, Pedro, Norfolk	58
2B	Dosch, Drew, Norfolk	36
3B	Fowler, Dustin, Scranton/Wilkes-Barre	8
	Albies, Ozzie, Gwinnett	8
HR	Brentz, Bryce, Pawtucket	31
RBI	Hoskins, Rhys, Lehigh Valley	91
SAC	May, Jacob, Charlotte	17
BB	Crawford, J.P., Lehigh Valley	79
HBP	Shaffer, Richie, Columbus	12
SO	Cozens, Dylan, Lehigh Valley	194
SB	Fields, Roemon, Buffalo	43
CS	Fields, Roemon, Buffalo	14
AB/SO	Shuck, J.B., Rochester	9.86

FIELDING

C PCT	Alfaro, Jorge, Lehigh Valley	.997
PO	Holaday, Bryan, Toledo	701
A	Rodriguez, Eddy, Scranton/W-	67
DP	Holaday, Bryan, Toledo	11
E	Holaday, Bryan, Toledo	11
PB	Garver, Mitch, Rochester	9
	Alfaro, Jorge, Lehigh Valley	9
1B PCT	Navarro, Efren, Toledo	.997
PO	Gillaspie, Casey, Durham, Charlotte	899
A	Tellez, Rowdy, Buffalo	67
DP	Rodriguez, Nellie, Columbus	101
E	Tellez, Rowdy, Buffalo	11
2B PCT	Infante, Omar, Toledo	.977
PO	Infante, Omar, Toledo	209
A	Infante, Omar, Toledo	304
DP	Infante, Omar, Toledo	73
E	Infante, Omar, Toledo	12
3B PCT	Dosch, Drew, Norfolk	.916
PO	Dosch, Drew, Norfolk	69
A	Dosch, Drew, Norfolk	181
DP	Ruiz, Rio, Gwinnett	19
E	Dixon, Brandon, Louisville	24
SS PCT	Ryan, Brendan, Toledo	.985
PO	Ryan, Brendan, Toledo	153
A	Adames, Willy, Durham	307
DP	Adames, Willy, Durham	74
E	Adames, Willy, Durham	24
OF PCT	Williams, Mason, Scranton/W-B	1.000
PO	Fields, Roemon, Buffalo	259
A	Shuck, J.B., Rochester	11
A	Schafer, Logan, Norfolk	11
DP	Bogusevic, Brian, Pawtucket	3
	Rodriguez, Ronny, Columbus	3
	Smith, Mallex, Durham	3
E	Brentz, Bryce, Pawtucket	8

PITCHING

G	Kensing, Logan, Toledo	66
GS	Yarbrough, Ryan, Durham	26
	Morimando, Shawn, Columbus	26
	Hutchison, Drew, Indianapolis	26
GF	Beato, Pedro, Lehigh Valley	48
SV	Beato, Pedro, Lehigh Valley	33
W	Slegers, Aaron, Rochester	15
L	Danish, Tyler, Charlotte	14
	Thompson, Jake, Lehigh Valley	14
IP	Hutchison, Drew, Indianapolis	159
	Morimando, Shawn, Columbus	159
H	Morimando, Shawn, Columbus	177
R	Danish, Tyler, Charlotte	107
ER	Plutko, Adam, Columbus	89
HB	Reed, Cody, Louisville	10
BB	Fulmer, Carson, Charlotte	65
SO	Yarbrough, Ryan, Durham	159
SO/9	Honeywell, Brent, Durham	11.06
SO/9(RP)	Adams, Austin, Syracuse	13.88
BB/9	Eshelman, Tom, Lehigh Valley	0.97
WP	Reed, Cody, Louisville	13
BK	Fulmer, Carson, Charlotte	3
HR	Kendrick, Kyle, Pawtucket	24
	Plutko, Adam, Columbus	24
AVG	Adams, Chance, Scranton/W-B	.197

PACIFIC COAST LEAGUE TRIPLE-A

BY KYLE GLASER

The Memphis Redbirds knew early on they had a special team on their hands. The Cardinals' Triple-A affiliate won six of their first seven games to open the season, and at the end of April began an 11-game winning streak that put them 10 games over .500 barely a month into the year.

The rest was just domination on top of more domination. The Redbirds went 91-50 during the regular season, the second-best record in all of the minor leagues. They finished their historic season with their first Pacific Coast League championship since 2009 with dramatic Game 5 wins in both the semifinals against Colorado Springs (Brewers) and the championship round against El Paso (Padres).

Top prospects Luke Weaver, Paul DeJong, Carson Kelly and Harrison Bader led Memphis early before ascending to St. Louis. Jack Flaherty, Tyler O'Neill and Jose Adolis Garcia led the band of midseason reinforcements that propelled the Redbirds to a 22-6 record in July. And in the playoffs, recent top draft picks Dakota Hudson, Zac Gallen and Ryan Helsley came up and locked down the title with sterling starting pitching performances.

There were plenty of other stars outside of Memphis. Mets top prospects Amed Rosario and Dominic Smith posted banner seasons at Las Vegas before receiving their first big league callups in August. Fresno's Derek Fisher, Oklahoma City's Alex Verdugo and Colorado Springs' Brett Phillips excelled in the outfield before joining the Astros, Dodgers and Brewers, respectively, down the stretch. Texas' Willie Calhoun and Oakland's Franklin Barreto also made their big league debuts in 2017 after starring in the PCL. Fresno's A.J. Reed hit 34 home runs to lead the minors.

The PCL's award winners were largely older and had previous major league experience. Reno's Christian Walker, 26, was named MVP after hitting .309 with 32 homers and 114 RBIs. Oklahoma City's Wilmer Font, 27, won pitcher of the year after leading the PCL in ERA (3.42) and strikeouts (178). El Paso's Nick Buss, 30, won the batting title with a .348 average.

The year also marked the final one for Colorado Springs as a Triple-A club. San Antonio is taking its place in the PCL, while Colorado Springs will become host to a Rookie-level affiliate.

TOP 20 PROSPECTS

1. Alex Reyes, RHP, Memphis (Cardinals)
2. Willson Contreras, C, Iowa (Cubs)
3. Jose De Leon, RHP, Oklahoma City (Dodgers)
4. Orlando Arcia, SS, Colorado Springs (Brewers)
5. Jeff Hoffman, RHP, Albuquerque (Rockies)
6. Joey Gallo, 3B/1B, Round Rock (Rangers)
7. Hunter Renfroe, OF, El Paso (Padres)
8. A.J. Reed, 1B, Fresno (Astros)
9. Joe Musgrove, RHP, Fresno (Astros)
10. Jharel Cotton, RHP, Okla. City (Dodgers)/Nash. (Athletics)
11. Josh Hader, LHP, Colorado Springs (Brewers)
12. Albert Almora, OF, Iowa (Cubs)
13. Manuel Margot, OF, El Paso (Padres)
14. Teoscar Hernandez, OF, Fresno (Astros)
15. Hunter Dozier, 3B, Omaha (Royals)
16. Brock Stewart, RHP, Oklahoma City (Dodgers)
17. Jeimer Candelario, 3B, Iowa (Cubs)
18. Daniel Mengden, RHP, Nashville (Athletics)
19. Brandon Nimmo, OF, Las Vegas (Mets)
20. Anthony Banda, LHP, Reno (D-backs)

OVERALL STANDINGS

American Northern	W	L	PCT	GB	Manager(s)	Attendance	Average	Last Pennant
Colorado Springs Sky Sox (Brewers)	80	57	.584	—	Rick Sweet	265,095	4,208	1995
Oklahoma City Dodgers (Dodgers)	72	69	.511	10	Bill Haselman	444,224	6,533	1965
Omaha Storm Chasers (Royals)	69	72	.489	13	Brian Poldberg	358,777	6,533	2014
Iowa Cubs (Cubs)	67	72	.482	14	Marty Pevey	535,660	7,763	Never
American Southern	**W**	**L**	**PCT**	**GB**	**Manager(s)**	**Attendance**	**Average**	**Last Pennant**
Memphis Redbirds (Cardinals)	91	50	.645	—	Stubby Clapp	350,007	5,073	2017
Nashville Sounds (Athletics)	68	71	.489	22	Ryan Christenson	593,679	8,861	2005
Round Rock Express (Rangers)	66	72	.478	23 ½	Jason Wood	610,681	8,724	Never
New Orleans Baby Cakes (Marlins)	55	83	.399	34 ½	Arnie Beyeler	349,883	5,554	2001
Pacific Northern	**W**	**L**	**PCT**	**GB**	**Manager(s)**	**Attendance**	**Average**	**Last Pennant**
Reno Aces (D-backs)	80	62	.563	—	Jerry Narron	347,502	4,894	2012
Fresno Grizzlies (Astros)	77	65	.542	3	Tony DeFrancesco/Dan Radison	428,341	6,208	Never
Tacoma Rainiers (Mariners)	66	76	.465	14	Pat Listach	374,951	5,434	2010
Sacramento River Cats (Giants)	64	77	.454	15 ½	Dave Brundage	562,237	8,032	2008
Pacific Southern	**W**	**L**	**PCT**	**GB**	**Manager(s)**	**Attendance**	**Average**	**Last Pennant**
El Paso Chihuahuas (Padres)	73	69	.514	—	Rod Barajas	544,668	7,894	2016
Salt Lake Bees (Angels)	72	70	.507	1	Keith Johnson	483,202	6,903	1979
Albuquerque Isotopes (Rockies)	68	73	.482	4 ½	Glenallen Hill	542,502	7,978	1994
Las Vegas 51s (Mets)	56	86	.394	17	Pedro Lopez	359,059	5,057	1998

Semifinals: El Paso defeated Reno 3-1 and Memphis defeated Colorado Springs 3-2 in best-of-five series. **Finals:** Memphis defeated El Paso 3-2 in a best-of-five series.

PACIFIC COAST LEAGUE STATISTICS

CLUB BATTING

	AVG	G	AB	R	H	2B	3B	HR	RBI	BB	SO	SB	OBP	SLG
Colorado Springs	.291	137	4675	818	1361	295	50	125	759	488	1034	99	.361	.456
Salt Lake	.290	142	4959	801	1440	275	40	102	745	560	896	173	.365	.424
Reno	.290	142	4977	858	1442	294	70	158	812	466	1046	83	.351	.472
Albuquerque	.287	141	4888	730	1402	275	79	130	702	390	1043	102	.341	.455
El Paso	.283	142	4930	804	1395	273	63	179	768	478	1173	117	.349	.473
Fresno	.282	142	4874	853	1374	266	33	200	805	554	1090	88	.359	.473
Memphis	.278	141	4826	714	1341	278	22	164	683	461	1040	84	.348	.447
Las Vegas	.275	142	4930	690	1356	273	33	146	647	466	1103	48	.341	.433
Omaha	.270	141	4752	628	1284	229	34	132	585	399	1018	119	.330	.416
Round Rock	.266	138	4690	656	1249	243	21	139	615	440	1115	67	.335	.416
Iowa	.264	139	4606	649	1216	287	24	114	612	464	1066	102	.335	.411
Sacramento	.263	141	4842	608	1272	268	22	126	577	385	1133	104	.320	.405
Oklahoma City	.262	141	4707	675	1234	256	29	147	628	469	1065	78	.334	.423
Nashville	.262	139	4739	655	1240	226	35	159	613	455	1217	95	.333	.425
Tacoma	.260	142	4689	639	1220	244	28	131	609	517	1033	118	.337	.408
New Orleans	.254	138	4606	568	1170	221	27	100	527	422	989	97	.321	.379

CLUB PITCHING

	ERA	G	CG	SHO	SV	IP	H	R	ER	HR	BB	SO	AVG
Memphis	3.77	141	1	0	41	1251	1216	566	524	118	366	1121	.256
Sacramento	4.23	141	0	0	37	1245	1315	671	585	120	462	1034	.272
New Orleans	4.24	138	1	0	26	1194	1143	634	563	140	497	1045	.254
Oklahoma City	4.26	141	0	0	37	1232	1229	638	583	115	440	1277	.259
Nashville	4.37	139	2	0	28	1229	1278	670	597	102	411	1050	.267
Colorado Springs	4.54	137	1	0	25	1181	1253	658	596	146	430	1003	.274
Omaha Storm	4.61	141	1	0	33	1232	1290	697	631	152	469	1098	.268
Tacoma	4.69	142	5	3	35	1214	1238	679	633	135	384	1072	.262
Iowa	4.75	139	2	2	42	1208	1285	701	637	150	461	1087	.274
Albuquerque	4.91	141	1	0	27	1242	1365	723	678	165	449	1064	.281
Salt Lake	4.94	142	0	0	30	1258	1324	762	690	133	498	1078	.272
Round Rock	5.02	138	2	1	31	1196	1327	719	667	157	504	1005	.283
El Paso	5.13	142	2	1	31	1247	1406	789	711	160	538	995	.286
Reno	5.19	142	1	0	41	1260	1391	782	726	160	515	1064	.281
Las Vegas	5.40	142	1	0	26	1249	1495	831	749	159	436	958	.297
Fresno	5.52	142	0	0	37	1241	1441	826	761	140	554	1110	.291

CLUB FIELDING

	PCT	PO	A	E	DP
Memphis	.985	4634	1360	92	346
Round Rock	.984	4389	1355	94	400
Oklahoma City	.984	4446	1320	97	314
New Orleans	.982	4405	1372	106	317
Salt Lake	.982	4674	1377	112	382
Albuquerque	.981	4567	1453	118	325
Fresno	.981	4612	1394	119	389
Omaha	.980	4647	1228	123	294
Iowa	.979	4400	1464	124	358
El Paso	.979	4646	1460	131	381
Colorado Springs	.979	4355	1387	124	396
Nashville	.979	4498	1368	127	349
Las Vegas	.979	4644	1462	134	357
Tacoma	.978	4550	1274	131	264
Reno	.978	4587	1476	137	410
Sacramento	.978	4532	1493	138	427

INDIVIDUAL BATTING

Batter, Club	AVG	G	AB	R	H	2B	3B	HR	RBI	BB	SO	SB
Buss, Nick, El Paso	.348	114	353	53	123	19	8	11	55	27	54	9
De Jesus Jr., Ivan, Colorado Springs	.345	112	412	67	142	30	4	7	65	33	75	3
Tauchman, Mike, Albuquerque	.331	110	420	82	139	30	8	16	80	40	73	16
Smith, Dominic, Las Vegas	.330	114	457	77	151	34	2	16	76	39	87	1
Kemp, Tony, Fresno	.329	118	504	95	166	23	9	10	62	35	43	24
Rosario, Amed, Las Vegas	.328	94	393	66	129	19	7	7	58	23	67	19
Cordero, Franchy, El Paso	.326	93	390	68	127	21	18	17	64	23	118	15
Arcia, Oswaldo, Reno	.326	93	341	79	111	25	5	24	87	45	86	0
Schwindel, Frank, Omaha	.321	99	392	51	126	30	0	17	72	10	68	0
Orf, Nate, Colorado Springs	.320	125	434	103	139	32	11	9	65	54	75	7

INDIVIDUAL PITCHING

Pitcher, Club	W	L	ERA	G	GS	CG	SV	IP	H	R	ER	BB	SO
Font, Wilmer, Oklahoma City	10	8	3.42	25	25	0	0	134	114	52	51	35	178
Masterson, Justin, Oklahoma City	11	6	4.13	26	25	0	0	142	129	72	65	66	140
Carpenter, Ryan Albuquerque	10	9	4.15	27	25	1	0	156	161	74	72	39	161
Jokisch, Eric, Reno	8	8	4.21	28	21	0	0	135	139	70	63	42	91
Frankoff, Seth, Iowa	2	8	4.40	24	21	0	0	117	102	61	57	47	119
Martinez, David, Fresno	7	12	4.69	25	23	0	0	136	143	77	71	47	101
Rodriguez, Bryan, El Paso	8	8	4.90	26	20	1	0	127	157	76	69	37	63
Copeland, Scott, New Orleans	9	11	4.97	26	26	0	0	138	158	78	76	53	118
Perez, Williams, Iowa	7	10	5.01	23	23	1	0	120	122	74	67	51	102
Thornton, Trent, Fresno	8	4	5.09	21	20	0	0	115	137	71	65	23	88

ALL-STAR TEAM

C: Victor Caratini, Iowa. **1B:** Christian Walker, Reno. **2B:** Willie Calhoun, Oklahoma City/Round Rock. **3B:** Patrick Wisdom, Memphis. **SS:** Amed Rosario, Las Vegas. **OF:** Oswaldo Arcia, Reno; Derek Fisher, Fresno; Mike Tauchman, Albuquerque. **DH:** Renato Nunez, Nashville. **RHP:** Wilmet Font, Oklahoma City. **LHP:** Ryan Carpenter, Albuquerque. **RP:** Matt Carasiti, Albuquerque/Iowa. **Most Valuable Player:** Christian Walker, Reno. **Pitcher of the Year:** Wilmer Font, Oklahoma City. **Rookie of the Year:** Amed Rosario, Las Vegas. **Manager of the Year:** Stubby Clapp, Memphis

DEPARTMENT LEADERS

BATTING

OBP	Arcia, Oswaldo, Reno	.410
SLG	Arcia, Oswaldo, Reno	.639
OPS	Arcia, Oswaldo, Reno	1.049
R	Walker, Christian, Reno	104
H	Kemp, Tony, Fresno	166
TB	Walker, Christian, Reno	307
XBH	Walker, Christian, Reno	75
2B	Vargas, Ildemaro, Reno	35
3B	Cordero, Franchy, El Paso	18
HR	Reed, A.J., Fresno	34
RBI	Walker, Christian, Reno	114
SAC	Mondesi, Raul, Omaha	10
BB	Vogelbach, Daniel, Tacoma	76
HBP	Cunningham, Todd, Memphis, Ok. City	18
SO	O'Neill, Tyler, Tacoma, Memphis	151
SB	Andreoli, John, Iowa	26
	Ortega, Rafael, El Paso	26
	Wren, Kyle, Colorado Springs	26
CS	Burns, Billy, Omaha	11
	Valera, Breyvic, Memphis	11
AB/SO	Valera, Breyvic, Memphis	12.47

FIELDING

C PCT	Wilson, Bobby, Oklahoma City	.999
PO	Gale, Rocky, El Paso	687
A	Gale, Rocky, El Paso	64
DP	Sanchez, Tony, Salt Lake	9
E	Perez, Carlos, Salt Lake	8
PB	Centeno, Juan, Fresno	12
1B PCT	Guzman, Ronald, Round Rock	.993
PO	Walker, Christian, Reno	1025
A	Smith, Dominic, Las Vegas	94
DP	Guzman, Ronald, Round Rock	118
E	Reed, A.J., Fresno	10
2B PCT	Kemp, Tony, Fresno	.977
PO	Kemp, Tony, Fresno	189
A	Vargas, Ildemaro, Reno	279
DP	Vargas, Ildemaro, Reno	78
E	Wendle, Joey, Nashville	11
3B PCT	Wisdom, Patrick, Memphis	.944
PO	Wisdom, Patrick, Memphis	73
A	Wisdom, Patrick, Memphis	181
DP	Wisdom, Patrick, Memphis	26
E	Wisdom, Patrick, Memphis	15
SS PCT	Castro, Daniel, Albuquerque	.989
PO	Culberson, Charlie, Oklahoma City	137
A	Castro, Daniel, Albuquerque	298
DP	Castro, Daniel, Albuquerque	63
E	Barreto, Franklin, Nashville	18
OF PCT	Verdugo, Alex, Oklahoma City	1.000
PO	Bader, Harrison, Memphis	301
A	Starling, Bubba, Omaha	11
	Puello, Cesar, Round Rock, Salt Lake	11
DP	Decker, Jaff, Nashville	4
E	Brinson, Lewis, Colorado Springs	7
	Williamson, Mac, Sacramento	7
	Phillips, Brett, Colorado Springs	7

PITCHING

G	Rogers, Tyler, Sacramento	55
GS	Boscan, Wilfredo, Las Vegas	26
	Brooks, Aaron, Iowa	26
	Copeland, Scott, New Orleans	26
GF	Carasiti, Matt, Iowa	41
SV	Carasiti, Matt, Iowa	21
W	Masterson, Justin, Oklahoma City	11
	Scribner, Troy, Salt Lake	11
L	Knapp, Ricky, Las Vegas	13
	Boscan, Wilfredo, Las Vegas	13
IP	Carpenter, Ryan, Albuquerque	156
H	Brooks, Aaron, Iowa	192
R	Brooks, Aaron, Iowa	110
ER	Brooks, Aaron, Iowa	99
HB	Masterson, Justin, Oklahoma City	23
BB	Masterson, Justin, Oklahoma City	66
SO	Font, Wilmer, Oklahoma City	178
SO/9	Font, Wilmer, Oklahoma City	11.93
SO/9 (RP)	Comer, Kevin, Fresono	10.46
BB/9	Brooks, Aaron, Iowa, Colo. Springs	1.79
WP	Gagnon, Drew, Salt Lake	18
BK	Reyes, Arturo, Memphis	3
	Font, Wilmer, Oklahoma City	3
HR	Brooks, Aaron, Iowa	29
AVG	Font, Wilmer, Oklahoma City	.222

EASTERN LEAGUE DOUBLE-A

BY JOSH NORRIS

As the Red Sox unloaded their system over the past few winters to acquire closer Craig Kimbrel, reliever Tyler Thornburg and lefty ace Chris Sale, among others, Devers was one of the few jewels who remained. In 2017, everyone saw why. The 20-year-old blitzed the Eastern League, then made a short stop at Triple-A before providing enough of an impact in the big leagues to earn himself the starting third baseman's job on Boston's playoff roster.

His feel for hitting and power, plus improved defense at third base helped Devers lead another strong crop of prospects in the Eastern League.

Had he not fallen one plate appearance short of qualifying for the Top 20 after a quick promotion to Triple-A, Trenton shortstop Gleyber Torres would have given Devers a run for his money at the top spot. Instead, he provided a quick boost of offensive firepower to the league's best team in the regular season.

The Thunder finished with the league's best record at 92-48 and played their way into the Eastern League Championship Series. They got past Binghamton in the first round in series win that included a combined no-hitter between lefty Justus Sheffield and reliever Taylor Widener, who was making his first Double-A appearance.

In the ELCS, the Altoona Curve, backed by strong starting pitching from righthander Mitch Keller and lefty Brandon Waddell, swept their way to the franchise's second championship. The big blow in the decisive third game came from catcher Jin-De Jhang, whose three-run triple gave Altoona all the breathing room it needed.

Elsewhere in the Eastern League, a pair of high-rising outfielders found their way into the upper echelon of the Top 20. Nationals prospect Victor Robles, just 20 years old, started the year with high Class A Potomac but, like Devers with the Red Sox, finished the year with the Nationals in the playoffs. A potential 70-grade hitter on the 20-80 scouting scale, Robles also plays tremendous outfield defense with a well above-average throwing arm and burgeoning power as well.

Bowie, too, got a boost from the Carolina League in the second half. Outfielder Austin Hays, perhaps the breakout prospect of the season, did not miss a step when he hit the upper levels for the first time. In fact, Hays, the Orioles' third-rounder last year out Jacksonville, put up nearly identical numbers at both of his minor league stops. And like Robles, Hays found himself in the major leagues at season's end.

Off the field, Hartford put its ballpark saga to an end with the opening of Dunkin' Donuts Park after a yearlong delay that forced the Yard Goats on the road for all of 2016. With the new park, Hartford averaged more than 5,800 fans per game and placed third in the EL in attendance.

TOP 20 PROSPECTS

1. Rafael Devers, 3B, Portland (Red Sox)
2. Victor Robles, OF, Harrisburg (Nationals)
3. Austin Hays, OF, Bowie (Orioles)
4. Brendan Rodgers, SS/2B, Hartford (Rockies)
5. Francisco Mejia, C, Akron (Indians)
6. Scott Kingery, 2B, Reading (Phillies)
7. Chris Shaw, OF/1B, Richmond (Giants)
8. Jorge Mateo, SS/OF, Trenton (Yankees)
9. Anthony Alford, OF, New Hampshire (Blue Jays)
10. Miguel Andujar, 3B, Trenton (Yankees)
11. Justus Sheffield, LHP, Trenton (Yankees)
12. Domingo Acevedo, OF, Trenton (Yankees)
13. Michael Chavis, 3B, Portland (Red Sox)
14. Tanner Scott, LHP, Bowie (Orioles)
15. Ryan McMahon, 1B/2B, Hartford (Rockies)
16. D.J. Stewart, OF, Bowie (Orioles)
17. Erick Fedde, RHP, Harrisburg (Nationals)
18. Cedric Mullins, OF, Bowie (Orioles)
19. Beau Burrows, RHP, Erie (Tigers)
20. Christin Stewart, OF, Erie (Tigers)

OVERALL STANDINGS

Eastern Division	W	L	PCT	GB	Manager(s)	Attendance	Average	Last Pennant
Trenton Thunder (Yankees)	92	48	.657	—	Bobby Mitchell	349,013	5,133	2013
Binghamton Rumble Ponies (Mets)	85	54	.612	6½	Luis Rojas	190,765	3,289	1994
Reading Fightin Phils (Phillies)	72	68	.514	20	Greg Legg	411,698	6,054	2001
Portland Sea Dogs (Red Sox)	65	74	.468	26½	Carlos Febles	356,153	5,653	2006
Hartford Yard Goats (Rockies)	62	77	.446	29½	Jerry Weinstein	395,196	5,812	2001
New Hampshire Fisher Cats (Blue Jays)	59	80	.424	32½	Gary Allenson	284,108	4,735	2011

Western Division	W	L	PCT	GB	Manager(s)	Attendance	Average	Last Pennant
Altoona Curve (Pirates)	74	66	.529	—	Michael Ryan	294,486	4,395	2017
Bowie Baysox (Orioles)	72	68	.514	2	Gary Kendall	234,789	3,453	Never
Akron RubberDucks (Indians)	69	71	.535	5	Mark Budzinski	343,351	5,202	2016
Erie SeaWolves (Tigers)	65	75	.464	9	Lance Parrish	214,394	3,350	Never
Richmond Flying Squirrels (Giants)	63	77	.450	11	Kyle Haines	386,185	6,034	2014
Harrisburg Senators (Nationals)	60	80	.429	13	Matt LeCroy	262,872	3,983	1999

Semifinals: Trenton defeated Binghamton 3-1 and Altoona defeated Bowie 3-0 in best-of-five series. **Finals:** Altoona defeated Trenton 3-0 in a best-of-five series.

CLUB BATTING

	AVG	G	AB	R	H	2B	3B	HR	RBI	BB	SO	SB	OBP	SLG
Bowie	.283	140	4816	697	1361	268	21	143	661	429	940	68	.345	.436
Portland Sea	.264	139	4549	619	1202	239	18	126	578	413	1050	62	.331	.408
Trenton	.264	140	4560	659	1202	237	44	103	616	492	935	79	.339	.403
Erie	.261	140	4666	614	1218	236	29	146	573	429	1059	86	.327	.418
Reading	.261	140	4700	642	1226	240	30	153	590	423	1080	87	.326	.422
Binghamton	.260	139	4457	582	1159	222	20	66	540	503	918	111	.337	.363
Harrisburg	.258	140	4614	588	1189	225	21	109	538	468	1082	67	.330	.386
Altoona	.256	140	4666	584	1192	223	37	99	540	454	931	83	.327	.383
New Hampshire	.255	139	4460	564	1139	230	22	89	512	464	953	97	.331	.377
Akron	.251	140	4507	621	1132	227	26	144	589	482	1147	115	.330	.409
Richmond	.250	140	4591	523	1148	238	33	93	485	399	971	41	.313	.377
Hartford	.246	139	4506	549	1107	210	31	112	515	439	1145	111	.319	.381

CLUB PITCHING

	ERA	G	CG	SHO	SV	IP	H	R	ER	HR	BB	SO	AVG
Trenton	2.83	140	7	2	47	1211	1057	442	381	92	429	1160	.234
Binghamton	3.20	139	14	7	41	1177	1079	462	419	86	365	990	.245
Altoona	3.67	140	2	0	46	1238	1229	563	505	82	464	1046	.259
Reading	3.94	140	1	0	35	1214	1157	600	532	134	467	960	.254
Richmond	4.04	140	5	3	29	1201	1200	603	539	96	497	1032	.262
Bowie	4.10	140	3	0	36	1219	1226	610	556	126	491	1097	.262
Erie	4.22	140	4	1	38	1205	1250	643	565	128	397	1097	.266
Hartford	4.35	139	5	2	37	1203	1214	654	581	134	413	971	.262
Akron	4.43	140	3	0	39	1189	1214	664	585	125	397	958	.264
New Hampshire	4.47	139	2	0	26	1175	1182	650	584	133	496	962	.261
Harrisburg	4.50	140	4	0	38	1199	1257	671	599	136	441	899	.271
Portland	4.62	139	4	1	26	1170	1210	680	601	111	538	1039	.269

CLUB FIELDING

	PCT	PO	A	E	DP
Binghamton	.987	4362	1381	74	266
Bowie	.982	4573	1261	108	331
Altoona	.981	4526	1494	119	357
Richmond	.980	4412	1462	120	346
Reading	.980	4473	1460	122	376
Harrisburg	.979	4474	1465	125	372
Erie	.978	4478	1266	127	282
Portland	.978	4279	1349	126	351
Trenton	.978	4445	1316	129	313
Akron	.978	4444	1382	132	288
New Hampshire	.977	4389	1353	136	312
Hartford	.975	4415	1472	151	341

INDIVIDUAL BATTING

Batter, Club	AVG	G	AB	R	H	2B	3B	HR	RBI	BB	SO	SB
Rosa, Garabez, Bowie	.310	124	523	75	162	24	2	14	91	17	98	1
Tocci, Carlos, Reading	.307	113	430	59	132	19	7	2	48	29	66	4
Fuentes, Josh, Hartford	.307	122	414	48	127	28	7	15	72	24	92	8
Ficociello, Dominic, Erie	.306	90	330	53	101	21	2	7	39	42	87	10
Mars, Danny, Portland	.304	119	477	62	145	21	4	6	47	33	95	12
Estrada, Thairo, Trenton	.301	122	495	72	149	19	4	6	48	34	56	8
Mejia, Francisco, Akron	.297	92	347	52	103	21	2	14	52	24	53	7
Taylor, Kevin, Binghamton	.292	114	383	44	112	20	1	3	46	54	53	2
Hernandez, Yadiel, Harrisburg	.292	120	397	57	116	21	1	12	59	56	66	5
Gerber, Mike, Erie	.291	92	350	62	102	22	2	13	45	39	85	10

INDIVIDUAL PITCHING

Pitcher, Club	W	L	ERA	G	GS	CG	SV	IP	H	R	ER	BB	SO
Oswalt, Corey, Binghamton	12	5	2.28	24	24	2	0	134	118	40	34	40	119
Pannone, Thomas, Akron/New	7	3	2.92	20	20	1	0	117	98	43	38	29	110
Long, Lucas, Bowie	9	6	2.95	31	14	2	5	128	124	45	42	33	106
Coley, Austin, Altoona	6	4	3.01	29	23	0	0	144	144	49	48	31	114
Conlon, P.J., Binghamton	8	9	3.38	28	22	3	1	136	130	53	51	38	108
Anderson, Tanner, Altoona	10	8	3.38	30	19	0	0	133	134	54	50	33	97
Ramirez, Yefry, Bowie/Trenton	15	3	3.47	24	24	3	0	124	105	51	48	49	117
Simms, John, Harrisburg	5	6	3.54	19	19	0	0	112	96	46	44	28	87
Jannis, Mickey, Binghamton	8	7	3.60	21	21	2	0	122	115	56	49	38	83
McRae, Alex, Altoona	10	5	3.61	27	25	1	0	150	170	71	60	36	89

ALL-STAR TEAM

C: Francisco Mejia, Akron. **1B:** Edwin Espinal, Altoona. **2B:** Luis Guillorme, Binghamton. **3B:** Josh Fuentes, Hartford. **SS:** Thairo Estrada, Trenton. **OF:** Jeremy Barfield, Portland; Danny Mars, Portland; Christin Stewart, Erie. **DH:** Eric Haase, Akron. **UT:** Garabez Rosa, Bowie. **RHP:** Corey Oswalt, Binghamton. **LHP:** P.J. Conlon, Binghamton. **RP:** Shane Broyles, Hartford.

Most Valuable Player: Garabez Rosa, Bowie
Pitcher of the Year: Corey Oswalt, Binghamton
Rookie of the Year: Francisco Mejia, Akron
Manager of the Year: Bobby Mitchell, Trenton

DEPARTMENT LEADERS

BATTING

OBP	Ford, Mike, Trenton	.410
SLG	Barfield, Jeremy, Portland	.584
OPS	Barfield, Jeremy, Portland	.944
R	Stewart, D.J., Bowie	80
H	Rosa, Garabez, Bowie	162
TB	Stewart, Christin, Erie	243
XBH	Stewart, Christin, Erie	60
2B	Urena, Richard, New Hampshire	36
3B	Gindl, Caleb, Richmond	7
	Tocci, Carlos, Reading	7
	Fuentes, Josh, Hartford	7
HR	Stewart, Christin, Erie	28
RBI	Rosa, Garabez, Bowie	91
SAC	Davis, J.D., New Hampshire	11
BB	Ford, Mike, Trenton	76
HBP	McBroom, Ryan, New Hamp., Trenton	14
SO	Stewart, Christin, Erie	138
	Heidt, Gunnar, New Hampshire	138
SB	Stuart, Champ, Binghamton	35
CS	Reyes, Pablo, Altoona	14
	Weeks, Drew, Hartford	14
	Davis, J.D., New Hampshire	14
AB/SO	Hinojosa, C.J, Richmond	8.88

FIELDING

C PCT	Wynns, Austin, Bowie	.998
PO	Wynns, Austin, Bowie	740
A	Mejia, Francisco, Akron	86
DP	Jhang, Jin-De, Altoona	11
E	Read, Raudy, Harrisburg	10
PB	Plaia, Colton, Binghamton	16
1B PCT	Oberste, Matt, Binghamton	.997
PO	Bradley, Bobby, Akron	1028
A	Martin, Kyle, Reading	73
DP	Martin, Kyle, Reading	102
E	Rodriguez, Aderlin, Bowie	10
2B PCT	Krieger, Tyler, Akron	.967
PO	Krieger, Tyler, Akron	197
A	Krieger, Tyler, Akron	237
DP	Tobias, Josh, Portland	60
E	Krieger, Tyler, Akron	15
3B PCT	Fuentes, Josh, Hartford	.965
PO	Thompson, David, Binghamton	82
A	Fuentes, Josh, Hartford	252
DP	Fuentes, Josh, Hartford	28
E	Heidt, Gunnar, New Hampshire	17
SS PCT	Salcedo, Erick, Bowie	.966
PO	Abreu, Osvaldo, Harrisburg	187
A	Chang, Yu-Cheng, Akron	373
DP	Abreu, Osvaldo, Harrisburg	81
E	Abreu, Osvaldo, Harrisburg	29
	Simcox, A.J., Erie	29
OF PCT	Tromp, Jiandido, Reading	1.000
PO	Davis, J.D., New Hampshire	305
A	Weeks, Drew, Hartford	11
DP	Cole, Hunter, Richmond	4
E	Weeks, Drew, Hartford	9

PITCHING

G	Scioneaux, Tate, Altoona	47
	Cyr, Tyler, Richmond	47
	Broyles, Shane, Hartford	47
GS	Castellani, Ryan, Hartford	27
	Reid-Foley, Sean, New Hampshire	27
GF	Broyles, Shane, Hartford	37
SV	Broyles, Shane, Hartford	21
W	Ramirez, Yefry, Bowie	15
L	Ball, Trey, Portland	12
	Castellani, Ryan, Hartford	12
IP	Castellani, Ryan, Hartford	157
H	Alexander, Tyler, Erie	178
R	French, Parker, Hartford	108
ER	French, Parker, Hartford	91
HB	Castellani, Ryan, Hartford	12
BB	Greene, Conner, New Hampshire	83
SO	Castellani, Ryan, Hartford	132
SO/9	Ramirez, Yefry, Bowie, Trenton	8.47
SO/9(RP)	Isaacs, Dusty, New Hampshire	11.09
BB/9	Wynkoop, Jack, Hartford	1.32
WP	Greene, Conner, New Hampshire	13
	Castellani, Ryan, Hartford	13
BK	Buttrey, Ty, Portland	3
HR	Reid-Foley, Sean, New Hampshire	22
	French, Parker, Hartford	22
AVG	Pannone, Thomas, Akron, New Hamp.	.227

SOUTHERN LEAGUE DOUBLE-A

MINOR LEAGUES

BY MATT EDDY

Pitchers ruled the Double-A Southern League in 2017 to a greater degree than usual in the hitter-hostile circuit. No minor league in 2017 saw fewer runs scored per game (3.95), and no Double-A or Triple-A league featured a lower ERA (3.60) or OPS (.688) than the SL.

Against that backdrop, the exploits of 19-year-old Mississippi outfielder Ronald Acuna, the BA Minor League Player of the Year, and Pensacola third baseman Nick Senzel, the No. 2 pick in the 2016 draft, stood out. Birmingham outfielder Eloy Jimenez, acquired by the White Sox from the Cubs in the Jose Quintana trade, also excited observers in an 18-game trial. All three hitters rank as top 10 overall prospects in baseball.

Though Mississippi finished with the second-worst record in the SL, the Braves affiliate at one point featured three 19-year-olds in a league where the average player was 24. In addition to Acuna, who advanced to Triple-A on July 13, the Braves' rotation featured 2015 first-rounders Mike Soroka and Kolby Allard all season. The righthanded Soroka ranked second in the SL in ERA (2.75) and walk rate (2.0 per nine innings). Allard, a lefthander waylaid by back trouble in his draft year, proved his durability by leading the SL with 27 starts and ranking fifth with 129 strikeouts.

Though it couldn't match the prospect firepower of Mississippi, Chattanooga was the class of the league—and the Twins affiliate featured its share of future big league talent, too. The Lookouts led the SL in runs per game (4.71) and ERA (3.09) and finished with a plus-177 run differential that ranked fourth best in the full-season minor leagues. Chattanooga was declared co-champions, along with Pensacola, after Hurricane Irma threatened the southeast with heavy rain.

Chattanooga shortstop Nick Gordon ranked first in the SL in triples (eight) and third in hits (140) and runs (80) while batting .270/.341/.408. Outfielder LaMonte Wade showed the best strike-zone judgment in the SL and ranked third with 76 walks and a .397 on-base percentage.

Righthanders Fernando Romero and Felix Jorge and lefty Stephen Gonsalves paced the Lookouts' pitching staff, though the Twins bumped Gonsalves to Triple-A in August. Romero flashed three plus pitches and ranked fourth in the league with 8.6 strikeouts per nine innings.

TOP 20 PROSPECTS

1. Ronald Acuna, OF, Mississippi (Braves)
2. Nick Senzel, 3B, Pensacola (Reds)
3. Michael Kopech, RHP, Birmingham (White Sox)
4. Mike Soroka, RHP, Mississippi (Braves)
5. Luiz Gohara, LHP, Mississippi (Braves)
6. Austin Riley, 3B, Mississippi (Braves)
7. Luis Castillo, RHP, Pensacola (Reds)
8. Corbin Burnes, RHP, Biloxi (Brewers)
9. Nick Gordon, SS/2B, Chattanooga (Twins)
10. Kolby Allard, LHP, Mississippi (Braves)
11. Fernando Romero, RHP, Chattanooga (Twins)
12. Luis Ortiz, RHP, Biloxi (Brewers)
13. Tyler Mahle, RHP, Pensacola (Reds)
14. Stephen Gonsalves, LHP, Chattanooga (Twins)
15. Jaime Barria, RHP, Mobile (Angels)
16. Justin Williams, OF, Montgomery (Rays)
17. Dawel Lugo, 3B/SS, Jackson (Diamondbacks)
18. LaMonte Wade, OF, Chattanooga (Twins)
19. Max Fried, LHP, Mississippi (Braves)
20. Taylor Clarke, RHP, Jackson (D-backs)

STANDINGS: SPLIT SEASON

FIRST HALF

NORTH	W	L	PCT	GB
Chattanooga	42	28	.600	—
Jackson	37	33	.529	5
Montgomery	37	33	.529	5
Tennessee	36	33	.522	5½
Birmingham	26	43	.377	15½
SOUTH	**W**	**L**	**PCT**	**GB**
Pensacola	40	30	.571	—
Biloxi	36	33	.522	3½
Mississippi	34	36	.486	6
Mobile	30	39	.435	9½
Jacksonville	30	40	.429	10

SECOND HALF

NORTH	W	L	PCT	GB
Chattanooga	49	21	.700	—
Montgomery	39	31	.557	10
Jackson	34	36	.486	15
Tennessee	32	37	.464	16½
Birmingham	27	42	.391	21½
SOUTH	**W**	**L**	**PCT**	**GB**
Jacksonville	39	31	.557	—
Biloxi	35	33	.515	3
Mobile	34	36	.486	5
Pensacola	34	36	.486	5
Mississippi	24	44	.353	14

Playoffs—Semifinals: Chattanooga defeated Montgomery 3-2 and Pensacola defeated Jacksonville 3-0 in best-of-five series. **Finals:** Cancelled. Chattanooga, Pensacola declared co-champions.

OVERALL STANDINGS

North Division	W	L	PCT	GB	Manager(s)	Attendance	Average	Last Pennant
Chattanooga Lookouts (Twins)	91	49	.650	—	Jake Mauer	209,948	3,181	2017
Montgomery Biscuits (Rays)	76	64	.543	15	Brady Williams	228,376	3,409	2007
Jackson Generals (D-backs)	71	69	.507	20	J.R. House	120,695	1,775	2016
Tennessee Smokies (Cubs)	68	70	.493	22	Mark Johnson	313,796	4,981	2004
Birmingham Barons (White Sox)	53	85	.384	37	Julio Vinas	391,725	5,935	2013
South Division	**W**	**L**	**PCT**	**GB**	**Manager(s)**	**Attendance**	**Average**	**Last Pennant**
Pensacola Blue Wahoos (Reds)	74	66	.529	—	Pat Kelly	298,108	4,320	2017
Biloxi Shuckers (Brewers)	71	66	.518	1½	Mike Guerrero	167,151	2,572	Never
Jacksonville Jumbo Shrimp (Marlins)	69	71	.493	5	Randy Ready	325,743	5,171	2014
Mobile BayBears (Angels)	64	75	.460	9½	Sal Fasano	92,898	1,498	2012
Mississippi Braves (Braves)	58	80	.420	15	Luis Salazar	190,645	2,889	2008

CLUB BATTING

	AVG	G	AB	R	H	2B	3B	HR	RBI	BB	SO	SB	OBP	SLG
Jackson	.265	140	4694	626	1246	280	26	118	584	471	1037	69	.336	.412
Montgomery	.263	140	4729	647	1245	270	43	84	588	522	1083	159	.339	.392
Chattanooga	.255	140	4659	659	1190	242	32	90	615	610	1171	67	.347	.379
Mobile	.244	139	4515	532	1102	196	22	72	482	477	1009	136	.323	.345
Tennessee	.244	138	4438	549	1081	211	21	114	497	439	1088	44	.320	.378
Jacksonville	.243	140	4438	510	1076	197	34	86	470	476	1152	59	.321	.360
Biloxi	.235	137	4490	507	1056	211	20	96	470	391	1110	142	.305	.355
Mississippi	.233	138	4517	498	1052	191	27	98	462	405	1170	70	.301	.352
Birmingham	.232	138	4455	463	1034	188	20	96	428	424	1138	63	.304	.348
Pensacola	.229	140	4485	502	1029	222	26	82	462	485	1116	78	.310	.345

CLUB PITCHING

	ERA	G	CG	SHO	SV	IP	H	R	ER	HR	BB	SO	AVG
Chattanooga	3.09	140	2	1	46	1248	1095	482	429	75	469	1157	.237
Pensacola	3.14	140	4	3	45	1215	1057	468	424	88	438	1175	.236
Biloxi	3.19	137	5	5	43	1208	1036	496	428	84	462	1198	.233
Mississippi	3.56	138	5	1	32	1216	1066	559	481	77	562	1196	.237
Jacksonville	3.69	140	3	1	32	1185	1148	551	486	107	375	993	.254
Montgomery	3.74	140	1	1	37	1234	1116	586	513	123	518	1057	.243
Mobile	3.76	139	2	2	28	1222	1109	561	510	129	456	1053	.243
Tennessee	3.81	138	3	1	28	1187	1123	565	503	92	435	974	.250
Jackson	3.85	140	1	1	38	1222	1172	602	523	81	506	1130	.254
Birmingham	4.13	138	5	2	37	1193	1189	623	547	80	479	1141	.260

CLUB FIELDING

	PCT	PO	A	E	DP
Pensacola	.984	4459	1292	92	338
Chattanooga	.984	4575	1380	96	306
Tennessee	.983	4454	1337	102	324
Mobile	.982	4551	1329	111	316
Jacksonville	.981	4407	1368	113	312
Mississippi	.980	4430	1340	118	342
Montgomery	.979	4635	1379	128	356
Jackson	.979	4556	1326	129	325
Biloxi	.977	4445	1317	134	323
Birmingham	.976	4329	1388	143	304

INDIVIDUAL BATTING

Batter, Club	AVG	G	AB	R	H	2B	3B	HR	RBI	BB	SO	SB
Lee, Braxton, Montgomery/Jacksonville	.309	127	476	81	147	21	3	3	37	65	104	20
Rodriguez, Jonathan, Chattanooga	.308	119	434	87	134	31	0	21	76	80	113	2
Corcino, Edgar, Chattanooga	.302	102	401	54	121	19	1	6	50	38	66	4
Williams, Justin, Montgomery	.301	96	366	53	110	21	3	14	72	37	69	6
Wade, LaMonte, Chattanooga	.293	117	424	74	124	22	3	7	67	76	71	9
Reyes, Victor, Jackson	.292	126	479	59	140	29	5	4	51	27	80	18
Meneses, Joey, Mississippi	.292	108	360	44	105	13	0	9	45	38	81	0
Norwood, John, Jacksonville	.285	135	473	68	135	17	4	19	62	59	134	4
Vidal, David, Jacksonville	.285	107	376	53	107	26	1	10	41	45	70	1
McCarthy, Joe, Montgomery	.284	127	454	76	129	31	8	7	56	90	94	20

INDIVIDUAL PITCHING

Pitcher, Club	W	L	ERA	G	GS	CG	SV	IP	H	R	ER	BB	SO
Long, Grayson, Mobile	8	6	2.52	23	23	0	0	122	100	38	34	38	111
Soroka, Mike, Mississippi	11	8	2.75	26	26	0	0	154	133	58	47	34	125
McGuire, Deck, Pensacola	9	9	2.79	28	27	0	0	168	125	58	52	57	170
Kopech, Michael, Birmingham	8	7	2.87	22	22	0	0	119	77	45	38	60	155
Mazza, Chris, Jacksonville	4	7	3.01	28	26	0	0	147	138	56	49	41	93
Mujica, Jose, Montgomery	13	8	3.03	25	25	0	0	154	128	56	52	44	86
Wilkerson, Aaron, Biloxi	11	4	3.16	24	24	2	0	142	117	54	50	36	143
Allard, Kolby, Mississippi	8	11	3.18	27	27	2	0	150	146	62	53	45	129
Tomshaw, Matt, Jacksonville	13	6	3.48	27	27	1	0	163	170	66	63	36	114
Hedges, Zach, Tennessee	9	9	3.49	22	22	2	0	129	143	61	50	30	71

ALL-STAR TEAM

C: Nick Ciuffo, Montgomery. **1B:** Kevin Cron, Jackson. **2B:** David Bote, Tennessee. **3B:** Jason Vosler. **SS:** Nick Gordon, Chattanooga. **OF:** Edgar Corcino, Chattanooga; Braxton Lee, Montgomery/Jacksonville; Joe McCarthy, Montgomery; Justin Williams, Montgomery. **DH:** Jonathan Rodriguez, Chattanooga. **UT:** Zach Houchins, Mobile. **RHP:** Michael Kopech, Birmingham. **LHP:** Kolby Allard, Mississippi. **RP:** Gabriel Moya, Jackson/Chattanooga.

Most Valuable Player: Kevin Cron, Jackson

Most Outstanding Pitcher: Michael Kopech, Birmingham

Manager of the Year: Jake Mauer, Chattanooga

DEPARTMENT LEADERS

BATTING

OBP	Rodriguez, Jonathan, Chattanooga	.414
SLG	Rodriguez, Jonathan, Chattanooga	.525
OPS	Rodriguez, Jonathan, Chattanooga	.939
R	Rodriguez, Jonathan, Chattanooga	87
H	Lee, Braxton, Mont., Jacksonville	147
TB	Cron, Kevin, Jackson	256
XBH	Cron, Kevin, Jackson	60
2B	Kay, Grant, Montgomery	36
3B	Gordon, Nick, Chattanooga	8
	McCarthy, Joe, Montgomery	8
HR	Cron, Kevin, Jackson	25
RBI	Cron, Kevin, Jackson	91
SAC	Lee, Braxton, Mont., Jacksonville	11
	Trahan, Blake, Pensacola	11
BB	McCarthy, Joe, Montgomery	90
HBP	Vosler, Jason, Tennessee	20
	Nottingham, Jacob, Biloxi	20
SO	Lien, Connor, Mississippi	160
SB	Davis, Johnny, Biloxi	52
CS	Lee, Braxton, Mont., Jacksonville	13
AB/SO	Robbins, Mason, Birmingham	9.80

FIELDING

C PCT	Hudson, Joe, Pensacola	.997
PO	Nottingham, Jacob, Biloxi	692
A	Nottingham, Jacob, Biloxi	84
DP	Briceno, Jose, Mobile	8
E	Briceno, Jose, Mobile	12
PB	Hernandez, Oscar, Jackson	23
1B PCT	Ard, Taylor, Jacksonville	.993
PO	Cron, Kevin, Jackson	965
A	Cron, Kevin, Jackson	69
DP	Cron, Kevin, Jackson	94
E	Cron, Kevin, Jackson	10
	Barnum, Keon, Birmingham	10
2B PCT	Bote, David, Tennessee	.988
PO	Bote, David, Tennessee	195
A	Bote, David, Tennessee	314
DP	Bote, David, Tennessee	67
E	Demeritte, Travis, Mississippi	13
3B PCT	Vosler, Jason, Tennessee	.974
PO	White, T.J., Chattanooga	75
A	Vosler, Jason, Tennessee	185
DP	Vosler, Jason, Tennessee	20
	Anderson, Brian, Jacksonville	20
E	Riley, Austin, Mississippi	13
	Kay, Grant, Montgomery	13
SS PCT	Trahan, Blake, Pensacola	.982
PO	Moore, Dylan, Mississippi	189
A	Trahan, Blake, Pensacola	345
DP	Moore, Dylan, Mississippi	78
E	Penalver, Carlos, Tennessee	24
OF PCT	Reyes, Victor, Jackson	.997
PO	Davis, Johnny, Biloxi	332
A	Lee, Braxton, Mont., Jacksonville	18
DP	Reyes, Victor, Jackson	5
E	Aquino, Aristides, Pensacola	8

PITCHING

G	Harrison, Jordan, Montgomery	53
	Bird, Kyle, Montgomery	53
GS	Allard, Kolby, Mississippi	27
	Tomshaw, Matt, Jacksonville	27
	McGuire, Deck, Pensacola	27
GF	Ramsey, Matt, Biloxi	42
SV	Ramsey, Matt, Biloxi	27
W	Mujica, Jose, Montgomery	13
	Tomshaw, Matt, Jacksonville	13
	Underwood Jr., Duane, Tennessee	13
L	Adams, Spencer, Birmingham	15
IP	McGuire, Deck, Pensacola	168
H	Adams, Spencer, Birmingham	171
R	Adams, Spencer, Birmingham	80
ER	Adams, Spencer, Birmingham	75
HB	Mazza, Chris, Jacksonville	13
BB	Pike, Tyler, Mississippi	63
SO	McGuire, Deck, Pensacola	170
SO/9	Kopech, Michael, Birmingham	11.69
SO/9(RP)	Moya, Gabriel, Jackson, Chattanooga	13.42
BB/9	Gunkel, Joe, Jacksonville	1.64
WP	Scott, Tayler, Biloxi	13
	Stewart, Kohl, Chattanooga	13
BK	Garner, David, Tennessee	3
HR	Adams, Spencer, Birmingham	19
AVG	Kopech, Michael, Birmingham	.184

MINOR LEAGUES

TEXAS LEAGUE DOUBLE-A

BY JOHN MANUEL

Minor league dynasties are hard to find in modern baseball. But the Texas League has one, and baseball fans should take notice.

The Midland RockHounds, the Athletics affiliate, won their fourth straight TL title, the longest streak in the league since the Fort Worth Cats won six in a row from 1920-25. The last minor league team to win four straight league titles was the Harrisburg Senators, then the Expos affiliate, which won the Double-A Eastern League from 1996-99.

The last longer dynasty in the full-season minor leagues was Orioles affiliate Miami; the minor league Marlins won five straight Florida State League titles from 1968-72.

Righthander James Naile earned the victory in the playoff clincher for the second straight season, giving manager Fran Riordan a title in his first season with the RockHounds. Ryan Christenson managed the previous two champions, while Aaron Nieckula skippered the 2014 club.

Midland lost the first two games of the championship series before rallying to win the last three, two by shutout, including a 1-0 decision in Game Five. Naile threw six shutout innings to start it, and veteran minor leaguer Viosergy Rosa had an RBI single in the first inning for the game's only run. Rosa had a minors-best 16 RBIs in 10 postseason games.

Midland went just 67-71 overall and made the playoffs as a wild card, clinching a spot on the season's final day, after San Antonio won both halves of the TL's South Division. The Missions (78-62) had the league's best record. San Antonio led the league with a 3.28 team ERA with a rotation that included prospects such as lefthanders Eric Lauer and Joey Lucchesi at season's end. Teen shortstop Fernando Tatis Jr. joined the team in August and went 7-for-20 in the playoffs.

Springfield and Tulsa tied for the best overall record in the TL North, with Tulsa winning the second-half title. Northwest Arkansas won the first half title, so Springfield didn't make the postseason at all despite going 77-63 overall. Cardinals righthander Dakota Hudson was the league's pitcher of the year after winning the league's ERA title, while Tulsa's Matt Beatty, the league's batting champ, won the MVP award.

The Missions' Phillip Wellman was manager of the year, while a team highlight came in May, when righthander threw the club's first complete-game no-hitter since 1979. he walked one and struck out three while needing just 94 pitches.

TOP 20 PROSPECTS

1. Walker Buehler, RHP, Tulsa (Dodgers)
2. Kyle Tucker, OF, Corpus Christi (Astros)
3. A.J. Puk, LHP, Midland (Athletics)
4. Jack Flaherty, RHP, Springfield (Cardinals)
5. Luis Urias, 2B/SS, San Antonio (Padres)
6. Jorge Mateo, SS, Midland (Athletics)
7. Yohander Mendez, LHP, Frisco (Rangers)
8. Edwin Rios, 1B/3B, Tulsa (Dodgers)
9. Magneuris Sierra, OF, Springfield (Cardinals)
10. Dakota Hudson, RHP, Springfield (Cardinals)
11. Jose Adolis Garcia, OF, Springfield (Cardinals)
12. Rogelio Armenteros, RHP, Corpus Christi (Astros)
13. J.D. Davis, 3B, Corpus Christi (Astros)
14. Oscar Mercado, OF, Springfield (Cardinals)
15. Joey Lucchesi, LHP, San Antonio (Padres)
16. Eric Lauer, LHP, San Antonio (Padres)
17. Grant Holmes, RHP, Midland (Athletics)
18. Josh Naylor, 1B, San Antonio (Padres)
19. Foster Griffin, LHP, Northwest Arkansas (Royals)
20. Sandy Alcantara, RHP, Springfield (Cardinals)

STANDINGS: SPLIT SEASON

FIRST HALF

NORTH	W	L	PCT	GB
NW Arkansas	39	31	.557	—
Springfield	35	35	.500	4
Tulsa	33	37	.471	6
Arkansas	32	38	.457	7
SOUTH	**W**	**L**	**PCT**	**GB**
San Antonio	41	29	.586	—
Midland	35	35	.500	6
Corpus Christi	34	36	.471	7
Frisco	31	39	.443	10

SECOND HALF

NORTH	W	L	PCT	GB
Tulsa	44	26	.629	—
Springfield	42	28	.600	2
Arkansas	33	37	.471	11
NW Arkansas	28	42	.400	16
SOUTH	**W**	**L**	**PCT**	**GB**
San Antonio	37	33	.529	—
Corpus Christi	33	35	.485	3
Midland	32	36	.471	4
Frisco	29	41	.414	8

Playoffs—Semifinals: Midland defeated San Antonio 3-2 and Tulsa defeated NW Arkansas 3-2 in best-of-five series. **Finals:** Midland defeated Tulsa 3-2 in a best-of-five series.

OVERALL STANDINGS

North Division	W	L	PCT	GB	Manager(s)	Attendance	Average	Last Pennant
Springfield Cardinals (Cardinals)	77	63	.550	—	Johnny Rodriguez	331,259	4,801	2012
Tulsa Drillers (Dodgers)	77	63	.550	—	Ryan Garko/Scott Hennessey	374,976	5,597	1998
Northwest Arkansas Naturals (Royals)	67	73	.479	10	Vance Wilson	304,026	4,471	2010
Arkansas Travelers (Mariners)	65	75	.464	12	Daren Brown	328,347	4,975	2008
South Division	**W**	**L**	**PCT**	**GB**	**Manager(s)**	**Attendance**	**Average**	**Last Pennant**
San Antonio Missions (Padres)	78	62	.557	—	Phillip Wellman	305,351	4,557	2013
Corpus Christi Hooks (Astros)	67	71	.486	10	Rodney Linares	331,242	4,944	2006
Midland RockHounds (Athletics)	67	71	.486	10	Fran Riordan	282,146	4,211	2017
Frisco RoughRiders (Rangers)	60	80	.429	18	Joe Mikulik	470,003	6,812	2004

CLUB BATTING

	AVG	G	AB	R	H	2B	3B	HR	RBI	BB	SO	SB	OBP	SLG
Midland	.277	138	4733	668	1310	247	39	84	601	471	1013	108	.346	.399
Tulsa	.269	140	4786	672	1288	245	18	168	631	408	1125	97	.335	.433
Springfield	.264	140	4689	634	1236	244	21	117	588	464	1090	120	.335	.399
Arkansas	.262	140	4719	607	1237	222	17	80	562	458	1040	88	.334	.367
Northwest Arkansas	.260	140	4782	544	1244	189	24	80	506	310	1051	119	.312	.360
San Antonio	.253	140	4675	598	1183	218	21	100	552	431	1067	59	.323	.373
Frisco	.250	140	4799	545	1198	217	27	103	494	353	966	83	.307	.371
Corpus Christi	.242	138	4548	586	1099	203	19	143	542	507	1149	105	.324	.389

CLUB PITCHING

	ERA	G	CG	SHO	SV	IP	H	R	ER	HR	BB	SO	AVG
San Antonio	3.28	140	2	1	43	1249	1130	529	456	87	403	1186	.240
Tulsa	3.62	140	1	1	37	1231	1147	576	495	98	492	1135	.244
Springfield	3.62	140	3	1	34	1230	1182	562	495	111	445	987	.253
Corpus Christi	3.95	138	0	0	33	1202	1276	629	527	99	404	1095	.271
Northwest Arkansas	4.21	140	1	1	40	1228	1298	643	574	115	435	1022	.272
Midland	4.22	138	0	0	32	1209	1253	635	567	107	434	1010	.268
Arkansas	4.24	140	3	1	31	1214	1247	621	572	112	393	988	.265
Frisco	4.31	140	3	3	34	1244	1262	659	596	146	396	1078	.264

CLUB FIELDING

	PCT	PO	A	E	DP		PCT	PO	A	E	DP
Arkansas	.985	4542	1339	87	350	NW Arkansas	.979	4651	1348	127	375
Corpus Christi	.977	4382	1345	136	405	San Antonio	.979	4548	1352	125	279
Frisco	.981	4534	1474	117	412	Springfield	.979	4545	1371	127	394
Midland	.982	4429	1410	109	436	Tulsa	.975	4496	1364	153	309

INDIVIDUAL BATTING

Batter, Club	AVG	G	AB	R	H	2B	3B	HR	RBI	BB	SO	SB
Beaty, Matt, Tulsa	.327	116	438	61	143	31	1	15	69	35	54	3
Miller, Ian, Arkansas	.326	83	344	63	112	18	3	4	29	28	69	30
Boyd, B.J., Midland	.323	130	533	82	172	29	6	5	56	34	74	16
Schrock, Max, Midland	.321	106	417	55	134	19	1	7	46	34	42	4
Waldrop, Kyle, Arkansas	.303	109	412	61	125	28	0	10	68	37	86	4
Urias, Luis, San Antonio	.296	118	442	77	131	20	4	3	38	68	65	7
Garcia, Anthony, Springfield	.294	101	347	57	102	18	2	15	69	40	72	8
Mejia, Erick, Tulsa	.289	102	356	61	103	17	3	7	30	37	78	25
Kiner-Falefa, Isiah, Frisco	.289	129	513	58	148	31	3	5	48	41	72	17
Mercado, Oscar, Springfield	.287	120	477	76	137	20	4	13	46	32	112	38

INDIVIDUAL PITCHING

Pitcher, Club	W	L	ERA	G	GS	CG	SV	IP	H	R	ER	BB	SO
Hudson, Dakota, Springfield	9	4	2.53	18	18	1	0	114	111	38	32	34	77
Unsworth, Dylan, Arkansas	9	8	3.31	20	20	1	0	120	112	49	44	20	86
Gomber, Austin, Springfield	10	7	3.34	26	26	0	0	143	116	64	53	51	140
Ogando, Emilio, Northwest Arkansas	10	10	3.45	23	23	0	0	133	130	62	51	36	83
Fillmyer, Heath, Midland	11	5	3.49	29	29	0	0	150	158	66	58	51	115
Kennedy, Brett, San Antonio	13	7	3.70	26	26	0	0	141	133	62	58	38	134
Caughel, Lindsey, Arkansas	10	10	3.71	27	26	2	0	158	148	66	65	38	116
De Los Santos, Enyel, San Antonio	10	6	3.78	26	24	0	0	150	131	69	63	48	138
Mendez, Yohander, Frisco	7	8	3.79	24	24	1	0	138	114	60	58	43	124
Sborz, Josh, Tulsa	8	8	3.86	24	24	0	0	117	106	60	50	56	81

ALL-STAR TEAM

C: Jose Trevino, Frisco. **1B:** Viosergy Rosa, Midland. **2B:** Max Schrock, Midland. **3B:** J.D. Davis, Corpus Christi. **SS:** Luis Urias, San Antonio. **1B/3B:** Matt Beaty, Tulsa. **OF:** B.J. Boyd, Midland; Anthony Garcia, Springfield; Ian Miller, Arkansas. **RHP:** Dakota Hudson, Springfield; Trey Wingenter, San Antonio; Brett Kennedy, San Antonio; Matt Pearce, Springfield; Scott Barlow, Tulsa; Jack Flaherty, Springfield.

Most Valuable Player: Matt Beaty, Tulsa

Pitcher of the Year: Dakota Hudson, Springfield

Manager of the Year: Phillip Wellman, San Antonio

DEPARTMENT LEADERS

BATTING

OBP	Urias, Luis, San Antonio	.398
SLG	Davis, J.D., Corpus Christi	.510
OPS	Beaty, Matt, Tulsa	.883
R	Boyd, B.J., Midland	82
	Heineman, Scott, Frisco	82
H	Boyd, B.J., Midland	172
TB	Reyes, Franmil, San Antonio	235
XBH	Reyes, Franmil, San Antonio	53
2B	Beaty, Matt, Tulsa	31
	Kiner-Falefa, Isiah, Frisco	31
3B	Heineman, Scott, Frisco	7
	Mateo, Jorge, Midland	7
HR	Reyes, Franmil, San Antonio	25
RBI	Rosa, Viosergy, Midland	110
SAC	Lopez, Jack, Northwest Arkansas	7
BB	Singleton, Jon, Corpus Christi	107
HBP	Locastro, Tim, Tus	26
SO	Rosa, Viosergy, Midland	137
SB	Mercado, Oscar, Springfield (MO)	38
CS	Mercado, Oscar, Springfield (MO)	19
AB/SO	Schrock, Max, Midland	9.93

FIELDING

C PCT	Trevino, Jose, Frisco	.996
PO	Trevino, Jose, Frisco	762
A	Trevino, Jose, Frisco	64
DP	Stubbs, Garrett, Corpus Christi	6
	Dini, Nick, Northwest Arkansas	6
E	Ritchie, Jamie, Corpus Christi	9
PB	McGee, Stephen, San Antonio	12
1B PCT	Rosa, Viosergy, Midland	.992
PO	Rosa, Viosergy, Midland	1076
A	Rosa, Viosergy, Midland	71
DP	Rosa, Viosergy, Midland	130
E	Duenez, Samir, Northwest Arkansas	10
2B PCT	Schrock, Max, Midland	.986
PO	Schrock, Max, Midland	173
A	Schrock, Max, Midland	257
DP	Schrock, Max, Midland	83
E	Alvarez, Eliezer, Springfield	12
3B PCT	Wilson, Jacob, Springfield	.967
PO	Mejias-Brean, Seth, Arkansas	79
A	Wilson, Jacob, Springfield	167
DP	Davis, J.D., Corpus Christi	21
E	Tarsovich, Jordan, Midland	16
SS PCT	Wong, Joey, Arkansas	.980
PO	De Leon, Michael, Frisco	167
A	Wong, Joey, Arkansas	343
DP	De Leon, Michael, Frisco	82
E	De Leon, Michael, Frisco	20
OF PCT	Dewees Jr., Donald, NW Arkansas	.994
PO	Dewees Jr., Donald, NW Arkansas	335
A	Laureano, Ramon, Corpus Christi	16
DP	Laureano, Ramon, Corpus Christi	6
E	Tendler, Luke, Frisco	6
	Mercado, Oscar, Springfield	6

PITCHING

G	Copping, Corey, Tulsa	49
	Wingenter, Trey, San Antonio	49
GS	Fillmyer, Heath, Midland	29
	Ray, Corey, Northwest Arkansas	29
GF	Curtis, Zac, Arkansas	37
SV	Wingenter, Trey, San Antonio	20
W	Kennedy, Brett, San Antonio	13
L	Ray, Corey, Northwest Arkansas	12
	Holmes, Grant, Midland	12
	Wiles, Collin, Frisco	12
IP	Caughel, Lindsey, Arkansas	157
H	Jurado, Ariel, Frisco	188
R	Ray, Corey, Northwest Arkansas	97
ER	Ray, Corey, Northwest Arkansas	86
HB	Payano, Pedro, Frisco	16
BB	Holmes, Grant, Midland	61
SO	Holmes, Grant, Midland	150
SO/9	Holmes, Grant, Midland	9.10
SO/9(RP)	Sadzeck, Connor, Frisco	10.67
BB/9	Unsworth, Dylan, Arkansas	1.50
WP	Alcantara, Sandy, Springfield	20
BK	De Los Santos, Enyel, San Antonio	3
HR	Mendez, Yohander, Frisco	23
AVG	Gomber, Austin, Springfield	.219

CALIFORNIA LEAGUE HIGH CLASS A

BY KYLE GLASER

The 2017 California League looked very different than its predecessors. Gone were High Desert and Bakersfield, two long-standing franchises who contracted at the end of the 2016 and were replaced by expansion clubs in the Carolina League.

The Mariners purchased a controlling interest in the Modesto franchise and moved their affiliate there. Lancaster became a Rockies affiliate after operating as an Astros affiliate the previous eight seasons and serving as the training ground for Houston's future success.

While the makeup of the league shifted, the quality of play was as high as ever. Shortstop Brendan Rodgers (Lancaster), lefthander A.J. Puk (Stockton) and righthander Cal Quantrill (Lake Elsinore) lived up to their billing as Top-10 draft picks and shot through the league in the first half. Fellow first-rounders such as lefthander Eric Lauer (Lake Elsinore), catcher Will Smith (Rancho Cucamonga) and outfielder Kyle Lewis (Modesto) also performed, as did big-name international signees and a host of second and third-round selections.

It was Modesto that took the league title in its first year as a Mariners affiliate. The Nuts won the first-half North Division title and shared it in the second half before running through the postseason, sweeping Stockton in the semifinals and Lancaster in the championship round. Joe Rizzo, the Mariners 2016 second-round pick, was named championship series MVP after hitting .538 (7-for-13) with two doubles, a home run and four RBIs. Lewis, the Mariners 2016 first-rounder who missed the first half of the year recovering from a torn ACL, hit .429 with a 1.110 OPS in the title round.

Rancho Cucamonga's D.J. Peters was named league MVP after leading the league with an .886 OPS and finishing in the top five in in home runs (27), RBIs (82), walks (64) and total bases (259). Modesto righthander Nick Neidert, who was promoted to Double-A before the Nuts' championship run, earned pitcher of the year honors after going 10-3, 2.76 with 109 strikeouts against just 17 walks in 104.1 innings.

Rodgers, the third overall pick in 2015, posted a .387 batting average that was highest in the Cal League since Jose Altuve's .408 mark in 2011 (min. 230 PA). Rodgers did not amass enough plate appearances to qualify for the batting title however, so the award went to his Lancaster teammate Yonathan Daza, who hit .341.

TOP 20 PROSPECTS

1. Ryan Castellani, RHP, Modesto (Rockies)
2. Chris Shaw, 1B, San Jose (Giants)
3. Luis Urias, 2B/SS, Lake Elsinore (Padres)
4. Grant Holmes, RHP, Rancho/Stockton (Dodgers/A's)
5. Yusniel Diaz, OF, Rancho Cucamonga (Dodgers)
6. Michael Gettys, OF, Lake Elsinore (Padres)
7. Domingo Leyba, SS/2B, Visalia (D-backs)
8. Travis Demeritte, 2B, High Desert (Rangers)
9. Dinelson Lamet, RHP, Lake Elsinore (Padres)
10. Ariel Jurado, RHP, High Desert (Rangers)
11. Andrew Moore, RHP, Bakersfield (Mariners)
12. Dawel Lugo, 3B, Visalia (D-backs)
13. Johan Mieses, OF, Rancho Cucamonga (Dodgers)
14. Yency Almonte, RHP, Modesto (Rockies)
15. Drew Jackson, SS, Bakersfield (Mariners)
16. Josh Sborz, RHP, Rancho Cucamonga (Dodgers)
17. Franchy Cordero, OF, Lake Elsinore (Padres)
18. Jose Trevino, C, High Desert (Rangers)
19. Rodolfo Martinez, RHP, San Jose (Giants)
20. Ramon Laureano, OF, Lancaster (Astros)

STANDINGS: SPLIT SEASON

FIRST HALF

NORTH	W	L	PCT	GB
Modesto	39	31	.557	—
Stockton	36	34	.514	3
Visalia	36	34	.529	3
San Jose	30	40	.386	9
SOUTH	**W**	**L**	**PCT**	**GB**
Lancaster	38	32	.543	—
R. Cucamonga	36	34	.514	2
Lake Elsinore	35	35	.500	3
Inland Empire	30	40	.429	8

SECOND HALF

NORTH	W	L	PCT	GB
Stockton	35	35	.500	—
Modesto	35	35	.500	—
Visalia	33	37	.471	2
San Jose	32	38	.457	3
SOUTH	**W**	**L**	**PCT**	**GB**
Lancaster	41	29	.586	—
R. Cucamonga	40	30	.571	1
Inland Empire	35	35	.500	6
Lake Elsinore	29	41	.529	12

Playoffs—Semifinals: Modesto defeated Stockton 3-0 and Lancaster defeated Rancho Cucamonga 3-1 in best-of-five series. **Finals:** Modesto defeated Lancaster 3-0 in a best-of-five series.

OVERALL STANDINGS

North Division	W	L	PCT	GB	Manager(s)	Attendance	Average	Last Pennant
Modesto Nuts (Mariners)	74	66	.529	—	Mitch Canham	147,562	2,108	2017
Stockon Ports (Athletics)	71	69	.507	3	Rick Magnante	184,164	2,669	2008
Visalia Rawhide (D-backs)	69	71	.493	5	Shelley Duncan	126,419	1,806	1978
San Jose Giants (Giants)	62	78	.443	12	Nestor Rojas	163,373	2,368	2010
South Division	**W**	**L**	**PCT**	**GB**	**Manager(s)**	**Attendance**	**Average**	**Last Pennant**
Lancaster JetHawks (Rockies)	79	61	.564	—	Fred Osacio	169,237	2,418	2014
Rancho Cucamonga Quakes (Dodgers)	76	64	.543	3	Drew Saylor	171,622	2,452	2015
Inland Empire 66ers (Angels)	65	75	.464	14	Chad Tracy	202,336	2,891	2013
Lake Eisinore Storm (Padres)	64	76	.457	15	Edwin Rodriguez	199,661	2,894	2011

CALIFORNIA LEAGUE STATISTICS

CLUB BATTING

	AVG	G	AB	R	H	2B	3B	HR	RBI	BB	SO	SB	OBP	SLG
Lancaster	.308	140	4936	867	1519	296	61	116	788	408	980	313	.360	.463
Inland Empire	.265	140	4846	680	1285	256	51	95	616	500	1192	133	.340	.398
Rancho Cucamonga	.263	140	4824	732	1270	246	37	160	667	473	1389	77	.339	.429
Stockton	.263	140	4854	717	1277	238	36	156	677	486	1332	67	.335	.423
Modesto	.262	140	4839	676	1267	269	41	91	605	527	1121	121	.340	.391
San Jose	.256	140	4884	633	1252	266	32	124	592	335	1275	63	.310	.400
Lake Elsinore	.255	140	4806	630	1224	256	47	116	587	385	1341	71	.316	.400
Visalia	.247	140	4715	574	1165	238	41	83	522	382	1236	111	.309	.368

CLUB PITCHING

	ERA	G	CG	SHO	SV	IP	H	R	ER	HR	BB	SO	AVG
Visalia	3.79	140	0	0	33	1241	1159	597	523	112	462	1346	.247
Rancho Cucamonga	3.87	140	1	1	38	1246	1205	628	536	90	428	1314	.252
Lake Elsinore	3.94	140	5	1	29	1241	1298	637	543	87	388	1255	.269
Modesto	4.14	140	1	0	34	1266	1297	652	582	104	362	1263	.264
Stockton	4.33	140	0	0	34	1242	1249	689	598	141	386	1270	.258
San Jose	4.52	140	0	0	34	1239	1287	718	622	100	533	1134	.268
Inland Empire	5.04	140	1	0	37	1249	1378	798	699	139	463	1229	.280
Lancaster	5.18	140	0	0	34	1236	1386	790	711	168	474	1055	.283

CLUB FIELDING

	PCT	PO	A	E	DP
Modesto	.979	4639	1393	127	283
Visalia	.978	4440	1326	133	276
Lancaster	.977	4597	1420	141	347
Inland Eimpire	.976	4553	1361	147	317

	PCT	PO	A	E	DP
Stockton	.975	4524	1282	152	241
San Jose	.974	4489	1480	161	369
Lake Elsinore	.972	4526	1400	168	326
R. Cucamonga	.971	4536	1324	175	284

INDIVIDUAL BATING

Batter, Club	AVG	G	AB	R	H	2B	3B	HR	RBI	BB	SO	SB
Daza, Yonathan, Lancaster	.341	125	519	93	177	34	11	3	87	30	88	31
Hampson, Garrett, Lancaster	.327	127	533	113	174	24	12	8	70	56	77	51
Filia, Eric, Modesto	.326	128	491	63	160	28	5	5	59	65	45	9
Rogers, Wes, Lancaster	.319	123	461	94	147	37	7	9	82	45	85	70
Reynolds, Bryan, San Jose	.312	121	491	72	153	26	9	10	63	37	106	5
Howard, Ryan, San Jose	.306	127	526	59	161	21	0	9	50	23	81	7
Mariscal, Chris, Modesto	.305	85	325	52	99	13	6	7	49	44	75	6
Hilliard, Sam, Lancaster	.300	133	536	95	161	23	7	21	92	50	154	37
Siddall, Brett, Stockton	.300	117	440	78	132	23	0	21	68	33	104	3
Ramos, Roberto, Lancaster	.297	122	478	72	142	29	1	13	68	41	124	3

INDIVIDUAL PITCHING

Pitcher, Club	W	L	ERA	G	GS	CG	SV	IP	H	R	ER	BB	SO
Ferguson, Caleb, Rancho Cucamonga	9	4	2.87	25	24	0	0	122	113	48	39	55	140
Almonte, Jose, Visalia	11	8	3.55	27	27	0	0	139	129	62	55	66	162
Bray, Adam, Rancho Cucamonga	7	3	3.89	26	19	1	1	130	123	64	56	26	118
Lambert, Peter, Lancaster	9	8	4.17	26	26	0	0	142	147	75	66	30	131
Bannister, Nathan, Modesto	8	7	4.33	23	23	0	0	121	130	60	58	16	99
Menez, Conner, San Jose	7	7	4.41	23	22	0	0	114	127	64	56	50	99
Tinoco, Jesus, Lancaster	11	4	4.67	24	24	0	0	141	157	78	73	50	107
McClain, Reggie, Modesto	12	9	4.75	27	27	1	0	153	164	85	81	35	127
Rodriguez, Jose, Inland Empire	8	12	5.18	27	27	0	0	149	178	97	86	44	134
Pena, Luis, Inland Empire	6	10	5.28	25	25	1	0	131	138	84	77	58	148

ALL-STAR TEAM

C: Aramis Garcia, San Jose. **1B:** Ibandel Isabel, Rancho Cucamonga. **2B:** Garrett Hampson, Lancaster. **3B:** Jose Rojas, Inland Empire. **SS:** Ryan Howard, San Jose. **OF:** D.J. Peters, Rancho Cucamonga; Yonathan Daza, Lancaster; Wes Rogers, Lancaster. **DH:** Brett Siddall, Stockton. **UT:** Eric Filia, Modesto. **P:** Jose Almonte, Visalia; Nick Neidert, Modesto; Dylan Rheault, San Jose; Caleb Ferguson, Rancho Cucamonga.

Most Valuable Player: D.J. Peters, Rancho Cucamonga
Pitcher of the Year: Nick Neidert, Modesto
Manager of the Year: Mitch Canham, Modesto

DEPARTMENT LEADERS

BATTING

OBP	Filia, Eric, Modesto	.407
SLG	Peters, DJ, Rancho Cucamonga	.514
OPS	Peters, DJ, Rancho Cucamonga	.886
R	Hampson, Garrett, Lancaster	113
H	Daza, Yonathan, Lancaster	177
TB	Brown, Seth, Stockton	262
XBH	Peters, DJ, Rancho Cucamonga	61
2B	Curletta, Joey, Modesto	37
	Rogers, Wes, Lancaster	37
3B	Hampson, Garrett, Lancaster	12
HR	Brown, Seth, Stockton	30
RBI	Brown, Seth, Stockton	109
SAC	Burcham, Scott, Lancaster	9
BB	Filia, Eric, Modesto	65
HBP	Raley, Luke, Rancho Cucamonga	19
SO	Gettys, Michael, Lake Elsinore	191
SB	Rogers, Wes, Lancaster	70
CS	Hilliard, Sam, Lancaster	17
AB/SO	Filia, Eric, Modesto	10.91

FIELDING

C PCT	Winn, Matt, San Jose	.989
PO	Allen, Austin, Lake Elsinore	732
A	Rabago, Chris, Lancaster	83
DP	Ward, Taylor, Inland Empire	6
E	Rabago, Chris, Lancaster	10
PB	Winn, Matt, San Jose	22
1B PCT	Curletta, Joey, Modesto	.995
PO	Curletta, Joey, Modesto	883
A	Byler, Austin, Visalia	65
DP	Byler, Austin, Visalia	72
	Isabel, Ibandel, Rancho Cucamonga	72
	Ramos, Roberto, Lancaster	72
E	Isabel, Ibandel, Rancho Cucamonga	17
2B PCT	Baker, Chris, Lake Elsinore	.981
PO	Miller, Jalen, San Jose	140
A	Baker, Chris, Lake Elsinore	232
DP	Baker, Chris, Lake Elsinore	55
E	Miller, Jalen, San Jose	13
SS PCT	Arenado, Jonah, San Jose	.922
PO	Arenado, Jonah, San Jose	61
A	Arenado, Jonah, San Jose	198
DP	Rojas, Jose, Inland Empire	18
E	Arenado, Jonah, San Jose	22
3B PCT	Howard, Ryan, San Jose	.969
PO	Howard, Ryan, San Jose	147
A	Justus, Connor, Inland Empire	268
DP	Howard, Ryan, San Jose	63
E	White, Eli, Stockton	25
OF PCT	Hilliard, Sam, Lancaster	.992
PO	Daza, Yonathan, Lancaster	281
A	Brown, Seth, Stockton	13
	Hilliard, Sam, Lancaster	13
DP	Peters, DJ, Rancho Cucamonga	5
E	Moreno, Edwin, Lake Elsinore	11

PITCHING

G	Rheault, Dylan, San Jose	55
GS	Killian, Trey, Lancaster	28
GF	Rheault, Dylan, San Jose	45
SV	Rheault, Dylan, San Jose	21
W	McClain, Reggie, Modesto	12
L	Reyes, Mark, San Jose	13
IP	Killian, Trey, Lancaster	153
	McClain, Reggie, Modesto	153
H	Killian, Trey, Lancaster	191
R	Killian, Trey, Lancaster	116
ER	Killian, Trey, Lancaster	108
HB	Almonte, Jose, Visalia	17
BB	Reyes, Mark, San Jose	77
SO	Almonte, Jose, Visalia	162
SO/9	Almonte, Jose, Visalia	10.46
SO/9(RP)	Festa, Matthew, Modesto	12.79
BB/9	Bannister, Nathan, Modesto	1.19
WP	Krook, Matt, San Jose	21
BK	Duno, Angel, Stockton	3
	Lopez, Pablo, Modesto	3
HR	Killian, Trey, Lancaster	27
AVG	Almonte, Jose, Visalia	.243

CAROLINA LEAGUE HIGH CLASS A

BY JOSH NORRIS

This past season marked a new era in the Carolina League. Two teams—High Desert and Bakersfield—were contracted in the California League and subsequently moved east, where they became Down East (Rangers) and Buies Creek (Astros), respectively. Down East moved into Grainger Stadium, in Kinston, N.C., and Buies Creek began its two-year stay at Jim Perry Stadium, on the campus of Campbell University, before it moves into its permanent home in Fayetteville, N.C., in 2019.

Independent of that split, the Carolina and California Leagues decided to play separate all-star games, instead of the dual-league classic it had played since 1996. The Carolina League's version featured a highlight straight out of the movies, when Eloy Jimenez hit a ball that shattered a light stanchion during the league's home run derby.

That massive power is part of what propelled Jimenez, who was dealt from the Cubs to the White Sox in July, to the top spot in the league's Top 20 prospects ranking. Jimenez was the headliner in the package—which also included righthander Dylan Cease, first baseman Matt Rose and infielder Bryant Flete—that sent lefthander Jose Quintana to the Cubs for their playoff run.

Jimenez went off after he moved from Myrtle Beach to Winston-Salem, racking up a 1.092 OPS with 11 doubles and eight home runs in 110 at-bats before moving to Double-A Birmingham.

Jimenez also headlined a Winston-Salem club that gained a boatload of prospect power later in the year. Righthanders Alec Hansen and Dane Dunning joined the club after beginning the year in low Class A Kannapolis, and catcher Zack Collins spent most of the season with the Dash.

The season closed on an unusual note because of Hurricane Irma, which wreaked havoc across the southeastern part of the country. As a result, the winners of the two divsion series were awarded shares of the championship. Down East, which leapfrogged Buies Creek in a head-to-head series to make the playoffs on the season's last day, took one share after topping Myrtle Beach. Lynchburg, which got stellar starting pitching from righthander Triston McKenzie in the series-evening game, took the other. It was the league's first split championship since 1999, when Wilmington and Myrtle Beach were named co-champions.

TOP 20 PROSPECTS

1. Eloy Jimenez, OF, Winston-Salem (White Sox)
2. Victor Robles, OF, Potomac (Nationals)
3. Austin Hays, OF, Frederick (Orioles)
4. Kyle Tucker, OF, Buies Creek (Astros)
5. Franklin Perez, RHP, Buies Creek (Astros)
6. Triston McKenzie, RHP, Lynchburg (Indians)
7. Monte Harrison, OF, Carolina (Brewers)
8. Corbin Burnes, RHP, Carolina (Brewers)
9. Alec Hansen, RHP, Winston-Salem (White Sox)
10. Dane Dunning, RHP, Winston-Salem (White Sox)
11. Michael Chavis, 3B, Salem (Red Sox)
12. Willi Castro, SS, Lynchburg (Indians)
13. Zack Collins, C, Winston-Salem (White Sox)
14. Jake Gatewood, 1B/3B, Carolina (Brewers)
15. Lucas Erceg, 3B, Carolina (Brewers)
16. Adbert Alzolay, RHP, Myrtle Beach (Cubs)
17. Ryan Mountcastle, SS, Frederick (Orioles)
18. Daniel Johnson, OF, Potomac (Nationals)
19. Jorge Alcala, RHP, Buies Creek (Astros)
20. Freddy Peralta, RHP, Carolina (Brewers)

STANDINGS: SPLIT SEASON

FIRST HALF

NORTH	W	L	PCT	GB
Lynchburg	40	29	.58	—
Salem	40	29	.58	—
Wilmington	39	31	.557	1½
Potomac	33	37	.471	7½
Frederick	31	38	.449	9
SOUTH	**W**	**L**	**PCT**	**GB**
Myrtle Beach	43	27	.614	—
Carolina	36	32	.529	6
Buies Creek	37	33	.529	6
Down East	24	45	.348	18½
W-S	24	46	.343	19

SECOND HALF

NORTH	W	L	PCT	GB
Lynchburg	47	23	.671	—
Frederick	37	33	.529	10
Salem	33	37	.471	14
Potomac	30	40	.429	17
Wilmington	28	41	.406	18½
SOUTH	**W**	**L**	**PCT**	**GB**
Down East	38	32	.543	—
Buies Creek	37	32	.536	½
Carolina	37	33	.529	1
W-S	32	38	.457	6
Myrtle Beach	30	40	.429	8

Playoffs—Semifinals: Down East defeated Myrtle Beach 2-0 and Lynchburg defeated Frederick 2-1 in best-of-three series.
Finals: Cancelled. Lynchburg, Down East declared co-championships.

OVERALL STANDINGS

Northern Division	W	L	PCT	GB	Manager(s)	Attendance	Average	Last Pennant
Lynchburg Hillcats(Indians)	87	52	.626	—	Tony Mansolino	137,566	2,084	2017
Salem Red Sox (Red Sox)	73	66	.525	14	Joe Oliver	215,244	3,311	2013
Frederick Keys (Orioles)	68	71	.489	19	Keith Bodie	303,930	4,824	2011
Wilmington Blue Rocks (Royals)	67	72	.482	20	Jamie Quirk	230,677	3,845	1999
Potomac Nationals (Nationals)	63	77	.450	24½	Tripp Keister	236,010	3,869	2014
Southern Division	**W**	**L**	**PCT**	**GB**	**Manager(s)**	**Attendance**	**Average**	**Last Pennant**
Buies Creek Astros (Astros)	74	65	.489	—	Omar Lopez	30,518	517	Never
Carolina Mudcats (Brewers)	73	65	.482	½	Joe Ayrault	190,420	2,800	2006
Myrtle Beach Pelicans (Cubs)	73	67	.450	1½	Buddy Bailey	233,126	3,587	2016
Down East Wood Ducks (Rangers)	62	77	.446	12	Howard Johnson	145,780	2,025	2017
Winston-Salem Dash (White Sox)	56	84	.400	18½	Willie Harris	304,607	4,415	2003

CAROLINA LEAGUE STATISTICS

CLUB BATTING

	AVG	G	AB	R	H	2B	3B	HR	RBI	BB	SO	SB	OBP	SLG
Frederick	.266	139	4504	633	1199	249	15	126	571	389	1025	75	.332	.412
Salem	.259	139	4574	651	1185	275	27	93	580	485	1195	128	.335	.392
Lynchburg	.258	139	4591	645	1183	262	44	93	577	484	1132	145	.334	.395
Myrtle Beach	.252	140	4621	585	1165	191	24	101	514	410	1079	62	.319	.369
Down East	.251	139	4622	539	1159	225	23	90	489	342	973	120	.312	.368
Buies Creek	.250	139	4609	582	1152	215	45	86	536	531	1138	118	.331	.372
Potomac	.250	140	4519	570	1129	227	37	93	533	450	1157	99	.322	.378
Wilmington	.244	139	4553	522	1110	209	47	78	461	476	1109	111	.320	.362
Winston-Salem	.241	140	4516	581	1087	248	33	104	533	437	1163	75	.314	.379
Carolina	.240	138	4506	622	1081	247	27	101	556	503	1245	175	.323	.374

CLUB PITCHING

	ERA	G	CG	SHO	SV	IP	H	R	ER	HR	BB	SO	AVG
Lynchburg	3.21	139	3	1	42	1217	1045	509	434	94	365	1091	.232
Buies Creek	3.56	139	3	2	40	1217	1036	547	481	95	444	1263	.229
Wilmington	3.58	139	4	1	35	1201	1138	547	478	81	434	1128	.251
Myrtle Beach	3.65	140	4	2	42	1215	1166	583	493	88	430	1110	.252
Carolina	3.87	138	4	2	44	1200	1101	607	516	96	478	1134	.245
Salem	3.90	139	1	0	37	1205	1215	609	522	95	507	1159	.263
Potomac	3.94	140	2	0	30	1195	1179	590	523	96	432	1017	.258
Down East	4.05	139	1	0	35	1223	1185	612	550	112	444	1192	.254
Winston-Salem	4.31	140	4	3	27	1193	1186	669	571	97	450	1030	.261
Frederick	4.41	139	4	1	36	1167	1199	657	572	111	523	1092	.266

CLUB FIELDING

	PCT	PO	A	E	DP
Buies Creek	.981	4485	1224	113	260
Down East	.978	4532	1315	131	283
Lynchburg	.978	4453	1424	134	314
Potomac	.977	4415	1441	136	319
Wilmington	.976	4464	1345	146	305
Myrtle Beach	.974	4475	1379	156	297
Frederick	.974	4314	1273	150	316
Winston-Salem	.974	4367	1433	157	309
Carolina	.972	4435	1327	165	363
Salem	.972	4456	1280	165	341

INDIVIDUAL BATTING

Batter, Club	AVG	G	AB	R	H	2B	3B	HR	RBI	BB	SO	SB
Mountcastle, Ryan, Frederick	.314	88	360	63	113	35	1	15	47	14	61	8
Straw, Myles, Buies Creek	.295	114	437	81	129	17	7	1	41	87	70	36
La O, Luis, Down East	.292	124	476	57	139	23	2	8	53	21	50	11
Castro, Willi, Lynchburg	.290	123	469	69	136	24	3	11	58	28	90	19
Rifaela, Ademar, Frederick	.284	126	450	73	128	23	1	24	78	41	124	7
Alamo, Tyler, Myrtle Beach	.281	114	427	61	120	24	0	12	42	21	108	0
Franco, Wander, Wilmington	.279	129	481	52	134	19	8	4	46	25	92	5
Cervenka, Martin, Lynchburg	.278	112	400	59	111	24	4	8	57	42	103	1
Sundberg, Jack, Potomac	.277	110	393	56	109	14	1	1	28	52	110	24
Flete, Bryant, Myrtle Beach/W-S	.276	115	442	63	122	25	2	7	49	32	81	5

INDIVIDUAL PITCHING

Pitcher, Club	W	L	ERA	G	GS	CG	SV	IP	H	R	ER	BB	SO
Hartson, Brock, Lynchburg	6	5	3.06	23	19	0	1	129	104	51	44	31	88
Ponce, Cody, Carolina	8	8	3.38	22	22	1	0	120	130	64	45	25	94
McKenzie, Triston, Lynchburg	12	6	3.46	25	25	0	0	143	105	62	55	45	186
Dunning, Dane, Winston-Salem	6	8	3.51	22	22	2	0	118	114	62	46	36	135
Chiang, Shao-Ching, Lynchburg	8	8	3.67	19	19	2	0	123	122	61	50	22	81
Springs, Jeffrey, Down East	2	8	3.69	31	17	0	2	112	104	48	46	37	146
Benjamin, Wes, Down East	10	7	3.94	22	22	0	0	119	133	53	52	34	101
Puckett, A.J., Wilmington/W-S	10	7	3.98	25	25	0	0	136	142	67	60	51	119
Hatch, Thomas, Myrtle Beach	5	11	4.04	26	26	0	0	125	126	74	56	50	126
Blewett, Scott, Wilmington	7	10	4.07	27	27	1	0	153	153	76	69	52	129

ALL-STAR TEAM

C: Taylor Gushue, Potomac. **1B:** Josh Ockimey, Salem. **2B:** Sam Haggerty, Lynchburg. **3B:** Lucas Erceg, Carolina. **SS:** Ryan Mountcastle, Frederick. **OF:** Ademar Rifaela, Frederick; Myles Straw, Buies Creek; Eloy Jimenez, Winston-Salem. **UT:** Willi Castro, Lynchburg. **UT/OF:** Victor Robles, Potomac. **DH:** Sicnarf Loopstok, Lynchburg. **SP:** Triston McKenzie, Lynchburg. **RP:** Nate Griep, Carolina.
Most Valuable Player: Ademar Rifaela, Frederick
Pitcher of the Year: Triston McKenzie, Lynchburg
Manager of the Year: Tony Mansolino, Lynchburg

DEPARTMENT LEADERS

BATTING

OBP	Straw, Myles, Buies Creek	.412
SLG	Mountcastle, Ryan, Frederick	.542
OPS	Mountcastle, Ryan, Frederick	.885
R	Straw, Myles, Buies Creek	81
H	La O, Luis, Down East	139
TB	Rifaela, Ademar, Frederick	225
XBH	Mountcastle, Ryan, Frederick	51
2B	Gatewood, Jake, Carolina	36
3B	Haggerty, Sam, Lynchburg	13
HR	Rifaela, Ademar, Frederick	24
RBI	Erceg, Lucas, Carolina	81
SAC	Flores, Jecksson, Wilmington	21
BB	Clark, Trent, Carolina	98
HBP	Robles, Victor, Potomac	17
SO	Ray, Corey, Carolina	156
SB	Haggerty, Sam, Lynchburg	49
CS	Burt, D.J., Wilmington	13
	Haggerty, Sam, Lynchburg	13
AB/SO	La O, Luis, Down East	9.52

FIELDING

C PCT	Gushue, Taylor, Potomac	.991
PO	Rei, Austin, Salem	740
A	Higgins, P.J., Myrtle Beach	93
DP	Rogers, Jake, Buies Creek	8
E	McDowell, Max, Carolina	12
	Vallot, Chase, Wilmington	12
PB	Collins, Zack, Winston-Salem	16
1B PCT	Sagdal, Ian, Potomac	.996
PO	Sagdal, Ian, Potomac	837
A	Ockimey, Josh, Salem	54
DP	Sagdal, Ian, Potomac	71
E	Gatewood, Jake, Carolina	14
2B PCT	Haggerty, Sam, Lynchburg	.980
PO	Haggerty, Sam, Lynchburg	179
A	Haggerty, Sam, Lynchburg	212
	Flete, Bryant, Myrtle Beach, W-S	212
DP	Flete, Bryant, Myrtle Beach, W-S	54
E	Burt, D.J., Wilmington	15
3B PCT	Franco, Wander, Wilmington	.938
PO	Hodges, Jesse, Myrtle Beach	82
A	Franco, Wander, Wilmington	214
DP	Erceg, Lucas, Carolina	18
E	Hodges, Jesse, Myrtle Beach	20
SS PCT	Castro, Willi, Lynchburg	.953
PO	Aviles, Luis, Carolina	178
A	Castro, Willi, Lynchburg	340
DP	Castro, Willi, Lynchburg	69
E	Castro, Willi, Lynchburg	25
OF PCT	Carter, Jodd, Lynchburg	.996
PO	Matheny, Tate, Salem	293
A	Clark, Trent, Carolina	14
	Wiseman, Rhett, Potomac	14
	Myers, Connor, Myrtle Beach	14
	Martinez, Eddy, Myrtle Beach	14
DP	Straw, Myles, Buies Creek	7
E	Garcia, Robert, Myrtle Beach	11

PITCHING

G	Griep, Nate, Carolina	45
GS	Kent, Matthew, Salem	28
GF	Griep, Nate, Carolina	43
SV	Griep, Nate, Carolina	30
W	McKenzie, Triston, Lynchburg	12
L	Reyes, Luis, Potomac	13
IP	Kent, Matthew, Salem	164
H	Kent, Matthew, Salem	186
R	Kent, Matthew, Salem	90
ER	Alvarado, Cristian, Frederick	78
HB	Medeiros, Kodi, Carolina	20
BB	Peralta, Ofelky, Frederick	86
SO	McKenzie, Triston, Lynchburg	186
SO/9	McKenzie, Triston, Lynchburg	11.71
SO/9(RP)	Springs, Jeffrey, Down East	11.70
BB/9	Alvarado, Cristian, Frederick	1.41
WP	Peralta, Ofelky, Frederick	19
	Rodgers, Colin, Wilmington	19
BK	Peralta, Ofelky, Frederick	4
HR	Reyes, Luis, Potomac	19
AVG	McKenzie, Triston, Lynchburg	.204

MINOR LEAGUES

FLORIDA STATE LEAGUE HIGH CLASS A

BY JOHN MANUEL

Officially, the Florida State League had two champions, Palm Beach and Dunedin.

For the third time in the 21st Century, the FSL had co-champions. In 2017 it was due to the massive, looming presence of Hurricane Irma, which wound up hitting Florida with ferocity and causing damage estimated in the billions of dollars to the state and its economy.

Hurricanes cancelled the FSL postseason in 2004, while the Sept. 11 attacks cancelled postseasons across minor league baseball in 2001.

Dunedin's share of the championship was its first FSL title for the Blue Jays affiliate in its 17th postseason appearance since 1990. Palm Beach won its second championship and first since 2005.

The Cardinals earned their share with a 74-60 overall record, including a 40-27 record and first-half title. They beat second-half champ Fort Myers in the league semifinals, winning a pair of 3-2 games. In the clincher, the game-winning run scored on a bases-loaded hit by pitch, as Miracle reliever Thomas Hackmer hit Thomas Spitz with a 3-2 pitch. Righthander Jake Woodford, who won the league's ERA title (3.10), earned the win in the first game of the series with a six-inning, one-run performance.

Dunedin made the playoffs as a wild card, having the second-best record in the FSL North Division. Tampa, with a league-best 85-50 overall record, edged Clearwater by a game in the first half, then won by 10 games in the second half.

The Blue Jays had reinforcements in the second half with two of baseball's best prospects, shortstop Bo Bichette and third baseman Vladimir Guerrero Jr. The teenagers arrived together on Aug. 1 from low Class A Lansing, with Bichette ending up as the minor league batting champion while Guerrero led the minors in on-base percentage. They fit into a lineup that featured league all-star Connor Panas, whose 18 home runs led the league.

TOP 20 PROSPECTS

1. Vladimir Guerrero Jr., 3B, Dunedin (Blue Jays)
2. Bo Bichette, SS, Dunedin (Blue Jays)
3. Mitch Keller, RHP, Bradenton (Pirates)
4. Nick Senzel, 3B, Daytona (Reds)
5. Ke'Bryan Hayes, 3B, Bradenton (Pirates)
6. Austin Riley, 3B, Florida (Braves)
7. Dillon Tate, RHP, Tampa (Yankees)
8. Brent Rooker, OF/1B, Fort Myers (Twins)
9. Cole Tucker, SS, Bradenton (Pirates)
10. Ryan Helsley, RHP, Palm Beach (Cardinals)
11. Beau Burrows, RHP, Lakeland (Tigers)
12. Cornelius Randolph, OF, Clearwater (Phillies)
13. Seranthony Dominguez, RHP, Clearwater (Phillies)
14. Nick Solak, 2B, Tampa (Yankees)
15. JoJo Romero, LHP, Clearwater (Phillies)
16. Max Pentecost, C/1B, Dunedin (Blue Jays)
17. Franklyn Kilome, RHP, Clearwater (Phillies)
18. Ryan Boldt, OF, Charlotte (Rays)
19. Alex Jackson, C, Florida (Braves)
20. Brandon Lowe, 2B, Charlotte (Rays)

STANDINGS: SPLIT SEASON

FIRST HALF

NORTH	W	L	PCT	GB
Tampa	39	31	.557	—
Clearwater	38	32	.543	1
Daytona	33	32	.508	3½
Dunedin	34	35	.493	4½
Lakeland	30	36	.455	9
Florida	25	41	.379	12
SOUTH	**W**	**L**	**PCT**	**GB**
Palm Beach	40	27	.597	—
Bradenton	37	30	.552	3
Fort Myers	33	35	.485	7½
Jupiter	33	35	.485	7½
St. Lucie	33	35	.485	7½
Charlotte	31	37	.456	9½

SECOND HALF

NORTH	W	L	PCT	GB
Tampa	46	19	.708	—
Dunedin	38	31	.551	10
Lakeland	32	30	.516	12½
Clearwater	29	39	.426	18½
Florida	23	40	.365	22
Daytona	20	48	.294	27½
SOUTH	**W**	**L**	**PCT**	**GB**
Fort Myers	42	25	.627	—
Charlotte	38	29	.567	4
Bradenton	33	32	.508	8
Jupiter	34	33	.507	8
Palm Beach	34	33	.507	8
St. Lucie	30	40	.429	13½

Playoffs—Semifinals: Palm Beach defeated Fort Myers 2-0 and Dunedin defeated Tampa 2-1 in best-of-three series. **Finals:** Cancelled. Palm Beach, Dunedin declared co-champs.

The league's other big winner was St. Lucie, which capitalized on the presence of 2007 Heisman Trophy winner Tim Tebow in the second half to set a franchise attendance record. The Mets drew 132,359 fans, crushing the 2011 record of 105,379.

OVERALL STANDINGS

North Division	W	L	PCT	GB	Manager(s)	Attendance	Average	Last Pennant
Tampa Yankees (Yankees)	85	50	.630	—	Jay Bell	93,823	1,422	2010
Dunedin Blue Jays (Blue Jays)	72	66	.522	14½	John Schneider	38,956	573	2017
Clearwater Threshers (Phillies)	67	71	.486	19½	Shawn Williams	200,201	2,988	2007
Lakeland Flying Tigers (Tigers)	62	66	.484	19½	Andrew Graham	52,191	815	2012
Daytona Tortugas (Reds)	53	80	.398	31	Eli Marrero	136,224	2,064	2011
Florida Fire Frogs (Braves)	48	81	.372	34	Paul Runge/Rocket Wheeler	57,324	1,082	Never
South Division	**W**	**L**	**PCT**	**GB**	**Manager(s)**	**Attendance**	**Average**	**Last Pennant**
Fort Myers Miracle (Twins)	75	60	.556	—	Doug Mientkiewicz	121,438	2,024	2014
Palm Beach Cardinals (Cardinals)	74	60	.552	½	Dann Bilardello	58,832	934	2017
Bradenton Marauders (Pirates)	70	62	.530	3½	Gerardo Alvarez	79,331	1,301	1963
Charlotte Stone Cards (Rays)	69	66	.511	6	Michael Johns	120,685	1,916	2015
Jupiter Hammerheads (Marlins)	67	68	.496	8	Kevin Randel	69,064	1,046	1991
St. Lucie (Mets)	63	75	.457	13½	Chad Kreuter	132,359	2,005	2006

FLORIDA STATE LEAGUE STATISTICS

CLUB BATTING

	AVG	G	AB	R	H	2B	3B	HR	RBI	BB	SO	SB	OBP	SLG
Bradenton	.260	132	4360	580	1132	208	39	78	531	489	1009	160	.341	.379
Charlotte	.258	135	4447	572	1145	229	40	56	518	426	937	137	.327	.365
Dunedin	.255	138	4599	642	1173	198	34	83	579	486	1160	106	.332	.367
Florida	.255	129	4241	505	1081	189	30	72	448	318	1107	82	.318	.365
Clearwater	.254	138	4571	494	1159	199	26	104	453	354	1083	86	.314	.377
Tampa	.253	135	4510	562	1140	219	34	103	505	425	1090	138	.323	.385
St. Lucie	.252	138	4586	555	1154	239	23	78	507	455	1116	112	.330	.365
Palm Beach	.251	134	4482	522	1124	193	30	56	459	364	919	72	.314	.345
Fort Myers	.251	135	4427	572	1109	190	38	68	505	410	1055	96	.323	.357
Daytona	.249	133	4482	498	1115	204	22	76	461	329	1123	102	.307	.355
Lakeland	.236	128	4200	419	989	162	35	62	387	373	1038	106	.303	.335
Jupiter	.234	135	4507	464	1053	205	23	58	419	398	1236	79	.305	.328

CLUB PITCHING

	ERA	G	CG	SHO	SV	IP	H	R	ER	HR	BB	SO	AVG
Tampa	2.81	135	5	1	43	1199	1018	428	374	73	362	1215	.230
Jupiter	2.82	135	1	0	33	1212	1084	456	380	57	328	1079	.240
Lakeland	2.93	128	2	2	30	1134	1011	430	369	56	334	1127	.240
Clearwater	3.16	138	3	1	40	1199	1094	492	421	95	405	1191	.243
Palm Beach	3.30	134	4	2	39	1189	1160	518	436	59	416	996	.259
Fort Myers	3.45	135	2	0	31	1168	1110	492	447	72	409	1027	.254
Bradenton	3.59	132	0	0	33	1170	1074	512	467	84	375	1001	.245
Dunedin	3.65	138	2	0	35	1204	1174	592	488	74	464	1035	.255
Charlotte	3.98	135	1	0	39	1174	1146	590	519	82	422	942	.257
Daytona	4.09	133	2	0	24	1177	1134	626	535	92	459	1037	.253
St. Lucie	4.14	138	3	1	38	1217	1280	665	559	93	397	1128	.269
Florida	4.20	129	1	1	24	1094	1089	584	510	57	456	1095	.258

CLUB FIELDING

	PCT	PO	A	E	DP
Bradenton	.985	4250	1488	88	309
Tampa	.981	4346	1326	111	245
Fort Myers	.980	4308	1364	115	334
Lakeland	.979	4142	1230	114	288
Clearwater	.978	4400	1338	127	287
Charlotte	.978	4366	1346	129	336
Palm Beach	.978	4388	1505	133	398
Jupiter	.977	4397	1525	142	376
Daytona	.975	4312	1423	145	341
St. Lucie	.970	4522	1326	184	260
Florida	.969	3958	1250	166	302
Dunedin	.967	4427	1436	199	341

INDIVIDUAL BATTING

Batter, Club	AVG	G	AB	R	H	2B	3B	HR	RBI	BB	SO	SB
Lago, Alay, Florida	.303	113	416	47	126	20	4	6	46	22	65	6
Solak, Nick, Tampa	.301	100	346	56	104	17	4	10	44	53	76	13
Boldt, Ryan, Charlotte	.296	120	440	60	130	22	6	5	62	39	89	23
Maris, Peter, Charlotte	.290	104	359	52	104	13	3	6	33	39	42	13
Mazeika, Patrick, St. Lucie	.287	100	352	45	101	21	0	7	50	48	53	2
Laird, Mark, Clearwater	.286	105	406	56	116	16	5	2	27	29	65	11
Castro, Carlos, Florida	.283	96	361	41	102	18	1	10	58	8	92	3
Urena, Jhoan, St. Lucie	.282	122	458	72	129	34	2	11	62	60	114	17
Hayes, Ke'Bryan, Bradenton	.278	108	421	66	117	16	7	2	43	41	76	27
Panas, Connor, Dunedin	.276	114	402	64	111	20	3	18	55	41	99	4

INDIVIDUAL PITCHING

Pitcher, Club	W	L	ERA	G	GS	CG	SV	IP	H	R	ER	BB	SO
Woodford, Jake, Palm Beach	7	6	3.10	23	21	0	0	119	128	57	41	39	72
Helton, Bret, Bradenton	8	3	3.25	30	14	0	0	116	110	43	42	37	89
Romano, Jordan, Dunedin	7	5	3.39	28	26	0	0	138	141	65	52	54	138
Widener, Taylor, Tampa	7	8	3.39	27	27	0	0	119	87	53	45	50	129
Lopez, Eduar, Charlotte	9	9	3.63	27	21	0	0	144	152	67	58	40	82
Vasquez, Pedro, Bradenton	9	7	3.73	26	24	0	0	138	135	57	57	30	107
Squier, Scott, Jupiter	5	9	3.82	28	26	1	0	132	143	65	56	26	102
Dowdy, Kyle, Lakeland	8	12	3.83	25	22	0	0	134	142	68	57	28	121
Fisk, Conor, Dunedin	8	11	3.84	28	22	2	1	152	153	81	65	33	112
Crismatt, Nabil, St. Lucie	6	13	3.95	26	25	1	0	146	161	82	64	36	142

ALL-STAR TEAM

C: Patrick Mazeika, St. Lucie; Brett Sullivan, Charlotte. **1B:** Peter Alonso, St. Lucie. **2B:** Brandon Lowe, Charlotte. **3B:** Jhoan Urena, St. Lucie. **SS:** Cole Tucker, Bradenton. **OF:** Ryan Boldt, Charlotte; Logan Hill, Bradenton; Max Murphy, Fort Myers; Connor Panas, Dunedin. **DH:** Max Pentecost, Dunedin. **UT:** Nick Solak, Tampa. **SP:** Matt Hall, Lakeland; Ryan Helsley, Palm Beach; Jose Taveras, Clearwater; Pedro Vasquez, Bradenton. **RP:** Seth McGarry, Clearwater; Jeff Singer, Clearwater.

Most Valuable Player: Brandon Lowe, Charlotte

Pitcher of the Year: Ryan Helsley, Palm Beach

Manager of the Year: Jay Bell, Tampa

DEPARTMENT LEADERS

	BATTING	
OBP	Solak, Nick, Trenton	.397
SLG	Lowe, Brandon, Charlotte	.475
OPS	Solak, Nick, Trenton	.856
R	Biggio, Cavan, Dunedin	75
H	Mora, John, St. Lucie	133
TB	Garcia, Wilson, Clearwater	202
XBH	Wiel, Zander, Fort Myers	49
2B	Urena, Jhoan, St. Lucie	34
	Lowe, Brandon, Charlotte	34
3B	Hughston, Casey, Bradenton	9
	Seferina, Darren, Palm Beach	9
HR	Panas, Connor, Dunedin	18
RBI	Kelly, Juan, Dunedin	68
SAC	Hayes, Ke'Bryan, Bradenton	12
BB	Biggio, Cavan, Dunedin	74
HBP	Didder, Ray-Patrick, Florida	21
SO	Davidson, Braxton, Florida	155
SB	Tucker, Cole, Bradenton	36
CS	Seymour, Anfernee, Florida	17
AB/SO	Garcia, Wilson, Clearwater	9.00
	FIELDING	
C PCT	Rodriguez, David, Charlotte	.996
PO	Kelley, Christian, Bradenton	653
A	Kelley, Christian, Bradenton	97
DP	Perez, Arvicent, Lakeland	8
	Martinez, Jeremy, Palm Beach	8
E	Jackson, Alex, Florida	10
PB	Rodriguez, David, Charlotte	19
1B PCT	Chinea, Chris, Palm Beach	.995
PO	Craig, Will, Bradenton	855
A	Craig, Will, Bradenton	78
DP	Chinea, Chris, Palm Beach	88
E	Alonso, Peter, St. Lucie	18
2B PCT	Tolman, Mitchell, Bradenton	.978
PO	Biggio, Cavan, Dunedin	205
A	Biggio, Cavan, Dunedin	330
DP	Biggio, Cavan, Dunedin	76
E	Reyes, Angel, Jupiter	22
3B PCT	Hayes, Ke'Bryan, Bradenton	.974
PO	Urena, Jhoan, St. Lucie	55
A	Hayes, Ke'Bryan, Bradenton	245
DP	Hayes, Ke'Bryan, Bradenton	25
E	Urena, Jhoan, St. Lucie	22
SS PCT	Rodriguez, Alfredo, Daytona	.967
PO	Rodriguez, J.C., St. Lucie	183
A	Rodriguez, Alfredo, Daytona	325
DP	Rodriguez, Alfredo, Daytona	66
E	Rodriguez, J.C., St. Lucie	31
OF PCT	Laird, Mark, Clearwater	1.000
PO	Mora, John, St. Lucie	311
A	Drake, Blake, Palm Beach	13
	Spitz, Thomas, Palm Beach	13
	Didder, Ray-Patrick, Florida	13
DP	English, Tanner, Fort Myers	6
E	Seymour, Anfernee, Florida	9
	PITCHING	
G	Magliozzi, Johnny, St. Lucie Mets	44
	McGarry, Seth, Bradenton	44
GS	Widener, Taylor, Tampa	27
GF	McGarry, Seth, Bradenton	38
SV	Singer, Jeff, Clearwater	19
	McGarry, Seth, Bradenton	19
W	Church, Andrew, St. Lucie Mets	12
L	Crismatt, Nabil, St. Lucie Mets	13
IP	Fisk, Conor, Dunedin	152
H	Church, Andrew, St. Lucie Mets	183
R	Church, Andrew, St. Lucie Mets	85
ER	Church, Andrew, St. Lucie Mets	78
HB	Crawford, Jonathon, Daytona	15
BB	Crawford, Jonathon, Daytona	79
SO	Crismatt, Nabil, St. Lucie Mets	142
SO/9	Toussaint, Touki, Florida	10.51
SO/9(RP)	Lugo, Sandy, Daytona	11.47
BB/9	Church, Andrew, St. Lucie	1.48
WP	Lugo, Sandy, Daytona	16
BK	Sanchez, Ricardo, Florida	7
HR	Fisk, Conor, Dunedin	19
AVG	Widener, Taylor, Tampa	.206

MIDWEST LEAGUE LOW CLASS A

BY JOHN MANUEL

The Quad Cities River Bandits have been an Astros affiliate since 2013, and won their second championship in that span in 2017. The River Bandits won the second-half title in the Western Division and put up the second-best record in the league thanks to the league's best offense. The Bandits scored 743 runs, the only team to surpass 700, and ranked second with 139 home runs while slugging a league-high .419.

Catcher Chuckie Robinson had a strong first full season, leading the team with 32 doubles, 15 home runs and 77 RBIs, then capped his campaign with a 4-for-5 effort in the championship clincher. Robinson was the only Quad Cities player who played in the team's first regular-season game and its last game. Robinson hit four homers in nine playoff games, and the River Bandits outscored Fort Wayne 23-5 in the championship series sweep.

The other Midwest League top story was the prospect star power at the top of the league's prospect list. Lansing featured the team's most anticipated roster coming into the season, thanks to its big league progeny, and they lived up to the billing.

Shortstop Bo Bichette flirted with .400, hitting .384 in 70 games and ranking second in the league with 32 doubles to earn the league's MVP award. Third baseman Vladimir Guerrero Jr. hit a robust .316/.409/.480 for the Lugnuts and was promoted along with Bichette in July. Bichette went on to lead the minors in batting overall, at .362, while Guerrero led the minors in on-base percentage (.425). Speaking of big league progeny, Fort Wayne's Fernando Tatis Jr. broke out after Bichette and Guerrero were promoted, leading the league in OBP, while hitting .281/.390/.520 with 21 home runs before a late promotion to Double-A San Antonio.

TOP 20 PROSPECTS

1. Vladimir Guerrero Jr., 3B, Lansing (Blue Jays)
2. Fernando Tatis Jr., SS, Fort Wayne (Padres)
3. Bo Bichette, SS/2B, Lansing (Blue Jays)
4. Michel Baez, RHP, Fort Wayne (Padres)
5. Forrest Whitley, RHP, Quad Cities (Astros)
6. Taylor Trammell, OF, Dayton (Reds)
7. Jesus Sanchez, OF, Bowling Green (Rays)
8. Yordan Alvarez, 1B/OF, Quad Cities (Astros)
9. Isaac Paredes, SS, West Michigan (Tigers)
10. Marcus Wilson, OF, Kane County (D-backs)
11. Dylan Cease, RHP, South Bend (Cubs)
12. Jon Duplantier, RHP, Kane County (D-backs)
13. Jordan Hicks, RHP, Peoria (Cardinals)
14. Logan Allen, LHP, Fort Wayne (Padres)
15. Keibert Ruiz, C, Great Lakes (Dodgers)
16. Dustin May, RHP, Great Lakes (Dodgers)
17. Tyler Stephenson, C, Dayton (Reds)
18. Garrett Whitley, OF, Bowling Green (Rays)
19. Hudson Potts, 3B, Fort Wayne (Padres)
20. Daz Cameron, OF, West Michigan (Tigers)

STANDINGS: SPLIT SEASON

FIRST HALF

EASTERN	W	L	PCT	GB
W. Michigan	45	22	.672	—
Dayton	41	29	.586	5½
South Bend	39	30	.565	7
Lansing	37	29	.561	7½
Great Lakes	36	33	.522	10
Bowling Green	31	36	.463	14
Lake County	27	42	.391	19
Fort Wayne	26	44	.371	20½
WESTERN	**W**	**L**	**PCT**	**GB**
Kane County	39	28	.582	—
Cedar Rapids	39	31	.557	1½
Quad Cities	37	31	.544	2½
Beloit	32	37	.464	8
Clinton	31	36	.463	8
Burlington	31	38	.449	9
Peoria	30	39	.435	10
Wisconsin	26	42	.382	13½

SECOND HALF

EASTERN	W	L	PCT	GB
W. Michigan	46	23	.667	—
Fort Wayne	42	28	.600	4½
Bowling Green	41	29	.586	5½
South Bend	36	34	.514	10½
Great Lakes	33	37	.471	13½
Dayton	30	40	.429	16½
Lake County	27	43	.386	19½
Lansing	26	44	.371	20½
WESTERN	**W**	**L**	**PCT**	**GB**
Quad Cities	42	28	.600	—
Peoria	39	31	.557	3
Cedar Rapids	36	33	.514	6
Beloit	33	36	.478	8½
Clinton	33	37	.471	9
Kane County	33	37	.471	9
Wisconsin	33	37	.471	9
Burlington	29	41	.414	13

Playoffs—Semifinals: Quad Cities defeated Cedar Rapids 2-1 and Fort Wayne defeated Dayton 2-1 in best-of-three series.
Finals: Great Lakes defeated Fort Wayne 3-0 in a best-of-five series.

OVERALL STANDINGS

Eastern Division	W	L	PCT	GB	Manager(s)	Attendance	Average	Last Pennant
West Michigan Whitecaps (Tigers)	91	45	.669	—	Mike Rabelo	383,983	5,565	2015
South Bend Cubs (Cubs)	75	64	.540	17½	Jimmy Gonzalez	354,070	5,285	2005
Bowling Green Hot Rods (Rays)	72	65	.526	19½	Reinaldo Ruiz	179,839	2,855	Never
Dayton Dragons (Reds)	71	69	.507	22	Luis Bolivar	554,638	8,038	Never
Great Lakes Loons (Dodgers)	69	70	.496	23½	Jeremy Rodriguez	202,433	3,021	2017
Fort Wayne TinCaps (Padres)	68	72	.486	25	Anthony Contreras	409,253	5,931	2009
Lansing Lugnuts (Blue Jays)	63	73	.463	28	Cesar Martin	303,843	4,468	2003
Lake County Captains (Indians)	54	85	.388	38½	Larry Day	212,747	3,223	2010
Western Division	**W**	**L**	**PCT**	**GB**	**Manager(s)**	**Attendance**	**Average**	**Last Pennant**
Quad Cities River Bandits (Astros)	79	59	.572	—	Russ Steinhorn	230,006	3,286	2013
Cedar Rapids Kernels (Twins)	75	65	.536	5	Tommy Watkins	166,427	2,378	1994
Kane County Cougars (D-backs)	72	65	.526	6½	Butch Hobson	394,567	5,889	2014
Peoria Chiefs (Cardinals)	69	70	.496	10½	Chris Swauger	212,659	3,174	2002
Beloit Snappers (Athletics)	65	73	.471	14	Scott Steinmann	64,236	959	1995
Clinton LumberKings (Mariners)	64	73	.467	14½	P. Shine/D. Macias/T. Arnerich	121,302	1,838	2016
Burlington Bees (Angels)	60	79	.432	19½	Adam Melhuse	67.044	1,048	2008
Wisconsin Timber Rattlers (Brewers)	59	79	.428	20	Matt Erickson	230,326	3,438	2012

CLUB BATTING

	AVG	G	AB	R	H	2B	3B	HR	RBI	BB	SO	SB	OBP	SLG
Bowling Green	.271	137	4628	663	1255	242	32	95	606	453	1100	125	.341	.399
Lansing	.268	136	4665	685	1250	256	39	81	622	510	1079	113	.351	.392
West Michigan	.264	136	4613	637	1218	243	36	61	575	451	988	102	.335	.372
Quad Cities	.261	138	4660	743	1214	252	35	139	680	514	1121	111	.339	.419
South Bend	.258	139	4666	676	1205	246	48	72	583	507	1003	143	.338	.378
Peoria	.253	139	4642	581	1176	226	33	118	539	454	1125	107	.327	.393
Kane County	.252	137	4590	553	1155	241	32	58	492	413	1135	115	.321	.356
Beloit	.247	138	4605	580	1138	224	32	84	524	482	1168	87	.321	.364
Cedar Rapids	.247	140	4613	591	1139	224	57	112	552	395	1218	96	.314	.393
Clinton	.244	137	4623	566	1130	227	33	87	495	429	1224	144	.313	.364
Fort Wayne	.244	140	4619	629	1129	227	38	127	568	497	1365	126	.324	.393
Dayton	.243	140	4672	649	1136	233	42	112	593	492	1175	166	.322	.383
Burlington	.241	139	4559	536	1098	197	33	69	472	439	1024	120	.317	.344
Lake County	.240	139	4607	582	1105	210	28	153	534	368	1236	99	.301	.397
Great Lakes	.236	139	4589	607	1085	226	40	108	541	486	1294	114	.313	.374
Wisconsin	.226	138	4463	521	1009	216	29	86	463	413	1241	126	.299	.345

CLUB PITCHING

	ERA	G	CG	SHO	SV	IP	H	R	ER	HR	BB	SO	AVG
West Michigan	2.77	136	3	1	47	1221	1013	438	376	72	358	1260	.224
Cedar Rapids	3.26	140	3	2	35	1231	1085	514	446	87	397	1088	.236
Kane County	3.35	137	3	2	42	1216	1053	520	453	71	421	1176	.233
Beloit	3.55	138	1	0	30	1218	1145	567	480	79	416	1155	.249
Quad Cities	3.63	138	0	0	32	1220	1049	555	492	91	574	1275	.232
Bowling Green	3.72	137	1	0	35	1192	1084	561	493	98	499	1140	.244
Peoria	3.81	139	5	2	33	1224	1179	587	518	118	423	1097	.255
Great Lakes	3.86	139	2	0	31	1225	1118	632	525	86	535	1196	.241
South Bend	3.89	139	0	0	37	1239	1201	632	536	99	487	1151	.256
Clinton	4.00	137	1	0	32	1219	1212	631	542	97	397	1128	.259
Dayton	4.16	140	3	2	42	1246	1198	648	576	115	374	1184	.251
Fort Wayne	4.18	140	1	0	29	1223	1144	647	568	92	446	1307	.246
Burlington	4.18	139	0	0	32	1211	1186	661	563	88	498	1187	.258
Wisconsin	4.31	138	2	2	30	1202	1189	652	575	118	422	1141	.259
Lake County	4.85	139	1	0	28	1207	1274	758	651	124	502	1003	.271
Lansing	5.32	136	3	0	25	1195	1312	796	706	127	554	1008	.282

CLUB FIELDING

	PCT	PO	A	E	DP
Beloit	.972	4437	1400	170	349
Bowling Green	.978	4434	1261	130	285
Burlington	.971	4392	1369	175	373
Cedar Rapids	.976	4512	1439	146	328
Clinton	.974	4490	1373	155	319
Dayton	.974	4694	1247	157	241
Fort Wayne	.975	4471	1272	146	185
Great Lakes	.969	4466	1359	187	338

	PCT	PO	A	E	DP
Kane County	.974	4416	1346	152	286
Lake County	.974	4489	1421	161	377
Lansing	.975	4430	1404	151	361
Peoria	.978	4508	1387	135	333
Quad Cities	.977	4500	1147	133	286
South Bend	.968	4491	1566	199	375
West Michigan	.977	4443	1302	136	301
Wisconsin	.974	4448	1308	153	321

INDIVIUAL BATTING

Batter, Club	AVG	G	AB	R	H	2B	3B	HR	RBI	BB	SO	SB
Bichette, Bo, Lansing	.384	70	284	60	109	32	3	10	51	28	55	12
Sanchez, Jesus, Bowling Green	.305	117	475	81	145	29	4	15	82	32	91	7
Tenerowicz, Robbie, Bowling Green	.295	94	349	43	103	25	3	11	37	32	67	4
Wilson, Marcus, Kane County	.295	103	383	56	113	21	5	9	54	55	90	15
Hernandez, Ramon, Kane County	.294	114	445	46	131	21	2	13	72	20	87	3
Siri, Jose, Dayton	.293	126	498	92	146	24	11	24	76	33	130	46
Diaz, Lewin, Cedar Rapids	.292	122	466	47	136	33	1	12	68	25	80	2
Pinero, Danny, West Michigan	.289	120	422	61	122	26	4	4	56	57	68	5
Zammarelli III, Nick, Clinton	.282	109	401	48	113	26	3	6	44	36	111	6
Ayala, Luis, South Bend	.281	114	391	52	110	17	5	3	42	43	86	24

INDIVIDUAL PITCHING

Pitcher, Club	W	L	ERA	G	GS	CG	SV	IP	H	R	ER	BB	SO
Beeker, Clark, Cedar Rapids	11	3	2.03	20	20	2	0	129	102	34	29	17	84
McWilliams, Sam, Kane County	11	6	2.84	25	25	0	0	133	112	46	42	31	98
Idrogo, Eudis, West Michigan	7	7	3.01	23	23	1	0	135	130	52	45	28	100
Gutierrez, Alfred, West Michigan	10	7	3.06	24	20	1	1	126	101	51	43	23	127
Santillan, Tony, Dayton	9	8	3.38	25	24	0	0	128	104	57	48	56	128
Moss, Scott, Dayton	13	6	3.45	26	26	0	0	136	114	62	52	48	156
Altamirano, Xavier, Beloit	8	6	3.59	31	14	0	2	118	106	53	47	31	95
Jankins, Thomas, Wisconsin	9	8	3.62	27	24	0	0	142	141	66	57	32	121
May, Dustin, Great Lakes	9	6	3.88	23	23	0	0	123	121	60	53	26	113
Hudson, Bryan, South Bend	9	3	3.91	24	24	0	0	124	128	65	54	52	81

DEPARTMENT LEADERS

BATTING

OBP	Tatis Jr., Fernando, Fort Wayne	.390
SLG	Siri, Jose, Dayton	.530
OPS	Tatis Jr., Fernando, Fort Wayne	.910
R	Siri, Jose, Dayton	92
H	Siri, Jose, Dayton	146
TB	Siri, Jose, Dayton	264
XBH	Siri, Jose, Dayton	59
2B	Diaz, Lewin, Cedar Rapids	33
3B	Siri, Jose, Dayton	11
	Blankenhorn, Travis, Cedar Rapids	11
HR	Tapia, Emmanuel, Lake County	29
RBI	Sanchez, Jesus, Bowling Green	82
SAC	Woodrow, Danny, West Michigan	13
BB	Tatis Jr., Fernando, Fort Wayne	75
HBP	Sinay, Nick, Lansing	38
SO	Morgan, Gareth, Clinton	185
SB	Siri, Jose, Dayton	46
CS	Rengifo, Luis, Clinton, Bowling Green	17
AB/SO	Quevedo, Yojhan, Clinton	7.76

FIELDING

C PCT	Robinson, Chuckie, Quad Cities	.996
PO	Robinson, Chuckie, Quad Cities	709
A	Rortvedt, Ben, Cedar Rapids	84
DP	Theroux, Collin, Beloit	12
E	Quevedo, Yojhan, Clinton	13
PB	Hamilton, Caleb, Cedar Rapids	18
1B PCT	Diaz, Lewin, Cedar Rapids	.987
PO	Diaz, Lewin, Cedar Rapids	940
A	Diaz, Lewin, Cedar Rapids	59
DP	Morgan, Brennan, Burlington	91
	Tapia, Emmanuel, Lake County	91
E	Tapia, Emmanuel, Lake County	17
2B PCT	Peguero, Yeiler, South Bend	.957
PO	Peguero, Yeiler, South Bend	172
A	Peguero, Yeiler, South Bend	275
DP	Peguero, Yeiler, South Bend	66
E	Peguero, Yeiler, South Bend	20
3B PCT	Potts, Hudson, Fort Wayne	.962
PO	Potts, Hudson, Fort Wayne	69
A	Rizzo, Joe, Clinton	185
DP	Rizzo, Joe, Clinton	19
E	Rizzo, Joe, Clinton	22
SS PCT	Wakamatsu, Luke, Lake County	.963
PO	Tatis Jr., Fernando, Fort Wayne	163
A	Wakamatsu, Luke, Lake County	286
DP	Wakamatsu, Luke, Lake County	66
E	Tatis Jr., Fernando, Fort Wayne	25
OF PCT	Thomas, Cody, Great Lakes	.991
PO	Siri, Jose, Dayton	310
A	Persico, Luke, Beloit	16
DP	Morgan, Gareth, Clinton	5
	Olivares, Edward, Lansing	5
E	Ayala, Luis, South Bend	11

PITCHING

G	Kuhnel, Joel, Dayton	48
GS	Aiken, Brady, Lake County	27
GF	Siri, Dalbert, Lake County	36
SV	Lujan, Hector, Cedar Rapids	17
W	Rondon, Manuel, South Bend	14
L	Garcia, Danny, Clinton	13
	Aiken, Brady, Lake County	13
	Miniard, Micah, Lake County	13
IP	Jankins, Thomas, Wisconsin	142
H	Garcia, Danny, Clinton	168
R	Miniard, Micah, Lake County	109
ER	Miniard, Micah, Lake County	102
HB	Miniard, Micah, Lake County	14
BB	Aiken, Brady, Lake County	101
SO	Moss, Scott, Dayton	156
SO/9	Rosenberg, Kenny, Bowling Green	10.53
SO/9(RP)	Mendez, Deivy, Bowling Green	13.66
BB/9	Newsome, Ljay, Clinton	1.11
WP	Diaz, Denis, Lansing	18
BK	Manoah, Erik, Burlington	8
HR	Hillman, Juan, Lake County	22
AVG	Gutierrez, Alfred, West Michigan	.213

ALL-STAR TEAM

C: Chuckie Robinson, Quad Cities. **1B:** Emmanuel Tapia, Lake County. **2B:** Robbie Tenerowicz, Bowling Green. **3B:** Vladimir Guerrero Jr., Lansing. **SS:** Bo Bichette, Lansing. **OF:** Jose Siri, Dayton; Jesus Sanchez, Bowling Green; Marcus Wilson, Kane County. **DH:** Li-Jen Chu, Lake County. **RHP:** Clark Beeker, Cedar Rapids; Sam McWilliams, Kane County. **LHP:** Gregory Soto, West Michigan. **RP:** Tommy Eveld, Kane County; Wyatt Short, South Bend. **Most Valuable Player:** Bo Bichette, Lansing. **Prospect of the Year:** Bo Bichette, Lansing. **Manager of the Year:** Mike Rabelo, West Michigan

SOUTH ATLANTIC LEAGUE LOW CLASS A

BY J.J. COOPER

The 2017 season on the field will be remembered as the year that Greenville finally won a South Atlantic League title.

The Red Sox low Class A affiliate edged Charleston in the semifinals and then topped Kannapolis 3-1 in the best-of-five championship series. It was Greenville's first Sally League title since 1970, when the league was still known as the Western Carolinas League.

But around the league, the year will be remembered as the year of Tim Tebow. The former Heisman Trophy winner spent the first half of the season playing for Columbia and drawing exceptional crowds. Tebow's presence helped the Fireflies draw 54,000 more fans than they did last year in their first year in the city in a brand-new stadium. Hagerstown drew more than 25 percent of its attendance for the entire season during the four games where Tebow was in town.

While it was a good year at the gate, it was a down year for prospects around the league. Usually the Sally League's top prospects are the best of the best. Just this decade we've seen Luis Severino, Jose Fernandez, Gary Sanchez, Bryce Harper and Manny Machado rank among the top five prospects on various year's Sally League Top 20s.

However for a second consecutive season, managers and scouts were a little disappointed in the caliber of prospects around the league. The modest debut seasons for 2016 top pick Mickey Moniak and fellow first-rounders Riley Pint, Jay Groome and Blake Rutherford played a part in that general malaise.

There were some memorable performances, however, as Augusta's Domenic Mazza and Lakewood's Nick Fanti both threw nine-inning no-hitters in 2017. White Sox first-round pick Jake Burger hit for the cycle with Kannapolis and Hagerstown's Carter Kieboom and Delmarva's Collin Woody each had a three-homer game.

TOP 20 PROSPECTS

1. Sixto Sanchez, RHP, Lakewood (Phillies)
2. Estevan Florial, OF, Charleston (Yankees)
3. Leody Taveras, OF, Hickory (Rangers)
4. Alec Hansen, RHP, Kannapolis (White Sox)
5. Cristian Pache, OF, Rome (Braves)
6. Ian Anderson, RHP, Rome (Braves)
7. Andres Gimenez, SS, Columbia (Mets)
8. Carter Kieboom, SS, Hagerstown (Nationals)
9. Colton Welker, 3B, Asheville (Rockies)
10. Adonis Medina, RHP, Lakewood (Phillies)
11. Bryse Wilson, RHP, Rome (Braves)
12. Micker Adolfo, OF, Kannapolis (White Sox)
13. Daniel Johnson, OF, Hagerstown (Nationals)
14. Joey Wentz, LHP, Rome (Braves)
15. Riley Pint, RHP, Asheville (Rockies)
16. Jake Burger, 3B, Kannapolis (White Sox)
17. Mickey Moniak, OF, Lakewood (Phillies)
18. Blake Rutherford, OF, Kannapolis (White Sox)
19. Sheldon Neuse, SS/3B, Hagerstown (Nationals)
20. Brian Miller, OF, Greensboro (Marlins)

STANDINGS: SPLIT SEASON

FIRST HALF

NORTH	W	L	PCT	GB
Kannapolis	39	29	.574	—
Lakewood	40	30	.571	—
Hagerstown	38	31	.551	1½
Greensboro	37	31	.544	2
West Virginia	30	36	.455	8
Delmarva	29	39	.426	10
Hickory	27	43	.386	13

SOUTH	W	L	PCT	GB
Greenville	41	28	.594	—
Columbia	40	28	.588	½
Rome	38	32	.543	3½
Lexington	34	35	.493	7
Charleston	34	36	.486	7½
Asheville	29	39	.426	11½
Augusta	23	42	.354	16

SECOND HALF

NORTH	W	L	PCT	GB
Greensboro	38	30	.559	—
West Virginia	39	31	.557	—
Hickory	37	33	.529	2
Hagerstown	35	32	.522	2½
Lakewood	33	36	.478	5½
Delmarva	30	39	.435	8½
Kannapolis	29	40	.420	9½

SOUTH	W	L	PCT	GB
Charleston	42	27	.609	—
Asheville	39	31	.557	3½
Greenville	38	32	.543	4½
Rome	36	33	.522	6
Augusta	32	38	.457	10½
Lexington	28	40	.412	13½
Columbia	28	42	.400	14½

Playoffs—Semifinals: Kannapolis defeated Greensboro 2-0 and Greenville defeated Charleston 2-1 in best-of-three-series. **Finals:** Greenville defeated Kannapolis 3-1 in a best-of-five series.

OVERALL STANDINGS

Northern Division	W	L	PCT	GB	Manager(s)	Attendance	Average	Last Pennant
Greensboro Grasshoppers (Marlins)	75	61	.551	—	Todd Pratt	350,743	5,235	2011
Hagerstown Suns (Nationals)	73	63	.537	2	Patrick Anderson	84,181	1,380	Never
Lakewood BlueClaws (Phillies)	73	66	.525	3½	Marty Malloy	338,544	5,208	2010
West Virginia Power (Pirates)	69	67	.507	6	Wyatt Toregas	133,679	2,057	1990
Kannapolis Intimidators (White Sox)	68	69	.496	7½	Justin Jirschele	69,112	1,080	2005
Hickory Crawdads (Rangers)	64	76	.457	13	Spike Owen	136,225	2,129	2015
Delmarva Shorebirds (Orioles)	59	78	.431	16½	Ryan Minor	207,131	3,236	2001

Southern Division	W	L	PCT	GB	Manager(s)	Attendance	Average	Last Pennant
Greenville Drive (Red Sox)	79	60	.568	—	Darren Fenster	328,222	4,899	2017
Charleston RiverDogs (Yankees)	76	63	.547	3	Pat Osborn	305,622	4,494	Never
Rome Braves (Braves)	74	65	.532	5	Randy Ingle	161,444	2,374	2016
Asheville Tourists (Rockies)	68	70	.493	10½	Warren Schaeffer	184,019	2,706	2014
Columbia Fireflies (Mets)	68	70	.493	10½	Jose Leger	315,034	4,773	2013
Lexington Legends (Royals)	62	75	.453	16	Scott Thorman	281,210	4,326	2001
Augusta GreenJackets (Giants)	55	80	.407	22	Carlos Valderrama	178,269	2,743	2008

CLUB BATTING

	AVG	G	AB	R	H	2B	3B	HR	RBI	BB	SO	SB	OBP	SLG
Asheville	.266	138	4714	660	1255	292	30	115	597	333	1108	229	.326	.414
Charleston	.261	139	4580	610	1194	227	28	71	551	426	1020	100	.328	.369
Hagerstown	.258	137	4443	643	1147	253	32	112	582	414	1036	110	.326	.405
Lexington	.258	138	4601	656	1187	258	26	111	593	399	1210	155	.324	.398
West Virginia	.256	136	4464	592	1142	228	28	92	546	359	1024	79	.323	.381
Hickory	.254	140	4674	601	1185	213	41	92	536	324	1103	89	.310	.376
Rome	.252	139	4785	567	1205	198	47	48	492	368	1144	157	.316	.343
Greenville	.250	139	4710	601	1177	231	26	87	533	413	1182	147	.320	.365
Greensboro	.246	136	4435	584	1093	210	34	70	529	425	1195	135	.322	.357
Kannapolis	.245	137	4564	561	1117	213	32	84	522	386	1204	46	.314	.361
Augusta	.243	135	4427	514	1076	214	22	72	445	368	1070	149	.312	.350
Lakewood	.243	139	4586	543	1114	222	32	84	484	324	1078	92	.301	.360
Delmarva	.240	137	4616	544	1108	229	31	77	492	341	1243	91	.304	.353
Columbia	.234	138	4504	541	1055	189	32	67	474	466	1170	127	.314	.335

CLUB PITCHING

	ERA	G	CG	SHO	SV	IP	H	R	ER	HR	BB	SO	AVG
Charleston	3.07	139	3	0	46	1203	1043	483	410	55	370	1252	.232
Rome	3.19	139	3	2	31	1258	1172	541	446	60	400	1254	.247
Lakewood	3.26	139	4	3	36	1208	1030	505	438	65	363	1231	.230
Kannapolis	3.44	137	4	0	31	1207	1072	548	461	57	371	1170	.238
Greenville	3.48	139	2	1	40	1245	1113	546	482	90	403	1246	.239
Columbia	3.45	138	8	1	32	1204	1120	575	461	62	410	1061	.246
West Virginia	3.62	136	6	3	30	1180	1031	554	475	93	391	1110	.235
Greensboro	3.66	136	5	3	29	1185	1101	548	482	133	326	1091	.246
Delmarva	3.79	137	0	0	29	1204	1210	613	507	94	354	1000	.261
Asheville	3.90	138	3	0	31	1229	1288	631	533	93	323	1102	.271
Augusta	3.94	135	3	2	23	1173	1153	638	513	56	461	1029	.257
Hickory	4.14	140	0	0	34	1204	1192	666	554	96	436	1151	.257
Hagerstown	4.32	137	3	1	32	1163	1224	643	558	111	317	1052	.268
Lexington	4.72	138	3	0	34	1213	1306	726	636	117	421	1038	.276

CLUB FIELDING

	PCT	PO	A	E	DP
Greensboro	.980	4298	1363	115	290
Greenville	.980	4454	1433	120	252
Lakewood	.978	4331	1321	128	223
West Virginia	.976	4321	1387	143	277
Delmarva	.975	4465	1394	151	290
Kannapolis	.973	4343	1399	157	280
Hagerstown	.973	4303	1285	156	283

	PCT	PO	A	E	DP
Charleston	.973	4334	1346	160	221
Rome	.973	4549	1492	171	373
Lexington	.972	4513	1410	174	307
Hickory	.971	4382	1393	170	304
Columbia	.970	4427	1344	178	248
Asheville	.970	4442	1496	186	320
Augusta	.965	4367	1311	205	275

INDIVIDUAL BATTING

Batter, Club	AVG	G	AB	R	H	2B	3B	HR	RBI	BB	SO	SB
Rivera, Emmanuel, Lexington	.310	122	464	60	144	27	5	12	72	31	87	8
Nelson, James, Greensboro	.309	102	395	41	122	31	3	7	59	26	106	6
Baur, Albert, West Virginia	.299	106	392	56	117	31	0	8	65	41	84	0
Florial, Estevan, Charleston	.297	91	344	64	102	21	5	11	43	41	124	17
Ventura, Randy, Rome	.294	95	381	46	112	7	1	1	16	24	83	29
Cedrola, Lorenzo, Greenville	.285	92	354	47	101	18	3	4	34	11	48	19
Abreu, Willie, Asheville	.283	119	477	73	135	32	6	14	78	26	93	40
Billingsley, Cole, Delmarva	.282	120	461	66	130	24	3	3	31	44	97	27
Pache, Cristian, Rome	.281	119	469	60	132	13	8	0	42	39	104	32
Espinal, Santiago, Greenville	.281	123	492	64	138	18	4	4	46	39	67	20

INDIVIDUAL PITCHING

Pitcher, Club	W	L	ERA	G	GS	CG	SV	IP	H	R	ER	BB	SO
Wells, Alex, Delmarva	11	5	2.38	25	25	0	0	140	118	49	37	10	113
Wilson, Bryse, Rome	10	7	2.50	26	26	1	0	137	105	45	38	37	139
Fanti, Nick, Lakewood	9	2	2.54	21	21	1	0	120	87	37	34	28	121
Wentz, Joey, Rome	8	3	2.60	26	26	0	0	132	99	44	38	46	152
Requena, Alejandro, Ashville/Lakewood	9	4	2.74	21	21	0	0	128	109	49	39	25	104
Perez, Freicer, Charleston	10	3	2.84	24	24	0	0	124	96	53	39	45	117
Falter, Bailey, Lakewood	8	7	2.99	21	21	0	0	114	117	41	38	23	105
Mazza, Domenic, Augusta	7	9	3.01	19	19	3	0	120	109	47	40	20	97
Medina, Adonis, Lakewood	4	9	3.01	22	22	0	0	120	103	47	40	39	133
King, Michael, Greensboro	11	9	3.14	26	25	2	0	149	141	55	52	21	106

ALL-STAR TEAM

C: Roldani Baldwin, Greenville. **1B:** Darick Hall, Lakewood. **2B:** Jake Noll, Hagerstown. **3B:** Emmanuel Rivera, Lexington. **SS:** Jose Gomez, Asheville. **OF:** Willie Abreu, Asheville; Estevan Florial, Charleston; Daniel Johnson, Hagerstown. **UT/INF:** James Nelson, Greensboro. **UT/OF:** Jake Ring, Delmarva. **DH:** Micker Adolfo, Kannapolis. **RHP:** Bryse Wilson, Rome. **LHP:** Joey Wentz, Rome. **RP:** Will Hibbs, Lakewood. **Coach:** Dan Meyer, Rome.

Most Valuable Player: Darick Hall, Lakewood
Most Outstanding Pitcher: Joey Wentz, Rome
Most Outstanding Prospect: Estevan Florial, Charleston
Manager of the Year: Darren Fenster, Greenville

DEPARTMENT LEADERS

BATTING

OBP	Munoz, Carlos, West Virginia	.386
SLG	Hall, Darick, Lakewood	.533
OPS	Hall, Darick, Lakewood	.872
R	Perkins, Blake, Hagerstown	105
H	Rivera, Emmanuel, Lexington	144
TB	Hall, Darick, Lakewood	227
XBH	Hall, Darick, Lakewood	56
2B	Ring, Jake, Delmarva	36
3B	Tejeda, Anderson, Hickory	9
HR	Hall, Darick, Lakewood	27
RBI	Hall, Darick, Lakewood	96
SAC	Bird, Corey, Greensboro	17
BB	Perkins, Blake, Hagerstown	72
HBP	Woody, Collin, Delmarva	35
SO	Lee, Khalil, Lexington	171
SB	Hill, Tyler, Greenville	42
CS	Lee, Khalil, Lexington	18
AB/SO	Castillo, Diego, Charleston	9.08

FIELDING

C PCT	Rindfleisch, Jarett, Greensboro	.997
PO	Baldwin, Roldani, Greenville	781
A	Baldwin, Roldani, Greenville	103
DP	Viloria, Meibrys, Lexington	11
E	Ewing, Skyler, Augusta	12
PB	Sands, Donny, Charleston	22
1B PCT	Tubbs, Tucker, Greenville	.997
PO	Palmeiro, Preston, Delmarva	1028
A	Baur, Albert, West Virginia	67
DP	Palmeiro, Preston, Delmarva	86
E	Vizcaino, Jose Jr., Augusta	12
2B PCT	Brito, Daniel, Lakewood	.977
PO	Beltre, Kelvin, Augusta	199
A	Beltre, Kelvin, Augusta	289
DP	Josephina, Kevin, Rome	77
E	Josephina, Kevin, Rome	22
3B PCT	Williams, Luke, Lakewood	.948
PO	Woody, Collin, Delmarva	82
A	Williams, Luke, Lakewood	216
DP	Hoekstra, Kurt, Rome	17
	Woody, Collin, Delmarva	17
E	Rivera, Emmanuel, Lexington	21
SS PCT	Castellano, Angelo, Lexington	.972
PO	Pintor, Luis, Greensboro	190
A	Espinal, Santiago, Greenville	324
DP	Pintor, Luis, Greensboro	68
E	Tejeda, Anderson, Hickory	24
OF PCT	Billingsley, Cole, Delmarva	.996
PO	Perkins, Blake, Hagerstown	304
A	Pache, Cristian, Rome	17
DP	Pache, Cristian, Rome	8
E	Fabian, Sandro, Augusta	12

PITCHING

G	Fernandez, Julian, Asheville	51
GS	Santos, Antonio, Asheville	27
	Walker, Jeremy, Rome	27
GF	Ruotolo, Patrick, Augusta	43
SV	Hibbs, Will, Lakewood	20
W	Mills, McKenzie, Hagerstown	12
L	Nelson, Nick, Charleston	12
	Gomez, Ofreidy, Lexington	12
IP	Humpal, Lucas, Delmarva	150
H	Santos, Antonio, Asheville	200
R	Santos, Antonio, Asheville	101
ER	Santos, Antonio, Asheville	88
HB	Davila, Garrett, Lexington	18
BB	Woods, Stephen, Augusta	64
SO	Escobar, Luis, West Virginia	168
SO/9	Escobar, Luis, West Virginia	11.48
SO/9(RP)	Blackham, Matt, Columbia	13.02
BB/9	Wells, Alex, Delmarva	0.64
WP	Pint, Riley, Asheville	26
BK	Orozco, Jio, Charleston	7
HR	Beggs, Dustin, Greensboro	23
AVG	Fanti, Nick, Lakewood	.200

NEW YORK-PENN LEAGUE SHORT-SEASON

BY J.J. COOPER

In a league that saw a number of 2017 first-round picks make their pro debuts, Hudson Valley's Brendan McKay was both the most prominent and the highest draft pick.

He also was a unique experiment. McKay, the 2017 Baseball America College Player of the Year, was one of the top two-way players in the country coming into the draft. But unlike virtually everyone else, he kept pitching and hitting when he reached pro ball.

The Rays worked out a system where McKay played first base or designated hitter during the week and took Wednesday's off to throw a side session off the mound. Then every Sunday, he served as the team's starting pitcher, which allowed him to get both innings and at-bats.

McKay was more effective on the mound than at the plate, but the two-way star, second baseman Vidal Brujan and shortstop Taylor Walls helped lead Hudson Valley to its first title since 2012. Hudson Valley had lost in the finals last year.

Brujan led the league in runs scored (51), total bases (108) and hits (74).

The Renegades knocked off Staten Island in the first round, then swept a pair of games against Vermont to win the league title. Drew Strotman threw six scoreless innings in the deciding game of the championship.

McKay was one of the few first-round picks who saw enough playing time in the league to qualify for the Top 20 Prospects list. There were a large number of impressive pitchers who failed to throw enough innings to qualify, including righthanders Will Crowe, Tanner Houck, Jonathan Loasiga and J.B. Bukauskas and lefthanders Seth Romero, David Peterson and Jay Groome.

The Yankees were knocked out in the first round of the playoffs by Hudson Valley but Staten Island finished with the best record in the league (46-29) and had the most talented roster as far as the number of big league prospects. Led by righthander Jorge Guzman, the Staten Island pitching staff was filled with hard-throwing starters and relievers with big league potential.

Staten Island led the league with a 2.64 ERA that was nearly .3 runs better than any other team in the league. Their 11 shutouts were also easily a league best.

Williamsport also had a talented roster, led by first-round pick Adam Haseley and outfielder Jhailyn Ortiz while the one-two-punch of Nolan Jones and Will Benson gave Mahoning Valley (Indians) sluggers to fear.

TOP 20 PROSPECTS

1. Brendan McKay, 1B/LHP, Hudson Valley (Rays)
2. Jorge Guzman, RHP, Staten Island (Yankees)
3. Jhailyn Ortiz, OF, Williamsport (Phillies)
4. Matt Manning, RHP, Connecticut (Tigers)
5. Vidal Brujan, 2B, Hudson Valley (Rays)
6. Adam Haseley, OF, Williamsport (Phillies)
7. Greg Deichmann, OF, Vermont (Athletics)
8. Nolan Jones, 3B, Mahoning Valley (Indians)
9. Trevor Stephan, RHP, Staten Island (Yankees)
10. Will Benson, OF, Mahoning Valley (Indians)
11. Tobias Myers, RHP, Hudson Valley (Rays)
12. Evan Mendoza, 3B, State College (Cardinals)
13. Kyle Young, LHP, Williamsport (Phillies)
14. Juan De Paula, RHP, Staten Island (Yankees)
15. Samad Taylor, 2B, Mahoning Valley (Indians)
16. Oswaldo Cabrera, SS/2B, Staten Island (Yankees)
17. Cameron Bishop, LHP, Aberdeen (Orioles)
18. Michael Baumann, RHP, Aberdeen (Orioles)
19. Tristan Gray, SS/2B, West Virginia (Pirates)
20. Spencer Howard, RHP, Williamsport (Phillies)

OVERALL STANDINGS

McNamara Division	W	L	PCT	GB	Manager(s)	Attendance	Average	Last Pennant
Staten Island Yankees (Yankees)	46	29	.613	—	Julio Mosquera	71,401	2,040	2011
Hudson Valley Renegades (Rays)	44	32	.579	2½	Craig Albernaz	147,936	3,998	2017
Aberdeen IronBirds (Orioles)	41	34	.547	5	Kevin Bradshaw	130,823	3,964	1983
Brooklyn Cyclones (Mets)	24	52	.316	22½	Edgardo Alfonzo	186,853	5,190	2001
Pinckney Division	**W**	**L**	**PCT**	**GB**	**Manager(s)**	**Attendance**	**Average**	**Last Pennant**
Mahoning Valley Scrappers (indians)	44	29	.603	—	Luke Carlin	107,894	2,997	2004
State College Spikes (Cardinals)	40	35	.533	5	Joe Kruzel	123,401	3,247	2016
West Virginia Black Bears (Pirates)	40	35	.533	5	Brian Esposito	75,064	2,029	2015
Williamsport Crosscutters (Phillies)	37	37	.500	7½	Pat Borders	61,082	1,797	2003
Auburn Doubledays (Nationals)	30	45	.400	15	Jerad Head	46,132	1,281	2007
Batavia Muckdogs (Marlins)	30	45	.400	15	Mike Jacobs	27,389	806	2008
Stedler Division	**W**	**L**	**PCT**	**GB**	**Manager(s)**	**Attendance**	**Average**	**Last Pennant**
Vermont Lake Monsters (Athletics)	42	33	.560	—	Aaron Nieckula	82,674	2,362	1996
Connecticut Tigers (Tigers)	37	35	.514	3½	Gerald Laird	73,439	2,225	1998
Tri-City ValleyCats (Astros)	34	39	.466	7	Morgan Ensberg	142,922	4,083	2013
Lowell Spinners (Red Sox)	33	42	.440	9	Iggy Suarez	126,565	3,516	Never

Semifinals: Vermont defeated Mahoning Valley 2-0 and Hudson Valley defeated Staten Island 2-1 in best-of-three series. **Finals:** Hudson Valley defeated Vermont 2-0 in a best-of-three series.

CLUB BATTING

	AVG	G	AB	R	H	2B	3B	HR	RBI	BB	SO	SB	OBP	SLG
State College	.262	75	2579	356	676	133	18	30	322	242	531	34	.333	.363
Aberdeen	.255	75	2460	329	628	123	18	26	295	248	677	76	.328	.352
Mahoning Valley	.252	73	2498	311	630	121	17	37	282	199	665	43	.315	.359
Hudson Valley	.247	76	2515	334	620	109	24	30	278	231	585	60	.321	.345
Williamsport	.242	74	2425	283	587	133	17	45	250	199	600	51	.312	.367
Vermont	.242	75	2510	319	607	107	19	34	283	242	600	47	.315	.340
Auburn	.242	75	2609	325	630	119	16	42	280	253	676	58	.317	.348
West Virginia	.240	75	2544	324	611	121	31	36	289	251	650	80	.318	.355
Connecticut	.233	72	2312	281	539	85	12	24	243	219	624	59	.304	.311
Brooklyn	.232	76	2419	241	560	104	12	17	202	235	643	100	.309	.306
Staten Island	.232	75	2315	273	536	107	12	29	238	247	601	51	.314	.326
Batavia	.231	76	2475	298	572	113	16	22	244	272	711	50	.316	.316
Lowell	.231	75	2388	268	551	92	22	20	238	231	660	47	.309	.313
Tri-City	.216	73	2338	290	506	104	19	58	251	266	668	89	.304	.352

CLUB PITCHING

	ERA	G	CG	SHO	SV	IP	H	R	ER	HR	BB	SO	AVG
Staten Island	2.64	75	1	0	28	640	499	232	188	21	205	702	.212
Mahoning Valley	2.92	73	0	0	23	648	546	271	210	34	240	663	.228
Vermont Lake	3.01	75	2	0	21	666	551	265	223	45	244	608	.224
Aberdeen	3.13	75	1	0	22	641	523	281	223	26	225	696	.219
Hudson Valley	3.14	76	0	0	23	667	541	287	233	25	266	670	.222
West Virginia	3.32	75	1	0	19	680	635	294	251	35	169	617	.243
State College	3.40	75	1	0	20	665	669	317	251	37	260	624	.263
Williamsport	3.43	74	0	0	24	642	554	290	245	22	281	688	.231
Connecticut	3.47	72	1	0	20	607	580	290	234	19	220	505	.250
Lowell	3.52	75	0	0	15	644	604	313	252	33	233	597	.245
Tri-City	3.61	73	0	0	19	629	537	291	252	22	290	737	.230
Auburn	3.87	75	0	0	15	677	710	367	291	43	225	549	.266
Batavia	4.16	75	1	0	14	650	667	370	300	44	214	611	.261
Brooklyn	4.18	76	2	0	15	639	637	364	297	44	263	624	.258

CLUB FIELDING

	PCT	PO	A	E	DP
West Virginia	.973	2494	762	90	126
State College	.972	2405	821	93	221
Hudson Valley	.972	2402	769	93	199
Tri-City	.970	2222	674	89	155
Aberdeen	.970	2258	771	95	149
Vermont	.969	2412	775	102	183
Mahoning Valley	.968	2330	757	102	184

	PCT	PO	A	E	DP
Brooklyn	.968	2274	753	101	107
Staten Island	.967	2304	711	102	151
Williamsport	.967	2269	767	103	144
Connecticut	.965	2236	681	105	143
Auburn	.965	2485	782	118	189
Batavia	.964	2333	752	117	148
Lowell	.963	2349	729	118	145

INDIVIDUAL BATTING

Batter, Club	AVG	G	AB	R	H	2B	3B	HR	RBI	BB	SO	SB
Mendoza, Evan, State College	.370	41	162	34	60	14	3	3	28	16	33	1
Breazeale, Ben, Aberdeen	.318	57	195	29	62	14	0	5	32	37	56	3
Jones, Nolan, Mahoning Valley	.317	62	218	41	69	18	3	4	33	43	60	1
Gonzalez, Yariel, State College	.305	56	213	27	65	12	0	2	42	18	33	2
Craport, Trevor, Aberdeen	.302	52	179	31	54	15	3	3	30	21	36	4
McCoy, Mason, Aberdeen	.301	53	186	34	56	11	3	1	29	26	28	4
Rasquin, Walter, Brooklyn	.300	63	243	41	73	21	1	1	19	13	40	32
Perez, Angel, Hudson Valley	.291	59	220	31	64	6	3	3	19	12	51	3
Lopez, Joshua, State College	.285	52	186	21	53	11	0	5	27	15	44	0
Brujan, Vidal, Hudson Valley	.285	67	260	51	74	15	5	3	20	34	36	16

INDIVIDUAL PITCHING

Pitcher, Club	W	L	ERA	G	GS	CG	SV	IP	H	R	ER	BB	SO
Reyes, Denyi, Lowell	9	0	1.45	15	0	0	0	62	52	13	10	7	53
Hightower, Scooter, West Virginia	4	1	1.94	16	15	0	0	88	77	30	19	9	80
Franklin, Austin, Hudson Valley	4	2	2.21	13	13	0	0	69	51	21	17	31	71
Perez, Sam, Batavia	4	2	2.21	14	14	0	0	77	69	20	19	13	53
Guzman, Jorge, Staten Island	5	3	2.30	13	13	1	0	67	51	21	17	18	88
Linares, Resly, Hudson Valley	3	3	2.35	13	12	0	0	61	36	20	16	23	60
Vasquez, Gregori, Mahoning Valley	5	3	2.38	14	14	0	0	76	67	20	20	13	57
Castano, Daniel, State College	9	3	2.57	14	14	1	0	91	87	33	26	13	81
Wallace, Gavin, West Virginia	3	2	2.65	15	13	0	0	68	60	26	20	5	41
Andueza, Ivan, Vermont	6	3	2.75	14	7	2	0	72	59	31	22	22	50

DEPARTMENT LEADERS

BATTING

OBP	Jones, Nolan, Mahoning Valley	.430
SLG	Ortiz, Jhailyn, Williamsport	.560
OPS	Jones, Nolan, Mahoning Valley	.912
R	Brujan, Vidal, Hudson Valley	51
H	Brujan, Vidal, Hudson Valley	74
TB	Brujan, Vidal, Hudson Valley	108
XBH	Jones, Nolan, Mahoning Valley	25
2B	Rasquin, Walter, Brooklyn	21
3B	Pineda, Andy, Tri-City	7
	Oliva, Jared, West Virginia	7
HR	Benson, Will, Mahoning Valley	10
RBI	Gonzalez, Yariel, State College	42
SAC	Oliva, Jared, West Virginia	9
BB	Jones, Nolan, Mahoning Valley	43
HBP	Jones, Thomas, Batavia	14
SO	Jones, Thomas, Batavia	94
SB	Rasquin, Walter, Brooklyn	32
CS	Siri, Raul, West Virginia	13
AB/SO	Tansel, Deion, Hudson Valley	9.10

FIELDING

C PCT	Carrillo, Jean, Aberdeen	.997
PO	Law, Zacrey, Hudson Valley	449
A	Carrillo, Jean, Aberdeen	56
DP	Lopez, Joshua, State College	7
E	Duran, Rodolfo, Williamsport	9
PB	Lopez, Jason, Staten Island	17
1B PCT	Cantu, Ulysses, Mahoning Valley	.987
PO	Cantu, Ulysses, Mahoning Valley	426
A	Cantu, Ulysses, Mahoning Valley	31
	Ripken, Ryan, Aberdeen	31
DP	Cantu, Ulysses, Mahoning Valley	39
E	Lameda, Raiwinson, Lowell	9
2B PCT	Brujan, Vidal, Hudson Valley	.967
PO	Brujan, Vidal, Hudson Valley	109
A	Brujan, Vidal, Hudson Valley	182
DP	Brujan, Vidal, Hudson Valley	48
E	Moesquit, Kirvin, Aberdeen	10
	Brujan, Vidal, Hudson Valley	10
3B PCT	Toffey, Will, Vermont	.930
PO	Meregildo, Omar, Auburn	47
A	Toffey, Will, Vermont	102
DP	Mendoza, Evan, State College	15
E	Jones, Nolan, Mahoning Valley	22
SS PCT	Peterson, Cole, Connecticut	.974
PO	Peterson, Cole, Connecticut	100
A	Four tied with	175
E	Garcia, Wilkerman, Staten Island	18
OF PCT	Hurst, Scott, State College	1.000
	Oliva, Jared, West Virginia	1.000
PO	Jones, Thomas, Batavia	123
A	Aybar, Yoan, Lowell	9
DP	Three tied with	3
E	Three tied with	7

PITCHING

G	Echols, Riley, Mahoning Valley	23
	Ramirez, Luis, Williamsport	23
	Chen, Ping-Hsueh, Mahoning Valley	23
GS	Five tied with	15
GF	Ramirez, Luis, Williamsport	18
SV	Ramirez, Luis, Williamsport	11
W	Castano, Daniel, State College	9
	Reyes, Denyi, Lowell	9
L	Three tied with	7
IP	Castano, Daniel, State College	91
H	Mulford, Jonathon, State College	87
	Castano, Daniel, State College	87
R	Balestrieri, Paul, State College	46
	Blanco, Argenis, Vermont	46
ER	Johnson, Trent, Brooklyn	41
	Blanco, Argenis, Vermont	41
HB	Cubilete, Sergio, West Virginia	9
	Vogel, Matt, Hudson Valley	9
BB	Mulford, Jonathon, State College	45
SO	Guzman, Jorge, Staten Island	88
SO/9	Garcia, Julian, Williamsport	12.30
SO/9(RP)	Teaney, Jonathan, Maho. Valley	15.13
BB/9	Wallace, Gavin, West Virginia	0.66
WP	Three tied with	16
BK	Three tied with	4
HR	Blanco, Argenis, Vermont	10
AVG	Linares, Resly, Hudson Valley	.171

NORTHWEST LEAGUE SHORT-SEASON

BY JOHN MANUEL

Vancouver joined the Northwest League in 2000 after a long stretch as a Triple-A Pacific Coast League franchise. By 2011, the Canadians had found their home as a Blue Jays affiliate.

And the Jays have turned Vancouver into a dynasty. The C's won their fourth Northwest League title in their seven years in the league. Vancouver had the league's best overall record at 43-33, then went 5-1 in the playoffs, winning the championship series 3-1 over Eugene.

Manager Rich Miller helped lead the team to the title in 2011 as interim manager and won it all in 2017, while also earning manager of the year honors. However, the Jays let Miller go after the season ended.

The key hit in the Game Four championship clincher, a 2-1 victory, came off the bat of Toronto's first 2017 draft pick, shortstop Logan Warmoth. His two-run single in the fourth inning drove home two, and the Canadians staff made it hold up. Vancouver used five pitchers overall, with William Ouellette getting the final out for his third playoff save.

Toronto's other first-round pick, righthander Nate Pearson, dominated in limited time and had 14 strikeouts while allowing only one run in two playoff starts. Vancouver also led the league in attendance for the third straight season.

Eugene was a worthy adversary, having finished two games back of Hillsboro overall in the South Division in the regular season before sweeping the Hops in the first round of the playoffs.

The Emeralds had a prospect-heavy pitching staff, particularly in the playoffs, featuring righty Jose Albertos for a pair of starts. Eugene pitchers limited hitters to a .171 average and had 61 strikeouts in 52 playoff innings and still lost out to the Canadians.

Five pitchers ranked among the league's top 10 prospects—four in the top five—and for good reason. The league's hitters, forced to contend with Cole Ragans' changeup, upper-90s fastballs from Jhoan Duran and Albertos and the poise and command of Adrian Morejon and Javier Assad, managed to hit just .253/.327/.368 collectively. Pearson, who flirts with triple-digit velocity, didn't have enough innings to qualify for this list.

While those arms stand out, there was no shortage of positional talent either—particularly up the middle. The likes of Daulton Varsho, Riley Adams and Miguel Amaya made catching a strength in the league. However, 2016 12th-round pick Ryan Kirby, a 22-year-old for Salem-Keizer (which had the league's worst record), won the MVP award.

TOP 20 PROSPECTS

1. Cole Ragans, LHP, Spokane (Rangers)
2. Pavin Smith, 1B, Hillsboro (D-backs)
3. Jhoan Duran, RHP, Hillsboro (D-backs)
4. Jose Albertos, RHP, Eugene (Cubs)
5. Adrian Morejon, LHP, Tri-City (Padres)
6. Logan Warmoth, SS, Vancouver (Blue Jays)
7. Drew Ellis, 3B, Hillsboro (D-backs)
8. Aramis Ademan, SS, Eugene (Cubs)
9. Javier Assad, RHP, Eugene (Cubs)
10. Daulton Varsho, C, Hillsboro (D-backs)
11. Riley Adams, C, Vancouver (Blue Jays)
12. Alex Speas, RHP, Spokane (Rangers)
13. Miguel Aparicio, OF, Spokane (Rangers)
14. Eudy Ramos, 3B/1B, Hillsboro (D-backs)
15. Matt Whatley, C, Spokane (Rangers)
16. Miguel Amaya, C, Eugene (Cubs)
17. Sean Bouchard, 1B, Boise (Rockies)
18. Malique Ziegler, OF, Salem-Keizer (Giants)
19. Kevin Vlcuna, SS, Vancouver (Blue Jays)
20. Reggie Pruitt, OF, Vancouver (Blue Jays)

STANDINGS: SPLIT SEASON

FIRST HALF

NORTH	W	L	PCT	GB
Vancouver	21	17	.553	—
Tri-City	20	18	.526	1
Everett	17	21	.447	4
Spokane	16	22	.421	5
SOUTH	**W**	**L**	**PCT**	**GB**
Hillsboro	22	16	.579	—
Eugene	21	17	.553	1
Boise	19	19	.500	3
Salem-Keizer	16	22	.421	6

SECOND HALF

NORTH	W	L	PCT	GB
Spokane	23	15	.605	—
Vancouver	22	16	.579	1
Tri-City	20	18	.526	3
Everett	19	19	.500	4
SOUTH	**W**	**L**	**PCT**	**GB**
Hillsboro	19	19	.500	—
Boise	18	20	.474	1
Eugene	18	20	.474	1
Salem-Keizer	13	25	.342	6

Playoffs—Semifinals: Eugene defeated Hillsboro 2-0 and Vancouver defeated Spokane 2-0 in best-of-three series. **Finals:** Vancouver defeated Eugene 3-1 in a best-of-five series.

OVERALL STANDINGS

North Division	W	L	PCT	GB	Manager(s)	Attendance	Average	Last Pennant
Vancouver Canadians (Blue Jays)	43	33	.566	—	Rich Miller	239,527	6,303	2017
Tri-City Dust Devils (Padres)	40	36	.526	3	Ben Fritz	86,461	2,275	Never
Spokane Indians (Rangers)	39	37	.513	4	Matt Hagen	196,653	5,315	2008
Everett AquaSox (Mariners)	36	40	.474	7	Jose Moreno	110,161	2,899	2010
South Division	**W**	**L**	**PCT**	**GB**	**Manager(s)**	**Attendance**	**Average**	**Last Pennant**
Hillsboro Hops (D-backs)	41	35	.539	—	Shawn Roof	128,416	3,379	2015
Eugene Emeralds (Cubs)	39	37	.513	2	Jesus Feliciano	125,297	3,297	2016
Boise Hawks (Rockies)	37	39	.487	4	Scott Little	121,455	3,196	2004
Salem-Keizer Volcanoes (Giants)	29	47	.382	12	Jolbert Cabrera	81,011	2,132	2009

NORTHWEST LEAGUE STATISTICS

CLUB BATTING

	AVG	G	AB	R	H	2B	3B	HR	RBI	BB	SO	SB	OBP	SLG
Salem-Keizer	.267	76	2622	390	699	109	20	38	341	243	678	138	.336	.367
Boise	.265	76	2657	413	705	116	16	63	360	270	701	95	.338	.392
Everett	.258	76	2659	420	687	134	32	65	376	242	706	55	.325	.406
Vancouver	.250	76	2610	344	653	121	22	25	293	265	653	83	.331	.342
Eugene	.249	76	2604	335	647	131	25	34	286	252	683	102	.324	.357
Hillsboro	.247	76	2617	404	647	140	21	38	353	300	646	70	.333	.360
Spokane	.247	76	2588	347	638	142	16	64	305	197	655	37	.312	.388
Tri-City	.240	76	2575	310	617	117	26	23	255	260	731	86	.317	.332

CLUB PITCHING

	ERA	G	CG	SHO	SV	IP	H	R	ER	HR	BB	SO	AVG
Tri-City	3.05	76	0	0	12	679	589	293	230	28	201	764	.231
Eugene	3.24	76	0	0	20	695	603	324	250	28	270	761	.231
Hillsboro	3.71	76	0	0	13	679	591	326	280	46	220	677	.234
Vancouver	3.80	76	0	0	22	679	625	345	287	48	240	647	.244
Spokane	3.88	76	0	0	22	678	646	363	292	48	290	761	.247
Boise	4.48	76	0	0	15	683	761	429	340	42	234	557	.283
Everett	4.58	76	0	0	21	676	746	432	344	57	257	664	.276
Salem-Keizer	4.99	76	1	0	14	680	732	451	377	53	317	622	.275

CLUB FIELDING

	PCT	PO	A	E	DP
Hillsboro	.975	2425	822	82	149
Vancouver	.971	2531	732	99	153
Salem-Keizer	.970	2516	798	102	158
Tri-City	.966	2457	753	112	121
Eugene	.964	2485	761	120	143
Boise	.963	2461	885	129	191
Spokane	.961	2394	787	128	161
Everett	.955	2496	770	153	129

WINDIVIDUAL BATTING

Batter, Club	AVG	G	AB	R	H	2B	3B	HR	RBI	BB	SO	SB
Baldwin, Logan, Salem-Keizer	.342	50	184	38	63	11	2	3	25	13	42	17
Johnson, Bryce, Salem-Keizer	.329	57	222	41	73	5	2	0	16	17	52	25
Smith, Pavin, Hillsboro	.318	51	195	34	62	15	2	0	27	27	24	2
Adams, Johnny, Everett	.316	52	209	39	66	12	0	5	37	17	44	4
Varsho, Daulton, Hillsboro	.311	50	193	36	60	16	3	7	39	17	30	7
Linkous, Steven, Boise	.308	63	250	50	77	5	1	1	24	39	54	37
Adams, Riley, Vancouver	.305	52	203	26	62	16	1	3	35	18	50	1
McLaughlin, Matt, Boise	.305	51	200	36	61	13	0	1	20	31	43	7
Helder, Eugene, Everett	.304	70	286	44	87	14	5	2	43	19	44	7
Edgeworth, Danny, Boise	.303	61	234	32	71	14	0	3	47	21	56	6

INDIVIDUAL PITCHING

Pitcher, Club	W	L	ERA	G	GS	CG	SV	IP	H	R	ER	BB	SO
Sheckler, Ben, Tri-City	3	3	2.60	13	12	0	0	72	70	32	21	19	60
Thompson, Tyree, Spokane	5	1	3.15	13	13	0	0	68	63	25	24	22	44
Woods, Stetson, Salem-Keizer	3	2	3.36	14	12	0	0	64	59	29	24	21	48
Phillips, Tyler, Spokane	4	2	3.45	13	13	0	0	73	78	33	28	11	78
Torres, Andres, Everett	7	2	3.65	15	15	0	0	74	82	36	30	22	64
Assad, Javier, Eugene	5	6	4.23	13	13	0	0	66	69	34	31	21	72
Benitez, Julio, Salem-Keizer	1	7	4.30	14	14	1	0	69	85	44	33	12	35
Keele, Tyler, Hillsboro	5	5	4.32	15	14	0	0	75	63	44	36	27	72
Luna, Ryan, Boise	4	4	4.41	13	10	0	0	69	82	46	34	18	50
Nunez, Juan, Vancouver	2	8	5.05	14	12	0	0	62	57	45	35	30	53

ALL-STAR TEAM

C: Daulton Varsho, Hillsboro. **1B:** Ryan Kirby, Salem-Keizer. **2B:** Bret Boswell, Boise. **3B:** Danny Edgeworth, Boise. **SS:** Camden Duzenack, Hillsboro. **OF:** Steven Linkous, Boise; Bryce Johnson, Salem-Keizer; Miguel Aparicio, Spokane. **DH:** Riley Adams, Vancouver. **P:** Jesus Camargo, Eugene; Cole Ragans, Spokane; Ben Sheckler, Tri-City; Andres Torres, Evertt; Stetson Woods, Salem-Keizer.

Most Valuable Player: Ryan Kirby, Salem-Keizer

Pitcher of the Year: Andres Torres, Everett

Manager of the Year: Rich Miller, Vancouver

DEPARTMENT LEADERS

BATTING

OBP	Linkous, Steven, Boise	.409
SLG	Varsho, Daulton, Hillsboro	.534
OPS	Varsho, Daulton, Hillsboro	.902
R	Kirby, Ryan, Salem-Keizer	51
H	Helder, Eugene, Everett	87
TB	Boswell, Bret, Boise	118
XBH	Rosa, Joseph, Everett	26
	Varsho, Daulton, Hillsboro	26
2B	O'Banion, Austin, Spokane	17
3B	Carter, Tre, Tri-City	11
HR	Terry, Curtis, Spokane	12
RBI	Kirby, Ryan, Salem-Keizer	65
SAC	Burgos, Aldemar, Tri-City	8
BB	Linkous, Steven, Boise	39
HBP	O'Banion, Austin, Spokane	14
SO	Carter, Tre, Tri-City	95
SB	Linkous, Steven, Boise	37
CS	Linkous, Steven, Boise	16
AB/SO	Smith, Pavin, Hillsboro	8.13

FIELDING

C PCT	Washington, Jalen, Tri-City	.987
PO	Amaya, Miguel, Eugene	399
A	Amaya, Miguel, Eugene	54
DP	Amaya, Miguel, Eugene	6
E	Gonzalez, Hidekel, Boise	8
PB	Calabrese, Rob, Salem-Keizer	14
1B PCT	Clemens, Kacy, Vancouver	1.000
PO	Kirby, Ryan, Salem-Keizer	566
A	Pena, Onil, Everett	35
DP	Kirby, Ryan, Salem-Keizer	43
E	Terry, Curtis, Spokane	11
	Pena, Onil, Everett	11
2B PCT	Boswell, Bret, Boise	.963
PO	Boswell, Bret, Boise	104
A	Boswell, Bret, Boise	159
DP	Boswell, Bret, Boise	33
E	Rosa, Joseph, Everett	12
3B PCT	Helder, Eugene, Everett	.952
PO	Helder, Eugene, Everett	50
A	Edgeworth, Danny, Boise	88
DP	Helder, Eugene, Everett	11
E	Filiere, Austin, Eugene	14
SS PCT	Geraldo, Manuel, Salem-Keizer	.956
PO	Geraldo, Manuel, Salem-Keizer	97
A	Geraldo, Manuel, Salem-Keizer	183
DP	McLaughlin, Matt, Boise	33
E	McLaughlin, Matt, Boise	19
	Torres, Chris, Everett	19
OF PCT	Johnson, Bryce, Salem-Keizer	1.000
PO	Ziegler, Malique, Salem-Keizer	160
A	Andrade, Greifer, Everett	10
DP	Ziegler, Malique, Salem-Keizer	3
	Singleton, Chris, Eugene	3
E	Pruitt, Reggie, Vancouver	8

PITCHING

G	Bunal, Mike, Boise	25
	Westphal, Ethan, Boise	25
GS	Torres, Andres, Everett	15
GF	Ouellette, William, Vancouver	20
SV	Ouellette, William, Vancouver	13
W	Suarez, Michael, Everett	7
	Torres, Andres, Everett	7
L	Nunez, Juan, Vancouver	8
IP	Keele, Tyler, Hillsboro	75
H	Benitez, Julio, Salem-Keizer	85
R	Santiago, Jose, Everett	51
ER	Santiago, Jose, Everett	42
HB	Nunez, Juan, Vancouver	11
BB	Santiago, Jose, Everett	36
SO	Ragans, Cole, Spokane	87
SO/9	Assad, Javier, Eugene	9.82
SO/9(RP)	Aquino, Luis, Eugene	13.93
BB/9	Phillips, Tyler, Hickory, Spokane	1.36
WP	Nunez, Juan, Vancouver	12
BK	Torres, Andres, Everett	5
	Speas, Alex, Spokane	5
HR	Aker, Mitchell, Hillsboro	8
AVG	Keele, Tyler, Hillsboro	.229

APPALACHIAN LEAGUE ROOKIE

BY JUSTIN PERLINE

The Elizabethton Twins took home their league-leading 11th championship title this summer, besting Greeneville and Pulaski with a pair dominant performances. Left fielder Mark Contreras, the Twins' ninth-round pick, powered the offense in the final series. He compiled two hits, including a home run, in each game of the best-of-three series.

Elizabethton was awash with stars, earning three of the top ten spots in this year's Top 20 rankings. Had he qualified, righthander Brusdar Graterol would have likely joined Wander Javier, Brent Rooker and Akil Baddoo atop the list. And further down, players like Andrew Bechtold and second-baseman Jose Miranda have a chance to surface in the majors as competitive infielders.

Talented major leaguers are almost always flowing out of Appalachia and the league has the good fortune of counting Craig Kimbrel (Braves, '08), Jose Altuve (Astros, '08/'09), and Carlos Correa (Astros, '12) among its many alumni. Rookies who finally made their way to the show and carved out hefty roles this year include German Marquez (Rays, '13), Paul DeJong (Cardinals, '15), and Ozzie Albies (Braves, '14).

This summer's class of prospects featured many highly-regarded international amateurs, but lacked the stateside amateur draft impact from years prior. The highest selection to play in the Appy League was supplemental first-rounder Rooker, who sustained his college dominance for 22 games in Elizabethton before being promoted to the Florida State League. The only second rounders to see time in the league were Drew Waters (Braves) and, briefly, Mark Vientos (Mets).

Kevin Maitan ranked as the No. 1 international prospect coming out of Venezuela in 2016, and was one of the youngest players to compete in the league after skipping the DSL as a 17-year-old. Both Seuly Matias and Wander Javier ranked highly a year prior, earning Top 10 rankings as amateurs and progressing their toolsets into more actionable baseball skills. Many of this year's talent didn't come from pedigreed international competition, though. Players like William Contreras, Mc Gregory Contreras, and Joel Peguero signed for just $10,000 for a chance to realize their baseball dreams.

The Appalachian League MVP, Ryan Noda, displayed considerable ability to impact the game. He compiled 25 more walks than the next closest batter and maintained an outrageous .364 batting average, never dipping below .400 until mid-August. Pitcher of the year Randy Pondler (Blue Jays) hailed from the same Bluefield team that won 46 games en route to the Eastern Division lead. The Nicaraguan lefthander held opponents to a .220 average, allowing just a 2.51 ERA over 57.1 innings.

Joining the current class of teams in 2018 will be a new Reds affiliate that is set to replace the Astros following their departure from Greeneville, Tenn.

TOP 20 PROSPECTS

1. Kevin Maitan, SS, Danville (Braves)
2. Wander Javier, SS, Elizabethon (Twins)
3. Seuly Matias, OF, Burlington (Royals)
4. Ronaldo Hernandez, C, Princeton (Rays)
5. Brent Rooker, OF/1B, Elizabethton (Twins)
6. Luis Medina, RHP, Pulaski (Yankees)
7. Akil Baddoo, OF, Elizabethton (Twins)
8. Kyle Muller, LHP, Danville (Braves)
9. Drew Waters, OF, Danville (Braves)
10. William Contreras, C, Danville (Braves)
11. Gilberto Celestino, OF, Greeneville (Astros)
12. Ryan Noda, 1B/OF, Bluefield (Blue Jays)
13. Braeden Ogie, LHP, Bristol (Pirates)
14. Alvaro Sejias, RHP, Johnston City (Cardinals)
15. Deivi Garcia, RHP Pulaski (Yankees)
16. Juan Uriarte, C, Kingsport (Mets)
17. Andrew Bechtold, 3B, Elizabethton (Twins)
18. Michael Gigliotti, OF, Burlington (Royals)
19. Mc Gregory Contreras, OF, Bluefield (Blue Jays)
20. Joel Peguero, RHP, Princeton (Rays)

OVERALL STANDINGS

Eastern Division	W	L	PCT	GB	Manager(s)	Attendance	Average	Last Pennant
Bluefield Blue Jays (Blue Jays)	46	22	.676	—	Dennis Holmberg	21,595	697	2001
Pulaski Yankees (Yankees)	41	26	.612	4½	Luis Dorante	77,880	2,360	2013
Danville Braves (Braves)	36	32	.529	10	Nestor Perez	32,634	1,045	2009
Princeton Rays (Rays)	31	36	.463	14½	Danny Sheaffer	17,690	536	1994
Burlington Royals (Royals)	29	39	.426	17	Omar Ramirez	34,483	1,045	1993
Western Division	**W**	**L**	**PCT**	**GB**	**Manager(s)**	**Attendance**	**Average**	**Last Pennant**
Elizabethton Twins (Twins)	41	27	.603	—	Ray Smith	18,746	586	2017
Greeneville Astros (Astros)	33	34	.493	7½	Danny Ortega	35,305	1,139	2015
Johnson City Cardinals (Cardinals)	33	34	.493	7½	Roberto Espinoza	29,742	901	2016
Kingsport Mets (Mets)	29	37	.439	11	Luis Rivera	29,742	901	1995
Bristol Pirates (Pirates)	17	49	.258	23	Miguel Perez	20,813	671	2002

Semifinals: Pulaski defeated Bluefield 2-1 and Elizabethton defeated Greeneville 2-1 in best-of-three series. **Finals:** Elizabethton defeated Pulaski 2-0 in a best-of-three series.

APPALACHIAN LEAGUE STATISTICS

CLUB BATTING

	AVG	G	AB	R	H	2B	3B	HR	RBI	BB	SO	SB	OBP	SLG
Elizabethton	.288	68	2344	432	674	127	15	69	387	264	542	39	.365	.443
Bluefield	.283	68	2325	410	658	126	24	44	353	222	543	44	.355	.415
Kingsport	.275	66	2279	365	626	122	17	47	324	223	515	35	.343	.405
Princeton	.267	67	2335	389	623	134	18	48	329	225	542	74	.346	.401
Burlington	.262	68	2303	327	604	108	25	42	288	203	540	55	.328	.386
Danville	.260	68	2285	328	595	124	16	53	286	225	631	51	.330	.398
Bristol	.249	66	2214	303	552	122	17	31	278	268	644	68	.340	.362
Johnson City	.249	67	2245	337	558	114	11	55	289	252	533	42	.334	.383
Greeneville	.246	67	2177	322	536	83	8	43	273	221	524	51	.326	.351
Pulaski	.242	67	2160	323	522	100	6	57	281	231	596	61	.324	.373

CLUB PITCHING

	ERA	G	CG	SHO	SV	IP	H	R	ER	HR	BB	SO	AVG
Danville Braves	3.71	68	0	0	18	593	557	309	244	32	222	570	.243
Bluefield Blue Jays	3.81	68	0	0	26	602	584	322	255	44	197	572	.252
Elizabethton Twins	3.86	68	0	0	12	595	529	303	255	47	240	598	.236
Pulaski Yankees	4.20	67	0	0	24	577	543	328	269	55	236	654	.250
Greeneville Astros	4.37	67	0	0	13	573	583	335	278	41	239	594	.261
Burlington Royals	4.59	68	1	0	18	588	624	375	300	50	209	523	.269
Johnson City Cardinals	4.60	67	0	0	20	587	606	369	300	49	271	611	.267
Kingsport Mets	4.92	66	0	0	12	574	606	373	314	47	263	543	.270
Bristol Pirates	5.24	66	0	0	6	572	647	421	333	54	232	474	.282
Princeton Rays	5.53	67	0	0	9	581	669	401	357	70	225	471	.292

CLUB FIELDING

	PCT	PO	A	E	DP
Pulaski	.971	2040	632	81	176
Elizabethton	.970	2120	683	88	166
Princeton	.969	2103	772	93	194
Bluefield	.968	2186	715	95	166
Burlington	.964	2179	632	104	145
Kingsport	.964	2123	659	103	152
Johnson City	.963	2128	656	106	146
Greeneville	.960	2101	609	113	127
Danville	.956	2154	638	128	116
Bristol	.950	2114	703	149	171

INDIVIDUAL BATTING

Batter, Club	AVG	G	AB	R	H	2B	3B	HR	RBI	BB	SO	SB
Noda, Ryan, Bluefield	.365	66	214	62	78	18	3	7	39	59	60	7
Terrazas, Rigoberto, Kingsport	.348	54	210	45	73	16	2	3	24	25	31	1
Rodriguez, Yorman, Bluefield	.346	57	240	36	83	11	0	3	36	7	25	2
Lagrange, Wagner, Kingsport	.335	45	185	27	62	10	1	4	40	15	18	2
Hernandez, Ronaldo, Princeton	.332	54	223	42	74	22	1	5	40	16	39	2
Gigliotti, Michael, Burlington	.329	42	155	30	51	8	3	3	30	32	21	15
Nunez, Oliver, Burlington	.321	59	221	44	71	10	3	2	20	22	36	19
Pinder, Chase, Johnson City	.320	50	169	35	54	9	1	3	21	31	39	5
Lantigua, Edison, Bristol	.307	48	176	28	54	14	2	4	18	30	62	8
Uriarte, Juan, Kingsport	.305	52	200	36	61	13	1	5	36	15	31	0

INDIVIDUAL PTICHING

Pitcher, Club	W	L	ERA	G	GS	CG	SV	IP	H	R	ER	BB	SO
Pondler, Randy, Bluefield	4	1	2.51	12	11	0	0	57	46	20	16	11	42
Piechota, Evan, Bristol	1	2	2.95	16	7	0	1	58	58	22	19	6	51
Javier, Odalvi, Danville	4	2	3.14	13	13	0	0	63	61	22	22	22	50
Colina, Edwar, Elizabethton	3	5	3.34	12	11	0	0	59	48	26	22	29	56
Paulino, Hansel, Greeneville	4	3	3.48	13	10	0	0	54	53	27	21	15	54
Hellinger, Jaret, Danville	4	2	3.64	13	7	0	1	54	44	23	22	20	41
Hernandez, Carlos, Kingsport	3	3	4.62	12	11	0	0	64	64	45	33	28	59
Robles, Domingo, Bristol	4	8	4.83	14	14	0	0	69	75	49	37	16	51
Seijas, Alvaro, Johnson City	4	3	4.97	12	12	0	0	63	79	42	35	20	63
Webb, Nathan, Burlington	3	5	5.28	12	12	1	0	58	61	42	34	22	44

ALL-STAR TEAM

C: William Contreras, Danville. **1B:** Ryan Noda, Bluefield. **2B:** Irving Lopez, Johnson City. **3B:** Rigoberto Terrazas, Kingsport. **SS:** Jose Miranda, Elizabethton. **OF:** Michael Gigliotti, Burlington; Chase Pinder, Johnson City; Wagner Lagrange, Kingsport. **DH:** Luis Bandes, Johnson City. **UT:** Edison Lantigua, Bristol. **RHP:** Edwar Colina, Elizabethton. **LHP:** Randy Pondler, Bluefield. **RP:** Ty Tice, Bluefield.

Most Valuable Player: Ryan Noda, Bluefield
Pitcher of the Year: Randy Pondler, Bluefield
Manager of the Year: Luis Dorante, Pulaski

DEPARTMENT LEADERS

BATTING

OBP	Noda, Ryan, Bluefield	.507
SLG	Noda, Ryan, Bluefield	.575
OPS	Noda, Ryan, Bluefield	1.082
R	Noda, Ryan, Bluefield	62
H	Rodriguez, Yorman, Bluefield	83
TB	Noda, Ryan, Bluefield	123
XBH	Smith, Kevin, Bluefield	34
2B	Smith, Kevin, Bluefield	25
3B	Young, Chavez, Bluefield	7
HR	Miranda, Jose, Elizabethton	11
	Dirocie, Anthony, Kingsport	11
RBI	Bandes, Luis, Johnson City	49
	Hair, Trey, Princeton	49
SAC	Navarro, Jesus, Bluefield	10
BB	Noda, Ryan, Bluefield	59
HBP	Bohanek, Cody, Greeneville	15
SO	Dirocie, Anthony, Kingsport	93
SB	Amador, Wilson, Greeneville	20
CS	Five tied with	6
AB/SO	Jimenez, Melvin, Bristol	10.47

FIELDING

C PCT	Uriarte, Juan, Kingsport	.995
PO	Torres, Saul, Pulaski	375
A	Hernandez, Ronaldo, Princeton	70
DP	Rodriguez, Julio, Johnson City	4
	Torres, Saul, Pulaski	4
E	Torres, Saul, Pulaski	7
PB	Torres, Saul, Pulaski	18
1B PCT	Davis, Devin, Princeton	.991
PO	Davis, Devin, Princeton	411
A	Wagaman, Eric, Pulaski	36
DP	Davis, Devin, Princeton	40
E	Wagaman, Eric, Pulaski	10
2B PCT	Manzanarez, Angel, Kingsport	.982
PO	Hair, Trey, Princeton	125
A	Hair, Trey, Princeton	138
DP	Hair, Trey, Princeton	46
E	Marquez, Jose, Burlington	11
	Valaika, Nick, Bristol	11
3B PCT	Terrazas, Rigoberto, Kingsport	.935
PO	Westmoreland, Brody, Greeneville	51
A	Terrazas, Rigoberto, Kingsport	102
DP	Terrazas, Rigoberto, Kingsport	9
E	Whalen, Brady, Johnson City	16
SS PCT	Rutherford, Zach, Princeton	.975
PO	Smith, Kevin, Bluefield	89
A	Smith, Kevin, Bluefield	200
DP	Smith, Kevin, Bluefield	40
E	Moreno, Hansel, Kingsport	20
OF PCT	Pinder, Chase, Johnson City	1.000
PO	Dirocie, Anthony, Kingsport	148
A	Lagrange, Wagner, Kingsport	8
	Celestino, Gilberto, Greeneville	8
DP	Matias, Seuly, Burlington	3
	Peurifoy, Ryan, Bristol	3
E	Amador, Wilson, Greeneville	10

PITCHING

G	Tice, Ty, Bluefield	23
	Patterson, Jacob, Johnson City	23
GS	Robles, Domingo, Bristol	14
GF	Tice, Ty, Bluefield	22
SV	Tice, Ty, Bluefield	12
W	Goodbrand, Kyle, Princeton	7
L	Robles, Domingo, Bristol	8
IP	Robles, Domingo, Bristol	69
H	Ramirez, Edwar, Johnson City	83
R	Ramirez, Edwar, Johnson City	54
ER	Ramirez, Edwar, Johnson City	46
	Zabaleta, Ezequiel, Kingsport	46
	Casadilla, Franyel, Johnson City	46
HB	Javier, Odalvi, Danville	11
BB	Schlesener, Jacob, Johnson City	38
SO	Seijas, Alvaro, Johnson City	63
SO/9	Seijas, Alvaro, Johnson City	8.95
SO/9(RP)	Walsh, Jake, Johnson City	12.39
BB/9	Piechota, Evan, Bristol	0.93
WP	Salazar, Paul, Johnson City	16
BK	Five tied with	3
HR	Ramirez, Edwar, Johnson City	10
	Zabaleta, Ezequiel, Kingsport	10
	Casadilla, Franyel, Johnson City	10
AVG	Colina, Edwar, Elizabethton	.219

MINOR LEAGUES

PIONEER LEAGUE ROOKIE

BY BILL MITCHELL

It was all about the offense in the eight-team Rookie-level Pioneer League this year, with 16 of the top 20 prospects being position players. The league with the most favorable hitting conditions in affiliated ball was even crazier this year and finished with a line of .293/.370/.457. Ogden hit .319 and slugged .513 as a team.

The Raptors, a Dodgers affiliate, slugged their way to a historic league championship, winning the first title in franchise history. The Ogden Dodgers won four straight PL titles from 1966-69, but that team moved away in 1974.

Ogden was guided to its historic title by manager Mark Kertenian, who was in his first season as a minor league manager after starting his career in the college coaching ranks. He led a team that included an exciting group of outfielders that briefly included Jeren Kendall, as well as Brayan Morales, who led the league with 29 stolen bases, Starling Heredia and Romer Cuardado.

After finishing the first half in second place in the South Division, Ogden won the second half title and then swept Orem in the semifinals. Ogden went on to beat Great Falls, two games to one, to win the league championship. The Raptors had most recently appeared in the PL finals in 2012, the last of three straight defeats in the championship series.

Great Falls first baseman Anthony Villa was named the circuit's MVP. In his second season with Great Falls, the 23-year-old hit .314/.453/.619 and led the PL in OPS (1.073). Orem righthander Elvin Rodriguez was named pitcher of the year. He went 5-1, 2.50 and struck out 49 batters in 54 innings. He was six innings shy of qualifying for the ERA title, but his 2.50 mark was the best of any pitcher to throw at least 35 innings. His strong year caught the eye of the Tigers, who acquired him in September as a player to be named later to complete the trade that sent Justin Upton to the Angels in August.

Despite the gaudy hitting totals in the PL, the overall level of talent was down in the league this year. The only 2017 first-round picks to appear on the circuit were righthander Hunter Greene (Billings), Kendall and outfielder Jo Adell (Orem). Of the three, Adell was the only player trio to log enough time in the league to qualify for the top prospect rankings.

After beginning his pro career in the Rookie-level Arizona League, Adell arrived in Orem in mid-August. He was a part of a prospect-laden team, with his Owlz teammates Brandon Marsh, Leonardo Rivas and Chris Rodriguez all earning spots on the top prospects list, as well.

TOP 20 PROSPECTS

1. Jo Adell, OF, Orem (Angels)
2. Chris Rodriguez, RHP, Orem (Angels)
3. Tristen Lutz, OF, Helena (Brewers)
4. Brandon Marsh, OF, Orem (Angels)
5. Starling Heredia, OF, Ogden (Dodgers)
6. Ryan Vilade, SS, Grand Junction (Rockies)
7. Pedro Gonzalez, OF, Grand Junction (Rockies)
8. K.J. Harrison, C, Helena (Brewers)
9. Leonardo Rivas, SS, Orem (Angels)
10. Jeter Downs, SS, Billings (Reds)
11. Eduardo Diaz, OF, Missoula (D-backs)
12. Andy Yerzy, C, Missoula (D-backs)
13. Stuart Fairchild, OF, Billings (Reds)
14. Janser Lara, RHP, Idaho Falls (Royals)
15. Packy Naughton, LHP, Billings (Reds)
16. Tommy Doyle, RHP, Grand Junction (Rockies)
17. Romer Cuadrado, OF, Ogden (Dodgers)
18. Payton Henry, C, Helena (Brewers)
19. Joey Rose, 3B, Missoula (D-backs)
20. Antonio Pinero, SS, Helena (Brewers)

STANDINGS: SPLIT SEASON

FIRST HALF

NORTH	W	L	PCT	GB
Missoula	19	19	.500	—
Billings	18	19	.486	½
Great Falls	15	23	.395	4
Helena	15	23	.395	4
SOUTH	**W**	**L**	**PCT**	**GB**
Orem	26	11	.703	—
Ogden	23	15	.605	3½
Grand Junct.	18	20	.474	8½
Idaho Falls	17	21	.447	9½

SECOND HALF

NORTH	W	L	PCT	GB
Great Falls	19	19	.500	—
Missoula	19	19	.500	—
Billings	18	20	.474	1
Helena	13	25	.342	6
SOUTH	**W**	**L**	**PCT**	**GB**
Ogden	24	14	.632	—
Orem	23	15	.605	1
Grand Junct.	20	18	.526	4
Idaho Falls	16	22	.421	8

Playoffs—Semifinals: Ogden defeated Orem 2-0 and Great Falls defeated Missoula 2-0 in best-of-three series. **Finals:** Ogden defeated Great Falls 2-1 in best-of-three series.

OVERALL STANDINGS

North Division	W	L	PCT	GB	Manager(s)	Attendance	Average	Last Pennant
Missoula Osprey (D-backs)	38	38	.500	—	Mlke Benjamin	71,936	1,893	2015
Billings Mustangs (Reds)	36	39	.480	1½	Ray Martinez	110,311	2,903	2014
Great Falls Voyagers (White Sox)	34	42	.447	4	Tim Esmay	47,260	1,244	2013
Helena Brewers (Brewers)	28	48	.368	10	Nestor Corredor	33,843	891	2010
South Division	**W**	**L**	**PCT**	**GB**	**Manager(s)**	**Attendance**	**Average**	**Last Pennant**
Orem Owlz (Angels)	49	26	.653		Tom Nieto	55,981	1,513	2016
Ogden Raptors (Dodgers)	47	29	.618	2½	Mark Kertenian	128,348	3,378	2017
Grand Junction Rockies (Rockies)	38	38	.500	11½	Frank Gonzales	79,547	2,150	Never
Idaho Falls Chukars (Royals)	33	43	.434	16½	Justin Gemoll	90,816	2,390	2013

PIONEER LEAGUE STATISTICS

CLUB BATTING

	AVG	G	AB	R	H	2B	3B	HR	RBI	BB	SO	SB	OBP	SLG
Ogden	.319	76	2747	587	875	168	27	104	531	320	649	115	.394	.513
Orem	.316	76	2783	607	879	165	32	67	540	372	535	72	.403	.470
Idaho Falls	.300	76	2740	537	823	168	35	50	486	317	538	129	.379	.442
Grand Junction	.298	76	2682	509	799	150	35	115	447	253	670	94	.366	.509
Missoula	.294	76	2715	462	798	171	34	77	414	247	584	47	.361	.467
Great Falls	.276	76	2684	440	740	150	20	72	400	309	638	36	.359	.427
Billings	.272	76	2637	441	717	113	33	66	381	252	613	92	.342	.415
Helena	.267	76	2671	414	714	129	11	74	370	285	701	49	.347	.407

CLUB PITCHING

	ERA	G	CG	SHO	SV	IP	H	R	ER	HR	BB	SO	AVG
Great Falls	4.73	76	0	0	11	677	770	457	356	63	261	546	.286
Billings	4.80	76	0	0	15	671	703	424	358	50	319	656	.267
Ogden	5.46	76	0	0	23	670	772	489	407	62	327	675	.288
Orem	5.54	76	0	0	15	677	731	453	417	87	326	689	.276
Missoula	5.77	76	0	0	21	664	803	517	426	102	236	598	.296
Helena	5.88	76	0	0	14	673	784	514	440	85	315	604	.291
Grand Junction	5.90	76	0	0	15	668	845	528	438	84	256	567	.306
Idaho Falls	6.91	76	0	0	16	671	937	615	515	92	315	593	.329

CLUB FIELDING

	PCT	PO	A	E	DP
Orem	.971	2415	818	96	193
Billings	.965	2398	781	114	209
Helena	.964	2448	789	121	192
Great Falls	.963	2483	878	130	223
Ogden	.962	2392	831	127	222
Grand Junctino	.958	2458	834	144	202
Idaho Falls	.953	2469	807	163	233
Missoula	.953	2433	779	160	146

INDIVIDUAL BATTING

Batter, Club	AVG	G	AB	R	H	2B	3B	HR	RBI	BB	SO	SB
Miller, Darrell, Idaho Falls	.376	48	186	45	70	18	0	5	43	25	25	0
Mendoza, Shael, Grand Junction	.364	55	231	54	84	13	4	5	35	20	38	25
Guzman, Manuel, Orem	.360	60	228	46	82	13	5	5	40	41	28	7
Rinn, Robby, Idaho Falls	.355	69	282	58	100	22	2	6	59	36	35	3
Hunter, Torii, Orem	.352	52	213	48	75	10	3	1	28	23	44	13
Yurchak, Justin, Great Falls	.345	60	223	46	77	13	1	8	27	43	33	1
Sugilio, Andy, Billings	.345	62	235	45	81	13	4	3	40	17	33	20
Cuadrado, Romer, Ogden	.335	64	260	54	87	12	5	9	60	30	74	11
Maciel, Gabriel, Missoula	.323	52	217	40	70	14	1	3	25	24	34	9
Dedelow, Craig, Great Falls	.321	60	249	40	80	21	3	12	54	12	39	5

INDIVIDUAL PITCHING

Pitcher, Club	W	L	ERA	G	GS	CG	SV	IP	H	R	ER	BB	SO
Von Ruden, Kyle, Great Falls	4	4	4.27	15	15	0	0	86	95	57	41	17	63
Mondile, Tyler, Billings	4	4	4.35	15	12	0	0	68	82	40	33	23	48
Agar, Brandon, Great Falls	7	2	5.01	15	15	0	0	83	104	57	46	20	42
Comito, Chris, Great Falls	3	7	5.09	15	15	0	0	76	100	59	43	24	41
Alecis, Luis, Billings	6	6	5.11	16	11	0	0	62	54	38	35	39	61
Muller, Brady, Missoula	7	7	5.22	15	15	0	0	79	96	61	46	22	73
De Jesus, Jhon, Billings	2	4	5.79	15	15	0	0	61	62	42	39	30	58
Valdespina, Justin, Grand Junction	3	6	5.97	15	15	0	0	75	110	59	50	25	40
McKay, David, Idaho Falls	6	5	6.49	14	14	0	0	79	104	62	57	18	68
Panayotovich, Adam, Great Falls	1	5	6.50	16	9	0	0	64	95	53	46	22	43

ALL-STAR TEAM

C: Hendrik Clementina, Ogden/Bilings; Luiz Paz, Ogden. **1B:** Robby Rinn, Idaho Falls. **2B:** Shael Mendoza, Grand Junction. **3B:** Joey Rose, Missoula. **SS:** Alan Trejo, Grand Junction. **OF:** Craig Dedelow, Great Falls; Casey Golden, Grand Junction; Ryan Vega, Orem. **DH:** Darrell Miller, Idaho Falls; Anthony VIlla, Great Falls. **P:** Abraham Almonte, Missoula; Nelson Hernandez, Helena; Isaac Mattson, Orem; Elvin Rodriguez, Orem; Kyle Von Ruden, Great Falls. **Manager:** Tom Nieto, Orem.

Most Valuable Player: Anthony Villa, Great Falls

Pitcher of the Year: Elvin Rodriguez, Orem

DEPARTMENT LEADERS

BATTING

OBP	Guzman, Manuel, Orem	.459
	Miller, Darrell, Idaho Falls	.459
SLG	Marcelino, Ramon, Grand Junction	.657
OPS	Villa, Anthony, Great Falls	1.073
R	Fukofuka, Amalani, Idaho Falls	66
H	Rinn, Robby, Idaho Falls	100
TB	Marcelino, Ramon, Grand Junction	159
XBH	Marcelino, Ramon, Grand Junction	38
2B	Rinn, Robby, Idaho Falls	22
3B	De La Trinidad, Ernie, Missoula	8
HR	Golden, Casey, Grand Junction	20
RBI	Paz, Luis, Ogden	63
SAC	Pinero, Antonio, Helena	9
	Brown, Nolan, Great Falls	9
BB	Villa, Anthony, Great Falls	52
HBP	Golden, Casey, Grand Junction	12
SO	McClanahan, Chad, Helena	78
SB	Morales, Brayan, Ogden	29
CS	Mendoza, Shael, Grand Junction	9
AB/SO	Pina, Keinner, Orem	9.74

FIELDING

C PCT	Pina, Keinner, Orem	.998
PO	Pina, Keinner, Orem	366
A	Pina, Keinner, Orem	66
DP	Nolan, Nate, Great Falls	6
E	Fermin, Freddy, Idaho Falls	12
PB	Yerzy, Andy, Missoula	13
1B PCT	Marshall, Montrell, Billings	.993
PO	Rinn, Robby, Idaho Falls	527
A	Spanberger, Chad, Grand Junction	37
DP	Rinn, Robby, Idaho Falls	66
E	Rinn, Robby, Idaho Falls	12
2B PCT	Mendoza, Shael, Grand Junction	.919
PO	Mendoza, Shael, Grand Junction	110
A	Lopez, Alejo, Billings	145
DP	Blackman, Tate, Great Falls	38
E	Mendoza, Shael, Grand Junction	21
3B PCT	Straub, Tyler, Idaho Falls	.906
PO	Santana, Leandro, Billings	38
A	Santana, Leandro, Billings	112
DP	Santana, Leandro, Billings	16
E	Santana, Leandro, Billings	19
SS PCT	Pinero, Antonio, Helena	.938
PO	Pinero, Antonio, Helena	95
A	Dutto, Max, Great Falls	190
DP	Dutto, Max, Great Falls	40
E	Dutto, Max, Great Falls	18
	Downs, Jeter, Billings	18
3B PCT	Gordon, Miles, Billings	.990
PO	Fukofuka, Amalani, Idaho Falls	149
A	Cuadrado, Romer, Ogden	8
	Golden, Casey, Grand Junction	8
DP	Three tied with	3
E	Three tied with	8

PITCHING

G	Valdez, Jefry, Grand Junction	27
GS	Nine tied with	15
GF	Valdez, Jefry, Grand Junction	25
SV	Almonte, Abraham, Missoula	11
W	Agar, Brandon, Great Falls	7
	Muller, Brady, Missoula	7
L	Pinto, Julio, Idaho Falls	8
IP	Von Ruden, Kyle, Great Falls	86
H	Valdespina, Justin, Grand Junction	110
R	Pinto, Julio, Idaho Falls	80
ER	Pinto, Julio, Idaho Falls	70
HB	Pinto, Julio, Idaho Falls	12
BB	Pinto, Julio, Idaho Falls	47
SO	Muller, Brady, Missoula	73
SO/9	Alecis, Luis, Billings	8.90
SO/9(RP)	Bennett, Connor, Billings	14.19
BB/9	Von Ruden, Kyle, Great Falls	1.77
WP	Cespedes, Francis, Ogden	19
BK	Seven tied with	2
HR	Lin, Kai-Wei, Missoula	15
AVG	Alecis, Luis, Billings	.241

ARIZONA LEAGUE ROOKIE

BY BILL MITCHELL

The AZL Cubs overcame a slow start to the-season in order to capture their first Arizona League championship since 2002. After starting the season slowly with a 9-19 first-half record, the Cubs shifted into high gear and finished one game ahead of the Angels for the second-half lead in the East. The Cubs rolled through the playoffs, dispatching the Brewers and Dodgers in single-game qualifying rounds before taking two of three from the Giants in the championship series.

Earning league MVP honors was Padres second baseman Esteury Ruiz, who started the season with the Royals before being included in a July trade made to strengthen Kansas City's big league pitching staff. Ruiz led all AZL hitters with a .350 batting average, while Cuban southpaw Ramon Perez (Padres) recorded a league-best 2.66 ERA.

In terms of prospects, this year's crop was perhaps the deepest in the Arizona League's 30-year history. The quality and quanity was aided in part by a new high in the number of teams in the league, with the Padres adding a second AZL squad to bring the total to 15.

In all, nine first round picks from the 2017 MLB Draft made their pro debuts in the Arizona League, with all but one (Jake Burger, White Sox) getting enough playing time to qualify for the Top 20 prospect list. The other eight first rounders—MacKenzie Gore (Padres), Austin Beck (Athletics), Keston Hiura (Brewers), Jo Adell (Angels), Nick Pratto (Royals), Heliot Ramos (Giants), Bubba Thompson (Rangers) and Chris Seise (Rangers)—all rank among the league's best prospects. In addition, Kyle Lewis, the Mariners 2016 first round pick, spent the early part of the season in the Arizona League on a rehab assignment while he continued his recovery from knee surgery.

TOP 20 PROSPECTS

1. MacKenzie Gore, LHP, Padres
2. Jo Adell, OF, Angels
3. Heliot Ramos, OF, Giants
4. Keston Hiura, DH, Brewers
5. Hans Crouse, RHP, Rangers
6. Bubba Thompson, OF, Rangers
7. Gabriel Arias, SS, Padres
8. Austin Beck, OF, Athletics
9. Nick Pratto, 1B, Royals
10. Esteury Ruiz, 2B, Padres
11. Tristen Lutz, OF, Brewers
12. Chris Sise, SS, Rangers
13. M.J. Melendez, C, Royals
14. Lazaro Armenteros, OF, Athletics
15. Jacob Gonzalez, 3B, Giants
16. Luis Campusano, C, Padres
17. Jordy Barley, SS, Padres
18. Jose Soriano, RHP, Angels
19. Nick Allen, SS, Athletics
20. Nelson Velazquez, OF, Cubs

STANDINGS: SPLIT SEASON

FIRST HALF

EAST	W	L	PCT	GB
Giants	20	8	.714	—
Angels	15	13	.536	5
Athletics	13	15	.464	7
D-backs	12	16	.429	8
Cubs	9	19	.321	11
CENTRAL	**W**	**L**	**PCT**	**GB**
Brewers	19	9	.679	—
Dodgers	18	10	.643	1
Reds	11	16	.407	7½
White Sox	11	17	.393	8
Indians	8	20	.286	11
WEST	**W**	**L**	**PCT**	**GB**
Mariners	17	11	.607	—
Padres	15	13	.536	2
Padres 2	15	13	.536	2
Rangers	13	14	.481	3½
Royals	13	15	.464	4

SECOND HALF

EAST	W	L	PCT	GB
Cubs	16	12	.571	—
Angels	15	13	.536	1
Giants	14	14	.500	2
Athletics	13	15	.464	3
D-backs	12	16	.429	4
CENTRAL	**W**	**L**	**PCT**	**GB**
Dodgers	19	9	.679	—
White Sox	19	9	.679	—
Brewers	14	14	.500	5
Reds	11	17	.393	8
Indians	10	18	.250	12
WEST	**W**	**L**	**PCT**	**GB**
Rangers	17	11	.607	—
Padres 2	15	12	.556	1½
Mariners	14	13	.519	2½
Royals	13	15	.464	4
Padres	10	18	.357	7

Playoffs—Quarterfinals: Cubs defeated Brewers, and Rangers defeated Mariners, in one-game playoffs. **Semifinals:** Cubs defeated Dodgers, and Giants defeated Rangers, in one-game playoffs. **Finals:** Cubs defeated Giants 2-1 in a best-of-three series.

OVERALL STANDINGS

East Division	W	L	PCT	GB	Manager(s)	Last Pennant
Giants	34	22	.607	—	Hector Borg	2013
Angels	30	26	.536	4	Dave Stapleton	Never
Athletics	26	30	.464	8	Webster Garrison	2001
Cubs	25	31	.446	9	Carmelo Martinez	2017
Diamondbacks	24	32	.429	10	Javier Colina	Never
Central Division	**W**	**L**	**PCT**	**GB**	**Manager(s)**	**Last Pennant**
Dodgers	37	19	.661	—	John Shoemaker	2011
Brewers	33	23	.589	4	Rafael Neda	2010
White Sox	30	26	.536	7	Ryan Newman	2015
Reds	23	33	.400	14½	Jose Nieves	Never
Indians	15	41	.268	22	Anthony Medrano	2014
West Division	**W**	**L**	**PCT**	**GB**	**Manager(s)**	**Last Pennant**
Mariners	31	24	.564	—	Zac Livingston	2016
Padres 2	30	25	.545	1	Michael Collins	Never
Rangers	30	25	.545	1	Matt Siegel	2012
Royals	26	30	.464	5½	Darryl Kennedy	Never
Padres	25	31	.446	6½	Shaun Cole	2006

ARIZONA LEAGUE STATISTICS

CLUB BATTING

	AVG	G	AB	R	H	2B	3B	HR	RBI	BB	SO	SB	OBP	SLG
Giants	.282	56	1917	314	540	110	29	28	257	172	442	66	.353	.413
White Sox	.275	56	1858	304	511	89	30	26	259	234	418	39	.368	.397
Rangers	.269	55	1899	334	511	98	26	30	280	246	528	75	.360	.396
Padres 2	.264	56	1937	347	512	108	32	20	296	260	529	41	.359	.384
Brewers	.264	56	1939	343	511	108	21	29	275	237	502	90	.356	.386
Mariners	.262	56	1918	349	502	104	38	37	301	272	567	92	.362	.414
Dodgers	.261	56	1881	337	491	115	25	42	301	238	486	54	.354	.416
Reds	.257	55	1888	275	486	87	21	16	227	156	492	64	.326	.351
Royals	.253	56	1876	297	475	94	36	26	246	188	527	98	.330	.383
Padres	.249	56	1889	298	470	99	21	29	247	222	558	63	.334	.370
Athletics	.244	56	1890	280	461	86	32	18	221	215	487	62	.329	.352
Angels	.244	56	1877	266	457	76	35	24	211	194	508	65	.321	.360
D-backs	.242	56	1872	252	453	79	37	18	208	183	520	55	.318	.353
Cubs	.235	56	1866	246	439	112	15	30	199	167	485	51	.303	.360
Indians	.233	56	1902	266	443	96	22	35	220	169	524	39	.305	.362

CLUB PITCHING

	ERA	G	CG	SHO	SV	IP	H	R	ER	HR	BB	SO	AVG
Dodgers	3.39	56	0	0	15	491	398	231	185	38	175	504	.218
Angels	3.60	56	0	0	14	493	416	245	197	17	198	511	.227
Rangers	3.77	55	0	0	8	485	448	251	203	17	212	552	.245
Cubs	3.95	56	0	0	11	489	497	289	215	27	185	494	.259
Giants	3.96	56	0	0	13	491	483	281	216	31	200	503	.253
Athletics	4.05	56	0	0	14	491	468	279	221	17	174	525	.248
White Sox	4.14	56	1	1	9	485	463	276	223	28	218	414	.254
Mariners	4.19	56	0	0	11	497	493	286	231	29	192	513	.259
Brewers	4.54	56	0	0	18	500	550	310	252	32	196	494	.276
D-backs	4.77	56	1	1	16	483	502	337	256	30	212	456	.264
Royals	4.78	56	1	0	11	488	519	328	259	32	198	442	.269
Padres 2	4.86	56	0	0	12	495	525	348	267	30	252	529	.270
Reds	4.88	55	0	0	8	472	492	328	256	25	225	523	.263
Padres	4.85	56	0	0	13	485	488	337	261	27	253	561	.256
Indians	5.45	56	0	0	10	485	520	382	294	28	263	552	.270

CLUB FIELDING

	PCT	PO	A	E	DP
White Sox	.968	1763	620	78	170
Mariners	.966	1775	596	84	126
Rangers	.962	1702	522	89	138
Dodgers	.961	1766	541	93	114
Cubs	.961	1757	575	95	118
Angels	.960	1777	541	96	90
Brewers	.959	1814	593	102	128
Padres 2	.956	1767	546	106	127
D-backs	.956	1765	574	108	160
Giants	.954	1800	555	113	87
Athletics	.954	1773	573	114	111
Royals	.954	1766	597	115	126
Padres	.951	1719	525	116	73
Indians	.950	1719	542	120	75
Reds	.948	1719	491	122	87

INDIVIDUAL BATTING

Batter, Club	AVG	G	AB	R	H	2B	3B	HR	RBI	BB	SO	SB
Ruiz, Esteury, Padres/Royals	.350	52	206	45	72	20	10	4	39	13	54	26
Ramos, Heliot, Giants	.348	35	138	33	48	11	6	6	27	10	48	10
Gonzalez, Jacob, Giants	.339	46	168	23	57	15	1	1	21	16	23	0
Costello, Ryan, Mariners	.331	44	142	31	47	13	3	8	38	26	38	3
Munguia, Ismael, Giants	.331	42	142	31	47	7	4	1	19	17	18	8
Jacobs, Justin, Rangers	.326	48	181	37	59	9	2	2	27	33	37	8
Bautista, Mariel, Reds	.320	36	147	29	47	9	1	0	20	5	24	16
Pineda, Gleyvin, Angels	.316	40	133	20	42	7	1	0	14	18	29	4
Martinez, Renae, D-backs	.313	37	134	20	42	4	1	5	30	13	22	1
Mastrobuoni, Marcus, Cubs	.308	41	133	25	41	13	0	6	22	19	18	1

INDIVIDUAL PITCHING

Pitcher, Club	W	L	ERA	G	GS	CG	SV	IP	H	R	ER	BB	SO
Perez, Ramon, Padres 2	2	2	2.66	12	9	0	0	51	37	21	15	33	48
Lewis, Zach, White Sox	6	1	2.72	12	8	1	0	53	46	18	16	13	45
Parke, John, White Sox	3	2	2.77	14	10	0	0	68	65	27	21	9	46
Soriano, Jose, Angels	2	2	2.94	12	10	0	0	49	43	23	16	14	37
Smith, Ricardo, Reds	4	4	3.33	13	6	0	0	54	63	34	20	17	61
Vargas, Jesus, Dodgers	4	3	3.38	14	11	0	0	5	51	30	22	9	49
Taugner, Christian, Brewers	2	4	3.74	14	3	0	0	4	53	28	19	8	50
Carrera, Faustino, Cubs	2	4	3.88	10	9	0	0	51	48	26	22	9	30
Colorado, Alfredo, Cubs	3	4	3.91	11	5	0	0	5	54	25	22	18	49
Hernandez, Kenny, D-backs	2	4	4.03	13	5	0	0	58	63	38	26	16	59

ALL-STAR TEAM

C: Sam Huff, Rangers; Marcus Mastrobuoni, Cubs. **1B:** Tyreque Reed, Rangers. **2B:** Esteury Ruiz, Padres. **3B:** Jacob Gonzalez, Giants. **SS:** Chris Seiwse, Rangers. **OF:** Heliot Ramos, Giants; Justin Jacobs, Rangers; Diego Rincones, Giants. **DH:** Pat McInerney, Brewers. **RHP:** Zach Lewis, White Sox; Olbis Parra, Giants. **LHP:** John Parke, White Sox; Joey Marciano, Giants.

DEPARTMENT LEADERS

BATTING

OBP	Hoover, Connor, Mariners	.481
SLG	Ramos, Heliot, Giants	.645
OPS	Costello, Ryan, Mariners	1.064
R	Lujano, Jesus, Brewers	50
H	Ruiz, Esteury, AZL Royals, AZL Padres	72
TB	Ruiz, Esteury, AZL Royals, AZL Padres	124
XBH	Ruiz, Esteury, AZL Royals, AZL Padres	34
2B	Ruiz, Esteury, AZL Royals, AZL Padres	20
3B	Ruiz, Esteury, AZL Royals, AZL Padres	10
HR	Huff, Sam, Rangers	9
	McInerney, Pat, Brewers	9
RBI	Garcia, Ryan, Mariners	44
SAC	Bradshaw, Montae, Royals	6
	Gregorio, Osmy, Mariners	6
	James, Tyler, Royals	6
BB	Hoover, Connor, Mariners	43
HBP	Rivera, Laz, White Sox	16
SO	Marriaga, Jesus, D-backs	78
SB	James, Tyler, Royals	31
CS	Ward, Je'Von, Brewers	7
	Rosario, Eguy, Padres 2	7
AB/SO	Cintron, Jancarlos, D-backs	10.56

FIELDING

C PCT	Huff, Sam, Rangers	.985
PO	Fernandez, Juan, Padres, Padres 2	303
A	Mastrobuoni, Marcus, Cubs	37
DP	Mastrobuoni, Marcus, Cubs	5
E	Ventura, Francisco, Rangers	8
PB	Homza, Jonny, Padres	15
1B PCT	McInerney, Pat, Brewers	.997
PO	Pratto, Nick, Royals	443
A	Pratto, Nick, Royals	45
DP	Hickman, Michael, White Sox	41
E	Pratto, Nick, Royals	11
2B PCT	Hoover, Connor, Mariners	.987
PO	Ruiz, Esteury, Royals, Padres	79
A	Ruiz, Esteury, Royals, Padres	119
DP	James, Tyler, Royals	21
	Sosa, Lenyn, White Sox	21
	Cintron, Jancarlos, D-backs	21
E	Ruiz, Esteury, Royals, Padres	14
3B PCT	Garcia, Julio, Angels	.904
PO	Medina, Angel, Royals	25
A	Kennedy, Buddy, D-backs	82
DP	Kennedy, Buddy, D-backs	12
E	Medina, Angel, Royals	24
SS PCT	Perez, Cristian, Royals	.959
PO	Perez, Cristian, Royals	69
A	Perez, Cristian, Royals	162
DP	Perez, Cristian, Royals	32
E	Barley, Jordy, Padres	30
OF PCT	Henry, Robert, Brewers	.988
PO	Marriaga, Jesus, D-backs	115
A	Four tied with	6
DP	Henry, Robert, Brewers	3
E	Ward, Je'Von, Brewers	9

PITCHING

G	Parra, Olbis, Giants	20
	Guzman, Jonathan, Padres	20
GS	Saucedo, Bryan, White Sox	13
GF	Lee, Slater, Athletics	14
SV	Bencomo, Edwuin, Padres 2	7
	Parra, Olbis, Giants	7
W	Lewis, Zach, White Sox	6
L	Valdez, Luis, Indians	7
	Cruz, Wilfry, D-backs	7
IP	Parke, John, White Sox	68
H	Greenwalt, Jake, Giants	70
R	Valdez, Luis, Indians	50
ER	Saucedo, Bryan, White Sox	43
HB	Valdez, Luis, Indians	12
BB	Saucedo, Bryan, White Sox	37
SO	Mota, Juan, Indians	73
SO/9	Oviedo, Luis, Indians	12.19
SO/9(RP)	Doval, Camilo, Giants	14.20
BB/9	Parke, John, White Sox	1.19
WP	Mota, Juan, Indians	19
BK	Natera, Jose, Angels	5
HR	Greenwalt, Jake, Giants	10
AVG	Perez, Ramon, Padres 2	.208

GULF COAST LEAGUE ROOKIE

BY BEN BADLER

The Yankees split their Gulf Coast League players into two teams in 2017, and the ensuing results showed why they needed so many roster spots.

While the Yankees West club finished with a winning record (32-27), they didn't make the playoffs as they finished third in the division behind the Phillies and Blue Jays, respectively. Yankees East, however, won the Northeast Division and won the GCL championship, defeating the Nationals 5-4 in the decisive third game of the finals.

The Yankees, Phillies and Nationals all won their divisions with teams rich on talented teenage prospects, particularly from Latin America. The Phillies (36-22), who had the best record during the regular season, were strong up the middle with shortstop Jonathan Guzman and center fielder Simon Muzziotti.

Two 17-year-old Yankees shortstops impressed scouts—Jose Devers (a cousin of Red Sox third baseman Rafael Devers) and Oswald Peraza—while left fielder Canaan Smith also had a strong debut by leading the GCL in walks after signing out of high school as a fourth-round pick in June.

The Nationals' regular season success stood out given how many first-year, 17-year-old international players they had playing key roles on the team, particularly in the infield with Luis Garcia, Yasel Antuna and Jose Sanchez.

Among the top-tier prospects in the league, the talent level was down from where it was a year ago, when outfielders Mickey Moniak (Phillies), Juan Soto (Nationals) and Jesus Sanchez (Rays), as well as righthanders Sixto Sanchez (Phillies) and Matt Manning (Tigers) were in the league. Like Moniak the previous year, the GCL did again have the No. 1 overall pick in the draft, with Twins shortstop Royce Lewis easily taking No. 1 prospect honors in the league after an impressive debut.

The league's MVP, Pirates first baseman/outfielder Mason Martin, went from under the radar to legitimate prospect by the season's end. Signed out of high school as a 17th-round pick in 2017, Martin immediately looked like a late-round gem by leading the league in on-base percentage, slugging and home runs, showing a promising combination of patience and plus power to all fields.

TOP 20 PROSPECTS

1. Royce Lewis, SS, Twins
2. Lolo Sanchez, OF, Pirates
3. Shane Baz, RHP, Pirates
4. Luis Garcia, 2B/SS, Nationals
5. Yasel Antuna, SS/3B, Nationals
6. Mason Martin, 1B/OF, Pirates
7. Simon Muzziotti, OF, Phillies
8. Jonathan Guzman, SS, Phillies
9. Elehuris Montero, 3B, Cardinals
10. Mark Vientos, SS/3B, Mets
11. Francisco Morales, RHP, Phillies
12. Jairo Solis, RHP, Astros
13. Blayne Enlow, RHP, Twins
14. Oswald Peraza, SS, Yankees
15. Yunior Severino, 2B, Braves
16. Yefri del Rosario, RHP, Braves
17. Michael Mercado, RHP, Rays
18. Jonathan Machado, OF, Cardinals
19. Jose Devers, SS, Yankees
20. Sam McMillan, C, Tigers

OVERALL STANDINGS

Eastern Division	W	L	PCT	GB	Manager(s)	Last Pennant
Nationals	34	22	.607	—	Josh Johnson	2009
Marlins	32	23	.582	1½	John Pachot	Never
Astros	27	27	.500	6	Wladimir Sutil	Never
Cardinals	26	29	.473	7½	Steve Turco/Erick Almonte	2016
Mets	19	37	.339	15	Jose Carreno	Never
Northeastern Division	**W**	**L**	**PCT**	**GB**	**Manager(s)**	**Last Pennant**
Yankees East	33	27	.555	—	Luis Sojo	2017
Braves	31	28	.525	1½	Barrett Kleinknecht	2003
Pirates	26	34	.433	7	Bob Herold	2012
Tigers East	14	45	.237	18½	Jesus Garces	Never
Northwestern Division	**W**	**L**	**PCT**	**GB**	**Manager(s)**	**Last Pennant**
Phillies	36	22	.621	—	Roly de Armas	2010
Blue Jays	35	25	.583	2	Luis Hurtado	Never
Yankees West	32	27	.542	4½	Marc Bombard	2011
Tigers West	29	28	.509	6½	Rafeal Gil	Never
Southern Division	**W**	**L**	**PCT**	**GB**	**Manager(s)**	**Last Pennant**
Twins	35	23	.603	—	Ramon Borrego	Never
Orioles	28	32	.467	8	Carlos Tosca	Never
Rays	28	32	.467	8	Jim Morrison	Never
Red Sox	27	31	.466	8	Tom Kotchman	2015

Semifinals: Nationals defeated Twins and Yankees East defeated Phillies in one-game playoffs. **Finals:** Yankees East defeated Nationals 2-1 in a best-of-three series.

GULF COAST LEAGUE STATISTICS

CLUB BATTING

	AVG	G	AB	R	H	2B	3B	HR	RBI	BB	SO	SB	OBP	SLG
Phillies	.267	58	1934	310	517	110	15	25	279	186	313	60	.340	.379
Tigers West	.260	57	1901	280	494	66	13	24	230	195	420	87	.342	.346
Braves	.259	59	1977	278	511	107	17	21	233	197	455	58	.336	.362
Nationals	.254	56	1799	256	457	76	17	15	197	182	360	44	.331	.340
Twins	.253	58	1828	299	462	87	21	29	257	199	449	88	.338	.371
Red Sox	.252	58	1848	271	465	76	9	16	212	245	483	53	.359	.329
Orioles	.251	60	1965	283	494	113	17	20	259	239	397	50	.345	.357
Cardinals	.249	55	1745	276	435	91	16	29	243	217	407	32	.340	.370
Pirates	.249	60	1968	260	489	94	26	34	233	218	439	46	.332	.375
Yankees West	.247	59	1894	291	467	84	17	34	250	232	462	64	.341	.363
Blue Jays	.245	60	1986	260	487	88	20	20	226	186	495	52	.321	.340
Mets	.245	54	1835	215	450	93	13	14	181	171	421	42	.315	.333
Astros	.244	54	1698	230	414	82	21	28	196	191	407	38	.331	.366
Marlins	.241	55	1781	273	430	78	22	23	231	194	461	63	.324	.349
Tigers East	.234	59	1816	208	424	66	16	14	178	173	415	49	.308	.311
Rays	.231	60	1845	231	427	93	15	18	192	183	450	74	.316	.327
Yankees East	.231	60	1794	218	414	73	13	15	189	250	425	73	.339	.311

CLUB PITCHING

	ERA	G	CG	SHO	SV	IP	H	R	ER	HR	BB	SO	AVG
Blue Jays	2.86	60	1	1	15	525	467	222	167	21	178	480	.237
Phillies	3.01	58	0	0	10	490	437	205	164	18	216	428	.241
Braves	3.18	59	0	0	12	513	456	237	181	17	215	428	.236
Yankees East	3.18	60	1	1	13	489	451	220	173	22	144	443	.243
Nationals	3.20	56	0	0	12	473	399	221	168	26	165	431	.225
Rays	3.47	60	0	0	14	498	422	230	192	25	206	423	.227
Astros	3.53	54	0	0	11	446	425	240	175	21	186	428	.248
Yankees West	3.64	59	0	0	15	493	473	259	199	33	174	476	.250
Marlins	3.67	55	0	0	10	470	428	244	192	13	207	373	.239
Twins	3.74	58	0	0	19	488	415	257	203	19	246	437	.229
Cardinals	3.97	55	0	0	11	458	509	266	202	26	149	398	.281
Tigers West	4.05	57	0	0	17	495	471	296	223	16	235	461	.250
Red Sox	4.24	58	0	0	15	484	500	280	228	13	209	433	.269
Mets	4.25	56	1	1	8	470	425	279	222	23	248	426	.241
Pirates	4.56	60	0	0	16	518	534	334	262	30	230	356	.265
Orioles	4.61	60	0	0	13	512	511	317	262	26	205	486	.262
Tigers East	4.90	59	0	0	8	483	514	332	263	30	245	352	.270

CLUB FIELDING

	PCT	PO	A	E	DP
Red Sox	.974	1763	579	63	130
Twins	.973	1776	556	66	146
Phillies	.970	1789	584	73	145
Rays	.969	1807	633	78	134
Orioles	.967	1839	612	83	147
Yankees East	.966	1764	582	83	104
Blue Jays	.966	1919	579	89	119
Cardinals	.963	1693	505	84	114
Tigers East	.962	1837	582	96	152

	PCT	PO	A	E	DP
Marlins	.962	1715	598	92	121
Yankees West	.962	1804	533	93	126
Astros	.961	1615	521	86	127
Nationals	.961	1712	535	91	111
Pirates	.960	1936	632	107	165
Braves	.960	1919	558	104	108
Mets	.960	1727	502	94	114
Tigers West	.959	1820	566	101	142\

INDIVIDUAL BATTING

Batter, Club	AVG	G	AB	R	H	2B	3B	HR	RBI	BB	SO	SB
Abbadessa, Dominic, Blue Jays	.340	39	147	30	50	4	3	0	10	7	14	11
Castellanos, Pedro, Red Sox	.339	52	186	27	63	14	1	2	30	10	15	0
Pelletier, Ben, Phillies	.333	46	171	21	57	13	1	3	26	8	30	1
Robles, Alex, Twins	.324	50	182	30	59	6	0	3	29	8	14	10
Bryant, Taylor, Cardinals	.324	43	136	22	44	11	1	1	21	27	27	2
Lozada, Everlouis, Red Sox	.315	44	159	26	50	9	2	0	20	18	27	6
Hogan, Max, Orioles	.310	40	129	32	40	11	5	2	28	32	17	2
Martin, Mason, Pirates	.307	39	127	37	39	8	0	11	22	32	41	2
Robertson, Will, Orioles	.303	53	211	32	64	19	0	2	40	11	26	7
Garcia, Luis, Nationals	.302	49	199	25	60	8	3	1	22	9	32	11

INDIVIDUAL PITCHING

Pitcher, Club	W	L	ERA	G	GS	CG	SV	IP	H	R	ER	BB	SO
Suniaga, Carlos, Twins	4	0	1.69	11	6	0	1	48	36	11	9	12	38
Vilera, Jaison, Mets	3	1	1.88	11	8	1	0	62	43	18	13	17	56
Garcia, Pedro, Twins	6	2	2.59	10	3	0	0	49	26	15	14	17	41
Nicacio, Winston, Cardinals	4	3	2.61	11	8	0	0	52	57	24	15	16	39
Rodriguez, Jesus, Tigers East	3	3	3.26	11	11	0	0	58	59	31	21	10	27
Hernandez, Tony, Yankees East	3	5	3.44	11	9	0	0	52	52	27	20	14	45
Rijo, Luis, Yankees East	4	3	3.50	11	7	1	0	54	51	23	21	9	55
Rosario, Sandro, Phillies	1	4	4.22	11	7	0	0	49	66	29	23	19	37
Pirela, Brian, Cardinals	3	4	4.50	11	8	0	0	54	60	33	27	23	37
Gonzalez, Junior, Cardinals	2	2	4.70	12	8	0	0	59	75	41	31	19	29

DEPARTMENT LEADERS

BATTING

OBP	Martin, Mason, Pirates	.457
SLG	Martin, Mason, Pirates	.630
OPS	Martin, Mason, Pirates	1.087
R	Sanchez, Lolo, Pirates	42
H	Robertson, Will, Orioles	64
TB	Castro, Rodolfo, Pirates	90
XBH	Montero, Elehuris, Cardinals	22
	Severino, Yunior, Braves	22
	Castro, Rodolfo, Pirates	22
2B	Robertson, Will, Orioles	19
3B	Muzziotti, Simon, Phillies	6
HR	Martin, Mason, Pirates	11
RBI	Robertson, Will, Orioles	40
	Rodriguez, Benjamin, Twins	40
SAC	Gonzalez, Gerardo, GCL Tigers E., GCL Tiger W.	7
BB	Smith, Canaan, Yankees East	46
HBP	Colon, Andre, Red Sox	14
SO	Severino, Yunior, Braves	61
SB	Granadillo, Guillermo, Mets	17
CS	De La Cruz, Isrrael, Tigers West	10
AB/SO	Markham, Kevin, Phillies	15.56

FIELDING

C PCT	Moore, Kipp, Phillies	.992
PO	Danner, Hagen, Blue Jays	234
A	Narvaez, Carlos, Yankees West	30
DP	Hurtado, Pedro, Tigers East	7
E	Danner, Hagen, Blue Jays	7
PB	Silverio, Gresuan, Tigers East	16
1B PCT	Escarra, J.C., Orioles	.998
PO	Escarra, J.C., Orioles	472
A	Escarra, J.C., Orioles	23
DP	Escarra, J.C., Orioles	49
E	Vizcaino, Nicholas, Braves	8
2B PCT	Theran, Jose, Blue Jays	.984
PO	Suarez, Kervin, Red Sox	82
A	Aranda, Jonathan, Rays	116
DP	Gonzalez, Brayan, Phillies	30
E	Severino, Yunior, Braves	10
3B PCT	Lozada, Everlouis, Red Sox	.965
PO	Montero, Elehuris, Cardinals	41
A	Schneider, Davis, Blue Jays	84
DP	Yahn, Willy, Orioles	8
	Tademo, Victor, Twins	8
	Salas, Jose, Tigers West	8
E	Vasquez, Braulio, Braves	17
SS PCT	De Los Santos, Luis, Blue Jays	.948
PO	Leon, Luis, Rays	64
A	Peraza, Oswald, Yankees West	108
DP	Guzman, Jonathan, Phillies	25
E	Antuna, Yasel, Nationals	20
OF PCT	Stone, Jake, Rays	1.000
	Robertson, Will, Orioles	1.000
	Sanchez, Lolo, Pirates	1.000
PO	Vital, Santiago, Tigers East	127
A	Markham, Kevin, Phillies	8
DP	Santos, Allan, Tigers East	4
E	Sparks, Lamar, Orioles	6

PITCHING

G	Four tied with	18
GS	Six tied with	11
GF	Naughton, Timothy, Orioles	16
SV	Naughton, Timothy, Orioles	7
W	Garcia, Pedro, Twins	6
	Silva, Manuel, Phillies	6
L	Escalona, Edgar, Tigers East	7
IP	Vilera, Jaison, Mets	62
H	Gonzalez, Junior, Cardinals	75
R	Three tied with	41
ER	Reuss, Grant, Tigers West	33
HB	Four tied with	9
BB	Reuss, Grant, Tigers West	41
SO	Vilera, Jaison, Mets	56
SO/9	Campos, Yeizo, Mets	9.59
SO/9(RP)	Stock, Dylan, Tigers West	11.48
BB/9	Rijo, Luis, Yankees East	1.50
WP	Reuss, Grant, Tigers West	13
BK	Morales, Francisco, Phillies	5
HR	Pirela, Brian, Cardinals	8
AVG	Garcia, Pedro, Twins	.152

DOMINICAN SUMMER LEAGUE

BY BEN BADLER

After the final out of Dominican Summer League championship, both the winning and losing teams decided to run onto the field to celebrate together, causing what was certainly an unusual sight.

But while the two teams were opponents for one, championship-deciding game, it was the Dodgers' two DSL clubs that faced each other in the title matchup. The Dodgers2 ended up winning the championship, taking the title with a 6-1 victory over Dodgers1. Pitching was key to the success for both Dodgers clubs, as the Dodgers1 ranked third in the league with a 2.63 team ERA, while Dodgers2 ranked 10th in ERA at 3.17.

The Twins leaned more heavily on their offense (2nd in the league in runs scored) to win the South Division, while the Mets2 were the most balanced team in the league—fourth in runs scored and third in runs allowed—to win the San Pedro Division. The Red Sox tied the Dodgers1 for first place in the DSL Northwest despite having been banned from making international signings the previous year as a penalty for what Major League Baseball determined was international bonus pool circumvention.

Giants outfielder Alexander Canario, 17, was one of the bright young talents in the league. Signed for just $60,000 in 2016, Canario batted .294/.391/.464 in 66 games in his professional debut. Rockies outfielder Yolki Pena also showed an advanced bat for a 17-year-old in his first season, batting .302/.411/.387 in 62 games with more walks (40) than strikeouts (34).

PLAYOFFS—Division Series: Mariners1 defeated Rockies 2-0 and Red Sox2 defeated D-Backs 2-0 in best-of-three series. **Semifinals:** Rangers1 defeated Red Sox2 2-0 and Red Sox1 defeated Mariners1 2-1 in best-of-three series. **Finals:** Red Sox1 defeated Rangers1 3-1 in a best-of-five series.

NORTH

TEAM	W	L	PCT	GB
Dodgers2	44	28	.611	—
Rangers1	42	28	.600	1
Rays2	41	30	.577	2 ½
Cubs1	37	33	.529	6
Pirates	36	34	.514	7
Indians	29	41	.414	14
Astros Orange	27	44	.380	16 ½
Indians/Brewers	26	44	.371	17

NORTHWEST

TEAM	W	L	PCT	GB
Red Sox1	47	24	.662	—
Dodgers1	47	24	.662	—
Marlins	40	29	.580	6
Athletics	40	32	.556	7 ½
Astros Blue	38	33	.535	9
Royals	30	40	.429	16 ½
Rays1	23	48	.324	24
Braves	18	53	.254	29

SAN PEDRO

TEAM	W	L	PCT	GB
Mets2	50	21	.704	—
Rangers2	46	25	.648	4
Phillies White	45	26	.634	5
Cubs2	34	37	.479	16
Rojos	30	40	.429	19 ½
Brewers	28	43	.394	22
Tigers	26	44	.371	23 ½
D-backs2	24	47	.338	26

SOUTH

TEAM	W	L	PCT	GB
Twins	49	22	.690	—
Mets1	44	27	.620	5
Rockies	36	35	.507	13
Angels	35	35	.500	13 ½
Phillies Red	32	39	.451	17
Cardinals	30	40	.429	18 ½
Yankees	29	42	.408	20
Nationals	28	43	.394	21

BASEBALL CITY

TEAM	W	L	PCT	GB
Blue Jays	44	26	.629	—
Giants	41	30	.577	3 ½
Reds	41	30	.577	3 ½
D-backs1	36	35	.507	8 ½
White Sox	34	37	.479	10 ½
Orioles	32	37	.464	11 ½
Mariners	30	40	.429	14
Padres	24	47	.338	20 ½

INDIVIDUAL BATTING LEADERS

PLAYER, TEAM	AVG	G	AB	R	H	2B	3B	HR	RBI	BB	SO	SB
Yanqui, Yoel, D-backs1	.373	50	169	31	63	13	5	2	28	29	34	11
Romero, Yoel, Mets2	.364	67	239	47	87	10	4	2	35	31	32	17
Hidalgo, Luis, Cubs1	.353	54	190	34	67	17	0	5	44	16	21	7
Pena, Andrison, Rangers1	.344	48	163	29	56	17	3	4	37	31	18	4
Rodriguez, Ramiro, Astros Orange	.342	49	164	33	56	8	3	5	23	27	18	8
Herrera, Ivan, Cardinals	.335	49	170	21	57	15	0	1	27	18	36	2
Beltre, Ramon, White Sox	.335	42	176	33	59	12	2	3	24	15	25	7
Sanchez, Aldenis, Rays2	.333	50	189	33	63	8	0	1	21	14	33	23
Torres, Nicolas, Phillies White	.333	69	240	40	80	13	4	0	28	11	31	11
Santana, Luis, Mets2	.325	65	237	47	77	12	8	3	52	34	22	16

INDIVIDUAL PITCHING LEADERS

PLAYER, TEAM	W	L	ERA	G	GS	CG	SV	IP	H	R	ER	BB	SO
Aponte, Leonel, Phillies Red/Phillies White	7	1	0.77	15	13	1	1	81	55	10	7	9	69
Vargas, Didier, Cubs2	4	2	0.99	14	14	0	0	64	44	19	7	23	55
Infante, Angello, Athletics	3	1	1.06	14	9	1	0	68	59	11	8	5	54
Calderon, Alexander, Athletics	6	1	1.35	14	9	0	0	60	40	16	9	20	56
Espinal, Erik, Mariners	5	2	1.40	20	5	0	2	58	44	12	9	6	51
Ferrebus, Emilio, Cubs2	5	3	1.54	12	12	0	0	64	52	18	11	19	58
Castillo, Juan, Rangers1	5	1	1.65	11	11	1	0	60	42	12	11	19	35
Ramirez, Miguel, Mets1	6	2	1.76	14	14	0	0	67	57	18	13	3	53
Valenzuela, Jose, Reds	5	5	1.79	15	15	1	0	75	62	23	15	21	62
Gudino, Norwith, Giants	6	1	1.82	13	13	0	0	74	62	18	15	10	83

MINOR LEAGUE BEST TOOLS

	International League	Pacific Coast League	Eastern League	Southern League	Texas League	California League	Carolina League	Florida State League	Midwest League	South Atlantic League
Best Batting Prospect	Yoan Moncada Charlotte	Amed Rosario Las Vegas	Francisco Mejia Akron	Ronald Acuna Mississippi	Edwin Rios Tulsa	Brendan Rodgers Lancaster	Austin Hays Frederick	Nick Senzel Daytona	Bo Bichette Lansing	Juan Soto Hagerstown
Best Power Prospect	Rhys Hoskins Lehigh Valley	Renato Nunez Nashville	Christin Stewart Erie	Kevin Cron Jackson	J.D. Davis Corpus Christi	D.J. Peters R. Cucamonga	Eloy Jimenez Winston-Salem	Logan Hill Bradenton	Emmanuel Tapia Lake County	Daniel Johnson Hagerstown
Best Strike-Zone Judment	Rhys Hoskins Lehigh Valley	Alex Verdugo Oklahoma City	Mike Ford Trenton	LaMonte Wade Chattanooga	Ian Miller Arkansas	Tyler Ramirez Stockton	Zack Collins Winston-Salem	Brett Sullivan Charlotte	Zack Short South Bend	Brett Cumberland Rome
Best Baserunner	Tyler Wade Scranton/W-B	Ketel Marte Reno	Scott Kingery Reading	Mauricio Dubon Biloxi	Ian Miller Arkansas	Wes Rogers Lancaster	Sam Haggerty Lynchburg	Cole Tucker Bradenton	Lucius Fox Bowling Green	Cristian Pache Rome
Fastest Baserunner	Ozzie Albies Gwinnett	Terrance Gore Omaha	Champ Stuart Binghamton	Johnny Davis Biloxi	Magneuris Sierra Springfield	Wes Rogers Lancaster	Victor Robles Potomac	Jorge Mateo Tampa	Jose Siri Dayton	Randy Ventura Rome
Best Pitching Prospect	Chance Adams Scranton/W-B	Luke Weaver Memphis	Justus Sheffield Trenton	Michael Kopech Birmingham	Walker Buehler Tulsa	A.J. Puk Stockton	Triston McKenzie Lynchburg	Mitch Keller Bradenton	Dylan Cease South Bend	Sixto Sanchez Lakewood
Best Fastball	Zack Burdi Charlotte	Frankie Montas Nashville	Conner Greene New Hampshire	Michael Kopech Birmingham	Walker Buehler Tulsa	Yadier Alvarez R. Cucamonga	Alec Hansen Winston-Salem	Taylor Hearn Bradenton	Dylan Cease South Bend	Sixto Sanchez Lakewood
Best Breaking Pitch	Tyler Glasnow Indianapolis	Josh Staumont Omaha	Colten Brewer Trenton	Dillon Maples Tennessee	Walker Buehler Tulsa	A.J. Puk Stockton	Triston McKenzie Lynchburg	Matt Hall Lakeland	Dylan Cease South Bend	Jay Groome Greenville
Best Changeup	Brent Honeywell Durham	John Gant Memphis	Yency Almonte Hartford	Jordan Guerrero Birmingham	Rogelio Arementeros Corpus Christi	Cal Quantrill Lake Elsinore	Thomas Pannone Lynchburg	Trevor Richards Jupiter	Austin Sodders West Michigan	JoJo Romero Lakewood
Best Control	Tom Eshelman Lehigh Valley	Trevor Oaks Oklahoma City	Domingo Acevedo Trenton	Tyler Mahle Pensacola	Matt Pearce Springfield	Nick Neidert Modesto	Shane Bieber Lynchburg	Kyle Dowdy Lakeland	Mike O'Reilly Peoria	Alex Wells Delmarva (Orioles)
Best Reliever	Kevin Shackelford Louisville	Jimmie Sherfy Reno	Tyler Cyr Richmond	Jimmy Herget Pensacola	Trey Wingenter San Antonio	Matt Festa Modesto	Richard Lovelady Wilmington	Jeff Singer Clearwater	Jason Foley West Michigan	Trevor Lane Charleston
Best Defensive C	Elias Diaz Indianapolis	Carson Kelly Memphis	Francisco Mejia Akron	Michael Perez Jackson	Garrett Stubbs Corpus Christi	Will Smith Rancho Cucamonga	Austin Rei Salem	Brian Navarreto Fort Myers	Keibert Ruiz Great Lakes	Ali Sanchez Columbia
Best Defensive 1B	Efren Navarro Toledo	Matt Olson Nashville	Edwin Espinal Altoona	Joe McCarthy Montgomery	Casey Grayson Springfield	Josh Naylor Lake Elsinore	Jake Gatewood Carolina	Brian Navarreto Charlotte	Stefan Trosclair Peoria	Carlos Munoz West Virgina
Best Defensive 2B	Ozzie Albies Gwinnett	Ildemaro Vargas Reno	Scott Kingery Reading	David Bote Tennessee	Luis Urias San Antonio	Garrett Hampson Lancaster	Danny Mendick Winston-Salem	Shed Long Daytona	Gavin Lux Great Lakes	Daniel Brito Lakewood
Best Defensive 3B	Giovanny Urshela Columbus	Matt Chapman Nashville	Rafael Devers Portland	Brian Anderson Jacksonville	J.D. Davis Corpus Christi	Jose Rojas Inland Empire (Angels)	Lucas Erceg Carolina	Nick Senzel Daytona	Adrian Rondon Bowling Green	Sheldon Neuse Hagerstown
Best Defensive SS	Willy Adames Durham	Amed Rosario Las Vegas	Kevin Newman Altoona	Nick Gordon Chattanooga	Richie Martin Midland	Brendan Rodgers Lancaster	Nicky Lopez Wilmington	Alfredo Rodriguez Daytona	Jermaine Palacios Cedar Rapids	Andres Gimenez Columbia
Best Infield Arm	Willy Adames Durham	Amed Rosario Las Vegas	Brendan Rodgers Hartford	Dawel Lugo Jackson	J.D. Davis Corpus Christi	Sergio Alcantara Visalia	Lucas Erceg Carolina	Ke'Bryan Hayes Bradenton	Fernando Tatis Jr. Fort Wayne	Sheldon Neuse Hagerstown
Best Defensive OF	Dustin Fowler Scranton/W-B	Lewis Brinson Colorado Springs	Greg Allen Akron	Braxton Lee Jacksonville	Magneuris Sierra Springfield	Yonathan Daza Lancaster	Victor Robles Potomac	Tanner English Fort Myers	Jose Siri Dayton	Cristian Pache Rome
Best Outfield Arm	Willy Garcia Charlotte	Alex Verdugo Oklahoma City	Elvis Escobar Altoona	Aristides Aquino Pensacola	Ramon Laureano Corpus Christi	Michael Gettys Lake Elsinore	Victor Robles Potomac	Blake Drake Palm Beach	Eleardo Cabrera Bowling Green	Christian Pache Rome
Most Exciting Player	Yoan Moncada Charlotte	Derek Fisher Fresno	Francisco Mejia Akron	Ronald Acuna Mississippi	Walker Buehler Tulsa	Brendan Rodgers Lancaster	Victor Robles Potomac	Ronald Acuna Florida	Bo Bichette Lansing	Estevan Florial Charleston
Best Manager Prospect	Jared Sandberg Durham	Stubby Clapp Memphis	Kyle Haines Richmond	Jake Mauer Chattanooga	Johnny Rodriguez Springfield	Drew Saylor Rancho Cucamonga	Willie Harris Winston-Salem	Jay Bell Tampa	Luis Bolivar Dayton	Warren Schaeffer Asheville

Franchises Worth Honoring

Triple-A

FRESNO (PACIFIC COAST)

The most successful minor league promotion over the last few years unquestionably belongs to the Fresno Tacos, er, Grizzlies. What started in 2015 as novel idea—wearing taco jerseys every Tuesday home game—has blossomed into a merchandise empire complete with its own website apart from the traditional team store.

"It's funny what ideas you can come up at 1 a.m. after an eight-game homestand when everybody's delirious," Grizzlies GM Derek Franks said. "You can come up with some interesting stuff, and we're really happy that it's caught on and caught fire."

The tacos theme has its roots in Fresno's annual taco truck throwdown, which brings scads of the area's vendors out to Chukchansi Park to sell their wares to hungry fans.

Thanks to Franks and promotions wizard Sam Hansen, tacos and baseball are connected in Fresno.

Double-A

READING (EASTERN)

Reading has a tradition of excellence. It has won two Freitas Awards prior to this year's. GM Scott Hunsicker credited an atmosphere of "continuity and community" established by owner Craig Stein and former GM Chuck Domino.

Just look at the staff: Reading has more than 170 employees who have worked for the team for at least a decade. Hunsicker himself has been with the organization since 1992, starting as an intern before moving up the ladder to GM, and there are many employees who predate him. The staff oozes with a sense of pride and ownership. FirstEnergy Stadium is their home.

"It was like that when I got here as an intern, and it's like that now," Hunsicker said, "and it's one of the things we're proudest of."

Class A

CHARLESTON (SOUTH ATLANTIC)

The credit card company won't stop calling Nate Kurant. He jokes that he might make a spreadsheet with all of the purchases it's rejected during the team's effort to put on a show for its fans.

Like the time he bought $4,000 worth of silly string. Obviously fraud, right? Or when he tried to buy $150 in circus peanuts at a candy store. Canceled—nobody would do that. Or the time he tried to rent a giraffe.

Whether the team wins or loses, Charleston fans can expect a captivating night at the yard. They may even see something they've never seen before. That's the goal for Kurant and the rest of the staff, to maintain creativity and constantly try new ideas. They want to wow their audience.

That formula isn't changing any time soon.

Short-Season

HILLSBORO HOPS (NORTHWEST)

It's been five years since Oregon added a third team to the Northwest League, joining Eugene and Salem-Keizer. In that half-decade, the Hillsboro Hops have established themselves as one of the minor leagues' most innovative franchises.

The team's ascent culminated this summer when it hosted the annual Northwest/Pioneer League all-star game at Ron Tonkin Field. The game itself was a success too, and featured the home team's Daulton Varsho driving in the game's tying run.

General manager K.L. Wombacher and the Hops have followed the trend set by other minor league clubs and used their merchandise to tie in to other local trends.

They've also found tremendous success on the field, too. The Hops won back-to-back NWL championships in 2014-15 and made the playoffs the next two seasons as well.

PREVIOUS 10 WINNERS

TRIPLE-A	DOUBLE-A	CLASS A	SHORT-SEASON
2007: Albuquerque (Pacific Coast)	**2007:** Frisco (Texas)	**2007:** Lake Elsinore (California)	**2007:** Missoula (Pioneer)
2008: Columbus (International)	**2008:** Birmingham (Southern)	**2008:** Greensboro (South Atlantic)	**2008:** Greeneville (Appalachian)
2009: Iowa (Pacific Coast)	**2009:** New Hamshire (Eastern)	**2009:** San Jose (California)	**2009:** Tri-City (New York-Penn)
2010: Louisville (International)	**2010:** Corpus Christi (Texas)	**2010:** Lynchburg (Carolina)	**2010:** Idaho Falls (Pioneer)
2011: Colo. Springs (Pacific Coast)	**2011:** Harrisburg (Eastern)	**2011:** Fort Wayne (Midwest)	**2011:** Vancouver (Northwest)
2012: Lehigh Valley (International)	**2012:** N-West Arkansas (Texas)	**2012:** Greenville (South Atlantic)	**2012:** Billings (Pioneer)
2013: Indianapolis (International)	**2013:** Tulsa (Texas)	**2013:** Clearwater (Florida State)	**2013:** State College (NY-Penn)
2014: Charlotte (International)	**2014:** Montgomery (Southern)	**2014:** West Michigan (Midwest)	**2014:** Brooklyn (NY-Penn)
2015: Salt Lake (Pacific Coast)	**2015:** Richmond (Eastern)	**2015:** Myrtle Beach (Carolina)	**2015:** Grand Junction (Pioneer)
2016: Round Rock (Pacific Coast)	**2016:** Pensacola (Southern)	**2016:** San Bernardino (California)	**2016:** Pulaski (Appalachian)

ARIZONA FALL LEAGUE

BY BILL MITCHELL

Peoria Javelinas outfielder Ronald Acuña led the Arizona Fall League with 7 home runs, posted an outstanding .325/.414/.639 slash line, and received the Joe Black MVP Award as the league's top player prior to the AFL's annual championship game. All for a player who is just 19.

So what else could the Atlanta Braves top prospect and Baseball America's Minor League Player of the Year do to top his outstanding Fall League season? How about going 2-for-4 with four RBIs in the championship game to lead the Javelinas to an 8-2 victory over the Mesa Solar Sox? Acuña was certainly the biggest star of the game played at Scottsdale Stadium in front of 3,255 fans.

Peoria was heavily favored entering the championship game after capturing the West division with an 18-12 record. The Javelinas roster unquestionably contained the AFL's best collection of prospects and that strength showed in the win over East division champion Mesa.

With that impressive array of players at his disposal, Peoria manager Luis Salazar (Braves) didn't have to come up with an elaborate game plan.

"I didn't have any strategy for these guys," Salazar said. "They came here to play, to enjoy themselves and to have a great time. The main thing is that I gave the guys the confidence .... I never lost confidence in them even when we were down two runs."

Mesa got its only lead of the game in the top half of the first inning, jumping on Peoria starter T.J. Zeuch (Blue Jays) for two early runs when Mesa's first three hitters—Victor Robles (Nationals), Jaycob Brugman (Athletics) and Sheldon Neuse (Athletics)—all singled, followed by a sacrifice fly from Kody Eaves (Tigers). But a nifty double play started by Peoria shortstop Luis Urias (Padres) snuffed the rally.

Zeuch settled down after that first inning, using his four-pitch mix and 93-94 mph fastball to blank the Solar Sox hitters through the rest of his 5.2 innings.

Zeuch's pitches were a bit flat and he was getting his four-seam fastball up in the zone in the first inning, which got him into the early trouble.

"He made a lot of mistakes and he paid for it," Salazar said. "(After the first inning) he moved the ball around and kept the ball down."

After Peoria got on the board with one run in the bottom of the second inning on a Urias sacrifice fly, it was time for Acuña to go to work. His line-drive single to center tied the game in the bottom of the third and a bases-loaded single in the fourth knocked in a pair of runs to boost the Javelinas' lead to 6-2.

Salazar, who managed Acuña at Double-A Mississippi this year, was used to seeing Acuña come through in clutch situations.

"You don't see a young hitter like Acuña very often," Salazar said. "He's going to hit...in a clutch situation, I have 100 percent confidence in this guy."

Peoria added two more insurance runs in the bottom of the eighth on back-to-back triples by Jonathan Davis (Blue Jays) and Michael Chavis (Red Sox), followed by a sacrifice fly from Acuña.

Zeuch earned the win, with the loss going to Mesa starter Alec Mills (Cubs). Another key to the Peoria win was the outstanding work of relievers Andrew Case (Blue Jays), Andres Munoz (Padres) and Art Warren (Mariners), each of whom held the Solar Sox hitless over the last 3 1/3 innings.

Warren's performance capped an outstanding AFL season in which the 24-year-old right-hander didn't give up a run over 11.1 innings.

Mariners prospect Eric Filia was awarded the Arizona Fall League's Dernell Stenson Sportsmanship Award prior to the championship game. Named in memory of the former AFL player who was tragically murdered in 2003 while a member of the Scottsdale Scorpions, the award has been given annually since 2004 to the league's player who best exemplifies unselfishness, hard work and leadership.

Filia led all AFL hitters in batting average (.408), on-base percentage (.483), OPS (1.088) and reached base in each of his 22 games, while Austin Riley (Braves) topped all hitters with a .657 slugging percentage. Acuña led the league in home runs (7), Sheldon Neuse (Athletics) was tops in RBIs (23), and Victor Reyes (Diamondbacks) stole the most bases (12).

The AFL assignment was important for the 25-year-old Filia, who got a late start to his pro career after spending two years on the sidelines during his five seasons at UCLA, and he accomplished what he came to Arizona to do.

"Just coming out each and every day, playing hard and learning as much as I can," Filia said, adding that he got valuable experience at first base in order to add to his versatility.

Relievers Ryan Eades (Twins) and J.D. Hammer (Phillies) led all qualifying pitchers with identical 0.66 ERAs, while Max Fried (Braves) recorded the most strikeouts (32).

STANDINGS

East	W	L	PCT	GB
Mesa Solar Sox	16	13	0.552	—
Salt River Rafters	13	15	0.464	2 ½
Scottsdale Scorpions	12	17	0.414	4
West	**W**	**L**	**PCT**	**GB**
Peoria Javelinas	18	12	0.600	—
Glendale Desert Dogs	16	14	0.533	2
Surprise Saguaros	13	17	0.433	5

INDIVIDUAL BATTING LEADERS

(Minimum 2 Plate Appearances/League Games)

PLAYER	TEAM	AVG	G	AB	R	H	HR	RBI
Eric Filia	Peoria	.408	22	76	15	31	1	13
Nicky Lopez	Surprise	.383	20	81	15	31	2	10
Will Smith	Glendalde	.371	18	62	12	23	2	16
Francisco Mejia	Glendalde	.365	15	63	12	23	2	8
Andrew Knizner	Surprise	.358	17	67	8	24	3	12
Kevin Kaczmarski	Scottsdale	.351	20	77	12	27	1	11
Braxton Lee	Salt River	.347	20	75	9	26	0	7
Thairo Estrada	Scottsdale	.342	20	79	13	27	1	10
Kody Eaves	Mesa	.337	22	83	14	28	3	9
David Bote	Mesa	.333	19	69	13	23	4	14

INDIVIDUAL PITCHING LEADERS

(Minimum .4 Innings Pitched/League Games)

PLAYER	TEAM	W	L	ERA	IP	H	BB	SO
Ryan Eades	Surprise	2	0	0.66	13.2	14	3	13
J.D. Hammer	Glendalde	0	0	0.66	13.2	4	7	11
Kyle Regnault	Scottsdale	0	1	0.71	12.2	9	3	17
Andrew Vasquez	Surprise	0	0	1.42	12.2	9	5	14
Mitch Keller	Glendalde	4	0	1.52	23.2	19	5	13
Max Fried	Peoria	3	1	1.73	26	15	8	32
Kirby Bellow	Salt River	1	0	1.80	15	10	3	17
Mickey Jannis	Scottsdale	1	3	2.33	27	23	5	24
Andrew Sopko	Glendalde	2	2	2.37	19	18	7	11
Brandon Waddell	Glendalde	1	0	2.57	14	13	4	15

GLENDALE DESERT DOGS

NAME	AVG	AB	R	H	2B	3B	HR	RBI	BB	SO	SB
Beaty, Matt	.242	66	8	16	6	0	2	10	2	10	0
Bradley, Bobby	.230	74	10	17	2	1	2	6	2	32	0
Cabral, Edgar	.298	47	2	14	2	0	0	4	3	13	0
Diaz, Yusniel	.303	66	10	20	2	1	1	10	6	9	2
Green, Zach	.258	62	10	16	4	0	2	6	4	20	0
Hill, Logan	.239	67	8	16	5	1	2	14	8	18	1
Kramer, Kevin	.200	60	9	12	1	0	2	6	9	20	1
Krieger, Tyler	.175	57	3	10	6	0	0	3	6	18	0
Mejia, Francisco	.365	63	12	23	1	0	2	8	2	6	0
Mendick, Danny	.290	69	5	20	4	0	1	10	2	13	4
Peters, DJ	.190	42	8	8	2	1	3	7	4	20	1
Polo, Tito	.267	30	5	8	0	0	0	1	1	10	4
Randolph, Cornelius	.239	71	10	17	4	1	0	8	7	20	2
Smith, Will	.371	62	12	23	4	1	2	16	10	18	0
Tilson, Charlie	.188	32	4	6	2	0	0	4	7	7	1
Tolman, Mitchell	.197	61	6	12	5	0	1	6	8	18	0
Tom, Ka'ai	.275	40	10	11	3	0	2	3	10	15	0
Zavala, Seby	.326	46	7	15	2	0	1	7	6	11	0

NAME	W	L	ERA	G	GS	SV	IP	H	BB	SO	AVG
Anderson, Isaac	0	0	2.19	9	0	0	12.1	14	5	12	.292
Angulo, Argenis	0	1	9.00	9	0	0	8.0	11	10	8	.324
Bettencourt, Trevor	0	1	10.13	8	0	1	8.0	10	3	9	.294
Boyle, Michael	2	0	3.46	10	0	0	13.0	10	3	11	.213
Brady, Sean	2	1	2.78	6	6	0	22.2	22	5	16	.247
Brown, Aaron	0	0	3.00	3	0	0	3.0	5	2	2	.385
Brubaker, J.T.	0	1	2.63	8	0	0	13.2	15	2	16	.278
Cleavinger, Garrett	0	1	6.35	11	0	0	11.1	14	4	10	.311
Covey, Dylan	1	1	5.25	3	3	0	12.0	16	4	6	.333
Eubank, Luke	0	0	5.79	10	0	0	9.1	12	3	9	.333
Foster, Matt	1	1	7.94	9	0	0	11.1	20	1	8	.385
Fry, Jace	0	0	3.38	8	0	0	8.0	6	1	10	.207
Garcia, Elniery	1	2	5.79	4	4	0	14.0	15	4	13	.268
Hammer, J.D.	0	0	0.66	10	0	3	13.2	4	7	11	.093
Hearn, Taylor	2	0	3.06	8	4	0	17.2	14	8	14	.230
Keller, Mitch	4	0	1.52	6	6	0	23.2	19	5	13	.226
Linares, Leandro	0	0	6.43	7	0	0	7.0	12	3	2	.364
Sopko, Andrew	2	2	2.37	6	6	0	19.0	18	7	11	.250
Spitzbarth, Shea	0	0	4.91	10	0	1	11.0	11	2	19	.250
Waddell, Brandon	1	0	2.57	9	1	1	14.0	13	4	15	.236
Walsh, Connor	0	3	8.74	10	0	1	11.1	11	8	13	.250

MESA SOLAR SOX

NAME	AVG	AB	R	H	2B	3B	HR	RBI	BB	SO	SB
Alvarez, Yordan	.313	16	1	5	0	1	0	1	1	6	0
Bote, David	.333	69	13	23	2	0	4	14	5	14	1
Brugman, Jaycob	.182	33	4	6	2	0	0	2	8	8	1
Burks, Charcer	.236	72	12	17	7	0	0	7	8	19	2
Eaves, Kody	.337	83	14	28	5	2	3	9	6	23	1
Gibson, Cam	.200	75	8	15	5	1	0	10	9	24	4
Gushue, Taylor	.143	49	4	7	0	0	2	3	2	15	0
Gutierrez, Kelvin	.350	40	6	14	0	1	1	9	7	10	1
Johnson, Daniel	.217	69	10	15	3	1	0	5	5	11	5
Murphy, Sean	.309	68	8	21	4	0	0	9	10	7	0
Neuse, Sheldon	.314	86	20	27	7	0	5	23	7	16	0
Ramirez, Tyler	.059	17	4	1	0	0	1	1	3	6	0
Rice, Ian	.311	45	5	14	7	0	0	7	7	11	0
Robles, Victor	.244	41	10	10	1	0	3	7	10	9	7
Simcox, A.J.	.194	103	13	20	6	1	2	13	5	29	2
Tanielu, Nick	.000	5	0	0	0	0	0	0	0	2	0
Tucker, Kyle	.214	84	15	18	6	1	0	9	9	22	2
Vosler, Jason	.210	81	11	17	4	0	2	13	12	24	0

NAME	W	L	ERA	G	GS	SV	IP	H	BB	SO	AVG
Alzolay, Adbert	0	1	6.17	7	0	0	11.2	11	3	13	.244
Araujo, Pedro	0	0	1.74	9	0	3	10.1	5	2	15	.143
Bacus, Dakota	0	1	5.23	8	0	0	10.1	12	2	14	.279
Blackwood, Nolan	2	0	1.59	9	0	1	11.1	6	3	16	.146
Bragg, Sam	0	1	4.82	9	0	1	9.1	12	1	6	.308
Cordero, Jimmy	2	0	1.50	9	0	0	12.0	11	2	13	.244
Deetz, Dean	0	1	4.91	8	0	0	11.0	9	4	23	.214
Ecker, Mark	0	0	0.00	4	0	0	5.1	3	0	7	.167
Ferrell, Riley	1	0	4.66	9	0	0	9.2	6	9	7	.188
Houston, Zac	1	0	0.00	9	0	0	11.1	4	1	18	.105
McCurry, Brendan	0	1	4.05	5	0	0	6.2	6	3	5	.261
McGowin, Kyle	3	1	4.79	6	6	0	20.2	31	0	27	.352
Mills, Alec	1	3	3.91	6	6	0	23.0	26	6	20	.289
Moreno, Gerson	0	0	2.61	8	0	1	10.1	10	3	12	.250
Ravenelle, Adam	0	0	7.94	5	0	0	5.2	7	2	4	.304
Romero, Miguel	1	0	7.59	9	0	0	10.2	20	3	7	.392
Shore, Logan	1	1	6.00	6	6	0	24.0	35	2	18	.343
Stinnett, Jake	0	0	1.80	7	0	0	10.0	6	3	14	.182
Turnbull, Spencer	2	2	3.74	6	6	0	21.2	25	6	19	.284
Valdez, Framber	1	1	3.20	6	6	0	19.2	24	8	14	.300
Williams, Austen	1	0	10.67	9	0	0	14.1	23	3	13	.371

PEORIA JAVELINAS

NAME	AVG	AB	R	H	2B	3B	HR	RBI	BB	SO	SB
Acuna, Ronald	.325	83	22	27	5	0	7	16	12	22	2
Bishop, Braden	.232	56	12	13	2	1	0	6	4	13	2
Chavis, Michael	.261	92	17	24	6	1	4	17	7	20	0
Davis, Jonathan	.295	78	15	23	6	0	1	13	9	15	7
De La Guerra, Chad	.255	51	7	13	1	1	2	8	4	13	0
DeCarlo, Joe	.130	23	2	3	0	0	0	2	1	6	0
Filia, Eric	.408	76	15	31	4	4	1	13	12	7	0
Guerra, Javier	.261	46	7	12	1	1	1	5	3	13	0
Gurriel, Lourdes	.291	79	10	23	7	0	3	11	1	11	2
Jackson, Alex	.263	80	15	21	5	0	5	16	4	23	0
James, Jared	.250	48	7	12	2	2	0	2	8	9	0
Lewis, Kyle	.375	8	3	3	2	0	0	1	1	1	0
Naylor, Josh	.304	79	10	24	6	0	3	14	3	14	2
Pentecost, Max	.195	41	5	8	1	0	1	4	4	17	1
Reyes, Franmil	.167	30	3	5	1	1	1	4	0	7	0
Riley, Austin	.300	70	11	21	5	1	6	18	4	21	1
Tobias, Josh	.261	46	6	12	2	0	0	5	3	13	0
Urias, Luis	.315	54	11	17	5	2	0	9	14	5	0

NAME	W	L	ERA	G	GS	SV	IP	H	BB	SO	AVG
Bednar, David	1	0	1.13	7	0	0	8.0	1	0	7	.040
Buttrey, Ty	0	0	2.16	7	0	1	8.1	9	3	10	.250

NAME	W	L	ERA	G	GS	SV	IP	H	BB	SO	AVG
Case, Andrew	2	0	0.00	8	0	1	10.0	8	1	6	.205
Clouse, Corbin	0	1	7.36	9	0	0	11.0	11	6	15	.244
Festa, Matthew	0	0	7.88	8	0	0	8.0	10	5	11	.303
Fried, Max	3	1	1.73	6	6	0	26.0	15	8	32	.163
Gillies, Darin	0	0	6.14	7	0	0	7.1	10	4	7	.323
Graham, Josh	0	0	6.97	9	0	0	10.1	16	2	11	.356
Keel, Jerry	1	0	4.91	8	2	0	14.2	17	7	11	.298
Lockett, Walker	2	1	5.40	6	6	0	25.0	30	9	22	.294
McAvoy, Kevin	0	0	6.30	8	0	0	10.0	9	8	6	.250
McClelland, Jackson	0	0	7.20	8	0	1	10.0	13	2	8	.317
Munoz, Andres	0	0	1.04	9	0	0	8.2	4	2	11	.138
Owens, Henry	3	3	8.86	6	6	0	21.1	24	13	15	.304
Povse, Max	1	2	4.56	6	6	0	25.2	28	6	25	.280
Poyner, Bobby	0	1	3.60	7	0	0	10.0	10	1	10	.263
Toussaint, Touki	1	1	10.38	8	0	0	8.2	7	7	14	.212
Warren, Art	3	0	0.00	9	0	3	11.1	5	4	12	.132
Weir, T.J.	0	0	1.59	5	0	1	5.2	4	0	5	.190
Young, Danny	0	1	16.43	8	0	0	7.2	21	3	7	.500
Zeuch, T.J.	1	1	3.44	5	4	0	18.1	14	4	15	.212

SALT RIVER RAFTERS

NAME	AVG	AB	R	H	2B	3B	HR	RBI	BB	SO	SB
Daza, Yonathan	.318	66	14	21	2	1	0	6	1	9	11
Erceg, Lucas	.250	52	4	13	3	1	1	5	2	14	0
Gatewood, Jake	.095	42	4	4	1	0	0	1	6	18	2
Harrison, Monte	.283	53	12	15	2	0	5	14	4	20	5
Lee, Braxton	.347	75	9	26	2	1	0	7	4	14	8
Mooney, Peter	.278	72	7	20	2	0	0	5	4	9	2
Mountcastle, Ryan	.244	82	11	20	4	0	3	14	4	19	2
Mundell, Brian	.262	84	11	22	4	1	1	8	16	11	2
Nunez, Dom	.091	44	3	4	2	0	0	1	1	12	0
Perez, Michael	.208	53	1	11	1	0	0	5	4	13	0
Ray, Corey	.231	78	11	18	4	0	1	7	8	19	6
Reinheimer, Jack	.324	68	11	22	3	1	0	2	9	15	0
Reyes, Victor	.316	79	8	25	3	2	0	9	2	12	12
Santander, Anthony	.208	72	8	15	4	1	1	15	2	18	1
Vigil, Rodrigo	.417	24	2	10	4	0	1	7	1	1	0
Wilkerson, Steve	.317	82	15	26	3	5	1	10	9	14	2

NAME	W	L	ERA	G	GS	SV	IP	H	BB	SO	AVG
Akin, Keegan	1	1	2.76	9	1	0	16.1	10	5	13	.169
Almonte, Yency	0	1	6.97	9	0	0	10.1	18	8	12	.383
Atkinson, Ryan	1	2	3.00	6	6	0	21.0	19	15	23	.247
Bellow, Kirby	1	0	1.80	11	0	0	15.0	10	3	17	.189
Broyles, Shane	0	0	2.25	8	0	3	8.0	8	3	7	.267
Del Pozo, Miguel	0	0	8.76	10	0	0	12.1	14	7	9	.286
Farris, James	0	0	11.57	9	0	0	9.1	16	4	9	.381
Gonzalez, Luis	2	0	0.00	9	0	1	9.2	5	2	6	.152
Griep, Nate	0	0	5.40	11	0	1	11.2	14	4	12	.292
Houser, Adrian	1	1	3.38	4	4	0	10.2	13	2	11	.317
Jemiola, Zach	2	1	2.74	6	6	0	23.0	22	9	19	.265
Liranzo, Jesus	0	0	11.57	4	0	0	4.2	7	6	3	.350
Lopez, Yoan	0	0	0.00	3	0	0	3.0	5	0	3	.357
Meisinger, Ryan	1	0	0.00	4	0	0	6.0	1	0	0	.056
Meyer, Ben	0	3	4.11	10	0	0	15.1	20	5	18	.303
Needy, James	1	0	4.67	6	4	0	17.1	17	7	17	.258
Ortega, Jorge	0	1	8.53	6	0	0	6.1	13	3	2	.394
Perrin, Jon	2	1	4.70	9	3	0	15.1	19	8	10	.306
Poche, Colin	1	0	3.31	11	0	0	16.1	11	8	21	.183
Scott, Tanner	0	2	12.54	5	3	0	9.1	11	11	7	.297
Squier, Scott	0	2	5.40	9	3	0	15.0	16	6	9	.281
Torres-Costa, Quintin	0	0	4.50	10	0	0	14.0	18	5	16	.321

SCOTTSDALE SCORPIONS

NAME	AVG	AB	R	H	2B	3B	HR	RBI	BB	SO	SB
Bell, Brantley	.215	65	6	14	3	0	0	6	2	25	3
Duggar, Steven	.263	76	17	20	3	0	3	7	12	21	9
Estrada, Thairo	.342	79	13	27	2	1	1	10	3	19	3
Florial, Estevan	.286	70	14	20	5	2	0	4	10	29	2
Garcia, Aramis	.259	54	4	14	1	0	1	12	1	15	0
Guillorme, Luis	.289	45	4	13	3	0	0	3	3	1	0
Holder, Kyle	.333	45	5	15	3	1	1	6	2	4	0
Kaczmarski, Kevin	.351	77	12	27	4	0	1	11	5	20	2
McKinney, Billy	.279	68	8	19	5	1	1	20	11	16	1
Montgomery, Troy	.231	78	14	18	2	3	0	10	6	20	3
Nido, Tomas	.184	49	3	9	4	0	1	7	5	13	0
Shaw, Chris	.158	19	1	3	0	0	0	0	3	2	0
Sparks, Taylor	.274	73	11	20	1	1	4	15	4	33	3
Thaiss, Matt	.266	64	11	17	3	1	0	7	11	24	4
Thompson, David	.328	58	11	19	7	2	1	5	4	11	1
Trahan, Blake	.231	52	5	12	1	0	0	3	7	10	4
Tromp, Chadwick	.316	38	3	12	1	0	1	4	1	7	0
Ward, Taylor	.000	4	0	0	0	0	0	0	0	2	0
Wass, Wade	.042	24	0	1	0	0	0	0	1	14	0

NAME	W	L	ERA	G	GS	SV	IP	H	BB	SO	AVG
Abreu, Albert	1	2	2.60	6	6	0	27.2	21	14	23	.219
Bates, Nathan	2	1	2.38	8	0	0	11.1	10	1	7	.250
Bautista, Wendolyn	0	2	9.82	6	6	0	22.0	34	6	11	.362
Beede, Tyler	0	1	4.50	4	4	0	16.0	16	4	11	.267
Bender, Joel	0	0	7.59	8	0	0	10.2	14	9	7	.341
Bernardino, Brennan	0	1	0.90	6	0	0	10.0	6	3	7	.171
Carroll, Cody	0	0	0.00	9	0	4	11.2	2	5	18	.056
Cyr, Tyler	0	1	5.63	8	0	0	8.0	8	2	5	.250
De Los Santos, Samil	2	0	13.94	7	0	0	10.1	14	12	5	.326
Ehret, Jake	1	1	1.74	7	0	0	10.1	6	5	13	.182
Gregorio, Joan	1	0	5.87	8	3	0	15.1	19	5	9	.311
Hofacket, Adam	1	1	15.63	5	0	0	6.1	12	3	6	.387
Jannis, Mickey	1	3	2.33	6	6	0	27.0	23	5	24	.223
Lillis-White, Conor	0	0	13.50	1	0	0	0.2	3	3	2	.600
Peterson, Tim	1	0	0.87	7	0	0	10.1	6	2	6	.171
Pobereyko, Matt	0	0	0.00	8	0	1	11.2	7	1	13	.175
Regnault, Kyle	0	1	0.71	8	0	1	12.2	9	3	17	.196
Schwaab, Andrew	0	1	6.35	9	0	0	11.1	14	7	8	.326
Sheffield, Justus	2	2	3.10	5	5	0	20.1	14	3	22	.192
Snelten, D.J.	0	0	2.25	8	0	0	12.0	9	5	11	.209

SURPRISE SAGUAROS

NAME	AVG	AB	R	H	2B	3B	HR	RBI	BB	SO	SB
Dini, Nick	.211	38	6	8	1	0	0	6	5	3	0
Hernandez, Elier	.206	68	10	14	4	0	1	6	7	16	0
Knizner, Andrew	.358	67	8	24	3	0	3	12	4	11	0
La O, Luis	.196	51	3	10	1	0	2	7	3	4	0
Lopez, Nicky	.383	81	15	31	5	2	2	10	7	14	3
Lowe, Brandon	.224	58	13	13	3	1	2	5	9	14	1
Mercado, Oscar	.264	87	9	23	5	0	0	11	14	18	6
Miller, Sean	.255	55	7	14	1	0	0	7	3	10	2
Morgan, Josh	.429	28	3	12	1	0	2	7	5	3	0
Nogowski, John	.188	32	4	6	4	0	0	2	3	7	0
O'Neill, Michael	.286	70	12	20	6	0	2	12	3	14	4
Padlo, Kevin	.259	85	14	22	3	2	0	14	8	22	1
Paul, Chris	.292	72	15	21	3	1	2	10	3	20	0
Perez, Yanio	.301	83	13	25	5	0	2	9	6	22	0
Sosa, Edmundo	.305	59	10	18	1	1	0	7	3	12	0
Sullivan, Brett	.313	48	6	15	3	2	0	11	4	5	0
Wade, LaMonte	.238	63	8	15	3	1	2	8	9	10	1

NAME	W	L	ERA	G	GS	SV	IP	H	BB	SO	AVG
Alcantara, Sandy	1	2	4.20	5	5	0	15.0	11	8	14	.208
Bodner, Jacob	0	1	4.22	11	0	2	10.2	10	4	9	.244
Bruce, Steven	0	1	6.00	1	1	0	3.0	8	0	2	.500
Choplick, Adam	1	1	4.50	10	0	1	12.0	11	7	6	.244
Davis, Tyler	2	0	4.50	5	5	0	14.0	14	1	4	.250
Dykstra, James	0	0	0.00	4	0	0	5.0	3	0	5	.167
Eades, Ryan	2	0	0.66	10	1	0	13.2	14	3	13	.259
Ferguson, Tyler	0	1	6.35	9	0	0	11.1	16	6	6	.333
Hackimer, Tom	0	1	2.31	10	0	0	11.2	8	7	10	.200
Hicks, Jordan	0	2	6.32	9	1	0	15.2	20	6	16	.323
Jay, Tyler	0	0	5.59	10	0	0	9.2	13	5	11	.325
Jones, Spencer	0	0	8.03	9	0	0	12.1	15	5	11	.313
Ledbetter, David	2	0	2.00	3	3	0	9.0	7	1	5	.206
Lovvorn, Zach	1	1	6.43	6	6	0	21.0	29	7	14	.319
Lucas, Josh	1	2	5.25	12	0	1	12.0	14	3	13	.298
Moss, Benton	0	1	3.18	5	2	0	11.1	15	1	7	.319
Ramirez, Roel	0	1	10.24	9	0	0	9.2	19	4	7	.422
Reyes, Arturo	0	0	6.23	10	0	1	13.0	18	2	12	.340
Ruxer, Jared	1	0	3.75	9	0	0	12.0	10	9	12	.227
Smith, Burch	1	2	3.98	6	6	0	20.1	12	11	29	.176
Tenuta, Matt	1	1	6.39	10	0	0	12.2	17	3	11	.309
Vasquez, Andrew	0	0	1.42	11	0	0	12.2	9	5	14	.191

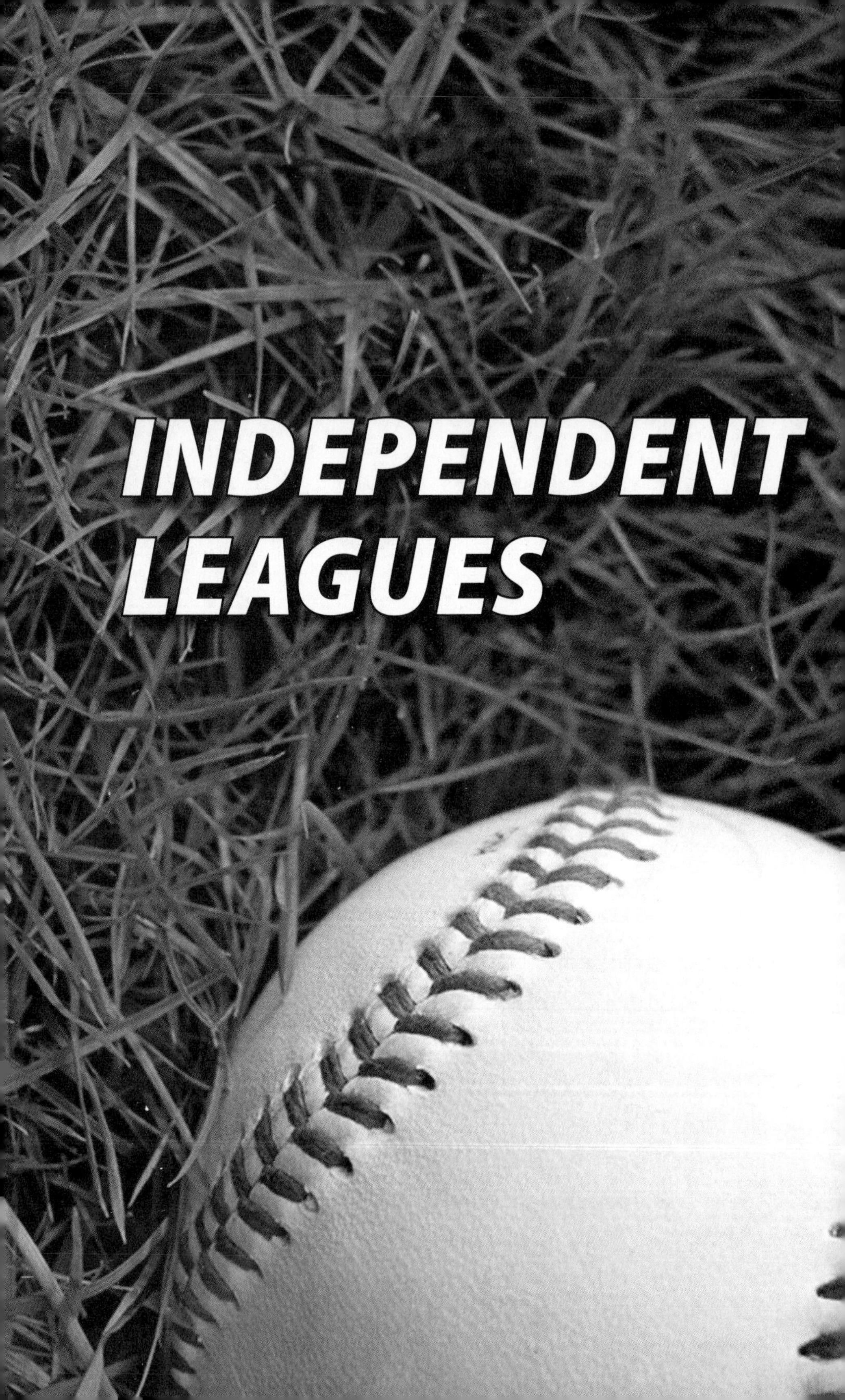

INDEPENDENT LEAGUES

Indy Leagues Swap Growth for Stability

Independent baseball in 2017 is on a treadmill.

It's a nice, reliable treadmill, but no matter how hard the indy leagues run to get ahead, they end up in about the same spot where they started.

The four longest-lived independent leagues–the Atlantic, American Association, Can-Am and Frontier Leagues–all draw roughly the same amount of fans from year to year. This year, the four leagues announced attendance of 5.86 million fans in 2017. That's the lowest announced attendance for the four leagues since 2010, but it's also just 30,000 fewer fans than last year's attendance. This decade the big four have peaked at 6.65 millon in attendance in 2012 and have slowly seen some erosion since then. The leagues actually average more fans per team, but there are less franchises than there were five years ago.

Next year, the American Association will add the Chicago Dogs in a brand new stadium in Rosemont, Ill. The new team fits perfectly in the geography of the league and should be an excellent draw.

But it's arrival was needed to avoid fielding a travel team, as it helps the league replace the losses of Joplin and Amarillo in recent years.

While Rosemont is arriving, the city of Wichita has announced an attempt to build a new stadium to bring an affiliated team to town. If they are successful, it would leave the league's Wichita Wingnuts homeless. Wichita's arrival into the league in 2008 was a big addition, but in part the Wingnuts helped cover the loss of the Coastal Bend Aviators, which were pushed out by the arrival of the affiliated Corpus Christi Hooks.

When the Atlantic League added the Sugar Land Skeeters in 2010, the team was supposed to be part of a four-team expansion into Texas. Eight seasons later, the Skeeters remain a solid draw, but they also remain the only Texas team in a league otherwise based on the Eastern seaboard.

That's the state of indy ball in its third decade. At its upper levels, there's plenty of stability. But nowadays it's also somewhat static. New markets help replace failing markets, but any idea of significant expansion, something that was often a topic of discussion a decade ago, has been replaced by the idea of maintaining.

Below the big four, the Pecos League, Pacific Association and United States Professional Baseball League have also found some stability in different ways.

York's Alonzo Harris is 2017 Independent Leagues Player of the Year.

The USPBL expanded to four teams playing at a lone stadium in 2017 while the Pecos League added California League refugees Bakersfield and High Desert. The Pacific Association has managed to survive year after year in the difficult California market despite modest attendance figures.

The Empire Professional Baseball League returned for a second season in 2017 while the new Thoroughbred League debuted, although it did so with no official statistics.

INDEPENDENT ATTENDANCE, 2017

Announced attendance for the four largest independent leagues.

LEAGUE	TOTAL ATTENDANCE	AVERAGE
American Association	2,071,325	3,945
Atlantic League	1,866,910	3,322
Frontier League	1,288,542	2,373
Can-Am League	631,144	2,111

INDEPENDENT LEAGUES

York's Harris Adds Power To His Speedy Resume

PLAYER OF THE YEAR

The York Revolution rolled to the Atlantic League title with a roster filled with big names.

There were former big leaguers like Alexi Casilla and Jose Arredondo and former top prospects in Joel Guzman, Carlos Triunfel and Jared Mitchell.

But the best player on the team and the best player in the Atlantic League was a 39th-round draft pick of the Mets who never made it above Double-A in affiliated ball.

Alonzo Harris had been released by the Mets in 2013. He made an 11-game cameo with the Marlins high Class A team in 2014 before beginning his life in indy ball.

And in the process, he's turned himself into a much better player than the one he was in affiliated ball.

Harris hit for New Jersey in the Can-Am League. He then moved on to the American Association's St. Paul Saints, where he hit for average and power. Jumping up to the Atlantic League this year, he proved to be the league's best player, hitting .315/.381/.530 while leading the Revolution to the Atlantic League title.

For all that, Harris is Baseball America's 2017 Independent Leagues Player of the Year. He led the Atlantic League in runs (89), finished fourth in home runs (23), sixth in steals (31), eighth in RBIs (73) and second in slugging percentage.

"I say some players have six tools. He has six tools because he's a good guy too. He's a good clubhouse guy. He can run. He has a strong arm. He can hit for average. He can hit for power. And he can play multiple positions," York manager Mark Mason said.

"Not many guys you can hit leadoff who can hit 20-30 home runs. He can bunt for a hit in one at-bat and then hit the next one over the center field fence."

It's that newly developed power that gives a pretty good argument for Harris, 28, to get another try at affiliated ball. In parts of five seasons in full season leagues in affiliated ball, Harris hit 21 home runs. He's hit 15, 15 and 23 in his past three years in indy ball.

As Harris sees it, the speed has always been there and so has the power, but it's been in the past few years that he's learned how to use his hands in a way that allows him to drive the ball more often.

"It's all about quick hands. When you learn how to use your hands, it's as simple as that. With the Mets, I hit home runs but not a lot of home runs like the last three years. I always had a little power, but the Mets, they didn't want me to...I had an aggressive swing. They thought I was trying to hit it over the fence at all times," Harris said. "They thought I was trying to hit home runs, but I've been swinging like this since coach pitch. The power numbers, I guess it's daddy strength now. I've got two kids."

Harris says he still has the near top of the scale speed that he had when he was younger to go with his newfound ability to drive the ball over the wall.

He also showed plenty of versatility this season. Harris played 44 games at second base, 37 games in left field, 16 in center field and 14 in right field, as he bounced around to wherever the Revolution needed someone on that night.

Harris' best fit is in the outfield–he has the speed to run down balls in the gaps in center–but he's equally adept in either corner outfield spot. But with the Revolution needing someone who could also move into the dirt, Harris was happy to dodge baserunners while turning double plays. It just meant he spent extra time ensuring that his arm handled the wear and tear of moving back and forth between the infield and outfield.

"He's just a good team guy. He's someone who says 'I'll do whatever you need me to do,'" Mason said.

PREVIOUS WINNERS

2007: Darryl Brinkley, OF, Calgary (Northern)
2008: Patrick Breen, OF, Orange County (Golden)
2009: Greg Porter, OF, Wichita (American Association)
2010: Beau Torbert, OF, Sioux Falls (American Association)
2011: Chris Collabello, 1B, Worcester (Can-Am League)
2012: Blake Gailen, OF, Lancaster (Atlantic)
2013: C.J. Ziegler, 1B, Wichita (American Association)
2014: Balbino Fuenmayor, 1B, Quebec (Can-Am League)
2015: Joe Maloney, OF, Rockland (Can-Am League)
2016: Art Charles, 1B, New Jersey (Can-Am League)
Full list: BaseballAmerica.com/awards

AMERICAN ASSOCIATION

The final game of Winnipeg's second straight championship was anti-climatic. Winnipeg beat Wichita 18-2 in the deciding Game 5. Shawn Pleffner hit for the cycle in Game 5. Goldeyes starter Edwin Carl got the Game 5 win.

While the final game was anti-climatic, there was plenty of drama before then. Winnipeg needed 17 innings to beat Wichita, 4-3, to stay alive in Game 4. Winnipeg had also rallied from one-run down to beat Lincoln with back-to-back bases loaded walks to clinch the semifinals series win.

With the title, Winnipeg has become the first American Association team to win back-to-back titles in the decade since Fort Worth won titles in 2006 and 2007. Winnipeg also won the title in 2012. All three of those titles have come under the leadership of manager Rick Forney.

STANDINGS

NORTH DIVISION	W	L	PCT	GB
Winnipeg Goldeyes	62	38	.620	—
Fargo-Moorhead RedHawks	57	43	.570	5
St Paul Saints	48	52	.480	14
Sioux Falls Canaries	45	55	.450	17
CENTRAL DIVISION	**W**	**L**	**PCT**	**GB**
Lincoln Saltdogs	58	41	.586	—
Gary SouthShore RailCats	57	43	.570	1 ½
Kansas City T-Bones	57	43	.570	1 ½
Sioux City Explorers	46	54	.460	12 ½
SOUTH DIVISION	**W**	**L**	**PCT**	**GB**
Wichita Wingnuts	61	38	.616	—
Cleburne Railroaders	47	53	.470	14 ½
Texas AirHogs	43	57	.430	18 ½
Salina Stockade	18	82	.180	43 ½

Playoffs: Semifinals—Wichita defeated Gary 3-0 and WInnipeg defeated Lincoln 3-1 in best-of-5 series. **Finals**—Winnipeg defeated Wichita 3-2 in best-of-5 series.

Attendance: St Paul 406,501; Winnipeg 219,556; Kansas City 211,599; Gary SouthShore 181,612; Fargo-Moorhead 176,086; Lincoln 172,712; Wichita 157,995; Sioux Falls 113,506; Cleburne 103,264; Texas 65,672; Sioux City 58,407.

All-Star Team: C: Martin Medina, Wichita. **1B:** Matt Chavez, Wichita. **2B:** Cesar Valera, Lincoln. **3B:** Wes Darvill, Winnipeg. **SS:** Andrew Sohn, Winnipeg. **OF:** Josh Romanski, Winnipeg; Anthony Gallas, St. Paul and Richard Prigatano, Wichita. **DH:** David Bergin, Winnipeg.

Player of the Year: Josh Romanski, Winnipeg. **Pitcher Of The Year:** Tyler Alexander, Fargo-Moorhead. **Relief Pitcher Of The Year:** Cody Winiarski, Kansas City. **Defensive Player Of The Year:** Tony Campana, Sioux City. **Manager Of The Year:** Bobby Brown, Lincoln. **Rookie Of The Year:** Colin Walsh, Gary.

INDIVIDUAL BATTING LEADERS

PLAYER, TEAM	AVG	AB	R	H	HR	RBI	SB
Shawn Pleffner, Winnipeg	.340	391	61	133	10	76	0
Matt Chavez, Wichita	.330	330	55	109	17	84	0
Cesar Valera, Lincoln	.327	391	70	128	4	52	9
Josh Romanski, Winnipeg	.324	404	74	131	11	81	10
David Bergin, Winnipeg	.323	365	74	118	20	77	0
Curt Smith, Lincoln	.322	348	56	112	11	62	3
Colin Willis, Gary	.319	301	54	96	8	49	15
Brady Shoemaker, St. Paul	.318	305	71	97	21	57	1
Richard Prigatano, Wichita	.316	339	67	107	8	61	34
Denis Phipps, Texas	.314	315	38	99	10	58	6

INDIVIDUAL PITCHING LEADERS

PITCHER, TEAM	W	L	ERA	IP	H	BB	SO
Bennett Parry, Lincoln	3	2	1.93	79	71	27	62
Tyler Alexander, F-M	8	6	2.07	148	112	51	167
Kevin McGovern, Winnipeg	13	3	2.56	144	115	45	118
Grady Wood, Sioux Falls	8	3	2.71	133	108	24	117
Tyler Herron, F-M	9	3	2.92	108	96	27	95
Scott Carroll, Kansas City	8	3	2.94	98	83	17	78
Ryan Kussmaul, Wichita	5	5	3.06	82	63	16	97
Charlie Rosario, Winnipeg	11	5	3.06	159	148	40	132
Eddie Medina, Wichita	9	3	3.09	90	81	25	68
Jared Mortensen, Kansas City	8	1	3.29	82	79	25	77

CLEBURNE RAILROADERS

PLAYER	AVG	AB	R	H	HR	RBI	BB	SO	SB	CS
Pyles, D	.360	86	6	31	2	19	5	6	0	1
Van Stratten, N	.313	147	20	46	1	20	19	12	7	1
Ahart, D	.308	52	9	16	0	7	2	15	0	3
Glasser, M	.282	347	70	98	3	33	41	40	18	5
Zarraga, S	.272	136	18	37	3	17	22	20	4	1
Gonzalez, M	.268	380	63	102	4	27	64	58	30	9
Mesa, O	.268	112	13	30	1	10	15	26	6	4
Balet, P	.265	136	10	36	0	20	4	23	0	0
Valentin, G	.263	373	33	98	4	69	25	38	2	1
Grant-Parks, B	.261	157	15	41	1	18	11	33	0	0
Escobar, E	.256	125	11	32	1	8	12	24	0	1
Johnson, A	.251	263	23	66	2	26	22	43	12	5
Abeita, M	.250	80	5	20	0	4	7	12	0	0
Huth, K	.236	318	30	75	3	38	17	57	11	5
Polston, A	.212	241	25	51	3	21	37	70	5	3
Courson, H	.194	72	9	14	1	4	5	12	0	0
Land, J	.185	27	2	5	0	1	3	9	0	0
Tierney, B	.184	163	20	30	2	8	10	27	2	0

PLAYER	W	L	ERA	G	SV	IP	H	BB	SO
Upperman, C	2	2	2.18	35	0	37	27	18	31
Abreu, W	2	0	2.83	40	25	41	27	12	56
Cox, C	4	2	2.96	37	0	52	43	19	66
Hodges, J	3	2	3.08	6	0	35	32	17	21
Mincey, P	10	8	3.32	21	0	138	135	21	81
Beeler, B	1	0	3.32	23	0	46	40	13	33
Rodriguez, A	5	7	3.38	21	0	98	85	51	95
Mathis, W	1	1	3.54	11	0	20	17	6	24
Galbraith, L	3	2	3.88	9	0	44	47	13	16
Quintero, B	0	1	4.23	4	0	17	23	6	24
Mouzakes, D	5	6	4.38	17	0	82	97	37	71
Misell, C	2	1	4.41	22	0	37	41	17	37
Arias, S	2	4	4.45	7	0	36	36	11	36
Martinez, J	2	6	4.50	13	0	66	67	23	57
Lee, H	1	3	5.82	16	0	56	62	30	35
Farfan, O	3	4	5.83	26	0	42	47	25	28
Perez, W	1	1	6.27	5	0	14	18	11	8
Chudacoff, J	0	1	10.50	6	0	12	18	7	9

FARGO-MOORHEAD REDHAWKS

PLAYER	AVG	AB	R	H	HR	RBI	BB	SO	SB	CS
DeLuca, J	.367	30	5	11	1	6	5	12	0	0
Ahart, D	.292	315	60	92	8	30	31	59	11	7
Grayson, C	.290	221	32	64	5	41	24	47	26	10
Medina, Y	.279	337	44	94	2	27	29	39	8	4
Valerio, C	.275	324	46	89	12	47	35	51	1	2
Kang, K	.270	356	54	96	11	50	46	95	1	2
Tierney, B	.265	151	13	40	2	11	8	30	1	1
Posso, J	.257	105	12	27	1	10	9	24	0	0
De La Cruz, K	.249	225	27	56	9	35	18	38	8	4
Mazzola, J	.239	360	54	86	15	57	47	111	5	2
Adams, T	.230	204	34	47	9	30	17	59	9	3
Delfino, M	.225	160	16	36	5	18	14	37	2	0
Schwartz, M	.211	38	5	8	0	2	9	5	0	0
Fox, D	.205	127	10	26	0	5	12	29	4	2
Pineda, R	.195	118	20	23	6	16	12	37	2	1
Carter, K	.192	120	16	23	5	18	21	42	2	0
Bryan, V	.182	33	3	6	1	3	3	14	1	1
Wiley, B	.150	40	5	6	0	3	12	14	2	0

PLAYER	W	L	ERA	G	SV	IP	H	BB	SO
Alexander, T	8	6	2.06	21	0	148	112	51	167
Prendergast, Z	2	0	2.07	4	0	26	18	8	25
Herron, T	9	3	2.91	15	0	108	96	27	95

	W	L	ERA	G	SV	IP	H	BB	SO
Tate, R	3	3	2.97	25	3	33	40	17	39
Pimentel, C	5	1	3.37	6	0	37	34	12	29
Almarante, J	6	7	3.78	21	0	133	141	36	118
Weathers, C	4	2	3.89	34	18	37	28	26	57
Solomon, W	5	5	4.47	24	2	105	113	40	69
ONeal, M	2	3	4.54	6	0	38	44	15	19
Stirewalt, T	1	2	4.67	3	0	17	17	8	9
McNutt, T	4	3	5.10	38	4	42	45	28	46
Thompson, T	4	3	5.17	37	1	49	63	18	46
Dennis, W	0	0	5.29	20	0	34	44	11	21
Mouzakes, D	2	2	5.89	4	0	18	21	8	14
Pacillo, A	1	1	6.27	22	0	14	16	11	9
Waite, B	0	2	8.71	3	0	10	13	8	8
McPartland, C	1	0	9.25	3	0	12	15	6	4

GARY SOUTHSHORE RAILCATS

PLAYER	AVG	AB	R	H	HR	RBI	BB	SO	SB	CS
Cheky Jr., A	.354	113	24	40	1	19	9	10	6	1
Willis, C	.319	301	54	96	8	49	43	54	15	3
Crosby, A	.291	244	26	71	3	24	22	42	6	5
Del Valle, J	.283	46	0	13	0	7	4	12	0	0
Martinez, F	.275	313	39	86	2	66	37	47	5	0
Sullivan, T	.275	40	2	11	0	3	1	9	1	1
Holland, J	.271	140	16	38	0	10	21	26	10	0
Newell, C	.264	193	35	51	2	19	23	28	2	0
Harris, C	.263	304	44	80	5	29	26	86	27	7
Fabio, C	.260	77	8	20	0	7	12	13	3	1
Santiesteban, R	.257	210	22	54	2	25	24	37	4	1
DeJesus, A	.254	228	25	58	2	19	11	61	9	2
Havrilak, J	.250	40	6	10	0	5	6	3	1	0
Goodman, K	.246	244	36	60	5	33	24	79	13	6
Fitzgerald, R	.239	289	39	69	7	20	23	64	8	2
Wilson, R	.239	272	40	65	0	17	52	70	14	3
Gimenez, W	.226	195	15	44	2	25	11	23	0	0
Gonzalez, J	.197	61	6	12	0	5	7	20	0	0
Alfonso, J	.133	60	4	8	0	5	3	16	0	0

PLAYER	W	L	ERA	G	SV	IP	H	BB	SO
Minor, D	3	1	1.47	7	0	37	20	6	41
Myers, S	2	0	1.65	11	1	16	11	1	16
De Leon, J	9	2	1.74	33	10	52	43	10	46
Johnson, D	4	4	2.25	34	12	44	44	7	36
Pautsch, M	1	0	3.15	4	0	20	22	3	8
Galbraith, L	0	0	3.37	9	0	13	13	6	3
Gunn, A	8	5	3.47	25	0	153	182	25	100
Rosario, C	8	5	3.65	19	0	118	118	28	89
McKenzie, J	4	4	3.72	14	0	77	80	17	42
Diaz, C	2	1	3.82	21	4	42	25	17	63
Mathys, J	0	1	3.85	20	0	33	32	7	31
Pinales, C	0	1	3.85	22	1	33	37	11	17
Pratt, J	1	3	3.97	8	0	11	11	5	5
Misell, C	0	1	4.09	7	0	11	12	5	10
Fowler, J	0	1	4.44	18	0	28	29	8	24
Harris, T	0	1	4.50	5	0	14	17	4	9
Torres-Perez, B	5	3	5.57	15	0	63	76	28	48
Costa, A	2	4	6.46	10	0	47	65	12	21
Fritze, R	5	1	7.89	19	1	22	20	17	19

KANSAS CITY T-BONES

PLAYER	AVG	AB	R	H	HR	RBI	BB	SO	SB	CS
Pennell, T	.393	28	9	11	1	3	4	6	0	0
Kjerstad, D	.379	66	15	25	0	6	1	9	1	0
Hunter, C	.360	175	32	63	9	29	19	13	5	2
Walters, Z	.347	75	14	26	6	20	3	7	0	0
Lemon, M	.294	402	60	118	8	45	26	48	3	0
Keyes, K	.294	364	69	107	24	81	61	95	4	0
Petty, K	.264	261	48	69	10	39	29	62	9	1
Jackson, J	.264	178	24	47	6	22	13	30	2	0
McDonald, C	.259	112	13	29	4	15	5	30	1	0
Edgerton, J	.255	259	29	66	7	33	18	63	8	1
Rojas, L	.251	171	23	43	5	24	10	54	0	0
Player	AVG	AB	R	H	HR	RBI	BB	SO	SB	CS
Mack, C	.247	292	38	72	10	48	54	68	3	1
Chavez, Z	.237	118	15	28	2	8	13	12	0	1
Brady, P	.231	91	9	21	1	8	10	22	0	1
Horan, T	.229	118	14	27	5	14	12	33	0	0
Garcia, O	.220	168	28	37	0	12	16	27	12	2
Rockett, D	.220	50	6	11	1	5	5	11	0	0
Correa, C	.214	28	3	6	1	5	3	8	0	0
Vasquez, N	.204	49	8	10	4	12	3	10	0	0
Newton, E	.187	166	19	31	1	11	12	44	1	0
Pena, J	.169	130	18	22	4	15	19	49	1	0
Caldwell, T	.167	60	6	10	0	2	11	23	0	0
Kivett, R	.150	40	4	6	0	1	4	6	3	0
Hendrix, P	.122	41	1	5	0	4	1	9	0	1

PLAYER	W	L	ERA	G	SV	IP	H	BB	SO
Winiarski, C	5	1	1.89	47	21	52	43	9	66
Sides, G	2	3	2.40	45	3	49	32	22	71
Usui, K	1	0	2.61	9	1	10	5	5	15
Carroll, S	8	3	2.93	15	0	98	83	17	78
Walters, J	2	3	3.00	26	0	42	42	15	42
Lowery, J	2	1	3.11	14	0	17	14	8	25
Sergey, M	5	4	3.30	13	0	76	60	31	80
Mascheri, R	3	2	3.31	43	0	54	42	28	59
Smith, M	2	2	3.37	44	1	51	45	22	62
Paula, L	7	2	3.45	35	1	68	53	35	51
Blackford, A	1	3	3.47	4	0	23	26	9	23
Perez, G	8	6	4.62	21	0	107	112	50	114
Drummond, C	6	3	4.85	18	0	98	107	53	78
Morgenstern, Z	1	1	5.31	10	1	20	26	14	11
Perry, C	3	4	6.01	16	0	76	69	54	74
Mortensen, J	0	0	7.50	2	0	12	18	3	13
Brooks, A	1	2	9.52	12	0	17	31	5	15
Waltrip, B	0	3	19.46	5	0	14	33	13	13

LINCOLN SALTDOGS

PLAYER	AVG	AB	R	H	HR	RBI	BB	SO	SB	CS
Valera, C	.327	391	70	128	4	52	32	60	9	4
Smith, C	.322	348	56	112	11	62	57	53	3	0
Robbins, J	.302	169	24	51	7	23	17	41	8	4
Mendonca, T	.291	158	22	46	6	28	7	40	1	1
Maggio, N	.288	177	19	51	7	35	16	49	2	0
Oduber, R	.286	353	47	101	17	60	18	90	3	3
Ricardo, D	.270	248	24	67	6	29	14	79	0	0
Jacobs, B	.249	373	51	93	12	49	45	82	8	1
Ibarra, C	.243	304	46	74	7	37	47	64	2	2
Adams, T	.243	140	22	34	8	23	14	52	4	5
Johnson, M	.225	191	33	43	4	15	25	31	8	5
Dean, B	.225	173	23	39	5	19	14	36	10	3
Marin, I	.218	216	30	47	0	9	27	40	6	3
OBrien, B	.207	29	7	6	0	1	4	8	4	1
Martinez, J	.180	50	6	9	3	7	7	9	0	0

PLAYER	W	L	ERA	G	SV	IP	H	BB	SO
McVey, C	1	1	1.62	36	3	33	30	13	48
McAfee, B	4	1	1.67	6	0	43	35	8	24
Parry, B	3	2	1.92	13	0	79	71	27	62
Martis, S	4	1	2.00	7	0	40	30	11	32
Crosby, C	0	0	2.16	16	0	17	11	12	17
Bunda, J	10	1	2.48	41	1	51	38	15	40
Wagner, M	3	3	2.84	39	21	44	42	17	35
Kourtis, D	1	2	3.39	26	1	53	58	25	34
Gordon, D	9	4	3.46	19	0	114	96	44	97
Webster, S	5	4	3.56	17	0	101	105	13	82
Pimentel, C	1	2	3.81	11	0	31	30	12	31
Martinez, F	2	3	4.00	35	0	45	35	24	30
Rowland, R	2	1	4.40	4	0	16	16	10	14
Smith, B	0	1	4.62	2	0	12	16	7	4
Gomez, L	4	3	4.65	21	0	29	37	7	27
Pimentel, Ca	7	4	4.67	14	0	85	84	26	88
McKendall, B	1	3	5.78	5	0	19	20	15	13
Portland, M	1	0	5.85	8	0	20	21	12	22
Frazier, P	0	2	9.00	4	0	12	16	8	7

SALINA STOCKADE

PLAYER	AVG	AB	R	H	HR	RBI	BB	SO	SB	CS
Moroney, J	.294	194	18	57	1	16	10	40	0	3
Meyer, K	.278	320	27	89	3	28	19	51	1	2
Randle, J	.265	68	8	18	1	13	8	17	2	2
Heck, J	.258	310	36	80	1	24	30	51	10	0
Baker, J	.253	332	32	84	8	35	6	56	2	0
Woodard, R	.252	262	35	66	5	22	18	73	20	8
Aldrich, D	.241	158	13	38	4	19	3	45	0	1
Olivas, A	.235	255	22	60	1	12	12	32	3	7
Garza, F	.235	102	8	24	0	13	4	24	4	2
Coffman, C	.233	292	35	68	10	32	37	80	2	0
Epperson, C	.233	30	3	7	0	3	1	7	0	0
Paris, T	.226	146	16	33	1	8	15	29	2	1
Trowbridge, L	.224	214	24	48	1	22	23	38	8	8
Caillouet, J	.214	341	36	73	8	32	20	53	12	1
Miller, J	.176	34	2	6	0	2	5	8	0	0
Cuyos, B	.162	37	3	6	0	1	5	11	0	0
Haskins, M	.161	31	4	5	0	1	2	17	1	0
Ferguson, E	.156	32	3	5	0	0	0	4	1	0
Blanke, M	.147	34	1	5	1	1	2	14	0	0

PLAYER	W	L	ERA	G	SV	IP	H	BB	SO
Herr, T	1	2	3.45	32	6	42	37	26	55
Sunnafrank, D	0	1	4.65	14	0	19	19	13	17
Hodges, J	3	6	4.90	13	0	88	87	39	48
Strayer, C	1	2	4.95	12	0	16	19	8	9
Mannebach, T	2	7	5.13	13	0	61	59	45	42
Cummins, C	0	3	5.16	31	1	45	53	17	33
Gates, D	1	2	5.51	14	0	31	34	12	19
Cody, C	1	2	5.62	3	0	16	18	3	10
Eaton, J	0	2	5.71	9	0	17	17	9	21
Smith, B	3	11	6.44	17	0	96	114	39	56
Hunter, S	0	2	6.56	17	0	25	23	9	29
Koenig, J	1	4	7.06	5	0	22	25	16	6
Bach, C	2	8	7.61	22	0	67	68	68	67
Cummings, J	1	7	7.81	11	0	53	66	37	49
Fazzini, T	1	1	8.02	18	0	25	32	18	17
Looney, T	0	3	8.03	13	0	28	31	19	22
Blackmon, T	0	4	8.60	7	0	23	30	28	12
Thurber, T	0	4	8.73	6	0	23	36	8	17
Robinson, J	0	5	8.92	15	0	37	47	27	28
Agnew-Wieland, S	0	3	10.80	8	0	20	34	9	13

SIOUX CITY EXPLORERS

PLAYER	AVG	AB	R	H	HR	RBI	BB	SO	SB	CS
Nogowski, J	.402	117	20	47	4	28	18	17	3	1
Garcia, E	.308	130	14	40	3	18	7	21	0	0
Samson, N	.302	255	43	77	4	43	20	16	12	5
Campana, T	.301	395	59	119	1	23	33	43	35	13
Kelly, D	.294	160	16	47	1	23	17	23	2	2
Washington, L	.293	355	53	104	12	57	45	70	4	3
Ray, J	.289	343	60	99	6	49	45	47	22	2
Ogle, T	.287	244	37	70	12	44	31	58	1	2
Gleason, D	.273	128	8	35	1	16	12	47	1	0
Bennie, J	.264	178	27	47	3	14	21	56	9	0
Lang, M	.258	349	64	90	5	42	29	78	18	1
Flair, N	.254	63	7	16	1	9	6	17	0	0
Alvarez, B	.241	58	7	14	0	5	6	21	0	0
Davis, J	.236	127	12	30	1	12	14	33	2	2
Jackson, D	.214	56	5	12	1	5	10	19	0	1
Vavra, T	.206	136	10	28	0	6	6	25	1	1
Gonzalez, J	.200	85	9	17	1	9	8	31	2	1
Vitters, J	.185	173	15	32	2	10	6	49	0	1

PLAYER	W	L	ERA	G	SV	IP	H	BB	SO
Needy, J	1	0	2.93	3	0	15	21	5	20
Francescon, P	4	3	2.95	39	18	49	51	8	32
McCanna, K	5	0	2.95	27	0	40	38	21	51
Picht, K	2	4	3.89	34	0	79	75	41	66
Flores, R	4	5	4.26	44	2	78	65	40	93
Orosey, B	3	4	4.34	31	0	50	44	20	57
Rossman, B	0	2	4.54	20	1	36	35	23	30
Johnson, H	3	9	4.90	22	2	116	135	49	90
Forsythe, C	6	8	5.44	20	0	114	135	42	87
Sneed, K	6	5	5.60	18	0	104	125	40	71
Heyer, K	3	5	5.74	11	0	47	58	34	32
Powell, C	2	3	6.08	16	0	37	45	11	29
Vernia, J	3	2	6.11	6	0	35	41	18	25
Eaton, T	3	0	6.33	14	0	27	31	7	29
White, A	0	2	7.76	7	0	24	31	13	20

SIOUX FALLS CANARIES

PLAYER	AVG	AB	R	H	HR	RBI	BB	SO	SB	CS
Henry, J	.302	324	71	98	29	72	48	74	1	0
Jacobs, C	.293	362	45	106	21	63	47	121	2	0
Morrison, T	.289	311	53	90	10	47	31	77	21	6
Reynolds, B	.283	389	61	110	16	68	36	110	34	6
Schmit, B	.274	354	54	97	4	44	28	53	20	7
Fiala, P	.265	245	28	65	5	30	21	50	1	1
Motl, D	.256	320	52	82	0	41	38	93	37	4
Mele, L	.247	89	9	22	2	7	6	26	1	2
Gretz, A	.244	221	27	54	3	22	34	37	1	0
Wolfe, T	.236	89	17	21	3	12	15	31	2	1
Marr, B	.225	213	34	48	2	13	26	51	9	0
Guinn, B	.213	141	13	30	1	10	10	29	0	1
Falsetti, M	.210	176	26	37	2	11	24	57	0	2
Vavra, T	.179	123	15	22	3	8	9	25	3	0
Popkins, D	.107	28	0	3	0	2	2	15	0	0

PLAYER	W	L	ERA	G	SV	IP	H	BB	SO
Jones, J	3	3	2.57	36	2	42	32	17	47
Wood, G	8	3	2.71	19	0	133	108	24	117
Woeck, A	4	1	3.15	40	3	51	49	19	62
Thompson, D	3	4	3.66	41	0	47	56	18	38
Hellquist, B	4	2	3.75	14	0	50	49	21	28
Bircher, J	5	6	4.59	20	0	125	135	42	87
Ortega, J	4	8	4.82	45	17	47	46	23	44
Nordgren, M	5	8	4.95	19	0	116	159	28	44
Blank, N	2	2	5.00	39	1	45	37	27	52
Marks, T	3	8	5.65	19	0	100	133	26	68
Morrow, B	2	6	6.13	20	0	91	124	29	60
Ferrell, J	2	3	7.57	15	0	19	24	16	20

ST. PAUL SAINTS

PLAYER	AVG	AB	R	H	HR	RBI	BB	SO	SB	CS
Johnson, D	.346	52	12	18	3	12	13	11	0	0
Shoemaker, B	.318	305	71	97	21	57	55	49	1	0
Gallas, A	.306	304	62	93	19	65	34	75	8	0
Burzynski, B	.292	48	7	14	0	4	9	14	3	0
Thomas, T	.287	349	52	100	18	54	27	104	7	3
Hanson, N	.281	405	49	114	13	66	30	49	1	0
Colwell, T	.281	274	50	77	5	23	23	45	22	1
Delfino, M	.275	204	20	56	0	22	9	41	4	1
Carter, K	.271	221	31	60	9	32	27	67	12	0
Oh, D	.265	223	32	59	5	29	23	36	3	0
Almadova, B	.255	196	31	50	4	27	14	42	17	3
Garrett, M	.254	181	21	46	3	24	26	72	0	0
Gould, J	.250	88	9	22	2	6	8	21	0	0
Vavra, T	.237	114	17	27	1	11	7	20	1	1
Buerkle, B	.234	94	9	22	0	6	9	30	0	1
Goihl, J	.220	41	3	9	0	1	3	10	0	0
Caldwell, T	.194	62	10	12	3	11	6	22	1	1
Kristoffersen, J	.178	247	25	44	2	17	28	89	0	1
Lubach, T	.176	68	6	12	3	5	5	32	0	1

PLAYER	W	L	ERA	G	SV	IP	H	BB	SO
Rosin, S	0	0	0.00	15	9	16	6	2	17
Thielbar, C	2	1	2.01	17	1	22	13	4	23
Hawkins, C	0	1	2.70	18	0	20	13	12	19
Nittoli, V	2	3	3.32	34	3	46	43	19	55
Hamburger, M	13	6	3.55	23	0	172	193	34	115
Waite, B	4	5	3.60	17	0	77	73	46	51
Frosch, K	4	1	3.61	35	1	42	38	18	42
Gutierrez, A	0	1	4.09	2	0	11	9	10	5
Malm, J	1	3	4.19	12	1	39	37	11	22
Zimmerman, R	7	7	5.32	17	0	98	101	59	68
Peterson, B	4	2	5.55	24	0	36	31	20	46

PLAYER	W	L	ERA	G	SV	IP	H	BB	SO
Hoppe, J	1	3	5.56	14	0	44	53	10	32
Creasy, J	4	5	5.68	11	0	57	72	20	49
Crenshaw, D	2	2	5.96	5	0	32	33	10	24
Little, C	0	1	5.97	25	0	41	45	19	31
Straka, J	3	4	6.01	10	0	55	74	21	37
Williams, C	0	1	7.36	6	0	15	18	11	9
Schuld, M	1	2	7.46	7	0	25	38	12	17
Vieitez, I	0	2	11.32	7	1	10	18	3	6

TEXAS AIRHOGS

PLAYER	AVG	AB	R	H	HR	RBI	BB	SO	SB	CS
Phipps, D	.314	315	38	99	10	58	31	68	6	3
Scott, L	.300	347	38	104	7	49	46	85	6	3
Rondon, A	.283	321	52	91	1	26	45	61	60	7
Grider, C	.283	247	51	70	5	23	26	54	37	4
Weems, B	.259	320	35	83	8	43	36	66	0	1
Wagner, R	.256	262	35	67	3	22	15	34	9	2
Ragira, B	.242	165	17	40	2	17	12	28	2	0
Thurber, C	.241	199	28	48	6	32	36	59	8	2
Sealey, T	.215	307	36	66	1	21	15	65	10	8
Taylor, J	.215	195	17	42	0	16	21	54	3	0
Willard, R	.210	248	23	52	1	29	27	73	3	3
Miller, M	.206	180	15	37	3	13	8	28	1	0
Luce, J	.151	53	3	8	0	2	3	18	1	1
Monger, C	.136	81	4	11	0	2	5	37	5	1

PLAYER	W	L	ERA	G	SV	IP	H	BB	SO
Tasin, R	3	1	1.14	22	5	24	18	9	33
Mortensen, J	8	1	2.57	15	0	70	61	22	64
Russell, J	3	1	2.79	9	0	58	62	6	46
Drummond, C	1	1	3.14	2	0	14	11	5	12
Gomez, L	1	2	3.37	10	0	40	33	16	23
Bremer, T	4	5	3.39	13	0	77	70	24	62
Bozeman, T	6	6	3.50	25	0	110	95	45	116
Freeman, M	4	4	3.67	19	0	86	71	54	77
Waltrip, B	1	4	3.85	21	0	49	46	34	52
Gomez, R	1	2	3.93	7	0	16	15	3	10
Morris, J	1	3	4.27	32	1	40	34	30	41
Contreras, C	1	3	4.27	7	0	34	27	18	35
De La Cruz, L	1	5	4.30	37	12	38	24	25	37
Blanco, J	2	2	4.84	34	3	39	37	11	52
Hilton, K	1	2	4.93	11	0	35	45	11	30
Firth, S	2	5	5.07	16	0	50	49	29	46
Kubitza, A	1	4	7.18	16	1	46	61	30	32
Mendoza, M	1	1	9.00	7	0	11	11	14	8

WICHITA WINGNUTS

PLAYER	AVG	AB	R	H	HR	RBI	BB	SO	SB	CS
Chavez, M	.330	330	55	109	17	84	39	85	0	0
Fisher, Z	.330	185	31	61	9	40	10	32	0	0
Prigatano, R	.316	339	67	107	8	61	42	93	34	4
Medina, M	.314	325	51	102	6	51	35	45	4	1
Stringer, C	.307	398	88	122	5	44	55	50	18	3
Kain, H	.307	218	39	67	3	31	29	37	12	4
Mittelstaedt, T	.303	350	83	106	9	75	83	84	27	6
Clevlen, B	.302	361	77	109	9	78	51	102	4	0
Sullivan, T	.289	90	16	26	0	9	7	10	3	3
Morris, J	.250	40	12	10	0	4	6	12	1	0
Vargas, L	.242	355	48	86	4	46	23	83	14	7
Salgado, B	.236	348	43	82	5	45	28	96	1	0
Phillips, W	.188	48	7	9	1	4	6	12	0	0

PLAYER	W	L	ERA	G	SV	IP	H	BB	SO
Goossen-Brown, J	0	1	1.62	34	0	44	29	16	36
Gutierrez, D	1	1	1.68	4	0	16	15	4	11
Devine, M	3	4	2.25	44	2	44	35	11	34
Boyle, A	1	1	2.56	35	1	39	33	12	44
Campbell, J	3	1	2.91	34	0	34	40	7	23
Kussmaul, R	5	5	3.06	23	4	82	63	16	97
Medina, E	9	3	3.08	17	0	90	81	25	68
Kane, T	12	1	3.34	25	0	102	101	28	64
Boshers, A	11	4	3.71	22	0	128	134	22	67
Cooper, J	8	2	3.97	20	0	109	109	31	76
Harvey, S	2	4	4.61	39	11	39	39	18	38
Gould, G	0	1	4.78	11	0	26	26	9	19
Pratt, J	1	1	4.85	18	0	30	43	5	18
Brown, T	4	5	5.93	10	0	58	86	10	29
Wilson, J	0	1	6.56	11	0	12	16	7	10

WINNIPEG GOLDEYES

PLAYER	AVG	AB	R	H	HR	RBI	BB	SO	SB	CS
Pleffner, S	.340	391	61	133	10	76	39	62	0	0
Turgeon, C	.339	62	14	21	0	10	10	12	1	0
Romanski, J	.324	404	74	131	11	81	46	51	10	3
Bergin, D	.323	365	74	118	20	77	55	90	0	0
Ebert, J	.316	158	24	50	2	13	12	23	4	1
Darvill, W	.309	376	53	116	4	49	28	43	30	3
Sohn, A	.302	388	88	117	11	45	44	86	30	6
Rohm, D	.279	394	64	110	6	47	47	63	3	4
Suarez, A	.274	84	10	23	0	5	10	21	1	0
Abercrombie, R	.272	404	72	110	16	82	30	110	20	5
Katz, M	.268	314	55	84	19	66	43	73	2	2
Grider, C	.141	85	8	12	0	1	4	26	3	2

PLAYER	W	L	ERA	G	SV	IP	H	BB	SO
Capellan, V	4	4	1.25	50	5	50	35	13	75
Rosario, C	3	0	1.33	6	0	40	30	12	43
McGovern, K	13	3	2.55	21	0	144	115	45	118
Mathews, K	3	2	2.63	33	0	41	36	20	33
Chaffee, R	3	3	3.25	45	21	47	35	20	53
Lambson, M	7	3	3.98	39	1	61	66	12	61
Carl, E	9	4	4.6	19	0	117	119	46	103
OBrien, M	10	5	4.64	23	0	132	147	50	80
Dodson, Z	5	7	5.13	21	0	124	139	45	98
Minor, D	0	0	5.22	21	0	21	20	4	24
Rutckyj, E	2	0	5.57	22	1	21	25	13	21
Nuding, Z	2	6	6.82	12	0	63	85	27	22

ATLANTIC LEAGUE

For the third time this decade, the York Revolution are Atlantic League champions.

York swept Long Island in the championship round. Telvin Nash hit a two-run home run in the eighth inning of Game 3 to give the Revolution a 3-2 win over Long Island.

York came from behind in all three games of the championship series. The title was York manager Mark Mason's first as manager. He previously had been part of the Revolution's 2010 and 2011 championship teams as the team's pitching coach.

STANDINGS

FREEDOM DIVISION	W	L	PCT	GB
Lancaster Barnstormers	76	64	.543	—
York Revolution	68	72	.486	8
Southern Maryland Blue Crabs	67	73	.479	9
Sugar Land Skeeters	67	73	.479	9
LIBERTY DIVISION	**W**	**L**	**PCT**	**GB**
Bridgeport Bluefish	76	64	.543	—
Somerset Patriots	74	65	.532	1 ½
Long Island Ducks	73	67	.521	3
New Britain Bees	58	81	.417	17 ½

PLAYOFFS: Semifinals—Long Island defeated Somerset 3-1 and York defeated Southern Maryland 3-1 in best-of-5 series. **Finals**—York defeated Long Island 3-0 in best-of-5 series.

Attendance: Somerset 342,231; Long Island 341,830; Sugar Land 317,721; Lancaster 255,251; York 212,624; Southern Maryland 210,007; Bridgeport 196,917; New Britain 194,744.:

All-Star Team: C: Isaias Tejeda, York. **1B:** Michael Snyder, Southern Maryland. **2B:** Josh Prince, Sugar Land. **3B:** Jovan Rosa, New Britain. **SS:** Luis Hernandez, Bridgeport. **OF:** Alonzo Harris, York; Marc Krauss, Long Island; Sean Halton, Lancaster. **DH:** Kyle Roller, Somerset. **SP:** Gaby Hernandez, Southern Maryland. **RP:** Chase Huchingson, York. **Closer:** Cody Eppley, Southern Maryland.

PLAYER OF THE YEAR: Alonzo Harris, York. **PITCHER OF THE YEAR:** Gaby Hernandez, Southern Maryland. **MANAGER OF THE YEAR:** Ross Peeples, Lancaster.

INDIVIDUAL BATTING LEADERS

PLAYER, TEAM	AVG	AB	R	H	HR	RBI	SB
D'arby Myers, Bridgeport	.337	359	63	121	4	43	31
Sean Burroughs, Bridgeport	.328	335	42	110	3	41	4
Kyle Roller, Somerset	.326	313	61	102	22	77	0
Tony Abreu, Bridgeport	.315	356	46	112	3	47	3
Alonzo Harris, York	.315	460	89	145	23	73	31
Giovanny Alfonzo, Long Island	.309	362	39	112	4	45	10
Elmer Reyes, Long Island	.302	467	42	141	5	56	1
Garrett Weber, Lancaster	.302	377	62	114	15	52	3
Isaias Tejeda, York	.300	483	62	145	17	78	2
Jovan Rosa, New Britain	.300	530	59	159	15	72	0

INDIVIDUAL PITCHING LEADERS

PITCHER, TEAM	W	L	ERA	IP	H	BB	SO
Gaby Hernandez, S. Maryland	11	4	2.80	141	122	39	150
Jake Hale, S. Land	11	6	3.24	153	156	39	86
John Brownell, Long Island	10	5	3.44	146	140	51	96
Matt Larkins, Long Island	9	7	3.69	156	155	42	139
Brett Marshall, S. Land	10	7	3.79	164	152	80	95
Dave Kubiak, Somerset	5	10	3.83	113	95	34	117
Daryl Thompson, S. Maryland	9	7	3.87	159	153	27	135
Brian Grening, S. Maryland	9	8	3.91	166	190	26	92
Drew Hayes, S. Maryland	8	8	3.94	123	123	52	96
Kyle Simon, New Britain	12	11	3.95	171	194	42	91

BRIDGEPORT BLUEFISH

PLAYER	AVG	AB	R	H	HR	RBI	BB	SO	SB	CS
Callaspo, A	.344	128	22	44	4	15	16	19	0	1
Myers, D	.337	359	63	121	4	43	18	47	31	8
Burroughs, S	.328	335	42	110	3	41	39	30	4	0
Abreu, T	.315	356	46	112	3	47	16	51	3	0
Gil, J	.305	269	44	82	3	43	25	54	5	4
Fields, D	.297	296	54	88	12	51	37	90	1	2
Lambo, A	.293	239	31	70	5	33	25	54	2	2
Hernandez, L	.280	464	58	130	5	43	46	66	12	4
Cuevas, J	.279	498	64	139	7	49	30	67	12	4
Galvez, J	.277	441	68	122	16	77	48	99	10	5
Dotel, W	.271	166	21	45	4	22	13	40	4	6
Nina, A	.264	258	28	68	5	36	18	36	7	3
Guillen, O	.253	281	30	71	2	29	20	39	5	6
Molina, G	.222	180	21	40	5	19	16	30	0	0
Rosa, A	.218	188	22	41	2	16	13	43	4	2
Nessy, S	.206	136	10	28	3	13	10	41	1	0

PLAYER	W	L	ERA	G	SV	IP	H	BB	SO
Perez, W	0	1	1.71	22	1	21	14	5	25
Carpenter, D	1	3	1.91	39	30	38	27	12	45
Ramirez, E	5	2	2.16	31	2	33	36	6	30
Moran, B	1	0	2.32	29	0	19	8	9	33
Roibal, R	4	2	2.52	10	0	46	37	18	50
Badamo, T	4	3	2.62	11	0	62	61	29	39
Rearick, C	4	1	3.02	9	0	48	40	16	60
Pestano, V	1	1	3.25	26	1	28	27	5	30
Riordan, C	7	3	3.29	14	0	93	95	11	88
Britton, D	4	1	3.68	34	0	29	30	12	19
Grotz, Z	4	3	3.77	67	2	74	84	30	80
DeJiulio Jr., F	4	5	3.93	59	0	66	68	21	63
Brewer, C	8	6	4.11	25	0	140	160	53	115
Lara, R	9	11	4.30	25	0	142	159	57	97
Delcarmen, M	3	2	4.39	59	9	57	62	26	54
Albaladejo, J	7	6	4.44	16	0	99	113	27	103
Seaton, R	2	4	5.15	11	0	58	75	26	40
Parra, M	3	4	5.87	9	0	46	60	19	43

LANCASTER BARNSTORMERS

PLAYER	AVG	AB	R	H	HR	RBI	BB	SO	SB	CS
Coronado, N	.333	207	32	69	6	38	14	36	16	6
Hobson, K	.326	239	42	78	21	61	29	42	1	1
Player	AVG	AB	R	H	HR	RBI	BB	SO	SB	CS
Sandford, D	.324	238	46	77	0	26	32	53	45	13
Gailen, B	.323	192	39	62	8	30	29	27	9	4
Garner, C	.320	219	37	70	8	46	10	54	4	3
Ahrens, K	.319	69	12	22	3	17	2	8	1	0
Weber, G	.302	377	62	114	15	52	43	83	3	2
Clevenger, S	.293	205	19	60	3	17	21	17	1	1
Amaral, B	.293	215	27	63	3	26	7	46	4	4
Robinson, T	.287	327	56	94	7	39	48	57	17	3
Frias, V	.277	253	33	70	5	30	25	41	12	6
Gindl, C	.271	314	39	85	10	54	39	60	5	3
Milledge, L	.270	311	42	84	1	36	30	42	14	4
Halton, S	.267	506	79	135	26	90	50	115	3	1
Noel, R	.261	207	42	54	2	17	25	48	34	4
De La Rosa, A	.255	318	33	81	3	38	15	76	2	0
Bell, J	.247	162	30	40	7	23	28	51	4	1
Zawadzki, L	.221	86	12	19	2	11	10	18	4	0
Clark, T	.176	148	16	26	1	11	7	63	5	2

PLAYER	W	L	ERA	G	SV	IP	H	BB	SO
Burawa, D	2	2	7.78	22	0	20	21	14	24
Villanueva, E	5	1	2.72	7	0	36	34	10	32
Shuman, S	3	1	2.91	62	2	59	47	22	73
Anderson, J	3	1	3.00	56	0	60	43	39	74
Carter, A	5	3	3.12	59	31	58	54	14	61
Moskos, D	6	3	3.26	58	0	52	44	21	50
Downing, K	2	1	3.31	54	1	57	45	37	53
Munson, K	2	3	3.43	59	1	58	52	33	74
Reed, N	2	4	3.52	11	0	66	65	15	62
Kuchno, J	3	1	4.05	25	0	33	27	12	32
Hively, R	6	0	4.52	55	0	62	60	19	70
Bergesen, B	9	9	4.74	25	0	137	172	27	84
Lewis, R	9	11	4.98	27	0	144	192	59	118
Evans, B	6	3	5.05	17	0	93	111	19	92
Hall, C	2	3	5.06	27	4	27	28	4	48
Gardner, J	3	4	5.95	10	0	48	70	29	32
Leverett, J	7	8	6.29	28	0	123	168	47	93
Shirley, T	3	5	6.57	15	0	63	85	32	41
Gonzalez, L	0	2	7.54	7	0	23	33	13	12

LONG ISLAND DUCKS

PLAYER	AVG	AB	R	H	HR	RBI	BB	SO	SB	CS
Alfonzo, G	.309	362	39	112	4	45	12	72	10	2
Reyes, E	.302	467	42	141	5	56	29	93	1	2
Krauss, M	.282	429	75	121	21	84	83	96	4	1
Hinshaw, J	.275	80	12	22	1	8	6	24	0	0
Pacheco, J	.273	150	22	41	3	22	14	26	4	0
Ford, L	.269	294	34	79	9	31	25	53	0	1
Cleary Jr., D	.265	476	59	126	3	46	36	98	25	4
Pyles, D	.264	53	2	14	0	4	0	5	0	0
Songco, A	.263	472	66	124	24	81	41	128	1	2
Gotay, R	.261	226	32	59	6	28	47	45	3	0
Lyons, D	.248	371	47	92	7	37	45	71	4	2
Vega, A	.245	163	35	40	3	19	24	68	10	4
Reimold, N	.238	63	6	15	2	7	10	23	2	0
Lentini, F	.234	278	41	65	3	15	6	35	28	2
Berry, Q	.228	101	16	23	0	9	12	21	15	3
Burg, A	.225	382	48	86	12	42	32	105	1	0
Puckett, C	.223	112	10	25	3	12	15	20	1	0

PLAYER	W	L	ERA	G	SV	IP	H	BB	SO
Tsao, C	1	1	1.52	18	7	18	13	10	19
Aardsma, D	1	2	2.01	23	9	22	13	9	31
Diaz, A	5	6	2.25	57	15	56	48	22	66
Fuller, J	1	0	2.29	18	0	16	12	6	20
Marsh, M	0	0	2.45	10	0	18	15	6	23
Alvarez, H	2	1	3.09	7	0	32	34	14	13
Melville, T	3	4	3.44	9	0	47	41	18	48
Brownell, J	10	5	3.44	24	0	146	140	51	96
Dunning, J	2	3	3.64	14	0	49	54	14	43
Crider, P	1	5	3.64	63	0	49	45	27	54
Larkins, M	9	7	3.69	27	0	156	155	42	139
Treece, Z	6	2	3.83	53	0	61	60	28	72
Rogers, R	6	1	3.93	58	2	66	58	30	40
Simon, A	2	3	4.55	12	1	55	54	13	48
OGrady, D	5	7	4.64	36	0	105	102	52	80
Perez, R	8	7	4.72	22	0	109	127	27	83
Hirsch, H	0	1	4.95	7	0	16	16	13	16
Wilson, T	2	2	5.47	24	1	25	22	16	26
Levine, T	3	3	5.85	23	0	60	80	21	36

PLAYER	W	L	ERA	G	SV	IP	H	BB	SO
De La Rosa, E	3	1	6.38	15	0	18	28	11	10
Lannan, J	1	0	6.65	19	0	23	29	12	27

NEW BRITAIN BEES

PLAYER	AVG	AB	R	H	HR	RBI	BB	SO	SB	CS
Hinshaw, J	.328	204	26	67	1	18	19	45	12	3
Rosa, J	.300	530	59	159	15	72	46	99	0	0
Walton, J	.290	414	43	120	13	52	9	90	2	2
Griffin, J	.278	403	46	112	13	64	39	103	3	0
Maddox, C	.274	519	67	142	12	83	26	86	1	0
Crouse, M	.261	491	86	128	20	68	52	160	40	14
Kajimoto, Y	.256	360	39	92	3	25	22	65	7	6
Skelton, J	.255	392	69	100	14	33	101	143	17	5
Bierfeldt, C	.238	450	61	107	23	64	60	140	1	1
Carrillo, S	.231	117	10	27	0	8	8	35	2	0
Baca, M	.208	289	21	60	2	19	18	81	6	4
Villaescusa, I	.194	72	8	14	1	3	1	14	0	0
McGuiggan, J	.187	230	21	43	3	16	22	59	1	2

PLAYER	W	L	ERA	G	SV	IP	H	BB	SO
Coleman, C	2	2	2.49	23	0	43	35	15	49
Marzi, A	5	5	2.84	12	0	70	72	21	46
Gilblair, S	2	3	2.89	37	21	37	42	11	29
Hepple, M	2	2	3.23	43	0	56	49	38	61
Roe, N	7	6	3.63	59	1	79	79	24	60
Simon, K	12	11	3.94	28	0	171	194	42	91
Nappo, G	3	2	3.97	14	0	68	73	27	49
Shimo, B	4	4	4.10	53	0	72	58	26	61
Fry, B	1	3	4.31	67	0	65	57	29	53
Greenwood, N	5	6	4.37	15	0	82	107	19	41
Lee, M	3	6	4.55	16	0	81	85	38	60
League, B	2	3	4.56	44	1	43	52	20	38
Pettibone, J	2	8	5.34	23	0	103	137	37	63
Beimel, J	3	2	5.57	22	6	21	33	9	14
Fornataro, E	0	2	5.85	15	0	40	47	25	19
Jarvis, J	1	4	6.86	18	0	38	54	11	17
Dupra, B	4	10	7.03	28	0	104	124	53	61

SOMERSET PATRIOTS

PLAYER	AVG	AB	R	H	HR	RBI	BB	SO	SB	CS
Richardson, D	.333	69	6	23	0	6	4	10	5	1
Trapp, J	.327	162	25	53	1	21	13	36	10	6
Roller, K	.326	313	61	102	22	77	55	84	0	0
Sands, J	.319	144	32	46	13	45	15	32	0	0
Marrero, C	.295	146	20	43	3	24	32	30	0	0
Gonzalez, Y	.291	299	29	87	3	31	33	55	0	2
Rosario, O	.282	298	41	84	6	42	25	39	16	5
Pacchioli, J	.281	299	61	84	0	30	46	39	35	2
Bortnick, T	.273	245	30	67	2	30	27	49	11	2
Eggleston, A	.263	331	46	87	4	41	60	45	12	1
Rodriguez, A	.257	405	57	104	1	32	50	52	14	8
Golson, G	.255	165	21	42	4	26	6	41	4	0
Grayson, C	.250	96	13	24	2	10	13	24	2	2
Kelly, S	.250	340	52	85	1	31	38	52	25	12
Guzman, C	.249	454	41	113	6	56	42	75	10	5
Ford, D	.243	70	13	17	1	10	7	19	9	1
Donachie, A	.239	226	21	54	2	24	35	51	5	1
Minicozzi, M	.239	251	34	60	8	36	26	70	0	0
LaHair, B	.228	92	10	21	0	4	20	22	0	0
Racusin, Z	.222	54	5	12	0	4	4	5	3	0

PLAYER	W	L	ERA	G	SV	IP	H	BB	SO
Antonini, M	2	1	1.61	9	0	39	22	10	47
Antolin, D	1	3	2.07	21	4	22	18	3	29
Laffey, A	1	1	2.82	4	0	22	16	5	19
Teasley, R	7	2	2.85	14	0	76	71	14	49
Below, D	5	1	2.88	46	0	62	65	9	58
Newby, K	3	4	3.37	38	1	35	28	17	35
Wright, J	3	1	3.46	47	0	52	52	18	45
Kubiak, D	5	10	3.83	21	0	113	95	34	117
Darnell, L	4	2	3.85	12	0	47	54	8	35
Nieves, E	3	6	3.94	16	0	73	79	37	63
Shaban, R	4	5	4.02	51	11	47	42	17	39
Atkins, M	4	3	4.06	11	0	62	58	13	59
Achter, A	3	2	4.07	22	0	35	35	10	38
Molleken, D	3	2	4.18	26	3	24	24	11	28
Irvine, L	9	4	4.25	25	0	135	138	55	89
Root, C	1	3	4.56	16	0	47	49	27	32
Johnson, P	2	2	4.76	7	0	23	20	8	28
Oliver, W	8	6	4.78	23	0	115	127	41	119
Williams, J	2	4	4.90	11	0	48	50	18	32
Gouin, A	3	1	4.95	24	0	36	33	12	28

SOUTHERN MARYLAND BLUE CRABS

PLAYER	AVG	AB	R	H	HR	RBI	BB	SO	SB	CS
Rodriguez, D	.364	280	37	102	6	50	16	40	2	2
Hoes, L	.312	234	30	73	3	30	27	42	6	1
Brown, G	.298	121	21	36	4	15	6	25	12	3
Lozada, J	.298	379	52	113	5	29	37	73	26	8
Wilson, Z	.282	301	46	85	14	52	37	70	1	2
Snyder, M	.280	460	71	129	25	72	52	100	2	0
Garcia, E	.260	534	69	139	3	33	34	65	11	5
Muno, D	.254	59	9	15	1	4	15	16	4	0
Vaughn, C	.252	453	71	114	13	63	64	119	17	3
Alen, L	.245	265	19	65	5	30	25	14	2	1
Cone, Z	.242	454	55	110	10	46	20	136	22	7
Palmeiro, P	.236	365	36	86	11	49	35	106	0	0
Nathans, T	.233	103	11	24	4	17	10	25	4	1
Kahoohalahala, K	.224	58	8	13	2	4	2	14	0	1
Bistagne, B	.209	196	13	41	1	16	15	40	9	3
Wiggins, R	.153	177	15	27	4	14	7	69	0	0

PLAYER	W	L	ERA	G	SV	IP	H	BB	SO
De Fratus, J	3	1	1.40	4	0	26	26	3	22
Eppley, C	2	4	2.42	58	32	56	47	17	54
Hernandez, G	11	4	2.80	23	0	141	122	39	150
Beal, J	6	4	3.35	59	2	59	58	13	55
Hebner, C	4	1	3.50	50	0	44	32	26	58
Thornton, Z	2	4	3.62	47	2	45	58	14	33
Carson, R	3	4	3.78	58	0	57	58	18	38
Thompson, D	9	7	3.86	26	0	158	153	27	135
Grening, B	9	8	3.91	27	0	166	190	26	92
Hayes, D	8	8	3.94	23	0	123	123	52	96
Runion, S	3	2	4.38	52	1	53	53	20	49
McCoy, P	2	5	4.76	11	0	62	67	24	38
Stem, C	2	3	5.00	30	0	54	57	29	39
Russo, D	2	4	5.25	30	0	63	65	35	40
Fornataro, E	0	7	6.39	9	0	38	53	26	24
Robertshaw, B	0	2	7.20	13	0	15	20	8	10

SUGAR LAND SKEETERS

PLAYER	AVG	AB	R	H	HR	RBI	BB	SO	SB	CS
Rodriguez, W	.333	288	34	96	3	28	30	33	5	0
Wilkins, A	.318	154	26	49	13	34	23	39	2	0
Gillespie, C	.302	169	25	51	5	26	21	28	12	1
Olivera, H	.289	173	20	50	2	15	7	17	0	0
Ramsey, C	.275	131	19	36	3	27	11	30	3	1
Barfield, J	.274	135	25	37	9	21	17	35	1	0
Giansanti, A	.273	465	49	127	9	52	27	63	31	5
Ahrens, K	.272	408	48	111	9	51	19	59	6	1
Prince, J	.263	471	75	124	11	52	85	103	55	12
Nelson, C	.261	92	10	24	2	11	7	17	1	0
Benson, J	.254	429	59	109	8	40	30	105	17	7
Scott, T	.253	415	49	105	12	58	45	77	0	1
Cordero, A	.246	345	29	85	4	37	13	58	6	1
Zawadzki, L	.242	124	17	30	5	16	10	33	5	0
Pounds, B	.218	317	45	69	11	35	45	80	0	1
Miller, D	.216	292	51	63	7	35	38	58	13	2
Thon, D	.205	73	10	15	3	7	9	23	4	3

PLAYER	W	L	ERA	G	SV	IP	H	BB	SO
Rodriguez, A	1	0	1.68	3	0	16	16	6	12
Paulino, F	4	5	1.97	39	16	41	25	13	50
Nix, M	9	5	2.23	19	0	101	66	35	75
Talbot, M	9	3	3.02	21	0	110	98	30	108
Hale, J	11	6	3.23	24	0	153	156	39	86
Haynes, M	2	5	3.39	55	13	50	44	30	57
DePaula, J	0	1	3.40	41	2	40	38	21	37

Marshall, B	10	7	3.79	28	0	164	152	80	95
Haley, T	3	2	4.05	48	0	47	49	24	38
Treibt, C	0	0	4.18	20	0	24	28	10	22
Maine, S	1	1	4.54	39	0	34	31	15	35
Gleason, S	4	7	4.55	28	0	87	94	26	46
Zinicola, Z	1	3	4.65	10	0	19	29	6	12
Johnston, A	2	5	4.78	52	0	47	59	11	28
Blevins, B	7	7	4.84	27	0	134	157	39	95
Richardson, D	1	4	5.02	48	4	43	34	29	62
Reed, E	1	1	5.10	26	1	25	34	10	23
Corpas, M	0	5	5.81	27	0	26	42	17	22
Drabek, K	1	3	8.33	6	0	27	37	12	16

YORK REVOLUTION

PLAYER	AVG	AB	R	H	HR	RBI	BB	SO	SB	CS
Casilla, A	.358	246	46	88	4	34	14	40	6	3
Harris, A	.315	460	89	145	23	73	48	95	31	13
Tejeda, I	.300	483	62	145	17	78	35	80	2	2
Mitchell, J	.295	421	66	124	14	62	55	122	24	6
Nash, T	.282	177	30	50	16	39	22	55	0	0
Varona, D	.277	202	25	56	4	36	9	52	3	5
Cruz, L	.276	232	32	64	5	29	21	63	1	2
Witherspoon, T	.275	447	68	123	8	48	42	142	19	10
Franco, A	.274	259	36	71	4	21	13	49	1	1
Triunfel, C	.271	218	29	59	8	28	14	42	1	2
Dent, R	.266	402	48	107	5	46	44	86	6	4
Burgess, M	.264	436	59	115	17	66	48	105	0	1
Constanza, J	.235	102	14	24	0	6	7	17	3	1
Guzman, J	.232	125	12	29	4	17	8	32	0	0
Robinson, D	.225	129	12	29	0	9	15	34	7	7
Pounds, B	.208	106	13	22	3	15	13	37	0	0
Simpson, C	.199	176	27	35	6	22	24	67	0	0

PLAYER	W	L	ERA	G	SV	IP	H	BB	SO
Martin, J	0	0	0.98	18	4	18	9	10	27
Huchingson, C	4	3	1.35	57	5	53	39	22	43
Van Meter, J	4	2	2.57	55	1	63	45	23	64
Allen, B	1	3	2.98	59	19	60	56	23	45
Click, M	3	1	3.00	58	0	57	45	21	55
Gomez, R	4	4	3.25	41	2	39	30	16	47
Westphal, L	2	7	3.35	45	1	46	44	18	64
Buchanan, H	2	2	3.40	38	0	40	35	35	33
Gause, J	10	4	3.67	19	0	91	87	45	74
Ezell, J	0	1	3.78	9	0	17	15	7	10
Gailey, F	14	9	4.11	28	0	153	150	58	112
Mateo, V	6	9	4.38	26	0	142	167	46	62
Janas, S	5	5	4.63	23	0	126	140	49	52
Williamson, L	6	9	5.20	27	0	130	164	59	49
Gaynor, J	1	2	6.20	16	0	29	42	10	16
Partch, C	3	5	6.39	20	1	56	77	20	43
Harris, T	1	2	8.17	8	0	25	33	18	20

CAN-AM LEAGUE

By Quebec's standards, the past three seasons had been a drought of historic proportions. After winning five straight league titles from 2009-2013, Quebec failed to make the playoffs in 2014 and had been knocked out in the first round in each of the past two years. But the Capitales dominated the league in 2017. Led by Patrick Scalabrini, Quebec finished with the best record in the league and placed seven players on the 11-man all-star team.

STANDINGS	W	L	PCT	GB
Quebec Capitales	65	35	.650	—
Rockland Boulders	64	35	.646	½
New Jersey Jackals	55	45	.550	10
Sussex County Miners	45	54	.455	19 ½

STANDINGS	W	L	PCT	GB
Ottawa Champions	42	56	.429	22
Trois-Rivieres Aigles	39	61	.390	26
Cuban National Team	5	16	.238	20 ½
Dominican Republic	2	15	.118	21 ½

PLAYOFFS: Semifinals—Rockland defeated New Jersey 3-1 and Quebec defeated Sussex County 3-0 in best-of-5 series.

Finals—Quebec defeated Rockland 3-0 in best-of-5 series.

Attendance: Rockland 145,005; Quebec 141,923; Ottawa 92,654; New Jersey 91,892; Sussex County 80,442; Trois-Rivieres 79,228.

All-Star Team: C: Maxx Tissenbaum, Quebec. **1B:** Jordan Lennerton, Quebec. **2B:** Dylan Tice, Rockland. **3B:** Yurisbel Gracial, Quebec. **SS:** Yordan Manduley, Quebec. **OF:** Johnny Bladel, New Jersey; Joe Maloney, Rockland; Kalian Sams, Quebec. **DH:** Brian Burgamy, New Jersey.

Player of the Year: Joe Maloney, Rockland. **Pitcher Of The Year:** Lazaro Blanco, Quebec. **Relief Pitcher Of The Year:** Nolan Becker, Quebec. **Defensive Player Of The Year:** Mike Fransoso, Rockland. **Manager Of The Year:** Patrick Scalabrini, Quebec. **Rookie Of The Year:** Mike Montville, Rockland.

INDIVIDUAL BATTING LEADERS

PLAYER, TEAM	AVG	AB	R	H	HR	RBI	SB
Yosvani Alarcon, Cuba	.433	60	11	26	0	8	0
Johnny Bladel, New Jersey	.345	391	95	135	8	55	32
Max Tissenbaum, Quebec	.340	306	70	104	13	61	0
Yurisbel Gracial, Quebec	.332	377	73	125	13	65	14
Dylan Tice, Rochester	.327	373	72	122	5	49	32
Jordan Lennerton, Quebec	.324	355	71	115	14	82	2
Jefferson Delgado, Cuba	.323	65	5	21	0	9	0
Javier Herrera, T.R.	.323	365	72	118	15	62	6
Alexander Ayala, T.R.	.320	362	41	116	7	47	1
Jose M. Rosario, D.R.	.317	60	9	19	2	10	2

INDIVIDUAL PITCHING LEADERS

PITCHER, TEAM	W	L	ERA	IP	H	BB	SO
Frank Luis Medina, Cuba	0	0	2.55	18	19	7	10
Lazaro Blanco, Quebec	11	4	2.98	118	99	39	118
Yariel Rodriguez, Cuba	1	1	3.13	23	16	15	22
Karl Gelinas, Quebec	9	3	3.27	129	115	25	91
Arik Sikula, Quebec	12	5	3.28	129	117	33	119
David Richardson, New Jersey	7	4	3.36	118	120	54	119
Gianni Zayas, Sussex	9	10	3.43	108	104	39	72
Justin Topa, Rockland	14	3	3.50	111	104	26	80
Markus Solbach, Rockland	11	4	3.60	123	130	20	95
Joe Maher, Quebec	8	5	3.85	108	109	41	88

CUBA NATIONAL TEAM

PLAYER	AVG	AB	R	H	HR	RBI	BB	SO	SB	CS
Alarcon, Y	.433	60	11	26	0	8	4	8	0	0
C.Torriente, J	.370	46	5	17	0	4	2	3	1	0
Torriente, J	.344	32	2	11	0	5	2	4	0	0
Delgado, J	.323	65	5	21	0	9	0	6	0	0
Aviles, G	.318	44	6	14	1	5	3	13	0	0
Gonzalez, R	.301	83	10	25	1	9	3	7	1	0
Gonzalez, N	.292	65	3	19	0	4	5	10	2	0
Samon, Y	.289	90	13	26	1	9	3	11	0	0
Cespedes, Y	.273	77	9	21	0	7	5	25	3	0
Laza, D	.233	43	5	10	1	6	2	5	0	0
Mesa, V	.214	84	9	18	1	5	7	11	2	1
Martinez, A	.182	33	3	6	0	1	1	9	0	0

PLAYER	W	L	ERA	G	SV	IP	H	BB	SO
Medina, F	0	0	2.54	9	0	18	19	7	10
Rodriguez, Y	1	1	3.13	8	0	23	16	15	22
Zulueta, Y	0	0	6.17	6	0	12	17	10	8
Garcia, U	0	4	6.23	5	0	22	32	10	17
Banos, B	1	2	6.92	3	0	13	20	4	9
Yera, Y	1	2	8.23	5	0	20	27	13	21
Duquesne, D	1	2	9.00	4	0	15	22	5	6
Nunez, L	0	4	6.63	7	0	20	23	12	21
Peralta, S	1	2	6.75	9	0	16	20	5	16
Lopez, R	0	2	8.52	4	0	19	21	8	12
Campos, F	1	0	9.67	9	0	18	24	13	20

DOMINICAN REPUBLIC

PLAYER	AVG	AB	R	H	HR	RBI	BB	SO	SB	CS
Rosario, J	.317	60	9	19	2	10	4	19	2	1
Salcedo, E	.304	69	12	21	4	8	5	17	3	0
Brito, A	.293	41	7	12	0	0	2	11	1	0
Taveras, D	.277	47	5	13	0	8	4	7	0	0

PLAYER	AVG	AB	R	H	HR	RBI	BB	SO	SB	CS
Perez, N	.261	46	6	12	2	7	7	17	0	1
Matos, S	.218	55	3	12	1	4	3	12	1	2
Crousset, J	.200	55	6	11	1	5	4	14	0	0
Gomez, G	.179	56	6	10	2	9	11	19	0	0
Polonia, R	.150	40	5	6	1	5	3	8	1	0

PLAYER	W	L	ERA	G	SV	IP	H	BB	SO
Hernandez, L	0	1	5.10	9	1	12	16	6	11
Nunez, L	0	4	6.63	7	0	20	23	12	21
Peralta, S	1	2	6.75	9	0	16	20	5	16
Lopez, R	0	2	8.52	4	0	19	21	8	12
Campos, F	1	0	9.67	9	0	18	24	13	20

NEW JERSEY JACKALS

PLAYER	AVG	AB	R	H	HR	RBI	BB	SO	SB	CS
Bladel, J	.345	391	95	135	8	55	56	60	32	10
Richardson, D	.321	196	35	63	4	20	8	26	10	1
Burgamy, B	.313	384	63	120	12	83	46	64	10	2
Gregor, C	.303	251	56	76	12	74	61	32	11	2
Stock, R	.297	165	28	49	8	40	9	26	1	0
Charles, A	.295	44	8	13	3	11	4	20	0	0
Sandoval, R	.285	386	81	110	8	46	54	106	7	5
Brennan, T	.272	305	48	83	8	48	35	89	11	1
Joynt, B	.260	346	43	90	3	45	25	95	1	2
Vargas, Y	.253	253	29	64	1	29	21	65	5	0
Casper, M	.241	162	20	39	0	13	14	42	2	3
Retz, R	.241	191	37	46	4	23	15	40	5	3
Dunigan, J	.233	90	8	21	4	10	7	30	1	1
Martin, A	.233	215	33	50	9	30	28	66	2	0
Rockett, D	.150	40	3	6	0	3	5	10	0	1

PLAYER	W	L	ERA	G	SV	IP	H	BB	SO
Jose, J	0	4	2.30	21	0	27	29	4	31
Gercken, N	2	2	2.70	43	1	47	35	24	47
Cruz, F	4	2	2.82	7	0	51	43	11	55
Richardson, D	7	4	3.35	20	0	118	120	54	119
Hellweg, J	2	3	3.78	36	19	38	38	16	62
McEachern, K	3	3	4.03	40	0	51	53	17	42
Pavlik, I	10	5	4.25	20	0	114	137	32	99
Sosa, L	9	4	4.34	20	0	124	137	42	107
Loosen, M	2	0	4.50	4	0	20	23	9	17
DeLuca, E	3	2	4.61	39	1	51	49	31	81
Arneson, Z	1	2	4.78	37	0	47	52	18	49
Parish, M	4	3	5.60	9	0	53	75	15	35
Caceres, A	6	7	6.34	18	0	84	73	86	93
Gil, I	2	4	7.26	21	1	40	51	17	23

OTTAWA CHAMPIONS

PLAYER	AVG	AB	R	H	HR	RBI	BB	SO	SB	CS
Boucher, S	.296	341	56	101	7	51	66	56	14	1
Helms, M	.296	348	48	103	6	32	22	52	6	2
Gillies, T	.294	262	46	77	11	50	22	70	8	2
Nyisztor, S	.293	294	52	86	3	43	24	41	13	5
Chambers, A	.290	62	7	18	1	7	2	8	3	0
Brown, S	.287	366	53	105	7	62	39	73	13	5
Grauer, D	.283	286	45	81	8	46	28	64	4	0
Pierre, G	.283	321	46	91	7	44	19	64	8	3
Oropesa, R	.265	272	28	72	5	41	28	53	0	0
Venditti, A	.262	42	1	11	1	4	3	10	0	0
Bick, D	.251	359	64	90	7	36	33	85	22	5
Helms, C	.250	56	12	14	1	3	4	20	2	1
Nordgren, T	.250	152	22	38	3	17	14	20	0	0
Bistagne, B	.203	64	10	13	1	7	9	7	8	0
Fischer, B	.139	36	5	5	0	4	3	9	1	0

PLAYER	W	L	ERA	G	SV	IP	H	BB	SO
Gapp, N	2	3	1.89	15	2	38	25	10	49
Price, J	1	0	3.50	13	1	18	17	11	18
Cortright, G	2	2	3.66	17	4	20	20	8	8
Cordero, D	8	6	3.90	17	0	101	97	39	88
Borkowski, S	9	7	4.38	20	0	123	117	53	117
Aumont, P	5	8	4.51	17	0	116	128	30	103
Chrismon, A	8	7	4.73	20	0	125	149	43	93
Cooper, A	0	0	5.03	15	0	20	24	9	17
Gil, Y	2	7	5.55	16	0	79	92	29	76
Sanchez, R	1	5	6.27	27	4	47	59	17	35
Peterson, P	0	3	6.30	4	0	20	21	9	19
Tulley, M	1	2	7.29	7	0	25	32	17	11
Eggnatz, A	1	2	7.71	14	0	21	20	18	19
Motta, C	0	0	8.01	12	0	21	20	22	6
Luna, A	1	0	8.40	7	0	15	27	10	16

QUEBEC CAPITALES

PLAYER	AVG	AB	R	H	HR	RBI	BB	SO	SB	CS
Tissenbaum, M	.344	302	69	104	13	59	30	31	0	1
Gracial, Y	.333	372	71	124	13	65	37	50	14	2
Lennerton, J	.328	351	71	115	14	82	76	55	2	0
Fuenmayor, B	.310	42	4	13	1	6	6	9	0	0
Manduley, Y	.309	333	52	103	1	37	18	27	8	4
Sams, K	.291	285	63	83	23	70	25	71	14	3
Craig-St-Louis, P	.283	304	54	86	5	27	41	67	7	3
McOwen, J	.278	334	49	93	12	57	28	61	9	7
Fontaine, L	.262	103	13	27	2	14	5	20	0	1
Richardson, D	.257	70	8	18	0	4	4	21	0	0
Malo, J	.250	44	9	11	0	2	4	5	0	0
Ehrlich, A	.247	296	34	73	0	26	30	55	0	2
Knecht, M	.242	273	36	66	5	43	38	98	11	6
Oldham, T	.235	81	8	19	1	6	2	19	4	2
Rockett, D	.231	108	12	25	5	26	9	31	0	2

PLAYER	W	L	ERA	G	SV	IP	H	BB	SO
Becker, N	5	1	1.14	37	24	39	21	14	45
Blanco, L	11	4	2.98	19	0	118	99	39	118
Lee, B	4	3	3.05	21	0	74	75	24	67
Gelinas, K	9	3	3.27	20	0	129	115	25	91
Sikula, A	12	5	3.27	22	0	129	117	33	119
Bayless, T	2	1	3.50	38	4	44	39	18	52
Maher, J	8	5	3.84	21	0	108	109	41	88
Moeller, M	3	3	4.32	35	0	42	32	31	53
Elliott, A	4	2	4.41	35	0	51	47	16	53
Gouvea, M	1	3	5.40	6	0	32	35	13	23
Shergill, J	2	1	5.60	24	0	35	31	15	15
Yuhl, K	2	2	7.54	5	0	23	35	5	23

ROCKLAND BOULDERS

PLAYER	AVG	AB	R	H	HR	RBI	BB	SO	SB	CS
Smith, J	.327	165	34	54	12	35	33	39	4	1
Tice, D	.327	373	72	122	5	49	46	42	32	8
Regis, C	.299	308	52	92	14	58	28	65	8	5
Bennie, J	.297	64	15	19	0	7	7	19	0	0
Maloney, J	.282	373	84	105	35	101	45	111	18	2
McDonald, J	.273	381	66	104	5	56	45	59	6	5
Fransoso, M	.272	312	58	85	4	38	68	68	30	7
Nidiffer, M	.271	266	50	72	12	56	48	65	1	0
Arribas, D	.255	153	23	39	5	25	18	31	3	0
Montville, M	.238	340	65	81	13	50	60	103	13	4
Wilson, A	.222	162	31	36	2	24	29	44	5	1
Mogues, M	.217	115	12	25	4	25	18	30	1	0
Herceg, A	.195	195	27	38	3	21	11	40	1	0

PLAYER	W	L	ERA	G	SV	IP	H	BB	SO
Guaipe, M	3	0	2.04	22	14	22	9	5	31
Fischer, D	3	1	3.00	4	0	15	13	8	15
Elias, E	0	1	3.10	23	0	29	26	12	21
Lawrence, T	1	1	3.41	45	2	63	53	20	46
Topa, J	14	3	3.49	20	0	111	104	26	80
Salazar, R	5	3	3.53	13	0	64	66	17	62
Solbach, M	11	4	3.59	19	0	123	130	20	95
Kostalos, M	4	3	3.64	44	2	54	59	31	42
Riefenhauser, C	5	1	3.81	23	0	54	49	27	45
Velasquez, J	3	3	4.03	29	12	29	27	12	21
Farina, A	3	1	4.45	28	0	36	39	12	21
Budkevics, B	6	3	5.62	17	0	90	98	32	59
Carmain, C	6	3	5.97	17	0	78	87	25	55
Kaufman, A	0	5	6.21	7	0	38	37	15	24
Byers, J	0	2	6.62	8	0	18	19	15	8

SUSSEX COUNTY MINERS

PLAYER	AVG	AB	R	H	HR	RBI	BB	SO	SB	CS
Lopez, C	.356	73	11	26	0	6	5	9	0	1
Austin, J	.349	169	28	59	1	21	16	22	20	6
Retherford, C	.340	50	11	17	1	6	9	7	2	0
Silva, R	.305	390	53	119	4	57	8	59	26	8
Irving, N	.297	158	29	47	4	25	24	59	2	0
Chambers, A	.295	183	32	54	2	10	30	24	14	3
Baum, J	.291	326	43	95	8	48	30	71	20	5
Nyisztor, S	.281	32	3	9	0	3	3	8	3	1
Colon, A	.265	264	35	70	4	28	37	51	14	9
Schwartz, M	.255	51	10	13	1	7	7	8	0	0
Trapp, J	.253	150	15	38	1	16	3	37	15	5
McDonald, C	.251	227	24	57	10	37	21	42	4	1
Duran, J	.248	294	39	73	9	41	36	93	5	3
Giarraputo, N	.242	194	29	47	8	27	14	44	1	2
Mederos, J	.210	300	39	63	3	25	38	85	23	3
Fernandez, J	.208	236	36	49	10	36	34	76	8	4
Rockett, D	.177	79	12	14	2	6	11	13	3	3
Mayer, B	.167	54	8	9	1	3	5	25	0	1

PLAYER	W	L	ERA	G	SV	IP	H	BB	SO
Carela, D	1	0	3.10	23	0	38	28	19	31
Zayas, G	9	10	3.42	25	0	108	104	39	72
Muhammad, E	3	1	3.45	40	2	44	34	28	36
DeLaCruz, S	0	0	3.62	19	0	22	19	16	23
Demchak, A	0	1	3.94	31	1	30	29	13	24
Kerski, K	6	5	4.10	24	3	83	86	25	61
Roth, B	1	2	4.68	5	0	25	22	9	23
Brockett, A	2	2	4.93	28	4	35	42	9	23
Regas, K	6	7	5.05	21	2	93	105	30	72
Tamburino, M	6	5	5.09	21	0	117	116	37	115
Heesch, M	0	2	5.40	6	0	30	41	9	14
Kaufman, A	0	4	5.48	8	0	43	61	11	24
McCoy, M	4	4	5.50	43	8	52	53	27	61
Roder, K	3	5	5.66	13	0	62	75	20	41
Suk, M	0	1	9.98	13	0	24	45	3	17

EMPIRE LEAGUE

TEAM	W	L	PCT	GB
Old Orchard Beach Surge	34	28	.548	—
Plattsburgh Redbirds	34	28	.548	—
Puerto Rico Islanders	29	29	.500	3
Sullivan Explorers	23	35	.397	9

Playoffs: Plattsburgh defeated Old Orchard 7-4 in championship game.

FRONTIER LEAGUE

Schaumburg has turned itself into the Frontier League's most prominent power. Led by manager Jamie Bennett and outfielder David Harris, the Boomers won their third Frontier League title in five years. The Boomers are the first team to win three league titles in the 25 year history of the league.

EAST DIVISION	W	L	PCT	GB
Schaumburg Boomers	66	30	.688	—
Washington Wild Things	53	43	.552	13
Windy City ThunderBolts	51	45	.531	15
Lake Erie Crushers	45	51	.469	21
Joliet Slammers	42	54	.438	24
Traverse City Beach Bums	37	59	.385	29
Florence Freedom	61	35	.635	—

WEST DIVISION	W	L	PCT	GB
Evansville Otters	52	44	.542	9
River City Rascals	50	46	.521	11
Normal CornBelters	48	48	.500	13
Southern Illinois Miners	39	57	.406	22
Gateway Grizzlies	32	64	.333	29

Playoffs: Semifinals-Schaumburg defeated Evansville 3-1 and Florence defeated Washington 3-1 in best-of-5 series. **Finals–** Schaumburg defeated Florence 3-1 in best-of-5 series.

Attendance: Schaumburg 160,644; Southern Illinois 151,521; Gateway 148,176; Traverse City 119,544; Evansville 100,337; Joliet 100,160; River City 94,958; Lake Erie 94,035; Florence 87,545; Windy City 78,585; Washington 77,233; Normal 75,804.

All-Star Team: C: Dane Phillips, Evansville. **1B:** Kane Sweeney, Washington. **2B:** Josh Allen, Evansville. **3B:** Jose Brizuela, Florence. **SS:** Santiago Chirino, Normal. **OF:** Jeff Gardner, Evansville; David Harris, Schaumburg; Coco Johnson, Windy City. **DH:** Blake Brown, Gateway. **SP:** Max Duval, Evansville. **RP:** Brian Loconsole, Windy City.

Most Valuable Player: David Harris, Schaumburg. **Pitcher of the Year:** Max Duval, Evansville. **Rookie of the Year:** Kyano Cummings, Evansville. **Manager of the Year:** Jamie Bennett, Schaumburg.

INDIVIDUAL BATTING LEADERS

PLAYER, TEAM	AVG	AB	R	H	HR	RBI	SB
Santiago Chirino, Normal	.357	395	60	141	3	60	3
David Harris, Schaumburg	.344	288	55	99	13	65	13
Dane Phillips, Evansville	.338	361	65	122	14	66	0
Jordan Brower, Florence	.335	358	58	120	8	63	16
Matt Hearn, Gateway	.331	296	51	98	0	23	30
Jim Kerrigan, River City	.328	250	47	82	10	47	17
L.J. Kalawaia, Lake Erie	.326	239	39	78	2	19	13
Will Kengor, Traverse City	.324	262	33	85	14	58	4
Ridge Hoopii-Haslam, Joliet	.321	315	59	101	9	47	18
Jose Brizuela, Florence	.321	280	49	90	13	59	6

INDIVIDUAL PITCHING LEADERS

PITCHER, TEAM	W	L	ERA	IP	H	BB	SO
Max Duval, Evansville	8	2	2.28	87	58	27	113
Jordan Kurokawa, Lake Erie	7	4	2.53	117	101	26	79
Jake Fisher, Windy City	10	7	2.80	138	126	29	120
Scott Sebald, Normal	9	2	2.89	109	104	29	87
Luc Rennie, Evansville	7	5	2.91	77	71	39	66
Shawn Blackwell, Normal	7	5	2.92	89	74	36	102
Trevor Foss, Washington	12	5	3.06	132	114	32	88
Cody Gray, Florence	10	4	3.24	114	110	26	94
Jordan Kraus, Florence	10	5	3.28	124	118	50	98
Lars Liguori, Schaumburg	9	4	3.44	99	101	31	82

EVANSVILLE OTTERS

PLAYER	AVG	AB	R	H	HR	RBI	BB	SO	SB	CS
Phillips, D	.338	361	65	122	14	66	42	54	0	0
Schultz, J	.317	322	55	102	11	61	49	75	3	0
Allen, J	.310	345	83	107	15	47	66	78	12	4
Long, R	.286	185	35	53	2	11	42	27	3	1
Sweeney, C	.281	114	14	32	3	16	6	49	2	0
Gardner, J	.278	335	61	93	23	86	46	97	10	2
Walker, N	.273	143	17	39	1	13	11	17	3	0
Soat, B	.262	256	34	67	7	38	27	70	13	10
Riopedre, C	.261	345	43	90	5	47	14	51	22	7
Yamaguchi, K	.258	93	10	24	1	13	11	17	4	0
Montano, L	.242	120	18	29	2	8	15	46	0	1
Segovia, A	.233	253	50	59	14	45	44	48	0	0

PLAYER	W	L	ERA	G	SV	IP	H	BB	SO
Cummings, K	4	2	1.22	50	7	74	57	20	58
Little, C	0	1	1.76	9	0	15	10	5	12
Duval, M	8	2	2.27	14	0	87	58	27	113
Etsell, R	2	2	2.42	5	0	26	23	10	18
McCurry, R	4	1	2.73	26	17	26	17	19	30
Rennie, L	7	5	2.90	13	0	77	71	39	66
Baez, F	5	4	3.69	15	0	85	75	39	104
Ackerman, H	8	6	4.74	15	0	91	104	26	88
Broussard, J	1	3	4.76	37	0	57	63	26	70
Cook, B	1	1	4.80	8	0	15	20	6	14
Freeman, H	2	1	5.17	19	1	31	35	21	27
Tasin, R	0	0	5.28	17	0	15	24	13	15
Ibarra, D	3	2	5.94	7	0	36	47	16	35
Weedman, S	5	4	6.27	22	0	66	57	56	61
Lunsford, T	0	2	7.17	7	0	21	22	31	18
Utterback, A	0	0	7.20	14	0	15	13	13	11
Sweet, A	2	2	7.96	15	0	20	26	10	19

FLORENCE FREEDOM

PLAYER	AVG	AB	R	H	HR	RBI	BB	SO	SB	CS
Berges, K	.341	82	14	28	4	14	8	13	0	0
Brower, J	.335	358	58	120	8	63	27	59	16	6
Brizuela, J	.321	280	49	90	13	59	34	46	6	5
Mercurio, A	.295	305	53	90	6	52	25	49	18	0
Fraga, D	.288	375	70	108	2	34	60	51	24	11
Oldham, T	.286	248	45	71	6	28	33	41	28	2
Godbold, A	.283	293	47	83	5	47	35	74	12	6
Cuthrell, C	.252	325	60	82	11	56	71	76	8	4
Braff, O	.248	105	20	26	4	17	13	34	4	1
Wobrock, A	.242	314	33	76	0	28	30	65	6	8
Morris, M	.239	92	18	22	1	5	16	26	7	2
Vail, G	.225	240	26	54	9	50	20	83	8	6
Rinsky, R	.200	70	10	14	0	10	17	15	0	0

PLAYER	W	L	ERA	G	SV	IP	H	BB	SO
Pobereyko, M	1	1	1.00	17	10	18	8	5	38
Longwith, L	3	0	2.45	4	0	22	14	5	13
Wilson, J	2	0	2.59	17	1	17	16	8	17
Torres-Perez, B	6	2	2.81	10	0	61	56	25	52
Perez, P	1	0	2.86	21	12	22	19	9	17
Hagen, S	4	1	2.90	6	0	40	37	7	20
Anderson, M	6	2	2.95	10	0	49	39	22	44
McGrath, P	0	1	3.13	30	1	23	16	8	21
Gray, C	10	4	3.23	18	0	114	110	26	94
Kraus, J	10	5	3.27	18	0	124	118	50	98
Brunner, S	0	1	3.88	20	0	44	40	22	30
Berges, K	3	1	4.50	17	1	18	25	4	12
Vocca, T	9	6	4.50	18	0	100	100	43	76
Zamora, E	3	1	4.59	24	3	47	47	25	40
Bickett, E	0	0	4.90	18	0	15	11	5	12
Anthony, M	1	2	5.40	16	0	15	16	6	15

GATEWAY GRIZZLIES

PLAYER	AVG	AB	R	H	HR	RBI	BB	SO	SB	CS
Hearn, M	.331	296	51	98	0	23	25	41	30	10
Brown, B	.300	340	62	102	18	69	70	95	9	2
McClure, T	.295	312	40	92	6	41	15	61	14	4
McKeithan, J	.289	187	21	54	5	22	24	44	0	1
Livesay, C	.273	297	43	81	0	24	57	60	20	7
Sakurai, B	.254	177	19	45	4	21	15	38	5	1
Massoni, C	.250	136	17	34	5	27	26	37	0	0
Osuna, R	.244	82	9	20	2	16	7	26	0	0
Lees, B	.234	94	9	22	2	10	5	25	0	0
Simmons, C	.234	154	11	36	3	11	19	27	0	0
Rogers, E	.233	262	42	61	7	32	45	75	10	2
Mattlage, G	.222	90	11	20	2	15	5	32	1	0
Hranec, J	.215	163	13	35	4	11	11	39	0	0
Gillespie, B	.203	59	5	12	3	7	2	16	0	0
Caronia, A	.203	74	6	15	0	6	2	17	3	1
Lavy, Z	.186	113	10	21	1	18	5	39	0	0
Holst, D	.183	175	16	32	2	12	20	29	2	0

PLAYER	W	L	ERA	G	SV	IP	H	BB	SO
Elwood, M	3	1	3.05	42	1	59	52	24	70
Earls, K	1	4	3.69	30	7	32	26	15	32
Molesky, V	8	7	3.84	21	1	129	118	34	120
Cable, T	4	4	3.91	32	0	46	33	45	46
West, J	3	8	4.93	26	0	104	109	38	102
Landsheft, W	4	8	5.06	15	0	80	79	47	64
Reynoso, J	1	0	5.11	21	0	32	31	18	36
Sigman, J	0	0	5.59	19	0	27	30	13	31
Anderson, W	2	14	5.85	20	0	111	138	51	69
Shalberg, D	0	3	6.08	5	0	24	23	16	15
Kisena, A	3	5	6.61	13	0	68	77	36	59
Craig, D	1	5	7.59	10	0	43	54	40	31
Eggnatz, A	0	2	10.22	5	0	22	36	20	14

JOLIET SLAMMERS

PLAYER	AVG	AB	R	H	HR	RBI	BB	SO	SB	CS
Merrigan, J	.333	111	21	37	1	8	12	29	3	3
Hoopii-Haslam, R	.321	315	59	101	9	47	24	74	18	10
Rodriguez, M	.312	369	62	115	11	46	31	52	3	1
Silva, J	.310	168	30	52	10	35	31	32	7	4
Gomez, E	.292	319	56	93	9	47	40	53	2	0
Bolin, T	.280	236	31	66	8	31	8	50	20	4
Zardon, D	.274	318	35	87	7	50	20	66	2	2
Meadows, C	.269	134	14	36	0	18	15	29	0	1
Rodriguez, A	.267	101	16	27	1	16	11	22	0	1
Navin, S	.254	193	29	49	5	29	29	63	2	3
Gonzalez, D	.239	138	18	33	1	11	15	12	4	4
Diaz, L	.235	115	19	27	0	15	13	30	2	0
Lero, D	.228	123	16	28	1	11	14	31	0	1
Shoulders, R	.207	227	35	47	10	34	37	77	4	2
Pollakov, S	.200	80	7	16	0	9	17	19	2	1

PLAYER	W	L	ERA	G	SV	IP	H	BB	SO
Wellander, J	1	3	2.27	31	3	36	22	9	47
McKenna, B	1	1	2.45	28	0	37	20	23	33
Lara, C	2	3	2.82	32	19	35	35	16	29
Cruz, L	5	5	3.22	12	0	61	52	25	67
Wozniak, C	1	2	3.41	5	0	26	29	13	16
Uherek, N	0	3	3.50	6	0	26	28	9	21
Janisse, S	6	3	3.61	21	1	62	63	24	54
Von Schamann, D	5	8	4.05	19	0	122	140	23	89
Zellner, A	1	4	4.17	13	0	32	22	17	19
Bryant, S	5	6	5.69	21	0	104	121	37	78
Ortiz, J	4	3	5.94	19	1	53	61	13	29
House, T	3	3	6.51	16	0	68	96	22	42
Hoffman, S	1	2	6.75	4	0	23	23	7	22
Russ, G	2	0	6.96	19	3	21	26	14	18
Strobel, T	1	2	7.31	7	0	16	27	8	6
Concepcion, D	1	4	8.62	18	0	40	61	20	43

LAKE ERIE CRUSHERS

PLAYER	AVG	AB	R	H	HR	RBI	BB	SO	SB	CS
Kalawaia, L	.326	239	39	78	2	19	29	41	13	6
Simonetti, C	.303	175	20	53	5	21	14	57	0	0
DeLaRosa, B	.297	74	8	22	1	11	3	16	1	0
Hurley, S	.263	331	65	87	15	58	63	95	5	0
Dean, J	.260	388	61	101	18	53	28	83	17	1
Murray, B	.256	219	33	56	11	30	15	57	10	0
OBrien, A	.241	108	21	26	6	15	14	37	0	0
McAdams, J	.238	193	25	46	6	25	5	58	8	2
Lenahan, C	.227	309	38	70	11	50	20	88	2	4
Lubach, T	.223	148	23	33	7	23	10	38	1	0
Oliver, C	.211	332	40	70	11	36	47	107	18	9
Norris, P	.210	224	27	47	0	18	36	70	5	1
Hofmann, C	.186	86	10	16	2	6	9	30	5	4
Casper, M	.176	91	2	16	0	7	4	13	0	1

PLAYER	W	L	ERA	G	SV	IP	H	BB	SO
Kurokawa, J	7	4	2.53	18	0	117	101	26	79
Deeg, N	3	3	3.13	7	0	37	25	17	31
Sinibaldi, J	5	2	3.15	36	0	60	48	13	73
Utterback, A	0	0	3.31	14	0	19	15	10	17
Klotz, M	1	3	3.75	10	0	38	35	22	31
Caballero, J	5	5	3.85	13	0	75	56	42	64
Quintana, A	4	4	4.36	10	0	56	51	24	50
Hagen, S	4	4	4.43	14	0	87	93	25	78
Jagodzinski, C	3	5	4.45	34	18	34	46	9	31
Reed, C	3	6	4.74	18	2	85	101	21	70
Lucio, S	2	2	4.84	29	1	26	21	25	34
Lobdell, P	4	5	4.98	11	0	65	67	19	35
Arciniega, M	2	1	5.13	26	1	54	58	16	54
Heddinger, J	0	3	7.96	5	0	26	43	9	14

NORMAL CORNBELTERS

PLAYER	AVG	AB	R	H	HR	RBI	BB	SO	SB	CS
Chirino, S	.357	395	60	141	3	60	31	37	3	5
Fletcher, J	.318	340	42	108	3	44	16	39	18	4
Dudley, A	.309	311	55	96	11	65	58	59	2	0
Hakes, B	.279	122	17	34	5	21	9	38	1	0
Solorzano, J	.277	191	26	53	5	21	7	29	5	5
Ruiz, Y	.268	351	73	94	6	32	32	61	34	7
Cedeno, D	.263	338	39	89	0	33	32	56	7	5

PLAYER	AVG	AB	R	H	HR	RBI	BB	SO	SB	CS
Torres, M	.262	313	35	82	3	42	21	29	2	1
Meadows, N	.259	351	49	91	12	57	51	91	0	0
Lepre, C	.249	221	33	55	3	28	72	29	0	0
Morris, T	.188	154	30	29	2	14	20	50	16	2

PLAYER	W	L	ERA	G	SV	IP	H	BB	SO
Gendron, C	3	1	0.82	21	5	33	20	12	27
Herrera, A	3	0	2.66	18	0	27	21	8	18
Sebald, S	9	2	2.89	22	1	109	104	29	87
Blackwell, S	7	5	2.92	36	11	89	74	36	102
Portland, M	1	1	3.12	12	0	40	27	32	48
Carillo, F	2	6	3.25	32	3	39	37	17	47
Vivas, J	5	4	3.58	14	0	88	86	36	69
Gillies, C	7	10	4.25	20	0	121	118	55	90
De La Rosa, E	3	6	4.97	14	0	76	78	31	60
Ihrig, T	1	2	5.52	6	0	29	34	9	17
De Marte, J	2	1	5.53	20	0	28	23	13	36
Nootbaar, N	2	1	5.57	15	0	21	16	21	24
Hasenbeck, M	0	1	6.75	15	0	24	28	15	24
Wheatley, B	2	3	7.06	5	0	22	27	16	9

RIVER CITY RASCALS

PLAYER	AVG	AB	R	H	HR	RBI	BB	SO	SB	CS
Kerrigan, J	.328	250	47	82	10	47	11	46	17	5
Kronenfeld, P	.301	153	25	46	7	30	15	31	7	0
Ludy, J	.288	340	36	98	7	49	44	61	1	0
Merjano, J	.285	354	53	101	10	52	10	54	24	7
Freeman, C	.283	336	57	95	10	45	30	60	4	3
Silver, J	.282	358	57	101	7	51	36	62	17	2
Jurgella, M	.260	358	50	93	11	54	41	59	16	8
Martinez, B	.240	271	46	65	15	39	46	66	4	1
Morales, J	.227	308	42	70	6	46	47	59	16	7
Thomas, B	.216	310	67	67	10	41	56	114	49	5
Love, T	.169	77	11	13	0	10	9	31	6	1

PLAYER	W	L	ERA	G	SV	IP	H	BB	SO
Zgardowski, J	3	3	1.33	34	3	34	12	15	40
Mincey, C	1	2	1.76	28	11	31	25	14	37
Kennedy, N	0	3	2.55	52	4	42	45	8	27
Hernandez, H	8	8	3.64	19	0	121	105	50	117
Warner, A	2	0	3.74	6	0	34	34	12	32
Ludwig, D	6	4	3.91	19	0	106	119	22	76
Sneed, Z	5	1	3.99	9	0	47	52	19	43
Laster, L	2	2	4.02	17	0	47	47	22	30
Paesano, A	1	1	4.15	23	0	17	21	9	8
Gregory, R	9	5	4.45	21	0	103	109	24	66
Chavarria, M	4	4	4.96	35	2	45	36	27	34
Hoffmann, N	0	2	5.59	13	0	27	35	12	17
Koons, T	4	5	5.69	19	0	92	114	31	61
Rynard, S	2	0	6.38	22	0	18	25	18	9
Swagerty, S	0	2	7.46	14	1	16	14	18	15

SCHAUMBURG BOOMERS

PLAYER	AVG	AB	R	H	HR	RBI	BB	SO	SB	CS
Spivey, S	.417	187	51	78	10	50	37	27	6	2
Pinkston, T	.403	62	11	25	1	9	4	9	0	0
Harris, D	.344	288	55	99	13	65	27	65	13	4
Weigel, Z	.315	286	59	90	8	53	46	55	7	7
Ruchim, K	.315	365	83	115	5	40	48	58	10	3
Holland, J	.301	133	21	40	1	20	15	24	2	3
Godfrey, S	.287	363	55	104	9	59	21	95	14	3
Brodbeck, A	.274	117	20	32	1	11	15	29	3	2
Parenty, J	.272	232	22	63	0	31	16	33	9	2
Gardiner, J	.261	318	58	83	3	47	36	44	11	4
Towns, K	.259	135	29	35	5	26	13	24	2	1
Keller, J	.251	207	25	52	4	38	26	55	1	1
Oddo, N	.234	145	16	34	2	14	12	28	1	1
OMalley, R	.229	118	14	27	2	15	12	32	2	0
Shoulders, R	.211	76	14	16	2	9	16	21	0	1
Cannella, C	.196	112	9	22	1	11	16	17	1	3

PLAYER	W	L	ERA	G	SV	IP	H	BB	SO
Kines, G	5	1	1.30	7	0	41	30	13	53
Kelly, G	1	0	1.77	35	3	41	17	25	56
Hauser, J	4	1	1.80	9	0	40	35	12	31
Fowler, K	5	2	1.84	12	1	49	33	18	51
Westwood, K	3	1	2.05	31	3	39	34	13	36
Joyce, J	2	3	2.67	40	16	40	25	27	65
Kenilvort, A	3	1	3.09	19	7	20	18	6	27
Liguori, L	9	4	3.44	18	0	99	101	31	82
McDonnell, R	1	1	3.60	39	1	40	26	28	59
Quintero, B	4	2	4.00	8	0	45	49	16	47
Hopkins, K	9	5	4.19	18	0	103	104	38	86
Wozniak, C	2	1	4.26	12	0	63	59	24	41
Wood, M	4	3	4.61	15	0	51	62	18	39
Kerr, A	5	1	5.03	17	0	20	24	11	19
DeYoung, D	1	2	5.80	30	0	40	36	26	48
Jamison, P	0	0	5.81	6	0	22	22	20	18
Costa, A	4	2	5.81	10	0	48	59	9	27

SOUTHERN ILLINOIS MINERS

PLAYER	AVG	AB	R	H	HR	RBI	BB	SO	SB	CS
Germaine, B	.298	57	5	17	0	7	8	7	0	0
Lindley, L	.291	258	40	75	0	14	15	36	24	5
Massey, C	.289	350	55	101	2	43	48	47	12	4
Wiley, B	.264	254	39	67	3	20	26	67	7	2
Earley, N	.264	341	43	90	11	45	53	45	2	3
Martin, W	.261	92	7	24	0	12	7	18	0	0
Cortina, R	.258	163	16	42	4	26	23	35	3	1
Chigbogu, J	.252	107	16	27	4	19	11	32	1	0
Wertz Jr., K	.250	88	14	22	5	18	10	20	2	0
Lashley, R	.250	364	41	91	13	66	13	58	1	0
Moore, B	.230	204	27	47	2	18	18	25	4	2
Plant, C	.218	78	12	17	0	5	10	22	0	0
Sluder, R	.211	123	17	26	3	13	9	28	1	0
Critelli, A	.210	157	16	33	1	12	14	43	1	1
Massoni, C	.188	197	20	37	4	20	31	41	0	0
McKeithan, J	.184	76	9	14	2	12	5	17	0	0

PLAYER	W	L	ERA	G	SV	IP	H	BB	SO
Grana, K	0	0	1.11	22	0	24	12	12	42
Young, P	0	0	2.20	17	0	16	9	12	32
Werner, J	3	1	2.43	39	22	41	21	19	56
Dubsky, A	3	1	3.01	27	0	54	42	24	58
Stubblefield, T	6	2	3.07	12	0	67	56	23	55
Tinius, K	2	4	3.17	45	1	51	53	23	42
Parish, M	4	4	3.69	9	0	46	44	22	17
Washington, C	3	6	4.17	15	0	84	108	18	47
Cooper, Z	6	10	4.44	19	0	105	98	42	94
Rowland, R	2	3	4.59	6	0	33	35	12	22
Palacios, N	0	2	4.90	28	0	33	33	21	29
Sessions, C	2	7	4.96	23	2	91	104	34	47
Gibbons, E	5	4	6.50	15	0	55	58	23	52
Lobdell, P	2	3	7.81	5	0	25	32	8	13

TRAVERSE CITY

PLAYER	AVG	AB	R	H	HR	RBI	BB	SO	SB	CS
Kengor, W	.324	262	33	85	14	58	18	54	4	3
Patterson, S	.311	344	60	107	16	56	48	81	4	4
Rivera, A	.287	324	37	93	10	59	19	72	11	7
Rivera, O	.286	133	18	38	1	10	9	12	2	2
Patrick, K	.241	195	20	47	3	12	12	47	0	1
Montgomery, J	.225	169	14	38	4	20	10	29	0	0
DeBlieux, J	.217	350	54	76	1	23	46	81	18	5
Murphy, N	.211	161	18	34	3	19	18	41	4	2
Fields, A	.210	272	35	57	5	24	44	95	21	9
Lowery, L	.202	84	10	17	3	12	4	29	2	1
Trail, E	.202	114	17	23	3	16	9	32	1	0
Files, Z	.190	63	2	12	1	4	8	25	2	1
Stidham, J	.189	74	4	14	1	4	10	28	2	3
Brugnoni, G	.185	108	17	20	4	9	14	51	0	0
Garvey, R	.174	86	13	15	1	7	3	27	2	0
Hauser, J	.168	107	9	18	0	5	9	22	3	1
Alexander, Q	.145	76	4	11	0	2	9	32	0	0

PLAYER	W	L	ERA	G	SV	IP	H	BB	SO
Oquendo, E	1	0	2.12	27	7	30	14	19	39
Mello, J	0	1	3.48	20	0	31	33	16	22
Havird, J	5	7	3.53	18	0	104	114	31	81
Knudsen, K	2	0	4.18	34	0	52	49	30	44
Lopez, R	3	11	4.18	19	0	105	120	35	56
Williams, M	2	2	4.27	32	4	40	35	21	54
Over, D	4	3	4.37	42	2	47	57	25	38
Bayliss*, B	3	6	4.42	10	0	59	58	17	39
Champlin, K	7	9	4.44	18	0	103	138	22	69
Lanning, J	0	3	5.33	21	9	29	28	13	29
Ezell, J	1	1	5.40	12	1	15	9	15	11
Gallardo, A	6	7	6.41	26	1	81	101	35	62
Toribio, J	1	1	7.23	11	1	19	23	12	19
Ball, J	1	2	7.98	13	0	24	32	7	11
Abel, N	1	3	8.16	7	0	29	38	15	15
Reed, D	0	1	8.59	5	0	15	21	10	11

WASHINGTON WILD THINGS

PLAYER	AVG	AB	R	H	HR	RBI	BB	SO	SB	CS
Harris, J	.299	187	31	56	5	25	20	31	18	3
Sweeney, K	.296	297	62	88	15	61	87	90	2	2
Jackson, B	.294	388	61	114	16	76	18	69	8	2
Brown, R	.275	385	65	106	1	33	36	60	29	4
Pollock, K	.255	243	45	62	11	41	39	48	1	2
Roa, H	.247	356	54	88	15	62	19	81	4	0
Peoples-Walls, K	.246	264	23	65	2	45	13	56	9	2
Fidanza, J	.245	110	11	27	1	15	3	23	3	1
Bohn, J	.233	163	24	38	2	16	29	46	1	3
Reese, K	.217	157	26	34	5	20	3	24	0	1
Hill, M	.214	295	47	63	13	39	44	107	0	0
Fernandez, A	.168	119	19	20	2	14	16	42	6	2

PLAYER	W	L	ERA	G	SV	IP	H	BB	SO
Condra-Bogan, J	1	0	1.17	11	1	15	10	3	15
Eaton, J	1	0	2.21	12	1	20	16	7	23
Strecker, Z	5	5	2.33	44	20	62	56	17	40
Gibbons, E	3	2	2.97	6	0	36	31	11	33
Trimarco, F	0	0	3.00	8	0	15	9	2	11
Foss, T	12	5	3.06	20	0	132	114	32	88
Adkins, D	5	1	3.37	39	1	51	36	25	50
Cunningham, C	10	3	3.45	20	0	125	120	46	64
Bradley, T	2	3	3.60	21	1	40	46	21	35
OKeefe, B	3	5	3.96	18	0	73	78	27	65
Garkow, T	2	1	4.21	4	0	21	17	4	26
Burns, A	4	3	4.33	19	1	71	74	37	56
Smyth, M	0	0	4.69	9	0	15	13	6	8
Ravert, J	1	1	5.06	14	0	21	23	19	14
Stanton, C	2	3	6.95	10	0	34	50	9	17
Schwartz, J	1	2	9.00	7	0	21	29	6	19
Belicek, T	1	3	10.95	6	0	23	35	11	19

WINDY CITY THUNDERBOLTS

PLAYER	AVG	AB	R	H	HR	RBI	BB	SO	SB	CS
Krane, R	.321	165	22	53	3	26	11	33	5	6
Johnson, C	.297	374	60	111	7	48	39	60	57	6
Zier, T	.296	382	50	113	5	46	25	52	15	6
LaLonde, R	.281	334	38	94	5	47	22	46	1	1
Balkwill, L	.268	317	46	85	20	64	41	83	2	0
Bass, C	.251	179	25	45	4	25	26	42	0	1
Wood, K	.249	281	48	70	7	30	52	93	2	2
Walker, K	.225	377	55	85	6	31	44	97	48	13
Player	AVG	AB	R	H	HR	RBI	BB	SO	SB	CS
Beck, B	.224	335	36	75	4	42	19	94	7	7
Dundon, A	.157	89	14	14	2	4	13	32	6	0
Kerian, D	.151	126	14	19	1	10	18	34	0	1
Krug, W	.123	73	10	9	0	3	9	21	5	4

PLAYER	W	L	ERA	G	SV	IP	H	BB	SO
Muller, B	5	1	1.36	7	0	46	34	9	41
Kuzminsky, S	3	2	1.42	32	1	32	23	12	42
Von Ruden, K	1	2	1.94	5	0	32	27	10	20
Loconsole, B	1	4	2.23	42	27	44	36	12	55
Fisher, J	10	7	2.80	20	0	138	126	29	120
Jaeger, J	0	1	3.37	21	0	27	30	8	14
Glick, J	6	2	3.51	34	0	33	24	14	30
Murphy, T	1	0	3.60	15	0	20	26	9	14
Landsheft, W	2	2	3.73	5	0	31	26	11	21
Chapman, C	5	6	3.86	20	0	121	113	50	113
Westcott, Z	8	5	4.23	19	0	115	116	36	88
Ledet, P	1	2	4.88	12	0	28	26	13	29
Chigas, C	0	3	5.90	28	0	43	48	17	37
Lowe, A	0	1	6.51	19	0	19	18	13	22
Santiago, T	3	4	6.58	13	0	55	73	14	45
Robison, D	2	2	7.26	7	0	26	30	23	9

PACIFIC ASSOCIATION

STANDINGS	W	L	PCT	GB
Sonoma Stompers	52	26	.667	—
Vallejo Admirals	36	42	.462	16
Pittsburg Diamonds	36	42	.462	16
San Rafael Pacifics	32	46	.410	20

Playoffs—Vallejo defeated Sonoma 11-8 in championship game.

PECOS LEAGUE

MOUNTAIN	W	L	PCT	GB
Alpine Cowboys	43	18	.705	—
Roswell Invaders	41	22	.651	3
Trinidad Triggers	36	24	.600	6 ½
Santa Fe Fuego	32	27	.542	10
Garden City Wind	19	43	.306	24 ½
White Sands Pupfish	13	50	.206	31

PACIFIC	W	L	PCT	GB
Tucson Saguaros	46	14	.767	—
Bakersfield Train Robbers	37	25	.597	10
High Desert Yardbirds	36	27	.571	11 ½
California City Whiptails	28	36	.438	20
Hollywood Stars	20	39	.339	25 ½
Monterey Amberjacks	18	44	.290	29

Playoffs—First Round-Roswell defeated Trinidad 2-1; High Desert defeated Bakersfield 2-0 in best-of-3 series. **Semifinals**—High Desert defeated Tucson 2-1 and Roswell defeated Alpine 2-1 in best-of-3 series. **Finals**—High Desert defeated Roswell 2-0 in best-of-3 series.

U.S. PROFESSIONAL BASEBALL LEAGUE

EAST	W	L	PCT	GB
Eastside	28	25	.528	—
Utica	26	27	.491	2

WEST	W	L	PCT	GB
Birmingham-Bloomfield	29	24	.547	—
Westside	24	31	.436	6

Playoffs— Birmingham-Bloomfield defeated Eastside 5-2 in championship game.

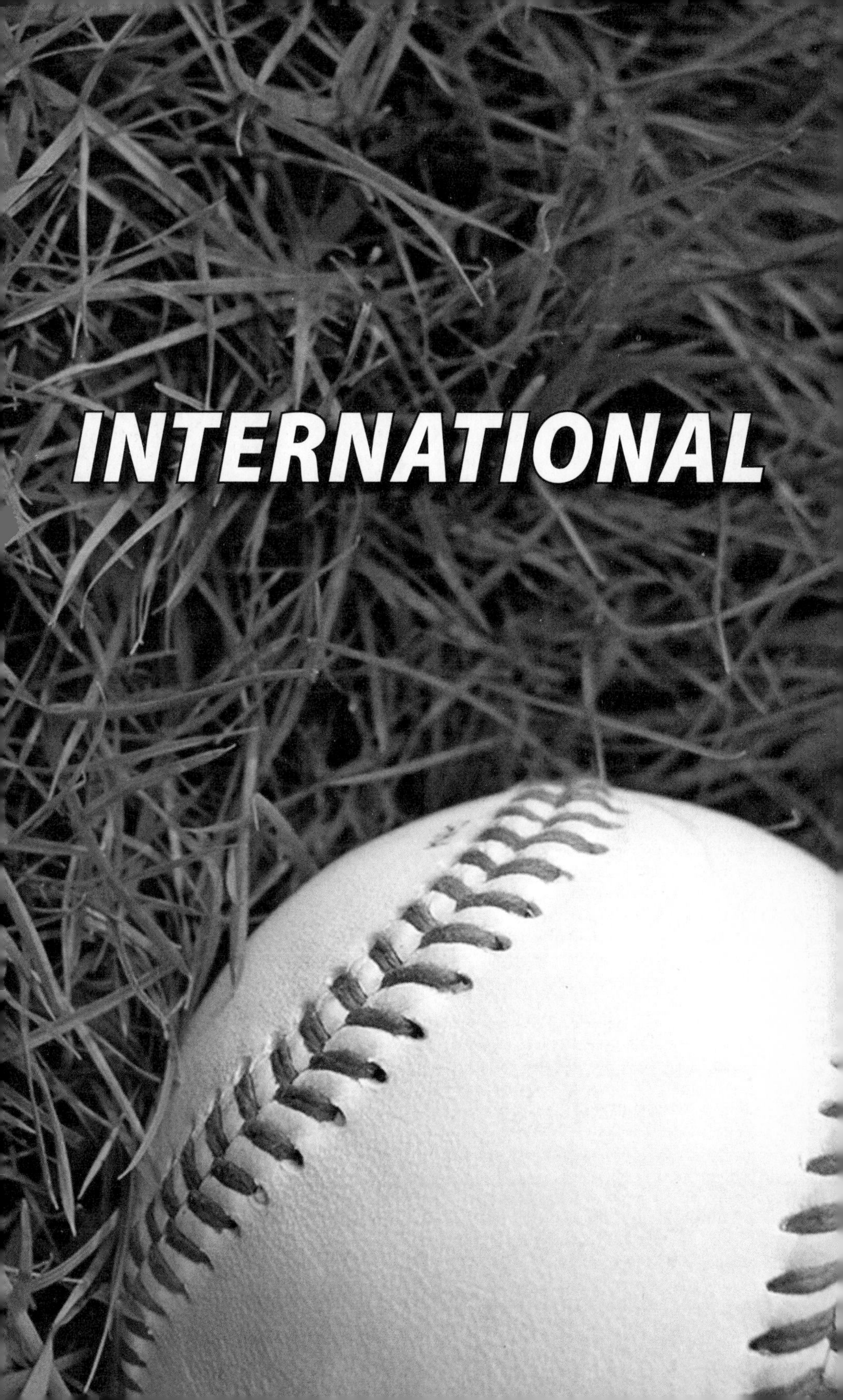
INTERNATIONAL

U.S. Kicks Off Historic Year With WBC Victory

BY KYLE GLASER

There was something different about this United States World Baseball Classic team. That much was apparent early on.

Its predecessors had been characterized largely by passivity, stoicism and, ultimately, disappointing finishes. Whether it was their two second-round eliminations or their fourth-place finish in 2009, one could hardly tell at times if the U.S. had won or lost a game based on their players' reactions.

With accomplished but famously restrained veterans such as Derek Jeter, Chipper Jones and David Wright leading their teams, the U.S. simply didn't project the energy or enthusiasm needed to compete in the two and a half week sprint that is the WBC.

And then this team came along. It was younger, less proven, hungrier than those that came before it. Before long, the narrative that U.S. players simply didn't care about the WBC was quickly rendered incompatible with the current group.

There was Eric Hosmer, pounding his chest and faux-ripping his shirt, a la Superman, after big hits. There was Adam Jones, leaping and crashing into walls and letting out roars for all to hear after he'd brought the crowd to its feet. There was Marcus Stroman, shimmying his shoulders and exuding his incomparable swag on the mound. There were unheralded relievers Pat Neshek and Tyler Clippard and Luke Gregerson, pumping their fists and letting out exhortations of joy after escaping key jams. There were Christian Yelich and Andrew McCutchen, flashing giant smiles after every key hit or big play.

This team was different. This team wanted something. And this team had the potent mix of passion, desire and talent to channel it into concrete results. By the time they were done, they had claimed the World Baseball Classic championship for the United States for the first time.

"The way this team came together and just went out every night and did anything we can to win, it was special to be a part of. It was the most fun I've ever had playing baseball," said Yelich, the Marlins' 25-year-old outfielder. "I think we just all had a common goal when we came here. There was only one thing on our mind, (which) was to win this thing and to do whatever we can to win. I think that helped us come together."

ALEX TRAUTWIG/WBCI/MLB PHOTOS VIA GETTY IMAGES

Eric Hosmer and Team USA won their first World Baseball Classic title.

Things began inauspiciously for Team USA in the first round in Miami. It labored through a 3-2, 10-inning win against Colombia and blew a five-run lead in its next contest, a 7-5 loss to the defending champion Dominicans in front of a raucous, pro-D.R. crowd.

It was at that point manager Jim Leyland made a choice. The 72-year-old looked around his locker room and saw a self-motivated group dissatisfied with how it had played. Rather than go for a big speech, Leyland decided to let his team be.

"We just kind of stayed the course," Leyland said. "You know, these teams are good. There's no rah-rah stuff or anything. Our guys, everybody knows what's at stake."

The U.S. bashed undermanned Canada 8-0 in the final game of pool play to punch its ticket to the second round in San Diego, where the

Dominican Republic, Venezuela and Puerto Rico awaited.

It was in San Diego where the U.S. discovered its identity. It was there it became a team that was going to fight, was going to play with everything, was going to go down swinging.

Against Venezuela, the U.S. fell behind 2-1 but scored three runs in the eighth on dramatic homers by Jones and Hosmer for the comeback victory. Team USA trailed 4-0 and 6-3 against Puerto Rico, but fought back to make it a 6-5 game with the tying run on third base. Though they lost, it was another emotional comeback effort on display.

American fans picked up on it and responded. A sellout crowd packed Petco Park for Team USA's second-round finale against the Dominican Republic, a winner-take-all elimination game. Whereas U.S. fans had been outnumbered and drowned out at other venues, in San Diego they showed up in droves and didn't stop screaming. The stars and stripes flew, the "U-S-A" chants never stopped and the decibel level never dipped below "loud."

"Atmosphere was great. It was huge," right fielder McCutchen said. "Crowds were big, crowds were great, and they were intense. I definitely felt we had the advantage up here in San Diego."

That hit a crescendo against the D.R. In the bottom of the seventh, with the U.S. nursing a 4-2 lead, Manny Machado hit a long fly ball to center field that looked like a home run off the bat. Jones raced back and to his left in center field. He curved slightly as he approached the 396-foot sign and ran out of room. In one athletic motion, he leaped as high as his 31-year-old body would allow, stretched his left arm as high and wide as it would go … and made The Catch to rob Machado of the home run.

The sellout crowd exploded. Jones contorted his body in all sorts of celebratory motions. Clippard on the mound raised his arms and screamed "Oh my God." In that moment, any notion that American players and fans didn't care about the WBC died a sudden death.

"At the end of the day I'm not representing the Orioles, Cutch ain't representing the Pirates, we're not representing the Marlins, we're representing the entire United States," Jones said the night of The Catch. "And that right there is pretty special."

The U.S. never trailed en route to a 2-1 semifinal victory over Japan as games shifted to Dodger Stadium, playing flawless defense despite a rain-soaked infield.

And then came the finale. Puerto Rico was the standard-bearer for the tournament to that point. With teamwide bleached blond hair, stars such as Carlos Correa, Francisco Lindor and Yadier Molina, and infectious energy, Puerto Rico ran roughshod through the tournament field to a 7-0 record entering the finals, with a raucous, drum-banging fan base following them to every city along the way.

The U.S. had one player who could match that energy and put him on the mound: Stroman, the irrepressible 5-foot-8 righthander whose motto is "Height Don't Measure Heart."

With the U.S. in the finals for the first time, Stroman soaked up all the energy and emotion he could from the crowd of 51,565, and performed like he was, indeed, the best pitcher in the world.

The 25-year-old took a no-hitter into the seventh inning and faced the minimum through six. He shimmied after striking out Enrique Hernandez to end the third. He snagged a comebacker from Lindor in the fourth and flicked it over to first base

USA BASEBALL

2017 WORLD BASEBALL CLASSIC
LOS ANGELES

FINAL STANDINGS

1. United States **3.** Japan
2. Puerto Rico **4.** Netherlands

FINAL STATISTICS

BATTING

PLAYER	AVG	AB	R	H	2B	3B	HR	RBI	BB	SO	SB
Alex Bregman	.500	4	0	2	0	0	0	0		1	0
Brandon Crawford	.385	26	3	10	3	1	0	6		1	0
Eric Hosmer	.385	26	6	10	3	0	1	5		1	1
Christian Yelich	.310	29	7	9	4	0	0	3		8	0
Ian Kinsler	.267	30	6	8	1	0	1	3		6	0
Jonathan Lucroy	.267	15	1	4	0	0	0	1		3	0
Buster Posey	.267	15	2	4	0	0	2	4		2	0
Andrew McCutch.	.238	21	1	5	1	0	0	5		7	0
Giancarlo Stanton	.227	22	3	5	2	0	1	4		10	0
Adam Jones	.200	35	4	7	2	0	2	5		6	0
Nolan Arenado	.161	31	6	5	1	0	1	3		11	0
Paul Goldschmidt	.077	13	2	1	0	0	0	0		3	0
Josh Harrison	.000	5	0	0	0	0	0	0		1	0
Daniel Murphy	.000	6	0	0	0	0	0	0		2	0

PITCHING

PITCHERS	W	L	ERA	SV	G	IP	H	BB	SO
Chris Archer	0	0	0.00	0	1	4	0	0	3
Sam Dyson	1	0	0.00	0	5	6	0	0	4
Luke Gregerson	0	0	0.00	3	4	4	0	1	3
Jake McGee	0	0	0.00	0	2	1	1	1	2
Mark Melancon	0	0	0.00	0	1	1	1	1	1
Pat Neshek	1	0	0.00	0	5	5	4	1	4
Drew Smyly	0	0	0.00	1	1	5	3	0	8
Danny Duffy	2	0	1.13	0	2	8	8	1	8
Tyler Clippard	1	0	2.08	0	3	4	2	1	6
Nate Jones	0	0	2.25	0	4	4	1	2	3
Marcus Stroman	1	1	2.35	0	3	15	12	2	9
Daniel Robertson	0	0	2.45	0	4	4	4	0	2
Tanner Roark	0	0	5.06	0	2	5	5	3	1
Mychal Givens	0	0	7.71	0	3	2	4	1	5
Andrew Miller	0	1	13.50	0	4	3	3	1	5

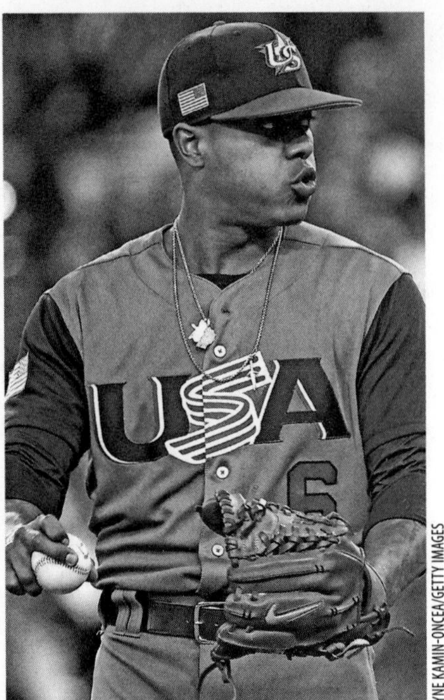

JAYNE KAMIN-ONCEA/GETTY IMAGES

Marcus Stroman posted a 2.35 ERA to be named the WBC tournament MVP.

like he didn't have a care on Earth. He walked off the mound in the seventh, biting his lip and nodding his head, letting the whole world know he had just been untouchable.

It was cocky. It was bold.

It was exactly what was needed to silence Puerto Rico's dugout and fans, a task no one had accomplished before, and in the process robbed the opponent of its greatest power source. Stroman took it and made the energy his own, and before long the "U-S-A" chants and cheers rained down on him as he departed with a 7-0 lead to put the U.S. in position to win the title, which it did with an 8-0 victory.

"There was more emphasis on just winning for America," said Stroman, who was named tournament MVP. "Obviously, this is our first win. We've had a few early exits in the past. So each and every guy came into this with one goal, and that was to win it. There was no one who kind of went about it lackadaisical. Everyone was into every single pitch."

The heroes were many for Team USA on its title run. Hosmer hit .385/.500/.615. Brandon Crawford slashed .385/.429/.577. Sam Dyson didn't allow a hit in six scoreless innings of relief. Gregerson converted three save opportunities without allowing a hit.

Jones, McCutchen, Ian Kinsler and Giancarlo Stanton all took turns playing offensive standout. Team USA recorded a 2.25 ERA and .191 opponent average.

Every single player was committed. The emotions were visible, the performance measurable, the results undeniable.

The United States was finally World Baseball Classic champion."

"I don't mean this to sound wrong, but for the most part, up until this point, the other countries were probably into this event a little bit more than the United States," Leyland said. "But in talking to our players, I know they're going to spread the word. I've had some players already tell me this is the greatest experience of their life."

Jewish Cinderella

The early storyline of the World Baseball Classic was Team Israel, which had never before gotten out of qualifying. Few expected them to even win a single game.

But riding a roster of largely Jewish-American minor leaguers like Ike Davis, Nate Freiman, and Josh Zeid, Israel stunned the world when by going 3-0 to win their pool, including massive upsets over perennial powers South Korea and the Netherlands. The run continued with another shocking win over Cuba in the second round. In a matter of one week, Israel went from a token entrant to one win shy of the semifinals. They fell short by losing their final two games of the second round, but their Cinderella run cemented Israel's place in the upper levels of international baseball.

The Kids Are All Right

The USA 18-and-under National Team not only won the U18 World Cup, but did so in dominating fashion. Team USA ran roughshod through the tournament field, going 9-0 and outscoring the opposition 60-5. Their 8-0 win over South Korea in the championship game secured the title in Thunder Bay, Ontario, Canada.

It was the fourth straight U18 World Cup championship for Team USA.

The pitchers were the stars of the tournament. Righthander Ethan Hankins (Forsyth, Ga.) pitched 12 innings with one run allowed and 27 strikeouts. Lefthander Matthew Liberatore (Peoria, Ariz.) pitched 12 scoreless innings with 13 strikeouts. Righthander Brandon Dieter (Covina, Calif.) pitched 10 scoreless with 10 punchouts.

Outfielder Alek Thomas (Chicago) hit .363 and first baseman Triston Casas (Pembroke Pines, Fla.) had three homers and 13 RBIs to lead the offense.

Tijuana scores first title game

The Tijuana Toros (Bulls) had never won the Mexican League championship since the franchise was launched in 2004. The Two Laredos Owls, the franchise that moved to Tijuana, had won it all in 1989, but the Toros lost in their first trip to the finals in 2016.

The 2017 edition of the Toros put an end to the frustrations and were Mexico's best team from start to finish. They posted a .691 winning percentage during the regular season, including a 40-16 home record, and cruised to the North Division title, despite the fact that five teams in the division won 60 or more games.

Tijuana needed six games to get past its first-round playoff series against Aguascalientes, and similarly needed six games in the semifinals to beat Monterrey. The Toros completed their run with a five-game championship series victory, capped by a grand slam by former Mets farmhand Dustin Martin in the third inning of game five. That led to a 15-3 runaway win in the clincher as the Toros avenged last year's championship series loss and defeated Puebla.

Martin was one of several key imports on the Tijuana lineup, including former Nationals outfielder Corey Brown, who led the club with 24 home runs and 85 RBIs while ranking second with 19 stolen bases. He also hit .313 with five homers in the postseason. Martin pitched in with 81 walks and a team-high 24 steals, while former Southern California outfielder Cyle Hankerd—who last played in the affiliated minors in 2013—hit .321 with 17 homers, then slugged five more in the postseason.

On the mound, lefthander Carlos Hernandez made a splash in his first Mexican League season, going 10-2, 2.67 to rank fourth in the circuit in ERA. Hernandez, a former Athletics and Rockies farmhand, was the Toros' top regular-season starter along with Miguel Pena (11-2, 2.77), but veterans Alex Sanabia and Horacio Ramirez combined to earn five of the team's 12 playoff wins.

Cuban outfielder Yadir Drake, a 27-year-old who spent parts of two seasons in the Dodgers system, won the league batting title at .385 in his first season with Durango.

Former White Sox and Blue Jays farmhand Nestor Molina, 28, won the league ERA title in his first full Mexican League season. The Venezuelan righthander went 12-3, 1.89, ranked second with 124 strikeouts and led the league with three complete games.

STANDINGS & LEADERS

NORTH	W	L	PCT	GB
Toros de Tijuana	76	34	.691	—
Sultanes de Monterrey	68	41	.624	7 ½
Acereros del Norte	67	41	.620	8
Rieleros de Aguascalientes	64	46	.582	12
Vaqueros Union Laguna	60	49	.550	15 ½
Diablos Rojos del Mexico	57	52	.523	18 ½
Saraperos de Saltillo	44	64	.407	31
Generales de Durango	43	66	.394	32 ½
SOUTH	**W**	**L**	**PCT**	**GB**
Leones de Yucatan	63	42	.600	—
Pericos de Puebla	56	54	.509	9 ½
Tigres de Quintana Roo	49	56	.467	14
Rojos del Aguila de Veracruz	48	57	.457	15
Bravos de Leon	45	60	.429	18
Piratas de Campeche	43	63	.406	20 ½
Guerreros de Oaxaca	40	67	.374	24
Olmecas de Tabasco	38	69	.355	26

Playoffs: Elimination Game—Leon defeated Veracruz. First Round–Monterrey defeated Monclova 4-0; Yucatan defeated Leon 4-0; Puebla defeated Quintana Roo 4-0 and Tijuana defeated Aquascalientes 4-2 in best-of-7 series. **Semifinals**—Tijuana defeated Monterrey 4-2 and Pueblca defeated Yucatan 4-1 in best-of-7 series. **Finals**—Tijuana defeated Puebla 4-1 in best-of-7 series.

PLAYER, TEAM	AVG	AB	R	H	2B	3B	HR	RBI	BB	SO	SB
Drake, Yadir, DUR	.385	260	46	100	21	2	14	61	28	39	6
Mayora, Daniel, MTY	.370	327	57	121	20	0	9	43	31	52	11
Borbon, Julio, PUE	.365	337	71	123	14	3	5	37	33	40	20
Valdez, Jesus, LAG	.363	350	67	127	26	2	16	61	32	39	3
Almonte, Zoilo, MTY	.355	442	78	157	33	1	15	70	46	84	0
Greene, Justin, MVA	.354	384	89	136	18	2	13	45	44	80	51
Roberson, Chris, MTY	.344	416	79	143	35	6	16	63	37	64	18
Chavez, Endy, PUE	.343	385	56	132	18	0	5	59	34	31	1
Lugo, Francisco, YUC	.342	365	62	125	13	1	8	55	18	44	8
Castillo, Jesus, AGS	.342	409	79	140	24	0	20	82	67	63	9
Zazueta, Amadeo, MVA	.341	405	60	138	26	2	9	64	21	42	8
Urias, Ramon, MEX	.340	388	91	132	29	3	19	79	41	75	12
Perez, Jairo, DUR	.336	342	57	115	20	0	14	65	21	41	12
Dotel, Welington, LAG	.333	306	64	102	16	6	9	44	23	63	17
Terrazas, Ivan, MEX	.332	322	44	107	28	0	5	60	20	45	1
Valdespin, Jordany, TAB	.332	265	48	88	13	4	4	37	35	34	15
Arredondo, Jesus, PUE	.332	398	71	132	33	1	15	87	42	65	8

PLAYER, TEAM	W	L	ERA	G	IP	H	R	ER	HR	BB	SO
Molina, Nestor, VER	12	3	1.89	23	153	128	40	32	6	37	124
Samayoa, Jose, YUC	11	2	2.29	22	110	95	32	28	4	38	77
Pina, Jose, VER	7	7	2.64	18	112	96	36	33	6	31	74
Hernandez, Carlos, TIJ	10	2	2.67	18	98	94	32	29	4	15	65
Lowey, Josh, MVA	8	5	2.69	20	127	115	46	38	4	36	146
Roenicke, Josh, PUE	7	5	2.70	21	120	129	43	36	8	28	103
Pena, Miguel, TIJ	11	2	2.77	20	107	97	33	33	8	34	83
Negrin, Yoanner, YUC	11	4	2.93	21	129	115	46	42	5	31	93
Gonzalez, Edgar, MTY	6	2	2.94	19	95	97	38	31	2	23	52
Acosta, Octavio, MEX	14	1	2.99	21	123	115	41	41	10	46	102
Silva, Walter, LEO	8	9	3.07	21	117	121	51	40	4	36	59
Astorga, Alejandro, TAB	4	12	3.26	22	116	122	54	42	8	40	82
Rodriguez, Francisco, YUC	8	6	3.34	18	97	104	38	36	8	33	53
Ortega, Pablo, TIG	10	9	3.43	21	134	141	59	51	14	33	85
Flores, Manuel Al, VER	8	7	3.59	22	130	133	57	52	9	25	96
Valdez, Salvador, TAB	2	9	3.69	21	100	121	51	41	5	25	46
De La Cruz, Frankie, SAL	11	4	3.79	20	126	110	60	53	9	44	91
Valdez, Rolando, CAM	9	5	3.87	20	121	127	59	52	14	30	73

JAPAN

Fukuoka's Dominance Continues

For the third time in four seasons, the Fukuoka SoftBank Hawks are the kings of Nippon Professional Baseball.

It was a fitting title for the best team in the league. Fukuoka won an NPB-best 94 games during the regular season, winning the Pacific League by 13 1/2 games.

This is nothing new for Fukuoka. They have won four titles this decade and now have eight Japan Series titles overall.

The Hawks had a well-balanced roster. Yuki Yanagita did a little bit of everything offensively, finishing second in the league with a .310 batting average with 31 home runs and 14 steals and a league-best .589 slugging percentage. Slugger Alfredo Despaigne added a league-best 35 home runs and 103 RBIs.

MASTERPRESS/GETTY IMAGES

Shohei Otani

But as good as the Fukuoka lineup was, its pitching staff was even better. Dennis Sarfate was a dominating closer, going 2-2, 1.09 with 54 saves in 66 games. Kodai Senga (13-4, 2.64), Nao Higashihama (16-5, 2.65) and Rick Van Den Hurk (13-7, 3.24) gave the Hawks a trio of aces. All three ranked among the league's ERA leaders while showing durabilty and the stuff to miss bats.

It was Sarfate who was the hero in the deciding Game Six of the Japan Series.

Seiichi Uchikawa homered in the ninth inning to tie the game, keeping the Yokohama DeNA Baystars from forcing a deciding Game Seven. But all that did was tie up the game.

Sarfate kept the Baystars scoreless for three innings–he worked exclusively in one-inning stints during the season. He was named the Japan Series MVP.

That gave Keizo Kawashima the opportunity he needed. In the 11th, Kawashima's sayanora single drove in Akira Nakamura for the championship-deciding run.

"To be honest, my mind went blank, and then I realized we just won the Japan Series," manager Kimiyasu Kudo told Jason Coksrey of the Japan Times. "In an instant, everything we went through, including the tough times, was playing out in my mind, and I had tears in my eyes. But we've done it, and I'm thankful the players were able to make it happen."

Although their playoffs ended two wins short of a title, it was still a very successful year for the Baystars. Led by Central League batting champ Toshiro Miyazaki and manager Alex Ramirez, Yokohama made its first Japan Series appearance since 1998.

With a 60-83 record, Hokkaido didn't come close to making the playoffs, but the Fighters were still a focus of attention thanks to young two-way star Shohei Otani.

An ankle injury cost Otani plenty of time on the mound, but he still managed to hit .332/.403/.540 in 202 at-bats and he also went 3-2, 3.20 in five starts. This was statistically the worst season Otani has had since he broke out as a 19-year-old in 2014, but that did little to dim expectations for a righthander who is considered the best pitcher in the world who is not pitching in Major League Baseball.

As the 2017 season ended, Otani was expected to investigate being posted and coming to the U.S., but he faced several hurdles. Most notably, the posting system agreement between the NPB and MLB had expired and negotiations for a new system had bogged down. Also, Otani would be forgoing potentially hundreds of millions of dollars by opting to come to the States before his age 25 season.

Under MLB's current collective bargaining agreement players under age 25 coming from a foreign league are subject to international bonus restrictions and can only sign a minor league contract. Under such rules, Otani would be limited to a likely seven figure contract offer. If he was a full free agent, he would be expected to land a $100+ million deal.

CENTRAL LEAGUE

Team	W	L	T	PCT	GB
Hiroshima Carp	88	51	4	.633	—
Hanshin Tigers	78	61	4	.561	10
Yokohama DeNA Baystars	73	65	5	.529	14 ½
Yomiuri Giants	72	68	3	.514	16 ½
Chunichi Dragons	59	79	5	.428	28 ½
Yakult Swallows	45	96	2	.319	44

Climax Series Playoffs–First Stage: Yokohama defeated Hanshin 2-1 in best-of-3 series. **Final Stage:** Yokohama defeated Hiroshima 4-1 in best-of-7 series.

JAPAN

INDIVIDUAL BATTING LEADERS

PLAYER	AVG	AB	R	H	2B	3B	HR	RBI	SB
Miyazaki, Toshiro, Baystars	.323	480	53	155	28	1	15	62	0
McGehee, Casey, Giants	.315	523	67	165	48	1	18	77	4
Oshima, Yohei, Dragons	.313	476	50	149	20	3	3	29	23
Abe, Tomohiro, Carp	.310	413	63	128	17	4	4	49	17
Maru, Yoshihiro, Carp	.308	556	109	171	35	3	23	92	13
Lopez, Jose, Baystars	.301	569	72	171	42	0	30	105	0
Suzuki, Seiya, Carp	.300	437	85	131	28	1	26	90	16
Toritani, Takashi, Tigers	.293	488	57	143	23	3	4	41	8
Sakamoto, Hayato, Giants	.291	539	82	157	30	0	15	61	14
Itoi, Yoshio, Tigers	.290	427	60	124	16	0	17	62	21

REMAINING U.S., CANADIAN & LATIN PLAYERS

PLAYER, TEAM	AVG	AB	R	H	2B	3B	HR	RBI	SB
Eldred, Brad, Carp	.265	344	40	91	11	0	27	78	0
Batista, Xavier, Carp	.256	125	21	32	5	0	11	26	0
Balentien, Wladimir, Swallows	.254	445	60	113	14	1	32	80	0
Rogers, Jason, Tigers	.252	123	15	31	7	0	5	23	0
Viciedo, Dayan, Dragons	.250	332	43	83	11	1	18	49	4
Pena, Ramiro, Carp	.216	37	2	8	1	0	0	2	0
Green, Dean, Swallows	.194	72	5	14	2	0	2	8	0
Campbell, Eric, Tigers	.191	47	5	9	2	0	1	5	0
Cruz, Luis, Giants	.156	32	2	5	1	0	0	3	0
Messenger, Randy, Tigers	.136	44	3	6	1	0	1	2	0
Ciriaco, Audy, BayStars	.074	27	1	2	1	0	0	0	0

INDIVIDUAL PITCHING LEADERS

PITCHER	W	L	ERA	G	IP	H	HR	BB	SO
Sugano, Tomoyuki, Giants	17	5	1.59	25	187	129	10	31	171
Mikolas, Miles, Giants	14	8	2.25	27	188	162	10	23	187
Messenger, Randy, Tigers	11	5	2.39	22	143	134	5	44	155
Nomura, Yusuke, Carp	9	5	2.78	25	155	152	12	38	106
Imanaga, Shota, Baystars	11	7	2.98	24	148	115	13	52	140
Akiyama, Takumi, Tigers	12	6	2.99	25	160	158	15	16	123
Taguchi, Kazuto, Giants	13	4	3.01	26	171	159	14	49	122
Osera, Daichi, Carp	10	2	3.65	24	146	143	12	43	109
Buchanan, David, Swallows	6	13	3.66	25	160	158	19	56	112
Valdes, Raul, Dragons	6	9	3.76	23	146	139	13	47	83

REMAINING NORTH AMERICAN & LATINO PLAYERS

PLAYER, TEAM	W	L	ERA	G	SV	IP	H	BB	SO
Jackson, Jay, Carp	2	2	2.03	60	1	62	43	19	55
Mathieson, Scott, Giants	4	4	2.24	59	2	68	52	18	79
Mikolas, Miles, Giants	14	8	2.25	27	0	188	162	23	187
Norberto, Jordan, Dragons	6	4	2.30	18	0	74	52	35	66
Patton, Spencer, BayStars	4	3	2.70	62	7	60	50	19	66
Dolis, Rafael, Tigers	4	4	2.71	63	37	63	53	17	85
Lueke, Josh, Swallows	4	6	2.97	61	7	61	54	19	70
Wieland, Joe, BayStars	10	2	2.98	21	0	133	114	37	112
Brasier, Ryan, Carp	2	1	3.00	26	1	30	32	8	19
Escobar, Edwin, BayStars	1	3	3.44	27	2	34	33	11	33
Guilmet, Preston, Swallows	1	1	3.62	28	0	55	49	15	57
Valdes, Raul, Dragons	6	9	3.76	23	0	146	139	47	83
Johnson, Kris, Carp	6	3	4.01	13	0	76	79	25	53
Klein, Phil, BayStars	2	3	4.75	7	0	36	35	22	27
Mendoza, Luis, Tigers	0	2	5.14	4	0	21	22	6	15
Ohlendorf, Ross, Swallows	0	1	5.50	4	0	18	18	11	15
Rondon, Jorge, Dragons	0	0	5.79	4	0	5	7	2	4
Araujo, Elvis, Dragons	1	0	6.48	6	0	8	9	3	6
Mendez, Roman, Tigers	0	0	6.52	8	0	10	12	3	9
Hagens, Bradin, Carp	0	0	6.60	11	0	15	24	7	10

PACIFIC LEAGUE

Team	W	L	T	PCT	GB
Fukuoka SoftBank Hawks	94	49	0	.657	—
Saitama Seibu Lions	79	61	3	.564	13 ½
Tohoku Rakuten Golden Eagles	77	63	3	.550	15 ½
Orix Buffaloes	63	79	1	.444	30 ½
Hokkaido Nippon Ham Fighters	60	83	0	.420	34
Chiba Lotte Marines	54	87	2	.383	39

CLIMAX SERIES PLAYOFFS—First Stage: Tohoku defeated Saitama 2-1 in best-of-3 series. **Final Stage:** Fukuoka defeated Tohoku 4-2 in best-of-7 series.

INDIVIDUAL BATTING LEADERS

PLAYER	AVG	AB	R	H	2B	3B	HR	RBI	SB
Akiyama, Shogo, Lions	.322	575	106	185	38	5	25	89	16
Yanagita, Yuki, Hawks	.310	448	95	139	30	1	31	99	14
Mogi, Eigoro, Eagles	.296	398	64	118	25	2	17	47	3
Nishikawa, Haruki, Fighters	.296	541	82	160	26	6	9	44	39
Akaminai, Ginji, Eagles	.293	529	55	155	30	0	3	60	2
Asamura, Hideto, Lions	.291	574	78	167	34	1	19	99	5
Nakajima, Hiroyuki, Buffaloes	.285	431	36	123	19	0	9	49	0
Peguero, Carlos, Eagles	.281	463	67	130	17	1	26	75	3
Koyano, Eiichi, Buffaloes	.277	470	41	130	14	1	6	47	0
Matsumoto, Go, Fighters	.274	402	46	110	17	0	5	33	6

REMAINING NORTH AMERICAN & LATINO PLAYERS

PLAYER, TEAM	AVG	AB	R	H	2B	3B	HR	RBI	SB
Marrero, Chris, Buffaloes	.290	283	39	82	15	1	20	50	1
Morel, Brent, Buffaloes	.276	98	9	27	8	0	1	11	0
Romero, Stefen, Buffaloes	.274	390	55	107	13	0	26	66	2
Despaigne, Alfredo, Hawks	.262	478	66	125	15	0	35	103	3
Santos, Roel, Marines	.250	180	22	45	10	0	3	8	5
Pena, Wily Mo, Marines	.242	219	24	53	14	0	15	38	0
Mejia, Ernesto, Lions	.241	345	34	83	18	0	19	53	1
Amador, Japhet, Eagles	.237	417	35	99	9	0	23	65	0
Laird, Brandon, Fighters	.229	503	56	115	18	1	32	90	0
Paredes, Jimmy, Marines	.219	269	31	59	9	0	10	26	1
Duffy, Matt, Marines	.201	164	15	33	8	1	6	18	0
Cruz, Luis, Eagles	.162	37	2	6	2	0	0	2	0
Jensen, Kyle, Hawks	.083	12	2	1	0	0	1	1	0

INDIVIDUAL PITCHING LEADERS

PITCHER	W	L	ERA	G	IP	H	HR	BB	SO
Kikuchi, Yusei, Lions	16	6	1.97	26	188	122	16	49	217
Norimoto, Takahiro, Eagles	15	7	2.57	25	186	148	11	48	222
Senga, Kodai, Hawks	13	4	2.64	22	143	107	15	46	151
Higashihama, Nao, Hawks	16	5	2.64	24	160	135	17	44	139
Kishi, Takayuki, Eagles	8	10	2.76	26	176	141	19	38	189
van den Hurk, Rick, Hawks	13	7	3.24	25	153	127	18	47	162
Mima, Manabu, Eagles	11	8	3.26	26	171	155	18	33	134
Futaki, Kota, Marines	7	9	3.39	23	143	136	14	35	128
Kaneko, Chihiro, Buffaloes	12	8	3.47	27	184	160	21	56	141
Nogami, Ryoma, Lions	11	10	3.63	24	144	128	10	24	113

REMAINING NORTH AMERICAN & LATINO PLAYERS

PLAYER, TEAM	W	L	ERA	G	SV	IP	H	BB	SO
Sarfate, Dennis, Hawks	2	2	1.09	66	54	66	34	10	102
Martin, Chris, Fighters	0	2	1.19	40	1	38	21	6	34
Germen, Gonzalez, Buffaloes	2	1	2.68	44	3	47	44	24	51
Herrmann, Frank, Eagles	3	1	2.72	56	1	53	48	13	58
Schlitter, Brian, Lions	1	5	2.83	64	0	64	58	29	23
Dickson, Brandon, Buffaloes	8	9	3.24	25	0	136	144	42	86
Wolfe, Brian, Lions	9	4	3.73	23	0	125	132	36	74
Mendoza, Luis, Fighters	3	7	3.97	20	0	100	106	38	56
Standridge, Jason, Marines	4	6	4.32	14	0	77	84	38	52
West, Matt, Buffaloes	0	0	4.50	2	0	2	1	3	0
Coke, Phillip, Buffaloes	2	3	4.56	6	0	24	30	10	16
Escobar, Edwin, Fighters	1	2	5.64	14	0	22	31	13	19
Garces, Frank, Lions	2	2	6.39	18	0	31	29	18	21
Fife, Stephen, Lions	1	1	6.86	5	0	21	32	13	11
Corrales, Josh, Eagles	0	0	15.00	1	0	3	5	6	3

KOREA

Kia Prevails

The Kia Tigers won their first Korean Series title in eight seasons in 2017, when it knocked off the Doosan Bears with a relatively easy run through the playoffs.

Kia had the best record in the regular season as well. They were led by league batting champ Kim Sun Bin, as well as slugger Choi Hyoung Woo, who led all players with 26 home runs.

Kia's Yang Hyeon Jong was named the league's MVP after he went 20-6, 3.44. Kia's pitching staff was especially deep as Hector Noesi and Pat Dean also excelled.

The 2017 season also marked the end for Lee Seung Yeop. One of the best sluggers in KBO history, Lee finished his career with a KBO-best 465 home runs over 15 seasons.

STANDINGS & LEADERS

TEAM	W	L	T	PCT	GB
Kia Tigers	87	56	1	.608	—
Doosan Bears	84	57	3	.596	2
Lotte Giants	80	62	2	.563	6 ½
NC Dinos	79	62	3	.560	7
SK Wyverns	75	68	1	.524	12
LG Twins	69	72	3	.489	17
Nexen Heroes	69	73	2	.486	17 ½
Hanwha Eagles	61	81	2	.430	25 ½
Samsung Lions	55	84	5	.396	30
KT Wix	50	94	0	.347	37 ½

PLAYOFFS: First round-NC defeated Lotte 3-2 in best-of-5 series. **Second round-**Doosan defeated NC 3-1 in best-of-5 series. **Championship-**Kia defeated Doosan 4-1 in best-of-7 series.

INDIVIDUAL BATTING LEADERS

PLAYER, TEAM	AVG	AB	R	H	2B	3B	HR	RBI	SB
Kim, Sun Bin, Kia	.370	476	84	176	34	1	5	64	4
Park, Kun Woo, Doosan	.366	483	91	177	40	2	20	78	20
Park, Min Woo, NC	.363	388	84	141	25	4	3	47	11
Na, Sung Bum, NC	.347	498	103	173	42	2	24	99	17
Park, Yong Taik, LG	.344	509	83	175	23	2	14	90	4
Choi, Hyoung Woo, Kia	.342	514	98	176	36	3	26	120	0
Kim, Jae Hwan, Doosan	.340	544	110	185	34	2	35	115	4
Rosario, Wilin, Hanwha	.339	445	100	151	30	1	37	111	10
Son, A Seop, Lotte	.335	576	113	193	35	4	20	80	25
Seo Geon Chang, Nexen	.332	539	87	179	28	3	6	76	15
Choi, Jeong, SK	.316	430	89	136	18	1	46	113	1
Ruf, Darin, .	315	515	90	162	38	0	31	124	2

INDIVIDUAL PITCHING LEADERS

PLAYER, TEAM	W	L	ERA	G	IP	H	BB	SO
Feierabend, Ryan, KT	8	10	3.04	26	160	153	31	132
Chang, Won Jun, Doosan	14	9	3.14	29	180	172	51	125
Hacker, Eric, NC	12	7	3.42	26	160	159	29	97
Cha, Woo Chan, LG	10	7	3.43	28	176	171	38	157
Yang, Hyeon Jong, KIA	20	6	3.44	31	193	209	45	158
Noesi, Hector, KIA	20	5	3.48	30	202	221	45	149
Kelly, Merrill, SK	16	7	3.60	30	190	204	45	189
Park, Se Woong, Lotte	12	6	3.68	28	171	170	56	117
Raley, Brooks, Lotte	13	7	3.80	30	187	199	44	156
Sosa, Henry, LG	11	11	3.88	30	185	189	38	153

TAIWAN

Spruill Helps Lamigo To Title

The Lamigo Monkeys won their fourth title since 2012 as they pounded Chinatrust Brother Elephants in three straight games after losing the Taiwan Series opener.

Zeke Spruill helped lead Lamigo all season as the Monkeys' ace went 15-4, 2.56.

The Taiwan Series outcome wasn't surprising as Brother Elephants left five star players off their postseason roster after rumors abounded in local media that there were players who were insubordinate to manager Cory Snyder. Several players went public with their complaints about Snyder's more American style of management. The team then benched two more players during the playoffs.

As soon as the season was over, the Chinatrust Brother Elephants released those seven players for what it announced were "disciplinary problems."

STANDINGS & LEADERS

TEAM	W	L	PCT	GB
Lamigo Monkeys	35	25	.583	—
Uni-President 7-Eleven Lions	34	26	.567	1
Fubon Guardians	28	32	.467	7
Chinatrust Brothers Elephants	23	37	.383	12

INDIVIDUAL BATITNG LEADERS

NAME, TEAM	AVG	AB	R	H	2B	3B	HR	RBI	SB
Wang Bai Rong, Lamigo	.407	437	107	178	33	1	31	101	16
Chen Jie Xian, Fubon	.387	437	113	169	34	5	3	48	17
Lin Yi Chuan, EDA	.353	385	62	136	23	1	17	71	4
Su Zhi Jie, 7-Eleven	.351	356	67	125	31	2	17	77	9
Chih Hsien Chiang, BE	.335	349	55	117	24	1	21	74	3
Hung Yu Lin, Lamigo	.331	393	69	130	28	0	18	77	1
Che Hsuan Lin, EDA	.323	347	60	112	24	1	7	48	3
Hu Jin Long, Fubon	.322	351	52	113	23	3	11	71	3
Chen Chun Xiu, Lamigo	.321	355	74	114	26	3	16	78	15
Ssu Chi Chou, BE	.317	325	58	103	27	2	1	35	9

INIDVIDUAL PITCHING LEADERS

NAME, TEAM	W	L	ERA	G	IP	H	BB	SO
Mike Loree, Fubon	16	4	2.18	25	161	131	32	154
Zeke Spruill, Lamigo	15	4	2.56	26	172	151	45	150
Darin Downs, Lamigo	10	3	3.49	25	150	146	52	143
Bryan Woodall, BE	13	8	3.63	26	174	188	32	135
Bruce Billings, 7-Eleven	13	10	4.17	26	145	133	63	148
Zack Segovia, Lamigo	16	5	4.20	27	165	177	45	129
Orlando Roman, BE	4	8	4.46	23	137	156	43	107
Scott Richmond, Fubon	7	7	4.53	30	137	156	45	118
Kevin Cheng, BE	5	8	4.58	35	126	148	29	87
Wang Yi Zheng, Lamigo	9	7	4.60	22	125	131	58	116

Rimini Wins Again

BY HARVEY SAHKER

The Rimini Pirates swept San Marino three games to none to win the Italy Series. It was Rimini's thirteenth national championship.

Dominican pitcher Jose Rosario (2-0, 0.00) dominated for Rimini in the brief series. A former Marlins minor leaguer, the 31-year old righty allowed three hits in 9.2 innings in the championship series.

Fourth place finishers in the regular season, Rimini faced first place Bologna in a best-of-five semi-final. The series went the distance, with the away team getting the win in all five games.

Several former big leaguers made their Italian Baseball League debuts in 2017 with some faring much better than others.

Cesar Jimenez

JAMIE SCHWABEROW/RICH CLARKSON AND ASSOCIATES, LLC

One successful MLB alumnus was southpaw Cesar Jimenez, who pitched in parts of six seasons with the Mariners, Phillies and Brewers between 2006 and 2015. The 32-year old Venezuelan joined Nettuno in June and was a key member of the pitching staff down the stretch (1-0, 1.53, 3 saves).

San Marino signed Fernando Nieve just before the end of the regular season. Formerly a member of the Astros and Mets, Nieve spent most of the 2017 campaign in the Mexican League. Nieve made four appearances in the postseason (1-1, 0.96) for San Marino and logged nineteen strikeouts in just 9.1 innings.

Infielder Jose Castillo signed with Parma in June. A veteran of 592 big league games with the Prates, Giants and Astros between 2004 and 2008, Castillo hit just .238 in 18 games for Parma.

Mark Teahen came out of retirement and spent the entire season with Padova. Teahen was a member of Team Canada at the 2009 World Baseball Classic and played over 800 big league games for the Royals, White Sox and Blue Jays. He last played pro ball in 2013. Teahen led the IBL with 29 walks but batted .211 in 33 games. Padova hit .199 as a team.

Osman Marval won his second IBL batting crown. A former Braves minor leaguer who has found significant success in Italy, Marval hit .384 to win his first title, with Parma in 2012. The 30-year old Venezuelan batted .464 for Bologna in 2017. That was the highest batting average in the league since Federico Bassi hit .477 for Modena in 1998. Marval also led the IBL in runs, hits, RBIs and on-base percentage.

San Marino hurler Carlos Quevedo (10-3, 2.05) led the IBL in wins and strikeouts (113). The 28-year-old Venezuelan spent seven seasons in the Astros minor league system.

Matteo Bocchi pitched a seven-inning no-hitter for Bologna in the European Cup. Bologna defeated the Rouen Huskies of France 14-0 in the game. The ten-run lead "mercy rule" was invoked after Rouen batted in the top of the seventh. Bocchi struck out 8 and walked 1 in the game. Earlier in the season, Bologna hurler Andrea Pizziconi threw a seven-inning one-hitter against Novara.

STANDINGS & LEADERS

TEAM	W	L	GB
Bologna	25	9	—
San Marino	24	10	1
Nettuno	22	12	3
Rimini	20	14	5
Parma	16	18	9
Novara	15	19	10
Padova	10	24	15
Padule	4	30	21

PLAYOFFS: Semifinals—Rimini defeated Bologna 3-2 and San Marino defeated Nettuno 3-0 in best-of-5 series. **Finals**—Rimini defeated San Marino 3-0 in best-of-5 series.

INDIVIDUAL BATTING LEADERS

PLAYER, TEAM	AVG	AB	R	H	2B	3B	HR	RBI
Marval, Osman, BOL	.464	125	36	58	10	0	7	40
Angulo, Oscar, NOV	.415	135	29	56	14	2	10	27
Bermudez, Ronald, NET	.403	134	25	54	11	2	2	25
Flores, Jose, BOL	.377	130	30	49	17	0	2	39
Nosti, Nick, BOL	.372	121	33	45	9	1	0	16
Epifano, Erik, RSM	.370	100	22	37	11	2	3	19
Colagrossi, Leonardo, NET	.352	88	10	31	7	1	0	13
Alarcon, Yordanis, PDU	.349	109	14	38	6	0	0	18
Vaglio, Alessandro, BOL	.336	128	28	43	10	1	0	18
Ferrini, Jose, RSM	.325	123	22	40	3	2	0	21

INDIVIDUAL PITCHING LEADERS

PLAYER, TEAM	W	L	ERA	SV	IP	H	R	ER	BB	SO
Rivero, Raul, BOL	5	0	1.23	1	44	28	8	6	10	53
Morellini, Yuri, NET	5	2	1.47	4	49	33	11	8	14	30
Jimenez, Cesar, NET	1	0	1.53	3	35	24	8	6	6	51
Pizziconi, Andrea, BOL	6	3	1.71	0	68	47	20	13	30	56
Aristil, Jonnathan, NOV	4	5	1.72	3	63	44	15	12	24	88
Quevedo, Carlos, RSM	10	3	2.05	0	92	65	25	21	28	113
Crepaldi, Filippo, BOL	4	1	2.38	1	34	21	11	9	13	36
Richetti, Carlos, RIM	4	3	2.40	0	64	63	28	17	11	37
Rosario, Jose, RIM	6	4	2.56	0	77	66	29	22	31	72
Uviedo, Ronald, NET	9	6	2.60	0	97	94	37	28	33	9

Neptunus Wins Fifth Straight

BY HARVEY SAHKER

Neptunus defeated the Amsterdam Pirates four games to one to win their fifth straight Holland Series. The Rotterdam club won a record seven consecutive Dutch national titles between 1999 and 2005. It was the first Series win for Ronald Jaarsma, who took over as Neptunus skipper after the 2016 campaign.

Reliever Loek van Mil won Games One and Five, saved Game Four and won the Holland Series MVP award. A 7-foot-1 righty, van Mil played in the minors from 2006 to 2016 and made it as high as AAA in the Indians, Angels, Reds and Twins organizations. Van Mil, 33, also had a stint in Japan's Pacific League. He appeared in four Holland Series games, striking out eight, walking none and posting a 2.16 ERA in 8.1 innings.

SHUGO TAKEMI/WBCI/MLB PHOTOS VIA GETTY IMAGES

Loek Van Mil

Righty Orlando Yntema threw a two-hitter in Game Two of the Series, a 12-0 Neptunus win. The 31-year old former Giants farm hand missed most of the regular season after having a tumor removed from one of his parathyroid glands in the spring. Yntema spent several days in intensive care and didn't make his 2017 Dutch Major League debut until July 29.

With Yntema unavailable, 44-year-old righty Elton Koeiman stepped into the breach and had a fantastic regular season (9-2, 2.73). Koeiman, a Curacao native, played in his first DML game in 1994.

Amsterdam's pitching staff was led by Rob Cordemans (10-0, 1.58). Cordemans, 42, topped the DML in wins, opponents' batting average (.180) and WHIP (0.77) after bouncing back from a shoulder injury that limited him in 2016. Cordemans has been the dominant pitcher in Dutch baseball for more than two decades, but his 2017 season ranked among his best efforts.

The DML operated with only seven teams in 2017. Haarlem based Kinheim opted to drop down one tier after the end of the 2016 season and no other club took their place. As a result of Kinheim's self-imposed relegation, the DML was missing slugger Bryan Engelhardt. The eight-time league home run leader and Kinheim veteran could be back in the DML in 2018. Engelhardt left Kinheim midway through the 2017 season and joined Amersfoort, who have been promoted to the top flight along with The Hague Storks.

Neptunus' dominance didn't end with their league title. They also won the 2017 European Cup. They claimed the continental club championship after defeating Bologna 7-3 in the final of the five-day tournament, which took place in Regensburg, Germany. It was their ninth European title and the second in three seasons. It was also the fifteenth European Cup crown for a Dutch club. The competition dates back to 1963. It was also the third consecutive season that a Dutch team has won the European Cup title.

STANDINGS & LEADERS

Team	W	L	T	GB
Amsterdam Pirates	29	6	1	—
Neptunus	26	9	1	3
HCAW	20	14	2	8 ½
Hoofddorp Pioniers	20	14	2	8 ½
DSS	13	23	0	16 ½
UVV	7	26	3	21
Oosterhout Twins	6	29	1	23
Semi-Final Round	**W**	**L**	**T**	**GB**
Neptunus	14	4	0	—
L&D Amsterdam Pirates	13	5	0	1
Hoofddorp Pioniers	6	12	0	8
HCAW	3	15	0	11

INDIVIDUAL BATTING LEADERS

(Mimimum 2.7 PA/Team Game)

PLAYER, TEAM	AVG	AB	R	H	2B	3B	HR	RBI
Dille, Benjamin, NEP	.448	116	30	52	7	1	0	22
Rombley, Danny,AMS	.390	118	31	46	10	0	5	40
Lampe Gilmer,AMS	.374	115	34	43	12	0	5	29
Vanden Meer, Stijn,NE	.369	122	43	45	7	4	0	21
Draijer, Remco,AMS	.362	130	37	47	7	1	3	17
Diaz, Christian,NEP	.359	131	30	47	9	2	2	32
Arends, Jeffrey,PIO	.357	112	15	40	7	0	5	31
Fernandes, Daniel,NEP	.356	132	31	47	12	2	1	27
Berkenbosch, Kenny,AMS	.336	110	23	37	11	1	3	26
Daantji, Shaldimar,NEP	.336	113	27	38	10	3	3	24

INDIVIDUAL PITCHING LEADERS

(Minimum 0.8 IP/Team Game)

PLAYER, TEAM	W	L	ERA	SV	IP	H	R	ER	BB	SO
Heijstek, Kevin, AMS	8	0	1.26	0	78	69	15	11	15	72
Cordemans, Rob, AMS	10	0	1.58	0	74	46	13	13	11	68
Huijer, Lars, PIO	4	3	2.01	0	72	60	23	16	23	78
Timmermans, Kaj, HCA	5	5	2.30	0	82	81	29	21	22	46
Ploeger, Jim, HCA	5	3	2.36	0	69	44	22	18	28	66
Koeiman, Elton, NEP	9	2	2.73	0	69	66	32	21	19	37
Markwell, Diegomar, NEP	9	2	3.01	0	81	60	32	27	29	45
Schel, Robin, AMS	7	1	3.09	0	58	53	20	20	15	41
Pfau, Chris, PIO	5	2	3.39	0	66	70	34	25	25	51
Delemarre, Ian, HCA	6	2	3.44	0	65	81	34	25	29	24

Granma Wins First Title

As the trickle of players leaving Cuba to try to make it to Major League Baseball turned into a torrent and eventually a flood, what remains for Cuba's Serie Nacional continues to be watered down, year after year.

The turnover the league sees from players leaving has understandably affected the caliber of play on the field. Yulieski Gurriel was the league's batting champ during the 2015-2016 season. He was playing for the Astros by the time the 2016-2017 season began. Similarly, Ciego de Avila outfielder Luis Robert, one of top young players in the league in 2016-2017, left after the season and has signed with the White Sox.

Luis Robert

BILL MITCHELL

All the departing talent has had one other effect. It's made traditional powers like Industriales (which has a Serie Nacional-record 12 titles) and Santiago de Cuba (eight league titles) into also-rans and has allowed previous bottom dwellers to rise up.

Led by Osvaldo Abreu and Lazaro Cedeno at the plate and Lazaro Blanco on the mound, Granma won its first ever Serie Nacional title. Granma's previous best finish was a third-place finish in 1989.

For Matanzas fans, the 2016-2017 season seemed all too repetitive. Once again, Matanzas dominated the regular season and once again they fell short in the playoffs. Matanzas has finished with the best regular season record in the league in each of the past four seasons, but it's yet to win a title.

Led by batting champ Jefferson Delgado and Yordanis Samon, Matanzas went an incredible 42-3 during the first phase of the regular season. Once teams were bulked up by additions from the teams eliminated in the first half, Matanzas' advantage was largely negated, but Matanzas' 28-17 record was still the best in the second half.

But Matanzas was knocked out in Game 7 of the semifinals by Granma, who then went on to sweep Ciego de Avila in the finals.

STANDINGS

Team	W	L	PCT	GB
Matanzas	70	20	.778	—
Ciego De Avila	56	34	.622	14
Villa Clara	52	38	.578	18
Granma	50	40	.556	20
Holquin	43	47	.478	27
Camaguey	39	51	.433	31

ELIMINATED IN FIRST HALF

Team	W	L	PCT	GB
Las Tunas	23	22	.512	19
Isla de la Juventud	23	22	.512	19
Guantanamo	23	22	.512	19
Industriales	21	23	.478	20 ½
Pinar del Rio	18	25	.419	23
Cienfuegos	18	27	.400	24
Artemisa	18	27	.400	24
Santiago de Cuba	14	30	.319	27 ½
Santi Spiritus	13	31	.296	28 ½
Mayabeque	11	33	.250	30 ½

INDIVIDUAL BATTING LEADERS

PLAYER, TEAM	AVG	OBP	SLG	AB	R	H	HR	RBI
Jefferson Delgado, MTZ	.446	.514	.554	148	32	66	3	22
Giorbis Duvergel, GTM	.400	.524	.600	115	19	46	5	23
Osvaldo Abreu, GRA	.398	.472	.503	161	31	64	1	17
Yordanis Samon, MTZ	.398	.467	.526	171	31	68	4	39
Luis Robert, CAV	.392	.522	.671	158	44	62	10	34
Ariel Sanchez, MTZ	.376	.473	.504	141	25	53	2	25
Frederic Cepeda, SSP	.373	.485	.560	134	18	50	6	22
Leonel Segura, CMG	.373	.435	.494	166	32	62	2	19
Alexander Ayala, CMG	.373	.465	.521	169	28	63	5	40
Leonardo Urgelles, IJV	.372	.472	.579	145	27	54	6	38
Dainier Galvez, IJV	.370	.449	.506	162	27	60	2	27
Lazaro Cedeño, GRA	.367	.474	.519	158	28	58	5	35
William Saavedra, PRI	.363	.451	.514	146	22	53	2	21
Edilse Silva La, SCU	.363	.466	.503	157	25	57	4	23
Raul Reyes, VCL	.362	.406	.450	149	19	54	2	18
Jorge Antonio Jhonson, LTU	.360	.410	.433	150	18	54	0	16
Michel Enrique, IJV	.357	.452	.452	115	16	41	1	17
Rigoberto Gomez, IJV	.356	.429	.397	146	22	52	0	15
Yorbert Sanchez, IND	.350	.391	.358	123	16	43	0	12
Anibal Medina, MTZ	.350	.416	.547	137	36	48	6	29

INDIVIDUAL PITCHING LEADERS

PLAYER, TEAM	W	L	ERA	SV	IP	H	R	ER	BB	SO
Erly Casanova, PRI	2	1	0.90	0	50	41	9	5	22	36
Yoanni Yera, MTZ	9	0	1.75	0	67	63	16	13	11	66
Lazaro Blanco, GRA	7	2	1.78	0	76	70	20	15	25	44
Freddy Asiel Alvarez, VCL	5	1	1.82	0	64	56	13	13	17	50
Alain Sanchez, VCL	5	3	2.09	0	65	56	24	15	23	36
Vladimir Garcia, CAV	9	1	2.25	0	84	78	25	21	26	55
Jose Ramon Rodriguez, CMG	7	2	2.30	0	55	39	14	14	18	28
Yoendris Montero, SCU	2	4	2.41	1	52	47	20	14	21	29
Jonder Martinez, MTZ	7	0	2.51	0	75	77	25	21	14	42
Miguel Lahera, ART	5	3	2.59	0	56	55	23	16	14	33
Ramon Licor, MTZ	3	0	2.63	0	48	43	18	14	19	33
Luis Manuel Castro, MAY	5	3	2.67	0	67	65	21	20	21	28
Carlos A. Santsteban, HOL	6	3	2.67	1	78	78	25	23	27	21
Arbelio Quiroz, CMG	4	5	2.84	1	44	50	23	14	25	26
Robelio Carrillo, VCL	5	1	2.88	0	56	53	23	18	16	21
Yariel Rodriguez, CMG	5	2	2.92	0	71	53	24	23	41	43
Noelvis Entenza, IND	4	1	3.06	1	47	42	19	16	24	20
Yudiel Rodriguez, LTU	2	3	3.08	1	53	62	25	18	15	25
Pedro Angel Alvarez, SSP	3	3	3.25	2	44	45	18	16	18	29
Yoalkis Cruz, LTU	7	2	3.43	0	66	69	29	25	8	28

RONALDO SCHEMIDT/AFP/GETTY IMAGES

Puerto Rico celebrates its first Caribbean Series title in the 21st century.

Puerto Rico shuts out Mexico to claim title

The last time Puerto Rico had won a Caribbean Series title, most of Puerto Rican's current big league stars were toddlers, so it's fair to call Puerto Rico's much-celebrated title long overdue.

David Vidal and Ivan DeJesus Jr., were the Series heroes for Puerto Rico. Vidal hit .417 with a series-best three home runs while DeJesus led all Caribbean Series hitters with a .500 average (11-for-22) and a series-best five runs.

In the championship game, Puerto Rico shut down Mexico's lineup for a narrow 1-0 win in 10 innings. Jonathan Morales' sacrifice fly drove in the lone run, scoring Yadiel Rivera.

While Puerto Rico soared, it was a very disappointing series for the Dominican Republic squad. The Dominican Republic club went 0-4 in the tournament and has now gone six years since it's last Caribbean Series title. The Dominican Republic had won six of the previous 10 tiles before that.

AUSTRALIAN BASEBALL LEAGUE

Team	W	L	PCT	GB
Melbourne Aces	26	14	.650	—
Adelaide Bite	23	17	.575	3
Brisbane Bandits	21	18	.538	4 ½
Canberra Cavalry	20	20	.500	6
Sydney Blue Sox	15	24	.385	10 ½
Perth Heat	14	26	.350	12

Semifinals: Brisbane defeated Adelaide 2-1 in best-of-3 series. **Finals:** Brisbane defeated Melbourne 2-0 in best-of-3-series.

PLAYER, TEAM	AVG	AB	R	H	2B	3B	HR	RBI	BB	SO	SB
Dening, Mitch, ADE	.340	147	21	50	9	0	6	27	14	15	1
Whitefield, Aaron, BRI	.338	157	34	53	12	0	4	15	10	37	20
Collins, Roman, MEL	.336	146	25	49	11	1	3	22	17	27	5
Perkins, Robbie, CAN	.331	121	16	40	10	1	5	21	7	26	1
Moanaroa, Boss, CAN	.331	118	17	39	7	0	3	17	7	16	0
Kelly, Scott, CAN	.326	138	21	45	6	1	0	12	16	23	13
Kennelly, Tim, PER	.323	124	23	40	13	0	6	17	14	18	6
Nilsson, Mitch, BRI	.317	126	25	40	5	0	7	24	18	21	2
Hughes, Luke, PER	.313	128	21	40	9	0	6	15	25	30	3
Almonte, Josh, CAN	.310	126	24	39	9	2	2	14	9	30	12

PLAYER, TEAM	W	L	ERA	G	SV	IP	H	BB	SO	AVG
Hamburger, Mark, MEL	5	1	1.90	11	0	76	61	14	86	.216
Cohen, Louis, CAN	4	0	2.61	7	0	41	33	10	37	.214
Ruzic, Dushan, MEL	4	2	2.96	11	0	46	46	15	29	.272
O'Loughlin, Jack, ADE	3	3	3.02	9	0	42	51	7	22	.305
Guinard, Sean, CAN	4	2	3.21	10	0	48	41	28	30	.240
Foss, Trevor, SYD	2	3	3.57	10	0	58	60	18	56	.259
DeGraaf, Josh, CAN	2	4	3.83	11	0	45	45	19	32	.253
Williams, Matthew, ADE	4	2	3.86	20	1	37	29	10	50	.212
Champlin, Kramer, BRI	2	4	4.37	9	0	47	49	6	34	.266
Anderson, Craig, SYD	4	3	4.44	10	0	53	58	17	32	.272

DOMINICAN LEAGUE

Team	W	L	PCT	GB
Gigantes del Cibao	27	23	.540	—
Tigres del Licey	26	24	.520	1
Aguilas Cibaenas	25	25	.500	2
Leones del Escogido	25	25	.500	2
Toros del Este	24	26	.480	3
Estrellas Orientales	23	27	.460	4

Round Robin: Aguilas and Licey advance. **Finals:** Licey defeats Aguilas 5-4 in best-of-9 series.

PLAYER, TEAM	AVG	AB	R	H	2B	3B	HR	RBI	BB	SO	SB
Rodriguez, Ronny, AGU	.306	160	24	49	10	3	3	12	14	33	2
Torres, Ramon, GIG	.306	157	26	48	9	1	4	16	10	21	2
Sosa, Ruben, ESC	.299	144	20	43	3	3	0	24	24	21	11

Perez, Juan, AGU	.291	172	23	50	13	0	0	24	13	30	2
Hernandez, Marco, LIC	.286	133	18	38	4	1	4	16	4	25	2
Krizan, Jason, EST	.284	134	12	38	6	1	2	14	31	21	1
Tavarez, Aneury, EST	.283	152	18	43	3	0	3	13	13	25	6
Rojas Jr., Mel, LIC	.270	148	19	40	7	4	2	17	4	41	2
Lake, Junior, EST	.264	174	20	46	10	2	2	18	23	33	7
Hernandez, Anderson, LIC	.264	148	16	39	4	0	0	10	17	21	0

INDIVIDUAL PITCHING LEADERS

PLAYER, TEAM	W	L	ERA	G	SV	IP	H	BB	SO	AVG
Marte, Kelvin, ESC	5	1	1.44	11	0	62	43	12	25	.195
Bueno, Francisley, AGU	4	2	1.64	10	0	49	39	16	23	.224
Asher, Alec, GIG	2	1	2.14	8	0	42	27	5	21	.180
Candelario, Alexis, EST	2	3	2.19	10	0	49	40	15	38	.222
Valdes, Raul, TOR	5	2	2.36	9	0	50	42	10	27	.223
MacLane, Evan, EST	3	3	2.37	10	0	49	46	6	26	.245
Elias, Roenis, AGU	2	3	2.47	10	0	44	38	19	37	.241
Evans, Bryan, TOR	2	3	2.61	11	0	52	38	12	37	.205
Doyle, Terry, GIG	4	3	2.70	11	0	43	34	17	37	.222
Valdez, Cesar, LIC	2	5	3.67	10	0	42	43	7	27	.264

MEXICAN PACIFIC LEAGUE

Team	W	L	PCT	GB
Mayos de Navojoa	39	29	.574	—
Caneros de los Mochis	38	30	.559	1
Aguilas de Mexicali	37	31	.544	2
Tomateros de Culiacan	36	32	.529	3
Naranjeros de Hermosillo	34	34	.500	5
Yaquis de Obregon	30	37	.448	8 ½
Venados de Mazatlan	29	39	.426	10
Charros de Jalisco	28	39	.418	10 ½

Playoffs: First Round-Los Mochis defeated Mazatlan 4-1; Mexicali defeated Navojoa 4-2 and Hermosillo defeated Culiacan 4-3 in best-of-7 series. **Semifinals**—Los Mochis defeated Culiacan 4-3 and Mexicali defeated Hermosillo 4-3 in best-of-7 series. **Finals**—Mexicali defeated Los Mochis 4-2 in best-of-7 series.

PLAYER, TEAM	AVG	AB	R	H	2B	3B	HR	RBI	BB	SO	SB
Juarez, Luis, MXC	.364	198	28	72	19	1	5	30	24	22	1
Castro, Leandro, MOC	.347	216	38	75	14	2	4	22	13	35	10
Rodriguez, Jose Manuel, JAL	.335	263	35	88	25	0	8	34	20	38	3
Roberson, Chris, MXC	.332	241	34	80	18	2	5	25	29	25	9
Rodriguez Salazar, Isaac, MOC	.314	264	44	83	14	0	4	26	31	33	8
Mustelier, Ronnier, CUL	.314	239	41	75	28	0	6	43	28	22	4
Murillo, Agustin, JAL	.312	218	34	68	9	0	5	32	33	21	8
Meneses, Joey, CUL	.308	234	33	72	9	1	7	46	16	47	0
Valdez, Jesus, JAL	.307	202	24	62	7	0	6	25	18	29	0
Castillo, Jesus, NAV	.302	212	32	64	8	0	7	46	38	37	1

PLAYER, TEAM	W	L	ERA	G	SV	IP	H	BB	SO	AVG
Barreda, Manny, MOC	4	3	2.20	12	0	70	44	31	66	.178
Velazquez, Hector, NAV	9	3	2.32	14	0	85	78	16	87	.246
Oramas, Juan Pablo, HER	4	3	2.39	14	0	79	69	26	46	.242
Lopez, Arturo, OBR	5	2	2.41	13	0	75	65	23	48	.230
Delgado, Efren, MXC	5	7	3.36	13	0	72	65	23	60	.241
Dodson, Zack, NAV	6	5	3.49	14	0	80	77	28	65	.253
Rodriguez, Daniel, CUL	4	6	3.50	13	0	75	74	16	61	.260
Alexander, Tyler, JAL	4	5	3.57	12	0	68	57	20	72	.230
Arballo, Julian, MOC	6	3	3.88	13	0	70	73	36	53	.282

PUERTO RICAN LEAGUE

Team	W	L	PCT	GB
Cangrejeros de Santurce	28	12	.700	—
Indios de Mayaguez	26	14	.650	2
Criollos de Caguas	19	21	.475	9
Gigantes de Carolina	16	24	.400	12
Tiburones de Aguadilla	11	29	.275	17

Playoffs: Semifinals-Santurce defeated Carolina 4-1 and Caguas defeated Mayaguez 4-2 in best-of-7 series. **Finals**—Caguas defeated Santurce 5-3 in best-of-9 wseries.

PLAYER, TEAM	AVG	AB	R	H	2B	3B	HR	RBI	BB	SO	SB
Ortiz, Danny, MAY	.340	144	19	49	3	2	2	16	11	12	0
Rivera, Emmanuel, MAY	.330	109	8	36	7	1	0	8	12	11	1
Corporan, Carlos, CAR	.321	106	15	34	6	1	1	17	8	21	1
De Jesus Jr., Ivan, SAN	.302	139	17	42	3	2	2	14	17	20	4
Fuentes, Reymond, AGU	.292	137	17	40	8	3	2	12	11	19	6
Navarro, Rey, CAG	.290	138	15	40	8	1	0	16	16	17	1
Padilla, Jorge, CAG	.289	97	9	28	5	0	1	11	15	20	2
Garcia, Anthony, CAR	.280	143	11	40	10	0	1	12	11	20	4
Soto, Neftali, SAN	.279	147	18	41	8	0	4	13	10	28	1
Balaguert, Yasiel, CAR	.277	119	12	33	4	1	1	10	8	29	1

PLAYER, TEAM	W	L	ERA	G	SV	IP	H	BB	SO	AVG
Flores, Adalberto, SAN	4	0	0.95	11	0	57	42	8	43	.210
Lopez, Jorge, MAY	1	1	1.56	9	0	35	17	13	32	.145
Del Valle, Frank, SAN	2	2	1.67	13	0	32	25	11	31	.219
Santiago, Andres, SAN	2	2	1.69	16	0	37	23	13	25	.173
Santiago, Mario, CAR	4	1	1.85	8	0	49	41	6	33	.224
Roibal, Reinier, SAN	3	2	1.87	11	0	53	47	17	39	.237
Burgos, Hiram, MAY	4	1	2.05	10	0	48	36	9	43	.213
Soto, Giovanni, CAR	4	3	2.05	9	0	48	42	9	31	.239
Grills, Evan, SAN	4	2	2.09	8	0	43	42	4	28	.263
Brownell, John, CAG	1	3	2.12	7	0	34	25	16	17	.207

VENEZUELAN WINTER LEAGUE

Team	W	L	PCT	GB
Cardenales de Lara	39	24	.619	—
Caribes de Anzoategui	34	29	.540	5
Aguilas del Zulia	33	30	.524	6
Bravos de Margarita	30	33	.476	9
Tiburones de La Guaira	30	33	.476	9
Tigres de Aragua	30	33	.476	9
Navegantes del Magallanes	29	34	.460	10
Leones del Caracas	27	36	.429	12

Playoffs: First round-Zulia defeated Aragua 4-0; Caribes defeated La Guaira 4-3; Lara defeated Margarita 4-3. Second chance-La Guaira defeated Aragua 2-0. **Semifinals**—Zulia defeated Caribe 4-1 and Lara defeated La Guaira 4-1 in best-of-7 series. **Finals**—Zulia defeated Lara 4-1 in best-of-7 series.

PLAYER, TEAM	AVG	AB	R	H	2B	3B	HR	RBI	BB	SO	SB
Perez, Hernan, ARA	.373	169	30	63	9	2	3	22	6	20	7
Diaz, Yandy, CAR	.371	151	24	56	9	3	2	18	20	26	1
Tabata, Jose, MAG	.367	188	31	69	13	2	4	35	21	29	6
Valera, Breyvic, MAR	.356	219	40	78	13	6	7	28	24	18	11
Montero, Jesus, LAR	.338	228	30	77	13	0	7	46	13	36	1
Urshela, Giovanny, ZUL	.337	169	23	57	16	0	3	33	5	16	1
Arraez, Luis, MAG	.335	182	31	61	8	6	0	22	15	15	5
Querecuto, Juniel, LAR	.335	200	28	67	13	5	1	19	14	25	3
Castillo, Jose, LAG	.332	214	14	71	10	2	3	27	18	19	0

PLAYER, TEAM	W	L	ERA	G	SV	IP	H	BB	SO	AVG
Cuevas, William, LAG	6	0	2.08	11	0	61	43	16	58	.200
Rivero, Raul, LAR	7	1	2.17	13	0	79	71	19	61	.247
Martinez, Jorge, LAR	6	2	2.33	13	0	66	57	11	43	.232
Molina, Nestor, LAR	5	3	2.7	13	0	63	61	24	35	.258
Bibens-Dirkx, Austin, ARA	3	4	3.04	13	0	68	69	13	42	.257
Pino, Yohan, ARA	4	3	3.39	14	0	72	67	16	38	.249
Lively, Mitch, MAG	5	1	3.43	12	0	60	66	18	34	.283
Youman, Shane, ORI	2	3	4.15	13	0	61	64	17	37	.287
Bencomo, Omar, MAR	4	3	4.21	14	0	68	75	14	48	.286
Boscan, Wilfredo, ZUL	1	6	4.24	11	0	51	64	8	29	.312

COLLEGE

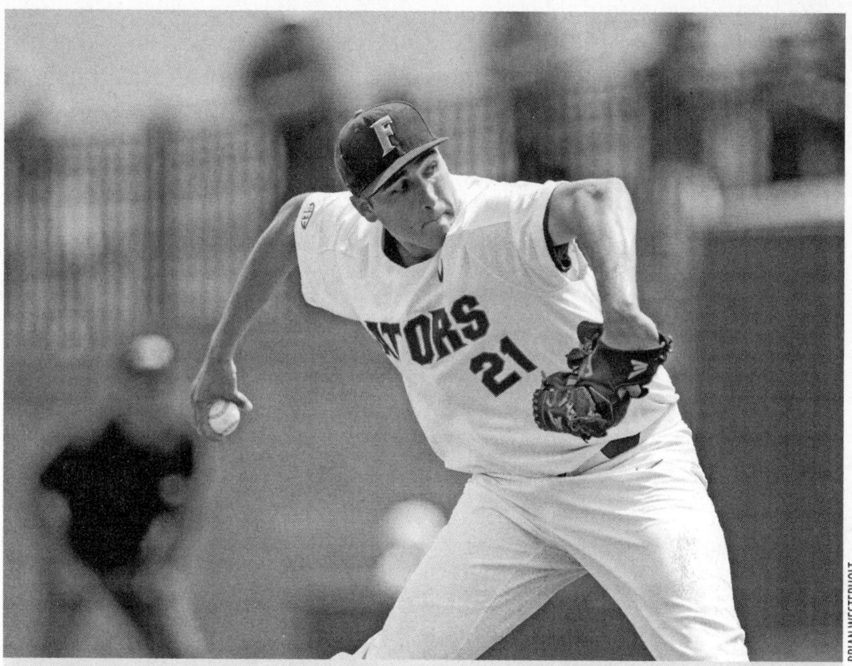

BRIAN WESTERHOLT

Florida righthander Alex Faedo was named College World Series Most Outstanding Player.

Florida Fulfills Promise With First CWS Title

BY TEDDY CAHILL

OMAHA

As fireworks lit up the Omaha skyline above TD Ameritrade Park and blue and orange streamers soared over the infield, Florida fell into a raucous dogpile between the mound and first base.

Florida had just defeated Louisiana State, 6-1, on June 27 in Game 2 of the College World Series finals to complete a sweep and win the first national championship in program history. Righthander Alex Faedo was named Most Outstanding Player after two dominant starts in the first week of the tournament carried the Gators to the finals.

The victory left coach Kevin O'Sullivan, who has led the Gators to Omaha six times in the last eight seasons, speechless even an hour after the final out.

"You never know how you're going to feel when you get the last out in the College World Series, and I'm still kind of numb," he said. "Just overwhelmed with emotions for our players."

Florida (52-19) relied on its elite rotation all spring and throughout the CWS. But because of how the schedule fell, the Gators were unable to start any of their trio of Faedo, Brady Singer and Jackson Kowar in Game 2. Instead, Florida called on freshman righthander Tyler Dyson, typically its setup man, to make just his second career start against LSU lefthander Jared Poche', the winningest pitcher in program history.

Dyson outdueled Poche', holding the Tigers (52-20) to one run on three hits and two walks in six innings. He turned a lead over to closer Michael Byrne as he had done so many times this season.

"I didn't get much sleep last night, thinking about this game," Dyson said. "I just went out there and executed the pitch call."

LSU, however, didn't make anything easy for Florida. The Gators grabbed an early lead with one run in both of the first two innings, but they were unable to expand it against Poche'. And the Tigers' potent offense threatened late in the game.

After scoring once in the seventh, LSU got run-

COACHING CAROUSEL

SCHOOL	IN (PREVIOUS JOB)	OUT (REASON/NEW JOB)
Alabama	Brad Bohannon (Auburn assistant)	Greg Goff (fired)
California	Mike Neu (Pacific head coach)	Dave Esquer (Stanford head coach)
Canisius	Matt Mazurek (Canisius assistant)	Mike McRae (VCU assistant)
Cincinnati	Scott Googins (Xavier head coach)	Ty Neal (resigned)
Citadel	Tony Skole (East Tennessee State head coach)	Fred Jordan (retired)
College of Charleston	Chad Holbrook (South Carolina head coach)	Matt Heath (fired)
Dayton	Jayson King (Army assistant)	Tony Vittorio (resigned)
East Tennessee State	Joe Pennucci (Stony Brook assistant)	Tony Skole (Citadel head coach)
Incarnate Word	Patrick Hallmark (Missouri assistant)	Danny Heep (resigned)
LaSalle	David Miller (Penn Charter School, Pa., head coach)	Mike Lake (fired)
Louisiana-Monroe	Mike Federico (Southern Mississippi assistant)	Bruce Peddie (fired)
Manhattan	Mike Cole (Fairfield assistant)	Jim Duffy (Rutgers assistant)
Maryland	Rob Vaughn (Maryland assistant)	John Szefc (Virginia Tech head coach)
Maryland-Eastern Shore	Brian Hollaman (Parkside HS, Md., head coach)	Charlie Goens (fired)
Massachusetts	Matt Reynolds (Washington College, Md., head coach)	Mike Stone (retired)
Norfolk State	Keith Shumate* (Norfolk State assistant)	Claudell Clark (resigned)
North Florida	Tim Parenton (Rays, short-season)	Smoke Laval (fired)
Oklahoma	Skip Johnson (Oklahoma assistant)	Pete Hughes (resigns)
Pacific	Ryan Garko (Dodgers, Double-A)	Mike Neu (California head coach)
Santa Clara	Rusty Filter (Stanford assistant)	Dan O'Brien (resigned)
South Carolina	Mark Kingston (South Florida head coach)	Chad Holbrook (resigned)
South Florida	Billy Mohl (South Florida assistant)	Mark Kingston (South Carolina head coach)
Southern	Kerrick Jackson (former Missouri assistant)	Roger Cador (retired)
Stanford	Dave Esquer (California head coach)	Mark Marquess (retired)
Tennessee	Tony Vitello (Arkansas assistant)	Dave Serrano (resigned)
Texas-Rio Grande Valley	Derek Matlock (West Virginia assistant)	Manny Mantrana (resigned)
Towson	Matt Tyner (Richmond assistant)	Mike Gottlieb (fired)
Virginia Tech	John Szefc (Maryland head coach)	Patrick Mason (fired)
Xavier	Billy O'Conner (Xavier assistant)	Scott Googins (Cincinnati head coach)

**interim head coach*

ners on first and third with no outs to start the eighth. Byrne struck out Antoine Duplantis, the Tigers' three-hole hitter, before O'Sullivan called on Kowar, who was slated to start if the series went to three games. Kowar got All-American Greg Deichmann to hit a grounder to first baseman J.J. Schwarz, who threw home to get Kramer Robertson, who had taken off from third base on contact.

"It was a heads-up play," O'Sullivan said. "He made a perfect throw. Quick feet. Probably saved the game, to be honest with you."

Florida scored four insurance runs in the bottom of the eighth against electric LSU freshman righthander Zack Hess. Deacon Liput drove in two runs in the inning and finished the night 2-for-5 with a run and three RBIs to celebrate his 21st birthday in style.

Kowar returned to the mound in the ninth and got the final three outs with little drama. He had last pitched June 23 against Texas Christian and was in line to start Game 3. But he went to O'Sullivan before Game 2 and told his coach that he had a few innings in him if he was needed. O'Sullivan said before that conversation, he had not thought about using Kowar, but he wanted to do anything he could to wrap up the series in two games to avoid LSU ace Alex Lange, who was also in line to start Game 3.

"Sometimes you make these decisions and they don't work out, and you look like a fool," O'Sullivan said. "And sometimes you make them and the players make you look like you're smart."

O'Sullivan has looked smart far more often than not in his 10 years at Florida. He has led the Gators to the CWS six times in the last eight years and turned the program into a powerhouse both for on-field production and player development.

But despite the parade of All-Americans and first-round draft picks that have come through Gainesville in the last decade, including stars such as Brian Johnson, Logan Shore and Mike Zunino, O'Sullivan had not been able to break through to win the program's first title. That changed a year after Florida went 0-2 in Omaha with what might have been one of its most talented teams ever, a team that was the No. 1 national seed and had eight players drafted in the top 10 rounds.

All eight of those players signed, leaving several holes for the Gators to replace this year. They lacked the depth many of O'Sullivan's teams have had, with injuries throughout the spring testing their depth even further. Florida's offense never truly clicked, and it ended the season without a .300 hitter. As a team, the Gators hit .259/.355/.378.

Through it all, Florida found a way to win. The Gators won 19 one-run games, the most in the nation, thanks in large part to its defense and Byrne, who set a program record with 19 saves. Most importantly, Florida was always able to rely on its rotation.

Faedo went 9-2, 2.26, earned All-America honors and was drafted 18th overall by the Tigers. Singer, a sophomore who is an early favorite to be the first overall pick in next year's draft, went 9-5, 3.21, while Kowar, his classmate, went 12-1, 4.08.

"What happens when we have pitching like we do, there's never a really long stretch of losses," O'Sullivan said. "You'll lose a game or two, but then you get back on the winning side of things because your pitching is what it is."

As good as they had been during the regular season, Faedo and Singer found another level during the postseason. The righthanders combined to go 4-0, 1.27 with 43 strikeouts and nine walks in 28.1 innings in the CWS.

Singer won Game 1 of the finals, striking out 12 batters in seven innings. Faedo was so good in the first half of the CWS that he didn't need to appear in the finals to win the MOP. He struck out 22 batters in 14.1 scoreless innings over two starts against TCU, and he won the game that clinched Florida's spot in the finals.

Faedo said being named MOP made Florida's victory even better.

"It's amazing," he said. "I can't even describe it. I never thought I would get to that point."

The same cannot be said for the Gators. For years, particularly in recent seasons once they got rolling under O'Sullivan, many have expected them to break through for a national championship.

To have now finally won it all says a lot about O'Sullivan, athletic director Scott Stricklin said.

"We've had 10 sports win team national titles and as good as baseball's been, it has not done that before now," he said. "To be able to put that banner up at the baseball facility—'national champions'—it's really special."

The Gators will be able to hang that banner at McKethan Stadium, fulfilling the program's ultimate promise.

"I'm just really happy for these guys because they deserve it and they're the ones who go out there and play," O'Sullivan said. "We'll let it sink in and we'll enjoy this for a little bit."

Oregon State Falls Short

They could've been the greatest team of all-time. And maybe they still are. Maybe with the right formulas, in the right context, with the right analysis, the 2017 Oregon State Beavers will still stand favorably among the elites. Their 56-6 record is a program-best. Their .903 winning percentage is the fourth-best in NCAA history, just shy of Arizona State's .914 mark in 1972—when the college game had far less parity. They led the country in team ERA at 1.93—almost a full run better than the next-closest team. They went a record-

RPI RANKINGS

The Ratings Percentage Index is an important tool used by the NCAA in selecting at-large teams for the 64-team Division I tournament. The NCAA now releases its RPI rankings during the season. These were the top 100 finishers for 2016. A team's rank in the final Baseball America Top 25 is indicated in parentheses, and College World Series teams are in bold.

Rank	Team	Record	Rank	Team	Record
1.	**Oregon State** (3)	56-6	51.	Old Dominion	37-21
2.	**Florida** (1)	52-19	52.	Dallas Baptist	42-21
3.	**Louisiana St.** (2)	51-20	53.	San Diego	35-18
4.	**Tex. Christian** (4)	50-18	54.	Nebraska	35-22
5.	North Carolina (11)	49-14	55.	Louisiana-Lafayette	35-21
6.	**Louisville** (6)	53-12	56.	Brigham Young	38-21
7.	Texas Tech (12)	45-17	57.	Florida Atlantic	35-21
8.	**Florida State** (6)	46-23	58.	Charlotte	34-24
9.	Kentucky (9)	43-23	59.	Tennessee	27-25
10.	Wake Forest (13)	43-20	60.	Coastal Carolina	37-19
11.	S. Mississippi (16)	50-16	61.	Bethune-Cookman	36-25
12.	Arkansas (19)	45-19	62.	Binghamton	30-13
13.	Stanford (15)	42-16	63.	Jacksonville	36-24
14.	Long Beach St. (8)	42-20	64.	California	25-29
15.	Clemson (23)	42-21	65.	UCLA	30-27
16.	Virginia (21)	43-16	66.	Kansas	30-28
17.	Texas (24)	39-24	67.	Loyola Marymount	38-18
18.	Vanderbilt (18)	36-25	68.	Rhode Island	31-22
19.	Houston (22)	42-21	69.	Utah	27-24
20.	West Virginia	36-26	70.	St. Mary's	37-20
21.	Mississippi St. (14)	40-27	71.	Xavier	34-27
22.	Missouri St. (17)	43-20	72.	Minnesota	36-21
23.	South Florida	42-19	73.	San Diego State	42-21
24.	Baylor	34-23	74.	New Mexico	30-27
25.	**Cal St. Fullerton** (7)	39-24	75.	Oral Roberts	43-16
26.	Central Florida	40-22	76.	Georgia Tech	27-28
27.	North Carolina St.	36-25	77.	Mercer	39-17
28.	Arizona	38-21	78.	Michigan State	29-23
29.	Oklahoma	35-24	79.	Liberty	32-23
30.	SE Louisiana	37-22	80.	Iowa	37-22
31.	South Carolina	35-25	81.	East Carolina	32-28
32.	South Alabama	40-21	82.	Tulane	27-31
33.	**Texas A&M** (10)	41-23	83.	Washington	28-26
34.	Indiana	34-24	84.	Boston College	25-28
35.	Florida Gulf Coast	43-20	85.	Georgia	25-32
36.	Yale	34-18	86.	Fla. International	31-27
37.	Mississippi	32-25	87.	Georgia Southern	38-21
38.	Sam Houston St. (20)	44-23	88.	Tennessee Tech	41-21
39.	Auburn (25)	37-26	89.	Oregon	30-25
40.	Michigan	42-17	90.	Winthrop	34-24
41.	Rice	33-31	91.	Duke	30-28
42.	Connecticut	33-25	92.	Kent State	37-18
43.	Miami	30-27	93.	Seton Hall	29-24
44.	Maryland	38-23	94.	Davidson	35-26
45.	McNeese State	36-20	95.	Cincinnati	28-30
46.	St. John's	42-13	96.	Va. Commonwealth	35-22
47.	Louisiana Tech	36-20	97.	Texas-San Antonio	29-28
48.	Oklahoma State	30-27	98.	Kansas State	29-26
49.	Missouri	36-23	99.	Illinois-Chicago	38-17
50.	Gonzaga	33-20	100.	Wright State	38-21

breaking 27-3 in Pacific-12 Conference games. They put together two 23-game winning streaks, carrying the latter into the College World Series.

But there's one milestone the 2017 Beavers don't have, and can never get:

A national title.

It turns out the Beavers' last streak was the one that did them in—two straight losses.

For the first time in 2017, the Beavers in the College World Series lost back-to-back games, both against Louisiana State, the eventual national runner-up. The last, a 6-1 loss on June 24, spelled the end of a nearly flawless season. For 60 games, Oregon State could do little wrong. For a two-game stretch in Omaha, little went right.

After LSU closer Zack Hess threw his final pitch and the final out at second base was made, after both teams exchanged handshakes on the field, junior infielders Michael Gretler and K.J. Harrison and coach Pat Casey took the post-game dais and showed little in the way of emotion—mostly a look of disbelief. A week before, when Oregon State came back to beat Cal State Fullerton, the Beavers talked after the game about how the thought of losing never crosses their minds. And for good reason. In 2017, losing rarely happened.

"I told the guys, 'It's a tough day when you've had such a great year,'" Casey said. "And now is not the time to really think about that or talk about it, but I know there will be a time when they get to sit back and reflect and realize what they accomplished.

"And I know they're not satisfied. But they'll feel better about it in a few days. I can tell you that."

The final two days of its season were, in many ways, a shocking turn of events given Oregon State's near-perfect season and the fact that the Beavers routed the same LSU team earlier in the tournament, 13-1.

Tigers coach Paul Mainieri knows as much as anyone that even the best clubs can stumble in the postseason.

"It's unbelievable what (the Beavers) did this year," Mainieri said. "To lose four games out of 60 when they came here, you don't do that accidentally . . . It's hard to do that. It's like once in a blue moon something like that happens. And you pretty much think of them like they're invincible, that they don't have any weaknesses. And they don't.

"They have a very balanced team. They pitched

COLLEGE WORLD SERIES CHAMPIONS

YEAR	CHAMPION	COACH	RECORD	RUNNER-UP	MOST OUTSTANDING PLAYER
1948	Southern California	Sam Barry	40-12	Yale	None selected
1949	Texas*	Bibb Falk	23-7	Wake Forest	Charles Teague, 2B, Wake Forest
1950	Texas	Bibb Falk	27-6	Washington State	Ray VanCleef, OF, Rutgers
1951	Oklahoma*	Jack Baer	19-9	Tennessee	Sid Hatfield, 1B/P, Tennessee
1952	Holy Cross	Jack Barry	21-3	Missouri	Jim O'Neill, P, Holy Cross
1953	Michigan	Ray Fisher	21-9	Texas	J.L. Smith, P, Texas
1954	Missouri	Hi Simmons	22-4	Rollins	Tom Yewcic, C, Michigan State
1955	Wake Forest	Taylor Sanford	29-7	Western Michigan	Tom Borland, P, Oklahoma State
1956	Minnesota	Dick Siebert	33-9	Arizona	Jerry Thomas, P, Minnesota
1957	California*	George Wolfman	35-10	Penn State	Cal Emery, 1B/P, Penn State
1958	Southern California	Rod Dedeaux	35-7	Missouri	Bill Thom, P, Southern California
1959	Oklahoma State	Toby Greene	27-5	Arizona	Jim Dobson, 3B, Oklahoma State
1960	Minnesota	Dick Siebert	34-7	Southern California	John Erickson, 2B, Minnesota
1961	Southern California*	Rod Dedeaux	43-9	Oklahoma State	Littleton Fowler, P, Oklahoma State
1962	Michigan	Don Lund	31-13	Santa Clara	Bob Garibaldi, P, Santa Clara
1963	Southern California	Rod Dedeaux	37-16	Arizona	Bud Hollowell, C, Southern California
1964	Minnesota	Dick Siebert	31-12	Missouri	Joe Ferris, P, Maine
1965	Arizona State	Bobby Winkles	54-8	Ohio State	Sal Bando, 3B, Arizona State
1966	Ohio State	Marty Karow	27-6	Oklahoma State	Steve Arlin, P, Ohio State
1967	Arizona State	Bobby Winkles	53-12	Houston	Ron Davini, C, Arizona State
1968	Southern California*	Rod Dedeaux	42-12	Southern Illinois	Bill Seinsoth, 1B, Southern California
1969	Arizona State	Bobby Winkles	56-11	Tulsa	John Dolinsek, OF, Arizona State
1970	Southern California	Rod Dedeaux	51-13	Florida State	Gene Ammann, P, Florida State
1971	Southern California	Rod Dedeaux	53-13	Southern Illinois	Jerry Tabb, 1B, Tulsa
1972	Southern California	Rod Dedeaux	50-13	Arizona State	Russ McQueen, P, Southern California
1973	Southern California*	Rod Dedeaux	51-11	Arizona State	Dave Winfield, OF/P, Minnesota
1974	Southern California	Rod Dedeaux	50-20	Miami	George Milke, P, Southern California
1975	Texas	Cliff Gustafson	56-6	South Carolina	Mickey Reichenbach, 1B, Texas
1976	Arizona	Jerry Kindall	56-17	Eastern Michigan	Steve Powers, DH/P, Arizona
1977	Arizona State	Jim Brock	57-12	South Carolina	Bob Horner, 3B, Arizona State
1978	Southern California*	Rod Dedeaux	54-9	Arizona State	Rod Boxberger, P, Southern California
1979	Cal State Fullerton	Augie Garrido	60-14	Arkansas	Tony Hudson, P, Cal State Fullerton
1980	Arizona	Jerry Kindall	45-21	Hawaii	Terry Francona, OF, Arizona
1981	Arizona State	Jim Brock	55-13	Oklahoma State	Stan Holmes, OF, Arizona State
1982	Miami	Ron Fraser	57-18	Wichita State	Dan Smith, P, Miami

great. Great defense. Offensively, they had table-setters, power guys. They had it all. But you still have to go out and play the games"

Perhaps the CWS would've turned out differently had lefthander Luke Heimlich—who removed himself from the team following a report from The Oregonian that he pleaded guilty to felony child molestation as a teenager—been available. Heimlich went 11-1 and led the country with a 0.76 ERA. He likely would've gotten the ball in one of the games against LSU.

There are a multitude of factors one could point toward for the Beavers' unraveling, but the Beavers weren't finger-pointing after the fact.

"I love all these guys so much," Gretler said. "It's been an unbelievable season. And I think that's just a testament to how much we love each other. We're truly brothers. I mean, I look forward to every 6 a.m. weight room, every practice, every game. Every moment I get to spend with these guys is very special. And that's what I'm going to remember the most, is the relationships."

Many of those relationships will remain intact. The Beavers often fielded a lineup with six freshmen and sophomores, and the returning core of infielders Madrigal and Grenier, catcher Adley Rutschman and center fielder Steven Kwan means the Beavers should once again be one of the most talented teams up the middle next spring.

But the Beavers weren't looking ahead. They weren't looking behind. They were looking squarely at the loss they never thought would come.

"I think to a man, they'd tell you that we've played better baseball, that's for sure," Casey said. "But I told them that there will be a time rather shortly that you'll realize what you did and how amazing of a season you had and how you guys fought through so many things. And you're playing in the College World Series and playing a really, really good team.

"We couldn't get that thing turned around, the momentum. And we were down a little bit there with a couple bullets. And we just never could get anything going. But I do think they'll reflect on this in a short period of time, and it will be something that they'll be very proud of."

Marquess Retires After Storied Career

Mark Marquess announced last June he would

YEAR	CHAMPION	COACH	RECORD	RUNNER-UP	MOST OUTSTANDING PLAYER
1983	Texas	Cliff Gustafson	66-14	Alabama	Calvin Schiraldi, P, Texas
1984	Cal State Fullerton	Augie Garrido	66-20	Texas	John Fishel, OF, Cal State Fullerton
1985	Miami*	Ron Fraser	64-16	Texas	Greg Ellena, DH, Miami
1986	Arizona	Jerry Kindall	49-19	Florida State	Mike Senne, OF, Arizona
1987	Stanford	Mark Marquess	53-17	Oklahoma State	Paul Carey, OF, Stanford
1988	Stanford	Mark Marquess	46-23	Arizona State	Lee Plemel, P, Stanford
1989	Wichita State	Gene Stephenson	68-16	Texas	Greg Brummett, P, Wichita State
1990	Georgia	Steve Webber	52-19	Oklahoma State	Mike Rebhan, P, Georgia
1991	Louisiana State*	Skip Bertman	55-18	Wichita State	Gary Hymel, C, Louisiana State
1992	Pepperdine*	Andy Lopez	48-11	Cal State Fullerton	Phil Nevin, 3B, Cal State Fullerton
1993	Louisiana State	Skip Bertman	53-17	Wichita State	Todd Walker, 2B, Louisiana State
1994	Oklahoma*	Larry Cochell	50-17	Georgia Tech	Chip Glass, OF, Oklahoma
1995	Cal State Fullerton*	Augie Garrido	57-9	Southern California	Mark Kotsay, OF/P, Cal State Fullerton
1996	Louisiana State*	Skip Bertman	52-15	Miami	Pat Burrell, 3B, Miami
1997	Louisiana State*	Skip Bertman	57-13	Alabama	Brandon Larson, SS, Louisiana State
1998	Southern California	Mike Gillespie	49-17	Arizona State	Wes Rachels, 2B, Southern California
1999	Miami*	Jim Morris	50-13	Florida State	Marshall McDougall, 2B, Florida State
2000	Louisiana State*	Skip Bertman	52-17	Stanford	Trey Hodges, RHP, Louisiana State
2001	Miami*	Jim Morris	53-12	Stanford	Charlton Jimerson, OF, Miami
2002	Texas*	Augie Garrido	57-15	South Carolina	Huston Street, RHP, Texas
2003	Rice	Wayne Graham	58-12	Stanford	John Hudgins, RHP, Stanford
2004	Cal State Fullerton	George Horton	47-22	Texas	Jason Windsor, RHP, Cal State Fullerton
2005	Texas*	Augie Garrido	56-16	Florida	David Maroul, 3B, Texas
2006	Oregon State	Pat Casey	50-16	North Carolina	Jonah Nickerson, RHP, Oregon State
2007	Oregon State*	Pat Casey	49-18	North Carolina	Jorge Reyes, RHP, Oregon State
2008	Fresno State	Mike Batesole	47-31	Georgia	Tommy Mendonca, 3B, Fresno State
2009	Louisiana State	Paul Mainieri	56-17	Texas	Jared Mitchell, OF, Louisiana State
2010	South Carolina	Ray Tanner	54-16	UCLA	Jackie Bradley Jr., OF, South Carolina
2011	South Carolina*	Ray Tanner	55-14	Florida	Scott Wingo, 2B, South Carolina
2012	Arizona*	Andy Lopez	48-17	South Carolina	Robert Refsnyder, OF, Arizona
2013	UCLA*	John Savage	49-17	Mississippi State	Adam Plutko, RHP, UCLA
2014	Vanderbilt	Tim Corbin	51-21	Virginia	Dansby Swanson, 2B, Vanderbilt
2015	Virginia	Brian O'Connor	44-24	Vanderbilt	Josh Sborz, RHP, Virginia
2016	Coastal Carolina	Gary Gilmore	55-18	Arizona	Andrew Beckwith, RHP, Coastal Carolina
2017	Florida	Kevin O'Sullivan	52-19	Louisiana State	Alex Faedo, RHP, Florida

**Undefeated*

COLLEGE ALL-AMERICA TEAM

FIRST TEAM

POS.	NAME	YEAR	AVG	OBP	SLG	AB	R	H	HR	RBI	BB	SO	SB
C	David Banuelos,Long Beach State	Jr.	.289	.368	.468	201	31	58	7	29	17	45	5
1B	Brent Rooker, Mississippi State	R-Jr.	.387	.495	.810	248	60	96	23	82	48	58	18
2B	Nick Madrigal. Oregon State	So.	.380	.449	.532	237	53	90	4	40	27	16	16
3B	Jake Burger, Missouri State	Jr.	.328	.443	.648	247	69	81	22	65	43	38	3
SS	Logan Warmoth, North Carolina	Jr.	.336	.404	.554	271	60	91	10	49	28	47	18
OF	Greg Deichmann, Louisiana State	Jr.	.308	.417	.579	266	54	82	19	73	51	62	7
OF	Stuart Fairchild, Wake Forest	Jr.	.360	.439	.636	261	65	94	17	67	31	54	21
OF	Adam Haseley, Virginia	Jr.	.390	.491	.659	223	68	87	14	56	44	21	10
DH	Keston Hiura, UC Irvine	Jr.	.442	.567	.693	199	48	88	8	42	50	38	9
UT	Brendan McKay, Louisville	Jr.	.341	.457	.659	223	57	76	18	57	45	39	2

POS.	NAME	YEAR	W	L	ERA	G	CG	SV	IP	H	BB	SO	AVG
SP	J.B. Bukauskas, North Carolina	Jr.	9	1	2.53	15	0	0	93	62	37	116	.188
SP	Steven Gingery, Texas Tech	So.	10	1	1.58	15	0	0	91	60	29	107	.186
SP	Cory Abbott, Loyola Marymount	Jr.	11	2	1.74	15	2	0	98	61	28	130	.173
SP	Jake Thompson, Oregon State	R-Jr.	14	1	1.96	20	1	0	128	85	40	119	.189
RP	Josh Hiatt, North Carolina	R-Fr.	4	2	1.90	32	0	13	52	31	20	64	.168
RP	Wyatt Marks, Louisiana-Lafayette	Jr.	2	1	2.28	30	0	7	59	29	25	100	.144
UT	Brendan McKay, Louisville	Jr.	11	3	2.56	17	0	0	109	77	35	146	.198

SECOND TEAM

POS.	NAME	YEAR	AVG	OBP	SLG	AB	R	H	HR	RBI	BB	SO	SB
C	Joey Morgan, Washington	Jr.	.324	.427	.500	182	28	59	5	45	30	35	1
1B	Evan White, Kentucky	Jr.	.373	.453	.637	212	48	79	10	41	25	31	5
2B	Braden Shewmake, Texas A&M	Fr.	.328	.374	.529	274	47	90	11	69	15	31	11
3B	Drew Ellis, Louisville	R-So.	.355	.448	.701	231	56	82	20	61	40	40	6
SS	Kevin Merrell, South Florida	Jr.	.384	.464	.569	216	48	83	7	38	29	31	19
OF	Garrett McCain, Oklahoma State	Jr.	.388	.491	.549	224	53	87	4	43	29	33	19
OF	Will Robertson, Davidson	Sr.	.333	.399	.632	258	61	86	18	48	20	33	4
OF	Matt Wallner, Southern Mississippi	Fr.	.336	.463	.655	235	56	79	19	63	45	50	4
DH	J.J. Matijevic, Arizona	Jr.	.383	.436	.633	240	57	92	10	65	23	38	9
UT	Taylor Braley, Southern Mississippi	Jr.	.313	.461	.587	230	62	72	17	61	63	50	6

POS.	NAME	YEAR	W	L	ERA	G	CG	SV	IP	H	BB	SO	AVG
SP	Tyler Holton, Florida State	So.	10	3	2.34	18	2	0	119	43	31	144	.178
SP	Alex Faedo, Florida	Jr.	9	2	2.26	20	0	0	123	95	42	157	.210
SP	Alex Lange, Louisiana State	Jr.	10	5	2.97	19	4	0	124	106	48	150	.229
SP	Kyle Wright, Vanderbilt	Jr.	5	6	3.40	16	1	0	103	82	31	121	.216
RP	Lincoln Henzman, Louisville	Jr.	3	0	1.67	27	0	16	37	22	10	37	.169
RP	Colton Hock, Stanford	Jr.	6	1	2.08	27	0	16	48	36	11	35	.211
UT	Taylor Braley, Southern Mississippi	Jr.	7	2	3.40	14	0	0	82	81	22	78	.263

THIRD TEAM

POS.	NAME	YEAR	AVG	OBP	SLG	AB	R	H	HR	RBI	BB	SO	SB
C	Daulton Varsho, Wisconsin-Milwaukee	Jr.	.362	.490	.643	199	47	72	11	39	46	39	10
1B	Gavin Sheets, Wake Forest	Jr.	.317	.424	.629	240	57	76	21	84	46	37	1
2B	Riley Mahan, Kentucky	Jr.	.336	.392	.618	262	58	88	15	67	22	56	9
3B	Jake Scheiner, Houston	Jr.	.346	.432	.667	243	50	84	18	64	27	41	8
SS	Jeremy Eierman, Missouri State	So.	.313	.431	.675	243	67	76	23	68	41	61	17
OF	D.J. Artis, Liberty	So.	.359	.532	.552	181	58	65	6	45	62	30	23
OF	Jeren Kendall, Vanderbilt	Jr.	.307	.372	.556	261	59	80	15	53	24	74	20
OF	Tristan Pompey, Kentucky	So.	.361	.463	.541	266	96	18	10	45	46	56	9
DH	Jake Adams, Iowa	Jr.	.335	.417	.747	245	55	82	29	72	29	57	5
UT	Jake Meyers, Nebraska	Jr.	.297	.439	.349	195	52	58	1	16	39	31	20

POS.	NAME	YEAR	W	L	ERA	G	CG	SV	IP	H	BB	SO	AVG
SP	Griffin Canning, UCLA	Jr.	7	4	2.34	17	4	0	119	93	32	140	.213
SP	David Peterson, Oregon	Jr.	11	4	2.51	15	1	0	100	88	15	140	.237
SP	J.P Sears, The Citadel	Jr.	7	3	2.64	14	2	0	95	69	27	142	.204
SP	Casey Mize, Auburn	So.	8	2	2.04	13	2	0	84	66	9	109	.210
RP	Michael Byrne, Florida	So.	4	5	1.67	38	0	19	75	64	15	93	.229
RP	Nate Harris, Louisiana Tech	Sr.	9	1	2.31	22	3	8	94	79	11	94	.226
UT	Jake Meyers, Nebraska	Jr.	8	2	3.42	14	1	0	84	86	9	57	.265
UT	Adam Haseley, Virginia	So.	9	3	1.73	23	1	0	78	54	21	48	.194

retire at the end of the 2017 season, his 41st season as Stanford's coach. The Cardinal produced a strong final season for its legendary coach, going 42-16 and earning the No. 8 national seed. But their run came up short of their goal to return to Omaha, instead ending with a loss to Cal State

Fullerton in the Stanford Regional final.

It was a frustratingly quick end for Marquess and his players too. The Cardinal entered the postseason as one of the hottest teams in the country having won 21 of their previous 23 games. They were hosting a regional for the first time since 2012.

After the loss, Marquess came out of the dugout to one final ovation from the home crowd, as Fullerton coach Rick Vanderhook and his team tipped their caps towards the retiring legend. And as Marquess made his way across the field for the press conference, the Titans' fans and players gave the Stanford coach a standing ovation that Marquess said meant a lot to him.

"I have the utmost respect for coach Marquess," Vanderhook said. "I've been in this game for a while and I've had the pleasure of coaching with or against guys like him and Augie Garrido and Gene Stephenson and now they are all gone. Do I want to see Mark go? No."

Despite the fact that he had just finished his last day at work at the only job he had known for the past 40 years, Marquess was in good spirits after the game. He joked about everything from coaching little league to doing his second guessing from the comfort of the bleachers now. He made it a point to thank everyone in sight, including but not limited to, his wife, his daughters, his players, the school operations staff, the NCAA officials and even some of the veteran reporters who had been covering the team for years.

COLLEGE WORLD SERIES

STANDINGS

BRACKET ONE	W	L
Louisiana State	4	1
Oregon State	2	2
Florida State	1	2
Cal State Fullerton	0	2
BRACKET TWO	**W**	**L**
Florida	3	1
Texas Christian	3	2
Louisville	1	2
Texas A&M	0	2

CWS FINALS (BEST OF THREE)

June 26: Florida 4, Louisiana State 3
June 27: Florida 6, Louisiana State 1

ALL-TOURNAMENT TEAM

C: Michael Papierski, Louisiana State. **1B:** Drew Mendoza, Florida State. **2B:** Nick Madrigal, Oregon State. **3B:** Dylan Busby, Florida State. **SS:** Timmy Richards, Cal State Fullerton. **OF:** Antoine Duplantis, Louisiana State; Austin Langworthy, Florida; Zach Watson, Louisiana State. **DH:** Brendan McKay, Louisville. **P:** *Alex Faedo, Florida; Brady Singer, Florida.

**Named Most Outstanding Player.*

BATTING

(Minimum 8 PA)

PLAYER	AVG	AB	R	H	2B	3B	HR	RBI	SB
Matt Henderson, FSU	.556	9	0	5	0	0	0	1	0
Blake Kopetsky, TAMU	.375	8	2	3	2	0	0	1	0
Devin Hairston, Louisville	.364	11	1	4	0	0	0	1	0
Josh Stowers, Louisville	.364	11	1	4	1	0	0	1	0
Drew Mendoza, FSU	.364	11	3	4	0	0	2	2	0
Connor Wanhanen, TCU	.357	14	2	5	1	0	0	2	1
Zach Watson, LSU	.346	26	5	9	1	0	1	2	2
Nick Madrigal, OSU	.333	15	1	5	1	0	0	4	0
Colby Fitch, Louisville	.333	12	0	4	1	0	0	4	0
Timmy Richards, CSF	.333	6	2	2	0	0	2	5	0

PITCHING

(Minimum 6 IP)

PITCHER	W-L	ERA	G	SV	IP	H	BB	SO
Alex Faedo, Florida	2-0	0.00	2	0	14	5	6	22
Michael Byrne, Florida	0-0	0.00	4	3	7	9	0	9
Kaylor Chafin, TAMU	0-0	0.00	2	0	7	4	0	8
Sean Wymer, TCU	1-0	0.00	2	1	6	2	0	7
Caleb Gilbert, LSU	1-0	0.90	2	0	10	6	3	11
Tyler Dyson, Florida	1-0	1.23	2	0	7	3	2	4
Brian Howard, TCU	1-0	1.29	1	0	7	5	0	12
Jared Poche', LSU	2-1	1.65	3	0	16	16	3	9
Brady Singer, Florida	2-0	2.57	2	0	14	14	3	21
Alex Lange, LSU	1-0	3.38	2	0	13	9	8	16

Buffalo Cuts Program, Akron, Boise State To Restart Theirs

Buffalo announced in April it would cut baseball, as well as men's soccer, men's swimming and diving and women's rowing, following the 2017 school year.

Buffalo is the third school in the last three years to cut baseball and the second from the Mid-American Conference to do so. Akron, a fellow MAC school, cut baseball following the 2015 season and North Dakota eliminated its program last year.

Buffalo has cut baseball once before. The program began in 1949 and was shuttered in 1987. Baseball returned in 2000 following the school's move to Division I and the MAC. The Bulls have had just one winning season since their return to the diamond, going 33-24 in 2013.

Buffalo has always been in a tough position in the MAC. The Bulls have just 6.5 scholarships and are competing in a conference against teams that are fully funded with 11.7 scholarships. But coach Ron Torgalski, who has been on the coaching staff since its return, has kept Buffalo competitive despite its limitations.

The Bulls went 17-34 in their final season.

Meanwhile, Akron and Boise State announced plans to restart their previously shuttered programs. Akron plans to bring baseball back for the 2019 season, while Boise State, which last had a baseball team in 1980, is eying a return the following year. Akron will also add a women's lacrosse team, while Boise State helped clear the way for baseball by cutting wrestling.

REGIONALS

JUNE 1-5

64 teams, 16 four-team, double-elimination tournaments. Winners advance to super regionals.

CORVALLIS, ORE.

Host: Oregon State (No. 1 national seed).
Participants: No. 1 Oregon State (49-4), No. 2 Nebraska (35-20-1), No. 3 Yale (32-16), No. 4 Holy Cross (23-27).
Champion: Oregon State (3-0).
Runner-up: Yale (2-2).

CLEMSON S,C.

Host: Clemson.
Participants: No. 1 Clemson (39-19), No. 2 Vanderbilt (33-22-1), No. 3 St. John's (42-11), No. 4 UNC Greensboro (35-22).
Champion: Vanderbilt (3-1).
Runner-up: Clemson (3-2).

STANFORD, CALIF.

Host: Stanford (No. 8 national seed).
Participants: No. 1 Stanford (40-14), No. 2 Cal State Fullerton (34-21), No. 3 Brigham Young (37-19), No. 4 Sacramento State (32-27).
Champion: Cal State Fullerton (3-0).
Runner-up: Stanford (2-2).

LONG BEACH, CALIF.

Host: Long Beach State.
Participants: No. 1 Long Beach State (37-17), No. 2 Texas (37-22), No. 3 UCLA (30-25), No. 4 San Diego State (41-19).
Champion: Long Beach State (4-1).
Runner-up: Texas (2-2).

BATON ROUGE, LA.

Host: Louisiana State (No. 4 national seed).
Participants: No. 1 Louisiana State (43-17), No. 2 Southeastern Louisiana (36-20), No. 3 Rice (31-29), No. 4 Texas Southern (20-32).
Champion: Louisiana State (3-0).
Runner-up: Rice (2-2).

HATTIESBURG, MISS.

Host: Southern Mississippi.
Participants: No. 1 Southern Mississippi (47-14), No. 2 Mississippi State (36-24), No. 3 South Alabama (39-19), No. 4 Illinois-Chicago (39-15).
Champion: Mississippi State (4-1).
Runner-up: Southern Mississippi (2-2).

LUBBOCK, TEXAS

Host: Texas Tech (No. 5 national seed).
Participants: No. 1 Texas Tech (43-15), No. 2 Arizona (37-19), No. 3 Sam Houston State (40-20), No. 4 Delaware (34-21).
Champion: Sam Houston State (4-1).
Runner-up: Texas Tech (2-2).

TALLAHASSEE, FLA.

Host: Florida State.
Participants: No. 1 Florida State (39-20), No. 2 Central Florida (40-20), No. 3 Auburn (35-24), No. 4 Tennessee Tech (40-19).
Champion: Florida State (4-1).
Runner-up: Auburn (2-2).

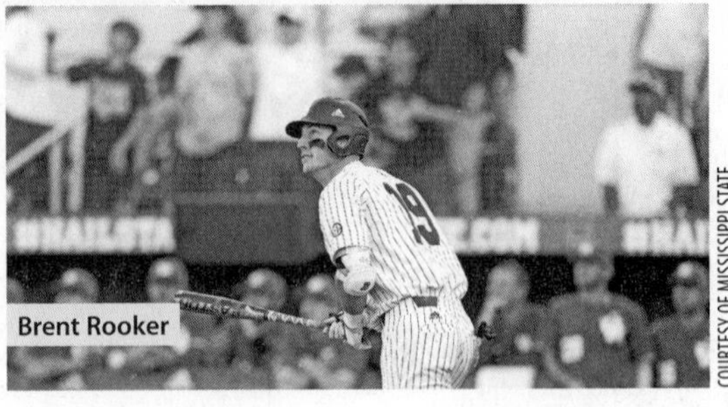
Brent Rooker

COURTESY OF MISSISSIPPI STATE

GAINESVILLE, FLA.

Host: Florida (No. 3 national seed).
Participants: No. 1 Florida (42-16), No. 2 South Florida (41-17), No. 3 Bethune-Cookman (33-23), No. 4 Marist (32-21).
Champion: Florida (3-1).
Runner-up: Bethune-Cookman (2-2).

WINSTON-SALEM, N.C.

Host: Wake Forest.
Participants: No. 1 Wake Forest (39-18), No. 2 West Virginia (34-24), No. 3 Maryland (37-21), No. 4 Maryland-Baltimore County (23-23).
Champion: Wake Forest (3-0).
Runner-up: West Virginia (2-2).

FORT WORTH, TEXAS

Host: Texas Christian (No. 6 national seed).
Participants: No. 1 Texas Christian (42-16), No. 2 Virginia (41-14), No. 3 Dallas Baptist (40-19), No. 4 Central Connecticut State (36-20).
Champion: Texas Christian (3-0).
Runner-up: Dallas Baptist (2-2).

FAYETTEVILLE, ARK.

Host: Arkansas.
Participants: No. 1 Arkansas (42-17), No. 2 Missouri State (40-17), No. 3 Oklahoma State (30-25), No. 4 Oral Roberts (42-14).
Champion: Missouri State (3-1).
Runner-up: Arkansas (3-2).

CHAPEL HILL, N.C.

Host: North Carolina (No. 2 national seed).
Participants: No. 1 North Carolina (47-12), No. 2 Florida Gulf Coast (42-18), No. 3 Michigan (42-15), No. 4 Davidson (32-24).
Champion: Davidson (3-0).
Runner-up: North Carolina (2-2).

HOUSTON

Host: Houston.
Participants: No. 1 Houston (40-19), No. 2 Baylor (34-21), No. 3 Texas A&M (36-21), No. 4 Iowa (38-20).
Champion: Texas A&M (3-0).
Runner-up: Houston (2-2).

LOUISVILLE

Host: Louisville (No. 7 national seed).
Participants: No. 1 Louisville (47-10), No. 2 Oklahoma (34-22), No. 3 Xavier (32-25), No. 4 Radford (27-30).
Champion: Louisville (3-0).
Runner-up: Xavier (2-2).

LEXINGTON, KY.

Host: Kentucky.
Participants: No. 1 Kentucky (39-20), No. 2 Indiana (33-22-2), No. 3 North Carolina State (34-23), No. 4 Ohio (30-26).
Champion: Kentucky (4-1).
Runner-up: North Carolina State (2-2).

SUPER REGIONALS

JUNE 9-12

16 teams, best-of-three series.
Winners advance to College World Series.

VANDERBILT AT OREGON STATE

Site: Corvallis, Ore.
Oregon State wins 2-0, advances to CWS.

CAL STATE FULLERTON AT LONG BEACH STATE

Site: Long Beach, Ca.
Cal State Fullerton wins 2-1, advances to CWS.

MISSISSIPPI STATE AT LOUISIANA STATE

Site: Baton Rouge, La.
Louisiana State wins 2-0, advances to CWS.

SAM HOUSTON STATE AT FLORIDA STATE

Site: Tallahassee, Fla.
Florida State wins 2-0, advances to CWS.

WAKE FOREST AT FLORIDA

Site: Gainesville, Fla.
Florida wins 2-1, advances to CWS.

MISSOURI STATE AT TEXAS CHRISTIAN

Site: Fort Worth, Texas.
Texas Christian wins 2-0, advances to CWS.

KENTUCKY AT LOUISVILLE

Site: Louisville
Louisville wins 2-0, advances to CWS.

DAVIDSON AT TEXAS A&M

Site: College Station, Texas.
Texas A&M wins 2-0, advances to CWS.

McKay Caps Storied Career

PLAYER OF THE YEAR

BY TEDDY CAHILL

Even after Brendan McKay dyed his hair blond along with his teammates before Louisville began the Atlantic Coast Conference tournament, nobody would confuse the lefthander/first baseman with Robert Redford. But Redford's Hollywood looks are about the only thing separating McKay from becoming "The Natural."

Baseball appears to come easily to McKay. In his senior year at his Pittsburgh-area high school, he had a 72-inning scoreless streak. At Louisville, he has been a staple of the rotation and the middle of the lineup throughout his career.

Brendan McKay

He spent two summers playing for USA Baseball's Collegiate National Team. He was Freshman of the Year in 2015 and has earned first-team All-America honors for three straight seasons. He's just the third player to do so in Baseball America's 37-year history, joining Texas' Greg Swindell (1984-86) and Oklahoma State's Robin Ventura (1986-88).

McKay's junior season was his best. He went 11-3, 2.56 with 146 strikeouts in 109 innings on the mound and hit .341/.457/.659 with 18 home runs. He helped lead Louisville to the College World Series and the ACC regular season title. For his sensational season and two-way talent, McKay is the 2017 College Player of the Year.

McKay has considerable physical talents, but his mental capabilities played a big role in his success as well. He shouldered a hefty burden for the Cardinals but never allowed the pressure to overwhelm him.

"Baseball's hard as it is, just being a regular player," McKay said. "If you put any extra pressure on yourself, it can take even more of a toll. That's when you play your best, when you're free and you've got a clear mind and you're just doing your thing out there."

While Louisville had high hopes for McKay, he first had to prove he belonged in the mix on the mound and in the lineup. He quickly did both. He opened his freshman year in the bullpen and earned four saves before moving into the rotation about a month into the season. He became a regular in the lineup in the first few weeks of the spring.

McKay has improved in nearly every aspect of the game. Indiana coach Chris Lemonis was Louisville's recruiting coordinator when McKay committed. He said McKay has surpassed expectations.

"He just keeps getting better and better," Lemonis said. "It's scary. I've never seen the kid have a bad week."

Louisville coach Dan McDonnell is not shy about declaring McKay the best player in program history. He is a transformative talent and has played a critical role in Louisville winning the ACC title in two of its first three years in the league.

Winning drives McKay more than any individual records, awards or his draft position.

"He just wants to win," McDonnell said. "He loves to compete. We're so blessed to have him."

PREVIOUS WINNERS

1982: Jeff Ledbetter, OF/LHP, Florida State
1983: Dave Magadan, 1B, Alabama
1984: Oddibe McDowell, OF, Arizona State
1985: Pete Incaviglia, OF, Oklahoma State
1986: Casey Close, OF, Michigan
1987: Robin Ventura, 3B, Oklahoma State
1988: John Olerund, 1B/LHP, Wash. St.
1989: Ben McDonald, RHP, Louisiana State
1990: Mike Kelly, OF, Arizona State
1991: David McCarthy, 1B, Stanford
1992: Phil Nevin, 3B, Cal State Fullerton
1993: Brooks Kieschnick, DH/RHP, Texas
1994: Jason Varitek, C, Georgia Tech
1995: Todd Helton, 1B/LHP, Tennessee
1996: Kris Benson, RHP, Clemson
1997: J.D. Drew, OF, Florida State
1998: Jeff Austin, RHP, Stanford
1999: Jason Jennings, RHP, Baylor
2000: Mark Teixeira, 3B, Georgia Tech
2001: Mark Prior, RHP, Southern California
2002: Khalil Greene, SS, Clemson
2003: Rickie Weeks, 2B, Southern
2004: Jered Weaver, RHP, Long Beach St.
2005: Alex Gordon, 3B, Nebraska
2006: Andrew Miller, LHP, North Carolina
2007: David Price, LHP, Vanderbilt
2008: Buster Posey, C/RHP, Florida State
2009: Stephen Strasburg, RHP, San Diego St.
2010: Anthony Rendon, 3B, Rice
2011: Trevor Bauer, RHP, UCLA
2012: Mike Zunino, C, Florida
2013: Kris Bryant, 3B, San Diego
2014: A.J. Reed, 1B/LHP, Kentucky
2015: Andrew Benintendi, OF, Arkansas
2016: Kyle Lewis, OF, Mercer

McDonnell Builds Powerhouse

BY MICHAEL LANANNA

Louisville coach Dan McDonnell had only been home from Omaha for a couple of days, yet he was already planning his next move. July is no time for rest.

McDonnell had his eyes on the Futures Game in Miami, where 2016 first-rounder Corey Ray will play. He thought about sticking around for the major league Home Run Derby, too, in case 2010 Louisville draftee Adam Duvall participated again. He sent a text to Brendan McKay, the No. 4 overall pick and 2017 College Player of the Year, to congratulate him on the $7.005 million bonus he just signed.

Dan McDonnell

Those players are all products of the McDonnell Era, a few of the pillars that have helped propel Louisville baseball into elite territory. McDonnell is quick to credit those players and his assistant coaches for Louisville's success. And while they've all played crucial roles, it's no coincidence that the Cardinals have emerged as a national power under the guidance of McDonnell—Baseball America's College Coach of the Year. The award reflects a decade of excellence.

Since McDonnell took over the program in 2007, Louisville has the third-most wins of any school in the country. In the last five years, no team has more wins. After making only one NCAA Tournament appearance previously, in 2002, the Cardinals have made 10 appearances in McDonnell's 11 seasons. This year marked Louisville's fourth trip to the College World Series—all under McDonnell, including his debut season.

He came to Louisville after spending six years as Mississippi's recruiting coordinator under Mike Bianco. The eight years before that, McDonnell coached under Fred Jordan at the Citadel, where he'd played for the 1990 CWS team. There he soaked up the toughness and work ethic required to thrive at a military school.

Louisville quickly has evolved into one of the country's top programs in terms of player development. The Cardinals have achieved those feats while mainly recruiting Kentucky, Pennsylvania and the Midwest, particularly Illinois. Those areas aren't known as baseball hotbeds, but McDonnell and his staff help mold those recruits into winners with the culture they've established at Louisville.

The Cardinals this year finished 53-12 and earned the No. 7 national seed. They won the Atlantic Coast Conference's Atlantic Division for the third time in the three years since joining the ACC in 2015. The Cardinals lost eight players to the draft this June, but McDonnell is not ready to call 2018 a rebuilding year.

"Sometimes it is what it is, we are who we are, and we're only going to be able to go so far," he said. "But I don't know if I can sleep with myself if I didn't think I challenged these guys, pushed these guys and at least gave them every opportunity to believe that they'd have a chance to win a national championship."

McDonnell hasn't stopped dreaming those big dreams. And why should he?

They keep coming true.

PREVIOUS WINNERS

1982: Gene Stephenson, Wichita State
1983: Barry Shollenberger, Alabama
1984: Augie Garrido, Cal State Fullerton
1985: Ron Polk, Mississippi State
1986: Skip Bertman, LSU/Dave Snow, LMU
1987: Mark Marquess, Stanford
1988: Jim Brock, Arizona State
1989: Dave Snow, Long Beach State
1990: Steve Webber, Georgia
1991: Jim Hendry, Creighton
1992: Andy Lopez, Pepperdine
1993: Gene Stephenson, Wichita State
1994: Jim Morris, Miami
1995: Pat Murphy, Arizona State
1996: Skip Bertman, Louisiana State
1997: Jim Wells, Alabama
1998: Pat Murphy, Arizona State
1999: Wayne Graham, Rice
2000: Ray Tanner, South Carolina
2001: Dave Van Horn, Nebraska
2002: Augie Garrido, Texas
2003: George Horton, Cal State Fullerton
2004: David Perno, Georgia
2005: Rick Jones, Tulane
2006: Pat Casey, Oregon State
2007: Dave Serrano, UC Irvine
2008: Mike Fox, North Carolina
2009: Paul Mainieri, Louisiana State
2010: Ray Tanner, South Carolina
2011: Kevin O'Sullivan, Florida
2012: Mike Martin, Florida State
2013: John Savage, UCLA
2014: Tim Corbin, Vanderbilt
2015: Brian O'Connor, Virginia
2016: Jim Schlossnagle, Texas Christian

Wallner Stars At Southern Miss

FRESHMAN OF THE YEAR

BY TEDDY CAHILL

Matt Wallner spent the first few weeks of his freshman year at Southern Mississippi sweating out the heat. The big outfielder/righthander had moved from his hometown of Forest Lake, Minn., to Hattiesburg, where each successive day felt like the hottest and most humid of his life.

By the spring, however, Wallner was making opponents sweat out games against Southern Miss. The freshman became the Golden Eagles' center fielder and a key cog in the heart of its lineup, hitting .346/.463/.655 with 19 home runs. He made nine appearances on the mound, going 2-0, 1.84 with three saves. Wallner helped the Golden Eagles to their most successful season since their 2009 College World Series run. For his spectacular season, Wallner is the 2017 Freshman of the Year.

Matt Wallner

Facing Northeastern on Opening Day, Wallner hit a double off the center-field wall on the first pitch he saw during his college career.

"That lifted a weight off my back, and I felt like I got moved into it with my first swing of the season," he said. "That was kind of relieving."

Wallner didn't slow down the rest of the season. He set the program's freshman records for home runs and RBIs (63).

Wallner said he still sees plenty of room for improvement, starting with staying healthy all season so that he can spend more time on the mound after a hip injury kept him from pitching much of the second half.

PREVIOUS WINNERS

1983: Rafael Palmeiro, OF, Mississippi State
1984: Greg Swindell, LHP, Texas
1985: Jack McDowell, RHP, Stanford
1986: Robin Ventura, 3B, Oklahoma State
1987: Paul Carey, OF, Stanford
1988: Kirk Dressendorfer, RHP, Texas
1989: Alex Fernandez, RHP, Miami
1990: Jeffrey Hammonds, OF, Stanford
1991: Brooks Kieschnick, RHP/DH, Texas
1992: Todd Walker, 2B, Louisiana State
1993: Brett Laxton, RHP, Louisiana State
1994: R.A. Dickey, RHP, Tennessee
1995: Kyle Peterson, RHP, Stanford
1996: Pat Burrell, 3B, Miami
1997: Brian Roberts, SS, North Carolina
1998: Xavier Nady, 2B, California
1999: James Jurries, 2B, Tulane
2000: Kevin Howard, 3B, Miami
2001: Michael Aubrey, OF/LHP, Texas
2002: Stephen Drew, SS, Florida State
2003: Ryan Braun, SS, Miami
2004: Wade LeBlanc, LHP, Alabama
2005: Joe Savery, LHP, Rice
2006: Pedro Alvarez, 3B, Vanderbilt
2007: Dustin Ackley, 1B, North Carolina
2008: Chris Hernandez, LHP, Miami
2009: Anthony Rendon, 3B, Rice
2010: Matt Purke, LHP, Texas Christian
2011: Colin Moran, 3B, North Carolina
2012: Carlos Rodon, LHP, N.C. State
2013: Alex Bregman, SS, Louisiana State
2014: Zack Collins, C, Miami
2015: Brendan McKay, LHP/1B, Louisville
2016: Seth Beer, OF, Clemson

FRESHMAN ALL-AMERICA TEAMS

FIRST TEAM

POS.		AVG	OBP	SLG	AB	R	H	HR	RBI	SB
C	Shea Langeliers, Baylor	.313	.388	.540	211	43	66	10	38	1
1B	Andrew Vaughn, California	.349	.414	.555	218	36	76	12	50	1
2B	Braden Shewmake, Texas A&M	.328	.374	.529	274	47	90	11	69	11
3B	Josh Jung, Texas Tech	.306	.395	.453	245	55	75	6	43	2
SS	Cam Shepherd, Georgia	.307	.354	452	241	29	74	5	28	5
OF	Dominic Fletcher, Arkansas	.291	.356	.495	220	44	64	12	37	1
OF	Grant Little, Texas Tech	.335	.405	.476	206	52	69	2	34	6
OF	Matt Wallner, So. Mississippi	.336	.463	.655	235	56	79	19	63	4
DH	Ashton McGee, North Carolina	.327	.417	.484	223	45	73	7	46	1
UT	Kevin Milam, St. Mary's	.313	.397	.547	214	45	67	12	55	0

		W	L	ERA	G	SV	IP	H	BB	SO	BAA
SP	Gianluca Dalatri, North Carolina	7	3	3.34	15	0	97	90	19	85	.245
SP	Shane McClanahan, So. Florida	4	2	3.28	14	0	74	48	35	104	.185
SP	Sean Mooney, St. John's	8	2	1.71	16	0	100	70	16	88	.196
SP	Eric Walker, Louisiana State	8	2	3.48	17	0	96	83	23	78	.233
RP	Josh Hiatt, North Carolina	4	2	1.90	32	13	52	31	20	64	.168
RP	Kenyon Yovan, Oregon	1	1	1.97	22	15	32	26	6	36	.213
UT	Kevin Milarm, St. Mary's	3	1	2.27	22	9	40	27	11	31	.191

SECOND TEAM

C–James Free, Pacific (.343-14-54). **1B**–Drew Mendoza, Florida State (.263-8-31). **2B**–Michael Massey, Illinois (.330-6-36). **3B**–Nick Quintana, Arizona (.293-6-38). **SS**–Logan Davidson, Clemson (.286-12-41). **OF**–Spencer Brickhouse, East Carolina (.310-10-28; Carlos Cortes, South Carolina (.286-12-41); Zach Watson, Louisiana State (.313-8-35). **DH**–Brad Debo, North Carolina State (.335-4-43). **UT**–Rylan Thomas, Central Florida (.303-14-53; 1-0, 0.00, 8 IP, 10 SO). **SP**–Nick Bennett, Louisville (5-0, 2.70, 63 IP, 59 SO); Tyler Blohm, Maryland (8-63, 3.48, 75 IP, 71 SO); Nick Lodolo, Texas Christian (5-1, 4.28, 74 IP, 69 SO); Zack Thompson (8-3, 3.45, 76 IP, 96 SO). **RP**–Jake Mulholland, Oregon State (6-1, 1.31, 48 IP, 41 SO); Riley Self, Mississippi State (5-2, 3.72, 48 IP, 60 SO).

NCAA DIVISION I LEADERS

HITTING (Minimum 140 at-bats)

BATTING AVERAGE

RK.	PLAYER, TEAM	CLASS	AVG	OBP	SLG	G	AB	2B	3B	HR	RBI	BB	SO	SB
1.	Keston Hiura, UC Irvine	Jr.	.442	.567	.693	56	199	24	1	8	42	50	38	9
2.	Eli Boggess, Morehead State	Jr.	.425	.487	.599	55	207	11	2	7	40	19	14	3
3.	Adam Groesbeck, Air Force	Sr.	.410	.460	.649	50	222	23	3	8	42	17	31	9
4.	Marshawn Taylor, Grambling	Jr.	.402	.477	.471	51	204	12	1	0	38	29	20	16
5.	Brock Hale, BYU	So.	.395	.481	.672	51	195	14	2	12	48	27	31	5
6.	Randell Kanemaru, Columbia	Jr.	.395	.435	.625	38	152	14	0	7	42	11	29	2
7.	Trevor Putzig, Tennessee Tech	Jr.	.394	.441	.568	56	236	23	0	6	52	22	22	1
8.	Troy Dixon, St. John's	Sr.	.394	.473	.525	49	160	12	0	3	35	23	23	0
9.	Andrew Moritz, UNC Greensboro	So.	.392	.450	.513	59	240	8	6	3	38	24	22	16
10.	Will Schneider, Morehead State	Sr.	.391	.486	.622	59	238	14	4	11	49	36	38	2
11.	Adam Haseley, Virginia	Jr.	.390	.491	.659	58	223	16	1	14	56	44	21	10
12.	Ryan Grotjohn, Cal State Bakersfield	Sr.	.390	.459	.512	56	213	15	4	1	42	23	20	6
13.	Garrett McCain, Oklahoma State	Jr.	.388	.491	.549	57	224	14	5	4	43	29	33	19
14.	Brent Rooker, Mississippi State	Jr.	.387	.495	.810	67	248	30	3	23	82	48	58	18
15.	Alec Skender, Southern Illinois Edwardsville	Sr.	.386	.444	.493	52	215	15	1	2	24	21	22	13
16.	Kevin Merrell, South Florida	Jr.	.384	.464	.569	52	216	11	4	7	36	29	31	19
17.	J.J. Matijevic, Arizona	Jr.	.383	.436	.633	59	240	30	0	10	65	23	38	9
18.	Caleb Webster, UNC Greensboro	Fr.	.383	.414	.517	51	201	14	5	1	40	14	17	2
19.	Josh Evans, Stephen F. Austin	Jr.	.383	.440	.638	51	149	8	0	10	38	17	15	0
20.	Bryson Bowman, Western Carolina	Sr.	.381	.470	.619	56	218	15	2	11	59	37	31	9
21.	Nick Madrigal, Oregon State	So.	.380	.449	.532	60	237	20	2	4	40	27	16	16
22.	Bradley Haslam, Air Force	Sr.	.380	.440	.620	49	213	19	1	10	51	21	24	5
23.	Matt McCann, Fairleigh Dickinson	Sr.	.379	.453	.451	46	182	7	3	0	30	23	22	25
24.	Raphael Gladu, Louisiana Tech	Sr.	.378	.439	.579	56	233	19	2	8	55	24	26	3
25.	Ryan Flick, Tennessee Tech	Jr.	.377	.461	.727	58	231	24	0	19	74	37	62	1
26.	Brent Sakurai, New Mexico State	Sr.	.377	.427	.571	57	231	15	9	4	41	21	28	9
27.	Nazier McILwain, Coppin State	So.	.377	.463	.510	41	151	11	0	3	33	25	33	3
28.	Jonah Todd, Auburn	Jr.	.376	.460	.471	63	242	13	5	0	37	37	28	9
29.	Danny Wright, Southeast Missouri State	Fr.	.376	.472	.567	51	178	13	3	5	36	26	36	9
30.	John Valente, St. John's	Jr.	.375	.437	.464	54	224	10	2	2	35	23	14	9
31.	Dan Holst, Southeast Missouri State	Sr.	.375	.509	.601	55	208	13	2	10	55	49	39	13
32.	Michael Donadio, St. John's	Sr.	.374	.473	.547	55	214	15	5	4	38	38	42	10
33.	Bryce Brown, Jackson State	Jr.	.374	.514	.448	49	163	7	1	1	33	36	36	27
34.	Aaron Arruda, Fresno State	Jr.	.373	.448	.643	60	244	17	2	15	67	31	59	1
35.	T.J. Nichting, Charlotte	Sr.	.373	.411	.529	58	244	15	4	5	49	17	22	16
36.	Jared Mang, New Mexico	So.	.373	.433	.573	57	241	17	2	9	62	20	27	4
37.	Evan White, Kentucky	Jr.	.373	.453	.637	53	212	24	1	10	41	25	31	5
38.	Michael Anatasia, New Jersey Institute of Technology	So.	.373	.463	.507	42	150	14	3	0	29	24	38	7
39.	David Metzgar, Cal State Bakersfield	Sr.	.372	.425	.465	55	215	10	5	0	36	24	14	18
40.	Andrew Penner, Cal State Bakersfield	Jr.	.372	.456	.401	54	207	4	1	0	32	26	26	6
41.	Alfonso Rivas, Arizona	So.	.371	.483	.531	58	213	13	0	7	63	39	36	3
42.	Tim Graul, Penn	Sr.	.371	.431	.600	45	175	16	3	6	41	13	28	6
43.	Ryan Brennan, Fairleigh Dickinson	Sr.	.370	.440	.580	46	181	17	0	7	45	20	27	12
44.	Dallas Carroll, Utah	Sr.	.369	.465	.591	51	198	17	3	7	52	35	19	12
45.	Jack Zoellner, New Mexico	Sr.	.368	.470	.663	50	193	19	1	12	56	37	26	5
46.	Jared Young, Old Dominion	Jr.	.367	.441	.580	58	226	19	4	7	34	15	19	9
47.	Trevor McCauley, Niagara	Jr.	.367	.448	.500	44	150	14	0	2	29	12	39	7
48.	Dominic DiCaprio, Rice	So.	.366	.438	.508	63	238	16	0	6	49	27	40	2
49	Tyler Zabojnik, Air Force	Jr.	.366	.433	.595	53	232	23	3	8	47	23	48	4
50.	Adonis Lao, Bethune-Cookman	Jr.	.366	.390	.421	57	216	10	1	0	31	8	34	3
51.	Mark Contreras, UC Riverside	Sr.	.366	.427	.558	42	172	11	8	2	22	17	30	7
52.	Ryan Kemp, Middle Tennessee	Jr.	.366	.419	.622	42	164	16	1	8	29	14	20	9
53.	Logan Farrar, Virginia Commonwealth	Sr.	.365	.450	.543	55	230	17	0	8	32	27	23	4
54.	Mason Fishback, New Mexico State	Jr.	.365	.417	.564	53	211	16	1	8	52	11	44	3
55.	Cutter McDowell, Lamar	Sr.	.365	.472	.556	46	178	22	0	4	31	31	37	9
56.	Dallas Oliver, Florida A&M	Jr.	.365	.443	.407	52	167	7	0	0	19	19	21	3
57.	Braxton Morris, Morehead State	Jr.	.364	.437	.516	59	225	17	1	5	47	15	33	3
58.	Cody Den Beste, Prairie View	Sr.	.364	.437	.561	56	214	16	7	4	36	13	30	12
59.	Allen Smoot, San Francisco	Sr.	.364	.470	.459	57	209	14	0	2	39	39	34	4
60.	Ben Fisher, Eastern Kentucky	Sr.	.363	.455	.762	56	223	14	0	25	72	38	35	0
61.	Dylan Hardy, South Alabama	So.	.363	.424	.498	58	215	10	2	5	30	21	50	18
62.	Tommy Richter, College of Charleston	Jr.	.363	.441	.441	53	204	9	2	1	26	24	32	5
63.	Daniel McFarland, Eastern Kentucky	Jr.	.363	.438	.516	51	190	12	1	5	25	18	25	5
64.	Brandon Melendez, North Carolina A&T	Jr.	.363	.439	.446	46	157	8	1	1	24	21	45	14
65.	Phil Caulfield, Loyola Marymount	Sr.	.362	.438	.477	54	218	12	2	3	35	30	30	9
66.	Daulton Varsho, Milwaukee	Jr.	.362	.490	.643	54	199	11	6	11	39	46	39	10
67.	Jon Rosoff, Army West Point	Jr.	.362	.464	.454	56	196	10	1	2	35	29	26	9
68.	Russell Williams, Air Force	Sr.	.362	.430	.592	47	174	10	3	8	41	17	41	5

69.	Tristan Pompey, Kentucky	So.	.361	.464	.541	66	266	18	0	10	45	46	56	9
70.	Reed Rohlman, Clemson	Jr.	.361	.448	.542	62	227	21	1	6	34	26	33	1
71.	Luis Gonzalez, New Mexico	Jr.	.361	.500	.589	55	219	22	2	8	42	58	32	14
72.	Paul Witt, Virginia Commonwealth	Fr.	.361	.429	.425	55	219	11	0	1	36	14	30	2
73.	Ernie De La Trinidad, UNLV	So.	.361	.465	.559	55	202	9	5	7	30	21	32	12
74.	Stuart Fairchild, Wake Forest	Jr.	.360	.439	.636	63	261	19	1	17	67	31	54	21
75.	Justin Jones, UNLV	Sr.	.360	.424	.591	56	203	16	2	9	50	23	34	8
76.	D.J. Artis, Liberty	So.	.359	.532	.552	52	181	13	2	6	45	62	30	23
77.	Shaine Hughes, Monmouth	Sr.	.359	.441	.519	47	181	14	0	5	30	20	21	5
78.	Tyler Jones, Air Force	Sr.	.359	.471	.706	43	170	17	0	14	59	29	38	3
79.	Dane Myers, Rice	Jr.	.358	.425	.545	62	246	12	5	8	43	24	54	13
80.	Jack Owens, Virginia Tech	So.	.358	.424	.504	55	240	16	2	5	28	18	41	9
81.	Hunter Williams, Tulane	Sr.	.357	.404	.574	58	244	18	1	11	41	18	43	5
82.	Collin Thacker, Gardner-Webb	Sr.	.357	.406	.545	55	224	15	0	9	46	17	23	2
83.	JT Thomas, Mercer	Jr.	.357	.454	.624	55	210	20	0	12	62	23	45	2
84.	David Hensley, San Diego State	Jr.	.357	.409	.486	59	210	16	1	3	31	17	35	7
85.	Charlie Carpenter, South Carolina Upstate	Jr.	.357	.441	.592	48	196	13	0	11	46	23	40	0
86.	Drew Wiss, Air Force	So.	.357	.447	.481	48	154	13	3	0	26	20	40	4
87.	Alex McKenna, Cal Poly	So.	.356	.420	.483	56	236	11	2	5	31	21	45	13
88.	Jesse Berardi, St. John's	Jr.	.356	.456	.462	55	225	10	1	4	47	38	35	12
89.	Travis Swaggerty, South Alabama	So.	.356	.484	.571	58	219	12	1	11	60	49	45	19
90.	Trevor Peterson, Utah Valley	Jr.	.356	.425	.461	54	219	12	1	3	20	23	41	7
91.	Lamar Briggs, Jackson State	Jr.	.356	.422	.470	55	219	17	4	0	46	21	26	14
92.	Tanner Allison, Western Michigan	Jr.	.356	.432	.574	53	216	18	1	9	68	25	31	3
93.	Joe Hoscheit, Northwestern	Sr.	.356	.436	.557	56	194	14	2	7	45	27	29	3
94.	Drew Ellis, Louisville	Jr.	.355	.448	.701	65	231	18	1	20	61	40	40	6
95.	Jake Lumley, Canisius	Sr.	.355	.436	.461	57	228	12	3	2	21	29	40	17
96.	Bobby Campbell, George Washington	Sr.	.355	.423	.532	58	220	15	0	8	43	26	14	2
97.	Jack Gethings, Fairfield	So.	.355	.429	.430	55	214	7	3	1	40	28	21	13
98.	Ben Spitznagel, UNC Greensboro	Sr.	.355	.440	.460	54	211	11	4	1	33	30	19	12
99.	Vinny Capra, Richmond	Jr.	.355	.420	.488	51	211	14	1	4	19	21	25	5
100.	Adam McGinnis, Western Illinois	Sr.	.355	.471	.566	48	166	17	0	6	37	28	13	8

ON-BASE PERCENTAGE

RANK, PLAYER, POS., TEAM	OBP
1. Keston Hiura, INF, UC Irvine	.567
2. D.J. Artis, OF, Liberty	.532
3. Bryce Brown, OF, Jackson St.	.514
4. Dan Holst, OF, SE Missouri St.	.509
5. Luis Gonzalez, OF, New Mexico	.500
6. Brent Rooker, OF, Mississippi State	.495
7. Garrett McCain, OF, Oklahoma State	.491
8. Adam Haseley, OF, Virginia	.491
9. Daulton Varsho, C, Milwaukee	.490
10. Eli Boggess, INF/OF, Morehead St.	.487

SLUGGING PERCENTAGE

RANK, PLAYER, POS., TEAM	SLG
1. Brent Booker, OF, Mississippi State	.810
2. Niko Hulsizer, OF, Morehead State	.775
3. Ben Fisher, INF, Eastern Kentucky	.762
4. Jake Adams, 1B, Iowa	.747
5. Patrick Robinson, OF, Harvard	.738
6. Austin Listi, OF, Dallas Baptist	.735
7. Ryan Flick, 1B, Tennessee Tech	.727
8. Jack Hranec, 1B, Murray State	.717
9. Nick Egil, C, Belmont	.715
10. Tyler Jones, OF, Air Force	.706

RUNS BATTED IN

RANK, PLAYER, POS., TEAM	RBI
1. Gavin Sheets, INF, Wake Forest	84
2. Niko Hulsizer, OF, Morehead State	82
Quincy Nieporte, INF, Florida State	82
Brent Rooker, OF, Mississippi State	82
5. Pavin Smith, 1B, Virginia	77
6. Ryan Flick, 1B, Tennessee Tech	74
7. Greg Deichmann, OF, Louisiana State	73
8. Jake Adams, 1B, Iowa	72
Ben Fisher, INF, Eastern Kentucky	72
Taylor Schwaner, INF, SE Louisiana	72

HOME RUNS

RANK, PLAYER, POS., TEAM	HR
1. Jake Adams, 1B, Iowa	29
2. Niko Hulsizer, OF, Morehead State	27
3. Ben Fisher, INF, Eastern Kentucky	25
4. Austin Listi, OF, Dallas Baptist	24
5. Jeremy Eierman, INF, Missouri State	23
Brent Rooker, OF, Mississippi State	23
7. Jake Burger, INF, Missouri State	22
8. Casey Golden, OF, UNC Wilmington	21
Gavin Sheets, INF, Wake Forest	21
10. Johnny Aiello, INF, Wake Forest	20
Austin Bush, INF, UC Santa Barbara	20
Drew Ellis, 3B, Louisville	20
Nick Rivera, INF, Florida Gulf Coast	20
Evan Skoug, C, Texas Christian	20
Chad Spanberger, C, Arkansas	20

DOUBLES

RANK, PLAYER, POS., TEAM	2B
1. J.J. Matijevic, INF, Arizona	30
Brent Rooker, OF, Mississippi State	30
3. Hunter Hargrove, INF, Texas Tech	26
4. Greg Lambert, OF, Southern Illinois	25
Brett Minnick, INF, Northern Colorado	25
Jared Olivia, OF, Arizona	25
Zach Rutherford, INF, Old Dominion	25
8. Dylan Burdeaux, INF, S Mississippi	24
Ryan Flick, 1B, Tennessee Tech	24
Keston Hiura, INF, UC Irvine	24
Fabian Pena, C, Manhattan	24
Hunter Strong, OF, Central Arkansas	24
Evan White, INF, Kentucky	24

TRIPLES

RANK, PLAYER, POS., TEAM	R
1. Brent Sakurai, INF, New Mexico State	9
2. Gage Canning, OF, Arizona State	8
Mark Contreras, INF, UC Riverside	8
Toby Handley, OF, Stony Brook	8
Kevin Markham, OF, Texas San Antonio	8
Tyler Panno, INF, Bryant	8
7. Roderick Bynum, OF, Northern Illinois	7
Cody Den Beste, OF, Prairie View	7
Jake McCarthy, OF, Virginia	7
Demetrius Sims, SS, Bethune-Cookman	7
Johnny Slater, OF, Michigan	7
Hunter Slater, OF, Southern Mississippi	7
Connor Smith, INF, Western Michigan	7
Antwaun Tucker, INF, Longwood	7
Billy Wilson, OF, Loyola Marymount	7

STOLEN BASES

RANK, PLAYER, POS., TEAM	SB	CS
1. Drew Butler, INF, Campbell	39	5
Robbie Podorsky, OF, McNeese	39	5
3. Zach Weatherford, OF, Wright State	36	6
4. Bryce Johnson, OF, Sam Houston St	33	7
Connor Kopach, INF, S Illinois	33	7
6. Wesley Drain, INF, Grambling	31	5
Michael Gigliotti, OF, Lipscomb	31	5
8. Brandon Hughes, P, Michigan St	30	6
9. Drew Avans, OF, SE Louisiana	28	4
10. Jake McCarthy, OF, Virginia	27	2

RUNS

RANK, PLAYER, POS., TEAM	R
1. Kramer Robertson, INF, Lousiana State	85
2. Taylor Walls, INF, Florida State	82
3. Brennon Anderson, 2B, Brigham Young	71
Ben Fisher, INF, Eastern Kentucky	71
5. Tristan Pompey, OF, Kentucky	70
6. Jake Burger, INF, Missouri State	69
Jameson Hannah, OF, Dallas Baptist	69
Niko Hulsizer, OF, Morehead State	69
9. Adam Haseley, OF, Virgina	68
Alex Junior, OF, Tennessee Tech	68

HITS

RANK, PLAYER, POS., TEAM	H
1. Dylan Burdeaux, INF, S Mississppi	102
2. Tristan Pompey, OF, Kentucky	96
Brent Rooker, OF, Mississippi State	96
4. Stuart Fairchild, OF, Wake Forest	94
Andrew Moritz, OF, UNC Greensboro	94
6. Brian Miller, OF, North Carolina	93
Jonathan Pryor, OF, Wake Forest	93
Trevor Putzig, INF, Tennessee Tech	93
Will Schneider, OF, Morehead State	93
10. Bryce Johnson, OF, Sam Houston St	92
J.J. Matijevic, INF, Arizona	92

TOTAL BASES

RANK, PLAYER, POS., TEAM	TB
1. Brent Rooker, OF, Mississippi State	201
2. Niko Hulsizer, OF, Morehead State	193
3. Jake Adams, 1B, Iowa	183
4. Austin Listi, OF, Dallas Baptist	175
5. Ben Fisher, INF, Eastern Kentucky	170
6. Ryan Flick, 1B, Tennessee Tech	168
7. Stuart Fairchild, OF, Wake Forest	166
8. Jeremy Eierman, INF, Missouri State	164
9. Will Robertson, OF, Davidson	163
10. Dylan Burdeaux, INF, S Mississippi	162
Drew Ellis, 3B, Louisville	162
Riley Mahan, INF, Kentucky	162
Jake Scheiner, INF, Houston	162

WALKS

RANK, PLAYER, POS., TEAM	BB
1. Taylor Walls, INF, Florida State	67
2. Seth Beer, OF, Clemson	64
3. Taylor Braley, INF, Southern Mississippi	63
4. D.J. Artis, OF, Liberty	62
5. Nick Rivera, INF, Florida Gulf Coast	59
6. Luis Gonzalez, OF, New Mexico	58
7. Nelson Maldonado, INF, Florida	53
8. Ryan Cleveland, INF, Georgia Southern	52
Dean Lockery, 2B, Central Conn State	52
10. Elijah Brown, INF, Sacred Heart	51
Greg Deichmann, OF, Louisana State	51
Michael Gigliotti, OF, Lipscomb	51

TOUGHEST TO STRIKE OUT

RANK, PLAYER, POS., TEAM	AB/SO
1. Ernie Clement, INF, Virginia	36.3
2. Zach Racusin, OF, Georgetown	22.5
3. Aaron Barnett, C, Pepperdine	19.1
4. Pavin Smith, 1B, Virginia	19
5. Tanner Chauncey, SS, BYU	18.9
6. Robbie Podorsky, OF, McNeese	18.1
7. Kevin Radziewicz, C, Fairfield	17.9
8. Ryan Rotondo, INF, Maryland E Shore	17.6
9. Kyle Adams, C, Richmond	16.4
10. Conner Fikes, OF, Stephen F. Austin	16.2

HIT BY PITCH

RANK, PLAYER, POS., TEAM	HBP
1. Evan Warden, INF, Purdue	30
2. Rudy Karre, INF, Kansas	27
3. Jake Bakamus, INF, Arkansas State	24
Harry Shipley, INF, Purdue	24
5. James Stea, OF, Valparaiso	23
6. Jake Bivens, INF, Michigan	22
Cornelius Copeland, INF, Jackson State	22
Cole Hallum, OF, Campbell	22
Parker Phillips, INF, Austin Peay	22
10. Taylor Beene, INF, Sam Houston State	21
Cole Freeman, INF, Lousiana State	21
Austen Zente, OF, High Point	21

SACRIFICE BUNTS

RANK, PLAYER, POS., TEAM	SH
1. Jackson Ware, INF, Mercer	22
2. Taylor Beene, INF, Sam Houston State	18
3. Matt Beaird, C, Coastal Carolina	17
Riley McKnight, INF, Sam Houston St	17
5. Roman Baisa, OF, Ball State	16
Cole Freeman, INF, Louisiana State	16
Jansen McCurdy, OF, Central Arkansas	16
Evan McDonald, SS, Georgia Southern	16
Brett Rasso, OF, St. Mary's	16
10. Brock Deatherage, OF, NC State	15
Connor Heady, INF, Kentucky	15
Andrew Selby, OF, George Washington	15

SACRIFICE FLIES

RANK, PLAYER, POS., TEAM	SF
1. Sam Fragale, INF, Virginia Tech	12
2. Austin Dennis, INF, Middle Tennesee	10
Frankie Gregoire, OF, Marist	10
Jake Kuzbel, INF, Georgetown	10
David Metzgar, INF, Cal St Bakersfield	10
Ricky Ramirez, P, McNeese	10
7. Scott Ota, INF, Illinois-Chicago	9
8. Matthew Alford, INF, NW State	8
Angelo Altavilla, INF, Nebraska	8
Bryson Bowman, OF, Western Carolina	8
Taylor Braley, INF, Southern Mississippi	8
Ernie Clement, INF, Virginia	8
Micah Coffey, INF, Minnesota	8
Parker Coss, INF, UC Irvine	8
Conor Grammes, INF, Xavier	8
Ryan Hall, INF, William & Mary	8
David Hamilton, INF, Texas	8
Joe Hoscheit, OF, Northwestern	8
Matt Morrow, INF, Wright State	8
Derrick Mount, INF, SE Louisana	8
Quincy Nieporte, INF, Florida State	8
John Valente, INF, St. John's	8

PITCHING (Minimum 40 innings pitched)

RK.	PITCHER, TEAM	CLASS	W	L	ERA	G	GS	SV	IP	H	R	ER	BB	SO
1.	Sam Bordner, Louisville	So.	2	0	0.41	23	0	3	44	16	2	2	10	39
2.	Ross Learnard, Purdue	Jr.	6	0	0.58	27	0	4	46	30	3	3	10	37
3.	Luke Heimlich, Oregon State	Jr.	11	1	0.76	16	16	0	118	70	13	10	22	128
4.	Jake Mulholland, Oregon State	Fr.	7	1	1.20	28	0	6	52	34	8	7	12	44
5.	Jose Tirado, Jackson State	Fr.	4	1	1.27	23	0	8	43	30	7	6	14	46
6.	Clarke Schmidt, South Carolina	Jr.	4	2	1.34	9	9	0	60	41	15	9	18	70
7.	Will Vest, Stephen F. Austin	Fr.	3	0	1.38	31	0	1	46	38	12	7	18	46
8.	Brett Conine, Cal State Fullerton	So.	0	1	1.39	31	0	15	45	35	10	7	6	43
9.	Beau Sulser, Dartmouth	Sr.	6	1	1.40	7	7	0	45	31	10	7	5	52
10.	Andrew Crane, Troy	Jr.	6	2	1.47	16	8	0	61	43	13	10	16	60
11.	Ryan Testani, Seton Hall	Sr.	2	2	1.47	27	0	4	43	30	9	7	7	23
12.	Steven Gingery, Texas Tech	So.	10	1	1.58	15	15	0	91	60	21	16	29	107
13.	Miguel Ausua, Oral Roberts	Jr.	11	3	1.65	16	15	0	93	80	22	17	30	85
14.	Michael Byrne, Florida	So.	4	5	1.67	38	3	19	76	64	20	14	15	93
15.	Brendan Jenkins, San Francisco	So.	0	4	1.70	30	1	3	42	43	15	8	12	41
16.	Sean Mooney, St. John's	Fr.	8	2	1.71	16	13	0	100	70	23	19	16	88
17.	Kutter Crawford, Florida Gulf Coast	Jr.	7	1	1.71	15	13	1	84	59	27	16	31	99
18.	Cory Abbott, Loyola Marymount	Jr.	11	2	1.74	15	15	0	98	61	27	19	28	130
19.	Matt Kent, Xavier	So.	5	2	1.74	23	0	2	47	46	12	9	11	34
20.	Colie Bowers, South Carolina	So.	5	1	1.74	25	0	4	41	19	10	8	16	48
21.	Ethan Decaster, Creighton	Jr.	4	2	1.77	24	0	5	46	37	11	9	12	36
22.	Wyatt Mills, Gonzaga	Sr.	2	2	1.79	22	0	12	40	40	10	8	4	58
23.	Joey Murray, Kent State	So.	6	1	1.80	14	14	0	75	55	22	15	32	110
24.	Nathan Wrighter, Bryant	So.	2	0	1.80	26	0	1	40	34	13	8	13	28
25.	Colton Laws, Charlotte	So.	7	2	1.87	15	15	0	96	76	24	20	13	94
26.	Will Gaddis, Furman	Jr.	9	3	1.89	17	14	1	105	81	27	22	16	89
27.	Beau Ridgeway, Texas	So.	2	2	1.89	37	0	12	52	35	12	11	14	40
28.	Josh Hiatt, North Carolina	Fr.	4	2	1.90	32	0	13	52	31	13	11	20	64
29.	Spencer Howard, Cal Poly	So.	8	1	1.95	17	12	1	88	72	31	19	23	97
30.	Austin Bizzle, Alabama State	Sr.	7	1	1.95	26	2	4	74	53	23	16	20	78
31.	Logan Salow, Kentucky	Sr.	2	5	1.95	31	0	12	55	37	23	12	17	73
32.	Jake Thompson, Oregon State	Jr.	14	1	1.96	20	19	0	129	85	29	28	40	119
33.	Danny Marsh, Wagner	Sr.	6	2	1.96	13	13	0	78	58	24	17	38	69

34.	Kenton Hering, Florida Gulf Coast	Sr.	7	3	1.96	30	1	7	60	51	19	13	19	77
35.	Devin Hemmerich, Norfolk State	Sr.	10	2	1.97	13	13	0	105	75	27	23	16	118
36.	Gunner Leger, Louisiana-Lafayette	Jr.	10	2	1.97	15	15	0	91	66	24	20	24	84
37.	J.B. Olson, Oklahoma	Sr.	5	1	1.99	31	0	8	45	45	12	10	13	46
38.	Will Kobos, George Washington	Fr.	4	1	1.99	18	2	3	41	27	12	9	15	42
39.	Ken Waldichuk, Saint Mary's	Fr.	3	4	2.00	22	2	3	45	37	13	10	16	51
40.	Jeff Schank, Butler	Sr.	4	2	2.01	10	10	0	67	50	19	15	23	74
41.	Walter Borkovich, Michigan State	Sr.	4	3	2.01	27	1	0	58	50	18	13	14	36
42.	Logan Gilbert, Stetson	So.	10	0	2.02	15	12	0	89	65	23	20	26	107
43.	Denton Norman, Lipscomb	Sr.	4	4	2.02	25	3	7	49	35	13	11	15	45
44.	Matt Meyer, Jacksonville	So.	4	4	2.03	21	0	3	40	28	13	9	17	43
45.	Trey Cumbie, Houston	So.	10	2	2.04	15	15	0	101	91	30	23	15	82
46.	Casey Mize, Auburn	So.	8	2	2.04	13	12	0	84	66	26	19	9	109
47.	Robert Broom, Mercer	So.	8	2	2.04	31	0	1	62	42	16	14	23	82
48.	Tyler Zuber, Arkansas State	Sr.	6	1	2.06	25	0	6	52	29	12	12	16	80
49.	Dave Smith, Long Beach State	Sr.	9	2	2.07	17	14	0	91	98	23	21	11	41
50.	Colton Hock, Stanford	Jr.	6	1	2.08	27	0	16	48	36	11	11	11	35
51.	Ron Marinaccio, Delaware	Jr.	4	3	2.09	22	8	3	65	45	17	15	22	68
52.	Chris Enns, Quinnipiac	Jr.	4	2	2.09	16	7	0	52	51	23	12	18	37
53.	Sean Wymer, Texas Christian	So.	6	4	2.10	30	0	2	56	35	16	13	10	66
54.	Bryan Warzek, New Orleans	So.	8	3	2.12	15	15	0	102	90	34	24	33	94
55.	Ryan Weiss, Wright State	So.	8	1	2.13	15	14	1	89	78	22	21	20	80
56.	Blaise Whitman, Rhode Island	Sr.	4	1	2.13	27	0	1	42	26	16	10	15	44
57.	Andrew Cabezas, Miami	So.	5	3	2.14	35	0	3	63	52	24	15	23	80
58.	Mason Marshall, Brigham Young	Sr.	3	2	2.14	29	0	2	46	46	18	11	16	45
59.	J.T. Newton, Houston Baptist	Jr.	7	0	2.15	23	0	6	54	51	16	13	17	43
60.	Caleb Gilbert, Louisiana State	So.	7	1	2.16	28	5	3	58	40	17	14	12	67
61.	Codie Paiva, Loyola Marymount	So.	6	0	2.16	24	2	5	58	49	19	14	11	52
62.	Jake Dahlberg, Illinois-Chicago	Sr.	10	2	2.17	16	16	0	104	58	30	25	35	78
63.	Drew Carlton, Florida State	Jr.	5	4	2.17	36	1	7	62	65	22	15	15	58
64.	Paul Balestrieri, Cornell	Sr.	5	4	2.18	9	9	0	58	50	23	14	15	36
65.	Adam Wolf, Louisville	So.	6	0	2.18	24	0	1	41	30	11	10	14	35
66.	Griffin Roberts, Wake Forest	So.	2	5	2.19	29	0	8	53	30	18	13	32	80
67.	Nate Pawelczyk, Winthrop	So.	7	2	2.23	16	11	1	77	53	23	19	32	69
68.	Vitaly Jangols, Rhode Island	Fr.	7	1	2.23	15	9	2	61	52	25	15	12	25
69.	Jake Fromson, Missouri State	Jr.	8	3	2.25	37	8	3	76	46	24	19	18	88
70.	Wyatt Burns, Samford	Jr.	5	1	2.25	28	0	12	48	41	13	12	9	44
71.	Alex Faedo, Florida	Jr.	9	2	2.26	20	19	1	124	95	39	31	42	157
72.	Jeb Bargfeldt, Miami	Jr.	7	3	2.28	15	15	0	87	62	24	22	29	61
73.	Connor Van Hoose, Bucknell	Jr.	6	6	2.28	13	13	0	83	67	32	21	19	97
74.	Jake Roehn, Ohio	Jr.	4	4	2.28	30	0	15	43	39	13	11	13	48
75.	Wyatt Marks, Louisiana-Lafayette	Jr.	2	1	2.28	30	0	7	59	29	20	15	25	100
76.	Joe Cavallaro, South Florida	Jr.	5	3	2.28	30	0	5	59	48	16	15	19	77
77.	Cody Eckerson, Niagara	Jr.	6	2	2.29	12	11	0	55	45	21	14	29	50
78.	Grant Anderson, McNeese State	So.	8	0	2.30	31	0	1	63	54	18	16	20	56
79.	Trent Shelton, Cal Poly	Jr.	1	1	2.30	28	3	0	43	35	13	11	8	42
80.	Nate Harris, Louisiana Tech	Sr.	9	1	2.31	22	9	8	94	79	29	24	11	94
81.	Jared Janczak, Texas Christian	So.	9	2	2.31	15	15	0	93	60	28	24	24	102
82.	Jake Reindl, Arkansas	So.	4	1	2.31	24	0	3	51	39	16	13	16	49
83.	Brandon Eisert, Oregon State	Fr.	5	0	2.31	21	0	4	47	32	14	12	19	50
84.	Morgan Cooper, Texas	Jr.	6	3	2.32	16	15	0	89	66	26	23	33	110
85.	Kaylor Chafin, Texas A&M	Jr.	7	2	2.33	33	1	3	77	57	27	20	16	72
86.	Tyler Holton, Florida State	So.	10	3	2.34	18	18	0	119	77	43	31	31	144
87.	Griffin Canning, UCLA	Jr.	7	4	2.34	17	17	0	119	93	34	31	32	140
88.	Levi Stoudt, Lehigh	Fr.	4	5	2.34	12	12	0	62	61	24	16	22	45
89.	Joe LaSorsa, St. John's	Fr.	7	1	2.34	21	0	1	50	42	18	13	14	39
90.	Nick Sandlin, Southern Mississippi	So.	10	2	2.38	29	0	8	57	41	17	15	29	80
91.	Naithen Dewsnap, CS Bakersfield	Jr.	3	1	2.39	31	0	14	49	39	15	13	7	60
92.	Kyle Zurak, Radford	Sr.	4	4	2.40	25	4	9	60	51	26	16	22	73
93.	Aaron Fletcher, Houston	Jr.	2	1	2.40	21	0	8	41	38	13	11	10	41
94.	Keegan Thompson, Auburn	Jr.	7	4	2.41	15	15	0	93	67	31	25	17	75
95.	Will Ethridge, Mississippi	Fr.	2	2	2.41	19	4	1	41	32	15	11	11	50
96.	Peter Strzelecki, South Florida	Jr.	3	4	2.42	14	14	0	67	55	33	18	27	62
97.	Tyler Thorne, Stanford	Sr.	4	1	2.42	29	0	2	52	42	16	14	20	43
98.	Austin Gardner, Texas-Arlington	Jr.	2	1	2.42	29	1	2	45	36	14	12	10	55
99.	Frank German, North Florida	So.	8	1	2.43	14	14	0	81	75	27	22	25	76
100.	Alec Bettinger, Virginia	Sr.	8	0	2.43	21	0	1	63	38	20	17	31	71

WINS

RANK, PITCHER, TEAM	W
1. Jake Thompson, Oregon State	14
2. Jackson Kowar, Florida	12
Brian Howard, Texas Christian	12
Jared Poche, Louisiana State	12
5. Luke Heimlich, Oregon State	11
Cory Abbott, Loyola Marymount	11
Scott Politz, Yale	11
Miguel Ausua, Oral Roberts	11
Brendan McKay, Louisville	11
Sean Hjelle, Kentucky	11
David Peterson, Oregon	11
Connor Seabold, Cal State Fullerton	11

SAVES

RANK, PITCHER, TEAM	SV
1. Michael Byrne, Florida	19
2. Durbin Feltman, Texas Christian	17
3. Lincoln Henzman, Louisville	16
Colton Hock, Stanford	16
Brian Glowicki, Minnesota	16

6.	Kenyon Yovan, Oregon	15
	Ryan Netemeyer, Southern Illinois	15
	Jake Roehn, Ohio	15
	Brett Conine, Cal State Fullerton	15
10.	Tommy Doyle, Virginia	14
	Ryan Lefner, Saint Louis	14
	John Russell, Connecticut	14
	Sam Donko, Virginia Commonwealth	14
	Naithen Dewsnao, Cal St Bakersfield	14
	Spencer Price, Mississippi State	14
	Stephen Villines, Kansas	14

STRIKEOUTS

RANK, PITCHER, TEAM		SO
1.	Alex Faedo, Florida	157
2.	Alex Lange, Lousiana State	150
3.	Brendan McKay, Louisville	146
4.	Tyler Holton, Florida State	144
5.	J.P. Sears, The Citadel	142
6.	Griffin Canning, UCLA	140
	David Peterson, Oregon	140
8.	Eli Morgan, Gonzaga	138
9.	Brandon Marsonek, Alabama A&M	137
10.	Cory Abbott, Loyola Marymount	130

STRIKEOUTS PER NINE

RANK, PITCHER, TEAM		SO/9
1.	Wyatt Marks, Lousiana-Lafayette	15.17
2.	James Karinchak, Bryant	13.66
3.	J.P. Sears, The Citadel	13.41
4.	Zac Lowther, Xavier	13.28
5.	Joey Murray, Kent State	13.20
6.	David Peterson, Oregon	12.56
7.	Eli Morgan, Gonzaga	12.34
8.	Shane McClanahan, South Florida	12.32
9.	Tim Cate, Connecticut	12.13
10.	Brendan McKay, Louisville	12.06

FEWEST HITS PER NINE

RANK, PITCHER, TEAM		H/9
1.	Wyatt Marks, Lousiana-Lafayette	4.40
2.	Jake Dahlberg, Illinois-Chicago	5.04
3.	Zac Lowther, Xavier	5.18
4.	Gregory Veliz, Miami	5.28
5.	Luke Heimlich, Oregon State	5.32
6.	Alec Bettinger, Virginia	5.43
7.	Jake Fromson, Missouri State	5.57
8.	Cory Abbott, Loyola Marymount	5.58
9.	Shane McClanahan, South Florida	5.68
10.	James Karinchak, Bryant	5.72

FEWEST WALKS PER NINE

RANK, PITCHER, TEAM		BB/9
1.	Brandon Hagerla, Central Arkansas	0.71
2.	Jeffrey Passantino, Lipscomb	0.84
3.	Jake Meyers, Nebraska	0.96
4.	Ryan Askew, Mercer	0.97
	Casey Mize, Auburn	0.97
6.	Lucas Rollins, Saint Joseph's	0.98
7.	Beau Sulser, Dartmouth	1.00
8.	Dakota Mills, Sam Houston State	1.01
9.	Grant Schuermann, Furman	1.02
10.	Colton Rendon, Winthrop	1.05

TEAM LEADERS

SCORING

RANK, TEAM		G	R	R/G
1.	Morehead State	59	525	8.9
2.	Air Force	53	465	8.8
3.	New Mexico	58	497	8.6
4.	Southern Mississippi	66	544	8.2
5.	Tennessee Tech	62	504	8.1
6.	Birimingham Young	59	477	8.1
7.	South Alabama	61	488	8.0
8.	New Mexico State	57	453	7.9
9.	Jackson State	56	440	7.9
10.	Virginia	59	459	7.8
11.	Murray State	59	456	7.7
12.	Arizona	59	453	7.7
13.	Wake Forest	63	481	7.6
14.	Fresno State	60	455	7.6
15.	Lousiana Tech	56	418	7.5
16.	Delaware	57	422	7.4
17.	St. John's	55	406	7.4
18.	Dallas Baptist	63	464	7.4
19.	Kentucky	66	484	7.3
20.	UNC Greensboro	60	438	7.3
21.	Florida State	69	502	7.3
22.	Mercer	56	405	7.2
23.	East Tennessee State	59	426	7.2
24.	McNeese	57	410	7.2
25.	Louisville	65	464	7.1
RANK, TEAM		**G**	**R**	**R/G**
26.	Texas Tech	62	442	7.1
27.	North Carolina	63	449	7.1
28.	Southeast Missouri State	55	388	7.1
29.	Liberty	55	386	7.0
30.	Wofford	58	406	7.0
31.	Florida Atlantic	57	397	7.0
32.	Eastern Kentucky	56	386	6.9
33.	Missouri State	63	433	6.9
34.	Old Dominion	58	398	6.9
35.	Yale	52	356	6.8
36.	Oral Roberts	59	402	6.8
37.	Navy	54	366	6.8
38.	Austin Peay	58	391	6.7
39.	Alabama State	56	377	6.7
40.	Furman	61	410	6.7
41.	Western Carolina	56	376	6.7
42.	Eastern Illinois	56	375	6.7
43.	Lousiana State	72	482	6.7
44.	San Diego State	63	421	6.7
45.	James Madison	51	339	6.6
46.	S. Illinois Edwardsville	52	345	6.6
47.	Texas Christian	68	451	6.6
48.	Charlotte	58	384	6.6
49.	Coastal Carolina	57	377	6.6
50.	Sam Houston State	67	443	6.6

BATTING AVERAGE

RANK, TEAM		AVG
1.	Air Force	.344
2.	Morehead State	.332
3.	St. John's	.323
4.	New Mexico State	.322
5.	Virginia	.321
6.	UNC Greensboro	.320
7.	Biringham Young	.319
8.	New Mexico	.318
9.	Jackson State	.318
10.	Fresno State	.317

HOME RUNS

RANK, TEAM		HR
1.	Wake Forest	106
2.	Tennessee Tech	99
3.	Dallas Baptist	97
4.	Southern Mississippi	90
5.	UNC Wilmington	85
6.	Virginia Tech	84
	Murray State	84
	Austin Peay	84
9.	Arkansas	83
	Eastern Illinois	83
	Morehead State	83

DOUBLES

RANK, TEAM		2B
1.	Air Force	153
2.	Kentucky	148
3.	Tennessee Tech	144
4.	Dallas Baptist	143
5.	New Mexico	141
6.	Southern Mississippi	140
	North Carolina State	140
8.	Louisiana Tech	137
9.	Fresno State	136
10.	Arizona	133
	Texas Tech	133

TRIPLES

RANK, TEAM		3B
1.	UNC Greensboro	33
2.	New Mexico State	31
3.	Sam Houston State	28
4.	Texas Tech	26
	Houston	26
	Northeastern	26
	Wright State	26
8.	Navy	25
9.	Delaware	24
10.	Fresno State	23

SLUGGING PERCENTAGE

TEAM, RANK		SLG
1.	Air Force	.556
2.	Tennessee Tech	.520
3.	Morehead State	.519
4.	Dallas Baptist	.517
5.	Wake Forest	.509
6.	Fresno State	.503
7.	New Mexico State	.501
8.	New Mexico	.498
9.	Southern Mississippi	.497
10.	Birmingham Young	.491

STOLEN BASES

TEAM, RANK		SB	CS
1.	Jackson State	141	19
2.	Wright State	130	31
3.	Michigan	125	29
4.	Wofford	124	25
5.	Southeastern Louisana	118	36
6.	Lipscomb	111	24
7.	Texas Christian	108	23
8.	Central Florida	106	16
	Texas Southern	106	33
10.	Norfolk State	105	30

WALKS

RANK, TEAM		BB
1.	Florida State	396
2.	South Alabama	373
3.	Southern Mississippi	356
4.	Texas Christian	354
5.	Missouri State	351
6.	Liberty	341
7.	North Carolina	321
8.	New Mexico	320
9.	Florida	313
10.	Kentucky	310

PITCHING Earned Run Average

RANK, TEAM	ERA
1. Oregon State	1.93
2. Illinois-Chicago	2.65
3. Louisville	2.92
4. North Carolina	2.96
5. Central Florida	3.00
6. Oral Roberts	3.06
7. Long Beach State	3.07
8. St. John's	3.11
9. Texas	3.15
10. South Florida	3.24
11. Louisiana Lafayette	3.33
12. Stanford	3.35
13. Seton Hall	3.38
14. UCLA	3.41
15. Houston	3.43
16. Kent State	3.43
17. Florida	3.45
18. Loyola Marymount	3.46
19. Michigan	3.46
20. Texas A&M	3.48
21. Binghamton	3.50
22. Hawaii	3.58
23. Clemson	3.59
24. Louisana State	3.59
25. Ole Miss	3.60
26. North Florida	3.60
27. Arkansas	3.61
28. Jackson State	3.61
29. Cal State Fullerton	3.64
30. Cal Poly	3.65
31. Rhode Island	3.65
32. North Dakota State	3.66
33. Missouri	3.67
34. Vanderbilt	3.71
35. Butler	3.71
36. South Carolina	3.72
37. Florida Gulf Coast	3.72
38. Gonzaga	3.73
39. Texas Tech	3.73
40. Nebraska	3.73
41. Florida State	3.75
42. Wright State	3.75
43. Missouri State	3.77
44. Miami	3.77
45. Michigan State	3.79
46. Sam Houston State	3.80
47. Stetson	3.80
48. Fairfield	3.80
49. Creighton	3.81
50. Connecticut	3.84

STRIKEOUTS PER NINE

TEAM, RANK	K/9
1. South Florida	10.1
2. Connecticut	10.1
3. Longwood	9.9
4. Arkansas	9.9
5. Stetson	9.7
6. San Diego	9.7
7. The Citadel	9.6
8. Louisiana Lafayette	9.6
9. Michigan	9.5
10. Texas Christian	9.5

FEWEST WALKS PER NINE

RANK, TEAM	BB/9
1. Hawaii	2.25
2. Clemson	2.26
3. Houston	2.28
4. Long Beach State	2.44
5. College of Charleston	2.55
6. Cal State Fullerton	2.55
7. Oregon State	2.59
8. Furman	2.61
9. Dartmouth	2.63
10. Oregon	2.65

FIELDING

FIELDING PERCENTAGE

RANK, TEAM	FPCT
1. Illinois-Chicago	.984
2. Michigan	.983
3. Washington	.982
4. Texas	.982
5. Cincinnati	.982
6. George Washington	.982
7. Stony Brook	.981
8. Florida	.981
9. Mississippi State	.980
10. Cal State Fullerton	.980
11. South Alabama	.980
12. Ohio	.980
13. UCLA	.980
14. Louisana State	.980
15. Stanford	.980
16. Long Beach State	.979
17. Southern California	.979
18. North Carolina	.979
19. Oral Roberts	.979
20. Charlotte	.979
21. Indiana	.979
22. San Diego State	.979
23. Minnesota	.978
24. Iowa	.978
25. UNC Greensboro	.978
26. Louisiana Tech	.978
27. Indiana State	.978
28. Wake Forest	.978
29. Oregon State	.978
30. Southern Illinois-Edwardsville	.978
31. Louisiana Lafayette	.978
32. Sacramento State	.978
33. Oklahoma	.978
34. Texas Tech	.978
35. UC Irvine	.978
36. Xavier	.977
37. Nebraska	.977
38. Arkansas	.977
39. San Francisco	.976
40. Old Dominion	.976
41. Vanderbilt	.976
42. South Florida	.976
43. San Diego	.976
44. Northeastern	.975
45. Auburn	.975
46. Tennessee Tech	.975
47. St. Bonaventure	.975
48. Texas A&M	.975
49. Hartford	.975
50. Louisville	.975

DOUBLE PLAYS

RANK, TEAM	DP
1. Fresno State	73
2. San Diego State	67
Iowa	67
4. Texas	65
Tulane	65
6. George Washington	63
7. Nevada	61
Eastern Illinois	61
9. Illinois	60
Florida	60
Nebraska	60

1. FLORIDA

Coach: Kevin O'Sullivan. **Record:** 52-19

PLAYER, POS., YEAR	AVG	OBP	SLG	AB	R	2B	3B	HR	RBI	SB
Baker, Andrew, OF, Fr.	.154	.290	.192	26	4	1	0	0	0	0
Bell, Keenan, OF, Fr.	.283	.327	.391	92	15	4	0	2	12	3
Bodrato, Austin, OF, Fr.	.143	.333	.143	7	2	0	0	0	1	1
Byrne, Michael, P, So.	.000	.500	.000	1	0	0	0	0	0	0
Guthrie, Dalton, INF, Jr.	.273	.349	.356	253	39	9	0	4	23	11
Hicks, Christian, INF, Jr.	.282	.328	.398	216	30	11	1	4	27	6
Horvath, Nick, OF, Jr.	.186	.341	.214	70	12	2	0	0	6	6
India, Jonathan, INF, So.	.274	.354	.429	212	38	15	0	6	34	13
Kolozsvary, Mark, C, Jr.	.276	.381	.440	116	20	8	1	3	26	2
Langworthy, Austin, OF, Fr.	.238	.352	.352	193	37	10	0	4	26	7
Larson, Ryan, OF, Sr.	.279	.369	.416	190	31	9	1	5	24	7
Liput, Deacon, INF, So.	.227	.313	.314	255	32	9	2	3	37	12
Moldonado, Nelson, INF, So.	.299	.449	.433	201	40	9	0	6	32	4
McMullen, Kirby, OF, Fr.	.000	.500	.000	1	1	0	0	0	0	0
Milchin, Garrett, INF, Fr.	.182	.269	.318	22	1	0	0	1	7	0
Reese, Blake, INF, So.	.233	.378	.260	73	12	2	0	0	11	4
Rivera, Mike, C, Jr.	.238	.346	.358	151	23	7	1	3	28	1
Schwarz, J.J., C, Jr.	.259	.351	.444	259	43	12	0	12	56	6

PITCHER, YEAR	W	L	ERA	G	GS	SV	IP	H	BB	SO
Baker, Andrew, Fr.	1	2	8.03	18	1	0	12	23	7	16
Bodrato, Austin, Fr.	0	0	18.00	1	0	0	1	0	4	0
Brown, Nate, Fr.	1	0	4.74	10	4	0	19	24	11	15
Byrne, Michael, So.	4	5	1.67	38	3	19	76	64	15	93
Dyson, Tyler, Fr.	4	0	3.23	24	2	2	39	30	10	47
Faedo, Alex, Jr.	9	2	2.26	20	19	1	124	95	42	157
Horvath, Nick, Jr.	3	0	3.68	27	0	1	29	35	8	23
Kowar, Jackson, So.	12	1	4.08	19	18	1	108	116	44	84
Langworthy, Austin, Fr.	1	1	3.71	7	1	0	17	17	4	11
Lee, David, Jr.	0	0	0.00	2	0	0	2	0	0	3
Long, Nick, Fr.	0	0	11.25	5	1	0	8	14	7	7
Maye, Cole, Fr.	0	0	12.27	5	0	0	4	8	3	4
McMullen, Kirby, Fr.	3	0	5.32	16	1	0	22	19	13	22
Milchin, Garrett, Fr.	4	2	3.29	19	2	1	27	21	12	18
Rubio, Frank, Sr.	1	1	4.15	24	0	2	30	35	7	20
Singer, Brady, So.	9	5	3.21	20	19	0	126	120	32	129

2. LOUISIANA STATE

Coach: Paul Mainieri. **Record:** 52-20

PLAYER, POS., YEAR	AVG	OBP	SLG	AB	R	2B	3B	HR	RBI	SB
Adams, Bryce, INF, Sr.	.238	.292	.619	21	4	2	0	2	5	0
Breaux, Brennan, OF, So.	.176	.263	.324	34	9	0	1	1	2	0
Coomes, Nick, INF, Jr.	.303	.401	.402	132	20	7	0	2	24	1
Deichmann, Greg, INF, Jr.	.308	.417	.579	266	54	15	0	19	73	7
Duplantis, Antoine, OF, So.	.316	.358	.400	285	50	14	2	2	61	19
Freeman, Cole, INF, Sr.	.315	.416	.404	270	54	14	2	2	61	19
Jordan, Beau, OF, Jr.	.268	.351	.381	168	30	7	0	4	29	0
Papierski, Michael, C, Jr.	.256	.401	.477	176	37	6	0	11	39	4
Poche, Jared, P, Sr.	.000	.000	.000	1	0	0	0	0	0	0
Reid, Chris, INF, So.	.208	.394	.208	24	4	0	0	0	3	0
Robertson, Kramer, INF, Sr.	.307	.403	.472	290	85	18	3	8	43	9
Romero, Jordan, C, Sr.	.229	.302	.292	96	11	3	0	1	12	0
Slaughter, Jake, INF, Fr.	.257	.358	.351	148	22	5	0	3	26	2
Smith, Josh, INF, Fr.	.281	.407	.409	242	52	16	0	5	48	5
Templet, Mason, INF, Fr.	.000	.000	.000	6	0	0	0	0	0	0
Watson, Zach, INF, Fr.	.317	.376	.507	221	42	9	3	9	27	12
Woley, Rankin, INF, Fr.	.267	.327	.400	45	8	4	1	0	5	0

PITCHER, YEAR	W	L	ERA	G	GS	SV	IP	H	BB	SO
Bain, Austin, Jr.	1	0	4.74	20	0	0	25	21	19	32
Beck, Matthew, Fr.	1	0	3.65	20	2	0	25	14	11	21
Bush, Nick, Fr.	1	1	3.75	23	0	0	24	20	19	22
Frederick, Blair, Fr.	0	0	10.12	5	0	0	3	3	5	3
Gilbert, Caleb, So.	7	1	2.16	28	5	3	58	40	12	67
Hess, Zack, Fr.	7	1	3.12	30	6	4	61	39	30	83
Kiel, Hunter, Jr.	0	0	18.47	10	0	0	6	8	8	9
Lange, Alex, Jr.	10	5	2.97	19	19	0	124	106	48	150
Newman, Hunter, Sr.	1	1	2.51	26	0	10	28	20	20	27
Norman, Doug, Sr.	0	0	5.40	3	0	0	3	4	1	3
Peterson, Todd, Fr.	3	1	4.19	22	3	0	34	32	16	21
Poche, Jared, Sr.	12	4	3.17	20	19	0	113	99	39	76
Reese, Will, Fr.	0	0	4.05	7	0	0	6	4	4	7
Reynolds, Russell, Sr.	1	2	8.50	15	1	0	18	22	14	14
Strall, Collin, Sr.	0	2	4.61	12	0	0	13	25	4	13
Walker, Eric, Fr.	8	2	3.48	17	17	0	95	83	23	78

3. OREGON STATE

Coach: Pat Casey. **Record:** 56-6

PLAYER, POS., YEAR	AVG	OBP	SLG	AB	R	2B	3B	HR	RBI	SB
Anderson, Jack, OF, R-Jr.	.281	.401	.339	171	33	5	1	1	30	3
Armstrong, Andy, INF, Fr.	.286	.444	.333	21	6	1	0	0	4	0
Atwood, Andy, INF, So.	.239	.313	.324	71	11	3	0	1	12	3
Cary, Elliott, OF, R-So.	.233	.314	.300	90	13	4	1	0	11	0
Donahue, Christian, INF, Jr.	.258	.357	.333	132	28	8	1	0	18	9
Engelbrekt, Max, P, R-Sr.	.000	.000	.000	1	0	0	0	0	0	0
Grenier, Cadyn, INF, So.	.275	.393	.435	200	34	5	6	5	37	6
Gretler, Michael, INF, Jr.	.301	.364	.468	216	34	13	4	5	33	1
Harrison, K.J., INF, Jr.	.313	.382	.498	217	30	13	0	9	43	7
Jones, Preston, OF, Fr.	.333	.462	.571	21	14	3	1	0	4	2
Kwan, Steven, OF, So.	.331	.440	.400	160	32	6	1	1	18	8
Larnach, Trevor, OF, So.	.303	.421	.429	198	32	16	0	3	48	2
Madrigal, Nick, INF, So.	.380	.449	.532	237	53	20	2	4	40	16
Malone, Tyler, INF, Fr.	.256	.441	.279	43	8	1	0	0	5	2
Mendazona, George, INF, Fr.	.000	.154	.000	11	1	0	0	0	1	0
Rutschman, Adley, C, Fr.	.234	.322	.306	209	38	7	1	2	33	5
Taylor, Zak, C, So.	.232	.279	.268	56	6	2	0	0	6	0

PITCHER, YEAR	W	L	ERA	G	GS	SV	IP	H	BB	SO
Britton, Jordan, So.	2	0	2.45	9	3	0	22	17	7	16
Eisert, Brandon, Fr.	5	0	2.31	21	0	4	47	32	19	50
Engelbrekt, Max, R-Sr.	3	0	0.43	17	0	5	21	9	7	20
Fehmel, Bryce, So.	6	3	3.87	15	14	0	81	69	22	49
Gambrell, Grant, Fr.	1	0	2.93	13	0	1	15	10	13	10
Heimlich, Luke, Jr.	11	1	0.76	16	16	0	118	70	22	128
Hickey, Mitch, Jr.	0	0	4.91	7	0	1	4	6	4	3
Mulholland, Jake, Fr.	7	1	1.20	28	0	6	52	34	12	44
Paul, Tommy, So.	0	0	4.50	2	0	0	2	2	1	2
Rasmussen, Drew, R-So.	3	0	1.00	8	4	2	27	19	5	26
Thompson, Jake, R-Jr.	14	1	1.96	20	19	0	129	85	40	119
Tweedt, Sam, R-So.	3	0	2.50	14	6	0	36	34	6	31
Verburg, Mitchell, Fr.	1	0	0.93	14	0	2	10	6	4	8

4. TEXAS CHRISTIAN

Coach: Jim Schlossnagle. **Record:** 50-18

PLAYER, POS., YEAR	AVG	OBP	SLG	AB	R	2B	3B	HR	RBI	SB
Baker, Luken, INF, So.	.317	.454	.528	161	39	8	1	8	41	2
Barzilli, Elliott, INF, Sr.	.242	.304	.367	256	42	14	0	6	31	6
Brown, Nolan, OF, R-Sr.	.277	.369	.388	242	50	14	2	3	35	26
Franson, Trent, INF, So.	.286	.444	.286	7	1	0	0	0	0	0
Hesse, Mason, INF, Sr.	.182	.282	.303	33	4	1	0	1	10	2
Humphreys, Zach, INF, Fr.	.267	.379	.396	101	25	3	2	2	19	3
Ingraham, Austin, OF, Jr.	.143	.333	.143	14	0	0	0	0	1	0
Landestoy, Michael, INF, R-Jr.	.197	.269	.282	71	11	3	0	1	6	3
Merrill, Ryan, INF, Sr.	.243	.333	.372	218	42	8	1	6	43	17
Skoug, Evan, C, Jr.	.272	.378	.544	261	59	11	0	20	71	3
Wade, Austen, OF, Jr.	.332	.441	.486	247	54	17	3	5	40	16
Wanhanen, Connor, OF, Jr.	.281	.430	.341	135	34	6	1	0	16	11
Warner, Cam, INF, Sr.	.284	.364	.384	268	51	12	0	5	49	10
Watson, Josh, OF, So.	.239	.370	.309	230	35	11	1	1	38	7
Williams, Evan, OF, R-Sr.	.174	.333	.239	46	4	1	1	0	8	2

PITCHER, YEAR	W	L	ERA	G	GS	SV	IP	H	BB	SO
Boyles, Austin, R-Fr.	2	0	5.68	15	0	0	19	16	6	25
Brown, Dalton, So.	0	0	5.62	10	0	1	8	7	6	11

PITCHER, YEAR	W	L	ERA	G	GS	SV	IP	H	BB	SO
Burnett, Ryan, Jr.	0	0	7.56	9	0	0	8	12	2	5
Coughlin, Cal, Fr.	1	0	1.59	23	0	0	23	17	11	22
Eissler, Jake, Fr.	4	0	5.02	18	1	1	38	49	12	38
Feltman, Durbin, So.	2	2	3.64	29	0	17	30	23	15	37
Green, Haylen, Fr.	2	1	3.10	15	2	0	20	11	9	24
Horton, Dalton, So.	0	1	9.00	6	3	0	13	21	4	14
Howard, Brian, Sr.	12	3	3.77	19	19	0	105	86	35	113
Janczak, Jared, R-So.	9	2	2.31	15	15	0	93	60	24	102
King, Charles, Fr.	1	3	5.44	20	1	1	46	56	17	37
Lodolo, Nick, Fr.	5	1	4.35	17	15	0	79	76	28	72
Morris, Trey, Fr.	2	0	5.65	17	0	0	29	37	7	24
Traver, Mitchell, R-Sr.	4	1	3.89	12	12	0	44	32	22	53
Wymer, Sean, So.	6	4	2.10	30	0	2	56	35	10	66

5. LOUISVILLE

Coach: Dan McDonnell. **Record:** 53-12

PLAYER, POS., YEAR	AVG	OBP	SLG	AB	R	2B	3B	HR	RBI	SB
Bollmer, Michael, 1B, Sr.	.278	.278	.444	18	3	0	0	1	4	0
Ellis, Drew, INF, Jr.	.355	.448	.701	231	56	18	1	20	61	6
Fitch, Colby, C, Jr.	.259	.372	.464	239	42	12	2	11	47	3
Fitzgerald, Tyler, INF, Fr.	.208	.303	.272	125	20	6	1	0	11	4
Hairston, Devin, INF, Jr.	.309	.356	.421	259	50	16	2	3	52	3
Henzman, Lincoln, P, Jr.	.000	.000	.000	1	0	0	0	0	0	0
Lavey, Justin, 3B, Fr.	.345	.486	.586	29	7	2	1	1	5	1
Lyman, Colin, OF, Sr.	.285	.376	.364	214	39	8	1	1	32	15
Mann, Devin, INF, So.	.268	.363	.434	235	52	11	8	8	44	9
McKay, Brendan, INF, Jr.	.341	.457	.659	223	57	15	18	18	57	2
Oreiente, Danny, OF, Fr.	.500	.500	1.000	2	0	1	0	0	0	0
Pinkham, Zeke, C, So.	.173	.211	.269	52	3	2	1	1	10	0
Rumoro, Pat, C, So.	.200	.333	.200	10	0	0	0	0	1	0
Snider, Jake, INF, Fr.	.286	.333	.393	56	12	1	1	1	11	2
Stowers, Josh, OF, So.	.313	.422	.507	201	50	15	6	6	34	22
Summers, Ryan, OF, Sr.	.210	.329	.258	62	13	3	0	0	4	9
Taylor, Logan, OF, Sr.	.271	.391	.360	225	56	13	1	1	42	22
Wyatt, Logan, INF, Fr.	.167	.273	.222	18	4	1	0	0	4	0

PITCHER, YEAR	W	L	ERA	G	GS	SV	IP	H	BB	SO
Bennett, Nick, Fr.	5	1	3.18	15	13	0	65	59	13	61
Bordner, Sam, So	2	0	0.41	23	0	3	44	16	10	39
Dale, Chandler, Jr.	0	0	0.00	10	0	0	8	4	5	7
Elliott, Adam, Fr.	2	0	2.14	22	0	0	34	25	9	31
Henzman, Lincoln, Jr.	3	0	1.67	27	0	16	38	22	10	37
Hoeing, Bryan, So.	0	0	5.06	11	4	1	21	27	13	18
Hummel, Shane, Sr.	4	1	4.60	10	4	0	16	24	2	13
Martin, Rabon, Jr.	4	1	4.88	15	2	0	24	22	10	19
McAvene, Michael, Fr.	1	1	4.15	7	5	0	17	17	15	26
McClure, Kade, Jr.	8	4	3.58	18	18	0	103	81	36	111
McKay, Brendan, Jr.	11	3	2.56	17	17	0	109	77	35	146
Smiddy, Shay, Fr.	1	0	3.48	15	2	0	21	17	16	21
Sparger, Jake, Sr.	5	1	3.72	20	0	1	29	34	6	21
Thomspon, Riley, So.	1	0	4.02	14	0	0	16	14	9	23
Wolf, Adam, So.	6	0	2.18	24	0	1	41	30	14	35

6. FLORIDA STATE

Coach: Mike Martin. **Record:** 46-23

PLAYER, POS., YEAR	AVG	OBP	SLG	AB	R	2B	3B	HR	RBI	SB
Aplin, Rhett, OF, Jr.	.322	.434	.524	143	34	9	1	6	24	4
Busby, Dylan, INF, Jr.	.315	.399	.597	248	58	21	2	15	65	10
Bussey, Bryan, C, Sr.	.267	.400	.333	15	4	1	0	0	1	0
Carlton, Drew, P, Jr.	.000	.000	.000	1	0	0	0	0	0	0
Cavanaugh, Kyle, 1B, R-Jr.	.190	.292	.333	21	3	0	0	1	1	0
Daughtry, Tyler, INF, Fr.	.209	.412	.314	86	19	6	0	1	13	3
Derr, Nick, INF, Fr.	.225	.401	.283	120	31	2	1	1	17	6
Flowers, J.C., OF, Fr.	.235	.359	.300	213	44	4	2	2	32	7
Henderson, Matt, INF, Sr.	.297	.448	.318	179	35	7	0	0	22	8
Holton, Tyler, OF, So.	.244	.300	.378	45	8	0	0	2	9	0
Kwiatkowski, Clayton, P, Fr.	.000	.000	.000	1	0	0	0	0	0	0
Lueck, Jackson, OF, Fr.	.318	.405	.507	211	41	11	1	9	54	6
Mejia, Ryan, OF, Fr.	.333	.400	.333	9	1	0	0	0	4	0
Mendoza, Drew, INF, Fr.	.270	.400	.534	148	33	9	0	10	33	3
Nieporte, Quincy, 1B, Sr.	.302	.378	.510	255	41	20	0	11	82	0
Petrey, Donovan, OF, Fr.	.158	.385	.158	19	2	0	0	0	4	0
Raleigh, Cal, C, So.	.227	.330	.398	264	5	16	1	9	39	1
Truluck, Hank, INF, Sr.	.222	.417	.407	27	8	2	0	1	2	1
Walls, Steven, OF, Jr.	.216	.328	.294	51	7	1	0	1	8	0
Walls, Taylor, INF, Fr.	.273	.421	.423	260	82	9	3	8	47	10
Zirzow, Will, P, R-Jr.	1.000	1.000	1.000	1	0	0	0	0	0	0

PITCHER, YEAR	W	L	ERA	G	GS	SV	IP	H	BB	SO
Byrd, Alec, Sr.	4	2	4.05	36	0	1	33	33	18	37
Carlton, Drew, Jr.	5	4	2.17	36	1	7	62	65	15	58
Haney, Chase, So.	3	2	4.26	33	0	0	32	31	8	26
Holton, Tyler, So.	10	3	2.34	18	18	0	119	77	31	144
Karp, Andrew, R-So.	2	3	4.48	18	12	0	66	65	18	70
Kwiatkowski, Clayton, Fr.	1	0	2.45	18	0	0	22	17	12	22
Parrish, Drew, Fr.	6	3	4.52	19	15	0	92	80	29	93
Reitz, Brandon, Fr.	0	0	6.00	3	0	0	3	3	2	3
Sands, Cole, So.	6	4	5.40	18	17	0	83	87	29	72
Stewart, Grant, Fr.	1	0	4.91	10	0	0	11	13	7	14
Voyles, Ed, R-Jr.	1	1	6.10	8	2	1	10	16	1	7
Voyles, Jim, Sr.	4	0	4.46	26	0	0	36	40	21	39
Wells, Steven, Jr.	0	0	2.70	6	0	0	3	8	1	3
Zirzow, Will, R-Jr.	3	1	2.58	20	4	0	45	31	19	52

7. CAL STATE FULLERTON

Coach: Rick Vanderhook. **Record:** 39-24

PLAYER, POS., YEAR	AVG	OBP	SLG	AB	R	2B	3B	HR	RBI	SB
Bryant, Taylor, INF, R-Jr.	.266	.378	.378	222	36	16	0	3	35	2
Cardenas, Ruben, OF, So.	.293	.354	.552	58	11	4	1	3	18	3
Cope, Daniel, C, Fr.	.276	.417	.448	29	4	2	0	1	2	0
Hildebrandt, Tristan, INF, Jr.	.133	.212	.233	60	8	3	0	1	5	0
Hudgins, Chris, C, Jr.	.240	.288	.398	171	24	10	1	5	33	3
Hunter, Cullen, OF, Sr.	.264	.341	.415	193	32	7	2	6	30	11
Hurst, Scott, OF, Jr.	.328	.419	.575	247	56	15	5	12	40	7
LaForte, Hank, INF, So.	.247	.314	.325	154	17	4	4	0	19	3
McLellan, J.T., 1B, Jr.	.143	.419	.143	28	6	0	0	0	5	0
Pacheco, Niko, C, R-Jr.	.181	.268	.319	72	6	5	1	1	12	0
Pavletich, Jake, INF, R-So.	.178	.275	.311	45	4	3	0	1	7	0
Persinger, Dillon, INF, Jr.	.287	.412	.378	209	42	8	1	3	31	18
Prescott, Chris, OF, Jr.	.228	.305	.260	127	17	2	1	0	7	3
Richards, Timmy, INF, Sr.	.309	.389	.486	181	31	10	2	6	31	0
Romero, Boston, INF, Jr.	.167	.250	.194	36	2	1	0	0	2	0
Valenzuela, Sahid, INF, Fr.	.314	.366	.377	223	31	5	3	1	24	3
Weisz, Zach, OF, R-Fr.	.333	.500	.667	12	5	1	0	1	4	0
Weller, Zach, INF, Fr.	.225	.360	.450	40	11	1	1	2	11	0

PITCHER, YEAR	W	L	ERA	G	GS	SV	IP	H	BB	SO
Brown, Dillon, Fr.	1	1	3.18	14	1	1	23	18	9	11
Cha, Erik, R-Fr.	1	1	4.85	17	0	1	26	31	6	11
Conine, Brett, So.	0	1	1.39	31	0	15	45	35	6	43
Eastman, Colton, So.	2	0	2.14	9	7	1	34	14	16	37
Gavin, John, Jr.	8	2	2.67	18	17	0	104	89	34	90
Gibbs, Maxwell, Sr.	1	3	7.71	14	1	0	9	13	6	7
Hurst, Scott, Jr.	0	0	0.00	2	0	0	2	3	0	1
Pabich, Jack, Jr.	1	3	6.10	20	1	0	31	31	8	26
Rios, Josh, R-Fr.	0	0	18.00	3	0	0	2	6	0	2
Seabold, Connor, Jr.	11	5	2.96	18	18	0	128	124	23	122
Velasquez, Gavin, So.	4	3	4.45	18	8	0	63	70	19	34
Wills, Joe, Jr.	4	2	9.19	13	7	0	32	43	14	30
Workman, Blake, So.	6	3	2.89	27	3	1	62	64	18	54

8. LONG BEACH STATE

Coach: Troy Buckley. **Record:** 42-20

PLAYER, POS., YEAR	AVG	OBP	SLG	AB	R	2B	3B	HR	RBI	SB
Banuelos, David, C, Jr.	.289	.368	.468	201	31	9	3	7	29	5
Colacchio, Domenic, UTL, So.	.220	.319	.244	41	4	1	0	0	5	0
Duran, Jarren, C, So.	.308	.375	.393	224	47	9	5	0	27	19
Gimenez, Matt, INF, R-Sr.	.174	.231	.174	23	2	0	0	0	1	0
Huffman, Laine, INF, Jr.	.294	.372	.369	160	22	4	1	2	26	4
Jackson, Daniel, 1B, Sr.	.277	.358	.382	238	37	13	0	4	33	8
Lundquist, Brock, OF, Jr.	.277	.388	.429	231	31	13	5	4	26	10
Mercadel, Tristan, OF, R-Jr.	.034	.263	.034	29	4	0	0	0	0	0
Montelongo, M., INF, Jr.	.154	.298	.154	39	6	0	0	0	1	1
Muzzi, Alex, OF, Sr.	.150	.320	.200	20	1	1	0	0	2	0

PLAYER, POS., YEAR	AVG	OBP	SLG	AB	R	2B	3B	HR	RBI	SB
Nellis, Jeff, INF, Sr.	.000	.250	.000	3	0	0	0	0	0	0
Nelson, Garrett, OF, R-So.	.183	.238	.258	93	11	3	2	0	8	2
Notch, Joey, C, Sr.	.400	.625	.500	10	0	1	0	0	3	1
Rasmussen, Luke, OF, Jr.	.246	.362	.315	203	34	11	0	1	33	7
Romano, Ramsey, INF, Jr.	.313	.340	.382	249	25	11	0	2	39	5
Sanchez, Joey, OF, Jr.	.095	.208	.143	21	3	1	0	0	3	1
Stotler, Brooks, OF, So.	.226	.327	.376	93	12	3	4	1	6	5
Tancas, Lucas, INF, R-Jr.	.304	.371	.491	230	42	12	2	9	37	8

PITCHER, YEAR	W	L	ERA	G	GS	SV	IP	H	BB	SO
Advocate, Josh, R-Sr.	3	1	1.86	27	0	5	39	28	7	38
Baayoun, Zak, Fr.	3	0	3.22	31	0	0	22	15	12	28
Castro, John, Fr.	0	3	6.09	13	5	0	34	35	11	24
Fields, Matt, Fr.	2	0	3.31	5	2	0	16	19	4	11
Jones, A.J., Jr.	1	2	2.36	6	6	0	27	22	6	24
McCaughan, Darren, Jr.	9	2	2.50	17	17	0	122	82	20	104
Radcliffe, Tyler, R-So.	1	0	3.52	9	1	0	23	24	3	19
Riley, Connor, Fr.	2	1	3.00	25	0	0	24	17	16	25
Rivera, Chris, So.	1	2	2.60	26	0	13	35	21	14	47
Sanchez, Sebastian, Jr.	0	2	7.15	9	1	0	11	12	4	4
Sheaks, John, Jr.	8	4	4.09	17	17	0	88	84	28	55
Smith, Dave, Sr.	9	2	2.07	17	14	0	91	98	11	41
Spacke, Dylan, Fr.	0	0	0.00	3	0	0	2	1	2	0
Villalobos, Eli, So.	3	1	3.48	24	0	3	31	24	14	27

9. KENTUCKY

Coach: Nick Mingione. **Record:** 43-23

PLAYER, POS., YEAR	AVG	OBP	SLG	AB	R	2B	3B	HR	RBI	SB
Becker, Luke, INF, Jr.	.287	.422	.467	167	48	9	0	7	46	7
Bellini, Joey, INF, Fr.	.000	.000	.000	2	0	0	0	0	0	0
Carson, Marcus, OF, Sr.	.303	.398	.474	234	50	13	3	7	39	8
Collett, T.J., C, Fr.	.087	.192	.217	23	1	0	0	1	6	0
Cottam, Kole, C, So.	.319	.380	.505	188	34	12	1	7	44	0
Gei, Marshall, INF, So.	.200	.200	.200	5	2	0	0	0	2	0
Heady, Connor, INF, Sr.	.276	.399	.419	210	47	9	0	7	32	2
Heyer, Luke, INF, Jr.	.262	.342	.492	65	12	6	0	3	12	1
Lewis, Zeke, INF, R-Fr.	.000	.500	.000	5	12	0	0	0	0	0
Mahan, Riley, INF, Jr.	.336	.392	.618	262	58	23	3	15	67	9
Marshall, Tyler, INF, Jr.	.293	.425	.343	140	22	4	0	1	29	1
McNeill, Gunnar, 1B, Sr.	.258	.314	.419	31	4	2	0	1	6	0
Pompey, Tristan, OF, So.	.361	.464	.541	266	70	18	0	10	45	9
Reks, Zach, OF, Sr.	.352	.461	.471	244	44	16	2	3	44	15
Squires, Troy, C, Jr.	.305	.427	.391	151	25	10	0	1	26	5
White, Evan, 1B, Jr.	.373	.453	.637	212	48	24	1	10	41	5
Wilson, Storm, OF, Sr.	.167	.325	.233	30	7	2	0	0	7	1

PITCHER, YEAR	W	L	ERA	G	GS	SV	IP	H	BB	SO
Cleary, Colton, Sr.	1	0	5.86	24	0	2	28	10	10	29
Doerries, Mark, R-Jr.	0	0	0.00	4	0	0	2	1	1	3
Hamilton, Jake, R-So.	0	0	4.50	2	0	0	2	1	1	3
Hjelle, Sean, So.	11	4	3.89	18	17	0	109	99	33	102
Keen, Austin, R-Fr.	0	0	3.68	11	0	0	7	9	9	1
Lewis, Justin, So.	6	4	3.56	17	16	0	91	77	27	72
Logue, Zach, Jr.	7	5	4.97	18	15	0	87	93	25	88
Machamer, Chris, Fr.	2	0	3.18	24	0	1	34	14	14	39
Maley, Alec, Jr.	0	0	5.59	13	0	0	10	10	10	9
McNeill, Gunnar, Sr.	0	0	13.50	1	0	0	2	0	0	3
Pop, Zach, Jr.	1	1	3.48	22	0	0	21	14	14	20
Salow, Logan, Sr.	2	6	1.95	31	0	12	55	17	17	73
Schaenzer, Brad, Jr.	5	0	3.46	23	5	0	52	15	15	42
Smith, Josh, So.	0	0	27.00	4	0	0	1	3	3	3
Thompson, Zack, Fr.	8	3	3.45	20	13	1	76	50	38	96

10. TEXAS A&M

Coach: Rob Childress. **Record:** 41-23

PLAYER, POS., YEAR	AVG	OBP	SLG	AB	R	2B	3B	HR	RBI	SB
Bedford, Cole, C, So.	.301	.351	.438	176	24	13	1	3	26	3
Blake, Cam, OF, Fr.	.214	.389	.214	56	5	0	0	0	9	0
Choruby, Nick, OF, Sr.	.321	.441	.415	246	55	10	2	3	33	11
Coleman, Hunter, C, Fr.	.283	.380	.441	152	29	7	1	5	22	0
Davis, Joel, INF, Sr.	.249	.356	.378	201	40	4	2	6	30	7
Foster, Logan, C, Fr.	.280	.333	.489	186	33	13	4	6	24	3
Gillman, Tommy, INF, Fr.	.222	.364	.222	9	4	0	0	0	2	0
Gutierrez, Jorge, INF, Fr.	.214	.337	.417	84	13	3	1	4	16	2
Homan, Austin, INF, Sr.	.218	.313	.273	216	31	10	1	0	28	5
Janca, George, INF, So.	.261	.309	.416	226	40	9	4	6	30	3
Kopetsky, Blake, OF, Sr.	.302	.350	.412	199	33	12	2	2	20	4
Lichty, Tim, OF, Jr.	.000	.000	.000	6	0	0	0	0	1	0
Pennington, Walker, OF, Sr.	.215	.319	.354	158	24	8	1	4	35	7
Schoenvogel, Baine, C, Jr.	.250	.417	.536	28	7	2	0	2	4	0
Shewmake, Braden, INF, Fr.	.328	.374	.529	274	47	18	2	11	69	11
Stanley, Coll, OF, R-Fr.	.154	.389	.231	13	4	1	0	0	1	0

PITCHER, YEAR	W	L	ERA	G	GS	SV	IP	H	BB	SO
Bayless, Tristen, Fr.	0	0	3.00	2	0	1	3	1	2	4
Chafin, Kaylor, Jr.	17	2	2.33	33	1	3	77	57	16	72
Cole, Mason, Fr.	1	0	0.00	2	0	0	3	2	1	2
Doxakis, John, Fr.	4	3	5.44	25	7	0	50	45	23	51
Gonzalez, Lee May, Jr.	1	0	4.50	6	0	0	8	7	5	11
Hill, Brigham, Jr.	8	3	3.15	17	16	0	100	88	31	111
Kilkenny, Mitchell, So.	3	3	3.67	26	5	7	56	66	18	56
Kolek, Stephen, So.	4	5	3.79	16	16	0	90	85	24	82
Larkins, Turner, Jr.	1	2	3.37	9	5	0	27	24	11	20
Martin, Corbin, Jr.	7	4	3.80	24	13	0	88	89	38	95
Miner, Landon, Fr.	1	0	2.55	17	0	1	25	16	6	16
Richardson, Kyle, Fr.	0	0	8.53	6	1	0	6	8	7	6
Ruffcorn, Jason, Fr.	0	0	2.61	12	0	0	10	6	5	10
Sherrod, Cason, Jr.	4	1	2.89	30	0	4	44	30	26	38

11. NORTH CAROLINA

Coach: Mike Fox. **Record:** 49-14

PLAYER, POS., YEAR	AVG	OBP	SLG	AB	R	2B	3B	HR	RBI	SB
Busch, Michael, INF, Fr.	.213	.351	.320	122	18	7	0	2	21	2
Datres, Kyle, INF, So.	.266	.393	.430	214	45	12	1	7	49	4
Freeman, Ike, INF, Fr.	.178	.291	.311	45	13	3	0	1	8	0
Gahagan, Zack, INF, Jr.	.238	.371	.394	193	44	9	0	7	40	6
Greenfield, Aaron, OF, Fr.	.000	.000	.000	1	0	0	0	0	0	0
Illies, Brendan, C, So.	.222	.462	.444	9	0	2	0	0	3	0
Jones, Utah, INF, So.	.000	.091	.000	10	1	0	0	0	0	0
Ladowski, Josh, OF, So.	.333	.391	.333	21	5	0	0	0	4	0
Lynn, Tyler, OF, Sr.	.313	.420	.511	176	39	8	3	7	38	6
Martorano, Brandon, C, Fr.	.070	.212	.070	43	5	0	0	0	5	0
McGee, Ashton, INF, Fr.	.340	.429	.510	206	44	10	2	7	44	1
Miller, Brian, INF, Jr.	.340	.413	.508	256	57	16	3	7	47	22
Pate, Adam, OF, Sr.	.140	.359	.175	57	12	2	0	0	7	2
Riley, Brandon, OF, So.	.301	.391	.459	209	43	7	4	6	49	10
Roberts, Cody, C, So.	.251	.348	.348	187	41	10	1	2	25	5
Warmoth, Logan, INF, Jr.	.349	.417	.569	255	59	19	5	9	45	18

PITCHER, YEAR	W	L	ERA	G	GS	SV	IP	H	BB	SO
Aker, Cole, So.	1	1	2.30	9	3	0	16	8	13	18
Attainese, Zach, Fr.	0	0	0.00	9	0	0	3	1	4	1
Baum, Tyler, Fr.	6	0	2.65	15	14	0	58	44	23	43
Bergner, Austin, Fr.	4	2	3.22	25	3	1	45	35	25	41
Bukauskas, J.B., Jr.	9	0	2.02	14	14	0	89	56	33	111
Dalatri, Luca, Fr.	6	3	3.50	14	14	0	90	85	17	79
Daniels, Brett, Jr.	5	0	2.75	26	0	0	39	34	20	33
Gay, Trevor, So.	1	0	3.97	15	0	0	11	10	7	13
Hiatt, Josh, R-Fr.	4	2	2.09	31	0	13	47	28	18	60
Hutchinson, Rodney, So.	7	4	3.90	30	1	1	58	55	17	53
Morgan, Jason, Jr.	3	0	4.10	16	7	0	42	41	20	33
Odum, Evan, Fr.	0	0	99.00	1	0	0	0	3	1	0
Sugg, Taylor, So.	1	0	1.54	16	2	0	23	19	13	14
Weiss, Bo, Fr.	0	0	2.93	14	1	0	15	15	7	14

12. TEXAS TECH

Coach: Tim Tadlock. **Record:** 45-17

PLAYER, POS., YEAR	AVG	OBP	SLG	AB	R	2B	3B	HR	RBI	SB
Beck, Connor, OF, Jr.	.289	.345	.382	76	12	2	1	1	9	3
Berglund, Michael, C, Fr.	.307	.369	.391	179	23	7	1	2	27	2
Bernstein, Matt, C, So.	.500	.500	.500	2	0	0	0	0	0	0
Davis, Michael, INF, Jr.	.269	.358	.446	175	38	9	2	6	29	3
Farhat, Cody, OF, So.	.343	.438	.569	137	32	10	6	3	22	7
Garcia, Orlando, INF, Jr.	.305	.386	.550	220	42	9	3	13	62	9

PLAYER, POS., YEAR	AVG	OBP	SLG	AB	R	2B	3B	HR	RBI	SB
Gardner, Tanner, INF, Jr.	.305	.395	.485	200	38	17	2	5	33	6
Hargrove, Hunter, INF, Sr.	.343	.423	.535	245	56	26	3	5	51	7
Jung, Josh, INF, Fr.	.306	.395	.453	245	55	14	2	6	43	2
Klein, Brian, INF, Fr.	.266	.291	.405	79	16	3	1	2	20	0
Koelzer, Clay, C, Fr.	.263	.333	.316	38	4	2	0	0	4	0
Little, Grant, INF, Fr.	.335	.405	.476	206	52	17	3	2	34	6
Long, Ryan, INF, Sr.	.322	.432	.475	183	38	11	1	5	26	3
Lyons, Anthony, OF, Sr.	.364	.500	.545	11	0	0	1	0	4	0
McMillon, John, INF, Fr.	.229	.299	.586	70	14	1	0	8	14	0
Paradoski, Trevor, INF, Fr.	.167	.167	.167	6	1	0	0	0	1	0
Rheams, Zach, INF, Jr.	.133	.322	.289	45	8	1	0	2	6	1
Sancez, Kholeton, C, Sr.	.417	.533	.500	24	10	2	0	0	7	2
Warren, Cameron, INF, So.	.182	.250	.273	22	3	2	0	0	4	0

PITCHER, YEAR	W	L	ERA	G	GS	SV	IP	H	BB	SO
Davis, Andrew, Fr.	0	0	2.70	3	0	0	3	0	2	3
Dusek, Dylan, Jr.	0	0	7.47	11	0	2	16	23	1	9
Freeman, Caleb, Fr.	0	1	8.83	11	2	0	17	25	15	15
Gingery, Steven, So.	10	1	1.58	15	15	0	91	60	29	107
Gonzalez, John Henry, Fr.	2	3	6.52	13	9	0	39	44	33	28
Harpenau, Ty, So.	0	0	6.53	10	0	1	21	26	12	25
Jung, Josh, Fr.	0	0	81.00	1	0	0	0	2	1	0
Killian, Caleb, Fr.	6	0	3.55	19	1	2	38	25	23	35
Lanning, Erikson, So.	3	1	3.12	17	7	0	40	40	17	18
Martin, Davis, So.	4	2	3.07	9	9	0	44	43	10	37
McDonald, Jake, Fr.	0	1	5.31	14	3	0	20	23	15	17
McMillion, John, Fr.	2	0	1.75	24	0	5	26	12	20	29
Mushinski, Parker, Jr.	3	2	2.15	31	0	6	38	24	25	47
Patterson, Jacob, Jr.	5	1	3.86	30	1	2	51	47	25	63
Quezada, Jose, Jr.	6	4	3.55	24	0	4	38	33	16	52
Shetter, Ryan, So.	4	1	3.71	15	15	0	70	66	27	74

13. WAKE FOREST

Coach: Tom Walter. **Record:** 43-20

PLAYER, POS., YEAR	AVG	OBP	SLG	AB	R	2B	3B	HR	RBI	SB
Aiello, Johnny, INF, So.	.328	.417	.643	244	57	17	0	20	53	4
Breazeale, Ben, C, Sr.	.333	.399	.540	237	50	16	0	11	51	0
DiPonzio, Nick, OF, Fr.	.190	.244	.357	42	8	1	0	2	7	3
Fairchild, Stuart, OF, Jr.	.360	.439	.636	261	65	19	1	17	67	21
Frick, Patrick, INF, Fr.	.294	.379	.333	51	6	2	0	0	3	0
Harvey, Logan, C, So.	.263	.386	.362	213	43	12	0	3	26	0
Long, Christian, OF, Fr.	.087	.185	.087	23	1	0	0	0	1	0
Maronpot, Keegan, OF, Jr.	.214	.318	.409	220	39	5	1	12	41	1
Mascolo, Chase, INF, Fr.	.333	.429	.333	6	0	0	0	0	0	0
Mueller, Jake, INF, So.	.345	.413	.430	258	58	16	0	2	34	6
Pryor, Jonathan, OF, Sr.	.354	.447	.479	263	55	21	0	4	35	5
Seal, Zach, INF, Fr.	.400	.625	.700	10	5	0	0	1	5	0
Sheets, Gavin, INF, Jr.	.317	.424	.629	240	57	10	1	21	84	1
Steel, Bruce, INF, R-So.	.264	.383	.533	182	37	10	0	13	38	5

PITCHER, YEAR	W	L	ERA	G	GS	SV	IP	H	BB	SO
Bach, Carter, Fr.	2	0	3.26	18	0	0	19	14	17	19
Dee, Rhyse, Fr.	0	0	4.50	3	0	0	2	3	2	3
Dunshee, Parker, Sr.	9	1	3.91	17	17	0	104	98	30	111
Farish, Chris, R-Jr.	0	0	5.89	24	0	0	18	18	9	32
Hearn, Bobby, R-Fr.	1	0	9.82	3	0	0	4	4	1	4
Johnson, Parker, R-Jr.	0	0	0.00	2	0	0	2	2	1	2
Johnstone, Connor, Sr.	8	0	3.61	16	15	0	92	86	33	69
Kubrak, Shane, Fr.	0	0	6.75	5	0	0	3	2	2	3
Loepprich, Drew, Jr.	3	3	5.84	18	5	0	45	51	18	36
McCarren, John, Sr.	5	4	4.91	29	4	2	51	56	15	39
McSweeney, Morgan, Fr.	5	1	3.50	25	1	0	36	40	18	48
Peluse, Colin, Fr.	5	1	3.54	20	7	1	41	31	12	37
Roberts, Griffin, So.	2	5	2.19	29	0	8	53	30	32	80
Sellers, Donnie, Jr.	3	5	4.71	17	14	0	84	83	29	60
Supple, Rayne, So.	0	0	6.75	10	0	0	8	5	18	11
White, Holden, Fr.	0	0	3.38	8	0	0	3	1	3	5

14. MISSISSIPPI STATE

Coach: Andy Cannizaro. **Record:** 40-27

PLAYER, POS., YEAR	AVG	OBP	SLG	AB	R	2B	3B	HR	RBI	SB
Alexander, Luke, INF, So.	.222	.295	.343	198	30	9	0	5	21	5
Barlow, Trysten, p, R-Fr.	.500	.667	.500	2	0	0	0	0	0	0
Blaylock, Brant, OF, R-Fr.	.193	.272	.325	83	14	1	2	2	10	2
Bragg, Harrison, INF, Jr.	.290	.333	.484	62	10	3	0	3	10	0
Brown, Cody, INF, R-Sr.	.323	.433	.539	217	46	14	3	9	42	10
Gordon, Cole, 1B, R-So.	.158	.258	.316	57	5	0	0	3	9	0
Gridley, Ryan, INF, Jr.	.327	.393	.457	269	60	15	1	6	39	7
Jolly, Trey, P, Jr.	.000	.000	.000	1	2	0	0	0	0	0
Lovelady, Josh, C, R-Sr.	.215	.305	.288	163	21	7	1	1	21	0
MacNamee, Elijah, OF, So.	.267	.315	.344	180	22	6	1	2	22	4
Mangum, Jake, OF, So.	.324	.380	.385	278	51	15	1	0	26	14
Marrero, Elih, C, So.	.000	.167	.000	10	1	0	0	0	1	0
McQuary, Denver, INF, Fr.	.000	.000	.000	1	0	0	0	0	0	0
Pilkington, Konnor, P, So.	.000	.000	.000	1	0	0	0	0	0	0
Poole, Tanner, OF, R-Jr.	.224	.290	.309	165	20	3	1	3	14	11
Price, Spencer, P, So.	1.000	1.000	1.000	1	0	0	0	0	0	0
Rooker, Brent, OF, R-Jr.	.387	.495	.810	248	60	30	3	23	82	18
Skelton, Dustin, INF, Fr.	.206	.295	.235	68	1	2	0	0	10	0
Stovall, Hunter, INF, So.	.288	.345	.375	160	30	6	1	2	18	4
Vansau, Hunter, OF, So.	.297	.377	.356	118	10	5	1	0	14	0

PITCHER, YEAR	W	L	ERA	G	GS	SV	IP	H	BB	SO
Ashcraft, Graham, Fr.	2	0	5.62	10	5	0	24	24	16	25
Barlow, Trysten, R-Fr.	0	2	5.23	26	0	0	21	16	25	28
Barton, Jacob, Jr.	2	0	6.57	23	0	0	37	40	18	26
Billingsley, Jacob, R-Jr.	2	3	4.78	16	13	0	53	44	38	52
Blaylock, Brant, R-Fr.	1	0	7.50	5	0	0	6	7	5	4
Breaux, Kale, So.	0	0	54.00	1	0	0	1	5	1	0
Cyr, Ryan, So.	0	1	6.46	6	2	0	15	17	9	14
Ford, Parker, R-Fr.	0	1	13.50	9	0	0	7	15	5	5
Gordon, Cole, R-So.	2	3	5.69	19	9	1	55	47	30	59
Jolly, Trey, Jr.	3	1	6.75	24	0	1	29	31	21	22
Mahoney, Andrew, Jr.	0	0	8.00	9	0	0	9	14	8	8
Mangum, Jake, So.	2	1	6.46	6	5	1	15	15	7	9
McQuary, Denver, Fr.	3	4	5.20	21	8	0	55	41	50	40
Pilkington, Konnor, So.	8	5	3.08	17	17	0	108	76	47	111
Plumlee, Peyton, So.	6	1	4.01	26	8	1	74	71	31	54
Price, Spencer, So.	4	1	2.91	31	0	14	34	24	19	40
Rigby, Ryan, Jr.	0	1	0.00	5	0	0	4	6	1	4
Rooker, Brent, R-Jr.	0	0	27.00	1	0	0	0	1	1	0
Self, Riley, Fr.	5	2	3.72	31	0	8	48	44	20	60
Smith, Blake, Sr.	0	1	18.00	2	0	0	2	2	5	1

15. STANFORD

Coach: Mark Marquess. **Record:** 42-16

PLAYER, POS., YEAR	AVG	OBP	SLG	AB	R	2B	3B	HR	RBI	SB
Bakst, Daniel, INF, Fr.	.311	.369	.439	196	23	16	0	3	38	0
Branton, Beau, INF, Jr.	.000	.000	.000	5	1	0	0	0	0	0
Brodey, Quinn, OF, Jr.	.314	.371	.556	239	41	17	4	11	51	3
Carter, Bryce, C, Jr.	.111	.111	.111	9	0	0	0	0	0	0
Daschbach, Andrew, INF, Fr.	.183	.269	.250	60	7	4	0	0	3	1
Decker, Matter, C, Sr.	.000	.000	.000	7	1	0	0	0	0	0
Diekroeger, Mikey, INF, Jr.	.262	.323	.326	141	16	7	1	0	14	1
Dunlap, Alex, INF, Sr.	.274	.365	.393	84	8	4	0	2	10	0
Handley, Maverick, C, Fr.	.257	.390	.367	109	26	10	1	0	13	3
Hoerner, Nico, INF, So.	.307	.357	.406	251	43	18	2	1	33	2
Kinamon, Duke, INF, So.	.284	.365	.379	211	38	11	0	3	22	15
Klein, Jack, OF, Sr.	.293	.354	.408	157	20	9	0	3	21	1
Kuet, Jesse, INF, Jr.	.333	.372	.359	78	14	2	0	0	12	1
Matthiessen, Will, INF, Fr.	.000	1.000	.000	0	0	0	0	0	0	0
Molfetta, Christian, C, So.	.500	.500	.500	2	4	0	0	0	1	1
Stowers, Kyle, OF, Fr.	.103	.182	.205	39	2	1	0	1	4	0
Wilson, Alec, OF, So.	.212	.235	.303	33	6	3	0	0	3	0
Winaker, Matt, OF, Jr.	.308	.432	.514	208	53	14	1	9	45	3
Wulff, Brandon, OF, So.	.231	.325	.385	143	24	4	0	6	23	2

PITCHER, YEAR	W	L	ERA	G	GS	SV	IP	H	BB	SO
Bubic, Kris, So.	7	6	2.79	15	15	0	90	79	31	96
Castellanos, Chris, Sr.	9	3	3.28	15	15	0	99	95	15	56
Grech, Zach, Fr.	0	0	9.00	3	0	0	3	4	3	1
Hanewich, Brett, Sr.	2	1	5.00	11	2	1	27	22	18	26

PITCHER, YEAR	W	L	ERA	G	GS	SV	IP	H	BB	SO
Hock, Colton, Jr.	6	1	2.08	27	0	16	48	36	11	35
Klein, Jack, Sr.	0	0	0.00	1	0	0	1	0	0	1
Little, Jack, Fr.	0	0	23.14	4	0	0	2	5	5	4
Matthiessen, Will, Fr.	3	0	2.33	20	0	3	39	31	9	32
Miller, Erik, Fr.	5	2	3.65	17	13	1	62	62	21	34
Styles, John Henry, Jr.	0	0	99.00	1	0	0	0	2	0	0
Summerville, Andrew, Jr.	5	2	4.10	15	13	0	75	83	20	69
Thorne, Tyler, Sr.	4	1	2.42	29	0	2	52	42	20	43
Weisenberg, Keith, Jr.	1	0	4.22	17	0	0	21	17	10	19

16. SOUTHERN MISSISSIPPI

Coach: Scott Berry. **Record:** 50-16

PLAYER, POS., YEAR	AVG	OBP	SLG	AB	R	2B	3B	HR	RBI	SB
Bowen, Bryant, C, R-Fr.	.337	.422	.568	95	20	7	0	5	20	0
Boyd, LeeMarcus, INF, Jr.	.289	.345	.434	235	48	18	2	4	42	10
Braley, Taylor, INF, Jr.	.313	.461	.587	230	62	12	0	17	61	6
Burdeaux, Dylan, INF, Sr.	.337	.409	.535	303	67	24	0	12	69	21
Cooper, Storme, INF, So.	.255	.423	.372	94	26	2	0	3	21	5
Donaldson, Cole, C, So.	.256	.345	.333	156	31	4	1	2	19	3
Guidry, Matthew, INF, R-Fr.	.363	.484	.559	102	33	6	1	4	33	2
Hadley, Tracy, INF, Sr.	.252	.346	.370	119	18	8	0	2	25	3
Irby, Mason, OF, Jr.	.338	.433	.449	263	62	20	3	1	40	6
Keating, Daniel, OF, Jr.	.261	.368	.522	161	32	9	0	11	31	11
Maack, Casey, INF, Jr.	.253	.286	.448	87	21	3	1	4	14	2
Slater, Hunter, OF, R-So.	.312	.446	.477	218	58	10	7	4	39	5
Viaene, Jake, C, Jr.	.324	.439	.588	34	10	3	0	2	7	0
Wallner, Matt, OF, Fr.	.336	.463	.655	235	56	14	2	19	63	4

PITCHER, YEAR	W	L	ERA	G	GS	SV	IP	H	BB	SO
Braley, Taylor, Jr.	7	2	3.40	14	13	0	82	81	22	78
Carroll, Cody, Fr.	0	0	11.93	8	5	0	14	26	5	13
Davis, Jake, Jr.	0	0	4.70	9	0	0	8	9	5	8
Driver, Trent, Jr.	2	1	5.58	28	1	0	31	40	9	30
Jones, Cooper, Jr.	0	0	0.00	2	0	0	5	4	1	3
Keys, J.C., So.	3	3	5.56	16	8	0	55	54	25	48
McCarty, Kirk, Jr.	10	2	3.52	17	17	0	100	94	22	103
Mikell, Calder, So.	0	0	6.75	11	2	0	12	13	13	13
Millet, Austin, R-Fr.	0	2	8.64	8	0	0	8	10	7	9
Nelms, Alex, Fr.	1	0	5.30	14	1	0	19	22	5	15
Powers, Stevie, So.	3	0	5.13	30	2	2	33	39	14	24
Roberts, Hayden, Jr.	5	2	4.30	20	10	1	73	75	27	86
Sandlin, Nick, So.	10	2	2.38	29	0	8	57	41	29	80
Smith, Colt, Jr.	6	2	3.36	23	6	0	67	69	17	43
Stevens, Hunter, Sr.	1	0	1.23	5	1	0	7	7	4	7
Tweedy, Sean, Fr.	0	0	3.00	11	0	0	9	8	3	8
Wallner, Matt, Fr.	2	0	1.84	9	0	3	15	8	7	15

17. MISSOURI STATE

Coach: Keith Guttin. **Record:** 43-20

PLAYER, POS., YEAR	AVG	OBP	SLG	AB	R	2B	3B	HR	RBI	SB
Brown, Matt, INF, Jr.	.091	.412	.212	33	5	1	0	1	3	0
Burger, Jake, INF, Jr.	.328	.443	.648	247	69	13	0	22	65	3
Duffy, Jack, OF, Fr.	.222	.344	.285	158	21	8	1	0	17	7
Eierman, Jeremy, INF, So.	.313	.431	.675	243	67	15	2	23	68	17
Geha, Logan, C, R-Fr.	.203	.429	.297	64	20	3	0	1	10	3
Graham, Blake, OF, Sr.	.309	.421	.543	162	28	11	0	9	34	0
Jefferson, Alex, OF, Sr.	.227	.361	.318	220	39	11	0	3	22	9
Meyer, Aaron, INF, Sr.	.292	.372	.441	161	24	10	1	4	30	1
Millas, Drew, C, Fr.	.224	.281	.282	174	15	7	0	1	29	3
Paulsen, Justin, INF, Sr.	.322	.406	.478	245	47	17	0	7	49	1
Privitera, John, INF, R-Fr.	.235	.364	.247	81	17	1	0	0	8	2
Rowley, Danny, INF, Sr.	.200	.200	.200	5	0	0	0	0	1	0
Ruff, Landan, OF, Jr.	.280	.393	.440	50	17	3	1	1	10	2
Skalnik, Ryan, INF, Jr.	.205	.319	.333	39	3	2	0	1	10	0
Steinmetz, Hunter, OF, So.	.300	.414	.427	253	60	11	0	7	42	10
Turner, Trey, OF, Jr.	.000	.125	.000	7	0	0	0	0	0	0
Whetstone, Ben, INF, R-Fr.	.050	.208	.050	20	1	0	0	0	1	0

PITCHER, YEAR	W	L	ERA	G	GS	SV	IP	H	BB	SO
Coleman, Dylan, So.	8	3	4.80	18	16	0	99	85	50	106
Dame, Hunter, Fr.	0	0	9.00	3	0	0	2	4	1	1
Fromson, Jake, Jr.	8	3	2.25	37	0	3	76	46	18	88
Gonnerman, Kolton, Jr.	0	0	11.12	4	1	0	6	7	6	4
Knight, Austin, Jr.	3	2	3.97	15	8	0	59	54	26	41
Knutson, Jordan, Sr.	8	4	4.53	23	15	1	93	96	21	90
Lochner, Jake, So.	1	0	4.97	13	0	0	13	12	8	13
McAlister, Tyler, Fr.	0	1	9.31	10	1	0	10	16	13	11
Moore, Alex, Fr.	0	0	2.61	10	0	0	10	11	5	7
Still, Doug, Jr.	8	3	2.88	17	17	0	103	98	27	89
Tallman, Justin, R-Fr.	0	0	0.00	1	0	0	1	1	0	1
Turner, Trey, Jr.	2	0	2.03	7	0	0	13	4	4	22
Witherspoon, Nate, Fr.	4	3	4.29	15	5	0	42	43	15	40
Young, Bryan, Sr.	1	1	1.53	25	0	8	29	12	17	47

18. VANDERBILT

Coach: Tim Corbin. **Record:** 36-25

PLAYER, POS., YEAR	AVG	OBP	SLG	AB	R	2B	3B	HR	RBI	SB
Bleday, J.J., OF, Fr.	.256	.384	.341	164	23	8	0	2	22	0
Brewer, Alex, INF, Fr.	.000	.167	.000	15	1	0	0	0	1	0
Coleman, Ro, OF, Sr.	.290	.347	.328	131	20	3	1	0	8	7
Delay, Jason, C, Sr.	.309	.381	.444	207	31	18	2	2	41	1
Duvall, Ty, C, Fr.	.375	.516	.500	24	6	3	0	0	6	0
Fentress, Kiambu, OF, R-Fr.	.250	.250	.250	4	0	0	0	0	0	0
Grisanti, Walker, OF, So.	.267	.333	.333	30	7	2	0	0	4	0
Hayes, Reed, OF, Jr.	.276	.375	.362	163	30	10	2	0	36	4
Infante, Julian, INF, So.	.315	.387	.518	251	51	16	1	11	66	0
Jones, Alonzo, INF, So.	.221	.357	.295	95	19	3	2	0	10	3
Kaiser, Connor, INF, So.	.222	.316	.284	194	32	7	1	1	18	4
Kendall, Jeren, OF, Jr.	.307	.372	.556	261	59	10	5	15	53	20
Paul, Ethanm inf, So.	.251	.336	.412	199	34	15	1	5	27	5
Ray, Harrison, INF, Fr.	.244	.333	.333	78	16	2	1	1	12	2
Scott, Stephen, OF, So.	.227	.347	.311	119	25	4	0	2	11	3
Toffey, Will, INF, Fr.	.354	.475	.602	206	55	13	1	12	64	5

PITCHER, YEAR	W	L	ERA	G	GS	SV	IP	H	BB	SO
Conger, Maddux, So.	2	1	4.96	15	3	0	33	35	17	28
Day, Chandler, So.	7	2	3.78	13	12	0	52	44	21	53
Fellows, Drake, Fr.	3	3	3.30	16	10	1	63	54	17	68
Gillis, Jackson, Fr.	0	0	3.60	16	0	0	15	9	11	19
Hayes, Reed, Jr.	0	2	5.75	21	0	7	20	22	13	25
King, Zach, Fr.	2	1	2.56	25	0	0	39	24	17	31
McGarry, Matt, So.	0	0	8.59	5	0	0	7	2	12	8
Murfee, Pennm, R-Jr.	0	1	4.91	10	0	0	11	10	4	6
Raby, Patrick, So.	10	4	2.73	16	16	0	105	89	30	87
Ruppenthal, Matt, Jr.	3	3	3.17	21	4	3	54	40	19	45
Sandborn, Michaelm, Fr.	0	0	0.00	3	0	0	3	0	1	3
Snider, Collin, Jr.	3	2	5.40	21	1	1	33	37	16	29
Stover, Paxton, Jr.	1	0	6.41	15	0	0	20	16	18	21
Wright, Kyle, Jr.	5	6	3.40	16	16	0	103	82	31	121

19. ARKANSAS

Coach: Dave Van Horn. **Record:** 45-19

PLAYER, POS., YEAR	AVG	OBP	SLG	AB	R	2B	3B	HR	RBI	SB
Arledge, Jake, OF, Sr.	.300	.420	.390	210	47	6	2	3	30	7
Biggers, Jax, INF, So.	.338	.423	.498	213	48	14	4	4	37	3
Bonfield, Luke, OF, Jr.	.294	.366	.448	248	41	9	1	9	49	1
Burch, Matt, INF, Fr.	.156	.206	.219	32	2	2	0	0	0	0
Chadwick, Cannon, p, Sr.	.000	1.000	.000	0	1	0	0	0	0	0
Cole, Eric, OF, So.	.282	.349	.413	206	31	12	0	5	25	3
Fletcher, Dominic, OF, Fr.	.291	.356	.495	220	44	7	1	12	37	1
Gates, Jared, INF, Jr.	.246	.328	.418	122	19	3	0	6	14	0
Gosser, Alex, C, Sr.	.259	.313	.407	27	6	1	0	1	4	0
Kenley, Jack, INF, Fr.	.133	.278	.167	30	5	1	0	0	2	1
Koch, Grant, C, So.	.264	.358	.498	235	40	14	1	13	42	1
Lee, Evan, OF, Fr.	.333	.451	.405	42	12	3	0	0	8	1
McFarland, Jordan, INF, Fr.	.271	.366	.357	70	14	0	0	2	10	1
Shaddy, Carson, INF, R-Jr.	.279	.383	.450	222	48	10	2	8	40	6
Spanberger, Chad, INF, Jr.	.305	.389	.619	239	54	13	1	20	67	2
Williams, Jaxon, INF, Fr.	.245	.333	.327	49	7	2	1	0	14	0
Wilson, Hunter, INF, Jr.	.310	.394	.310	29	3	0	0	0	6	0

PITCHER, YEAR	W	L	ERA	G	GS	SV	IP	H	BB	SO
Stephan, Trevor, Jr.	6	3	2.87	16	16	0	91	73	20	120
Knight, Blaine, So.	8	4	3.28	17	16	0	91	75	20	96

PITCHER, YEAR	W	L	ERA	G	GS	SV	IP	H	BB	SO
Cronin, Matt, Fr.	3	1	2.00	15	0	1	18	8	12	31
Reindl, Jake, So.	4	1	2.31	24	0	3	51	39	16	49
Kopps, Kevin, R-Fr.	3	1	3.31	22	5	2	49	46	18	40
Lee, Evan, Fr.	0	0	3.60	15	1	2	15	12	6	17
Heiss, Brenden, Fr.	0	0	3.60	4	0	0	5	3	3	3
Murphy, Kacey, So.	5	1	3.65	19	10	0	49	43	21	68
Chadwick, Cannon, Sr.	4	3	3.66	24	0	2	32	24	12	38
Scroggins, Cody, So.	0	0	3.86	3	0	0	2	3	1	1
Loseke, Barrett, So.	3	0	4.21	15	2	0	26	23	17	28
Taccolini, Dominic, Fr.	4	1	4.24	20	5	2	51	41	27	49
Alberius, Josh, R-Sr.	3	4	4.55	23	9	2	55	64	16	48
Denton, Angus, Fr.	0	0	5.23	8	0	0	10	10	3	10
Kostyshock, Jacob, Fr.	1	0	6.75	6	0	0	5	6	6	6
Rogers, Weston, So.	1	0	7.11	12	0	0	13	13	8	14
Campbell, Isaiah, So.	0	0	40.50	1	0	0	1	3	1	1

20. SAM HOUSTON STATE

Coach: Matt Deggs. **Record:** 44-23

PLAYER, POS., YEAR	AVG	OBP	SLG	AB	R	2B	3B	HR	RBI	SB
Adams, Austin, INF, Fr.	.000	.333	.000	2	0	0	0	0	0	0
Austin, Cross, INF, Fr.	.118	.105	.118	17	0	0	0	0	2	0
Beene, Taylor, INF, Sr.	.292	.417	.361	202	36	6	1	2	40	7
Biles, Josh, OF, So.	.250	.391	.472	36	3	3	1	1	7	0
Chisolm, Blake, INF, Jr.	.343	.466	.551	178	42	17	4	4	35	1
Freqia, Andrew, INF, So.	.302	.356	.450	278	47	10	5	7	48	14
Grisham, Jaxxon, INF, So.	.255	.377	.327	110	24	3	1	1	15	3
Harp, Clayton, OF, So.	.289	.379	.436	225	45	12	3	5	50	6
Hearn, Hunter, OF, So.	.326	.395	.447	215	42	12	4	2	42	3
Johnson, Bryce, OF, Jr.	.350	.453	.433	263	63	12	5	0	43	33
McKnight, Riley, INF, So.	.238	.349	.317	164	36	4	3	1	22	11
Miles, Lance, INF, R-Sr.	.280	.363	.353	218	36	13	0	1	33	8
Odom, Mac, OF, So.	.234	.413	.234	47	19	0	0	0	7	8
Rojas, Robie, C, Sr.	.342	.408	.498	243	46	15	1	7	45	7
Southerland, Hunter, C, R-Jr.	.412	.444	.471	17	1	1	0	0	4	0
VanDyke, Nate, INF, Jr.	.000	.100	.000	8	0	0	0	0	2	0
Williams, Mike, OF, Fr.	.208	.296	.250	24	1	1	0	0	0	1

PITCHER, YEAR	W	L	ERA	G	GS	SV	IP	H	BB	SO
Backhus, Kyle, Fr.	4	4	4.19	28	6	2	58	56	28	64
Ballew, Seth, R-So.	6	3	4.03	18	14	0	74	77	34	60
Cameron, Colin, So.	0	0	5.09	15	1	1	18	15	7	21
Cannon, Jordan, So.	2	0	3.04	21	1	0	24	27	6	12
Chisolm, Blake, Jr.	0	0	0.00	2	0	0	1	1	0	0
Cooper, Riley, R-Jr.	4	3	3.38	24	0	1	51	42	12	45
Demco, Brad, Fr.	0	0	3.44	14	1	0	18	17	16	21
Donica, Heath, Sr.	9	3	2.53	17	16	0	110	86	32	109
Hammel, Mark, Jr.	1	0	6.59	13	0	0	14	17	7	11
Mikolajchak, Nick, Fr.	0	4	3.38	32	0	13	29	30	10	32
Mills, Dakota, R-Jr.	7	3	4.54	22	13	1	71	79	8	56
Robinson, Dominic, Fr.	1	0	4.21	24	1	3	36	45	15	36
Sequeira, Gabriel, Fr.	0	1	5.56	8	1	0	11	12	6	8
Wesneski, Hayden, Fr.	10	2	3.93	19	13	0	85	87	25	47

NO. 21 VIRGINIA

Coach: Brian O'Connor. **Record:** 43-16

PLAYER, POS., YEAR	AVG	OBP	SLG	AB	R	2B	3B	HR	RBI	SB
Blakely, Drew, INF, Fr.	.250	.348	.250	20	2	0	0	0	4	0
Clement, Ernie, INF, Jr.	.315	.345	.366	254	56	5	1	2	34	14
Cody, Charlie, OF, Jr.	.254	.407	.507	67	17	5	0	4	16	3
Coman, Robbie, C, R-Sr.	.347	.402	.492	199	28	14	0	5	40	3
Comer, Cameron, INF, So.	.105	.227	.105	19	1	0	0	0	1	0
Eikhoff, Nate, INF, So.	.278	.336	.357	126	26	7	0	1	15	1
Harrison, Jalen, OF, Fr.	.143	.400	.571	7	5	0	0	1	1	0
Haseley, Adam, OF, Jr.	.390	.491	.659	223	68	16	1	14	56	10
Knight, Caleb, INF, Jr.	.301	.474	.469	113	32	5	1	4	20	1
McCarthy, Jake, OF, So.	.338	.425	.506	237	57	11	7	5	36	27
Novak, Justin, INF, Jr.	.295	.377	.388	129	24	9	0	1	14	3
Richardson, Cayman, INF, Fr.	.231	.302	.282	39	8	0	1	0	2	0
Simmons, Cameron, OF, So.	.352	.432	.563	213	47	14	2	9	57	9
Smith, Pavin, 1B, Jr.	.342	.427	.570	228	53	11	1	13	77	2
Weber, Andy, INF, So.	.278	.349	.396	187	35	8	4	2	43	4

PITCHER, YEAR	W	L	ERA	G	GS	SV	IP	H	BB	SO
Bettinger, Alec, Sr.	8	0	2.43	21	0	1	63	38	31	71
Casey, Derek, Jr.	5	2	3.79	14	14	0	71	68	21	58
Donahue, Grant, So.	1	0	3.86	12	0	0	14	13	8	13
Doyle, Tommy, Jr.	3	1	1.87	23	0	14	34	28	10	38
Harrington, Chesdin, So.	3	2	2.41	18	2	0	37	21	12	38
Haseley, Adam, Jr.	7	1	3.58	11	11	0	65	58	18	53
Lynch, Daniel, So.	7	5	5.00	14	14	0	77	86	29	45
Murdock, Noah, Fr.	3	1	3.32	11	7	0	38	30	20	21
Nicholson, Bobby, Fr.	0	0	6.28	10	1	0	14	16	10	13
Paisley, Teddy, Fr.	0	0	0.00	1	0	0	0	0	0	0
Roberts, Jake, Sr.	0	0	7.04	15	0	0	15	14	14	21
Shambora, Tyler, Sr.	0	0	10.50	6	0	0	6	10	3	2
Sousa, Bennett, Jr.	3	0	4.09	24	0	0	33	25	15	44
Sperling, Evan, So.	3	3	7.51	15	10	0	38	28	30	44
Tedder, Jackson, Fr.	0	0	27.00	2	0	0	1	3	2	1
Wilson, Riley, Jr.	0	1	5.52	12	0	0	15	16	11	21

22. HOUSTON

Coach: Todd Whitting. **Record:** 42-21

PLAYER, POS., YEAR	AVG	OBP	SLG	AB	R	2B	3B	HR	RBI	SB
Bielamowicz, Tyler, P, Fr.	.267	.388	.384	86	17	3	2	1	16	1
Champion, Wendell, INF, R-Fr.	.258	.415	.452	31	10	1	1	1	4	2
Coldiron, Copper, INF, Jr.	.245	.355	.283	53	6	2	0	0	6	4
Davis, Joe, INF, So.	.299	.368	.451	244	36	9	2	8	46	1
Etzel, Landon, OF, Fr.	.258	.378	.355	31	11	0	0	1	6	0
Fuentes, Rey, INF, So.	.258	.343	.387	31	3	2	1	0	5	0
Grimsley, John, OF, R-So.	.217	.294	.304	46	5	1	0	1	3	3
Hollis, Connor, INF, Jr.	.266	.387	.369	203	39	9	3	2	30	5
Julks, Corey, UTL, Jr.	.335	.426	.572	215	38	12	6	9	45	15
Lockhart, Lael, INF, Fr.	.276	.393	.356	174	36	9	1	1	27	5
Monacy, Jordan, INF, Fr.	.192	.323	.212	52	9	1	0	0	3	0
Padgett, Grayson, UTL, So.	.309	.402	.414	191	41	10	2	2	40	7
Scheiner, Jake, INF, Jr.	.346	.432	.667	243	50	18	3	18	64	8
Slaughter, Nick, C, Fr.	.282	.318	.436	39	2	0	0	2	12	0
Triolo, Jared, INF, Fr.	.271	.360	.372	218	39	12	2	2	17	7
Wong, Connor, INF, Jr.	.287	.379	.494	265	61	13	3	12	36	26

PITCHER, YEAR	W	L	ERA	G	GS	SV	IP	H	BB	SO
Bielamowicz, Tyler, Fr.	0	0	5.06	5	0	0	5	3	3	5
Bond, Nolan, So.	2	1	3.60	13	1	0	25	35	3	15
Cumbie, Trey, So.	10	2	2.04	15	15	0	101	91	15	82
Fletcher, Aaron, R-So.	2	1	2.40	21	0	8	41	38	10	41
Henry, Carter, Fr.	2	1	5.58	14	6	0	40	44	18	40
Hurdsman, Brayson, Fr.	5	2	3.41	18	3	0	34	29	10	30
Kanada, David, Fr.	0	0	54.00	2	0	0	1	5	1	0
King, John, Sr.	8	1	3.11	13	12	0	81	85	10	40
Pulido, Joey, Jr.	2	3	3.98	21	0	2	41	39	15	42
Romero, Seth, Jr.	4	5	3.51	10	7	0	49	46	20	85
Ullom, Mitch, So.	6	3	3.57	16	16	0	96	99	28	51
Villarreal, Fred, Fr.	1	2	4.25	14	3	2	42	44	8	14

23. CLEMSON

Coach: Monte Lee. **Record:** 42-21

PLAYER, POS., YEAR	AVG	OBP	SLG	AB	R	2B	3B	HR	RBI	SB
Beer, Seth, OF, So.	.298	.478	.606	218	51	17	1	16	53	2
Bryant, K.J., OF, R-So.	.211	.318	.316	38	9	2	1	0	2	3
Byrd, Grayson, INF, R-So.	.284	.345	.344	183	22	6	1	1	20	3
Cox, Andrew, 1B, R-Sr.	.280	.347	.401	232	29	10	0	6	35	5
Cromwell, Patrick, INF, Jr.	.203	.313	.290	69	6	0	0	2	5	1
Davidson, Logan, INF, Fr.	.286	.388	.473	241	56	9	0	12	41	10
Greene, Jordan, INF, So.	.263	.332	.308	198	21	9	0	0	18	5
Jackson, Weston, OF, R-Sr.	.248	.346	.489	133	26	4	2	8	31	2
Jolly, Robert, C, Jr.	.280	.371	.393	107	26	9	0	1	15	2
Pinder, Chase, OF, Jr.	.305	.419	.464	223	59	16	0	7	32	13
Renwick, Adam, INF, Jr.	.000	.200	.000	4	1	0	0	0	0	0
Rohlman, Reed, OF, R-Jr.	.361	.448	.542	227	44	21	1	6	34	1
Wharton, Drew, OF, Jr.	.214	.277	.238	42	3	1	0	0	6	1
Wilkie, Kyle, C, Fr.	.235	.371	.294	51	5	1	1	0	5	0
Williams, Chris, INF, Jr.	.261	.320	.572	180	29	14	0	14	51	2

PITCHER, YEAR	W	L	ERA	G	GS	SV	IP	H	BB	SO
Andrews, Patrick, R-Sr.	0	0	4.22	21	0	1	21	27	4	22
Barnes, Charlie, Jr.	5	5	3.20	16	16	0	101	98	22	113
Beasley, Jeremy, Jr.	1	2	5.79	23	0	1	23	18	13	26
Campbell, Paul, Jr.	0	0	5.19	5	2	0	9	10	6	13
Crawford, Brooks, So.	4	0	1.23	17	0	0	22	20	7	22
Eubanks, Alex, R-So.	7	6	4.09	18	16	0	106	104	15	104
Gilliam, Ryey, So.	3	1	2.57	27	0	4	35	29	14	50
Griffith, Owen, Fr.	1	2	1.23	12	0	0	15	8	3	14
Hennessy, Jacob, Fr.	2	1	3.82	26	0	3	31	32	11	37
Jackson, Tyler, R-Sr.	9	1	3.56	19	13	0	83	82	10	68
Krall, Pat, Sr.	8	3	3.50	17	16	1	90	101	25	64
Marr, Travis, Fr.	0	0	0.00	1	0	0	1	0	0	2
Miller, Mitchell, Fr.	0	0	22.09	6	0	0	4	6	6	4
Miller, Ryan, Jr.	1	0	3.09	11	0	1	12	9	2	11
Schnell, Alex, Jr.	1	0	2.51	13	0	0	14	15	5	9
Spiers, Carson, Fr.	0	0	3.00	3	0	0	3	4	0	3

24. TEXAS

Coach: David Pierce. **Record:** 39-24

PLAYER, POS., YEAR	AVG	OBP	SLG	AB	R	2B	3B	HR	RBI	SB
Baker, Joe, INF, Jr.	.250	.250	.250	12	3	0	0	0	1	0
Boswell, Bret, INF, R-Jr.	.273	.384	.444	198	34	13	0	7	33	5
Bucey, Trace, OF, Fr.	.222	.286	.278	18	2	1	0	0	3	0
Cantu, Michael, C, Jr.	.222	.308	.419	117	14	5	0	6	17	0
Clemens, Kacy, INF, Sr.	.305	.414	.532	220	48	14	0	12	49	10
Clemens, Kody, INF, So.	.241	.356	.365	170	21	6	0	5	23	2
Gurwitz, Zane, OF, Sr.	.305	.366	.397	131	18	3	0	3	15	4
Hamilton, David, INF, Fr.	.218	.305	.292	202	30	11	2	0	20	14
Jones, Travis, INF, Jr.	.253	.393	.401	217	40	18	1	4	32	14
Mathis, Patrick, OF, Jr.	.245	.376	.432	139	23	5	0	7	19	6
McCann, Michael, C, R-So.	.268	.346	.321	112	12	4	1	0	16	4
McKenzie, Jake, INF, Jr.	.143	.294	.214	14	1	1	0	0	2	0
Rand, Tyler, OF, So.	.143	.242	.179	28	11	1	0	0	3	5
Reynolds, Ryan, INF, Fr.	.212	.346	.347	193	22	11	0	5	25	1
Shaw, Tate, OF, R-So.	.239	.358	.370	92	17	6	0	2	14	3
Sosa, Andres, INF, Fr.	.100	.250	.100	10	1	0	0	0	0	0
Todd, Austin, OF, Fr.	.276	.359	.359	145	24	7	1	1	19	2

PITCHER, YEAR	W	L	ERA	G	GS	SV	IP	H	BB	SO
Cooper, Morgan, R-Jr.	6	3	2.32	16	15	0	89	66	33	110
Henley, Blair, Fr.	4	5	4.23	17	10	0	62	61	25	47
Johnston, Kyle, Jr.	3	2	3.56	17	12	2	73	63	39	52
Kennedy, Nick, So.	8	2	3.02	19	9	0	54	51	20	59
Kingham, Nolan, So.	10	4	2.84	16	13	0	92	80	24	67
Malmin, Jon, Sr.	1	0	4.30	10	0	0	15	18	7	13
Mayes, Connor, Jr.	1	2	6.00	13	4	0	27	20	16	22
McKenzie, Jake, Jr.	1	1	3.24	10	0	1	17	12	4	11
O'Hara, Beau, So.	0	0	7.11	6	0	1	6	7	4	4
Ridgeway, Beau, So.	2	2	1.89	37	0	12	52	35	14	40
Robinson, Parker Joe, R-So.	0	1	1.93	7	0	0	9	6	6	4
Roliard, Kevin, Fr.	0	0	0.00	5	0	0	5	4	7	3
Schimpf, Tyler, R-So.	0	0	1.56	12	0	0	17	11	7	13
Shugart, Chase, So.	3	2	3.43	29	0	0	42	39	22	30

25. AUBURN

Coach: Butch Thompson. **Record:** 37-26

PLAYER, POS., YEAR	AVG	OBP	SLG	AB	R	2B	3B	HR	RBI	SB
Anthony, Josh, INF, Jr.	.266	.375	.352	233	37	14	0	2	39	7
Davis, Conor, INF, Fr.	.282	.359	.368	163	22	11	0	1	29	1
Decker, Bo, OF, R-Sr.	.259	.337	.358	81	10	5	0	1	14	3
Estes, Jay, INF, Jr.	.276	.346	.379	232	39	19	1	1	29	6
Gillikin, Sam, OF, R-Sr.	.213	.351	.319	47	9	2	0	1	4	0
Haecker, Damon, INF, Sr.	.234	.412	.297	64	7	4	0	0	10	2
Holland, Will, INF, Fr.	.209	.299	.343	134	23	7	1	3	18	4
Ingram, Dylan, INF, R-Jr.	.258	.382	.448	194	36	13	0	8	39	0
Jarvis, Luke, INF, R-Jr.	.276	.313	.443	185	34	10	3	5	27	7
Johnson, Jeremy, OF, R-Fr.	.229	.322	.271	48	9	2	0	0	8	1
Logan, Blake, C, Sr.	.250	.335	.361	144	25	5	1	3	19	0
McGuffin, Bowen, OF, Jr.	.245	.341	.309	110	15	7	0	0	9	2
Robert, Daniel, UTL, Sr.	.290	.402	.429	217	33	11	2	5	42	11
Rojas, Mike, C, So.	.267	.389	.333	15	4	1	0	0	3	0
Shaffer, J.J., OF, Sr.	.000	.143	.000	6	4	0	0	0	0	2
Todd, Jonah, OF, Jr.	.376	.460	.471	242	56	13	5	0	37	9

PITCHER, YEAR	W	L	ERA	G	GS	SV	IP	H	BB	SO
Anderson, Elliott, Fr.	1	0	6.39	14	0	0	13	20	8	9
Camacho, Christian, Fr.	2	3	5.45	12	8	0	36	42	9	26
Coker, Calvin, Jr.	3	3	3.78	31	0	2	52	54	12	41
Daniel, Davis, Fr.	4	3	5.89	17	16	0	70	75	26	61
Davis, Kevin, R-Jr.	0	0	0.00	1	0	0	1	0	0	1
Gahm, Joe, Fr.	0	0	36.00	1	0	0	1	3	1	0
Herndon, Corey, Jr.	1	1	5.45	24	0	2	35	41	23	18
Hillhouse, Trevor, Fr.	0	0	0.00	1	0	0	0	1	1	1
Klobosits, Gabe, Sr.	0	1	5.18	17	4	0	33	45	11	20
Lipscomb, Cole, R-Sr.	4	0	3.44	23	1	6	55	45	13	50
Malczewski, Welby, R-So.	0	0	13.50	3	0	0	2	4	2	2
Mitchell, Andrew, R-Jr.	5	4	5.14	23	4	3	35	30	23	27
Mize, Casey, So.	8	2	2.04	13	12	0	84	66	9	109
Robert, Daniel, Sr.	1	0	2.16	6	0	1	8	4	4	11
Sprinkle, Daniel, So.	0	4	14.66	10	1	0	12	21	9	12
Thompson, Keegan, R-Jr.	7	4	2.41	15	15	0	93	67	17	75
Warner, Grant, Jr.	0	0	54.00	1	0	0	0	2	2	0
Watson, Ryan, Fr.	1	1	5.17	22	2	0	31	39	11	22

CONFERENCE STANDINGS & LEADERS

NCAA regional teams in bold. Conference category leaders in bold.
*Team won conference's automatic regional bid. #Category leader who did not qualify for batting or pitching title.

COLLEGE

AMERICA EAST CONFERENCE

	Conference		Overall	
	W	L	W	L
Binghamton	15	4	30	13
* Maryland-Baltimore County	11	9	23	25
Stony Brook	12	10	26	26
Albany	10	13	26	26
Massachusetts-Lowell	10	13	22	26
Maine	8	12	25	29
Hartford	8	13	20	30

All-Conference Team: C—Hunter Dolshun, Sr., Maryland-Baltimore County. **1B**—David MacKinnon, Sr., Hartford. **2B**—Justin Drpich, Sr., Binghamton. **3B**—Justin Yurchak, So., Binghamton. **SS**—Ben Bengtson, Jr., Hartford. **OF**—Connor Powers, Jr., Albany; Ashton Bardzell, Jr., Hartford; Toby Handley, Sr., Stony Brook. **DH**—Cam Climo, Fr., Massachusetts-Lowell. **UTIL**—Dylan Resk, So., Stony Brook. **SP**—Nick Gallagher, So., Binghamton; Jacob Wloczewski, Jr., Binghamton; Andrew Ryan, Jr., Massachusetts-Lowell; Brian Herrmann, Fr., Stony Brook; **RP**—Dominic Savino, So. Albany; **Player of the Year:** Toby Handley, Stony Brook. **Pitcher of the Year:** Nick Gallagher, Binghamton. **Freshman of the Year:** Christian Torres, Maryland-Baltimore County. **Coach of the Year:** Tim Sinicki, Binghamton.

INDIVIDUAL BATTING LEADERS

(Minimum 140 At-Bats)

	AVG	OBP	SLG	AB	2B	3B	HR	RBI	SB
Ashton Bardzell, Hartford	.343	.457	.619	181	13	5	9	43	9
Toby Handley, Stony Brook	.342	.466	.587	196	17	8	5	34	18
Christopher Bec, Maine	.340	.426	.465	200	20	1	1	26	15
Hunter Dolshun, UMBC	.333	.406	.604	144	12	0	9	34	0
Andrew Casali, UMBC	.332	.367	.481	187	16	3	2	19	12
David MacKinnon, Hartford	.327	.403	.385	208	12	0	0	18	5
Kevin Donati, Albany	.327	.382	.495	196	13	4	4	34	6
C.J. Krowiak, Binghamton	.326	.390	.480	175	14	2	3	18	13
Collin Stack, UMBC	.326	.383	.375	144	5	1	0	21	6
Ben Bengtson, Hartford	.323	.401	.479	167	7	2	5	36	7
Connor Powers, Albany	.323	.398	.484	186	17	2	3	29	0
Justin Yurchak, Binghamton	.320	.474	.442	147	9	0	3	26	0
Jason Agresti, Binghamton	.320	.358	.517	147	14	0	5	27	0
Jeremy Pena, Maine	.319	.371	.491	226	13	4	6	32	9
Colby Maiola, UMass-Lowell	.319	.397	.512	166	10	2	6	35	14
Nick Campana, Hartford	.307	.339	.450	202	11	3	4	23	11
Andruw Gazzola, Stony Brook	.304	.399	.433	171	16	3	0	14	3
Casey Baker, Stony Brook	.302	.404	.439	189	8	3	4	37	15
Jamie Switalski, UMBC	.294	.403	.497	163	17	2	4	27	0
Brandon Janofsky, Stony Brook	.290	.349	.338	145	3	2	0	17	11
Christian Torres, UMBC	.287	.341	.382	157	9	0	2	29	0
Tyler Schwanz, Maine	.284	.377	.457	208	12	3	6	38	4
Evan Harasta, Albany	.280	.373	.317	186	7	0	0	24	0
Eddie Posavec, Binghamton	.275	.372	.349	149	6	1	1	18	4
Steve Passatempo, UMass-Lowell	.271	.359	.463	177	13	0	7	35	1

INDIVIDUAL PITCHING LEADERS

(Minimum 40 Innings Pitched)

	W	L	ERA	G	SV	IP	H	BB	SO
Dominic Savino, Albany	5	3	2.48	27	7	58	50	24	32
Nick Gallagher, Binghamton	8	3	2.67	13	0	71	54	32	58
Jack McClure, Albany	4	1	2.70	11	0	53	46	22	35
Collin Duffley, Umass-Lowell	5	3	2.74	15	0	69	50	30	71
Andrew Ryan, Umass-Lowell	5	3	2.88	13	0	74	56	28	57
Jacob Wloczewski, Binghamton	4	2	2.91	12	0	62	50	17	55
Nick Wegmann, Binghamton	4	5	3.19	13	0	63	59	20	43
Brian Hermann, Stony Brook	4	3	3.27	15	0	81	68	32	54
Justin Courtney, Maine	4	5	3.46	15	0	87	87	33	67
Greg Marino, Stony Brook	2	3	3.68	16	0	60	60	29	58
Jonah Normandeau, Maine	2	6	3.78	13	0	66	72	30	39
Brendan Smith, Albany	1	5	3.92	18	0	56	62	25	41
Nick Kuzia, Umass-Lowell	2	5	4.18	15	0	58	62	28	54
Nick Silva, Maine	2	5	4.36	15	0	64	52	47	62
Michael Austin, UMBC	4	3	4.37	18	1	66	74	22	47
Matt Chanin, UMBC	4	6	4.47	13	0	65	60	24	44
Connor Lewis, Hartford	3	4	4.64	13	0	53	62	23	37
Brian Stepniak, Hartford	3	4	4.75	15	0	59	67	17	40
Bret Clarke, Stony Brook	3	3	4.87	13	0	64	78	40	51
Jacob Christian, UMBC	5	3	5.23	16	1	61	66	22	55
Aaron Pinto, Stony Brook	5	4	5.44	20	3	41	34	18	48
Kevin Kernan, Stony Brook	4	1	5.61	10	0	44	42	21	39
Kenny McLean, Albany	4	2	5.91	13	0	48	53	24	33
Joe Vanderplas, UMBC	3	4	6.22	15	1	41	47	10	28
Sam Turcotte, Stony Brook	1	1	6.30	14	0	43	49	30	40

AMERICAN ATHLETIC CONFERENCE

	Conference		Overall	
	W	L	W	L
Central Florida	15	9	40	22
* Houston	15	9	42	21
Connecticut	14	10	33	25
South Florida	14	10	42	19
Tulane	13	11	27	31
Cincinnati	10	14	28	30
Memphis	8	16	30	29
East Carolina	7	17	32	28

All-Conference Team: C—Travis Watkins, Sr., East Carolina. **1B**—Hunter Williams, Sr., Tulane. **2B**—Charlie Yorgen, Sr., East Carolina. **3B**—Eric Tyler, Sr., East Carolina. **SS**—Kevin Merrell, Jr., South Florida. **OF**—Eli Putnam, Sr., Central Florida; Corey Julks, Jr., Houston; Chris Carrier, Sr, Memphis. **DH**—Luke Borders, Sr., South Florida. **UTIL**—Jake Scheiner, Jr., Houston. **SP**—Robby Howell, Sr., Central Florida; Tim Cate, So., Connecticut; Mason Feole, Fr., Connecticut; Trey Cumbie, So., Houston. **RP**—Bryce Tucker, So., Central Florida. **Players of the Year:** Jake Scheiner, Houston; Hunter Williams, Tulane. **Pitchers of the Year:** Robby Howell, Central Florida; Trey Cumbie, Houston. **Freshmen of the Year:** Rylan Thomas, Central Florida; Mason Feole, Connecticut. **Coach of the Year:** Greg Lovelady, Central Florida.

INDIVIDUAL BATTING LEADERS

(Minimum 140 At-Bats)

	AVG	OBP	SLG	AB	2B	3B	HR	RBI	SB
Kevin Merrell, South Florida	.384	.464	.569	216	11	4	7	38	19
Hunter Williams, Tulane	.360	.408	.582	239	18	1	11	40	5
R.J. Thomspon, Cincinnati	.350	.426	.493	223	18	1	4	28	3
Jake Scheiner, Houston	.346	.432	.667	243	18	3	18	64	8
Duke Stunkel Jr., South Florida	.344	.430	.456	195	16	0	2	24	4
Eric Tyler, East Carolina	.343	.401	.488	242	17	0	6	38	6
Travis Watkins, East Carolina	.340	.379	.526	247	14	1	10	49	5
Charlie Yorgen, East Carolina	.339	.438	.483	230	14	2	5	38	8
Corey Julks, Houston	.335	.426	.572	215	12	6	9	45	15
Luke Borders, South Florida	.333	.426	.500	228	11	3	7	49	5
Chris Carrier, Memphis	.330	.438	.641	206	16	0	16	50	10
Willy Yahn, Connecticut	.317	.376	.434	189	12	2	2	26	6
Eli Putnam, Central Flordia	.315	.380	.496	248	17	2	8	39	16
Spencer Brickhouse, E Carolina	.310	.385	.513	197	8	1	10	28	2
Grayson Padgett, Houston	.309	.402	.414	191	10	2	2	40	7
Tyler Webb, Memphis	.305	.389	.474	213	16	1	6	25	3
Kyle Marsh, Central Florida	.304	.375	.504	230	20	4	6	51	1
Rylan Thomas, Central Florida	.303	.359	.530	234	11	0	14	53	9
Anthony Prato, Connecticut	.303	.376	.386	228	10	3	1	33	14
Lex Kaplan, Tulane	.302	.424	.542	192	17	1	9	27	3
Joe Davis, Houston	.299	.368	.451	244	9	2	8	46	1
Grant Witherspoon, Tulane	.299	.373	.420	224	10	1	5	36	10
Coco Montes, South Florida	.293	.358	.394	246	13	0	4	30	2
Trent Turner, Memphis	.292	.365	.460	226	12	1	8	44	7
Luke Hamblin, Central Florida	.292	.412	.389	226	13	3	1	35	19

INDIVIDUAL PITCHING LEADERS

(Minimum 40 Innings Pitched)

	W	L	ERA	G	SV	IP	H	BB	SO
Trey Cumbie, Houston	10	2	2.04	15	0	101	91	15	82
Joe Cavallaro, South Florida	5	3	2.28	30	5	59	48	19	77
Aaron Fletcher, Houston	2	1	2.40	21	8	41	38	10	41
Peter Strzelecki, South Florida	3	4	2.42	14	0	67	55	27	62
Chris Williams, Central Florida	5	4	2.65	23	0	78	61	20	48
Phoenix Sanders, South Florida	6	2	2.78	16	0	97	89	25	109
Jason Bahr, Central Florida	0	2	2.97	24	1	61	42	15	98
John King, Houston	8	1	3.11	13	0	81	85	10	40
Shane McClanahan, South Fla.	4	2	3.20	15	0	76	48	36	104
Jake Agnos, East Carolina	3	3	3.22	16	0	64	58	32	64
Joseph Sheridan, Central Fla.	10	4	3.25	17	0	72	74	24	64
Tim Cate, Connecticut	4	3	3.33	12	0	76	78	31	102
D.J. Roberts, South Florida	3	0	3.35	11	0	46	51	12	32
Mason Feole, Connecticut	7	4	3.38	15	0	83	78	30	75
Chris Holba, East Carolina	4	2	3.38	14	1	43	46	8	47
David Orndorff, Cincinnati	5	4	3.41	21	7	63	66	15	40
Robby Howell, Central Florida	10	1	3.50	16	0	103	94	42	94
Seth Romero, Houston	4	5	3.51	10	0	49	46	20	85
Mitch Ullom, Houston	6	3	3.57	16	0	96	99	28	51
William Montgomerie, Conn.	6	3	3.73	15	0	89	88	40	116
Jonathan Bowlan, Memphis	4	5	3.75	18	1	84	72	30	78
Chase Solesky, Tulane	5	3	3.84	25	0	68	73	26	40
J.P. France, Tulane	5	5	3.84	15	0	96	100	30	73
olton Hathcock, Memphis	3	4	3.94	26	11	48	55	26	62
Tyler Smith, East Carolina	2	0	3.95	27	0	43	44	13	26

ATLANTIC COAST CONFERENCE

	Conference		Overall	
Atlantic Division	W	L	W	L
Louisville	23	6	53	12
Wake Forest	19	11	43	20
Clemson	17	13	42	21
North Carolina State	16	14	36	25
* Florida State	14	14	46	23
Boston College	11	19	25	28
Notre Dame	10	20	26	32

	Conference		Overall	
Coastal Division	W	L	W	L
North Carolina	23	7	49	14
Virginia	18	12	43	16
Miami	16	13	31	27
Duke	12	18	30	28
Georgia Tech	11	19	27	28
Virginia Tech	9	21	23	32
Pittsburgh	9	21	23	30

All-Conference Team: C—Ben Breazeale, Sr., Wake Forest. **1B**—Pavin Smith, Jr. Virginia. **2B**—Wade Bailey, Jr., Georgia Tech. **3B**—Drew Ellis, Jr., Louisville. **SS**—Logan Warmoth, Jr., North Carolina. **OF**—Brian Miller, Jr., North Carolina; Adam Haseley, Jr., Virginia; Stuart Fairchild, Jr., Wake Forest; Reed Rohlman, Jr., Clemson. **UTIL**—Brendan McKay, Jr., Louisville. **SP**—Tyler Holton, So., Florida State; Brendan McKay, Jr., Louisville; J.B. Bukauskas, Jr., North Carolina. **RP**—Lincoln Henzman, Jr., Louisville; Josh Hiatt, Fr., North Carolina. **Player of the Year:** Brendan McKay, Louisville. **Pitcher of the Year:** J.B. Bukauskas, North Carolina. **Freshman of the Year:** Ashton McGee, North Carolina. **Coach of the Year:** Dan McDonnell, Louisville.

INDIVIDUAL BATTING LEADERS

(Minimum 140 At-Bats)

	AVG	OBP	SLG	AB	2B	3B	HR	RBI	SB
Adam Haseley, Virginia	.390	.491	.659	223	16	1	14	56	10
Reed Rohlman, Clemson	.361	.448	.542	227	21	1	6	34	1
Stuart Fairchild, Wake Forest	.360	.439	.636	261	19	1	17	67	21
Jack Owens, Virginia Tech	.358	.424	.504	240	16	2	5	28	9
Drew Ellis, Louisville	.355	.448	.701	231	18	1	20	61	6
Jonathan Pryor, Wake Forest	.354	.447	.479	263	21	0	4	35	5
Cameron Simons, Virgina	.352	.432	.563	213	14	2	9	57	9
Robbie Coman, Virgina	.347	.402	.492	199	14	0	5	40	3
Wade Bailey, Georgia Tech	.347	.420	.538	236	21	3	6	38	6
Jake Mueller, Wake Forest	.345	.413	.430	258	16	0	2	34	6
Brian Miller, North Carolina	.343	.422	.502	271	16	3	7	49	24
Pavin Smith, Virgina	.342	.427	.570	228	11	1	13	77	2
Tom Stoffel, Virgina Tech	.342	.410	.563	222	21	2	8	49	0
Brendan McKay, Louisville	.341	.457	.659	223	15	1	18	57	2
Jack McCarthy, Virginia	.338	.425	.506	237	11	7	5	36	27
Austin White, Georgia Tech	.338	.410	.434	198	14	1	1	25	1
Trevor Craport, Georgia Tech	.336	.399	.502	235	20	2	5	30	8
Logan Warmoth, NC	.336	.404	.554	271	19	5	10	49	18
Brad Debo, NC State	.335	.387	.493	215	18	2	4	43	0
Ben Breazeale, Wake Forest	.333	.399	.540	237	16	0	11	51	0
Jake Alu, Boston College	.331	.384	.386	166	9	0	0	23	12
Matt Vierling, Notre Dame	.330	.398	.549	224	20	4	7	42	7
Johnny Aiello, Wake Forest	.328	.417	.643	244	17	0	20	53	4
Ashton McGee, North Carolina	.327	.417	.484	223	10	2	7	46	1
Jimmy Herron, Duke	.326	.412	.474	230	17	1	5	39	17

INDIVIDUAL PITCHING LEADERS

(Minimum 40 Innings Pitched)

	W	L	ERA	G	SV	IP	H	BB	SO
Sam Bordner, Louisville	2	0	0.41	23	3	44	16	10	39
Josh Hiatt, North Carolina	4	2	1.90	32	13	52	31	20	64
Andrew Cabezas, Miami	5	3	2.14	35	3	63	52	23	80
Drew Carlton, Florida State	5	4	2.17	36	7	62	65	15	58
Adam Wolf, Louisville	6	0	2.18	24	1	41	30	14	35
Griffin Roberts, Wake Forest	2	5	2.19	29	8	53	30	32	80
Jeb Bargfeldt, Miami	7	3	2.28	15	0	87	62	29	61
Tyler Holton, Florida State	10	3	2.34	18	0	119	77	31	144
Alec Bettinger, Virginia	8	0	2.43	21	1	63	38	31	71
J.B. Bukauskas, North Carolina	9	1	2.53	15	0	93	62	37	116
Brendan McKay, Louisville	11	3	2.56	17	0	109	77	35	146
Tyler Baum, North Carolina	7	0	2.57	16	0	63	47	27	47
Wil Zirzow, Florida State	3	1	2.58	20	0	45	31	19	52
Sean Guenther, Notre Dame	2	6	2.64	24	7	58	58	19	69
Brett Daniels, North Carolina	5	0	2.68	27	0	40	34	20	33
Johnny Piedmonte, NC State	7	0	2.77	15	0	62	49	21	42
Charlie Vorsheck, Notre Dame	5	0	2.88	17	0	41	28	14	31
Austin Bergner, North Carolina	4	2	3.00	27	1	48	35	25	45
Nick Bennett, Louisville	5	1	3.18	15	0	65	59	13	61
Sam Mersing, Pittsburgh	3	2	3.18	26	3	51	53	9	42
Charlie Barnes, Clemson	5	5	3.20	16	0	101	98	22	113
Ryan Day, Duke	4	3	3.30	13	0	74	64	17	43
	W	**L**	**ERA**	**G**	**SV**	**IP**	**H**	**BB**	**SO**
Zac Ryan, Georgia Tech	3	5	3.33	27	5	46	40	22	42
Luca Dalatri, North Carolina	7	3	3.34	15	0	97	90	19	85
Gregory Veliz, Miami	6	4	3.39	12	0	61	36	33	66

ATLANTIC SUN CONFERENCE

	Conference		Overall	
	W	L	W	L
Jacksonville	16	5	36	24
Stetson	15	6	27	29
* Florida Gulf Coast	13	8	42	18
North Florida	12	9	33	24
Kennesaw State	10	11	25	32
Lipscomb	9	12	28	28
South Carolina-Upstate	7	14	24	31
NJIT	2	19	9	40

All-Conference Team: C—Charlie Carpenter, Jr., South Carolina-Upstate. **1B**—Austin Upshaw, Jr., Kennesaw State. **2B**—Grant Williams, Jr., Kennesaw State. **3B**—Alex Merritt, Sr., North Florida. **SS**—Julio Gonzalez, Jr., Florida Gulf Coast. **OF**—Taylor Allum, Jr., Kennesaw State; Yahir Gurrola, Jr., North Florida; Nathan Koslowski, Sr., Jacksonville. **DH**—Nick Rivera, Sr., Florida Gulf Coast. **SP**—Logan Gilbert, So., Stetson; Kutter Crawford, Jr., Florida Gulf Coast; Frank German, So., North Florida. **RP**—Matthew Naylor, Sr., North Florida. **Player of the Year:** Nick Rivera, Florida Gulf Coast. **Pitcher of the Year:** Logan Gilbert, Stetson. **Freshman of the Year:** Richie Garcia, Florida Gulf Coast. **Coach of the Year:** Chris Hayes, Jacksonville.

INDIVIDUAL BATTING LEADERS

(Minimum 140 At-Bats)

	AVG	OBP	SLG	AB	2B	3B	HR	RBI	SB
Michael Anastasia, NJIT	.373	.463	.507	150	14	3	0	29	7
Charlie Carpenter, USC Upstate	.357	.441	.592	196	13	0	11	45	0
Patrick Ervin, North Florida	.354	.439	.392	189	7	0	0	24	0
Alex Merritt, North Florida	.343	.400	.452	230	17	1	2	43	3
Julio Gonzalez, Fla Gulf Coast	.337	.421	.492	246	15	4	5	39	1
Austin Upshaw, Kennesaw St	.333	.383	.518	222	17	0	8	41	1
Nathan Koslowski, Jacksonville	.328	.405	.447	253	18	0	4	46	5
Yahir Gurrola, North Florida	.320	.373	.541	244	19	4	9	51	10
Taylor Allum, Kennesaw State	.319	.435	.590	188	6	0	15	46	2
Jacob Koos, Stetson	.317	.402	.352	230	6	1	0	22	23
Chris Thibideau, North Florida	.317	.377	.507	221	18	0	8	37	14
Chris Berry, North Florida	.310	.425	.398	171	6	0	3	33	1
Ruben Someillan, Jacksonville	.310	.357	.348	155	6	0	0	15	3
Grant Williams, Kennesaw St	.305	.375	.359	223	7	1	1	29	6
Zeke Dodson, Lipscomb	.304	.403	.430	207	13	2	3	37	4
Nick Rivera, Florida Gulf Coast	.304	.452	.585	217	8	1	17	55	0
Mike Spooner, Stetson	.303	.380	.412	211	8	0	5	43	8
J.J. Shimko, USC Upstate	.300	.417	.435	207	16	3	2	35	7
Angel Camacho, Jacksonville	.299	.350	.433	194	8	0	6	34	0
Jack Gonzalez, Stetson	.298	.371	.453	181	8	1	6	28	2
Cade Sorrellis, Lipscomb	.298	.426	.369	198	5	0	3	42	12
Gage Morey, Florida Gulf Coast	.296	.422	.360	189	4	1	2	23	11
Devon Ortiz, USC Upstate	.296	.364	.366	213	11	2	0	23	10
Griffin Helms, Kennesaw State	.296	.383	.453	159	9	2	4	27	7
Justin Etts, NJIT	.288	.340	.390	177	9	0	3	31	4

INDIVIDUAL PITCHING LEADERS

(Minimum 40 Innings Pitched)

	W	L	ERA	G	SV	IP	H	BB	SO
Kutter Crawford, Fa Gulf Coast	7	1	1.71	15	1	84	59	31	99
Logan Gilbert, Stetson	10	0	2.02	15	0	89	65	26	107
Denton Norman, Lipscomb	4	4	2.02	25	7	49	35	15	45
Matt Meyer, Jacksonville	4	2	2.03	21	3	40	28	17	43
Kenton Hering, Fla Gulf Coast	7	3	2.04	29	6	57	49	19	75
Frank German, North Florida	8	1	2.43	14	0	81	75	25	76
Tony Dibrell, Kennesaw State	7	4	2.45	14	0	96	77	39	103
Casey Kulina, Jacksonville	6	1	2.46	15	0	88	74	34	78
Jack Perkins, Stetson	7	5	2.71	17	1	100	89	30	108
Cooper Bradford, North Florida	1	4	2.79	19	1	52	57	21	53
Brooks Wilson, Stetson	4	7	3.01	18	0	108	87	38	127
Austin Drury, North Florida	6	2	3.03	12	0	74	63	30	61
Michael Baumann, Jacksonville	6	3	3.09	14	0	87	70	35	97
Jeffery Passantino, Lipscomb	4	3	3.09	15	0	96	94	9	95
Mason Ward, Kennesaw State	4	2	3.26	9	0	50	42	14	40
Josh Dye, Florida Gulf Coast	7	4	3.32	17	0	87	88	12	71
Garrett Anderson, Fla Gulf Coast	7	1	3.43	16	3	76	81	21	61
Chris Gau, Jacksonville	2	4	3.96	13	0	75	83	16	69
Brady Puckett, Lipscomb	8	6	4.10	15	0	101	106	23	70
Gabe Friese, Kennesaw State	3	2	4.33	18	3	54	53	25	44
Conner Campbell, USC Upstate	3	5	4.34	23	2	58	64	16	51
Mario Leon, Florida Gulf Coast	4	2	4.58	14	0	57	67	19	64
Peyton Gray, Florida Gulf Coast	5	3	4.60	19	9	63	64	25	60
Bryan Hathaway, USC Upstate	3	3	4.68	27	0	58	68	29	32
Kevin Hickey, USC Upstate	4	7	4.73	17	13	70	79	25	48

ATLANTIC 10 CONFERENCE

	Conference W	Conference L	Overall W	Overall L
Virginia Commonwealth	19	5	35	22
Rhode Island	17	6	31	22
St. Bonaventure	15	8	26	22
George Washington	14	10	31	27
Saint Louis	12	10	35	22
* Davidson	13	11	35	24
George Mason	13	11	26	33
Saint Joseph's	12	12	21	25
Fordham	11	12	27	24
Dayton	9	15	20	35
Massachusetts	8	16	15	32
Richmond	6	17	17	36
La Salle	4	20	10	41

All-Conference Team: C—Deon Stafford, Jr., Saint Joseph's. **1B**—Darian Carpenter, Sr., Virginia Commonwealth. **2B**—Chris Hess, Jr., Rhode Island. **3B**—Matt O'Neil, Sr., Rhode Island. **SS**—Cole Peterson, Jr., St. Bonaventure. **OF**—Will Robertson, Sr., Davidson; Joey Bartosic, Sr., George Washington; Mike Corin, Sr., Rhode Island; Logan Farrar, Sr., Virginia Commonwealth. **DH**—Trevor Kelly, Jr., George Mason. **SP**—Aaron Phillips, Jr., St. Bonaventure; Jimmy Murphy, Gr., Fordham. **RP**—Sam Donko, Sr., Virginia Commonwealth. **Player of the Year:** Logan Farrar, Virginia Commonwealth. **Pitcher of the Year:** Aaron Phillips, St. Bonaventure. **Freshman of the Year:** Paul Witt, Virginia Commonwealth. **Coach of the Year:** Larry Sudbrook, St. Bonaventure.

INDIVIDUAL BATTING LEADERS

(Minimum 140 At-Bats)

	AVG	OBP	SLG	AB	2B	3B	HR	RBI	SB
Logan Farrar, VCU	.369	.455	.551	225	17	0	8	32	4
Paul Witt, VCU	.364	.433	.430	214	11	0	1	36	2
Vinny Capra, Richmond	.355	.420	.488	211	14	1	4	19	5
Bobby Campbell, GW	.355	.423	.532	220	15	0	8	43	2
Jordan Powell, Rhode Island	.352	.403	.427	213	10	0	2	27	6
Chris Hess, Rhode Island	.347	.414	.581	222	22	3	8	48	12
Robbie Metz, GW	.339	.379	.424	224	10	3	1	32	13
Will Robertson, Davidson	.336	.405	.644	247	18	2	18	46	4
Joey Bartosic, GW	.333	.395	.405	237	14	0	1	26	24
Nate Fassnacht, GW	.332	.407	.453	214	11	0	5	29	9
Daniel Brumbaugh, Richmond	.332	.402	.485	202	11	4	4	37	7
Cole Peterson, St. Bonaventure	.330	.405	.476	191	16	3	2	17	24
Matt Maul, St. Joseph's	.328	.375	.373	177	5	0	1	12	10
Logan Driscoll, George Mason	.323	.413	.479	167	10	2	4	38	5
Eric Jones, Davidson	.316	.392	.460	237	7	0	9	36	2
James Morisano, Saint Louis	.316	.379	.578	187	11	1	12	37	4
Alex Gransback, VCU	.314	.376	.399	153	7	0	2	28	5
Luke Stampfl, Fordham	.313	.375	.513	150	11	2	5	22	2
Trent Leimkuehler, Saint Louis	.313	.342	.463	227	20	1	4	37	3
Brain Fortier, Davidson	.313	.377	.580	243	18	1	15	53	0
Alec Acosta, Davidson	.312	.382	.418	237	10	0	5	30	0
Matt O'Neil, Rhode Island	.310	.356	.575	200	10	2	13	51	7
Mark Donadio, Fordham	.309	.395	.446	175	11	2	3	28	7
Austin Constantini, La Salle	.304	.380	.357	171	5	2	0	13	6
Nick Reeser, Saint Louis	.303	.400	.373	185	7	0	2	26	2

INDIVIDUAL PITCHING LEADERS

(Minimum 40 Innings Pitched)

	W	L	ERA	G	SV	IP	H	BB	SO
Will Kobos, GW	4	1	1.99	18	3	41	27	15	42
Blaise Whitman, Rhode Island	4	1	2.13	27	1	42	27	15	42
Vitaly Jangols, Rhode Island	7	1	2.23	15	2	61	52	12	25
Jimmy Murphy, Fordham	6	7	2.59	13	0	94	76	27	85
Miller Hogan, Saint Louis	8	3	2.70	15	0	90	95	23	78
Tyler Zombro, George Mason	6	5	2.78	15	0	104	108	16	76
Sam Donko, VCU	3	3	2.81	25	14	51	47	9	57
Brooks Vial, VCU	9	4	2.82	16	0	93	92	33	84
Durin O'Linger, Davidson	9	3	2.97	19	1	109	118	29	90
Tim Brennan, St. Joseph's	4	4	2.97	12	0	76	71	11	60
Aaron Phillips, St. Bonaventure	9	2	3.04	15	0	101	77	45	90
Eddie Muhl, GW	2	3	3.04	24	10	47	44	25	22
Elliott Raimo, GW	8	3	3.20	15	0	90	70	25	73
Layne Looney, Richmond	3	6	3.21	15	0	62	56	50	65
Josh Garner, Saint Louis	1	1	3.22	16	1	45	35	26	43
Tyler Swiggart, GW	2	2	3.31	16	0	35	34	9	18
Lucas Rollins, Saint Joseph's	2	1	3.33	10	1	46	45	5	25
Kevin Piersol, Dayton	2	4	3.33	21	2	54	53	30	50
Brady Renner, GW	8	5	3.42	15	0	84	89	21	38
Sean Thompson, VCU	7	4	3.46	15	1	83	72	31	77
Justin Lasko, UMass	3	6	3.69	13	0	83	94	20	62
Luke Reilly, La Salle	2	6	3.75	13	0	82	84	25	77
Brooks Knapek, UMass	2	3	3.86	8	0	42	47	24	35
Reiss Knehr, Fordham	3	3	3.91	13	0	74	63	38	86
Benjamin Dum, VCU	3	1	3.92	23	0	44	45	11	27

BIG EAST CONFERENCE

	Conference W	Conference L	Overall W	Overall L
Creighton	11	4	24	25
St. John's	13	5	42	13
* Xavier	10	6	34	27
Seton Hall	10	8	29	24
Butler	7	10	31	20
Villanova	5	13	14	33
Georgetown	4	14	27	28

All-Conference Team: C—Troy Dixon, Sr, St. John's. **1B**—John Valente, Jr., St. John's. **2B**—Josh Shaw, So., St. John's. **3B**—Rylan Bannon, Jr., Xavier. **SS**—Jesse Berardi, Jr., St. John's. **OF**—Tyler Houston, Jr., Butler; Anthony Brocato, Jr., St. John's; Michael Donadio, Sr., St. John's. **DH**—Jake Kuzbel, Sr., Georgetown. **SP**—Rollie Lacy, Jr., Creighton; Sean Mooney, Fr., St. John's; Zach Prendergast, Sr., Seton Hall; Hunter Schryver, Sr., Villanova, Sr.; Zac Lowther, Jr., Xavier. **RP**—Matt Kent, So., Xavier. **Player of the Year:** Rylan Bannon, Xavier. **Pitcher of the Year:** Sean Mooney, St. John's. **Freshman of the Year:** Sean Mooney, St. John's. **Coaching Staff of the Year:** Ed Blankmeyer, St. John's.

INDIVIDUAL BATTING LEADERS

(Minimum 140 At-Bats)

	AVG	OBP	SLG	AB	2B	3B	HR	RBI	SB
Troy Dixon, St. John's	.394	.473	.525	160	12	0	3	35	0
John Valente, St. John's	.375	.437	.464	224	10	2	2	35	9
Michael Donadio, St. John's	.374	.473	.547	214	15	5	4	38	10
Jesse Berardi, St. John's	.356	.456	.462	225	10	1	4	47	12
Zach Racusin, Georgetown	.342	.409	.409	225	8	2	1	34	10
Conor Grammes, Xavier	.341	.381	.500	232	14	1	7	41	2
Rylan Bannon, Xavier	.339	.449	.633	221	14	3	15	50	17
Jake Kuzbel, Georgetown	.335	.394	.517	209	13	5	5	43	3
Michael Derenzi, Georgetown	.330	.397	.457	221	7	3	5	44	12
Michael Hartnagel, Butler	.328	.405	.464	192	16	2	2	28	3
Matt Toke, Seton Hall	.321	.411	.378	156	5	2	0	25	2
Jamie Galazin, St. John's	.319	.378	.446	204	10	5	2	34	12
Gui Gingras, St. John's	.318	.399	.503	151	9	2	5	37	0
Anthony Brocato, St. John's	.317	.400	.550	180	16	1	8	47	1
Jordan Lucio, Georgetown	.310	.397	.339	171	5	0	0	26	1
Robbie Knightes, St. John's	.301	.337	.370	173	8	2	0	28	0
Mike Alescio, Seton Hall	.298	.372	.416	161	14	1	1	20	12
Gehrig Parker, Butler	.294	.381	.494	170	13	3	5	33	4
Jake Bernstein, Georgetown	.290	.377	.332	217	6	0	1	23	5
Josh Shaw, St. John's	.288	.350	.384	219	13	1	2	33	2
Tyler Houston, Butler	.287	.379	.540	202	13	1	12	38	18
Will LaRue, Xavier	.285	.394	.370	200	6	1	3	27	26
Sammy Stevens, Georgetown	.283	.397	.462	145	14	0	4	36	0
Todd Czinege, Villanova	.283	.353	.402	184	7	3	3	25	5
Isaac Collins, Creighton	.282	.380	.344	163	2	1	2	11	11

INDIVIDUAL PITCHING LEADERS

(Minimum 40 Innings Pitched)

	W	L	ERA	G	SV	IP	H	BB	SO
Ryan Testani, Seton Hall	2	2	1.47	27	4	43	30	7	23
Sean Mooney, St. John's	8	2	1.71	16	0	100	70	16	88
Matt Kent, Xavier	5	2	1.74	23	2	47	46	11	34
Ethan Decaster, Creighton	4	2	1.77	24	5	46	37	12	36
Jeff Schank, Butler	4	2	2.01	10	0	67	50	23	74
Joe LaSorsa, St. John's	7	1	2.34	21	1	50	42	14	39
Hunter Schryver, Villanova	4	6	2.44	12	0	74	56	37	91
Joe Kelly, St. John's	3	1	2.45	25	2	48	42	10	26
Kevin Magee, St. John's	4	1	2.45	10	0	40	32	10	40
Rollie Lacy, Creighton	5	2	2.54	15	0	89	86	18	83
Garrett Christman, Butler	3	2	2.60	11	1	55	38	12	54
Zac Lowther, Xavier	5	5	2.92	15	0	83	48	33	123
Zach Prendergast, Seton Hall	7	4	3.07	16	0	91	84	16	69
Connor Mitchell, Butler	3	3	3.36	10	0	59	42	26	46
Cullen Dana, Seton Hall	5	3	3.40	15	0	79	79	32	81
Garrett Schilling, Xavier	6	4	3.57	15	0	86	79	27	52
Chris Morris, Seton Hall	3	2	3.57	10	0	40	28	37	44
Ryan Doty, Villanova	2	7	3.82	17	1	61	77	20	39
Jeff Albrecht, Creighton	5	6	3.93	16	0	76	72	26	63
Kevin Superko, Georgetown	6	3	4.15	13	0	78	78	19	43
Nick Leonard, Georgetown	5	3	4.19	19	0	62	77	20	39
Ryan Pepiot, Butler	4	4	4.39	13	0	66	53	41	79
Brad Kirschner, Xavier	4	3	4.44	28	0	51	62	25	39
Mike Sgaramella, Villanova	0	1	4.50	18	0	40	56	20	22
Keith Rogalla, Creighton	2	5	4.54	12	0	71	61	35	70

BIG SOUTH CONFERENCE

	Conference W	Conference L	Overall W	Overall L
Winthrop	17	7	34	24
Liberty	16	8	32	23
Presbyterian	15	9	32	29
High Point	13	11	30	23
* Radford	11	13	27	32
UNC Asheville	11	13	25	32
Gardner-Webb	11	13	25	30
Campbell	10	14	25	32
Charleston Southern	9	15	22	29
Longwood	7	17	19	34

All-Conference Team: C—T.J. Richardson, Jr., Presbyterian. **INF**—Sammy Taormina, Sr., Liberty; Collin Thacker, Sr., Gardner-Webb; Mitch Spires, Jr., Winthrop; Jason Miller, So., Charleston Southern. **OF**—D.J. Artis, So., Liberty; Danny Sullivan, Sr., Gardner-Webb; Anthony Paulsen, R-Sr., Winthrop. **UTIL**—Danny Hrbek, Sr., Radford. **DH**—Cole Hallum, Sr., Campbell. **SP**—Zack Ridgely, Jr., Radford. Colten Rendon, Fr., Winthrop; Nate Pawelczyk, So., Winthrop. **RP**—Kyle Zurak, Sr., Radford. **Player of the Year:** D.J. Artis, Liberty. **Pitcher of the Year:** Zack Ridgely, Radford. **Freshman of the Year:** Colten Rendon, Winthrop. **Coach of the Year:** Tom Riginos, Winthrop.

INDIVIDUAL BATTING LEADERS

(Minimum 140 At-Bats)

	AVG	OBP	SLG	AB	2B	3B	HR	RBI	SB
D.J. Artis, Liberty	.359	.532	.552	181	13	2	6	45	23
Collin Thacker, Gardner-Webb	.357	.406	.545	224	15	0	9	46	2
Anthony Paulsen, Winthrop	.344	.452	.493	221	14	2	5	25	1
Mitch Spires, Winthrop	.342	.402	.462	225	14	2	3	36	5
Jason Miller, Charleston Southern	.340	.397	.438	203	10	2	2	30	12
Matthew Barefoot, Campbell	.335	.400	.537	227	22	0	8	49	7
T.J. Richardson, Presbyterian	.335	.402	.452	155	12	0	2	25	2
Blake Schunk, High Point	.326	.399	.438	144	13	0	1	22	5
Danny Sullivan, Gardner-Webb	.317	.417	.623	199	10	0	17	44	1
Drew Butler, Campbell	.317	.426	.398	221	8	2	2	33	38
Glen Casaceli, Presbyterian	.316	.416	.362	177	3	1	1	19	8
Jeff Hahs, Campbell	.313	.422	.552	192	14	1	10	44	10
Nick Wise, Presbyterian	.313	.335	.476	166	9	0	6	24	3
Sammy Taormina, Liberty	.311	.411	.534	219	15	2	10	55	1
Spencer Horwitz, Radford	.311	.384	.481	206	11	0	8	34	7
Kyle Butler, Radford	.308	.344	.392	227	13	0	2	33	8
Michael Osinski, Longwood	.308	.360	.443	201	14	2	3	36	13
Nick Guimbarda, Presbyterian	.305	.391	.463	203	16	2	4	31	8
Brett Auckland, Presbyterian	.303	.388	.439	198	7	1	6	38	4
Trey McDyre, Liberty	.301	.400	.380	166	5	1	2	40	1
Antwaun Tucker, Longwood	.298	.365	.449	198	7	7	3	23	15
Babe Thomas, Winthrop	.297	.393	.495	212	10	1	10	47	4
Zach Minnick, Campbell	.294	.389	.463	160	10	1	5	25	1
Hunter Lipscomb, Winthrop	.292	.363	.402	219	4	1	6	61	4
Jake Barbee, Liberty	.290	.406	.447	217	15	2	5	50	3

INDIVIDUAL PITCHING LEADERS

(Minimum 40 Innings Pitched)

	W	L	ERA	G	SV	IP	H	BB	SO
Nate Pawelczyk, Winthrop	7	2	2.23	16	1	77	53	32	69
Kyle Zurak, Radford	4	4	2.40	25	9	60	51	22	73
Matt Hodges, High Point	5	1	2.74	24	6	49	34	20	54
Shane Quarterley, Liberty	3	2	2.79	21	1	48	45	11	41
Zack Ridgely, Radford	7	5	2.84	15	0	95	75	12	85
Daniel Johnson, Charleston So.	1	1	2.85	18	1	41	38	10	59
Evan Mitchell, Liberty	6	2	2.93	15	0	74	69	38	49
Drew Daczkowski, High Point	6	4	3.29	14	0	77	65	31	70
Brian Kehner, Presbyterian	4	3	3.33	15	0	95	96	14	70
Eric Miles, Presbyterian	8	1	3.36	23	2	70	76	13	48
Steven Farkas, Longwood	2	3	3.38	11	0	51	52	17	58
Hayden Deal, Presbyterian	4	4	3.45	14	0	78	70	34	78
Bradley Hallman, Gardner-Webb	4	6	3.49	15	0	98	93	29	53

Name	W	L	ERA	G	SV	IP	H	BB	SO
Wes Noble, Campbell	4	2	3.52	22	0	61	47	35	61
Riley Arnone, Winthrop	3	2	3.53	29	4	51	55	19	30
Cody Wager, Longwood	4	5	3.54	15	0	76	77	21	91
Zach Peek, Winthrop	5	1	3.70	24	0	56	52	21	41
Spencer Orr, UNC Asheville	2	5	3.72	13	0	75	80	28	71
Andrew Gottfried, High Point	4	3	3.86	12	0	56	44	21	48
Reece Green, Winthrop	5	4	3.89	15	0	90	98	26	69
Harry Thomas, Campbell	2	2	3.93	23	2	55	54	28	44
Joe Johnson, High Point	6	2	3.94	41	2	59	56	24	49
Ryan Sande, Radford	0	4	3.97	15	0	45	52	20	31
Austin Gerber, Radford	4	4	3.98	24	1	54	53	9	33
Garret Price, Liberty	5	1	3.99	21	1	59	55	27	57

BIG TEN CONFERENCE

	Conference W	Conference L	Overall W	Overall L
Nebraska	16	7	35	22
Michigan	16	8	42	17
Minnesota	15	8	36	20
* Iowa	15	9	39	22
Maryland	15	9	37	22
Indiana	14	9	34	24
Northwestern	13	11	26	29
Purdue	12	12	29	27
Michigan State	10	14	29	23
Illinois	9	15	23	28
Ohio State	8	16	22	34
Rutgers	7	16	19	34
Penn State	4	20	18	37

All-Conference Team: C—Cole McDevitt, So., Minnesota. **1B**—Jake Adams, Jr., Iowa. **2B**—Ako Thomas, So., Michigan. **3B**—Drew Lugbauer, Jr., Michigan. **SS**—Michael Brdar, Sr., Michigan. **OF**—Jack Yalowitz, So., Illinois; Marty Costes, Jr., Maryland; Joe Hoscheit, Sr., Northwestern. **DH**—Scott Schreiber, Jr., Nebraska. **UTIL**—Jake Meyers, Jr., Nebraska. **SP**—Brian Shaffer, Jr., Maryland; Oliver Jaskie, Jr., Michigan; Lucas Gilbreath, Jr., Minnesota. **RP**—Jackson Lamb, Jr., Michigan. **Player of the Year:** Jake Adams, Iowa. **Pitcher of the Year:** Brian Shaffer, Maryland. **Freshman of the Year:** Tyler Blohm, Maryland. **Coach of the Year:** Darin Erstad, Nebraska.

INDIVIDUAL BATTING LEADERS

(Minimum 140 At-Bats)

	AVG	OBP	SLG	AB	2B	3B	HR	RBI	SB
Ako Thomas, Michigan	.363	.472	.406	160	7	0	0	21	22
Luke Pettersen, Minnesota	.356	.414	.393	191	7	0	0	28	1
Bryce Kelly, Michigan State	.353	.416	.436	156	7	3	0	21	13
Joe Hoscheit, Northwestern	.349	.432	.527	186	14	2	5	42	3
Dominic Canzone, Ohio State	.343	.390	.458	166	4	3	3	36	13
Jake Adams, Iowa	.335	.417	.747	245	14	0	29	72	5
Jack Yalowitz, Illinois	.335	.409	.590	200	9	3	12	44	10
Jordan Kozicky, Minnesota	.335	.432	.491	161	11	1	4	28	3
Micah Coffey, Minnesota	.333	.391	.475	198	15	2	3	44	3
Scott Schreiber, Nebraska	.330	.376	.494	233	15	1	7	51	0
Michael Massey, Illinois	.330	.360	.483	209	12	1	6	36	4
Brandon Hughes, Michigan St	.330	.382	.473	203	12	1	5	35	30
Brandon Gum, Maryland	.330	.449	.445	191	8	1	4	33	12
Mike Carter, Rutgers	.329	.397	.470	219	14	1	5	33	9
Mason McCoy, Iowa	.328	.394	.474	253	18	2	5	34	7
Skyler Hunter, Purdue	.323	.355	.388	201	9	2	0	34	8
Mart Costes, Maryland	.322	.424	.528	233	9	3	11	44	5
Zach Jancarski, Maryland	.320	.432	.440	225	14	2	3	26	20
Toby Hanson, Minnesota	.316	.348	.463	231	14	4	4	56	3
Angelo Altavilla, Nebraska	.316	.407	.406	212	14	1	1	39	2
Michael Brdar, Michigan	.315	.375	.416	238	11	2	3	37	19
Tony Butler, Indiana	.314	.418	.454	207	15	1	4	30	7
Tre' Gantt, Ohio State	.314	.426	.426	204	13	2	2	18	14
A.J. Lee, Maryland	.314	.389	.486	185	8	0	8	35	15
Terrin Vavra, Minnesota	.313	.368	.424	198	8	4	2	19	7

INDIVIDUAL PITCHING LEADERS

(Minimum 40 Innings Pitched)

	W	L	ERA	G	SV	IP	H	BB	SO
Ross Learnard, Purdue	6	0	0.58	27	4	46	30	10	37
Walter Borkovich, Michigan St	4	3	2.01	27	0	58	68	29	83
Alex Troop, Michigan State	8	3	2.47	14	0	84	68	29	83
Josh Martsching, Iowa	5	1	2.54	29	8	46	35	10	46
Robbie Palkert, Nebraska	0	0	2.61	24	2	41	35	12	39
Lucas Gilbreath, Minnesota	5	2	2.66	14	0	81	52	32	92
Brian Shaffer, Maryland	7	4	2.66	16	0	108	88	18	109
Cal Krueger, Indiana	5	2	2.82	22	1	61	59	21	37
Sam Lawrence, Northwestern	4	3	2.93	22	2	46	48	11	24
Seth Kinker, Ohio State	3	1	2.95	24	7	58	56	32	48
Ryan Erickson, Iowa	4	3	3.00	16	1	75	78	24	58
Ryan Selmer, Maryland	2	2	3.05	27	8	41	44	12	26
Cooper Wetherbee, Northwestern	4	3	3.17	20	1	71	66	18	32
Reggie Meyer, Minnesota	5	1	3.18	19	2	57	40	9	57
Zach Daniels, Iowa	7	3	3.22	24	1	50	55	25	55
Josh Davis, Northwestern	4	2	3.29	12	0	52	49	12	37
Jake Meyers, Nebraska	8	2	3.42	14	0	84	86	39	88
Sal Biasi, Penn State	5	5	3.48	14	0	72	47	25	87
Nick Gallagher, Iowa	8	2	3.48	15	0	96	96	29	49
Derek Burkamper, Nebraska	6	6	3.53	15	0	71	79	32	67
Tyler Blohm, Maryland	8	6	3.63	15	0	72	62	31	119
Jake Lowery, Michigan State	2	4	3.71	22	0	51	43	16	70
Chad Luensmann, Nebraska	3	4	3.74	27	8	43	39	21	33
Oliver Jaskie, Michigan	8	3	3.77	16	0	93	83	31	119
Hank Christie, Northwestern	5	3	3.82	14	0	78	85	18	49

BIG 12 CONFERENCE

	Conference W	Conference L	Overall W	Overall L
Texas Tech	16	8	45	17
Texas Christian	16	8	50	18
Oklahoma	12	11	35	24
West Virginia	12	12	36	26
Baylor	12	12	34	23
Texas	11	12	39	24
Kansas	11	13	30	28
* Oklahoma State	8	14	30	27
Kansas State	8	16	29	26

All-Conference Team: C—Evan Skoug, Jr., Texas Christian. **INF**—Aaron Dodson, Sr., Baylor; Garrett Benge, Jr., Oklahoma State; Cam Warner, Sr., Texas Christian; Orlando Garcia, Jr., Texas Tech; Hunter Hargrove, Sr., Texas Tech. **OF**—Steele Walker, So., Oklahoma; Garrett McCain, Jr., Oklahoma State; Austen Wade, Jr., Texas Christian; Cody Farhat, So., Texas Tech. **DH**—Brylie Ware, So., Oklahoma. **UTIL**—Braden Zarbnisky, So., West Virginia. **P**—Troy Montemayor, Jr., Baylor; Stephen Villines, Sr., Kansas; Jared Janczak, So., Texas Christian; Morgan Cooper, Jr., Texas; Nolan Kingham, So., Texas; Steven Gingery, So., Texas Tech. **Players of the Year:** Evan Skoug, Texas Christian; Hunter Hargrove, Texas Tech. **Pitcher of the Year:** Steven Gingery, Texas Tech. **Newcomers of the Year:** Montana Parsons, Baylor; Brylie Ware, Oklahoma. **Coach of the Year:** Steve Rodriguez, Baylor.

INDIVIDUAL BATTING LEADERS

(Minimum 140 At-Bats)

	AVG	OBP	SLG	AB	2B	3B	HR	RBI	SB
Garrett McCain, Oklahoma St	.388	.491	.549	224	14	5	4	43	19
Will Brennan, Kansas State	.350	.453	.388	183	7	0	0	27	8
Aaron Dodson, Baylor	.344	.403	.587	189	9	2	11	42	0
Hunter Hargrove, Texas Tech	.343	.423	.535	245	26	3	5	51	7
Grant Little, Texas Tech	.335	.405	.476	206	17	3	2	34	6
Steele Walker, Oklahoma	.333	.413	.541	222	16	3	8	51	2
Austen Wade, TCU	.332	.441	.486	247	17	3	5	40	10
Renae Martinez, Oklahoma	.323	.399	.510	192	15	0	7	37	3
Ryan Long, Texas Tech	.322	.432	.475	183	11	1	5	26	3
Cameron Thompson, Kansas St	.318	.409	.418	220	8	4	2	33	12
Ivan Gonzalez, West Virginia	.317	.359	.444	205	9	1	5	29	4
Luken Baker, TCU	.317	.454	.528	161	8	1	8	41	2
Kyle Davis, West Virginia	.316	.405	.526	234	13	3	10	44	1
Matt McLaughlin, Kansas	.314	.420	.469	207	19	2	3	39	6
Shea Langliers, Baylor	.313	.388	.540	211	14	2	10	38	1
Matt Menard, Baylor	.313	.380	.404	208	10	0	3	28	4
Darius Hill, West Virginia	.307	.355	.422	244	14	1	4	46	5
Michael Berglund, Texas Tech	.307	.369	.391	179	7	1	2	27	2

	AVG	OBP	SLG	AB	2B	3B	HR	RBI	SB
Josh Jung, Texas Tech	.306	.395	.453	245	14	2	6	43	2
Richard Cunningham, Baylor	.306	.365	.518	170	15	3	5	29	2
Kacy Clemens, Texas	.305	.414	.532	220	14	0	12	49	10
Tamer Garnder, Texas Tech	.305	.395	.485	200	17	2	5	33	6
Orlando Garcia, Texas Tech	.305	.386	.550	220	9	3	13	62	9
Garrett Benge, Oklahoma St	.304	.437	.533	214	11	4	10	53	5
Cole Austin, West Virginia	.302	.345	.459	242	13	2	7	44	9

INDIVIDUAL PITCHING LEADERS

(Minimum 40 Innings Pitched)

	W	L	ERA	G	SV	IP	H	BB	SO
Steven Gingery, Texas Tech	10	1	1.58	15	0	91	60	29	107
Beau Ridgeway, Texas	2	2	1.89	37	12	52	35	14	40
J.B. Olson, Oklahoma	5	1	1.99	31	8	45	45	13	46
Sean Wymer, TCU	6	4	2.10	30	2	56	35	10	66
Jared Janczak, TCU	9	2	2.31	15	0	93	60	24	102
Morgan Cooper, Texas	6	3	2.32	16	0	89	66	33	110
Stephen Villines, Kansas	1	2	2.70	32	14	43	42	5	54
Blake Weiman, Kansas	5	1	2.80	30	0	45	45	5	55
Nolan Kingham, Texas	10	4	2.84	16	0	92	80	24	67
Michael Grove, West Virginia	3	1	2.87	9	0	47	29	15	61
Kyle Hill, Baylor	3	3	2.98	30	0	42	36	32	54
Nick Kennedy, Texas	8	2	3.02	19	0	54	51	20	59
Montana Parsons, Baylor	5	4	3.06	15	0	88	88	38	71
Carson Teel, Oklahoma State	5	4	3.06	28	3	65	53	20	77
Alek Manoah, West Virginia	1	1	3.07	19	2	56	43	33	45
Davis Martin, Texas Tech	4	2	3.07	9	0	44	43	10	37
Erikson Lanning, Texas Tech	3	1	3.12	17	0	40	40	17	18
Chase Shugart, Texas	3	2	3.43	29	3	42	39	22	30
Devon Perez, Oklahoma	6	2	3.50	14	0	64	66	11	81
Taylor Turski, Kansas	3	4	3.51	13	0	74	59	32	68
Jake Irvin, Oklahoma	6	3	3.53	13	0	71	64	29	75
Kyle Johnston, Texas	3	2	3.56	17	2	73	63	39	52
Zack Leban, Kansas	3	3	3.57	28	1	40	39	14	37
Parker Rigler, Kansas State	4	4	3.67	14	0	76	69	44	51
Ryan Shetter, Texas Tech	4	1	3.71	15	0	70	66	27	74

BIG WEST CONFERENCE

	Conference W	Conference L	Overall W	Overall L
* Long Beach State	20	4	42	20
Cal Poly	16	8	28	28
Cal State Fullerton	15	9	39	24
Cal State Northridge	12	12	26	29
Hawaii	10	14	28	23
UC Davis	10	14	21	30
UC Irvine	9	15	23	33
UC Santa Barbara	8	16	24	32
UC Riverside	8	16	22	32

All-Conference Team: C—David Banuelos, Jr., Long Beach State. **1B**—Austin Bush, Jr., UC Santa Barbara. **2B**—Sahid Valenzuela, Fr., Cal State Fullerton. **3B**—Ramsey Romano, Jr., Long Beach State. **SS**—Kyle Marinconz, So., Cal Poly. **OF**—Alex McKenna, So., Cal Poly; Scott Hurst, Jr., Cal State Fullerton; Mark Contreras, Sr., UC Riverside. **DH**—Keston Hiura, Jr., UC Irvine. **UTIL**—Dillon Persinger, Jr., Cal State Fullerton. **SP**—Spencer Howard, So., Cal Poly; Connor Seabold, Jr., Cal State Fullerton; Darren McCaughan, Jr., Long Beach State. **RP**—Josh Advocate, Sr., Long Beach State. **CP**—Brett Conine, So., Cal State Fullerton. **Player of the Year:** Keston Hiura, UC Irvine. **Pitcher of the Year:** Darren McCaughan, Long Beach State. **Freshman of the Year:** Dylan Thomas, Hawaii. **Coach of the Year:** Troy Buckley, Long Beach State.

INDIVIDUAL BATTING LEADERS

(Minimum 140 At-Bats)

	AVG	OBP	SLG	AB	2B	3B	HR	RBI	SB
Keston Hiura, UC Irvine	.442	.567	.693	199	24	1	8	42	9
Mark Contreras, UC Riverside	.366	.427	.558	172	11	8	2	22	7
Alex McKenna, Cal Poly	.356	.420	.483	236	11	2	5	31	13
Scott Hurst, Cal State Fullerton	.328	.419	.575	247	15	5	12	40	7
Michael Sanderson, Cal Poly	.323	.384	.434	189	10	1	3	26	1
Mikey Duarte, UC Irvine	.320	.395	.448	194	17	1	2	25	3
Sahid Valenzuela, Cal St Fullerton	.314	.366	.377	223	5	3	1	24	3
Ryan Anderson, UC Davis	.313	.372	.483	201	14	1	6	39	7
Ramsey Romano, Long Beach St	.313	.340	.382	249	11	0	2	39	5
Ryan Hooper, UC Davis	.310	.392	.476	168	8	1	6	29	9
Colton Burns, UC Santa Barbara	.308	.422	.389	185	6	0	3	16	5
Jarren Duran, Long Beach St	.308	.375	.393	224	9	5	0	27	19
Bradlee Beesley, Cal Poly	.305	.376	.399	203	13	3	0	14	4
Lucas Tancas, Long Beach State	.304	.371	.491	230	12	2	9	37	8
Austin Bush, UC Santa Barbara	.303	.372	.654	211	14	0	20	60	0
Timmy Richards, Cal St Fullerton	.302	.383	.478	182	10	2	6	31	0
Nolan Bumstead, Cal St Northridge	.302	.388	.422	192	11	0	4	25	1
Dylan Vchulek, Hawaii	.302	.381	.351	202	8	1	0	23	12
Kenny Corey, UC Santa Barbara	.299	.381	.395	147	8	3	0	20	4
Alvaro Rubalcaba, Cal St Northridge	.299	.425	.437	174	5	2	5	27	16
Ignacio Diaz, UC Davis	.297	.373	.348	155	5	0	1	20	1
Colby Schultz, UC Riverside	.296	.372	.408	223	15	2	2	19	3
Cameron Olson, UC Davis	.296	.380	.516	159	7	2	8	24	4
Tommy Jew, UC Santa Barbara	.295	.352	.447	190	9	4	4	30	9
Josh Rojas, Hawaii	.294	.404	.541	170	15	6	5	25	5

INDIVIDUAL PITCHING LEADERS

(Minimum 40 Innings Pitched)

	W	L	ERA	G	SV	IP	H	BB	SO
Brett Conine, Cal St Fullerton	0	1	1.39	31	15	45	35	6	43
Spencer Howard, Cal Poly	8	1	1.95	17	1	88	72	23	97
Dave Smith, Long Beach State	9	2	2.07	17	0	91	98	11	41
Trent Shelton, Cal Poly	1	1	2.30	28	0	43	35	8	42
Darren McCaughan, Long Beach St	9	2	2.50	17	0	122	82	20	104
John Gavin, Cal State Fullerton	8	2	2.67	18	0	104	89	34	90
Connor O'Neil, Cal St Northridge	5	4	2.70	27	7	50	35	27	63
Michael Clark, Cal Poly	5	0	2.77	30	11	49	34	17	36
Slater Lee, Cal Poly	4	2	2.86	20	2	44	39	15	54
Blake Workman, Cal St Fullerton	6	3	2.89	27	1	62	64	18	54
Erich Uelmen, Cal Poly	4	8	2.93	15	0	98	95	23	100
Connor Seabold, Cal St Fullerton	11	5	2.96	18	0	128	124	23	122
Dominic DeMiero, Hawaii	4	5	3.23	13	0	75	80	11	41
Brendan Hornug, Hawaii	6	6	3.25	15	0	108	114	18	89
Alex Fagalde, UC Riverside	7	4	3.39	15	0	80	70	27	63
Louis Raymond, UC Irvine	5	5	3.54	15	0	94	114	20	54
Justin Mullins, UC Davis	4	3	3.55	13	0	84	78	29	38
Neil Uskali, Hawaii	6	4	3.59	15	0	83	92	16	44
Tei Vanderford, Cal St Northridge	5	4	3.77	14	0	98	94	33	69
Matt Blais, UC Davis	1	3	3.86	17	1	58	60	26	32
Ben Brecht, UC Santa Barbara	4	2	3.99	14	0	59	73	13	39
Samuel Myers, Cal St Northridge	6	6	4.08	15	0	90	72	27	85
John Sheaks, Long Beach State	8	4	4.09	17	0	88	84	28	55
Jackson Rees, Hawaii	5	2	4.11	14	0	81	87	34	39
Andrew Weston, Cal St Northridge	5	4	4.16	13	0	89	103	23	51

COLONIAL ATHLETIC ASSOCIATION

	Conference W	Conference L	Overall W	Overall L
Northeastern	16	7	29	25
UNC Wilmington	16	8	30	29
William & Mary	15	8	32	25
* Delaware	15	9	34	23
Charleston	13	11	28	31
Elon	12	12	24	32
James Madison	7	17	24	27
Hofstra	7	17	14	37
Towson	6	18	20	34

All-Conference Team: C—Ryan Jeffers, So., UNC Wilmington. **1B**—Nick Patten, So., Delaware. **2B**—Cullen Large, Jr., William & Mary. **3B**—Tommy Richter, Jr., College of Charleston. **SS**—Ryne Ogren, So., Elon. **3B**—Tommy Richter, Jr., College of Charleston. **OF**—Jordan Glover, Sr., Delaware; Casey Golden, Sr., UNC Wilmington; Logan McRae, So., College of Charleston. **UTIL**—Teddy Cillis, Jr., Hofstra. **DH**—Nick Feight, Jr., UNC Wilmington. **SP**—Kyle Brnovich, Fr., Elon; Alex Royalty, So., UNC Wilmington. **RP**—Burk Fitzpatrick, Sr., Delaware. **Player of the Year:** Casey Golden, UNC Wilmington. **Pitcher of the Year:** Alex Royalty, UNC Wilmington. **Freshman of the Year:** Kyle Brnovich, Elon. **Coach of the Year:** Mike Glavine, Northeastern.

INDIVIDUAL BATTING LEADERS

(Minimum 140 At-Bats)

	AVG	OBP	SLG	AB	2B	3B	HR	RBI	SB
Tommy Richter, Charleston	.363	.441	.441	204	9	2	1	26	5
Ryne Ogren, Elon	.350	.411	.498	223	21	0	4	33	3
Jeremy Ake, Delawre	.347	.427	.460	202	12	1	3	44	1
Jordan Glover, Delaware	.339	.425	.575	186	8	3	10	49	24
Richie Palacios, Towson	.338	.417	.502	213	14	3	5	29	19
Doug Trimble, Delaware	.338	.411	.495	222	15	1	6	49	11
Cullen Large, William & Mary	.338	.419	.507	226	16	2	6	39	5
Brandon Raquet, William & Mary	.337	.433	.506	178	13	4	3	25	6
Adam Sisk, James Madison	.337	.449	.560	193	10	0	11	41	14
Calvin Scott, Delaware	.332	.436	.473	184	13	2	3	41	1
Kyle McPherson, James Madison	.330	.404	.520	200	12	1	8	27	6
Ryan Jeffers, UNC Wilmington	.328	.422	.604	192	19	2	10	32	0
Brian Mayer, Delaware	.324	.386	.648	142	11	1	11	39	0
Brian Mims, UNC Wilmington	.320	.397	.502	231	14	2	8	37	6
Ryder Miconi, William & Mary	.318	.433	.531	192	14	0	9	45	3
Steven Foster, Hofstra	.317	.368	.465	202	17	2	3	20	8
Cam Hanley, Northeastern	.316	.381	.469	209	7	5	5	43	2
Nick Tierno, Delaware	.314	.410	.416	185	5	4	2	22	2
Nick Patten, Delaware	.312	.446	.580	205	9	2	14	54	8
Logan McRae, Charleston	.310	.412	.602	216	12	0	7	63	0
Casey Golden, UNC Wilmington	.310	.402	.646	226	13	0	21	42	6
Ryan Hall, William & Mary	.308	.383	.481	214	17	1	6	41	3
Kevin Mohollen, Delaware	.307	.429	.454	218	13	5	3	31	8
Vito Friscia, Hofstra	.305	.404	.532	154	9	1	8	33	2
Kyle Jackson, Elon	.304	.374	.551	214	17	0	12	50	9

INDIVIDUAL PITCHING LEADERS

(Minimum 40 Innings Pitched)

	W	L	ERA	G	SV	IP	H	BB	SO
Ron Marinaccio, Delaware	4	3	2.09	22	3	65	45	22	68
Nate Borges, Northeastern	5	3	2.93	15	0	58	52	26	51
Kyle Brnovich, Elon	6	5	3.10	15	0	90	67	41	103
Alex Royalty, UNC Wilmington	9	2	3.20	15	0	98	86	25	106
Jordan Barrett, Elon	4	5	3.22	17	0	78	58	32	100
Mike Fitzgerald, Northeastern	4	1	3.29	16	4	66	56	26	60
Nathan Ocker, Charleston	4	1	3.29	21	4	55	44	7	63
Carter Love, Charleston	3	4	3.39	26	2	74	66	14	72
Brandon Walter, Delaware	4	5	3.42	9	0	55	53	16	61
Burk Fitzpatrick, Delaware	2	1	3.47	25	6	49	46	20	48
Brian Christian, Northeastern	7	3	3.59	16	0	83	71	35	85
Evan Sisk, Charleston	5	2	3.72	15	0	75	75	26	47
David Marriggi, Towson	4	6	4.18	17	3	47	52	24	44
Austin Easter, UNC Wilmington	1	1	4.20	28	3	45	36	27	48
James Meeker, Delaware	6	2	4.25	16	2	42	43	16	30
Matt Colon, James Madison	1	1	4.28	27	0	40	39	17	33
Daniel Powers, William & Mary	6	4	4.31	16	1	77	79	12	60
Ryan Conroy, Elon	4	6	4.40	14	0	74	81	25	62
Nick Spadafino, Delaware	7	3	4.46	16	0	77	71	31	49
Josh Silvestri, James Madison	3	4	4.47	13	0	56	63	34	46
Bailey Ober, Charleston	7	2	4.50	10	0	56	56	11	73
Bodie Sheehan, William & Mary	6	5	4.58	15	0	90	81	20	78
Nick Raquet, William & Mary	2	2	4.66	16	0	77	79	45	95
Colton Harlow, James Madison	3	3	4.66	14	0	75	85	22	70
Kevin Milley, Delaware	4	3	4.71	14	0	63	77	40	51

CONFERENCE USA

	Conference		Overall	
	W	L	W	L
Southern Mississippi	25	5	50	16
Old Dominion	19	11	37	21
Charlotte	18	12	34	24
Florida Atlantic	18	12	35	21
Louisiana Tech	17	13	36	20
* Rice	16	14	33	21
Florida International	15	15	31	27
Texas-San Antonio	15	15	29	28
Marshall	12	18	25	29
Middle Tennessee State	10	20	24	31
Alabama-Birmingham	9	21	24	31
Western Kentucky	6	24	16	39

All-Conference Team: C—Brent Diaz, Sr., Louisiana Tech. **INF—**Dylan Burdeaux, Sr., Southern Mississippi; Tyler Frank, Sr., Florida Atlantic; Zach Rutherford, Jr., Old Dominion; Jared Young, Jr., Old Dominion. **OF—**T.J. Nichting, Sr., Charlotte; Raphael Gladu, Sr., Louisiana Tech; Sam Finfer, Sr., Marshall. **DH—**Aaron Aucker, Jr., Middle Tennessee. **UTIL—**Taylor Braley, Jr., Southern Mississippi. **SP—**Adam Bainbridge, Sr., Old Dominion; Nate Harris, Sr., Louisiana Tech; Colton Laws, So., Charlotte; Kirk McCarty, Sr., Southern Mississippi. **RP—**Nick Sandlin, So., Southern Mississippi; Colt Smith, Jr., Southern Mississippi. **Player of the Year:** Dylan Burdeaux, Southern Mississippi. **Pitcher of the Year:** Nate Harris, Louisiana Tech. **Freshman of the Year:** Matt Wallner, Southern Mississippi. **Coach of the Year:** Scott Berry, Southern Mississippi.

INDIVIDUAL BATTING LEADERS

(Minimum 140 At-Bats)

	AVG	OBP	SLG	AB	2B	3B	HR	RBI	SB
Raphael Gladu, Louisiana Tech	.378	.439	.579	233	19	2	8	55	3
T.J. Nichting, Charlotte	.367	.409	.518	251	15	4	5	51	17
Jared Young, Old Dominion	.367	.441	.580	226	19	4	7	34	9
Ryan Kemp, Middle Tenn.	.366	.419	.622	164	16	1	8	29	9
Dominic DiCaprio, Rice	.366	.438	.508	238	16	0	6	49	2
Aaron Aucker, Middle Tenn.	.359	.448	.641	156	10	2	10	41	0
Dane Myers, Rice	.358	.425	.545	246	12	5	8	43	13
Riley Delgado, Middle Tenn.	.352	.427	.464	233	15	1	3	33	0
Jordan Washam, Louisana Tech	.350	.416	.574	223	19	2	9	44	10
Brett Netzer, Charlotte	.347	.426	.508	242	16	4	5	45	5
Matt Wallner, Southern Miss.	.346	.469	.671	243	15	2	20	67	4
Sean Ullrich, Lousiana Tech	.344	.455	.490	192	20	1	2	32	6
Shane Hanon, Marshall	.342	.392	.426	190	10	0	2	33	9
Kyle Battle, Old Dominion	.341	.419	.425	167	8	0	2	36	6
Brad Jarreau, Middle Tenn.	.340	.371	.488	162	4	1	6	31	5
Sam Finfer, Marshall	.338	.410	.692	201	17	0	18	51	8
Mason Irby, Southern Miss.	.338	.438	.446	269	20	3	1	40	6
Kevin Markham, UTSA	.338	.411	.553	228	21	8	4	37	5
Zach Jarrett, Charlotte	.337	.391	.549	246	8	1	14	47	8
Tyler Frank, Florida Atlantic	.336	.448	.540	235	15	0	11	43	6
Zach Rutherford, Old Dominion	.332	.397	.472	235	25	1	2	56	7
Austin Langham, Fla Atlantic	.332	.443	.462	208	10	1	5	39	2
Brent Diaz, Lousiana Tech	.332	.433	.581	217	19	4	9	48	3
Ben Brookover, UTSA	.331	.418	.423	163	7	1	2	32	3
Brewer Hicklen, UAB	.328	.422	.586	186	12	6	8	31	17

INDIVIDUAL PITCHING LEADERS

(Minimum 40 Innings Pitched)

	W	L	ERA	G	SV	IP	H	BB	SO
Colton Laws, Charlotte	7	2	1.87	15	0	96	76	13	94
Nate Harris, Lousiana Tech	9	1	2.31	22	8	94	79	11	94
Nick Sandlin, Southern Miss.	10	2	2.38	29	8	57	41	29	80
Karl Craigie, UTSA	7	1	2.66	26	1	47	41	32	39
Zach Flanagan, Charlotte	3	3	2.85	10	0	54	65	7	47
Matt Brooks, Charlotte	7	4	3.14	23	2	63	52	12	58
Colt Smith, Southern Miss.	6	2	3.36	21	0	67	69	17	43
Taylor Braley, Southern Miss.	7	2	3.40	14	0	82	81	22	78
John Wilson, Old Dominion	6	1	3.41	12	0	58	45	14	35
Tyler Giovanoni, UTSA	4	3	3.41	14	1	69	53	25	55
Kirk McCarty, Southern Miss.	9	2	3.52	17	0	100	94	22	103
Adam Bainbridge, Old Dominion	7	4	3.53	15	0	97	96	19	75
Thomas Johns, UAB	3	3	3.59	26	0	68	72	37	49
Tyler Myrick, Fla International	6	2	3.73	15	0	72	71	28	57
Glenn Otto, Rice	7	4	3.77	26	8	60	50	29	81
Cameron Linick, Lousiana Tech	3	2	3.88	20	0	58	60	23	41
Dane Myers, Rice	1	5	3.98	16	1	54	49	31	37
Steven Dressler, UTSA	4	4	3.99	17	0	68	70	27	47
Kent Hasler, Lousiana Tech	5	3	3.99	18	4	56	52	17	54
Zach Esquivel, Rice	6	5	4.00	23	1	83	87	46	63
Garrett Whitlock, UAB	3	6	4.03	17	2	60	57	24	44
Kevin Elder, Western Kentucky	3	2	4.07	20	2	55	57	15	43
Matt Canterino, Rice	5	5	4.13	17	0	96	67	49	111
Sam Sinnen, Old Dominion	3	4	4.21	15	1	94	102	31	48
Hayden Roberts, Southern Miss.	5	2	4.22	21	7	79	78	27	89

HORIZON LEAGUE

	Conference W	Conference L	Overall W	Overall L
*Illinois-Chicago	22	8	39	17
Wright State	21	9	38	21
Northern Kentucky	17	13	25	33
Valparaiso	13	15	24	29
Oakland	11	19	17	40
Milwaukee	10	18	22	32
Youngstown State	9	21	15	40

All-Conference Team: C—Rob Calabrese, Jr., Illinois-Chicago. **1B**—Trey Ganns, Jr., Northern Kentucky. **2B**—Matt Morrow, Jr., Wright State. **3B**—Ben Chally, Jr., Milwaukee. **SS**—Cody Bohanek, Sr., Illinois-Chicago. **OF**—T.J. Alas, Sr., Northern Kentucky; Jake Richmond, Jr., Northern Kentucky; Tyler Pagano, Oakland. **DH**—Chad Roberts, Northern Kentucky. **SP**—Jay Peters, Sr., Milwaukee; Jake Dahlbergh, Sr., Illinois-Chicago; Ryan Weiss, Fr., Wright State. **RP**—Alex Padilla, So., Illinois-Chicago. **Player of the Year:** Rob Calabrese, Illinois-Chicago. **Pitcher of the Year:** Jake Dahlberg, Illinois-Chicago. **Freshman of the Year:** Ryan Weiss, Wright State. **Coach of the Year:** Mike Dee, Illinois-Chicago.

INDIVIDUAL BATTING LEADERS

(Minimum 140 At-Bats)

	AVG	OBP	SLG	AB	2B	3B	HR	RBI	SB
Daulton Varsho, Milwaukee	.362	.490	.643	199	11	6	11	39	10
Rob Calabrese, Illinois-Chicago	.353	.425	.583	204	23	0	8	53	3
Trey Ganns, Northern Kentucky	.348	.449	.633	221	19	1	14	57	0
Zach Sterry, Oakland	.346	.441	.643	185	14	1	13	44	7
Tyler Pagano, Oakland	.333	.376	.554	231	18	0	11	49	5
Matt Morrow, Wright State	.333	.427	.487	228	14	3	5	38	13
T.J. Alas, Northern Kentucky	.331	.404	.587	242	20	0	14	48	2
Chris Kelly, Milwaukee	.327	.383	.426	202	9	4	1	26	12
Ben Chally, Milwaukee	.327	.394	.421	171	10	3	0	23	4
Emerson Misch, Oakland	.319	.358	.456	204	17	1	3	31	6
Sam Shaikin, Valparaiso	.317	.412	.471	189	13	2	4	29	1
David Cronin, Illinois-Chicago	.313	.429	.435	214	4	2	6	32	14
Dominic Mercurio, N Kentucky	.308	.381	.459	185	8	1	6	31	1
Giovanni Garbella, Valparaiso	.302	.366	.488	172	17	0	5	32	5
Will Haueter, N Kentucky	.301	.355	.362	196	9	0	1	27	1
Seth Gray, Wright State	.300	.350	.416	233	13	4	2	37	19
Cody Bohanek, Illinois-Chicago	.297	.411	.448	212	11	0	7	47	8
Jake Richmond, N Kentucky	.296	.407	.474	230	12	1	9	29	8
Jake Hanson, Valparaiso	.291	.355	.374	206	14	0	1	30	2
Brandon Gibis, Illinois-Chicago	.291	.348	.352	165	5	1	1	24	3
Chad Jacob, Valparaiso	.291	.380	.426	141	8	1	3	18	2
James Stea, Valparaiso	.290	.420	.475	200	9	2	8	32	21
Gabe Snyder, Wright State	.289	.379	.570	228	17	4	13	49	12
Nico Padovan, Youngstown St	.284	.371	.343	204	9	0	1	24	5
Lorenzo Arcuri, Youngstown St	.284	.344	.433	194	8	3	5	24	13

INDIVIDUAL PITCHING LEADERS

(Minimum 40 Innings Pitched)

	W	L	ERA	G	SV	IP	H	BB	SO
Ryan Weiss, Wright State	8	1	2.13	15	1	89	78	20	80
Jake Dahlberg, Illinois-Chicago	10	2	2.17	16	0	104	58	35	78
Jacob Key, Illinois-Chicago	6	0	2.44	12	0	52	45	23	31
Danny Sexton, Wright State	8	2	2.78	14	1	91	83	23	69
Zane Collins, Wright State	7	5	2.83	15	0	92	75	35	77
Jon Tieman, Valparaiso	4	1	2.93	20	7	46	46	15	51
Reid Birlinghair, Illinois-Chicago	7	5	3.10	15	0	93	74	25	81
Jack Andersen, Illinois-Chicago	5	2	3.30	13	0	71	69	18	51
Jay Peters, Milwaukee	8	2	3.32	15	0	103	95	27	82
Austin Schulfer, Milwaukee	6	5	3.72	13	0	82	78	28	70
Jeremy Randolph, Wright State	4	2	3.76	17	1	53	52	16	35
Jeremy Quinlan, Youngstown St	3	0	3.95	9	0	41	38	12	24
Cameron Ross, N Kentucky	6	2	4.02	36	5	63	61	29	47
Nate Schweers, Oakland	3	2	4.47	22	3	50	53	19	37
Ellis Foreman, Valparaiso	2	2	4.47	20	0	46	60	7	26
Jake Lee, Oakland	2	6	4.71	15	0	86	97	28	86
Joe King, Youngstown State	3	8	4.72	29	6	61	81	29	26
Brandon Parr, Milwaukee	2	6	4.91	17	3	44	51	19	32
Jordan Menfee, N Kentucky	1	3	5.18	22	0	49	56	35	31
Mario Losi, Valparaiso	2	4	5.44	15	0	91	104	28	48
Wes Gordon, Valparaiso	2	4	5.80	9	0	40	58	11	24
Conor Bowers, Oakland	2	3	5.86	11	0	51	59	23	41
Trevor Swaney, Wright State	3	4	5.91	16	1	46	55	18	23
Grant Inman, Valparaiso	4	6	5.94	13	0	53	64	26	37
Adam Reuss, Milwaukee	2	6	5.95	14	0	59	65	34	49

IVY LEGAUE

Rolfe Division	Conference W	Conference L	Overall W	Overall L
*Yale	16	4	34	18
Dartmouth	11	9	22	17
Harvard	7	13	19	23
Brown	6	14	13	24

Gehrig Division	Conference W	Conference L	Overall W	Overall L
Pennsylvania	12	8	23	22
Columbia	12	8	18	23
Cornell	9	11	21	17
Princeton	7	13	12	28

All-Conference Team: C—Josh Huntley, Sr., Brown. **1B**—Marc Sredojevic, Sr., Brown. **2B**—Kyle Bartelman, Sr., Columbia. **3B**—Randell Kanemaru, Jr., Columbia. **SS**—Ryan Krainz, Jr., Cornell. **OF**—Rob Henry, Sr., Brown; Julian Bury, Fr., Columbia; Tim Graul, Sr., Penn. **UTIL**—Patrick Robinson, So., Harvard. **DH**—Benny Wanger, So., Yale. **SP**—Beau Sulser, Sr., Dartmouth; Jake Cousins, Sr., Penn; Scott Politz, So., Yale. **RP**—Peter Lannoo, Sr., Cornell. **Player of the Year:** Randell Kanemaru, Columbia. **Pitcher of the Year:** Beau Sulser, Dartmouth. **Rookie of the Year:** Julian Bury, Columbia. **Coach of the Year:** John Stuper, Yale.

INDIVIDUAL BATTING LEADERS

(Minimum 140 At-Bats)

	AVG	OBP	SLG	AB	2B	3B	HR	RBI	SB
Randell Kanemaru, Columbia	.395	.435	.625	152	14	0	7	42	2
Tim Graul, Pennslyvania	.371	.431	.600	175	16	3	6	41	6
Kyle Bartelman, Columbia	.349	.369	.568	146	7	2	7	33	2
Tim DeGraw, Yale	.343	.428	.439	198	10	3	1	42	17
Richard Slenker, Yale	.342	.443	.473	184	12	0	4	40	3
Julian Bury, Columbia	.333	.408	.427	150	14	0	0	17	2
Kyle Holbrook, Dartmouth	.329	.395	.461	152	8	0	4	31	2
Michael Ketchmark, Dartmouth	.329	.408	.527	146	12	1	5	25	2
Matt Feinstein, Dartmouth	.327	.380	.379	153	6	1	0	21	6
Sean Phelan, Pennsylvania	.323	.383	.473	167	13	0	4	31	1
Sam Grigo, Brown	.313	.360	.427	150	9	4	0	21	2
Simon Whiteman, Yale	.311	.367	.410	161	7	0	3	23	11
Nick Hernandez, Princeton	.307	.354	.453	150	6	2	4	24	4
Tommy Wagner, Cornell	.296	.343	.355	152	2	2	1	22	1
Chris Adams, Pennsylvania	.292	.354	.363	171	9	0	1	20	7
Andrew Murnane, Pennsylvania	.292	.373	.370	154	8	2	0	14	8
Quinn Hoffman, Harvard	.288	.323	.392	153	9	2	1	15	5
Harrison White, Yale	.285	.380	.386	158	8	1	2	21	1
Dustin Shirley, Dartmouth	.281	.350	.379	153	6	3	1	24	5
Matt O'Neill, Pennsylvania	.281	.341	.445	146	6	0	6	23	3
Ben Porter, Columbia	.280	.378	.393	150	9	1	2	25	8
Matt McGeagh, Pennsylvania	.279	.325	.463	147	12	0	5	20	0
Matt Tola, Pennsylvania	.252	.305	.316	155	7	0	1	12	1
Trevor Johnson, Dartmouth	.250	.387	.386	140	3	2	4	21	17
Dai Dai Otaka, Yale	.245	.272	.305	151	14	0	0	17	2

INDIVIDUAL PITCHING LEADERS

(Minimum 40 Innings Pitched)

	W	L	ERA	G	SV	IP	H	BB	SO
Beau Sulser, Dartmouth	6	1	1.40	7	0	45	31	5	52
Paul Balestrieri, Cornell	5	4	2.18	9	0	58	50	15	36
Michael Danielak, Dartmouth	7	2	2.64	9	0	58	57	10	55
Christian Taugner, Brown	4	4	2.70	9	0	60	62	12	35
Jake Cousins, Pennsylvania	7	2	3.15	11	0	69	72	21	59
Max Ritchie, Brown	1	6	3.22	9	0	59	65	11	39
Scott Politz, Yale	11	2	3.23	13	0	92	86	21	75
Mike Reitcheck, Pennsylvania	4	4	3.46	11	0	65	64	9	40
Chad Powers, Princeton	1	3	3.93	9	0	50	57	14	41
Josh Simpson, Columbia	4	3	4.02	10	0	56	65	14	38
Ben Gross, Princeton	3	5	4.20	9	0	49	56	13	48
Gabe Kleiman, Pennsylvania	3	0	4.23	9	0	45	47	20	24

	W	L	ERA	G	SV	IP	H	BB	SO
Cole O'Connor, Dartmouth	4	2	4.27	9	0	46	57	9	24
Ty Wiest, Columbia	2	3	4.32	10	0	42	40	14	54
Simon Rosenblum-Larson, Harvard	3	4	4.42	9	0	53	56	28	54
Adam Bleday, Pennsylvania	2	5	4.77	11	1	60	61	26	74
Ian Miller, Harvard	3	5	4.87	10	0	61	58	20	44
Kumar Nambiar, Yale	4	1	5.06	16	2	43	52	12	34
Kevin Stone, Harvard	4	2	5.27	10	0	56	57	25	25
Chris Giglio, Princeton	3	3	5.28	10	0	44	59	17	56
Justin Lewis, Cornell	3	2	5.32	9	0	46	49	14	20
Eric Brodkowitz, Yale	6	3	5.50	14	0	72	82	37	56
Reid Anderson, Brown	1	4	5.80	10	1	40	45	26	34
Noah Zavolas, Harvard	3	6	5.95	9	0	56	80	15	41
Tim Willittes, Cornell	4	3	6.12	10	0	50	64	18	34

METRO ATLANTIC ATHLETIC CONFERENCE

	Conference W	Conference L	Overall W	Overall L
Fairfield	17	7	31	24
Canisius	16	8	35	22
* Marist	16	8	32	23
Iona	14	10	25	26
Niagara	12	12	24	24
Rider	12	12	24	28
Manhattan	12	12	18	34
Siena	11	13	20	27
Monmouth	11	13	20	28
Quinnipiac	11	13	18	32
Saint Peter's	0	24	0	38

All-Conference Team: C—Fabian Pena, So., Manhattan. **1B**—Joe Drpich, Jr., Siena. **2B**—Jordan Bishop, Jr., Siena. **3B**—Jack Gethings, So., Fairfield. **SS**—Jake Lumley, Sr., Canisius. **OF**—Frankie Gregoire, So., Marist; Tanner Kirwer, Jr., Niagara; Dan Swain, Sr., Siena. **DH**—Liam Scafariello, So., Quinnipiac. **UTIL**—Liam Wilson, Jr., Canisius. **SP**—Gavin Wallace, Jr., Fairfield; Charlie Jerla, Jr., Marist; Cody Eckerson, Jr., Niagara; Nick Margevicius, Jr., Rider. **RP:** Jake Finkel, Jr., Iona. **Player of the Year:** Jake Lumley, Canisius. **Pitcher of the Year:** Charlie Jerla, Marist. **Rookie of the Year:** Matt Brash, Niagara. **Coach of the Year:** Pat Carey, Iona.

INDIVIDUAL BATTING LEADERS

(Minimum 140 At-Bats)

	AVG	OBP	SLG	AB	2B	3B	HR	RBI	SB
Trevor McCauley, Niagara	.367	.448	.500	150	14	0	2	29	7
Jack Gethings, Fairfield	.364	.436	.440	209	7	3	1	40	13
Shaine Hughes, Monmouth	.359	.441	.519	181	14	0	5	30	5
Jake Lumley, Canisius	.355	.436	.461	228	12	3	2	21	17
Joe Drpich, Siena	.346	.411	.577	182	10	1	10	46	1
Greg Cullen, Niagara	.341	.414	.451	182	8	3	2	33	7
Tyler Kapuscinski, Marist	.335	.440	.410	173	8	1	1	15	3
Brendan Bisset, Manhattan	.335	.406	.422	185	11	1	1	29	3
Tanner Kirwer, Niagara	.335	.430	.469	194	20	0	2	29	23
Liam Wilson, Canisius	.333	.414	.486	216	16	4	3	37	2
Ryan Stekl, Canisius	.333	.422	.490	210	17	2	4	41	12
Fabian Pena, Manhattan	.330	.384	.502	203	24	1	3	32	4
Drew Arciuolo, Fairfield	.329	.396	.410	222	5	2	3	32	16
Troy Scocca, Fairfield	.328	.405	.540	198	17	2	7	46	5
Dan Swain, Siena	.324	.407	.559	204	11	5	9	36	9
Brian Kelly, Siena	.323	.405	.443	158	7	0	4	22	7
Fran Kinsey, Iona	.317	.390	.399	183	6	3	1	38	6
Peter Battaglia, Niagara	.317	.423	.467	180	11	2	4	48	7
Jordan Bishop, Siena	.313	.369	.394	160	13	0	0	24	0
Kevin Radziewicz, Fairfield	.311	.412	.403	196	9	0	3	42	2
Andrew Rouse, Marist	.311	.391	.417	206	13	0	3	34	12
Matt Forlow, Manhattan	.305	.393	.463	177	11	4	3	30	8
Randy Taveras, Marist	.303	.406	.430	165	7	1	4	24	17
Matt Batten, Quinnipiac	.302	.362	.456	169	15	1	3	24	10
Christ Conley, Canisius	.299	.468	.420	157	8	1	3	41	0

INDIVIDUAL PITCHING LEADERS

(Minimum 40 Innings Pitched)

	W	L	ERA	G	SV	IP	H	BB	SO
Chris Enns, Quinnipiac	4	2	2.09	16	0	52	51	18	37
Cody Eckerson, Niagara	6	2	2.29	12	0	55	45	29	50
Nate Mascellino, Niagara	1	4	2.67	16	1	57	55	25	32
Scott Boches, Marist	6	5	2.72	16	0	86	82	28	85
Matthew Brash, Niagara	5	1	2.79	17	2	77	72	27	63
Nick Margevicius, Rider	6	4	2.81	13	0	86	86	20	78
Bill Maier, Iona	8	5	2.85	13	0	85	96	21	59
Patrick Ryan, Iona	5	3	3.00	14	0	69	60	33	44
Gavin Wallace, Fairfield	8	5	3.08	14	0	91	88	13	76
Sean Keenan, Marist	6	1	3.14	18	1	92	69	44	89
Tony Romanelli, Marist	2	2	3.24	23	0	42	27	15	47
John Signore, Fairfield	7	2	3.26	14	0	86	73	17	76
Joe DeRosa, Iona	2	5	3.34	14	0	67	67	8	38
Mike Bonaiuto, Fairfield	3	5	3.40	27	5	50	60	16	41
Taylor Luciana, Quinnipiac	4	6	3.48	12	0	54	55	25	33
Andrew Sipowicz, Canisius	6	3	3.48	18	1	83	69	23	65
John Parisi, Marist	3	3	3.70	19	1	41	42	17	37
Joe Molettiere, Monmouth	3	5	3.74	19	1	55	54	22	55
J.P. Stevenson, Canisius	9	5	3.75	15	0	94	89	21	69
Kyle Dube, Fairfield	6	2	3.84	14	0	77	80	23	59
Charlie Jerla, Marist	9	2	4.08	13	0	71	68	23	69
Daniel Procopio, Niagara	6	4	4.19	12	0	58	43	27	75
Zachary Sloan, Canisius	4	2	4.31	17	0	65	72	33	58
Tom Cosgrove, Manhattan	5	7	4.38	14	0	84	82	35	105
Dylan D'Anna, Siena	3	3	4.50	17	5	42	43	27	49

MID-AMERICAN CONFERENCE

Eastern Division	Conference W	Conference L	Overall W	Overall L
Kent State	18	6	36	18
* Ohio	13	11	31	28
Bowling Green	9	15	15	33
Miami (Ohio)	8	16	22	34
Buffalo	8	16	17	34

Western Division	Conference W	Conference L	Overall W	Overall L
Central Michigan	16	8	30	26
Ball State	14	10	30	27
Eastern Michigan	14	10	23	35
Western Michigan	12	12	24	27
Northern Illinois	11	13	17	37
Toledo	9	15	16	40

All-Conference Team: C—Robert Greenman, Sr., Central Michigan. **1B**—Dylan Rosa, Jr., Kent State. **2B**—Sean Kennedy, Sr., Ball State. **3B**—Chris Kwitzer, Jr., Buffalo. **SS**—Ben Haefner, Jr., Buffalo. **OF**—Luke Burch, Sr., Kent State; Spencer Ibarra, Sr., Ohio; Tanner Allison, Jr., Western Michigan. **DH**—Tyler Harris, Sr., Miami. **At-Large**—Daniel Jipping, Jr., Central Michigan. **SP**—Sam Delaplane, Sr., Eastern Michigan; Joey Murray, So., Kent State; Eli Kraus, Jr., Kent State; Michael Klein, Jr., Ohio. **RP**—Jake Roehn, Jr., Ohio. **Player of the Year:** Tanner Allison, Western Michigan. **Pitcher of the Year:** Joey Murray, Kent State. **Freshman of the Year:** Jake Wilson, Bowling Green. **Freshman Pitcher of the Year:** Tyler Hankins, Central Michigan. **Coach of the Year:** Jeff Duncan, Kent State.

INDIVIDUAL BATTING LEADERS

(Minimum 140 At-Bats)

	AVG	OBP	SLG	AB	2B	3B	HR	RBI	SB
Tanner Allison, Western Mich	.356	.432	.574	216	18	1	9	68	3
Luke Burch, Kent State	.350	.441	.489	223	15	2	4	25	13
Chris Kwitzer, Buffalo	.348	.420	.510	155	9	2	4	30	2
Connor Smith, Western Mich	.339	.394	.480	221	11	7	2	35	8
Haffey, Miami (Ohio)	.338	.422	.581	222	13	1	13	39	3
Caleb Stayton, Ball State	.331	.455	.436	163	8	0	3	35	0
Mason Mamarella, Kent State	.330	.441	.405	215	6	5	0	26	18
Sean Kennedy, Ball State	.329	.386	.566	228	16	1	12	50	1
Nick Vogelmeier, Western Mich	.329	.429	.407	216	11	0	2	26	1
Ben Haefner, Buffalo	.326	.435	.426	190	6	2	3	37	2
Spencer Ibarra, Ohio	.325	.398	.542	240	14	1	12	38	2
Brian Dudek, Buffalo	.324	.429	.497	173	10	4	4	37	4

Player	AVG	OBP	SLG	AB	2B	3B	HR	RBI	SB
Matt Eppers, Ball State	.321	.394	.460	224	13	6	2	36	9
Dylan Rosa, Kent State	.314	.406	.638	185	14	2	14	50	4
Connor Callery, Ohio	.312	.360	.339	218	3	0	1	23	3
Daniel Jipping, Central Mich	.309	.422	.560	207	17	1	11	61	4
Alex Goodwin, Western Mich	.309	.383	.382	178	11	1	0	25	2
Daniel Robinson, Central Mich	.305	.389	.362	246	7	2	1	39	22
Jake Wilson, Bowling Green	.305	.387	.348	187	5	0	1	31	8
Tim Dalporto, Kent State	.304	.353	.369	217	8	0	2	32	0
Rudy Rott, Ohio	.303	.395	.504	234	14	0	11	50	1
Evan Kratt, Central Michigan	.302	.386	.337	199	5	1	0	30	1
Nate Grys, Western Michigan	.302	.373	.453	192	11	0	6	39	0
Righter, Bowling Green	.301	.357	.482	193	17	0	6	29	0
Michael Klein, Ohio	.300	.368	.490	210	10	3	8	38	2

INDIVIDUAL PITCHING LEADERS

(Minimum 40 Innings Pitched)

Player	W	L	ERA	G	SV	IP	H	BB	SO
Joey Murray, Kent State	6	1	1.80	14	0	75	55	32	110
Jake Roehn, Ohio	4	4	2.28	30	15	43	39	13	48
Ernst, Miami (Ohio)	3	2	2.63	20	4	55	42	21	42
Eli Kraus, Kent State	8	3	2.69	14	0	94	78	21	73
B.J. Butler, Ball State	4	4	2.74	11	1	66	64	16	52
Nick Floyd, Ball State	2	2	2.81	19	1	48	40	27	40
Ross Achter, Toledo	3	4	3.21	11	0	56	65	26	60
Sam Delaplane, Eastern Mich	4	3	3.27	20	0	85	83	32	92
Michael Klein, Ohio	5	3	3.48	14	0	67	67	26	31
Joe Hawks, Northern Illinois	4	6	3.61	14	0	77	76	32	75
Tom Colletti, Ohio	4	3	3.66	27	0	64	44	23	56
Kyle Mallwitz, Western Mich	5	3	3.66	26	0	93	83	39	79
T.J. Baker, Ball State	1	2	3.70	26	6	41	39	15	50
Jared Skolnicki, Kent State	5	2	3.71	18	2	51	48	16	42
Schwartz, Miami (Ohio)	3	5	3.78	20	1	69	54	30	63
Tyler Hankins, Central Mich	6	1	3.83	15	0	92	100	28	51
Pat Leatherman, Central Mich	7	4	3.86	15	0	86	84	39	83
Connor Wollersheim, Kent State	2	1	3.91	16	2	51	47	23	46
Brendan Burns, Ball State	4	3	3.94	16	2	46	36	20	54
Colin Brockhouse, Ball State	3	2	3.98	10	0	41	31	19	40
Brad Allen, Eastern Michigan	2	7	4.03	16	0	92	90	47	59
Colton Bradley, Central Mich	6	2	3.10	28	10	48	38	23	39
Cory Blessing, Ohio	3	1	4.12	25	0	44	34	18	55
Donovin Sims, Northern Illinois	5	4	4.12	14	0	72	84	26	35
Kenny Ogg, Ohio	3	1	4.22	28	0	43	50	19	29

MID-EASTERN CONFERENCE

Northern Division	Conference W	Conference L	Overall W	Overall L
Norfolk State	16	7	26	22
Delaware State	14	10	22	25
Maryland-Eastern Shore	9	15	12	40
Coppin State	8	15	11	31

Southern Division	Conference W	Conference L	Overall W	Overall L
* Bethune-Cookman	15	8	36	25
North Carolina A&T	15	9	28	25
Florida A&M	14	10	27	26
North Carolina Central	12	11	22	28
Savannah State	3	21	12	39

All-Conference Team: C—Adan Ordonez, Jr., North Carolina A&T. **1B**—Danny Rodriguez, So., Bethune-Cookman. **2B**—Corey Joyce, Fr., North Carolina Central. **3B**—Jameel Edney, Jr., Bethune-Cookman. **SS**—Demetrius Sims, Jr., Bethune-Cookman. **OF**—Myles Sowell, Jr., North Carolina A&T; Adonis Lao, Jr., Bethune-Cookman; Brian Beard, Sr., Norfolk State. **UTIL**—Alex Mauricio, Jr., Norfolk State. **SP**—Devin Hemmerich, Sr., Norfolk State; Anthony Maldonado, Fr., Bethune-Cookman. **RP**—Noah Dyals, Jr., North Carolina AT&T. **Player of the Year:** Alex Mauricio, Norfolk State. **Pitcher of the Year:** Devin Hemmerich, Norfolk State. **Freshman of the Year:** Corey Joyce, North Carolina Central. **Coach of the Year:** Ben Hall, North Carolina A&T.

INDIVIDUAL BATTING LEADERS

(Minimum 140 At-Bats)

Player	AVG	OBP	SLG	AB	2B	3B	HR	RBI	SB
Nazier McIlwain, Coppin State	.377	.463	.510	151	11	0	3	33	3
Adonis Lao, Bethune-Cookman	.366	.390	.421	216	10	1	0	31	3
Dallas Oliver, Florida A&M	.365	.443	.407	167	7	0	0	19	3
Brandon Melendez, N.C. A&T	.363	.442	.446	157	8	1	1	24	14
Myles Sowell, N.C. A&T	.356	.403	.500	174	6	5	3	29	11
Carter Williams, N.C. Central	.351	.427	.459	205	14	1	2	26	12
Evan Regez, Delaware State	.348	.432	.373	158	4	0	0	20	5
Greg White, N.C. A&T	.348	.429	.425	181	12	1	0	19	15
Alex Mauricio, Norfolk State	.345	.427	.528	142	17	3	1	27	11
Corey Joyce, N.C. Central	.344	.417	.513	189	11	3	5	43	5
Justin Burrel, Nolfork State	.333	.381	.450	171	9	4	1	30	14
Brian Beard, Nolfork State	.332	.400	.446	184	13	4	0	23	18
Danny Rodriguez, Bethune-Cookman	.330	.382	.555	227	18	0	11	46	0
Demetrius Sims, Bethune-Cookman	.323	.412	.430	223	7	7	1	23	13
Kaycee Reese, Florida A&M	.318	.444	.371	151	3	1	1	17	1
Nate Sterijevski, Bethune-Cookman	.310	.376	.458	155	9	1	4	33	3
Jameel Edney, Bethune-Cookman	.309	.404	.500	230	21	4	5	41	1
Kyle Gerdts, Savannah State	.306	.362	.376	173	10	1	0	29	9
Ben Ellzey, Florida A&M	.303	.403	.415	188	6	0	5	29	0
Jalen Atterbury, Savannah St	.303	.387	.377	175	11	1	0	13	18
Willis McDaniel, Florida A&M	.302	.410	.411	192	8	2	3	31	14
McCarthy, Florida A&M	.299	.358	.485	204	12	1	8	51	0
Adan Ordonez, N.C. A&T	.299	.369	.471	174	12	0	6	52	1
Ryan Rotondo, UMES	.297	.322	.333	195	4	0	1	26	11
Jake Raby, N.C. Central	.295	.367	.418	146	12	0	2	31	1

INDIVIDUAL PITCHING LEADERS

(Minimum 40 Innings Pitched)

Player	W	L	ERA	G	SV	IP	H	BB	SO
Devin Hemmerich, Norfolk St	10	2	1.97	13	0	105	75	16	118
Chase Anderson, Norfolk State	6	2	2.82	19	1	77	72	25	77
Lane DeLeon, Delaware State	4	6	2.84	13	0	70	66	27	57
Anthony Maldonado, Bethune-Cookman	8	4	3.02	16	1	86	70	31	61
Thomas Nicoll, Florida A&M	3	3	3.24	24	3	42	40	16	36
Devin Sweet, N.C. Central	4	3	3.33	12	0	68	63	31	61
Sean McGrath, Delaware State	5	2	3.41	13	0	63	60	30	59
Tyler Norris, Bethune-Cookman	9	1	3.42	15	0	84	66	33	64
Ryan Anderson, Florida A&M	4	3	3.45	16	0	91	101	24	56
Alex Mauricio, Norfolk State	4	4	3.49	11	0	59	57	27	55
Wesley Martin, UMES	3	4	3.54	14	0	69	66	38	26
Tyler Krull, Bethune-Cookman	5	2	3.74	19	0	55	58	16	31
Zach Mills, UMES	3	5	3.86	15	0	56	55	37	45
Aubrey McCarthy, Florida A&M	7	4	4.07	16	0	77	79	30	42
Trevor McKenna, Savannah St	2	6	4.57	12	0	65	66	37	51
Landon Fraley, N.C. Central	4	2	4.68	11	0	42	41	22	30
Krystian Negron, Coppin State	1	4	4.68	9	1	42	44	12	46
Garrett Lawson, Delaware St	6	4	4.72	13	0	74	71	35	58
Travis Dill, Delaware State	2	6	4.97	22	4	54	75	14	46
Josh Bottenfield, N.C. A&T	5	4	5.10	22	8	65	88	20	37
Alexis Herrera, Bethune-Cookman	4	1	5.17	24	1	47	50	21	36
Jonathan Mauricio, Norfolk St	3	5	5.26	14	1	63	73	28	36
Jonathan Figueroa, N.C. Central	4	5	5.37	12	0	62	74	29	60
Marcello Betances, N.C. A&T	5	6	5.40	14	0	72	81	46	58
Austin Robinson, Savannah St	1	7	5.40	12	0	72	89	31	47

MISSOURI VALLEY CONFERENCE

Team	Conference W	Conference L	Overall W	Overall L
Missouri State	18	1	43	20
* Dallas Baptist	15	6	42	21
Indiana State	12	9	29	26
Southern Illinois	10	10	27	30
Wichita State	10	11	28	30
Evansville	8	12	18	39
Bradley	6	14	20	31
Illinois State	2	18	16	40

All-Conference Team: C—Garrett Wolforth, So., Dallas Baptist. **1B**—Austin Listi, Sr., Dallas Baptist. **2B**—Aaron Meyer, Sr., Missouri State. **3B**—Jake Burger, Jr., Missouri State; Alec Bohm, So., Wichita State. **SS**—Jeremy Eierman, So., Missouri State. **OF**—Tony Rosselli, Sr.,

Indiana State; Jameson Hannah, So., Dallas Baptist; Greg Lambert, Jr., Southern Illinois. **DH**—Blake Graham, Sr., Missouri State. **SP**—Zach Lewis, Sr., Wichita State; Connor Strain, Sr., Evansville; Doug Still, Jr., Missouri State. **RP**—Jake Fromson, Jr., Missouri State; Seth Elledge, Jr., Dallas Baptist. **Player of the Year:** Jake Burger, Missouri State. **Pitcher of the Year:** Jake Fromson, Missouri State. **Newcomer of the Year:** Doug Still, Missouri State. **Freshman of the Year:** Brendan Dougherty, Bradley. **Coach of the Year:** Keith Guttin, Missouri State

INDIVIDUAL BATTING LEADERS

(Minimum 140 At-Bats)

	AVG	OBP	SLG	AB	2B	3B	HR	RBI	SB
Devlin Granberg, Dallas Baptist	.359	.439	.564	181	12	2	7	47	6
Austin Listi, Dallas Baptist	.336	.454	.735	238	23	0	24	55	1
Matt Duce, Dallas Baptist	.333	.424	.554	222	18	2	9	55	1
Greg Lambert, S Illinois	.329	.393	.551	225	25	2	7	52	11
Jameson Hannah, Dallas Baptist	.328	.411	.530	268	19	4	9	38	9
Tony Rosselli, Indiana State	.328	.392	.602	186	9	6	10	41	8
Jake Burger, Missouri State	.328	.443	.648	247	13	0	22	65	3
Owen Miller, Illinois State	.325	.351	.498	249	19	3	6	48	6
Justin Paulsen, Missouri State	.322	.406	.478	245	17	0	7	49	1
Tyler Friis, Indiana State	.322	.405	.422	180	11	2	1	23	14
Greyson Jenista, Wichita State	.320	.413	.509	228	14	1	9	41	6
Ryan Smith, Southern Illinois	.317	.407	.385	205	8	0	2	24	20
Jeremy Eierman, Missouri State	.313	.431	.675	243	15	2	23	68	17
Blake Graham, Missouri State	.309	.421	.543	162	11	0	9	34	0
Tim Millard, Dallas Baptist	.308	.410	.543	234	17	1	12	62	4
Brendan Dougherty, Bradley	.305	.387	.359	167	9	0	0	15	2
Alec Bohm, Wichita State	.305	.385	.519	233	13	2	11	40	5
Andrew Tanous, Evansville	.303	.361	.442	231	18	1	4	31	2
Luke Mangieri, Bradley	.300	.376	.414	203	13	2	2	35	6
Hunter Steinmetz, Missouri St	.300	.414	.427	253	11	0	7	42	10
Trey Hair, Evansville	.297	.411	.498	219	21	1	7	43	8
Trey Vickers, Wichita State	.296	.351	.398	226	7	2	4	32	1
Jordan Boyer, Wichita State	.295	.379	.448	183	15	2	3	42	1
Aaron Meyer, Missouri State	.292	.372	.441	161	10	1	4	30	1
Dane Giesler, Indiana State	.291	.391	.593	199	7	1	17	49	0

INDIVIDUAL PITCHING LEADERS

(Minimum 40 Innings Pitched)

	W	L	ERA	G	SV	IP	H	BB	SO
Jake Fromson, Missouri State	8	3	2.25	37	3	76	46	18	88
Connor Strain, Evansville	2	5	2.62	14	0	69	62	38	68
Damon Olds, Indiana State	1	2	2.85	24	1	41	32	16	44
Doug Still, Missouri State	8	3	2.88	17	0	103	98	27	89
Zach Lewis, Wichita State	4	4	3.07	15	0	82	60	32	64
Dalton Higgins, Dallas Baptist	7	1	3.15	30	6	40	38	17	40
Chad Whitmer, S Illinois	6	3	3.46	15	0	104	102	26	95
Jimmy Frouse, Dallas Baptist	5	0	3.71	25	0	44	33	24	40
Patric Schnieders, Evansville	5	6	3.95	15	0	82	65	51	96
Austin Knight, Missouri State	3	2	3.97	15	0	59	54	26	41
Travis Stone, Dallas Baptist	2	3	3.98	29	0	52	57	13	33
J. McKinney, Indiana State	5	1	4.09	16	1	55	45	35	68
Tyler Ward, Indiana State	4	5	4.16	14	0	84	90	15	58
Brady Huffman, Illinois State	4	5	4.20	17	0	64	66	26	52
Nate Witherspoon, Missouri St	4	3	4.29	15	0	42	43	15	40
MD Johnson, Dallas Baptist	6	2	4.43	18	0	69	80	29	57
Jordan Knutson, Missouri State	8	4	4.53	23	1	93	96	21	90
Michael Baird, Southern Illinois	4	4	4.56	13	0	79	79	22	51
Joey Marciano, Southern Illinois	3	3	4.70	12	0	46	31	43	56
Cole Cook, Bradley	8	6	4.77	18	0	77	89	24	38
Jordan Martinson, Dallas Baptist	9	4	4.78	17	0	81	77	35	76
Dylan Coleman, Missouri State	8	3	4.80	18	0	99	85	50	106
Ryan Kaeffaber, Indiana State	4	6	5.10	16	1	55	64	15	41
Ray Gaither, Dallas Baptist	9	4	5.11	17	0	76	80	40	68
Jack Landwehr, Illinois State	8	3	5.12	24	2	63	74	19	57

MOUNTAIN WEST CONFERENCE

	Conference W	Conference L	Overall W	Overall L
New Mexico	19	9	30	27
* San Diego State	20	10	42	21
Fresno State	18	12	35	25
Nevada	13	16	19	36
Air Force	12	17	27	26
San José State	10	18	19	35
Nevada-Las Vegas	10	20	20	36

All-Conference Team: 1B—Aaron Arruda, Jr., Fresno State; Jack Zoellner, Sr., New Mexico. **3B**—Bradley Haslam, Sr., Air Force; Jesse Medrano, Sr., Fresno State; Carl Stajduhar, Jr., New Mexico. **SS**—Danny Sheehan, Sr., San Diego State. **OF**—Adam Groesbeck, Sr., Air Force; Jared Mang, So., New Mexico; Tyler Adkison, Jr., San Diego State. **SP**—Ricky Tyler Thomas, Jr., Fresno State; Mark Nowaczewski, Jr., Nevada; Dominic Purpura, Sr., San Diego State; Brett Seeburger, Sr., San Diego State. **Players of the Year:** Jack Zoellner, New Mexico; Danny Sheehan, San Diego State. **Pitcher of the Year:** Brett Seeburger, San Diego State. **Freshmen of the Year:** Carter Bins, Fresno State; Bryson Stott, Nevada-Las Vegas. **Coach of the Year:** Ray Birmingham, New Mexico.

INDIVIDUAL BATTING LEADERS

(Minimum 140 At-Bats)

	AVG	OBP	SLG	AB	2B	3B	HR	RBI	SB
Adam Groesbeck, Air Force	.410	.460	.649	222	23	3	8	42	9
Bradley Haslam, Air Force	.380	.440	.620	213	19	1	10	51	5
Jared Mang, New Mexico	.373	.433	.573	241	17	2	9	62	4
Aaron Arruda, Fresno State	.373	.448	.643	244	17	2	15	67	1
Jack Zoellner, New Mexico	.368	.470	.663	193	19	1	12	56	5
Tyler Zabojnik, Air Force	.366	.433	.595	232	23	3	8	47	4
Russell Williams, Air Force	.362	.430	.592	174	10	3	8	41	5
E. De La Trinidad, UNLV	.361	.465	.559	202	9	5	7	30	12
Luis Gonzalez, New Mexico	.361	.500	.589	219	22	2	8	42	14
Justin Jones, UNLV	.360	.424	.591	203	16	2	9	50	8
Tyler Jones, Air Force	.359	.471	.706	170	17	0	14	59	3
David Hensley, San Diego St	.357	.409	.486	210	16	1	3	31	7
Drew Wiss, Air Force	.357	.447	.481	154	13	3	0	26	4
Carl Stajduhar, New Mexico	.350	.453	.650	237	16	2	17	69	3
Jesse Medrano, Fresno State	.346	.390	.543	243	19	4	7	45	6
Danny Sheehan, San Diego St	.344	.430	.504	250	17	1	7	54	11
Nic Ready, Air Force	.340	.359	.591	235	22	2	11	53	2
Tyler Adkison, San Diego State	.337	.445	.648	196	14	1	15	64	7
Scott Silva, Fresno State	.335	.372	.533	257	19	1	10	50	4
Alan Trejo, San Diego State	.332	.402	.440	268	17	0	4	36	10
Andrew Brown, San Diego St	.332	.372	.438	217	12	1	3	37	7
Jake Stone, Fresno State	.332	.424	.550	238	15	2	11	54	6
Payton Squier, UNLV	.329	.398	.410	222	9	0	3	33	1
Danny Collier, New Mexico	.328	.418	.480	198	13	4	3	51	6
Grant Fennell, Nevada	.328	.405	.456	180	13	2	2	24	3

INDIVIDUAL PITCHING LEADERS

(Minimum 40 Innings Pitched)

	W	L	ERA	G	SV	IP	H	BB	SO
C.J. Saylor, San Diego State	3	0	2.45	32	13	40	31	15	51
Jorge Fernandez, San Diego St	3	1	2.79	23	2	48	44	19	35
Marcus Reyes, San Diego St	4	2	2.96	27	0	55	49	14	40
Jacob Erickson, San Diego St	5	3	3.67	34	0	49	51	9	35
Ryan Holloway, Air Force	3	2	3.83	24	4	47	45	34	54
Dominic Purpura, San Diego St	6	3	4.25	16	0	89	109	19	45
Brett Seeburger, San Diego St	10	3	4.53	15	0	93	101	30	69
Tyler Stevens, New Mexico	7	6	4.81	15	0	97	106	27	102
Fred Schlichtholz, Fresno State	3	5	4.82	31	2	62	57	28	64
Edgar Gonzalez, Fresno State	6	4	4.83	21	5	73	75	41	72
Ricky Tyler Thomas, Fresno St	8	4	4.86	17	0	91	84	52	100
Mark Nowaczewski, Nevada	6	6	4.89	15	0	99	111	38	53
Josh Goldberg, San José State	2	5	4.91	29	6	44	53	15	38
Dominic Topoozian, Fresno St	4	2	4.97	30	2	63	73	16	45
Harrison Pyatt, San Diego St	3	2	5.23	22	0	41	47	14	41
Trevor Charpie, Nevada	3	7	5.23	15	0	96	114	29	69
Riley Ohl, Nevada	3	3	5.29	13	0	49	57	25	29
Rickey Ramirez, Fresno State	3	6	5.30	19	2	88	105	30	68
Larry Quaney, UNLV	1	3	5.40	9	1	45	54	14	18
Johnathon Tripp, New Mexico	6	2	5.42	15	0	83	102	22	55
Cody Thompson, San Diego St	2	2	5.81	20	0	67	69	28	49

	W	L	ERA	G	SV	IP	H	BB	SO
Matt Brown, San José State	4	6	5.94	15	0	73	58	64	62
Jake Swiech,San José State	1	5	5.95	17	0	65	84	16	37
Paul Richy, UNLV	4	4	6.06	18	0	68	73	22	20
Garrett Poole, UNLV	3	7	6.20	14	0	74	98	25	27
Joseph Balfour, San José State	1	4	6.25	19	2	45	57	17	23

NORTHEAST CONFERENCE

	Conference W	Conference L	Overall W	Overall L
Bryant	20	6	29	26
* Central Connecticut State	21	7	36	22
Wagner	13	12	22	28
Sacred Heart	14	13	23	36
Long Island-Brooklyn	12	14	22	28
Fairleigh Dickinson	8	18	12	34
Mount St. Mary's	5	23	8	39

All-Conference Team: C—Mickey Gasper, Jr., Bryant. **1B**—Ryan Brennan, Sr., Fairleigh Dickinson. **2B**—Dean Lockery, Jr., Central Connecticut State. **3B**—Ryan Costello, Jr., Central Connecticut State. **SS**—Matt McCann, Sr., Fairleigh Dickinson. **OF**—Nick Angelini, So., Bryant; Franklin Jennings, Sr., Central Connecticut State; Anthony Godino, Jr., Wagner. **DH**—Mitch Guilmette, Jr., Central Connecticut State. **SP**—Austin Goeke, Sr., Wagner; Danny Marsh, Sr., Wagner; Steve Theetge, So., Bryant. **RP**—Jared Gallagher, So., Central Connecticut State. **Player of the Year:** Mickey Gasper, Bryant. **Pitcher of the Year:** Steve Theetge, Bryant. **Freshman of the Year:** Jimmy Titus, Bryant. **Coach of the Year:** Charlie Hickey, Central Connecticut State.

INDIVIDUAL BATTING LEADERS

(Minimum 140 At-Bats)

	AVG	OBP	SLG	AB	2B	3B	HR	RBI	SB
Matt McCann, Fairleigh Dickinson	.379	.453	.451	182	7	3	0	30	25
Ryan Brennan, Fairleigh Dickinson	.370	.440	.580	181	17	0	7	45	12
Phil Capra, Wagner	.351	.453	.541	185	10	2	7	42	5
Mickey Gasper, Bryant	.342	.470	.528	193	11	2	7	53	3
Andrew Turner, LIU-Brooklyn	.339	.431	.545	165	14	1	6	37	2
Evan McDonald, Fairleigh Dickinson	.333	.393	.541	159	12	0	7	34	3
Mitch Guilmette, CCSU	.331	.429	.435	154	8	1	2	35	1
Dean Lockery, CCSU	.330	.459	.473	224	22	2	2	30	6
Anthony Godino, Wagner	.328	.443	.569	174	13	4	7	37	17
Franklin Jennings, CCSU	.327	.384	.403	211	6	5	0	21	13
Nick Angelini, Bryant	.318	.419	.512	211	15	4	6	36	19
P.J. DeFilippo, Sacred Heart	.315	.396	.443	203	12	1	4	44	8
Dom Paiotti, LIU-Brooklyn	.310	.396	.422	187	10	1	3	26	17
Sean Mazzio, Wagner	.303	.394	.454	185	9	2	5	27	11
Ted Shaw, Sacred Heart	.300	.383	.352	227	7	1	1	21	14
Tyler Coleman, CCSU	.298	.409	.393	191	9	3	1	30	3
Vaughn Parker, Mount St. Mary's	.298	.357	.383	141	3	0	3	22	0
Freddy Sabido, Wagner	.297	.347	.509	175	6	2	9	31	2
Jimmy Titus, Bryant	.296	.368	.500	216	16	2	8	42	0
Ryan Costello, CCSU	.296	.423	.532	216	22	1	9	52	2
Keith Klebart, Sacred Heart	.295	.381	.411	224	17	0	3	37	7
Austin Markmann, Sacred Heart	.293	.394	.429	140	5	1	4	28	1
Charles Misiano, LIU-Brooklyn	.290	.418	.366	186	7	2	1	30	19
Tyler Post, Mount St. Mary's	.290	.378	.475	162	15	0	5	33	2
Buddy Dewaine, CCSU	.290	.348	.370	162	8	1	1	26	4

INDIVIDUAL PITCHING LEADERS

(Minimum 40 Innings Pitched)

	W	L	ERA	G	SV	IP	H	BB	SO
Nathan Wrighter, Bryant	2	0	1.80	26	1	40	34	13	28
Danny Marsh, Wagner	6	2	1.96	13	0	78	58	38	69
Austin Goeke, Wagner	6	2	2.55	14	0	85	54	44	83
Jack Patterson, Bryant	4	0	2.90	14	3	40	35	18	38
Craig Lacey, Bryant	0	1	3.46	19	0	42	39	23	30
James Karinchak, Bryant	6	3	3.65	13	0	57	36	34	86
Jackson Aldam, Sacred Heart	1	1	3.80	29	0	47	59	17	25
Steve Theetge, Bryant	8	5	3.86	15	0	82	72	38	60
Brendan Smith, CCSU	5	8	4.06	15	0	89	109	19	62
Patrick Clyne, LIU-Brooklyn	4	1	4.18	19	0	60	54	32	42
Baylor Sundahl, Sacred Heart	4	6	4.21	23	1	83	86	43	49
Brent Teller, Sacred Heart	4	3	4.43	19	1	81	91	39	58
Mike Appel, CCSU	4	4	4.52	16	0	76	76	39	49
Douglas Molnar, Wagner	3	4	4.63	19	1	45	54	12	18
James Taubl, Sacred Heart	5	8	4.85	20	0	89	122	30	64
Vito Morgese, Bryant	4	5	4.89	13	0	53	66	21	28
Ron Grant, CCSU	4	2	5.54	14	0	67	78	33	45
Chris Mormile, Wagner	1	3	5.61	15	1	59	54	51	59
Jordan Lawson, Mount St. Mary's	1	8	5.76	19	0	80	110	26	40
Danny Demetrops, Fairleigh Dickson	3	5	5.80	11	0	64	82	28	41
Nick Freijomil, LIU-Brooklyn	4	5	5.89	15	0	66	72	35	33
John Sostarich, Sacred Heart	4	6	6.19	17	0	52	53	49	34
Michael Collins, Mount St. Mary's	1	7	6.59	12	0	57	67	32	43
Jackson Svete, LIU-Brooklyn	5	4	6.83	18	0	58	75	28	33
Evan Layne, Fairleigh Dickinson	3	4	7.21	18	0	49	67	35	45.

OHIO VALLEY CONFERENCE

	Conference W	Conference L	Overall W	Overall L
* Tennessee Tech	23	7	41	21
Morehead State	18	11	36	23
Jacksonville State	17	13	30	26
Belmont	17	13	31	29
Southeast Missouri	16	14	29	26
Murray State	15	15	29	30
Austin Peay	13	16	28	30
Tennessee-Martin	12	18	25	30
Eastern Illinois	12	18	21	35
SIU-Edwardsville	11	19	23	29
Eastern Kentucky	10	20	24	32

All-Conference Team: C—Brock Weimer, So., SIU-Edwardsville. **1B**—Ben Fisher, Sr., Eastern Kentucky. **2B**—Jimmy Govern, So., Eastern Illinois. **3B**—Eli Boggess, Jr., Morehead State. **SS**—David Garza, Jr., Tennessee Tech. **OF**—Niko Hulsizer, So., Morehead State; Brandon Gutzler, Jr., Murray State; Dan Holst, Sr., Southeast Missouri State. **DH**—Nick Egli, Sr., Belmont. **UTIL**—Alex Robles, Sr., Austin Peay State. **SP**—Joe McGuire, Sr., Jacksonville State; Aaron Leasher, Jr., Morehead State; Dylan King, So., Belmont. **RP**—Ethan Roberts, So., Tennessee Tech. **Players of the Year:** Ben Fisher, Eastern Kentucky; Niko Hulsizer, Morehead State. **Pitcher of the Year:** Joe McGuire, Jacksonville State. **Rookie of the Year:** Davis Sims, Murray State. **Coach of the Year:** Matt Bragga, Tennessee Tech.

INDIVIDUAL BATTING LEADERS

(Minimum 140 At-Bats)

	AVG	OBP	SLG	AB	2B	3B	HR	RBI	SB
Eli Boggess, Morehead State	.425	.487	.599	207	11	2	7	40	3
Trevor Putzig, Tennessee Tech	.394	.441	.568	236	23	0	6	52	1
Will Schneider, Morehead St	.391	.486	.622	238	14	4	11	49	2
Alec Skender, SIU-Edwardsville	.386	.444	.493	215	15	1	2	24	13
Ryan Flick, Tennessee Tech	.377	.461	.727	231	24	0	19	74	1
Danny Wright, SE Mo. State	.376	.472	.567	178	13	3	5	36	9
Dan Holst, SE Mo. State	.375	.509	.601	208	13	2	10	55	13
Braxton Morris, Morehead St	.364	.437	.516	225	17	1	5	47	3
Ben Fisher, Eastern Kentucky	.363	.455	.762	223	14	0	25	72	0
Daniel McFarland, E Kentucky	.363	.438	.516	190	12	1	5	25	5
Alex Holderbach, E Kentucky	.355	.433	.618	186	12	2	11	49	3
Chris Osborne, SE Mo. State	.354	.429	.585	229	18	4	9	51	3
Brandon Gutzler, Murray State	.353	.426	.626	238	17	0	16	71	5
Nick Egli, Belmont	.353	.458	.715	207	17	2	18	54	7
Tanner Wessling, Tenn-Martin	.350	.419	.484	217	12	4	3	39	9
Niko Hulsizer, Morehead State	.349	.435	.775	249	21	2	27	82	3
Jack Hranec, Murray State	.349	.385	.717	166	9	2	16	53	0
Alex Robles, Austin Peay	.347	.414	.551	225	12	2	10	47	11
Tyler Albright, Tenn-Martin	.343	.422	.488	207	13	1	5	38	4
Rafael Bournigal, Belmont	.337	.430	.472	193	18	1	2	31	8
Dan Kerwin, Tennessee-Martin	.337	.382	.568	199	16	0	10	38	6
Jimmy Govern, Eastern Illinois	.335	.382	.589	185	12	1	11	50	6
Matt Cogen, Belmont	.332	.403	.472	235	17	2	4	32	9
Dre Gleason, Austin Peay	.332	.439	.572	208	14	0	12	56	0
Joseph Duncan, E Illinois	.331	.372	.524	254	14	4	9	47	18

INDIVIDUAL PITCHING LEADERS

(Minimum 40 Innings Pitched)

	W	L	ERA	G	SV	IP	H	BB	SO
Joe McGuire, Jacksonville St	8	1	3.20	15	0	65	49	17	48
Dylan King, Belmont	3	5	4.07	14	0	84	93	25	108
Aaron Leasher, Morehead St	9	3	4.19	15	0	92	88	32	105

	W	L	ERA	G	SV	IP	H	BB	SO
Josh Rye, Austin Peay	6	4	4.34	17	0	66	64	19	53
Justin Murphy, SE Mo. State	7	3	4.55	16	0	95	101	20	49
Kyle Klotz, Belmont	3	3	4.94	46	1	62	64	30	43
Derrick Adams, Jacksonville St	7	3	5.04	15	0	86	92	45	94
Michael Wood, Tennessee Tech	8	4	5.08	17	0	90	100	24	80
Alex Evans, Tennessee-Martin	8	5	5.11	28	4	69	78	25	73
Caleb Johnson, E Kentucky	2	3	5.14	23	7	56	67	21	49
Curtis Wilson, Morehead State	4	4	5.16	15	2	68	94	12	57
Tyler Vaughn, Belmont	4	9	5.22	16	0	100	117	31	96
Dalton Westfall, Tenn-Martin	5	6	5.24	14	0	81	77	62	81
Clay Chandler, SE Mo. State	8	3	5.31	16	1	85	112	22	64
Peyton Cain, Tennessee-Martin	1	6	5.45	22	1	73	88	23	48
Nelson Martz, SIU-Edwardsville	7	5	5.56	13	0	79	91	26	66
Colton Pate, Jacksonville State	2	7	5.67	16	0	73	81	32	75
Jake Usher, Tennessee Tech	5	3	5.72	15	0	72	73	34	58
Austin Dubsky, Murray State	4	7	5.76	16	0	70	73	42	62
Zach Neff, Austin Peay	1	3	5.76	23	3	59	76	15	57
Jake Piekos, Eastern Kentucky	3	5	5.92	16	0	59	53	22	62
Ryan Dills, Murray State	5	4	6.21	15	0	87	116	20	95
Brock Fulkerson, SIU-Edwardsville	4	7	6.32	14	0	84	111	13	69
Winston Cannon, Tenn Martin	5	4	6.71	13	0	59	62	45	47
Alex Robles, Austin Peay	6	8	6.75	23	3	73	87	26	85

PACIFIC-12 CONFERENCE

	Conference W	Conference L	Overall W	Overall L
* Oregon State	27	3	56	6
Stanford	21	9	42	16
UCLA	19	11	30	27
Arizona	16	14	38	21
Utah	15	15	27	24
California	15	15	25	29
Washington	14	16	28	26
Oregon	12	18	30	25
Washington State	10	20	24	29
Arizona State	8	22	23	32
Southern California	8	22	21	34

All-Conference Team: C—Cesar Salazar, So., Arizona; Joey Morgan, Jr., Washington. **1B**—Sean Bouchard, Jr., UCLA; K.J. Harrison, Jr., Oregon State; J.J. Matijevic, Jr., Arizona; Andrew Vaughn, Fr., California; Matt Winaker, Jr., Stanford. **2B**—Duke Kinamon, So., Stanford; Nick Madrigal, So., Oregon State. **3B**—Dallas Carroll, Sr., Utah; Shane Matheny, Jr., Washington State. **SS**—Cadyn Grenier, So., Oregon State; Nico Hoerner, So., Stanford; Kyle Kasser, Jr., Oregon; Frankie Rios, Sr., Southern California. **OF**—Jack Anderson, Jr., Oregon State; Gage Canning, So., Arizona State; M.J. Hubbs, Sr., Washington; DaShawn Keirsey Jr., So., Utah; Lars Nootbaar, So., Southern California; Jared Oliva, Jr., Arizona. **RHP**—Noah Bremer, Jr., Washington; Griffin Canning, Jr., UCLA; Colton Hock, Jr., Stanford; Jon Olsen, So., UCLA; Jayson Rose, Jr., Utah; Jake Thompson, Jr., Oregon State; Kenyon Yovan, Fr., Oregon State. **LHP**—J.C. Cloney, Sr., Arizona; Luke Heimlich, Jr., Oregon State; David Peterson, Jr., Oregon. **Player of the Year:** Nick Madrigal, Oregon State. **Pitcher of the Year:** Luke Heimlich, Oregon State. **Freshman of the Year:** Andrew Vaughn, California. **Coach of the Year:** Pat Casey, Oregon State.

INDIVIDUAL BATTING LEADERS

(Minimum 140 At-Bats)

	AVG	OBP	SLG	AB	2B	3B	HR	RBI	SB
J.J. Matijevic, Arizona	.383	.436	.633	240	30	0	10	65	9
Nick Madrigal, Oregon State	.380	.449	.532	237	20	2	4	40	16
Alfonso Rivas, Arizona	.371	.483	.531	213	13	0	7	63	3
Dallas Carroll, Utah	.369	.465	.591	198	17	3	7	52	12
Frankie Rios, USC	.354	.418	.451	206	13	2	1	26	4
Kyle Kasser, Oregon	.352	.435	.408	213	9	0	1	23	6
Andrew Vaughn, California	.349	.414	.555	218	7	1	12	50	1
Gage Canning, Arizona State	.332	.366	.538	223	12	8	6	29	9
Steven Kwan, Oregon State	.331	.440	.400	160	6	1	1	18	8
Brandon Perez, USC	.328	.387	.398	210	11	0	1	23	3
DaShawn Keirsey Jr., Utah	.327	.388	.461	217	10	5	3	31	9
Jeffrey Mitchell Jr., California	.325	.405	.437	206	12	1	3	23	11
Joey Morgan, Washington	.324	.427	.500	182	15	1	5	45	1
Mitchell Morimoto, Arizona	.323	.420	.407	167	7	2	1	24	4
Jared Olivia, Arizona	.321	.385	.498	243	25	3	4	54	10
Tyrus Greene, California	.317	.385	.393	145	8	0	1	10	3
Cameron Eden, California	.315	.361	.472	178	8	1	6	24	6
Quinn Broedy, Stanford	.314	.371	.556	239	17	4	11	51	3
K.J. Harrison, Oregon State	.313	.382	.498	217	13	0	9	43	7
Lars Nootbaar, USC	.313	.419	.510	198	6	6	7	34	2
Daniel Bakst, Stanford	.311	.369	.439	196	16	0	3	38	0
Cal Stevenson, Arizona	.311	.448	.461	193	11	3	4	30	5
Shane Matheny, Washington St	.309	.408	.471	191	16	3	3	34	5
Matt Winaker, Stanford	.308	.432	.514	208	14	1	9	45	3
Andres Alvarez, Washington St	.308	.381	.374	195	13	0	0	19	6

INDIVIDUAL PITCHING LEADERS

(Minimum 40 Innings Pitched)

	W	L	ERA	G	SV	IP	H	BB	SO
Luke Heimlich, Oregon State	11	1	0.76	16	0	118	70	22	128
Jake Mulholland, Oregon State	7	1	1.20	28	6	52	34	12	44
Jake Thomspon, Oregon State	14	1	1.96	20	0	129	85	40	119
Colton Hock, Stanford	6	1	2.08	27	16	48	36	11	35
Brandon Eisert, Oregon State	5	0	2.31	21	4	47	32	19	50
Griffin Canning, UCLA	7	4	2.34	17	0	119	93	32	140
Tyler Thorne, Stanford	4	1	2.42	29	2	52	42	20	43
David Peterson, Oregon	11	4	2.51	15	0	100	88	15	140
Scott Burke, UCLA	0	3	2.51	35	5	43	36	18	47
Jake Bird, UCLA	5	5	2.75	18	0	56	45	22	42
Cameron Ming, Arizona	7	2	2.78	21	2	78	68	24	60
Kris Bubic, Stanford	7	6	2.79	15	0	90	79	31	96
Jon Olsen, UCLA	7	1	2.86	16	0	85	61	31	80
Tanner Thomas, Utah	4	0	2.91	23	2	43	43	15	31
Noah Bremer, Washington	6	3	3.15	15	0	103	89	36	103
Matt Mercer, Oregon	6	7	3.16	15	0	88	79	30	59
Chris Castellanos, Stanford	9	3	3.28	15	0	99	95	15	56
Michael Flynn, Arizona	5	0	3.29	22	1	52	41	13	49
Jayson Rose, Utah	8	3	3.35	15	0	94	85	43	82
Joe DeMers, Washington	6	3	3.35	15	0	99	114	25	65
J.C. Cloney, Arizona	6	2	3.38	14	0	83	84	17	65
Cody Anderson, Washington St	5	4	3.40	15	0	79	68	23	58
Moises Ceja, UCLA	2	5	3.52	21	0	61	62	20	42
Greg Minier, Washington	2	2	3.53	33	1	43	48	14	41
Eder Erives, Arizona State	1	5	3.62	17	3	60	52	30	44

PATRIOT LEAGUE

	Conference W	Conference L	Overall W	Overall L
Navy	16	4	37	17
* Holy Cross	12	8	24	29
Army	10	10	25	31
Bucknell	10	10	21	28
Lehigh	8	12	21	29
Lafayette	4	16	8	44

All-Conference Team: C—Jon Rosoff, Jr., Army. **1B**—Anthony Critelli, Sr., Holy Cross. **2B**—Kris Lindner, Sr., Army. **3B**—Sam Clark, Jr., Bucknell. **SS**—Travis Blue, Sr., Navy. **OF**—Brett Smith, Sr., Bucknell; Jacen Nalesnik, Sr., Lehigh; Leland Saile, Sr., Navy; Logan Knowles, Jr., Navy. **DH**—Connor Donovan, Sr., Lehigh; John Selsor, Jr., Lafayette. **SP**—Connor Van Hoose, Jr., Bucknell; Kyle Condry, Sr., Navy. **RP**—Jett Meenach, Sr., Navy. **Player of the Year:** Travis Blue, Navy. **Pitcher of the Year:** Kyle Condry, Navy. **Rookie of the Year:** Austin Masel, Holy Cross. **Coach of the Year:** Jim Foster, Army.

INDIVIDUAL BATTING LEADERS

(Minimum 140 At-Bats)

	AVG	OBP	SLG	AB	2B	3B	HR	RBI	SB
Jon Rosoff, Army	.362	.464	.454	196	10	1	2	35	9
Travis Blue, Navy	.344	.421	.502	209	16	4	3	43	14
Logan Knowles, Navy	.335	.440	.459	209	14	6	0	23	16
Steven Cohen, Lafayette	.331	.420	.534	178	15	3	5	16	8
Zach Biggers, Navy	.331	.394	.528	142	10	3	4	22	2
Sam Clark, Bucknell	.328	.383	.563	174	12	1	9	37	1
Leland Saile, Navy	.326	.414	.540	187	9	2	9	58	0
Jacen Nalesnik, Lehigh	.321	.397	.606	193	14	1	13	39	9
Brett Smith, Bucknell	.318	.400	.472	195	17	2	3	26	5
Anthony Critelli, Holy Cross	.317	.367	.561	189	13	0	11	41	0
Danny Rafferty, Bucknell	.313	.422	.416	166	15	1	0	28	1
John McCarthy, Army	.308	.351	.433	208	9	1	5	39	17

David Young, Lehigh	.303	.359	.497	165	11	0	7	34	1
John Selsor, Lafayette	.301	.327	.461	193	19	0	4	35	1
Jacob Williamson, Navy	.296	.364	.441	186	12	0	5	25	4
Austin Masel, Holy Cross	.294	.356	.403	211	11	0	4	28	4
Dan Leckie, Lafayette	.291	.363	.454	141	8	0	5	18	4
Bill Schlich, Holy Cross	.291	.381	.417	199	13	0	4	23	3
Alex Woinsky, Lafayette	.288	.341	.455	156	11	0	5	21	0
Quentin Bubb, Lafayette	.285	.381	.344	186	6	1	1	24	12
Kris Linder, Army	.284	.399	.432	176	11	3	3	33	11
Luke Johnson, Bucknell	.283	.365	.398	166	11	1	2	24	3
Stephen Born, Navy	.281	.382	.396	192	12	2	2	36	9
Connor Donovan, Lehigh	.280	.384	.507	150	8	1	8	30	0
Christian Hodge, Navy	.275	.335	.418	153	6	2	4	25	1

INDIVIDUAL PITCHING LEADERS

(Minimum 40 Innings Pitched)

	W	L	ERA	G	SV	IP	H	BB	SO
Levi Stoudt, Lehigh	4	5	2.34	12	0	62	61	22	45
Kyle Condry, Navy	6	2	2.97	12	0	70	67	22	58
Mike Castellani, Bucknell	6	1	3.49	13	0	77	79	18	57
Jason Reynolds, Lehigh	3	5	3.68	11	0	51	56	21	48
Noah Song, Navy	6	4	3.77	12	0	74	68	25	85
George Capen, Holy Cross	9	1	3.88	30	3	53	57	17	61
Tyler Giovinco, Army	5	5	4.17	27	0	69	76	17	48
Brendan King, Holy Cross	5	7	4.18	17	0	93	80	36	68
Andrew Sauer, Navy	2	1	4.26	14	0	44	37	20	31
Joe Cravero, Holy Cross	2	5	4.46	17	1	77	76	26	73
Jeremy Mortensen, Army	2	5	4.61	15	1	55	59	18	49
Jacob Carte, Army	2	6	4.94	14	1	47	42	20	38
Jack Simpson, Bucknell	0	1	4.95	17	1	40	45	17	27
Carter Van Gytenbeek, Army	2	1	5.04	17	4	45	39	28	42
Trevor Houck, Lafayette	2	8	5.16	12	0	66	84	17	40
George Coughlin, Navy	4	3	5.40	11	0	60	61	22	51
Phil Reese, Holy Cross	2	7	5.74	23	0	53	64	12	35
Blake Walters, Army	0	2	6.38	20	1	42	49	16	16
Connor Jones, Lafayette	1	3	6.41	27	0	46	62	21	25
Brett Kreyer, Lafayette	0	7	6.54	10	0	54	65	20	31
Jeff Gottesman, Bucknell	3	5	6.67	12	1	54	56	30	28
Justin Finan, Holy Cross	3	3	7.54	16	0	45	74	12	23
David Giusti, Lafayette	1	8	8.94	15	0	50	68	28	32

SOUTHEASTERN CONFERENCE

	Conference		Overall	
Eastern Division	W	L	W	L
Florida	21	9	42	16
Kentucky	19	11	39	20
Vanderbilt	15	13	33	22
Missouri	14	16	36	23
South Carolina	13	17	35	25
Eastern Division	W	L	W	L
Georgia	11	19	25	32
Tennessee	7	21	27	25

	Conference		Overall	
Western Division	W	L	W	L
* Louisana State	21	9	43	17
Arkansas	18	11	42	17
Mississippi State	17	13	36	24
Texas A&M	16	14	36	21
Auburn	16	14	35	24
Mississippi	14	16	32	25
Alabama	5	24	19	34

All-Conference Teams: C—Grant Koch, So., Arkansas. **1B**—Brent Rooker, Jr., Mississippi State. **2B**—Braden Shewmake, Fr., Texas A&M. **3B**—Jordan Rodgers, Sr., Tennessee. **SS**—Ryan Gridley, Jr., Mississippi State. **OF**—Greg Deichmann, Jr., Louisiana State; Tristan Pompey, So., Kentucky; Jeren Kendall, Jr., Vanderbilt. **DH**—Michael Curry, So., Georgia. **SP**—Kyle Wright, Jr., Vanderbilt; Sean Hjelle, So., Kentucky; Alex Lange, Jr., Louisiana State. **RP**—Logan Salow, Sr., Kentucky. **Player of the Year:** Brent Rooker, Mississippi State. **Pitcher of the Year:** Sean Hjelle, Kentucky. **Freshman of the Year:** Braden Shewmake, Texas A&M. **Coach of the Year:** Nick Mingione, Kentucky.

INDIVIDUAL BATTING LEADERS

(Minimum 140 At-Bats)

	AVG	OBP	SLG	AB	2B	3B	HR	RBI	SB
Brent Rooker, Miss. State	.387	.495	.810	248	30	3	23	82	18
Jonah Todd, Auburn	.376	.460	.471	242	13	5	0	37	9
Evan White, Kentucky	.373	.453	.637	212	24	1	10	41	5
Tristan Pompey, Kentucky	.361	.464	.541	266	18	0	10	45	9
Will Toffey, Vanderbilt	.354	.475	.602	206	13	1	12	64	5
Zach Reks, Kentucky	.352	.461	.471	244	16	2	3	44	15
Jax Biggers, Arkansas	.338	.423	.498	213	14	4	4	37	3
Riley Mahan, Kentucky	.336	.392	.618	262	23	3	15	67	9
Braden Shewmake, Texas A&M	.328	.374	.529	274	18	2	11	69	11
Ryan Gridley, Miss. State	.327	.393	.457	269	15	1	6	39	7
Jake Magnum, Miss. State	.324	.380	.385	278	15	1	0	26	14
Cody Brown, Miss. State	.323	.433	.539	217	14	3	9	42	10
Jordan Rodgers, Tennessee	.322	.390	.512	205	10	1	9	35	8
Nick Choruby, Texas A&M	.321	.441	.415	246	10	2	3	33	11
Kole Cottam, Kentucky	.319	.380	.505	188	12	1	7	44	0
Zach Watson, LSU	.317	.376	.507	221	9	3	9	37	12
Antoine Duplantis, LSU	.316	.358	.400	285	14	2	2	61	19
Cole Freeman, LSU	.315	.416	.404	270	14	2	2	41	19
Julian Infante, Vanderbilt	.315	.387	.518	251	16	1	11	66	0
Tucker Bradley, Georgia	.314	.376	.365	156	8	0	0	10	7
Will Golsan, Mississippi	.312	.372	.407	221	12	0	3	22	7
Jeff Moberg, Tennessee	.311	.386	.517	209	10	3	9	33	5
Jason Delay, Vanderbilt	.309	.381	.444	207	18	2	2	41	1
Greg Deichmann, LSU	.308	.417	.579	266	15	0	19	73	7
Cam Shepard, Georgia	.307	.354	.452	241	16	2	5	28	5

INDIVIDUAL PITCHING LEADERS

(Minimum 40 Innings Pitched)

	W	L	ERA	G	SV	IP	H	BB	SO
Clarke Schmidt, South Carolina	4	2	1.34	9	0	60	41	18	70
Michael Byrne, Florida	4	5	1.67	38	19	76	64	15	93
Colie Bowers, South Carolina	5	1	1.74	25	4	41	19	16	48
Logan Salow, Kentucky	2	5	1.95	31	12	55	37	17	73
Casey Mize, Auburn	8	2	2.04	13	0	84	66	9	109
Caleb Gilbert, LSU	7	1	2.16	28	3	58	40	12	67
Alex Faedo, Florida	9	2	2.26	20	1	124	95	42	157
Jake Reindl, Arkansas	4	1	2.31	24	3	51	39	16	49
Kaylor Chafin, Texas A&M	7	2	2.33	33	3	77	57	16	72
Keegan Thompson, Auburn	7	4	2.41	15	0	93	67	17	75
Will Ethridge, Mississippi	2	2	2.41	19	1	41	32	11	50
T.J. Sikkema, Missouri	8	2	2.72	22	4	79	52	18	81
Josh Reagan, South Carolina	6	2	2.72	27	2	56	49	19	51
Patrick Raby, Vanderbilt	10	4	2.73	16	0	105	89	30	87
Andy Toelken, Missouri	5	3	2.80	16	0	71	59	24	52
Trevor Stephan, Arkansas	6	3	2.87	16	0	91	73	20	120
Cason Sherrod, Texas A&M	4	1	2.89	30	4	44	30	26	38
Alex Lange, LSU	10	5	2.97	19	0	124	106	48	150
Adam Hill, South Carolina	3	6	3.04	14	0	77	56	39	87
Ryan Rolison, Mississippi	6	3	3.06	19	0	62	57	24	64
Konnor Pilkington, Miss. State	8	5	3.08	17	0	108	76	47	111
Zach Hess, LSU	7	1	3.12	30	4	61	39	30	83
Brigham Hill, Texas A&M	8	3	3.15	17	0	100	88	31	111
Jared Poché, LSU	12	4	3.17	20	0	114	99	39	76
Matt Ruppenthal, Vanderbilt	3	3	3.17	21	3	54	40	19	45

SOUTHERN CONFERENCE

	Conference		Overall	
	W	L	W	L
Mercer	17	6	39	17
Western Carolina	15	8	28	28
* UNC Greensboro	14	10	36	24
Furman	14	10	33	28
Wofford	13	11	28	30
Samford	11	13	33	26
East Tennessee State	9	15	30	29
Virginia Military Institute	7	17	24	34
The Citadel	7	17	16	35

All-Conference Team: C—Hagen Owenby, Jr., East Tennessee State. **1B**—Brett Hash, Sr., Wofford. **2B**—Danny Edgeworth, Sr., Mercer; Nobu Suzuki, Sr., Western Carolina. **3B**—Caleb Webster, Fr., UNC

Greensboro. **SS**—Ryan Hagan, Sr., Mercer. **OF**—Andrew Moritz, So., UNC Greensboro; Tyler Tharp, Sr., Virginia Military Institute; Bryson Bowman, Sr., Western Carolina. **SP**—J.P. Sears, Jr., Citadel; Will Gaddis, Jr., Furman. **RP**—Robert Broom, So., Mercer. **Player of the Year:** Bryson Bowman, Western Carolina. **Pitcher of the Year:** J.P. Sears, Citadel. **Freshman of the Year:** Caleb Webster, UNC Greensboro. **Coach of the Year:** Craig Gibson, Mercer.

INDIVIDUAL BATTING LEADERS

(Minimum 140 At-Bats)

	AVG	OBP	SLG	AB	2B	3B	HR	RBI	SB
Andrew Moritz, UNC Greensboro	.392	.450	.513	240	8	6	3	38	16
Caleb Webster, UNC Greensboro	.383	.414	.517	201	14	5	1	40	2
Bryson Bowman, W Carolina	.381	.470	.619	218	15	2	11	59	9
McClain Bradley, Wofford	.365	.437	.606	170	15	1	8	35	17
Matt Pita, VMI	.364	.429	.583	151	10	1	7	28	4
J.T. Thomas, Mercer	.357	.454	.624	210	20	0	12	62	2
Ben Spitznagel, UNC Greensboro	.355	.440	.460	211	11	4	1	33	12
Hunter Parker, E Tenn. State	.351	.427	.427	211	13	0	1	34	10
Chris Cook, East Tenn. State	.350	.424	.550	260	22	0	10	42	19
Tyler Tharp, VMI	.348	.444	.647	221	12	3	16	40	8
Hagen Owenby, E Tenn. State	.346	.438	.573	234	12	1	13	51	1
Brett Pope, Western Carolina	.342	.399	.465	243	12	3	4	28	15
Brandon Elmy, Furman	.341	.390	.559	220	15	0	11	49	0
Christian Bailey, E Tenn. State	.337	.381	.477	243	18	2	4	48	3
Sky Overton, Furman	.336	.416	.485	235	15	1	6	39	13
Taylor Garris, Samford	.333	.376	.441	186	8	0	4	30	2
Carter Grote, Furman	.332	.427	.534	247	16	5	8	56	5
Danny Edgeworth, Mercer	.332	.421	.519	214	14	1	8	46	3
Landon Kay, Furman	.332	.394	.550	211	11	1	11	37	7
Alex Hanson, Mercer	.332	.429	.461	193	11	1	4	35	21
Ayrton Schafer, Samford	.331	.411	.634	145	9	1	11	38	1
Nobu Suzuki, Western Carolina	.330	.424	.459	194	11	1	4	35	5
T.J. Dixon, Samford	.326	.401	.417	242	11	4	1	41	23
Aaron Maher, East Tenn. State	.324	.391	.473	256	17	3	5	41	15
Brett Hash, Wofford	.320	.410	.547	225	12	0	13	53	9

INDIVIDUAL PITCHING LEADERS

(Minimum 40 Innings Pitched)

	W	L	ERA	G	SV	IP	H	BB	SO
Will Gaddis, Furman	9	3	1.89	17	1	105	81	16	89
Robert Broom, Mercer	8	2	2.04	31	1	62	42	23	82
Wyatt Burns, Samford	5	1	2.25	28	12	48	41	9	44
J.P. Sears, Citadel	7	3	2.64	14	0	95	69	27	142
Cody Shelton, Samford	5	3	2.69	15	0	64	55	22	59
Bryan Sammons, W Carolina	8	3	3.02	16	1	104	84	41	108
Josh Winder, VMI	7	6	3.59	15	0	108	100	19	112
Korey Anderson, W Carolina	0	2	3.92	30	5	44	43	28	46
Ryan Simpler, East Tenn. State	6	4	3.99	14	0	90	97	26	96
Heath Hawkins, Furman	4	3	4.07	29	2	49	52	15	46
Andrew Wantz, UNC Greensboro	6	4	4.08	27	5	68	56	26	64
Matt Frisbee, UNC Greensboro	8	4	4.10	17	0	97	87	30	74
Grant Schuermann, Furman	7	4	4.19	16	0	97	105	11	60
Jack Maynard, UNC Greensboro	3	3	4.24	23	3	68	66	26	80
Ryan Bennett, VMI	6	1	4.31	23	5	48	48	20	52
Matt Ellmyer, Wofford	1	3	4.36	21	2	54	62	13	30
Mikhail Cazenave, Samford	5	7	4.38	15	0	88	92	20	73
Bryce Hensley, UNC Greensboro	7	8	4.71	18	0	92	96	33	80
Blake Smith, East Tenn. State	4	6	4.83	17	0	91	114	34	87
Kevin Coulter, Mercer	5	3	4.86	15	1	70	88	17	47
Austin Higginbotham, Wofford	6	5	4.88	17	0	94	105	29	66
Adam Scott, Wofford	6	6	4.92	15	0	93	104	24	108
Will Abbott, Citadel	1	7	4.96	13	0	65	62	37	58
Billy Greenfield, Furman	2	1	4.98	35	3	47	61	8	40
Ryan Askew, Mercer	4	2	5.06	14	0	84	121	9	54

SOUTHLAND CONFERENCE

	Conference		Overall	
	W	L	W	L
McNeese State	22	8	37	20
Southeastern Louisiana	20	10	37	21
* Sam Houston State	19	11	44	23
Houston Baptist	18	12	29	25
Central Arkansas	17	13	34	25
Stephen F. Austin	17	13	29	28
Lamar	16	14	33	25
New Orleans	16	14	30	29
Nicholls State	15	15	29	27
Texas A&M-Corpus Christi	14	16	22	32
Northwestern State	10	20	20	34
Incarnate Word	8	22	20	35
Abilene Christian	3	27	13	43

All-Conference Team: C—Robie Rojas, Sr., Sam Houston State. **1B**—Hunter Strong, So., Central Arkansas. **2B**—Joe Provenzano, Jr., McNeese State. **3B**—Taylor Schwaner, Jr., Southeastern Louisiana. **SS**—Taylor Beene, Sr., Sam Houston State. **DH**—Josh Evans, Jr., Stephen F. Austin. **OF**—Shane Selman, So., McNeese State; Bryce Johnson, Jr., Sam Houston State; Russell Crippen, Sr., Abilene Christian. **UTIL**—Ricky Ramirez, Sr., McNeese State. **P**—Heath Donica, Sr., Sam Houston State; Mac Sceroler, Jr., Southeastern Louisiana; Shawn Semple, Jr., New Orleans. **Player of the Year:** Taylor Schwaner, Southeastern Louisiana. **Pitcher of the Year:** Heath Donica, Sam Houston State. **Freshman of the Year:** Hayden Wesneski, Sam Houston State. **Coach of the Year:** Justin Hill, McNeese State.

INDIVIDUAL BATTING LEADERS

(Minimum 140 At-Bats)

	AVG	OBP	SLG	AB	2B	3B	HR	RBI	SB
Josh Evans, Stephen F. Austin	.383	.440	.638	149	8	0	10	38	0
Cutter McDowell, Lamar	.365	.472	.556	178	22	0	4	31	9
Luis Trevino, Abilene Christian	.360	.414	.502	225	18	1	4	43	1
Hunter Strong, Central Ark	.351	.433	.514	245	24	2	4	47	2
Russell Crippen, Abilene Christian	.350	.421	.585	217	21	0	10	42	6
Bryce Johnson, Sam Houston St.	.350	.453	.433	263	12	5	0	43	33
John Cable, New Orleans	.349	.429	.464	209	13	1	3	32	2
E. Gonzalez, Incarnate Word	.347	.422	.432	176	13	1	0	19	4
Ricky Ramirez, McNeese State	.345	.462	.498	203	22	3	1	53	5
Robin Adames, Lamar	.344	.413	.493	227	13	0	7	58	1
Blake Chisolm, Sam Houston St.	.343	.466	.551	178	17	4	4	35	1
Robie Rojas, Sam Houston St.	.342	.408	.498	243	15	1	7	45	7
David Fry, Northwestern State	.340	.430	.591	203	21	0	10	44	2
J. Provenzano, McNeese State	.336	.437	.498	211	12	2	6	54	4
Shane Selman, McNeese State	.333	.367	.615	162	16	1	14	59	8
Grant DeVore, Lamar	.333	.418	.383	211	8	0	0	25	5
Taylor Schwaner, SE La.	.332	.453	.668	213	15	4	16	72	17
Spencer Halloran, Houston Baptist	.329	.403	.465	217	12	4	3	32	11
Zac Michener, Stephen F. Austin	.327	.381	.544	211	15	1	10	55	4
Dalton Stark, Texas A&M-CC	.327	.386	.469	144	15	3	3	32	5
Juan Givan, Nicholls State	.326	.410	.417	215	8	1	1	21	5
Hunter Hearn, Sam Houston St.	.326	.395	.447	191	12	4	2	42	3
Zane Otten, Houston Baptist	.325	.371	.393	211	7	3	0	18	18
Nick Ramos, Stephen F. Austin	.322	.410	.379	235	12	0	0	37	2
Robbie Podorsky, McNeese St	.319	.397	.455	207	7	5	5	28	39

INDIVIDUAL PITCHING LEADERS

(Minimum 40 Innings Pitched)

	W	L	ERA	G	SV	IP	H	BB	SO
Will Vest, Stephen F. Austin	3	0	1.38	31	1	46	38	18	46
Bryan Warzek, New Orleans	8	3	2.12	15	0	102	90	33	94
J.T. Newton, Houston Baptist	7	0	2.15	23	6	54	51	17	43
Grant Anderson, McNeese State	8	0	2.30	31	1	63	54	20	56
Heath Donica, Sam Houston St.	9	2	2.53	17	0	110	86	32	109
Brandon Hagerla, Central Ark	9	3	2.84	22	2	76	75	6	35
Tanner Driskill, Lamar	4	3	2.87	27	6	78	62	14	63
Shawn Semple, New Orleans	8	3	3.07	15	0	94	92	20	109
Corey Gaconi, Southeastern La.	7	5	3.08	16	0	108	101	14	70
Austin Sanders, McNeese State	7	2	3.26	15	0	86	84	33	67
Zach Carter, Houston Baptist	7	3	3.28	19	2	71	65	25	46
Daniel Endsley, Houston Baptist	3	2	3.29	17	1	68	68	28	46
Mark Moyer, Central Arkansas	7	3	3.38	16	0	85	75	31	48
Riley Cooper, Sam Houston St.	4	3	3.38	24	0	51	42	12	45
Cole Stapler, Nicholls State	7	6	3.44	14	0	97	84	30	85
Addison Russ, Houston Baptist	2	6	3.62	15	0	92	90	43	79
Alex Ernestine, Nicholls State	2	4	3.65	25	1	69	74	26	50
Rhett Deaton, McNeese State	8	3	3.78	14	0	79	82	25	48
Chris Cooper, Texas A&M-CC	5	4	3.78	25	7	64	63	22	58
Tyler Gray, Central Arkansas	6	6	3.80	19	0	88	91	34	89
Mac Sceroler, Southeastern La.	9	2	3.81	16	0	102	84	34	110

	W	L	ERA	G	SV	IP	H	BB	SO
Will Brand, Central Arkansas	4	1	3.86	15	1	47	50	19	37
Mike Hanchar, Nicholls State	4	4	3.89	17	0	83	75	34	80
Hayden Wesneski, Sam Houston St.	10	2	3.93	19	0	85	87	25	47
Reeves Martin, New Orleans	3	4	3.94	30	3	62	64	23	47

SOUTHWESTERN ATHLETIC CONFERENCE

	Conference		Overall	
Eastern Division	**W**	**L**	**W**	**L**
Jackson State	20	4	38	17
Alabama State	18	6	31	25
Alabama A&M	9	15	12	45
Alcron State	7	17	12	33
Mississippi Valley State	6	18	7	34

	Conference		Overall	
Western Division	**W**	**L**	**W**	**L**
Grambling State	15	9	22	30
* Texas Southern	14	10	20	34
Prairie View	11	13	20	37
Southern	10	14	17	25
Arkansas-Pine Bluff	10	14	15	31

All-Conference Team: C—Chris Biocic, Sr., Alabama State. **1B**—Gustavo Rios, Jr., Alabama State. **2B**—Wallace Rios Jimenez, Jr., Alcorn State. **3B**—Jesus Santana, Jr., Jackson State. **SS**—Marshawn Taylor, Jr., Grambling State. **OF**—Cody Den Beste, Sr., Prairie View A&M; Lamar Briggs, Jr., Jackson State; Bryce Brown, Jr., Jackson State. **DH**—Cage Cox, Fr., Alabama State. **SP**—Miguel Yrigoyen, Sr., Jackson State; Tyler Howe, Sr., Alabama State. **RP**—Brandon Marsonek, Sr., Alabama A&M. **Player of the Year:** Marshawn Taylor, Grambling State. **Pitcher of the Year**: Tyler Howe, Alabama State. **Freshman of the Year:** Cage Cox, Alabama State. **Coach of the Year:** James Cooper, Grambling State.

INDIVIDUAL BATTING LEADERS

(Minimum 140 At-Bats)

	AVG	OBP	SLG	AB	2B	3B	HR	RBI	SB
Marshawn Taylor, Grambiling St	.402	.477	.471	204	12	1	0	38	16
Bryce Brown, Jackson State	.374	.514	.448	163	7	1	1	33	27
Cody Den Beste, Prairie View	.364	.437	.561	214	16	7	4	36	12
Lamar Briggs, Jackson State	.356	.422	.470	219	17	4	0	46	14
Cage Cox, Alabama State	.350	.409	.547	214	17	2	7	44	4
C.J. Newsome, Jackson State	.340	.426	.494	162	15	5	0	27	25
John Pope, Southern	.339	.424	.558	165	12	0	8	43	1
Gustavo Rios, Aabama State	.332	.405	.574	202	17	1	10	50	0
Diandre Amion, Alabama State	.331	.411	.398	166	6	1	1	29	2
Cornelius Copeland, Jackson St	.330	.468	.443	185	17	2	0	42	17
Daniel Barnett, Grambling St	.319	.441	.497	185	15	0	6	47	9
Gerrek Jimenez, Tex Southern	.315	.338	.385	143	6	2	0	18	14
Gaudencio Lucca, Tex Southern	.314	.460	.549	175	13	5	6	29	11
Sam Campbell, Jackson State	.314	.407	.410	156	6	0	3	30	6
Tray Bell, Grambiling State	.313	.402	.313	179	10	0	5	47	5
Cornelious Woods, Ala A&M	.309	.371	.309	165	12	4	1	22	0
Rios Jimenez, Alcorn State	.308	.445	.308	146	4	0	0	22	2
Sergio Esparza, Ark.-Pine Bluff	.304	.353	.304	168	8	1	2	28	6
Wesley Reyes, Jackson State	.299	.372	.406	187	10	2	2	31	4
Kirt Cormier, Alcorn State	.298	.374	.417	151	9	0	3	21	1
Kamren Dukes, Texas Southern	.292	.405	.400	195	9	3	2	30	16
Corbin Jamison, Prairie View	.289	.346	.423	194	11	3	3	27	15
Carlos Ocasio, Alabama State	.288	.373	.415	229	11	0	6	37	11
Jesus Santata, Jackson State	.288	.379	.525	198	15	1	10	65	8
Bobby Johnson, Southern	.284	.368	.358	148	11	0	0	21	7

INDIVIDUAL PITCHING LEADERS

(Minimum 40 Innings Pitched)

	W	L	ERA	G	SV	IP	H	BB	SO
Jose Tirado, Jackson State	4	1	1.27	23	8	43	30	14	46
Austin Bizzle, Alabama State	7	1	1.95	26	3	74	53	20	78
Mark Watson, Jackson State	4	3	2.63	19	0	41	38	25	47
Jacob Snyder, Southern	4	2	2.89	13	0	56	54	23	29
Brandon Marsonek, Ala A&M	3	8	2.91	38	5	111	97	60	137
Miguel Yrigoyen, Jackson State	9	2	2.93	13	0	89	86	27	65
Issac O'Bear, Grambiling State	5	4	3.17	16	0	77	87	26	42
Carlos Lopez, Alcorn State	4	4	3.33	16	1	54	59	18	43
Tyler Howe, Alabama State	8	4	3.51	14	0	95	97	35	103
Jonathan Aponte, Jackson Ste	8	2	3.57	14	0	86	83	33	54
Jake Waters, Ark.-Pine Bluff	3	3	3.62	18	1	55	49	34	36
Jordan Bolden, Jackson State	8	3	3.71	16	0	80	80	36	66
Tanner Raiburn, Grambling St	4	2	3.76	13	0	77	74	32	84
Burke Echelmeier, Alabama St	6	4	4.11	13	0	70	82	32	59
Patrick Coffin, Alabama State	4	0	4.14	18	1	50	51	19	41
Darrien Williams, Prairie View	4	4	4.28	12	1	67	59	47	63
Troy Lewis, Southern	4	5	4.29	18	5	42	36	18	42
Edgar Sanchez, Praire View	4	5	4.91	16	2	88	101	20	51
Zac Uecker, Mississippi Valley St.	1	7	5.16	12	0	61	73	39	59
Daniel Beizer, Grambling State	4	6	5.22	22	0	60	69	28	51
Seth Oliver, Texas Southern	3	5	5.25	16	0	86	88	49	69
Sm. Arrington, Miss Valley St.	3	5	5.29	15	0	63	85	12	45
Harold Myles, Southern	2	5	5.32	13	0	68	80	28	50
C.J. Lewington, Ark.-Pine Bluff	1	3	5.37	17	1	54	62	34	31
Daniel Franklin, Southern	3	5	5.64	12	0	67	79	29	53

SUMMIT LEAGUE

	Conference		Overall	
	W	**L**	**W**	**L**
* Oral Roberts	25	4	43	16
North Dakota State	19	11	31	25
South Dakota State	18	12	26	24
Western Illnois	12	15	18	32
Omaha	9	19	12	40
Fort Wayne	4	26	9	43

All-Conference Team: C—Adam McGinnis, Sr., Western Illinois. **1B**—Brent Williams, Sr., Oral Roberts. **2B**—Nick Roark, Jr., Oral Roberts. **3B**—Cal Hernandez, So., Oral Roberts. **SS**—Dylan Snypes, Jr., Oral Roberts. **OF**—Logan Busch, Jr., North Dakota State; Noah Cummings, Jr., Oral Roberts; Michael Hungate, Sr., Oral Roberts. **DH**—Grant Suponchick, So., Nebraska-Omaha. **UTIL**—Trevor McCuthchin, So., Oral Roberts. **SP**—Miguel Ausua, Jr., Oral Roberts; Justin McGregor, Jr., Oral Roberts; Josh McMinn, So., Oral Roberts. **RP**—Chris Halbur, Sr., South Dakota State. **Player of the Year:** Noah Cummings, Oral Roberts. **Pitcher of the Year:** Ausua, Oral Roberts. **Newcomer of the Year:** Dylan Snypes, Oral Roberts. **Coach of the Year:** Ryan Folmar, Oral Roberts.

INDIVIDUAL BATTING LEADERS

(Minimum 140 At-Bats)

	AVG	OBP	SLG	AB	2B	3B	HR	RBI	SB
Adam McGinnis, W Illinois	.355	.471	.566	166	17	0	6	37	8
Nick Smith, S.D. State	.340	.410	.414	191	10	2	0	16	7
Jake Weber, Fort Wayne	.331	.384	.450	160	11	1	2	16	6
Dylan Snypes, Oral Roberts	.325	.393	.438	242	19	3	0	39	9
Matt Johnson, S.D. State	.325	.415	.589	197	16	0	12	40	0
Johnathan Fleek, W Illinois	.325	.390	.380	166	4	1	1	28	9
Noah Cummings, Oral Roberts	.321	.378	.567	240	14	0	15	70	4
Jackson Boyce, Fort Wayne	.318	.441	.479	192	13	3	4	30	23
Mitch Ellis, Western Illinois	.310	.369	.380	171	5	2	1	17	6
Nick Roark, Oral Roberts	.307	.418	.404	225	11	1	3	36	12
Mason Pierzchalski, N.D. State	.305	.350	.405	220	13	3	1	36	0
Logan Busch, N.D. State	.303	.435	.447	188	12	3	3	30	1
Matt Whatley, Oral Roberts	.302	.446	.509	212	11	0	11	49	10
Michael Hungate, Oral Roberts	.302	.350	.455	222	15	2	5	31	15
Newt Johnson, S.D. State	.302	.386	.432	192	16	0	3	40	1
Cal Hernandez, Oral Roberts	.299	.376	.360	214	10	0	1	27	2
Trevor McCutchin, Oral Roberts	.299	.331	.497	147	9	1	6	26	2
Ben Peterson, N.D. State	.296	.404	.503	199	12	1	9	35	8
Sam Palensky, Omaha	.289	.384	.315	197	3	1	0	12	7
Grant Suponchick, Omaha	.287	.374	.366	164	7	0	2	22	0
Luke Ringhofer, S.D. State	.286	.398	.347	196	9	0	1	23	2
Sam Grellner, Oral Roberts	.284	.374	.521	169	12	2	8	33	2
Bennett Hostetler, N.D. State	.279	.332	.347	190	5	1	2	26	5
Jacob Dickson, Fort Wayne	.275	.328	.363	160	6	1	2	25	1
J.T. Core, N.D. State	.274	.361	.366	164	9	0	2	23	0

INDIVIDUAL PITCHING LEADERS

(Minimum 40 Innings Pitched)

	W	L	ERA	G	SV	IP	H	BB	SO
Miguel Ausua, Oral Roberts	11	3	1.65	16	0	93	80	30	85
Josh McMinn, Oral Roberts	9	3	2.47	16	0	91	86	30	75
Bryce Hanson, S.D. State	4	1	2.93	20	1	46	40	18	53
Derek Feige, S.D. State	5	3	2.98	23	0	45	45	21	36

	W	L	ERA	G	SV	IP	H	BB	SO
Justin McGregor, Oral Roberts	9	0	2.99	18	0	81	82	26	69
Grant Glaze, Oral Roberts	3	0	3.26	27	1	47	36	22	50
Chris Coles, N.D. State	4	3	3.07	19	4	44	43	20	32
Jordan Harms, N.D. State	4	7	3.15	15	0	71	62	34	62
Reed Pfannenstein, N.D. State	7	4	3.39	15	0	93	99	28	63
Preston Church, Western Illinois	3	5	3.82	13	0	64	54	33	52
Payton Kinney, Omaha	3	3	3.88	16	0	51	39	31	56
Ethan Kenkel, S.D. State	4	1	4.23	14	0	55	55	27	29
Brandon Phelps, Fort Wayne	1	3	4.42	21	2	53	57	32	51
Brett Mogen, S.D. State	0	3	4.56	16	0	49	51	16	39
Luke Lind, N.D. State	5	4	4.79	15	0	83	68	24	92
Ian Koch, Western Illinois	5	5	4.86	16	0	87	96	43	65
Sam Murphy, Omaha	3	8	4.98	16	0	78	97	33	69
Mitchell Ley, Fort Wayne	2	4	5.93	14	1	58	69	29	36
Jake Weber, Fort Wayne	0	8	5.93	14	0	69	101	29	36
Jordan Martin, Fort Wayne	2	8	6.40	14	0	72	106	27	55
Javin Drake, Western Illinois	3	5	6.47	13	0	56	66	22	42
Corey Binger, Omaha	3	11	6.75	16	0	63	86	17	45
Damian Helm, Fort Wayne	2	4	7.61	21	1	60	86	25	44
Grant Suponchick, Omaha	0	4	8.44	17	2	43	60	15	24

SUN BELT CONFERENCE

	Conference		Overall	
Eastern Division	**W**	**L**	**W**	**L**
Coastal Carolina	22	7	37	19
* South Alabama	22	8	40	21
Georgia Southern	18	12	38	21
Troy	16	14	31	25
Eastern Division	**W**	**L**	**W**	**L**
Georgia State	10	20	22	33
Appalachian State	8	22	19	36

	Conference		Overall	
Western Division	**W**	**L**	**W**	**L**
Texas-Arlington	20	10	30	25
Louisiana-Lafayette	19	10	35	21
Arkansas State	13	16	28	27
Texas State	13	17	29	30
Arkansas-Little Rock	11	18	21	34
Louisiana-Monroe	6	24	12	43

All-Conference Team: C—Jared Barnes, Jr., South Alabama. **1B**—Kevin Woodall Jr., Jr., Coastal Carolina. **2B**—Brandon Lockridge, So., Troy. **3B**—Joe Robbins, Sr., Louisiana-Lafayette. **SS**—Drew LaBounty, Jr., South Alabama. **OF**—Billy Cooke, Jr., Coastal Carolina; Travis Swaggerty, So., South Alabama; Theodore Hoffman, Jr., Texas State. **DH**—Omar Salinas, Jr., Texas-Arlington. **UTIL**–Anthony Herrera, Sr., Louisiana-Monroe. **SP**—Alex Cunningham, Sr., Coastal Carolina; Gunner Leger, Jr., Louisiana-Lafayette; Andrew Crane, Jr., Troy. **RP**—Wyatt Marks, Jr., Louisiana-Lafayette. **Player of the Year:** Billy Cooke, Coastal Carolina. **Pitcher of the Year:** Gunner Leger, Louisiana-Lafayette. **Freshman of the Year:** Cory Wood, Coastal Carolina. **Newcomer of the Year:** Andrew Crane, Jr., Troy. **Coach of the Year:** Darin Thomas, Texas-Arlington.

INDIVIDUAL BATTING LEADERS

(Minimum 140 At-Bats)

	AVG	OBP	SLG	AB	2B	3B	HR	RBI	SB
Travis Swaggerty, South Ala.	.361	.487	.567	208	11	1	10	56	19
Dylan Hardy, South Ala.	.358	.421	.488	201	10	2	4	28	18
Billy Cooke, Coastal Carolina	.353	.479	.587	201	15	1	10	37	21
Theodore Hoffman, Texas St	.349	.406	.614	249	16	1	16	56	14
Brandon Lockridge, Troy	.344	.396	.498	241	13	3	6	39	11
Joe Schrimpf, Arkansas State	.343	.474	.528	178	11	2	6	44	1
Jonathan Ortega, Texas State	.339	.410	.502	239	15	3	6	45	22
Brendan Donovan, South Ala.	.338	.445	.577	201	17	2	9	46	8
Omar Salinas, Texas-Arlington	.333	.439	.559	195	11	0	11	44	2
Wood Myers, Coastal Carolina	.330	.393	.476	212	11	1	6	43	11
Hunter Owens, Ark.-Little Rock	.329	.404	.514	222	17	3	6	40	6
Will Olson, Texas-Arlington	.322	.439	.408	174	9	0	2	28	2
Jared Barnes, South Alabama	.320	.416	.605	172	10	0	13	50	2
Nick Gatewood, Ga. Southern	.319	.370	.482	141	8	0	5	22	
0 Jordan Gore, Coastal Carolina	.318	.389	.415	217	12	0	3	29	3
Turner Francis, La.-Monroe	.317	.371	.428	208	10	2	3	25	3
Matt Vernon, App. State	.316	.368	.513	228	15	3	8	31	4
Steven Sensley, La.-Lafayette	.314	.417	.576	191	11	3	11	46	6
Steven Curry, Ga. Southern	.312	.426	.355	234	10	0	0	21	4
Cameron Knight, Ark.-Little Rock	.310	.390	.437	174	12	2	2	23	0
Logan Baldwin, Ga. Southern	.308	.370	.444	214	13	2	4	36	13
Drew LaBounty, South Ala.	.308	.453	.459	185	16	0	4	41	7
Spencer Hemphill, La.-Monroe	.308	.390	.395	185	10	0	2	18	0
Trevor Davis, Troy	.306	.401	.492	193	16	1	6	45	5
Riley Pittman, Ark.-Little Rock	.305	.344	.494	174	7	1	8	34	0

INDIVIDUAL PITCHING LEADERS

(Minimum 40 Innings Pitched)

	W	L	ERA	G	SV	IP	H	BB	SO
Andrew Crane, Troy	6	2	1.47	16	0	61	43	16	60
Gunner Leger, La.-Lafayette	10	2	1.97	15	0	91	66	24	84
Tyler Zuber, Arkansas State	6	1	2.06	25	6	52	29	16	80
Wyatt Marks, La.-Lafayette	2	1	2.28	30	7	59	29	25	100
Austin Gardner, Tex-Arlington	2	1	2.42	29	2	45	36	10	55
Jack Burk, La.-Lafayette	2	4	2.45	11	0	40	38	7	33
Landon Hughes, Ga. Southern	6	2	2.51	28	8	43	26	16	55
Bobby Holmes, Coastal Carolina	5	3	2.51	23	3	43	43	21	38
Alex Cunningham, Coastal Caro	7	2	2.63	15	0	106	75	24	117
Anthony Herrera, La.Monroe	1	5	2.63	22	7	41	32	13	47
Hogan Harris, La.-Lafayette	5	2	2.66	13	0	68	45	34	87
Trae Patterson, Texas-Arlington	7	4	2.75	16	0	98	90	22	73
Matt Peacock, South Ala.	3	3	2.88	25	10	50	41	17	55
Justin Garcia, Ark.-Little Rock	2	1	3.02	33	2	42	23	26	56
Jakob Hernandez, Tex-Arlington	6	1	3.28	13	0	80	72	35	89
Seth Shuman, Ga. Southern	8	0	3.34	14	1	57	54	17	49
Reed Howell, App. State	1	2	3.38	25	5	43	45	20	39
Cory Malcom, Ark.-Little Rock	4	5	3.46	16	0	96	91	19	109
Evan Guillory, La.-Lafayette	4	3	3.57	19	0	63	56	24	49
Colin Schmid, App. State	6	7	3.61	14	0	87	98	26	79
Cole Townsend, Ark.-Little Rock	2	1	3.70	13	0	41	39	20	35
Hunter Gaddis, Ga. Southern	4	4	3.72	15	0	75	63	19	67
Randy Bell, South Ala.	6	3	3.75	15	0	98	108	19	93
Zack Hopeck, Coastal Carolina	5	2	3.79	13	0	62	62	15	50
Tanner Kirby, Arkansas State	4	2	4.01	27	2	49	49	30	43

WEST COAST CONFERENCE

Conference			Overall	
	W	**L**	**W**	**L**
Loyola Marymount	20	7	38	18
* Brigham Young	20	7	38	21
Gonzaga	20	7	33	20
Saint Mary's	18	9	37	20
San Diego	18	9	35	18
San Francisco	11	16	29	28
Santa Clara	9	18	13	40
Pepperdine	8	19	20	32
Pacific	6	21	18	34
Portland	5	22	10	41

All-Conference Team: C—Riley Adams, Jr., San Diego; Bronson Larsen, Sr., Brigham Young. **INF**—Jake Brodt, Jr., Santa Clara; Phil Caulfield, Sr., Loyola Marymount; Edward Haus, So., St. Mary's; Jamey Smart, Jr., Loyola Marymount; Allen Smoot, Sr., San Francisco. **OF**—Joey Fiske, Jr., St. Mary's. **DH**—Aaron Barnett, Sr., Pepperdine; Colton Shaver, Jr., Brigham Young. **SP**—Cory Abbott, Jr., Loyola Marymount; Eli Morgan, Jr., Gonzaga; Nick Sprengel, So., San Diego. **Player of the Year:** Riley Adams, San Diego. **Pitcher of the Year:** Cory Abbott, Jr., Loyola Marymount. **Freshman of the Year:** Kevin Milam, St. Mary's. **Coach of the Year:** Mark Machtolf, Gonzaga.

INDIVIDUAL BATTING LEADERS

(Minimum 140 At-Bats)

	AVG	OBP	SLG	AB	2B	3B	HR	RBI	SB
Brock Hale, BYU	.395	.481	.672	195	14	2	12	48	5
Allen Smoot, San Francisco	.364	.470	.459	209	14	0	2	39	4
Phil Caulfield, Loyola Mary.	.362	.438	.477	218	12	2	3	35	9
Jay Schuyler, San Diego	.352	.405	.521	213	18	0	6	32	4
Brennon Anderson, BYU	.346	.422	.512	260	23	1	6	40	9
James Free II, Pacfiic	.343	.407	.652	181	14	0	14	54	1
Jake Brodt, Santa Clara	.338	.375	.532	216	21	0	7	39	1
Nate Faveo, BYU	.337	.397	.554	166	9	3	7	46	2
Edward Haus, Saint Mary's	.335	.398	.520	221	21	1	6	44	1

Joey Fiske, Saint Mary's	.332	.392	.412	238	12	2	1	31	18
Bronson Larsen, BYU	.330	.426	.621	206	10	1	16	63	1
Jamey Smart, Loyola Mary.	.326	.398	.460	215	11	0	6	41	3
Niko Decolati, Loyala Mary.	.320	.426	.432	206	11	0	4	24	12
Keaton Kringlen, BYU	.318	.383	.442	242	11	2	5	55	3
Daniel Schneemann, BYU	.317	.376	.418	249	13	3	2	38	10
Tanner Chauncey, BYU	.317	.371	.394	246	10	0	3	43	1
Matt Sinatro, San Francisco	.314	.418	.398	226	9	2	2	37	22
Hunt Mercado-Hood, San Diego	.314	.404	.536	220	18	2	9	38	6
Brandon Shearer, Loyola Mary.	.314	.373	.398	194	9	2	1	37	3
Steven Chavez, Loyola Mary.	.314	.355	.408	169	11	1	1	21	0
Sam Brown, Gonzaga	.313	.395	.378	217	8	3	0	22	4
Kevin Milam, Saint Mary's	.313	.397	.547	214	14	0	12	55	0
Riley Adams, San Diego	.312	.424	.564	202	12	0	13	47	2
Michael Perri, San Francisco	.312	.374	.460	215	17	0	5	22	6
Justin Jacobs, Gonzaga	.309	.404	.412	204	12	0	3	38	3

INDIVIDUAL PITCHING LEADERS

(Minimum 40 Innings Pitched)

	W	L	ERA	G	SV	IP	H	BB	SO
Brendan Jenkins, San Francisco	0	4	1.70	30	3	42	43	12	41
Cory Abbott, Loyola Mary.	11	2	1.74	15	0	98	61	28	130
Wyatt Mills, Gonzaga	2	2	1.79	22	12	40	40	4	58
Ken Waldichuk, Saint Mary's	3	4	2.00	22	3	45	37	16	51
Mason Marshall, BYU	3	2	2.14	29	2	46	46	16	45
Codie Paiva, Loyola Mary.	6	0	2.16	24	5	58	49	11	52
Thomas Ponticelli, San Fran.	4	2	2.45	13	0	70	62	10	65
Kiko Garcia, Pepperdine	4	1	2.53	20	1	43	43	9	25
Troy Conyers, San Diego	2	1	2.70	25	13	47	38	13	65
Giuseppe Benedetti, Loyola Mary.	4	0	2.74	16	0	43	45	10	15
Eli Morgan, Gonzaga	10	2	2.86	14	0	101	80	31	138
Brenton Arriaga, Loyola Mary.	7	2	2.93	14	0	89	83	18	66
Kevin Baker, Portland	3	6	3.03	14	1	62	67	21	79
Paul Richan, San Diego	5	2	3.05	18	0	77	84	21	73
Justin Vernia, Gonzaga	7	3	3.11	14	0	90	88	20	59
Benji Post, San Francisco	7	2	3.29	26	0	63	49	31	40
Nick Sprengel, San Diego	9	1	3.29	15	0	82	77	33	86
Calvin LeBrun, Gonzaga	1	1	3.56	22	3	48	50	12	39
Ryan Wilson, Pepperdine	2	7	3.61	14	0	90	87	34	72
Hayden Rogers, BYU	9	2	3.63	16	0	92	93	23	49
Louis Crow, San Diego	3	2	3.67	21	2	49	55	21	41
Ricky Reynoso, Pacific	5	7	3.75	15	0	74	77	25	56
Sam Hellinger, Gonzaga	4	3	3.79	23	2	40	50	9	25
Jake Valdez, Saint Mary's	4	3	3.81	17	1	76	80	23	61
Vince Arobic, Pacific	4	4	3.86	24	7	42	43	20	44

WESTERN ATHLETIC CONFERENCE

	Conference		Overall	
	W	L	W	L
Grand Canyon	20	4	29	25
New Mexico State	19	5	35	22
Cal State Bakersfield	14	10	31	24
* Sacramento State	12	12	32	29
Utah Valley	11	13	18	36
Northern Colorado	10	14	24	29
Seattle	8	16	20	35
Texas-Rio Grande Valley	7	17	26	38
Chicago State	7	17	11	41

All-Conference Teams: C—Mason Fishback, Jr., New Mexico State. **1B**—Ian Evans, Jr., Grand Canyon. **2B**—David Metzgar, Sr., Cal State Bakersfield. **3B**—Tyler Wyatt, So., Grand Canyon. **SS**—Ryan Grotjohn, Sr., Cal State Bakersfield. **OF**—Garrison Schwartz, Jr., Grand Canyon; Tom Lerouge, Jr., Grand Canyon; Dan Hetzel, Sr., New Mexico State. At-Large: Ian Dawkins, Jr., Sacramento State; L.J. Hatch, Sr., New Mexico State; Kyle Bradish, So., New Mexico State. **SP**—Max Carter, Sr., Cal State Bakersfield; Parker Brahms, Fr., Sacramento State. **RP**—A.J. Franks, Sr., Grand Canyon. **Player of the Year:** Garrison Schwartz, Grand Canyon. **Pitcher of the Year:** Max Carter, Cal State Bakersfield. **Freshman of the Year:** Parker Brahms, Sacramento State. **Coach of the Year:** Andy Stankiewicz, Grand Canyon.

INDIVIDUAL BATTING LEADERS

(Minimum 140 At-Bats)

	AVG	OBP	SLG	AB	2B	3B	HR	RBI	SB
Ryan Grotjohn, CS Bakersfield	.390	.459	.512	213	15	4	1	42	6
Brent Sakurai, N.M. State	.377	.427	.571	231	15	9	4	41	9
David Metzgar, CS Bakersfield	.372	.425	.465	215	10	5	0	36	18
Andrew Penner, CS Bakersfield	.372	.456	.401	207	4	1	0	32	6
Mason Fishback, N.M. State	.365	.417	.564	211	16	1	8	52	3
Trevor Peterson, Utah Valley	.356	.425	.461	219	12	1	3	20	7
Tom Lerough, Grand Canyon	.349	.390	.432	169	9	1	1	27	6
Austin Botello, N.M. State	.345	.434	.524	229	17	3	6	55	2
Jackson Overlund, Utah Valley	.342	.436	.580	193	22	3	6	34	4
Mahlik Jones, CS Bakersfield	.341	.389	.411	214	6	3	1	49	9
Ian Dawkins, Sacramento St	.340	.401	.439	262	11	3	3	29	15
Austin Bull, Grand Canyon	.339	.436	.404	218	9	1	1	21	6
Austin Lively, Seattle	.335	.416	.404	188	10	0	1	31	4
Jack Pauley, Northern Colorado	.332	.372	.561	214	21	2	8	46	4
Ian Evans, Grand Canyon	.323	.407	.485	198	15	1	5	46	3
Dan Hetzel, N.M. State	.322	.436	.630	208	18	2	14	67	1
L.J. Hatch, N.M. State	.321	.408	.498	215	15	4	5	36	14
Conrad McMahon, UTRGV	.317	.393	.354	189	5	1	0	23	11
Aaron Strossma, Seattle	.317	.405	.438	224	8	2	5	41	19
Jose Garcia, UTRGV	.317	.453	.519	183	12	2	7	33	9
Matt Sullivan, Chicago State	.314	.352	.402	169	8	2	1	19	3
Tristen Carranza, N.M. State	.314	.424	.649	185	12	1	16	52	1
Max Carter, CS Bakersfield	.311	.397	.350	206	5	0	1	34	3
Tyler Watt, Grand Canyon	.309	.388	.408	152	7	1	2	21	4
Joseph Collazo, UTRGV	.307	.418	.434	189	10	1	4	41	8

INDIVIDUAL PITCHING LEADERS

(Minimum 40 Innings Pitched)

	W	L	ERA	G	SV	IP	H	BB	SO
Naithen Dewsnap, CS Bakersfield	3	1	2.39	31	14	49	39	7	60
A.J. Franks, Grand Canyon	4	0	2.60	34	4	62	59	8	39
Carter Johnson, UTRGV	5	5	2.70	14	0	80	64	26	87
Austin Root, Sacramento State	2	0	2.70	30	3	57	56	9	37
Jonathan Groff, N.M. State	8	6	3.10	16	0	87	83	32	65
Parker Brahms, Sacramento St	8	4	3.13	17	0	98	81	26	63
Kyle Bradish, N.M. State	8	2	3.20	15	0	84	62	49	89
Justin Dillon, Sacramento St	5	8	3.36	19	0	112	91	26	108
Jake Repavich, Grand Canyon	6	4	3.80	14	0	88	90	16	57
Isaiah Moten, CS Bakersfield	4	4	3.90	23	0	58	56	21	29
Max Carter, CS Bakersfield	8	2	3.94	14	0	94	88	17	66
Jake Wong, Grand Canyon	5	3	4.00	14	0	79	77	25	51
Jack Schneider, Grand Canyon	7	0	4.11	11	0	50	43	19	32
Aaron Hamilton, N Colorado	6	5	4.14	17	1	76	78	30	67
Matthew McHugh, N.M. State	4	2	4.24	26	0	57	58	24	48
Aaron Charles, CS Bakersfield	4	1	4.29	9	0	42	48	13	25
Joe Baier, CS Bakersfield	3	3	4.44	19	1	49	57	28	30
ake Prizina, Seattle	5	3	4.44	20	1	103	101	31	65
Andrew Garcia, UTRGV	4	3	4.45	18	0	85	110	32	63
Jake Perkins, CS Bakersfield	2	7	4.54	14	0	77	93	31	64
Marco Briones, Utah Valley	3	1	4.74	22	0	44	57	16	31
Marcel Renteria, N.M. State	7	3	4.78	15	0	79	81	30	86
Tyler Oldenberg, Seattle	4	1	4.91	21	1	59	71	18	44
Austin Roberts, Sacramento St	4	1	4.95	19	0	64	61	40	44
Jacob Howard, N Colorado	3	0	4.96	25	2	45	60	24	39

SMALL COLLEGES

BY OWEN MCCUE AND JUSTIN PERLINE

NCAA DIVISION II

West Chester (Pa.) coach Jad Prachniak came into the 2017 NCAA Division II College World Series, held in Grand Prairie, Texas, unbeaten in the CWS. He left the same way. Prachniak, who won a national championship in his first year with West Chester in 2012, helped guide the Golden Rams to their second title in six years.

West Chester won all four of its games at the CWS, beating UC San Diego, 5-2, in the title game. Golden Rams closer Josh McClain allowed one run in four innings of relief in the championship game and went 2-0, 1.86 to win the tournament's most outstanding player award.

UC San Diego righthander Kyle Goodbrand dominated in the tournament. He tossed a complete-game shutout in UC San Diego's 10-0 semifinal win and allowed six hits and struck out six in 11 scoreless innings overall.

DIVISION II WORLD SERIES

Site: Grand Prairie, Texas.
Participants: Colorado Mesa (50-12); Delta State, Miss. (45-13); Lindenwood, Mo. (40-20); North Georgia (46-12); Quincy, Ill. (37-23); St. Thomas Aquinas, N.Y. (44-17); UC San Diego (44-19); West Chester, Penn. (44-12).
Champion: West Chester.
Runner-up: UC San Diego.
Outstanding player: Josh McClain, RHP, West Chester.

LEADERS

BATTING AVERAGE (Minimum 140 at bats)

RK. PLAYER, POS., TEAM	CLASS	AVG	OBP	SLG
1. Justin Childers, 1B, Ohio Dominican	Jr.	.451	.526	.846
2. David Vinsky, OF, Northwood (Mich.)	Fr.	.449	.483	.642
3. Dylan Harris, 3B, St. Leo (Fla.)	Sr.	.448	.472	.593
4. Alex DeLaCruz, DH, Eastern New Mexico	Jr.	.441	.522	.672
5. Cal Gentry, 3B, Georgia College	Fr.	.441	.487	.533
6. Zack Shannon, 1B, Delta State (Miss.)	Jr.	.434	.498	.758
7. Tyler Curtis, 3B, Lynn (Fla.)	Sr.	.433	.518	.733
8. Chad Frazier, SS, Concord (W.V.)	Jr.	.428	.511	.608
8. Josh Newell, OF, Regis (Colo.)	Sr.	.428	.495	.716
10. Kevin Santa, SS, Tampa	Sr.	.423	.502	.581

EARNED RUN AVERAGE (Minimum 40 innings pitched)

RK. PITCHER, TEAM	CLASS	W	L	ERA
1. Jacob Blank, Augustana (S.D.)	Jr.	10	0	0.78
2. Kyle Leahy, Colorado Mesa	Fr.	13	0	1.41
3. Roscoe Blackburn, Malone (Ohio)	Jr.	4	2	1.42
3. Cam Monagle, Merrimack (Mass.)	So.	2	0	1.42
5. John Holland, Felician (N.J.)	Sr.	8	1	1.43
6. Tim Kennedy, New Haven (Conn.)	Jr.	7	0	1.43
7. Joshua Hurford, Malone (Ohio)	Jr.	7	0	1.48
8. T.J. Santiago, Adelphi (N.Y.)	Sr.	8	3	1.51
9. David Palmer, New Haven (Conn.)	Jr.	8	1	1.51
10. Dalton Roach, Minnesota State	Jr.	10	1	1.56

CATEGORY LEADERS: BATTING

DEPT.	PLAYER, POS., TEAM	CLASS	G	TOTAL
OBP	* Max Hogan, 3B, Missouri Southern State	Sr.	55	.528
SLG	* Justin Childers, 1B, Ohio Dominican	Jr.	48	.846
R	Nick Beinlich, OF, Belmont Abbey (N.C.)	Jr.	54	76
H	David Vinsky, OF, Northwood (Mich.)	Fr.	59	109
2B	Dylan Jones, OF, Flagler (Fla.)	Sr.	55	27
3B	Dion Williams, of, Arkansas-Fort Smith	Jr.	56	11
HR	Michael Rothmund, 1b, Illinois-Springfield	Jr.	54	24
RBI	Zack Shannon, 1b, Delta State (Miss.)	Jr.	57	88
SB	Randy Norris, of, Winston-Salem State (N.C.)	So.	58	47

**Minimum 140 at bats*

CATEGORY LEADERS: PITCHING

DEPT.	PITCHER, TEAM	CLASS	TOTAL
W	Kyle Leahy, Colorado Mesa	Fr.	13
L	Sam Beattie, Oklahoma Panhandle	Sr.	11
	Alex Ruxlow, Fort Hays State (Kan.)	Jr.	11
SV	Gibson Russ, Central Oklahoma	Sr.	15
	Nick Vourmard, Cal State Stanislaus	Sr.	15
G	Nikko Pablo, Northwest Missouri State	Sr.	34
	Jonathan Porter, West Alabama	Sr.	34
IP	Brendan Feldmann, Lindenwood (Mo.)	Sr.	121
SO	Marshall Kasowski, West Texas A&M	Jr.	165
SO/9	* Marshall Kasowski, West Texas A&M	Jr.	15.91
BB/9	* Kellen Sheppard, Point Loma (Calif.)	Sr.	.72
WHIP	* Dalton Roach, Minnesota State	Jr.	.76

**Minimum 40 IP*

NCAA DIVISION III

California Lutheran won the final two games of the championship series in Appleton, Wis., to earn its first championship. Tournament MVP Miguel Salud pitched the final three innings to close out the title game and earn his 14th save of the season. Salud had three saves in four CWS appearances, striking out nine in 7.1 innings.

Division III World Series

Site: Appleton, Wisc.
Participants: California Lutheran (40-11); Concordia (Ill.) (34-13); Massachusetts-Boston (38-12); North Central, Ill. (31-18); Oswego State, N.Y. (32-11); Roanoke, Va. (35-19); Washington & Jefferson, Pa. (42-13); Wheaton, Mass. (27-17).
Champion: Cal Lutheran.
Runner-up: Washington & Jefferson.
Outstanding player: Miguel Salud, RHP, Cal Lutheran.

LEADERS

BATTING AVERAGE (Minimum 120 at bats)

RK. PLAYER, POS., TEAM	CLASS	AVG	OBP	SLG
1. Trevor Mears, OF, Wesley (Del.)	Sr.	.500	.568	.772
1. Wyatt Ulrich, OF, St. John's (Minn.)	Fr.	.500	.523	.566
3. Garet Griffin, SS, Mitchell (Conn.)	Jr.	.496	.556	.752
4. Ian Mikowski, OF, Adrian (Mich.)	Sr.	.472	.580	.551
5. Vince Rebar, 2B, Marywood (Pa.)	Sr.	.464	.497	.717

EARNED RUN AVERAGE (Minimum 30 IP)

RK. PITCHER, TEAM	CLASS	W	L	ERA
1. Josh Fleming, Webster (Mo.)	Jr.	8	1	0.67
2. Phil Mary, Mount Union (Ohio)	So.	9	0	0.78
3. Bryan Kaufman, Massachusetts-Boston	Jr.	3	0	1.03
4. Billy Dimlow, Emory (Ga.)	So.	6	2	1.09
5. Ryan Obin, Wentworth (Mass.)	So.	5	3	1.13

CATEGORY LEADERS: BATTING

DEPT.	PLAYER, POS., TEAM	CLASS	G	TOTAL
OBP	* Ian Mikowski, OF, Adrian (Mich.)	Sr.	47	.580
SLG	* Tanner Nishioka, OF, Pomona-Pitzer (Calif.)	Sr.	39	.888
HR	Tanner Nishioka, OF, Pomona-Pitzer (Calif.)	Sr.	39	18
RBI	Chris Zapata, C, Centenary (La.)	Jr.	45	71
SB	Nate Lynch, OF, Earlham (Ind.)	Sr.	43	47

**Minimum 120 at bats*

CATEGORY LEADERS: PITCHING

DEPT.	PITCHER, TEAM	CLASS	TOTAL
W	Felix Minjarez, Redlands (Calif.)	Jr.	12
	Tommy Parsons, Adrian (Mich.)	Jr.	12
SV	Miguel Salud, California Lutheran	Jr.	14
	T.J. Storer, Ohio Northern	Jr.	14
SO	Jimi Keating, Spalding (Ky.)	Jr.	124

NAIA

Lewis-Clark State (Idaho) continued its dominance of National Association of Intercollegiate Athletics by capturing its third straight title. It was the Warriors' 19th national title, which leads all NAIA programs.

The host Warriors, who came into the tournament as the No. 5 seed, defeated No. 2 Faulkner (Ala.), 6-4, in the championship game in Lewiston, Idaho, in a rematch of last year's final.

NAIA WORLD SERIES

Site: Lewiston, Idaho.
Participants: Faulkner, Ala., (54-12); Keiser, Fla., (43-21); Lewis-Clark State, Idaho, (40-14); Missouri Baptist (45-16); Oklahoma City (50-10); Science & Arts, Okla., (45-17); The Master's, Calif., (41-23); William Carey, Miss., (45-20).
Champion: Lewis-Clark State.
Runner-up: Faulkner.
Outstanding player: J.J. Robinson, DH, Lewis-Clark State.

LEADERS

BATTING AVERAGE (Minimum 140 at bats)

RK. PLAYER, POS., TEAM	CLASS	AVG	OBP	SLG
1. Andrew Warner, C, Columbia (Mo.)	Jr.	.478	.583	.872
2. Trevor Achenbach, SS, Oklahoma Wesleyan	Sr.	.476	.532	.847
3. Ernesto Lizardi, C, Wayland Baptist (Texas)	Sr.	.474	.539	.617
4. Will Price, OF, Oklahoma Wesleyan	Sr.	.460	.506	.912
5. Glen McClain, 1B, Indiana Tech	So.	.457	.528	.700

EARNED RUN AVERAGE (Minimum 40 innings pitched)

RK. PITCHER, TEAM	CLASS	W	L	ERA
1. Matt Burleton, Marian (Ind.)	So.	8	2	1.17
2. Damon Proctor, Northwestern Ohio	Sr.	13	0	1.50
3. Enrique Zamora, Reinhardt (Ga.)	Sr.	8	0	1.73
4. Zach Mahoney, Mayville State (N.D.)	Sr.	7	3	1.89
5. Josh Arnold, Purdue Northwest (Ind.)	Jr.	3	1	1.92

CATEGORY LEADERS: BATTING

DEPT.	PLAYER, POS., TEAM	CLASS	G	TOTAL
OBP	* Andrew Warner, C, Columbia (Mo.)	Jr.	51	.583
SLG	* Will Price, OF, Oklahoma Wesleyan	Sr.	63	.912
HR	Will Price, OF, Oklahoma Wesleyan	Sr.	63	28
RBI	Will Price, OF, Oklahoma Wesleyan	Sr.	63	101
SB	Tra'mayne Holmes, 3B, Faulkner (Ala.)	Jr.	65	59

Minimum 140 at bats

CATEGORY LEADERS: PITCHING

DEPT.	PITCHER, TEAM	CLASS	TOTAL
W	Kyle Chavez, Talladega (Ala.)	Sr.	13
	Torrey Escamilla, Midland (Neb.)	Jr.	13
	Damon Proctor, Northwestern Ohio	Sr.	13
	Grant Wolfram, Davenport (Mich.)	So.	13
SO	Ben Madison, Central Baptist (Ark.)	So.	129
	Damon Proctor, Northwestern Ohio	So.	129

NJCAA DIVISION I

Chipola (Fla.) JC team claimed its first national championship since 2007 with a 15-6 championship victory over San Jacinto (Texas) JC in Grand Junction, Colo. Chipola had previously lost to San Jac, causing it to fall into the losers' bracket, but the Indians' offense proved unstoppable. Chipola scored 85 runs in the tournament, six more than the previous record of 79 set by Southern Idaho JC in 1984.

NJCAA Division I World Series

Site: Grand Junction, Colo.
Participants: Chipola, Fla., (51-9); Cowley County, Kan., (45-18); Crowder, Mo., (54-14); Dyersburg State, Tenn., (48-9); Florence-Darlington Tech, S.C., (42-19); McLennan, Texas, (52-13); San Jacinto, Texas, (48-17); Southern Nevada (45-18); Wabash Valley, Ill., (50-15); Wallace-Dothan, Ala., (43-21).
Champion: Chipola.
Runner-up: San Jacinto.
Outstanding player: Jose Caballero, SS, Chipola.

LEADERS

BATTING AVERAGE (Minimum 140 at bats)

RK. PLAYER, POS., TEAM	CLASS	AVG	OBP	SLG
1. Michael Helman, 2B, Hutchinson (Kan.)	So.	.487	.567	.829
2. Luis Pelayo, OF, Connors State (Okla.)	Fr.	.459	.550	.668
3. Connor Quick, 1B, North Central Missouri	Fr.	.458	.527	.633
4. Miguel Medina, SS, ASA-Brooklyn	Fr.	.455	.508	.610
5. Peyton Sorrels, 2B, Harford (Md.)	So.	.451	.495	.747

EARNED RUN AVERAGE (Minimum 40 innings pitched)

RK. PITCHER, TEAM	CLASS	W	L	ERA
1. Ryan Beard, Southern Idaho	So.	5	1	0.84
2. Braden Scott, Olney Central (Ill.)	Fr.	8	1	1.23
3. Luis Sanchez Tejada, ASA-Brooklyn	Fr.	7	2	1.24
4. Casey Cobb, Chattahoochee Valley (Ala.)	Fr.	10	4	1.29
5. Troy Newell, Jefferson (Mo.)	So.	11	1	1.40

CATEGORY LEADERS: BATTING

DEPT.	PLAYER, POS., TEAM	CLASS	G	TOTAL
OBP	* Tre Todd, C, Harford (Md.)	So.	56	.577
SLG	* Reynaldo Rivera, 1B/OF, Chipola (Fla.)	So.	59	.865
HR	Dalton Reed, 1B, Seminole State (Okla.)	Fr.	58	26
RBI	Jake Northern, 3B, Connors State (Okla.)	Fr.	59	100
SB	Ian Raidy, 2B, South Mountain (Ariz.)	Fr.	55	49

Minimum 140 at bats

CATEGORY LEADERS: PITCHING

DEPT.	PITCHER, TEAM	CLASS	TOTAL
W	Seth Hougesen, Dyersburg State (Tenn.)	So.	14
L	Cooper Harris, Vernon (Texas)	Fr.	11
SV	Taylor Floyd, Grayson (Texas)	Fr.	16
IP	Eric Ligda, Arizona Western	So.	109
SO	Tommy Romero, Eastern Florida State	So.	145

NJCAA DIVISION II

After losing in its first game of the Series in Enid, Okla., Kankakee (Ill.) JC rattled off six straight wins to grab its first national title. Kankakee used a seven-run fifth inning to take down Mercer County (N.J.) JC, 11-5, in the championship game.

NJCAA DIVISION II WORLD SERIES

Site: Enid, Okla.
Participants: Connecticut-Avery Point (29-16); Hinds, Miss., (34-18); Kankakee, Ill., (54-11-1); Lansing, Mich., (41-17); Mercer County, N.J., (48-14); Murray State, Okla., (48-14-1); Parkland, Ill. (52-9-1); Phoenix (43-22); Pitt, N.C., (42-9); Southeast, Neb., (40-20).
Champion: Kankakee.
Runner-up: Mercer County.
Outstanding player: Matt Littrell, 2B, Kankakee.

LEADERS

BATTING AVERAGE (Minimum 140 at bats)

RK. PLAYER, POS., TEAM	CLASS	AVG	OBP	SLG
1. Tyreque Reed, 1B/OF, Itawamba (Miss.)	So.	.504	.638	.943
2. Bailey Peterson, SS, Kellogg (Mich.)	Fr.	.473	.590	.836
3. Jacob Gleason, OF, Jackson (Mich.)	So.	.470	.545	.780
4. Bailey Walker, OF, Northeast Mississippi	So.	.465	.538	.683
5. Chandler Jenkins, OF, Catawba Valley (N.C.)	So.	.460	.516	.868

EARNED RUN AVERAGE (Minimum 40 IP)

RK. PITCHER, TEAM	CLASS	W	L	ERA
1. Dennis Brady, Mercer County (N.J.)	So.	11	2	0.96
2. Joe Funkhouser, Kirkwood (Iowa)	So.	5	3	1.53
3. Ben Stiglets, Jones County (Miss.)	So.	11	0	1.59
4. Justin Walke, Pitt (N.C.)	So.	7	2	1.66
5. Brian Rourke, Frederick (Md.)	So.	10	1	1.80

CATEGORY LEADERS: BATTING

DEPT.	PLAYER, POS., TEAM	CLASS	G	TOTAL
OBP *	Tyreque Reed, 1B/OF Itawamba (Miss.)	So.	47	.638
SLG *	Dalton Bealmer, OF, Metropolitan-Longview (Mo.)	Fr.	52	1.029
HR	Dalton Bealmer, OF, Metropolitan-Longview (Mo.)	Fr.	52	26
RBI	Dalton Bealmer, OF, Metropolitan-Longview (Mo.)	Fr.	52	82
SB	Nick Daley, OF, Chandler-Gilbert (Ariz.)	So.	55	57

**Minimum 140 at bats*

CATEGORY LEADERS: PITCHING

DEPT.	PITCHER, TEAM	CLASS	TOTAL
W	Logan Robbins, Jones County (Miss.)	So.	12
L	Charles Morris, New River (Va.)	Fr.	10
SV	Jake Suddreth, Mesa (Ariz.)	Fr.	16
IP	Jared Flores, Northern Oklahoma	So.	95
SO	Brady Schanuel, Parkland (Ill.)	So.	130

NJCAA DIVISION III

Tyler (Texas) JC cruised to its fourth straight national championship, defeating Niagara County (N.Y.) JC, 5-1, in the final in Greeneville, Tenn. The Apaches outscored opponents 25-9 in four games.

NJCAA DIVISION III WORLD SERIES

Site: Greeneville, Tenn.
Participants: Century, Minn., (35-14); Cumberland County, N.J., (55-8); Delta, Mich., (35-23); Niagara County, N.Y., (45-10); Northampton, Pa., (35-9); Prince George's, Md., (33-15-1); Surry, N.C., (29-24-1); Tyler, Texas, (41-20);
Champion: Tyler.
Runner-up: Niagara County.
Outstanding player: Taylor Broadway, DH/RHP, Tyler.

LEADERS

BATTING AVERAGE (Minimum 120 at bats)

RK. PLAYER, POS., TEAM	CLASS	AVG	OBP	SLG
1. Jeff Charles, C, Lehigh Carbon (Pa.)	So.	.488	.585	.816
2. Ryan Collins, SS, Northern Essex (Mass.)	Fr.	.458	.526	.695
3. Blaine McCullars, OF, Richland (Texas)	So.	.448	.515	.569
4. Brandon Henshaw, SS, Genesee (N.Y.)	So.	.447	.524	.654
5. Jake Hansen, OF/RHP, Anoka-Ramsey (Minn.)	Fr.	.446	.523	.620

EARNED RUN AVERAGE (Minimum 30 IP)

RK. PITCHER, TEAM	CLASS	W	L	ERA
1. Joseph Murphy, Suffolk County (N.Y.)	So.	6	1	1.21
2. Francisco Colon, Riverland (Minn.)	So.	7	0	1.34
3. Christian Young, Niagara County (N.Y.)	So.	6	2	1.57
4. Corey Imbriano, Northern Essex (Mass.)	Fr.	6	1	1.67
5. Zach Rustad, Century (Minn.)	So.	6	1	1.69

CALIFORNIA JCS

Grossmont JC won its first state championship with a 10-6 win against defending state champ Santa Rosa JC in the California Community College Athletic Association title game in Fresno.

CALIFORNIA CC ATHLETIC ASSOCIATION

Site: Fresno, Calif.
Participants: El Camino (40-11), Grossmont (38-8-1), Ohlone (42-7), Santa Rosa (38-11).
Champion: Grossmont.
Runner-up: Santa Rosa.
Outstanding player: Hayden Shenefield, RHP, Grossmont.

LEADERS

BATTING AVERAGE (Minimum 120 at bats)

RK. PLAYER, POS., TEAM	CLASS	AVG	OBP	SLG
1. Cristian Montes, OF, Glendale	So.	.450	.524	.608
2. Cabot Van Til, OF, Grossmont	So.	.449	.545	.669
3. Ryan Ruley, OF, Ohlone	So.	.435	.500	.740
4. Mike Bowes, OF, Mission	So.	.434	.480	.623
5. Joey Cooper, OF, Palomar	So.	.434	.516	.566

EARNED RUN AVERAGE (Minimum 30 IP)

RK. PITCHER, TEAM	CLASS	W	L	ERA
1. Eric Schreter, Butte	So.	6	0	0.58
2. Andrew Quezada, Cypress	So.	9	2	1.17
3. James Giambalvo, Glendale	So.	3	2	1.40
4. Kobe Portillo, Fresno	Fr.	7	2	1.42
5. Ryan Semon, Palomar	Fr.	9	0	1.54

NORTHWEST ATHLETIC CONFERENCE

Lower Columbia (Wash.) JC captured its second Northwest CC title in the past three years. The Red Devils now have 12 baseball championships.

NORTHWEST ATHLETIC CONFERENCE

Site: Longview, Wash.
Participants: Columbia Basin, Wash., (35-15); Everett, Wash., (37-13); Lane, Ore., (28-21); Linn-Benton, Ore., (30-12); Lower Columbia, Wash., (40-10); Mount Hood, Ore., (18-25); Tacoma, Wash., (30-17); Walla Walla, Wash., (30-20).
Champion: Lower Columbia.
Runner-up: Everett.
Outstanding player: Ricky Muzzy, 2B, Lower Columbia.

LEADERS

BATTING AVERAGE (Minimum 120 at bats)

RK. PLAYER, POS., TEAM	CLASS	AVG	OBP	SLG
1. Collin Runge, SS, Chemeketa (Ore.)	So.	.406	.510	.494
2. Cole McKenzie, OF, Yakima Valley (Wash.)	Fr.	.396	.530	.532
3. Austin Shenton, 3B, Bellevue (Wash.)	Fr.	.395	.494	.600
4. Jace McKinney, OF, Mount Hood (Ore.)	So.	.385	.429	.460
5. Peter Perkins, OF, Tacoma (Wash.)	So.	.379	.446	.483

EARNED RUN AVERAGE (Minimum 30 IP)

RK. PITCHER, TEAM	CLASS	W	L	ERA
1. Mac McCarty, Pierce (Wash.)	So.	4	4	0.99
2. Garrett Westberg, Tacoma (Wash.)	So.	6	1	1.15
3. Nick Flesher, Spokane (Wash.)	So.	6	4	1.55
4. Jesse Davis, Lane (Ore.)	Fr.	4	5	1.81
5. Hunter French, Columbia Basin (Wash.)	Fr.	10	1	1.82

COLLEGE SUMMER BASEBALL

BY TEDDY CAHILL

USA Baseball's Collegiate National Team did not have a roster as rich in prospects as it has had in some previous years, but it had a strong summer on the field. Team USA went 10-4 against international opposition and won all three of its series, beating Taiwan, Cuba and Japan.

The CNT won its first seven international games, sweeping a four-game series against Taiwan before winning the first three games against Cuba. It has now won the annual series against Cuba three years in a row and has won all three of the friendship series played on American soil since the series was restarted six years ago.

Team USA finished the summer with a taut series against Japan. After falling behind 2 games to 1, the CNT won back-to-back 3-1 games to finish the summer with a flourish.

Playing Cuba is a highlight of the schedule every year for both teams, even though the Cuban national team is not quite its former self, thanks to so many of those defections draining top talent off the island. Cuba didn't make it out of the first round of the World Baseball Classic this March, and the national team went 5-16 against Can-Am League competition before taking on Team USA.

Higinio Velez, the Cuban federation president and former team manager who won silver in the 2000 Olympics and gold in 2004, said the Cubans enjoy playing the American college players every year."

"Go back to when only (amateurs) were on the national teams," Velez said via translator, "and we have had many important games, many times where we have had to fight the Collegiate National Team over many gold medals."

Outfielder Steele Walker (Oklahoma) was named MVP of the Taiwan and Cuba series and hit .333/.417/.514 with two home runs and seven stolen bases in 20 games."You take pride in wearing the USA," he said. "It kind of has a different meaning, bigger than yourself that you can beat another country."

Walker and outfielder Travis Swaggerty (South Alabama) teamed up at the top of the order to help lead Team USA offensively. Swaggerty hit .328/.449/.406 with six stolen bases in a breakout summer. Catcher Grant Koch (Arkansas) led the team in hitting with a .372/.500/.535 line.

A year after producing a team ERA of 1.81, Team USA was again strong on the mound in 2017. The staff combined for a 2.15 team ERA and a 198-to-58 strikeout-to-walk ratio. Lefthanders Steven Gingery (Texas Tech) and Konnor Pilkington (Mississippi State) were the CNT's top starters and combined to go 2-0, 1.91 in nine appearances (seven starts).

COLLEGIATE NATIONAL TEAM STATS

Year indicates 2014-15 class standing

PLAYER, POS.	YEAR	SCHOOL	AVG	OBP	SLG	G	AB	R	H	2B	3B	HR	RBI	BB	SO	SB
Grant Koch, C	Jr.	Arkansas	.372	.500	.535	20	43	9	16	1	0	2	9	10	11	1
Steele Walker, OF	Jr.	Oklahoma	.333	.417	.514	20	72	13	24	5	1	2	11	10	15	7
Travis Swaggerty, OF	Jr.	South Alabama	.328	.449	.406	19	64	15	21	3	1	0	7	11	18	6
Nick Madrigal, SS/2B	Jr.	Oregon State	.258	.292	.323	15	62	8	16	1	0	1	4	3	6	8
Andrew Vaughn, 1B	So.	California	.242	.320	.364	19	66	6	16	3	1	1	9	7	16	2
Seth Beer, OF	Jr.	Clemson	.232	.368	.304	19	56	5	13	1	0	1	13	6	8	0
Jake McCarthy, OF	Jr.	Virginia	.232	.317	.321	20	56	13	13	3	1	0	6	6	16	3
Braden Shewmake, 2B	So.	Texas A&M	.209	.327	.302	17	43	5	9	2	1	0	6	5	7	2
Nick Meyer, C	Jr.	Cal Poly	.188	.350	.250	15	16	1	3	1	0	0	2	3	3	0
Tyler Frank, 3B/OF	Jr.	Florida Atlantic	.162	.298	.216	15	37	7	6	2	0	0	7	6	7	1
Cadyn Grenier, SS	Jr.	Oregon State	.158	.333	.289	14	38	7	6	2	0	1	2	7	13	2
Jeremy Eierman, 3B	Jr.	Missouri State	.125	.182	.225	18	40	5	5	4	0	0	6	2	10	1

PITCHER, POS.	YEAR	SCHOOL	W	L	ERA	G	SV	IP	H	R	ER	BB	SO	AVG
Patrick Raby, RHP	Jr.	Vanderbilt	3	0	0.00	6	0	19	8	1	0	5	15	.125
Ryley Gilliam, RHP	Jr.	Clemson	1	1	0.00	9	3	8	4	5	0	2	9	.148
Casey Mize, RHP	Jr.	Auburn	1	0	0.00	2	0	7	5	0	0	0	8	.192
Tyler Holton, LHP	Jr.	Florida State	2	0	0.69	4	0	13	11	2	1	2	14	.224
Tim Cate, LHP	Jr.	Connecticut	0	0	0.75	5	0	12	3	2	1	4	20	.081
Dallas Woolfolk, RHP	Jr.	Mississippi	1	0	0.87	10	4	10	4	2	1	7	13	.118
Steven Gingery, LHP	Jr.	Texas Tech	2	0	1.12	4	0	16	9	2	2	4	9	.176
Jon Olsen, RHP	Jr.	UCLA	1	0	2.61	6	0	10	13	3	3	2	15	.302
Konnor Pilkington, LHP	Jr.	Mississippi State	0	0	2.65	5	0	17	11	6	5	5	12	.183
Nick Sprengel, LHP	Jr.	San Diego	1	0	2.89	10	0	9	2	3	3	8	12	.067
Gianluca Dalatri, RHP	So.	North Carolina	0	1	3.27	3	0	11	9	4	4	2	10	.231
Bryce Tucker, LHP	Jr.	Central Florida	0	1	4.50	10	0	10	5	7	5	6	18	.152
Jake Irvin, RHP	Jr.	Oklahoma	1	0	5.14	2	0	7	5	4	4	4	10	.208

Brewster Wins Cape Title

Brewster completed an improbable run through the playoffs to win the Cape Cod League championship for the second time in franchise history and the first time since 2000.

East Division rivals Orleans and Yarmouth-Dennis were again two of the most talented teams on the Cape and posted the league's two best regular-season records. But the Whitecaps upended both in the playoffs before defeating Bourne, 2 games to 1, in the finals.

Brewster's victory snapped Y-D's three-year run as champions. The Red Sox had been attempting to become the first team to win four straight titles since Cotuit did so from 1972-75.

The Cape had a strong Tobacco Road feel this summer, as Duke outfielders Griffin Conine and Jimmy Herron swept the All-Star Game MVP honors and righthander Tyler Baum (North Carolina) won the pitching triple crown, going 5-1, 2.72 with 41 strikeouts.

This summer also marked John Schiffner's final season as manager of Chatham, ending his run of 25 seasons at the club's helm. When his career came to a close when the Anglers lost in the first round of the playoffs, Schiffner was the longest-tenured and winningest coach in the Cape's history. He will join the coaching staff at Maine, working with head coach Nick Derba, who played for Schiffner and later coached with him at Chatham.

Schiffner took over Chatham in 1993 and went on to coach more than 100 major leaguers and 39 first-round draft picks. He won 541 games and won the league title in 1996 and 1998. He was also portrayed by Golden Globe winner Brian Dennehy in the 2001 movie, "Summer Catch," which was set in Chatham.

SUMMER LEAGUE ROUNDUP

■ The **St. Cloud Rox** won their first-ever Northwoods League championship in three games over the **Battle Creek Bombers**. The **Wisconsin Rapids Rafters** easily had the best regular season record, going 52-20, but the Bombers knocked them off with a 6-1 victory to reach the championship series. The Rox beat the **Mankato Moondogs** 5-2 in 12 innings to set up the final matchup. After St. Cloud beat **Battle Creek** 7-5 in the first game of the championship series, Battle Creek pulled out a 3-2 win in 10 innings in Game 2. The Rox clinched the series with a 5-3 win in Game 3, with Nick Morreale (Georgetown) and Jackson Rose (Minnesota) combining for three scoreless, hitless innings of relief for St. Cloud.

■ The **Orange County Riptide** rode some of the top prospects in the California Collegiate League to win its first ever championship. The Riptide, managed by Tyger Pederson (brother of Joc), defeated the **Healdsburg Prune Packers**, 5-3, in the winner-take-all championship game. **Arkansas'** Dominic Fletcher, **Delta (Calif.) CC's** Beau Philip and **Lewis-Clark State (Idaho)** JC's Joey Parente helped anchor the top of the Riptide's championship-winning lineup. Orange County also had some of the league's top arms, including **Pacific** lefthander Ricky Reynoso, **Brown** righty Will Tomlinson and **Virginia** lefty Jordan Dosey.

■ The **Gastonia Grizzlies** claimed their second ever Coastal Plains League championship after defeating **Wilmington** in a best-of-three series. Evan Wise's squad entered the CPL playoffs as the No. 4 seed in the Western Conference but more than proved its dominance by sweeping through three different teams without a loss.

■ For the second consecutive year and fourth time in the league's seven-year history, the **Nashua Silver Knights** claimed the Futures Collegiate Baseball League championship this summer. It seemed to be a case of deja vu for the Sliver Knights, who swept the **Worcester Bravehearts** in the best-of-three championship series for the second straight year. Righthanded reliever Kyle Murphy (Jr., Northeastern) won the 2017 FCBL Playoff MVP award, totaling four saves in four scoreless relief appearances during Nashua's flawless postseason run.

■ **Brazos Valley** won their fifth straight Texas Collegiate League championship in walk-off fashion, completing a two-game sweep of **Acadiana** with a ninth-inning single from Ryan Benavidez (Arkansas-Little Rock). The championship capped an incredible summer for the Bombers, who finished the season with a 34-18 record. Brazos Valley, coached the last two years by Trey Porras, rode a seven-inning start from Michigan State's Mike Mokma in game one, and TCL player of the year Jared Mang (New Mexico) scored the winning run in game two after leading off the ninth inning with a double.

■ **Bethesda** rolled over **Baltimore** in three games to claim the Ripken Collegiate League title for the second straight year. In the decisive game, the Big Train rode a strong outing by East Carolina righthander Tyler Smith, while Smith's catcher, Justin Morris (Maryland), provided the offense. Morris' three-run double in the fourth inning gave the Big Train an early lead, and the defending champs held on to win, 4-2.

■ The **Mohawk Valley DiamondDawgs** won the Perfect Game Collegiate League title with an impressive playoff run. Following an upset victory over the loaded No. 1 seed **Amsterdam Mohawks**, Mohawk Valley, the No. 3 seed, advanced out of the East and went on to defeat the **Jamestown Jammers** in three games. Russ Olive (Massachusetts-Lowell) drove in nine runs in six playoff games for Mohawk Valley.

■ **Liberal** and **Hays** battled down to the wire for the Jayhawk League title and in fact finished tied at 30-12 overall, but Liberal won the title by virtue of a 4-2 head-to-head record against Hays. Both teams advanced to the National Baseball Congress World Series, with third-place **Derby** (28-14) and fourth-place **Great Bend** (23-19) joining them. Though Hays didn't win the title, its coach, Frank Leo, achieved a significant milestone when he earned his 1,000th win with the Larks on June 14.

COLLEGE SUMMER LEAGUES

For players who played for multiple teams: 1: Stats with first team. 2: Stats with second team. 3: Stats with third team. T: combined stats.

CAPE COD LEAGUE

East Division	W	L	T	PTS
Orleans Firebirds	29	15	0	58
Yarmouth-Dennis Red Sox	27	16	1	55
Brewster White Caps	21	21	2	44
Chatham Anglers	21	23	0	42
Harwich Mariners	15	28	1	31
West Division	**W**	**L**	**T**	**PTSa**
Falmouth Commodores	24	19	1	49
Cotuit Kettleers	22	21	1	45
Bourne Braves	22	22	0	44
Wareham Gatemen	18	25	1	37
Hyannis Harbor Hawks	16	25	3	35

Championship: Brewster defeated Bourne 2-1 in best-of-three championship series.

Top 50 Prospects: 1. Greyson Jenista, OF (Jr., Wichita State). **2.** Griffin Conine, OF (Jr., Duke). **3.** Ryan Rolison, LHP (So., Mississippi). **4.** Logan Gilbert, RHP (Jr., Stetson). **5.** Tyler Baum, RHP (So., North Carolina). **6.** Tristan Pompey, OF (Jr., Kentucky). **7.** Alec Bohm, 3B/1B (Jr., Wichita State). **8.** Tanner Dodson, OF/RHP (Jr., California). **9.** Kris Bubic, LHP (Jr., Stanford). **10.** Zack Hess, RHP (So., Louisiana State). **11.** Austin Bergner, RHP (So., North Carolina). **12.** Shea Langiliers, C (So., Baylor). **13.** Jimmy Herron, OF (Jr., Duke). **14.** Jonathan India, 3B (Jr., Florida). **15.** Matt Mercer, RHP (Jr., Oregon). **16.** Hunter Bishop, OF (So., Arizona State). **17.** Nico Hoerner, 2B/SS (Jr., Stanford). **18.** Adam Hill, RHP (Jr., South Carolina). **19.** Alex McKenna, OF (Jr., Cal Poly). **20.** Jake Mangum, OF (Jr., Mississippi State). **21.** Griffin Roberts, RHP (Jr., Wake Forest). **22.** Drew Mendoza, 3B/SS (So., Florida State). **23.** Graeme Stinson, LHP (So., Duke). **24.** Cameron Bishop, LHP (SIGNED: Orioles). **25.** Carlos Cortes, OF (So., South Carolina). **26.** Antoine Duplantis, OF (Jr., Louisiana State). **27.** Josh Stowers, OF (Jr., Louisville). **28.** Kyle Bradish, RHP (Jr., New Mexico). **29.** Cole Sands, RHP (Jr., Florida State). **30.** Josiah Gray, RHP (Jr., Le Moyne, N.Y.). **31.** Jason Bilous, RHP (Jr., Coastal Carolina). **32.** Hogan Harris, LHP (Jr., Louisiana-Lafayette). **33.** Adley Rutschman, C (So., Oregon State). **34.** Daniel Lynch, LHP (Jr., Virginia). **35.** Sam Bordner, RHP (Jr., Louisville). **36.** Alfonso Rivas, 1B/OF (Jr., Arizona). **37.** Johnny Aiello, 3B (Jr., Wake Forest). **38.** Jake Wong, RHP (Jr., Grand Canyon). **39.** Justin Hooper, LHP (Jr., UCLA). **40.** John Rooney, LHP (Jr., Hofstra). **41.** Josh Smith, SS/3B (So., Louisiana State). **42.** Tony Locey, RHP (So., Georgia). **43.** Ryan Feltner, RHP (Jr., Ohio State). **44.** Logan Davidson, SS (So., Clemson). **45.** Ford Proctor, SS (Jr., Rice). **46.** Tyler Frank, SS/2B (Jr., Florida Atlantic). **47.** Connor Kaiser, SS (Jr., Vanderbilt). **48.** Justin Montgomery, RHP (Jr., Cal Baptist). **49.** Nick Dunn, 2B (Jr., Maryland). **50.** Jack DeGroat, RHP (Jr., Liberty).

INDIVIDUAL BATTING LEADERS

Player, Pos., Team	AVG	AB	R	H	2B	3B	HR	RBI	SB
Tanner Dodson, RHP/OF, Wareham	.365	96	12	35	8	1	1	14	2
Alec Bohm, 3B, Falmouth	.351	154	23	54	10	0	5	28	1
Jimmy Herron, OF, Orleans	.338	154	26	52	10	0	4	19	13
Nick Dunn, 2B, Brewster	.333	123	20	41	7	1	1	16	3
Griffin Conine, OF, Cotuit	.329	164	32	54	5	1	9	28	3
George Janca, SS, Falmouth	.327	110	14	36	6	1	5	12	1
Grant Williams, 2B, Bourne	.326	135	22	44	7	0	0	13	3
Jake Mangum, OF, Hyannis	.319	113	14	36	3	1	0	8	11
Clayton Daniel, 2B, Falmouth	.316	174	31	55	10	1	2	18	9
Niko Decolati, 3B, Orleans	.311	122	22	38	5	0	1	12	3

INDIVIDUAL PITCHING LEADERS

Player, Team	W	L	ERA	SV	IP	H	BB	SO
Austin Bergner, Chatham	3	1	1.16	0	31	24	11	30
Kris Bubic, Yarmouth-Dennis	4	1	1.65	0	32.2	23	7	41
Logan Gilbert, Stetson	1	2	1.72	0	31.1	24	4	31
Griffin Roberts, Wareham	0	0	1.97	0	32	22	6	35
Nick Sandlin, Hyannis	1	1	1.99	3	31.2	19	14	39
Daniel Lynch, Orleans	4	0	2.08	0	30.1	25	3	25
Joey Matulovich, Wareham	2	2	2.35	0	30.2	26	4	26
Matt Mercer, Falmouth	4	1	2.64	0	30.2	22	9	31
Tyler Baum, Harwich	5	1	2.72	0	43	36	10	41
Tony Locey, Brewster	4	2	2.75	0	36	28	14	38

BOURNE

Batting	AVG	AB	R	H	2B	3B	HR	RBI	SB
Jake Alu, 3b	.217	23	4	5	1	0	0	1	2
Andy Atwood, ss	.170	53	7	9	1	0	1	5	0
Spencer Brickhouse, 1b	.276	58	6	16	2	1	0	5	1
Turner Brown, ss/2b	.238	42	7	10	1	0	1	3	1
Jeremy Eierman, ss	.133	15	2	2	0	0	2	2	1
Tyler Fitzgerald, ss	.169	65	8	11	1	0	1	6	0
Andrew Fregia, ss	.182	110	11	20	2	1	3	11	8
Jameson Hannah, of	.265	132	15	35	7	1	1	16	8
Drew La Bounty, ss/2b	.000	7	2	0	0	0	0	0	0
Lyle Lin, c	.283	138	8	39	5	0	0	21	1
Logan McRae, of	.227	22	0	5	0	0	0	2	0
Richie Palacios, ss	.278	133	21	37	8	1	1	16	6
Anthony Prato, ss	.318	22	5	7	0	0	0	1	1
Kevin Radziewicz, c	.261	46	7	12	2	0	0	3	0
Scott Schreiber, of	.255	145	17	37	5	0	3	17	1
Zac Susi, c	.267	75	12	20	3	0	3	10	0
Jared Triolo, 3b	.250	100	12	25	7	0	1	12	0
Grant Williams, 2b	.326	135	22	44	7	0	0	13	3
Grant Witherspoon, of	.234	141	21	33	11	1	2	19	10

Pitching	W	L	ERA	G	SV	IP	H	BB	SO
Luis Alvarado	2	1	0.92	7	1	20	10	7	18
Andy Atwood	0	0	0.00	1	0	1	0	0	1
Tyler Barss	0	0	18.00	2	1	2	6	1	3
Nick Bennett	0	2	7.50	3	0	12	18	4	8
Daniel Bies	3	2	3.09	7	0	32	36	10	27
Tim Cate	0	0	5.40	1	0	5	6	1	7
Dylan Coleman	0	1	5.87	3	0	8	10	5	10
Andrew Crane	0	2	5.95	5	0	20	31	5	16
Brian Eichhorn	3	2	3.34	7	0	30	28	5	25
Ryan Feltner	1	0	0.00	13	8	15	10	7	15
Ray Gaither	1	0	5.79	3	0	5	7	2	5
Carter Henry	0	0	3.38	2	0	3	2	3	3
Zack Hess	0	0	2.61	3	0	10	10	7	10
Bryan Hoeing	1	1	4.91	6	0	15	14	5	16
Christopher Holba	0	2	4.91	4	0	18	17	13	14
Nick Johnson	2	0	3.57	10	0	18	16	7	20
Eli Kraus	1	0	2.49	5	0	25	25	7	17
Sean Leland	1	1	4.29	11	0	21	21	5	20
Chad Luensmann	1	1	3.92	11	3	21	23	5	19
Kyle Marman	0	2	3.98	10	2	21	22	6	24
Kyle Martin	0	1	18.00	2	0	2	3	2	1
Ian Miller	0	0	4.15	3	0	4	4	7	5
Zach Mort	1	1	6.52	5	0	10	9	4	9
Jack Nelson	0	1	10.13	2	0	3	2	2	1
P.J. Poulin	2	1	1.66	14	0	22	15	7	23
Ronnie Rossomando	0	1	14.9	6	0	10	22	7	8
Christian Ryder	2	0	5.65	9	0	14	24	3	9
Ryan Simpler	0	0	2.46	5	0	11	9	3	9
Baylor Sundahl	0	0	10.8	1	0	2	4	2	0
Blake Whitney	1	0	0.00	1	0	2	0	0	2

BREWSTER

Batting	AVG	AB	R	H	2B	3B	HR	RBI	SB
Hunter Bishop, OF	.212	104	15	22	5	1	1	11	8
Marty Costes, OF	.293	92	18	27	3	1	5	23	7
Michael Curry, DH	.280	93	17	26	3	0	2	15	0
Kyle Datres, 3B	.225	111	21	25	3	1	1	9	5
Troy Dixon, 2B	.000	3	2	0	0	0	0	0	2
Nick Dunn, 2B	.333	123	20	41	7	1	1	16	3
Devin Foyle, OF	.191	47	10	9	1	0	0	1	0
Zack Gahagan, 2B	.220	50	7	11	0	0	0	2	3
Mickey Gasper, C	.305	128	22	39	7	1	5	30	1
Chris Givin, SS/2B	.250	4	1	1	0	0	0	1	0
A.J. Graffanino, SS	.256	121	14	31	2	1	0	15	6
Darius Hill, OF	.232	69	6	16	6	0	0	10	1
Julian Infante, 1B	.238	80	5	19	4	0	1	12	1
Justin Kunz, C	.237	59	10	14	4	0	3	9	0

	AVG	AB	R	H	2B	3B	HR	RBI	SB
Christian Molfetta, 2B	.267	60	7	16	3	0	0	11	1
Anthony Prato, SS/2B	.000	3	0	0	0	0	0	0	0
Pete Schuler, C/1B	.400	10	1	4	0	0	0	2	0
Connor Smith, SS	.233	86	15	20	0	0	0	4	4
Travis Swaggerty, OF	.250	8	0	2	0	0	0	0	0
Chandler Taylor, OF	.230	113	28	26	5	0	9	26	8
Cesar Trejo, SS	.303	33	4	10	2	0	1	5	0
Steele Walker, OF	.280	25	1	7	0	0	1	4	1

Pitching	W	L	ERA	G	SV	IP	H	BB	SO
Ryan Avidano	1	1	2.84	8	0	25	30	9	21
Matthew Beck	0	0	10.80	6	2	10	19	9	6
Sam Bordner	0	1	1.35	8	0	13	8	6	14
Ryan Broom	1	1	0.44	11	3	20	16	3	25
Ryan Cyr	0	0	4.50	2	0	2	1	2	2
Davis Daniel	2	1	5.28	4	0	15	18	8	13
Joe DeMers	1	1	1.80	12	1	20	24	4	19
Connor Higgins	1	2	2.75	4	0	20	19	7	14
Stephen Jones	1	0	9.00	3	0	4	5	1	1
Zach Linginfelter	0	0	0.00	3	0	3	1	2	3
Tony Locey	4	2	2.75	8	0	36	28	14	38
Chris Machamer	2	0	1.35	3	1	7	3	2	6
J.R. McDermott	2	2	2.81	6	0	26	22	9	23
Conor McNamara	1	0	3.38	3	0	5	5	2	4
Troy Miller	0	1	7.71	2	0	5	7	1	4
Paul Milto	0	1	4.45	11	0	30	29	11	22
Joe Molettiere	0	4	4.50	9	0	34	39	15	20
Andy Pagnozzi	1	0	7.94	4	0	6	8	2	5
C.J. Pruitt	0	0	0.00	1	0	1	0	0	0
Drew Reveno	0	1	4.97	4	1	13	16	4	13
Zach Schneider	0	0	4.50	2	0	4	2	2	3
Bradley Spooner	0	0	5.75	4	0	16	22	6	9
Jonathan Stiever	3	1	4.45	10	0	28	33	2	25
Will Tribucher	1	2	4.10	11	0	26	22	20	30

CHATHAM

Batting	AVG	AB	R	H	2B	3B	HR	RBI	SB
Johnny Aiello, 3B	.306	62	9	19	3	0	1	8	3
D.J. Artis, OF	.250	28	5	7	0	0	0	3	1
Kyle Baker, OF	.273	11	3	3	0	0	0	0	1
Bobby Brennan, OF	.125	8	0	1	0	0	0	2	0
Donovan Casey, OF	.294	17	0	5	1	0	0	1	0
Austin Edens, 1B	.111	18	4	2	0	0	0	2	0
Landon Kay, OF	.133	30	2	4	0	0	0	3	1
Mason Koppens, OF	.304	115	16	35	10	0	0	10	5
Shea Langeliers, C	.234	128	15	30	8	2	6	21	0
Colby Maiola, OF	.000	5	0	0	0	0	0	0	0
John Mazza, C	.000	1	0	0	0	0	0	0	0
Ashton McGee, 2B	.141	71	5	10	0	1	0	4	1
Jacob Olsen, OF	.308	91	16	28	11	0	2	14	2
Jake Palomaki, OF	.175	120	23	21	3	0	1	10	6
Nick Patten, 1B	.217	138	20	30	5	0	3	21	1
Fabian Pena, C	.275	80	9	22	3	0	2	12	2
Jeremy Pena, SS	.228	127	20	29	3	0	3	13	2
Antonio Ralat, SS	.228	57	6	13	0	0	0	4	0
Cody Roberts, C	.157	70	6	11	0	0	1	5	0
Josh Shaw, 2B	.283	127	12	36	2	0	0	16	5
Josh Stowers, OF	.250	84	15	21	2	0	2	15	12
Jimmy Titus, SS	.136	22	0	3	0	0	0	2	0

Pitching	W	L	ERA	G	SV	IP	H	BB	SO
Jeff Belge	1	2	4.05	7	0	27	21	18	24
Austin Bergner	3	1	1.16	7	0	31	24	11	30
Cameron Bishop	1	1	0.82	3	0	11	7	2	15
Bo Burrup	0	1	10.13	3	0	5	9	5	3
Jack DeGroat	1	0	0.00	11	3	14	4	7	28
R.J. Freure	2	2	4.42	12	0	18	18	10	25
Josiah Gray	1	1	4.85	12	3	13	13	3	21
Dan Hammer	1	3	9.00	7	0	23	39	9	20
Ryan Hedrick	1	0	13.50	4	0	6	8	3	6
Adam Hill	0	1	2.77	3	0	13	10	4	7
Rodney Hutchison	2	0	0.71	9	2	25	20	6	14
Reiss Knehr	0	1	10.13	10	0	16	19	11	15
Justin Lasko	2	0	2.79	4	0	19	17	2	14
Joseph Lienhard	1	0	2.29	7	0	20	13	6	21
Taylor Luciani	0	1	2.16	2	0	8	4	4	4
Daniel Metzdorf	3	0	2.46	11	0	18	20	7	15
Eli Nabholz	0	1	2.35	5	1	8	8	6	10
Andre Pallante	0	1	1.20	11	0	15	9	5	15
Jack Perkins	0	3	4.97	6	0	25	24	11	22
Nick Rand	0	0	4.00	12	0	18	17	7	17
John Signore	1	0	1.80	1	0	5	2	1	5
Nick Silva	0	1	6.75	2	0	4	6	1	5
Jacob Stevens	0	2	4.32	7	0	25	31	15	17
Adam Wolf	1	1	2.19	10	2	12	13	6	19

COTUIT

Batting	AVG	AB	R	H	2B	3B	HR	RBI	SB
Luke Alexander, SS	.272	114	11	31	3	0	4	17	2
Chandler Avant, SS	.213	122	17	26	3	1	3	15	2
Mitchell Bigras, 1B	.176	17	2	3	1	0	0	0	1
Griffin Conine, OF	.329	164	32	54	5	1	9	28	3
Clark Cota, RHP	.000	1	0	0	0	0	0	0	0
John Cresto, SS	.266	94	12	25	7	0	3	15	2
Christian Demby, OF/RHP	.200	5	0	1	0	0	0	0	0
Thomas Dillard, 1B/OF	.213	75	11	16	3	0	2	8	2
Daniel Gardner, OF	.000	1	0	0	0	0	0	0	0
Ivan Gonzalez, C	.188	48	8	9	3	0	0	3	0
Alex Hanson, OF	.000	1	0	0	0	0	0	0	0
Greyson Jenista, OF	.310	142	25	44	4	0	3	16	9
Brett Kinneman, OF	.207	121	22	25	5	1	2	15	10
Zack Kone, 1B/3B	.232	125	16	29	2	1	2	13	6
Miles Lewis, OF	.230	74	8	17	2	0	0	7	3
Gian Martellini, C	.195	87	11	17	4	0	3	16	0
Blake Reese, 2B/SS	.000	2	0	0	0	0	0	1	1
Josh Rolette, C	1.000	1	1	1	1	0	0	0	0
Adam Scott, LHP	.000	1	0	0	0	0	0	0	0
Ako Thomas, 2B	.333	12	4	4	1	0	0	1	2
Michael Toglia, OF	.240	121	18	29	6	0	6	25	2
Andrew Turner, 3B	.000	3	0	0	0	0	0	0	0
Jayce Vancena, RHP	.000	1	0	0	0	0	0	0	0
Terrin Vavra, SS	.279	68	12	19	4	0	1	10	4

Pitching	W	L	ERA	G	SV	IP	H	BB	SO
Joshua Andrews	1	1	9.00	2	0	1	3	0	0
Jason Bilous	0	1	5.18	9	0	33	25	30	37
Michael Byrne	0	0	0.69	6	1	13	8	4	13
Chase Cohen	3	2	2.92	9	0	25	20	9	19
Zane Collins	4	2	2.25	11	0	28	31	8	23
Clark Cota	2	2	2.50	11	3	18	11	7	24
Noah Davis	1	1	2.81	5	0	16	22	7	12
Christian Demby	0	0	3.45	13	1	16	10	2	14
Thomas Dillard	0	0	0.00	1	0	2	1	0	4
Jacob Erickson	0	0	12.71	3	0	6	8	3	4
Justin Hooper	2	1	2.31	6	0	23	22	4	21
David Inman	1	0	7.11	5	0	6	11	4	5
Kyle Kemp	0	1	6.48	12	0	17	17	17	17
Dylan King	0	0	3.00	2	0	9	6	4	12
Brett Kinneman	0	0	4.50	1	0	2	2	0	1
Austin Kitchen	1	2	3.05	7	0	21	25	6	20
Taylor Lehman	1	0	2.38	6	0	11	15	4	8
Mark Moclair	0	1	30.38	2	0	3	8	6	4
Brian Rapp	1	0	3.86	8	1	19	11	13	23
Stephen Schoch	0	0	4.50	2	0	4	4	0	4
Adam Scott	2	1	4.05	6	0	20	21	5	13
Luke Shilling	0	0	27.00	1	0	1	2	2	1
Chase Shugart	0	1	4.18	11	3	24	31	10	24
Sheth Shuman	1	2	6.35	8	0	23	27	8	19
Mitch Stallings	0	2	8.00	5	0	9	15	3	8
Jayce Vancena	2	1	3.80	14	2	24	22	7	16

FALMOUTH

Batting	AVG	AB	R	H	2B	3B	HR	RBI	SB
Marty Bechina, 3B/OF	.262	126	29	33	8	2	8	28	8
Austin Biggar, C	.143	21	2	3	0	0	1	2	1
Ellis Bitar, OF	1.000	1	0	1	0	0	0	0	0
Alec Bohm, 3B/1B	.351	154	23	54	10	0	5	28	1
Joshua Breaux, C/RHP	.271	133	19	36	9	0	6	24	1

Willie Burger, C	.196	56	4	11	5	0	1	8	1
Clayton Daniel, 2B	.316	174	31	55	10	1	2	18	9
Logan Davidson, SS	.210	124	19	26	4	0	1	8	3
Zeke Dodson, 2B/3B	.097	31	3	3	1	0	1	1	0
Chris Fowler, 1B	.000	1	0	0	0	0	0	0	0
George Janca, SS	.327	110	14	36	6	1	5	12	1
Austin Langworthy, OF/LHP	.243	74	14	18	1	0	0	11	0
Trevor Larnach, OF	.308	104	13	32	9	1	1	15	0
Deacon Liput, 2B	.000	4	0	0	0	0	0	0	0
Jackson McGowan, 1B/RHP	.357	14	2	5	0	0	0	3	0
Cameron O'Neill, 2B	.279	68	10	19	5	0	4	13	0
Adley Rutschman, C	.164	67	6	11	1	0	0	4	1
Lee Solomon, OF	.088	34	4	3	0	0	0	3	2
Hunter Steinmetz, OF	.288	132	23	38	7	1	4	18	17
Josh Watson, OF	.250	48	7	12	0	0	1	1	2
Dale Wickham, OF	.077	13	1	1	0	0	0	0	0

Pitching	W	L	ERA	G	SV	IP	H	BB	SO
Derrick Adams	2	1	1.91	14	1	28	29	3	25
Tyler Blohm	1	2	4.60	7	0	29	28	15	25
Kyle Bradish	2	0	2.57	5	0	21	21	8	28
Joshua Breaux	0	0	0.00	3	1	3	0	2	8
Luke Corbin	0	0	15.00	2	0	3	8	3	0
Connor Eason	1	0	5.40	3	0	7	7	9	10
Will Ethridge	0	1	1.29	10	0	14	13	4	12
Dalton Feeney	0	2	2.19	6	0	25	18	12	23
Durbin Feltman	0	0	1.69	5	0	5	3	3	10
Israel Fuentes	0	0	2.16	6	0	8	10	2	10
Brian Gadsby	0	1	6.30	16	0	20	25	8	19
Jordan Gubelman	0	1	19.29	2	0	5	9	7	5
Ian Koch	3	2	3.72	14	0	19	14	5	21
Austin Langworthy	0	0	0.00	2	0	2	2	0	1
Zachary Leban	1	0	8.49	8	0	12	15	8	12
Ryan Leckich	0	0	0.00	1	0	2	2	0	0
James McArthur	1	2	3.10	7	0	29	29	11	19
Parker McFadden	0	0	9.00	2	0	3	3	6	5
Jackson McGowan	0	0	18.00	2	0	2	4	2	0
Matt Mercer	4	1	2.64	6	0	31	22	9	31
Mitchell Miller	1	1	2.57	10	2	21	13	7	29
Matthew Murphy	0	0	0.00	1	0	1	1	0	2
Jack Pabich	2	0	10.80	4	0	5	3	5	3
Robbie Peto	1	2	7.36	8	1	22	21	22	21
Scott Politz	2	2	4.80	4	0	15	20	5	6
Thomas Ponticelli	2	1	6.23	9	0	13	16	5	13
Cole Sands	1	0	3.71	6	0	17	14	4	21
Cody Shelton	0	0	0.00	2	0	8	5	2	5
Ryan Zeferjahn	0	0	2.40	13	6	15	5	9	20

HARWICH

Batting	AVG	AB	R	H	2B	3B	HR	RBI	SB
Joey Bart, C	.167	30	1	5	2	0	0	1	0
Max Burt, SS	.205	117	12	24	4	0	1	4	1
Nick Dalesandro, C/OF	.267	101	14	27	6	0	0	12	4
Brad Debo, C	.233	120	10	28	7	0	1	13	0
Antoine Duplantis, OF	.265	102	14	27	10	1	2	6	4
Jake Farrell, 1B/OF	.059	17	1	1	0	0	0	1	0
Jonathan India, 3B	.273	66	9	18	5	0	1	3	5
Jake McCarthy, OF	.387	31	11	12	2	1	1	6	5
Owen Miller, SS	.333	6	0	2	1	0	0	0	0
Travis Moniot, SS	.179	39	6	7	2	0	0	2	1
Andrew Moritz, OF	.243	111	15	27	4	0	0	11	5
Kyler Murray, OF	.170	47	4	8	2	0	1	5	4
Justin Novak, 3B	.192	52	4	10	1	0	0	8	2
Ryan Ogren, 3B	.263	99	11	26	3	0	0	7	1
Cam Simmons, OF	.200	100	15	20	2	2	1	12	4
Josh Smith, SS/3B	.382	76	12	29	1	0	3	12	5
Cobie Vance, 2B/3B	.279	140	11	39	3	2	1	21	7
Jordan Verdon, 1B	.188	85	5	16	2	0	1	7	1
Matt Vierling, OF	.182	99	7	18	4	1	1	11	1
Dwayna Williams-Sutton, OF	.148	27	5	4	1	0	0	0	1

Pitching	W	L	ERA	G	SV	IP	H	BB	SO
Jake Agnos	1	1	6.17	6	0	23	25	17	31
Cole Aker	1	4	4.24	13	1	23	17	21	26
Peyton Alford	0	0	5.40	2	0	3	4	0	1
Tyler Baum	5	1	2.72	7	0	43	36	10	41
Jacob Billingsley	1	3	3.94	6	0	30	30	18	27
Logan Browning	0	2	4.15	8	2	13	14	5	8
Brian Christian	2	2	6.44	8	0	29	31	10	19
Nick Dalesandro	0	0	0.00	1	0	4	4	1	2
Cullen Dana	1	0	6.00	7	0	15	17	8	11
Matthew Frisbee	0	2	4.50	6	0	24	32	12	21
Chris Gau	1	2	8.04	9	0	28	40	7	30
Dylan Grove	0	1	3.00	3	0	12	8	2	9
Austin Hansen	2	1	4.68	14	2	25	25	11	22
Tim Herrin	0	1	5.23	7	0	21	23	11	20
Cal Krueger	0	0	4.61	10	0	14	12	6	11
Mitchell Powers	0	2	16.88	3	0	3	2	3	1
Zach Reid	0	0	4.50	4	0	4	4	10	1
Theodore Rodliff	0	2	3.66	14	3	20	21	5	13
Jamie Sara	0	2	2.03	7	0	13	7	8	10
Noah Song	0	1	2.70	2	0	10	12	2	9
Chris Vallimont	0	0	81.00	1	0	1	6	0	1
John Witkowski	1	1	3.00	10	0	27	29	6	24

HYANNIS

Batting	AVG	AB	R	H	2B	3B	HR	RBI	SB
Micah Coffey, SS	.282	131	15	37	5	0	2	12	0
Griffin Dey, 1B	.250	8	3	2	0	0	1	2	0
Dominic DiCaprio, C	.202	84	7	17	7	0	0	8	0
Brendan Donovan, 3B	.138	87	12	12	3	0	2	11	0
Tyler Frank, SS/2B	.262	65	5	17	6	1	1	13	1
Reece Hampton, OF	.284	169	19	48	9	2	1	17	10
Ismael Herrera, C	.000	1	0	0	0	0	0	0	0
Dakota Julylia, SS/2B	.286	14	3	4	0	0	0	1	1
Ethan Larrison, RHP	.000	5	0	0	0	0	0	0	0
Reid Leonard, SS/3B	.130	23	4	3	1	0	0	2	1
Jake Mangum, OF	.319	113	14	36	3	1	0	8	11
Cole Murphy, 1B	.100	10	0	1	0	0	0	0	0
Robert Neustrom, OF	.302	96	16	29	5	0	4	18	2
Ryan Olenek, OF/1B	.283	113	14	32	5	0	1	10	1
Chris Proctor, C	.295	78	10	23	2	1	1	12	2
Ford Proctor, SS/2B	.260	127	16	33	6	1	2	18	0
Daniel Robinson, OF	.294	136	20	40	7	0	2	15	10
Thomas Russo, 2B/OF	.077	13	2	1	0	0	0	0	0
Blake Sanderson, RHP	.000	1	0	0	0	0	0	0	0
Brandt Stallings, OF	.176	17	2	3	0	0	0	1	0
Connor Stephens, OF	.000	1	0	0	0	0	0	0	0
Hunter Stovall, 2B	.238	143	17	34	6	0	1	12	5
Joseph Sullivan, B	.000	1	0	0	0	0	0	0	0
Cesar Trejo, SS	.107	28	3	3	1	0	0	2	0

Pitching	W	L	ERA	G	SV	IP	H	BB	SO
Trysten Barlow	0	2	8.37	14	0	24	26	17	18
Michael Brettell	3	3	4.74	9	0	44	50	11	31
Wyatt Burns	0	1	8.53	4	0	6	10	2	4
Ricky Constant	0	0	4.36	10	0	10	9	11	10
Kevin Coulter	0	6	7.11	8	0	25	40	7	22
Brooks Crawford	1	0	4.68	7	0	25	23	13	16
Austin Drury	1	0	0.00	1	0	5	2	1	4
Ryley Gilliam	0	1	10.39	1	0	4	6	1	2
Connor Green	0	1	7.91	12	0	19	27	13	19
Chase Haney	2	0	0.00	3	0	5	1	0	2
James Harrington	0	1	12.27	6	0	7	12	8	6
M.D. Johnson	1	3	9.16	5	0	19	28	16	18
Kevin Kernan	0	0	4.50	1	0	2	2	1	2
Ethan Larrison	1	2	4.85	17	1	26	33	12	20
Jordan Martinson	1	2	6.00	5	0	21	25	3	18
Matthew Mervis	0	0	9.82	2	0	4	3	4	1
Ryan Olenek	0	0	36.00	1	0	1	3	2	1
Ryan Rigby	0	0	4.36	6	0	10	10	2	5
Blake Sanderson	0	0	13.50	1	0	2	5	0	1
Nick Sandlin	1	1	1.99	19	3	32	19	14	39
Marc Stewart	0	0	11.57	3	0	2	4	1	4
Nick Swan	0	0	3.00	4	0	6	7	0	4
Christian Tripp	2	0	2.67	19	4	27	27	8	34
Davis Vainer	0	2	7.58	14	0	19	29	11	13
Tyler Vaughn	1	0	0.82	2	0	11	11	0	9
Ryan Weiss	2	0	2.52	14	1	25	20	4	27

ORLEANS

Batting	AVG	AB	R	H	2B	3B	HR	RBI	SB
Cole Austin, SS	.263	19	4	5	1	0	0	1	0
Niko Decolati, 3B	.311	122	22	38	5	0	1	12	3
Romy Gonzalez, 2B	.318	110	20	35	9	0	4	17	10
Preston Grand Pre, SS	.000	4	0	0	0	0	0	0	0
Jaxx Groshans, C	.291	117	17	34	3	0	4	17	1
Austin Hale, C	.220	50	3	11	2	0	1	8	0
Jimmy Herron, OF	.338	154	26	52	10	0	4	19	13
Jeff Houghtby, SS	.173	104	9	18	4	0	0	10	0
Cooper Johnson, C	.182	11	1	2	0	0	0	0	0
Devin Mann, 2B	.500	4	0	2	0	0	0	1	0
Lars Nootbaar, OF/1B	.252	111	15	28	1	1	0	4	1
Steven Passatempo, OF	.227	88	11	20	3	0	4	16	1
Ethan Paul, 2B	.304	135	24	41	6	0	4	17	7
Brandon Riley, OF	.254	118	18	30	5	2	0	17	3
Cesar Salazar, C	.229	96	9	22	2	0	4	13	2
Stephen Scott, OF	.300	120	25	36	8	1	7	33	2
Brandon Shearer, 3B	.227	22	5	5	0	0	0	0	2
Kevin Strohschein, OF	.247	89	10	22	4	0	1	11	2

Pitching	W	L	ERA	G	SV	IP	H	BB	SO
Canaan Cropper	0	0	9.00	1	0	1	0	3	1
Brett Daniels	0	0	3.77	13	1	29	20	6	23
Chandler Day	1	1	3.86	9	0	21	20	16	21
Cody Deason	1	0	1.19	12	1	23	12	11	32
Logan Gilbert	1	2	1.72	7	0	31	24	4	31
Jackson Goddard	0	2	3.86	2	0	7	9	4	3
Josh Hiatt	4	2	2.74	18	6	23	11	10	26
J.T. Hintzen	2	0	1.96	16	2	23	15	3	23
Parker Kelly	0	1	4.34	14	0	19	15	6	22
Daniel Lynch	4	0	2.08	6	0	30	25	3	25
Joey Murray	4	2	4.31	8	0	31	26	8	29
Ryan Orr	0	0	0.00	2	0	2	4	1	3
Ryan Rolison	4	0	1.93	6	0	28	15	10	35
Kevin Smith	1	2	3.50	4	0	18	11	7	15
Graeme Stinson	0	1	2.46	12	0	18	11	8	32
Taylor Sugg	2	1	5.54	11	0	26	27	11	18
Riley Thompson	2	0	3.00	5	0	6	6	6	6
Bryce Tucker	0	0	0.00	3	0	3	2	0	3
Brooks Wilson	2	0	1.71	11	2	21	12	6	20
Jake Wong	1	1	2.66	16	1	20	12	3	22

WAREHAM

Batting	AVG	AB	R	H	2B	3B	HR	RBI	SB
Jake Anchia, C	.219	105	10	23	3	0	5	20	1
Nick Angelini, OF	.208	53	8	11	2	1	1	4	2
Ben Baird, SS	.160	75	8	12	2	0	0	4	0
Luke Bonfield, OF	.172	64	6	11	2	0	2	11	0
Giovanni Dingcong, OF	.200	5	1	1	0	0	1	3	0
Tanner Dodson, OF/RHP	.365	96	12	35	8	1	1	14	2
Joe Drpich, 1B	.750	4	2	3	1	0	1	2	0
Jarren Duran, 2B	.281	114	19	32	6	2	0	10	10
Nate Fassnacht, SS	.222	27	2	6	1	0	0	3	1
Kyle Kasser, SS	.297	128	16	38	3	0	0	14	4
Kyle Knauth, C	.000	5	0	0	0	0	0	0	0
Steven Kwan, OF	.304	102	14	31	4	0	0	13	8
Brandon Lockridge, 2B	.208	24	2	5	0	0	0	1	1
Willie MacIver, C	.258	159	23	41	6	0	2	16	16
Robert Metz, 2B	.272	125	17	34	4	1	0	7	4
Tristan Pompey, OF	.230	87	7	20	2	1	2	15	5
Blake Sabol, C	.177	113	14	20	2	1	2	8	7
Andrew Shadid, OF	.242	33	3	8	1	0	0	3	2
Randy Taveras, SS	.000	4	0	0	0	0	0	0	0
John Toppa, OF	.281	139	19	39	3	1	0	12	4
Garrett Zech, OF	.333	3	1	1	0	0	0	0	0

Pitching	W	L	ERA	G	SV	IP	H	BB	SO
John Amendola	1	0	0.00	1	0	1	0	0	2
Frankie Bartow	0	0	1.50	3	0	6	4	1	5
Jordan Britton	1	1	6.92	5	0	13	20	7	12
Blakely Brown	0	0	11.81	2	0	5	10	2	3
Brad Case	0	0	9.00	1	0	1	2	1	0
Brett Conine	1	0	1.00	8	3	9	5	1	18
Peyton Culbertson	0	1	8.71	5	1	10	14	2	14
Tanner Dodson	1	2	3.70	8	1	24	26	5	16
Mason Feole	1	3	4.94	8	0	24	28	11	24
Riley Gates	0	3	7.84	11	0	10	13	11	12
Franklin German	0	0	3.55	11	0	13	18	3	17
Justin Glover	2	1	1.13	4	0	16	11	3	9
Justin Hagenman	0	1	12.46	2	0	4	10	0	3
Aaron Hernandez	1	0	0.90	5	0	10	7	4	11
Miller Hogan	3	0	1.08	6	0	25	14	7	23
Barrett Loseke	0	0	19.80	4	0	5	7	9	3
Joey Matulovich	2	2	2.35	7	0	31	26	4	26
Justin Montgomery	3	2	3.14	9	0	29	27	12	28
John Murphy	0	0	16.88	2	0	3	5	2	2
Will Neely	0	1	2.31	9	0	12	13	7	12
Ben Olson	0	0	0.00	2	0	2	2	0	1
Samuel Nepiarsky	0	0	0.00	1	0	2	1	0	3
Darrien Ragins	0	0	3.86	2	0	2	4	2	3
Dalton Roach	1	1	5.23	9	0	10	12	1	16
Griffin Roberts	0	0	1.97	8	0	32	22	6	35
Andrew Ryan	0	0	1.50	3	0	6	4	3	6
Cody Smith	0	0	5.79	4	0	5	6	1	7
Fitzpatrick Stadler	1	3	3.72	9	0	19	16	7	13
Chris Weiss	0	0	6.00	2	0	3	4	2	3
Brendan White	0	0	27.00	1	0	2	6	0	1
Grant Wolfram	0	3	4.19	10	0	19	16	7	18
Noah Zavolas	0	1	0.64	9	0	28	22	4	31

YARMOUTH-DENNIS

Batting	AVG	AB	R	H	2B	3B	HR	RBI	SB
Daniel Amaral, OF	.000	5	0	0	0	0	0	0	0
Michael Cassala, RHP/C	.189	37	2	7	1	0	0	1	0
Charlie Concannon, OF	.077	13	0	1	0	0	0	1	0
Carlos Cortes, OF	.268	138	21	37	5	1	4	21	4
Kole Cottam, C	.277	47	6	13	1	0	1	5	0
Jake Crawford, 3B/RHP	.167	6	0	1	0	0	0	0	0
Jonah Davis, OF	.167	18	4	3	1	0	0	1	0
Dominic DeRenzo, C/OF	.273	11	1	3	1	0	0	1	0
Tyler Depreta-Johnson, SS	.182	11	1	2	1	0	0	2	0
Edward Haus, OF	.500	6	1	3	1	0	0	0	1
Nico Hoerner, SS/2B	.300	160	25	48	7	0	6	28	15
Kyle Isbel, OF	.265	151	32	40	6	1	2	19	13
Cooper Johnson, C	.000	7	0	0	0	0	0	0	0
Connor Kaiser, SS	.300	100	17	30	9	1	2	16	8
Christian Koss, SS/2B	.309	94	13	29	4	0	1	10	4
Cody Martin, C	.300	10	3	3	0	0	0	2	0
Alex McKenna, OF	.298	124	16	37	9	2	0	16	7
Drew Mendoza, 3B/SS	.171	82	4	14	1	0	1	8	0
Luke Miller, 3B/OF	.302	96	15	29	5	0	3	12	7
Carter Pharis, 3B	.280	75	10	21	4	0	1	9	3
Nick Quintana, 3B	.200	105	13	21	4	0	6	14	0
Alfonso Rivas, 1B/OF	.276	116	14	32	6	0	3	11	3
Christopher Sharpe, OF	.000	7	1	0	0	0	0	1	0
Jake Slaughter, 2B/3B	.225	40	6	9	2	0	0	2	3
Darren Trainor, C	.222	27	4	6	1	0	1	5	0

Pitching	W	L	ERA	G	SV	IP	H	BB	SO
Cameron Beauchamp	0	0	2.08	2	0	4	4	0	3
Karl Blum	1	3	3.60	14	0	20	16	9	27
Tim Brennan	1	2	3.96	7	0	29	39	8	31
Kris Bubic	4	1	1.65	6	0	33	23	7	41
Michael Cassala	1	0	1.80	7	0	10	10	2	10
Nick Gallagher	0	0	3.86	7	0	16	17	7	15
Tanner Graham	1	1	5.89	12	0	18	26	6	17
Hogan Harris	0	1	1.50	4	0	18	10	12	24
Tommy Henry	1	0	5.93	8	0	14	19	7	15
Karl Kauffmann	1	1	1.27	9	1	21	14	12	17
Riley McCauley	2	0	1.72	14	8	16	7	6	27
Josh McMinn	4	3	4.50	8	0	38	36	11	21
Brendan Nail	2	0	1.04	16	3	26	15	14	32
Hunter Parsons	1	1	6.75	13	1	15	15	6	12
Andrew Quezada	4	0	1.50	7	0	18	16	3	17
John Rooney	1	2	4.38	7	0	37	33	15	29
Grant Schuermann	0	0	0.00	1	0	1	0	0	0

	W	L	ERA	G	SV	IP	H	BB	SO
Brent Teller	0	0	0.00	2	0	3	2	2	3
Troy Terzi	1	0	0.00	4	1	7	5	1	7
Spencer Van Scoyoc	2	1	3.12	7	0	26	20	12	20
Jacob Wloczewski	0	0	3.52	8	0	8	5	5	9

ALASKA LEAGUE

	W	L	PCT	GB
Mat-Su Miners	30	14	.682	—
Anchorage Bucs	24	20	.545	6
Anchorage Glacier Pilots	20	24	.455	10
Peninsula Oilers	19	25	.432	11
Chugiak Chinooks	17	27	.386	13

Championship: Mat-Su defeated Anchorage 2-1 in best-of-three series.

Top 10 Prospects: 1. Quin Cotton, OF, Mat-Sun (So., Grand Canyon). **2.** John Doxakis, LHP, Mat-Su (So., Texas A&M). **3.** Todd Lott, OF, Anchorage (So., Louisiana-Lafayette). **4.** Logan Boyer, RHP, Anchorage (So., San Diego State). **5.** Armani Smith, INF/OF, Anchorage (So., UC Santa Barbara). **6.** Josh Green, RHP, Mat-Su (Sr., Southeastern Louisiana). **7.** Elijah MacNamee, OF, Mat-Su (Jr., Mississippi State). **8.** Ray Kerr, LHP, Peninsula (Jr., Lassen JC, Calif.). **9.** Eli Villalobos, RHP, Anchorage Glacier (Jr., Long Beach State). **10.** Thaddeus Ward, RHP, Mat-Su (Jr., Central Florida).

INDIVIDUAL BATTING LEADERS

	AVG	AB	R	H	2B	3B	HR	RBI	SB
Quinn Cotton, OF, Mat-Su	.347	147	24	51	12	2	2	19	4
Rainer Ausmus, INF, Mat-Su	.341	44	6	15	3	0	1	6	0
Kellen Strahm, OF, Peninsula	.316	136	32	43	2	0	1	12	6
Elijah MacNamee, OF, Mat-Su	.315	111	15	35	8	1	3	24	1
Justin Ammons, OF, Mat-Su	.311	122	16	38	6	1	1	16	5
Andre Gregory, INF, Pilots	.306	111	19	34	1	1	2	12	3
Ian Evans, INF, Pilots	.301	123	18	37	6	1	0	13	6
Benjamin Wagner, INF, Penn.	.299	67	11	20	4	1	2	10	1
Will Brennan, OF, Pilots	.297	118	19	35	2	0	1	12	5
Todd Lott, OF, Anchorage	.294	136	24	40	10	2	2	14	8

INDIVIDUAL PITCHING LEADERS

	W	L	ERA	G	SV	IP	H	BB	SO
Spencer Hanson, Mat-Su	2	1	0.61	6	0	29	23	15	17
Max Karnos, Pilots	3	1	0.78	5	0	23	16	3	14
John Doxakis, Mat-Su	3	1	1.08	4	0	25	17	5	30
Raymond Kerr, Peninsula	4	2	1.13	9	0	48	31	10	43
Kyle Tyler, Pilots	4	0	1.29	6	0	35	25	6	47
Robert Winborne, Anchorage	2	1	1.37	19	3	20	16	5	20
Logan Boyer, Anchorage	2	2	1.52	10	1	30	13	19	43
Thaddeus Ward, Mat-Su	5	1	1.72	17	1	31	24	10	25
Steven Ledesma, Pilots	2	1	1.80	6	0	20	12	7	21
Calvin LeBrun, Mat-Su	4	2	2.11	9	0	43	40	5	33

ATLANTIC COLLEGIATE LEAGUE

	W	L	PCT	GB
Allentown Railers	23	9	.719	—
South Jersey Giants	25	10	.714	0½
Quakertown Blazers	19	15	.559	5
North Jersey Eagles	18	17	.514	6½
Trenton Generals	16	19	.457	8½
Jersey Pilots	14	22	.389	11
Staten Island Tide	13	22	.375	11½
Ocean Gulls	10	24	.294	14

Championship: Allentown defeated Quakertown 2-0 in best-of-three series.

Top 10 Prospects: 1. Levi Stoudt, RHP, Quakertown (So., Lehigh). **2.** Harrison Rutkowski, LHP, Trenton (Fr., Rutgers). **3.** Rhett Jacoby, RHP, Allentown (Jr., Moravian, Pa.). **4.** Jared Melone, 1B/3B, Allentown (Jr., West Chester). **5.** Jerry D'Andrea, LHP, Staten Island (Sr., Ramapo, N.J.). **6.** Shayne Fontana, OF, Jersey (Jr., Lynn, Fla.). **7.** Jim Bleming, SS/OF, Allentown (Sr., Lehigh). **8.** Jordan DiValerio, RHP, Quakertown (So., St. Joseph's). **9.** Jack Gloan, C/OF, South Jersey (So., Rowan-Gloucester, N.J.). **10.** Bobby Shannon, SS/2B, North Jersey (Jr., Ramapo, N.J.).

INDIVIDUAL BATTING LEADERS

	AVG	AB	R	H	2B	3B	HR	RBI	SB
Jared Melone, 3B, Allentown	.450	109	23	49	14	2	4	26	4
Dom D'Alessandro, C/1B. SJ	.382	136	31	52	6	1	15	49	0
Jack Goan, C, SJ	.378	111	31	42	9	0	6	30	0
Marc Chernin, C/3B, Ocean	.376	85	19	32	5	0	1	8	6
Devin Ruiz, OF/1B, SJ	.375	88	26	33	3	0	8	29	2
Matt Tancredi, Ocean	.372	94	17	35	4	0	0	11	14
Ryan Malloy, OF, Quakertown	.365	115	22	42	5	0	5	31	3
Luis Amaro, 1B/3B, NJ	.359	92	25	33	6	1	8	27	2
Brian Kelly, 1B/3B, NJ	.355	110	10	39	3	1	2	22	6
P.J. Harrington, SI	.353	85	24	30	4	0	0	10	4

INDIVIDUAL PITCHING LEADERS

	W	L	ERA	G	SV	IP	H	BB	SO
Christian Scafidi, SJ	3	1	1.57	14	1	29	24	6	39
Jason Reynolds, SJ	5	0	2.13	10	0	38	28	14	52
Rhett Jacoby, Allentown	5	1	2.14	7	1	42	34	2	52
Dan Morrin, Allentown	3	1	2.49	7	0	43	34	4	50
Ryan Takcas, Trenton	2	2	3.00	6	0	33	39	23	21
Brett Lubreski, Jersey	3	1	3.06	7	0	50	44	18	35
Thomas Ambrosino, SI	4	1	3.11	8	0	46	47	16	41
Chad Cooperman, Allentown	3	2	3.12	7	0	43	43	8	45
Eddie Lehr, Jersey	2	3	3.13	10	0	55	48	30	42
Alex Mack, NJ	3	0	3.15	7	0	34	29	22	29

CAL RIPKEN COLLEGIATE LEAGUE

North Division	W	L	PCT	GB
Baltimore Redbirds	26	14	.650	—
Gaithersburg Giants	19	21	.475	7
Baltimore Dodgers	18	22	.450	8
Silver Spring-Takoma T Bolts	17	23	.425	9
Rockville Express	15	25	.375	11
South Division	**W**	**L**	**PCT**	**GB**
Bethesda Big Train	31	9	.775	—
Alexandria Aces	28	12	.700	3
Loudoun Riverdogs	17	23	.425	14
Herndon Braves	16	24	.400	15
D.C. Grays	13	27	.325	18

Championship: Bethesda defeated the Baltimore Redbirds 2-1 in best-of-three series.

Top 10 Prospects: 1. Parker Caracci, RHP, Baltimore Redbirds (So., Mississippi). **2.** Daniel Cabrera, OF, Gaitherburg (Fr., Louisiana State). **3.** Hayden Cantrelle, INF, Gaithersburg (Fr., Louisiana-Lafayette). **4.** Randy Bednar, OF, Baltimore Redbirds (Fr., Maryland). **5.** Jim Outman, OF, Bethesda (Jr., Sacramento State). **6.** Harrison Freed, OF, D.C. (So., Butler). **7.** Cole Zabowski, 1B, Baltimore Redbirds (So., Mississippi). **8.** Ciaran Devenney, C, Herndon (So., Delaware State). **9.** Zach Jancarski, OF, Bethesda (Sr., Maryland). **10.** Ken Waldichuck, LHP, Bethesda (Jr., St. Mary's).

INDIVIDUAL BATTING LEADERS

	AVG	AB	R	H	2B	3B	HR	RBI	SB
Richard Constantine, 1B, Herndon	.404	109	20	44	12	2	5	31	3
Lamar Briggs, OF/2B, D.C.	.400	135	22	54	5	0	2	24	8
Carl Colbert, INF, SS-T	.361	108	25	39	7	0	3	25	9
Zach Jancarski, OF, Bethesda	.347	98	23	34	2	0	3	17	15
James Outman, OF, Bethesda	.341	132	38	45	7	1	9	36	18
Kevin Milam, INF/RHP, Bethesda	.340	103	22	35	8	0	4	19	8
Daniel Cabrera, OF, GG	.339	124	22	42	7	0	3	21	11
Mack Nathanson, OF, AA	.336	128	23	43	13	1	4	36	9
Cayden Stover, inf, Herndon	.336	125	29	42	4	1	2	17	24
Cole Zabowski, inf, Redbirds	.336	107	14	36	3	0	1	19	2

INDIVIDUAL PITCHING LEADERS

	W	L	ERA	G	SV	IP	H	BB	SO
Ty Madrigal, Bethesda	5	1	0.55	6	0	32.2	25	13	34
Parker Caracci, Redbirds	7	0	0.70	20	5	38.2	16	12	48
Josh Hejka, Dodgers	3	2	0.95	8	1	38	25	9	29
Zach Attianese, Redbirds	2	1	1.31	8	0	34.1	18	13	32
Mark Michael, Dodgers	1	1	1.80	7	0	35	29	13	29
David Hutchison, GG	4	0	2.02	9	1	35.2	28	11	19
Matthew Dalke, D.C.	4	4	3.42	8	0	47.1	49	22	32

	W	L	ERA	G	SV	IP	H	BB	SO
Mark Tindall, AA	2	2	3.44	9	0	34	27	18	17
Zach Thompson, Redbirds	1	4	3.57	13	0	40.1	30	15	42
Huei-Sheng Lin, SS-T	3	2	3.65	7	0	37	45	10	28

CALIFORNIA COLLEGIATE LEAGUE

North Division	W	L	PCT	GB
Healdsburg Prune Packers	26	9	.743	—
Neptune Beach Pearl	25	10	.714	1
Rockville Rock Hounds	13	19	.406	11½
Auburn Wildcats	10	21	.323	14
Walnut Creek Crawdads	8	24	.250	16½
Central Division	**W**	**L**	**PCT**	**GB**
Santa Barbara Foresters	25	11	.694	—
Conejo Oaks	19	14	.576	4½
San Luis Obispo Blues	19	16	.543	5½
Ventura Halos	10	22	.313	13
South Division	**W**	**L**	**PCT**	**GB**
Orange County Riptide	26	10	.722	—
Arroyo Seco Saints	19	17	.528	7
Academy Barons	16	20	.444	10
Long Beach Legends	13	22	.371	12½
Southern California Catch	12	24	.333	14

Championship: Orange County defeated Healdsburg 2-1 in best-of-three series.

Top 10 Prospects: 1. Dominic Fletcher, OF, Orange County (So., Arkansas). **2.** Blair Henley, RHP, Santa Barbara (So., Texas). **3.** John McMillon, RHP, Santa Barbara (So., Texas Tech). **4.** Josh Jung, 3B, Santa Barbara (So., Texas Tech). **5.** Chase Gardner, LHP, Healdsburg (Jr., Connecticut). **6.** Evan Lee, LHP/OF, Santa Barbara (So., Arkansas). **7.** Garrett Gayle, RHP, Santa Barbara (So., Rice). **8.** James Free, C, Neptune Beach (So., Pacific). **9.** David Clawson, C, Santa Barbara (So., Brigham Young). **10.** Beau Phillips, SS, Orange County (So., San Joaquin Delta JC, Calif.).

INDIVIDUAL BATTING LEADERS

	AVG	AB	R	H	2B	3B	HR	RBI	SB
Dayton Provost, Ventura	.431	123	19	53	12	2	1	19	3
Cameron Warren, Healdsburg	.402	102	25	41	8	1	7	34	3
Blake Burton, Arroyo Seco	.395	124	20	49	8	1	5	32	4
Randy Rubio, Academy	.383	115	23	44	6	0	3	23	2
Max Smith, Rockville	.377	122	22	46	15	2	6	27	0
William Homza, Rockville	.375	104	21	39	7	0	4	27	1
Evan Lee, Santa Barbara	.375	72	13	27	6	2	0	15	9
Cole Brodnansky, Healdsburg	.370	100	17	37	6	0	2	25	1
Mickey Nunes, Rockville	.370	73	21	27	4	0	0	8	3
Christopher May, Ventura	.368	87	9	32	5	1	0	8	2

INDIVIDUAL PITCHING LEADERS

	W	L	ERA	G	SV	IP	H	BB	SO
Tanner Lawson, Santa Barbara	4	0	0.57	6	0	31	20	6	34
Evan Lee, Santa Barbara	2	0	0.86	8	2	21	13	8	28
Nathan Wiles, Santa Barbara	1	1	1.16	10	0	23	22	3	20
Chase Gardner, Healdsburg	4	0	1.42	6	0	32	14	15	38
Will Tomlinson, Orange County	3	0	1.42	13	4	25	15	6	22
Jackson Simonsgaard, Conejo	1	0	1.48	14	0	24	16	8	27
Ty Wiest, Santa Barbara	5	1	1.65	10	0	44	32	12	48
Blair Henley, Santa Barbara	3	1	1.69	5	0	32	17	2	30
Daniel Vasquez, Santa Barbara	2	0	1.71	6	0	32	29	5	29
Joseph Mercado, Academy	1	0	1.74	11	2	21	12	9	24

COASTAL PLAIN LEAGUE

East Division	W	L	PCT	GB
Fayetteville SwampDawgs	32	22	.593	—
Peninsula Pilots	32	23	.593	—
Wilmington Sharks	31	23	.574	1
Edenton Steamers	31	25	.554	2
Holly Springs Salamanders	25	30	.455	7½
Morehead City Marlins	25	30	.455	7½
Wilson Tobs	18	37	.327	14½
West Division	**W**	**L**	**PCT**	**GB**
Forest City Owls	36	18	.667	—
Savannah Bananas	30	25	.545	6½
High Point-Thomasville HiToms	29	25	.537	7
Gastonia Grizzlies	30	26	.536	7
Martinsville Mustangs	24	31	.436	12½
Florence RedWolves	23	30	.434	12½
Lexington County Blowfish	23	30	.434	12½
Asheboro Copperheads	20	35	.364	16½

Championship: Gastonia defeated Wilmington 2-0 in best-of-three series.

Top 10 Prospects: 1. Andre Nnebe, OF, Wilson (So., Santa Clara). **2.** Nick Podkul, 2B, Morehead City (Jr., Notre Dame). **3.** Matt Cronin, LHP, Holly Springs (So., Arkansas). **4.** Will Matthiessan, RHP, Morehead City (So., Stanford). **5.** Cory Wood, 2B, Holly Springs (So., Coastal Carolina). **6.** Chris Chatfield, OF, Forest City (Jr., South Florida). **7.** Connor Riley, RHP, Martinsville (So., Long Beach State). **8.** Jamie Galazin, OF/RHP, Edenton (Sr., St. John's). **9.** Connor Grant, OF, Forest City (Jr., North Greenville, S.C.). **10.** Tad Ratliff, RHP, Peninsula (SIGNED: Royals).

INDIVIDUAL BATTING LEADERS

	AVG	AB	R	H	2B	3B	HR	RBI	SB
Luke Morgan, Wilmington	.385	182	42	70	16	0	3	51	11
Evan Edwards, HP-Thomasville	.355	155	35	55	13	1	13	32	5
Jayson Newman, Fayetteville	.352	182	36	64	11	2	11	56	4
Harris Yett, Gastonia	.351	154	25	54	7	0	2	21	7
Seth Hoagland, Forest City	.347	124	27	43	7	2	5	28	6
Adam Sisk, Holly Springs	.343	134	30	46	7	1	5	22	11
Scott Dubrule, Peninsula	.338	130	21	44	4	1	1	14	15
Justin Dean, Wilmington	.337	199	57	67	12	2	1	13	27
Chandler Corley, Morehead City	.331	139	28	46	6	1	2	13	6
Drake McNamara, Peninsula	.330	176	27	58	12	1	8	42	5

INDIVIDUAL PITCHING LEADERS

	W	L	ERA	G	SV	IP	H	BB	SO
Jason Goe, HP-Thomasville	2	0	1.01	11	1	45	27	11	43
Zach Neff, Fayetteville	7	0	1.45	12	2	50	34	7	65
Clay Young, HP-Thomasville	2	0	1.53	11	0	47	29	13	59
Collin Liberatore, Peninsula	4	0	2.51	12	0	43	37	13	52
Nick Silber, HP-Thomasville	1	4	2.68	19	3	50	38	25	57
Nick Wegmann, Edenton	4	1	2.78	10	0	55	36	16	56
Alec Bivins, Forest City	5	2	2.81	9	0	48	50	8	47
Breydan Gorham, Wilmington	6	2	3.14	9	0	57	55	23	51
Devin Sweet, Asheboro	3	1	3.20	7	0	45	31	12	53
Bryan Cruse, Savannah	7	1	3.29	11	0	63	69	13	57

FLORIDA COLLEGIATE SUMMER LEAGUE

	W	L	PCT	GB
Sanford River Rats	30	12	0.714	—
Altamonte Springs Scorpions	19	17	1.514	8
Winter Park Diamond Dawgs	19	18	1.500	8½
Leesburg Lightning	19	19	1.487	9
Winter Garden Squeeze	16	21	0.432	1½
DeLand Suns	11	27	1.282	17

Championship: Sanford defeated Winter Park, 6-5, in championship game.

Top 10 Prospects: 1. Tyler Keysor, RHP, Leesburg (So., Eastern Florida State JC). **2.** Jacob Katzfey, 1B, Winter Park (So., Wichita State). **3.** Garrett Zech, OF, Altamonte Springs (Jr., South Florida). **4.** Ray Alejo, OF/INF, Altamonte Springs (So., Central Florida). **5.** Sadler Goodwin, INF/RHP, Winter Garden (Jr., Troy). **6.** Elih Marrero, C, Sanford (Jr., St. Thomas, Fla.). **7.** Brenton Burgess, RHP/3B, Leesburg (Jr., Middle Georgia). **8.** Ronny Orta, RHP, Sanford (Jr., Nova Southeastern, Fla.). **9.** John Jones, C/1B, Sanford (Sr., South Carolina). **10.** Brandon White, OF, Winter Park (So., West Virginia).

INDIVIDUAL BATTING LEADERS

	AVG	AB	R	H	2B	3B	HR	RBI	SB
Trace Thornal, SS, AS	.369	84	11	31	6	0	0	10	6
Omar Villaman, SS, Sanford	.345	119	17	41	6	0	2	12	7
Ray Alejo, OF, AS	.340	97	24	33	4	2	4	12	14
Kyle Guttveg, OF, WP	.331	121	20	40	6	2	4	21	5
Jacob Silverstein, OF, WG	.327	104	16	34	3	1	0	6	9
Jacob Katzfey, 1B, WP	.316	114	23	36	2	2	7	30	3
Camden Williamson, OF, Leesburg	.315	89	12	28	4	1	0	10	2
Cody Oerther, 2B, Sanford	.311	106	21	33	5	0	0	14	5

	AVG	AB	R	H	2B	3B	HR	RBI	SB
Drew Frederic, 3B, WG	.306	121	21	37	5	3	0	16	12
Daniel Rodriguez, SS, WP	.298	141	19	42	4	0	1	11	16

INDIVIDUAL PITCHING LEADERS

	W	L	ERA	G	SV	IP	H	BB	SO
David Litchfield, AS	3	2	1.04	13	2	35	20	7	24
Michael Johnson, Leesburg	3	2	1.59	11	0	45	35	10	20
Jared Cenal, AS	3	1	1.72	8	0	31	19	10	27
Dillon McCollough, DeLand	1	3	1.78	11	1	35	24	10	39
Vladimir Nunez, Sanford	3	3	1.99	10	0	41	36	18	37
Ryan Ashworth, WG	2	1	2.18	7	0	33	28	9	26
Lance Johnson, WG	2	1	2.38	20	1	34	29	5	27
Frank Follaco, Sanford	2	0	2.81	11	0	42	41	7	34
Hamp Skinner, Sanford	1	1	2.86	10	1	35	26	15	34
Christopher Moore, WG	1	2	3.00	9	0	36	39	3	25

FUTURES COLLEGIATE LEAGUE

East Division	W	L	PTS
Brockton Rox	32	21	67
Nashua Silver Knights	26	27	53
Martha's Vineyard Sharks	26	28	53
Seacoast Mavericks	25	29	50
North Shore Navigators	21	32	43
West Division	**W**	**L**	**PTS**
Wachusett Dirt Dawgs	29	23	58
Bristol Blues	28	22	56
Pittsfield Suns	26	27	53
Worcester Bravehearts	25	29	53

Championship: Nashua defeated Worcester 2-0 in best-of-three series.

Top 10 Prospects: 1. Phil Clarke, C, Martha's Vineyard (Fr., Vanderbilt). **2.** Jayson Gonzalez, INF, Bristol (Fr., Vanderbilt). **3.** Tyler Hardman, INF, Martha's Vineyard (Fr., Oklahoma). **4.** Zack Martin, RHP, Brockton (So., Notre Dame). **5.** Cade Cavalli, INF/RHP, Pittsfield (Fr., Oklahoma). **6.** Joe Gobillot, LHP, Seacoast (Fr., Vanderbilt). **7.** Aldrich De Jongh, OF, Brockton (So., Florida Atlantic). **8.** Billy DeVito, RHP, Worcester (Jr., Hartford). **9.** Joe Simeone, RHP, Wachusett (Fr., Connecticut). **10.** Garrett Blaylock, INF, Bristol (Fr., Vanderbilt).

INDIVIDUAL BATTING LEADERS

	AVG	AB	R	H	2B	3B	HR	RBI	SB
Cam Cook, INF, Nashua	.397	204	30	81	8	1	0	30	8
Jack Roberts, INF, MV	.374	174	34	65	11	0	3	28	7
Tyler Kapuscinski, 1B, NS	.360	125	28	45	8	2	1	26	1
Kyle Bonicki, INF, Nashua	.358	179	40	64	10	0	4	26	5
Kevin Doody, INF, Worcester	.353	153	26	54	0	0	0	14	23
Kevin Donati, INF, Pittsfield	.344	151	38	52	6	3	4	21	19
Phillip Clarke, C, MV	.337	169	29	57	12	0	4	32	3
Daane Berezo, INF, NS	.333	138	29	46	4	1	2	17	0
Greg Kocinski, INF, Worcester	.332	190	39	63	17	0	9	40	5
Kyle Simon, INF, Brockton	.329	164	39	54	13	3	8	39	4

INDIVIDUAL PITCHING LEADERS

	W	L	ERA	G	SV	IP	H	BB	SO
Austen Michel, NS	2	0	1.55	9	0	46	34	7	50
Billy Devito, Worcester	2	0	2.64	9	0	48	43	22	50
Mitch Holcomb, Pittsfield	3	1	2.86	11	0	50	59	22	42
Jonathan Gegetskas, Wachusett	5	3	3.40	10	0	53	38	18	52
Michael Genaro, Bristol	2	0	3.50	9	0	44	53	6	24
Malachi Emond, Bristol	1	2	3.83	8	0	42	46	20	37
Edward Baram, Wachusett	4	3	3.86	11	0	58	61	20	55
Austin Pope, Pittsfield	4	3	4.22	9	0	43	45	13	41
Willie Krajnik, Wachusett	5	3	4.28	11	0	55	67	23	47
Conor Bawiec, NS	1	6	4.41	11	0	49	55	12	33

GREAT LAKES LEAGUE

Northern Division	W	L	PCT	GB
Lake Erie Monarchs	27	15	.643	—
St. Clair Green Giants	22	19	.537	4½
Grand River Loggers	21	21	.500	6
Muskegon Clippers	18	23	.439	8½
Irish Hills Leprechauns	16	26	.381	11
Central Division	**W**	**L**	**PCT**	**GB**
Lima Locos	30	11	.732	—
Grand Lake Mariners	23	19	.548	7½
Licking County Settlers	19	21	.475	10½
Galion Graders	19	22	.463	11
Lorain County Ironmen	13	29	.310	17½
Southern Division	**W**	**L**	**PCT**	**GB**
Richmond Jazz	25	17	.595	—
Southern Ohio Copperheads	24	17	.585	0½
Cincinnati Steam	24	18	.571	1
Xenia Scouts	15	26	.366	9½
Hamilton Joes	14	26	.350	10

Championship: Lima defeated Grand Lake 2-1 in best-of-three series.

Top 10 Prospects: 1. Bailey Peterson, INF, Grand River (So., Michigan State). **2.** Vince Vanelle, RHP, Cincinnati (So., Florida Southwestern State JC). **3.** Jack Weisenburger, RHP/OF, Lake Erie (So., Michigan). **4.** Tyler Tolbert, SS, Lima (So., Alabama-Birmingham). **5.** Nate Grys, OF, Lake Erie (Jr., Western Michigan). **6.** Blaine Crimson, OF, Southern Ohio (Jr., Mississippi College). **7.** Braden Niksich, RHP, Grand Lake (So., Illinois State). **8.** Ryan Fournier, 2B, Lake Erie (So., Xavier). **9.** Bryce Kelley, OF/LHP, Muskegon (So., Michigan State). **10.** Christian Bullock, OF, Lake Erie (So., Michigan).

INDIVIDUAL BATTING LEADERS

	AVG	AB	R	H	2B	3B	HR	RBI	SB
Nate Grys, OF, Lake Erie	.400	145	34	58	13	2	6	35	0
Zachary Leone, C, Grand River	.398	128	31	51	10	0	7	34	0
Joe Aeilts, Grand Lake	.396	154	27	61	7	1	6	30	14
Chase Knodle, OF, Lorain County	.388	139	33	54	5	1	1	19	5
Alex Holderbach, INF, Cincinnati	.383	154	36	59	14	0	5	29	0
Chad Wagner, OF, Grand River	.383	133	46	51	13	3	3	18	5
Bailey Peterson, SS, Grand River	.374	131	34	49	7	1	12	40	11
Blaine Crim, 3B, Southern Ohio	.359	167	26	60	17	2	4	38	1
Alex Kerschner, OF, Lake Erie	.358	123	35	44	7	3	3	19	1
Dallas Beaver, C, Cincinnati	.356	163	35	58	11	1	3	28	2

INDIVIDUAL PITCHING LEADERS

	W	L	ERA	G	SV	IP	H	BB	SO
Landon Williams, Xenia	2	0	0.27	15	4	34	24	12	24
Joe Gahm, Lima	4	0	1.60	10	3	34	27	3	38
Aaron Ochsenbein, S. Ohio	3	0	1.62	9	2	39	27	14	52
Zach Graveno, Lima	3	0	1.91	7	0	38	31	10	24
Brad Croy, Lima	2	1	1.96	7	0	46	37	13	36
Brody Basilone, Galion	3	0	2.03	6	0	40	37	10	30
Hunter Brown, St. Clair	5	2	2.33	8	0	46	39	29	33
Tyler Whitbread, St. Clair	4	2	2.37	9	0	49	42	31	36
Luke Smith, Southern Ohio	4	1	2.47	7	0	44	32	10	18
Brian Taggett, Muskegon	1	1	2.60	18	3	35	28	19	31

HAMPTONS COLLEGIATE LEAGUE

	W	L	T	PTS
Westhampton Aviators	27	14	0	54
Long Island Road Warriors	24	16	1	49
Riverhead Tomcats	21	18	2	44
North Fork Ospreys	22	19	0	44
Shelter Island Bucks	18	22	1	37
Southampton Breakers	15	23	1	31
Sag Harbor Whalers	13	28	1	27

Championship: Long Island defeated Westhampton 2-0 in best-of-three series.

Top 10 Prospects: 1. Kyle Martin, RHP, Riverhead (So., Fordham). **2.** Nick Bottari, INF, Westhampton (Jr., Southeastern, Fla.). **3.** George Bell, OF, Riverhead (So., Connors State JC, Okla.). **4.** Shane McDonald, LHP, Long Island (Sr., Southern New Hampshire). **5.** Justin Lebek, OF, Sag Harbor (Jr., Davidson). **6.** Freddy Sabido, 1B/OF, Riverhead (So., Wagner). **7.** Jacob Stracner, OF, Shelter Island (Jr., McNeese State). **8.** Matt Hansen, INF, Westhampton (Sr., Toledo). **9.** Nick Robinson, RHP, Shelter Island (So., Rhode Island). **10.** Tanner Propst, LHP, North Fork (Fr., Louisiana Tech).

INDIVIDUAL BATTING LEADERS

	AVG	AB	R	H	2B	3B	HR	RBI	SB
Nick Bottari, 1B, Westhampton	.454	97	23	44	10	0	10	38	1
Michael Calamari, INF, Sag Harbor	.411	129	18	53	9	0	1	24	1
Freddy Sabido, INF, Riverhead	.386	127	24	49	16	1	4	25	4
Alvin Melendez, OF, Riverhead	.369	149	34	55	9	0	2	18	16
Mike Sciorra, OF, North Fork	.365	115	24	42	8	1	1	15	4
Simon Whiteman, INF, Southampton	.347	118	24	41	4	0	1	10	19
Matt Hansen, INF, Westhampton	.333	141	33	47	10	4	6	40	9
Garrett Heaton, INF, Long Island	.330	97	18	32	1	0	1	19	3
George Bell, OF, Riverhead	.323	133	22	43	5	2	3	23	9
Brian Goulard, INF, Shelter Island	.319	119	26	38	4	0	6	28	16

INDIVIDUAL PITCHING LEADERS

	W	L	ERA	G	SV	IP	H	BB	SO
Evan Tubbs, Southampton	5	1	1.54	11	0	41	29	16	29
Connor McNamara, Shelter Island	3	1	1.78	7	0	35	27	9	36
Grant Young, Westhampton	5	1	1.93	11	0	37	35	14	27
Ray Weber, Long Island	3	4	1.94	9	0	46	35	11	42
Tim Kennedy, Long Island	4	1	2.16	8	0	42	43	14	46
Grant Schroeder, Southampton	2	2	2.33	9	1	39	45	11	10
Nick Robinson, Shelter Island	1	3	2.34	9	1	42	43	6	22
Brian Weissert, Westhampton	4	1	2.58	8	0	38	33	23	38
Darren Williams, Riverhead	3	1	2.61	7	0	38	25	16	32
Andrew Ciocia, North Fork	6	1	2.72	8	0	40	39	11	40

JAYHAWK LEAGUE

	W	L	PCT	GB
Liberal BeeJays	30	12	.714	—
Hays Larks	30	12	.714	—
Derby Twins	28	14	.667	2
Great Bend Bat Cats	23	19	.548	7
Dodge City A's	22	20	.524	8
El Dorado Broncos	20	22	.476	10
Haysville Aviators	11	31	.262	19
Oklahoma City Indians	4	38	.095	26

Championship: Liberal won regular season title.

Top 10 Prospects: 1. Colin Simpson, C, Hays (Jr., Oklahoma State). **2.** Gabe Constantine, LHP, Derby (So., Grayson JC, Texas). **3.** Tyler Starks, LHP, Hays (Jr., Stephen F. Austin). **4.** Benjamin Sems, SS, Great Bend (So., Kansas). **5.** Jaron Robinson, SS, Liberal (Jr., Murray State). **6.** Trevor Boone, OF, Hays (So., Oklahoma State). **7.** Chance Carner, RHP, Liberal (Jr., Murray State). **8.** Joe Corbett, RHP, Oklahoma City (Jr., West Texas A&M). **9.** Jordan Wilkerson, OF, Great Bend (Jr., Fort Hays State, Kan.). **10.** Clayton Rasbeary, OF, Hays (So., Grayson JC, Texas).

INDIVIDUAL BATTING LEADERS

	AVG	AB	R	H	2B	3B	HR	RBI	SB
Colin Simpson, C, Hays	.451	133	35	60	10	0	12	50	1
Cale O'Donnell, UTL, Liberal	.391	115	25	45	9	0	3	27	0
Troy Konwinski, UTL, Haysville	.387	111	6	43	7	1	2	19	2
Jaron Robinson, INF, Liberal	.372	137	30	51	5	2	6	29	0
Michael Uquiri, OF, Derby	.371	97	32	36	4	1	1	12	1
Bennett Hostetler, UTL, Dodge City	.366	164	41	60	8	1	2	39	2
Tyler Flores, of, Haysville	.351	151	32	53	19	2	6	22	0
Colton Onstott, c, Liberal	.347	118	24	41	18	0	4	30	0
Clayton Rasbeary, of, Hays	.346	136	36	47	10	0	5	30	1
Tucker Rohde, inf, Dodge City	.333	102	16	34	5	1	0	15	1

INDIVIDUAL PITCHING LEADERS

	W	L	ERA	G	SV	IP	H	BB	SO
Walter Pennington, Hays	2	1	2.30	7	0	43	33	11	22
Brick Knoten, Dodge City	3	1	2.41	18	1	34	32	14	29
Sam Beattie, Liberal	3	2	2.47	7	0	44	48	5	45
Chandler Coates, Hays	6	0	2.64	7	0	44	36	9	32
Jarrett Seaton, Great Bend	4	1	3.28	8	0	47	40	19	37
Alex Lopez, Hays	6	2	3.42	9	0	47	43	12	46
Hunter Larson, El Dorado	3	3	3.72	8	0	39	36	19	32
Mitch McIntyre, El Dorado	2	2	3.82	12	0	38	42	15	39
Taylor Kopplin, Haysville	1	4	3.83	8	0	40	43	8	31
Josh Riggs, El Dorado	3	1	3.98	11	0	43	45	18	38

MINK LEAGUE

North Division	W	L	PCT	GB
St. Joseph Mustangs	27	12	.684	—
Sedalia Bombers	25	16	.610	3
Chillicothe Mudcats	19	21	.475	8½
Clarinda A's	19	21	.475	8½
South Division	**W**	**L**	**PCT**	**GB**
Ozark Generals	23	17	.575	—
Nevada Griffons	21	21	.500	3
Jefferson City Renegades	16	24	.400	7
Joplin Outlaws	12	30	.286	12

Championship: St. Joseph defeated Ozark 2-1 in best-of-three series.

Top 10 Prospects: 1. Trey Harris, OF, Sedalia (Sr., Missouri). **2.** L.J. Hatch, SS, Nevada (SIGNED: Rockies). **3.** Mojo Hagge, OF, Clarinda (So., Nebraska). **4.** Kale Emshoff, C, Clarinda (So., Arkansas-Little Rock). **5.** Cole Evans,OF, Jefferson City (So., Iowa Western JC). **6.** Mike Million, OF, Jefferson City (Jr., Missouri Southern State). **7.** Nigel Nootbaar, RHP, Clarinda (No school). **8.** Jacob Voss, RHP, Jefferson City (Jr., Creighton). **9.** Ramger Iglesias, SS, Chillicothe (Sr., Bloomfield College, N.J.). **10.** Danny Mitchell, OF, Clarinda (So., Arkansas-Little Rock).

INDIVIDUAL BATTING LEADERS

	AVG	AB	R	H	2B	3B	HR	RBI	SB
Ryan Curtis, OF, Ozark	.394	175	38	69	13	2	2	47	7
Zack Ehlen, OF, Joplin	.374	147	36	55	7	1	0	23	20
Matt Delavega, C, Joplin	.347	147	24	51	8	1	4	41	3
Dalton Horstmeier, OF, Sedalia	.340	153	36	52	10	2	8	47	1
Justin Blasinki, OF, Chillicothe	.333	165	27	55	9	2	4	42	2
Danny Mitchell, OF, Clarinda	.333	201	44	67	12	1	3	36	27
Kainalu Pitoy, OF, Nevada	.319	160	26	51	11	1	5	27	6
Ramger Iglesias, INF, Chillicothe	.318	154	34	49	10	0	0	20	26
Bryce Bisenius, 1B, Chillicothe	.316	155	26	49	7	2	2	26	1
Kaleb DeLatorre, INF, Joplin	.308	159	28	49	4	2	1	18	4

INDIVIDUAL PITCHING LEADERS

	W	L	ERA	G	SV	IP	H	BB	SO
Nikko Pablo, St. Joseph	1	1	1.40	16	4	26	22	9	19
Louis Niemerg, Sedalia	0	4	1.69	15	6	21	12	8	25
Caleb Lasher, Jefferson City	2	1	1.69	5	0	21	14	16	9
Steve D'Amico, St. Joseph	5	1	1.80	8	0	55	39	22	66
Parker Kirkpatrick, Chillicothe	3	1	2.14	7	0	42	39	13	16
Osvaldo Raya, St. Joseph	5	1	2.38	7	0	42	38	14	29
Trenton Moeller, Joplin	1	2	2.38	16	4	23	27	8	19
Samuel Reed, Clarinda	4	2	2.49	20	3	22	17	10	32
Jake Fraze, Nevada	3	2	2.63	12	0	51	45	20	40
Mark Lesinski, Ozark	2	2	2.79	5	0	29	30	7	22

NEW ENGLAND COLLEGIATE LEAGUE

Northern Division	W	L	PCT	GB
Upper Valley Nighthawks	29	15	.659	0
Valley Blue Sox	26	18	.591	3
Keene Swamp Bats	20	24	.455	9
Winnipesaukee Muskrats	18	25	.419	10½
North Adams SteepleCats	18	26	.409	11
Vermont Mountaineers	18	26	.409	11
Sanford Mainers	17	27	.386	12
Southern Division	**W**	**L**	**PCT**	**GB**
Ocean State Waves	31	13	.705	0
Mystic Schooners	27	17	.614	4
Plymouth Pilgrims	25	19	.568	6
Newport Gulls	20	22	.476	10
Danbury Westerners	18	25	.419	12½
New Bedford Bay Sox	17	27	.386	14

Championship: Valley defeated Ocean State 2-0 in best-of-three series.

Top 10 Prospects: 1. Kameron Misner, OF, Newport (So., Missouri). **2.** Charles King, RHP, Newport (So., Texas Christian). **3.** Blake Whitney, RHP, North Adams (Sr., South Carolina Upstate). **4.** Dazon Cole, RHP, Valley (Jr., Central Michigan). **5.** Tommy Jew, OF, Mystic (So., UC Santa Barbara). **6.** Niko Hulszier, OF, Valley (Jr., Morehead State). **7.** Hernen Sardinas, 1B/OF, Plymouth (So., Maine). **8.** Jimmy Titus, SS, Ocean State (So., Bryant). **9.** Cam Alldred, LHP, Upper Valley (Jr., Cincinnati).

10. Giovanni Dingcong, OF, Danbury (Sr., St. Thomas Aquinas, Fla.).

INDIVIDUAL BATTING LEADERS

	AVG	AB	R	H	2B	3B	HR	RBI	SB
Kameron Misner, OF, Newport	.378	135	35	51	13	0	8	25	14
Nathaniel Eikhoff, 3B, Keene	.371	116	14	43	10	0	1	24	4
Koby Claborn, 1B, Winnipesaukee	.354	147	29	52	12	0	12	37	0
Randy Taveras, Danbury	.352	105	30	37	6	0	3	20	12
Shaine Hughes, 3B, Sanford	.349	129	22	45	8	0	4	24	3
Hernen Sardinas, OF, Plymouth	.345	119	23	41	10	1	7	28	3
Nicholas Mascelli, SS, Mystic	.344	163	28	56	14	0	6	21	7
Alexander Brewer, INF, Keene	.342	120	21	41	5	0	6	20	0
Anthony Godino, OF, Upper Valley	.336	143	30	48	9	3	9	32	11
Griffin Dey, INF, Danbury	.331	118	25	39	5	0	7	24	2

INDIVIDUAL PITCHING LEADERS

	W	L	ERA	G	SV	IP	H	BB	SO
Ashton Raines, Upper Valley	4	0	1.39	10	1	39	30	10	33
Kyle Mora, Newport	3	1	1.75	7	0	36	26	7	32
Brent Teller, New Bedford	3	3	1.93	9	0	37	34	17	32
Jake Dexter, Sanford	2	1	2.04	25	1	35	26	12	35
Blake Whitney, North Adams	1	3	2.08	9	0	52	36	13	80
Sonny Potter, Mystic	4	1	2.21	8	0	37	28	15	32
Cameron Alldred, Upper Valley	4	2	2.25	7	0	40	28	8	38
Danny Wirchansky, Upper Valley	4	1	2.52	7	0	39	31	8	26
Tim Elliott, Keene	6	1	2.53	9	0	43	34	10	42
Benjamin White, Plymouth	3	1	2.61	7	0	38	39	7	38

NORTHWOODS LEAGUE

North Division	W	L	PCT	GB
Mankato MoonDogs	44	28	.611	—
St. Cloud Rox	42	30	.583	2
Willmar Stingers	41	31	.569	3
Waterloo Bucks	39	33	.542	5
Eau Claire Express	39	33	.542	5
Bismarck Larks	31	40	.437	12½
La Crosse Loggers	31	40	.437	12½
Rochester Honkers	30	39	.435	12½
Duluth Huskies	31	41	.431	13
Thunder Bay Border Cats	27	43	.386	16
South Division	**W**	**L**	**PCT**	**GB**
Wisconsin Rapids Rafters	52	20	.722	—
Battle Creek Bombers	42	30	.583	10
Rockford Rivets	39	33	.542	13
Lakeshore Chinooks	38	34	.528	14
Madison Mallards	38	34	.528	14
Fond du Lac Dock Spiders	38	34	.528	14
Kenosha Kingfish	36	36	.500	16
Kalamazoo Growlers	28	44	.389	24
Wisconsin Woodchucks	26	46	.361	26
Green Bay Bullfrogs	23	49	.319	29

Championship: St. Cloud defeated Battle Creek 2-1 in best-of-three series.

Top 10 Prospects: 1. Zach Watson, OF, Rockford (So., Louisiana State). **2.** Tyler Dyson, RHP, Madison (So., Florida). **3.** Bryson Stott, SS, Wisconsin Rapids (So., Nevada-Las Vegas). **4.** Hunter Feduccia, C, Rockford (Jr., Louisiana State). **5.** Kenyon Yovan, RHP, Rochester (So., Oregon). **6.** Zach Zubia, 1B, Rochester (Fr., Texas). **7.** Michael Busch, INF, St. Cloud (So., North Carolina). **8.** Jake Guenther, OF, Wisconsin Rapids (So., Sacramento City JC). **9.** Daniel Ritcheson, RHP, Kalamazoo (Fr., San Diego State). **10.** Parker Sanburn, RHP, Lakeshore (SIGNED: Rangers).

INDIVIDUAL BATTING LEADERS

	AVG	AB	R	H	2B	3B	HR	RBI	SB
Connor Hollis, INF, Kalamazoo	.375	176	56	66	8	1	1	19	11
Ryan Stekl, INF, Wisconsin	.364	253	37	92	18	0	5	52	2
Bryson Scott, INF, Wisconsin	.352	284	72	100	17	1	3	51	26
Zac Taylor, OF, Madison	.350	180	37	63	13	0	7	33	18
Hunter Feduccia, C, Rockford	.348	184	43	64	18	1	8	41	0
Daniel Amaral, OF, Mankato	.347	167	41	58	13	7	0	27	23
Ryan Anderson, OF, Bismarck	.340	197	18	67	13	1	5	27	1
Cole Daily, SS, Madison	.338	284	72	96	8	2	1	31	19
Matthew Mika, INF, Lakeshore	.335	221	53	74	13	1	5	37	27
Alex Howard, INF, Battle Creek	.333	240	56	80	27	0	9	43	9

INDIVIDUAL PITCHING LEADERS

	W	L	ERA	G	SV	IP	H	BB	SO
Aaron Rozek, St. Cloud	6	1	2.39	10	0	64	48	17	78
Brett Newberg, Mankato	5	4	2.66	11	0	71	69	19	54
Jesse Slinger, Wisconsin	8	1	2.71	11	0	63	48	11	31
Tyler Steele, Bismarck	4	3	2.95	13	0	58	60	21	41
Connor Manous, Kalamazoo	4	2	3.07	11	0	59	48	18	57
Jack Eagan, Wisconsin	7	0	3.08	12	0	61	44	31	66
Andy Lalonde, Bismarck	4	5	3.27	13	0	66	62	29	56
Luke Eldred, Eau Claire	4	2	3.27	10	0	66	68	8	35
Tyler Lesley, Mankato	4	1	3.36	12	0	67	60	30	51
Matt Horkey, Madison	5	4	3.52	12	0	61	67	13	42

PERFECT GAME COLLEGIATE LEAGUE

East Division	W	L	PCT	GB
Amsterdam Mohawks	36	12	.750	—
Albany Dutchmen	33	16	.673	3½
Mohawk Valley DiamondDawgs	29	18	.617	6½
Saugerties Stallions	20	28	.417	16
Utica Blue Sox	18	30	.375	18
Glens Falls Dragons	17	33	.340	20
Oneonta Outlaws	14	30	.318	20
West Division	**W**	**L**	**PCT**	**GB**
Jamestown Jammers	34	15	.694	—
Geneva Red Wings	29	21	.580	5½
Elmira Pioneers	27	23	.540	7½
Onondaga Flames	23	26	.469	11
Newark Pilots	19	31	.380	15½
Adirondack Trail Blazers	16	32	.333	17½

Championship: Mohawk Valley defeated Jamestown 2-1 in best-of-three series.

Top 10 Prospects: 1. T.J. Collett, C, Amsterdam (So., Kentucky). **2.** Will Holland, SS, Amsterdam (So., Auburn). **3.** Houston Roth, RHP, Elmira (So., Mississippi). **4.** Tyler Mattison, RHP, Glens Falls (Fr., Bryant). **5.** Eric Rivera, OF, Amsterdam (So., Florida Atlantic). **6.** Mathieu Gauthier, RHP, Amsterdam (So., North Carolina State). **7.** Dustin Skelton, C, Amsterdam (So., Mississippi State). **8.** Greg Marino, RHP, Albany (So., Stony Brook). **9.** Brett Rodriguez, SS, Elmira (So., Wofford). **10.** Russ Olive, 1B, Mohawk Valley (So., Massachusetts-Lowell).

INDIVIDUAL BATTING LEADERS

	AVG	AB	R	H	2B	3B	HR	RBI	SB
John Valente, INF, Amsterdam	.422	147	37	62	13	1	2	26	11
Christ Conley, C, Jamestown	.382	123	43	47	13	0	5	27	1
Conor Grammes, INF, Elmira	.377	138	25	52	9	2	3	36	1
Marshall Gilbert, C, Elmira	.376	117	31	44	10	1	4	38	1
Jimmy Standohar, Jamestown	.346	133	36	46	6	2	0	19	15
John Conti, OF, Jamestown	.345	116	32	40	3	3	0	30	21
Allbry Major, UTL, Elmira	.336	122	28	41	12	0	2	21	3
Kyle Gallagher, OF, Onondaga	.336	137	25	46	6	1	0	24	4
Ayrton Schafer, OF, Elmira	.335	155	29	52	10	1	1	28	0
Brian Uliana, OF, Glens Falls	.335	170	31	57	5	4	0	13	9

INDIVIDUAL PITCHING LEADERS

	W	L	ERA	G	SV	IP	H	BB	SO
Matt Pierce, Albany	8	1	1.71	12	0	42	38	11	26
Thomas Lane, Amsterdam	3	2	2.30	10	0	43	30	32	48
Henry Martinez, Newark	3	2	2.43	8	0	41	36	18	51
Bradley Griggs, Jamestown	4	2	2.50	9	1	50	38	25	38
Alex Bellardini, Geneva	6	1	2.80	9	0	61	59	15	37
Dylan Leahy, Utica	3	3	3.43	7	0	42	37	20	25
Jonathan Hardy, Adirondack	2	4	3.56	9	0	48	58	10	22
Andrew Saalfrank, Amsterdam	7	0	3.68	8	0	44	31	14	48
Nathan Wrighter, Oneonta	3	4	3.75	11	0	48	52	14	39
Joe DeSarro, Mohawk Valley	5	1	3.78	8	0	48	35	21	45

PROSPECT LEAGUE

East Division	W	L	PCT	GB
Butler BlueSox	37	23	.617	—
West Virginia Miners	30	28	.517	6
Champion City Kings	29	29	.500	7
Chillicothe Paints	29	31	.483	8

	W	L	PCT	GB
Kokomo Jackrabbits	27	33	.450	10
West Division	**W**	**L**	**PCT**	**GB**
Lafayette Aviators	36	24	.600	—
Terre Haute Rex	32	28	.533	4
Danville Dans	31	29	.517	5
Springfield Sliders	26	34	.433	10
Quincy Gems	21	39	.350	15

Championship: Lafayette defeated Butler 2-1 in best-of-three series.

Top 10 Prospects: 1. Will Freeman, RHP, Kokomo (So., Jones County JC, Miss.). **2.** Connor Coward, RHP, Butler (Sr., Virginia Tech). **3.** Connor Curlis, LHP, Champion City (Jr., Ohio State). **4.** Brad Depperman, RHP, Lafayette (Sr., North Florida). **5.** Pat Ferguson, INF, Butler (So., Kent State). **6.** Nic Laio, RHP, Chillicothe (Jr., Western Michigan). **7.** Seth Gray, INF, Champion City (So., Wright State). **8.** Tanner Murhpy, OF, Butler (So., North Florida). **9.** Tanner Piechnick, C, Chillicothe (So., Ohio). **10.** Nic Webre, OF, Danville (Fr., Louisiana State).

INDIVIDUAL BATTING LEADERS

	AVG	AB	R	H	2B	3B	HR	RBI	SB
Austin Norman, OF, W. Virginia	.375	192	37	72	14	7	3	34	9
James Meeker, INF, Butler	.357	154	24	55	7	3	2	28	5
Imani Willis, OF, Kokomo	.354	158	27	56	7	6	3	21	24
Dougie Parks, INF, Lafayette	.346	211	51	73	22	1	8	60	0
James Govern, INF, Danville	.335	218	41	73	15	2	5	37	25
Michael Rothmund, INF, Danville	.335	161	42	54	13	2	11	47	1
Tanner Murphy, OF, Butler	.330	197	38	65	16	5	6	42	22
Logan Beaman, OF, Lafayette	.329	213	56	70	10	4	7	59	11
Dan Ward, INF, West Virginia	.328	180	37	59	13	3	9	42	18
Dalton Schumer, INF, Quincy	.327	208	54	68	14	3	13	53	13

INDIVIDUAL PITCHING LEADERS

	W	L	ERA	G	SV	IP	H	BB	SO
Brad Depperman, Lafayette	4	2	2.11	11	1	60	38	12	108
Daryin Lewis, Chillicothe	2	3	2.44	13	3	52	49	9	46
Austin Krizan, Terre Haute	6	0	2.56	16	0	56	44	23	39
Connor Curlis, Champion City	2	3	2.64	13	1	58	37	15	82
Andrew Reisinger, Chillicothe	4	0	2.91	10	0	53	59	15	50
Tyler Grauer, Terre Haute	2	3	3.00	11	0	60	54	17	79
Quentin Miller, Kokomo	4	3	3.42	13	0	50	39	21	55
Brad Wilson, Champion City	4	2	3.47	9	0	49	49	14	44
Nick Bucci, Butler	5	2	3.63	10	0	67	64	22	39
Danny Cody, Chillicothe	3	4	3.77	11	0	60	55	16	60

SUNBELT LEAGUE

East Division	**W**	**L**	**PCT**	**GB**
Atlanta Crackers	19	9	.679	—
Brookhaven Bucks	16	13	.552	3½
Gwinnett Tide	12	14	.462	6
Alpharetta Braves	8	15	.348	8½
West Division	**W**	**L**	**PCT**	**GB**
Sunbelt Patriots	22	7	.759	—
Carrollton Clippers	12	15	.444	9
Norcross Astros	10	15	.400	10
Phenix City Crawdads	5	16	.238	13

Championship: Sunbelt defeated Atlanta 2-0 in best-of-three series.

Top Five Prospects: 1. Michael Livingston, RHP, Sunbelt (Sr., Young Harris, Ga.). **2.** Coleman Williams, RHP, Norcross (So., Duke). **3.** Tucker Maxwell, OF, Norcross (So., Georgia). **4.** Hunter Caudelle, RHP, Gwinnett (Jr., Georgia Gwinnett). **5.** Zach Keenan, RHP, Atlanta (Fr., Middle Tennessee State).

INDIVIDUAL BATTING LEADERS

	AVG	AB	R	H	2B	3B	HR	RBI	SB
Jeremy Glore, OF, Atlanta	.361	108	21	39	5	0	0	14	12
Eriq White, 2B, Sunbelt	.346	81	17	28	4	0	2	10	7
Frank Wager, 1B, Phenix City	.343	67	6	23	5	0	2	15	0
Drew Lingo, OF, Phenix City	.339	62	8	21	8	1	2	12	1
Daino Deas, 2B, Brookhaven	.333	84	12	28	4	0	0	9	1
Connor Stutts, OF, Brookhaven	.328	64	13	21	4	2	1	7	2
Trenton Nash, INF, Alpharetta	.327	52	9	17	4	0	1	10	6
Tyler Adams, INF, Sunbelt	.325	80	17	26	7	0	4	13	6
Matthew Vaccaro, 1B, Carrollton	.324	71	9	23	4	0	0	14	2
Isaac Philips, OF, Carrollton	.321	81	17	26	5	0	0	9	8

INDIVIDUAL PITCHING LEADERS

	W	L	ERA	G	SV	IP	H	BB	SO
Scheldon Paulk, Norcross	0	2	0.88	13	0	31	26	3	27
Michael Livingston, Sunbelt	4	0	0.94	9	0	38	24	6	43
Lucas Cloud, Atlanta	2	1	0.99	14	0	27	19	7	30
Jake Watkins, Sunbelt	3	1	1.00	8	0	54	42	16	54
Chris Raasch, Atlanta	5	0	1.21	8	0	37	30	5	27
Tucker Plouffe, Gwinnett	2	0	1.50	7	0	36	22	7	37
Austin Goff, Carrollton	0	1	1.52	6	0	24	22	12	24
Jake Brace, Brookhaven	3	3	1.70	7	0	42	37	7	31
Tyler Sylvester, Gwinnett	2	2	1.88	7	0	29	23	20	30
Brooks Luther, Carrollton	3	2	1.90	14	4	24	19	7	23

TEXAS COLLEGIATE LEAGUE

	W	L	PCT	GB
Brazos Valley Bombers	34	18	.654	—
Victoria Generals	34	22	.607	2
Acadiana Cane Cutters	29	23	.558	5
Texarkana Twins	19	34	.358	15½
Texas Marshals	18	37	.327	17½

Championship: Brazos Valley defeated Arcadiana 2-0 in best-of-three series.

Top 10 Prospects: 1. Gunner Halter, INF, Texarkana (So., Seminole State JC, Okla.). **2.** Mike Mokma, RHP, Brazos Valley (So., Michigan State). **3.** Zac Leigh, RHP, Victoria (So., Texas State). **4.** Jack Kenley, INF, Victoria (So., Arkansas). **5.** Daniel Lahare, OF, Arcadiana (Jr., Louisiana-Lafayette). **6.** Hayden Marze, RHP, Arcadiana (Jr., Florida Southern). **7.** Glen McClain, 1B, Victoria (Jr., Indiana Tech). **8.** Jared Mang, OF, Brazos Valley (Jr., New Mexico). **9.** Alex Rodriguez, INF, Texarkana (Jr., Kentucky). **10.** Handsome Monica, C, Arcadiana (Sr., Louisiana-Lafayette).

INDIVIDUAL BATTING LEADERS

	AVG	AB	R	H	2B	3B	HR	RBI	SB
Brady Bell, INF, Acadiana	.358	137	30	49	8	0	3	28	5
Daniel Lahare, OF, Acadiana	.356	163	37	58	6	3	0	24	15
Jared Mang, OF, Brazos Valley	.349	149	27	52	10	1	3	26	12
Logan Bottrell, OF, Acadiana	.328	125	33	41	8	2	0	23	12
Thomas Jeffries, 1B, Brazos Valley	.328	134	22	44	3	0	0	10	15
Jack Kenley, INF, Victoria	.319	138	33	44	9	2	2	22	5
Glen McClain, INF, Victoria	.317	123	21	39	3	1	1	20	2
Gavin Bourgeois, OF, Acadiana	.311	119	40	37	4	1	0	15	18
Jonathon Artigues, SS, Acadiana	.309	123	24	38	3	0	1	14	11
Chase Calabuig, OF, Brazos Valley	.303	109	25	33	9	1	1	17	11

INDIVIDUAL PITCHING LEADERS

	W	L	ERA	G	SV	IP	H	BB	SO
Mike Mokma, Brazos Valley	5	2	2.78	10	0	58	47	12	29
Brandon Talley, Texas	1	2	3.05	9	0	44	32	20	35
Ben Donnell, Texarkana	3	6	3.07	10	0	62	55	20	36
Max Page, Acadiana	4	2	3.34	17	0	57	46	37	53
Jordan Hackett, Victoria	5	1	3.48	12	0	54	67	21	38
Chase Maddux, Brazos Valley	2	2	3.61	11	0	57	51	20	39
Jeremy Hammer, Texas	4	3	3.74	12	0	55	58	17	30
Calder Mikell, Texas	3	4	4.08	9	1	46	38	30	35
Billy Fogle, Texarkana	3	4	4.41	17	0	49	50	31	31
Jose Delmar, Texas	2	5	4.71	14	1	57	68	30	39

VALLEY LEAGUE

North Division	**W**	**L**	**PCT**	**GB**
Purcellville Cannons	26	16	.619	—
New Market Rebels	24	17	.585	1½
Strasburg Express	22	19	.537	3½
Winchester Royals	21	21	.500	5
Front Royal Cardinals	17	25	.405	9
Woodstock River Bandits	14	28	.333	12
South Division	**W**	**L**	**PCT**	**GB**
Charlottesville TomSox	32	10	.762	—
Harrisonburg Turks	21	21	.500	11
Waynesboro Generals	20	22	.476	12
Staunton Braves	19	23	.452	13
Covington Lumberjacks	14	28	.333	18

COLLEGE

Championship: Charlottesville defeated Strasburg 2-1 in best-of-three series.

Top 10 Prospects: 1. Zachary Peek, RHP, Strasburg (So., Winthrop). **2.** Dominic Canzone, OF, Front Royal (So., Ohio State). **3.** Tom Sutera, RHP, Purcellville (Jr., Siena). **4.** Vinnie Pasquantino, 1B, Charlottesville (So., Old Dominion). **5.** Luc Lipcius, OF, Front Royal (So., Tennessee). **6.** Nate Pawelczyk, RHP, New Market (Jr., Winthrop). **7.** Jake Washer, C, New Market (So., East Carolina). **8.** Brandon Quaranta, OF/1B, Strasburg (Sr., Philadelphia). **9.** Mike Wielansky, 2B/SS, Charlottesville (Jr., Wooster, Ohio). **10.** Cash Gladfelter, SS, Woodstock (Jr., Shippensburg, Pa.).

INDIVIDUAL BATTING LEADERS

	AVG	AB	R	H	2B	3B	HR	RBI	SB
Michael Wielansky, INF, CTS	.432	155	38	67	18	4	4	34	11
Dominic Canzone, OF, Front Royal	.404	114	28	46	3	2	3	23	17
Max Wood, OF, Staunton	.390	123	33	48	12	1	5	21	8
Danton Hyman, OF, Woodstock	.379	161	28	61	7	1	1	27	15
Jacob Rhinesmith, OF, New Market	.369	122	28	45	9	2	3	33	9
Trevin Esquerra, 1B, Purcellville	.362	152	25	55	11	3	8	33	0
McClain Bradley, OF, Waynesboro	.359	153	31	55	9	3	2	18	20
Ty Andrus, OF, Harrisonburg	.348	155	29	54	0	2	0	11	10
Dillon Reed, OF, Waynesboro	.347	167	30	58	9	1	0	23	18
Jake Washer, C, New Market	.346	133	36	46	10	0	5	35	0

INDIVIDUAL PITCHING LEADERS

	W	L	ERA	G	SV	IP	H	BB	SO
Thomas Sutera, Purcellville	6	0	1.57	15	3	34	26	10	39
Sean McCracken, CTS	2	0	1.66	8	0	38	27	9	27
Zachary Peek, Strasburg	4	1	1.80	9	0	35	25	6	40
Andy Crum, Purcellville	3	2	2.01	7	0	40	31	12	32
Mason Studstill, Harrisonburg	4	0	2.50	6	0	36	27	19	31
Grant Suponchick, Waynesboro	2	3	2.57	8	0	35	37	5	21
Nick Fuchs, Woodstock	3	3	2.72	9	0	43	35	20	53
Benjamin Dum, Strasburg	5	2	2.78	9	0	45	44	9	39
Dylan Hall, Strasburg	2	1	3.34	9	0	35	32	13	35
Payton Kinney, Waynesboro	4	0	3.41	9	0	37	38	12	32

WEST COAST LEAGUE

North Division	W	L	PCT	GB
Bellingham Bells	31	23	.574	—
Wenatchee AppleSox	29	25	.537	2
Victoria HarbourCats	29	25	.537	2
Kelowna Falcons	28	26	.519	3
Walla Walla Sweets	25	29	.463	6
Port Angeles Lefties	19	34	.358	11½
South Division	**W**	**L**	**PCT**	**GB**
Corvallis Knights	34	20	.630	—
Yakima Valley Pippins	28	26	.519	6
Cowlitz Black Bears	27	27	.500	7
Bend Elks	26	28	.481	8
Gresham GreyWolves	20	33	.377	13 ½

Championship: Corvallis defeated Victoria 2-1 in best-of-three series.

Top 10 Prospects: 1. Chris Lincoln, RHP, Walla Walla (So., UC Santa Barbara). **2.** Jordan Qsar, OF/RHP, Corvallis (Jr., Pepperdine). **3.** Chase Illig, C, Bellingham (So., West Virginia). **4.** Austin Shenton, 3B, Bellingham (So., Florida International). **5.** Louis Crow, RHP, Corvallis (So., San Diego). **6.** Devlin Granberg, OF, Cowlitz (Sr., Dallas Baptist). **7.** Holden Powell, RHP, Bellingham (Fr., UCLA). **8.** Darius Vines, RHP, Walla Walla (So., Yavapai JC, Ariz.). **9.** Jackson Thoreson, C, Gresham (Sr., St. Mary's). **10.** Chase Kaplan, LHP, Corvallis (Sr., Kansas).

INDIVIDUAL BATTING LEADERS

	AVG	AB	R	H	2B	3B	HR	RBI	SB
Austin Shenton, of, Bellingham	.409	193	36	79	15	1	4	47	3
Ryan Kim, of, Cowlitz	.375	144	33	54	7	2	5	27	9
J.J. Hancock, of, Walla Walla	.360	161	28	58	12	4	1	22	4
Chase Illig, c, Bellingham	.360	164	34	59	6	1	15	52	0
Hunter Vansau, of, Victoria	.359	131	28	47	8	1	8	34	6
Jacob Prater, inf, Wenatchee	.359	131	33	47	14	1	2	21	2
Lucas Denney, inf, Yakima Valley	.338	160	34	54	15	0	8	34	3
Taylor Wright, inf, Kelowna	.337	205	47	69	12	0	11	54	12
Tora Otsuka, of, Yakima Valley	.333	147	30	49	3	2	3	25	12
Austin Pinorini, c, Bellingham	.323	155	36	50	12	1	4	25	6

INDIVIDUAL PITCHING LEADERS

	W	L	ERA	G	SV	IP	H	BB	SO
Jack Owen, Victoria	4	1	1.02	8	0	44	29	14	48
Kris Jackson, Bend	6	3	2.43	10	0	63	61	20	49
Collin Maier, Wenatchee	6	1	2.68	9	0	54	48	22	38
Grant Larson, Bend	3	2	2.79	11	0	48	44	16	44
Cal Hehnke, Kelowna	4	0	3.17	11	0	54	57	17	52
Andrew Hansen, Gresham	6	2	3.49	10	0	59	65	15	43
Davis Baillie, Cowlitz	3	2	3.51	15	1	49	42	11	29
Holden Powell, Bellingham	4	3	3.69	10	0	46	34	26	43
Robert Reaser, Gresham	1	5	3.79	12	0	55	50	26	62
A.J. Landis, Yakima Valley	3	3	3.84	11	0	68	88	16	39

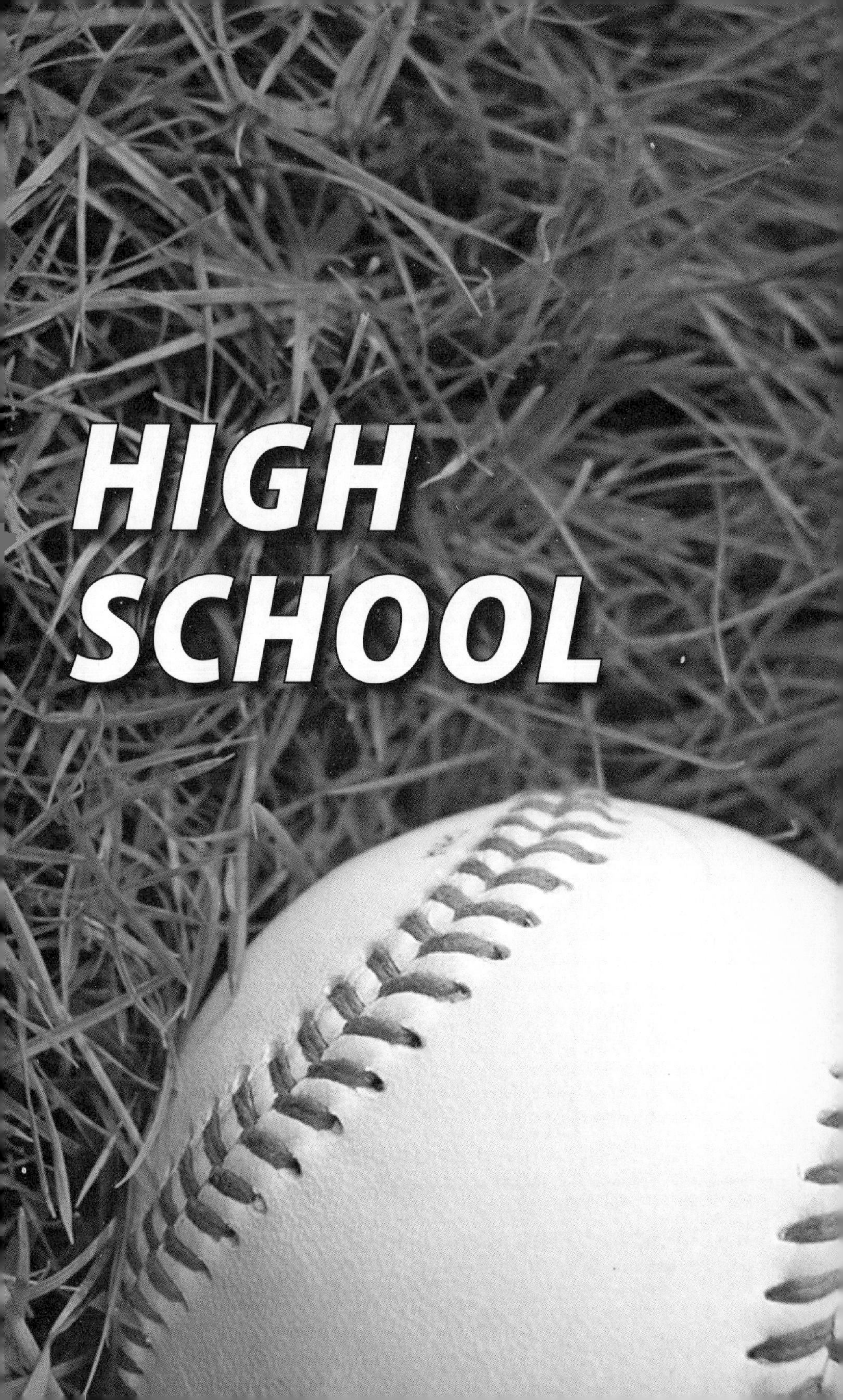
HIGH
SCHOOL

Shawnee (Okla.) High won its third-straight Oklahoma 5A state title in 2017.

Perfect 40-0 puts Shawnee at the top

BY CARLOS COLLAZO

When Todd Boyer first started with the Shawnee (Okla.) High baseball program it was as an assistant coach.

He watched as the Wolves began to form a baseball dynasty that would make the Oklahoma state tournament in 18 of the last 21 years.

In 2007, Boyer became the head coach of the program and continued that tradition of success.

Before the 2017 season began, Boyer had led the Wolves to a 236-130 record in his 10 years at the helm. He didn't know it at the time, but it would be his final year as Shawnee's head coach. And he would leave the program at an elite level—and with a season that he would never forget.

Led by senior catcher Jake Taylor—a future Oklahoma State player who was drafted in the 25th round by the Braves—Shawnee won 40 straight games this spring, en route to winning a third straight Oklahoma 5A state championship and the 2017 Baseball America Team of the Year award.

"What an incredible, great group of kids," Boyer said. "The thing is, this group of seniors won three state championships on the field. But they also won two academic state championships—what a well-rounded group.

"They've got good heads on their shoulders and are an extremely hard working group. And I couldn't be any prouder of any group that's come through."

Boyer has seen a lot of groups come through.

Since taking over as the head coach of Shawnee's program more than a decade ago, the Wolves missed the state tournament just three times.

And for the senior class, which includes Taylor and fellow four-year starters Tanner Sparks, A.J. Barron and Eli Davis as well as three-year starter Cole Payne, all they know is success. Each player has made the state tournament all four seasons of their high school careers, and each has won the 5A championship the last three years.

The group won 52-straight games, dating back to the championship season in 2016.

"What a legacy they've left," Boyer said. "I think what they've left for their teammates is they've had a great work ethic. And, you know, they were talented, but they were our hardest workers as well. They were the guys who were the first ones here and the last ones to leave, and they would work with our younger kids on some little things.

"That's what separates good teams from great

teams, doing all the little things right. This group paid attention to the details. So I think just the work ethic, and what it takes to be a great player, they've instilled that in some of our younger players."

That starts with Taylor, who hit .519/.594/.938 with nine home runs and 22 doubles. He was the rock of the team.

"He's got a good head on his shoulders," Boyer said. "He knows what it's all about . . .

"A quick story on Jake. One of our former players—Pat Presley—came through. He started for us for four years at shortstop. He has some young children now, around 10-12 years of age. Towards the end of the year we finished a ball game, and they came in the dugout after our game was over and asked Jake, 'Would you please sign our hats.' And Jake said, 'I'll tell you what, I'll sign your stuff, but first you have to sign mine.'

"He'd have every right to have a big ego, but he has none whatsoever. He's just an unbelievable player."

In addition to Taylor and Sparks, who led Shawnee with 12 home runs, the Wolves got a tremendous season out of junior Kade Self, who led the team in both slugging (.947) and on-base percentage (.629), while walking 34 times and striking out just 13.

For the season, Shawnee outscored their opponents 495-117, including a 12-7 win against Claremore (Okla.) High in the championship game.

"I just feel very blessed," Boyer said. "What a great opportunity for me to coach a great group of kids. I'm very, very proud of this group. It's just hard to put into words."

After the season, Boyer walked away from his head coaching job and took over as Shawnee's athletic director, where he'll have the opportunity to impact many more student-athletes. He'll miss the relationships with his players, and the coaches he's become friends with, but Boyer is leaving behind a legitimate high school dynasty. And what could be better than that?

"(My wife and I) sat down and talked a lot about it, prayed about it," Boyer said. "We just felt like it couldn't be better timing. You win three straight championships, you win 40 in a row to end the year.

"That's the storybook ending."

HIGH SCHOOL TOP 50

Rk.	School	Record
1.	Shawnee (Okla.) HS	40-0
2.	Archbishop McCarthy HS, Southwest Ranches, Fla.	29-2
3.	Calvary Christian HS, Clearwater, Fla.	30-0
4.	Woodlawn HS, Rison, Ark.	33-1
5.	La Cueva HS, Albuquerque, N.M.	28-1
6.	West Lauderdale HS, Collinsville, Miss.	33-3
7.	Jackson HS, Massillon, Ohio	29-1
8.	El Toro (Calif.) HS	27-7
9.	Pope HS, Marietta, Ga.	34-6
10.	Helena (Ala.) HS	38-6
11.	Etiwanda (Calif.) HS	27-3
12.	Riverdale Baptist HS, Marlboro, Md.	30-1
13.	Eastlake HS, Chula Vista, Calif.	32-4
14.	Basic HS, Henderson, Nev.	29-7
15.	Central HS, Baton Rouge, La.	31-13
16.	Deer Park (Texas) HS	36-8
17.	Etowah HS, Woodstock, Ga.	28-16
18.	Jefferson City (Mo.) HS	31-2
19.	Corona (Calif.) HS	24-10
20.	Loganville (Ga.) HS	30-13
21.	Clovis (Calif.) HS	25-7
22.	St. John Bosco HS, Bellflower, Calif.	27-8
23.	Timber Creek HS, Orlando	25-7
24.	Port Neches-Groves HS, Port Neches, Texas	22-7
25.	De La Salle HS, Concord, Calif.	21-8
26.	Rocky Mountain HS, Ft. Collins, Colo.	20-6
27.	Marist HS, Atlanta	25-17
28.	Reagan HS, San Antonio	35-8
29.	Buchanan HS, Clovis, Calif.	28-4
30.	Delbarton HS, Morristown, N.J.	21-7
31.	Lincoln HS, Tallahassee, Fla.	26-6
32.	Maize (Kan.) HS	22-3
33.	James Monroe Campus HS, Bronx, N.Y.	20-2
34.	West Monroe (La.) HS	38-3
35.	Nogales (Ariz.) HS	28-4
36.	Malvern (Pa.) Prep HS	25-6
37.	North Hall HS, Gainesville, Ga.	33-11
38.	Mater Dei HS, Santa Ana, Calif.	21-12
39.	Aurora (Mo.) HS	24-4
40.	Birmingham HS, Lake Balboa, Calif.	26-9
41.	Sheridan (Ariz.) HS	33-5
42.	St. John's HS, Shrewsbury, Mass.	26-3
43.	Turner Ashby HS, Bridgewater, Va.	22-2
44.	Saline (Miss.) HS	40-3
45.	El Dorado HS, Placentia, Calif.	21-9
46.	Pleasure Ridge Park HS, Louisville	43-5
47.	T.C. Roberson HS, Asheville, N.C.	31-3
48.	Cathedral HS, Indianapolis	29-0
49.	Cabot (Ark.) HS	25-7
50.	Brentwood (Tenn.) HS	30-10

Pitch Counts Sweep The Nation

Long before he was a Baltimore Oriole, Dylan Bundy was one of the best high school pitchers scouts had ever seen. In 2010 as a high school junior with a low-to-mid-90s fastball, the then 17-year-old carried his Owasso (Okla.) High team to a state runner-up finish, throwing 293 pitches over three games in four days as the Tulsa (Okla.) World noted at the time.

It was completely legal by Oklahoma Secondary School Activities Association rules. Those rules allowed a pitcher to pitch up to 10 innings in any single day or a complete game, no matter how many innings that game lasted (Dylan's older brother Bobby pitched 13 innings in an extra-inning game in 2007 (also noted by the Tulsa World). While Dylan Bundy's run with Owasso ended up one win short of a state title, fellow future big leaguer Dillon Overton was carrying

HIGH SCHOOL

Weatherford to a 4A state title by throwing 19 of the 22 innings Weatherford needed during the playoff run.

Coincidentally or not, both Bundy brothers and Overton have had Tommy John surgery since.

Oklahoma's next Bundy or Overton won't get the chance to be so heroic. And for that baseball can be thankful.

The 2017 season proved the start of whole new era of high school baseball. When it comes to pitch limits, high school baseball has entered the 21st century. After years of relying on innings limits (or in some states, no limits), high school state federations around the country have adopted pitch limits.

They didn't really have a choice. The National High School Federation mandated that each state adopt pitch limits of some sort. Only Massachussetts, which does not follow National High School Federation rules for baseball, has avoided adopting a pitch limit of any kind. Connecticut did not set an upper limit for the number of pitches a pitcher can throw in an outing, but did adopt days of rest limits.

"It's going to change the way we play baseball. We will give more kids opportunities and we are going to protect kids," said Elliot Hopkins, the director of educational services at the NHFS. Hopkins has served as the national federation's point person on baseball for 18 years.

It was just two years ago that Major League Baseball and USA Baseball announced the Pitch Smart program that brought together some of the nation's top sports medicine practitioners to put together recommendations to try keep young pitchers healthy. This is part of MLB commissioner Rob Manfred's "One Baseball" initiative where MLB is trying to take a larger role in guiding the sport at all levels. Among Pitch Smart's recommendations was a list of workload recommendations by age, all of which revolve around pitch counts.

In those two years, Pitch Smart has helped lead a revolution in arm care. Little League baseball had adopted pitch limits years ago, but as late as 2014, pitchers could spend the majority of their amateur careers on teams that did not adhere to pitch or days of rest limits.

Now two years later with high schools around the country adopting pitch limits, it's possible for a pitcher to make it to the major leagues without ever pitching for a team that didn't adhere to strict pitch limits.

Little League Baseball, Dixie Baseball and the National Amateur Baseball Foundation are among the youth leagues that are Pitch Smart compliant. On the showcase circuit, Perfect Game, East Coast Pro Showcase and Baseball Factory are all on board. Now high schools (and in many states, junior highs) have installed pitch limits as well. So has American Legion ball. And at the college level, some of the top summer college leagues, including the Cape Cod League, are Pitch Smart compliant. In pro ball, while there are no rules restricting pitch counts, no professional team allows its pitchers to ever throw much more than 110-120 pitches, no matter what the pitcher's age. In the minors, no young pitcher ever throws much more than 100 pitches.

"In a very short time, it's kind of become the known standard," said USA Baseball's Senior Director of Baseball Development Rick Riccobono, the organization's point person for Pitch Smart. "We're not there, but we're getting there."

Riccobono said that in one state in one recent year there were 186 instances of high school pitchers throwing more than 125 pitches in a game. There were 29 instances of a pitcher throwing over 150 pitches, 12 pitchers who threw 165 pitchers or more in a game and the top pitch count was 196.

There is no certainty that stricter pitch limits will reduce injuries. When it comes to pitching and pitching injuries, there are no absolutes, but the guidelines have been developed by some of the top names in sports medicine, including Dr. James Andrews, Dr. Glenn Fleisig, Dr. Neal ElAttrache and MLB Medical Director Dr. Gary Green.

The best research by the best medical minds believe that limiting workloads will help reduce injuries. In 2017, there are top youth, amateur showcase, high school baseball and summer college leagues that are all strictly following pitch limits with the realistic hope that by doing so, pitchers can stay healthier. The biggest remaining holdout is the college baseball level, where the NCAA seems unlikely to adopt any pitch limits anytime soon.

At the high school level, the new rules are expected to significantly change the way the game is played and managed.

Some coaches see the new pitch count limits as leveling the playing field. In the past, a coach who followed the latest recommendations for limiting young pitchers workloads was putting his team at a competitive disadvantage. The difference between top high school pitchers and the next best bullpen option is often quite significant. If one coach pulled his ace after 95 pitches while the opposing team let its ace go for 140+ pitches, the team that stuck with its ace often had the advantage.

Baseball players are competitive by nature. So are coaches. The temptation is always going to remain to send the ace out for one more inning.

But now there's no choice.

"I think it really takes the pressure off of us more than anything," Huntington Beach (Calif.) High coach Benji Medure said. "You just can't do it. Every coach reasons it and says 'you know it's his bullpen day.' With the new rule you just can't do it. There's no arguing with the kid who tries to convince you about one more batter. We have dealt with that with pitchers in the past where they don't want to come out. Now there is no question at all."

"For every call we've gotten from someone saying we're killing the sport, we get two saying 'Thank you, I feel like I lost the state championship because I refused to bring my starter from the day before in to close the next game because those are the principles under which I coach,' " Riccobono said.

The new rules will also force high school teams to develop deeper bullpens which will give more teenagers a chance to pitch.

"That gives kids roles. Instead of everyone trying to be the guy, what about that lefty on lefty guy who can get three outs? That's now huge for a team," Medure said.

"A good consequence is more participation. Most schools have three or four pitchers if you are lucky. Now you will have to have a bullpen," Hopkins said. "Looking back on it, we were smarter than we thought we were. More kids will get to play."

Eventually, these rules will likely tighten further. Currently the Pitch Smart guidelines would allow a pitcher to throw 25 pitches on Monday and then 90 pitches on Tuesday, a workload that goes far beyond what sports medicine experts would recommend. Some states will let 15 year olds throw up to 125 pitches in a game this year, or return from an 80-pitch outing after only two days off, workloads that would get many professional pitching coaches reprimanded or fired.

But this step forward is the big one for the nearly 500,000 high school baseball players around the country. It's one that may have effects for years to come.

"It feels like a watershed moment," Riccobono said. "If you're not on board by now, you're in danger of being late to the party."

Underclass Canes shock at Jupiter

No one would be surprised to hear that the two teams playing in the championship game of the 2017 World Wood Bat Association (WWBA) World Championship were represented by FTB and the Canes.

Routinely carrying some of the top talent into Jupiter, Fla., for the biggest amateur tournament in the country, both FTB and the Canes carried some of the highest-ranked prospects in the 2018 MLB Draft Class. Throughout the weekend leading up to Monday's championship, the FTB/SF Giants Scout Team and the Canes National team had their games attended by a pantheon of golf-cart-perched scouts.

But the Canes team representing the organization in the championship game wasn't the National team—the organization's A team, which rostered five top 50 prep draft prospects—but the C team, Canes Prospects.

And after a nine-inning 8-7 victory over FTB and the top-ranked prospect at the event, Nander De Sedas, it was Canes Prospects standing as the final team. A team made up almost entirely of underclassmen.

"It feels different," said Canes catcher C.J. Rodriguez, a 2019 Vanderbilt commit responsible for the winning run after leading off the top of the ninth with a double. "We're used to watching the older guys win everything, and this year they didn't get it done. So we had to step in for them.

"We said, 'We're here. Might as well just win it.'"

Much easier said, than done.

The Canes endured a brutal, grinding schedule where they played three games on Sunday, starting at 8 a.m., and another three starting Monday morning, culminating in the championship victory. Monday included two extra-inning games. First in the semi-final round when it took 11 innings to take down the AZ D-Backs Scout Team, 3-1, and immediately thereafter in the 9-inning matchup with FTB.

Rodriguez caught each inning of the extra-long games.

"I'm really tired," he said. "I really just want to go home and lay in my bed. But it's exciting to end the fall with the championship."

Rodriguez wasn't the only one who endured a long final 48 hours in Jupiter, though. Florida righthander Dylan Delucia—one of the few players on Canes Prospects who has yet to commit—was already back home in New Smyrna Beach, Fla., more than two hours north of Roger Dean Stadium.

After pitching once earlier in the tournament, Delucia had turned in his jersey, thanked coach Mike Petty and said his goodbye to all of his teammates. He assumed he was done in Jupiter for the year. But he got a call late Sunday night.

"(Coach Petty) called me up at 2:00 in the morning," Delucia said. "And he says, 'Dylan, how fast can you get here?' I said I can get there in two hours if you need it. So me and my mom

HIGH SCHOOL

AMATEUR/YOUTH CHAMPIONS 2017

ALL-AMERICAN AMATEUR BASEBALL ASSOCIATION (AAABA)

Event	Site	Champion	Runner-up
World Series (21U)	Johnstown, Pa.	New Orleans Boosters	Johnstown-2 Paul Carpenter Capital Advisors

AMATEUR ATHLETIC UNION (AAU)

Event	Site	Champion	Runner-up
9U	Orlando	Scorpions Baseball Club	Delaware Diamonds
10U	Orlando	Kangaroo Court	MC Mariners
11U Diamond (70-foot)	Orlando	SJ Young Guns	Southshore Rockets
11U Gold (70-foot)	Orlando	Florida Force	Space Coast Titans
12U	Orlando	Kangaroo Court	Team Swarm Elite
13U Diamond (90-foot)	Orlando	Gulf Coast Fury	Home Plate Chili Dogs Bonner
13U Gold (90-foot)	Orlando	Belmont Bombers	RI Rays
14U	Orlando	Florida Elite	Kings Baseball
15U	Vero Beach, Fla.	Indy Sharks	Wiregrass Cardinals
16/17U	Vero Beach, Fla.	Wiregrass Cardinals Red	Americus Travelers
18/19U	Vero Beach, Fla.	North Florida Black Sox	Boston Blue Jays

AMERICAN AMATEUR BASEBALL CONGRESS (AABC)

Event	Site	Champion	Runner-up
Pee Wee Reese (12U)	Shelton, Wash.	Shelton, Wash.	Las Cruces, N.M.
Sandy Koufax (14U)	Orange County, Calif.	CBA Dirtbags	Temecula Tar Heels
Ken Griffey, Jr. (15U)	Surprise, Ariz.	DBAT Tompkins	Ropes Thornton
Mickey Mantle (16U)	Waterbury, Conn.	Colton Nighthawks	Toronto Mets
Don Mattingly (17U)	Surprise, Ariz.	DBAT Matthews	AZ Pilots
Connie Mack (18U)	Farmington, N.M.	Midland Redskins	Danville Hoots
Stan Musial (19-and-over)	Seattle, Wash.	Farmington Frackers	En Fuego Sports

AMERICAN LEGION BASEBALL

Event	Site	Champion	Runner-up
World Series (19U)	Shelby, N.C.	Henderson, Nev., Post 40	Omaha, Neb., Post 1

BABE RUTH BASEBALL

Event	Site	Champion	Runner-up
Cal Ripken (10U)	Hammond, Ind.	West Raleigh, N.C.	Pearl City, Hawaii
Cal Ripken 12-year-old (60 feet)	Clemmons, N.C.	Ferndale, Wash.	Cedar Cliff, Pa.
Cal Ripken 13-year-old (70 feet)	Aberdeen, Md.	Japan	Atlantic Beach, Fla.
13-year-old	Mt. Home, Ark.	Tri-Valley, Calif.	Tallahassee, Fla.
14-year-old	Glen Allen, Va.	Pearl City, Hawaii	West Linn, Ore.
13-15-year-olds	Lawrenceburg, Tenn.	Tri-Valley, Calif.	Lawrenceburg, Tenn.
16-18-year-olds	Ephrata, Wash.	Mid-County, Texas	Cape Cod, Mass.

CONTINENTAL AMATEUR BASEBALL ASSOCIATION (CABA)

Event	Site	Champion	Runner-up
12U	Grapevine, Texas	Georgia Octane	East Cobb Astros
13U (60/90)	Northboro, Mass.	Legends Prospects	Nokona Chiefs
15U (Aluminum)	Jacksonville, Ill.	St. Louis Naturals	Minnesota Blizzard
16U (Aluminum)	Marietta, Ga.	Ontario Blue Jays	Georgia Jackets
16U (Wood)	Marietta, Ga.	East Cobb Astros 15U	East Cobb Athletics
16U (Wood)	Seattle	Enfuego Hawaii	Enfuego Washington
17U (Wood)	Charleston, S.C.	Knoxville Star Blue	Lexington BB
18U (Wood)	Charleston, S.C.	Midwest Prospects	Team Georgia
18U (Wood)	Seattle	Northeast Bandits	Mudville

LITTLE LEAGUE BASEBALL

Event	Site	Champion	Runner-up
Little League (11-12)	Williamsport, Pa.	Japan	Lufkin, Texas
Junior League (13-14)	Taylor, Mich.	Taiwan	Kennett Square, Pa.
Senior League (15-16)	Easley, S.C.	Latin America	Southeast
Intermediate (50/70)	Livermore, Calif.	Puerto Rico	East

zoomed down here, got here first game. (We) made a comeback, (won in the quarterfinals) and then got to (the semi-finals) and he said you've got the ball.

Delucia took the ball and shoved.

He threw 7.2 innings against a talented AZ D-backs Scout Team, striking out eight batters and walking one while allowing just one unearned run on 99 pitches before handing the ball to 2019 righthander Tyler Nesbitt. Nesbitt tossed 3.1 shutout innings before the Canes wound up winning in the eleventh inning.

Both the Canes and FTB were down to their final arms in the championship game, and both teams had to resort to pitching players whose futures are solidly in the batter's box, not on the

HIGH SCHOOL

NATIONAL AMATEUR BASEBALL FEDERATION (NBAF)

Event	Site	Champion	Runner-up
Rookie (10U)	New York	New York Bluebirds	NYC Titans
Freshman (12U)	Glen Cove, N.Y.	N.J. Axemen	Clarkstown Stars
Sophomore (14U)	Struthers, Ohio	Brooklyn Bonnie Paws, N.Y.	Baird Brothers, Ohio
Junior (16U)	Toledo, Ohio	Astro Falcons	HCYP Raiders.
High School (17U)	Jackson, Miss.	Jackson 96ers, Miss.	North MS Indians, Miss.
Senior (18U)	Struthers, Ohio	Jackson 96ers	Astro Falcons

PERFECT GAME/BCS FINALS

Event	Site	Champion	Runner-up
13U	Fort Myers, Fla.	D-BAT Elite, Kangaroo Court Roos (Co-Champions)	
14U	Fort Myers, Fla.	Team Elite 14U Nation	Tennessee Nationals
15U	Fort Myers, Fla.	Team Elite 15U Prime	Elite Squad 15U Prime
16U	Fort Myers, Fla.	5 Star National Burress	Top Tier Roos 16U Americans
17U	Fort Myers, Fla.	5 Star National Dobbs	Team Elite 17U Prime
18U	Fort Myers, Fla.	Next Level Baseball 18u	Nelson Baseball School 18u

PERFECT GAME/WORLD WOOD BAT ASSOCIATION SUMMER CHAMPIONSHIPS

Event	Site	Champion	Runner-up
14U	Cartersville, Ga.	Academy Select	Louisiana Tigers
15U	Cartersville, Ga.	East Coast Sox Select	Evoshield Bombers Texas
16U	Cartersville, Ga.	Banditos Scout Team	BPA
17U	Cartersville, Ga.	Canes 17U	Texas Twelve Maroon
18U	Cartersville, Ga.	East Cobb Astros	Game On West Braves

PONY BASEBALL

Event	Site	Champion	Runner-up
Mustang 9U	Walnut, Calif.	Los Alamitos, Calif.	Navajoa Sonora, Mexico
Mustang 10U	Youngsville, La.	Santa Clarita, Calif.	Tijuana, Baja Cali, Mexico
Bronco 11U	Chesterfield, Va.	AFCA Chicago	Simi Valley, Calif.
Bronco 12U	Los Alamitos, Calif.	Levittown, Puerto Rico	Tijuana, Baja Cali, Mexico
Pony 13U	Whittier, Calif.	Seoul, South Korea	Johnstown, Pa.
Pony 14U	Washington, Pa.	Covina, Calif.	Seoul, South Korea
Colt (15-16)	Lafayette, Ind.	Netherlands	Upland, Calif..
Palomino (17-18)	Santa Clara, Calif.	Los Gatos, Calif.	Santa Clara, Calif.

REVIVING BASEBALL IN INNER CITIES (RBI)

Event	Site	Champion	Runner-up
Junior (13-15)	Cincinnati	Philadelphia Phillies RBI	Chicago White Sox RBI
Senior (16-18)	Cincinnati	Hilo, Hawaii	Paterson, N.J.

U.S. SPECIALTY SPORTS ASSOCIATION (USSSA)

Event	Site	Champion	Runner-up
10U/Majors Elite	Orlando	Five Stars Tigers DeMarini	Alamo Drillers
11U/Majors Elite	Orlando	Wilson MVP	Boca Hitmen Ultra
12U/Majors Elite	Orlando	Genesis Baseball	Gamblers
13U/Majors Elite	Orlando	S.L. Select Crochet	Louisiana Tigers Purple
14U/Majors Elite	Orlando	Louisiana Tigers	Coqui Academy

USA BASEBALL

Event	Site	Champion	Runner-up
Tournament of Stars (18 & Under)	Cary, N.C.	Pride	Free
USA Baseball 17U—East	Palm Beach County, Fla.	Dallas Tigers	Texas Stix Baseball Club
USA Baseball 17U—West	Peoria, Ariz.	TB SoCal Adidas	Team California 2018s
USA Baseball 15U—East	Palm Beach County, Fla.	Top Tier Roos Americans	MVP Banditos
USA Baseball 15U—West	Peoria, Ariz.	BPA	GBG Marucci Navy
USA Baseball 14U—East	Palm Beach County, Fla.	Team Citius USA - Roland	Florida Stealth 2021
USA Baseball 14U—West	Peoria, Ariz.	TB SoCal	PBA

mound. Without Delucia's effort in the semifinals, the Canes might have had to go to position players earlier, and the first place trophy might never have been there's to claim.

Because of that, Delucia was named the World Championship's Most Valuable Pitcher.

"Ninety-nine pitches is a lot," Delucia said. "I don't usually do that. But it was one of those things where you felt it and you have to keep going . . . Friday was a rough day, (I started) off really bad. Walking the first batter, beaming the second, walking the third. So coming back, bouncing back to this was a really good outing.

"It was absolutely amazing. I've never been here, never played in a tournament like this. Truly a blessing to win this."

HIGH SCHOOL

Gifted Gore wraps up storied career

BY CARLOS COLLAZO

Twice before, in 2014 and 2015, the lefthander with the head-turning wind-up led his Whiteville High team to the North Carolina 1A state championship.

That lefthander, MacKenzie Gore, won the MVP award on both occasions.

After a 9-8 victory against Murphy High this spring, Whiteville again won the state championship. Yet again, Gore led the way and was on the verge of becoming the first three-time championship MVP in state history.

Only he didn't want it.

Throughout the tournament, Gore, the only senior on the Whiteville team, had received all the attention.

"They didn't get much shine," Gore said of his teammates. "Before Game 2 on Saturday, I said, 'Coach, you need to tell those people up there, when we win this thing I don't want the MVP.'"

He gave the award to someone else—Jake Harwood, the coach's son who picked up the win in the second game of the state championship."My time was done," Gore said. "I didn't really need an MVP to end it. I just needed a state championship."

For Coach Harwood, who had watched Gore develop as a person and a player for four years at Whiteville High, that moment meant everything.

"It meant to me a lot as a coach," he said. "It showed that we were doing something right here in Whiteville."

Gore's consistent excellence, selflessness and work ethic helped make him a three-time state champion, the No. 3 overall pick this year by the Padres and, now, the Baseball America High School Player of the Year.

The 6-foot-2 southpaw's stats jump off the page. He went 11-0 with a 0.19 ERA and allowed just three runs all season, only two of which were earned. Gore used a lethal four-pitch mix to strike out 158 batters over 74.1 innings. Perhaps most impressive, he had the same number of complete games (five) as walks.

During his four years in the North Carolina state playoffs, Gore went 15-0 and allowed just two earned runs in 99 innings. He feeds off of that playoff energy in the same way that he feeds off of the increased attention and scrutiny inherent with dozens of MLB scouts in attendance.Hammond remembers Gore's reaction to a large crowd during his first start of the 2017 season.

"He loves it," Hammond said, "The first start he has against West Columbus, which is a big rival for us, we look and there's 75 scouts there. And, hell, I'm a little shook."

"And he kind of looks at me in the bullpen and he's like, 'This is fun.'"

It hasn't all been that easy, though. Obviously naturally gifted, Gore didn't just stumble upon his success. He had to work for it. And he had to realize that he wasn't, in fact, the best.

Back in August 2016, Gore competed at Petco Park in the Perfect Game All-American Classic, along with the two players drafted ahead of him—Royce Lewis and Hunter Greene—as well as an entire host of talented players. In Gore's mind, some of those players were better than he was.

"I wanted to be the best player in the country," Gore said. "And when I played in the (Classic), I wasn't the best player in the country at that point. I just had a lot of work to do."

PLAYER OF THE YEAR

PREVIOUS WINNERS

1992: Preston Wilson, OF/RHP, Bamberg-Ehrhardt (S.C.) HS
1993: Trot Nixon, OF/LHP, New Hanover HS, Wilmington, N.C.
1994: Doug Million, LHP, Sarasota (Fla.) HS
1995: Ben Davis, C, Malvern (Pa.) Prep
1996: Matt White, RHP, Waynesboro Area (Pa.) HS
1997: Darnell McDonald, OF, Cherry Creek HS, Englewood, Colo.
1998: Drew Henson, 3B/RHP, Brighton (Mich.) HS
1999: Josh Hamilton, OF/LHP, Athens Drive HS, Raleigh, N.C.
2000: Matt Harrington, RHP Palmdale (Calif.) HS
2001: Joe Mauer, C, Cretin-Derham Hall HS, St. Paul, Minn.
2002: Scott Kazmir, LHP, Cypress Falls HS, Houston
2003: Jeff Allison, RHP, Veterans Memorial HS, Peabody, Mass.
2004: Homer Bailey, RHP, LaGrange (Texas) HS
2005: Justin Upton, SS, Great Bridge HS, Chesapeake, Va.
2006: Adrian Cardenas, SS/2B, Mons. Pace HS, Opa Locka, Fla.
2007: Mike Moustakas, SS, Chatsworth (Calif.) HS
2008: Ethan Martin, RHP/3B, Stephens County HS, Toccoa, Ga.
2009: Bryce Harper, C, Las Vegas HS
2010: Kaleb Cowart, RHP/3B, Cook HS, Adel, Ga.
2011: Dylan Bundy, RHP, Owasso (Okla.) HS
2012: Byron Buxton, OF, Appling County HS, Baxley, Ga.
2013: Clint Frazier, OF Loganville (Ga.) HS
2014: Alex Jackson, OF, Rancho Bernardo (Calif.) HS
2015: Kyle Tucker, OF, Plant HS, Tampa
2016: Mickey Moniak, OF, La Costa Canyon HS, Carlsbad, Calif.

2017 HIGH SCHOOL ALL-AMERICA TEAM

Jordon Adell
ALYSON BOYER RODE

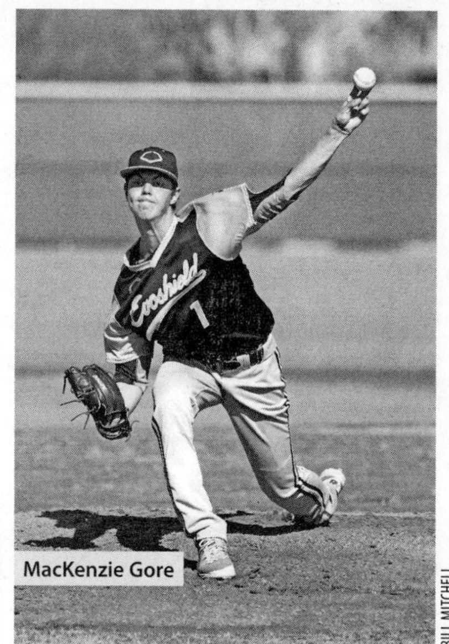
MacKenzie Gore
BILL MITCHELL

FIRST TEAM

Pos.	Name	High School	Yr.	AVG	AB	R	H	2B	3B	HR	RBI	SB	Drafted
C	Luis Campusano-Brac.	Cross Creek HS, Augusta, Ga.	Sr.	.622	90	44	56	13	2	6	27	—	Padres (2)
1B	Nick Pratto	Huntington Beach (Calif.) HS	Sr.	.326	92	31	30	6	1	7	19	—	Royals (1)
MIF	Royce Lewis	JSerra Catholic HS, San Juan Capistrano, Calif.	Sr.	.388	80	35	31	6	2	4	12	23	Twins (1)
MIF	Alika Williams	Rancho Bernardo HS, San Diego	Sr.	.402	112	35	45	14	2	3	23	28	Yankees (32)
MIF	Jeter Downs	Monsignor Pace HS, Miami	Sr.	.426	94	43	40	10	4	12	37	31	Reds (1s)
3B	Jacob Gonzalez	Chaparral HS, Scottsdale, Ariz.	Sr.	.489	90	38	44	14	1	7	48	3	Giants (2)
OF	Jordon Adell	Ballard HS, Louisville	Sr.	.563	96	53	54	9	0	25	61	21	Angels (1)
OF	Austin Beck	North Davidson HS, Lexington, N.C.	Sr.	.590	78	41	46	11	1	12	38	7	Athletics (1)
OF	Drew Waters	Etowah HS, Woodstock, Ga.	Sr.	.510	96	48	49	12	3	15	39	14	Braves (2)
UT	Hunter Greene	Notre Dame HS, Sherman Oaks, Calif.	Sr.	.324	102	23	33	6	2	6	28	2	Reds (1)

Pos.	Name	High School	Yr.	W	L	ERA	IP	H	R	ER	BB	SO	Drafted
RHP	Shane Baz	Concordia Lutheran HS, Tomball, Texas	Sr.	5	1	1.02	41	25	13	6	11	81	Pirates (1)
LHP	MacKenzie Gore	Whiteville (N.C.) HS	Sr.	11	0	0.19	75	25	3	2	5	158	Padres (1)
RHP	Michael Mercado	Westview HS, San Diego	Sr.	9	1	0.69	79	21	11	7	17	97	Rays (2)
LHP	Trevor Rogers	Carlsbad (N.M.) HS	Sr.	11	0	0.33	63	14	4	3	13	134	Marlins (1)
RHP	Alex Scherff	Colleyville (Texas) Heritage HS	Sr.	15	0	0.74	85	35	11	9	16	144	Red Sox (5)
UT	Hunter Greene	Notre Dame HS, Sherman Oaks, Calif.	Sr.	3	0	0.75	28	18	9	3	4	43	Reds (1)

SECOND TEAM

Pos.	Name	High School	Yr.	AVG	AB	R	H	2B	3B	HR	RBI	SB	Drafted
C	Sam McMillan	Suwannee HS, Live Oak, Fla.	Sr.	.494	77	20	38	14	1	7	30	5	Tigers (5)
1B	Nick Brueser	Hamilton HS, Scottsdale, Ariz.	Sr.	.344	96	27	33	9	1	6	24	—	Undrafted
MIF	Chris Seise	West Orange HS, Winter Garden, Fla.	Sr.	.444	90	37	40	8	5	8	29	12	Rangers (1)
MIF	Brice Turang	Santiago HS, Corona, Calif.	Jr.	.465	101	25	47	13	2	2	15	—	Undrafted
3B	Cory Acton	American Heritage HS, Plantation, Fla.	Jr.	.458	83	25	38	5	3	7	26	—	Undrafted
OF	Jacob Pearson	West Monroe (L.A.) HS	Sr.	.523	132	57	69	18	6	13	41	21	Angels (3)
OF	Heliot Ramos	Leadership Christian Academy, Guaynabo, P.R.	Sr.	.628	43	29	27	5	1	9	35	15	Giants (1)
OF	Connor Uselton	Southmoore HS, Oklahoma City	Sr.	.467	75	31	35	10	2	7	29	9	Pirates (2s)
UT	Hagen Danner	Huntington Beach (Calif.) HS	Sr.	.368	95	22	35	8	0	12	40	—	Blue Jays (2)

Pos.	Name	High School	Yr.	W	L	ERA	IP	H	R	ER	BB	SO	Drafted
RHP	Hans Crouse	Dana Hills HS, Dana Point, Calif.	Sr.	7	3	0.88	63	35	13	8	17	99	Rangers (2)
RHP	Blayne Enlow	St. Amant (La.) HS	Sr.	5	3	1.00	70	44	26	10	7	101	Phillies (2)
LHP	D.L. Hall	Valdosta (Ga.) HS	Sr.	6	2	1.36	51	24	13	10	25	105	Orioles (1)
RHP	Chris McMahon	West Chester (Pa.) Rustin HS	Sr.	8	0	0.77	54	31	10	6	5	83	Braves (33)
LHP	Matt Sauer	Righetti HS, Santa Maria, Calif.	Sr.	9	1	0.98	78	42	18	11	31	142	Yankees (2)
UT	Hagen Danner	Huntington Beach (Calif.) HS	Sr.	11	1	1.22	63	34	13	11	19	92	Blue Jays (2)

DRAFT

High School Talent Rises To Top Of Class

BY JOHN MANUEL

The drama went all the way down to the last minute. As the first round started and MLB Network started to roll from the draft show preview, into the draft proper, the first overall pick was still an unknown.

But with the clock passing 7 p.m. ET and the show about to start, Minnesota Twins chief baseball officer Derek Falvey and general manager Thad Levine finally had their man, and the rest of the first round could finally fall into place.

Minnesota took the top prep hitter available in Royce Lewis to kick-start the 2017 MLB draft, one that started with three consecutive high school players.

The Reds followed the Twins at No. 2 overall with another Los Angeles-area prep, righthander/shortstop Hunter Greene, the top-ranked player on Baseball America's Top 500 draft prospects. Then San Diego drafted North Carolina prep lefty MacKenzie Gore. Lewis and Greene became the first pair of L.A.-area preps to be drafted 1-2 in draft history.

BILL MITCHELL

Royce Lewis led off a trio of high school picks at the top of the 2017 draft.

But it was Lewis, No. 5 on the BA 500, who goes down in history as the first pick. He's been on the amateur baseball scene for years, having been MVP of Southern California's Trinity League in both his sophomore and junior seasons as well as this spring. Lewis has a chance to stay at shortstop, premium speed, power potential and a long track record, including hitting .500 with eight walks

FIRST-ROUND BONUS PROGRESSION

Teams continue to pay a premium for talent at the top of the draft. In 2017, teams paid first rounders an average bonus of $3,880,723, shattering the first-round record and setting a new record for the third year in a row. First-round bonuses have increased five times in six years of the bonus-pool era, and the increase of more than 25 percent was the largest since 1997.

After the first draft in 1965, first-round bonuses rose by an average of just 0.6 percent annually for the rest of the 1960s and 5.2 percent per year in the 1970s. Bonus inflation picked up in the 1980s, averaging 10.2 percent annually, and soared to 26.9 percent per year in the 1990s.

Below are the annual averages for first-round bonuses since the draft started in 1965. The 1996 total does not include four players who became free agents through a loophole in the draft rules.

YEAR	AVERAGE	CHANGE	YEAR	AVERAGE	CHANGE	YEAR	AVERAGE	CHANGE	YEAR	AVERAGE	CHANGE
1965	$42,516	—	1979	$68,094	0.20%	1993	$613,037	27.20%	2007	$2,098,083	8.50%
1966	$44,430	4.50%	1980	$74,025	8.70%	1994	$790,357	28.90%	2008	$2,458,714	17.20%
1967	$42,898	-3.40%	1981	$78,573	6.10%	1995	$918,019	16.10%	2009	$2,434,800	-1.00%
1968	$43,850	2.20%	1982	$82,615	5.10%	1996*	$944,404	2.90%	2010	$2,220,966	-8.80%
1969	$43,504	-0.80%	1983	$87,236	5.60%	1997	$1,325,536	40.40%	2011	$2,653,375	19.50%
1970	$45,230	3.90%	1984	$105,391	20.80%	1998	$1,637,667	23.10%	2012	$2,475,167	-6.70%
1971	$45,197	-0.10%	1985	$118,115	12.10%	1999	$1,809,767	10.50%	2013	$2,641,538	6.70%
1972	$44,952	-0.50%	1986	$116,300	-1.60%	2000	$1,872,586	3.50%	2014	$2,612,109	-1.10%
1973	$48,832	8.60%	1987	$128,480	10.50%	2001	$2,154,280	15.00%	2015	$2,774,945	6.23%
1974	$53,333	9.20%	1988	$142,540	10.90%	2002	$2,106,793	-2.20%	2016	$2,897,557	4.42%
1975	$49.33	-7.50%	1989	$176,008	23.50%	2003	$1,765,667	-16.20%	2017	$3,880,723	25.4%
1976	$49,631	0.60%	1990	$252,577	43.50%	2004	$1,958,448	10.90%			
1977	$48,813	-1.60%	1991	$365,396	44.70%	2005	$2,018,000	3.00%			
1978	$67,892	39.10%	1992	$481,893	31.90%	2006	$1,933,333	-4.20%			

and no strikeouts for USA Baseball's 18U national team last fall.

"I feel like I haven't grown into my man strength yet," Lewis said in describing himself to reporters on a conference call, "but you use speed for everything: defensively, offensively, and it helps with range. (Speed is) my favorite . . . because it never leaves you."

The Twins long considered a deep group of players for the first selection and narrowed it late to Lewis and Brendan McKay, the College Player of the Year out of Louisville. The Twins had a comfort level of signing Lewis, who signed quickly for $6,725,500. While that was just the fourth-largest bonus of the 2017 class, it's still the largest bonus for a No. 1 overall pick in the bonus-pool era, topping the $6.5 million the Diamondbacks gave Dansby Swanson in 2015.

McKay, the first college player picked, fell to fourth with the Rays. Lewis, Greene and Gore rounded out just the second trio of prep players picked 1-2-3 overall in the last 45 years. It happened previously in 1990, with position players Chipper Jones, Tony Clark and Mike Lieberthal.

While Twins officials said prior to the draft that signability would play a "significant role" in who went 1-1, scouting director Sean Johnson cited Lewis' talent first and foremost. In a draft class with little separation between top prospects, the Twins found reasons to put Lewis No. 1.

"Our group loved everything about Royce," Johnson said. "He's got a real chance to be a dynamic five-tool player. One thing that separated Royce in our room, beyond his tools, was his high character, instincts and baseball makeup.

"He's one of the best 'makeup' players I've had the chance to scout. He's got a great personality, and he's a natural leader."

Lewis said all of his role models have played shortstop and he hopes to stay there, but there are scouts who see center field as his best future position. Scouts also were split on several key two-way players in this year's draft class, and both Greene and McKay—the two most prominent two-way players—were afforded the chance to both hit and pitch as pros, at least early in their career.

The Reds let Greene DH in Rookie ball while building his arm back up, as he had not pitched in a game since April. He pitched briefly in August and worked exclusively as a pitcher in instructional league. Greene became the ninth high school right-hander drafted No. 2 overall, joining a group that includes J.R. Richard (1969), Josh Beckett (1999) and Jameson Taillon (2010).

"There have been discussions before about it and it was always 'We'd love to do both,'" Greene said on a post-draft conference call. The Los Angeles high schooler wound up signing just in time—Reds general manager Dick Williams said it was done 8 seconds before the July 12 deadline—for a $7,230,000 bonus. That was the largest bonus handed out in 2017, the largest since MLB started assigning bonus pools in 2012 and the largest bonus ever for a high school pitcher.

BONUS SPENDING BY TEAM

Teams combined to spend $248.6 million on draft bonuses in 2017, falling short of the $267.4 million mark set in 2016. Teams' total expenditure on draft bonuses initially fell when a new Collective Bargaining Agreement changed the draft rules when it went into effect in 2012, but bonuses have now exceeded the level they reached under the old system.

The CBA that went into effect in 2012 curtailed spending by instituting harsh penalties for teams that exceed their bonus pools by more than five percent. It also ended the practice of awarding major league contracts to draftees. But as revenues within the game have increased, so too have the bonus pools MLB allocates to teams for the first 10 rounds. As a result, overall spending in the draft has been allowed to increase over time.

Teams at the top of the draft and those with extra picks get more money in their pools, so it's no surprise the Twins and Reds led the industry in spending. The Twins had the top overall selection, while the Reds picked tree times in the first 38 picks. While no team came close to the record for spending under the current draft system, held by the Astros in 2015, the Twins spending in 2017 ranked sixth-most since 2012. At the opposite end of the spectrum, the Cardinals, who were ordered to surrender their first and second round picks to the Astros after an MLB investigation concluded a former Cardinals employee breached the Astros baseball operations database, spent the least amount of money since the Angels and Tigers in 2012.

TEAM	2017	2016	2015
Twins	$14,090,300	$8,532,900	$7,154,400
Reds	$13,665,300	$14,679,100	$9,018,050
Padres	$12,354,700	$14,886,045	$4,892,100
Athletics	$11,950,600	$11,001,300	$6,381,000
Brewers	$10,968,900	$11,136,264	$8,352,600
Rays	$10,912,800	$7,765,700	$7,946,400
Pirates	$10,418,300	$6,472,700	$8,485,000
Braves	$10,372,100	$15,516,300	$12,659,400
D-backs	$10,330,300	$6,116,900	$12,270,900
Marlins	$9,375,000	$7,219,900	$7,551,400
Phillies	$8,933,400	$14,990,300	$7,653,200
Astros	$8,913,300	$6,910,700	$19,103,000
Blue Jays	$8,642,500	$7,871,100	$4,848,800
Royals	$8,369,000	$5,047,000	$7,994,300
Angels	$8,251,000	$7,322,600	$5,835,800
White Sox	$7,957,000	$10,061,500	$5,977,600
Rangers	$7,893,200	$6,860,900	$10,728,300
Cubs	$7,655,100	$2,959,900	$8,335,700
Yankees	$6,937,800	$7,123,600	$9,442,800
Tigers	$6,837,300	$6,712,300	$7,606,700
Mariners	$6,732,800	$7,574,700	$5,368,600
Giants	$6,456,400	$4,825,200	$8,865,300
Orioles	$6,404,300	$8,106,900	$7,031,200
Mets	$6,064,500	$8,654,501	$4,268,700
Dodgers	$6,048,000	$11,275,800	$7,363,600
Red Sox	$5,927,000	$7,947,500	$7,589,000
Nationals	$5,533,800	$8,724,000	$4,982,800
Rockies	$4,477,600	$11,649,200	$14,415,900
Indians	$3,828,870	$8,934,100	$8,461,880
Cardinals	$2,248,100	$10,493,300	$8,247,400
Total	**$248,598,870**	**$267,351,610**	**$248,831,830**
Average	**$8,286,629**	**$8,911,720**	**$8,294,394**

The 2014 draft was the last time two high school pitchers went this high, when lefthander Brady Aiken and righthander Tyler Kolek went 1-2. Both have had Tommy John surgery and checkered careers to this point to put it mildly, but that didn't stop the Reds and Padres from aggressively pursuing prep arms with Greene and Gore.

"You have to be comfortable and willing to accept the risk of injury," said Padres special assistant Logan White, who hit with high school arms such as Chad Billingsley and famously Clayton Kershaw while running Dodgers drafts. "If you're going to try to get an ace, you have to be willing to draft pitching and accept the risk.

"But if you look around the big leagues at the aces, almost all of them are first-round picks, and often pretty high picks."

Meanwhile, the Rays let McKay DH and pitch after his college career—the most decorated in BA history—ended in the College World Series. The all-time strikeouts leader in Louisville history, McKay was announced as a first baseman at

HIGHEST BONUSES EVER

Only seven bonuses from 2012-2016 under the previous CBA ranked among the top bonuses in draft history, but 2017 was different. Three players received bonuses of at least $7 million, and five of the top 10 bonuses in draft history were handed out to the top five picks in 2017.

PLAYER, POS.	TEAM, YEAR (PICK)	BONUS
Gerrit Cole, rhp	Pirates, 2011 (No. 1)	$8,000,000
Stephen Strasburg, rhp	Nationals, 2009 (No. 1)	*$7,500,000
Bubba Starling, of	Royals, 2011 (No. 5)	+$7,500,000
Hunter Greene, rhp/ss	Reds, 2017 (No. 2)	$7,230,000
Brendan McKay, 1b/lhp	Rays, 2017 (No. 4)	$7,005,000
Kyle Wright, rhp	Braves, 2017 (No. 5)	$7,000,000
Royce Lewis, ss	Twins, 2017 (No. 1)	$6,725,000
Kris Bryant, 3b	Cubs, 2013 (No. 2)	$6,708,400
MacKenzie Gore, lhp	Padres, 2017 (No. 3)	$6,700,000
Carlos Rodon, lhp	White Sox, 2014 (No. 3)	$6,582,000
Jameson Taillon, rhp	Pirates, 2010 (No. 2)	$6,500,000
Dansby Swanson, ss	D-backs, 2015 (No. 1)	$6,500,000
Danny Hultzen, lhp	Marinters, 2011 (No. 2)	*$6,350,000
Mark Appel, rhp	Astros, 2013 (No. 1	$6,350,000
Donavan Tate, of	Padres, 2009 (No. 3)	+$6,250,000
Bryce Harper, of	Nationals, 2010 (No. 1)	*$6,250,000
Buster Posey, c	Giants, 2008 (No. 5)	$6,200,000
Nick Senzel, 3b	Reds, 2016 (No. 2)	$6,200,000
Tim Beckham, ss	Rays, 2008 (No. 1)	+$6,150,000
Justin Upton, ss	D-backs, 2005 (No. 1)	+$6,100,000
Mickey Moniak, of	Phillies, 2016 (No. 1)	$6,100,000
Matt Wieters, c	Orioles, 2007 (No. 5)	$6,000,000
Pedro Alvarez, 3b	Pirates, 2008 (No. 2)	*$6,000,000
Eric Hosmer, 1b	Royals, 2008 (No. 3)	$6,000,000
Dustin Ackley, of	Mariners, 2009 (No. 2)	*$6,000,000
Anthony Rendon, 3b	Nationals, 2011 (No. 6)	*$6,000,000
Byron Buxton, of	Twins, 2012 (No. 2)	$6,000,000
Tyler Kolek, rhp	Marlins, 2014 (No. 2)	$6,000,000
Alex Bregman, ss	Astros, 2015 (No. 2)	$5,900,000
David Price, lhp	Rays, 2007 (No. 1)	*$5,600,000
Brendan Rodgers, ss	Rockies, 2015 (No. 3)	$5,500,000
Austin Beck, of	Athletics, 2017 (No. 6)	$5,303,000

**Part of major league contract. +Bonus spread over multiple years under MLB two-sport provisions.*

MIKE JANES

The Reds took two-way talent Hunter Greene with the second overall pick

the podium by commissioner Rob Manfred, but McKay hit and pitched after signing for $7.005 million, helping lead short-season Hudson Valley to the New York-Penn League championship.

"If a guy can figure out how to handle his arm and his body and not get worn down and stay healthy, it could add a whole new level in having two-guys-in-one that can do both," McKay said. "The (Rays have) said we're going to experiment with it and see if it's a feasible thing to do."

McKay confirmed that there had been negotiations with the Twins about being the No. 1 selection. "They had offered a number that we felt we could get a better offer from another team or what not," he said. "It ultimately came down to, another team was able to give a better offer, so we went with that. I'm happy the ways things worked out. You got a good deal and you got a great organization to work with."

Gore at No. 3 and Vanderbilt's Kyle Wright, to the Braves at No. 5, were ultimately the players who did separate themselves a bit from the rest of the draft class, and they went in the first five picks. Wright signed for $7 million, joining Greene and McKay at the $7 million level. No other player signed for more than $5.4 million.

The only larger straight signing bonuses in draft history were all paid prior to the current bonus-pool era—Gerrit Cole's record $8 million at No. 1 overall in 2011, Stephen Strasburg ($7.5 million as part of a 2009 major league contract) and Bubba Starling ($7.5 million, 2011, on a two-sport bonus spread over multiple years).

Both Strasburg and Starling got bonuses as part of deals outlawed under the current system. But that system is paying out higher bonuses than ever at the top thanks to a healthy industry and the risk-reward calculus made by front offices around the game.

"The guys making the ultimate decisions believe there is less risk than (the high school pitcher) demographic) used to have," said Twins vice president of player personnel Mike Radcliff. "When you go through the process and see a guy with a ceiling as a No. 1 or No. 2 starter, that immediately has huge value . . . It's not just the present visual observations. There's way more that goes into the equation.

"It makes a lot more sense to take your shot at $5-$7 million than at $150 million."

NO. 1 OVERALL PICKS

YEAR	TEAM: PLAYER, POS., SCHOOL	BONUS
1965	Athletics: Rick Monday, of, Arizona State	$100,000
1966	Mets: Steve Chilcott, c, Antelope Valley HS, Lancaster, Calif.	$75,000
1967	Yankees: Ron Blomberg, 1b, Druid Hills HS, Atlanta	$65,000
1968	Mets: Tim Foli, ss, Notre Dame HS, Sherman Oaks, Calif.	$74,000
1969	Senators: Jeff Burroughs, of, Centennial HS, Long Beach	$88,000
1970	Padres: Mike Ivie, c, Walker HS, Atlanta	$75,000
1971	White Sox: Danny Goodwin, c, Peoria (Ill.) HS	Did Not Sign
1972	Padres: Dave Roberts, 3b, Oregon	$70,000
1973	Rangers: David Clyde, lhp, Westchester HS, Texas	*$65,000
1974	Padres: Bill Almon, ss, Brown	*$90,000
1975	Angels: Danny Goodwin, c, Southern	*$125,000
1976	Astros: Floyd Bannister, lhp, Arizona State	$100,000
1977	White Sox: Harold Baines, of, St. Michaels (Md.) HS	$32,000
1978	Braves: Bob Horner, 3b, Arizona State	*$162,000
1979	Mariners: Al Chambers, 1b, Harris HS, Harrisburg, Pa.	$60,000
1980	Mets: Darryl Strawberry, of, Crenshaw HS, Los Angeles	$152,500
1981	Mariners: Mike Moore, rhp, Oral Roberts	$100,000
1982	Cubs: Shawon Dunston, ss, Jefferson HS, New York	$135,000
1983	Twins: Tim Belcher, rhp, Mount Vernon Nazarene (Ohio)	Did Not Sign
1984	Mets: Shawn Abner, of, Mechanicsburg (Pa.) HS	$150,500
1985	Brewers: B.J. Surhoff, c, North Carolina	$150,000
1986	Pirates: Jeff King, 3b, Arkansas	$180,000
1987	Mariners: Ken Griffey Jr., of, Moeller HS, Cincinnati	$160,000
1988	Padres: Andy Benes, rhp, Evansville	$235,000
1989	Orioles: Ben McDonald, rhp, Louisiana State	*$350,000
1990	Braves: Chipper Jones, ss, The Bolles School, Jacksonville	$275,000
1991	Yankees: Brien Taylor, lhp, East Carteret HS, Beaufort, N.C.	$1,550,000
1992	Astros: Phil Nevin, 3b, Cal State Fullerton	$700,000
1993	Mariners: Alex Rodriguez, ss, Westminster Christian HS, Miami	*$1,000,000
1994	Mets: Paul Wilson, rhp, Florida State	$1,550,000
1995	Angels: Darin Erstad, of, Nebraska	$1,575,000
1996	Pirates: Kris Benson, rhp, Clemson	$2,000,000
1997	Tigers: Matt Anderson, rhp, Tigers	$2,505,000
1998	Phillies: Pat Burrell, 3b, Miami	*$3,150,000
1999	Devil Rays: Josh Hamilton, of, Athens Drive HS, Raleigh	$3,960,000
2000	Marlins: Adrian Gonzalez, 1b, Eastlake HS, Chula Vista, Calif.	$3,000,000
2001	Twins: Joe Mauer, c, Cretin-Derham Hall, St. Paul	$5,150,000
2002	Pirates: Bryan Bullington, rhp, Ball State	$4,000,000
2003	Devil Rays: Delmon Young, of, Camarillo (Calif.) HS	*$3,700,000
2004	Padres: Matt Bush, ss, Mission Bay HS, San Diego	$3,150,000
2005	Diamondbacks: Justin Upton, ss, Great Bridge HS, Chesapeake, Va.	$6,100,000
2006	Royals: Luke Hochevar, rhp, Fort Worth (American Association)	*$3,500,000
2007	Devil Rays: David Price, lhp, Vanderbilt	*$5,600,000
2008	Rays: Tim Beckham, ss, Griffin (Ga.) HS	$6,150,000
2009	Nationals: Stephen Strasburg, rhp, San Diego State	*$7,500,000
2010	Nationals: Bryce Harper, of, JC of Southern Nevada	*$6,250,000
2011	Pirates: Gerrit Cole, rhp, UCLA	$8,000,000
2012	Astros: Carlos Correa, ss, Puerto Rico Baseball Academy, Gurabo, P.R.	$4,800,000
2013	Astros: Mark Appel, rhp, Stanford	$6,350,000
2014	Astros: Brady Aiken, lhp, Cathedral Catholic, San Diego	Did Not Sign
2015	Diamondbacks: Dansby Swanson, ss, Vanderbilt	$6,500,000
2016	Phillies: Mickey Moniak, La Costa Canyon HS, Carlsbad, Calif.	$6,100,000
2017	Twins: Royce Lewis, JSerra Catholic HS, San Juan Capistrano, Calif.	$6,750,000

**Part of major league contract.*

Bonus Payments Soar

Teams spent $287,575,870 on signing bonuses overall, a new draft record. The '16 draft had the old mark at $267,451,610. The Collective Bargaining Agreement sets out parameters for draft bonus spending, so huge bonuses no longer come as a surprise, but it's still somewhat surprising that the three $7 million-plus bonuses helped push the first-round bonus average to $3,880,723.

That's an increase of more than 25 percent above the previous mark of $2,897,557 set in '16. That came mostly as a result of the compressed bonus structure set out in the new CBA.

The last time the first-round average rose at a higher rate was in 1997, coming off the free-agent loophole madness of 1996 that saw Matt White ($10.2 million) and Travis Lee ($10 million) blow bonus records out of the water when they became free agents.

This time, the change stemmed from the increase in bonus pool allotments being spread throughout the first round and concentrated less at the top. For example, the value of the No. 1 pick dropped from just over $9 million in 2016 to $7,770,700 for the top pick in 2017. The value for the No. 2 pick was down more than $500,000.

Also, fewer players signed below-slot bonuses in 2017. Of the 30 first-round picks in '17, 13 signed above-slot bonuses, six signed at slot and 11 signed for below-slot bonuses.

The breakdown for 2015 and 2016, under the previous CBA and first iteration of bonus pools, was almost identical. In both years, 11 of the first 30 picks signed at slot, with just five above-slot in 2016 and six in 2015.

Meanwhile, just three players taken in the first 10 rounds failed to sign, and two of them flunked physicals after intending to sign.

The 31st overall pick, Oregon State righthander Drew Rasmussen, had Tommy John surgery earlier in his career, and his physical with the Rays prompted the club to pull its bonus offer. Rasmussen had pitched well down the stretch for Oregon State's top-ranked team and was poised to start an elimination game in the College World Series before being passed over in a loss to LSU. He went back to Corvallis for school but wasn't expected to pitch in 2018 after having a second reconstructive elbow surgery. The Rays get a compensation pick in 2018, 32nd overall.

Righthander Jack Conlon, the Orioles' fourth-rounder, also didn't sign after traveling to Baltimore for his physical. The Orioles pulled their offer after the physical, and Conlon became a free agent. However, he didn't pass a physical with the Giants either and wound up attending Texas A&M. The only other unsigned player in the first 10 rounds, righthander JoJo Booker, spurned the Angels to attend South Alabama.

THE BONUS RECORD

Rick Monday, the No. 1 overall pick in baseball's first draft in 1965, signed with the Athletics for $100,000—a figure that no draftee bettered for a decade. The record has been broken many times since, with Gerrit Cole setting a new standard in 2011 when he signed for $8 million with the Pirates as the No. 1 overall pick and no draftee under the CBA has eclipsed him in the three years under the new rules. In fact, no signee during that timeframe has topped $7.3 million.

The list below represents only cash bonuses and doesn't include guaranteed money from major league deals, college scholarship plans or incentives. It also considers only players who signed with the clubs that drafted them and doesn't include draft picks who signed after being granted free agency, such as Bill Bordley ($200,000 from the Giants after the Reds selected him in the January 1979 draft) and Matt White ($10.2 million from the Devil Rays after the Giants chose him in the 1996 draft).

YEAR	PLAYER, POS., CLUB (ROUND)	BONUS
1965	Rick Monday, of, Athletics (1)	$100,000
1975	Danny Goodwin, c, Angels (1)	$125,000
1978	Kirk Gibson, of, Tigers (1)	$150,000
	* Bob Horner, 3b, Braves (1)	$162,000
1979	Todd Demeter, 1b, Yankees (2)	$208,000
1988	Andy Benes, rhp, Padres (1)	$235,000
1989	Tyler Houston, c, Braves (1)	$241,500
	* Ben McDonald, rhp, Orioles (1)	$350,000
	* John Olerud, 1b, Blue Jays (3)	$575,000
1991	Mike Kelly, of, Braves (1)	$575,000
	Brien Taylor, lhp, Yankees (1)	$1,550,000
1994	Paul Wilson, rhp, Mets (1)	$1,550,000
	Josh Booty, 3b, Marlins (1)	$1,600,000
1996	Kris Benson, rhp, Pirates (1)	$2,000,000
1997	Rick Ankiel, lhp, Cardinals (2)	$2,500,000
	Matt Anderson, rhp, Tigers (1)	$2,505,000
1998	* J.D. Drew, of, Cardinals (1)	$3,000,000
	* Pat Burrell, 3b, Phillies (1)	$3,150,000
	Mark Mulder, lhp, Athletics (1)	$3,200,000
	Corey Patterson, of, Cubs (1)	$3,700,000
1999	Josh Hamilton, of, Devil Rays (1)	$3,960,000
2000	Joe Borchard, of, White Sox (1)	$5,300,000
2005	Justin Upton, ss, Diamondbacks (1)	$6,100,000
2008	Tim Beckham, ss, Rays (1)	$6,150,000
	Buster Posey, c, Giants (1)	$6,200,000
2009	Donavan Tate, cf, Padres (1)	$6,250,000
	* Stephen Strasburg, rhp, Nationals (1)	$7,500,000
2011	Gerrit Cole, rhp, Pirates (1)	$8,000,000

**Part of major league contract.*

DRAFT

Tidbits & Trivia

■ Virginia and North Carolina had two players apiece picked in the first round. Cavaliers teammates Pavin Smith and Adam Haseley went back-to-back at picks seven and eight overall, with the Diamondbacks taking Smith, the first baseman with power and plate discipline, and the Phillies taking outfielder Haseley, who will finally get to give up pitching.

The Tar Heels saw ace righty J.B. Bukauskas fall a bit; the No. 6 overall player on the BA 500 fell to Houston with the No. 15 pick, a good fit for the slider-heavy righthander considering Houston's big league staff, which ranks last in the majors in fastball usage. Tar Heels shortstop Logan Warmoth went seven picks later as the No. 22 overall pick to the Blue Jays.

Vanderbilt joined the ACC schools with two first-round picks in Wright and outfielder Jeren Kendall, who wound up going at No. 23 overall to the Dodgers.

■ Four schools—Chipola (Fla.) JC, Michigan, Stanford and Texas—each had 11 players drafted, tied for most among colleges. Chipola (Fla.) JC had the highest pick among the schools in outfielder Rey Rivera, the Tigers' second-round pick, No. 57 overall. It was a record number of picks for the program that also won the NJCAA World Series and produced big leaguers such as Jose Bautista, Patrick Corbin and Russell Martin, among many others.

"We're just so happy for these players and their families," Chipola coach Jeff Johnson said. "They are all quality individuals who have worked hard to reach the top of their sport. We look forward to following their careers as they represent Chipola in professional baseball."

The Longhorns' top pick was second-rounder

Morgan Cooper, one of five Horns taken in the first eight rounds. The Wolverines, meanwhile, had only one player drafted in the first 10 rounds in lefthander Oliver Jaskie (Mariners) but set a school record with 11 players picked, the same number, coincidentally, that the school's football program produced in the spring's NFL draft.

Stanford's crop included third-round outfielder Quinn Brodey (Mets) and three other players in the first 10 rounds. Two Cardinal players didn't sign, including righthander Tristan Beck, an eligible sophomore who projected as a first-rounder coming into the season before missing the entire year with a back injury. He could be a first-rounder if healthy in 2018.

■ Lexington, N.C., prep outfielder Austin Beck, drafted sixth overall by the Athletics, joined Bukauskas, Warmoth and Gore to give the state of North Carolina four first-round picks, tying a state record. North Carolina had as many first-round picks as usual draft hot spots California and Florida. Tar Heels outfielder Brian Miller just missed joining them, being picked by the Marlins with the 36th overall selection.

Kentucky, meanwhile, produced three first-round picks for the second consecutive draft. The emergence of Louisville's program as a national power drove the rise in 2016, when the Cardinals produced a trio of first-rounders. In 2017, Louisville's McKay shared the stage with Louisville Ballard High outfielder Jo Adell (No. 10 overall) and Kentucky first baseman Evan White (No. 17 overall). Adell was the highest-drafted high school player from the Bluegrass State since Austin Kearns (No. 7 overall) in 1998.

The Padres drafted infielder Johnny Homza in the fifth round, making him the second-highest player ever drafted out of Alaska and the highest-drafted to sign. The only Alaskan drafted higher than Homza was righthander Brian Montalbo (fourth round, 2000). He broke the record as the highest signed Alaskan ever, previously set by Trajan Langdon in 1994. Langdon gained much more notoriety as a basketball player at Duke and later in the NBA.

BONUSES VS. PICK VALUES

Signing bonuses and assigned pick values have largely lined up since revamped draft rules were introduced as part of the Collective Bargaining Agreement in 2012. To give the worst teams extra spending power, the values for the selections at the top of the draft have been set higher than the perceived market value. In 2017, Hunter Greene was the first player selected to receive more than pick value at No. 2. Five of the top 10 picks received more than pick value, and three signed for slot.

Ultimately, the top 50 bonuses added up to $154.1 million, a little more than $6 million more than what MLB asigned to those picks. By comparison, when MLB unilaterally determined slot recommendations in the last year of the previous CBA (2011), the total of the first 50 bonuses ($120.5 million) dwarfed that of the top 50 slots ($70 millon).

PLAYER, POS., TEAM (ROUND/OVERALL PICK)	BONUS	PICK VALUE
1. Hunter Greene, RHP, Reds (1st round/No. 2)	$7,230,000	$7,193,200
2. Brendan McKay, 1B/LHP, Rays (1st round/No. 4)	$7,005,000	$6,153,600
3. Kyle Wright, RHP, Braves (1st round/No. 5)	$7,000,000	$5,707,300
4. Royce Lewis, SS, Twins (1st round/No. 1)	$6,725,000	$7,770,700
5. MacKenzie Gore, LHP, Padres (1st round/No. 3)	$6,700,000	$6,668,100
6. Austin Beck, OF, Athletics (1st round/No. 6)	$5,303,000	$5,303,000
7. Adam Haseley, OF, Phillies (1st round/No. 8)	$5,100,000	$4,780,400
8. Pavin Smith, 1B, Diamondbacks (1st round/No. 7)	$5,016,300	$5,016,300
9. Jo Adell, OF, Angels (1st round/No. 10)	$4,376,800	$4,376,800
10. Shane Baz, RHP, Pirates (1st round/No. 12)	$4,100,000	$4,032,000
11. Keston Hiura, 2B, UC Irvine (1st round/No. 9)	$4,000,000	$4,570,000
12. Jake Burger, 3B, White Sox (1st round/No. 11)	$3,700,000	$4,199,200
13. J.B. Bukauskas, RHP, Astros (1st round/No. 15)	$3,600,000	$3,588,200
14. Alex Faedo, RHP, Tigers (1st round/No. 18)	$3,500,000	$3,214,600
15. Nick Pratto, 1B, Royals (1st round/No. 14)	$3,450,000	$3,727,600
16. Trevor Rogers, LHP, Marlins (1st round/No. 13)	$3,400,000	$3,875,800
17. Evan White, 1B, Mariners (1st round/No. 17)	$3,125,000	$3,333,200
18. Heliot Ramos, OF, Giants (1st round/No. 19)	$3,101,700	$3,101,700
19. D.L. Hall, LHP, Orioles (1st round/No. 21)	$3,000,000	$2,892,400
20. David Peterson, LHP, Mets (1st round/No. 20)	$2,994,500	$2,994,500
21. Jeren Kendall, OF, Dodgers (1st round/No. 23)	$2,897,500	$2,702,700
22. Logan Warmoth, SS, Blue Jays (1st round/No. 22)	$2,820,200	$2,795,200
23. Seth Romero, LHP, Nationals (1st round/No. 25)	$2,800,000	$2,530,400
24. Tanner Houck, RHP, Red Sox (1st round/No. 24)	$2,614,500	$2,614,500
25. Matt Sauer, RHP, Yankees (2nd round/No. 54)	$2,497,500	$1,236,000
26. Nate Pearson, RHP, Blue Jays (1st round/No. 28)	$2,452,900	$2,302,900
27. Tristen Lutz, OF, Brewers (supp. 1st/No. 34)	$2,352,000	$1,983,600
28. Brendon Little, LHP, Cubs (1st round/No. 27)	$2,200,000	$2,373,300
29. Clarke Schmidt, RHP, Yankees (1st round/No. 16)	$2,184,300	$3,458,600
30. Michael Mercado, RHP, Rays (2nd round/No. 40)	$2,132,400	$1,714,500
31. Bubba Thompson, OF, Rangers (1st round/No. 26)	$2,100,000	$2,450,100
32. M.J. Melendez, C, Royals (2nd round/No. 52)	$2,097,500	$1,295,700
33. Chris Seise, SS, Rangers (1st round/No. 29)	$2,000,000	$2,238,900
34. Gavin Sheets, 1B, White Sox (2nd round/No. 49)	$2,000,000	$1,392,200
35. Sam Carlson, RHP, Mariners (2nd round/No. 55)	$2,000,000	$1,206,900
36. Blayne Enlow, RHP, Twins (3rd round/No. 76)	$2,000,000	$755,500
37. Nick Allen, SS, Athletics (3rd round/No. 81)	$2,000,000	$697,500
38. Brent Rooker, OF, Twins (supp. 1st/No. 35)	$1,935,300	$1,935,300
39. Alex Lange, RHP, Cubs (1st round/No. 30)	$1,925,000	$2,184,300
40. Steven Jennings, RHP, Pirates (2nd round/No. 42)	$1,900,000	$1,635,500
41. Brian Miller, OF, Marlins (supp. 1st/No. 36)	$1,888,800	$1,888,800
42. Jeter Downs, SS, Reds (supp. 1st/No. 32)	$1,822,500	$2,084,400
43. Stuart Fairchild, OF, Reds (2nd round/No. 38)	$1,800,300	$1,802,800
44. Kevin Merrell, SS, Athletics (supp. 1st/No. 33)	$1,800,000	$2,033,500
45. Greg Deichmann, OF, Athletics (2nd round/No. 43)	$1,700,000	$1,597,300
46. Joe Perez, 3B, Astros (2nd round/No. 53)	$1,600,000	$1,265,500
47. Blake Hunt, C, Padres (supp. 2nd/No. 69)	$1,600,000	$858,600
48. Drew Ellis, 3B, Diamondbacks (2nd round/No. 44)	$1,560,100	$1,560,100
49. Drew Waters, OF, Braves (2nd round/No. 41)	$1,500,000	$1,674,600
50. Mark Vientos, 3B, Mets (2nd round/No. 59)	$1,500,000	$1,094,700
Total	**$154,108,100**	**$147,862,500**

DRAFT 2017 # TOP 100 PICKS

TEAM. PLAYER, POS., SCHOOL — BONUS

1. Twins. Royce Lewis, SS, JSerra Catholic HS, San Juan Capistrano, Calif. $6,725,000
2. Reds. Hunter Greene, RHP, Notre Dame HS, Sherman Oaks, Calif. $7,230,000
3. Padres. MacKenzie Gore, LHP, Whiteville (N.C.) HS $6,700,000
4. Rays. Brendan McKay, 1B, Louisville $7,005,000
5. Braves. Kyle Wright, RHP, Vanderbilt $7,000,000
6. Athletics. Austin Beck, OF, North Davidson HS, Lexington, N.C. $5,303,000
7. Diamondbacks, Pavin Smith, 1B, Virginia $5,016,300
8. Phillies. Adam Haseley, OF, Virginia $5,100,000
9. Brewers. Keston Hiura, 2B, UC Irvine $4,000,000
10. Angels. Jo Adell, OF, Ballard HS, Louisville $4,376,800
11. White Sox. Jake Burger, 3b, Missouri State $3,700,000
12. Pirates, Shane Baz, RHP, Concordia Lutheran HS, Tomball, Texas. $4,100,000
13. Marlins. Trevor Rogers, LHP, Carlsbad (N.M.) HS $3,400,000
14. Royals. Nick Pratto,1B, Huntington Beach (Calif.) HS $3,450,000
15. Astros. J.B. Bukauskas, RHP, North Carolina $3,600,000
16. Yankees. Clarke Schmidt, RHP, South Carolina $2,184,300
17. Mariners. Evan White, 1B, Kentucky $3,125,000
18. Tigers. Alex Faedo, RHP, Florida $3,500,000
19. Giants. Heliot Ramos, OF, Leadership Christian Academy, Guaynabo, P.R. $3,101,700
20. Mets. David Peterson, LHP, Oregon $2,994,500
21. Orioles. D.L. Hall, LHP, Valdosta (Ga.) HS $3,000,000
22. Blue Jays. Logan Warmoth, SS, North Carolina $2,820,200
23. Dodgers. Jeren Kendall, OF, Vanderbilt $2,897,500
24. Red Sox. Tanner Houck, RHP, Missouri $2,614,500
25. Nationals. Seth Romero, LHP, Houston $2,800,000
26. Rangers. Bubba Thompson, OF, McGill-Toolen Catholic HS, Mobile, Ala. $2,100,000
27. Cubs. Brendon Little, LHP, State JC of Florida $2,200,000
28. Blue Jays. Nate Pearson, RHP, JC of Central Florida $2,452,900
29. Rangers. Chris Seise, SS, West Orange HS, Winter Garden, Fla. $2,000,000
30. Cubs. Alex Lange, RHP, Louisiana State $1,925,000
31. Rays. Drew Rasmussen, RHP, Oregon State .... Did not sign
32. Reds. Jeter Downs, SS, Pace HS, Miami Gardens $1,822,500
33. Athletics. Kevin Merrell, SS, South Florida $1,800,000
34. Brewers. Tristen Lutz, OF, Martin HS, Arlington, Texas $2,352,000
35. Twins. Brent Rooker, OF, Mississippi State $1,935,300
36. Marlins. Brian Miller, OF, North Carolina $1,888,800
37. Twins. Landon Leach, RHP, Pickering HS, Ajax, Ont. $1,400,000
38. Reds. Stuart Fairchild, OF, Wake Forest $1,800,300
39. Padres. Luis Campusano, C, Cross Creek HS, Augusta, Ga. $1,300,000
40. Rays. Michael Mercado, RHP, Westview HS, San Diego $2,132,400
41. Braves. Drew Waters, OF, Etowah HS, Woodstock, Ga $1,500,000
42. Pirates. Steven Jennings, RHP, Dekalb County HS, Smithville, Tenn. $1,900,000
43. Athletics. Greg Deichmann, OF, Louisiana State $1,700,000
44. Diamondbacks. Drew Ellis, 3B, Louisville $1,560,100
45. Phillies. Spencer Howard, RHP, Cal Poly $1,150,000
46. Brewers. Caden Lemons, RHP, Vestavia Hills (Ala.) HS $1,450,000
47. Angels. Griffin Canning, RHP, UCLA $1,459,200
48. Rockies. Ryan Vilade, 3B, Stillwater (Okla.) HS $1,425,400
49. White Sox. Gavin Sheets, 1B, Wake Forest $2,000,000
50. Pirates. Calvin Mitchell, OF, Rancho Bernardo HS, San Diego $1,357,300
51. Marlins. Joe Dunand, 3B, North Carolina State $1,200,000
52. Royals, M.J. Melendez, C, Westminster Christian School, Palmetto Bay, Fla. $2,097,500
53. Astros. Joe Perez, 3B, Archbishop McCarthy HS, Southwest Ranches, Fla. $1,600,000
54. Yankees. Matt Sauer, RHP, Righetti HS, Santa Maria, Calif. $2,497,500
55. Mariners. Sam Carlson, RHP, Burnsville (Minn.) HS $2,000,000

TOM PRIDDY

The A's took outfielder Austin Beck with the No. 6 overall pick in this year's draft

56. Astros. Corbin Martin, RHP, Texas A&M $1,000,000
57. Tigers. Rey Rivera, OF, Chipola (Fla.) JC $850,000
58. Giants. Jacob Gonzalez, 3B, Chaparral HS, Scottsdale, Ariz. $950,000
59. Mets. Mark Vientos, 3B, American Heritage HS, Plantation, Fla. $1,500,000
60. Orioles. Adam Hall, SS, A.B. Lucas SS, London, Ont. $1,300,000
61. Blue Jays. Hagen Danner, C, Huntington Beach (Calif.) HS $1,500,000
62. Dodgers. Morgan Cooper, RHP, Texas $867,500
63. Red Sox. Cole Brannen, OF, The Westfield School, Perry, Ga.. .... $1,300,000
64. Indians. Quentin Holmes, OF, McClancy Memorial HS, East Elmhurst, N.Y. $988,970
65. Nationals. Wil Crowe, RHP, South Carolina $946,500
66. Rangers. Hans Crouse, RHP, Dana Hills HS, Dana Point, Calif. $1,450,000
67. Cubs. Cory Abbott, RHP, Loyola Marymount $901,900
68. Diamondbacks. Daulton Varsho, C, Wisconsin-Milwaukee .. $881,100
69. Padres. Blake Hunt, C, Mater Dei HS, Santa Ana, Calif. $1,600,000
70. Rockies. Tommy Doyle, RHP, Virginia $837,300
71. Indians. Tyler Freeman, SS, Etiwanda HS, Rancho Cucamonga, Calif. $816,500
72. Pirates. Conner Uselton, OF, Southmoore HS, Oklahoma City $900,000
73. Royals. Evan Steele, LHP, Chipola (Fla.) JC $826,500
74. Orioles. Zac Lowther, LHP, Xavier $779,500
75. Astros. J.J. Matijevic, 2B, Arizona $700,000
76. Twins. Blayne Enlow, RHP, St. Amant (La.) HS $2,000,000
77. Reds. Jacob Heatherly, LHP, Cullman (Ala.) HS $1,047,500
78. Padres. Mason House, OF, Whitehouse (Texas) HS $732,200
79. Rays. Taylor Walls, SS, Florida State $612,500
80. Braves. Freddy Tarnok, RHP, Riverview (Fla.) HS $1,445,000
81. Athletics. Nick Allen, SS, Parker School, San Diego $2,000,000
82. Diamondbacks. Matt Tabor, RHP, Milton (Mass.) Academy $1,000,000
83. Phillies. Connor Seabold, RHP, Cal State Fullerton $525,000
84. Brewers. K.J. Harrison, C, Oregon State $667,000
85. Angels. Jacob Pearson, OF, West Monroe (La.) HS $1,000,000
86. Rockies. Will Gaddis, RHP, Furman $600,000
87. White Sox. Luis Gonzalez, OF, New Mexico $517,000
88. Pirates. Dylan Busby, 3B, Florida State $575,000
89. Marlins. Riley Mahan, 2B, Kentucky $525,000
90. Royals. Daniel Tillo, LHP, Iowa Western JC $557,500
91. Astros. Tyler Ivey, RHP, Grayson (Texas) JC $450,000
92. Yankees. Trevor Stephan, RHP, Arkansas $797,500
93. Mariners. Wyatt Mills, RHP, Gonzaga $125,000
94. Cardinals. Scott Hurst, OF, Cal State Fullerton $450,000
95. Tigers. Joey Morgan, C, Washington $564,000
96. Giants, Seth Corry, LHP, Lone Peak HS, Highland, Utah $1,000,000
97. Mets. Quinn Brodey, OF, Stanford $500,000
98. Orioles. Mike Baumann, RHP, Jacksonville $500,000
99. Blue Jays. Riley Adams, C, San Diego $542,400
100. Dodgers. Connor Wong, C, Houston $547,500

DRAFT

2017 CLUB-BY-CLUB SELECTIONS

ORDER OF SELECTION IN PARENTHESES PLAYERS SIGNED IN BOLD

ARIZONA DIAMONDBACKS (7)

1. Pavin Smith, 1B, Virginia
2. Drew Ellis, 3B, Louisville
2s. Daulton Varsho, C, Wisconsin-Milwaukee (Competitive balance Round 'B' pick—68th)
3. Matt Tabor, RHP, Milton (Mass.) Academy
4. Harrison Francis, RHP, Chiles HS, Tallahassee, Fla.
5. Buddy Kennedy, 3B, Millville (N.J.) Senior HS
6. Brian Shaffer, RHP, Maryland
7. Jose Caballero, SS, Chipola (Fla.) JC
8. Tim Susnara, C, Oregon
9. Cam Duzenack, SS, Dallas Baptist
10. Ryan Grotjohn, SS, Cal State Bakersfield
11. Tra'Mayne Holmes, OF, Faulkner (Ala.)
12. Matt Brill, RHP, Appalachian State
13. Riley Cabral, RHP, Chipola (Fla.) JC
14. Keshawn Lynch, 2B, State JC of Florida
15. Clayton Keyes, OF, Bishop Carroll HS, Calgary
16. Jeff Bain, RHP, Cal Poly Pomona
17. Trent Autry, RHP, Florence-Darlington Tech (S.C.) JC
18. Kevin Watson, OF, Beaverton (Ore.) HS
19. Ernie De La Trinidad, OF, Nevada-Las Vegas
20. Dominic Miroglio, C, San Francisco
21. Jack Maynard, RHP, UNC Greensboro
22. Cole Stapler, RHP, Nicholls State
23. Matt Peacock, RHP, South Alabama
24. Jancarlos Cintron, 2B, Nova Southeastern (Fla.)
25. Cole Bartlett, RHP, Missouri
26. Abraham Almonte, LHP, Philadelphia
27. Andrew Eyster, OF, Forest HS, Ocala, Fla.
28. James Johnson, RHP, Lamar
29. Tarik Skubal, LHP, Seattle
30. Ryan Dobson, OF, Fresno State
31. Cole Percival, RHP, Riverside (Calif.) Poly HS
32. Will Gorman, OF, Rochester Institute of Technology
33. Renae Martinez, C, Oklahoma
34. Dan Swain, OF, Siena
35. Zach Almond, C, Catawba (N.C.)
36. Boyd Vander Kooi, RHP, Skyline HS, Mesa, Ariz.
37. David Vasquez, SS, Douglas HS, Parkland, Fla.
38. Emerson Hancock, RHP, Cairo (Ga.) HS
39. Nathan Reynolds, SS, Louisiana-Monroe
40. Terence Connelly, 3B, UNC Wilmington

ATLANTA BRAVES (5)

1. Kyle Wright, RHP, Vanderbilt
2. Drew Waters, OF, Etowah HS, Woodstock, Ga.
3. Freddy Tarnok, RHP, Riverview (Fla.) HS
4. Troy Bacon, RHP, Santa Fe (Fla.) JC
5. Bruce Zimmerman, LHP, Mount Olive (N.C.)
6. Jordan Rodgers, 3B, Tennessee
7. Landon Hughes, RHP, Georgia Southern
8. John Curtis, LHP, Lenoir-Rhyne (N.C.)
9. Riley Delgado, SS, Middle Tennessee State
10. Jake Belinda, RHP, Lock Haven (Pa.)
11. Drew Lugbauer, C, Michigan
12. Hagen Owenby, C, East Tennessee State
13. Connor Simmons, LHP, Georgia Southern
14. Keith Weisenberg, RHP, Stanford
15. Austin Bush, 1B, UC Santa Barbara
16. Gary Schwartz, OF, Grand Canyon
17. Cutter Dyals, RHP, North Carolina A&T
18. Zack Soria, C, Florida International
19. Tanner Allison, LHP, Western Michigan
20. Justin Smith, OF, St. Johns River State (Fla.) JC
21. Connor Johnstone, RHP, Wake Forest
22. Justin Morhardt, C, Bryan (Tenn.)
23. Troy Conyers, LHP, San Diego
24. Jackson Lourie, RHP, Rhodes (Tenn.)
25. Jake Taylor, C, Shawnee (Okla.) HS
26. Charlie Carpenter, C, South Carolina-Upstate
27. Randy Bednar, OF, Landon School, Bethesda, Md.
28. Brett Brocoff, RHP, Desert Oasis HS, Las Vegas
29. Cade Cavalli, RHP, Bixby (Okla.) HS
30. Hayden Wynja, LHP, Heritage Christian School, Indianapolis
31. Ryan Miller, RHP, Clemson
32. Reid Detmers, LHP, Glenwood HS, Chatham, Ill.
33. Chris McMahon, RHP, West Chester (Pa.) Rustin HS
34. Ricky Negron, 3B, Tampa
35. Jason Rooks, OF, Walton HS, Marietta, Ga.
36. Chase Blueberg, RHP, Feather River (Calif.) JC
37. Dean Miller, OF, Riverside (Calif.) JC
38. Adam Groesbeck, OF, Air Force
39. Joe Sanchez, LHP, TERRA Environmental Research Institute, Miami
40. Baron Radcliff, OF, Norcross (Ga.) HS

BALTIMORE ORIOLES (23)

1. D.L. Hall, LHP, Valdosta (Ga.) HS
2. Adam Hall, SS, A.B. Lucas SS, London, Ont.
2s. Zac Lowther, LHP, Xavier (Competitive balance Round 'B' pick—74th)
3. Mike Baumann, RHP, Jacksonville
4. Jack Conlon, RHP, Clements HS, Sugar Land, Texas
5. Lamar Sparks, OF, Seven Lakes HS, Katy HS
6. Mason McCoy, SS, Iowa
7. Ben Breazeale, C, Wake Forest
8. Jimmy Murphy, RHP, Fordham
9. T.J. Nichting, OF, Charlotte
10. Josh Keaton, RHP, Adams State (Colo.)
11. Trevor Craport, 3B, Georgia Tech
12. Tucker Baca, LHP, St. Katherine (Calif.)
13. Reed Hayes, RHP, Vanderbilt
14. Cameron Ming, LHP, Arizona
15. J.C. Escarra, 1B, Florida International
16. Logan Allen, LHP, University HS, Orange City, Fla.
17. Greg Jones, SS, Cary (N.C.) HS
18. Jacob Brown, OF, Northeast Guilford HS, McLeansville, N.C
19. Adam Stauffer, RHP, Coatesville (Pa.) Area HS
20. Scott Burke, RHP, UCLA
21. Jose Montanez, C, Colegio Angel David HS, San Juan, P.R.
22. Luke Ringhofer, C, South Dakota State
23. Bryndan Arredondo, C, Lamar
24. Jason Willow, SS, Lambrick Park SS, Victoria, B.C.
25. Willy Yahn, 3B, Connecticut
26. Cameron Bishop, LHP, UC Irvine
27. Nick Vichio, RHP, Missouri Baptist
28. Zach Jarrett, OF, Charlotte
29. Matt Hammonds, LHP, Sonoma State (Calif.)
30. Will Robertson, OF, Davidson
31. Robbie Thorburn, OF, UNC Wilmington
32. Max Hogan, 2B, Missouri Southern State
33. Ryan Wilson, LHP, Pepperdine
34. Tim Naughton, RHP, North Carolina State
35. Keegan Collett, RHP, Northern Oklahoma JC
36. Tyler Coolbaugh, SS, Angelo State (Texas)
37. Cole Haring, OF, McLennan (Texas) JC
38. Bobby Miller, RHP, McHenry (Ill.) HS
39. Sam Glick, LHP, El Toro HS, Lake Forest, Calif.
40. Niko Leontarakis, RHP, Tallahassee (Fla.) JC

BOSTON RED SOX (26)

1. Tanner Houck, RHP, Missouri
2. Cole Brannen, OF, The Westfield School, Perry, Ga.
3. Brett Netzer, 2B, Charlotte
4. Jake Thompson, RHP, Oregon State
5. Alex Scherff, RHP, Colleyville (Texas) Heritage HS
6. Zach Schellenger, RHP, Seton Hall
7. Tyler Esplin, OF, IMG Academy, Bradenton, Fla.

8. Zach Sterry, 1B, Oakland
9. Tanner Nishioka, OF, Pomona-Pitzer (Calif.)
10. Jordan Wren, OF, Georgia Southern
11. Andre Colon, SS, Washburn Bilingual HS, Ponce, P.R.
12. Beau Hanna, C, Winder-Barrow HS, Winder, Ga.
13. Garrett Benge, 3B, Oklahoma State
14. Aaron Perry, RHP, Hurricane (W.Va.) HS
15. Marcus Ragan, OF, East Mississippi JC
16. Kutter Crawford, RHP, Florida Gulf Coast
17. Frankie Rios, SS, Southern California
18. Dominic LoBrutto, LHP, Florida International
19. Angel Gonzalez, OF, International Baseball Acad., Ceiba, P.R.
20. David Durden, OF, Emanuel County Institute, Twin City, Ga.
21. Lukas Young, RHP, Mobile
22. Hunter Haworth, RHP, Chico State (Calif.)
23. Donny Diaz, RHP, San Jacinto (Texas) JC
24. Charlie Madden, C, Mercer
25. Kory Behenna, LHP, Wingate (N.C.)
26. Trenton Denholm, RHP, Oak Ridge HS, El Dorado Hills, Calif.
27. Xavier LeGrant, 2B, Spartanburg Methodist (S.C.) JC
28. Oraj Anu, OF, The Next Level Academy, Longwood, Fla.
29. Tyler Dearden, OF, Rancocas Valley Regional HS, Mount Holly, N.J.
30. Andrew Carber, RHP, Chipola (Fla.) JC
31. Michael Osinski, 3B, Longwood
32. Taylor Ahearn, RHP, Cal State San Marcos
33. Tanner Raiburn, LHP, Grambling State
34. Luis Torres, OF, Colon HS, Santa Isabel, P.R.
35. Trey Ganns, 1B, Northern Kentucky
36. Rio Gomez, LHP, Arizona
37. Carson Teel, LHP, Oklahoma State
38. Jose Garcia, C, Doral Academy Prep HS, Miami
39. Ridge Chapman, RHP, Spartanburg Methodist (S.C) JC
40. Cody Masters, OF, Coppell (Texas) HS

CHICAGO CUBS (30)

1. Brendon Little, LHP, State JC of Florida
1. Alex Lange, RHP, Louisiana State (Compsenation for loss of Dexter Fowler as free agent––30th)
2. Cory Abbott, RHP, Loyola Marymount
3. Keegan Thompson, RHP, Auburn
4. Erich Uelmen, RHP, Cal Poly
5. Nelson Velazquez, OF, P.J. Education HS, Carolina, P.R.
6. Jeremy Estrada, RHP, Palm Desert (Calif.) HS
7. Ricky Tyler Thomas, LHP, Fresno State
8. Austin Filiere, 3B, Massachussetts Institute of Technology
9. Chris Carrier, OF, Memphis
10. Brian Glowicki, RHP, Minnesota
11. Rollie Lacy, RHP, Creighton
12. Ben Hecht, RHP, Wichita State
13. Austin Upshaw, 1B, Kennesaw State
14. Luis Vazquez, SS, Alberto Melendez Torres HS, Orocovis, P.R.
15. Jared Young, 2B, Old Dominon
16. Brandon Hughes, OF, Michigan State
17. Peyton Remy, RHP, Central Arizona JC
18. Casey Ryan, RHP, Hawaii
19. Chris Singleton, OF, Charleston Southern
20. Brendan King, RHP, Holy Cross
21. Sean Barry, RHP, San Diego
22. Skyler Messinger, SS, Niwot (Colo.) HS
23. Brady Miller, RHP, Western Oregon
24. Braxton Light, RHP, Wallace State (Ala.) JC
25. Mitch Stophel, RHP, King (Tenn.)
26. Bryce Bonnin, RHP, Barbers Hill HS, Mont Belvieu, Texas
27. Darius Vines, RHP, Oxnard (Calif.) JC
28. Kier Meredith, OF, Glenn HS, Kernersville, N.C.
29. Jake Steffens, RHP, Santa Clara
30. Cam Balego, SS, Mercyhurst (Pa.)
31. Ramsey Romano, 3B, Long Beach State
32. Hunter Ruth, RHP, Buchholz HS, Gainesville, Fla.
33. Joe Donovan, C, Westmont (Ill.) HS
34. Andrew Karp, RHP, Florida State
35. Ben Ramirez, SS, Eastlake HS, Chula Vista, Calif.
36. Tanner Allen, OF, UMS-Wright Prep, Mobile, Ala.
37. Alex Cornwell, LHP, Maranatha HS, Pasadena, Calif.
38. Russell Smith, LHP, Midlothian (Texas) HS
39. Cooper Coldiron, SS, Houston
40. Jeffrey Passantino, RHP, Lipscomb

CHICAGO WHITE SOX (12)

1. Jake Burger, 3B, Missouri State
2. Gavin Sheets, 1B, Wake Forest
3. Luis Gonzalez, OF, New Mexico
4. Lincoln Henzman, RHP, Louisville
5. Tyler Johnson, RHP, South Carolina
6. Kade McClure, RHP, Louisville
7. Evan Skoug, C, Texas Christian
8. Sam Abbott, 1B, Curtis HS, University Place, Wash.
9. Craig Dedelow, OF, Indiana
10. J.B. Olson, RHP, Oklahoma
11. Will Kincanon, RHP, Indiana State
12. Justin Yurchak, 3B, Binghamton
13. Tate Blackman, 2B, Mississippi
14. Alex Destino, OF, South Carolina
15. Tyler Frost, OF, Gonzaga
16. Logan Taylor, OF, Louisville
17. Blake Battenfield, RHP, Oklahoma State
18. Hunter Kiel, RHP, Louisiana State
19. Anthony Herron, RHP, Missouri State
20. David Cronin, 2B, Illinois-Chicago
21. John Parke, LHP, South Carolina
22. Joey Benitez, LHP, South Carolina-Aiken
23. Mikey Duarte, SS, UC Irvine
24. Vince Arobio, RHP, Pacific
25. Jose Garcia, OF, Texas-Rio Grande Valley
26. Michael Staudinger, OF, Azuza Pacific (Calif.)
27. J.J. Muno, SS, UC Santa Barbara
28. Laz Rivera, 2B, Tampa
29. Joe Mockbee, LHP, Michigan State
30. Ryan Erickson, LHP, Iowa
31. Parker Rigler, LHP, Kansas State
32. Greg Minier, LHP, Washington
33. Kevin George, LHP, Menlo (Calif.)
34. Michael McCormick, RHP, Eastern Illinois
35. Riley Crean, RHP, Bloomington (Ind.) North HS
36. Alex Widmer, RHP, Norwayne HS, Creston, Ohio
37. Ted Andrews, RHP, Tulane
38. Dylan Horvitz, C, New Trier HS, Winnetka, Ill.
39. Chance King, RHP, IMG Academy, Bradenton, Fla.
40. Angelo Smith, LHP, Richards HS, Oak Lawn, Ill.

CINCINNATI REDS (2)

1. Hunter Greene, RHP, Notre Dame HS, Sherman Oaks, Calif.
1s Jeter Downs, SS, Pace HS, Miami Gardens (Competitive balance Round 'A" pick––32nd)
2. Stuart Fairchild, OF, Wake Forest
3. Jacob Heatherly, LHP, Cullman (Ala.) HS
4. Cash Case, SS, The First Academy, Orlando
5. Mac Sceroler, RHP, Southeastern Louisiana
6. Tyler Buffet, RHP, Oklahoma State
7. Mark Kolozsvary, C, Florida
8. Connor Ryan, RHP, Illinois-Chicago
9. Packy Naughton, LHP, Virginia Tech
10. Robby Howell, RHP, Central Florida
11. Jared Solomon, RHP, Lackawanna (Pa.) JC
12. Tommy Mace, RHP, Sunlake HS, Land O' Lakes, Fla.
13. Ricky Karcher, RHP, Walters State (Tenn.) JC
14. Brody Wofford, OF, Chipola (Fla.) JC
15. Nate Scantlin, OF, Rose Hill (Kan.) HS
16. Ryan Nutof, RHP, Michigan
17. Jeffrey Harding, RHP, Chipola (Fla.) JC
18. John Ghyzel, RHP, Rochester (N.Y.)
19. Seth Lonsway, LHP, Celina (Ohio) HS
20. Blake Wiggins, 3B, JC of Southern Nevada
21. Christian Lindsay-Young, RHP, Niagara County (N.Y.) JC
22. Justin Bellinger, 1B, Duke
23. Adrian Chacon, RHP, Tampa
24. Anderson DeLeon, RHP, Iowa Central JC

DRAFT

25. Doug Norman, RHP, Louisiana State
26. Tyler Brown, RHP, Olentangy Orange HS, Lewis Center, Ohio
27. Clay Fisher, SS, UC Santa Barbara
28. Harrison Rutkowski, LHP Woodbridge (N.J.) HS
29. A.J. Bumpass, OF, Cincinnati
30. Garrett Shoenle, LHP, Northrop HS, Fort Wayne, Ind.
31. Dondrae Bremner, 2B, Bill Crothers SS, Markham, Ont.
32. Michael Bono, RHP, Santa Clara
33. Brady McConnell, SS, Merritt Island (Fla.) HS
34. R.J. Barnes, OF, Sycamore HS, Montgomery, Ohio
35. Stephen Keller, RHP, Hargrave HS, Huffman, Texas
36. Logan Chapman, RHP, Easley (S.C.) HS
37. Robert Touron, RHP, Gulliver Prep, Miami
38. Tyler Littlefield, SS, St. John Bosco HS, Bellflower, Calif.
39. Zack Gahagan, 3B, North Carolina
40. Ian Jenkins, OF, Collins Hill HS, Suwanee, Ga.

DRAFT

CLEVELAND INDIANS (27)

1. (Pick forfeited for signing of free agent Edwin Encarnacion)
2. Quentin Holmes, OF, McClancy Mem. HS, East Elmhurst, N.Y.
2s. Tyler Freeman, SS, Etiwanda HS, Rancho Cucamonga, Calif. (Competitive balance Round 'B' pick––71st)
3. Johnathan Rodriguez, OF, Beltran Base. Acad., Florida, P.R.
4. Ernie Clement, 2B, Virginia
5. Austen Wade, OF, Texas Christian
6. Mike Rivera, C, Florida
7. Kirk McCarty, LHP, Southern Mississippi
8. Eli Morgan, RHP, Gonzaga
9. James Karinchak, RHP, Bryant
10. Jesse Berardi, SS, St. John's
11. Matt Turner, LHP, Palmetto (Fla.) HS
12. Dante Mendoza, RHP, Torrance (Calif.) HS
13. Angel Lopez, C, Northampton (Pa.) JC
14. Oscar Serratos, SS, Grayson HS, Loganville, Ga.
15. Kyle Nelson, LHP, UC Santa Barbara
16. Nick Gallagher, RHP, Iowa
17. "Pedro Alfonseca, OF, Black Hawk (Ill.) JC "
18. Dillon Persinger, 2B, Cal State Fullerton
19. Josh Nashed, RHP, San Jose State
20. Jonathan Teaney, RHP, San Diego
21. Tyler Friis, 2B, Indiana State
22. Clark Scolamiero, OF, North Greenville (S.C.)
23. Jordan Scheftz, RHP, Central Florida
24. Riley Echols, RHP, Freed-Hardeman (Tenn.)
25. Chandler Ferguson, RHP, Jefferson HS, Lafayette, Ind.
26. Tommy DeJuneas, RHP, North Carolina State
27. Casey Opitz, C, Heritage HS, Littleton, Colo.
28. Michael Hendrickson, LHP, Michigan
29. Tre' Gantt, OF, Ohio State
30. Zach Draper, LHP, College of Idaho
31. Asa Lacy, LHP, Tivy HS, Kerrville, Texas
32. Mitch Reeves, OF, Florida Southern
33. Michael Cooper, 1B, Ridge Point HS, Missouri City, Texas
34. Cole Turney, OF, Travis HS, Richmond, Texas
35. Spencer Strider, RHP, Christian Academy of Knoxville
36. Jorge Arellano, LHP, Downey (Calif.) HS
37. Austin Martin, SS, Trinity Christian Academy, Jacksonville
38. Scott Kobos, LHP, St. Johns River State (Fla.) JC
39. Josh Rolette, C, Kansas State
40. Cole Kleszcz, OF, JC of the Canyons (Calif.)

COLORADO ROCKIES (11)

1. (Pick forfeited for signing of free agent Ian Desmond)
2. Ryan Vilade, 3B, Stillwater (Okla.) HS
2s. Tommy Doyle, RHP, Virginia (Competitive balance Round 'B' pick––70th)
3. Will Gaddis, RHP, Furman
4. Pearson McMahan, RHP, St. Johns River State (Fla.) JC
5. Nick Kennedy, LHP, Texas
6. Chad Spanberger, 1B, Arkansas
7. Lucas Gilbreath, LHP, Minnesota
8. Bret Boswell, 2B, Texas
9. Sean Bouchard, 1B, UCLA
10. Austin Bernard, C, Pepperdine
11. Hunter Williams, LHP, Washington (Frontier League)
12. Matt McLaughlin, SS, Kansas
13. Shameko Smith, RHP, Polk State (Fla.) JC
14. Nic Motley, C, McLennan (Texas) JC
15. Colton Hathcock, RHP, Memphis
16. Alan Trejo, SS, San Diego State
17. Jeff Bohling, 3B, Gonzaga
18. Garrett Schilling, RHP, Xavier
19. Joey Bartosic, OF, George Washington
20. Casey Golden, OF, UNC Wilmington
21. Nate Harris, RHP, Louisiana Tech
22. Daniel Jipping, OF, Central Michigan
23. Danny Edgeworth, 3B, Mercer
24. Jesse Lepore, RHP, Miami
25. Derrik Watson, RHP, Murray State
26. Aubrey McCarty, OF, Florida A&M
27. Brandon Lambright, RHP, Abilene Christian (Texas)
28. Brett Stephens, OF, UCLA
29. Todd Czinege, 2B, Villanova
30. Jeff Moberg, 2B, Tennessee
31. Reagan Biechler, LHP, Wichita State
32. Moises Ceja, RHP, UCLA
33. Alec Byrd, LHP, Florida State
34. Hayden Roberts, RHP, Southern Mississippi
35. James Notary, RHP, Broomfield (Colo.) HS
36. Michael Agis, RHP, Florida International
37. Tyler Hardman, 3B, Temescal Canyon HS, Lake Elsinore, Calif
38. Drake Davis, RHP, Rallston Valley HS, Arvada, Colo.
39. Colin Hall, OF, Wesleyan HS, Peachtree Corners, Ga.
40. George Stanley, C, Centennial HS, Peoria, Ariz.

DETROIT TIGERS (20)

1. Alex Faedo, RHP, Florida
2. Rey Rivera, OF, Chipola (Fla.) JC
3. Joey Morgan, C, Washington
4. Gio Arriera, RHP, Palm Beach State (Fla.) JC
5. Sam McMillan, C, Suwannee HS, Live Oak, Fla.
6. Dane Myers, RHP, Rice
7. Brad Bass, RHP, Notre Dame
8. Max Green, LHP, Pepperdine
9. Luke Burch, OF, Kent State
10. Garrett McCain, OF, Oklahoma State
11. Garett King, RHP, Cal Baptist
12. Will Vest, RHP, Stephen F. Austin State
13. Cole Peterson, SS, St. Bonaventure
14. Antoine Mistico, OF, Chandler (Ariz.) HS
15. Teddy Hoffman, OF, Texas State
16. Carson Lance, RHP, Lamar
17. Billy Lescher, RHP, Pennsylvania
18. Dylan Rosa, OF, Kent State
19. Ryan Karstetter, 3B, State JC of Florida
20. Dylan Burdeaux, 1B, Southern Mississippi
21. Jordan Pearce, 3B, Nevada
22. Colby Bortles, 3B, Mississippi
23. Mitch Stalsberg, LHP, Winona State (Minn.)
24. Jordan Knutson, LHP, Missouri State
25. Dylan Stock, RHP, Binghamton
26. Drew Crosby, LHP, Memphis
27. Jake Bivens, SS, Michigan
28. Cam Warner, 2B, Texas Christian
29. Grant Reuss, LHP, Michigan State
30. Kyle Thomas, RHP, Northwestern Ohio
31. Nick Storz, RHP, Poly Prep Country Day School, Brooklyn
32. Drew Carlton, RHP, Florida State
33. Jake Nelson, RHP, Pennsylvania
34. Ro Coleman, RHP, Vanderbilt
35. Jeff Criswell, RHP, Portage (Mich.) Central HS
36. Jesse Heikkinen, LHP, Holt (Mich.) HS
37. Shane Cooper, SS, Hutchinson (Kan.) JC
38. Steve Mann, OF, Detroit Country Day School, Beverly Hills, Mich.
39. Jack Leftwich, RHP, The Next Level Academy, Longwood, Fla.
40. Rhys Cratty, 2B, Langley (B.C.) SS

HOUSTON ASTROS (16)

1. **J.B. Bukauskas, RHP, North Carolina**
2. **Joe Perez, 3B, Archbishop McCarthy HS, S.W. Ranches, Fla.**
2. **Corbin Martin, RHP, Texas A&M** (Special compensation from the Cardinals for breach of MLB rules)
2s. **J.J. Matijevic, 2B, Arizona** (Special compensation from the Cardinals for breach of MLB rules; Competitive balance Round 'B' pick—75th)
3. **Tyler Ivey, RHP, Grayson (Texas) JC**
4. **Peter Solomon, RHP, Notre Dame**
5. **Nathan Perry, C, Bassett (Va.) HS**
6. **Jake Adams, 1B, Iowa**
7. **Parker Mushinski, LHP, Texas Tech**
8. **Corey Julks, OF, Houston**
9. **Mike Papierski, C, Louisiana State**
10. **Kyle Serrano, RHP, Tennessee**
11. Brandon Bielak, RHP, Notre Dame
12. **Jonathan Lacroix, OF, Seminole State (Okla.) JC**
13. **Jake Meyers, OF, Nebraska**
14. **Carlos Diaz, OF, Colegio Angel David HS, San Juan, P.R.**
15. **Kyle Davis, 2B, West Virginia**
16. **Adrian Tovalin, 3B, Azusa Pacific (Calif.)**
17. **Matt Ruppenthal, RHP, Vanderbilt**
18. **Tim Hardy, LHP, Tusculum (Tenn.)**
19. **Roman Garcia, 1B, San Diego**
20. **Hunter Martin, RHP, Tennessee**
21. **Chas McCormick, OF, Millersville (Pa.)**
22. **Patrick Mathis, OF, Texas**
23. Brett Bond, C, Missouri
24. **Alex House, RHP, Florida Atlantic**
25. Marty Costes, OF, Maryland
26. **Josh Rojas, 2B, Hawaii**
27. **Adam Bleday, LHP, Pennsylvania**
28. **Richard Slenker, 3B, Yale**
29. **Andres Santana, OF, Doral Academy Prep HS, Miami**
30. **Cody Bohanek, SS, Illinois-Chicago**
31. **Cole Watts, LHP, Skyline (Calif.) JC**
32. **Martin Figueroa, C, Rhode Island**
33. **Reid Russell, OF, Lamar**
34. **Noel Pinto, LHP, Connors State (Okla.) JC**
35. Trei Cruz, SS, Episcopal HS, Bellaire, Texas
36. Josh Breaux, C, McLennan (Texas) JC
37. **Matt Merrill, RHP, Oklahoma City (home school)**
38. Trey Cumbie, LHP, Houston
39. **Colton Shaver, 3B, Brigham Young**
40. Chase Farrell, RHP, Valencia HS, Santa Clarita, Calif.

KANSAS CITY ROYALS (15)

1. **Nick Pratto, 1B, Huntington Beach (Calif.) HS**
2. **M.J. Melendez, C, Westminster C. School, Palmetto Bay, Fla.**
2s. **Evan Steele, LHP, Chipola (Fla.) JC** (Competitve balance Round 'B' pick—73rd)
3. **Daniel Tillo, LHP, Iowa Western JC**
4. **Michael Gigliotti, OF, Lipscomb**
5. **Charlie Neuweiler, RHP, McClancy Mem. HS, E Elmhurst, N.Y.**
6. **Tyler Zuber, RHP, Arkansas State**
7. **Brewer Hicklen, OF, Alabama-Birmingham**
8. **Holden Capps, LHP, Central Oklahoma**
9. **J.C. Cloney, LHP, Arizona**
10. **Jordan Floyd, LHP, Kansas State**
11. **Sal Biasi, RHP, Penn State**
12. **Collin Snider, RHP, Vanderbilt**
13. Cason Sherrod, RHP, Texas A&M
14. **Isaiah Henry, RHP, North Shore HS, Houston**
15. **Robert Garcia, LHP, UC Davis**
16. **Chris Hudgins, C, Cal State Fullerton**
17. **Julio Gonzalez, SS, Florida Gulf Coast**
18. **Marlin Willis, LHP, McEachern HS, Powder Springs, Ga.**
19. Korry Howell, SS, Kirkwood (Iowa) JC
20. **Bryar Johnson, RHP, Carolina Forest HS, Myrtle Beach, S.C.**
21. **Isaiah Smith, OF, Battle Ground (Wash.) HS**
22. **Josh Mitchell, LHP, Pittburgh**
23. Matt Morales, SS, Palm Beach State (Fla.) JC
24. **Connor Mayes, RHP, Texas**
25. **Tyler James, OF, William Carey (Miss.)**
26. **Garrett Suchey, RHP, Alabama**
27. **Nick Hutchins, C, Southern Illinois**
28. **Tylor Fischer, RHP, Langham Creek HS, Houston**
29. **Travis Jones, OF, Texas**
30. **Adam Bainbridge, LHP, Old Dominion**
31. Justin Vought, C, Wyoming Valley West HS, Plymouth, Pa.
32. **Andrew Beckwith, RHP, Coastal Carolina**
33. **Damon Olds, RHP, Indiana State**
34. **Jack Klein, RHP, Stanford**
35. **Reed Rohlman, OF, Clemson**
36. **Brady Cox, C, Texas-Arlington**
37. Trevor Hauver, SS, Perry HS, Gilbert, Ariz.
38. **Montae Bradshaw, OF, Patrick Henry (Va.) JC**
39. Justin Mitchell, C, Platte County HS, Platte City, Mo.
40. Yaniel Ramos, SS, Beltran Baseball Academy, Florida, P.R.

LOS ANGELES ANGELS (10)

1. **Jo Adell, OF, Ballard HS, Louisville**
2. **Griffin Canning, RHP, UCLA**
3. **Jacob Pearson, OF, West Monroe (La.) HS**
4. **John Swanda, RHP, Roosevelt HS, Des Moines**
5. **Joseph Booker, RHP, Miller HS, Brewton, Ala.**
6. **Jonah Todd, OF, Auburn**
7. **Dennis Brady, RHP, Mercer County (N.J.) JC**
8. **Connor Riley, RHP, South Carolina-Aiken**
9. **Brett Hanewich, RHP, Stanford**
10. **Daniel Procopio, RHP, Niagara**
11. Jerryell Rivera, LHP, Beltran Baseball Academy, Florida, P.R.
12. **Keith Rogalla, RHP, Creighton**
13. **Kevin Williams, OF, Samford**
14. **Sam Fuller, RHP, Whitefield Academy, Mableton, Ga.**
15. Hunter Brittain, C, Miller HS, Brewton, Ala.
16. **Spencer Griffin, OF, Wharton County (Texas) JC**
17. **Caleb Scires, OF, Nevarro (Texas) JC**
18. **Tyler Stevens, RHP, New Mexico**
19. **Isaac Mattson, RHP, Pittsburgh**
20. Mitchell Traver, RHP, Texas Christian
21. Devon Perez, RHP, Oklahoma
22. **James Ziemba, LHP, Duke**
23. **Zac Ryan, RHP, Georgia Tech**
24. **Harrison Wenson, C, Michigan**
25. Matt McCann, SS, Farleigh Dickinson
26. **Zane Gurwitz, 2B, Texas**
27. **Brandon Sandoval, RHP, Vanguard**
28. Bernabe Camargo, SS, Galveston (Texas) JC
29. Cobi Johnson, RHP, Florida State
30. **Jeremy Beasley, RHP, Clemson**
31. **Jon Malmin, LHP, Texas**
32. **David MacKinnon, 1B, Hartford**
33. **Tyler Walsh, RHP, Belmont**
34. Weston Smith, RHP, O'Connor HS, Helotes, Texas
35. Brady Feigl, RHP, Mississippi
36. Steven Rivas, OF, Etiwanda HS, Rancho Cucamonga, Calif.
37. Peyton Glavine, LHP, Blesset Trinity Catholic HS, Roswell, Ga.
38. Jacob Rogers, 3B, Liberty HS, Henderson, Nev.
39. Josh Hatcher, OF, Lee County, Leesburg, Ga.
40. Matt Russell, RHP, Staley HS, Kansas City, Mo.

LOS ANGELES DODGERS (25)

1. **Jeren Kendall, OF, Vanderbilt**
2. **Morgan Cooper, RHP, Texas**
3. **Connor Wong, C, Houston**
4. **James Marinan, RHP, Park Vista HS, Lake Worth, Fla.**
5. **Riley Ottesen, RHP, Utah**
6. **Wills Montgomerie, RHP, Connecticut**
7. **Zach Pop, RHP, Kentucky**
8. **Rylan Bannon, 3B, Xavier**
9. **Connor Strain, RHP, Evansville**
10. **Zach Reks, OF, Kentucky**
11. **Jacob Amaya, SS, South Hills HS, West Covina, Calif.**
12. Andre Jackson, RHP, Utah

13. Marshall Kasowski, RHP, West Texas A&M
14. Josh McLain, OF, North Carolina State
15. Marcus Chiu, 2B, Marin (Calif.) JC
16. Evy Ruibal, RHP, Notre Dame
17. Nathan Witt, RHP, Michigan State
18. Max Gamboa, RHP, Pepperdine
19. Zach Willeman, RHP, Kent State
20. Donovan Casey, OF, Boston College
21. Joshua Rivera, SS, Beltran Baseball Academy, P.R.
22. Justin Hoyt, LHP, Jacksonville State
23. Connor Heady, SS, Kentucky
24. Preston Grand Pre, SS, California
25. Mark Washington, RHP, Lehigh
26. Devin Hemmerich, LHP, Norfolk State
27. Jeremy Arocho, SS, Old Mill HS, Millersville, Md.
28. Justin Lewis, LHP, Cornell
29. Deacon Liput, 2B, Florida
30. Chris Roller, OF, McLennan (Texas) JC
31. Hunter Mercado-Hood, OF, San Diego
32. Tyler Adkison, OF, San Diego State
33. Brett De Geus, RHP, Cabrillo (Calif.) JC
34. Dan Jagiello, RHP, Long Island-Post (N.Y.)
35. Colby Nealy, RHP, Washington State
36. Riley Richert, RHP, Howard (Texas) JC
37. Corey Merrill, RHP, Tulane
38. Preston White, OF, Birmingham-Southern
39. Logan White, C, Mountain Pointe HS, Phoenix
40. Clayton Andrews, LHP, Cabrillo (Calif.) JC

MIAMI MARLINS (14)

1. Trevor Rogers, LHP, Carlsbad (N.M.) HS
1s Brian Miller, OF, North Carolina (Competitive balance Round 'A' pick—36th)
2. Joe Dunand, 3B, North Carolina State
3. Riley Mahan, 2B, Kentucky
4. Colton Hock, RHP, Stanford
5. Ryan Lillie, RHP, UC Riverside
6. Taylor Braley, RHP, Southern Mississippi
7. Sean Guenther, LHP, Notre Dame
8. Jared Barnes, C, South Alabama
9. Cameron Baranek, OF, Hope International (Calif.)
10. Denis Karas, 3B, California
11. Dakota Bennett, LHP, Brewer HS, Somerville, Ala.
12. Josh Roberson, RHP, UNC Wilmington
13. Jan Mercado, C, Puerto Rico Baseball Academy, Gurabo, P.R.
14. Demetrius Sims, SS, Bethune-Cookman
15. Brady Puckett, RHP, Lipscomb
16. Gavin Fritz, RHP, Dallas Baptist
17. Dylan Cyphert, LHP, Gulf Coast State (Fla.) JC
18. Bryce Howe, RHP, Oral Roberts
19. Micah Brown, SS, Lewis-Clark State (Idaho)
20. Matt Givin, RHP, Rock Canyon HS, Lone Tree, Colo.
21. Ben Fisher, 1B, Eastern Kentucky
22. J.D. Osborne, C, Tampa
23. Tyler Curtis, 3B, Lynn (Fla.)
24. Montana Parsons, RHP, Baylor
25. Evan Estes, RHP, Merced (Calif.) JC
26. Gunner Leger, LHP, Lousiana-Lafayette
27. Doug Domnarski, LHP, Connecticut
28. Vincenzo Aiello, RHP, Oklahoma
29. Henry McAree, RHP, Lewis-Clark State (Idaho)
30. Michael Donadio, OF, St. John's
31. Harrison White, OF, Yale
32. Elliott Barzilli, 3B, Texas Christian
33. Kyle Farjad, LHP, Palm Beach State (Fla.) JC
34. Karl Craigie, LHP, Texas-San Antonio
35. Tyler Holton, LHP, Florida State
36. Josh Alberius, RHP, Arkansas
37. Jared Price, RHP, Maryland
38. Cody Roberts, C, North Carolina
39. Brandon Boone, RHP, St. Edward's (Texas)
40. Andrew Turner, 3B, Long Island

MILWAUKEE BREWERS (9)

1. Keston Hiura, 2B, UC Irvine
1s Tristen Lutz, OF, Martin HS, Arlington, Texas (Competitve balance Round 'A'—34th)
2. Caden Lemons, RHP, Vestavia Hills (Ala.) HS
3. K.J. Harrison, C, Oregon State
4. Brendan Murphy, LHP, Mundelein (Ill.) HS
5. Nick Egnatuk, 3B, Immaculata HS, Somerville, N.J.
6. Devin Hairston, SS, Louisville
7. Bowden Francis, RHP, Chipola (Fla.) JC
8. Jayson Rose, RHP, Utah
9. Dallas Carroll, 3B, Utah
10. Alec Bettinger, RHP, Virginia
11. Max Lazar, RHP, Coral Springs (Fla.) HS
12. Je'Von Carrier-Ward, OF, Gahr HS, Cerritos, Calif.
13. Abdiel Layer, SS, Colegio Angel David HS, San Juan, P.R.
14. Gage Workman, SS, Basha HS, Chandler, Ariz.
15. Christian Santana, RHP, American Heritage HS, Plantation, Fla.
16. Justin Bullock, RHP, South Granville HS, Creedmoor, N.C.
17. L.G. Castillo, OF, Lancaster (N.Y.) HS
18. Ledgend Smith, LHP, Binger-Oney HS, Binger, Okla
19. Noah Campbell, SS, Cardinal Gibbons HS, Raleigh, N.C.
20. Austin Rubick, RHP, Ventura (Calif.) JC
21. Dylan File, RHP, Dixie State (Utah)
22. Brandon Presley, LHP, Florida Southwestern State JC
23. Cam Robinson, RHP, University HS, Orange City, Fla.
24. Robbie Hitt, RHP, Quinnipiac
25. Karlos Morales, LHP, South Hills HS, West Covina, Calif.
26. Carson McCusker, OF, Folsom Lake (Calif.) JC
27. Cody Martin, RHP, Tampa
28. Roberto Delgado, RHP, Oklahoma City
29. Brent Diaz, C, Louisiana Tech
30. Cody Beckman, LHP, North Carolina State
31. Rylan Kaufman, LHP, Friendswood (Texas) HS
32. Miller Hogan, RHP, Saint Louis
33. Kyle Jacobsen, OF, Allatoona HS, Acworth, Ga.
34. Garrett Crochet, LHP, Ocean Springs (Miss.) HS
35. Davis Bradshaw, OF, McLaurin HS, Florence, Miss.
36. Kenny Corey, 3B, UC Santa Barbara
37. Christian Taugner, RHP, Brown
38. Robie Rojas, C, Sam Houston State
39. Robert Henry, OF, Brown
40. Trevor Koenig, LHP, St. Cloud (Minn.) Tech HS

MINNESOTA TWINS (1)

1. Royce Lewis, SS, JSerra Cath. HS, San Juan Capistrano, Calif.
1s Brent Rooker, OF, Mississippi State (Competitve balance Round 'A' pick—35th)
2. Landon Leach, RHP, Pickering HS, Ajax, Ont.
3. Blayne Enlow, RHP, St. Amant (La.) HS
4. Charlie Barnes, LHP, Clemson
5. Andrew Bechtold, 3B, Chipola (Fla.) JC
6. Ricky De La Torre, SS, P.R. Baseball Academy, Gurabo, P.R.
7. Ryley Widell, LHP, Central Arizona JC
8. Bryan Sammons, LHP, Western Carolina
9. Mark Contreras, OF, UC Riverside
10. Calvin Faucher, RHP, UC Irvine
11. Gabriel Rodriguez, OF, Colegio Angel David HS, San Juan, P.R.
12. Bailey Ober, RHP, College of Charleston
13. Jared Akins, OF, Fresno State
14. Derek Molina, RHP, Merced (Calif.) JC
15. Rickey Ramirez, RHP, Fresno State
16. Cade Smith, RHP, Mennonite Educat. Institue HS, Abbotsford, B.C.
17. Andy Cosgrove, C, North Carolina State
18. Colton Burns, OF, UC Santa Barbara
19. Jordan Gore, SS, Coastal Carolina
20. Tyler Gray, RHP, Central Arkansas
21. Colton Waltner, C, San Diego
22. C.J. Broussard, RHP, Cal State Los Angeles
23. Jared Finkel, RHP, Iona
24. T.J. Dixon, OF, Samford
25. Carson Crites, 2B, Southeast Louisiana
26. Jordan Spicer, RHP, Polk State (Fla.) JC

27. Chandler Taylor, OF, Alabama
28. Joe Record, RHP, UC Santa Barbara
29. Griffin Roberts, RHP, Wake Forest
30. Alex Robles, RHP, Austin Peay State
31. Luke Miller, 3B, Indiana
32. Nick Brown, RHP, William & Mary
33. J.J. Robinson, 1B, Lewis-Clark State (Idaho)
34. Max Meyer, RHP, Woodbury (Minn.) HS
35. Adam Oviedo, SS, Alvarado (Texas) HS
36. Josh McMinn, RHP, Oral Roberts
37. Patrick Bailey, C, Wesleyan Christian Academy, High Point, N.C.
38. Ben Rodriguez, C, Pepperdine
39. Jonny DeLuca, OF, Agoura HS, Agoura Hills, Calif.
40. Austin Bizzle, RHP, Alabama State

NEW YORK METS (22)

1. David Peterson, LHP, Oregon
2. Mark Vientos, 3B, American Heritage HS, Plantation, Fla.
3. Quinn Brodey, OF, Stanford
4. Tony Dibrell, RHP, Kennesaw State
5. Matt Winaker, OF, Stanford
6. Marcel Renteria, RHP, New Mexico State
7. Conner O'Neil, RHP, Cal State Northridge
8. Trey Cobb, RHP, Oklahoma State
9. Cannon Chadwick, RHP, Arkansas
10. Stephen Villines, RHP, Kansas
11. Jack Schneider, OF, Daviess County HS, Owensboro, Ky.
12. Bryce Hutchinson, RHP, DeLand (Fla.) HS
13. Nate Peden, RHP, University HS, Orange City, Fla.
14. Matt Duce, C, Dallas Baptist
15. Dylan Snypes, SS, Oral Roberts
16. Raphael Gladu, OF, Louisiana Tech
17. A.J. Labas, RHP, Trinity Christian Academy, Jacksonville
18. Carl Stajduhar, 3B, New Mexico
19. C.J. Van Eyk, RHP, Steinbrenner HS, Lutz, Fla.
20. Yadiel Flores, RHP, Puerto Rico Baseball Acad., Gurabo, P.R.
21. Aaron Ford, LHP, Tennessee Wesleyan
22. Josh Payne, RHP, West Texas A&M
23. Jose Sierra, LHP, Monroe (N.Y.) JC
24. Joey Cavallaro, RHP, South Florida
25. Laine Huffman, SS, Long Beach State
26. Gavin Garay, SS, St. Petersburg (Fla.) JC
27. Billy Oxford, RHP, Azusa Pacific (Calif.)
28. Jeremy Vasquez, 1B, Nova Southeastern (Fla.)
29. Liam McCall, RHP, First Coast HS, Jacksonville
30. Ian McWilliams, RHP, Beech HS, Hendersonville, Tenn.
31. Ryan Selmer, RHP, Maryland
32. Kaylor Chafin, LHP, Texas A&M
33. Mac Lozer, RHP, Michigan
34. Jake Eder, LHP, Calvary Christian Academy, Fort Lauderdale
35. Kyle Wilson, RHP, Crowder (Mo.) JC
36. Robby Kidwell, C, Brunswick (N.C.) JC
37. Josh Walker, LHP, New Haven (Conn.)
38. Daniel Alfonzo, 3B, Bayside (N.Y.) HS
39. Noah Nunez, RHP, Santana HS, Santee, Calif.
40. Ronnie Taylor, RHP, Allen Central HS, Eastern, Ky.

NEW YORK YANKEES (17)

1. Clarke Schmidt, RHP, South Carolina
2. Matt Sauer, RHP, Righetti HS, Santa Maria, Calif.
3. Trevor Stephan, RHP, Arkansas
4. Canaan Smith, OF, Rockwall-Heath HS, Rockwall, Texas
5. Glenn Otto, RHP, Rice
6. Dalton Lehnen, LHP, Augustana (S.D.)
7. Dalton Higgins, RHP, Dallas Baptist
8. Kyle Zurak, RHP, Radford
9. Austin Gardner, RHP, Texas-Arlington
10. Chad Whitmer, RHP, Southern Illinois
11. Shawn Semple, RHP, New Orleans
12. Steven Sensley, OF, Louisiana-Lafayette
13. Eric Wagaman, 1B, Orange Coast (Calif.) JC
14. Harold Cortijo, RHP, Riverdale Bap. HS, Upper Marlboro, Md.
15. Aaron McGarity, RHP, Virginia Tech
16. Ricky Surum, SS, Mount Olive (N.C.)
17. Chris Hess, 2B, Rhode Island
18. Garrett Whitlock, RHP, Alabama-Birmingham
19. Ron Marinaccio, RHP, Delaware
20. Ryan Lidge, C, Notre Dame
21. Bryan Blanton, RHP, Catawba (N.C.)
22. Janson Junk, RHP, Seattle
23. Colby Davis, RHP, Chaparral HS, Scottsdale, Ariz.
24. Pat DeMarco, OF, Winder-Barrow HS, Winder, Ga.
25. Riley Thompson, RHP, Louisville
26. Austin Crowson, LHP, Lane (Ore.) JC
27. Alex Mauricio, RHP, Norfolk State
28. Shane Roberts, RHP, Dwyer HS, Palm Beach Gardens, Fla.
29. Tristan Beck, RHP, Stanford
30. Jake Mangum, OF, Mississippi State
31. Jimmy Herron, OF, Duke
32. Alika Williams, SS, Rancho Bernardo HS, San Diego
33. Jacob Stevens, RHP, Boston College
34. Jordan Butler, LHP, Alonso HS, Tampa
35. Steven Williams, C, Deerfield-Windsor HS, Albany, Ga.
36. Andrew Abbott, LHP, Halifax County HS, South Boston, Va.
37. Tanner Burns, RHP, Decatur (Ala.) HS
38. Brent Burgess, RHP, Spartanburg Methodist (S.C.) JC
39. Andrew Nardi, LHP, Ventura (Calif.) JC
40. Hayden Cantrelle, SS, Teurlings Catholic HS, Lafayette, La.

OAKLAND ATHLETICS (6)

1. Austin Beck, OF, North Davidson HS, Lexington, N.C.
1s Kevin Merrell, SS, South Florida (Competitive balance Round 'A' pick––33rd)
2. Greg Deichmann, OF, Louisiana State
3. Nick Allen, SS, Parker School, San Diego
4. Will Toffey, 3B, Vanderbilt
5. Santis Sanchez, C, International Baseball Acad., Ceiba, P.R.
6. Logan Salow, LHP, Kentucky
7. Parker Dunshee, RHP, Wake Forest
8. Brian Howard, RHP, Texas Christian
9. Jared Poche', LHP, Louisiana State
10. Jack Meggs, OF, Washington
11. Ryan Gridley, SS, Mississippi State
12. Aaron Arruda, 1B, Fresno State
13. Wyatt Marks, RHP, Louisiana-Lafayette
14. Garrett Mitchell, OF, Orange (Calif.) Lutheran HS
15. Josh Reagan, LHP, South Carolina
16. Payton Squier, OF, Nevada-Las Vegas
17. Josh Falk, RHP, Pittsburgh
18. Mickey McDonald, OF, Illinois-Chicago
19. Michael Danielak, RHP, Dartmouth
20. Osvaldo Berrios, RHP, P.R. Baseball Acad., Gurabo, P.R.
21. Heath Donica, RHP, Sam Houston State
22. Bryce Conley, RHP, Georgia State
23. Malik Jones, RHP, Missouri Baptist
24. Slater Lee, RHP, Cal Poly
25. Hunter Hargrove, 1B, Texas Tech
26. Nate Webb, C, King HS, Riverside, Calif.
27. Ben Spitznagel, OF, UNC Greensboro
28. Pat Krall, LHP, Clemson
29. Adam Reuss, RHP, Wisconsin-Milwaukee
30. Cody Puckett, LHP, Middle Tennessee State
31. Brandon Withers, RHP, James Madison
32. Caleb Evans, RHP, Liberty
33. Jake Lumley, 2B, Canisus
34. Justin Jones, 2B, Nevada-Las Vegas
35. Cooper Goldby, C, Lewis-Clark State (Idaho)
36. Logan Farrar, OF, Virginia Commonwealth
37. Raymond Gill, 3B, Gulliver Prep, Miami
38. Wil Hoyle, 2B, Jordan HS, Durham, N.C.
39. Haydn King, LHP, Archbishop Mitty HS, San Jose
40. Jacob Hoffman, SS, Stanford

PHILADELPHIA PHILLIES (8)

1. **Adam Haseley, OF, Virginia**
2. **Spencer Howard, RHP, Cal Poly**
3. **Connor Seabold, RHP, Cal State Fullerton**
4. **Jake Scheiner, 3B, Houston**
5. **Ethan Lindow, LHP, Locust Grove (Ga.) HS**
6. **Dalton Guthrie, SS, Florida**
7. **Nick Maton, SS, Lincoln Land (Ill.) JC**
8. **Jhordany Mezquita, LHP, Hazelton, Pa. (No school)**
9. **Jack Zoellner, 1B, New Mexico**
10. **Connor Brogdon, RHP, Lewis-Clark State (Idaho)**
11. **Jake Holmes, SS, Pinnacle HS, Phoenix**
12. **David Parkinson, LHP, Mississippi**
13. **Colby Fitch, C, Louisville**
14. **Zach Warren, LHP, Tennessee**
15. **Alex Garcia, RHP, UC Santa Barbara**
16. **Kyle Dohy, LHP, Cal Poly Pomona**
17. **Austin Listi, OF, Dallas Baptist**
18. **Damon Jones, LHP, Washington State**
19. **Addison Russ, RHP, Houston Baptist**
20. Brady Schanuel, RHP, Parkland (Ill.) JC
21. **Jakob Hernandez, LHP, Texas-Arlington**
22. **Brian Mims, 2B, UNC Wilmington**
23. Shane Drohan, LHP, Cardinal Newman HS, West Palm Beach, Fla.
24. **Kevin Markham, OF, Texas-San Antonio**
25. **Jesus Azuaje, SS, Glendale (Ariz.) JC**
26. **Quincy Nieporte, 1B, Florida State**
27. **Yahir Gurrola, OF, North Florida**
28. Bill Sullivan, RHP, St. Mark's HS, Wilmington, Del.
29. **Bailey Cummings, RHP, San Jacinto (Texas) JC**
30. Matt Kroon, 3B, Central Arizona JC
31. **Danny Mayer, OF, Pacific**
32. **Sati Santa Cruz, RHP, Central Arizona JC**
33. **Ben Brown, RHP, Melville HS, East Setauket, N.Y.**
34. Kyle Hurt, RHP, Torrey Pines HS, San Diego
35. Brian Morrell, RHP, Shoreham-Wading River HS, Shoreham, N.Y.
36. Joe Breaux, OF, McClennan (Texas) JC
37. Eduoard Julien, 2B, Cardinal-Roy SS, Quebec City
38. Landon Gray, C, Weatherford (Texas) JC
39. **D.J. Stewart, 3B, Westminster Chris. Acad., Chesterfield, Mo.**
40. Paul Coumoulos, OF, Bishop McLaughlin Catholic HS, Spring Hill, Fla.

PITTSBURGH PIRATES (13)

1. **Shane Baz, RHP, Concordia Lutheran HS, Tomball, Texas**
2. **Steven Jennings, RHP, Dekalb County HS, Smithville, Tenn.** (Compensation for failure to sign 2016 second-round pick Nick Lodolo—42nd)

2\. **Calvin Mitchell, OF, Rancho Bernardo HS, San Diego**

2s. **Conner Uselton, OF, Southmoore HS, Oklahoma City** (Competitve balance Round 'B' pick—72nd)

3. **Dylan Busby, 3B, Florida State**
4. **Jason Delay, C, Vanderbilt**
5. **Deon Stafford, C, St. Joseph's**
6. **Cody Bolton, RHP, Tracy (Calif.) HS**
7. **Jared Oliva, OF, Arizona**
8. **Blake Weiman, LHP, Kansas**
9. **Bligh Madris, OF, Colorado Mesa**
10. **Beau Sulser, RHP, Dartmouth**
11. **Alex Manasa, RHP, Jackson (Mich.) JC**
12. Hunter Wolfe, SS, Walters State (Tenn.) JC
13. **Tristan Gray, 2B, Rice**
14. **Chris Sharpe, OF, Massachusetts-Lowell**
15. **Gavin Wallace, RHP, Fairfield**
16. **Hunter Stratton, RHP, Walters State (Tenn.) JC**
17. **Mason Martin, OF, Southridge HS, Kennewick, Wash.**
18. **Shea Murray, RHP, Ohio State**
19. **Jake Webb, RHP, Pittsburg (Kan.) HS**
20. **Will Reed, RHP, Harford (Md.) JC**
21. **Robbie Glendinning, SS, Missouri**
22. **Brett Pope, SS, Western Carolina**
23. **Ben Bengtson, SS, Hartford**
24. **Nick Valaika, SS, UCLA**
25. **Eddie Muhl, RHP, George Washington**
26. **Lucas Tancas, OF, Long Beach State**
27. David Lee, RHP, Florida
28. **Matt Seelinger, RHP, Farmingdale State (N.Y.)**
29. Brock Deatherage, OF, North Carolina State
30. **Manny Bejerano, C, Broward (Fla.) JC**
31. **Jesse Medrano, 3B, Fresno State**
32. **Hector Quinones, RHP, Midway (Ky.)**
33. **Ryan Valdes, RHP, South Florida**
34. **Mason Ward, LHP, Kennesaw State**
35. **Drew Fischer, RHP, Amherst (Mass.)**
36. Ryan Hoerter, RHP, Indian Trail HS, Kenosha, Wis.
37. **Kyle Watson, SS, Mississippi**
38. **Ryan Peurifoy, OF, Georgia Tech**
39. Mike Gretler, 3B, Oregon State
40. Tyler Osick, 3B, Chipola (Fla.) JC

ST. LOUIS CARDINALS (19)

1\. Pick forfeitted for signing free agent Dexter Fowler

2\. Pick forfeitted due to breach of MLB rules

2s. Pick forfeitted due to breach of MLB rules

3. **Scott Hurst, OF, Cal State Fullerton**
4. **Kramer Robertson, SS, Louisiana State**
5. **Zach Kirtley, 2B, St. Mary's**
6. **Zach Jackson, C, Winter Haven (Fla.) HS**
7. **Chase Pinder, OF, Clemson**
8. **Wilberto Rivera, RHP, Beltran Baseball Acad., Florida, P.R.**
9. **Evan Kruczynski, LHP, East Carolina**
10. **Brett Seeburger, LHP, San Diego State**
11. **Evan Mendoza, 3B, North Carolina State**
12. **Andrew Summerville, LHP, Stanford**
13. **Jacob Patterson, LHP, Texas Tech**
14. **Donivan Williams, 3B, Richards HS, Oak Lawn, Ill.**
15. **Terry Fuller, OF, Griffin (Ga.) HS**
16. **Jake Walsh, RHP, Florida Southern**
17. **Will Latcham, RHP, Coastal Carolina**
18. **Shane McCarthy, RHP, Seton Hall**
19. **Irving Lopez, 2B, Florida International**
20. **Brandon Benson, OF, Georgia College & State**
21. **Jake Dahlberg, LHP, Illinois-Chicago**
22. **Kevin Hamann, RHP, Lewis-Clark State (Idaho)**
23. **Evan Guillory, RHP, Louisiana-Lafayette**
24. Thomas St. Clair, RHP, Lenoir-Rhyne (N.C.)
25. **Patrick Dayton, LHP, Kent State**
26. **Paul Balestrieri, RHP, Cornell**
27. **Kodi Whitley, RHP, Mount Olive (N.C.)**
28. **C.J. Saylor, RHP, San Diego State**
29. **Wood Myers, 2B, Coastal Carolina**
30. **Alex Fagalde, RHP, UC Riverside**
31. Saul Garza, C, North HS, Edinburg, Texas
32. **Cameron Knight, C, Arkansas-Little Rock**
33. **Taylor Bryant, 2B, Cal State Fullerton**
34. **Cory Malcom, RHP, Arkansas-Little Rock**
35. **Alex Gallegos, RHP, Torrance (Calif.) HS**
36. **Michael Brdar, SS, Michigan**
37. Adam Kerner, C, Oaks Christian HS, Westlake Village, Calif.
38. **Jim Voyles, RHP, Florida State**
39. **Chris Hunt, RHP, Henderson State (Ark.)**
40. Austin Pollock, LHP, Lincoln HS, Tallahassee, Fla.

SAN DIEGO PADRES (3)

1. **MacKenzie Gore, LHP, Whiteville (N.C.) HS**
2. **Luis Campusano, C, Cross Creek HS, Augusta, Ga.**

2s. **Blake Hunt, C, Mater Dei HS, Santa Ana, Calif.** (Competitive balance Round 'B' pick—69th)

3. **Mason House, OF, Whitehouse (Texas) HS**
4. **Sam Keating, RHP, Canterbury HS, Fort Myers, Fla.**
5. **Jonny Homza, 3B, South HS, Anchorage**
6. **Aaron Leasher, LHP, Morehead State**
7. **Nick Margevicius, LHP, Rider**
8. **Olivier Basabe, SS, Faulkner (Ala.)**
9. **Alex Cunningham, RHP, Coastal Carolina**
10. **Dominic Taccolini, RHP, Arkansas**
11. **Chandler Newman, RHP, Chattahoochee Valley (Ala.) JC**

12. **Tom Cosgrove, LHP, Manhattan**
13. **Fred Schlichtholz, LHP, Fresno State**
14. **Vijay Miller, RHP, East Mississippi JC**
15. **Cole Bellinger, RHP, Hamilton HS, Chandler, Ariz.**
16. **Joey Cantillo, LHP, Kailua (Hawaii) HS**
17. **Jason Pineda, 1B, Monroe HS, Bronx, N.Y.**
18. Cam Sanders, RHP, Northwest Florida State JC
19. **Nick Feight, 1B, UNC Wilmington**
20. Duke Ellis, OF, Panola (Texas) JC
21. **Greg Lambert, OF, Southern Illinois**
22. Jake Lyons, RHP, Weatherford (Texas) JC
23. **Luis Roman, 3B, Texas Wesleyan**
24. **Harrison Simon, RHP, Loyola Marymount**
25. **Robbie Podorsky, OF, McNeese State**
26. Daniel Cabrera, OF, Parkview Baptist HS, Baton Rouge
27. Christian Robinson, OF, Viera High, Melbourne, Fla.
28. **Noel Vela, LHP, Veterans Memorial HS, Mission, Texas**
29. **Jalen Washington, C, Ohio State**
30. **Chandler Seagle, C, Appalachian State**
31. **Tyler Benson, OF, Bloomsburg (Pa.)**
32. **Matt Batten, SS, Quinnipiac**
33. **Caleb Boushley, RHP, Wisconsin-La Crosse**
34. Henry Marchese, OF, Stevenson HS, Lincolnshire, Ill.
35. Kevin Abel, rhp, Madison HS, San Diego
36. Shane Muntz, c, Malvern (Pa.) Prep HS
37. Logan Browning, lhp, Florida Southern
38. **Jeremy Smith, rhp, Southwestern Oklahoma State**
39. **Justin Paulsen, 1b, Missouri State**
40. Chad Stevens, 3b, Gig Harbor (Wash.) HS

SAN FRANCISCO GIANTS (21)

1. **Heliot Ramos, OF, Leadership Christ. Acad., Guaynabo, P.R.**
2. **Jacob Gonzalez, 3B, Chaparral HS, Scottsdale, Ariz.**
3. **Seth Corry, LHP, Lone Peak HS, Highland, Utah**
4. **Garrett Cave, RHP, Tampa**
5. **Jason Bahr, RHP, Central Florida**
6. **Bryce Johnson, OF, Sam Houston State**
7. **Logan Harasta, RHP, Buffalo**
8. **John Gavin, LHP, Cal State Fullerton**
9. **Aaron Phillips, RHP, St. Bonaventure**
10. **Rob Calabrese, C, Illinois-Chicago**
11. **Doug Still, LHP, Missouri State**
12. **Aaron Bond, OF, San Jacinto (Texas) JC**
13. **Tyler Schimpf, RHP, Texas**
14. **Michael Sexton, 3B, The Master's (Calif.)**
15. **Orlando Garcia, SS, Texas Tech**
16. **John Russell, RHP, Connecticut**
17. **Brac Warren, RHP, Oregon**
18. **Chris Corbett, C, Rollins (Fla.)**
19. **Frankie Tostado, OF, Oxnard (Calif.) JC**
20. Keaton Winn, RHP, Iowa Western JC
21. **Logan Baldwin, OF, Georgia Southern**
22. **Greg Jacknewitz, LHP, Xavier**
23. **Shane Matheny, 3B, Washington State**
24. **Nico Giarratano, SS, San Francisco**
25. **Franklin Van Gurp, RHP, Florida International**
26. **Kyle McPherson, SS, James Madison**
27. **Matt Brown, RHP, San Jose State**
28. **Peter Lannoo, RHP, Cornell**
29. Frank Rubio, RHP, Florida
30. Sean Watkins, OF, Cal State Los Angeles
31. **Keenan Bartlett, RHP, Richmond**
32. Blake Rivera, RHP, Wallace State (Ala.) JC
33. Peyton Maddox, C, Virginia Military Institute
34. **Conner Nurse, RHP, Ridge Community HS, Davenport, Fla.**
35. **Dalton Combs, OF, Huntington (Ind.)**
36. **Joey Marciano, LHP, Southern Illinois**
37. **Andy Rohloff, RHP, Central Florida**
38. Antonio Saldana, LHP, Joliet (Ill.) Catholic HS
39. Brad Dobzanski, RHP, Delsea Regional HS, Franklinville, N.J.
40. Liam Jenkins, RHP, Wabash Valley (Ill.) JC

SEATTLE MARINERS (18)

1. **Evan White, 1B, Kentucky**
2. **Sam Carlson, RHP, Burnsville (Minn.) HS**
3. **Wyatt Mills, RHP, Gonzaga**
4. **Seth Elledge, RHP, Dallas Baptist**
5. **David Banuelos, C, Long Beach State**
6. **Oliver Jaskie, LHP, Michigan**
7. **Max Roberts, LHP, Wabash Valley (Ill.) JC**
8. **Billy Cooke, OF, Coastal Carolina**
9. **Jorge Benitez, LHP, Puerto Rico Baseball Acad., Gurabo, P.R.**
10. **Randy Bell, RHP, South Alabama**
11. **J.P. Sears, LHP, The Citadel**
12. **Darren McCaughan, RHP, Long Beach State**
13. Luis Alvarado, RHP, Nebraska
14. Trevor Casanova, C, El Camino (Calif.) JC
15. **Tommy Romero, RHP, Eastern Florida State JC**
16. **Orlando Razo, LHP, UC Davis**
17. **Jamal Wade, RHP, Maryland**
18. Myles Christian, OF, Olive Branch (Miss.) HS
19. **Kevin Santa, SS, Tampa**
20. **Troy Dixon, C, St. John's**
21. **Connor Hoover, SS, North Georgia**
22. **Johnny Adams, SS, Boston College**
23. **Sam Delaplane, RHP, Eastern Michigan**
24. **Louis Boyd, SS, Arizona**
25. **Bryan Pall, RHP, Michigan**
26. **Austin Hutchison, RHP, Mount Olive (N.C.)**
27. **Collin Kober, RHP, McNeese State**
28. **Johnny Slater, OF, Southfield-Lat. HS, Lathrup Village, Mich.**
29. **Dave Gerber, RHP, Creighton**
30. **Scott Boches, RHP, Marist**
31. **Ryan Costello, 3B, Central Connecticut State**
32. **Ryan Garcia, 1B, Point Loma Nazarene (Calif.)**
33. **Chris Castellanos, LHP, Stanford**
34. **David Hesslink, LHP, Massachusetts Institute of Technology**
35. Hunter Lonigro, RHP, Connellsville (Pa.) Area HS
36. Heston Kjerstad, OF, Randall HS, Amarillo, Texas
37. Jesse Franklin, OF, Seattle Prep HS
38. Kolby Somers, LHP, Century HS, Hillsboro, Ore.
39. Jack Smith, SS, Mercer Island (Wash.) HS
40. Zachary Needham, 3B, Edmonds (Wa.) JC

DRAFT

TAMPA BAY RAYS (4)

1. **Brendan McKay, 1B, Louisville**

1s **Drew Rasmussen, RHP, Oregon State** (Competitive balance Round 'A' pick––31st)

2. **Michael Mercado, RHP, Westview HS, San Diego**
3. **Taylor Walls, SS, Florida State**
4. **Drew Strotman, RHP, Saint Mary's**
5. **Josh Fleming, LHP, Webster (Mo.)**
6. **Zach Rutherford, SS, Old Dominion**
7. **Hunter Schryver, LHP, Villanova**
8. **Riley O'Brien, RHP, College of Idaho**
9. **Andrew Gist, LHP, Georgia**
10. **Phoenix Sanders, RHP, South Florida**
11. Justin Lewis, RHP, Kentucky
12. **Carl Chester, OF, Miami**
13. **Erik Ostberg, C, Hartford**
14. **Vincent Byrd, 1B, Long Beach JC**
15. Bryce Brown, OF, Jackson State
16. Caleb Bolden, RHP, Pleasant Grove HS, Texarkana, Texas
17. **Chris Muller, RHP, Texas-San Antonio**
18. **Michael Smith, OF, San Jacinto (Texas) JC**
19. **Tyler Day, RHP, Colorado Mesa**
20. Andrew Quezada, RHP, Cypress (Calif.) JC
21. **Paul Campbell, RHP, Clemson**
22. **Alex Valverde, RHP, Miami Dade JC**
23. **Zack Mozingo, RHP, Mount Olive (N.C.)**
24. **Jordyn Muffley, C, Parkland (Ill.) JC**
25. **Andrew Miller, C, Southwest Tennessee JC**
26. Scott Schreiber, 1B, Nebraska
27. **Blake Pflughaupt, LHP, Galveston (Texas) JC**
28. **Justin Bridgman, SS, Nevada**

29. Ryan Askew, RHP, Mercer
30. Gavin Williams, RHP, Cape Fear HS, Fayetteville, N.C.
31. Chris Williams, C, Clemson
32. Seaver Whalen, 3B, Lewis-Clark State (Idaho)
33. Ivan Pelaez, LHP, Faulkner (Ala.)
34. Trey Hair, 2B, Evansville
35. Garrett Anderson, RHP, Florida Gulf Coast
36. Kyle Goodbrand, RHP, UC San Diego
37. Cole Cabrera, OF, Punahou HS, Honolulu
38. J.J. Schwarz, C, Florida
39. Jonathan Stroman, RHP, La Cueva HS, Albuquerque
40. Allen Smoot, 3B, San Francisco

TEXAS RANGERS (29)

1. Bubba Thompson, OF, McGill-Toolen Cath. HS, Mobile, Ala.
1. Chris Seise, SS, West Orange HS, Winter Garden, Fla. (Compensation for loss of free agent Ian Desmond––29th)
2. Hans Crouse, RHP, Dana Hills HS, Dana Point, Calif.
3. Matt Whatley, C, Oral Roberts
4. Ryan Dease, RHP, Next Level Acad., Altamonte Springs, Fla.
5. Jake Latz, LHP, Kent State
6. Noah Bremer, RHP, Washington
7. Joel Urena, LHP, Monroe (N.Y.) JC
8. Tyreque Reed, 1B, Itawamba (Miss.) JC
9. Tanner Gardner, OF, Texas Tech
10. John King, LHP, Houston
11. Obie Ricumstrict, SS, Mount Pleasant (Mich.) HS
12. Joey Jarneski, RHP, Hilo (Hawaii) HS
13. Seth Nordlin, RHP, Gateway (Ariz.) JC
14. Alex Eubanks, RHP, Clemson
15. Ricky Vanasco, RHP, Williston (Fla.) HS
16. Xavier Moore, RHP, Steele HS, Amherst, Ohio
17. Tyler Ratliff, 3B, Marshall
18. Chris Morris, RHP, Seton Hall
19. Nick Snyder, RHP, Indian River State (Fla.) JC
20. Josh Advocate, RHP, Long Beach State
21. Daniel Robert, RHP, Auburn
22. Kyle Keith, RHP, Lane (Ore.) JC
23. Myles McKisic, SS, American Heritage HS, Delray Beach, Fla.
24. Brooks Wilson, RHP, Stetson
25. Aaron Ashby, LHP, Crowder (Mo.) JC
26. Jordan Fowler, LHP, Dyer County HS, Newbern, Tenn.
27. Corey Stone, LHP, Mid-Carolina HS, Prosperity, S.C.
28. Jacob Hilton, RHP, Heritage HS, Littleton, Colo.
29. Blaine Knight, RHP, Arkansas
30. Ryan Dorow, SS, Adrian (Mich.)
31. Griff McGarry, RHP, Menlo HS, Atherton, Calif.
32. Will Moriarty, RHP, South Oldham HS, Crestwood, Ky.
33. Troy Newell, LHP, Jefferson (Mo.) JC
34. Edmond Americaan, OF, Chipola (Fla.) JC
35. Connor Higgins, LHP, Arizona State
36. William Jeffry, OF, Colegio Angel David HS, San Juan, P.R.
37. Spencer Smith, C, Northern HS, Durham, N.C.
38. Mark DiLuia, RHP, Marian Catholic HS, Chicago Heights, Ill.
39. Chad Bryant, RHP, Thomasville (Ala.) HS
40. Jordan Anderson, OF, Clemens HS, Madison, Ala.

TORONTO BLUE JAYS (24)

1. Logan Warmoth, SS, North Carolina
1. Nate Pearson, RHP, JC of Central Florida (Compensation for loss of free agent Edwin Encarnacion––28th)
2. Hagen Danner, C, Huntington Beach (Calif.) HS
3. Riley Adams, C, San Diego
4. Kevin Smith, SS, Maryland
5. Cullen Large, 2B, William & Mary
6. Brock Lundquist, OF, Long Beach State
7. Colton Laws, RHP, Charlotte
8. Kacy Clemens, 1B, Texas
9. Zach Logue, LHP, Kentucky
10. Justin Dillon, RHP, Sacramento State
11. Donnie Sellers, RHP, Wake Forest
12. Matt Shannon, RHP, Angelo State (Texas)
13. Brody Rodning, LHP, Minnesota State
14. P.K. Morris, 1B, Steinbrenner HS, Lutz, Fla.
15. Ryan Noda, OF, Cincinnati
16. Ty Tice, RHP, Central Arkansas
17. Kobie Russell, C, Waipahu (Hawaii) HS
18. Jordan Barrett, LHP, Elon
19. Cordell Dunn, C, Center Hill HS, Olive Branch, Miss.
20. Tanner Kirwer, OF, Niagra
21. Turner Larkins, RHP, Texas A&M
22. Gunnar Halter, SS, Seminole State (Okla.) JC
23. Daniel Richardson, RHP, Bishop Alemany HS, Mission Hills, Calif.
24. Colin Brockhouse, RHP, Ball State
25. Cooper Davis, OF, St. Aloysius Gonzaga SS, Mississauga, Ont.
26. D.J. Neal, OF, South Carolina-Sumter
27. Sam Weatherly, LHP, Howell (Mich.) HS
28. Davis Schneider, 3B, E. Regional HS, Voorhees Township, N.J.
29. Joe DiBenedetto, LHP, Nova Southeastern (Fla.)
30. Reilly Johnson, C, State JC of Florida
31. Graham Spraker, RHP, Quincy (Ill.)
32. Jacob Condra-Bogan, RHP, Georgia Southern
33. Matthew Gunter, LHP, Hawaii Pacific
34. Maverik Buffo, RHP, Brigham Young
35. Brandon Polizzi, OF, Cal State Dominguez Hills
36. Jonathan Cheshire, RHP, Davenport (Mich.)
37. Justin Watts, RHP, Southern Indiana
38. Marcus Reyes, LHP, San Diego State
39. Ben Fariss, RHP, Valencia HS, Santa Clarita, Calif.
40. Sean Ross, OF, Granite Hills HS, El Cajon, Calif.

WASHINGTON NATIONALS (28)

1. Seth Romero, LHP, Houston
2. Wil Crowe, RHP, South Carolina
3. Nick Raquet, LHP, William & Mary
4. Cole Freeman, 2B, Louisiana State
5. Brigham Hill, RHP, Texas A&M
6. Kyle Johnston, RHP, Texas
7. Jackson Tetreault, RHP, State JC of Florida
8. Jared Brasher, RHP, Samford
9. Alex Troop, LHP, Michigan State
10. Trey Turner, RHP, Missouri State
11. Justin Connell, OF, American Heritage HS, Plantation, Fla.
12. Jackson Stoeckinger, LHP, JC of Central Florida
13. Eric Senior, OF, Midland (Texas) JC
14. Anthony Peroni, C, Mercer County (N.J.) JC
15. Bryce Montes de Oca, RHP, Missouri
16. Jake Scudder, 1B, Kansas State
17. Jared Johnson, LHP, Palm Beach State (Fla.) JC
18. Nick Choruby, OF, Texas A&M
19. Jonathan Pryor, OF, Wake Forest
20. Jake Cousins, RHP, Pennsylvania
21. Leif Strom, RHP, Pierce (Wash.) JC
22. Nelson Galindez, LHP, Haines City (Fla.) HS
23. Jamori Blash, 1B, Cochise (Ariz.) JC
24. Timmy Richards, SS, Cal State Fullerton
25. Dave Smith, RHP, Long Beach State
26. Kameron Esthay, OF, Baylor
27. Darren Baker, SS, Jesuit HS, Carmichael, Calif.
28. Nic Perkins, C, Drury (Mo.)
29. Alex Dunlap, C, Stanford
30. Austin Guibor, OF, Fresno State
31. Jeremy McKinney, RHP, Indiana State
32. Phil Caulfield, 2B, Loyola Marymount
33. Adalberto Carrillo, C, Southern California
34. Bennett Sousa, LHP, Virginia
35. Jackson Cramer, 1B, West Virginia
36. Gabe Klobosits, RHP, Auburn
37. Kody Gratkowski, 3B, Fairhope (Ala.) HS
38. Jake Boone, SS, Torrey Pines HS, San Diego
39. Kai Nelson, OF, Fieldston HS, Bronx, N.Y.
40. Max Engelbrekt, LHP, Oregon State

APPENDIX

OBITUARIES

■ **Red Adams**, a righthander who pitched one season in the majors and had a long coaching career, died Jan. 18. He was 95.

Adams pitched 19 seasons professionally, spanning from 1939 to 1958, mostly in the Pacific Coast League. He made the majors for part of one season in 1946, appearing in eight games for the Cubs, all in relief, and going 0-1, 8.25. After his playing career ended, Adams, joined the Dodgers organization and had a long career as a scout (1959-68) and then as the big league team's pitching coach from 1969-80.

■ **Vic Albury**, a lefthander who pitched for the Twins from 1973-76, died April 18 in Tampa. He was 69.

Drafted in the ninth round of the 1965 MLB Draft by the Indians, Albury made 101 career appearances (37 starts) in his major league career, retiring with an 18-17 record and 193 strikeouts.

■ **Ruben Amaro Sr.**, a Gold Glove shortstop with the Phillies, died March 31. He was 81.

Amaro Sr. had an 11-year major league career with the Cardinals, Phillies, Yankees and Angels. After he retired as a player, he also served as a scout, coach and manager. He is a member of the Cuban and Mexican baseball halls of fame.

■ **John Barfield**, a lefthander who pitched in three big league seasons from 1989-91, died Dec. 24, 2016, in Little Rock, Ark. He was 52.

An 11th-round pick by the Rangers in 1986, Barfield reached the big leagues with Texas in Sept. 1989 and pitched in four games, two of them starts, with a 6.17 ERA in 11.2 innings.

■ **Vic Barnhart**, who played shortstop and third base for the Pirates from 1944-46, died April 13 in Hagerstown, Md. He was 94.

Barnhart played in 74 career games in the major leagues, notching 55 hits in 204 at-bats.

■ **Edward "Ed" Barnowski**, a righthander for the Orioles in 1965 and '66, died Oct. 17 in Naples, Fla. He was 74.

Barnowski appeared in six big league games, allowing two earned runs and striking out eight batters in 7.1 innings

■ **Don Baylor**, the 1979 American League MVP and a left fielder and first baseman for the Orioles, Athletics, California Angels, Yankees and Red Sox from 1970-88, died Aug. 7 in Austin, Tex. He was 68.

In 1979, Baylor won the AL MVP in a season in which he played all 162 games and hit .296/.371/.530 with 36 home runs and a league-best 139 RBIs. For his career, Baylor hit .260/.342/.436 and slugged 338 career home runs.

■ **Charlie Beamon**, a righthander who pitched in parts of three seasons in the majors from 1956-58, died May 3 in San Leandro, Calif. He was 81.

Beamon was just 21 years old when he made his major league debut with the Orioles in Sept. 1956 by appearing in a pair of games and allowing two runs in 13 innings. Aside from an early-season cup of coffee in Baltimore, he returned to the minors in 1957 before getting his most extensive big league time in 1958.

■ **Winston Blenckstone**, a long-time South Atlantic League franchise owner, died March 22. He was 72.

Blenckstone owned his SAL club from 1987-2001. Blenckstone moved the then-Florence Blue Jays to Myrtle Beach, S.C., when he purchased the team, but then moved them again to Hagerstown, Md., after Hagerstown's Double-A franchise moved to Bowie, Md.

■ **Bob Bowman**, an outfielder who played in five major league seasons from 1955-59, died Jan. 27. He was 85.

Bowman came up through the Phillies system starting in 1950 and reached the majors for the first time in 1955. He played in just nine big league games over the 1955 and '56 seasons but started to get regular time in the Phillies' outfield in 1957, when he batted .266 with six homers in 237 at-bats.

■ **Jackie Brown**, a righthander who pitched seven years in the big leagues in the 1970s, died Jan. 8 in Holdenville, Okla. He was 73.

After his playing days, he went on to a long career as a pitching coach in the major and minor leagues. His big league coaching stops included stints with the Rangers (1979 and 1981-83), White Sox (1992-95) and Devil Rays (2002).

■ **Mark Brownson**, a righthander who pitched three years in the big leagues from 1998-2000, died Feb. 1. He was 41.

Brownson made it to the big leagues as a 30th-round draft-and-follow pick of the Rockies in 1993. He debuted with Colorado in July 1998. He made two starts for the Rockies in '98, then seven starts for them in 1999, going 0-2, 7.89.

■ **Bob Bruce**, a righthander for three big league teams, died March 14. He was 83.

Bruce made his major league debut with the Tigers in 1959. He was traded to the Houston Colt .45's in 1962 and then to the Braves in 1967 in a deal that sent Eddie Mathews to the Astros. Bruce went 49-71, 3.85 in a nine-year career.

■ **Jim Bunning**, a Hall of Fame righthander who pitched for the Tigers, Phillies, Pirates and Dodgers from 1955-71, died May 26 in Edgewood, Kent. He was 85.

Bunning won 224 games in 519 career starts, including a career-high and American League-best 20 wins in 1957. Bunning also finsihed ninth in the AL MVP voting in 1957, which was followed a decade later by a second place finish in the National League Cy Young voting in 1967.

■ **Ralph "Putsy" Caballero**, a second baseman who played eight years in the major leagues in the 1940s and '50s, died Dec. 8, 2016. He was 89.

Caballero was the youngest player ever (16 years, 314 days) to play a game for the Phillies. Wartime necessities prompted the club to call him up on Sept. 14, 1944. He played in 15 big league games before his 20th birthday, getting brief stints in the majors in 1944, '45 and '47. He got his first extensive playing time in 1948, when he appeared in 113 games and hit .245 in 351 at-bats.

■ **Eddie Carnett**, an outfielder who played three years in the major leagues in the 1940s, died Nov. 4, 2016, in Ringling, Okla. He was 100, and the oldest living former major leaguer at the time of his passing.

Although Carnett was primarily an outfielder in the big leagues, he was a two-way player in the minors and made six pitching appearances among the 158 games he played in the majors. Carnett originally came up with the Boston Braves, making two pitching appearances for them in 1941. He got back to the majors in 1944 with the White Sox and received regular playing time in the outfield, batting .276 with 60 RBIs in 457 at-bats—he also pitched in two games.

■ **Paul Casanova**, a catcher for the Washington Senators and Braves from 1965-1974, died Aug. 12 in Miami. He was 75.

Casanova was an all-star for the Senators in 1967, when he hit nine home runs. With the Braves on Aug. 5, 1973, he caught Hall of Fame knuckleballer Phil Niekro's lone career no-hitter.

■ **Bob Cerv**, who was a left fielder for the Yankees, Kansas City Athletics, Angels and Astros from 1951-62, died April 6 in Blair, Neb. He was 91.

An all-star in 1958, Cerv also finished fourth in the American League MVP that same year, when he hit .305/.371/.592 with 38 home rns and 104 RBIs for the Kansas City Athletics. For his career, Cerv recorded 624 hits in 2,261 at-bats.

■ **Bill Champion**, a righthander who pitched eight years in the big leagues from 1969-76, died Jan. 7 in Shelby, N.C. He was 69.

Champion was just 21 years old when he debuted for the Phillies in June 1969. He was a regular in their rotation for the rest of that season, going 5-10, 5.01 in 117 innings. After spending most of the 1970 season back in the minor leagues, he returned to the Phillies full time in 1971. Champion spent the rest of his big league career splitting his time between starting and relieving. He had his best season in 1974, when he went 11-4, 3.62 in 162 innings. Champion went on to serve as a scout for the Cubs and later as a minor league pitching coach.

■ **Gene Conley**, who was a righthander for the Boston Braves, Milwaukee Braves, Phillies and Red Sox from 1952-63, died on July 4 in Foxborough, Mass. He was 86.

Conley was a three-time all-star and won 91 career games, including a career-best 14 wins in 1954 when he finished third in rookie of the year voting for the Milwaukee Braves. Conely made 214 career starts and 62 more relief apperances, totaling 1,589 innings and 888 career strikeouts.

■ **Marlan Coughtry**, a second baseman who played in parts of two major league seasons, died Nov. 8, 2016, in Vancouver, Wash. He was 82.

Coughtry made his big league debut as a 25-year-old with Boston in September 1960, going 3-for-19 over 15 games. After spending the entire 1961 season back in the minors, the Angels took him in the Rule 5 draft that winter. Coughtry went on to play for three different big league teams during the 1962 season, including the Angels, Kansas City Athletics and then the the Indians. Altogether, he hit .200 (7-for-35) in his three stops.

■ **Clarence "Chuck" Curn**, a righthander for the Pirates, Indians and Dodgers from 1957-59, died Oct. 21 in Lady Lake, Fla. He was 87.

Curn, also known as "Slim", made 25 career relief appearances in his big league career, including a career-best year in 1959, when he struck out 24 hitters and recorded a 4.99 ERA in 30.2 innings for the Dodgers.

■ **Darren Daulton**, who was a catcher, right fielder and first baseman for the Phillies and Marlins from 1983-97, died Aug. 6 in Clearwater, Fla. He was 55.

Daulton was a three-time all-star and finished in the top-10 in National League MVP voting on two different occassions, while also winning a Silver Slugger award in 1992. Daulton was an all-star and played in 147 games for the 1993 Phillies, who won the NL Pennant. For his career, Daulton hit .245/.357/.427 with 137 home runs in 1,161 games—1,109 of which came with the Phillies.

APPENDIX

OBITUARIES

■ **Melvin "Mel" Didier**, a longtime and well-respected scout who worked for the Dodgers, Tigers, Braves, Montreal Expos, Mariners, Diamondbacks, Indians, Orioles, Rangers, and, most recently, Blue Jays, died Sept. 11 in Phoenix. He was 90.

■ **James "Jim" Donohue**, a righthander who pitched in the major leagues for the Tigers, Angels and Twins in 1961 and '62, died Sept. 9 in St. Louis. He was 79.

Donohue made 70 career appearances (nine starts) during his two-year major league stint, ending his career with a 4.29 ERA and 116 strikeouts in 155 innings.

■ **Bob Drew**, a 25-year minor league executive best known as general manager of the Triple-A Rochester Red Wings, died March 19. He was 80.

■ **Enda Dummerth**, who played for the Minneapolis Millerettes and Racine Belles in the All-American Girls Professional Baseball League in 1944 and was honored by the Hall of Fame in 1988, died Oct. 8. She was 93.

■ **Bill Endicott**, an outfielder who played one sason in the big leagues in 1946, died Nov. 26, 2016, in Sacramento. He was 98.

Endicott played seven seasons of pro ball, sandwiched around four missed years because of World War II. His only big league time came in 1946, when he went 4-for-20 with three RBIs for the eventual World Series-champion Cardinals.

■ **Jack Faszholz**, a righthander with the Cardinals during the 1953 season, died March 25 in Belle, Mo. He was 89.

Faszholz made four appearances (one start) for the Cardinals, striking out seven and allowing nine earned runs in 12 innings.

■ **Bob Ferguson**, a righthander who appeared in nine games for the 1944 Reds, died May 23 in Wetumpka, Ala. He was 89.

■ **Dave "Boo" Ferriss**, a righthander who pitched six years in the majors from 1945-50, died Nov. 24 in Cleveland, Miss. He was 94.

Ferriss was spectacular as a rookie in 1945, going 21-10, 2.96. He didn't fall off in 1946 either, even with many of the sport's regulars returning from military service. Ferriss went 25-6, 3.25 for the Red Sox to help them to the 1946 AL pennant. He pitched a shutout against the Cardinals in Game Three of the World Series and got the start in Game Seven. He took no decision in the game the Red Sox famously lost on Enos Slaughter's mad dash.

Unfortunately, the combination of asthma and arm problems—Ferriss threw north of 260 innings in each of his two big seasons—derailed his career after 1946. He went just 12-11, 4.04 in 1947, and he would win just seven more games for the rest of his big league career. He went on to serve as head coach at Division II Delta State (Miss.) and took the program to the D-II College World Series three times (1977, 1978 and 1982).

Ferriss, a Mississippi native who also pitched collegiately at Mississippi State, was inducted into the state's sports hall of fame in 1961 and the Red Sox hall of fame in 2002.

■ **Daniel Flores**, a catcher and one of the most promising prospects in the Red Sox's farm system, died on Nov. 8. He was 17 years old.

Flores was considered one of the best young catchers to come out of Venezuela in years, with scouts long raving about his defensive ability. Many considered Flores the best international scouting prospect since Gary Sanchez and he ranked No. 2 on the Baseball America Top 50 International Prospects list this year.

According to the Red Sox, Flores died of complications from treatment for a cancer that was discovered just days before Flores' death.

■ **Todd Frohwirth**, a righthander for the Phillies, Orioles, Red Sox and California Angels from 1987-96, died March 26 in Waukesha, Wis. He was 54.

Frohwirth made 284 relief apperances in his major league career, recording 20 wins and 259 strikeouts in 418 innings.

■ **Phil Gagliano**, a second baseman who played 12 seasons in the big leagues from 1963-74, died Dec. 19, 2016, in Hollister, Mo. He was 74.

Gagliano served as a utility player for the dominant Cardinals teams of the 1960s, helping St. Louis win two World Series (1964 and 1967) and appear in another (1968).

■ **Ned Garver**, a 20-game winner for the 100-game loser St. Louis Browns in 1951, died Feb. 26. He was 91.

Garver was 129-157, 3.73 in 14 seasons with the Browns, Athletics, Tigers and Angels. Garver was best known as a durable starter on second-division teams. He led the league in losses in 1949 and led the league in complete games in back-to-back seasons in 1950 and 1951. His 20-12. 3.73 season in 1951 earned him an all-star berth and helped him finish second in the MVP race, impressive for a pitcher on a team that went 52-102 overall.

■ **Miguel Gonzalez**, an Orioles righthander who pitched in the Dominican Summer League this season, died Sept. 16 in the Dominican Republic. He was 21.

Gonzalez signed in 2014 and played three seasons in the DSL, making 38 appearances (13 starts). He died from injuries sustained in a car accident.

■ **Dallas Green**. a righthander for the Phillies, Washington Senators and Mets from 1960-67, died March 22 in Philadelphia. He was 82.

Greene pitched in 185 games during his big league career, making 46 starts and striking out 268 in 562 innings.

■ **Donald "Don" Gross**, a lefthander who pitched for the Reds and Pirates from 1955-60, died Aug. 10 in Mount Pleasant, Mich. He was 86.

Gross spent six seasons in the big leagues, working mostly as a reliever. He finished his career 20-22, 3.73 in 398 innings.

■ **John Gunther**, the head coach for Albuquerque's Sandia High, died March 15. He was 55.

Gunther had battled cancer for 15 months, but he kept coaching his team. That included running team workouts this year, according to the Albuquerque Journal. Gunther had coached the Sandia baseball team for six years and led them to two New Mexico state final appearances.

■ **Creighton Hale**, who was the president of Little League Baseball from 1973-94 as part of a nearly 60-year affiliation with the organization, died Oct. 8 in Williamsport, Pa. He was 93.

■ **Roy Halladay**, one of the sport's most decorated pitchers in recent momory, died in a plane crash in the Gulf of Mexico just off the coast of St. Petersburg, Fla. on Nov. 7. He was 40.

Halladay was a first-round pick (17th overall) by the Blue Jays in 1995 and went on to split his 16-year major league career between the Blue Jays and Phillies. Halladay retired with a 203-105 career record and 3.38 ERA, as well as 2,117 strikeouts in 2,749 innings. The 6-foot-6, 225-pound righthander was an eight-time all-star and won his first Cy Young Award with the Blue Jays in 2003 when he led the American League in wins, starts, complete games, shutouts, innings and strikeout-to-walkout ratio. Seven years later, Halladay won the National League Cy Young Award with the Phillies after leading the league in all of the aforementioned categories, expect starts.

Halladay was honored by Baseball America as the Major League Player of the Year in 2010, which is the same year he became just the second pitcher in history to throw a postseason no-hitter, which came on Oct. 6 during Game 1 of the NLDS against the Cincinnati Reds.

■ **Vern Handrahan**, a righthander who pitched in parts of two big league seasons in the 1960s, died Nov. 2 in Charlottetown, Prince Edward Island. He was 79.

Handrahan was 27 years old when he debuted with the A's in 1964 and went 0-1, 6.06 in 36 innings. He got back to the majors two years later, making 16 appearances, including one start, for the A's and went 0-1, 4.26. After his playing career, Handrahan was hired as a scout with the Montreal Expos.

■ **Bill Hands**, a righthander for four major league teams, died March 9. He was 76.

Hands pitched for the Giants (1965), Cubs (1966-72), Twins (1973-74) and Rangers (1974-75). He went 111-110 for his career with a 3.35 ERA.

■ **Charles "Mickey" Harrington**, whose only major league appearance was a pinch-running stint for the 1963 Phillies, died Sept. 20 in Hattiesburg, Miss. He was 82.

■ **Roy Hawes**, a first baseman who played for the Washington Senators in 1951 after a 14-year minor league career, died Oct. 9 in Ringgold, Ga. He was 91.

■ **Solomon "Solly" Hemus**, who played shortstop and second base for the Cardinals and Phillies from 1949-59, died Oct. 2 in Houston. He was 94.

Hemus ended his 11-year major league career with a .273/.390/.411 slash line, which included a total of 736 hits in 961 games. He was named the last player-manager in Cardinals franchise history in the fall of 1958 and remained with the organization until 1962. Also a coach for the Mets (1962-63) and Indians (1964-65), Hemus' last role came in 1966, when he served as the manager for the Jacksonville Suns, an affiliate of the Mets.

■ **John Herbold**, a member of the America Baseball Coaches Association Hall of Fame, died July 27 in Long Beach. He was 88.

Herbold won 455 games in 21 seasons at Cal State Los Angeles (1984-2004) after winning 483 games as a high school coach in the L.A. area.

■ **John Herrnstein**, who played for the Phillies, Cubs and Braves from 1962-66, died Oct. 3 in Chillicothe, Ohio. He was 79.

Herrnstein was the primary first baseman for the Phillies in 1964, when he set career highs in games (125), hits (71), home runs (six), RBIs (25) and batting average (.234).

■ **Mark Higgins**, a firstbaseman for the Indians during the 1989 season, died March 22 in Duluth, Ga. He was 53.

A first-round pick (seventh overall) by the

APPENDIX

Indians in the 1984 MLB Draft, Higgins appeared in six games during the '89 season, recording one hit in 10 at-bats.

■ **Garry Hill**, a righthander for the Braves during the 1969 season, died Sept. 20 in Charlotte. He was 70.

Hill was a first-round pick (eighth overall) by the Braves in 1967 out of North Carolina. He pitched in one game during his major league career, on June 12, 1969.

■ **John "Dave" Hilton**, who played second and third base for the Padres from 1972-75, died Sept. 17 in Scottsdale, Ariz. He was 67.

Hilton was the first overall pick in the January phase of the 1971 draft by the Padres. He ended his four-year major league career with a .213/.265/.298 slash line. He also founded the Arizona School of Baseball in Scottsdale.

■ **Greg Jelks**, a corner infielder who played in 10 games for the Phillies during the 1987 season, died Jan. 6 in Sydney, Australia. He was 55.

■ **Joe Kirrene**, a third baseman who played in parts of two seasons in the big leagues in 1950 and '54, died Oct. 19 in San Ramon, Calif. He was 85.

Kirrene was three days away from turning 19 when the White Sox decided to call him up for the final day of the 1950 season. He appeared in the second game of a doubleheader against the St. Louis Browns and went 1-for-4. He spent the next three years away from the sport serving in the Korean War.

■ **Robert Kloss**, a Tigers draft pick in 1966 and longtime high school baseball coach in the Detroit area, died Oct. 23. He was 69.

Kloss is a member of the Wayne State University athletics hall of fame. He ended his four-year collegiate career with a 2.26 ERA.

■ **Bob Kuzava**, a lefthander who pitched for the Indians, White Sox, Washington Senators, Yankees, Orioles, Phillies, Pirates and Cardinals from 1946-57, died May 15 in Wyandotte, Mich. He was 93.

Kuzava won 49 games in his 10-year major league career, including a career-high 11 wins for the Senators and Yankees in 1951. Kuzava finished fourth in the Rookie of the Year voting in 1949.

■ **Jim Landis**, an outfielder for the White Sox, Indians, Astros, Tigers, Red Sox and Kansas City Athletics from 1957-67, died Oct. 7 in Napa, Calif. He was 83.

Landis spent the majority of his 11-year career with the White Sox, including 1962 when he was American League all-star. He also won five Gold Glove awards from 1960-64, a streak that began one year after he finished 7th in the American League MVP voting in 1959.

■ **Jim Lehew**, a righthander who pitched in parts of two big league seasons from 1961-62, died Dec. 23, 2016, in Grantsville, Md. He was 79.

Lehew debuted with the Orioles in September 1961. He made two appearances in the final days of the '61 season, throwing two scoreless innings, and pitched in six games in the first half of the 1962 season. He didn't figure in any decisions but logged a 1.86 ERA in 9.2 innings.

■ **Don Lock**, an outfielder for the Phillies, Red Sox and Washington Senators from 1962-69, died Oct. 8 in Wichita. He was 81.

Lock led the American League in outfield assists in 1963, when he also finished sixth in the AL with 27 home runs. Lock then hit a career-high 28 home runs in 1964, before eventually ending his eight-year big league career with 122 home runs and a .238/.331/.417 slash line.

■ **Stu Locklin**, an outfielder who played in parts of two major league seasons in 1955 and '56, died Dec. 4, 2016, in Albuquerque. He was 88.

Locklin got his first big league time with the Indians in June 1955, his first season back in the game after missing three years to serve in the Korean War. He went 3-for-18 in 16 games for Cleveland that year and was briefly called up early in the 1956 season, playing in nine games.

■ **Harry MacPherson**, a righthander who pitched just one inning for the Boston Braves during the 1944 season, died on Feb. 19 in Englewood, Fla. He was 90.

■ **James "Jim" Marshall**, a former high school coach and scout with the Padres and Mets, died March 12 in Clearwater, Fla. He was 80.

Marshall played baseball and football at the University of Tampa before becoming the first baseball coach at Tampa's King High. With the Padres, Marshall helped sign No. 1 overall draft picks Bill Almon and Mike Ivie.

■ **Jim Marshall**, a former major leaguer and long-time scout, died March 12. He was 85.

Marshall spent five years in the majors as a first baseman/corner outfielder. He hit .242/.320/.388 in 962 plate appearances with the Orioles, Cubs, Giants, Mets and Pirates from 1958-62. After his big league career, Marshall played in Japan, which led to a second career as a scout. He served as a senior advisor for Pacific Rim operations for the Diamondbacks for more than a decade.

■ **Andy Marte**, a corner infielder for the Braves, Indians and Diamondbacks for parts of seven seasons from 2005-2014, died Jan 22 in

Casa de Alto, Dominican Republic. He was 33.

Marte, who was a former top prospect for the Braves and Red Sox, died in a car accident. In the early 2000's, Marte was one of the game's most promisng prospects, ranking among Baseball America's Top 100 prospects four times, including a high ranking of No. 9. During his major league career, Marte hit .218/.276/.358 in 307 games, never playing more than 80 games in a season.

■ **Lee May**, a first baseman and outfielder for the Reds, Astros, Orioles and Royals from 1965-82, died July 29 in Cincinnati. He was 74.

A three-time all-star, May played in 2,071 big league games before retiring at 39. He finished his career with 2,031 hits and 354 home runs.

■ **David "Dave" McDonald**, a lefthanded-hitting first baseman for the Yankees in 1969 and Montreal Expos in 1971, died May 19 in Pompano Beach, Fla. He was 73.

McDonald appeared in 33 games during his big league career, hitting .145 in 62 at-bats.

■ **Michael McQueen**, a lefthander with the Braves from 1969-72 and then with the Reds in 1974, died Oct. 9 in Batesville, Ark. He was 67.

McQueen was a fourth-round pick by the Braves in 1968 and recorded three saves to go with a career 4.66 ERA during five big league seasons.

■ **Sam Mele**, a former outfielder, first baseman, manager and scout, died May 1, in Quincy, Mass. He was 95.

Mele began his playing career with the Red Sox in 1947 and went on to have a 10-year major league career, playing for the Washington Senators, White Sox, Orioles, Indians and Reds. He led the AL with 36 doubles in 1951. After his playing career, Mele managed the Twins for seven years, leading Minnesota to the AL pennant in 1965.

■ **Eugene "Gene" Michael**, whose two stints as the Yankees' general manager included the 1981 AL pennant and acquiring or keeping the home-grown players at the heart of the 1990s Yankees dynasty, died Sept. 7 in Oldsmar, Fla. He was 79.

Michael, who carried the nickname "Stick" due to his listed 6-foot-2, 183-pound frame, had a 10-year major league career from 1966-75, when he played second base and shortstop for the Pirates, Dodgers, Yankees and Tigers. After a brief stint as the Yankees GM in 1980, Michael managed the Yankees from 1981-82 and served as a organizational scout from 1983-85. He then took over as the Cubs manager from 1986-87, finishing his career with a 206-200 managerial record.

Michael became the Yankees GM for a second time on Aug. 20, 1990, holding the position until October 1995. During that time, he oversaw the organization's rebuild from the AL's worst team in 1990, including the drafting and signing of the 1992 No. 6 pick Derek Jeter, as well as Andy Pettitte and Jorge Posada as draft-and-follows.

■ **Ed Mierkowicz**, who was a left fielder for the Tigers in 1945, '47 and '48 and then with the Cardinals in 1950, died May 19 in Rochester Hills, Mich. He was 93.

Mierkowicz played in 35 games at the major league level, notching 11 hits in 63 at-bats.

■ **Jerome "Jerry" Mileur**, who was the long-time owner of the Harrisburg Senators until selling the Double-A franchise in 1994, died Sept. 5 in Hadley, Ill. He was 83.

■ **Robert "Bob" Motley**, who was the last surviving umpire from the Negro Leagues and the first African-American to graduate from the renown Al Somers Umpire School, died Sept. 15. He was 94.

■ **Morris Nettles**, an outfielder who spent two years with the Angels, died Jan. 24. He was 64. Nettles hit .247/.310/.279 while playing all three outfield spots.

■ **Russ Nixon**, a catcher who played 12 years and later managed in the majors, died Nov. 8, 2016, in Cleves, Ohio. He was 81.

Nixon spent the bulk of his big league playing career as a backup catcher, appearing in 906 games spanning the 1957-68 seasons.

Nixon got into managing after his playing career wrapped up in 1968, including a 101-131 record during a two-year stint managing the Reds from 1982-83. He then moved on to the Braves organization and continuned managing in the minor leagues through 2005.

■ **Luis Olmo**, who was an outfielder and infielder for the Brooklyn Dodgers and Boston Braves for parts of six seasons from 1943-51, died April 28 in San Juan, Puerto Rico. He was 97.

Olmo finished his career with a .281/.319/.405 slashline, which including a career-best year in 1945 when he hit .313/.356/.462 with a National League-leading 13 triples.

■ **John Orsino**, a catcher who played seven years in the majors from 1961-67, died Nov. 2 in Sunny Isles Beach, Fla. He was 78.

Orsino broke into the majors with the Giants but played sparingly in his two stints with them—a combined 43 games in 1961 and '62. Traded to the Orioles after the 1962 season, he served as Baltimore's everyday catcher in 1963 and hit .272 with 19 homers. However, that was his only season with more than 250 at-bats. His average fell to .222 over 81 games played in 1964, and the Orioles traded him to the Washington Senators after the 1965 season. He played in 15 games for Washington from 1966-67.

■ **Bob Perry**, who was a centerfielder for the Angels from 1963-64, died July 2 in New Bern, N.C. He was 82. Perry played in 131 career games for the Angels, hitting .266/.310/.362 in 387 at-bats.

■ **Norman "Ed" Phillips**, a righthander for the Red Sox during the 1970 season, died Sept. 20 in Moody, Maine. He was 73.

Phillips was a 16th-round pick by the Red Sox in the 1966 draft and made 18 relief appearances with a 5.32 ERA during his one-year career.

■ **Jim Piersall**, a centerfielder for the Red Sox, Indians, Washington Senators, Mets and Angels from 1950-67, died June 3 in Wheaton, Ill. He was 87.

A two-time all-star and Gold Glove winner, Piersall hit .272/.332/.386 during his major league career, spanning 1,734 games and 5,890 at-bats.

■ **Ross Powell**, a lefthander for the Reds, Astros and Pirates from 1993-95, died Oct. 25 in Lucas, Texas. He was 49. Powell made 48 career appearances in the majors, striking out 42 batters in 53.1 innings.

■ **Joe Preseren**, a long-time minor league executive, died March 30. He was 58.

Preseren served as general manager of the Tulsa Drillers and Frederick Keys among his multiple stops. He was the 1999 Carolina League executive of the year.

■ **Rafael "Felo" Ramirez**, the Spanish-language radio voice of the Marlins since the team's inaugural season in 1993, died Aug. 21 in Miami. He was 94.

Ramirez, who had been hospitalized since he fell and struck his head getting off the team bus in April, earned the Ford C. Frick award in 2001, earning him a place in the Hall of Fame.

■ **Jim Reinebold**, a long-time high school and minor league baseball coach, died Feb. 8. He was 87. Reinebold was 646-289-4 as a high school coach at South Bend, Ind.'s Clay High and Greene Township (Ind.) High and won a state title at Clay in 1970. He also spent more than a decade as a minor league coach with the Diamondbacks, White Sox, Cubs and Athletics.

■ **Al Richter**, who played shortstop for the Red Sox in 1951 and 1953, died on Oct. 28 in Virginia Beach, Va. He was 90. Richter appeared in six games over two seasons for the Red Sox, recording one hit in 11 at-bats.

■ **John Rheinecker**, a left-hander who pitched in parts of two seasons for the Rangers, died July 18 in St. Louis. He was 38.

An Athletics supplemental first-round pick out of Southwest Missouri State in 2001, Rheinecker made 44 appearances for Texas in 2006 and 2007.

■ **Bob Sadowski**, a third baseman who played for four teams over parts of four seasons in the majors from 1960-63, died Jan. 6. He was 79.

■ **Colin Saunders**, the clubhouse manager for the Triple-A Durham Bulls for more than a decade, died March 5. He was 42.

Saunders became the Bulls' clubbie in 2003 and worked spring training every season before coming north with the team. Saunders also served as the Rays' Double-A Orlando clubbie.

■ **Paul Schaal**, who was a third baseman for the Angels and Royals from 1964-74, died Sept. 1 in Waikoloa, Hawaii. He was 74.

For his career Schaal hit .244/.341/.344 with 869 hits, including a career-best year in 1971 when he hit .274 with 11 home runs and 63 RBIs in 161 games with the Royals.

■ **Roy Sievers**, the 1949 American League Rookie of the Year, died April 3. He was 90.

Sievers had a distinguished 17-year big league career with the St. Louis Browns, Washington Senators, White Sox and Phillies and made five all-star teams. He led the AL with 42 home runs and 114 RBIs in 1957.

■ **Daryl Spencer**, an infielder for the Giants, Cardinals, Dodgers and Reds from 1952-63, died Jan. 2 in Wichita, Kan. He was 88.

Spencer played in 1,098 games during his 10-year major league career, hitting .244/.327/.380 with 105 home runs in 3,689 at-bats.

■ **Dick Starr**, a righthander who pitched five years in the big leagues from 1947-51, died Jan. 18 in Kittanning, Pa. He was 95.

Starr reached the big leagues in 1947 after coming up through the Yankees organization. He made a combined five appearances for New York from 1947-48 before being traded to the St. Louis Browns after the '48 season. He stayed in the majors full-time with the Browns, spending the 1949 season mostly in the bullpen before taking on more starting assignments in 1950.

■ **Herm Starrette**, a righthander for the Orioles from 1963-65, died June 2 in Statesville, N.C. He was 80.

Starrette made 27 apperances in his major league career, striking out 21 in 46 innings with a 2.54 ERA.

■ **Rick Stelmaszek**, who was a catcher for the

Washington Senators in 1971 and for the Rangers, California Angels and Cubs from 1973-74, died Nov. 6 in Chicago. He was 69.

Stelmaszek, who was an 11th-round pick by the Washington Senators in the 1967 MLB Draft, played in 60 major league games during his career, hitting .170/.302/.239 in 88 at-bats.

■ **Walt Streuli**, a catcher who played in parts of three seasons in the majors, died Jan. 19 in Greensboro, N.C. He was 81.

Streuli made his major league debut one day before his 19th birthday in September 1954 when he played the last three innings of a game for the Tigers against the Indians. He would go on to play in five games for Detroit over the next two seasons, getting his first big league hit in September 1955.

■ **Stanley "Stan" Swanson**, an outfielder for the Montreal Expos in 1971, died Sept. 1 in Fallbrook, Calif. He was 73. Swanson played 49 games for the Expos, hitting .245/.310/.330.

■ **Bob Talbot**, an outfielder who played for the Cubs from 1953-54, died Oct. 31 in Visalia, Calif. He was 90.

Talbot appeared in 122 games for the Cubs, including 114 in 1954 when he hit .241/.274/.305.

■ **Yordano Ventura**, a righthander for the Royals from 2013-16, died Jan. 22 in a car accident in Juan Adrian, Dominican Republic. He was 25.

Known for his blazing fastball, Ventura helped key the Royals to the 2015 World Series title, going 13-8, 4.08 that season. He made nine postseason starts during Kansas City's pennant-winning seasons in '14 and '15, going 1-2, 4.66 Overall, Ventura was 38-31, 3.89 since making his big league debut as a 22-year old in 2013.

■ **Gene Verble**, who was a middle infielder for the Washington Senators in 1951 and 1953, died Nov. 4 in Kannapolis, N.C. He was 89.

Verble played in 81 games during his career in the majors, hitting .202/.275/.237 in 198 at-bats.

■ **Hector Wagner**, a righthander for the Royals in 1990 and '91, died June 5 in Clifton, N.J. He was 48.

Wagner started seven games in his major league career, winning one start and striking out 19.

■ **Daniel "Danny" Walton**, an outfielder who played for six big league teams in parts of nine seasons from 1968-80, died Aug. 9 in Morgan, Utah. He was 70.

A 10th-round pick by the Astros in 1965, Walton reached Houston in 1968 and went on to play for the Brewers, Yankees, Twins, Dodgers and Rangers.

■ **Steve Waterbury**, a righthander who made five appearances for the Cardinals in 1976, died on May 19 in Marion, Ill. He was 65.

■ **Bill Webb**, one of the best television producers of baseball, died March 7. He was 70.

Webb, a long-time producer for Fox as well as SNY, was known for his technique of using close-ups of players and fans to show the tension in pressure-packed moments.

■ **Daniel Webb**, a righthander for the White Sox from 2013-16, died in an ATV accident Oct. 14 in Waverly, Tenn. He was 28.

Webb made 94 career relief appearances and recorded a 4.50 ERA. He saw his highest workload in 2014, when he went 6-5, 3.99 in 68 innings. The Blue Jays drafted Webb as an 18th-rounder in 2009 from Northwest Florida State JC.

■ **Brett Williams**, a first baseman at White Knoll High in Lexington, S.C. who had committed to play at South Carolina, died Jan. 17 in Columbia, S.C. He was 16.

■ **Ken Wright**, a righthander who pitched five years in the big leagues from 1970-74, died Jan. 21. He was 70.

Wright came up through the Boston system until being taken by the Royals in the 1969 Rule 5 draft. He saw regular action out of Kansas City's bullpen as a 23-year-old rookie in 1970. The club eventually traded him along with Lou Piniella to the Yankees after the '73 season, but he made just three apperances for New York.

■ **Thomas "Tom" Wright**, who was a major league outfielder for the Red Sox, White Sox, St. Louis Browns and Washington Senators from 1948-56, died Sept. 5 in Shelby, N.C. He was 93.

■ **Anthony Young**, a righthander for the Mets, Cubs and Astros from 1991-96, died June 27 in Houston. He was 51.

Young pitched in 181 games (51 starts) during his major league career, winning 15 games with a 3.89 ERA and striking out 245 in 460 innings.

■ **Dom Zanni**, a righthander pitcher for the Giants, White Sox and Reds for parts of seven seasons from 1958-66, died July 6 in Massapequa, N.Y. He was 85.

Zanni appeared in 111 major league games. mostly as a reliever, and finished his career 9-6, 3.79 with 148 strikeouts in 183 innings.

■ **Jose Zardon**, an outfielder for the Washington Senators in 1945, died on March 21 in Tamarac, Fla. He was 93.

■ **Robert "Bob" Zick**, a righthander for the Cubs in 1954, died June 12 in Sun City, Ariz. He was 90.

STATISTICS INDEX